ZIP CODE FINDER

RAND McNALLY
Chicago • New York • San Francisco

Reproducing or recording maps, tables, text listings, or any other material which appears in this publication by photocopying, electronic storage or retrieval, or by any other means, is prohibited.

The information in the *Zip Code Finder* was collected directly from the Rand McNally *1991 Commercial Atlas & Marketing Guide* and other Rand McNally products.

Hospital names and zip codes printed by permission of the American Hospital Association (Source: *AHA Guide to the Health Care Field,* published by the American Hospital Association, copyright 1989).

The *Rand McNally Zip Code Finder* and its contents are not affiliated with the U.S. Postal Service.

copyright © 1990 by Rand McNally & Company

All rights reserved

Printed in the United States of America

ISBN 528-20138-7

Rand McNally Zip Code Finder
Table of Contents

INTRODUCTION

The Meaning of Your Zip Code .... p.   5

Using The Zip Code Finder .... p.   6

Standard Address Abbreviations .... p.   7

Toll-Free Reservation Numbers .... p.   8

Telephone Area Code/Time Zone Tables .... p.   9 - 11

Telephone Area Code/Time Zone Map .... p. 12 - 13

Postal Rates and Regulations .... p. 14 - 18

Post Office Divisional Offices .... p. 19 - 21

BASIC LISTINGS AND
3-DIGIT ZIP CODE MAPS

State	3-Digit Map	Listings	State	3-Digit Map	Listings
Alabama	24-25	23	Iowa	188-189	187
Alaska	38-39	40	Kansas	196-197	195
Arizona	44-45	43	Kansas City		199
Phoenix		47	Kentucky	204-205	203
Arkansas	50-51	49	Louisville		213
California	60-61	59	Louisiana	222-223	221
Anaheim		59	New Orleans		227
Long Beach		69	Maine	232-233	231
Los Angeles		69	Maryland	240-241	242
San Diego		75	Baltimore		242
San Francisco		75	Massachusetts	256-257	258
Colorado	82-83	81	Boston		258
Denver		84	Michigan	268-269	267
Connecticut	88-89	90	Detroit		272
Delaware	240-241	95	Minnesota	286-287	285
District of Columbia	240-241	98	Minneapolis		291
Washington		98	St. Paul		293
Florida	102-103	104	Mississippi	298-299	297
Fort Lauderdale		107	Missouri	306-307	308
Miami		111	St. Louis		316
Orlando		112	Montana	320-321	319
Tampa		115	Nebraska	324-325	326
Georgia	118-119	120	Nevada	330-331	329
Atlanta		121	New Hampshire	334-335	333
Hawaii	132-133	131	New Jersey	340-341	339
Honolulu		131	Newark		347
Idaho	136-137	135	New Mexico	352-353	354
Illinois	140-141	142	New York	358-359	360
Chicago		145	Bronx		362
Indiana	168-169	167	Brooklyn		362
Indianapolis		175	Far Rockaway		366

State	3-Digit Map	Listings	State	3-Digit Map	Listings
Flushing		367	South Dakota	506-507	508
Jamaica		370	Tennessee	512-513	511
Long Island City		372	Memphis		522
New York City		374	Nashville		523
Staten Island		382	Texas	532-533	531
North Carolina	388-389	387	Dallas		537
Charlotte		391	Fort Worth		540
North Dakota	404-405	406	Houston		543
Ohio	410-411	409	San Antonio		551
Cincinnati		414	Utah	558-559	557
Cleveland		414	Vermont	562-563	561
Columbus		415	Virginia	568-569	567
Oklahoma	436-437	435	Norfolk		580
Oklahoma City		440	Washington	588-589	587
Oregon	444-445	443	Seattle		593
Pennsylvania	450-451	452	West Virginia	596-597	598
Philadelphia		478	Wisconsin	610-611	609
Pittsburgh		480	Milwaukee		619
Rhode Island	494-495	496	Wyoming	626-627	628
South Carolina	498-499	500			

MAJOR CITIES WITH 5-DIGIT ZIP CODE MAPS

City	5-Digit Map	City	5-Digit Map
Atlanta, GA	121	Minneapolis, MN	292
Boston, MA	259	New York, NY	375, 376
Chicago, IL	146	Philadelphia, PA	479
Dallas, TX	538	San Francisco, CA	76
Detroit, MI	273	St. Paul, MN	294
Kansas City, KS	200	Washington, DC	99
Los Angeles, CA	70		

THE MEANING OF YOUR ZIP CODE   5

INTRODUCTION

The Rand McNally *Zip Code Finder* is a complete and convenient reference containing zip code listings for more than 110,000 places in the United States. Arranged alphabetically by state, these listings enable you to quickly and easily find zip codes. The *Zip Code Finder's* listings are visually enhanced by a detailed 3-digit zip code map for each state. These maps show the location of towns and cities within Zip Code Sectional Areas.

Listings for 50 major U.S. cities include zip codes for selected hospitals, military installations, hotels/motels, colleges, universities and financial institutions. The Washington, D.C. listing additionally includes zip codes for government offices.

Included in the listings is a telephone number for each multiple zip code city. By using this number, you can readily determine which of the city's zip codes you need. Five-digit zip code maps display zip code boundaries for each of thirteen multiple zip code cities.

The Rand McNally *Zip Code Finder* saves you time and money. Information provided on postal rates and regulations, plus the locations of post office division offices, helps you to mail economically and efficiently. Convenient listings of toll-free numbers for car rentals, airline reservations and hotel/motel accommodations place these services at your fingertips. In addition, telephone area code lists provide a helpful and economical reference when placing long-distance calls.

THE MEANING OF YOUR ZIP CODE

Zip codes, set up to improve mail distribution, define areas within the U.S.

The country is divided into ten geographic regions that consist of three or more states. Each of these regions is assigned a number 0-9. This number is the first digit of your zip code.

Within the ten geographic regions, states are further divided into smaller geographic units. The second and third digits of your zip code identify these units.

Together, the first three digits of your zip code identify either a particular Sectional Center or Multi-Coded City. Sectional Centers and Multi-Coded Cities have similar postal functions. A Sectional Center, usually the natural center of local transportation, is a large post office serving smaller surrounding post offices. The Multi-Coded City is a main city post office which serves its stations and branches within the city's neighborhoods.

The final two digits of your zip code identify the post offices served by the Sectional Center <u>or</u> branches and stations served by the city post office.

The example below further illustrates the meaning of a 5-digit zip code:

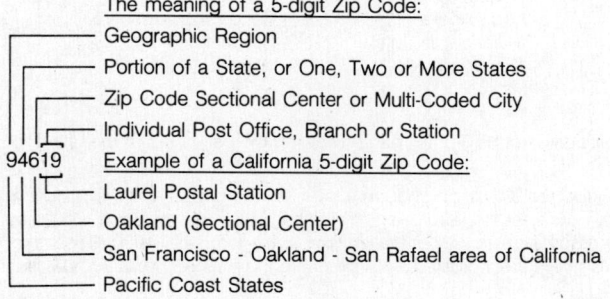

USING THE ZIP CODE FINDER

Using the Rand McNally *Zip Code Finder* is easy. If you have the name of a city or town, but don't know its zip code, check the basic listings.

The basic listings are organized by state. Cities and towns are arranged alphabetically within each state.

Since it is not uncommon for the name of a city or town to occur more than once within a state, the *Zip Code Finder* differentiates between such cities or towns in several ways. First, if a city or town has the same name as another city or town, but is located in a different county, the *Zip Code Finder* will list the county in which the city or town is located. The county will be listed in parenthesis following the name of the city or town for all places that have a name which is identical to the name of another place within the same state. For example:

      Altamont (Effingham County).......................   62411
      Altamont (Madison County).........................   62035

In most cases, listing the county in which a city or town is located will differentiate between places with the same name. However, since the *Zip Code Finder* also lists townships and "towns,"* places that are "part of" other places, places that are defined by the Bureau of the Census, and several other types of localities, additional differentiation is also shown in parenthesis following the name of the place. For example:

      Ashford   06278
      Ashford (Town)..........   06250

In this case, the first listing refers to a single community that has the same name as the larger civil division which contains it and several other communities or places as well. The zip code for the larger civil division is shown in the second listing.

For places with more than one zip code, the *Zip Code Finder* provides the *range* of zip codes as shown below:

      Belleville   62220-25
      For specific Belleville Zip Codes
      call (618) 233-0291

In this example, the hyphenated numbers indicate the zip code range for Belleville. To obtain the zip code for a specific address within this multi-coded city, telephone the number shown.

In addition to the telephone number for zip code information, a 5-digit zip code map is provided for each of the following cities:

- Atlanta, GA
- Boston, MA
- Chicago, IL
- Dallas, TX
- Detroit, MI
- Kansas City, KS
- Los Angeles, CA
- Minneapolis, MN
- New York, NY
- Philadelphia, PA
- San Francisco, CA
- St. Paul, MN
- Washington, DC

The 5-digit zip code map appears on the first full page following the beginning of the listing for each city shown above.

The *Zip Code Finder* also includes 3-digit zip code maps for the fifty states and the District of Columbia. Cities, counties, county seats, and 3-digit Sectional Areas are all shown on these maps. In addition, these maps provide a population key based on the 1980 Census of Population, and Sectional Centers are indicated by a circle around their respective population symbols.

Zip Codes for selected hospitals, military installations, hotels, motels, banks, savings and loans, colleges, and universities are also listed for the 50 largest U.S. cities.

* In certain states, the civil divisions know as "townships" or "towns" have significant local importance. These civil divisions frequently include several distinct communities or places, and one of these places may bear the same name as the civil division. In the *Zip Code Finder*, "townships" are included in the listings for Illinois, Indiana, Michigan, Ohio, New Jersey and Pennsylvania, and "towns" are included for Connecticut, Maine, Massachusetts, New Hampshire, New York, Rhode Island, Vermont and Wisconsin.

STANDARD ABBREVIATIONS FOR ADDRESSES

Listed below are two-letter state abbrevations which can be used in addressing mail.

Two-Letter State Abbreviations

Alabama AL	Kentucky KY	North Dakota ND
Alaska AK	Louisiana LA	Ohio OH
Arizona AZ	Maine ME	Oklahoma OK
Arkansas AR	Maryland MD	Oregon OR
California CA	Massachusetts MA	Pennsylvania PA
Colorado CO	Michigan MI	Rhode Island RI
Connecticut CT	Minnesota MN	South Carolina SC
Delaware DE	Mississippi MS	South Dakota SD
District of Columbia DC	Missouri MO	Tennessee TN
Florida FL	Montana MT	Texas TX
Georgia GA	Nebraska NE	Utah UT
Hawaii HI	Nevada NV	Vermont VT
Idaho ID	New Hampshire NH	Virginia VA
Illinois IL	New Jersey NJ	Washington WA
Indiana IN	New Mexico NM	West Virginia WV
Iowa IA	New York NY	Wisconsin WI
Kansas KS	North Carolina NC	Wyoming WY

SELECTED TOLL - FREE RESERVATION NUMBERS

To save you time and facilitate your reservations needs, the following toll-free reservation numbers are provided for selected lodging accommodations, car rental services and major airlines. (All numbers listed were effective at time of publication.)

AIRLINES

American
800-433-7300

Braniff
800-BRANIFF

Continental
800-525-0280

Delta
800-221-1212

Eastern
800-EASTERN

Northwest
800-225-2525

Pan American
800-221-1111

TWA
800-221-2000

United
800-241-6522

U.S. Air
800-428-4322

HOTEL/MOTELS

Best Western
International, Inc.
800-528-1234

Days Inn
800-325-2525

Embassy Suites
800-362-2779

Fairmont Hotels
800-527-4727

Guest Quarters
800-424-2900

Harley Hotels
800-321-2323

Helmsley Hotels
800-221-4982

Holiday Inns
800-HOLIDAY

Howard Johnson's
Motor Lodges
800-654-2000

Hyatt Hotels Corp
800-228-9000

Marriott
800-228-9290

Omni/Supranational
Hotels
800-843-6664

Preferred Hotels
800-323-7500

Quality Inns
800-228-5151

Radisson Hotels Int'l
800-333-3333

Ramada Inns, Inc.
800-228-2828

Regent International
Hotels
800-545-4000

Sheraton Hotels
& Motor Inns
800-325-3535

Stouffer Hotels & Resorts
800-468-3571

Westin Hotels
800-228-3000

CAR RENTAL COMPANIES

Agency Rent-A-Car
800-321-1972
800-362-1794 (Ohio only)

Alamo Rent-A-Car
800-327-9633

Allstate Rent-A-Car
800-634-6186 (except NV)

American International
Rent-A-Car
800-527-0202

Avis Reservations Center
800-331-1212 (Domestic)
800-331-1084 (International)

Budget Rent-A-Car
800-527-0700

Enterprise Rent-A-Car
800-325-8007

Hertz Corporation
800-654-3131

Holiday Payless
Rent-A-Car Int'l Inc.
800-237-2804

National Car Rental
800-328-4567

Sears Rent-A-Car
800-527-0770

Thrifty Rent-A-Car
800-367-2277

Value Rent-A-Car
800-327-2501

TELEPHONE AREA CODE AND TIME ZONE INFORMATION

The following tables list telephone area codes used in the United States. The first table is arranged in alphabetical order by state. The second table lists telephone area codes in numerical order.

The United States (including Alaska and Hawaii) is divided longitudinally into six time zones. If you were traveling from east to west, you would pass through the time zones in the following order: Eastern Standard Time (EST), Central Standard Time (CST), Mountain Standard Time (MST), Pacific Standard Time (PST), Alaska Time (AK), and Hawaii Time (HI).

Each time you enter a new time zone, it becomes one hour earlier. When it is 5 p.m. Eastern Standard Time (EST), it is 4 p.m. Central Standard Time (CST), 3 p.m. Mountain Standard Time (MST), etc. For your convenience, the appropriate time zone is listed in parentheses after each area code below. The map on pages 12 and 13 details the time zone boundaries.

Aphabetical List of Telephone Area Codes

Alabama	205
Montgomery (CST)	205
Alaska (AK-HI)	907
Juneau (AK)	907
Arizona (MST)	602
Phoenix (MST)	602
Arkansas	501
Little Rock (CST)	501
California	
Bakersfield (PST)	805
Eureka (PST)	707
Fresno (PST)	209
Los Angeles (PST)	213
Pasadena (PST)	818
Riverside (PST)	714
Sacramento (PST)	916
San Diego (PST)	619
San Francisco (PST)	415
San Jose (PST)	408
Colorado	
Colorado Springs (MST)	719
Denver (MST)	303
Connecticut	203
Hartford (EST)	203
Delaware	302
Dover (EST)	302
District of Columbia	202
Washington (EST)	202
Florida (CST,EST)	
Jacksonville (EST)	904
Miami (EST)	305
Orlando (EST)	407
St. Petersburg (EST)	813
Tallahassee (EST)	904
Georgia	
Atlanta (EST)	404
Savannah (EST)	912
Hawaii (HI)	808
Honolulu (AK-HI)	808
Idaho (MST,PST)	208
Boise (MST)	208
Illinois	
Chicago (CST)	312
Aurora (CST)	708
Peoria (CST)	309
Rockford (CST)	815
Springfield (CST)	217
West Frankfort (CST)	618
Indiana (CST,EST)	
Evansville (EST)	812
Indianapolis (EST)	317
South Bend (EST)	219
Iowa	
Council Bluffs (CST)	712
Des Moines (CST)	515
Dubuque (CST)	319
Kansas (CST,MST)	
Topeka (CST)	913
Wichita (CST)	316
Kentucky (CST,EST)	
Covington (EST)	606
Frankfort (EST)	502
Louisville (EST)	502
Louisiana	
Baton Rouge (CST)	504
New Orleans (CST)	504
Shreveport (CST)	318
Maine	207
Augusta (EST)	207
Maryland	301
Annapolis (EST)	301
Massachusetts	
Boston (EST)	617
Lowell (EST)	508
Springfield (EST)	413
Michigan (CST,EST)	
Detroit (EST)	313
Escanaba (EST)	906
Grand Rapids (EST)	616
Lansing (EST)	517
Minnesota	
Duluth (CST)	218
Minneapolis (CST)	612
Rochester (CST)	507
St. Paul (CST)	612
Mississippi	601
Jackson (CST)	601

TELEPHONE AREA CODE AND
TIME ZONE INFORMATION, CONT'D.

Aphabetical List of Telephone Area Codes, continued

Missouri
    Jefferson City (CST) 314
    Kansas City (CST) 816
    St. Louis (CST) 314
    Springfield (CST) 417
Montana 406
    Helena (MST) 406
Nebraska (CST,MST)
    Lincoln (CST) 402
    North Platte (CST) 308
    Omaha (CST) 402
Nevada 702
    Carson City (PST) 702
New Hampshire 603
    Concord (EST) 603
New Jersey
    Newark (EST) 201
    Trenton (EST) 609
New Mexico 505
    Santa Fe (MST) 505
New York
    Albany (EST) 518
    Binghamton (EST) 607
    Buffalo (EST) 716
    Hempstead (EST) 516
    New York (EST) 212
    New York (EST) 718
    White Plains (EST) 914
North Carolina
    Charlotte (EST) 704
    Raleigh (EST) 919
North Dakota (CST,MST) 701
    Bismark (CST) 701
Ohio
    Cincinnati (EST) 513
    Cleveland (EST) 216
    Columbus (EST) 614
    Toledo (EST) 419
Oklahoma
    Oklahoma City (CST) 405
    Tulsa (CST) 918
Oregon (MST,PST) 503
    Salem (PST) 503

Pennsylvania
    Erie (EST) 814
    Harrisburg (EST) 717
    Philadelphia (EST) 215
    Pittsburgh (EST) 412
Rhode Island 401
    Providence (EST) 401
South Carolina 803
    Columbia (EST) 803
South Dakota (CST,MST) 605
    Pierre (CST) 605
Tennessee (CST,EST)
    Memphis (CST) 901
    Nashville (CST) 615
Texas (CST,MST)
    Abilene (CST) 915
    Amarillo (CST) 806
    Austin (CST) 512
    Beaumont (CST) 409
    Dallas (CST) 214
    Fort Worth (CST) 817
    Houston (CST) 713
    San Antonio (CST) 512
Utah 801
    Salt Lake City (MST) 801
Vermont 802
    Montpelier (EST) 802
Virginia
    Richmond (EST) 804
    Roanoke (EST) 703
Washington
    Olympia (PST) 206
    Seattle (PST) 206
    Spokane (PST) 509
West Virginia
    Charleston (EST) 304
Wisconsin
    Eau Claire (CST) 715
    Madison (CST) 608
    Milwaukee (CST) 414
Wyoming 307
    Cheyenne (MST) 307

Numerical List of Telephone Area Codes

Area Code	Location (Time Zone)
201	New Jersey (EST)
202	District of Columbia (EST)
203	Connecticut (EST)
205	Alabama (CST)
206	Washington (PST)
207	Maine (EST)
208	Idaho (MST,PST)
209	California (PST)

Area Code	Location (Time Zone)
212	New York (EST)
213	California (PST)
214	Texas (CST)
215	Pennsylvania (EST)
216	Ohio (EST)
217	Illinois (CST)
218	Minnesota (CST)
219	Indiana (CST,EST)

TELEPHONE AREA CODE AND TIME ZONE INFORMATION, CONT'D.

Numerical List of Telephone Area Codes, continued

Area Code	Location (Time Zone)	Area Code	Location (Time Zone)
301......	Maryland (EST)	608......	Wisconsin (CST)
302......	Delaware (EST)	609......	New Jersey (EST)
303......	Colorado (MST)	612......	Minnesota (CST)
304......	West Virginia (EST)	614......	Ohio (EST)
305......	Florida (EST)	615......	Tennessee (CST,EST)
307......	Wyoming (MST)	616......	Michigan (EST)
308......	Nebraska (CST,MST)	617......	Massachusetts (EST)
309......	Illinois (CST)	618......	Illinois (CST)
312......	Illinois (CST)	619......	California (PST)
313......	Michigan (EST)	701......	North Dakota (CST,MST)
314......	Missouri (CST)	702......	Nevada (PST)
315......	New York (EST)	703......	Virginia (EST)
316......	Kansas (CST,MST)	704......	North Carolina (EST)
317......	Indiana (EST)	707......	California (PST)
318......	Louisiana (CST)	708......	Illinois (CST)
319......	Iowa (CST)	712......	Iowa (CST)
401......	Rhode Island (EST)	713......	Texas (CST)
402......	Nebraska (CST,MST)	714......	California (PST)
404......	Georgia (EST)	715......	Wisconsin (CST)
405......	Oklahoma (CST)	716......	New York (EST)
406......	Montana (MST)	717......	Pennsylvania (EST)
407......	Florida (EST)	718......	New York (EST)
408......	California (PST)	719......	Colorado (MST)
409......	Texas (CST)	800......	Inward Watts
412......	Pennsylvania (EST)	801......	Utah (MST)
413......	Massachusetts (EST)	802......	Vermont (EST)
414......	Wisconsin (CST)	803......	South Carolina (EST)
415......	California (PST)	804......	Virginia (EST)
417......	Missouri (CST)	805......	California (PST)
419......	Ohio (EST)	806......	Texas (CST)
501......	Arkansas (CST)	808......	Hawaii (AK-HI)
502......	Kentucky (CST,EST)	812......	Indiana (CST,EST)
503......	Oregon (MST,PST)	813......	Florida (EST)
504......	Louisiana (CST)	814......	Pennsylvania (EST)
505......	New Mexico (MST)	815......	Illinois (CST)
507......	Minnesota (CST)	816......	Missouri (CST)
508......	Massachusetts (EST)	817......	Texas (CST)
509......	Washington (PST)	818......	California (PST)
512......	Texas (CST)	901......	Tennessee (CST)
513......	Ohio (EST)	904......	Florida (CST,EST)
515......	Iowa (CST)	906......	Michigan (CST,EST)
516......	New York (EST)	907......	Alaska (AK-HI)
517......	Michigan (EST)	912......	Georgia (EST)
518......	New York (EST)	913......	Kansas (CST,MST)
601......	Mississippi (CST)	914......	New York (EST)
602......	Arizona (MST)	915......	Texas (CST,MST)
603......	New Hampshire (EST)	916......	California (PST)
605......	South Dakota (CST,MST)	918......	Oklahoma (CST)
606......	Kentucky (EST)	919......	North Carolina (EST)
607......	New York (EST)		

12 TELEPHONE AREA CODE/TIME ZONE MAP

TELEPHONE AREA CODE/TIME ZONE MAP 13

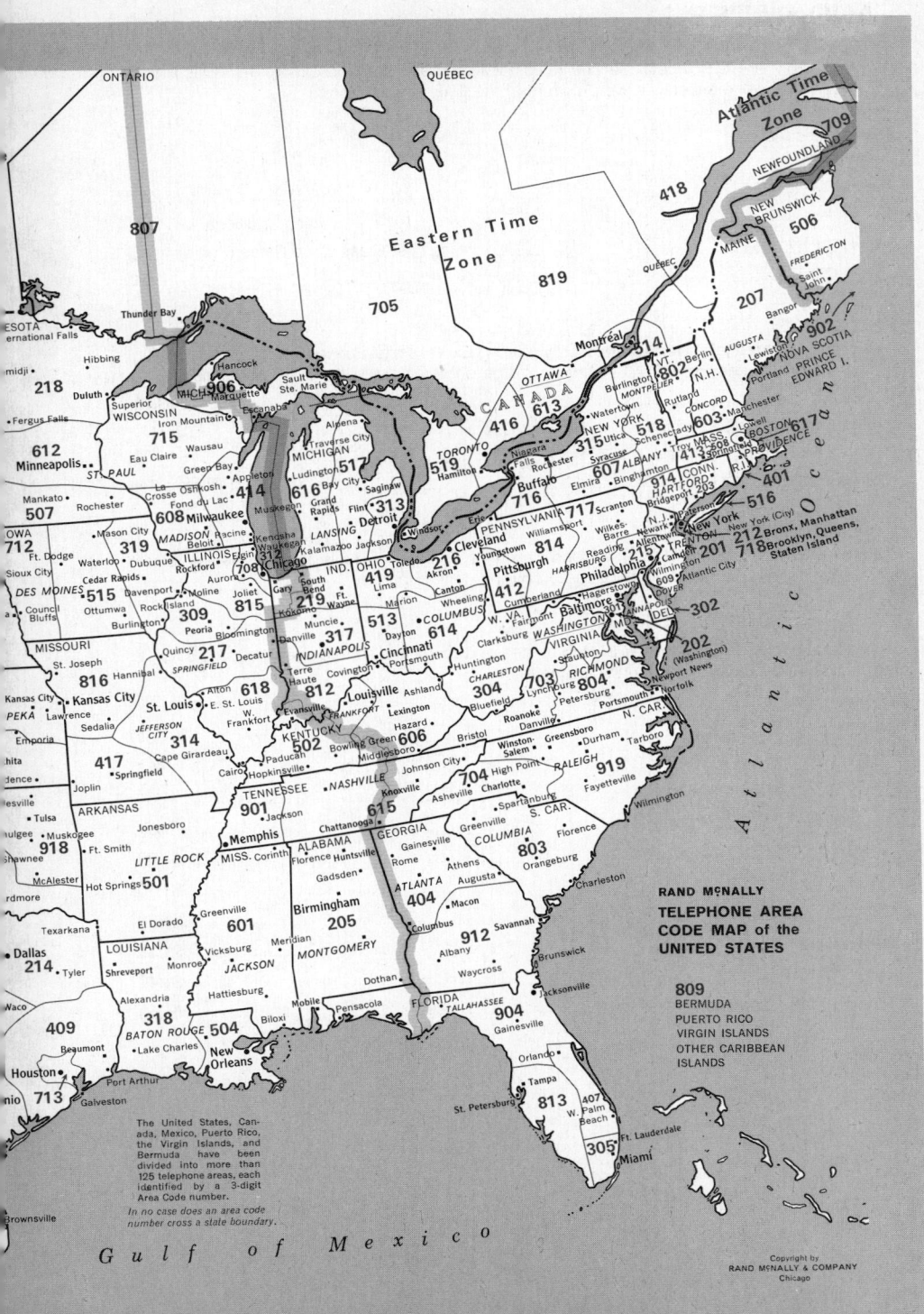

DOMESTIC POSTAL REGULATIONS AND RATES

Listed below are U.S. Postal Service rates for First-Class, Second-Class, Third-Class, and Express Mail. (All rates shown were current at the time of publication.)

First-Class Mail
Letters
11 oz. or less .... first oz. 25¢
each additional oz. 20¢
Over 11 oz. .... Use First Class Zone Rates (Priority Mail)
Post Cards .... 15¢

Express Mail
Packages that are taken to a postal facility offering Express Mail Service, and addressed to an area which also has Express Mail Service, will be delivered next day to the addressee.
½ lb. or less $8.75
Over 1 lb. and up to 2 lbs. $12.00
Over 2 lbs. and up to 5 lbs. $15.00
6 lbs. up to 70 lbs. .... Consult Postmaster

Second-Class Mail
Newspapers and periodicals with second-class mail privileges. Rate is applicable single piece third- or fourth-class rate for copies mailed by the general public.

Third-Class Mail
Circulars, books, catalogs, other printed matter, and merchandise, etc. weighing less than 16 oz. Over 16 oz., mail at the fourth-class rate.
Single Piece Rate
0 to 1 oz. .... 25¢
Over 1 to 2 ozs. .... 45¢
Over 2 to 3 ozs. .... 65¢
Over 3 to 4 ozs. .... 85¢
Over 4 to 6 ozs. $1.00
Over 6 to 8 ozs. $1.10
Over 8 to 10 ozs. $1.20
Over 10 to 12 ozs. $1.30
Over 12 to 14 ozs. $1.40
Over 14 but less than 16 ozs. $1.50

SMALL PARCEL RATES

Ground service rates for packages of 1 to 20 pounds are shown for the U.S. Postal Service, United Parcel Service (UPS), and Roadway Package System (RPS). Air freight rates for packages of 1 to 5 pounds and express letters, are also shown for selected air freight companies. (All rates shown were current at the time publication.)

In order to use the ground zone rate charts presented below for the U.S. Postal Service, United Parcel Service (UPS), and Roadway Package System (RPS), you will need to contact the carrier of your choice and request the zone chart that applies to your specific geographic location. This chart will enable you to determine the zone which corresponds to the destination of your parcel. Contact your local post office or UPS office; RPS may be contacted by calling the toll-free number which appears beneath the RPS Ground Zones Chart.

GROUND SERVICE RATES

United States Post Office Parcel Post Rates

First-Class Zone Rates (Priority Mail): All first-class mail weighting over 12 oz. Maximum weight is 70 lbs., size is limited to 108 inches in combined length and girth.

Weight over 12 oz. and not exceeding	Local 1, 2 & 3	4	5	6	7	8
1 #	$ 2.40	$ 2.40	$ 2.40	$ 2.40	$ 2.40	$ 2.40
2 #	2.40	2.40	2.40	2.40	2.40	2.40
3 #	2.74	3.16	3.45	3.74	3.96	4.32
4 #	3.18	3.75	4.13	4.53	4.92	5.33
5 #	3.61	4.32	4.86	5.27	5.81	6.37
6 #	4.15	5.08	5.71	6.31	6.91	7.66
7 #	4.58	5.66	6.39	7.09	7.80	8.67
8 #	5.00	6.23	7.07	7.87	8.68	9.68
9 #	5.43	6.81	7.76	8.66	9.57	10.69
10 #	5.85	7.39	8.44	9.44	10.45	11.70
11 #	6.27	7.97	9.12	10.22	11.33	12.71
12 #	6.70	8.55	9.81	11.01	12.22	13.72
13 #	7.12	9.12	10.49	11.79	13.10	14.73
14 #	7.55	9.70	11.17	12.57	13.99	15.74
15 #	7.97	10.28	11.86	13.36	14.87	16.75
16 #	8.39	10.86	12.54	14.14	15.75	17.75
17 #	8.82	11.44	13.22	14.92	16.64	18.76
18 #	9.24	12.01	13.90	15.70	17.52	19.77
19 #	9.67	12.59	14.59	16.49	18.41	20.78
20 #	10.09	13.17	15.27	17.27	19.29	21.79

For additional rate information, call your local Post Office.

SMALL PARCEL RATES, CONT'D.

United Parcel Service (UPS)

Ground Zones

Weight not to exceed	2	3	4	5	6	7	8
1 #	$ 1.63	$ 1.77	$ 1.93	$ 2.01	$ 2.09	$ 2.19	$ 2.28
2 #	1.64	1.78	2.16	2.28	2.46	2.62	2.81
3 #	1.72	1.93	2.34	2.53	2.77	3.03	3.28
4 #	1.81	2.08	2.53	2.72	3.04	3.35	3.69
5 #	1.90	2.17	2.62	2.85	3.23	3.61	4.01
6 #	1.99	2.21	2.68	2.93	3.33	3.77	4.23
7 #	2.07	2.23	2.73	3.01	3.47	3.97	4.47
8 #	2.16	2.27	2.81	3.21	3.74	4.29	4.87
9 #	2.27	2.38	2.96	3.39	4.00	4.61	5.27
10 #	2.35	2.49	3.09	3.56	4.23	4.93	5.64
11 #	2.45	2.60	3.23	3.78	4.48	5.27	6.08
12 #	2.56	2.74	3.40	3.99	4.79	5.62	6.50
13 #	2.63	2.86	3.58	4.21	5.08	5.99	6.93
14 #	2.67	2.99	3.77	4.42	5.36	6.33	7.36
15 #	2.74	3.11	3.93	4.65	5.64	6.70	7.79
16 #	2.81	3.24	4.10	4.88	5.94	7.05	8.22
17 #	2.86	3.37	4.27	5.09	6.22	7.40	8.65
18 #	2.95	3.49	4.44	5.31	6.50	7.76	9.07
19 #	3.06	3.64	4.62	5.52	6.80	8.12	9.50
20 #	3.18	3.77	4.79	5.75	7.08	8.46	9.93

For additional rate information, contact your local United Parcel Service office.

Roadway Package System (RPS)

Ground Zones

Weight not to exceed	2	3	4	5	6	7	8
1 #	$ 1.63	$ 1.77	$ 1.93	$ 2.01	$ 2.09	$ 2.19	$ 2.28
2 #	1.64	1.78	2.16	2.28	2.46	2.62	2.81
3 #	1.72	1.93	2.34	2.53	2.77	3.03	3.28
4 #	1.81	2.08	2.53	2.72	3.04	3.35	3.69
5 #	1.90	2.17	2.62	2.85	3.23	3.61	4.01
6 #	1.99	2.21	2.68	2.93	3.33	3.77	4.23
7 #	2.07	2.23	2.73	3.01	3.47	3.97	4.47
8 #	2.16	2.27	2.81	3.21	3.74	4.29	4.87
9 #	2.27	2.38	2.96	3.39	4.00	4.61	5.27
10 #	2.35	2.49	3.09	3.56	4.23	4.93	5.64
11 #	2.45	2.60	3.23	3.78	4.48	5.27	6.08
12 #	2.56	2.74	3.40	3.99	4.79	5.62	6.50
13 #	2.63	2.86	3.58	4.21	5.08	5.99	6.93
14 #	2.67	2.99	3.77	4.42	5.36	6.33	7.36
15 #	2.74	3.11	3.93	4.65	5.64	6.70	7.79
16 #	2.81	3.24	4.10	4.88	5.94	7.05	8.22
17 #	2.86	3.37	4.27	5.09	6.22	7.40	8.65
18 #	2.95	3.49	4.44	5.31	6.50	7.76	9.07
19 #	3.06	3.64	4.62	5.52	6.80	8.12	9.50
20 #	3.18	3.77	4.79	5.75	7.08	8.46	9.93

For additional rate information, call 1-800-ROADPAK.

SMALL PARCEL RATES, CONT'D.

AIR FREIGHT RATES FOR SELECTED PRIVATE CARRIERS

With the exception of UPS, most private carriers offer a variety of services, including overnight and second-day delivery. Most provide free envelopes and shipping containers and offer discounts for drop-off by the sender.

All of the private carriers listed provide pick-up as well as delivery. Most have drop-off boxes available in convenient locations. Next-day air and second-day air delivery times vary by carrier.

For your convenience in obtaining additional information on rates for heavier shipments, multiple shipments and frequent shipper discounts, toll-free numbers have been included in the rate tables. (All rates shown were current at the time of publication. Rates are subject to change without notice.)

United Parcel Service (UPS)

Overnight Letter

Weight (lbs.)	Prices All States
	$9.00

Next-Day Air (Per Pkg.)

Weight (lbs.)	Prices (48 States & Hawaii)
1	$12.00
2	13.00
3	14.25
4	15.25
5	16.50

2nd-Day Air (Per Pkg.)

Weight (lbs.)	Prices 48 States	Hawaii & Alaska
1	$4.00	$ 6.50
2	5.00	8.00
3	5.50	9.00
4	6.00	10.50
5	7.00	11.50

Federal Express (1-800-238-5355)

Overnight Letter

Weight (lbs.)	Price *
up to 8 oz.	$15.50

Early Morning Services (Priority/Courier-Pak Service) (Per Pkg.)

Weight (lbs.)	Prices *
1	$22.50
2	24.25
3	27.00
4	29.75
5	32.50

One-to-Two Day Service (Per Pkg.)

Weight (lbs.)	Prices *
1	$15.50
2	16.50
3	17.50
4	18.50
5	19.50

Airbourne (1-800-328-4937; Washington state 1-800-562-2227)

Overnight Letter

Weight (lbs.)	Price *
up to 8 oz.	$14.00

Express "One" Pkg. Charges NEXT DAY AIR (Per Pkg/Door to Door)

Weight (lbs.)	Prices *
1	$14.00
2	25.00
3	30.00
4	36.00
5	38.00

SMALL PARCEL RATES, CONT'D.

Emery (1-800-HI-EMERY)
For specific rate information, call Emery's 800 number above.

Burlington Air Express (1-800-CALL-BAX)
For specific rate information, call 1-800-528-8110.

* Prices not applicable for shipments from Continental U.S. to or between Alaska and Hawaii.
  Contact the "800" numbers for further information.

U.S. POSTAL SERVICE FIELD DIVISION OFFICES

The following is a list of Marketing and Communications Directors for each of the Postal Services 74 divisions. In the event that you have questions about mailing procedures, rates or regulations, contact the appropriate divisional office. The listings below were current at the time of publication and are subject to change.

NORTHEAST REGION

Albany, NY Division
Director, Marketing & Communications
Barry Brennan (518) 452-2472

Boston, MA Division
Director, Marketing & Communications
Lois A. Murphy (617) 654-5700

Brooklyn, NY Division
Director, Marketing & Communications
Lois Wertemberger (718) 834-3307

Buffalo, NY Division
Director, Marketing & Communications
Nicholas A. Fabozzi (716) 846-2505

Caribbean Division
Director, Marketing & Communications
Ivan O. Puig (809) 766-5058

Hartford, CT Division
Director, Marketing & Communications
Bruce Parmiter (203) 524-6077

Hicksville, NY Division
Director, Marketing & Communications
Salvatore Sparacino (516) 755-2770

Manchester, NH Division
Director, Marketing & Communications
Paul Beaver (603) 644-3816

Newark, NJ Division
Director, Marketing & Communications
Sidney McAbee (201) 669-0770

New Brunswick, NJ Division
Director, Marketing & Communications
John McCarthy (201) 819-3602

New York, NY Division
Director, Marketing & Communications
John L. Ghisoni (212) 330-3070

Providence, RI Division
Director, Marketing & Communications
Spiro Kyriakakis (401) 838-6958

Queens, NY Division
Director, Marketing & Communications
Betty A. Rowe (718) 321-5088

Springfield, MA Division
Acting Director, Marketing & Communications
Dickey Rustin (413) 731-0504

Westchester, NY Division
Director, Marketing & Communications
Theresa Whalen (914) 345-1238

EASTERN REGION

Baltimore, MD Division
Director, Marketing & Communications
John J. Dials (301) 347-4516

Charleston, WV Division
Director, Marketing & Communications
Carolyn B. Drury (304) 340-4235

Cincinnati, OH Division
Director, Marketing & Communications
M. Lee Terry (513) 684-5489

Cleveland, OH Division
Director, Marketing & Communications
Jacqueline A. Sue (216) 443-4076

Columbia, SC Division
Director, Marketing & Communications
James R. Smith, Jr. (803) 731-5900

Columbus, OH Division
Director, Marketing & Communications
Edlen G. Johnson (614) 469-4412

Greensboro, NC Division
Acting Director, Marketing & Communications
Dee Zane (919) 668-1208

Harrisburg, PA Division
Acting Director, Marketing & Communications
Bill Brady (717) 231-3700

Louisville, KY Division
Director, Marketing & Communications
Dennis W. Patti (502) 454-1788

Philadelphia, PA Division
Director, Marketing & Communications
Richard F. Nye (215) 895-8810

Pittsburgh, PA Division
Director, Marketing & Communications
James S. Gall (412) 359-7851

U.S. POSTAL SERVICE FIELD DIVISION OFFICES, CONT'D.

EASTERN REGION, CONT'D.

Richmond, VA Division
Director, Marketing & Communications
Gail Sonnenberg (804) 775-6137

South Jersey Division
Director, Marketing & Communications
Michael E. Kurtzman (609) 933-4245

Southern MD Division
Director, Marketing & Communications
Kent B. Smith (301) 499-7561

SOUTHERN REGION

Atlanta, GA Division
Director, Marketing & Communications
(404) 765-7254

Birmingham, AL Division
Director, Marketing & Communications
Albert W. Young (205) 521-0416

Dallas, TX Division
Director, Marketing & Communications
Gerald R. Carr (214) 819-7179

Houston, TX Division
Director, Marketing & Communications
Richard M. Sanchez (713) 226-3713

Jackson, MS Division
Director, Marketing & Communications
Robert Rankin (601) 968-0505

Jacksonville, FL Division
Director, Marketing & Communications
Cheryl Pawlowski (904) 359-2929

Little Rock, AR Division
Director, Marketing & Communications
Paul D. Watkins (501) 371-0301

Memphis, TN Division
Director, Marketing & Communications
John V. Rountree (901) 521-2182

Miami, FL Division
Director, Marketing & Communications
Marjorie M. Brown (305) 470-0232

Nashville, TN Division
Director, Marketing & Communications
Robert C. Wilfong (615) 885-9113

New Orleans, LA Division
Director, Marketing & Communications
Anthony J. Brescia (504) 589-1117

Oklahoma City, OK Division
Director, Marketing & Communications
(405) 278-6111

San Antonio, TX Division
Director, Marketing & Communications
Richard W. Stephens (512) 657-8500

Tampa, FL Division
Director, Marketing & Communications
Virginia L. Ramos (813) 877-0825

CENTRAL REGION

Chicago, IL Division
Director, Marketing & Communications
Helen G. Rogers, Jr. (312) 765-3034

Denver, CO Division
Director, Marketing & Communications
Richard Abell (303) 297-6112

Des Moines, IA Division
Director, Marketing & Communications
Samuel C. Gonzalez (515) 283-7593

Detroit, MI Division
Director, Marketing & Communications
Marilyn Terrell (313) 226-8634

Grand Rapids, MI Division
Director, Marketing & Communications
Earl S. Douglas (616) 776-6156

Indianapolis, IN Division
Director, Marketing & Communications
Bernard A. Dargo (317) 464-6452

Kansas City, MO Division
Director, Marketing & Communications
Nathan Henderson (816) 374-9170

Milwaukee, WI Division
Director, Marketing & Communications
William J. Matheson (414) 287-2520

Minneapolis, MN Division
Director, Marketing & Communications
John J. Kelliher (612) 349-4992

North Suburban, IL Division
Director, Marketing & Communications
Wayne J. Gardner (708) 451-5780

U.S. POSTAL SERVICE FIELD DIVISION OFFICES, CONT'D.

CENTRAL REGION, CONT'D.

Omaha, NE Division
Director, Marketing & Communications
Donald R. Warner (402) 348-2550

St. Louis, MO Division
Director, Marketing & Communications
Robert W. Roberts (314) 436-4505

St. Paul, MN Division
Director, Marketing & Communications
M. Lee Terry (612) 293-3326

South Suburban, IL Division
Director, Marketing & Communications
Steven E. Onstot (708) 563-5565

Wichita, KS Division
Director, Marketing & Communications
Larry Dingman (316) 946-4615

WESTERN REGION

Anchorage, AK Division
Director, Marketing & Communications
Margaret Parsons (907) 261-5418

Honolulu, HI Division
Director, Marketing & Communications
Glen Sakagawa (808) 423-3808

Long Beach, CA Division
Director, Marketing & Communications
Rufus F. Porter (213) 432-5611

Los Angeles, CA Division
Director, Marketing & Communications
Ronald G. Barco (213) 586-1475

Oakland, CA Division
Director, Marketing & Communications
Linda A. Deaktor (415) 874-8293

Phoenix, AZ Division
Director, Marketing & Communications
Ronald C. Abalos (602) 225-3100

Portland, OR Division
Director, Marketing & Communications
Barbara VanArsdall (503) 294-2305

Sacramento, CA Division
Director, Marketing & Communications
E. Jackson Bryant (916) 923-3141

Salt Lake City, UT Division
Director, Marketing & Communications
Warren Philips (801) 974-2304

San Diego, CA Division
Director, Marketing & Communications
Gerald W. Vega (619) 221-3326

San Francisco, CA Division
Director, Marketing & Communications
Dolores M. Farrelly (415) 550-5276

San Jose, CA Division
Director, Marketing & Communications
(408) 723-6100

Santa Ana, CA Division
Director, Marketing & Communications
(714) 662-6223

Seattle, WA Division
Director, Marketing & Communications
Peter A. Craft (206) 442-6032

Tucson, AZ Division
Director, Marketing & Communications
Polo J. Martinez, Jr. (602) 325-9815

Van Nuys, CA Division
Director, Marketing & Communications
Arthur O. Martinez (818) 908-6960

Abanda-Blountsville ALABAMA 23

Name	ZIP
Abanda	36274
Abbeville	36310
Abel	36258
Abercrombie	35042
Aberfoil	36089
Abernant	35440
Abernathy	36264
Acipcoville (Part of Birmingham)	35207
Ackerville	36768
Acmar	35094
Active	36793
Ada	36069
Adamsburg	35967
Adamsville	35005
Addison	35540
Adger	35006
Adler	36779
Ai	36264
Aimwell	36782
Airport Highlands (Part of Birmingham)	35206
Akron	35441
Alabama City (Part of Gadsden)	35904
Alabama Fork	35611
Alabama Port	36523
Alabama Shores	35660
Alabaster	35007
Alaga	36343
Alberta	36720
Alberta City (Part of Tuscaloosa)	35401
Alberton	36453
Albertville	35950
Alder Springs	35950
Aldrich	35115
Aldridge	35580
Aldridge Grove	35650
Alexander City	35010
Alexandria	36250
Alexis	35960
Aliceville	35442
Allen	36419
Allens Crossroads	35175
Allenton	36768
Allenton Station	36768
Allenville (Hale County)	36738
Allenville (Marengo County)	36738
Allgood	35013
Allsboro	35616
Allsop	36272
Alma	36501
Almeria	36089
Almond	36276
Alpine (De Kalb County)	35984
Alpine (Talladega County)	35014
Altadena Valley	35243
Alton	35015
Altoona	35952
America	35580
Andalusia	36420
Anderson (Etowah County)	35901
Anderson (Lauderdale County)	35610
Andrews Chapel	35619
Angel	36265
Annemanie	36721
Anniston	36201-06
For specific Anniston Zip Codes call (205) 236-6355	
Anniston Army Depot	36201
Ansley	36081
Antioch (Calhoun County)	36253
Antioch (Covington County)	36420
Antioch (Pike County)	36081
Appleton	36426
Aqua Vista	35645
Aquilla	36558
Arab	35016
Ararat	36921
Arbacoochee	36264
Arbor Acres (Part of Huntsville)	35810
Ardell	35053
Ardilla (Part of Dothan)	36301
Ardmore	35739
Ardmore Highway (Part of Huntsville)	35805
Argo	35173
Argo Heights	35550
Arguta	36360
Ariton	36311
Arkadelphia	35033
Arkwright (Part of Vincent)	35178
Arley	35541
Arlington	36722
Armstead	35121
Armstrong	36089
Arona	35957
Arrowhead	36109

Name	ZIP
Arrowwood (Part of Tuscaloosa)	35405
Asberry	36272
Asbury (Dale County)	36360
Asbury (Marshall County)	35950
Ashbank	35578
Ashby	35035
Ashford	36312
Ashland (Clay County)	36251
Ashland (Madison County)	35811
Ashridge	35565
Ashville	35953
Aspel	35768
Athens	35611
Atkinson	36784
Atmore	36502
Attalla	35954
Atwood	35571
Auburn	36830-49
For specific Auburn Zip Codes call (205) 821-3754	
Augustin	36701
Aurora	35957
Aurora Springs	35616
Austinville (Part of Decatur)	35601
Autaugaville	36003
Avalon Park (Part of Hueytown)	35020
Avant	36033
Avery (Part of Stevenson)	35772
Avoca	35653
Avon	36312
Avondale (Part of Birmingham)	35222
Avondale Mill (Part of Alexander City)	35010
Avondale Village (Part of Pell City)	35125
Avon Park (Part of Birmingham)	35234
Awin	36768
Axis	36505
Ayres	35126
Babbie	36420
Bacon Level	36274
Bagley	35062
Bailey Springs	35645
Baileyton	35019
Baileytown	35019
Baker Hill	36004
Bald Hill	36375
Baldwin Farms	36083
Balkum	36345
Ballplay	35901
Bangor	35079
Bankhead (De Kalb County)	35984
Bankhead (Walker County)	35580
Banks	36005
Bankston	35542
Barachias (Part of Montgomery)	36064
Barber	36312
Barfield	36266
Barlow	36558
Barlow Bend	36545
Barnes	36311
Barnesville	35570
Barnett Chapel	35572
Barnett Crossroads	36426
Barney	35550
Barnisdale Forest (Part of Birmingham)	35215
Barnwell	36532
Barrytown	36908
Barton	35616
Basham	35640
Bashi	36784
Basin	36323
Bass	35772
Bassetts Creek	36585
Batesville	36053
Battelle	35989
Battens Crossroads	36316
Battleground	35179
Battles Wharf	36532
Bay Minette	36507
Bayou La Batre	36509
Bay Shore Junction (Part of Prichard)	36610
Bayside (Part of Decatur)	35603
Bay Springs	35960
Bayview	35005
Bazemore	35559
Beachwood Park (Part of Birmingham)	35212
Beamon	36360
Bean Rock	35175
Bear Creek	35543
Bear Point	36561
Beasons Mill	36264
Beatrice	36425

Name	ZIP
Beaty Crossroads (Part of Ider)	35981
Beauregard	36801
Beaverton	35544
Beaver Town	35442
Beck	36420
Beehive	36865
Bel Air (Jefferson County)	35210
Bel Air (Mobile County)	36616
Bel Air Mall (Part of Mobile)	36616
Belforest	36526
Belgreen	35653
Belk	35545
Bellamy	36901
Bellefontaine	36567
Bellefonte	35752
Bellefountaine	36582
Bellemeade	35630
Belle Mina	35615
Belleville	36401
Bellevue (Part of Gadsden)	35901
Bell Springs	35622
Bellview	36726
Bellwood (Geneva County)	36313
Bellwood (Jefferson County)	35064
Belmont	35470
Beloit	36759
Beltline (Part of Decatur)	35601
Belview Heights (Part of Tuscumbia)	35674
Bemiston (Part of Talladega)	35160
Bendale (Part of Birmingham)	35217
Benevola	35466
Benoit	35550
Bentley Hills (Part of Mountain Brook)	35216
Benton	36785
Ben Vines Gap (Part of Maytown)	35118
Berkley	35748
Berlin	35055
Bermuda (Conecuh County)	36401
Bermuda (Monroe County)	36460
Berney Points (Part of Birmingham)	35211
Berry	35546
Bertha	36353
Bessemer	35020-23
For specific Bessemer Zip Codes call (205) 428-9163	
Bessemer Gardens (Part of Hueytown)	35020
Bessemer Homestead (Part of Bessemer)	35020
Bessie	35062
Bessie Junction	35062
Bethany	35452
Bethel (Barbour County)	36311
Bethel (Cullman County)	35055
Bethel (Limestone County)	35620
Bethlehem	36046
Beulah (Covington County)	36467
Beulah (Greene County)	35469
Beulah (Lee County)	36854
Beverly Station (Part of Birmingham)	35211
Bexar	35570
Bibbville	35188
Biddle Crossroads (Part of Henagar)	35978
Bigbee	36510
Big Creek	36301
Big Oak	35645
Big Springs	35188
Billingsley	36006
Billy Goat Hill	35960
Birdine	36740
Birdsong	35055
Birmingham	35201-61
For specific Birmingham Zip Codes call (205) 521-0451	
Birmingham Green (Part of Birmingham)	35237
Birwat (Part of Tarrant)	35217
Bishop	35616
Biven	35214
Black	36314
Blackankle	35768
Black Creek	35207
Black Diamond	35023
Black Rock	36042
Blacksher	36507
Blackwood	36345
Bladon Springs	36919
Blanche	35973
Blanton	36854
Bleecker	36874
Blossburg	35073
Blount Springs	35079
Blountsville	35031

24 ALABAMA

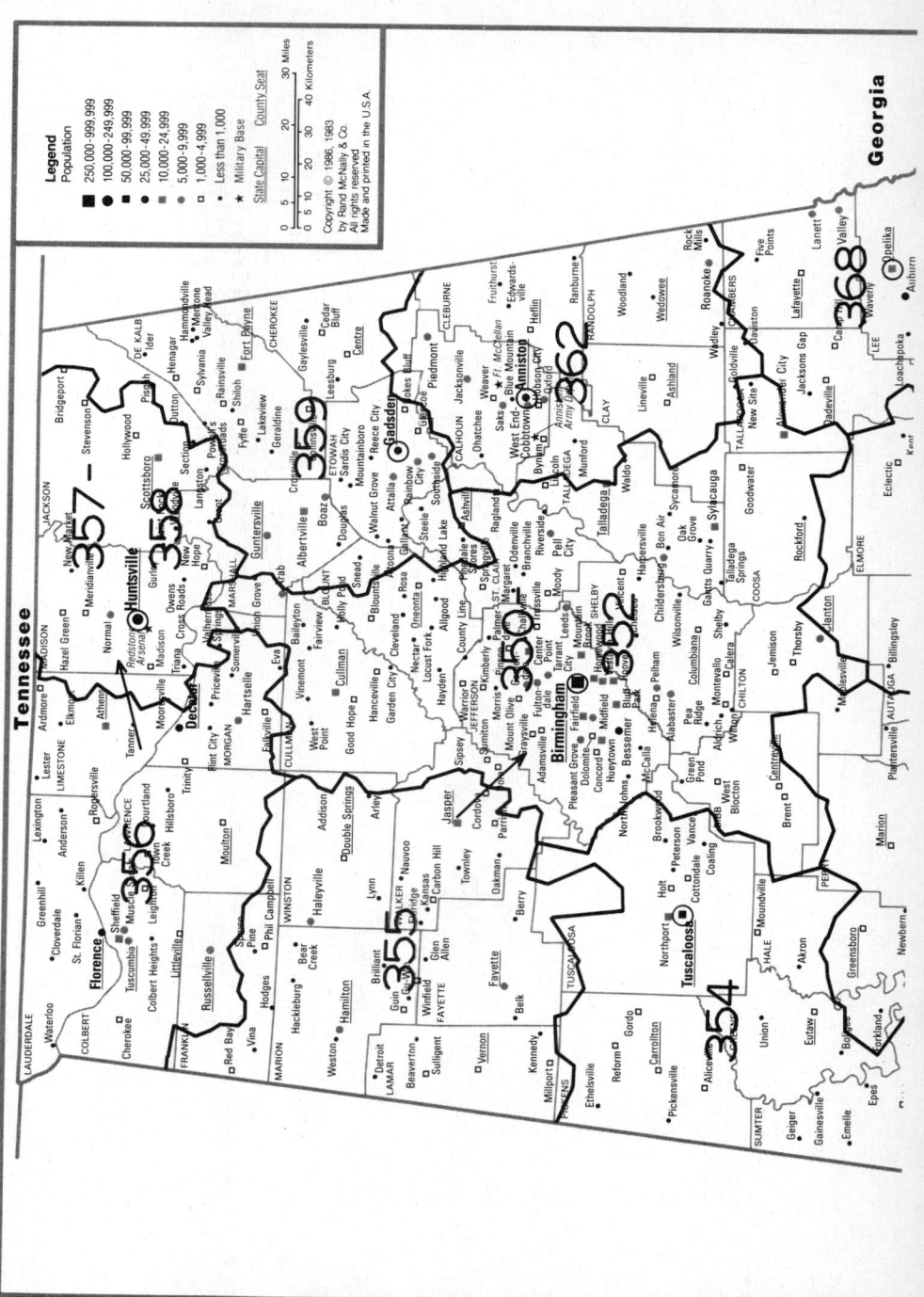

ALABAMA 25

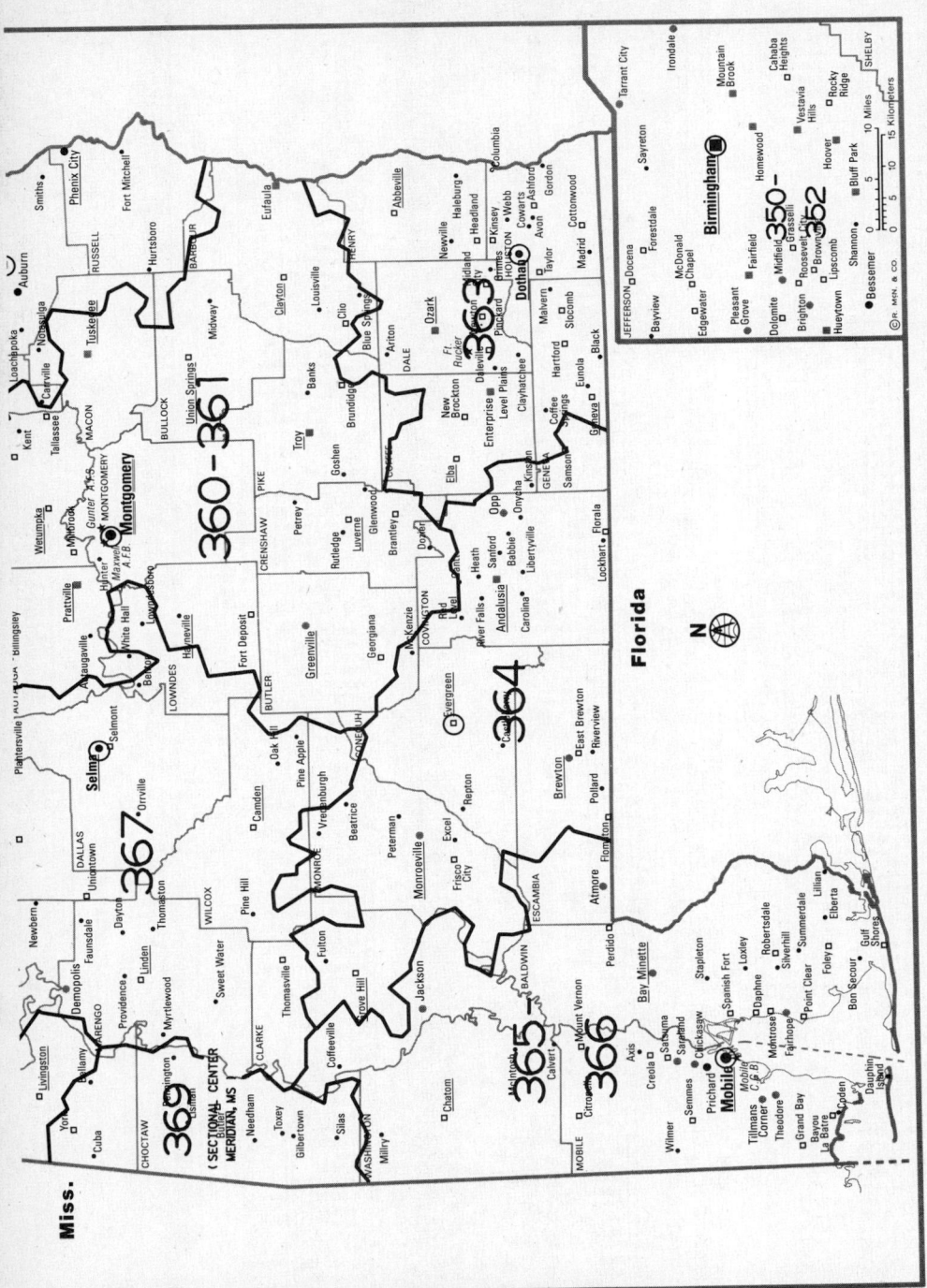

26 ALABAMA Blow Gourd-Chelsea

Name	ZIP
Blow Gourd	35049
Blue Creek	35023
Blue Creek Junction (Part of Bessemer)	35020
Blue Mountain	36201
Blue Pond	35959
Blue Ridge Estates	35226
Blues Old Stand	36061
Blue Spring (Part of Huntsville)	35810
Blue Springs (Barbour County)	36017
Blue Springs (Blount County)	35031
Blue Springs (Covington County)	36467
Blue Springs Garden	35811
Bluff	35555
Bluff Park	35226
Bluff Spring	36251
Bluff Springs	36323
Blufftton	30138
Boar Tush	35565
Boaz	35957
Bobo (Fayette County)	35594
Bobo (Madison County)	35773
Boiling Springs	36271
Boldo	35501
Boley Springs	35546
Boligee	35443
Bolinger	36903
Bolivar	35740
Bolling	36033
Bomar	35960
Bon Air	35032
Bonita	36749
Bonneville	35611
Bonnie Doone	35611
Bon Secour	36511
Booth	36008
Boot Hill	36048
Boothtown	36521
Boozer Heights (Part of Oxford)	36201
Borden Springs	36262
Borden Wheeler Springs	36262
Borom	36860
Boston (Part of Brilliant)	35548
Boswell	36081
Bowles	36401
Bowmans Crossroads	35744
Boyd	35470
Boyd Crossing	35490
Boykin (Escambia County)	36426
Boykin (Wilcox County)	36723
Boyles (Part of Birmingham)	35217
Boylston (Part of Montgomery)	36110
Boys Ranch	36761
Bradford	35089
Bradley	36420
Bradleyton	36041
Braggs	36761
Branchville	35120
Brandontown (Part of Huntsville)	35805
Brannon Springs	36271
Brannon Stand	36301
Brantley (Crenshaw County)	36009
Brantley (Dallas County)	36701
Brantleyville	35114
Bremen	35033
Brent	35034
Brewersville	35470
Brewton	36426-27
For specific Brewton Zip Codes call (205) 867-3560	
Briar Hill	36035
Brick	35660
Bridgeport	35740
Bridgeville	35442
Bridlewood Forest Estates	35215
Brierfield	35035
Brighton	35020
Bright Star	35980
Brilliant	35548
Brisco Store	35772
Broadmoor (Part of Bessemer)	35020
Bromley	36507
Brompton	35094
Brookhurst (Jefferson County)	35215
Brookhurst (Madison County)	35810
Brookland	36453
Brookley (Part of Mobile)	36605
Brooklyn (Coffee County)	36467
Brooklyn (Conecuh County)	36429
Brooklyn (Cullman County)	35083
Brooks	36456

Name	ZIP
Brookside	35036
Brooksville (Blount County)	35031
Brooksville (Morgan County)	35670
Brookwood	35444
Brookwood Forest (Part of Athens)	35611
Brookwood Village (Part of Homewood)	35209
Broomtown	35973
Broughton	36274
Browns	36759
Brownsboro	35741
Browns Corner	35773
Browns Crossroad	36310
Browns Crossroads	36360
Browntown (Jackson County)	35978
Brown Town (Mobile County)	39451
Brownville (Clay County)	35072
Brownville (Conecuh County)	36401
Brownville (Jefferson County)	35211
Brownville (Tuscaloosa County)	35476
Bruceville	36089
Brundidge	36010
Brunnet Heights	35217
Brushy Pond	35033
Bryant	35958
Bryant's Lower Landing	36579
Bryce Hospital (Part of Tuscaloosa)	35401
Buchanan Peninsula	35616
Buckhorn (Madison County)	35761
Buckhorn (Pike County)	36081
Buck Island Shores	35976
Bucks	36512
Bucksnort	35747
Buena Vista	36425
Buena Vista Highlands (Part of Homewood)	35209
Buffalo	36862
Buggs Chapel	35763
Buhl	35446
Bull City	35468
Bullock	36009
Bullock Correctional Facility	36089
Burchfield	35444
Burgreen Corners	35758
Burks Gardens (Part of Tuscaloosa)	35401
Burkville	36752
Burl	36753
Burlington	36078
Burningtree Estates (Part of Decatur)	35603
Burningtree Mountain (Morgan County)	35603
Burns	36272
Burnsville	36701
Burnt Corn	36431
Burntout	35593
Burnwell	35038
Burstall (Part of Bessemer)	35020
Bushy Creek	36033
Butler	36904
Butler Springs	36030
Buttston	36853
Buyck	36080
Bynum	36253
Caddo	35673
Caffee Junction	35111
Cahaba	36767
Cahaba Heights	35243
Cahaba Hills (Part of Leeds)	35094
Cahaba River Estates	35020
Calcis	35178
Caldwell	35146
Caledonia	36753
Calera	35040
Calhoun	36047
Calumet	35580
Calvert	36513
Camden	36726
Camelot (Part of Huntsville)	35803
Cameronsville	35772
Campbell	36727
Campbells Crossroads	36266
Campbellville	35063
Camp Hill	36850
Camp Oliver	35130
Canoe	36502
Cantebury Heights (Part of Mobile)	36609
Cantelous Spur	36113
Canton Bend	36726
Capell	36726
Capitol Heights (Part of Montgomery)	36107

Name	ZIP
Capps	36353
Capshaw	35742
Carbon Hill	35549
Cardiff	35041
Carlisle	35957
Carlowville	36761
Carlton	36515
Carns	35746
Carolina	36420
Carolyn (Part of Montgomery)	36106
Carpenter	36507
Carriger	35611
Carr Mill	36251
Carrollton	35447
Carrville (Part of Tallassee)	36023
Carson	36548
Carter Grove	35750
Cartersville	35967
Cartwright	35620
Carver Court (Part of Tuskegee)	36088
Casemore	36742
Casey	36701
Castleberry	36432
Catalpa	36081
Catherine	36728
Catoma	36108
Cavalry Hill (Part of Huntsville)	35805
Cave Spring (Etowah County)	35954
Cave Spring (Madison County)	35763
Cave Springs	35674
Cecil	36013
Cedar Bluff	35959
Cedar Cove	35453
Cedar Fork	36482
Cedar Grove (Baldwin County)	36542
Cedar Grove (Covington County)	36420
Cedar Grove (Jackson County)	35772
Cedar Hill (Fayette County)	35555
Cedar Hill (Limestone County)	35739
Cedar Hill Estates	35674
Cedar Plains	35622
Cedar Point	35760
Cedar Springs	36265
Cedrum	35549
Center	35565
Centercrest	35215
Centergrove	35670
Center Hill (Cullman County)	35077
Center Hill (Lauderdale County)	35648
Center Hill (Limestone County)	35773
Center Point (Clarke County)	36524
Center Point (Jefferson County)	35215
Center Point Gardens	35215
Center Springs	35172
Center Star	35645
Centerville	36401
Centerwood Estates	35215
Central (Cullman County)	35055
Central (Elmore County)	36024
Central City	36330
Central Crossroads	35978
Central Heights	35633
Central Highlands (Part of Birmingham)	35206
Central Mills	36773
Centre	35960
Centreville	35042
Century Plaza (Part of Birmingham)	35210
Ceramic (Part of Phenix City)	36867
Chalkville	35215
Chalybeate Springs	35643
Champion	35121
Chance	36751
Chancellor	36316
Chandler Springs	35160
Chapel Hill (Chambers County)	36862
Chapel Hill (Jefferson County)	35216
Chapman	36015
Chapman Heights (Part of Huntsville)	35810
Chase	35811
Chastang	36560
Chatom	36518
Chelsea (Madison County)	35801

ALABAMA 27 Chelsea-Docena

Place	ZIP
Chelsea (Shelby County)	35043
Cherokee	35616
Cherokee Bluffs	36078
Cherokee Forest (Part of Mountain Brook)	35223
Cherry Grove	35611
Chesson	36029
Chesterfield	30731
Chestnut	36425
Chestnut Grove	36010
Chetopa	35139
Chickasaw	36611
Chigger Hill	35971
Childersburg	35044
Chilton	36451
China	36401
China Grove	36081
Chinneby	36268
Chisholm (Part of Montgomery)	36110
Choccolocco	36254
Choctaw Bluff	36545
Choctaw City	36904
Choctaw Corner (Part of Thomasville)	36784
Chosea Springs	36201
Christiana	36258
Chrysler	36550
Chulafinnee	36264
Chunchula	36521
Circlewood (Part of Tuscaloosa)	35405
Citronelle	36522
Claiborne	36470
Clairmont Springs	35160
Clanton	35045
Clarksville	36524
Claud	36024
Clay	35048
Clay City	36532
Clayhatchee	36322
Clayhill	36784
Claysville	35976
Clayton	36016
Clear Springs	35121
Clearview (Covington County)	36028
Clearview (Crenshaw County)	36041
Cleveland (Blount County)	35049
Cleveland (Fayette County)	35542
Cleveland Crossroads	35072
Cliff Haven (Part of Sheffield)	35660
Clift Acres (Madison County)	35758
Clinton	35448
Clintonville	36351
Clio	36017
Clisby Park (Part of Montgomery)	36104
Clopton	36317
Cloverdale (Jefferson County)	35215
Cloverdale (Lauderdale County)	35617
Cloverdale (Mobile County)	36541
Cloverdale (Montgomery County)	36105
Cloverdale (Tuscaloosa County)	35401
Cloverdale Heights	35630
Cloverland (Part of Montgomery)	36105
Clowers Crossroads	36010
Clubview Heights (Part of Gadsden)	35901
Coal Bluff	36769
Coalburg	35068
Coal City	35131
Coal Fire	35481
Coaling	35449
Coalmont	35114
Coal Valley	35579
Coatopa	35470
Cobb City (Part of Glencoe)	35905
Cobbs Ford	36025
Cobb Town	36201
Cochrane	35442
Coden	36523
Cody	35555
Coffee Junction	35111
Coffee Springs	36318
Coffeeville	36524
Cohasset	36474
Coker	35452
Colbert Heights	35674
Cold Springs (Cullman County)	35033
Cold Springs (Elmore County)	36022

Place	ZIP
Coldwater (Calhoun County)	36260
Coldwater (Cleburne County)	36262
Cole Spring	35622
Collbran	35967
Collins Chapel	35045
Collinsville	35961
Collirene	36785
Coloma	35960
Colonial Gardens	35759
Colonial Heights (Part of Tuscumbia)	35674
Colony (Cullman County)	35077
Colony (Tuscaloosa County)	35476
Columbia	36319
Columbiana	35051
Columbus City	35976
Colwell	35905
Comer	36053
Concord (Blount County)	35049
Concord (Fayette County)	35555
Concord (Jefferson County)	35023
Congo	35959
Conifer	36078
Consul	36728
Cook Springs	35052
Cool Springs	35953
Coon Creek	35063
Coopers	35045
Coosa Court (Part of Childersburg)	35044
Coosada	36020
Coosa River	36022
Copeland	36558
Copeland Bridge	35961
Copper Springs	35120
Coppinville (Part of Enterprise)	36330
Corcoran (Part of Troy)	36081
Cordova	35550
Corinth (Bullock County)	36081
Corinth (Cullman County)	35179
Corinth (Randolph County)	36278
Corner	35180
Cornhouse	36274
Cornwall Furnace	35959
Corona	35579
Cortelyou	36585
Cotaco	35670
Cottage Grove	35089
Cottage Hill (Jefferson County)	35127
Cottage Hill (Mobile County)	36609
Cottondale	35453
Cottonton	36851
Cottontown	35646
Cotton Valley	36083
Cottonville	35747
Cottonwood	36320
Country Club Acres (Part of Athens)	35611
Country Club Estates (Madison County)	35201
Country Club Estates (Mobile County)	36608
Country Club Village (Part of Mobile)	36608
Country Estates (Jefferson County)	35215
Country Estates (Madison County)	36108
County Line (Blount County)	35172
County Line (Covington County)	36453
County Line (Pike County)	36034
Courtland	35618
Covin	35555
Cowarts	36321
Cox Beach (Part of Satsuma)	36572
Coxey	35611
Coy	36435
Cragford	36255
Crane Hill	35053
Crawford (Mobile County)	36608
Crawford (Russell County)	36867
Creek Stand	36089
Creeltown	35063
Creola	36525
Crescent Heights (Part of Lipscomb)	35020
Crestline (Part of Mountain Brook)	35213
Crestline Gardens (Part of Birmingham)	35210
Crestline Heights (Part of Mountain Brook)	35213
Crestline Park (Part of Birmingham)	35213
Crestview (Part of Mobile)	36609

Place	ZIP
Crestview Gardens (Part of Pell City)	35125
Crestwood (Part of Huntsville)	35807
Creswell	35078
Crews	35586
Crichton (Part of Mobile)	36607
Crockett Junction	35118
Cromwell	36906
Crooked Oak	35674
Cropwell (Part of Pell City)	35054
Crosby	36343
Cross Key	35620
Crossroads (Baldwin County)	36507
Cross Roads (Clarke County)	36570
Crossroads (Marshall County)	35976
Crosston	35126
Crossville (De Kalb County)	35962
Crossville (Lamar County)	35592
Crudup (Part of Reece City)	35954
Crumley Chapel	35214
Cuba	36907
Cullman	35055-56
For specific Cullman Zip Codes call (205) 734-6633	
Cullomburg	36919
Cunningham (Clarke County)	36727
Cunningham (Pickens County)	35442
Curry (Talladega County)	36268
Curry (Walker County)	35501
Currytown	36350
Curtis	36323
Curtiston (Part of Attalla)	35954
Cusseta	36852
Cypress	35474
Cyril	36912
Dadeville	36853
Daisy City	35214
Daleville	36322
Dallas (Blount County)	35172
Dallas (Madison County)	35801
Damascus (Coffee County)	36323
Damascus (Escambia County)	36426
Dancy	35442
Dancy Quarter (Part of Decatur)	35603
Danley	36323
Danville	35619
Danway	36801
Daphne	36526
Dargin	35040
Darlington	36726
Darwin Downs (Part of Huntsville)	35801
Dauphin Island	36528
Davis Hills (Part of Huntsville)	35805
Daviston	36256
Davisville	36083
Dawes	36601
Dawson	35963
Dawsons Mill	36749
Dayton	36731
De Armanville	36257
Deason Hill	35550
Deatsville	36022
Deavertown	35049
Decatur	35601-03
For specific Decatur Zip Codes call (205) 355-1211	
Deer Park	36529
DeFoor	35565
Delchamps	36523
Delmar	35551
Delta	36258
Demopolis	36732
Dempsey	35653
Deposit	35761
Detroit	35552
Devenport	36047
Dexter	36092
Diamond	35976
Dickert	36276
Dickinson	36436
Dillard	36360
Dilworth	35063
Dime	35581
Dixiana	35126
Dixie	36420
Dixieland	36867
Dixie Springs	35579
Dixon Corner	36544
Dixons Mills	36736
Dixonville	36426
Docena	35060

28 ALABAMA Dock-Forest Park

Name	ZIP
Dock	36037
Dogtown	35549
Dolcito (Part of Tarrant)	35217
Doliska (Part of Dora)	35130
Dolomite	35061
Dolonah	35023
Dora	35062
Doster	36311
Dothan	36301-04
For specific Dothan Zip Codes call (205) 794-8567	
Double Bridges (Henry County)	36310
Double Bridges (Marshall County)	35957
Doublehead	36862
Double Springs	35553
Douglas (De Kalb County)	35967
Douglas (Marshall County)	35964
Douglasville (Part of Birmingham)	35207
Downing	36052
Downs	36039
Downtown (Madison County)	35801
Downtown (Montgomery County)	36104
Downtown (Tuscaloosa County)	35401
Dozier	36028
Draper Correctional Center	36025
Drewry	36460
Drummond	35063
Dry Forks	36726
Dry Valley	35096
Dublin	36069
Duck Nest Springs	36268
Ducksprings	35954
Dudley	35490
Dudleyville	36850
Duke	36279
Dulin	35594
Duncan Crossroads	35771
Duncanville	35456
Dundee	36344
Dunn	36081
Dunns	36420
Dupree	36312
Dutton	35744
Duval (Part of Opp)	34467
Dyas	36507
Dyers Crossroads	35055
Eady City (Part of Valley)	36854
Eagle	35540
Earlytown	36453
Eastaboga	36260
East Birmingham (Part of Birmingham)	35204
East Boyles (Part of Birmingham)	35217
East Brewton	36426
Eastbrook (Part of Montgomery)	36109
East Brookwood	35444
Eastdale (Part of Montgomery)	36117
Eastdale Mall (Part of Montgomery)	36109
Eastern Valley	35020
East Gadsden (Part of Gadsden)	35903
East Hampton (Part of Athens)	35611
East Haven	35215
East Irondale (Part of Irondale)	35210
East Killen (Part of Killen)	35645
East Lake (Part of Birmingham)	35206
East Point	35055
East Side (Part of Tuscaloosa)	35404
East Tallassee (Part of Tallassee)	36023
East Thomas (Part of Birmingham)	35204
Eastwood (Blount County)	35121
Eastwood (Jefferson County)	35224
Eastwood Mall (Part of Birmingham)	35234
Ebenezer	35179
Echo	36350
Echola	35457
Echols Crossroads	35670
Echols Hills (Part of Huntsville)	35801
Eclectic	36024
Eddy (Part of Arab)	35016
Eden (Part of Pell City)	35125
Edgefield (Barbour County)	36016

Name	ZIP
Edgefield (Jackson County)	35772
Edgemont (Part of Homewood)	35209
Edgemont Park (Part of Homewood)	35209
Edgewater	35224
Edmonton Heights (Part of Huntsville)	35810
Edna	36922
Edwardsville	36261
Edwin	36317
Egypt	35952
Eight Mile (Part of Prichard)	36613
Elamville	36311
Elba	36323
Elberta	36530
Eldridge	35554
Elgin	35652
Eliska	36480
Elkmont	35620
Elkwood	38449
Ellards	35034
Elliotsville (Part of Alabama)	35007
Ellisville (Baldwin County)	36551
Ellisville (Cherokee County)	35960
Elmore	36025
Elmore Correctional Facility	36025
Elrod	35458
Elsanor	36567
Elsmeade (Part of Montgomery)	36116
Elting (Part of Florence)	35630
Elyton (Part of Birmingham)	35204
Emelle	35459
Emerald Shores	35630
Empire	35063
Englewood	35405
English Village (Jefferson County)	35223
English Village (Madison County)	35802
Enon (Bullock County)	36053
Enon (Cullman County)	35179
Enon (Houston County)	36376
Enon (Pike County)	36005
Ensley (Part of Birmingham)	35218
Enterprise (Coffee County)	36330-31
For specific Enterprise Zip Codes call (205) 347-8472	
Enterprise (Chilton County)	36091
Eoda	36420
Eoline	35042
Epes	35460
Equality	36026
Erin	36266
Escambia Correctional Center	36503
Escatawpa	36584
Estelle	36726
Estes Crossroads	36272
Estillfork	35745
Ethel	36081
Ethelsville	35461
Euclid Estates (Part of Mountain Brook)	35217
Eufaula	36027
Eulaton	36201
Eunola	36340
Eureka	35772
Eutaw	35462
Eva	35621
Evansboro	36913
Evansville	35441
Evergreen (Autauga County)	36006
Evergreen (Conecuh County)	36401
Ewell	36360
Excel	36439
Exmoor	36782
Fabius	35966
Fackler	35746
Fadette	36375
Fairdale	35042
Fairfax (Part of Valley)	36854
Fairfield (Covington County)	36420
Fairfield (Jefferson County)	35064
Fairfield (Lawrence County)	35650
Fairfield Highlands (Part of Midfield)	35064
Fairford	36553
Fairhope	36532-33
For specific Fairhope Zip Codes call (205) 928-8251	
Fairmont	35811
Fairoaks	35477
Fairview (Chilton County)	35045
Fairview (Coffee County)	36323
Fairview (Conecuh County)	36401
Fairview (Cullman County)	35055
Fairview (De Kalb County)	35963
Fairview (Jefferson County)	35208

Name	ZIP
Fairview (Limestone County)	35611
Fairview (Marion County)	35564
Fairview (Mobile County)	36587
Fairview (Morgan County)	35601
Fairview (St. Clair County)	35131
Fairview (Winston County)	35540
Fairview West	35077
Falkville	35622
Fannie	36441
Farill	35959
Farley (Part of Huntsville)	35802
Farmersville	36761
Farmville	36801
Fatama	36726
Faunsdale	36738
Fayette	35555
Fayetteville	35150
Federal Prison Camp	36112
Fergusons Cross Roads	35972
Fernbank	35576
Fernland	36541
Fernwood Estates	35215
Fieldstown (Part of Gardendale)	35071
Fig Tree	36749
Finchburg	36444
Finley Crossing	36784
Fisher Crossroads (Part of Fort Payne)	35967
Fishhead	36258
Fish Pond	35643
Fish River	36555
Fisk	35750
Fitzpatrick	36029
Five Points (Blount County)	35049
Five Points (Chambers County)	36855
Five Points (Cleburne County)	36264
Five Points (Dale County)	36352
Five Points (Dallas County)	36767
Five Points (Elmore County)	36025
Five Points (Houston County)	36320
Five Points (Lawrence County)	35619
Five Points (Madison County)	35773
Five Points (Marshall County)	35755
Five Points (Walker County)	35501
Five Points East (Part of Irondale)	35210
Five Points West Shopping City (Part of Birmingham)	35208
Flat Creek	35130
Flat Rock (Clay County)	36266
Flat Rock (Jackson County)	35966
Flat Top	35062
Flatwood (Montgomery County)	36110
Flatwood (Walker County)	35549
Flatwood (Wilcox County)	36728
Fleetwood	35453
Fleming Meadows (Part of Huntsville)	35802
Flemington Heights (Part of Huntsville)	35802
Fleta	36043
Flint City	35601
Flomaton	36441
Florala	36442
Floral Crest	35774
Florence	35630-33
For specific Florence Zip Codes call (205) 764-6961	
Florette	35670
Flower Hill	35643
Floyd	36024
Foley	36535-36
For specific Foley Zip Codes call (205) 943-7211	
Ford City	35660
Forest	35461
Forest Brook Estates	35226
Forestdale (Jefferson County)	35214
Forester	36067
Forester Chapel	36276
Forest Hill (Part of Mobile)	36608
Forest Hills (Calhoun County)	36201
Forest Hills (Jefferson County)	35064
Forest Hills (Lauderdale County)	35630
Forest Hills (Talladega County)	35044
Forest Home	36030
Forest Park (Jefferson County)	35222

Forest Park-Henagar **ALABAMA** 29

Name	ZIP
Forest Park (Mobile County)	36608
Forkland	36740
Forkville	35565
Forney	35960
Fort Benning	31905
Fort Dale	36037
Fort Davis	36031
Fort Deposit	36032
Fort McClellan (Calhoun County)	36205
Fort Mitchell	36856
Fort Morgan	36542
Fort Payne	35967
Fort Rucker (Dale County)	36362
Fosheeton	35010
Fosters	35463
Fostoria	36761
Fountain	36460
Fountain Heights (Part of Birmingham)	35204
Four Mile	35186
Fowlers Crossroads	35542
Fowl River	36582
Fox	35401
Frances Heights (Part of Fultondale)	35068
Francisco	37345
Francis Mill	36271
Frankfort	35653
Franklin (Macon County)	36083
Franklin (Monroe County)	36444
Frankville	36538
Fredonia	36855
Freemanville	36502
Fremont	36749
French Mill	35611
Fridays Crossing	35121
Friendship (Covington County)	36467
Friendship (Elmore County)	36078
Friendship (Montgomery County)	36036
Frisco	36010
Frisco City	36445
Frisco Quarters (Part of Jasper)	35501
Frost (Part of Centreville)	35042
Fruitdale	36539
Fruithurst	36262
Fullers Crossroads	36049
Fullerton	35973
Fulton	36446
Fulton Bridge (Part of Hamilton)	35570
Fultondale	35068
Fulton Road (Part of Mobile)	36605
Fulton Springs (Part of Fultondale)	35068
Furman	36741
Fyffe	35971
Gadsden	35901-05
For specific Gadsden Zip Codes call (205) 547-6391	
Gadsden Mall (Part of Gadsden)	35901
Gainer	36477
Gainestown	36540
Gainesville	35464
Gallant	35972
Gallion	36742
Gamble	35501
Gandys Cove	35622
Gann Crossroad	35981
Gantt	36038
Gantts Junction (Part of Sylacauga)	35150
Gantts Quarry	35150
Garden	35442
Garden City	35070
Gardendale	35071
Garden Highlands	35211
Gardiners Gin	35550
Garland	36456
Garrards Crossroads	36375
Garth	35764
Gary Springs	35042
Garywood	35023
Gasque	36542
Gastonburg	36728
Gate City (Part of Birmingham)	35212
Gaylesville	35973
Gay Meadows (Part of Montgomery)	36111
Geiger	35459
Genery	35020
Geneva	36340
Gentilly Forest (Part of Vestavia Hills)	35216
Georgetown	36521
Georgia (Part of Hartselle)	35640

Name	ZIP
Georgiana	36033
Gerald (Part of Level Plains)	36322
Geraldine	35974
Germania (Part of Birmingham)	35211
Gibsonville	36251
Gilbert Crossroads	35963
Gilbertown	36908
Gilbertsboro	35647
Giles	35188
Gilliam Springs (Part of Arab)	35016
Gilmore	35020
Gipsy	35620
Girard (Part of Phenix City)	36867
G.K.Fountain Correctional Center	36502
Gladstone	35806
Glass (Part of Valley)	36854
Gleandean (Part of Auburn)	36830
Glen Allen	35559
Glen City (Part of Pell City)	35125
Glencoe (Etowah County)	35905
Glencoe (Jefferson County)	35213
Glen Hills (Part of Bessemer)	35020
Glen Mary	35577
Glenn Acres	36608
Glen Oaks (Part of Fairfield)	35064
Glenville	36871
Glenwood	36034
Gnatville	36272
Godwin Estates	35215
Goldbranch	35183
Golden Springs (Part of Anniston)	36201
Gold Mine	35548
Gold Ridge (Cullman County)	35055
Gold Ridge (Lee County)	36879
Goldville	36255
Gonce	35772
Good Hope (Cullman County)	35055
Good Hope (Elmore County)	36024
Goodman	36330
Good Springs (Limestone County)	35610
Goodsprings (Walker County)	35560
Goodwater	35072
Goodway	36449
Goodyear (Part of Gadsden)	35903
Goose Pond Crossroads (Part of Scottsboro)	35768
Gordo	35466
Gordon	36343
Gordon Heights (Part of Lipscomb)	35020
Gordonsville	36785
Gorgas	35580
Goshen	36035
Gosport	36482
Graball (Part of Abbeville)	36310
Grady	36036
Graham	36263
Grand Bay	36541
Grangeburg	36343
Grant	35747
Grantley	36272
Granttown	36268
Grasselli (Part of Birmingham)	35211
Grassy	35016
Gravel Hill (Part of Russellville)	35653
Gravelly Springs	35630
Graymont (Part of Birmingham)	35204
Grays Chapel	35745
Grayson	35572
Graystone	35013
Graysville	35073
Grayton	36271
Greeley	35111
Green Acres (Part of Birmingham)	35228
Greenbrier (Lauderdale County)	35630
Greenbrier (Limestone County)	35758
Green Chapel	35971
Greenhill	35630
Green Lantern (Part of Montgomery)	36111
Green Meadows	36067
Green Pond	35074
Greensboro	36744
Greens Chapel	35049

Name	ZIP
Greensport	35953
Green Valley (Etowah County)	35903
Green Valley (Jefferson County)	35216
Greenville	36037
Greenwood (Clarke County)	36451
Greenwood (Jefferson County)	35020
Greenwood (Macon County)	36088
Greenwycke Village (Part of Huntsville)	35802
Griffith Bend	35160
Grimes	36301
Grove Hill	36451
Groveoak	35975
Grove Park (Jefferson County)	35209
Grove Park (Talladega County)	35044
Grovewood Estates	36108
Guerryton	36860
Guest	35967
Guin	35563
Gulf Crest	36521
Gulf Shores	36542
Gum Pond	35621
Gum Spring	35640
Gum Springs	35031
Guntersville	35976
Gurley	35748
Guthery Crossroads	35053
Gu-Win	35563
Hackleburg	35564
Hackneyville	35010
Hacoda	36442
Hagler	35456
Haleburg	36319
Haleyville	35565
Half Acre	36763
Halls Crossroads	36445
Halltown	35582
Halsell	36912
Hamburg (Perry County)	36759
Hamburg (Wilcox County)	36768
Hamilton	35570
Hamilton Crossroads	36010
Hammondville	35989
Hamner	35460
Hampden	36722
Hanceville	35077
Hancock Crossroads	35771
Hannah (Part of Athens)	35611
Hannon	36860
Hanover	35136
Hardaway	36039
Harkins Crossroads	36251
Harlem Heights (Part of Hueytown)	35023
Harmony (Covington County)	36420
Harmony (Lawrence County)	35650
Harmony (Marshall County)	35950
Harpersville	35078
Harrell	36759
Harriman Park (Part of Birmingham)	35207
Harrisburg (Bibb County)	35034
Harrisburg (St. Clair County)	35125
Harrisville	35952
Hartford	36344
Hartselle	35640
Harvest	35749
Hatchechubbee	36858
Hatton	35672
Havana	35474
Hawk	36280
Hawthorn	36585
Hayden	35079
Haynes	36067
Haynes Crossing	35772
Hayneville	36040
Haysland (Part of Huntsville)	35802
Haysland Estates (Part of Huntsville)	35802
Hays Mill	35620
Haywood	36280
Hazel Green	35750
Hazen	36767
Headland	36345
Healing Springs	36558
Heath	36420
Hebron	35747
Hector	36029
Heflin	36264
Heiberger	36756
Helena	35080
Helicon (Crenshaw County)	36036
Helicon (Winston County)	35541
Henagar	35978

30 ALABAMA Henderson-Lakeview

Name	ZIP
Henderson	36035
Hendrick Mill	35121
Hendrix	35121
Henryville	35976
Henson Springs	35544
Herbert	36401
Heron Bay	36523
Hester Heights (Part of Russellville)	35653
Hickory	35442
Hickory Flat	36274
Hickory Grove	35650
Hickory Hills (Lauderdale County)	35630
Hickory Hills (Morgan County)	35603
Hideaway Hills	35645
Higdon	35979
High Bluff	36344
Highland (Part of Lineville)	36266
Highland Home	36041
Highland Lake	35121
Highland Park (Part of Montgomery)	36107
Highmound	35980
High Point (De Kalb County)	35989
High Point (Marshall County)	35950
High Ridge	36089
Hightogy	35592
Hightower	36263
Hillandale (Part of Huntsville)	35805
Hillard	35587
Hillman	35020
Hillman Gardens	35020
Hillman Park	35020
Hillsboro (Lawrence County)	35643
Hillsboro (Madison County)	35761
Hillsdale (Part of Jasper)	35501
Hilltop (Part of Bessemer)	35020
Hillview	35214
Hinton	39355
Hirsch	36871
Hissop	35089
Hobbs Island	35803
Hobgood	35674
Hoboken (Barbour County)	36027
Hoboken (Marengo County)	36782
Hobson	36518
Hobson City	36201
Hodge	35744
Hodges	35571
Hodges Store	35619
Hodgesville	36301
Hodgewood	36921
Hogglesville	35474
Hog Jaw	35016
Hokes Bluff	35903
Holiday Homes (Part of Huntsville)	35807
Holiday Park Estates	35215
Holland Gin	35620
Holley Crossroads	36272
Hollins	35082
Hollis Crossroads	36264
Holly Grove	35587
Holly Pond	35083
Holly Springs	35146
Hollytree	35751
Hollywood (Jackson County)	35752
Hollywood (Jefferson County)	35209
Holman	36503
Holman Prison	36502
Holt	35404
Holt Junction (Part of Tuscaloosa)	35401
Holtville	36022
Holy Trinity	36859
Homewood	35209
Honoraville	36042
Hoods Crossroads	35121
Hoover (Jefferson County)	35216
Hoover (Madison County)	35749
Hope Hull	36043
Hopewell (Cherokee County)	35959
Hopewell (Cleburne County)	36264
Hopewell (De Kalb County)	35950
Hopewell (Jefferson County)	35020
Hoppes	36535
Hornady	36039
Horn Hill	36467
Horton	35980
Hortons Mill	35121
Houston	35572
Howard	35549
Howells Cross Roads	35960
Howelton	35952
Howton	35453

Name	ZIP
Hubbertville (Part of Glen Allen)	35555
Hudson Gardens (Part of Lipscomb)	35020
Hudson Settlement	35501
Hueytown	35023
Hueytown Crest (Part of Hueytown)	35020
Huffman (Part of Birmingham)	35215
Huffman Gardens (Part of Birmingham)	35215
Hugo	36783
Huguley	36854
Hulaco	35087
Hull (Part of Sumiton)	35063
Humpton	35776
Hunter (Part of Montgomery)	36108
Huntsville	35801-24
For specific Huntsville Zip Codes call (205) 772-0211	
Huntsville Park (Part of Huntsville)	35807
Hurricane	36507
Hurtsboro	36860
Hustleville	35950
Hustontown	35645
Huxford	36543
Hyatt	35980
Hybart	36444
Hytop	35768
Idaho	36251
Ider	35981
Independence	36067
Indian Creek	36061
Indian Hill (Part of Childersburg)	35044
Indian Hills	35244
Indian Springs (Lauderdale County)	35630
Indian Springs (Mobile County)	36613
Indian Valley	35244
Industrial City (Part of Hueytown)	35023
Industry	36033
Inglenook (Part of Birmingham)	35217
Ingram	35474
Inland	35121
Inmanfield	35540
Ino	36453
Institute	36778
Interburan Heights (Part of Fairfield)	35064
Inverness	36089
Ironaton	36268
Iron City	36201
Irondale	35210
Irvington	36544
Isabella	36750
Isbell	35653
Ishkooda (Part of Birmingham)	35211
Isney	36919
Ivalee	35954
Ivanhoe (Part of Birmingham)	35222
Jachin	36910
Jack	36346
Jackson (Choctaw County)	36921
Jackson (Clarke County)	36545
Jackson Heights (Part of Mobile)	36609
Jackson Oak	36526
Jacksons Gap	36861
Jacksonville	36265
Jack Springs	36502
Jagger	35578
Jamestown	35973
Jamesville	36879
Jarrett (Part of Valley)	36854
Jasper	35501-02
For specific Jasper Zip Codes call (205) 384-5516	
Java	36010
Jay Villa	36401
Jeddo	36480
Jeff	35806
Jefferson (Marengo County)	36745
Jefferson Hills (Part of Birmingham)	35217
Jefferson Park	35210
Jemison	35085
Jena	35480
Jenifer	36268
Jericho	36756
Jernigan	36851
Jerusalem Heights	35405
Joe Wheeler Dam	35672

Name	ZIP
Johnsons Crossing	35077
Johnsonville	36401
Jones	36749
Jonesboro (Baldwin County)	36526
Jonesboro (Franklin County)	35653
Jonesboro (Jefferson County)	35020
Jones Chapel	35055
Jones Crossroads	35611
Jones Valley (Part of Birmingham)	35211
Jones Valley Estates (Part of Huntsville)	35802
Joppa	35087
Joquin	36035
Jordan (Elmore County)	36092
Jordan (Washington County)	36518
Jordans Mill	35593
Josephine	36530
Joseph Springs	36201
Josie	36005
Julia Tutwiler Prison for Women	36092
Kahatchie	35044
Kansas	35573
Kaolin (Part of Phenix City)	36867
Kaulton (Part of Tuscaloosa)	35401
Keego	36426
Keener	35954
Kellerman	35468
Kelly	36322
Kelly Springs (Part of Dothan)	36301
Kellyton	35089
Kendale Gardens	35630
Kennedy	35574
Kent (Elmore County)	36045
Kent (Pike County)	36035
Kenwood	35226
Ketona (Part of Tarrant)	35217
Key	35960
Keyno	35089
Keys Mill	35761
Keystone (Part of Pelham)	35007
Keyton	36330
Kilby (Part of Montgomery)	36114
Kilby Corrections Facility	36109
Kilgore	35062
Killen	35645
Killough Springs (Part of Birmingham)	35235
Kilpatrick	35950
Kimberly	35091
Kimbrel	35111
Kimbrough	36769
Kincheon	35045
Kings Landing (Baldwin County)	36567
Kings Landing (Dallas County)	36775
Kingston (Part of Birmingham)	35234
Kingsway Terrace (Part of Birmingham)	35206
Kingtown	35652
Kingville	35574
Kinsey	36301
Kinston	36453
Kinterbish	36907
Kirbytown	35755
Kirk	35466
Kirkland	36426
Kirklands Crossroads	36345
Kirks Grove	35960
Klein	35078
Klondike	35580
Knightens Crossroads	36272
Knoxville	35469
Koenton	36558
Kowaliga Beach	35010
Krafton (Part of Prichard)	36610
Kyles	35746
Kymulga	35014
Laceys Chapel	35020
Laceys Spring	35754
Lacon	35622
Ladiga	36272
Ladonia	36867
Lafayette	36862
Lagoon Park (Part of Montgomery)	36117
Lake Coves	35630
Lake Drive Estates (Part of Homewood)	35209
Lake Forest	36526
Lakeside Acres	35645
Lakeside Highlands (Part of Florence)	35630
Lakeview (De Kalb County)	35971
Lakeview (Marshall County)	35976

Lakeview Highlands-Midway ALABAMA 31

	ZIP		ZIP		ZIP
Lakeview Highlands (Part of Muscle Shoals)	35660	Little Texas	36083	Madrid	36320
Lakewood (Jefferson County)	35234	Littleton (Etowah County)	35954	Magazine (Part of Mobile)	36610
		Littleton (Jefferson County)	35073	Magnolia	36754
		Littleville (Colbert County)	35653	Magnolia Beach (Part of Fairhope)	36532
Lakewood (Limestone County)	35611	Littleville (Winston County)	35565	Magnolia Springs	36555
		Live Oak Landing	36507	Magnolia Terminal	36722
Lakewood (Madison County)	35810	Livingston	35470	Majestic	35116
		Loachapoka	36865	Malbis	36526
Lakewood Estates (Part of Bessemer)	35020	Loango	36474	Malcolm	36556
		Locke Crossroads	35620	Mall, The (Part of Huntsville)	35801
Lamison	36728	Lockhart	36455	Malone	36276
Land	36904	Lock Six	35645	Malta	36502
Landersville	35650	Lock Three	35652	Malvern	36349
Lands Crossroads (Part of Rainsville)	35986	Locust Fork	35097	Mamie	36052
		Loflin	36851	Manack	36752
Lane Springs	35616	Logan	35098	Manchester	35501
Lanett	36863	Logton	36081	Manila	36586
Langdale (Part of Valley)	36854	Lola City	35173	Manley Crossroads	35758
Langston	35755	Lomax	35045	Manningham	36037
Langtown	35650	London (Conecuh County)	36432	Mansion View	35630
Laniers	35014	London (Montgomery County)	36064	Mantua	35462
Lapine (Crenshaw County)	36041	Long Island	35958	Maple Hill	38449
Lapine (Montgomery County)	36046	Longleaf Estates (Part of Decatur)	35603	Maplesville	36750
La Place	36075			Maplewood (Jefferson County)	35094
Larkinsville	35768	Longview (Cullman County)	35179		
Larkwood	35215	Longview (Shelby County)	35137	Maplewood (Madison County)	35758
Lasca	36784	Longwood (Part of Huntsville)	35801		
Latham	36579			Marble City Heights (Part of Sylacauga)	35150
Lathamville	35962	Loop (Cherokee County)	35959		
Lattiwood	35950	Loop (Mobile County)	36606	Marble Valley	35150
Lauderdale Beach	35630	Loree	36401	Marbury	36051
Laurendine	36582	Lott	36613	Marcoot	36862
Lavaca	36911	Lottie	36502	Margaret	35112
Lawley	36793	Louisville	36048	Margerum	35616
Lawrence	35959	Love Hill	36312	Marietta	35579
Lawrence Cove	35621	Lovelace Crossroads	35630	Marion	36756
Lawrence Mill	35555	Loveless	35967	Marion Junction	36759
Lawrenceville	36310	Loveless Park	35020	Markeeta	35094
Leatherwood	36201	Lovick	35173	Marl	36477
Lebanon (Cleburne County)	36269	Lower Peach Tree	36751	Marley Mill	36360
Lebanon (De Kalb County)	35961	Lowery	36453	Marlow	36580
Lecta	36264	Lowerytown	35184	Mars Hill (Part of Florence)	35630
Leeds	35094	Low Gap	35120	Martins (Part of Birmingham)	35208
Leeds Mineral Well (Part of Leeds)	35094	Lowndesboro	36752		
		Lowry Mill	36346	Martintown	35752
Leesburg	35983	Loxley	36551	Martinville	36502
Leesdale (Part of Falkville)	35622	Loxley Heights	36551	Martling	35950
Leggtown	35620	Lucille	35184	Marvel	35115
Le Grand	36105	Lugo	36027	Marvyn	36801
Leighton	35646	Lumbull	35543	Marylee	35501
Lenlock (Part of Anniston)	36201	Luttrell	35971	Maryville	35954
Lenox	36454	Luverne	36049	Massey	35619
Leon	36028	Lydia	35967	Masterson Mill	35650
Leroy	36548	Lyeffion	36401	Mathews	36052
Leslie	36790	Lynn	35575	Mattawana	35121
Lester	35647	Lynn Crossing	35073	Maud	35616
Letcher	35776	Lynndale (Part of Montgomery)	36105	Maxine	35130
Letchers	36201			Maxwell	35401
Letohatchee	36047	Lynn Haven (Part of Tuscaloosa)	35404	Maxwellborn	36272
Level Plains	36322			Maxwell Heights (Part of Montgomery)	36113
Levelroad	36276	Lynns Park	35550		
Levert	36779	Lytle	36477	Mayes Crossroads	35901
Lewis	36350	Mabson	36360	Mayfair (Jefferson County)	35209
Lewisburg (Part of Birmingham)	35207	McCalla	35111	Mayfair (Madison County)	35801
		McClure Town	36081	Maylene (Part of Alabaster)	35114
Lewiston	35462	McCollum	35501	Maynards Cove	35768
Lexington	35648	McCord Crossroads	35960	Maysville	35748
Liberty (Blount County)	35031	McCulley Hill	35184	Maytown	35118
Liberty (Butler County)	36037	McCullough	36502	Meadow Crossroads	36874
Liberty (De Kalb County)	35957	McDonald Chapel	35224	Meadow Hills (Part of Huntsville)	35810
Liberty City	36866	McDowell	35470		
Liberty Highlands	35210	Macedonia (Cleburne County)	36273	Mechanicsville	36874
Liberty Hill (Franklin County)	35581			Media	35062
Liberty Hill (Jackson County)	35966	Macedonia (Jackson County)	35771	Meeksville	36081
				Megargel	36457
Libertyville	36420	Macedonia (Montgomery County)	36036	Mehama	35653
Lightwood	36022			Mellow Valley	36255
Ligon Springs	35653	Macedonia (Walker County)	35501	Melrose (Conecuh County)	36401
Lillian	36549	McElderry	36268	Melrose (Pickens County)	35471
Lily Flag (Part of Huntsville)	35802	McFarland Mall (Part of Tuscaloosa)	35405	Melton	36776
Lime	36274			Meltonsville	35755
Lime Kiln	35616	McGhees Bend	35960	Melville	35541
Limestone	36460	McGinty (Part of Valley)	36854	Melvin	36913
Lim Rock	35776	McIntosh	36553	Memphis	39353
Lincoln (Madison County)	35810	McKenzie	36456	Mentone	35984
Lincoln (Talladega County)	35096	McKestes	35963	Mercury	35811
Lincoya Estates (Part of Vestavia Hills)	35216	McKinley	36728	Meridianville	35759
		McLarty	35980	Merry	36064
Lindbergh	35073	McLendon	36851	Mertz (Part of Mobile)	36606
Linden	36748	McMullen	35442	Mexboro	36445
Lineville	36266	Macon	36271	Mexia	36458
Linwood	36081	McQueen	36067	Mexia Crossing	36264
Lipscomb	35020	McShan	35471	Micaville	36879
Lisman	36912	McVay	36451	Middle Brooks Cross Roads	36271
Little Oak	36081	McVille	35950	Middleton	35228
Little River (Baldwin County)	36550	McWilliams	36753	Midfield	36350
Little River (Cherokee County)	35959	Madison	35758	Midland City	36350
		Madison Crossroads	35772	Midtown (Part of Mobile)	36640
Little Rock	36502	Madison Square Mall (Part of Huntsville)	35806	Midway (Bullock County)	36053
Little Shawmut	36863				

32 ALABAMA Midway-Oakleigh Estates

Name	ZIP
Midway (Butler County)	36042
Midway (Chilton County)	36051
Midway (Clay County)	35072
Midway (Lawrence County)	35650
Midway (Monroe County)	36768
Miflin	36530
Mignon	35150
Miles (Part of Fairfield)	35064
Millbrook	36054
Miller	36748
Millers Ferry	36760
Millertown	36613
Millerville	36267
Millport	35576
Milry	36558
Mills Quarter's	36535
Milltown	36862
Mill Village (Part of Guntersville)	35976
Milstead	36075
Milton	36749
Mineral Springs	35085
Minooka	35040
Minor	35224
Minor Terrace (Part of Childersburg)	35044
Minter	36761
Minvale (Part of Fort Payne)	35967
Mitchell	36029
Mitchell Town	35645
Mobile	36601-95
For specific Mobile Zip Codes call (205) 694-5917	
Mobile Festival Centre (Part of Mobile)	36609
Mobile Junction	35023
Moffett	36587
Mollie	36906
Molloy	35586
Mon Louis	36523
Monroeville	36460-61
For specific Monroeville Zip Codes call (205) 743-3475	
Monrovia	35806
Montague	35740
Monterey	36030
Monterey Heights	36877
Monte-Sano (Part of Birmingham)	35228
Montevallo	35115
Monte Vista (Part of Gadsden)	35901
Montgomery	36101-99
For specific Montgomery Zip Codes call (205) 244-7500	
Montgomery Mall (Part of Montgomery)	36116
Monticello	36005
Montrose	36559
Moody	35094
Moorefield	36862
Moores Bridge	35476
Moores Crossroad	35971
Moores Crossroads	36274
Moores Mill	35811
Mooresville	35649
Moreland	35572
Morgan (Part of Bessemer)	35020
Morgan City	35175
Moriah	35136
Morningside	35215
Morris	35116
Morvin	36762
Moshat	35960
Mosses	36040
Mossy Grove	36081
Mostellers	35143
Motley	36276
Moulton	35650
Moulton Heights (Part of Decatur)	35601
Moundville	35474
Mountainboro	35957
Mountain Brook (Jefferson County)	35223
Mountain Brook (Madison County)	35801
Mountain Brook Village (Part of Mountain Brook)	35223
Mountain Chest (Part of Guntersville)	35976
Mountain Creek	36051
Mountain Grove	35031
Mountain Home	35673
Mountain Park (Part of Birmingham)	35217
Mountain View (Part of Guntersville)	35976
Mountain Woods (Part of Vestavia Hills)	35216

Name	ZIP
Mountain Woods Park (Part of Vestavia Hills)	35216
Mount Andrew	36053
Mount Carmel (Jackson County)	35740
Mount Carmel (Marshall County)	35976
Mount Carmel (Montgomery County)	36046
Mount Hebron (Greene County)	35443
Mount Hebron (Marshall County)	35957
Mount Hester	35616
Mount Hope	35651
Mount Ida	36009
Mount Jefferson	36801
Mount Meigs	36057
Mount Nebo	36785
Mount Olive (Coosa County)	35072
Mount Olive (Jefferson County)	35117
Mount Pleasant (Coffee County)	36330
Mount Pleasant (Monroe County)	36480
Mount Rozell	35647
Mount Sinai	36113
Mount Star	35653
Mount Sterling	36904
Mount Union	36401
Mount Vernon (Cullman County)	35179
Mount Vernon (De Kalb County)	35967
Mount Vernon (Fayette County)	35555
Mount Vernon (Mobile County)	36560
Mount Willing	36032
Mount Zion	36069
Muck City	35650
Mud Creek (Jackson County)	35752
Mud Creek (Jefferson County)	35006
Mulga	35118
Mulga Mine	35118
Munford	36268
Murphy	35677
Murrays Chapel	35146
Muscadine	36269
Muscadine Junction	36269
Muscle Shoals	35661
Muscoda	35020
Mynot	35616
Myrick Chapel	36022
Myrtlewood	36763
Nadawah	36726
Naftel	36046
Nanafalia	36764
Nances Creek	36272
Napier Field	36301
Napoleon	36280
Nat	35776
Natchez	36425
Nathan (Part of Arley)	35541
Natural Bridge	35577
Nauvoo	35578
Navco (Part of Mobile)	36605
Nebo	35758
Nectar	35049
Needham	36915
Needmore (Marshall County)	35957
Needmore (Pike County)	36081
Needmore (Winston County)	35565
Neel	35640
Neenah	36726
Nellie	36726
Neshota (Part of Mobile)	36605
Nesmith (Cullman County)	35055
Ne Smith (Lawrence County)	35672
Nettleboro	36436
Newbern	36765
Newberry Crossroads	35960
New Brashier Chapel	35950
New Brockton	36351
Newburg	35653
New Castle	35119
New Center	35640
New Dora (Part of Dora)	35062
Newell	36270
New Georgia	35540
New Haven	35758
New Hill (Part of Lipscomb)	35020
New Home	35978
New Hope (Coffee County)	36010

Name	ZIP
New Hope (Cullman County)	35083
New Hope (Jackson County)	35768
New Hope (Madison County)	35760
New Hope (Shelby County)	35243
New Hopewell	36264
New Lexington	35546
New London	35054
New Market	35761
New Moon	35973
New Prospect (Autauga County)	36051
New Prospect (Hale County)	35441
New Sharon	35750
New Site	35010
Newsome (Part of Rainsville)	35986
Newton (Dale County)	36352
Newton (Houston County)	36301
Newtonville	35555
Newtown (Franklin County)	35653
New Town (Jackson County)	35772
Newville	36353
Nichburg	36475
Nicholsville	36784
Nitrate City	35660
Nixburg	36026
Nix Mill	35581
Nixons Chapel	35980
Noah	35960
Nokomis	36502
Nolandale (Part of Madison)	35758
Nolan Hills (Part of Madison)	35758
Normal (Part of Huntsville)	35762
Normandale Shopping Center (Part of Montgomery)	36111
North Arab (Part of Arab)	35016
North Athens (Part of Athens)	35611
North Birmingham (Part of Birmingham)	35207
North Courtland	35618
North Daye Hill	35749
North Elmore	36025
North Florence (Part of Florence)	35630
North Highlands (Part of Hueytown)	35020
North Johns	35006
North Mobile (Part of Chickasaw)	36611
Northport	35476
Northside (Part of Dothan)	36304
Northside Acres	35806
Northside Mall (Part of Dothan)	36303
North Smithfield Estates	35214
North Smithfield Manor (Part of Birmingham)	35207
North Vinemont	35179
North Walter	35055
Northwood Hills (Part of Florence)	35630
Norton	35803
Norwood (Part of Birmingham)	35234
Notasulga	36866
Nottingham	35014
Nuckols	36856
Nymph	36401
Oak	36535
Oak Bowery	36862
Oak Crossing (Part of Leeds)	35094
Oakdale	35611
Oakdale Acres	35611
Oak Grove (Autauga County)	36067
Oak Grove (Chilton County)	35085
Oak Grove (Franklin County)	35653
Oak Grove (Jefferson County)	35006
Oak Grove (Limestone County)	35739
Oak Grove (Mobile County)	36613
Oak Grove (Talladega County)	35150
Oak Hill (De Kalb County)	35962
Oak Hill (Wilcox County)	36766
Oakhurst (Part of Birmingham)	35207
Oakland	35630
Oakleigh Estates (Part of Gadsden)	35901

Oak Level-Praco **ALABAMA** 33

Name	ZIP
Oak Level	36262
Oakman	35579
Oakmulgee	36793
Oak Ridge (Morgan County)	35640
Oak Ridge (St. Clair County)	35125
Oak Ridge Park (Part of Birmingham)	35212
Oakville (Jefferson County)	35206
Oakville (Lawrence County)	35619
Oakwood (Part of Bessemer)	35020
Oakwood College	35896
Oakworth (Part of Decatur)	35601
Oaky Grove	36353
Oaky Streak	36037
Octagon	36748
Odena	35150
Oden Ridge	35621
Odenville	35120
Odom	36456
Ofelia	36266
Ohatchee	36271
Old Bethel	35646
Old Burleson	35593
Old Davistown	36201
Old Fabius	35966
Oldfield (Part of Sylacauga)	35150
Old Jonesboro	35215
Old Kingston	36067
Old Maylene (Part of Alabaster)	35114
Old Monrovia	35806
Old Nauvoo	35653
Old Samuel	36908
Old Spring Hill	36742
Old Texas	36768
Old Town (Conecuh County)	36401
Old Town (Dallas County)	36785
Oleander	35175
Oliver	35652
Ollie	36460
Olney	35442
Olustee	36081
Omaha	36274
O'Neal	35611
Oneonta	35121
Onycha	36467
Opelika	36801-03
For specific Opelika Zip Codes call (205) 745-3561	
Opine (Clarke County)	36784
Opine (Covington County)	36467
Opp	36561
Orange Beach	36561
Orchard (Part of Mobile)	36618
Ord (Part of Gadsden)	35901
Orion	36081
Orrville (Dallas County)	36767
Orrville (Limestone County)	35671
Osanippa	36854
Osborn	36779
Oswichee	36856
Our Town	35010
Overbrook	35150
Overlook (Part of Mobile)	36608
Overton	35210
Owassa	36401
Owens Cross Roads	35763
Owenton (Part of Birmingham)	35204
Oxford	36203
Oxford Lake (Part of Oxford)	36201
Oxmoor	35211
Oyster Bay	36535
Ozark	36360-61
For specific Ozark Zip Codes call (205) 774-5200	
Painter	35962
Paint Rock	35764
Palestine	36262
Palmerdale	35123
Palmers Crossroads	36480
Palmetto	35481
Palmetto Beach	36542
Palos	35130
Panola (Crenshaw County)	36046
Panola (Sumter County)	35477
Pansey	36370
Paran	36274
Park City	36526
Parkdale	35072
Park Hill (Part of Pell City)	35125
Parkland (Part of Jasper)	35501
Parkway City (Part of Huntsville)	35801
Parkway Estates (Part of Huntsville)	35802
Parkwood	35020

Name	ZIP
Parrish	35580
Partridge Crossroads	35180
Patsburg	36049
Patton	35579
Patton Chapel (Part of Hoover)	35216
Paul	36469
Pauls Hill	35020
Pawnee	35217
Peacock	36451
Pea Ridge (Escambia County)	36426
Pea Ridge (Fayette County)	35546
Pea Ridge (Madison County)	35801
Pea Ridge (Marion County)	35563
Pea Ridge (Shelby County)	35115
Pearson	35456
Pebble	35565
Peeks Corner	35961
Peeks Hill	36271
Peets Corner	35611
Pelham	35124
Pelham Heights (Part of Anniston)	36201
Pell City	35125
Penfield Heights (Part of Birmingham)	35217
Penn	35619
Pennington	36916
Pennsylvania (Part of Satsuma)	36572
Penton	36862
Pentonville	35136
Pepperell (Part of Opelika)	36801
Perdido	36562
Perdido Beach	36530
Perdue Hill	36470
Perote	36061
Perry Chapel	36586
Perry Store	36453
Perryville	36701
Peterman	36471
Peterson	35478
Petersville	35633
Petrey	36062
Petronia	36785
Pettusville	35620
Peytonia Points	35660
Phalin	35456
Phelan	35055
Phenix City	36867-68
For specific Phenix City Zip Codes call (205) 298-7871	
Phil Campbell	35581
Phillips Estates (Part of Bessemer)	35020
Phillipsville	36507
Phoenixville (Part of Birmingham)	35221
Pickensville	35447
Pickering	36758
Piedmont (Calhoun County)	36272
Piedmont (Madison County)	35801
Piedmont Springs	36272
Pierce	36587
Pigeon Creek	36037
Pike Road	36064
Pikeville	35768
Pilgrims Rest (Part of Southside)	35901
Pinckard	36371
Pinder Hill	35772
Pine Apple	36768
Pine Beach	36542
Pinebelt	36767
Pine Dale (Limestone County)	35739
Pinedale (Montgomery County)	36106
Pinedale Acres (Lauderdale County)	35645
Pinedale Acres (Limestone County)	35611
Pinedale Shores	35953
Pine Flat	36022
Pine Grove (Baldwin County)	36507
Pine Grove (Bullock County)	36053
Pine Grove (Cherokee County)	35960
Pine Grove (Lee County)	36801
Pine Grove (Tallapoosa County)	36850
Pine Hill (Randolph County)	36263
Pine Hill (Wilcox County)	36769
Pine Level (Autauga County)	36022
Pine Level (Coffee County)	36323
Pine Level (Montgomery County)	36065

Name	ZIP
Pine Mountain	35133
Pine Orchard	36471
Pine Ridge	35967
Pineview (Part of Irondale)	35210
Pinewood Terrace (Part of Childersburg)	35044
Piney	35960
Piney Bend	35593
Piney Chapel	35611
Piney Grove (Lawrence County)	35619
Piney Grove (Marion County)	35548
Piney Woods	36262
Pinkeyville	35072
Pinkney City	35214
Pinnell	36850
Pinson	35126
Pintlalla	36043
Pisgah (Jackson County)	35765
Pisgah (Limestone County)	35773
Pisgah (Montgomery County)	36036
Pittsview	36871
Plainview (Cleburne County)	36264
Plainview (De Kalb County)	35986
Plant City	36863
Plantersville (Dallas County)	36758
Plantersville (Talladega County)	35014
Plateau (Part of Prichard)	36610
Plaza De Malaga (Part of Mobile)	36685
Pleasant Acres	35811
Pleasant Gap	36272
Pleasant Grove (Chilton County)	35085
Pleasant Grove (Jackson County)	35772
Pleasant Grove (Jefferson County)	35127
Pleasant Grove (Marshall County)	35950
Pleasant Hill (Barbour County)	36027
Pleasant Hill (Choctaw County)	36908
Pleasant Hill (Dallas County)	36701
Pleasant Hill (Escambia County)	36502
Pleasant Hill (Franklin County)	35585
Pleasant Hill (Jefferson County)	35020
Pleasant Home	36420
Pleasant Plains	36312
Pleasant Ridge (Franklin County)	35653
Pleasant Ridge (Greene County)	35462
Pleasant Ridge (Pike County)	36034
Pleasant Site	35582
Pletcher	36750
Plevna	35761
Poarch	36502
Pocahontas	35549
Pogo	35582
Point Clear	36564
Polk	36785
Pollard	36441
Pollards Bend	35983
Ponderosa Estates	36575
Ponders	36853
Pondville	35034
Pool	35619
Pooles Crossroads	36274
Pools Crossroads	35045
Pope	36769
Poplarridge	35760
Poplar Springs (Marshall County)	35950
Poplar Springs (Winston County)	35578
Port Birmingham	35118
Porter	35005
Portersville	35961
Posey Mill	35565
Poseys Crossroads	36067
Postoak	36089
Potash	36274
Potter	36701
Powderly (Part of Birmingham)	35211
Powderly Hills (Part of Birmingham)	35211
Powell's Crossroads	35971
Powers	35474
Powhatan	35118
Powledge	36874
Praco	35130

34 ALABAMA Prairie-Scottsboro

Name	ZIP
Prairie	36771
Prairieville	36742
Pratt City (Part of Birmingham)	35214
Prattmont (Part of Prattville)	36067
Pratts	36016
Prattville	36067
Prescott	35125
Preston	35768
Prestwick	36548
Priceville	35601
Prichard	36610
Pride	35674
Primitive Ridge	35184
Princeton	35766
Pronto	36081
Prospect	35578
Providence (Butler County)	36033
Providence (Cullman County)	35179
Providence (Marengo County)	36742
Providence (Walker County)	35579
Prudence	36871
Pruitton	35630
Pulaski Pike (Part of Huntsville)	35810
Pullight	35548
Pumpkin Center (De Kalb County)	35967
Pumpkin Center (Morgan County)	35619
Pumpkin Center (Walker County)	35130
Pushmataha	36912
Putnam	36784
Pyriton	36266
Queenstown	35173
Quintard Mall (Part of Oxford)	36201
Quinton	35130
Quintown	35130
Rabb	36401
Rabbittown (Calhoun County)	36272
Rabbit Town (Marshall County)	35950
Rabbittown (Winston County)	35565
Rabun	36507
Ragland	35131
Raimund	35020
Rainbow	35758
Rainbow City	35901
Rainbow Mountain Heights (Madison County)	35758
Rainsville	35986
Ralph	35480
Ramer	36069
Ranburne	36273
Randolph	36792
Range	36473
Rash	35772
Rayburn (Part of Guntersville)	35976
Read's Mill	36279
Red Bank	35672
Red Bay	35582
Reddock Springs	36037
Red Eagle Honor Farm	36101
Red Hill (Blount County)	35063
Red Hill (Elmore County)	36078
Red Hill (Marshall County)	35976
Redland Heights	36854
Red Level	36474
Redmont Park (Part of Mountain Brook)	35213
Red Ore	35020
Red Rock	35674
Red Rock Junction	35616
Redstone Arsenal (Madison County)	35808
Redstone Arsenal (Madison County)	35809
Redtown	36502
Reece City	35954
Reedtown (Part of Russellville)	35653
Reeltown	36078
Reform	35481
Regency (Part of Florence)	35630
Regent Forest	35226
Rehobeth	36301
Rehoboth	36720
Reid	36611
Remlap	35133
Renfroe	35160
Reno	35111
Repton	36475
Republic	35214
Rhoades	36453

Name	ZIP
Rhodesville	35630
Rice	35201
Richmond	36761
Richmond Hills (Part of Tuscumbia)	35674
Rideout Village (Part of Huntsville)	35806
Riderwood	36904
Ridgecrest	36105
Ridgeville (Butler County)	36030
Ridgeville (Etowah County)	35954
Ringgold	35973
Ripley	35611
Riverbend	35184
Riverdale (Part of Mentone)	35984
River Falls	36476
Rivermont (Colbert County)	35660
Rivermont (Lauderdale County)	35630
River Park	36532
Riverside (Blount County)	35031
Riverside (St. Clair County)	35135
Riverton	35616
River View (Chambers County)	36854
Riverview (Chambers County)	36854
Riverview (Escambia County)	36426
Riverview (Tuscaloosa County)	35401
Riverwood (Part of Tuscaloosa)	35406
Roanoke	36274
Roanoke Junction (Part of Opelika)	36801
Roba	36089
Robbins Crossroads	35062
Roberta	35040
Roberts	36420
Robertsdale	36567
Robinsons	36752
Robinson Springs	36025
Robinsonville	36502
Robinwood	35217
Rock City (Jackson County)	35771
Rock City (Marion County)	35594
Rockdale	35020
Rocket	35808
Rockford	35136
Rock Hill	36426
Rock House	35771
Rockledge	35954
Rock Mills	36274
Rock Run	36272
Rock Spring (Part of Glencoe)	35905
Rock Spring Quarry (Part of Glencoe)	35905
Rock Springs (Blount County)	35031
Rock Springs (Choctaw County)	36904
Rock Stand	36274
Rockville	36545
Rockwest	36726
Rockwood	35653
Rocky Head	36311
Rocky Hill	35672
Rocky Hollow	35550
Rocky Ridge	35243
Rodentown	35957
Roebuck (Part of Birmingham)	35206
Roebuck Crest Estates (Part of Birmingham)	35215
Roebuck Forest (Part of Birmingham)	35235
Roebuck Gardens (Part of Birmingham)	35235
Roebuck Park (Part of Birmingham)	35215
Roebuck Plaza	35235
Roebuck Springs (Part of Birmingham)	35206
Roebuck Terrace (Part of Birmingham)	35206
Roeton	36010
Rogersville	35652
Rolling Hills (Part of Decatur)	35603
Rollins	36022
Romar Beach	36561
Rome	36420
Romulus	35446
Roosevelt City	35020
Roper	35173
Rosa	35121
Rosalie	35765
Roseboro	37328
Rosebud	36766

Name	ZIP
Rosedale (Part of Homewood)	35209
Rose Hill (Covington County)	36028
Rose Hill (Jefferson County)	35210
Rosemont (Part of Birmingham)	35221
Rose Park (Part of Florence)	35630
Rosinton	36567
Rossland City	35555
Round Hill	36784
Round Mountain	35959
Rowells Crossroad	36879
Roxana	36879
Royal	35031
Ruffner (Part of Irondale)	35210
Russell Heights (Part of Leeds)	35094
Russell Mill (Part of Alexander City)	35010
Russell Village (Part of Decatur)	35603
Russellville	35653
Rutan	36518
Ruth	35016
Rutherford	36860
Rutledge	36071
Rutledge Heights (Jefferson County)	35064
Rutledge Heights (Madison County)	35816
Ryan	35115
Ryan Crossroads	35087
Ryland	35767
Saco	36081
Safford	36773
Saginaw	35137
Sahama Village (Part of Tuscaloosa)	35401
St. Bernard	35055
St. Clair	35752
St. Clair Correctional Facility	35120
St. Clair Springs	35146
St. Elmo	36568
St. Florian	35630
Saints Crossroads	35653
St. Stephens	36569
Saks (Calhoun County)	36201
Salem (Dallas County)	36767
Salem (Fayette County)	35546
Salem (Lee County)	36874
Salem (Limestone County)	35620
Salitpa	36570
Samantha	35482
Samford University (Part of Homewood)	35229
Samson	36477
Samuels Chapel	35952
Sandfield	36081
Sandfort	36875
Sandhurst Park (Part of Huntsville)	35802
Sand Rock	35961
Sandtown	35546
Sandusky (Part of Birmingham)	35214
Sandy Creek	36850
Sandy Ridge	36047
Sanford	36420
Sanie	35120
San Souci Beach (Part of Bayou La Batre)	36509
Santuck	36092
Sapps	35447
Saragossa	35578
Saraland	36571
Saratoga (Part of Albertville)	35950
Sardine	36441
Sardis (Bullock County)	36089
Sardis (Dallas County)	36775
Sardis (Walker County)	35550
Sardis City	35957
Sardis Springs	35611
Satsuma	36572
Saucer	36030
Saville	36041
Sawyerville	36776
Sayre	35139
Scant City	35016
Scarce Grease	35647
Scenic Heights (Part of Gadsden)	35901
Schenks	36279
Schmits Mill	35096
Schuster Springs	36768
Scotland	36471
Scotrock (Part of Alabaster)	35007
Scott City	35094
Scottland	36089
Scottsboro	35768

Scranage-The Highlands ALABAMA 35

Name	ZIP
Scranage	36502
Scranton	36313
Scyrene	36436
Seaboard	36522
Seacliff (Part of Fairhope)	36532
Seale	36875
Sealy Springs (Part of Cottonwood)	36320
Searight	36028
Searles	35444
Section	35771
Segco	35580
Selbrook	36108
Selfville	35133
Sellers	36046
Sellersville	36318
Selma	36701-02
For specific Selma Zip Codes call (205) 874-4678	
Selma Mall (Part of Selma)	36701
Selmont	36701
Selmont-West Selmont	36701
Seman	36024
Seminole	36567
Semmes	36575
Service	36919
Seven Hills	36601
Seymour Bluff	36542
Shacklesville	36033
Shades Crest Estates	35226
Shady Grove (Clay County)	35072
Shady Grove (Coffee County)	36323
Shady Grove (Franklin County)	35581
Shady Grove (Pike County)	36035
Shady Lane (Part of Huntsville)	35810
Shanghai	35611
Shannon	35142
Shawmut (Part of Valley)	36854
Shawnee	36726
Sheffield	35660-62
For specific Sheffield Zip Codes call (205) 383-0252	
Shelby	35143
Shellhorn	36081
Sherman Heights (Part of Anniston)	36201
Sherwood Forest (Part of Florence)	35630
Sherwood Park (Part of Huntsville)	35206
Shiloh (De Kalb County)	35967
Shiloh (Marengo County)	36754
Shiloh (Pike County)	36005
Shinebone	36266
Shingle	35581
Shoals Acres	35645
Shopton	36029
Short Creek	35118
Shorter	36075
Shorterville	36373
Shortleaf (Part of Demopolis)	36732
Shottsville	35570
Shreve	36456
Sico	35150
Siddonsville	36738
Sigma	36319
Sikesville	36276
Silas	36919
Siloam	36907
Siluria (Part of Alabaster)	35144
Silver Cross	36919
Silverhill	36576
Silver Run	36268
Simcoe	35055
Simmons Crossroads	36879
Simmsville	35043
Sims Chapel	36553
Simsville	36089
Sipsey	35584
Six Mile	35035
Six Way	35603
Skaggs Corner (Part of Ider)	35978
Skeggs Crossroads	35072
Skinem	35750
Skinnerton	36401
Skipperville	36374
Skirum	35963
Skyline	35768
Skyline Acres	35758
Skyline Estates	35226
Sky Ranch	35226
Skyview (Part of Bessemer)	35020
Slackland	35901
Slocomb	36375
Smithfield (Part of Birmingham)	35204
Smith Hill	35184

Name	ZIP
Smith Institute	35957
Smiths	36877
Smiths Crossroads (Part of Glencoe)	35901
Smithson	35020
Smithsonia	35630
Smut Eye	36061
Smyer	36727
Smyrna	36301
Snead	35952
Snoddy	35462
Snowdoun	36105
Snow Hill	36778
Snowtown	35062
Socapatoy	35089
Society Hill	36801
Soleo	35072
Somerville	35670
South (Covington County)	36474
South (Montgomery County)	36116
South Calera (Part of Calera)	35040
South Gadsden (Part of Gadsden)	35901
South Gate Mall (Part of Muscle Shoals)	35660
South Guntersville (Part of Guntersville)	35976
South Haleyville (Part of Haleyville)	35565
South Highlands (Part of Birmingham)	35205
South Lowell	35501
Southmont (Part of Montgomery)	36105
South Orchard	36582
South Park Estates (Part of Huntsville)	35802
South Sheffield (Part of Tuscumbia)	35674
Southside	35901
Southtown (Part of Guntersville)	35976
Southwood (Part of Homewood)	35209
Souwilpa	36919
Spanish Fort	36527
Speake	35619
Speed	36026
Speeds Water Mill	35466
Speigener	36022
Spivey's	36535
Sprague	36069
Springbrook (Part of Tuscaloosa)	35405
Springdale (Part of Tarrant)	35217
Springdale Mall (Part of Mobile)	36606
Springfield (Clarke County)	36784
Springfield (Lauderdale County)	35652
Springfield (Randolph County)	36274
Spring Garden	36275
Spring Hill (Barbour County)	36053
Spring Hill (Mobile County)	36608
Springhill (Pike County)	36081
Spring Hill (Walker County)	35549
Spring Valley (Colbert County)	35674
Spring Valley (Montgomery County)	36116
Springville	35146
Springville Lake Estates	35146
Sprott	36779
Spruce Pine	35585
Standard	35580
Standing Rock	36855
Stanley	36420
Stansel	35481
Stanton	36790
Stapleton	36578
Star	35576
State Line	36320
Statesville (Autauga County)	36701
Statesville (Bibb County)	35184
Steele	35987
Steele Crossing	37328
Steelwood	36551
Steenson Hollow (Part of Muscle Shoals)	35660
Steiner (Part of Montgomery)	36111
Sterrett	35147
Stevenson	35772
Stewart	35441
Stewartsville	35150
Stills Cross Road	36081
Stockdale	36268
Stockton	36579
Stokeley (Part of Andalusia)	36420

Name	ZIP
Stokes	35456
Stones	36054
Stoney Point	36022
Stough	35555
Straight Mountain	35121
Strata	36046
Strawberry	35016
Stroud	36855
Studdards Crossroads	35549
Sturkie	36862
Suggsville	36482
Sulligent	35586
Sulphur Springs (Blount County)	35079
Sulphur Springs (De Kalb County)	30738
Sulphur Springs (Jackson County)	35966
Sulphur Springs (Madison County)	35761
Sumiton	35148
Summerdale	36580
Summerfield	36701
Summit	35031
Summit Farm	35023
Sumterville	35460
Sunflower	36581
Sunny Cove	36582
Sunny South	36769
Sunset Cove (Part of Huntsville)	35802
Sunset Mill Village (Part of Selma)	36701
Sunset Shores	36535
Sun Valley	35215
Surginer	36754
Susan Moore	35952
Suspension	36089
Suttle	36701
Swaim	35764
Swancott	35758
Swearengin	35768
Sweet Water	36782
Sycamore	35149
Sylacauga	35150
Sylvan Grove	36350
Sylvania	35988
Sylvan Springs	35118
Tabernacle (Coffee County)	36351
Tabernacle (Houston County)	36301
Tabor	35901
Taft	35973
Taits Gap	35121
Talladega	35160
Talladega Springs	35150
Tallahatta Springs	36784
Tallapoosa City (Part of Tallassee)	36023
Tallassee	36078
Tallaweka (Part of Tallassee)	36078
Talucah	35775
Tanner	35671
Tanner Crossroads	35671
Tanner Heights (Part of Hartselle)	35640
Tanner Williams	36587
Tanyard (Bullock County)	36061
Tanyard (St. Clair County)	35125
Tarentum	36010
Tarpley (Part of Birmingham)	35211
Tarrant	35217
Tarrant Heights	35217
Tasso	36767
Tattlersville	36524
Taylor	36301
Taylors Crossroads	36274
Taylorville	35405
Teals Crossroads	36311
Teasleys Mill	36052
Tecumseh	30138
Teddy	36426
Tenant	36274
Ten Broeck (Part of Lakeview)	35971
Tennala	35960
Tennille	36010
Tensaw	36579
Terese (Part of Eufaula)	36027
Terry Heights (Part of Huntsville)	35805
Texasville	36016
Thach	35501
Tharptown	35653
Thatch	35620
The Cedars (Part of Florence)	35630
The Highlands (Etowah County)	35901

36 ALABAMA The Highlands-Whitehead

Place	ZIP
The Highlands (Madison County)	35810
Theodore	36582
The Ridge	36460
Thomas (Autauga County)	36067
Thomas (Jefferson County)	35214
Thomas Acres (Part of Bessemer)	35020
Thomas F. Station Correctional Center	36025
Thomas Hill (Part of Sylacauga)	35150
Thomaston	36783
Thomasville	36784
Thompson	36089
Thorn Hill	35565
Thornton	36853
Thorntontown	35652
Thorsby	35171
Three Notch	36053
Threet	35617
Thurston	36340
Tibbie	36583
Tilden	36761
Till	36033
Tiller Crossroads	36850
Tillery Crossroads	36854
Tillmans Corner (Mobile County)	36619
Tinela	36481
Titus	36080
Toadvine	35020
Toddtown	36451
Tompkinsville	36916
Toney	35773
Toonersville	35652
Toulminville (Part of Mobile)	36610
Town Creek	35672
Townley	35587
Toxey	36921
Trade	35053
Trafford	35172
Travis Bridge	36401
Tredegar	36265
Trenton	35774
Triana	35758
Trickem	36785
Trimble	35055
Trinity	35673
Trotwood Park (Part of Birmingham)	35206
Troy	36081
Trussville	35173
Tuckabatchie	36078
Tuckahoe Heights (Part of Gadsden)	35901
Tucker Crossroads	35959
Tumbleton	36345
Tunnel Springs	36471
Tupelo	35768
Turkestan	36753
Turkey Branch	36555
Turkeytown	35901
Turner Crossroads	36351
Tuscaloosa	35401-06 35486-87
For specific Tuscaloosa Zip Codes call (205) 553-6415	
Tuscumbia	35674
Tuskegee	36083
Tuskegee Institute (Part of Tuskegee)	36088
Twilley Town	35130
Twin	35563
Twin Oaks (Part of Montgomery)	36123
Twinsprings	36027
Tyler	36785
Tyler Crossroads	36048
Tyson	36043
Tysonville	36075
Uchee	36858
Underwood (Lauderdale County)	35630
Underwood (Shelby County)	35115
Underwood Crossroads	35646
Underwood-Petersville	35630
Union (Etowah County)	35957
Union (Greene County)	35462
Union (Henry County)	36310
Union (Morgan County)	35670
Union (Tallapoosa County)	36853
Union Academy	36330
Union Grove (Chilton County)	35085
Union Grove (Cullman County)	35083
Union Grove (Jefferson County)	35005
Union Grove (Marshall County)	35175

Place	ZIP
Union Hill (Cleburne County)	36273
Union Hill (Limestone County)	35610
Union Hill (Morgan County)	35622
Union Springs	36089
Uniontown	36786
Unity (Autauga County)	36006
Unity (Coosa County)	35183
Unity (Tuscaloosa County)	35401
Universal Heights	35404
University (Part of Tuscaloosa)	35486
University Mall (Part of Tuscaloosa)	35401
University of Montevallo (Part of Montevallo)	35115
University of South Alabama (Part of Mobile)	36608
Upper Coalburg	35068
Upper Green Hill	35630
Upshaw	35540
Uriah	36480
Valdosta (Part of Tuscumbia)	35674
Valhermoso Springs	35775
Vallegrande	36701
Valley	36854
Valley Creek	35020
Valley Creek Junction	36758
Valley Head	35989
Valley View	35640
Vance	35490
Vanderbilt (Part of Birmingham)	35204
Vandiver	35176
Vangale	36782
Vaughn	36579
Vaughn Corners	35758
Verbena	36091
Verlie (Part of Alabaster)	35007
Vernledge	36049
Vernon	35592
Vernontown	35184
Vestavia Hills	35216
Vestavia Hills Centre (Part of Vestavia Hills)	35216
Vesthaven (Part of Vestavia Hills)	35216
Veterans Hospital (Part of Tuscaloosa)	35401
Veto	35620
Vick (Part of Centreville)	35042
Victoria	36323
Vida	36067
Vidette	36049
Vienna	35442
Viewpoint	35963
Vigo	36272
Village Creek (Part of Birmingham)	35207
Village Springs	35126
Villula	36871
Vina	35593
Vincent	35178
Vinegar Bend	36584
Vine Hill	36758
Vineland	36784
Vineland Park (Part of Hueytown)	35020
Vinemont	35179
Vinesville (Part of Birmingham)	35208
Vinnette	36201
Virginia	35020
Virginia Shores	35560
Vocation	36480
Volanta (Part of Fairhope)	36532
Vredenburgh	36481
Vulcan City (Part of Birmingham)	35207
Waco	35653
Wacoochee Valley	36874
Wadley	36276
Wadsworth	36022
Wagar	36585
Wagarville	36585
Wahouma (Part of Birmingham)	35206
Walco (Part of Sylacauga)	35150
Waldo	35160
Walker Chapel (Part of Fultondale)	35068
Walkers Corner	35055
Walker Springs	36586
Walkerton (Part of Pell City)	35125
Wallace	36426
Walley	36584
Wallsboro	36092
Wall Street	35758
Walnut Grove	35990
Walnut Hill	36853

Place	ZIP
Walnut Park (Part of Gadsden)	35904
Walter	35077
Wannville	35752
Ward	36922
Ware	36078
Warrenton	35976
Warrior	35180
Warriorstand	36089
Warsaw	35477
Waterford (Part of Newton)	36352
Waterloo	35677
Water Valley	36908
Watson (Cherokee County)	35973
Watson (Jefferson County)	35187
Watsonville	36753
Watts Mill	36266
Wattsville	35182
Waugh	36109
Waverly	36879
Wawbeek	36502
Wayne	36782
Wayside	35594
Weatherly Heights (Part of Huntsville)	35802
Weaver	36277
Webb	36376
Webb Addition (Part of Scottsboro)	35768
Webster Chapel	35901
Wedgewood	36108
Wedgworth	36776
Wedowee	36278
Weed Crossroad	36009
Weeden Heights (Part of Florence)	35630
Weeks	36453
Wegra	35130
Wehadkee	36274
Wellington	36279
Welti	35055
Wende	36860
Wenonah (Part of Birmingham)	35211
Weogufka	35183
Weoka	36092
Wessington	35040
West (Part of Huntsville)	35805
West Alexandria	36250
West Bend	36524
West Blocton	35184
West End (Calhoun County)	36201
West End (Jefferson County)	35211
West End (Montgomery County)	36104
West End-Cobbtown	36201
West Ensley	35224
Western Hills (Part of Mobile)	36618
Western Hills Estates	35749
Western Hills Mall (Part of Fairfield)	35064
West Greene (Greene County)	35491
West Highlands (Part of Hueytown)	35023
West Huntsville (Part of Huntsville)	35807
West Jefferson	35130
West Lake Highlands (Part of Bessemer)	35020
Westlake Mall (Part of Bessemer)	35020
Westlawn (Part of Huntsville)	35807
West Monroeville (Part of Monroeville)	36460
Weston	35570
Westover	35185
West Point	35055
West Pratt (Part of Dora)	35062
West Sayre	35062
West Selmont	36701
West Side (Jefferson County)	35020
West Side (Montgomery County)	36108
West Wellington	36279
Westwood	35005
Wetumpka	36092
Whatley	36482
Wheat	35053
Wheeler	35618
Wheelerville (Part of Mobile)	36608
Whistler (Part of Mobile)	36612
White City (Autauga County)	36051
White City (Cullman County)	35077
White Hall	36040
Whitehead	35652

Whitehouse-Zoar **ALABAMA** 37

	ZIP		ZIP		ZIP
Whitehouse	35565	Wilsonville	35186	Woodmont (Part of Hueytown)	35020
Whitehouse Forks	36507	Wilton	35187	Woodstock	35188
Whiteoak (Colbert County)	35646	Wimberly	36921	Woodstock Junction	35188
White Oak (Henry County)	36310	Winburn	35094	Woodville	35776
Whiteoak (Marshall County)	35950	Windham Springs	35546	Woodward	35020
White Plains (Calhoun County)	36201	Windsor Highlands (Part of Homewood)	35209	Woolfolk	36268
White Plains (Chambers County)	36862	Winfield	35594	Wren	35650
Whites Bluff	36767	Wing	36483	Wright	35677
Whitesboro	35957	Wingard	36035	Wright Crossroads (Lee County)	36830
Whitesburg Estates (Part of Huntsville)	35802	Winn	36545	Wyatt	35130
Whites Chapel	35173	Winninger	35776	Wylam (Part of Birmingham)	35224
Whites Gap	36265	Winslow	36003	Wynnville	35952
Whitesville	35957	Winterboro	35014	Yantley	36912
Whitfield	36925	Winton	35670	Yarbo	36558
Whitney (Part of Ashville)	35953	Wolf Creek	35125	Yelling Settlement	36526
Whiton	35962	Wolf Springs	35672	Yellow Bluff	36769
Whorton	35960	Womack Hill	36908	Yellow Creek Falls	35959
Wicksburg	36352	Woodaire Estates	35215	Yellowleaf	35186
Wiggins (Part of Babbie)	36420	Woodbluff	36727	Yellow Pine	36539
Wigginsville	35611	Wooddale	35244	Yerkwood	35062
Wiginton	35564	Woodford	35470	York	36925
Wilburn	35033	Woodland (Macon County)	36866	Youngblood	36081
Wiley (Montgomery County)	36105	Woodland (Randolph County)	36280	Youngs Chapel	35901
Wiley (Tuscaloosa County)	35501	Woodland Forest	35405	Yucca	35966
Wilkes (Part of Midfield)	35064	Woodland Lake	35111	Yupon	36555
Wilkinstown	36081	Woodlawn (Part of Birmingham)	35212	Zimco	36451
Williamstown	35580	Woodlawn Heights (Franklin County)	35653	Zion (Montgomery County)	36047
Willowbrook (Part of Huntsville)	35802	Woodlawn Heights (Jefferson County)	35212	Zion (Pickens County)	35466
Willow Springs	36092	Woodley Park (Part of Montgomery)	36116	Zion City (Part of Birmingham)	35207
Wills Crossroads	36310	Woodmeadow (Part of Hoover)	35226	Zion Heights (Part of Birmingham)	35207
Wills Valley	35967			Zip City	35630
Wilmer	36587			Zoar	36323
Wilson Lake Shores	35660				
Wilson Quarters	36303				

ALASKA

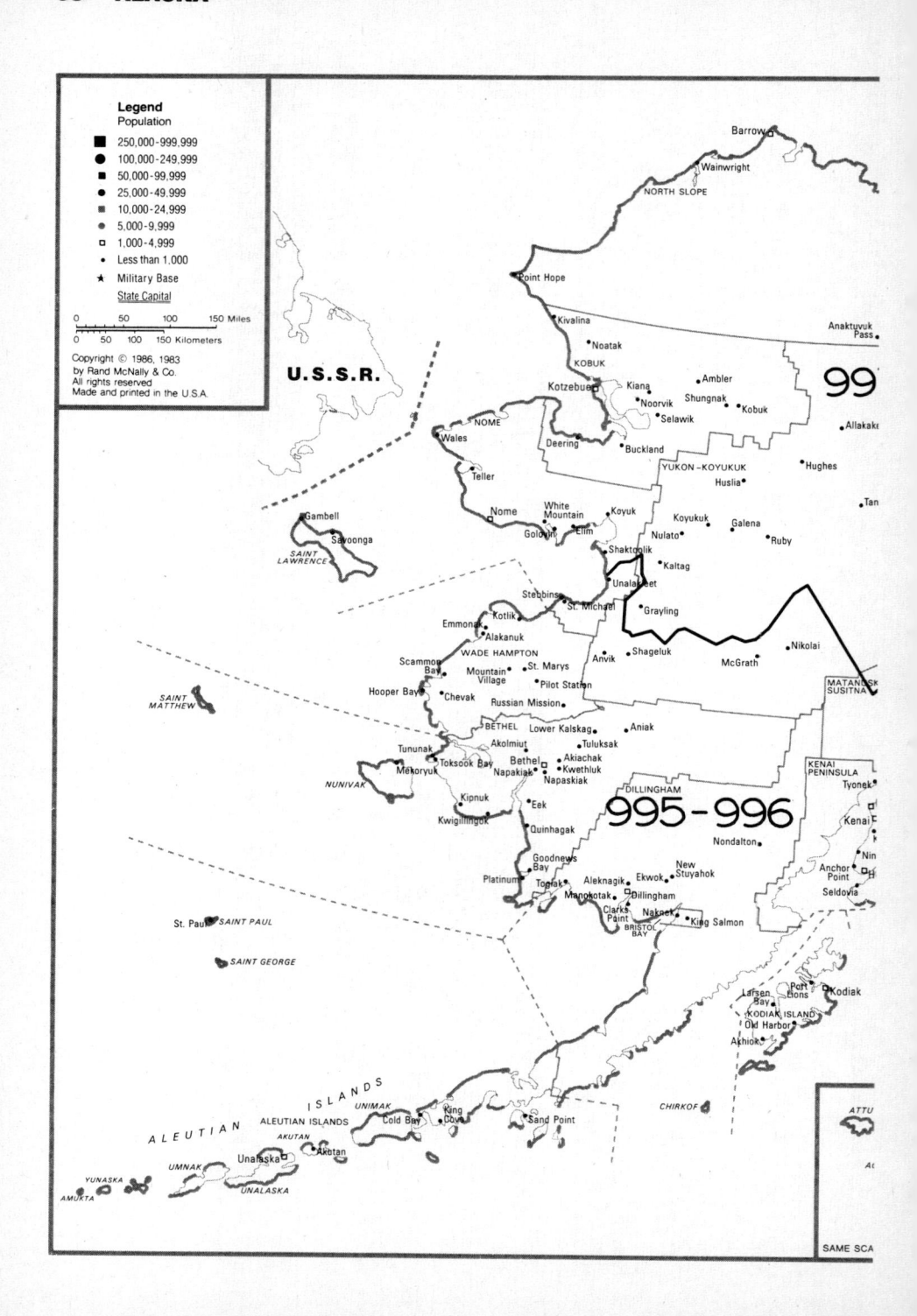

ALASKA 39

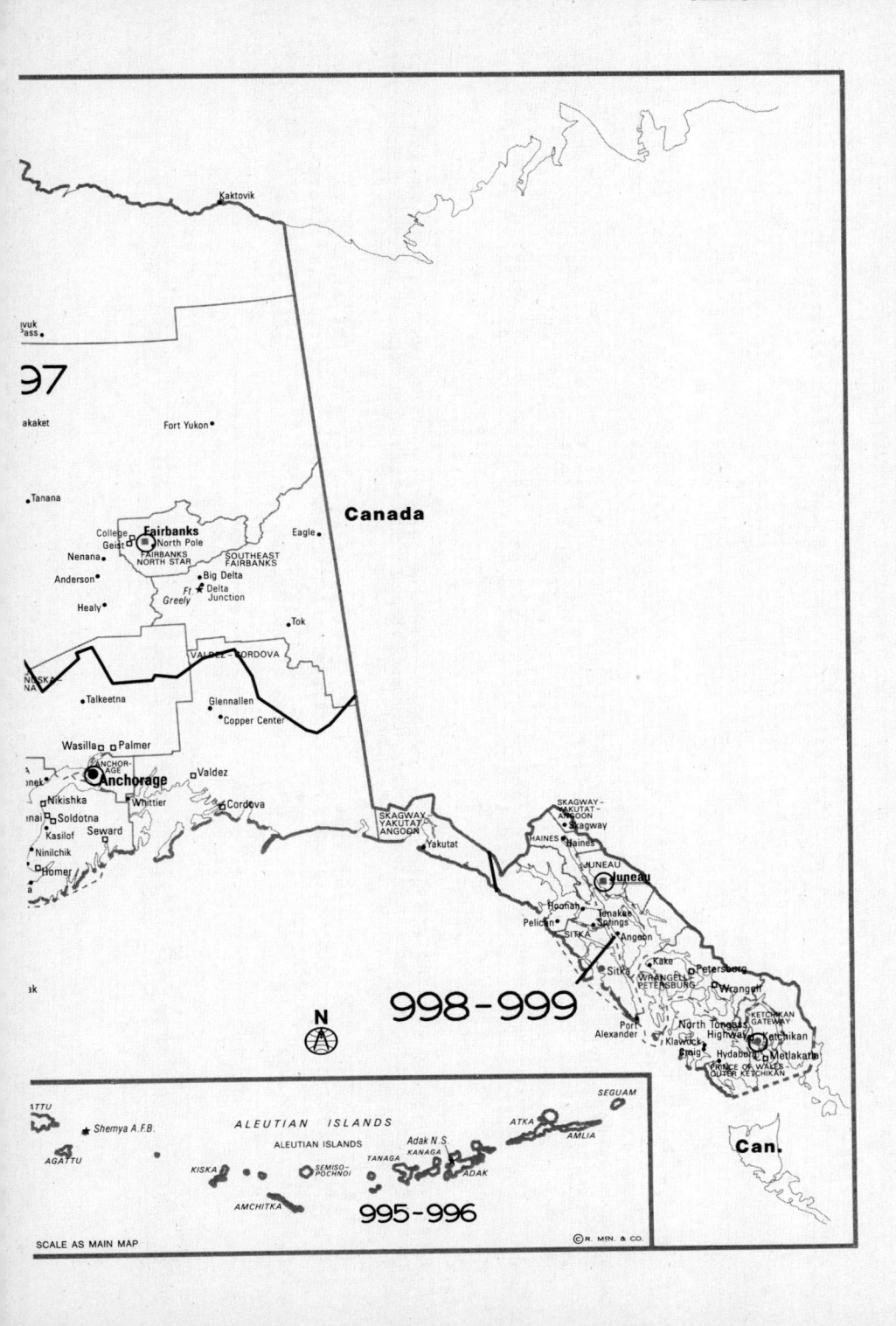

ALASKA Adak Naval Station-Lake Minchumina

Place	ZIP
Adak Naval Station	98791
Adak Station	98791
Akhiok	99615
Akiachak	99551
Akiak	99552
Akutan	99553
Alakanuk	99554
Alatna (Part of Allakaket)	99720
Aleknagik	99555
Alexander Creek	99502
Alitak	99615
Allakaket	99720
Ambler	99786
Amook	99697
Anaktuvuk Pass	99721
Anchorage	99501-40
For specific Anchorage Zip Codes call (907) 564-2842	
Anchorage 5th Avenue Shopping Center (Part of Anchorage)	99501
Anchor Point	99556
Anderson	99744
Angoon	99820
Aniak	99557
Annette	99926
Anvik	99558
Arctic Village	99722
Atka	99502
Atmautluak	99559
Atqasuk	99791
Attu	99502
Auke Bay (Part of Juneau)	99821
Aurora (Part of Fairbanks)	99701
Aurora Lodge	99701
Baranof (Part of Sitka)	99833
Barrow	99723
Bartlett Cove	99826
Beaver	99724
Belkofski	99612
Bell Island Hot Springs	99901
Bethel	99559
Bettles Field	99726
Big Delta	99737
Big Horn	99701
Big Lake	99652
Birch Creek	99740
Birch Estates	99701
Birchwood (Part of Anchorage)	99567
Bird Creek (Part of Anchorage)	99540
Bjerremark (Part of Fairbanks)	99701
Black Sand	99689
Bluff	99784
Bodenburg Butte	99645
Border	99780
Boswell Bay	99574
Boundary	99790
Boyd	99701
Brevig Mission	99785
Broadmoor Acres	99701
Brooks Lodge	99613
Browerville (Part of Barrow)	99723
Buckland	99727
Campbell (Anchorage Borough)	99503
Campbell (Prince of Wales-Outer Ketchikan Census Division)	99901
Campion Station	99741
Candle	99752
Cantwell	99729
Cape Lisburne (North Slope Borough)	99766
Cape Newenham	99651
Cape Newenham Air Force Station	99651
Cape Pole	99901
Cape Romanzof Air Force Station	99559
Cape Yakataga	99574
Carlanna (Part of Ketchikan)	99901
Central	99730
Chalkyitsik	99788
Chandalar	99701
Charcoal Point (Part of Ketchikan)	99901
Chase	99676
Chatanika	99701
Chatham (Part of Sitka)	99801
Chefornak	99561
Chena Hot Springs	99701
Chernofski	99685
Chevak	99563
Chickaloon	99674
Chicken	99732
Chignik	99564
Chignik Lagoon	99565
Chignik Lake	99564

Place	ZIP
Chisana	99588
Chistochina	99586
Chitina	99566
Chuathbaluk	99557
Chugiak (Part of Anchorage)	99567
Circle	99733
Circle Hot Springs	99730
Clam Gulch	99568
Clarks Point	99569
Clear	99704
Clearwater Ranch	99737
Clover Pass	99901
Coffman Cove	99550
Cohoe	99610
Cold Bay	99571
College (Fairbanks North Star Borough)	99708
College (Fairbanks North Star Borough)	99701
Collegiate Park	99701
Colorado	99501
Cooper Landing	99572
Copper Center	99573
Cordova	99574
Cosna	99756
Cottonwood	99687
Council	99762
Craig	99921
Crooked Creek	99575
Deadhorse	99734
Debar Shopping Center (Part of Anchorage)	99501
Deering	99736
Delta Junction	99737
Denali National Park	99755
Derby Tract (Part of Fairbanks)	99701
Dillingham	99576
Dot Lake	99737
Douglas (Part of Juneau)	99824
Downtown (Anchorage Borough)	99501
Downtown (Fairbanks North Star Borough)	99707
Dunbar	99760
Duncan Canal	99833
Dutch Harbor	99692
Eagle	99738
Eagle River (Part of Anchorage)	99577
Eagle Village	99738
Eastchester (Part of Anchorage)	99520
Edna Bay	99901
Eek	99578
Egegik	99579
Eielson AFB	99702
Eielson Air Force Base	99702
Eklutna (Part of Anchorage)	99567
Eklutna Housing Project (Part of Anchorage)	99645
Ekuk	99576
Ekwok	99580
Elfin Cove	99825
Elim	99739
Emmonak	99581
English Bay	99603
Eska	99674
Ester	99725
Eureka (Matanuska-Susitna Borough)	99645
Eureka (Yukon-Koyukuk Census Division)	99756
Evansville	99726
Excursion Inlet	99826
Eyak	99574
Fairbanks	99701
	99706-16
For specific Fairbanks Zip Codes call (907) 474-0722	
False Pass	99583
Farewell	99627
Fire Lake (Part of Anchorage)	99577
Fishhook Junction	99645
Flat	99584
Fort Greely (Southeast Fairbanks Census Division)	98733
Fort Wainwright (Part of Fairbanks)	99703
Fortymile Roadhouse	99737
Fort Yukon	99740
Four Corners	99645
Fox	99701
Fritz Cove (Part of Juneau)	99824
Fritz Creek	99603
Funter Bay	99801
Gakona	99586
Galena	99741

Place	ZIP
Gambell	99742
Ganes Creek	99675
Geist	99701
Girdwood (Part of Anchorage)	99587
Glennallen	99588
Goat Creek	99645
Gold Creek	99676
Golovin	99762
Goodnews Bay	99589
Goodnews Mining Camp	99651
Graehl (Part of Fairbanks)	99701
Granite Mountain	99762
Grayling	99590
Gulkana	99586
Gulkana Airport	99588
Gustavus	99826
Haines	99827
Halibut Cove	99603
Hamilton	99620
Hamilton Acres (Part of Fairbanks)	99701
Happy Valley	99555
Harding Lake	99701
Hawk Inlet	99850
Haycock	99753
Healy	99743
Healy Lake	99737
Herring Cove	99901
Hogatza	99701
Holy Cross	99602
Homer	99603
Hoonah	99829
Hooper Bay	99604
Hope	99605
Houston	99694
Hughes	99745
Huslia	99746
Hydaburg	99922
Hyder	99923
Igiugig	99613
Iliamna	99606
Indian (Part of Anchorage)	99540
Indian Mountain	99745
Indian River	99720
Island Homes (Part of Fairbanks)	99701
Ivanof Bay	99613
Jakolof Bay	99695
Jennie M.	99701
Johnston (Part of Fairbanks)	99701
Juneau	99801-03
	99821-24
For specific Juneau Zip Codes call (907) 586-7138	
Kachemak	99603
Kake	99830
Kako	99657
Kaktovik	99747
Kalakaket Creek Radio Relay Site	99741
Kalifonsky	99610
Kalskag	99607
Kaltag	99748
Karluk	99608
Kasaan	99901
Kashegelok	99668
Kasigluk	99609
Kasilof	99610
Kenai	99611
Kenai Lake	99572
Kenai Packers Cannery (Part of Kenai)	99611
Kennicott	99588
Ketchikan	99901
Ketchikan East	99901
Kiana	99749
King Cove	99612
King Salmon	99613
Kipnuk	99614
Kivalina	99750
Klawock	99925
Klukwan	99827
Knik	99687
Knudson Cove	99901
Kobuk	99751
Kodiak	99615
Kodiak Station	99615
Kokhanok	99606
Kokrines	99768
Koliganek	99576
Kongiganak	99559
Kotlik	99620
Kotzebue	99752
Koyuk	99753
Koyukuk	99754
Kupreanof	99833
Kustatan	99682
Kwethluk	99621
Kwigillingok	99622
Lake Minchumina	99757

ALASKA

Name	ZIP
Lake Nancy	99688
Lakloey Hill	99701
Larsen Bay	99624
Lawing	99664
Lemeta (Part of Fairbanks)	99701
Lemon Creek (Part of Juneau)	99801
Lena Cove (Part of Juneau)	99801
Levelock	99625
Lime Village	99627
Little Diomede	99762
Little Port Walter	99835
Livengood	99701
Long	99768
Long Island	99687
Lost River (Nome County)	99762
Lost River (Skagway-Yakutat-Angoon County)	99689
Lower Kalskag	99626
Lower Mendenhall Valley (Part of Juneau)	99801
Lower Tonsina	99573
McCarthy	99695
McGrath	99627
Mack	99701
McKinley Acres	99701
Manley Hot Springs	99756
Manokotak	99628
Mansfield Village	99760
Marshall	99585
Marvel Creek	99557
Mary's Igloo	99778
Matanuska	99645
May Creek	99588
Meade River	99723
Medfra	99627
Meekins Roadhouse	99645
Mekoryuk	99630
Mellicks Trading Post	99668
Mendeltna Lodge	99645
Mendenhall (Part of Juneau)	99803
Mendenhall Flats (Part of Juneau)	99801
Mentasta Lake	99780
Metlakatla	99926
Meyers Chuck	99903
Minto	99758
Montana	99676
Moose Creek	99701
Moose Pass	99631
Moser Bay	99697
Mountain Point	99901
Mountain View (Part of Anchorage)	99508
Mountain Village	99632
Mount Edgecumbe (Part of Sitka)	99835
Mud Bay	99901
Murphy Dome	99701
Naknek	99633
Napakiak	99634
Napaskiak	99559
Nelson Lagoon	99501
Nenana	99760
Nenana Native Village (Part of Nenana)	99760
Newhalen	99606
New Stuyahok	99636
Newtok	99559
Nightmute	99690
Nikishka	99635
Nikolai	99691
Nikolski	99638
Nikshka Number Two	99611
Ninilchik	99639
Noatak	99761
Nome	99762
Nondalton	99640
Noorvik	99763
North Douglas (Part of Juneau)	99824
North Kenai	99611
North Pole	99705
North Tongass Highway	99901
Northway	99764
Northway Village	99764
North Whale Pass	99550
Nuiqsut	99789
Nulato	99765
Nunaka Valley (Part of Anchorage)	99504
Nunapitchuk	99641
Nyac	99642
Odiak Slough (Part of Cordova)	99574
Okagamute	99607
Old Andreafski	99658
Old Harbor	99643
Old Ninilchik	99639
Old Tyonek	99682
Old Valdez (Part of Valdez)	99686

Name	ZIP
Olnes	99701
Oscarville	99559
Ouzinkie	99644
Palmer	99645
Paradise Hill	99602
Parks	99697
Paxson	99737
Pederson Point	99633
Pedro Bay	99647
Pelican	99832
Peninsula Point	99901
Pennock Island	99901
Perkinsville	99762
Perryville	99648
Petersburg	99833
Peters Creek (Part of Anchorage)	99567
Pilot Point	99649
Pilot Station	99650
Pitkas Point	99658
Pittman	99687
Platinum	99651
Pleasant Harbor	99697
Point Baker	99927
Point Barrow DEW Station	99723
Point Higgins	99901
Point Hope	99766
Point Lay	99759
Point Retreat	99801
Point Whiteshed	99574
Portage (Part of Anchorage)	99501
Portage Creek	99576
Port Alexander	99836
Port Alsworth	99653
Port Armstrong	99836
Port Ashton	99574
Port Bailey	99697
Port Clarence	99762
Port Graham	99603
Port Heiden	99549
Port Lions	99550
Portlock	99663
Port Moller	99695
Port Williams	99697
Potter (Part of Anchorage)	99501
Prudhoe Bay	99734
Quartz Creek	99572
Queen	99576
Quinhagak	99655
Rainbow (Part of Anchorage)	99501
Rampart	99767
Red Devil	99656
Red Salmon	99633
Rego	99701
Rodman (Part of Sitka)	99835
Rogers Park (Part of Anchorage)	99501
Ruby	99768
Russian Mission	99657
St. George Island	99660
St. Marys	99658
St. Marys Mission (Part of St. Marys)	99658
St. Michael	99659
St. Paul	99660
Salamatof	99611
Salcha	99714
Salmon Creek (Part of Juneau)	99801
Sand Lake (Part of Anchorage)	99522
Sand Point	99661
Savoonga	99769
Saxman	99901
Saxman East	99901
Scammon Bay	99662
Scow Bay	99833
Seal Bay	99697
Selawik	99770
Seldovia	99663
Seward	99664
Shageluk	99665
Shaktoolik	99771
Shanley (Part of Fairbanks)	99701
Sheldon Point	99666
Shemya Air Force Base	99501
Shemya Station	99501
Shishmaref	99772
Shoreline Drive	99901
Shungnak	99773
Silver Tip	99631
Sitka	99835
Sitkinak	99697
Situk	99689
Skagway	99840
Skwentna	99667
Slana	99586
Slaterville (Part of Fairbanks)	99701
Sleetmute	99668
Snowball	99701

Name	ZIP
Snug Harbor	99572
Soldotna	99669
Solomon	99762
Sourdough	99586
South (Part of Anchorage)	99511
South Bjerremark	99701
South Naknek	99670
Sparrevohn Station	99557
Spenard (Part of Anchorage)	99509
Sprucewood	99701
Squaw Harbor	99661
Stebbins	99671
Steese	99710
Sterling	99672
Stevens Village	99774
Stony River	99557
Summit	99729
Summit Lodge	99586
Sunnyside	99832
Sunshine	99501
Suntrana	99743
Sutton	99674
Takotna	99675
Taku Lodge (Part of Juneau)	99801
Talkeetna	99676
Tanacross	99776
Tanana	99777
Tatalina Station	99627
Tatitlek	99677
Tazlina	99588
Tee Harbor (Part of Juneau)	99801
Telida	99627
Teller	99778
Tenakee Springs	99841
Terror Bay	99697
Tetlin	99779
Thane (Part of Juneau)	99801
Thorne Bay	99919
Tin City	99783
Togiak	99678
Tok	99780
Tokeen	99901
Toksook Bay	99637
Tonsina	99573
Totem Bight	99901
Totem Park	99701
Trapper Creek	99683
Tuluksak	99679
Tuntutuliak	99680
Tununak	99681
Turnagain (Part of Anchorage)	99503
Turnagain By-the-Sea (Part of Anchorage)	99503
Turnagain Heights (Part of Anchorage)	99503
Twin Hills	99576
Two Rivers	99716
Tyonek	99682
Uganik	99697
Ugashik	99613
Umiat	99701
Umkumute	99690
Unalakleet	99684
Unalaska	99685
Ungalik	99684
University Center (Part of Anchorage)	99504
University Park	99701
Upper Kalskag	99607
Upper Mendenhall Valley (Part of Juneau)	99801
Upper Nickeyville (Part of Ketchikan)	99901
U.S. Coast Guard Station	99619
Usibelli	99743
Usibelli Mine	99743
Valdez	99686
Vank Island	99929
Venetie	99781
View Cove	99901
Wacker	99928
Wainwright	99782
Wales	99783
Ward Cove	99928
Wasilla	99687
Waterfall	99901
West Fairwest	99701
Westgate (Part of Fairbanks)	99701
West Juneau (Part of Juneau)	99801
West Point	99697
Westwood	99701
White Mountain	99784
Whites Crossing	99688
Whitney (Part of Anchorage)	99506
Whittier	99693
Wilcox	99701

ALASKA Wilcox Estates-Zachar Bay

	ZIP		ZIP		ZIP
Wilcox Estates	99701	Woodland Park (Part of Anchorage)	99503	Yakutat	99689
Wild Lake	99726			Yankee Creek	99675
Willow	99688	Wood River	99576	Zachar Bay	99697
Wiseman	99726	Wrangell	99929		

Adamana-Forest Lakes ARIZONA 43

Name	ZIP
Adamana	86025
Adamsville	85232
Agua Caliente	85333
Agua Linda	85640
Aguila	85320
Ahwatukee (Part of Phoenix)	85044
Ajo	85321
Akchin (Pima County)	85634
Akchin (Pinal County)	85239
Alamo Crossing	85357
Alchesay Flat	85941
Ali Chuk	85634
Ali Molina	85634
Allentown	86506
Alpine	85920
Amado	85645
Anegam	85634
Apache	88056
Apache Flats	85613
Apache Grove	85534
Apache Ho (Part of Apache Junction)	85220
Apache Junction	85217-20
For specific Apache Junction Zip Codes call (602) 982-2121	
Apache Wells	85205
Arcadia (Part of Phoenix)	85018
Arcosanti	86333
Arivaca	85601
Arizola	85222
Arizona City	85223
Arizona Shores	85344
Arizona State Prison Complex-Douglas (Cochise County)	85607
Arizona State Prison Complex-Perryville (Maricopa County)	85338
Arizona State Prison Complex-Tucson (Pima County)	85706
Arizona State Prison Complex-Florence (Pinal County)	85232
Arizona State Prison-Safford	85546
Arizona Sunsites	85625
Arlington	85322
Artesa	85634
Artesia	85546
Ash Fork	86320
Avondale	85323
Avondale-Goodyear (Part of Avondale)	85323
Aztec	85333
Baby Rock	86033
Bacobi	86030
Bagdad	86321
Bakerville (Part of Bisbee)	85603
Bapchule	85221
Bayless Shopping Center (Part of Apache Junction)	85220
Beardsley	85373
Beautys Estates	85621
Beaver Dam	86432
Bella Vista Estates (Part of Sierra Vista)	85635
Bellemont	86015
Ben Franklin (Part of Phoenix)	85080
Benson	85602
Beyerlville	85621
Biltmore Fashion Park (Part of Phoenix)	85016
Bisbee	85603
Bisbee Junction	85603
Bitahochee	86031
Bitter Springs	86036
Black Canyon City	85324
Black Hills (Part of Clarkdale)	86324
Blackwater	85228
Blue	85922
Bonita	85643
Bouse	85325
Bowie	85605
Boys Ranch	85225
Braemer (Part of Peoria)	85381
Branding Iron	85701
Brenda	85348
Bridge Canyon Country Estates	86337
Bridgeport	86326
Briggs Townsite (Part of Bisbee)	85603
Buckeye	85326
Buckhorn	85205
Buena Vista	85546
Bullhead City	86430
Bumble Bee	86333
Burnt Water	86512

Name	ZIP
Bushman Acres	86047
Bylas	85530
Cactus (Part of Phoenix)	85032
Cactus Flat	85546
Cactus Forest	85232
Calva	85530
Camelview Plaza (Part of Scottsdale)	85251
Cameron	86020
Camp Creek	85331
Camp Verde	86322
Camp Verde Indian Reservation	86322
Cane Beds	86022
Canelo	85611
Canyon Day	85941
Capitol (Part of Phoenix)	85009
Carefree	85377
Carmen	85640
Carrizo	85901
Casa Blanca	85221
Casa Grande	85222
Casas Adobes	85704
Cascabel	85602
Cashion	85329
Castle Hot Springs	85342
Castle Rock Shores	85344
Catalina	85738
Catalina Foothills	85718
Cave Creek	85331
Cedar Creek	85941
Cedar Ridge	86020
Centerville (Part of Clarkdale)	86324
Central	85531
Central Heights	85501
Central Heights-Midland City	85532
Chambers	86502
Chandler	85224-27 85248-49
For specific Chandler Zip Codes call (602) 963-6643	
Chandler Heights	85227
Cherry	86327
Chevelon	86001
Chiawuli Tak	85634
Chilchinbito	86033
Childs	85321
Chinle	86503
Chino Valley	86323
Chloride	86431
Choulic	85634
Christmas	85292
Chris-Town Center (Part of Phoenix)	85015
Chuichu	85222
Cibecue	85911
Cibola	85334
Cienega Springs	85344
Circle City	85342
Citrus Gardens	85201
Clarkdale	86324
Claypool	85532
Clay Springs	85923
Cleator	86333
Clifton	85533
Coal Mine Mesa	86045
Cobblestone Village (Part of Peoria)	85381
Cochise	85606
Cocopah Indian Reservation	85350
College (Part of Tucson)	85722
Colonnade, The (Part of Phoenix)	85016
Colorado City	86021
Colorado River Indian Reservation	85344
Commerce (Part of Phoenix)	85003
Comobabi	85634
Concho	85924
Congress	85332
Continental	85640
Coolidge	85228
Coolidge Dam	85542
Co-op Village	85339
Copper Mines	86040
Copper Queen (Part of Bisbee)	85603
Cordes Lakes	86333
Cork	85536
Cornfields	86505
Cornville	86325
Coronada Foothills Estates	85718
Corona de Tucson	85726
Coronado (Part of Tucson)	85711
Coronado Unit	86047
Cortaro	85652
Cottonwood	86326
Cottonwood Station	86503
Country Life	85201

Name	ZIP
Cove	87420
Covered Wells	85634
Cowlic	85634
Cow Springs	86044
Crane	85365
Crestview (Part of Bisbee)	85603
Cross Canyon	86511
Crown King	86343
Cuckelbur	85222
Cutter	85501
Dam View	85344
Date	85332
Dateland	85333
Davis Dam	86430
Davis-Monthan AFB	85707
Davis-Monthan Air Force Base	85707
Deer Valley (Part of Phoenix)	85023
Del Rio	86323
Dennehotso	86535
Desert (Part of Mesa)	85206
Desert Carmel	85222
Desert Harbor (Part of Peoria)	85381
Desert Hills	86403
Desert Sands	85208
Desert View	86023
Dewey	86327
Diamond Valley	86301
Dilkon	86047
Discovery at the Orchard (Part of Peoria)	85381
Dolan Springs	86441
Dome	85365
Don Luis (Part of Bisbee)	85603
Dos Cabezas	85643
Double Adobe	85617
Douglas	85607-08
For specific Douglas Zip Codes call (602) 364-3631	
Downtown (Coconino County)	86001
Downtown (Maricopa County)	85281
Downtown (Maricopa County)	85003
Downtown (Mohave County)	86402
Downtown (Pima County)	85701
Dragoon	85609
Drake	86334
Dreamland-Velda Rose	85205
Dreamland Villa	85205
Drexel Heights	85706
Dudleyville	85292
Duncan	85534
Dysart	85345
Eagar	85925
Eagle Creek	85533
East Flagstaff (Part of Flagstaff)	86001
East Fork	85943
East Plantsite (Part of Clifton)	85540
Eden	85535
Ehrenberg	85334
El Con Regional Shopping Center (Part of Tucson)	85716
Eleven Mile Corner	85222
Elfrida	85610
Elgin	85611
El Mirage (Maricopa County)	85335
El Mirage (Maricopa County)	85201
Eloy	85231
El Pueblecito (Part of Yuma)	85364
Emery Park (Part of Tucson)	85706
Empire Landing	85344
Fairbank	85621
Falcon Estates	85203
Federal Correctional Institution (Maricopa County)	85027
Federal Correctional Institution (Pima County)	85706
Federal Prison Camp	85546
Fiesta Mall (Part of Mesa)	85202
Fiesta Park	85201
Fishers Landing	85365
Flagstaff	86001-16
For specific Flagstaff Zip Codes call (602) 527-2440	
Flecha Caida Estates	85718
Florence	85232
Florence Junction	85219
Forbing Park (Part of Prescott)	86301
Forest Lakes	85931

44 ARIZONA

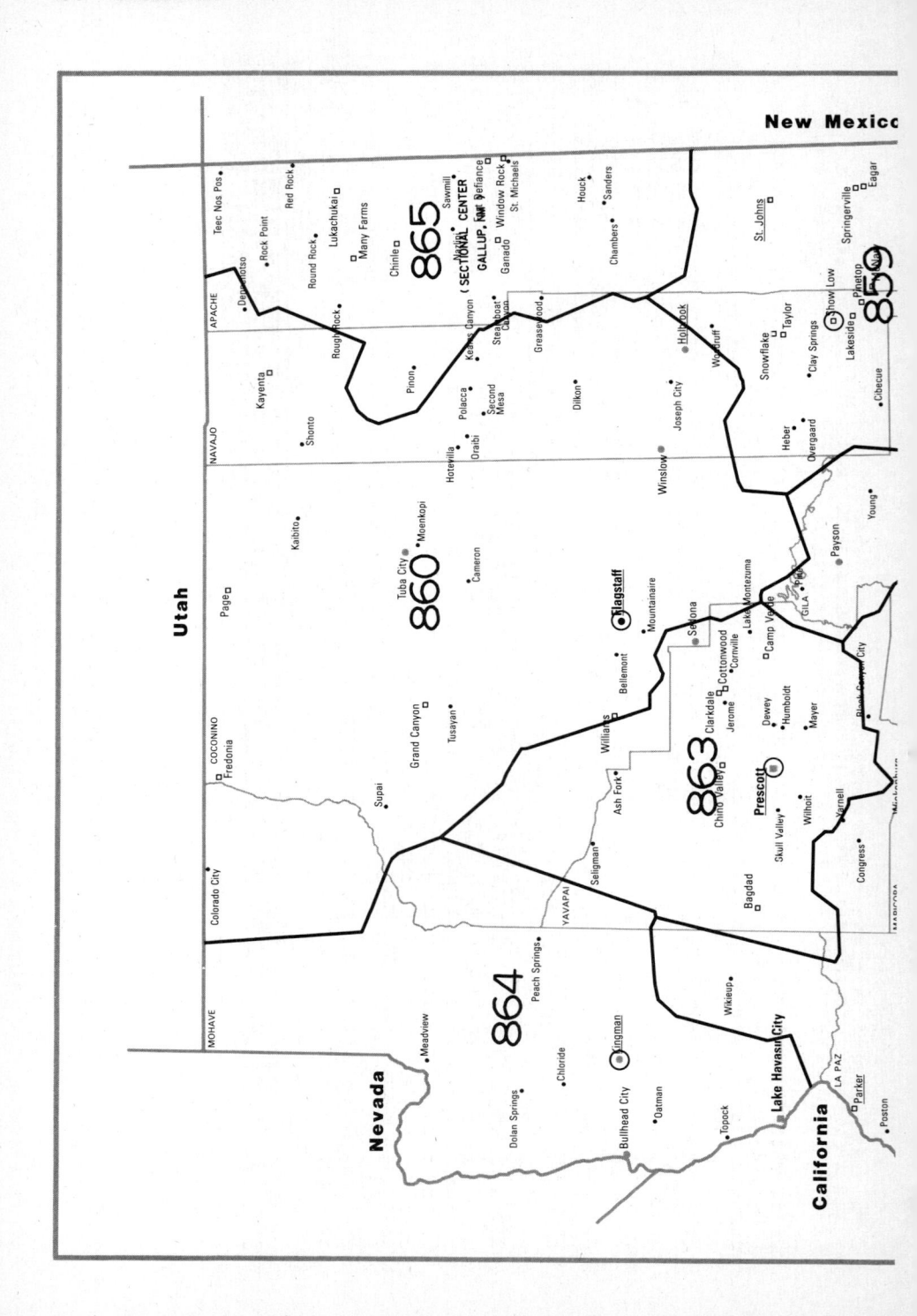

ARIZONA 45

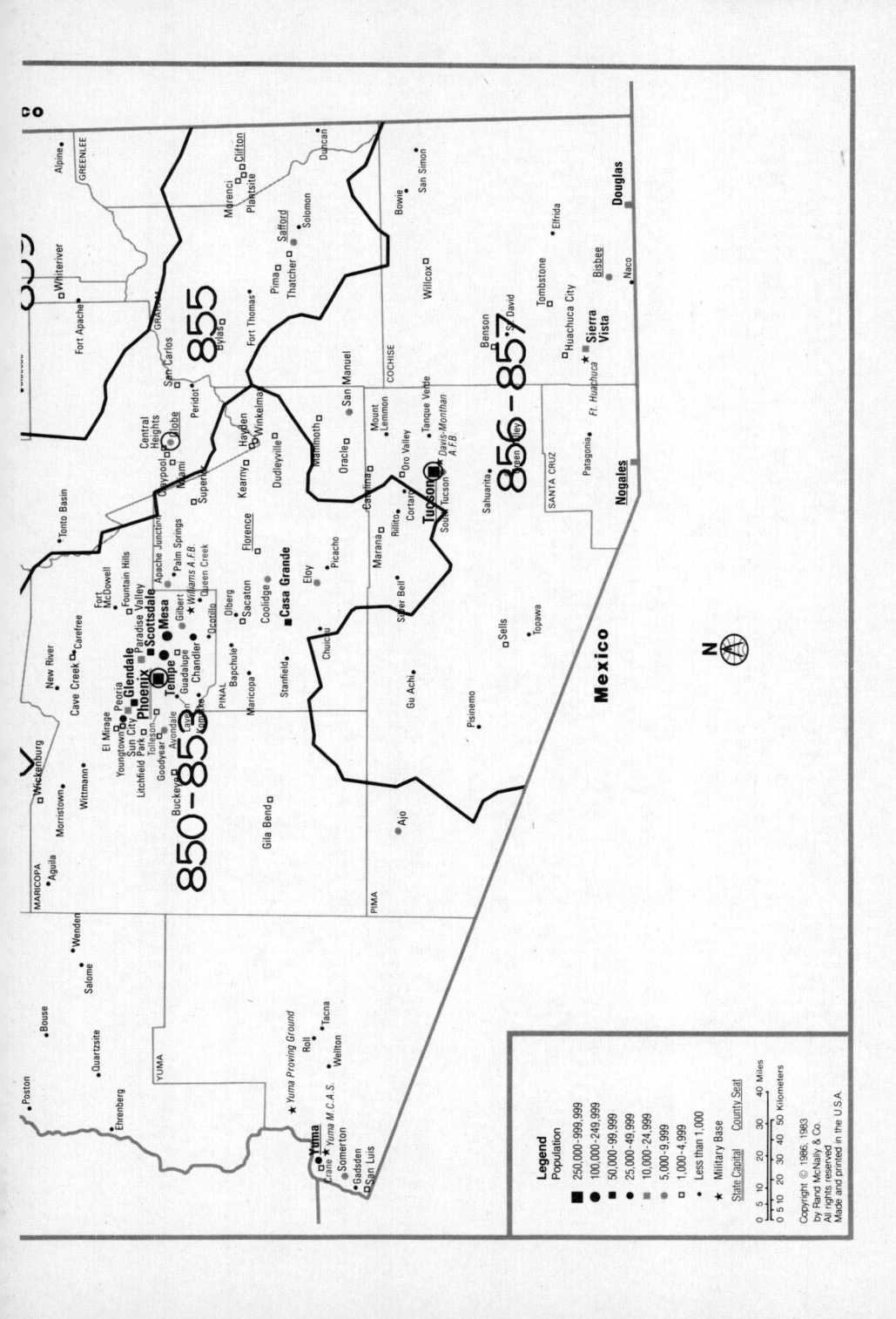

ARIZONA Fort Apache-Nutrioso

Location	ZIP
Fort Apache	85926
Fort Apache Indian Reservation	85941
Fort Apache Junction	85941
Fort Defiance	86504
Fort Grant	85643
Fort Lowell (Part of Tucson)	85715
Fort McDowell	85257
Fort McDowell Indian Reservation	85251
Fort Mohave (Part of Bullhead City)	86427
Fort Thomas	85536
Fountain East	85201
Fountain Hills	85269
Fountain of the Sun	85208
Foxfire (Part of Peoria)	85381
Foxwood (Part of Peoria)	85381
Franklin	85534
Fredonia	86022
Fresnal Canyon	85634
Friendly Corners	85231
Fry (Part of Sierra Vista)	85635
Gadsden	85336
Galena (Part of Bisbee)	85603
Ganado	86505
Geronimo	85536
Gibson	85321
Gila Bend	85337
Gila Bend Indian Reservation	85634
Gila Crossing	85339
Gila River Indian Reservation	85247
Gilbert	85234
Gisela	85541
Gladden	85320
Gleeson	85610
Glendale	85301-12
For specific Glendale Zip Codes call (602) 842-0099	
Glen Ilah	85362
Globe	85501-02
For specific Globe Zip Codes call (602) 425-2381	
Goldfield	85219
Goodyear	85338
Goodyear Farms (Part of Litchfield Park)	86340
Graham	85552
Grand Canyon	86023
Grand Canyon Caverns	86434
Grand Canyon Estates	86023
Grand View	86301
Grasshopper Junction	86401
Gray Mountain	86016
Greasewood	86505
Greasewood Springs	86507
Greaterville	85637
Green Valley	85614
Greenway (Part of Glendale)	85306
Greer	85927
Gripe	85546
Groom Creek	86301
Gu Achi	85634
Guadalupe	85283
Gunsight	85321
Gu Oidak	85634
Guthrie	85533
Gu Vo	85634
Hacienda De Valencia	85201
Hackberry	86411
Hamilton Corner	85248
Hano	86042
Happy Jack	86024
Harcuvar	85348
Harmony Villa	85201
Hassayampa	85343
Havana Nakya	85634
Havasupai Indian Reservation	86435
Hawkins	85332
Hawley Lake	85930
Hayden	85235
Hayden Junction	85235
Heber	85928
Hereford	85615
Hermits Rest	86023
Hickiwan	85634
Hidden Springs	86020
Highland Park	85603
Highland Pines	86301
Higley	85236
Hillside	86301
Hilltop	85632
Ho-Kay-Gan	86301
Holbrook	86025-29
For specific Holbrook Zip Codes call (602) 524-3311	
Holiday	85344
Hollywood	85546

Location	ZIP
Hope	85348
Hopi (Part of Scottsdale)	85258
Hopi Indian Reservation	86039
Horn	85333
Horse Mesa	85290
Horse Thief	86333
Hotason Vo	85634
Hotevilla	86030
Houck	86506
Huachuca City	85616
Huachuca Terrace (Part of Bisbee)	85603
Hualapai	86412
Hualapai Indian Reservation	86434
Hubbell	86505
Humboldt	86329
Hunt	85924
Hunters Point	86511
Hyder	85333
Immanuel Mission	86514
Indian Gardens	86336
Indian Ridge Estates	85715
Indian School (Part of Phoenix)	85014
Indian Wells	86031
Inscription House	86044
Inspiration	85532
Iron Springs	86330
Jackrabbit	85222
Jackson Acres	86301
Jacob Lake	86022
Jade Park North (Part of Phoenix)	85308
Jakes Corner	85541
Jeddito	86034
Jerome	86331
Johnson	85609
Joseph City	86032
Juniper Heights	86301
Kaibab	86022
Kaibab Indian Reservation	86022
Kaibito	86053
Kaihon Kug	85634
Kaka	85634
Kansas Settlement	85643
Katherine	86430
Kayenta	86033
Keams Canyon	86034
Kearny	85237
Kelvin	85237
Kerwo	85634
Kingman	86401-02
For specific Kingman Zip Codes call (602) 753-2480	
Kinlichee	86505
Kino (Part of Tucson)	85705
Kino Hills	85621
Kino Springs	85621
Kinsley Ranch	85640
Kirkland	86332
Kirkland Junction	86332
Klagetoh	86505
Klondyke	85643
Kofa (Part of Yuma)	85364
Kohatk	85634
Komatke	85339
Ko Vaya	85634
Kykotsmovi Village	86039
Lake Havasu City	86403
Lake Mead City	86444
Lake Mead Ranchers	86401
Lake Mohave	86430
Lake Montezuma	86342
Lakeside (La Paz County)	85344
Lakeside (Navajo County)	85929
Lampliter Village (Part of Clarkdale)	86324
La Palma	85222
Las Ligas	85323
Laveen	85339
Lees Ferry	86036
Leisure World	85206
Leupp	86035
Leupp Corner	86047
Liberty	85326
Ligurta	85356
Lincon	85634
Litchfield Greens (Part of Litchfield Park)	85340
Litchfield Park	85340
Little Acres	85501
Littlefield	86432
Little Tucson	85634
Lizard Acres	85373
Lochiel	85624
Loma Linda	85619
Lone Star	85546
Long Valley	86001
Los Arcos Mall (Part of Scottsdale)	85257
Los Gatos	85251

Location	ZIP
Lowell (Part of Bisbee)	85603
Lower Miami	85539
Low Mountain	86503
Lukachukai	86507
Luke AFB	85309
Luke Air Force Base	85309
Lukeville	85341
Lupton	86508
Lynx Estates (Part of Prescott Valley)	86301
McDowell (Part of Phoenix)	85008
McGees Settlement	85736
McGuireville	86335
McNary	85930
McNeal	85617
Madera Canyon	85706
Mammoth	85618
Many Farms	86538
Marana	85653
Marble Canyon	86036
Maricopa	85239
Maricopa Indian Reservation	85247
Maricopa Village	85339
Mariposa Manor	85621
Martinez Lake	85364
Maryvale (Part of Phoenix)	85031
Mayer	86333
Meadow Brook (Part of Yuma)	85364
Meadview	86444
Mennonite Mission	86505
Mesa	85201-16
For specific Mesa Zip Codes call (602) 969-9171	
Mesa Del Oro	85219
Mescal	85602
Metrocenter (Part of Phoenix)	85021
Mexican Town	85321
Mexican Water	86514
Miami	85539
Miami Gardens	85539
Middle Verde (Part of Camp Verde)	86322
Midland City	85501
Miller Valley (Part of Prescott)	86301
Miracle Valley	85615
Miramonte Acres (Part of Bisbee)	85603
Mishongnovi	86043
Mobile	85239
Moccasin	86022
Moenave	86045
Moenkopi	86045
Mohave Valley	86440
Morenci (Greenlee County)	85540
Mormon Lake	86038
Morristown	85342
Mountainaire	86001
Mountain View (Cochise County)	85603
Mountain View (Maricopa County)	85213
Mount Elden (Part of Flagstaff)	86001
Mount Lemmon	85619
Munds Park	86017
Na-Ah-Tee Canyon	86025
Naco	85620
N A U (Northern Arizona University) (Part of Flagstaff)	86011
Navajo	86509
Navajo Depot Activity	86015
Navajo Indian Reservation	86515
Navajo Mountain Trading Post	86044
Navajo Spring	86036
Navajo Station	86505
Nazlini	86540
Nelson	86434
New Hope	85201
New Oraibi	86039
New River	85029
New Tucson (Part of Tucson)	85714
Nicksville	85615
Nogales	85621
Nogales West	85621
Nolia	85634
Normal Junction (Part of Tempe)	85281
Northeast (Part of Phoenix)	85016
Northern Hills	85704
North Komelik	85634
Northridge Park	86314
North Rim	86052
Northwest (Part of Phoenix)	85017
Nortons Corner	85225
Nutrioso	85932

Oak Creek-Sun Lakes **ARIZONA** 47

	ZIP
Oak Creek	86341
Oak Knoll Village	86301
Oak Springs	86511
Oasis Park (Part of Apache Junction)	85220
Oatman	86433
Ocotillo	85248
Octave	85332
Olberg	85247
Old Columbine	85546
Old Oraibi	86039
Oracle	85623
Oracle Foot Hill Estates	85704
Oracle Junction	85738
Orange Grove Estates	85704
Oro Valley	85704
Osborn (Part of Phoenix)	85013
Overgaard	85933
Page	86040
Page Springs	86325
Palm Springs (Part of Apache Junction)	85219
Palominas	85615
Palomino Acres	85234
Palo Verde	85343
Pan Tak	85634
Papago (Part of Scottsdale)	85257
Papago Indian Reservation	85634
Paradise	85632
Paradise Valley	85253
Paradise Valley Mall (Part of Phoenix)	85032
Park Central Mall (Part of Phoenix)	85013
Parker	85344
Parker Creek	85501
Park Mall (Part of Tucson)	85711
Parks	86018
Patagonia	85624
Paulden	86334
Paul Spur	85607
Payson	85541
Peach Springs	86434
Pearce	85625
Peeples Valley	86332
Peoria	85345
	85380-82
For specific Peoria Zip Codes call (602) 979-1841	
Peralta Estates	85219
Peridot	85542
Perkinsville	86323
Perryville	85326
Petrified Forest National Park	86028
Phoenix	85001-82
For specific Phoenix Zip Codes call (602) 225-3434	

COLLEGES & UNIVERSITIES

DeVry Institute of Technology-Phoenix	85021
University of Phoenix	85012

FINANCIAL INSTITUTIONS

Century Bank	85012
Chase Bank of Arizona	85012
Citibank (Arizona)	85012
First Interstate Bank of Arizona, N.A.	85003
Merabank, A Federal Savings Bank	85012
Security Pacific Bank Arizona	85002
Sentinel Savings & Loan Association of Arizona	85018
Southwest Savings & Loan Association	85012
Sun State Savings & Loan Association	85018
Thunderbird Bank	85012
The Valley National Bank of Arizona	85004
Western Savings & Loan Association	85016

HOSPITALS

Arizona State Hospital	85008
Carl T. Hayden Veterans Administration Medical Center	85012
Good Samaritan Medical Center	85006
Humana Hospital-Phoenix	85016
John C. Lincoln Hospital and Health Center	85020
Maricopa Medical Center	85008
St. Joseph's Hospital and Medical Center	85013

	ZIP
HOTELS/MOTELS	
Arizona Biltmore	85016
Embassy Suites	85016
Embassy Suites Camelhead	85008
Doubletree Hotel	85008
Holiday Inn-Corporate Center	85029
Hyatt Regency Phoenix	85004
La Mancha Athletic Club & Resort Hotel	85013
Phoenix Sheraton	85001
The Pointe at Squaw Peak	85020
Ramada Inn Metrocenter	85029
Sheraton Greenway Inn	85023

MILITARY INSTALLATIONS

Arizona Air National Guard, FB6021	85034
Pia Oik	85634
Picacho	85241
Pima	85543
Pine	85544
Pinedale	85934
Pine Lake	86401
Pine Springs	86506
Pinetop (Part of Pinetop-Lakeside)	85935
Pinetop-Lakeside	85935
Pinnacle Peak Village	85255
Pinon	86510
Pioneer (Part of Mesa)	85210
Pirtleville	85626
Pisinemo	85634
Plantsite	85540
Plaza Del Rio (Part of Peoria)	85381
Polacca	86042
Poland Junction	86333
Pomerene	85627
Ponderosa Park	86301
Portal	85632
Porter Creek Estates	85929
Porter Mountain Estates	85929
Poston	85371
Prescott	86301-14
For specific Prescott Zip Codes call (602) 778-1890	
Prescott Valley	86314
Presidential Estates	85616
Prinston Park	85234
Pumpkin Center	85553
Quartzsite	85346
Queen Creek	85242
Queen Valley	85219
Querino	86506
Rainbow Valley	85326
Ranch del Sol	85234
Rancho del Rio	85344
Randolph	85222
Reata Pass	85251
Redington	85602
Red Lake	86046
Red Mesa	86514
Red Rock (Apache County)	87420
Red Rock (Pinal County)	85245
Red Valley	86544
Rillito	85654
Rimrock	86335
Rincon (Part of Tucson)	85710
Rio Rico	85621
Rio Salado (Part of Phoenix)	85074
Rio Verde	85255
Riverside Stage Stop	85237
Riverside Terrace	85704
Riviera (Part of Bullhead City)	86442
Rock Point	86503
Rock Springs	85026
Roll	85347
Roosevelt	85545
Roosevelt Estates	85545
Roosevelt Resort	85545
Rough Rock	86503
Round Rock	86503
Royal Estates	85621
Rye	85541
Sacate	85221
Sacaton	85221
Sacaton Flats	85247
Sacred Mountain	86001
Safford	85546
Saginaw (Part of Bisbee)	85603
Sahuarita	85629
Sahuarita Heights	85629
St. David	85630
St. Johns	85936
St. Michaels	86511
Salado	85936
Salina	86503

	ZIP
Salome	85348
Salt River Indian Reservation	85257
Salt River Powder District Camp	85545
San Carlos	85550
San Carlos Indian Reservation	85550
Sanchez	85546
Sanders	86512
Sand Springs	86039
San Jose (Cochise County)	85603
San Jose (Graham County)	85546
San Lucy Village	85337
San Luis (Pima County)	85634
San Luis (Yuma County)	85349
San Manuel	85631
San Miguel	85634
San Pedro	85634
San Rafael Terrace (Part of Bisbee)	85603
San Simon	85632
Santa Cruz	85339
Santa Maria (Maricopa County)	85009
Santa Maria (Yavapai County)	85332
Santan	85247
Santa Rita	85640
San Xavier	85746
San Xavier Indian Reservation	85634
Sasabe	85633
Sawmill	86549
Schuckk	85634
Schuchuli	85634
Scottsdale	85250-71
For specific Scottsdale Zip Codes call (602) 949-7100	
Scottsdale Fashion Square (Part of Scottsdale)	85251
Second Mesa	86043
Sedona	86336
Seligman	86337
Sells	85634
Sentinel	85333
Shaw Butte (Part of Phoenix)	85071
Sheldon	85534
Sherwood (Part of Mesa)	85214
Shipolovi	86043
Shongopovi	86043
Shonto	86054
Shopishk	85634
Show Low	85901
Shumway	85901
Sichomovi	86042
Sierra Bonita	85643
Sierra Vista	85635-36
For specific Sierra Vista Zip Codes call (602) 458-2540	
Sil Nakaya	85634
Site Six (Part of Lake Havasu City)	86403
Skull Valley	86338
Skyline Bel Aire Estates	85718
Skyway Village	85205
Smoke Signal	86503
Snowflake	85937
Solomon	85551
Somerton	85350
Sonoita	85637
Sonora Town	85234
South Bisbee	85603
South Central (Part of Phoenix)	85040
Southgate Mall (Part of Yuma)	85364
South Komelik	85634
South Santan	85247
South Tucson	85713
Springerville	85938
Spring Valley	86333
Stanfield	85272
Stanton	85332
Stargo	85540
Star Valley	85541
Steamboat Canyon	86505
Stoneman Lake	86024
Strawberry	85544
Student Union (Part of Tucson)	85720
Sun (Part of Tucson)	85719
Sun City	85351
	85372-75
For specific Sun City Zip Codes call (602) 974-3623	
Sun City West	85375
Sunflower	85201
Sunizona	85625
Sun Lakes	85224

48 ARIZONA Sunnyslope-Yuma Proving Ground

Name	ZIP
Sunnyslope (Part of Phoenix)	85020
Sunrise	86047
Sunrise Springs	86505
Sunset	85643
Sunset Acres	85603
Sunshine Acres (Part of Mesa)	85201
Sun Terra Acres	85234
Suntown (Part of Peoria)	85381
Sun Valley	86029
Supai	86435
Superior	85273
Superstition Estates (Part of Apache Junction)	85220
Supi Oidak	85634
Surprise	85374
Sweetwater (Apache County)	87401
Sweetwater (Maricopa County)	85326
Sweetwater (Pinal County)	85221
Swift Trail Junction	85546
Tacna	85352
Tapco	86324
Tat Momoli	85634
Tatria Toak	85634
Taylor	85939
Teec Nos Pos	86514
Tees To	86047
Tempe	85280-85
For specific Tempe Zip Codes call (602) 220-0258	
Temple Bar Marina	86443
Tes Nez Iah	86033
Thatcher	85552
Theba	85337
The Gap	86020
Thomas Mall (Part of Phoenix)	85018
Three Points	85714
Three Way	85534
Tierra Madre	85234
Tintown (Part of Bisbee)	85603
Tolani	86047
Tolleson	85353
Toltec (Part of Eloy)	85231
Tombstone	85638
Tonalea	86044
Tonopah	85354
Tonto Basin	85553
Topawa	85639
Topock	86436
Toreva	86043
Tortilla Flat	85290
Totopitk	85634
Tovrea (Part of Phoenix)	85034
Tower Plaza Mall (Part of Phoenix)	85018
Toyei	86505
Tremaine	85224

Name	ZIP
Tri-City Mall (Part of Mesa)	85201
Truxton	86434
Tsaile	86556
Tubac	85646
Tuba City (Coconino County)	86045
Tucson	85701-51
For specific Tucson Zip Codes call (602) 620-5142	
Tucson Country Club Estates	85715
Tucson Estates	85715
Tucson National Estates	85704
Tumacacori	85640
Turkey Flat	85546
Tusayan	86023
Tusconita	85706
Twin Arrows (Part of Flagstaff)	86001
Twin Buttes	85629
Twin Knolls	85207
Two Story	86511
University of Arizona (Part of Tucson)	85717
Upper Greasewood Trading Post	86507
Upper Wheatfields	86556
Utting	85348
Vahki	85221
Vail	85641
Vaiva Vo	85634
Valencia	85326
Valentine	86437
Valley Farms	85291
Valley West Mall (Part of Glendale)	85301
Vamori	85634
Vandenberg Village	85708
Vaya Chin	85634
Velda Rose Estates	85205
Velda Rose Gardens	85201
Ventana	85634
Ventana Lakes (Part of Peoria)	85382
Venture Out	85201
Vernon	85940
Vicksburg	85348
Village Meadows (Part of Sierra Vista)	85635
Waddell	85355
Wagoner	86332
Wahak Hotrontk	85634
Wahweap	86040
Walker	86301
Walnut Grove	86332
Walpi	86042
Warren (Part of Bisbee)	85603
Washington (Part of Phoenix)	85021
Washington Camp	85624
Wellton	85356

Name	ZIP
Wenden	85357
Westbrook Village (Part of Peoria)	85382
West Chandler (Part of Chandler)	85224
Westgate	85611
Westgreen Estates (Part of Peoria)	85345
West Plaza Shopping Center (Part of Phoenix)	85017
Westridge (Part of Phoenix)	85033
Westridge Mall (Part of Phoenix)	85033
West Sedona	86340
Westward Quest	85201
Wheatfields	86515
Whipple (Part of Prescott)	86313
Whippoorwill	86503
Whispering Hills (Part of Sierra Vista)	85635
White Clay	86504
White Cone	86025
White Mountain Lake	85912
Whiteriver (Navajo County)	85941
White Tanks	85326
Why	85321
Wickenburg	85358
Wide Ruins	86502
Wikieup	85360
Wilhoit	86332
Willcox	85643
Williams	86046
Williams AFB	85240
Williams Air Force Base	85240
Willow Beach	86445
Willow Canyon	85619
Willow Valley Estates	86440
Window Rock	86515
Winkelman	85292
Winona	86001
Winslow	86047
Winwood	85603
Wittmann	85361
Wood Hills	85616
Woodruff	85942
Woodsprings	86505
Yarnell	85362
Yava	86301
Yavapai Indian Reservation	86301
York	85534
Young	85554
Youngtown	85363
Yucca	86438
Yuma	85364-69
For specific Yuma Zip Codes call (602) 783-2124	
Yuma Marine Corps Air Station	85369
Yuma Proving Ground (Yuma County)	85364

Abbott-Canehill ARKANSAS 49

	ZIP		ZIP		ZIP
Abbott	72944	Batesville	72501-03	Blytheville Junction (Part of	
Aberdeen	72134	For specific Batesville Zip Codes		Blytheville)	72315
Acorn	71953	call (501) 793-6828		Board Camp	71932
Ada	72001	Battlefield	71801	Bodcaw	71858
Adkins Lake	71601	Baucum	72117	Bolding	71747
Adona	72001	Bauxite	72011	Boles	72926
Agnos	72513	Baxter	71638	Bonanza	72901
Alabam	72740	Bay	72411	Bondsville	72354
Albert Pike (Part of Hot		Bayou Meto (Arkansas		Bonnerdale	71933
Springs National Park)	71913	County)	72160	Bono (Craighead County)	72416
Albion	72143	Bayou Meto (Lonoke		Bono (Faulkner County)	72058
Alco	72610	County)	72086	Booker	72117
Alexander (Greene County)	72450	Bay Village	72324	Booneville	72927
Alexander (Pulaski County)	72002	Bear Creek Springs	72601	Booster	72645
Algoa	72112	Bearden	71720	Boothe	72927
Alicia	72410	Bear Hollow Village	72901	Boston	72752
Alix	72820	Beaty	72736	Boswell	72516
Allbrook	71851	Beaudry	71949	Botkinburg	72031
Alleene	71820	Beaver	72613	Boughton	71857
Allison	72560	Beaver Shores	72756	Bowen	71940
Allport	72046	Beck	72348	Bowman	72437
Alma	72921	Becton	72036	Boxley	72742
Almond	72550	Beebe	72012	Boyd (Lafayette County)	71845
Almyra	72003	Bee Branch	72013	Boyd (Miller County)	71837
Alonzo	72534	Beech Grove	72412	Boydell	71658
Alpena	72611	Beedeville	72014	Boydsville	72461
Alpine	71920	Beirne	71721	Boynton	72438
Alread	72031	Bellaire	71638	Bradford	72020
Altheimer	72004	Bella Vista	72712	Bradley	71826
Alto	72354	Bellefonte	72601	Brady (Part of Little Rock)	72205
Altus	72821	Belle Meade	72348	Bragg City	71726
Aly	72857	Belleville	72824	Brakebill	72444
Amagon	72005	Bells Chapel	72823	Branch	72928
Amanca	72376	Bellville	71846	Brasfield	72017
Amboy (Part of North Little		Belton	71852	Bredlow Corner	72046
Rock)	72114	Ben	72530	Brentwood	72959
Amity	71921	Bengall	72112	Brewer	72044
Amy	71701	Ben Gay	72466	Brickeys	72320
Andy	72376	Ben Hur	72856	Briggsville	72828
Annieville	72434	Ben Lomond	71823	Brighton	72450
Antioch (Perry County)	72070	Benton	72015	Bright Star	71834
Antioch (White County)	72012	Bentonville	72712-14	Brightwater	72756
Antoine	71922	For specific Bentonville Zip Codes		Brinkley	72021
Aplin	72126	call (501) 273-2722		Brister	71740
Appleton	72822	Benton Work Release and		Brockett	72455
Apt	72401	Pre Release Center	72015	Brockwell	72517
Arbor Grove	72433	Bergman	72615	Brookland	72417
Ard	72834	Berryville	72616	Brown	72442
Arden	71822	Beryl	72032	Brown Springs	72104
Arkadelphia	71923	Bethany	71833	Brownstown	71846
Arkana	71826	Bethel	72450	Brownsville	72067
Arkansas City	71630	Bethel Heights	72764	Bruins	72348
Arkinda	71836	Bethesda	72501	Brumley	72032
Arkola	72940	Beulah	72017	Brummitt	72160
Arlberg	72031	Bexar	72515	Bruno	72618
Armorel	72310	Bidville	72959	Brush Creek	72084
Armstrong	72482	Bigelow	72016	Brutonville	72479
Armstrong Springs	72143	Big Flat	72617	Bryant	72022
Ashdown	71822	Big Fork	71953	Buckeye	72438
Asher (Madison County)	72727	Biggers	72413	Buckner	71827
Asher (Pulaski County)	72204	Big Lake	72442	Buck Range	71851
Ash Flat	72513	Big Springs	72657	Buckville	71956
Athelstan	72370	Billingsley's Corner	71866	Buena Vista	71764
Athens	71971	Billstown	71958	Buffalo City	72653
Atkins	72823	Bingen	71852	Buie	72129
Atlanta	71740	Birdell	72455	Bullfrog Valley	72837
Attica	72455	Birdeye	72314	Bull Shoals	72619
Aubrey	72311	Birdsong	72386	Bunney	72414
Augusta	72847	Bird Town	72157	Burdette	72321
Aurelle	72006	Birta	72853	Burg	71833
Aurora	71765	Biscoe	72017	Burlington	72662
Austin (Conway County)	72740	Bismarck	71929	Burnville	72936
Austin (Lonoke County)	72031	Blackburn	72959	Buroak	72650
Auvergne	72007	Blackfish	72346	Busch	72632
Avilla	72112	Black Fork	71953	Bussey	71860
Avoca	72002	Blackland	71836	Butlerville	72176
Avon	72711	Black Oak (Craighead		Butterfield	72104
Back Gate	71832	County)	72414	Byron	72576
Baker	71639	Black Oak (Poinsett County)	72415	Cabot	72023
Balch	72482	Black Rock	72415	Caddo Gap	71935
Bald Knob	72009	Black Springs	71960	Caddo Valley	71923
Baldwin (Part of Fayetteville)	72010	Blackton	72069	Cain	72946
Ballard	72701	Blackville	72112	Calamine	72469
Band Mill	72513	Blackwell	72823	Caldwell	72322
Banks	72517	Blakely	71931	Cale	71828
Banner	71631	Blakemore	72046	Caledonia	71749
Barber	72523	Blevins	71825	Calhoun	71753
Bard	72927	Bloomer	72933	Calico Rock	72519
Bardstown	72450	Bloomfield	72734	Calion	71724
Barfield	72350	Blossom	72392	Calmer	71665
Barling	72315	Blue Ball	72833	Calumet	72315
Barney	72923	Blue Eye	65611	Camark	71701
Barton	72047	Blue Hill	72118	Camden	71701
Bashe (Part of Fort Smith)	72312	Blue Mountain	72826	Cammack Village	72207
Bass	72901	Blue Springs	71901	Camp	72520
Bassett	72612	Bluff City	71722	Campbell Station	72473
Batavia	72313	Bluffton	72827	Camp Joseph T. Robinson	72205
Bates	72601	Blytheville	72315-19	Canaan	72650
	72924	For specific Blytheville Zip Codes		Cane Creek	72150
		call (501) 763-3690		Canehill	72717

50 ARKANSAS

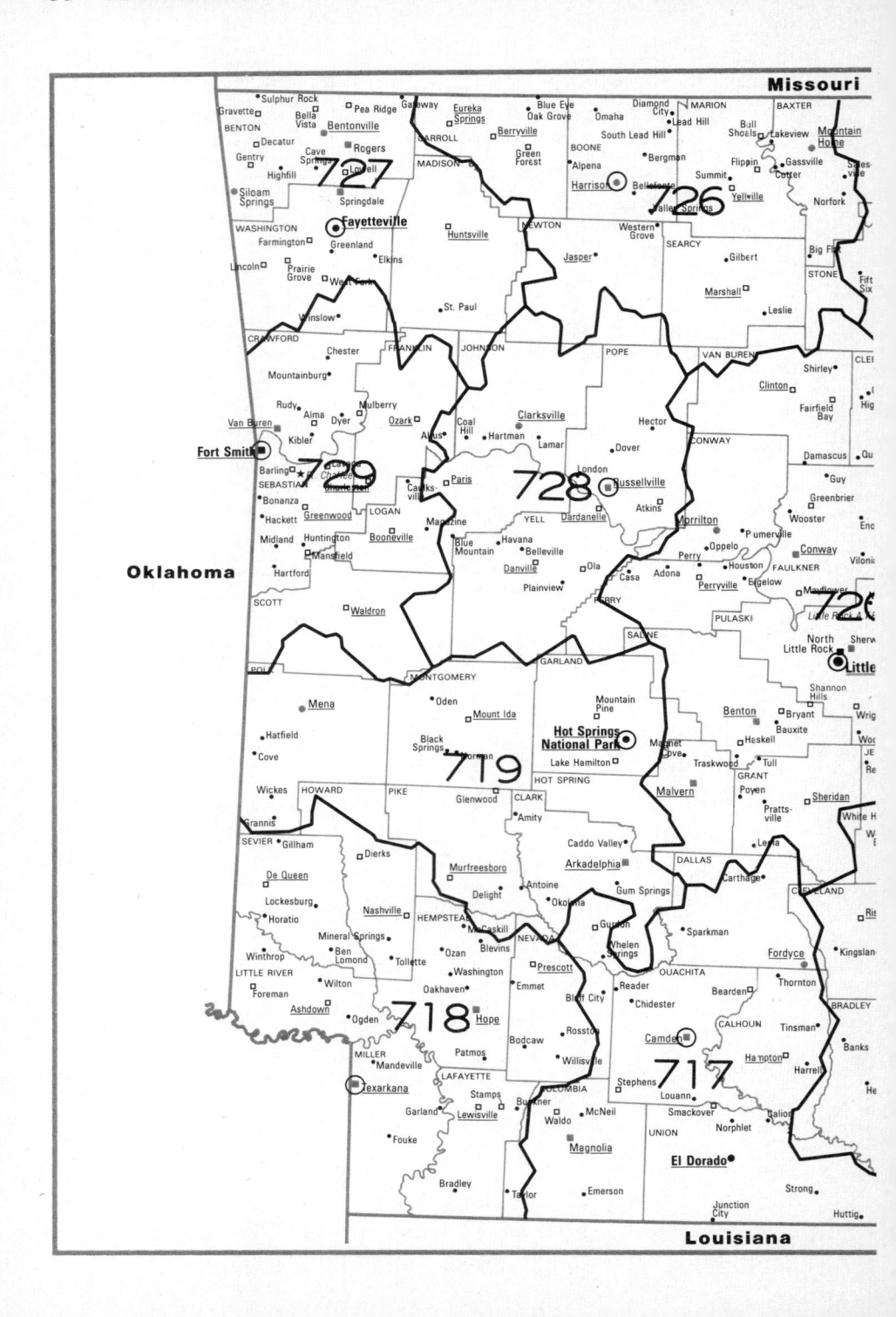

ARKANSAS 51

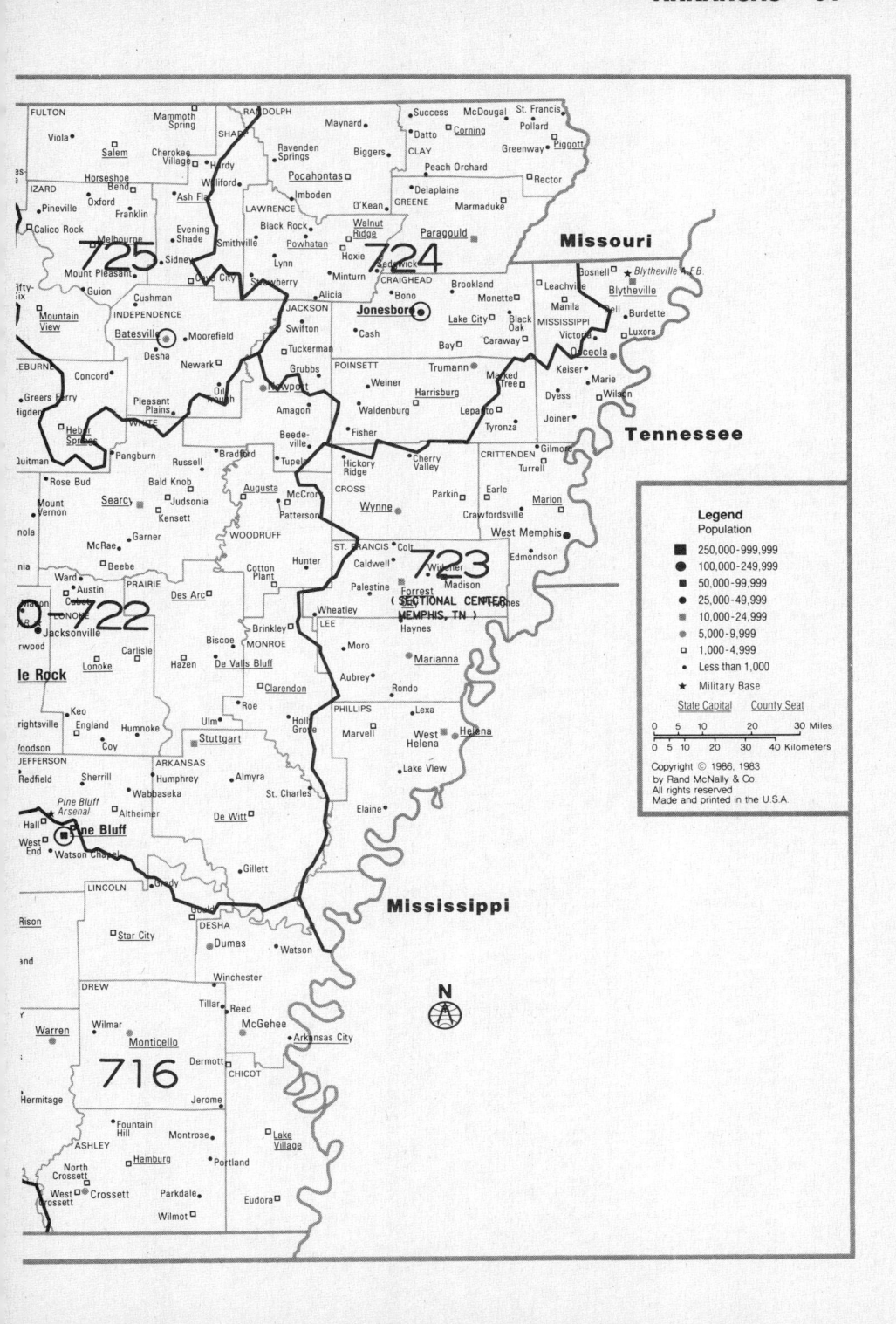

52 ARKANSAS Caney-Elkins

	ZIP		ZIP		ZIP
Caney (Faulkner County)	72032	Clarkridge	72623	Danville	72833
Caney (Hot Spring County)	71929	Clarks Corner	72394	Dardanelle	72834
Caney (Nevada County)	71858	Clarksville	72830	Datto	72424
Caney Valley	71921	Clay	72143	Dayton	72940
Canfield	71845	Clear Lake (Grant County)	72150	Dean	72616
Cantwell	72422	Clear Lake (Mississippi County)	72315	De Ann	71801
Capps	72601			Deans Market	72921
Capps City	71069	Cleveland	72030	Dean Springs	72921
Caraway	72419	Clifty	72756	Decatur	72722
Carbon City	72855	Clinton	72031	Deckerville	72386
Carden Bottoms	72834	Clover Bend	72433	Deep Elm	71653
Careyville	71765	Clow	71855	Deer	72628
Carlile Highland	72653	Clyde	72717	Deerfield	72328
Carlisle	72024	Coaldale	74937	Delaney	72727
Carmel	71671	Coal Hill	72832	Delaplaine	72425
Carmi	72438	Coffeeville	72020	Delaware	72835
Carolan	72927	Coffman (Greene County)	72450	Delfore	72438
Carroll's Corner	72442	Coffman (Lawrence County)	72433	Delight	71940
Carrollton	72611	Coleman	71655	Dell	72426
Carryville	72454	Cole Spur	71643	De Luce	72042
Carson Lake	72370	Colfax	72653	Denmark	72020
Carter Cove Use Area	72857	College City	72476	Dennard	72629
Carthage	71725	Collegehill	71752	Denning	72821
Casa	72025	College Station	72053	Dennison Heights	72527
Cash	72421	Collegeville	72002	Denver	72638
Cass	72949	Collins	71634	Denwood	72386
Casscoe	72026	Colt	72326	De Queen	71832
Catalpa	72854	Columbus	71831	Dermott	71638
Catcher	72956	Combs	72721	De Roche	71929
Catholic Point	72027	Cominto	71655	Des Arc	72040
Cato	72114	Compton	72624	Desha	72527
Catron	72367	Concord	72523	Detonti	72011
Caulksville	72951	Congo	72015	De Valls Bluff	72041
Cauthron (Logan County)	72927	Connells Point	72366	Dewey	72121
Cauthron (Scott County)	72958	Conway	72032	De Witt	72042
Cavanaugh (Part of Fort Smith)	72901	Copper Mine	72756	Dialton	71665
		Cord	72524	Diamond Bay	72531
Cave City	72521	Corinth	72824	Diamond Cave	72666
Cave Creek	72501	Corley	72855	Diamond City	72644
Cave Springs	72718	Cornerstone	72004	Diamondhead	71913
Cecil	72930	Cornerville	71667	Dian (Part of Prescott)	71857
Cedar Creek	72950	Cornhill	71846	Diaz	72043
Cedar Grove	72534	Corning	72422	Dierks	71833
Cedarville	72932	Cotter	72626	Dillen	72854
Center	72542	Cotton Plant	72036	Dixie (Craighead County)	72437
Center Hill (Greene County)	72450	Cottonwood Corner (Craighead County)	72447	Dixie (Woodruff County)	72006
Center Hill (White County)	72143			Doddridge	71834
Center Point (Clark County)	71743	Cottonwood Corner (Mississippi County)	72370	Dogpatch	72648
Center Point (Howard County)	71852			Dogtown	71832
		Council	72320	Dogwood	72315
Center Point (Prairie County)	72064	Cove	71937	Dollarway (Part of Pine Bluff)	71602
		Cowell	72856		
Center Ridge (Clark County)	71921	Cowlingsville	71846	Dolph	72528
Center Ridge (Conway County)	72027	Coy	72037	Donaldson	71941
		Cozahome	72639	Dongola	72650
Centerton	72719	Crabtree	72031	Doniphan	72143
Center Valley	72801	Cravens	72949	Dora	72956
Centerville (Faulkner County)	72058	Crawfordsville	72327	Double Bridges	72358
		Creigh	72366	Douglas Corner	72205
Centerville (Hempstead County)	71835	Crigler	71667	Dover	72837
		Crockett	72454	Dowdy	72524
Centerville (Yell County)	72829	Crocketts Bluff	72038	Drakes Creek	72740
Central (Clark County)	71923	Crosses	72701	Drasco	72530
Central (Hot Spring County)	72104	Crossett	71635	Driggs	72943
Central (Sevier County)	71842	Crossroads (Cleburne County)	72131	Driver	72329
Central Baptist College (Part of Conway)	72032			Dryden	72401
		Cross Roads (Hot Spring County)	71933	Dryfork	72740
Central City (Garland County)	71913			Dublin	72863
		Cross Roads (Izard County)	72566	Duff	72675
Central City (Sebastian County)	72941	Crossroads (Jackson County)	72112	Dumas	71639
				Durham	72727
Central Mall (Part of Fort Smith)	72901	Cross Roads (Little River County)	71866	Durian	72104
				Dutch Mills	72744
Cerrogordo	71866	Cross Roads (Logan County)	72863	Dutton	72760
Chambersville	71766			Dyer	72935
Chapel Hill	71832	Cross Roads (Madison County)	72738	Dyess	72330
Charleston	72933			Eagle Mills	71720
Charlotte	72501	Crossroads (Prairie County)	72040	Eagleton	71953
Chasewood Landing	71969	Crossroads (Sebastian County)	72944	Earle	72331
Chatfield	72323			East Black Oak	72386
Chelford	72386	Crumpler	72644	East Camden	71701
Cherokee City	72734	Crumrod	72328	East End	72065
Cherokee Village	72525	Crystal Hill	72118	Eaton	72458
Cherokee Village-Hidden Valley	72525	Crystal Springs	71968	Ebenezer	71764
		Crystal Springs Landing	71968	Ebony	72364
Cherry Hill (Perry County)	72126	Cullendale (Part of Camden)	71701	Echo	72927
Cherry Hill (Polk County)	71953	Culpeper	72031	Economy	72823
Cherry Valley	72324	Cumi	72544	Eden Isle	72543
Chester	72934	Cummins Unit	71644	Edgemont	72044
Chickalah	72834	Curtis	71728	Edmondson	72332
Chicot Junction	71640	Cushman	72526	Efay (Part of Fayetteville)	72701
Chicot Terrace (Part of Little Rock)	72209	Cypert	72366	Eglantine	72153
		Cypress Valley	72156	Egypt	72427
Chidester	71726	Dabney	72110	Elaine	72333
Childress	72447	Dacus (Part of West Memphis)	72301	El Dorado	71730-31
Chimes	72645			For specific El Dorado Zip Codes call (501) 863-7571	
Chismville	72943	Daisy	71950		
Choctaw	72028	Dalark	71923	Elevenpoint	72455
Cincinnati	72769	Dallas	71953	Elgin	72112
Clarendon	72029	Dalton	72455	Elizabeth	72531
Clarkedale	72325	Damascus	72039	Elkins	72727

ARKANSAS 53

	ZIP		ZIP		ZIP
Elk Ranch	72632	Forty Four	72585	Gravelridge (Bradley County)	71631
Elliott	71701	Forum	72740	Gravel Ridge (Pulaski County)	72076
Ellison	72152	Fouke	71837	Graves Chapel	71846
Elm Springs	72728	Fountain Hill	71642	Gravesville	72039
Elm Store	65778	Fountain Lake	71901	Gravette	72736
Elmwood	72601	Fourche	72016	Gray Rock	72855
Elnora	72455	Fourmile Hill	72143	Grays	72101
El Paso	72045	Fox	72051	Graysoh	72927
Emanuel	72003	Francis	72601	Greasy Corner	72346
Emerson	71740	Franklin	72536	Greenbrier	72058
Emmet	71835	Free Hope	71753	Greene High	72450
Empire	71661	Frenchmans Bayou	72338	Greenfield	72432
Enders	72131	Frenchport	71701	Green Forest	72638
Engelberg	72455	Friendship (Columbia County)	71860	Green Hill	71675
England	72046	Friendship (Hot Spring County)	71942	Greenland	72737
English	72004	Friley	72752	Green Tree	72031
Enola	72047	Fritz	72461	Greenway	72430
Enterprise	72901	Fryatt	72554	Greenwood (Franklin County)	72949
Eros	72633	Frys Mill	72365	Greenwood (Sebastian County)	72936
Erwin	72112	Fulton	71838	Greers Ferry	72067
Ethel	72048	Furlow	72086	Gregory	72059
Etna	72949	Gaines Landing	71653	Grider	72370
Etowah	72428	Gainesville	72436	Griffith Spring	71667
Euclid Heights (Part of Hot Springs National Park)	71901	Gainsboro	72501	Griffithtown	71923
Eudora	71640	Gaither	72601	Griffithville	72060
Eula	72675	Galla Rock	72823	Grubbs	72431
Eureka Springs	72632	Gallatin	72761	Guernsey	71801
Evansville	72729	Galloway	72117	Guion	72540
Evening Shade (Hempstead County)	71801	Gamaliel	72537	Gum Springs (Clark County)	71923
Evening Shade (Sharp County)	72532	Gammon	72364	Gum Springs (Newton County)	72641
Evening Star	72425	Gardner	71765	Gurdon	71743
Everton	72633	Garfield	72732	Guy	72061
Excelsior	72936	Garland City	71839	Hackett	72937
Fairbanks	72131	Garland Springs	72111	Hagarville	72839
Fairfield (Part of Little Rock)	72209	Garner	72052	Half Moon	72315
Fairfield Bay	72088	Garret Grove	72368	Halley	71638
Fair Oaks	72397	Garrett	72846	Halley Junction	71638
Fairview (Chicot County)	71653	Garrett Bridge	71639	Halliday	72443
Fairview (Lonoke County)	72086	Gassville	72635	Hamburg	71646
Fairview (Marion County)	72650	Gaston	71957	Hamil	72460
Fairview (Ouachita County)	71701	Gateway	72733	Hamilton	72024
Fairview (Sevier County)	71841	Gaylor	72657	Hammonsville	72111
Fairwood	71901	Geneva	71832	Hampton	71744
Falcon	71827	Genoa	71840	Hanover	72541
Falls Chapel	71846	Gentry	72734	Happy	72143
Fallsville	72854	George Creek	72687	Happy Bend	72823
Fancy Hill	71935	Georgetown (Madison County)	72773	Happy Corners	72438
Farelly Lake	72160	Georgetown (Pope County)	72847	Hardin	71602
Fargo	72021	Georgetown (White County)	72143	Hardy	72542
Farmington	72730	Gepp	72538	Hargrave Corner	72461
Farmville	71671	Geridge	72046	Harmon (Boone County)	72601
Farville	72417	Gethsemane	72004	Harmon (Washington County)	72701
Fayetteville	72701-03	Gibbs	71969	Harmontown	72501
For specific Fayetteville Zip Codes call (501) 442-8286		Gibson (Craighead County)	72401	Harmony (Columbia County)	71753
Felsenthal	71747	Gibson (Pulaski County)	72076	Harmony (Johnson County)	72830
Felton	72360	Gieseck	72373	Harmony (Madison County)	72740
Fender	72476	Gifford	72104	Harmony (White County)	72143
Fendley	71921	Gilbert	72636	Harmony Grove	71701
Fenter	72167	Gilchrist	72358	Harness	72645
Ferguson	72328	Giles Spur	72476	Harrell	71745
Ferguson Crossroads	71837	Gilkey	72853	Harriet	72639
Fern	72946	Gillett	72055	Harrisburg	72432
Ferndale	72208	Gillham	71841	Harrison	72601-02
Fifty-Six	72533	Gilmore	72339	For specific Harrison Zip Codes call (501) 741-3473	
Figure Five	72956	Gin City	71826	Hartford	72938
Finch	72450	Gladden	72331	Hartman	72840
Fisher (Craighead County)	72421	Gleason	72032	Hartwell	72740
Fisher (Poinsett County)	72429	Glencoe	72539	Harvey	72841
Fitzgerald	72112	Glendale	71667	Haskell	72015
Fitzhugh	72006	Glen Rose	72104	Hasty	72640
Fivemile	72530	Glenwood	71943	Hatchie Coon	72472
Flag	72645	Gobblers Point	72080	Hatfield	71945
Flat Rock	72847	Gobell	72366	Hattieville	72063
Flint Springs	72583	Gold Creek	72032	Hatton	71946
Flippin	72634	Golden City	72927	Havana	72842
Floodway	72442	Golden Lake	72395	Hayley	72040
Floral	72534	Gold Lake Estates	72032	Haynes	72341
Florence	71655	Goobertown	72417	Hazen	72064
Floyd	72143	Goodwin	72340	Heafer	72331
Fomby	71822	Goose Camp	72840	Healing Springs	72712
Fontaine	72416	Goshen	72735	Heart	72539
Fordyce	71742	Gosnell	72319	Heber Springs	72543
Foreman	71836	Gould	71643	Hebron	71660
Forest Grove (Columbia County)	71740	Gourd	71639	Hector	72843
Forest Grove (Lafayette County)	71861	Gourd Neck	72101	Helena	72342
Forest Park (Part of Little Rock)	72207	Grady	71644	Helena Crossing (Part of Helena)	72342
Formosa	72031	Grand Glaise	72020	Helena Junction	72355
Forrest City	72335	Grandview	72616	Hempwallace	71964
Fort Chaffee	72905	Grange	72521	Henderson	72544
Fort Douglas	72854	Grannis	71944	Henderson College (Part of Arkadelphia)	71923
Fort Lynn	71837	Grapevine	72057	Hendrix College (Part of Conway)	72032
Fort Smith	72901-17	Graphic	72921		
For specific Fort Smith Zip Codes call (501) 484-6370		Grassy Lake Bottom	72331		
		Gravel Hill (Van Buren County)	72030		
		Gravel Hill (White County)	72136		
		Gravelly	72838		

54 ARKANSAS Hensley-Lundell

Name	ZIP
Hensley	72065
Herbine	71665
Hergett	72401
Heritage Estates	72653
Herman	72401
Hermitage (Bradley County)	71647
Hermitage (Pulaski County)	72206
Herndon	72401
Hervey	75502
Heth	72346
Hickeytown	72847
Hickman	72315
Hickoria	72422
Hickory Flat	72121
Hickory Hill	72110
Hickory Plains	72066
Hickory Ridge	72347
Hickory Valley	72521
Hicks	72366
Hicks Station	72394
Hidden Valley	72542
Higden	72067
Higgins (Part of Little Rock)	72206
Higginson	72068
Highfill	72734
Highland	72542
Hill Creek	72127
Hillcrest (Johnson County)	72830
Hillcrest (Pulaski County)	72205
Hilleman	72101
Hilltop	72482
Hilo	71647
Hindsville	72738
Hiram	72179
Hiwasse	72739
Hobbs Spur	72952
Holiday Island	72632
Holland	72173
Hollis	72857
Holly Corner	72461
Holly Grove	72069
Holly Island	72461
Holly Springs (Dallas County)	71763
Holly Springs (White County)	72143
Hollywood	71923
Holman	72846
Holub	72360
Homan	75502
Homewood	72025
Hon	72958
Hooker	72450
Hope	71801
Hopewell (Cleburne County)	72137
Hopewell (Greene County)	72443
Hopewell (Lawrence County)	72433
Hopper	71935
Horatio	71842
Horseshoe	72112
Horseshoe Bend	72512
Horseshoe Lake	72348
Horton	72326
Hot Springs Mall (Part of Hot Springs National Park)	71901
Hot Springs National Park	71901-14
For specific Hot Springs National Park Zip Codes call (501) 623-7704	
Hot Springs Village	71901
	71909
For specific Hot Springs Village Zip Codes call (501) 922-1394	
Houston	72070
Howell	72071
Hoxie	72433
Huff	72501
Huffman	72315
Hughes	72348
Hulbert (Part of West Memphis)	72301
Humnoke	72072
Humphrey	72073
Hunt	72844
Hunter	72074
Huntington	72940
Huntsville	72740
Hurricane Grove	71957
Hutchinson	72534
Huttig	71747
Hydrick	72324
Ida	72546
Imboden	72434
Indiandale (Part of Hot Springs National Park)	71901
Indianhead Lake Estates (Part of North Little Rock)	72116
Indian Springs	72002

Name	ZIP
Industrial (Part of Little Rock)	72209
Ingalls	71647
Ingleside	72112
Ingram	72455
Ink	71953
Ione	72927
Island Town	72112
Iuka	72519
Ivan	71748
Ivesville	72207
Ivy	71725
Jackson Heights (Part of Jacksonville)	72076
Jacksonport	72075
Jacksonville	72076
Jamestown (Independence County)	72501
Jamestown (Johnson County)	72830
Japton	72740
Jasper	72641
Jefferson	72079
Jefferson Square (Part of Pine Bluff)	71601
Jeffersonville	72360
Jeffery	72118
Jennette	72327
Jennie	71649
Jenny Lind	72903
Jenson	72937
Jericho	72327
Jerome	71650
Jerrett	72444
Jersey	71651
Jerusalem	72080
Jessieville	71949
Jesup	72466
Joan	71923
Johnson	72741
Johnstown	72112
Johnsville	71647
Joiner	72350
Jolliff Store	72442
Jonesboro	72401-03
For specific Jonesboro Zip Codes call (501) 972-8400	
Jones Mill	72105
Jonesville	71837
Jonquil	72346
Joplin	71957
Jordan	72519
Joy	72143
Joyce City	71762
Joyland Park	72927
Judd Hill	72472
Judsonia	72081
Julius	72327
Jumbo	72556
Junction City	71749
Kahoka	72560
Kansas	71772
Kearney	72132
Kedron	71665
Keiser	72351
Kellum	71832
Kelso	71674
Kenova	71762
Kensett	72082
Kent	71701
Kentucky	72015
Kenwood	72823
Keo	72083
Kerlin	71753
Kerr	72142
Kibler	72956
Kimberley	71958
Kindall	72374
Kings	71841
Kingsland	71652
Kingston (Madison County)	72742
Kingston (Yell County)	72853
Kingswood Estates	72653
Kingtown	72366
Kirby	71950
Kirkland	71751
Knob	72436
Knobel	72435
Knoxville	72845
Koch Ridge	72031
Lacey	71655
Laconia	72379
La Crosse	72584
Ladd	71601
Ladelle	71655
Lafe	72436
Lafferty	72561
La Grange	72352
Lake Catherine	71901
Lake City	72437
Lake Dick	72004

Name	ZIP
Lake Elmdale	72764
Lake Hamilton	71913
Lakeport	71653
Lakeside (Garland County)	71901
Lakeside (Ouachita County)	71701
Lakeside Terrace	72653
Lakeview (Baxter County)	72642
Lake View (Craighead County)	72437
Lake View (Phillips County)	72342
Lake Village	71653
Lakeway	72687
Lakewood	72004
Lakewood Estates	75501
Lamar	72846
Lamartine	71770
Lambert	71929
Lambrook	72353
Landers	72472
Landis	72650
Laneburg	71844
Langford	72004
Langley	71952
Lanieve	72416
Lansing	72327
Lanty	72063
La Pile	71765
Larkin	72584
Larue	72756
Latour	72355
Lavaca	72941
Lawson	71750
Leachville	72438
Lead Hill	72644
Lebanon	71846
Lee Creek	72934
Lehi	72364
Leitner (Part of Pine Bluff)	71601
Lemsford	72442
Leola	72084
Leonard	72461
Lepanto	72354
Leslie	72645
Lester	72437
Letona	72085
Lewisville	71845
Lexa	72355
Lexington	72031
Liberty	72835
Liberty Hall	72834
Liberty Valley	72010
Lick Mountain	72027
Light	72439
Limedale	72501
Limestone	72628
Lincoln	72744
Linder	72058
Linwood	71659
Lisbon	71730
Little Flock	72756
Little Italy	72016
Little Red	72121
Little River	72442
Little River Country Club	71866
Little Rock	72201-31
For specific Little Rock Zip Codes call (501) 375-8148	
Little Rock Air Force Base	72099
Locke	72946
Lockesburg	71846
Locust Bayou	71701
Locust Grove	72550
Lodge Corner	72160
Lodi	71943
Logan	72761
Lollie	72106
London	72847
Lonelm	72947
Lone Pine	72650
Lono	72084
Lonoke	72086
Lonsdale	72087
Lookout	72756
Lookout Store	72134
Lorado	72401
Lorine	72455
Lost Bridge	72732
Lost Cane	72442
Lost Corner	72080
Louann	71751
Louise	72376
Lowell	72745
Lower Boydsville	72461
Lower Poplar Ridge	72414
Low Gap	72641
Luber	72560
Lucas	72927
Ludwig	72830
Lumber	71770
Luna	71653
Lundell	72367

Lunenburg-Oaklawn ARKANSAS 55

Name	ZIP
Lunenburg	72556
Lunsford	72437
Lurton	72856
Lutherville	72846
Luxora	72358
Lynn	72440
Mabelvale (Part of Little Rock)	72103
McAlmont	72117
McArthur	71654
McCain Mall (Part of North Little Rock)	72116
McCaskill	71847
McClelland	72006
McCormick	72472
McCrory	72101
McDonald	72373
McDougal	72441
Macedonia (Columbia County)	71753
Macedonia (Conway County)	72063
Macey	72447
McFadden	72347
McGehee	71654
McGintytown	72058
McHue	72501
McJester	72121
McKamie	71860
Macks	72112
McMilan Corner	71653
McNab	71838
McNeil	71752
Macon	72076
Macon Lake	71653
McRae	72102
Madding	72004
Madison	72359
Magazine	72943
Magic Springs	72650
Magness	72553
Magnet Cove	72104
Magnolia	71753
Main Street (Part of North Little Rock)	72119
Mallet Town	72157
Mallory Spur	72323
Malvern	72104
Mammoth Spring	72554
Mandalay	72442
Mandeville	75501
Manfred	71935
Mangrum	72414
Manila	72442
Manning	71763
Mansfield	72944
Many Island	72554
Maple Corner	72374
Maple Grove	72472
Maple Springs	72564
Marble	72740
Marcella	72555
Marche	72118
Marianna	72360
Marie	72395
Marion	72364
Marked Tree	72365
Marmaduke	72443
Marsena	72650
Marshall	72650
Mars Hill	71860
Martindale	72204
Martinville	72204
Marvell	72366
Marvinville	72842
Marysville	71753
Mason Valley	72712
Masonville	71654
Massard (Part of Fort Smith)	72901
Maumee	72675
Maumelle	72118
Maxville	72521
Mayfield	72701
Mayflower	72106
Maynard	72444
Maysville	72747
Mazarn	71933
Meadow Cliff	72335
Meeks Settlement	71962
Melbourne	72556
Mellwood	72367
Melrose	72550
Mena	71953
Menifee	72107
Meridian	71635
Meroney	71643
Merrivale (Part of Little Rock)	72204
Mesa	72041
Metalton	72616
Middlebrook	72444

Name	ZIP
Middleton	72027
Midland	72945
Midway (Baxter County)	72651
Midway (Hot Spring County)	71941
Midway (Howard County)	71852
Midway (Jackson County)	72479
Midway (Lafayette County)	71845
Midway (Logan County)	72865
Midway (Nevada County)	71857
Midway (White County)	72568
Midway Corner	72376
Milford	71846
Mill Creek (Pope County)	72801
Mill Creek (Sebastian County)	72901
Miller	71836
Milligan Ridge	72442
Milltown	72936
Milo	71646
Mineral	71841
Mineral Springs	71851
Minorca	72444
Minturn	72445
Mist	71646
Mitchell	72583
Mitchellville	71639
Mixon	72927
Moark	72422
Moko	72557
Monarch	72687
Monette	72447
Monkey Run	72635
Monnie Springs	72135
Monroe	72108
Montana	72840
Monte Ne Shores	72756
Monterey	72373
Monticello	71655
Montongo	71655
Montreal	72940
Montrose	71658
Moore	72856
Moore Camp	71822
Moorefield	72501
Moreland	72801
Morgan	72118
Morganton	72013
Morning Star (Garland County)	71901
Morning Star (Searcy County)	72650
Morning Sun	72143
Moro	72368
Morobay	71651
Morrilton	72110
Morrison Bluff	72863
Morriston	72576
Morrow	72749
Morton	72101
Mosby Spur	72328
Moscow	71659
Mosley	72834
Mossville	72641
Mounds (Crittenden County)	72376
Mounds (Greene County)	72461
Mountainburg	72946
Mountain Crest	72727
Mountain Fork	71953
Mountain Home	72653
Mountain Pine	71956
Mountain Springs	72023
Mountain Top	72949
Mountain Valley	71901
Mountain View	72560
Mount Comport	72701
Mount Elba	71660
Mount Gayler	72959
Mount George	72833
Mount Hersey	72633
Mount Holly	71758
Mount Ida	71957
Mount Judea	72655
Mount Moriah	71958
Mount Olive (Bradley County)	71647
Mount Olive (Conway County)	72127
Mount Olive (Izard County)	72556
Mount Olive (Washington County)	72727
Mount Pisgah	72143
Mount Pleasant	72561
Mount Sherman	72641
Mount Tabor	71956
Mount Vernon (Faulkner County)	72111
Mount Vernon (Johnson County)	72840
Mozart	72051
Muddyfork	71852
Mulberry	72947

Name	ZIP
Murfreesboro	71958
Murphys Corner	72112
Mustin Lake	71701
Myron	72513
Nady	72166
Nail	72628
Nashville	71852
Nathan	71852
Natural Dam	72948
Natural Steps	72135
Naylor	72173
Neal Springs	71842
Nebo	71667
Needham	72437
Needmore	72958
Nella	71953
Nelsonville	72466
Nettleton (Part of Jonesboro)	72401
Neuhardt	72376
Newark	72562
New Augusta (Part of Augusta)	72006
New Blaine	72851
Newburg	72556
New Dixie	72016
New Edinburg	71660
Newell	71730
New Gascony	72004
New Hope (Drew County)	71655
New Hope (Independence County)	72501
Newhope (Pike County)	71959
New Hope (Pope County)	72801
New London	71765
Newnata	72657
Newport	72112
New Spadra	72830
New Summit (Part of Benton)	72011
New Town (Crawford County)	72921
Newtown (Jefferson County)	72004
Nimmo	72143
Nimmons	72461
Nimrod	72126
Noble Lake	71601
Nodena	72395
Noland	72455
Norfork	72658
Norman	71960
Norphlet	71759
Norristown (Part of Russellville)	72801
North Bingen	71852
North Cedar (Part of Pine Bluff)	71601
North Crossett	71635
North Dardanelle	72834
Northern Ohio	72365
North Heights (Part of Texarkana)	75502
North Hughes	72348
North Lewisville (Part of Lewisville)	71845
North Little Rock	72114-20
For specific North Little Rock Zip Codes call (501) 758-1707	
Northpoint	72135
Northwest Arkansas Mall (Part of Fayetteville)	72701
Norvell (Part of Earle)	72331
Nuckles	72020
Number Nine	72315
Nunley	71953
Oak Forest (Lee County)	72360
Oak Forest (Pulaski County)	72201
Oak Grove (Carroll County)	72660
Oak Grove (Clark County)	71728
Oak Grove (Hot Spring County)	72104
Oak Grove (Little River County)	71822
Oak Grove (Lonoke County)	72007
Oak Grove (Nevada County)	71858
Oak Grove (Perry County)	72070
Oak Grove (Pope County)	72801
Oak Grove (Pulaski County)	72118
Oak Grove (Sevier County)	71846
Oak Grove (Washington County)	72764
Oak Grove Heights	72443
Oakhaven	71801
Oak Hill	71822
Oakland	72661
Oakland Heights (Part of Russellville)	72801
Oaklawn (Part of Hot Springs National Park)	71901

56 ARKANSAS Oak Park-Rondo

	ZIP
Oak Park (Part of Pine Bluff)	71603
Oark	72852
Oconee	72455
Oden	71961
O'Donnell Bend	72358
Ogden	71853
Ogemaw	71764
Oil Trough	72564
O'Kean	72449
Okolona	71962
Ola	72853
Old Alabam	72740
Old Austin	72007
Old Grand Glaise	72020
Old Hickory	72063
Old Jenny Lind	72901
Old Joe	72659
Old Town	72389
Old Union	71730
Old Weona	72472
Oliver	72958
Oliver Springs	72952
Olmstead	72116
Olvey	72601
Olyphant	72020
Oma	71964
Omaha	72662
Omega	72834
Onda	72774
One Horse Store	72160
Oneida	72369
Onia	72663
Onyx	72857
Opal (Polk County)	71953
Opal (White County)	72012
Oppelo	72110
Optimus	72519
Orion	72132
Orlando	71660
Osage	72638
Osage Mills	72712
Osceola	72370
Ott	65626
Otto	72173
Otwell	72401
Ouachita	71763
Ouachita College (Part of Arkadelphia)	71923
Overcup (Conway County)	72110
Overcup (Woodruff County)	72101
Owensville	72087
Oxford	72565
Oxley	72645
Ozan	71855
Ozark	72949
Ozark Acres	72482
Ozark Lithia	71901
Ozone	72854
Pace City	71751
Palestine	72372
Palmyra	71667
Pangburn	72121
Pankey (Part of Little Rock)	72207
Panther Forest	71653
Paragould	72450-51
For specific Paragould Zip Codes call (501) 236-7636	
Paraloma	71846
Paris	72855
Parkdale	71661
Parkers Chapel	71730
Parkers-Iron Springs	72206
Park Grove	72029
Park Hill (Part of North Little Rock)	72116
Park Hill Terrace	75501
Parkin	72373
Park Place	72320
Park Plaza (Part of Little Rock)	72205
Parks	72950
Parma	72044
Parnell	72023
Paron	72122
Parthenon	72666
Pastoria	72152
Patmos	71801
Patrick	72727
Patsville	71647
Patterson	72123
Pauls	72416
Pauls Switch	72416
Pawheen	72438
Payneway	72472
Peach Orchard	72453
Pearcy	71964
Pea Ridge (Benton County)	72751
Pea Ridge (Desha County)	71674
Pearson	72131
Pecan Point	72350
Pedro	72761

	ZIP
Peel	72668
Pelsor	72856
Pencil Bluff	71965
Pendleton	71639
Penjur	72348
Pennington	72005
Pennys	71846
Penrose	72101
Peppers Landing	72041
Perla	72104
Perry	72125
Perrytown	71801
Perryville	72126
Peterpender	72933
Pettigrew	72752
Pettus	72086
Pettyville	72442
Pfeiffer	72501
Philadelphia	72401
Philander Smith College (Part of Little Rock)	72203
Phillips Bayou	72360
Phoenix Village (Part of Fort Smith)	72901
Pickens (Desha County)	71662
Pickens (White County)	72143
Pickering	71730
Piercetown	72641
Piggott	72454
Pike City	71958
Pilgrims Rest	72764
Pindall	72669
Pine Bluff	71601-13
For specific Pine Bluff Zip Codes call (501) 536-3535	
Pine Bluff Arsenal	71601
Pine Bluff Southeast (Part of Pine Bluff)	71601
Pine City	72069
Pine Grove	71763
Pine Grove Valley	72944
Pine Ridge	71966
Pine Valley	72521
Pineville	72566
Piney (Garland County)	71901
Piney (Johnson County)	72847
Piney Grove	71845
Pinnacle	72135
Pisgah (Pike County)	71940
Pisgah (Yell County)	72834
Pitman	72444
Pitts	72421
Plainfield	71740
Plainview (White County)	72081
Plainview (Yell County)	72857
Plant	72031
Pleasant Grove (Craighead County)	72401
Pleasant Grove (Stone County)	72567
Pleasant Grove (Van Buren County)	72030
Pleasant Hill (Crawford County)	72947
Pleasant Hill (Cross County)	72396
Pleasant Hill (Garland County)	71901
Pleasant Hill (Nevada County)	71857
Pleasant Plains	72568
Pleasant Valley (Faulkner County)	72058
Pleasant Valley (Izard County)	72519
Pleasant Valley (Lafayette County)	71826
Pleasant Valley (Perry County)	72016
Pleasant View	72949
Pleasure Heights	72745
Plumerville	72127
Plunketts	72017
Pocahontas	72455
Point Cedar	71921
Pollard	72456
Ponca	72670
Pontoon	72025
Poplar Grove	72374
Portia	72457
Portland	71663
Posey	72392
Possum Grape	72020
Postelle	72366
Post Oak	71658
Potter	71953
Potter Junction	71953
Pottsville	72858
Poughkeepsie	72569
Powhatan	72458
Poyen	72128
Prairie Creek	72756

	ZIP
Prairie Grove	72753
Prairie View	72863
Prattsville	72129
Prescott	71857
Preston	72032
Preston Ferry	72134
Price Place	65729
Prim	72130
Princeton	71725
Process City	71832
Proctor	72376
Promised Land (Mississippi County)	72315
Promised Land (Poinsett County)	72472
Providence	72081
Provo	71846
Pruitt	72648
Pumpkin Bend	72101
Pyatt	72672
Quarry Heights	72826
Quinn	71730
Quitman	72131
Rainbow Island	72121
Ralph	72687
Rambo Riveria	72756
Ramsey	71742
Ranger	72824
Ratcliff	72951
Ratio	72333
Ravanna	75556
Ravenden	72459
Ravenden Springs	72460
Rawlison	72348
Reader	71726
Readland	71640
Rea Valley	72634
Rector	72461
Redfield	72132
Redland	71857
Red Leaf	71653
Red Onion	72447
Red Rock	72655
Red Star	72752
Red Wing	71832
Reed	71670
Reedville	71639
Relfs Bluff	71667
Remmel	72112
Rena	72956
Republican	72058
Revel	72006
Rex	72031
Reydell	72133
Reyno	72462
Rich	72021
Richardson	72004
Richland (Part of Little Rock)	72205
Richland View	72727
Richmond	71822
Richwood (Clark County)	71923
Richwood (Lawrence County)	72476
Ridgeway	72601
Rio Vista	72010
Risher	72421
Rison	71665
Rivercliff Estates	72756
Riverdale	72941
River Mountain	72835
Riverside	72101
Rivervale	72377
Riverview	72110
Rixey (Part of North Little Rock)	72117
Robertsville	72063
Robinson	72761
Rob Roy	72004
Rock Hill	71846
Rockport	72104
Rock Springs	71675
Rockwell (Garland County)	71901
Rockwell (Garland County)	71913
Rocky	71953
Rocky Hill	72629
Rocky Mound (Hempstead County)	71801
Rocky Mound (Miller County)	71837
Rodney	72519
Roe	72134
Rogers	72756-57
For specific Rogers Zip Codes call (501) 636-3301	
Rohwer	71666
Roland	72135
Rolla	72104
Romance	72136
Rondo (Lee County)	72355
Rondo (Miller County)	75502

Rosa-Twentythree ARKANSAS 57

Name	ZIP
Rosa	72358
Rosboro	71921
Rose Bud	72137
Rose City (Part of North Little Rock)	72117
Roseland	72442
Rose Meadow (Part of Little Rock)	72206
Roseville	72949
Rosie	72571
Ross	72846
Rosston	71858
Rotan	72370
Round Mountain	72025
Round Pond	72378
Rover	72860
Rowell	71665
Roy	71852
Royal	71968
Royal Oak	72103
Rubicon	72015
Rudy	72952
Rule	72638
Rumley	72645
Rupert	72031
Russell	72139
Russellville	72801
Rutherford	72501
Rye	71665
Sacred Heart	72840
Saddle	72554
Saffell	72572
Sage	72573
Saginaw	71941
St. Charles	72140
St. Francis	72464
St. Joe	72675
St. Matthews	71752
St. Paul	72760
St. Vincent	72063
Salado	72575
Salem (Fulton County)	72576
Salem (Pike County)	71943
Salem (Saline County)	72015
Salesville	72653
Saltillo	72032
Salus	72854
Sand Hill	72040
Sandtown	72501
Sandy Bend	71765
Sandyland	71762
Sandy Ridge	72315
Saratoga	71859
Sardis	72011
Savoy	72701
Schaal	71851
Schaberg	72946
Schug	72450
Scotland	72141
Scott	72142
Scottsville	72843
Scranton	72863
Screeton	72064
Searcy	72143
Seaton	72046
Seaton Dump	72046
Sedgwick	72465
Selma	71670
Seyppel	72348
Shady	71953
Shady Grove (Fulton County)	72583
Shady Grove (Johnson County)	72830
Shady Grove (Mississippi County)	72442
Shady Grove (Nevada County)	71857
Shady Grove (Poinsett County)	72472
Shakertown	71923
Shannon	72455
Shannondale	72348
Shannon Hills	72103
Shannonville	72331
Sharman	71860
Sharum	72425
Shearerville	72346
Shelbyville	72521
Shell Lake	72346
Sheppard	71838
Sheridan	72150
Sherrill	72152
Sherwood	72116
Sherwood Hills	72105
Shiloh (Howard County)	71851
Shiloh (Pope County)	72801
Shippen	72351
Shirley	72153
Shoffner	72112
Shover Springs	71801

Name	ZIP
Sidney	72577
Sidon	72137
Signal Hill	72560
Siloam Springs	72761
Silver	71957
Silver Ridge	71846
Sims	71969
Simsboro	72348
Sitka	72482
Skunkhollow	72032
Slaytonville	72937
Slonikers Mill	72372
Slovak	72160
Smackover	71762
Smale	72021
Smearney	71647
Smiths Corner	72368
Smithville	72466
Snow	72687
Snowball	72650
Snow Hill	71751
Snow Lake	72379
Snyder	71658
Social Hill	72104
Solgohachia	72156
Sonora	72764
South Crossett (Part of Crossett)	71635
Southern Hills	72601
Southern State College (Part of Magnolia)	71753
South Fort Smith (Part of Fort Smith)	72906
South Jacksonville (Part of Jacksonville)	72117
Southland	72355
South Lead Hill	72601
South Ozark	72949
South Sheridan	72150
South Shore Park	72543
South Side (Independence County)	72501
South Side (Pulaski County)	72206
Southside (Van Buren County)	72013
Spadra	72830
Sparkman	71763
Spence Junction	72856
Spirit Lake	71845
Springdale	72764-65
For specific Springdale Zip Codes call (501) 751-4441	
Springfield	72157
Springhill (Faulkner County)	72058
Spring Hill (Hempstead County)	71801
Spring Lake Estates	72653
Springtown	72767
Spring Valley (Pulaski County)	72210
Spring Valley (Washington County)	72764
Stacy (Crittenden County)	72384
Stacy (Poinsett County)	72472
Stamps	71860
Standard-Umsted	71762
Stanford	72450
Star City	71667
Stark (Part of Greers Ferry)	72067
State Capitol (Part of Little Rock)	72201
State College of Arkansas (Part of Conway)	72032
State Line (Columbia County)	71740
State Line (Lafayette County)	71861
State Services	72158
State University (Part of Jonesboro)	72467
Staves	71665
Stelltown	71940
Stephens	71764
Steprock	72159
Stevens Creek	72010
Stevens Landing	72472
Stokes	72455
Stonewall	72450
Stony Point	72070
Story	71970
Strangers Home	72410
Strawberry (Johnson County)	72830
Strawberry (Lawrence County)	72469
Stringtown	71842
Strong	71765
Stump City	72346
Sturkie	72578
Stuttgart	72160
Subiaco	72865

Name	ZIP
Success	72470
Sugar Grove	72927
Sugarloaf Lake	72937
Sulphur City	72701
Sulphur Rock	72579
Sulphur Springs (Benton County)	72768
Sulphur Springs (Jefferson County)	71603
Sulphur Springs (Yell County)	72834
Summers	72769
Summit	72677
Sumpter	71647
Sunnydale	72159
Sunny Hill (Part of Searcy)	72143
Sunset (Crittenden County)	72364
Sunset (Washington County)	72959
Sunshine (Ashley County)	71661
Sunshine (Garland County)	71968
Supply	72444
Sutton	71835
Swain	72628
Swan Lake	72004
Sweden	72004
Sweethome (Montgomery County)	71957
Sweet Home (Pulaski County)	72164
Swifton	72471
Sycamore Bend	72348
Sylamore	72556
Sylvan Hills (Part of Sherwood)	72116
Sylvania	72176
Tafton	72183
Tafton-Wrightsville	72183
Talley	71740
Tamo	71644
Tarry	71667
Tate	72927
Taylor	71861
Tech (Part of Russellville)	72801
Tennessee	71655
Texarkana	75502
Thebes	71658
Thida	72165
Thompson Grove	72348
Thornburg	72126
Thorney	72727
Thornton	71766
Three Brothers	72653
Three Creeks	71749
Three Way	72370
Tichnor	72166
Tillar	71670
Tilly	72679
Tilton	72347
Timber Lake Manor	72531
Timbo	72680
Tinsman	71767
Toad Suck	72016
Togo	72373
Tokio	71852
Toledo	71665
Tollette	71851
Tollville	72041
Toltec	72142
Tomahawk	72675
Tomato	72381
Tomberlin	72046
Toneyville (Part of Jacksonville)	72076
Tongin	72320
Tontitown	72770
Trammellville	72461
Traskwood	72167
Treasure Hills	72032
Treat	72854
Trenton	72374
Trippe	71654
Troy	71764
Trumann	72472
Tuck (Part of Jonesboro)	72401
Tucker	72168
Tuckerman	72473
Tuckertown	72321
Tucker Unit	72168
Tulip	71725
Tull	72015
Tully	72472
Tulot	72472
Tumbling Shoals	72581
Tupelo	72169
Turkey Scratch	72366
Turner	72383
Turrell	72384
Tuttle	72727
Twentythree	72010

58 ARKANSAS Twin Lakes-Zion Hill

	ZIP		ZIP		ZIP
Twin Lakes (Part of Little Rock)	72201	Walnut Ridge	72476	Whitmore	72394
Twin Springs	72205	Walnut Springs	71842	Whitton	72386
Twist	72385	Walters	72438	Wickes	71973
Tyro	71639	Waltreak	72833	Wideman	72585
Tyronza	72386	Wampler Spur (Part of Pine Bluff)	71601	Widener	72394
Ulm	72170	Ward	72176	Wiederkehr Village	72821
Umpire	71971	Wardell	72350	Wilburn	72179
Union (Fulton County)	72576	Warm Springs	72478	Wild Cherry	72576
Union (Sevier County)	71832	Warner	71701	Wildwood	72346
Unionhill	72020	Warren	71671	Williamson	71842
Uniontown	72955	Washburn	72936	Williford	72482
Unity	71852	Washington	71862	Willisville	71864
University Mall (Part of Little Rock)	72205	Washita	71957	Willow	72084
University of Arkansas at Monticello (Part of Monticello)	71655	Watalula	72949	Wilmar	71675
		Waterloo	71858	Wilmot	71676
		Watkins Corner	72366	Wilson (Mississippi County)	72395
Uno	72421	Watson	71674	Wilson (Pope County)	72823
Urbana	71768	Watson Chapel (Part of Pine Bluff)	71601	Wilton	71865
Urbanette	72616	Wattensaw	72086	Winchester	71677
Ursula	72933	Waveland	72867	Windamere (Part of Little Rock)	72201
Vail	72438	Wayton	72628	Winesburg	72401
Valley Gin	71837	Webb City	72949	Winfield	72958
Valley Springs	72682	Weber	72166	Winfrey	72959
Valley View	72401	Wedington	72701	Wing	72857
Van	72042	Wedington Woods	72701	Winslow	72959
Van Buren	72956	Weiner	72479	Winston Terrace (Part of Little Rock)	72201
Vandervoort	71972	Welcome	71861	Winthrop	71866
Vanity Corner	72143	Welcome Home	72650	Wirth	72554
Vanndale	72387	Weldon	72112	Wiseman	72587
Varner Unit	71644	Weona	72472	Witcherville	72940
Vaughn	72712	Weona Junction	72472	Witherspoon	71923
Velvet Ridge	72010	Wesley	72773	Witter	72776
Vendor	72683	Wesley Chapel	72110	Wittsburg	72396
Verona	72618	Wesson	71749	Witts Springs	72686
Vesta	72933	West Bauxite (Part of Bauxite)	72011	Wiville	72101
Veterans Administration Facility (Part of North Little Rock)	72114	West Camden Heights (Part of Camden)	71701	Wolf Bayou	72530
				Woodberry	71744
Vick	71647	West Crossett	71635	Woodland	72830
Victoria	72370	West End (Part of Pine Bluff)	71601	Woodland Corner	72315
Village	71769			Woodland Heights (Part of Little Rock)	72201
Vilonia	72173	Western Grove	72685	Woodland Hills (Fulton County)	72542
Vimy Ridge	72002	West Fork	72774		
Vincent	72327	West Gum Springs (Part of Gum Springs)	71923	Woodland Hills (Saline County)	72002
Vine Prairie	72947				
Vineyard	72360	West Hartford	72938	Woodrow	72130
Vineygrove	72753	West Helena	72390	Woodson	72180
Viola	72583	West Line	74734	Wooster	72181
Violet Hill	72584	West Marche	72118	Worden	72010
Vista Shores	72732	West Memphis	72301	Worthen (Part of Pottsville)	72858
Wabash	72389	West Pangburn	72543	Wright	72182
Wabbaseka	72175	West Point (Benton County)	72734	Wrights Corner	72010
Wakefield Village (Part of Little Rock)	72201	West Point (White County)	72178	Wrightsville	72183
		West Ridge	72391	Wrightsville Unit	72183
Walcott	72474	Westville	72956	Wycamp	72390
Waldenburg	72475	Westwood (Part of Little Rock)	72201	Wye	72016
Waldo	71770			Wyman	72701
Waldron	72958	Wharton	72740	Wynne	72396-97
Walker (Columbia County)	71753	Wheatley	72392	For specific Wynne Zip Codes call (501) 238-2131	
Walker (White County)	72143	Wheeler	72775		
Walkers Creek	71861	Wheeling	72576	Wyola	72959
Walkerville	71740	Whelen Springs	71772	Yale	72752
Wallace	71836	Whispering Springs	72067	Yancopin	71674
Walnut	72854	Whistleville	72442	Yancy	71855
Walnut Corner (Greene County)	72416	Whitaker	72432	Yarbro	72315
		White	71635	Yardelle	72685
Walnut Corner (Phillips County)	72312	Whitecliffs (Little River County)	71846	Y City	71965
Walnut Grove (Clay County)	72435	White Cliffs (Sevier County)	71846	Yellow Bayou	71653
Walnut Grove (Independence County)	72524	White Hall (Jefferson County)	71602	Yellville	72687
				Yocana	71953
Walnut Grove (Van Buren County)	72031	Whitehall (Lee County)	72320	Yoestown	72921
		Whitehall (Poinsett County)	72432	Yorktown	71678
Walnut Grove (Washington County)	72730	Whiteoak	72949	Zent	72021
		Whitetown	71961	Zinc	72601
Walnut Grove (Yell County)	72842	Whiteville	72635	Zion	72556
Walnut Hill	71826			Zion Hill	72110

Abalone Cove-Bayview Park   CALIFORNIA   59

Name	ZIP
Abalone Cove (Part of Rancho Palos Verdes)...	90274
Aberdeen	93526
Academy	93612
Acampo	95220
Acasia Acres	93277
Actis Gardens	93501
Acton	93510
Adelaida	93446
Adelanto	92301
Adin	96006
Adobe Corners	92392
Aerial Acres	93523
Aetna Springs	94567
Afton	95920
Ager	96064
Agnew (Part of Santa Clara)	95054
Agoura Hills	91301
Agua Caliente	95476
Agua Caliente Indian Reservation	92262
Agua Dulce	91350
Aguanga	92302
Ahwahnee	93601
Airbase (Part of Santa Maria)	93454
Airport (Part of Oakland)...	94614
Alabama Hills	93545
Alameda	94501
Alamo (Contra Costa County)	94507
Alamo Oaks (Part of Danville)	94526
Alamorio	92227
Albany	94706
Alberhill	92330
Albion	95410
Alcatraz (Part of San Francisco)	94123
Alderbrook Tract (Part of Cupertino)	95014
Aldercroft Heights	95030
Alderpoint	95411
Alder Springs	93602
Alessandro (Part of Riverside)	92508
Alexander Valley	95441
Alhambra	91801-99
For specific Alhambra Zip Codes call (818) 289-9101	
Alhambra General Mail Facility	91897-98
For specific Alhambra General Mail Facility Zip Codes call (818) 289-9101	
Alhambra Valley	94553
Alisal (Part of Salinas)	93905
Alleghany	95910
Allendale	95688
Allensworth	93219
Alliance (Part of Arcata)	95521
Almaden Plaza (Part of San Jose)	95118
Almaden Valley (Part of San Jose)	95120
Almanor (Plumas County)	95923
Almanor (Plumas County)	95947
Almondale	93553
Almonte	94941
Alondra	90249
Alpaugh	93201
Alpine	92001
Alpine Heights	92001
Alpine Village (Riverside County)	92262
Alpine Village (Tulare County)	93265
Alta	95701
Altadena	91001-02
For specific Altadena Zip Codes call (818) 794-1147	
Alta Heights (Part of Napa)	94558
Alta Hill	95945
Al Tahoe (Part of South Lake Tahoe)	95702
Alta Loma (Part of Cucamonga)	91701
Alta Sierra (Kern County)	93285
Alta Sierra (Nevada County)	95949
Altaville (Part of Angels Camp)	95221
Alta Vista	93514
Alto (Part of Mill Valley)...	94941
Alton	95540
Alturas	96101
Alum Rock	95127
Alvarado (Part of Union City)	94587
Alviso (Part of San Jose)...	95002
Amador City	95601
Amarillo Beach	90265

Name	ZIP
Ambassador (Part of Los Angeles)	90005
Ambler Park	93901
Amboy	92304
Ambrose	94565
American Canyon	94589
American House	95981
Amphibious Base (Naval Amphibious Base, Coronado)	92155
Anaheim	92801-25
For specific Anaheim Zip Codes call (714) 520-2600	
FINANCIAL INSTITUTIONS	
El Camino Bank	92805
United California Savings Bank	92806
HOTELS/MOTELS	
Anaheim Hilton & Towers	92802
Sheraton-Anaheim Hotel...	92802
Anaheim Hills (Part of Anaheim)	92808
Anaheim Plaza (Part of Anaheim)	92801
Anchor Bay	95445
Anderson	96007
Anderson Springs	95461
Andrew Jackson (Part of San Diego)	92115
Angels Camp	95222
Angelus Oaks	92305
Angiola	93212
Angwin	94508
Annapolis	95412
Annex III (Part of Los Angeles)	91405
Antelope	95678
Antelope Acres	93534
Antioch	94509
Antonio	93437
Anza	92306
Applegate	95703
Apple Valley	92307-08
For specific Apple Valley Zip Codes call (619) 247-7819	
Aptos	95003
Arbolada (Part of Ojai)	93023
Arbuckle	95912
Arcade (Los Angeles County)	90052
Arcade (Sacramento County)	95821
Arcadia	91006-07
For specific Arcadia Zip Codes call (818) 446-4678	
Arcata	95521
Arch Beach Heights (Part of Laguna Beach)	92651
Arden	95825
Arden-Arcade	95821
Arden Fair Mall (Part of Sacramento)	95815
Arden Town	95825
Ardmore (Part of South Gate)	90280
Arena	95301
Argus	93562
Arleta (Part of Los Angeles)	91331
Arlington (Part of Riverside)	92503
Arlington Heights Estate...	95934
Arlynda Corners	95536
Armistead	93527
Armona	93202
Army Point	94510
Army Terminal (Part of Oakland)	94626
Arnold	95223
Arnold Heights	92508
Aromas	95004
Arrowbear Lake	92382
Arrowhead Highlands	92325
Arroyo Grande	93420-21
For specific Arroyo Grande Zip Codes call (805) 489-5923	
Arroyo Vista (Part of Dublin)	94566
Artesia	90701-03
For specific Artesia Zip Codes call (213) 860-6694	
Artois	95913
Arvin (Kern County)	93203
Arvin (Kern County)	93308
Ash Creek	96057
Ashland	94541
Asilomar (Part of Pacific Grove)	93950
Aspendell	93514
Asti	95425

Name	ZIP
Atascadero	93422-23
For specific Atascadero Zip Codes call (805) 466-1103	
Athens	90047
Atherton	94027
Athlone	95333
Atlanta	95366
Atwater	95301
Atwood (Part of Placentia)	92601
Auberry	93602
Auburn	95603-04
For specific Auburn Zip Codes call (916) 885-7944	
August	95201
Avalon	90704
Avalon Village (Part of Carson)	90744
Avenal	93204
Avery	95224
Avila Beach	93424
Avocado Heights	91746
Azusa	91702
Baden (Part of South San Francisco)	94080
Badger	93603
Bailey (Part of Whittier)	90601
Baker	92309
Baker Ranch	95631
Bakersfield	93301-89
For specific Bakersfield Zip Codes call (805) 861-4346	
Bakersfield East	93305
Bakersfield Plaza (Part of Bakersfield)	93308
Bakersfield South	93304
Balance Rock	93260
Balboa (Part of Newport Beach)	92661
Balboa Island (Part of Newport Beach)	92662
Balch Camp	93649
Balderson Station	95634
Baldwin Hills Regional Shopping Mall (Part of Los Angeles)	90067
Baldwin Lake	92314
Baldwin Park	91706
Baldy Mesa	92369
Ballarat	93562
Ballard	93463
Ballico	95303
Balls Ferry	96007
Baltimore Park (Part of Larkspur)	94939
Bandini (Part of Commerce)	90022
Bangor	95914
Bankhead Springs	92034
Banner	92036
Banning	92220
Banta	95304
Barber City (Part of Westminster)	92683
Bard	92222
Bardsdale	93015
Barona	92040
Barona Ranch Indian Reservation	92040
Barrett	92017
Barrington (Part of Los Angeles)	90049
Barron Park (Part of Palo Alto)	94306
Barstow	92310-12
For specific Barstow Zip Codes call (619) 296-8494	
Barstow Colony	93705
Barton (Part of Fresno)	93702
Base Line (Part of San Bernardino)	92410
Bassett	91746
Bassetts	96125
Bass Lake	93604
Batavia	95620
Baxter	95704
Bay (Part of Big Bear Lake)	92315
Bay Fair Mall (Part of San Leandro)	94578
Bayliss	95943
Bayo Vista	94572
Bay Park (Part of San Diego)	92110
Bayshore (Part of Brisbane)	94005
Bayshore Mall (Part of Eureka)	95501
Bayside	95524
Bayview (Humboldt County)	95501
Bay View (San Francisco County)	94124
Bayview Park (Contra Costa County)	94806

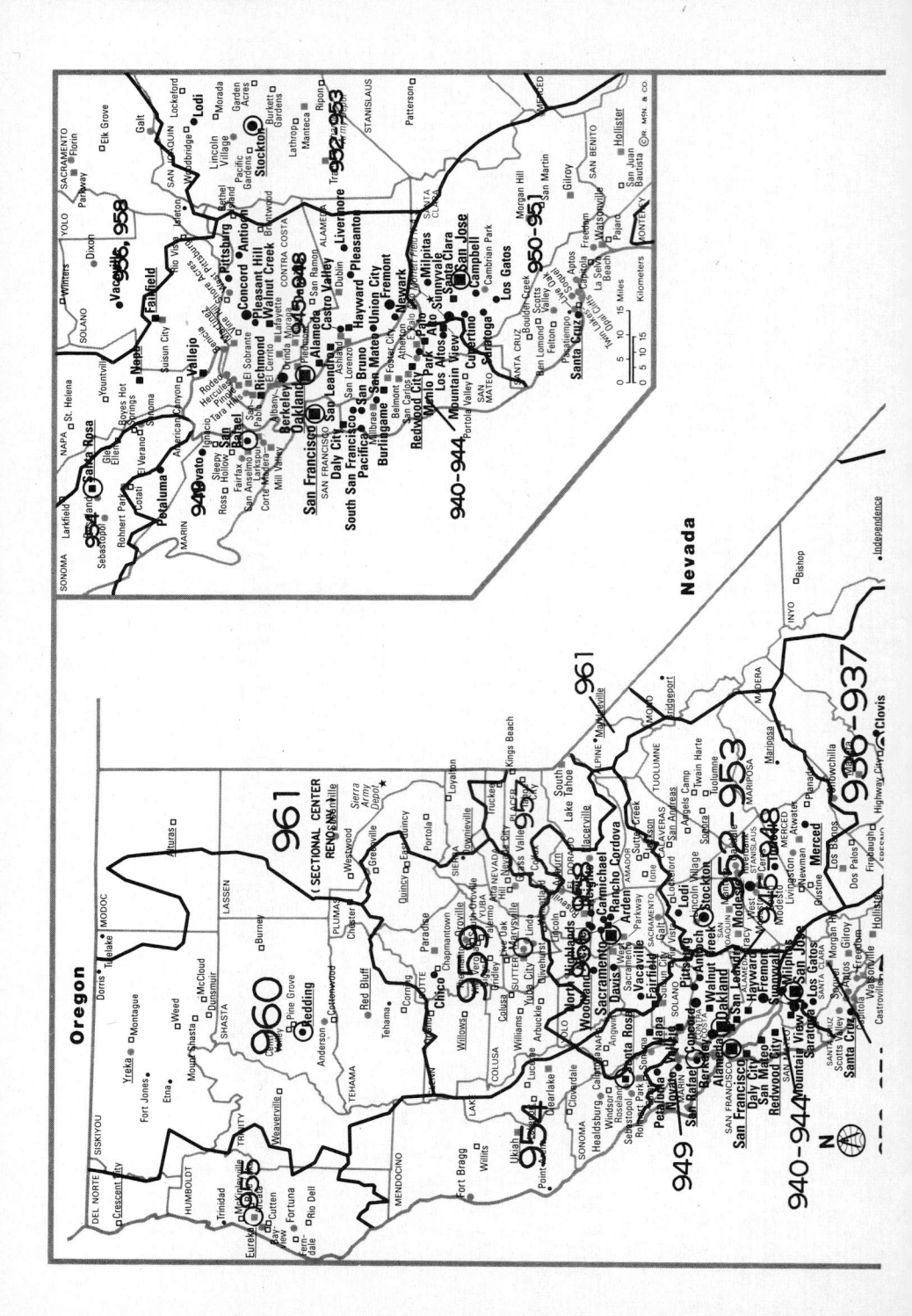

CALIFORNIA

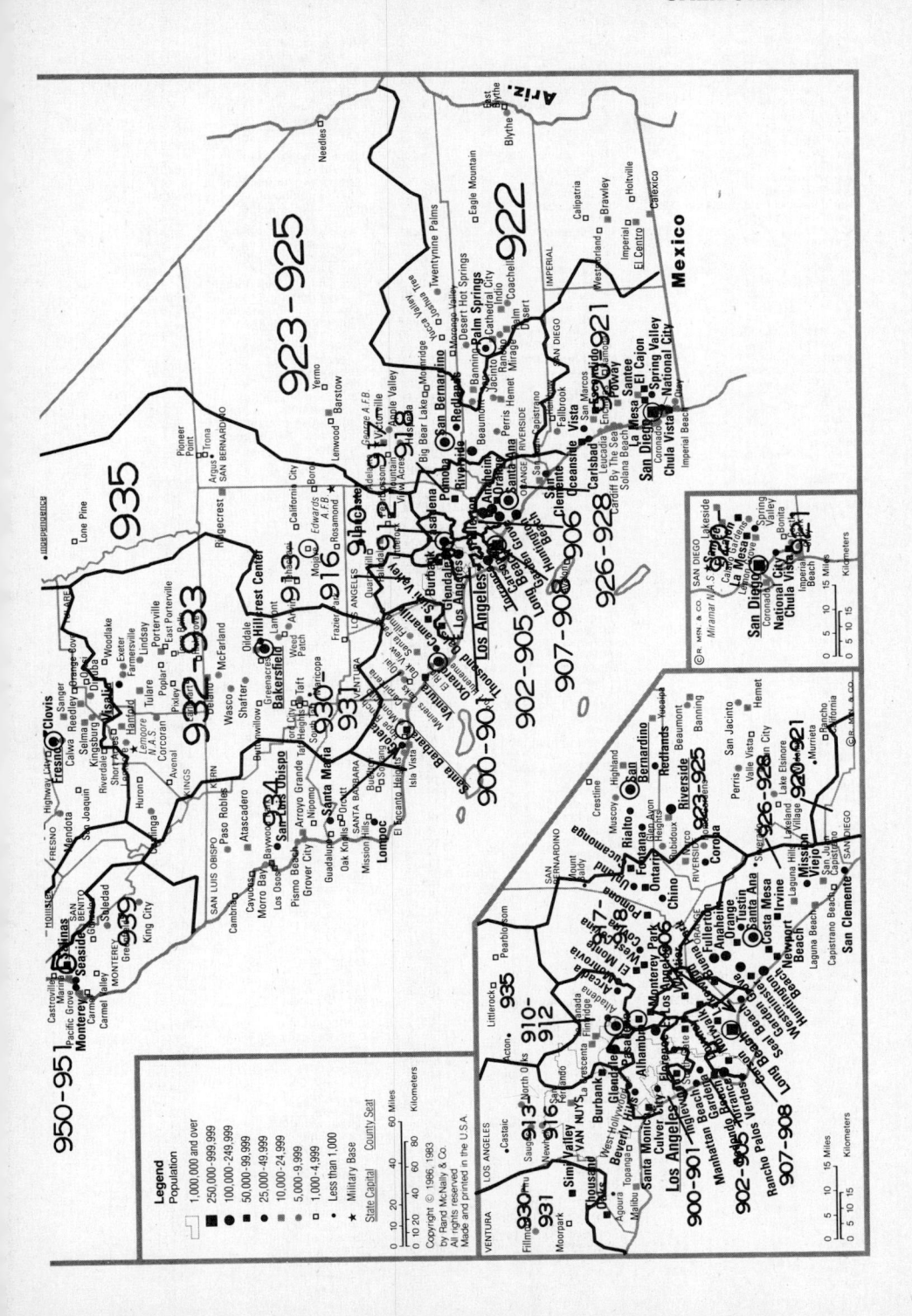

CALIFORNIA 61

62 CALIFORNIA   Bay View Park-Calaveras

Name	ZIP
Bay View Park (Monterey County)	93955
Baywood-Los Osos	93402
Baywood Park	93402
Beach Center (Part of Huntington Beach)	92648
Beale AFB East	95903
Beale Air Force Base	95903
Beale West	95903
Bear Creek	95340
Bear River	95603
Bear River Lake	95666
Bear River Pines	95945
Bear Valley (Alpine County)	95223
Bear Valley (Mariposa County)	95338
Beaumont	92223
Beckwourth	96129
Bee Rock	93426
Bel Aire Estates (Part of Tiburon)	94920
Belden	95915
Bell	90201
Bella Vista (Contra Costa County)	94565
Bella Vista (Kern County)	93240
Bella Vista (Los Angeles County)	90022
Bella Vista (Shasta County)	96008
Belle Haven (Part of Menlo Park)	94025
Belleview	95370
Bellflower	90706-07
For specific Bellflower Zip Codes call (213) 560-2931	
Bell Gardens	90201
Bell Mountain	92392
Belltown	92509
Bellview (Part of Rio Dell)	95562
Bel Marin Keys	94947
Belmont	94002
Belridge Farms	93251
Belvedere (Los Angeles County)	90022
Belvedere (Marin County)	94920
Belvedere Gardens	90022
Belvedere-Tiburon (Part of Belvedere)	94920
Belvernon Gardens (Part of Tiburon)	94920
Benbow	95440
Bend	96080
Ben Hur	93653
Benicia	94510
Ben Lomond	95005
Benton	93512
Berenda	93637
Berkeley	94701-10
For specific Berkeley Zip Codes call (415) 649-3100	
Berkeley Highlands	94707
Bernal (Part of San Francisco)	94110
Berry Creek	95916
Berryessa (Part of San Jose)	95132
Berryessa Park	94558
Berry Hill Estates (Part of Rancho Palos Verdes)	90274
Berteleda	95531
Bertsch Terrace	95531
Bethany Park (Part of Scotts Valley)	95066
Bethel Island	94511
Betteravia	93454
Beverly Center (Part of Los Angeles)	90048
Beverly Hills	90209-13
For specific Beverly Hills Zip Codes call (213) 276-3161	
Bicentennial (Part of Los Angeles)	90048
Bieber	96009
Big Bar	96010
Big Basin	95006
Big Bear	92315
Big Bear City	92314
Big Bear Highlands	92386
Big Bear Lake	92315
Big Bend	96011
Big Chief	95734
Big Creek	93605
Big Flat	96091
Biggs	95917
Big Lagoon Park	95570
Big Meadows	95223
Big Oak Flat	95305
Big Pine	93513
Big Pine Indian Reservation	93513
Big River	92242
Big Springs	96064

Name	ZIP
Big Sur	93920
Big Trees	95018
Bijou (Part of South Lake Tahoe)	95702
Bijou Park (Part of South Lake Tahoe)	95702
Binghamton	95620
Biola	93606
Birch Hill	92060
Birch Meadow Acres	95945
Birdcage Walk	95610
Bird Rock (Part of San Diego)	92037
Birds Landing	94512
Bishop	93514-15
For specific Bishop Zip Codes call (619) 873-3526	
Bishop Acres	93263
Bishop Indian Reservation	93514
Bitterwater	93930
Bixby (Part of Long Beach)	90807
Black Meadow Landing	92267
Black Point	94947
Blackrock	93526
Blackstone (Part of Fresno)	93710
Blackwells Corner	93249
Blairsden	96103
Blanco	93901
Blocksburg	95414
Bloomfield	94952
Bloomfield Acres (Part of Arcata)	95521
Bloomington	92316
Blossom Hill (Part of San Jose)	95123
Blossom Valley (Part of Mountain View)	94040
Blue Canon	95715
Blue Hills (Part of Saratoga)	95070
Blue Jay	92317
Blue Lake	95525
Bluff Creek	95546
Blythe	92225-26
For specific Blythe Zip Codes call (619) 922-6157	
Bodega	94922
Bodega Bay	94923
Bodfish	93205
Bohemia	95945
Bolinas	94924
Bolsa (Part of Westminster)	92683
Bolsa Knolls	93901
Bombay Beach	92257
Bonadelle Ranchos	93637
Bonadelle Ranchos-Madera Ranchos	93637
Bonds Corner	92250
Bonita (Madera County)	93637
Bonita (San Diego County)	92002
Bonnie Bell	92282
Bonny Doon	95060
Bonnyview (Part of Redding)	96001
Bonsall	92003
Boonville	95415
Bootjack	95338
Boron	93516
Borosolvay	93562
Borrego Springs	92004
Borrego Wells	92004
Bostonia (Part of El Cajon)	92021
Boston Ravine (Part of Grass Valley)	95945
Boulder Creek	95006
Boulder Oaks	92062
Boulder Park	92034
Boulevard	92005
Bouquet Canyon (Part of Santa Clarita)	91350
Bowling Green	95815
Bowman	95604
Box Springs	92507
Boyes Hot Springs	95416
Boyle (Part of Los Angeles)	90033
Boys Republic	91710
Brackney	95005
Bradbury	91010
Bradford (Part of Hayward)	94541
Bradley	93426
Brandeis	93064
Branscomb	95417
Brawley	92227
Bray	96058
Brea	92621-22
For specific Brea Zip Codes call (714) 529-3000	
Brea Mall (Part of Brea)	92621
Brentwood	94513
Briceburg	95345
Briceland	95440
Bridgehead	94509

Name	ZIP
Bridgeport (Mariposa County)	95338
Bridgeport (Mono County)	93517
Bridgeville	95526
Brisbane	94005
Bristol (Part of Santa Ana)	92703
Broadmoor	94015
Broadway (Sacramento County)	95818
Broadway (San Mateo County)	94010
Broadway Manchester (Part of Los Angeles)	90003
Broadway Plaza (Part of Walnut Creek)	94596
Brockway	95719
Broderick (Part of West Sacramento)	95605
Brookdale	95007
Brookhurst Center (Part of Anaheim)	92804
Brooks	95606
Brookside Park (Part of Portola Valley)	94028
Browns Corner (Part of Woodland)	95695
Browns Valley	95918
Brownsville	95919
Brundage (Part of Bakersfield)	93307
Bryant (Part of Long Beach)	90805
Bryn Mawr (Part of Loma Linda)	92318
Bryson	93426
Bryte (Part of West Sacramento)	95605
Buckeye (Part of Redding)	96001
Buckhorn Lodge	95666
Buckingham Park	95451
Buck Meadows	95321
Bucks Bar	95667
Bucks Lake	95971
Bucks Lake Lodge	95971
Bucktail	96052
Buellton	93427
Buena (Part of Vista)	92083
Buena Park	90620-24
For specific Buena Park Zip Codes call (714) 523-1960	
Buena Park Mall (Part of Buena Park)	90620
Buenaventura Plaza (Part of Ventura)	93003
Buena Vista (Amador County)	95640
Buena Vista (Sonoma County)	95476
Buffalo Hill	95634
Buhach	95340
Bummerville	95255
Burbank	91501-10
For specific Burbank Zip Codes call (818) 846-3155	
Burbank	95128
Burkett Acres (Part of Stockton)	95205
Burkett Gardens	95205
Burlingame	94010-11
For specific Burlingame Zip Codes call (415) 342-7694	
Burlingame Hills	94010
Burney	96013
Burnt Ranch	95527
Burrel	93607
Burrough	93667
Burson	95225
Butano Canyon	94060
Butte City	95920
Butte Creek	95926
Butte Meadows	95942
Buttonwillow	93206
Byron	94514
Cabazon	92230
Cabin Cove	93271
Cabrillo (Part of Long Beach)	90810
Cabrillo Estates	93402
Cache Creek	93501
Cachuma Village	93101
Cadiz	92319
Cahuilla	92306
Cahuilla Estates	92306
Cahuilla Hills	92260
Cahuilla Indian Reservation	92343
Cairns Corner	93247
Cajon Junction	92403
Calabasas	91302
Calabasas Highlands	91302
Calabasas Park	91302
Calaveras (Part of Stockton)	95207

Calaveras Yacht and Country Club Estates-Civic Center CALIFORNIA 63

Place	ZIP
Calaveras Yacht and Country Club Estates	95204
Calaveritas	95249
Calavo Gardens	92041
Calexico	92231-32
For specific Calexico Zip Codes call (619) 357-2982	
Calexico Lodge	92005
Calico	92398
Cal-Ida	95922
Caliente	93518
California City	93504-05
For specific California City Zip Codes call (619) 373-2162	
California Correctional Institution (Kern County)	93561
California Correctional Center (Lassen County)	96130
California Hot Springs	93207
California Medical Facility	95688
California Polytechnic State University-San Luis Obispo	93407
California Rehabilitation Center (Part of Norco)	91720
California State Prison-Amador	95640
California Valley	93453
Calimesa	92320
Calipatria	92233
Calistoga	94515
Calla	95336
Callahan	96014
Calpella	95418
Calpine	96124
Calville	95521
Calwa	93725
Camanche Lake	95640
Camarillo	93010-11
For specific Camarillo Zip Codes call (805) 482-8894	
Camarillo Heights (Ventura County)	93010
Cambria	93428
Cambrian Park	95124
Camden	93242
Camellia (Part of Sacramento)	95819
Cameo Acres (Part of Danville)	94526
Cameron Corners	92006
Cameron Creek Colony	93277
Cameron Park	95682
Camino	95709
Camino Heights	95709
Campbell	95008-09
For specific Campbell Zip Codes call (408) 378-2153	
Campbell Hot Springs	96126
Camp Conifer	93271
Camp Connell	95223
Camp Evers (Part of Scotts Valley)	95066
Camp Meeker	95419
Camp Nelson	93208
Campo	92006
Campo Indian Reservation	92006
Campo Seco	95226
Camp Pendleton	92055
Camp Pendleton Marine Corps Base	92055
Camp Pendleton North	92055
Camp Pendleton South	92055
Camp Richardson	95702
Camp Sierra	93664
Camp St. Michael	95455
Camp Ten	95634
Campton Heights (Part of Fortuna)	95540
Camptonville	95922
Camp Wishon	93265
Camulos	93040
Canby	96015
Canebrake	93255
Canoga Annex (Part of Los Angeles)	91304
Canoga Park	91303-09
For specific Canoga Park Zip Codes call (818) 340-7525	
Cantil	93519
Cantua Creek	93608
Canyon	94516
Canyon Country (Part of Santa Clarita)	91351
Canyondam	95923
Canyon Lake	92380
Capay (Glenn County)	95963
Capay (Yolo County)	95607
Capetown	95536
Capistrano Beach	92624
Capistrano Highlands	92653

Place	ZIP
Capital Hill (Part of Paso Robles)	93446
Capitola	95010
Capitol Square (Part of San Jose)	95133
Carbona	95376
Carbon Beach	90265
Carbon Canyon	91710
Cardiff By The Sea (Part of Encinitas)	92007
Cardwell (Part of Fresno)	93704
Caribou	95965
Carlotta	95528
Carlsbad	92008-09
For specific Carlsbad Zip Codes call (619) 729-2456	
Carlton Hills (Part of Santee)	92071
Carmel	93921-23
For specific Carmel Zip Codes call (408) 625-4411	
Carmel-By-The-Sea (Part of Carmel)	93921
Carmel Highlands	93923
Carmel Hills	93923
Carmel Point	93923
Carmel Valley	93924
Carmel Woods	93923
Carmenita (Part of Santa Fe Springs)	90670
Carmet	94923
Carmichael	95608-09
For specific Carmichael Zip Codes call (916) 483-8568	
Carnelian Bay	95711
Carpinteria	93013
Carquinez Heights (Part of Vallejo)	94590
Carriage Hills	92077
Carrick Addition	96094
Carson	90749
Carson Hill	95222
Carson Mall (Part of Carson)	90745
Cartago	93549
Caruthers	93609
Carvin Creek Homesites	96126
Casa Correo (Part of Concord)	94521
Casa de Oro	92077
Casa de Oro-Mount Helix	92077
Cascadel Woods	93643
Casitas Springs	93001
Casmalia	93429
Caspar	95420
Cassel	96016
Castaic	91310
Castella	96017
Castellammare (Part of Los Angeles)	90272
Castle Air Force Base	95342
Castle Garden	95342
Castle Park	92011
Castle Park-Otay	92011
Castlewood	94566
Castro Valley	94546
Castroville	95012
Catalina (Part of Pasadena)	91106
Cathedral City	92234-35
For specific Cathedral City Zip Codes call (619) 328-2270	
Catheys Valley	95306
Cawelo	93308
Cayucos	93430
Cazadero	95421
Cecilville	96027
Cedar (Part of Lancaster)	93534
Cedarbrook	93641
Cedar Crest	93605
Cedar Flat	95711
Cedar Glen	92321
Cedar Grove (El Dorado County)	95709
Cedar Grove (Fresno County)	93633
Cedarpines Park	92322
Cedar Ridge (Nevada County)	95924
Cedar Ridge (Tuolumne County)	95370
Cedar Slope	93265
Cedar Stock	96052
Cedarville	96104
Cedarville Indian Reservation	96104
Centerpoint Mall (Part of Oxnard)	93033
Centerville (Alameda County)	94536
Centerville (Fresno County)	93657
Central City Mall (Part of San Bernardino)	92401

Place	ZIP
Central District (Part of Pomona)	91769
Central Valley	96019
Centre	95860
Century City (Part of Los Angeles)	90067
Century City Shopping Center (Part of Los Angeles)	90067
Ceres	95307
Cerritos	90703
Cerro Villa Heights (Part of Villa Park)	92667
Chalfant	93514
Challenge	95925
Chambless	92319
Champagne Fountain (Part of Saratoga)	95070
Channel Islands (Part of Oxnard)	93030
Chapmantown	95926
Chapman Woods	91107
Chappo	92055
Charleston	93635
Charter Oak	91724
Chatsworth	91311-13
For specific Chatsworth Zip Codes call (818) 341-9551	
Chatsworth Lake Manor	91311
Chawanakee	93602
Cheeseville	96037
Chemeketa Park	95030
Chemeketa Park-Redwood Estates	95030
Cherokee (Butte County)	95965
Cherokee (Nevada County)	95959
Cherokee Strip	93263
Cherry Creek Acres	95949
Cherryland	94541
Cherry Valley	92223
Chester	96020
Chestnut (Part of South San Francisco)	94080
Chicago Park	95712
Chico	95926-28
For specific Chico Zip Codes call (916) 343-5531	
Chico North	95926
Chico West	95926
Chilcoot	96105
Childs Meadows	96061
Chili Bar	95667
China (Part of San Francisco)	94108
China Camp	94901
China Lake	93555
China Lake Naval Weapons Center	93555
Chinatown (Part of San Francisco)	94108
Chinese Camp	95309
Chino	91708-10
For specific Chino Zip Codes call (714) 627-3631	
Chinowths Corner (Part of Visalia)	93277
Chiriaco Summit	92201
Cholame	93431
Chowchilla	93610
Christofferson	93610
Chrome	95963
Chualar	93925
Chula Vista	92010-13
For specific Chula Vista Zip Codes call (619) 422-9221	
Chula Vista Shopping Center (Part of Chula Vista)	92010
Church of God Colony	93648
Cima	92323
Cisco	95728
Citrus	91702
Citrus Heights	95610-11
For specific Citrus Heights Zip Codes call (916) 725-2060	
City Hall (Part of San Francisco)	94102
City Heights (Part of San Diego)	92105
City of Industry	91744
City Shopping Center, The (Part of Orange)	92668
City Terrace	90063
Civic Center (Fresno County)	93721
Civic Center (Los Angeles County)	91401
Civic Center (Marin County)	94903
Civic Center (Orange County)	90633

64 CALIFORNIA Civic Center-Desert Shores

Name	ZIP
Civic Center (Orange County)	92701
Civic Center Annex (Part of Oakland)	94612
Clairemont (Part of San Diego)	92117
Clam Beach	95521
Claremont	91711
Clarksburg	95612
Clarksville	95682
Clay	95638
Clayton	94517
Clear Creek (Lassen County)	96137
Clear Creek (Siskiyou County)	96039
Clearlake	95422
Clearlake Highlands-Clearlake Park	95422
Clearlake Oaks	95423
Clearlake Park (Part of Clearlake)	95424
Clearlake Riviera	95451
Clements	95227
Cleone	95437
Cliff Haven (Part of Newport Beach)	92660
Clifton	90277
Clingans Junction	93646
Clinter (Part of Fresno)	93703
Clinton	95642
Clio	96106
Clipper Gap	95603
Clipper Mills	95930
Cloverdale (Shasta County)	96007
Cloverdale (Sonoma County)	95425
Clovis	93612-13
For specific Clovis Zip Codes call (209) 299-3118	
Clyde	94520
Coachella	92236
Coalinga	93210
Coarsegold	93614
Cobb	95426
Cockatoo Grove (Part of Chula Vista)	92010
Coddington Center (Part of Santa Rosa)	95406
Coddingtown (Part of Santa Rosa)	95406
Codora	95970
Coffee Creek	96091
Cohasset	95926
Coit	93640
Cold Fork	96080
Cole (Part of West Hollywood)	90046
Coleville	96107
Colfax	95713
College City	95931
College Grove Center (San Diego County)	92115
College Heights (Kern County)	93305
College Heights (San Bernardino County)	91786
College Heights (Santa Cruz County)	95003
College Park (Part of Thousand Oaks)	91360
College Plaza (Part of Oceanside)	92056
Collegeville	95206
Collier (Part of Los Angeles)	91307
Collierville	95220
Collinsville	94585
Colma (San Mateo County)	94014
Coloma	95613
Colonial (Part of Sacramento)	95820
Colonial Juarez (Part of Fountain Valley)	92708
Colony	92363
Colorado River Indian Reservation	85344
Colton	92324
Columbia	95310
Columbus (Part of Bakersfield)	93306
Colusa	95932
Commerce	90040
Commonwealth (Part of Fullerton)	92632
Community Center (Part of Simi Valley)	93065
Comptche	95427
Compton	90220-24
For specific Compton Zip Codes call (213) 494-2371	
Concepcion	93436

Name	ZIP
Concord	94518-24
For specific Concord Zip Codes call (415) 687-1500	
Concord Naval Weapons Station	94520
Conejo	93662
Conejo Valley (Part of Thousand Oaks)	91360
Confidence	95370
Consumne	95683
Convict Lake	93514
Cool	95614
Coopers Corner	95220
Copco	96044
Copperopolis	95228
Corbin Village (Part of Los Angeles)	91364
Corcoran	93212
Cordelia	94585
Corning	96021
Corona	91718-20
For specific Corona Zip Codes call (714) 737-0451	
Corona Del Mar (Part of Newport Beach)	92625
Coronado	92118
Coronado Naval Amphibious Base	92155
Corona Mall (Part of Corona)	91720
Coronita	91720
Corral Beach	90265
Corralitos	95076
Correctional Training Facility	93960
Corte Madera (Marin County)	94925
Coso Junction	93542
Costa Mesa	92626-28
For specific Costa Mesa Zip Codes call (714) 546-5330	
Cotati	94931
Cotners Corners	92307
Cottage Springs	95223
Cotton Center	93257
Cottonwood	96022
Coulterville	95311
Country Club	95204
Country Club Centre	95825
Country Club Estates	93401
Country Club Plaza	95825
Country Modern	93501
County East Mall (Part of Antioch)	94509
Court (Part of Martinez)	94553
Courtland	95615
Covelo	95428
Covina	91722-24
For specific Covina Zip Codes call (818) 966-8391	
Covington Mill	96052
Cowan Heights	92705
Cowell (Part of Concord)	94520
Coy Flat	93208
Coyote (Part of San Jose)	95013
Craf	92359
Crafton	92359
Crenshaw (Part of Los Angeles)	90008
Crenshaw-Imperial (Part of Inglewood)	90303
Crescent City	95531
Crescent Mills	95934
Crescent North	95531
Cressey	95312
Crest	92021
Crestline	92325
Crestmore	92316
Crestmore Heights	92509
Creston	93432
Crest Park	92326
Crestview Village	95608
Crockett	94525
Cromberg	96103
Crossroads (Part of Santa Rosa)	95401
Crossroads Plaza (Part of Pico Rivera)	90661
Crowley (Part of Visalia)	93277
Crowley Lake	93546
Crown Point (Part of San Diego)	92109
Crows Landing	95313
Crutcher (Part of Paramount)	90723
Crystal Court (Part of Costa Mesa)	92626
Crystal Cove	92651
Cucamonga	91730
Cudahy	90201
Cuesta-by-the-Sea	93402

Name	ZIP
Culver City	90230-33
For specific Culver City Zip Codes call (213) 391-6374	
Cummings	95454
Cunningham	95472
Cupertino	95014-16
For specific Cupertino Zip Codes call (408) 252-6798	
Curry Village	95389
Curtiss Heights (Part of Arcata)	95521
Cutler	93615
Cutten	95534
Cuyama	93214
Cypress	90630
Cypress South (Part of Cypress)	90630
Daggett	92327
Dairyville	96080
Dales	96080
Daly City	94014-17
For specific Daly City Zip Codes call (415) 756-2303	
Dana	96028
Dana Point	92629
Danby	92332
Danville	94526
Daphnedale Park	96101
Dardanelle	95314
Darrah	95338
Darwin	93522
Daulton	93637
Davenport	95017
Davis	95616-17
For specific Davis Zip Codes call (916) 753-3496	
Davis Creek	96108
Day	96056
Dayton	95926
Daywalt	95472
Deane Brothers	91350
Dearborn Park	94060
Death Valley	92328
Death Valley Junction	92328
Decoto (Part of Union City)	94587
Deep Springs	89010
Deer Creek	96061
Deer Lick Springs	96076
Deer Park (Napa County)	94576
Deer Park (Santa Cruz County)	95003
Del Aire (Los Angeles County)	90250
Del Amo (Part of Torrance)	90503
Del Amo Fashion Center (Part of Torrance)	90503
Delano	93215-16
For specific Delano Zip Codes call (805) 725-8742	
Del Dios	92025
Delevan	95988
Delft Colony	93618
Delhi	95315
Delkern	93307
Delleker	96122
Del Loma	96010
Del Mar (San Diego County)	92014
Del Mar (Santa Cruz County)	95060
Del Mesa	94904
Del Monte Forest	93953
Del Monte Heights (Part of Seaside)	93955
Del Monte Park	93950
Del Monte Shopping Center (Part of Monterey)	93940
Del Paso Heights (Part of Sacramento)	95838
Del Rey	93616
Del Rey Oaks	93940
Del Rio Woods	95448
Del Rosa (Part of San Bernardino)	92404
Del Sur	93534
Delta (Part of Stockton)	95202
De Luz	92028
Del Valle (Part of Los Angeles)	90015
Delways	95695
Democrat Hot Springs	93301
Denair	95316
Denny	95527
Denverton	94585
Derby Acres	93224
Descanso	92016
Desert	92309
Desert Beach	92254
Desert Center	92239
Desert Hot Springs	92240
Desert Lake	93516
Desert Shores	92274

Desert View Highlands-Fairview **CALIFORNIA** 65

	ZIP		ZIP		ZIP
Desert View Highlands	93550	East Compton (Los Angeles County)	90221		95758-59
Des Moines (Part of La Habra)	90631	East Firebaugh	93622	For specific Elk Grove Zip Codes call (916) 685-5700	
Deuel Vocational Institution	95376	East Fresno (Part of Fresno)	93727	Elkhorn	95012
Devils Den	93204	Eastgate (Part of Beverly Hills)	90211	Elkhorn Village (Part of West Sacramento)	95605
Devore	92407	East Gridley	95948	Elk River	95501
Devore Heights	92407	East Guernewood	95446	Elk River Corners	95501
Diablo	94528	East Hemet	92343	Ellwood	93118
Diamond (Part of Santa Ana)	92704	East Highlands	92346	El Macero (Part of Davis)	95618
Diamond Bar	91765	East Irvine	92650	Elmhurst (Part of Oakland)	94603
Diamond Heights (Part of San Francisco)	94131	East La Mirada	90638	Elmira	95625
Diamond Springs	95619	Eastland Shopping Center (Part of West Covina)	91790	El Mirador	93247
Diamond Springs Heights	95619	East Linda	95901	El Mirage	92301
Di Giorgio	93217	East Long Beach (Part of Long Beach)	90804	El Modena (Part of Orange)	92667
Dillon Beach	94929	East Los Angeles	90022	El Monte	91731-34
Dimond (Part of Oakland)	94602	East Lynwood (Part of Lynwood)	90262	For specific El Monte Zip Codes call (818) 443-8995	
Dinkey Creek	93664	Eastmont (Part of Oakland)	94605	El Monte (Part of Concord)	94521
Dinsmore	95526	Eastmont Mall (Part of Oakland)	94605	El Monte Center (Part of El Monte)	91732
Dinuba	93618	East Nicolaus	95622	El Monte Park	92040
Discovery Bay	94513	Easton	93706	Elm View	93609
Dixon	95620	East Orosi	93647	Elmwood (Part of Berkeley)	94705
Dobbins	95935	East Palo Alto (San Mateo County)	94303	El Nido	95317
Dockweiler (Part of Los Angeles)	90007	East Palo Alto (Santa Clara County)	94303	El'Portal (Contra Costa County)	94806
Doheny Park	92624	East Pasadena (Part of Pasadena)	91107	El Portal (Mariposa County)	95318
Dollar Ranch (Part of Walnut Creek)	94595	East Porterville	93257	El Porto Beach (Part of Manhattan Beach)	90266
Dolomite	93545	East Quincy	95971	El Pueblo	94565
Dominguez (Part of Carson)	90810	East Richmond	94805	El Rio	93030
Dominguez Hills (Part of Carson)	90801	Eastridge Shopping Center (Part of San Jose)	95122	El Rio Villa	95694
Donlon (Part of Oxnard)	93030	East San Diego (Part of San Diego)	92105	El Segundo	90245
Donner	95737	East Santa Cruz (Part of Santa Cruz)	95060	El Segundo Station (Part of El Segundo)	90245
Donner Lake	95734	Eastside Acres	93622	El Sereno (Part of Los Angeles)	90026
Don Pedro Camp	95329	Eastside Ranch	93622	El Sobrante	94803
Dorrington	95223	East Stockton (Part of Stockton)	95205	El Sueno	93110
Dorris	96023	East Tustin	92705	El Toro	92630
Dos Palos	93620	East Vallejo (Part of Vallejo)	94590	El Toro Marine Corps Air Station	92709
Dos Rios	95429	East Ventura (Part of Ventura)	93003	El Toro Station	92709
Douglas City	96024	Eastview	90734	El Verano	95433
Douglas Flat	95229	Echo Lake	95721	Elverta	95626
Downey	90240-42	Echo Park (Part of Los Angeles)	90026	El Viejo (Part of Modesto)	95354
For specific Downey Zip Codes call (213) 923-5345		Edendale (Part of Los Angeles)	90026	Emandal	95490
Downieville	95936	Edgemar (Part of Pacifica)	94044	Emerald Bay	92651
Downtown (Kern County)	93303	Edgemont (Lassen County)	96114	Emerald Lake	94062
Downtown (Los Angeles County)	90266	Edgemont (Riverside County)	92508	Emeryville	94608
Downtown (Los Angeles County)	91502	Edgemont Acres	93523	Emigrant Gap	95715
Downtown (Riverside County)	92501	Edgewater Estates	92077	Empire	95319
Downtown (San Bernardino County)	92401	Edgewood	96094	Encanto (Part of San Diego)	92114
Downtown (San Bernardino County)	91761	Edison	93220	Encinal (Part of Sunnyvale)	94087
Downtown (San Diego County)	92101	Edmundson Acres	93203	Encinitas	92023-24
Downtown (Tuolumne County)	95370	Edwards (Wherry Housing)	93523-24	For specific Encinitas Zip Codes call (619) 753-6446	
Downtown Plaza (Part of Sacramento)	95814	For specific Edwards Zip Codes call (805) 258-5811		Encino (Part of Los Angeles)	91316
Doyle (Lassen County)	96109	Edwards AFB	93523	Enterprise (Part of Redding)	96001
Doyle (Tulare County)	93258	Edwards Air Force Base	93523	Escalle (Part of Larkspur)	94939
Drakesbad	96020	Edwards Estates	93523	Escalon	95320
Dryden Flight Research Center	93523	Edwards Palisades	95554	Escondido	92025-27
Drytown	95699	Eel Rock	95709	For specific Escondido Zip Codes call (619) 745-1912	
Duarte	91010	Eight Mile House	95446	Escondido Junction (Part of Oceanside)	92054
Dublin	94568	El Bonita	92019-22	Escondido Village Mall (Part of Escondido)	92025
Ducor	93218	El Cajon		Esparto	95627
Dulzura	92017	For specific El Cajon Zip Codes call (619) 442-0727		Esplanade, The	93030
Duncans Mills	95430	El Camino	96035	Essex	92332
Dunlap	93621	El Camino North Shopping Center (Part of Oceanside)	92054	Estrella	93451
Dunlap Acres	92399	El Casco Lake	92373	Estudillo (Part of San Leandro)	94577
Dunmovin	93542	El Centro	92243-44	Etiwanda (Part of Cucamonga)	91739
Dunneville Corners	95023	For specific El Centro Zip Codes call (619) 352-2494		Etna	96027
Dunnigan	95937	El Cerrito (Contra Costa County)	94530	Ettersburg	95440
Dunsmuir	96025	El Cerrito (Riverside County)	91720	Eucalyptus Hills	92040
Durham	95938	El Cerrito Plaza (Part of El Cerrito)	94530	Eugene	95230
Dustin Acres	93268	Elders Corner	95603	Eureka	95501-02
Dutch Flat	95714	Elderwood	93286	For specific Eureka Zip Codes call (707) 442-1768	
Eagle Lake Resort	96130	El Dorado	95623	Exeter	93221
Eagle Mountain	92239	El Dorado Hills	95630	Fairfax (Kern County)	93307
Eagle Rock (Part of Los Angeles)	90041	Eldridge	95431	Fairfax (Marin County)	94930
Eagle Rock Plaza (Part of Los Angeles)	90041	El Encanto Heights	93117	Fairfield	94533
Eagle Tree	95690	El Granada	94018	Fairhaven	95564
Eagleville	96110	Elizabeth Lake	93550	Fairmead	93610
Earlimart	93219	Elk	95432	Fairmont	93534
Earp	92242	Elk Creek	95939	Fairmont Terrace	94577
East Anaheim Shopping Center (Part of Anaheim)	92806	Elk Grove	95624	Fairmount (Part of El Cerrito)	94530
East Applegate	95703			Fair Oaks (Sacramento County)	95628
East Bakersfield (Part of Bakersfield)	93305			Fair Oaks (San Luis Obispo County)	93420
East Baldy Mesa	92369			Fairview (Alameda County)	94542
East Blythe	92225				

66 CALIFORNIA Fairview-Graham

Name	ZIP
Fairview (Fresno County)	93657
Fairview (Trinity County)	96052
Fairview (Tulare County)	93238
Falk	95501
Fallbrook	92028
Fallbrook Junction	92055
Fallbrook Mall (Part of Los Angeles)	91307
Fallen Leaf	95716
Falling Springs	91702
Fallon	94952
Fall River Mills	96028
Fallsvale	92339
Famoso	93250
Fancher	93702
Farmers Market (Part of Los Angeles)	90036
Farmersville	93223
Farmington	95230
Fashion Island (Part of Newport Beach)	92660
Fashion Valley Center (Part of San Diego)	92108
Fawnskin	92333
Fay Creek	93283
Feather Falls	95940
Feather River	96020
Feather River Inn	96103
Feather River Park	96103
Federal (Los Angeles County)	90012
Federal (Los Angeles County)	91723
Federal (Orange County)	92805
Federal Building (San Francisco County)	94102
Federal Building (Ventura County)	93030
Federal Correctional Institution	94566
Federal Prison Camp	93516
Federal Terrace (Part of Vallejo)	94590
Fellows	93224
Felton (Santa Cruz County)	95041
Felton (Santa Cruz County)	95018
Felton Grove	95018
Fernbridge	95540
Fernbrook	92065
Ferndale	95536
Fern Valley	92349
Fernwood	90290
Fetters Hot Springs	95476
Fetters Hot Springs-Agua Caliente	95476
Fickle Hill	95521
Fiddletown	95629
Fieldbrook	95521
Fields Landing	95537
Fig Garden	93704
Fig Garden Village	93704
Figueroa (Part of Los Angeles)	91001
Fillmore	93015
Finley	95435
Firebaugh	93622
Fire Mountain	96061
Firestone (Part of South Gate)	90280
Firestone Park	90001
First Street (Part of Oceanside)	92054
Fish Camp	93623
Fish Springs	93513
Fisk (Part of San Francisco)	94122
Fitchburg (Part of Oakland)	94621
Five Brooks	94950
Five Mile Terrace	95667
Five Points (Fresno County)	93624
Five Points (San Diego County)	92110
Flinn Springs	92021
Flintridge (Part of La Canada Flintridge)	91011
Florence	90001
Florence-Graham	90001
Florin	95828
Florin Mall (Part of Sacramento)	95823
Floriston	96111
Flosden Acres (Part of Vallejo)	94590
Flournoy	96029
Flower Village	93305
Fly in Acres	95223
Folsom	95630
Folsom Junction (Part of Folsom)	95630
Fontana	92334-36
For specific Fontana Zip Codes call (714) 822-8039	

Name	ZIP
Foothill Farms	95841
Forbestown	95941
Ford City	93268
Forest	95910
Foresta	95389
Forest Falls	92339
Forest Glen	96041
Foresthill	95631
Forest Home (Amador County)	95669
Forest Home (San Bernardino County)	92339
Forest Knolls	94933
Forest Park	95006
Forest Ranch	95942
Forest Springs (Nevada County)	95949
Forest Springs (Santa Cruz County)	95006
Forestville	95436
Forks of Salmon	96031
Forrest Park	91350
Fort Baker	94965
Fort Barry	94965
Fort Bidwell	96112
Fort Bidwell Indian Reservation	96112
Fort Bragg	95437
Fort Cronkhite	94965
Fort Dick	95538
Fort Goff	96086
Fort Hunter Liggett	93928
Fort Independence Indian Reservation	93526
Fort Irwin	92310
Fort Jones	96032
Fort Mason (Part of San Francisco)	94123
Fort McArthur (Part of Los Angeles)	90731
Fort Miley (Part of San Francisco)	94121
Fort Mohave Indian Reservation	92363
Fort Ord	93941
Fort Ord Village (Part of Seaside)	93941
Fort Seward	95411
Fort Sutter (Part of Sacramento)	95816
Fortuna	95540
Fort Yuma	85364
Fort Yuma Indian Reservation	92283
Foster City	94404
Fountainhead Springs	93257
Fountain Valley	92708
Four Corners (Madera County)	93637
Four Corners (San Bernardino County)	92277
Four Corners (San Bernardino County)	93516
Fouts Springs	95979
Fowler	93625
Fox Creek	95528
Fox Hills (Part of Culver City)	90233
Fox Hills Mall (Part of Culver City)	90230
Foy (Part of Los Angeles)	90017
Franciscan Park (Part of Daly City)	94014
Franklin	95758
Frazier Park	93225
Fredericksburg	96120
Freedom	95019
Freestone	95472
Fremont	94536-39
For specific Fremont Zip Codes call (415) 792-8654	
Fremont Fashion Center (Part of Fremont)	94538
Fremont Hub Shopping Center (Part of Fremont)	94538
French Camp	95231
French Corral	95960
French Gulch	96033
Fresh Pond	95726
Freshwater	95501
Freshwater Corners	95501
Fresno	93701-94
For specific Fresno Zip Codes call (209) 478-7700	
Fresno Fashion Fair (Part of Fresno)	93710
Friant	93626
Friendly Hills	92252
Fruitland	95554
Fruitridge	95820
Fruitvale (Alameda County)	94601

Name	ZIP
Fruitvale (Kern County)	93308
Fruto	95988
Fullerton	92631-35
For specific Fullerton Zip Codes call (714) 525-3893	
Fulton	95439
Gabilan (Part of Salinas)	93906
Gabilan Acres	93901
Galleria at South Bay, The (Part of Redondo Beach)	90278
Gallinas	94903
Galt	95632
Garberville	95440
Gardena	90247-49
For specific Gardena Zip Codes call (213) 327-9114	
Garden Acres (San Joaquin County)	95205
Garden Farms	93422
Garden Gate Village	95014
Garden Grove	92640-45
For specific Garden Grove Zip Codes call (714) 537-1331	
Garden Valley	95633
Garden Village (Part of Daly City)	94015
Garey	93454
Garfield	93205
Garlock	93554
Gasoline Alley	95603
Gas Point	96022
Gasquet	95543
Gateway (Los Angeles County)	90232
Gateway (Nevada County)	95734
Gaviota	93117
Gazelle	96034
Geary (Part of San Francisco)	94108
Gene	92267
Genesee	95983
Genesee Plaza (Part of San Diego)	92111
George AFB	92392
George Air Force Base	92394
Georgetown	95634
George Washington (Part of San Diego)	92103
Gerber	96035
Geyser Resort	95425
Geyserville	95441
Gilman Hot Springs	92383
Gilroy	95020-21
For specific Gilroy Zip Codes call (408) 842-2550	
Glamis	92227
Glassell (Part of Los Angeles)	90065
Glen Arbor	95005
Glen Avon	92509
Glenbrook Heights	95945
Glenburn	96028
Glencoe	95232
Glencove (Part of Vallejo)	94590
Glendale	91201-14
For specific Glendale Zip Codes call (818) 502-3202	
Glendale Galleria (Part of Glendale)	91210
Glendora	91740
Glen Ellen	95442
Glenhaven	95443
Glen Martin	92305
Glenn	95943
Glennville	93226
Glenoaks (Part of Burbank)	91504
Glenshire	95734
Glenview (Los Angeles County)	90290
Glenview (San Diego County)	92021
Glorietta (Part of Orinda)	94563
Goffs	92332
Golden Hill (Part of San Diego)	92102
Gold Flat	95959
Gold Gulch	95018
Gold Hill	95667
Gold River	95670
Gold Run	95717
Goleta	93117
Gonzales	93926
Goodyears Bar	95944
Gordon Valley	94585
Gorman	93243
Goshen	93227
Government Island (Part of Alameda)	94501
Graeagle	96103
Graham	90002

Granada Hills-Ingot CALIFORNIA 67

	ZIP		ZIP		ZIP
Granada Hills (Part of Los Angeles)	91344	Haskell Creek Homesites	96126	Hollywood Beach (Part of Oxnard)	93030
Grand Central (Part of Glendale)	91201	Haskins Resort	95971	Hollywood-by-the-Sea (Part of Oxnard)	93030
Grand Lake (Part of Oakland)	94610	Hat Creek	96040	Hollywood Riviera (Part of Torrance)	90277
Grand Terrace	92324	Hathaway Pines	95233	Holmes	95569
Grandview	92311	Hatton Fields	93923	Holt	95234
Grandview-Palos Verdes (Part of Rancho Palos Verdes)	90274	Havasu Lake	92363	Holtville	92250
		Havilah	93518	Holy City	95026
		Hawaiian Gardens	90716	Home Garden	93239
Grangeville	93230	Hawkins Bar	95563	Home Gardens	91720
Granite Bay Vista	95678	Hawkinsville	96097	Homeland	92348
Granite Hill	95945	Hawthorne	90250-51	Homestead (Kern County)	93527
Graniteville	95959	For specific Hawthorne Zip Codes call (213) 676-2284		Homestead (Riverside County)	92306
Grantville (Part of San Diego)	92120	Hawthorne Plaza (Part of Hawthorne)	90250	Homestead (San Joaquin County)	95206
Grass Valley	95945	Hayfork	96041	Homestead Valley	94941
Graton	95444	Hayward	94540-46	Homewood	95718
Grayson	95363	For specific Hayward Zip Codes call (415) 783-2440		Honby	91350
Greeley	93307	Hayward Highlands (Part of Hayward)	94542	Honcut	95965
Greeley Hill	95311	Hazard	90063	Honer Plaza (Part of Santa Ana)	92706
Green (Part of Los Angeles)	90037	Healdsburg	95448	Honeydew	95545
Greenacres	93308	Heber	92249	Hood	95639
Green Brae	94904	Helena	96042	Hooker	96022
Greenbrook (Part of Danville)	94526	Helendale	92342	Hookston (Part of Pleasant Hill)	94523
Greenfield	93927	Helm	93627	Hoopa	95546
Greenmead (Part of Los Angeles)	90059	Hemet	92343-44	Hoopa Valley Indian Reservation	95546
Green Meadows	95616	For specific Hemet Zip Codes call (714) 658-3263		Hope Ranch	93105
Greenspot	92359	Henderson (Part of Porterville)	93258	Hopeton	95369
Green Valley	91350	Henderson Center (Part of Eureka)	95501	Hope Valley	96120
Green Valley Estates	94585	Henderson Village	95240	Hopland	95449
Green Valley Lake	92341	Hendy Woods	95466	Hornbrook	96044
Greenview	96037	Henley	96044	Hornitos	95325
Greenview Acres (Part of Arcata)	95521	Henleyville	96021	Horse Creek	96045
Greenville	95947	Herald	95638	Horton Plaza (Part of San Diego)	92101
Greenwich Village (Part of Thousand Oaks)	91360	Hercules	94547	Hot Springs	95984
Greenwood	95635	Herlong	96113	Howard Landing	95690
Grenada	96038	Hermosa Beach	90254	Howest (Part of Burlingame)	94010
Gridley	95948	Hernandez	95023	Hub City (Part of Compton)	90220
Griffith (Part of Los Angeles)	90039	Herndon	93711	Hudson (Part of Modesto)	95355
Grimes	95950	Hesperia	92345	Hughes (Part of Fresno)	93705
Grizzly Flats	95636	Heyer	94544	Hughson	95326
Grossmont (San Diego County)	92041	Hickman	95323	Humboldt Bay CGAS	95521
Grove Highlands (Part of Pacific Grove)	93950	Hidden Hills	91302	Hume	93628
Groveland	95321	Hidden Meadows	92025	Humphreys Station	93612
Grover City	93433	Hidden Valley	95650	Hunters Valley	95325
Guadalupe	93434	Highgrove	92507	Huntington (Part of Huntington Beach)	92646
Gualala	95445	Highland	92346	Huntington Beach	92646-49
Guasti	91743	Highland Manor	93308	For specific Huntington Beach Zip Codes call (714) 847-5665	
Guatay	92031	Highland Park (Kern County)	93308	Huntington Center (Part of Huntington Beach)	92647
Guerneville	95446	Highland Park (Los Angeles County)	90042	Huntington Lake	93629
Guernewood Park	95446	Highway City	93706	Huntington Park	90255
Guernsey	93230	Highway Highlands (Part of Glendale)	91214	Huron	93234
Guinda	95637	Hilarita (Part of Tiburon)	94920	Hyampom	96046
Gustine	95322	Hillcrest (Los Angeles County)	90301	Hydesville	95547
Hacienda	95436	Hillcrest (San Diego County)	92103	Idlewild (Del Norte County)	95543
Hacienda Heights	91745	Hillcrest Center (Part of Bakersfield)	93306	Idlewild (Tulare County)	93260
Haiwee	93549	Hillcrest Park	94590	Idria	95023
Halcyon	93420	Hillsborough	94010	Idyllwild	92349
Hales Grove	95455	Hillsdale (Part of San Mateo)	94403	Idyllwild-Pine Cove	92349
Half Moon Bay	94019	Hillsdale Shopping Center (Part of San Mateo)	94403	Idywood Acres (Part of Walnut Creek)	94596
Hall (Part of Union City)	94587	Hills Flat	95945	Ignacio (Marin County)	94947
Halloran Springs	92309	Hilltop (Contra Costa County)	94806	Igo	96047
Halls Corner	93245	Hilltop (Kern County)	93307	Imola	94558
Hallwood	95901	Hillview (Part of San Jose)	95121	Imperial	92251
Hamburg	96045	Hilmar	95324	Imperial Beach	92032
Hamilton (Part of Palo Alto)	94301	Hilt	96044	Imperial Crest (Part of Norwalk)	90650
Hamilton City	95951	Hilton	95436	Incline	95318
Hammer Ranch (Part of Stockton)	95210	Hinkley	92347	Independence	93526
Hammil	93514	Hiouchi Valley	95531	Indian Beach	95443
Hammonton	95901	Hirschdale	95734	Indian Creek	95466
Hancock (Part of Los Angeles)	90044	Hi Vista	93534	Indian Falls	95952
Hanford	93230-32	Hoaglin	95495	Indian Hill Mall (Part of Pomona)	91767
For specific Hanford Zip Codes call (209) 582-2507		Hobart (Part of Vernon)	90058	Indian Lakes Estates	93614
Happy Camp	96039	Hobart Mills	95734	Indian Mission	93602
Harbison Canyon	92020	Hodge	92311	Indianola	95501
Harbor City (Part of Los Angeles)	90710	Holiday (Part of Anaheim)	92802	Indian Wells	92260
Harbor Side	92012	Holiday Forest	92386	Indio	92201-02
Hardman Center (Part of Riverside)	92504	Holiday Lake (Part of Morgan Hill)	95037	For specific Indio Zip Codes call (619) 347-3442	
Hardwick	93230	Hollister	95023-24	Industrial (Part of Santa Ana)	92705
Harlem Springs (Part of Highland)	92346	For specific Hollister Zip Codes call (408) 637-3350		Inglenook	95437
Harmony	93435	Hollydale (Los Angeles County)	90280	Ingleside (Part of San Francisco)	94112
Harmony Grove	92025	Hollydale (Sonoma County)	95436	Inglewood	90301-12
Harris	95440	Hollywood (Part of Los Angeles)	90028	For specific Inglewood Zip Codes call (213) 301-1230	
Harrison Park	92036				
Hartland	93603				
Harvard	92398			Ingot	96008

68 CALIFORNIA Inland Center-Lincoln Heights

Location	ZIP
Inland Center (Part of San Bernardino)	92408
Inverness	94937
Inverness Park	94956
Inyokern	93527
Ione	95640
Iowa Hill	95713
Irish Beach	95459
Iron Mountain	92242
Irvine	92713-20
For specific Irvine Zip Codes call (714) 474-0307	
Irvington (Part of Fremont)	94538
Irwin	95324
Irwindale	91706
Irwin Estates	92311
Island Mountain	95440
Isla Vista	93117
Isleton	95641
Ivanhoe	93235
Ivanpah	92309
Jacinto Grange	95943
Jackson	95642
Jackson Gate (Part of Jackson)	95642
Jacumba	92034
Jalama	93436
Jamesburg	93924
Jamestown	95327
Jamul	92035
Janesville	96114
Jarbo	95965
Jarvis Landing (Part of Newark)	94560
Jelly	96080
Jenner	95450
Jenny Lind	95236
Jesmond Dene	92025
Jimtown	95448
Johannesburg	93528
John Adams (Part of San Diego)	92116
Johnsondale	93238
Johnson Park	96013
Johnstonville	96130
Johnstown	92020
Johnsville	96103
Jolon	93928
Jonesville	95942
Joshua Tree	92252
Julian (San Diego County)	92036
Junction City	96048
June Lake	93529
June Lake Junction	93529
Juniper Hills	93543
Juniper Lake Resort	96020
Juniper Springs	92348
Kaiser Center (Part of Oakland)	94612
Kaiser's Eagle Mountain	92239
Kaweah	93237
Keddie	95952
Keeler	93530
Keene	93531
Kelly	96020
Kelsey	95643
Kelseyville	95451
Kelso	92351
Kennedy Meadow	95370
Kennedy Ranch	95449
Kensington	94707
Kensington Park (Part of San Diego)	92116
Kentfield	94904
Kentwood-In-The Pines	92036
Kent Woodlands	94904
Kenwood	95452
Keough Hot Springs	93514
Kerman	93630
Kern Homes	93308
Kernvale	93240
Kernville	93238
Keswick	96001
Kettleman City	93239
Kevet (Part of Santa Paula)	93060
Keyes	95328
Kilkare Woods	94586
King (Part of Santa Ana)	92706
King City	93930
King Island	95209
King Salmon	95501
Kings Beach	95719
Kingsburg	93631
Kingvale	95728
Kirkville	95645
Kirkwood (Alpine County)	95646
Kirkwood (Tehama County)	96021
Kirkwood Meadows	95646
Kit Carson	95644
Klamath	95548
Klamath Glen	95548

Location	ZIP
Klamath River	96050
Klinefelter	92363
Kneeland	95549
Knightsen	94548
Knights Ferry	95361
Knights Landing	95645
Knob	96076
Knowles	93653
Konocti	95451
Korbel	95550
Krug (Part of St. Helena)	94574
Kyburz	95720
La Barr Meadows	95949
La Canada (Part of La Canada Flintridge)	91011
La Canada Flintridge	91011
La Costa	90265
La Costa Beach	90265
La Crescenta	91214
La Crescenta-Montrose	91214
La Cresta (Kern County)	93305
La Cresta (San Diego County)	92020
La Cumbre Plaza (Part of Santa Barbara)	93105
Ladera	94028
Ladera Heights	90045
Lafayette	94549
La Grange	95329
Laguna Beach	92651-54
For specific Laguna Beach Zip Codes call (714) 494-4122	
Laguna Dam	85364
Laguna Hills (Orange County)	92653
Laguna Hills Mall	92653
Laguna Lake (Part of San Luis Obispo)	93405
Laguna Niguel	92677
Lagunitas	94938
Lagunitas-Forest Knolls	94933
La Habra	90631-33
For specific La Habra Zip Codes call (714) 992-5620	
La Habra Fashion Square (Part of La Habra)	90631
La Habra Heights	90631
La Honda	94020
Lairport (Part of El Segundo)	90245
La Jolla	92037-38
For specific La Jolla Zip Codes call (619) 454-7139	
La Jolla (Part of Placentia)	92670
La Jolla Indian Reservation	92025
Lake Alpine	95223
Lake Arrowhead (San Bernardino County)	92352
Lake Arrowhead (San Bernardino County)	92317
Lake Christopher (Part of South Lake Tahoe)	95702
Lake City	96115
Lake Elsinore	92330-31
For specific Lake Elsinore Zip Codes call (714) 674-3720	
Lake Forest	95730
Lakehead	96051
Lake Henshaw	92070
Lake Hills Estates	95630
Lake Hughes	93532
Lake Isabella	93240
Lake Kirkwood	95646
Lakeland Village	92330
Lake Los Angeles	93550
Lake Madera Country Estates	93637
Lake Marie Estates	93455
Lake Mary	93546
Lake Morena Village	92006
Lake Murray (Part of San Diego)	92119
Lake of the Pines	95603
Lake of the Woods	93225
Lake Pillsbury Homesites	95469
Lake Pillsbury Resort	95469
Lakeport	95453
Lake San Marcos	92069
Lakeshore	93634
Lakeshore Lodge	95971
Lakeside	92040
Lakeside Farms	92040
Lake Tamarisk	92239
Lakeview (Kern County)	93307
Lakeview (Riverside County)	92353
Lakeview (San Diego County)	92040
Lakeville	94954
Lakewood	90711-16
For specific Lakewood Zip Codes call (213) 866-1741	

Location	ZIP
Lakewood Center Mall (Part of Lakewood)	90712
La Loma (Part of Modesto)	95350
La Mesa	92041-44
For specific La Mesa Zip Codes call (619) 466-3283	
La Mirada	90637-38
For specific La Mirada Zip Codes call (714) 521-0787	
La Mirada Mall (Part of La Mirada)	90638
Lamont	93241
Lanare	93656
Lancaster	93534-39
For specific Lancaster Zip Codes call (805) 948-1691	
Landers	92284
Land Park (Part of Sacramento)	95822
Landscape (Part of Berkeley)	94707
Lansdale (Part of San Anselmo)	94960
La Palma	90623
La Panza	93453
La Patera	93117
La Porte	95981
La Puente	91744-49
For specific La Puente Zip Codes call (818) 968-9311	
La Quinta	92253
Larabee Ranch	95569
La Riviera	95826
Larkfield	95401
Larkspur	94939
Larson Tract	93240
Larwin Plaza (Part of Vallejo)	94590
Las Cruces	93117
La Selva Beach	95076
Las Flores (Los Angeles County)	90265
Las Flores (Tehama County)	96035
La Sierra (Part of Riverside)	92505
Las Lomas	95076
Las Posas Estates	93010
Lathrop	95330
La Tijera (Part of Los Angeles)	90043
Laton	93242
Latrobe	95682
Laurel (Part of Oakland)	94619
Laurel Canyon (Part of Los Angeles)	91605
Laurel Plaza (Part of Los Angeles)	91606
Laurelwood (Part of Los Angeles)	91604
La Verne	91750
La Vina	93637
Lawndale	90260-61
For specific Lawndale Zip Codes call (213) 679-0121	
Lawndale	95452
Lawrence (Part of Danville)	94506
Laws	93514
Layman	96103
Laytonville	95454
Lazy Acre	93311
Lebec	93243
Ledgewood	94585
Lee	96020
Lee Vining	93541
Leggett	95455
Le Grand	95333
Leisure Town (Part of Vacaville)	95688
Leisure World (Part of Seal Beach)	90740
Lemoncove	93244
Lemon Grove	92045
Lemon Heights	92705
Lemoore	93245
Lemoore Naval Air Station	93245
Lemoore Station	93245
Lennox	90304
Lenwood	92311
Leona Valley	93550
Leucadia (Part of Encinitas)	92024
Lewiston	96052
Liberty Acres	90250
Liberty Farms	95620
Libfarm	95620
Likely	96116
Lily Valley	95255
Limco	93060
Lincoln	95648
Lincoln Acres	92047
Lincoln Heights (Part of Los Angeles)	90031

Lincoln Village-Los Nietos CALIFORNIA 69

	ZIP
Lincoln Village (Los Angeles County)	90810
Lincoln Village (San Joaquin County)	95207
Linda	95901
Linda Vista (San Diego County)	92111
Linda Vista (Santa Clara County)	95127
Lind Cove	93221
Linden	95236
Linden Avenue (Part of South San Francisco)	94080
Lindenwood (Part of Menlo Park)	94027
Lindsay	93247
Lingard	95333
Linnell	93277
Litchfield	96117
Little Lake	93542
Little Morongo Heights	92256
Little Norway	95721
Little Reed Heights (Part of Tiburon)	94920
Littleriver	95456
Littlerock	93543
Little Shasta	96064
Little Valley	96053
Live Oak (Santa Cruz County)	95062
Live Oak (Sutter County)	95953
Live Oak Acres (Tehama County)	96080
Live Oak Acres (Ventura County)	93022
Live Oak Canyon	91750
Live Oak Springs	92062
Livermore	94550
Livingston	95334
Llano	93544
Lobitos	94019
Lobo (Part of Stanton)	90680
Loch Lomond	95426
Locke	95690
Lockeford	95237
Lockhart	92347
Lockwood	93932
Lodge Pole	93262
Lodi	95240-42
For specific Lodi Zip Codes call (209) 369-9545	
Lodoga	95979
Logan Heights (Part of San Diego)	92113
Loleta	95551
Loma (Part of Long Beach)	90814
Loma Linda	92354
Loma Mar	94021
Loma Portal (Part of San Diego)	92110
Loma Rica	95901
Lomas Santa Fe (Part of Solana Beach)	92075
Loma Verda (Part of Novato)	94947
Lomita	90717
Lomita Park (Part of San Bruno)	94066
Lompico	95018
Lompoc	93436
London	93618
Lone Pine	93545
Lone Pine Indian Reservation	93545
Long Barn	95335
Long Beach	90745-47
	90749-99
	90801-88
For specific Long Beach Zip Codes call (213) 494-2371	

COLLEGES & UNIVERSITIES

California State University-Long Beach	90840

FINANCIAL INSTITUTIONS

Farmers & Merchants Bank of Long Beach	90802
Guardian Savings & Loan Association	90803
Harbor Bank	90802
National Bank of Long Beach	90807

HOSPITALS

Dominguez Medical Center	90805
Long Beach Community Hospital	90804
Memorial Medical Center	90806
St. Mary Medical Center	90801

	ZIP
Veterans Administration Medical Center	90822

HOTELS/MOTELS

Golden Sails Hotel	90803
Hyatt Edgewater at Long Beach Marina	90803
Queen Mary Hotel	90801
Ramada Inn	90804

MILITARY INSTALLATIONS

Long Beach Naval Shipyard	90822
Naval Regional Contracting Center	90822
Naval Supply Center Detachment	90822
Supervisor of Shipbuilding, Conversion and Repair, Long Beach	90822
United States Property and Fiscal Office for California, Long Beach CSMS	90822
11th Coast Guard District, Long Beach	90822
Long Beach Plaza (Part of Long Beach)	90802
Longvale	95490
Longview	93553
Lonoak	93930
Lonoke (Part of Gilroy)	95020
Lookout	96054
Loomis	95650
Loomis Corners	96001
Loraine	93518
Loree Estates	95014
Los Alamitos	90720-21
For specific Los Alamitos Zip Codes call (213) 431-6546	
Los Alamitos Naval Air Station	90720
Los Alamos	93440
Los Altos	94022-24
For specific Los Altos Zip Codes call (415) 948-6000	
Los Altos Hills	94022
Los Altos Shopping Center (Part of Long Beach)	90815
Los Amigos (Part of Downey)	90240
Los Angeles	90001-99
	90101-99
For specific Los Angeles Zip Codes call (213) 586-1737	

COLLEGES & UNIVERSITIES

California State University-Los Angeles	90032
Loyola Marymount University	90045
Mount Saint Mary's College	90049
Northrop University	90045
Occidental College	90041
University of California-Los Angeles	90024
University of Southern California	90089

FINANCIAL INSTITUTIONS

American International Bank	90017
The Bank of California, National Association	90071
Bankers Trust Company of California, National Association	90071
Bel-Air Savings & Loan Association	90049
Brentwood Square Savings & Loan Association	90049
California Commerce Bank	90017
California Federal Savings & Loan Association	90036
California Korea Bank	90006
California Overseas Bank	90010
Canadian Imperial Bank of Commerce (California)	90071
Capital Bank of California	90067
Cathay Bank	90012
Community Bank	90065
Dai-Ichi Kangyo Bank of California	90017
East-West Federal Bank, F.S.B.	90012
Family Savings & Loan Association	90016
Far East National Bank	90012
1st Business Bank	90071
First Interstate Bank, Ltd.	90017

	ZIP
First Interstate Bank of California	90017
First Los Angeles Bank	90067
First Network Savings Bank	90067
First Public Savings Bank	90012
Founders Savings & Loan Association	90008
General Bank	90012
Guardian Bank	90017
Hancock Savings & Loan Association	90004
Hanmi Bank	90019
Highland Federal Savings & Loan Association of Los Angeles	90042
Home Savings of America, F.A.	90010
Marathon National Bank	90064
Mercantile National Bank	90067
Metrobank, National Association	90024
Mitsui Manufacturers Bank	90071
Security Pacific Asian Banking Corporation, National Association	90017
Security Pacific National Bank	90071
Southwest Savings & Loan Association	90036
Standard Savings Bank	90012
Sterling Bank	90010
Tokai Bank of California	90014
Union Bank	90071
Union Federal Savings & Loan Association	90013
Western Bank	90024

HOSPITALS

California Medical Center-Los Angeles	90015
Cedars-Sinai Medical Center	90048
Childrens Hospital of Los Angeles	90054
Hospital of the Good Samaritan	90017
Kaiser Foundation Hospital-Sunset	90027
King-Drew Medical Center	90059
LAC-University of Southern California Medical Center	90033
St. Vincent Medical Center	90057
University of California at Los Angeles Medical Center	90024
Veterans Administration Medical Center-West Los Angeles	90073

HOTELS/MOTELS

The Beverly Plaza Hotel	90048
The Biltmore Hotel	90071
Holiday Inn-Crowne Plaza	90045
Holiday Inn-Downtown	90017
Hyatt Regency Los Angeles	90017
Hyatt Wilshire	90010
Le Parc Hotel	90069
Los Angeles Hilton & Towers	90017
Mayfair Hotel	90017
The New Otani Hotel & Garden	90012
Sheraton Grande	90071
Sheraton Plaza La Reina Hotel	90045
Sheraton Town House	90010
University Hilton-Los Angeles	90007
The Westin Bonaventure	90071

MILITARY INSTALLATIONS

Los Angeles Air Force Station	90009
Military Airlift Command	90045
United States Army Engineer District, Los Angeles	90053
Los Banos	93635
Los Berros	93420
Los Cerritos Center (Part of Cerritos)	90701
Los Coyotes Indian Reservation	92086
Los Deltos	93622
Los Feliz (Part of Los Angeles)	90027
Los Gatos	95030-32
For specific Los Gatos Zip Codes call (408) 354-6666	
Los Molinos	96055
Los Nietos	90606

CALIFORNIA Los Angeles

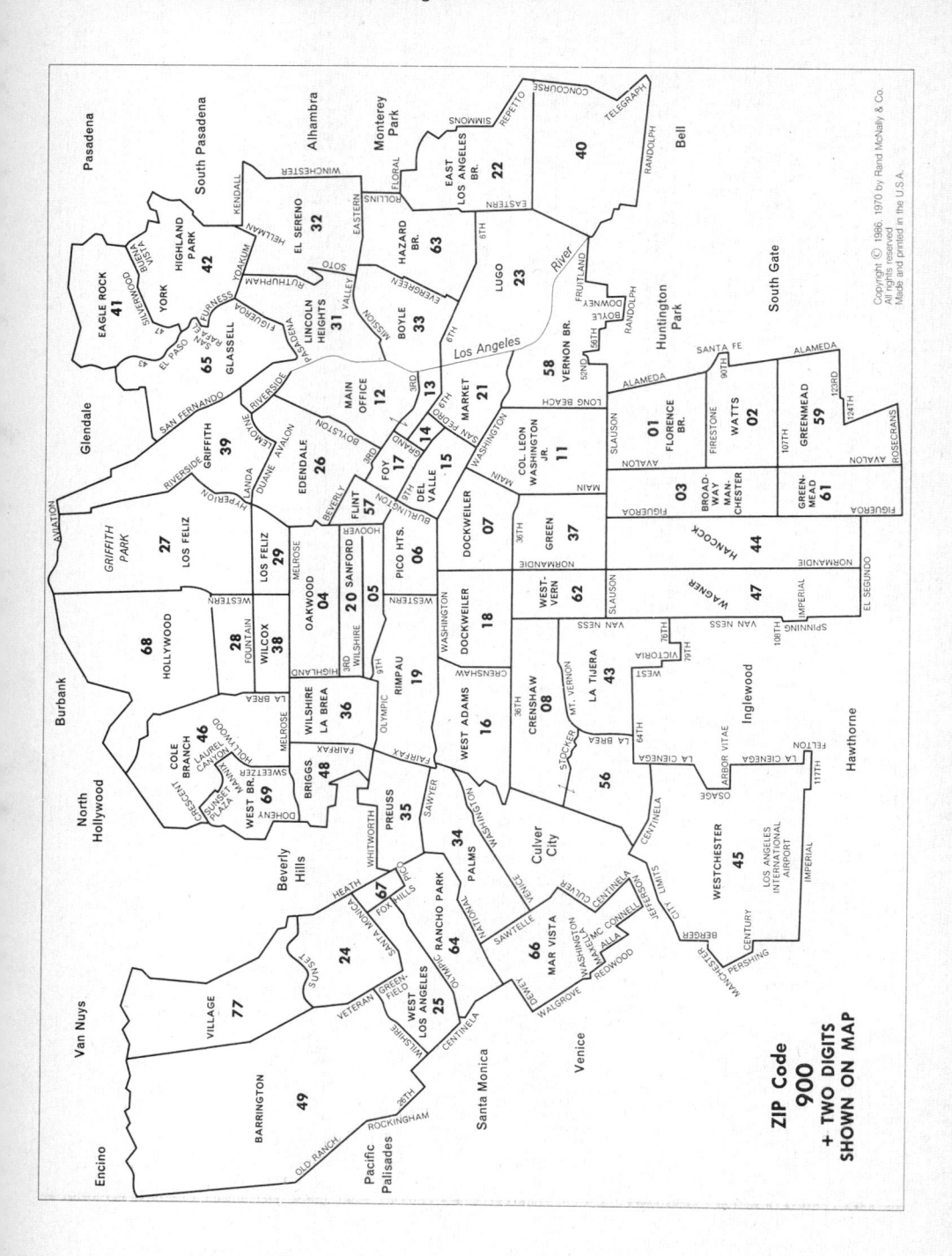

Los Olivos-Mojave Heights **CALIFORNIA** 71

Name	ZIP
Los Olivos	93441
Los Osos	93402
Los Ranchitos	94903
Los Serranos	91709
Lost Hills	93249
Lost Lake	92225
Los Trancos Woods	94028
Los Tules	92086
Lotus	95651
Lovelock	95954
Lower Echo Lake	95721
Lower Lake	95457
Lowrey	96080
Loyalton	96118
Loyola (Part of Los Altos)	94022
Lucas Valley	94903
Lucas Valley-Marinwood	94903
Lucerne	95458
Lucerne Valley	92356
Lugo (Part of Los Angeles)	90023
Lugonia (Part of Redlands)	92375
Lunada Bay (Part of Palos Verdes Estates)	90274
Lundy	93541
Lushmeadows Mountain Estates	95338
Luther Burbank (Part of Santa Rosa)	95402
Lyman Springs	96075
Lynwood	90262
Lynwood Gardens (Part of Lynwood)	90262
Lytle Creek	92358
McArthur	96056
McCann	95569
McClellan Air Force Base	95652
McCloud	96057
Macdoel	96058
McFarland	93250
McHie	96080
McIntyre Park	92225
McKeon	95631
McKinleyville	95521
McKittrick	93251
McKnight Acres	94590
McLaren (Part of San Francisco)	94134
Maclay (Part of San Fernando)	91340
McMillan Manor (Part of Oxnard)	93030
Madeline	96119
Madera	93637-39
For specific Madera Zip Codes call (209) 673-9288	
Madera Acres	93637
Madera Country Club Estates	93637
Madera Highlands	93637
Madera Ranchos	93637
Madison	95653
Madonna Road Plaza (Part of San Luis Obispo)	93405
Mad River	95552
Madrone (Part of Morgan Hill)	95037
Magalia	95954
Magnolia (Imperial County)	92227
Magnolia (Santa Barbara County)	93111
Magnolia Center (Part of Riverside)	92506
Magnolia Park (Part of Burbank)	91505
MainPlace/Santa Ana (Part of Santa Ana)	92701
Malaga	93725
Malibu	90264-65
For specific Malibu Zip Codes call (213) 456-2018	
Malibu Beach	90265
Malibu Bowl	90265
Malibu Canyon Homes	91302
Mall at Northgate, The (Part of San Rafael)	94903
Mall at Weberstown, The (Part of Stockton)	95207
Mall of Orange, The (Part of Orange)	92665
Malott (Part of El Cerrito)	94530
Mammoth Lakes	93546
Manchester	95459
Manchester Center (Part of Fresno)	93726
Manhattan Beach	90266
Manhattan Village (Part of Manhattan Beach)	90266
Manila	95521
Manka's Corners	94585
Manlove	95826
Manor (Part of Fairfax)	94930

Name	ZIP
Manteca	95336
Manton	96059
Manzana	95444
Manzanita	95948
Manzanita Indian Reservation	92005
Maple Creek	95550
Maravilla Park	90022
Marcelina (Part of Torrance)	90501
March AFB	92508
March Air Force Base	92508
Marcus Foster (Part of Oakland)	94624
Maricopa	93252
Marina (Monterey County)	93933
Marina (San Francisco County)	94123
Marina Del Rey	90292
Marin City	94965
Marin Country Club Estates (Part of Novato)	94947
Marine Corps Air Station (H)	92709
Marine Corps Logistics Support Base, Pacific	92311
Marine Corps Supply Center, West Yermo Area	92398
Mariner (Part of Seal Beach)	90740
Marinwood	94903
Mariposa	95338
Market (Part of Los Angeles)	90021
Marklee Village	96120
Markleeville	96120
Marloma (Part of Rolling Hills Estates)	90274
Marne (Part of City of Industry)	91743
Marshall	94940
Marshall Station	93612
Martell	95654
Martinez	94553
Martins Beach	94019
Mar Vista (Part of Los Angeles)	90066
Marysville	95901
Massack	95971
Mather AFB	95655
Mather Air Force Base	95655
Mather Heights	95655
Maxwell	95955
Mayflower Village	91016
Maywood	90270
Meadowbrook	92370
Meadowbrook Woods	92326
Meadow Lake Park	95734
Meadow Lakes	93602
Meadowsweet (Part of Corte Madera)	94925
Meadow Valley	95956
Meadow Vista	95722
Mead Valley	92370
Mecca	92254
Medicine Lake Lodge	96134
Meeks Bay	95733
Meiners Oaks	93023
Meiners Oaks-Mira Monte	93023
Melbourne	95427
Melody Oaks	95642
Meloland	92243
Melsons Corner	95684
Melvin (Part of Clovis)	93612
Mendocino	95460
Mendosama	95463
Mendota	93640
Menifee	92380
Menlo Park	94025-28
For specific Menlo Park Zip Codes call (415) 323-0038	
Mentone	92359
Merced	95339-44
For specific Merced Zip Codes call (209) 723-1063	
Merced Falls	95369
Merced Mall (Part of Merced)	95340
Meridian	95957
Mesa Camp	93514
Mesa Center (Part of Costa Mesa)	92627
Mesa Grande	92070
Mesa Verde	92225
Metro (Part of Sacramento)	95814
Metropolitan (Humboldt County)	95540
Metropolitan (Los Angeles County)	90014
Mettler	93301
Mexican Colony	93263
Michigan Bluff	95631
Michillinda	91107
Mid City (Part of Stockton)	95202

Name	ZIP
Midco (Part of Santa Maria)	93454
Middlefield Road	94061
Middle River	95234
Middletown	95461
Midpines	95345
Midtown (Part of Chico)	95926
Midway City	92655
Mikon (Part of West Sacramento)	95605
Milford	96121
Millbrae	94030
Millbrae Meadows (Part of Millbrae)	94030
Mill City	93546
Mill Creek	96061
Mill Creek Park	92359
Millers Corners	93637
Mills College (Part of Oakland)	94613
Mills Orchard	95951
Mill Valley	94941-42
For specific Mill Valley Zip Codes call (415) 388-8656	
Millville	96062
Milo	93265
Milpas (Part of Santa Barbara)	93103
Milpitas	95035-36
For specific Milpitas Zip Codes call (408) 262-2322	
Milton	95230
Mineral	96063
Mineralking	93271
Minkler	93657
Mint Canyon (Part of Santa Clarita)	91350
Mirabel Heights	95436
Mirabel Park	95436
Miracle Hot Springs	93301
Miracle Manor	93501
Miracle Mile (Part of Los Angeles)	90036
Miraleste (Part of Rancho Palos Verdes)	90274
Mira Loma	91752
Miramar (San Diego County)	92145
Miramar (San Mateo County)	94018
Mira Mesa (Part of San Diego)	92126
Miramonte (Fresno County)	93641
Mira Monte (Ventura County)	93023
Miranda	95553
Mira Vista (Part of Richmond)	94805
Mission (San Francisco County)	94110
Mission (San Luis Obispo County)	93406
Mission (Santa Clara County)	95051
Mission Annex (Part of San Francisco)	94103
Mission Beach (Part of San Diego)	92109
Mission City Annex (Part of Los Angeles)	91345
Mission Highlands	95476
Mission Hills (Los Angeles County)	91345
Mission Hills (San Diego County)	92103
Mission Hills (Santa Barbara County)	93436
Mission Rafael (Part of San Rafael)	94901
Mission San Jose (Part of Fremont)	94539
Mission Valley Center (Part of San Diego)	92108
Mission Viejo	92691
Mission Viejo Mall (Part of Mission Viejo)	92691
Missouri Triangle	93251
Mitchell Mill	95257
Mi-Wuk Village	95346
Moccasin	95347
Mococo (Part of Martinez)	94553
Modesto	95350-56
For specific Modesto Zip Codes call (209) 523-8326	
Modjeska	92667
Moffett Field Naval Air Station	94035
Mohave Manor	92311
Mojave	93501-02
For specific Mojave Zip Codes call (805) 824-4561	
Mojave Heights (Part of Victorville)	92392

72 CALIFORNIA Mojave Knolls-Oak Knolls

	ZIP
Mojave Knolls	93501
Mokelumne Hill	95245
Monarch Bay	92677
Monmouth	93725
Mono Hot Springs	93642
Mono Lake	93541
Mono Village	93517
Mono Vista	95370
Monrovia	91016
Monson	93618
Montague	96064
Montair (Part of Danville)	94526
Montalvin Manor	94806
Montalvo (Part of Ventura)	93003
Montara	94037
Monta Vista	95014
Montclair	91763
Montclair Plaza (Part of Montclair)	91763
Montebello	90640
Montebello Gardens (Part of Pico Rivera)	90660
Montebello Town Center (Part of Montebello)	90640
Montecito	93108
Monte Nido	91302
Monterey	93940
Monterey Park	91754
Monte Rio	95462
Monte Rosa	95446
Montesano	95446
Monte Sereno	95030
Monte Toyon	95003
Montgomery Creek	96063
Montgomery Village (Part of Santa Rosa)	95405
Montrose	91020
Moody (Part of Cypress)	90630
Moonridge	92315
Moonstone	95570
Moorpark	93020-21
For specific Moorpark Zip Codes call (805) 529-1771	
Moorpark Home Acres	93021
Morada	95205
Moraga	94556
Morena	92040
Moreno (Part of Moreno Valley)	92313
Moreno Valley	92387-88
For specific Moreno Valley Zip Codes call (714) 656-2590	
Morgan Hill	95037-38
For specific Morgan Hill Zip Codes call (408) 779-2484	
Mormon Bar	95338
Morningside Park (Part of Inglewood)	90305
Morongo Indian Reservation	92220
Morongo Valley	92256
Morro Bay	93442-43
For specific Morro Bay Zip Codes call (805) 772-2361	
Morro Palisades	93402
Moss Beach	94038
Mossdale	95330
Moss Landing	95039
Mountain Center	92361
Mountain Gate	96003
Mountain House (Alameda County)	95376
Mountain House (Butte County)	95916
Mountain Mesa	93240
Mountain Pass	92366
Mountain Ranch	95246
Mountain Spring	92034
Mountain View	94039-43
For specific Mountain View Zip Codes call (415) 967-5721	
Mountain View	93307
Mountain View Acres	92392
Mount Aukum	95656
Mount Baldy	91759
Mount Bullion	95338
Mount Eden (Part of Hayward)	94557
Mount Hamilton	95140
Mount Hannah Lodge	95451
Mount Hebron	96058
Mount Helix	92041
Mount Hermon	95041
Mount Laguna	92048
Mount Shasta	96067
Mount Shasta Mall (Part of Redding)	96003
Mount Signal	92231
Mount View	94553
Mount Whitney	93545
Mount Wilson	91023
Mugginsville	96032

	ZIP
Muir (Part of Willits)	95490
Muir Beach	94965
Muir Woods	94941
Murietta	93640
Murphys	95247
Murray Park (Part of Larkspur)	94939
Murrieta	92362
Murrieta Hot Springs	92362
Muscoy	92405
Myers Flat	95554
Myrtletown	95501
Nadeau	90001
Napa	94558-59
For specific Napa Zip Codes call (707) 255-1791	
Napa Junction	94590
Nashville	95623
National City	92050
Navajo (Part of San Diego)	92119
Naval (Part of Port Hueneme)	93043
Naval Air Facility	92243
Naval Air Station (Alameda County)	94501
Naval Air Station (Kings County)	93245
Naval Amphibious Base, Coronado (Amphibious Base)	92155
Naval Regional Medical Center	92055
Naval Weapons Station (Contra Costa County)	94520
Naval Weapons Station (Orange County)	90740
Navarro	95463
Navelencia	93654
Nebo	92311
Nebo Center	92311
Needles	92363
Nelson	95958
Nestor (Part of San Diego)	92053
Nevada City	95959
New Almaden	95042
Newark	94560
New Auberry	93602
Newberry Springs	92365
Newburg	95540
Newbury Park (Part of Thousand Oaks)	91320
Newcastle	95658
New Cuyama	93254
Newell	96134
Newhall (Part of Santa Clarita)	91321
Newhall Ranch (Part of Santa Clarita)	91350
New Helvetia (Part of Sacramento)	95815
Newman	95360
New Monterey (Part of Monterey)	93940
New Park Mall (Part of Newark)	94560
New Pine Creek	97635
Newport Beach	92658-63
For specific Newport Beach Zip Codes call (714) 640-8720	
Newport Center Fashion Island (Part of Newport Beach)	92660
Newtown (El Dorado County)	95667
Newtown (Nevada County)	95959
Newville	95963
Nicasio	94946
Nice	95464
Nichols	94565
Nicolaus	95659
Nigger Hill	95667
Nightingale	92361
Niguel Terrace	92677
Niland	92257
Niles (Part of Fremont)	94536
Nimshew	95954
Nipinnawassee	93601
Nipomo	93444
Nipton	92364
Nob Hill (Part of San Francisco)	94108
Noe Valley (Part of San Francisco)	94114
No Mirage	92259
Norco	91760
Nord	95926
Norden	95724
Normal Heights (Part of San Diego)	92116
North (Part of Los Angeles)	91342

	ZIP
North Auburn	95603
North Bay View Park (Part of Seaside)	93955
North Beach (Part of San Francisco)	94133
North Belridge	93429
North Berkeley (Part of Berkeley)	94709
North Bloomfield	95959
North Clairemont (Part of San Diego)	92107
North Columbia	95959
North County Fair (Part of Escondido)	92025
Northcrest (Part of Crescent City)	95531
North Cucamonga (Part of Cucamonga)	91730
North Downey (Part of Downey)	90240
Northeast Modesto (Part of Modesto)	95350
North Edwards	93523
North Elsinore (Part of Lake Elsinore)	92330
Northern California Women's Facility	95213
North Fair Oaks	94025
North Fillmore (Part of Fillmore)	93015
North Fork	93643
North Gardena	90247
North Glendale (Part of Glendale)	91202
North Highlands	95660
North Hollywood	91601-16
For specific North Hollywood Zip Codes call (818) 503-0695	
North Inglewood (Part of Inglewood)	90302
North Island Naval Air Station	92135
North Loma Linda (Part of Loma Linda)	92354
North Long Beach (Part of Long Beach)	90805
North Oakland (Part of Oakland)	94609
North Oaks	91350
North Palm Springs	92258
North Park (Part of San Diego)	92104
North Redondo Beach (Part of Redondo Beach)	90278
North Richmond	94804
Northridge	91323-28
For specific Northridge Zip Codes call (818) 394-4475	
Northridge Center (Part of Salinas)	93906
Northridge Fashion Center (Part of Los Angeles)	91324
North Sacramento (Part of Sacramento)	95815
North San Juan	95960
North Seal Beach (Part of Seal Beach)	90740
North Shore	92254
North Torrance (Part of Torrance)	90504
North Valley Plaza (Part of Chico)	95926
North Whittier	91746
North Whittier Heights	91745
Norwalk	90650-52
For specific Norwalk Zip Codes call (213) 868-3247	
Norwalk Manor (Part of Norwalk)	90650
Norwalk Square (Part of Norwalk)	90650
Novato	94947-49
For specific Novato Zip Codes call (415) 897-3171	
Noyo	95437
Nubieber	96068
Nuevo	92367
Nummi (Part of Fremont)	94538
Nut Tree (Part of Vacaville)	95696
Nyland Acres	93030
Oak Bottom	96095
Oakdale	95361
Oak Glen	92399
Oak Grove (Butte County)	95965
Oak Grove (San Diego County)	92302
Oakhills	93907
Oakhurst	93644
Oak Knoll Hills	95014
Oak Knolls	93454

Oakland-Pine Flat CALIFORNIA 73

Name	ZIP
Oakland	94601-62
For specific Oakland Zip Codes call (415) 874-8200	
Oakley	94561
Oakmont (Part of Santa Rosa)	95405
Oak Park (Sacramento County)	95817
Oak Park (San Luis Obispo County)	93446
Oak Park (Ventura County)	91301
Oakridge Mall (Part of San Jose)	95122
Oak Run	96069
Oaks (Part of Arroyo Grande)	93420
Oaks, The (Part of Thousand Oaks)	91360
Oak Shores	93426
Oak View	93022
Oakville	94562
Oakwood (Part of Los Angeles)	90004
Oasis	89010
O'Brien	96070
Occidental	95465
Ocean Beach (Part of San Diego)	92107
Oceano	93445
Ocean Park (Part of Santa Monica)	90405
Oceanside	92054-56
For specific Oceanside Zip Codes call (619) 433-8711	
Ocean View (San Francisco County)	94112
Ocean View (Sonoma County)	94923
Ocotillo	92259
Ocotillo Wells	92004
Oildale	93308
Ojai	93023
Olancha	93549
Old Fellows Park	95446
Old Fort Jim	95667
Old Gilroy	95020
Old Hopland	95449
Old Mammoth (Part of Mammoth Lakes)	93546
Old River	93309
Old San Diego (Part of San Diego)	92110
Old Station	96071
Old Towne (Part of Tehachapi)	93561
Old Towne Mall (Part of Torrance)	90503
Oleander	93725
Olema	94950
Oleum	94572
Olinda (Orange County)	92621
Olinda (Shasta County)	96007
Olive (Part of Orange)	92665
Olivehurst	95961
Olivenhain (Part of Encinitas)	92024
Olympia	95018
Olympic (Part of Beverly Hills)	90212
Olympic Valley	95730
Omo Ranch	95684
O'Neals	93645
One Hundred Palms	92274
Ono	96001
Ontario	91761-62
For specific Ontario Zip Codes call (714) 983-1873	
Onyx	93255
Opal Cliffs	95062
Ophir	95603
Orange	92664-69
For specific Orange Zip Codes call (714) 997-1255	
Orange Cove	93646
Orangefair Mall (Part of Fullerton)	92632
Orange Glen (Part of Escondido)	92027
Orange Heights (Part of Upland)	91786
Orangehurst (Part of Fullerton)	92633
Orange Park Acres	92667
Orangevale	95662
Orangewood (Part of Pasadena)	91105
Orcutt	93455
Ordbend	95943
Oregon City	95965
Oregon House	95962
Orick	95555

Name	ZIP
Orinda	94563
Orinda Village (Part of Orinda)	94563
Orland	95963
Orleans	95556
Ormand	92509
Oro Fino	96032
Oro Grande	92368
Oro Loma	93622
Orosi (Tulare County)	93647
Oroville	95965-66
For specific Oroville Zip Codes call (916) 533-4515	
Osbourne (Part of Los Angeles)	90028
Otay	92010
Otay Mesa (Part of Chula Vista)	92154
Otterbein	91745
Outingdale	95684
Oval (Part of Visalia)	93291
Owenyo	93545
Oxnard	93030-35
For specific Oxnard Zip Codes call (805) 485-6722	
Oxnard Beach (Part of Oxnard)	93030
Pabrico (Part of Union City)	94587
Pachappa	92506
Pacheco	94553
Pacific (Part of Long Beach)	90806
Pacifica	94044
Pacific Beach (Part of San Diego)	92109
Pacific Gardens	95204
Pacific Grove	93950
Pacific Grove Acres (Part of Pacific Grove)	93950
Pacific House	95726
Pacific Manor (Humboldt County)	95521
Pacific Manor (San Mateo County)	94044
Pacific Missile Test Center-Point Mugu	93042
Pacific Palisades (Part of Los Angeles)	90272
Pacific Villas	90272
Pacoima	91331-33
For specific Pacoima Zip Codes call (818) 896-7491	
Paddison Square (Part of Norwalk)	90652
Paicines	95043
Paintersville	95615
Pajaro	95076
Pala	92059
Pala Mesa Village	92028
Palermo	95968
Pallett	93563
Palm City (Part of Palm Desert)	92260
Palmdale	93550-51
For specific Palmdale Zip Codes call (805) 947-4134	
Palmdale East	93550
Palm Desert	92260-61
For specific Palm Desert Zip Codes call (619) 568-5803	
Palm Desert Town Center (Part of Palm Desert)	92260
Palmer Creek	95540
Palms (Part of Los Angeles)	90034
Palm Springs	92262-64
For specific Palm Springs Zip Codes call (619) 325-9631	
Palm Springs Mall (Part of Palm Springs)	92262
Palm Wells	92256
Palo Alto	94301-09
For specific Palo Alto Zip Codes call (415) 321-4310	
Palo Cedro	96073
Paloma	95252
Palomares	94546
Palomar Mountain	92060
Palomar Park	94062
Palos Verdes Estates	90274
Palos Verdes Peninsula (Part of Rolling Hills Estates)	90274
Palo Verde	92266
Palo Vista (Part of Vista)	92083
Panoche	95043
Panorama Heights (Orange County)	92705
Panorama Heights (Tulare County)	93260
Panorama Mall (Part of Los Angeles)	91402
Pappas	93640

Name	ZIP
Paradise	95969
Paradise Cay (Part of Tiburon)	94920
Paradise Hills (Part of San Diego)	92139
Paradise Park	95060
Paramount	90723
Parchers Camp	93514
Park (Part of Berkeley)	94702
Park Central (Part of Alameda)	94501
Parker Dam	92267
Parkfield	93451
Parkmoor (Part of San Jose)	95128
Parksdale	93637
Parkside (Part of San Francisco)	94116
Park Siding (Part of Petaluma)	94952
Parkway	95823
Parkway Estates	95823
Parkway Plaza (Part of El Cajon)	92020
Parkway-Sacramento South	95823
Parkwood	93637
Parlier	93648
Pasadena	91101-09
For specific Pasadena Zip Codes call (818) 304-7183	
Pasatiempo	95060
Paskenta	96074
Paso Robles	93446-47
For specific Paso Robles Zip Codes call (805) 238-4904	
Patata (Part of South Gate)	90280
Patrick Creek	95543
Patricks Point	95570
Patterson (Stanislaus County)	95363
Patterson (Tulare County)	93277
Patton	92369
Patton Village	96113
Pauma Valley	92061
Paxton	95952
Paynes Creek	96075
Paynesville	96120
Peanut	96041
Pearblossom	93553
Peardale	93550
Pearland	93527
Pearsonville	93953
Pebble Beach	95546
Pecwan	92509
Pedley	92509
Pedro Valley (Part of Pacifica)	94044
Peninsula Center (Part of Rolling Hills Estates)	90274
Peninsula Village	96137
Penngrove	94951
Pennington	95953
Penn Valley	95946
Penryn	95663
Pentz	95965
Pepperwood	95565
Peralta Hills	92667
Perkins	95826
Perris	92370
Perry (Los Angeles County)	90603
Perry (Santa Clara County)	95037
Pescadero	94060
Petaluma	94952-54
For specific Petaluma Zip Codes call (707) 762-0051	
Peters	95236
Petrolia	95558
Pheasant Hill	93065
Phelan	92371
Phelps Corner	92035
Phillipsville	95559
Philo	95466
Pico (Part of Pico Rivera)	90660
Pico Heights (Part of Los Angeles)	90006
Pico Rivera	90660-61
For specific Pico Rivera Zip Codes call (213) 942-7008	
Piedmont (Alameda County)	94611
Piedra	93649
Piercy	95467
Pierpoint Springs	93208
Pike	95960
Pilot Hill	95664
Pine Cove (Riverside County)	92349
Pine Cove (Trinity County)	96052
Pinecrest	95364
Pinedale (Part of Fresno)	93650
Pine Flat	93207

74 CALIFORNIA Pine Grove-Rockport

Location	ZIP
Pine Grove (Amador County)	95665
Pine Grove (Lake County)	95426
Pine Grove (Mendocino County)	95420
Pine Grove (Shasta County)	96079
Pine Hills (Humboldt County)	95501
Pine Hills (San Diego County)	92036
Pinehurst	93641
Pine Mountain Club	93225
Pine Mountain Lake	95321
Pine Ridge	93602
Pine Valley	92062
Pinnacles	95043
Pinole	94564
Pinon Hills	92372
Pinyon Crest	92262
Pinyon Pines	92361
Pioneer	95666
Pioneer Point	93562
Pioneertown	92268
Piru	93040
Pismo Beach	93448-49
For specific Pismo Beach Zip Codes call (805) 773-2191	
Pittsburg	94565
Pittville	96056
Pixley	93256
Placentia	92670
Placerville	95667
Plainsburg	95333
Plainview	93267
Planada	95365
Planehaven	95652
Plantation	95421
Plaster City	92269
Platina	96076
Playa (Part of Laguna Beach)	92652
Playa Del Rey (Part of Los Angeles)	90293
Playa Vista (Part of Los Angeles)	90094
Playmor	92011
Plaza (Los Angeles County)	91101
Plaza (Orange County)	92666
Plaza (Santa Clara County)	94086
Plaza Camino Real (Part of Carlsbad)	92008
Plaza Center (Part of Ontario)	91762
Plaza Pasadena (Part of Pasadena)	91101
Pleasant Grove	95668
Pleasant Hill	94523
Pleasanton	94566
Pleasant Valley	95667
Pleasant View	93260
Plymouth	95669
Poinsettia Tract	94565
Point Arena	95468
Point Dume	90265
Point Loma (Part of San Diego)	92106
Point Mugu	93042
Point Pleasant	95624
Point Reyes Station	94956
Point Richmond (Part of Richmond)	94807
Poker Flat	95228
Pollock Pines	95726
Pomona	91765-69
For specific Pomona Zip Codes call (714) 623-4476	
Pond	93280
Pondosa	96057
Pope Valley	94567
Poplar	93258
Port Costa	94569
Porter Ranch (Part of Los Angeles)	91326
Porterville	93257-58
For specific Porterville Zip Codes call (209) 784-4272	
Porterville Development Center	93257
Porterville West	93257
Port Hueneme	93041
Port Kenyon	95536
Portola	96122
Portola Valley	94028
Port San Luis	93424
Portuguese Bend (Part of Rancho Palos Verdes)	90274
Posey	93260
Poso Park	93260
Post Office Annex (Part of Burlingame)	94010
Posts	93920

Location	ZIP
Potrero (San Diego County)	92063
Potrero (San Francisco County)	94110
Potter Valley	95469
Poway	92064
Power Tract	93283
Pozo	93453
Prather	93651
Prattville	95923
Presidential Heights (Part of San Clemente)	92672
Preston Heights (Part of Arcata)	95521
Preuss (Part of Los Angeles)	90035
Priest Valley	93210
Princeton (Colusa County)	95970
Princeton (San Mateo County)	94019
Princeton-by-the-Sea	94019
Proberta	96078
Project City	96079
Promenade Mall (Part of Los Angeles)	91367
Prosser Lakeview Estates	95734
Prunedale	93907
Pruneyard, The (Part of Campbell)	95008
Pudding Creek	95437
Puente Junction (Part of City of Industry)	91744
Puerco Beach	90265
Pulga	95965
Pumpkin Center	93309
Putah Creek Park	94558
Quail Valley	92380
Quaking Aspen	93265
Quartz Hill	93536
Quincy	95971
Quincy-East Quincy	95971
Quintette	95634
Quito (Part of Saratoga)	95070
Rackerby	95972
Radec	92343
Rafael Village (Part of Novato)	94947
Rail Road Flat	95248
Rainbow	92028
Raisin	93652
Ralph	95370
Ramirez (Part of Los Angeles)	90037
Ramona	92065
Ramos Village	95336
Ranch, The (Part of Scotts Valley)	95066
Rancheria	95449
Ranch House	92055
Ranchita	92066
Rancho Bernardo (Part of San Diego)	92128
Rancho Buena	96022
Rancho California	92390
Rancho Cordova	95670
Rancho Del Mar	94590
Rancho Del Rey	92011
Rancho La Costa	92008
Rancho Mirage	92270
Rancho Murieta	95683
Rancho Palos Verdes	90274
Rancho Park (Part of Los Angeles)	90064
Rancho Penasquitos (Part of San Diego)	92129
Rancho Rinconado	95014
Rancho San Diego	92041
Rancho Santa Fe	92067
Randall Island	95615
Randolph	96126
Randsburg	93554
Ravendale	96123
Ravenswood (Part of East Palo Alto)	94303
Rawhide	95370
Rawson	96080
Raymond	93653
Red Bank	96080
Red Bluff	96080
Redcrest	95569
Redding	96001-03
For specific Redding Zip Codes call (916) 246-5503	
Red Hill	92705
Redlands	92373-75
For specific Redlands Zip Codes call (714) 793-2171	
Redlands Heights (Part of Redlands)	92373
Red Mountain	93558

Location	ZIP
Redondo Beach	90277-78
For specific Redondo Beach Zip Codes call (213) 376-2472	
Reds Meadow	93546
Red Top	95340
Redway	95560
Redwood City	94061-65
For specific Redwood City Zip Codes call (415) 368-4181	
Redwood Estates	95044
Redwood Grove	95006
Redwood Lodge	95437
Redwood Retreat	95020
Redwood Terrace	94020
Redwood Valley	95470
Reedley	93654
Relief	95959
Requa	95548
Rescue	95672
Reseda (Part of Los Angeles)	91335
Rheem (Part of San Pablo)	94806
Rheem Valley (Part of Moraga)	94570
Rialto	92376-77
For specific Rialto Zip Codes call (714) 875-1522	
Rice	92225
Richardson Springs	95973
Richfield	96021
Richgrove	93261
Richmond	94801-08
For specific Richmond Zip Codes call (415) 232-9709	
Richmond (Part of San Francisco)	94118
Richvale	95974
Ridgecrest	93555
Riego	95626
Rimcrest (Part of Palm Springs)	92264
Rimforest	92378
Rimpau (Part of Los Angeles)	90019
Rimrock	92268
Rincon	92061
Rincon Annex (Part of San Francisco)	94119
Rincon Valley (Part of Santa Rosa)	95405
Rio Bonito	95917
Rio Bravo	93306
Rio Dell (Humboldt County)	95562
Rio Dell (Sonoma County)	95436
Rio Del Mar	95003
Rio Linda	95673
Rio Nido	95471
Rio Oso	95674
Rio Vista	94571
Ripley	92272
Ripon	95366
Ripperdan	93637
Rivera (Part of Pico Rivera)	90660
Riverbank	95367
Riverbank Army Ammunition Plant	95367
Riverdale	93656
River Kern	93238
River Oaks	95045
River Pines	95675
River Road	95350
Riverroad Estates	93637
Riverside	92501-19
For specific Riverside Zip Codes call (714) 351-6686	
Riverside (Part of Newport Beach)	92663
Riverside Grove	95006
Riverside Park	95528
Riverside Plaza (Part of Riverside)	92506
Riverview (Kern County)	93308
Riverview (San Diego County)	92040
Riverview Farms	92040
Riviera Cliff	95204
Roads End	93238
Robbins	95676
Robertsville (Part of San Jose)	95118
Robinsons Corner	95965
Robles Del Rio	93924
Rob Roy Junction	95003
Rockaway Beach (Part of Pacifica)	94044
Rock Creek	95965
Rock Crest	95980
Rock Haven	93664
Rocking Horse Ranchos	90731
Rocklin	95677
Rockport	95488

Rockridge-San Francisco CALIFORNIA 75

	ZIP
Rockridge (Part of Oakland)	94618
Rockville	94585
Rodeo	94572
Rodgers Flat	95980
Rogina Heights	95482
Rohnert Park	94927-28
For specific Rohnert Park Zip Codes call (707) 585-2074	
Rohnerville	95540
Rolinda	93706
Rolling Hills (Los Angeles County)	90274
Rolling Hills (Riverside County)	92306
Rolling Hills Estates (Los Angeles County)	90274
Rolling Hills Estates (San Luis Obispo County)	93401
Rolling Hills Plaza (Part of Torrance)	90505
Rolling Hills Riviera	90731
Rollingwood	94806
Romie Lane (Part of Salinas)	93901
Romoland	92380
Roosevelt Corner	93534
Roosevelt Terrace	94590
Rosamond	93560
Rose Bowl (Part of Pasadena)	91103
Rosedale	93308
Roseland	95407
Rosemead	91770
Rosemead Square (Part of Rosemead)	91770
Rosemont (Sacramento County)	95826
Rosemont (San Diego County)	92065
Roseville	95678
Rosewood (Part of Eureka)	95501
Ross	94957
Ross Corner	92222
Rossmoor	90720
Rossmoor Business Center (Part of Seal Beach)	90740
Rossmoor Highlands (Part of Los Alamitos)	90720
Rough And Ready	95975
Round Hill Country Club	94507
Round Mountain	96084
Round Valley	93514
Round Valley Indian Reservation	95428
Rovana	93514
Rowland (Part of City of Industry)	91743
Rowland Heights	91748
Rubidoux (Riverside County)	92509
Rucker	95020
Rumsey	95679
Running Springs	92382
Rupert	95901
Russian River Terrace	95436
Ruth	95526
Rutherford	94573
Ryde	95680
Sabre City	95678
Sacramento	94203-99
	95801-66
For specific Sacramento Zip Codes call (916) 921-0280	
Sacramento South	95820
Sage	92343
Sage Valley	96113
St. Bernard	96061
St. Francis Heights (Part of Daly City)	94015
St. Helena	94574
St. James Park (Part of San Jose)	95113
St. Johns	93286
St. Marys College (Part of Moraga)	94575
St. Matthew (Part of San Mateo)	94401
Salida	95368
Salinas	93901-15
For specific Salinas Zip Codes call (408) 422-8687	
Salinas Resort	95451
Salmon Creek	94923
Saltdale	93519
Salton City	92274
Salton Sea Beach	92274
Saltus	92304
Salvador (Part of Napa)	94558
Salyer	95563
Samoa	95564
San Andreas	95249

	ZIP
San Anselmo	94960
San Antonio Heights	91786
San Antonio Shopping Center (Part of Mountain View)	94040
San Ardo	93450
San Benito	95043
San Bernardino	92401-27
For specific San Bernardino Zip Codes call (714) 884-3626	
San Bruno	94066
San Carlos (San Diego County)	92119
San Carlos (San Mateo County)	94070
San Clemente	92672-74
For specific San Clemente Zip Codes call (714) 492-3494	
Sand City	93955
Sand Hill	94561
San Diego	**92101-99**
For specific San Diego Zip Codes call (619) 574-0477	

COLLEGES & UNIVERSITIES

National University	92108
Point Loma Nazarene College	92106
San Diego State University	92182
United States International University	92131
University of San Diego	92110

FINANCIAL INSTITUTIONS

The Bank of Rancho Bernardo	92128
The Bank of San Diego	92101
First National Bank	92101
Flagship Federal Savings & Loan Association	92122
Girard Savings Bank	92122
International Savings Bank	92108
Peninsula Bank of San Diego	92106
San Diego National Bank	92112
San Diego Trust & Savings Bank	92101

HOSPITALS

Kaiser Foundation Hospital	92120
Mercy Hospital and Medical Center	92103
Naval Hospital	92134
Sharp Cabrillo Hospital	92110
Sharp Memorial Hospital	92123
University of California San Diego Medical Center	92103
Veterans Administration Medical Center	92161

HOTELS/MOTELS

Bahia Resort Hotel	92109
Best Western Seven Seas Lodge	92108
Catamaran Resort Hotel	92109
Dana Inn & Marina	92109
Hyatt Islandia	92109
Park Manor Hotel	92103
Ramada Inn	92108
San Diego Hilton Beach & Tennis Resort	92109
Sheraton Grand on Harbor Island	92101
Sheraton Harbor Island Hotel-East	92101
The Westgate Hotel	92101

MILITARY INSTALLATIONS

Coast Guard Air Station, San Diego	92101
Defense Subsistence Office, San Diego	92112
Fuel Department, Point Loma Annex, Naval Supply Center	92132
Marine Corps Recruiting Depot, San Diego	92140
Naval Air Station, Miramar	92145
Naval Air Station, North Island	92135
Naval Hospital, San Diego	92134
Naval Ocean Systems Center	92152
Naval Supply Center, San Diego	92132
Naval Training Station, San Diego	92133
San Diego International Airport, Lindbergh Field, Air Force Facility	92101

	ZIP
Supervisor of Shipbuilding, Conversion and Repair, San Diego	92136
San Diego Country Estates	92065
San Dimas	91773
Sandy Korner	92274
San Felipe	95023
San Fernando	91340-46
For specific San Fernando Zip Codes call (818) 365-0683	
Sanford (Part of Los Angeles)	90005
San Francisco	**94101-88**
For specific San Francisco Zip Codes call (415) 550-6500	

COLLEGES & UNIVERSITIES

Golden Gate University	94105
San Francisco State University	94132
University of California Hastings College of Law	94102
University of California-San Francisco	94143
University of San Francisco	94117

FINANCIAL INSTITUTIONS

Bank of America National Trust & Savings Association	94104
The Bank of California, National Association	94104
Bank of Canton of California	94111
Bank of San Francisco	94111
Bank of the Orient	94104
Bank of Trade	94133
California Savings & Loan, A Federal Association	94120
Central Bank	94104
Continental Savings of America, A Savings & Loan Association	94103
Golden Coin Savings & Loan Association	94108
Hamilton Savings Bank, F.S.B.	94111
Home Federal Savings & Loan Association of San Francisco	94108
Homestead Savings, A Federal Savings & Loan Association	94121
Pacific Bank, National Association	94104
Pacific Coast Savings & Loan Association of America	94111
Redwood Bank	94111
Sanwa Bank California	94111
Security Pacific Asian Bank	94111
The Sumitomo Bank of California	94104
Union Bank	94104
United Savings Bank, F.S.B.	94102
Wells Fargo Bank, N.A.	94163

HOSPITALS

Kaiser Foundation Hospital	94115
Laguna Honda Hospital and Rehabilitation Center	94116
Letterman Army Medical Center	94129
Mount Zion Hospital and Medical Center	94115
Pacific Presbyterian Medical Center	94118
San Francisco General Hospital Medical Center	94110
St. Francis Memorial Hospital	94109
St. Mary's Hospital and Medical Center	94117
University of California, San Francisco Medical Center	94143
Veterans Administration Medical Center	94121

HOTELS/MOTELS

Best Western Americania	94103
Hyatt on Union Square	94108
The Mark Hopkins Inter-Continental	94108
Miyako Hotel	94115
Park 55 Hotel	94102
San Francisco Airport Hilton	94128
San Francisco Marriott Fisherman's Wharf	94133
Sir Francis Drake	94102

76 CALIFORNIA San Francisco

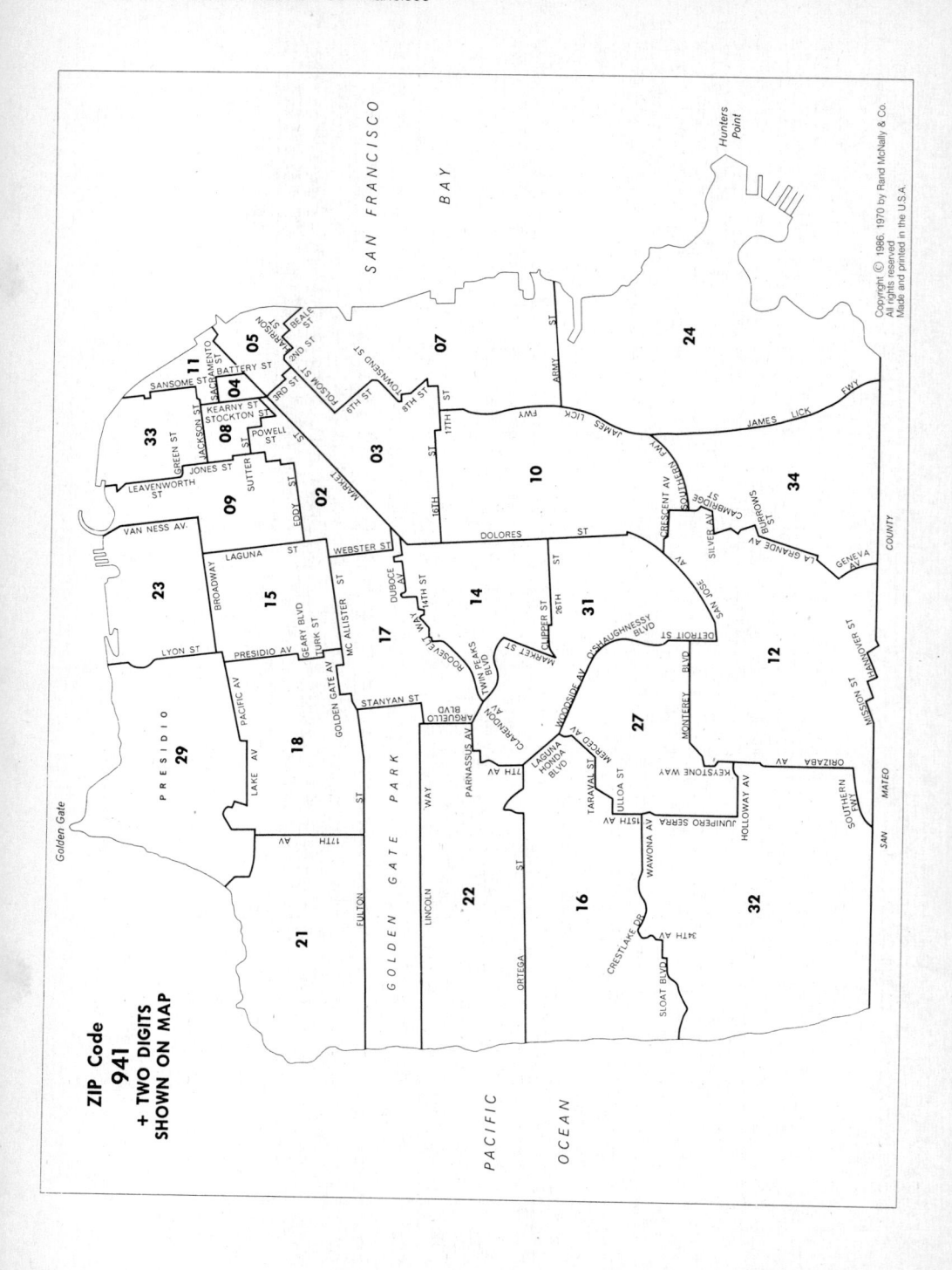

San Francisco-Smoke Tree **CALIFORNIA** 77

	ZIP
The Stanford Court Hotel	94108
MILITARY INSTALLATIONS	
Coast Guard Air Station, San Francisco	94128
Coast Guard Industrial Base, Yerba Buena Island	94130
Letterman Army Medical Center	94129
Naval Station, Treasure Island	94130
Presidio of San Francisco	94129
San Francisco International Airport, Air Force Facility	94128
United States Army Engineer District, San Francisco	94105
San Francisco Recreation Camp	95655
San Gabriel	91775-78
For specific San Gabriel Zip Codes call (818) 287-9661	
Sanger	93657
San Geronimo	94963
San Gregorio	94074
San Jacinto	92383
San Joaquin	93660
San Joaquin River Club	95385
San Jose	95101-96
For specific San Jose Zip Codes call (608) 452-0660	
San Jose (recreation area)	95321
San Juan Bautista	95045
San Juan Capistrano	92690-93
For specific San Juan Capistrano Zip Codes call (714) 364-5020	
San Juan Plaza (Part of San Juan Capistrano)	92675
San Lawrence Terrace	93451
San Leandro	94577-79
For specific San Leandro Zip Codes call (415) 483-0550	
San Lorenzo	94580
San Lorenzo Park	95006
San Lucas	93954
San Luis Obispo	93401-12
For specific San Luis Obispo Zip Codes call (805) 543-1882	
San Luis Rey (Part of Oceanside)	92068
San Luis Rey Heights	92028
San Marcos	92069
San Marin (Part of Novato)	94947
San Marino	91108
San Martin	95046
San Mateo	94401-04
For specific San Mateo Zip Codes call (415) 349-2301	
San Mateo Fashion Island (Part of San Mateo)	94404
San Miguel	93451
San Onofre	92672
San Pablo	94806
San Pasqual	92025
San Pedro	90731-34
For specific San Pedro Zip Codes call (213) 831-3246	
San Quentin	94964
San Rafael	94901-15
For specific San Rafael Zip Codes call (415) 459-0944	
San Ramon	94583
San Ramon Village (Part of Dublin)	94568
San Roque (Part of Santa Barbara)	93105
San Simeon	93452
San Simeon Acres	93452
Santa Ana	92701-08
	92711-12
	92721-28
For specific Santa Ana Codes call (714) 662-6345	
Santa Ana Heights	92701
Santa Ana Marine Corps Air Facility	92709
Santa Anita Fashion Park (Part of Arcadia)	91006
Santa Barbara	93101-90
For specific Santa Barbara Zip Codes call (805) 564-2266	
Santa Clara	95050-55
For specific Santa Clara Zip Codes call (408) 296-1881	
Santa Clarita	91321-22
	91350-51
	91354-55
	91380-86
For specific Santa Clarita Zip Codes call (805) 254-1684	

	ZIP
Santa Cruz	95060-67
For specific Santa Cruz Zip Codes call (408) 426-5200	
Santa Cruz Gardens	95060
Santa Fe Plaza	90605
Santa Fe Springs	90670-71
For specific Santa Fe Springs Zip Codes call (213) 868-3731	
Santa Margarita	93453
Santa Maria	93454-56
For specific Santa Maria Zip Codes call (805) 922-1911	
Santa Maria Town Center (Part of Santa Maria)	93454
Santa Monica	90401-06
For specific Santa Monica Zip Codes call (213) 393-0716	
Santa Monica Canyon (Part of Los Angeles)	90406
Santa Monica Place (Part of Santa Monica)	90401
Santa Nella	95322
Santa Paula	93060
Santa Rita (Monterey County)	93901
Santa Rita (Santa Barbara County)	93436
Santa Rita Park	93661
Santa Rosa	95401-09
For specific Santa Rosa Zip Codes call (707) 528-8763	
Santa Rosa Indian Reservation	92343
Santa Rosa Island Air Force Station	93041
Santa Rosa Plaza (Part of Santa Rosa)	95401
Santa Susana (Part of Simi Valley)	93063
Santa Venetia	94901
Santa Western (Part of Los Angeles)	90072
Santa Ynez	93460
Santa Ysabel	92070
Santa Ysabel Indian Reservation	92070
Santee	92071
San Ysidro (Part of San Diego)	92173
Saranap	94596
Saratoga	95070-71
For specific Saratoga Zip Codes call (408) 867-3086	
Sather Gate (Part of Berkeley)	94704
Saticoy (Part of Ventura)	93004
Sattley	96124
Saugus (Part of Santa Clarita)	91350
Sausalito	94965-66
For specific Sausalito Zip Codes call (415) 332-4656	
Saviers (Part of Oxnard)	93033
Sawyers Bar	96027
Scenic Brook Estates	95370
Scenic Center (Part of Modesto)	95350
Scheelite	93514
Scheideck	93252
Schellville	95476
Scotia	95565
Scotland	92358
Scott Bar	96085
Scotts Valley	95066-67
For specific Scotts Valley Zip Codes call (408) 438-0121	
Seacliff	95003
Seahaven	94937
Seal Beach	90740
Seal Beach Naval Weapons Station	90740
Seal Cove	94038
Searles Valley	93562
Seaside	93955
Sebastiani (Part of Sonoma)	95476
Sebastopol	95472-73
For specific Sebastopol Zip Codes call (707) 823-3191	
Sebastopol	95960
Sedco Hills	92330
Seeley	92273
Seiad Valley	96086
Selby	94572
Selma	93662
Seneca	95923
Sepulveda (Part of Los Angeles)	91343
Sequoia Crest	93265
Sequoia Mall (Part of Visalia)	93277
Sequoia National Park	93262

	ZIP
Serena Park	93013
Serra Mesa (Part of San Diego)	92123
Serramonte (Part of Daly City)	94015
Serramonte Center (Part of Daly City)	94015
Sespe	93015
Seven Oaks	92305
Seville	93277
Shady Glen	95713
Shafter	93263
Shandon	93461
Sharpe Army Depot	95330
Sharp Park (Part of Pacifica)	94044
Shasta	96087
Shaver Lake	93664
Shaver Lake Heights	93664
Shaver Lake Point	93664
Shaw City (Part of Fresno)	93704
Sheepranch	95250
Sheldon	95624
Shell Beach (Part of Pismo Beach)	93449
Shelter Cove (Humboldt County)	95489
Shelter Cove (San Mateo County)	94044
Sheridan	95681
Sherman Island	94571
Sherman Oaks (Part of Los Angeles)	91403
Sherman Oaks Fashion Square (Part of Los Angeles)	91423
Sherman Oaks Galleria (Part of Los Angeles)	91403
Sherwin Plaza (Part of Mammoth Lakes)	93546
Sherwood (Part of Salinas)	93906
Sherwood Forest	94803
Sherwood Mall (Part of Stockton)	95207
Shingle Springs	95682
Shingletown	96088
Shively	95565
Shore Acres	94565
Short Acres	93230
Shoshone	92384
Sierra (Part of Fresno)	93703
Sierra Army Depot	96113
Sierra Brooks	96118
Sierra Cedars	93664
Sierra City	96125
Sierra Conservation Center	95327
Sierra Heights	93247
Sierra Madre	91024
Sierra Pines	89439
Sierra Sky Park (Part of Fresno)	93711
Sierra Village No.1	95346
Sierraville	96126
Signal Hill	90806
Silverado	92676
Silver City	93271
Silver Fork	95720
Silver Lake	95666
Silver Strand (Part of Oxnard)	93030
Simi Valley	93062-65
For specific Simi Valley Zip Codes call (805) 526-1331	
Simmler	93453
Simms (Marin County)	94901
Simms (San Joaquin County)	95366
Sisquoc	93454
Sites	95979
Skaggs Island	95476
Skyforest	92385
Skyhigh	95223
Skyline East	92311
Skyline North	92311
Sky Londa (Part of Woodside)	94062
Sky Valley	92240
Sleepy Hollow (Marin County)	94960
Sleepy Hollow (San Bernardino County)	91710
Slide Inn	95335
Sloat	96103
Sloughhouse	95683
Smartville	95977
Smiley Heights (Part of Redlands)	92373
Smiley Park	92382
Smithflat	95667
Smith River	95567
Smoke Tree (Part of Palm Springs)	92262

78 CALIFORNIA Snelling-Temecula

	ZIP		ZIP		ZIP
Snelling	95369	Spring Valley	92077-78	Sunnyslope (Butte County)	95914
Snow Creek	92282	For specific Spring Valley Zip Codes call (619) 670-9815		Sunnyslope (Riverside County)	92509
Snowline	95709			Sunnyvale	94086-89
Soboba Hot Springs	92383	Spring Valley Lake	92392	For specific Sunnyvale Zip Codes call (408) 732-0121	
Soda Bay	95451	Springville	93265		
Soda Springs	95728	Spruce Point	95501	Sunnyvale Town Center (Part of Sunnyvale)	94086
Solana Beach	92075	Spurgeon (Part of Santa Ana)	92701		
Solano Mall (Part of Fairfield)	94533	Squaw Valley	93675	Sunny Vista (Part of Chula Vista)	92010
Soledad	93960	Squirrel Valley	93240		
Solemint (Part of Santa Clarita)	91350	Stadium (Part of Anaheim)	92825	Sunol	94586
		Stafford	95565	Sunrise Mall	95610
Solvang	93463	Stamoules	93640	Sunrise Oasis (Part of Palm Springs)	92262
Somerset	95684	Standard	95373		
Somesbar	95568	Standish	96128	Sunrise Vista	95451
Somis	93066	Stanford	94305	Sunset (Humboldt County)	95521
Sonoma	95476	Stanford Shopping Center (Part of Palo Alto)	94304	Sunset (San Francisco County)	94122
Sonoma Vista	95476				
Sonora	95370	Stanton	90680	Sunset Beach (Orange County)	90742
Sonora Junction	93517	State Capitol (Part of Sacramento)	95814		
Soquel	95073			Sunset Beach (Santa Cruz County)	95076
Sorensens	96120	Stateline (Part of South Lake Tahoe)	95729		
Soto (Part of Huntington Park)	90255			Sunset Cliffs (Part of San Diego)	92107
		State Street (Part of Huntington Park)	90255		
Soulsbyville	95372			Sunset Hills	91745
South Alhambra (Part of Alhambra)	91803	Steele Park	94558	Sunset Terrace	93402
		Steinbeck (Part of Salinas)	93901	Sunset Tract	93022
South Belridge	93251	Stent	95370	Sunset View	95945
South Berkeley (Part of Berkeley)	94703	Stephens (Part of Santa Fe Springs)	90670	Sunset Whitney Ranch (Part of Rocklin)	95677
South Coast Plaza and Town Center (Part of Costa Mesa)	92626	Sterling Park	94014	Sunshine Homes	91350
		Stevinson	95374	Sunshine Summit	92302
		Stewarts Point	95480	Sunvalley (Contra Costa County)	94520
South Corona (Part of Corona)	91720	Stewart Springs	96094		
		Stine Station (Part of Bakersfield)	93309	Sun Valley (Los Angeles County)	91352
South Dos Palos	93665				
South Downey (Part of Downey)	90242	Stinson Beach	94970	Sun Village (Part of Palmdale)	93550
		Stirling City	95978		
Southeastern (Part of San Diego)	92113	Stockdale (Part of Bakersfield)	93309	Surf	93436
				Surfside (Part of Seal Beach)	90743
South El Monte	91733	Stockton	95201-13		
South Fontana (Part of Fontana)	92335	For specific Stockton Zip Codes call (209) 983-6317		Susana Knolls (Part of Simi Valley)	93063
				Susanville	96130
South Fork (Humboldt County)	95569	Stonegate (Part of Portola Valley)	94028	Sutter	95982
				Sutter Creek	95685
South Fork (Madera County)	93643	Stonehurst (Part of Oakland)	94603	Sutter Hill	95685
South Fork (Mariposa County)	95318			Sutter Island	95615
		Stone Lagoon	95570	Sutter Street (Part of San Francisco)	94104
South Gardena (Part of Gardena)	90247	Stonestown (Part of San Francisco)	94132		
				Swanton	95017
South Gate	90280	Stonewood Shopping Center (Part of Downey)	90241	Sweet Brier	96017
South Hills (Part of West Covina)	91791			Sweetwater	95451
		Stonyford	95979	Sycamore (Colusa County)	95957
South Laguna	92677	Storey	93637	Sycamore (Contra Costa County)	94526
South Lake	93240	Storrie	95980		
South Lake Tahoe	95702	Stovepipe Wells	92328	Sylmar (Part of Los Angeles)	91345
	95705-08	Stratford	93266		
For specific South Lake Tahoe Zip Codes call (916) 544-2208		Strathmore	93267	Sylvia Park	90290
		Strawberry (El Dorado County)	95720	Table Bluff	95551
Southland Shopping Center (Part of Hayward)	94545			Taft	93268
		Strawberry (Tuolumne County)	95375	Taft Heights	93268
South Leggett	95455			Tahoe City	95730
South Main (Part of Santa Ana)	92707	Strawberry Point	94941	Tahoe Keys (Part of South Lake Tahoe)	95702
		Strawberry Valley	95981		
South Modesto	95350	Stuart	92055	Tahoe Paradise	95705-08
South Oroville (Butte County)	95965	Studebaker (Part of Norwalk)	90650	For specific Tahoe Paradise Zip Codes call (916) 577-8187	
		Studio City (Part of Los Angeles)	91604		
South Pasadena	91030			Tahoe Pines	95718
Southport (Part of West Sacramento)	95691	Suburban Acres	96080	Tahoe Valley (Part of South Lake Tahoe)	95731
		Success	93257		
South San Francisco	94080-83	Sugarloaf	92386	Tahoe Vista	95732
For specific South San Francisco Zip Codes call (415) 588-2855		Sugarloaf Mountain Park	93260	Tahoma	95733
		Sugar Pine (Madera County)	93644	Talica (Part of Oceanside)	92054
South San Gabriel	91770	Sugar Pine (Tuolumne County)	95346	Talmage	95481
South San Jose Hills	91744			Tamalpais-Homestead Valley	94941
South San Leandro (Part of San Leandro)	94578	Suisun City	94585		
		Sulphur Springs	93060	Tamalpais Valley	94941
South Shafter	93263	Sultana	93666	Tamarack	95223
South Shore Shopping Center (Part of Alameda)	94501	Summer Home	95336	Tambs Station	95370
		Summerhome Park	95436	Tanforan (Part of South San Francisco)	94080
South Taft	93268	Summerland	93067		
South Turlock	95380	Summit	92345	Tanforan Park (Part of San Bruno)	94066
South Whittier	90605	Summit City	96089		
South Whittier Heights	90605	Sun City	92380-81	Tangair	93437
South Yuba City	95991	For specific Sun City Zip Codes call (714) 679-1737		Tanglewood	95018
Spanish Flat (El Dorado County)	95633			Tara Hills	94564
		Sunfair	92252	Tara Hills-Montalvin Manor	94806
Spanish Flat (Napa County)	94558	Sunkist (Part of Anaheim)	92806	Tarpey	93727
Spanish Hills	91720	Sunland (Part of Los Angeles)	91040	Tarzana (Part of Los Angeles)	91356
Spanish Ranch	95956				
Spaulding Tract	96130	Sunny Brae (Part of Arcata)	95521	Tassajara Hot Springs	93924
Spicer City	93206	Sunnybrook	95640	Taurusa	93277
Spreckels	93962	Sunny Hills (Part of Fullerton)	92632	Taylorsville	95983
Spring Creek Tract	95731			Tecate	92080
Springfield	95370	Sunnymead	92388	Tecnor	96058
Spring Garden	95971	Sunnyside (Fresno County)	93727	Tecopa	92389
Spring Hill	95945	Sunnyside (Placer County)	95730	Tecopa Hot Springs	92389
Springstowne (Part of Vallejo)	94591	Sunnyside (San Diego County)	92002	Tehachapi	93561
				Tehama	96090
		Sunnyside-Tahoe City	95730	Temecula	92390

Temelec-Waddington **CALIFORNIA** 79

Name	ZIP
Temelec	95476
Temple City	91780
Templeton	93465
Tennant	96058
Tent City (Part of Coronado)	92118
Terminal Annex (Part of Los Angeles)	90054
Terminous	95240
Termo	96132
Terra Bella	93270
Terra Linda (Part of San Rafael)	94901
Tewksbury Heights	94805
Textile (Part of Los Angeles)	90015
The Falls	93604
The Forks (Madera County)	93604
The Forks (Mendocino County)	95482
The Geysers	95425
The Hermitage	95455
The Oaks	95945
The Pines	93604
Thermal	92274
Thermalito	95965
The Sea Ranch	95497
Thomas Mountain	92361
Thornton	95686
Thousand Oaks	91359-62
For specific Thousand Oaks Zip Codes call (805) 497-8661	
Thousand Palms	92276
Three Arch Bay	92677
Three Point	93532
Three Rivers	93271
Three Rocks	93608
Tiburon	94920
Tierra Buena	95991
Tierra del Sol	92005
Tionesta	96134
Tipton	93272
Tivy Valley	93657
Tobin	95965
Tocaloma	94950
Todd Valley	95631
Todos Santos (Part of Concord)	94522
Tollhouse	93667
Toluca Lake (Part of Los Angeles)	91602
Tomales	94971
Toms Place	93514
Tonyville	93247
Toolville	93221
Topanga	90290
Topanga Beach	90265
Topanga Oaks	90290
Topanga Park	90290
Topanga Plaza (Part of Los Angeles)	91303
Topa Topa	93060
Topaz	96133
Top of the World (Part of Laguna Beach)	92651
Tormey	94572
Torrance	90501-10
For specific Torrance Zip Codes call (213) 328-9363	
Torres-Martinez Indian Reservation	92274
Torrey Pines Homes (Part of San Diego)	92037
Tower (Part of Fresno)	93728
Town and Country (Riverside County)	92388
Town and Country (Sacramento County)	95821
Town Center (Part of Visalia)	93291
Toyon	96019
Trabuco Canyon	92678
Tracy	95376-78
For specific Tracy Zip Codes call (209) 835-4774	
Tranquillity	93668
Traver	93673
Tres Pinos	95075
Trevarno (Part of Livermore)	94550
Trigo	93637
Trimmer	93657
Trinidad	95570
Trinity Alps	96052
Trinity Center	96091
Trinity Village	95527
Triple R Estates	93257
Trona	93562
Tropico (Part of Glendale)	91204
Tropico Village	93560
Trowbridge	95659
Truckee	95734

Name	ZIP
Tujunga (Part of Los Angeles)	91042
Tulare	93274-75
For specific Tulare Zip Codes call (209) 686-1594	
Tulare East	93274
Tulare Northwest	93274
Tulelake	96134
Tule River Indian Reservation	93257
Tunitas	94109
Tuolumne	95379
Tuolumne Meadows	95389
Tupman	93276
Turlock	95380-81
For specific Turlock Zip Codes call (209) 632-3801	
Tustin	92680-81
For specific Tustin Zip Codes call (714) 544-5170	
Tustin Foothills	92680
Tuttle	95340
Tuttletown	95370
Tuxedo Country Club Estates	95204
Tuxedo Park (Part of Stockton)	95204
T.V. Bell (Part of Merced)	95340
Twain	95984
Twain Harte	95383
Tweedy (Part of South Gate)	90280
Twentynine Palms	92277-78
For specific Twentynine Palms Zip Codes call (619) 367-3501	
Twentynine Palms Base	92278
Twentynine Palms Marine Corps Base	92278
Twentytwo Mile House	93637
Twin Bridges	95735
Twin Creeks	95120
Twin Lakes	95060
Twin Oaks	92069
Twin Peaks	92391
Two Rock Coast Guard Station	94952
Tyler Mall (Part of Riverside)	92503
Ukiah	95482
Ulmar (Part of Livermore)	94550
Union (Part of Napa)	94558
Union City	94587
Union Hill	95945
Universal City	91608
University (Orange County)	92716
University (Santa Barbara County)	93107
University City (Part of San Diego)	92122
University Heights	94025
University of California-Davis	95616
University of Santa Clara (Part of Santa Clara)	95050
University Towne Centre (Part of San Diego)	92121
Upland	91785-86
For specific Upland Zip Codes call (714) 981-2824	
Upper Lake	95485
Uptown (Part of San Bernardino)	92405
Vaca (Part of Vacaville)	95687
Vacation	95446
Vacaville	95687-88
For specific Vacaville Zip Codes call (707) 448-3516	
Valencia (Part of Santa Clarita)	91354
Valinda	91744
Valla (Part of Santa Fe Springs)	90670
Vallco Fashion Park (Part of Cupertino)	95014
Vallecito	95251
Vallecitos Town Center (Part of San Marcos)	92069
Vallejo	94589-92
For specific Vallejo Zip Codes call (707) 642-4441	
Vallemar (Part of Pacifica)	94044
Valle Vista (Alameda County)	94541
Valle Vista (Riverside County)	92343
Valley Acres	93268
Valley Center	92082
Valleydale	91702
Valley Estates	93283
Valley Fair (Part of San Jose)	95128
Valley Ford	94972
Valley Home	95384

Name	ZIP
Valley Lake Ranchos	93637
Valley of Enchantment	92325
Valley of the Moon	92325
Valley Plaza (Imperial County)	92243
Valley Plaza (Kern County)	93304
Valley Plaza (Los Angeles County)	91606
Valley Springs	95252
Valley View Park	92325
Valley Village (Part of Los Angeles)	91607
Valona	94525
Val Verde Park	91350
Valyermo	93563
Vandenberg AFB	93437
Vandenberg Air Force Base	93437
Vandenberg Village	93436
Van Nuys	91401-36
For specific Van Nuys Zip Codes call (818) 908-6608	
Vanowen (Part of Los Angeles)	91405
Venice	90291-96
For specific Venice Zip Codes call (213) 396-3191	
Ventucopa	93252
Ven-tu Park (Part of Thousand Oaks)	91320
Ventura	93001-07
For specific Ventura Zip Codes call (805) 643-5457	
Verdemont	92402
Verdi	89439
Verdugo City (Part of Glendale)	91046
Verdugo Viejo (Part of Glendale)	91206
Vernalis	95385
Vernon	90058
Verona	95659
Verona Landing	95659
Veteran Heights	94508
Veterans Administration	90073
Veterans Bureau Hospital (Part of Palo Alto)	94304
Veterans Home (Part of Yountville)	94599
Veterans Hospital (Part of Los Angeles)	91343
Victor	95253
Victoria Court (Part of Santa Barbara)	93101
Victoria Park (Part of Carson)	90247
Victorville	92392-93
For specific Victorville Zip Codes call (619) 245-7723	
Victory Center (Part of Los Angeles)	91606
Vidal (San Bernardino County)	92225
View Park	90043
View Park-Windsor Hills	90043
Viking (Part of Long Beach)	90808
Village (Part of Los Angeles)	90024
Villa Grande	95486
Villa Park	92667
Villa Verona	95965
Vina	96092
Vineburg	95487
Vine Hill	94553
Vine Hill-Pacheco	94553
Vintage Faire Mall (Part of Modesto)	95356
Vinton	96135
Vinvale (Part of South Gate)	90280
Viola	96088
Virginia Colony	93021
Virner	95634
Visalia	93277-79
For specific Visalia Zip Codes call (209) 732-8073	
Visalia Mall (Part of Visalia)	93277
Visitacion (Part of San Francisco)	94134
Vista	92083-84
For specific Vista Zip Codes call (619) 726-0772	
Vista Del Mar (Part of San Clemente)	92672
Vista del Morro	93402
Vista Grande	93637
Vista La Mesa (Part of La Mesa)	92041
Vista Park	93307
Volcano	95689
Volta	93635
Vorden	95690
Waddington	95536

80 CALIFORNIA Wagner-Zenia

Name	ZIP
Wagner (Part of Los Angeles)	90047
Wagy Flats	93240
Walerga	95660
Walker (Los Angeles County)	90201
Walker (Mono County)	96107
Walker Landing	95690
Wallace	95254
Walnut	91789
Walnut Creek	94593-98
For specific Walnut Creek Zip Codes call (415) 935-1842	
Walnut Creek West	94598
Walnut Grove	95690
Walnut Heights	94596
Walnut Park	90255
Walteria (Part of Torrance)	90505
Warm Springs (Part of Fremont)	94539
Warner Ranch	92388
Warner Springs	92086
Wasco	93280
Washington (Los Angeles County)	91104
Washington (Los Angeles County)	90011
Washington (Nevada County)	95986
Washington Flat	95543
Washington Manor (Part of San Leandro)	94579
Waterford	95386
Waterloo	95205
Watson (Part of Carson)	90744
Watsonville	95076-77
For specific Watsonville Zip Codes call (408) 724-2262	
Watts (Part of Los Angeles)	90002
Watts Valley	93667
Waukena	93282
Waverly Heights (Part of Thousand Oaks)	91360
Wawona	95389
Weaverville	96093
Webster Street (Part of Alameda)	94501
Weed	96094
Weed Patch	93241
Weimar	95736
Weitchpec	95546
Weldon	93283
Wendel	96136
Weott	95571
West (Part of West Hollywood)	90069
West Adams (Part of Los Angeles)	90016
West Arcadia (Part of Arcadia)	91006
West Athens	90247
West Butte	95953
West Carson	90502
Westchester (Part of Los Angeles)	90045
West Compton	90220
West Covina	91790-93
For specific West Covina Zip Codes call (818) 962-8611	
West Covina Fashion Plaza (Part of West Covina)	91790
Westend	93562
Western Pacific Mole (Part of Oakland)	94607
Western Village	93501
Westfield (Part of Rancho Palos Verdes)	90274
West Garden Grove (Part of Garden Grove)	92645
Westgate (Santa Clara County)	95117
Westgate (Ventura County)	91360
Westgate Mall (Part of San Jose)	95129
West Guernewood	95446
Westhaven (Fresno County)	93245
Westhaven (Humboldt County)	95570
West Hollywood	90069
Westlake (San Mateo County)	94014
Westlake (San Mateo County)	94015
Westlake Shopping Center (Part of Daly City)	94015
Westlake Village (Los Angeles County)	91361
Westlake Village (Ventura County)	91360

Name	ZIP
Westley	95387
West Los Angeles (Part of Los Angeles)	90025
West Menlo Park	94025
Westminster	92683-84
For specific Westminster Zip Codes call (714) 898-4929	
Westminster Mall (Part of Westminster)	92683
West Modesto	95351
Westmont	90044
Westmorland	92281
West Palm Springs	92282
West Parlier	93648
West Pittsburg (Contra Costa County)	94565
West Point	95255
Westport	95488
West Portal (Part of San Francisco)	94127
West Puente Valley	91744
West Sacramento	95691
West Saticoy (Part of Ventura)	93001
Westside (San Bernardino County)	92411
Westside (Stanislaus County)	95350
Westside Pavilion (Part of Los Angeles)	90074
West Truckee	95737
Westvern (Part of Los Angeles)	90062
West Whittier	90606
West Whittier-Los Nietos	90606
Westwood (Lassen County)	96137
Westwood (Los Angeles County)	90024
Westwood Manor	96001
Westwood Village (Part of Arcata)	95521
Wheatland	95692
Wheeler Ridge	93301
Wherry Housing	93523
Whiskeytown	96095
Whispering Pines (Lake County)	95461
Whispering Pines (San Diego County)	92036
White Hall	95726
White Oak (Part of Los Angeles)	91416
White Pines	95223
White River (Tulare County)	93257
White River (Tulare County)	93207
White Rock	95630
Whitethorn	95489
White Water	92282
Whitley Gardens	93446
Whitlow	95554
Whitmore	96096
Whitmore Hot Springs	93546
Whitner Heights	93648
Whittier	90601-12
For specific Whittier Zip Codes call (213) 698-9921	
Whittier Quad Shopping Center (Part of Whittier)	90605
Whittwood Mall (Part of Whittier)	90603
Wiest	92227
Wilbur Springs	95987
Wilcox (Part of Los Angeles)	90038
Wildflower	93662
Wildomar	92395
Wildwood (Santa Cruz County)	95006
Wildwood (Trinity County)	96001
Wilfred	95401
Willaura Estates	95949
William H. Taft (Part of San Diego)	92117
Williams	95987
Willits	95490
Willow Brook	90222
Willow Creek (Humboldt County)	95573
Willow Creek (Plumas County)	96020
Willow Ranch	96108
Willows	95988
Willow Springs (Kern County)	93560
Willow Springs (Mono County)	93517
Willow Springs (Tuolumne County)	95372

Name	ZIP
Willow Valley	95959
Will Rogers (Part of Santa Monica)	90403
Wilmar (Part of Rosemead)	91770
Wilmington (Part of Los Angeles)	90744
Wilmington Park (Part of Los Angeles)	90744
Wilseyville	95257
Wilsona	93534
Wilson Acres	96080
Wilsona Gardens	93534
Wilsonia	93633
Wilton	95693
Winchester	92396
Windsor	95492
Windsor Hills	90052
Windy Acres	93283
Winnetka (Part of Los Angeles)	91306
Winter Gardens	92040
Winterhaven	92283
Winters	95694
Winterwarm	92028
Winton	95388
Wise (Part of El Segundo)	90245
Wiseburn (Part of Hawthorne)	90250
Wishon	93669
Witch Creek	92065
Witter Springs	95493
Wofford Heights	93285
Wolf	95603
Wonderland	96003
Woodacre	94973
Woodbridge	95258
Woodcrest	92504
Woodfords	96120
Woodlake	93286
Woodland	95695
Woodland Hills	91364-72
For specific Woodland Hills Zip Codes call (818) 347-4056	
Woodleaf	95925
Woodruff Avenue (Part of Bellflower)	90706
Woodside	94062
Woodside Glens (Part of Woodside)	94062
Woodson Bridge Estates	96021
Woodville	93258
Woodward Park (Part of Fresno)	93729
Woody	93287
Workman (Part of South Gate)	90280
Worldway Postal Center (Part of Los Angeles)	90009
Wrights Lake	95720
Wrightwood	92397
Wyandotte	95965
Wynola	92070
Wyntoon	96091
Yale (Part of Hemet)	92343
Yankee Hill	95965
Yankee Jims	95631
Yerba Buena Island (Part of San Francisco)	94130
Yermo	92398
Yettem	93670
Ygnacio Valley (Part of Walnut Creek)	94598
Yolanda (Part of San Anselmo)	94960
Yolo	95697
Yorba (Part of Pomona)	91767
Yorba Linda	92686
York (Part of Los Angeles)	90050
Yorkville	95494
Yosemite Lodge	95389
Yosemite National Park	95389
Yountville	94599
Yreka	96097
Yuba City	95991-92
For specific Yuba City Zip Codes call (916) 673-9153	
Yuba City Farm Labor Center	95991
Yucaipa (San Bernardino County)	92399
Yucca Valley	92284-86
For specific Yucca Valley Zip Codes call (619) 365-3855	
Zamora	95698
Zayante	95018
Zenia	95495

Acres Green-Crisman **COLORADO** 81

	ZIP		ZIP		ZIP
Acres Green	80124	Berthoud Falls	80438	Central City	80427
Adams	80022	Berthoud Pass	80452	Chaddsford (Part of Aurora)	80014
Adams City (Part of Commerce City)	80022	Bethune	80805	Chama	81126
Agate	80101	Beulah	81023	Chambers Square (Part of Aurora)	80011
Aguilar	81020	Beverly Hills	80104	Chapel Hills	80907
Airport Mail Facility (Part of Denver)	80207	Big Bend	81092	Chatfield Estates	80123
Akron	80720	Big Elk Meadows	80540	Chautauqua (Part of Boulder)	80302
Alameda (Part of Lakewood)	80215	Black Forest	80908	Cheraw	81030
Alamosa	81101-02	Black Hawk	80422	Cherry Creek (Part of Denver)	80206
For specific Alamosa Zip Codes call (719) 589-4908		Blanca	81123	Cherry Creek Shopping Center (Part of Denver)	80206
		Blende	81006		
		Blue Mountain	81610		
Alamosa East	81101	Blue Mountain Estates	80401	Cherry Hills Crest	80120
Alcott (Part of Denver)	80212	Blue Ridge	80424	Cherry Hills Manor	80120
Alder	81155	Blue River	80424	Cherry Hills Village	80110
Allenspark	80510	Blue Valley	80452	Cherry Knolls	80120
Allison	81137	Bonanza City	81155	Cherry Park	80110
Alma	80420	Boncarbo	81024	Cherry Valley	80116
Almont	81210	Bond	80423	Cherrywood Village	80120
Alpine (Chaffee County)	81236	Bondad	81301	Cheyenne Canon (Part of Colorado Springs)	80907
Alpine (Rio Grande County)	81154	Boone	81025		
Altura (Part of Aurora)	80011	Boulder	80301-08		
Altura Annex (Part of Aurora)	80011	For specific Boulder Zip Codes call (303) 938-1100		Cheyenne Wells	80810
		Boulder Heights	80302	Chimney Rock	81127
Alvin	80758	Bountiful	81140	Chipita Park	80809
American City	80427	Bovina	80818	Chivington	81031
Ames	81426	Bowie	81428	Chromo	81128
Amherst	80721	Bow Mar	80120	Chula Vista	80401
Andersonville (Part of Fort Collins)	80521	Boxelder Estates	80521	Cimarron	81220
		Boyero	80806	Cimarron Hills	80906
Angel Acres	80433	Bracewell	80631	Cinderella City (Part of Englewood)	80110
Antlers	81650	Brandon	81026		
Anton	80801	Branson	81027	Citadel, The (Part of Colorado Springs)	80909
Antonito	81120	Breckenridge	80424		
Apache City	81089	Breen	81326	Clark	80428
Apex	80427	Brewster	81226	Clifton	81520
Appleton	81501	Briargate (Part of Colorado Springs)	80918	Climax	80429
Applewood (Jefferson County)	80401			Coal Creek	81221
		Brigadoon Glen	80501	Coaldale	81222
Applewood Village (Part of Wheat Ridge)	80033	Briggsdale	80611	Coalmont	80430
		Brighton	80601	Cokedale	81032
Arabian Acres	80816	Bristol	81028	Collbran	81624
Arapahoe	80802	Broadmoor (Part of Colorado Springs)	80906	College Heights (Part of Durango)	81301
Arapahoe Park (Part of Greenwood Village)	80112				
		Broadway Estates	80120	Colona	81401
Arboles	81121	Broken Arrow Acres	80433	Colorado City (El Paso County)	80904
Aristocrat Ranchettes	80621	Brook Forest	80439		
Arlington	81021	Brook Forest Estates	80439	Colorado City (Pueblo County)	81019
Aroya	80862	Brookridge	80120		
Arriba	80804	Brookside	81212	Colorado Mountain Estates	80816
Arriola	81323	Brookvale	80439	Colorado Sierra	80401
Arvada	80001-05	Broomfield	80020-21	Colorado Springs	80901-99
For specific Arvada Zip Codes call (303) 421-2200		For specific Broomfield Zip Codes call (303) 466-1711		For specific Colorado Springs Zip Codes call (303) 570-5377	
Aspen	81611-15	Brownlee	80480	Colorado Technical College	80907
For specific Aspen Zip Codes call (303) 925-7523		Brownsville	80026	Columbine (Jefferson County)	80123
		Brush	80723		
		Buckeye	80549	Columbine (Jefferson County)	80120
Aspen-Gerbaz	81611	Buckingham (Part of Fort Collins)	80521		
Aspen Park	80433			Columbine (Routt County)	80428
Association Camp	80511	Buckingham Plaza (Part of Aurora)	80012	Columbine Hills	80120
Atwood	80722			Columbine Knolls	80120
Ault	80610	Buckingham Square (Part of Aurora)	80012	Columbine Knolls South	80123
Aurora	80010-19			Columbine Manor	80120
	80040-46	Buda	80513	Columbine Valley	80123
For specific Aurora Zip Codes call (303) 364-9215		Buena Vista	81211	Commerce City	80022
		Buena Vista Correctional Facility	81211	Como	80432
Aurora Mall (Part of Aurora)	80012			Conejos	81129
Austin (Part of Orchard City)	81410	Buffalo Creek	80425	Conifer	80433
		Buford	81641	Conifer Mountain	80433
Avon	81620	Burland Ranchettes	80470	Conifer Park	80433
Avondale	81022	Burlington	80807	Cope	80812
Bailey	80421	Burns	80426	Copper Mountain	80443
Bakersville	80476	Byers	80103	Copper Spur	80423
Baldwin	81230	Caddoa	81044	Cornish	80611
Balltown	81228	Cadet	80841	Coronado	80229
Barnesville	80624	Cahone	81320	Cortez	81321
Barr	80601	Calhan	80808	Cory (Part of Orchard City)	81414
Bartlett	81090	California Oil Camp	81648	Cotopaxi	81223
Barton	81041	Camp Bird	81427	Country Acres	80534
Basalt	81621	Camp George West	80401	Country Club Estates	80521
Battlement Mesa	81636	Campion	80537	Country Club Park	80303
Baxterville	81132	Campo	81029	Cowdrey	80434
Bayfield	81122	Canfield	80026	Cragmor (Part of Colorado Springs)	80907
Beacon Hill	80860	Canon	81120		
Bear Valley (Part of Denver)	80227	Canon City	81212	Craig	81625-26
Bear Valley Shopping Center (Part of Denver)	80227	Capitol Hill (Part of Denver)	80218	For specific Craig Zip Codes call (303) 824-5795	
		Capulin	81124		
Beaver Ridge	80440	Carbondale	81623	Craig South Highlands	81625
Bedrock	81411	Cardiff	81601	Crawford	81415
Beecher Island	80758	Carr	80612	Creede	81130
Belle Plain (Part of Pueblo)	81001	Cascade	80809	Crescent	80401
Bellvue	80512	Castle Rock	80104	Crested Butte	81224
Belmar (Part of Lakewood)	80226	Castlewood (Arapahoe County)	80120	Crestmoor (Part of Glendale)	80222
Belmont (Part of Pueblo)	81001				
Bendemeer Valley	80439	Cattle Creek	81623	Crestone	81131
Bennett	80102	Cedar	81431	Crestwoods	80424
Bergen Park	80439	Cedar Cove	80537	Crews	80911
Berthoud (Larimer County)	80513	Cedaredge	81413	Cripple Creek	80813
Berthoud (Weld County)	80513	Center	81125	Crisman	80302

COLORADO

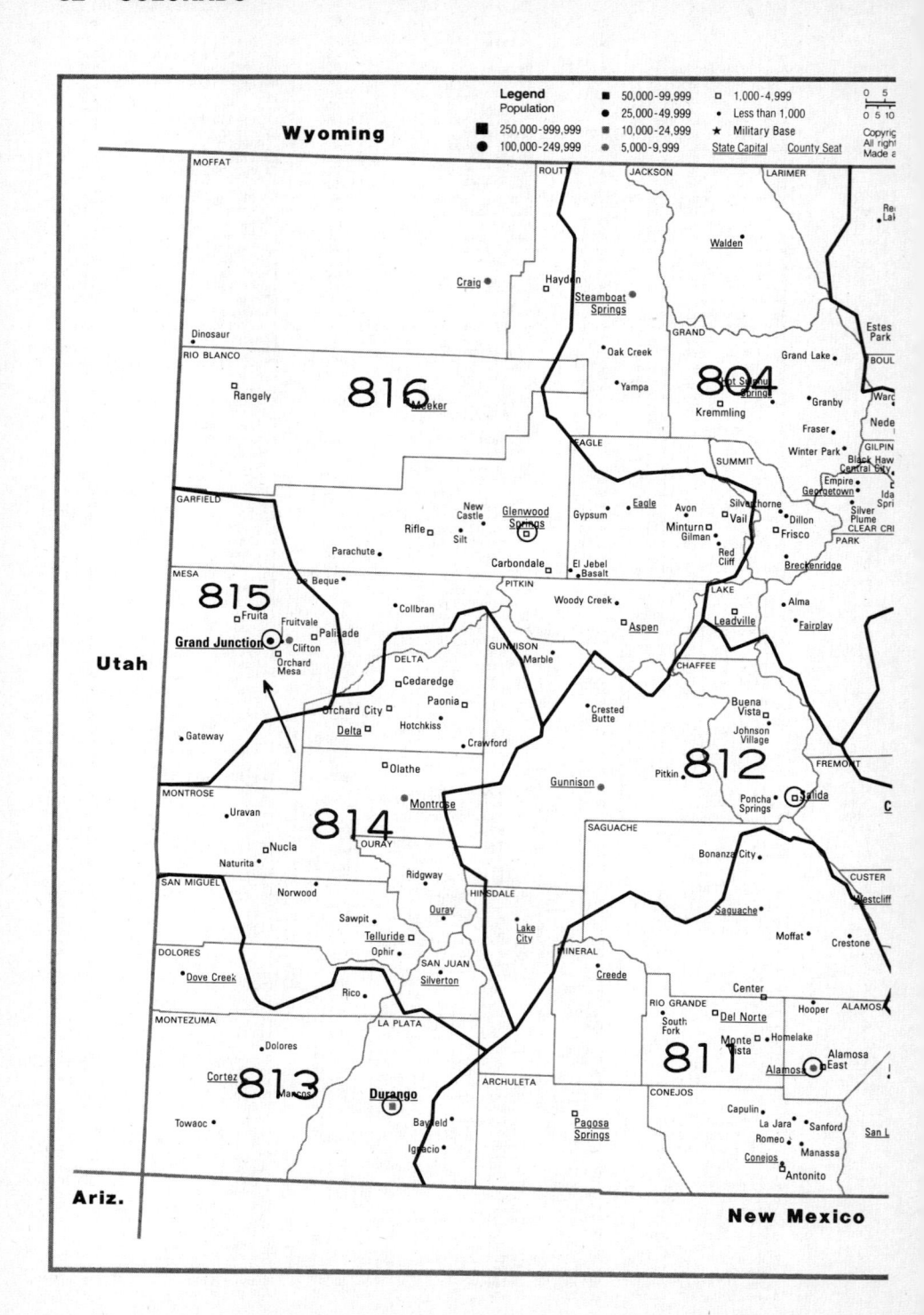

COLORADO 83

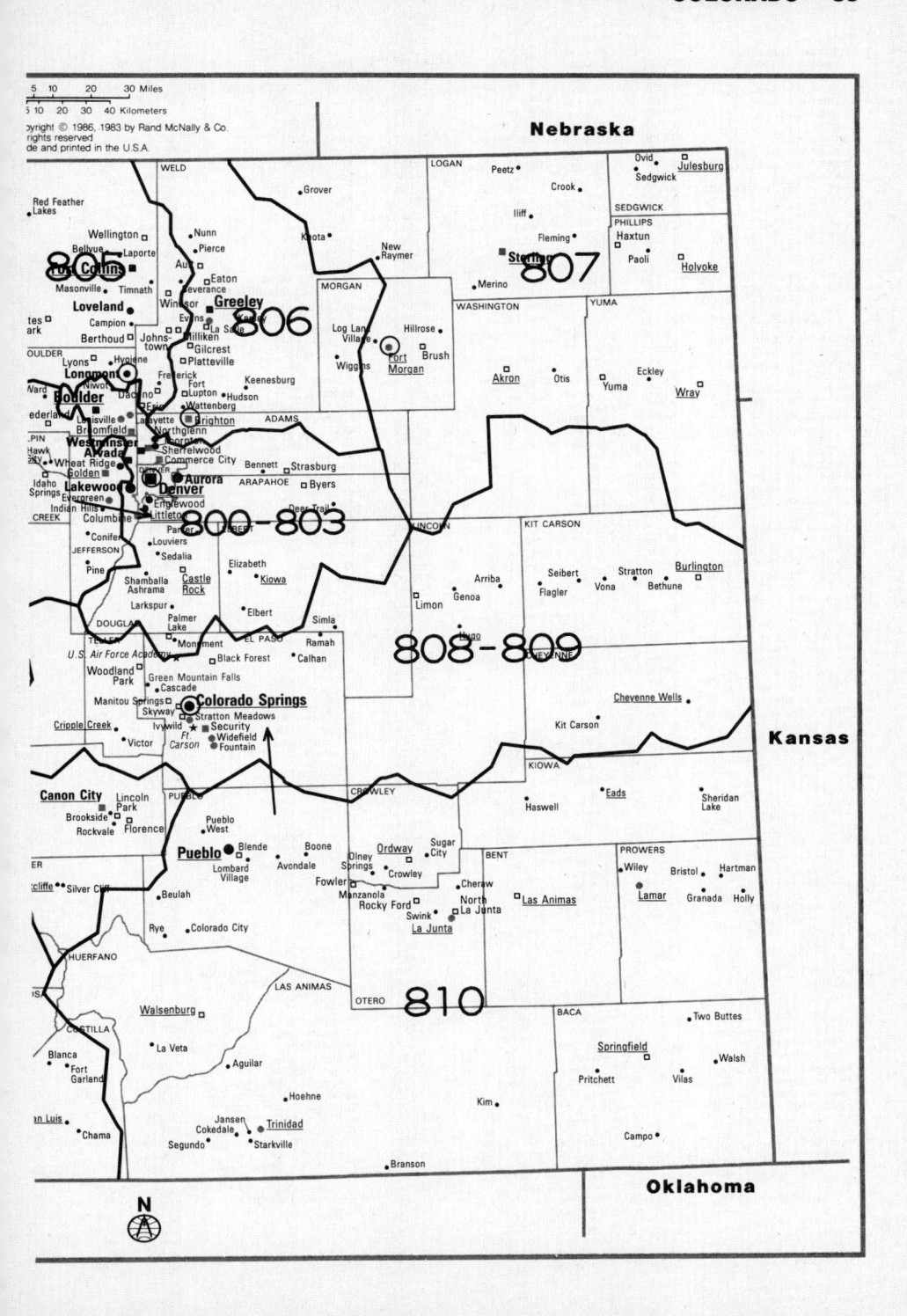

COLORADO Crook-Gulnare

Location	ZIP
Crook	80726
Crossroads Mall (Part of Boulder)	80301
Crowley	81033
Crystola	80863
Cuchara	81055
Cuerna Verde	81069
Dacono	80514
Dailey	80728
De Beque	81630
Deckers	80135
Deepcreek	80428
Deer Creek Valley Ranchos	80470
Deer Park	80467
Deer Trail	80105
Delhi	81059
Del Norte	81132
Delta	81416
Denver	80201-95
For specific Denver Zip Codes call (303) 297-6000	

COLLEGES & UNIVERSITIES

Metropolitan State College	80204
Regis College	80221
University of Colorado at Denver	80202
University of Colorado Health Sciences Center	80262
University of Denver	80208

FINANCIAL INSTITUTIONS

Bank Western, Federal Savings Bank	80202
Central Bank of Denver	80202
Cherry Creek National Bank	80206
Colorado National Bank of Denver	80202
Colorado State Bank of Denver	80202
Denver National Bank	80202
First Colorado Bank and Trust, National Association	80222
First Federal Savings Bank of Colorado	80226
First Interstate Bank of Denver, N.A.	80270
First National Bank of Southeast Denver	80210
Guaranty Bank & Trust Co.	80202
Lakeside National Bank	80212
Mountain States Bank	80218
Silverado Banking, Savings & Loan Association	80210
United Bank of Bear Valley, National Association	80227
United Bank of Denver, National Association	80274
United Bank of Lakewood, National Association	80226

HOSPITALS

AMI Presbyterian-St. Luke's Medical Center	80203
Denver Health and Hospitals	80204
Mercy Medical Center	80206
Porter Memorial Hospital	80210
Rose Medical Center	80220
Saint Joseph Hospital	80218
St. Anthony Hospital Systems	80204
University Hospital	80262
Veterans Administration Medical Center	80220

HOTELS/MOTELS

The Brown Palace Hotel	80202
The Denver Marriott Hotel-City Center	80202
Embassy Suites Hotel	80202
Governor's Court Hotel	80203
The Oxford Hotel	80202
Radisson Hotel Denver	80202
Westin Hotel, Tabor Center	80202

MILITARY INSTALLATIONS

Air Force Accounting and Finance Center	80279
Denver Merchandise Mart	80216
Derby	80022
Derby Junction	80426
Devine	81001
Dillon	80435
Dinosaur	81610
Divide	80814
Dolores	81323
Dome Rock	80441

Location	ZIP
Dorey Lakes	80401
Dory Hill	80401
Dotsero	81637
Dove Creek	81324
Downieville	80436
Downtown (Part of Englewood)	80110
Drake	80515
Drakes (Part of Fort Collins)	80521
Dream House Acres	80120
Dry Creek Basin	81431
Dumont	80436
Dupont	80024
Durango	81301-02
For specific Durango Zip Codes call (303) 247-3434	
Eads	81036
Eagle	81631
Eastlake (Adams County)	80614
Eastlake (Pueblo County)	81004
East Portal	80474
Eastridge (Part of Aurora)	80014
Eastridge South (Part of Aurora)	80014
East Weston	81091
Eaton	80615
Echo Lake	80452
Eckert (Part of Orchard City)	81418
Eckley	80727
Edgemont (Part of Lakewood)	80401
Edgewater	80214
Edison	80864
Edith	81128
Edler	81073
Edwards	81632
Egnar	81325
Elbert	80106
Eldora	80466
Eldorado Springs	80025
Elephant Park	80439
Eleven Mile Village	80827
Elizabeth	80107
El Jebel	81628
Elk Creek Acres	80470
Elk Creek Highlands	80470
Elkdale	80478
Elkhorn Acres	80470
Elk Springs	81633
Elkton	80860
Ellicott	80808
El Moro	81082
El Rancho	80401
El Vado	80302
Elwell	80534
Emma (Eagle County)	81623
Emma (Pitkin County)	81623
Empire	80438
Englewood	80110-12, 80150-56
For specific Englewood Zip Codes call (303) 761-0474	
Erie	80516
Erie Air Park (Part of Erie)	80516
Escalante Forks	81416
Estes Park	80517
Estrella	81101
Evans	80620
Evanston	80530
Evergreen (Jefferson County)	80439
Ever Green Hills	80439
Evergreen West	80439
Fairplay	80440
Fairview	81069
Fairview Estates	80123
Fairway Estates	80521
Falcon	80908
Falcon Estates	80908
Falfa	81301
Fall Creek	81430
Farisita	81037
Farmers	80631
Federal Correctional Institution	80110
Federal Heights	80221
Fenders	80465
Ferncliff	80510
Firestone	80520
First View	80810
Flagler	80815
Fleming	80728
Flintwood Hills	80116
Florence	81226
Florissant	80816
Florissant Heights	80816
Fondis	80106
Foothills Fashion Mall (Part of Fort Collins)	80525
Forest Hills	80401

Location	ZIP
Fort Carson (El Paso County)	80913
Fort Collins	80521-26
For specific Fort Collins Zip Codes call (303) 482-2837	
Fort Garland	81133
Fort Logan (Part of Sheridan)	80236
Fort Lupton	80621
Fort Lyon	81038
Fort Morgan	80701
Fountain	80817
Fountain Valley School	80911
Fowler	81039
Fox Creek	81120
Foxton	80441
Franktown	80116
Fraser	80442
Frederick	80530
Friendship Ranch	80470
Friendship Ranch Estates	80470
Frisco	80443
Fruita	81521
Fruitvale	81504
Galeton	80622
Garcia	81134
Garden City	80631
Gardner	81040
Garfield	81227
Gateway (Arapahoe County)	80014
Gateway (Mesa County)	81522
Gato	81147
Gem Village	81122
Genesee	80401
Genoa	80818
Georgetown	80444
Gilcrest	80623
Gill	80624
Gilman	81645
Glade Park	81523
Glen Comfort	80515
Glendale	80222
Glendevey	82063
Glenelk	80470
Glen Haven	80532
Glen Isle	80421
Glen Park (Part of Palmer Lake)	80133
Glentivar	80440
Glenwood Springs	81601-02
For specific Glenwood Springs Zip Codes call (303) 945-5611	
Golden	80401-03
For specific Golden Zip Codes call (303) 278-8537	
Golden Acres (Part of Longmont)	80501
Goldfield	80860
Gold Hill	80302
Goodnight	81005
Goodrich	80653
Gould	80480
Granada	81041
Granby	80446
Grand Junction	81501-06
For specific Grand Junction Zip Codes call (303) 241-3809	
Grand Lake	80447
Grand Mesa	81413
Grandview	81301
Grandview Estates	80134
Granite	81228
Grant	80448
Gray's Mary Greenwood	81069
Greeley	80631-34
For specific Greeley Zip Codes call (303) 353-0398	
Greeley Mall (Part of Greeley)	80631
Greenland	80118
Green Mountain (Part of Lakewood)	80228
Green Mountain Camp	80459
Green Mountain Estates (Part of Lakewood)	80228
Green Mountain Falls	80819
Green Mountain Village (Part of Lakewood)	80228
Green Towers	81069
Green Valley Acres	80433
Greenway Park	80020
Greenwood (Custer County)	81253
Greenwood (Pueblo County)	81069
Greenwood Village	80111
Greystone	81640
Grizzly	81601
Grover	80729
Guadalupe	81129
Guffey	80820
Gulnare	81042

Gunbarrel-Naturita **COLORADO** 85

	ZIP		ZIP		ZIP
Gunbarrel (Boulder County)	80501	Keenesburg	80643	Loveland	80537-39
Gunbarrel Estates	80501	Kelim	80537	For specific Loveland Zip Codes call (303) 667-0344	
Gunbarrel Greens	80301	Kelker (Part of Colorado Springs)	80906	Loveland Heights	80515
Gunnison	81230	Kellytown (Douglas County)	80125	Lubers	81057
Gypsum	81637	Ken Caryl	80123	Lucerne	80646
Hahns Peak	80428		80127	Ludlow	81082
Hale	80735	For specific Ken Caryl Zip Codes call (303) 798-2461		Lyons	80540
Halfway House	81220			Lyons Park Estates	80540
Hallcraft Town Houses (Part of Lakewood)	80228	Keota	80729	McClave	81057
Hamilton	81638	Kersey	80644	McClellands (Part of Fort Collins)	80521
Hanover	80909	Keystone	80435	McCoy (Chaffee County)	81201
Happy Canyon	80104	Kim	81049	McCoy (Eagle County)	80463
Hardin	80644	Kingsborough (Part of Aurora)	80017	McElmo	81321
Harmony (Part of Fort Collins)	80521	Kingsborough South (Part of Aurora)	80012	Mack	81525
Harris Park (Adams County)	80036	Kings Corner	80537	Madison Hill (Part of Westminster)	80030
Harris Park (Park County)	80470	Kiowa	80117	Madrid	81082
Hartman	81043	Kipling Hills	80123	Magnolia	80466
Hartsel	80449	Kipling Villas	80123	Maher	81421
Hasty	81044	Kirk	80824	Manassa	81141
Haswell	81045	Kit Carson	80825	Mancos	81328
Hawley	81067	Kittredge	80457	Mancos Creek	81321
Haxtun	80731	Kline	81326	Mandalay Gardens	80021
Hayden	81639	Knaus	80634	Manitou Springs	80829
Hazeltine Heights	80640	Knob Hill (Part of Colorado Springs)	80910	Manzanola	81058
Heather Ridge (Part of Aurora)	80014	Koen	81041	Marble	81623
Heatherwood	80301	Kornman	81052	Marshall	80302
Heeney	80459	Kremmling	80459	Marshdale Park	80439
Henderson	80640	Kuhlmann Heights	80401	Marvel	81329
Hereford	80732	Kutch	80832	Mary Jane	80480
Heritage Place	80110	K-Z Ranchettes	80470	Maryvale	80442
Hermosa	81301	Lafayette	80026	Mason Corner	80631
Herzman Mesa	80439	La Garita	81132	Masonic Park	81154
Hesperus	81326	Laird	80758	Masonville	80541
Hiawatha Camp	82901	La Jara	81140	Massadona	81610
Hidden Valley	80439	La Junta	81050	Masters	80649
Hideaway Park (Part of Winter Park)	80482	La Junta Gardens	81050	Matheson	80830
High Chateau Ranches	80816	Lakeborough	80235	Maxeyville	81144
Highland Acres	80631	Lake City	81235	Maybell	81640
Highland Hills	80634	Lake George	80827	Mayday	81326
Highland Lake	80651	Lakeside	80212	Maysville	81201
Highland Lakes	80814	Lakeside Mall (Part of Wheat Ridge)	80212	May Valley	81052
Highland Park	80470	Lake View	80401	Mead	80542
Highlands (Part of Denver)	80211	Lakewood	80215	Meadow Brook Heights	80120
Highlands Ranch	80126	Lamar	81052	Meadowood (Part of Aurora)	80013
High-Mar (Part of Boulder)	80303	La Montana Mesa	80816	Medina Plaza	81091
Hi-Land Acres	80601	Laporte	80535	Meeker	81641
Hill N' Park	80631	La Posta	81301	Meeker Park	80510
Hillrose	80733	Lariat (Part of Monte Vista)	81144	Meredith	81642
Hillside	81232	Larkspur	80118	Merino	80741
Hilltop	80134	La Salle	80645	Mesa	81643
Hiwan Hills	80439	Las Animas	81054	Mesa Verde National Park	81330
Hoehne	81046	Lasauses	81151	Mesita	81152
Hoffman Heights (Part of Aurora)	80012	Las Mesitas	81120	Messex	80741
Holiday Hills	80863	Last Chance	80757	Milliken	80543
Holly	81047	La Valley	81153	Milner	80487
Holyoke	80734	La Veta	81055	Mineral Hot Springs	81143
Homelake	81135	Lawson	80452	Minnequa (Part of Pueblo)	81007
Hooper	81136	Lay	81625	Minnequa Heights (Part of Pueblo)	81007
Hotchkiss	81419	Lazear	81420	Minturn	81645
Hot Sulphur Springs	80451	Leadville	80461	Mirage	81143
Howard	81233	Leadville North	80461	Mission Viejo (Part of Aurora)	80013
Howells (Part of Littleton)	80120	Leawood	80123	Model	81059
Hoyt	80654	Lebanon	81323	Moffat (Moffat County)	81638
Hudson	80642	Leisure Living	80516	Moffat (Saguache County)	81143
Hugo	80821	Lewis	81327	Mogote	81120
Husted	80840	Leyden	80401	Molina	81646
Hyde	80743	Liberty Bell Village	81435	Montbello (Part of Denver)	80239
Hygiene	80533	Limon	80828	Montclair (Part of Denver)	80220
Hyland Hills	80439	Lincoln Park	81212	Monte Vista	81144
Hyland Knolls	80634	Lindon	80740	Montezuma	80435
Idaho Springs	80452	Littleton	80120-27	Montrose	81401-02
Idalia	80735		80160-62	For specific Montrose Zip Codes call (303) 249-6654	
Idledale	80453	For specific Littleton Zip Codes call (303) 798-2461			
Ignacio	81137			Monument	80132
Iliff	80736	Livengood Hills	80134	Monument Lake Park	81091
Ilse	81212	Livermore	80536	Moore Dale	80421
Indian Creek	80816	Lobatos	81120	Morgan	81140
Indian Hills	80454	Lochbuie	80601	Morrison	80465
Indian Springs Village	80470	Lochwood (Part of Lakewood)	80215	Mosca	81146
Ione	80621	Log Lane Village	80701	Mountain Park	80401
Irondale	80022	Loma	81524	Mountain View (Jefferson County)	80212
Ivywild (Part of Colorado Springs)	80906	Loma Linda	81301	Mountain View (Larimer County)	80521
Jamestown	80455	Lombard Village	81006	Mountain View Acres	81101
Jansen	81082	Lone Pine Estates	80465	Mountain View Lakes	80470
Jaroso	81138	Longmont	80501-02	Mount Crested Butte	81225
Jefferson	80456	For specific Longmont Zip Codes call (303) 776-2135		Mount Massive Lakes	80461
Jefferson Heights	80456			Mount Princeton Hot Springs	81236
Joes	80822	Longview	80441	Mount Vernon Club Place	80401
Johnson Village	81211	Lookout Mountain	80401	Mutual	81089
Johnstown	80534	Loretto Heights (Part of Denver)	80236	Nast	81642
Juanita	81147	Los Fuertes	81153	Nathrop	81236
Julesburg	80737	Louisville	80027	Naturita	81422
Kahler	80513	Louviers	80131		
Kaibab	81631				
Karval	80823				

86 COLORADO Nederland-Stoneham

Name	ZIP
Nederland	80466
Nevadaville	80427
New Castle	81647
New Raymer	80742
Nighthawk	80135
Nine Mile Corner	80026
Niwot	80544
Nob Hill	80122
North Avondale	81022
North Boulder (Part of Boulder)	80302
North Cherry Creek Valley	80231
North Delta	81416
North End (Part of Colorado Springs)	80907
Northglenn	80233
Northglenn Mall (Part of Northglenn)	80233
North La Junta	81050
North Pecos	80221
North Pole	80809
North Valley Shopping Center (Part of Thornton)	80229
North Washington Heights	80229
North Yard (Part of Denver)	80221
Norwood	81423
Nucla	81424
Numa	81063
Nunn	80648
Nutria	81147
Oak Creek	80467
Oak Grove	81401
Oehlmann Park	80433
Ohio	81237
Olathe	81425
Olney Springs	81062
Olympus Heights	80515
Ophir	81426
Orchard	80649
Orchard City	81410
Orchard Mesa	81501
Ordway	81063
Ormandale	81005
Ortiz	81120
Otis	80743
Ouray	81427
Ovid	80744
Oxford	81137
Pactolus	80401
Padroni	80745
Pagosa	81147
Pagosa Springs	81147
Paisaje	81120
Palisade	81526
Palmer Lake	80133
Palos Verdes	80123
Palos Verdes East	80110
Pandora	81435
Paoli	80746
Paonia	81428
Parachute	81635
Paradox	81429
Paragon Estates	80303
Park Center	81212
Park City	80420
Parker	80134
Park Hill (Part of Denver)	80207
Park Vista Estates	80908
Parlin	81239
Parshall	80468
Peaceful Valley	80540
Peagreen	81416
Peak Seven West	80424
Peckham	80645
Peetz	80747
Penitentiary (Part of Canon City)	81212
Penrose	81240
Peyton	80831
Pheasant Run (Part of Aurora)	80015
Phippsburg	80469
Pierce	80650
Pine	80470
Pinebrook Hills	80302
Pinecliffe	80471
Pine Crest (Part of Palmer Lake)	80133
Pine Hills	80132
Pine Nook	80135
Pine Park Estates	80465
Pinewood Springs	80540
Pinnacle Park	80631
Pinon	81008
Pinon Acres	81301
Pinon Canyon	81082
Pitkin	81241
Placerville	81430
Plateau City	81624
Platner	80743
Platoro	81144

Name	ZIP
Platteville	80651
Plaza	81132
Pleasant View (Jefferson County)	80401
Pleasant View (Montezuma County)	81331
Poncha Springs	81242
Ponderosa	80424
Ponderosa Hills	80134
Ponderosa Park	80107
Poudre Park	80521
Powderhorn	81243
Powder Wash	82901
Pritchett	81064
Proctor	80736
Prospect Heights	81212
Prospect Valley	80643
Prowers	81052
Pryor	81065
Pueblo	81001-19
For specific Pueblo Zip Codes call (303) 544-0132	
Pueblo Army Depot	81001
Pueblo Dam	81003
Pueblo Mall (Part of Pueblo)	81008
Pueblo West	81007
Punkin Center	80821
Quincy (Part of Aurora)	80015
Radium	80423
Ragged Mountain	81434
Rainbow Valley	80814
Ramah	80832
Rand	80473
Rangely	81648
Rangeview Estates (Boulder County)	80501
Range View Estates (Weld County)	80631
Rattlesnake Buttes	81089
Raymond	80540
Read	81416
Red Cliff	81649
Red Feather Lakes	80545
Redlands	81503
Redmesa	81326
Red Rock Ranch	80132
Redstone	81623
Redvale	81431
Red Wing	81066
Rembrandt Place	80121
Rezago	81082
Richfield	81140
Rico	81332
Ridgeview Hills	80122
Ridgway	81432
Rifle	81650
Rinn	80501
Rio Blanco	81650
Riverside	80540
Roberta	81050
Rockvale	81244
Rocky Ford	81067
Rocky Mountain Arsenal	80022
Rogers Mesa	81419
Roggen	80652
Roland Valley	80470
Rollinsville	80474
Romeo	81148
Rosedale (Part of Garden City)	80631
Rosita	81252
Roswell (Part of Colorado Springs)	80907
Rowena	80455
Roxborough Park	80125
Royal Gorge	81246
Royal Ranch	80470
Ruedi	81621
Rulison	81635
Rush	80833
Russell Gulch	80427
Rustic	80512
Rye	81069
Rye Ranchettes	81069
Sable (Part of Aurora)	80011
Saguache	81149
Saint Charles Mesa	81006
St. Elmo	81236
St. Petersburg	80728
Salida	81201
Salina	80302
Salt Creek (Part of Pueblo)	81006
San Acacio	81150
San Antonio	81120
Sand Creek (Part of Commerce City)	80022
Sandown (Part of Denver)	80216
Sanford	81151
Sangre De Cristo Ranches	81133
San Isabel	81069
San Juan	81070

Name	ZIP
San Luis	81152
San Pablo	81153
San Pedro	81153
Santa Fe (Denver County)	80204
Santa Fe (Pueblo County)	81003
Sapinero	81247
Sarcillo	81082
Sarcillo Canon	81091
Sargents	81248
Sargents School	81144
Sawpit	81430
Security	80911
Security-Widefield	80911
Sedalia	80135
Sedgwick	80749
Segundo	81070
Seibert	80834
Semper	80021
Severance	80546
Shadow Mountain	80447
Shadows North	80424
Shaffers Crossing	80433
Shamballa Ashrama	80135
Shauano Vista	81201
Shaw Heights	80030
Shaw Heights Mesa	80030
Shawnee	80475
Sheridan	80110
Sheridan Lake	81071
Sherrelwood (Adams County)	80221
Sherrelwood Estates	80221
Silt	81652
Silver Cliff	81249
Silver Creek	80446
Silver Heights	80104
Silver Plume	80476
Silver Shekel	80424
Silver Springs	80470
Silver Spruce	80301
Silverthorne	80498
Silverton	81433
Simla	80835
Singleton	80475
Skyland Village (Part of Westminster)	80030
Skyline	80222
Sky Village	80465
Skyway (El Paso County)	80906
Skyway (Mesa County)	81643
Skyway Estates (Part of Colorado Springs)	80906
Skyway Park (Part of Colorado Springs)	80906
Slater	81653
Slick Rock	81333
Smeltertown	81201
Smoky Hill (Part of Aurora)	80015
Snowmass	81654
Snowmass Village	81615
Snow Mountain Ranch	80446
Snyder	80750
Somerset	81434
South Boulder (Part of Boulder)	80303
South Canon (Part of Canon City)	81212
South Denver (Part of Denver)	80209
Southern Ute Indian Reservation	81137
South Fork	81154
Southglenn (Arapahoe County)	80122
South Park City (Part of Fairplay)	80440
South Platte	80441
South Roggen	80652
Southwind	80120
Southwood	80120
Spanish Colony	80631
Spanish Village	80644
Spar City	81130
Sparks	82901
Sphinx Park	80470
Spivak (Part of Lakewood)	80214
Springfield	81073
Spring Valley	80814
Sprucedale	80439
Squaw Point	81324
Stanley Park	80439
Starkville	81074
Steamboat 1981	80477
Steamboat Plaza (Part of Steamboat Springs)	80488
Steamboat Springs	80487
Steamboat Village (Part of Steamboat Springs)	80487
Sterling	80751
Stockyards (Part of Denver)	80216
Stoneham	80754

Stoner-Yuma **COLORADO** 87

	ZIP		ZIP		ZIP
Stoner	81323	Troutdale	80439	Waterton	80125
Stonewall	81091	Trout Haven	80814	Watkins	80137
Stonington	81075	Trout Lake	81426	Wattenberg	80621
Strasburg	80136	Truckton	80864	Waverly	81101
Stratmoor (El Paso County)	80906	Trujillo	81147	Welby (Adams County)	80229
Stratmoor Hills	80906	Trumbull	80135	Weldona	80653
Stratton	80836	Twin Forks	80454	Wellington	80549
Stratton Meadows (Part of Colorado Springs)	80906	Twin Lakes	81251	Wellshire (Part of Denver)	80222
		Twin Rock	80816	Wellsville	81201
Stratton Park (Part of Colorado Springs)	80907	Twin Spruce	80401	West (Part of Greeley)	80634
		Two Buttes	81084	Westcliffe	81252
Stringtown	80461	Tyrone	81059	West End (Part of Colorado Springs)	80904
Sugar City	81076	Unaweep	81527		
Sugarloaf	80302	Uncompahgre	81401	Western Hills	80221
Summit Cove	80435	Union	80750	West Farm	81052
Summitville	81132	Union Stockyards (Part of Denver)	80216	Westland Center (Part of Lakewood)	80215
Sunbeam	81640				
Sunnyside (Boulder County)	80466	University (Part of Boulder)	80309	Westminster	80030-31
Sunnyside (La Plata County)	81301	University Hills Mall (Part of Denver)	80222		80035-36
Sunnyslopes	80020			For specific Westminster Zip Codes call (303) 429-0340	
Sunset (Part of Pueblo)	81005	University Park (Part of Denver)	80210		
Sunshine	80302			Westminster East	80221
Superior	80027	Uravan	81422	Westminster Mall (Part of Westminster)	80030
Surrey Ridge	80104	USAF Academy	80840-41		
Sutank	81623	For specific USAF Academy Zip Codes call (719) 472-1818		Weston	81091
Swallows	81003			Westridge	80634
Swede Corners	81149	Ute Heights	81201	West Vail (Part of Vail)	81657
Sweetwater	81637	Ute Mountain Indian Reservation	81334	Westwood (Part of Denver)	80219
Swink	81077			Westwood Lake	80863
Swissvale	81201	Utleyville	81064	Wetmore	81253
Switzerland Village	80470	Vail	81657-58	Wheat Ridge	80033-34
Tabernash	80478	For specific Vail Zip Codes call (303) 476-5217		For specific Wheat Ridge Zip Codes call (303) 421-2855	
Tallahassee School	81212				
Tamarron	81301	Vallecito	81122	Wheeler	80401
Tanglewood Acres	81252	Valley Hi Mountain Estates	80816	White Pine	81248
Tarryall	80827	Valley of Blue	80424	Whitewater	81527
Taylor Park	81210	Vancorum	81422	Widefield	80911
Telluride	81435	Velasquez Plaza	81091	Wiggins	80654
Templeton (Part of Colorado Springs)	80936	Vernon	80755	Wild Horse (Cheyenne County)	80862
		Victor	80860		
Ten Mile Vista	80424	Viejo San Acacio	81150	Wild Horse (Pueblo County)	81001
Tennyson Heights (Part of Fort Collins)	80521	Vigil	81091	Wiley	81092
		Vilas	81087	Willard	80741
Terminal Annex (Part of Denver)	80217	Village East (Part of Aurora)	80012	Williamsburg (Fremont County)	81226
		Villa Grove	81155		
Texas Creek	81250	Villa Italia Center (Part of Lakewood)	80226	Williamsburg (Jefferson County)	80127
Thatcher	81059				
The Meadows	80127	Villegreen	81049	Willowbrook	80465
The Mesa	80904	Vineland	81001	Willow Creek	80110
The Pinery	80134	Virginia Dale	80535	Willow Gulch	81423
The Shadows	80424	Vista Grande (Part of Colorado Springs)	80918	Wilson Lake Estates	80816
The Springs	80906			Windsor	80550
Thomasville	81642	Vista Verde	80120	Windsor Gardens (Part of Denver)	80231
Thornton	80229	Vollmar	80621		
Thurman	80801	Vona	80861	Winter Park (Grand County)	80482
Tiffany	81137	Vroman	81067	Wolcott	81655
Timbers (Part of Aurora)	80014	Waconda Hills	80132	Wondervu	80401
Timnath	80547	Wagner Manor	80302	Woodglen (Part of Thornton)	80229
Timpas	81050	Wagon Wheel Gap	81154		
Tincup	81210	Wahatoya	81055	Woodland Acres	81069
Tiny Town	80465	Wah Keeney Park	80439	Woodland Park	80863
Tolland	80474	Wahketa Village	80701	Woodmar Village	80123
Toltec	81089	Walden	80480	Woodmoor	80908
Toponas	80479	Wallace Village	80021	Woodrow	80757
Tordal Estates	80424	Wallstreet	80302	Woody Creek	81656
Torres (Las Animas County)	81091	Walnut Hills	80112	Wray	80758
Torres (Rio Grande County)	81144	Walsenburg	81089	Yampa	80483
Towaoc	81334	Walsh	81090	Yellow Jacket	81335
Towner	81080	Waltonia	80515	Yoder	80864
Tranquil Acres	80863	Wamblee Park	80433	Yorkborough (Part of Thornton)	80229
Trimble	81301	Wamblee Valley	80433		
Trinchera	81081	Wandcrest Park	80470	Yuma	80759
Trinidad	81082	Ward	80481		

88 CONNECTICUT

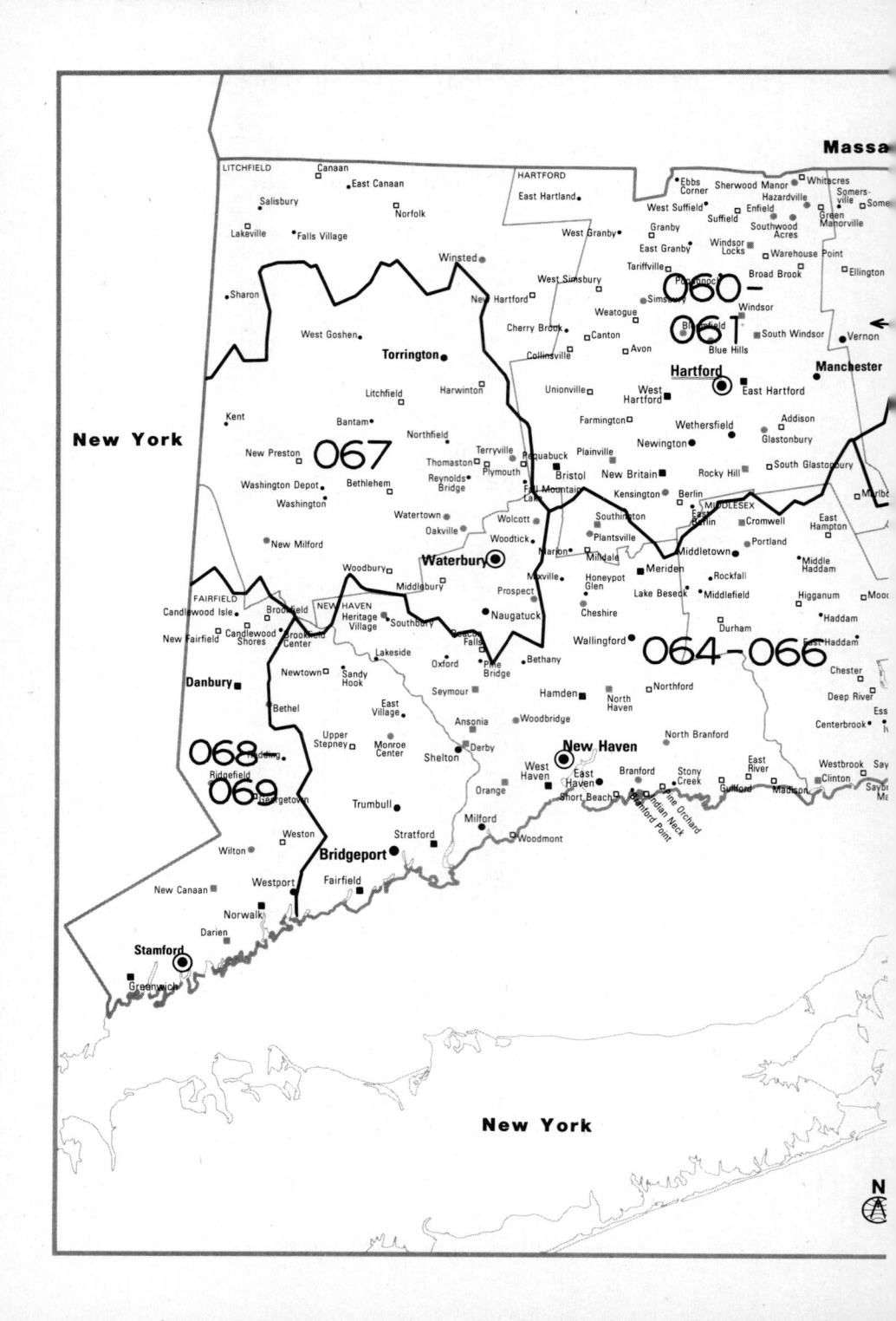

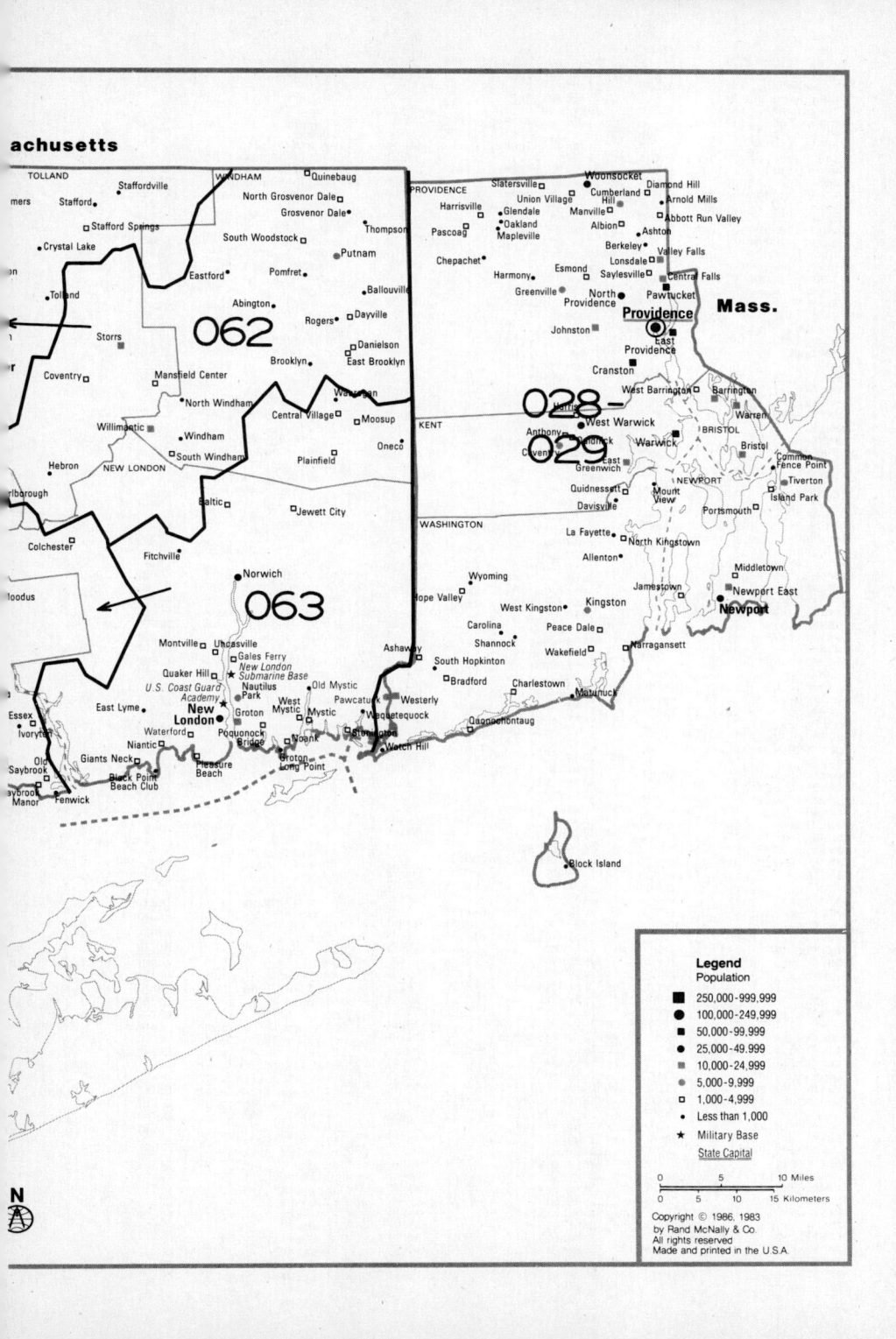

CONNECTICUT 89

90 CONNECTICUT Abington-Durham

Place	ZIP
Abington	06230
Addison	06033
Agua Vista (Part of Danbury)	06810
Aljen Heights	06339
Allerton Farms (Part of Naugatuck)	06770
Allington (Part of West Haven)	06516
Almyville	06354
Alpine	06810
Amenia Union	06069
Amesville	06031
Amity (Part of New Haven)	06525
Amston	06231
Andover	06232
Andover (Town)	06232
Ansonia (New Haven County)	06401
Ansonia (New Haven County) (Town)	06401
Ashford	06278
Ashford (Town)	06250
Ashford Lake	06250
Aspetuck	06880
Attawan Beach	06357
Attawaugan	06241
Atwoodville	06250
Avery Heights	06776
Avery Hill	06339
Avon	06001
Avon (Town)	06001
Baileyville	06455
Bakersville	06057
Ballouville	06233
Ball Pond	06812
Baltic	06330
Banksville	06830
Bantam	06750
Barkhamsted (Town)	06063
Barnum (Part of Bridgeport)	06605
Barry Square (Part of Hartford)	06134
Bartlett Corners	06375
Bayview (Part of Milford)	06460
Beacon Falls	06403
Beacon Falls (Town)	06403
Beardsley (Part of Bridgeport)	06606
Beaverbrook (Part of Danbury)	06810
Beckettville (Part of Danbury)	06810
Bedlam Corner	06256
Bel Aire Estates	06355
Belden (Part of Norwalk)	06850
Belle Haven	06830
Bell Island (Part of Norwalk)	06853
Belltown (Part of Stamford)	06906
Berkshire	06482
Berkshire Estates	06488
Berkshire Shopping Center (Part of Danbury)	06810
Berlin	06037
Berlin (Town)	06037
Beseck Lake	06455
Bethany	06525
Bethany (Town)	06525
Bethel (Town)	06801
Bethel	06801
Bethlehem	06751
Bethlehem (Town)	06751
Birch Groves	06776
Birch Hill	06757
Birch Meadow	06479
Birch Mountain	06040
Birchwood	06095
Birdland	06082
Bishop	06374
Bishops Corner	06137
Bissell	06074
Black Point	06357
Black Point Beach Club	06357
Bloomfield	06002
Bloomfield (Town)	06002
Blue Hills (Hartford County)	06132
Blue Hills (Hartford County)	06002
Boardman Manor	06776
Boardmans Bridge	06776
Bolton	06040
Bolton (Town)	06040
Bolton Center	06040
Bonny Brook	06776
Borough (Part of Groton)	06340
Botsford	06404
Boulder Lake	06413
Bozrah	06334
Bozrah (Town)	06334
Branchville	06829
Brandy Hill	06277
Branford	06405

Place	ZIP
Branford (Town)	06405
Branford Hills	06405
Branhaven Shopping Center	06405
Brendan Heights	06078
Bretton Heights (Part of Middletown)	06457
Bridgeport	06601-50
For specific Bridgeport Zip Codes call (203) 332-5337	
Bridgeport (Town)	06604
Bridgewater	06752
Bridgewater (Town)	06752
Brighton Beach	06371
Bristol (Hartford County)	06010
Bristol (Hartford County) (Town)	06010
Bristol Terrace (Part of Naugatuck)	06770
Broad Brook	06016
Bromica	06757
Brookfield	06804
Brookfield (Town)	06804
Brookfield Center	06804
Brooklyn	06234
Brooklyn (Town)	06234
Brook Valley (Part of Naugatuck)	06770
Bruce Park	06830
Brush Island	06820
Buckingham	06033
Buckland	06040
Bucks Corners	06073
Bulls Bridge	06785
Bunker Hill (Part of Waterbury)	06708
Burlington	06013
Burlington (Town)	06085
Burnside	06108
Burr Hill	06417
Burrville (Part of Torrington)	06790
Burwells Beach (Part of Milford)	06460
Byram	06830
Camp Bethel	06438
Camptown (Part of Derby)	06418
Canaan (Litchfield County)	06018
Canaan (Litchfield County) (Town)	06031
Candleset Cove	06776
Candlewood Hill	06441
Candlewood Hills	06810
Candlewood Isle	06812
Candlewood Knolls	06810
Candlewood Lake Club	06804
Candlewood Lake Estates	06784
Candlewood Orchards	06804
Candlewood Point	06776
Candlewood Shores	06804
Candlewood Springs	06776
Candlewood Trails	06776
Cannondale	06897
Canterbury	06331
Canterbury (Town)	06331
Canton	06019
Canton (Town)	06019
Canton Center	06020
Carl Robinson Correctional Institution	06082
Carmel Hill	06751
Castle Hill	02891
Cedar Beach (Part of Milford)	06460
Cedar Heights (Part of Danbury)	06810
Cedarhurst	06482
Cedar Knolls	06776
Cedar Lake (Part of Bristol)	06010
Cedar Land	06488
Center	06611
Centerbrook	06409
Center Groton	06340
Center Hill	06057
Centerville	06518
Centerville-Mount Carmel	06518
Central (Part of Hartford)	06103
Central Village	06332
Chaffeeville	06268
Chalkers Beach	06475
Chaplin	06235
Chaplin (Town)	06235
Chapman Beach	06498
Charcoal Ridge	06812
Cherry Brook	06020
Cherry Hill	06796
Cherrywood	06479
Cheshire	06410
Cheshire (Town)	06410
Chester	06412
Chester (Town)	06412
Chickahominy	06830

Place	ZIP
Chippens Hill (Part of Bristol)	06010
Christy Hill Estates	06335
Church Hill	06794
Churchwood	06357
Clam Island	06405
Clarks Corner	06256
Clarks Falls	06359
Clarksville	02891
Clearview Heights	06076
Clinton (Middlesex County) (Town)	06413
Clinton (Middlesex County)	06413
Clinton Beach	06413
Clintonville	06473
Cobalt	06414
Codfish Hill	06801
Colburn Hill	06076
Colchester	06415
Colchester (Town)	06415
Colebrook	06021
Colebrook (Town)	06021
Collinsville	06022
Colonial Manor	06360
Columbia	06237
Columbia (Town)	06237
Compo Beach	06880
Compo Hill	06880
Conantville	06226
Congamond Lakes	06093
Connecticut Correctional Institution (Hartford County)	06082
Connecticut Correctional Center (New Haven County)	06410
Connecticut Correctional Institution (Tolland County)	06071
Connecticut Post Mall (Part of Milford)	06460
Conning Towers	06340
Conning Towers-Nautilus Park	06340
Copaco Shopping Center	06002
Cornwall	06753
Cornwall (Town)	06753
Cornwall Bridge	06754
Cornwall Center	06796
Cornwall Hollow	06031
Cos Cob	06807
Cottage Grove	06002
Coventry	06238
Coventry (Town)	06238
Cranbury (Part of Norwalk)	06851
Cranska Village	06354
Crescent Beach	06357
Cromwell (Town)	06416
Cromwell	06416
Cromwell Hills	06416
Crystal Lake	06029
Daleville	06279
Damascus	06405
Danbury	06810-13
For specific Danbury Zip Codes call (203) 748-1230	
Danbury Fair (Part of Danbury)	06810
Danbury Quarter	06098
Danbury Shopping Center (Part of Danbury)	06810
Danielson	06239
Darien (Fairfield County) (Town)	06820
Darien (Fairfield County)	06820
Dayville	06241
Deep River	06417
Deep River (Town)	06417
Deer Island	06758
Deer Run Shores	06784
Derby (New Haven County)	06418
Derby (New Haven County) (Town)	06418
Derby Junction (Part of Derby)	06418
Derby Neck (Part of Derby)	06418
Devil's Backbone	06751
Devon (Part of Milford)	06460
Diamond Lake	06033
Dibble Hill	06796
Dickerman's Corner	06479
Doanville	06384
Dodgingtown	06470
Dolphin Gardens	06340
Double Beach	06405
Dowd's Corner	06019
Downersville	02891
Drakeville (Part of Torrington)	06790
Durham	06422
Durham (Town)	06422

Durham Center-Knollcrest **CONNECTICUT 91**

Location	ZIP
Durham Center	06422
Eagleville	06268
East Berlin	06023
East Bristol (Part of Bristol)	06010
East Brooklyn	06239
East Canaan	06024
East Cornwall	06759
East Derby (Part of Derby)	06418
East End (Part of Waterbury)	06705
Eastern Point (Part of Groton)	06340
East Farmington Heights	06032
East Farms (Part of Waterbury)	06705
Eastford	06242
Eastford (Town)	06242
East Glastonbury	06025
East Granby	06026
East Granby (Town)	06026
East Great Plain (Part of Norwich)	06360
East Haddam	06423
East Haddam (Town)	06423
East Haddam Landing	06423
East Hampton	06424
East Hampton (Town)	06424
East Hampton Center	06424
East Hartford (Hartford County) (Town)	06108
East Hartford (Hartford County)	06128
East Hartland	06027
East Haven (New Haven County) (Town)	06512
East Haven (New Haven County)	06512
East Hill	06019
East Killingly	06243
East Litchfield	06759
East Lyme	06333
East Lyme (Town)	06333
East Morris	06763
East Mountain (Part of Waterbury)	06706
East New London (Part of New London)	06320
East Norwalk (Part of Norwalk)	06601
Easton	06612
Easton (Town)	06612
East Plymouth	06786
East Port Chester	06830
East Putnam	06260
East River	06443
East Thompson	06277
East Village	06468
East Wallingford	06492
East Willington	06279
East Windsor	06088
East Windsor (Town)	06016
East Windsor Hill	06028
East Woodstock	06244
Ebbs Corner	06093
Edgewood (Hartford County)	06010
Edgewood (Tolland County)	06076
Ekonk	06354
Ekonk Hill	06384
Ellington	06029
Ellington (Town)	06029
Elliot	06259
Ellsworth	06069
Elm Hill	06111
Elmville	06241
Elmwood	06133
Elys Ferry	06371
Enders Island	06378
Enfield	06082
Enfield (Town)	06082
Enfield Square	06082
Enfield Street	06082
Essex	06426
Essex (Town)	06426
Ethel Acres	06351
Ettadore Park (Part of Milford)	06460
Fabyan	06245
Fairfield	06430-32
For specific Fairfield Zip Codes call (203) 255-4591	
Fairfield Hills Hospital	06470
Fairground (Part of Norwich)	06360
Fair Haven (Part of New Haven)	06513
Fair Lawn (Part of Waterbury)	06705
Fairmount (Part of Waterbury)	06706
Fairy Lake	06370
Fall Mountain (Part of Bristol)	06010

Location	ZIP
Fall Mountain Lake	06786
Falls Switch (Part of Norwich)	06360
Falls Village	06031
Farmington	06032
Farmington (Town)	06032
Far View Beach (Part of Milford)	06460
Federal (Part of New Haven)	06510
Federal Correctional Institution	06810
Fenwick	06475
Fenwood	06475
Ferris Estates	06776
Ferry Point	06475
Ferry View Heights	06335
Field Crest Estates	06355
Firetown	06070
Five City Plaza Shopping Center	06032
Five Points (Fairfield County)	06896
Five Points (Hartford County)	06035
Flanders	06757
Flax Hill (Part of Norwalk)	06850
Floral Park	06475
Floydville	06035
Forbes Village	06108
Forest Glen	06475
Forest Heights (Part of Milford)	06460
Forest Hills	06489
Forest Park	06248
Forestville (Part of Bristol)	06010
Fort Hill	06776
Fort Trumbull Beach (Part of Milford)	06460
Fox Den	06001
Foxon	06512
Franklin	06254
Franklin (Town)	06254
Franklin Square (Part of Norwich)	06360
Furnace Hollow	06076
Gales Ferry	06335
Gallows Hill	06896
Gaylordsville	06755
Georgetown (Fairfield County)	06829
Georgetown (Hartford County)	06479
Germantown (Part of Danbury)	06810
Giants Neck	06357
Giants Neck Heights	06357
Gildersleeve	06480
Gilead	06248
Gilman	06336
Glasgo	06337
Glastonbury	06033
Glastonbury (Town)	06033
Glen	06896
Glenbrook (Part of Stamford)	06906
Glenville	06830
Golden Spur	06385
Good Hill (rural) (Litchfield County)	06757
Good Hill (Litchfield County)	06798
Good Hill (New Haven County)	06483
Goodrich Heights	06416
Goodsell Point	06405
Goshen	06756
Goshen (Town)	06756
Goshen	06385
Goshen Hills	06249
Governor's Hill	06483
Granby	06035
Granby (Town)	06035
Granite Bay	06405
Grappaville	06750
Grassy Hill (Litchfield County)	06798
Grassy Hill (New London County)	06371
Grassy Plain	06801
Great Hammock	06475
Great Harbor	06437
Great Meadows	06810
Greenfield Hill	06430
Greenhaven Shores	02891
Green Manorville	06082
Greens Farms	06436
Greenville (Part of Norwich)	06360
Greenwich	06830-36
For specific Greenwich Zip Codes call (203) 869-3737	
Greystone	06786

Location	ZIP
Griswold (Town)	06351
Griswoldville	06109
Grosvenor Dale	06246
Groton	06340
Groton (Town)	06340
Groton Heights (Part of Groton)	06340
Groton Lake Shores	06357
Groton Long Point	06340
Grove Beach	06413
Gugliotti	06479
Guilford	06437
Guilford (Town)	06437
Guilford Lake	06437
Gurleyville	06268
Haddam	06438
Haddam (Town)	06438
Haddam Neck	06424
Hadlyme	06439
Hale Court	06880
Hallville	06360
Hamburg	06371
Hamden (New Haven County) (Town)	06514
Hamden (New Haven County)	06514
Hamden Plaza	06514
Hampton	06247
Hampton (Town)	06247
Hank Hills	06268
Hanover	06350
Happyland	06360
Harborview (Fairfield County)	06853
Harbor View (Middlesex County)	06413
Harrisons	06375
Harrisville	06281
Hartford	06101-99
For specific Hartford Zip Codes call (203) 524-6004	
Hartland (Town)	06027
Harwinton	06791
Harwinton (Town)	06790
Hawks Nest Beach	06371
Hawleyville	06440
Hawthorne Terrace (Part of Danbury)	06810
Hayden	06095
Hayestown (Part of Danbury)	06810
Hazardville	06082
Headquarters	06759
Hebron	06248
Hebron (Town)	06248
Heritage Village	06488
Hidden Lake	06441
Higganum	06441
Highland Park	06040
Hi-Ho Center (Part of Bridgeport)	06604
Hillside (Part of Bridgeport)	06610
Hitchcock Lake	06716
Holiday Homes (Part of Colchester)	06415
Hollywyle Park	06810
Holy Apostles College	06416
Honeypot Glen	06410
Hopeville (New Haven County)	06706
Hopeville (New London County)	06351
Horton Hill (Part of Naugatuck)	06770
Hotchkissville	06798
Huckleberry Hill	06001
Hungary Hill	06377
Huntington (Part of Shelton)	06484
Hydeville	06075
I-91 Exit 8 Mall (Part of New Haven)	06515
Indian Cove	06437
Indian Neck	06405
Ivoryton	06442
Jericho Hill	06371
Jewett City	06351
Jordan Village	06385
Kelseytown	06413
Kensington	06037
Kent	06757
Kent (Town)	06757
Kent Furnace	06757
Kenyonville	06282
Kilby (Part of New Haven)	06519
Killingly (Town)	06239
Killingly Center	06241
Killingworth	06417
Killingworth (Town)	06417
Kings Corner	06088
Knollcrest	06810

92 CONNECTICUT Knollwood-Plainville

	ZIP
Knollwood	06475
Lake Bashan	06423
Lake Beseck	06455
Lake Bungee	06282
Lake Garda	06013
Lake Hayward	06415
Lake Plymouth	06782
Lake Pocotopaug	06424
Lakeside (Litchfield County)	06758
Lakeside (New Haven County)	06488
Lakeview Terrace	06076
Lakeville	06039
Lakewood (Part of Waterbury)	06704
Lattins Landing (Part of Danbury)	06810
Laurel (Part of Middletown)	06457
Laurel Beach (Part of Milford)	06460
Laurel Hill (Part of Norwich)	06360
Laysville	06371
Lebanon	06249
Lebanon (Town)	06249
Ledyard	06339
Ledyard (Town)	06339
Leesville	06469
Leetes Island	06437
Leffingwell	06360
Liberty Hill	06249
Lime Rock	06039
Lisbon	06351
Lisbon (Town)	06351
Litchfield	06759
Litchfield (Town)	06759
Little Boston	06875
Little City	06441
Long Hill (Fairfield County)	06611
Long Hill (Middlesex County)	06457
Long Hill (New Haven County)	06704
Long Hill (New London County)	06340
Long Ridge (Part of Stamford)	06901
Lordship	06497
Lords Point	06378
Lydallville	06040
Lyme (New London County)	06371
Lyme (New London County) (Town)	06371
Lyons Plains	06880
Macedonia	06757
Madison	06443
Madison (Town)	06443
Manchester	06040-43
For specific Manchester Zip Codes call (203) 643-2735	
Manchester (Hartford County) (Town)	06040
Manchester (Hartford County)	06040
Manchester Green	06040
Mansfield (Town)	06250
Mansfield Center	06250
Mansfield City	06268
Mansfield Depot	06251
Mansfield Four Corners	06268
Mansfield Hollow	06250
Maple Hill	06111
Maplewood (Part of Derby)	06418
Marble Dale	06777
Margerie Manor (Part of Danbury)	06810
Marion	06444
Marlborough	06447
Marlborough (Town)	06447
Maromas (Part of Middletown)	06457
Mashapaug	06076
Mason Island	06355
Massapeag	06382
Mayberry Village	06108
Mechanicsville	06277
Melrose	06049
Melville Village	06430
Meriden (New Haven County)	06450
Meriden (New Haven County) (Town)	06450
Meriden Square (Part of Meriden)	06450
Merrow	06251
Mianus	06807
Middle Beach	06443
Middlebury	06762
Middlebury (Town)	06762
Middlefield	06455
Middlefield (Town)	06455
Middle Haddam	06456

	ZIP
Middletown (Middlesex County)	06457
Middletown (Middlesex County) (Town)	06460
Midway	06340
Milbrook	06830
Milford (New Haven County)	06460
Milford (New Haven County) (Town)	06460
Milford Lawns (Part of Milford)	06460
Millbrook	06518
Milldale	06467
Millington	06423
Mill Plain (Part of Danbury)	06810
Millville (Part of Naugatuck)	06770
Milton	06759
Mixville	06410
Mohegan	06382
Momauguin	06512
Monroe	06468
Monroe (Town)	06468
Monroe Center	06468
Montowese	06473
Montville	06353
Montville (Town)	06353
Montville Manor	06370
Moodus	06469
Moosup	06354
Morningside (Part of Milford)	06460
Morris	06763
Morris (Town)	06763
Morris Cove	06512
Mount Carmel	06518
Mount Hope	06250
Murphy Road Annex (Part of Hartford)	06114
Murray	06430
Myrtle Beach (Part of Milford)	06460
Mystic	06355
Naugatuck (New Haven County)	06770
Naugatuck (New Haven County) (Town)	06770
Naugatuck Gardens (Part of Milford)	06460
Naugatuck Valley Mall (Part of Waterbury)	06705
Nautilus Park	06340
Nepaug	06057
Newberry Corner (Part of Torrington)	06790
New Britain	06050-53
For specific New Britain Zip Codes call (203) 223-3681	
New Canaan (Fairfield County) (Town)	06840
New Canaan (Fairfield County)	06840
Newent	06351
New Fairfield	06812
New Fairfield (Town)	06810
Newfield (Fairfield County)	06607
Newfield Heights (Part of Middletown)	06457
Newhallville (Part of New Haven)	06511
New Hartford	06057
New Hartford (Town)	06057
New Haven	06511-36
For specific New Haven Zip Codes call (203) 782-7203	
Newington (Hartford County) (Town)	06111
Newington (Hartford County)	06111
Newington Junction	06111
New London (New London County)	06320
New London (New London County) (Town)	06320
New London Submarine Base	06349
New Milford	06776
New Milford (Town)	06776
New Preston	06777
New Preston-Marble Dale	06777
Newtown	06470
Newtown (Town)	06470
New Village	06374
Niantic	06357
Nichols	06611
Noank	06340
Noble (Part of Bridgeport)	06608
Norfolk	06058
Norfolk (Town)	06058
Noroton	06820
Noroton Heights	06820
North Ashford	06282
North Bloomfield	06002

	ZIP
North Branford	06471
North Branford (Town)	06471
North Bridgeport (Part of Bridgeport)	06601
North Canaan (Town)	06018
North Canton	06059
North Cornwall	06796
North End (Part of Waterbury)	06704
North Farms	06471
Northfield	06778
Northford	06472
North Franklin	06254
North Glenwood	06335
North Granby	06060
North Grosvenor Dale	06255
North Guilford	06437
North Haven (New Haven County) (Town)	06473
North Haven (New Haven County)	06473
North Kent	06757
North Mianus	06807
North Plain	06423
North Sterling	06377
North Stonington	06359
North Stonington (Town)	06359
North Thompsonville	06082
Northville	06776
North Westchester	06474
North Windham	06256
Norwalk	06850-56
For specific Norwalk Zip Codes call (203) 838-4881	
Norwich (New London County)	06360
Norwich (New London County) (Town)	06360
Norwich Hospital	06360
Norwichtown (Part of Norwich)	06360
Nut Plains	06437
Oakdale	06370
Oakdale Heights	06370
Oakdale Manor	06488
Oakland Gardens	06032
Oakville	06779
Oakwood Acres	06812
Occum (Part of Norwich)	06360
Old Greenwich	06870
Old Lyme	06371
Old Lyme (Town)	06371
Old Lyme Shores	06371
Old Mystic	06372
Old Saybrook	06475
Old Saybrook (Town)	06475
Old Saybrook Shopping Center	06475
Old State House (Part of Hartford)	06123
Oneco	06373
Orange (New Haven County) (Town)	06477
Orange (New Haven County)	06477
Orcutts	06076
Oronoke (Part of Waterbury)	06708
Oronoque	06497
Oswegatchie	06385
Overlook (Part of Waterbury)	06710
Owenoke	06880
Oxford	06483
Oxford (Town)	06483
Ox Hill (Part of Norwich)	06360
Oxoboxo Lake (New London County)	06370
Pachaug	06351
Palestine	06470
Palmertown	06353
Paradise Green	06497
Parcel Post (Part of Milford)	06460
Parkville (Part of Hartford)	06106
Pawcatuck	06379
Pemberwick	06830
Pequabuck	06781
Perkins Corner	06226
Phoenixville	06235
Pine Bridge	06403
Pine Grove (Litchfield County)	06031
Pine Grove (New London County)	06357
Pine Meadow	06061
Pine Orchard	06405
Pine Rock Park (Part of Shelton)	06484
Plainfield	06374
Plainfield (Town)	06374
Plainville (Hartford County) (Town)	06062

Plainville-Weatogue **CONNECTICUT** 93

Name	ZIP
Plainville (Hartford County)	06062
Plantsville	06479
Platts Mills (Part of Waterbury)	06706
Plaza (Part of Waterbury)	06704
Pleasant Acres (Part of Danbury)	06810
Pleasant Valley	06063
Pleasure Beach	06385
Plymouth	06782
Plymouth (Town)	06782
Point Beach (Part of Milford)	06460
Point O'Woods	06376
Pomfret	06258
Pomfret (Town)	06258
Pomfret Center	06259
Pomfret Landing	06259
Pond Point (Part of Milford)	06460
Ponset	06441
Pootatuck Park	06482
Poquetanuck	06360
Poquonock	06064
Poquonock Bridge	06340
Portland (Middlesex County) (Town)	06480
Portland (Middlesex County)	06480
Presidential	06082
Preston	06360
Preston (Town)	06360
Prospect (New Haven County) (Town)	06712
Prospect (New Haven County)	06712
Prospect Beach (Part of West Haven)	06516
Puddle Town	06022
Putnam	06260
Putnam (Town)	06260
Putnam Heights	06260
Putney	06497
Quaddick	06277
Quaker Farms	06483
Quaker Hill	06375
Quarryville	06040
Quebec	06239
Quinebaug	06262
Quinnipiac	06492
Rawson	06247
Redding (Town)	06875
Redding	06875
Redding Ridge	06876
Reynolds Bridge	06787
Ridgebury	06877
Ridgefield	06877
Ridgefield (Town)	06877
Ridgeway (Part of Stamford)	06905
Ridgewood	06413
Ridgewood Park	06385
Rising Corner	06093
Rivercliff (Part of Milford)	06460
River Glen	06032
Riverside (Fairfield County)	06878
Riverside (Fairfield County)	06482
Riverside (Hartford County)	06022
Riverside (New Haven County)	06483
Riversville	06830
Riverton	06065
Robertsville	06065
Rockfall	06481
Rock Ridge	06830
Rocky Hill (Hartford County) (Town)	06067
Rocky Hill (Hartford County)	06067
Rogers	06263
Round Hill	06830
Rowayton (Part of Norwalk)	06853
Roxbury	06783
Roxbury (Town)	06783
Roxbury Falls	06783
Sachem Head	06437
Salem	06415
Salem (Town)	06415
Salisbury	06068
Salisbury (Town)	06068
Samp Mortar	06430
Sandy Beach	06758
Sandy Hook	06482
Sanfordtown	06896
Saugatuck	06880
Saugatuck Shores	06880
Saunders Point	06357
Savin Rock (Part of West Haven)	06516
Saybrook Manor	06475
Saybrook Point	06475
Scantic	06088
Scitico	06082
Scotland	06264
Scotland (Town)	06264
Seaview Beach	06443

Name	ZIP
Secret Lake	06001
Seymour (New Haven County) (Town)	06483
Seymour (New Haven County)	06483
Shady Rest	06482
Shailerville	06438
Sharon	06069
Sharon (Town)	06069
Sharon Valley	06069
Shelton (Fairfield County)	06484
Shelton (Fairfield County) (Town)	06484
Sherman	06784
Sherman (Town)	06784
Sherman Corner	06256
Sherwood Manor	06082
Shippan Point (Part of Stamford)	06902
Short Beach	06405
Silver Beach (Part of Milford)	06460
Silver Lane	06138
Simsbury	06070
Simsbury (Town)	06070
Skiff Mountain	06757
Somers	06071
Somers (Town)	06071
Somersville	06072
Sound View	06371
South Britain	06487
Southbury	06488
Southbury (Town)	06488
South Canaan	06031
South Ellsworth	06069
South End (Fairfield County)	06902
South End (New Haven County)	06512
South Farms (Part of Middletown)	06457
South Glastonbury	06073
South Glenwoods	06335
Southington	06489
Southington (Town)	06489
South Kent	06785
South Killingly	06239
South Lyme	06376
South Manchester	06040
South Meriden (Part of Meriden)	06450
South Norwalk (Part of Norwalk)	06854
Southport	06490
South Wethersfield	06109
South Willington	06265
South Windham	06266
South Windsor	06074
South Windsor (Town)	06074
Southwood Acres	06082
South Woodstock	06267
Sport Hill	06612
Sprague (Town)	06330
Springdale (Part of Stamford)	06907
Spring Hill	06268
Spring Lake Village	06489
Stafford	06075
Stafford (Town)	06075
Stafford Springs	06076
Staffordville	06077
Stamford	06901-12
For specific Stamford Zip Codes call (203) 975-7657	
Stamford Town Center (Part of Stamford)	06901
Stanwich	06830
State Line	06076
Station A (Part of Hartford)	06126
Sterling	06377
Sterling (Town)	06377
Sterling Hill	06354
Stetson Corner	06234
Stevenson	06491
Stonington	06378
Stonington (Town)	06378
Stony Corners	06001
Stony Creek	06405
Storrs	06268
Straitsville (Part of Naugatuck)	06770
Stratfield	06432
Stratfield-Brooklawn	06430
Stratford (Fairfield County) (Town)	06497
Stratford (Fairfield County)	06497
Stratmore Farms	06492
Suburban Enfield Mall	06082
Suffield	06078
Suffield (Town)	06078
Summer Hill	06492
Sunrise Hill	06525

Name	ZIP
Taconic	06079
Taft Station (Part of Norwich)	06360
Taftville (Part of Norwich)	06380
Talcott Village	06032
Talcottville	06066
Talmadge Hill	06840
Tariffville	06081
Terminal (Part of New Haven)	06511
Terryville	06786
Thamesville (Part of Norwich)	06360
Thomaston	06787
Thomaston (Town)	06787
Thompson	06277
Thompson (Town)	06277
Titicus	06877
Tokeneke	06820
Tolland	06084
Tolland (Town)	06084
Torringford (Part of Torrington)	06790
Torrington (Litchfield County) (Town)	06790
Torrington (Litchfield County)	06790
Town Hill	06057
Town Plot Hill (Part of Waterbury)	06708
Trails Corner	06340
Trumbull (Fairfield County) (Town)	06612
Trumbull (Fairfield County)	06611
Trumbull Shopping Center	06611
Trumbull Shopping Park	06611
Turn of River (Part of Stamford)	06901
Turnpike	06066
Twin Lakes	06079
Tyler Lake Heights	06756
Uncasville	06382
Union	06076
Union (Town)	06076
Union City (Part of Naugatuck)	06770
Unionville	06085
Unity Plaza (Part of Hartford)	06140
Upper Stepney	06468
Vernon (Tolland County) (Town)	06066
Vernon (Tolland County)	06066
Vernon Center	06066
Versailles	06383
Versailles Station	06383
Village Hill	06249
Voluntown (Town)	06384
Voluntown	06384
Wailacks Point (Part of Stamford)	06902
Wallingford (New Haven County) (Town)	06492
Wallingford (New Haven County)	06492
Walnut Beach (Part of Milford)	06460
Walnut Hill	06333
Walnut Tree Hill	06482
Wamphassuc Point	06378
Wapping	06074
Warren	06754
Warren (Town)	06753
Warrenville	06278
Washington (Town)	06793
Washington Depot	06793-94
For specific Washington Depot Zip Codes call (203) 868-7474	
Washington Green	06793
Washington Hill	06059
Washington Square (Part of Norwich)	06360
Waterbury	06701-26
For specific Waterbury Zip Codes call (203) 574-6553	
Waterbury Plaza Shopping Center (Part of Waterbury)	06704
Waterford	06385
Waterford (Town)	06385
Waterside (Part of Stamford)	06901
Watertown	06795
Watertown (Town)	06795
Waterville (Part of Waterbury)	06704
Wauregan	06387
Wauwecus Hill (Part of Norwich)	06360
Weatogue	06089

94 CONNECTICUT — Webster Square Shopping Center-Zoar

Name	ZIP
Webster Square Shopping Center	06037
Weekeempee	06798
Welles Village	06033
Wells Quarter Village	06109
Wequetequock	02891
Wesleyan (Part of Middletown)	06457
West Ashford	06250
West Avon	06001
West Bantam	06750
Westbrook	06498
Westbrook (Town)	06498
Westchester	06415
West Cornwall	06796
West End (Part of Bristol)	06010
Westfarms	06032
West Farms Village (Part of New Britain)	06050
Westfield (Part of Middletown)	06457
Westford	06076
West Goshen	06756
West Granby	06090
West Hartford (Hartford County) (Town)	06107
West Hartford (Hartford County)	06127
West Hartland	06091
West Haven (New Haven County)	06516
West Haven (New Haven County) (Town)	06516
West Lakes	06437
West Mystic	06388
West Norwalk (Part of Norwalk)	06851
Weston	06883
Weston (Town)	06880
Westport	06880-83

For specific Westport Zip Codes call (203) 227-9569

Name	ZIP
West Putnam Avenue	06830
West Redding	06896
West Shore (Part of West Haven)	06516
West Side (Part of Norwich)	06360
West Side Hill (Part of Waterbury)	06708
West Simsbury	06092
West Stafford	06076
West Suffield	06093
West Thompson	06255
West Torrington (Part of Torrington)	06790
Westview Acres	06483
Westville (Part of New Haven)	06515
West Wauregan	06387
West Willington	06279
Westwood Park (Part of Norwich)	06360
West Woods	06069
West Woodstock	06281
Wethersfield (Hartford County) (Town)	06109
Wethersfield (Hartford County)	06129
Wethersfield Shopping Center	06109
Wheeler Farms (Part of Milford)	06460
Whigville	06013
Whipstick	06877
Whitacres	06082
White Sands Beach	06371
Whitneyville	06517
Wildermere Beach (Part of Milford)	06460
Williams Crossing	06249
Willimantic	06226

Name	ZIP
Willington (Town)	06279
Willington Hill	06279
Willow Point	06388
Wilsonville	06255
Wilton	06897
Wilton (Town)	06897
Winchester (Town)	06094
Winchester Center	06094
Windham	06280
Windham (Town)	06280
Winding Lanes	06001
Windsor	06095
Windsor (Town)	06095
Windsor Locks (Hartford County) (Town)	06096
Windsor Locks (Hartford County)	06096
Windsorville	06016
Winnipauk (Part of Norwalk)	06851
Winsted	06098
Winthrop	06417
Wolcott	06716
Wolcott (Town)	06716
Woodbridge (Town)	06525
Woodbridge	06525
Woodbury	06798
Woodbury (Town)	06798
Woodlake	06798
Woodmont	06460
Woodstock	06281
Woodstock (Town)	06281
Woodstock Valley	06282
Woodtick	06716
Woodville	06777
Yale (Part of New Haven)	06520
Yalesville	06492
Yantic (Part of Norwich)	06389
Zoar	06482

Adams Crossroads-Holly Oak **DELAWARE** 95

Name	ZIP
Adams Crossroads	19950
Adamsville	19950
Afton	19810
Alapocas	19803
Albertson Park	19808
Analine Village	19703
Andrewsville	19950
Anglesey	19807
Angola Beach	19951
Angola by the Bay	19958
Anne Acres	19971
Arden	19803
Ardencroft	19810
Ardentown	19810
Argo Corner	19963
Arundel	19808
Ashbourne Hills	19703
Ashland	19807
Ashley	19804
Atlanta	19933
Atlanta Estates	19973
Augustine Beach	19731
Avalon	19808
Bacon	19940
Bakers Choice	19946
Bakıton (Part of New Castle)	19720
Bayard	19945
Bay Berry Dunes	19930
Bay View Beach	19709
Bay View Park	19930
Bayville	19975
Bay Vista	19971
Bear	19701
Beaver Brook Apartments	19720
Beaverdam Heights	19973
Bellefonte	19809
Bellemoor	19802
Bellevue Manor	19809
Belltown	19958
Belmont Hall	19977
Belvidere	19804
Bestfield	19804
Bethany Beach	19930
Bethany Dunes	19930
Bethany Village	19930
Bethel	19931
Big Mills Bridge	19956
Big Oak Corners	19977
Big Pine	19950
Big Stone Beach	19963
Binns Village (Part of Newark)	19711
Birchwood Park	19711
Blackbird	19734
Blackiston	19938
Blackwater Village	19939
Blades	19973
Blue Hen Mall (Part of Dover)	19901
Blue Rock Manor	19803
Bowers	19946
Bowers Beach	19946
Boxwood	19804
Brack-Ex	19805
Brandywine	19810
Brandywine Estates	19703
Brandywine Springs Manor	19808
Brandywood	19810
Breezewood (Kent County)	19943
Breezewood (New Castle County)	19713
Brenford	19977
Briar Park	19901
Bridgeville	19933
Broadacres	19973
Broad Creek	19956
Broadkill Beach	19968
Brookbend	19713
Brookdale Heights	19934
Brookhaven	19711
Brookland Terrace	19805
Brookside (New Castle County)	19713
Brookview Apartments	19703
Brownsville	19952
Bull Pine Corners	19947
Bunting	19975
Buttonwood (Part of New Castle)	19720
Camden	19934
Camden-Wyoming (Part of Wyoming)	19934
Cannon	19933
Canterbury	19943
Capitol Green (Part of Dover)	19901
Capitol Park	19901
Cardiff	19810
Carlisle Village	19901
Carrcroft	19803
Carrcroft Crest	19803
Carter	19901
Castle Hills	19720
Catalina Gardens (Part of Newark)	19711
Cave Colony	19968
Cedar Beach	19963
Cedarbrook Acres	19977
Cedar Heights	19804
Centreville	19807
Chalfonte	19810
Channin	19803
Chapel Hill	19711
Chatham	19810
Chelsea Estates	19720
Cherokee Woods	19713
Chestnut Hill Estates	19713
Chestnut Knoll	19963
Cheswold	19936
Christiana	19702
Christiana Acres	19720
Clarksville	19970
Claymont (New Castle County)	19703
Claymont (New Castle County)	19702
Clayton	19938
Clearfield	19703
Clearview Manor	19720
Cleland Heights	19805
Clifton Park Manor	19802
Cocked Hat	19933
College Park (Part of Newark)	19711
Collins Park	19720
Colmar Manor	19977
Colonial Heights	19805
Colonial Park	19805
Columbia	19940
Concord	19973
Concord Mall	19803
Concord Manor	19803
Cool Spring	19968
Cooper Farm	19808
Cottonpatch Hill	19930
Country Club Estates	19963
Coventry	19720
Coverdale Crossroads	19933
Covered Bridge Farms	19711
Covey Creek	19958
Cragmere	19809
Cragmere Woods	19809
Craigs Mill	19973
Cranston Heights	19808
Crossgates (Part of Dover)	19901
Cross Keys	19966
Dagsboro	19939
Darley Woods	19810
Dartmouth Woods	19810
Deerhurst	19803
Delaplane Manor	19711
Delaware City	19706
Delaware Correctional Center	19977
Delaware Heights	19807
Del Haven Estates	19962
Delmar	19940
Del Park Manor	19808
Devon	19810
Devonshire	19810
Dewey Beach	19971
Diamond Acres	19939
Dobbinsville (Part of Castle)	19720
Dover	19901-03
For specific Dover Zip Codes call (302) 734-5821	
Dover AFB Housing Annex	19901
Dover Base Housing	19901
Doverbrook Gardens	19901
Dover Mall (Part of Dover)	19901
Downs Chapel	19938
Drummond North	19711
Dublin Hill	19933
Dunleith	19801
Dunlinden Acres	19805
Dupont Manor	19901
Du Ross Heights	19720
Dutch Acres	19958
Eastman Heights	19963
Eastover Hills (Part of Dover)	19901
Eberton	19901
Eden Park	19720
Edge Hill (Part of Dover)	19901
Edgehill Acres (Part of Dover)	19901
Edgemoor (New Castle County)	19809
Edgemoor (New Castle County)	19802
Edgemoor Gardens	19802
Edgemoor Terrace	19802
Edgewater Acres	19975
Edgewood Hills	19802
Edwardsville	19943
Ellendale	19941
Elmhurst	19804
Elsmere	19805
Elsmere Junction (Part of Elsmere)	19805
English Village	19711
Evergreen Acres	19963
Fairfax	19803
Fairfield Farms	19901
Fairmount	19951
Fairwinds	19701
Farmington	19942
Faulkland	19808
Faulkland Heights	19808
Faulkwoods	19810
Federal (Part of Newark)	19711
Felton	19943
Felton Heights	19943
Felton Manor	19943
Fenwick Island	19944
Fieldsboro	19734
Fireside Park	19713
Flemings Corner	19952
Flemings Landing	19734
Forest Brook Glen	19804
Forest Hills Park	19803
Four Seasons	19702
Foxhall Courtside	19901
Fox Hollow	19958
Frankford	19945
Frederica	19946
Galewood	19803
Garfield Park	19720
Gateway Farms	19707
Georgetown	19947
Ginns Corner	19734
Glasgow	19711
Glasgow Court	19702
Glasgow Pines	19702
Glen Burne Estates	19804
Glendale	19711
Glenville	19804
Goldey Beacom College	19808
Gordon Heights	19802
Gordy Estates	19804
Granogue	19807
Gravel Hill	19947
Graylyn Crest	19810
Green Acres	19803
Green Bank	19808
Greenbriar	19720
Greenshire	19703
Greentree	19703
Greenview	19901
Greenville	19807
Greenville Place	19807
Greenwood	19950
Gulls Nest	19930
Gumboro	19945
Guyencourt	19807
Gwinhurst	19809
Hall Estates	19963
Hamilton Park	19720
Hanbys Corner	19810
Harbeson	19951
Hardscrabble	19973
Harmony Hills	19711
Harrington	19952
Hartly	19953
Hayden Park	19804
Hearns Crossroads	19956
Hearns Mill	19973
Heather Woods	19702
Henlopen Acres	19971
Henry Clay	19807
Hickman	21629
Hickory Hill	19966
Hickory Ridge	19977
Highland Acres (Kent County)	19901
Highland Acres (Sussex County)	19958
Highland West	19808
High Point Park	19946
Hillcrest	19802
Hillside Acres	19943
Hillside Heights	19711
Hilltop Manor	19809
Hitchens Crossroads	19956
Hockessin	19707
Holiday Acres	19939
Hollandsville	19943
Holletts Corners	19938
Holloway Terrace	19720
Holly Oak (New Castle County)	19809

# 96 DELAWARE Holly Oak-Webb Manor

Name	ZIP
Holly Oak (Sussex County)	19973
Holly Oak Terrace	19809
Hollyville	19951
Houston	19954
Huntley	19901
Hyde Park	19808
Idela	19804
Indian Beach	19971
Indian Field	19810
Indian River Acres	19939
Iron Hill Apartments	19702
Ivy Ridge	19720
Jefferson Farms	19720
Jimtown	19958
Johnson	19975
Johnstown	19950
Jones Crossroads	19956
Keen-Wik	19975
Kenilworth	19703
Kenmore Park	19973
Kent Acres (Kent County)	19901
Kenton	19955
Kiamensi	19804
Kirkwood	19708
Kitts Hummock	19901
Klair Estates	19808
Kynlyn Apartments	19809
Lake Pines	19956
Lamatan	19711
Lancashire	19810
Lancaster Court	19805
Lancaster Village	19805
Laurel	19956
Lebanon	19901
Leedom Estates	19720
Leipsic	19901
Lewes	19958
Lewes Beach (Part of Lewes)	19958
Liftwood	19803
Limestone Acres	19808
Limestone Gardens	19808
Lincoln	19960
Lindenmere	19809
Little Creek	19961
Little Heaven	19946
Llangollen Estates	19720
London Village	19962
Longview Farms	19810
Lowe	19956
Lowes Crossroads	19966
Lumbrook (Part of Newark)	19711
Lynch Heights	19963
Lyndalia	19804
Lynnfield	19803
McClellandville	19711
McDaniel Heights	19803
Magnolia	19962
Manor	19720
Manor Park	19720
Manor Park Apartments	19720
Maplecrest	19808
Marabou Meadows	19702
Marshallton	19808
Marvels Crossroads	19952
Marydel	19964
Mastens Corner	19943
Mayfair (Part of Dover)	19901
Mayfield	19803
Mayview Manor	19720
Meadowbrook	19804
Meadowbrook Acres	19962
Meadowood	19711
Mechanicsville	19711
Meeting House Hill	19711
Melody Meadows	19702
Middleford	19973
Middlesex Beach	19930
Middletown	19709
Midvale	19720
Midway	19971
Milford	19963
Milford Cross Roads	19711
Millpond Acres	19958
Millsboro	19966
Millville	19970
Milton	19968
Minquadale	19720
Mispillion Light	19963
Mission	19966
Montchanin	19710
Monterey Farms	19720
Morris Estates (Part of Dover)	19901
Mount Cuba	19807
Mount Pleasant	19709
Naamans Gardens	19810
Naamans Manor	19810
Naamans Trailer Park	19703
Nanticoke Acres	19973
Nassau	19969

Name	ZIP
Newark	19711-15 -19725-26
For specific Newark Zip Codes call (302) 737-5770	
New Castle	19720
New Castle Manor (Part of New Castle)	19720
Newkirk Estates	19711
Newport	19804
Newport Heights	19804
Northcrest	19810
North Hills	19809
North Ridge	19703
North Seaford Heights	19973
Northshire	19810
North Star	19711
Northwest Dover Heights (Part of Dover)	19901
Northwood	19803
Oak Forest Estates	19953
Oak Grove (Kent County)	19901
Oak Grove (New Castle County)	19805
Oak Grove (Sussex County)	19973
Oak Hill	19805
Oak Lane Manor	19803
Oakley	19941
Oakmont	19720
Oak Orchard	19966
Ocean View	19970
Ocean Village	19930
Odessa	19730
Ogletown	19711
Old Furnace	19947
Omar	19945
Orchard Acres	19943
Overview Gardens	19720
Owens	19950
Owls Nest Estates	19807
Palm Springs Manor	19711
Paris Villa	19962
Pembrey	19803
Penarth	19803
Penn Acres	19720
Pennrock	19809
Penny Hill	19809
Pepper	19956
Pepperbox	19956
Perry Park	19810
Perth	19803
Petersburg	19979
Pickering Beach	19901
Pinetown	19958
Pine Tree Corners	19734
Piney Grove	19947
Pleasant Hill	19804
Pleasanton Acres	19901
Pleasantville	19720
Plymouth	19943
Polly Drummond	19711
Polly Drummond Hill	19711
Porter	19701
Port Mahon	19901
Port Penn	19731
Portsville	19956
Primehook Beach	19963
Quakertown	19958
Radnor Green	19703
Radnor Woods	19703
Rambleton Acres	19720
Ramblewood	19810
Redden	19947
Redden Crossroads	19947
Red Lion	19701
Reeves Crossing	19943
Rehoboth Beach	19971
Reliance	19973
Richardson Park	19804
Rising Sun	19934
Rising Sun-Lebanon	19901
Riverdale	19966
Riverside Gardens	19703
Riverview	19966
Robscott Manor	19713
Rockland	19732
Rodney Square (Part of Wilmington)	19801
Rodney Village (Kent County)	19901
Rodric Village	19901
Rogers Haven	19970
Rogers Manor (Part of New Castle)	19720
Rolling Hills	19804
Rolling Park	19703
Rosedale Beach	19966
Rose Gate	19720
Rose Hill	19720
Rose Hill Gardens	19720
Roselle	19805
Roseville Park	19711

Name	ZIP
Roxana	19945
Rutherford	19711
St. Georges	19733
Sandtown	19943
Sandy Brae	19958
Scottfield	19711
Scotts Corner	19933
Seabreeze	19971
Sea Del Estates	19930
Seaford	19973
Seaford Heights	19973
Sedgley Farms	19807
Seeneytown	19938
Selbyville	19975
Shady Lane	19901
Shaft Ox Corner	19966
Sharpley	19803
Shawnee Acres	19963
Shawtown (Part of New Castle)	19720
Shell Bridge	19956
Shellburne	19803
Sherwood (Part of Dover)	19901
Sherwood Acres	19945
Sherwood Park	19808
Shipley Heights	19803
Shortly	19947
Silverbrook	19805
Silver Lake Shores	19971
Silverside Heights	19809
Silview	19804
Simonds Gardens	19720
Slaughter Beach	19963
Smyrna	19977
Smyrna Landing (Part of Smyrna)	19977
Snug Harbor	19973
South Bethany	19930
South Bowers	19963
South Dover Acres (Part of Dover)	19901
Spruance City	19977
Stanton (New Castle County)	19804
Star Hill	19901
Star Hill-Briar Park	19901
Staytonville	19952
Stockdale	19703
Stockley	19947
Stockton	19720
Stoneybrook Apartments	19703
Stratford	19720
Surrey Park	19803
Sussex Correctional Institution	19947
Sussex Shores	19930
Swain Acres	19947
Swann Keys	19975
Swanwyck	19720
Swanwyck Estates	19720
Swanwyck Gardens	19720
Sycamore	19956
Sycamore Gardens	19711
Talleyville (New Castle County)	19803
Tanglewood	19713
Tarleton	19803
Taylor Estates	19901
Taylors Bridge	19734
The Beeches (Part of Dover)	19901
The Cedars	19808
The Island	19973
The Timbers	19803
Thomas Landing	19734
Thompsonville	19963
Tidbury Manor	19901
Todd Estates	19713
Towne Point (Part of Dover)	19901
Townsend	19734
Tuxedo Park	19804
Twin Eagle Farms	19938
Tybrook	19808
Union Street (Part of Wilmington)	19805
Valley Run	19810
Van Dyke Village (Part of New Castle)	19720
Varlano	19702
Vernon	19952
Village of Drummond Hill	19711
Village of Garrisons Lake	19977
Village of Windhover	19702
Villa Monterey	19809
Viola	19979
Voshells Cove	19901
Ward	19940
Washington Heights	19971
Washington Park (Part of New Castle)	19720
Webb Manor	19963

	ZIP		ZIP		ZIP
Webster Farms	19803	Willow Grove	19934	Woodcrest (New Castle County)	19804
Wedgewood Acres	19720	Willow Run	19805	Wooddale	19807
Weisman Acres	19963	Wilmington	19801-99	Woodenhawk	19950
Wellington Woods	19702	For specific Wilmington Zip Codes call (302) 323-3783		Woodland (New Castle County)	19805
Welshire	19803				
West Beach	19939	Wilmington College	19720	Woodland (Sussex County)	19973
Westfield	19804	Wilmington Manor (New Castle County)	19720	Woodland Beach	19977
West Haven	19807			Woodshade	19702
West Meadow	19711	Wilmington Manor Gardens	19720	Woods Haven	19963
Westover Hills	19807	Wilmont	19810	Woodside	19980
West Park	19807	Windermer	19804	Woodside East	19980
Westview	19804	Windsor Hills	19803	Woodside Hills	19809
Westwood Manor	19810	Windy Bush	19810	Woods Manor	19901
Whaleys Corners	19956	Windy Hills	19711	Workmans Corners	19947
Whaleys Crossroads	19956	Winterthur	19735	Wyoming	19934
Whiteleysburg	19943	Woodbine	19803	York Beach (Part of South Bethany)	19930
White Oak Farms (Part of Dover)	19901	Woodbrook (Kent County)	19901		
Whitesville	19940	Woodbrook (New Castle County)	19803	Yorklyn	19736
Williamsville (Kent County)	19954	Woodcrest (Kent County)	19901		
Williamsville (Sussex County)	19975				

98 DISTRICT OF COLUMBIA Anacostia-Washington

	ZIP
Anacostia (Part of Washington)	20020
Barnaby Terrace (Part of Washington)	20032
Benjamin Franklin (Part of Washington)	20004
Benning (Part of Washington)	20019
Blue Plains (Part of Washington)	20032
Bolling Air Force Base (Part of Washington)	20332
Brightwood (Part of Washington)	20011
Brightwood Park (Part of Washington)	20011
Brookland (Part of Washington)	20017
Calvert (Part of Washington)	20007
Cardinal (Part of Washington)	20017
Central (Part of Washington)	20005
Chillum (Part of Washington)	20011
Cleveland Park (Part of Washington)	20008
Colonial Village (Part of Washington)	20012
Columbia Heights (Part of Washington)	20009
Congress Heights (Part of Washington)	20032
Congress Park (Part of Washington)	20032
Customs House (Part of Washington)	20018
Douglas Dwellings (Part of Washington)	20020
Eagle (Part of Washington)	20016
Eckington (Part of Washington)	20002
Fairfax Village (Part of Washington)	20020
Farragut (Part of Washington)	20036
Fort Davis (Part of Washington)	20020
Fort Lincoln (Part of Washington)	20018
Fort McNair (Part of Washington)	20319
Friendship (Part of Washington)	20016
F Street (Part of Washington)	20004
Garfield Heights (Part of Washington)	20020
Georgetown (Part of Washington)	20007
Glover Park (Part of Washington)	20007
Good Hope (Part of Washington)	20020
Hillcrest (Part of Washington)	20020
Hoya (Part of Washington)	20007
Kalorama (Part of Washington)	20009
Kendall Green (Part of Washington)	20002
Knox Hill Dwellings (Part of Washington)	20020
Lamond (Part of Washington)	20011
Le Droit Park (Part of Washington)	20001
L'Enfant Plaza (Part of Washington)	20024
Les Champs (Part of Washington)	20037
McLean Gardens (Part of Washington)	20016
Manor Park (Part of Washington)	20011
Mid City (Part of Washington)	20005
Mount Pleasant (Part of Washington)	20010
Naval Research Laboratory (Part of Washington)	20375
Naylor Gardens (Part of Washington)	20020
Northeast (Part of Washington)	20002
Northwest (Part of Washington)	20015
Palisades (Part of Washington)	20016
Park View (Part of Washington)	20010

	ZIP
Petworth (Part of Washington)	20011
Philatelic Sales Division (Part of Washington)	20265
Randle (Part of Washington)	20020
Saint Elizabeth (Part of Washington)	20032
Shepherd (Part of Washington)	20032
Southeast (Part of Washington)	20003
Southwest (Part of Washington)	20024
Spring Valley (Part of Washington)	20016
State Department (Part of Washington)	20520
Techworld (Part of Washington)	20091
Temple Heights (Part of Washington)	20009
Tenleytown (Part of Washington)	20016
Terra Cotta (Part of Washington)	20011
The Palisades (Part of Washington)	20016
T Street (Part of Washington)	20009
Twentieth Street (Part of Washington)	20036
Twining (Part of Washington)	20020
U.S. Naval Station (Part of Washington)	20374
Walter Reed (Part of Washington)	20012
Washington	20001-99
	20101-99
	20201-99
	20301-72
(Government Offices)	20500-94
For specific Washington D.C. Zip Codes call (202) 682-9595	

COLLEGES & UNIVERSITIES

	ZIP
American University	20016
Catholic University of America	20064
Gallaudet University	20002
George Washington University	20052
Georgetown University	20057
Howard University	20059
University of the District of Columbia	20008

FINANCIAL INSTITUTIONS

	ZIP
American Security Bank, N.A.	20013
Citicorp Savings of Washington, D.C., F.A.	20006
Columbia First Federal Savings & Loan Association	20005
Crestar Bank, National Association	20005
Dominion Bank Of Washington, National Association	20005
First American Bank N.A.	20005
Home Federal Savings & Loan Association	20015
Independence Federal Savings Bank	20036
Industrial Bank of Washington	20011
Madison National Bank	20036
McLachlen National Bank	20005
The National Bank of Washington	20005
Oba Federal Savings & Loan Association	20004
The Riggs National Bank of Washington, DC	20074
Signet Bank, National Association	20036
Sovran Bank/DC National	20006
United National Bank of Washington	20019
Washington Federal Savings Bank	20016

GOVERNMENT OFFICES

	ZIP
ACTION	20525
Administrative Committee of the Federal Register	20408
Administrative Conference of the United States	20037
Administrative Office of the United States Courts	20544
Advisory Commission on Intergovernmental Relations	20575
Advisory Council on Historic Preservation	20004
African Development Foundation	20036
Agency for International Development	20523
American Battle Monuments Commission	20314
Appalachian Regional Commission	20235
Architect of the Capitol	20515
Architectural and Transportation Barriers Compliance Board	20202
Board for International Broadcasting	20036
Board of Foreign Scholarships	20547
Bureau of Alcohol, Tobacco and Firearms	20226
Bureau of Engraving and Printing	20228
Bureau of Prisons	20534
Central Intelligence Agency	20505
Citizens' Stamp Advisory Committee	20260
Commission of Fine Arts	20006
Commission on Civil Rights	20425
Commission on the Bicentennial of the United States Constitution	20503
Committee for the Implementation of Textile Agreements	20230
Committee on Foreign Investment in the United States	20220
Commodity Futures Trading Commission	20581
Congressional Budget Office	20515
Consumer Product Safety Commission	20207
Coordinating Council on Juvenile Justice and Delinquency Prevention	20531
Copyright Royalty Tribunal	20036
Council of Economic Advisors	20500
Council on Environmental Quality	20006
Defense Intelligence Agency	20340
Defense Investigative Service	20324
Defense Legal Services Agency	20301
Defense Mapping Agency	20305
Defense Nuclear Agency	20305
Defense Security Assistance Agency	20301
Delaware River Basin Commission	20240
Department of Agriculture	20250
Department of Commerce	20230
Department of Defense	20301
Department of Defense Computer Institute	20374
Department of Education	20202
Department of Energy	20585
Department of Health and Human Services	20201
Department of Housing and Urban Development	20410
Department of Justice	20530
Department of Labor	20210
Department of State	20520
Department of the Air Force	20330
Department of the Army	20310
Department of the Interior	20240
Department of the Navy	20350
Department of the Treasury	20220
Department of Transportation	20590
Development Coordination Committee	20523
Drug Enforcement Administration	20537
Endangered Species Committee	20240
Environmental Protection Agency	20460
Equal Employment Opportunity Commission	20507
Export Administration Review Board	20230

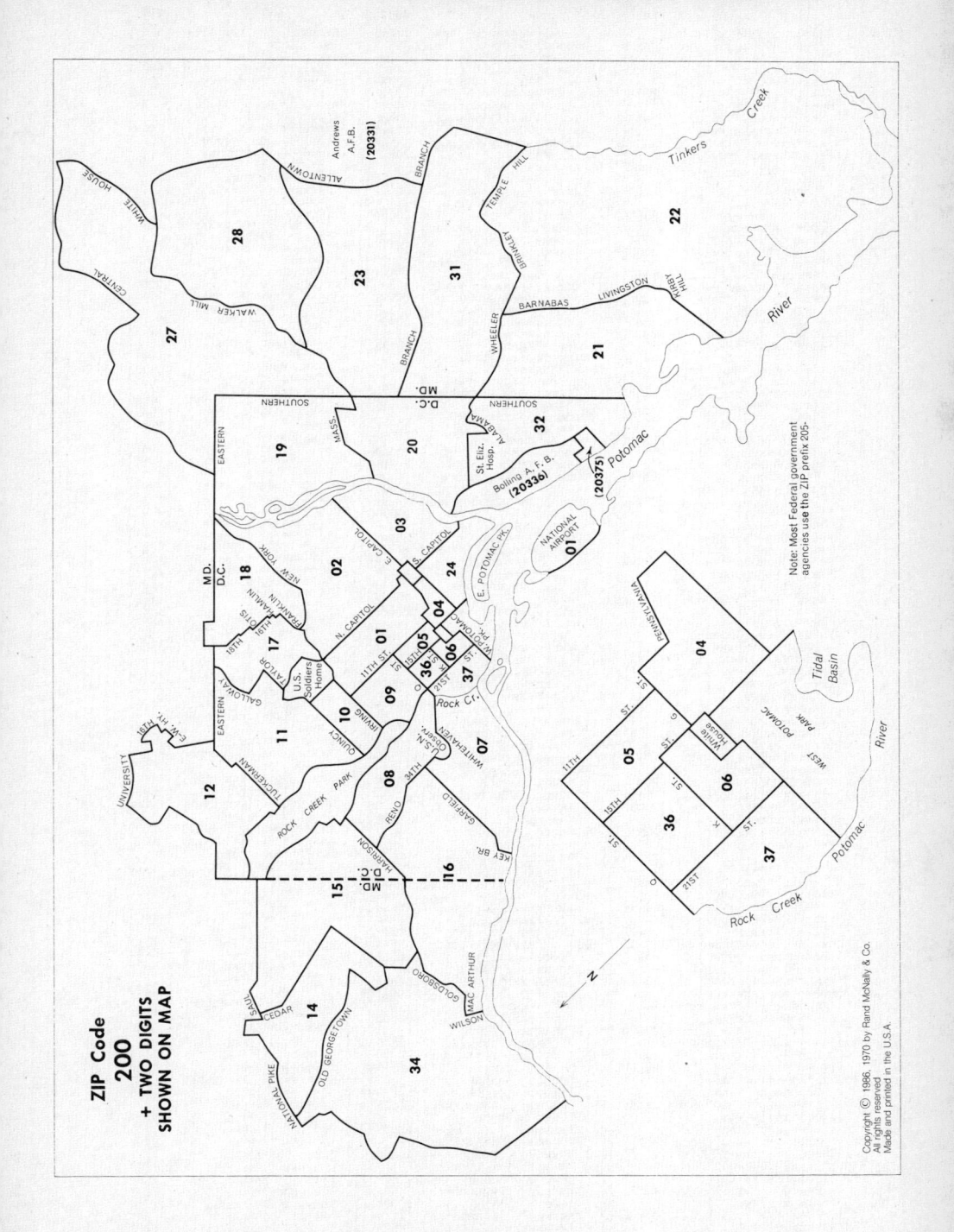

Washington **DISTRICT OF COLUMBIA** 99

100 DISTRICT OF COLUMBIA Washington

	ZIP		ZIP		ZIP
Export-Import Bank of the United States	20571	International Monetary Fund	20431	Panama Canal Commission	20036
Family Support Administration	20201	Interstate Commerce Commission	20423	Peace Corps	20526
Federal Aviation Administration	20591	Japan-United States Friendship Commission	20004	Pennsylvania Avenue Development Corporation	20004
Federal Bureau of Investigation	20535	Joint Board for the Enrollment of Actuaries	20220	Pension Benefit Guaranty Corporation	20006
Federal Communications Commission	20554	Legal Services Corporation	20024	Permanent Committee for the Oliver Wendell Holmes Devise	20540
Federal Deposit Insurance Corporation	20429	Library of Congress	20540	Postal Rate Commission	20268
Federal Election Commission	20463	Mailers Technical Advisory Committee	20260	President's Commission on Executive Exchange	20503
Federal Emergency Management Agency	20472	Marine Mammal Commission	20006	President's Committee on Employment of People with Disabilities	20036
Federal Financial Institutions Examination Council	20006	Maritime Administration	20590	President's Council on Integrity and Efficiency	20503
Federal Financing Bank	20220	Merit Systems Protection Board	20419	President's Foreign Intelligence Advisory Board	20500
Federal Highway Administration	20590	Migratory Bird Conservation Commission	20240	President's Intelligence Oversight Board	20500
Federal Home Loan Bank Board	20552	National Advisory Council on International Monetary and Financial Policies	20220	Public Buildings Service	20405
Federal Interagency Committee on Education	20202	National Aeronautics and Space Administration	20546	Railroad Retirement Board	20036
Federal Judicial Center	20005	National Archives and Records Administration	20408	Regulatory Information Service Center	20503
Federal Labor Relations Authority	20424	National Archives Trust Fund Board	20408	Research and Special Programs Administration	20590
Federal Library and Information Center Committee	20540	National Capital Planning Commission	20576	Saint Lawrence Seaway Development Corporation	20590
Federal Maritime Commission	20573	National Commission on Libraries and Information Science	20036	Securities and Exchange Commission	20549
Federal Mediation and Conciliation Service	20427	National Council on the Handicapped	20591	Selective Service System	20435
Federal Mine Safety and Health Review Commission	20006	National Credit Union Administration	20456	Senate	20510
Federal Property Resources Service	20405	National Defense University	20319	Small Business Administration	20416
Federal Railroad Administration	20590	National Endowment for the Arts	20506	Smithsonian Institution	20560
Federal Reserve System	20551	National Endowment for the Humanities	20506	Strategic Defense Initiative Organization	20301
Federal Supply Service	20406	National Highway Traffic Safety Administration	20590	Supreme Court of the United States	20543
Federal Trade Commission	20580	National Historical Publications and Records Commission	20408	Susquehanna River Basin Commission	20240
Financial Management Service	20227	National Labor Relations Board	20570	Task Force on Legal Equity for Women	21235
Foreign Claims Settlement Commission of the United States	20579	National Mediation Board	20572	Tennessee Valley Authority	20444
Franklin Delano Roosevelt Memorial Commission	20515	National Oceanic and Atmospheric Administration	20230	Textile Trade Policy Group	20506
Gallaudet University	20002	National Park Foundation	20037	Trade and Development Program	20523
General Accounting Office	20548	National Railroad Passenger Corporation(AMTRAK)	20001	Trade Policy Committee	20506
General Services Administration	20405	National Science Foundation	20550	United States Arms Control and Disarmament Agency	20451
Government Printing Office	20401	National Security Council	20506	United States Botanic Garden	20024
Graduate School, U.S. Department of Agriculture	20250	National Transportation Safety Board	20594	United States Coast Guard	20593
Harry S. Truman Scholarship Foundation	20006	National War College	20319	United States Customs Service	20229
Health Care Financing Administration	20201	Nuclear Regulatory Commission	20555	United States Information Agency	20547
House of Representatives	20515	Occupational Safety and Health Review Commission	20006	United States International Development Cooperation Agency	20523
Howard University	20001	Office of Administration	20500	United States International Trade Commission	20436
Immigration and Naturalization Service	20536	Office of Aviation Information Management	20590	United States Marine Corps	20380
Indian Arts and Crafts Board	20240	Office of Emergency Transportation	20590	United States National Commission for UNESCO	20520
Industrial College of the Armed Forces	20319	Office of Hazardous Materials Transportation	20590	United States Postal Service	20260
Information Resources Management Service	20405	Office of Human Development Services	20201	United States Savings Bonds Division	20226
Information Security Oversight Office	20405	Office of Management and Budget	20503	United States Secret Service	20223
Institute of Museum Service	20506	Office of Personnel Management	20415	United States Sentencing Commission	20004
Interagency Committee for the Purchase of United States Savings Bonds	20226	Office of Pipeline Safety	20550	United States Tax Court	20217
Interagency Committee on Handicapped Employees	20507	Office of Policy Development	20500	Urban Mass Transportation Administration	20590
Inter-American Defense Board	20441	Office of Science and Technology Policy	20506	Veterans Administration	20420
Inter-American Development Bank	20577	Office of Technology Assessment	20510	Veterans Day National Committee	20420
Internal Revenue Service	20224	Office of the Federal Inspector, Alaska Natural Gas Transportation System	20585	White House Commission on Presidential Scholars	20202
International Bank for Reconstruction and Development	20433	Office of the Special Counsel	20005	White House Office	20500
International Boundary Commission, United States and Canada	20001	Office of the United States Trade Representative	20506	*HOSPITALS*	
International Criminal Police Organization-United States National Central Bureau	20530	Office of the Vice President of the United States	20501	Capitol Hill Hospital	20002
International Finance Corporation	20433	Organization of American States	20006	District of Columbia General Hospital	20003
International Joint Commission-United States and Canada	20440	Overseas Private Investment Corporation	20527	George Washington University Hospital	20037
		Pan American Health Organization	20037	Georgetown University Medical Center	20007
				Greater Southeast Community Hospital	20032
				Howard University Hospital	20060
				Providence Hospital	20017
				Sibley Memorial Hospital	20016
				Veterans Administration Medical Center	20422
				Walter Reed Army Medical Center	20307

Washington Highlands-Woodridge — DISTRICT OF COLUMBIA

	ZIP		ZIP		ZIP
Washington Hospital Center	20010	Coast Guard Headquarters, Washington D.C.	20593	Walter Reed Medical Center	20307
HOTELS/MOTELS		Comptroller and Supply Department, Naval District, Washington Navy Yard	20374	Washington Highlands (Part of Washington)	20032
The Hay-Adams Hotel	20006			Washington Square (Part of Washington)	20036
Hyatt Regency Washington	20001				
The Jefferson Hotel	20036	Fort Lesley J. McNair	20319	Watergate (Part of Washington)	20037
JW Marriott Hotel at National Place	20004	Headquarters, United States Marine Corps, Navy Annex	20380	Wesley Heights (Part of Washington)	20016
The Mayflower-A Stouffer Hotel	20036	Marine Barracks	20390	West End (Part of Washington)	20037
Ramada Renaissance Hotel	20037	Military District of Washington D.C., Headquarters	20032	Woodley Park (Part of Washington)	20008
Sheraton Washington Hotel	20008				
The Watergate Hotel	20037	Naval Research Laboratory	20375	Woodley Road (Part of Washington)	20008
Wyndham Bristol Hotel	20037	Naval Security Station	20390	Woodridge (Part of Washington)	20018
MILITARY INSTALLATIONS		United States Property and Fiscal Office, Washington D.C.	20315		
Armed Forces Institute of Pathology	20307				
Bolling Air Force Base	20332				

102 FLORIDA

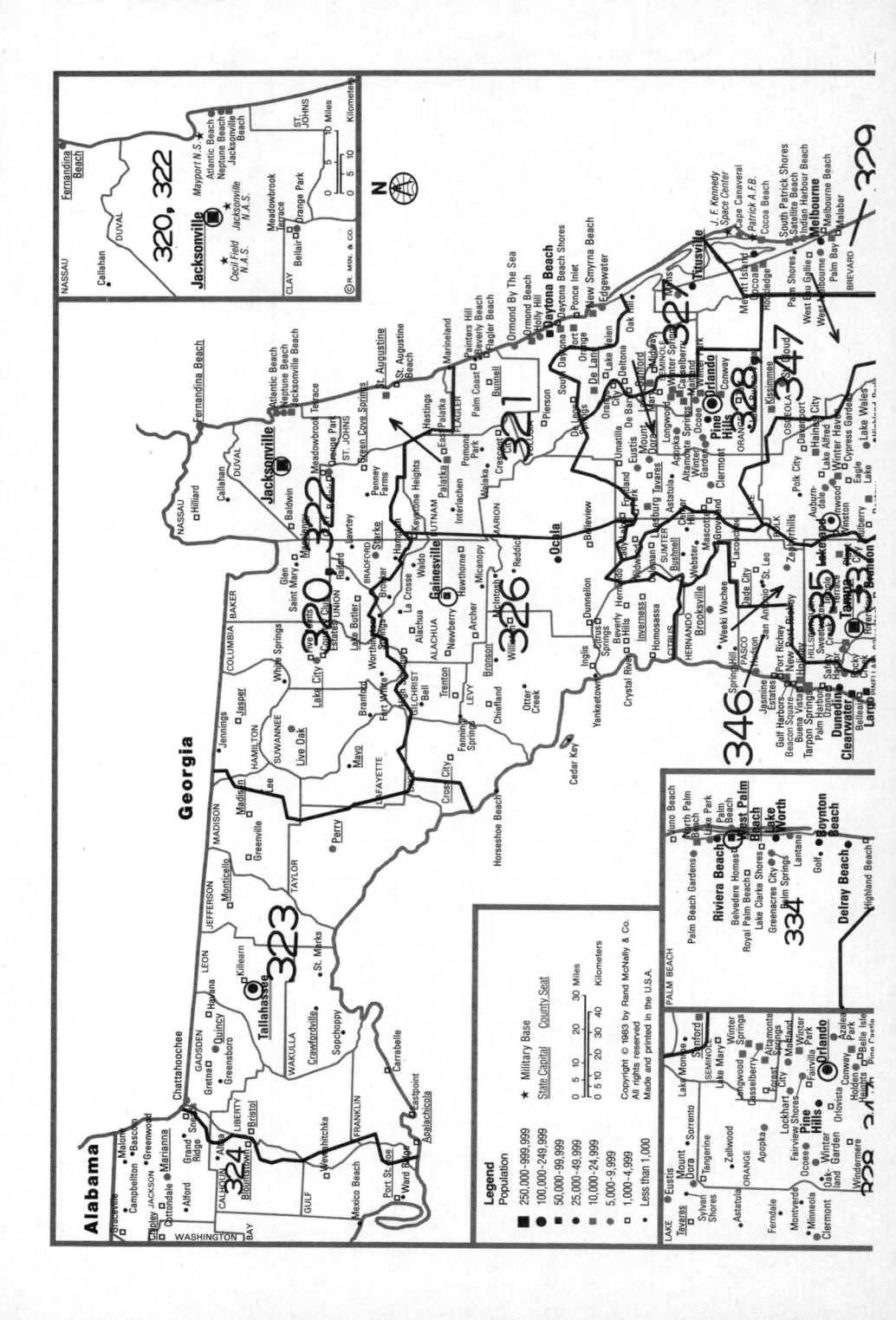

FLORIDA 103

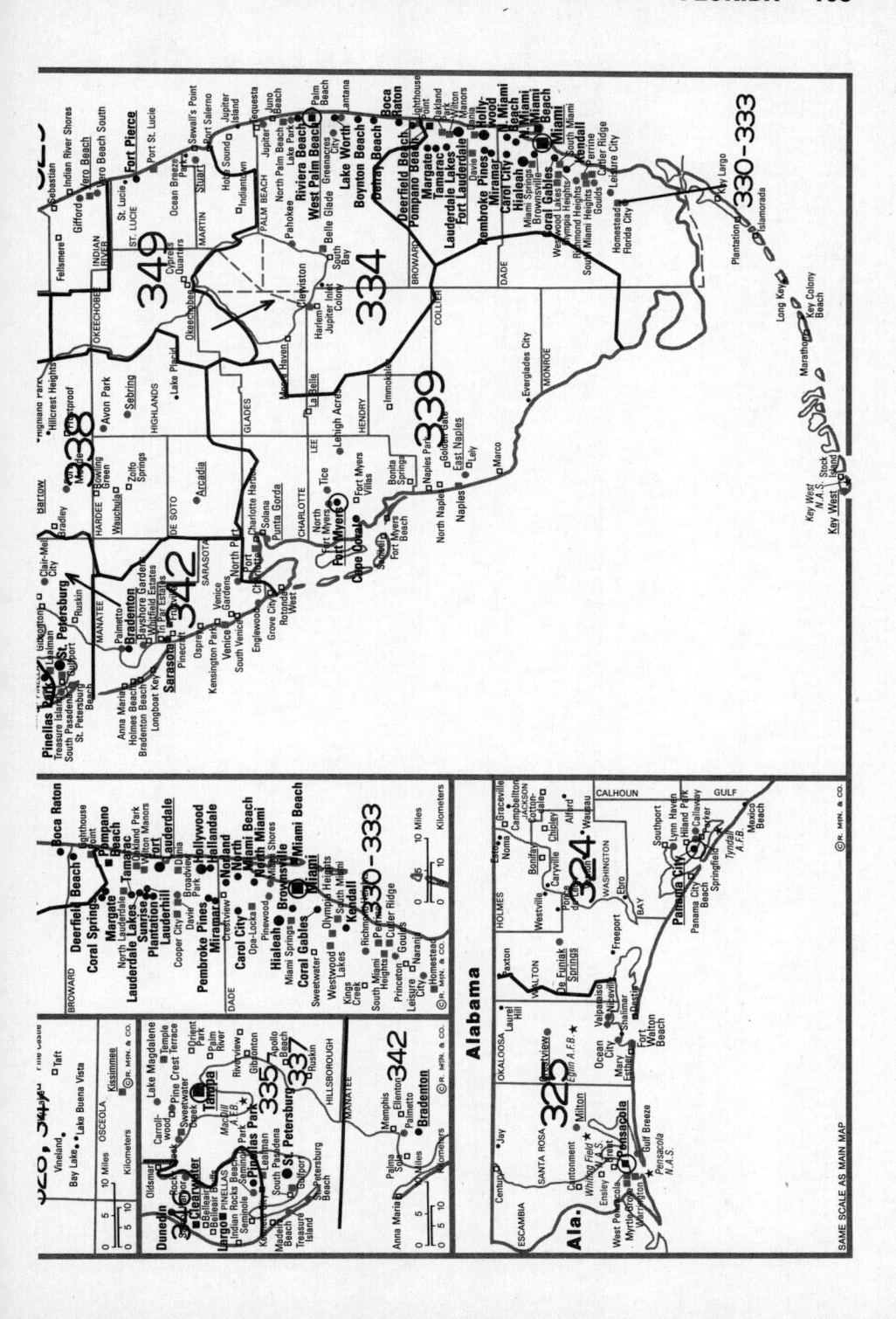

104 FLORIDA Abe Springs-Biscayne Gardens

Name	ZIP
Abe Springs	32424
Acline	33950
Acres of Diamond	32901
Adamsville (Hillsborough County)	33534
Adamsville (Sumter County)	34785
Airport Siding (Part of Jacksonville)	32229
Alachua	32615
Aladdin City	33187
Alafia	33566
Alameda (Part of West Miami)	33144
Alaqua	32433
Alderman Park (Part of Jacksonville)	32211
Alford	32420
Allandale	32127
Allanton	32401
Allapattah (Part of Miami)	33142
Allentown	32570
Alliance	32446
Alligator Lake	34772
Alligator Point Marina	32327
Aloma (Part of Winter Park)	32792
Alpine Heights	32433
Altamonte Mall (Part of Altamonte Springs)	32701
Altamonte Springs	32714-16
For specific Altamonte Springs Zip Codes call (407) 682-3977	
Altamonte Springs	32701
Alta Vista	33950
Altha	32421
Alton	32066
Altoona	32702
Altschul	32333
Alturas	33820
Alva	33920
Amelia City	32034
Amelia Island Plantation	32034
American Beach	32034
American Village (Part of Titusville)	32780
Anastasia (Part of St. Augustine)	32084
Anclote	34691
Anclote Acres	34680
Andalusia	32110
Andover Golf Estates	33169
Andover Lake Estates	33169
Andrews	32046
Angel City	32952
Angler Park	33037
Angus Valley	33544
Ankona	34982
Anna Maria	34216
Anona (Part of Largo)	34644
Anthony	32617
Antioch	33565
Apalachee Correctional Institution	32324
Apalachicola	32320
Apollo Beach	33572
Apopka	32703-04
For specific Apopka Zip Codes call (407) 886-2951	
Aquarina	32951
Araguey	32095
Arbor Hills (Part of Tallahassee)	32308
Arcadia	33821
Archer	32618
Argyle	32422
Aripeka	34679
Arlington (Part of Jacksonville)	32211
Arlington Green (Part of Jacksonville)	32211
Arlington Heights (Part of Jacksonville)	32211
Arlington Park (Part of Deerfield Beach)	33441
Arlingwood (Part of Jacksonville)	32211
Armstrong	32033
Arran	32327
Asbury Lake	32043
Ashton	34771
Ashville	32331
Astatula	34705
Astor	32102
Astoria Park	32303
Astor Park	32102
Astronaut Trail (Part of Titusville)	32796
Athena	32347
Atlantic Beach	32233
Atlantic Boulevard Estates (Part of Jacksonville)	32211

Name	ZIP
Atlantic Heights (Part of Miami Beach)	33139
Atlantis	33462
Auburn	32536
Auburndale	33823
Aucilla	32344
Audubon	32952
Aurantia	32754
Avalon Beach	32570
Aventura	33180
Avondale (Part of Jacksonville)	32204
Avon Park	33825
Avon Park Air Force Base	33825
Avon Park Correctional Institution	33825
Avon Park Lakes	33825
Azalea Park	32807
Azalea Terrace (Part of Jacksonville)	32216
Babson Park	33827
Bagdad	32530
Bahia Mar (Part of Fort Lauderdale)	33316
Bahia Shores (Part of St. Petersburg Beach)	33736
Baker (Bay County)	32401
Baker (Okaloosa County)	32531
Baker Correctional Institution	32072
Baker Settlement	32464
Bakersville	32092
Bal-Alex Estates	32561
Baldwin	32234
Bal Harbour	33154
Bal Harbour Shops (Part of Bal Harbour)	33154
Ballantine Manor	34243
Balm	33503
Bamboo	34748
Barberville	32105
Bar Dee Homes	34647
Bardin	32177
Bardmoor	34643
Bare Beach	33440
Barefoot Bay	32958
Barrineau Park	32533
Barry College (Part of Miami Shores)	33161
Barth	32533
Bartow	33830
Bascom	32423
Basinger	34972
Baskin	34648
Bassville Park	34748
Baum	32308
Bay Acres	34229
Bayard (Part of Jacksonville)	32224
Bay City	32320
Bay Crest (Hillsborough County)	33615
Bay Grove	32439
Bay Harbor (Part of Springfield)	32401
Bay Harbor Islands	33154
Bayhead (Bay County)	32466
Bay Head (Pasco County)	33525
Bayhill	33513
Bay Lake (Lake County)	34736
Bay Lake (Marion County)	32113
Bay Lake (Orange County)	32802
Bayonet Point	34667
Bayou George	32401
Bay Pines (Pinellas County)	34642
Bay Pines (Pinellas County)	33504
Bay Point	32407
Bayport	34607
Bayridge	32703
Bayshore	33917
Bay Shore Estates (Part of Venice)	34292
Bayshore Gardens	34207
Bayshore Manor	33917
Bayshore Park	33982
Bay Springs	32568
Bayview	32401
Bay Vista (Dade County)	33181
Bay Vista (Pinellas County)	33712
Bayway (Part of St. Petersburg)	33715
Baywood	32140
Baywood Village	34683
Beach (Indian River County)	32963
Beach (St. Lucie County)	34949
Beach Haven	32507
Beach Highlands	32459
Beachway (Part of Bradenton)	34209
Beachwood (Part of Jacksonville)	32250

Name	ZIP
Beacon Groves	34684
Beacon Hill	32456
Beacon Hills (Part of Jacksonville)	32211
Beacon Lakes	34652
Beacon Light (Part of Lighthouse Point)	33064
Beacon Square (Pasco County)	34652
Bealsville	33567
Bean City	33459
Bear Creek	32401
Bear Head	32433
Bear Lake	32703
Bearss Plaza	33612
Beasley	33872
Beauclere (Part of Jacksonville)	32217
Beauclere Manor (Part of Jacksonville)	32217
Beaver Creek	32531
Becker	32097
Beckhamtown	32640
Beeghly Heights (Part of Jacksonville)	32218
Bee Ridge	34233
Bel-Air (Part of Sanford)	32771
Bell	32619
Bellair	32073
Bell Air Carver Heights	32507
Bellair-Meadowbrook Terrace	32073
Bellair Plaza (Part of Daytona Beach)	32118
Bellair West	32073
Belleair	34616
Belleair Beach	34635
Belleair Bluffs	34640
Belleair Shore	34635
Belle Ayre Estates	32757
Belle Glade	33430
Belle Glade Camp	33430
Belle Haven	34615
Belle Isle	32809
Belleview (Escambia County)	32506
Belleview (Marion County)	32620
Belleview Heights	32620
Belleview Hills Manor	32691
Belleville	31636
Bellview	32506
Bellwood	32780
Belmont (Part of Clearwater)	34616
Belvedere (Part of West Palm Beach)	33405
Belvedere Homes	33401
Benbow	33440
Bennett	32466
Ben's Lake	32542
Benson Junction	32713
Bent Pine	32960
Bent Tree Village	34241
Bereah	33841
Berkshire Estates	34241
Berry	33868
Berrydale	32565
Bertha	32801
Bethany	34251
Bethel	32301
Bethlehem	32425
Bethune Beach	32169
Betmar Acres	33541
Betton Hills (Part of Tallahassee)	32312
Betts (Part of Panama City)	32401
Betty Lou Beach (Part of Panama City Beach)	32401
Beulah (Escambia County)	32533
Beulah (Orange County)	34787
Beverly Beach	32136
Beverly Hill	32665
Beverly Hills (Part of Jacksonville)	32208
Beverly Terrace	34234
Beville Heights	32601
Bevilles Corner	33513
Bid-A-Wee (Part of Panama City Beach)	32401
Big Bayou (Part of St. Petersburg)	33705
Big Coppitt Key	33040
Big Cypress	33440
Big Cypress Seminole Indian Reservation	33024
Big Pine Key	33043
Biltmore (Part of Jacksonville)	32205
Biltmore Beach	32401
Biscayne College	33054
Biscayne Gardens	33168

Biscayne One-Clear Springs **FLORIDA** 105

Name	ZIP
Biscayne One (Part of Miami)	33131
Biscayne Park	33161
Biscay Plaza Shopping Center (Part of Miami)	33138
Bithlo	32807
Black Acres (Part of Gainesville)	32601
Blackbottom	32234
Black Creek	32439
Black Jacks	32680
Blackman	32531
Black Rock	32097
Bland	32615
Blanton	33525
Blichton	32675
Bloomingdale	33594
Blountstown	32424
Bloxham	32304
Blue Gulf Beach	32459
Blue Inlet (Part of Boca Raton)	33431
Blue Lake	32720
Blue Mountain Beach	32454
Blue Springs	34797
Bluff Springs	32535
Boardman	32633
Boca Ciega (Part of Treasure Island)	33740
Boca Grande	33921
Boca Harbour (Part of Boca Raton)	33487
Boca Raton	33427-29
	33431-34
	33486-87
	33496-98
For specific Boca Raton Zip Codes call (305) 994-2700	
Boca Raton Mall (Part of Boca Raton)	33432
Boca West	33434
Bogia	32568
Bokeelia	33922
Bolton Hills (Part of Tallahassee)	32312
Bonaventure	33317
Bonifay	32425
Bonita Beach	33923
Bonita Shores	33923
Bonita Springs (Lee County)	33923
Bonnie Loch	33060
Bon Terra	32136
Bostwick	32007
Botts	32570
Boulevard (Dade County)	33132
Boulevard (Pinellas County)	34616
Boulougne	32046
Bowden (Part of Jacksonville)	32216
Bowling Green	33834
Boyd	32347
Boynton Beach	33424-26
	33435-37
For specific Boynton Beach Zip Codes call (305) 738-5220	
Boys Ranch	32060
Braden Castle (Part of Bradenton)	34208
Bradenton	34201-10
	34280-82
For specific Bradenton Zip Codes call (813) 746-4195	
Bradenton Beach	34217
Bradford	32428
Bradford Manor (Part of Tallahassee)	32303
Bradfordville	32308
Bradley	33835
Bradshaw Acres	34711
Brandon	33509-11
For specific Brandon Zip Codes call (813) 689-1616	
Branford	32008
Brannonville	32401
Bratt	32535
Brent (Escambia County)	32503
Brentwood (Part of Jacksonville)	32208
Brentwood Estates	34232
Briarwood Shores	33905
Brickell (Part of Miami)	33131
Bright (Part of Hialeah)	33010
Brighton	34972
Brighton Indian Reservation	33024
Briny Breezes	33483
Bristol	32321
Britton Plaza (Part of Tampa)	33611
Broadview	33068
Broadview Park	33314
Broadview-Pompano Park	33068

Name	ZIP
Broadwater (Part of St. Petersburg)	33711
Brock Crossroad	32463
Bronson	32621
Brooker	32622
Brooker Creek	34685
Brooklyn (Part of Jacksonville)	32204
Brookridge (Hernando County)	34613
Brook Ridge (Hernando County)	34601
Brooksville	34601-14
For specific Brooksville Zip Codes call (904) 799-4441	
Brockview (Part of Jacksonville)	32211
Browardale	33311
Broward Correctional Institution	33024
Broward Mall (Part of Plantation)	33388
Brownsdale	32565
Brownsville (Dade County)	33142
Brownsville (Escambia County)	32505
Browntown	32440
Brownville	33821
Bruce	32455
Bruceville	32688
Bryant	33439
Bryceville	32009
Brynwood	33901
Buccaneer Estates	33054
Buchanan	33890
Buckhorn	32358
Buckingham	33905
Buckingham West	32601
Buenaventura Lakes	34743
Buena Vista (Dade County)	33137
Buena Vista (Jackson County)	32460
Buena Vista (Orange County)	34787
Buena Vista (Pasco County)	34691
Buffalo Bluff	32189
Bunche Park	33054
Bunker (De Soto County)	33821
Bunker (Walton County)	32459
Bunker Creek	32454
Bunnell	32110
Burbank	32134
Burnett's Lake	32615
Bushnell	33513
Byrneville	32535
Calhoun Correctional Center	32424
Callahan	32011
Callaway	32401
Calusa Cove	33908
Camellia Gardens	32809
Cameron City	32771
Campbell	34746
Campbellton	32426
Camp Mack	33853
Camp Roosevelt	32674
Camps Mine	34601
Campton	32567
Campville	32640
Canaan	32771
Canal Point	33438
Candler	32111
Cannon Town	32531
Canova Beach	32937
Cantonment	32533
Cape Canaveral	32920
Cape Coral	33904
Cape Coral Central (Part of Cape Coral)	33915
Cape Haze	33946
Cape Orlando	32820
Cape Vista (Part of Bradenton)	34209
Capital Hills (Part of Tallahassee)	32308
Capitola	32301
Capps	32336
Capri Isle (Part of Treasure Island)	33740
Captiva	33924
Caribbean Key (Part of Boca Raton)	33487
Carleton	32640
Carl Fisher (Part of Miami Beach)	33139
Carlson	33538
Carlton Village	32159
Carol City (Dade County)	33055
Carr	32421
Carrabelle	32322
Carrabelle Beach	32322
Carraway	32177

Name	ZIP
Carrollwood	33618
Carters	33801
Carver (Part of Jacksonville)	32209
Carver Ranch Estates	33023
Carver Village	33060
Carwens Holmes	33060
Caryville	32427
Casa Bianco	32344
Casa Blanca (Part of Gulf Breeze)	32561
Casey Key	34275
Cason Inglis Acres	32649
Cassadaga	32706
Casselberry	32707-08
For specific Casselberry Zip Codes call (305) 339-5919	
Cassia	32726
Cedar Creek	32688
Cedar Grove	32401
Cedar Hammock	34207
Cedar Hills (Part of Jacksonville)	32210
Cedar Hills Estates (Part of Jacksonville)	32210
Cedar Key	32625
Cedar Lake Estates	32629
Cedar Point (Part of Jacksonville)	32218
Center City	34643
Center Hill	33514
Center Park (Part of Jacksonville)	32216
Central Plaza (Part of St. Petersburg)	33713
Central Shopping Plaza (Part of Miami)	33126
Century (Escambia County)	32535
Century (Escambia County)	36441
Century Corners	33409
Century Twenty One	33901
Century Village	33409
Cerrogordo	32464
Chain O'Lakes	32767
Chaires	32301
Channell	32757
Chantilly Acres	32606
Charlotte Harbor	33980
Charlotte Park	33950
Charlotte Square	33948
Chaseville (Part of Jacksonville)	32211
Chason	32421
Chassahowitzka	32650
Chatmar	32630
Chattahoochee	32324
Cherry Lake (Lake County)	32159
Cherry Lake (Madison County)	32331
Chester	32097
Chestnut Hill Ranches	32675
Chiefland	32626
Chipley	32428
Chipola (Calhoun County)	32421
Chipola (Jackson County)	32446
Chipola Park	32465
Chipola River Estates	32424
Choctaw	32454
Choctaw Beach	32439
Chokoloskee	33925
Chosen (Part of Belle Glade)	33430
Chosen Labor Camp (Part of Belle Glade)	33430
Christina	33801
Christmas	32709
Chuluota	32766
Chumuckla	32570
Cinco Bayou	32548
Cisky Park	34748
Citra	32113
Citronelle	32630
Citrus (Part of Inverness)	32650
Citrus Center	33471
'Citrus Park	33624
Citrus Springs	32630
Citrus Tower (Part of Clermont)	34711
City Of Sunrise	33313
City Point	32922
City View (Part of Fort Myers)	33901
Clair-Mel City	33619
Clarcona	32710
Clark	32643
Clarksville	32430
Clear Lake	32601
Clear Springs (Okaloosa County)	32567
Clear Springs (Walton County)	32567

106 FLORIDA Clearview-Drifton

	ZIP
Clearview (Part of St. Petersburg)	33701
Clearwater	34615-30
For specific Clearwater Zip Codes call (813) 441-4511	
Clearwater Beach (Part of Clearwater)	34630
Clearwater Coast Guard Air Station	34622
Clearwater Mall (Part of Clearwater)	34619
Clermont	34711-12
For specific Clermont Zip Codes call (904) 394-2423	
Cleveland (Charlotte County)	33982
Cleveland Street (Part of Clearwater)	34615
Clewiston	33440
Clifton (Part of Jacksonville)	32211
Cloud Lake	33406
Cluster Springs	32433
Coach Light Manor	33901
Coastal Systems Laboratory	32407
Coastland Center (Part of Naples)	33940
Cobbtown	32565
Cocoa	32922-27
For specific Cocoa Zip Codes call (305) 636-6565	
Cocoa Beach	32931-32
For specific Cocoa Beach Zip Codes call (407) 783-2544	
Cocoa West	32922
Coconut	33923
Coconut Creek	33060
Coconut Grove (Part of Miami)	33133
Cody	32344
Coldwater	32570
Colee (Part of Fort Lauderdale)	33301
Coleman	33521
College Park (Orange County)	32804
College Park (St. Johns County)	32033
College Point	32444
Collier City	33060
Collier Manor	33064
Collier Manor-Cresthaven	33064
Collins Park Estates	34982
Colonial Acres	33903
Colonial Gables	34232
Colonial Hills	34652
Colonial Manor (Part of Jacksonville)	32205
Colonial Plaza (Part of Orlando)	32803
Colonialtown (Part of Orlando)	32803
Columbia	32055
Columbia City	32055
Combee Settlement	33801
Compass Lake	32446
Conch Key	33001
Concord	32333
Conner	32688
Connersville	33830
Conway (Orange County)	32809
Cooks Hammock	32066
Cooper City	33328
Copans Road (Part of Pompano Beach)	33064
Copeland	33926
Cora	32565
Coral Cove	34231
Coral Estates (Part of Wilton Manors)	33305
Coral Gables	33134
Coral Gardens	34997
Coral Point (Part of Wilton Manors)	33305
Coral Ridge Shopping Plaza (Part of Fort Lauderdale)	33306
Coral Springs	33065
Coral Square (Part of Coral Springs)	33065
Coral Terrace	33157
Coral Way Village	33155
Coralwood (Part of Cape Coral)	33904
Coral Woods (Part of Oakland Park)	33307
Corkscrew	33934
Corley Island	34748
Cornwell	33857
Coronado (Part of New Smyrna Beach)	32169
Coronet	33566

	ZIP
Corry Station Naval Training Center	32511
Cortez (Manatee County)	34215
Cortez Road (Part of Bradenton)	34207
Cottage Hill	32533
Cottage Point	33901
Cottondale	32431
Cottonplant	32674
Country Club (Part of Port St. Lucie)	34952
Country Club Acres	33484
Country Club Estates (Columbia County)	32055
Country Club Estates (Lee County)	33901
Country Club Estates (Polk County)	33801
Country Club Manor	32771
Country Estates	34690
Countryside Mall (Part of Clearwater)	34621
Country Woods Estates	34240
Courtenay	32952
Cove (Part of Panama City)	32401
Cove Springs	34683
Cox	32424
Coytown (Part of Orlando)	32803
Crackertown (Part of Inglis)	32649
Crandall	32097
Crawford	32009
Crawfordville	32327
Crescent Beach (Sarasota County)	34242
Crescent Beach (St. Johns County)	32086
Crescent City	32112
Cresthaven (Broward County)	33064
Cresthaven (Palm Beach County)	33406
Crestview (Dade County)	33054
Crestview (Okaloosa County)	32536
Crewsville	33890
Crooked Lake Park	33853
Croom-A-Coochee	33597
Cross City	32628
Cross City Correctional Institution	32628
Cross County Mall (Part of West Palm Beach)	33409
Cross Creek	32640
Crossroads (Part of St. Petersburg)	33710
Crown Heights	32906
Crystal Beach (Okaloosa County)	32548
Crystal Beach (Pinellas County)	34681
Crystal Hill	32642
Crystal Lake (Polk County)	33803
Crystal Lake (Washington County)	32428
Crystal River	32629
Crystal Springs	33524
Cudjoe	33042
Cumbee	33801
Curlew	34698
Curtis Mill	32358
Cutler	33157
Cutler Ridge	33157
Cutler Ridge Mall	33189
Cypress (Broward County)	33060
Cypress (Jackson County)	32432
Cypress Gardens (Polk County)	33880
Cypress Isle	33852
Cypress Lake	33919
Cypress Point	32131
Cypress Quarters	34972
Cypress Village	33907
Dade City	33525-26
For specific Dade City Zip Codes call (904) 567-5179	
Dade City North	33525
Dade Correctional Institution	33030
Dadeland Mall	33156
Dalkeith	32465
Dallas	32691
Dames Point (Part of Jacksonville)	32226
Dames Point Junction (Part of Jacksonville)	32226
Dania	33004
Dania Indian Reservation	33004
Danks Corner	32691
Darby	33525
Darlington	32464
Daughtreys Creek	33903
Davenport	33837

	ZIP
Davie	33328
Day	32013
Daytona Beach	32114-24
For specific Daytona Beach Zip Codes call (904) 252-7657	
Daytona Beach Shores	32116
Daytona Highbridge Estates	32114
Daytona Mall (Part of Daytona Beach)	32114
Daytona Park Estates	32720
De Bary	32713
Deerfield Beach	33441-43
For specific Deerfield Beach Zip Codes call (305) 427-3600	
Deerland	32536
Deer Park	32901
Deer Point	32405
Deerwood (Part of Jacksonville)	32216
De Funiak Springs	32433
Dekle Beach	32347
Delaco	32536
De Land	32720-24
For specific De Land Zip Codes call (904) 734-7600	
De Land Highlands	32720
De Land Southwest	32720
De Leon Springs	32130
Delespine	32780
Dellwood	32442
Delray (Part of Delray Beach)	33483
Delray Beach	33444-47
	33483-84
For specific Delray Beach Zip Codes call (305) 276-6047	
Delray Beach Mall (Part of Delray Beach)	33483
Delray Gardens	33484
Delray Shores (Part of Delray Beach)	33483
Delray Square (Part of Delray Beach)	33445
Del Rio	33617
Deltona (Volusia County)	32725
Del Tura	33903
Denaud	33935
Denver	32112
De Soto Acres	34234
De Soto City	33870
DeSoto Correctional Institution	33821
Desoto Lakes	34235
DeSoto Square (Part of Bradenton)	34205
Destin	32541
Devils Garden	33440
Dewey Park (Part of Jacksonville)	32230
Dickerson City	32570
Dills	32344
Dinsmore (Part of Jacksonville)	32219
Diplomat Mall (Part of Hallandale)	33009
Dirego Park	32401
Dixie Grove	34690
Dixieland (Part of Lakeland)	33803
Dixie Ranch Acres	34972
Dixie Village (Part of Orlando)	32806
Doctors Inlet	32030
Doctor's Lake Estates	32073
Dogtown	32351
Dogwood Lake Estates	32425
Dona Vista	32784
Dorcas	32536
Douglas City	32351
Douglas Crossroads	32455
Dover	33527
Dover Shores (Part of Orlando)	32806
Dowling Park	32060
Downtown (Collier County)	33940
Downtown (Duval County)	32201
Downtown (Escambia County)	32501
Downtown (Hillsborough County)	33602
Downtown (Lee County)	33901
Downtown (Orange County)	32801
Downtown (Palm Beach County)	33432
Downtown (Volusia County)	32114
Drayton Island	32139
Dreamworld (Pinellas County)	34642
Dreamworld (Seminole County)	32771
Drexel	34639
Drifton	32344

Driftwood-Fort Lauderdale FLORIDA 107

	ZIP
Driftwood (Part of Hollywood)	33024
Druid Hills	32751
Duck Key	33050
Duette	33834
Dunbar Heights (Part of Fort Myers)	33901
Dundee	33838
Dunedin	34697-98
For specific Dunedin Zip Codes call (813) 733-5750	
Dunedin Isles (Part of Dunedin)	34698
Dunlawton (Part of Daytona Beach Shores)	32118
Dunnellon	32630
Dupont	32110
Dupont Center	32086
Dupree Gardens	34639
Durant	33530
Durant Estates	32601
Durham	32424
Durward (Part of Tallahassee)	32303
Duval (Part of Jacksonville)	32218
Dyal	32011
Eagle Lake	33839
Eagle Ridge	33912
Eagles Nest	33852
Earleton	32631
East Auburndale	33823
East Avenue (Part of Sarasota)	34237
Eastbrook	34787
Eastern Shores (Part of North Miami Beach)	33162
Eastgate (Leon County)	32308
Eastgate (Orange County)	32792
East Hill (Part of Pensacola)	32503
East Lake	33610
East Lake Harris Estates	34705
East Lake-Orient Park	33610
Eastlake Square	33610
Eastlake Weir	32133
East Lake Woodlands	34677
East Mulberry (Part of Mulberry)	33860
East Naples (Collier County)	33962
East Orlando Estates	32807
East Palatka	32131
Eastpoint	32328
East Rockland Key	33040
East Williston	32696
East Winter Haven	33880
Eaton Park	33840
Eatonville	32751
Eau Gallie (Part of Melbourne)	32935
Ebro	32437
Edgar	32149
Edgewater	32132
Edgewater Gulf Beach (Part of Panama City Beach)	32401
Edgewood (Duval County)	32207
Edgewood (Orange County)	32809
Edgewood Manor (Part of Jacksonville)	32208
Edinburg	32301
Edison	33547
Edison Center (Part of Miami)	33150
Edison Mall (Part of Fort Myers)	33901
Eglin AFB (Okaloosa County)	32542
Eglin Air Force Base (Okaloosa County)	32542
Eglin Village	32544
Egypt Lake	33614
Elder Springs	32771
El Dorado Acres	33923
Elfers (Pasco County)	34680
El Jobean	33927
Elkton	32033
Ellaville (Jackson County)	32426
Ellaville (Madison County)	32060
Ellenton	34222
Ellinor Village (Part of Ormond Beach)	32175
Ellison Acres	32168
Ellisville	32055
Ellzey	32683
Eloise	33880
Eloise Woods	33880
El Portal	33138
El Ranchero Village	34203
Elsi De Monde Heights	32446
Elwood Park	34208
Emery Riddle University (Part of Daytona Beach)	32114

	ZIP
Empire Point (Part of Jacksonville)	32201
Emporia	32180
Enchanted Park (Part of Jacksonville)	32210
Englewood	34223-24
For specific Englewood Zip Codes call (813) 474-3547	
Englewood Beach	34223
Englewood Manor	33460
Enon	32568
Ensley (Escambia County)	32504
Ensley (Escambia County)	32534
Enterprise	32725
Eridu	32331
Erin Park	33872
Errol Estates	32703
Escambia Farms	32531
Escondita Place	32506
Espanola	32110
Esquire Lake (Part of Pompano Beach)	33060
Estero	33928
Estero River Heights	33928
Estifanulga	32321
Esto	32425
Eucheeanna	32433
Euclid (Part of St. Petersburg)	33704
Eureka	32113
Eustis	32726-27
For specific Eustis Zip Codes call (904) 357-4530	
Eva	33802
Everglades City	33929
Evergreen	32097
Evinston	32633
Facil	32096
Factory Outlet Mall (Part of Orlando)	32819
Fairbanks	32601
Fairfield (Duval County)	32206
Fairfield (Marion County)	32634
Fair Gate (Part of Margate)	33063
Fairmont (Part of Jacksonville)	32216
Fairview Shores (Orange County)	32804
Fairvilla (Part of Orlando)	32804
Fairyland	32952
Falmouth	32060
Fanlew	32344
Fanning Springs	32680
Favorita	32110
Federal Correctional Institution	32304
Federal Point	32131
Fedhaven	33854
Felda	33930
Felicia	32642
Fellowship	32670
Fellsmere	32948
Fenholloway	32347
Fernandina Beach	32034
Fern Crest Village (Part of Davie)	33314
Ferndale	34729
Fern Park	32730
Ferry Pass (Escambia County)	32504
Ferry Pass (Escambia County)	32514
Festus	32344
Fiddlesticks	33912
Fidelis	32565
Fiesta Key	33001
Fifty Seventh Avenue	34207
Fisher Island (Part of Miami Beach)	33139
Fishermans Road	32767
Fish Lake	34744
Fivay Junction	34639
Five Points (Brevard County)	32922
Five Points (Columbia County)	32055
Five Points (Washington County)	32427
Flagler (Dade County)	33136
Flagler (Monroe County)	33040
Flagler Beach	32136
Flagler Estates	32145
Flamingo	33030
Flamingo Bay	33956
Fleming Heights	32808
Flemington	32686
Fletcher	33612
Floradale (Part of Jacksonville)	32209
Florahome	32140

	ZIP
Floral Bluff (Part of Jacksonville)	32211
Floral City	32636
Floral Park	33462
Flordale (Part of Jacksonville)	32209
Florence Lake	33883
Florence Villa (Part of Winter Haven)	33881
Floresta (Part of Boca Raton)	33486
Florida Beach (Part of Panama City Beach)	32401
Florida City	33034
Florida Correctional Institution	32663
Florida Gardens	33460
Florida Hills	32726
Floridana Beach	32951
Florida Ridge	32960
Florida Sector Command, Fourth U.S. Army Corps	32960
Florida Southern College (Part of Lakeland)	33801
Florida State Prison	32091
Florida State University (Part of Tallahassee)	32306
Floriland Mall (Part of Tampa)	33612
Florosa	32569
Flowersville	32567
Fluffy Landing	32439
Footman	32952
Forest City (Seminole County)	32751
Forest City (Seminole County)	32714
Forest Heights (Part of Tallahassee)	32303
Forest Hills (Hillsborough County)	33612
Forest Hills (Lake County)	32720
Forest Hills (Pasco County)	34690
Forest Lakes (Part of Sarasota)	34232
Forest Ridge (Part of Gainesville)	32601
Forest Ridge Village (Part of Fernandina Beach)	32034
Forrest Hills	32174
Fort Barrancas	32508
Fort Basinger	34972
Fort Caroline Club Estates (Part of Jacksonville)	32211
Fort Drum	34972
Fort George Island (Part of Jacksonville)	32226
Fort Green	33834
Fort Green Springs	33834
Fort Lauderdale	33301-51
For specific Fort Lauderdale Zip Codes call (305) 527-2074	

COLLEGES & UNIVERSITIES

Nova University	33314

FINANCIAL INSTITUTIONS

The Citizens and Southern National Bank of Florida	33394
Guardian Savings & Loan Association	33309
Sun Bank/South Florida, N.A.	33301

HOSPITALS

AMI North Ridge General Hospital	33334
Broward General Medical Center	33316
Florida Medical Center Hospital	33313
Holy Cross Hospital	33308

HOTELS/MOTELS

Best Western Ft. Lauderdale Inn	33308
Best Western Marina Inn & Yacht Harbor	33316
Days Inn Downtown	33312
Days Inn Lauderdale Surf	33316
Embassy Suites North	33309
Embassy Suites South	33316
Holiday Inn Coral Springs	33065
Holiday Inn I-95 Airport	33312
Holiday Inn Lauderdale-by-the-Sea	33308
Holiday Inn North	33309
Holiday Inn West	33319
Howard Johnson's Airport	33315

108 FLORIDA Fort Lonesome-Highland Park

Name	ZIP
Howard Johnson's Lauderdale-by-the-Sea	33308
Howard Johnson's North	33308
Howard Johnson's Oceans Edge Resort	33304
Travelodge	33304

MILITARY INSTALLATIONS

Name	ZIP
Naval Surface Warfare Center, Fort Lauderdale	33315
Fort Lonesome	33547
Fort McCoy	32134
Fort Meade	33841
Fort Myers	33901-19 33990-91
For specific Fort Myers Zip Codes call (813) 334-2116	
Fort Myers Beach	33931-32
For specific Fort Myers Beach Zip Codes call (813) 463-9151	
Fort Myers Shores	33905
Fort Myers Villas	33917
Fort Ogden	33842
Fort Pierce	34945-54 34981-88
For specific Fort Pierce Zip Codes call (305) 461-2460	
Fort Pierce Beach (Part of Fort Pierce)	34949
Fort Pierce Northwest	34947
Fort Pierce Shores	34949
Fort Pierce South	34982
Fort Taylor (Part of Key West)	33040
Fort Union	32060
Fort Walton Beach	32548
Fort White	32038
Forty Ninth Street (Part of St. Petersburg)	33707
Fountain	32438
Fountain Heights	33803
Four Mile Village	32459
Four Points (Part of West Palm Beach)	33406
Fowlers Bluff	32626
Foxcroft (Part of Tallahassee)	32308
Foxtown	33868
Francis	32177
Franklin Park	33916
Franklintown	32034
Franwood Pines	33445
Freeport	32439
Frink	32430
Frontenac	32959
Frostproof	33843
Fruit Cove	32223
Fruit Cove-Switzerland	32043
Fruitland	32112
Fruitland Park	34731
Fruitville	34232
Fuller Heights	33860
Fullerton (Part of Oak Hill)	32759
Fulton (Part of Jacksonville)	32211
Fussels Corner	33823
Gainesville	32601-14
For specific Gainesville Zip Codes call (904) 377-1912	
Gainesville Mall (Part of Gainesville)	32601
Gainesville North (Part of Gainesville)	32601
Galleria at Fort Lauderdale, The (Part of Fort Lauderdale)	33304
Galliver	32564
Galloway	33801
Galt City	33270
Gardena	32765
Garden City (Duval County)	32218
Garden City (Okaloosa County)	32536
Garden Grove	34609
Gardenia Gardens (Part of Tallahassee)	32312
Gardens of Gulf Cove	33953
Gardenville	33534
Gardner	33890
Garnier	32548
Garver Manor (Part of Jacksonville)	32209
Gaskin	32433
Gateway Mall (Part of St. Petersburg)	33702
Gateway Shopping Center (Part of Jacksonville)	32208
Geneva	32732
Georgetown (Lee County)	33907
Georgetown (Madison County)	32340

Name	ZIP
Georgetown (Putnam County)	32139
Georgiana	32952
Gibson	32333
Gibsonia	33805
Gibsonton	33534
Gifford	32960
Gillett	34221
Gilmore (Part of Jacksonville)	32211
Gladeview	33138
Glencoe (Volusia County)	32168
Glendale (Leon County)	32303
Glendale (Walton County)	32433
Glen Ridge	33406
Glen Saint Mary	32040
Glenvar Heights (Dade County)	33143
Glenwood (Bay County)	32401
Glenwood (Nassau County)	32097
Glenwood (Volusia County)	32722
Glory	32351
Glynlea (Part of Jacksonville)	32216
Golden Beach (Dade County)	33160
Golden Beach (Sarasota County)	34292
Golden Gate (Collier County)	33999
Golden Gate (Martin County)	34997
Golden Glades	33055
Golden Heights	32757
Golden Isle Park	32757
Golden Isles (Part of Hallandale)	33009
Goldenrod (Orange County)	32733
Golden Shores	33160
Gold Tree (Part of Sarasota)	34237
Golf	33436
Golfair (Part of Jacksonville)	32218
Golf Lake Estates	34203
Golfview	33406
Golfview Heights	33406
Gomez	33455
Gonzalez	32560
Goodbys Lake (Part of Jacksonville)	32217
Good Hope	32531
Goodland	33933
Goodno	33471
Gopher Ridge	32145
Gordon	32433
Gordon Chapel	32640
Gordonville	33830
Gotha	34734
Goulding	32503
Goulds	33170
Governor's Square Mall (Part of Tallahassee)	32301
Graceville	32440
Graham	32042
Grahamsville	32688
Grandin	32138
Grand Island	32735
Grand Park (Part of Jacksonville)	32219
Grand Ridge	32442
Grandview	32131
Grangers Mill	32055
Grant	32949
Grassy Key	33050
Gratigny (Part of North Miami)	33168
Gravce's	33872
Grayton Beach	32459
Greenacres City	33463
Greenbriar (Part of Sanford)	32771
Green Cove Springs	32043
Greenfield Manor (Part of Jacksonville)	32216
Green Hills (Bay County)	32438
Green Hills (Dade County)	33157
Greenland (Part of Jacksonville)	32224
Greensboro	32330
Greenville	32331
Greenway	32320
Greenwood (Jackson County)	32443
Greenwood (Santa Rosa County)	32565
Greenwood Hills	32303
Grenelefe	33844
Gretna	32332
Griffin	33801
Gross	32097
Grove City	34224
Groveland	34736

Name	ZIP
Grove Park (Alachua County)	32640
Grove Park (Duval County)	32216
Grove Park (Hillsborough County)	33614
Grove Park (Polk County)	33803
Grove Park Estates	33614
Gulf Beach	32507
Gulf Breeze	32561
Gulf City	33570
Gulf Cove	33953
Gulf Gate East	34238
Gulf Gate Estates	34231
Gulf Gate Mall	34231
Gulf Hammock	32639
Gulf Harbors	34652
Gulf Pines	32459
Gulfport	33707
Gulf Shores (Part of Venice)	34292
Gulf Stream	33483
Hacienda Village (Part of Davie)	33314
Hague	32601
Haines City	33844
Hainesworth	32615
Hainesworth Farm	32615
Hallandale	33009
Hamilton (Part of Pompano Beach)	33060
Hammock	32135
Hampton	32044
Hanson	32340
Harbinwood	32303
Harbor Bluffs	34640
Harbor East (Part of Boca Raton)	33431
Harbor Oaks	32127
Harbor Ridge	34990
Harbor Shores	34748
Harbor View (Charlotte County)	33980
Harborview (Duval County)	32208
Harbor View (Pinellas County)	34698
Harbour Heights	33983
Hardaway	32324
Hardeetown (Part of Chiefland)	32626
Hardin Heights	32324
Harlem	33440
Harmony Heights	34946
Harold	32563
Hart Haven (Part of Jacksonville)	32205
Harvey Heights	33901
Hastings	32145
Hatchbend	32008
Havana	32333
Haven Beach (Part of Indian Rocks Beach)	34635
Haverhill	33406
Haw Creek	32110
Hawthorne (Alachua County)	32640
Hawthorne (Lake County)	34748
Heathrow	32746
Hedges	32097
Heilbron Springs	32091
Henderson Creek	33961
Hendry Correctional Institution	33934
Heritage Farms	33912
Hermitage	32324
Hernando	32642
Hernando Beach	34607
Hernando City Heights	32642
Hernando Ridge	33525
Herndon (Part of Orlando)	32803
Hero	32097
Hesperides	33853
Hialeah	33010-16
For specific Hialeah Zip Codes call (305) 888-6491	
Hialeah Gardens	33016
Hialeah Lakes (Part of Hialeah)	33014
Hibernia	32043
Hibiscus	32757
Hickory Hill	32464
Hidden River	34240
Highland	32058
Highland Beach	33431
Highland City	33846
Highland Court Manor (Part of Gainesville)	32601
Highland Lakes	34684
Highland Park (Franklin County)	32320
Highland Park (Pinellas County)	34640
Highland Park (Polk County)	33853

Highland Park-Lake Haven Estates **FLORIDA** 109

Name	ZIP
Highland Park (Seminole County)	32771
Highlands (Broward County)	33064
Highlands (Duval County)	32218
Highlands Lakes	33825
Highlands Park Estates	33852
Highland View	32456
High Point (Hernando County)	34613
High Point (Pinellas County)	34620
High Ridge Estates	32656
High Springs	32643
Hiland Park (Bay County)	32405
Hildreth	32008
Hillcrest Heights	33827
Hilldale (Part of Tampa)	33614
Hilliard	32046
Hill N Dale	34602
Hillsboro Beach	33062
Hillsborough Correctional Institution	33569
Hinson	32333
Hinson Crossroads	32427
Hiway Park	33852
Hobe Sound	33455
Hogan (Part of Jacksonville)	32216
Holden Heights (Orange County)	32805
Holder	32645
Holiday (Pasco County)	34690
Holiday Gardens	34691
Holiday Harbor (Part of Jacksonville)	32224
Holiday Heights	33037
Holiday Hills	34653
Holiday Manor	33844
Holland Crossroads	32425
Holley	32561
Hollister	32147
Holly Ford (Part of Jacksonville)	32218
Holly Hill	32117
Holly Hills (Part of Tallahassee)	32303
Holly Point (Part of Orange Park)	32073
Hollywood	33019-29, 33081-84
For specific Hollywood Zip Codes call (305) 527-2074	
Hollywood Beach	32407
Hollywood Fashion Center (Part of Hollywood)	33021
Hollywood Hills (Part of Hollywood)	33021
Hollywood Mall (Part of Hollywood)	33021
Hollywood Seminole Indian Reservation	33024
Holmes Beach	34218
Holmes Correctional Institution	32425
Holmes Valley	32462
Holopaw	32901
Holt	32564
Homeland	33847
Homestead	33030-35, 33090-92
For specific Homestead Zip Codes call (305) 247-2641	
Homestead AFB	33039
Homestead Air Force Base	33039
Homestead Ridge	32308
Homosassa	32646
Homosassa Springs	32647
Honeyville	32465
Hopewell (Hillsborough County)	33567
Hopewell (Madison County)	32340
Horeshoe Acres	33471
Horseshoe Beach	32648
Hosford	32334
Houston	32060
Howey-in-the-Hills	34737
Hudson-Bayonet Point	34667
Hugh	32265
Hull	33821
Huntington	32112
Huntington Estates	32303
Hurlburt Field	32544
Hyde Grove (Part of Jacksonville)	32222
Hyde Park (Duval County)	32222
Hyde Park (Wakulla County)	32305
Hypoluxo	33460
Iddo	32331
Idylwild (Part of Gainesville)	32601
Ilexhurst (Part of Bradenton Beach)	34217
Immokalee	33934
Imperial Estates	32809

Name	ZIP
Indialantic	32903
Indian Bluff	32466
Indian Bluff Island	34683
Indian Creek	33154
Indian Hammock	34972
Indian Harbour Beach	32937
Indian Hills (Brevard County)	32922
Indian Hills (Glades County)	33471
Indian Lake Estates	33855
Indian Mound Village	32771
Indianola	32952
Indian Pass	32456
Indian River City (Part of Titusville)	32780
Indian River Correctional Institution	32960
Indian River Estates	34982
Indian River Shores	32963
Indian Rocks Beach	34635
Indian Shores	34635
Indiantown	34956
Indrio	34946
Inglis	32649
Inlet Beach	32407
Innerarity	32507
Interbay (Part of Tampa)	33611
Intercession City	33848
Interlachen	32148
Inverness	32650-52
For specific Inverness Zip Codes call (904) 726-2757	
Inverrary (Part of Lauderhill)	33313
Inwood (Jackson County)	32460
Inwood (Polk County)	33880
Iona Gardens	33901
Irvine	32686
Islamorada	33036
Island Grove	32654
Island Harbor	33946
Islandia	33131
Isleboro (Part of New Smyrna Beach)	32168
Isle of Palms (Part of Jacksonville)	32250
Isleworth	34786
Istachatta	34635
Istokpoga Shores	33857
Ives Estates (Dade County)	33162
Izagora	32427
Jackson Still	32433
Jacksonville	32201-98
For specific Jacksonville Zip Codes call (704) 355-7311	
Jacksonville ATO (Part of Jacksonville)	32229
Jacksonville Beach	32250
Jacksonville Heights (Part of Jacksonville)	32210
Jacksonville University (Part of Jacksonville)	32211
Jacob City	32431
Jamaica Bay	33912
Jamestown	32765
Jamie's	33853
Jan Phyl Village	33880
Jarrott	32344
Jasmine Estates (Pasco County)	34668
Jasper	32052
Jay	32565
Jena	32359
Jenada Isles (Part of Wilton Manors)	33305
Jennings	32053
Jensen Beach	34957-58
For specific Jensen Beach Zip Codes call (407) 334-1898	
Jerome	33926
Jessamine	33525
John F. Kennedy Space Center	32815
John's Lake	34787
Johnson	32640
Johnson's Corner	32767
John's Pass (Part of Madeira Beach)	33708
Jonathan's Landing	33458
Jonesville	32669
Judson	32693
June Park	32901
Juniper	32330
Juno Beach	33406
Jupiter	33468-69, 33477-78
For specific Jupiter Zip Codes call (407) 746-3620	
Jupiter	33458
Jupiter Inlet Colony	33458
Jupiter Island	33455
Kathleen	33849
Keaton Beach	32347

Name	ZIP
Kenansville	34739
Kendale Lakes	33183
Kendall (Dade County)	33156
Kendall Green	33060
Kendall Town & country	33183
Kendrick	32670
Kenneth City	33709
Kensington Park	34235
Key Biscayne	33149
Key Colony Beach	33051
Key Largo	33037
Key Largo Park	33037
Key Largo Village	33037
Keystone Heights	32656
Keystone Islands (Part of North Miami)	33161
Keysville	33547
Key West	33040-41
For specific Key West Zip Codes call (305) 294-2557	
Key West Naval Air Station	33040
Killarney	34740
Killarney Shores (Part of Jacksonville)	32216
Killearn	32303
Killearn Acres	32308
Killearn Lakes	32312
Kinard	32449
Kincaid Hills	32601
King Lake	32688
Kings Bay	33158
Kings Creek	33143
Kings Ferry	32046
Kingsley Lake	32091
Kingsley Village	32091
Kings Manor	33310
Kings Point	33484
Kings Road (Part of Jacksonville)	32205
Kingswood Manor (Brevard County)	32780
Kingswood Manor (Orange County)	32804
Kissimmee	34741-46, 34758-59
For specific Kissimmee Zip Codes call (407) 846-3121	
Kissimmee Park	34772
Klosterman	34689
Knights	33565
Knoxhill	32455
Korona	32110
Kossuthville	33823
Kynesville	32431
La Belle	33935
Lackawana Estates	32640
Lackawanna (Part of Jacksonville)	32210
Lacoochee	33537
La Crosse	32658
Lady Lake	32159
La Gorce Island (Part of Miami Beach)	33139
Lagrange	32780
Laguna Beach	32407
Laird	32439
Lake Alfred	33850
Lake Bird	32331
Lake Bradford	32301
Lake Brantley	32750
Lakebreeze	32303
Lake Bryant	32179
Lake Buena Vista	32830
Lake Butler	32054
Lake Cain Hills	32805
Lake Carroll	33618
Lake Charles	32688
Lake Charm (Part of Oviedo)	32765
Lake City	32055-56
For specific Lake City Zip Codes call (904) 752-3373	
Lake Clarke Shores	33406
Lake Como	32157
Lake Correctional Institution	34711
Lake Crescent Estates	32112
Lake Denton	33825
Lake Eaton	32688
Lake Forest (Broward County)	33023
Lake Forest (Duval County)	32208
Lake Forest Hills (Part of Jacksonville)	32208
Lake Frances (Part of Tavares)	32778
Lake Garfield	33830
Lake Geneva	32160
Lake Hamilton	33851
Lake Harbor	33459
Lake Harris Shores	32778
Lake Haven Estates	33872

110 FLORIDA Lake Helen-Melrose Park

Location	ZIP
Lake Helen	32744
Lake Jem	32745
Lake Joanna	32726
Lake Josephine	33872
Lake Juniata	32778
Lake Kathryn Estates	32707
Lake Kathryn Heights	32720
Lake Kathryn Village (Part of Casselberry)	32707
Lakeland	33801-13
For specific Lakeland Zip Codes call (813) 683-6245	
Lakeland Highlands	33801
Lakeland Mall (Part of Lakeland)	33801
Lake Letta	33825
Lake Lindsey	34601
Lake Lorraine	32569
Lake Lotela	33825
Lake Lou	32688
Lake Lucerne (Dade County)	33054
Lake Lucina (Part of Jacksonville)	32211
Lake Magdalene	33612
Lake Marian Highlands	34739
Lake Mary	32746
Lake Maude (Part of Winter Haven)	33880
Lake Mendelin Estates	32703
Lake Miona Heights	34785
Lake Monroe	32747
Lakemont	33825
Lake of the Hills	33853
Lake Ola	32757
Lake Panasoffkee	33538
Lake Park	33403
Lake Placid	33852
Lakeport	33471
Lake Rogers Isle (Part of Boca Raton)	33431
Lake Saunders	32757
Lake Shipp Heights	33880
Lake Shore (Part of Jacksonville)	32244
Lake Shore Estates	34684
Lakeside	32073
Lakeside Hills	32140
Lakes Mall (Part of Lauderdale Lakes)	33319
Lake Tarpon	34684
Lake Tarpon Mobile Homes	34684
Lake View Park	33843
Lake Wales	33853
Lake Weir	32179
Lake Winnott	32640
Lakewood (Duval County)	32207
Lakewood (Leon County)	32303
Lakewood (Walton County)	32433
Lakewood Park	34951
Lake Worth	33460-67
For specific Lake Worth Zip Codes call (305) 964-1102	
Lamont	32336
Lam Smith Crossroads	32425
Lanair Park	33462
Lanark Village	32323
Lancaster	32060
Land O'Lakes	34639
Lane View Estates	33872
Lantana (Palm Beach County)	33462
Lantana (Polk County)	33843
Largo	34640-49
For specific Largo Zip Codes call (813) 584-2191	
Larsen (Part of Jacksonville)	32216
Lauderdale-by-the-Sea	33308
Lauderdale Isles	33312
Lauderdale Lakes	33313
Lauderhill	33313
Lauderhill Mall (Part of Lauderhill)	33313
Laurel (Sarasota County)	34272
Laurel Grove (Part of Orange Park)	32073
Laurel Hill	32567
Laurel Park (Escambia County)	32505
Laurel Park (Orange County)	32809
Lawtey	32058
Lazy Lagoon	33982
Lazy Lake	33314
Lealman	33714
Lebanon	32630
Lecanto	32661
Lee	32059
Leesburg	34748-49

Location	ZIP
	34788-89
For specific Leesburg Zip Codes call (904) 787-3679	
Lehigh (Part of Tallahassee)	32301
Lehigh Acres	33970-71
For specific Lehigh Acres Zip Codes call (813) 369-2159	
Lehigh Acres	33936
Leisure City	33033
Leisure Lakes Estates	33852
Lely	33961
Lely Golf Estates	33961
Lemon Bluff	32764
Lemon Grove	33873
Leon (Part of Tallahassee)	32303
Leonards	32424
Leonia	32464
Leonton	32344
Leroy	32674
Lessie	32046
Leto	33614
Libby Heights (Part of Gainesville)	32601
Liberty	32433
Lido Beach (Part of St. Petersburg Beach)	33736
Lighthouse Point (Broward County)	33064
Lighthouse Point (Martin County)	34994
Lily	33865
Limestone (Hardee County)	33865
Limestone (Jefferson County)	32344
Limona	33510
Lincoln City (Part of Starke)	32091
Lincoln Estates (Part of Gainesville)	32601
Lincoln Road (Part of Miami)	33139
Lincoln Road Mall (Part of Miami Beach)	33139
Linda Loma	33901
Linden	33597
Lindgren Acres	33177
Lisbon	34748
Lithia (Hillsborough County)	33547
Lithia Square	33511
Little Acres	34736
Little Gasparilla	33946
Little Havana (Part of Miami)	33130
Little Lake City	32619
Little Red Water Lake	33825
Little River (Part of Miami)	33138
Little River Springs	32071
Little Sun Ray	33843
Little Torch Key	33042
Live Oak (Suwannee County)	32060
Live Oak (Washington County)	32462
Live Oak Island	32327
Lloyd	32337
Lochloosa	32662
Lock Arbor	32771
Lockhart	32810
Lockwood Ridge (Part of Sarasota)	34234
Londonderry	32808
Long Beach Resort (Part of Panama City Beach)	32401
Longboat Key	34228
Longdale (Part of Longwood)	32750
Long Hammock	32684
Long Key	33001
Longwood (Okaloosa County)	32579
Longwood (Seminole County)	32750
Lorida	33857
Los Robles (Part of Tallahassee)	32303
Lotus	32952
Loughman	33858
Lovedale	34623
Lovewood	32431
Lowell	32663
Lower Grand Lagoon	32401
Loxahatchee	33470
Lucerne Avenue (Part of Lake Worth)	33460
Lucerne Park	33880
Ludlam (Part of Miami)	33155
Lullwater Beach (Part of Panama City Beach)	32401
Lulu	32061
Lumberton	33540
Lundy	32177
Luraville	32060
Lutz	33549

Location	ZIP
Lynne	32688
Lynn Haven	32444
Mabel	33514
McAlpin	32062
McCall	33927
Macclenny	32063
Macclenny II	32063
McCoy Annex	32812
McDavid	32568
Macedonia	32424
McGregor Groves (Part of Fort Myers)	33919
McIntosh	32664
Mack Bayou	32459
McKinnon	32568
McLellen	32570
McMeekin	32640
McRae	32656
Madeira Beach	33708
Madison	32340
Magnet Cove	32333
Magnolia Beach	32401
Magnolia Gardens (Part of Jacksonville)	32209
Magnolia Springs	32043
Mainland (Part of Ormond Beach)	32174
Mainlands Center (Part of Pinellas Park)	34666
Maitland	32751
Malabar	32950
Malone	32445
Manalapan	33460
Manasota Key	34223
Manatee (Part of Bradenton)	34208
Mandarin (Part of Jacksonville)	32217
Mango	33550
Mango Hills	33584
Mangonia Park	33406
Mango-Seffner	33550
Marathon	33050
Marathon Shores	33052
Maravilla (Part of Fort Pierce)	34982
Marco	33937
Margate	33063
Margate Estates (Part of Margate)	33063
Marianna	32446
Marietta (Part of Jacksonville)	32205
Marineland	32086
Marion Correctional Institution	32663
Marion Oaks	32673
Market Square Mall (Part of Jacksonville)	32207
Martel	32670
Martin	32670
Martin Correctional and Vocational Center	34956
Mary Esther	32569
Masaryktown	34609
Mascotte	34753
Matlacha	33909
Matoaka	34270
Maxcy Quarters	33843
Maximo Moorings (Part of St. Petersburg)	33711
Maxville (Part of Jacksonville)	32265
Mayfair in the Grove (Part of Miami)	33133
Mayo	32066
Mayo Correctional Institution	32066
Mayo Junction	32066
Mayport (Part of Jacksonville)	32267
Meadowbrook (Clay County)	32073
Meadowbrook (Orange County)	32808
Meadowbrook Terrace	32073
Mecca	32771
Medart	32327
Medley	33166
Medulla	33803
Melaleuca Isle	33314
Melbourne	32901-10
	32934-40
For specific Melbourne Zip Codes call (305) 723-5135	
Melbourne Beach	32951
Melbourne Gardens (Part of Melbourne Village)	32901
Melbourne Shores	32951
Melbourne Village	32901
Melrose	32666
Melrose Park (Broward County)	33312

Melrose Park-North Miami **FLORIDA** **111**

	ZIP
Melrose Park (Columbia County)	32055
Memphis	34221
Meredith Manor	32750
Merritt Island	32952-54
For specific Merritt Island Zip Codes call (305) 453-1366	
Merritt Square	32952
Mexico Beach	32401
Miami	33101-99
	33201-69
For specific Miami Zip Codes Call (305) 470-0327	

COLLEGES & UNIVERSITIES

Barry University	33161

FINANCIAL INSTITUTIONS

American Savings & Loan Association of Florida	33169
Amerifirst Bank, A Federal Savings Bank	33131
Atico Savings Bank	33131
Barnett Bank of South Florida, N.A.	33131
Capital Bank	33141
Centrust Savings Bank	33131
Chase Federal Savings and Loan Association	33156
Citizens Federal Savings & Loan Association	33131
City National Bank of Florida	33101
Coconut Grove Bank	33133
Continental National Bank of Miami	33135
Coral Gables Federal Savings & Loan Association	33156
County National Bank of South Florida	33137
Creditbank	33137
Dadeland Bank	33156
Eagle National Bank of Miami	33132
Flagler Federal Savings & Loan Association	33132
Interamerican Federal Savings & Loan Association	33165
Intercontinental Bank	33131
Key Biscayne Bank and Trust Company	33149
Lincoln Savings & Loan Association	33129
Miami Savings Bank	33132
Northern Trust Bank of Florida, N.A.	33131
Ocean Bank	33126
Pacific National Bank	33131
Republic National Bank of Miami	33126
SafraBank	33132
Southeast Bank, N.A.	33131
Sun Bank/Miami, National Association	33131
Terrabank, National Association	33145
Totalbank	33145
United National Bank	33130

HOSPITALS

AMI Kendall Regional Medical Center	33175
Baptist Hospital of Miami	33176
Cedars Medical Center	33136
Golden Glades Regional Medical Center	33169
Humana Hospital-Biscayne	33180
James M. Jackson Memorial Hospital	33136
Mercy Hospital	33133
North Shore Medical Center	33150
South Miami Hospital	33143
Veterans Administration Medical Center	33125

HOTELS/MOTELS

Hyatt Regency Miami	33131
Marriott Hotel-Airport	33126
Miami Airport Hilton & Marina	33126
Radisson Mart Plaza Hotel	33126

MILITARY INSTALLATIONS

7th Coast Guard District, Miami	33130
Miami Beach	33139

	ZIP
Miami Beach Coast Guard Base	33139
Miami Coast Guard Station	33054
Miami Gardens	33023
Miami Gardens-Utopia-Carver	33023
Miami Lakes	33014
Miami Shores	33138
Miami Springs	33166
Micanopy	32667
Micco	32958
Miccosukee	32309
Middleburg	32068
Mid Town Plaza (Part of Sarasota)	34239
Midway (Gadsden County)	32343
Midway (Hillsborough County)	33565
Midway (Seminole County)	32771
Mill Bayou	32444
Millcreek	32092
Milligan	32537
Milltown	32456
Millview	32506
Millville (Part of Panama City)	32401
Milton	32570-71
For specific Milton Zip Codes call (904) 623-3807	
Milton East	32570
Mi-Lu Estates	32159
Mims	32754
Mineral Springs	32565
Minneola	34755
Mintons Corner	32904
Miracle City Mall (Part of Titusville)	32780
Miramar (Broward County)	33023
Miramar (Duval County)	32207
Miramar Beach	32541
Miramar Terrace (Part of Jacksonville)	32226
Mission City	32168
Mobile Gardens	34224
Mobile Haven Estates	33901
Mobile Home Park (Part of Sarasota)	34237
Modello	33030
Moffitt	33890
Molino	32577
Molino Crossroads	32533
Money Bayou	32456
Monroes Corner	32691
Montbrook	32696
Montclair	34748
Monteocha	32601
Monterey (Part of Jacksonville)	32211
Monticello	32344
Montverde	34756
Montverde Junction (Part of Montverde)	32757
Moore Haven	33471
Moreland Park	34785
Morningside Park	32809
Morning View	34748
Morrison Home	33406
Morriston	32668
Mosley Hall	32331
Moss Bluff	32179
Mossy Head	32434
Moultrie	32086
Moultrie Junction (Part of St. Augustine)	32084
Mountain Lake	33853
Mountain Park (Hernando County)	34601
Mount Carmel	32565
Mount Dora	32757
Mount Pleasant	32352
Mount Plymouth	32776
Mount Royal	32193
Mulat	32570
Mulberry	33860
Mullinsville	33843
Mullis City	33618
Munson	32570
Munson Island	33042
Murat Hills (Part of Tallahassee)	32304
Murdock	33938
Murray Hill (Part of Jacksonville)	32205
Myakka City	34251
Myakka Head	33865
Myakka River Manor (Part of North Port)	34287
Myakka Valley Ranchos	34241
Myerlee (Part of Fort Myers)	33919
Myrtis	32055
Myrtle Grove	32506

	ZIP
Nalcrest	33856
Naples	33939-42
	33961-64
For specific Naples Zip Codes call (813) 262-5411	
Naples Manor	33961
Naples Park	33963
Naranja	33032
Naranja-Princeton	33032
Narcoossee	34771
Nash	32336
Nashua	32189
Nassau Village	32011
Nassau Village-Ratcliff	32011
Nassauville	32034
National Gardens	32174
Naval Regional Medical Clinic	33040
Naval Training Center (Part of Orlando)	32813
Navarre	32569
Navy Point	32507
Neptune Beach	32233
Neptune Shores	34744
NETPDC	32509
Neukoms (Part of Zephyrhills)	33540
New Berlin (Part of Jacksonville)	32226
Newberry	32669
Newburn	32060
New Harmony	32433
New Hope (Holmes County)	32464
New Hope (Washington County)	32462
New Liberty City	33054
New Point Comfort	34223
Newport (Monroe County)	33037
Newport (Wakulla County)	32327
New Port Richey	34652-56
For specific New Port Richey Zip Codes call (813) 849-4333	
New Port Richey East	34653
New River (Bradford County)	32054
New River (Broward County)	33312
New River Correctional Institution	32083
New Smyrna Beach	32168-70
For specific New Smyrna Beach Zip Codes call (904) 427-1377	
Newtown Heights (Part of Sarasota)	34234
New Upsala	32771
New York	32565
Niceville	32578
Nichols	33863
Nobles (Part of Pensacola)	32504
Nobleton	34661
Nocatee	33864
Nokomis	34274-75
For specific Nokomis Zip Codes call (813) 488-1135	
Noma	32452
Noma Junction	32452
Norin Plaza (Part of North Miami)	33161
Norland	33169
Normandy (Dade County)	33141
Normandy (Duval County)	32205
Normandy Isle (Part of Miami Beach)	33139
Normandy Mall (Part of Jacksonville)	32205
Normandy Manor (Part of Jacksonville)	32205
Normandy Village (Part of Jacksonville)	32222
North Andrews Gardens	33308
North Babcock (Part of Melbourne)	32901
North Bay Village	33141
North Brooksville	34601
Northcliffe	32561
North Cocoa (Part of Cocoa)	32922
North Crest	32703
North De Land	32720
Northeast Florida State Hospital	32063
Northeast Park (Part of St. Petersburg)	33704
North Fort Myers (Lee County)	33903
North La Belle	33935
North Lauderdale	33068
North Meadowbrook Terrace	32073
North Merritt Island	32953
North Miami	33161

112 FLORIDA North Miami Beach-Parramore

	ZIP
North Miami Beach	33162
North Naples	33963
North Oak Hill (Part of Jacksonville)	32210
North Palm Beach	33408
North Port	34287
North Redington Beach	33708
North River Shores	34994
North Ruskin	33572
North Sarasota	34234
North Shore (Part of Jacksonville)	32208
North Shore Junction (Part of Jacksonville)	32208
Northside (Bay County)	32405
Northside (Sarasota County)	34234
North Winter Haven	33880
Northwood (Alachua County)	32605
Northwood (Palm Beach County)	33407
Northwood Mall (Part of Tallahassee)	32303
Northwood Plaza (Part of Clearwater)	34621
Norwood (Part of Jacksonville)	32208
NTC Annex	32812
Nutall Rise	32336
Oak	32670
Oak Crest (Alachua County)	32640
Oakcrest (Marion County)	32670
Oak Forest	32636
Oak Grove (Calhoun County)	32449
Oak Grove (Escambia County)	32568
Oak Grove (Gadsden County)	32324
Oak Grove (Gulf County)	32456
Oak Grove (Hardee County)	33873
Oak Grove (Lake County)	32159
Oak Grove (Okaloosa County)	32531
Oak Grove (Sumter County)	33597
Oak Grove Village	32696
Oak Harbor (Part of Jacksonville)	32233
Oak Haven (Part of Jacksonville)	32216
Oak Hill	32759
Oak Hill Park (Part of Jacksonville)	32210
Oakhurst (Part of Seminole)	34646
Oak Knoll Estates	32312
Oakland	34760
Oakland Hills	32810
Oakland Park (Broward County)	33334
Oakland Park (Lake County)	32757
Oakland Shores	32751
Oak Ridge	32809
Oaks Royal	33541
Oak Street (Part of Kissimmee)	34741
Oak Terrace	33860
Oakwood	32688
Oakwood Hills	32433
Oakwood Villa (Part of Jacksonville)	32211
O'Brien	32071
Ocala	32670-78
For specific Ocala Zip Codes call (904) 629-7146	
Ocala Park Ranch	32670
Ocala Ridge	32670
Ocala West (Part of Ocala)	32670
Ocean Breeze Park	34957
Ocean City	32548
Ocean Ridge	33435
Oceans (Part of Jacksonville Beach)	32250
Ocean View (Part of Miami Beach)	33140
Oceanway (Part of Jacksonville)	32218
Ocheesee	32442
Ochopee	33943
Ocoee	34761
Odessa	33556
Ojus (Dade County)	33163
Ojus (Dade County)	33180
Okahumpka	34762
Okaloosa Correctional Institution	32536
Okaloosa Island	32548
Okeechobee	34972-74
For specific Okeechobee Zip Codes call (813) 763-3616	
Oklawaha	32179

	ZIP
Old Callaway (Part of Callaway)	32401
Old Myakka	34240
Oldsmar	34677
Old Town	32680
Olustee	32072
Olympia Heights	33175
Omni International of Miami (Part of Miami)	33132
Ona	33865
Oneco	34264
O'Neil	32034
Opa-Locka	33054-56
For specific Opa-Locka Zip Codes call (305) 681-7489	
Opa-Locka North	33054
Open Air (Part of St. Petersburg)	33701
Orange	32321
Orange Bend	34748
Orange Blossom (Lake County)	34737
Orange Blossom (Orange County)	32805
Orange Blossom Estates	33872
Orange Blossom Gardens	34748
Orange Blossom Hills	32691
Orange Blossom Hills South	32691
Orange Blossom Mall (Part of Fort Pierce)	34947
Orange City	32763
Orange City Hills	32763
Orangedale (Polk County)	33801
Orangedale (St. Johns County)	32043
Orange Hammock	32110
Orange Harbor	33905
Orange Heights	32640
Orange Hill	32428
Orange Home	34786
Orange Lake	32681
Orange Lake Village (Part of Seminole)	34642
Orange Mills	32131
Orange Park	32073
Orange Park Mall (Part of Orange Park)	32073
Orange River Hills	33905
Orange Springs	32182
Orchid	32960
Orienta Gardens (Part of Altamonte Springs)	32701
Orient Park	33614
Oriole Beach	32561
Orlando	**32801-72**
For specific Orlando Zip Codes call (407) 850-6200	
COLLEGES & UNIVERSITIES	
University of Central Florida	32816
FINANCIAL INSTITUTIONS	
American Pioneer Savings Bank	32853
Firstate Financial, A Savings Bank	32803
The First, F.A.	32802
SunBank, National Association	32801
HOSPITALS	
Florida Hospital Medical Center	32803
Humana Hospital-Lucerne	32801
Orlando Regional Medical Center	32806
HOTELS/MOTELS	
Hilton Inn Florida Center	32819
Sheraton World	32821
MILITARY INSTALLATIONS	
Naval Research Laboratory, Underwater Sound Reference Detachment	32856
Naval Training Station, Orlando	32813
Navy and Marine Corps Reserve Center, Orlando	32803
Orlando Fashion Square (Part of Orlando)	32803
Orlovista	32811
Ormond Beach	32174-76
For specific Ormond Beach Zip Codes call (904) 677-0333	
Ormond By The Sea	32174
Ortega (Part of Jacksonville)	32210
Ortega Farms (Part of Jacksonville)	32220

	ZIP
Ortega Forest (Part of Jacksonville)	32230
Ortega Hills (Part of Jacksonville)	32230
Ortega Terrace (Part of Jacksonville)	32220
Osceola Heights (Part of Tallahassee)	32301
Osprey	34229
Osteen	32764
Otis (Part of Jacksonville)	32220
Otter Creek	32683
Overbrook Gardens	34223
Overstreet	32453
Oviedo	32765
Owens	33821
Oxford	32684
Oyster Bayou	34652
Ozello	32629
Ozona	34660
Pace	32570
Paddock Mall (Part of Ocala)	32674
Page Park	33901
Pahokee	33476
Painters Hill	32136
Paisley	32767
Palatka	32177
Palma Ceia (Part of Tampa)	33609
Palm Acres	33901
Palm Aire (Part of Pompano Beach)	33069
Palma Sola	34209
Palma Sola Park	34209
Palm Bay	32905
Palm Beach	33480
Palm Beach Gardens	33410
Palm Beach Mall (Part of West Palm Beach)	33401
Palm Beach Shores	33404
Palm City	34990
Palm Coast	32135
Palm Coast Plaza (Part of West Palm Beach)	33405
Palmdale	33944
Palmetto	34220-21
For specific Palmetto Zip Codes call (813) 722-1701	
Palmetto Estates (Dade County)	33157
Palmetto Point	33908
Palm Grove Colony (Hernando County)	34607
Palm Harbor	34682-85
For specific Palm Harbor Zip Codes call (813) 784-3203	
Palm Plaza	34233
Palm River	33619
Palm River-Clair Mel	33619
Palm River Estates	33999
Palm Shores	32935
Palm Springs	33460
Palm Springs Mile (Part of Hialeah)	33012
Palm Springs North	33015
Palm Valley	32082
Palm View	34221
Palm Village (Part of Hialeah)	33012
Paloma Park	33903
Panacea	32346
Panacea Park	32346
Panacoochee Retreats	33538
Panama City	32401-13
For specific Panama City Zip Codes call (904) 785-5280	
Panama City Beach	32407
Panama City Mall (Part of Panama City)	32405
Paola	32771
Paradise Bay	34210
Paradise Beach	32561
Paradise Island (Part of Treasure Island)	33740
Paradise Palms (Part of Boca Raton)	33486
Paradise Park	34946
Paradise Point	32629
Paradise Shores	33905
Paradise Village	33317
Park Avenue (Part of Tallahassee)	32302
Park City	33324
Park City West	33317
Parker	32401
Park Haven	33060
Parkland	33060
Parkside (Part of Tallahassee)	32303
Parmalee	34251
Parramore	32423

Parrish-Riviera Beach FLORIDA 113

Name	ZIP
Parrish	34219
Pass-a-Grille Beach (Part of St. Petersburg Beach)	33706
Patrick AFB North	32925
Patrick AFB South	32925
Patrick Air Force Base	32925
Paxon (Part of Jacksonville)	32205
Paxton	32538
Peaceful Acres	32630
Peace River Shores	33982
Peach Orchard	32618
Pecan Park (Part of Jacksonville)	32218
Pedro	32691
Pelican Bay	33963
Pelican Lake	33491
Pellis Springs	32331
Pembroke	33841
Pembroke Park	33009
Pembroke Pines	33024
Peniel	32177
Peninsula (Hillsborough County)	33609
Peninsula (Volusia County)	32118
Peninsular (Part of Ormond Beach)	32176
Penney Farms	32079
Pennsuco	33010
Pensacola	32501-26
	32573-76
	32581-98
For specific Pensacola Zip Codes call (904) 434-9184	
Pensacola Beach	32561
Pensacola Naval Air Station	32508
Pensacola Shores (Part of Gulf Breeze)	32561
Peoples City	32681
Peppertree Bay	34231
Peppertree Pointe	33908
Perrine	33157
Perry	32347
Peters	33157
Petes Island	32134
Phillipi Gardens	34231
Pickettville (Part of Jacksonville)	32205
Pickwick Park (Part of Jacksonville)	32217
Picnic	33547
Picolata	32092
Piedmont (Leon County)	32312
Piedmont (Orange County)	32703
Pierce	33860
Pierson	32180
Pine Air	33406
Pine Castle	32809
Pinecraft	34232
Pinecrest	33547
Pineda	32935
Pine Dale	33860
Pine Forest	32506
Pine Grove (Osceola County)	34771
Pine Grove (Suwannee County)	32060
Pine Hill Estates	32601
Pine Hills (Lake County)	32726
Pine Hills (Orange County)	32808
Pine Hills Center	32808
Pine Island (Calhoun County)	32424
Pine Island (Hernando County)	34607
Pine Island (Lee County)	33945
Pine Island Center	33991
Pine Lakes	32726
Pineland (Lee County)	33945
Pineland (Taylor County)	32347
Pineland Gardens (Part of Jacksonville)	32216
Pine Level	33821
Pinellas Park	34664-66
For specific Pinellas Park Zip Codes call (813) 546-0007	
Pinellas Square (Part of Pinellas Park)	34665
Pine Log	32437
Pine Manor	33907
Pineola	32636
Pine Ridge Country Estates	32665
Pine Shores	34231
Pinesville	32618
Pinetta	32350
Pineville	32568
Pinewood (Dade County)	33168
Pinewood Park	33168
Pioneer Village	33903
Pirate Harbor	33955
Pirates Wood	32097
Pittman (Holmes County)	32427

Name	ZIP
Pittman (Lake County)	32702
Placida	33946-47
For specific Placida Zip Codes call (813) 697-1511	
Placid Lakes	33852
Plantation (Broward County)	33317
Plantation (Monroe County)	33036
Plantation Acres	33314
Plantation Woods	32303
Plant City	33564-67
For specific Plant City Zip Codes call (813) 752-4111	
Platt	33821
Playland Isles	33314
Playland Village (Part of Davie)	33314
Pleasant Grove (Escambia County)	32507
Pleasant Grove (Hillsborough County)	33530
Pleasant Grove (Walton County)	32433
Pleasant Ridge	32433
Plummer (Part of Jacksonville)	32219
Plymouth	32768
Poinciana	34758-59
For specific Poinciana Zip Codes call (407) 846-3121	
Poinciana Place	33467
Point Baker	32570
Point Brittany (Part of St. Petersburg)	33715
Point La Vista (Part of Jacksonville)	32207
Point O' Rocks	34242
Point Washington	32454
Polk City	33868
Polk Correctional Institution	33868
Polly Town (Part of Jacksonville)	32218
Polo Club Estates	33406
Pomona Park	32181
Pompano Beach	33060-69
	33071-76
For specific Pompano Beach Zip Codes call (305) 942-0126	
Pompano Beach Highlands	33060
	33064
For specific Pompano Beach Highlands Zip Codes call (305) 942-0126	
Pompano Highlands West	33060
Pompano Park	33068
Pompano Square (Part of Pompano Beach)	33062
Ponce (Part of Coral Gables)	33134
Ponce de Leon	32455
Ponce Inlet	32127
Ponte Vedra	32082
Ponte Vedra Beach	32082
Poplar Head	32462
Port Charlotte	33952
Port Everglades (Part of Fort Lauderdale)	33316
Portland	32439
Port Malabar (Part of Palm Bay)	32905
Port Mayaca	33438
Port of Palm Beach (Part of Riviera Beach)	33404
Port of Palm Beach Junction (Part of Riviera Beach)	33404
Port Orange	32127
Port Richey	34667-74
For specific Port Richey Zip Codes call (813) 849-1233	
Port Salerno	34992
Port Sewall	34996
Port St. Joe	32456
Port St. John	32922
Port St. Lucie	34952
Port Tampa City (Part of Tampa)	33616
Pottsburg (Part of Jacksonville)	32216
Power Park (Part of Jacksonville)	32226
Prairie Creek Park	33982
Pretty Bayou	32401
Princeton	33032
Prine	33844
Produce (Part of Tampa)	33610
Progress Village	33619
Prospect	33309
Prospect Road (Part of Oakland Park)	33307
Prosperity	32464
Providence (Polk County)	33801

Name	ZIP
Providence (Union County)	32054
Pumpkin Center	34797
Punta Gorda	33948-55
	33980-83
For specific Punta Gorda Zip Codes call (813) 639-3395	
Punta Gorda Isles (Part of Punta Gorda)	33950
Punta Rassa	33908
Putnam Hall	32185
Quail Heights	33157
Quail Hollow	33544
Queens Cove	34947
Quincy	32351
Quinlan (Part of Jacksonville)	32218
Raccoon Key	33040
Raiford	32083
Rainbow Homes (Part of Delray Beach)	33444
Rainbow Lakes	32630
Rainbow Springs	32630
Raintree	32751
Raleigh	32696
Ralston Beach	33614
Ramrod Key	33042
Ratliff	32011
Ravenna Park (Part of Sanford)	32771
Ravenwood	34748
Rawls Park	33801
Reception and Medical Center	32054
Recruit Training Command	32813
Red Bay	32455
Reddick	32686
Red Head	32437
Redington Beach	33708
Redington Shores	33708
Redland	33031
Red Level	32629
Regal Oaks	34744
Regal Park	32670
Regency (Part of Jacksonville)	32211
Regency Park (Part of Jacksonville)	32203
Regency Square (Part of Jacksonville)	32211
Regional Seminary of Saint Vincent De Paul in Flor	33425
Remley Heights	32757
Remuda Ranch Grants	33933
Rerdell	33597
Rex	32640
Rexmere Village	33317
Ribault Manor (Part of Jacksonville)	32208
Rice Creek	32177
Richey Lakes	34653
Richloam	33597
Richmond Heights	33156
Richter Crossroads	32440
Ridge Harbor	33982
Ridge Manor	33525
Ridgeway	33903
Ridgewood (Alachua County)	32601
Ridgewood (Clay County)	32065
Ridgewood Estates	34232
Ridge Wood Heights	34231
Rileys Park	32757
Rio	34957
Riomar	32963
Rio Pinar Estates	32817
Ritta	33440
Riverdale (Hernando County)	33525
Riverdale (Lee County)	33905
Rivergate (Part of Ormond Beach)	32174
Riverhaven Village	32647
River Junction (Part of Chattahoochee)	32324
Riverland	33312
Riverland Village	33312
River Lawn	33905
River Park	34983
River Ranch	33853
River Ranch Shores	33853
River Retreats	32630
Riverside (Dade County)	33135
Riverside (Duval County)	32204
Riversink	32301
River Trails	33903
Riverview (Duval County)	32208
Riverview (Escambia County)	32501
Riverview (Hillsborough County)	33569
Riviera Beach	33404

114 FLORIDA Riviera Colony-South Gate Plaza

	ZIP		ZIP		ZIP
Riviera Colony	33961	Sandalwood (Part of Jacksonville)	32216	Sewall's Point	34996
Rixsford	32060	Sand Cut	33438	Shadeville	32327
Robin Hill	32701	Sanderson	32087	Shadow Lawn Estates	32601
Rock Bluff	32321	Sandestin	32541	Shady	32670
Rockdale	33157	Sand Lake (Part of Orlando)	32819	Shady Grove (Jackson County)	32442
Rockdale Keys	33157	Sandpiper Cove (Part of Destin)	32541	Shady Grove (Taylor County)	32357
Rock Harbor	33043	Sandy	34251	Shady Rest	32333
Rock Hill (Broward County)	33314	Sanford	32771-73	Shalimar	32579
Rock Hill (Okaloosa County)	32531	For specific Sanford Zip Codes call (407) 322-2892		Shamrock	32628
Rock Hill (Walton County)	32433	Sanford Farms	32771	Shangri-La (Part of Largo)	34640
Rock Hill (Washington County)	32428	Sanibel	33957	Shannon Forest (Part of Tallahassee)	32308
Rock Island Village	33314	San Jose (Part of Jacksonville)	32217	Shannon Wood	32601
Rockledge	32955-56	San Luis Ridge (Part of Tallahassee)	32303	Sharpes (Brevard County)	32922
For specific Rockledge Zip Codes call (407) 636-4177		San Marco (Part of Jacksonville)	32207	Sharpes (Brevard County)	32959
Rock Springs	32703	San Mateo (Duval County)	32218	Shawnee	33440
Rocky Creek	33615	San Mateo (Putnam County)	32187	Shell Point	32327
Ro-Len Lake Gardens (Part of Hallandale)	33009	San Pablo (Part of Jacksonville)	32250	Shell Point Village	33908
Rolling Acres	34602	San Souci (Part of Jacksonville)	32216	Sheltering Pines	33901
Rolling Hills (Duval County)	32205	San Souci Estates (Part of North Miami)	33161	Shenandoah (Part of Miami)	33145
Rolling Hills (Marion County)	32670	San Souci Lakes	33903	Sherman	34974
Rolling Hills (Polk County)	33860	Sans Souci	33982	Sherwood Forest (Part of Jacksonville)	32208
Rolling Oak Acres	33328	Santa Fe	32616	Sherwood Park (Part of Delray Beach)	33445
Rolling Ranches	32630	Santa Fe Lake	32631	Shiloh	32780
Romeo	32630	Santa Monica (Bay County)	32407	Shilow (Part of Plant City)	33567
Roosevelt Estates (Part of West Palm Beach)	33406	Santa Monica (Duval County)	32216	Shingle Creek	34746
Roosevelt Mall (Part of Jacksonville)	32210	Santa Rosa Beach	32459	Shockley Heights	32702
Rosedale	32324	Santa Rosa Mall (Part of Mary Esther)	32569	Shockley Hills	32702
Roseland	32957	Santos	32670	Siesta	34242
Rosemont	32805	Sarabay Acres	34229	Siesta Key	34242
Rosemont Hills	32804	Sarasota	34230-43	Siesta Lago	34746
Rosiwood	32625		34277-78	Silver Beach Heights	32784
Rotonda West	33947	For specific Sarasota Zip Codes call (813) 952-9720		Silver Sands (Part of Panama City Beach)	32407
Round Lake	32446	Sarasota Beach	34242	Silver Shores (Part of Lauderdale-by-the-Sea)	33308
Royal	34785	Sarasota Main Plaza (Part of Sarasota)	34236	Silver Springs (Marion County)	32688
Royal Gardens Estates	34207	Sarasota Springs	34232	Silver Springs (Okaloosa County)	32536
Royal Oak Hills (Part of Boca Raton)	33486	Sarasota Square (Sarasota County)	34238	Silver Springs Shores	32672
Royal Oaks (Part of Tallahassee)	32308	Saratoga	32189	Simmons Point	32346
Royal Palm Beach	33411	Sarno Plaza (Part of Melbourne)	32935	Singer Island (Part of Riviera Beach)	33404
Royal Palm Village	33908	Sasafrass Acres	32038	Sink Creek	32446
Royal Poinciana Park	32962	Satellite Beach	32937	Sipes	32771
Royals Cross Roads	32464	Satsuma	32189	Sirmans	32331
Rubonia	34221	Sawdust	32351	Skeen	32052
Runnymeade	32303	Sawgrass	32082	Skycrest (Part of Clearwater)	34625
Ruskin	33570-73	Scotland	32333	Sky Lake	32809
For specific Ruskin Zip Codes call (813) 645-1820		Scott Lake	33055	Skylake Mall	33162
Russell	32043	Scotts Ferry	32424	Skyland Heights (Part of Gainesville)	32601
Rutland	33538	Scottsmoor	32775	Skyland Meadows	32642
Saddlebunch Keys	33040	Scrambletown	32688	Skyline Hills	32159
Saddle Creek	34241	Seaglades	32507	Sky Top	34755
Safety Harbor	34695	Seagrove Beach	32454	Slaughter	33597
St. Andrews (Part of Panama City)	32401	Sea Ranch Lakes	33314	Slavia	32765
St. Armands (Part of Sarasota)	34236	Searstown (Part of Lakeland)	33801	Slones Ridge	34736
St. Augustine	32084-86	Searstown Mall (Part of Titusville)	32780	Snake Creek (Part of Miramar)	33023
For specific St. Augustine Zip Codes call (904) 829-8716		Seascape	32541	Snapper Creek Park	33143
St. Augustine Beach	32086	Seaside (Monroe County)	33070	Sneads	32460
St. Augustine Shores	32086	Seaside (Walton County)	32459	Snow Hill	32765
St. Augustine South	32086	Sebastian	32958	Snug Harbor	34996
St. Catherine	33513		32976-78	Socrum	33801
St. Cloud	34769-73	For specific Sebastian Zip Codes call (407) 589-4397		Solana	33950
For specific St. Cloud Zip Codes call (407) 892-3779		Sebastian Highlands (Part of Sebastian)	32958	Sopchoppy	32358
St. Georges Island	32328	Sebring	33870-72	Sorrento	32776
Saint James	32358	For specific Sebring Zip Codes call (813) 382-1151		Sorrento Shores	34229
St. James City	33956	Sebring Hills	33872	Sorrento Shores South	34275
Saint Joe Beach	32456	Sebring Shores	33870	South and East Junction (Part of Sanford)	32771
St. Johns Park (Duval County)	32210	Sebring Southgate (Part of Sebring)	33870	South Apopka (Orange County)	32703
St. Johns Park (Flagler County)	32110	Seffner	33584	South Arlington (Part of Jacksonville)	32216
Saint Johns River Estates	32771	Seminole (Okaloosa County)	32578	South Bay	33493
Saint Josephs	32771	Seminole (Pinellas County)	34642	South Beach (Part of Miami Beach)	33139
St. Leo	33574	Seminole Heights (Part of Tampa)	33603	Southboro (Part of West Palm Beach)	33405
St. Lucie	34946	Seminole Lake Country Club	34647	South Boyette	33547
St. Marks	32355	Seminole Mall (Part of Seminole)	34642	South Bradenton	34205
St. Petersburg	33701-84	Seminole Manor (Leon County)	32304	South Brooksville	34601
For specific St. Petersburg Zip Codes call (813) 323-6516		Seminole Manor (Palm Beach County)	33460	South Clermont	34711
St. Petersburg Beach	33706	Seminole Park	34647	South Cleviston	33440
St. Teresa	32358	Seville	32190	South Daytona	32121
Salem	32356			Southeast (Part of Winter Haven)	33880
Salt Springs	32113			South Fort Myers (Part of Fort Myers)	33901
Salvista	33903			Southgate	34239
Samoset	34208			South Gate Plaza (Part of Sarasota)	34239
Sampson City	32091				
Samsula	32168				
Samsula-Spruce Creek	32168				
San Antonio	33576				
San Blas	32456				
San Carlos Park	33912				
Sandalfoot Cove	33433				

South Gate Ridge-Tropical Shores Manor FLORIDA 115

	ZIP		ZIP		ZIP
South Gate Ridge (Sarasota County)	34233	Sunland Gardens	34947	*HOTELS/MOTELS*	
		Sunniland	33934		
South Jacksonville (Part of Jacksonville)	32207	Sun 'n Lakes Estates	33852	Days Inn Tampa Downtown	33602
		Sunny Breeze Harbour	33821	Guest Quarters Hotel	33609
South Lake Wales	33853	Sunny Hills	32428	Tampa Airport Marriott	33623
South Merritt Estates	32952	Sunny Isles	33160	Tampa Hilton Westshore	33602
South Miami	33143	Sunnyland	34233	Tampa Marriott Westshore	33607
South Miami Heights (Dade County)	33157	Sunnyside (Bay County)	32461	*MILITARY INSTALLATIONS*	
		Sunnyside (Lake County)	34748		
South Mulberry	33860	Sunnyside (Pasco County)	33541	MacDill Air Force Base	33608
South Palm Beach	33480	Sun Ray Homes	33843	Marine Corps Reserve Training Center, Tampa	33611
South Pasadena	33707	Sunrise (Part of Fort Lauderdale)	33304		
South Patrick (Part of Satellite Beach)	32937	Sunrise Golf Club Estates	34238	Tampa Bay Center (Part of Tampa)	33607
South Patrick Shores	32937	Sunset	33143	Tangelo Park	32809
South Pine Lakes	32726	Sunset Beach (Part of Treasure Island)	33740	Tangerine	32777
South Pointe	33919	Sunset Gardens	32901	Tanglewood	33907
South Ponte Vedra Beach	32082	Sunset Harbor	32691	Tang-O-Mar Beach	32541
Southport (Bay County)	32409	Sunset Island (Part of Miami Beach)	33139	Tarpon Lake Village	34685
Southport (Osceola County)	34746			Tarpon Springs	34688-91
South Punta Gorda Heights	33955	Sunset Point	33070	For specific Tarpon Springs Zip Codes call (813) 937-5741	
Southridge (Part of Jacksonville)	32216	Sunshine	33615		
		Sunshine Beach (Part of Treasure Island)	33708	Tarpon Woods	34685
South Sarasota	34239			Tarrytown	33597
South Sea Plantation	33924	Sunshine Mall (Part of Clearwater)	34616	Tavares	32778
South Shore	33440			Tavernier	33070
Southside (Broward County)	33316	Sunshine Ranches	33314	Taylor	32087
Southside (Lake County)	32784	Suntree	32935	Taylor Creek	34974
Southside (Polk County)	33803	Surf (Broward County)	33020	Tee and Green Estates	33982
Southside (Sarasota County)	34239	Surf (Wakulla County)	32340	Telogia	32360
		Surfside	33154	Temple Terrace	33617
Southside Estates (Part of Jacksonville)	32216	Suwanee Valley	32055	Tenille	32356
		Suwannee	32692	Tensulate (Part of Jacksonville)	32222
South Trail	34231	Suwannee Gardens	32680		
South Venice	34293	Suwannee River Park Estates	32060	Tequesta	33469
South Weeki Wachee	34606			Terra Ceia	34250
Southwest (Part of West Palm Beach)	33406	Suwannee Springs	32060	The Forest	33908
		Svea	32567	The Fountains	33467
Southwood	32809	Sweet Gum Head	32464	The Meadows (Lake County)	32702
Spanish River (Part of Boca Raton)	33431	Sweetwater (Dade County)	33152		
		Sweetwater (Duval County)	32222	The Meadows (Sarasota County)	34277
Sparr	32192	Sweetwater (Liberty County)	32321		
Spaulding (Part of Jacksonville)	32218	Sweetwater Creek	33614	Theresa Arbor	33617
		Sweetwater Oaks	32750	Theressa	32091
Spring Creek	32305	Switzerland	32043	Thomas City	32344
Springfield	32401	Sycamore	32351	Thompson	33070
Spring Glen (Part of Jacksonville)	32207	Sydney	33587	Thonotosassa	33592
		Sylvania	32462	Three Rivers	33222
Springhead	33566	Sylvan Shores (Highlands County)	33852	Three Rivers Estates	32038
Springhill (Columbia County)	32071			Thunderbird	33901
Spring Hill (Hernando County)	34606	Sylvan Shores (Lake County)	32757	Tice	33905
				Tierra Verde	33715
Spring Lake (Hernando County)	34602	Taft	32824	Tildenville	34787
		Tahitian Gardens	34691	Timberline Estates	32661
Spring Lake (Highlands County)	33870	Talisman Estates	33525	Timberwood Estates	34785
		Tallahassee	32301-17	Tiote	33853
Spring Park (Part of Jacksonville)	32207	For specific Tallahassee Zip Codes call (904) 877-4189		Tisonia (Part of Jacksonville)	32218
				Titusville	32780-83
Springside	32177	Tallahassee Mall (Part of Tallahassee)	32303	For specific Titusville Zip Codes call (305) 267-4826	
Springs Plaza	32779				
Spruce Creek	32119	Tallevast	34270	Tocoi Junction	32033
Spuds	32033	Talleyrand (Part of Jacksonville)	32206	Tomoka Estates	32174
Stanton	32195			Topes Farm	33852
Starke	32091	Tally Rand (Part of Jacksonville)	32226	Torchlite	34711
State Line	32426			Torrey	33834
Steele Church	32433	Tamami Village	33903	Towers (Part of Winter Park)	32792
Steinhatchee	32359	Tamarac	33321	Town and Country Estates (Part of Tallahassee)	32303
Stemper	33549	Tamiami	33144		
Stetson (Part of De Land)	32720		33165	Town and Country Plaza	32505
Stock Island	33040	For specific Tamiami Zip Codes call (305) 261-5102		Town and River Estates	33907
Streamline (Part of Pahokee)	33476			Town Center At Boca Raton (Part of Boca Raton)	33431
Stuart	34994-97	**Tampa**	33601-97		
For specific Stuart Zip Codes call (305) 287-2171		For specific Tampa Zip Codes call (813) 877-0717		Towne Mall (Part of Plantation)	33317
Stucky Still	34736			Town 'n' Country (Hillsborough County)	33615
Suburban Heights	32601	*COLLEGES & UNIVERSITIES*			
Suburban Hills (Part of Tallahassee)	32312	Tampa College	33614	Townsend	32066
		University of South Florida	33620	Trailer Estates	34207
Sugar Loaf Shores	33044	University of Tampa	33606	Trailer Haven (Part of Melbourne)	32901
Sugar Mill	32168				
Sugarmill Woods	32646	*FINANCIAL INSTITUTIONS*		Tranquility Park (Part of Winter Haven)	33880
Sulphur Springs (Part of Tampa)	33604	Bank of Tampa	33603		
		Barnett Bank of Tampa, N.A.	33602	Trapnell	33567
Sumatra	32335			Treasure Island (Dade County)	33141
Summerfield	32691	Bay Financial Savings Bank	33602		
Summer Haven	32086	Central Bank of Tampa	33677	Treasure Island (Lake County)	34748
Summerland Key	33042	First Florida Bank, National Association	33601		
Summer Place	32960			Treasure Island (Pinellas County)	33706
Summerport Beach	34787	NCNB National Bank of Florida	33602		
Sumner	32625			Trenton	32693
Sumter Correctional Institution	33513	Sun Bank of Tampa Bay	33602	Triangle (Part of Mount Dora)	32757
Sumterville	33585	*HOSPITALS*			
Sun City	33586			Triangle Acres	32757
Sun City Center	33573	James A. Haley Veterans Hospital	33612	Trilby	33593
Suncoast Estates	33903			Tri Par Estates	34234
Sun Haven	34231	St. Joseph's Hospital	33607	Tropic	32952
Suniland	33156	Tampa General Hospital	33601	Tropical Gulf Acres	33955
Sunlake	32735	University Community Hospital	33613	Tropical Shores Manor	32778
Sunland (Part of Sanford)	32771				

116 FLORIDA Tropicanna Mobile Manor-Yon's Lakeside Estates

	ZIP		ZIP		ZIP
Tropicanna Mobile Manor	33901	Wakulla Springs	32305	Whispering Hills Golf	
Tropic Isle (Part of Delray		Walden Lake (Part of Plant		Estates (Part of Titusville)	32780
Beach)	33483	City)	33567	Whispering Palms (Part of	
Turkey Creek	33567	Waldo	32694	Lake Worth)	33460
Turner River	33943	Wallace	32570	Whispering Pines (Madison	
Turquoise Beach	32459	Wall Springs	34683	County)	32340
Tuscanooga	34736	Walnut Hill	32568	Whispering Pines (Putnam	
Tuscowilla Acres	32751	Walton	34957	County)	32139
Tuskawilla	32708	Wannee	32619	White Acres (Part of	
Twin City Mall (Part of North		Ward Ridge	32456	Tallahassee)	32304
Palm Beach)	33408	Warm Mineral Springs	34287	White City (Gulf County)	32465
Twin Lake (Part of Tampa)	33604	Warrington	32507	White City (St. Lucie	
Twin Palms	33919	Washington Lake Estates		County)	34981
Two Egg	32423	(Part of Jacksonville)	32208	Whitehouse (Part of	
Two Mile	32320	Washington Park	33314	Jacksonville)	32220
Tyndall AFB (Bay County)	32403	Washington Shores (Part of		White Springs (Hamilton	
Tyrone Square (Part of St.		Orlando)	32805	County)	32096
Petersburg)	33710	Watertown (Columbia		White Springs (Liberty	
Uleta	33162	County)	32055	County)	32321
Umatilla	32784	Waterway Estates	33903	Whitfield Estates (Manatee	
Union Correctional		Wauchula	33873	County)	34243
Institution	32083	Wauchula Hills	33873	Whiting Field	32570
Union Park	32817	Waukeenah	32344	Whitney	34748
University (Alachua County)	32603	Wausau	32463	Whitney Beach (Part of	
University (Dade County)	33146	Waverly	33877	Longboat Key)	34228
University (Duval County)	32216	Weathersfield	32701	Wilbur-By-The-Sea	32127
University (Hillsborough		Webbs City (Part of St.		Wildwood	34785
County)	33620	Petersburg)	33701	Williamsburg (Part of	
University Mall (Broward		Webster	33597	Orlando)	32821
County)	33024	Weeki Wachee	34606	Williams Point	32922
University Mall (Escambia		Weeki Wachee Acres	34606	Willis Landing	32465
County)	32504	Weeki Wachee Gardens	34607	Williston	32696
University of South Florida	33620	Weirsdale	32195	Williston Highlands	32696
University of Tampa (Part of		Wekiva Springs (Seminole		Willow	34219
Tampa)	33606	County)	32750	Willow Oak	33860
University of West Florida	32514	Wekiwa Manor	32703	Wilson Corner (Seminole	
University Park (Part of		Wekiwa Springs	32703	County)	32771
Jacksonville)	32211	Welaka	32193	Wilson Corner (Sumter	
University Square (Part of		Welcome	33547	County)	33597
Tampa)	33612	Wellborn	32094	Wilson Place	32771
Upper Grand Lagoon	32401	Wellington	33414	Wilton Manors	33334
Upper Key Largo	33037	Wesley Chapel	33544	Wimauma	33598
USAF Hospital	32542	Wesley Manor	32223	Wimberly Estates	32601
Useppa Island	33924	West Augustine (Part of St.		Windermere	34786
Valkaria	32905	Augustine)	32095	Windover Farms	32780
Valparaiso	32580	West Bay (Bay County)	32407	Windsor	32601
Valrico	33594	West Bay (Duval County)	32219	Windy Hill (Part of	
Vamo	34231	West Bradenton	34205	Jacksonville)	32216
Venetia (Part of		Westchester (Dade County)	33136	Winewood (Part of	
Jacksonville)	32220	Westchester (Dade County)	33144	Tallahassee)	32301
Venetian Gardens	34275	West De Land	32720	Winfield	32055
Venetian Islands (Part of		West Eau Gallie	32935	Winston	33801
Miami Beach)	33139	West End (Calhoun County)	32424		33803
Venetian Isles	32561	West End (Jackson County)	32446	For specific Winston Zip Codes	
Venice	34284-87	Western Acres	33903	call (813) 688-9023	
	34292-93	West Farm	32340	Winter Beach	32971
For specific Venice Zip Codes call		West Frostproof	33843	Winter Garden	34787
(813) 485-9858		Westgate	33401	Winter Haven	33880-84
Venice East	34293	West Hills	32601	For specific Winter Haven Zip	
Venice Gardens	34293	West Holly Hill	32117	Codes call (813) 294-4157	
Venus	33960	West Hollywood	33023	Winter Haven Mall (Part of	
Verdie	32009	West Jacksonville (Part of		Winter Haven)	33880
Vermont Heights	32033	Jacksonville)	32220	Winter Park	32789-90
Verna	34251	Westlake (Part of			32792-93
Vernon	32462	Jacksonville)	32219	For specific Winter Park Zip	
Vero Beach	32960-68	West Lakes at Boca Raton	33433	Codes call (305) 647-3621	
For specific Vero Beach Zip		West Lake Wales	33853	Winter Park Estates	32792
Codes call (407) 567-5206		Westland Mall (Part of		Winter Park Mall (Part of	
Vero Beach Highlands	32960	Hialeah)	33012	Winter Park)	32789
Vero Beach South	32960	West Lantana (Part of		Winter Springs	32708
Vero Lake Estates	32960	Lantana)	33462	Withla	33868
Vero Shores	32960	West Little River	33147	Wonderwood (Part of	
Vicksburg	32401	West Melbourne	32901	Jacksonville)	32233
Victory Gardens	33170	West Miami	33174	Woodgate (Part of	
Vilano Beach	32095	Westmoreland Estates (Part		Tallahassee)	32312
Vilas	32304	of Gainesville)	32601	Woodland Acres (Part of	
Village Green (Alachua		Weston	33326	Jacksonville)	32211
County)	32601	West Palm Beach	33401-20	Woodland Drives (Part of	
Village Green (Brevard		For specific West Palm Beach Zip		Tallahassee)	32301
County)	32955	Codes call (407) 697-1933		Woodland Park	33902
Villager (Part of Boynton		West Palmetto Park (Part of		Woodlawn	32407
Beach)	33435	Boca Raton)	33486	Woodlawn Beach	32561
Villa Pines	33917	West Panama City Beach		Woods	32321
Villa Rica (Part of Boca		(Part of Panama City		Woodville (Bay County)	32401
Raton)	33487	Beach)	32407	Woodville (Leon County)	32362
Villas (Lee County)	33917	West Pensacola	32505	Woodward Avenue (Part of	
Villa Sabine	32561	West Scenic Park	33853	Tallahassee)	32304
Villa Tasso	32578	West Shore Plaza (Part of		Worthington Springs	32697
Virginia Gardens	33166	Tampa)	33609	Wright	32548
Vitis	33540	Westside (Part of Daytona		Wynnehaven Beach	32569
Volusia Mall (Part of		Beach)	32120	Wynwood (Part of Sanford)	32771
Daytona Beach)	32114	West Tampa (Part of		Yacht Harbor (Part of	
Wabash (Part of Lakeland)	33801	Tampa)	33607	Riviera Beach)	33404
Wabasso	32970	Westview	33168	Yalaha	34797
Wacahotta	32667	Westville	32464	Yankeetown	32698
Waccasassa Lake	32693	Westward	33414	Yatch Club Colony	33903
Wacissa	32361	Westwood (Duval County)	32210	Ybor City (Part of Tampa)	33605
Wahneta	33880	Westwood (Orange County)	32808	Yeehaw Junction	34972
Wahoo	33513	Westwood Acres	32674	Yellow Pine	32340
Wakulla	32327	Westwood Lakes	33165	Yelvington	32131
Wakulla Gardens	32327	Wewahitchka	32465	Yon's Lakeside Estates	32301

	ZIP
Yon's Subdivision	32456
York	32670
Youmans	33565
Youngstown	32466
Yukon (Part of Jacksonville)	32230
Yulee	32097
Yulee Heights	32097

	ZIP
Zellwood	32798
Zephyrhills	33539-44
For specific Zephyrhills Zip Codes call (813) 782-2013	
Zephyrhills Correctional Institution	33539

	ZIP
Zephyrhills North	33540
Zephyrhills South	33541
Zephyrhills West	33541
Zolfo Springs	33890
Zuber	32670

GEORGIA

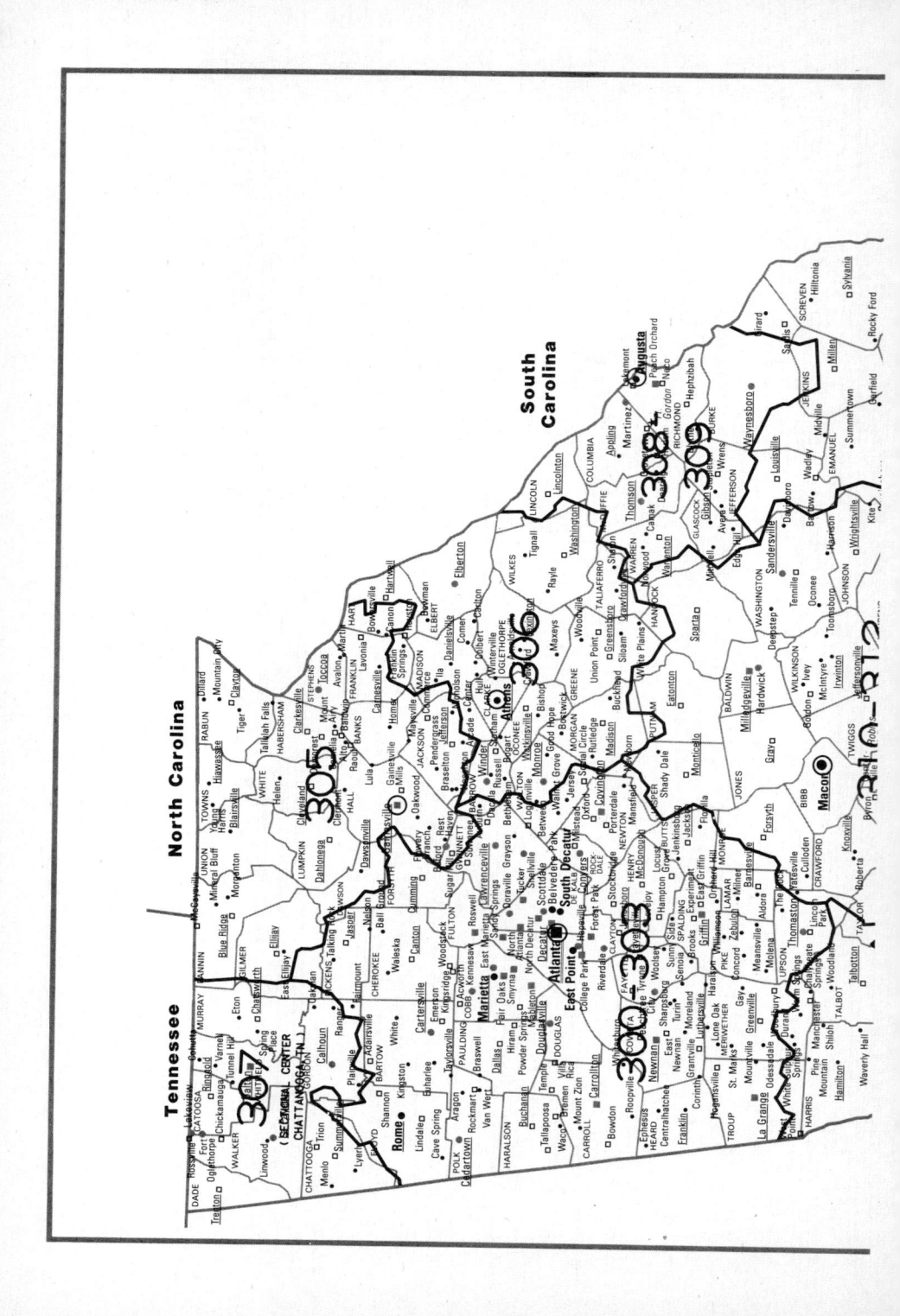

GEORGIA 119

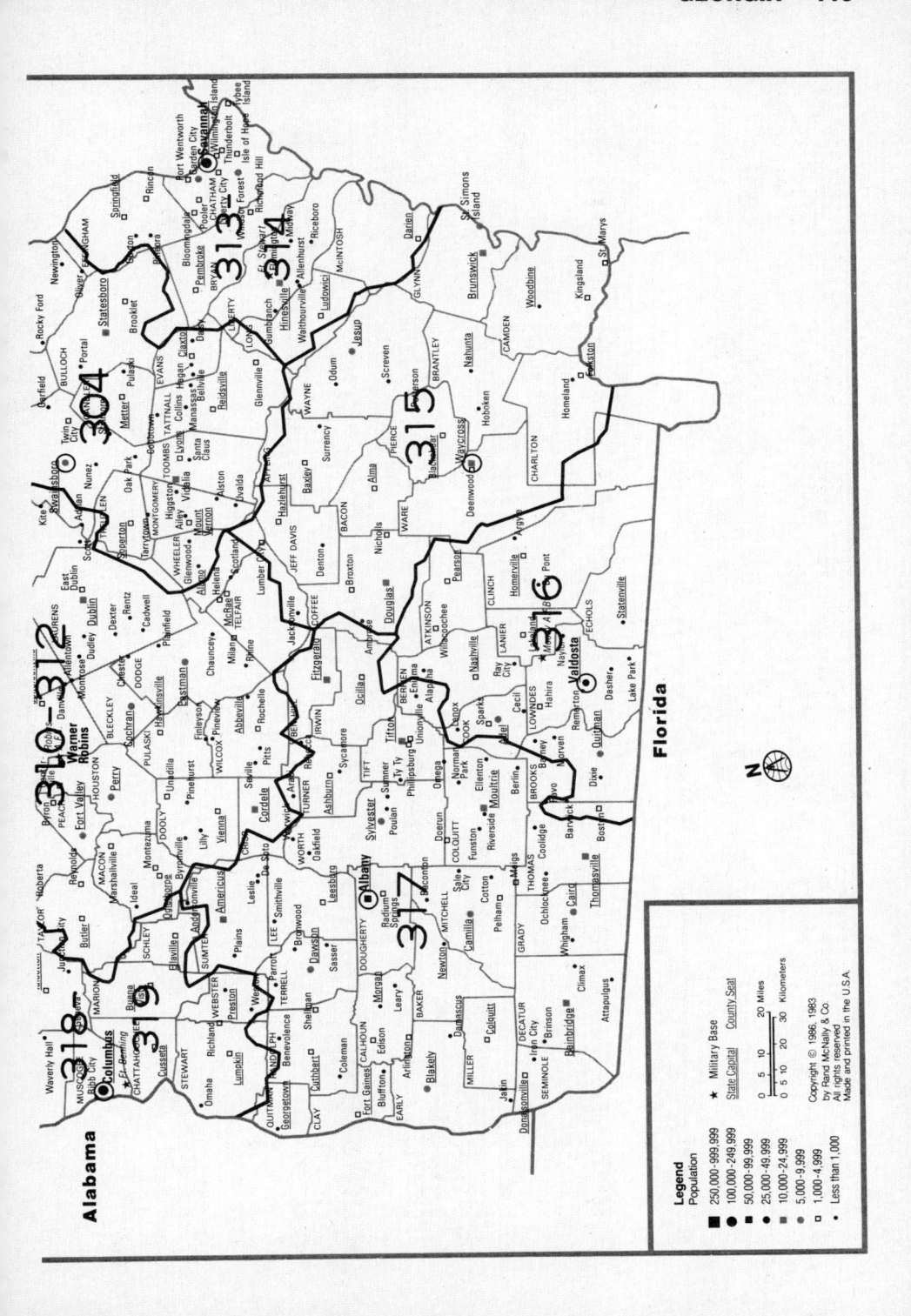

120 GEORGIA Aaron-Berkshire Woods

	ZIP
Aaron	30450
Abac	31794
Abba	31750
Abbeville	31001
Abbott	30207
Abbottsford	30240
Aberdeen (Part of Peachtree City)	30269
Acree	31791
Acworth	30101
Adairsville	30103
Adams Park (Fulton County)	30311
Adams Park (Twiggs County)	31020
Adamsville (Part of Atlanta)	30331
Adasburg	30673
Adel	31620
Adgateville	31038
Adrian	31002
Agnes	30817
Agnes Scott College (Part of Decatur)	30030
Aid	30521
Ailey	30410
Air Line	30516
Airport Mail Facility (Part of Atlanta)	30320
Airport Subdivision	31601
Akin	30415
Alamo	30411
Alapaha	31622
Albany	31701-07
For specific Albany Zip Codes call (912) 833-7600	
Albion Acres	30906
Alcovy	30209
Alcovy Shores	31064
Aldora	30204
Alexander	30456
Alfords	31791
Aline	30420
Allen City	30071
Allendale (Gwinnett County)	30245
Allendale (Muscogee County)	31904
Allenhurst	31301
Allentown	31003
Allenville	31639
Allenwood	31061
Allie	30222
Alma	31510
Almon	30209
Almond Park (Part of Atlanta)	30318
Alpharetta	30201-02
For specific Alpharetta Zip Codes call (404) 475-7235	
Alpine	30731
Alps Road (Part of Athens)	30604
Alston	30412
Altamaha	30453
Alta Vista (Part of Columbus)	31906
Altman	30467
Alto	30510
Alto Park	30161
Alvaton	30218
Amboy	31714
Ambrose	31512
Americus	31709
Amity	30817
Amos Mill	35967
Amsterdam	31734
Anderson City	31744
Andersonville	31711
Anguilla	31520
Ansley Estates	30274
Antioch (Polk County)	30125
Antioch (Troup County)	30240
Aonia	30673
Apalachee	30650
Apple Valley	30529
Appling	30802
Arabi	31712
Aragon	30104
Aragon Park	30901
Arcade	30549
Arch City	30701
Archery	31780
Arco	31520
Arcola	30415
Ardick	31331
Ardmore	31329
Ardsley Park (Part of Savannah)	31405
Argyle	31623
Arkwright	31204
Arlington	31713
Armstrong State College	31406
Armuchee	30105
Arnco Mills	30263

	ZIP
Arnoldsville	30619
Arp	31783
Arrowhead Village	30236
Ascalon	30738
Ashburn	31714
Ashford Park	30319
Ashintilly	31331
Ashland	30521
Athens	30601-13
For specific Athens Zip Codes call (404) 548-8357	
Atkinson	31543
Atlanta	30301-83
	31101-99
For specific Atlanta Zip Codes call (404) 762-7689	
COLLEGES & UNIVERSITIES	
Clark College	30314
Emory University	30322
Georgia Institute of Technology	30332
Georgia State University	30303
Mercer University in Atlanta	30341
Morris Brown College	30314
Oglethorpe University	30319
Spelman College	30314
FINANCIAL INSTITUTIONS	
Bank South, National Association	30302
Citizens Trust Bank	30303
First American Bank of Georgia	30328
The First National Bank of Atlanta	30383
First Union National Bank of Georgia	30303
Georgia Federal Bank, F.S.B.	30303
Home Federal Savings & Loan Association	30305
NCNB National Bank	30319
The Prudential Bank and Trust Company	30339
Southern Federal Savings & Loan Association of Georgia	30308
Trust Company Bank	30303
Trust Company Bank of Cobb County, N.A.	30339
HOSPITALS	
Crawford Long Memorial Hospital of Emory University	30365
Emory University Hospital	30322
Georgia Baptist Medical Center	30312
Grady Memorial Hospital	30335
HCA West Paces Ferry Hospital	30327
Northside Hospital	30042
Piedmont Hospital	30309
Saint Joseph's Hospital	30342
HOTELS/MOTELS	
The Atlanta Hilton & Towers	30043
Atlanta Marriott Perimeter Center	30346
Holiday Inn Buckhead	30026
Lanier Plaza Hotel & CC	30324
Omni International Hotel at CNN Center	30335
Pierremont Plaza Hotel	30308
Radisson Inn Dunwoody	30338
The Ritz-Carlton Atlanta	30303
Sheraton Atlanta Airport Hotel	30344
The Westin Peachtree Plaza	30343
MILITARY INSTALLATIONS	
Atlanta International Airport, Air Force Facility	30320
United States Army Engineer Division, South Atlantic	30335
United States Property and Fiscal Office for Georgia	30316
Atlanta Naval Air Station	30060
Attapulgus	31715
Attapulgus Station	31715
Attica	30606
Auburn	30203
Audubon	30735
Augusta	30901-19
For specific Augusta Zip Codes call (404) 724-7436	
Aumond Heights	30909

	ZIP
Aumond Place	30909
Auraria	30534
Austell	30001
Austin	30663
Autreyville	31768
Autumn Forest	30236
Avallon	30328
Avalon (Chatham County)	31406
Avalon (Stephens County)	30557
Avans	30752
Avera	30803
Avert Acres	31705
Avery	30114
Avondale (Bibb County)	31206
Avondale (McDuffie County)	30814
Avondale Estates	30002
Avondale Park (Part of Savannah)	31404
Avon Park (Part of Savannah)	31404
Axson	31624
Ayersville	30577
Baconton	31716
Bainbridge	31717
Bairdstown	30669
Baker Village (Part of Columbus)	31903
Baldwin	30511
Baldwinville	31812
Ball Ground (Cherokee County)	30107
Ball Ground (Murray County)	30705
Baltimore (Part of Washington)	30673
Banning	30185
Bannockburn	31639
Barksdale	31082
Barnesville	30204
Barnett	30821
Barnett Shoals	30605
Barney	31625
Barnsley	30145
Barretts	31602
Barrettsville	30534
Barrow Heights	30680
Bartletts Ferry	31808
Barton Village	30906
Bartonwoods	30307
Bartow	30413
Barwick	31720
Bascom	30467
Bass Crossroads	30230
Batesville	30523
Bath	30805
Battery Point	31404
Baughs Crossroads	31833
Baxley	31513
Bay	31756
Bayview	31316
Beach	31554
Beachton	31792
Beacon Heights	30650
Beallwood (Part of Columbus)	31904
Beaulieu	31406
Beaumont	30736
Beaverdale	30720
Beechwood Shopping Center (Part of Athens)	30606
Belair	30907
Belair Hills Estates	30909
Belfast	31324
Bellemeade	30906
Bellton (Part of Lula)	30554
Bellville	30414
Bellville Bluff	31331
Belmont (De Kalb County)	30035
Belmont (Hall County)	30507
Belmont Hills Shopping Center (Part of Smyrna)	30080
Belvedere	30032
Belvedere Park	30032
Belvedere Plaza	30032
Belvins Acres	30736
Bemiss	31602
Benedict	30125
Benevolence	31740
Ben Hill (Part of Atlanta)	30331
Benning Hills (Part of Columbus)	31903
Benning Park (Part of Columbus)	31903
Bentley Place	30741
Benton	30161
Bent Tree	30143
Berckman Hills	30909
Berckman Village	30909
Berkeley Lake	30136
Berkshire Woods (Part of Savannah)	31406

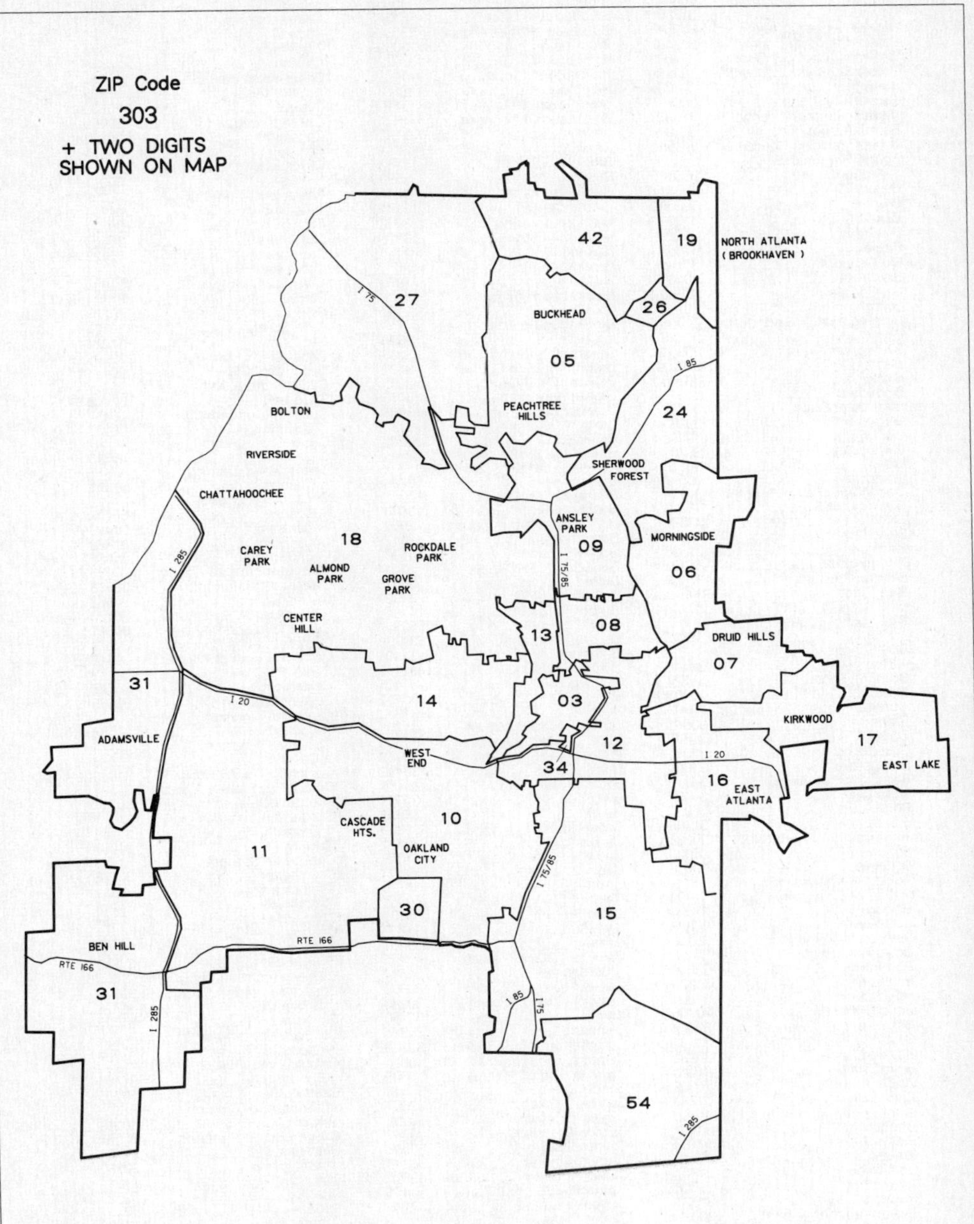
ZIP Code
303
+ TWO DIGITS
SHOWN ON MAP
42
19
NORTH ATLANTA
(BROOKHAVEN)
27
I 75
BUCKHEAD
26
05
I 85
PEACHTREE
HILLS
24
BOLTON
RIVERSIDE
SHERWOOD
FOREST
CHATTAHOOCHEE
ANSLEY
PARK
18
09
MORNINGSIDE
CAREY
PARK
ROCKDALE
PARK
I 285
ALMOND
PARK
GROVE
PARK
I 75/85
06
CENTER
HILL
08
13
DRUID HILLS
07
31
I 20
03
14
KIRKWOOD
ADAMSVILLE
12
17
WEST
END
I 20
34
EAST LAKE
16
EAST
ATLANTA
CASCADE
HTS.
10
11
OAKLAND
CITY
I 75/85
30
15
BEN HILL
RTE 166
RTE 166
31
I 85
I 75
I 285
54
I 285

Copyright © 1986, 1970 by Rand McNally & Co.
All rights reserved
Made and printed in the U.S.A.

122 GEORGIA Berlin-Chippewa Terrace

Name	ZIP
Berlin	31722
Berryton	30747
Berzelia	30814
Bethany	31762
Bethel (Jasper County)	31064
Bethel (Randolph County)	31740
Bethesda (Chatham County)	31406
Bethesda (Gwinnett County)	30245
Bethlehem	30620
Between	30655
Beulah (Hancock County)	31087
Beulah (Lincoln County)	30668
Beulah (Paulding County)	30153
Beulah Heights (Part of Atlanta)	30312
Beverly Hills	30741
Bexton	31259
Bibb City	31904
Bibb Mills	31029
Bickley	31554
Big Canoe	30143
Big Creek	30130
Big Springs	30240
Billarp	30187
Bingville (Part of Savannah)	31405
Birdie	30223
Birmingham	30201
Bishop	30621
Blackjack	32276
Blackshear	31516
Blackshear Place	30507
Blacksville	30253
Blackwells	30066
Blackwood	30701
Blaine	30175
Blairsville	30512
Blair Village (Part of Atlanta)	30354
Blakely	31723
Blandford	31326
Bland Villa	31015
Blitchton	31308
Bloomingdale	31302
Blowing Springs	37409
Blue Ridge	30513
Blue Spring	30736
Blue Springs (Dougherty County)	31707
Blue Springs (Screven County)	30446
Bluffton	31724
Blun	30401
Blundale	30401
Blythe	30805
Bogart	30622
Bold Spring	30655
Bolingbroke	31004
Bolton (Part of Atlanta)	30318
Bona Bella	31406
Bonair	30907
Bonaire	31005
Bonanza	30236
Bonds	31020
Boneville	30806
Booker Washington Heights (Part of Columbus)	31909
Boston	31626
Bostwick	30623
Bowdon	30108
Bowdon Junction	30109
Bowersville	30516
Bowman	30624
Box Springs	31801
Boyd Highlands	30736
Boydville	30577
Boykin	31737
Boynton	30736
Boys Estate	31520
Bradley	31032
Branchville	31730
Brantley	31803
Braselton	30517
Braswell	30153
Bremen	30110
Brentwood	31707
Brest	31716
Brewton	31021
Briarcliff (Part of Atlanta)	30329
Briarwood (Chatham County)	31408
Briarwood (Columbia County)	30907
Briarwood (Fulton County)	30344
Briarwood (Rockdale County)	30207
Briar Wood Estates	30060
Brick Store	30279
Bridgeboro	31705
Bridgeman Heights	31201
Brighton	31794
Brinson	31725
Brisbon	31324

Name	ZIP
Bristol	31518
Bristol Woods	30207
Broad	30668
Broadhurst	31545
Broadview (Part of Atlanta)	30324
Brockton	30506
Bronco	30728
Bronwood	31726
Brookfield	31727
Brookhaven (Bibb County)	31206
Brookhaven (Muscogee County)	31906
Brooklet	30415
Brooklyn	31825
Brooks	30205
Brookstore Place	30342
Brooksville	31740
Brookton	30501
Brookvale Estates	30736
Brookview	31406
Brookwood (Forsyth County)	30201
Brookwood (Laurens County)	31021
Brookwood (Richmond County)	30904
Browndale	31036
Browns (Baldwin County)	31061
Browns (Dade County)	30752
Brownsville	30133
Brownwood	30650
Broxton	31519
Brunswick	31520-22
For specific Brunswick Zip Codes call (912) 265-6186	
Brynwood	30909
Buchanan	30113
Buckhead (Fulton County)	30339
Buckhead (Morgan County)	30625
Budapest	30176
Buena Vista	31803
Buffington	30114
Buford	30518
Bullard	31020
Bulloch Crossroads	31816
Bunker Hill	30512
Burning Bush	30736
Burnside	31406
Burnside Island	31406
Burroughs	31405
Burwell	30117
Bushnell	31533
Butler (Dougherty County)	31705
Butler (Taylor County)	31006
Butler Manor	30905
Butts	30442
Byers Crossroads	30185
Byromville	31007
Byron	31008
Cabaniss	31029
Cadley	30821
Cadwell	31009
Cagle	30143
Cairo	31728
Caleb	30058
Calhoun	30701
Calvary	31729
Camak	30807
Camellia Terrace (Part of Savannah)	31404
Camelot (Clarke County)	30606
Camelot (Clayton County)	30236
Camilla	31730
Campania	30814
Campbellton	30213
Campton	30655
Campus (Part of Athens)	30605
Canal Lake	30512
Candler	30507
Candler-McAfee	30032
Cannon Crossing	30742
Cannon Gate	30907
Cannonville	30240
Canon	30520
Canoochee	30471
Canton	30114
Canton Plaza (Part of Marietta)	30066
Capel	31728
Capitol Hill (Part of Atlanta)	30334
Captolo	30467
Carbondale	30720
Carey Park (Part of Atlanta)	30318
Carl	30203
Carlton	30627
Carmel	30218
Carmichael Crossroads	30114
Carnegie	31740
Carnes Creek	30577
Carnesville	30521
Carnigan	31319

Name	ZIP
Carns Mill	30175
Caroline Park (Part of Columbus)	31904
Carrollton	30117
Carrs	31087
Carsonville	31827
Cartecay	30540
Carter Acres (Part of Columbus)	31903
Carters	30705
Carters Grove	30660
Cartersville	30120
Cary	31014
Cascade Heights (Part of Atlanta)	30311
Cascade Hills (Part of Columbus)	31904
Cash	30701
Cassandra	30707
Cassville	30123
Castle Park (Part of Valdosta)	31601
Cataula	31804
Catlett	30728
Cave Spring	30124
Cecil	31627
Cedar Creek Park	30605
Cedar Crossing	30436
Cedar Grove (Chatham County)	31406
Cedar Grove (De Kalb County)	30027
Cedar Grove (Fulton County)	30213
Cedar Grove (Laurens County)	31021
Cedar Grove (Walker County)	30707
Cedar Hammock	31406
Cedar Point	31332
Cedar Springs	31732
Cedartown	30125
Celeste	30673
Centennial	30663
Center (Bartow County)	30120
Center (Jackson County)	30601
Center (Toombs County)	30474
Center Hill (Part of Atlanta)	30318
Center Point	30179
Centerpost	30728
Centerville (Elbert County)	30635
Centerville (Gwinnett County)	30058
Centerville (Houston County)	31028
Centerville (Talbot County)	31812
Central City (Part of Atlanta)	30303
Centralhatchee	30217
Central Junction (Part of Garden City)	31408
Century	31763
Chalybeate Springs	31816
Chamberlain	30728
Chamblee	30341
Chambliss	31709
Chapel Hill	30134
Chappel	30257
Charing	31058
Charles (Stewart County)	31815
Charles (Toombs County)	30474
Charleston South	30906
Charlotteville	30473
Chastain	31738
Chatham City (Part of Garden City)	31408
Chatham Villa (Part of Garden City)	31408
Chatsworth	30705
Chattahoochee (Part of Atlanta)	30318
Chattahoochee Plantation	30067
Chatterton	31554
Chattoogaville	30730
Chauncey	31011
Checkero	30525
Chelsea	30731
Chennault	30668
Cherokee Forest	30188
Cherrylog	30522
Cheshire Bridge (Part of Atlanta)	30324
Chestatee	30130
Chester	31012
Chestnutflat	30728
Chestnut Mountain	30502
Chickamauga	30707
Chickasawhatchee	31742
Chicopee	30507
China Hill	31077
Chippewa Terrace (Part of Savannah)	31406

Choestoe-Eastman GEORGIA 123

Name	ZIP
Choestoe	30512
Chubtown	30124
Chula	31733
Cinderella Hills	30736
Cisco	30708
Civic Center (Part of Atlanta)	30308
Clarkdale	30020
Clarke Dale	30605
Clarkesville	30523
Clarksboro	30607
Clarkston	30021
Claxton	30417
Clayfields	31054
Clayton	30525
Clearview (Part of Savannah)	31401
Clem	30117
Clermont	30527
Cleveland	30528
Cliftondale	30337
Climax	31734
Clinchfield	31013
Clinton	31032
Cloudland	30731
Cloverdale	30738
Clubview Heights (Part of Columbus)	31906
Clyattville	31601
Clyo	31303
Coal Mountain	30130
Coastal Correctional Institution	31408
Cobb	31735
Cobb Centre Mall (Part of Smyrna)	30080
Cobbtown	30420
Cochran	31014
Coffee	31551
Coffee Bluff Plantation (Part of Savannah)	31406
Cogdell	31634
Cohutta	30710
Cohutta Springs	30711
Colbert	30628
Cole City	30752
Coleman	31736
Colemans Lake	30441
Colesburg	31569
Colfax	30458
College (Part of Fort Valley)	31030
College Heights (Dougherty County)	31705
College Heights (Muscogee County)	31906
College Park	30337
Collins	30421
Collinsville	30035
Colomokee	31723
Colonial Oaks (Part of Savannah)	31406
Colonial Place	31705
Colonial Village (Part of Savannah)	31406
Colony Park	30909
Colquitt	31737
Columbia Heights	30907
Columbus	31901-09
For specific Columbus Zip Codes call (404) 563-0100	
Columbus Square (Part of Columbus)	31908
Colwell	30541
Comer	30629
Commerce	30529
Concord (Pike County)	30206
Concord (Schley County)	31806
Coney	31015
Conley	30027
Constitution	30316
Conyers	30207-08
For specific Conyers Zip Codes call (404) 483-8378	
Cooksville	30230
Coolidge	31738
Cool Spring	31771
Cooper Creek Park (Part of Columbus)	31907
Cooper Heights	30707
Coopers	31031
Coosa	30129
Copeland	31077
Cordele	31015
Corinth	30230
Cornelia	30531
Cotton	31739
Cotton Hill	31767
Council	31631
Country Club Hills (Part of Augusta)	30904
Country Park	30906

Name	ZIP
Country Side (Part of Savannah)	31406
County Line (Barrow County)	30680
County Line (De Kalb County)	30032
County Line (Stewart County)	31815
Court Square (Part of Dublin)	31021
Covena	30401
Coverdale	31714
Covington	30209
Covington Mills (Part of Covington)	30209
Cox	31331
Coxs Crossing	30321
Crabapple	30201
Crandall	30711
Craneeater	30701
Cravey	31060
Crawford	30630
Crawfordville	30631
Crescent	31304
Crest	30286
Cresthill	31406
Crest Hill Gardens (Part of Savannah)	31406
Crestview	31713
Crestwell Heights	31204
Crosland	31771
Cross Keys (Part of Macon)	31201
Crossroads (Hart County)	30516
Crossroads (Liberty County)	31323
Crossroads at Stewart Lakewood, The (Part of Atlanta)	30315
Cruse	30245
Crystal Springs (Bibb County)	31201
Crystal Springs (Floyd County)	30105
Crystal Valley (Part of Columbus)	31907
Culloden	31016
Culverton	31087
Cumberland	30339
Cumming	30130
Curryville	30701
Curtis	30513
Cusseta	31805
Custer Terrace (Part of Columbus)	31905
Cuthbert	31740
Cypress Mills	31520
Dacula	30211
Daffin Heights (Part of Savannah)	31404
Dahlonega	30533
Daisy	30423
Dakota	31714
Dallas	30132
Dallas Heights	30906
Dallondale	30741
Dalton	30720-22
For specific Dalton Zip Codes call (404) 278-7450	
Damascus (Early County)	31741
Damascus (Gordon County)	30701
Dames Ferry	31046
Danburg	30668
Daniel	31324
Daniel Springs	30669
Danielsville	30633
Danville	31017
Darien	31305
Dasher	31601
Davisboro	31018
Davis Crossroads	30707
Dawesville	31792
Dawnville	30720
Dawson	31742
Dawsonville	30534
Days Crossroads	31751
Dearing	30808
Decatur	30030-37
For specific Decatur Zip Codes call (404) 378-8857	
Deenwood (Ware County)	31501
Deepstep	31082
Deer Run	32007
Deerwood Forest	30906
Deerwood Park	30032
Delhi	30668
Dellwood	30401
DeLowe (Part of East Point)	30344
Demorest	30535
Denmark	30415
Dennis	31024
Denton	31532
Denver	30217

Name	ZIP
De Soto	31743
De Soto Park	30161
Desser	31745
Devereux	31087
Dewberry	30741
Dewy Rose	30634
Dexter	31019
Dial	30513
Dialtown	30267
Diamond Hill	30628
Dickey	31746
Digbey	30205
Dillard	30537
Dillon	31792
Dinglewood (Part of Columbus)	31906
Dixie (Brooks County)	31629
Dixie (Newton County)	30209
Dixie Heights (Part of Albany)	31705
Dixie Union	31501
Dobbins Air Force Base	30060
Dock Junction	31520
Doctortown	31545
Doerun	31744
Doles	31791
Donald	31316
Donalsonville	31745
Donegal	30458
Donovan	31096
Doogan	30708
Dooling	31063
Doraville	30340
Dorchester (Liberty County)	31320
Dorchester (Richmond County)	30909
Dot	30108
Double Branches	30817
Doublegate	31707
Double Run	31072
Dougherty	30534
Douglas	31533
Douglasville	30133-35
For specific Douglasville Zip Codes call (404) 765-7261	
Dove Creek	30635
Dover	30424
Doverel	31742
Downtown (Fulton County)	30301
Downtown (Muscogee County)	31901
Doyle	31803
Draketown	30179
Dranesville	31803
Drayton	31092
Dresden	30263
Drew	30130
Drexel	30663
Druid Hills (De Kalb County)	30333
Dry Branch (Jenkins County)	30822
Dry Branch (Twiggs County)	31020
Dry Pond	30529
Dublin	31021
Dubois	31026
Ducktown	30130
Dudley	31022
Due West	30064
Duffee	31730
Dugdown	30140
Duluth	30136
Dumas	31824
Dunaire	30032
Duncan Park	37412
Dunwoody (De Kalb County)	30338
Du Pont	31630
Durand	31830
Dutch Island	31406
Eagle Cliff	37409
Eagle Grove	30520
East Albany (Part of Albany)	31701
Eastanollee	30538
East Armuchee	30728
East Athens	30683
East Atlanta (Part of Atlanta)	30316
East Boundary	30901
East Boynton	30736
East Columbus	31907
East Dublin	31021
East Edgewood (Part of Columbus)	31907
East Ellijay	30539
East Englewood (Part of Columbus)	31907
East Griffin	30223
East Highlands (Part of Columbus)	31901
East Juliette	31046
Eastman	31023

GEORGIA — Eastman Mills-Goss

Name	ZIP
Eastman Mills	31023
East Marietta	30062
East Meadow	30605
East Newnan	30263
East Point	30344
East Side (Part of Dalton)	30721
East Town (Part of Albany)	31705
East Trion (Part of Trion)	30753
Eastview	30904
Eastville	30621
Eastwood	30316
	30317
For specific Eastwood Zip Codes call (404) 373-4787	
Eatonton	31024
Ebernezer	30279
Echeconnee	31008
Echota	30701
Eden	31307
Edge Hill	30810
Edgemere (Part of Savannah)	31404
Edgemoor East	30236
Edgemoor West	30236
Edgewater (Part of Savannah)	31406
Edgewater Park (Part of Savannah)	31406
Edgewood (Columbia County)	30907
Edgewood (Muscogee County)	31907
Edison	31746
Edith	31631
Egypt	31329
Elberta (Houston County)	31093
Elberton	30635
Elder	30677
Eldorado	31794
Eldorendo	31737
Eleanor Village	31705
Elim	31316
Elizabeth (Part of Marietta)	30060
Elko	31025
Ellabell	31308
Ellaville	31806
Ellenton	31747
Ellenwood	30049
Ellerslie	31807
Ellijay	30540
Ellwood	30805
Elmodel	31770
Elza	30453
Embry Hills	30341
Emerson	30137
Emerson Park	31501
Emit	30458
Emma	30534
Emmalane	30442
Emory University	30322
Empire	31026
Englewood (Part of Columbus)	31907
Enigma	31749
Enon Grove	30217
Enterprise	30627
Ephesus	30217
Epworth	30541
Epworth Acres	31522
Esom Hill	30138
Etna	30138
Eton	30724
Euharlee	30120
Eulonia	31331
Evans	30809
Evansville	30240
Everett	31520
Everett Springs	30105
Evergreen	31707
Excelsior	30439
Executive Park	30347
Experiment (Spalding County)	30223
Experiment (Spalding County)	30212
Faceville	31717
Fairburn	30213
Fairchild	31745
Fairfax	31524
Fairfield (Part of Savannah)	31404
Fairlawn Acres (Part of Fort Oglethorpe)	30741
Fairmount	30139
Fair Oaks	30060
Fairplay (Douglas County)	30187
Fairplay (Morgan County)	30663
Fairview (Habersham County)	30535
Fairview (Walker County)	30741
Fairway Oaks (Part of Savannah)	31405

Name	ZIP
Fairway Village	30906
Fantasy Hills	37409
Fargo	31631
Farmdale	30467
Farmers High	30117
Farmington	30638
Farmville	30701
Farrar	31085
Fashion	30705
Faulkner	30107
Fayetteville	30214
Federal (Part of Albany)	31702
Federal Reserve (Part of Atlanta)	30303
Felton	30140
Fence	30203
Fernwood (Part of Savannah)	31404
Ficklin	30673
Ficklings Mill	31006
Fidele	30735
Fife	30213
Fincherville	30233
Findlay	31070
Finleyson	31071
Fish Creek	30125
Fitzgerald	31750
Fitzgerald Cotton Mill	31750
Fitzpatrick	31044
Five Forks (Gwinnett County)	30245
Five Forks (Thomas County)	31626
Five Points (Fulton County)	30303
Five Points (Lowndes County)	31601
Five Points (Macon County)	31063
Five Points (Marion County)	31803
Five Points (Randolph County)	31786
Five Points (Taylor County)	31006
Five Points (Treutlen County)	30457
Five Springs	30720
Flat Rock (Muscogee County)	31907
Flat Rock (Putnam County)	31024
Flat Shoals	30516
Fleetwood (Part of Savannah)	31404
Fleming	31309
Fleming Heights	30906
Flemington	31313
Flint	31716
Flint Hill	31826
Flint River	31711
Flint River Estates	30236
Flintside	31735
Flintstone	30725
Flintwood	30274
Flippen	30253
Floral Hill	30668
Flovilla	30216
Flowery Branch	30542
Floyd	30059
Floyd Springs	30105
Folkston	31537
Folsom	30103
Forest Estates	30909
Forest Lake (Part of Macon)	31204
Forest Park	30050-51
For specific Forest Park Zip Codes call (404) 363-1804	
Forest Park (Dougherty County)	31701
Forest Park (Richmond County)	30904
Forest River Farms (Part of Savannah)	31406
Forrest Hills (Part of Savannah)	31404
Forsyth	31029
Fort Benning	31905
Fort Benning South	31905
Fort Gaines	31751
Fort Gillem	30050
Fort Gordon (Richmond County)	30905
Fort Lamar	30633
Fort McAllister	31324
Fort Oglethorpe	30742
Fort Screven (Part of Tybee Island)	31328
Fortson (Part of Columbus)	31808
Fortsonia	30635
Fort Stewart (Liberty County)	31313
Fort Stewart (Liberty County)	31314
Fort Valley	31030
Foster Hills	30736
Fosters Mills	30161

Name	ZIP
Four Points (Part of Albany)	31705
Four Seasons	30207
Fowlstown	31752
Fox (Part of Rome)	30161
Foxboro	31601
Frances Hollow	30207
Franklin	30217
Franklin Springs	30639
Franklinton	31020
Frazier	31014
Free Home	30114
Friendship (Polk County)	30125
Friendship (Sumter County)	31709
Frolona	30217
Fruitland	31630
Fry	30555
Funston	31753
Furniture City	30001
Gabbettville	30240
Gaddistown	30572
Gaillard	31078
Gaines School	30605
Gainesville	30501-07
For specific Gainesville Zip Codes call (404) 532-3138	
Gainesville Mills	30501
Galloway	30513
Garden Acres Estates (Part of Pooler)	31322
Garden City	31408
Garden Lakes	30161
Garden Valley	31041
Gardi	31545
Gardner (Part of Oconee)	31067
Garfield	30425
Garnersville	31767
Garretta	31021
Gasco (Part of Atlanta)	30301
Gates City (Part of Atlanta)	30312
Gateway (Part of Thomasville)	31792
Gay	30218
Geneva	31810
Gentian (Part of Columbus)	31907
Georgetown (Chatham County)	31405
Georgetown (Quitman County)	31754
Georgetown Estates	30906
Georgia Diagnostic and Classification	30233
Georgia Southern (Part of Statesboro)	30458
Georgia Southwestern College (Part of Americus)	31709
Georgia State Prison	30453
Georgia Training and Development Center	30518
Georgia University (Part of Athens)	30602
Germany	30525
Gibson	30810
Gill	30668
Gillis Springs	30457
Gillsville	30543
Girard	30426
Gladesville	31064
Gladys	31622
Glasgow	31626
Glencliff	30286
Glen Haven	30032
Glenloch	30217
Glenloch Village (Part of Peachtree City)	30269
Glenmore	31501
Glenn	30217
Glenn Hills	30906
Glennville	30427
Glenwood (Floyd County)	30161
Glenwood (Wheeler County)	30428
Glenwood Hills	30032
Gloster	30245
Glynn Haven	31522
Goat Town	31082
Gobblers Hill	31805
Gober	30107
Godfrey	30650
Godwinsville	31023
Goggins	30204
Golden Isle	31410
Goldmine	30520
Goldsboro	31014
Goldson	31006
Goodes	30268
Good Hope	30641
Gorday	31791
Gordon	31031
Gordon Springs	30740
Gore	30747
Goss	30635

Gough-Kenwood GEORGIA 125

Name	ZIP
Gough	30811
Gracewood	30812
Grady	30125
Graham	31513
Grange	30434
Granite Hill	31087
Grantville	30220
Gratis	30655
Graves	31742
Gray	31032
Gray Hill	31833
Graymont (Part of Twin City)	30471
Grays	31404
Grayson	30221
Graysville	30726
Great Southwest Industrial Park (Part of Atlanta)	30336
Green Acres (Catoosa County)	30741
Green Acres (Chatham County)	31404
Green Acres (Clarke County)	30605
Green Acres Estate (Part of Dublin)	31021
Greenbriar (Part of Atlanta)	30331
Greenbrier	30909
Green Island Hills (Part of Columbus)	31904
Greenough	31716
Greensboro	30642
Greens Crossing	31641
Greens Cut	30906
Greenville (Camden County)	31548
Greenville (Meriwether County)	30222
Greenway (Emanuel County)	30441
Greenway (Fulton County)	30075
Greenwood	31730
Greenwood Forest	31649
Gresham Park	30316
Gresham Road (Part of Marietta)	30062
Greshamville	30650
Gresston	31023
Griffin	30223-24
For specific Griffin Zip Codes call (404) 227-2426	
Grimball Park	31406
Griswoldville	31201
Grizzletown	30101
Grooverville	31626
Grovania	31036
Groveland (Bryan County)	31321
Groveland (Chatham County)	31405
Grove Park (Chatham County)	31406
Grove Point	31405
Grovetown	30813
Gumbranch	31313
Gum Log	30512
Guysie	31510
Guyton	31312
Habersham	30544
Haddock	31033
Hagan	30429
Hahira	31632
Halcyondale	30467
Halfmoon Landing	31320
Halls	30145
Hallwood	31024
Halycon Bluff	31401
Hamilton	31811
Hammett	31078
Hampton	30228
Handy	30263
Haney	30124
Hannah	30187
Hannahs Mill (Upson County)	30286
Hannatown	31717
Hapeville	30354
Happy Hollow	30184
Haralson	30229
Harbins	30620
Harbor Creek	31410
Hardwick	31034
Harlem	30814
Harmony	31024
Harmony Church	31905
Harp	32232
Harrietts Bluff	31569
Harrington	31522
Harrisburg	30747
Harris City	30222
Harrison	31035
Harrisonville	30230
Harrock Hall	31406

Name	ZIP
Hartford	31036
Hartsfield	31756
Hartwell	30643
Harvest	30523
Haskins Crossing	31022
Hassier Mill	30740
Hatcher	31754
Hatley	31015
Hawkinsville	31036
Haylow	31630
Hayneville	31036
Hayston	30255
Hazlehurst	31539
Head River	30731
Heardville	30130
Hebardville	31501
Helen	30545
Helena	31037
Hemp	30560
Henderson	31025
Hentown	31723
Hephzibah	30815
Herndon	30441
Herod	31742
Hiawassee	30546
Hickory Bluff	31565
Hickory Flat (Banks County)	30554
Hickory Flat (Cherokee County)	30114
Hickory Level	30117
Hickox	31553
Hicks Circle	30207
Hidden Acres	30207
Higdon	30541
Higgston	30410
Highfalls	30233
Highgate	30909
Highland Heights	31709
Highland Mills	30223
Highland Park (Part of Savannah)	31406
High Point (Newton County)	30209
High Point (Walker County)	30707
High Shoals	30645
Hightower	30130
Hill City	30735
Hillcrest	30240
Hillman	30631
Hillsboro	31038
Hilltonia	30467
Hilton	31723
Hilton Heights (Part of Columbus)	31906
Hilyer	30240
Hinesville	31313
Hinkles	30738
Hinsonton	31765
Hinton	30143
Hiram	30141
Hi Roc Shores	30207
Hobby	31714
Hoboken	31542
Hogansville	30230
Holbrook	30130
Holcomb Bridge (Part of Roswell)	30076
Holland	30730
Hollingsworth	30510
Hollis	31778
Hollonville	30292
Holly Hills (Part of Columbus)	31906
Holly Springs (Cherokee County)	30142
Holly Springs (Jackson County)	30558
Hollywood	30523
Holt	31774
Homeland	31537
Homer	30547
Homerville	31634
Honey Creek	30207
Honora	30817
Hooker	30752
Hopeful	31730
Hopewell (Cherokee County)	30114
Hopewell (Harris County)	31822
Horns	31078
Hornsby	30901
Horseleg Estates	30161
Hortense	31543
Hoschton	30548
Houston Lake	31047
Houston Mall (Part of Warner Robins)	31093
Howard	31039
Howell	31636
Howell Mill (Part of Atlanta)	30325
Howells Transfer (Part of Atlanta)	30301

Name	ZIP
Howell Tower (Part of Atlanta)	30318
Huber	31201
Hubert	30415
Hudson Mill	31804
Huffaker	30161
Huffer	31533
Hughland	30438
Hulett	30117
Hull	30646
Hunter	30467
Huntington	31709
Hurst	30560
Hutchins	30630
Ideal	31041
Ila	30647
Imlac	30293
Imperial	31024
Inaha	31790
Indian Hills	30236
Indianola	31601
Indian Springs (Butts County)	30216
Indian Springs (Catoosa County)	30736
Industrial (Part of Atlanta)	30336
Industrial City of Gordon, Murray and Whitfield Co	30705
Inman	30232
Iron City	31759
Irwins	31089
Irwinton	31042
Irwinville	31760
Isabella	31791
Islandwood (Chatham County)	31410
Isle of Hope	31406
Ivey	31031
Ivy Log	30512
Jackson	30233
Jacksons Crossroads	30668
Jacksons Store	30668
Jacksonville (Telfair County)	31544
Jacksonville (Towns County)	30582
Jake	30182
Jakin	31761
Jamaica Estates	30907
James	31032
Jamestown	31501
Jarrell	31006
Jasper	30143
Jay Bird Springs	31011
Jefferson (Jackson County)	30549
Jefferson (Putnam County)	31024
Jeffersonville	31044
Jekyll Island	31520
Jenkinsburg	30234
Jersey	30235
Jerusalem (Camden County)	31568
Jerusalem (Pickens County)	30143
Jesup	31545
Jewell	31045
Jewtown	31522
Jinks	31717
Johnson Corner	30436
Johnson Crossroads	31822
Johnstonville	30204
Jolly	30292
Jones	31323
Jones Acres	31201
Jonesboro	30236-37
For specific Jonesboro Zip Codes call (404) 478-8286	
Jones Crossroads	31822
Jonesville	30108
Jordan City (Part of Columbus)	31904
Jot Em Down Store	31516
Joy Lake	30260
Juliette	31046
Junction City	31812
Juniper	31801
Juno	30534
Kansas	30182
Kathleen	31047
Keith	30755
Keithsburg	30114
Keller	31324
Kelley Hill	31905
Kelleytown	30253
Kelly	31085
Kemp	30401
Kenilworth	30909
Kennesaw	30144
Kensington	30707
Kensington Park (Part of Savannah)	31405
Kenwood (Fayette County)	30214

GEORGIA Kenwood-Mitchell

	ZIP
Kenwood (Muscogee County)	31909
Keysville	30816
Kibbee	30474
Kiker	30540
Kildare	30446
Killarney	31761
Kimbrough	31825
Kinderlou	31601
Kings	30209
Kings Bay	31547
Kingsboro	31811
Kingsland	31548
Kingsridge	30188
Kingston (Bartow County)	30145
Kingston (Richmond County)	30909
Kings Wood (Chatham County)	31401
Kingswood (Clarke County)	30606
Kings Wood (Richmond County)	30904
Kirkland (Atkinson County)	31642
Kirkland (Jeff Davis County)	31539
Kirkwood (Part of Moultrie)	31768
Kite	31049
Klondike (De Kalb County)	30058
Klondike (Houston County)	31036
Knott	30240
Knoxville	31050
Kramer	31001
Laboon	30641
La Crosse	31806
La Fayette	30728
La Grange	30240-41
For specific La Grange Zip Codes call (404) 882-1851	
Lake	30125
Lake Arrowhead	30183
Lake Capri Estates	30058
Lake Cindy	30228
Lake City	30260
Lake Creek	30125
Lake Hills	30263
Lake Howard	30728
Lake Iodeco	30236
Lakeland	31635
Lake Lanier Islands	30518
Lake Lucerne	30247
Lakemont (Rabun County)	30552
Lakemont (Richmond County)	30901
Lake Park	31636
Lakeshore Estates (Part of Gainesville)	30501
Lakeshore Mall (Part of Gainesville)	30501
Lakeside Park	31406
Lake Talmadge	30228
Lake Tara	30236
Lakeview (Bleckley County)	31014
Lakeview (Catoosa County)	30741
Lakeview (Peach County)	31030
Lakeview Estates	30207
Lakewood (Clarke County)	30605
Lakewood (Fulton County)	30315
Lakewood Heights (Part of Atlanta)	30315
Lamara Heights (Part of Savannah)	31405
Lamarville (Part of Savannah)	31405
Landrum	30534
Laney	31784
Lanier	31321
Laroche Park (Part of Savannah)	31404
Lashley	31005
Lathemtown	30114
Laurel Hills (Part of Columbus)	31907
La Vista	30329
Lavonia	30553
Lawrenceville	30243-46
For specific Lawrenceville Zip Codes call (404) 963-7118	
Lax	31774
Leaf	30528
Leah	30802
Leary	31762
Leathersville	30817
Lebanon	30146
Lee Correctional Institution	31763
Leefield	30458
Lee Pope	31030
Leesburg	31763
Lees Crossing	30240
Lees Mill	30214
Leland	30059
Leliaton	31650
Lena	30101

	ZIP
Lenox	31637
Lenox Square (Part of Atlanta)	30326
Leslie	31764
Lewis	30467
Lewiston	30809
Lexington	30648
Lexsy	30401
Liberty	30678
Liberty City (Part of Savannah)	31405
Liberty Hill	30257
Lifsey	30295
Lilburn	30247
Lilly	31051
Lillypond	30701
Limestone	31014
Lincoln Hills (Part of Columbus)	31904
Lincoln Park	30286
Lincolnton	30817
Lindale	30147
Lindbergh Plaza (Part of Atlanta)	30324
Lindsey Creek (Part of Columbus)	31907
Linesville	30631
Linton	31087
Linwood	30728
Lions Gate	30327
Listonia	31015
Lithia Springs	30057
Lithonia	30058
Little Five Points (Part of Atlanta)	30307
Little Miami	31601
Live Oak Gardens (Part of College Park)	30337
Livingston	30161
Lizella	31052
Loco	30817
Locust Grove	30248
Loftin	31816
Loganville	30249
Lollie	31021
Lone Oak	30230
Long Cane	30240
Lookout Mountain	30750
Lorane	31201
Lorenzo	31329
Lorwood (Part of Savannah)	31406
Lost Mountain	30073
Lothair	30457
Lotts	31519
Louise	30230
Louisville	30434
Louvale	31814
Lovejoy	30250
Lovett	31021
Lowell	30117
Lowndes Correctional Institution	31601
Lowry	30214
Lucile	31723
Lucius	30522
Ludowici	31316
Ludville	30175
Luella	30248
Lula	30554
Lulaton	31553
Lumber City	31549
Lumpkin	31815
Luthersville	30251
Luvdale	31701
Luxomni	30247
Lyerly	30730
Lyn Hills (Part of Columbus)	31904
Lynhurst	31406
Lynn	31717
Lynnwood	30741
Lyons	30436
Lytle	30707
Mableton (Cobb County)	30059
McAfee	30032
McBean	30906
McCaysville	30555
McCollum	30263
McCutchen	30740
McDaniels	30701
McDonald Acres	30741
McDonough	30253
Macedonia (Cherokee County)	30114
Macedonia (Towns County)	30546
McElroys Mill	30249
McGregor	30410
Machen	31064
McIntosh	31320
McIntosh Mill Village	30263
McIntyre	31054
McKinnon	31545

	ZIP
Macland	30073
Macon	31201-95
For specific Macon Zip Codes call (912) 741-8400	
Macon Correctional Center	31201
Macon Mall (Part of Macon)	31206
McPherson	30132
McRae	31055
McWhorter	30134
Madison	30650
Madola	30541
Madras	30254
Madray Springs	31545
Magby Gap	30752
Magnet	30207
Magnolia (Chatham County)	31404
Magnolia (Fulton County)	30318
Mallorysville	30668
Manassas	30438
Manchester	31816
Manor	31550
Mansfield	30255
Manta	31805
Marblehill	30148
Maretts	30553
Marietta	30060-68
For specific Marietta Zip Codes call (404) 424-0140	
Marietta Campground	30060
Marine Corps Supply Center	31704
Marion	31020
Marketplace at North DeKalb (Part of Decatur)	30033
Marlborough	30274
Marlow	31312
Marshallville	31057
Mars Hill	30101
Martech (Part of Atlanta)	30318
Martin	30557
Martinez (Columbia County)	30907
Massee	31620
Matt	30130
Matthews	30818
Mattox	31537
Mauk	31058
Maura Estates	30906
Maxeys	30671
Maxim	30817
Maxwell	31085
Mayday	31636
Mayfair (Part of Savannah)	31406
Mayfield	31087
Mayhaw	31723
Maysville	30558
Meadow Grove	30905
Meansville	30256
Mechanicsville	30340
Meeks	31049
Meigs	31765
Meinhard (Part of Port Wentworth)	31407
Meldrim	31318
Melrose	31636
Mendes	30427
Menlo	30731
Mercer University (Part of Macon)	31207
Meridian	31319
Merrillville	31738
Mershon	31551
Mesena	30819
Metasville	30673
Metcalf	31792
Metter	30439
Mica	30107
Middleton	30635
Midland (Part of Columbus)	31820
Midtown (Part of Atlanta)	30309
Midville	30441
Midway (Catoosa County)	30741
Midway (Liberty County)	31320
Midway (Tattnall County)	30427
Midway-Hardwick	31061
Milan	31060
Miles Park	30906
Milford	31762
Mill Creek	30740
Mill Creek Estates	30506
Milledgeville	31061
Millen	30442
Millers Mill	30281
Millhaven	30467
Millwood	31552
Milner	30257
Milstead	30207
Mineola	31602
Mineral Bluff	30559
Minnesota	31744
Mission Ridge (Part of Rossville)	30741
Mitchell	30820

Mize-Pendley Hills **GEORGIA** 127

	ZIP		ZIP		ZIP
Mize	30577	Nevils	31321	Ochillee	31905
Mizell	31006	Newark	31792	Ochlocknee	31773
Modoc	30401	Newborn	30262	Ochwalkee	30428
Molena	30258	New Branch	30436	Ocilla	31774
Moncrief	32301	New Cotton Mill (Part of		Oconee	31067
Moniac	31646	Canton)	30114	Oconee Heights	30607
Monroe	30655	New Elm	31768	Odessadale	30222
Montclair	30907	New England	30752	Odum	31555
Monteith (Part of Port		New Era	31709	Offerman	31556
Wentworth)	31407	New Georgia	30132	Ogeechee	30467
Montevideo	30635	New Holland	30501	Ogeechee Farms	31405
Montezuma	31063	New Home	30752	Ogeechee Road	31405
Montgomery	31406	New Hope (Gwinnett		Ogeecheeton (Part of	
Montgomery Correctional		County)	30245	Savannah)	31401
Institution	30445	New Hope (Lincoln County)	30817	Oglethorpe (Chatham	
Monticello (Jasper County)	31064	New Hope (Paulding		County)	31406
Monticello (Richmond		County)	30132	Oglethorpe (Macon County)	31068
County)	30906	Newington	30446	Oglethorpe Mall (Part of	
Montreal	30033	Newnan	30263-65	Savannah)	31406
Montrose	31065	For specific Newnan Zip Codes		Oglethorpe Park (Part of	
Moody AFB	31601	call (404) 253-2725		Savannah)	31405
Moody Field	31601	New Point	31780	Oglethorpe University	30319
Moons	30725	New Salem	30547	Ogletree Woods (Part of	
Moores	31021	Newton	31770	Columbus)	31904
Mora	31650	Newton Factory	30209	Ohoopee	30436
Moreland	30259	Newtown (Fulton County)	30201	Okefenokee	31501
Morgan	31766	New Town (Gordon County)	30701	Ola	30253
Morganton	30560	New Town (Wilkes County)	30673	Old Damascus	31741
Morganville	30757	New York (Part of Aragon)	30153	Old National (Part of	
Morningside (Fulton County)	30324	Neyami	31763	Atlanta)	30349
Morningside (Muscogee		Nicholasville	31713	Old South	30236
County)	31904	Nicholls	31554	Olive Branch	31827
Morningside Hills	30501	Nicholson	30565	Oliver	30449
Morris	31767	Nickelsville	31042	Olney	31308
Morris Brown (Part of		Nickleville	31797	Omaha	31821
Atlanta)	30314	Nickville	30634	Omega	31775
Morris Estates	30736	Noah's Station	30818	Oostanaula	30701
Morris Siding (Part of		Noble	30728	Ophir	30107
Atlanta)	30301	Noonday	30060	Orange	30114
Morrow	30260	Norcross	30071	Orchard Hill	30266
Mortons	31405		30091-93	Orchard Hills	30741
Morven	31638	For specific Norcross Zip Codes		Orianna	31002
Moultrie	31768	call (404) 448-2241		Orland	30457
Mountainbrook (Part of Pine		Norman	30668	Ormewood (Part of Atlanta)	30312
Mountain)	31822	Norman Park	31771	Oscarville	30506
Mountain City	30562	Normantown	30474	Osierfield	31750
Mountain Hill	31811	Norris	30828	Other	30132
Mountain Park (Fulton		Norristown	30447	Ottawa Estates (Part of	
County)	30075	North Atlanta (De Kalb		Bloomingdale)	31302
Mountain Park (Gwinnett		County)	30319	Owensboro	31079
County)	30087	North Canton	30114	Owltown	30512
Mountain View (Clayton		North Decatur	30033	Oxford	30267
County)	30321	North Druid Hills (De Kalb		Pace	30209
Mountain View (Walker		County)	30033	Pachitta	31740
County)	30741	North Dublin (Part of Dublin)	31021	Palmetto (Fulton County)	30268
Mount Airy	30563	North Elberton	30635	Palmetto (Oglethorpe	
Mount Berry	30149	Northgate	31907	County)	30627
Mount Bethel	30060	North Highland (Part of		Palmyra	31763
Mount Carmel	30728	Atlanta)	30306	Pancras	31061
Mount Olivet	30643	North Highlands (Part of		Panhandle	31076
Mount Pleasant (Banks		Columbus)	31904	Pannell	30655
County)	30547	North High Shoals	30645	Pantertown	30559
Mount Pleasant (Wayne		Northlake	30345	Panthersville	30032
County)	31543	Northridge (Part of Conyers)	30207	Paoli	30629
Mount Vernon (Montgomery		North Roswell (Part of		Paradise Park (Part of	
County)	30445	Roswell)	30075	Savannah)	31406
Mount Vernon (Walton		North Side (Part of Atlanta)	30305	Paradise Valley	30607
County)	30655	North West Point	31833	Parhams	30521
Mount Vernon (Whitfield		Norton Acres	30906	Parkchester (Part of	
County)	30740	Norwood	30821	Columbus)	31906
Mountville	30261	Note	31024	Park City (Part of Fort	
Mount Zion	30150	Nuberg	30634	Oglethorpe)	30741
Moxley	30477	Nunez	30448	Parkersburg	31406
Mulberry	30680	Oakdale	30080	Parkerville	31744
Mulberry Grove	31804	Oakfield	31772	Park Hill (Part of Gainesville)	30501
Mulberry Heights (Part of		Oak Forest	30236	Parkwood (Part of	
Albany)	31705	Oak Grove (Carroll County)	30117	Savannah)	31404
Mulberry Street (Part of		Oak Grove (Cherokee		Parrott	31777
Macon)	31201	County)	30101	Patillo	30233
Munnerlyn	30830	Oak Grove (De Kalb		Patten	31626
Murphy	31738	County)	30033	Patterson	31557
Murray Hills	30909	Oak Grove (Troup County)	31822	Pavo	31778
Murrays Crossroads	31806	Oakhaven	31707	Payne (Bibb County)	31201
Murrayville	30564	Oak Hill (Gilmer County)	30540	Payne (Cherokee County)	30101
Musella	31066	Oak Hill (Newton County)	30209	Peach Orchard	30906
Myrtle Grove	31324	Oakhurst (Part of Savannah)	31406	Peachtree	30909
Mystic	31769	Oakland	30218	Peachtree Center (Part of	
Nahunta	31553	Oakland City (Part of		Atlanta)	30343
Nails Creek	30521	Atlanta)	30301	Peachtree City	30269
Nance Springs	30720	Oakland Heights	30120	Peachtree Hills (Part of	
Nankipooh (Part of		Oakland Park (Part of		Atlanta)	30324
Columbus)	31909	Savannah)	31404	Peachtree Mall (Part of	
Naomi	30728	Oaklawn	30263	Columbus)	31909
Nashville	31639	Oakleaf Plantation	30067	Pearly	31021
National Hills	30904	Oakman	30732	Pearson	31642
Naylor	31641	Oak Mountain	31826	Pebble City	31784
Neal	30206	Oak Park	30401	Pedenville	30206
Nebo	30132	Oakwood	30566	Pelham	31779
Needmore	31630	Oasis	30513	Pembroke	31321
Neese	30646	Oatland Island	31410	Pendergrass	30567
Nelson	30151	Ocee	30201	Pendley Hills	30032

128 GEORGIA Penfield-Sautee-Nacoochee

	ZIP
Penfield	30669
Penia	31015
Pennick	31520
Pennington	30650
Pennville	30747
Peoples Still	31797
Perkins	30822
Perry	31069
Persimmon	30525
Petross	30474
Phelps	30720
Phillips	30907
Phillipsburg	31794
Philomath	30660
Phinizy	30802
Phipps Plaza (Part of Atlanta)	30326
Phoenix	31024
Pickard	30286
Piedmont	30204
Pierceville	37317
Pineboro	31768
Pine Chapel	30701
Pine Gardens (Part of Savannah)	31404
Pine Grove	31513
Pine Harbor	31331
Pine Hill (Part of Columbus)	31903
Pinehurst (Dooly County)	31070
Pinehurst (Henry County)	30281
Pine Lake	30072
Pineland	31630
Pine Log	30171
Pine Mountain (Harris County)	31822
Pine Mountain (Rabun County)	29664
Pine Mountain Valley	31823
Pineora	31312
Pine Park	31728
Pine Valley	30904
Pineview	31071
Pinewood Shores	30207
Piney Bluff	31565
Piney Grove	31808
Pin Point	31406
Pinson	30161
Pio Nono (Part of Macon)	31204
Pirkle Woods	30130
Pitts	31072
Pittsburg	30084
Plainfield	31073
Plains	31780
Plainview (Franklin County)	30521
Plainview (Whitfield County)	30720
Plainville	30733
Pleasant Hill (Fulton County)	30337
Pleasant Hill (Gwinnett County)	30136
Pleasant Hill (Talbot County)	31836
Pleasant Hill (Terrell County)	31742
Pleasant Valley (Bartow County)	30103
Pleasant Valley (Dooly County)	31092
Pocataligo	30633
Point Peter	30627
Pollards Corner	30802
Pomona	30223
Pond Spring	30707
Pooler	31322
Pope City	31079
Popes Ferry	31046
Poplar Springs	30113
Portal	30450
Porterdale	30270
Porter Springs	30533
Portland	30104
Port Royal	31324
Port Wentworth	31407
Port Wentworth Junction (Part of Port Wentworth)	31407
Postell	31201
Potterville	31076
Poulan	31781
Powder Springs	30073
Powell Place	31701
Powelton	31087
Powers Lake	30327
Powersville	31008
Prather	30673
Prattsburg	31039
Presley	30546
Preston	31824
Pretoria	31701
Price	30506
Pridgen	31519
Primrose	30222
Princeton (Part of Athens)	30601
Pringle	31035
Prior	30138

	ZIP
Pritchetts	31744
Privette Heights	30060
Pulaski	30451
Pumpkin Center	30814
Putnam	31803
Putney	31782
Pyles Marsh	31520
Pyne	30240
Queensland	31750
Quitman	31643
Rabbit Hill	31324
Rabun Gap	30568
Race Pond	31537
Radium Springs	31702
Raines	31015
Raleigh	30293
Ramhurst	30705
Randall	31815
Ranger	30734
Raoul	30510
Raulerson	31557
Ravenwood	30907
Raybon	31553
Ray City	31645
Rayle	30660
Raymond	30263
Raytown	30631
Rebecca	31783
Rebie	31012
Recovery	32324
Redan	30074
Redbud	30701
Red Clay	30710
Red Hill (Franklin County)	30557
Red Hill (Stewart County)	31825
Red Lane	30501
Red Oak	30272
Red Rock (Paulding County)	30101
Red Rock (Worth County)	31791
Red Stone	30549
Reed Creek	30643
Reese	30828
Reeves	30701
Regency Mall (Part of Augusta)	30904
Register	30452
Rehoboth	30033
Reidsboro	30292
Reidsville	30453
Reka	31321
Relay	30125
Remerton	31601
Renfroe	31805
Reno	31728
Rentz	31075
Reo	30740
Resaca	30735
Resseaus Crossroads	31024
Rest Haven	30518
Retreat	31323
Rex	30273
Reynolds	31076
Reynoldsville	31745
Rhine	31077
Riceboro	31323
Richfield (Part of Savannah)	31405
Richland	31825
Richmond Hill	31324
Richwood	31092
Rico	30268
Riddleville	31018
Ridgefield Heights (Part of Columbus)	31907
Ridgeville	31331
Ridgewood	30909
Rincon	31326
Ringgold	30736
Rio	30223
Rio Vista (Chatham County)	31406
Rio Vista (Dougherty County)	31705
Rising Fawn	30738
Riverdale	30274
Riverland Terrace (Part of Columbus)	31903
River Oaks	31410
River Road	31707
Rivers End (Part of Savannah)	31406
Riverside (Bibb County)	31204
Riverside (Colquitt County)	31768
Riverside (Floyd County)	30161
Riverside (Fulton County)	30318
Rivertown	30213
Riverturn	31745
Roanoke Acres	31750
Roberta	31078
Robertstown	30545
Robertsville	30707

	ZIP
Robins AFB	31098
Robins Air Force Base	31098
Robinson	30669
Rochelle	31079
Rock Branch	30635
Rockdale (Part of Atlanta)	30318
Rock Hill	31723
Rockingham	31510
Rockledge	30454
Rockmart	30153
Rock Spring	30739
Rockville	31024
Rocky Creek	30701
Rocky Face	30740
Rocky Ford	30455
Rocky Mount	30251
Rocky Plains	30209
Roddy	31014
Rogers	30529
Rogers Correctional Institution	30453
Rolling Green	30207
Rolling Meadows	30905
Rome	30161-64
For specific Rome Zip Codes call (404) 232-1073	
Roopville	30170
Roosterville	30170
Roper	31539
Ropers Crossroads	30809
Roscoe	30263
Rosebud	30249
Rosedale	30701
Rose Dhu	31406
Rose Hill (Chatham County)	31406
Rose Hill (Pike County)	30256
Rose Hill Heights (Part of Columbus)	31904
Rosemont	30802
Rosemont Park	30161
Rosier	30434
Rossignol Hill (Part of Garden City)	31408
Rossville	30741-42
For specific Rossville Zip Codes call (404) 866-1500	
Roswell	30075-77
For specific Roswell Zip Codes call (404) 993-6778	
Round Oak	31038
Rover	30292
Rowena	31713
Roxanna	31132
Royston	30662
Ruckersville	30635
Rudden	31024
Rupert	31081
Russell	30680
Russellville	31016
Rutledge	30663
Rydal	30171
Ryo	30139
St. Charles	30259
St. Clair	30816
St. George	31646
St. Marks	30230
St. Marys	31558
St. Marys Hills (Part of Columbus)	31906
St. Simons Island	31522
Sale City	31784
Salem	30638
Salem Arms	30906
Sanborn	31705
Sandalwood	31701
Sandersville	31082
Sandfly	31406
Sand Hill (Brooks County)	31778
Sand Hill (Carroll County)	30180
Sand Hill (Muscogee County)	31905
Sand Hills	30904
Sandtown	30673
Sandy Cross (Franklin County)	30662
Sandy Cross (Oglethorpe County)	30627
Sandy Plains	30075
Sandy Springs (Fulton County)	30328
Sanford (Madison County)	30646
Sanford (Stewart County)	31815
Santa Claus	30436
Sapelo Island	31327
Sapp	31014
Sardis	30456
Sargent	30275
Sasser	31785
Satolah	30525
Sautee-Nacoochee	30571

Savannah-Trickum GEORGIA 129

Name	ZIP
Savannah	31401-20
For specific Savannah Zip Codes call (912) 236-7851	
Savannah Gardens (Part of Savannah)	31404
Sawdust	30814
Sawhatchee	31723
Scarboro	30442
Scarbrough Cross Roads	30049
Scarlet	31569
Schatulga (Part of Columbus)	31820
Schlatterville	31501
Schley	31768
Scotland	31083
Scott	31002
Scottdale	30079
Scottsboro	31061
Screven	31560
Screvens Point	31410
Sea Island	31561
Sea Palms	31522
Sells	30548
Seney	30104
Senoia	30276
Sessoms	31554
Seville	31084
Seymour	31024
Shady Dale	31085
Shake Rag	30174
Shannon	30172
Sharon	30664
Sharon Park (Part of Garden City)	31408
Sharpe	30728
Sharpsburg	30277
Sharps Spur	30410
Sharp Top	30114
Shawnee	31329
Sheffield	30909
Shell Bluff	30830
Shellman	31786
Shellman Bluff	31331
Shelly	31778
Shenandoah	30265
Sheppards	30467
Sherwood (Clayton County)	30236
Sherwood (Richmond County)	30904
Sherwood Forest (Coweta County)	30263
Sherwood Forest (Floyd County)	30161
Shields Crossroads	30707
Shiloh (Harris County)	31826
Shiloh (Lowndes County)	31634
Shingler	31781
Shoal Creek	30553
Shoals	30820
Shurlington (Part of Macon)	31211
Sigsbee	31744
Silco	31537
Silica Hills	31705
Silk Hope	31401
Silk Mills	30635
Siloam	30665
Silver City	30506
Silver Creek	30173
Silver Crest	30906
Silver Pines	31206
Simpson	30217
Skidaway Island	31411
Skipperton	31206
Skyland	30319
Skyland Terrace (Part of Savannah)	31401
Sky Valley	30525
Smarr	31086
Smiths Crossroads	31823
Smithsonia	30628
Smithville	31787
Smyrna	30080-82
For specific Smyrna Zip Codes call (404) 436-5246	
Snake Nation	30513
Snapfinger	30035
Snapping Shoals	30029
Snead	30809
Snellville	30278
Snipesville	31532
Snug Harbor Estates	30504
Soapstick	30701
Social Circle	30279
Sofkee	31206
Somerset Park (Part of Savannah)	31406
Sonoraville	30701
Soperton	30457
South Augusta	30901
South Base (Part of Warner Robins)	31098

Name	ZIP
South Cobb	30001
Southdale	30906
South Decatur	30034
South DeKalb Mall	30034
Southern Tech (Part of Marietta)	30060
Southgate Villa	30906
South Glen	30236
Southlake Mall (Part of Morrow)	30260
Southland	30906
South Macon (Part of Macon)	31206
South Moultrie (Part of Moultrie)	31768
South Nellieville	30901
South Newport	31323
Southover (Part of Savannah)	31405
South Pooler	31322
Southside (Part of Savannah)	31419
Spanish Trace	30906
Spann	31096
Sparks	31647
Sparta	31087
Spence	31779
Spencer Hills	30741
Split Silk	30249
Spout Spring Crossroads	30542
Spring Bluff	31565
Springfield	31329
Spring Hill (Part of Savannah)	31404
Spring Place	30705
Springvale	31767
Springvale (railroad station)	31767
Springview Acres (Part of Gainesville)	30501
Staley Heights (Part of Savannah)	31406
Stanleys Store	30436
Stanton Woods	30207
Stapleton	30823
Stark	30233
Starr	30207
Starr's Mill	30214
Starrsville	30209
State College	31404
Statenville	31648
State Sanitarium	31061
Statesboro	30458
Statham	30666
Steadham Store	31717
Steadman	30176
Steam Mill	31745
Stellaville	30833
Stephens	30667
Stephensville	30752
Sterling	31520
Stevens Pottery	31031
Stewart	30209
Stewart Town	30752
Stilesboro	30120
Stillmore	30464
Stillwell	31329
Stilson	30415
Stockbridge	30281
Stockton	31649
Stockwood	30188
Stone Mountain	30083
	30086-88
For specific Stone Mountain Zip Codes call (404) 469-4544	
Stonewall (Part of Union City)	30349
Stoney Point	30170
Stovall (Habersham County)	30531
Stovall (Meriwether County)	30283
Stratford (Part of Atlanta)	30311
Stuckey	30428
Subligna	30747
Suches	30572
Sudie	30132
Sugar Hill (Gwinnett County)	30518
Sugar Hill (Hall County)	30507
Sugartown	30755
Sugar Valley	30746
Sulphur Springs	30738
Sulphur Springs Station	35967
Sumach	30705
Summertown	30466
Summerville	30747
Summit (Part of Twin City)	30471
Sumner	31789
Sumter	31709
Sunbury	31320
Sunny Acres	31701
Sunny Side (Spalding County)	30284
Sunnyside (Ware County)	31501

Name	ZIP
Sunset	31768
Sunset Heights (Part of Gainesville)	30501
Sunset Park (Part of Savannah)	31404
Sunset Village	30286
Sunsweet	31794
Surrency	31563
Sutalee	30184
Suttles Mill	30728
Suttons Corner	31746
Suwanee	30174
Swainsboro	30401
Swan Lake	30281
Swords	30625
Sybert	30817
Sycamore	31790
Sylvan Hills (Part of Atlanta)	30310
Sylvania	30467
Sylvester	31791
Talahi Island	31410
Talbotton	31827
Talking Rock	30175
Tallapoosa	30176
Tallulah Falls	30573
Talmo	30575
Talona	30175
Tanglewood (Clarke County)	30606
Tanglewood (Richmond County)	30909
Tarboro	31568
Tarrytown	30470
Tarver	31630
Tate	30177
Tate City	30525
Tatumsville (Part of Savannah)	31406
Tax	31826
Taylorsville	30178
Tazewell	31803
Teloga	30747
Temperance	31077
Temple	30179
Tennga	30751
Tennille	31089
Terrace Manor	30906
Terrell	31789
Texas	30217
Thalmann	31520
The Hill (Part of Augusta)	30904
The Landings	31411
The Rock	30285
Thomasboro	30455
Thomaston	30286
Thomasville (Fulton County)	30315
Thomasville (Thomas County)	31792
Thomas Woods	30906
Thompson	31601
Thompsons Mills	30548
Thompsonville	30738
Thomson	30824
Thornhedge	30274
Thrift	30442
Thunderbolt	31404
Thurston	30642
Thyatira	30549
Ticknor	31744
Tifton	31793-94
For specific Tifton Zip Codes call (912) 382-1511	
Tiger	30576
Tignall	30668
Tilton	30720
Timothy Estates	30606
Tippettville	31092
Tison	30427
Titus	30546
Toccoa	30577
Toccoa Falls	30598
Toco Hills	30329
Toledo	31646
Tom	31049
Toms Creek	30557
Toomsboro	31090
Topeka Junction	30285
Town and Country Acres	31707
Town and Country Shopping Center (Part of Marietta)	30060
Towns	31055
Townsend	31331
Traders Hill	31537
Trans	30728
Tremont	30907
Tremont Park (Part of Savannah)	31401
Trenton	30752
Trice	30286
Trickum	30755

GEORGIA Trimble-Zingara

	ZIP		ZIP		ZIP
Trimble	30230	Ware Correctional Institution	31501	Willard	31024
Trion	30753	Waresboro	31564	Williamson	30292
Troutman	31740	Wares Crossroads	30240	Williams Plaza (Part of	
Trudie	31557	Waresville	30217	Warner Robins)	31093
Tucker	30084-85	Waring	30720	Wilmington Island	31410
For specific Tucker Zip Codes call (404) 938-6920		Warm Springs	31830	Wilmington Park	31410
		Warner Robins	31088	Wilshire (Part of Savannah)	31406
Tugalo	30577		31098-99	Wilshire Estates (Part of	
Tugaloo (Part of Tallulah Falls)	30573	For specific Warner Robins Zip Codes call (912) 922-3121		Savannah)	31406
				Wilsons Church	30529
Tunnel Hill	30755	Warren Terrace	30741	Wilsonville	31554
Turin	30289	Warrenton	30828	Wimberly on the Marsh	31406
Turner City (Part of Albany)	31705	Warsaw	30201	Winchester	31057
Turners Rock	31406	Warthen	31094	Winchester Hills	30207
Turnerville	30580	Warwick	31796	Winder	30680
Tusculum	31329	Washington	30673	Windermere	30904
Tuxedo (Part of Atlanta)	30342	Waterloo	31733	Windsor	30249
Twin City	30471	Waterport	30249	Windsor Estates	30263
Twin Lakes	31636	Watkinsville	30677	Windsor Forest (Chatham County)	31406
Tybee Island	31328	Waverly (Camden County)	31565		
Tyrone (Fayette County)	30290	Waverly (Richmond County)	30909	Windsor Forest (Richmond County)	30904
Tyrone (Wilkes County)	30673	Waverly Hall	31831		
Ty Ty	31795	Waverly Park	30741	Windsor Park (Lowndes County)	31601
Tyus	30108	Wax	30104		
Unadilla	31091	Wayback	31746	Windsor Park (Muscogee County)	31904
Union (Marion County)	31803	Waycross	31501		
Union (Paulding County)	30179	Wayne Correctional Institution	31555	Windward (Part of Savannah)	31405
Union (Quitman County)	31754				
Union (Stewart County)	31821	Waynesboro	30830	Windy Ridge	30559
Unionburg	31794	Waynesville	31566	Winfield	30824
Union City	30291	Wayside	31032	Winokur	31537
Union Hill	30201	Webb	30201	Winona Park	31501
Union Point	30669	Weber	31639	Winston	30187
Unionville	31794	Welcome	30263	Winterville	30683
Unity	30521	Welcome Hill	30753	Withers	31630
University Heights	30605	Wenona	31015	Wofford Crossroads	30184
Upatoi (Part of Columbus)	31829	Weracoba Heights (Part of Columbus)	31906	Woodbine	31569
Upton	31533			Woodbury	30293
Upton Mill	31006	Wesley (Emanuel County)	30401	Woodcliff	30467
Uptonville	31537	Wesley (Taylor County)	31812	Woodgate	30909
Uvalda	30473	Wesleyan College (Part of Macon)	31201	Woodlake	30906
Vada	31734			Woodland	31836
Valdosta	31601-04	Wesleyan Estates	31204	Woodland Hills (Laurens County)	31021
For specific Valdosta Zip Codes call (912) 242-8201		West Augusta	30901		
		West Bainbridge (Part of Bainbridge)	31717	Woodland Hills (Walker County)	30741
Valley Forge	30906				
Valley View	37409	West Brow	30738	Woodlawn (Part of Savannah)	31408
Valona	31332	West Crossing	30176		
Vanceville	31794	West Dublin (Part of Dublin)	31021	Woodlawn Estates (Part of Columbus)	31909
Vandiver Heights	30060	West End (Floyd County)	30161		
Vanna	30662	West End (Fulton County)	30310	Woodlawn Terrace (Part of Garden City)	31408
Vans Valley	30161	Westgate (Part of Albany)	31707		
Van Wert	30153	Westgate Mall (Part of Macon)	31206	Woodridge Estates	31410
Varnell	30756			Woods Grove	30582
Vaughn	30223	Westgate Park	30607	Wood Station	30736
Veal	30108	West Georgia College (Part of Carrollton)	30117	Woodstock	30188
Veazey	30642			Woodville (Chatham County)	31401
Vega	30256	West Green	31567		
Veribest	30627	Westmont	30809	Woodville (Greene County)	30669
Vernonburg	31406	Westoak	30060	Woolsey	30214
Vernon View	31406	Weston	31832	Wooster	30218
Vesta	30627	West Point	31833	Wormsloe	31406
Veterans Hospital (Part of Augusta)	30909	West Rome (Part of Rome)	30161	Worth	31714
		West Savannah (Part of Savannah)	31401	Worthville	30233
Victoria	30188			Wray	31798
Victory	30108	Westside (Catoosa County)	30741	Wrens	30833
Victory Heights (Part of Savannah)	31404	Westside (Hall County)	30501	Wright Square (Part of Savannah)	31401
		West Valdosta	31601		
Vidalia	30474	West Vidalia (Part of Vidalia)	30474	Wrightsville	31096
Vidette	30434	Westwick	30909	Wymberly	31406
Vienna	31092	Westwood	31750	Wynngate	30907
View	30531	Wexwood	30274	Wynnton (Part of Columbus)	31906
Villanow	30728	Wheat Hill (Part of Garden City)	31408		
Villa Rica	30180			Yahoola	30533
Vineland	30909	Wheeler Heights	31201	Yates	30263
Vinings	30339	Whigham	31797	Yates Crossroads	30217
Vista-Grove	30033	Whistleville	30680	Yatesville	31097
Vulcan	30738	White	30184	Yellow Bluff Fishing Village	31320
Waco	30182	White Bluff (Part of Savannah)	31406	Yellow Dirt	30217
Wadley	30477			Yeomans	31742
Wahoo	30533	White City	30187	Yonah	30510
Walden	31206	White Hall	30605	Yonkers	31014
Waleska	30183	Whitehouse	30253	Ycrkville	30132
Walker Correctional Institution	30739	Whitemarsh Island	31404	Youngcane	30512
		White Oak	31568	Young Harris	30582
Walker Park	30655	White Plains	30678	Youngs	30125
Wallace	31036	Whitesburg	30185	Youngstown	30512
Wallaceville	30707	Whitestone	30175	Youth	30249
Walls Crossing	31806	White Sulphur Springs	31822	Zaidee	30457
Walnut Grove (Walker County)	30728	Whitesville	31833	Zebina	30833
Walnut Grove (Walton County)	30209	Whitworth	30553	Zebulon	30295
		Wilbanks Store	30711	Zenith	31078
Walnut Square (Part of Dalton)	30720	Wildwood	30757	Zetella	30223
		Wiley	30581	Zetto	31724
Walthourville	31333	Willacoochee	31650	Zingara	30207

Ahualoa-Kihei HAWAII 131

	ZIP
Ahualoa	96727
Ahuimano	96744
Ahuimano	96744
Aiea (Honolulu County)	96701
Aiea Heights	96701
Aiea Shopping Center	96701
Aikahi	96734
Aina Haina (Part of Honolulu)	96821
Alabama Village	96784
Alasaki Camp	96774
Alewa Heights (Part of Honolulu)	96819
Aliamanu (Part of Honolulu)	96818
Amauulu Camps	96720
Anahola	96703
Andrade	96783
Barbers Point Housing	96862
Barbers Point Naval Air Station	96706
Brigham Young University-Hawaii	96762
Camp 106	96727
Camp H.M. Smith Marine Corps Base	96861
Captain Cook	96704
Chinatown (Part of Honolulu)	96817
Chin Chuck	96710
Coconut Grove	96734
Coral Gardens	96744
Crestview	96797
Downtown (Hawaii County)	96720
Downtown (Honolulu County)	96813
Downtown (Maui County)	96767
Dowsett Highlands (Part of Honolulu)	96817
Eight and One-half Mile Camp	96749
Eightmile Camp	96749
Eleele (Kauai County)	96705
Elevenmile Homestead	96760
Ewa	96706
Ewa Beach	96706-07
For specific Ewa Beach Zip Codes call (808) 689-5033	
Fernandez Village	96706
Ford Island	96818
Foster Village	96771
Glenwood	96720
Haaheo	96720
Haena	96714
Haiku	96708
Haina	96727
Hakalau	96710
Halaula	96755
Halawa (Hawaii County)	96755
Halawa (Honolulu County)	96701
Halawa (Maui County)	96748
Halawa Heights	96701
Halawa Hills	96701
Haleiwa	96712
Halepalaoa Landing	96763
Haliimaile	96768
Hamoa	96713
Hana	96713
Hanalei	96714
Hanamaulu	96715
Hanapepe	96716
Hanapepe Heights	96716
Haou	96713
Happy Valley	96793
Hauula	96717
Hawaiian Ocean View Estates	96704
Hawaiian Village (Part of Honolulu)	96813
Hawaii Kai (Part of Honolulu)	96825
Hawaii National Park	96718
Hawi	96719
Hawi Camp 17	96719
Heeia	96744
Hickam Air Force Base	96818
Hickam Housing	96818
Highway Village	96728
Hilo	96720-21
For specific Hilo Zip Codes call (808) 935-2821	
Hoaeae	96797
Hokamahoe House Lot	96764
Holualoa	96725
Honaunau	96726
Honohina	96710
Honokaa	96727
Honokahua	96761
Honokai Hale	96706
Honokohau	96725
Honokowai	96761

	ZIP
Honolulu	96801-50
For specific Honolulu Zip Codes call (808) 423-3990	
COLLEGES & UNIVERSITIES	
Chaminade University of Honolulu	96816
Hawaii Pacific College	96813
University of Hawaii at Manoa	96822
FINANCIAL INSTITUTIONS	
American Savings Bank, FSB	96813
Bank of Hawaii	96846
Central Pacific Bank	96811
City Bank	96813
First Federal Savings & Loan Association of America	96813
First Hawaiian Bank	96813
First Interstate Bank of Hawaii	96814
Hawaii National Bank	96813
Honolulu Federal Savings & Loan Association	96813
International Savings & Loan Association, Limited	96813
Liberty Bank	96817
Pioneer Federal Savings Bank	96813
Territorial Savings & Loan Association	96813
HOSPITALS	
Kuakini Medical Center	96817
Queen's Medical Center	96813
HOTELS/MOTELS	
Ambassador Hotel of Waikiki	96815
Best Western Plaza Hotel Honolulu International Airport	96819
Best Western Waikiki Plaza Hotel	96815
The Breakers	96815
Colony Surf East Hotel	96815
Coral Reef Hotel	96815
Coral Seas Hotel	96815
Discovery Bay Resort	96815
Halekulani Hotel	96815
Hawaiian Monarch Hotel	96815
Hawaiian Regent	96815
Hawaiiana Hotel	96815
Hilton Hawaiian Village	96815
Holiday Inn-Honolulu Airport	96819
Holiday Inn-Waikiki Beach	96815
Hyatt Regency Waikiki	96815
Ilikai, The	96815
Ilima Hotel	96815
Kahala Hilton Hotel	96816
Miramar at Waikiki	96815
New Otani Kaimana Beach Hotel	96815
Outrigger East	96815
Outrigger Malia	96815
Outrigger Prince Kuhio	96815
Outrigger Surf	96815
Outrigger Waikiki Hotel	96815
Outrigger West	96815
Pacific Beach Hotel	96815
Pagoda Hotel	96814
Park Shore Hotel	96815
Quality Inn Waikiki-Diamond Head	96815
Quality Inn Waikiki-Pali	96815
Royal Hawaiian Hotel	96815
Sheraton Princess Kaiulani Hotel	96815
Sheraton-Waikiki	96815
Waikiki Beachcomber	96815
Waikikian On The Beach	96815
Honomakau	96755
Honomalino	96704
Honomu	96728
Honouliuli	96706
Honuapo	96772
Hookena	96704
Hoolehua	96729
Hoopuloa	96726
Huehue	96725
Huelo	96708
Iroquois Point	96706
Iwasaki Camp	96760
Kaaawa	96730
Kaahumanu Center	96732
Kaalaea	96744
Kaalawai (Part of Honolulu)	96821
Kaanapali	96761

	ZIP
Kaapahu	96776
Kaapoko Homesteads	96781
Kaauhuhu Homesteads	96719
Kaawanui Village	96769
Kahakuloa	96793
Kahala Mall (Part of Honolulu)	96816
Kahaluu (Hawaii County)	96725
Kahaluu (Honolulu County)	96744
Kahana (Honolulu County)	96717
Kahana (Maui County)	96761
Kahei Homesteads	96719
Kahua	96755
Kahuku (Hawaii County)	96772
Kahuku (Honolulu County)	96731
Kahului	96732-33
For specific Kahului Zip Codes call (808) 871-4710	
Kaiaakea	96773
Kaieie Homesteads	96781
Kailua (Honolulu County)	96734
Kailua (Maui County)	96708
Kailua Kona	96739-40
For specific Kailua Kona Zip Codes call (808) 329-1927	
Kai Malino	96704
Kaimu	96778
Kaimuki (Part of Honolulu)	96816
Kainaliu	96750
Kainalu	96748
Kaiwiki	96720
Kalae	96729
Kalaheo	96741
Kalamaula	96748
Kalaoa	96781
Kalaoa Homesteads	96725
Kalauao	96701
Kalaupapa	96742
Kalepoleopo	96753
Kalihi (Part of Honolulu)	96819
Kalihi Kai (Part of Honolulu)	96818
Kalihi Shopping Center (Part of Honolulu)	96819
Kalihiwai	96754
Kalopa Mauka	96727
Kaluaaha	96748
Kamaili	96778
Kamalo	96748
Kamehameha Heights (Part of Honolulu)	96819
Kamiloloa	96748
Kamooloa	96791
Kamuela	96743
Kaneohe	96744
Kaneohe Marine Corps Air Station	96863
Kaneohe State Hospital	96744
Kaniahiku Village	96778
Kapaa	96746
Kapaau	96755
Kapahulu (Part of Honolulu)	96815
Kapaia	96715
Kapaka	96747
Kapalama (Part of Honolulu)	96817
Kapehu	96780
Kapoho	96778
Kapulena	96727
Kaumakani	96747
Kaumalapau	96763
Kaumana	96720
Kaunakakai	96748
Kaupakalua	96708
Kaupo	96713
Kawaihae	96743
Kawaihua	96746
Kawailoa	96712
Kawailoa Beach	96712
Kawainui	96783
Kawanui	96750
Kawela (Honolulu County)	96731
Kawela (Maui County)	96748
Keaau	96749
Keaau Camp	96749
Keaau Ranch	96749
Kealakehe Homesteads	96740
Kealakekua	96750
Kealia	96751
Keanae	96708
Keauhou	96740
Keaukaha	96720
Keawakapu	96753
Keehia	96726
Keei	96774
Kehena	96778
Kekaha	96752
Kelawea	96761
Keokea (Hawaii County)	96704
Keokea (Maui County)	96790
Keolu Hills	96734
Kihalani Homestead	96780
Kihei	96753

HAWAII

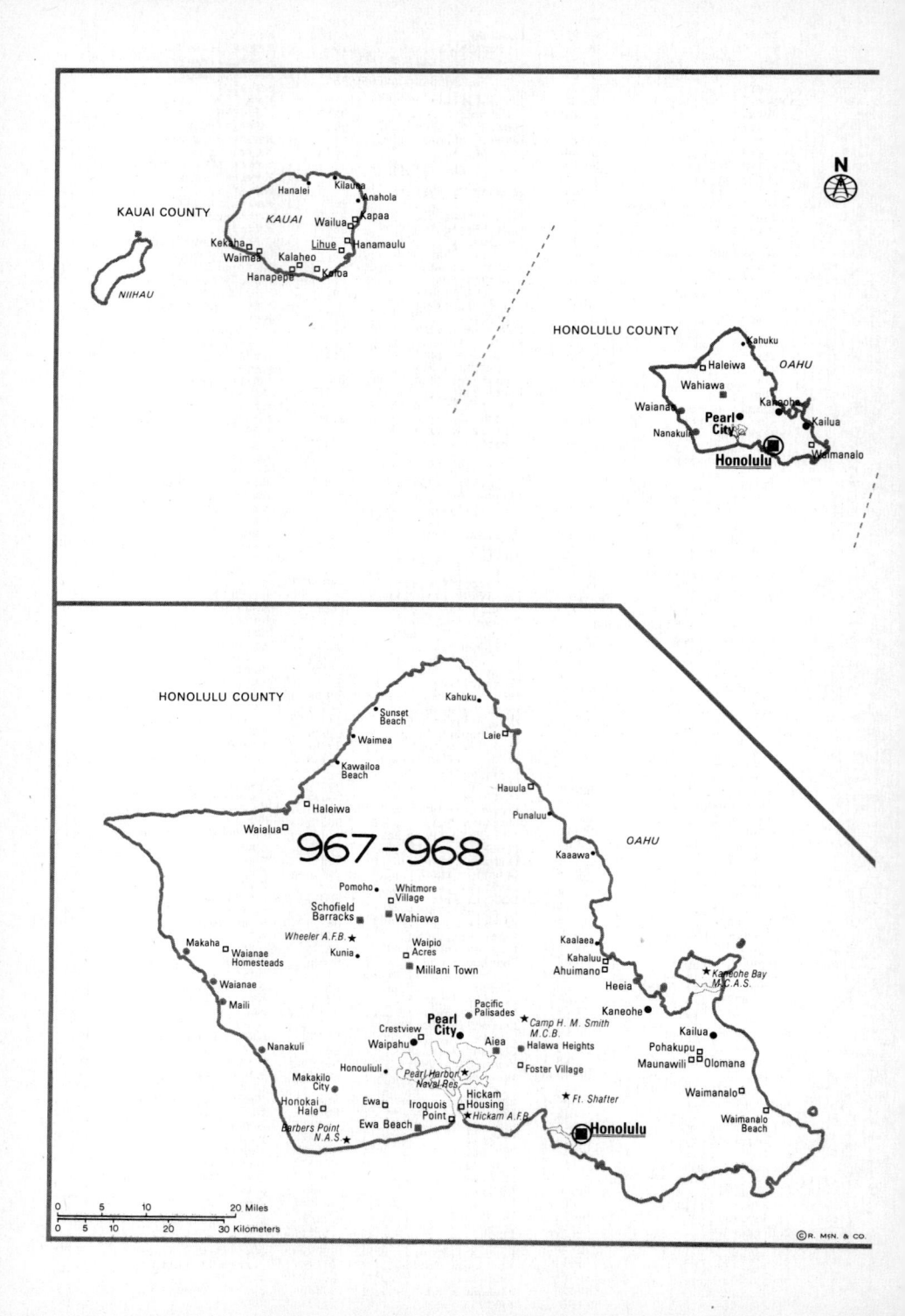

KAUAI COUNTY

- Hanalei
- Kilauea
- Anahola
- Kapaa
- Wailua
- Kekaha
- Lihue
- Hanamaulu
- Waimea
- Kalaheo
- Koloa
- Hanapepe

KAUAI

NIIHAU

HONOLULU COUNTY

- Kahuku
- Haleiwa
- Wahiawa
- Waianae
- Kaneohe
- Pearl City
- Kailua
- Nanakuli
- Honolulu
- Waimanalo

OAHU

967-968

HONOLULU COUNTY — OAHU

- Kahuku
- Sunset Beach
- Waimea
- Laie
- Kawailoa Beach
- Hauula
- Haleiwa
- Punaluu
- Waialua
- Kaaawa
- Pomoho
- Whitmore Village
- Schofield Barracks
- Wahiawa
- Makaha
- Wheeler A.F.B.
- Waipio Acres
- Kaalaea
- Waianae Homesteads
- Kunia
- Kahaluu
- Kaneohe Bay M.C.A.S.
- Mililani Town
- Ahuimano
- Waianae
- Heeia
- Maili
- Pacific Palisades
- Kaneohe
- Crestview
- Pearl City
- Camp H. M. Smith M.C.B.
- Nanakuli
- Waipahu
- Aiea
- Kailua
- Halawa Heights
- Pohakupu
- Makakilo City
- Honouliuli
- Foster Village
- Maunawili
- Olomana
- Honokai Hale
- Pearl Harbor Naval Res.
- Ewa
- Hickam Housing
- Ft. Shafter
- Waimanalo
- Barbers Point N.A.S.
- Iroquois Point
- Ewa Beach
- Hickam A.F.B.
- Honolulu
- Waimanalo Beach

0 5 10 20 Miles
0 5 10 20 30 Kilometers

©R. McN. & CO.

HAWAII 133

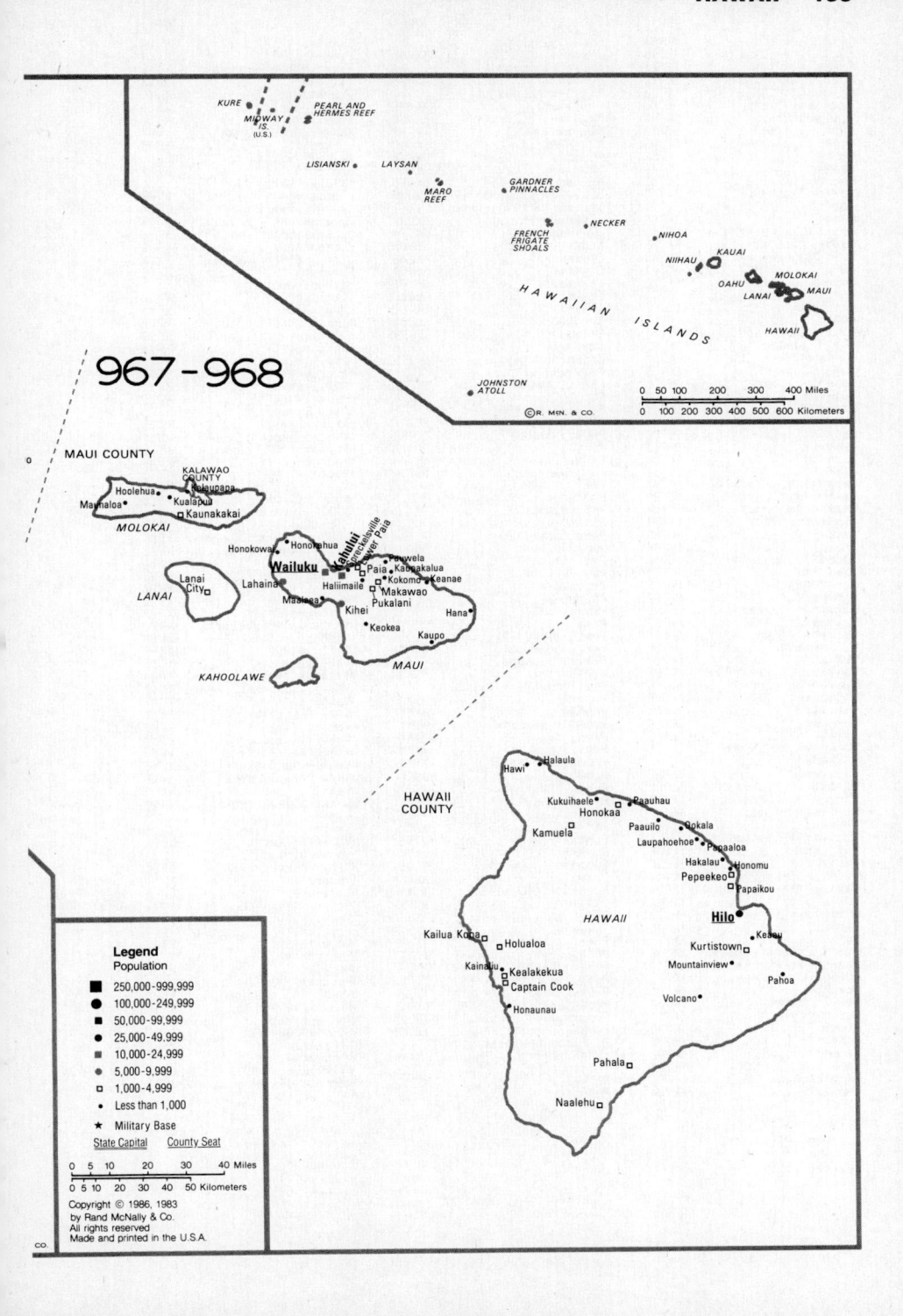

967-968

HAWAII Kilauea-Wood Valley Homesteads

	ZIP		ZIP		ZIP
Kilauea	96754	Naval Communication		Puunene	96784
Kilauea Military Camp	96718	Station	96786	Puunoa	96761
Kilauea Settlement	96785	Navy Cantonment (Part of		Puunui (Part of Honolulu)	96819
Kiolakaa Keaa Homesteads	96772	Honolulu)	96818	Puuohala	96793
Kipahulu	96713	Navy Terminal (Part of		Puu Waawaa	96740
Kipu (Kauai County)	96766	Honolulu)	96818	Puuwai	96769
Kipu (Maui County)	96757	Nawiliwili	96766	Renton Village	96706
Koali	96713	Newtown Estates	96782	Royal Hawaiian (Part of	
Koele	96763	Nine Miles	96749	Honolulu)	96815
Kokee	96752	Ninole	96773	St. Louis Heights (Part of	
Kokohahi	96744	Niulii	96755	Honolulu)	96822
Kokomo	96708	Niumalu	96766	Schofield Barracks	
Kolekole Beach Park	96710	Niu Valley (Part of Honolulu)	96816	(Honolulu County)	96786
Kolo	96704	Niu Valley Shopping Center		Spanish Village B	96784
Koloa	96756	(Part of Honolulu)	96821	Spreckelsville	96779
Kualapuu	96757	Niu Village	96774	Submarine Base	96818
Kualoa	96730	Numila	96705	Sunset Beach	96712
Kuhio Village	96743	Olinda	96768	Tantalus (Part of Honolulu)	96822
Kuhua	96761	Olomana	96734	Tenney	96706
Kukaiau	96776	Olowalu	96761	Timber Town (Part of	
Kukui	96771	Omao	96756	Honolulu)	96826
Kukuihaele	96727	Omapio	96790	Ualapue	96748
Kukuiula	96756	Onomea	96781	Ulumalu	96708
Kukui Village	96774	Ookala	96774	Ulupalakua	96790
Kula	96790	Opihikao	96778	Umikoa	96776
Kumukumu	96751	Orpheum Village	96779	Union Mill	96719
Kunia	96759	Paauhau	96775	University (Part of Honolulu)	96822
Kupolo	96766	Paauhau Mauka	96727	Upolu Point	96719
Kurtistown	96760	Paauilo	96776	Varona Village	96706
Lahaina	96761	Pacific Heights (Part of		Village Seven	96705
Lahaina Shopping Center	96761	Honolulu)	96817	Volcano	96785
Laie	96762	Pacific Palisades	96782	Wahiawa (Honolulu County)	96786
Lalakoa	96763	Pahala	96777	Wahiawa (Kauai County)	96705
Lanai City	96763	Pahoa	96778	Waiahole	96744
Lanikai	96734	Pahoehoe	96704	Waiaka	96743
Lanikai Heights	96734	Paia	96779	Waiakea	96720
Lau Hue Point	96720	Palama (Part of Honolulu)	96817	Waiakea Camps	96720
Laupahoehoe	96764	Palani Junction	96725	Waialae-Kahala (Part of	
Laupahoehoe Point	96764	Panaewa	96720	Honolulu)	96816
Lawai	96765	Papa (Hawaii County)	96704	Waialua (Honolulu County)	96791
Lihue	96766	Papaaloa	96780	Waialua (Maui County)	96748
Lihue Shopping Center	96766	Papaikou	96781	Waialua Mill	96791
Lower Paia	96779	Paukaa	96720	Waianae (Honolulu County)	96792
Lower Village	96706	Paukukalo	96793	Waianae Homesteads	96792
Lualualei	96792	Paumalu	96712	Waiau	96782
Lualualei Homesteads	96792	Pauwela	96708	Waiau View Estates	96782
Maalaea	96793	Peahi	96708	Waiawa Correctional Facility	96782
McGerrow Village	96786	Pearl City (Honolulu County)	96782	Waiehu	96793
McGrew Point	96701	Pearl City Heights	96782	Waiehu Village	96793
Maili	96792	Pearl Harbor Naval		Waihee	96793
Makaha	96792	Reservation	96818	Waikane	96744
Makakilo City	96706	Pearl Harbor Naval Supply		Waikapu	96793
Makapala	96755	Center	96818	Waikele	96797
Makawao	96768	Pepeekeo	96783	Waikiki (Part of Honolulu)	96815
Makaweli	96769	Pepeekeo Mill Camp	96783	Waikoloa Village	96743
Makena	96753	Pihana	96793	Wailea (Hawaii County)	96710
Makiki (Part of Honolulu)	96822	Piihonua	96720	Wailea (Maui County)	96753
Makiki Heights (Part of		Pohakea Homesteads	96776	Wailua (Kauai County)	96746
Honolulu)	96822	Pohakupu	96734	Wailua (Maui County)	96708
Mana	96752	Pohoiki	96778	Wailuku	96793
Market (Part of Honolulu)	96816	Poipu	96756	Wailupe (Part of Honolulu)	96821
Mark Twain Estates	96772	Pomoho	96786	Waimalu	96701
Maulua	96780	Port Allen	96705	Waimanalo	96795
Maunalani Heights (Part of		Portlock (Part of Honolulu)	96821	Waimanalo Beach	96795
Honolulu)	96816	Prince Kuhio Plaza	96720	Waimea (Honolulu County)	96712
Maunaloa	96770	Princeville	96722	Waimea (Kauai County)	96796
Maunalua (Part of Honolulu)	96816	Puako	96743	Wainaku	96720
Maunawili (Honolulu County)	96734	Pualaea Homestead	96764	Wainee	96761
Mikilua	96792	Pua Loke	96766	Wainiha	96714
Mililani Town	96789	Puhi	96766	Waiohinu	96772
Milolii	96726	Pukalani	96788	Waipahu	96797
Milo Village	96774	Pukoo	96748	Waipio	96727
Moanalua (Part of Honolulu)	96819	Pulehu	96790	Waipio Acres	96786
Moiliili (Part of Honolulu)	96814	Punaluu (Hawaii County)	96777	Waipouli	96746
Mokapu	96863	Punaluu (Honolulu County)	96717	Waipunalei Homesteads	96764
Mokuleia	96791	Puohala Village	96744	Wharf	96761
Momilani Estates	96782	Pupukea	96712	Wheeler Air Force Base	96854
Mountain View	96771	Puuanahulu	96725	Whitmore Village	96786
Muolea	96713	Puueo	96720	Wilhelmina Rise (Part of	
Naalehu	96772	Pu'uhonua o Honaunau		Honolulu)	96816
Nanakuli	96792	National Historical Park	96726	Woodlawn (Part of	
Napili	96761	Puu Hue	96719	Honolulu)	96816
Napili-Honokowai	96761	Puuiki	96713	Wood Valley Homesteads	96777
Napoopoo	96704	Puukolii	96761		

Aberdeen-Harvard IDAHO 135

Name	ZIP
Aberdeen	83210
Acequia	83350
Ahsahka	83520
Alameda (Part of Pocatello)	83201
Albion	83311
Aldape Heights (Part of Boise)	83701
Algoma	83860
Almo	83312
Alpha	83611
Alpine	83610
American Falls	83211
Ammon	83401
Anderson Dam	83647
Annis	83442
Antelope	83443
Apple Valley	83660
Arbon	83212
Archer	83440
Arco	83213
Argora	83423
Arimo	83214
Ashton	83420
Athol	83801
Atlanta	83601
Atomic City	83215
Avery	83802
Avon	83823
Baker	83467
Bancroft	83217
Banida	83263
Banks	83602
Bannock (Part of Pocatello)	83204
Basalt	83218
Basin	83346
Bates	83422
Bayview	83803
Beachs Corner	83401
Bear	83612
Bellevue	83313
Belmont	83801
Bench	83241
Benewah	83861
Bennington	83254
Berger	83301
Bern	83220
Big Creek	83677
Big Little Acres	83338
Big Springs (Part of Island Park)	83433
Black Cloud	83873
Blackfoot	83221
Black Lake	83861
Blackrock	83245
Blaine	83843
Blanchard	83804
Bliss	83314
Bloomington	83223
Boise	83701-13
For specific Boise Zip Codes call (208) 383-4211	
Boise Airport (Part of Boise)	83715
Boise Heights (Part of Boise)	83702
Boise Town Square (Part of Boise)	83701
Bone	83401
Bonners Ferry	83805
Borah (Part of Boise)	83702
Bovill	83806
Bowmont	83651
Box Canyon (Part of Island Park)	83429
Bradley (Part of Kellogg)	83837
Bridge	83342
Bruneau	83604
Bruneau Valley	83604
Buhl	83316
Buist	83243
Burgdorf	83638
Burke	83873
Burley	83318
Burmah	83349
Burton	83440
Butler Bay	83861
Butte City	83213
Cabinet	83811
Cache	83452
Calder	83808
Caldwell	83605-06
For specific Caldwell Zip Codes call (208) 459-7489	
Caldwell Labor Camp	83605
Cambridge (Bannock County)	83234
Cambridge (Washington County)	83610
Cameron	83537
Cape Horn	83821
Care-Free Estates	83318
Carey	83320

Name	ZIP
Careywood	83809
Carlin Bay	83833
Carmen	83462
Cascade	83611
Castleford	83321
Cataldo	83810
Cathedral Pines	83340
Cavendish	83537
Central	83217
Central Cove	83676
Challis	83226
Chatcolet	83851
Cherry Creek	83252
Cherry Lane (Part of Boise)	83705
Chester	83421
Chesterfield	83217
Chilco	83801
Chubbuck	83202
Churchill	83318
Clagstone	83856
Clark Fork	83811
Clarkia	83812
Clawson	83452
Clayton	83227
Clearwater	83539
Clementsville	83346
Cleveland	83263
Cliffs	97910
Clifton	83228
Clover	83316
Coats	83350
Cobalt	83229
Cocolalla	83813
Coeur d'Alene	83814
Coeur d'Alene Indian Reservation	83851
Colburn	83865
Cold House	83636
Cole Village (Part of Boise)	83704
Collister (Part of Boise)	83703
Coltman	83401
Columbus Park (Part of Boise)	83705
Conda	83230
Conkling Park	83876
Conner	83342
Coolin	83821
Corral	83322
Cotterel	83323
Cottonwood	83522
Council	83612
Country Club Mall (Part of Idaho Falls)	83401
Country Club Manor (Part of Boise)	83705
Country Club Terrace (Part of Boise)	83705
Craigmont	83523
Crescent	83537
Crouch	83602
Crystal	83672
Culdesac	83524
Cuprum	83612
Curry	83328
Dalton Gardens	83814
Daniels	83252
Darlington	83231
David Taylor Research Center, Acoustic Research Detachment	83803
Davis Acres (Part of Garden City)	83704
Dayton	83232
Deary	83823
Declo	83323
Deep Creek	83316
Delta	83873
Denton (Part of Boise)	83704
Denver	83530
Desmet	83824
Dietrich	83324
Dingle	83233
Dixie	83525
Doles	83605
Donnelly	83615
Dover	83825
Downey	83234
Driggs	83422
Drummond	83420
Dubois	83423
Duck Valley Indian Reservation	89832
Dudley	83810
Eagle (Ada County)	83616
Eagle (Shoshone County)	83874
Eagle Rock (Part of Idaho Falls)	83402
Easley Hot Springs	83340
East Hope	83836
East Kamiah	83539

Name	ZIP
East Lewiston (Part of Lewiston)	83501
Eastport	83826
Eaton	83672
Echo Beach	83858
Eddiville	83814
Eden	83325
Edmonds	83440
Egin	83445
Elba	83326
Elk City	83525
Elk River	83827
Ellis	83235
Elmira	83862
Emida	83861
Emmett	83617
Enaville	83839
Enkraft	83350
Enrose	83605
Excelsior Beach	83858
Fairfield	83327
Fairview (Franklin County)	83263
Fairview (Twin Falls County)	83316
Fall Creek (Elmore County)	83647
Fall Creek (Idaho County)	83530
Falls City	83338
Featherville	83647
Felt	83424
Fenn	83531
Ferdinand	83526
Fernan Lake Village	83814
Fernwood	83830
Filer	83328
Firth	83236
Fish Haven	83287
Fort Hall	83203
Fort Hall Indian Reservation	83203
Fox Creek	83455
Franklin (Ada County)	83704
Franklin (Franklin County)	83237
Franklin Park (Part of Boise)	83704
Fraser	83544
Freedom	83120
Fruitland	83619
Fruitvale	83620
Galena	83340
Gannett	83313
Gardena	83629
Garden City	83704
Garden Valley	83622
Garfield	83401
Garwood	83835
Gem	83873
Genesee	83832
Geneva	83238
Georgetown	83239
Gibbonsville	83463
Gibson	83221
Gibson City (Part of Pinehurst)	83850
Gifford	83541
Glendale	83263
Glengary	83864
Glenns Ferry	83623
Glenwood (Clearwater County)	83544
Glenwood (Idaho County)	83536
Golden	83530
Gooding	83330
Goodrich	83612
Goshen	83274
Grace	83241
Grand Teton Mall (Part of Idaho Falls)	83401
Grandview (Bingham County)	83210
Grand View (Owyhee County)	83624
Grangemont	83544
Grangeville	83530
Granite	83801
Grant	83401
Grasmere	83604
Gray	83285
Greencreek	83533
Greenleaf	83626
Greenwood	83335
Greer	83544
Gross	83657
Groveland	83221
Gwenford	83252
Hagerman	83332
Hailey	83333
Hamer	83425
Hamilton Corner	83655
Hammett	83627
Hampton	83857
Hansen	83334
Harpster	83539
Harrison	83833
Harvard	83834

IDAHO

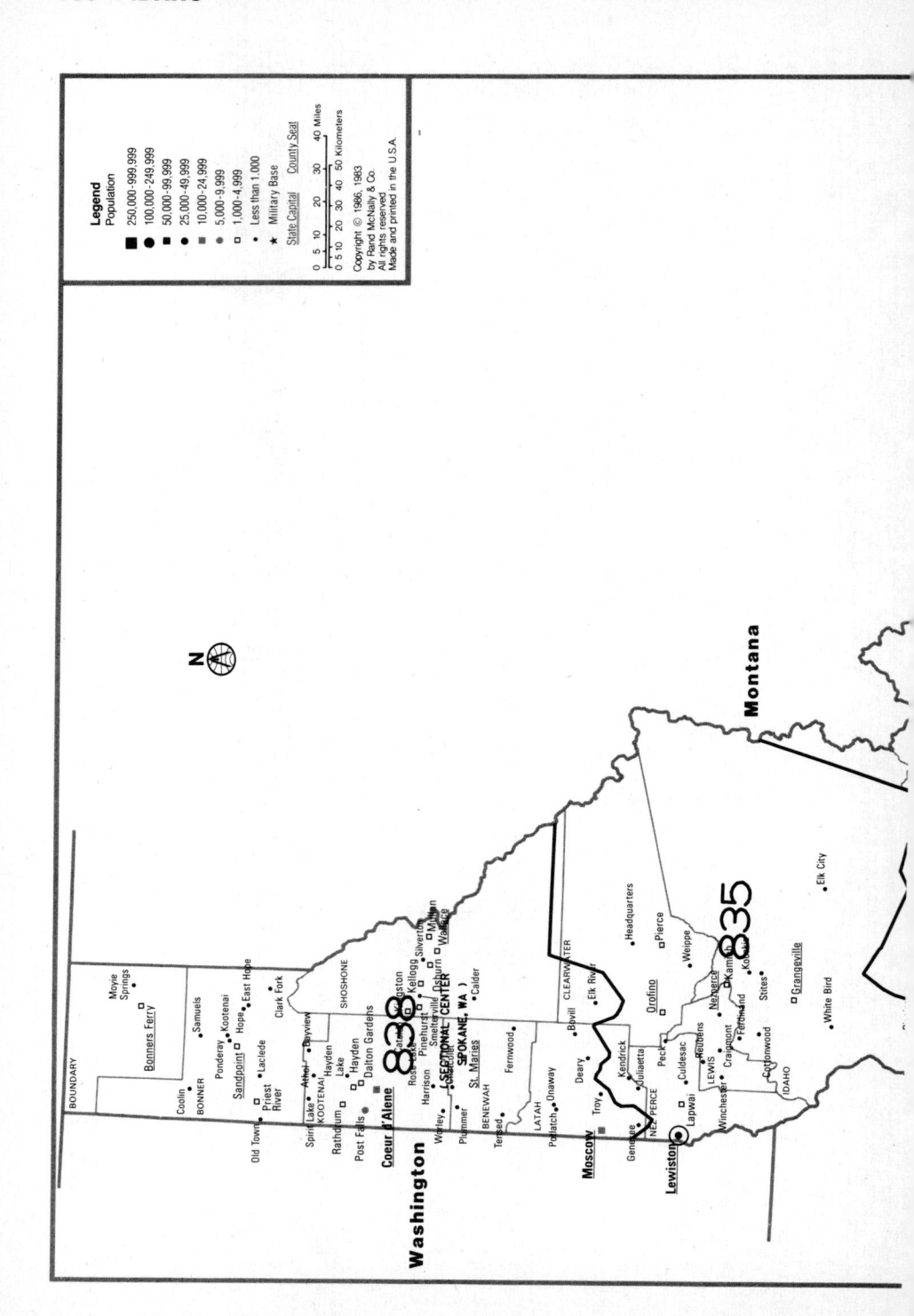

Legend
Population
- ■ 250,000-999,999
- ■ 100,000-249,999
- ■ 50,000-99,999
- ■ 25,000-49,999
- ● 10,000-24,999
- ● 5,000-9,999
- ○ 1,000-4,999
- · Less than 1,000
- ★ Military Base

State Capital County Seat

0 10 20 30 40 Miles
0 5 10 20 30 40 50 Kilometers

Copyright © 1966, 1983
by Rand McNally & Co.
All rights reserved
Made and printed in the U.S.A.

Washington

Montana

BOUNDARY
Moyie Springs
Bonners Ferry
Samuels
Coolin
Ponderay · Kootenai
Sandpoint · Hope · East Hope
Clark Fork
Laclede
BONNER
Priest River
Old Town
Bayview
Spirit Lake · Athol
Rathdrum
KOOTENAI · Hayden
Post Falls · Hayden Lake · Dalton Gardens
Coeur d'Alene
Rose... Kellogg Silverton
Worley Harrison Pinehurst Smelterville Osburn Wallace
Plummer SHOSHONE
SECTIONAL CENTER
(SPOKANE, WA)
St. Maries · Calder
BENEWAH
Fernwood
Tensed
Potlatch · Onaway
LATAH
Deary
Moscow Troy
Genesee Kendrick Juliaetta
Lewiston Lapwai Peck
NEZ PERCE Culdesac
Winchester LEWIS Reubens
Craigmont
Cottonwood Ferdinand
Nezperce Kamiah
Kooskia
Grangeville
White Bird
IDAHO
Stites
CLEARWATER
Bovill
Elk River
Headquarters
Pierce
Weippe
Orofino
Elk City

IDAHO 137

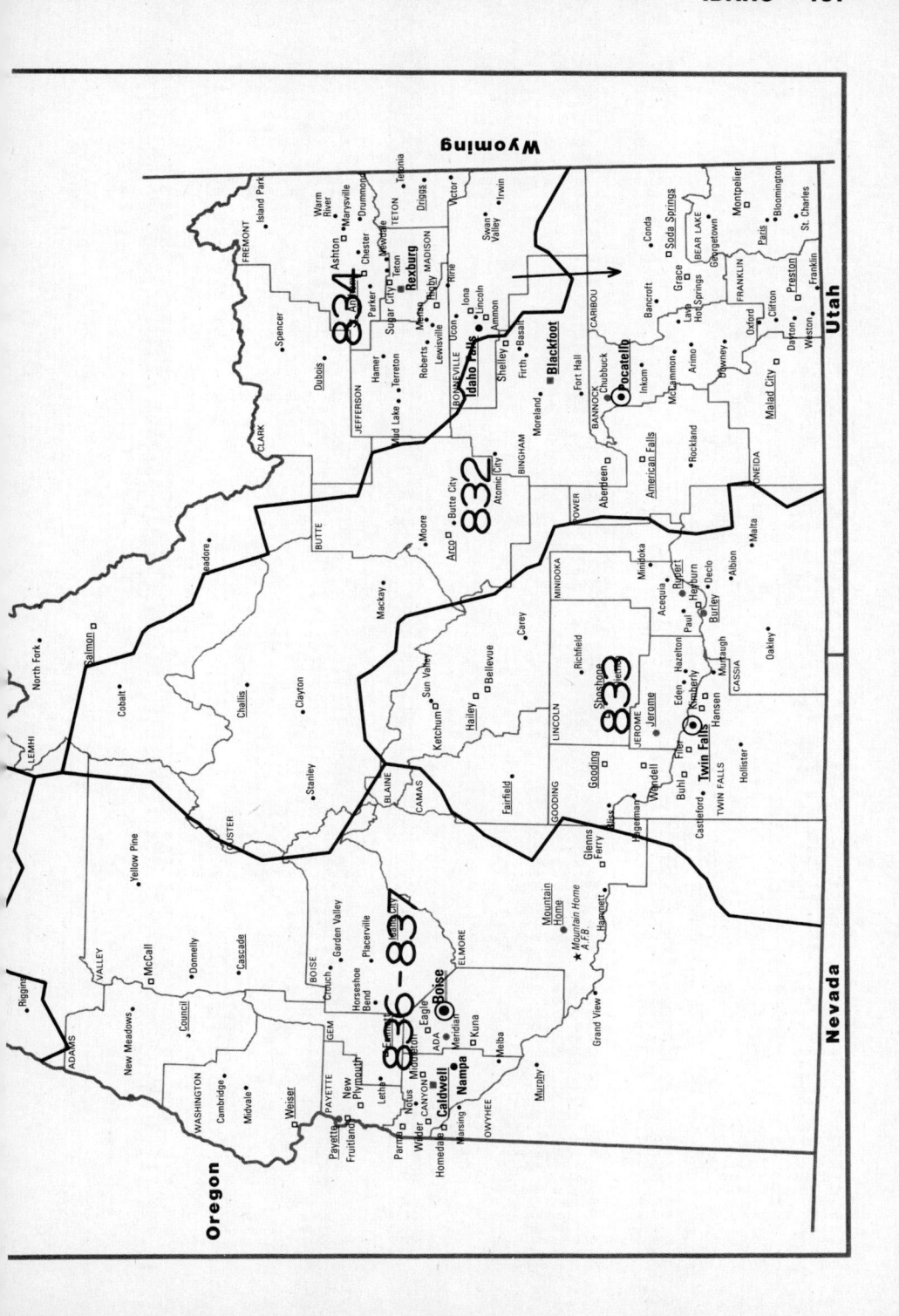

138 IDAHO Hatwai-Rockford

Name	ZIP
Hatwai	83501
Hauser	83854
Havens	83221
Hayden	83835
Hayden Lake	83835
Hazelton	83335
Headquarters	83534
Heglar	83211
Heise	83443
Helmer	83823
Heman	83445
Henry	83230
Hess Point	83821
Heyburn	83336
Hibbard	83440
Highlands (Part of Boise)	83702
Hill City	83337
Hillview (Part of Ammon)	83401
Holbrook	83243
Hollister	83301
Home Acres (Part of Boise)	83704
Homedale	83628
Honeysuckle Hills	83835
Hop (Part of Greenleaf)	83626
Hope	83836
Hornet	83612
Horseshoe Bend	83629
Hot Spring Landing	83313
Howe	83244
Huetter	83854
Hulen Meadows	83340
Humphrey	83446
Hunt	83325
Huston	83630
Hyland Park (Part of Pocatello)	83201
Idaho City	83631
Idaho Falls	83401-15
For specific Idaho Falls Zip Codes call (208) 523-3650	
Idahome	83323
Idman	83423
Indian Cove	83627
Indian Hills (Part of Pocatello)	83204
Indian Valley	83632
Inkom	83245
Iona	83427
Irwin	83428
Island Park	83429
Jackson	83350
Jacques	83524
Jamestown	83274
Jerome	83338
Joel	83843
Johnny Creek (Part of Pocatello)	83204
Jonathan	83672
Judge Town	83546
Juliaetta	83535
Juniper	84336
Kamiah	83536
Karcher Mall (Part of Nampa)	83651
Kellogg	83837
Kendrick	83537
Ketchum	83340
Keuterville	83538
Kidder	83539
Kilgore	83423
Kimball	83236
Kimberly	83341
King Hill	83633
Kingston	83839
Knowlton Heights	83605
Kooskia	83539
Kootenai	83840
Kuna	83634
Labelle	83442
Laclede	83841
Lake Creek	83876
Lake Fork	83635
Lakeview	83803
Lamont	83420
Lanark	83260
Lancaster Terrace (Part of Boise)	83702
Lane	83810
Lapwai	83540
Lardo (Part of McCall)	83638
Last Chance Resort (Part of Island Park)	83429
Lava Hot Springs	83246
Leadore	83464
Leland	83537
Lemhi	83465
Lenore	83541
Leslie	83255
Letha	83636
Lewiston	83501

Name	ZIP
Lewiston Orchards (Part of Lewiston)	83501
Lewisville	83431
Liberty	83260
Lidy Hot Springs	83423
Lincoln	83401
Linden	83537
Linrose	83286
Lone Pine	83464
Lookout	83541
Lorenzo	83442
Lost River (Butte County)	83255
Lost River (Custer County)	83231
Lowell	83539
Lower Stanley	83278
Lowman	83637
Lucile	83542
Lund	83217
Lyman	83440
McArthur	83847
McCall	83638
McCammon	83250
McGuires (Part of Post Falls)	83854
Mackay	83251
Macks Inn (Part of Island Park)	83433
Magic City	83313
Magic Resort	83352
Malad City	83252
Malta	83342
Mapleton	83263
Marion	83346
Marley (Part of Richfield)	83349
Marshcenter	83214
Marsing	83639
Marysville	83420
May	83253
Meadow Creek	83805
Meadows	83654
Meadowville	83276
Medimont	83842
Melba	83641
Menan	83434
Meridian	83642
Mesa	83643
Mica	83814
Midas	83864
Middleton	83644
Midvale	83645
Miller Creek Settlement	89832
Milltown	83861
Milo	83401
Minidoka	83343
Minkcreek	83263
Montana Junction (Part of Pocatello)	83201
Monteview	83435
Montour	83617
Montpelier	83254
Moore	83255
Mora	83634
Moravia	83805
Moreland	83256
Morgans Alley (Part of Lewiston)	83501
Moscow	83843
Mountain Home	83647
Mountain Home AFB (Elmore County)	83648
Mountain Home Air Force Base (Elmore County)	83648
Mountain View (Part of Boise)	83704
Mount Idaho	83530
Moyie Springs	83845
Mud Lake	83450
Mullan	83846
Murphy	83650
Murray	83874
Murtaugh	83344
Myrtle	83535
Naf	83342
Nampa	83651-53
	83686-87
For specific Nampa Zip Codes call (208) 466-8938	
Naples	83847
Naval Administration Unit, Idaho Falls	83401
Neeley	83211
New Centerville	83631
Newdale	83436
New Meadows	83654
New Plymouth	83655
New Sweden	83402
Nezperce	83543
Nez Perce Indian Reservation	83540
Niter	83241
Nordman	83848

Name	ZIP
Norland	83343
North Fork	83466
North Idaho Correctional Institution	83522
North Lewiston (Part of Lewiston)	83501
North Shoshone	83352
Northside (Ada County)	83702
Northside (Gem County)	83617
Notus	83656
Nounan	83254
Nuclear Power Training Unit, Idaho Falls	83401
Oakley	83346
Obsidian	83340
Ola	83657
Old Town	83822
Onaway	83855
Oreana	83650
Orofino	83544
Orogrande	83525
Osburn	83849
Osgood	83402
Outlet Bay	83856
Ovid	83260
Oxford	83263
Page	83868
Palisades	83437
Palouse Empire Mall (Part of Moscow)	83843
Paradise Hot Springs	83647
Paris	83261
Park	83823
Parker	83438
Parma	83660
Patterson	83253
Paul	83347
Payette	83661
Pearl	83616
Peck	83545
Pedee (Part of Chatcolet)	83851
Pegram	83254
Pella	83318
Peterson Corners	83553
Picabo	83348
Pierce	83546
Pine	83647
Pinehurst (Adams County)	83654
Pinehurst (Shoshone County)	83850
Pine Ridge	83612
Pine Ridge Mall (Part of Pocatello)	83201
Pingree	83262
Pinto Point	83821
Pioneerville	83631
Placerville	83666
Plano	83440
Pleasantview	83252
Plummer	83851
Pocatello	83201-06
For specific Pocatello Zip Codes call (208) 233-0800	
Polaris (Part of Osburn)	83849
Pollock	83547
Ponderay	83852
Ponds Resort (Part of Island Park)	83429
Porthill	83853
Post Falls	83854
Potlatch	83855
Potlatch Junction	83855
Prairie	83647
Preston	83263
Prichard	83873
Priest River	83856
Princeton	83857
Raft River	83211
Ramsdell (Part of Chatcolet)	83851
Rathdrum	83858
Raymond	83114
Redfish Lake	83278
Red River Hot Springs	83525
Reno	83423
Reubens	83548
Rexburg	83440
Reynolds	83650
Richfield	83349
Riddle	83604
Rigby	83442
Riggins	83549
Ririe	83443
Riverdale	83263
Riverside (Bingham County)	83221
Riverside (Canyon County)	83605
Riverside (Clearwater County)	83544
Roberts	83444
Robin	83214
Rock Creek	83334
Rockford	83221

Rockford Bay-Yellow Pine **IDAHO 139**

	ZIP		ZIP		ZIP
Rockford Bay	83814	Southside (Part of Boise)	83706	Twin Falls	83301-03
Rockland	83271	Southwick	83537	For specific Twin Falls Zip Codes call (208) 733-4380	
Rocky Bar	83647	Spalding	83551		
Rocky Point (Benewah County)	83851	Spencer	83446	Twin Groves	83445
		Spirit Lake	83869	Twin Lakes	83858
Rocky Point (Bonner County)	83821	Springdale	83318	Twinlow	83858
		Springfield	83277	Tyhee	83201
Rogerson	83302	Squirrel	83447	Ucon	83454
Rose	83221	Standrod	83342	Unity	83318
Roseberry	83615	Stanley	83278	University (Part of Moscow)	83843
Rose Lake	83810	Star	83669	Ustick (Part of Boise)	83702
Roseworth	83321	Starrhs Ferry	83318	Valley View Heights (Part of Lewiston)	83501
Roswell	83660	State Line	83854		
Roy	83271	Sterling	83210	Victor	83455
Rupert	83350	Stites	83552	View	83318
Sagle	83860	Stoddard	83641	Viola	83872
St. Anthony	83445	Stone	83280	Virginia	83234
St. Charles	83272	Sugar City	83448	Waha	83501
St. Joe	83861	Sunbeam	83278	Wallace	83873
St. John	83252	Sunnydell	83440	Wapello	83221
St. Leon	83401	Sunnyside (Bonner County)	83864	Wardboro	83254
St. Maries	83861	Sunnyside (Shoshone County)	83837	Wardner	83837
Salem	83440			Warm Lake	83611
Salmon	83467	Sunnyslope	83605	Warm River	83420
Samaria	83252	Sun Valley	83353-54	Warren	83671
Samuels	83862	For specific Sun Valley Zip Codes call (208) 622-5265		Washoe	83661
Sanders	83870			Wayan	83285
Sandpoint	83862-65	Swanlake	83281	Webb	83540
For specific Sandpoint Zip Codes call (208) 263-2716		Swan Valley	83449	Weippe	83553
		Sweet	83670	Weiser	83672
Santa	83866	Sweetwater	83540	Weitz	83605
Selle	83864	Syringa	83539	Wendell	83355
Sharon	83260	Taber	83281	Westgate Acres (Part of Boise)	83704
Shelley	83274	Talache	83860		
Shelton	83401	Tamarack	83612	Westlake	83526
Sherwood Beach	83821	Taylor	83401	Westmond	83860
Shoshone	83352	Teakean	83537	Westmoreland (Part of Boise)	83704
Shoup	83469	Tendoy	83468		
Silver City	83650	Tenmile	83642	West Mountain	83611
Silver Creek Plunge	83602	Tensed	83870	Weston	83286
Silver Sands Beach	83858	Terreton	83450	White Bird	83554
Silverton	83867	Teton	83451	Whitney (Ada County)	83705
Skyline (Part of Idaho Falls)	83401	Tetonia	83452	Whitney (Franklin County)	83263
Slate Creek	83554	Thatcher	83283	Wilder	83676
Slickpoo	83524	Thomas	83221	Wilford	83445
Small	83423	Thomas Junction	83221	Winchester	83555
Smelter Heights (Part of Kellogg)	83837	Thornton	83440	Winder	83263
		Three Creek	83302	Wolf Lodge	83814
Smelterville	83868	Topaz	83246	Wolverine	83236
Smiths Ferry	83602	Transfer (Part of Lewiston)	83501	Woodland	83536
Soda Springs	83276	Treasureton	83263	Woodland Park	83873
Soldiers Home (Part of Boise)	83704	Trestle Creek	83836	Woodruff	83252
		Triumph	83333	Woodville	83274
South Boise (Part of Boise)	83706	Troy	83871	Worley	83876
South Gate Plaza (Part of Lewiston)	83501	Turner Bay	83833	Yellow Pine	83677
		Tuttle	83314		
South Park (Part of Pocatello)	83201				

ILLINOIS

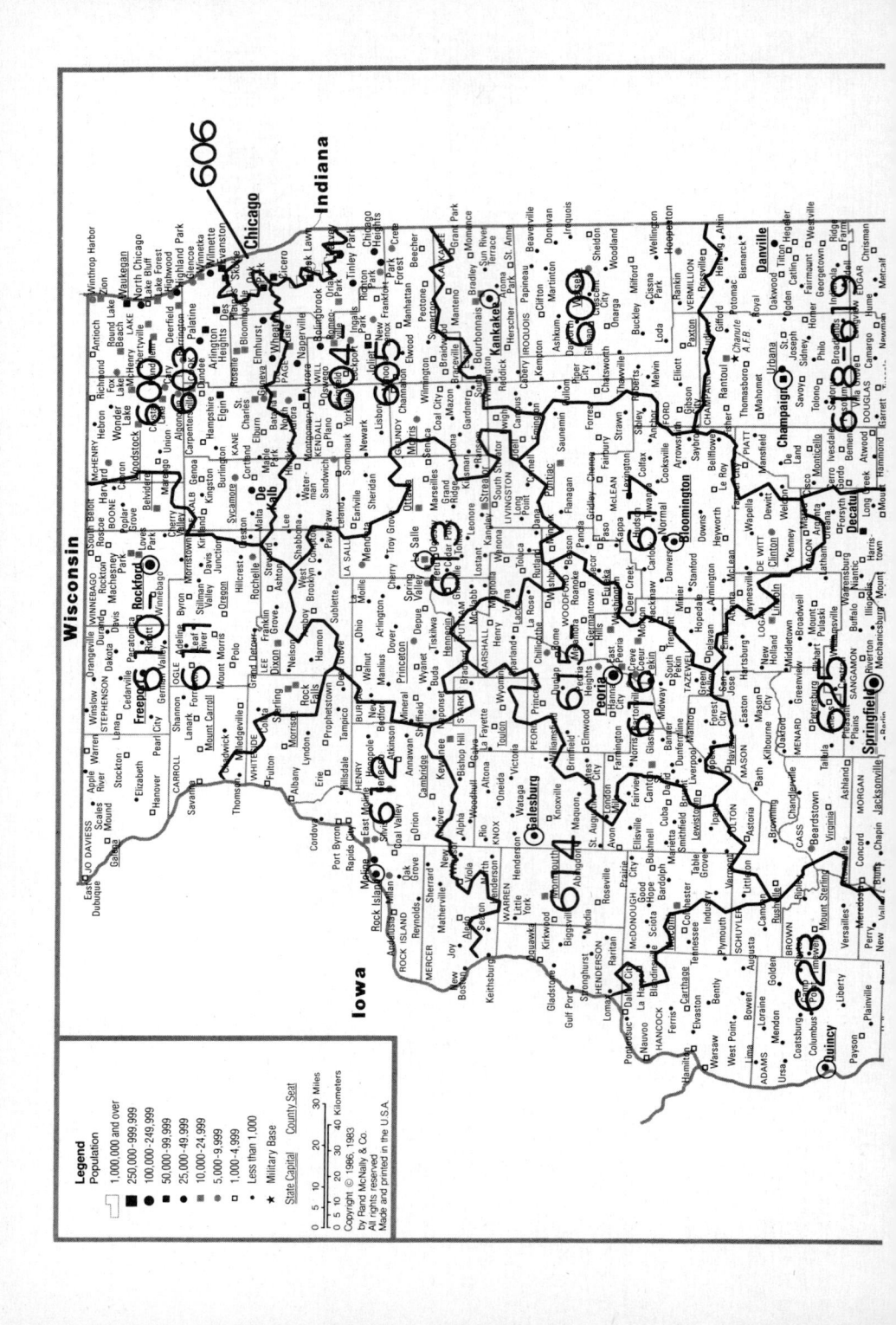

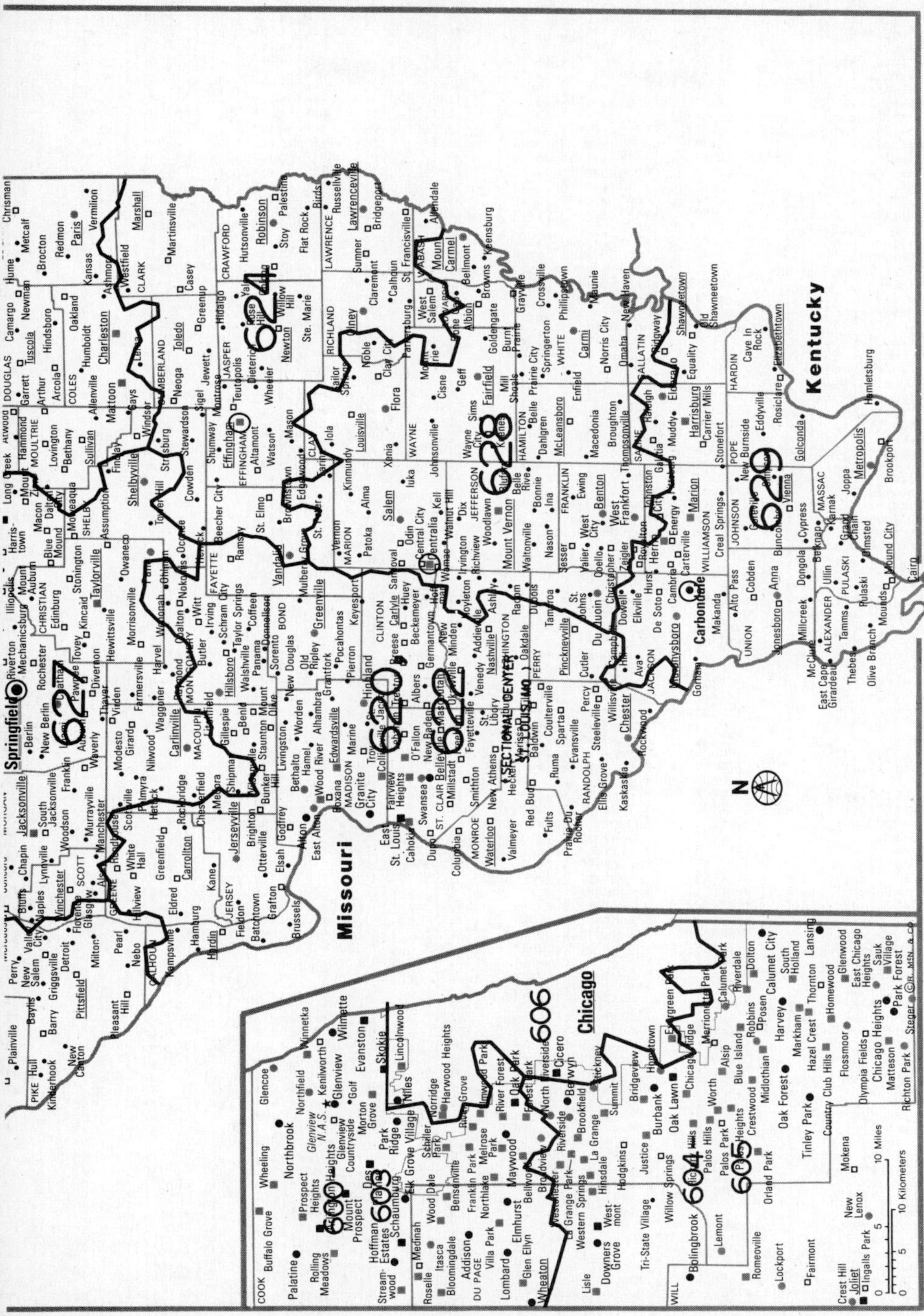
Missouri
Kentucky
Chicago
Springfield
Carbondale
N
10 Miles
10 Kilometers
©R. MCN. & CO.

142 ILLINOIS Abingdon-Batchtown

Name	ZIP
Abingdon	61410
Abington (Township)	61476
Acacia Acres	60525
Acme Station (Part of Bartonville)	61607
Adair	61411
Adams (Adams County)	62347
Adams (La Salle County) (Township)	60531
Adams Corner	62410
Addieville	62214
Addison (Township)	60101
Addison	60101
Adeline	61047
Aden	62895
Adrian	62310
Aero Estates	60564
Aetna (Coles County)	61938
Aetna (Logan County) (Township)	61749
Afolkey	61018
Afton (Township)	60115
Agnew	61081
Airport	61074
Airport Heights	61607
Akin	62805
Akron (Township)	61559
Alan Dale	62035
Alba (Township)	61235
Albany	61230
Albany (Township)	61230
Albers	62215
Albion	62806
Alden	60001
Alden (Township)	60001
Aldridge	62998
Aledo	61231
Alexander	62601
Alexis	61412
Algonquin	60102
Algonquin (Township)	60102
Algonquin Shores	60102
Algonquin Trails (Part of Mount Prospect)	60056
Alhambra	62001
Alhambra (Township)	62001
Allen (La Salle County) (Township)	60470
Allen (Mason County)	62682
Allen (Whiteside County)	61071
Allendale	62410
Allen Grove (Township)	62682
Allens Corners	60140
Allentown	61568
Allenville	61951
Alierton	61810
Allin (Township)	61774
Allison (Township)	62439
Alma	62807
Alma (Township)	62807
Almora	60123
Almora Heights	60123
Alorton	62207
Alpha	61413
Alsey	62610
Alsip	60658
Alsip Woods (Part of Alsip)	60658
Alta	61614
Altamont (Effingham County)	62411
Altamont (Madison County)	62035
Alto (Township)	60553
Alton (Madison County) (Township)	62002
Alton (Madison County)	62002
Altona	61414
Alton Square (Part of Alton)	62002
Alto Pass	62905
Altorf	60914
Alvin	61811
Alworth	61088
Amboy	61310
Amboy (Township)	61310
Amenia	61856
America	62996
Americana Village (Part of Glendale Heights)	60139
Ames	62277
Amity (Township)	61319
Anchor	61720
Anchor (Township)	61720
Anchorage (Part of Glenview)	60026
Ancient Tree (Part of Northbrook)	60062
Ancona	61311
Andalusia	61232
Andalusia (Township)	61232
Anderman Acres	60544
Anderson (Township)	62441
Anderson Lake	61501

Name	ZIP
Andover	61233
Andover (Township)	61233
Andres	60468
Andrew	62707
Anna	62906
Anna Mental Health and Developmental Center	62906
Annapolis	62413
Annawan	61234
Annawan (Township)	61234
Antioch	60002
Antioch (Township)	60002
Appanoose (Township)	62354
Apple Canyon Lake	61001
Applegate (Part of Schaumburg)	60194
Apple River	61001
Apple River (Township)	61001
Appleton	61428
Appletree (Part of Country Club Hills)	60477
Apple Valley (Part of Glenview)	60025
Appoaloosa West	60119
Aptakisic	60069
Arboretum East	60137
Arboretum Villages (Part of Lisle)	60532
Arboretum West	60137
Arbor Trails (Part of Park Forest)	60466
Arbury Hills	60448
Arcadia	62650
Archer	62707
Archie	61876
Arcola	61910
Arcola (Township)	61910
Arenzville	62611
Arenzville (Township)	62611
Argenta	62501
Argo (Part of Summit)	60501
Argo Fay	61053
Argyle	61011
Arispie (Township)	61368
Arlington	61312
Arlington Heights	60004-07
For specific Arlington Heights Zip Codes call (708) 253-7456	
Arlington Ridge (Part of Arlington Heights)	60004
Armington	61721
Armstrong	61812
Arnold	62650
Aroma (Township)	60901
Aroma Park	60910
Aroma Park Northwest	60901
Arrington (Township)	62886
Arrowhead (Du Page County)	60187
Arrowhead (Kankakee County)	60914
Arrowhead (McDonough County)	61455
Arrowhead Hills	60543
Arrowsmith (Township)	61772
Arrowsmith	61722
Arrow Wood	62035
Artesia (Township)	60918
Arthur	61911
Asbury (Township)	62871
Ashburn (Part of Chicago)	60652
Ash Grove (Iroquois County) (Township)	60953
Ash Grove (Shelby County) (Township)	61957
Ashkum	60911
Ashkum (Township)	60911
Ashland	62612
Ashland (Township)	62612
Ashley	62808
Ashley (Township)	62808
Ashmore	61912
Ashmore (Township)	61912
Ashton	61006
Ashton (Township)	61006
Assumption	62510
Assumption (Township)	62510
Astoria	61501
Astoria (Township)	61501
Athens	62613
Athensville	62082
Athensville (Township)	62082
Atkinson	61235
Atkinson (Township)	61235
Atlanta	61723
Atlanta (Township)	61723
Atlas	62370
Atlas (Township)	62370
Atlee Ogles	62223
Atrium (Part of Elmhurst)	60126
Atterbury	62675

Name	ZIP
Attila	62974
Atwater	62511
Atwood	61913
Atwood Heights (Part of Alsip)	60658
Auburn (Township)	62615
Auburn (Clark County) (Township)	62441
Auburn (Sangamon County)	62615
Auburn Park (Part of Chicago)	60620
Auburn Woods (Part of Palatine)	60067
Audubon (Township)	62075
Augsburg	62885
Augusta	62311
Augusta (Township)	62311
Aurora	60504-07
For specific Aurora Zip Codes call (708) 897-2221	
Aurora (Township)	60505
Austin (Cook County)	60644
Austin (Macon County) (Township)	62573
Austin View	60463
Aux Sable (Township)	60447
Ava	62907
Avalon Park (Part of Chicago)	60619
Avena	62458
Avena (Township)	62458
Avery Hill	62223
Aviston	62216
Avoca (Township)	61739
Avon (Fulton County)	61415
Avon (Lake County) (Township)	60030
Avondale (Part of Chicago)	60641
Ayers (Township)	61816
Babcock	61244
Babson (Part of St. Charles)	60174
Babylon	61415
Baden Baden (Part of Pierron)	62273
Bader	62624
Baileyville	61007
Bainbridge (Township)	62639
Baker	60531
Baker Lake	60010
Bakerville	62864
Balcom	62906
Bald Bluff (Township)	61476
Bald Hill (Township)	62883
Baldwin	62217
Baldwin Beach	62644
Bales Lake	60948
Ball (Township)	62629
Ballou	60481
Banner (Township)	61520
Banner (Effingham County) (Township)	62461
Banner (Fulton County)	61520
Bannister	62881
Bannockburn	60015
Barclay	62561
Bardolph	61416
Bargerville	62960
Barnett (De Witt County) (Township)	61727
Barnett (Montgomery County)	62056
Barnhill	62809
Barnhill (Township)	62809
Barr (Macoupin County) (Township)	62674
Barr (Sangamon County)	62613
Barren (Township)	62812
Barrington	60010-11
For specific Barrington Zip Codes call (708) 381-0514	
Barrington Center (Part of Barrington Hills)	60010
Barrington Highlands	60010
Barrington Hills	60010
Barrington Square (Part of Hoffman Estates)	60195
Barrington Woods	60074
Barrow	62082
Barry	62312
Barry (Township)	62312
Barstow	61236
Bartelso	62218
Bartlett	60103
Bartonville	61607
Basco	62313
Base (Part of Rantoul)	61866
Batavia	60510
Batavia (Township)	60510
Batavia Highlands (Part of Batavia)	60510
Batchtown	62006

Bates-Bradley ILLINOIS 143

Name	ZIP
Bates	62670
Batestown	61832
Bath	62617
Bath (Township)	62617
Bay City	62938
Bayle	62080
Baylestown	62033
Baylis	62314
Bay View Gardens	61611
Beach Park	60085
Beacon Hill (Part of Chicago Heights)	60411
Bear Creek (Christian County) (Township)	62556
Bear Creek (Hancock County) (Township)	62313
Beardstown	62618
Beardstown (Township)	62618
Bear Grove (Township)	62471
Bearsdale	62526
Beason	62512
Beau Bien (Part of Lisle)	60532
Beaucoup	62263
Beaucoup (Township)	62263
Beaver (Township)	60931
Beaver Creek (Bond County)	62246
Beaver Creek (Hamilton County) (Township)	62887
Beaver Valley (Boone County)	61008
Beaver Valley (Cook County)	60462
Beaverville	60912
Beaverville (Township)	60912
Beckemeyer	62219
Bedford (Pike County)	62361
Bedford (Wayne County) (Township)	62823
Bedford Park	60638
Beecher	60401
Beecher City	62414
Beechville	62006
Beecreek	62361
Beh Lake Estates	61038
Bel Air Gardens (Part of Glenview)	60025
Belgium	61883
Belgium Row	61858
Belknap	62908
Bellair	62449
Belle Prairie (Township)	61731
Belle Prairie City	62828
Belle Rive	62810
Belleview	62045
Belleville	62220-25
For specific Belleville Zip Codes call (618) 233-0391	
Belleville (Township)	62221
Bellevue	61604
Bellflower	61724
Bellflower (Township)	61724
Bellmont	62811
Bell Plain (Township)	61541
Bell Ridge	61944
Belltown	62092
Bellwood Lane (Part of Glenview)	60025
Bellwood	60104
Bel-Mar Estates	61008
Belmont (Township)	60970
Belmont Acres	60970
Belmont Road (Part of Downers Grove)	60515
Belmont Village	62035
Beltrees	62022
Belvidere	61008
Belvidere (Township)	61008
Belvidere Mall (Part of Waukegan)	60085
Bement	61813
Bement (Township)	61813
Benedale Green (Part of Lisle)	60532
Benevolent Heights	62220
Benld	62009
Bennington (Edwards County)	62476
Bennington (Marshall County) (Township)	61369
Bensenville	60106
Benson	61516
Bentley	62321
Benton	62812
Benton (Franklin County) (Township)	62812
Benton (Lake County) (Township)	60096
Benton City Park	62812
Ben Town	61701

Name	ZIP
Bent Tree Village (Part of Elgin)	60120
Benwick (Part of Schaumburg)	60194
Berdan	62016
Bergen	53525
Berger (Part of Dolton)	60419
Berkeley	60163
Berkland Heights	61341
Berlin (Bureau County) (Township)	61312
Berlin (Sangamon County)	62670
Bernadotte	61441
Bernadotte (Township)	61441
Bernice (Part of Lansing)	60438
Berreman (Township)	61053
Berry (Sangamon County)	62563
Berry (Wayne County) (Township)	62850
Berryville (Richland County)	62419
Berryville (Union County)	62952
Bertinetti Lake	62568
Berwick	61417
Berwick (Township)	61417
Berwyn (Cook County) (Township)	60402
Berwyn (Cook County)	60402
Bethalto	62010
Bethany	61914
Bethel (McDonough County) (Township)	61415
Bethel (Morgan County)	62628
Bethel (Vermilion County)	61870
Bethlehem	62411
Beulah Heights (Part of Eldorado)	62930
Be-Ver Kreek	61008
Beverly	62312
Beverly (Township)	62312
Beverly Hills (Part of Chicago)	60642
Beverly Manor (Part of Washington)	61571
Beyers Lake Addition	62557
Bible Grove	62858
Bible Grove (Township)	62858
Biddleborn	62257
Big Bay	62960
Big Foot	60033
Big Grove (Township)	60541
Biggs	62633
Biggsville	61418
Biggsville (Township)	61418
Big Hollow	60041
Big Mound (Township)	62837
Bigneck	62349
Big Rock	60511
Big Rock (Township)	60511
Big Spring (Township)	62447
Billett	62439
Bingham	62011
Binghampton	61310
Binney	62074
Bird (Township)	62630
Birds	62415
Birkbeck	61727
Birmingham	62367
Birmingham (Township)	62367
Bishop (Effingham County) (Township)	62424
Bishop (Mason County)	61532
Bishop Hill	61419
Bishop Quarter Lane (Part of Oak Park)	60301
Bismarck	61814
Bissell	62707
Black	62806
Blackberry (Township)	60119
Blackberry Heights	60538
Blackberry Woods	60554
Blackhawk (Township)	61264
Blackhawk Heights (Part of Clarendon Hills)	60514
Blackhawk Island	61125
Black Hawk Springs	60545
Blackstone	61313
Blaine	61065
Blair (Clay County) (Township)	62858
Blair (Livingston County)	60961
Blair (Randolph County)	62286
Blairsville (Hamilton County)	62859
Blairsville (Williamson County)	62918
Blandinsville	61420
Blandinsville (Township)	61420
Blissville (Township)	62894
Block	61877
Blodgett (Part of Highland Park)	60035
Bloom (Township)	60411

Name	ZIP
Bloomfield (Adams County)	62338
Bloomfield (Edgar County)	61924
Bloomfield (Johnson County)	62995
Bloomingdale	60108
Bloomingdale (Township)	60108
Bloomington	61701-04
For specific Bloomington Zip Codes call (309) 663-8484	
Bloomington City (Township)	61701
Bloomington Heights	61701
Blossom Hill (Part of Cary)	60013
Blount (Township)	61832
Blue Fountain	62035
Blue Island	60406
Blue Island Junction (Part of Chicago)	60617
Blue Island Junction (Part of Blue Island)	60406
Blue Mound (Macon County)	62513
Blue Mound (Macon County) (Township)	62514
Blue Mound (McLean County) (Township)	61730
Blue Point	62401
Blue Ridge	61854
Blue Ridge (Township)	61854
Bluff City (Fayette County)	62471
Bluff City (Schuyler County)	62624
Bluffdale (Greene County) (Township)	62027
Bluffdale (Henderson County)	61437
Bluff Hall	62360
Bluffs	62621
Bluffside	62236
Bluff Springs	62622
Bluff Springs (Township)	62622
Bluff View Park (Part of Caseyville)	62232
Bluford	62814
Blyton	61477
Boaz	62956
Boden	61281
Bogan's (Part of Effingham)	62401
Bogota	62448
Bohleysville	62260
Bois d'Arc (Township)	62533
Boles	62909
Bolingbrook	60439
Boling Green (Part of Bolingbrook)	60439
Bolivia	62545
Bolo (Township)	62808
Bolton	61032
Bond (Township)	62439
Bondville	61815
Bone Gap	62815
Bonfield	60913
Bongard	61864
Bonnie	62816
Bonnie Brea	60441
Bonpas (Township)	62419
Bonus (Township)	61038
Boody	62514
Boone (Township)	61012
Boos	62448
Booster Station	62269
Borton	61917
Boskydell	62901
Boulder	62283
Boulder Hill	60538
Boulevard Manor (Part of Cicero)	60650
Bourbon	61953
Bourbon (Township)	61953
Bourbonnais	60914
Bourbonnais (Township)	60914
Bowdre (Township)	61910
Bowen	62316
Bowes	60123
Bowlesville (Township)	62984
Bowling (Township)	61264
Bowling Green (Township)	62422
Boyd	62830
Boyleston	62837
Boynton (Township)	61734
Braceville	60407
Braceville (Township)	60407
Bradbury	62468
Bradford (Lee County) (Township)	61006
Bradford (Stark County)	61421
Bradfordton	62707
Bradley (Grundy County)	60450
Bradley (Jackson County) (Township)	62907
Bradley (Kankakee County)	60915

144 ILLINOIS Braeside-Carmi

Place	ZIP
Braeside (Part of Highland Park)	60035
Braidwood	60408
Brainerd (Part of Chicago)	60620
Branding	62013
Brandywine	60181
Branigar Estates	60007
Breckenridge	62563
Breeds	61520
Breese	62230
Breese (Township)	62230
Bremen (Cook County) (Township)	60426
Bremen (Randolph County)	62233
Brementowne Mall (Part of Tinley Park)	60477
Brenton (Township)	60959
Brentwood (Part of Des Plaines)	60016
Brentwood Estates	60074
Brereton	61520
Brettwood (Part of Decatur)	62526
Briar Bluff	61240
Briarbrook Village (Part of Wheaton)	60187
Briarcliffe (Part of Wheaton)	60187
Briarcliffe Knolls (Part of Wheaton)	60187
Briarcliff Estates (Part of Bourbonnais)	60914
Briarwick	61938
Briarwood	61107
Briarwoods Estates (Part of Deerfield)	60015
Briarwood Trace	62901
Brickman Manor (Part of Mount Prospect)	60056
Brickyard, The (Part of Chicago)	60634
Bridgelane	61265
Bridgeport	62417
Bridgeport (Township)	62417
Bridgeview	60455
Bridgeway Addition (Part of Moline)	61265
Bridle Creek Estates	60175
Brierwood	60175
Bright Oaks (Part of Cary)	60013
Brighton	62012
Brighton (Township)	62012
Brighton Park (Part of Chicago)	60632
Brimfield	61517
Brimfield (Township)	61517
Brisbane	60451
Bristol	60512
Bristol (Township)	60512
Bristol Lake	60560
Bristol Ridge	60560
Broadlands	61816
Broadmoor	61421
Broadview	60153
Broadway (Part of Rockford)	61106
Broadwell	62634
Broadwell (Township)	62634
Brocton	61917
Brooke Estates (Part of Highland Park)	60035
Brookeridge	60515
Brookfield (Cook County)	60513
Brookfield (La Salle County) (Township)	60470
Brook Forest (Part of Oak Brook)	60521
Brookforest North	60435
Brookhaven	61277
Brookhaven Manor (Part of Darien)	60559
Brookhill	60048
Brooklyn (Township)	62367
Brooklyn (Lee County) (Township)	61318
Brooklyn (Schuyler County)	62367
Brookport	62910
Brooks	62040
Brookside (Clinton County) (Township)	62801
Brookside (Kane County)	60175
Brooks Isle	61061
Brookview	61614
Brookville	61064
Brookville (Township)	61064
Brookwood (Cook County)	60008
Brookwood (Cook County)	60070
Brookwood (Kane County)	60174
Brookwood Estates (Part of Wood Dale)	60191
Brothers	61858
Broughton (Hamilton County)	62817
Broughton (Livingston County) (Township)	60934
Brouillets Creek (Township)	61924
Brown (Township)	61845
Brownfield	62911
Browning (Township)	62624
Browning (Franklin County) (Township)	62812
Browning (Schuyler County)	62624
Browns	62818
Brownstown	62418
Brownsville	62821
Brownwood	61747
Brubaker	62807
Bruce (La Salle County) (Township)	61364
Bruce (Moultrie County)	61951
Brunning	60441
Brunswick	62534
Brushy (Township)	62935
Brushy Mound (Township)	62033
Brussels	62013
Bryant	61519
Bryce	60953
Bryn Mawr (Part of Chicago)	60649
Buck (Township)	61944
Buckeye (Township)	61013
Buckhart (Christian County) (Township)	62531
Buckhart (Sangamon County)	62545
Buckheart (Township)	61563
Buckhorn (Brown County)	62353
Buckhorn (Brown County) (Township)	62375
Buckingham	60917
Buckley	60918
Buckner	62819
Bucks	61745
Buda	61314
Budd	61313
Buena Vista (Saline County)	62946
Buena Vista (Schuyler County) (Township)	62681
Buena Vista (Stephenson County)	61032
Buffalo (Ogle County) (Township)	61064
Buffalo (Sangamon County)	62515
Buffalo Grove (Cook County)	60089
Buffalo Grove (Ogle County)	61064
Buffalo Hart	62515
Buffalo Hart (Township)	62515
Buffalo Prairie	61237
Buffalo Prairie (Township)	61237
Bull Creek	60048
Bullock Addition	61241
Bull Valley	60098
Bulpitt	62517
Buncombe	62912
Bungay	62887
Bunker Hill	62014
Bunker Hill (Township)	62014
Bunkum (Part of Fairview Heights)	62208
Bunsenville	61846
Burbank	60459
Burches	60914
Bureau (Bureau County)	61315
Bureau (Bureau County) (Township)	61379
Burgess (Bond County) (Township)	62275
Burgess (Mercer County)	61231
Burksville (Monroe County)	62298
Burlington	60109
Burlington (Township)	60109
Burnham	60633
Burnham Mill (Part of Elgin)	60123
Burns (Township)	61443
Burnside (Cook County)	60617
Burnside (Hancock County)	62318
Burnside's Lakewood (Part of Richton Park)	60646
Burnt Prairie	62820
Burnt Prairie (Township)	62821
Burritt (Township)	61088
Burr Oak (Part of Blue Island)	60406
Burr Oaks (Part of Joliet)	60435
Burrowsville	61929
Burr Ridge	60521
Burt	61721
Burton	62301
Burton (Adams County) (Township)	62301
Burton (McHenry County) (Township)	60081
Burtons Bridge	60050
Burtonview	62656
Bush (Jackson County)	62901
Bush (Williamson County)	62924
Bushnell	61422
Bushnell (Township)	61422
Bushton	61920
Butler (Montgomery County)	62015
Butler (Vermilion County) (Township)	60960
Butler Grove (Township)	62015
Butterfield	60148
Butterfield West	60137
Button (Township)	60960
Buyssse Addition	61240
Buzzville	62644
Byron	61010
Byron (Township)	61010
Byron Hills (Ogle County)	61010
Byron Hills (Rock Island County)	61275
Cabery	60919
Cable	61281
Cache	62913
Cadiz	62931
Cadwell	61911
Cahokia (Macoupin County) (Township)	62023
Cahokia (St. Clair County)	62206
Cairo	62914
Caledonia	61011
Caledonia (Township)	61011
Calhoun	62419
Calumet (Cook County)	60429
Calumet (Cook County) (Township)	60406
Calumet City	60409
Calumet Harbor (Part of Chicago)	60633
Calumet Park	60643
Calvin	62827
Camargo	61919
Camargo (Township)	61919
Cambria	62915
Cambridge	61238
Cambridge (Township)	61238
Cambridge (Part of Libertyville)	60048
Camden	62319
Camden (Township)	62319
Camelot	62401
Cameo Terrace (Part of Wheeling)	60090
Cameron	61423
Campbell Hill	62916
Campbells Island	61244
Camp Epworth	61038
Camp Ground	62864
Camp Grove	61424
Camp Logan	60099
Camp Point	62320
Camp Point (Township)	62320
Campton (Township)	60183
Campus	60920
Campus Walk (Part of Elgin)	60120
Camridge West (Part of Mundelein)	60060
Candlewood Estates	61853
Canoe Creek (Township)	61257
Canteen (Township)	62204
Canterbury Lane (Part of Glenview)	60025
Canterbury Shopping Center (Part of Markham)	60426
Canton	61520
Canton (Township)	61520
Cantrall	62625
Capital (Township)	62707
Capitol (Part of Springfield)	62701
Capri Gardens	60074
Capri Village	60074
Capron	61012
Carbon (Part of O'Fallon)	62269
Carbon Cliff	61239
Carbondale	62901-03
For specific Carbondale Zip Codes call (618) 457-3800	
Carbon Hill	60416
Cardiff	60420
Carlinville	62626
Carlinville (Township)	62626
Carlock	61725
Carlsburg	62069
Carlyle	62231
Carlyle (Township)	62231
Carlysle (Part of Schaumburg)	60194
Carman	61425
Carman (Township)	61425
Carmi	62821
Carmi (Township)	62821

Carol Stream-Chicago ILLINOIS 145

	ZIP		ZIP		ZIP
Carol Stream	60188	Channahon (Township)	60410	University of Chicago	60637
Carpenter	62025	Channahon	60410	University of Illinois at	
Carpentersville	60110	Channel Lake	60002	Chicago	60680
Carriage Creek (Part of Richton Park)	60466	Chantilly (Part of Highland Park)	60035	*FINANCIAL INSTITUTIONS*	
Carriage Park	60543	Chapin	62628	Amalgamated Trust &	
Carriage Way Court	60074	Chapman	62032	Savings Bank	60603
Carrier Mills	62917	Charleston	61920	American National Bank	
Carriers Mills (Township)	62917	Charleston (Township)	61920	and Trust Company of	
Carrigan (Clinton County)	62231	Charlotte	60921	Chicago	60690
Carrigan (Marion County) (Township)	62875	Charlotte (Township)	60921	Associated Bank	60601
Carroll (Township)	61870	Charlotte Hills	62274	Avondale Federal Savings Bank	60602
Carroll Addition (Champaign County)	61801	Charter Grove	60178	Bank of Commerce &	
Carroll Addition (Ford County)	60936	Chasco	62923	Industry	60631
Carrollton	62016	Chateau Terrace	62221	Bank of Ravenswood	60640
Carrollton (Township)	62016	Chatham (Township)	62629	Bell Federal Savings & Loan Association	60603
Carrollwood (Part of Wood River)	62095	Chatham (Cook County)	60619	Belmont National Bank of Chicago	60657
Carson (Township)	62080	Chatham (Sangamon County)	62629	Beverly Bank	60643
Carterville	62918	Chatham Manor (Part of Buffalo Grove)	60089	Boulevard Bank National Association	60611
Carthage	62321	Chatsworth	60921	Calumet Federal Savings & Loan Association	60617
Carthage (Township)	62321	Chatsworth (Township)	60921	Capitol Bank and Trust	60639
Carthage Lake	61425	Chatton	62346	Capitol Federal Bank	60641
Cartter	62853	Chauncey	62466	Central Federal Savings & Loan Association	60650
Cartwright (Township)	62677	Chautauqua	62028	Chesterfield Federal Savings & Loan Association	60643
Cary	60013	Chautauqua Park (Mason County)	62644	Chicago City Bank & Trust Company	60621
Casey	62420	Chautauqua Park (Menard County)	62675	The Chicago-Tokyo Bank	60602
Casey (Township)	62420	Chebanse	60922	Citicorp Savings of Illinois, A Federal Savings & Loan Association	60603
Caseyville (Township)	62232	Chebanse (Township)	60927	Clearing Bank	60638
Caseyville	62232	Checkrow	61415	Cole Taylor Bank/Drovers	60609
Casner (Jefferson County) (Township)	62898	Chelsea Cove (Part of Wheeling)	60090	Cole Taylor Bank/Ford City	60652
Casner (Macon County)	62552	Cheltenham (Part of Chicago)	60649	Colonial Bank & Trust Company	60634
Cass (Township)	61477	Chemung	60033	Columbia National Bank of Chicago	60656
Castellean Lower	61021	Chemung (Township)	60033	Commercial National Bank of Chicago	60625
Castellean Upper	61021	Cheney Grove (Township)	61770	Continental Bank National Association	60604
Castleton	61426	Cheneyville	60942	Cook County Federal Savings & Loan Association	60659
Cataloga 2	60123	Chenoa	61726	The Cosmopolitan National Bank of Chicago	60610
Catatoga	60123	Chenoa (Township)	61726	Cragin Federal Savings & Loan Association	60639
Catlin	61817	Chenot Place	62221	Damen Savings & Loan Association	60609
Catlin (Township)	61817	Cherry	61317	Devon Bank	60645
Cave (Township)	62890	Cherry Grove-Shannon (Township)	61046	Drexel National Bank	60616
Cave In Rock	62919	Cherry Hill	60431	Enterprise Savings Bank F.A.	60606
Cayuga	61764	Cherry Hills (Champaign County)	61821	The Exchange National Bank of Chicago	60603
Cazenovia	61545	Cherry Hills (Kane County)	60506	Fidelity Federal Savings & Loan Association of Chicago	60641
Cazenovia (Township)	61545	Cherry Point	61924	The First Commercial Bank	60626
Cedar (Township)	61410	Cherryvale Mall (Part of Cherry Valley)	61016	First Federal Savings of Hegewisch	60633
Cedar Glen	60543	Cherry Valley (Township)	61016	The First National Bank of Chicago	60670
Cedar Grove	62959	Cherry Valley	61016	First National Bank of Cicero	60650
Cedar Island	60020	Cherrywood (Christian County)	62568	First National Bank of Evergreen Park	60642
Cedar Meadows	62269	Cherrywood (Will County)	60439	The First National Bank of Lincolnwood	60645
Cedar Park	62040	Chester (Logan County) (Township)	62656	First National Bank of Niles	60648
Cedar Point	61316	Chester (Randolph County)	62233	First of America Bank-Golf Mill	60648
Cedar Run (Part of Wheeling)	60090	Chesterfield (Township)	62630	First Security Federal Savings Bank	60622
Cedarville	61013	Chesterfield (Cook County)	60619	First Security Trust & Savings Bank	60635
Centaur Estate	61008	Chesterfield (Macoupin County)	62630	First State Bank of Chicago	60656
Center Hill	61053	Chesterville	61911	The Harris Trust and Savings Bank of Chicago	60603
Centerville (Calhoun County)	62036	Chestline	62314	Heritage/Pullman Bank & Trust Company	60628
Centerville (Knox County)	61485	Chestnut (Knox County) (Township)	61544	Hoyne Savings & Loan Association	60630
Centerville (Macoupin County)	62685	Chestnut (Logan County)	62518	Hyde Park Bank & Trust Company	60615
Centerville (Piatt County)	61854	**Chicago**	60601-66	Independence Bank of Chicago	60619
Centerville (White County)	62821		60680-91	Irving Federal Savings & Loan Association	60618
Central (Township)	62246	For specific Chicago Zip Codes call (312) 765-3585		Jefferson State Bank	60630
Central City (Grundy County)	60407	*COLLEGES & UNIVERSITIES*		Lake Shore National Bank	60611
Central City (Marion County)	62801	Chicago State University	60628	Lakeside Bank	60604
Centralia	62801	Columbia College	60605		
Centralia (Township)	62801	De Paul University	60604		
Central Park	61832	DeVry Institute of Technology-Chicago	60618		
Central Street (Part of Evanston)	60201	Illinois Institute of Technology	60616		
Centre, The (Part of Park Forest)	60466	The John Marshall Law School	60604		
Centreville (Township)	62207	Keller Graduate School of Management	60606		
Centreville	62207	Loyola University of Chicago	60611		
Century Oaks (Part of Elgin)	60123	Moody Bible Institute	60610		
Century Oaks West (Part of Elgin)	60123	Mundelein College	60660		
Cerro Gordo	61818	North Park College	60625		
Cerro Gordo (Township)	61818	Northeastern Illinois University	60625		
Chadwick	61014	Roosevelt University	60605		
Chalfin Bridge	62244	Rush University	60612		
Chalmers (Township)	61455	Saint Xavier College	60655		
Chambersburg	62323	School of the Art Institute of Chicago	60603		
Chambersburg (Township)	62323				
Chambord (Part of Oak Brook)	60521				
Champaign	61820-21				
For specific Champaign Zip Codes call (217) 373-5200					
Champaign City (Township)	61820				
Champlin	61739				
Chana	61015				
Chandlerville	62627				
Chandlerville (Township)	62627				

146 ILLINOIS Chicago

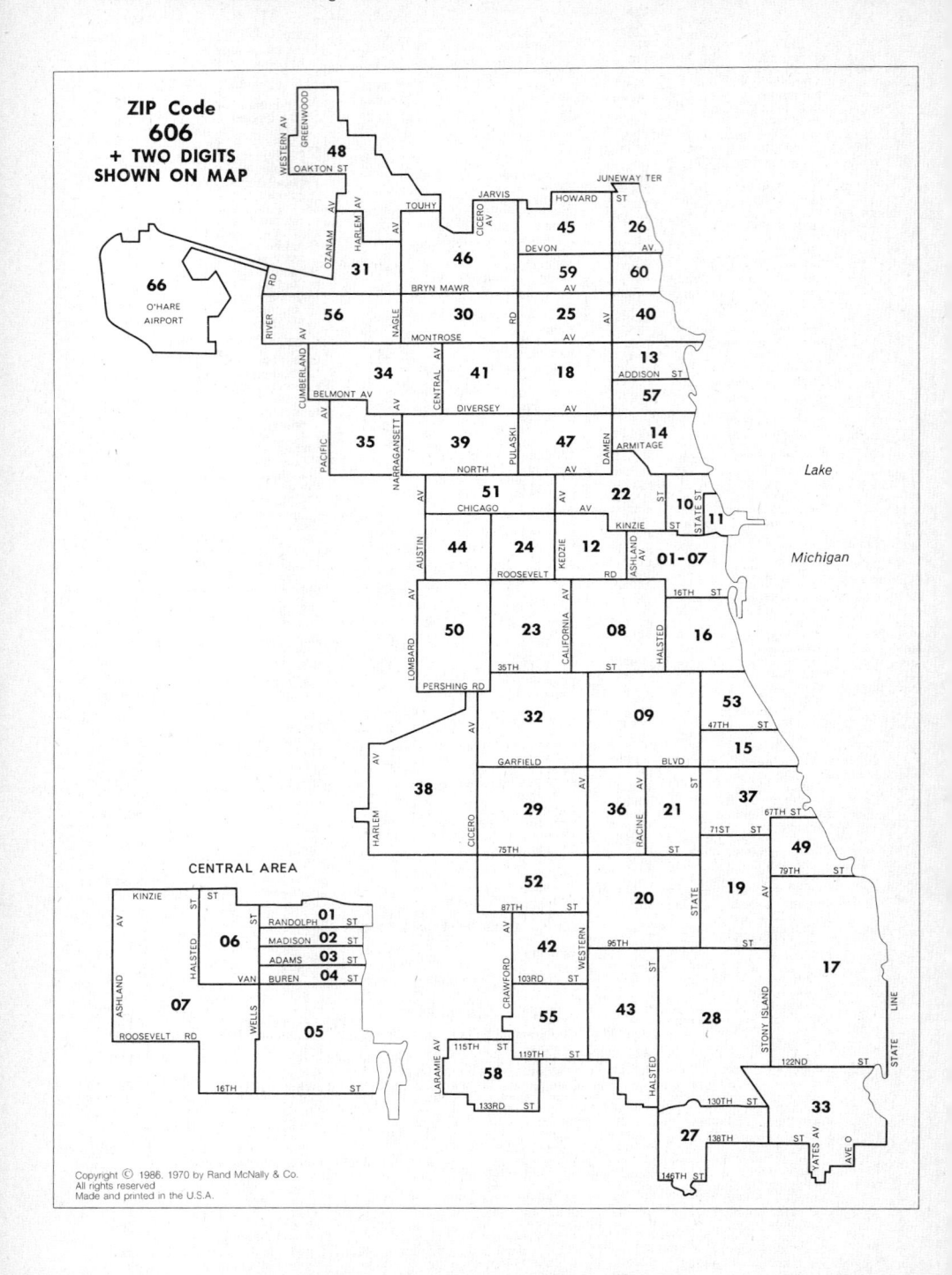

ZIP Code 606 + TWO DIGITS SHOWN ON MAP

Chicago Heights-Colonial Gardens ILLINOIS 147

	ZIP
Lake View LaSalle Bank	60657
LaSalle National Bank	60603
LaSalle National Northwest Bank	60641
Liberty Federal Savings & Loan Association of Chicago	60659
Liberty Savings	60647
Lincoln National Bank	60613
Lincoln Park Federal Savings & Loan Association	60613
Madison Bank & Trust Company	60606
Manufacturers Bank	60622
Marquette National Bank	60636
Merchandise National Bank of Chicago	60654
Michigan Avenue National Bank of Chicago	60602
The Mid-City National Bank of Chicago	60607
Midwest Bank and Trust Company	60635
Midwest Securities Trust Company	60605
Mount Greenwood Bank	60655
The National Security Bank of Chicago	60622
NBD/Chicago Bank	60601
Northern Trust Bank/O'Hare, N.A.	60631
The Northern Trust Company	60675
Northwestern Savings & Loan Association	60647
Norwood Federal Savings Bank	60646
Old Kent Bank-Chicago	60606
Park National Bank of Chicago	60618
Parkway Bank & Trust Company	60656
Pathway Financial, A Federal Association	60602
Peerless Federal Savings & Loan Association of Chicago	60630
Peterson Bank	60659
Pioneer Bank & Trust Company	60639
St. Paul Federal Bank for Savings	60635
Seaway National Bank of Chicago	60619
Second Federal Savings & Loan Association of Chicago	60623
Security Federal Savings & Loan Association of Chicago	60622
South Chicago Bank	60617
The South Shore Bank of Chicago	60649
Standard Federal Savings & Loan Association of Chicago	60632
The Steel City National Bank of Chicago	60617
United Savings of America	60652
Uptown National Bank of Chicago	60640
Western Savings & Loan Association	60630

HOSPITALS

Chicago Osteopathic Medical Center	60615
Children's Memorial Hospital	60614
Columbus Hospital	60614
Cook County Hospital	60612
Edgewater Hospital	60660
Grant Hospital of Chicago	60614
Holy Cross Hospital	60629
Illinois Masonic Medical Center	60657
Jackson Park Hospital	60649
Louis A. Weiss Memorial Hospital	60640
Mercy Hospital and Medical Center	60616
Michael Reese Hospital and Medical Center	60616
Mount Sinai Hospital Medical Center of Chicago	60608
Northwestern Memorial Hospital	60611
Our Lady of Resurrection Medical Center	60634

	ZIP
Ravenswood Hospital Medical Center	60640
Resurrection Hospital	60631
Rush-Presbyterian-St. Luke's Medical Center	60612
Saint Mary of Nazareth Hospital Center	60622
South Chicago Community Hospital	60617
St. Elizabeth's Hospital	60622
St. Joseph Hospital and Health Center	60657
University of Chicago Hospitals	60637
University of Illinois Hospital	60612
Veterans Administration Lakeside Medical Center	60611
Veterans Administration West Side Medical Center	60612

HOTELS/MOTELS

Ambassador East Hotel	60610
The Chicago Hilton and Towers	60605
The Congress Hotel of Chicago	60605
The Drake	60611
Holiday Inn-Mart Plaza	60654
Hyatt Regency Chicago in Illinois Center	60601
Knickerbocker-Chicago Hotel	60611
Marriott-Chicago O'Hare	60631
The Mayfair Regent	60611
The O'Hare Hilton	60666
Palmer House and Towers	60690
Park Hyatt on Water Tower Square	60611
The Ritz-Carlton	60611
The Tremont	60611
The Westin Hotel	60611

MILITARY INSTALLATIONS

Illinois Air National Guard, FB6121	60666
United States Army Engineer District, Chicago	60606
928th Tactical Airlift Group, O'Hare Air Reserve Forces Facility	60666

Chicago Heights	60411
Chicago Lawn (Part of Chicago)	60629
Chicago Ridge	60415
Chicago Ridge Mall (Part of Chicago Ridge)	60415
Chicken Bristle	61953
Chili (Hancock County)	62380
Chili (Hancock County) (Township)	62380
Chillicothe (Township)	61523
Chillicothe	61523
Chilon Chalet (Part of Chicago Heights)	60411
China (Township)	61310
Chinatown (Part of Maryville)	62062
Chippendale (Part of Barrington)	60010
Chippewa	60658
Chippewa Ridge (Part of Alsip)	60658
Chittenden (Part of Gurnee)	60031
Chittyville (Part of Herrin)	62948
Chouteau (Township)	62040
Chrisman	61924
Christopher	62822
Christy (Township)	62466
Churchill (Part of Hoffman Estates)	60195
Churchville (Part of Bensenville)	60126
Cicero (Cook County)	60650
Cicero (Cook County) (Township)	60650
Cimic (Part of Divernon)	62530
Cincinnati (Pike County) (Township)	62343
Cincinnati (Tazewell County) (Township)	61554
Cinnamon Creek (Part of Bolingbrook)	60439
Circle Drive	61364
Circle Park	62565
Cisco	61830
Cisne	62823
Cissna Park	60924
Citation Lake Estates	60062
City Park (Part of Taylorville)	62568
Claburn (Part of Chicago)	60617

	ZIP
Clank	62988
Clare	60111
Claremont	62421
Claremont (Township)	62421
Clarence	60960
Clarendon Hills	60514
Clarion (Township)	61330
Clark Center	62441
Clarksburg	62565
Clarksburg (Township)	62565
Clarksdale	62556
Clarksville (Clark County)	62441
Clarksville (McLean County)	61753
Clarmin	62257
Clay City	62824
Clay City (Township)	62824
Claypool	60450
Clays Prairie	61944
Clayton	62324
Clayton (Adams County) (Township)	62324
Clayton (Woodford County) (Township)	61516
Claytonville	60926
Clearing (Cook County)	60638
Clear Lake (Township)	62707
Clear Lake (Cass County)	62622
Clear Lake (Sangamon County)	62707
Cleburne	62865
Clement (Township)	62252
Clements	62638
Cleone	62442
Cleveland	61241
Clifton	60927
Clifton Terrace	62035
Clifty Heights	62959
Clinch	62832
Clinton (De Kalb County) (Township)	60556
Clinton (De Witt County)	61727
Clintonia (Township)	61727
Clover (Township)	61490
Cloverdale (Du Page County)	60103
Cloverdale (Tazewell County)	61611
Cloverleaf (Madison County)	62060
Cloverleaf (Rock Island County)	61265
Clybourn (Part of Chicago)	60610
Clyde (Cook County)	60650
Clyde (Whiteside County) (Township)	61270
Coach Homes of Willow Bend (Part of Rolling Meadows)	60008
Coach Light Manor (Part of Mount Prospect)	60056
Coal City	60416
Coal Hollow	61356
Coalton	62075
Coal Valley	61240
Coal Valley (Township)	61240
Coatsburg	62325
Cobblestone	60025
Cobblewood (Part of Northbrook)	60062
Cobden	62920
Coe (Township)	61275
Coello	62825
Coffeen	62017
Colby Point	60050
Colchester	62326
Colchester (Township)	62326
Coldbrook (Warren County)	61423
Coldbrook (Warren County) (Township)	61401
Cold Spring (Township)	62571
Colehour (Part of Chicago)	60617
Coleman	60177
Coles	61928
Coleta	61017
Colfax (Champaign County) (Township)	61851
Colfax (McLean County)	61728
College Hills Mall (Part of Normal)	61761
College Park (Part of Elgin)	60123
College View	60441
Collins (Will County)	60544
Collins (Winnebago County)	61080
Collinsville	62234
Collinsville (Township)	62234
Collison	61831
Colmar	62327
Coloma (Township)	61071
Colona	61241
Colona (Township)	61241
Colonial Gardens	61111

148 ILLINOIS Colonial Manor-Deep Woods

	ZIP
Colonial Manor (Part of Mount Prospect)	60056
Colonial Ridge	60016
Colonial Village (Madison County)	62035
Colonial Village (Will County)	60439
Colonial Village (Winnebago County)	61108
Colony Grove	61853
Colony Park (Part of Carol Stream)	60188
Colony Point (Part of Deerfield)	60015
Colp	62921
Columbia	62236
Columbia Village	61801
Columbus	62328
Columbus (Township)	62320
Colusa	62329
Colvin Park	60145
Como	61081
Compromise (Township)	61862
Compton	61318
Compton Pines	60175
Conant	62274
Concord (Adams County) (Township)	62324
Concord (Bureau County) (Township)	61361
Concord (Iroquois County) (Township)	60945
Concord (Morgan County)	62631
Condit (Township)	61840
Confidence	62418
Congerville	61729
Congress Park (Part of Brookfield)	60513
Conlogue	61944
Conover	60560
Conrad	62036
Continental Village (Part of Waukegan)	60085
Cooks Mills	61931
Cooksville	61730
Cooper (Township)	62563
Cooperstown	62353
Cooperstown (Township)	62353
Copley (Township)	61485
Cora	62280
Coral	60152
Coral (Township)	60180
Coral Gable (Part of O'Fallon)	62269
Cordova	61242
Cordova (Township)	61242
Corinth	62890
Cornell	61319
Cornerville	62935
Cornland	62519
Cornwall (Township)	61235
Cortese	60901
Cortland	60112
Cortland (Township)	60112
Corwin (Township)	62666
Costin (Part of Bloomington)	61701
Cottage (Township)	62946
Cottagegrove	62930
Cottage Hills	62018
Cotton Hill (Township)	62563
Cottonwood (Cumberland County) (Township)	62468
Cottonwood (Gallatin County)	62871
Coulterville	62237
Council Hill	61075
Council Hill (Township)	61075
Council Hill Station	61075
Country Acres (La Salle County)	61360
Country Acres (St. Clair County)	62220
Country Aire (Jefferson County)	62864
Country Aire (Kane County)	60120
Country Club	61938
Country Club Acres	62626
Country Club Heights	61938
Country Club Hills	60478
Country Club Manor (Part of Country Club Hills)	60477
Country Club Place	62223
Country Club Terrace	62220
Country Courts	61265
Country Estates	61254
Country Fair (Part of Champaign)	61821
Country Gardens (Part of Prospect Heights)	60070
Country Heights (Part of Mount Vernon)	62864

	ZIP
Country Knolls (Kane County)	60123
Country Knolls (Knox County)	61410
Country Lake	60563
Country Lake Estates	62613
Country Manor (Coles County)	61938
Country Manor (Effingham County)	62401
Country Manor (Henry County)	61254
Country Orchard	61938
Countryside (Cook County)	60525
Countryside (Kane County)	60560
Countryside (Kendall County)	60560
Countryside (Lake County)	60047
Countryside Estates	60922
Countryside Lake	60060
Countryside Manor	60048
Country Squire (Part of Urbana)	61801
Country Squire Estates	61032
Countryview Estates (Kane County)	60118
Country View Estates (Will County)	60565
Covel	61701
Coventry (Part of Crystal Lake)	60014
Coventry East (Part of Crystal Lake)	60014
Coventry West (Part of Crystal Lake)	60014
Covington	62271
Covington (Township)	62271
Covington Manor	60089
Cow Bell Lane	62274
Cowden	62422
Cowling	62863
Crab Orchard	62959
Crab Orchard Estates	62901
Cragin (Part of Chicago)	60639
Cragin Junction (Part of Chicago)	60639
Craig Manor (Part of Des Plaines)	60016
Crainville	62918
Cramers	61529
Crane Creek (Township)	62633
Cravat	62801
Crawford Countryside (Part of Matteson)	60443
Creal Springs	62922
Creek (Township)	61750
Creekside (Cook County)	60008
Creekside (Cook County)	60443
Creekwood	60439
Crenshaw	62959
Crescent (Township)	60953
Crescent City	60928
Cress Creek (Part of Naperville)	60563
Crest Haven (Part of Fairview Heights)	62221
Crest Hill	60435
Creston	60113
Crestview	60970
Crestview Terrace (Part of Fairfield)	62837
Crestwood	60445
Crestwood Estates	62959
Crete	60417
Crete (Township)	60417
Creve Coeur	61611
Cricket Hill (Part of Matteson)	60443
Crisp	62895
Crittenden (Township)	61880
Crocketts Estates	60041
Crook (Township)	62859
Crooked Creek (Cumberland County) (Township)	62428
Crooked Creek (Jasper County) (Township)	62432
Crooked Lake	60046
Crooked Lake Oaks	60046
Cropsey	61731
Cropsey (Township)	61731
Cross County Mall (Part of Mattoon)	61938
Crossroads (Johnson County)	62995
Crossroads (St. Clair County)	62232
Crossroad Terrace (Part of Fairview Heights)	62232
Crossville	62827
Crouch (Township)	62895

	ZIP
Crown Estates (Part of Elmhurst)	60126
Cruger	61530
Cruger (Township)	61530
Crystal Gardens (Part of Crystal Lake)	60014
Crystal Lake (Jersey County)	62012
Crystal Lake (Madison County)	62035
Crystal Lake (McHenry County)	60014
Crystal Lake Estates	60014
Crystal Lawns	60435
Crystal Manor (Part of Crystal Lake)	60014
Crystal Point Mall (Part of Crystal Lake)	60014
Crystal Vista (Part of Crystal Lake)	60014
Cuba (Fulton County)	61427
Cuba (Lake County) (Township)	60010
Cullom	60929
Cumberland (Part of Des Plaines)	60016
Cumberland Green (Part of St. Charles)	60174
Cumberland Heights (Part of Fairfield)	62837
Cumberland Highlands (Part of Des Plaines)	60016
Cunningham (Township)	61801
Cunningham Courts (Part of Palatine)	60067
Curran	62670
Curran (Township)	62670
Custer (Township)	60481
Custer Park	60481
Cutler	62238
Cypress	62923
Cypress Gardens	62901
D'Adrian Gardens	62035
Daggetts	61053
Dahinda	61428
Dahlgren	62828
Dahlgren (Township)	62828
Dailey	61862
Dakota	61018
Dakota (Township)	61018
Dale (Hamilton County)	62829
Dale (McLean County) (Township)	61772
Dale Valley	61853
Dallasania	62917
Dallas City	62330
Dallas City (Township)	62330
Dalton City	61925
Dalzell	61320
Damiansville	62215
Dana	61321
Danada North (Part of Wheaton)	60187
Danada West (Part of Wheaton)	60187
Danforth	60930
Danforth (Township)	60930
Danvers	61732
Danvers (Township)	61732
Danville	61832-34
For specific Danville Zip Codes call (217) 446-9440	
Danville Junction (Part of Danville)	61832
Danway	61341
Darien	60559
Darmstadt	62255
Darrow	60966
Darwin	62477
Darwin (Township)	62477
Davis	61019
Davis Junction	61020
Dawson (McLean County) (Township)	61737
Dawson (Sangamon County)	62520
Dawson Park	60953
Daysville	61061
Dayton	61350
Dayton (Township)	61350
Dearborn Heights (Part of Oak Lawn)	60453
Decatur	62521-26
For specific Decatur Zip Codes call (217) 428-4474	
Decker (Township)	62868
Decorra	61480
Deep Lake	60046
Deep Spring Woods	60097
Deep Woods (Part of Mundelein)	60060

Deerbrook Mall-Effingham ILLINOIS 149

Name	ZIP
Deerbrook Mall (Part of Deerfield)	60015
Deer Creek	61733
Deer Creek (Township)	61733
Deerfield (Township)	60035
Deerfield (Fulton County) (Township)	61431
Deerfield (Lake County)	60015
Deer Grove	61243
Deering (Part of Chicago)	60610
Deering City	62896
Deer Lake	60010
Dee Road (Part of Park Ridge)	60068
Deer Park (La Salle County) (Township)	61348
Deer Park (Lake County)	60010
Deer Plain	62013
Deer Run	60175
Deerwood Estates	62471
Degognia (Township)	62950
De Kalb	60115
De Kalb (Township)	60115
Delafield	62859
De Land	61839
Delavan	61734
Delavan (Township)	61734
Del-Bar	61520
Delhi	62052
Dellwood Highlands	60441
Del Mar Woods	60015
DeLong	61436
Del Rey	60968
Delwood	62946
Dement (Township)	61068
Denison (Township)	62460
Denmark	62238
Denning (Township)	62896
Dennison	62423
Denny	62832
Denver (Hancock County)	62321
Denver (Richland County) (Township)	62868
Depue	61322
Derby (Ford County)	60936
Derby (Saline County)	62947
Derinda (Township)	61028
Derinda Center	61028
Derry (Township)	62312
Deselm	60950
De Soto	62924
De Soto (Township)	62924
Des Plaines	60016-19
For specific Des Plaines Zip Codes call (708) 827-5591	
Des Plaines Manor (Part of Des Plaines)	60016
Des Plaines Terrace (Part of Des Plaines)	60016
Detroit	62332
Detroit (Township)	62332
Devereux Heights (Part of Springfield)	62707
Devonshire (Part of Des Plaines)	60018
Dewey	61840
Dewitt	61735
De Witt (Township)	61735
Dewmaine	62918
Dexter	62411
Diamond	60416
Diamond City	62859
Diamond Lake	60060
Diamond Town	62274
Dieterich	62424
Dillon	61568
Dillon (Township)	61568
Dillsburg	61866
Dimmick (Township)	61301
Diona	62428
Disco	61450
Diswood	62988
Divernon	62530
Divernon (Township)	62530
Divide	62889
Division Street (Part of Chicago)	60651
Dix (Ford County) (Township)	60933
Dix (Jefferson County)	62830
Dixmoor	60406
Dixon	61021
Dixon (Township)	61021
Dixon Springs	62943
Dobbins Downs	61801
Dodds (Township)	62864
Doddsville	61452
Dollville	62571
Dolson (Township)	61944
Dolton	60419
Dongola	62926

Name	ZIP
Donnellson	62019
Donovan	60931
Dora (Township)	61925
Dorans	61938
Dorchester	62020
Dorchester (Township)	62009
Dorr (Township)	60098
Dorris Heights (Part of Harrisburg)	62946
Dorsey	62021
Douglas (Clark County) (Township)	62441
Douglas (Effingham County) (Township)	62401
Douglas (Iroquois County) (Township)	60938
Douglas (Knox County)	61572
Douglas (St. Clair County)	62243
Douglas Park	61081
Dover	61323
Dover (Township)	61356
Dow	62022
Dowell	62927
Downers Fairview (Part of Downers Grove)	60515
Downers Grove	60515-17
For specific Downers Grove Zip Codes call (708) 969-2001	
Downers Grove (Township)	60559
Downers Grove Estates	60515
Downey (Part of North Chicago)	60064
Downs (Township)	61736
Downs	61736
Downtown (Adams County)	62301
Downtown (Part of Des Plaines)	60016
Downtown (Part of Northbrook)	60062
Downtown (Du Page County)	60137
Downtown (Jackson County)	62901
Downtown (La Salle County)	61301
Downtown (McLean County)	61701
Downtown (Sangamon County)	62701
Downtown (Winnebago County)	61101
Drake	62092
Dresden Acres	60450
Drexel (Part of Cicero)	60650
Drivers	62898
Druce Lake	60046
Drummer (Township)	60936
Drury (Township)	52761
Dry Grove (Township)	61732
Dry Point (Township)	62422
Dubois	62831
Du Bois (Township)	62831
Duck Lake Woods	60041
Dudley	61944
Dudleyville	62246
Duncan (Mercer County) (Township)	61231
Duncan (Stark County)	61559
Duncans Mills	61542
Duncanville	62454
Dundas	62425
Dundee (Kane County)	60118
Dundee (Kane County) (Township)	60118
Dunfermline	61524
Dunham (Township)	60033
Dunhurst (Part of Wheeling)	60090
Dunkel	62557
Dunlap	61525
Dunlap Lake (Part of Edwardsville)	62025
Dunleith (Township)	61025
Dunn	61951
Dunning (Part of Chicago)	60634
Du Page (Township)	60441
Dupo	62239
Du Quoin	62832
Durand	61024
Durand (Township)	61024
Durham (Hancock County)	62330
Durham (Hancock County) (Township)	62330
Durley Camp	62246
Dutch Creek Woodlands	60050
Dutch Hollow (Part of Belleville)	62221
Duvall	62565
Dwight	60420
Dwight (Township)	60420
Dwight Correctional Center	60420
Dykersburg	62987

Name	ZIP
Eagarville	62023
Eagle (Township)	61364
Eagle Creek (Township)	62934
Eagle Heights	60123
Eagle Lake	60401
Eagle Park	62060
Eagle Point (Township)	61064
Eagle Point Bay	62939
Earl (Township)	60518
Earl Estates	60554
Earlville	60518
East Alton	62024
East Bend (Township)	61840
East Brooklyn	60474
East Cape Girardeau	62957
East Carondelet	62240
East Clinton	61252
East Dubuque	61025
East Dundee	60118
East Eldorado (Township)	62930
Eastern (Township)	62812
East Fork (Clinton County) (Township)	62283
East Fork (Montgomery County) (Township)	62017
East Fulton	61252
East Galena (Township)	61036
East Galesburg	61430
Eastgate	62881
East Gillespie	62033
East Grove (Township)	61349
East Hannibal	62343
East Hardin	62031
East Hazel Crest	60429
East Keokuk (Part of Hamilton)	62341
Eastland Mall (Part of Bloomington)	61701
East Lincoln (Township)	62656
East Loon Lake	60002
East Lynn	60932
East Meadowbrook	62067
East Meadowview (Part of Bradley)	60915
East Moline	61244
East Nelson (Township)	61951
East Newbern	62022
East Oakland (Township)	61943
Easton	62633
East Peoria	61611
East River	60964
East Rockford (Part of Rockford)	61110
East Side (Cook County)	60617
East Side (Kankakee County)	60954
East St. Louis	62201-08
For specific East St. Louis Zip Codes call (618) 875-0200	
East Wenona	61377
Eastwood Manor	60050
Eaton	62454
Eberle	62424
Echo Lake	60047
Eckard	62644
Eddyville	62928
Edelstein	61526
Eden (La Salle County) (Township)	61370
Eden (Peoria County)	61536
Eden (Randolph County)	62286
Eden Park	62933
Edford (Township)	61254
Edgar	61924
Edgar (Township)	60118
Edgebrook (Cook County)	60646
Edgebrook (De Kalb County)	60178
Edgemont (Part of East St. Louis)	62203
Edgewater Beach	62231
Edgewood (Champaign County)	61801
Edgewood (Effingham County)	62426
Edgewood (Woodford County)	61530
Edgewood Heights	61008
Edgington	61284
Edgington (Township)	61284
Edinburg	62531
Edison Park (Part of Chicago)	60631
Edison Square (Part of Waukegan)	60085
Edwards	61528
Edwardsville	62025
Edwardsville (Township)	62025
Edwardsville Junction (Part of Edwardsville)	62025
Effingham	62401

150 ILLINOIS Effner-Flint

Name	ZIP
Effner	60966
Egan	61047
Egyptian Hills	62922
Egyptian Shores	62922
Eight Mile Prairie	62918
Eighty-Seventh Street (Part of Chicago)	60619
Eighty-Third Street (Part of Chicago)	60617
Eiker Addition	61448
Eileen (Part of Coal City)	60416
Ela (Township)	60047
Elam Lake	61951
Elba (Gallatin County)	62871
Elba (Knox County) (Township)	61489
Elba Center	61572
Elbridge	61944
Elbridge (Township)	61944
Elburn	60119
Elco	62929
El Dara	62312
Eldena	61324
Elderville	62313
Eldorado (McDonough County) (Township)	61411
Eldorado (Saline County)	62930
Eldred	62027
Eleanor	61453
Eleroy	61027
Elgin	60120-23
For specific Elgin Zip Codes call (708) 741-0725	
Elgin Estates	60123
Eliza	61272
Eliza (Township)	61272
Elizabeth	61028
Elizabeth (Township)	61028
Elizabethtown	62931
Elk (Township)	62932
Elk Grove (Township)	60007
Elk Grove Village	60009
Elkhart	62634
Elkhart (Township)	62634
Elkhorn (Township)	62353
Elkhorn Grove (Township)	61051
Elk Prairie (Township)	62816
Elk Ridge Villa (Part of Mount Prospect)	60056
Elkton	62268
Elkville	62932
Ellery	62833
Ellington (Adams County)	62301
Ellington (Adams County) (Township)	62301
Elliott	60933
Elliottstown	62424
Ellis	61865
Ellis Grove	62241
Ellison (Township)	61478
Ellisville	61431
Ellisville (Township)	61431
Ellsworth	61737
Ellwood Greens	60135
Elm Estates (Part of Elmhurst)	60126
Elm Grove (Township)	61554
Elmhurst	60126
Elmira	61483
Elmira (Township)	61483
Elmore	61451
El Morro (Part of Oak Forest)	60452
Elm River (Township)	62842
Elmwood	61529
Elmwood (Township)	61529
Elmwood Park	60635
El Paso	61738
El Paso (Township)	61738
El-Rancho	60901
Elsah	62028
Elsah (Township)	62028
Elsdon (Part of Chicago)	60632
El Sierra (Part of Downers Grove)	60515
Elva	60115
Elvaston	62334
El Vista (Cook County)	60452
El Vista (Peoria County)	61604
Elwin	62532
Elwood (Vermilion County) (Township)	61870
Elwood (Will County)	60421
Embarrass (Township)	61949
Emden	62635
Emerald Green (Part of Warrenville)	60555
Emerald Park	60050
Emerald Terrace	62223
Emerson	61081
Emerson City	62883

Name	ZIP
Eminence (Township)	61721
Emington	60934
Emma	62834
Emma (Township)	62834
Emmet (Township)	61455
Empire (Township)	61752
Empire Hills	60175
Enchanted Forest	61604
Energy	62933
Enfield	62835
Enfield (Township)	62835
Engelmann (Township)	62258
England Heights	62901
Englewood (Part of Chicago)	60621
English (Township)	62052
Enion	62644
Enos	62626
Enright	61738
Enterprise	62823
Eola	60519
Eppards Point (Township)	61764
Epworth	62821
Equality	62934
Equality (Township)	62934
Erie	61250
Erie (Township)	61250
Erienna (Township)	60450
Erin (Township)	61027
Erontenac	60118
Esmen (Township)	60460
Esmond	60129
Essex (Kankakee County)	60935
Essex (Stark County) (Township)	60935
Essex (Township)	61491
Estate Lane (Part of Glenview)	60025
Etherton	62966
Eubanks	62301
Euclid Lake (Part of Mount Prospect)	60056
Eureka	61530
Evans (Marshall County)	61377
Evans (Marshall County) (Township)	61377
Evanston	60201-04
For specific Evanston Zip Codes call (708) 328-6201	
Evansville	62242
Evarts	61067
Evergreen Park	60642
Evergreen Plaza (Part of Evergreen Park)	60642
Ewing	62836
Ewing (Township)	62836
Exeter	62621
Exline	60901
Expo Park (Part of Hoffman Estates)	60192
Eylar	61769
Ezra	62896
Factory Outlet Mall (Part of Kankakee)	60901
Fairbanks	61937
Fairbury	61739
Fair City	62952
Fairdale	60146
Fairfield (Bureau County) (Township)	61283
Fairfield (Lake County)	60047
Fairfield (Wayne County)	62837
Fairfield Heights	61032
Fair Grange	61920
Fair Haven	61014
Fairhaven (Township)	61014
Fairland	61956
Fairman	62882
Fairmont	60441
Fairmont City	62201
Fairmount (Madison County)	62002
Fairmount (Massac County)	62960
Fairmount (Pike County) (Township)	62314
Fairmount (Vermilion County)	61841
Fair Oaks (Cook County)	60103
Fair Oaks (Du Page County)	60185
Fair Oaks (Kane County)	60175
Fairview (Township)	61432
Fairview (Part of Fairview Heights)	62232
Fairview (Christian County)	62568
Fairview (Cook County)	60176
Fairview (Fulton County)	61432
Fairview Addition	62930
Fairview Avenue (Part of Downers Grove)	60515
Fairview Gardens (Part of Mount Prospect)	60056
Fairview Heights	62208

Name	ZIP
Fairway	61401
Fairway Estates (Cook County)	60462
Fairway Estates (Du Page County)	60187
Fall Creek	62360
Fall Creek (Township)	62360
Fall River (Township)	61350
Falmouth	62448
Fancher	62444
Fancy Creek (Township)	62684
Fancy Prairie	62613
Fandon	62326
Fargo	62375
Farina	62838
Farmer City	61842
Farmers (Township)	61482
Farmersville	62533
Farmingdale (Du Page County)	60559
Farmingdale (Sangamon County)	62677
Farmingdale South (Part of Darien)	60559
Farmingdale Terrace (Part of Darien)	60559
Farmingdale Village (Part of Darien)	60559
Farmington (Township)	61531
Farmington (Kane County)	60174
Farmington (Lake County)	60047
Farmington (Coles County)	62440
Farmington (Fulton County)	61531
Farm Ridge (Township)	61325
Farmsted (Part of Naperville)	60565
Farnsworth (Part of Waukegan)	60088
Farrington (Township)	62814
Farrow	61605
Fayette (Greene County)	62044
Fayette (Livingston County) (Township)	61775
Fayetteville	62258
Fayetteville (Township)	62258
Fayville	62990
Federal Penitentiary	62959
Feehanville (Part of Mount Prospect)	60056
Felix (Township)	60416
Felker (Part of Washington)	61571
Fenton	61251
Fenton (Township)	61251
Fergestown	62959
Fernway (Part of Orland Park)	60462
Ferrel	61944
Ferrin	62231
Ferris	62336
Fiatt	61433
Ficklin	61953
Fiday View	60435
Fidelity	62030
Fidelity (Township)	62030
Field (Township)	62889
Fieldcrest (Part of Oak Forest)	60452
Fieldon	62031
Fields West	61821
Fifty-Fifth Street (Part of Chicago)	60615
Fifty-Ninth Street (Part of Chicago)	60637
Fifty-Seventh Street (Part of Chicago)	60637
Fillmore	62032
Fillmore (Township)	62032
Filson	61910
Findlay	62534
Finley Square Mall (Part of Downers Grove)	60515
Finney Heights	62801
First Pommier	60964
Fisher	61843
Fishhook	62314
Fithian	61844
Five Islands Park	60177
Flag Center	61068
Flagg	61068
Flagg (Township)	61068
Flamingo Estates	62286
Flanagan	61740
Flannigan (Township)	62890
Flat Branch (Township)	62550
Flat Rock	62427
Flatville	61878
Flat Woods	62985
Fletcher	61730
Flickerville	60914
Flint (Township)	62340

Flora-Glen Park **ILLINOIS** **151**

	ZIP		ZIP		ZIP
Flora (Boone County) (Township)	61008	Fox Valley Center (Part of Aurora)	60505	Garfield Park (Part of Chicago)	60624
Flora (Clay County)	62839	Fox Valley East (Part of Aurora)	60505	Garland	61917
Floraville	62298	Fox Valley Villages (Part of Aurora)	60505	Garrett	61913
Florence (Stephenson County) (Township)	61032	Frankfort (Franklin County)	62896	Garrett (Township)	61913
Florence (Will County) (Township)	60481	Frankfort (Will County)	60423	Gary Gardens	60188
Florence (Pike County)	62363	Frankfort	60423	Gas Light Village	60450
Florence (Stephenson County)	61032	Frankfort Heights (Part of West Frankfort)	62840	Gateway Yard (Part of East St. Louis)	62207
Florid	61327	Franklin (De Kalb County) (Township)	60146	Gays	61928
Flossmoor	60422	Franklin (Morgan County)	62638	Geff	62842
Flossmoor Highlands (Part of Flossmoor)	60422	Franklin Grove	61031	Genesee (Township)	61270
Flowerfield Acres (Part of Lombard)	60148	Franklin Park	60131	Geneseo (Township)	61254
Floyd (Township)	61423	Franklin Square	60423	Geneseo	61254
Fondulac (Tazewell County) (Township)	61611	Franklinville	60098	Geneseo Hills	61254
Fon-Du-Lac (Will County)	60544	Frederick	62639	Geneva	60134
Foosland	61845	Frederick (Township)	62639	Geneva (Township)	60134
Ford City Shopping Center (Part of Chicago)	60652	Freeburg	62243	Genoa	60135
Fordham (Part of Chicago)	60619	Freeburg (Township)	62243	Genoa (Township)	60135
Ford Heights	60411	Freedom (Carroll County) (Township)	61046	Gent City	62959
Forest Acres	62201	Freedom (La Salle County) (Township)	61350	Gentry Acres	62918
Forest City	61532	Freeman Spur	62841	Georgetown (Township)	61846
Forest City (Township)	61532	Freeport (Stephenson County)	61032	Georgetown (Carroll County)	61046
Forest Estates	60067	Freeport (Stephenson County) (Township)	61032	Georgetown (McDonough County)	61455
Forest Gardens	60084	Fremont (Township)	60060	Georgetown (Vermilion County)	61846
Forest Glen (Part of Chicago)	60630	Fremont Center	60060	Gerald	61812
Foresthaven	60045	Fremont Junction (Part of Hanover Park)	60103	Gerlaw	61435
Forest Heights (Part of Chicago Heights)	60411	Frenchman's Cove (Part of Arlington Heights)	60004	German (Township)	62421
Forest Hill (Part of Chicago)	60652	French Village (Part of Fairview Heights)	62208	Germantown	62245
Forest Hills Estates	62471	Frentress Lake	61025	Germantown (Township)	62245
Forest Homes	62018	Friends Creek (Township)	62501	Germantown	61548
Forest Lake	60047	Friendsville	62863	Germantown Hills	61548
Forest Manor	60441	Frisco	62836	German Valley	61039
Forest Park	60130	Frog City	62913	Germanville (Township)	60921
Forest River	60056	Frogtown (Clinton County)	62231	Gibson City	60936
Forest View	60402	Frogtown (Washington County)	62271	Gibsonia	62954
Forest View Hills (Part of Oak Forest)	60452	Frontenac	60563	Gifford	61847
Forman	62908	Frontenac Place	62035	Gila	62445
Forrest	61741	Frost	62901	Gilberts	60136
Forrest (Township)	61741	Fruit	62025	Gilchrist	61486
Forrestal Village (Part of North Chicago)	60088	Fruitland	61265	Gilead	62006
Forreston	61030	Fry's Wheatland View	60565	Gillespie	62033
Forreston (Township)	61030	Fulton	61252	Gillespie (Township)	62033
Forsyth	62535	Fulton (Township)	61252	Gillespie Lakes	62033
Fort Dearborn (Part of Chicago)	60610	Fults	62244	Gillum	61701
Fort Gage	62241	Funkhouser	62401	Gilman	60938
Fort Russell (Township)	62010	Funks Grove	61754	Gilmer (Township)	62328
Forty-Seventh Street (Part of Chicago)	60615	Funks Grove (Township)	61754	Gilmore	62443
Foss Acres (Part of Waukegan)	60088	Future City	62914	Gilmore Lake	62236
Foster (Madison County) (Township)	62002	Fyre Lake	61281	Gilson	61436
Foster (Marion County) (Township)	62807	Gages Lake	60030	Ginger Creek (Part of Oak Brook)	60521
Fosterburg	62002	Galatia	62935	Ginger Hill (Part of Milan)	61264
Foster Pond	62298	Galatia (Township)	62935	Girard	62640
Fountain	62295	Gale	62990	Girard (Township)	62640
Fountain Bluff (Township)	62950	Galena	61036	Givins (Part of Chicago)	60620
Fountain Creek	60942	Galena Oaks	61028	Gladstone	61437
Fountain Creek (Township)	60942	Galesburg	61401-02	Gladstone (Township)	61437
Fountain Gap	62236	For specific Galesburg Zip Codes call (309) 342-6165		Gladstone Commons (Part of Mount Prospect)	60056
Fountain Green	62321	Galesburg City (Township)	61401	Gladstone Park (Part of Chicago)	60630
Fountain Green (Township)	62321	Galesville	61854	Glasford	61533
Four Lakes	60532	Gallagher	62450	Glasgow	62694
Four Mile (Township)	62895	Galnipper Place	62047	Glass Works (Part of Alton)	62002
Fowler	62338	Galt	61252	Glen (Part of Glen Carbon)	62034
Fox (Township)	60560	Galton	61910	Glen Acres (Part of Rosemont)	60018
Fox (Jasper County) (Township)	62448	Galva	61434	Glenarm	62536
Fox (Kendall County)	60560	Galva (Township)	61434	Glen Arms	60041
Fox Chase (Part of St. Charles)	60174	Ganeer (Township)	60954	Glenavon	61724
Foxcroft	60137	Ganntown	62943	Glenayre (Part of Glenview)	60025
Foxfield	60175	Garber	60936	Glenayre Gardens (Part of Glenview)	60025
Fox Lake	60020	Gardena (Part of East Peoria)	61611	Glenbrook Countryside	60062
Fox Lake Hills	60046	Garden Heights	62946	Glenburn	61858
Fox Lake Vista	60081	Garden Hill (Township)	62899	Glen Carbon	62034
Fox Lawn	60560	Garden Hills (Part of Champaign)	61821	Glencoe	60022
Fox Point (Part of Barrington)	60010	Garden Homes	60655	Glendale (Pope County)	62985
Fox Ridge (Part of South Elgin)	60177	Garden of Eden	60954	Glendale (Rock Island County)	61282
Fox River Bluffs 2	60118	Garden Plain	61252	Glendale Gardens (Part of Wood River)	62024
Fox River Estates	60174	Garden Plain (Township)	61252	Glendale Heights	60139
Fox River Gardens	60560	Garden Prairie	61038	Glen Ellyn	60137-38
Fox River Grove	60021	Garden Quarter (Part of Elgin)	60123	For specific Glen Ellyn Zip Codes call (708) 469-1060	
Fox River Heights	60174	Gardner (Grundy County)	60424	Glen Ellyn Countryside	60137
Fox River Valley Gardens	60010	Gardner (Sangamon County) (Township)	62677	Glen Ellyn Woods	60137
		Gardspoint	62863	Glengarry (Part of Geneva)	60134
		Garfield (Grundy County) (Township)	60424	Glen Hill (Part of Glendale Heights)	60139
		Garfield (La Salle County)	61377	Glenn	62280
				Glennshire (Part of Lake Zurich)	60047
				Glen Oak	60137
				Glen Park	60551

152 ILLINOIS Glen Ridge-Hastings

Name	ZIP
Glen Ridge (Part of Matteson)	60443
Glenshire (Part of Glenview)	60025
Glenview (Cook County)	60025
Glen View (St. Clair County)	62269
Glenview Countryside	60025
Glenview Estates	60025
Glenview Naval Air Station	60026
Glenview Terrace (Part of Glenview)	60025
Glenview Woodlands	60025
Glenwood	60425
Glenwood Estates (Part of Glenwood)	60425
Glenwood Plaza (Part of Glenwood)	60425
Godfrey	62035
Godfrey (Township)	62035
Godley	60407
Golconda	62938
Gold (Township)	61344
Golden	62339
Golden Acres	60025
Golden Eagle	62036
Golden Gardens (Part of Centreville)	62206
Goldengate	62843
Golden Highridge (Part of Des Plaines)	60016
Golden Lilly	62914
Golden Manor (Part of Des Plaines)	60016
Gold Hill (Township)	62984
Golena Knolls	61523
Golf	60029
Golf Mill Shopping Center (Part of Niles)	60648
Golfview Hills	60521
Goode (Township)	62884
Goodenow	60401
Goodfarm (Township)	60424
Goodfield	61742
Good Hope	61438
Goodrich	60913
Goodwine	60939
Goofy Ridge	61567
Goose Creek (Township)	61839
Goose Lake (Township)	60444
Gordons	62454
Goreville	62939
Gorham	62940
Goshen (Township)	61483
Gossett	62869
Grafton (Jersey County)	62037
Grafton (McHenry County) (Township)	60142
Graham Correctional Center	62049
Grand Chain	62941
Grand Crossing (Part of Chicago)	60619
Grand Detour	61021
Grand Detour (Township)	61021
Grand Prairie (Township)	62898
Grand Rapids (Township)	61325
Grand Ridge	61325
Grand Tower	62942
Grand Tower (Township)	62942
Grandview (Township)	61944
Grandview (Sangamon County)	62707
Grandview (Woodford County)	61611
Grandview (Carroll County)	61285
Grandview (Edgar County)	61944
Grandville (Township)	62481
Grandwood Park	60031
Grange	61872
Granite City (Madison County)	62040
Granite City (Madison County) (Township)	62040
Grant (Lake County) (Township)	60041
Grant (Vermilion County) (Township)	60942
Grantfork	62249
Grant Park	60940
Grantsburg	62943
Granville	61326
Granville (Township)	61326
Grape Creek	61832
Grass Lake (Lake County)	60002
Gray (Township)	62844
Grayland (Part of Chicago)	60641
Graymont	61743
Graymoor (Part of Olympia Fields)	60461
Grayslake	60030
Grays Siding	61858
Grayville	62844

Name	ZIP
Green Acres (McDonough County)	61455
Green Acres (Sangamon County)	62707
Greenbriar (Part of New Lenox)	60451
Greenbriar Addition	62918
Greenbrook Country (Part of Hanover Park)	60103
Greenbush	61415
Greenbush (Township)	61415
Greene (Mercer County) (Township)	61486
Greene (Woodford County) (Township)	61516
Greenfield (Greene County)	62044
Greenfield (Grundy County) (Township)	60474
Green Garden (Township)	60423
Greenleaf Hills	61842
Green Meadows (Cook County)	60103
Green Meadows (Kane County)	60510
Green Oak	61356
Green Oaks	60048
Greenpond	62361
Green River	61241
Green Rock	61241
Greentree (Part of Libertyville)	60048
Greenup	62428
Greenup (Township)	62428
Green Valley (Du Page County)	60148
Green Valley (Tazewell County)	61534
Greenview	62642
Greenville (Bond County)	62246
Greenville (Bureau County) (Township)	61376
Greenwich	60901
Greenwood (Township)	60098
Greenwood (Christian County) (Township)	62546
Greenwood (McHenry County)	60098
Greenwood Acres	61840
Greenwood Meadows	62035
Greer	60973
Gresham (Part of Chicago)	60620
Gridley	61744
Gridley (Township)	61744
Grigg	62278
Griggsville	62340
Griggsville (Township)	62340
Grimes Addition	61081
Grimsby	62940
Grinnell	62908
Grisham (Township)	62077
Griswold	60929
Gromers Woods	60120
Gross	62931
Grove (Township)	62448
Grove, The (Part of Downers Grove)	60517
Grove City	62531
Groveland (Township)	61535
Groveland (La Salle County) (Township)	61358
Groveland (Tazewell County)	61535
Grover (Township)	62837
Grupe	62401
Guilford (Jo Daviess County)	61036
Guilford (Jo Daviess County) (Township)	61028
Gulf Port	52601
Gurnee	60031
Guthrie	60936
Hadley	62312
Hadley (Township)	62312
Haegers Bend	60102
Hafer	62918
Hagaman	62630
Hagarstown	62247
Hagener (Township)	62618
Hahnaman (Whiteside County)	61243
Hahnaman (Whiteside County) (Township)	61283
Haines (Township)	62853
Hainesville	60030
Haldane	61030
Hale (Township)	61462
Half Day	60069
Hall (Township)	61362
Hallidayboro	62932
Hallock (Iroquois County)	60973

Name	ZIP
Hallock (Peoria County) (Township)	61526
Hallville	61727
Halsey Village (Part of Waukegan)	60088
Halsted Street (Part of Chicago)	60608
Hamburg (Bond County)	62262
Hamburg (Calhoun County)	62045
Hamel	62046
Hamel (Township)	62046
Hamilton (Hancock County)	62341
Hamilton (Lee County) (Township)	61349
Hamlet	61231
Hamletsburg	62944
Hammond	61929
Hampshire	60140
Hampshire (Township)	60140
Hampshire Manor (Part of Hampshire)	60140
Hampton	61256
Hampton (Township)	61256
Hampton Court (Part of Country Club Hills)	60477
Hancock (Township)	62321
Hanna (Township)	61254
Hanna City	61536
Hannon (Part of Taylorville)	62568
Hanover (Township)	61041
Hanover (Cook County) (Township)	60103
Hanover (Jo Daviess County)	61041
Hanover Highlands (Part of Hanover Park)	60103
Hanover Park	60103
Hanover Park-Ontaroville (Part of Hanover Park)	60103
Hanover Square (Part of Hanover Park)	60103
Hanson	62080
Hanson Park (Part of Chicago)	60639
Happy Hills	60175
Happy Hollow Lake	61428
Harbor Dell	62035
Harbor Estates	60010
Harco	62945
Hardin (Calhoun County)	62047
Hardin (Pike County) (Township)	62355
Harding	60518
Hardinville	62449
Harlem (Township)	61111
Harlem (Stephenson County) (Township)	61032
Harlem (Winnebago County)	61111
Harlem Avenue (Part of Berwyn)	60402
Harlem-Irving Plaza (Part of Chicago)	60634
Harmon	61042
Harmon (Township)	61042
Harmony (Hancock County) (Township)	62321
Harmony (Jefferson County)	62864
Harmony (McHenry County)	60140
Harmony Village (Part of Wheeling)	60090
Harp (Township)	61727
Harper	61030
Harpster	61845
Harris (Fulton County) (Township)	61459
Harris (Piatt County)	61842
Harrisburg	62946
Harrisburg (Township)	62946
Harrison (Township)	61072
Harrison (Jackson County)	62966
Harrison (Winnebago County)	61072
Harrisonville (Grundy County)	60416
Harrisonville (Monroe County)	62295
Harristown	62537
Harristown (Township)	62537
Harter (Township)	62839
Hartford	62048
Hartland	60098
Hartland (Township)	60098
Hartsburg	62643
Harvard	60033
Harvard Hills	61571
Harvel	62538
Harvel (Township)	62538
Harvey	60426
Harwood (Township)	61847
Harwood Heights	60656
Hastings	61810

ILLINOIS

Name	ZIP
Hatcher Woods	60450
Havana	62644
Havana (Township)	62644
Haw Creek (Township)	61458
Hawthorn Center (Part of Vernon Hills)	60060
Hawthorne (Part of Cicero)	60650
Hawthorne (Part of Chicago)	60623
Hawthorne (White County) (Township)	62821
Hawthorn Woods	60047
Hawthrone Hills	62864
Hayes	61953
Hayford (Part of Chicago)	60652
Haymarket (Part of Chicago)	60606
Haypress	62027
Hazel Crest	60429
Hazelcrest Highlands (Part of Hazel Crest)	60429
Hazel Dell	62428
Hazelgreen (Part of Alsip)	60482
Hazelhurst	61064
Hazelwood	61254
Hazelwood Heights	61254
Hazelwood West	61254
Headyville	62424
Healy (Part of Chicago)	60639
Heapsville	61425
Heartville	62401
Heathercrest (Part of Northbrook)	60062
Heatherfield	60450
Heatherlea	60074
Heathsville	62427
Hebron	60034
Hebron (Township)	60034
Hecker	62248
Hegeler	61832
Hegewisch (Part of Chicago)	60633
Helena	62466
Helmar	60541
Helvetia (Township)	62249
Heman	62573
Henderson	61439
Henderson (Township)	61439
Henderson	62033
Henderson Grove	61401
Hendryx Manor	61614
Hennepin	61327
Hennepin (Township)	61327
Henning	61848
Henry	61537
Henry (Township)	61537
Hensley (Township)	61820
Henton	62565
Herald	62845
Heralds Prairie (Township)	62869
Herbert	60145
Herborn	62465
Heritage (Part of Moline)	61265
Heritage Estates (Part of Bourbonnais)	60914
Hermon	61458
Hermosa (Part of Chicago)	60639
Herod	62947
Herrick	62431
Herrick (Township)	62431
Herrin	62948
Herscher	60941
Hersman	62353
Hervey City	62549
Hettick	62649
Hewittville	62568
Heyworth	61745
Hickory (Township)	62624
Hickory Falls	60097
Hickory Grove	62301
Hickory Hill (Township)	62895
Hickory Hills (Cook County)	60457
Hickory Hills (Piatt County)	61884
Hickory Hollow	60118
Hickory Point (Macon County) (Township)	62526
Hickory Point (Shelby County)	62565
Hickoryville	63673
Hicks	62947
Hidalgo	62432
Hidden Creek	60074
Hidden Hills	61455
Higginsville	61865
High Knob	60187
High Lake	60185
Highland (Grundy County) (Township)	60437
Highland (Madison County)	62249
Highlander	62901
Highland Haven	60123
Highland Hills	60148
Highland Lake	60030
Highland Park (Lake County)	60035
Highland Park (Marion County)	62881
Highlands (Cook County)	60411
Highlands (Du Page County)	60521
Highlands-Clarks	60543
Highland Shores	60097
Highlawn (Part of Riverdale)	60627
High Meadows	61607
High Point (Part of Hoffman Estates)	60195
Highview Estates	60514
Highway Village (Part of East Peoria)	61611
Highwood (Lake County)	60040
Highwood (St. Clair County)	62221
Highwood Terrace (Part of Belleville)	62221
Hilcrest	62089
Hildreth	61876
Hill Correctional Center	61401
Hillcrest (Calhoun County)	62045
Hillcrest (Christian County)	62568
Hillcrest (Cook County)	60439
Hillcrest (Douglas County)	61953
Hillcrest (Henry County)	61254
Hillcrest (Ogle County)	61068
Hillcrest Shopping Center (Part of Crest Hill)	60435
Hildale Villages (Part of Hoffman Estates)	60195
Hillerman	62941
Hillery	61832
Hillery-Batestown	61832
Hillsboro	62049
Hillsboro (Township)	62049
Hillsdale	61257
Hillside (Cook County)	60162
Hillside (Kankakee County)	60901
Hillside-Berkeley (Part of Hillside)	60162
Hillside Mall (Part of Hillside)	60162
Hillside Manor	60901
Hill Top	62675
Hillview	62050
Hillyard (Township)	62676
Himrod	61883
Hinckley	60520
Hindsboro	61930
Hinsdale	60521-22
For specific Hinsdale Zip Codes call (708) 990-4224	
Hinswood (Part of Darien)	60559
Hire (Township)	62326
Hitt	61051
Hittle (Township)	61721
Hodgetown	62865
Hodgkins	60525
Hoffman	62250
Hoffman Estates	60195
Hoffmann Edition	60924
Holbrook	60411
Holcomb	61043
Holden	62832
Holder	61736
Holiday Hills	60050
Holiday Shores	62025
Holland	62414
Holland (Township)	62414
Hollandia	62221
Hollenback	60450
Hollendale (Part of South Holland)	60473
Holliday	62414
Hollis (Township)	61607
Hollowayville	61356
Hollydale (Part of Homewood)	60430
Hollywood (Part of Brookfield)	60513
Hollywood Heights	62232
Hollywood Ridge (Part of Wheeling)	60090
Holmes Center	61523
Homberg	62938
Home Gardens (Part of Danville)	61832
Homer (Champaign County)	61849
Homer (Will County) (Township)	60441
Homerican Villas (Part of Des Plaines)	60016
Homestead (Part of O'Fallon)	62269
Hometown	60456
Homewood (Cook County)	60430
Homewood (Rock Island County)	61265
Homewood Acres	60430
Homewood Shores (Part of Homewood)	60430
Homewood Terrace (Part of Homewood)	60430
Honegger	61741
Honey Bend	62056
Honey Creek (Adams County) (Township)	62325
Honey Creek (Crawford County) (Township)	62427
Honey Creek (Ogle County)	61015
Honey Point (Township)	62056
Hononegah Heights	61073
Hoodville	62859
Hookdale	62284
Hoopeston	60942
Hoopole	61258
Hoosier (Township)	62858
Hope (La Salle County) (Township)	61334
Hope (Vermilion County)	61812
Hopedale	61747
Hopedale (Township)	61747
Hopewell (Marshall County)	61565
Hopewell (Marshall County) (Township)	61540
Hop Hollow	62035
Hopkins (Township)	61081
Hopkins Park	60944
Hopper	61480
Horace	61924
Horatio Gardens	60069
Hord	62858
Hornsby	62056
Horseshoe	62934
Houston (Adams County) (Township)	62339
Houston (Randolph County)	62286
Howardton	62942
Howe (Part of Depue)	61322
Howe Terrace	60010
Hoyleton	62803
Hoyleton (Township)	62803
Hubbard Woods (Cook County)	60093
Hubbard Woods (Marion County)	62801
Hubly	62642
Hudgens	62959
Hudson	61748
Hudson (Township)	61748
Huegely	62803
Huey	62252
Hugh's Addition	62684
Hugo	61953
Hull	62343
Humboldt	61931
Humboldt (Township)	61931
Hume (Edgar County)	61932
Hume (Whiteside County) (Township)	61071
Humm Wye	62938
Humrick	61870
Hunt City	62480
Hunt City (Township)	62480
Hunter (Boone County)	61011
Hunter (Edgar County)	61944
Hunter (Edgar County) (Township)	61944
Hunter Trail (Part of Oak Brook)	60521
Huntington (Part of Naperville)	60540
Huntington Commons (Part of Mount Prospect)	60056
Huntington Park (Part of Elgin)	60120
Huntinton Park	62035
Huntley	60142
Huntsville	62344
Huntsville (Township)	62344
Hurlbut (Township)	62634
Hurricane (Township)	62080
Hurst	62949
Hutchins Park	61103
Hutsonville	62433
Hutsonville (Township)	62433
Hutton	61920
Hutton (Township)	61920
Hyde Park (Part of Chicago)	60653
Idaville Corner	60924
Ideal	61285
Idlewild	60030
Idlewood	62864
Iliana	47982
Illiana Heights	60954
Illini (Township)	62573
Illinois City	61259

154 ILLINOIS Illinois Veterans Home-La Grange Highlands

Name	ZIP
Illinois Veterans Home (Part of Quincy)	62301
Illiopolis	62539
Illiopolis (Township)	62539
Imbs	62240
Imperial	60048
Ina	62846
Independence (Pike County)	62363
Independence (Saline County) (Township)	62946
Indian Creek (Lake County)	60060
Indian Creek (White County) (Township)	62869
Indian Grove (Township)	61739
Indian Head Park	60525
Indian Hill (Cook County)	60093
Indian Hill (Du Page County)	60563
Indian Hills (Cook County)	60411
Indian Hills (Jo Daviess County)	61025
Indian Oaks (Kankakee County)	60914
Indian Oaks (Will County)	60439
Indianola	61850
Indian Point (Knox County) (Township)	61410
Indian Point (Lake County)	60002
Indian Point (Menard County)	62613
Indian Prairie (Township)	62823
Indian Ridge (McHenry County)	60097
Indian Ridge (Piatt County)	61884
Indiantown (Township)	61421
Indian Trail Estates	60015
Industrial Park	62864
Industry	61440
Industry (Township)	61440
Ingalls Park	60431
Ingalton	60185
Ingleside (Lake County)	60041
Ingleside Shores	60041
Ingraham	62434
Ingram Hill	62946
International Village (Cook County)	60194
International Village (Du Page County)	60148
International Village (Will County)	60439
Inverness	60067
Inverness on the Ponds (Part of Inverness)	60067
Iola	62847
Ipava	61441
Irene	61016
Irishtown (Township)	62253
Irondale (Part of Chicago)	60617
Iroquois (Iroquois County)	60945
Iroquois (Iroquois County) (Township)	60928
Irving	62051
Irving (Township)	62051
Irving Park (Part of Chicago)	60641
Irvington	62848
Irvington (Township)	62848
Irwin	60901
Isabel (Edgar County)	61943
Isabel (Fulton County) (Township)	61542
Island Grove (Jasper County)	62467
Island Grove (Sangamon County) (Township)	62677
Island Lake	60042
Itasca	60143
Itasca Ranchettes	60143
Iuka	62849
Iuka (Township)	62849
Ivanhoe (Cook County)	60627
Ivanhoe (Lake County)	60060
Ivanhoe (Will County)	60439
Ivanhoe Estates	61801
Ivesdale	61851
Ivy Glen (Part of Aurora)	60506
Ivy Heights (Part of Wood River)	62024
Jackson (Effingham County) (Township)	62401
Jackson (Will County) (Township)	60421
Jackson Park (Part of Chicago)	60637
Jacksonville	62650-51
For specific Jacksonville Zip Codes call (217) 245-2149	
Jacksonville Correctional Center	62650
Jacob	62950
Jalapa	62054
Jamaica	61841

Name	ZIP
Jamaica (Township)	61841
Jamesburg	61865
Jamestown (Clinton County)	62275
Jamestown (Perry County)	62238
Janesville	62435
Jarvis (Township)	62294
Jasper (Township)	62837
Jefferson (Cook County)	60630
Jefferson (Stephenson County) (Township)	61062
Jefferson Square Mall (Part of Joliet)	60436
Jeffries	62951
Jeiseyville	62568
Jenkins	61727
Jerome	62707
Jersey (Township)	62052
Jerseyville	62052
Jewett	62436
Jimtown	61872
Johannisburg	62296
Johannisburg (Township)	62296
Johnsburg	60050
Johnson (Christian County) (Township)	62568
Johnson (Clark County) (Township)	62420
Johnsonville	62850
Johnston City	62951
Johnstown	62440
Joliet	60431-36
For specific Joliet Zip Codes call (815) 741-7813	
Jonathan Creek (Township)	61911
Jones (Coles County)	61938
Jones (Cook County)	60452
Jonesboro	62952
Jones Ridge	62280
Jonesville	61348
Joppa	62953
Jordan (Township)	61081
Joshua (Township)	61432
Joslin	61257
Joy	61260
Joywood Farms Estates	62028
Jubilee (Township)	61559
Junction	62954
Junction City	62882
Justice	60458
Kampsville	62053
Kane	62054
Kane (Township)	62054
Kaneville	60144
Kaneville (Township)	60144
Kangley	61364
Kankakee	60901
Kankakee (Township)	60901
Kankakee Valley	60964
Kansas	61933
Kansas (Township)	61933
Kansas (Township)	61725
Kappa	61738
Karbers Ridge	62955
Karnak	62956
Kasbeer	61328
Kaskaskia (Fayette County) (Township)	62892
Kaskaskia (Randolph County)	63673
Kaskaskia Heights	62217
Kaskaskia River	62231
Kaufman	62001
Kedron	62934
Kedzie (Part of Chicago)	60623
Kedzie Grace (Part of Chicago)	60618
Keene (Township)	62349
Keenes	62851
Keeneyville	60172
Keensburg	62852
Keith (Township)	62878
Keithsburg	61442
Keithsburg (Township)	61442
Kell	62853
Kellart Lake	60924
Kellerville	62324
Kelleyville (Part of Westville)	61883
Kelly (Township)	61412
Kemp	61910
Kemper	62063
Kempton	60946
Kendall (Township)	60560
Kendall Hills	62024
Keneddy	61080
Kenilwicke	60067
Kenilworth	60043
Kenney	61749
Ken Rock	61109
Kensington (Part of Chicago)	60628

Name	ZIP
Kensington Junction (Part of Chicago)	60628
Kent	61044
Kent (Township)	61044
Kenton (Part of Chicago)	60644
Kentucky	61944
Kenwood (Champaign County)	61821
Kenwood (Cook County)	60615
Keptown	62411
Kernan	61364
Kerr (Township)	61847
Kerton (Township)	62644
Kewanee	61443
Kewanee (Township)	61443
Keyesport	62253
Keyesport Landing	62253
Key West (Part of Niles)	60016
Kickapoo	61528
Kickapoo (Township)	61528
Kidd	62277
Kidley	61924
Kilbourne	62655
Kilbourne (Township)	62655
Kildeer	60047
Kimberly Heights	60477
Kincaid	62540
Kinderhook	62345
Kinderhook (Township)	62345
King (Township)	62546
Kingdom	61021
Kingman	62463
Kings	61045
Kings Cove (Part of Deerfield)	60015
Kings Island (Part of Fox Lake)	60020
Kings Park (Part of Bolingbrook)	60439
Kingston (Township)	60145
Kingston (Adams County)	62312
Kingston (De Kalb County)	60145
Kingston Mines	61539
Kingswood	60175
Kinkaid (Township)	62907
Kinmundy	62854
Kinmundy (Township)	62854
Kinsman	60437
Kirkland	60146
Kirksville	61951
Kirkwood	61447
Kishwaukee Glen	61109
Klein Acres (Part of Rantoul)	61866
Klendworth Addition	61250
Klondike (Alexander County)	62914
Klondike (Lake County)	60002
Klondyke	62466
Knapp's Noll	61072
Knight Prairie (Township)	62859
Knollcrest (Part of Hazel Crest)	60429
Knollwood (Christian County)	62568
Knollwood (Lake County)	60047
Knollwood (Lake County)	60044
Knollwood (Sangamon County)	62684
Knottingham (Part of Downers Grove)	60515
Knox (Township)	61448
Knoxville	61448
Kortcamp (Part of Schram City)	62049
Kraft Addition	62812
Kriegh Addition	61448
Kristal Lake Ranch	61032
Kuhn	62025
La Clede	62426
La Clede (Township)	62426
Lacon	61540
Lacon (Township)	61540
La Crosse	61450
Ladd	61329
Laenna (Township)	62548
Lafayette (Coles County) (Township)	61938
Lafayette (Ogle County) (Township)	61006
Lafayette (Randolph County)	63673
La Fayette (Stark County)	61449
La Fontaine (Part of Glenview)	60025
Lafox	60147
Lagrange (Bond County) (Township)	62019
La Grange (Brown County)	62378
La Grange (Cook County)	60525
La Grange Highlands	60525

La Grange Park-Lively Grove ILLINOIS 155

Name	ZIP
La Grange Park	60525
La Grange Road (Part of La Grange)	60525
Laguna Woods	60462
La Harpe	61450
La Harpe (Township)	61450
La Hogue	60938
Lake (Clinton County)	62283
Lake (Clinton County) (Township)	62801
Lake Barrington	60010
Lake Bluff	60044
Lake Boulevard Addition	61832
Lake Bracken	61401
Lake Briarwood	60004
Lake Camelot	61547
Lake Carlinville	62626
Lake Catherine	60002
Lake Centralia	62801
Lake Charleston	61920
Lake Charlotte	60174
Lake City	61937
Lakecrest (Montgomery County)	62049
Lake Crest (Williamson County)	62922
Lake Estates	62959
Lake Forest	60045
Lake Forest Estates (Part of Belleville)	62221
Lake Fork (Logan County)	62541
Lake Fork (Logan County) (Township)	62548
Lake Holiday	60548
Lakehurst Shopping Center (Part of Waukegan)	60085
Lake in the Hills	60102
Lake in the Woods	60515
Lake Iroquois	60948
Lake Ka-Ho	62069
Lake Killarney	60013
Lake Lancelot	61547
Lakeland Hills (Jackson County)	62901
Lakeland Hills (St. Clair County)	62221
Lakeland Park (Part of McHenry)	60050
Lake Lawrence	47591
Lake Louise	61010
Lake Lynwood (Cook County)	60411
Lake Lynwood (Henry County)	61262
Lake Mantero	60950
Lake Marie	60002
Lake Marion	60110
Lake Mattoon	62447
Lakemoor	60050
Lake Oakland	61943
Lake of the Winds (Part of Wheeling)	60090
Lake of the Woods (Champaign County)	61820
Lake of the Woods (Peoria County)	61525
Lake Pana	62557
Lake Park (Champaign County)	61821
Lake Park (Cook County)	60615
Lake Park Estates	60067
Lake Park Forest	60067
Lake Petersburg	62675
Lake Piasa	62012
Lake Ranier	62626
Lake Sara	62401
Lakeshore Acres	62231
Lakeside Knolls	62049
Lakeside Villas (Part of Wheeling)	60090
Lake Summerset	61019
Lake Tacoma	62901
Lake Tara Estates	60118
Lake Thunderbird	61560
Lakeview (Part of Chicago)	60613
Lakeview Acres	62234
Lakeview Estate	62881
Lakeview Estates (Jefferson County)	62864
Lake View Estates (Williamson County)	62958
Lakeview Heights (Part of Fairfield)	62837
Lake Villa	60046
Lake Villa (Township)	60046
Lake Wildwood	61336
Lake Williamson	62626
Lakewood (Township)	62438
Lakewood (Cook County)	60466
Lakewood (Du Page County)	60185

Name	ZIP
Lakewood (Madison County)	62035
Lakewood (McHenry County)	60014
Lakewood (Shelby County)	62438
Lakewood Park	62901
Lakewood Shores	60481
Lakewood Village (Part of Carpentersville)	60110
Lake Zurich	60047
Lamard (Township)	62842
Lamb	62919
Lambert	60439
La Moille	61330
La Moille (Township)	61349
Lamoine (Township)	61415
Lamotte (Township)	62451
Lamplighter (Part of Towanda)	61776
Lanark	61046
Lancaster (Stephenson County) (Township)	61032
Lancaster (Wabash County)	62855
Landers (Part of Chicago)	60652
Landes	62466
Landings, The (Part of Lansing)	60438
Lane	61750
Lanesville	62515
Lanesville (Township)	62515
Langleyville	62568
Lansing	60438
Laona (Township)	61024
La Place	61936
La Prairie (Adams County)	62346
La Prairie (Marshall County) (Township)	61523
La Prairie Center	61565
Larchland	61462
Larkdale (Lake County)	60084
Larkdale (Macon County)	62521
Larkinsburg (Township)	62426
La Rose	61541
La Salle	61301
La Salle (Township)	61301
Latham	62543
Latona	62479
Laura	61451
La Vergne (Part of Berwyn)	60402
Lawndale (Logan County)	61751
Lawndale (McLean County) (Township)	61728
Lawn Ridge	61526
Lawrence (Lawrence County) (Township)	62439
Lawrence (McHenry County)	60033
Lawrenceville	62439
Lawrencewood Shopping Center (Part of Niles)	60648
Layton	62681
Leaf River	61047
Leaf River (Township)	61047
Leaverton Park	62451
Lebanon	62254
Lebanon (Township)	62254
Le Claire (Part of Edwardsville)	62025
Ledford	62946
Lee (Brown County) (Township)	62375
Lee (Fulton County) (Township)	61470
Lee (Lee County)	60530
Lee Center	61331
Lee Center (Township)	61331
Leech (Township)	62833
Leeds	61377
Leef (Township)	62249
Leepertown (Township)	61315
Leesburg	61501
Leesville	60964
Lehigh	60901
Leisure Lea	60543
Leisure Village (Part of Fox Lake)	60020
Leland	60531
Leland Grove	62707
Leland Lake	62650
Lemont	60439
Lemont (Township)	60439
Le Moyne (Part of Chicago)	60638
Lena	61048
Lenox (Township)	61462
Lenzburg	62255
Lenzburg (Township)	62257
Leonard	60938
Leon Corners	61277
Leonore	61332
L'Erable	60927
Lerna	62440

Name	ZIP
Le Roy (Boone County) (Township)	61012
Le Roy (McLean County)	61752
Levan (Township)	62966
Levee (Township)	62343
Leverett	61821
Lewistown	61542
Lewistown (Township)	61542
Lewood	60544
Lexington	61753
Lexington (Township)	61753
Leyden (Township)	60131
Liberty	62347
Liberty (Township)	62347
Liberty (Effingham County) (Township)	62414
Liberty (Saline County)	62946
Liberty Acres	60048
Liberty Lake (Part of Libertyville)	60048
Liberty Park	60559
Libertyville	60048
Libertyville (Township)	60048
Lick	62629
Lick Creek	62912
Licking (Township)	62449
Lidice (Part of Crest Hill)	60435
Lightsville	61047
Lilac Circle Homes (Part of Lombard)	60148
Lilly	61755
Lily Cache	60544
Lily Cache Acres	60544
Lily Lake	60151
Lilymoor	60050
Lima	62348
Lima (Township)	62348
Limerick	61349
Limestone (Kankakee County) (Township)	60901
Limestone (Peoria County)	61607
Limestone (Peoria County) (Township)	61604
Lincoln (Logan County)	62656
Lincoln (Ogle County) (Township)	61064
Lincoln Addition (Part of Wood River)	62095
Lincoln Correctional Center	62656
Lincoln Developmental Center	62656
Lincoln Estates	60423
Lincoln Gardens (Part of Alton)	62002
Lincoln Highway (Part of Olympia Fields)	60461
Lincoln Hills	60137
Lincoln Mall (Part of Matteson)	60443
Lincoln Park (Part of Chicago)	60614
Lincolnshire (Lake County)	60069
Lincolnshire (Will County)	60417
Lincolnshire Fields	61821
Lincolnwood	60645
Lincolnwood Hills	60451
Lincolnwood Town Center (Part of Lincolnwood)	60645
Lindenhurst	60046
Lindenhurst Estates (Part of Lindenhurst)	60046
Lindenwood	61049
Linder (Township)	62016
Linn (Wabash County)	62410
Linn (Woodford County) (Township)	61570
Linrose Heights	62216
Lintner	61929
Lioncrest (Part of Richton Park)	60466
Lis	62448
Lisbon	60541
Lisbon (Township)	60541
Lisbon Center	60541
Lisle	60532
Lisle (Township)	60532
Litchfield (Kankakee County)	60954
Litchfield (Montgomery County)	62056
Literberry	62660
Little America	61542
Little Indian	62691
Little Mackinaw (Township)	61759
Little Rock	60545
Little Rock (Township)	60545
Little Swan Lake	61415
Littleton	61452
Littleton (Township)	61452
Little York	61453
Lively Grove	62268

156　ILLINOIS　Lodge-Meadowbrook West

	ZIP		ZIP		ZIP
Lodge	61856	McCook	60525	Mardell Manor	61607
Logan (Edgar County)	61924	McCormick	62987	Marengo	60152
Logan (Franklin County)	62856	McCullom Lake	60050	Marengo (Township)	60152
Logan (Peoria County) (Township)	61536	McCully	61764	Marietta	61459
Logan Correctional Center	62656	McDowell	61764	Marigold	62242
Logan Square (Part of Chicago)	60647	Macedonia	62860	Marina Terrace	60543
Log Cabin Camp	60954	McGirr	60556	Marina Village	60543
Lomax	61454	McHenry	60050	Marine	62061
Lomax (Township)	61454	McHenry (Township)	60050	Marine (Township)	62061
Lombard	60148	McHenry Shores (Part of McHenry)	60050	Marion (Lee County) (Township)	61310
Lombardville	61421	Machesney Park	61111	Marion (Ogle County) (Township)	61015
London Mills	61544	Machesney Park Mall (Part of Machesney Park)	61111	Marion (Williamson County)	62959
Lone Grove (Township)	62880	MacIntoch	61364	Marion Circle	60554
Lone Tree	61368	McIntosh	60123	Marion Country Club	62959
Long Branch (Mason County)	62644	McKee (Township)	62347	Marion Hills (Part of Darien)	60559
Long Branch (Saline County) (Township)	62935	McKeen	62441	Marissa	62257
Long Creek	62521	McKendree (Township)	61832	Marissa (Township)	62257
Long Creek (Township)	62521	Mackinaw (Township)	61755	Mark	61340
Long Grove	60047	Mackinaw	61755	Market Place (Part of Champaign)	61820
Long Lake	60041	Mackler Heights (Part of Chicago Heights)	60411	Markham (Cook County)	60426
Long Meadow (Part of Downers Grove)	60515	McLean	61754	Markham (Morgan County)	62628
Long Point	61333	McLeansboro	62859	Markham City (Part of Bluford)	62814
Long Point (Township)	61333	McLeansboro (Township)	62859	Marley (Edgar County)	61944
Longshadow	60175	McNabb	61335	Marley (Will County)	60448
Longview	61852	Macomb (McDonough County) (Township)	61438	Marlow	62872
Longwood Farms (Part of Chicago Heights)	60411	Macomb (McDonough County)	61455	Marnico Village	62650
Longwood Manor	60563	Macomb City (Part of)	61455	Maroa	61756
Loogootee	62857	Macon (Bureau County) (Township)	61314	Maroa (Township)	61756
Looking Glass (Township)	62265	Macon (Macon County)	62544	Marquette Heights	61554
Lookout Point	60097	Macoupin	62676	Marrowbone (Township)	61914
Loon Lake	60002	McQueen	60185	Mars (Part of Chicago)	60639
Loop (Part of Chicago)	60604	McVey	62640	Marseilles	61341
Loraine (Adams County)	62349	Madison (Madison County)	62060	Marshall	62441
Loraine (Henry County) (Township)	61277	Madison (Richland County) (Township)	62450	Marshall (Township)	62441
Loran	61062	Madonnaville	62298	Marston	61279
Loran (Township)	61062	Maeystown (Monroe County)	62256	Martin (Crawford County) (Township)	62454
Lords' Park Manor (Part of Elgin)	60120	Magnet	61938	Martin (McLean County) (Township)	61728
Lorenzo	60481	Magnolia	61336	Martinsburg	62363
Loretto	60460	Magnolia (Township)	61336	Martinsburg (Township)	62363
Lorraine Park (Part of Wheaton)	60187	Mahomet	61853	Martinsville	62442
Lostant	61334	Mahomet (Township)	61853	Martinsville (Township)	62442
Lost Lake	61070	Maine (Cook County) (Township)	60016	Martinton	60951
Lost Nation	61021	Maine (Grundy County) (Township)	60444	Martinton (Township)	60951
Lotus	61845	Main Post Office (Part of Chicago)	60607	Mary Crest (Part of Country Club Hills)	60477
Lotus Woods	60081	Main Street (Part of Evanston)	60202	Marydale	62231
Lou Del	62298	Makanda	62958	Marydale Manor (Part of Dolton)	60419
Loudon (Township)	62414	Makanda (Township)	62958	Maryland (Ogle County)	61064
Louis Joliet Mall (Part of Joliet)	60435	Malden	61337	Maryland (Ogle County) (Township)	61007
Louisville	62858	Malibu Village	62901	Mary Meadows	60175
Louisville (Township)	62858	Mallard West (Part of Schaumburg)	60194	Maryville	62062
Love (Township)	61870	Malone (Township)	61534	Mascoutah	62258
Lovejoy (Iroquois County) (Township)	60973	Malta	60150	Mascoutah (Township)	62258
Lovejoy (St. Clair County)	62059	Malta (Township)	60150	Mason	62443
Loves Park	61111	Malvern	61270	Mason (Township)	62443
Lovington	61937	Manchester (Boone County) (Township)	61011	Mason City (Township)	62664
Lovington (Township)	61937	Manchester (Scott County)	62663	Mason City	62664
Lowder	62662	Manhattan	60442	Massbach	61028
Lowe (Township)	61911	Manhattan (Township)	60442	Massilon (Township)	62883
Lowell	61370	Manito	61546	Matanzas Beach	62644
Lowpoint	61545	Manito (Township)	61546	Matherville	61263
Loxa	61938	Manlius	61338	Matteson	60443
Lucas (Township)	62424	Manlius (Bureau County) (Township)	61338	Mattoon (Township)	61938
Ludlow	60949	Manlius (La Salle County) (Township)	61360	Mattoon	61938
Ludlow (Township)	60949	Mannheim (Part of Franklin Park)	60131	Maud	62863
Lukin (Township)	62417	Mannon	61272	Maunie	62861
Lumaghi Heights	62234	Mansfield	61854	Maxwell (Township)	62661
Luther	62664	Manteno	60950	May (Christian County) (Township)	62567
Lyman (Township)	60962	Manteno (Township)	60950	May (Lee County) (Township)	61367
Lynchburg (Township)	62617	Manville	61339	Mayberry (Township)	62817
Lyndon	61261	Maplebrook (Part of Naperville)	60565	Mayfair (Cook County)	60630
Lyndon (Township)	61261	Maple Grove	62476	Mayfair (Tazewell County)	61550
Lynn (Henry County) (Township)	61262	Maple Lane	61081	Mayfield (Township)	60178
Lynn (Knox County) (Township)	61414	Maple Park	60151	Maynard Lake	61821
Lynn Center	61262	Maple Point	62428	Mays	61944
Lynn Gardens	60901	Maples Mill	61542	Maysville	62340
Lynnville (Morgan County)	62650	Mapleton	61547	Maytown	61310
Lynnville (Ogle County) (Township)	61049	Maplewood (Cook County)	60647	Mayview	61801
Lynnwood (Cook County)	60411	Maplewood (St. Clair County)	62206	Maywood	60153-54
Lynnwood (Kendall County)	60543	Maplewood Estates	61520	For specific Maywood Zip Codes call (708) 344-4243	
Lynnwood (La Salle County)	61354	Maquon	61458	Mazon	60444
Lynwood	60411	Maquon (Township)	61458	Mazon (Township)	60444
Lyons	60534	Marblehead	62301	Meacham (Township)	62854
Lyons (Township)	60525	Marcelline	62376	Meadowbrook (Madison County)	62010
Lyons (Part of Belgium)	61883	Marcoe	62864	Meadowbrook (McDonough County)	61455
McCall	62321			Meadowbrook East (Part of Wheeling)	60090
McClellan (Township)	62894			Meadowbrook West (Part of Wheeling)	60090
McClure	62957				
McClusky	62052				
McConnell	61050				

Mayfair-Muncie **ILLINOIS** 157

Name	ZIP
Mayfair (Tazewell County)	61550
Mayfield (Township)	60178
Maynard Lake	61821
Mays	61944
Maysville	62340
Maytown	61801
Mayview	61310
Maywood	60153-54
For specific Maywood Zip Codes call (708) 344-4243	
Mazon	60444
Mazon (Township)	60444
Meacham (Township)	62854
Meadowbrook (Madison County)	62010
Meadowbrook (McDonough County)	61455
Meadowbrook East (Part of Wheeling)	60090
Meadowbrook West (Part of Wheeling)	60090
Meadowdale (Part of Carpentersville)	60110
Meadowdale Shopping Center (Part of Carpentersville)	60110
Meadow Heights (Part of Collinsville)	62234
Meadow Knolls (Part of Schaumburg)	60194
Meadowlake	61821
Meadows	61726
Meadowview (Kane County)	60175
Meadowview (Kankakee County)	60901
Mechanicsburg	62545
Mechanicsburg (Township)	62545
Medalist Park (Part of Palatine)	60067
Media	61460
Media (Township)	61460
Medina (Township)	61523
Medinah	60157
Medinah on the Lake (Part of Bloomingdale)	60108
Medora	62063
Meeks	61846
Meersman	61244
Melrose (Township)	62478
Melrose (Adams County) (Township)	62301
Melrose (Clark County)	62478
Melrose Park	60160-63
For specific Melrose Park Zip Codes call (708) 343-2150	
Melville	62035
Melvin	60952
Menard	62259
Mendon	62351
Mendon (Township)	62351
Mendota	61342
Mendota (Township)	61342
Menominee (Township)	61025
Menominee (Jo Daviess County)	61025
Meppen	62064
Mercer (Township)	61231
Merchandise Mart (Part of Chicago)	60654
Meredosia	62665
Meriden	61342
Meriden (Township)	61342
Meridian (Township)	62283
Meridian Heights (Part of Mounds)	62964
Mermet	62908
Merna	61758
Merriam	62837
Merrimac	62295
Merrionette Park	60655
Merritt	62650
Merry Oaks	61244
Mesa Lake	62855
Metamora	61548
Metamora (Township)	61548
Metcalf	61940
Metropolis	62960
Mettawa	60048
Meyer (Adams County)	62379
Meyer (Kankakee County)	60901
Meyerbrook	60545
Meyers Bay (Part of Fox Lake)	60050
Michael	62065
Middlebury (Part of Barrington Hills)	60010
Middle Creek (Hancock County)	62321
Middlecreek (Kane County)	60175
Middlefork (Township)	61865
Middle Grove	61531
Middleport (Township)	61970
Middlesworth	62565
Middletown	62666
Midland City	61727
Midland Hills	62958
Midlothian	60445
Midway (Madison County)	62067
Midway (Massac County)	62960
Midway (Tazewell County)	61554
Midway (Vermilion County)	61883
Midwest (Part of Chicago)	60612
Midwest Club (Part of Oak Brook)	60521
Milan (De Kalb County) (Township)	60550
Milan (Macon County) (Township)	62544
Milan (Rock Island County)	61264
Mildred	62707
Miles Station	62012
Milford	60953
Milford (Township)	60953
Milks Grove (Township)	60941
Millbrook (Kendall County)	60536
Millbrook (Peoria County) (Township)	61451
Millburn	60046
Millcreek	62961
Milledgeville	61051
Miller (Township)	61360
Miller Addition	61250
Miller City	62962
Miller Lake	62864
Millersburg	61231
Millersburg (Township)	61260
Millerville	62557
Miller Woods	60411
Millhurst	60545
Millington	60537
Mills (Township)	62246
Mill Shoals	62862
Mill Shoals (Township)	62862
Mill Spring	62035
Millstadt	62260
Millstadt (Township)	62260
Milmine	61855
Milo (Bureau County) (Township)	61421
Milo (Bureau County)	61421
Milton (Du Page County) (Township)	60187
Milton (Pike County)	62352
Mindale	62319
Mineral	61344
Mineral (Township)	61344
Mineral Springs	61081
Minier	61759
Minonk	61760
Minonk (Township)	61760
Minooka	60447
Missal	61364
Mission (Township)	60551
Mission Hills	60062
Mississippi (Township)	62022
Missouri (Township)	62353
Mitchell	62040
Mitchellsville	62917
Mitchie	62295
Mobet Meadows	61275
Mobile City	61401
Moccasin	62411
Moccasin (Township)	62411
Mode	62444
Modena	61491
Modesto	62667
Modoc	62261
Moecherville	60504
Mohawk (Part of Bensenville)	60106
Mokena	60448
Moline	61265
Moline (Township)	61265
Momence	60954
Momence (Township)	60954
Mona (Township)	60964
Monee	60449
Monee (Township)	60449
Money Creek (Township)	61753
Monica	61559
Monmouth	61462
Monmouth (Township)	61462
Monroe (Township)	61052
Monroe Center	61052
Monroe City	62298
Mont	62025
Montague Forest	60123
Mont Clare (Part of Chicago)	60639
Montebello (Township)	62341
Monterey	61520
Monterey Village (Part of University Park)	60466
Montezuma	62361
Montezuma (Township)	62361
Montgomery (Crawford County) (Township)	62427
Montgomery (Kane County)	60538
Montgomery (Woodford County) (Township)	61733
Monticello	61856
Monticello (Township)	61856
Montmorency (Township)	61071
Montrose	62445
Moon Lake Village (Part of Hoffman Estates)	60195
Moonshine	62442
Moores Prairie (Township)	62810
Mooseheart	60539
Moraine Valley Facility (Part of Bridgeview)	60455
Morea	62451
Morehaven	61073
Morgan (Township)	61943
Morgan Park (Part of Chicago)	60643
Morgan's Gate	60067
Moriah	62420
Moro	62067
Moro (Township)	62067
Morris	60450
Morris (Township)	60450
Morris Hills (Part of Collinsville)	62234
Morrison	61270
Morrisonville	62546
Morristown (Henry County)	61274
Morristown (Winnebago County)	61109
Morseville	61085
Morton	61550
Morton (Township)	61550
Morton Grove	60053
Morton Park (Part of Cicero)	60650
Moser Highlands (Part of Naperville)	60540
Mosquito (Township)	62547
Mossville	61552
Mound (Effingham County) (Township)	62411
Mound (McDonough County) (Township)	61455
Mound City	62963
Mounds	62964
Mountain (Township)	62946
Mountain Glen	62920
Mount Auburn	62547
Mount Auburn (Township)	62547
Mount Carbon	62966
Mount Carmel	62863
Mount Carroll	61053
Mount Carroll (Township)	61053
Mount Clair	62035
Mount Clare	62033
Mount Erie	62446
Mount Erie (Township)	62446
Mount Greenwood (Part of Chicago)	60655
Mount Hope (Township)	61754
Mount Joy	61723
Mount Morris	61054
Mount Morris (Township)	61054
Mount Olive	62069
Mount Olive (Township)	62069
Mount Palatine	61334
Mount Pleasant (Union County)	62912
Mount Pleasant (Whiteside County) (Township)	61270
Mount Prospect	60056
Mount Prospect Gardens (Part of Mount Prospect)	60056
Mount Prospect Plaza (Part of Mount Prospect)	60056
Mount Pulaski	62548
Mount Pulaski (Township)	62548
Mount Sterling	62353
Mount Sterling (Township)	62353
Mount Vernon	62864
Mount Vernon (Township)	62864
Mount Zion	62549
Mount Zion (Township)	62549
Moweaqua	62550
Moweaqua (Township)	62550
Mozier	62070
Mozier Landing	62045
Mt. Vernon	61025
Muddy	62965
Mulberry Grove	62262
Mulberry Grove (Township)	62262
Mulkeytown	62865
Muncie	61857

158 ILLINOIS Mundelein-Oak Manor

	ZIP		ZIP		ZIP
Mundelein	60060	Newman	61942	North Henderson	
Mundelein Ridge Estates		Newman (Township)	61942	(Township)	61466
(Part of Mundelein)	60060	Newmansville	62612	North Hills	60060
Munson (Township)	61238	Newmansville (Township)	62612	Northlake	60164
Munster	61364	New Memphis (Clinton		North Lakewood	62881
Murdock	61941	County)	62266	Northland Mall (Part of	
Murdock (Township)	61941	New Milford	61109	Sterling)	61081
Murphy Acres	60435	New Minden	62263	North Libertyville Estates	60048
Murphysboro	62966	New Palatine	62297	North Litchfield (Township)	62056
Murphysboro (Township)	62966	New Philadelphia	61459	Northmore	62035
Murrayville	62668	Newport (Lake County)		Northmore Heights (Part of	
Myers Lake	62568	(Township)	60083	Effingham)	62401
Mylith Park	60050	Newport (Madison County)	62060	North Mounds	62964
Myrtle	61047	New Salem (Township)	62357	North Muddy (Township)	62479
Naausay (Township)	60560	New Salem (McDonough		North Okaw (Township)	61938
Nachusa	61057	County) (Township)	61482	North Oregon	61061
Nachusa (Township)	61057	New Salem (Pike County)	62357	North Otter (Township)	62690
Nameoki (Madison County)	62040	Newton (Jasper County)	62448	North Palmyra (Township)	62667
Nameoki (Madison County)		Newton (Whiteside County)		North Park	61111
(Township)	62040	(Township)	61250	North Park Mall (Part of Villa	
Nameoki Village Shopping		Newtown (Livingston		Park)	60181
Center (Part of Granite		County) (Township)	61311	North Pekin	61554
City)	62040	Newtown (Vermilion County)	61858	North Plato	60140
Nantucket Cove (Part of		New Trier (Township)	60093	Northpoint Estates	60914
Schaumburg)	60194	New Virginia	62951	Northpoint Shopping Center	
Naperville	60540	New Windsor	61465	(Part of Arlington Heights)	60004
	60563-67	Niantic	62551	North Prairie Acres	61953
For specific Naperville Zip Codes		Niantic (Township)	62551	North Riverside	60546
call (708) 717-2662		North Illinois Fair		North Riverside Park Mall	
Naperville (Township)	60540	Association (Part of North		(Part of North Riverside)	60546
Naplate	61350	Aurora)	60542	North Shoreland	62959
Naples	62665	Niles	60648	North Suburban Facility	60197-99
Nashua (Township)	61061	Niles (Township)	60076	For specific North Suburban Facility	
Nashville	62263	Nilwood	62672	Zip Codes call (708) 451-2400	
Nashville (Township)	62263	Nilwood (Township)	62640	Northtown (Part of Chicago)	60645
Nason	62866	Nineteenth Avenue (Part of		North Towne Mall (Part of	
Natalie Estates (Part of Oak		Melrose Park)	60160	Rockford)	61103
Forest)	60452	Niota	62358	North Venice (Part of	
National Stock Yards	62071	Nippersink Terrace	60081	Venice)	62090
Natrona	62682	Nixon (Township)	61882	Northville (Township)	60551
Nauvoo	62354	Nixon's Greenwood-Central	60025	Northwood	61801
Nauvoo (Township)	62354	Noble	62868	Northwoods (De Kalb	
Navajo Hills (Part of Palos		Noble (Township)	62868	County)	60135
Heights)	60463	Nokomis	62075	North Woods (Du Page	
Neadmore	62442	Nokomis (Township)	62075	County)	60185
Nebo	62355	Nolle Hill	62036	Northwoods (St. Clair	
Nebraska (Township)	61760	Nora	61059	County)	62269
Neelys	62621	Nora (Township)	61059	Northwoods Place (Part of	
Nekoma	61490	Nordic Acres	61008	East Alton)	62024
Nelson	61058	Nordic Park	60143	Northwoods Shopping	
Nelson (Township)	61058	Normal	61761	Center (Part of Peoria)	61613
Neoga (Township)	62447	Normal (Township)	61761	Norton (Township)	60917
Neoga	62447	Normal Junction (Part of		Nortonville	62668
Neponset	61345	Normal)	61761	Norway	60551
Neponset (Township)	61345	Norman (Township)	60450	Norwood (Mercer County)	61412
Nerska (Part of Chicago)	60632	Normandale	61554	Norwood (Peoria County)	61604
Nettle Creek (Township)	60541	Normandy	61376	Norwood Park (Cook	
Neunert	62950	Normandy Heights	62864	County)	60631
Nevada (Township)	60460	Normandy Hill (Part of		Norwood Park (Cook	
Nevins	61944	Northbrook)	60062	County) (Township)	60656
Newark	60541	Normandy Villa (Part of		Nottingham Park (Part of	
New Athens (Township)	62264	Chicago Heights)	60411	Bridgeview)	60638
New Athens	62264	Norpaul (Part of Franklin		Nottingham Woods	60119
New Baden	62265	Park)	60131	Novak Park	60174
New Bedford	61346	Norridge	60656	Nubbin Ridge	62835
New Berlin	62670	Norris	61553	Nunda (Township)	60012
New Berlin (Township)	62670	Norris City	62869	Nutwood	62031
Newbern	62022	North (Part of Evanston)	60201	Oak	62947
New Blossom Hill (Part of		North Alton (Part of Alton)	62002	Oak Bluff Estates	61038
Cary)	60013	North Arm	61944	Oak Brook (Du Page	
New Boston	61272	North Aurora	60542	County)	60521
New Boston (Township)	61272	North Barrington	60010	Oakbrook (Macoupin	
Newburg (Macon County)	62501	Northbelt Homesites (Part of		County)	62626
Newburg (Pike County)		Belleville)	62221	Oakbrook Center (Part of	
(Township)	62363	Northbrook	60062	Oak Brook)	60521
New Burnside	62967	Northbrook Court (Part of		Oakbrook Terrace	60181
Newby	61938	Northbrook)	60062	Oakdale (Township)	62268
New Camp	62921	Northbrook Knolls (Part of		Oakdale (Cook County)	60619
New Canton	62356	Northbrook)	60062	Oakdale (Washington	
Newcastle	62987	Northbrook West	60062	County)	62268
New Century Town (Part of		North Chicago	60064	Oakdale Woods	60106
Vernon Hills)	60060	North Chillicothe (Part of		Oakford	62673
New City	62563	Chillicothe)	61523	Oak Forest	60452
New Columbia	62943	North Dixon (Part of Dixon)	61021	Oak Grove (Madison	
Newcomb (Township)	61853	Northeast (Township)	62339	County)	62035
New Delhi	62052	Northern (Township)	62860	Oak Grove (Rock Island	
New Dennison	62959	Northern Heights	61010	County)	61264
New Douglas	62074	Northern Hills	61032	Oak Hill	61518
New Douglas (Township)	62074	Northfield	60093	Oak Hills	62232
Newell (Township)	61832	Northfield (Township)	60025	Oak Hills Estates	61008
New Hanover	62298	Northfield Woods	60025	Oak Knolls	60118
New Hartford	62363	North Fork (Township)	62979	Oakland (Coles County)	61943
New Haven	62867	Northgate (Part of Hanover		Oakland (Schuyler County)	
New Haven (Township)	62867	Park)	60103	(Township)	62681
New Hebron	62454	Northgate Shopping Center		Oak Lawn	60453-59
New Holland	62671	(Part of Aurora)	60506	For specific Oak Lawn Zip Codes	
New La Grange	62378	North Glen Ellyn	60137	call (708) 598-6305	
New Lebanon	60140	North Hampton	61523	Oaklawn (Part of Danville)	61832
New Lenox	60451	North Harvey (Part of		Oakley	62552
New Lenox (Township)	60451	Harvey)	60426	Oakley (Township)	62552
New Liberty	62910	North Henderson	61466	Oak Manor	60545

Oak Meadows-Penn ILLINOIS 159

Name	ZIP
Oak Meadows	60185
Oak Park	60301-05
For specific Oak Park Zip Codes call (708) 848-7900	
Oak Park (Township)	60302
Oak Ridge	61548
Oak Run	61428
Oak Spring Woods	60048
Oakwood (Township)	61858
Oakwood (Du Page County)	60559
Oakwood (Henderson County)	61437
Oakwood (Peoria County)	61605
Oakwood (Vermilion County)	61858
Oakwood Acres (Part of Geneseo)	61254
Oakwood Hills	60013
Oakwood Shores	60097
Obed	62510
Oblong	62449
Oblong (Township)	62449
Oconee	62553
Oconee (Township)	62553
Ocoya	61764
Odell	60460
Odell (Township)	60460
Odgen	62863
Odin	62870
Odin (Township)	62870
O'Fallon	62269
O'Fallon (Township)	62269
Ogden	61859
Ogden (Township)	61859
Ogden Park (Part of Chicago)	60636
Oglesby	61348
O'Hare Airport (Part of Chicago)	60666
Ohio	61349
Ohio (Township)	61349
Ohio Grove (Township)	61231
Ohlman	62076
Oil Center (Part of Centralia)	62801
Oilfield	62420
Okaw (Township)	62534
Okawville	62271
Okawville (Township)	62271
Oklahoma Addition	62451
Old Camp	62921
Old Du Quoin	62832
Oldenburg	62024
Olde Salem (Part of Hanover Park)	60103
Old Farm (Part of Naperville)	60563
Old Gilchrist	61231
Old Kane	62054
Old Marissa (Part of Marissa)	62257
Old Mill Creek	60083
Old Mill Grove (Part of Lake Zurich)	60047
Old Niota	62358
Old Orchard Shopping Center (Part of Skokie)	60077
Old Pearl	62361
Old Ripley	62275
Old Ripley (Township)	62275
Old Shawneetown	62984
Old Stonington	62567
Oldtown (McLean County) (Township)	61701
Oldtown (Saline County)	62987
Olena	61480
Olio (Township)	61530
Olive (Township)	62058
Olive Branch	62969
Oliver	62441
Olivet	61846
Olmsted	62970
Olney	62450
Olney (Township)	62450
Olympia Fields	60461
Olympia Gardens	60411
Olympic Terrace (Part of Naperville)	60540
Olympic Village (Part of Chicago Heights)	60411
Omaha	62871
Omaha (Township)	62871
Omega	62849
Omega (Township)	62849
Omphghent (Township)	62097
Onarga	60955
Onarga (Township)	60955
Oneco	61060
Oneco (Township)	61060
One Hundred Forty-Seventh Street (Part of Harvey)	60426

Name	ZIP
One Hundred Third Street (Part of Chicago)	60628
Oneida	61467
Ontario (Township)	61467
Ontario Street (Part of Chicago)	60611
Ontarioville	60103
Opdyke	62872
Opheim	61468
Ophir (Township)	61342
Oquawka	61469
Oquawka (Township)	61469
Ora (Township)	62971
Oran (Township)	62512
Orange (Clark County) (Township)	62442
Orange (Knox County) (Township)	61436
Orange Prairie	61614
Orangeville	61060
Oraville	62971
Orchard (Township)	62850
Orchard Acres	60014
Orchard Estates	60187
Orchard Heights	62450
Orchard Mines	61607
Orchard Place (Part of Des Plaines)	60018
Orchard Valley	60031
Orchardville	62899
Oreana	62554
Oregon	61061
Oregon (Township)	61061
Orel (Township)	62895
Orient	62874
Orion (Fulton County) (Township)	61520
Orion (Henry County)	61273
Orland (Township)	60462
Orland Hills (Cook County)	60477
Orland Hills (Cook County)	60462
Orland Park	60462
Orland Park Place (Part of Orland Park)	60462
Orland Square (Part of Orland Park)	60462
Orleans	62601
Orleans Terrace (Part of Addison)	60101
Orvil (Township)	62635
Osage (Franklin County)	62983
Osage (La Salle County) (Township)	61377
Osbernville	62513
Osborn	61257
Osceola (Stark County)	61345
Osceola (Stark County) (Township)	61421
Osco	61274
Osco (Township)	61274
Oskaloosa	62899
Oskaloosa (Township)	62899
Osman	61843
Ospur	61727
Ossami Lake (Part of Morton)	61550
Oswego	60543
Oswego (Township)	60543
Otego (Township)	62418
Ottawa	61350
Ottawa (Township)	61350
Otter Creek (Jersey County) (Township)	62052
Otter Creek (La Salle County) (Township)	61364
Otterville	62037
Otto	60922
Otto (Township)	60922
Otto Mall (Part of Chicago Heights)	60411
Ottville	61362
Outter Creek	62031
Owaneco	62555
Owego (Township)	61764
Owen (Township)	61103
Oxford (Township)	61413
Oxville	62621
Ozark	62972
Pacesetter Park (Part of South Holland)	60473
Paderborn	62298
Padua	61737
Painesville	62948
Palatine	60067
Palatine (Township)	60067
Palermo	61876
Palestine (Crawford County)	62451
Palestine (Woodford County) (Township)	61771
Palmer	62556
Palmyra (Lee County)	61021

Name	ZIP
Palmyra (Lee County) (Township)	61021
Palmyra (Macoupin County)	62674
Paloma	62359
Palos (Township)	60464
Palos Gardens	60463
Palos Heights	60463
Palos Hills	60465
Palos Park	60464
Palos Westgate (Part of Palos Heights)	60463
Palsgrove	61053
Pam Anne Estates	60025
Pana	62557
Pana (Township)	62557
Panama	62077
Pankeyville	62946
Panola	61738
Panola (Township)	61738
Panther Creek (Township)	62627
Papineau	60956
Papineau (Township)	60956
Paradise	61938
Paradise (Township)	61938
Paradise Acres	62918
Paris	61944
Paris (Township)	61944
Park City	60085
Parker (Clark County) (Township)	62474
Parker (Johnson County)	62922
Parkersburg	62452
Parkfield Terrace	62206
Park Forest	60466
Park Hills (Part of Effingham)	62401
Parkhome (Part of Cicero)	60650
Park Lane	60964
Park Manor (Part of Chicago)	60619
Park Meadows (Part of Rolling Meadows)	60008
Park Ridge	60068
Parkville	61872
Parkway (Part of North Riverside)	60546
Parkwood (Part of Elgin)	60120
Parkwood Village (Part of Elgin)	60120
Parnell	61842
Parrish	62890
Parrish Addition	62930
Partridge (Township)	61545
Partridge Hill (Part of Hoffman Estates)	60195
Passport	62868
Patoka	62875
Patoka (Township)	62875
Patterson	62078
Patterson (Township)	62078
Patterson Heights	62035
Patterson Springs	61919
Patton (Ford County) (Township)	60957
Patton (Wabash County)	62863
Pattonsburg	61369
Paulton	62959
Pavillion	60560
Pawnee	62558
Pawnee (Township)	62558
Paw Paw (De Kalb County) (Township)	60518
Paw Paw (Lee County)	61353
Paxton	60957
Paynes Point	61015
Payson	62360
Payson (Township)	62360
Peach Orchard (Township)	60952
Pea Ridge (Township)	62375
Pearl	62361
Pearl (Township)	62361
Pearl City	61062
Pebble Beach	60450
Pecan Grove	62031
Pecatonica	61063
Pecatonica (Township)	61063
Peerless	60544
Pekin	61554-55
For specific Pekin Zip Codes call (309) 346-7878	
Pekin Heights (Part of Pekin)	61554
Pekin Mall (Part of Pekin)	61554
Pella (Township)	60959
Pembroke (Township)	60964
Pendleton (Township)	62810
Penfield	61862
Penn (Shelby County) (Township)	62550
Penn (Stark County) (Township)	61421

160 ILLINOIS Pennsylvania-Raddle

	ZIP
Pennsylvania (Township)	62664
Penny Oaks (Part of Macomb)	61455
Penrose	61081
Peoria	61601-56
For specific Peoria Zip Codes call (309) 671-8813	
Peoria City (Township)	61601
Peoria Heights	61614
Peotone	60468
Peotone (Township)	60468
Pepper Tree	60067
Pequot (Part of Coal City)	60416
Percy	62272
Perdueville	60957
Perks	62973
Perry	62362
Perry (Township)	62362
Perryton (Township)	61279
Perryville	61016
Persifer (Township)	61436
Peru	61354
Peru (Township)	61354
Peru Mall (Part of Peru)	61354
Pesotum	61863
Pesotum (Township)	61863
Peters (Part of Glen Carbon)	62034
Petersburg (Menard County)	62675
Petersburg (St. Clair County)	62269
Peters Creek	62931
Peterson Avenue (Part of Chicago)	60646
Petite Lake	60002
Petrolia	62417
Petty (Township)	62466
Pharoah's Gardens	62932
Pheasant Creek (Part of Northbrook)	60062
Pheasant Hollow	60187
Pheasant Meadows	60401
Pheasant Ridge (Will County)	60448
Pheasant Ridge (Will County)	60544
Phelps	62240
Phenix (Township)	61254
Philadelphia	62612
Philadelphia (Township)	62612
Phillippe (Part of Rolling Meadows)	60008
Phillips (Township)	62827
Phillipstown	62827
Philo	61864
Philo (Township)	61864
Phinney	61801
Phoenix	60426
Piasa (Jersey County) (Township)	62012
Piasa (Macoupin County)	62079
Piasa Hills	62035
Picadilly Terrace	60514
Pickaway (Township)	61914
Pierce (Township)	60151
Pierceburg	62449
Pierron	62273
Pierson	61929
Piety Hill	61348
Pigeon Grove (Township)	60924
Pike (Livingston County) (Township)	61726
Pike (Pike County)	62370
Pilot (Kankakee County) (Township)	60941
Pilot (Vermilion County) (Township)	61831
Pilot Grove (Township)	62318
Pilot Knob (Township)	62263
Pilsen (Part of Chicago)	60608
Pinckneyville	62274
Pine Creek (Township)	61064
Pinecrest	60435
Pine Grove	60450
Pinelands	60174
Pine Meadow (Part of Bolingbrook)	60439
Pine Ridge	61254
Pine Rock (Township)	61015
Pingree Grove	60140
Pinkstaff	62439
Pin Oak (Township)	62025
Pioneer Acres	61025
Pioneer Terrace	60115
Piopolis	62859
Piper City	60959
Pisgah	62650
Pistakee Bay	60050
Pistakee Heights (Part of Fox Lake)	60050

	ZIP
Pistakee Highlands (McHenry County)	60050
Pistakee Hills	60050
Pistaqua Heights	60050
Pitchin	60924
Pitman (Township)	62572
Pittsburg (Fayette County)	62471
Pittsburg (Williamson County)	62974
Pittsfield	62363
Pittsfield (Township)	62363
Pittwood	60970
Pixley (Township)	62868
Plainfield	60544
Plainfield (Township)	60544
Plainfield Acres	60544
Plainview	62676
Plainville	62365
Plano	60545
Plato (Township)	60170
Plato Center	60170
Plattville	60560
Playfield (Part of Crestwood)	60445
Plaza (Part of Belleville)	62223
Pleasant (Township)	61441
Pleasant Dale (Part of Burr Ridge)	60525
Pleasantdale Estates	60439
Pleasant Grove (Coles County) (Township)	62440
Pleasant Grove (Johnson County)	62912
Pleasant Hill (Township)	62366
Pleasant Hill (Du Page County)	60188
Pleasant Hill (Jackson County)	62901
Pleasant Hill (McLean County)	61753
Pleasant Hill (Pike County)	62366
Pleasant Hills	60172
Pleasant Mound	62284
Pleasant Mound (Township)	62284
Pleasant Plains	62677
Pleasant Ridge (Livingston County) (Township)	61747
Pleasant Ridge (Madison County)	62234
Pleasant Run (Part of Wheeling)	60090
Pleasant Vale (Township)	62356
Pleasant Valley (Township)	61085
Pleasant View (Macon County) (Township)	62513
Pleasant View (Schuyler County)	62681
Plumfield	62896
Plum Grove Countryside (Part of Rolling Meadows)	60008
Plum Grove Estates	60067
Plum Grove Hills (Part of Rolling Meadows)	60008
Plum Grove Village (Part of Rolling Meadows)	60008
Plum Grove Woods	60067
Plum Hill	62263
Plum Hill (Township)	62214
Plum Hollow	61021
Plymouth	62367
Plymouth Farms (Part of Vernon Hills)	60060
Poag	62025
Pocahontas	62275
Poe	62278
Point Pleasant (Township)	61473
Point West (Part of Lombard)	60148
Polk (Township)	62626
Polo	61064
Pomona	62975
Pomona (Township)	62975
Pond	62995
Pontiac	61764
Pontiac (Township)	61764
Pontiac (Part of Fairview Heights)	62232
Pontiac Correctional Center	61764
Pontiac Station (Part of Fairview Heights)	62208
Pontoon Beach	62040
Pontoosuc	62330
Pontoosuc (Township)	62330
Pope (Township)	62875
Poplar City	62633
Poplar Grove	61065
Poplar Grove (Township)	61065
Poplar Grove	61244
Port Byron	61275
Port Byron (Township)	61275
Port Jackson	62427

	ZIP
Portland (Whiteside County) (Township)	61277
Portland (Whiteside County)	61277
Port Ridge (Part of Lockport)	60441
Posen (Cook County)	60469
Posen (Washington County)	62263
Posey	62231
Post Oak	62418
Potomac	61865
Pottawatawi Highlands (Part of Tinley Park)	60477
Pottstown	61614
Powder Creek	62223
Powder Mill Woods	62220
Powellton	62358
Prairie (Crawford County) (Township)	62442
Prairie (Edgar County) (Township)	61924
Prairie (Hancock County) (Township)	62321
Prairie (Randolph County)	62278
Prairie (Shelby County) (Township)	62463
Prairie Center	61350
Prairie City	61470
Prairie City (Township)	61470
Prairie Court (Part of Oak Park)	60301
Prairie Creek (Township)	62635
Prairie Du Long (Township)	62243
Prairie du Pont	62240
Prairie Du Rocher	62277
Prairie Estates	62675
Prairie Green (Du Page County)	60187
Prairie Green (Iroquois County) (Township)	60942
Prairie Grove	60050
Prairie Home	62550
Prairie Ridge (Part of Hoffman Estates)	60195
Prairieton (Township)	62550
Prairietown	62097
Prairie View	60069
Prairieville	61021
Preemption	61276
Preemption (Township)	61276
Prentice	62612
Presswood Hills	62274
Prestbury	60506
Preston (Randolph County)	62242
Preston (Richland County) (Township)	62450
Preston Heights	60431
Prestwick	60423
Prickett (Part of Edwardsville)	62025
Princeton	61356
Princeton (Township)	61356
Princeville	61559
Princeville (Township)	61559
Proctor	60936
Prophetstown	61277
Prophetstown (Township)	61277
Prospect	61866
Prospect Heights	60070
Prospect Meadows (Part of Mount Prospect)	60056
Prospect Park (Part of Fairview Heights)	62208
Providence	61368
Provincetown (Part of Country Club Hills)	60477
Proving Ground	61074
Proviso (Township)	60160
Prudential Plaza (Part of Chicago)	60601
Pruett	62458
Pujol	63673
Pulaski	62976
Pulleys Mill	62939
Pullman (Part of Chicago)	60628
Pullman Junction (Part of Chicago)	60617
Putnam (Fulton County) (Township)	61427
Putnam (Putnam County)	61560
Quarry (Township)	62037
Quatoga	62035
Quincy	62301-06
For specific Quincy Zip Codes call (217) 224-4950	
Quincy Mall (Part of Quincy)	62301
Quiver (Township)	62644
Quiver Beach	62644
Raccoon (Township)	62801
Racine Avenue (Part of Chicago)	60628
Raddle	62950

Radford-Ross ILLINOIS 161

Name	ZIP
Radford	62550
Radnor (Township)	61525
Radom	62876
Rainbow Hills	60174
Rakers Addition	62216
Raleigh	62977
Raleigh (Township)	62977
Ramona Place	62035
Ramsey	62080
Ramsey (Township)	62080
Randhurst Shopping Center (Part of Mount Prospect)	60056
Randolph	61745
Randolph (Township)	61745
Randolph Street (Part of Chicago)	60601
Range	62864
Rankin	60960
Ransom	62470
Ransom Ridge Estates (Part of Park Ridge)	60068
Rantoul	61866
Rantoul (Township)	61866
Rapatee	61544
Rapids City	61278
Rardin	61920
Raritan	61471
Raritan (Township)	61471
Rasmunsen Addition	60936
Raven	61924
Ravenswood (Part of Chicago)	60625
Ravinia (Part of Highland Park)	60035
Ravinia Park (Part of Highland Park)	60035
Rawalts	61520
Rawlins (Township)	61036
Ray	62681
Raymond (Township)	62560
Raymond (Champaign County) (Township)	61852
Raymond (Montgomery County)	62560
Reader	62630
Reading	61311
Reading (Township)	61311
Rector (Township)	62930
Red Bud	62278
Reddick	60961
Redmon	61949
Red Oak	61032
Red Oak Terrace (Part of Highland Park)	60035
Reed (Township)	60408
Reed City	61547
Reeds Station	62924
Rees	62638
Reevesville	62943
Regency Grove	60515
Regency Terrace (Part of Bloomingdale)	60108
Reilly	60960
Reily Lake	62241
Rellswood Hills	61008
Renault	62279
Renchville	61523
Rend City	62812
Reno	62246
Rentchler	62221
Reseda (Part of Palatine)	60067
Resthaven	60481
Reynolds (Lee County) (Township)	61006
Reynolds (Rock Island County)	61279
Reynoldsburg	62991
Reynoldsville	62952
Rice (Jo Daviess County) (Township)	61036
Rice (Perry County)	62274
Rice Lake	61401
Rich (Township)	60450
Richards	60151
Richardson	61801
Richardson Estates	62365
Richfield	62365
Richfield (Township)	62365
Richland (La Salle County) (Township)	61334
Richland (Marshall County) (Township)	61570
Richland (Sangamon County)	62677
Richland (Shelby County) (Township)	62465
Richland Grove (Township)	61281
Richmond	60071
Richmond (Township)	60071
Richmond Estates (Part of Oak Forest)	60452

Name	ZIP
Richton Hills (Part of Richton Park)	60466
Richton Park	60471
Richview	62877
Richview (Township)	62877
Richwood (Township)	62031
Richwoods (Crawford County)	62451
Richwoods (Peoria County) (Township)	61614
Ricks (Township)	62546
Ridge (Township)	62565
Ridgecrest	60450
Ridge Farm	61870
Ridgefield	60012
Ridgeland (Township)	60968
Ridgemoor (Part of Willowbrook)	60521
Ridge Prairie Heights (Part of O'Fallon)	62269
Ridgeville	60955
Ridgewood (Part of Western Springs)	60558
Ridgewood East	60452
Ridgewood West (Part of Oak Forest)	60452
Ridgway	62979
Ridgway (Township)	62979
Ridott	61067
Ridott (Township)	61067
Rieuf's Meadows	61341
Riffel	62858
Riggston	62694
Riley (Township)	61038
Riley Center	60152
Rinard	62878
Ring Neck	60543
Ringwood	60072
Rio	61472
Rio (Township)	61472
Ripley	62353
Ripley (Township)	62353
Rising Sun	62821
Ritchason Addition	62896
Ritchie	60481
Riverair	62035
Riverdale (Cook County)	60627
Riverdale (Winnebago County)	61073
River Forest (Cook County)	60305
River Forest (Cook County) (Township)	60305
River Glen	60010
River Grange Lakes	60175
River Grove	60171
River Heights (Part of Danville)	61832
River Isle	60954
River Oaks Center (Part of Calumet City)	60409
River Reach	61008
River Ridge	60560
Riverside (Township)	60546
Riverside (Adams County) (Township)	62301
Riverside (Cook County)	60546
Riverside Island (Part of Fox Lake)	60020
Riverside Lawns	60546
Riverside Park	60050
Riverton	62561
Riverview (Carroll County)	61285
Riverview (Lee County)	61021
Riverview (Whiteside County)	61071
Riverview Heights	60543
Riverwoods	60015
Rivoli (Township)	61465
Roaches	62898
Roachtown	62260
Roanoke	61561
Roanoke (Township)	61561
Robbins	60472
Robbs	62985
Robein (Part of East Peoria)	61611
Roberts (Ford County)	60962
Roberts (Marshall County) (Township)	61375
Roberts Park (Part of Bridgeview)	60453
Robin Hill (Part of Joliet)	60435
Robinson	62454
Robinson (Township)	62454
Rob Roy Country Club (Part of Prospect Heights)	60070
Roby	62545
Rochelle	61068
Rochester (Sangamon County)	62563
Rochester (Sangamon County) (Township)	62563

Name	ZIP
Rochester (Wabash County)	62863
Rock	62938
Rockbridge	62081
Rockbridge (Township)	62081
Rock City	61070
Rock Creek (Adams County)	62301
Rock Creek (Hancock County) (Township)	62321
Rock Creek (Hardin County)	62919
Rock Creek-Lima (Township)	61046
Rockdale	60436
Rock Falls	61071
Rockford	61101-32
For specific Rockford Zip Codes call (815) 229-4811	
Rockgate Estates	62035
Rock Grove	61070
Rock Grove (Township)	61070
Rock Island	61201-04
For specific Rock Island Zip Codes call (309) 793-7200	
Rock Island Arsenal	61299
Rockport	62370
Rock River Terrace	61010
Rock Run (Township)	61019
Rockton	61072
Rockton (Township)	61072
Rockvale (Township)	61061
Rock Vale Heights	61010
Rockville (Township)	60950
Rockwell (Part of La Salle)	61301
Rockwood	62280
Rocky Run (Township)	62373
Rodden	61041
Rogers (Township)	60946
Rogers Park (Part of Chicago)	60660
Rolling Acres (Champaign County)	61866
Rolling Acres (Peoria County)	61614
Rolling Green	61938
Rolling Hills (Clinton County)	62293
Rolling Hills (Piatt County)	61884
Rolling Meadows (Cook County)	60008
Rolling Meadows (McDonough County)	61455
Rollo	60518
Rome (Jefferson County) (Township)	62830
Rome (Peoria County)	61562
Rome Heights	61523
Romeoville	60441
Romine (Township)	62849
Rondout	60044
Roodhouse	62082
Roodhouse (Township)	62082
Rooks Creek (Township)	61764
Rooney Heights	60435
Roosevelt Road (Part of Chicago)	60607
Roots	62277
Root Spring	60013
Ropers Landing	62938
Rosamond	62083
Rosamond (Township)	62083
Roscoe	61073
Roscoe (Township)	61073
Rose (Township)	62565
Rosebud	62938
Rosecrans	60083
Rosedale	62031
Rosedale (Township)	62031
Rosefield (Township)	61529
Rose Hill (Cook County)	60640
Rose Hill (Du Page County)	60515
Rose Hill (Jasper County)	62432
Rose Lake (Part of Fairmont City)	62201
Roseland (Part of Chicago)	60628
Rose Lawn (Part of Chicago)	60628
Roselle	60172-73
For specific Roselle Zip Codes call (708) 885-6515	
Rosemont (Cook County)	60018
Rosemont (St. Clair County)	62204
Roseville	61473
Roseville (Township)	61473
Rosewood	62024
Rosewood Heights	62024
Rosiclare	62982
Roslyn	62462
Ross (Edgar County) (Township)	61924
Ross (Pike County) (Township)	62366

162 ILLINOIS Ross-Shore Heights Manor

	ZIP
Ross (Vermilion County) (Township)	60963
Rossville	60963
Round Barn (Part of Champaign)	61821
Round Grove (Livingston County) (Township)	60420
Round Grove (Whiteside County)	61270
Round Knob	62960
Round Lake	60073
Round Lake Beach	60073
Round Lake Heights	60073
Round Lake Park	60073
Round Prairie	62823
Rountree (Township)	62094
Rowe	61764
Roxana	62084
Roxanne	62901
Roxbury	61353
Royal	61871
Royal Lake Resort (Bond County)	62262
Royal Lake Resort (Clinton County)	62231
Royal Lakes (Macoupin County)	62685
Royal Lakes (Marion County)	62870
Royal Oaks	61032
Royalton	62983
Rozetta (Henderson County)	61469
Rozetta (Henderson County) (Township)	61447
Rubicon (Township)	62044
Rudement	62946
Ruma	62278
Rural (Rock Island County) (Township)	61240
Rural (Shelby County) (Township)	62510
Rush (Township)	61085
Rushville	62681
Rushville (Township)	62681
Russell	60075
Russell (Township)	47591
Russellville	47591
Rutland (Kane County) (Township)	60120
Rutland (La Salle County)	61358
Rutland (La Salle County) (Township)	61341
Rutledge (Township)	61752
Ruyle (Township)	62063
Sabina	61722
Sacramento	62835
Sadorus	61872
Sadorus (Township)	61872
Sag Bridge	60439
Saidora	62627
Sailor Springs	62879
St. Albans (Township)	62380
St. Anne	60964
St. Anne (Township)	60964
St. Anne Woods	60964
St. Augustine	61474
St. Charles	60174-75
For specific St. Charles Zip Codes call (708) 584-2318	
St. Clair (Township)	62221
St. Clair Square (Part of Fairview Heights)	62208
St. David	61563
St. Elmo	62458
St. Francis (Township)	62467
St. Francisville	62460
St. George	60914
St. Jacob	62281
St. Jacob (Township)	62281
St. James	62857
St. James Estates (Part of Sauk Village)	60411
St. Joe	62298
St. Johns	62832
St. Joseph	61873
St. Joseph (Township)	61873
St. Joseph's	60557
St. Libory	62282
Ste. Marie	62459
Ste. Marie (Township)	62459
St. Mary	62367
St. Mary (Township)	62367
St. Marys	62401
Saint Morgan	62293
St. Paul	62885
St. Peter	62880
St. Regis (Part of Lombard)	60148
St. Rose	62230
St. Rose (Township)	62293
Salem (Township)	62881

	ZIP
Salem (Carroll County) (Township)	61046
Salem (Knox County) (Township)	61572
Salem (Marion County)	62881
Salina (Township)	60913
Saline (Township)	62249
Saline Landing	62919
Saline Mines	62984
Salisbury	62677
Salt Creek (Township)	62664
Samoth	62943
Samsville	62476
Sand Barrens	62460
Sandburg Mall (Part of Galesburg)	61401
Sandoval	62882
Sandoval (Township)	62882
Sandpebble Walk (Part of Wheeling)	60090
Sand Prairie (Township)	61534
Sandra Heights (Part of Chicago Heights)	60411
Sand Ridge	62940
Sand Ridge (Township)	62940
Sandusky	62988
Sandwich	60548
Sandwich (Township)	60548
Sangamon (Macon County)	62521
Sangamon (Piatt County) (Township)	61884
Sangamon Heights	61853
Sangamon Valley (Township)	62618
San Jose	62682
Santa Anna (Township)	61842
Santa Fe (Township)	62218
Santa Fe Park	60521
Saratoga (Grundy County) (Township)	60450
Saratoga (Marshall County) (Township)	61537
Saratoga (Union County)	62906
Saratoga Center	61537
Sargent (Township)	61943
Sato	62907
Sauganash (Part of Chicago)	60646
Sauget	62201
Sauk Village	60411
Saunemin	61769
Saunemin (Township)	61769
Savanna	61074
Savanna (Township)	61074
Savoy	61874
Sawyerville	62085
Say Brook (Du Page County)	60563
Saybrook (McLean County)	61770
Scales Mound	61075
Scales Mound (Township)	61075
Scarboro	60553
Schaeferville	61554
Schapville	61028
Schaumburg	60172-73
	60192-95
For specific Schaumburg Zip Codes call (708) 885-6500	
Schaumburg (Township)	60194
Schaumburg Green (Part of Schaumburg)	60194
Scheller	62883
Schiller Park	60176
Schram City	62049
Schrodt	62863
Schulines	62286
Schwer	60953
Sciota	61475
Sciota (Township)	61475
Scioto Mills	61076
Scotland (Edgar County)	61924
Scotland (McDonough County) (Township)	61455
Scotsboro	62959
Scott (Champaign County) (Township)	61875
Scott (Ogle County) (Township)	61020
Scott AFB	62225
Scott Air Force Base	62225
Scottsburg	61422
Scottswood	61801
Scottville	62683
Scottville (Township)	62683
Seagaert	61354
Seaton	61476
Seatonville	61359
Seco Park	60115
Secor	61771
Seeger (Part of Des Plaines)	60016
Seehorn	62343

	ZIP
Sefton (Township)	62418
Selby (Township)	61322
Selmaville	62881
Seminary (Fayette County) (Township)	62471
Seminary (Richland County)	62450
Senachwine (Township)	61560
Seneca (La Salle County)	61360
Seneca (McHenry County) (Township)	60098
Sepo	61542
Serena	60549
Serena (Township)	60549
Sesser	62884
Seven Hickory (Township)	61920
Seven Hills (Part of Lindenhurst)	60046
Seville	61477
Seward (Township)	61077
Seward (Kendall County) (Township)	60447
Seward (Winnebago County)	61077
Sexson Corner	61928
Seymour	61875
Shabbona	60550
Shabbona (Township)	60550
Shabbona Grove	60518
Shadetree (Part of Oak Forest)	60452
Shadow Lawn	60954
Shady Acres	62665
Shady Beach	61254
Shady Grove	62910
Shady Hill	60010
Shafter (Fayette County)	62471
Shafter (Fayette County) (Township)	62471
Shakerag	62951
Shale City	61231
Shanghai City	61412
Shannon	61078
Sharon (Township)	62080
Sharpsburg	62568
Shattuc	62283
Shaw	60073
Shawnee (Township)	62984
Shawnee Correctional Center	62995
Shawneetown	62984
Shaws	61310
Shaws Point (Township)	62511
Sheffield	61361
Sheffield Park (Part of Schaumburg)	60194
Shelbyville	62565
Shelbyville (Township)	62565
Sheldon	60966
Sheldon (Township)	60966
Sheldons Grove	62624
Shepherd	62343
Sherburnville	60940
Sheridan (La Salle County)	60551
Sheridan (Logan County) (Township)	62671
Sheridan Correctional Center	60551
Sheridan Village (Part of Peoria)	61614
Sherman (Mason County) (Township)	62633
Sherman (Sangamon County)	62684
Sherrard	61281
Sherwood Forest (Part of Wood Dale)	60191
Sherwood Oaks	60120
Sherwood on the Fox (Part of Carpentersville)	60110
Shields (Jefferson County)	62851
Shields (Lake County) (Township)	60045
Shiloh (Edgar County) (Township)	61917
Shiloh (Jefferson County) (Township)	62864
Shiloh (St. Clair County)	62221
Shiloh Hill	62916
Shiloh Valley (Township)	62221
Shipman	62685
Shipman (Township)	62685
Shippingsport	61348
Shires of Inverness	60067
Shirland	61079
Shirland (Township)	61079
Shirley	61772
Shoal Creek (Township)	62086
Shobonier	62885
Shokokon	61425
Shore Acres	61071
Shore Heights Manor	60543

Shore Hills-Sumpter ILLINOIS 163

Name	ZIP
Shore Hills	60097
Shores of Shining Waters (Part of Carol Stream)	60188
Shorewood (Kankakee County)	60964
Shorewood (Will County)	60435
Shull's Urban Estates (Part of Rantoul)	61866
Shumway	62461
Sibley	61773
Sicily	62558
Sidell	61876
Sidell (Township)	61876
Sidney	61877
Sidney (Township)	61877
Sigel	62462
Sigel (Township)	62462
Signal Hill	62223
Silver Creek (Township)	61032
Silver Lake	60013
Silver Ridge	61061
Silvis	61282
Silvis Heights (Part of Silvis)	61282
Simpson (Johnson County)	62985
Simpson (White County)	62827
Sims	62886
Sims Western Acres	62707
Sinclair	62650
Six Mile (Township)	62999
Sixty-seventh Street (Part of Chicago)	60649
Sixty Six Court	60452
Sixty-Third Street (Part of Chicago)	60637
Skokie	60076-77
For specific Skokie Zip Codes call (708) 676-2200	
Slap Out	62849
Sleepy Hollow	60118
Smallwood (Township)	62448
Smithboro	62284
Smithfield	61477
Smithshire	62285
Smithton	62285
Smithton (Township)	61536
Smithville	62617
Snicarte	62477
Snyder	60401
Sollitt	60080
Solon Mills	61820
Somer (Township)	60521
Somerset (Du Page County)	60521
Somerset (Jackson County) (Township)	62966
Somerset (McHenry County)	60014
Somerset (Saline County)	62946
Somonauk	60552
Somonauk (Township)	60552
Songer (Township)	62899
Sonora (Township)	62354
Sorento	62086
South (Part of Evanston)	60202
South Addison (Part of Villa Park)	60181
South Barrington	60010
South Bartonville (Part of Bartonville)	61607
South Beloit	61080
South Chicago (Part of Chicago)	60617
South Chicago Heights	60411
South Crouch (Township)	62859
South Danville (Part of Danville)	61832
South Deering (Part of Chicago)	60617
South Dixon (Township)	61021
South Elgin	60177
Southern Hills	62901
Southern Illinois University	62026
Southern View	62707
South Fillmore (Township)	62032
South Flannigan (Township)	62890
South Fork (Township)	62540
South Grove (Township)	60146
South Holland	60473
South Homer (Township)	61849
South Hurricane (Township)	62011
South Jacksonville	62650
South Litchfield (Township)	62056
South Lockport (Part of Lockport)	60441
South Macon (Township)	62544
South Moline (Township)	61244
South Moline Gardens (Part of Moline)	61265
Southmore	62035
Southmore Heights	62411
South Mounds (Part of Mounds)	62964
South Muddy (Township)	62448
South Oak Park (Part of Oak Park)	60304
South Ottawa (Township)	61350
South Otter (Township)	62674
South Palmyra (Township)	62674
Southpark Mall (Part of Moline)	61265
South Pekin	61564
Southport	61517
South Rock Island (Township)	61201
South Rome	61523
South Ross (Township)	61848
South Roxana	62087
South Shore (Part of Chicago)	60649
South Streator	61364
South Twigg (Township)	62817
South Waukegan (Part of North Chicago)	60064
Southwest (Township)	62466
South Wheatland (Township)	62532
South Wilmington	60474
Space Valley	60521
Spanish Court (Part of Highland Park)	60035
Spankey	62031
Sparks Hill	62931
Sparland	61565
Sparta (Knox County) (Township)	61488
Sparta (Randolph County)	62286
Spaulding (Cook County)	60120
Spaulding (Sangamon County)	62561
Speer	61479
Spencer	60451
Spencer Heights	62964
Spillertown	62959
Spin Lake	61732
Sportsman Lake	62881
Spring (Township)	61008
Spring Arbor Lake	62901
Spring Bay (Township)	61611
Spring Bay	61611
Spring Creek (Township)	62355
Springerton	62887
Springfield	62701-94
For specific Springfield Zip Codes call (217) 788-7200	
Springfield (Township)	62702
Spring Garden	62846
Spring Garden (Township)	62846
Spring Grove (McHenry County)	60081
Spring Grove (Warren County) (Township)	61412
Springhaven	62035
Spring Hill	61250
Spring Hill Mall (Part of Dundee)	60118
Spring Lake (Champaign County)	61853
Spring Lake (Tazewell County) (Township)	61546
Spring Lake (Tazewell County)	61546
Spring Point (Township)	62462
Spring Valley	61362
Squaw Grove (Township)	60520
Squaw Prairie Estate	61008
Stable	62918
Stainfield	60545
Staleys	61821
Standard	61363
Standard City	62686
Stanford (Clay County) (Township)	62824
Stanford (McLean County)	61774
Stanton (Township)	61873
Stanton Point	60041
Stark	61559
Starks	60140
Starnes	62707
State Line	62423
State Park Place	62201
State Street (Part of Chicago)	60628
Staunton	62088
Staunton (Township)	62088
Stavanger	61360
Steel City	62812
Steeleville	62288
Steeple Run	60540
Steger	60475
Stelle	60919
Sterling (Township)	61081
Sterling	61081
Sterling Place (Part of Caseyville)	62232
Steuben (Township)	61565
Stevenson (Township)	62881
Steward	60553
Stewardson	62463
Stickney	60402
Stickney (Township)	60402
Stillman Valley	61084
Stillmeadow	60119
Stillwell	62380
Stiritz	62896
Stites (Township)	62059
Stockland (Township)	60967
Stockland	60967
Stockton	61085
Stockton (Township)	61085
Stock Yards (Part of Chicago)	60609
Stolletown	62231
Stone	62931
Stone Church	62296
Stonefort (Township)	62987
Stonefort	62987
Stonehenge	60178
Stonelake (Part of Woodstock)	60098
Stone Park	60165
Stoneyville	61350
Stonington	62567
Stonington (Township)	62567
Stony Island Avenue (Part of Chicago)	60649
Stookey (Township)	62221
Storeyland	62035
Storybrook	60512
Stoy	62464
Strasburg	62465
Stratford	61064
Stratford Hills (Part of Elmhurst)	60126
Stratford Park	61821
Stratford Square (Part of Bloomingdale)	60108
Stratton (Edgar County) (Township)	61944
Stratton (Jefferson County)	62814
Strawberry Hill	61270
Strawn	61775
Streamwood	60103
Streator	61364
Streator Junction (Part of Eureka)	61530
Stringtown	62450
Stronghurst	61480
Stronghurst (Township)	61480
Stubblefield	62246
Sublette	61367
Sublette (Township)	61367
Suburban Estates	60515
Suburban Heights	62801
Suez (Township)	61412
Sugar Brook (Part of Bolingbrook)	60439
Sugar Creek (Township)	62293
Sugar Grove	60554
Sugar Grove (Township)	60554
Sugar Grove	61231
Sugar Island	60922
Sugar Loaf (St. Clair County)	62240
Sugar Loaf (St. Clair County) (Township)	62240
Sullivan (Township)	61951
Sullivan (Livingston County) (Township)	60929
Sullivan (Moultrie County)	61951
Sullivant (Township)	61773
Summerdale (Part of Chicago)	60640
Summerfield	62289
Summerhill (Cook County)	60062
Summer Hill (Cook County)	60120
Summer Hill (Pike County)	62372
Summerlakes (Part of Warrenville)	60555
Summersville (Part of Mount Vernon)	62864
Summerville	62063
Summit (Cook County)	60501
Summit (Effingham County) (Township)	62461
Summit-Argo (Part of Summit)	60501
Summit Heights	62089
Summum	61501
Sumner (Kankakee County) (Township)	60940
Sumner (Lawrence County)	62466
Sumner (Warren County) (Township)	61453
Sumpter (Township)	62468

164 ILLINOIS Sunbeam-Valley Lo

	ZIP		ZIP		ZIP
Sunbeam	61231	Thebes Junction (Part of Thebes)	62990	Trago Lake	62839
Sunbury (Livingston County)	61313	The Burg	61318	Tremont (Township)	61568
Sunbury (Livingston County) (Township)	61313	The Clusters (Part of Bolingbrook)	60439	Tremont (Madison County)	62035
Sunfield	62832	The Covered Bridges (Part of Carol Stream)	60188	Tremont (Tazewell County)	61568
Sunny Acres (Champaign County)	61853	The Fairway of Country Lakes (Part of Naperville)	60563	Trenton	62293
Sunny Acres (Kankakee County)	60950	The Greens of Woodgate (Part of Matteson)	60443	Trilla	62469
Sunny Crest	60430	The Grove Shopping Center (Part of Elk Grove Village)	60007	Trimble	62454
Sunnydale	61021	The Knolls	60175	Triple Lance Heights	62901
Sunny Hill	61273	The Laurels (Part of Justice)	60458	Tri-State Village	60521
Sunny Hill Estates	61273	The Ledges	61073	Triumph	61371
Sunny Hills Estates	60515	The Meadows	60532	Triumvera	60025
Sunnyland (Tazewell County)	61571	The Old Farm	61821	Trivoli	61569
Sunny Land (Will County)	60435	Third Lake	60046	Trivoli (Township)	61569
Sunnyside (McHenry County)	60050	Thomas	61283	Trout Valley (Part of Cary)	60013
Sunnyside (Williamson County)	62948	Thomasboro	61878	Trowbridge	62447
Sunnyside Acres	62531	Thomas Eddition	61364	Troxel	60151
Sun Prairie Seed	61873	Thomasville	62533	Troy (Madison County)	62294
Sun Ridge (Part of Hoffman Estates)	60195	Thompson (Township)	61001	Troy (Will County) (Township)	60435
Sunrise Ridge (Part of Romeoville)	60441	Thompson Addition	61241	Troy Grove	61372
Sun River Terrace	60964	Thompsonville	62890	Troy Grove (Township)	61372
Sunset Acres (Lake County)	60048	Thomson	61285	Tru Lock Acres	61455
Sunset Acres (Stephenson County)	61032	Thornhill (Part of Carol Stream)	60187	Trumbull	62821
Sunset Harbor	62959	Thornton	60476	Truro (Township)	61489
Sunset Hills (Part of Roselle)	60172	Thornton (Township)	60476	Tullamore (Part of Mundelein)	60060
Sunset Lake	62640	Thornton Junction (Part of South Holland)	60473	Tunbridge (Township)	61749
Sunset Trailer Park (Part of Glenview)	60025	Thornwilde (Part of Warrenville)	60555	Tunnel Hill	62991
Sutter	62373	Thunderbird Lake	62012	Turnberry	60014
Sutton	60010	Tice	62675	Tuscola	61953
Sutton Point (Part of Northbrook)	60062	Ticona	61370	Tuscola (Township)	61953
Swan (Township)	61473	Tierra Grande (Part of Country Club Hills)	60477	Twelvemile Corner	61318
Swan Creek	61473	Tilden	62292	Twenty-Second Street (Part of Chicago)	60616
Swansea	62221	Tilton	61833	Twenty-Seventh Street (Part of Chicago)	60616
Swanwick	62237	Timber (Township)	61533	Twenty-Third Street (Part of Chicago)	60616
Swedona	61262	Timberbrook	61254	Twigg (Township)	62829
Sweetwater	62642	Timbercrest (Part of Schaumburg)	60194	Twilight Terrace	62221
Swiss Valley (Part of Crete)	60417	Timber Lake (Carroll County)	61053	Twin City (Part of Champaign)	61801
Swissville (Part of Dixon)	61021	Timber Lake (Lake County)	60010	Twin Creek Acres	61010
Swygert	61764	Timberlake Estate	62568	Twin Lakes	62294
Sycamore	60178	Timberlake Estates	60521	Twin Oaks (Part of Joliet)	60435
Sycamore (Township)	60178	Timberlake Village (Part of Mount Prospect)	60056	Tyrone (Township)	62822
Sylvan Hill	60462	Timber Lane	61008	Udina	60123
Sylvan Lake	60060	Timberline	60435	Ulah	61238
Symerton	60481	Timber Ridge (Cook County)	60457	Ullin	62992
Symmes (Township)	61944	Timber Ridge (Du Page County)	60190	Union (Cumberland County) (Township)	62428
Table Grove	61482	Timber Terrace	60115	Union (Effingham County) (Township)	62424
Tabor	61778	Timber Trails (Part of Oak Brook)	60521	Union (Fulton County) (Township)	61415
Taggert Woods	62626	Timber View (Champaign County)	61801	Union (Livingston County) (Township)	60460
Talkington (Township)	62692	Timberview (Champaign County)	61853	Union (Logan County)	62635
Tall Trees (Part of Glenview)	60025	Time	62363	Union (McHenry County)	60180
Tallula	62688	Timewell	62375	Union Center	62428
Tamalco	62253	Timothy	62428	Union Grove	61270
Tamalco (Township)	62253	Tinley Park	60477	Union Grove (Township)	61270
Tamarac (Part of Flossmoor)	60422	Tinley Terrace (Part of Tinley Park)	60477	Union Hill (Kankakee County)	60969
Tamaroa	62888	Tioga	62351	Union Hill (St. Clair County)	62232
Tamms	62988	Tipton	62298	Union Stock Yards (Part of Chicago)	60609
Tampico	61283	Tiskilwa	61368	Uniontown	61572
Tampico (Township)	61283	Todds Mill	62263	Unionville (Massac County)	62910
Tanbark (Part of Tinley Park)	60477	Todds Point	61914	Unionville (Vermilion County)	61883
Tanglewood (Part of Hanover Park)	60103	Todds Point (Township)	61914	Unionville (Whiteside County)	61270
Tate (Township)	62935	Toledo	62468	Unity (Alexander County)	62993
Tatumville	62988	Tolono	61880	Unity (Piatt County) (Township)	61913
Taylor (Township)	61021	Tolono (Township)	61880	University (Part of Urbana)	61801
Taylor Ridge	61284	Toluca	61369	University Heights (Part of Charleston)	61920
Taylor Springs	62089	Tomahawk Bluff	61301	University Mall (Part of Carbondale)	62901
Taylorville	62568	Tompkins (Township)	61447	University Park	60466
Taylorville (Township)	62568	Toms Prairie	62837	Upper Alton (Part of Alton)	62002
Techny	60082	Tonica	61370	Uptown (Part of Chicago)	60640
Teheran	62664	Tonti	62881	Urbain	62822
Temple Hill	62938	Tonti (Township)	62881	Urban (Part of Taylorville)	62568
Tenerelli	60511	Topeka	61567	Urbana (Champaign County)	61801
Tennessee	62374	Toronto	62707	Urbana (Champaign County) (Township)	61801
Tennessee (Township)	62374	Toulon	61483	Urbandale	62914
Terminal Junction (Part of Rock Island)	61201	Toulon (Township)	61483	Ursa	62376
Terra Cotta	60014	Tovey	62570	Ursa (Township)	62376
Terre Haute	61454	Towanda	61776	Ustick (Township)	61270
Terre Haute (Township)	61454	Towanda (Township)	61776	Utica	61373
Teutopolis	62467	Tower Hill	62571	Utica (Township)	61373
Teutopolis (Township)	62467	Tower Hill (Township)	62571	Vale Vue Acres	62650
Texas (Township)	61727	Tower Lakes	60010	Valier	62891
Texas City	62930	Town and Country	62901	Valley (Township)	61491
Texico	62889	Towne Oaks	61535	Valley City	62340
Thackeray	62859	Tradewinds	60115	Valley Lo (Part of Glenview)	60025
Thawville	60968				
Thayer	62689				
Thebes	62990				

Valley View-West Salem **ILLINOIS** 165

	ZIP
Valley View (De Kalb County)	60145
Valley View (Du Page County)	60137
Valley View (Kane County)	60174
Valley View (Tazewell County)	61611
Valmeyer	62295
Van Burensburg	62032
Van Buren Street (Part of Chicago)	60601
Vance (Township)	61841
Vandalia	62471
Vandalia (Township)	62471
Vandalia Correctional Center	62471
Van Orin	61374
Varna	61375
Velma	62568
Venedy (Township)	62296
Venedy (Washington County)	62296
Venetian Village (Lake County)	60046
Venice	62090
Venice (Township)	62090
Venice Crossing (Part of Venice)	62090
Vera	62080
Vergennes	62994
Vergennes (Township)	62994
Vermilion (Edgar County)	61955
Vermilion (La Salle County) (Township)	61370
Vermilion Grove	61870
Vermilion Heights	61832
Vermilionville	61370
Vermillion Estates	61764
Vermont	61484
Vermont (Township)	61484
Vernon (Lake County) (Township)	60069
Vernon (Marion County)	62892
Vernon Hills	60061
Verona	60479
Versailles	62378
Versailles (Township)	62378
Versailles-on-the-Lake (Part of Schaumburg)	60194
Veterans Administration Medical Center	60064
Vets Row	61523
Vevay Park	62420
Vicic (Part of East Peoria)	61611
Victor (Township)	60556
Victoria	61485
Victoria (Township)	61485
Vienna (Grundy County) (Township)	60479
Vienna (Johnson County)	62995
Village Mall (Part of Danville)	61832
Village Square	60515
Village Square Mall (Part of Effingham)	62401
Villa Grove	61956
Villa Grove Junction (Part of Villa Grove)	61956
Villa Hills	62223
Villa Marie	62035
Villa Park	60181
Villa Ridge	62996
Villas Salceda (Part of Northbrook)	60062
Villa Verde (Part of Buffalo Grove)	60090
Villa West	60462
Villa Westbrook (Part of Macomb)	61455
Vincennes Trail	60954
Vinegar Hill (Township)	61036
Viola (Lee County) (Township)	61318
Viola (Mercer County)	61486
Virden	62690
Virden (Township)	62690
Virgil	60182
Virgil (Township)	60182
Virginia	62691
Virginia (Township)	62691
Volo	60073
Vonachen Knolls	61523
Von Glenn Acres	61010
Voorhies	61813
Vulcan (Part of East Carondelet)	62240
Wabash (Township)	62441
Wacker (Carroll County)	61053
Wacker (Kendall County)	60560
Waddams (Township)	61050
Waddams Grove	61048

	ZIP
Wade (Clinton County) (Township)	62231
Wade (Jasper County) (Township)	62448
Wadsworth	60083
Waggoner	62572
Wakefield	62448
Waldo (Township)	61744
Walker (Township)	62373
Walkerville	62050
Walkerville (Township)	62050
Wall (Township)	60948
Wallace (Township)	61350
Wallingford	60442
Walnut	61376
Walnut (Township)	61376
Walnut Grove (Township)	61438
Walnut Grove (Knox County) (Township)	61414
Walnut Grove (McDonough County)	61470
Walnut Hill	62893
Walnut Park	62231
Walnut Prairie	62477
Walpole	62817
Walsh	62297
Walshville	62091
Walshville (Township)	62091
Waltham (La Salle County)	61373
Waltham (La Salle County) (Township)	61373
Walton	61021
Waltonville	62894
Wamac	62801
Wanda	62025
Wanlock	61231
Wapella	61777
Wapella (Township)	61777
Wards Grove (Township)	61048
Ware	62952
Warner	61273
Warren (Jo Daviers County)	61087
Warren (Lake County) (Township)	61087
Warren (Township)	60031
Warren G. Murray Developmental Center	62801
Warrenhurst (Part of Warrenville)	60555
Warren Park (Part of Cicero)	60650
Warrensburg	62573
Warrenville	60555
Warsaw (Hancock County)	62379
Warsaw (Hancock County) (Township)	62379
Wartburg	62298
Wartrace	62943
Wasco	60183
Washburn	61570
Washington (Tazewell County) (Township)	61571
Washington (Will County) (Township)	60401
Washington (Carroll County) (Township)	61074
Washington (Tazewell County)	61571
Washington Heights (Part of Chicago)	60628
Washington Park	62204
Washington Square Mall (Part of Homewood)	60430
Wasson	62930
Wataga	61488
Waterford (Du Page County)	60521
Waterford (Fulton County) (Township)	61542
Waterloo	62298
Waterman	60556
Water Tower Place (Part of Chicago)	60611
Watertown (Part of East Moline)	61244
Watervalley	62920
Watseka	60970
Watson	62473
Watson (Township)	62473
Wauconda	60084
Wauconda (Township)	60084
Waukegan	60085-87
For specific Waukegan Zip Codes call (708) 662-6800	
Wauponsee (Township)	60450
Waverly	62692
Waycinden Park	60016
Wayne (Township)	60185
Wayne	60184
Wayne Center	60185
Wayne City	62895
Waynesville	61778

	ZIP
Waynesville (Township)	61778
Weathersfield (Part of Schaumburg)	60194
Weaver	62423
Webber (Township)	62814
Webster	62321
Webster Park (Part of Spring Valley)	61362
Wedgewood Estates	62293
Wedron	60557
Weedman	61842
Wee-Ma-Tuk Hills	61427
Weldon	61882
Welge	62288
Weller (Township)	61238
Wellington	60973
Wellington Heights	60435
Wells	62871
Wendelin	62448
Wenona	61377
Wenonah	62075
Wentworth Avenue (Part of Calumet City)	60409
Wesley (Tazewell County)	61611
Wesley (Will County) (Township)	60481
West (Effingham County) (Township)	62458
West (McLean County) (Township)	61722
Westaway	60504
Westbrook	61853
Westbrook Estates (Part of O'Fallon)	62269
West Brooklyn	61378
West Brook Village (Part of Macomb)	61455
Westbury (Part of Bolingbrook)	60439
Westchester	60153
West Chicago	60185
West City	62812
West Clinton Estates	62265
Westdale Gardens	60126
West Deerfield (Township)	60015
West End	62890
Western (Township)	61273
Western Avenue (Cook County)	60612
Western Avenue (Cook County)	60608
Western Knolls	62707
Western Mound (Township)	62630
Western Springs	60558
Westervelt	62574
Westfield (Township)	62474
Westfield (Part of Joliet)	60435
Westfield (Bureau County) (Township)	61312
Westfield (Clark County)	62474
West Frankfort	62896
West Frankfort Lake	62896
West Galena (Township)	61036
Westgate	62959
West Glen (Part of Peoria)	61614
West Glenview	60025
West Hallock	61526
West Jersey	61483
West Jersey (Township)	61483
West Kankakee (Part of Kankakee)	60901
West Lake (Crawford County)	62454
Westlake (Du Page County)	60139
West Lake Forest (Part of Lake Forest)	60045
West Liberty	62475
West Lincoln (Township)	62656
West Meadowview (Part of Kankakee)	60901
West Miltmore	60046
Westmont	60559
Westmore (Part of Lombard)	60148
Weston	61726
West Peoria	61604
West Peoria (Township)	61604
West Point (Hancock County)	62380
West Point (Morgan County)	62650
West Point (Stephenson County) (Township)	61048
Westport (Knox County)	61401
Westport (Lawrence County)	47591
West Pullman (Part of Chicago)	60628
Westridge (Cook County)	60070
West Ridge (Douglas County)	61953
West Salem	62476

166 ILLINOIS West Sandford-Zurich Heights

	ZIP
West Sandford	61944
West Twenty-Second St. (Part of Chicago)	60650
West Union	62477
Westville	61883
Westwood (Part of Addison)	60101
West York	62478
Wetaug	62926
Wethersfield (Township)	61277
Wetzel	61944
Wheatfield (Township)	62231
Wheatland (Bureau County) (Township)	61368
Wheatland (Fayette County) (Township)	62418
Wheatland (Will County) (Township)	60544
Wheaton	60187-89
For specific Wheaton Zip Codes call (708) 668-3530	
Wheaton Center (Part of Wheaton)	60187
Wheeler	62479
Wheeling (Township)	60090
Wheeling	60090
Whiskey Corners	60071
Whiskey Creek	60185
Whispering Hills	60050
Whispering Oaks (Part of Lake Forest)	60045
Whitaker	60940
Whiteash	62959
White City	62069
White Cliffs	62035
Whitefield	61537
Whitefield (Township)	61537
White Hall (Township)	62092
Whitehall (Cook County)	60056
White Hall (Greene County)	62092
White Heath	61884
White Oak (Township)	61725
White Oaks	61021
White Oaks Bay	60097
White Oaks Mall (Part of Springfield)	62704
White Pigeon	61270
White Pines	60106
White Post	62093
White Rock (Township)	61045
White Rock (Lee County)	61021
White Rock (Ogle County)	61015
Whites Addition	61244
Whitford Place	62035
Whitley (Township)	61928
Whitmore (Township)	62501
Whittington	62897
Wichert	60964
Wicker Park (Part of Chicago)	60622
Wickmore	62035
Wideview	60175
Wieisbrook	62918
W. I. Junction (Part of Chicago)	60621
Wilbern	61570
Wilberton (Township)	62885
Wilbur Heights	61821
Wilcox (Clay County)	62824
Wilcox (Hancock County) (Township)	62379
Wildrose	60174
Wildwood (Cook County)	60628
Wildwood (Kane County)	60504
Wildwood (Lake County)	60030 / 60081
For specific Wildwood (Lake County) Zip Codes call (708) 223-2787	
Wildwood Addition (Part of Moline)	61265
Wildwood Valley	60123
Will (Township)	60468
Willard (Alexander County)	62962
Willard (St. Clair County)	62269
Willeys	62568
Williams (Township)	62693
Williamsburg	61937
Williamsfield	61489
Williamson	62088
Williams Park	60084
Williams Place	62035
Williamsville	62693
Willisville	62997
Willow	61085
Willoway (Part of Naperville)	60540
Willoway Manor (Part of Willowbrook)	60521
Willow Branch (Township)	61830
Willowbrook (Du Page County)	60521
Willowbrook (Kendall County)	60512

	ZIP
Willow Brooke	61080
Willow Creek (Township)	60530
Willow Estates (De Kalb County)	60135
Willow Estates (Iroquois County)	60912
Willow Hill	62480
Willow Hill (Township)	62480
Willow's East (Part of Glenview)	60025
Willow Springs	60480
Willow Wood (Part of Palatine)	60067
Wilmette	60091
Wilmington	60481
Wilmington (Township)	60481
Wilshire Bluffs Estate	61008
Wilson (Township)	61777
Wilson Avenue (Part of Chicago)	60640
Wilson Heights	62234
Wilsonville	62093
Wilton (Township)	60442
Wilton Center	60442
Winchester	62694
Winden Oak	60119
Windham Manor (Part of Northbrook)	60062
Windings	60175
Windsor	61957
Windsor (Township)	61957
Windsor Estates West (Part of Mount Prospect)	60056
Windsor Park (Champaign County)	61801
Windsor Park (Cook County)	60649
Windsor Square (Part of Peoria)	61614
Wine Hill	62288
Winfield	60190
Winfield (Township)	60185
Wing	61741
Winkle	62237
Winnebago	61088
Winnebago (Township)	61088
Winneshiek	61032
Winnetka	60093
Winslow	61089
Winslow (Township)	61089
Winston Hills (Part of Woodridge)	60515
Winston Park (Part of Palatine)	60067
Winston Park Northwest (Part of Palatine)	60067
Winston Park South (Part of Country Club Hills)	60477
Winston Plaza Shopping Center (Part of Melrose Park)	60160
Winston Village (Part of Bolingbrook)	60439
Winston Woods (Part of Bolingbrook)	60439
Winterrowd	62424
Winthrop Harbor	60096
Wireton (Part of Blue Island)	60406
Witt	62094
Witt (Township)	62094
Woburn	62246
Wolf Lake	62998
Womac	62626
Wonder Lake (McHenry County)	60097
Wonder View	60097
Wonder Woods	60097
Woodbine	61085
Woodbine (Township)	61085
Woodborough (Part of Homewood)	60430
Woodburn	62014
Woodbury	62445
Woodbury (Township)	62445
Wood Dale (Du Page County)	60191
Wooddale (Peoria County)	61607
Wooded Shores	60097
Woodfield (Part of Schaumburg)	60195
Woodford	61516
Woodford Heights	61548
Woodgate	60178
Wood Hill (Part of University Park)	60466
Woodhill Estates	61038
Woodhull	61490
Woodland (Carroll County) (Township)	61053
Woodland (Fulton County) (Township)	61501

	ZIP
Woodland (Iroquois County)	60974
Woodland (Kankakee County)	60954
Woodland Addition	61350
Woodland Heights (Part of Streamwood)	60103
Woodland Hills (Part of Batavia)	60510
Woodland Lake	61817
Woodland Shores	61021
Woodlawn (Cook County)	60637
Woodlawn (Jefferson County)	62898
Woodlawn Heights	61081
Woodmere (Part of Libertyville)	60048
Woodridge	60517
Wood River	62095
Wood River (Township)	62095
Woodruff (Part of Chicago)	60619
Woods Edge	61801
Woodside (Township)	62703
Woodside Estates (Part of Oak Brook)	60521
Woodson	62695
Woodstock (McHenry County)	60098
Woodstock (Schuyler County) (Township)	62681
Woodview Manor (Part of Prospect Heights)	60070
Woodville (Township)	62027
Woodworth	60953
Woody	62016
Woodyard (Edgar County)	61924
Woodyard (Fayette County)	62885
Wooster Lake	60041
Woosung	61091
Woosung (Township)	61091
Worden	62097
Worth	60482
Worth (Cook County) (Township)	60482
Worth (Woodford County) (Township)	61548
Wrights	62098
Wrights (Township)	62098
Wrights Corner	62414
Wyanet	61379
Wyanet (Township)	61379
Wynoose	62868
Wyoming (Lee County) (Township)	61353
Wyoming (Stark County)	61491
Wysox (Township)	61051
Wythe (Township)	62373
Xenia	62899
Xenia (Township)	62899
Yale	62481
Yankee Ridge	61801
Yantisville	62534
Yard Center (Part of Dolton)	60419
Yates (Township)	61726
Yates City	61572
Yatesville	62612
Yellowhead (Township)	60940
Yeoward Addition	61071
York (Clark County) (Township)	62477
York (Du Page County) (Township)	60181
York (Carroll County) (Township)	61285
York (Clark County)	62477
York Center	60148
Yorkfield	60126
Yorkshire Woods (Part of Oak Brook)	60521
Yorktown (Bureau County)	61283
Yorktown (Henry County) (Township)	61277
Yorktown Shopping Center (Part of Lombard)	60148
Yorkville	60560
Young America (Township)	61940
Young Hickory (Township)	61544
Youngstown	61473
Zanesville (Township)	62572
Zearing	61337
Zeigler	62999
Zenith	62899
Zif (Township)	62824
Zion (Carroll County)	61074
Zion (Lake County)	60099
Zion (Lake County) (Township)	60099
Zuma (Township)	61257
Zurich Heights (Part of Lake Zurich)	60047

Abbey Dell-Blue Lake **INDIANA** **167**

	ZIP		ZIP		ZIP
Abbey Dell	47469	Arcadia	46030	Beattys Corner	46360
Aberdeen	47040	Arcana	46952	Beaver (Newton County)	
Abington	47330	Arcola	46704	(Township)	47963
Abington (Township)	47330	Arctic Springs (Part of		Beaver (Pulaski County)	
Aboite	46783	Jeffersonville)	47130	(Township)	46996
Aboite (Township)	46804	Arda	47567	Beaver City	47922
Acme	47274	Ardmore	46628	Becks Grove	47235
Acton (Part of Indianapolis)	46259	Argos	46501	Becks Mill	47167
Adams (Township)	47272	Ari	47723	Bedford	47421
Adams (Hamilton County)		Ar'les Acres	46060	Bedford Heights (Part of	
(Township)	46069	Arlington (Monroe County)	47401	Bedford)	47421
Adams (Madison County)		Arlington (Rush County)	46104	Beecamp	47250
(Township)	46056	Arlington Park	46815	Beech Brook	46176
Adams (Morgan County)	46151	Armiesburg	47862	Beech Creek (Township)	47459
Adams (Morgan County)		Armstrong	47712	Beech Grove (Marion Co.)	46107
(Township)	46151	Armstrong (Township)	47712	Beech Grove (Morgan Co.)	46151
Adams (Parke County)		Armuth Acres	47203	Beechwood	47137
(Township)	47872	Arney	47431	Bee Ridge	47834
Adams (Ripley County)		Aroma	46031	Bell Center	47925
(Township)	47041	Arrowhead Park	46580	Bellefountain	47371
Adams (Warren County)		Art	47834	Belle Union	46120
(Township)	47975	Arthur	47598	Belleview	47250
Adams (Allen County)		Artic	46721	Belleville	46118
(Township)	46774	Ashboro	47840	Bellmore	47830
Adams (Carroll County)		Asherville	47834	Bell Rohr Park	46538
(Township)	47960	Ash Grove	47920	Belmont (Brown County)	47448
Adams (Cass County)		Ashland (Henry County)	47362	Belmont (Henry County)	47362
(Township)	46988	Ashland (Morgan County)		Belshaw	46356
Adams (Decatur County)	47240	(Township)	46151	Ben Davis (Part of	
Adamsboro	46947	Ashley	46705	Indianapolis)	46241
Adams Lake	46795	Athens	46912	Bengal	46131
Adams Mill	46920	Atherton	47874	Benham	47042
Addison (Township)	46176	Atkinsonville	47868	Bennetts	46901
Addmore (Part of		Atlanta	46031	Bennettsville	47143
Clarksville)	47130	Attica	47918	Bennington	47011
Ade	47922	Atwood	46502	Benton	46526
Advance	46102	Aubbeenaubbee (Township)	46975	Benton (Elkhart County)	
Ainsworth	46342	Auburn	46706	(Township)	46526
Air Mail Field (Part of		Auburn Junction	46706	Benton (Monroe County)	
Indianapolis)	46241	Augusta (Marion County)	46268	(Township)	46526
Akron	46910	Augusta (Pike County)	47598	Bentonville	47322
Alamo	47916	Aultshire (Part of Muncie)	47302	Benwood	47834
Albany	47320	Aurora	47001	Berlien	46703
Albion	46701	Austin	47102	Berne	46711
Albion (Township)	46701	Avalon Hills (Part of		Berwick Manor (Part of	
Aldine	46366	Indianapolis)	46250	Shelbyville)	46176
Alert	47283	Avery	46041	Bethany	46111
Alexandria	46001	Avilla	46710	Bethel (Posey County)	
Alfont	46040	Avoca	47420	(Township)	47616
Alford	47567	Avon	46168	Bethel (Wayne County)	47341
Alfordsville	47553	Avondale	46952	Bethel Village	47201
Algers	47567	Ayr	46550	Bethlehem (Township)	47104
Alida	46391	Ayrshire	47598	Bethlehem (Cass County)	
Allen (Miami County)		Azalia	47232	(Township)	46988
(Township)	46951	Babcock	46383	Bethlehem (Clark County)	47104
Allen (Noble County)		Bacon (Part of Indianapolis)	46220	Between-the-Lakes Park	46538
(Township)	46755	Baileys Corner	47978	Beverly Shores	46301
Allendale	47802	Bainbridge (Dubois County)		Bicknell	47512
Allens Acres	46077	(Township)	47546	Big Creek (Township)	47929
Allensville	47011	Bainbridge (Putnam County)	46105	Bigger (Township)	47265
Allisonville (Part of		Baker (Township)	47433	Big Lake	46725
Indianapolis)	46250	Bakers Corners	46069	Big Springs	46069
Allman	46158	Bakertown	46701	Billingsville	47353
Alma Lake	47834	Balbec	47369	Billtown	47834
Alpine	47331	Baldwin Heights (Part of		Billville	47834
Alquina	47331	Princeton)	47670	Bippus	46713
Alta	47854	Bandon	47514	Birdseye	47513
Alto	46902	Banquo	46940	Birmingham	46951
Alton	47137	Banta	46106	Black (Township)	47620
Altona	46738	Bar-Barry Heights (Part of		Blackhawk (Allen County)	46805
Alvarado	46742	West Lafayette)	47906	Blackhawk (Vigo County)	47866
Amber Valley	47803	Barbee	46562	Blackhawk Beach	46383
Ambia	47917	Bargersville	46106	Blackhawk Forest	46805
Amboy	46911	Barkley (Township)	47978	Blackiston Heights (Part of	
Americus	47905	Barnaby Acres	47201	Clarksville)	47130
Ames (Part of		Barnard	46172	Blackiston Mill	47130
Crawfordsville)	47933	Barr (Township)	47519	Blackiston Village (Part of	
Amity	46131	Barrick Corner	47841	Clarksville)	47130
Amo	46103	Bartlettsville	47421	Black Oak (Part of Gary)	46406
Anderson	46011-18	Bartley	47805	Blaine	47371
For specific Anderson Zip Codes		Barton (Township)	47613	Blairsville	47638
call (317) 643-3356		Bartonia	47390	Blanford	47831
Anderson (Township)	46016	Bass Lake (Starke County)	46534	Blocher	47138
Anderson (Perry County)		Batesville	47006	Bloomfield (Greene County)	47424
(Township)	47586	Bath	47010	Bloomfield (Lagrange	
Anderson (Rush County)		Bath (Township)	47010	County) (Township)	46761
(Township)	46156	Battle Ground	47920	Bloomfield (Spencer Co.)	47611
Anderson (Warrick County)		Baugh City	47610	Bloomingdale	47832
(Township)	47630	Baugo (Township)	46514	Blooming Grove	47012
Andersonville	47024	Bayfield	46562	Blooming Grove (Township)	47012
Andrews	46702	Beal	47591	Bloomingport	47355
Angola	46703	Bean Blossom (Brown Co.)	46160	Bloomington	47401-08
Annandale Estates	47448	Bean Blossom (Monroe		For specific Bloomington Zip	
Annapolis	47832	County) (Township)	47429	Codes call (812) 334-4030	
Anoka	46947	Bear Branch	47018	Blountsville	47354
Ansley Acres	46804	Bearcreek (Township)	47326	Blue Creek (Adams County)	
Anthony	47302	Beard	46041	(Township)	46772
Antioch	46041	Beardstown	46996	Blue Creek (Franklin	
Antiville	47371	Bear Lake	46701	County)	47041
Apache Acres	47805	Beatrice	46341	Blue Lake	46723
Arba	47355				

168 INDIANA

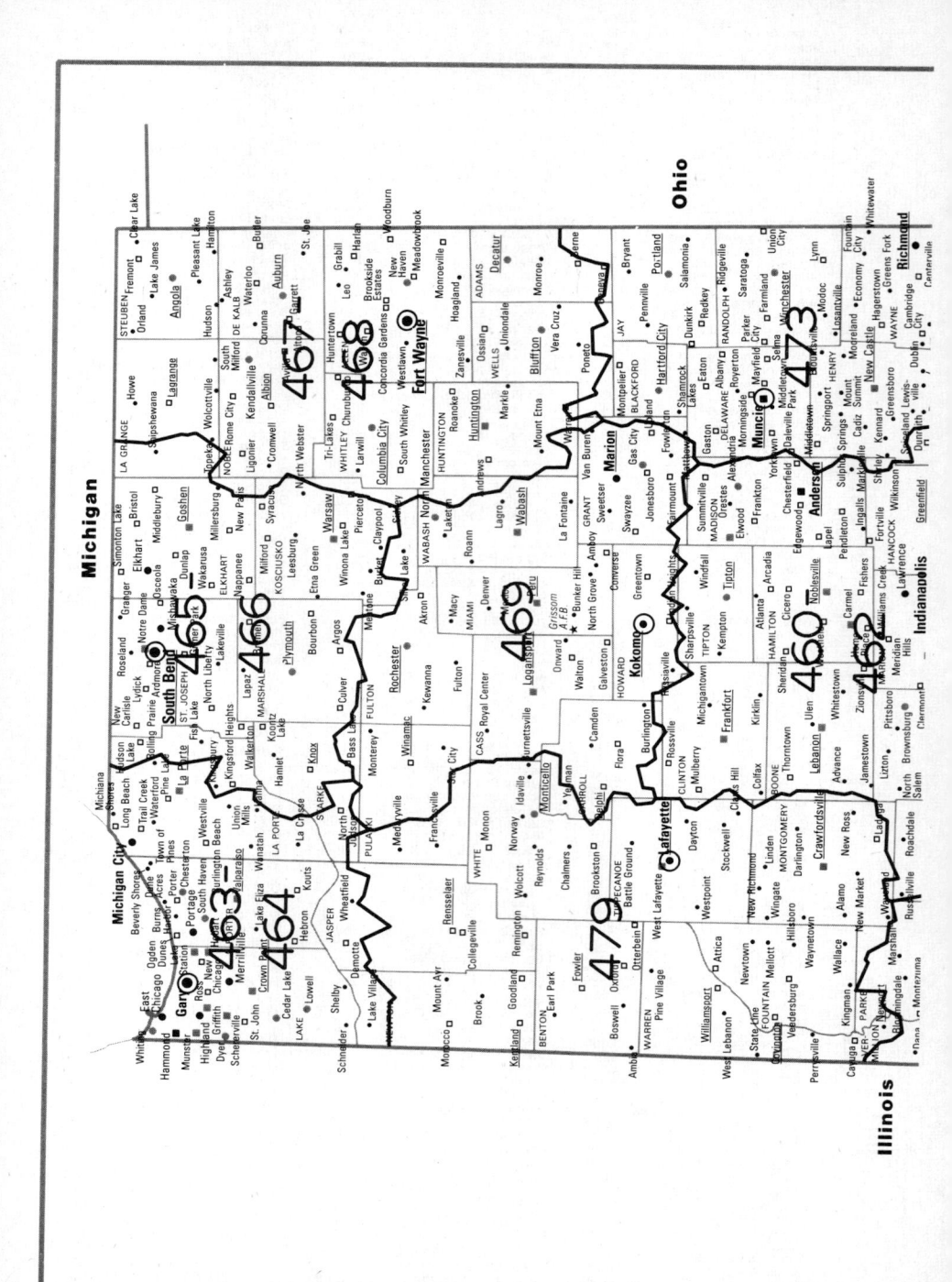

INDIANA 169

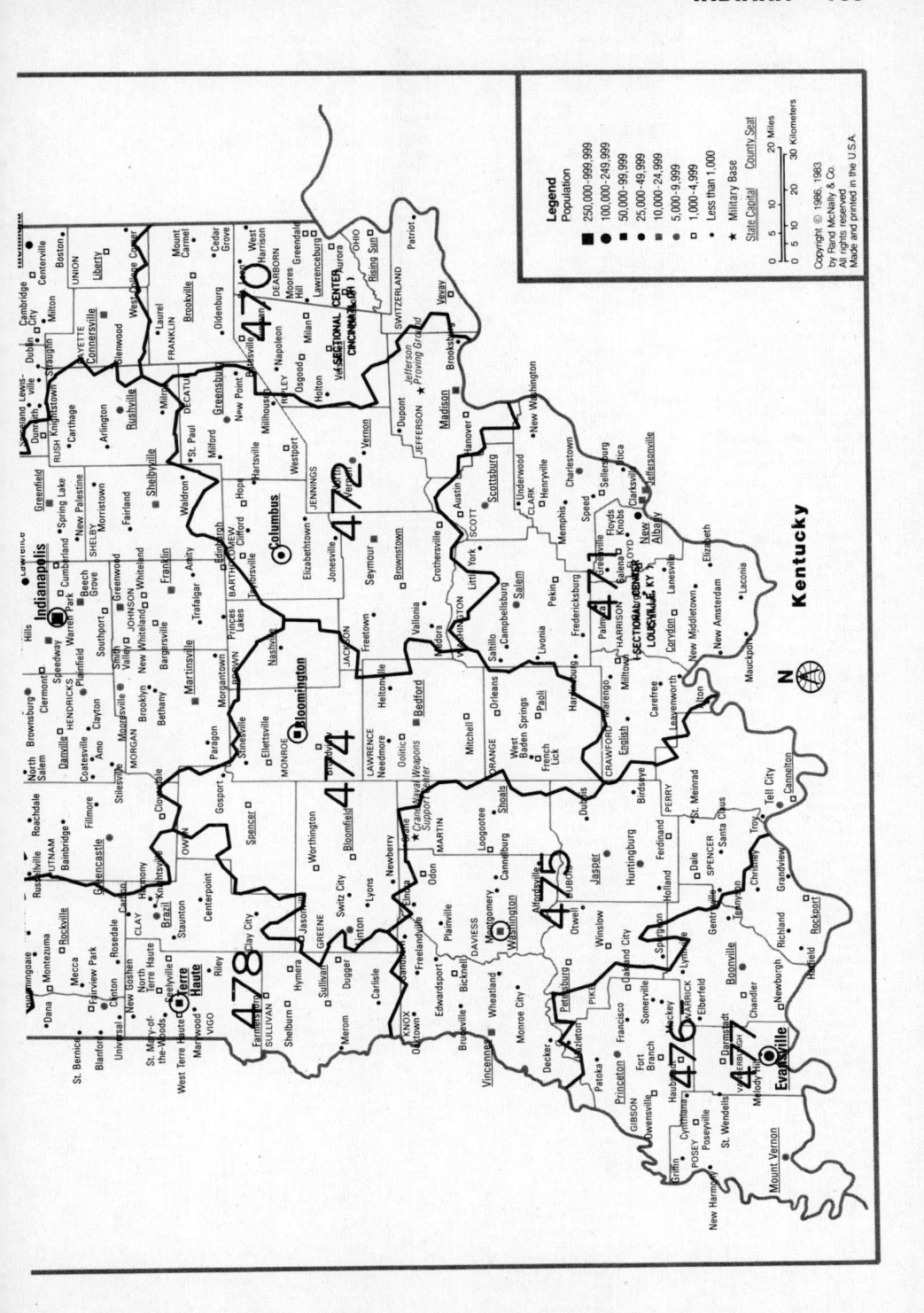

170 INDIANA Blue Lake-Cemar Estates

Name	ZIP
Blue Lake	46723
Blue Ridge	46176
Blue River (Hancock County) (Township)	46140
Blue River (Harrison County) (Township)	47115
Blue River (Henry County) (Township)	47360
Blue River (Johnson County) (Township)	46124
Bluff Point	47371
Bluffs	46151
Bluffton	46714
Bobtown	47274
Bogard (Township)	47568
Boggstown	46110
Bogle Corner	47438
Bolivar (Township)	47970
Bonnell	47022
Bonnenburger	47130
Bono	47446
Bono (Township)	47446
Boon (Township)	47601
Boone (Cass County) (Township)	46978
Boone (Crawford County) (Township)	47137
Boone (Dubois County) (Township)	47546
Boone (Harrison County) (Township)	47135
Boone (Madison County) (Township)	46036
Boone (Porter County) (Township)	46341
Boone Grove	46302
Boonville	47601
Borden	47106
Boston	47324
Boston (Township)	47324
Boswell	47921
Boundary	47371
Bourbon	46504
Bourbon (Township)	46504
Bowers	47940
Bowerstown	46750
Bowling Green	47833
Bowman	47567
Bowman Acres (Part of Greenfield)	46140
Boxley	46069
Boyleston	46057
Bracken	46750
Bradford	47107
Bradford Village (Part of Marion)	46952
Bradley	47611
Bramble	47553
Branchville	47514
Branchville Training Center	47586
Brandywine (Hancock County) (Township)	46140
Brandywine (Shelby County) (Township)	46126
Braytown	47043
Brazil	47834
Brazil (Township)	47834
Breezewood	46952
Breezewood Park	47302
Breezy Point	47960
Bremen	46506
Brems	46534
Brendan Wood (Part of Lebanon)	46052
Brendonwood (Part of Indianapolis)	46226
Brent Woods (Part of Shelbyville)	46176
Bretzville	47542
Brewersville	47265
Brewington Woods	47302
Briarwood	46157
Brice	47371
Brick Chapel	46135
Bridgeport (Part of Indianapolis)	46231
Bridgeton	47836
Brierwood Hills	46804
Bright	47025
Brighton	46746
Brightwood (Part of Indianapolis)	46218
Brimfield	46720
Brinckley	47340
Bringhurst	46913
Bristol	46507
Bristow	47515
Broadlands	47805
Broad Ripple (Part of Indianapolis)	46220
Broadview (Grant County)	46952

Name	ZIP
Broadview (Lawrence County)	47421
Broadview (Monroe County)	47401
Bromer	47452
Brook	47922
Brookfield	46126
Brook Haven	46952
Brook Knoll (Part of Bedford)	47421
Brooklyn	46111
Brookmoor	46158
Brooks	46060
Brooksburg	47250
Brookside Estates (Allen County)	46805
Brookside Estates (Vigo County)	47802
Brookston	47923
Brook Trails	46637
Brookville	47012
Brookville (Township)	47012
Brookville Heights	46163
Brookwood (Part of Warsaw)	46580
Broom Hill	47106
Brown (Hancock County) (Township)	47384
Brown (Hendricks County) (Township)	46112
Brown (Montgomery County) (Township)	47933
Brown (Morgan County) (Township)	46158
Brown (Ripley County) (Township)	47250
Brown (Washington County) (Township)	47108
Brownsburg	46112
Browns Crossing	46151
Brownstown (Township)	47220
Brownstown (Crawford County)	47118
Brownstown (Jackson County)	47220
Browns Valley	47933
Brownsville	47325
Brownsville (Township)	47325
Bruce Lake	46939
Bruceville	47516
Brummitt Acres	46304
Brunswick (Part of Gary)	46406
Brunswick	46303
Brushy Prairie	46761
Bryant	47326
Bryantsburg	47250
Bryantsville	47446
Buck Creek (Hancock County) (Township)	46140
Buck Creek (Tippecanoe County)	47924
Buckeye	46792
Buckskin	47613
Bucktown	47838
Bud	46131
Buddha	47421
Buena Vista	47024
Buffalo	47925
Buffaloville	47550
Buffington (Part of Gary)	46406
Bufkin	47620
Bugtown	47633
Bullocktown	47601
Bunker Hill (Fayette County)	47331
Bunker Hill (Knox County)	47591
Bunker Hill (Miami County)	46914
Bunker Hill (Washington County)	47167
Burdick	46304
Burglen Hills (Part of Tell City)	47586
Burket	46508
Burlington	46915
Burlington (Township)	46915
Burlington Beach	46383
Burnett	47805
Burnettsville	47926
Burney	47222
Burns City	47553
Burns Harbor	46304
Burnsville	47201
Burr Oak (Marshall County)	46511
Burr Oak (Noble County)	46701
Burrows	46916
Busseron	47561
Busseron (Township)	47561
Butler (De Kalb County)	46721
Butler (De Kalb County) (Township)	46763
Butler (Franklin County) (Township)	47006

Name	ZIP
Butler (Miami County) (Township)	46970
Butler Center	46738
Butlerville	47223
Byrneville	47122
Byron	46371
Caborn	47620
Cadiz	47362
Caesar Creek (Township)	47018
Cagle Mill	47868
Cain (Township)	47949
Cairo	47906
Cale	47581
California (Township)	46534
Calumet (Township)	46402
Calverrtville	47424
Cambria	46041
Cambridge City	47327
Camby (Part of Indianapolis)	46113
Camden	46917
Cammack	47302
Campbell (Jennings County) (Township)	47023
Campbell (Warrick County) (Township)	47610
Campbellsburg	47108
Campbelltown	47598
Canaan	47224
Candleglo Village	46176
Candle Light Village (Part of Columbus)	47201
Cannelburg	47519
Cannelton	47520
Cannelton Heights (Part of Cannelton)	47520
Canton	47167
Carbon	47837
Carbondale	47993
Cardonia	47834
Carefree	47137
Carey (Part of Noblesville)	46060
Carlisle	47838
Carlos City	47355
Carmel	46032
Carp	47460
Carpenter (Township)	47977
Carpentersville	46172
Carr (Clark County) (Township)	47143
Carr (Jackson County) (Township)	47260
Carriage Estates (Bartholomew County)	47201
Carriage Estates (Hancock County)	46163
Carrollton	46913
Carrollton (Township)	46929
Carter (Township)	47523
Cartersburg	46114
Carthage	46115
Carwood	47106
Cascade Heights (Part of Bloomington)	47401
Cass (Township)	47882
Cass (Township)	47960
Cass (Clay County) (Township)	47868
Cass (Dubois County) (Township)	47541
Cass (Greene County) (Township)	47449
Cass (La Porte County) (Township)	46390
Cass (Ohio County) (Township)	47040
Cass (Pulaski County) (Township)	47957
Cass (Sullivan County)	47882
Cassville	46901
Castleton	46250
Castleton Square (Part of Castleton)	46250
Cataract	47460
Cates	47952
Catlin	47872
Cato	47598
Cayuga	47928
Cedar Canyons	46825
Cedar Creek (Allen County) (Township)	46741
Cedar Creek (De Kalb County)	46738
Cedar Creek (Lake County) (Township)	46356
Cedar Grove	47016
Cedar Lake	46303
Cedar Point	47960
Cedar Shores	46741
Cedarville	46741
Celestine	47521
Cemar Estates	47805

Cementville-Corydon INDIANA 171

Name	ZIP
Cementville (Part of Jeffersonville)	47130
Centenary	47842
Centennial	47952
Center (Benton County) (Township)	47944
Center (Boone County) (Township)	46052
Center (Clinton County) (Township)	46041
Center (Dearborn County) (Township)	47001
Center (Delaware County) (Township)	47302
Center (Gibson County) (Township)	47649
Center (Grant County) (Township)	46952
Center (Greene County) (Township)	47424
Center (Hancock County) (Township)	46140
Center (Hendricks County) (Township)	46122
Center (Howard County)	46902
Center (Howard County) (Township)	46902
Center (Jay County)	47371
Center (Jennings County) (Township)	47265
Center (La Porte County) (Township)	46350
Center (Lake County) (Township)	46307
Center (Marion County) (Township)	46204
Center (Marshall County) (Township)	46563
Center (Martin County) (Township)	47553
Center (Porter County) (Township)	46383
Center (Posey County) (Township)	47620
Center (Ripley County) (Township)	47037
Center (Rush County) (Township)	46148
Center (Starke County) (Township)	46534
Center (Union County) (Township)	47353
Center (Vanderburgh County) (Township)	47710
Center (Warrick County)	47601
Center (Wayne County) (Township)	47330
Centerpoint	47840
Center Square	47043
Centerton	46116
Center Valley	46158
Centerville (Spencer County)	47611
Centerville (Wayne County)	47330
Central	47110
Central Barren	47161
Centre (Township)	46614
Century Consumer Mall (Part of Merrillville)	46410
Ceylon	46740
Chain O'Lakes	46628
Chalmers	47929
Chambersburg	47454
Champlin Meadows (Part of Martinsville)	46151
Chandler	47610
Chapel Bluff (Part of Columbus)	47201
Chapel Hill (Marion County)	46224
Chapelhill (Monroe County)	47436
Chapel Manor (Part of Merrillville)	46410
Charlemac Village (Part of Indianapolis)	46259
Charlestown	47111
Charlestown (Township)	47111
Charle Sumac Estates (Part of Indianapolis)	46259
Charlottesville	46117
Chase	47921
Chelsea	47138
Cherokee Terrace	47130
Cherry Grove	47933
Chester (Wabash County) (Township)	46962
Chester (Wayne County)	47374
Chester (Wells County) (Township)	46781
Chesterfield	46017
Chesterton (Hamilton County)	46280

Name	ZIP
Chesterton (Porter County)	46304
Chesterville	47032
Chestnut Hill (Part of Chesterton)	46304
Chestnut Ridge	47274
Chicago Avenue (Part of East Chicago)	46312
Chili	46926
China	47250
Chippewa (Part of South Bend)	46614
Chrisney	47611
Christiansburg	47201
Christmas Lake Village (Part of Santa Claus)	47579
Churubusco	46723
Cicero (Hamilton County)	46034
Cicero (Tipton County) (Township)	46031
Cicero Heights	46072
Cincinnati	47424
Circle Park	46742
Circleville	46173
Clare	46060
Clark (Johnson County) (Township)	46142
Clark (Montgomery County) (Township)	47954
Clark (Perry County) (Township)	47515
Clarksburg	47225
Clarks Hill	47930
Clarks Landing	46742
Clarksville (Clark County)	47130
Clarksville (Hamilton County)	46060
Clay (Bartholomew County) (Township)	47201
Clay (Carroll County) (Township)	46923
Clay (Cass County) (Township)	46947
Clay (Dearborn County) (Township)	47032
Clay (Decatur County) (Township)	47240
Clay (Hamilton County) (Township)	46032
Clay (Hendricks County) (Township)	46121
Clay (Howard County) (Township)	46901
Clay (Kosciusko County) (Township)	46580
Clay (Lagrange County) (Township)	46761
Clay (Miami County) (Township)	46914
Clay (Morgan County) (Township)	46111
Clay (Owen County) (Township)	47460
Clay (Pike County) (Township)	47640
Clay (Spencer County) (Township)	47579
Clay (St. Joseph County) (Township)	46637
Clay (Wayne County) (Township)	47345
Clay City (Clay County)	47841
Clay City (Spencer County)	47550
Claypool	46510
Claysville	47108
Clayton	46118
Clear Creek (Huntington County) (Township)	46750
Clear Creek (Monroe County)	47426
Clear Creek (Monroe County) (Township)	47401
Clear Lake (Township)	46737
Clear Lake	46737
Clear Spring (Jackson County)	47220
Clearspring (Lagrange County) (Township)	46571
Clermont	46234
Clermont Heights	46112
Cleveland (Elkhart County) (Township)	46514
Cleveland (Hancock County)	46140
Cleveland (Whitley County) (Township)	46787
Clifford	47226
Clifty (Township)	47246
Clifty Village	47203
Clinton (Township)	47842
Clinton (Boone County) (Township)	46052

Name	ZIP
Clinton (Cass County) (Township)	46947
Clinton (Decatur County) (Township)	47240
Clinton (Elkhart County) (Township)	46526
Clinton (La Porte County) (Township)	46382
Clinton (Putnam County) (Township)	46135
Clinton (Vermillion County)	47842
Clinton Falls	46135
Cloud Crest Hills	47448
Cloverdale	46120
Cloverdale (Township)	46120
Cloverland	47834
Clover Village	46126
Clunette	46538
Clymers	46947
Coal Bluff	47874
Coal City	47427
Coal Creek (Fountain County)	47932
Coal Creek (Montgomery County) (Township)	47994
Coalmont	47845
Coatesville	46121
Cochran (Part of Aurora)	47001
Coe	47598
Coesse	46725
Coesse Corners	46725
Coffey	47448
Cofield Corner	47040
Colburn	47931
Colburn Acres	46536
Cold Springs (Dearborn County)	47032
Cold Springs (Steuben County)	46742
Colfax (Clinton County)	46035
Colfax (Newton County) (Township)	46349
Collamer	46787
College Corner (Jay County)	47371
College Corner (Union County)	45003
College Hill (Part of Logansport)	46947
College Mall (Part of Bloomington)	47401
College Meadows	46240
Collegeville	47978
Collett	47371
Collins	46725
Coloma	47872
Colonial Hills	47630
Colonial Park	47802
Colonial Village	46040
Columbia (Township)	47331
Columbia (Gibson County) (Township)	47660
Columbia (Jennings County) (Township)	47265
Columbia (Whitley County) (Township)	46725
Columbia (Dubois County) (Township)	47527
Columbia (Fayette County)	47331
Columbia City	46725
Columbus	47201-03
For specific Columbus Zip Codes call (812) 378-2089	
Commercial Place (Part of Greencastle)	46135
Commiskey	47227
Como	47371
Concord (Township)	46785
Concord (De Kalb County)	46706
Concord (Elkhart County) (Township)	46514
Concord (Tippecanoe County)	47905
Concordia Gardens	46825
Connersville	47331
Connersville (Township)	47331
Continental Camp	47616
Converse	46919
Cook (Part of Cedar Lake)	46303
Cool Spring (Township)	46360
Coolwood Acres	46383
Cope	46151
Coppess Corner	46772
Cordry Lake	46164
Corn Brook	47203
Cornettsville	47568
Correct	47042
Cortland	47228
Corunna	46730
Cory	47846
Corydon	47112

172 INDIANA Cosperville-Ellis

Name	ZIP
Cosperville	46794
Cottage Grove	47353
Cotton (Township)	47011
Country Club Gardens	46804
Country Club Heights	46011
Country Club Meadows (Part of Evansville)	47710
Countryside Estates	46805
Country Terrace	47302
Country Village	47303
Courter	46970
Coveyville	47421
Covington	47932
Covington Dells	46804
Covington Plaza (Part of Fort Wayne)	46804
Cowan	47302
Coxville	47874
Craig (Township)	47043
Craig Highlands	46060
Craigville	46731
Crandall	47114
Crane	47522
Crane Naval Depot	47522
Crane Naval Weapons Support Center	47522
Crawfordsville	47933
Cree Lake	46755
Crest Manor (Part of South Bend)	46614
Crestmoor (Part of Shelbyville)	46176
Creston	46356
Crestview	46383
Crestview Heights	46158
Crestwood (Part of Fort Wayne)	46804
Crete	47355
Crisman (Part of Portage)	46368
Critchfield	46142
Crocker (Part of Chesterton)	46383
Crompton Hill	47842
Cromwell	46732
Crooked Lake	46703
Cross Plains	47017
Crothersville	47229
Crown Center	46157
Crown Colony	46816
Crown Point	46307
Crows Nest	46208
Crumley Crossing	47336
Crump Estates (Part of Columbus)	47201
Crumstown	46554
Crystal	47527
Cuba (Allen County)	46741
Cuba (Bartholomew County)	46124
Cuba (Owen County)	47460
Culver	46511
Culver Military Academy (Part of Culver)	46511
Cumback	47501
Cumberland	46229
Cunot	46120
Curby	47118
Curry (Township)	47879
Curryville (Adams County)	46731
Curryville (Sullivan County)	47879
Curtisville	46036
Cutler	46920
Cuzco	47432
Cyclone	46041
Cynthiana	47612
Cypress	47712
Dabney	47023
Daggett	47427
Daisy Hill	47106
Dale	47523
Daleville	47334
Dallas (Township)	46702
Dalton	47346
Dalton (Township)	47346
Dana	47847
Danville	46122
Darlington	47940
Darmstadt	47711
Darrough Chapel	46901
Davis (Fountain County) (Township)	47918
Davis (La Porte County)	46360
Davis (Starke County) (Township)	46532
Daylight	47711
Dayton	47941
Dayville	47630
Deacon	46994
De Camp Gardens	46516
Decatur (Adams County)	46733
Decatur (Marion County) (Township)	46241
Decker (Knox County)	47524

Name	ZIP
Decker (Knox County) (Township)	47524
Deedsville	46921
Deep River	46342
Deer Creek (Carroll County)	46917
Deer Creek (Carroll County) (Township)	46923
Deer Creek (Cass County) (Township)	46932
Deer Creek (Miami County) (Township)	46959
Deerfield (Bartholomew County)	47201
Deerfield (Randolph County)	47380
Deerfield (Vigo County)	47802
Deer Park	46310
Deers Mills	47989
De Gonia	47601
Delaware (Township)	47037
Delaware (Delaware County) (Township)	47320
Delaware (Hamilton County) (Township)	46060
Delaware (Ripley County)	47037
Delong	46922
Delp	47905
Delphi	46923
Deming	46034
Democrat (Township)	46920
Demotte	46310
Denham	46925
Denmark	47427
Denver	46926
Depauw	47115
Deputy	47230
Derby	47525
Desoto	47302
Devon Park (Part of Muncie)	47304
Devonshire (Part of Lawrence)	46226
Dewey (Township)	46348
Diamond	47874
Diamond Lake	46794
Diamond Valley (Part of Evansville)	47710
Dick Johnson (Township)	47834
Dike (Part of Princeton)	47670
Dillman	46792
Dillsboro	47018
Diplomat Plaza (Part of Fort Wayne)	46806
Disko	46982
Dixon	46773
Doans	47424
Dodd	47587
Dodds Bridge	47849
Dogwood	47135
Dolan	47401
Domestic	46714
Donaldson	46513
Dongola	47660
Doolittle Mills	47118
Door Village	46350
Dover (Boone County)	46052
Dover (Dearborn County)	47022
Dover Hill	47581
Dovers View	46072
Dowden Acres	47802
Downtown (Delaware County)	47305
Downtown (Howard County)	46901
Downtown (Lake County)	46402
Downtown (Tippecanoe County)	47902
Dreamwold Heights	46637
Dresden	47453
Dresser	47885
Drexel Gardens (Part of Indianapolis)	46241
Driftwood (Township)	47281
Dublin	47335
Dubois	47527
Dubois Crossroads	47527
Duck Creek (Township)	46036
Dudley (Township)	47387
Dudleytown	47274
Duff	47542
Dugger	47848
Dundee	46001
Dune Acres	46304
Dune Acres Station (Part of Dune Acres)	46304
Duneland Beach	46360
Dunfee	46818
Dunkirk (Cass County)	46947
Dunkirk (Jay County)	47336
Dunlap (Elkhart County)	46514
Dunlapsville	47353
Dunn	47944
Dunnington	47944
Dunns Bridge	46380

Name	ZIP
Dunreith	47337
Dupont	47231
Durbin	46060
Dutch Town (Part of Garrett)	46738
Dyer	46311
Eagle (Township)	46077
Eagle Creek (Township)	46341
Eagledale Plaza Shopping Center (Part of Indianapolis)	46222
Eagle Hollow	47250
Eagletown	46074
Eagle Village	46077
Eaglewood Estates	46077
Earle	47711
Earlham (Part of Richmond)	47374
Earl Park	47942
East Cedar Lake (Part of Cedar Lake)	46303
East Chicago	46312
East Clifford	47203
East Columbus (Part of Columbus)	47201
East Enterprise	47019
Eastern Heights (Part of Bloomington)	47401
Eastgate (Bartholomew County)	47201
Eastgate (Clark County)	47130
East Gate (Hancock County)	46040
Eastgate (Marion County)	46219
Eastgate Consumer Mall (Part of Indianapolis)	46219
East Glenn	47803
Eastland Gardens (Part of Fort Wayne)	46816
Eastland Mall (Part of Evansville)	47715
East Monticello	47960
East Mount Carmel	47665
East Oolitic	47421
East Park (Part of Frankfort)	46041
Eastridge Manor	47203
East Shelburn (Part of Shelburn)	47879
East Shoals (Part of Shoals)	47581
East Union	46031
Eastwich (Part of Lafayette)	47901
Eaton	47338
Echo Heights (Part of Muncie)	47302
Eckerty	47116
Economy	47339
Eddy	46795
Eden (Hancock County)	46140
Eden (Lagrange County) (Township)	46571
Edgerton	46797
Edgewater	46383
Edgewood (Bartholomew County)	47201
Edgewood (La Porte County)	46360
Edgewood (Lawrence County)	47421
Edgewood (Madison County)	46011
Edgewood (Marion County)	46227
Edgewood Park	46818
Edinburgh	46124
Edison Park (Part of South Bend)	46615
Edna Mills	46065
Edwardsport	47528
Edwardsville	47150
Eel (Township)	46947
Eel River (Allen County) (Township)	46723
Eel River (Hendricks County) (Township)	46165
Effner	60966
Ege	46763
Ehrmandale	47805
Ekin	46031
Elberfeld	47613
El Dorado	46142
Elizabeth	47117
Elizabethtown	47232
Elizaville	46052
Elkhart	46514-17
For specific Elkhart Zip Codes call (219) 293-5502	
Elkhart (Elkhart County) (Township)	46526
Elkhart (Noble County) (Township)	46794
Elkinsville	47448
Ellettsville	47429
Ellis	47848

Elliston-Gilboa INDIANA 173

Name	ZIP
Elliston	47424
Elmdale	47933
Elmira	46761
Elmore (Township)	47529
Elmwood (Part of Peru)	46970
Elnora	47529
Elrod	47018
Elston	47905
Elwood	46036
Elwren	47401
Eminence	46125
Emison	47530
Emma	46571
Emporia	46056
Enchanted Hills	46732
Englewood (Part of Bedford)	47421
English	47118
English Lake	46366
Enochsburg	47240
Enos	47963
Enos Corners	47660
Epsom	47568
Epworth Forest	46555
Erie	46970
Erie (Township)	46970
Ervin (Township)	46929
Etna (Kosciusko County) (Township)	46524
Etna (Whitley County)	46725
Etna Green	46524
Etna-Troy (Township)	46764
Eugene	47928
Eugene (Township)	47928
Eureka	47635
Evanston	47531
Evansville	47701-37
For specific Evansville Zip Codes call (812) 429-3300	
Evergreen Acres (Part of Clarksville)	47130
Everroad Park East (Part of Columbus)	47203
Everroad Park West (Part of Columbus)	47203
Everton	47331
Ewing (Part of Brownstown)	47220
Fair Acres (Part of Salem)	47167
Fairbank (Township)	47849
Fairbanks	47849
Fairfield (De Kalb County) (Township)	46730
Fairfield (Franklin County) (Township)	47012
Fairfield (Tippecanoe County) (Township)	47904
Fairfield Center	46730
Fair Grounds (Part of Indianapolis)	46205
Fairland	46126
Fairlawn (Part of Columbus)	47201
Fairmount	46928
Fairmount (Township)	46928
Fair Oaks	47943
Fairplay (Township)	47465
Fairview	47331
Fairview (Township)	47331
Fairview (Randolph County)	47373
Fairview (Switzerland County)	47011
Fairview Park	47842
Fairwood Hills (Part of Indianapolis)	46256
Fall Creek (Hamilton County) (Township)	46064
Fall Creek (Henry County) (Township)	47356
Fall Creek (Madison County) (Township)	46011
Falmouth	46127
Farlen	47562
Farmers	47431
Farmersburg	47850
Farmers Retreat	47018
Farmersville	47620
Farmland	47340
Farrabee	47167
Farrville	46952
Fayette (Boone County)	46052
Fayette (Vigo County) (Township)	47885
Fayetteville	47421
Federal (Part of Indianapolis)	46204
Fenn Haven	47586
Ferdinand	47532
Ferdinand (Township)	47532
Ferguson Hill	47885
Fewell Rhoades	46151
Fiat	47326
Fickle	46041

Name	ZIP
Fields	46158
Fifteenth Avenue (Part of Gary)	46407
Fillmore	46128
Fincastle	46712
Finley (Township)	47170
Finly	46129
Fishers	46038
Fishersburg	46051
Fisher's Woodland	46060
Fish Lake (La Porte County)	46574
Fish Lake (Lagrange County)	46761
Five Points (Marion County)	46239
Five Points (Morgan County)	46158
Five Points (Whitley County)	46725
Flat Rock (Bartholomew County) (Township)	47201
Flat Rock (Shelby County)	47234
Flat Rock Park	47201
Flat Rock Park North (Part of Columbus)	47201
Fleming	47274
Fletcher Lake	46939
Flint	46703
Flintwood (Part of Columbus)	47201
Flora (Carroll County)	46929
Flora (Miami County)	46970
Florence	47020
Florida (Madison County)	46011
Florida (Parke County) (Township)	47874
Floyd (Township)	46121
Floyds Knobs	47119
Folsomville	47614
Fontanet	47851
Foraker	46526
Foresman	47922
Forest	46039
Forest (Township)	46039
Forest Hill	47240
Forest Park (Part of Columbus)	47201
Forest Park Beach	46742
Forest Park Heights	47401
Forest Park North (Part of Columbus)	47201
Forest Ridge (Allen County)	46804
Forest Ridge (Grant County)	46952
Forest Ridge Estates	46804
Forrest Hills	46036
Fort Branch	47648
Fort Ritner	47430
Fortville	46040
Fort Wayne	46801-99
For specific Fort Wayne Zip Codes call (219) 427-7311	
Foster	47932
Fountain	47918
Fountain City	47341
Fountain Park (Jasper County)	47977
Fountain Park (Steuben County)	46742
Fountain Square (Part of Indianapolis)	46203
Fountaintown	46130
Fowler	47944
Fowlerton	46930
Foxglen	46060
Fox Hill	46113
Fox Lake	46703
Fox Ridge	46135
Francesville	47946
Francisco	47649
Frankfort	46041
Franklin (Township)	46131
Franklin (Kosciusko County) (Township)	46910
Franklin (Marion County) (Township)	46239
Franklin (Montgomery County) (Township)	47940
Franklin (Owen County) (Township)	47431
Franklin (Pulaski County) (Township)	46996
Franklin (Putnam County) (Township)	46172
Franklin (Randolph County) (Township)	47380
Franklin (Ripley County) (Township)	47031
Franklin (Washington County) (Township)	47167
Franklin (Wayne County)	47346
Franklin (Wayne County) (Township)	47341

Name	ZIP
Franklin (De Kalb County) (Township)	46721
Franklin (Floyd County) (Township)	47117
Franklin (Grant County) (Township)	46952
Franklin (Harrison County) (Township)	47136
Franklin (Hendricks County) (Township)	46180
Franklin (Henry County) (Township)	47352
Franklin (Johnson County)	46131
Franklin Hills (Part of Tell City)	47586
Frankton	46044
Fredericksburg	47120
Fredonia	47137
Freedom	47431
Freeland Park	47944
Freelandville	47535
Freeman	47460
Freeport	46161
Freetown	47235
Fremont (Township)	46737
Fremont	46737
French (Adams County) (Township)	46714
French (Ohio County)	47001
French Lake	47802
French Lick	47432
French Lick (Township)	47432
Frenchtown	47115
Friendship	47021
Friendswood	46113
Fritchton	47591
Fritz Corner	47585
Fruitdale	46160
Fugit (Township)	47240
Fulda	47536
Fulton (Fountain County) (Township)	47932
Fulton (Fulton County)	46931
Furnace	47424
Furnessville	46304
Gadsden	46052
Galena (Floyd County)	47119
Galena (La Porte County) (Township)	46371
Galveston	46932
Gambill	47848
Gar Creek	46774
Garden Acres (Boone County)	46071
Garden Acres (Monroe County)	47401
Garden City	47201
Garfield (Part of Indianapolis)	46203
Garrett	46738
Gary	46401-11
For specific Gary Zip Codes call (219) 886-8011	
Gasburg	46158
Gas City	46933
Gaston	47342
Gatchel	47586
Gatesville	46164
Gateway Shopping Center (Part of Richmond)	47374
Gatewood (Part of Muncie)	47304
Gaynorsville	47240
Geetingsville	46041
Gem	46140
Geneva (Adams County)	46740
Geneva (Jennings County) (Township)	47273
Geneva (Shelby County)	47234
Gentryville	47537
Georgetown (Township)	47122
Georgetown	47340
Georgetown (Allen County)	46741
Georgetown (Cass County)	46947
Georgetown (Floyd County)	47122
Georgia	47446
Georgia Heights (Part of Merrillville)	46410
Gerald	47520
German (Bartholomew County) (Township)	47201
German (Marshall County) (Township)	46506
German (St. Joseph County) (Township)	46628
German (Vanderburgh County) (Township)	47712
Germantown	47272
Gessie	47974
Gibson (Township)	47170
Gifford	47978
Gilboa (Township)	47944

174 INDIANA Gilead-Haskells

	ZIP
Gilead	46951
Gill (Township)	47861
Gillam (Township)	46392
Gilman	46001
Gilmer Park	46624
Gilmour	47438
Gingrich	47960
Gings	46173
Giro	47640
Glen Aire	47803
Glenbrook Square (Part of Fort Wayne)	46805
Glendale	47558
Glendale Center (Part of Indianapolis)	46220
Glendale Lake	46952
Glen Eden	46703
Glenhall	47992
Glenns Valley (Part of Indianapolis)	46217
Glen Park (Part of Gary)	46409
Glenview	47203
Glenwood	46133
Glenwood Acres	47620
Glenwood Park (Part of Fort Wayne)	46805
Glezen	47567
Gnaw Bone	47448
Goblesville	46750
Goff	46952
Golden Acres	46815
Golden Hill	47960
Golden Lake	46779
Goldsmith	46045
Golfview Estates	47130
Goodland	47948
Goose Lake	46725
Goshen (Elkhart County)	46526
Goshen (Scott County)	47170
Gospel Grove	47803
Gosport	47433
Gowdy	46173
Grabill	46741
Graceland Heights (Part of Hagerstown)	47346
Grafton	47620
Graham (Township)	47230
Graham Valley	47601
Graham Woods	46304
Grammer	47236
Grandview (Monroe County)	47401
Grandview (Spencer County)	47615
Grandview Lake	47201
Grandview Village	47150
Granger	46530
Grant (Benton County) (Township)	47944
Grant (De Kalb County) (Township)	46793
Grant (Greene County) (Township)	47465
Grant (Newton County) (Township)	47948
Grant City	47384
Grantsburg	47123
Granville	47338
Grass (Township)	47611
Grass Creek	46935
Grasselli (Part of East Chicago)	46312
Grassy Fork (Township)	47274
Gravel Beach	46747
Gravelton	46542
Grayford	47265
Graysville	47852
Green (Grant County) (Township)	46928
Green (Hancock County) (Township)	46040
Green (Madison County) (Township)	46048
Green (Marshall County) (Township)	46501
Green (Morgan County) (Township)	46151
Green (Noble County) (Township)	46763
Green (Randolph County) (Township)	47368
Green (Wayne County) (Township)	47393
Green Acres	46410
Greenbriar (Marion County)	46260
Greenbriar (Putnam County)	46135
Greenbrier	47601
Greencastle	46135
Greencastle (Township)	46135
Green Center	46701
Greendale (Allen County)	46805

	ZIP
Greendale (Dearborn County)	47025
Greene (Jay County) (Township)	47371
Greene (Parke County) (Township)	47989
Greene (St. Joseph County) (Township)	46614
Greenfield (Hancock County)	46140
Greenfield (Lagrange County) (Township)	46746
Greenfield (Orange County) (Township)	47118
Greenfield Estates	46952
Greenfield Mills	46746
Greenhill	47970
Greenleaf Manor (Part of Elkhart)	46514
Green Meadows (Shelby County)	46126
Green Meadows (Tippecanoe County)	47906
Greenoak	46975
Greensboro	47344
Greensboro (Township)	47344
Greensburg	47240
Greensfork (Randolph County) (Township)	47335
Greens Fork (Wayne County)	47345
Greentown	46936
Green Tree Mall (Part of Clarksville)	47130
Greenvalley	46060
Greenview	46815
Greenville (Floyd County)	47124
Greenville (Wells County) (Township)	47124
Greenville	46781
Greenwood (Johnson County)	46142
Greenwood (Lagrange County)	46795
Greenwood Park Mall (Part of Greenwood)	46142
Greer (Township)	47613
Gregg (Township)	46157
Greybrook Lake	47868
Griffin	47616
Griffith	46319
Grissom AFB (Miami County)	46971
Grissom A F B (Miami County)	46971
Groomsville	46049
Groveland	46105
Grovertown	46531
Guilford (Dearborn County)	47022
Guilford (Hendricks County) (Township)	46168
Guion	47872
Gurley Corner	47038
Guthrie (Lawrence County)	47421
Guthrie (Lawrence County) (Township)	47467
Guy	46936
Gwynneville	46144
Hacienda Village	46805
Hackleman	46928
Haddon (Township)	47838
Hadley	46121
Hagerstown	47346
Halbert (Township)	47581
Haleysbury	47281
Hall (Dubois County) (Township)	47546
Hall (Morgan County)	46157
Halteman Village (Part of Muncie)	47304
Hamblen (Township)	46164
Hamburg (Clark County)	47172
Hamburg (Franklin County)	47036
Hamilton (Clinton County)	46058
Hamilton (Delaware County) (Township)	47302
Hamilton (Jackson County) (Township)	47274
Hamilton (Madison County)	46011
Hamilton (Steuben County)	46742
Hamilton (Sullivan County) (Township)	47882
Hamilton Park	47302
Hamilton Village	47303
Hamlet	46532
Hammond	46320-27
For specific Hammond Zip Codes call (219) 932-1519	
Hammond (Township)	47615
Hamor Heights	47203
Hancock	47115

	ZIP
Handy	47401
Hanfield	46952
Hanging Grove (Township)	47978
Hangman Crossing	47274
Hanna	46340
Hanna (Township)	46340
Hanover	47243
Hanover (Township)	47243
Hanover (Lake County) (Township)	46303
Hanover (Shelby County) (Township)	46161
Hanover Beach	47243
Happy Hollow Heights (Part of West Lafayette)	47906
Harbison (Township)	47527
Harbor (Part of East Chicago)	46312
Hardinsburg (Dearborn County)	47025
Hardinsburg (Washington County)	47125
Hardscrabble	46051
Harlan	46743
Harmony (Clay County)	47853
Harmony (Posey County) (Township)	47631
Harmony (Union County) (Township)	47331
Harper	47283
Harris (Township)	46530
Harrisburg	47331
Harris City	47240
Harrison (Bartholomew County) (Township)	47201
Harrison (Blackford County) (Township)	47359
Harrison (Boone County) (Township)	46052
Harrison (Cass County) (Township)	46947
Harrison (Clay County) (Township)	47841
Harrison (Daviess County) (Township)	47501
Harrison (Dearborn County) (Township)	47060
Harrison (Delaware County) (Township)	47302
Harrison (Elkhart County) (Township)	46526
Harrison (Fayette County) (Township)	47331
Harrison (Harrison County) (Township)	47122
Harrison (Henry County) (Township)	47384
Harrison (Howard County) (Township)	46979
Harrison (Knox County) (Township)	47591
Harrison (Kosciusko County) (Township)	46502
Harrison (Miami County) (Township)	46911
Harrison (Morgan County) (Township)	46151
Harrison (Owen County) (Township)	47433
Harrison (Pulaski County) (Township)	46939
Harrison (Spencer County) (Township)	47532
Harrison (Union County) (Township)	47353
Harrison (Vigo County) (Township)	47807
Harrison (Wayne County) (Township)	47327
Harrison (Wells County) (Township)	46714
Harrison Hills (Part of Columbus)	47201
Harrison Lake	47201
Harristown	47167
Harrisville	47390
Harrodsburg	47434
Hart (Township)	47619
Hartford (Adams County) (Township)	46740
Hartford (Ohio County)	47001
Hartford City	47348
Hartford Place (Part of Columbus)	47201
Hartleyville	47421
Hartsdale (Part of Schererville)	46375
Hartsville	47244
Harveysburg	47952
Hashtown	47424
Haskells	46390

Hastings-Island Park INDIANA 175

	ZIP
Hastings	46542
Hatfield	47617
Haubstadt	47639
Haw Creek (Township)	47246
Hawthorne Hills	46307
Hayden	47245
Haymond	47006
Haysville	47546
Hazelrigg	46052
Hazelwood (Allen County)	46805
Hazelwood (Hendricks County)	46118
Hazelwood (Shelby County)	46176
Hazleton	47640
Headlee	47960
Heath	47905
Heather Heights (Part of Columbus)	47201
Heather Hills (Part of Indianapolis)	46229
Heaton Lake	46514
Hebron	46341
Hedrick	47993
Heilman	47523
Helmcrest (Part of Fortville)	46040
Helmer	46744
Helmsburg	47435
Helt (Township)	47847
Heltonville	47436
Hemlock	46937
Hemlock Lakes	47952
Henderson	46173
Hendricks (Johnson County)	46142
Hendricks (Shelby County) (Township)	46176
Hendricksville	47459
Henry (Fulton County) (Township)	46910
Henry (Henry County) (Township)	47362
Henryville	47126
Hensley (Township)	46181
Herbst	46952
Heritage Lake	46128
Herr	46052
Hessen Cassel	46806
Hesston	46350
Hessville (Part of Hammond)	46323
Heth (Township)	47110
Heusler	47712
Hibbard	46511
Hibernia	47111
Hibernia Mills	47933
Hickory Grove (Township)	47984
Hickory Hills	46952
Hideaway Lake	47952
Highbanks	46555
High Lake	46701
Highland (Franklin County) (Township)	47012
Highland (Greene County) (Township)	47424
Highland (Lake County)	46322
Highland (Vanderburgh County)	47710
Highland (Vermillion County)	47854
Highland (Vermillion County) (Township)	47974
Highland Meadows	46952
Highland Village (Part of Bloomington)	47401
Highwoods (Part of Indianapolis)	46222
Hiker Trace (Part of Columbus)	47201
Hildebrand Village	46176
Hill and Dale (Part of Sellersburg)	47172
Hillcrest (Bartholomew County)	47201
Hillcrest (Harrison County)	47112
Hillcrest (Porter County)	46383
Hillcrest Circle (Part of Bedford)	47421
Hillendale	47006
Hillham	47432
Hillisburg	46046
Hills And Dales	47383
Hillsboro (Fountain County)	47949
Hillsboro (Henry County)	47362
Hillsdale (Vanderburgh County)	47711
Hillsdale (Vermillion County)	47854
Hillview Estates	47201
Hindostan Falls	47581
Hindustan	47401
Hitchcock	47167
Hi-View (Part of South Bend)	46624

	ZIP
Hoagland	46745
Hobart	46342
Hobart (Township)	46342
Hobbieville	47462
Hobbs	46047
Hoffman Lake	46580
Hogan (Township)	47001
Hogtown	47140
Holaday Hills and Dales	46032
Holiday Lakes	46738
Holiday Park	46902
Holland	47541
Hollandsburg	47872
Hollybrook Lake	47433
Holly Hills	47802
Holton	47023
Home Corner	46952
Homecroft	46227
Home Place	46240
Homer	46146
Homestead (Part of Greendale)	47025
Honey Creek (Henry County)	47356
Honey Creek (Howard County) (Township)	46979
Honey Creek (Vigo County) (Township)	47802
Honey Creek (White County) (Township)	47980
Honeyville	46571
Hoosier Acres (Part of Bloomington)	47401
Hoosier Highlands	47868
Hoosierville	47834
Hoover	46947
Hope	47246
Hopewell (De Kalb County)	46706
Hopewell (Johnson County)	46131
Horace	47240
Horton	46069
Houston	47235
Hovey	47620
Howard (Howard County) (Township)	46901
Howard (Parke County)	47985
Howard (Parke County) (Township)	47859
Howard (Washington County) (Township)	47167
Howe	46746
Howell (Part of Evansville)	47712
Howesville	47438
Hubbell	47427
Hubbells Corner	47041
Hudson (La Porte County) (Township)	46552
Hudson (Steuben County)	46747
Hudson Lake	46552
Hudsonville	47558
Huff (Township)	47615
Huffman	47588
Hull Addition	46072
Hunter (Part of Indianapolis)	46239
Huntersville (Part of Batesville)	47006
Huntertown	46748
Huntingburg	47542
Huntington (Township)	46750
Huntington	46750
Huntsville (Madison County)	46064
Huntsville (Randolph County)	47358
Huron	47437
Hyde Park	47302
Hymera	47855
Hyndsdale	46151
Idaho (Part of Terre Haute)	47802
Idaville	47950
Ijamsville	46962
Imperial Gardens	46815
Imperial Hills (Part of Greenwood)	46227
Independence	47918
Independence Hill (Part of Merrillville)	46410
Indiana Army Ammunition Plant	47111
Indiana Beach	47960
Indiana Oaks	47172
Indianapolis	46201-90
For specific Indianapolis Zip Codes call (317) 464-6150	

COLLEGES & UNIVERSITIES

	ZIP
Butler University	46208
Indiana University-Purdue University at Indianapolis	46202
Marian College	46222
University of Indianapolis	46227

FINANCIAL INSTITUTIONS

	ZIP
Bank One, Indianapolis, National Association	46277
First of America Bank-Indianapolis	46224
The INB National Bank	46266
Merchants National Bank and Trust Company of Indianapolis	46255
Peoples Bank & Trust Company	46204
Railroadmen's Federal Savings & Loan Association	46204
Security Savings Association	46204
Shelby Federal Savings Bank	46203
Union Federal Savings Bank	46204

HOSPITALS

	ZIP
Community Hospitals of Indiana	46219
Indiana University Hospitals	46223
Methodist Hospital of Indiana	46206
Richard L. Roudebush Veterans Administration Medical Center	46202
St. Vincent Hospital and Health Care Center	46260
William N. Wishard Memorial Hospital	46202

HOTELS/MOTELS

	ZIP
Adam's Mark Hotel	46241
The Canterbury Hotel	46225
Embassy Suites Indianapolis-Downtown	46204
Hilton at the Circle	46204
Holiday Inn-Southeast	46203
Indianapolis Airport Hilton	46241
Indianapolis Marriott	46219
Radisson Plaza Hotel Indianapolis	46240

MILITARY INSTALLATIONS

	ZIP
Naval Avionics Center	46219
United States Property and Fiscal Office for Indiana	46241
United States Property and Fiscal Office, Camp Atterbury	46241
Indianapolis Union Stock Yards (Part of Indianapolis)	46241
Indiana State Farm	46135
Indiana State Reformatory	46064
Indiana State University Evansville Campus	47712
Indian Creek (Lawrence County) (Township)	47421
Indian Creek (Monroe County) (Township)	47401
Indian Creek (Pulaski County) (Township)	46985
Indian Creek Settlement	47512
Indianhead Lake	46122
Indian Heights	46902
Indian Hills	47201
Indian Lake (De Kalb County)	46730
Indian Lake (Marion County)	46226
Indianola	46795
Indian Springs	47581
Indian Village (Noble County)	46732
Indian Village (St. Joseph County)	46637
Industry (Part of Muncie)	47302
Ingalls	46048
Inglefield (Part of Darmstadt)	47618
Innisdale	46001
Inverness	46703
Inwood	46563
Iona	47591
Ireland	47545
Ironton	47581
Iroquois (Township)	47922
Irvington (Part of Indianapolis)	46219
Irvington Plaza Shopping Center (Part of Indianapolis)	46219
Island Park (Kosciusko County)	46580
Island Park (Steuben County)	46742

176 INDIANA Iva-Ladoga

	ZIP
Iva	47564
Ivanhoe (Part of Indianapolis)	46219
Ivy Hills (Part of Indianapolis)	46220
Jackson (Allen County) (Township)	46773
Jackson (Bartholomew County) (Township)	47274
Jackson (Blackford County) (Township)	47348
Jackson (Boone County) (Township)	46147
Jackson (Brown County) (Township)	47448
Jackson (Carroll County) (Township)	46917
Jackson (Cass County) (Township)	46932
Jackson (Clay County) (Township)	47834
Jackson (Clinton County) (Township)	46041
Jackson (De Kalb County) (Township)	46706
Jackson (Dearborn County) (Township)	47041
Jackson (Decatur County) (Township)	47283
Jackson (Dubois County) (Township)	47542
Jackson (Elkhart County) (Township)	46553
Jackson (Fayette County) (Township)	47331
Jackson (Fountain County) (Township)	47949
Jackson (Greene County) (Township)	47462
Jackson (Hamilton County) (Township)	47030
Jackson (Hancock County) (Township)	46140
Jackson (Harrison County) (Township)	47161
Jackson (Howard County) (Township)	46936
Jackson (Huntington County) (Township)	46783
Jackson (Jackson County) (Township)	47274
Jackson (Jay County) (Township)	47326
Jackson (Kosciusko County) (Township)	46566
Jackson (Madison County) (Township)	46011
Jackson (Miami County) (Township)	46919
Jackson (Morgan County) (Township)	46160
Jackson (Newton County) (Township)	47963
Jackson (Orange County) (Township)	47432
Jackson (Owen County) (Township)	46120
Jackson (Parke County) (Township)	47837
Jackson (Porter County) (Township)	46304
Jackson (Putnam County) (Township)	46172
Jackson (Randolph County) (Township)	47390
Jackson (Ripley County) (Township)	47034
Jackson (Rush County) (Township)	46115
Jackson (Shelby County) (Township)	46176
Jackson (Spencer County) (Township)	47537
Jackson (Starke County) (Township)	46534
Jackson (Steuben County) (Township)	46703
Jackson (Sullivan County) (Township)	47855
Jackson (Tippecanoe County) (Township)	47901
Jackson (Washington County) (Township)	47165
Jackson (Wayne County) (Township)	47327
Jackson (Wells County) (Township)	46991
Jackson (White County) (Township)	47926
Jacksonburg	47327
Jackson Hill	47879

	ZIP
Jackson Park	47302
Jacksons	46072
Jacksonville	47842
Jalapa	46952
Jamestown (Township)	46737
Jamestown (Boone County)	46147
Jamestown (Steuben County)	46737
Jasonville	47438
Jasper	47546-47
For specific Jasper Zip Codes call (812) 634-5050	
Jay City	47326
Jefferson (Adams County) (Township)	46711
Jefferson (Allen County) (Township)	46773
Jefferson (Boone County) (Township)	46071
Jefferson (Carroll County) (Township)	46923
Jefferson (Cass County) (Township)	46978
Jefferson (Clinton County) (Township)	46041
Jefferson (Dubois County) (Township)	47513
Jefferson (Elkhart County) (Township)	46526
Jefferson (Grant County) (Township)	46989
Jefferson (Greene County) (Township)	47471
Jefferson (Henry County) (Township)	47388
Jefferson (Huntington County) (Township)	46792
Jefferson (Jay County) (Township)	47371
Jefferson (Kosciusko County) (Township)	46550
Jefferson (Miami County) (Township)	46970
Jefferson (Morgan County) (Township)	46151
Jefferson (Newton County) (Township)	47951
Jefferson (Noble County) (Township)	46701
Jefferson (Owen County) (Township)	47427
Jefferson (Pike County) (Township)	47564
Jefferson (Pulaski County) (Township)	46996
Jefferson (Putnam County) (Township)	46120
Jefferson (Sullivan County) (Township)	47838
Jefferson (Switzerland County) (Township)	47043
Jefferson (Tipton County) (Township)	46072
Jefferson (Washington County) (Township)	47108
Jefferson (Wayne County) (Township)	47346
Jefferson (Wells County) (Township)	46777
Jefferson (Whitley County) (Township)	46725
Jefferson Proving Ground	47250
Jeffersonville	47130-31
For specific Jeffersonville Zip Codes call (812) 284-4834	
Jennings (Crawford County) (Township)	47137
Jennings (Fayette County) (Township)	47331
Jennings (Owen County) (Township)	46120
Jennings (Scott County) (Township)	47102
Jericho	47848
Jerome	46936
Jessups	47874
Jewell Village	47201
Jimtown	46514
Jockey	47637
Johnsburg	47542
Johnson (Clinton County) (Township)	46041
Johnson (Crawford County) (Township)	47116
Johnson (Gibson County)	47665
Johnson (Gibson County) (Township)	47639
Johnson (Knox County) (Township)	47591
Johnson (La Porte County) (Township)	46574

	ZIP
Johnson (Lagrange County) (Township)	46796
Johnson (Ripley County) (Township)	47042
Johnson (Scott County) (Township)	47230
Johnsonville	47993
Johnstown (Greene County)	47471
Johnstown (Knox County)	47512
Jolietville	46069
Jonesboro	46938
Jonestown	47842
Jonesville	47247
Joppa	46158
Jordan (Jasper County) (Township)	47978
Jordan (Owen County)	47868
Jordan (Warren County) (Township)	47993
Judah	47421
Judson (Howard County)	46901
Judson (Parke County)	47856
Judyville	47993
Julietta (Part of Indianapolis)	46239
Junction (Part of Peru)	46970
Kalorama Park	46538
Kankakee (Jasper County) (Township)	46374
Kankakee (La Porte County) (Township)	46371
Karwick (Part of Michigan City)	46360
Kasson	47712
Keener (Township)	46310
Kellerville	47527
Kelso (Township)	47022
Kempton	46049
Kendallville	46755
Kennard	47351
Kent (Jefferson County)	47250
Kent (Warren County) (Township)	47982
Kentland	47951
Kentwood (Part of Frankfort)	46041
Kenwood	47885
Kersey	46310
Kewanna	46939
Keyser (Township)	46738
Keystone	46759
Kilmore	46041
Kimmell	46760
Kinder	46106
Kingman	47952
Kingsbury	46345
Kingsford Heights	46346
Kingsland	46777
Kingston	47240
Kingswood Terra	47802
Kirkland (Township)	46733
Kirklin	46050
Kirklin (Township)	46050
Kirkpatrick	47955
Kirksville	47401
Kirkville	47649
Kitchell	47353
Klemmes Corner	47012
Klondyke (Parke County)	47862
Klondyke (Vermillion County)	47842
Knapp Lake	46732
Knight (Township)	47711
Knighthood Grove	46176
Knighthood Village	46176
Knight Ridge	47401
Knightstown	46148
Knightstown Lake	46148
Knightsville	47857
Kniman	46392
Knob Hill	47711
Knox (Jay County) (Township)	47336
Knox (Starke County)	46534
Kokomo	46901-04
For specific Kokomo Zip Codes call (317) 455-8300	
Koleen	47439
Koontz Lake	46574
Kossuth	47167
Kouts	46347
Kramer	47918
Kreitsburg	46311
Kriete Corners	47274
Kurtz	47249
Kyana	47575
Kyle	47001
Laconia	47135
La Crosse	46348
Ladoga	47954

Lafayette-Mace INDIANA 177

Name	ZIP
Lafayette	47901-06
For specific Lafayette Zip Codes call (317) 448-9245	
Lafayette (Allen County) (Township)	46783
Lafayette (Floyd County) (Township)	47119
Lafayette (Madison County) (Township)	46011
Lafayette (Owen County) (Township)	47460
Lafayette Square (Part of Indianapolis)	46254
La Fontaine	46940
Lagrange	46761
Lagro	46941
Lagro (Township)	46941
Lake (Allen County) (Township)	46818
Lake (Kosciusko County) (Township)	46982
Lake (Newton County) (Township)	46349
Lake Bodona	46158
Lake Bruce	46939
Lake Cicott	46942
Lakecrest (Part of Noblesville)	46060
Lake Dalecarlia	46356
Lake Dilldear	47018
Lake Edgewood	46151
Lake Eliza	46383
Lake Everett	46808
Lake Front (Part of Whiting)	46394
Lake Hart	46158
Lake Hills	46375
Lake Holiday	47933
Lake James	46703
Lakeland (Part of Michigan City)	46360
Lake Latonka	46511
Lake Lincoln	47552
Lake Manitou	46975
Lake Maxine	47456
Lake McCoy	47240
Lake Mohee	47348
Lake Noji	47802
Lake of the Four Seasons	46307
Lake of the Woods	46506
Lake Park	46552
Lakeside	46795
Lakeside Park (Part of Warsaw)	46580
Lake Station	46405
Lake Sullivan	47882
Laketon	46943
Lakeview (Franklin County)	47024
Lakeview (Lagrange County)	46795
Lake View (Porter County)	46383
Lakeview Estates	47802
Lake Village	46349
Lakeville	46536
Lake Wood (Grant County)	46952
Lakewood (Vigo County)	47802
Lakewood (White County)	47960
Lakewood Hills (Part of Evansville)	47711
Lamar	47550
Lamb	47043
Lamb Lake	46181
Lamong	46069
Lamplighter	46060
Lancaster	46750
Lancaster (Huntington County) (Township)	46750
Lancaster	47250
Lancaster (Jefferson County) (Township)	47250
Lancaster (Wells County) (Township)	46714
Lancaster Park	47401
Landess	46944
Lane (Township)	47637
Lanesville	47136
Lantana Estate (Part of Shelbyville)	46176
Lantern Park	47302
Laotto	46763
Lapaz	46537
La Paz Junction	46563
Lapel	46051
La Porte	46350
Larimer Hill	47885
Larwill	46764
Lasalle Square (Part of South Bend)	46601
Laud	46725
Laughery (Township)	47006
Lauramie (Township)	47930
Laurel	47024

Name	ZIP
Laurel (Township)	47024
Lawndale (Part of Evansville)	47715
Lawrence	46226
Lawrence (Township)	46226
Lawrenceburg	47025
Lawrenceburg (Township)	47025
Lawrenceport	47446
Lawrenceville	47041
Lawton	46996
Laynecrest (Part of Muncie)	47304
Leases Corner	46950
Leavenworth	47137
Lebanon	46052
Lee	47978
Leesburg	46538
Leesville	47421
Leininger Acres	46072
Leipsic	47452
Leisure	46036
Leiters Ford	46945
Lena	47834
Leo	46765
Leopold	47551
Leopold (Township)	47551
Leota	47170
Leroy	46355
Letts	47240
Letts Corner	47240
Lewis (Clay County) (Township)	47438
Lewis (Vigo County)	47858
Lewisburg	47335
Lewis Creek	47234
Lewisville (Henry County)	47352
Lewisville (Morgan County)	46120
Lexington (Township)	47138
Lexington (Carroll County)	46920
Lexington (Scott County)	47138
Liber	47371
Liberty (Carroll County) (Township)	46916
Liberty (Crawford County) (Township)	47140
Liberty (Delaware County) (Township)	47383
Liberty (Fulton County) (Township)	46931
Liberty (Grant County) (Township)	46952
Liberty (Hendricks County) (Township)	46118
Liberty (Henry County) (Township)	47362
Liberty (Howard County) (Township)	46901
Liberty (Parke County) (Township)	47985
Liberty (Porter County) (Township)	46383
Liberty (Shelby County) (Township)	46182
Liberty (St. Joseph County) (Township)	46554
Liberty (Tipton County) (Township)	46068
Liberty (Union County) (Township)	47353
Liberty (Union County) (Township)	47353
Liberty (Wabash County) (Township)	46940
Liberty (Warren County) (Township)	47918
Liberty (Wells County) (Township)	46766
Liberty (White County) (Township)	47925
Liberty Center	46766
Liberty Hills	46804
Liberty Mills	46946
Liberty Park	46307
Libertyville	47885
Licking (Township)	47348
Liggett	47885
Ligonier	46767
Lilly Dale	47586
Lima (Township)	46746
Limberlost Hills	47803
Limedale	46135
Lincoln (Cass County)	46994
Lincoln (Hendricks County) (Township)	46112
Lincoln (La Porte County) (Township)	46365
Lincoln (Newton County) (Township)	46310
Lincoln (St. Joseph County) (Township)	46574
Lincoln (White County) (Township)	47950
Lincoln City	47552

Name	ZIP
Lincoln Heights (Clark County)	47130
Lincoln Heights (Madison County)	46001
Lincoln Hills	46383
Lincoln Park (Part of Clarksville)	47130
Lincoln Village (Part of Merrillville)	46410
Lincolnville	46992
Linden	47955
Linden Park (Part of Muncie)	47303
Lindenwood (Part of Indianapolis)	46227
Linkville	46563
Linn Grove	46769
Linnsburg	47933
Linton (Greene County)	47441
Linton (Vigo County) (Township)	47802
Linwood (Madison County)	46001
Linwood (Marion County)	46201
Lippe	47620
Lisbon	46755
Little	47567
Little Acres	47274
Little Point	46180
Little Saint Louis	47115
Little York	47139
Liverpool (Part of Lake Station)	46408
Livonia	47108
Lizton	46149
Locke	46550
Locke (Township)	46550
Lockhart (Township)	47585
Lockport	47926
Lodi	47952
Logan	47060
Logan (Township)	47060
Logan (Fountain County) (Township)	47918
Logan (Pike County) (Township)	47567
Logansport	46947
Logansport State Hospital	46947
London	46126
London Heights	46126
Long Acres	46176
Long Beach	46360
Long Lake	46962
Long Lake Island	46383
Longview Beach	47130
Loogootee	47553
Lookout	47041
Loon Lake	46725
Lorane	46725
Loree	46914
Losantville	47354
Lost Creek (Township)	47803
Lost River (Township)	47432
Lottaville (Part of Merrillville)	46410
Lotus	47353
Lovett	47265
Lovett (Township)	47265
Lowell (Bartholomew County)	47201
Lowell (Lake County)	46356
Lower Sunset Park	47960
Loyal	46975
Luce (Township)	47617
Lucerne	46950
Ludwig Park (Part of Fort Wayne)	46825
Lukens Lake	46974
Luray	47386
Luther	46787
Lutheran Lake	47274
Lydick	46628
Lyford	47874
Lynhurst	46241
Lynn (Posey County) (Township)	47620
Lynn (Randolph County)	47355
Lynnville	47619
Lyons	47443
Lyonsville	47331
McBride Heights	47130
McCarthy Addition (Part of Alexandria)	46001
McCarty	46142
McClellan (Township)	47963
Mc Col Place (Part of Salem)	47167
McCool (Part of Portage)	46368
McCordsville	46055
McCoysburg	47978
McCutchanville	47711
McDaniel	46151
Mace	47933

178 INDIANA Mac-Fair-Mar-Monroe

	ZIP		ZIP		ZIP
Mac-Fair-Mar	46947	Markland	47020	Michigantown	46057
McGrawsville	46911	Markland Mall (Part of Kokomo)	46902	Mickleyville (Part of Indianapolis)	46241
Mackey	47654	Markle	46770	Middle (Township)	46167
McKinley	47108	Markleville	46056	Middleboro	47374
McKinley Town and Country Shopping Center (Part of Mishawaka)	46545	Marlin Hills	47401	Middlebury	46540
		Marquette Farm	47805	Middlebury (Township)	46540
McNatts	47359	Marquette Mall (Part of Michigan City)	46360	Middlefork (Clinton County)	46041
Macy	46951			Middlefork (Jefferson County)	47231
Madison (Township)	47250	Marrs (Township)	47620		
Madison (Montgomery County) (Township)	47933	Marrs Center	47620	Middletown (Henry County)	47356
		Marshall (Lawrence County) (Township)	47421	Middletown (Shelby County)	46182
Madison (Morgan County) (Township)	46158	Marshall (Parke County)	47859	Middletown Park	47302
		Marshfield	47956	Midland	47445
Madison (Pike County) (Township)	47567	Mars Hill (Part of Indianapolis)	46241	Midway (Elkhart County)	46526
				Midway (Jefferson County)	47250
Madison (Putnam County) (Township)	46135	Marshtown	46939	Midway (Spencer County)	47601
		Martin Heights (Part of Salem)	47167	Midwest (Part of Portage)	46368
Madison (St. Joseph County) (Township)	46614			Mier	46919
		Martinsburg	47165	Mifflin	47118
Madison (Tipton County) (Township)	46072	Martinsville	46151	Milan (Allen County) (Township)	46797
		Martz	47841		
Madison (Washington County) (Township)	47108	Maryland	47802	Milan (Ripley County)	47031
		Marysville (Clark County)	47141	Milan Center	46774
Madison (Allen County) (Township)	46773	Marysville (Pike County)	47598	Milford (Decatur County)	47240
		Marywood	47802	Milford (Kosciusko County)	46542
Madison (Carroll County) (Township)	46923	Matlock Heights (Part of Bloomington)	47401	Milford (Lagrange County) (Township)	46795
Madison (Clinton County) (Township)	46058				
		Matthews	46957	Milford Junction	46542
Madison (Daviess County) (Township)	47562	Mattix Corner	46041	Mill (Township)	46933
		Mauckport	47142	Mill Creek (Fountain County) (Township)	47952
Madison (Dubois County) (Township)	47546	Maumee (Township)	46797		
		Mauzy	46173	Mill Creek (Hamilton County)	46060
Madison (Jay County) (Township)	45846	Max	46052		
		Maxinkuckee	46511	Mill Creek (La Porte County)	46365
Madison (Jefferson County)	47250	Maxville	47340	Milledgeville	46052
Madison State Hospital	47250	Maxwell (Hancock County)	46154	Miller (Dearborn County) (Township)	47025
Magley	46733	Maxwell (Morgan County)	46151		
Magnet	47555	Mayfield (Part of Muncie)	47302	Miller (Lake County)	46403
Mahalasville	46151	Maynard (Part of Munster)	46321	Millersburg (Elkhart County)	46543
Mahon	46750	Mays	46155	Millersburg (Hamilton County)	46030
Majenica	46750	Maysville	47501		
Malden	46383	Maywood (Part of Indianapolis)	46241	Millersburg (Orange County)	47454
Malott Park (Part of Indianapolis)	46205			Millersburg (Warrick County)	47610
		M-Dee Acres	46550	Millersville (Part of Lawrence)	46226
Maltersville	47542	Meadowbrook (Allen County)	46774		
Manchester	47001			Mill Grove (Blackford County)	47348
Manchester (Township)	47001	Meadowbrook (Tippecanoe County)	47901		
Manhattan	46135			Millgrove (Steuben County) (Township)	46776
Manilla	46150	Meadowood (Elkhart County)	46514		
Manor Woods	46804			Millhousen	47261
Mansfield	47872	Meadowood (Marion County)	46224	Milligan	47872
Manson	46041			Milltown	47145
Manville	47250	Meadowood Estates	46036	Millville	47362
Maplecrest Shopping Center (Part of Kokomo)	46902	Meadows (Part of Terre Haute)	47803	Milners Corner	46140
				Milo	46991
Maple Lane	46635	Meadows Shopping Center (Part of Indianapolis)	46205	Milroy (Jasper County) (Township)	47978
Maples	46806				
Mapleton (Part of Indianapolis)	46208	Meadowview	46947	Milroy (Rush County)	46156
		Mead Village (Part of Columbus)	47201	Milton (Jefferson County) (Township)	47250
Maple Valley	46117				
Maplewood (Hendricks County)	46122	Mecca	47860	Milton (Ohio County)	47018
		Mechanicsburg (Boone County)	46050	Milton (Wayne County)	47357
Maplewood (Vigo County)	47885			Mineral	47424
Maplewood Park	46805	Mechanicsburg (Henry County)	47356	Mineral Springs	46538
Marco	47443			Mishawaka	46544-45
Marengo	47140	Medaryville	47957	For specific Mishawaka Zip Codes call (219) 255-9691	
Mariah Hill	47556	Medford	47302		
Marietta	46176	Medina (Township)	47970	Mitchell	47446
Marineland Gardens	46567	Medora	47260	Mitchelltree (Township)	47581
Marion	46952-53	Meiks	46176	Mitchellville (Part of Indianapolis)	46201
For specific Marion Zip Codes call (317) 668-8191		Mellott	47958		
		Melody Acres (Part of Warsaw)	46580	Mixerville	47010
Marion (Township)	46176			Moberly	47115
Marion (Allen County) (Township)	46745	Melody Hill	47711	Modesto	47401
		Meltzer	46176	Modoc	47358
Marion (Pike County) (Township)	47590	Memphis	47143	Mohawk	46140
		Mentone	46539	Mongo	46771
Marion (Boone County) (Township)	46069	Mentor	47513	Monitor	47905
		Meridian Hills	46260	Monmouth	46733
Marion (Putnam County) (Township)	46128	Merom (Sullivan County)	47861	Monon	47959
		Merriam	46701	Monon (Township)	47959
Marion (Decatur County) (Township)	47261	Merrillville	46410	Monoquet	46580
		Metamora (Township)	47030	Monroe	46772
Marion (Shelby County)	46176	Metamora	47030	Monroe (Township)	46711
Marion (Dubois County) (Township)	47546	Metea	46950	Monroe (Allen County) (Township)	46773
		Metz	46703		
Marion (Hendricks County) (Township)	46122	Mexico	46958	Monroe (Carroll County) (Township)	46929
		Miami (Cass County) (Township)	46947		
Marion (Jasper County) (Township)	47978			Monroe (Clark County) (Township)	47126
		Miami (Miami County)	46959		
Marion (Jennings County) (Township)	47270	Miami Bend	46947	Monroe (Delaware County) (Township)	47302
		Miami Trails Addition	46614		
Marion (Lawrence County) (Township)	47446	Michaelsville	46952	Monroe (Grant County) (Township)	46952
		Michiana Shores	49117		
Marion (Owen County) (Township)	47455	Michigan (Clinton County) (Township)	46057	Monroe (Howard County) (Township)	46979
Marion Heights	47885				
Marion Manor (Part of Valparaiso)	46383	Michigan (La Porte County) (Township)	46360	Monroe (Jefferson County) (Township)	47250
				Monroe (Kosciusko County) (Township)	46580
		Michigan City	46360		

Monroe-Oak Grove **INDIANA** 179

Name	ZIP
Monroe (Madison County) (Township)	46001
Monroe (Morgan County) (Township)	46157
Monroe (Pike County) (Township)	47584
Monroe (Pulaski County) (Township)	46996
Monroe (Putnam County) (Township)	46135
Monroe (Randolph County) (Township)	47368
Monroe (Tippecanoe County)	47901
Monroe (Washington County) (Township)	47167
Monroe City	47557
Monroe Manor	46350
Monroeville	46773
Monrovia	46157
Montclair	46149
Monterey	46960
Monterey Village (Part of Noblesville)	46060
Montezuma	47862
Montgomery (Daviess County)	47558
Montgomery (Gibson County) (Township)	47665
Montgomery (Jennings County) (Township)	47230
Montgomery (Owen County) (Township)	47460
Monticello	47960
Montmorenci	47962
Montpelier	47359
Moonlight Bay	46779
Moonville	46001
Moore	46721
Moorefield (Marion County)	46222
Moorefield (Switzerland County)	47250
Mooreland	47360
Moores Hill	47032
Mooresville	46158
Moral (Township)	46126
Moran	46041
Morgan (Harrison County) (Township)	47164
Morgan (Owen County) (Township)	47868
Morgan (Porter County) (Township)	46383
Morgan Park (Part of Chesterton)	46304
Morgantown	46160
Morningside (Part of Muncie)	47302
Morocco	47963
Morris	47033
Morristown	46161
Morton	46135
Moscow	46156
Mott Station	47161
Mound (Township)	47932
Mounds Mall (Part of Anderson)	46013
Mount Auburn (Shelby County)	46124
Mount Auburn (Wayne County)	47327
Mount Ayr	47964
Mount Carmel (Franklin County)	47012
Mount Carmel (Washington County)	47108
Mount Comfort	46140
Mount Etna	46750
Mount Healthy	47201
Mount Meridian	46135
Mount Olympus	47640
Mount Pisgah	46761
Mount Pleasant (Delaware County)	47302
Mount Pleasant (Delaware County) (Township)	47396
Mount Pleasant (Johnson County)	46131
Mount Pleasant (Martin County)	47553
Mount Pleasant (Perry County)	47559
Mounts	47665
Mount Sinai	47032
Mount Sterling	47043
Mount Summit	47361
Mount Vernon	47620
Mount Zion	46792
Mud Center (Part of Evansville)	47712
Mudlavia Springs	47918

Name	ZIP
Mulberry	46058
Mull	47394
Muncie	47302-08
For specific Muncie Zip Codes call (317) 286-9600	
Muncie Mall (Part of Muncie)	47303
Munster	46321
Muren	47598
Murray	46714
Nabb	47147
Napoleon	47034
Nappanee	46550
Nashville	47448
Navilleton	47119
Nead	46970
Nebraska	47262
Needham	46162
Needham (Township)	46126
Needmore (Brown County)	47448
Needmore (Lawrence County)	47421
Negangards Corner	47031
Nevada	46068
Nevada Mills	46703
Nevins (Township)	47851
New Albany	47150-51
For specific New Albany Zip Codes call (812) 948-0649	
New Alsace	47022
New Amsterdam	47110
Newark	47459
Newark Village (Part of Carmel)	46032
New Augusta (Part of Indianapolis)	46268
New Bellsville	47201
Newbern	47201
Newberry	47449
New Boston (Harrison County)	47117
New Boston (Spencer County)	47531
New Britton	46060
New Brunswick	46052
Newburgh	47629-30
For specific Newburgh Zip Codes call (812) 853-3707	
New Burlington	47302
Newbury (Township)	46565
New Carlisle	46552
Newcastle (Fulton County) (Township)	46975
New Castle (Henry County)	47362
New Chicago	46342
New Columbus	46011
New Corydon	47326
New Durham (Township)	46350
New Elizabethtown	47274
New Elliott	46319
New Fairfield	47012
New Farmington	47274
New Frankfort	47170
New Garden (Township)	47374
New Goshen	47863
New Harmony	47631
New Haven	46774
New Hope	47601
Newland	47978
New Lebanon	47864
New Lisbon (Henry County)	47366
New Lisbon (Randolph County)	47390
New London	46979
New Marion	47023
New Market	47965
New Maysville	46172
New Middletown	47160
New Mount Pleasant	47371
New Palestine	46163
New Paris	46553
New Philadelphia	47167
New Pittsburg	47390
New Point	47263
Newport	47966
New Richmond	47967
New Ross	47968
New Salem	46173
New Salisbury	47161
New Santa Fe	46970
Newton (Township)	47615
Newtonville	47969
Newtown	47969
New Trenton	47035
Newville	46721
Newville (Township)	46721
New Washington	47162
New Waverly	46961
New Whiteland	46184
New Winchester	46122
Nibbyville	46507

Name	ZIP
Niles (Township)	47338
Nine Mile Place	46809
Nineveh	46164
Nineveh (Township)	46164
Nisbet	47639
Noble (Cass County) (Township)	46947
Noble (Jay County) (Township)	47371
Noble (La Porte County) (Township)	46382
Noble (Noble County) (Township)	46796
Noble (Rush County) (Township)	46173
Noble (Shelby County) (Township)	47234
Noble (Wabash County) (Township)	46992
Noblesville	46060
Noblesville (Township)	46060
Noblitt Falls (Part of Columbus)	47201
Nora (Part of Indianapolis)	46240
Nora Plaza (Part of Indianapolis)	46240
Norland Park	46706
Normal	46986
Norman	47264
Normanda	46072
Normandy Addition (Part of Muncie)	47302
Norristown	47234
North (Lake County) (Township)	46312
North (Marshall County) (Township)	46506
Northaven (Part of Jeffersonville)	47130
North Bend (Township)	46534
Northcliff	47201
North Columbus (Part of Columbus)	47201
Northcrest Shopping Center (Part of Fort Wayne)	46805
North Crows Nest	46208
North Delphi	46923
Northeast (Township)	47452
Northern Meadows	46077
Northfield	46077
Northfield Village (Part of Lebanon)	46052
North Gate	47201
North Grove	46911
North Harbor (Part of Noblesville)	46060
North Hayden	46356
North Judson	46366
North Liberty	46554
North Madison (Part of Madison)	47250
North Manchester	46962
North Oaks	46714
North Ogilville	47201
North Park (Bartholomew County)	47280
North Park (Vanderburgh County)	47710
North Park Mall (Part of Marion)	46952
North Ridge Village	46240
North Salem	46165
North Terre Haute	47805
North Vernon	47265
North Webster	46555
Northwest (Township)	47469
Northwood (Elkhart County)	46550
Northwood (Putnam County)	46135
Northwood (Vigo County)	47805
Northwood Hills	46032
North Wood Park	46383
Norton	47432
Nortonsburg	47201
Norway	47960
Norwood Addition (Part of Muncie)	47304
Notre Dame	46556
Nottingham	47359
Nottingham (Township)	47359
Nulltown	47331
Numa	47874
Nyesville	47872
Nyona Lake	46951
Oakcrest	47201
Oakdale (Part of Peru)	46970
Oakford	46965
Oak Forest	47012
Oak Grove (Benton County) (Township)	47971
Oak Grove (Starke County)	46511

180 INDIANA Oak Grove-Pleasant

	ZIP		ZIP		ZIP
Oak Grove (Vigo County)	47802	Owasco	46065	Perry (Lawrence County)	
Oak Hill	47660	Owen (Clark County)		(Township)	47462
Oakland City	47660	(Township)	47111	Perry (Marion County)	
Oaklandon (Part of Lawrence)	46226	Owen (Clinton County) (Township)	46041	(Township)	46227
Oaklawn Terrace (Part of Jeffersonville)	47130	Owen (Jackson County) (Township)	47220	Perry (Martin County) (Township)	47553
Oak Park (Clark County)	47130	Owen (Warrick County)		Perry (Miami County) (Township)	46974
Oaktown	47561	(Township)	47614	Perry (Monroe County)	
Oakville	47367	Owensburg	47453	(Township)	47401
Oakwood	46742	Owensville	47665	Perry (Noble County)	
Oakwood Commons	46952	Oxford	47971	(Township)	46767
Oakwood Park	46567	Packertown	46510	Perry (Tippecanoe County)	
Oakwood Shores	46742	Paint Mill Lake	47802	(Township)	47901
Oatsville	47567	Palestine (Franklin County)	47012	Perry (Vanderburgh County)	
Ober	46534	Palestine (Kosciusko County)	46539	(Township)	47712
Occident	46115	Palmer	46307	Perry (Wayne County) (Township)	47339
Ockley	46923	Palmyra (Harrison County)	47164	Perry Crossing	47172
Odell	47918	Palmyra (Knox County)		Perry Manor (Part of Indianapolis)	46227
Odon	47562	(Township)	47591	Perrysburg	46951
Ogden	46148	Paoli	47454	Perrysville	47974
Ogden Dunes	46368	Paoli (Township)	47454	Pershing (Jackson County)	
Ogilville	47201	Papakeechie Lake	46567	(Township)	47235
Ohio (Bartholomew County) (Township)	47201	Paradise	47630	Pershing (Wayne County)	47370
Ohio (Crawford County) (Township)	47137	Paradise Lakes	46151	Perth	47837
Ohio (Spencer County) (Township)	47635	Paragon	46166	Peru	46970
Ohio (Warrick County) (Township)	47610	Paris	47230	Peru (Township)	46970
Ohio Falls (Part of Clarksville)	47130	Paris Crossing	47270	Petersburg	47567
Oil (Township)	47576	Parish Grove (Township)	47944	Peterson	46733
Old Bargersville	46106	Park	47424	Peters Switch	47274
Old Bath	47012	Parker City	47368	Petersville	47201
Oldenburg	47036	Parkersburg	47954	Petroleum	46778
Old Milan	47031	Parkers Settlement	47638	Pettit	47905
Old Otto	47162	Park Fletcher (Part of Indianapolis)	46241	Pheasant Run	46819
Old Pekin (Part of Pekin)	47165	Park Forest Estates (Part of Columbus)	47201	Philadelphia	46140
Old St. Louis	47246	Parkmor (Part of Elkhart)	46514	Philomath	47325
Old Stone	47630	Park Ridge (Part of Bloomington)	47401	Phlox	46936
Old Tip Town	46570	Parkside (Part of Columbus)	47201	Pickard	46050
Oldtown (Part of Lawrenceburg)	47025	Park View Heights (Part of Peru)	46970	Pierce (Township)	47167
Old Watson (Part of Jeffersonville)	47130	Parkway Hills	46804	Pierceton	46562
Olean	47042	Parkwood	47130	Pierceville	47039
Olive (Elkhart County) (Township)	46573	Parr	47978	Pierre Moran (Part of Elkhart)	46514
Olive (St. Joseph County) (Township)	46552	Pate	47040	Pierson (Township)	47802
Oliver	47620	Patoka (Crawford County) (Township)	47175	Pigeon (Vanderburgh County) (Township)	47708
Olive Street (Part of South Bend)	46619	Patoka (Dubois County) (Township)	47542	Pigeon (Warrick County) (Township)	47523
Omega	46030	Patoka (Gibson County)	47666	Pike (Boone County)	46052
Ontario	46746	Patoka (Gibson County) (Township)	47670	Pike (Jay County) (Township)	47371
Onward	46967	Patoka (Pike County) (Township)	47598	Pike (Marion County) (Township)	46254
Oolitic	47451	Patricksburg	47455	Pike (Ohio County) (Township)	47011
Ora	46968	Patriot	47038	Pike (Warren County) (Township)	47991
Orange	47331	Patronville	47635	Pikes Peak	47201
Orange (Township)	47331	Patton	47960	Pikeville	47590
Orange (Noble County) (Township)	46755	Patton Hill	47421	Pilot Knob	47145
Orange (Rush County) (Township)	46173	Patton Lake	46151	Pimento	47866
Orangeville	47452	Paw Paw (Township)	46974	Pine (Benton County) (Township)	47970
Orangeville (Township)	47542	Paxton	47865	Pine (Porter County) (Township)	46360
Orchard Heights	46624	Paynesville	47243	Pine (Warren County) (Township)	47975
Orchard Park	46280	Peabody	46725	Pine Grove Estates	47006
Oregon (Clark County) (Township)	47141	Pearsontown	47140	Pine Lake	46350
Oregon (Starke County) (Township)	46574	Pecksburg	46118	Pine Valley	47454
Oregon Heights (Part of Hobart)	46405	Peerless	47421	Pine Village	47975
Orestes	46063	Pekin	47165	Pinhook (La Porte County)	46350
Oriole	47551	Pelzer	47601	Pinhook (Lawrence County)	47421
Orland	46776	Pence	47973	Pinola	46350
Orleans	47452	Pendleton	46064	Pipe Creek (Madison County) (Township)	46036
Orleans (Township)	47452	Penn (Jay County) (Township)	47369	Pipe Creek (Miami County) (Township)	46914
Orleans Southwest	46902	Penn (Parke County) (Township)	47832	Pittsboro	46167
Ormas	46725	Penn (St. Joseph County) (Township)	46544	Pittsburg	46923
Osborn Landing	46580	Penn Meadows	46544	Plain (Township)	46538
Osceola	46561	Penn Park	46742	Plainfield	46168
Osgood	47037	Penntown	47041	Plainville	47568
Osolo (Township)	46514	Pennville (Jay County)	47369	Plano	46151
Ossian	46777	Pennville (Wayne County)	47327	Plato	46761
Oswego	46538	Peoga	46181	Plattsburg	47281
Otis	46367	Peoria (Franklin County)	45056	Pleasant (Allen County) (Township)	46798
Otisco	47163	Peoria (Miami County)	46970	Pleasant (Grant County) (Township)	46952
Otsego (Township)	46742	Peppertown	47030	Pleasant (Johnson County) (Township)	46131
Otterbein	47970	Perkinsville	46011	Pleasant (La Porte County) (Township)	46350
Otter Creek (Ripley County) (Township)	47023	Perry (Allen County) (Township)	46748	Pleasant (Porter County) (Township)	46347
Otter Creek (Vigo County) (Township)	47805	Perry (Boone County) (Township)	46052	Pleasant (Steuben County) (Township)	46703
Otter Lake	46703	Perry (Clay County) (Township)	47846		
Otter Village	47023	Perry (Clinton County) (Township)	46041		
Otto	47162	Perry (Delaware County) (Township)	47302		
Otwell	47564				

Pleasant-Ross INDIANA 181

Name	ZIP
Pleasant (Switzerland County)	47224
Pleasant (Wabash County) (Township)	46962
Pleasant Gardens	46171
Pleasant Lake	46779
Pleasant Mills	46780
Pleasant Plain	47692
Pleasant Run (Township)	47436
Pleasant Valley	46544
Pleasant View	46126
Pleasant View Village	46124
Pleasantville	47838
Pleasure Valley	46182
Plevna	46901
Plummer	47424
Plum Tree	46792
Plymouth	46563
Poe	46819
Point (Township)	47620
Point Commerce	47471
Point Idalawn	47468
Point Isabel	46928
Poland	47868
Polk (Huntington County) (Township)	46750
Polk (Marshall County) (Township)	46574
Polk (Monroe County) (Township)	47436
Polk (Washington County) (Township)	47165
Poneto	46781
Pontiac	47837
Popcorn	47462
Portage	46368
Portage (Porter County) (Township)	46368
Portage (St. Joseph County) (Township)	46601
Porter (Porter County)	46304
Porter (Porter County) (Township)	46383
Portersville	47546
Port Fulton (Part of Jeffersonville)	47130
Portland	47371
Portland Mills	46135
Posey (Clay County) (Township)	47834
Posey (Fayette County) (Township)	47331
Posey (Franklin County) (Township)	47024
Posey (Harrison County) (Township)	47117
Posey (Rush County) (Township)	46104
Posey (Switzerland County) (Township)	47038
Posey (Washington County) (Township)	47120
Poseyville	47633
Pottawattomie Park	46360
Pottersville	47460
Powers	47371
Prairie (Henry County) (Township)	47360
Prairie (Kosciusko County) (Township)	46580
Prairie (La Porte County) (Township)	46340
Prairie (Tipton County) (Township)	46049
Prairie (Warren County) (Township)	47921
Prairie (White County) (Township)	47923
Prairie City	47834
Prairie Creek	47869
Prairie Creek (Township)	47869
Prairieton	47870
Prairieton (Township)	47870
Prairie Village	47802
Prather	46151
Preble	46782
Preble (Township)	46733
Prescott	46176
Presidential Village	46803
Pretty Lake	46795
Prince Hall Plaza (Part of Marion)	46952
Princes Lakes	46164
Princeton (Gibson County)	47670
Princeton (White County) (Township)	47995
Progress	47302
Progress Acres	47805
Prospect	47469
Providence	46106

Name	ZIP
Publico (Part of New Albany)	47150
Puckett	46952
Pulaski	46996
Pumpkin Center	47170
Purcell	47591
Purdue University	47906
Purdue University North Central Campus	46391
Putnamville	46170
Pyrmont	46923
Quail Meadows Estates (Part of Batesville)	47006
Queensville	47265
Quercus Grove	47040
Quincy	47456
Raber	46725
Raccoon (Parke County) (Township)	47874
Raccoon (Putnam County)	46172
Radioville	47957
Radley	46938
Radnor	46923
Raglesville	47562
Ragsdale	47573
Railroad (Township)	46374
Rainbow (Part of Indianapolis)	46222
Rainsville	47918
Raleigh	46173
Ramsey	47166
Randolph (Ohio County) (Township)	47040
Randolph (Tippecanoe County) (Township)	47981
Raub	47976
Ravenswood	46240
Ravinamy	47906
Ray (Franklin County) (Township)	47036
Ray (Morgan County) (Township)	46166
Ray (Steuben County)	46737
Raymond	47010
Rays Crossing	46176
Raysville	46148
Reception Diagnostic Center	46168
Red Bridge	46911
Red Bush	47630
Redding (Township)	47274
Reddington	47274
Redkey	47373
Redmond Park	46567
Reed Station	47302
Reelsville	46171
Reeve (Township)	47553
Rego	47125
Reiffsburg	46714
Remington	47977
Reno	46121
Rensselaer	47978
Reo	47635
Republican (Township)	47138
Reserve (Township)	47862
Retreat	47229
Rexville	47250
Reynolds	47980
Riceville	47513
Richey Park	47960
Rich Grove (Township)	46996
Richland (Township)	46173
Richland (Spencer County)	47634
Richland (Steuben County) (Township)	46703
Richland (Benton County) (Township)	47942
Richland (De Kalb County) (Township)	46730
Richland (Fountain County) (Township)	47969
Richland (Fulton County) (Township)	46975
Richland (Grant County) (Township)	46952
Richland (Greene County) (Township)	47424
Richland (Jay County) (Township)	47373
Richland (Madison County) (Township)	46011
Richland (Miami County) (Township)	46970
Richland (Monroe County) (Township)	47429
Richland (Rush County)	46173
Richland (Whitley County) (Township)	46764
Richmond	47374-75
For specific Richmond Zip Codes call (317) 966-7631	

Name	ZIP
Richmond Square (Part of Richmond)	47374
Richmond State Hospital	47374
Richvalley	46992
Riddie	47118
Ridgemede (Part of Bloomington)	47401
Ridgeport	47424
Ridgeview (Part of Peru)	46970
Ridgeview Heights	46806
Ridgeville	47380
Ridgeway	46809
Ridinger Lake	46562
Rigdon	46036
Riley	47871
Riley (Township)	47871
Rileysburg	47932
Riley Village (Part of Shelbyville)	46176
Ripley (Montgomery County) (Township)	47933
Ripley (Pulaski County)	46996
Ripley (Rush County) (Township)	46115
Rising Sun	47040
Risse (Part of Frankfort)	46041
Rivare	46733
River Forest	46011
Riverhaven	46802
River Ridge	47111
Riverside (Clark County)	47130
Riverside (Fountain County)	47918
Riverton	47861
River Vale	47446
Riverview	47849
Riverview Acres	47201
Riverwood	46060
Riviera Plaza (Part of Fort Wayne)	46815
Roachdale	46172
Roann	46974
Roanoke	46783
Robb (Township)	47633
Robertsdale (Part of Hammond)	46394
Robinson (Township)	47638
Robinwood	47803
Roble Woods	46383
Rob Roy	47918
Rochester	46975
Rochester (Township)	46975
Rock Creek (Township)	46750
Rockcreek (Township)	46714
Rock Creek (Bartholomew County) (Township)	47232
Rock Creek (Carroll County) (Township)	46923
Rock Creek (Huntington County)	46750
Rockdale	47060
Rockfield	46977
Rockford (Jackson County)	47274
Rockford (Wells County)	46714
Rock Island (Part of Indianapolis)	46268
Rock Lake	46910
Rocklane	46142
Rockport	47635
Rockville	47872
Rocky Fork Lake	47834
Rocky Ripple	46208
Roland	47469
Roll	47348
Rolling Acres	47601
Rolling Hill Estates (Part of Schererville)	46410
Rolling Hills (Allen County)	46804
Rolling Hills (Clark County)	47111
Rolling Hills (Grant County)	46952
Rolling Prairie	46371
Rolling Ridge (Part of Shelbyville)	46176
Rollins	47581
Rome	47574
Rome City	46784
Romney	47981
Romona	47460
Root (Township)	46733
Roseburg (Grant County)	46952
Roseburg (Union County)	47353
Rosedale	47874
Rosedale Hills (Part of Indianapolis)	46227
Rose Hill Gardens	47805
Rose-Hulman Institute of Technology	47803
Roseland	46635
Roselawn	46372
Rosewood	47117
Ross (Clinton County) (Township)	46041

182 INDIANA Ross-Speedway

Name	ZIP
Ross (Lake County) (Township)	46410
Ross (Lake County)	46408
Rosston	46077
Rosstown	47201
Rossville	46065
Roth Park	47960
Round Grove (Township)	47923
Round Lake	46755
Royal Center	46978
Royal Oaks	46815
Royalton	46077
Royal View	47201
Royer Lake	46761
Royerton	47302
Royerton Park	47303
Royville	46845
Rugby	47246
Rural	47394
Rushville	46173
Rushville (Township)	46173
Russell (Township)	46172
Russell Lake	46077
Russellville	46175
Russels Point	46742
Russiaville	46979
Rustic Hills	47630
Rutherford (Township)	47553
Rutland	46563
Ryan Place	47620
Rykers Ridge	47250
Saddle Lake	46733
Sagers Lake	46383
Sagunay Lake	46371
St. Anthony	47575
St. Bernice	47875
St. Croix	47576
St. Henry	47532
St. James	47639
St. Joe	46785
St. John (Lake County)	46373
St. John (Township)	46373
St. John (Warrick County)	47613
St. Johns	46738
St. Joseph (Allen County) (Township)	46805
St. Joseph (Vanderburgh County)	47712
St. Leon	47060
St. Louis Crossing	47201
St. Marks (Dubois County)	47575
St. Marks (Perry County)	47586
St. Mary-of-the-Woods	47876
St. Marys (Adams County) (Township)	46733
St. Marys (Floyd County)	47119
St. Marys (St. Joseph County)	46556
St. Maurice	47240
St. Meinrad	47577
St. Omer	47272
St. Paul	47272
St. Peters	47012
St. Philip	47620
St. Thomas	47591
St. Wendells	47712
Salamonia	47381
Salamonie (Township)	46792
Salem (Township)	46747
Salem	47167
Salem (Delaware County) (Township)	47334
Salem (Jay County)	47390
Salem (Pulaski County) (Township)	47946
Salem Center	46747
Salem Heights	46350
Saline City	47840
Salt Creek (Decatur County) (Township)	47240
Salt Creek (Franklin County) (Township)	47024
Salt Creek (Jackson County) (Township)	47235
Salt Creek (Monroe County) (Township)	47401
Salt Creek Commons	46383
Saltillo	47108
Saluda	47243
Saluda (Township)	47243
Samaria	46181
Sandborn	47578
Sand Creek (Bartholomew County) (Township)	47232
Sand Creek (Decatur County) (Township)	47283
Sand Creek (Jennings County) (Township)	47265
Sandcut	47805
Sanders	47401
Sandford	47877

Name	ZIP
Sand Ridge	47635
Sandusky	47240
Sandy Beach	47960
Sandy Hook (Part of Columbus)	47201
Sandytown	47842
San Jacinto	47223
San Pierre	46374
Santa Claus	47579
Santa Fe	46970
Saratoga	47382
Sardinia	47283
Savah	47620
Scenic Heights	47586
Scenic Hill	47553
Schaefer Lake	47246
Schererville	46375
Schneider	46376
Schnellville	47580
Scipio (Allen County) (Township)	45813
Scipio (Franklin County)	45053
Scipio (Jennings County)	47273
Scipio (La Porte County) (Township)	46350
Scircleville	46041
Scotchtown	47848
Scotland	47457
Scott (Kosciusko County) (Township)	46550
Scott (Lagrange County)	46565
Scott (Montgomery County) (Township)	47933
Scott (Steuben County) (Township)	46703
Scott (Vanderburgh County) (Township)	47711
Scott City	47879
Scottsburg (Pike County)	47660
Scottsburg (Scott County)	47170
Scottsdale Mall (Part of South Bend)	46612
Scottsville	47106
Searcy Crossroads	47038
Sedalia	46067
Sedan	46793
Seelyville	47878
Sellersburg	47172
Sellers Lake	46562
Selma	47383
Selvin	47523
Servia	46980
Sevastopol	46510
Seward (Township)	46510
Sexton	46173
Seymour	47274
Shadeland (Grant County)	46952
Shadeland (Tippecanoe County)	47905
Shady Hills	46952
Shady Hills Estates	46952
Shady Lawn	46307
Shady Nook	46795
Shady Side (Part of Burns Harbor)	46304
Shaffer Woods	47303
Shamrock Lakes	47348
Shannondale	47933
Sharon	46929
Sharpsville	46068
Shawnee (Township)	47987
Shawswick (Township)	47421
Shawville	47805
Sheddfield (Part of Hammond)	46320
Sheffield (Township)	47901
Sheffield Woods (Part of Indianapolis)	46229
Shelburn	47879
Shelburne	46151
Shelby (Jefferson County) (Township)	47250
Shelby (Lake County)	46377
Shelby (Ripley County) (Township)	47250
Shelby (Shelby County) (Township)	46176
Shelby (Tippecanoe County) (Township)	47906
Shelbyville	46176
Shepardsville	47880
Sheridan (Hamilton County)	46069
Sheridan (La Porte County)	46360
Sherwood Forest (Part of Indianapolis)	46240
Shideler	47338
Shields	47274
Shiloh Village	47201
Shipshewana	46565
Shirkieville	47885
Shirley	47384

Name	ZIP
Shoals	47581
Shoe Lake	46538
Shore Acres (Part of Indianapolis)	46201
Shoreland Hills	46360
Siberia	47515
Sidney	46566
Silver Creek (Township)	47172
Silver Hills (Part of New Albany)	47150
Silver Lake	46982
Silver Lakes Estates	47130
Silverville	47470
Silverwood	47952
Simonton Lake	46514
Sims (Township)	46983
Sims (Bartholomew County)	47201
Sims (Grant County)	46983
Sitka	47960
Skelton (Township)	47637
Skinner Lake	46701
Sleepy Hollow	46182
Sleeth	46923
Sloan	47993
Smartsburg	47933
Smedley	47108
Smith (Greene County) (Township)	47471
Smith (Posey County) (Township)	47612
Smith (Whitley County) (Township)	46723
Smithfield (De Kalb County) (Township)	46793
Smithfield (Delaware County)	47383
Smithland	46176
Smithson	47980
Smith Valley	46142
Smithville	47458
Smyrna	47250
Smyrna (Township)	47250
Snow Hill	47394
Solitude	47620
Solsberry	47459
Somerset	46984
Somerville	47683
South Bend	46601-80
For specific South Bend Zip Codes call (219) 282-8400	
South Bethany	47201
South Boston	47167
South Calumet Avenue (Part of Hammond)	46324
South Center	46532
Southeast (Township)	47140
Southeast Grove	46341
Southeast Manor	46126
South Edgewood (Part of Edgewood)	46011
South Gate (Franklin County)	47060
Southgate (La Porte County)	46360
South Harbor (Part of Noblesville)	46060
South Haven	46383
South Lake	47885
Southlake Mall (Part of Merrillville)	46410
South Marion (Part of Marion)	46952
South Milford	46786
Southmoor (Part of Merrillville)	46410
South Mud Lake	46951
South Park	46567
South Peru (Part of Peru)	46970
Southport	46227
South Raub	47905
South Salem	47390
Southtown Mall (Part of Fort Wayne)	46806
South Wanatah	46390
South Washington	47501
Southwest	46526
South Whitley	46787
Southwick Village	46816
Southwood (La Porte County)	46360
Southwood (Vigo County)	47802
Spades	47041
Sparksville	47260
Sparta	47032
Sparta (Township)	47032
Sparta (Township)	46760
Spartanburg	47355
Spearsville	46181
Speed	47172
Speedway	46224

Name	ZIP
Speedway Shopping Center (Part of Speedway)	46224
Speicher	46992
Spelterville	47805
Spencer (De Kalb County) (Township)	46788
Spencer (Harrison County) (Township)	47115
Spencer (Jennings County) (Township)	47265
Spencer (Owen County)	47460
Spencerville	46788
Spiceland	47385
Spiceland (Township)	47385
Spice Valley (Township)	47437
Spraytown	47274
Springersville	47325
Springfield (Allen County) (Township)	46743
Springfield (Franklin County) (Township)	45056
Springfield (La Porte County) (Township)	46360
Springfield (Lagrange County) (Township)	46771
Springfield (Posey County)	47620
Spring Grove	47374
Spring Grove Heights (Part of Spring Grove)	47374
Spring Hill	46208
Spring Hill Estates	47802
Spring Lake	46140
Springport	47386
Springtown	46122
Spring Valley Estates	47802
Springville (La Porte County)	46350
Springville (Lawrence County)	47462
Springwood	47805
Spurgeon	47584
Spurgeons Corner	47235
Stacer	47639
Stafford (De Kalb County) (Township)	46721
Stafford (Greene County) (Township)	47578
Stampers Creek (Township)	47454
Stanford	47463
Star City	46985
Stardust Village	46060
Starlight	47106
State Line (Vigo County)	47885
State Line (Warren County)	47982
Staunton	47881
Stavetown	47012
Stearleyville	47834
Steele (Township)	47501
Steen (Township)	47597
Steinbarger Lake	46784
Steinmeir Estates (Part of Indianapolis)	46250
Stendal	47585
Sterling (Crawford County) (Township)	47118
Sterling (Fountain County)	47987
Steuben (Steuben County) (Township)	46705
Steuben (Warren County) (Township)	47993
Steubenville	46705
Stevenson	47610
Stewart	47993
Stewartsville	47633
Stilesville	46180
Stillwell	46351
Stinesville	47464
Stockdale	46974
Stockton (Township)	47441
Stockwell	47983
Stone	47394
Stonebluff	47987
Stoneburner Landing	46580
Stonecrest	46952
Stonegate Square (Part of Newburgh)	47630
Stone Head	47448
Stones Crossing	46142
Stoney Creek (Henry County) (Township)	47360
Stoney Creek (Randolph County) (Township)	47368
Stonington	47446
Stony Creek (Township)	46051
Stony Lonesome	47201
Stony Ridge	46538
Story	47448
Straughn	47387
Strawtown	46060
Stringtown (Boone County)	46052
Stringtown (Hancock County)	46140
Stroh	46789
Sugar Creek (Boone County) (Township)	46071
Sugar Creek (Clinton County) (Township)	46050
Sugar Creek (Hancock County) (Township)	46163
Sugar Creek (Montgomery County) (Township)	46035
Sugar Creek (Parke County) (Township)	47859
Sugar Creek (Shelby County)	46126
Sugar Creek (Shelby County) (Township)	46110
Sugar Creek (Vigo County) (Township)	47885
Sugar Ridge (Township)	47840
Sullivan	47882
Sulphur	47174
Sulphur Springs	47388
Suman	46383
Sumava Resorts	46379
Summit Grove	47842
Summit Ridge (Part of Fort Wayne)	46805
Summitville	46070
Sundown Manor	46158
Sunman	47041
Sunnybrook Acres	46805
Sunnymeadow	46815
Sunnymede (Allen County)	46803
Sunnymede (Wabash County)	46992
Sunnymede Woods	46803
Sunny Slopes	47401
Sunset Acres	46514
Sunset Parkway (Part of Seymour)	47274
Sunset Village	47111
Sunshine Gardens (Part of Indianapolis)	46217
Sunview	46040
Surprise	47274
Sussex Woods (Part of Hobart)	46342
Swan	46763
Swan (Township)	46763
Swanington	47944
Swayzee	46986
Sweetser	46987
Sweetwater Lake	46164
Switz City	47465
Sycamore	46936
Sycamore Hills	46036
Sycamore Knolls	47802
Sycamore Park	47885
Sylvan Hills	46952
Sylvania	47832
Sylvan Manor	46383
Syndicate	47842
Syracuse	46567
Tab	47917
Tabertown (Part of Seelyville)	47878
Talbot	47984
Tall Timbers	46952
Talma	46975
Tampico	47220
Tangier	47985
Tanglewood (Part of New Haven)	46774
Taswell	47175
Taylor (Greene County) (Township)	47424
Taylor (Harrison County) (Township)	47117
Taylor (Howard County) (Township)	46901
Taylor (Owen County) (Township)	47460
Taylors	47905
Taylorsville	47280
Tecumseh	47885
Teegarden	46574
Tee Lake	46350
Tefft	46380
Tell City	47586
Temple	47118
Templeton	47986
Tennyson	47637
Terhune	46069
Terrace Bay	47960
Terrace Lake (Part of Columbus)	47201
Terre Haute	47801-08
For specific Terre Haute Zip Codes call (812) 231-9414	
Tetersburg	46072
Texas (Part of Aurora)	47001
Thayer	46381
The Hamlet	47303
Thomas Lake	46135
Thomaston	46390
Thorncreek (Township)	46725
Thornhope	46985
Thorntown	46071
Thurman	46774
Tilden	46122
Tillman	46773
Timbercrest (Allen County)	46804
Timbercrest (Cass County)	46947
Timberhurst	46795
Tiosa	46975
Tippecanoe (Township)	46570
Tippecanoe (Pulaski County) (Township)	46960
Tippecanoe (Tippecanoe County) (Township)	47906
Tippecanoe (Carroll County) (Township)	46923
Tippecanoe (Kosciusko County) (Township)	46555
Tippecanoe (Marshall County)	46570
Tippecanoe Mall (Part of Lafayette)	47905
Tipton (Cass County) (Township)	46994
Tipton (Tipton County)	46072
Tipton Park (Part of Columbus)	47201
Toad Hop	47885
Tobin (Township)	47574
Tobinsport	47587
Tocsin	46790
Toledo	46750
Tolleston (Part of Gary)	46404
Toll Gate Heights	46714
Tomahawk Village (Part of Indianapolis)	46224
Topeka	46571
Toto	46534
Townley	46773
Town of Pines	46360
Tracy	46532
Traders Point (Part of Indianapolis)	46278
Trafalgar	46181
Trail Creek	46360
Travisville	46714
Treaty	46992
Tremont	46304
Trenton	47348
Trevlac	47448
Trier Ridge Park	46806
Tri-Lakes	46725
Trilobi Hills (Part of Lawrence)	46226
Trinity	47326
Trinity Springs	47581
Troy (Township)	47588
Troy (De Kalb County) (Township)	46721
Troy (Fountain County) (Township)	47932
Troy (Perry County)	47588
Tudor	47201
Tulip	47424
Tunker	46787
Tunnel Hill	47118
Tunnelton	47467
Turkey Creek (Township)	46567
Turkey Creek Meadows (Part of Merrillville)	46410
Turkey Track	46151
Turman (Township)	47882
Turner	47834
Twelve Mile	46988
Twelve Points (Part of Terre Haute)	47804
Twin Branch (Part of Mishawaka)	46544
Twin Brooks (Part of Indianapolis)	46227
Twin Crest	47201
Twin Lakes	46563
Twin Oaks Lake	46160
Tyner	46572
Ulen	46052
Underwood	47177
Underwood Meadows	46036
Union (Adams County) (Township)	46733
Union (Benton County) (Township)	47944
Union (Boone County) (Township)	46069
Union (Clark County) (Township)	47143

184 INDIANA Union-Washington

	ZIP		ZIP		ZIP
Union (Clinton County) (Township)	46041	Vallyd Acres	46816	Wallen	46806
Union (Crawford County) (Township)	47123	Valparaiso	46383-84	Wall Lake	46776
		For specific Valparaiso Zip Codes call (219) 462-2180		Walnut	46501
Union (De Kalb County) (Township)	46706	Van (Part of Logansport)	46947	Walnut (Township)	46501
		Vanada Camps	47630	Walnut (Township)	47933
Union (Delaware County) (Township)	47302	Van Bibber Lake	46135	Walnut Gardens	47960
		Van Buren (Township)	46991	Walnut Grove	46030
Union (Elkhart County) (Township)	46550	Van Buren (Grant County)	46991	Walnut Heights	47421
		Van Buren (Kosciusko County) (Township)	46542	Walnut Ridge (Clark County)	47130
Union (Fulton County) (Township)	46939	Van Buren (Lagrange County) (Township)	46540	Walnut Ridge (Jennings County)	47265
Union (Gibson County) (Township)	47648	Van Buren (Madison County) (Township)	46070	Walton	46994
Union (Hendricks County) (Township)	46149	Van Buren (Monroe County) (Township)	47401	Waltz (Township)	46992
				Wanamaker (Part of Indianapolis)	46239
Union (Howard County) (Township)	46936	Van Buren (Pulaski County) (Township)	46985	Wanatah	46390
Union (Huntington County) (Township)	46750	Van Buren (Shelby County) (Township)	46176	Ward (Township)	47380
				Warren (Clinton County) (Township)	46039
Union (Jasper County) (Township)	47943	Van Buren (Brown County) (Township)	47448	Warren (Huntington County)	46792
Union (Johnson County) (Township)	46106	Van Buren (Clay County) (Township)	47837	Warren (Huntington County) (Township)	46713
Union (La Porte County) (Township)	46346	Van Buren (Daviess County) (Township)	47553	Warren (Marion County) (Township)	46219
Union (Madison County) (Township)	46017	Van Buren (Fountain County) (Township)	47932	Warren (Putnam County) (Township)	46135
Union (Marshall County) (Township)	46511	Van Buren Park	47401	Warren (St. Joseph County) (Township)	46552
Union (Miami County) (Township)	46921	Vandalia	47460	Warren (Warren County) (Township)	47918
		Vanmeter Park	46996	Warren Park	46219
Union (Montgomery County) (Township)	47933	Vawter Park	46567	Warrenton	47639
		Veale (Township)	47501	Warrington	46186
Union (Ohio County) (Township)	47001	Veedersburg	47987	Warsaw	46580
		Velpen	47590	Washington (Township)	47501
Union (Parke County) (Township)	47872	Vera Cruz	46714	Washington (Dearborn County) (Township)	47001
Union (Perry County) (Township)	47555	Vermillion (Township)	47966	Washington (Decatur County) (Township)	47240
		Vermillion Acres	47885		
Union (Pike County)	47640	Vermont	46901	Washington (Delaware County) (Township)	47342
Union (Porter County) (Township)	46342	Verne	47591		
		Vernon (Township)	47282	Washington (Elkhart County) (Township)	46507
Union (Randolph County) (Township)	47355	Vernon (Wabash County)	46940		
		Vernon (Washington County) (Township)	47108	Washington (Gibson County) (Township)	47640
Union (Rush County) (Township)	46173	Vernon (Hancock County) (Township)	46040	Washington (Grant County) (Township)	46952
Union (Shelby County) (Township)	46150	Vernon (Jackson County) (Township)	47229	Washington (Greene County) (Township)	47443
Union (St. Joseph County) (Township)	46536	Vernon (Jennings County)	47282	Washington (Hamilton County) (Township)	46074
Union (Tippecanoe County) (Township)	47901	Versailles	47042		
		Veterans Administration Medical Center (Part of Marion)	46952	Washington (Harrison County) (Township)	47110
Union (Union County) (Township)	45003	Vevay	47043	Washington (Hendricks County) (Township)	46122
Union (Vanderburgh County) (Township)	47712	Vicksburg	47441	Washington (Jackson County) (Township)	47274
		Victor	47401		
Union (Wells County) (Township)	46777	Vienna	47170	Washington (Knox County) (Township)	47516
		Vienna (Township)	47170		
Union (White County) (Township)	47960	Vigo (Township)	47512	Washington (Kosciusko County) (Township)	46562
		Vilas	47460		
Union (Whitley County) (Township)	46725	Vincennes (Township)	47591	Washington (La Porte County) (Township)	46350
		Vincennes	47591		
Union City	47390	Virgie	47978	Washington (Marion County) (Township)	46220
Uniondale	46791	Vistula	46507		
Union Mills	46382	Volga	47250	Washington (Miami County) (Township)	46970
Unionport	47340	Wabash (Adams County) (Township)	46740		
Uniontown (Jackson County)	47229	Wabash (Fountain County) (Township)	47932	Washington (Monroe County) (Township)	47401
Uniontown (Perry County)	47515	Wabash (Gibson County) (Township)	47665	Washington (Morgan County) (Township)	46151
Unionville (railroad station)	47401				
Unionville	47468	Wabash (Jay County) (Township)	47326	Washington (Newton County) (Township)	47922
Universal	47884				
University Heights (Delaware County)	47303	Wabash (Parke County) (Township)	47860	Washington (Noble County) (Township)	46760
University Heights (Marion County)	46227	Wabash (Tippecanoe County) (Township)	47906	Washington (Owen County) (Township)	47460
University Park Mall (Part of Mishawaka)	46545	Wabash (Wabash County)	46992	Washington (Parke County) (Township)	47859
Upland	46989	Wabash Shores (Part of West Lafayette)	47906		
Upper Long Lake	46701			Washington (Pike County) (Township)	47567
Upper Sunset Park	47960	Wadena	47944		
Upton	47620	Wadesville	47638	Washington (Porter County) (Township)	46383
Urbana	46990	Wakarusa	46573		
Urbandale	46902	Wakefield Village	46755	Washington (Putnam County) (Township)	46171
Urmeyville	46131	Wakeland	46166		
Utah (Part of Aurora)	47001	Wake Robin Fields	46304	Washington (Randolph County) (Township)	47394
Utica	47130	Walden	46805		
Utica (Township)	47130	Waldron	46182	Washington (Ripley County) (Township)	47031
Valeene	47125	Waldron Lake	46794		
Valentine	46761	Walesboro	47201	Washington (Rush County) (Township)	46127
Valley Acres	46952	Walford Manor	47130		
Valley Brook (Marion County)	46229	Walker (Jasper County) (Township)	47978	Washington (Shelby County) (Township)	46176
Valley Brook (Wabash County)	46992	Walker (Rush County) (Township)	46146	Washington (Starke County) (Township)	46534
Valley City	47110	Walker Park	46538		
Valley Mills (Part of Indianapolis)	46241	Walkerton	46574	Washington (Tippecanoe County) (Township)	47924
Valley View Hills	46514	Walkerville (Part of Shelbyville)	46176	Washington (Warren County) (Township)	47993
Vallonia	47281	Wallace	47988		

Washington-York INDIANA 185

	ZIP		ZIP		ZIP
Washington (Adams County) (Township)	46733	Wells	46970	Wildwood	46952
Washington (Allen County) (Township)	46808	Wellsboro	46382	Wildwood Lake	47454
		Wellsburg	46714	Wilfred	47879
Washington (Blackford County) (Township)	47348	West (Township)	46563	Wilkinson	46186
		Westacres	47302	Williams (Adams County)	46733
Washington (Boone County) (Township)	46071	West Atherton	47874	Williams (Lawrence County)	47470
		West Baden Springs	47469	Williamsburg	47393
Washington (Brown County) (Township)	47448	West Brook Acres (Part of Batesville)	47006	Williams Creek	46240
		West Brook Downs	47401	Williamsport	47993
Washington (Carroll County) (Township)	46947	Westchester (Jay County)	47371	Williamstown	47240
		Westchester (Porter County) (Township)	46304	Willisville	47567
Washington (Cass County) (Township)	46994			Willow Branch	46187
		West College Corner	45003	Willowbrook Estates	46151
Washington (Clark County) (Township)	47162	West Creek (Township)	46356	Willow Creek (Part of Portage)	46368
		West Elwood	46036	Willow Valley	47581
Washington (Clay County) (Township)	47833	Western Acres (Part of Chesterton)	46304	Wills (Township)	46371
Washington (Clinton County) (Township)	46041	Western Hills (Part of Mount Vernon)	47620	Wilmington (De Kalb County) (Township)	46721
Washington (Daviess County)	47501	Westfield	46074	Wilmington (Dearborn County)	47001
		West Fork	47178	Wilmot	46562
Washington (Washington County) (Township)	47167	West Franklin	47620	Wilshire (Part of Frankfort)	46041
		West Harrison	47060	Wilson (Clark County)	47106
Washington (Wayne County) (Township)	47357	West Haven	46580	Wilson (Porter County)	46368
		West Hill	46383	Wilson (Shelby County)	46176
Washington (Whitley County) (Township)	46725	West Indianapolis (Part of Indianapolis)	46221	Wilson Lake	46725
				Winamac	46996
Washington Center	46725	West Lafayette	47906	Winchester	47394
Washington Place (Part of Indianapolis)	46219	Westland	46140	Windemere Lake	47885
		Westlawn	46804	Windfall	46076
Washington Square (Part of Indianapolis)	46229	West Lebanon	47991	Windom	47581
		West Liberty	46936	Windsor	47368
Washington Square Mall (Part of Evansville)	47715	West Middleton	46995	Windsor Village (Part of Indianapolis)	46219
		Westmoor (Part of Fort Wayne)	46804	Winfield	46307
Washington Trails (Part of Indianapolis)	46229	West Muncie (Part of Yorktown)	47396	Winfield (Township)	46307
Waterford	46360			Wingate	47994
Waterford Mills	46526	West Newton (Part of Indianapolis)	46183	Winona	46534
Waterloo (Township)	47331			Winona Lake	46590
Waterloo (De Kalb County)	46793	West Noblesville (Part of Noblesville)	46060	Winslow	47598
Waterloo (Fayette County)	47331			Winthrop	47918
Waterswolde	46825	West Peru (Part of Peru)	46970	Wirt	47250
Wathen Heights	47130	West Petersburg (Part of Petersburg)	47567	Wirt Station	47250
Watson	47130			Witmer Manor	46795
Waugh	46075	Westphalia	47596	Witts	47353
Wauhob Lake	46383	West Point (Howard County)	46901	Wolcott	47995
Waveland	47989			Wolcottville	46795
Waverly	46151	Westpoint (Tippecanoe County)	47992	Wolff	46151
Waverly Woods	46151			Wolflake	46796
Wawaka	46794	West Point (White County) (Township)	47980	Wonder Lake	47802
Wawpecong	46901			Wood (Township)	47106
Waymansville	47201	Westport	47283	Woodbridge (Part of Bloomington)	47407
Wayne (Allen County) (Township)	46806	Westport Addition	47302		
		Westside (Part of Aurora)	47001	Woodburn	46797
Wayne (Bartholomew County) (Township)	47201	West Terre Haute	47885	Woodbury	46055
		Westville	46391	Woodcrest	46151
Wayne (Fulton County) (Township)	46939	Westville Correctional Center	46391	Woodgate	47802
				Woodgate East	47802
Wayne (Hamilton County) (Township)	46060	Westwood	47362	Woodland	46619
		Wey Lake	47834	Woodland Heights	46952
Wayne (Henry County) (Township)	46148	Wheatfield	46392	Woodland Lake	46160
		Wheatfield (Township)	46392	Woodland Park (Delaware County)	47302
Wayne (Huntington County) (Township)	46940	Wheatland	47597		
		Wheatonville	47613	Woodland Park (Lagrange County)	46795
Wayne (Jay County) (Township)	47371	Wheeler	46393		
		Wheeling (Carroll County)	46929	Woodland Trace (Part of Carmel)	46032
Wayne (Kosciusko County) (Township)	46590	Wheeling (Delaware County)	47342		
		Whiskey Run (Township)	47145	Woodlawn Heights	46011
Wayne (Marion County) (Township)	46241	Whitaker	46166	Woodmar Mall (Part of Hammond)	46320
		Whitcomb	47012		
Wayne (Montgomery County) (Township)	47990	Whitcomb Heights	47885	Woodridge	47803
		White Cloud	47112	Woodruff	46795
Wayne (Noble County) (Township)	46755	Whitehall	47401	Woodruff Place (Part of Indianapolis)	46201
		Whiteland	46184		
Wayne (Owen County) (Township)	47433	Whiteoak	47598	Woodville	46304
		White Post (Township)	47957	Woodville Hills	47401
Wayne (Randolph County) (Township)	47390	White Ridge	46952	Wooster (Kosciusko County)	46562
		White River (Gibson County) (Township)	47666		
Wayne (Starke County) (Township)	46366			Wooster (Scott County)	47138
		White River (Hamilton County) (Township)	46031	Worth (Township)	46075
Wayne (Tippecanoe County) (Township)	47992			Worthington	47471
		White River (Johnson County) (Township)	46142	Wright (Township)	47441
Wayne (Wayne County) (Township)	47374			Wrights Corners	47001
		White River (Randolph County) (Township)	47394	Wyatt	46595
Wayne Center	46755			Wynnedale	46208
Waynedale (Part of Fort Wayne)	46809	White River Bluffs (Part of Bedford)	47421	Yankeetown	47630
				Yeddo	47952
Waynesburg	47244	Whites Crossing	47441	Yellowbanks	46555
Waynesville	47201	Whitestown	46075	Yellow Creek Lake	46510
Waynetown	47990	Whitesville	47933	Yeoman	47997
Wea (Township)	47901	Whitewater (Franklin County) (Township)	47060	Yockey	47446
Webster (Township)	47392			Yoder	46798
Webster (Harrison County) (Township)	47112	Whitewater (Wayne County)	47374	York (Steuben County) (Township)	46703
		Whitfield	47553		
Webster (Wayne County)	47392	Whiting	46394	York (Switzerland County) (Township)	47020
Wegan	47220	Wickliffe	47116		
Wehmeir	47201	Widner (Township)	47561	York (Benton County) (Township)	47942
Weisburg	47041	Wilbur	46151		
Wellington Heights (Part of Shelbyville)	46176	Wildcat (Township)	46076	York (Dearborn County) (Township)	47022
		Wilders	46348		

INDIANA York-Zulu

Name	ZIP
York (Elkhart County) (Township)	46507
York (Noble County) (Township)	46701
York (Steuben County)	46737
Yorktown	47396
Yorkville	47022
Young	46158
Young America	46998
Youngs Corner	47012
Youngs Creek	47454
Youngstown	47802
Youngstown Acres	47802
Youngstown Meadows	47802
Youngstown Shopping Center (Part of Jeffersonville)	47130
Yountsville	47933
Yule Estates (Part of Alexandria)	46001
Zanesville	46799
Zelma	47264
Zenas	47223
Zionsville	46077
Zoar	47585
Zulu	46773

Abingdon-Coralville IOWA 187

Name	ZIP	Name	ZIP	Name	ZIP
Abingdon	52533	Belmond	50421	Carroll	51401
Ackley	50601	Beloit	51240	Carson	51525
Ackworth	50001	Bennett	52721	Carter Lake	51510
Adair	50002	Benton	50835	Cartersville	50469
Adaza	50050	Bentonsport	52565	Cascade	52033
Adel	50003	Berkley	50220	Casey	50048
Afton	50830	Bernard	52032	Casino Beach	50588
Agency	52530	Bertram	52401	Castalia	52133
Ainsworth	52201	Berwick	50032	Castana	51010
Akron	51001	Bethlehem	50238	Cedar	52543
Albert City	50510	Bettendorf	52722	Cedar Bluff	52772
Albia	52531	Bevington	50033	Cedar Falls	50613
Albion	50005	Big Mound	52630	Cedar Rapids	52401-09
Alburnett	52202	Big Rock	52725	For specific Cedar Rapids Zip Codes call (319) 399-2900	
Alden	50006	Bingham	51601		
Alexander	50420	Birmingham	52535	Cedar Valley	52358
Algona	50511	Bladensburg	52501	Cedar View	50616
Alleman	50007	Blairsburg	50034	Centerdale	52776
Allendorf	51330	Blairstown	52209	Center Grove (Part of Dubuque)	52001
Allerton	50008	Blakesburg	52536		
Allison	50602	Blanchard	51630	Center Junction	52212
Alpha	52130	Blencoe	51523	Center Point	52213
Alta	51002	Blockton	50836	Centerville (Appanoose County)	52544
Alta Vista	50603	Bloomfield	52537		
Alton	51003	Blue Grass	52726	Centerville (Boone County)	50036
Altoona	50009	Bluff Park (Part of Montrose)	52639	Central (Part of Davenport)	52801
Alvord	51230			Central City	52214
Amana	52203	Bluffton	52101	Central College (Part of Pella)	50219
Amber	52205	Bode	50519		
Amboy	50208	Bolan	50448	Central Heights (Part of Mason City)	50401
Ames	50010	Bonair	52155		
Anamosa	52205	Bonaparte	52620	Centralia	52068
Anderson	51652	Bondurant	50035	Chapin	50427
Andover	52701	Boone	50036	Chariton	50049
Andrew	52030	Booneville	50038	Charles City	50616
Anita	50020	Botna	51454	Charleston	52619
Ankeny	50021	Bouton	50039	Charlotte	52731
Anthon	51004	Boxholm	50040	Charter Oak	51439
Aplington	50604	Boyd	50659	Chatsworth	51011
Arcadia	51430	Boyden	51234	Chelsea	52215
Archer	51231	Boyer	51448	Cherokee	51012
Aredale	50605	Braddyville	51631	Chester	52134
Argyle	52619	Bradford	50041	Chickasaw	50645
Arion	51520	Bradgate	50520	Chillicothe	52548
Arispe	50831	Brainard	52141	Church	52151
Arlington	50606	Brandon	52210	Churchville	50211
Armstrong	50514	Brayton	50042	Churdan	50050
Arnolds Park	51331	Brazil	52574	Cincinnati	52549
Artesian	50677	Breda	51436	Clare	50524
Arthur	51431	Bremer	50677	Clarence	52216
Asbury	52001	Bridgewater	50837	Clarinda	51632
Ashton	51232	Brighton	52540	Clarion	50525
Aspinwall	51432	Bristow	50611	Clarkdale	52544
Atalissa	52720	Britt	50423	Clarksville	50619
Athelstan	50836	Bronson	51007	Clayton	52049
Atkins	52206	Brooklyn	52211	Clayton Center	52043
Atlantic	50022	Brooks	50841	Clearfield	50840
Attica	50138	Brunsville	51008	Clear Lake	50428
Auburn	51433	Brushy	50532	Cleghorn	51014
Audubon	50025	Bryant	52727	Clemons	50051
Augusta	52658	Bryantsburg	50641	Clermont	52135
Aurelia	51005	Buchanan	52772	Cleves	50601
Aureola	50653	Buckcreek	50674	Climbing Hill	51015
Aurora	50607	Buckeye	50043	Clinton	52732
Austinville	50608	Buck Grove	51528	Clio	50052
Avery	52531	Buckingham	50612	Clive	50322
Avoca	51521	Buffalo	52728	Cloverdale	51249
Avon	50047	Buffalo Center	50424	Cloverhills (Part of West Des Moines)	50265
Avon Lake	50047	Buffalo Heights	52728		
Ayrshire	50515	Burchinal	50469	Clutier	52217
Badger	50516	Burlington	52601	Coalville	50501
Bagley	50026	Burnside	50521	Coburg	51566
Baldwin	52207	Burr Oak	52131	Coggon	52218
Balltown	52073	Burt	50522	Coin	51636
Bancroft	50517	Bussey	50044	Colesburg	52035
Bangor	50258	Cairo	52738	Colfax	50054
Bankston	52045	Calamus	52729	College Springs	51637
Barnes City	50027	Calhoun	51555	College Square Mall (Part of Cedar Falls)	50613
Barnum	50518	California Junction	51555		
Barrett Superette	50164	Callender	50523	Collins	50055
Bartlett	51655	Calmar	52132	Colo	50056
Bassett	50645	Calumet	51009	Colonial Village (Part of West Des Moines)	50265
Batavia	52533	Camanche	52730		
Battle Creek	51006	Cambria	50060	Columbia	50057
Baxter	50028	Cambridge	50046	Columbus City	52737
Bayard	50029	Camp Dodge	50111	Columbus Junction	52738
Beacon	52534	Canby	50048	Colwell	50620
Beaconsfield	50030	Canton	52309	Commerce (Part of West Des Moines)	50265
Beaman	50609	Cantril	52542		
Beaver	50031	Capital Square (Part of Des Moines)	50393	Conesville	52739
Beaverdale (Part of Des Moines)	50310			Confidence	52569
		Capitol Heights	50317	Conger	50240
Beaverdale Heights	52655	Carbon	50839	Conover	52132
Beckwith	52556	Carl	50841	Conrad	50621
Bedford	50833	Carlisle	50047	Conroy	52220
Beebeetown	51546	Carmel	51247	Conway	50833
Beech	50225	Carnarvon	51437	Cool	50125
Bel Air Beach	50588	Carnes	51003	Coon Rapids	50058
Belknap	52537	Carney	51637	Cooper	50059
Belle Plaine	52208	Carnforth	52347	Coppock	52654
Bellevue	52031	Carpenter	50426	Coralville	52241

IOWA

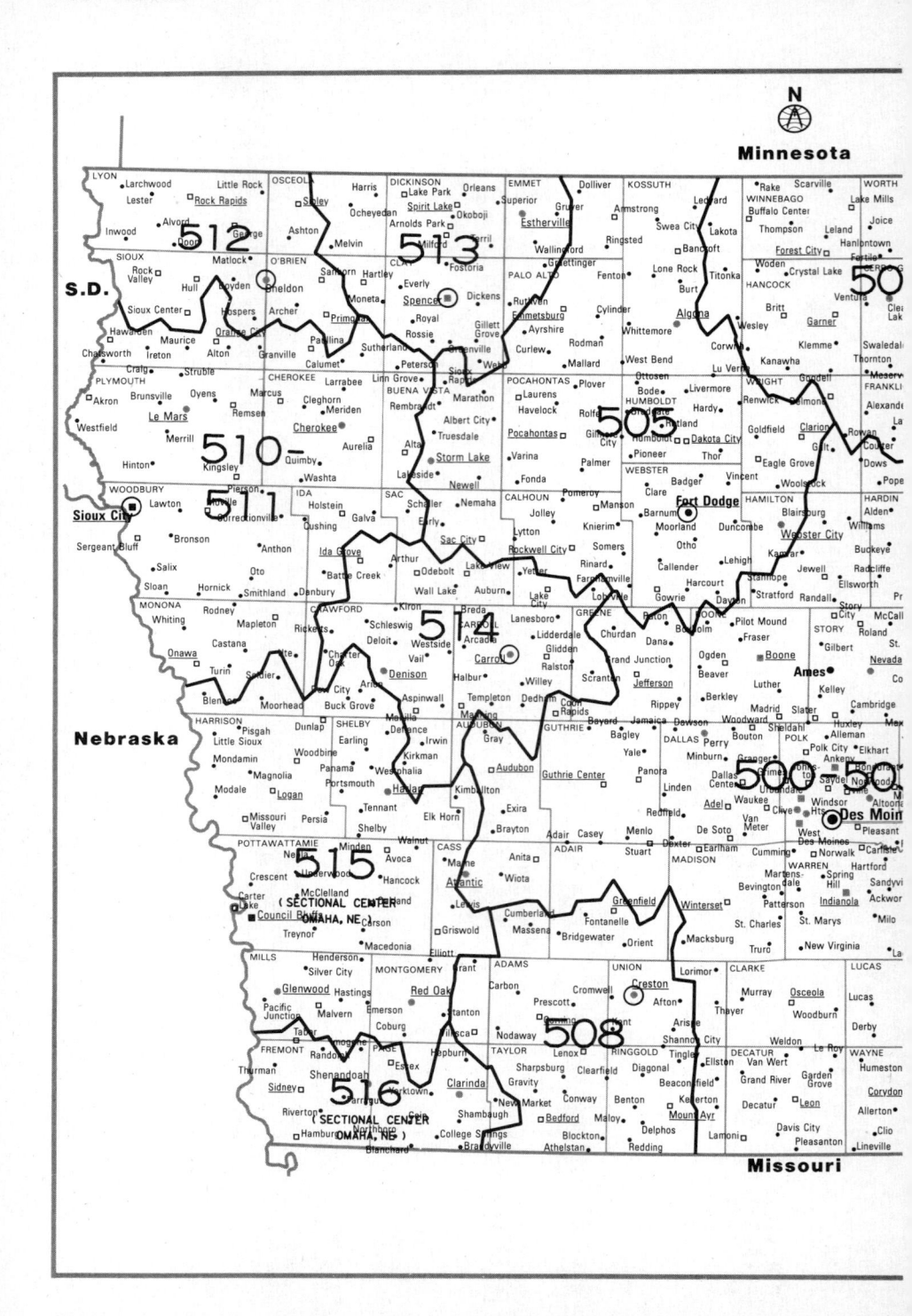

IOWA 189

190 IOWA Corley-Grinnell

	ZIP		ZIP		ZIP
Corley	51537	Dubuque	52001-04	Finchford	50647
Cornelia	50525	For specific Dubuque Zip Codes call (319) 582-3674		First Street (Part of Cedar Rapids)	52407
Cornell	50585			Fiscus	50025
Corning	50841	Duck Creek Plaza (Part of Bettendorf)	52722	Five Points	52073
Correctionville	51016	Dumont	50625	Flagler	50138
Corwith	50430	Dunbar	50158	Florenceville	52136
Corydon	50060	Duncan	50423	Floris	52560
Cosgrove	52322	Duncombe	50532	Floyd	50435
Cotter	52738	Dundee	52038	Folletts	52730
Cottonville	52054	Dunkerton	50626	Fonda	50540
Coulter	50431	Dunlap	51529	Fontanelle	50846
Council Bluffs	51501-03	Durango	52073	Forbush	52544
For specific Council Bluffs Zip Codes call (712) 325-0630		Durant	52747	Forest City	50436
		Durham	50119	Fort Atkinson	52144
Covington	52324	Dutchtown	52057	Fort Dodge	50501
Craig	51017	Dyersville	52040	Fort Dodge Junction (Part of Fort Dodge)	50501
Crandalls Lodge	51360	Dysart	52224		
Cranston	52754	Eagle Center	50701	Fort Madison	52627
Crawfordsville	52621	Eagle Grove	50533	Fostoria	51340
Crescent	51526	Eagle Point (Part of Dubuque)	52001	Four Corners	52635
Cresco	52136			Franklin	52625
Creston	50801	Earlham	50072	Frankville	52162
Crestwood (Part of Windsor Heights)	50311	Earling	51530	Fraser	50036
		Earlville	52041	Fredericksburg	50630
Crocker	50226	Early	50535	Frederika	50631
Cromwell	50842	East Amana	52203	Fredonia	52738
Crossroads Center (Part of Waterloo)	50703	East Des Moines (Part of Des Moines)	50309	Freeman	50401
				Freeport	52101
Crossroads Mall (Part of Fort Dodge)	50501	East Fourteenth Street (Part of Des Moines)	50316	Fremont	52561
				Froelich	52047
Croton	52626	East Pleasant Plain	52540	Fruitland	52749
Crystal Lake	50432	Eddyville	52553	Fulton	52060
Cumberland	50843	Edgewood	52042	Galesburg	50232
Cumming	50061	Edgewood Park (Part of Bettendorf)	52722	Galland	52639
Curlew	50527			Galt	50101
Cushing	51018	Edna	51246	Galva	51020
Cylinder	50528	Egralharve	51360	Gambrill	52756
Dahlonega	52501	Elberon	52225	Garber	52048
Dakota City	50529	Eldon	52554	Garden City	50102
Dallas (Part of Melcher)	50062	Eldora	50627	Garden Grove	50103
Dallas Center	50063	Eldorado	52175	Gardiner	50039
Dana	50064	Eldridge	52748	Garnavillo	52049
Danbury	51019	Elgin	52141	Garner	50438
Danville	52623	Elkader	52043	Garrison	52229
Darbyville	52544	Elkhart	50073	Garwin	52632
Davenport	52801-09	Elk Horn	51531	Gaza	51245
For specific Davenport Zip Codes call (319) 322-5991		Elkport	52044	Geneva	50633
		Elk Run Heights	50701	George	51237
Davis City	50065	Elliott	51532	Georgetown	52531
Dawson	50066	Ellston	50074	Germantown	51046
Dayton	50530	Ellsworth	50075	German Valley	50480
Daytonville	52356	Elma	50628	Germanville	52540
Dean	52572	Elon	52170	Giard	52157
Decatur	50067	Elrick	52653	Gibson	50104
Decorah	52101	Elvira	52732	Gifford	50259
Dedham	51440	Elwood	52226	Gilbert	50105
Deep River	52222	Ely	52227	Gilbertville	50634
Defiance	51527	Emeline	52207	Gillett Grove	51341
Delaware	52036	Emerson	51533	Gilman	50106
Delhi	52223	Emery	50401	Gilmore City	50541
Delmar	52037	Emmetsburg	50536	Gladbrook	50635
Deloit	51441	Enterprise	50073	Glasgow	52556
Delphos	50844	Epworth	52045	Glendale Acres	51503
Delta	52550	Essex	51638	Glendon	50164
Denison	51442	Estherville	51334	Glenwood	51534
Denmark	52624	Evans	52577	Glidden	51443
Denver	50622	Evansdale	50707	Goddard	50054
Depew	50528	Evanston	50532	Goldfield	50542
Derby	50068	Evergreen	52804	Goodell	50439
Des Moines	50301-95	Everly	51338	Goose Lake	52750
For specific Des Moines Zip Codes call (515) 283-7500		Ewart	50171	Gowrie	50543
		Exira	50076	Grace Hill	52353
De Soto	50069	Exline	52555	Graettinger	51342
Dewar	50623	Fairbank	50629	Graf	52073
Dewey	50853	Fairfax	52228	Grafton	50440
De Witt	52742	Fairfield	52556	Grand (Part of Des Moines)	50309
Dexter	50070	Fair Ground (Part of Dubuque)	52001	Grand Junction	50107
Diagonal	50845			Grand Mound	52751
Dickens	51333	Fairmount Park (Part of Council Bluffs)	51503	Grand River	50108
Dike	50624			Grandview	52752
Dillon	50158	Fairport	52761	Granger	50109
Dinsdale	50669	Fairview	52205	Granger Homesteads	50109
Dixon	52745	Fanslers	50115	Granite	51241
Dodge Park (Part of Council Bluffs)	51501	Farley	52046	Grant	50847
		Farlin	50077	Grant Wood (Part of Bettendorf)	52722
Dodgeville	52650	Farmersburg	52047		
Dolliver	50531	Farmington	52626	Granville	51022
Donahue	52746	Farnhamville	50538	Gravity	50848
Donnan	52142	Farragut	51639	Gray	50110
Donnellson	52625	Farrar	50161	Greeley	52050
Doon	51235	Farson	52563	Green Castle	50054
Dorchester	52140	Faulkner	50601	Greene	50636
Douds	52551	Fayette	52142	Greenfield	50849
Dougherty	50433	Fenton	50539	Greenfield Plaza	50315
Douglas	52175	Ferguson	50078	Green Island	52051
Dow City	51528	Fern	50665	Green Mountain	50637
Downey	52358	Fernald	50201	Greenville	51343
Dows	50071	Fertile	50434	Greenwood Acres	50021
Drakesville	52552	Festina	52143	Grimes	50111
		Fillmore	52033	Grinnell	50112

Griswold-Mall of the Bluffs IOWA 191

	ZIP		ZIP		ZIP
Griswold	51535	Inwood	51240	Larchwood	51241
Grundy Center	50638	Ionia	50645	Larrabee	51029
Gruver	51344	Iowa Army Ammunition		Latimer	50452
Guernsey	50172	Plant	52638	Laurel	50141
Gunder	52162	Iowa Center	50161	Laurens	50554
Guss	50857	Iowa City	52240-46	Lawler	52154
Guthrie Center	50115	For specific Iowa City Zip Codes		Lawn Hill	50206
Guttenberg	52052	call (319) 354-1560		Lawton	51030
Halbur	51444	Iowa Falls	50126	Leando	52551
Hale	52230	Iowa State University (Part		Lebanon (Sioux County)	51250
Hamburg	51640	of Ames)	50010	Lebanon (Van Buren	
Hamill	52625	Ira	50127	County)	52565
Hamilton	50116	Ireton	51027	Le Claire	52753
Hamlin	50117	Ironhills	52060	Ledyard	50556
Hampton	50441	Irving	52208	Leeds (Part of Sioux City)	51108
Hancock	51536	Irvington	50560	Le Grand	50142
Hanford	50401	Irwin	51446	Lehigh	50557
Hanley	50240	Ivy	50009	Leighton	50143
Hanlontown	50444	Jackson Junction	52150	Leland	50453
Hanover	51002	Jacksonville	51537	Le Mars	51031
Hansell	50640	Jamaica	50128	Lenox	50851
Harcourt	50544	James	51108	Leon	50144
Hardy	50545	Jamison	50210	Le Roy	50123
Harlan	51537	Janesville	50647	Lester	51242
Harper	52231	Jefferson	50129	Letts	52754
Harpers Ferry	52146	Jerico	50659	Lewis	51544
Harris	51345	Jerome	52544	Liberty	50210
Harrisburg	52620	Jesup	50648	Liberty Center	50145
Hartford	50118	Jewell	50130	Libertyville	52567
Hartley	51346	Joetown	52247	Lidderdale	51452
Hartwick	52232	Johnston	50131	Lime City	52778
Harvard	50008	Johnston Station (Part of		Lime Springs	52155
Harvey	50119	Johnston)	50131	Linby	52580
Haskins	52201	Joice	50446	Lincoln	50652
Hastings	51540	Jolley	50551	Lincoln Center	50841
Hauntown	52732	Jordan	50036	Lindale Mall (Part of Cedar	
Havelock	50546	Julien	52001	Rapids)	52402
Haven	52339	Juniata	50588	Linden	50146
Haverhill	50120	Kalo	50569	Lineville	50147
Hawarden	51023	Kalona	52247	Linn Grove	51033
Hawkeye	52147	Kamrar	50132	Linwood (Part of Buffalo)	52805
Hawleyville	51632	Kanawha	50447	Lisbon	52253
Hawthorne	51566	Kellerton	50133	Liscomb	50148
Hayesville	52562	Kelley	50134	Little Cedar	50454
Hayfield	50438	Kellogg	50135	Littleport	52055
Hazleton	50641	Kendallville	52136	Little Rock	51243
Hedrick	52563	Kennedy Mall (Part of		Little Sioux	51545
Henderson	51541	Dubuque)	52001	Littleton	50648
Hepburn	51632	Kensett	50448	Little Turkey	52154
Herndon	50128	Kent	50850	Livermore	50558
Herrold	50111	Keokuk	52632	Livingston	52549
Hesper	52101	Keomah	52577	Lockridge	52635
Hiawatha	52233	Keosauqua	52565	Logan	51546
Hickman Road (Part of		Keota	52248	Logansport	50036
Urbandale)	50322	Kesley	50649	Lohrville	51453
High	52203	Keswick	50136	Lone Rock	50559
Highland Center	52501	Keystone	52249	Lone Tree	52755
Highland Park (Part of Des		Key West	52001	Long Grove	52756
Moines)	50333	Kilbourn	52535	Lorah	50022
Highlandville	52149	Killduff	50137	Lorimor	50149
High Point	50103	Kimballton	51543	Lost Nation	52254
Highview	50595	Kingsley	51028	Lourdes	50628
Hills	52235	Kingston	52637	Loveland	51555
Hillsboro	52630	Kinross	52250	Lovilia	50150
Hinton	51024	Kirkman	51447	Lovington	50322
Hiteman	52531	Kirkville	52566	Lowden	52255
Hobarton	50511	Kiron	51448	Lowell	52645
Hocking	52531	Klemme	50449	Low Moor	52757
Holbrook	52325	Klinger	50668	Luana	52156
Holiday Lake	52211	Knierim	50552	Lucas	50151
Holland	50642	Knittel	50668	Lundstrom Heights	50021
Holly Springs	51026	Knoke	50553	Luther	50152
Holmes	50525	Knoxville	50138	Luther Manor (Part of	
Holstein	51025	Knoxville Estates	50138	Bettendorf)	52722
Holy Cross	52053	Konigsmark	52401	Luton	51052
Homer	50595	Kossuth	52637	Lu Verne	50560
Homestead	52236	Koszta	52208	Luxemburg	52056
Honey Creek	51542	Lacelle	50213	Luzerne	52257
Hopeville	50174	Lacey	50207	Lyman	51535
Hopkinton	52237	Lacona	50139	Lynnville	50153
Hornick	51026	Ladora	52251	Lyons (Clinton County)	52732
Horton	50677	La Fayette	52202	Lyons (Linn County)	52302
Hospers	51238	Lake Canyada	52804	Lytton	50561
Houghton	52631	Lake City	51449	McCallsburg	50154
Hubbard	50122	Lake Mills	50450	McCausland	52758
Hudson	50643	Lake Park	51347	McClelland	51548
Hull	51239	Lakeside	50588	Macedonia	51549
Humboldt	50548	Lake View	51450	McGregor	52157
Humeston	50123	Lakewood	50211	McIntire	50455
Huntington	51334	Lakota	50451	Macksburg	50155
Hurstville	52060	Lambs Grove	50208	McNally	51027
Hutchins	50423	Lamoille	50158	Macy	50601
Huxley	50124	Lamoni	50140	Madison (Part of Council	
Iconium	52571	Lamont	50650	Bluffs)	51503
Ida Grove	51445	La Motte	52054	Madrid	50156
Imogene	51645	Lanesboro	51451	Magnolia	51550
Independence	50644	Langdon	51301	Maine	52571
Indian Creek (Part of		Langworthy	52252	Malcom	50157
Marion)	52302	Lansing	52151	Mallard	50562
Indianola	50125	Lanyon	50544	Mall of the Bluffs (Part of	
Industry	50540	La Porte City	50651	Council Bluffs)	51503

192 IOWA Malone-Pleasantville

	ZIP		ZIP		ZIP
Malone	52742	Monti	52218	Odebolt	51458
Maloy	50852	Monticello	52310	Oelwein	50662
Malvern	51551	Montour	50173	Ogden	50212
Manawa (Part of Council Bluffs)	51501	Montpelier	52759	Okoboji	51355
		Montrose	52639	Old Balltown	52073
Manchester	52057	Mooar	52632	Olds	52647
Manilla	51454	Moorhead	51558	Old Town	51351
Manly	50456	Moorland	50566	Olin	52320
Manning	51455	Moran	50276	Olivet	50143
Manson	50563	Moravia	52571	Ollie	52576
Maple Heights	50616	Morley	52312	Onawa	51040
Maple Hill	50514	Morningside (Part of Sioux City)	51106	Oneida	52057
Maple River	51401			Onslow	52321
Mapleton	51034	Morning Sun	52640	Ontario (Part of Ames)	50010
Maquoketa	52060	Morrison	50657	Oralabor	50021
Marathon	50565	Morse	52240	Oran	50664
Marble Rock	50653	Morton Mills	50864	Orange (Part of Waterloo)	50701
Marcus	51035	Moscow	52760	Orange City	51041
Marengo	52301	Moulton	52572	Orchard	50460
Marietta	50158	Mount Auburn	52313	Orient	50858
Marion	52302	Mount Ayr	50854	Orilla	50061
Mark	52537	Mount Carmel	51401	Orleans	51360
Marne	51552	Mount Etna	50855	Osage	50461
Marquette	52158	Mount Joy	52804	Osborne	52043
Marquisville	50313	Mount Pleasant	52641	Osceola	50213
Marsh	52659	Mount Sterling	52573	Osgood	50536
Marshalltown	50158	Mount Union	52644	Oskaloosa	52577
Marshalltown Mall (Part of Marshalltown)	50158	Mount Vernon	52314	Ossian	52161
		Mount Zion	52565	Osterdock	52035
Martelle	52305	Moville	51039	Otho	50569
Martensdale	50160	Munterville	52536	Otley	50214
Martinsburg	52568	Murphy	50677	Oto	51044
Martinstown	52575	Murray	50174	Otranto	50472
Marysville	50116	Muscatine	52761	Otter Creek	52079
Mason City	50401	Muscatine Mall (Part of Muscatine)	52761	Otterville	50644
Masonville	50654			Ottosen	50570
Massena	50853	Mystic	52574	Ottumwa	52501
Massey	52001	Napier	50010	Ottumwa Junction (Part of Ottumwa)	52501
Massillon	52255	Nashua	50658		
Matlock	51244	Nashville	52060	Owasa	50126
Maurice	51036	Nemaha	50567	Oxford	52322
Maxwell	50161	Neola	51559	Oxford Junction	52323
May City	51349	Nevada	50201	Oxford Mills	52323
Maynard	50655	Nevinville	50801	Oyens	51045
Maysville	52773	New Albin	52160	Pacific Junction	51561
Mechanicsville	52306	New Boston	52619	Packard	50619
Mederville	52043	Newburg	50112	Packwood	52580
Mediapolis	52637	Newell	50568	Painted Rocks	50214
Medora	50125	New Era	52761	Palmer	50571
Melbourne	50162	Newhall	52315	Palm Grove	50501
Melcher	50163	New Hampton	50659	Palmyra	50047
Melrose	52569	New Hartford	50660	Palo	52324
Meltonville	50472	New Haven	50461	Panama	51562
Melvin	51350	Newkirk	51238	Panora	50216
Menlo	50164	New Liberty	52765	Panorama Park	52722
Meriden	51037	New London	52645	Paralta	52336
Merle Hay Mall (Part of Des Moines)	50310	New Market	51646	Paris (Davis County)	52552
		New Providence	50206	Paris (Linn County)	52214
Meroa	50461	New Sharon	50207	Parkersburg	50665
Merrill	51038	Newton	50208	Park Hills	50214
Meservey	50457	New Vienna	52065	Parkview	52748
Methodist Camp	51360	New Virginia	50210	Parnell	52325
Meyer	50455	Nichols	52766	Paton	50217
Middle	52307	Noble	52641	Patterson	50218
Middleburg	51041	Nodaway	50857	Paullina	51046
Middletown	52638	Nora Springs	50458	Payne	51640
Midlands Mall (Part of Council Bluffs)	51503	Nora Springs Junction (Part of Nora Springs)	50458	Pekin	52580
				Pella	50219
Midvale	50124	Northboro	51647	Peoria	50219
Midway (Floyd County)	50616	North Branch	50002	Peosta	52068
Midway (Linn County)	52302	North Buena Vista	52066	Percival	51648
Miles	52064	North English	52316	Perkins	51239
Milford	51351	North Grand Mall (Part of Ames)	50010	Perlee	52556
Miller	50438			Perry	50220
Millersburg	52308	North Liberty	52317	Pershing	50221
Millerton	50165	Northpark Mall (Part of Davenport)	52806	Persia	51563
Millnerville	51062			Peru	50222
Millville	52052	North Side (Part of Sioux City)	51104	Petersburg	52040
Milo	50166			Peterson	51047
Milton	52570	North Wall Lake (Part of Wall Lake)	51466	Petersville	52731
Minburn	50167			Pierceville	52565
Minden	51553	North Washington	50661	Pierson	51048
Mineola	51554	Northwest (Linn County)	52405	Pilot Grove	52648
Mineral Ridge	50036	Northwest (Scott County)	52804	Pilot Mound	50223
Minerva	50005	Northwood	50459	Pioneer	50541
Mingo	50168	Norwalk	50211	Piper	50579
Missouri Valley	51555	Norway	52318	Pisgah	51564
Mitchell	50461	Norwich	51601	Pittsburg	52565
Mitchellville	50169	Norwood	50151	Pitzer	50072
Modale	51556	Norwoodville	50317	Plainfield	50666
Moingona	50036	Numa	52575	Plain View	52773
Mona	50472	Nyman	51566	Plano	52581
Mondamin	51557	Oakdale (Part of Coralville)	52319	Plaza Hills (Part of Windsor Heights)	50311
Moneta	51346	Oakland	51560		
Monmouth	52309	Oakland Acres	50112	Pleasantgrove	52645
Monona	52159	Oakland Mills	52641	Pleasant Hill	50301
Monroe	50170	Oakley	50049	Pleasanton	50065
Monteith	50115	Oakville	52646	Pleasant Plain	52540
Monterey	52537	Oakwood	50653	Pleasant Prairie	52761
Montezuma	50171	Oasis	52358	Pleasant Valley	52767
Montgomery	51360	Ocheyedan	51354	Pleasantville	50225

	ZIP		ZIP		ZIP
Plover	50573	Runnells	50237	Spaulding	50801
Plymouth	50464	Russell	50238	Spencer	51301
Pocahontas	50574	Ruthven	51358	Sperry	52650
Polk City	50226	Rutland	50582	Spillville	52168
Pomeroy	50575	Ryan	52330	Spirit Lake	51360
Popejoy	50227	Sabula	52070	Spragueville	52074
Portland	50401	Sac and Fox Indian		Springbrook	52075
Portsmouth	51565	Reservation	52339	Springdale	52358
Postville	52162	Sac City	50583	Spring Grove	52601
Powersville	50636	Sageville	52001	Spring Hill	50125
Prairieburg	52219	St. Ansgar	50472	Springville	52336
Prairie City	50228	St. Anthony	50239	Spruce Hills Village (Part of	
Prairie Grove	52655	St. Benedict	50511	Bettendorf)	52722
Prescott	50859	St. Catherines	52001	Stacyville	50476
Preston	52069	St. Charles	50240	Stanhope	50246
Primghar	51245	St. Donatus	52071	Stanley	50671
Primrose	52625	St. Joseph	50519	Stanton	51573
Princeton	52768	St. Lucas	52166	Stanwood	52337
Prole	50229	St. Marys	50241	Stanzel	50849
Promise City	52583	St. Olaf	52072	State Center	50247
Prospect Hill (Part of		St. Paul	52657	Steamboat Rock	50672
Burlington)	52601	Salem	52649	Stennett	51566
Protivin	52163	Salina	52556	Sterling	52070
Pulaski	52584	Salix	51052	Stiles	52537
Quarry	50158	Sanborn	51248	Stilson	50423
Quasqueton	52326	Sand Springs	52237	Stockport	52651
Quimby	51049	Sandusky	52632	Stockton	52769
Radcliffe	50230	Sandyville	50001	Stone City	52205
Rake	50465	Santiago	50169	Storm Lake	50588
Ralston	51459	Saratoga	52167	Story City	50248
Randalia	52164	Saude	52154	Stout	50673
Randall	50231	Savannah	52537	Strahan	51540
Randolph	51649	Sawyer	52627	Stratford	50249
Rands	50579	Saydel	50313	Strawberry Point	52076
Rathbun	52544	Saylorville	50313	Stringtown	50851
Raymar	50701	Scarville	50473	Struble	51057
Raymond	50667	Schaller	51053	Stuart	50250
Readlyn	50668	Schleswig	51461	Suburban Heights	52556
Reasnor	50232	Schley	52136	Sully	50251
Redding	50860	Sciola	50864	Sulphur Springs	50588
Redfield	50233	Scotch Grove	52331	Summerset	50125
Red Line	51447	Scotch Ridge	50047	Summitville	52632
Red Oak	51566	Scranton	51462	Sumner	50674
Red Rock Lakeview	50138	Searsboro	50242	Sunbury	52778
Reinbeck	50669	Sedan	52544	Sunshine	52544
Rembrandt	50576	Selma	52588	Superior	51363
Remsen	51050	Seneca	50539	Sutherland	51058
Renwick	50577	Seney	51031	Sutliff	52253
Rhodes	50234	Sergeant Bluff	51054	Swaledale	50477
Riceville	50466	Sewal	50060	Swan	50252
Richards	50579	Sexton	50483	Swea City	50590
Richland	52585	Seymour	52590	Swedesburg	52652
Richmond	52247	Shaffton	52730	Sweetland Center	52761
Rickardsville	52073	Shambaugh	51651	Swisher	52338
Ricketts	51460	Shannon City	50861	Tabor	51653
Ridgeport	50036	Sharon Center	52240	Taintor	50253
Ridgeway	52165	Sharpsburg	50862	Talleyrand	52248
Rinard	50587	Shawondasse	52001	Tama	52339
Ringsted	50578	Sheffield	50475	Tara	50501
Rippey	50235	Shelby	51570	Teeds Grove	52771
Rising Sun	50317	Sheldahl	50243	Templar Park	51360
Ritter	51201	Sheldon	51201	Templeton	51463
Riverdale	52722	Shell Rock	50670	Ten Mile	52727
River Heights	52240	Shellsburg	52332	Tennant	51574
River Junction	52755	Shenandoah	51601	Tenville	50864
Riverside (Washington		Sheridan	50157	Tenville Junction	50864
County)	52327	Sherrill	52073	Terril	51364
Riverside (Woodbury		Sherwood	50579	Thayer	50254
County)	51109	Shipley	50201	Thirty	52544
River Sioux	51545	Shueyville	52404	Thompson	50478
Riverton	51650	Siam	50833	Thor	50591
Riverview Release Center	50208	Sibley	51249	Thornburg	50255
Roberts	50569	Sidney	51652	Thornton	50479
Robertson	50601	Sigourney	52591	Thorpe	52057
Robins	52328	Silver City	51571	Thurman	51654
Robinson	52330	Sinclair	50665	Ticonic	51010
Rochester	52772	Sioux Center	51250	Tiffin	52340
Rock Creek	50461	Sioux City	51101-11	Timberland Heights (Part of	
Rockdale (Part of Dubuque)	52001	For specific Sioux City Zip Codes		Ames)	50010
Rock Falls	50467	call (712) 277-6411		Tingley	50863
Rockford	50468	Sioux Rapids	50585	Tipton	52772
Rock Rapids	51246	Six Mile	52732	Titonka	50480
Rock Valley	51247	Slater	50244	Toddville	52341
Rockwell	50469	Slifer	50543	Toeterville	50481
Rockwell City	50579	Sloan	51055	Toledo	52342
Rodman	50580	Smithland	51056	Toolesboro	52653
Rodney	51051	Soldier	51572	Toronto	52343
Roelyn	50566	Solon	52333	Tracy	50256
Roland	50236	Somers	50586	Traer	50675
Rolfe	50581	South Amana	52334	Trenton	52641
Rome	52642	South Des Moines (Part of		Treynor	51575
Rose Hill	52586	Des Moines)	50315	Triboji Beach	51360
Roselle	51401	South English	52335	Tripoli	50676
Ross	50025	Southern Hills Mall (Part of		Troy	52537
Rossie	51357	Sioux City)	51101	Troy Mills	52344
Rossville	52159	South Muscatine (Part of		Truax	52553
Rowan	50470	Muscatine)	52761	Truesdale	50592
Rowley	52329	South Ottumwa (Part of		Truro	50257
Royal	51357	Ottumwa)	52501	Turin	51059
Rubio	52585	Southridge Mall (Part of Des		Turkey River	52052
Rudd	50471	Moines)	50315	Twin View Heights	52333

194 IOWA Udell-Zwingle

Location	ZIP
Udell	52593
Ulmer	51450
Underwood	51576
Union	50258
Union Center	51031
Union Mills	50207
Unionville	52594
University Heights	52240
University Park	52595
University Place (Part of Des Moines)	50311
Urbana	52345
Urbandale	50322
Ute	51060
Utica	52651
Vail	51465
Valeria	50054
Valley West Mall (Part of West Des Moines)	50265
Van Cleve	50162
Vandalia	50228
Van Horne	52346
Van Meter	50261
Van Wert	50262
Varina	50593
Ventura	50482
Vernon	52565
Vernon Springs	52136
Vernon View	52401
Veterans Administration Medical Center (Part of Knoxville)	50138
Victor	52347
Villisca	50864
Vincennes	52619
Vincent	50594
Vining	52348
Vinton	52349
Viola	52350
Volga	52077
Volney	52159
Voorhies	50643
Wadena	52169
Wahpeton	51351
Walcott	52773
Wales	51533
Walford	52351
Walker	52352
Wallingford	51365
Wall Lake	51466
Walnut	51577
Walnut City	52574
Wapello	52653

Location	ZIP
Ware	50546
Washburn	50706
Washington	52353
Washta	51061
Waterloo	50701-07
For specific Waterloo Zip Codes call (319) 291-7400	
Waterville	52170
Watkins	52354
Waubeek	52214
Waucoma	52171
Waukee	50263
Waukon	52172
Waukon Junction	52146
Waupeton	52073
Waverly	50677
Wayland	52654
Webb	51366
Webster (Keokuk County)	52355
Webster (Madison County)	50273
Webster City	50595
Welch Avenue (Part of Ames)	50010
Weldon	50264
Wellman	52356
Wellsburg	50680
Welton	52774
Wesley	50483
West	52357
West Bend	50597
West Branch	52358
West Broadway (Part of Council Bluffs)	51501
West Burlington	52655
West Chester	52359
Westdale Mall (Part of Cedar Rapids)	52404
West Des Moines	50265
Western College	52404
Westfield	51062
Westgate	50681
West Grove	52538
West Le Mars	51031
West Liberty	52776
West Okoboji	51351
Weston	51576
Westphalia	51578
West Point	52656
Westside	51467
West Spencer	51338
West Storm Lake (Part of Storm Lake)	50588

Location	ZIP
West Union	52175
Westwood	52641
Wever	52658
What Cheer	50268
Wheatland	52777
White Oak	50073
Whiting	51063
Whittemore	50598
Whitten	50269
Whittier	52336
Wichita	50115
Wick	50240
Wildwood Camp	52756
Willey	51401
William Penn College (Part of Oskaloosa)	52577
Williams	50271
Williamsburg	52361
Williamson (Adams County)	50859
Williamson (Lucas County)	50272
Williamstown	52247
Wilton	52778
Windham	52322
Windsor Heights	50311
Winfield	52659
Winnebago Heights	50401
Winterset	50273
Winthrop	50682
Wiota	50274
Wiscotta	50233
Woden	50484
Wood	52042
Woodbine	51579
Woodburn	50275
Woodland	50103
Woodward	50276
Woodward State Hospital-School	50276
Woolstock	50599
Worthington	52078
Wright	52577
Wyman	52621
Wyoming	52362
Yale	50277
Yarmouth	52660
Yetter	51433
Yorktown	51656
Zaneta	50643
Zearing	50278
Zion	50858
Zook Spur	50156
Zwingle	52079

Abbyville-Deerfield **KANSAS** 195

	ZIP		ZIP		ZIP
Abbyville	67510	Belvidere	67015	Castleton	67501
Abilene	67410	Belvue	66407	Catharine	67627
Ada	67414	Bendena	66008	Cato	66711
Adams (Kingman County)	67128	Benedict	66714	Cave	67952
Admire	66830	Bennington	67422	Cawker City	67430
Agenda	66930	Bentley	67016	Cedar (Johnson County)	66018
Aggieville Shopping Center		Benton (Butler County)	67017	Cedar (Smith County)	67628
(Part of Manhattan)	66502	Bern	66408	Cedar Bluffs	67749
Agra	67621	Berryton	66409	Cedar Point	66843
Agricola	66871	Berwick	66534	Cedar Vale	67024
Akron	67156	Beulah	66743	Centerville	66014
Alamota	67830	Beverly	67423	Centralia	66415
Albert	67511	Big Bow	67855	Centropolis	66067
Alden	67512	Big Springs	66050	Chanute	66720
Alexander (Rush County)	67513	Bird City	67731	Chapman (Dickinson	
Aliceville	66093	Birmingham	66436	County)	67431
Allen (Lyon County)	66833	Bismarck Grove (Part of		Charleston (Gray County)	67853
Alma	66401	Lawrence)	66044	Chase	67524
Almena	67622	Bison	67520	Chautauqua	67334
Altamont	67330	Black Wolf	67490	Cheney	67025
Alta Vista	66834	Blaine (Pottawatomie		Cherokee (Crawford	
Alton	67623	County)	66549	County)	66724
Altoona	66710	Blair	66090	Cherryvale	67335
Americus	66835	Blakeman	67730	Chetopa (Labette County)	67336
Ames	66931	Bloom (Ford County)	67833	Chicopee	66762
Amy	67850	Bloomington (Butler County)	67010	Child's Acres	67101
Andale	67001	Bloomington (Osborne		Chiles	66071
Andover	67002	County)	67473	Chisholm (Part of Wichita)	67217
Angelus	67738	Blue Mound	66010	Cicero	67152
Angola	67337	Blue Rapids (Marshall		Cimarron	67835
Anna	66701	County)	66411	Circleville	66416
Anness	67106	Bluff City	67018	Civic Center (Part of	
Anson	67152	Bogue	67625	Kansas City)	66101
Antelope	66858	Boicourt	66075	Claflin	67525
Anthony (Harper County)	67003	Bolton (Montgomery		Clare	66061
Antioch	66083	County)	67301	Claudell	67628
Antonino	67601	Bonita	66061	Clay Center (Clay County)	67432
Arcadia	66711	Bonner Springs	66012	Clayton	67629
Argentine (Part of Kansas		Bonnie Brae (Part of		Clearfield	67025
City)	66106	Wichita)	67207	Clearview City	66019
Argonia	67004	Bonnie Ridge	67401	Clearwater	67026
Arkansas City	67005	Boyle	66088	Clements	66843
Arlington	67514	Brainerd	67154	Clifton	66937
Arma	66712	Brazilton	66743	Climax	67137
Armourdale (Part of Kansas		Bremen	66412	Clinton	66046
City)	66105	Brenham	67059	Clonmel	67149
Arnold	67515	Brenner Heights (Part of		Clyde	66938
Arrington	66436	Kansas City)	66104	Coalvale	66711
Arthur Heights (Part of Bel		Brewster	67732	Coats	67028
Aire)	67220	Bridgeport	67416	Codell	67630
Arvonia	66523	Bronson	66716	Coffeyville	67337
Asherville	67420	Brookhaven Estates	67230	Colby	67701
Ash Grove	67481	Brookridge (Part of		Coldwater	67029
Ashland (Clark County)	67831	Overland Park)	66212	Collyer	67631
Ashland (Riley County)	66502	Brookville	67425	Colony (Anderson County)	66015
Ashton	67051	Brookwood Shopping		Columbus	66725
Assaria	67416	Center (Part of Topeka)	66614	Colwich	67030
Atchison	66002	Brownell	67521	Concordia	66901
Atchison Mall (Part of		Browns Spur	67068	Conway (McPherson	
Atchison)	66002	Buckeye	67410	County)	67460
Athol	66932	Bucklin	67834	Conway Springs	67031
Atlanta (Cowley County)	67008	Bucyrus	66013	Coolidge	67836
Attica (Harper County)	67009	Buffalo (Wilson County)	66717	Copeland	67837
Atwood	67730	Buhler	67522	Corbin (Montgomery	
Aubry	66085	Bunker Hill	67626	County)	67335
Auburn	66402	Burden	67019	Corbin (Sumner County)	67032
Augusta (Butler County)	67010	Burdett	67523	Corinth Square Shopping	
Aulne	66861	Burdick	66838	Center (Part of Prairie	
Aurora	67417	Burlingame	66413	Village)	66208
Aurora Park (Part of Bel		Burlington (Coffey County)	66839	Corning (Nemaha County)	66417
Aire)	67220	Burns	66840	Corwin	67061
Axtell	66403	Burr Oak (Jewell County)	66936	Cottonwood Falls	66845
Baileyville	66404	Burrton	67020	Council Grove (Morris	
Bala	66531	Busby	67349	County)	66846
Baldwin City	66006	Bush City	66032	Countryside	66222
Bancroft	66428	Bushong	66833	County Acres (Part of	
Barclay	66523	Bushton	67427	Wichita)	67212
Barker (Part of Kansas City)	66104	Buxton	66736	Courtland	66939
Barnard	67418	Byers	67021	Covert	67651
Barnes	66933	Cairo	67035	Cow Town (Part of Wichita)	67203
Bartlett	67332	Caldwell (Sumner County)	67022	Coyville	66727
Basehor	66007	Calista	67121	Craig	66215
Bassett	66749	Callahan (Part of Wichita)	67209	Crestline	66728
Bavaria	67401	Calvert	67622	Croweburg	66756
Baxter Springs	66713	Cambridge	67023	Cruppers Corner	67501
Bayard	66039	Camp Forsyth	66442	Cuba	66940
Bazar	66845	Camp Funston	66442	Cullen Village (Part of	
Bazine	67516	Camp Naish	66111	Topeka)	66619
Beagle	66064	Campus	67748	Cullison	67124
Beardsley	67730	Camp Whiteside	66442	Culver	67484
Beattie	66406	Canada (Marion County)	66861	Cummings	66016
Beaumont	67012	Caney (Montgomery		Cunningham	67035
Beaver (Barton County)	67517	County)	67333	Cunningham Highlands	
Beeler	67518	Canton (McPherson County)	67428	(Part of Overland Park)	66204
Bel Aire	67220	Capaldo	66762	Curranville	66756
Bellaire	66952	Carbondale	66414	Dalton	67152
Belle Plaine	67013	Carlton	67429	Damar	67632
Belleville (Republic County)	66935	Carlyle	66749	Danville	67036
Belmont (Kingman County)	67014	Carneiro	67425	Dartmouth	67530
Beloit (Mitchell County)	67420	Carona	66773	Dearing	67340
Belpre	67519	Cassoday	66842	Deerfield	67838

KANSAS

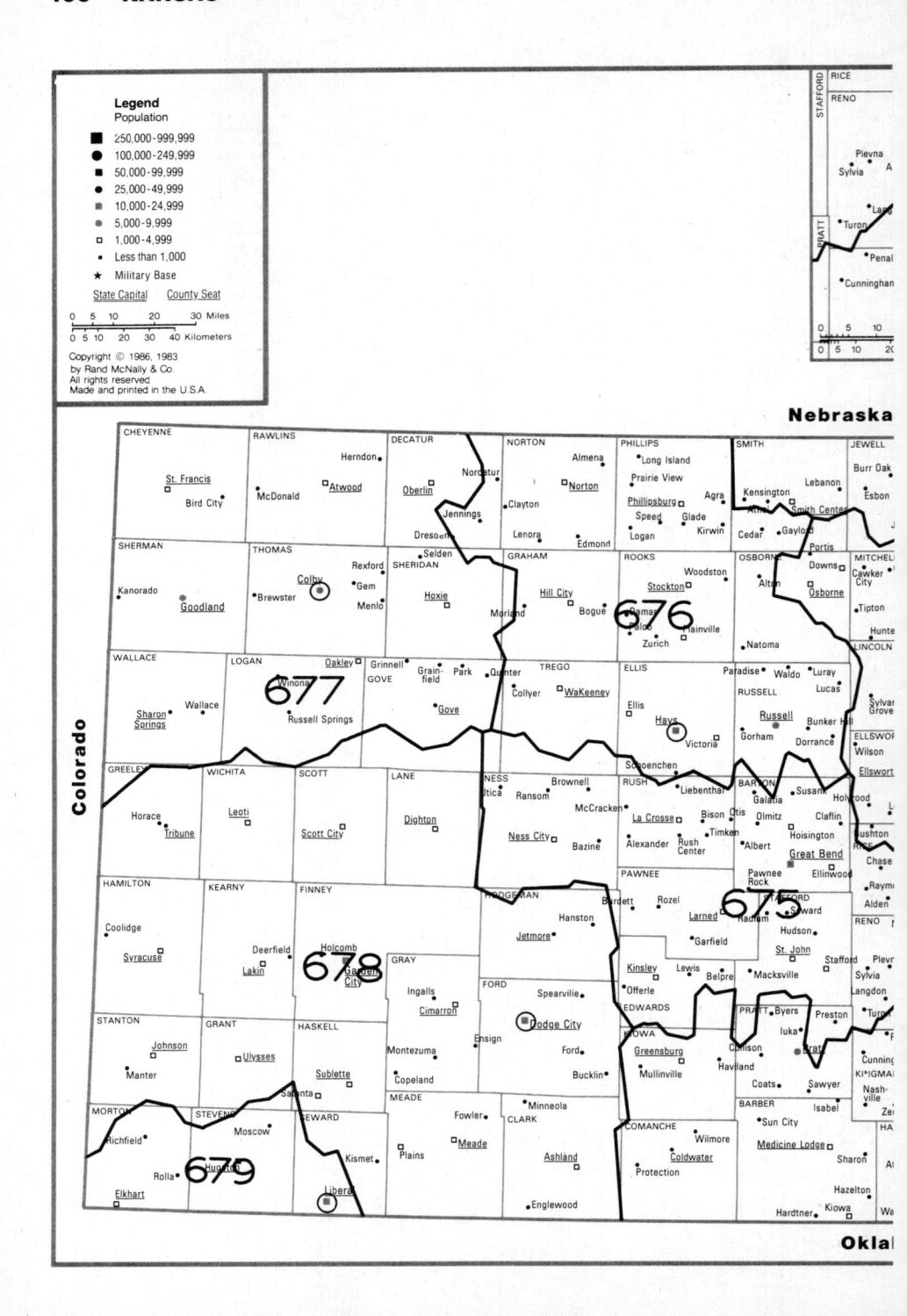

Legend
Population
- ■ 250,000-999,999
- ● 100,000-249,999
- ● 50,000-99,999
- ● 25,000-49,999
- ● 10,000-24,999
- ● 5,000-9,999
- □ 1,000-4,999
- · Less than 1,000
- ★ Military Base

State Capital   County Seat

0 5 10 20 30 Miles
0 5 10 20 30 40 Kilometers

Copyright © 1986, 1983
by Rand McNally & Co.
All rights reserved
Made and printed in the U.S.A.

Nebraska

Colorado

Oklahoma

KANSAS 197

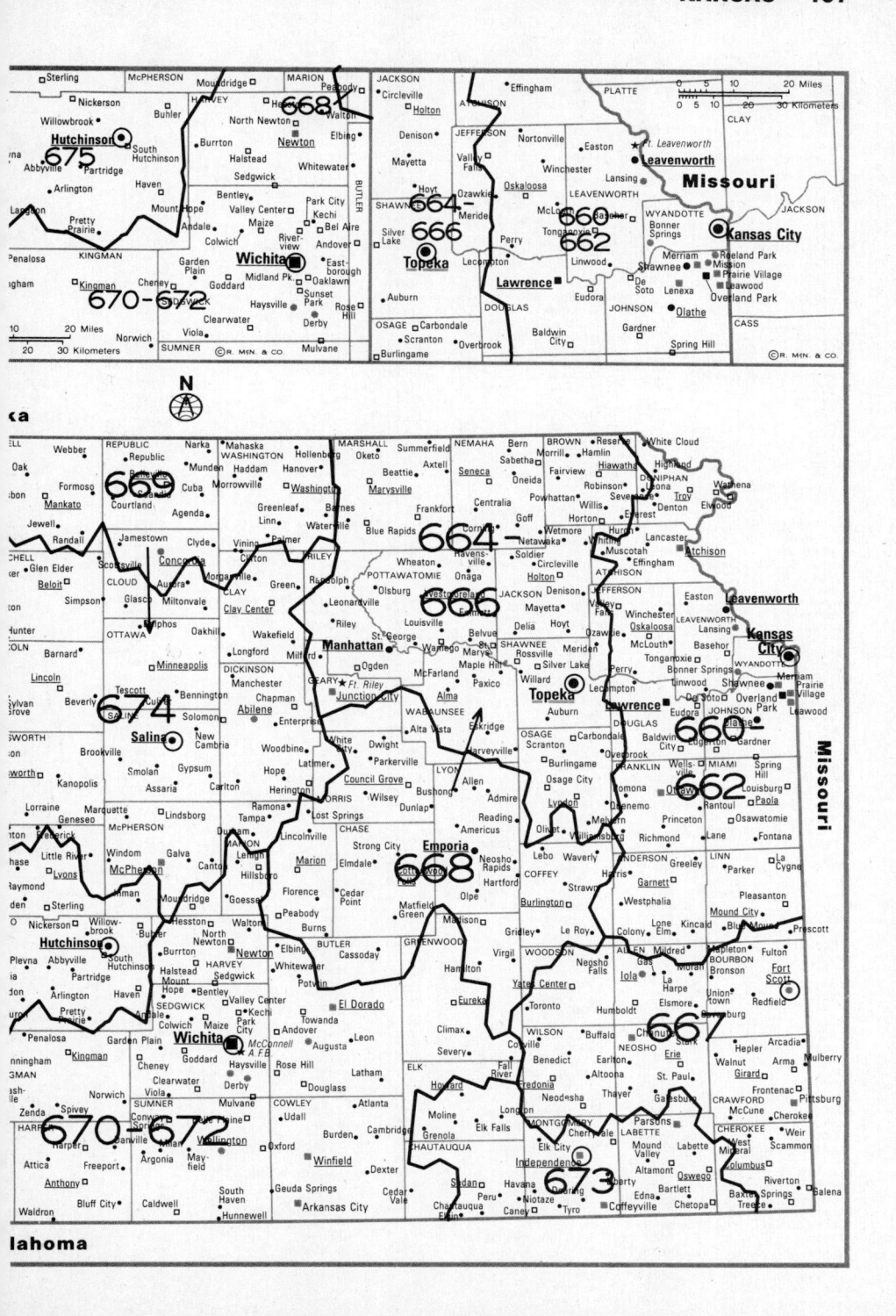

198 KANSAS De Graff-Iola

	ZIP		ZIP		ZIP
De Graff	66840	Farlinville	66014	Halford	67701
Delavan	66847	Farmington (Atchison		Hallowell	66725
Delia	66418	County)	66023	Halls Summit	66871
Delphos	67436	Faulkner	67336	Halstead (Harvey County)	67056
Denison	66419	Federal Penitentiary	66048	Hamilton	66853
Denmark	67455	Fellsburg	67552	Hamlin	66434
Dennis	67341	Fleming	66762	Hammond	66701
Densmore	67633	Floral	67156	Hanover (Washington	
Denton	66017	Florence	66851	County)	66945
Denton-McWorter Addition	67101	Flush	66535	Hanston	67849
Derby	67037	Fontana	66026	Hardtner	67057
Dermot	67954	Ford	67842	Harlan (Smith County)	67641
De Soto	66018	Forest Hills (Part of Wichita)	67206	Harper (Harper County)	67058
Detroit	67410	Forest Lake (Part of		Harris	66032
Devon	66701	Edwardsville)	66113	Hartford	66854
Dexter	67038	Formoso	66942	Harveyville	66431
Diamond Springs	66838	Fort Dodge	67843	Haskell (Douglas County)	66044
Dighton	67839	Fort Leavenworth	66027	Havana	67347
Dillwyn	67557	Fort Riley	66442	Haven	67543
Dispatch	67430	Fort Riley-Camp Whiteside	66442	Havensville	66432
Dodge City	67801	Fort Riley North	66442	Haverhill	67010
Doniphan	66002	Fort Scott	66701	Haviland	67059
Dorrance	67634	Fostoria (Osage County)	66413	Hays	67601
Douglass	67039	Fostoria (Pottawatomie		Haysville	67060
Dover	66420	County)	66426	Hazelton	67061
Downs (Osborne County)	67437	Four Corners	66537	Healy	67850
Downtown (Part of Wichita)	67202	Fowler	67844	Hedville	67401
Dresden	67635	Fox Town	66756	Heizer	67530
Drury	67022	Frankfort	66427	Hepler	66746
Dubuque	67634	Franklin (Crawford County)	66735	Herington	67449
Duluth	66521	Frederick	67444	Heritage Hills	66002
Dundee	67530	Fredonia	66736	Herkimer (Marshall County)	66433
Dunkirk	66762	Freeport	67049	Herndon	66739
Dunlap	66846	Friend	67845	Hesper	66025
Duquoin	67058	Frontenac	66762	Hessdale	66401
Durham (Marion County)	67438	Fulton	66738	Hesston	67062
Dwight	66849	Furley	67147	Hewins	67024
Earlton	66720	Gage Center (Part of		Hiattville	66701
East Bank (Part of Iola)	66749	Topeka)	66604	Hiawatha (Brown County)	66434
Eastborough	67206	Galatia	67565	Hickok	67880
East Forbes	66620	Galena	66739	Hickory Acres	66512
Eastgate Shopping Center		Galesburg (Neosho County)	66740	Hicrest (Part of Topeka)	66605
(Part of Wichita)	67207	Galva	67443	Hidden Lakes (Part of	
Easton	66020	Garden City (Finney		Wichita)	67212
Eastshore	66861	County)	67846	Highland (Doniphan County)	66035
Edgerton	66021	Garden Plain	67050	Highland Park (Part of	
Edmond	67636	Gardner	66030	Topeka)	66605
Edna	67342	Gardner Lake	66030	Hill City	67642
Edson	67733	Garfield (Pawnee County)	67529	Hillcrest Shopping Center	
Edwardsville	66113	Garland	66741	(Part of Lawrence)	66044
Effingham	66023	Garnett	66032	Hillsboro	67063
Elbing	67041	Gas	66742	Hillsdale	66036
El Dorado	67042	Gaylord	66738	Hillside (Part of Wichita)	67208
El Dorado Honor Camp	67042	Gem	67734	Hitschmann	67525
Elgin	67361	Geneseo	67444	Hoge	66086
Elk City	67344	Geuda Springs	67051	Hoisington	67544
Elk Falls	67345	Girard	66743	Holcomb	67851
Elkhart	67950	Glade	67639	Holland (Dickinson County)	67410
Ellinwood	67526	Glasco	67445	Hollenberg	66946
Ellis (Ellis County)	67637	Glendale	67425	Holliday (Part of Shawnee)	66218
Ellsworth (Ellsworth County)	67439	Glen Elder	67446	Holliday Square Shopping	
Elmdale	66850	Glen Park (Part of Kansas		Center (Part of Topeka)	66611
Elmhurst (Part of Overland		City)	66102	Holton	66436
Park)	66204	Glenville (Part of Wichita)	67217	Holyrood	67450
Elmo	67451	Goddard	67052	Home (Marshall County)	66438
Elmont	66618	Goessel	67053	Homewood	66095
Elsmore	66732	Goff	66428	Hope	67451
Elwood (Doniphan County)	66024	Golden Belt Spur (Part of		Hopewell	67557
Elyria	67460	Salina)	67401	Horace	67879
Emmeram	67671	Goodland	67735	Horton	66439
Emmett (Pottawatomie		Goodrich	66072	Howard	67349
County)	66422	Gorham	67640	Hoxie	66740
Empire City (Part of Galena)	66739	Gove	67736	Hoyt	66440
Empire Junction (Part of		Grainfield	67737	Hudson	67545
Galena)	66739	Granada	66550	Hugoton	67951
Emporia (Lyon County)	66801	Grand Summit	67023	Humboldt (Allen County)	66748
Englevale	66756	Grandview (Wyandotte		Hunnewell	67140
Englewood	67840	County)	66012	Hunter	67452
Ensign	67841	Grandview Plaza	66441	Huron	66038
Enterprise (Dickinson		Grantville	66429	Huscher	66901
County)	67441	Great Bend (Barton County)	67530	Hutchinson	67501-05
Erie	66733	Greeley (Anderson County)	66033	For specific Hutchinson Zip Codes	
Esbon	66941	Green (Clay County)	67447	call (316) 662-1295	
Eskridge	66423	Greenbush	66743	Hutchinson Mall (Part of	
Eudora	66025	Greenleaf	66943	Hutchinson)	67501
Eureka (Greenwood		Greensburg	67054	Idana	67432
County)	67045	Greenwich	67055	Imes	66079
Eureka City Lake	67045	Greenwich Heights	67207	Independence (Montgomery	
Everest	66424	Grenola	67346	County)	67301
Fairfax (Wyandotte County)	66115	Gretna	67661	Indian Creek (Johnson	
Fairmount (Leavenworth		Gridley	66852	County)	66207
County)	66048	Grigston	67871	Indian Ridge	66512
Fairport	67665	Grinnell	67738	Indian Springs Shopping	
Fairview (Brown County)	66425	Gross	66711	Center (Part of Kansas	
Fairway	66205	Grove (Shawnee County)	66539	City)	66102
Fall Leaf	66052	Groveland	67546	Indian Valley	66608
Fall River (Greenwood		Gypsum (Saline County)	67448	Indian Village	67337
County)	67047	Hackney	67156	Industry	67410
Falun	67442	Haddam	66944	Ingalls	67853
Fanning	66087	Haggard	67835	Inman	67546
Farlington	66734	Half Mound	66088	Iola (Allen County)	66749

KANSAS

	ZIP
Ionia	66949
Iowa Point	66035
Isabel	67065
Iuka	67066
Jacobs Creek Landing	66854
Jamestown	66948
Jarbalo	66048
Jayhawk (Part of Lawrence)	66046
Jefferson (Montgomery County)	67301
Jennings	67643
Jetmore	67854
Jewell	66949
Johnson (Stanton County)	67855
Junction City	66441
Juniata	67423
Kackley	66948
Kalloch	67337
Kalvesta	67856
Kanona	67749
Kanopolis	67454
Kanorado	67741
Kansas City	66101-19

For specific Kansas City Zip Codes call (913) 573-2655

COLLEGES & UNIVERSITIES

University of Kansas Medical Center	66103

FINANCIAL INSTITUTIONS

Anchor Savings Association	66112
Brotherhood Bank and Trust Co	66101
Citizens Bank & Trust of Kansas City	66103
Home State Bank of Kansas City, Kansas	66101
Inter-State Federal Savings and Loan Association of Kansas City	66101
Security Bank of Kansas City	66101
Sun Savings Association, F.A.	66112

HOSPITALS

Bethany Medical Center	66102
Providence-St. Margaret Health Center	66112
University of Kansas Hospital	66103

HOTELS/MOTELS

Best Western Flamingo Motel	66102
Best Western Hallmark Inn	66103
La Quinta Motor Inn - Lenexa	66215
Kansas State Penitentiary	66043
Kansas State University of Agriculture and Applied	66506
Keats	66502
Kechi	67067
Keene	66423
Kellogg	67156
Kelly	66538
Kendall	67857
Kennekuk	66439
Kenneth (Johnson County)	66223
Kensington	66951
Kickapoo	66048
Kickapoo Indian Reservation	66439
Kimball	66733
Kimeo	66943
Kincaid	66039
Kingman (Kingman County)	67068
Kingsdown	67858
Kinsley (Edwards County)	67457
Kiowa	67070
Kipp	67401
Kirkwood	66762
Kiro	66539
Kirwin	67644
Kismet	67859
Labette (Labette County)	67356
La Crosse	67548
La Cygne	66040
Lafontaine	66750
La Harpe	66751
Lake Chaparral	66056
Lake City	67071
Lake Kahola	66846
Lake of the Forest (Part of Bonner Springs)	66012
Lake Quivira	66106
Lake Shore (Ellsworth County)	67454

	ZIP
Lake Shore (Jefferson County)	66070
Lakeshore (Shawnee County)	66605
Lakeside Acres Addition	67208
Lakeside Village	66070
Lakeview Heights	67230
Lake Wabaunsee	66401
Lakewood Hills	66070
Lakin (Kearny County)	67860
Lamont (Greenwood County)	66855
Lancaster	66041
Lane (Franklin County)	66042
Langdon	67549
Langley	67464
Lanham	68415
Lansing	66043
Larkinburg	66436
Larned (Pawnee County)	67550
Larned State Hospital	67550
Latham	67072
Latimer	67449
Lawrence	66044-46

For specific Lawrence Zip Codes call (913) 843-1681

Lawton	66781
Leavenworth	66048
Leawood	66206
Lebanon	66952
Lebo	66856
Lecompton	66050
Lehigh	67073
Le Loup	66091
Lenape	66052
Lenexa	66215
Lenexa Plaza (Part of Lenexa)	66215
Lenora	67645
Leon	67074
Leona	66532
Leonardville	66449
Leoti	67861
Leoville	67757
Le Roy	66857
Levant	67743
Lewis (Edwards County)	67552
Liberal	67901-05

For specific Liberal Zip Codes call (316) 624-4031

Liberty (Montgomery County)	67351
Liebenthal	67553
Lillis	66544
Lincoln (Lincoln County)	67455
Lincolnville	66858
Lindsborg	67456
Linn	66953
Linn Valley Lakes	66040
Linwood	66052
Little River (Rice County)	67457
Lone Elm	66039
Lone Star (Douglas County)	66046
Longford	67458
Long Island	67647
Longton	67352
Loretta	67520
Lorraine	67459
Lost Springs	66859
Louisburg (Miami County)	66053
Louisville	66450
Lovewell	66942
Lowell (Cherokee County)	66713
Lowemont	66020
Lucas	67648
Ludell	66744
Luray	67649
Lydia	67861
Lyndon	66451
Lyons	67554
McConnell Air Force Base	67221
McCracken	67556
McCune	66753
McDonald	67745
McFarland	66501
Mackie	66725
Macksville	67557
McLouth	66054
McPherson (McPherson County)	67460
Madison	66860
Mahaska	66955
Maize	67101
Manchester	67463
Manhattan (Riley County)	66502
Mankato	66956
Manning	67871
Manter	67862
Maple City	67102
Maple Hill	66507
Mapleton	66754

	ZIP
Marienthal	67863
Marietta	66518
Marion (Marion County)	66861
Marion County Lake	66861
Marmaton (Bourbon County)	66701
Marquette	67464
Marysville (Marshall County)	66508
Matfield Green	66862
Mayetta	66509
Mayfield	67103
Meade	67864
Mecca Acres	67230
Medicine Lodge	67104
Medina	66073
Medora	67502
Melrose	67336
Melvern	66510
Menlo	67746
Mentor	67465
Mercier	66439
Meriden	66512
Merriam	66203
Metcalf South Shopping Center (Part of Overland Park)	66212
Michigan (Osage County)	66528
Midland (Part of Wichita)	67216
Midland Park	67216
Midway (Kingman County)	67111
Midway (Rawlins County)	67739
Milan	67105
Milberger	67665
Mildred	66039
Milford	66514
Millbrook (Sedgwick County)	67212
Miller	66868
Milton (Sumner County)	67106
Miltonvale	67466
Mingo	67701
Minneapolis	67467
Minneola	67865
Mission (Johnson County)	66205
Mission Hills	66205
Mission Shopping Center (Part of Mission)	66222
Mission Woods	66205
Mitchell (Rice County)	67554
Modoc	67866
Moline	67353
Monmouth (Crawford County)	66753
Monrovia	66023
Montana (Labette County)	67356
Montara	66619
Montezuma	67867
Monticello (Part of Shawnee)	66218
Mont Ida	66091
Montrose	66956
Monument	67747
Moran	66755
Moray	66087
Morehead	66776
Morganville	67468
Morland	67650
Morrill	66515
Morrowville	66958
Morse	66061
Moscow	67952
Mound City	66056
Moundridge	67107
Mound Valley	67354
Mount Hope	67108
Mount Vernon	67025
Mulberry (Crawford County)	66756
Mullinville	67109
Mulvane	67110
Muncie (Part of Kansas City)	66111
Munden	66959
Munger (Part of Wichita)	67208
Munjor	67601
Murdock (Kingman County)	67111
Muscotah	66058
Narka	66960
Nashville	67112
Natoma	67651
Navarre	67469
Neal	66863
Nekoma	67559
Neodesha (Wilson County)	66757
Neosho Falls	66758
Neosho Rapids	66864
Ness City	67560
Netawaka	66516
Neuchatel	66521
Neutral	66725
New Albany	66759
New Almelo	67652

200 KANSAS Kansas City

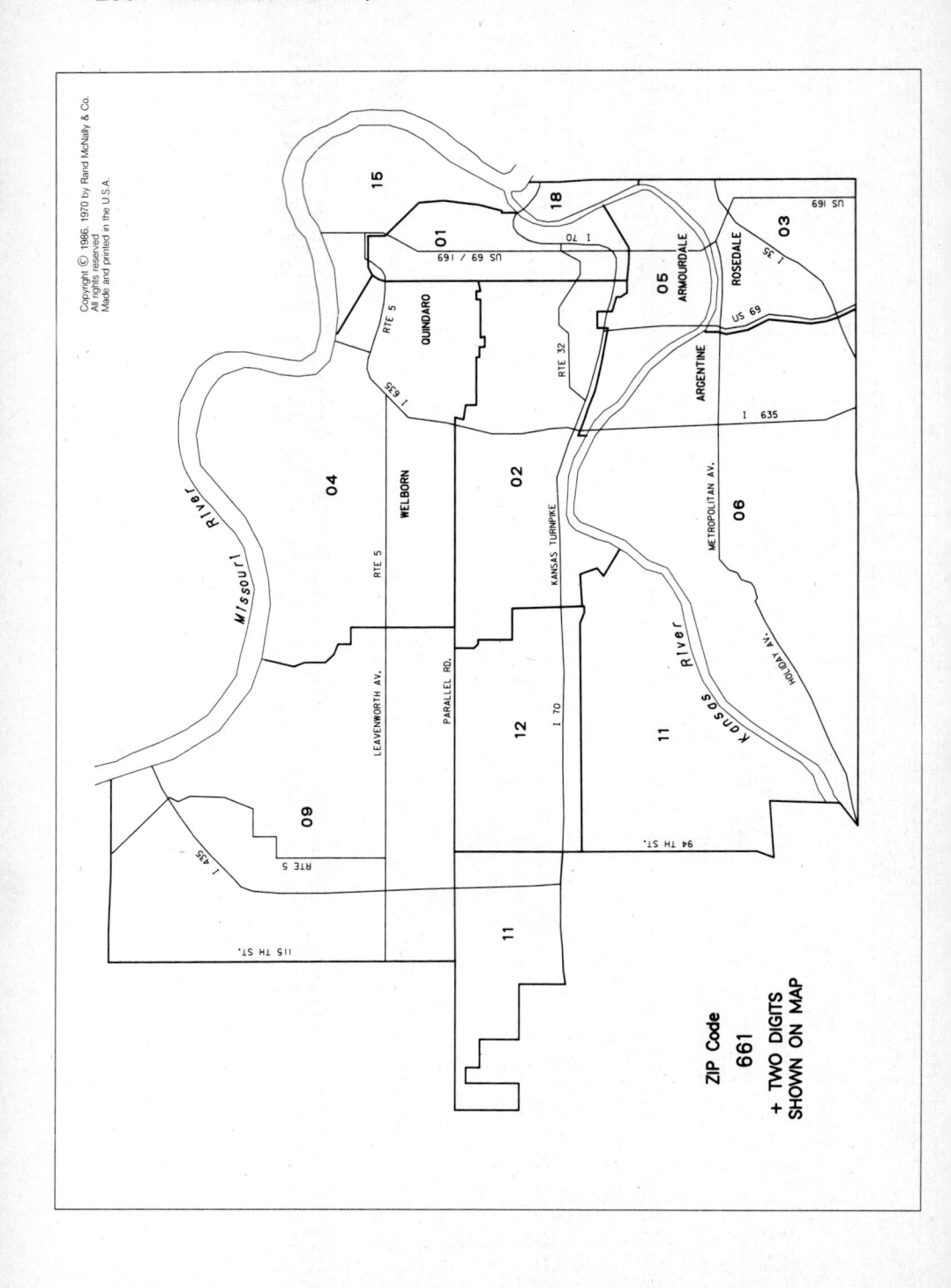

Newbury-Spring Grove **KANSAS** 201

	ZIP		ZIP		ZIP
Newbury	66526	Petrolia	66720	Ruleton	67735
New Cambria	67470	Pfeifer	67660	Rush Center	67575
New Lancaster	66040	Phillipsburg (Phillips County)	67661	Russell (Russell County)	67665
Newman	66073	Pickrell Corner	67010	Russell Springs	67755
New Salem	67156	Piedmont	67122	Sabetha	66534
Newton (Harvey County)	67114	Pierceville	67868	Saffordville	66801
Nickerson	67561	Pilsen	66861	St. Benedict	66538
Nicodemus	67625	Piper	66109	St. Francis	67756
Niles	67480	Piqua	66761	St. George	66535
Niotaze	67355	Pittsburg (Crawford County)	66762	St. John	67576
Norcatur	67653	Plains	67869	St. Joseph	66938
Normandie Shopping Center (Part of Wichita)	67206	Plainville	67663	St. Leo	67112
Northbranch	66936	Pleasant Grove (Douglas County)	66046	St. Mark	67030
Northern Hills	66608	Pleasanton	66075	St. Marys	66536
North Newton	67117	Plevna	67568	Saint Marys	67050
North Osage City (Part of Osage City)	66523	Plymell	67846	St. Mary's College (Part of Leavenworth)	66048
North Topeka (Part of Topeka)	66608	Plymouth (Lyon County)	66801	St. Pats	66002
North Wichita (Part of Wichita)	67204	Polk	66743	St. Paul	66771
Norton (Norton County)	67654	Pomona	66076	St. Peter	67650
Nortonville	66060	Portis	67474	St. Theresa	67861
Norway	66961	Portland	67140	Salina	67401-02
Norwich	67118	Potawatomi Indian Reservation	66439	For specific Salina Zip Codes call (913) 827-3695	
Oakhill	67472	Potter	66077	Sand Spring	67410
Oakland (Shawnee County)	66616	Potwin	67123	Sanford	67550
Oaklawn	67216	Powhattan	66527	Sarcoxie (Leavenworth County)	66052
Oakley	67748	Prairie View	67664	Satanta	67870
Oak Park Mall (Part of Overland Park)	66216	Prairie Village	66208	Saunders	67862
Oak Valley	67352	Prairie Village Shopping Center (Part of Prairie Village)	66208	Savonburg	66772
Oberlin	67749	Pratt	67124	Sawyer	67134
Ocheltree	66083	Prescott	67767	Saxman	67579
Odin	67562	Preston	67569	Scammon	66773
Offerle	67563	Pretty Prairie	67570	Scandia	66966
Ogallah	67656	Princeton	66078	Schoenchen	67667
Ogden (Riley County)	66517	Prospect (Butler County)	67042	Schulte	67215
Oketo	66518	Prospect Park	67215	Scipio	66032
Olathe	66061-62	Protection	67127	Scott City	67871
For specific Olathe Zip Codes call (913) 764-0375		Purcell	66638	Scottsville	67477
Olivet	66856	Quenemo	66528	Scranton	66537
Olmitz	67564	Quincy	66870	Sedan	67361
Olpe	66865	Quinter	67752	Sedgwick	67135
Olsburg	66520	Radium	67551	Seguin	67740
Onaga	66521	Radley	66762	Selden	67757
Oneida	66522	Rago	67128	Selkirk	67861
Opolis	66760	Ramona	67475	Selma	66039
Orchard Park (Part of Parsons)	67357	Ranch Mart Shopping Center (Part of Leawood)	66206	Seneca	66538
Osage City	67523	Randall	66963	Severance	66081
Osawatomie (Miami County)	66064	Randolph	66554	Severy	67137
Osborne (Osborne County)	67473	Ransom	67572	Seward (Stafford County)	67577
Oskaloosa	66066	Rantoul	66079	Shady Bend	67455
Ost	67108	Raymond	67573	Shady Brook	67449
Oswego (Labette County)	67356	Reading	66868	Shallow Water	67871
Otego	66936	Reager	67654	Sharon	67138
Otis	67565	Redel	66085	Sharon Springs	67758
Ottawa (Franklin County)	66067	Redfield	66769	Sharpe	66871
Ottumwa	66839	Red Wing	67544	Shaw	66733
Overbrook	66524	Reece	67045	Shawnee (Johnson County)	66203
Overland Park	66204	Reno (Leavenworth County)	66086	Shawnee Mission	66201-27
Oxford (Sumner County)	67119	Republic	66964	For specific Shawnee Mission Zip Codes call (913) 831-5302	
Ozawkie	66070	Reserve	66434	Sherman (Cherokee County)	67356
Packers (Part of Kansas City)	66105	Rexford	67753	Sherwin	66725
Padonia	66434	Rice	66901	Sherwood Estates	66604
Page City	67764	Richfield	67953	Shields	67874
Palco	67657	Richland (Shawnee County)	66409	Silverdale	67005
Palmer	66962	Richmond	66080	Silver Lake	66539
Paola (Miami County)	66071	Richter	66067	Simpson	67478
Paradise (Russell County)	67658	Riley	66531	Sitka (Clark County)	67831
Park (Gove County)	67751	Ringer (Part of Wichita)	67212	Skiddy	66872
Park City	67219	Ringo	66743	Skidmore	66773
Park East	67208	Riverdale	67152	Smith Center	66967
Parker (Linn County)	66072	Riverside (Sedgwick County)	67203	Smolan	67479
Parkerville	66846	Riverton	66770	Soldier (Jackson County)	66540
Parklane Shopping Center (Part of Wichita)	67218	Riverview (Sedgwick County)	67204	Solomon (Dickinson County)	67480
Parsons	67357	Robert L. Roberts (Part of Kansas City)	66104	Somerset	66071
Partridge	67566	Robinson	66532	South Dodge (Part of Dodge City)	67801
Patterson	67020	Rock (Cowley County)	67131	Southeast (Part of Wichita)	67218
Pauline (Part of Topeka)	66619	Rock Creek (Jefferson County)	66512	Southgate Shopping Center (Part of Liberal)	67901
Pawnee Plaza Mall (Part of Wichita)	67211	Rocky Ford	66502	South Haven	67140
Pawnee Rock	67567	Roeland Park	66203	South Hoisington	67544
Paxico	66526	Rolla	67954	South Hutchinson	67505
Peabody	66866	Rolling Hills (Part of Wichita)	67212	South Mound	67357
Pearl	67431	Rome	67152	South Radley	66762
Peck	67120	Roper	66714	South Seneca Gardens (Part of Wichita)	67217
Peck Addition	66605	Rosalia	67132	Sparks	66035
Penalosa	67121	Rose	67783	Spearville	67876
Pence	67871	Rosedale (Part of Kansas City)	66103	Speed	67661
Pen Dennis	67874	Rose Hill	67133	Spivey	67142
Penokee	67659	Roseland	66773	Springdale (Leavenworth County)	66020
Peoria	66067	Rosewood (Part of Parsons)	67357	Springdale (Sedgwick County)	67230
Perry (Jefferson County)	66073	Rossville	66533	Spring Grove (Part of Galena)	66739
Perth	67152	Roxbury	67476		
Peru	67360	Rozel	67574		

KANSAS Spring Hill-Zurich

Location	ZIP
Spring Hill (Johnson County)	66083
Stafford	67578
Stanley	66223
Stanton (Miami County)	66064
Stark	66775
State House (Part of Topeka)	66603
Sterling (Rice County)	67579
Stilwell	66085
Stippville	66725
Stockton	67669
Stony Point (Part of Kansas City)	66111
Strauss	66753
Strawn	66839
Strong City	66869
Studley	67759
Stull	66050
Stuttgart	67670
Sublette	67877
Suburban Heights (Part of Independence)	67301
Sugar Valley	66056
Summerfield	66541
Sun City	67143
Sunnydale	67147
Sunset Park (Part of Haysville)	67060
Suppesville	67106
Susank	67580
Sweetbriar Shopping Center (Part of Wichita)	67204
Sycamore (Montgomery County)	67363
Sylvan Grove	67481
Sylvia	67581
Syracuse	67878
Talmage	67482
Talmo	66935
Tampa	67483
Tanglewood Lake	66040
Tasco	67740
Tecumseh	66542
Terra Heights (Part of Topeka)	66609
Tescott	67484
Thayer	66776
The Dell (Part of Wichita)	67209
Thompsonville	66073
Timken	67582
Tipton	67485
Tonganoxie	66086
Topeka	66601-99
For specific Topeka Zip Codes call (913) 295-9100	
Toronto	66777
Towanda	67144
Tower Grove (Part of Overland Park)	66204
Towne East Square (Part of Wichita)	67207
Towne West Square (Part of Wichita)	67209
Trading Post	66075
Traer	67749
Travel Air	67206
Treece	66778
Trego Center	67672
Tribune	67879
Trousdale	67059
Troy (Doniphan County)	66087
Turck	66725
Turkville	67663
Turner (Part of Kansas City)	66106
Turon	67583
Twin Lakes Shopping Center (Part of Wichita)	67203
Tyro	67364

Location	ZIP
Udall	67146
Ulysses	67880
Uniontown	66779
University (Crawford County)	66762
University (Douglas County)	66044
Urbana	66720
Utica	67584
V.A. Hospital (Part of Topeka)	66622
Valeda	67337
Valencia	66604
Valley Center (Sedgwick County)	67147
Valley Falls	66088
Varner	67068
Vassar	66543
Venango	67464
Verdi	67480
Vermillion (Marshall County)	66544
Vernon (Woodson County)	66783
Vesper	67455
Victoria	67671
Vilas	66720
Village Square, The (Part of Dodge City)	67801
Vine Creek	67458
Vining	66937
Vinland	66006
Viola	67149
Virgil	66870
Vliets	66545
Voda	67631
Wabaunsee	66547
Waco (Sedgwick County)	67120
Wagon Wheel Ranch	67010
Wagstaff	66071
Wakarusa (Shawnee County)	66546
WaKeeney	67672
Wakefield	67487
Waldo	67673
Waldron	67150
Walker (Ellis County)	67674
Wallace	67761
Walnut (Crawford County)	66780
Walton	67151
Wamego	66547
Washburn University (Part of Topeka)	66621
Washington (Washington County)	66968
Waterloo (Kingman County)	67111
Waterville	66548
Wathena	66090
Watson	66542
Wauneta	67024
Waverly	66871
Wayne (Republic County)	66930
Wayside	67301
Wea	66013
Webber	66970
Webster (Rooks County)	67669
Wego-Waco	67216
Weir	66781
Welborn (Part of Kansas City)	66104
Welda	66091
Wellington (Sumner County)	67152
Wells (Ottawa County)	67488
Wellsford	67059
Wellsville	66092
Weskan	67762
Wesleyan (Part of Salina)	67401
Westboro (Part of Topeka)	66604
West Coffeyville	67337
Westfall	67455
Westlink Shopping Center (Part of Wichita)	67212

Location	ZIP
Westlink Village (Part of Wichita)	67212
West Mineral	66782
Westmoreland	66549
Westphalia	66093
Westport (Part of Wichita)	67217
West Shore	66512
Westway Shopping Center (Part of Wichita)	67217
Westwood	66205
Westwood Hills	66205
Wetmore	66550
Wheaton	66551
Wheatridge Addition (Part of Wichita)	67212
Wheeler	67756
White Church (Part of Kansas City)	66109
White City	66872
White Cloud	66094
White Lakes Shopping Center (Part of Topeka)	66611
Whitewater	67154
Whiting	66552
Wichita	67201-78
For specific Wichita Zip Codes call (316) 946-4511	
Wichita State University (Part of Wichita)	67208
Wilburton	67950
Wilder Junction	66018
Willard	66604
Williamsburg	66095
Williamstown	66073
Willis	66435
Willowbrook	67501
Willowdale (Kingman County)	67142
Wilmore	67155
Wilmot	67131
Wilroads Gardens	67801
Wilsey	66873
Wilson	67490
Winchester	66097
Windom	67491
Windsor Park	67207
Windthorst	67876
Winfield (Cowley County)	67156
Winfield State Hospital and Training Center	67156
Winifred	66427
Winona	67764
Winway (Part of Parsons)	67357
Wolcott (Part of Kansas City)	66109
Womer	66952
Wonsevu	66840
Woodbine	67492
Woodruff	67661
Woods	67951
Woodston	67675
Worden	66006
Wright	67882
Wyandotte West (Part of Kansas City)	66112
Xenia	66716
Yaggy	67501
Yale	66762
Yates Center	66783
Yocemento	67601
Yoder	67585
Zarah (Part of Shawnee)	66218
Zeandale	66502
Zenda	67159
Zenith	67578
Zook	67550
Zurich	67676

Aaron-Bethesda KENTUCKY 203

Name	ZIP
Aaron	42601
Abbott	40006
Abegall	41044
Aberdeen	42201
Absher	42728
Access	41164
Acorn	42510
Acton	42718
Acup	41751
Adaburg	42347
Adair	42348
Adairville	42202
Adams	41201
Adamson	41517
Add	41224
Addison	40143
Adeline	41129
Aden	41142
Adolphus	42120
Aetnaville	42368
Aflex	41529
Ages	40801
Ages-Brookside	40801
Airport Gardens	41701
Ajax	41722
Akers (Part of Cumberland)	40823
Akersville	42133
Albany	42602
Alberta	41031
Albia	42567
Alcalde	42511
Alcorn	40447
Alexandria	41001
Algonquin Manor (Part of Louisville)	40211
Alhambra	41055
Aliceton	40328
Alka	41562
Allais (Part of Hazard)	41701
Allegre	42203
Allen	41601
Allendale	42782
Allen Springs	42122
Allensville	42204
Allock	41710
Almo	42020
Almo Heights	42020
Alonzo	42120
Alpha	42603
Alpine	42519
Alta	42358
Alton	40342
Alton Station	40342
Altro	41306
Alumbaugh	40336
Alum Springs	40440
Alva	40863
Alvaton	42122
Amandaville	42711
Amba	41635
Amburgey	41801
Ammie	40962
Ammons	40170
Amos	42153
Anchorage	40223
Anco	41711
Anderson	42268
Andyville	40157
Anna	42270
Anneta	42754
Annville	40402
Ano	42510
Ansel	42553
Antepast	40987
Anthoston	42420
Antioch Mills	41003
Antioch Shores	42519
Anton	42431
Apex	42464
Aqua Shores	40065
Arat	42717
Arch	42724
Argillite	41121
Argo	41568
Argyle	42516
Arista	42718
Arjay	40902
Arkansas Creek	41649
Arkle	40734
Arlington (Carlisle County)	42021
Arlington (Madison County)	40475
Arlington Heights (Part of Frankfort)	40601
Armstrong Hill	41164
Arnett	41314
Arnold	42349
Arrington Corner	42348
Arrowood	41316
Artemus	40903
Arthur	42210
Arthurmable	41430

Name	ZIP
Artville	40387
Arvel	40447
Ary	41712
Ashbyburg	42456
Ashcamp	41512
Asher	40803
Ashers Fork	40962
Ashland	41101-05
For specific Ashland Zip Codes call (606) 327-2121	
Ashlock	38551
Askin	42343
Asphalt	42210
Atchison	42718
Athens (Part of Lexington)	40502
Athertonville	42748
Athol	41307
Atkinstown	40434
Atlanta	40741
Atoka	40422
Atwood	41063
Auburn	42206
Audobon Acres	42301
Audubon Park	40213
Augusta	41002
Ault	41164
Aurora	42048
Austerlitz	40361
Austin	42123
Auxier	41602
Avawam	41713
Avoca	40223
Avon (Part of Lexington)	40505
Avondale (Part of Paducah)	42001
Avondale Heights (Part of Paducah)	42001
Axtel	40103
Ayers	40769
Bachelors Rest	41040
Backusburg	42054
Bagdad	40003
Bailey Creek	40828
Bailey Mine	41168
Baileys Branch	42151
Baileys Switch	40905
Bainbridge	42215
Baizetown	42349
Baker Branch	41263
Bakerton	42711
Bald Hill	41041
Baldrock	40741
Baldwin	40475
Balkan	40977
Ballard	40342
Ballardsville	40014
Balltown	40051
Baltimore	42066
Bancroft (Jefferson County)	40222
Bancroft (Muhlenberg County)	42345
Bandana	42022
Bandy	42567
Bank Lick	41094
Banner	41603
Bancck	42261
Baptist	41301
Barbourmeade	40222
Barbourville	40906
Barcreek	40972
Bardo	40831
Bardstown	40004
Bardstown Junction	40165
Bardwell	42023
Barefoot	40311
Bark Camp	40701
Barkley Field	42001
Barlow	42024
Barnesburg	42501
Barnes Store	42445
Barnetts Creek	41256
Barnrock	41219
Barnsley	42431
Barnyard	40935
Barrallton	40165
Barren River	42101
Barrier	42633
Barr Street (Part of Lexington)	40507
Barterville	40311
Barwick	41306
Bascom	41171
Bashford Manor Mall (Part of West Buechel)	40218
Basil	42742
Basin Springs	40146
Baskett	42402
Bass	42733
Bath	41836
Battle	40400
Battle Run	41039
Battletown	40104

Name	ZIP
Baughman	40911
Baughman Heights (Part of Danville)	40422
Baxter (Harlan County)	40806
Baxter (Jefferson County)	40204
Bayfork	42122
Bayou	42081
Bays	41310
Bays Branch	41222
Bealers Knob	42371
Beals	42451
Bear Branch	41714
Bear Grass (Part of Louisville)	40218
Beartown	41176
Bearville	41740
Bear Wallow	42127
Beattyville	41311
Beaumont	42124
Beaumont Park (Part of Lexington)	40502
Beauty	41203
Beaver	41604
Beaver Bottom	41522
Beaver Dam	42320
Beaver Junction (Part of Allen)	41601
Beaverlick	41094
Becknerville	40391
Becks Store	42715
Beckton	42141
Beda	42347
Bedford	40006
Bee	42729
Beech (Breathitt County)	41306
Beech (Harlan County)	40964
Beechburg	41093
Beech Creek	42321
Beech Fork	41756
Beech Grove (Bullitt County)	40150
Beech Grove (McLean County)	42322
Beechland	42256
Beechmont	42323
Beechville	42129
Beechwood	40359
Beechwood Village	40207
Beechy	41175
Beefhide	41537
Beelerton	42041
Bee Lick	40419
Bee Spring	42207
Beetle	41143
Bel-Air (Part of Winchester)	40391
Belcher	41513
Belcourt	42456
Belcraft	41858
Belfry	41514
Belknap	41342
Belknap Beach	40059
Bell City (Elliott County)	41171
Bell City (Graves County)	42040
Bell County Forestry Camp	40977
Bellefonte	41101
Bellemeade	40222
Bellepoint (Part of Frankfort)	40601
Belleview	41005
Bellevue	41073
Bellewood	40207
Bell Farm	42647
Bells Run	42378
Belltown	40033
Belmont (Bullitt County)	40150
Belmont (Harrison County)	41031
Belton	42324
Ben Bow	41230
Bengal	42718
Benham	40807
Benito	40849
Bennettstown	42236
Benson	40601
Bent	42501
Benton	42025
Berea	40403
Berea College (Part of Berea)	40404
Berlin	41043
Bernice	40932
Bernstadt	40741
Berry	41003
Berrys Lick	42268
Berrytown	40223
Bertha	40734
Bethanna	41401
Bethany (Jefferson County)	40272
Bethany (Wolfe County)	41313
Bethel (Bath County)	40306
Bethel (Jessamine County)	40356
Bethelridge	42516
Bethesda	42633

KENTUCKY

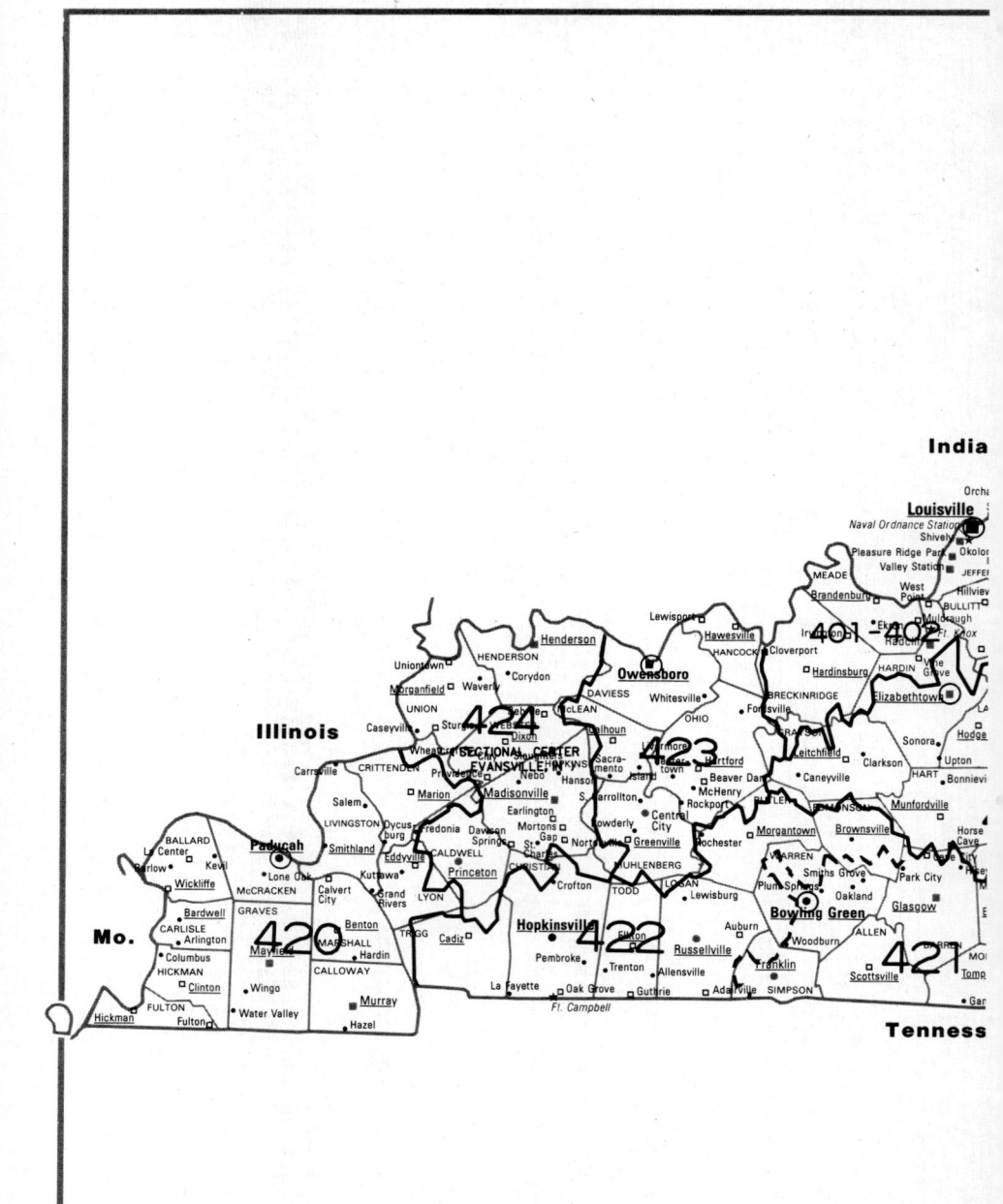

KENTUCKY

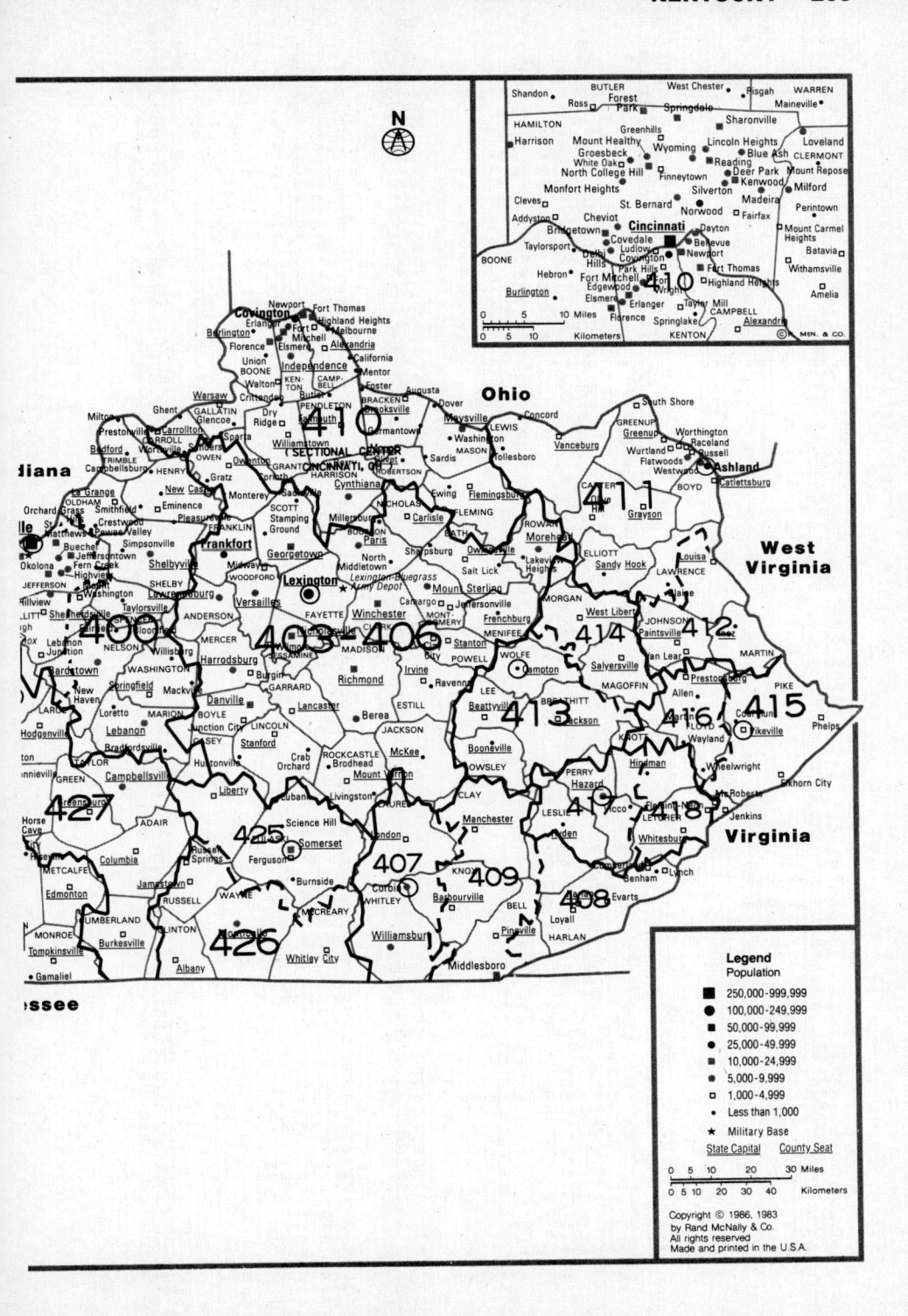

206 KENTUCKY Bethlehem-Cadentown

	ZIP
Bethlehem	40007
Betsey	42633
Betsy Layne	41605
Beulah (Hickman County)	42039
Beulah (Hopkins County)	42408
Beulah Heights	42607
Beverly	40913
Beverly Hills (Part of Danville)	40422
Bevier	42337
Bevinsville	41606
Bewleyville	40146
Biddle	40324
Big Bear Creek	42025
Big Bone	41091
Big Branch	41522
Big Clifty	42712
Big Creek	40914
Big Eddy	40601
Big Fork	41777
Biggs	41524
Bighill	40405
Big Laurel	40808
Big Ready	42275
Big Rock	41777
Big Sandy Junction (Part of Catlettsburg)	41129
Big Shoals	41501
Big Spring	40106
Bigstone	41171
Big Woods	40387
Billows	42501
Bimble	40915
Birdie	40342
Birdsville	42081
Birk City	42301
Biscayne	41812
Bishop (Part of Lexington)	40505
Black Bottom	40828
Blackburn Correctional Complex	40504
Black Diamond (Part of Drakesboro)	42337
Blackey	41804
Blackford	42403
Black Gnat	42718
Black Gold	42285
Black Jack	42134
Black Mountain	40847
Black Rock	42754
Black Snake	40863
Blackwater	40741
Bladeston	41004
Blaine	41124
Blair	40823
Blairs Mills	41472
Blake	41314
Blanche	40902
Blanchet	41010
Blandville	42026
Blaze	41472
Bledsoe	40810
Blevins	41124
Blincoe	40037
Bloomfield	40008
Bloomingdale	40391
Bloomington (Grayson County)	42754
Bloomington (Magoffin County)	41475
Bloss	40456
Blowing Spring	42743
Blowing Springs	42729
Blue Bank	41041
Blue Diamond	41719
Blue Grass (Part of Lexington)	40503
Bluegrass Estates	40422
Bluehole	40917
Blue John	42519
Blue Level	42274
Blue Lick Springs	40311
Blue Moon	41655
Blue Ridge Manor	40223
Blue River	41607
Blue Spring	42211
Bluestone	40351
Blue Water Estates	42211
Bluff Boom	42743
Bluff City	42420
Blythe	42151
Board Tree	41528
Boaz	42027
Bobbs	41260
Bobs Creek	40815
Bobtown	40403
Bohon	40330
Boiling Spring	42101
Boldman	41501
Boles	42167
Boltsfork	41168

	ZIP
Bolyn	41630
Bon	40769
Bon Air Hills (Part of Frankfort)	40601
Bonanza	41653
Bonayer	42160
Bond	40407
Bondurant	42050
Bondville	40372
Boneyville	40484
Bon Haven (Part of Winchester)	40391
Bonnie Brae	40065
Bonnieville	42713
Bonny	41332
Bonnyman	41719
Booker	40069
Boone	40403
Boone Heights	40906
Boonesboro (Clark County)	40475
Boonesboro (Madison County)	40475
Booneville	41314
Boons Camp	41204
Bordley	42404
Boreing	40740
Borowick Farms	40031
Boston (Butler County)	42268
Boston (Nelson County)	40107
Boston (Pendleton County)	41006
Botland	40004
Botto	40944
Bourbon	42501
Bourbon Furnace	40360
Bourne	40444
Bouty	40769
Bow	42714
Bowen	40309
Bowling Green	42101-04
For specific Bowling Green Zip Codes call (502) 782-4202	
Boyce	42122
Boyd	41003
Boyds Crossing	42782
Boyds Landing	42055
Boydsville	42079
Boydtown	40324
Bracht	41030
Bracktown (Part of Lexington)	40505
Bradford	41043
Bradfordsville	40009
Bradshaw	40434
Brady (Part of Morehead)	40351
Brainard	41465
Bramlett	42743
Brandenburg (Meade County)	40108
Brandy Keg	41653
Brassfield	40385
Braxton	40330
Brazil	40447
Breadens Creek	40927
Breathitt	41340
Breckinridge	41031
Breckinridge Center	42437
Breeding	42715
Bremen	42325
Brent (Part of Fort Thomas)	41075
Brentsville	40361
Brentwood (Part of Madisonville)	42431
Brewers	42025
Briartown	40069
Briarwood	40222
Briarwood Manor (Part of Bowling Green)	42103
Bridgeport	40601
Bridge Street (Part of Paducah)	42001
Bridgeville	41004
Briensburg	42025
Brighton (Part of Lexington)	40505
Brightshade	40962
Brinegar	41164
Brinkley	41805
Bristol Oakes	40299
Bristow	42101
Britmark	42220
Broad Bottom	41501
Broad Fields	40207
Broad Ford	42726
Broadview Manor	40601
Broadwell	41031
Brodhead	40409
Broeck Point	40201
Bromley (Kenton County)	41016
Bromley (Owen County)	41086
Bromo	40456
Bronston	42518

	ZIP
Brookhaven (Part of Lexington)	40502
Brooklyn	42209
Brooks	40109
Brookside	40801
Brooksville	41004
Broughtentown	40419
Browder	42326
Brownies Creek	40856
Browning	42274
Brownings Corner	41040
Browningtown	40165
Brownsboro	40014
Brownsboro Farm	40222
Brownsboro Road Shopping Center (Part of Windy Hills)	40207
Brownsboro Village	40222
Browns Fork	41720
Browns Grove	42071
Brown's Valley	42376
Brownsville (Edmonson County)	42210
Brownsville (Fulton County)	42050
Brownwood Manor	42301
Bruin	41125
Brush Grove	40040
Brutus	40972
Bryan	42629
Bryants Store	40921
Bryantsville	40410
Buchanan	41129
Buck Creek	41314
Buckettown	40475
Buckeye	40444
Buck Grove	40117
Buckhorn	41721
Buckingham	41636
Buckner	40010
Buechel	40218
Buel	42327
Buena Vista (Garrard County)	40444
Buena Vista (Harrison County)	41031
Buena Vista (Lewis County)	41179
Buena Vista (Marshall County)	42044
Buffalo (Larue County)	42716
Buffalo (Trigg County)	42211
Buford	42376
Bug	42602
Bugtussle	42140
Bulan	41722
Bull Creek	41653
Bullittsville	41005
Bummer	40460
Burdick	42718
Burdine (Part of Jenkins)	41517
Burfield	42633
Burgin	40310
Burke (Elliott County)	41171
Burke (Henry County)	40057
Burkesville	42717
Burkhart	41315
Burk Hollow	40769
Burkley	42021
Burkshire Terrace	40214
Burlington	41005
Burna	42028
Burnaugh	41129
Burnetta	42544
Burning Fork (Magoffin County)	41405
Burning Fork (Pike County)	41501
Burning Springs	40962
Burnside	42519
Burnwell	41518
Burr	40456
Burton	41612
Burtonville	41189
Bush	40724
Bushong	42167
Bushtown	40330
Buskirk (Morgan County)	41406
Buskirk (Pike County)	41544
Busseyville	41230
Busy	41723
Butler (Franklin County)	40601
Butler (Pendleton County)	41006
Butterfly	41719
Buttimer Hill (Part of Frankfort)	40601
Buttonsberry	42350
Bybee	40385
Bypro	41612
Cabell	42633
Cabot	42343
Caddo	41040
Cadentown (Part of Lexington)	40505

Cadiz-Corinth KENTUCKY 207

	ZIP		ZIP		ZIP
Cadiz	42211	Cedar Brook	41031	Clifford	41230
Cains Store	42544	Cedarcrest	42532	Clifton	40383
Cairo	42420	Cedar Flat	42129	Clifty	42216
Calana Shores	41097	Cedar Grove (Pulaski County)	42501	Climax	40456
Caldwell	41033	Cedar Grove (Todd County)	42220	Clinton	42031
Caldwell Manor (Part of Danville)	40422	Cedar Heights Park	42291	Clintonville	40361
Caleast	40475	Cedar Hill Heights	42518	Clio	40769
Caledonia	42232	Cedar Spring	42160	Closplint	40927
Calf Creek	41224	Cedar Springs	42164	Clover Bottom	40447
Calhoun	42327	Cedarville (Pike County)	41522	Cloverdale (Part of Frankfort)	40601
California	41007	Cedarville (Rockcastle County)	40456	Clover-Darby	40927
Calla	40336	Center	42214	Cloverleaf (Part of Louisville)	40216
Callaboose	41301	Centerfield	40014	Cloverport	40111
Callaway	40977	Center Point	42167	Clovertown	40831
Calloway	40456	Center Ridge	42071	Cloyds Landing	42752
Calmes	40391	Centertown	42328	Cluttts	40823
Calvary	40033	Centerview	40145	Clyffeside (Part of Ashland)	41101
Calvert City	42029	Centerview Rough River	40145	Coakley	42743
Calvin	40813	Central Avenue (Part of Paducah)	42001	Coalgood	40818
Camargo	40353	Central City	42330	Coal Run	41501
Cambridge	40220	Centreville	42324	Coalton	41168
Cambridge Shores	42044	Ceralvo	42369	Cobb	42445
Camelia	42086	Cerulean	42215	Cobhill	40415
Camelot (Part of St. Matthews)	40222	Chad	40823	Coburg	42743
Campbellsburg	40011	Chalybeate	42171	Codyville (Part of Hardinsburg)	40143
Campbellsville	42718-19	Chambers	42348	Coe	42167
For specific Campbellsville Zip Codes call (502) 465-4251		Chance	42728	Cofer	42129
Camp Dick Robinson	40444	Chandlers Chapel	42206	Cogswell	40351
Camp Dix	41127	Chandlerville	41257	Colby Hills	40391
Camp Kennedy	40444	Chapel Hill	42120	Coldiron	40819
Camp Nelson	40444	Chaplin	40012	Cold Spring	41076
Camp Pleasant	40601	Chapman	41230	Cold Spring-Highland Heights (Part of Highland Heights)	41076
Camp Shantituck	40165	Chappell	40816	Coldstream	40202
Camp Springs	41059	Charleston	42408	Coldwater	42071
Campton	41301	Charleswood	40229	Coleman	41553
Canada	41519	Charley	41230	Colemansville	41003
Canby	41010	Charters	41179	Coles Bend	42171
Cane Creek	40741	Chatham	41002	Colesburg	40150
Cane Valley	42720	Chavies	41727	Coletown (Part of Lexington)	40502
Caney	41407	Cheap (Part of Flatwoods)	41144	Colfax	41049
Caneyville	42721	Chenault	40170	College (Part of Berea)	40403
Canmer	42722	Chenoa	40977	College Heights (Part of Bowling Green)	42101
Cannel City	41408	Chenowee	41339	College Hill	40385
Cannon	40923	Cherokee (Jefferson County)	40205	College Park (Part of Frankfort)	40601
Cannonsburg	41101	Cherokee (Lawrence County)	41180	Collista	41222
Canoe	41316	Cherry	42071	Colly	41815
Canton	42212	Cherrywood Village	40207	Colmar	40965
Canton Heights Estates	42211	Chesnutburg	40962	Colo	42501
Canyon Falls	41311	Chestnut Gap	41314	Colonial Terrace	40222
Capital Heights (Part of Frankfort)	40601	Chestnut Grove	40065	Colson	41858
Capito	40965	Chevrolet	40817	Columbia	42728
Carbondale	42408	Chevy Chase (Part of Lexington)	40502	Columbus	42032
Carbon Glow	41832	Chicken Bristle	40484	Colville	41031
Carcassonne	41804	Chilesburg (Part of Lexington)	40505	Combs	41729
Cardinal Hills (Part of Frankfort)	40601	Chloe	41501	Comer	42327
Cardinal Valley (Part of Lexington)	40503	Choateville	40601	Concord (Fleming County)	41041
Cardwell	40330	Christianburg	40065	Concord (Lewis County)	41131
Carlisle	40311	Christine	42728	Concord (Pendleton County)	41040
Carmen	41522	Christopher	41701	Concordia	40157
Carntown	41006	Christy	40351	Conder	41514
Carpenter	40906	Church	42754	Confederate	42038
Carr Creek	41847	Cinda	41728	Confederate Estates	40014
Carrie	41725	Cinderella Estates	40229	Confluence	41730
Carrollton	41008	Cisco	41410	Congleton (Lee County)	41311
Carrs	41179	Cisselville	40069	Congleton (McLean County)	42327
Carrsville	42081	Clabber Bottom	40324	Conkling	41314
Carter	41128	Clare	42134	Conley	41411
Carthage	41007	Clarence	42567	Connersville	41031
Cartwright	42602	Clark Hill	41164	Conoloway	42726
Carver	41409	Clarksburg	41179	Conrad	42501
Cary	40977	Clarkson	42726	Consolation	40003
Casey	42261	Clark Station	40023	Constance	41009
Casey Creek	42723	Clark Street (Part of Paducah)	42001	Constantine	40114
Caseyville	42459	Claryville	41001	Conway	40417
Cash	42784	Claxton	42408	Cooktown	42123
Casky	42240	Clay	42404	Cool Springs	42320
Cassaday	42103	Clay City	40312	Cooper	42633
Castlewood (Part of Lexington)	40505	Clayhole	41317	Co Operative	42647
Castner (Part of.Louisville)	40206	Clay Lick	40337	Cooperstown	42276
Catalpa	41230	Claymour	42220	Coopersville	42611
Catawba	41040	Claypool	42103	Copebranch	41339
Cat Creek	40380	Claysville	41064	Coral Hill	42141
Catlettsburg	41129	Clay Village	40065	Coral Ridge (Jefferson County)	40118
Caudell	41858	Clear Creek	40977	Corbin	40701-02
Causey	41777	Clear Creek Springs	40977	For specific Corbin Zip Codes call (606) 528-3912	
Cave City	42127	Clearfield	40313	Cordell	41124
Cavehill	42274	Clear Run	42347	Cordia	41701
Cave Ridge	42129	Cleaton	42332	Cordova	41010
Cave Spring	42276	Clementsville	42539	Corey	41142
Cawood	40815	Clemons	41719	Corinth (Grant County)	41010
Cayce	42041	Cleopatra	42327	Corinth (Logan County)	42276
Cecil	42001	Clermont	40110		
Cecilia	42724	Cliff (Part of Prestonsburg)	41653		
Cedar Bluff	42445				

208 KENTUCKY Cork-Earlington

	ZIP
Cork	42129
Corn Creek	40006
Corners	40146
Cornette	40729
Cornettsville	41731
Cornishville	40330
Corydon	42406
Costelow	42276
Cote	40828
Cottageville	41179
Cottle	41412
Cottonburg	40475
Country Club Heights	41056
Country Lane Estates	40601
Country Manor	40065
Countryside	40059
Country Village	40014
Counts Cross Roads	41164
Covedale	41179
Covington	41011-18
For specific Covington Zip Codes call (606) 261-4425	
Cowan	41039
Cow Creek (Estill County)	40472
Cowcreek (Owsley County)	41314
Coxs Creek	40013
Coxton	40831
Crab Orchard	40419
Cracker	41649
Crailhope	42214
Craintown	41041
Crane Nest	40906
Cranetown	40324
Craney	40351
Cranks	40820
Cranston	40351
Crawford (Laurel County)	40741
Crawford (Perry County)	41719
Crayne	42033
Craynor	41614
Creal	42764
Creekmore	42649
Creekside	40222
Creekville	40962
Creelsboro	42629
Crenshaw	40071
Crescent Hill (Part of Louisville)	40206
Crescent Park	41017
Crescent Springs	41016
Cressmont	41311
Crestmoor (Part of Bowling Green)	42101
Creston	42539
Crestview	41076
Crestview Hills	41017
Crestview Hills Mall (Part of Crestview Hills)	41017
Crestwood (Fayette County)	40503
Crestwood (Franklin County)	40601
Crestwood (Oldham County)	40014
Creswell	42411
Crider	42445
Crittenden	41030
Crix	40313
Croakes	40069
Crockett (Bell County)	40977
Crockett (Morgan County)	41413
Crocus	42741
Crofton	42217
Croley	42031
Cromona	41810
Cromwell	42333
Cropper	40057
Crossgate	40222
Cross Keys	40065
Crossland	42049
Cross Roads	42256
Crown	41811
Crowtown	42445
Crummies	40815
Crutchfield	42041
Crystal	40420
Crystal Lake	40031
Cuba	42066
Cubage	40856
Cub Run	42729
Culbertson	41129
Cullen	42437
Culver	41211
Culvertown	40051
Cumberland	40823
Cumberland City	42602
Cumberland College (Part of Williamsburg)	40769
Cumminsville	41004
Cundiff	42730
Cunningham (Carlisle County)	42035

	ZIP
Cunningham (Hickman County)	42031
Cupio	40177
Curdsville (Daviess County)	42334
Curdsville (Mercer County)	40310
Curt	41339
Custer	40115
Cutshin	41732
Cutuno	41439
Cuzick	40475
Cyclone	42166
Cynthiana	41031
Dabney	42501
Dabolt	40421
Dahl	42501
Daisy	41733
Dal	40769
Dalesburg (Breathitt County)	41314
Dalesburg (Fleming County)	41041
Dalton	42445
Damron	41572
Dan (Menifee County)	40387
Dan (Ohio County)	42349
Dana	41615
Danby	42276
Daniel Boone	42442
Daniels Creek	41265
Danleytown	41144
Dants	40037
Danville	40422
Darfork	41701
Dartmont	40828
Davella	41214
David	41616
Davis	40370
Davis Branch	41129
Davisburg	40977
Davis Cross Roads	42268
Davison Station	42361
Davisport	41262
Davistown (Garrard County)	40444
Davistown (Woodford County)	40347
Dawson Springs	42408
Day	41858
Dayhoit	40824
Daylight	42408
Daysboro	41332
Daysville	42276
Dayton	41074
Deane	41812
Deatsville	40016
Debord	41214
Decker	42721
DeCoursey (Part of Taylor Mill)	41015
Decoy	41321
Dee Acres	42366
Deep Spring (Part of Lexington)	40505
Deering Heights	40272
Deer Lick	42256
Defiance	41760
Defoe	40017
Defries	42722
Dehart	41472
De Koven	42459
Delafield (Part of Bowling Green)	42101
Delaplain	40324
Delaware	42373
Delia	41097
Dellville	40011
Delmer	42544
Delphia	41735
Delta	42613
Delvinta	41311
Dema	41859
Democrat	41858
De Mossville	41033
Demplytown	40014
Denison	42729
Denney	42633
Dennis	42276
Denniston	40316
Denton	41132
Denver	41215
Depoy	42336
Dermont	42301
Devon	41042
Devondale (Part of Graymoor-Devondale)	40222
Dewdrop	41171
Dewitt	40930
Dexter	42036
Dexterville	42261
Diablock	41701
Diamond	42404
Diamond Springs	42256
Dice	41736
Dimple	42261

	ZIP
Dingus	41417
Dinwood	41619
Dione	40823
Dishman Springs	40906
Disputanta	40456
Dix Fork	41564
Dixie (Harlan County)	40849
Dixie (Henderson County)	42406
Dixie (Kenton County)	41017
Dixie Bend	42558
Dixie Manor Shopping Center	40258
Dixie Plantation (Part of Lexington)	40505
Dixon	42409
Dixville	40330
Dizney	40825
Dobbins	41180
Dock	41653
Doddy	42164
Doe Creek	40336
Doe Run	40108
Doe Valley Estates	40108
Dogcreek	42729
Dogtown	42025
Dog Walk (Lincoln County)	40419
Dogwalk (Ohio County)	42766
Dogwood	42051
Donaldson	42211
Donansburg	42743
Donerail (Part of Lexington)	40505
Dongola	41858
Dony	41647
Dortha	40701
Dorton	41520
Dorton Branch	40977
Do Stop	42721
Dot	42202
Dougan Town (Part of Burkesville)	42717
Douglas	41560
Douglass Hills	40243
Dover	41034
Downtown (Part of Louisville)	40201
Doylesville	40475
Dozier Heights (Part of Madisonville)	42431
Draffenville	42025
Draffin	41521
Drake	42128
Drakesboro	42337
Draper	40828
Drennon Springs	40011
Dressen (Part of Harlan)	40831
Dreyfus	40426
Drift	41619
Dripping Spring	42171
Drip Rock	40336
Druid Hills	40207
Drum	42501
Dry Creek	41862
Dryfork (Barren County)	42131
Dry Fork (Pike County)	41561
Dryhill	41749
Dry Ridge	41035
Dublin	42039
Dubre	42731
Duckers	40347
Duckrun	40769
Duco	41465
Duff	42754
Duganville	40330
Dukedom	42085
Dukes	42348
Dulaney	42445
Duluth	40403
Dunbar	42219
Duncan (Casey County)	40442
Duncan (Mercer County)	40330
Duncannon	40475
Dundee	42338
Dunham (Part of Jenkins)	41537
Dunlap	41524
Dunleary	41522
Dunmor	42339
Dunnville	42528
Dunraven	41754
Durbin	41129
Durbintown	41003
Duval	40324
Dwale	41621
Dwarf	41739
Dycusburg	42037
Dyer	40115
Dykes	42501
Eadsville	42633
Eagle Creek	40363
Eagle Hill	41046
Eagle Station	41083
Earlington	42410

Earnestville-Foxport KENTUCKY 209

Name	ZIP
Earnestville	41314
East Bernstadt	40729
Easterday	41008
Eastern	41622
East Fork	42129
East Frankfort (Part of Frankfort)	40601
East Hickman	40356
East Jenkins (Part of Jenkins)	41537
Eastland (Part of Maysville)	41056
Eastland Park (Fayette County)	40505
Eastland Park (Warren County)	42103
Eastland Shopping Center (Part of Lexington)	40505
East McDowell	41647
Easton	42343
East Pineville	40977
East Point	41216
East Union	40311
Eastview	42732
Eastwood (Franklin County)	40601
Eastwood (Jefferson County)	40018
Ebenezer (Mercer County)	40372
Ebenezer (Monroe County)	42167
Ebenezer (Muhlenberg County)	42337
Eberle	40447
Echo	42154
Echols	42340
Echo Point	42518
Echo Valley	40031
Eddyville	42038
Eddyville Shores	42038
Edenton	40475
Edgewater	41534
Edgewood	41017
Edmonton	42129
Edna	41419
Edsel	41180
Edwards	42256
Eglon	40447
Egypt	40430
Eighty Eight	42130
Ekron	40117
Elamton	41472
Elba	42327
Elcomb	40831
Eldridge	41149
Eifie	42766
Elgin	42501
Eli	42642
Elihu	42501
Elizabeth	40361
Elizabethtown	42701-02
For specific Elizabethtown Zip Codes call (502) 765-7310	
Elizaville	41037
Elkatawa	41339
Elk Creek	40023
Elkfork	41421
Elk Horn	42733
Elkhorn City	41522
Elk Lake Shore	40359
Elkton	42220
Ella	42728
Ellington	42752
Elliottville	40317
Ellisburg	40437
Elliston (Grant County)	41171
Elliston (Madison County)	40475
Ellisville	40311
Ellmitch	42343
Ellwood	41538
Elmburg	40057
Elmer Davis Lake	40359
Elmrock	41640
Elmville	40379
Elna	41219
Elsie	41422
Elsinore	40601
Elsmere	41018
Elswick	41538
Elva	42082
Elys	40939
Emanuel	40734
Emerling	40854
Emerson	41135
Eminence	40019
Emlyn	40730
Emma	41653
Emmalena	41740
Empire	42442
Endee	41314
Endicott	41626
End of Line	41667
Engle	41727
English	41008

Name	ZIP
Ennis	42337
Enon	42411
Ensor	42301
Enterprise	41164
Eolia	40826
Epleys	42276
Epperson	42001
Epson	41439
Epworth	41189
Eriline	40931
Erlanger	41018
Ermine	41815
Erose	40970
Esco	41501
Essie	40827
Estep	41230
Estesburg	40489
Estill	41627
Esto	42642
Ethridge	41095
Etna	42567
Etoile	42131
Etterwood	40324
Etty	41572
Eubank	42567
Eunice	42728
Evanston	41340
Evarts	40828
Eveleigh	42754
Ever	41465
Everett (Logan County)	42256
Everett (Todd County)	42280
Evergreen	40601
Eversole	41314
Ewing	41039
Ewingford	40006
Ewington	40353
Exie	42743
Ezel	41425
Faber	40701
Fagan	40322
Fairbanks (Graves County)	42079
Fairbanks (Owen County)	40359
Fairdale (Jefferson County)	40118
Fairdealing	42025
Fairfield (Breckinridge County)	40144
Fairfield (Nelson County)	40020
Fair Grounds (Part of Maysville)	41056
Fairland	42602
Fairlane Acres	40065
Fairmeade	40207
Fairmont	42404
Fairplay	42735
Fairview (Anderson County)	40342
Fairview (Boyd County)	41101
Fairview (Christian County)	42221
Fairview (Fleming County)	41039
Fairview (Kenton County)	41015
Fairview (Lyon County)	42038
Fairview (Whitley County)	40769
Fairview Heights (Part of Frankfort)	40601
Fairview Hill	41146
Fairway (Part of Lexington)	40502
Falcon	41426
Fall Rock	40932
Fallsburg	41230
Falls of Rough	40119
Falmouth	41040
Fancy Farm	42039
Fannin	41171
Fariston	40741
Farler	41774
Farmers	40351
Farmers Mill	40817
Farmersville	42445
Farmington	42040
Farraday	41855
Farristown	40403
Faubush	42532
Faulconer	40422
Faxon	42071
Faye	41171
Fayette Mall (Part of Lexington)	40503
Faywood	40383
Fearisville	41179
Fearsville	42240
Feathersburg	42733
Federal Correctional Institution	41101
Fedscreek	41524
Fee	40863
Feliciana	42085
Felty	40962
Fencroft	40272
Fentress McMahon	40119
Fenwick	40069
Ferguson (Logan County)	42276

Name	ZIP
Ferguson (Pulaski County)	42533
Ferguson Creek (Part of Pikeville)	41501
Fern Creek (Jefferson County)	40291
Ferndale	40977
Fernleaf	41034
Fern View	40291
Ferrells Creek	41513
Fielden	41177
Fieldstone Acres	40065
Figg	40065
Fillmore	41323
Fincastle	40222
Finchville	40022
Finley	42736
Finney	42141
Firebrick	41137
Firmantown	40383
Fisher	42754
Fisherville	40023
Fishtrap	41557
Fiskburg	41033
Fisty	41743
Fitch	41164
Fitchburg	40472
Five Forks	41230
Fivemile	41339
Fixer	41397
Flag Fork	40601
Flag Spring	41007
Flaherty	40175
Flanary	41548
Flat	41301
Flat Fork	41427
Flatgap	41219
Flat Lick	40935
Flat Rock (Caldwell County)	42411
Flat Rock (McCreary County)	42653
Flat Rock (Rockcastle County)	40460
Flat Rock (Simpson County)	42134
Flatwoods	41139
Fleet	42140
Fleming (Part of Fleming-Neon)	41840
Fleming-Neon	41840
Flemingsburg	41041
Flemingsburg Junction	41041
Flener	42261
Fletcher	40741
Flingsville	41030
Flint Springs	42349
Flippin	42167
Floral	42348
Florence	41042
Florress	41472
Flosie	42613
Flournoy	42437
Floyd	42567
Floydsburg	40014
Fogertown	40936
Folsom	41035
Folsomdale	42051
Fonde	40940
Fonthill	42642
Foraker	41429
Ford	40320
Fords Branch	41526
Fordsville	42343
Forest Cottage	42717
Forest Grove	40391
Forest Hill (Part of Paducah)	42001
Forest Hills (Jefferson County)	40299
Forest Hills (Kenton County)	41015
Forest Hills (Pike County)	41527
Forkton	42167
Forrest Park (Part of Winchester)	40391
Fort Campbell	42223
Fort Campbell North	42223
Fort Knox (Hardin County)	40121
Fort Mitchell	41017
Fort Spring (Part of Lexington)	40504
Fort Thomas	41075
Fort Wright	41011
Foster	41043
Fount	40999
Fountain Run	42133
Four Corners	40162
Fourmile	40939
Four Oaks	41040
Fourseam	41701
Fox	40336
Foxboro	40223
Fox Chase	40165
Fox Creek	40342
Foxport	41093

210 KENTUCKY Foxtown-Harlan Gas

Name	ZIP
Foxtown	40447
Frakes	40940
Frances	42064
Francisville	41048
Frankfort	40601-22
For specific Frankfort Zip Codes call (502) 223-3447	
Franklin	42134-35
For specific Franklin Zip Codes call (502) 586-3322	
Franklin Cross Roads	42724
Franklin Mines	42064
Franklinton	40057
Frazer	42618
Fraziertown	40014
Fredericktown	40069
Fredonia	42411
Fredville	41430
Freeburn	41528
Freedom	42157
Freetown	42140
Free Union	42409
Fremont	42001
Frenchburg	40322
Fresh Meadows	40824
Frew	41776
Friendly Hills	40219
Frisby	42633
Fritz	41431
Frogtown (Fayette County)	40383
Frogtown (Marion County)	40033
Frogue	42714
Frozen Creek	41339
Fruithill	42217
Fry	42743
Fuget	41220
Fulgham	42031
Fulton	42041
Fultz	41143
Funston	42634
Furnace	40472
Fusonia	41774
Future City	42053
Gabbard	41364
Gabe	42743
Gadberry	42735
Gage	42056
Gainesville	42164
Gainesway (Part of Lexington)	40502
Gallup	41230
Galveston	41629
Gamaliel	42140
Gapcreek	42603
Gap in Knob	40165
Gapville	41433
Gardenside (Part of Lexington)	40504
Garden Springs (Part of Lexington)	40504
Garden Village	41501
Gardnersville	41033
Garfield	40140
Garlin	42728
Garner (Boyd County)	41168
Garner (Knott County)	41817
Garrard	40941
Garrett (Floyd County)	41630
Garrett (Meade County)	40117
Garrettsburg	42236
Garrison	41141
Garvin Ridge	41164
Gascon	42129
Gaskill (Part of Jenkins)	41537
Gasper	42206
Gates	40351
Gatewood	42348
Gatliff	40769
Gatun	40806
Gausdale	40906
Gaybourn	40383
Gays Creek	41745
Geddes	42134
Geneva (Henderson County)	42406
Geneva (Lincoln County)	40437
Gentrys Mill	42728
Georges Creek	41264
Georgetown (Harlan County)	40843
Georgetown (Scott County)	40324
Germantown	41044
Gertrude	41004
Gesling	41128
Gest	40057
Gethsemane	40051
Ghent	41045
Gibbs	40906
Gifford	41465
Gilbertsville (Marshall County)	42044

Name	ZIP
Gillem Branch	41219
Gilley	41818
Gillmore	41327
Gilpin	42539
Gilreath	42635
Gilstrap	42349
Gimlet	41164
Girdler	40943
Girkin	42101
Gishton	42325
Glasgow	42141-42
For specific Glasgow Zip Codes call (502) 651-8859	
Gleanings	40052
Glenarm	40014
Glencoe	41046
Glendale	42740
Glen Dean	40141
Glengary	40118
Glensboro	40342
Glens Fork	42741
Glen Springs	41179
Glenview (Daviess County)	42301
Glenview (Jefferson County)	40025
Glenview (Shelby County)	40065
Glenview Heights	40222
Glenview Hills	40222
Glenview Manor	40222
Glenville	42376
Glo	41666
Globe	41164
Glomawr	41701
Goddard	41093
Goering	42348
Goffs Corner	40391
Goforth	41040
Goins	40763
Goldbug	40769
Gold City	42134
Golden Ash	40831
Golden Meadows	40272
Golden Pond	42211
Golo	42054
Goochtown	42567
Goodluck	42129
Goodnight	42127
Goodwater	42501
Goody	41529
Goose Creek	40222
Goose Rock	40944
Gordon	41819
Gordon Ford	41412
Gordonsville	42276
Goshen	40026
Gott	42101
Grab	42743
Grace	40962
Gracey	42232
Gradyville	42742
Graefenburg	40601
Graham	42344
Graham Hill	42420
Grahamville	42086
Grahn	41142
Grancer	42287
Grand Rivers	42045
Grandview (Part of Tompkinsville)	42167
Grandview Heights (Part of Frankfort)	40601
Grange City	41049
Grangertown	42459
Grants Lick	41001
Grapevine (Part of Madisonville)	42431
Grassy Creek	41332
Grassy Lick	40353
Gratz	40327
Gravel Switch	40328
Gray	40734
Gray Hawk	40434
Graymoor-Devondale	40222
Grays Branch	41144
Grays Knob	40829
Grayson	41143
Grayson Springs	42726
Graysville	40146
Greasy Creek	41562
Great Crossing	40324
Grear	41472
Greeley	40420
Green	41164
Green Acres (Part of Danville)	40422
Greenbriar (Daviess County)	42301
Greenbriar (Marion County)	40033
Greenbriar (Oldham County)	40031
Greenbrier	40489
Greencastle	42270
Greendale (Part of Lexington)	40505

Name	ZIP
Green Fields Estates	40391
Green Grove	42714
Green Hall	41328
Green Hill (Jackson County)	40402
Greenhill (Warren County)	42103
Green Hills	42728
Greenland Park	40065
Greenmount	40741
Greenough	41534
Green River	42374
Green Road	40946
Greensburg	42743
Green Spring	40222
Greenup	41144
Greenville	42345
Greenwood (McCreary County)	42634
Greenwood (Pendleton County)	41006
Greenwood (Warren County)	42104
Greenwood Mall (Part of Bowling Green)	42104
Grefco	41164
Gregory	42633
Gregoryville	41143
Gresham	42743
Grethel	41631
Grider	42717
Griderville	42127
Griffin	42640
Griffith	42301
Griffytown (Part of Middletown)	40243
Grove Center	42437
Grubbs	42031
Grundy	42501
Guage	41329
Gubser Mill	41007
Guerrant	41339
Guffie	42327
Gulfco (Part of Ashland)	41101
Gullett	41441
Gulnare	41501
Gulston	40830
Gum Sulphur	40419
Gum Tree	42167
Gunlock	41632
Gunns Chapel	40444
Guston	40142
Guthrie	42234
Guthrie's Ridge	42752
Guy	42101
Gwinn Island	40422
Gypsy	41438
Habit	42366
Hackley	40444
Haddix	41331
Hadensville	42234
Hadley	42235
Hager	41439
Hagerhill	41222
Hail	42501
Halcom	41171
Haldeman	40329
Halfway	42150
Halifax	42164
Hall (Jessamine County)	40356
Hall (Knott County)	41840
Hallie	41821
Halls Gap	40489
Halls Store	42263
Halo	41633
Hamlin	42046
Hammackville	42286
Hammonville	42757
Hampton	42047
Hampton Manor (Part of Winchester)	40391
Handshoe	41640
Hanly	40356
Hannah	41124
Hansford	40456
Hanson	42413
Happy	41746
Happy Acre	42642
Happy Landing	40403
Hardburly	41747
Hardin	42048
Hardinsburg	40143
Hardin Springs	42712
Hard Money	42001
Hardshell	41348
Hardwick	42618
Hardy	41531
Hardyville	42746
Hare	40729
Hargett	40336
Harlan	40831
Harlan Crossroads	42167
Harlan Gas	40831

Harmony-Jenkinsville **KENTUCKY** 211

Name	ZIP
Harmony	40359
Harmony Lake Estates	40059
Harmony Village	40059
Harned	40144
Harold	41635
Harper	41465
Harreldsville	42256
Harrington Mill Estates	40065
Harris	41179
Harris Grove	42071
Harrisonville	40076
Harrodsburg	40330
Harrods Creek	40027
Hart	40741
Hartford	42347
Hartley	41572
Harveyton	41719
Harvy	42025
Haskingsville	42743
Hatcher	42718
Hatfield	41514
Hatton	40601
Hawesville	42348
Hayes	41040
Haynesville	42368
Hays	42171
Hays Crossing	40351
Hayslen	41719
Hayward	41173
Haywood	42141
Hazard	41701
Hazel	42049
Hazel Green	41332
Hazel Patch	40729
Head of Cedar	40379
Head of Grassy	41135
Headquarters	40311
Hearin	42404
Heath	42086
Hebbardsville	42420
Hebron	41048
Hebron Estates	40165
Hecla	42410
Hector	40962
Hedgeville	40444
Heekin	41097
Heenon	41545
Heflin	42347
Hegira	42717
Heidelberg	41333
Heidrick	40949
Heiner	41722
Helechawa	41332
Helena	41055
Hellier	41534
Helton	40840
Hemp Ridge	40076
Henderson	42420
Hendricks	41441
Hendron	42001
Henry Clay (Fayette County)	40502
Henry Clay (Pike County)	41542
Henryville	40311
Henshaw	42437
Hensley (Breckinridge County)	40146
Hensley (Clay County)	40962
Herbert	42368
Herd	40435
Hermitage Hills (Part of Lexington)	40505
Hermon	42234
Herndon (Christian County)	42236
Herndon (Scott County)	40324
Herron Hill	41189
Heselton	41179
Hesler	40359
Hestand	42151
Hi Acres (Part of Lexington)	40505
Hickman	42050
Hickman Hill	40601
Hickory	42051
Hickory Flat	42134
Hickory Grove (Cumberland County)	42752
Hickory Grove (McCreary County)	42638
Hickory Hill	40201
Hidalgo	42633
Hide-A-Way Hills	40359
High Bridge	40390
High Falls	41301
Highgrove	40013
High Knob	40402
Highland (Lincoln County)	40484
Highland (Simpson County)	42134
Highland Heights	41076
Highplains	40106
High Point	42086
Highsplint	40828
High Top	40741

Name	ZIP
Highview (Jefferson County)	40228
Highview (Ohio County)	42320
Highway	42602
Hignite	40965
Hi Hat	41636
Hikes Point (Part of Louisville)	40220
Hilda	40351
Hillcrest	40475
Hillendale	41095
Hill-N-Dale	40065
Hill Ridge	40299
Hills and Dales	40222
Hillsboro	41049
Hillsdale	42134
Hillside	42330
Hilltop (Fleming County)	41039
Hilltop (Grant County)	41097
Hilltop (Logan County)	42202
Hill Top (McCreary County)	42647
Hillview (Bullitt County)	40229
Hillview (Edmonson County)	42207
Hilton	41701
Hima	40951
Himyar	40906
Hinda Heights (Part of Lexington)	40502
Hindman	41822
Hinkle	40953
Hinkleville	42056
Hinton	41010
Hippo	41637
Hiram	40823
Hisel	40447
Hiseville	42152
Hislope	42544
Hitchins	41146
Hite	41649
Hitesville	42437
Hobson	42718
Hode	41267
Hodgenville	42748
Hogue	42553
Holbrook	41097
Holiday Hills (Part of Lexington)	40502
Holland	42153
Holliday	41474
Hollonville	41301
Hollow Bill	42256
Hollow Creek	40228
Hollybush	41823
Hollyhill	42635
Hollyvilla	40118
Hollywood (Part of Lexington)	40502
Holmes Mill	40843
Holt (Breckinridge County)	40143
Holt (Lawrence County)	41230
Holt (Muhlenberg County)	42332
Holy Cross	40037
Homer	42276
Honaker	41639
Honeybee	42634
Honey Fork	41513
Hooktown	41031
Hootentown	40391
Hope	40334
Hopeful Heights (Part of Florence)	41042
Hopewell	41143
Hopkinsville	42240-41
For specific Hopkinsville Zip Codes call (502) 886-5259	
Hopson	42445
Horntown	42642
Horse Branch	42349
Horse Cave	42749
Horse Creek Junction	40962
Horse Lick	40341
Horton	42320
Hoskinston	40844
Hosman	40977
Houston	41314
Houston Acres	40220
Hovious Ridge	42723
Howard	40177
Howards Creek	41331
Howardstown	40028
Howel	42262
Howe Valley	42724
Hubble	40444
Hubbs	40921
Huddy	41535
Hudgins	42782
Hudson	40145
Hueys Corners	41091
Hueysville	41640
Huff	42250
Hulen	40845
Humble	42642

Name	ZIP
Hummel	40492
Hunnewell	41121
Hunt	40391
Hunter	41641
Hunters	40004
Hunters Grove	40258
Hunters Hollow	40165
Hunters Trace	40216
Huntertown	40383
Huntington Woods	40601
Huntsville	42251
Hurley	40447
Hurricane Hills	40107
Hurst	41301
Hurstborne Estates	40222
Hurstbourne	40222
Hurstbourne Acres	40220
Hustonville	40437
Hutch	40965
Hutchison	40361
Hyattsville	40444
Hyden	41749
Hydro	42171
Iberia	42726
Ibex	41164
Ice	41858
Ida	42602
Idamay	41311
Idle Hour (Part of Lexington)	40502
Idlewild	41005
Iisley	42408
Independence	41051
Independence Station	41051
Index	41472
Indiancreek	40734
Indian Fields	40391
Indian Hills (Boyle County)	40422
Indian Hills (Carroll County)	41008
Indian Hills (Hardin County)	42701
Indian Hills (Jefferson County)	40207
Indian Hills (Russell County)	42642
Indian Hills (Scott County)	40324
Indian Hills (Warren County)	42103
Indian Hills Cherokee Section	40207
Indian Lake	42348
Indian Trail Square	40219
Inez	41224
Ingle	42536
Ingleside	42053
Ingram	40955
Insco	42276
Insko	41443
Inverness Estates	40601
Iron Hill	41143
Iron Hill Camp	42055
Ironville	41101
Iroquois (Part of Louisville)	40214
Iroquois Heights	40214
Iroquois Vista (Part of Louisville)	40214
Irvine	40336
Irvington	40146
Irvins Store	42642
Island	42350
Island City	41338
Isom	41824
Isonville	41149
Iuka	42045
Ivel	41642
Ivis	41822
Ivor	41007
Ivy Grove	40939
Ivyton	41444
Jabez	42532
Jackhorn	41825
Jacks Creek	40931
Jackson	41339
Jacksonville (Bourbon County)	40361
Jacksonville (Shelby County)	40003
Jackstown	40311
Jacktown	40009
Jacobs	41150
Jamboree	41536
Jamestown	42629
Jarvis	40906
Jason	41714
Jason Ridge	42519
Jasper Bend	41828
Jax	41751
Jeff	40299
Jeffersontown	40299
Jeffersonville	40337
Jeffrey	42157
Jellico	40769
Jellicocreek	40769
Jenkins	41537
Jenkinsville	40040

212 KENTUCKY Jenn'y Creek-Little Dixie

	ZIP		ZIP		ZIP
Jenn'y Creek	41215	Kidder	42518	Layman	40819
Jenson	40977	Kidds Crossing	42611	Laynesville	41635
Jep Hill	40456	Kidds Store	40437	Leach	41129
Jeptha	41472	Kiddville	40353	Leafdale	42748
Jeremiah	41826	Kildav	40828	Leander	41228
Jericho (Henry County)	40068	Kilgore	41168	Leatha	41473
Jericho (Larue County)	42748	Kimbrell	40336	Leatherwood	41756
Jerico	42256	Kimper	41539	Lebanon	40033
Jeriel	41143	Kinchloes Bluff	42330	Lebanon Junction	40150
Jessietown	40033	Kingbee	42516	Leburn	41831
Jetson	42252	Kings Creek	41858	Leckieville	41529
Jett	40601	Kings Forest	40165	Lecta	42141
Jetts Creek	41314	Kingsley	40205	Ledbetter	42058
Jewell City	42456	Kings Mountain	40442	Ledocio	41201
Jimtown (Fayette County)	40505	Kingston (Fayette County)	40505	Lee City	41342
Jimtown (Washington County)	40069	Kingston (Madison County)	40403	Leeco	41343
Jinks	40336	Kingswood	40144	Leesburg	41031
Job	41225	Kinniconick	41179	Lees Lick	41031
Jock	42207	Kino	42141	Leestown (Part of Frankfort)	40601
Johnetta	40460	Kirbyton	42023	Lee Villa Circles	40165
Johns Creek	41265	Kirk	40143	Legrand	42749
Johnson Bottom	41528	Kirkland	40330	Leighton	40336
Johnsontown	40272	Kirkmansville	42220	Leitchfield	42754-55
Johns Run	41152	Kirksey	42054	For specific Leitchfield Zip Codes call (502) 259-3087	
Johnsville	41043	Kirksville	40475		
Jonancy	41538	Kirkwood	40372	Leitchfield Crossing	42765
Jonestown (Part of Lexington)	40505	Kirkwood Springs	42408	Lejunior	40849
		Kiserton	40361	Lemon	42327
Jonesville (Grant County)	41052	Kite	41828	Lemons Mill	40324
Jonesville (Hart County)	42757	Kitts	40831	Lenarue	40818
Jonican	41557	Knifley	42753	Lennut	41729
Joppa	42728	Knob Lick	42154	Lenore	40013
Jordan	38261	Knobview	40065	Lenox	41447
Josephine	40370	Knottsville	42366	Lenoxburg	41040
Joy	42047	Knowlton	40380	Leon	41143
Joyes	40065	Knoxfork	40906	Lerose	41344
J'Town Shopping Center (Part of Jeffersontown)	40299	Knoxville	41097	Lesbas	40741
		Kodak	41773	Leslie	42717
Juan	41339	Kona	41829	Letcher	41832
Judio	42752	Korea	40387	Letitia	41175
Judson	40444	Kosmosdale	40272	Levee	40337
Judyville	40311	Kragon	41339	Level Green	40456
Julien	42232	Kris	41666	Levi	41314
Julip	40769	Kronos	42328	Levias	42064
Jumbo	40484	Krypton	41754	Lewis	40828
Junction City	40440	Kuttawa	42055	Lewisburg (Logan County)	42256
Justell	41605	Kyrock	42285	Lewisburg (Mason County)	41056
Justice	42256	Labascus	42539	Lewis Creek	40810
Justiceville	41501	La Center	42056	Lewisport	42351
Kaler	42051	Lacey	41465	Lexie	41301
Kaliopi	41749	Lacie	40075	Lexington	40501-96
Kansas	42069	Lackey	41643	For specific Lexington Zip Codes call (606) 231-6700	
Karlus	42629	Lacon	42712		
Katharyn	40177	Laden	40865	Lexington-Bluegrass Army Depot	40507
Kavanaugh	41129	La Fayette	42254		
Kayjay	40906	La Grange	40031	Lexington Mall (Part of Lexington)	40502
Keaton	41226	Lair	41031		
Keavy	40737	Lake	40741	Liberty (Casey County)	42539
Keefer	41010	Lake Carnico	40311	Liberty (Webster County)	42409
Keene	40339	Lake City	42045	Liberty Heights (Fayette County)	40505
Keeneland	40223	Lake Dreamland	40216		
Kehoe	41141	Lake Louisvilla	40014	Liberty Heights (Nicholas County)	40311
Keith	40846	Lakeside Park	41017		
Kelat	41003	Lakeview Acres (Part of Lexington)	40502	Liberty Road	41472
Kellacey	41472			Lick Branch	41472
Kelly	42240	Lakeview Heights	40351	Lickburg	41465
Kellyville	42728	Lakeville	41465	Lick Creek	41540
Keltner	42761	Lakeway Shore	42071	Lick Fork	40313
Kemp	42761	Lamasco	42038	Licking River	41472
Ken Acres	40065	Lamb	42155	Lick Skillet (Logan County)	42265
Kendall Springs	40360	Lambert	41636	Lickskillet (Meade County)	40175
Kenmont	41751	Lambric	41340	Lida	40741
Kennianna	42046	Lamero	40341	Liggett	40831
Keno	42558	Lamont (McCracken County)	42053	Ligon	41604
Kensee	40769			Liletown	42743
Kenshores	42046	Lamont (Perry County)	41727	Lily	40740
Kenton	41053	Lancaster	40444	Limaburg	41005
Kenton Hills	41011	Lancelot Estates	40324	Limestone	41164
Kentontown	41064	Lancer (Part of Prestonsburg)	41653	Limestone Springs	40165
Kenton Vale	41015			Limeville	41175
Kentucky Correctional Institution for Women	40056	Landsaw	41301	Limp	42732
		Langdon Place	40222	Lincoln	40962
Kentucky Oaks Mall (Part of Paducah)	42001	Langley	41645	Lincoln Ridge	40067
		Langnau	40741	Lincolnshire	40220
Kentucky State Reformatory	40031	Lansdowne (Part of Lexington)	40502	Lindseyville	42257
Kenvir	40847			Linefork	41833
Kenwick (Part of Lexington)	40502	Larkslane	41817	Linton	42211
Kenwood	41220	Latonia (Part of Covington)	41015	Linwood (Grayson County)	42726
Kerby Knob	40441	Latonia Lakes	41015	Linwood (Hart County)	42757
Kernie	41439	Laura	41250	Lionilli	41537
Kern Orchard	42459	Laurel	41144	Lisletown	40391
Kessinger	42765	Laurel Creek	40962	Lisman	42404
Keswick	40769	Laurel Fork	40940	Litsey	40069
Kettle	42752	Laurel Gap	41129	Littcarr	41834
Kettlecamp	41522	Laurel Ridge	42259	Little	41346
Kettle Island	40958	Lawhorn Hill	42539	Little Barren	42743
Kevil	42053	Lawrenceburg	40342	Little Bear Creek	42044
Kewanee	41526	Lawrenceville (rural)	41097	Little Creek	40902
Keysburg	42204	Lawrenceville	41010	Little Cypress	42029
Keyser Heights	41501	Lawson	41339	Little Dixie	41501
		Lawton	41153		

Little Georgetown-Memphis Junction KENTUCKY 213

	ZIP		ZIP		ZIP
Little Georgetown (Part of Lexington)	40504	NKC Hospitals	40202	Mammoth Cave	42259
Little Hickman	40356	Saints Mary and Elizabeth Hospital	40215	Manchester	40962
Little Mount	40071	Veterans Administration		Manco	41534
Little Muddy	42261	Medical Center	40202	Manda	42333
Little Needmore	40422			Mangum	42516
Little Rock	40311	*HOTELS/MOTELS*		Manila	41233
Little Sandy	41171	The Brown-A Hilton Hotel	40202	Manitou	42436
Little Tar Springs	42348	Brownsboro Inn	40207	Mannington	42217
Little Texas (Part of Lexington)	40504	Galt House	40202	Mannsville	42758
Littleton	40962	Hyatt Regency Louisville	40202	Manor Creek	40222
Little Valley	42442	Seelbach/Doubletree Hotel	40202	Manse	40461
Littrell	42752			Manton (Floyd County)	41648
Livermore	42352	*MILITARY INSTALLATIONS*		Manton (Washington County)	40037
Livia	42327	Kentucky Air National Guard, FB6161	40213	Manuel	41701
Livingston	40445	Naval Ordnance Station, Louisville	40214	Maple Grove (Jefferson County)	40229
Lloyd	41156	United States Army Engineer District, Louisville	40201	Maple Grove (Trigg County)	42211
Load	41144			Maple Mount	42356
Lockards Creek	40941			Maplesville	40741
Lockport	40036			Marcellus	40444
Lockwood Estates	40014	Lovelaceville	42060	Marcum	40962
Locust	40045	Lovely	41231	Marcus	41003
Locust Grove (Clark County)	40391	Lowell	40461	Maretburg	40456
Locust Grove (Pendleton County)	41040	Lower Gillmore	41327	Mariba	40345
Locust Hill	40144	Lower Hunters	40216	Mariemont	40258
Lodiburg	40146	Lower Kings Addition	41175	Marion	42064
Logana	40356	Lower Pompey	41501	Mark	42501
Logansport	42261	Lowes	42061	Marksbury	40444
Logantown	40484	Lowmansville	41232	Marlowe	41858
Loglick	40391	Loyall	40854	Marrowbone	42759
Log Mountain	40977	Lucas	42156	Marshall	41056
Logville	41465	Lucile	41171	Marshallville	41452
Lola	42059	Lucky Fork	41364	Marshes Siding	42631
Lombard	40380	Lucky Stop	40337	Martha	41159
London	40741	Ludlow	41016	Martha Mills	41041
Lone	41347	Luner	40456	Martin	41649
Lone Oak	42001	Lusby's Mill	40359	Martinsville	42159
Lone Star	42713	Luther Luckett Correctional Complex	40031	Martwick	42330
Long Fork	41572	Luzon	42409	Mary	41301
Longlick	40379	Lykins	41401	Mary Alice	40964
Long Ridge	40359	Lynch	40855	Marydale	41018
Long Run	40023	Lyndale	40391	Marydell	40751
Long View	42701	Lyndon	40222	Maryhill Estates	40207
Longview Estates	40422	Lynn	41144	Maryville (Part of Hillview)	40229
Lookout	41542	Lynncamp	40701	Mashfork	41465
Loradale (Part of Lexington)	40505	Lynn City	42372	Mason (Grant County)	41054
Loretto	40037	Lynn Grove	42071	Mason (Magoffin County)	41465
Lost Creek	41348	Lynnview	40213	Masonic Home (Part of Louisville)	40041
Lost River	42101	Lynnville	42063	Masonville	42376
Lot	40769	Lyons	40051	Massac	42001
Lothair (Part of Hazard)	41701	Lytten	41157	Matanzas	42328
Lotus	40016	Mac	42718	Matlock	42104
Louden	40769	McAfee	40330	Matthew	41472
Louellen	40828	McAndrews	41543	Mattingly	40111
Louisa	41230	McBrayer	40342	Mattoon	42064
Louisville	**40201-99**	McCarr	41544	Mattoxtown	40505
For specific Louisville Zip Codes call (502) 454-1650		McClure	41250	Maud	40069
		McCombs	41545	Maulden	40486
COLLEGES & UNIVERSITIES		McCreary	40444	Mavity	41129
Southern Baptist Theological Seminary	40280	McCreight	40999	Maxie	40769
Spalding University	40203	McDaniels	40152	Maxine	42776
University of Louisville	40292	McDowell	41647	Maxwell	42376
		Macedonia (Breathitt County)	41370	Mayfield	42066
FINANCIAL INSTITUTIONS		Macedonia (Christian County)	42217	Mayflower	41501
Citizens Fidelity Bank and Trust Company	40202			Mayking	41837
The Cumberland Federal Savings Bank	40202	Macedonia (Jackson County)	40447	Maynard	42164
First Kentucky Trust Company	40202	Maceo	42355	Mayo	40330
First National Bank of Louisville	40202	McGowan	42445	Mayo Village	41501
Future Federal Savings Bank	40207	McHenry	42354	Mays Lick	41055
Great Financial Federal	40270	McKee	40447	Maysville	41056
Liberty National Bank and Trust Company of Louisville	40202	McKinney	40448	Maytown	41472
		McKinneysburg	41040	Maywood	40484
Mid-America Bank of Louisville and Trust Company	40201	Mackville	40040	Mazie	41160
		Mc Neely Lake	40229	Meador	42164
Republic Bank & Trust Company	40202	McQuady	40153	Meadow Branch	41301
		McRoberts	41835	Meadowbrook (Clark County)	40391
Stock Yards Bank & Trust Company	40206	McVeigh	41546	Meadowbrook (Shelby County)	40065
		McVille	41005	Meadowbrook Farm	40223
HOSPITALS		McWhorter	40741	Meadow Creek	40759
Baptist Hospital East	40207	Madisonville	42431	Meadowrun	40065
Humana Hospital-Audubon	40217	Madrid	42754	Meadowthorpe (Part of Lexington)	40505
Humana Hospital-Suburban	40207	Magan	42343	Meadow Vale	40222
Humana Hospital-University of Louisville	40202	Maggard	41465	Meadowview	40475
Jewish Hospital	40202	Maggie	42211	Meadowview Estates	40220
Methodist Evangelical Hospital	40201	Magnolia	42757	Meally	41234
		Magoffin	41464	Means	40346
		Main Street (Part of Pikeville)	41501	Medora	40272
		Majestic	41547	Meece	42511
		Major	41314	Meeting Creek	42732
		Malaga	41301	Melber	42069
		Mallie	41836	Melbourne	41059
		Mall in St. Matthews, The (Part of St. Matthews)	40207	Meldrum	40965
		Malone	41451	Mell	42743
		Maloneton	41158	Melody Lake	40051
				Melvin	41650
				Memphis Junction	42101

214 KENTUCKY Mendota Village-Norwood

Name	ZIP
Mendota Village	41222
Mentor	41007
Meredith	42754
Meridian	41006
Merrimac	40009
Merry Oaks	42171
Mershons	40729
Meshack	42167
Meta	41501
Mexico	42064
Midas	41640
Middleburg	42541
Middlefork	40447
Middlesboro	40965
Middleton	42134
Middleton Heights (Part of Shelbyville)	40065
Middletown (Jefferson County)	40243
Middletown (Madison County)	40403
Middletown (Russell County)	42629
Midland (Bath County)	40371
Midland (Muhlenberg County)	42325
Midway (Calloway County)	42049
Midway (Crittenden County)	42064
Midway (Meade County)	40142
Midway (Woodford County)	40347
Milburn	42070
Mildred	40447
Milford	41061
Millard	41562
Mill Creek	41055
Milledgeville	40437
Miller (Fulton County)	42050
Miller (Nicholas County)	40311
Millersburg	40348
Millers Creek	42472
Millerstown	42726
Million	40475
Mill Pond	40962
Millport	42372
Mills	40970
Millseat	41101
Mill Springs	42632
Millstone	41838
Milltown (Adair County)	42761
Milltown (Nicholas County)	40350
Millville	40601
Millwood	42762
Milner	40383
Milo	41262
Milton	40045
Mima	41456
Minerva	41062
Miniard	41763
Minnie	41651
Minor Lane Heights	40213
Minorsville	40379
Mintonville	42539
Miracle	40856
Mistletoe	41351
Mitchellsburg	40452
Mize	41352
Moberly	40475
Mockingbird Valley	40207
Moct	41385
Modoc	42714
Molus	40819
Monford	42252
Monica	41362
Monitor	40006
Monkeys Eyebrow	42056
Monroe	42746
Montclair (Fayette County)	40502
Montclair (Shelby County)	40065
Monterey	40359
Montgomery	42211
Montgomerys Mill	42743
Monticello	42633
Montpelier	42763
Montrose (Part of Lexington)	40505
Montrose Park (Part of Frankfort)	40601
Mooleyville	40143
Moon	41457
Moon Lake Estates	40324
Moorefield	40350
Moores Creek	40402
Moores Ferry	40371
Mooresville	40069
Moorland	40223
Moorman	42357
Moranburg	41056
Morcoal	41543
Morehead	40351
Moreland	40437
Morgan	41040

Name	ZIP
Morganfield	42437
Morgantown	42261
Morningglory	41031
Morning View	41063
Morrill	40455
Morris Fork	41314
Mortiner Station	42202
Mortons Gap	42440
Mortonsville	40383
Moscow	42031
Moseleyville	42301
Mossy Bottom	41501
Motley	42103
Mount Aerial	42128
Mountain Ash	40769
Mountain Top	41164
Mountain Valley	41339
Mount Auburn	41006
Mount Carmel	41041
Mount Eden	40046
Mount Gilead (Green County)	42743
Mount Gilead (Monroe County)	42167
Mount Hermon	42157
Mount Lebanon	40356
Mount Olive (Casey County)	42566
Mount Olive (Lee County)	41311
Mount Olivet	41064
Mount Pisgah	42633
Mount Pleasant (Ohio County)	42333
Mount Pleasant (Trimble County)	40006
Mount Salem	40437
Mount Sherman	42764
Mount Sterling	40353
Mount Tabor (Larue County)	42716
Mount Tabor (Todd County)	42220
Mount Union	42120
Mount Vernon (Rockcastle County)	40456
Mount Vernon (Scott County)	40324
Mount Victor	42104
Mount Victory	42501
Mount Washington	40047
Mount Zion (Allen County)	42164
Mount Zion (Grant County)	41035
Mount Zion (Pulaski County)	42553
Mousie	41839
Moutardier	42754
Mouthcard	41548
Moxley	40363
Mozelle	40858
Mud Camp	42717
Muddy Ford	40324
Mud Lick	42167
Muir (Part of Lexington)	40505
Mulberry	40065
Muldraugh	40155
Mulfordtown	42459
Mullikin Junction	42028
Mullins	40456
Mullins Addition	41501
Mummie	40486
Munfordville	42765
Murl	42633
Murphyfork	41332
Murphysville	41056
Murray	42071
Murray Hill	40222
Muses Mills	41065
Music	41168
Myers	40311
Myra	41549
Mystic	40146
Nancy	42544
Naomi	42544
Napfor	41754
Napier	40810
Naples	41101
Napoleon	41046
Narco (Part of Lexington)	40505
Narrows	42358
Narvel	42603
Nashtown	41189
Natlee	41010
Natural Bridge	40376
Nazareth	40048
Neafus	42766
Neave	41040
Nebo (Hopkins County)	42441
Nebo (Muhlenberg County)	42345
Ned	41339
Needmore (Ballard County)	42053
Needmore (Boyle County)	40422
Needmore (Caldwell County)	42445
Needmore (Madison County)	40426

Name	ZIP
Needmore (Shelby County)	40022
Nelse	41550
Nelson	42330
Nelsonville	40107
Neon (Part of Fleming-Neon)	41840
Neon Junction	41840
Neosheo	42134
Nepton	41039
Nerinx	40049
Nero	41265
Nevada	40330
Nevelsville	42653
Nevin	40342
Nevisdale	40754
New	40359
New Allen (Part of Allen)	41601
Newburg (Jefferson County)	40218
Newby	40475
New Camp	25661
New Castle	40050
New Columbus	41010
Newcombe	41149
New Concord	42076
New Cypress (Hickman County)	42031
New Cypress (Muhlenberg County)	42345
Newfound	40972
Newfoundland	41162
Newgarden	40121
New Haven	40051
New Hope	40052
New Liberty	40355
Newman	42301
New Market	40033
Newport	41071-76
For specific Newport Zip Codes call (606) 291-5250	
Newport Shopping Center (Part of Newport)	41071
New Providence	42049
New Roe	42120
New Salem (Crittenden County)	42064
New Salem (Lincoln County)	40437
Newstead	42240
New Stithton	40121
Newt	42743
Newtown	40324
New Zion (Jackson County)	40447
New Zion (Scott County)	40505
Niagara	42420
Nicholasville	40356
Nichols (Bullitt County)	40177
Nichols (Hickman County)	42031
Nicholson (Kenton County)	41051
Nicholson (Trigg County)	42215
Nickell	41332
Nigh	41524
Nina	40444
Nineteen	42320
Ninevah	40342
Nippa	41240
Noble	41317
Nobob	42166
Nocreek	42347
Noctor	41357
Node	42214
Noetown (Part of Middlesboro)	40965
Noland	40336
Nolansburg	40870
Nolin	42776
Nolin Lake Estates	42726
Nonesuch	40383
Nonnel	42337
Nora	42602
Norbourne Estates	40207
Norfleet	42544
Normal (Part of Ashland)	41101
Normal Heights (Part of Frankfort)	40601
Normandy	40071
North (Part of Lexington)	40505
North Corbin (Knox County)	40701
North Corbin (Laurel County)	40701
Northfield	40222
North Irvine	40336
North Lexington (Part of Lexington)	40505
North Middletown	40357
North Pleasureville (Part of Pleasureville)	40057
Northpoint Training Center	40310
Northtown	42749
Norton Branch	41168
Nortonville	42442
Norwood (Jefferson County)	40222

Norwood-Port Royal KENTUCKY 215

Name	ZIP
Norwood (Pulaski County)	42553
Nuckols	42352
Nugent Cross Roads	40383
Nugym	40902
Number One	42633
Oakdale (Breathitt County)	41339
Oakdale (McCracken County)	42001
Oak Forest	42164
Oak Grove (Christian County)	42262
Oak Grove (Ohio County)	42333
Oak Hill (Hopkins County)	42442
Oak Hill (Pulaski County)	42501
Oakland	42159
Oakland Mills	40311
Oaklawn Estates	41222
Oak Level	42025
Oakley	40729
Oak Ridge (Edmonson County)	42207
Oak Ridge (Kenton County)	41015
Oaks (Bell County)	40813
Oaks (Ohio County)	42343
Oak Street (Part of Louisville)	40210
Oakton	42077
Oakville	42263
O'Bannon	40223
Octavia	41543
Oddville	41031
Odessa	40360
Offutt	41237
Ogle	40962
Oil City	42141
Oil Springs	41238
Oil Valley	42633
O. K.	42567
Okolona	40219
Olaton	42361
Old Brownsboro Place	40222
Old Christianburg	40003
Old Cypress	42031
Old Flat Lick	40935
Oldham	40077
Oldham Acres	40059
Old Landing	41358
Old Olga	42629
Old Orchard	40447
Old Pine Grove	40391
Old Taylor Place	40026
Oldtown	41163
Old Volney	42265
Olga	42629
Olin	40447
Olive	42025
Olive Branch (Fleming County)	41041
Olive Branch (Shelby County)	40065
Olive Hill	41164
Oliver	41156
Ollie	42264
Olmstead	42265
Olney	42408
Olympia	40358
Olympia Springs	40358
Omaha	41843
Omega	40324
Oneida	40972
Oneonta	41007
Ono	42642
Onton	42455
Open Gates (Part of Lexington)	40503
Ophir	41459
Oppy	41231
Orangeburg	41056
Orchard Grass Hills	40031
Ordinary	41162
Oregon	40372
Orinoco	41514
Orkney	41647
Orlando	40460
Orr	41180
Ortiz	42455
Orville	40057
Osborn	41635
Oscaloosa	41858
Oscar	42056
Otas (Part of Corbin)	40701
Otia	42167
Ottawa	40409
Ottenheim	40489
Otter Pond	42445
Oven Fork	40861
Overlook (Part of Eddyville)	42038
Ovesen Heights	42748
Owensboro	42301-03
For specific Owensboro Zip Codes call (502) 684-2301	

Name	ZIP
Owensboro East (Part of Owensboro)	42301
Owensboro West (Part of Owensboro)	42301
Owensby	42629
Owenton	40359
Owingsville	40360
Owsley	41501
Oxford	40324
Ozark	42728
Pactolus	41143
Paducah	42001-03
For specific Paducah Zip Codes call (502) 444-7272	
Paint Lick	40461
Paintsville	41240
Palestine	41091
Palma	42025
Palmer	40336
Panama	41472
Panco	40972
Panola	40385
Panorama Shores	42071
Panther	42376
Paris	40361-62
For specific Paris Zip Codes call (606) 987-4500	
Park City	42160
Parkers Lake	42634
Park Hills	41015
Park Lake	41093
Parksville	40464
Parkway Village	40213
Parmleysville	42640
Parnell	42633
Parrot	40465
Partridge	40862
Pascal	42746
Patesville	42348
Pathfork	40863
Patrick	41230
Patsey	40380
Pauley (Part of Pikeville)	41501
Pauline	42276
Paw Paw	41551
Paxton	41385
Payne Gap	41552
Paynes	40505
Payneville	40157
Payton	41332
Peabody	40914
Peachgrove	41006
Peach Orchard	41230
Peak	40324
Peaks Mill	40601
Pea Ridge (Scott County)	40379
Pea Ridge (Todd County)	42220
Pearl	40940
Pearman	42726
Peasticks	40360
Pebble	40360
Pebworth	41359
Pecksridge	41041
Peden Mill	42134
Peedee	42236
Pelfrey	40313
Pellville	42364
Pellyton	42728
Pembroke	42266
Pence	41313
Penchem	42286
Pendleton	40055
Penile	40272
Penn Run No. One	40201
Penny (Calloway County)	42071
Penny (Pike County)	41501
Pennyrile Mall (Part of Hopkinsville)	42240
Penrod	42365
Peonia	42726
Peoples	40467
Perry Park	40363
Perryville	40468
Persimmon Grove	41001
Persimon	42167
Petersburg	41080
Petersville	41179
Petra	41004
Petrie	42348
Petroleum	42120
Petros	42274
Pettit	42301
Pewee Valley	40056
Peytona	40065
Peyton Creek	41501
Peytonsburg	42768
Peytons Store	40437
Peytontown	40475
Phelps	41553
Phillipsburg	42736
Philpot	42366

Name	ZIP
Phyllis	41554
Picadome (Part of Lexington)	40503
Pickett (Adair County)	42761
Pickett (Shelby County)	40022
Pierce	42743
Pierce Acres	40272
Pigeon	41501
Pigeonroost	40962
Pike View	42757
Pikeville	41501
Pilgrim	41250
Pilot Oak	42085
Pilotview	40391
Pinchem	40391
Pinckard	40383
Pinckneyville	42078
Pine Bluffs	42046
Pine Grove (Clark County)	40470
Pine Grove (Laurel County)	40740
Pine Hill	40456
Pine Knob	42721
Pine Knot	42635
Pine Meadows (Part of Lexington)	40504
Pine Mountain	40810
Piner	41063
Pine Ridge	41360
Pine Top	41843
Pineville	40977
Piney Fork	42064
Piney Grove	42501
Pink	40356
Pinnacle	41358
Pinsonfork	41555
Pioneer Village	40165
Pippa Passes	41844
Piqua	41064
Pisgah	40383
Piso	41501
Pitts	40472
Pittsburg	40755
Plainview (Part of Jeffersontown)	40224
Plank	40978
Plano	42104
Plantation	40222
Plato	42501
Pleasant Hill (Butler County)	42273
Pleasanthill (Mercer County)	40330
Pleasant Hill (Pendleton County)	41006
Pleasant Home	40359
Pleasant Ridge	42376
Pleasant Valley	41039
Pleasant View	40769
Pleasure Ridge Park (Jefferson County)	40258
Pleasureville (Fleming County)	41093
Pleasureville (Henry County)	40057
Plummers Landing	41081
Plummers Mill	41093
Plum Springs	42101
Plumville	41056
Plymouth Village	40207
Poindexter	41031
Pointer	42544
Point Leavell	40444
Point Pleasant	42328
Polin	40040
Polksville	40371
Polkville	42159
Polly	41858
Pomeroyton	40365
Pomp	41472
Ponderosa (Fayette County)	40324
Ponderosa (Grayson County)	42726
Pondsville	42171
Pongo	40456
Poole	42444
Poortown	40356
Pope	42128
Poplar	41128
Poplar Corner	40033
Poplar Flat	41189
Poplar Grove (Fleming County)	41041
Poplar Grove (McLean County)	42372
Poplar Grove (Owen County)	41046
Poplar Highlands	41169
Poplar Hills	40218
Poplar Plains	41041
Poplarville	42501
Porter	40370
Portland (Adair County)	42761
Portland (Pendleton County)	41033
Port Royal	40058

216 KENTUCKY Portsmouth-Sandgap

	ZIP		ZIP		ZIP
Portsmouth	41339	Redwine	41477	Rolling Hills (Shelby County)	40065
Possum Trot	42029	Reed	42451	Rollington (Part of Pewee Valley)	40056
Potters	41230	Reeds Crossing	40475	Rome	42301
Potters Fork	41537	Reedville	41143	Romine	42718
Pottsville (Graves County)	42051	Reedyville	42275	Rookwood (Part of Lexington)	40505
Pottsville (Washington County)	40069	Regina	41559	Roscoe	41171
Poverty	42327	Region	42275	Roseburg	42729
Powderly	42367	Reidland	42001	Rose Crossroads	42629
Powells Creek	41501	Reid Village	40353	Rosefork	41301
Powersburg	42633	Relief	41472	Rose Hill (Carter County)	41164
Powersville	41004	Rella	40902	Rose Hill (Mercer County)	40330
Prairie Village	40272	Renaker	41003	Rose Terrace	40121
Prater	41164	Render	42320	Rosetta	40146
Pratt	42455	Renfro Valley	40473	Roseville (Barren County)	42141
Preachersville	40419	Renfrow	42349	Roseville (Hancock County)	42368
Preece	41224	Repton	42064	Rosewood	42345
Premium	41845	Revelo	42638	Rosine	42370
Prentiss	42320	Rex	42746	Ross	41059
Press	41339	Rexville	41332	Rossland	40734
Preston	40366	Reynolds Station	42368	Rosslyn	40380
Preston Estates	41240	Reynoldsville	40374	Rosspoint	40806
Prestonsburg	41653	Rhea	40806	Rothwell	40322
Prestonville	41008	Rheber	42528	Roundhill (Edmonson County)	42275
Prewitt	40353	Rhoda	42210	Round Hill (Madison County)	40475
Price	41636	Rhodelia	40161	Roundstone	40456
Prices Mill	42202	Ribolt	41189	Rouse (Part of Covington)	41014
Pricetown (Casey County)	42539	Rice Station	40336	Rousseau	41366
Pricetown (Fayette County)	40502	Ricetown	41364	Routt	40299
Priceville	42765	Riceville (Fulton County)	42041	Rowdy	41367
Pride	42404	Riceville (Johnson County)	41258	Rowena	42629
Primrose	41362	Richardson	41253	Rowland (Lincoln County)	40484
Princess	41101	Richardsville	42270	Rowland (McCracken County)	42001
Princeton	42445	Richelieu	42206	Rowlandtown (Part of Paducah)	42001
Printer	41655	Richland	42431	Rowletts	42772
Pritchardsville	42141	Richlawn	40207	Roxana	41848
Privett	40486	Richmond	40475	Royal	42726
Proctor	41311	Rich Pond	42104	Royalton	41464
Prospect	40059	Richwood	41094	Royrader	40402
Prosperity	42207	Ridgeview Heights (Part of Independence)	41051	Royville	42642
Providence (Jessamine County)	40503	Ridgeway	40849	Ruckerville	40391
Providence (Knox County)	40906	Riley	40328	Ruddels Mills	41031
Providence (Simpson County)	42134	Rineyville	40162	Ruin	41171
Providence (Trimble County)	40011	Ringgold	42501	Rumsey	42371
Providence (Webster County)	42450	Ringos Mills	41049	Rural	25687
Provo	42267	Risner	41649	Rush	41168
Pruden	37851	Ritchie	41701	Russell	41169
Pryors	42066	Ritner	42639	Russell Heights (Part of Russell)	41169
Pryors Chapel	42066	Rivals	40071	Russell Springs	42642
Pryse	40471	River	41254	Russellville	42276
Public	42501	River Bluff	40059	Ruth	42501
Pueblo	42633	River Bluff Farms	40059	Rutland	41031
Pulaski	42567	Riverfront (Part of Louisville)	40270	Ryan	41093
Pulliam	40078	River Oaks	42765	Ryland	41015
Pumpkin Center	42445	River Ridge	40828	Ryland Heights	41015
Puncheon	41828	Riverside	42101	Sacramento	42372
Purdy	42728	Riverside Gardens	40216	Sadieville	40370
Putney	40865	Riverton (Part of Greenup)	41144	Sadler	42754
Pyramid	41637	Riverview	42001	St. Catharine	40061
Pyrus	42742	Riverview Estates (Part of Harrodsburg)	40330	St. Charles	42453
Quail	40409	Riverwood	40222	St. Dennis	40216
Quality	42268	Road Junction	41522	St. Elmo	42266
Queens	41179	Roaring Spring	42211	St. Francis	40062
Quicksand	41363	Roark	40979	St. Helens	41368
Quincy	41166	Robards	42452	St. John	42701
Quinton	42518	Robinson	41031	St. Johns	42001
Rabbit Hash	41097	Robinson Creek	41560	St. Joseph (Daviess County)	42373
Rabbit Ridge	42441	Robinsville	40475	St. Joseph (Marion County)	40060
Raccoon	41557	Robinswood	40207	St. Mary	40063
Raceland	41169	Rob Roy	42320	St. Matthews	40207
Radcliff	40159-60	Rochester	42273	St. Paul (Grayson County)	42754
For specific Radcliff Zip Codes call (502) 351-3688		Rockbridge	42167	St. Paul (Lewis County)	41170
Radcliff (Part of Lexington)	40505	Rockcastle	42211	St. Regis Park	40220
Ragland	42053	Rockdale (Boyd County)	41101	St. Vincent	42437
Railton	42160	Rockdale (Owen County)	40359	Saldee	41369
Ralph	42378	Rockfield	42274	Salem (Livingston County)	42078
Randolph	42129	Rock Haven	40175	Salem (Russell County)	42642
Ransom	41531	Rockholds	40759	Salleeton	40033
Rapids	42134	Rockhouse	41561	Salmon	42134
Raven	41861	Rockland	42101	Saloma	42718
Ravenna	40472	Rockport	42369	Salt Gum	40980
Raymond	40176	Rock Springs	42406	Salt Lick	40371
Raywick	40060	Rockybranch	42640	Salt River (Part of Shepherdsville)	40165
Ready	42721	Rocky Hill (Barren County)	42141	Saltwell	40311
Rectorville	41056	Rocky Hill (Edmonson County)	42163	Salvisa	40372
Red Bird (Bell County)	40913	Rodburn	40351	Salyersville	41465
Redbird (Whitley County)	40769	Rodgers Park	41570	Sample	40163
Redbud	40828	Roederer Farm Center	40031	Samuels	40013
Redbush	41219	Roff	40178	Sandcliff	42633
Red Cross	42160	Rogers	41365	Sandefur Crossing	42320
Redfox	41847	Rogers Chapel	40380	Sanders	41083
Red Hill (Allen County)	42164	Rogers Gap	40324	Sandgap	40481
Red Hill (Daviess County)	42376	Rogersville (Part of Radcliff)	40160		
Red Hill (Hardin County)	40175	Rolling Acres (Part of Frankfort)	40601		
Redhouse	40475	Rollingburg	42743		
Redlick	42129	Rolling Fields	40207		
Red River	42202	Rolling Hills (Jefferson County)	40222		

Sand Hill-Stony Fork Junction KENTUCKY 217

Name	ZIP
Sand Hill (Estill County)	40336
Sand Hill (Harlan County)	40823
Sand Hill (Warren County)	42101
Sand Springs (Jackson County)	40447
Sand Springs (Rockcastle County)	40456
Sandy City (Part of Catlettsburg)	41129
Sandy Hook	41171
Sano	42728
Sarah	41171
Saratoga	42445
Sardis	41056
Sargent-Sturgeon	42301
Sassafras	41759
Sassafras Ridge	42050
Saul	40981
Savage	42602
Savage Branch	41129
Savoy	40769
Savoyard	42749
Sawyer	42643
Saxton	40769
Saylor	40840
Scale	42025
Scalf	40982
Schley	42202
Schochon	42202
Schultztown	42320
Schweizer	42134
Science Hill	42553
Scot (Part of Cumberland)	40823
Scottown	42340
Scottsburg	42445
Scotts Station	40065
Scottsville	42164
Scoville	41314
Scranton	40322
Scuddy	41760
Seaville	40330
Sebastians Branch	41370
Sebree	42455
Seco	41849
Sedalia	42079
Seitz	41466
Select	42333
Seminary	42602
Seminary Village (Part of Louisville)	40206
Semiway	42371
Seneca Gardens	40205
Senterville	41522
Se Ree	40164
Sergent	41858
Settle	42164
Settlers Point	40059
Seventy Six	42602
Sewell	41385
Sewellton	42629
Sextons Creek	40983
Seymour	42749
Shadeland (Part of Lexington)	40503
Shady Acres	42518
Shady Grove (Crittenden County)	42064
Shady Grove (Metcalfe County)	42214
Shadynook	41031
Shafter	42501
Shannon	41055
Sharer	42235
Sharkey	41049
Sharon	41002
Sharondale	41514
Sharon Grove	42280
Sharpe	42025
Sharpsburg	40374
Sharpsville	40330
Shawhan	41031
Shawnee Estates (Part of Bowling Green)	42104
Shawneetown (Part of Lexington)	40503
Shearer Valley	42633
Shelbiana	41562
Shelby (Part of Louisville)	40217
Shelby City (Part of Junction City)	40422
Shelby Gap	41563
Shelbyville	40065
Shepherdsville	40165
Shepola	42544
Sherburne	41041
Sheridan	42064
Sherman	41035
Sherwood Shores	42044
Shetland	40383
Shiff	40324
Shiloh	42071

Name	ZIP
Shipley	42602
Shively	40216
Shoal	41730
Shop Branch	40447
Shopville	42554
Shore Acres	40601
Short Creek	42721
Short Town	40828
Shreve	42343
Shrewsbury	42721
Sibert	40962
Sidell	40962
Sideview	40353
Sideway	41164
Sidney	41564
Siler (Knox County)	40701
Siler (Whitley County)	40763
Silerville	42649
Silica	41153
Siloam	41175
Silver	42320
Silver City	42261
Silver Creek	40403
Silver Grove	41085
Silverhill	41467
Simmons	42354
Simpson	41301
Simpsonville	40067
Sims Fork	40902
Sinai	40342
Sinks	40456
Sirocco	40108
Sitka	41255
Sizerock	41762
Skibo	42345
Skillman	42348
Skinnersburg	40379
Skullbuster	40379
Skylight	40059
Skyline	41821
Slade	40376
Slat	42633
Slate Lick	40403
Slater	42087
Slate Valley	40360
Slaughters	42456
Slavans	42653
Slemp	41763
Slickford	42633
Slick Rock	42141
Sligo	40055
Sloan	41653
Sloans Valley	42555
Smilax	41764
Smile	40351
Smith	40867
Smithfield	40068
Smithland	42081
Smith Mills	42457
Smiths Creek	41164
Smiths Grove	42171
Smith Town	42647
Smithview	42721
Smithwood	42076
Smoky Valley	41164
Snell	42501
Snow	42602
Snow Hill	40065
Soft Shell	41831
Soldier	41173
Somerset	42501-02
For specific Somerset Zip Codes call (606) 678-5712	
Sonora	42776
Sorgho	42301
South	42754
South Buffalo	42716
South Carrollton	42374
South Columbus	42032
South Corbin (Part of Corbin)	40701
South Dixie	40272
Southdown	41815
South Elkhorn (Part of Lexington)	40503
South Fork (Breathitt County)	41339
South Fork (Lincoln County)	40437
Southfork (Owsley County)	41314
Southgate	41071
South Higginsport	41002
South Highlands	42066
South Hill	42261
South Irvine	40336
South Marshall	42048
South Park	40118
South Park View	40219
South Portsmouth	41174
South Ripley	41034
South Shore	41175
Southshores	40065

Name	ZIP
South Union	42283
Southville	40065
South Wallins	40873
South Williamson	41503
Southwire	42348
Spa	42256
Spanglin	41171
Spann	42633
Sparksville	42728
Sparta	41086
Spears	40502
Speck	42723
Speedwell	40475
Speight	41565
Spence (Part of Newport)	41071
Spencer	40353
Spencer Ridge	41311
Spider	41843
Spindletop	40324
Spiro	40456
Spottsville	42458
Spring Creek	40962
Springdale (Jefferson County)	40222
Springdale (Mason County)	41056
Springfield	40069
Spring Grove	42437
Springhill (Hickman County)	42031
Springhill (Warren County)	42101
Springlake (Kenton County)	41015
Springlake (Madison County)	40475
Spring Lake Farms	40299
Springlee	40207
Spring Lick	42779
Spring Mill	40228
Spring Station	40347
Springval	40324
Spring Valley	40216
Sprout	40350
Spruce Pine	40874
Sprule	40906
Spurlington	42718
Spurlock	40987
Squib	42501
Squiresville	40359
Stab	42557
Stacy Fork	41472
Staffordsburg	41051
Staffordsville	41256
Stambaugh	41257
Stamping Ground	40379
Standiford (Part of Louisville)	40209
Standing Rock	41343
Stanfill	40831
Stanford	40484
Stanley	42375
Stanton	40380
Stanville	41659
Stark	41176
Star Mills	42740
State Line	42050
Static	42602
Station Camp	40336
Stay	41311
Stearns	42647
Stedmantown	40601
Steele	41566
Steff	42780
Stella (Calloway County)	42071
Stella (Magoffin County)	41465
Stephens	41177
Stephensburg	42781
Stephensport	40170
Stepstone	40360
Steubenville	42648
Stewart	40330
Stewart Acres	42320
Stewartsville	41097
Stiles	40028
Stillwater	41301
Stinnett	40868
Stinnettsville	40146
Stinson	41143
Stites	40177
Stockholm	42257
Stone	41567
Stone Hedge Estates	40324
Stonestreet	40272
Stonewall (Bracken County)	41004
Stonewall (Scott County)	40370
Stonewall Estates (Fayette County)	40503
Stonewall Estates (Franklin County)	40601
Stoneybrook	40391
Stoney Fork	40988
Stoney Point	41034
Stony Fork Junction (Part of Middlesboro)	40965

218 KENTUCKY Stoops-Verda

	ZIP
Stoops	40353
Stop	42633
Stopover	41568
Stormking	41701
Stovall	42160
Straight Creek	40977
Strait Creek	41132
Strathmoor Gardens	40205
Strathmoor Manor	40205
Strathmoor Village	40205
Straw	42259
Strawberry	42511
Stricklett	41179
Stringtown (Anderson County)	40342
Stringtown (Boone County)	41048
Stringtown (Grant County)	41003
Stringtown (Madison County)	40475
Stringtown (Magoffin County)	41465
Stringtown (McLean County)	42372
Stringtown (Mercer County)	40330
Stringtown (Muhlenberg County)	42372
Strunk	42649
Stubblefield	42088
Sturgeon	41314
Sturgis	42459
Sublett	41465
Sublimity City	40741
Subtle	42129
Sudith	40371
Sugar Bay	41095
Sugar Grove	42261
Sugar Hill	42501
Sugartit	41042
Sullivan	42460
Sulphur	40070
Sulphur Lick	42166
Sulphur Springs	42358
Sulphur Well (Jessamine County)	40356
Sulphur Well (Metcalfe County)	42129
Summer Shade	42166
Summersville	42782
Summit (Boyd County)	41101
Summit (Hardin County)	42783
Sumpter	42633
Sunfish	42284
Sunny Acres (Part of Taylor Mill)	41015
Sunnybrook	42633
Sunny Corner	42348
Sunnydale	42358
Sunny Hills (Part of Frankfort)	40601
Sunnyside	42101
Sunrise	41031
Sunset	41049
Sunshine (Greenup County)	41175
Sunshine (Harlan County)	40831
Susie	42633
Sussex Estates	40356
Suterville	40379
Sutherland	42376
Sutton (Fleming County)	41041
Sutton (Pike County)	41562
Suwanee	42055
Swain	42635
Swallowfield	40601
Swamp Branch	41258
Swampton	41464
Swanee Shores	41097
Swan Lake	40906
Swanpond	40906
Sweeden	42285
Sweeneyville	42718
Sweet Owen	40359
Switzer	40601
Sycamore	40222
Sycamore Estates	40383
Sylvandell	41031
Sylvania	40258
Symbol	40729
Symsonia	42082
Tabernacle	42220
Tablow	40330
Tacky Town	40988
Taffy	42347
Taft	41314
Talbert	41377
Talcum	41765
Tallega	41378
Talmage	40330
Tanksley	40962
Tanner	42748
Tannery	41179
Tar Fork	40111

	ZIP
Tar Hill	42754
Tarkiln	41124
Tarryon Number One	42055
Tates Creek Estates	40356
Tateville	42558
Tatham Springs	40078
Tatumsville	42044
Taulbee	41385
Taylor Mill	41015
Taylor Mines	42320
Taylorsport	41048
Taylors Store	42049
Taylorsville	40071
Teaberry	41660
Tedders	40906
Teddy	42539
Teetersville	40831
Teges	40972
Temperance	42134
Temple Hill	42141
Ten Broeck	40201
Teresita	40359
Terry Manor	42258
Terryville	41159
Texas	40069
Texola	40471
Thealka	41240
The Colony (Fayette County)	40504
The Colony (Franklin County)	40601
Thelma	41260
The Meadows (Part of Lexington)	40505
The Moors Camp	42044
The Ridge	41171
Thomas	41626
Thorn Hill (Franklin County)	40601
Thornhill (Jefferson County)	40222
Thornton	41855
Thorobred Acres	40222
Thoroughbred Acres	40065
Thousandsticks	41766
Threeforks (Martin County)	41261
Threeforks (Warren County)	42159
Threelinks	40456
Three Mile	41144
Three Point	40815
Three Springs (Hart County)	42746
Three Springs (Warren County)	42104
Thruston	42301
Thurlow	42743
Tidalwave	40701
Tierra Linda (Part of Frankfort)	40601
Tilden	42409
Tilford	42721
Tiline	42083
Tilton	41041
Timber Lake	42518
Timberwood Lake Shores	41010
Tina	41740
Tinsley	40977
Tiny Town	42234
Tiptop	41409
Toddspoint	40065
Toddville	40444
Toler	41569
Toliver	41332
Tollesboro	41189
Tolliver Town	41810
Tolu	42084
Tomahawk	41262
Tompkinsville	42167
Tonieville	42748
Toonerville	41548
Topmost	41862
Topton	40741
Torrent	41396
Totz	40870
Toulouse	41723
Touristville	42633
Tousey	40119
Tower Heights	40065
Town and Country (Daviess County)	42301
Town and Country (Logan County)	42276
Tracy	42133
Trailwood Lakes	40003
Tram	41663
Trammel	42164
Trapp	40391
Trappist	40051
Travellers Rest	41314
Treasure Island	40229
Tremont	40873
Trent	41301
Trenton	42286
Tress Shop	42220

	ZIP
Tribbey	41722
Tribune	42064
Tri City	42040
Trigg Furnace	42211
Trimble	42544
Trinity	41179
Trinity Station	41179
Trisler	42343
Tri-State (Part of Catlettsburg)	41129
Trosper	40995
Troublesome	41712
Troy	40383
Tucker	40229
Tuckertown	42159
Tuggleville	40863
Tunnel Hill	42701
Turfland Mall (Part of Lexington)	40504
Turin	41314
Turkey	41314
Turkey Creek	41570
Turkey Foot	40370
Turkeytown	40419
Turners Station	40075
Turnersville	40484
Turnertown (Butler County)	42268
Turnertown (Simpson County)	42134
Tutor Key	41263
Tuttle	40741
Tway (Part of Harlan)	40831
Twentysix	41472
Twila	40873
Twin Lakes	41091
Twin Oaks (Fayette County)	40503
Twin Oaks (Jefferson County)	40216
Tyewhoppety	42216
Tygarts Valley	41144
Tyler (Part of Paducah)	42001
Tyner	40486
Typo	41771
Tyrone	40342
Ula	42501
Ulvah	41731
Ulysses	41264
Union	41091
Union City	40475
Union Hall	40472
Union Mills	40356
Union Ridge	42365
Union Star	40171
Uniontown	42461
Unity (Part of Ashland)	41101
University (Calloway County)	42071
University (Fayette County)	40506
Uno	42749
Upchurch	42602
Upper Elk	41568
Upper Hunters	40216
Upper Kings Addition	41175
Upper Tygart	41178
Upton	42784
Urban	40962
Utica	42376
Utility	42348
Uttingertown (Part of Lexington)	40505
Uz	41858
Vada	41383
Valeria	41301
Valley Downs	40272
Valley Gardens	40258
Valley Hill	40069
Valley Oak	42501
Valley Station (Jefferson County)	40272
Valley View (Bracken County)	41002
Valley View (Madison County)	40475
Valley Village	40272
Van	41858
Vanarsdell	40330
Vance	40075
Vanceburg	41179
Vancleve	41385
Vanderburg	42409
Vandetta	42413
Vanhook	42501
Van Lear (Johnson County)	41265
Vanzant	40119
Varilla	40813
Varney	41571
Veech	40022
Veechdale	40067
Venters	41522
Vento (Part of Upton)	42784
Verda	40828

KENTUCKY 219

Name	ZIP
Verne	40769
Vernon	42151
Verona	41092
Versailles	40383
Vertrees	42785
Vest	41772
Vester	42728
Vicco	41773
Vicksburg	42083
Victory	40729
Villa Hills	41016
Vincent	41386
Vine Grove	40175
Vine Grove Junction (Part of Radcliff)	40160
Vineyard	40356
Viola	42051
Viper	41774
Virden	40312
Virgie	41572
Visalia	41015
Volga	41266
Vortex	41301
Wabaco	42713
Wabash	41701
Wabd	40456
Waco	40385
Waddy	40076
Wadesboro	42048
Wagersville	40336
Wagner	40317
Waite	42603
Wakefield	40071
Walden	40759
Waldo	41632
Wales	41572
Walker	40997
Walkertown (Part of Hazard)	41701
Wallaceton	40461
Wallingford	41093
Wallins Creek	40873
Wallonia	42211
Wallsend (Part of Pineville)	40977
Walltown	40489
Walnut Grove (Allen County)	42120
Walnut Grove (Pulaski County)	42563
Waltersville	40312
Walton	41094
Waltz	40351
Wanamaker	42455
Waneta	40488
Warbranch	40874
Warco	41645
War Creek	41339
Warfield	41267
Warnock	41144
Warren	40906
Warsaw	41095
Washington	41096
Wasioto	40977
Watauga	42602
Waterford	40071
Watergap	41653
Water Valley	42085
Waterview	42786
Watkinsville	40379
Watterfern Hills	40291
Watterson Park	40213
Watts	41348
Watts Creek	40769
Waverly	42462
Waverly Hills	40258
Wax	42787
Wayland	41666
Waynesburg	40489
Weaverton (Part of Henderson)	42420
Webbs	42743
Webbs Cross Roads	42642
Webbville	41180
Weberstown	42364
Webster	40176
Wedonia	41055
Weeksbury	41667
Weir	42345
Welborn	42501
Welchburg	40486
Welchs Creek	42287
Welcome	42261
Weldon	40108
Wellhope	40456
Wellington (Jefferson County)	40205
Wellington (Menifee County)	40387
Wells	42330
Wellsburg	41043
Wells Landing	40422
Wendover	41775
Wentz	41731

Name	ZIP
Wesco	42431
Wesleyan Park (Part of Winchester)	40391
Wesleyville	41164
Westbend	40388
West Buechel	40218
West Clifty	42754
West Danville (Part of Danville)	40422
Western	42050
Western Kentucky Farm Center	42038
Western State Hospital	42240
West Fairview	41101
West Frankfort (Part of Frankfort)	40601
West Garrett	41630
Westgate Meadows (Part of Frankfort)	40601
West Irvine	40336
Westland Mall	40258
West Liberty	41472
West Louisville	42377
Weston	40311
West Paducah	42086
West Paris (Part of Paris)	40361
West Point	40177
Westport	40077
West Prestonsburg (Part of Prestonsburg)	41668
West Royalton	41465
West Russell (Part of Flatwoods)	41169
West Somerset (Part of Somerset)	42564
Westvaco	42087
West Van Lear	41268
Westview	40178
West Viola	42051
West Wheatcroft (Part of Wheatcroft)	42463
West Wind Park	40258
Westwood (Boyd County)	41101
Westwood (Jefferson County)	40220
Weymouth	42041
Wheatcroft	42463
Wheatley	40389
Wheeler	40906
Wheelersburg	41473
Wheelwright	41669
Whick	41390
Whipple	40977
Whipps Millgate	40223
Whipps Mill Village	40222
Whispering Hills	40219
Whitaker (Floyd County)	41216
Whitaker (Letcher County)	41849
Whitco	41858
White City (Hopkins County)	42464
White City (Larue County)	42748
White Hall	40475
Whitehouse	41269
White Lily	42501
White Mills	42788
White Oak (Garrard County)	40444
White Oak (Morgan County)	41474
White Oak Junction	42647
White Plains (Allen County)	42164
White Plains (Hopkins County)	42464
Whitepost	25687
White Run	42349
Whites	40403
Whitesburg	41858
White Sulphur (Caldwell County)	42411
White Sulphur (Scott County)	40324
Whitesville	42378
White Tower	41051
White Villa	41063
Whitewood	42743
Whitfield	40071
Whitley City	42653
Wiborg	42653
Wickliffe	42087
Wicks Well	42431
Widecreek	41391
Wilbur	41124
Wild Cat	40962
Wilder	41076
Wilderness Road	42259
Wildie	40492
Wildwood	40222
Wilhurst	41385
Willailla	40409
Willard	41181
Williams (Morgan County)	41474
Williams (Ohio County)	42354
Williamsburg	40769

Name	ZIP
Williamsport	41271
Williams Station	42404
Williamstown	41097
Willisburg	40078
Willow (Bracken County)	41004
Willow (Lee County)	41358
Willow Creek	40222
Willowcrest	40601
Willow Grove	41043
Willow Shade	42169
Willowtown	42718
Willow Tree	40472
Wilmore	40390
Wilson	42406
Wilsonville (Boyle County)	40422
Wilsonville (Spencer County)	40023
Wilstacy	41339
Wilton	40771
Winchester	40391
Wind Cave	40494
Winding Falls	40207
Winding Way (Part of Frankfort)	40601
Windsor	42565
Windy	42655
Windy Hill	42349
Windy Hills	40207
Windyville	42210
Wingo	42088
Winifred	41219
Winslow Park	42064
Winston	40495
Winwright	41501
Wiscoal	41711
Wisconsin	41711
Wisdom	42129
Wisemantown	40336
Wises Landing	40006
Wiswell	42071
Wittensville	41274
Witt Springs	40336
Wofford	40769
Wolf	41164
Wolf Coal	41393
Wolf Creek	40104
Wolf Lick	42256
Wolfpit	41522
Wolverine	41339
Wonder	41626
Wonnie	41475
Woodbine	40771
Woodburn	42170
Woodbury	42288
Woodhill	40219
Woodlake	40601
Woodland Estates	41240
Woodland Hills	40243
Woodlands (Part of Frankfort)	40601
Woodlawn (Campbell County)	41076
Woodlawn (McCracken County)	42001
Woodlawn (Nelson County)	40004
Woodlawn-Oakdale	42001
Woodlawn Park	40207
Woodman	41574
Woodrow	40140
Woods (Floyd County)	41653
Woods (Harlan County)	40828
Woodsbend	41472
Woodson Bend	42518
Woodsonville	42749
Woodstock	42501
Woodville	42053
Woolcott	41004
Wooleyville	42718
Woollum	40999
Wooton	41776
Worthington (Greenup County)	41183
Worthington (Jefferson County)	40222
Worthington Hills	40201
Worthville	41098
Wray Gap	42633
Wrights	42718
Wrightsburg	42327
Wrigley	41477
Wurtland	41144
Wyett	41171
Wyman	42327
Yaden	40769
Yancey	40831
Yatesville	41230
Yeaddiss	41777
Yeager (Knox County)	40915
Yeager (Pike County)	41501
Yeaman	42361
Yellow Rock	41311

KENTUCKY Yelvington-Zula

	ZIP
Yelvington	42355
Yerkes	41778
Yesse	42164
Yocum	41472
York	41175
Yorktown	41501
Yosemite	42566
Younger Creek	42701

	ZIP
Youngs Creek	40701
Youngtown	42261
Yuma	42733
Zachariah	41396
Zag	41472
Zandale (Part of Lexington)	40503
Zebulon	41501
Zelda	41230

	ZIP
Zion (Grant County)	41035
Zion (Henderson County)	42420
Zion (Todd County)	42234
Zion Hill	40347
Zoe	41397
Zoneton (Part of Pioneer Village)	40165
Zula	42603

Abbeville-Calcasieu **LOUISIANA** 221

Name	ZIP
Abbeville	70510-11
For specific Abbeville Zip Codes call (318) 893-2972	
Abby Plantation	70301
Aben	70346
Abington	71052
Abita Springs	70420
Acadia	70301
Acadia Academy	70535
Acme	71316
Acy	70774
Ada	71080
Addis	70710
Adeline	70544
Adner	71037
Advance (Part of Hodge)	71247
Afton	71282
Aimwell	71401
Airline Park	70003
Airview Terrace (Part of Alexandria)	71301
Ajax	71450
Akers	70421
Albania	70544
Albany	70711
Alberta	71016
Alco	71446
Alden Bridge	71006
Alexandria	71301-15
For specific Alexandria Zip Codes call (318) 484-4625	
Alexandria Mall (Part of Alexandria)	71301
Alfalfa	71409
Alfords	70720
Alice B	70538
Alice C	70538
Allemand	70360
Allen	71469
Allendale	70767
Alliance	70037
Allon	70760
Alluvial City	70085
Aloha	71417
Aloysia	70788
Alsen	70807
Alto	71269
Alton	70458
Alvin Callender	70037
Ama	70031
Amelia	70340
Amite	70422
Anacoco	71403
Anandale	71301
Andrew	70548
Andrew Guillot Subdivision	70076
Angelina	70301
Angie	70426
Annadale	70788
Antioch (Claiborne Parish)	71040
Antioch (Lincoln Parish)	71275
Antonia	71467
Antonio	70767
Antrim	71064
Arabi	70032
Ararat	70601
Arbroth	70720
Arcadia	71001
Archibald	71218
Archie	71343
Arcola	70456
Ardoyne	70360
Argo	71344
Argyle	70360
Arizona	71040
Arklatex (Part of Mooringsport)	71060
Arlington	70808
Armistead	71019
Arnaudville	70512
Ashland (Natchitoches Parish)	71002
Ashland (Terrebonne Parish)	70360
Ashley	71282
Ashton	70538
Athens	71003
Atlanta	71404
Attakapas Landing	70390
Audubon (Part of Baton Rouge)	70806
Audubon Terrace	70808
Augusta (Iberville Parish)	70788
Augusta (Plaquemines Parish)	70037
Avalon	70392
Avandale	71366
Avery Island	70513
Avondale	70094
Aycock	71001
Azucena	71375
Bagdad	71417

Name	ZIP
Bains	70775
Baker	70714
Baldwin	70514
Ball	71405
Bancroft	70653
Bankers	70582
Banks	70807
Banks Springs	71418
Baptist	70403
Barataria	70036
Barber Spur	70586
Bardel	71269
Barnet Springs (Part of Ruston)	71270
Barron	71328
Barton	70346
Basile	70515
Baskin	71219
Baskinton	71219
Bastrop	71220-21
For specific Bastrop Zip Codes call (318) 281-2672	
Batchelor	70715
Baton Rouge	70801-98
For specific Baton Rouge Zip Codes call (504) 381-0372	
Batree	70090
Bawcomville	71291
Bayou Barbary	70754
Bayou Blue	70360
Bayou Cane	70359
Bayou Chicot	70586
Bayou Crab	70390
Bayou Current	71353
Bayou Gauche	70030
Bayou Goula	70716
Bayou Pigeon	70764
Bayou Sale	70538
Bayou Sorrel	70764
Baywood	70739
Beach Grove	71277
Beachview (Part of Kenner)	70065
Bear Creek	71008
Bear Skin	71266
Beaver	71463
Bee Bayou	71269
Beech Springs	71247
Beekman	71220
Beggs	71322
Bel	70658
Belah	71371
Belair	70040
Belair Cove	70586
Belcher	71004
Bell City	70630
Belle Amie	70345
Belle Chasse	70037
Belledeau	71341
Belle Place	70552
Belle Point	70084
Belle River	70339
Belle Rose	70341
Belle Terre (Assumption Parish)	70346
Belle Terre (Iberville Parish)	70764
Belleview	70570
Bellevue (Bossier Parish)	71037
Bellevue (Caldwell Parish)	71418
Bellfontaine	70815
Bell Helene	70734
Bellwood	71468
Belmont (Sabine Parish)	71406
Belmont (St. James Parish)	70743
Belmont (West Baton Rouge Parish)	70767
Benson	71419
Bentley	71407
Benton	71006
Bermuda	71456
Bernice	71222
Bertie	70390
Bertrandville (Assumption Parish)	70390
Bertrandville (Plaquemines Parish)	70040
Berwick	70342
Bethany	71007
Bienville	71008
Big Bend	71318
Big Branch	70445
Big Cane	71356
Big Creek	71328
Big Island	71219
Big Woods	70668
Billeaud	70518
Bissonnet	70003
Bivens	70653
Blackburn	71038
Black Hawk	71373
Blade	71342
Blanchard	71009

Name	ZIP
Blanche	71433
Blanks	70717
Blankston	71202
Blond	70433
Bluff Creek	70722
Bob Acres	70560
Bodcau	71037
Bodoc	71329
Bogalusa	70427-29
For specific Bogalusa Zip Codes call (504) 735-5921	
Bohemia	70082
Bolden	71358
Boleyn	71450
Bolinger	71064
Bolivar	70444
Bonaire	70808
Bond	71463
Bonfouca	70458
Bonita	71223
Bon Marche Mall (Part of Baton Rouge)	70806
Bon Secour	70086
Book	71343
Boone's Corner	70605
Boothville	70038
Bordelonville	71320
Borgne Mouth	70092
Borodino	71355
Bosco	71202
Boscoville	70570
Bossier City	71111-13
	71171-72
For specific Bossier City Zip Codes call (318) 746-1481	
Boston	70533
Boudreaux Canal	70344
Bourg	70343
Boutte	70039
Boyce	71409
Braithwaite	70040
Branch	70516
Breard (Part of Monroe)	71203
Breaux Bridge	70517
Breezy Hill	71467
Brewtons Mill	71031
Bridge City	70094
Brignac	70737
Bristol	70584
Brittany	70718
Broadmoor (Lafayette Parish)	70501
Broadmoor (Orleans Parish)	70125
Broadmoor (Terrebonne Parish)	70360
Broadview (Part of Baton Rouge)	70815
Brooks	70760
Brouillette	71351
Broussard	70518
Brown	71016
Brownell	71295
Brownfields	70811
Brown Heights	70714
Brownlee	71111
Brownsville-Bawcomville	71291
Brownville (Caldwell Parish)	71418
Brownville (Ouachita Parish)	71291
Brule	70372
Brule Guillot	70301
Bruly La Croix	70788
Bruly Saint Martin	70341
Brusle Saint Vincent	70390
Brusly	70719
Bryant (Part of New Iberia)	70560
Bryceland	71014
Buckeye	71321
Buckner	71269
Bueche	70720
Buhler	70663
Bull Run	70395
Bunkie	71322
Buras	70041
Buras-Triumph	70041
Burkplace	71016
Burr Ferry	71403
Burroughs	71418
Burwood	70091
Burton Lane	70086
Bush	70431
Bushes	71295
Bywaters (Part of New Orleans)	70117
Caddo (Part of Oil City)	71061
Caddo Station	71082
Cade	70519
Cadeville	71238
Caernarvon	70040
Caffery	70538
Caicasieu (Allen Parish)	71433
Calcasieu (Rapides Parish)	71433

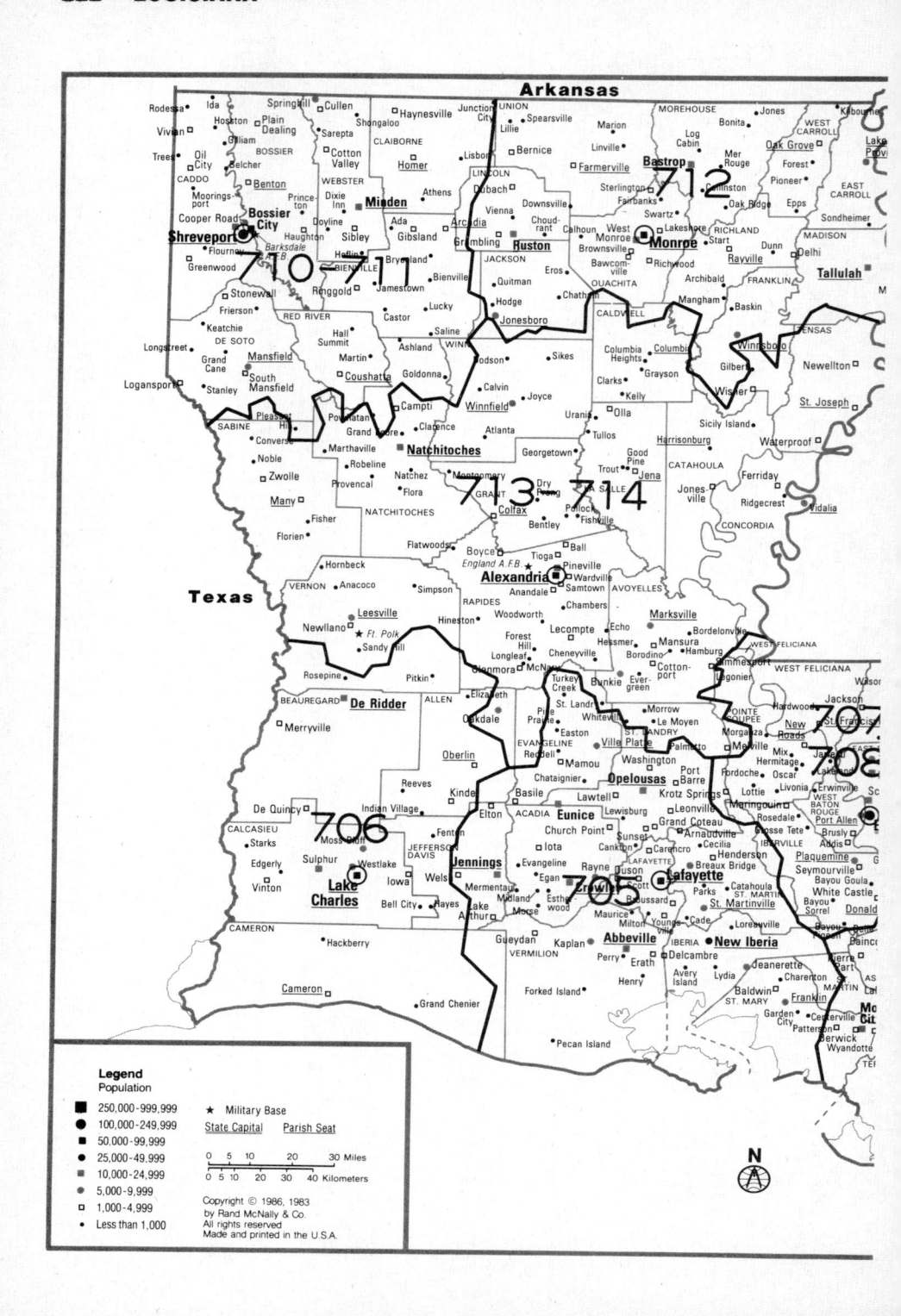

LOUISIANA

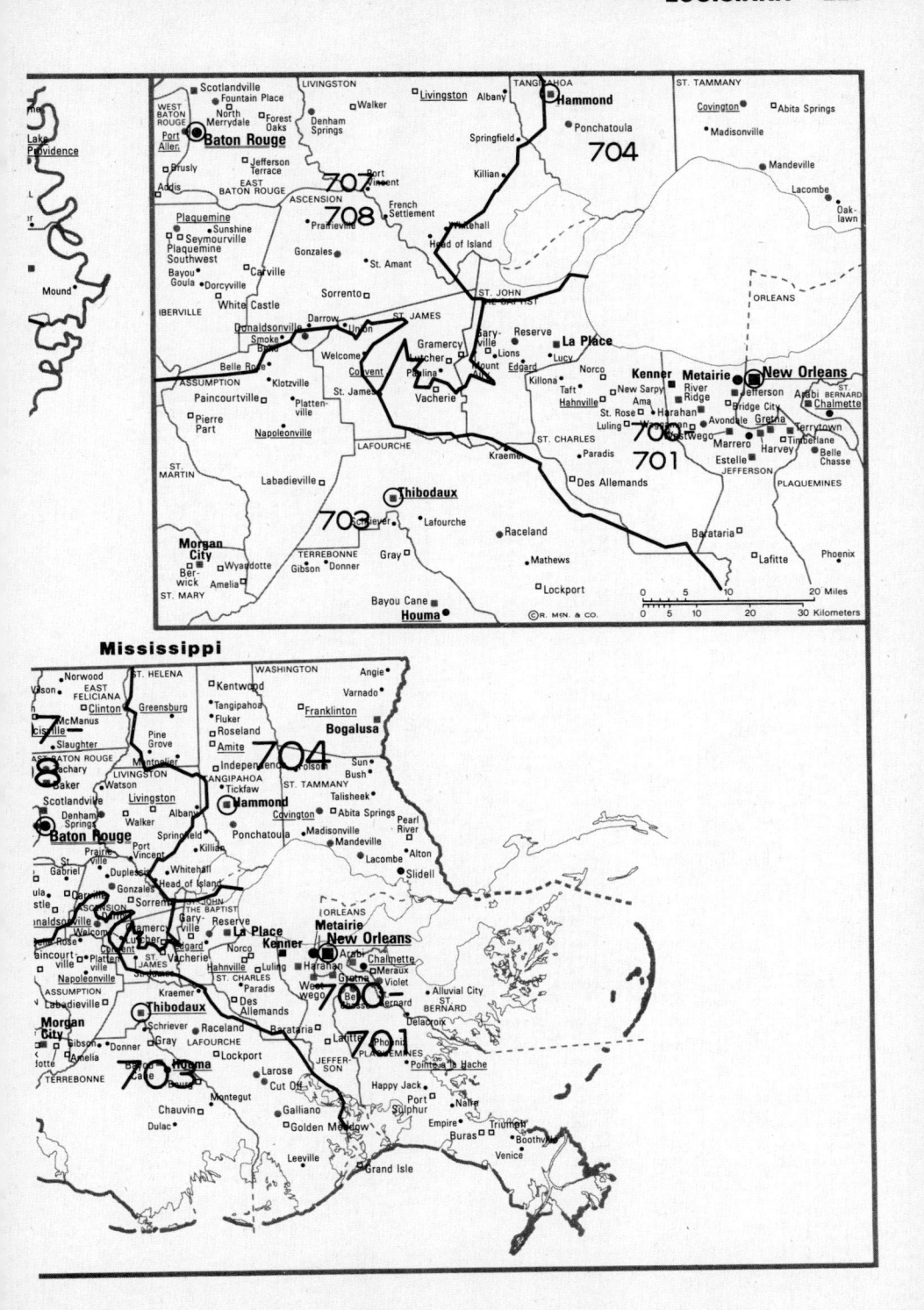

LOUISIANA 223

224 LOUISIANA Calhoun-Ebenezer

Name	ZIP
Calhoun	71225
Calumet	70392
Calvin	71410
Camelia Gardens	71301
Cameron	70631
Camp Beauregard	71301
Camperdown	70538
Campti	71411
Cancienne	70390
Canebrake	71334
Caney	71446
Cankton	70584
Cannonburg	70788
Capitan	70592
Capitol (Part of Baton Rouge)	70804
Caplis	71111
Carencro	70520
Carlisle	70042
Carlton	71225
Carlyss	70663
Carmel	71052
Caroline	70552
Carrollton (Part of New Orleans)	70118
Carrollton Central Plaza (Part of New Orleans)	70118
Carrolwood	70068
Carterville	71064
Carthage Bluff Landing	70462
Cartwright	71227
Carville	70721
Caspiana	71115
Castle Village	71301
Castor	71016
Catahoula	70582
Catherine	70716
Cat Island	71436
Catuna	71052
Cavett	71004
Cecile	71105
Cecilia	70521
Cedar Crest	70816
Cedar Glen	70811
Cedar Grove (Assumption Parish)	70372
Cedar Grove (Caddo Parish)	71106
Cedar Grove (Plaquemines Parish)	70037
Cedarton	71227
Centenary (Part of Shreveport)	71104
Center Point	71323
Centerville (Evangeline Parish)	71367
Centerville (St. Mary Parish)	70522
Central (East Baton Rouge Parish)	70811
Central (St. James Parish)	70723
Central (Terrebonne Parish)	70360
Chacahoula	70395
Chackbay	70301
Chalmette	70043-44
For specific Chalmette Zip Codes call (504) 271-4173	
Chalmette Vista	70043
Chamale Cove (Part of Slidell)	70460
Chamberlin	70767
Chambers	71346
Chandler Park	71301
Charenton	70523
Charles Park (Part of Alexandria)	71301
Charlotte	70560
Chase	71324
Chataignier	70524
Chateau Village (Part of Kenner)	70065
Chatham	71226
Chatman Town	70090
Chauvin	70344
Chef Menteur (Part of New Orleans)	70126
Cheneyville	71325
Cheniere	71291
Cherokee Court	70123
Cherokee Village	71301
Cherry Grove	70655
Chesbrough	70444
Chestnut	71070
Chickama	71346
Chickasaw	71263
Chinchuba	70448
Chipola	70441
Chloe	70647
Choctaw (Iberville Parish)	70767
Choctaw (Lafourche Parish)	70301
Chopin	71412
Choudrant	71227

Name	ZIP
Choupique (Lafourche Parish)	70301
Choupique (St. Mary Parish)	70538
Chula	70372
Church Point	70525
Church Spur	70390
Cinclare	70767
Cindy Park	70075
Claiborne (Ouachita Parish)	71291
Claiborne (St. Tammany Parish)	70433
Claibourne Gardens	70094
Clare	71429
Clarence	71414
Clarks	71415
Clay	71270
Clayton	71326
Clayton Junction (Part of Clayton)	71326
Clearview Shopping Center	70002
Clearwater	71325
Clifton (Rapides Parish)	71455
Clifton (Washington Parish)	70438
Clinton	70722
Clio	70449
Clotilda	70394
Cloutierville	71416
Clovelly Farms	70345
Cocodrie	70344
Cocoville	71350
Coker	71052
Coleman	71282
Colfax	71417
Colgrade	71483
College (Part of Hammond)	70401
Collinsburg	71064
Collinston	71229
Colonial Heights	71109
Colquitt	71038
Columbia (Caldwell Parish)	71418
Columbia (St. John the Baptist Parish)	70049
Columbia Heights	71418
Como	71295
Concession	70037
Concord	71263
Constance Beach	70631
Consuella	71375
Coptreras	70085
Convent	70723
Converse	71419
Conway	71260
Coon	70715
Cooper Road	71107
Coopers	71446
Copenhagen	71418
Cora	71444
Corbin (Part of Walker)	70785
Corey	71202
Corinth	71235
Cornerview	70737
Cornor	39669
Cortableau	70577
Cortana Mall (Part of Baton Rouge)	70815
Coteau Holmes	70582
Coteau Rodaire	70512
Cotton Plant	71435
Cottonport	71327
Cotton Valley	71018
Couchwood	71018
Coulon Plantation	70301
Country Club Subdivision	70301
Coushatta	71019
Covington	70433-34
For specific Covington Zip Codes call (504) 892-2421	
Covington Country Club Estates	70433
Cow Island	70510
Cravens	70656
Creedmoor	70085
Creole	70632
Crescent (Iberville Parish)	70764
Crescent (Terrebonne Parish)	70360
Creston	71020
Crew Lake	71269
Crews	71454
Crichton	71019
Cross-Road	71435
Crossroads (Lincoln Parish)	71235
Cross Roads (Red River Parish)	71019
Crowley	70526-27
For specific Crowley Zip Codes call (318) 783-2370	
Crown Point	70072
Crowville	71230
Crozier	70360
Cullen	71021

Name	ZIP
Curry	71483
Curtis	71112
Cut Off	70345
Cypremort	70538
Cypress (Natchitoches Parish)	71420
Cypress (Ouachita Parish)	71291
Cypress Gardens (St. Bernard Parish)	70075
Cypress Gardens (Terrebonne Parish)	70360
Cypress Island	70582
Daigleville (Part of Houma)	70360
Dalcour	70040
Danville	71008
D'Arbonne	71227
Darlington	70441
Darnell	71266
Darrow	70725
Daspit	70560
Davant	70046
Dean	71260
Dean Chapel	71291
De Broeck Landing	71106
Deerford	70791
Deer Park	71373
Dehlco	71269
Delacroix (St. Bernard Parish)	70085
Delacroix (St. Martin Parish)	70582
Del Bueno Park	70075
Delcambre	70528
Delhi	71232
Delta	71233
Delta Farms	70374
Denham Springs	70726-27
For specific Denham Springs Zip Codes call (504) 665-5435	
Dennis Mills	70726
Denson	70449
Dent Terrace	70808
De Quincy	70633
De Ridder	70634
Derry	71421
Des Allemands	70030
De Selle	71301
Dess	71429
Destrehan	70047
Devalls	70767
Deville	71328
Dewdrop	71220
Diamond	70083
Dixie	71107
Dixie Acres	71280
Dixie Gardens	71105
Dixie Inn	71055
Dixon Correctional Institute	70748
Dodson	71422
Donaldsonville	70346
Donner	70352
Dorcyville	70788
Douglas	71227
Downsville	71234
Downtown (Caddo Parish)	71101
Downtown (Ouachita Parish)	71201
Downtown (Rapides Parish)	71301
Downtown (St. Mary Parish)	71380
Doyle (Part of Livingston)	70754
Doyline	71023
Drew (Calcasieu Parish)	70605
Drew (Ouachita Parish)	71291
Dry Creek	70637
Dry Prong	71423
Dubach	71235
Dubberly	71024
Duckroost	70774
Dufresne	70070
Dukedale	71006
Dulac	70353
Dunbarton	71334
Dunn	71236
Duplessis	70728
Dupont (Avoyelles Parish)	71329
Dupont (Pointe Coupee Parish)	70783
Duson	70529
Dutch Town	70734
Dykesville	71038
Easleyville	70441
Eastgate Plaza (Part of Shreveport)	71108
East Hammond	70401
East Hodge	71247
East Louisiana State Hospital	70748
Easton	70586
East Point	71025
East Side (Part of Lake Charles)	70601
Eastside Columbia	71418
Ebenezer	70526

Echo-Hico **LOUISIANA** 225

	ZIP		ZIP		ZIP
Echo	71330	Fort Jesup	71449	Grand Coteau	70541
Eden	71371	Fort Necessity	71243	Grand Ecore	71457
Edgard	70049	Fort Polk	71459	Grand Isle	70358
Edgefield	71019	Fort Polk North	71459	Grand Lake	70605
Edgerly	70668	Fort Polk South	71459	Grand Point	70763
Edna	70648	Fortune Fork	71282	Grand Prairie	70589
Effie	71331	Fosters (Part of Bossier		Grand River	70764
Egan	70531	City)	71111	Grangeville	70422
Elam	71378	Fosters Canal	70083	Grant	70644
Elba	71353	Foules	71326	Gray	70359
Eliza	70764	Fourborge	70586	Gray Point	70586
Elizabeth	70638	Four Corners	70538	Grayson	71435
Ellendale	70360	Four Forks (Caddo Parish)	71046	Green Acres (Concordia	
Ellis	70526	Four Forks (Richland Parish)	71259	Parish)	71373
Ellsworth	70360	Fowler	71240	Green Acres (East Baton	
Elmer (Lafourche Parish)	70301	Francis Place	70075	Rouge Parish)	70811
Elmer (Rapides Parish)	71424	Franklin	70538	Green Acres (St. Charles	
Elmfield	70390	Franklinton	70438	Parish)	70030
Elm Grove	71051	Fred	70791	Green Gables	71360
Elm Hall	70390	Freetown (Assumption		Greenlaw	70444
Elm Hall Junction	70390	Parish)	70390	Green Lawn (Part of	
Elm Park	70775	Freetown (St. Mary Parish)	70538	Kenner)	70065
Elton	70532	French Settlement	70733	Green Lawn Terrace (Part	
Empire	70050	Frenier	70068	of Kenner)	70065
Encalade	70083	Friendship	71008	Greensburg	70441
Energy (Part of Lafayette)	70598	Frierson	71027	Greenwell Springs	70739
England Air Force Base	71311	Frisco	70755	Greenwood (Caddo Parish)	71033
Englewood	71282	Frogmore	71335	Greenwood (St. Mary	
English Turn	70040	Frost	70754	Parish)	70380
Enola	70390	Frost Town	71234	Greenwood (Terrebonne	
Enon	70438	Fryeburg	71039	Parish)	70356
Enterprise (Catahoula		Fullerton	70642	Greenwood Park	71108
Parish)	71425	Fulton	70657	Gretna	70053-54
Enterprise (Iberia Parish)	70544	Funston	71049	For specific Gretna Zip Codes call	
Eola	71322	Gaars Mill	71422	(504) 362-5610	
Epps	71237	Gahagan	71019	Grosse Tete	70740
Erath	70533	Galbraith	71447	Gueydan	70542
Eros	71238	Galion	71223	Gulf Outport (Part of New	
Erwinville (West Baton		Galliano	70354	Orleans)	70146
Rouge Parish)	70729	Galva	70421	Gullett	70422
Essen Heights	70808	Galvez	70769	Gum Ridge	71264
Estelle	70072	Gandy Spur	71429	Gurley	70730
Esther	70510	Gansville	71422	Haaswood	70452
Estherwood	70534	Garden City	70540	Hackberry	70645
Ethel	70730	Gardner	71431	Hacketts Corner	70630
Eunice	70535	Garland	71322	Hackley	70438
Eureka	71234	Garyville	70051	Hagewood	71457
Eva	71354	Gassoway	71254	Hahnville	70057
Evangeline	70537	Gayles	71105	Haile	71260
Evans	70639	Ged	70668	Haire	70548
Evelyn	71052	Geismar	70734	Half Way (Assumption	
Evergreen (Avoyelles		Gentilly (Part of New		Parish)	70346
Parish)	71333	Orleans)	70122	Halfway (Red River Parish)	71019
Evergreen (Webster Parish)	71055	Georgetown	71432	Hall Summit	71034
Evergreen Fashion Square	70808	Georgeville	70443	Hamburg	71339
Extension	71239	Georgia	70390	Hammet	71373
Fairbanks	71240	Getty Camp	70091	Hammond	70401-04
Fairlane	70360	Gheens	70355	For specific Hammond Zip Codes	
Fairmont	71417	Gibbstown	70630	call (504) 345-6014	
Fairview	71373	Gibsland	71028	Hanna	71019
Farmer Spur (Part of		Gibson	70356	Hanson City (Part of	
Vienna)	71270	Gilark	71055	Kenner)	70062
Farmerville	71241	Gilbert	71336	Happy Jack	70083
Faubourg	70589	Gilleyville	71269	Harahan	70123
Felixville	70722	Gilliam	71029	Hardwood	70775
Fellowship	71371	Gillis	70611	Hargis	71454
Fenris	70554	Girard	71269	Hargrove	70633
Fenton	70640	Glade	71343	Harlem (Plaquemines	
Ferriday	71334	Glencoe	70538	Parish)	70046
Ferry Lake	71061	Glen Dale	70049	Harlem (Vermilion Parish)	70510
Fields	70653	Glenmora	71433	Harmon	71036
Fifth Ward	71351	Glenwild	70342	Harrisonburg	71340
Fillmore	71037	Glenwood	70390	Harvey	70058-59
Fisher	71426	Gloria	70037	For specific Harvey Zip Codes call	
Fishville	71467	Gloster	71030	(504) 366-2626	
Fiske	71263	Glynn	70736	Hathaway	70532
Five Forks	71483	Godchaux	70394	Haughton	71037
Flat Creek	71479	Godchaux Community	70068	Hawthorne	71446
Flatwoods	71427	Gold Dust	71322	Hayes	70646
Flora	71428	Golden Meadow	70357	Haynesville	71038
Florence	70538	Golden Star Plantation	70090	Hazelwood	70577
Florien	71429	Goldman	71375	Head of Island	70449
Florissant	70085	Goldonna	71031	Hearn Island	71418
Flournoy	71109	Goldridge	70788	Hebert	71436
Floyd	71266	Gonzales	70737	Hecker	70647
Fluker	70436	Goodbee	70433	Heflin	71039
Foley (Allen Parish)	70655	Good Hope	70079	Helena	71366
Foley (Assumption Parish)	70390	Good Pine	71342	Henderson	70517
Folsom	70437	Goodwill	71263	Henfer Park	70123
Fondale	71201	Goodwood	71353	Henry	70533
Forbing	71106	Gordon	71038	Hermitage	70749
Fordoche	70732	Gorum	71434	Hessmer	71341
Foreman	70815	Goudeau	71338	Hester	70743
Forest	71242	Gouldsboro (Part of Gretna)	70053	Hewes	70762
Forest Glen	70445	Grambling	71245	Hickory (Avoyelles Parish)	71327
Forest Hill	71430	Gramercy	70052	Hickory (St. Tammany	
Forest Oaks	70815	Grand Bayou	71052	Parish)	70452
Forest Park	71291	Grandbois	70343	Hickory Grove	71328
Forked Island	70510	Grand Caillou	70360	Hickory Valley	71473
Forksville	71225	Grand Cane	71032	Hicks	71437
Fort De Russy	71351	Grand Chenier	70643	Hico	71235

226 LOUISIANA Higginbotham-Longleaf

	ZIP
Higginbotham	70525
Highland Acres	70123
Highland Park (Ouachita Parish)	71201
	71291
For specific Highland Park (Ouachita Parish) Zip Codes call (318) 387-6161	
Highland Park (Terrebonne Parish)	70360
Highland Park Heights	70808
Highland Road	70808
Highway Park (Part of Kenner)	70065
Hi-Land	70092
Hillaryville	70725
Hillsdale	70422
Hilltop	71268
Hilly	71235
Hineston	71438
Hobart	70769
Hodge	71247
Hohen Solms	70788
Holden	70744
Holiday Park	70502
Holloway	71328
Holly	71032
Holly Beach	70631
Hollybrook	71254
Holly Grove	71378
Holly Ridge (Richland Parish)	71269
Holly Ridge (Tensas Parish)	71375
Hollywood (Calcasieu Parish)	70663
Hollywood (Terrebonne Parish)	70360
Hollywood (West Feliciana Parish)	70775
Holmwood	70647
Holum	71435
Home Place	70083
Homer	71040
Hopedale	70085
Hope Villa	70808
Hornbeck	71439
Horse Bluff Landing	70462
Hosston	71043
Hotwells	71409
Houltonville	70447
Houma	70360-64
For specific Houma Zip Codes call (504) 868-3800	
Howard	71105
Hubertville (Part of Jeanerette)	70544
Hudson	71422
Hughes	71006
Humphreys	70356
Hundley	70535
Hunter	71052
Huron	70512
Hurricane	71003
Husser	70442
Hutton	71446
Hyde (Part of Simmesport)	71369
Hymel	70090
Iberville	70776
Ida	71044
Idlewild (St. Mary Parish)	70392
Idlewild (Terrebonne Parish)	70364
Ikes	70634
Independence	70443
Indian Bayou	70578
Indian Mound	70739
Indian Village (Allen Parish)	70648
Indian Village (Ouachita Parish)	71225
Industrial (Part of Shreveport)	71107
Ingleside	70390
Innis	70747
Inniswold	70809
International Trade Mart (Part of New Orleans)	70130
Intracoastal City	70510
Iota	70543
Iowa	70647
Irish Bend	70538
Irma	71457
Ironton	70083
Isabel	70427
Isle Labbe	70582
Istrouma (Part of Baton Rouge)	70805
Ivan	71006
Jackson	70748
Jackson Road	70748
Jacoby	70753
Jamestown	71045
Janie	71412

	ZIP
Jarreau	70749
Jay	70374
Jeanerette	70544
Jean Lafitte	70067
Jefferson (Jefferson Parish)	70121
Jefferson (Lafayette Parish)	70501
Jefferson Island	70560
Jefferson Terrace	70808
Jena	71342
Jennings	70546
Jesuit Bend	70037
Jewella (Part of Shreveport)	71109
Jigger	71249
Johnson (St. John the Baptist Parish)	70049
Johnson (St. Mary Parish)	70538
Johnson Ridge	70301
Johnson's Bayou	70631
Johnson Street	70001
Jones	71250
Jonesboro	71251
Jonesburg	71269
Jones Park (Part of Kenner)	70065
Jonesville	71343
Jordan Hill	71483
Joyce	71440
Junction	70653
Junction City	71749
Kadesh	71454
Kahns	70767
Kaplan	70548
Katy	70538
Keatchie	71046
Kedron	70422
Keithville	71047
Kelly	71441
Kellys	71270
Kendale	70062
Kendrick's Ferry	71336
Kenilworth	70085
Kenmore	70757
Kennedy Heights	70094
Kenner	70062-65
For specific Kenner Zip Codes call (504) 469-1506	
Kenner Junction (Part of Kenner)	70062
Kentwood	70444
Kickapoo	71030
Kilbourne	71253
Killian	70462
Killona	70066
Kinder	70648
King Hill	71019
Kingston	71032
Kingsville	71360
Kiroli Woods	71291
Kisatchie	71468
Kleinpeter	70808
Klondyke	70343
Klotzville	70341
Kolin	71360
Kolter (Part of Keatchie)	71046
Koran	71037
Kraemer	70371
Krotz Springs	70750
Kurthwood	71443
Laark	71250
Labadieville	70372
Labarre	70751
Lacamp	71444
Lacassine	70650
Lachute	71115
Lacombe	70445
Lacour	70715
Lafayette	70501-09
For specific Lafayette Zip Codes call (318) 269-4800	
Lafayette Square (Part of New Orleans)	70130
Lafayette Woods	70360
Lafitte	70067
Lafourche	70301
Lagan	70086
Lagonda	70380
Lake	70769
Lake Arthur	70549
Lake Bruin	71366
Lake Charles	70601-29
For specific Lake Charles Zip Codes call (318) 439-3631	
Lake End	71019
Lake Forest (Part of New Orleans)	70187
Lake Judge Perez	70083
Lakeland	70752
Lake Providence	71254
Lakeshore	71201
Lakeside (Cameron Parish)	70542
Lakeside (Rapides Parish)	71360

	ZIP
Lakeside Shopping Center	70002
Lakeview (Caddo Parish)	71107
Lakeview (Natchitoches Parish)	71456
Lakeview (Orleans Parish)	70124
Lamar	71232
Lamourie	71346
Lampman (Part of Abbeville)	70510
Landay Gautreaux Subdivision	70301
Lapine	71291
La Place	70068-69
For specific La Place Zip Codes call (504) 652-6662	
Laran	71765
La Reusitte	70037
Larose	70373
Larto	71344
Latanier	71346
Laurel Grove	70301
Laurel Hill	39669
Laurel Lea	70808
Laurel Ridge	70788
Laurel Valley Plantation	70301
Lawhon	71045
Lawtell	70550
Lazy Acres	70360
Leander	71445
Lebeau	71345
Le Blanc	70651
Le Bleu	70601
Lecompte	71346
Lee Bayou	71326
Lee Heights	71360
Lees Creek	70427
Lees Landing	70454
Leesville	71446
Leeville	70357
Legonier	70753
Leighton	70301
Leland	71368
Leleux	70560
Lemannville	70346
Le Moyen	71347
Lena	71447
Leonville	70551
Leroy	70555
Leton	71072
Lettsworth	70753
Levert	70582
Levins	71334
Lewisburg (St. Landry Parish)	70525
Lewisburg (St. Tammany Parish)	70448
Lewiston	70444
Lewistown	70394
Liberty	71225
Liberty Hill	71008
Libuse	71348
Liddieville	71295
Lillie	71256
Linda Lee	70726
Lindsay	70748
Link	70516
Linton	71006
Linville	71260
Linwood	70514
Lions	70068
Lisbon	71048
Lismore	71343
Litroe	71260
Little Caillou	70344
Little Creek	71371
Little Prairie	70769
Little Texas	70390
Live Oak	70037
Live Oak Hills	70433
Live Oak Manor	70094
Liverpool	70441
Livingston	70754
Livonia	70755
Lobdell	70767
Lockhart	71277
Lockport (Lafourche Parish)	70374
Lockport Heights	70374
Locust Ridge	71366
Logansport	71049
Log Cabin	71220
Logtown	71201
Lonepine	71367
Lone Star (Iberville Parish)	70788
Lone Star (St. Charles Parish)	70070
Longbridge (Avoyelles Parish)	71327
Long Bridge (Lafayette Parish)	70501
Longlake	71418
Longleaf	71448

Long Straw-New Orleans LOUISIANA 227

	ZIP		ZIP		ZIP
Long Straw	71227	Marthaville	71450	Mount Lebanon	71028
Longstreet	71049	Martin	71019	Mount Moriah	71226
Longview	71295	Martin Park (Part of		Mount Olive	71268
Longville	70652	Alexandria)	71301	Mount Sinai	71038
Longwood (Caddo Parish)	71060	Mason	71295	Mount Union	71277
Longwood (East Baton		Mathews	70375	Mount Zion (Lincoln Parish)	71235
Rouge Parish)	70780	Maurepas	70449	Mount Zion (Winn Parish)	71454
Loranger	70446	Maurice	70555	Mowata	70535
Loreauville	70552	Maxie	70526	Mudville	71432
Lorelein	71336	Mayfair (Part of Baton		Mulberry	70360
Lottie	70756	Rouge)	70808	Myrtle Grove (Iberville	
Louisiana Army Ammunition		Mayna	71343	Parish)	70764
Plant	71102	Meadowbrook	70056	Myrtle Grove (Plaquemines	
Louisiana Correctional and		Meadow Park Heights	71108	Parish)	70083
Industrial School		Meaux	70510	Naborton	71052
(Beauregard Parish)	70633	Mechanicsville (Part of		Nairn	70041
Louisiana Correctional		Houma)	70360	Naomi	70037
Institute for Women		Meeker	71346	Napoleonville	70390
(Iberville Parish)	70776	Melder	71451	Napoleonville Junction (Part	
Louisiana Tech (Part of		Melrose	71452	of Thibodaux)	70301
Ruston)	71272	Melville	71353	Naquin	70301
Louisville (Part of Monroe)	71207	Meraux	70075	Natalbany	70451
Lower Bonne Idee	71264	Mermentau	70556	Natchez	71456
Lower Texas	70390	Mer Rouge	71261	Natchitoches	71457-58
Lower Vacherie	70090	Merryville	70653	For specific Natchitoches Zip	
Loyds Bridge	71325	Messick	71019	Codes call (318) 352-2161	
Lozes	70560	Metairie	70001-11	Neal Landing	70462
Lucas	71105	For specific Metairie Zip Codes		Nebo	71342
Lucky	71008	call (504) 831-7750		Negreet	71460
Lucy	70049	Methvin	71019	Nesser	70815
Ludington (Part of De		Michoud (Part of New		Newellton	71357
Ridder)	70634	Orleans)	70129	New Era	71354
Ludvine	70374	Mid City (Part of New		Newhope	71266
Lukeville	70719-22	Orleans)	70119	New Iberia	70560-62
For specific Lukeville Zip Codes		Midland	70557	For specific New Iberia Zip Codes	
call (504) 749-2900		Midway (Bossier Parish)	71006	call (318) 364-4568	
Lula	71052	Midway (La Salle Parish)	71342	New Light (Richland Parish)	71259
Luling	70070	Midway (Rapides Parish)	71430	Newlight (Tensas Parish)	71357
Luna	71291	Midway (St. Mary Parish)	70538	Newllano	71461
Lunita	70661	Midway (Webster Parish)	71071		
Lutcher	70071	Milldale	70791	**New Orleans**	70101-95
Lydia	70569	Millerton	71038	For specific New Orleans Zip	
Lyons Point	70526	Millerville (Acadia Parish)	70543	Codes call (504) 589-1111	
MacArthur Village (Part of		Millerville (East Baton Rouge		*COLLEGES & UNIVERSITIES*	
Alexandria)	71301	Parish)	70815		
McBride	70360	Millikin	71254	Dillard University	70122
McCall	70346	Milly Plantation	70764	Louisiana State University	
McClendon	70438	Milton	70558	Medical Center	70112
McCrea	70715	Mimosa Park	70070	Loyola University	70118
McDade	71051	Minden	71055	New Orleans Baptist	
McGinty	71250	Mineral Springs (Lincoln		Theological Seminary	70126
McIlhenny	70513	Parish)	71235	Southern University at New	
McIntyre	71055	Mineral Springs (Ouachita		Orleans	70126
McKneeley	70732	Parish)	71225	Tulane University of	
McLeod	70374	Minerva	70360	Louisiana	70118
McManus	70748	Minorca	71334	University of New Orleans	70148
McNary	71433	Mira	71059	Xavier University of	
McNeely	71417	Mire	70578	Louisiana	70125
McNeese University (Part of		Mitchell	71419		
Lake Charles)	70609	Mittie	70654	*FINANCIAL INSTITUTIONS*	
Madewood	70390	Mix	70760	American Bank & Trust Co.	70130
Madisonville	70447	Modeste	70376	Citizens Homestead	
Magda	71301	Moisant Airport (Part of		Association	70130
Magnolia (Assumption		Kenner)	70141	Dixie Savings & Loan	
Parish)	70341	Moncla	71351	Association	70130
Magnolia (East Baton		Monette Ferry	71447	Fidelity Homestead	
Rouge Parish)	70739	Monroe	71201-13	Association	70112
Magnolia (Livingston Parish)	70744	For specific Monroe Zip Codes		Fifth District Savings & Loan	
Magnolia (Natchitoches		call (318) 387-6161		Association	70114
Parish)	71456	Montcalm	71275	First Federal Savings Bank	
Magnolia (Plaquemines		Montegut	70377	of New Orleans	70127
Parish)	70083	Monterey	71354	First National Bank of	
Magnolia (Terrebonne		Montgomery	71454	Commerce	70112
Parish)	70360	Monticello	71254	Hibernia National Bank	70130
Magnolia Park	71417	Montpelier	70422	Southern Savings Bank	70130
Magnolia Woods (Part of		Montrose	71457	Whitney National Bank	70130
Baton Rouge)	70808	Montz	70068		
Maitland	71326	Mooringsport	71060	*HOSPITALS*	
Major (Part of New Roads)	70760	Mora	71455	Charity Hospital at New	
Mallard Junction	70647	Morbihan	70560	Orleans	70140
Mamou	70554	Moreauville	71355	Hotel Dieu Hospital	70112
Manchester	70647	Moreland	71301	Ochsner Foundation	
Mandalay	70360	Morgan City	70380-81	Hospital	70121
Mandeville	70448	For specific Morgan City Zip		Southern Baptist Hospital	70115
Mangham	71259	Codes call (504) 384-0277		Touro Infirmary	70115
Manifest	71343	Morganza	70759	Tulane University Hospital	
Mansfield	71052	Morningside (Part of		and Clinics	70112
Mansura	71350	Shreveport)	71108	Veterans Administration	
Many	71449	Morrisonville	70764	Medical Center	70146
Maplewood (Part of		Morrow	71356		
Sulphur)	70663	Morse	70559	*HOTELS/MOTELS*	
Marcel	70560	Morvant	70301	Holiday Inn-Crowne Plaza	70130
Marco	71447	Morville	71373	Hotel Marie Antoinette	70130
Maringouin	70757	Moss Bluff	70611	Hotel Meridien New Orleans	70130
Marion	71260	Moss Lake	70663	Hyatt Regency New	
Marksville	71351	Mossville	70663	Orleans	70140
Marrero	70072-73	Mot	71064	New Orleans Hilton	
For specific Marrero Zip Codes		Mound	71282	Riverside and Towers	70140
call (504) 341-1741		Mount Airy	70076	Omni Hotel/Royal Orleans	70140
Marsalis	71003	Mount Carmel	71429	Royal Sonesta Hotel	70140
Mars Hill	71404	Mount Hermon	70450		

228 LOUISIANA New Roads-Rosefield

Name	ZIP
Sheraton New Orleans Hotel & Towers	70130
The Westin Canal Place	70130

MILITARY INSTALLATIONS

Name	ZIP
Louisiana Air National Guard	70143
MTMC Western Area Gulf Outport	70146
Naval Support Activity	70142
New Orleans International Airport, Moisant Airfield, Air Force Facility	70141
Supervisor of Shipbuilding, Conversion and Repair, New Orleans	70142
United States Army Engineer District, New Orleans	70160
United States Property and Fiscal Office for Louisiana	70146
8th Coast Guard District, New Orleans	70130
8th Marine Corps District	70130
926th Tactical Fighter Group	70143
New Roads	70760
New Rockdale	71052
Newton	70601
New Verda	71404
Nibletts Bluff	70668
Nicholas	70560
Nicholls University (Part of Thibodaux)	70301
Nickel	71465
Ninock	71051
Noble	71462
Noles Landing	71073
Norah	70374
Norco	70079
Normandy Park	70094
Norris Springs	71368
Northeast Louisiana University (Part of Monroe)	71209
Northgate Mall (Part of Lafayette)	70501
North Hodge	71247
North Merrydale	70812
North Monroe	71201
North Plaquemine (Part of Plaquemine)	70764
North Shore	70458
North Shore Beach	70458
North Slidell (Part of Slidell)	70458
Northwestern (Part of Natchitoches)	71457
Norton Shop	71072
Norwood	70761
Notleyville	70512
Notnac	71357
Numa	70560
Nunez	70548
Oakdale	71463
Oak Forest	70356
Oak Grove (Ascension Parish)	70769
Oak Grove (Cameron Parish)	70643
Oak Grove (Grant Parish)	71417
Oak Grove (Lincoln Parish)	71275
Oak Grove (Sabine Parish)	71419
Oak Grove (West Carroll Parish)	71263
Oak Hills Place	70808
Oakland	71260
Oaklawn (St. Mary Parish)	70538
Oaklawn (St. Tammany Parish)	70445
Oakley	70390
Oak Manor	70815
Oaknolia	70777
Oak Ridge	71264
Oaks	71038
Oakshire Manor	70364
Oakville	70037
Oakwood Shopping Center (Part of Gretna)	70053
Oberlin	70655
Oil Center (Part of Lafayette)	70501
Oil City	71061
Okaloosa	71238
Old Athens	71003
Oldfield	70785
Old Lafitte	70067
Old Shongaloo	71072
Olive Branch	70777
Oliver (Part of Hammond)	70401
Olivier	70560

Name	ZIP
Olla	71465
Ollie	70037
Omega	71276
Opelousas	70570-71

For specific Opelousas Zip Codes call (318) 942-2421

Name	ZIP
Orange Grove Plantation	70301
Oretta	70633
Oscar	70762
Ossun	70583
Ostrica	70041
Otis	71466
Ouachita City	71280
Oubre (Part of Loreauville)	70552
Oxford (De Soto Parish)	71052
Oxford (St. Mary Parish)	70538
Pace	71055
Packton	71483
Paincourtville	70391
Palmetto	71358
Palo Alto	70346
Panchoville	70532
Panola	71254
Paradis	70080
Paradise	71360
Paradise Manor	70123
Parhams	71343
Park Manor	70003
Parks	70582
Parkside Manor	70123
Park Vista (Part of Opelousas)	70570
Patoutville	70544
Patterson	70392
Paulina	70763
Pearl River	70452
Peason	71429
Pecan Grove	70094
Pecaniere	70512
Pecan Island	70548
Pecan Place	70764
Peck	71368
Pelican	71063
Perkins	70633
Perry	70575
Perryville	71220
Phoenix	70042
Pickering	71446
Pierre Bossier Mall (Part of Bossier City)	71112
Pierre Part	70339
Pierre Part Settlement	70339
Pilottown	70081
Pine	70438
Pine Coupee	71427
Pine Grove (Ouachita Parish)	71201
Pine Grove (St. Helena Parish)	70453
Pine Island	70532
Pine Oak Terrace (Part of Shreveport)	71108
Pine Prairie	70576
Pineville	71360-61

For specific Pineville Zip Codes call (318) 442-3254

Name	ZIP
Pioneer	71266
Pitkin	70656
Pitreville	70525
Plain Dealing	71064
Plains	70791
Plainview	70427
Plaisance	70570
Plantation Acres	71301
Plaquemine	70764-65

For specific Plaquemine Zip Codes call (504) 687-2282

Name	ZIP
Plaquemine Southwest	70764
Plattenville	70393
Plaucheville	71362
Plaza in Lake Forest, The (Part of New Orleans)	70127
Pleasant Hill (Bienville Parish)	71028
Pleasant Hill (Sabine Parish)	71065
Pleasant Hills	70811
Pleasant Valley	71234
Plettenberg	70775
Point	71234
Point Au Chien	70377
Point Blue	70586
Pointe a la Hache	70082
Pointe Coupee	70760
Point Pleasant	71220
Poland	71301
Pollock	71467
Ponchatoula	70454
Ponchatoula Beach	70454
Pontchartrain Beach (Part of New Orleans)	70122
Poole	71051

Name	ZIP
Poplar Grove	70767
Portage	70512
Port Allen	70767
Port Barre	70577
Port Barrow (Part of Donaldsonville)	70346
Port Eads	70091
Porters Curve	70450
Porterville	71071
Port Fourchon	70357
Port Gardner	70791
Port Hickey	70791
Port Manchac	70421
Port of West Saint Mary	70538
Port Sulphur	70083
Port Vincent	70726
Potash	70083
Pot Cove	70586
Poufette	70560
Powhatan	71066
Poydras	70085
Prairie Ronde	70570
Prairieville	70769
Pratt	71028
Presque Isle	70363
Pride	70770
Prien	70605
Prien Lake Mall (Part of Lake Charles)	70601
Princeton	71067
Promised Land	70040
Prospect (Grant Parish)	71423
Prospect (St. Charles Parish)	70078
Provencal	71468
Providence	70062
Puckett	70791
Pumpkin Center	70403
Punkin Center	71247
Quaid	71343
Quimby	71282
Quitman	71268
Raceland	70394
Ragley	70657
Ramah	70757
Rambin	71063
Randolph	71256
Rapides	71409
Ratliff	70390
Rattan	71429
Rayne	70578
Rayville	71269
Readhimer	71070
Red Chute	71037
Reddell	70580
Red Gum	71334
Redland (Bossier Parish)	71064
Redland (Evangeline Parish)	70554
Red Oaks	70815
Reeves	70658
Reggio	70085
Reids	70656
Remy	70763
Reserve	70084
Rhinehart	71363
Rhymes	71269
Riceville	70542
Richard	70525
Richardson	70438
Richmond	71282
Richohoc	70538
Richwood	71201
Rideau Settlement	71358
Ridge	70578
Ridgecrest	71334
Ridgewood	70739
Rienzi Plantation	70301
Ringgold	71068
Rio	70427
Risinger Woods	71107
Riverlands	70068
River Ridge	70123
Riverton	71418
Riverwood	70433
Roanoke	70581
Robeline	71469
Robert	70455
Robson	71105
Rock	71447
Rock Hill	71423
Rocky Branch	71241
Rocky Mount	71064
Rodessa	71069
Rogers	71342
Romeville	70723
Roosevelt	71276
Rosa	71364
Rosedale (Assumption Parish)	70390
Rosedale (Iberville Parish)	70772
Rosefield	71435

LOUISIANA 229

Name	ZIP
Roseland	70456
Rosepine	70659
Rougon	70773
Rousseau	70394
Roxana	71301
Roy	71016
Ruby	71365
Rum Center	71256
Ruple	71038
Rural Park	70123
Ruston	71270-73
For specific Ruston Zip Codes call (318) 255-3791	
Ruth	70517
Rynella	70560
Sadie	71260
Sadou	70529
Sailes	71028
St. Amant	70774
St. Benedict	70457
St. Bernard	70085
St. Bernard Grove	70075
St. Charles	70301
St. Clair	70040
St. Claude Heights	70032
St. Elmo	70725
St. Francisville	70775
St. Gabriel	70776
St. Genevieve	71373
St. Gertrude	70433
St. James	70086
St. Joe	70452
St. John	70301
St. Joseph	71366
St. Landry	71367
St. Martinville	70582
St. Maurice	71471
St. Rosalie	70037
St. Rose	70087
St. Tammany	70445
St. Thomas	70390
Saline	71070
Samstown	70788
Samtown	71301
Sandy Hill	71446
Sardis (Sabine Parish)	71419
Sardis (Winn Parish)	71483
Sarepta	71071
Satsuma	70754
Savoy	70535
Scarsdale	70040
Schriever	70395
Scotlandville	70807
Scott	70583
Searcy	71371
Sebastapol	70085
Sellers	70079
Selma	71432
Sentell	71107
Serena	71343
Seymourville	70764
Shadyside	70538
Shamrock	71469
Sharon	71235
Sharon Hills	70811
Sharp	71447
Shaw	71373
Shelburn	71254
Shelton	71220
Sherburne	70750
Sheridan	70438
Sherwood	71435
Shiloh (Tangipahoa Parish)	70422
Shiloh (Union Parish)	71222
Shongaloo	71072
Shreve City Shopping Center (Part of Shreveport)	71105
Shreveport	71101-10
	71115-66
For specific Shreveport Zip Codes call (318) 677-2334	
Shrewsbury	70121
Shuteston	70570
Sibley (Lincoln Parish)	71227
Sibley (Webster Parish)	71073
Sicard (Part of Monroe)	71201
Sicily Island	71368
Siegle	71291
Sieper	71472
Sikes	71473
Sikes Ferry	71072
Silverwood	70546
Simmesport	71369
Simms	71467
Simpson	71474
Simsboro	71275
Singer	70660
Siracusaville	70380
Slacks	70757
Slagle	71475
Slaughter	70777
Slidell	70458-61
For specific Slidell Zip Codes call (504) 643-5338	
Sligo	71112
Smithfield	70767
Smith Ridge	70344
Smoke Bend	70346
Socola	70083
Soileau	70655
Somerset	71357
Sondheimer	71276
Soniat	70788
Sorrell	70544
Sorrento	70778
South Acres	70663
South Bend	70538
Southdown	70360
Southeast (Part of Baton Rouge)	70808
Southeast Louisiana Hospital	70448
Southern	70813
Southfield (Part of Shreveport)	71105
South Fort Trailer Park	71459
South Kenner	70094
South Lafourche	70357
South Mansfield	71052
South Park (Caddo Parish)	71118
South Park (Rapides Parish)	71301
South Park Mall (Part of Shreveport)	71118
South Pass	70091
Southport	70121
South Sherwood (Part of Baton Rouge)	70816
Southside (Part of Lafayette)	70503
Southwestern University (Part of Lafayette)	70504
Spaulding	71441
Spearsville	71277
Spencer	71280
Spillman	70748
Splane Place (Part of West Monroe)	71291
Spokane	71334
Springcreek	70444
Springfield	70462
Spring Hill (Jackson Parish)	71251
Springhill (Washington Parish)	70438
Springhill (Webster Parish)	71075
Springridge (Caddo Parish)	71047
Spring Ridge (Sabine Parish)	71065
Springville (Livingston Parish)	70754
Springville (Red River Parish)	71019
Standard	71465
Stanley	71049
Star	70037
Starhill	70748
Staring (Part of Baton Rouge)	70801
Starks	70661
Start	71279
State Line	70438
Stella	70040
Stephensville	70380
Sterlington	71280
Stevensdale	70815
Stevenson	71220
Stonewall	71136
Stoney Point	70438
Stonypoint	70739
Stumpf's Westside Shopping Center (Part of Gretna)	70053
Sugarcreek	71001
Sugartown	70662
Sulphur	70663-64
For specific Sulphur Zip Codes call (318) 625-2214	
Summerfield	71079
Summer Grove (Part of Shreveport)	71118
Summerville	71465
Sun	70463
Sunnybrook	70814
Sunny Hill	70438
Sunrise	70767
Sunset	70584
Sunshine	70780
Sun Spur	71232
Supreme	70390
Susan Park (Part of Kenner)	70062
Swampers	71295
Swartz	71281
Sweet Lake	70630
Swords	70525
Taconey	71373
Taft	70057
Talisheek	70464
Talla Bena	71276
Tallulah	71282-84
For specific Tallulah Zip Codes call (318) 574-0295	
Tangipahoa	70465
Tanglewood (East Baton Rouge Parish)	70811
Tanglewood (Rapides Parish)	71301
Tannehill	71422
Tate Cove	70586
Taylor	71080
Taylor Hill	71447
Taylortown (Bossier Parish)	71051
Taylortown (Union Parish)	71277
Tchefuncte Estates	70433
Temple	71474
Tendal	71282
Terry	71263
Terrytown	70053
Theriot	70397
The Rock	71417
Thibodaux	70301-02
For specific Thibodaux Zip Codes call (504) 447-3737	
Thomas	70438
Thomastown	71282
Thornwell	70549
Three Oaks	70032
Three Rivers Heights	70433
Tickfaw	70466
Tidewater Camp	70091
Tigerville	70049
Timberlane (Jefferson Parish)	70053
Timber Trails	71360
Tioga	71477
Toca	70085
Toomey	70668
Topsy	70601
Torbert (sta.) (Pointe Coupee Parish)	70781
Torbert (Pointe Coupee Parish)	70781
Toro	71429
Torras	70753
Tower Park (Part of Leesville)	71446
Town and Country	71201
Transylvania	71286
Trees	71082
Tremont	71227
Trenton	71052
Trinity (Catahoula Parish)	71343
Trinity (Iberville Parish)	70772
Triumph	70041
Tropical Bend	70050
Trout	71371
Trout-Goodpine	71342
Truxno	71260
Tullos	71479
Tunica	70782
Turkey Creek	70585
Turnerville (Part of Plaquemine)	70764
Twin Oaks	71223
Uncle Sam	70792
Union	70723
Union Church	71268
Union Hill (Rapides Parish)	71433
Union Hill (Winn Parish)	71483
Union Landing	70754
Union Springs	71419
Unionville	71235
University (Part of Baton Rouge)	70803
Upland	71220
Upstream	70123
Urania	71480
Utility	71343
Vacherie	70090
Valmar	70075
Valverda	70757
Vanceville	71111
Varnado	70467
Vatican	70520
Vaughn	71220
Velma	70422
Venice	70091
Ventress	70783
Verda	71481
Verdun	70754
Verdunville	70538
Vernon	71270
Verret	70085

LOUISIANA

Veterans Administration Hospital-Zylks

	ZIP		ZIP		ZIP
Veterans Administration Hospital (Part of Shreveport)	71101	Waterproof (Terrebonne Parish)	70360	Wildwood (East Baton Rouge Parish)	70808
Vick	71372	Watson	70786	Willhite	71234
Vidalia	71373	Waverly	71232	Williams	71105
Vidrine	70586	Waxia	70589	Williana	71423
Vienna	71270	Weil	71301	Willow Glen	71301
Vieux Carre (Part of New Orleans)	70112	Welcome	70086	Wills Point	70040
		Weldon	71222	Wilmer	70444
Village East	70360	Welsh	70591	Wilshire Park	71301
Village St. George	70808	Wemple	71052	Wilson	70789
Ville Platte	70586	Westdale	71105	Wilsona	71366
Vincent Landing	70663	Western Kraft	71411	Wilson Point	71301
Vincent Park	70075	West Ferriday	71334	Wilton Subdivision	71107
Vinton	70668	Westfield	70390	Winnfield	71483
Violet (St. Bernard Parish)	70092	Westlake	70669	Winnsboro	71295
		Westminster	70809	Wisner	71378
Vista Village Regional Shopping Center (Part of Opelousas)	70570	West Monroe	71291-94	Womack (Jackson Parish)	71226
		For specific West Monroe Zip Codes call (318) 387-8821		Womack (Red River Parish)	71068
				Woodardville	71068
Vivian	71082	Weston	71251	Woodhaven	70466
Vixen	71418	Westover	70767	Woodland	70083
Voorhies	71355	West Pointe a la Hache	70083	Woodlawn (Assumption Parish)	70390
Vowells Mill	71469	Westport	70656		
Wade Correctional Center	71038	Westside (Rapides Parish)	71301	Woodlawn (Jefferson Davis Parish)	70647
Wadesboro	70454	West Slidell (Part of Slidell)	70460		
Waggaman (Jefferson Parish)	70094	Westwego	70094-96	Woodlawn (Plaquemines Parish)	70040
		For specific Westwego Zip Codes call (504) 341-2411			
Wakefield	70784			Woodlawn (Terrebonne Parish)	70360
Waldheim	70433	Weyanoke	70787		
Walker (Jackson Parish)	71251	Whatley Landing	71371	Woodside	71353
Walker (Livingston Parish)	71785	Wheeling	71454	Woodville	71270
Wallace	70049	White	70301	Woodworth	71485
Wallace Ridge	71343	White Castle	70788	Wyandotte	70380
Walls	70720	Whitehall (La Salle Parish)	71342	Wyatt	71251
Walters	71343	Whitehall (Livingston Parish)	70449	Yellow Pine	71073
Ward	71463	White Hall (St. James Parish)	70723	Youngsville	70592
Warden	71232			Zachary	70791
Wardview	71064	White Hills	70714	Zebedee	71269
Wardville (Morehouse Parish)	71220	White Sulphur Springs	71371	Zenoria	71371
		Whiteville	71322	Zion	71432
Wardville (Rapides Parish)	71360	Whittington	71301	Zion City (Part of Baton Rouge)	70811
Warnerton	70438	Wickland Terrace	70815		
Warsaw Landing	70462	Wickliffe	70783	Zwolle	71486
Washington	70589	Wildsville	71377	Zylks	71069
Waterloo	70783	Wildwood (Assumption Parish)	70390		
Waterproof (Tensas Parish)	71375				

Abbot-Clinton MAINE 231

	ZIP		ZIP		ZIP
Abbot (Town)	04406	Belmont (Town)	04915	Bustins Island	04013
Abbotts Mill	04219	Belmont Corner	04915	Buxton (Town)	04093
Abbot Village	04406	Benedicta	04733	Buxton Center	04093
Acadia Terrace	04785	Benton	04910	Byron	04275
Acton	04001	Benton (Town)	04910	Byron (Town)	04275
Acton (Town)	04001	Benton Falls	04901	Calais	04619
Addison	04606	Benton Station	04937	Caldwel Corner	04281
Addison (Town)	04606	Bernard	04612	Caldwell Corner	04281
Admiralty Village	03904	Berry Mills	04224	Cambridge	04923
Airport Mall (Part of Bangor)	04401	Berwick	03901	Cambridge (Town)	04923
Albion	04910	Berwick (Town)	03901	Camden	04843
Albion (Town)	04910	Bethel	04217	Camden (Town)	04843
Alexander	04619	Bethel (Town)	04217	Campbell (Part of Presque	
Alexander (Town)	04619	Biddeford	04005	Isle)	04769
Alfred	04002	Biddeford Pool (Part of		Camp Ellis (Part of Saco)	04072
Alfred (Town)	04002	Biddeford)	04006	Canaan	04924
Alfred Mills	04002	Bingham	04920	Canaan (Town)	04924
Allagash (Town)	04774	Bingham (Town)	04920	Canton	04221
Allagash	04774	Birch Harbor	04613	Canton (Town)	04221
Allens Mills	04938	Birch Island	04011	Canton Point	04221
Alna	04535	Black Point	04074	Cape Cottage	04107
Alna (Town)	04535	Blackstrap	04105	Cape Elizabeth	
Alna Center	04535	Blackwell	04950	(Cumberland County)	
Alton (Town)	04468	Blaine	04734	(Town)	04107
Amherst	04605	Blaine (Town)	04734	Cape Elizabeth	
Amherst (Town)	04605	Blaisdell Corners	04027	(Cumberland County)	04107
Amity (Town)	04465	Blake Corner	04250	Cape Neddick	03902
Andover	04216	Blanchard	04406	Cape Porpoise	04014
Andover (Town)	04216	Blanchard (Town)	04406	Capitol Island	04538
Anson	04911	Blue Hill	04614	Caratunk	04925
Anson (Town)	04911	Blue Hill (Town)	04614	Caratunk (Town)	04925
Appleton	04862	Blue Hill Falls	04615	Cardville	04418
Appleton (Town)	04862	Blue Point	04074	Caribou	04736
Argyle (Town)	04468	Bolsters Mills	04040	Caribou Road (Part of	
Aroostook Farm (Part of		Bonny Eagle	04093	Presque Isle)	04769
Presque Isle)	04769	Boothbay	04537	Carmel	04419
Arrowsic (Town)	04530	Boothbay (Town)	04537	Carmel (Town)	04419
Arundel (Town)	04046	Boothbay Harbor (Lincoln		Carrabassett	04947
Ashdale	04565	County)	04538	Carrabassett Valley (Town)	04947
Ashland	04732	Boothbay Harbor (Lincoln		Carroll	04487
Ashland (Town)	04732	County) (Town)	04538	Carroll (Town)	04487
Ashville	04607	Boothbay Park (Part of		Carson	04786
Athens	04912	Saco)	04072	Carthage	04224
Athens (Town)	04912	Bowdoin	04008	Carthage (Town)	04224
Atkinson (Town)	04426	Bowdoin (Town)	04008	Cary	04465
Atkinson Corner	04426	Bowdoinham	04008	Cary (Town)	04465
Atkinson Mills	04426	Bowdoinham (Town)	04008	Casco	04015
Atlantic	04608	Bowerbank (Town)	04426	Casco (Town)	04015
Auburn	04210-12	Bradford	04410	Cash Corner (Part of South	
For specific Auburn Zip Codes call		Bradford (Town)	04410	Portland)	04106
(207) 786-0604		Bradford Center	04410	Castine	04421
Auburn Mall (Part of		Bradley	04411	Castine (Town)	04421
Auburn)	04210	Bradley (Town)	04411	Castle Hill (Town)	04757
Auburn Plains (Part of		Bremen (Town)	04551	Caswell (Town)	04750
Auburn)	04210	Brewer	04412	Cathance	04086
Augusta	04330-38	Bridgewater	04735	Cedar Grove	04342
For specific Augusta Zip Codes		Bridgewater (Town)	04735	Center Lebanon	04027
call (207) 623-8054		Bridgton	04009	Center Lovell	04016
Aurora	04408	Bridgton (Town)	04009	Center Minot	04258
Aurora (Town)	04408	Brighton	04912	Center Montville	04941
Avon (Town)	04966	Brighton (Town)	04912	Center Vassalboro	04989
Back Narrows	04537	Bristol	04539	Centerville	04623
Bailey Island	04003	Bristol (Town)	04539	Centerville (Town)	04623
Baileyville (Town)	04694	Brixham	03909	Central Aroostook (Town)	04760
Baker Corner	04082	Broad Cove	04572	Central Hancock (Town)	04640
Balch Pond	03830	Brookhaven	04062	Central Somerset (Town)	04920
Bald Head	03907	Brooklin	04616	Chamberlain	04541
Baldwin (Town)	04024	Brooklin (Town)	04616	Chapman	04757
Bancroft	04497	Brooks	04921	Chapman (Town)	04757
Bancroft (Town)	04497	Brooks (Town)	04921	Charleston	04422
Bangor	04401	Brooksville (Town)	04617	Charleston (Town)	04422
Bangor Mall (Part of		Brooksville (Hancock		Charleston Correctional	
Bangor)	04401	County)	04617	Facility	04422
Bar Harbor	04609	Brookton	04413	Charlotte (Town)	04666
Bar Harbor (Town)	04609	Brown Corner (Aroostook		Chases Pond	03909
Baring	04619	County)	04750	Chebeague Island	04017
Baring (Town)	04619	Brown Corner (Waldo		Chelsea	04330
Bar Mills	04004	County)	04915	Chelsea (Town)	04345
Barnard (Town)	04414	Brownfield (Town)	04010	Cherryfield	04622
Barrett (Part of Caribou)	04736	Brownfield (Oxford County)	04010	Cherryfield (Town)	04622
Bartlett Mills	04043	Brownville	04414	Chester	04458
Basin Mills	04473	Brownville (Town)	04414	Chester (Town)	04458
Bass Harbor	04653	Brownville Junction	04415	Chesterville	04938
Batchelders Crossing	04350	Brunswick	04011	Chesterville (Town)	04938
Bath	04530	Brunswick (Town)	04011	Chesuncook	04441
Bay Point	04548	Brunswick Naval Air Station	04011	Chicopee	04038
Bayside (Hancock County)	04605	Brunswick Station	04011	China	04926
Bayside (Waldo County)	04915	Bryant Pond	04219	China (Town)	04926
Bayview (Part of Saco)	04072	Buckfield	04220	Chisholm	04239
Bayville	04536	Buckfield (Town)	04220	Christmas Cove	04568
Beals	04611	Bucks Harbor	04618	Cider Hill	03909
Beals (Town)	04611	Bucksport	04416	City Point (Part of Belfast)	04915
Beans Corner	04225	Bucksport (Town)	04416	Clapboard Island	04105
Beaver Cove (Town)	04441	Bunganuc Landing	04011	Clark Island	04859
Beaver Dam	03901	Bunkers Harbor	04613	Clarks Mill	04042
Beddington (Town)	04622	Burkettville	04574	Clay Hill	03902
Beech Ridge	03909	Burlington	04417	Clayton Lake	04737
Belfast	04915	Burlington (Town)	04417	Cliff Island (Part of Portland)	04019
Belgrade	04917	Burnham	04922	Clifton	04428
Belgrade (Town)	04917	Burnham (Town)	04922	Clifton (Town)	04428
Belgrade Lakes	04918	Burnt Meadow Pond	04041	Clinton	04927

232 MAINE

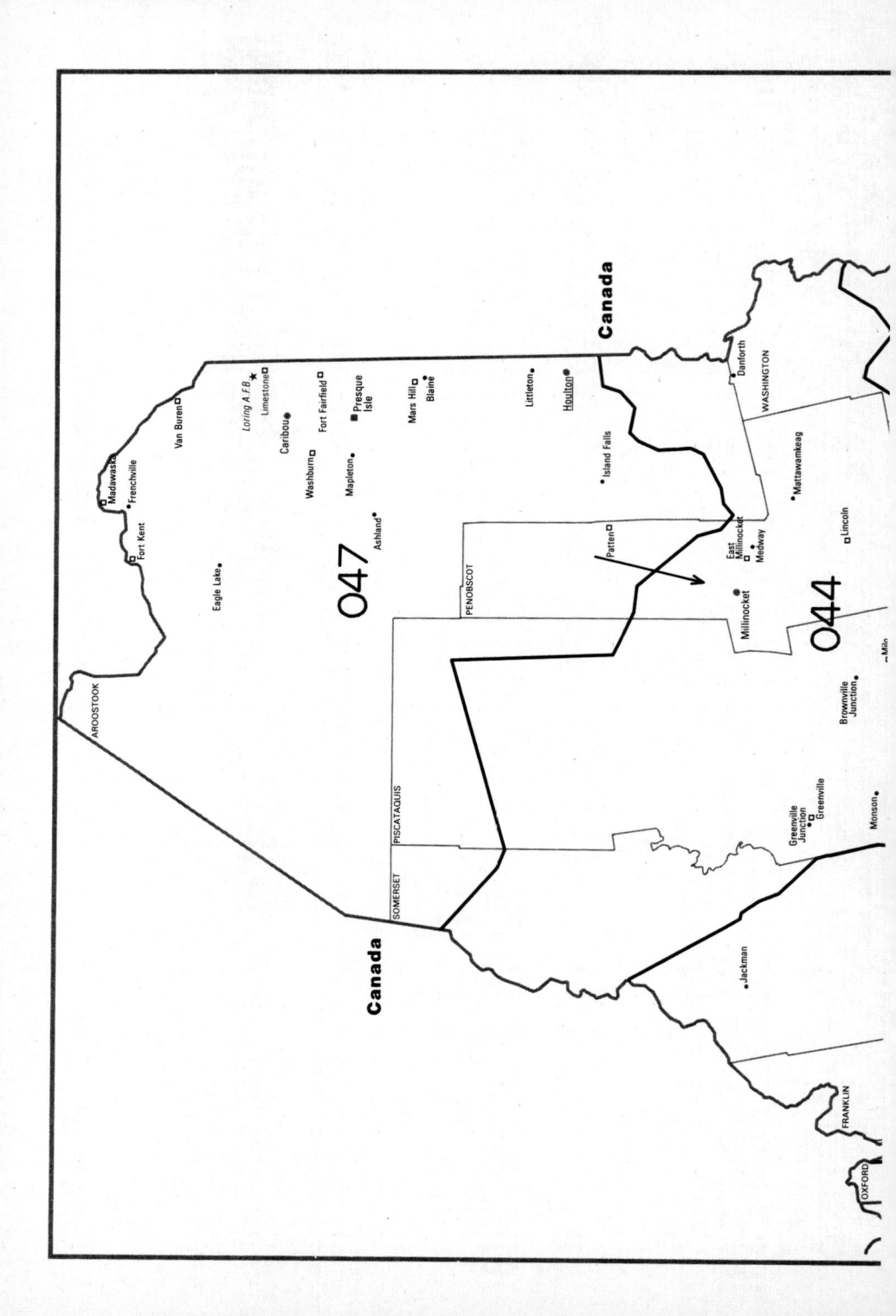

MAINE 233

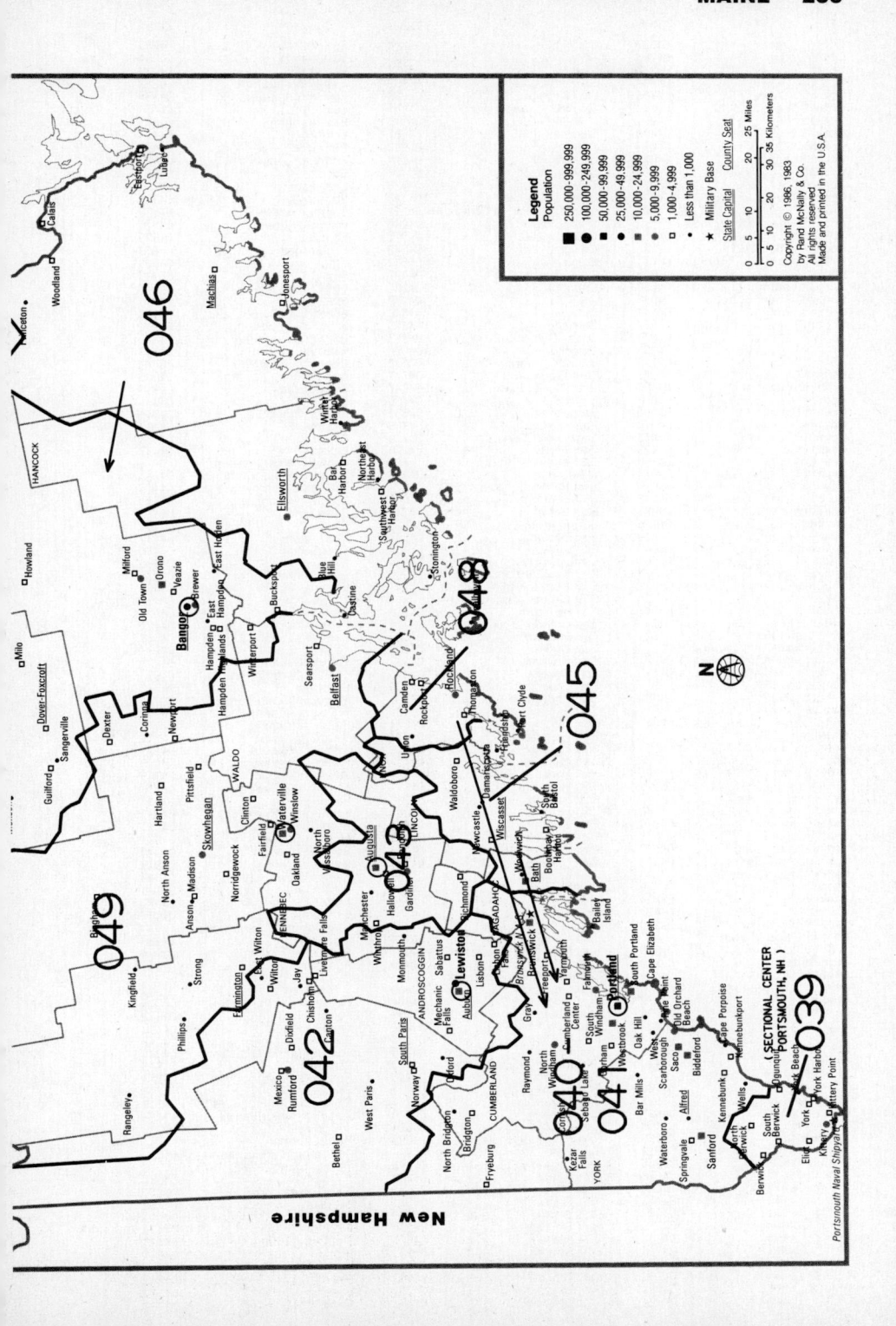

234 MAINE Clinton-Freeport

	ZIP		ZIP		ZIP
Clinton (Town)	04927	Dixfield Center	04224	East Vassalboro	04935
Cobbs Bridge	04260	Dixmont	04932	East Warren	04864
Coburn Gore	04936	Dixmont (Town)	04932	East Waterboro	04030
Codyville (Town)	04490	Dixmont Center	04932	East Waterford	04233
Colby	04736	Dog Corner	04038	East Wilton	04234
Colby College (Part of		Dog Island Corner (Part of		East Winn	04455
Waterville)	04901	Belfast)	04915	East Winthrop	04343
Coles Corner	04496	Dogtown	04967	Eaton	04424
Columbia (Town)	04623	Dorman	04643	Eddington	04428
Columbia Falls	04623	Douglas Hill	04024	Eddington (Town)	04428
Columbia Falls (Town)	04623	Dover-Foxcroft	04426	Eden	04672
Concordville	03910	Dover-Foxcroft (Town)	04426	Edes Falls	04055
Connor (Town)	04736	Dover South Mills	04426	Edgecomb	04556
Convene	04091	Downtown (Part of Portland)	04112	Edgecomb (Town)	04556
Cooks Corner (Cumberland		Drake Corner	04849	Edinburg (Town)	04448
County)	04011	Drakes Island	04090	Edmunds	04628
Cooks Corner (Waldo		Dresden	04342	Eggemoggin	04650
County)	04987	Dresden (Town)	04342	Egypt	04605
Cooks Mills	04015	Drew (Town)	04497	Eliot	03903
Cooper (Town)	04638	Dryden	04225	Eliot (Town)	03903
Coopers Corner	04046	Dry Mills	04039	Elizabeth Park	04106
Coopers Mills	04341	Ducktrap	04849	Ellingswood Corner	04456
Coplin (Town)	04982	Dunkertown	04270	Elliottsville (Town)	04464
Corea	04624	Dunns Corner	04355	Ellis Pond	04235
Corinna	04928	Durgintown	04020	Ellsworth	04605
Corinna (Town)	04928	Durham (Town)	04032	Ellsworth Falls (Part of	
Corinna Center	04928	Dyer Brook	04747	Ellsworth)	04605
Corinth (Town)	04427	Dyer Brook (Town)	04747	Embden (Town)	04958
Cornish	04020	E (Town)	04758	Emery Mills	04031
Cornish (Town)	04020	Eagle Island	04683	Emerys Corner	04048
Cornville	04976	Eagle Lake	04739	Empire	04258
Cornville (Town)	04976	Eagle Lake (Town)	04739	Enfield	04433
Costigan	04423	East Andover	04226	Enfield (Town)	04433
Cote Corner	04750	East Auburn (Part of		English (Part of Presque	
Country Living	04073	Auburn)	04210	Isle)	04769
Cousins Island	04096	East Baldwin	04024	Estabrook Settlement	04465
Coventry North	04048	East Benton	04910	Estcourt Station	04741
Cranberry Isles	04625	East Bethel	04217	Estes Lake	04073
Cranberry Isles (Town)	04625	East Blue Hill	04629	Etna	04434
Crawford (Town)	04619	East Boothbay	04544	Etna (Town)	04434
Crescent Lake	04015	Eastbrook	04634	Etna Center	04434
Criehaven (Town)	04851	Eastbrook (Town)	04634	Eustis	04936
Crockett Corner	04069	East Buckfield	04220	Eustis (Town)	04936
Crossman Corner	04252	East Central Franklin (Town)	04947	Exeter	04435
Crouseville	04738	East Central Washington		Exeter (Town)	04435
Crystal	04747	(Town)	04628	Exeter Center	04435
Crystal (Town)	04747	East Corinth	04427	Exeter Mills	04427
Cumberland (Town)	04021	East Denmark	04022	Fairbanks	04938
Cumberland Center		East Dixfield	04227	Fairfield	04937
(Cumberland County)	04021	East Dixmont	04932	Fairfield (Town)	04937
Cumberland Foreside	04110	East Dover	04426	Fairfield Center	04937
Cumberland Mills (Part of		East Eddington	04428	Fairmount	04742
Westbrook)	04092	East Edgecomb	04556	Falmouth (Cumberland	
Cundys Harbor	04011	East Exeter	04427	County) (Town)	04105
Curtis Corner	04263	East Franklin	04634	Falmouth (Cumberland	
Cushing	04563	East Friendship	04547	County)	04105
Cushing (Town)	04563	East Fryeburg	04010	Falmouth Foreside	04105
Cutler	04626	East Hampden	04401	Falmouth Shopping Center	04105
Cutler (Town)	04626	East Hancock (Town)	04408	Farmingdale	04345
Cutts Island	03905	East Harpswell	04011	Farmingdale (Town)	04345
Cyr (Town)	04785	East Hebron	04238	Farmington	04938
Daigle	04743	East Hiram	04041	Farmington (Town)	04938
Dallas (Town)	04970	East Holden	04429	Farmington Falls	04940
Damariscotta	04543	East Knox	04986	Farwells Corner	04988
Damariscotta (Town)	04543	East Lamoine	04605	Fayette	04349
Damariscotta Mills	04553	East Lebanon	04027	Fayette (Town)	04349
Damariscotta-Newcastle	04543	East Limington	04049	Fayette Corner	04349
Damascus	04419	East Livermore	04228	Felch Corner	04048
Danforth	04424	East Lowell	04433	Ferry Beach (Part of Saco)	04072
Danforth (Town)	04424	East Machias	04630	Fish Street	04037
Danville (Part of Auburn)	04223	East Machias (Town)	04630	Five Corners (Androscoggin	
Danville Corner (Part of		East Madison	04976	County)	04256
Auburn)	04210	East Millinocket (Penobscot		Five Corners (York County)	03906
Dark Harbor	04848	County) (Town)	04430	Five Islands	04548
Davenport Cove	04424	East Millinocket (Penobscot		Five Points (Part of	
Davis Island	04556	County)	04430	Biddeford)	04005
Days Ferry	04579	East Monmouth	04364	Fletchers Landing	04605
Dayton (Town)	04005	East Newport	04933	Forest City	04413
Deblois	04622	East New Portland	04961	Fort Fairfield	04742
Deblois (Town)	04622	East Northport	04915	Fort Fairfield (Town)	04742
Dedham	04429	Easton (Town)	04740	Fort Hill (Part of Biddeford)	04005
Dedham (Town)	04429	Easton (Aroostook County)	04740	Fort Kent	04743
Deering (Part of Presque		Easton Center	04740	Fort Kent (Town)	04743
Isle)	04769	East Orland	04431	Fort Kent Mills	04744
Deer Isle	04627	East Orrington	04474	Fort Kent Village	04743
Deer Isle (Town)	04627	East Otisfield	04270	Fortunes Rocks (Part of	
Delano Park	04106	East Palermo	04354	Biddeford)	04005
Denmark	04022	East Parsonsfield	04028	Fosters Corner	
Denmark (Town)	04022	East Peru	04229	(Cumberland County)	04062
Dennistown (Town)	04945	East Pittston	04345	Fosters Corner (Waldo	
Dennysville	04628	East Poland	04230	County)	04921
Dennysville (Town)	04628	Eastport	04631	Four Corners (Aroostook	
Derby	04463	East Raymond	04071	County)	04750
Detroit	04929	East Sebago	04029	Four Corners (York County)	04043
Detroit (Town)	04929	East Stoneham	04231	Frankfort	04438
Dexter	04930	East Sullivan	04607	Frankfort (Town)	04438
Dexter (Town)	04930	East Sumner	04220	Franklin	04634
Dickey	04774	East Surry	04605	Franklin (Town)	04634
Dickvale	04290	East Thorndike	04986	Freedom	04941
Dixfield	04224	East Troy	04987	Freedom (Town)	04941
Dixfield (Town)	04224	East Union	04862	Freeport	04032

Freeport-Limington **MAINE** **235**

Name	ZIP
Freeport (Town)	04032
Frenchboro (Hancock County) (Town)	04635
Frenchboro (Hancock County)	04635
Frenchville (Town)	04745
Frenchville (Aroostook County)	04745
Frenchville (Aroostook County)	04732
Friendship	04547
Friendship (Town)	04547
Frye	04235
Fryeburg	04037
Fryeburg (Town)	04037
Fryeburg Center	04037
Fryeburg Harbor	04037
Gardiner	04345
Garfield (Town)	04732
Garland	04939
Garland (Town)	04939
Georgetown	04548
Georgetown (Town)	04548
Gerrishville	04693
Gilbertville	04221
Gilead	04217
Gilead (Town)	04217
Glantz Corner	04062
Glenburn (Town)	04401
Glenburn Center	04401
Glen Cove	04846
Glendon	04572
Glenmere	04860
Glenwood (Town)	04497
Goodings (Part of Presque Isle)	04769
Good Will-Hinckley School	04944
Goodwins Mills	04005
Goose Rocks Beach	04046
Gorham	04038
Gorham (Town)	04038
Gotts Island	04653
Gould Landing	04401
Gouldsboro	04607
Gouldsboro (Town)	04607
Grand Beach	04064
Grand Falls (Town)	04417
Grand Isle	04746
Grand Isle (Town)	04746
Grand Lake Stream	04637
Grand Lake Stream (Town)	04637
Granite Hill (Part of Hallowell)	04347
Grass Corner	04750
Gray (Town)	04039
Gray (Cumberland County)	04039
Grays Corner	04676
Great Diamond Island (Part of Portland)	04109
Great Falls (Part of Auburn)	04210
Great Pond	04408
Great Pond (Town)	04408
Great Works (Part of Old Town)	04468
Greeley Landing	04426
Greenbush	04467
Greenbush (Town)	04467
Greene	04236
Greene (Town)	04236
Greenfield	04423
Greenfield (Town)	04423
Green Lake	04429
Greens Corner	04988
Greenville	04441
Greenville (Town)	04441
Greenville	04441
Greenville Junction	04442
Greenwood	04289
Greenwood (Town)	04289
Grimes Mill (Part of Caribou)	04736
Grindstone	04460
Grindstone Neck	04693
Grove	04638
Groveville	04038
Guerette	04783
Guilford	04443
Guilford (Town)	04443
Guillemette	04073
Guinea Corner (Part of Biddeford)	04005
Hackett Mills	04258
Haldale	04986
Hallowell	04347
Hall Quarry	04660
Hamlin	04785
Hamlin (Town)	04785
Hammond (Town)	04730
Hampden	04444
Hampden (Town)	04444
Hampden	04444
Hampden Highlands	04444

Name	ZIP
Hancock	04640
Hancock (Town)	04640
Hancock Point	04640
Hanover	04237
Hanover (Town)	04237
Harborside	04642
Hardings	04011
Harmon Beach	04075
Harmons Corner (Part of Auburn)	04210
Harmony	04942
Harmony (Town)	04942
Harpswell (Town)	04079
Harpswell Center	04079
Harrimans Point	04578
Harrington	04643
Harrington (Town)	04643
Harrison	04040
Harrison (Town)	04040
Hartford	04221
Hartford (Town)	04221
Hartland	04943
Hartland (Town)	04943
Hartsfords Point	04442
Harts Neck	04860
Hatch's Corner	04342
Haven	04616
Haynesville	04446
Haynesville (Town)	04446
Head of Tide (Part of Belfast)	04915
Head Tide	04535
Hebron	04238
Hebron (Town)	04238
Hebron Station	04238
Hendricks Harbor	04576
Hermon	04401
Hermon (Town)	04401
Hermon Center	04401
Heron Island	04568
Hersey (Town)	04765
Hibberts (Town)	04341
Higgins Beach	04074
Higginsville	04450
Highland (Town)	04961
Highland Lake (Part of Westbrook)	04092
Highland Lake Vista	04062
Highpine	04090
Hills Beach (Part of Biddeford)	04005
Hillside	04024
Hinckley	04944
Hiram	04041
Hiram (Town)	04041
Hodgdon	04730
Hodgdon (Town)	04730
Holden	04429
Holden (Town)	04429
Hollandville	04048
Hollis (Town)	04042
Hollis Center	04042
Holmes Mill (Part of Belfast)	04915
Hope	04847
Hope (Town)	04847
Houghton	04275
Houlton	04730
Houlton (Town)	04730
Howes Corner	04282
Howland (Penobscot County) (Town)	04448
Howland (Penobscot County)	04448
Hoyttown	04654
Hudson	04449
Hudson (Town)	04449
Hulls Cove	04644
Hunnewell Hill	04074
Hunts Corner	04217
Hutchins Corner	04942
Indian Island	04468
Indian Point	04660
Indian River	04606
Indian Township Passamaquoddy Indian Reservation	04668
Industrial (Part of Presque Isle)	04769
Industry (Town)	04938
Ingall's Hill	04009
Intervale	04260
Irish Settlement	04424
Island Falls	04747
Island Falls (Town)	04747
Isle au Haut	04645
Isle Au Haut (Town)	04645
Isle of Springs	04549
Islesboro	04848
Islesboro (Town)	04848
Islesford	04646
Jackman	04945

Name	ZIP
Jackman (Town)	04945
Jackson	04921
Jackson (Town)	04921
Jackson Corners	04921
Jacksonville	04630
Jay	04239
Jay (Town)	04239
Jefferson	04348
Jefferson (Town)	04348
Jemtland	04783
Jonesboro	04648
Jonesboro (Town)	04648
Jones Corner	04354
Jonesport	04649
Jonesport (Town)	04649
Kalers Corner	04572
Keegan	04785
Kelleyland	04694
Kendalls Corner (Part of Belfast)	04915
Kenduskeag	04450
Kenduskeag (Town)	04450
Kennebago Lake	04970
Kennebec	04654
Kennebunk	04043
Kennebunk (Town)	04043
Kennebunk Beach	04043
Kennebunk Landing	04043
Kennebunk Lower Village	04046
Kennebunkport	04046
Kennebunkport (Town)	04046
Kennedy Terrace	04785
Kents Hill	04349
Kezar Falls	04047
Kingfield	04947
Kingfield (Town)	04947
Kingman	04451
Kingman (Town)	04451
Kingsbury (Town)	04942
Kinney Shores (Part of Saco)	04072
Kittery	03904
Kittery (Town)	03904
Kittery Point	03905
Knights Landing	04414
Knightville (Part of South Portland)	04106
Knowles Corner	04780
Knox (Town)	04986
Knox Center	04986
Knox Corner	04986
Knox Station	04986
Kokadjo	04441
Lagrange	04453
Lagrange (Town)	04453
Lake Arrowhead Estates	04061
Lake City	04843
Lake Moxie	04985
Lake View (Town)	04463
Lakeville (Town)	04487
Lakewood	04976
Lambert Lake	04454
Lamoine (Town)	04605
Lamoine	04605
Lamoine Beach	04605
Lamoine Corner	04605
Larone	04937
Larrabee	04655
Lawry	04547
Lebanon (Town)	04027
Lee	04455
Lee (Town)	04455
Leeds	04263
Leeds (Town)	04263
Leeds Junction	04263
Levant	04456
Levant (Town)	04456
Lewiston	04240-43
For specific Lewiston Zip Codes call (207) 783-8551	
Lewiston Junction (Part of Auburn)	04210
Lewiston Lower (Part of Lewiston)	04240
Lewiston Mall (Part of Lewiston)	04240
Lewiston Upper (Part of Lewiston)	04240
Libby Hill (Part of Gardiner)	04345
Liberty	04949
Liberty (Town)	04949
Lille	04749
Lily Bay	04441
Limerick	04048
Limerick (Town)	04048
Limerick Mills	04048
Limestone	04750-51
For specific Limestone Zip Codes call (207) 325-4838	
Limington	04049

236 MAINE Limington-North Parsonsfield

	ZIP		ZIP		ZIP
Limington (Town)	04049	Masardis	04759	Newcastle	04553
Lincoln (Town)	04457	Masardis (Town)	04759	Newcastle (Town)	04553
Lincoln (Oxford County) (Town)	03579	Mason Bay	04649	Newfield	04056
Lincoln (Penobscot County)	04457	Mast Landing	04032	Newfield (Town)	04056
Lincoln Center	04458	Matinicus	04851	New Gloucester	04260
Lincoln Mills	04928	Matinicus Isle (Town)	04851	New Gloucester (Town)	04260
Lincolnville	04849	Mattawamkeag	04459	Newhall	04062
Lincolnville (Town)	04849	Mattawamkeag (Town)	04459	New Harbor	04554
Lincolnville Center	04850	Maxfield (Town)	04453	New Limerick	04761
Linekin	04544	Mayberry Hill	04015	New Limerick (Town)	04761
Linneus	04730	Mayville	04217	Newport	04953
Linneus (Town)	04730	Mechanic Falls (Androscoggin County) (Town)	04256	Newport (Town)	04953
Lisbon	04250			New Portland	04954
Lisbon (Town)	04250			New Portland (Town)	04954
Lisbon Center	04251	Mechanic Falls (Androscoggin County)	04256	Newry (Oxford County)	04261
Lisbon Falls	04252			Newry (Oxford County) (Town)	04261
Lisbon-Lisbon Center	04250	Meddybemps	04657		
Litchfield	04350	Meddybemps (Town)	04657	New Sharon	04955
Litchfield (Town)	04350	Medford	04453	New Sharon (Town)	04955
Litchfield Corners	04350	Medford (Town)	04453	New Sweden	04762
Litchfield Plains	04350	Medford Center	04453	New Sweden (Town)	04762
Little Deer Isle	04650	Medomak	04551	Newtown (Part of Biddeford)	04005
Little Falls	04082	Medway	04460		
Little Falls-South Windham	04082	Medway (Town)	04460	New Vineyard	04956
Littlefield (Part of Auburn)	04210	Melvin Heights	04843	New Vineyard (Town)	04956
Littlefield Corner (Part of Auburn)	04210	Mercer	04957	Nicolin (Part of Ellsworth)	04605
		Mercer (Town)	04957	Nobleboro	04555
Little Machias	04626	Merepoint	04053	Nobleboro (Town)	04555
Littleton	04730	Merrill (Town)	04780	Norridgewock	04957
Littleton (Town)	04730	Mexico	04257	Norridgewock (Town)	04957
Livermore	04253	Mexico (Town)	04257	North Alfred	04002
Livermore (Town)	04253	Middledam	04216	North Amity	04465
Livermore Falls	04254	Middle Intervale	04217	North Anson	04958
Livermore Falls (Town)	04254	Milbridge	04658	North Auburn (Part of Auburn)	04210
Locke Mills	04255	Milbridge (Town)	04658		
Long Beach (Cumberland County)	04075	Milford	04461	North Augusta (Part of Augusta)	04330
		Milford (Town)	04461		
Long Beach (York County)	03910	Milliken Mills	04064	North Baldwin	04024
Longcove	04857	Millinocket (Penobscot County) (Town)	04462	North Bancroft	04424
Long Island (Part of Portland)	04050			North Bangor (Part of Bangor)	04401
		Millinocket (Penobscot County)	04462		
Lookout	04645	Milltown (Part of Calais)	04619	North Bath (Part of Bath)	04530
Loring AFB	04751	Milo	04463	North Belgrade	04963
Loring Air Force Base	04751	Milo (Town)	04463	North Berwick	03906
Lovell	04051	Milton (Oxford County)	04219	North Berwick (Town)	03906
Lovell (Town)	04051	Milton (Oxford County) (Town)	04219	North Blue Hill	04614
Lowell	04433			North Bradford	04410
Lowell (Town)	04433	Minot	04258	North Bridgton	04057
Lower Dennysville	04628	Minot (Town)	04258	North Brooklin	04661
Lubec	04652	Minturn	04659	North Brooksville	04617
Lubec (Town)	04652	Molunkus	04451	North Buckfield	04220
Lucerne-In-Maine	04429	Monarda	04776	North Castine	04472
Ludlow (Town)	04730	Monhegan	04852	North Chesterville	04938
Ludlow	04730	Monhegan (Town)	04852	North Cutler	04630
Lyman (Town)	04005	Monmouth	04259	North Dixmont	04932
Lynchville	04231	Monmouth (Town)	04259	North East Carry	04478
McFarlands Corner	04941	Monroe	04951	Northeast Harbor	04662
Machias	04654	Monroe (Town)	04951	Northeast Piscataquis (Town)	04462
Machias (Town)	04654	Monroe Center	04951		
Machiasport	04655	Monson	04464	Northeast Somerset (Town)	04920
Machiasport (Town)	04655	Monson (Town)	04464	North Edgecomb	04556
Mackworth Island	04105	Monticello	04760	North Ellsworth (Part of Ellsworth)	04605
Mackworth Point	04105	Monticello (Town)	04760		
MacMahan	04548	Montsweag	04578	Northern Maine Junction	04401
Macwahoc	04451	Montville (Town)	04941	North Fairfield	04937
Macwahoc (Town)	04451	Moody	04054	North Falmouth	04105
Madawaska	04756	Moody Beach	04054	Northfield	04654
Madawaska (Town)	04756	Moosehead	04442	Northfield (Town)	04654
Madawaska Lake	04783	Moose River	04945	North Franklin (Town)	04936
Madison	04950	Moose River (Town)	04945	North Fryeburg	04058
Madison (Town)	04950	Moro (Town)	04780	North Gorham	04075
Madrid	04966	Morrill	04952	North Gray	04039
Madrid (Town)	04966	Morrill (Town)	04952	North Guilford	04443
Magalloway (Town)	03579	Morris Corner	04750	North Harpswell	04079
Maine Mall (Part of South Portland)	04106	Morse Corners	04928	North Haven	04853
		Moscow (Town)	04920	North Haven (Town)	04853
Mainstream	04942	Moscow	04920	North Hermon	04401
Mallison Falls	04082	Mount Chase (Town)	04765	North Hill	04220
Manchester	04351	Mount Desert	04660	North Islesboro	04848
Manchester (Town)	04351	Mount Desert (Town)	04660	North Jay	04262
Manset	04656	Mount Pisgah	04538	North Lamoine	04605
Maple Grove	04742	Mount Vernon	04352	North Lebanon	04027
Mapleton	04757	Mount Vernon (Town)	04352	North Leeds	04263
Mapleton (Town)	04757	Murphy Corner	04578	North Limington	04049
Maplewood	04095	Muscongus	04551	North Livermore	04254
Mariaville	04605	Muscongus Bay	04555	North Lovell	04231
Mariaville (Town)	04605	Naples	04055	North Lubec	04652
Marion	04628	Naples (Town)	04055	North Lyndon (Part of Caribou)	04736
Marlboro	04605	Nashville (Town)	04732		
Marrtown	04548	Naskeag	04616	North Monmouth	04265
Marshfield	04654	Naval Air Station	04011	North Monroe	04951
Marshfield (Town)	04654	Naval Communications Unit	04630	North Newcastle	04553
Mars Hill	04758	Naval Shipyard	03801	North New Portland	04961
Mars Hill (Town)	04758	Nequasset	04579	North Norway	04268
Mars Hill-Blaine	04758	Newagen	04552	North Orland	04429
Marshville	04643	New Auburn (Part of Auburn)	04210	North Orrington	04474
Marston Corner (Part of Auburn)	04210			North Oxford (Town)	03579
		Newburgh	04444	North Palermo	04354
Martin	04547	Newburgh (Town)	04444	North Paris	04289
Martinsville	04860	New Canada (Town)	04743	North Parsonsfield	04047

North Penobscot-St. Francis MAINE 237

Name	ZIP
North Penobscot (Hancock County)	04476
North Penobscot (Penobscot County) (Town)	04462
North Perry	04667
Northport (Town)	04849
Northport	04849
North Pownal	04069
North Raymond	04274
North Scarborough	04074
North Searsmont	04973
North Searsport	04974
North Sebago	04029
North Sedgwick	04676
North Shapleigh	04060
North Sullivan	04664
North Turner	04266
North Vassalboro	04962
North Wade	04786
North Waldoboro	04572
North Warren	04864
North Washington (Town)	04686
North Waterboro	04061
North Waterford	04267
North Wayne	04284
Northwest Aroostook (Aroostook County)	04770
Northwest Aroostook (Aroostook County) (Town)	04788
Northwest Bethel	04217
Northwest Hancock (Town)	04408
Northwest Piscataquis (Town)	04441
Northwest Somerset (Town)	04945
North Whitefield	04353
North Windsor	04361
North Woodstock	04219
North Yarmouth (Town)	04021
Norumbega	04617
Norway	04268
Norway (Town)	04268
Norway Center	04268
Norway Lake	04268
Number Four	04051
Oakfield	04763
Oakfield (Town)	04763
Oak Hill (Androscoggin County)	04273
Oak Hill (Cumberland County)	04074
Oakland	04963
Oakland (Town)	04963
Oak Point	04605
Oak Ridge (Part of Biddeford)	04005
Oak Terrace	03904
Ocean Park	04063
Ocean Point	04544
Oceanview Harbor	04074
Oceanville	04681
Ogontz	04478
Ogunquit (York County) (Town)	03907
Ogunquit (York County)	03907
Olamon	04467
Olde Mill Brook	04074
Old Orchard Beach (York County) (Town)	04064
Old Orchard Beach (York County)	04064
Old Town	04468
Onawa	04443
Oquossoc	04964
Orffs Corner	04572
Orient	04471
Orient (Town)	04471
Orland	04472
Orland (Town)	04472
Orono (Penobscot County)	04473
Orono (Penobscot County) (Town)	04473
Orono (Penobscot County)	04473
Orrington	04474
Orrington (Town)	04474
Orrington Center	04474
Orrs Island	04066
Osborn (Town)	04605
Otis (Hancock County)	04605
Otis (Hancock County) (Town)	04605
Otisfield	04270
Otisfield (Town)	04270
Otter Creek	04665
Owls Head	04854
Owls Head (Town)	04854
Oxbow	04764
Oxbow (Town)	04764
Oxford (Town)	04270
Oxford	04270

Name	ZIP
Paine Corner	04281
Palermo	04354
Palermo (Town)	04354
Palmyra	04965
Palmyra (Town)	04965
Paris	04271
Paris (Town)	04271
Parker Head	04562
Parkman	04443
Parkman (Town)	04443
Parsonsfield	04048
Parsonsfield (Town)	04028
Passadumkeag	04475
Passadumkeag (Town)	04475
Passamaquoddy Indian Township Indian Reservation (Town)	04668
Passamaquoddy Pleasant Point Indian Reservation (Town)	04667
Patten	04765
Patten (Town)	04765
Peabbles Cove	04107
Peaks Island (Part of Portland)	04108
Pea Ridge	04458
Pejepscot	04067
Pelton Hill (Part of Augusta)	04330
Pemaquid	04558
Pemaquid Beach	04554
Pemaquid Harbor	04558
Pemaquid Point	04554
Pembroke	04666
Pembroke (Town)	04666
Penley's Corner (Part of Auburn)	04210
Penobscot	04476
Penobscot (Town)	04476
Penobscot Indian Island Indian Reservation (Town)	04468
Perham	04766
Perham (Town)	04766
Perkins (Town)	04357
Perry (Town)	04667
Perry (Aroostook County)	04769
Perry (Washington County)	04667
Perrys Corner	04048
Peru	04290
Peru (Town)	04290
Peter Dana Point	04668
Phair (Part of Presque Isle)	04769
Phillips	04966
Phillips (Town)	04966
Phippsburg	04562
Phippsburg (Town)	04562
Pigeon Hill	04658
Pike Corner	04015
Pine Cliff	04576
Pine Hill	03902
Pine Park	04064
Pine Point	04074
Pittsfield	04967
Pittsfield (Town)	04967
Pittston	04345
Pittston (Town)	04345
Pittston Farm	04478
Plaisted	04767
Plantation Number Fourteen (Town)	04628
Plantation Number Twenty-one (Town)	04668
Pleasant Beach	04858
Pleasantdale (Part of South Portland)	04106
Pleasant Hill (Cumberland County)	04105
Pleasant Hill (Cumberland County)	04032
Pleasant Hill (Cumberland County)	04074
Pleasant Lake	04619
Pleasant Point	04563
Pleasant Point Indian Reservation	04667
Pleasant Pond	04925
Pleasant Ridge (Town)	04920
Pleasantville	04864
Plummer Island	04074
Plymouth	04969
Plymouth (Town)	04969
Poland	04273
Poland (Town)	04273
Poland Spring	04274
Pond Cove	04107
Poors Mills (Part of Belfast)	04915
Popham Beach	04562
Portage	04768
Portage Lake (Town)	04768
Port Clyde	04855
Porter	04068
Porter (Town)	04068

Name	ZIP
Porterfield	04047
Porter Landing	04032
Portland	04101-12
For specific Portland Zip Codes call (207) 871-8411	
Portsmouth Naval Shipyard	03801
Pownal	04069
Pownal (Town)	04069
Pownal Center	04069
Pratt Corner	04281
Prentiss	04487
Prentiss (Town)	04487
Presque Isle	04769
Prides Corner (Part of Westbrook)	04092
Princeton	04668
Princeton (Town)	04668
Promenade Mall (Part of Lewiston)	04240
Promised Land	04273
Prospect	04981
Prospect (Town)	04981
Prospect Ferry	04981
Prospect Harbor	04669
Prouts Neck	04074
Pulpit Harbor	04853
Pumpkin Valley	04009
Quimby	04770
Quoddy Village (Part of Eastport)	04631
Randolph (Kennebec County) (Town)	04345
Randolph (Kennebec County)	04345
Rangeley	04970
Rangeley (Town)	04970
Raymond	04071
Raymond (Town)	04071
Rayville	04270
Razorville	04574
Reach	04627
Readfield (Town)	04355
Readfield (Kennebec County)	04355
Red Beach (Part of Calais)	04619
Redding	04292
Reed (Town)	04497
Reeds	04966
Richmond	04357
Richmond (Town)	04357
Richmond Mill	04284
Richville	04075
Ridlonville	04257
Rileys	04239
Ripley	04930
Ripley (Town)	04930
Ripley	04643
Riverside	04330
Riverview (Part of Presque Isle)	04769
Robbinston	04671
Robbinston (Town)	04671
Robinhood	04530
Robinson	04758
Robinson Corner	04240
Robyville	04450
Rockland	04841
Rockport	04856
Rockport (Town)	04856
Rockville	04841
Rockwood	04478
Rogers Corners	04987
Rome	04957
Rome (Town)	04957
Roque Bluffs	04654
Roque Bluffs (Town)	04654
Ross Corner	04087
Round Pond	04564
Roxbury	04275
Roxbury (Town)	04275
Royal Corner (Part of Auburn)	04210
Rumford	04276
Rumford (Town)	04276
Rumford Center	04278
Rumford Corner	04219
Rumford Junction (Part of Auburn)	04210
Rumford Point	04279
Sabattus	04280
Sabattus (Town)	04280
Sabbathday Lake	04274
Saco	04072
St. Agatha	04772
St. Agatha (Town)	04772
St. Albans	04971
St. Albans (Town)	04971
St. David	04773
St. Francis	04774
St. Francis (Town)	04774

MAINE St. Francis College-Van Buren

Name	ZIP
St. Francis College (Part of Biddeford)	04005
St. George	04857
St. George (Town)	04857
St. John	04743
St. John (Town)	04743
St. Josephs College	04062
Salem	04983
Salmon Falls	04004
Salsbury Cove	04672
Sanderson Corners	04349
Sandhill Corner	04341
Sandy Beach	04401
Sandy Creek	04009
Sandy Point	04972
Sandy River (Town)	04970
Sandy River Beach	04649
Sanford	04073
Sanford (Town)	04073
Sangerville	04479
Sangerville (Town)	04479
Sargentville	04673
Saunders (Part of Presque Isle)	04769
Scarboro Beach	04074
Scarborough	04074
Scarborough (Town)	04074
Scituate	03909
Scotland	03909
Scott (Part of Presque Isle)	04769
Scribners Mill	04040
Seabury	03909
Seal Cove	04674
Seal Harbor	04675
Searsmont	04973
Searsmont (Town)	04973
Searsport	04974
Searsport (Town)	04974
Seawall	04656
Sebago (Town)	04029
Sebago Lake	04075
Sebasco	04565
Sebasco Estates	04565
Sebec	04481
Sebec (Town)	04481
Sebec Corners	04426
Sebec Lake	04482
Seboeis	04448
Seboeis (Town)	04448
Seboomook	04478
Seboomook Lake (Town)	04478
Sedgwick	04676
Sedgwick (Town)	04676
Shady Nook	03830
Shaker Village	04274
Shapleigh	04076
Shapleigh (Town)	04076
Shaw Mills	04075
Shawmut	04975
Sheepscot	04578
Sheridan	04775
Sherman	04776
Sherman (Town)	04776
Sherman Mills	04776
Shermans Corner	04949
Sherman Station	04777
Shin Pond	04765
Shirley (Town)	04485
Shirley Mills	04485
Sidney	04330
Sidney (Town)	04330
Silver Ridge	04776
Simonton Corners	04843
Simpson Corners	04932
Sinclair	04779
Skillings Corner	04210
Skowhegan	04976
Skowhegan (Town)	04976
Slab City (Oxford County)	04231
Slab City (Waldo County)	04849
Small Point	04567
Smithfield	04978
Smithfield (Town)	04978
Smithville	04680
Smyrna (Town)	04780
Smyrna Center	04780
Smyrna Mills	04780
Soldier Pond	04781
Solon	04979
Solon (Town)	04979
Somerville	04341
Somerville (Town)	04341
Sorrento	04677
Sorrento (Town)	04677
Sound	04660
South Acton	04001
South Addison	04606
South Andover	04216
South Arm	04216
South Aroostook (Town)	04730
South Bancroft	04424
South Berwick	03908
South Berwick (Town)	03908
South Blue Hill	04615
South Brewer (Part of Brewer)	04412
South Bridgton	04009
South Bristol	04568
South Bristol (Town)	04568
South Buxton	04038
South Casco	04077
South China	04358
South Corinth	04427
South Deer Isle	04681
South Dover	04426
South Durham	04032
Southeast Piscataquis (Town)	04463
South Eliot	03903
South Exeter	04928
South Franklin (Town)	04224
South Freeport	04078
South Gardiner (Part of Gardiner)	04359
South Gorham	04038
South Gouldsboro	04678
South Gray	04039
South Hancock	04605
South Harpswell	04079
South Hiram	04080
South Hollis	04042
South Hope	04862
South Jefferson	04553
South Lagrange	04453
South Lebanon	04027
South Levant	04456
South Lewiston (Part of Lewiston)	04240
South Liberty	04949
South Limington	04048
South Lincoln	04457
South Livermore	04254
South Lubec	04652
South Monmouth	04259
South Montville	04949
South Newcastle	04556
South Orland	04472
South Orrington	04474
South Oxford (Town)	04267
South Paris	04281
South Parsonsfield	04048
South Penobscot	04476
Southport	04576
Southport (Town)	04576
South Portland	04106
South Princeton	04668
South Rangeley	04964
South Rumford	04276
South Sanford	04073
South Side	03909
South Surry	04684
South Thomaston	04858
South Thomaston (Town)	04858
South Trescott	04652
South Union	04864
South Waldoboro	04572
South Warren	04864
South Waterford	04081
South West Bend	04252
Southwest Harbor	04679
Southwest Harbor (Town)	04679
Southwest Harbor Coast Guard Base	04679
South Windham	04082
South Windsor	04363
South Woodstock	04289
South Woodville	04458
Spears Corner	04345
Spragueville (Part of Presque Isle)	04769
Springfield	04487
Springfield (Town)	04487
Springvale	04083
Spruce Head	04859
Spruce Head Island	04859
Spruce Point	04538
Spruce Shores	04544
Squa Pan	04732
Square Lake (Town)	04743
Squirrel Island	04570
Stacyville	04782
Stacyville (Town)	04782
Standish	04084
Standish (Town)	04084
Starboard	04618
Starks	04911
Starks (Town)	04911
State Road	04769
Steep Falls	04085
Stetson	04488
Stetson (Town)	04488
Steuben	04680
Steuben (Town)	04680
Stevens Corner	03830
Stevensville	04742
Stickney Corner	04574
Stillwater (Part of Old Town)	04489
Stockholm	04783
Stockholm (Town)	04783
Stockton Springs	04981
Stockton Springs (Town)	04981
Stoneham (Town)	04231
Stonington	04681
Stonington (Town)	04681
Stover Corner	04617
Stow	04058
Stow (Town)	04058
Stratton	04982
Stricklands	04263
Strong	04983
Strong (Town)	04983
Sullivan	04664
Sullivan (Town)	04664
Summerhaven (Part of Augusta)	04330
Summit (Town)	04417
Sumner (Town)	04292
Sunset	04683
Sunshine	04627
Surfside	04064
Surry	04684
Surry (Town)	04684
Sutton Island	04662
Swans Island	04685
Swans Island (Town)	04685
Swanville	04915
Swanville (Town)	04915
Sweden (Aroostook County)	04762
Sweden (Oxford County) (Town)	04040
Tacoma	04350
Tainter Corner	04224
Tallwood	04355
Talmadge (Town)	04492
Tatnic	03906
Temple	04984
Temple (Town)	04984
Temple Heights	04915
Tenants Harbor	04860
The Forks (Town)	04985
The Kingdom	04941
The Ridge	04009
Thomaston (Town)	04861
Thomaston	04861
Thompson's Point	04055
Thorndike	04986
Thorndike (Town)	04986
Thorndike Center	04986
Thornton Heights (Part of South Portland)	04106
Todds Corner	04930
Topsfield	04490
Topsfield (Town)	04490
Topsham	04086
Topsham (Town)	04086
Tory Hill	04038
Town Farm Hill	04040
Town Hill	04609
Town House Corners	04046
Tracy Corners	04606
Trainor Corner	04345
Trap Corner	04289
Tremont (Town)	04653
Trenton	04605
Trenton (Town)	04605
Trevett	04571
Troutdale	04985
Troy	04987
Troy (Town)	04987
Troy Center	04987
Turbats Creek	04046
Turner	04282
Turner (Town)	04282
Turner Center	04283
Turnpike Mall (Part of Augusta)	04330
Twelve Corners	04254
Twombly (Town)	04417
Union	04862
Union (Town)	04862
Unionville	04622
Unity (Town)	04988
Unity (Kennebec County) (Town)	04988
Unity (Waldo County)	04988
University Bookstore	04473
Upper Abbot	04406
Upper Frenchville	04784
Upper Gloucester	04260
Upton	04261
Upton (Town)	04261
Van Buren	04785

Van Buren-Youngtown **MAINE** 239

	ZIP		ZIP		ZIP
Van Buren (Town)	04785	West Bath (Town)	04530	Whitefield (Town)	04362
Vanceboro	04491	West Bethel	04286	White Rock	04038
Vanceboro (Town)	04491	West Boothbay Harbor	04575	Whites Corner	04260
Vassalboro	04989	West Bowdoin	04287	Whiting	04691
Vassalborough (Town)	04989	West Bridgton	04009	Whiting (Town)	04691
Veazie (Penobscot County)		Westbrook	04092	Whitney (Town)	04487
(Town)	04401	West Brooklin	04616	Whitneyville	04692
Veazie (Penobscot County)	04401	West Brooksville	04617	Whitneyville (Town)	04692
Verona	04416	West Buxton	04093	Wildes District	04046
Verona (Town)	04416	West Central Franklin		Wildwood Park	04110
Vienna	04360	(Town)	04285	Wiley's Corner	04861
Vienna (Town)	04360	West Charleston	04422	Williamsburg	04414
Viking Village	04217	West Corinth	04427	Willimantic	04443
Vinalhaven	04863	West Cumberland	04021	Willimantic (Town)	04443
Vinalhaven (Town)	04863	West Denmark	04010	Wilson Corner (Part of	
Wade (Town)	04786	West Durham	04069	Ellsworth)	04605
Waite	04492	West Ellsworth (Part of		Wilsons Mills	03579
Waite (Town)	04492	Ellsworth)	04605	Wilton	04294
Waites Landing	04105	West End (Part of Portland)	04102	Wilton (Town)	04294
Waldo	04915	West Enfield	04493	Windham (Cumberland	
Waldo (Town)	04915	West Falmouth	04105	County)	04062
Waldoboro	04572	West Farmington	04992	Windham (Cumberland	
Waldoboro (Town)	04572	Westfield	04787	County) (Town)	04062
Wales (Town)	04280	Westfield (Town)	04787	Windham Center	04062
Wales Corner	04280	West Forks	04985	Windham Hill	04062
Walkers Mill	04217	West Forks (Town)	04985	Windsor	04363
Wallagrass	04781	West Franklin	04634	Windsor (Town)	04363
Wallagrass (Town)	04781	West Fryeburg	04037	Winkumpaugh Corners (Part	
Walnut Hill	04021	West Gardiner (Town)	04345	of Ellsworth)	04605
Walpole	04573	West Georgetown	04548	Winn	04495
Waltham	04605	West Gorham	04038	Winn (Town)	04495
Waltham (Town)	04605	West Gouldsboro	04607	Winnecook	04922
Wards Cove	04075	West Gray	04039	Winnegance	04530
Wardtown	04032	West Harpswell	04079	Winslow	04901
Warren (Town)	04864	West Harrington	04643	Winslow (Town)	04901
Warren (Knox County)	04864	West Hollis	04042	Winslows Mills	04572
Washburn	04786	West Jonesport	04649	Winter Harbor	04693
Washburn (Town)	04786	West Kennebunk	04094	Winter Harbor (Town)	04693
Washburn Junction (Part of		West Lebanon	04027	Winterport	04496
Presque Isle)	04769	West Leeds	04263	Winterport (Town)	04496
Washington	04574	West Levant	04456	Winterville	04788
Washington (Town)	04574	West Lovell	04051	Winterville (Town)	04788
Waterboro	04087	West Lubec	04652	Winthrop	04364
Waterboro (Town)	04087	Westmanland (Town)	04783	Winthrop (Town)	04364
Waterboro Center	04030	West Mills	04938	Winthrop Center	04364
Waterford	04088	West Minot	04288	Wiscasset	04578
Waterford (Town)	04088	West Mount Vernon	04352	Wiscasset (Town)	04578
Waterman Beach	04858	West Newfield	04095	Wonsqueak Harbor	04613
Water Street (Part of		West Old Town (Part of Old		Woodfords (Part of	
Augusta)	04330	Town)	04468	Portland)	04103
Waterville	04901	Weston	04424	Woodland (Aroostook	
Waverly	04967	Weston (Town)	04424	County) (Town)	04736
Wayne	04284	West Paris	04289	Woodland (Washington	
Wayne (Town)	04284	West Paris (Town)	04289	County)	04694
Webster (Penobscot		West Pembroke		Woodmans Mills	04973
County)	04473	(Washington County)	04666	Woodstock (Town)	04219
Webster (Penobscot		West Penobscot	04476	Woodville (Town)	04458
County) (Town)	04487	West Peru	04290	Woolwich	04579
Webster Corner	04250	Westpoint	04565	Woolwich (Town)	04579
Weeks Mills	04361	West Poland	04291	Worthley Pond	04229
Welchville	04270	Westport	04578	Wyman (Franklin County)	
Welcomes Corner (Part of		Westport (Town)	04578	(Town)	04982
Auburn)	04210	West Princeton	04668	Wyman (Washington	
Weld	04285	West Rockport	04865	County)	04658
Weld (Town)	04285	West Scarborough	04074	Wytopitlock	04497
Wellington	04942	West Seboois	04462	Yarmouth	04096
Wellington (Town)	04942	West Southport	04576	Yarmouth (Town)	04096
Wells	04090	West Stonington	04681	York	03909
Wells (Town)	04090	West Sullivan	04689	York (Town)	03909
Wells Beach	04090	West Sumner	04292	York Beach	03910
Wells Branch	04090	West Surry	04605	York Center	03909
Wesley	04686	West Tremont	04690	York Cliffs	03902
Wesley (Town)	04686	West Trenton	04605	York Harbor	03911
West Appleton	04949	West Waldoboro	04572	York Heights	03909
West Athens	04912	West Washington	04341	Youngs Corner (Part of	
West Auburn (Part of		West Winterport	04496	Auburn)	04210
Auburn)	04210	Whitefield	04362	Youngtown	04850
West Baldwin	04091				

MARYLAND / DELAWARE / DC

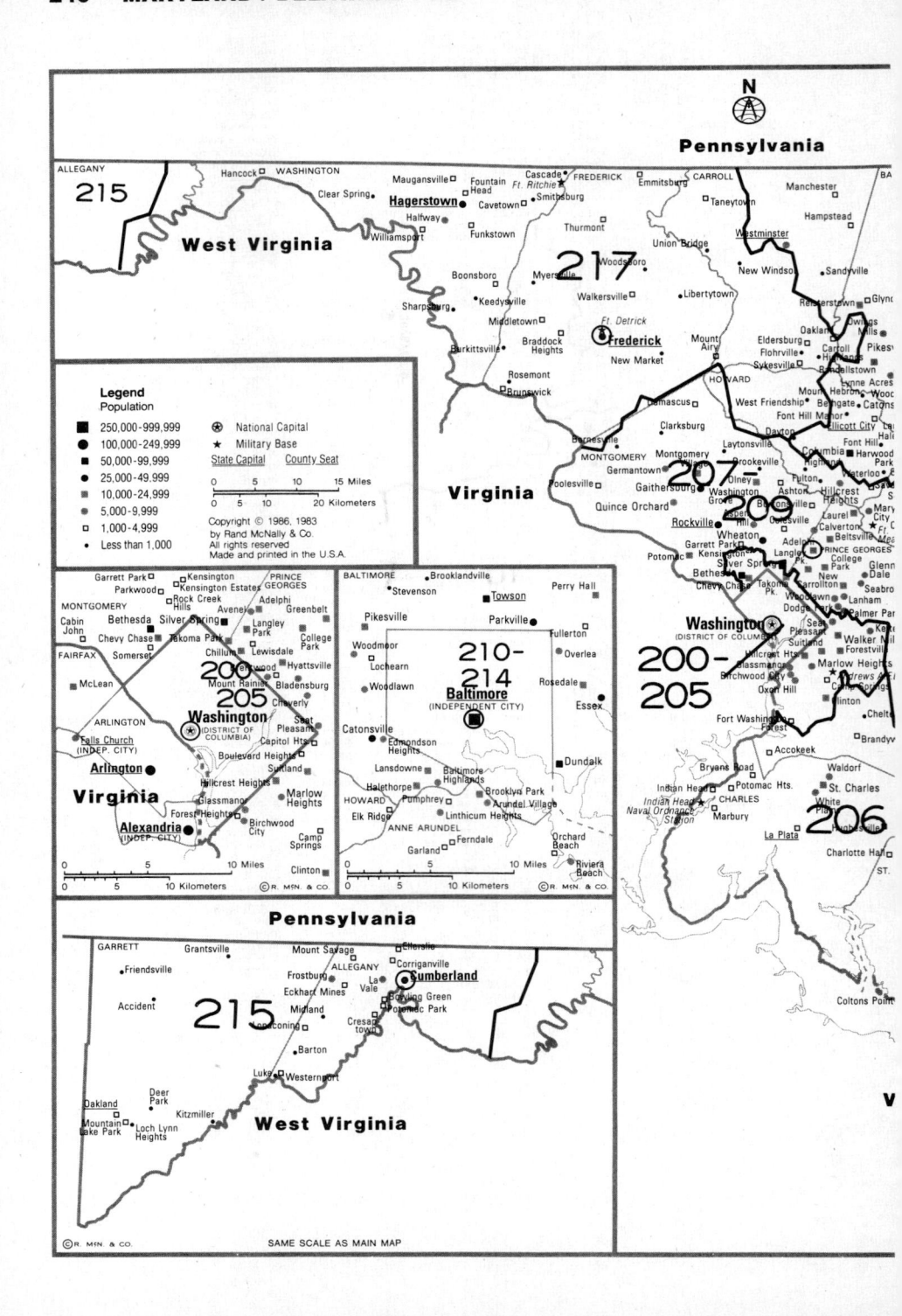

MARYLAND / DELAWARE / DC   241

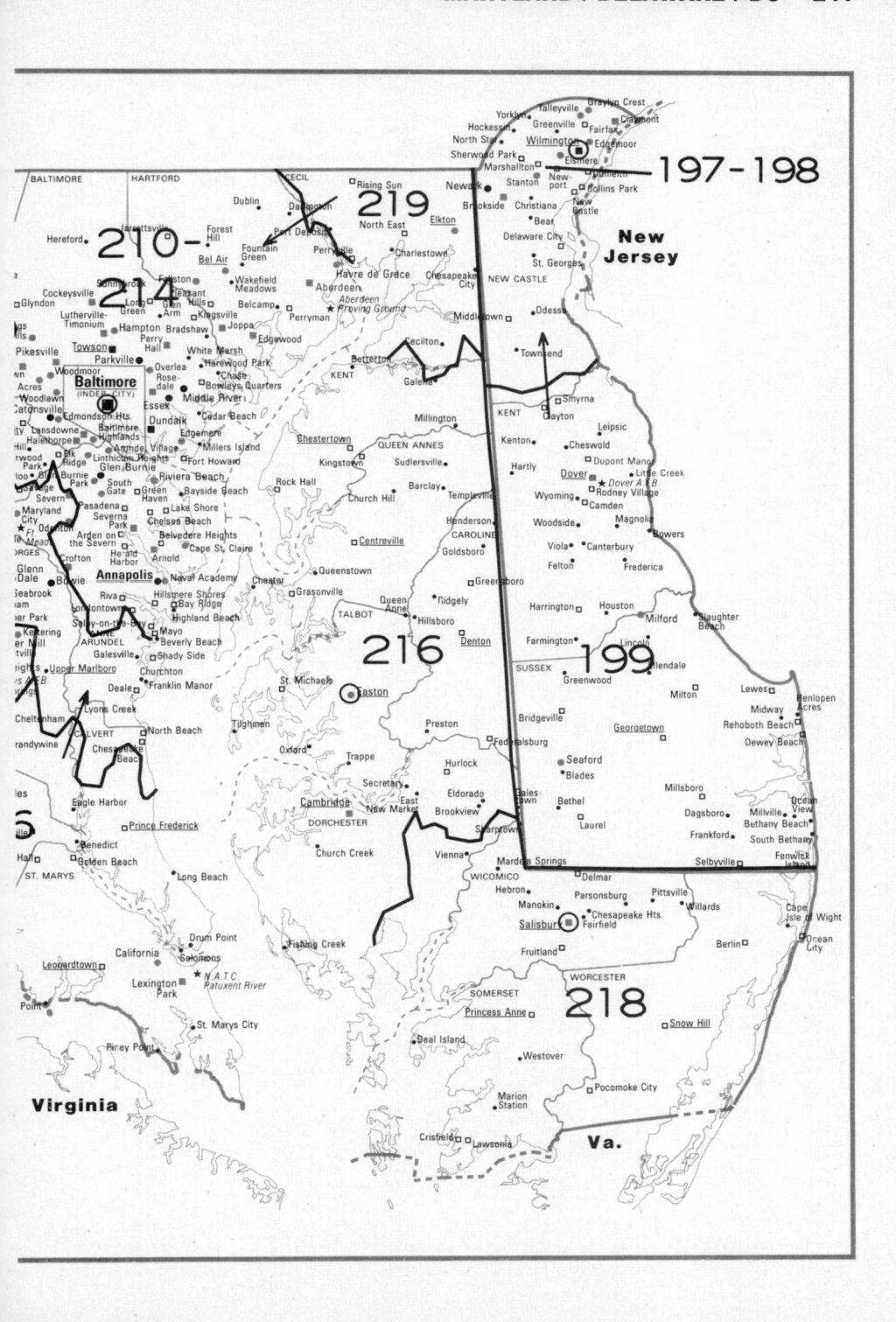

242 MARYLAND Abell-Bay Ridge

Name	ZIP
Abell	20606
Aberdeen	21001
Aberdeen Proving Ground (Harford County)	21005
Abingdon	21009
Academy Heights	21228
Academy Junction	21113
Accident	21520
Accokeek	20607
Accokeek Acres	20607
Accokeek Groves	20607
Acco Park	20607
Adamstown	21710
Adams Woods	20783
Adelina	20678
Adelphi (Prince George's County)	20783
Adelphi Hills	20783
Adelphi Manor	20783
Ady	21154
Aero Acres	21220
Aikin	21903
Airey	21613
Albantown	21074
Albeth Heights	21163
Aldino	21001
Alesia	21107
Allanwood	20906
Allegany	21532
Allegany Grove	21502
Allen	21810
Allenford	21043
Allens Fresh	20632
Allenwood	21801
Allenwood Acres	20748
Allview	21043
Allview Estates	21046
Alpha	21104
Alpine Beach	21122
Altamont	21561
Alta Vista	20817
Alta Vista Gardens	20814
Alta Vista Terrace	20814
Amberly	21401
Amberly of Kings Court	21237
Amber Meadows (Part of Bowie)	20716
Amcelle Acres	21502
American Cities	21044
American Corners	21632
Ammendale	20705
Anchorage	21401
Ancient Oak	20878
Ancient Oak North	20878
Andersontown	21629
Andover Estates	20692
Andrew Hills	20748
Andrews	21626
Andrews AFB	20331
Andrews Air Force Base	20331
Andrews Air Force Base Hospital	20331
Andrews Estates	20746
Andrews Manor	20746
Annapolis	21401-05
For specific Annapolis Zip Codes call (301) 263-9292	
Annapolis Junction	20701
Annapolis Rock	21797
Anneslie	21204
Antietam (Washington County)	21782
Apple Green	20754
Apple Grove	20744
Appleton Acres	21921
Appletown	21713
Appliance Park-East (Part of Baltimore)	21045
Appolds	21778
Aquasco	20608
Aragona Village	20744
Arbutus	21227
Arden on the Severn	21032
Ardmore	20785
Ardwick	20785
Argonne Hills	20755
Argyle Park	20901
Arlington (Part of Baltimore)	21215
Armagh	21204
Arnold (Anne Arundel County)	21012
Arnold Heights	20746
Arnoldtown	21718
Arrowhead (Howard County)	21046
Arrow Head (Montgomery County)	20879
Arrowood	20817
Arundel Gardens	21225
Arundel Hills	21090
Arundel on the Bay	21403

Name	ZIP
Arundel Plaza	21146
Arundel View	21054
Arundel Village	21225
Asbury Methodist Home (Part of Gaithersburg)	20877
Ashburton	20817
Asher Glade	21531
Ashland	21030
Ashton	20861
Ashton Pond	20861
Ashton-Sandy Springs	20861
Asleigh	20817
Aspen Hill (Montgomery County)	20906
Aspen Hill Park	20853
Aspen Knolls	20853
Athol	21837
Atholton	21043
Atholton Manor	21043
Augusta	21758
Aurora Hills	21108
Auth Village	20746
Autrey Park (Part of Rockville)	20850
Autumn Hill	21043
Avalon Shores	20764
Avenue	20609
Avilton	21539
Avondale Grove	20782
Ayrlawn	20814
Back Bay Beach	20778
Back River	21223
Back River Highlands	21221
Baden	20613
Bainbridge Naval Training Center	21904
Bakersville	21713
Bald Eagle	20613
Baldwin	21013
Baldwin Hill	21108
Baldwins' Hills South	21032
Ballard	20735
Ballard Gardens	21220
Baltimore	21201-99
For specific Baltimore Zip Codes call (301) 347-4430	
COLLEGES & UNIVERSITIES	
College of Notre Dame of Maryland	21210
Coppin State College	21216
Johns Hopkins University	21218
Loyola College	21210
Maryland Institute College of Art	21217
University of Maryland-Baltimore Professional Schools	21201
FINANCIAL INSTITUTIONS	
American National Savings Association, F.A.	21201
Arundel Federal Savings & Loan Association	21225
Atlantic Federal Savings Bank	21213
Augusta Savings & Loan Association, Inc.	21201
Baltimore County Savings Bank, F.S.B.	21236
The Bank of Baltimore	21203
Bradford Federal Savings Bank	21212
The Carrollton Bank of Baltimore	21201
Chase Bank of Maryland	21202
Citibank (Maryland), National Association	21202
Commercial Credit Bank	21236
Equitable Bank, N.A.	21201
Fairfax Savings & Loan Association	21202
The First National Bank of Maryland	21201
Greater Baltimore Savings & Loan Association	21201
Hamilton Federal Savings & Loan Association	21214
Harbor Federal Savings & Loan Association	21224
Leeds Federal Savings & Loan Association	21229
Loyola Federal Savings & Loan Association	21201
Maryland National Bank	21202
Mercantile-Safe Deposit & Trust Company	21202
NCNB National Bank of Maryland	21201
Provident Bank of Maryland	21202

Name	ZIP
Rosedale Federal Savings & Loan Association	21206
Signet Bank/Maryland	21202
HOSPITALS	
Francis Scott Key Medical Center	21224
Franklin Square Hospital Center	21237
Good Samaritan Hospital of Maryland	21239
Greater Baltimore Medical Center	21204
Harbor Hospital Center	21230
Johns Hopkins Hospital	21205
Levindale Hebrew Geriatric Center and Hospital	21215
Liberty Medical Center	21215
Mercy Medical Center	21202
Sinai Hospital of Baltimore	21215
St. Agnes Hospital of The City of Baltimore	21229
St. Joseph Hospital	21204
Union Memorial Hospital	21218
University of Maryland Medical System	21201
Veterans Administration Medical Center	21218
HOTELS/MOTELS	
Baltimore Marriott	21201
Baltimore Ramada Hotel	21207
Best Western Harbor City Inn	21230
Brookshire Hotel	21202
Cross Keys	21210
Holiday Inn-Belmont	21207
Holiday Inn Downtown-Inner Harbor	21201
The Hotel Belvedere	21202
Hyatt Regency Baltimore-Inner Harbor	21202
International Hotel	21240
Master Hosts Inn	21201
Omni Inner Harbor Hotel	21201
The Peabody Court	21201
Quality Inn-West	21228
Sheraton Inner Harbor Hotel	21201
Sheraton Johns Hopkins Inn	21231
Society Hill Hotel	21201
Tremont Hotel	21202
Tremont Plaza Hotel	21202
MILITARY INSTALLATIONS	
Air Force Publications Distribution Center	21220
Baltimore Outport, MTMC Dundalk Marine Terminal	21222
Baltimore Washington International Airport, Air Force Facility	21240
Coast Guard Yard, Curtis Bay	21226
Maryland Air National Guard, FB6191	21220
United States Army Engineer District, Baltimore	21203
United States Army Publications Center	21220
Baltimore Corner	21640
Baltimore Highlands	21227
Banks O'Dee	20664
Bannockburn	20814
Bannockburn Estates	20817
Bannockburn Heights	20817
Barclay	21607
Barefoot Acres	20619
Bar Harbor	21122
Bark Hill	21791
Barksdale	21921
Barnaby Manor	20744
Barnaby Run Estates	20745
Barnaby Village	20745
Bar Neck	21671
Barnes Corner	21917
Barnesville	20838
Barnesville (rural)	20842
Barrelville	21545
Barstow	20610
Bartholows	21771
Barton	21521
Bartonsville	21701
Battery Park	20814
Battle Grove	21222
Bayberry	21012
Bay City	21666
Bay Highlands	21403
Baynesville	21204
Bay Ridge	21403

MARYLAND 243
Bayside Beach-Burgundy Estates

Name	ZIP
Bayside Beach	21122
Bay View (Baltimore Indep. City)	21224
Bay View (Cecil County)	21901
Bay View Estates	21919
Beachville	20684
Beachwood Forest	21122
Beachwood Grove	21122
Beachwood on the Burley	21401
Beacon Heights	20737
Beacon Hill	21401
Beale Manor	21403
Beall Estates	20716
Beallsville	20839
Beantown	20601
Bear Creek Junction	21222
Beaufort Park	20759
Beauty Beach	21061
Beaver Creek	21740
Beaver Dam	21851
Beaverdam Estates	20785
Beaver Heights	20743
Beckleysville	21074
Bedford	20708
Bedford Road	21502
Bedfordshire	20854
Bel Air (Allegany County)	21502
Bel Air (Harford County)	21014
Belair (Prince George's County)	20715
Bel Air Acres (Charles County)	20601
Bel Air Acres (Harford County)	21014
Belair Buckingham (Part of Bowie)	20715
Belair Chapel Forge (Part of Bowie)	20715
Belair Foxhill (Part of Bowie)	20715
Belair Heather Hills (Part of Bowie)	20715
Belair Idlewild (Part of Bowie)	20715
Belair Kenilworth (Part of Bowie)	20715
Belair Longridge (Part of Bowie)	20715
Bel Air North	21050
Belair Overbrook (Part of Bowie)	20715
Belair Rockledge (Part of Bowie)	20715
Belair Shopping Center (Part of Bowie)	20715
Belair Somerset (Part of Bowie)	20715
Bel Air South	21014
Belair Tulip Grove (Part of Bowie)	20715
Belair White Hall (Part of Bowie)	20715
Belair Yorktown (Part of Bowie)	20715
Bel Alton	20611
Belcamp	21017
Belhaven	21122
Belleair Estates	20744
Belle Farm Estates	21208
Bellefonte	20735
Belle Grove	21766
Bellemead	20784
Belleview Estates	21146
Bellevue	21662
Bellevue Estates	20607
Bells Mill Village	20854
Bellwood Park	20601
Belmar	21206
Bel Pre Estates	20906
Bel Pre Park	20906
Bel Pre Woods	20853
Beltsville	20704-05
For specific Beltsville Zip Codes call (301) 937-3355	
Beltsville Heights	20705
Beltway Plaza (Part of Greenbelt)	20770
Belvedere Heights	21012
Bembe Beach	21403
Benedict	20612
Benevola	21713
Bennsville	20601
Ben Oaks	21146
Benson	21018
Bentley Springs	21120
Bentons Pleasure	21619
Berkley	21034
Berkshire	20747
Berlin	21811
Berrett	21784
Berry	20601
Berrywood	21122

Name	ZIP
Berwyn (Part of College Park)	20740
Berwyn Heights	20740
Bestgate	21401
Bethany Manor	21043
Bethel (Carroll County)	21048
Bethel (Cecil County)	21915
Bethel (Frederick County)	21701
Bethel (Garrett County)	21550
Bethesda	20813-17
For specific Bethesda Zip Codes call (301) 652-7401	
Bethgate	21043
Bethlehem	21609
Betterton	21610
Beulah	21643
Beverly Beach	21106
Beverly Farms	20854
Big Pines	20850
Big Pool	21711
Big Spring	21722
Bigwoods	21678
Billingsley Forest	20640
Birchwood City	20745
Birchwood Gardens	20708
Birdlawn	20744
Bird River Beach	21220
Birdsville	20776
Birmingham Estates	20705
Birmingham Terrace	20705
Bishop	21813
Bishops Head	21611
Bishopville	21813
Bitter Sweet	21403
Bittinger	21522
Bivalve	21814
Black Horse	21161
Blackrock Estates	20874
Blacks Corner	21157
Blackwater	21622
Bladensburg	20710
Bladenwoods (Part of Bladensburg)	20710
Blair	20910
Blenheim	21131
Bloomfield	21701
Blooming Rose Settlement	21531
Bloomington	21523
Bloomsbury	21228
Blossom Hills	21122
Blueball	21921
Blueberry Hills	20855
Blue Hill (Part of Hancock)	21750
Blue Mount	21111
Blue Mountain (Frederick County)	21788
Blue Mountain (Washington County)	21783
Blue Ridge Manor	20902
Blue Ridge View	21157
Blythedale	21903
Bolivar Heights	21769
Bolton	20601
Bond Mill Park	20707
Bonds	20607
Bon Haven	21401
Bonnie Acres	21043
Bonnie Brae	21784
Bonnie Brook	21613
Bonnie Knob (Part of Woodsboro)	21798
Bonnie Ridge	21209
Boonsboro	21713
Borden Shaft	21532
Borden Yard	21532
Boring	21020
Boulevard Heights	20743
Boulevard Park	21122
Bowens	20678
Bowie	20715-16
For specific Bowie Zip Codes call (301) 464-0707	
Bowie State College	20715
Bowleys Quarters	21220
Bowling Green	21502
Bowlings Alley	20622
Boxhill North	21014
Boxiron	21829
Boxwood Village (Part of Greenbelt)	20770
Boyds	20841
Boyer Mill Heights	21774
Bozman	21612
Bradbury Heights	20743
Bradbury Park	20746
Braddock	21701
Braddock Estates (Part of Frostburg)	21532
Braddock Heights	21714
Bradley Farms	20854
Bradley Hills	20817

Name	ZIP
Bradley Hills Grove	20817
Bradley Woods	20817
Bradshaw	21021
Braebrook Village	20770
Bramble Hills	21157
Branchville (Part of College Park)	20740
Brandwine Farms	21047
Brandywine	20613
Brandywine Country	20772
Brandywine Heights	20613
Breathedsville	21740
Breezewood Farms	21163
Breezy Point	20732
Breezy Point Beach	21221
Brentwood	20722
Breton Beach	20650
Briarcrest Heights	21755
Briarwood (Charles County)	20601
Briarwood (Prince George's County)	20708
Briddletown	21811
Bridewell	20794
Bridgeport (Frederick County)	21787
Bridgeport (Washington County)	21740
Bridgetown	21636
Bright Oaks	21014
Brighton (Baltimore County)	21207
Brighton (Montgomery County)	20833
Brightview Woods	21108
Brightwood Acres	21740
Brinkleigh	21043
Brinkleigh Manor	21043
Brinkley Manor	20748
Brinklow	20862
Bristol	20711
Broad Creek	21160
Broadmoor	21030
Broad Run	21718
Broadview	20748
Broadview Acres	21701
Broadwater Estates	20744
Broadwater Point	20733
Broadwood Manor (Part of Rockville)	20851
Brock Bridge	20707
Brock Hall	20772
Brock Hall Estates	20772
Brock Hall Gardens	20772
Brock Hall Manor	20772
Brookdale	20815
Brookdale Heights	21801
Brooke-Jane Manor	20735
Brooke Manor	20745
Brookemanor Estates	20853
Brookeville	20833
Brook Hill	21701
Brooklandville	21093
Brooklyn (Part of Baltimore)	21225
Brooklyn-Curtis Bay	21225
Brooklyn Park (Anne Arundel County)	21225
Brookmead	20874
Brookmead North	20874
Brookmont	20816
Brookside Forest	20901
Brookside Manor	20782
Brookview	21659
Brookville Knolls	20833
Brookwood	20772
Brookwood Estates	20646
Broomes Island	20615
Browns Corner	21617
Brownsville (Queen Anne's County)	21617
Brownsville (Washington County)	21715
Browns Woods Villa	21401
Bruceville (Carroll County)	21757
Bruceville (Talbot County)	21673
Brunswick	21716
Bryans Road (Charles County)	20616
Bryantown (Charles County)	20617
Bryantown (Queen Anne's County)	21658
Bryant Square	21044
Bryant Woods	21044
Buckeystown	21717
Buckingham View	21157
Buck Lodge	20783
Bucktown	21613
Budds Creek	20659
Buena Vista	20678
Buffalo Run	21531
Burgundy Estates (Part of Rockville)	20851

244 MARYLAND Burgundy Knolls-Clinton Grove

	ZIP		ZIP		ZIP
Burgundy Knolls (Part of Rockville)	20850	Carroll Heights (Part of Hagerstown)	21740	Cherry Hill (Part of College Park)	20740
Burgundy Village (Part of Rockville)	20850	Carroll Highlands	21784	Cherry Hill (mobile home park)	20705
Burkittsville	21718	Carroll Island	21220	Cherrywalk	21830
Burning Tree Estates	20817	Carroll Knolls	20910	Chesaco Park	21237
Burning Tree Manor	20817	Carroll Manor (Part of Takoma Park)	20912	Chesapeake Beach	20732
Burns Corner (Part of Aberdeen)	21001	Carrollton	21157	Chesapeake City	21915
Burnt Mills	20901	Carrollton Manor	21146	Chesapeake Estates	21666
Burnt Mills Hills	20901	Carrollwood	21220	Chesapeake Heights	21801
Burnt Mills Knolls	20901	Carrollwood Estate	21157	Chesapeake Isle	21901
Burnt Mills Manor	20901	Carsins Run	21001	Chesapeake Landing	21620
Burnt Mills Village	20901	Carsondale	20706	Chesapeake Ranch Estates	20657
Burrisville	21617	Carter Hill (Part of Rockville)	20850	Chesapeake Terrace	21222
Burrsville	21629	Carvel Beach	21226	Cheshaven	21919
Burtner	21713	Carver Heights	20653	Chester	21619
Burtonsville	20866	Cascade	21719	Chesterfield	21032
Bush	21009	Cascade-Highfield	21719	Chesterfield Gardens	21122
Bushs Corner	21132	Cashell Estates	20855	Chester Harbor	21620
Bushwood	20618	Casselman	21536	Chester River Beach	21638
Butler	21023	Castle Marina	21619	Chestertown	21620
Butlertown	21678	Castleton	21034	Chesterville	21651
Buttercup Estates	21794	Catchpenny	21856	Chesterville Forest	21651
Buttonwood Beach	21919	Catoctin	21755	Chestnut Grove (Frederick County)	21701
Byford Knolls	20895	Catoctin Furnace	21788	Chestnut Grove (Washington County)	21756
Bynum	21050	Catoctin View	21771	Chestnut Hill (Baltimore County)	21204
Bynum Ridge	21050	Catonsville	21228	Chestnut Hill (Harford County)	21050
Byrdtown	21817	Catonsville Heights	21228	Chestnut Hill (Howard County)	21043
Cabin Creek	21643	Catonsville Manor	21207	Chestnut Hill Estates	21043
Cabin John	20818	Cavalier Country	20754	Chestnut Hills	20705
Cabin John-Brookmont	20816	Cavetown	21720	Chestnut Ridge (Baltimore County)	21117
Cabin John Park	20818	Cayots	21915	Chestnut Ridge (Prince George's County)	20737
Cactus Hill	20607	Cearfoss	21740	Cheverly	20785
Cadillac Homes	21061	Cecilton	21913	Cheverly Manor	20785
California (St. Mary's County)	20619	Cedar Acres	21044	Chevy Chase (Montgomery County)	20815
Callaway	20620	Cedar Beach	21221	Chevy Chase Lake	20815
Caltor Manor	20744	Cedar Grove	20874	Chevy Chase Manor	20815
Calvary	21028	Cedar Grove Beach	21631	Chevy Chase Section Five	20815
Calvert (Baltimore Indep. City)	21202	Cedar Hall	21851	Chevy Chase Section Three	20815
Calvert (Cecil County)	21901	Cedar Haven	20608	Chevy Chase Terrace	20815
Calvert Beach	20685	Cedar Heights	20743	Chevy Chase View	20895
Calvert Manor	20607	Cedarhurst (Anne Arundel County)	20764	Chevy Chase Village	20815
Calverton	20705	Cedarhurst (Carroll County)	21048	Chewsville	21721
Cambria	21131	Cedarhurst Acres	21830	Chicamuxen	20640
Cambridge	21613	Cedarhurst-on-the-Bay	20764	Childs	21916
Cambridge Estates	20735	Cedar Lawn	21740	Chillum (Prince George's County)	20783
Camden (Baltimore Indep. City)	21201	Cedarmere	21117	Chillum Estates	20783
Camden (Wicomico County)	21810	Cedar Park (Part of Annapolis)	21401	Chillum Heights	20783
Camelback Village	20832	Cedar Spring	21014	Chillum Manor	20783
Camelot (Harford County)	21014	Cedartown	21863	Chingville	20620
Camelot (Prince George's County)	20769	Cedarville	20613	Choptank	21655
Camotop	20854	Centennial	21043	Christs Rock	21613
Campbell	21813	Centennial Estates	21043	Church Creek	21622
Campbelltown	21813	Center Court	20879	Church Hill (Frederick County)	21773
Camp Springs (Prince George's County)	20748	Centerville	21754	Church Hill (Queen Anne's County)	21623
Camp Springs Forest	20748	Centreville	21617	Churchill Town Sector	20874
Campus Hills	21204	Ceresville	21701	Churchton	20733
Canada Hill	21773	Chadwick Manor	21207	Churchville	21028
Canal	21904	Chalfone Manor	21043	Cinnamon Ridge	20772
Candlewood Park	20855	Chalk Point	20778	Cissel Farms	20777
Cannon Acres	21613	Champ	21853	Claggettsville	20872
Canton (Part of Baltimore)	21224	Chance	21816	Claiborne	21624
Cape Anne	20733	Chaney	20754	Claremont (Part of Baltimore)	21223
Cape Arthur	21146	Chaneyville	20736	Clarksburg	20871
Cape Estate	21012	Chaneyville Farm Estates	20639	Clarks Landing	20636
Cape Isle of Wight	21842	Chapel	21601	Clarksville	21029
Cape Loch Haven	21037	Chapel Gate	21113	Clarksville Ridge	21029
Cape May Beach	21221	Chapel Hill	20744	Clarysville	21532
Cape St. Claire	21401	Chapel Hill Estates	20610	Clayton Manor	21085
Cape St. John	21401	Chapel Oaks	20743	Clearfield	21157
Capital Estates	20695	Chapelview	21043	Clear Spring	21722
Capitol Heights	20743	Chaptico	20621	Clearview	21040
Capitol Hills	21061	Charles Manor	21047	Clearview Manor	20745
Capitol Plaza (Part of Landover Hills)	20784	Charlesmont	21222	Clearview Village	21122
Capitol View Park	20910	Charlestown (Allegany County)	21539	Clearwater Beach	21226
Capri Estate	21012	Charlestown (Cecil County)	21914	Clements	20624
Captains Hill	21842	Charlestown Manor Beach	21901	Clifford (Part of Baltimore)	21230
Carderock Springs	20817	Charlesville	21701	Cliffs City	21620
Cardiff	21024	Charlotte Hall (St. Mary's County)	20622	Clifton	21701
Carea	17321	Charlton	21722	Clifton-East End (Part of Baltimore)	21213
Carlos (Allegany County)	21532	Charred Oak Estates	20817	Clifton on the Potomac	20664
Carlson Spring	20747	Chartley	21136	Clifton Park	20901
Carlton East	20706	Chartridge	21146	Clinton (Prince George's County)	20735
Carmichael	21658	Chartwell	21146	Clinton Acres	20613
Carmody Hills	20743	Chase	21027	Clinton Estates	20735
Carmody Hills-Pepper Mill Village	20743	Chateau Valley	21043	Clinton Gardens	20735
Carney (Baltimore County)	21234	Chatham	20783	Clinton Grove	20735
Carney Grove	21234	Chattolanee	21117		
Carney Heights	21234	Chelsea Beach	21122		
Carole Highlands	20783	Chelsea Woods (Part of Greenbelt)	20770		
Carpenter Point	21903	Cheltenham	20623		
Carroll (Part of Baltimore)	21229	Cheltenham Forest	20735		
Carroll County Trails	21048	Chelten Park	20735		
		Cherry Hill (Cecil County)	21921		
		Cherry Hill (Harford County)	21154		

Clinton Hills-Edgewater Village **MARYLAND** **245**

	ZIP
Clinton Hills	20735
Clinton Park	20735
Clinton Vista	20735
Clinton Woods	20735
Clopper	20878
Cloverfields	21666
Clover Hill	21701
Cloverlea	21106
Cloverly (Montgomery County)	20904
Club of Stedwick	20879
Clubside	20879
Clydesdale Acres	21048
Cobb Island	20625
Cockeysville (Baltimore County)	21030
Cohasset	20814
Cohill Estates	21750
Cokesburg	21851
Cokesbury	21904
Cold Spring Estates	20854
Coleman	21678
Colesville (Montgomery County)	20904
Colesville Farm Estates	20904
Colesville Gardens	20904
Colesville Manor	20904
Colesville Park	20904
College (Part of Westminster)	21157
College Estates (Part of Frederick)	21701
College Gardens (Part of Rockville)	20850
College Heights Estates	20783
College Park	20740-41
For specific College Park Zip Codes call (301) 345-1714	
College Park Woods (Part of College Park)	20740
College View	20902
Colmar Manor	20722
Colonial Acres (Cecil County)	21921
Colonial Acres (Harford County)	21014
Colonial Gardens	21228
Colonial Heights	21502
Colonial Park (Baltimore County)	21207
Colonial Park (Washington County)	21740
Colonial Village	21208
Colony Ridge	21113
Colora	21917
Coltons Point	20626
Columbia	21044-46
For specific Columbia Zip Codes call (301) 381-0121	
Columbia Beach	20764
Columbia Hills	21043
Columbia Park	20785
Colvilla	21157
Compton	20627
Comus	20842
Concord	21632
Congressional Forest Estates	20817
Connecticut Avenue Estates	20902
Connecticut Avenue Hills	20902
Connecticut Avenue Park	20906
Connecticut Gardens	20902
Conowingo	21918
Conowingo Village	21918
Contee	20708
Cooksville	21723
Coopersville	21023
Coopstown	21050
Copenhaver	20854
Copperville (Carroll County)	21787
Copperville (Talbot County)	21601
Coral Hills (Prince George's County)	20743
Corbett (Baltimore County)	21111
Corbett (Washington County)	21740
Cordova	21625
Cornersville	21613
Cornfield Harbor	20687
Corriganville	21524
Costen	21851
Cottage City	20722
Country Club Acres	21550
Country Club Estate	21061
Country Club Manor	21061
Country Club Park	21093
Country Club Village	20814
Country Place	20866
Country Road Estates	20754
Courthouse (Part of Rockville)	20850

	ZIP
Courtleigh	21133
Cove	21520
Coventry	21234
Cove Point	20657
Covers Corner	21776
Cowentown	21921
Coxby Estates	21037
Cox Creek Acres	21619
Crabtree	21561
Craigtown	21904
Cranberry	21157
Crapo	21626
Creagerstown	21788
Crellin	21550
Cremona	20659
Cresaptown	21502
Crescendo	21676
Cresthaven	20903
Crestleigh	21043
Crestview	20814
Crestview Manor	20735
Crestwood (Anne Arundel County)	21090
Crestwood (Wicomico County)	21801
Crestwood Acres	21040
Creswell	21014
Crisfield	21817
Crisp (Part of Baltimore)	21225
Criswood Manor	21029
Crocheron	21627
Crofton	21114
Cromwood	21234
Croom	20772
Crosby	21661
Crowder	21043
Crownsville	21032
Crownsville Hospital Center	21032
Croydon Park (Part of Rockville)	20850
Crumpton	21628
Crystal Beach	21919
Cub Hills	21234
Cuckhold Creek	20664
Cumberland	21501-05
For specific Cumberland Zip Codes call (301) 722-8190	
Curtis Bay (Part of Baltimore)	21225
Cypress Creek	21146
Dailsville	21613
Daisy	21797
Dalton	21043
Damascus	20872
Dameron	20628
Dames Quarter	21820
Dam No. 4	21782
Daniel	21797
Daniels Park (Part of College Park)	20740
Danville	21557
Danwood	21801
Darcy Manor	20746
Dares Beach	20678
Dargan	25425
Darleigh Manor	21236
Darlington	21034
Darnestown	20874
Darryl Gardens	21162
Daugherty Town	21817
Davidsonville	21035
Dawson	26726
Dawsonville	20841
Day	21797
Daysville	21793
Dayton	21036
Deale	20751
Deale Beach	20751
Deal Island	21821
Deanwood Park	20743
Decatur Heights (Part of Bladensburg)	20710
Deep Creek	21012
Deep Creek Lake	21541
Deep Landing Estates	20639
Deerfield (Harford County)	21034
Deerfield (Montgomery County)	20817
Deerfield Run	20708
Deer Harbour	21801
Deer Park (Garrett County)	21550
Deer Park (Montgomery County)	20877
Deer Park (Prince George's County)	20748
Deer Park Estates	21048
Deer Park Heights	20748
Deers Head	21801
Defense Heights (Baltimore County)	21222

	ZIP
Defense Heights (Prince George's County)	20784
Delight	21117
Dellmont	21048
Delmar	21875
Delmont	21144
Den Lee Acres	20735
Dennings	21776
Dennis Grove Apartments	20745
Denton	21629
Derwood	20855
Detmold	21539
Detour	21725
Devonshire Forest	21093
Diamond Farms (Part of Gaithersburg)	20878
Dickerson	20842
Discovery	21793
District Heights-Forestville	20747
Dodge Park	20785
Dogwood Flats	21521
Dogwood Hills	21204
Dominion	21619
Doncaster	20640
Doncaster Village	21234
Donleigh	21046
Donnybrook	21204
Dorceytown	21771
Dorchester Estates	20735
Dorsey	21227
Dorseys Regard	20879
Doubs	21710
Dowell	20629
Downsville	21795
Drayden	20630
Dresden Green	20706
Drexel Woods	21228
Druid (Part of Baltimore)	21217
Drumcliff	20636
Drumeldra Hills	20904
Drum Point	20657
Drury	20711
Drybranch	21161
Dry Run	21722
Dublin	21034
Dufief	20878
Dulaney Village	21204
Dulls Corner	21401
Dumbarton	21208
Dumbarton Heights	21208
Dunbrook	21122
Dundalk	21222
Dundalk Shopping Center	21222
Dundalk-Sparrows Point	21222
Dundee Village	21220
Dunkirk	20754
Dunlaney Village	21093
Dunloggin	21043
Dunwood	21085
Dupont Heights	20746
Dynard	20621
Eagle Harbor	20608
Eakles Mill	21756
Earleigh Heights	21146
Earleville	21919
Earlton	21078
East Columbia Park	20785
Eastfield	21222
East Fort Foote Village	20744
East Meadow	20745
East New Market	21631
Easton	21601
Easton Point	21601
Eastover Knolls	20745
East Park Village	21061
Eastpines	20737
Eastpoint	21222
Eastpoint Mall	21224
Eastport (Part of Annapolis)	21403
East Riverdale (Prince George's County)	20737
East Springbrook	20904
Eastview (Carroll County)	21048
Eastview (Frederick County)	21701
Eastview Estates	21048
Eckhart Mines	21528
Eden	21822
Eder	21921
Edesville	21661
Edgemere (Baltimore County)	21221
Edgemont (Frederick County)	21701
Edgemont (Washington County)	21783
Edgemoor	20814
Edgewater	21037
Edgewater Beach	21037
Edgewater Village	21040

246 MARYLAND Edgewood-Gist

Name	ZIP
Edgewood (Frederick County)	21701
Edgewood (Harford County)	21040
Edgewood (Montgomery County)	20814
Edgewood Arsenal	21040
Edgewood Meadows	21040
Edmondson Heights	21207
Edmondson Ridge	21228
Edmonston	20781
Ednor	20905
Ednor Acres	20904
Elberon	20854
Elder Hill	21531
Eldersburg (Carroll County)	21784
Eldorado	21659
Elioak	21044
Elk Mills	21920
Elkmore	21921
Elk Neck	21901
Elk Ranch Park	21921
Elk Ridge	21227
Elkton	21921
Elkton Heights (Part of Elkton)	21921
Elktonia	21401
Elkton Landing (Part of Elkton)	21921
Elkwood Estates	21921
Ellerslie	21529
Ellerton	21773
Ellicott City (Howard County)	21043
Ellicott Mills (Baltimore County)	21228
Ellicott Mills (Howard County)	21043
Elliott	21869
Elmwood	21206
Elvaton Acres	21108
Elvatone Town	21061
Elwood	21643
Emmitsburg	21727
Emmorton	21009
Emory Church	21155
Emory Grove (Baltimore County)	21071
Emory Grove (Montgomery County)	20877
Emory Hills	21048
Engles Mill	21520
Englewood	20785
English Manor	20853
English Village	20814
Enterprise Estates	20716
Enterprise Shopping Center	20706
Epping Forest	21401
Ernstville	21711
Essex	21221
Estonian Estates	20772
Etchison	20877
Eudowood	21204
Eutaw Forest	20601
Evanston	20747
Evergreen Estates	21146
Evergreen Hills	21048
Evergreen Overlook	20745
Evergreen Park	21221
Evergreen Valley Estates	21043
Evitts Creek	21502
Ewell	21824
Ewingville	21620
Fahrney Keedy Memorial Home	21713
Fairbank	21671
Fairfield (Baltimore Indep. City)	21226
Fairfield (Carroll County)	21157
Fairfield Knolls	20747
Fairgreen	20772
Fairgreen Acres	21740
Fair Haven	20754
Fairhaven on the Bay	20754
Fair Hill	21921
Fairidge	20877
Fairknoll	20905
Fairland (Montgomery County)	20904
Fairland Acres	20866
Fairland Heights	20904
Fairlee	21620
Fairmont	21014
Fairmount	21871
Fairmount Heights	20743
Fair Play	21733
Fairview (Anne Arundel County)	20707
Fairview (Anne Arundel County)	21122
Fairview (Washington County)	21722

Name	ZIP
Fairview Estates	20904
Fairway	21014
Fairway Hills	20812
Fairway Island	20879
Fallsmont	21047
Fallston	21047
Family Estates	20743
Farmington (Cecil County)	21911
Farmington (Montgomery County)	20815
Farmsbrook	21701
Faulkner	20632
Faulkner Ridge	21044
Fawsett Farms	20854
Feagaville	21701
Federal Hill	21084
Federalsburg	21632
Felicity Cove	20764
Fellowship Forest	21204
Ferdinand Heights	21061
Ferndale (Anne Arundel County)	21061
Fernglen Manor	21061
Fernwood (Montgomery County)	20817
Fernwood (Prince George's County)	20737
Fernwood (mobile home park) (Prince George's County)	20743
Fiddlersburg	21740
Figgs Landing	21863
Finksburg	21048
Finzel	21532
Fishing Creek	21634
Fleishman Village	20746
Flickersville	21756
Flintstone	21530
Flohrville	21784
Florence	21797
Flower Valley	20853
Flower Valley Estates	20853
Fontana Village	21237
Font Hill	21043
Font Hill Manor	21043
Forest Estates	20910
Forest Glen	20910
Forest Greens	21001
Forest Heights	20745
Forest Hill	21050
Forest Knolls (Montgomery County)	20901
Forest Knolls (Prince George's County)	20744
Forest Lake	21050
Forest Lawn	21014
Forest Manor	20747
Forest Oaks	21784
Forest Park	20705
Forestville (Prince George's County)	20747
Forestville Estates	20747
Forge Acres	21128
Forge Heights	21128
Fork	21051
Forrest Hall	20659
Fort Foote Estates	20747
Fort Foote Village	20744
Fort George G. Meade	20755
Fort Howard (Baltimore County)	21052
Fort Meade (Anne Arundel County)	20755
Fort Ritchie (Washington County)	21719
Fort Sumner	20816
Fort Washington Estates	20744
Fort Washington Forest	20744
Foundry Siding (Part of Westernport)	21562
Fountaindale	21769
Fountain Green	21014
Fountain Green Heights	21014
Fountain Head	21740
Fountain Mills	21754
Fountain Rock (Part of Walkersville)	21793
Fountain Valley	21157
Four Locks	21722
Four Seasons Estates	21113
Four Winds	21204
Fowblesburg	21155
Fowlers Concord	20747
Fox Chapel	20874
Fox Chapel North	20874
Fox Chase	21061
Foxhall	20906
Foxhall Estates	21035
Fox Hills	20854
Fox Hills West	20854
Foxley Manor	21620

Name	ZIP
Fox Rest	20708
Fox Rest South	20708
Foxridge	21078
Fox Run Estates	20735
Foxville	21780
Franklin (Part of Baltimore)	21223
Franklin Manor Beach	20733
Franklin Manor on-the-Bay	20733
Franklin Park	20852
Franklin Square	20744
Franklinville (Baltimore County)	21087
Franklinville (Frederick County)	21788
Frederick	21701
Frederick Junction	21701
Frederick Shopping Center (Part of Frederick)	21701
Frederick Towne Mall (Part of Frederick)	21701
Frederick Village	21228
Freedom Forest	21784
Freeland	21053
Free State Mall (Part of Bowie)	20715
Frenchtown	21903
Friendly (Prince George's County)	20744
Friendly Farms	20744
Friends Creek	21727
Friendship (Anne Arundel County)	20758
Friendship (Frederick County)	21791
Friendship (Worcester County)	21811
Friendship Heights	20813
Friendship Park	21740
Friendsville	21531
Frizzelburg	21157
Frostburg	21532
Frostown	21769
Fruitland	21826
Fullerton	21206
Fulton	20759
Fulton Junction (Part of Baltimore)	21217
Funkstown	21734
Furnace Branch	21061
Gaither	21735
Gaithersburg	20877-79, 20882-86
For specific Gaithersburg Zip Codes call (301) 948-1894	
Galena	21635
Galestown	19973
Galesville	20765
Gallant Green	20601
Gamber	21048
Gambrills	21054
Gannon	21562
Gapland	21736
Garfield	21783
Garland	21061
Garrett Forest	20906
Garrett Park	20896
Garrett Park Estates	20895
Garretts Mill	21758
Garrison	21055
Gatts Corner	21106
Gayfields	20906
George Island Landing	21864
Georgetown (Anne Arundel County)	20794
Georgetown (Cecil County)	21930
Georgetown (mail Chestertown) (Kent County)	21620
Georgetown (mail Georgetown) (Kent County)	21930
Georgetown Estates	20852
Georgetown Village	20812
Georgian Forest	20902
Germantown	20874-75
For specific Germantown Zip Codes call (301) 428-3839	
Germantown (Montgomery County)	20874
Germantown (Worcester County)	21811
Germantown Estates	20874
Germantown Park	20874
Germantown View	20874
Gibson Island	21056
Gibson Manor	21014
Gilmore	21532
Gingerville Manor Estates	21037
Girdletree	21829
Gist	21784

Glade Towne-High Ridge MARYLAND 247

Place	ZIP
Glade Towne (Part of Walkersville)	21793
Gladstone Acres	21034
Glassmanor	20745
Glazewood Manor (Part of Takoma Park)	20912
Glebe Heights	21037
Glenallen	20902
Glenarden	20706
Glen Arm	21057
Glen Brook	21043
Glenbrook Knolls	20814
Glenbrook Village	20814
Glen Burnie (Anne Arundel County)	21061
Glen Burnie Mall	21061
Glen Burnie Park	21061
Glencoe (Baltimore County)	21152
Glencoe (Kent County)	21645
Glen Cove	20816
Glendale (Baltimore County)	21204
Glendale (Wicomico County)	21801
Glendale Heights	20769
Glen Echo	20812
Glen Echo Heights	20816
Glenelg	21737
Glen Ellen	21204
Glen Elyn	21047
Glen Farms	19711
Glen Gardens	21061
Glen Hills	20850
Glen Isle	21401
Glen Kyle	19711
Glenmar (Baltimore County)	21220
Glenmar (Howard County)	21043
Glen Mar Park	20814
Glen Mary Heights (Part of Elkton)	21921
Glenmont (Baltimore County)	21239
Glenmont (Montgomery County)	20902
Glenmont Park	20906
Glenmore	21061
Glen Morris	21136
Glenn Dale	20769
Glenn Heights	21078
Glen Oaks	20854
Glenora Hills (Part of Rockville)	20850
Glen Park	20854
Glen Ridge	20784
Glenside Park	21234
Glenville	21034
Glen Westover	19711
Glen Willows	20743
Glenwood (Harford County)	21014
Glenwood (Howard County)	21738
Glenwood Estates	21738
Glenwood Park	20706
Glover Acres	21157
Glymont	20640
Glyndon	21071
Goddard	20770
Goddard Space Flight Center	20770
Golden Beach	20659
Golden Hill	21622
Golden Ring	21237
Golden Ring Mall	21237
Goldsboro	21636
Golf Club Shores	21811
Golts	21635
Good Acres (Part of Hagerstown)	21740
Good Hope	20905
Goodwill	21851
Gorman	26720
Gortner	21550
Goshen	20879
Goshen Estates	20879
Gotts	21032
Govans (Part of Baltimore)	21212
Governors Run	20676
Graceham	21788
Graceton	21160
Grahamtown	21532
Granby Woods	20855
Grand Bel Manor	20906
Grandview	21784
Granite	21163
Grantsville	21536
Grasonville	21638
Gratitude	21661
Gray Haven	21222
Gray Manor	21222
Gray Rock	21043
Grayton	20662
Greater Capitol Heights	20743
Great Mills	20634

Place	ZIP
Green Acres (Harford County)	21085
Green Acres (Montgomery County)	20817
Greenbelt	20770
Greenberry Hills	21740
Greenbriar	21713
Greenbrier (Part of Greenbelt)	20770
Greendale Estates	21047
Greenfield	20735
Greenfield Mills	21710
Green Glade	21561
Green Haven (Anne Arundel County)	21122
Green Hill	21856
Green Hill Acres	21740
Green Meadows (Charles County)	20616
Green Meadows (Prince George's County)	20782
Greenmount	21074
Green Ridge (Allegany County)	21766
Green Ridge (Baltimore County)	21093
Greenridge (Harford County)	21014
Greensboro	21639
Greensburg	21783
Green Spring Hills	21085
Greentop Manor	21030
Greentree (Anne Arundel County)	21061
Greentree (Montgomery County)	20879
Green Tree Manor	20817
Greenvale Village	21783
Green Valley	21771
Greenview Knolls	20653
Greenwich Forest	20814
Greenwood Acres	21401
Greenwood Farms	20777
Greenwood Forest	20706
Gregg Neck	21635
Greystone Manor (Part of Hagerstown)	21740
Grimesville	21053
Grosstown	20637
Grove	21655
Grove Hill	21701
Guilford	20794
Guilford Manor	21225
Gum Springs	20868
Gum Springs Farm	20868
Gunners Lake Village	20874
Gunpowder (Baltimore County)	21021
Gunpowder (Harford County)	21010
Gunpowder Estates	21128
Gwenlee Estates	21738
Gwynn	21043
Gwynn Acres	21043
Gwynnbrook	21117
Gwynn Oak (Part of Baltimore)	21207
Hack Point	21919
Hacks Point Acre	21919
Hagerstown	21740
Halethorpe	21227
Halfway (Washington County)	21740
Halfway Manor	21740
Hallett Heights	21863
Halley Estates	20695
Halpine Village	20852
Hambleton Estates	21140
Hamilton (Part of Baltimore)	21214
Hamilton Park (Part of Hagerstown)	21740
Hamlet North	20855
Hammondell Heights	21108
Hammond Park	20707
Hampden (Part of Baltimore)	21211
Hampshire Knolls	20783
Hampstead	21074
Hampton (Baltimore County)	21204
Hampton Gardens	21204
Hance Point	21901
Hancock	21750
Hanesville	21678
Hanover (Anne Arundel County)	21076
Hanover (Howard County)	21076
Hanson Valley View	20744
Hansonville	21701
Harbor View (Anne Arundel County)	21037

Place	ZIP
Harborview (Queen Anne's County)	21619
Hardesty Estates	21035
Harewood	21220
Harewood Park	21220
Harford Estates	21050
Harford Farms	21234
Harford Furnace	21014
Harford Hills	21234
Harford Mall (Part of Bel Air)	21014
Harford Park	21234
Harford Square	21040
Harmans	21077
Harmony (Caroline County)	21655
Harmony (Frederick County)	21769
Harmony Grove	21701
Harmony Hall	20744
Harmony Hills	20906
Harness Woods	21403
Harney	21787
Harpers Choice	21044
Harpers Corner	20659
Harpers Mill	21108
Harris Heights	21061
Harrison Ferry	21643
Harrisonville	21133
Harrisville (Carroll County)	21771
Harrisville (Cecil County)	21917
Harundale	21061
Harundale Mall	21061
Harvest Hills	21047
Harwood (Anne Arundel County)	20776
Har-Wood (Howard County)	21227
Harwood Estates	20748
Harwood Park	21227
Havenwood Hills	21783
Haverhill	21234
Havre de Grace	21078
Havre de Grace Heights	21078
Hawbottom	21769
Hawkeye	21631
Hayes Landing	21811
Hazelhurst	21561
Hazelmoor	21919
Head of the Creek	21856
Hearn Bailey Farm	21801
Heather Heights	21784
Heather Hill Apartments	20748
Hebbville	21207
Hebron	21830
Helen	20635
Helen Estates	20635
Henderson	21640
Henryton	21080
Herald Harbor	21032
Herald Square	21207
Hereford	21111
Heritage Farm	20854
Heritage Harbor	21401
Heritage Hills	21061
Heritage Walk	20852
Hermanville	20653
Hermitage Park	20906
Hernwood Heights	21133
Herrington Manor	21550
Hickman	21629
Hickory	21014
Hickory Hills (Part of Bel Air)	21014
Hickory Ridge	21044
Hicksburg	21631
Hidden Point	21401
High Bridge	20715
High Bridge Estates	20715
Highfield (Montgomery County)	20879
Highfield (Washington County)	21719
Highland (Frederick County)	21773
Highland (Howard County)	20777
Highland Beach	21403
Highland Park (Prince George's County)	20743
Highland Park (Worcester County)	21811
Highlands	20854
Highlands of Olney	20832
Highland Stone	20854
Highlandtown (Part of Baltimore)	21224
High Meadows	21770
High Point (Anne Arundel County)	21122
High Point (Montgomery County)	20814
High Point Heights (Prince George's County)	20705
Highpoint Heights (Prince George's County)	20705
High Point Manor	21014
High Ridge	20707

248 MARYLAND High Ridge Park-Lanham

Place	ZIP
High Ridge Park	20707
High View	21771
High-View Estates (Carroll County)	21102
Highview Estates (Howard County)	21043
Highview on the Bay	20779
Hillandale (Montgomery County)	20903
Hillandale Forest	20907
Hillandale Heights	20903
Hillcrest (Anne Arundel County)	21225
Hill Crest (Montgomery County)	20912
Hillcrest (Prince George's County)	20748
Hillcrest Estates	20748
Hillcrest Heights (Howard County)	20707
Hillcrest Heights (Prince George's County)	20748
Hillcrest Terrace	20748
Hillendale Shopping Center	21204
Hillmead	20817
Hillmeade	20769
Hillmeade Manor	20769
Hillsboro	21641
Hillsborough	20707
Hillside	21157
Hillsmere Estates	21403
Hillsmere Shores	21403
Hills Point	21613
Hill Top	20693
Hillwood Manor	20783
Hobbs	21629
Hoffman	21532
Holabird (Part of Baltimore)	21224
Holbrook	21133
Holiday Acres	21783
Holiday Beach	20732
Holiday Hills	21044
Holiday Park	20906
Holland Cliff Shores	20639
Holland Heights	21801
Hollaway Estates	20772
Hollinsworth Manor (Part of Elkton)	21921
Holly Beach	21221
Holly Gaf. Acres	20636
Holly Hall Terrace	21921
Holly Hill Harbor	21037
Holly Lake Estates	21801
Holly Spring	20747
Holly Tree	20601
Hollywood (Prince George's County)	20740
Hollywood (St. Mary's County)	20636
Hollywood Beach	21915
Hollywood Estates (Part of College Park)	20740
Hollywood Park	20904
Hollywood Shores	20636
Holmehurst	20715
Home Acres	20705
Homecrest	20906
Homestead Estates	20904
Homewood (Allegany County)	21502
Homewood (Montgomery County)	20895
Honga	21622
Hood College (Part of Frederick)	21701
Hoods Mill	21723
Hoopersville	21634
Hope Hill	21701
Hopewell	21817
Hopkins Mead	21029
Horizon Run	20877
Houcksville	21074
Howard Heights	21043
Howardville	21208
Hoyes Run	21531
Hudson	21613
Hughesville	20637
Hungerford Towne (Part of Rockville)	20852
Hunt Club Estates (Charles County)	20601
Hunt Club Estates (Howard County)	21227
Hunt Crest Estates	21204
Hunters Harbor	21122
Hunters Hill	21093
Hunters Ridge	20610
Huntersville	20659
Hunting Hills	20639
Hunting Lodge	21234
Hunting Park	21801
Huntington Terrace	20814
Huntingtown	20639
Huntsmoor	21227
Huntsville	20785
Hunt Valley	21031
Hunt Valley Mall	21030
Hurlock	21643
Hurry	20621
Hutton	21550
Huyett	21740
Hyattstown	20871
Hyattsville	20780-89
For specific Hyattsville Zip Codes call (301) 699-8905	
Hyde Park (Baltimore County)	21221
Hyde Park (Wicomico County)	21801
Hydes	21082
Hynesboro	20706
Hynson	21632
Idlewild	20764
Idlewylde	21204
Ijamsville	21754
Ilchester	21043
Imperial Gardens	21133
Indian Creek Estates	20622
Indian Head	20640
Indian Head Manor	20616
Indian Head Naval Ordnance Station	20640
Indian Head Plant	20640
Indian Queen East	20744
Indian Queen Estates	20744
Indian River Estates	20659
Indian Springs (Frederick County)	21701
Indian Springs (Washington County)	21711
Indiantown	21863
Ingleside	21644
Inverness	21222
Inverness Forest	20854
Inverness Woods	20854
Iron Hill	21920
Ironshire	21811
Ironsides	20643
Isabella Park	20783
Island Creek	20685
Island View Beach	21221
Issue	20645
Iverson Mall	20748
Ivy Hills	21043
Ivytown	21601
Jackson	21903
Jacksonville (Baltimore County)	21131
Jacksonville (Somerset County)	21817
Jacktown	21613
Jacobsville	21122
Jarrettsville	21084
Jefferson	21755
Jefferson Heights (Prince George's County)	20743
Jefferson Heights (Washington County)	21740
Jennings	21536
Jersey Heights (Wicomico County)	21801
Jerusalem (Baltimore County)	21087
Jerusalem (Frederick County)	21773
Jerusalem (Montgomery County)	20837
Jessup	20794
Jesterville	21814
Jewell	20754
Johnsontown	21620
Johnstown	20688
Johnsville (Carroll County)	21784
Johnsville (Frederick County)	21791
Jones	21146
Jonestown	21655
Joppa	21085
Joppa Heights	21234
Joppatowne	21085
Joppa View	21128
Josenhans Corner	21221
Joyce Acres	21012
Kalma Ridge	21032
Kalmia	21014
Kalmia Farms	21036
Kalten Acres	21157
Kastle Estates	20735
Kaywood Gardens (Part of Mount Rainier)	20712
Keedysville	21756
Keeler Glade	21531
Keifer	25434
Kemp Mill Estates	20902
Kemp Mill Farms	20902
Kempton	26292
Kemptown	21770
Ken Gar	20895
Kennedyville	21645
Kensington	20895
Kensington Estates	20895
Kensington Heights	20902
Kensington View	20895
Kent Island Estates	21666
Kentland (Prince George's County)	20785
Kentmore Park	21645
Kentmorr	21666
Kent Village	20785
Kenwood (Baltimore County)	21206
Kenwood (Montgomery County)	20815
Kenwood Beach	20676
Kerby Hills	20744
Kettering	20772
Kettering Estate Park	20772
Keymar	21757
Keysers Ridge	21536
Keystone Manor	20747
Keysville	21787
Kilbirnie Estates	21801
Kilbourn Estates	20748
Kilmarock	20912
Kimberly Gardens	20708
Kings Contrivance	21045
Kings County	21087
Kings Creek Estate	20772
Kingsford	20716
Kings Grove	21529
Kings Manor	20695
Kings Park	21208
Kings Ransom	21113
Kings Ridge	21234
Kingston	21871
Kingston Manor	20772
Kingstown	21620
Kingsville	21087
Kingwood Common	21207
Kirkham	21601
Kirkwood	20782
Kitzmiller	21538
Klej Grange	21851
Knapps Meadow	21539
Knettishall	21204
Knollview	21043
Knollwood (Baltimore County)	21204
Knollwood (Prince George's County)	20783
Knoxville	21758
Kump Station	21787
Ladiesburg	21759
Lakeland (Anne Arundel County)	21146
Lakeland (Prince George's County)	20740
Lake Linganore	21701
Lake Normandy Estates	20854
Lake Roland	21209
Lake Shore (Anne Arundel County)	21122
Lakeside Manor	21801
Lakeside Park	21740
Lakeside Terrace	20854
Lakeside Vista	21085
Lakeview (Howard County)	20707
Lakeview (Montgomery County)	20817
Lakewood	21801
Lakewood Estates (Calvert County)	20754
Lakewood Estates (Montgomery County)	20850
Lancaster	20601
Land-O-Lakes	20636
Landon Woods	20817
Landover (Prince George's County)	20784-85
For specific Landover (Prince George's County) Zip Codes call (301) 699-8905	
Landover (Prince George's County)	20785
Landover Estates	20784
Landover Hills	20784
Landover Knolls	20785
Landover Park (Part of Cheverly)	20785
Lane Beach	20650
Langley Park (Prince George's County)	20783
Lanham	20706

Lanham Heights-Merrymount **MARYLAND** 249

Name	ZIP
Lanham Heights	20706
Lanham-Seabrook (Prince George's County)	20706
Lanham Woods	20706
Lansdowne	21227
Lansdowne-Baltimore Highlands	21227
Lantz	21780
Lapidum	21078
La Plata	20646
Lappans	21733
Larchmont Knolls	20895
Largo (Prince George's County)	20772
Largo/Kettering	20775
Largo Knolls	20772
Laurel	20707-08
For specific Laurel Zip Codes call (301) 498-1400	
Laurel Acres	21122
Laurel Brook	21047
Laureldale	21234
Laurel Grove	20659
Laurel Pines	20708
Laurel Shopping Center (Part of Laurel)	20707
Laurel Wood	20708
La Vale	21502
La Vale-Narrows Park	21502
Lawndale Acres	21048
Lawsonia	21817
Lawyer Heights	21788
Layhill	20906
Layhill Gardens	20906
Layhill Village	20906
Laytonia	20877
Laytonsville	20879
Lees Woods	21014
Legion Avenue (Part of Annapolis)	21401
Le Gore	21757
Leisure World	20906
Leitersburg	21740
Leon	20711
Leonardtown	20650
Leslie	21901
Level	21078
Lewis Corner	21811
Lewisdale	20783
Lewis Heights	20783
Lewis Spring Manor	20735
Lewistown (Frederick County)	21701
Lewistown (Talbot County)	21625
Lexington Park (St. Mary's County)	20653
Liberty Grove	21918
Liberty Manor	21207
Libertytown (Frederick County)	21762
Libertytown (Worcester County)	21811
Lime Kiln	21701
Linchester	21655
Lincoln Avenue	21740
Lincoln Heights (Part of Salisbury)	21801
Lincoln Manor	21102
Lincoln Park (Part of Rockville)	20850
Lindamoor on the Severn	21401
Linden	20907
Linden Chapel Hills	21036
Lineboro	21088
Linhigh	21206
Linkwood	21835
Linsey Acres	20748
Linsted on the Severn	21146
Linthicum	21090
Linthicum Heights	21090
Linthicum Hills	21090
Linthicum Oaks	21090
Linwood (Carroll County)	21764
Linwood (Howard County)	21043
Linwood Village	21122
Lipins Corner	21122
Lisbon	21765
Little Orleans	21766
Little Washington	20747
Livingston Grove	20607
Llandaff	21601
Lloyds	21613
Loartown	21532
Lochearn (Baltimore County)	21207
Loch Haven	21234
Loch Hill	21212
Loch Lynn Heights	21550
Loch Raven	21234
Loch Raven Heights	21234
Loch Raven Village	21234

Name	ZIP
Locust Grove (Allegany County)	21502
Locust Grove (Kent County)	21645
Locust Grove (Washington County)	21779
Locust Grove Beach	20732
Locust Grove Station	21788
Locust Hill Estates	20814
Locust Valley	21769
Lodgecliffe	21613
Lodge Forest	21222
Lonaconing	21539
Londontown	21037
Londontowne	21037
London Woods	20743
Lone Oak	20814
Long	21502
Long Bar Harbor	21009
Long Beach	20685
Long Beach-Calvert Beach	20685
Long Corner	21771
Longfellow	21043
Longfield Estates	20747
Long Green	21092
Long Meadow	21784
Long Meadow Estates	20814
Long Meadow Shopping Center (Part of Hagerstown)	21740
Long Meadow West	21208
Long Point	21122
Long Reach	21045
Longview Beach	20618
Longwood	20817
Longwoods	21601
Lord	21532
Lord Calvert Estates	20639
Loreley	21162
Loretta Heights	21401
Lothian	20711
Louisville	21048
Lou Mar Estates	21009
Love Point	21666
Loveville	20656
Lower Magothy Beach	21146
Lower Marlboro	20736
Loyola (Part of Baltimore)	21210
Lucas Heights	21502
Luke	21540
Lusby	20657
Lusby Crossroads	21401
Lute	20906
Lutherville	21093
Lutherville-Timonium	21093
Lutz Hill	21237
Luxmanor	20852
Lynch	21646
Lynch Point	21222
Lynnbrook (Anne Arundel County)	21225
Lynnbrook (Charles County)	20601
Lynne Acres	21207
Lyons Creek (Anne Arundel County)	20711
Lyons Creek (Calvert County)	20754
Lyons Homes	21222
Mac Alpine	21043
McCahill Estates	20707
McCanns Corner	21154
McComas Beach	21550
McCoole	26726
McDaniel	21647
Mc Daniel City	20601
Mac Donald Farms	20639
McDonogh	21208
Mc Donogh Park	21133
Maceys Corner	21146
McHenry	21541
McKaig	21771
McKay Beach	20650
Mc Kendree	20879
McKenney Hills	20910
McKinleyville	21661
McKinstrys Mill	21791
Maddox	20621
Madison	21677
Madonna	21084
Madonna Manor	21084
Magnolia	21101
Magnolia Springs	20784
Magothy Beach	21122
Magothy Park Beach	21122
Mago Vista Beach	21012
Magruder Landing	20613
Main Street (Part of Salisbury)	21801
Malcolm	20601
Mall in Columbia, The	21043
Malvern	21204
Manchester	21102

Name	ZIP
Manchester Estates	20746
Manhattan Woods	21146
Manokin (Somerset County)	21836
Manokin (Wicomico County)	21801
Manor	21111
Manor Lake	20853
Manor Park	20853
Manor View	21057
Manor Woods	20853
Maple Crest (Baltimore County)	21220
Maplecrest (Carroll County)	21157
Maple Park	21801
Maple Plains	21801
Mapieside (Part of Cumberland)	21502
Maple View	21157
Mapleville (Frederick County)	21771
Mapleville (Washington County)	21713
Maplewood (Howard County)	21043
Maplewood (Montgomery County)	20814
Maplewood (Prince George's County)	20744
Marbury	20658
Mardela Springs	21837
Margate	21061
Mariners	21817
Marion Station	21838
Marley	21061
Marley Heights	21061
Marley Station	21061
Marling Farms	21619
Marlow Heights	20748
Marlton	20772
Marlywood	21204
Marriottsville	21104
Mars Estates	21221
Marshall Hall	20616
Marshalls Corner	20646
Marston	21776
Martinsburg	20842
Martins Woods	20706
Marwood	21061
Marydel	21649
Maryland City (Anne Arundel County)	20707
Maryland Correctional Institution for Women (Anne Arundel County)	20794
Maryland Correctional Pre-Release System (Anne Arundel County)	20794
Maryland Line	21105
Maryland Park	20743
Maryland Point	20662
Marymount	20814
Maryvale (Part of Rockville)	20850
Marywood	21050
Masons Beach	20751
Mason Springs	20640
Massey	21650
Mattapex	21666
Mattapony (Part of Bladensburg)	20710
Matthews	21601
Maugansville	21767
Mayberry	21157
Maydale	20868
Mayfield (Anne Arundel County)	21113
Mayfield (Howard County)	21043
Mayo (Anne Arundel County)	21106
Mays Chapel	21093
Mays Chapel Village	21093
Meadowbrook (Part of Bowie)	20715
Meadowbrook Estates	20874
Meadowcliff	21057
Meadowland	21093
Meadowood	20904
Meadowood of Davidsonville	21035
Meadowvale Manor	21078
Meadowview Park	21921
Mechanicsville	20659
Medford	21776
Melitota	21620
Mellwood Hills	20772
Melody Acres	20622
Melrose	21102
Melson	21875
Merchants (Part of Baltimore)	21201
Merrimack Park	20817
Merritt Heights	21801
Merrymount	21207

250 MARYLAND Michigan Park Hills-Olive

Place	ZIP
Michigan Park Hills	20782
Middleborough	21221
Middlebrook	20874
Middleburg	21768
Middlepoint	21773
Middle River	21220
Middlesex	21221
Middlesex Shopping Center	21221
Middleton Valley	20748
Middletown (Baltimore County)	21053
Middletown (Frederick County)	21769
Middletown Heights	21769
Midland	21542
Midlothian	21543
Milford	21207
Milford Mill	21207
Milford Park	21207
Milford Ridge	21207
Millbrook (Part of Laurel)	20707
Mill Creek South	20855
Mill Creek Towne	20707
Mill Creek Towne East	20855
Miller	21532
Millers	21107
Millers Island	21219
Millersville	21108
Mill Green	21154
Millington	21651
Millison Plaza	20653
Mill Point	20621
Mill Point Shores	20621
Millrace	21108
Mill Run	21562
Mills Choice	20879
Millwood	20743
Millwood Towne	20743
Mimosa Cove	20751
Minefield	21154
Mitchell Manor	21550
Mitchellville	20716-17
For specific Mitchellville Zip Codes call (301) 249-2511	
Mondawmin/Metro Plaza (Part of Baltimore)	21215
Monie	21853
Monkton	21111
Monrovia	21770
Montego (Part of Ocean City)	21842
Montevideo (Anne Arundel County)	21076
Montevideo (Howard County)	20794
Montgomery Knolls	21043
Montgomery Square	20854
Montgomery Village (Montgomery County)	20879
Montgomery White Oak	20904
Montpelier	20708
Montpelier Woods	20708
Montrose	20852
Monumental	21227
Mooresfield	20759
Morgan	21797
Morgantown (Allegany County)	21532
Morgantown (Charles County)	20664
Morganza	20660
Morningside	20746
Moscow	21521
Mount Aetna	21740
Mountain	21085
Mountaindale	21788
Mountain Lake Park	21550
Mountain View	21157
Mountain View Estates	20878
Mountain Wood	21122
Mount Airy	21771
Mount Briar	21756
Mount Carmel	21122
Mount Clare (Part of Baltimore)	21223
Mount De Sales	21228
Mount Harmony	20736
Mount Hebron	21043
Mount Hermon	21801
Mount Hope (Part of Baltimore)	21215
Mount Lena	21713
Mount Olive	21771
Mount Pleasant (Frederick County)	21701
Mount Pleasant (Washington County)	21713
Mount Pleasant (Wicomico County)	21874
Mount Pleasant Beach	21122
Mount Rainier	20712

Place	ZIP
Mount Saint Mary's College	21727
Mount Savage	21545
Mount Vernon	21853
Mount Victoria	20661
Mountview	21104
Mountville	21701
Mount Washington (Part of Baltimore)	21209
Mount Westley	21863
Mount Zion (Caroline County)	21649
Mount Zion (Frederick County)	21701
Mount Zoar	21918
Mousetown	21713
Muirkirk	20705
Mulberry Hills	21401
Murray Hills	20745
Myersdale (Part of Hancock)	21750
Myersville	21773
Nanjemoy	20662
Nanticoke	21840
Narrows	21638
Narrows Park	21502
National Naval Medical Center	20814
Naval Academy	21402
Naval Air Facility	20390
Naval Ordnance Station	20640
Naval Surface Weapons Center	20903
Naylor	20772
Neavitt	21652
Needwood Estates	20855
Neeld Estates	20639
Neelsville	20874
Neilwood	20852
New Addition	21758
Newark	21841
New Birmingham Manor	20866
Newburg	20664
New Carrollton	20784
Newcomb	21653
New Germany	21536
New Hampshire Estates	20903
New Hampshire Gardens (Part of Takoma Park)	20912
Newhope	21874
New London	21771
New Mark Commons (Part of Rockville)	20850
New Market (Frederick County)	21774
New Market (St. Mary's County)	20622
New Market View	21771
New Midway	21775
New Orchard Estates	20772
Newport	20622
Newport Hills	20895
Newton	21655
Newton Village	20781
Newtown (Kent County)	21678
Newtown (Talbot County)	21625
New Valley	21918
New Windsor	21776
Nikep	21546
Nob Hill (Howard County)	21043
Nob Hill (Montgomery County)	20903
Nomira Heights (Part of Elkton)	21921
Norbeck	20906
Normandy Heights	21043
Normans	21666
Norris Corner	21009
Norrisville	21161
Northampton (Baltimore County)	21093
Northampton (Prince George's County)	20772
Northamton	20772
North Barnaby	20745
North Beach	20714
North Beach Park	20714
North Bethesda	20814
North Branch	21502
North Brentwood	20722
North Chevy Chase	20815
North College Park (Part of College Park)	20740
North Deale	20751
North East	21901
Northeast Heights	21901
North Englewood	20785
Northern (Part of Hagerstown)	21740
North Forestville	20747
North Fort Foote Village	20744
North Glade	21561

Place	ZIP
North Indian Head Estates	20616
North Junction (Part of Hagerstown)	21740
North Kensington	20902
North Laurel (Howard County)	21784
North Laurel (Howard County)	20707
North Laurel Park	20707
North Linthicum	21090
North Ocean City (Part of Ocean City)	21842
North Point	21222
North Point Village	21222
North Potomac Vista	20745
Northridge Manor	21740
North Roblee Acres	20772
North Sherwood Forest	20904
Northshire	21222
North Shore	21122
North Springbrook	20904
North Wellham	21061
Northwest Park (Montgomery County)	20814
Northwest Park (Montgomery County)	20903
Northwood (Part of Baltimore)	21239
Northwood Park	20901
Northwood Village	20901
Norwood Corner	20906
Norwood Estates	20905
Notch Cliff	21057
Nottingham	21237
Nottingham Woods	21236
Oak Acres	21701
Oak Court	21401
Oakcrest	20707
Oakcrest Towers	20743
Oakdale	20853
Oak Estates	20622
Oak Forest	21228
Oak Hollow	21122
Oakhurst	20866
Oakington	21078
Oakland (Baltimore County)	21053
Oakland (Carroll County)	21784
Oakland (Garrett County)	21550
Oakland (Prince George's County)	20747
Oakland Acres	20622
Oakland Mills	21045
Oakland Park	21133
Oakland Terrace	20895
Oaklawn	20744
Oakleigh	21234
Oakleigh Forest	21146
Oakleigh Manor	21234
Oaklyn Manor	21085
Oakmont	20814
Oak Orchard	20735
Oak Park (Baltimore County)	21227
Oak Park (Garrett County)	21550
Oak Ridge	21740
Oak Springs	20868
Oak Summit	21234
Oak View	20903
Oakville (Somerset County)	21853
Oakville (St. Mary's County)	20659
Oakwood	21918
Oakwood Knolls	20817
Ocean City	21842
Ocean City Harbor	21842
Ocean Pines	21811
Odenton (Anne Arundel County)	21113
Odenton Gardens	21113
Odenton Heights	21113
Odenton Park	21113
Odyssey	20754
Oella	21043
Old Bay Trail	20772
Old Country Estates	21146
Olde Colonial Woods	20832
Olde Fort Village	20744
Olde Towne Village (Part of District Heights-Forestville)	20747
Old Farm	20852
Old Field (Dorchester County)	21622
Oldfield (Frederick County)	21791
Old Field (Montgomery County)	20854
Old Fort Hills	20744
Old Glory Beach	21061
Old Salem Village	20904
Old Severna Park	21146
Oldtown	21555
Olive	21758

Oliver Beach-Raynor Heights **MARYLAND** 251

	ZIP		ZIP		ZIP
Cliver Beach	21220	Perry Point	21902	Porterstown	21756
Olivet	20657	Perrys Corner	21638	Port Herman	21915
Olivet Hill	21637	Perry View	21128	Port Republic	20676
Olney (Montgomery County)	20832	Perryville	21903	Port Tobacco	20677
Olney Mills	20832	Perrywood Estates	20866	Port Tobacco Riviera	20677
Olney Square	20832	Perry Wright	20640	Potomac (Montgomery	
Orangeville (Part of		Petersburg	21643	County)	20851
Baltimore)	21224	Petersville	21758	Potomac (Montgomery	
Oraville	20659	Pfeiffer Corners	21043	County)	20854
Orchard Beach	21226	Pheasant Run	20708	Potomac Commons	20854
Orchard Hills (Baltimore		Phoenix	21131	Potomac Falls Estates	20854
County)	21093	Picketts Corner	21797	Potomac Green	20854
Orchard Hills (Washington		Pike (Part of Rockville)	20852	Potomac Heights (Charles	
County)	21740	Pikesville (Baltimore County)	21208	County)	20640
Oregon	21030	Pilot Town	21918	Potomac Heights	
Oriole	21853	Pindell	20711	(Washington County)	21740
Otter Point	21009	Pine Cliff	21701	Potomac Hills	20854
Overlea (Baltimore County)	21206	Pinecrest (Part of Takoma		Potomac Park	21502
Owen Brown	21045	Park)	20912	Potomac Park-Bowling	
Owings	20736	Pinedale	21128	Green	21502
Owings Beach	20751	Pinefield	20601	Potomac Ranch	20854
Owings Mills (Baltimore		Pine Grove	21801	Potomac Shores (Charles	
County)	21117	Pine Grove Village	21122	County)	20677
Owings Wood	20714	Pine Hill Estates	20601	Potomac Shores (St. Mary's	
Oxford	21654	Pinehurst Estates	20744	County)	20650
Oxon Hill (Prince George's		Pinehurst on the Bay	21122	Potomac View	20664
County)	20745	Pine Knoll	21157	Potomac View Estates	20854
Oxon Hill Village	20745	Pine Knoll Terrace	21801	Potomac Village	20854
Oxon Run Hills	20748	Pineleigh	21204	Potomac Vista	20745
Oyster Harbor	21401	Pine Orchard Meadows	21043	Potomac Woods (Part of	
Padonia	21030	Pine Ridge	21234	Rockville)	20854
Pagetts Corner	20748	Pinesburg	21795	Pot Spring	21093
Paint Branch Estates	20904	Pines on the Severn	21012	Powder Mill Estates	20783
Paint Branch Farm	20904	Pinewiff Beach	21037	Powder Mill Village	20705
Palmer Park	20785	Pinewood Hill	20744	Powellville	21852
Palmers Corner	20744	Piney Glen Farms	20854	Powhatan Beach	21122
Palmetto	21853	Piney Grove	21766	Powhattan Mill	21207
Paradise	21228	Piney Point	20674	Prathertown	20879
Paradise Beach	21122	Pinto	21556	Presidential Park	20783
Paramount	21740	Pioneer City	21144	Presidential Towers	20783
Paramount Manor	21740	Piscataway	20607	Presley Manor	20784
Paris	20736	Piscataway Bay	20744	Preston	21655
Parkertown	21811	Piscataway Estates	20744	Preston Manor	21009
Parker Wharf	20685	Piscataway Hills	20744	Price	21656
Park Hall (St. Mary's		Pisgah	20640	Priceville	21152
County)	20667	Pittsville	21850	Prince Frederick	20678
Park Hall (Washington		Plainfield	21801	Princess Anne	21853
County)	21713	Plane Number Four	21771	Princeton	20746
Parkhead	21711	Pleasant Fields	20874	Principio Furnace	21903
Parkhurst Manor	21801	Pleasant Grove (Baltimore		Prophecy	20744
Parkland	20747	County)	21136	Prospect Knolls	20715
Parkland Apartments	20747	Pleasant Grove (Frederick		Prospect Walk	21044
Parkland Terrace	20746	County)	21771	Providence (Baltimore	
Park Mills	21710	Pleasant Hill (Baltimore		County)	21204
Park Overlook	20855	County)	21117	Providence (Cecil County)	21921
Parkridge	20877	Pleasant Hill (Cecil County)	21921	Public Landing	21863
Parkside	20814	Pleasant Hills	21087	Pumphrey (Anne Arundel	
Parkside Estates	20855	Pleasant Point	21061	County)	21227
Parkton	21120	Pleasant Ridge	21157	Puncheon Landing	21851
Parktowne	21234	Pleasant Springs	20613	Putnam	21050
Parkview	20735	Pleasant Valley (Allegany		Putty Hill	21236
Parkville	21234	County)	21502	Pylesville	21132
Park West	21061	Pleasant Valley (Carroll		Quail Ridge	21227
Parkwood	20814	County)	21157	Quail Run	20878
Parole	21401	Pleasant Valley (Washington		Quaint Acres	20904
Parrsville	21771	County)	21783	Quaker Ridge	20772
Parsonsburg	21849	Pleasant View (Frederick		Quantico	21856
Partridge Place	20879	County)	21710	Queen Anne	21657
Pasadena (Anne Arundel		Pleasant View (Howard		Queen Anne Colony	21666
County)	21122	County)	21043	Queens Chapel Manor (Part	
Patapsco	21048	Pleasantville (Anne Arundel		of Hyattsville)	20782
Patterson (Part of Baltimore)	21231	County)	21061	Queenstown (Prince	
Patuxent	21113	Pleasantville (Washington		George's County)	20712
Patuxent Beach	20619	County)	25425	Queenstown (Queen Anne's	
Patuxent Institution	20794	Pleasant Walk	21773	County)	21658
Patuxent Manor	21035	Plumgar	20874	Queenswood	20772
Patuxent Naval Air Test		Plum Point	20639	Quince Orchard	
Center	20670	Pocomoke City	21851	(Montgomery County)	20878
Patuxent Palisades	20754	Pointer Ridge (Part of		Quince Orchard	
Patuxent Park	20653	Bowie)	20716	(Montgomery County)	20877
Patuxent River	20670	Point Lookout	20687	Quincy Manor	20784
Peach Orchard Heights	20866	Point of Rocks	21777	Rabbit Town	21869
Peachwood	20905	Point of Rocks Estates	21777	Radiant Valley	20784
Peacock Corners	21651	Poland	21562	Ramblewood Village	20735
Pearl	21701	Pomfret	20675	Ramgate	20744
Pectonville	21711	Pomona	21620	Ranchleigh (Baltimore	
Pendennis Mount	21401	Pomonkey	20640	County)	21209
Peninsula General Hospital		Ponder Cove	21037	Ranchleigh (Baltimore	
(Part of Salisbury)	21801	Pondsville	21783	Indep. City)	21209
Pen Mar	21719	Pooks Hill	20814	Randalia	21915
Pen-Mar Shopping Center	20747	Poole	21034	Randallstown (Baltimore	
Penn Mary Junction (Part of		Poolesville	20837	County)	21133
Baltimore)	21224	Popes Creek	20664	Randle Cliff Beach	20732
Pepper Mill Village	20743	Poplar Grove	21154	Randolph Farms	20852
Perry Hall (Baltimore		Poplar Hill Estates	20735	Randolph Hills	20852
County)	21128	Poplar Knob	21788	Random Heights	21157
Perry Hall Estates	21236	Poplar Springs	21771	Raspeburg (Part of	
Perry Hall Manor	21128	Port Covington (Part of		Baltimore)	21206
Perry Hall Shopping Center	21128	Baltimore)	21230	Rawlings	21557
Perry Hall Village	21128	Port Deposit	21904	Rawlings Heights	21557
Perryman	21130	Porters Park	21221	Raynor Heights	21090

252 MARYLAND Rayville-Shane

	ZIP
Rayville	21120
Red Coat Woods	20854
Reddings Corner	21678
Redford Estates	20744
Red Hill	20658
Redhouse	21550
Redland (Montgomery County)	20855
Red Point	21901
Reeder Development (Part of Frederick)	21701
Reese	21157
Reese Manor	21157
Regal Estates	20754
Regency Estates	20852
Regent Park	20854
Regent Square (Part of Rockville)	20850
Rehobeth	21857
Reid	21740
Reids Grove	21659
Reisterstown	21136
Reisterstown Road Plaza (Part of Baltimore)	21215
Relay	21227
Reliance	19973
Rest Haven	20751
Revell	21012
Revere Park	21234
Reynolds	21562
Rhodesdale	21659
Rhodes Point	21858
Riawakin Acres	21830
Richards Oak	21917
Ricmar	21801
Riderwood	21139
Riderwood Hills	21139
Ridge	20680
Ridge Lake	21043
Ridgeleigh	21234
Ridgely	21660
Ridgeview	21077
Ridgeville (Part of Mount Airy)	21771
Ridgeway	21144
Ridgeway Estates	20743
Ridgley Park	21784
Riding Woods	21122
Riggins Corner	21622
Ringgold	21740
Rio Vista	21663
Ripley	20646
Ripplewood	21207
Rippling Ridge	21061
Rising Sun	21911
Rison	20658
Ritchie	20747
Ritchie Heights	20747
Ritchie Manor	20747
Riva	21140
Rivendell	21146
River Bend	20744
River Bend Estates	20744
River Club Estates	21037
Riverdale (Prince George's County)	20737-38
For specific Riverdale Zip Codes call (301) 699-8859	
Riverdale (Anne Arundel County)	21146
Riverdale Heights	20737
Riverdale Hills	20737
River Falls	20854
River Forest	20744
River Meadows	21043
River Ridge Estates	20745
Riverside	20662
River Springs	20609
Riverton	21837
Riverview Manor	21401
Riverview Village (Part of Indian Head)	20640
Riverwood (Anne Arundel County)	21035
Riviera Beach (Anne Arundel County)	21122
Riviera Isle	21122
Robbins	21626
Roberts	21623
Roberts Glen	20854
Robinson	21146
Robinwood	21740
Roblee Acres	20772
Rockawalking Village	21801
Rockaway Beach	21221
Rock Creek Forest	20815
Rock Creek Gardens	20815
Rock Creek Highlands	20895
Rock Creek Hills	20895
Rock Creek Manor	20853
Rock Creek Palisades	20895

	ZIP
Rock Creek Village	20853
Rockcrest (Part of Rockville)	20851
Rockdale	21207
Rock Hall (Frederick County)	21790
Rock Hall (Kent County)	21661
Rock Hill Beach	21122
Rockland (Howard County)	21043
Rockland (Montgomery County)	20850
Rockland Run	21209
Rock Point	20682
Rock Run	21078
Rockshire (Part of Rockville)	20850
Rockshire Square (Part of Rockville)	20850
Rockshire Village (Part of Rockville)	20850
Rockview Beach	21122
Rockville	20850-59
For specific Rockville Zip Codes call (301) 424-2600	
Rockville Estates (Part of Rockville)	20850
Rockwell	21228
Rocky Gorge Estates	20707
Rocky Ridge	21778
Rocky Springs	21701
Rodgers Forge	21204
Rogers Heights	20781
Rohrersville (Washington County)	21779
Rohrersville (Washington County)	21756
Roland Park (Part of Baltimore)	21210
Rolling Acres (Howard County)	21043
Rolling Acres (Prince George's County)	20623
Rolling Acres (St. Mary's County)	20622
Rolling Green	21028
Rolling Hills (Anne Arundel County)	21401
Rolling Hills (Carroll County)	21784
Rolling Knolls	21401
Rolling Ridge (Carroll County)	21157
Rolling Ridge (Prince George's County)	20743
Rolling Terrace	20912
Rolling Terrace Estates	20912
Rollingwood	20815
Rollins Park (Part of Rockville)	20852
Rolphs	21620
Romancoke on the Bay	21666
Rosaryville Estates	20772
Rosecroft	20744
Rosecroft Park	20744
Rosedale (Baltimore County)	21237
Rosedale Estates	20744
Rosedale Park	20815
Rose Haven	20714
Rose Hill Estates	20817
Rosemary Hills	20910
Rosemont (Baltimore County)	21225
Rosemont (Frederick County)	21758
Rosemont (Montgomery County)	20877
Rose Valley Estates	20744
Rossville (Baltimore County)	21237
Round Acres	21047
Round Bay	21146
Round Hill	21701
Roundtop	21750
Rover Mill Estates	21794
Rowlandsville	21918
Roxboro (Part of Rockville)	20850
Roxbury Correctional Institution	21740
Royal Beach	21122
Royal Oak (Talbot County)	21662
Royal Oak (Wicomico County)	21856
Rugby Hall	21012
Ruhl	21053
Rumbley	21871
Rumsey Island	21085
Running Brook	21044
Rustic Acres	21801
Rusty Acres	20866
Ruthsburg	21617
Rutledge	21047
Ruxton	21204
Ryceville	20659
Sabillasville	21780

	ZIP
Sackertown	21817
St. Andrews Estates	20619
St. Anthony	21727
St. Aubins Heights (Part of Easton)	21601
St. Augustine	21915
St. Charles	20601
St. Clement Shores	20650
St. Denis	21227
St. George Island	20674
St. Georges	21071
St. George's Park	20690
St. Helena	21222
St. Inigoes	20684
St. James (Washington County)	21781
St. James (Worcester County)	21851
St. Jeromes	20628
St. Johns Manor	21043
St. Johns Village	21043
St. Leonard	20685
St. Margarets	21401
St. Margarets Farm	21401
St. Mark's	21758
St. Martins	21811
St. Marys City	20686
St. Michaels	21663
St. Stephen	21853
Salem	21869
Salisbury	21801-03
For specific Salisbury Zip Codes call (301) 742-9261	
Salisbury Mall (Part of Salisbury)	21801
Samples Manor	25425
Sams Creek	21776
Sanders Park	21122
Sandgates	20659
Sand Spring	21531
Sandy Acres	21613
Sandy Bottom	21620
Sandy Hook	21758
Sandy Spring	20860
Sandy Spring Estates	20707
Sandy Spring Meadows	20860
Sandyville	21048
Sang Run	21541
Sanmar	21713
Sansbury Park	20747
Santa Fe Acres	21801
Santo Domingo	21837
Sassafras	21637
Satyr Hill	21234
Saunders Point	21037
Savage	20763
Savage-Guilford	20763
Scaggsville	20707
Scarboro (Harford County)	21154
Scarboro (Worcester County)	21863
Schnaders Shores	21122
Schultz	20735
Scientists Cliffs	20676
Scotland (Montgomery County)	20854
Scotland (St. Mary's County)	20687
Scotland Beach	20687
Scrabbletown	21106
Seabrook	20706
Seabrook Acres	20706
Seabrook Park Estates	20706
Seat Pleasant	20743
Sebring	21043
Secretary	21664
Security (Baltimore County)	21207
Security (Washington County)	21740
Security Square	21207
Selassie Villa	20764
Selby-on-the-Bay (Anne Arundel County)	21037
Selbysport	21531
Seneca	20837
Seneca Park	20874
Sequioa	20868
Severn	21144
Severna Forest	21146
Severna Park	21146
Severn Grove	21401
Severn Heights	21146
Severnside	21401
Sewell	21009
Sewells Orchard	21045
Shad Point	21801
Shady Dale	20659
Shady Oaks	20778
Shady Side	20764
Shallmar	21538
Shane	21161

Sharewood Acres-Tolchester Beach MARYLAND 253

Name	ZIP
Sharewood Acres	20794
Sharonville	21122
Sharon Woods	20879
Sharperville	20601
Sharpsburg	21782
Sharpstown	21661
Sharptown	21861
Shavox	21801
Shawsville	21161
Shawsville Acres	21161
Shelltown	21838
Shervettes Corner	21784
Sherwood (Kent County)	21635
Sherwood (Talbot County)	21665
Sherwood Forest (Anne Arundel County)	21405
Sherwood Forest (Montgomery County)	20904
Sherwood Forest (Prince George's County)	20772
Sherwood Manor (Prince George's County)	20715
Sherwood Manor (Wicomico County)	21801
Shetland Hills	21093
Shiloh (Charles County)	20664
Shiloh (Dorchester County)	21643
Shipley	21090
Shookstown	21701
Shore Acres	21012
Shoreham Beach	21037
Shoreland	21061
Shorwood Estates	21637
Showell	21862
Sierra Manor	21801
Sillery Bay	21122
Siloam	21822
Silver Gate Village	21236
Silver Grove	21740
Silver Hill	20746
Silver Hill Park	20746
Silver Meadow	21128
Silver Rock (Part of Rockville)	20850
Silver Run	21157
Silver Sands	21061
Silver Spring	20901-12
For specific Silver Spring Zip Codes call (301) 588-9068	
Silver Valley	20746
Simpsonville	21150
Sinepuxent	21811
Singerly	21916
Skidmore	21401
Skipton	21625
Skyline	20746
Skyline Additions	20746
Sky Valley	21561
Slabtown	21545
Sligo Park Knolls	20901
Smallwood	21157
Smithsburg	21783
Smithville (Caroline County)	21632
Smithville (Dorchester County)	21669
Smoketown	21713
Smugglers Cove	21146
Snowden Manor	21157
Snowden Oaks	20708
Snow Hill	21863
Snow Hill Manor	20708
Snug Harbor (Anne Arundel County)	20764
Snug Harbor (Worcester County)	21811
Snydersburg	21074
Social Security Administration	21207
Society Hill	20650
Sollers Homes	21222
Sollers Point	21222
Solley Heights	21061
Solomons	20688
Somerset	20815
Sonoma	20814
South (Part of Baltimore)	21230
Southampton	20653
South Cheverly Forest	20784
South Cumberland (Part of Cumberland)	21502
Southdown Shores	21037
Southeast (Part of Baltimore)	21224
Southerland	20601
Southern Garden Apartments	20032
Southern Maryland Facility	20743-48
	20790-91
For specific Southern Maryland Facility Zip Codes call (202) 682-9595	

Name	ZIP
South Fort Foote Village	20744
South Gate (Anne Arundel County)	21061
South Haven	21401
South Kensington	20895
Southland Hills	21204
South Laurel (Prince George's County)	20708
South Laurel (Prince George's County)	20707
South Lawn	20745
South Layhill	20906
South Piscataway	20607
South River Park	21037
South Salisbury (Part of Salisbury)	21801
South Tantallon	20748
Southview	20745
South Woodside Park	20910
Sparks	21152
Sparks Glencoe	21152
Sparrows Point	21219
Spaulding Heights	20747
Spence	21863
Spencerville	20868
Spielman	21733
Spoolsville	21769
Springbrook (Baltimore County)	21133
Springbrook (Montgomery County)	20904
Springbrook Forest	20902
Springbrook Manor	20904
Springbrook Village	20904
Springdale (Baltimore County)	21030
Springdale (Prince George's County)	20706
Springdale Gardens	20706
Springfield	20814
Spring Gap	21560
Spring Garden Estates	21793
Spring Grove	21837
Spring Hill	21830
Springhill Acres	21801
Springhill Lake (Part of Greenbelt)	20770
Springlake	20817
Spring Meadow	21084
Spring Mills	21157
Spring Valley	21740
Squires Woods	20744
Stablersville	21161
Stafford	21034
Stanbrook	21222
Stansbury Estates	21220
Stansbury Manor	21220
Starkeys Corner	21623
Starr	21617
Stemmer's Run	21220
Stepney	21001
Steuart Level	21037
Stevenson	21153
Stevensville	21666
Stewartown	20879
Stillmeadows	21144
Still Pond	21667
Stockton	21864
Stonecrest	21043
Stonegate	20905
Stone Haven	21061
Stoneleigh	21212
Stoneybrook Estates	20906
Stony Beach	21226
Stony Run	21076
Stratford	21093
Strathmore At Bel Pre	20906
Strathmore Estates	20906
Stratton Woods	20817
Strawberry Hills Estates	20616
Strawbridge Estates	21784
Strawleigh	21701
Street	21154
Stronghold	20842
Suburban Acres	21801
Suburbia	21061
Sudbrook Park	21208
Sudlersville	21668
Sugarland	20837
Sugarloaf Estates	21710
Suitland	20746
Suitland-Silver Hill	20746
Sullivan Heights	21157
Summerhill (Anne Arundel County)	21032
Summerhill (Montgomery County)	20837
Summit Farms	21237
Summit Park	21209
Sumner	20816
Sunair (Part of Salisbury)	21801

Name	ZIP
Sunderland	20689
Sunny Acres	20747
Sunnybrook	21131
Sunnybrook Hills	21131
Sunny Isle of Kent	21666
Sunrise	20744
Sunrise Beach	21032
Sunset Acres	21740
Sunset Beach	21122
Sunset Heights	21801
Sunset Hills	21701
Sunset Knoll	21122
Sunshine	20833
Sunshine Acres	20639
Sun Valley	21061
Surratt Gardens	20735
Susquehanna Hills	21078
Sussex Square	21108
Sutton Acres	20677
Swallow Falls	21550
Swan Creek	21001
Swanton	21561
Sweet Air Manor	21013
Sweetser Heights	21090
Sycamore Acres	20853
Sycamore Heights	21740
Sykesville	21784
Sylmar	21911
Sylvan View	21122
Table Rock	26720
Takoma Park	20912
Tall Timbers	20690
Tammany Manor	21795
Tanager Forest	21108
Taneytown	21787
Tanglewood	21401
Tantallon (Prince George's County)	20744
Tantallon North	20744
Tantallon on the Potomac	20748
Tantallon Square	20744
Tanterra	20833
Tanyard	21655
Tarquin Village	20735
Taylor Mill Village	21801
Taylors Island	21669
Taylorsville	21771
Taylorville	21811
Temple Heights	20748
Temple Hills (Prince George's County)	20748
Temple Hills Park	20748
Templeton Estates	20737
Templeton Manor	20737
Templeville	21670
Temple Woods	20744
Terrace Gardens	21012
Terrace View Estates	21225
Texas	21030
Thayerville	21550
The Colony	20874
The Crest of Wickford	20852
The Downs	21401
The Glen	20854
The Hamlet	20815
The Highlands	21061
The Lakes	21093
The Meadows	20639
The Oaks (Calvert County)	20639
The Oaks (Howard County)	21043
Theodore	21911
The Orchards	21043
The Pines	20772
The Points	20879
Thomas Choice	20879
Thomas Run	21014
Thomas Town	21629
Thompson Corner	20659
Thompsontown	21631
Thomson Estates	21921
Thornleigh	21139
Thornwood Knoll	20744
Thorwood Park	21234
Thunder Hill	21045
Thurmont	21788
Thurston	20842
Tilden Woods	20852
Tilghman	21671
Tilghmanton	21713
Timber Grove	21117
Timber Ridge (Anne Arundel County)	21076
Timber Ridge (Carroll County)	21157
Timberview	21227
Timonium	21093
Tintop Hill	20650
Tobytown	20854
Todd Village	21048
Toddville	21672
Tolchester Beach	21620

254 MARYLAND Tollgate-Wildwood Hills

Name	ZIP
Tollgate	21117
Tompkinsville	20664
Tonytank	21801
Tower Acres	20707
Tower Garden on the Bay	21666
Town Creek	25434
Town Creek Estates	20619
Town Creek Manor	20653
Town Crest	20855
Towne and Country North	21030
Towne Center	20708
Town Point	21915
Townsend	20735
Townsontown Centre	21204
Towson	21204
Towson Estates	21204
Towson Marketplace	21204
Towson Park	21204
Towson Plaza Shopping Center	21204
Tracys Landing	20779
Trappe (St. Mary's County)	20628
Trappe (Talbot County)	21673
Trappe (Worcester County)	21811
Trappe Station	21654
Travilah	20854
Treetops	21122
Trengall Acres	21740
Trent Hall	20659
Trenton	21155
Trescher Heights	21502
Triple Lakes	21502
Troutville	21798
Truman Heights	20748
Tulip Hill (Frederick County)	21701
Tulip Hill (Montgomery County)	20816
Tunis Mills	21601
Turkey Neck	21561
Turkey Point (Anne Arundel County)	21037
Turkey Point (Baltimore County)	21221
Turnbull Estates	21037
Turners Station	21222
Tuscarora	21790
Tuxedo (Part of Cheverly)	20785
Tuxedo Colony	20785
Twinbrook (Part of Rockville)	20851
Twinbrook Estates	20601
Twin Brook Forest (Part of Rockville)	20851
Twinbrook Park (Part of Rockville)	20851
Twin Harbors	21012
Tyaskin	21865
Tydings on the Bay	21401
Tylerton	21866
Tyrone	21157
Ulmsted Acres	21012
Ulmsted Estate	21012
Ulmsted Gardens	21012
Ulmsted Point	21012
Union Bridge	21791
Union Corner	21636
Union Mills	21157
Uniontown	21157
Unionville (Baltimore County)	21092
Unionville (Frederick County)	21792
Unionville (Talbot County)	21601
Unionville (Worcester County)	21851
Unity	20833
University City	20783
University Gardens	20783
University Hills	20783
University Park	20784
Upperco	21155
Upper Crossroads	21047
Upper Fairmount	21867
Upper Falls	21156
Upper Ferry Estates	21801
Upper Hill	21867
Upper Homewood	21502
Upper Marlboro	20772-75
For specific Upper Marlboro Zip Codes call (301) 627-4330	
Urbana	21701
Utica	21788
Vale	21014
Vale Summit	21532
Valley Crest	21093
Valley Lee	20692
Valley Mede	21043
Valley Stream Estates	20866
Valley View (Howard County)	21043

Name	ZIP
Valley View (Prince George's County)	20744
Valleywood (Baltimore County)	21093
Valleywood (Wicomico County)	21801
Van Bibber	21040
Van Bibber Manor	21040
Van Lear Manor	21795
Vansville	20705
Venice on the Bay	21122
Venton	21853
Vernon	21161
Veterans Administration Medical Center	21902
Victory Villa	21220
Vienna	21869
Viers Mill Village	20906
View More Acres	21701
Villa Cresta	21234
Village of Vanderway	21234
Villages of Montpelier	20708
Villa Heights	20784
Villa Monticello	21723
Villa Nova	21207
Villa Toscano	21122
Villa Verdi	21054
Waggaman Heights	20748
Wakefield (Baltimore County)	21093
Wakefield (Carroll County)	21776
Wakefield Meadows	21014
Walbrook (Part of Baltimore)	21216
Waldon Woods	20735
Waldorf	20601-04
For specific Waldorf Zip Codes call (301) 645-5231	
Walker Hill	20707
Walker Mill (Prince George's County)	20743
Walker Mill Estates	20743
Walkersville	21793
Wallington Estates	20747
Wallville	20685
Walnut Hill	20877
Walnut Ridge	21157
Walnut Woods	20852
Walston	21849
Walter Heights	20748
Wango	21801
Warburton Oaks	20744
Wards Chapel	21133
Warfieldburg	21157
Warfield Estates	21738
Warington Hills (Part of Indian Head)	20640
Warlinda	20646
Warren	21030
Warwick	21912
Washington Grove	20880
Waterbury	21032
Waterloo	21227
Wateroak Point	21122
Watersville	21771
Waterview	21840
Watkins Glen	20854
Waverly (Part of Baltimore)	21218
Wayside	20664
Webster Village	21078
Weems Creek	21401
Weisburg	21161
Welcome	20693
Welhams	21061
Wellington Estates	20707
Wenona	21870
Wesley	21626
Wesmond (Part of Poolesville)	20837
West Baltimore (Part of Baltimore)	21227
West Beach (Part of Chesapeake Beach)	20732
West Bethesda	20817
Westboro	20814
West Bowie (Part of Bowie)	20715
Westchester (Baltimore County)	21228
Westchester (Montgomery County)	20902
Westchester Estates	20748
Westchester Park (Part of College Park)	20740
West Denton	21629
West Edmondale	21229
West Elkridge	21227
West End (Part of Annapolis)	21401
West End Park (Part of Rockville)	20850
Westerlea	21228
Westernport	21562

Name	ZIP
Western Shores Estates	20676
West Friendship	21794
Westgate	20816
West Gate Woods	20706
West Hills (Baltimore County)	21207
West Hills (Frederick County)	21701
West Hyattsville (Part of Hyattsville)	20782
Westlake (Wicomico County)	21801
West Lanham Estates	20784
West Lanham Hills	20784
West Laurel Acres	20707
West Liberty	21161
West Magothy Manor	21012
Westminster (Carroll County)	21157
Westminster (Montgomery County)	20852
Westminster South	21157
Westmore (Part of Rockville)	20850
Westmoreland Hills	20816
West Nottingham	21917
West Ocean City	21842
Westover	21871
Westowne	21229
Westphalia Estates	20772
Westphalia Woods	20772
West River	20778
West Severna Park	21146
West Shady Side	20764
West Shore	21106
West Twin River Beach	21220
Westview	21801
Westview Mall	21228
Westview Park	21228
West View Shores	21919
West Vindex	21538
Westwood	20613
Westwood Estates (Charles County)	20601
Westwood Estates (Prince George's County)	20623
Wetipquin	21856
Weverton	21758
Wexford	21012
Whaleysville	21872
Wheaton	20902
Wheaton Crest	20902
Wheaton Forest	20902
Wheaton-Glenmont	20902
Wheaton Hills	20902
Wheaton Plaza Regional Center	20902
Wheaton Woods	20853
Whetstone	20879
Whipporwill Estates	21122
Whiskey Bottom	20707
Whiteburg	21863
White Crystal Beach	21919
Whitefield Knolls	20706
Whitefield Woods	20706
White Flint	20895
White Flint Park	20895
Whiteford	21160
White Hall (Baltimore County)	21161
Whitehall (Prince George's County)	20607
Whitehall Beach	21401
Whitehall Manor	20814
Whitehaven	21856
Whitehouse Heights	20785
White Landing	20613
Whiteleysburg	21639
White Marsh	21162
White Oak (Montgomery County)	20904
White Oak (Montgomery County)	20901
White Oak Manor	20904
White Oak Park	20904
White Oak Shopping Center	20904
White Oak Tower	20904
White Plains	20695
White Point Beach	20650
White Rock	21701
White Sands	20657
Whiton	21863
Wicomico	20622
Wicomico Beach	20664
Wilburn Estates	20743
Wilde Lake	21044
Wildercroft	20737
Wild Rose Shores	21403
Wild Wood Beach	21221
Wildwood Estates	20735
Wildwood Hills	20817

Wildwood Manor-Zittlestown **MARYLAND** 255

Name	ZIP
Wildwood Manor	20817
Wildwoods	21133
Wielinor Estates	21037
Willards	21874
Willerburn Acres	20854
Williamsburg	21643
Williamsburg Estates	20772
Williamsburg Gardens	20854
Williamsburg Village	20832
Williamsbury	21207
Williamsport (Washington County)	21795
Williams Wharf	20685
Williston	21629
Willoughby Beach	21040
Willow Beach Colony	20732
Willowbrook (Montgomery County)	20854
Willowbrook (Prince George's County)	20783
Willow Lake	20708
Wilson	21722
Wilson Hills	20906
Wilson Point	21220
Wiltondale	21204
Wilton Farm Acres	21043
Winchester on the Severn	21401
Winchester Park	21157
Windbrook	20735
Windham Manor (Montgomery County)	20904
Windham Manor (Wicomico County)	21801
Winding Brook Village	21921
Windmere Acres	20763

Name	ZIP
Windsor	21207
Windsor Estates	21717
Windsor Heights (Part of Westminster)	21157
Windsor Terrace	21207
Winfield (Carroll County)	21157
Winfield (Howard County)	21044
Winfield Heights	21157
Wingate	21675
Wingates Point	21675
Winsor Hills	20854
Winterest	21161
Wiseburg	21762
Wisperren Oaks	21676
Wittman	21773
Wolfsville	21773
Wolverton Park	20735
Woodacres	20816
Woodberry Forest	20748
Woodbine	21797
Woodbrook	21212
Woodburn	20817
Wood Creek	21045
Woodcroft	21234
Woodensburg	21136
Woodfield	20877
Woodford	21044
Woodhaven	20817
Woodhaven Park	20646
Woodland	21532
Woodland Acres	20619
Woodland Point	20664
Woodlands	21133
Woodlane	20748
Woodlark	20784

Name	ZIP
Woodlawn (Baltimore County)	21207
Woodlawn (Cecil County)	21904
Woodlawn (Prince George's County)	20784
Woodlawn Heights	21061
Woodmont	20815
Woodmoor (Baltimore County)	21207
Woodmoor (Montgomery County)	20901
Woodmoor (Washington County)	21740
Wood Point	21740
Woodsboro	21798
Woods Corner	20748
Woodside	20901
Woodside Park	20901
Woodstock	21163
Woodville	21771
Woolford	21677
Worthington	21043
Worthington Heights	21014
Worthington Valley	21071
Worton	21678
Wrights Crossing	21532
Wye Mills	21679
Wyngate	20814
Wynne Wood	21227
Yarrowsburg	21758
Yellow Springs	21701
Yorkshire Knolls	20743
Zion	21901
Zittlestown	21713

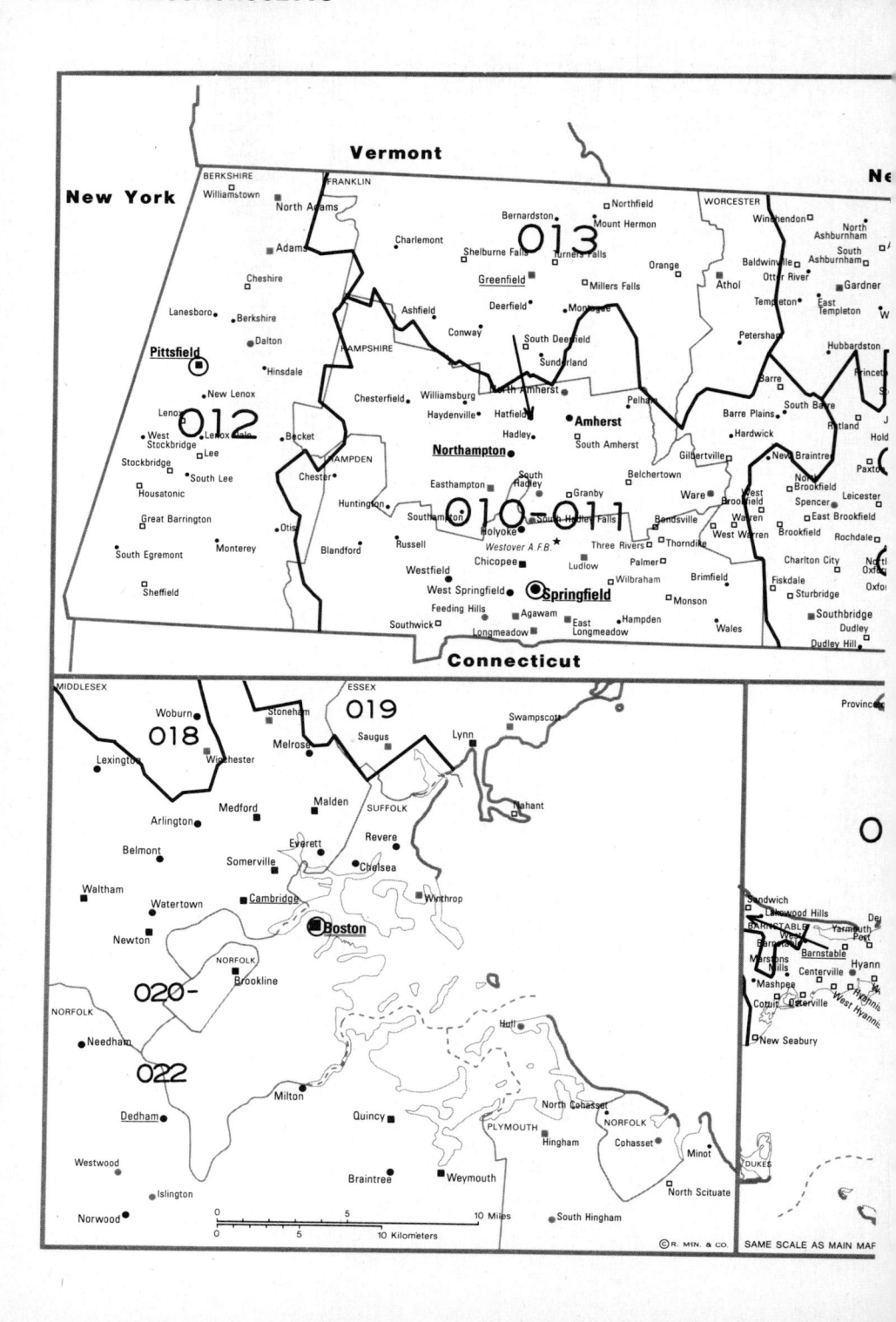

MASSACHUSETTS

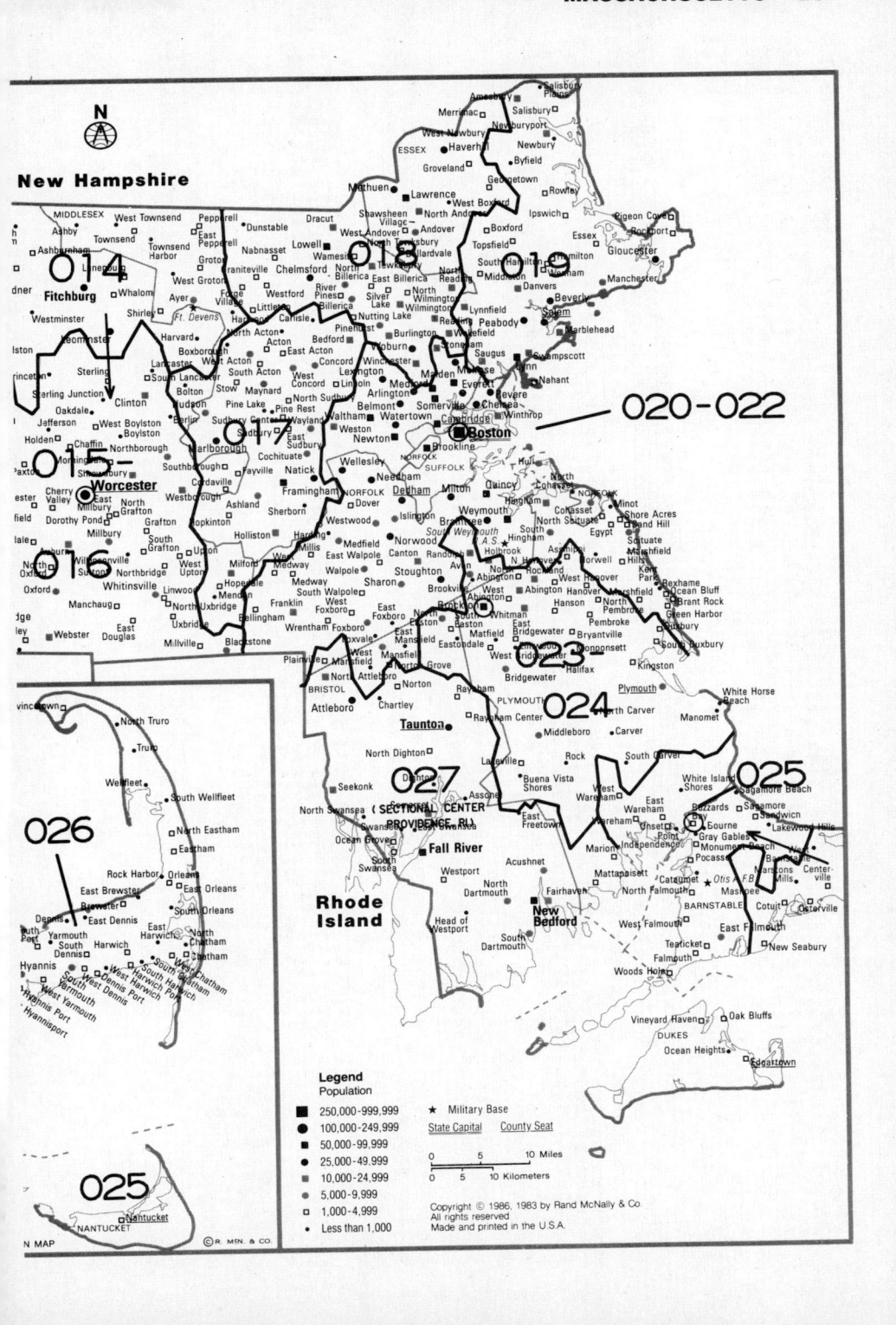

MASSACHUSETTS 257

258 MASSACHUSETTS Aberdeen-Boston

	ZIP
Aberdeen (Part of Boston)	02135
Abington (Plymouth County)	02351
Abington (Plymouth County) (Town)	02351
Acapesket	02536
Accord	02018
Acoaxet	02801
Acton	01720
Acton (Town)	01720
Acton Center	01720
Acushnet	02743
Acushnet (Town)	02743
Adams (Berkshire County) (Town)	01220
Adams (Berkshire County)	01220
Adamsdale	02760
Adams Shore (Part of Quincy)	02169
Adamsville	01340
Agawam	01001
Agawam (Town)	01001
Agawam Beach	02571
Agawam Shopping Center	01001
Airport Mail Facility (Part of Boston)	02109
Aldenville (Part of Chicopee)	01013
Alford	01230
Alford (Town)	01230
Allendale (Part of Pittsfield)	01201
Allendale Shopping Center (Part of Pittsfield)	01201
Allerton	02045
Allston (Part of Boston)	02134
Amesbury (Essex County)	01913
Amesbury (Essex County) (Town)	01913
Amesbury (Essex County)	01913
Amesbury Center	01913
Amherst	01002-04
For specific Amherst Zip Codes call (413) 549-0523	
Amrita	02534
Andover	01810
Andover (Town)	01810
Annisquam (Part of Gloucester)	01930
Antassawamock Beach	02739
Apponagansett Village	02748
Arlington (Middlesex County) (Town)	02174
Arlington (Middlesex County)	02174
Arlington Heights	02175
Armory (Part of Springfield)	01101
Army Materials and Mechanics Research Center	02172
Arsenal Mall	02172
Ashburnham	01430
Ashburnham (Town)	01430
Ashby	01431
Ashby (Town)	01431
Ashdod	02332
Ashfield	01330
Ashfield (Town)	01330
Ashland (Middlesex County)	01721
Ashland (Middlesex County) (Town)	01721
Ashley Falls	01222
Ashley Heights	02717
Ashmont (Part of Boston)	02124
Assinippi	02339
Assonet	02702
Assonet Bay Shores	02702
Assumption College (Part of Worcester)	01609
Astor (Part of Boston)	02123
Athol (Worcester County) (Town)	01331
Athol (Worcester County)	01331
Athol Junction (Part of Springfield)	01101
Atlantic (Part of Quincy)	02169
Attleboro	02703
Attleboro Falls	02763
Auburn (Worcester County) (Town)	01501
Auburn (Worcester County)	01501
Auburndale (Part of Newton)	02166
Auburn Shopping Mall	01501
Avon (Norfolk County) (Town)	02322
Avon (Norfolk County)	02322
Ayer	01432-33
For specific Ayer Zip Codes call (617) 772-2083	
Ayer (Middlesex County) (Town)	01432
Ayer (Middlesex County)	01432

	ZIP
Ayers Village (Part of Haverhill)	01830
Babson Park	02157
Back Bay Annex (Part of Boston)	02115
Bakers Grove	01473
Bakers Island (Part of Salem)	01970
Baldwinville	01436
Ballardvale	01810
Baptist Corner	01370
Barkerville (Part of Pittsfield)	01201
Barnstable	02630
Barnstable (Town)	02630
Barre	01005
Barre (Town)	01005
Barre Plains	01606
Barrowsville	02766
Bass Point	01908
Bass River	02664
Bass Rocks (Part of Gloucester)	01930
Bay State (Part of Northampton)	01060
Bay State Correctional Center	02056
Baystate West Shopping Center (Part of Springfield)	01103
Bayview (Bristol County)	02748
Bayview (Essex County)	01930
Beach (Part of Revere)	02151
Beachmont (Part of Revere)	02151
Beach Point	02652
Beachwood	01262
Beacon Hill (Part of Boston)	02108
Beaver Brook (Middlesex County)	02154
Beaver Brook (Worcester County)	01602
Becket	01223
Becket (Town)	01223
Becket Center	01011
Bedford (Middlesex County) (Town)	01730
Bedford (Middlesex County)	01730
Bedford Springs	01730
Beechwood	02025
Belcher Square	01230
Belchertown	01007
Belchertown (Town)	01007
Belchertown State School	01007
Bellingham (Norfolk County) (Town)	02019
Bellingham (Norfolk County)	02019
Bell Rock (Part of Malden)	02148
Belmont (Middlesex County) (Town)	02178
Belmont (Middlesex County)	02178
Belvidere (Part of Lowell)	01852
Bennetts Corner	02379
Berkley	02780
Berkley (Town)	02780
Berkshire	01224
Berkshire Heights	01230
Berlin	01503
Berlin (Town)	01503
Bernardston	01337
Bernardston (Town)	01337
Beverly	01915
Beverly Cove (Part of Beverly)	01915
Beverly Farms (Part of Beverly)	01915
Beverly Junction (Part of Beverly)	01915
Big Pond	01029
Billerica	01821-22
For specific Billerica Zip Codes call (508) 663-8301	
Birch Island	01570
Blackinton (Part of North Adams)	01247
Black Rock	02025
Blackstone	01504
Blackstone (Town)	01504
Blandford	01008
Blandford (Town)	01008
Bleachery (Part of Lowell)	01852
Bleachery (Part of Waltham)	02154
Blissville	01364
Bloomingdale (Part of Worcester)	01604
Blue Hills	02186
Blush Hollow	01243
Bolton	01740
Bolton (Town)	01740
Bondsville	01009
Boston	02101-99

	ZIP
	02201-99
For specific Boston Zip Codes call (617) 654-5768	
COLLEGES & UNIVERSITIES	
Berklee College of Music	02215
Boston University	02215
Emerson College	02116
Massachusetts College of Art	02215
Massachusetts College of Pharmacy and Allied Health Sciences	02115
Northeastern University	02115
School of the Museum of Fine Arts	02115
Suffolk University	02108
University of Massachusetts at Boston	02125
Wentworth Institute of Technology	02115
FINANCIAL INSTITUTIONS	
Advantage Bank for Savings	02152
Bank of Boston	02108
Bank of New England, N.A.	02109
BayBank Boston, N.A.	02110
BayBank Harvard Trust Company	02138
Boston Safe Deposit and Trust Company	02108
Boston Trade Bank	02109
Braintree Savings Bank	02184
Brookline Savings Bank	02146
Brown Brothers Harriman & Co	02109
Cambridge Port Savings Bank	02139
Capitol Bank and Trust Company	02114
Coolidge Bank and Trust Company	02116
East Boston Savings Bank	02128
Eliot Savings Bank	02109
1st American Bank for Savings	02125
First Mutual Bank of Savings	02199
The First National Bank of Boston	02110
Greater Boston Bank (A Co-Operative Bank)	02135
Grove Bank for Savings	02146
Guaranty-First Trust Company	02108
Hibernia Savings Bank	02108
Hyde Park Savings Bank	02136
Malden Trust Company	02148
The Massachusetts Company, Inc.	02110
Medford Savings Bank	02155
Neworld Bank for Savings	02110
Olympic International Bank and Trust Company	02210
Pioneer Financial, A Co-Operative Bank	02148
The Provident Institution for Savings in the Town of Boston	02111
Shawmut Bank, National Association	02211
South Boston Savings Bank	02127
South Weymouth Savings Bank	02190
State Street Bank and Trust Company	02110
Stoneham Savings Bank	02180
United States Trust Company	02108
University Bank, National Association	02161
Waltham Savings Bank	02154
Watertown Savings Bank	02172
Weymouth Savings Bank	02188
Workingmens Co-Operative Bank	02110
HOSPITALS	
Beth Israel Hospital	02215
Boston City Hospital	02118
Brigham and Women's Hospital	02115
Carney Hospital	02124
Children's Hospital	02115
Faulkner Hospital	02130
Hebrew Rehabilitation Center for Aged	02131
Lemuel Shattuck Hospital	02130
Massachusetts General Hospital	02114

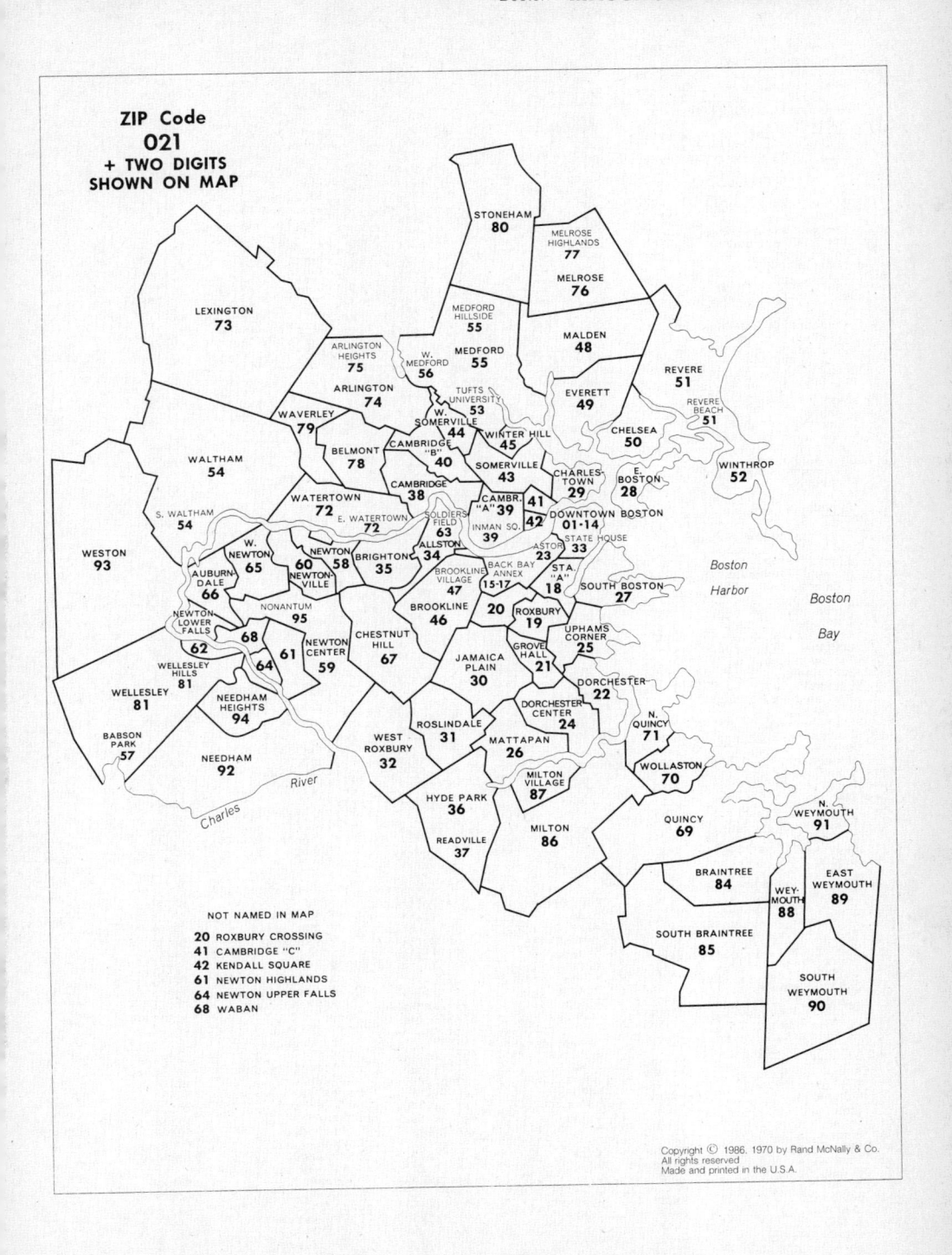

Boston **MASSACHUSETTS** **259**

ZIP Code
021
+ TWO DIGITS
SHOWN ON MAP

STONEHAM 80
MELROSE HIGHLANDS 77
MELROSE 76
LEXINGTON 73
MEDFORD HILLSIDE 55
MALDEN 48
ARLINGTON HEIGHTS 75
W. MEDFORD 56
MEDFORD 55
ARLINGTON 74
TUFTS UNIVERSITY 53
EVERETT 49
REVERE 51
WAVERLEY 79
W. SOMERVILLE 44
WINTER HILL 45
CHELSEA 50
REVERE BEACH 51
WALTHAM 54
BELMONT 78
CAMBRIDGE "B" 40
SOMERVILLE 43
CHARLESTOWN 29
E. BOSTON 28
WINTHROP 52
S. WALTHAM 54
CAMBRIDGE 38
CAMBR. "A" 39
CAMBR. 41
DOWNTOWN BOSTON 01-14
WATERTOWN 72
SOLDIERS FIELD 63
INMAN SQ. 39
42
WESTON 93
E. WATERTOWN 72
ALLSTON 34
ASTOR 23
STATE HOUSE 33
W. NEWTON 65
NEWTON 58
BRIGHTON 35
BROOKLINE VILLAGE 47
BACK BAY ANNEX 15-17
STA. "A" 18
Boston Harbor
AUBURNDALE 66
NEWTONVILLE 60
BROOKLINE 46
20
ROXBURY 19
SOUTH BOSTON 27
NEWTON LOWER FALLS 62
NONANTUM 95
CHESTNUT HILL 67
JAMAICA PLAIN 30
GROVE HALL 21
UPHAMS CORNER 25
Boston Bay
68
NEWTON CENTER 59
61
64
WELLESLEY HILLS 81
DORCHESTER 22
N. QUINCY 71
WELLESLEY 81
NEEDHAM HEIGHTS 94
ROSLINDALE 31
WEST ROXBURY 32
MATTAPAN 26
DORCHESTER CENTER 24
BABSON PARK 57
NEEDHAM 92
HYDE PARK 36
MILTON VILLAGE 87
WOLLASTON 70
Charles River
READVILLE 37
MILTON 86
QUINCY 69
N. WEYMOUTH 91
BRAINTREE 84
WEYMOUTH 88
EAST WEYMOUTH 89
SOUTH BRAINTREE 85
SOUTH WEYMOUTH 90

NOT NAMED IN MAP
20 ROXBURY CROSSING
41 CAMBRIDGE "C"
42 KENDALL SQUARE
61 NEWTON HIGHLANDS
64 NEWTON UPPER FALLS
68 WABAN

Copyright © 1986, 1970 by Rand McNally & Co.
All rights reserved
Made and printed in the U.S.A.

260 MASSACHUSETTS Boston-Dunstable

	ZIP
New England Deaconess Hospital	02215
New England Medical Center	02111
Spaulding Rehabilitation Hospital	02114
St. Elizabeth's Hospital of Boston	02135
University Hospital	02118
Veterans Administration Medical Center	02130

HOTELS/MOTELS

Boston Park Plaza Hotel & Towers	02117
Le Hotel Meridien Boston	02110
The Ritz-Carlton, Boston	02117
Sheraton-Boston Hotel	02199
The Westin Hotel, Copley Place	02116

MILITARY INSTALLATIONS

Army Materials Technology Laboratory	02172
Coast Guard Support Center, Boston	02109
Naval Air Station, South Weymouth	02190
Naval Recruiting District, Boston	02210
Supervisor of Shipbuilding, Conversion and Repair, Boston	02210
United States Army Engineer Division, New England	02254

Boston College (Part of Newton)	02167
Boston University (Part of Boston)	02215
Bourne (Town)	02532
Bourne (Barnstable County)	02532
Bournedale	02532
Boxborough	01719
Boxborough (Town)	01719
Boxford	01921
Boxford (Town)	01921
Boylston	01505
Boylston (Town)	01505
Bradford (Part of Haverhill)	01830
Bradstreet	01038
Braintree (Norfolk County) (Town)	02184
Braintree (Norfolk County)	02184
Braintree Highlands	02184
Braleys	02717
Bramanville	01527
Brant Rock	02020
Brayton Point	02725
Brewster	02631
Brewster (Town)	02631
Briarwood Beach	02571
Bridgewater	02324
Bridgewater (Town)	02324
Brier Neck (Part of Gloucester)	01930
Brigadoon Village	01949
Briggsville	01247
Brighton (Part of Boston)	02135
Brightside (Part of Holyoke)	01040
Brightwood (Part of Springfield)	01107
Brimfield	01010
Brimfield (Town)	01010
Brittan Square (Part of Worcester)	01605
Broadway (Part of Malden)	02148
Brockton	02401-03
For specific Brockton Zip Codes call (508) 559-1800	
Brookfield	01506
Brookfield (Town)	01506
Brookline (Norfolk County) (Town)	02146
Brookline (Norfolk County)	02146
Brookline Hill	02146
Brookline Village	02147
Brooks Place	02379
Brookville	02343
Brownell Corner	02790
Browns Point	01950
Brushwood	02038
Bryantville	02327
Buckland	01338
Buckland (Town)	01338
Buena Vista Shores	02346
Buffington Corner	02725
Buffumville	01540
Bullardville	01475

	ZIP
Burlington (Middlesex County) (Town)	01803
Burlington (Middlesex County)	01803
Burlington Mall	01803
Burncoat (Part of Worcester)	01606
Buzzards Bay	02532
Byfield	01922
Cabot (Part of Newton)	02158
Cambridge	02138
Campello (Part of Brockton)	02403
Campground Landing	02651
Camp Grounds	01564
Canterbury Estates	02563
Canton (Norfolk County) (Town)	02021
Canton (Norfolk County)	02021
Canton Junction	02021
Cape Cod Mall	02601
Carletonville (Part of Salem)	01970
Carlisle	01741
Carlisle (Town)	01741
Carver	02330
Carver (Town)	02330
Castle Hill (Part of Salem)	01970
Cataumet	02534
Cathedral (Part of Boston)	02118
Cedar Bushes	02345
Cedarville	02532
Center (Middlesex County)	01801
Center (Plymouth County)	02360
Centerville (Barnstable County)	02632
Centerville (Essex County)	01915
Central Village	02790
Centralville (Part of Lowell)	01850
Chadwick Square (Part of Worcester)	01605
Chaffin	01520
Chandler Hill (Part of Worcester)	01609
Chapel Hill Estates	02359
Chappaquiddick Island	02539
Chappaquoit	02574
Charlemont	01339
Charlemont (Town)	01339
Charles River Grove	02019
Charles Street (Part of Boston)	02114
Charlestown (Part of Boston)	02129
Charlton	01507
Charlton (Town)	01507
Charlton City	01508
Charlton Depot	01509
Chartley	02712
Chaseville	01570
Chatham	02633
Chatham (Town)	02633
Chelmsford (Middlesex County)	01824
Chelmsford (Middlesex County) (Town)	01824
Chelsea	02150
Cherry Brook	02193
Cherry Valley	01611
Cheshire	01225
Cheshire (Town)	01225
Cheshire Harbor	01220
Chester	01011
Chester (Town)	01011
Chester Center	01011
Chesterfield	01012
Chesterfield (Town)	01012
Chestnut Hill (Part of Newton)	02167
Chicopee	01013-22
For specific Chicopee Zip Codes call (413) 332-9451	
Chicopee Center (Part of Chicopee)	01020
Chilmark	02535
Chilmark (Town)	02535
Chiltonville	02360
Churchill Shores	02346
City Mills	02056
City Point (Part of Boston)	02127
Clarendon Hills (Part of Boston)	02131
Clarksburg (Town)	01247
Clayton	06018
Clematis Brook (Part of Waltham)	02154
Clevelandtown	02539
Clicquot	02054
Cliftondale	01906
Clinton (Worcester County) (Town)	01510
Clinton (Worcester County)	01510
Cochesett	02379

	ZIP
Cochituate	01778
Cohasset	02025
Cohasset (Town)	02025
Cohasset Army Ammunition Activity	02043
Cold Spring	01253
Cole Corner	02043
College Hill (Part of Worcester)	01610
Collinsville	01826
Colonial Park	01570
Colrain	01340
Colrain (Town)	01340
Coltsville (Part of Pittsfield)	01201
Columbus Park (Part of Worcester)	01603
Cominsville	01542
Concord	01742
Concord (Town)	01742
Congamond	01077
Conomo	01929
Conway	01341
Conway (Town)	01341
Cooks Brook Beach	02651
Cooleyville	01355
Copley Place (Part of Boston)	02116
Cordaville	01772
Cotley (Part of Taunton)	02780
Cottage Hill	02152
Cottage Park	02152
Cotuit	02635
Country View Estates	02038
Court Park	02152
Coury Heights	02743
Cow Yard	02748
Craigville	02636
Craigville Beach	02636
Crescent Beach (Plymouth County)	02739
Crescent Beach (Suffolk County)	02151
Crescent Mills	01050
Crooks Corner	02019
Cummaquid	02637
Cummington	01026
Cummington (Town)	01026
Cushman	01002
Cuttyhunk	02713
Dalton	01226-27
For specific Dalton Zip Codes call (413) 684-0364	
Danvers (Essex County) (Town)	01923
Danvers (Essex County)	01923
Danversport	01923
Dartmouth	02714
Dartmouth (Town)	02714
Davisville	02536
Dawson	01520
Dedham (Norfolk County) (Town)	02026
Dedham (Norfolk County)	02026
Dedham Mall	02026
Deerfield	01342
Deerfield (Town)	01342
Deer Island (Part of Boston)	02152
Dennis	02638
Dennis (Town)	02638
Dennis Port	02639
Devenscrest	01432
Devereux	01945
Dighton	02715
Dighton (Town)	02715
Division Street (Part of New Bedford)	02744
Dodge	01507
Dorchester (Part of Boston)	02122
Dorchester Center (Part of Boston)	02124
Dorchester Lower Mills (Part of Boston)	02124
Dorothy Manor	01527
Dorothy Pond	01527
Douglas	01516
Douglas (Town)	01516
Dover	02030
Dover (Town)	02030
Dracut (Middlesex County) (Town)	01826
Dracut (Middlesex County)	01826
Drury	01343
Drury Square	01501
Dry Pond	02072
Dudley	01570
Dudley (Town)	01570
Dudley Hill	01570
Dunstable	01827
Dunstable (Town)	01827

Duxbury-Harwood MASSACHUSETTS 261

	ZIP		ZIP		ZIP
Duxbury	02331-32	Elmdale	01569	Georgetown (Town)	01833
For specific Duxbury Zip Codes call (617) 934-5551		Elm Grove	01340	Germantown (Part of Quincy)	02169
		Elm Square	02379	Gilbertville	01031
Duxbury (Town)	02332	Elmwood (Hampden County)	01040	Gill (Town)	01376
Dwight	01007	Elmwood (Plymouth County)	02337	Gillett Corner	01077
Eagleville	01364	Endicott	02026	Gleasondale	01775
East Acton	01720	Erving	01344	Glendale	01229
East Arlington	02174	Erving (Town)	01344	Glen Echo	02072
East Billerica	01821	Essex	01929	Glen Grove	01508
East Blackstone	01504	Essex (Town)	01929	Glen Grove Annex	01508
East Boston (Part of Boston)	02128	Essex (Part of Boston)	02112	Glenridge	02030
East Boxford	01921	Everett	02149	Gloucester	01930-31
East Braintree	02184	Factory Hollow	01002	For specific Gloucester Zip Codes call (508) 283-0474	
East Brewster	02631	Fairfield Mall (Part of Chicopee)	01020		
East Bridgewater	02333			Goodrichville	01462
East Bridgewater (Town)	02333	Fairhaven (Bristol County) (Town)	02719	Goshen	01032
East Brimfield	01010	Fairhaven (Bristol County)	02719	Goshen (Town)	01032
East Brookfield	01515	Fairlawn	01545	Gosnold (Town)	02713
East Brookfield (Town)	01515	Fairmount (Part of Boston)	02136	Goss Heights	01050
East Cambridge (Part of Cambridge)	02138	Fairview (Part of Chicopee)	01020	Goulding Village	01331
East Carver	02355	Fall River	02720-26	Grafton	01519
East Charlemont	01370	For specific Fall River Zip Codes call (508) 675-7438		Grafton (Town)	01519
East Chelmsford	01824			Granby	01033
East Dedham	02026	Falls	01075	Granby (Town)	01033
East Deerfield	01342	Falmouth	02540-41	Graniteville	01886
East Dennis	02641	For specific Falmouth Zip Codes call (508) 548-1071		Granville	01034
East Douglas	01516			Granville (Town)	01034
East Fairhaven	02719	Falmouth (Town)	02540	Granville Center	01034
East Falmouth	02536	Falmouth Heights	02540	Gray Gables	02532
Eastfield Mall (Part of Springfield)	01109	Farley	01344	Great Barrington	01230
		Farm Hill	02180	Great Barrington (Town)	01230
East Foxboro	02035	Farnams	01225	Great Brook Valley (Part of Worcester)	01605
East Freetown	02717	Farnumsville	01560	Greenbush	02040
East Gloucester (Part of Gloucester)	01930	Faulkner (Part of Malden)	02148	Greendale (Part of Worcester)	01606
East Greenfield	01301	Fayville	01745	Greenfield	01301-02
Eastham	02642	Federal (Part of Worcester)	01601	For specific Greenfield Zip Codes call (413) 773-3654	
Eastham (Town)	02642	Feeding Hills	01030		
Easthampton (Hampshire County) (Town)	01027	Felchville	01760	Greenfield Center	01301
		Fellsway (Part of Medford)	02155	Green Harbor	02041
Easthampton (Hampshire County)	01027	Fentonville	01069	Green Harbor-Cedar Crest	02041
East Harwich	02645	Fields Corner (Part of Boston)	02122	Greenlodge	02026
East Holliston	01746	Fieldston	02065	Green Ridge Park	01226
East Junction (Part of Attleboro)	02703	Findlen	02026	Greenview Estates	02035
		First Cliff	02066	Greenville	01542
East Lee	01238	Fiskdale	01518	Greenwood	01880
East Leverett	01054	Fitchburg	01420	Greenwood Manor Estates	02359
East Longmeadow (Hampden County) (Town)	01028	Five Corners	02356	Greylock (Part of North Adams)	01247
		Flint (Part of Fall River)	02723		
		Florence (Part of Northampton)	01060	Griswoldville	01340
East Longmeadow (Hampden County)	01028			Grosvenor Corner	01844
		Florida	01343	Groton	01450
East Lynn (Part of Lynn)	01904	Florida (Town)	01343	Groton (Town)	01450
East Mansfield	02031	Forbes Park	02019	Grove Hall (Part of Boston)	02121
Eastdale	02738	Fore River (Part of Quincy)	02169	Groveland	01834
East Marion	02346	Forestdale	02644	Groveland (Town)	01834
East Middleboro	02346	Forestdale Estates	02359	Hadley	01035
East Millbury	01527	Forest Hills (Part of Boston)	02130	Hadley (Town)	01035
East Milton	02186	Forest Lake	01069	Halfway Pond	02532
East Northfield	01360	Forest Park (Part of Springfield)	01108	Halifax	02338
Easton	02334			Halifax (Town)	02338
Easton (Town)	02334	Forest River (Part of Salem)	01970	Halifax Beach	02338
Eastondale	02375	Forge Village	01886	Hamilton	01936
East Orleans	02643	Fort Banks (U.S. Army) (inactive)	02152	Hamilton (Town)	01936
East Otis	01029			Hamilton (Part of Worcester)	01604
East Pembroke	02359	Fort Bellingham	02019	Hamilton Beach	02571
East Pepperell	01463	Fort Devens (Middlesex County)	01433	Hampden	01036
East Princeton	01541			Hampden (Town)	01036
East Sandwich	02537	Fort Devens (Worcester County)	01433	Hampshire Mall	01035
East Saugus	01906			Hampton Mills	01027
East Springfield (Part of Springfield)	01101	Fort Heath	02152	Hancock	01237
		Foundry Village	01340	Hancock (Town)	01237
East Sudbury	01776	Foxboro	02035	Hancock Village	02146
East Swansea	02777	Foxborough (Town)	02035	Hanover	02339
East Taunton (Part of Taunton)	02718	Foxvale	02035	Hanover (Town)	02339
		Framingham (Middlesex County) (Town)	01701	Hanover Center	02339
East Templeton	01438			Hanover Street (Part of Boston)	02113
Eastview Park (Part of Waltham)	02154	Framingham (Middlesex County)	01701		
				Hanson	02341
East Village	01570	Framingham Center	01701	Hanson (Town)	02341
Eastville	02557	Franklin (Norfolk County) (Town)	02038	Happy Hills	02019
East Walpole	02032			Harbor Beach	02739
East Wareham	02538	Franklin (Norfolk County)	02038	Harbour Mall (Part of Fall River)	02721
East Watertown	02172	Franklin Park (Part of Revere)	02151		
East Weymouth	02189			Harding	02052
East Windsor	01270	Freetown (Town)	02702	Hardwick	01037
East Woburn (Part of Woburn)	01801	Fresh Pond (Part of Cambridge)	02138	Hardwick (Town)	01037
				Harrubs Corner	02367
Eddyville	02346	Freshwater Cove (Part of Gloucester)	01930	Harthaven	02557
Edgartown	02539			Hartsville	01230
Edgartown (Town)	02539	Fuller Shores	02346	Harvard	01451
Edgemere	01545	Furnace Pond Colony	02359	Harvard (Town)	01451
Edgewater Estates	02359	Furnace Village	02334	Harvard Square (Part of Cambridge)	02138
Edgeworth (Part of Malden)	02148	Galleria at Worcester Center (Part of Worcester)	01608		
Egleston Square (Part of Boston)	02116			Harwich	02645
		Gardner	01440	Harwich (Town)	02645
Egremont (Town)	01252	Gay Head	02535	Harwich	02645
Egypt	02066	Gay Head (Town)	02535	Harwich Port	02646
Ellisville	02532	Georgetown	01833	Harwood	01460

262 MASSACHUSETTS Hastings-Medway

Name	ZIP
Hastings	02193
Hatchville	02536
Hatfield	01038
Hatfield (Town)	01038
Hathorne	01937
Haverhill	01830-35
For specific Haverhill Zip Codes call (508) 373-5643	
Hawley	01339
Hawley (Town)	01339
Haydenville	01039
Head of Westport	02790
Heath	01346
Heath (Town)	01346
Heaven Heights	02717
Hebronville (Part of Attleboro)	02703
Hemlocks	02346
Hickory Hills Lake	01462
Hicksville	02747
Highland (Part of Springfield)	01109
Highland Lake	02056
Highland Park (Part of Holyoke)	01040
Highlands (Hampden County)	01040
Highlands (Middlesex County)	01851
Hillcrest Acres	02790
Hilltop Acres	02346
Hingham (Town)	02043
Hingham (Plymouth County)	02043
Hingham Center	02043
Hinsdale	01235
Hinsdale (Town)	01235
Hinsdale Estates	02019
Hodges Village	01540
Holbrook (Norfolk County)	02343
Holbrook (Norfolk County) (Town)	02343
Holden	01520
Holden (Town)	01520
Holland	01010
Holland (Town)	01550
Holliston (Middlesex County) (Town)	01746
Holliston (Middlesex County)	01746
Holly Woods	02739
Holyoke	01040-41
For specific Holyoke Zip Codes call (413) 534-4577	
Holyoke Mall at Ingleside (Part of Holyoke)	01040
Hoosac Tunnel	01367
Hopedale (Worcester County) (Town)	01747
Hopedale (Worcester County)	01747
Hopkinton	01748
Hopkinton (Town)	01748
Horseneck Beach	02790
Hortonville	02777
Houghs Neck (Part of Quincy)	02169
Houghtonville	01247
Housatonic	01236
Hovey's Corner	01463
Howe	01949
Hubbardston	01452
Hubbardston (Town)	01452
Huckleberry Corner	02576
Huckleberry Shores	02346
Hudson (Town)	01749
Hudson	01749
Hull (Plymouth County) (Town)	02045
Hull (Plymouth County)	02045
Humarock	02047
Huntington	01050
Huntington (Town)	01050
Hyannis (Barnstable County)	02601
Hyannis Port	02647
Hyde Park (Part of Boston)	02136
Idlewell	02188
Idlewood	02747
Indian Mound Beach	02532
Indian Orchard (Part of Springfield)	01151
Indian Shore	02346
Ingleside (Part of Holyoke)	01040
Inman Square (Part of Cambridge)	02139
Interlaken	01266
Ipswich	01938
Ipswich (Town)	01938
Island Creek	02332
Islington	02090
Jamaica Plain (Part of Boston)	02130

Name	ZIP
Jefferson	01522
Jefferson Shores	02532
Jeffries Point (Part of Boston)	02128
John Fitzgerald Kennedy (Part of Boston)	02114
John W. Mc Cormack (Part of Boston)	02109
Katama	02539
Kearney Square (Part of Lowell)	01852
Kempton Croft	02747
Kendal Green	02193
Kendall Square (Part of Cambridge)	02142
Kenmore (Part of Boston)	02215
Kent Park	02050
Kenwood	01826
Killdeer Island	01570
Kingsbury Beach	02642
Kings Forest	01921
Kingston	02364
Kingston (Town)	02364
Knightville	01050
Knollmere	02719
Konkapot	01244
Lafayette Place (Part of Boston)	02111
Lagoon Heights	02557
Lake Attitash	01913
Lake Forest Park	01760
Lake Hiawatha	02019
Lake Mattawa	01364
Lake Pleasant	01347
Lakeside (Bristol County)	02790
Lakeside (Plymouth County)	02346
Lake Street	02174
Lakeview (Middlesex County)	02154
Lake View (Worcester County)	01604
Lakeview Heights	02717
Lakeview Terrace (Part of Pittsfield)	01201
Lakeville	02346
Lakeville (Town)	02346
Lakewood (Part of Pittsfield)	01201
Lakewood Hills	02537
Lakewood Park	01473
Lambs Grove	01562
Lancaster	01523
Lancaster (Town)	01523
Lanesboro	01237
Lanesborough (Town)	01237
Lanesville (Part of Gloucester)	01930
Lane Village	01430
Larrywaug	01262
Laurel Park (Part of Northampton)	01060
Laurence G. Hanscom Air Force Base	01731
Lawrence	01840-45
For specific Lawrence Zip Codes call (508) 691-4500	
Le Count Hollow	02663
Lee	01238
Lee (Town)	01238
Leeds (Part of Northampton)	01053
Leicester	01524
Leicester (Town)	01524
Leino Park	01473
Lenox	01240
Lenox (Town)	01240
Lenox Dale	01242
Leominster	01453
Leverett	01054
Leverett (Town)	01054
Lexington (Middlesex County) (Town)	02173
Lexington (Middlesex County)	02173
Leyden (Town)	01301
Liberty Tree Mall	01923
Lincoln	01773
Lincoln (Town)	01773
Lincoln Center	01773
Lincoln Square (Part of Worcester)	01601
Linden (Part of Malden)	02148
Lindenwood	02180
Linwood	01525
Lithia	01032
Little Acres	02327
Little Harbor Beach	02571
Little Nahant	01908
Little Neck (Bristol County)	02777
Little Neck (Essex County)	01938
Little River (Part of Westfield)	01085

Name	ZIP
Littleton	01460
Littleton (Town)	01460
Lobsterville	02535
Lockerville	01760
Locks Village	01072
Long Beach	01930
Long Hill Acres	02359
Long Island Hospital (Part of Boston)	02169
Longmeadow (Hampden County) (Town)	01106
Longmeadow (Hampden County)	01106
Long Plain	02743
Long Pond Village	02532
Longwood	02146
Loudville	01027
Lovell Corners	02188
Lowell	01850-54
For specific Lowell Zip Codes call (508) 934-0500	
Lower Mills (Part of Boston)	02126
Lower Village	01775
Ludlow (Hampden County) (Town)	01056
Ludlow (Hampden County)	01056
Ludlow (Worcester County)	01603
Lunds Corner (Part of New Bedford)	02745
Lunenburg	01462
Lunenburg (Town)	01462
Lynn	01901-08
For specific Lynn Zip Codes call (617) 595-5700	
Lynnfield (Essex County) (Town)	01940
Lynnfield (Essex County)	01940
Lynnhurst	01906
Lyonsville	01340
Madaket	02554
Magnolia (Part of Gloucester)	01930
Mahkeenac Heights	01240
Main Street	02532
Malden	02148
Manchaug	01526
Manchester (Town)	01944
Manchester-By-The-Sea	01944
Manleys Corner	02379
Manomet	02345
Manomet Beach	02345
Manomet Bluffs	02345
Mansfield	02048
Mansfield (Town)	02048
Maple Park	01844
Maplewood (Middlesex County)	02148
Maplewood (Worcester County)	01536
Mara Vista	02536
Marblehead (Essex County) (Town)	01945
Marblehead (Essex County)	01945
Marblehead Neck	01945
Marion	02738
Marion (Town)	02738
Marlboro	01833
Marlborough	01752
Marshfield	02050
Marshfield (Town)	02050
Marshfield Hills	02051
Marstons Mills	02648
Mashnee Island	02532
Mashpee	02649
Mashpee (Town)	02649
Masons Corner	02717
Massachusette Correctional Institution	02366
Massachusetts Correctional Institution (Middlesex County)	01701
Massachusetts Correctional Institution (Norfolk County)	02071
Massachusetts Correctional Institution (Plymouth County)	02324
Matfield	02379
Mattapan (Part of Boston)	02126
Mattapoisett	02739
Mattapoisett (Town)	02739
Maynard (Middlesex County) (Town)	01754
Maynard (Middlesex County)	01754
Mayo Beach	02667
Medfield	02052
Medfield (Town)	02052
Medford	02155
Medway	02053
Medway (Town)	02053

MASSACHUSETTS 263
Meeting House Hill-Otis

Name	ZIP
Meeting House Hill (Part of Boston)	02122
Megansett	02556
Melrose	02176
Melrose Highlands (Part of Melrose)	02177
Menauhant	02536
Mendon	01756
Mendon (Town)	01756
Menemsha	02552
Merrick	01089
Merrimac	01860
Merrimac (Town)	01860
Merrimack College	01845
Merrimacport	01860
Merrymount (Part of Quincy)	02169
Methuen (Essex County) (Town)	01844
Methuen (Essex County)	01844
Methuen Mall	01844
Middleboro	02346
Middleborough (Town)	02346
Middlefield (Town)	01243
Middlefield (Hampshire County)	01243
Middleton (Essex County) (Town)	01949
Middleton (Essex County)	01949
Midland	02019
Mile Oak Center	01095
Milford (Worcester County) (Town)	01757
Milford (Worcester County)	01757
Millbury	01527
Millbury (Town)	01527
Millers Falls	01349
Millerville	01504
Millis	02054
Millis (Town)	02054
Millis-Clicquot	02054
Mill River	01244
Millville (Worcester County) (Town)	01529
Millville (Worcester County)	01529
Millville Center	01529
Milton (Norfolk County) (Town)	02186
Milton (Norfolk County)	02186
Milton Center	02186
Milton Village	02187
Minot	02055
Mirror Lake	02093
Mishaum Point	02748
M.I.T. (Part of Cambridge)	02139
Monomoy	02554
Monponsett	02350
Monroe (Town)	01350
Monroe Bridge	01350
Monson	01057
Monson (Town)	01057
Montague	01351
Montague (Town)	01351
Montague City	01376
Montello (Part of Brockton)	02403
Monterey	01245
Monterey (Town)	01245
Montgomery	01085
Montgomery (Town)	01085
Montserrat (Part of Beverly)	01915
Montville	01255
Monument Beach	02553
Moores Corner	01054
Morningdale	01505
Morrills	02062
Morseville	01760
Mount Auburn	02172
Mount Bowdoin (Part of Boston)	02121
Mount Hermon	01354
Mount Saint James (Part of Worcester)	01610
Mount Tom	01027
Mount Washington	12517
Mount Washington (Town)	12517
Myricks	02718
Mystic Grove	01507
Mystic Wharf (Part of Boston)	02109
Nabnasset	01886
Nahant (Essex County) (Town)	01908
Nahant (Essex County)	01908
Nantucket	02554
Nantucket (Town)	02554
Nashaquitsa	02535
Natick (Middlesex County) (Town)	01760
Natick (Middlesex County)	01760
Natick Development Center	01760
Natick Laboratories	01760
Natick Mall	01760

Name	ZIP
Needham (Norfolk County) (Town)	02192
Needham (Norfolk County)	02192
Needham Heights	02194
Nelsons Grove	02346
Nelsons Shores	02346
Neponset (Part of Boston)	02122
New Ashford	01237
New Ashford (Town)	01237
New Bedford	02740-48
For specific New Bedford Zip Codes call (508) 966-8523	
New Boston	01255
New Braintree	01531
New Braintree (Town)	01531
Newbury	01951
Newbury (Town)	01950
Newburyport	01950-52
For specific Newburyport Zip Codes call (508) 462-4403	
New England Shopping Center	01906
New Lenox	01240
New Marlboro	01230
New Marlborough (Town)	01230
New Salem	01355
New Salem (Town)	01355
New Seabury	02649
Newton	02158
Newton Center (Part of Newton)	02159
Newton Highlands (Part of Newton)	02161
Newton Lower Falls (Part of Newton)	02162
Newton Upper Falls (Part of Newton)	02164
Newtonville (Part of Newton)	02160
New Town	02258
New Village	01588
Nobska Beach	02571
Nonantum (Part of Newton)	02195
Nonquitt	02748
Noquochoke	02790
Norfolk	02056
Norfolk (Town)	02056
North (Part of New Bedford)	02746
North Abington	02351
North Acton	01720
North Adams	01247
North Adams Junction (Part of Pittsfield)	01201
North Amherst	01059
Northampton	01060-61
For specific Northampton Zip Codes call (413) 584-0960	
North Andover (Essex County) (Town)	01845
North Andover (Essex County)	01845
North Andover Center	01845
North Ashburnham	01430
North Attleboro	02760-63
For specific North Attleboro Zip Codes call (508) 699-7556	
North Attleborough (Town)	02760
North Bellingham	02019
North Beverly (Part of Beverly)	01915
North Billerica	01862
North Blandford	01008
Northborough	01532
Northborough (Town)	01532
Northbridge	01534
Northbridge (Town)	01534
Northbridge Center	01588
North Brighton (Part of Boston)	02135
North Brookfield	01535
North Brookfield (Town)	01535
North Cambridge (Part of Cambridge)	02138
North Carver	02355
North Chatham	02650
North Chelmsford	01863
North Chester	01050
North Cohasset	02025
North Dartmouth	02747
North Dartmouth Mall	02747
North Dighton	02764
North Duxbury	02332
North Eastham	02651
North Easton	02356
North Egremont	01252
Northey Point (Part of Salem)	01970
North Falmouth	02556
Northfield	01360
Northfield (Town)	01360

Name	ZIP
Northgate Shopping Center (Part of Revere)	02151
North Grafton	01536
North Hadley	01035
North Hancock	01267
North Hanover	02339
North Harwich	02645
North Hatfield	01066
North Lakeville	02346
North Lancaster	01523
North Leominster (Part of Leominster)	01453
North Leverett	01054
North Littleton	01460
North Marshfield	02059
North Middleboro	02346
North Milford	01757
North Natick	01760
North New Salem	01364
North Orange	01364
North Otis	01253
North Oxford	01537
North Pembroke	02358
North Pepperell	01463
North Plymouth	02360
North Plympton	02364
North Quincy (Part of Quincy)	02171
North Randolph	02368
North Reading (Middlesex County) (Town)	01864
North Reading (Middlesex County)	01864
North Rehoboth	02769
North Rutland	01543
North Salem (Part of Salem)	01970
North Saugus	01906
North Scituate (Plymouth County)	02060
Northshore Shopping Center (Part of Peabody)	01960
North Sommerville (Part of Somerville)	02143
North Stoughton	02072
North Sudbury	01776
North Swansea	02777
North Tewksbury	01876
North Tisbury	02568
North Truro	02652
North Uxbridge	01538
North Waltham (Part of Waltham)	02154
North Weymouth	02191
North Wilmington	01887
North Woburn (Part of Woburn)	01801
North Worcester (Part of Worcester)	01606
Norton	02766
Norton (Town)	02766
Norton Grove	02061
Norwell	02161
Norwell (Town)	02161
Norwood (Norfolk County) (Town)	02062
Norwood (Norfolk County)	02062
Norwood Central	02062
Nutting Lake	01865
Oak Bluffs (Dukes County) (Town)	02557
Oak Bluffs (Dukes County)	02557
Oakdale (Hampden County)	01040
Oakdale (Norfolk County)	02026
Oakdale (Worcester County)	01583
Oak Grove (Part of Malden)	02148
Oakham	01068
Oakham (Town)	01068
Oak Island (Part of Revere)	02151
Oakland Vale	01906
Ocean Bluff	02065
Ocean Bluff-Brant Rock	02020
Ocean Grove	02777
Ocean Heights	02539
Ocean Spray	02152
Old City	01474
Old Common	01527
Old Furnace	01031
Oldham Pines	02359
Oldham Village	02359
Old Silver Beach	02556
Old Sturbridge Village	01566
Onset	02558
Orange	01364
Orange (Town)	01364
Orient Heights (Part of Boston)	02128
Orleans	02653
Orleans (Town)	02653
Osceola	01254
Osterville	02655
Otis	01253

MASSACHUSETTS Otis-Shrewsbury

Name	ZIP
Otis (Town)	01253
Otis Air Force Base	02542
Otter River	01436
Overbrook	02181
Oxford	01540
Oxford (Town)	01540
Oyster Harbors	02655
Packard Heights	01331
Padanaram Village	02748
Pages Beach	01430
Painting Island	02738
Pakachoag	01501
Palmer	01069
Palmer (Town)	01069
Park Street (Part of Medford)	02155
Parkwood Beach	02571
Patuisset	02559
Pawtucketville (Part of Lowell)	01854
Paxton	01612
Paxton (Town)	01612
Payson Park	02172
Peabody	01960-61
For specific Peabody Zip Codes call (508) 531-5400	
Pelham	01002
Pelham (Town)	01002
Pembroke	02359
Pembroke (Town)	02359
Pembroke Heights	02358
Pepperell	01463
Pepperell (Town)	01463
Perryville	02769
Peru	01235
Peru (Town)	01235
Petersham	01366
Petersham (Town)	01366
Phelps Mills (Part of Peabody)	01960
Phillipston	01331
Phillipston (Town)	01331
Phillipston Four Corners	01331
Pierceville	02576
Piety Corner (Part of Waltham)	02154
Pigeon Cove	01966
Pilgrim Heights	02652
Pilgrim Pines Estates	02327
Pilgrim Village	02019
Pine Bluffs	02346
Pinefield	01938
Pine Grove (Part of Northampton)	01060
Pinehurst	01866
Pinehurst Beach	02571
Pine Island	01951
Pine Island Lake	01060
Pine Lake	01776
Pine Point (Part of Springfield)	01101
Pine Rest	01776
Piney Point Beach	02738
Pingryville	01460
Pittsfield	01201-03
For specific Pittsfield Zip Codes call (413) 442-6961	
Plainfield	01070
Plainfield (Town)	01070
Plainville (Hampshire County)	01002
Plainville (Norfolk County)	02762
Plainville (Norfolk County) (Town)	02762
Pleasant Lake	02645
Plimptonville	02081
Plumbush	01951
Plum Island (Part of Newburyport)	01950
Plummer Corner	01588
Plymouth	02360-61
For specific Plymouth Zip Codes call (508) 746-0058	
Plympton	02367
Plympton (Town)	02367
Pocasset	02559
Pocomo	02554
Podunk	01515
Point Independence	02532
Point of Pines (Part of Revere)	02151
Point Pleasant	01570
Point Shirley	02152
Polpis	02554
Pomponotto Pines	02333
Ponakin Mill	01523
Pond Village (Barnstable County)	02652
Pond Village (Barnstable County)	02630
Pondville (Norfolk County)	02093
Pondville (Plymouth County)	02532
Pondville (Worcester County)	01501
Pontoosuc Gardens (Part of Pittsfield)	01201
Pope Beach	02719
Popponesset Beach	02649
Potoosuc Lake	01237
Precinct	02346
Prentice Gardens	01588
Prides Crossing (Part of Beverly)	01965
Princeton	01541
Princeton (Town)	01541
Priscilla Beach	02360
Provincetown (Barnstable County)	02657
Provincetown (Barnstable County) (Town)	02657
Provincetown (Barnstable County)	02657
Provincetown Wharf	02657
Prudential Center (Part of Boston)	02199
Quaise	02554
Queen Lake	01331
Quidnet	02554
Quincy	02169
Quincy Adams (Part of Quincy)	02169
Quincy Center (Part of Quincy)	02169
Quincy Point (Part of Quincy)	02169
Quinsigamond Village (Part of Worcester)	01607
Quissett	02540
Rakeville	02019
Randolph (Norfolk County) (Town)	02368
Randolph (Norfolk County)	02368
Raynham	02767
Raynham (Town)	02767
Raynham Center	02768
Reading (Middlesex County) (Town)	01867
Reading (Middlesex County)	01867
Readville (Part of Boston)	02137
Redstone Shopping Center	02180
Rehoboth	02769
Rehoboth (Town)	02769
Renfrew	01220
Reservoir	02146
Revere	02151
Revere Beach (Part of Revere)	02151
Rexhame	02050
Rice Square (Part of Worcester)	01604
Richmond	01254
Richmond (Town)	01254
Richmond Furnace	01254
Rings Island	01950
Rio Vista	01862
Risingdale	01230
Riverdale (Essex County)	01930
Riverdale (Norfolk County)	02026
Riverdale (Worcester County)	01534
Rivermoor	02066
River Pines	01821
Riverside (Essex County)	01830
Riverside (Franklin County)	01376
Riverside (Hampden County)	01040
Riverside (Plymouth County)	02558
Riverview (Essex County)	01930
Riverview (Middlesex County)	02154
Roberts (Part of Waltham)	02154
Rochdale	01542
Rochester	02770
Rochester (Town)	02770
Rock	02346
Rockdale	01236
Rock Harbor	02653
Rockland (Plymouth County) (Town)	02370
Rockland (Plymouth County)	02370
Rockport	01966
Rockport (Town)	01966
Rocks Village (Part of Haverhill)	01830
Rock Valley (Part of Holyoke)	01040
Rockville	02054
Rocky Hill	01757
Rolling Acres Estates	01886
Roosterville	01255
Roslindale (Part of Boston)	02131
Rowe	01367
Rowe (Town)	01367
Rowley	01969
Rowley (Town)	01969
Roxbury (Part of Boston)	02119
Roxbury Crossing (Part of Boston)	02120
Royalston	01368
Royalston (Town)	01368
Russell	01071
Russell (Town)	01071
Russellville	01085
Rutland	01543
Rutland (Town)	01543
Saconesset Hills	02540
Sagamore	02561
Sagamore Beach	02562
Sagamore Highlands	02562
Salem	01970-71
For specific Salem Zip Codes call (508) 744-8600	
Salem Neck (Part of Salem)	01970
Salem State College (Part of Salem)	01970
Salisbury	01952
Salisbury (Town)	01950
Salisbury Beach	01950
Salisbury Heights (Part of Worcester)	01609
Salisbury Plains	01950
Salters Point	02748
Sandersdale	01550
Sand Hill	02066
Sandisfield	01255
Sandisfield (Town)	01255
Sandwich	02563
Sandwich (Town)	02563
Sandy Beach (Norfolk County)	02025
Sandy Beach (Worcester County)	01543
Santuit	02635
Sassaquin (Part of New Bedford)	02745
Saugus (Essex County) (Town)	01906
Saugus (Essex County)	01906
Saugus Center	01906
Saundersville	01560
Savin Hill (Part of Boston)	02125
Savoy	01256
Savoy (Town)	01256
Saxonville	01701
Scituate	02066
Scituate (Town)	02066
Scorton Shores	02537
Scott Hill Acres	02019
Searstown Mall (Part of Leominster)	01453
Searsville	01096
Sea View	02050
Second Cliff	02066
Seekonk (Bristol County) (Town)	02771
Seekonk (Bristol County)	02771
Segreganset	02715
Shaker Village	01451
Sharon (Norfolk County) (Town)	02067
Sharon (Norfolk County)	02067
Sharon Heights	02067
Shattuckville	01369
Shawkemo	02554
Shawsheen Heights	01810
Shawsheen Village	01810
Sheffield	01257
Sheffield (Town)	01257
Shelburne	01370
Shelburne (Town)	01370
Shelburne Falls	01370
Sheldonville	02070
Shell Beach	02739
Shepardville	02762
Sherborn	01770
Sherborn (Town)	01770
Sherwood Forest (Berkshire County)	01223
Sherwood Forest (Bristol County)	02743
Shimmo	02554
Shirley	01464
Shirley (Town)	01464
Shirley Center	01464
Shoppers' World	01701
Shore Acres (Bristol County)	02748
Shore Acres (Plymouth County)	02066
Shrewsbury (Worcester County) (Town)	01545

Shrewsbury-Warren Terrace MASSACHUSETTS 265

	ZIP		ZIP		ZIP
Shrewsbury (Worcester County)	01545	South Salem (Part of Salem)	01970	Tewksbury (Town)	01876
Shutesbury	01072	South Sandisfield	01255	Tewksbury Hospital	01876
Shutesbury (Town)	01072	South Sandwich	02563	Texas	01537
Siasconset	02564	South Shore Plaza	02184	The Green	02346
Silver Beach	02565	South Springfield (Part of Springfield)	01101	The Pines	01866
Silver Hill	02193	South Stoughton	02072	Thomastown	02346
Silver Lake (Middlesex County)	01887	South Sutton	01516	Thorndike	01079
Silver Lake (Plymouth County)	02360	South Swansea	02777	Three Rivers	01080
Silver Shell Beach	02719	South Truro	02666	Thumpertown Beach	02651
Silver Spring Beach	02651	South Uxbridge	01569	Tihonet	02571
Simon's Rock of Bard College	01230	Southville	01772	Tinkertown	02332
Sippewisset	02540	South Walpole	02071	Tinkhamtown	02739
Sixteen Acres (Part of Springfield)	01101	South Waltham (Part of Waltham)	02154	Tisbury (Town)	02568
Smith Highlands (Part of Chicopee)	01020	South Wareham	02571	Tobeys Island	02553
Smiths Ferry (Part of Holyoke)	01040	South Wellfleet	02663	Tolland	01034
Smoke Rise Heights	02777	South Westport	02790	Tolland (Town)	01034
Snug Harbor	02332	South Weymouth	02190	Tonset	02653
Soldiers Field (Part of Boston)	02163	South Weymouth Naval Air Station	02190	Topsfield	01983
Somerset (Bristol County) (Town)	02725	Southwick	01077	Topsfield (Town)	01983
Somerset (Bristol County)	02725	Southwick (Town)	01077	Touisset	02777
Somerset Centre	02725	South Williamstown	01267	Town Crest Village	01225
Somerville	02143	South Wilmington (Part of Woburn)	01801	Town Hall	02341
South (Part of Fall River)	02724	South Worthington	01050	Townsend	01469
South Acton	01720	South Yarmouth	02664	Townsend (Town)	01469
South Amherst	01002	Spencer	01562	Townsend Harbor	01469
Southampton	01073	Spencer (Town)	01562	Tozier Corner	01844
Southampton (Town)	01073	Spindleville	01747	Tri-Town Shopping Center	02021
South Ashburnham	01466	Springdale (Part of Holyoke)	01040	Truro	02666
South Ashfield	01330	Springdale Mall (Part of Springfield)	01101	Truro (Town)	02666
South Athol	01331	Springfield	01101-05	Tufts University (Part of Medford)	02153
South Attleboro (Part of Attleboro)	02703		01107-52	Tully	01331
South Barre	01074	For specific Springfield Zip Codes call (413) 785-6300		Turkey Hill Shores	01543
South Bellingham	02019	Springfield Plaza (Part of Springfield)	01104	Turners Falls	01376
South Berlin	01549	Squantum (Part of Quincy)	02171	Turnpike	01545
South Billerica	01730	Standish (Part of Taunton)	02780	Twin City Plaza (Part of Fitchburg)	01420
South Bolton	01740	Staples Shore	02346	Tyngsboro	01879
Southborough	01772	State House (Part of Boston)	02133	Tyngsborough (Town)	01879
Southborough (Town)	01772	State Line	01266	Tyringham	01264
South Boston (Part of Boston)	02127	Sterling	01564	Tyringham (Town)	01264
South Braintree	02184	Sterling (Town)	01564	Union Market	02172
Southbridge (Worcester County) (Town)	01550	Sterling Junction	01564	Union Point	01570
Southbridge (Worcester County)	01550	Stetson Road	02359	Unionville (Norfolk County)	02038
South Byfield	01922	Stevens Corner	01201	Unionville (Worcester County)	01520
South Carver	02366	Still River	01467	University Park (Part of Worcester)	01605
South Charlton	01507	Stockbridge	01262	Uphams Corner (Part of Boston)	02125
South Chatham	02659	Stockbridge (Town)	01262	Upton	01568
South Chelmsford	01824	Stoneham (Middlesex County) (Town)	02180	Upton (Town)	01568
South Dartmouth	02748	Stoneham (Middlesex County)	02180	Upton-West Upton	01568
South Deerfield	01373	Stoneville (Franklin County)	01344	Uxbridge	01569
South Dennis	02660	Stoneville (Worcester County)	01501	Uxbridge (Town)	01569
South Duxbury	02332	Stony Brook	02193	Vallersville	02532
Southeastern Correctional Center	02324	Stoughton (Norfolk County) (Town)	02072	Valley View	02019
South Easton	02375	Stoughton (Norfolk County)	02072	Van Deusenville	01236
South Egremont	01258	Stow	01775	Varnumtown	01826
Southfield	01259	Stow (Town)	01775	Veterans Administration Hospital (Part of Boston)	02130
South Foxboro	02035	Sturbridge	01566	Victory Hill (Part of Pittsfield)	01201
South Framingham	01701	Sturbridge (Town)	01566	Village	02053
South Georgetown	01833	Sudbury	01776	Village Mall, The	02021
South Grafton	01560	Sudbury (Town)	01776	Village of Nagog Woods	01718
South Groveland	01834	Sudbury Center	01776	Vineyard Haven	02568
South Hadley	01075	Summit (Part of Worcester)	01606	Vineyard Highlands	02557
South Hadley (Town)	01075	Sunderland	01375	Waban (Part of Newton)	02168
South Hadley Falls	01075	Sunderland (Town)	01375	Wachusett (Part of Fitchburg)	01420
South Hamilton	01982	Sunderland (Part of Worcester)	01604	Wakeby	02563
South Hanover	02339	Sunken Meadow Beach	02651	Wakefield (Middlesex County) (Town)	01880
South Harwich	02661	Sunnyside	01570	Wakefield (Middlesex County)	01880
South Hingham	02043	Surfside	02554	Wakefield Center	01880
South Lakeville	02346	Sutton	01527	Wakefield Junction	01880
South Lancaster	01561	Sutton (Town)	01527	Wales	01081
South Lawrence (Part of Lawrence)	01842	Swampscott (Essex County) (Town)	01907	Wales (Town)	01081
South Lee	01260	Swampscott (Essex County)	01907	Wallis Street (Part of Peabody)	01960
South Lowell	01876	Swansea	02777	Walnut Hill (Part of Woburn)	01801
South Lynnfield	01940	Swansea (Town)	02777	Walpole	02081
South Mashpee	02649	Swansea Center	02777	Walpole (Town)	02081
South Middleboro	02346	Sweets Corner	01267	Walpole Mall, The	02032
South Milford	01747	Swift River	01026	Waltham	02154
South Natick	01760	Swifts Beach	02571	Waltham Highlands (Part of Waltham)	02154
South Orleans	02662	Symmes Corner	01890	Wamesit	01876
South Peabody (Part of Peabody)	01960	Tafts Corner	01562	Wampun Corner	02093
South Postal Annex (Part of Boston)	02109	Tahanto Beach	02559	Wapping	01342
South Quincy (Part of Quincy)	02169	Tapleyville	01923	Waquoit	02536
South Rehoboth	02769	Tatnuck (Part of Worcester)	01602	Ward Hill (Part of Haverhill)	01830
South Royalston	01331	Taunton	02780	Ware	01082
		Teaticket	02536	Ware (Town)	01082
		Templeton	01468	Wareham	02571
		Templeton (Town)	01468	Wareham (Town)	02571
		Tewksbury	01876	Wareham Center	02571
				Warren	01083
				Warren (Town)	01083
				Warren Terrace	02359

266 MASSACHUSETTS Warrentown-Zylonite

Location	ZIP
Warrentown	02346
Warwick (Town)	01364
Warwick	01364
Washington	01223
Washington (Town)	01223
Watertown (Middlesex County) (Town)	02172
Watertown (Middlesex County)	02172
Waterville (Plymouth County)	02346
Waterville (Worcester County)	01475
Watuppa (Part of Fall River)	02721
Wauwinet	02554
Waverley	02179
Wawela Park	01570
Wayland	01778
Wayland (Town)	01778
Wayside Inn	01776
Webster (Worcester County) (Town)	01570
Webster (Worcester County)	01570
Webster Square (Part of Worcester)	01603
Wedgemere	01890
Weir Village (Part of Taunton)	02780
Wellesley (Norfolk County) (Town)	02181
Wellesley (Norfolk County)	02181
Wellesley Farms	02181
Wellesley Fells	02181
Wellesley Hills	02181
Wellfleet	02667
Wellfleet (Town)	02667
Wellington (Part of Medford)	02155
Wellville	01430
Wendell	01379
Wendell (Town)	01379
Wendell Depot	01380
Wenham (Essex County) (Town)	01984
Wenham (Essex County)	01984
West Abington	02351
West Acton	01720
West Andover	01810
West Auburn	01501
West Barnstable	02668
West Becket	01238
West Bedford	01730
West Berlin	01503
West Billerica	01862
Westborough (Worcester County) (Town)	01581
Westborough (Worcester County)	01581
West Boxford	01885
West Boylston	01583
West Boylston (Town)	01583
West Bridgewater	02379
West Bridgewater (Town)	02379
West Brimfield	01069
West Brookfield	01585
West Brookfield (Town)	01585
West Cambridge (Part of Cambridge)	02138
West Chatham	02669
West Chelmsford	01863
Westchester (Part of Worcester)	01605
West Chesterfield	01084
West Chop	02573
West Concord	01742
West Cummington	01026
Westdale	02333
West Deerfield	01342
West Dennis	02670
West Dudley	01550
West Duxbury	02332
West Falmouth	02574
West Farms (Part of Northampton)	01060
Westfield	01085-86
For specific Westfield Zip Codes call (413) 562-2221	
West Fitchburg (Part of Fitchburg)	01420
Westford	01886
Westford (Town)	01886
West Foxboro	02035
Westgate Mall (Part of Brockton)	02401
West Gloucester (Part of Gloucester)	01930
West Granville	01034
West Groton	01472
Westhampton	01027
Westhampton (Town)	01027
West Hanover	02339
West Harwich	02671
West Hatfield	01088
West Hawley	01339
West Hingham	02043
West Hyannisport	02672
Westlands	01824
West Leominster (Part of Leominster)	01453
West Leyden	01337
West Lynn (Part of Lynn)	01905
West Manchester	01944
West Mansfield	02048
West Medford (Part of Medford)	02156
West Medway	02053
West Millbury	01586
Westminster	01473
Westminster (Town)	01473
West Natick	01760
West New Boston	01255
West Newbury	01985
West Newbury (Town)	01985
West Newton (Part of Newton)	02165
Weston (Middlesex County) (Town)	02193
Weston (Middlesex County)	02193
West Otis	01245
Westover Air Force Base	01022
West Peabody (Part of Peabody)	01960
West Pelham	01002
Westport (Town)	02790
Westport	02790
Westport Factory	02790
Westport Point	02791
West Quincy (Part of Quincy)	02169
West Roxbury (Part of Boston)	02132
West Royalston	01331
West Side (Part of Worcester)	01602
West Somerville (Part of Somerville)	02144
West Springfield	01089-90
West Sterling	01564
West Stockbridge	01266
West Stockbridge (Town)	01266
West Stockbridge Center	01266
West Stoughton	02072
West Sutton	01527
West Tatnuck (Part of Worcester)	01602
West Tisbury	02575
West Tisbury (Town)	02575
West Townsend	01474
West Upton	01587
Westview	02038
Westville (Part of Taunton)	02780
West Walpole	02081
West Wareham	02576
West Warren	01092
West Watertown	02172
West Whately	01039
West Wind Shores	02532
Westwood	02090
Westwood (Town)	02090
West Worthington	01098
West Wrentham	02070
West Yarmouth	02673
Wethersfield	02019
Weymouth (Norfolk County) (Town)	02188
Weymouth (Norfolk County)	02188
Weymouth Heights	02188
Weymouth Landing	02188
Whalom	01420
Whately (Town)	01093
Whately (Franklin County)	01373
Whately (Franklin County)	01093
Wheelockville	01569
Wheelwright	01094
White City	01747
White City Shopping Center	01545
White Horse Beach	02381
White Island Shores	02538
White Oaks	01267
Whitinsville	01588
Whitman (Plymouth County) (Town)	02382
Whitman (Plymouth County)	02382
Whittenton (Part of Taunton)	02780
Wigginsville (Part of Lowell)	01850
Wilbraham	01095
Wilbraham (Town)	01095
Wilkinsonville	01527
Williamsburg	01096
Williamsburg (Town)	01096
Williamstown	01267
Williamstown (Town)	01267
Williamsville (Berkshire County)	01236
Williamsville (Worcester County)	01452
Wilmington (Middlesex County)	01887
Wilmington (Middlesex County) (Town)	01887
Wilson (Part of Gloucester)	01930
Winchendon	01475
Winchendon (Town)	01475
Winchendon Springs	01477
Winchester (Middlesex County) (Town)	01890
Winchester (Middlesex County)	01890
Winchester Highlands	01890
Windsor	01270
Windsor (Town)	01270
Winmere	01803
Winnecunnet	02766
Winslows	02062
Winter Hill (Part of Somerville)	02145
Winthrop (Suffolk County) (Town)	02152
Winthrop (Suffolk County)	02152
Winthrop Highlands	02152
Woburn	01801
Wollaston (Part of Quincy)	02170
Woodland Park	01501
Woods Hole	02543
Woods Hole Coast Guard Base	02543
Woodville	01784
Worcester	01601-15
For specific Worcester Zip Codes call (508) 795-3666	
Woronoco	01097
Woronoco Heights	01097
Worthington	01098
Worthington (Town)	01098
Worthington Center	01098
Wrentham	02093
Wrentham (Town)	02093
Wyben	01085
Wyoming (Part of Melrose)	02176
Yankee Orchards (Part of Pittsfield)	01201
Yarmouth	02675
Yarmouth (Town)	02675
Yarmouth Port	02675
Zoar	01367
Zylonite	01220

Abscota-Bedford **MICHIGAN** 267

	ZIP		ZIP		ZIP
Abscota	49029	Andrews	49104	Baie de Wasai	49783
Ackerson Lake	49201	Ann Arbor	48103-08	Bailey	49303
Acme	49610	For specific Ann Arbor Zip Codes		Bainbridge (Township)	49022
Acme (Township)	49610	call (313) 665-1100		Bainbridge Center	49022
Ada	49301	Ann Arbor (Township)	48105	Bakertown	49107
Ada (Township)	49301	Antioch (Township)	49688	Baldwin (Delta County) (Township)	49872
Adair	48062	Antoine (Part of Iron Mountain)	49801	Baldwin (Iosco County) (Township)	48770
Adams (Arenac County) (Township)	48659	Antrim (Antrim County)	49659	Baldwin (Lake County)	49304
Adams (Hillsdale County) (Township)	49262	Antrim (Shiawassee County) (Township)	48418	Baltic	49905
Adams (Houghton County) (Township)	49963	Antwerp (Township)	49065	Baltimore (Barry County) (Township)	49058
Adams Park	49097	Anvil Location	49911	Baltimore (Ontonagon County)	49912
Adamsville	49112	Aplin Beach	48706	Banat	49821
Addison (Lenawee County)	49220	Applegate	48401	Bancroft	48414
Addison (Oakland County) (Township)	48367	Arbela (Township)	48746	Banfield	49017
Adrian (Lenawee County)	49221	Arborland Consumer Mall (Part of Ann Arbor)	48104	Bangor (Bay County) (Township)	48706
Adrian (Lenawee County) (Township)	49221	Arbutus Beach	49735	Bangor (Van Buren County)	49013
Advance	49712	Arcada (Township)	48801	Bangor (Van Buren County) (Township)	49103
Aetna (Mecosta County) (Township)	49336	Arcade (Part of Ann Arbor)	48104	Bangor Township	48706
Aetna (Missaukee County) (Township)	48632	Arcadia (Township)	49613	Bankers	49242
Aetna (Newaygo County)	49412	Arcadia (Lapeer County) (Township)	48412	Banks (Township)	49729
Afton	49705	Arcadia (Manistee County)	49613	Banksons Lake	49065
Agate	49967	Arenac (Township)	48749	Bannister	48807
Agnew	49460	Argentine	48451	Baraga	49908
Ahmeek	49901	Argentine (Township)	48451	Baraga (Township)	49908
Airport Forest	48625	Argyle	48410	Barbeau	49710
Akron	48701	Argyle (Township)	48410	Barker Creek	49690
Akron (Township)	48701	Arlington (Township)	49013	Bark River	49807
Alabaster	48763	Armada	48005	Bark River (Township)	49807
Alabaster (Township)	48763	Armada (Township)	48005	Bar Lake	49660
Alaiedon (Township)	48854	Armstrong Corners	49079	Barnard	49720
Alamo	49009	Arnheim	49958	Barnes Lake-Millers Lake	48421
Alamo (Township)	49009	Arnold	49819	Baroda	49101
Alanson	49706	Artesia Beach	48656	Baroda (Township)	49101
Alaska	49302	Arthur (Township)	48617	Barron Lake	49120
Alba	49611	Arvon (Township)	49962	Barry (Township)	49060
Albee (Township)	48655	Ash (Township)	48117	Barryton	49305
Albert (Township)	49756	Ashland (Township)	49327	Barton (Township)	49338
Alberta	49946	Ashland Center	49327	Barton City	48705
Albion (Calhoun County)	49224	Ashley	48806	Barton Hills	48105
Albion (Calhoun County) (Township)	49224	Ashmore	48767	Barton Lake	49097
Albion (Houghton County)	49913	Ashton	49655	Base Line Lake	49055
Alcona (Alcona County)	48740	Askel	49958	Bass Lake	49449
Alcona (Alcona County) (Township)	48721	Assyria	49021	Batavia	49036
Alden	49612	Assyria (Township)	49021	Batavia (Township)	49036
Algansee (Township)	49082	Athens	49011	Batavia Center	49036
Alger	48610	Athens (Township)	49011	Bates (Grand Traverse County)	49690
Algoma (Township)	49341	Atlanta	49709	Bates (Iron County) (Township)	49935
Algonac	48001	Atlantic Mine	49905	Bath	48808
All Bright Shores	48612	Atlas	48411	Bath (Township)	48808
Allegan (Allegan County)	49010	Atlas (Township)	48438	Battle Creek	49015-17
Allegan (Allegan County) (Township)	49010	Attica	48412	For specific Battle Creek Zip Codes call (616) 965-3284	
Allen	49227	Attica (Township)	48412	Bauer	49426
Allen (Township)	49227	Atwood	49729	Baw Beese Lake	49242
Allendale (Township)	49401	Auburn	48611	Bay (Township)	49712
Allendale (Clare County)	48625	Auburn Hills	48321	Bay City	48706-08
Allendale (Ottawa County)	49401	Au Gres (Arenac County)	48703	For specific Bay City Zip Codes call (517) 895-5555	
Allen Park	48101	Au Gres (Arenac County) (Township)	48703	Bay de Noc (Township)	49878
Allenton	48002	Augusta (Kalamazoo County)	49012	Bay Mills (Township)	49715
Allenville	49760	Augusta (Washtenaw County) (Township)	48191	Bay Mills	49715
Allis (Township)	49765	Aura	49946	Bay Mills Indian Reservation	49715
Allouez	49805	Aurelius	48854	Bay Port	48720
Allouez (Township)	49805	Aurelius (Township)	48854	Bayshore	49711
Alma	48801	Aurora (Part of Ironwood)	49938	Bay View	49770
Almeda Beach	48653	Au Sable	48750	Beachwood	48654
Almena	49079	Au Sable (Iosco County) (Township)	48750	Beacon	49814
Almena (Township)	49079	Au Sable (Roscommon County) (Township)	48653	Beacon Hill	49905
Almer (Township)	48723	Au Sable River Park	48656	Beadle Lake	49017
Almira (Township)	49630	Austin (Hillsdale County)	49232	Beal City	48858
Almont	48003	Austin (Marquette County)	49841	Bear Creek (Township)	49770
Almont (Township)	48003	Austin (Mecosta County) (Township)	49346	Bearinger (Township)	49759
Aloha	49721	Austin (Sanilac County) (Township)	48475	Bear Lake (Township)	49614
Aloha (Township)	49721	Austin Center	48475	Bear Lake (Hillsdale County)	49242
Alpena (Alpena County)	49707	Austin Lake (Part of Portage)	49081	Bear Lake (Kalkaska County) (Township)	49646
Alpena (Alpena County) (Township)	49707	Au Train	49806	Bear Lake (Manistee County)	49614
Alpena Junction (Part of Alpena)	49707	Au Train (Township)	49806	Beaugrand (Township)	49721
Alpha	49902	Auvinen Corner	49938	Beaver (Bay County) (Township)	48611
Alpine	49321	Avalon Beach	48161	Beaver (Newaygo County) (Township)	49309
Alpine (Township)	49321	Averill	48640	Beaver Creek (Township)	48653
Alston	49958	Avery (Township)	49709	Beaverdam	49464
Alto	49302	Avoca	48006	Beaver Grove	49855
Altona	49336	Avondale	49631	Beaverton (Gladwin County)	48612
Alverno	49721	Azalia	48110	Beaverton (Gladwin County) (Township)	48612
Amador	48422	Bach	48759	Bedford	49020
Amasa	49903	Backus (Township)	48656	Bedford (Calhoun County) (Township)	49017
Amber (Township)	49431	Backus Beach	48762		
Amble	49329	Bad Axe	48413		
Amboy (Township)	49232	Bagley (Menominee County)	49821		
Anchorville	48004	Bagley (Otsego County) (Township)	49735		
Andersonville	48350				

268 MICHIGAN

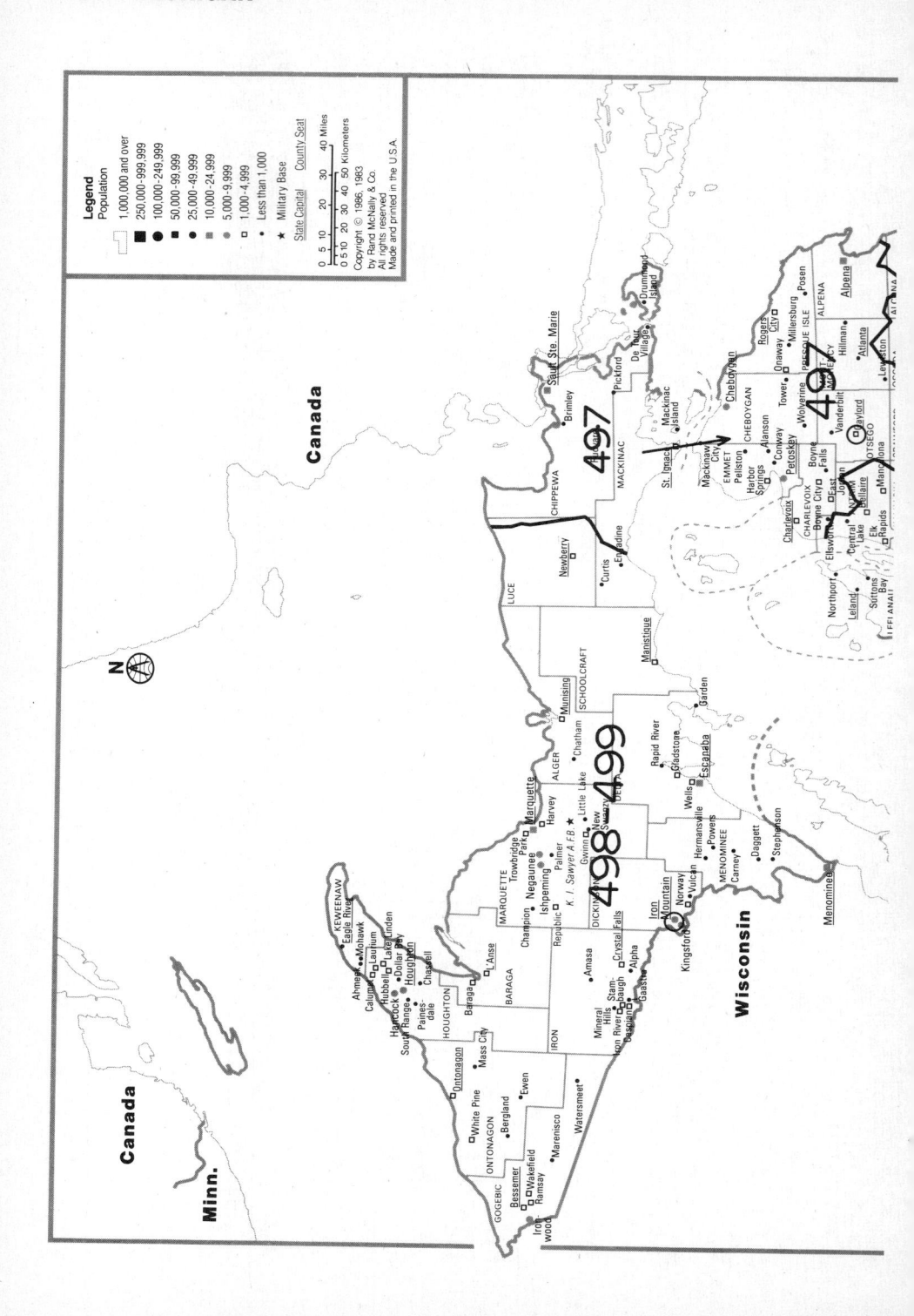

MICHIGAN 269

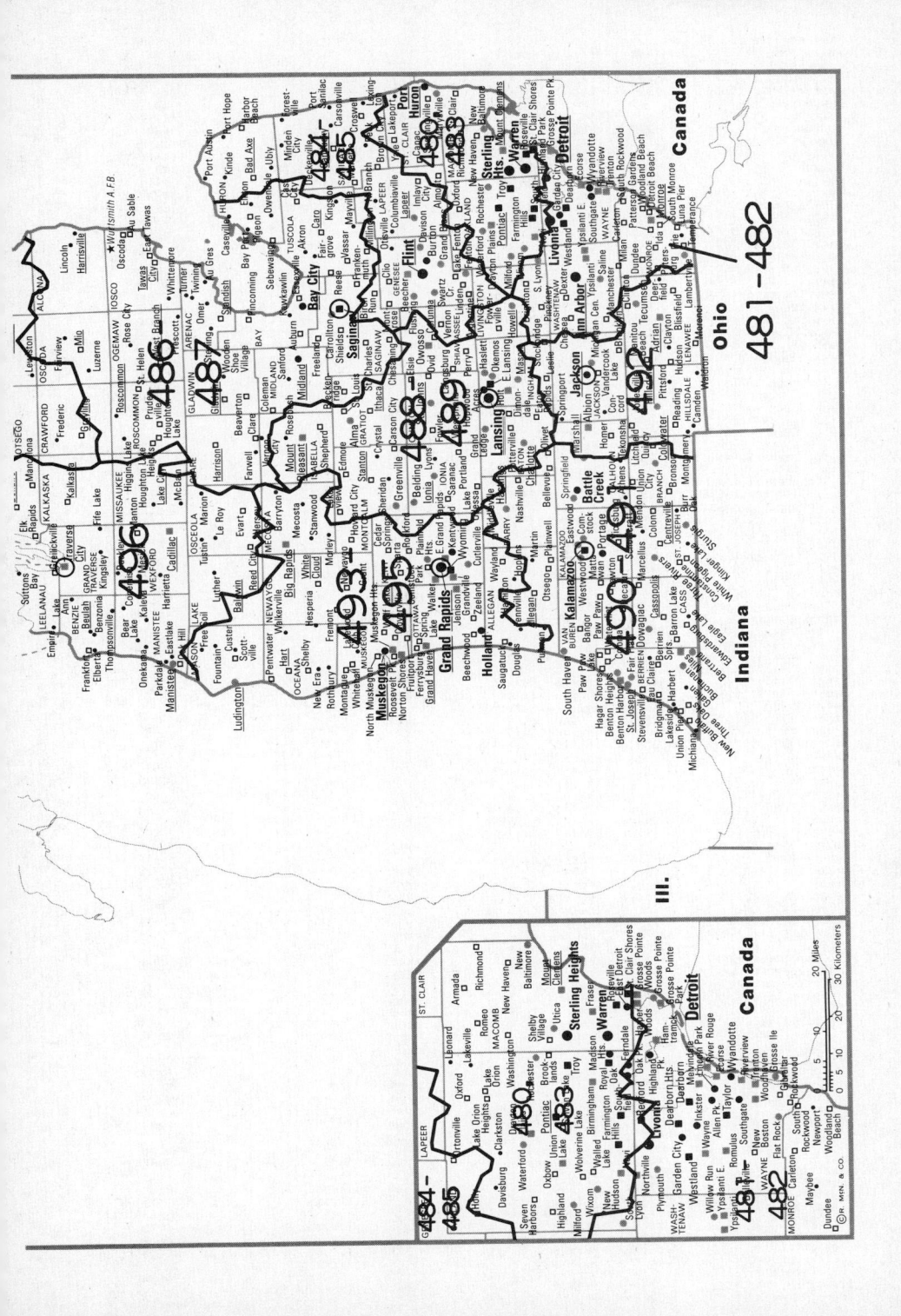

270 MICHIGAN Bedford-Caledonia

	ZIP		ZIP		ZIP
Bedford (Monroe County) (Township)	48182	Bitely	49309	Brighton (Livingston County)	48116
Beebe	48847	Black Lake Bluffs	49765	Brighton (Livingston County) (Township)	48116
Beecher	48458	Blackman (Township)	49202	Briley (Township)	49709
Beechwood (Iron County)	49909	Black River	48721	Brimley	49715
Beechwood (Ottawa County)	49423	Black River Harbor	49938	Brinton	48632
Belding	48809	Blaine (Benzie County) (Township)	49635	Bristol	49688
Belknap (Township)	48743	Blaine (St. Clair County)	48032	Britton	49229
Bell	49707	Blair (Township)	49684	Broad Acres	48043
Bellaire	49615	Blanchard	49310	Brockway	48097
Belleville	48111	Blaney Park	49836	Brockway (Township)	48097
Bellevue	49021	Blendon (Township)	49426	Brohman	49312
Bellevue (Township)	49021	Bliss	49755	Bronson (Branch County)	49028
Bell Oak	48892	Bliss (Township)	49755	Bronson (Branch County) (Township)	49028
Belmont	49306	Blissfield	49228	Brookfield	48813
Belsay (Part of Burton)	48503	Blissfield (Township)	49228	Brookfield (Eaton County) (Township)	48813
Belvedere	49720	Bloomer (Township)	48811	Brookfield (Huron County) (Township)	48754
Belvidere (Township)	48886	Bloomfield (Huron County) (Township)	48468	Brooklyn	49230
Bendon	49643	Bloomfield (Missaukee County) (Township)	49651	Brooks (Township)	49337
Bengal (Township)	48879	Bloomfield (Oakland County) (Township)	48302	Brookside	49412
Bennington	48867	Bloomfield Glens	48322	Brookville	48170
Bennington (Township)	48867	Bloomfield Hills	48302-04	Broomfield (Township)	49340
Benona (Township)	49455	For specific Bloomfield Hills Zip Codes call (313) 642-7030		Brown (Township)	49660
Bentheim	49419	Bloomfield Hills North	48302	Brown City	48416
Bentley (Bay County)	48613	Bloomfield Township	48302	Brownlee Park	49017
Bentley (Gladwin County) (Township)	48652	Bloomfield Town Square	48302	Brownstown (Township)	48134
Bentleys Corners	49245	Bloomfield Village	48010	Brownsville	49031
Benton (Cheboygan County) (Township)	49721	Bloomingdale	49026	Brownwood Lake	49079
Benton (Eaton County) (Township)	48876	Bloomingdale (Township)	49026	Bruce (Chippewa County) (Township)	49783
Benton Charter (Township)	49022	Blue Jacket	49913	Bruce (Macomb County) (Township)	48065
Benton Harbor	49022-23	Blue Lake (Kalkaska County) (Township)	49646	Bruce Crossing	49912
For specific Benton Harbor Zip Codes call (616) 926-8227		Blue Lake (Muskegon County) (Township)	49461	Bruningville	49779
Benton Heights	49022	Blue Water Beach	48450	Brunswick	49313
Benzonia	49616	Bluff Beach	49099	Brutus	49716
Benzonia (Township)	49616	Blumfield (Township)	48757	Buchanan (Berrien County)	49107
Bergland	49910	Blumfield Corners	48757	Buchanan (Berrien County) (Township)	49107
Bergland (Township)	49910	Boardman (Township)	49680	Buckeye (Township)	48624
Berkley	48072	Bohemia (Township)	49965	Buckley	49620
Berlamont	49026	Boichott Acres	48906	Bucks Corners	49449
Berlin (Ionia County) (Township)	48846	Bois Blanc (Township)	49775	Buel (Township)	48422
Berlin (Monroe County) (Township)	48166	Bolles Harbor	48161	Buena Vista Charter (Township)	48601
Berlin (St. Clair County) (Township)	48002	Bombay	48640	Bullock Creek	48640
Berne	48755	Boon	49618	Bumbletown	49805
Berrien (Township)	49102	Boon (Township)	49618	Bunker Hill	49251
Berrien Center	49102	Bootjack	49945	Bunker Hill (Township)	49251
Berrien Springs	49103	Borculo	49464	Bunny Run	48362
Bertrand (Berrien County)	49120	Boston (Houghton County)	49930	Burdell (Township)	49688
Bertrand (Berrien County) (Township)	49120	Boston (Ionia County) (Township)	48881	Burdickville	49664
Berville	48002	Bostwick Lake	49341	Burgess	49720
Bessemer (Gogebic County)	49911	Bourret (Township)	48610	Burleigh (Township)	48770
Bessemer (Gogebic County) (Township)	49959	Bowens Mills	49333	Burley Corner	49017
Bete Grise	49950	Bowne (Township)	49302	Burlington	49029
Bethany (Township)	48880	Boyne City	49712	Burlington (Calhoun County) (Township)	49029
Bethany Beach	49125	Boyne Falls	49713	Burlington (Lapeer County) (Township)	48727
Bethel (Township)	49028	Boyne Valley (Township)	49713	Burnips	49314
Betzer	49271	Bradley	49311	Burns (Township)	48418
Beulah	49617	Brady (Kalamazoo County) (Township)	49097	Burnside (Township)	48416
Beverly Hills (Marquette County)	49866	Brady (Saginaw County) (Township)	48649	Burr Oak	49030
Beverly Hills (Oakland County)	48009	Brampton	49837	Burr Oak (Township)	49030
Big Bay	49808	Brampton (Township)	49837	Burt (Alger County) (Township)	49839
Big Creek (Township)	48647	Branch (Mason County)	49402	Burt (Cheboygan County) (Township)	49721
Biggs Settlement	48647	Branch (Mason County) (Township)	49458	Burt (Saginaw County)	48417
Big Prairie (Township)	49349	Brandon (Township)	48462	Burtchville (Township)	48060
Big Rapids (Mecosta County)	49307	Brandywine Lake	49055	Burt Lake	49717
Big Rapids (Mecosta County) (Township)	49307	Brant	48614	Burton (Genesee County)	48509
Big Rock	49709	Brant (Township)	48614	Burton (Shiawassee County)	48867
Billings (Township)	48612	Brassar	49783	Burton-Northeast (Part of Burton)	48509
Bingham (Clinton County) (Township)	48879	Bravo	49408	Burton-Southeast (Part of Burton)	48529
Bingham (Huron County) (Township)	48475	Breckenridge	48615	Bushnell (Township)	48884
Bingham (Leelanau County) (Township)	49684	Breedsville	49027	Butler (Township)	49082
Bingham Farms	48010	Breen (Township)	49834	Butman (Township)	48624
Birch Beach	48450	Breezy Beach	49099	Butterfield (Township)	48632
Birch Creek	49858	Breitung (Township)	49876	Butternut	48811
Birch Run	48415	Brent Creek	48433	Byron (Kent County) (Township)	49315
Birch Run (Township)	48415	Brethren	49619	Byron (Shiawassee County)	48418
Birchwood (Berrien County)	49115	Bretton Woods	48917	Byron Center	49315
Birchwood (Cheboygan County)	49721	Brevort (Mackinac County)	49760	Cadillac	49601
Birmingham	48009-12	Brevort (Mackinac County) (Township)	49760	Cadmus	49231
For specific Birmingham Zip Codes call (313) 646-4431		Bridgehampton (Township)	48419	Cady	48044
Birmingham Farms	48010	Bridgeport	48722	Calcite (Part of Rogers City)	49779
Bismarck (Township)	49779	Bridgeport (Township)	48722	Calderwood	49967
		Bridgeton	49327	Caldwell (Township)	49651
		Bridgeton (Township)	49327	Caledonia (Kent County) (Township)	49316
		Bridgeville	48879	Caledonia (Shiawassee County) (Township)	48817
		Bridgewater	48115		
		Bridgewater (Township)	48158		
		Bridgman	49106		
		Brightmoor (Part of Detroit)	48223		

Caledonia-Cornell **MICHIGAN** 271

	ZIP		ZIP		ZIP
Caledonia (Alcona County) (Township)	48762	Ceresco	49033	Cleon (Township)	49625
Caledonia (Kent County)	49316	Chamberlains	49067	Cleveland (Township)	49664
California	49255	Champion	49814	Clifford	48727
California (Township)	49255	Champion (Township)	49814	Climax	49034
Calumet	49913	Chandler (Charlevoix County) (Township)	49712	Climax (Township)	49034
Calumet (Township)	49913			Clinton	49236
Calvin (Township)	49031	Chandler (Huron County) (Township)	48731	Clinton (Township)	49236
Calvin Center	49031			Clinton (Macomb County) (Township)	48043
Cambria	49242	Channing	49815		
Cambria (Township)	49242	Chapin	48841	Clinton (Oscoda County) (Township)	48619
Cambridge (Township)	49265	Chapin (Township)	48841		
Cambridge Junction	49230	Charleston (Kalamazoo County) (Township)	49053	Clinton Township	48043
Camden	49232			Clinton Village	48906
Camden (Township)	49232	Charleston (Sanilac County)	48456	Clio	48420
Campbell (Township)	48815	Charlevoix (Charlevoix County)	49720	Cloverdale	49035
Campbells Corner	48367			Cloverville	49444
Campbells Corners	48661	Charlevoix (Charlevoix County) (Township)	49720	Clyde (Allegan County) (Township)	49408
Camp Grayling	49739				
Canada Corners	49318	Charlotte	48813	Clyde (Oakland County)	48356
Canada Creek Ranch	49709	Charlton (Township)	49751	Clyde (St. Clair County) (Township)	48049
Canada Shores	49036	Chase	49623		
Canal (Part of Sault Ste. Marie)	49783	Chase (Township)	49623	Coats Grove	49058
		Chassell	49916	Coddes Beach	49765
Canandaigua	49235	Chassell (Township)	49916	Cody (Part of Flint)	48507
Canfield Beach	49765	Chatham	49816	Coe	48880
Cannon (Township)	49341	Chatham Corners (Part of Chatham)	49816	Coe (Township)	48880
Cannonsburg	49317			Cohoctah	48816
Canton	48187	Chauncey	49306	Cohoctah (Township)	48816
Canton (Township)	48184	Cheboygan	49721	Cohoctah Center	48816
Capac	48014	Chelsea	48118	Cold Springs (Township)	49646
Caribou Lake	49725	Cherry Beach	48039	Coldwater (Branch County)	49036
Carland	48810	Cherry Bend	49684	Coldwater (Branch County) (Township)	49036
Carleton	48117	Cherry Grove (Township)	49601		
Carlisle	49508	Cherry Hill	48187	Coldwater (Isabella County) (Township)	48632
Carlshend	49885	Cherry Island (Part of Rockwood)	48173		
Carlton (Township)	49058			Coleman	48618
Carlton Center	49325	Cherryland Mall (Part of Traverse City)	49684	Colfax (Benzie County) (Township)	49683
Carmel (Township)	48813				
Carney	49812	Cherry Valley (Township)	49623	Colfax (Huron County) (Township)	48413
Caro	48723	Chesaning	48616		
Carp Lake	49718	Chesaning (Township)	48616	Colfax (Mecosta County) (Township)	49307
Carp Lake (Emmet County) (Township)	49718	Cheshire (Township)	49010		
		Cheshire Center	49010	Colfax (Oceana County) (Township)	49459
Carp Lake (Ontonagon County) (Township)	49953	Chester	48813		
		Chester (Township)	48813	Colfax (Wexford County) (Township)	49663
Carrollton (Saginaw County) (Township)	48724	Chester (Otsego County) (Township)	49735		
				College Park (Part of Detroit)	48221
Carrollton (Saginaw County)	48724	Chester (Ottawa County) (Township)	49403		
Carr Settlement	49402			College Town	48706
Carson City	48811	Chesterfield (Macomb County)	48045	Colling	48767
Carsonville	48419			Collins	48851
Cascade	49506	Chesterfield (Macomb County) (Township)	48047	Coloma (Berrien County)	49038
Cascade (Township)	49506			Coloma (Berrien County) (Township)	49038
Casco (Allegan County) (Township)	49090	Chestonia (Township)	49611		
		Chicagoan Lake	49920	Colon (Township)	49040
Casco (St. Clair County) (Township)	48062	Chicora	49010	Colon	49040
		Chief Lake	49645	Columbia (Jackson County) (Township)	49230
Case (Township)	49759	Chikaming (Township)	49116		
Caseville	48725	China (Township)	48079	Columbia (Tuscola County) (Township)	48767
Caseville (Township)	48725	Chippewa (Chippewa County) (Township)	49790		
Cash	48471			Columbia (Van Buren County) (Township)	49056
Casnovia	49318	Chippewa (Isabella County) (Township)	48858		
Casnovia (Township)	49318			Columbiaville	48421
Caspian	49915	Chippewa (Mecosta County) (Township)	49320	Columbus (Luce County) (Township)	49853
Cass City	48726				
Cassidy Lake Technical School	48118	Chippewa Lake	49320	Columbus (St. Clair County) (Township)	48062
		Chippewa Vista	49305		
Cassopolis	49031	Chocolay (Township)	49855	Colwood	48767
Castle Park	49423	Christie Lake	49064	Comins (Oscoda County)	48619
Castleton (Township)	49073	Christmas	49862	Comins (Oscoda County) (Township)	48621
Cathro	49707	Churchill (Muskegon County)	49441		
Cato (Township)	48850			Commerce	48387
Cedar (Leelanau County)	49621	Churchill (Ogemaw County) (Township)	48661	Commerce (Township)	48382
Cedar (Osceola County) (Township)	49631			Comstock	49041
		Circle Pine Center	49046	Comstock (Township)	49041
Cedar Bluff	49090	Cisco Lake	49969	Comstock Park	49321
Cedar Creek (Barry County)	49046	Clam Lake (Township)	49601	Concord	49237
Cedar Creek (Muskegon County) (Township)	49457	Clam River	49615	Concord (Township)	49237
		Clam Union (Township)	48632	Condit	49245
		Clare	48617	Cone	48160
Cedar Creek (Wexford County) (Township)	49663	Clarence (Township)	49224	Conklin	49403
		Clarendon	49245	Connorville	49968
Cedar Lake (Montcalm County)	48812	Clarendon (Township)	49245	Constantine	49042
		Clarion	49713	Constantine (Township)	49042
Cedar Lake (Van Buren County)	49067	Clark (Township)	49719	Convis (Township)	49017
		Clarklake	49234	Conway (Emmet County)	49722
Cedar River	49813	Clarkston	48346-48	Conway (Livingston County) (Township)	48836
Cedar Springs	49319	For specific Clarkston Zip Codes call (313) 625-0032.			
Cedarville (Mackinac County)	49719			Cooks	49817
		Clarksville	48815	Cooks Corners	48809
Cedarville (Menominee County) (Township)	49813	Clawson	48017	Cooper (Township)	49007
		Clay (Township)	48001	Cooper Center	49007
Cement City	49233	Claybanks (Township)	49452	Coopersville	49404
Centennial Heights	49913	Clayton (Arenac County) (Township)	48659	Copemish	49625
Center (Township)	49769			Copenhagen	49854
Center Line	48015	Clayton (Genesee County) (Township)	48473	Copper City	49917
Centerville (Township)	49621			Copper Harbor	49918
Central	49950	Clayton (Lenawee County)	49235	Coral	49322
Central Lake	49622	Clear Lake	48661	Corey	49093
Central Lake (Township)	49622	Clearwater (Township)	49676	Corinne	49838
Centreville	49032	Clement (Township)	48610	Cornell	49818

272 MICHIGAN Cornell-Easton

Name	ZIP
Cornell (Township)	49818
Corrections Camp Program	49240
Corunna	48817
Corwith (Township)	49795
Coryell Islands	49719
Cottage Grove	48653
Cottage Park	49724
Cottrellville (Township)	48039
Court (Part of Kalamazoo)	49007
Courtland (Township)	49341
Courtland Center (Part of Burton)	48509
Covert	49043
Covert (Township)	49043
Covington	49919
Covington (Township)	49919
Cranbrook (Part of Bloomfield Hills)	48303
Crescent Lake Estates	48327
Crisp	49423
Crockery (Township)	49448
Crofton	49680
Crooked Lake (Barry County)	49046
Crooked Lake (Livingston County)	48116
Crossroads, The (Part of Portage)	49081
Cross Village	49723
Cross Village (Township)	49723
Croswell	48422
Croton	49337
Croton (Township)	49337
Croton Heights	49337
Crump	48634
Crystal	48818
Crystal (Montcalm County) (Township)	48818
Crystal (Oceana County) (Township)	49420
Crystal Beach	49036
Crystal Falls (Iron County) (Township)	49920
Crystal Falls (Iron County)	49920
Crystal Lake (Township)	49635
Crystal Valley	49420
Cumber	48475
Cumming (Township)	48635
Cunard	49847
Curran	48728
Curtis (Alcona County) (Township)	48737
Curtis (Mackinac County)	49820
Curtisville	48761
Custer (Mason County) (Township)	49405
Custer (Sanilac County) (Township)	48471
Custer (Antrim County) (Township)	49659
Custer (Mason County)	49405
Cutlerville	49508
Dafter	49724
Dafter (Township)	49724
Daggett	49821
Daggett (Township)	49821
Dailey	49031
Dallas (Township)	48835
Dalton	49445
Dalton (Township)	49445
Damon	48654
Danby (Township)	48890
Danish Landing	49738
Dansville	48819
Darragh	49646
Davis	48094
Davisburg	48350
Davison (Genesee County)	48423
Davison (Genesee County) (Township)	48423
Day (Township)	48852
Dayton (Berrien County)	49113
Dayton (Newaygo County) (Township)	49412
Dayton (Tuscola County) (Township)	48744
Dayton Center	49412
Dealno	48703
Dearborn	48120-26
For specific Dearborn Zip Codes call (313) 337-4711	
Dearborn Heights	48127
Decatur	49045
Decatur (Township)	49045
Decker	48426
Deckerville	48427
Deep River (Township)	48659
Deerfield (Livingston County) (Township)	48451

Name	ZIP
Deerfield (Mecosta County) (Township)	49336
Deerfield (Isabella County) (Township)	48858
Deerfield (Lapeer County) (Township)	48421
Deerfield (Lenawee County)	49238
Deerfield Center (Isabella County)	48858
Deerfield Center (Livingston County)	48451
Deer Park	49868
Deerton	49822
Deford	48729
Dehoco	48175
Delaware (Township)	49456
Delhi (Township)	48842
Delray (Part of Detroit)	48217
Delta (Township)	48917
Delta Mills	48917
Delton	49046
Delwin	48858
Denmark (Township)	48758
Denton (Roscommon County) (Township)	48651
Denton (Wayne County)	48111
Denver (Isabella County) (Township)	48858
Denver (Newaygo County) (Township)	49421
Derby	49127
Detour (Township)	49725
De Tour Village	49725
Detroit	**48201-44**
For specific Detroit Zip Codes call (313) 271-6544	
COLLEGES & UNIVERSITIES	
Marygrove College	48221
Mercy College of Detroit	48219
University of Detroit	48221
FINANCIAL INSTITUTIONS	
Comerica Bank-Detroit	48226
Detroit Federal Savings & Loan Association	48226
First Federal of Michigan	48226
First of America Bank-Southeast Michigan	48226
Manufacturers National Bank of Detroit	48243
National Bank of Detroit	48226
HOSPITALS	
Children's Hospital of Michigan	48201
Detroit Receiving Hospital and University Health Center	48201
Detroit-Macomb Hospital Corporation	48214
Grace Hospital	48235
Harper Hospital	48201
Henry Ford Hospital	48202
Holy Cross Hospital	48234
Hutzel Hospital	48201
Mount Carmel Mercy Hospital	48235
North Detroit General Hospital	48212
Samaritan Health Center	48213
Sinai Hospital of Detroit	48235
St. John Hospital and Medical Center	48236
HOTELS/MOTELS	
Hotel Pontchartrain	48226
Hotel St. Regis	48202
Marriott Airport	48242
The Westin Hotel	48243
MILITARY INSTALLATIONS	
Coast Guard Base, Detroit	48207
Detroit Marine Terminal, Inc.	48218
United States Army Engineer District, Detroit	48231
United States Army Engineer District, Detroit Area Office	48209
Detroit Beach	48161
Detroit River (Part of Detroit)	48222
Devereaux	49224
Devils Lake	49253
De Witt (Clinton County)	48820
De Witt (Clinton County) (Township)	48820
Dexter (Washtenaw County)	48130
Dexter (Washtenaw County) (Township)	48169

Name	ZIP
Diamond Lake	49349
Diamond Shores	49031
Diamond Springs	49419
Dice Corners	48640
Dickson (Township)	49619
Diffin	49891
Dighton	49688
Dimondale	48821
Diorite	49814
Disco	48315
Dixboro	48105
Dodgeville	49921
Dollar Bay	49922
Dollar Settlement	49715
Dollarville	49868
Dolph	49632
Donaldson	49783
Donken	49965
Donoghue Beach	49707
Doriva Beach	49721
Dorr	49323
Dorr (Township)	49323
Doster	49080
Doughertys Corners	49009
Douglas	49406
Douglass (Township)	48888
Dover (Lake County) (Township)	49656
Dover (Lenawee County) (Township)	49235
Dover (Otsego County) (Township)	49738
Dowagiac	49047
Dowling	49050
Downington	48427
Downtown (Genesee County)	48502
Downtown (Ingham County)	48924
Downtown (Midland County)	48640
Doyle (Township)	49840
Drayton Plains	48330
Drenthe	49464
Drummond (Township)	49726
Drummond Island	49726
Dryburg	49780
Dryden	48428
Dryden (Township)	48428
Dublin	49689
Duck Lake (Allegan County)	49055
Duck Lake (Calhoun County)	49224
Duel	48640
Duffield	48473
Dukes	49885
Duncan (Township)	48131
Dundee	48131
Dundee (Township)	48131
Dunham Lake	48092
Dunningville	49010
Duplain	48879
Duplain (Township)	48831
Durand	48429
Dutton	49316
Dwight (Township)	48445
Eagle	48822
Eagle (Township)	48822
Eagle Harbor	49950
Eagle Harbor (Township)	49950
Eagle Lake (Cass County)	49112
Eagle Lake (Van Buren County)	49079
Eagle Point	49031
Eagle River	49924
East Bay (Township)	49684
Eastbrook Mall (Part of Grand Rapids)	49508
East China (Township)	48039
East Cooper	49004
East Dayton	48723
East Detroit	48021
Eastgate Shopping Center (Part of Roseville)	48066
East Gilead	49028
East Grand Rapids	49506
East Houghton (Part of Houghton)	49931
East Jordan	49727
East Kingsford	49801
Eastlake	49626
Eastland Center (Part of Harper Woods)	48225
East Lansing	48823-26
For specific East Lansing Zip Codes call (517) 351-3205	
East Leroy	49051
Eastmanville	49404
Easton (Ionia County) (Township)	48846
Easton (Shiawassee County)	48867

Detroit **MICHIGAN** 273

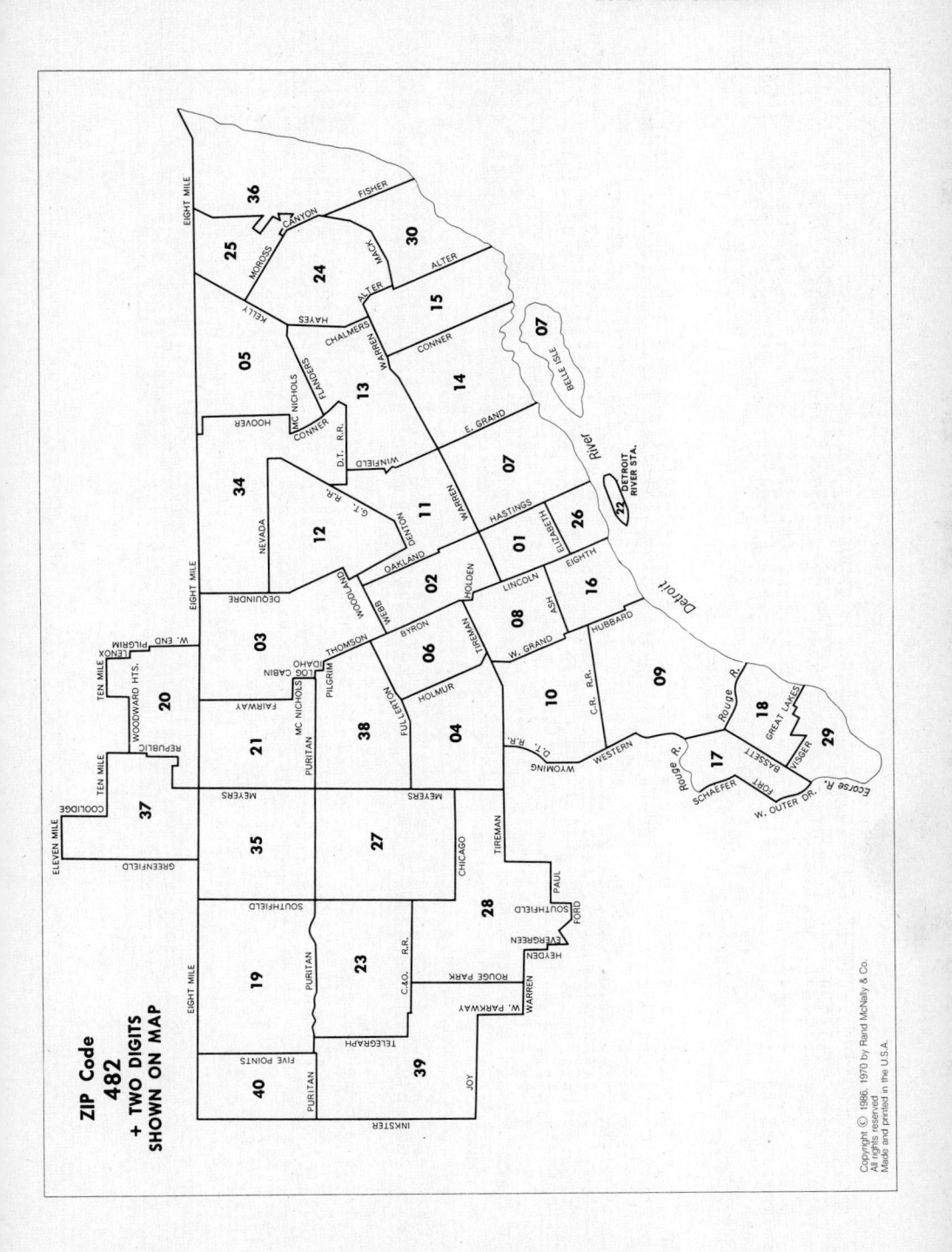

274 MICHIGAN East Paris-Frost Corners

Place	ZIP
East Paris (Part of Kentwood)	49508
Eastport	49627
East Rockwood	48173
East Saugatuck	49419
East Sebewa	48890
East Side (Saginaw County)	48601
East Tawas	48730
Eastview	48065
Eastwood	49001
Eaton (Township)	48813
Eaton Rapids (Eaton County)	48827
Eaton Rapids (Eaton County) (Township)	48827
Eau Claire	49111
Eben Junction	49825
Echo (Township)	49622
Eckerman	49728
Eckford	49245
Eckford (Township)	49245
Ecorse	48229
Eden (Ingham County)	48854
Eden (Lake County) (Township)	49644
Eden (Mason County) (Township)	49454
Edenville (Township)	48620
Edenville	48620
Edgemont Park	48917
Edgerton	49341
Edmore	48829
Edwards (Township)	48661
Edwardsburg	49112
Edwards Corners	49067
Egelston (Township)	49442
Eight Point Lake	48632
Elba (Township)	48446
Elba (Gratiot County) (Township)	48807
Elba (Lapeer County)	48446
Elberta	49628
Elbridge (Township)	49459
Elizabeth Lake Estates	48327
Elk (Lake County) (Township)	49644
Elk (Sanilac County) (Township)	48466
Elkland (Township)	48726
Elk Rapids	49629
Elk Rapids (Township)	49629
Elkton	48731
Ellington (Township)	48723
Ellis (Township)	49705
Ellsworth (Antrim County)	49729
Ellsworth (Lake County) (Township)	49656
Elmdale	48815
Elmer (Oscoda County) (Township)	48647
Elmer (Sanilac County) (Township)	48471
Elm Hall	48830
Elmira	49730
Elmira (Township)	49730
Elm River (Township)	49965
Elmwood (Leelanau County) (Township)	49684
Elmwood (Tuscola County) (Township)	48726
Elo	49958
Eloise (Part of Westland)	48185
Elsie	48831
Elwell	48832
Ely (Township)	49814
Emerson (Township)	48615
Emmet (Township)	49017
Emmett	48022
Emmett (Township)	48022
Empire	49630
Empire (Township)	49630
Engadine	49827
Ensign	49878
Ensign (Township)	49878
Ensley (Township)	49329
Ensley Center	49343
Enterprise (Township)	49667
Entrican	48888
Epoufette	49762
Epsilon	49770
Erie	48133
Erie (Township)	48133
Erwin (Township)	49938
Escanaba (Delta County)	49829
Escanaba (Delta County) (Township)	49829
Essex (Township)	48879
Essexville	48732
Estey	48652
Estral Beach	48166
Eureka (Clinton County)	48833

Place	ZIP
Eureka (Montcalm County) (Township)	48838
Evangeline (Township)	49712
Evans	49319
Evans Lake	49287
Evart (Osceola County)	49631
Evart (Osceola County) (Township)	49631
Eveline (Township)	49727
Everett (Township)	49349
Evergreen (Montcalm County) (Township)	48884
Evergreen (Sanilac County) (Township)	48426
Evergreen Acres	48161
Evergreen Shores	49781
Ewen	49925
Ewing (Township)	49880
Excelsior (Township)	49646
Exeter (Township)	48159
Eyedywild Beach	49735
Fabius (Township)	49093
Factoryville	49066
Fairbanks (Township)	49817
Fairfax	49040
Fairfield	49221
Fairfield (Lenawee County) (Township)	49221
Fairfield (Shiawassee County) (Township)	48831
Fairgrove	48733
Fairgrove (Township)	48733
Fairhaven (Huron County) (Township)	48720
Fair Haven (St. Clair County)	48023
Fairlane Town Center (Part of Dearborn)	48121
Fair Plain (Berrien County)	49022
Fairplain (Montcalm County) (Township)	48838
Fairplain Plaza	49022
Fairport	49817
Fairview	48621
Fairview Heights	48197
Faithorn	49892
Faithorn (Township)	49892
Falmouth	49632
Fargo	48006
Farmers Creek	48455
Farmington	48331-36
For specific Farmington Zip Codes call (313) 474-9409	
Farmington Hills	48331-34
For specific Farmington Hills Zip Codes call (313) 553-3910	
Farrandville	48420
Farwell	48622
Fawn River	49091
Fawn River (Township)	49091
Fayette (Delta County)	49817
Fayette (Hillsdale County) (Township)	49250
Federal (Part of Saginaw)	48606
Federal Correctional Institution	48160
Felch	49831
Felch (Township)	49831
Felch Mountain	49801
Fenkell (Part of Detroit)	48238
Fennville	49408
Fenton (Genesee County)	48430
Fenton (Genesee County) (Township)	48430
Fenwick	48834
Ferndale	48220
Ferris (Township)	48891
Ferry	49455
Ferry (Township)	49455
Ferrysburg	49409
Fibre	49780
Fife Lake	49633
Fife Lake (Township)	49633
Filer (Township)	49660
Filer City	49634
Filion	48432
Fillmore (Township)	49423
Fillmore	49423
Findlay	49030
Fisher (Part of Wyoming)	49509
Fisher Building (Part of Detroit)	48211
Fisherville	48611
Fitchburg	49285
Five Lakes	48446
Five Points	48867
Flat Rock (Delta County)	49837
Flat Rock (Wayne County)	48134
Flint	48501-32
For specific Flint Zip Codes call (313) 257-1574	

Place	ZIP
Flint (Township)	48532
Florence (Township)	49042
Florida	49913
Flowerfield	49093
Flowerfield (Township)	49093
Floyd	48640
Flushing (Genesee County)	48433
Flushing (Genesee County) (Township)	48433
Flynn (Township)	48453
Foote Site Village	48750
Ford Lake	49410
Ford River (Township)	49829
Ford River (railroad station) (Delta County)	49807
Ford River (Delta County)	49829
Forest (Cheboygan County) (Township)	49792
Forest (Genesee County) (Township)	48463
Forest (Missaukee County) (Township)	49651
Forester	48419
Forester (Township)	48419
Forest Grove	49426
Forest Grove Station	49426
Forest Hill	48801
Forest Hills	49506
Forest Home (Township)	49615
Forest Lake	49862
Forestville	48434
Fork (Township)	49305
Forsyth (Township)	49833
Fort Dearborn (Part of Dearborn)	48124
Fort Gratiot (Township)	48060
Fortune Lake	49920
Foster (Township)	48661
Foster City	49834
Fosters	48415
Fostoria	48435
Fountain	49410
Fountain Park	49266
Four Mile Corner	49868
Fowler	48835
Fowlerville	48836
Fox	49813
Fox Creek (Part of Detroit)	48215
Francisco	49240
Frandor Shopping Center (Part of Lansing)	48917
Frankenlust (Township)	48706
Frankenmuth (Saginaw County)	48734
Frankenmuth (Saginaw County) (Township)	48734
Frankentrost	48601
Frankfort	49635
Franklin (Clare County) (Township)	48625
Franklin (Houghton County) (Township)	49930
Franklin (Lenawee County) (Township)	49287
Franklin (Oakland County)	48025
Franklin Mine	49930
Fraser (Bay County) (Township)	48634
Fraser (Macomb County)	48026
Freda	49905
Frederic	49733
Frederic (Township)	49733
Fredonia (Township)	49068
Freedom (Township)	48158
Freeland	48623
Freeman (Township)	48632
Freeport	49325
Free Soil	49411
Free Soil (Township)	49411
Freiburger	48475
Fremont (Isabella County) (Township)	49310
Fremont (Newaygo County)	49412
Fremont (Saginaw County) (Township)	48655
Fremont (Sanilac County) (Township)	48097
Fremont (Tuscola County) (Township)	48744
French Landing (Part of Romulus)	48174
Frenchtown (Marquette County)	49849
Frenchtown (Monroe County) (Township)	48161
French Town (Oceana County)	49449
Friendship (Township)	49740
Frontier	49239
Frost (Township)	48625
Frost Corners	48875

Fruitland-Harrisville **MICHIGAN** **275**

Name	ZIP
Fruitland (Township)	49461
Fruitport (Township)	49415
Fruitport	49415
Fruitport Siding (Part of Norton Shores)	49444
Fulton (Gratiot County) (Township)	48871
Fulton (Kalamazoo County)	49052
Fulton (Keweenaw County)	49950
Fulton Center	48871
Gaastra	49927
Gagetown	48735
Gaines	48436
Gaines (Genesee County) (Township)	48436
Gaines (Kent County) (Township)	49508
Galesburg	49053
Galien	49113
Galien (Township)	49113
Ganges	49408
Ganges (Township)	49408
Garden	49835
Garden (Township)	49835
Garden City	48135
Garden Corners	49817
Gardendale	48060
Gardenville	49783
Gardner	49821
Garfield (Bay County) (Township)	48634
Garfield (Clare County) (Township)	49684
Garfield (Grand Traverse County) (Township)	49684
Garfield (Kalkaska County) (Township)	49633
Garfield (Mackinac County) (Township)	49827
Garfield (Newaygo County) (Township)	49337
Garnet	49762
Garth	49878
Gay	49928
Gaylord	49735
General Post Office (Part of Detroit)	48233
Genesee	48437
Genesee (Township)	48437
Geneva (Midland County) (Township)	48618
Geneva (Van Buren County) (Township)	49056
Genoa (Township)	48116
Georgetown (Township)	49426
Gera	48734
Germfask	49836
Germfask (Township)	49836
Gerrish (Township)	48653
Gibraltar	48173
Gibson (Allegan County)	49423
Gibson (Bay County) (Township)	48613
Gilbo Corners	49679
Gilchrist	49762
Gilead	49028
Gilead (Township)	49028
Gilford	48736
Gilford (Township)	48736
Gilmore (Benzie County) (Township)	49628
Gilmore (Isabella County) (Township)	48622
Gingellville	48359
Girard	49036
Girard (Township)	49036
Gladstone	49837
Gladwin (Gladwin County)	48624
Gladwin (Gladwin County) (Township)	48624
Glen Arbor	49636
Glen Arbor (Township)	49636
Glencoe Hills Apartments (Part of Ann Arbor)	48108
Glendale	49079
Glendora	49107
Glen Haven	49621
Glenn	49416
Glenn Haven Shores	49090
Glennie	48737
Glenn Shores	49090
Glenside (Part of Norton Shores)	49441
Glenwood	49047
Gobles	49055
Goetzville	49736
Goiden (Township)	49436
Golfcrest	48161
Goodar (Township)	48761
Goodells	48027
Good Hart	49737

Name	ZIP
Goodison	48306
Goodland (Township)	48444
Goodrich	48438
Goodwell (Township)	49349
Gordon Beach	49129
Gordonville	48640
Gore (Township)	48468
Gotts Corners	48725
Gould City	49838
Gourley (Township)	49812
Gowen	49326
Graafschap	49423
Grace	49759
Graham Lake	49017
Grand Beach	49117
Grand Blanc (Genesee County)	48439
Grand Blanc (Genesee County) (Township)	48439
Grand Haven (Ottawa County)	49417
Grand Haven (Ottawa County) (Township)	49417
Grand Island (Township)	49862
Grand Junction	49056
Grand Ledge	48837
Grand Marais	49839
Grand Rapids	49501-99
For specific Grand Rapids Zip Codes call (616) 776-1415	
Grand Rapids (Township)	49505
Grand River (Part of Detroit)	48208
Grand View Acres	48167
Grand View Beach (Cheboygan County)	49749
Grandview Beach (Monroe County)	48145
Grandville	49418
Grant (Cheboygan County) (Township)	49721
Grant (Clare County) (Township)	48617
Grant (Grand Traverse County) (Township)	49647
Grant (Huron County) (Township)	48726
Grant (Iosco County) (Township)	48763
Grant (Keweenaw County) (Township)	49918
Grant (Mason County) (Township)	49411
Grant (Mecosta County) (Township)	49307
Grant (Newaygo County)	49327
Grant (Newaygo County) (Township)	49327
Grant (Oceana County) (Township)	49452
Grant (St. Clair County) (Township)	48032
Grant Center	49307
Grape	48161
Grass Lake (Township)	49240
Grass Lake (Gladwin County)	48624
Grass Lake (Jackson County)	49240
Grassmere	48731
Gratiot (Part of Detroit)	48207
Grattan	48809
Grattan (Township)	48809
Gravel Lake	49065
Grawn	49637
Grayling (Crawford County)	49738
Grayling (Crawford County) (Township)	49738
Great Lake Beach	48450
Great Lakes Bible College	48917
Great Western (Part of Crystal Falls)	49920
Greeley	49753
Green (Alpena County) (Township)	49753
Green (Mecosta County) (Township)	49338
Green (Ontonagon County)	49953
Greenbush	48738
Greenbush (Alcona County) (Township)	48738
Greenbush (Clinton County) (Township)	48833
Greendale (Township)	48883
Greenfield Village (Part of Dearborn)	48124
Green Lake (Allegan County)	49316
Green Lake (Grand Traverse County) (Township)	49684
Greenland	49929

Name	ZIP
Greenland (Township)	49929
Greenleaf (Township)	48726
Green Oak (Township)	48116
Green River	49659
Greenville	48838
Greenwood (Clare County) (Township)	48625
Greenwood (Marquette County)	49849
Greenwood (Oceana County) (Township)	49412
Greenwood (Ogemaw County)	48610
Greenwood (Oscoda County) (Township)	49756
Greenwood (St. Clair County) (Township)	48097
Greenwood (Wexford County) (Township)	49663
Gregory	48137
Greilickville	49684
Gresham	48813
Grim (Township)	48652
Grind Stone City	48467
Groos	49837
Groscap	49781
Grosse Ile (Wayne County) (Township)	48138
Grosse Ile (Wayne County)	48138
Grosse Pointe	48236
Grosse Pointe (Township)	48236
Grosse Pointe Farms	48236
Grosse Pointe Park	48230
Grosse Pointe Shores	48236
Grosse Pointe Woods	48225
Grosvenor	49228
Grout (Township)	48624
Groveland (Township)	48462
Gulliver	49840
Gull Lake	49083
Gunplain (Township)	49080
Gustin (Township)	48740
Gwinn	49841
Hadley	48440
Hadley (Township)	48455
Hagar (Township)	49038
Hagar Shores	49039
Hagensville	49779
Hagerman Lake	49935
Haight (Township)	49912
Hale	48739
Halfway Corners	48441
Hamburg	48139
Hamburg (Township)	48169
Hamilton (Allegan County)	49419
Hamilton (Clare County) (Township)	48625
Hamilton (Gratiot County) (Township)	48847
Hamilton (Van Buren County) (Township)	49045
Hamlin (Eaton County) (Township)	48827
Hamlin (Mason County) (Township)	49431
Hammond Bay	49759
Hampton (Township)	48732
Hamtramck	48212
Hancock (Houghton County)	49930
Hancock (Houghton County) (Township)	49930
Handy (Township)	48836
Hannah	49649
Hanover	49241
Hanover (Jackson County) (Township)	49241
Hanover (Wexford County) (Township)	49620
Harbert	49115
Harbor Beach	48441
Harbor Point	49740
Harbor Springs	49740
Harbor View	49777
Hardwood	49807
Haring (Township)	49601
Harlan	49625
Harlem	49423
Harper (Part of Detroit)	48213
Harper Woods	48225
Harrietta	49638
Harris	49845
Harris (Township)	49845
Harrisburg	49451
Harrison (Clare County)	48625
Harrison (Macomb County) (Township)	48045
Harrison Beach	49854
Harrison Township	48045
Harrisville (Alcona County)	48740

276 MICHIGAN Harrisville-Kensington

Name	ZIP
Harrisville (Alcona County) (Township)	48740
Harsens Island	48028
Hart (Oceana County)	49420
Hart (Oceana County) (Township)	49420
Hartford (Van Buren County)	49057
Hartford (Van Buren County) (Township)	49057
Hartland	48353
Hartland (Township)	48353
Hartwick (Township)	49631
Harvard	49319
Harvey	49855
Haslett	48840
Hastings (Barry County)	49058
Hastings (Barry County) (Township)	49058
Hatton (Township)	48625
Hautala Corner	49938
Hawes (Township)	48742
Hawkhead	49416
Hawkins	49677
Hawks	49743
Hay (Township)	48624
Hayes (Charlevoix County) (Township)	49720
Hayes (Clare County) (Township)	48625
Hayes (Otsego County) (Township)	49735
Haynes (Township)	48742
Hazelhurst Camp	49115
Hazel Park	48030
Hazelton (Township)	48433
Heath (Township)	49419
Hebron (Township)	49755
Helena (Township)	49612
Hell	48169
Helmer	49853
Helps	49873
Hemans	48426
Hematite (Township)	49903
Hemlock	48626
Henderson (Shiawassee County)	48841
Henderson (Wexford County) (Township)	49641
Hendricks (Township)	49762
Henrietta (Township)	49259
Henry Street (Part of Norton Shores)	49441
Herman	49946
Hermansville	49847
Herron	49744
Hersey	49639
Hersey (Township)	49639
Hesperia	49421
Hessel	49745
Hetherton	49751
Hiawatha (Township)	49854
Hickory Corners	49060
Higgins (Township)	48653
Higgins Lake	48627
Highland	48356-57
For specific Highland Zip Codes call (313) 887-2211	
Highland (Township)	49665
Highland Lakes	48167
Highland Park (Kalamazoo County)	49083
Highland Park (Wayne County)	48203
Highway	49913
Hi Hill Villa	48360
Hill (Township)	48739
Hillcrest	49938
Hillcrest Orchard	48145
Hilliards	49328
Hillman	49746
Hillman (Township)	49746
Hillsdale (Hillsdale County)	49242
Hillsdale (Hillsdale County) (Township)	49242
Hinchman	49103
Hinton (Township)	48850
Hockaday	48624
Hodunk	49094
Holland	49422-24
For specific Holland Zip Codes call (616) 396-5201	
Holland (Missaukee County) (Township)	48632
Holland (Ottawa County) (Township)	49423
Holloway	49229
Holly	48442
Holly (Township)	48442
Holmes (Township)	49821
Holt	48842

Name	ZIP
Holton	49425
Holton (Township)	49425
Home (Montcalm County) (Township)	48829
Home (Newaygo County) (Township)	49309
Home Acres (Part of Wyoming)	49508
Homer	49245
Homer (Calhoun County) (Township)	49245
Homer (Midland County) (Township)	48640
Homestead (Benzie County) (Township)	49640
Homestead (Chippewa County)	49783
Hongore Bay	49765
Honor	49640
Hooper	49080
Hope (Township)	48628
Hope (Barry County) (Township)	49058
Hope (Midland County)	48628
Hopkins	49328
Hopkins (Township)	49328
Hopkinsburg	49328
Hopwood Acres	48912
Horr	48893
Horton (Jackson County)	49246
Horton (Ogemaw County) (Township)	48661
Houghton (Houghton County)	49931
Houghton (Keweenaw County) (Township)	49924
Houghton Lake	48629
Houghton Lake Heights	48630
Houghton Point	48629
Howard (Township)	49120
Howard City	49329
Howardsville	49067
Howell	48843-44
For specific Howell Zip Codes call (517) 546-2560	
Hoxeyville	49641
Hubbard Lake	49747
Hubbardston	48845
Hubbell	49934
Hudson (Charlevoix County) (Township)	49730
Hudson (Lenawee County)	49247
Hudson (Lenawee County) (Township)	49247
Hudson (Mackinac County) (Township)	49762
Hudsonville	49426
Hulbert	49748
Hulbert (Township)	49748
Humboldt (Township)	49814
Hume (Township)	48467
Hunters Creek	48446
Huntington Woods	48070
Huron (Huron County) (Township)	48467
Huron (Wayne County) (Township)	48164
Huron Gardens	48341
Huronia Heights	48450
Huron Mountain	49808
Hurontown	49931
Huron Valley Men's Facility	48197
Huron Valley Women's Facility	48197
Hylas	49807
Ida	48140
Ida (Township)	48140
Idlewild	49642
Imlay (Township)	48444
Imlay City	48444
Imperial Heights	49861
Ina	49688
Independence (Township)	48346
Indianfield (Part of Portage)	49081
Indianfields (Township)	48723
Indian Lake	49047
Indian River	49749
Indiantown	48601
Ingalls	49848
Ingallston (Township)	49893
Ingersoll (Township)	48623
Ingham (Township)	48819
Ingleside	49755
Inkster	48141
Inland (Township)	49643
Inland Corners	49643
Interior (Township)	49967
Interlochen	49643
Inverness (Township)	49721
Inwood (Township)	49817
Ionia (Ionia County)	48846

Name	ZIP
Ionia (Ionia County) (Township)	48846
Ionia Temporary Facility	48846
Iosco (Township)	48836
Ira (Township)	48023
Iron Mountain	49801
Iron River (Iron County)	49935
Iron River (Iron County) (Township)	49935
Irons	49644
Ironton	49720
Ironwood (Gogebic County)	49938
Ironwood (Gogebic County) (Township)	49938
Irving	49058
Irving (Township)	49058
Isabella (Delta County)	49878
Isabella (Isabella County) (Township)	48878
Isabella Indian Reservation	48858
Isadore	49621
Ishpeming (Marquette County)	49849
Ishpeming (Marquette County) (Township)	49849
Ithaca	48847
Iva	48626
Ivanrest (Part of Grandville)	49418
Jackson	49201-04
For specific Jackson Zip Codes call (517) 789-2400	
Jacobsville	49945
Jam	48637
James (Township)	48603
Jamestown	49427
Jamestown (Township)	49426
Jasper (Lenawee County)	49248
Jasper (Midland County) (Township)	48880
Jeddo	48032
Jefferson (Cass County) (Township)	49112
Jefferson (Hillsdale County) (Township)	49266
Jefferson (Jackson County)	49230
Jefferson (Wayne County)	48214
Jenison	49428-29
For specific Jenison Zip Codes call (616) 457-2600	
Jennings	49651
Jericho Corners	49090
Jerome (Hillsdale County)	49249
Jerome (Midland County) (Township)	48657
Jessieville (Part of Ironwood)	49938
Johannesburg	49751
Johnstown (Township)	49050
Jones	49061
Jonesfield (Township)	48637
Jonesville	49250
Joppa	49051
Jordan (Township)	49729
Joyfield (Benzie County) (Township)	49616
Joyfield (Wayne County)	48228
Juddville	48817
Jugville	49349
Juhl	48453
Juniata (Tuscola County)	48744
Juniata (Tuscola County) (Township)	48768
Kaiserville	48137
Kalamazoo	49001-09
For specific Kalamazoo Zip Codes call (616) 388-7211	
Kalamazoo (Township)	49004
Kalamo	49096
Kalamo (Township)	49096
Kaleva	49645
Kalkaska	49646
Kalkaska (Township)	49646
Karlin	49647
Kasson (Township)	49664
Kawkawlin	48631
Kawkawlin (Township)	48631
Kearney (Township)	49615
Kearsarge	49942
Keego Harbor	48320
Keeler	49057
Keeler (Township)	49057
Keene (Township)	48881
Kegomic	49770
Kellogg	49010
Kelloggsville (Part of Kentwood)	49508
Kellys Corners	49451
Kelsey Lake	49031
Kendall	49062
Kenockee (Township)	48006
Kensington (Part of Detroit)	48224

Kent City-Mackinaw City **MICHIGAN** 277

Name	ZIP
Kent City	49330
Kenton	49943
Kentwood	49508
Kerby	48817
Kessington	49112
Kewadin	49648
Keweenaw Bay	49944
Keystone	49684
Kibbie Corners	49090
Killarney Beach	48706
Killmaster	48740
Kilmanagh	48759
Kimball (Township)	48074
Kincheloe	49788
Kinde	48445
Kinderhook	49036
Kinderhook (Township)	49036
King Arthur's Court	48906
Kingsford	49801
Kingsley	49649
Kings Mill	48461
Kingston	48741
Kingston (Township)	48729
Kinneville	48827
Kinross	49752
Kinross (Township)	49752
Kinross Correctional Facility	49788
Kipling	49837
K.I.Sawyer AFB	49843
K. I. Sawyer Air Force Base	49843
Kissipee	49751
Kiva	49891
Klacking (Township)	48654
Klinger Lake	49091
Klingville	49916
Klondike	49421
Kneeland	48647
Knollwood Park	49203
Kochville (Township)	48604
Koehler (Township)	49705
Koss	49887
Koylton (Township)	48741
Krakow (Township)	49776
La Branch	49873
Lacey	49021
Lachine	49753
Lac La Belle	49950
Lacota	49063
Lafayette (Township)	48662
Lagoon Beach	48706
La Grange	49031
La Grange (Township)	49031
Laing	48472
Laingsburg	48848
Laird (Township)	49952
Lake (Benzie County) (Township)	49640
Lake (Clare County)	48632
Lake (Huron County) (Township)	48725
Lake (Lake County) (Township)	49304
Lake (Macomb County) (Township)	48236
Lake (Menominee County) (Township)	49821
Lake (Missaukee County) (Township)	49651
Lake (Roscommon County) (Township)	48629
Lake Angeline (Part of Ishpeming)	49849
Lake Angelus	48326
Lake Ann	49650
Lake Charter (Township)	49106
Lake City	49651
Lake Fenton	48430
Lakefield (Luce County) (Township)	49853
Lakefield (Saginaw County) (Township)	48637
Lake George	48633
Lakeland	48143
Lake Lansing	48840
Lake Leelanau	49653
Lake Linden	49945
Lake Margrethe	49738
Lake Mine	49948
Lake Nepessing	48446
Lake Odessa	48849
Lake Orion	48360-62
For specific Lake Orion Zip Codes call (313) 693-8368	
Lake Orion Heights	48362
Lake Pleasant	48412
Lakeport	48060
Lake Roland	49968
Lakeside (Berrien County)	49116
Lakeside (Huron County)	48467
Lakeside (Macomb County)	48313
Lakeside Landing	48430

Name	ZIP
Laketon (Township)	49445
Laketown (Township)	49423
Lakeview (Berrien County)	49129
Lakeview (Calhoun County)	49015
Lakeview (Montcalm County)	48850
Lakeview Square (Part of Battle Creek)	49017
Lakeville	48366
Lakewood (Kalamazoo County)	49002
Lakewood (Monroe County)	48157
Lakewood Club	49457
Lamar (Part of Wyoming)	49509
Lambertville	48144
Lambs	48027
Lamont	49430
Lamotte (Township)	48426
Lanewood (Part of Chelsea)	48118
Langston	48888
L'Anse (Township)	49946
L'Anse	49946
L'Anse Indian Reservation	55401
Lansing	48901-33
For specific Lansing Zip Codes call (517) 337-8711	
Lansing (Township)	48912
Lapeer (Lapeer County)	48446
Lapeer (Lapeer County) (Township)	48446
Laporte	48623
Larkin (Township)	48640
Larson Beach	48762
La Salle	48145
La Salle (Township)	48145
La Salle Gardens	48341
Lathrup Village	48076
Laurium	49913
Lawrence	49064
Lawrence (Township)	49064
Lawson	49885
Lawton	49065
Layton Corners	48118
Leaton	48858
Leavitt (Township)	49459
Lebanon (Township)	48845
Ledyard (Part of Grand Rapids)	49523
Lee (Allegan County) (Township)	49450
Lee (Calhoun County) (Township)	49068
Lee (Midland County) (Township)	48640
Lee Center	49076
Leelanau (Township)	49670
Leighton (Township)	49316
Leisure	49090
Leland	49654
Leland (Township)	49654
Lemon Park	49097
Lennon	48449
Lennon Green Estates	48449
Lenox (Township)	48062
Leonard	48367
Leoni	49201
Leoni (Township)	49201
Leonidas	49066
Leonidas (Township)	49066
Le Roy (Township)	49655
Leroy (Calhoun County) (Township)	49051
Leroy (Ingham County) (Township)	48892
Le Roy (Osceola County)	49655
Les Cheneaux Club	49719
Leslie (Ingham County)	49251
Leslie (Ingham County) (Township)	49251
Level Park	49017
Level Park-Oak Park	49017
Levering	49755
Lewiston	49756
Lewisville	48468
Lexington	48450
Lexington (Township)	48450
Lexington Heights	48450
Liberty	49233
Liberty (Township)	49234
Liberty (Washtenaw County)	48107
Liberty (Wexford County) (Township)	49663
Liberty Corners	48144
Lilley (Township)	49309
Lima (Township)	48118
Lima Center	48130
Lime Island	49736
Limestone	49816
Limestone (Township)	49816
Lincoln (Alcona County)	48742

Name	ZIP
Lincoln (Arenac County) (Township)	48658
Lincoln (Berrien County) (Township)	49127
Lincoln (Clare County) (Township)	48633
Lincoln (Huron County) (Township)	48432
Lincoln (Isabella County) (Township)	48883
Lincoln (Midland County) (Township)	48640
Lincoln (Newaygo County) (Township)	49349
Lincoln (Osceola County) (Township)	49677
Lincoln Park (Muskegon County)	49441
Lincoln Park (Wayne County)	48146
Linden	48451
Linden Hills	49042
Linkville	48755
Linwood (Bay County)	48634
Linwood (Wayne County)	48206
Linwood Beach	48634
Lisbon	49403
Liske	49743
Litchfield (Hillsdale County)	49252
Litchfield (Hillsdale County) (Township)	49252
Littlefield (Township)	49706
Little Lake	49833
Little Point Sable	49455
Little Traverse (Township)	49740
Livernois (Part of Detroit)	48210
Livingston (Township)	49735
Livonia	48150-54
For specific Livonia Zip Codes call (313) 425-8050	
Livonia Mall (Part of Livonia)	48152
Loch Alpine	48103
Locke (Township)	48895
Lockport (Township)	49032
Lodi (Kalkaska County)	49646
Lodi (Washtenaw County) (Township)	48103
Logan (Mason County) (Township)	49402
Logan (Ogemaw County) (Township)	48756
London (Township)	48159
Long Lake (Clare County)	48625
Long Lake (Grand Traverse County) (Township)	49684
Long Lake (Ionia County)	48865
Long Lake (Iosco County)	48743
Long Lake Shores	48323
Long Point	49721
Long Rapids (Township)	49753
Longrie	49887
Loomis	48617
Loretto	49852
Lost Lake Woods	48762
Loud (Township)	48619
Lovells	49738
Lovells (Township)	49738
Lowell (Kent County)	49331
Lowell (Kent County) (Township)	49331
Lucas	49657
Ludington	49431
Lulu	48140
Lum	48452
Luna Pier	48157
Lupton	48635
Luther	49656
Luzerne	48636
Lyndon (Township)	48118
Lynn (Township)	48416
Lyon (Oakland County) (Township)	48167
Lyon (Roscommon County) (Township)	48653
Lyon Lake	49068
Lyons	48851
Lyons (Township)	48851
Mable	49690
Macatawa	49434
McBain	49657
McBrides	48852
McCords	49302
McDonald	49013
McFarlands	49880
McGregor	48427
McIntyre Landing	49738
McIvor	48748
Mackinac Island	49757
Mackinaw (Township)	49701
Mackinaw City	49701

278 MICHIGAN McKinley-Moscow

Name	ZIP
McKinley (Emmet County) (Township)	49769
McKinley (Huron County) (Township)	48755
McKinley (Oscoda County)	48647
McLean	49412
McLeods Corner	49868
McMillan (Luce County)	49853
McMillan (Luce County) (Township)	49868
McMillan (Ontonagon County) (Township)	49925
McMillan Corner	49853
Macomb	48044
Macomb (Township)	48044
Macomb Mall (Part of Roseville)	48066
Macon	49236
Macon (Township)	49236
Madison (Township)	49221
Madison Center (Part of Madison Heights)	48071
Madison Heights	48071
Mancelona	49659
Mancelona (Township)	49659
Manchester	48158
Manchester (Township)	48158
Manistee (Manistee County)	49660
Manistee (Manistee County) (Township)	49660
Manistique (Schoolcraft County)	49854
Manistique (Schoolcraft County) (Township)	49854
Manitou Beach (Lenawee County)	49253
Manitou Beach (Presque Isle County)	49779
Manitou Beach-Devils Lake	49253
Manlius (Township)	49408
Manning	49721
Mansfield (Township)	49920
Mansfield	49881
Manton	49663
Maple (Part of Dearborn)	48126
Maple City	49664
Maple Forest (Township)	49738
Maple Grove	49073
Maple Grove (Township)	49073
Maple Grove (Manistee County) (Township)	49645
Maple Grove (Saginaw County) (Township)	48460
Maple Grove Corners	49090
Maple Hill	49339
Maple Lake (Part of Paw Paw)	49079
Maple Rapids	48853
Maple Ridge (Alpena County) (Township)	49707
Maple Ridge (Arenac County)	48766
Maple Ridge (Delta County) (Township)	49880
Maple River (Township)	49716
Mapleton (Grand Traverse County)	49684
Mapleton (Midland County)	48640
Maple Valley (Montcalm County) (Township)	49347
Maple Valley (Roscommon County)	48656
Maple Valley (Sanilac County) (Township)	48416
Marathon (Township)	48421
Marcellus	49067
Marcellus (Township)	49067
Marengo	49224
Marengo (Township)	49224
Marenisco	49947
Marenisco (Township)	49947
Marilla (Township)	49625
Marine City	48039
Marion (Township)	49665
Marion (Saginaw County) (Township)	48614
Marion (Sanilac County) (Township)	48426
Marion (Charlevoix County) (Township)	49720
Marion (Livingston County) (Township)	48843
Marion (Osceola County)	49665
Marion Springs	48614
Markey (Township)	48629
Marlette	48453
Marlette (Township)	48453
Marne	49435
Marquette (Mackinac County) (Township)	49774
Marquette (Marquette County)	49855
Marquette (Marquette County) (Township)	49855
Marshall (Calhoun County)	49068
Marshall (Calhoun County) (Township)	49068
Martin	49070
Martin (Township)	49070
Martiny (Township)	49342
Marysville	48040
Mason (Arenac County) (Township)	48766
Mason (Cass County) (Township)	49112
Mason (Houghton County)	49930
Mason (Ingham County)	48854
Masonville (Township)	49878
Mass City	49948
Mastodon (Township)	49902
Matchwood (Township)	49925
Matherton	48845
Mathias (Township)	49891
Mattawan	49071
Matteson (Township)	49028
Matteson Lake	49028
Max Myers Addition	49120
Maybee	48159
Mayfield (Grand Traverse County)	49666
Mayfield (Grand Traverse County) (Township)	49649
Mayfield (Lapeer County) (Township)	48446
Mayflower	49913
Mayville	48744
Maywood	49878
Meade (Huron County) (Township)	48432
Meade (Macomb County)	48048
Meade (Mason County) (Township)	49411
Meads Landing	48629
Mears	49436
Meauwataka	49601
Mecosta (Mecosta County)	49332
Mecosta (Mecosta County) (Township)	49346
Medina	49247
Medina (Township)	49247
Melita	48659
Mellen (Township)	49648
Melrose (Township)	49796
Melstrand	49884
Melvin	48454
Melvindale	48122
Memphis	48041
Mendon	49072
Mendon (Township)	49072
Menominee (Menominee County)	49858
Menominee (Menominee County) (Township)	49858
Menonaqua Beach	49740
Mentha	49055
Mentor (Cheboygan County) (Township)	49799
Mentor (Oscoda County) (Township)	48647
Meredith	48624
Meridian (Township)	48823
Meridian Mall	48864
Merrill (Newaygo County) (Township)	49309
Merrill (Saginaw County)	48637
Merriman	49801
Merritt (Bay County) (Township)	48747
Merritt (Missaukee County)	49667
Merriweather	49947
Merson	49010
Mesick	49668
Metamora	48455
Metamora (Township)	48455
Metropolitan	49801
Metropolitan Airport (Part of Romulus)	48242
Metropolitan Airport South Terminal (Part of Romulus)	48242
Metz	49776
Metz (Township)	49776
Meyer (Township)	49847
Miami Park	49090
Michiana	49117
Michigamme	49861
Michigamme (Township)	49861
Michigan Center	49254
Michigan Reformatory	48846
Michigan State University Residence Halls (Ingham County)	48825
Michigan State University (Ingham County)	48824
Michigan Training Unit	48846
Middlebelt (Part of Romulus)	48174
Middle Branch (Township)	49665
Middlebury (Township)	48866
Middleton	48856
Middle Village	49737
Middleville	49333
Midland	48640-41
For specific Midland Zip Codes call (517) 631-6580	
Midland Park	49060
Mikado	48745
Mikado (Township)	48745
Milan (Monroe County) (Township)	48160
Milan (Washtenaw County)	48160
Milford	48380-82
For specific Milford Zip Codes call (313) 684-0775	
Milford (Township)	48381
Millbrook	49334
Millbrook (Township)	49334
Millburg	49022
Millecoquins	49827
Millen (Township)	48705
Millersburg	49759
Millett	48917
Milleville Beach	48173
Mill Grove	49010
Millington	48746
Millington (Township)	48746
Mill Lake	49055
Mills (Houghton County)	49934
Mills (Midland County) (Township)	48652
Mills (Ogemaw County) (Township)	48756
Mills (Sanilac County)	48427
Millville	49285
Milnes	49250
Milton (Antrim County) (Township)	49648
Milton (Cass County) (Township)	49120
Minards Mill	49269
Minden (Township)	48456
Minden City	48456
Mineral Hills	49935
Minor Beach	49854
Mio	48647
Missaukee Park	49651
Mitchell (Township)	48728
M & M Plaza (Part of Menominee)	49858
Moddersville	48632
Moffatt (Township)	48610
Mohawk	49950
Moline	49335
Moltke (Township)	49779
Monitor (Township)	48706
Monongahela Location	49920
Monroe (Monroe County)	48161
Monroe (Monroe County) (Township)	48161
Monroe (Newaygo County) (Township)	49349
Monroe Center	49637
Montague (Muskegon County)	49437
Montague (Muskegon County) (Township)	49437
Montcalm (Township)	48838
Monterey (Township)	49010
Monterey Center	49010
Montgomery	49255
Montmorency (Township)	49746
Montrose	48457
Montrose (Township)	48457
Moore (Township)	48471
Moore Park	49093
Moorestown	49651
Mooreville	48160
Moorland	49451
Moorland (Township)	49451
Moran (Mackinac County)	49760
Moran (Mackinac County) (Township)	49781
Morenci	49256
Morgan	49073
Morgan Corners	49017
Morley	49336
Morrice	48857
Morseville	48415
Morton (Township)	49332
Moscow	49257
Moscow (Township)	49257

Mosherville-Otter Lake **MICHIGAN** 279

Name	ZIP
Mosherville	49258
Mosherville Station	49250
Motley	49952
Mott Park (Part of Flint)	48504
Mottville	49099
Mottville (Township)	49099
Mound Spring	49091
Mountain Beach	49460
Mount Clemens	48043-46
For specific Mount Clemens Zip Codes call (313) 465-1936	
Mount Clemens Southeast	48043
Mount Elliott (Part of Detroit)	48234
Mount Forest	48650
Mount Forest (Township)	48650
Mount Haley (Township)	48637
Mount Morris (Genesee County)	48458
Mount Morris (Genesee County) (Township)	48458
Mount Pleasant	48858-59
	49090
For specific Mount Pleasant Zip Codes call (517) 773-3653	
Mount Vernon	48306
Mueller (Township)	49840
Muir	48860
Mullet (Township)	49791
Mullet Lake	49761
Mulliken	48861
Mundy (Township)	48507
Munger	48747
Munising (Alger County)	49862
Munising (Alger County) (Township)	49895
Munith	49259
Munro (Township)	49755
Munson	49256
Muskegon	49440-45
For specific Muskegon Zip Codes call (616) 722-7292	
Muskegon (Township)	49445
Muskegon Heights	49444
Muskegon Mall (Part of Muskegon)	49440
Mussey (Township)	48014
Muttonville	48062
Nadeau	49863
Nadeau (Township)	49863
Nagel Corner	49743
Nahma	49864
Nahma (Township)	49864
Napoleon	49261
Napoleon (Township)	49261
Nashville	49073
Nathan	49821
National (Part of Crystal Falls)	49920
National City	48748
National Mine	49865
Naubinway	49762
Nazareth (Part of Kalamazoo)	49074
Needmore	48813
Neeley	49080
Negaunee (Marquette County)	49866
Negaunee (Marquette County) (Township)	49866
Nelson (Kent County) (Township)	49343
Nelson (Saginaw County)	48626
Nessen City	49683
Nester (Township)	48624
Nestoria	49861
New Allouez	49901
Newark (Gratiot County) (Township)	48847
Newark (Oakland County)	48442
Newaygo	49337
New Baltimore	48047
Newberg (Township)	49061
Newberry	49868
New Boston	48164
New Bristol Location	49920
New Buffalo (Berrien County)	49117
New Buffalo (Berrien County) (Township)	49117
New Era	49446
Newfield (Township)	49421
New Greenleaf	48726
New Haven (Gratiot County) (Township)	48889
New Haven (Macomb County)	48048
New Haven (Shiawassee County) (Township)	48867
New Holland	49423
New Hudson	48165
Newkirk (Township)	49656

Name	ZIP
Newland	49660
New Lothrop	48460
Newport	48166
New Richmond	49447
New Salem	49315
New Swanzy	49841
Newton (Calhoun County) (Township)	49017
Newton (Mackinac County) (Township)	49838
New Troy	49119
Nicholsville	49067
Niles (Berrien County)	49120
Niles (Berrien County) (Township)	49120
Nirvana	49623
Nisula	49952
Noble (Township)	49028
Noordeloos	49423
Norman (Township)	49689
North Adams	49262
North Allis (Township)	49765
North Bell	48815
North Blendon	49426
North Bradley	48618
North Branch (Township)	48461
North Branch	48461
North Dorr	49323
Northeast (Part of Livonia)	48152
North End (Part of Detroit)	48202
North Epworth	49431
Northfield (Township)	48189
Northgate	49505
North Kent Mall	49505
North Lake (Lapeer County)	48464
North Lake (Marquette County)	49849
North Lake (Van Buren County)	49055
North Lakeport	48060
Northland	49869
Northland Shopping Center (Part of Southfield)	48075
North Manitou	49654
North Morenci	49256
North Muskegon	49445
North Paynesville	49912
North Plains (Township)	48845
Northport	49670
Northport Point	49670
North Shade (Township)	48856
North Shores	48145
North Side (Part of Flint)	48505
North Star	48862
North Star (Township)	48862
North Street	48049
Northview	49505
Northville (Kent County)	49505
Northville (Wayne County)	48167
Northville (Wayne County) (Township)	48167
Northville Commons	48167
Northville Regional Psychiatric Hospital	48167
Northwestern (Part of Detroit)	48204
North Wheeler	48662
Northwood	49007
Norton Shores	49441
Norvell	49263
Norvell (Township)	49263
Norwalk	49660
Norway (Dickinson County)	49870
Norway (Dickinson County) (Township)	49892
Norwich (Missaukee County) (Township)	49651
Norwich (Newaygo County) (Township)	49307
Norwood	49720
Norwood (Township)	49720
Nottawa (Township)	49075
Nottawa (Isabella County) (Township)	48858
Nottawa (St. Joseph County)	49075
Novesta (Township)	48729
Novi	48374-77
For specific Novi Zip Codes call (313) 394-2100	
Novi (Township)	48375
Nunda (Township)	49799
Nunica	49448
Oakfield (Township)	48838
Oak Grove (Livingston County)	48863
Oak Grove (Otsego County)	49735
Oak Grove (Roscommon County)	48653
Oak Hill	49660
Oakhurst	48701

Name	ZIP
Oakland (Allegan County)	49419
Oakland (Oakland County) (Township)	48363
Oakley	48649
Oak Manor	49120
Oak Park (Calhoun County)	49017
Oak Park (Oakland County)	48237
Oak Shade Park	49230
Oakville	48160
Oakwood (Oakland County)	48371
Oakwood (St. Joseph County)	49099
Oakwood (Wayne County)	48122
Oceola (Township)	48843
Ocqueoc (Presque Isle County)	49759
Ocqueoc (Presque Isle County) (Township)	49759
Oden	49764
Odessa (Township)	48849
Odgers Location	49920
Ogden (Township)	49228
Ogden Center	49228
Ogemaw (Township)	48661
Ogemaw Springs	48661
Oil City	48883
Okemos	48864
Old Mission	49673
Old Redford (Part of Detroit)	48219
Olive (Clinton County) (Township)	48879
Olive (Ottawa County) (Township)	49460
Olive Center	49423
Olive Hills	49460
Oliver (Huron County) (Township)	48731
Oliver (Kalkaska County) (Township)	49646
Olivet (Eaton County)	49076
Olson	48640
Omena	49674
Omer	48749
Onaway	49765
Oneida (Township)	48837
Onekama	49675
Onekama (Township)	49675
Onondaga	49264
Onondaga (Township)	49264
Onota (Township)	49822
Onsted	49265
Ontonagon	49953
Ontonagon (Township)	49953
Ontwa (Township)	49112
Orange (Ionia County) (Township)	48846
Orange (Kalkaska County) (Township)	49646
Orangeville	49080
Orangeville (Township)	49080
Orchard Beach	49721
Orchard Lake	48323-24
For specific Orchard Lake Zip Codes call (313) 682-0222	
Orchard Park (Part of Battle Creek)	49017
Oregon (Township)	48446
Orient (Township)	49679
Orion	48360-62
Orleans	48865
Orleans (Township)	48865
Oronoko (Township)	49103
Ortonville	48462
Osceola	49913
Osceola (Township)	49913
Osceola (Township)	49631
Oscoda	48750
Oscoda (Township)	48750
Oscoda Indian Mission	48745
Oshtemo	49077
Oshtemo (Township)	49077
Osier	49878
Oskar	49931
Osseo	49266
Ossineke (Alpena County)	49766
Ossineke (Alpena County) (Township)	49747
Otisco (Township)	48809
Otisville	48463
Otsego (Allegan County)	49078
Otsego (Allegan County) (Township)	49078
Otsego Lake	49735
Otsego Lake (Township)	49735
Ottawa Beach	49423
Ottawa Center	49404
Ottawa Lake	49267
Otterburn (Part of Swartz Creek)	48473
Otter Lake	48464

280 MICHIGAN Otto-Renaissance Center

	ZIP
Otto (Township)	49421
Overisel	49423
Overisel (Township)	49423
Ovid (Township)	48866
Ovid (Branch County) (Township)	49036
Ovid (Clinton County)	48866
Owasippe	49457
Owendale	48754
Owosso (Shiawassee County)	48867
Owosso (Shiawassee County) (Township)	48867
Owosso Junction (Part of Owosso)	48867
Oxford	48370-71
For specific Oxford Zip Codes call (313) 628-2557	
Oxford (Township)	48371
Ozark	49760
Paavola	49930
Painesdale	49955
Paka Plaza (Part of Jackson)	49202
Palestine	49887
Palisades Park	49043
Palmer	49871
Palms	48465
Palmyra	49268
Palmyra (Township)	49268
Palo	48870
Paradise (Chippewa County)	49768
Paradise (Grand Traverse County) (Township)	49649
Parchment	49004
Paris (Huron County) (Township)	48470
Paris (Mecosta County)	49338
Parisville	48470
Park (Ottawa County) (Township)	49423
Park (St. Joseph County) (Township)	49093
Parkdale	49660
Parkers Corners	48836
Park Grove (Part of Detroit)	48205
Park Lake	48808
Park Plaza (Part of Lincoln Park)	48146
Park Shore Resort	49031
Parkville	49093
Parma	49269
Parma (Township)	49224
Parnell	49301
Parshallville	48430
Partello	49076
Patterson Gardens (Monroe County)	48161
Patterson Lake	48169
Paulding	49912
Pavilion (Township)	49088
Paw Paw	49079
Paw Paw (Township)	49079
Paw Paw Lake	49038
Payment	49783
Paynesville	49912
Peacock	49644
Peacock (Township)	49644
Peaine (Township)	49782
Pearl	49408
Pearl Beach (Branch County)	49036
Pearl Beach (St. Clair County)	48052
Pearl Grange	49022
Peck	48466
Pelkie	49958
Pellston	49769
Peninsula (Township)	49684
Penn	49031
Penn (Township)	49031
Pennellwood	49103
Pennfield	49017
Pennfield (Township)	49017
Penobscot (Part of Detroit)	48226
Pentland (Township)	49868
Pentoga	49920
Pentwater	49449
Pentwater (Township)	49449
Pequaming	49431
Pere Marquette (Township)	49449
Perkins	49872
Perrinton	48871
Perronville	49873
Perry (Shiawassee County)	48872
Perry (Shiawassee County) (Township)	48872
Perry Acres	48360
Perry Lake Heights	48462
Peshawbestown	49682

	ZIP
Peters	48039
Petersburg	49270
Petoskey	49770
Pewabic	49930
Pewamo	48873
Phillipsville	49805
Phoenix (Keweenaw County)	49950
Phoenix (Oakland County)	48342
Phoenix Correctional Facility	48170
Pickford	49774
Pickford (Township)	49774
Pier Cove	49090
Pierport	49614
Pierson	49339
Pierson (Township)	49339
Pigeon	48755
Pinckney	48169
Pinconning (Bay County)	48650
Pinconning (Bay County) (Township)	48650
Pine (Township)	48888
Pine Bluffs	48653
Pine Creek	49051
Pine Grove	49055
Pine Grove (Township)	49055
Pine River (Arenac County)	48658
Pine River (Gratiot County) (Township)	48801
Pine Run	48420
Pine Stump Junction	49868
Piney Woods	48625
Pinnebog	48445
Pinora (Township)	49677
Pioneer (Township)	49651
Pipestone (Township)	49111
Pittsburg	48867
Pittsfield (Township)	48108
Pittsford	49271
Pittsford (Township)	49271
Plainfield (Iosco County) (Township)	48739
Plainfield (Kent County) (Township)	49321
Plainfield (Livingston County)	48137
Plainfield Heights	49505
Plainwell	49080
Platte (Township)	49640
Pleasant Lake (Hillsdale County)	49266
Pleasant Lake (Jackson County)	49272
Pleasant Lake (Washtenaw County)	48158
Pleasanton (Township)	49614
Pleasant Plains (Township)	49304
Pleasant Ridge	48069
Pleasant Valley	48880
Pleasant View (Township)	49740
Plymouth (Gogebic County)	49968
Plymouth (Wayne County)	48170
Plymouth (Wayne County) (Township)	48170
Pogy	49639
Point Au Gres	48703
Pointe Aux Barques	48467
Pointe Aux Barques (Township)	48467
Pointe aux Peaux Farms	48166
Pointe aux Pins	49775
Point Nipigon	49721
Pokagon	49047
Pokagon (Township)	49047
Polkton (Township)	49404
Pomona	49625
Pompeii	48874
Ponchartrain Shores	49781
Ponshewaing	49706
Pontiac	48322-25
	48340-43
For specific Pontiac Zip Codes call (313) 338-4511	
Portage (Houghton County) (Township)	49921
Portage (Kalamazoo County)	49081
Portage (Mackinac County) (Township)	49820
Portage Entry	49916
Portage Lake	48169
Port Austin	48467
Port Austin (Township)	48467
Port Austin Air Force Station	48467
Porter (Cass County) (Township)	49042
Porter (Midland County) (Township)	48615
Porter (Van Buren County) (Township)	49065

	ZIP
Port Gypsum (Part of Tawas City)	48763
Port Hope	48468
Port Huron	48060-61
For specific Port Huron Zip Codes call (313) 984-4121	
Portland (Ionia County)	48875
Portland (Ionia County) (Township)	48875
Port Sanilac	48469
Port Sheldon	49460
Port Sheldon (Township)	49460
Portsmouth (Township)	48708
Posen	49776
Posen (Township)	49776
Poseyville	48640
Potters Lake	48423
Potterville	48876
Powell (Township)	49808
Powers	49874
Prairie Ronde (Township)	49087
Prairieville	49046
Prairieville (Township)	49080
Prattville	49273
Prescott	48756
Presque Isle	49777
Presque Isle (Township)	49777
Princeton	49841
Prosper	49632
Prudenville	48651
Pulaski	49241
Pulaski (Township)	49241
Pulawski (Township)	49776
Pullman	49450
Putnam (Township)	48169
Quanicassee	48733
Quarry	48720
Quimby	49058
Quincy	49082
Quincy (Branch County) (Township)	49082
Quincy (Houghton County) (Township)	49930
Quincy Mine	49930
Quinnesec	49876
Rabbit Bay	49945
Rabbits Back	49781
Raber	49736
Raber (Township)	49736
Raco	49778
Rainy Beach	49765
Raisin (Township)	49221
Raisinville (Township)	48161
Ralph	49877
Rambaultown	49913
Ramsay	49959
Ranch Acres	49456
Randall Lake	49036
Randville	49801
Rankin	48473
Ransom	49266
Ransom (Township)	49266
Rapid City	49676
Rapid River (Delta County)	49878
Rapid River (Kalkaska County) (Township)	49659
Rapson	48413
Rathbone	48615
Rattle Run	48079
Ravenna	49451
Ravenna (Township)	49451
Ravenswood	48917
Ray (Branch County)	46737
Ray (Macomb County) (Township)	48048
Ray Center	48048
Raymond Corners	49656
Reading (Hillsdale County)	49274
Reading (Hillsdale County) (Township)	49274
Readmond (Township)	49723
Redding (Township)	48625
Redford (Wayne County)	48239
Redford (Wayne County) (Township)	48239
Redford A	48240
Redman	48468
Red Oak	49756
Red Park	49660
Redridge	49931
Reed City	49677
Reeder (Township)	49651
Reeds Lake (Part of East Grand Rapids)	49506
Reeman	49412
Reese	48757
Regional Shopping Center	48043
Remus	49340
Renaissance Center (Part of Detroit)	48243

Reno-Sherwood Corners **MICHIGAN** 281

	ZIP		ZIP		ZIP
Reno (Township)	48770	Ross (Township)	49012	Sawyer	49125
Republic	49879	Rothbury	49452	Sawyer Lake	49815
Republic (Township)	49879	Round Lake (Lenawee County)	49253	Schaffer	49807
Rescue	48735			Schoolcraft (Township)	49087
Resort (Township)	49770	Round Lake (Mason County)	49410	Schoolcraft (Houghton County) (Township)	49087
Rexton	49762				
Reynolds (Township)	49329	Rousseau	49948	Schoolcraft (Kalamazoo County)	49087
Rhodes	48652	Rowes Corner	48158		
Rich (Township)	48744	Roxand (Township)	48837	Schuck Island	48759
Richfield (Genesee County) (Township)	48423	Royal Oak	48067-73	Schultz	49058
		For specific Royal Oak Zip Codes call (313) 546-7108		Scio (Township)	48130
Richfield (Roscommon County) (Township)	48656			Sciota (Township)	48848
		Royal Oak (Township)	48220	Scipio (Township)	49250
Richfield Center	48423	Royal Oak Beach	49721	Scott Correctional Facility	48170
Richland	49083	Royalton (Township)	49085	Scottdale	49085
Richland (Township)	49083	Rubicon (Township)	48468	Scott Lake	49927
Richland (Missaukee County) (Township)	49657	Ruby	48027	Scotts	49088
		Rudyard	49780	Scottville	49454
Richland (Montcalm County) (Township)	48891	Rudyard (Township)	49780	Sears	49679
		Rumely	49826	Sears Lincoln Park Shopping Center (Part of Lincoln Park)	48146
Richland (Ogemaw County) (Township)	48756	Rush (Township)	48841		
		Rush Lake	48169	Sebewa (Township)	48875
Richland (Saginaw County) (Township)	48626	Rusk	49464	Sebewa Center	48875
		Russell Island	48001	Sebewaing	48759
Richmond (Macomb County)	48062	Russellville	48423	Sebewaing (Township)	48759
		Rust	49746	Secord (Township)	48624
Richmond (Macomb County) (Township)	48062	Rust (Township)	49746	Seidler Corners	48611
		Ruth	48470	Selfridge Air Force Base	48045
Richmond (Marquette County) (Township)	49871	Rutland (Township)	49058	Selkirk	48661
		Ryan	48637	Selma (Township)	49601
Richmond (Osceola County) (Township)	49677	Sac Bay	49817	Seneca	49280
		Saddle Lake	49056	Seneca (Township)	49280
Richmondville	48427	Sage (Township)	48624	Seneca Location	49950
Richville	48758	Saginaw	48601-08	Seney	49883
Ridgeway	49275	For specific Saginaw Zip Codes call (517) 771-5725		Seney (Township)	49883
Ridgeway (Township)	49275			Senter	49922
Riga	49276	Saginaw (Township)	48603	Seven Harbors	48356
Riga (Township)	49276	Saginaw Valley State College	48604	Seven-Mile & Mack Shopping Center (Part of Detroit)	48236
Riley (Clinton County) (Township)	48820				
		Sagola	49881		
Riley (St. Clair County) (Township)	48022	Sagola (Township)	49881	Seven Oaks (Part of Detroit)	48235
		St. Anthony	48182	Seville (Township)	48832
Riley Center	48022	St. Charles	48655	Seymour Square (Part of Grand Rapids)	49510
Ripley	49930	St. Charles (Township)	48655		
Riverdale	48877	St. Clair (St. Clair County)	48079	Shabbona	48426
River Rouge	48218	St. Clair (St. Clair County) (Township)	48079	Shady Shores	48635
Riverside (Berrien County)	49084			Shadyside	49266
Riverside (Missaukee County) (Township)	49657	St. Clair Shores	48080-82	Shafer Location	49920
		For specific St. Clair Shores Zip Codes call (313) 775-5050		Shaftsburg	48882
Riverside Correctional Facility	48846			Shanghai Corners	49111
		St. Helen	48656	Sharon (Township)	48158
Riverton (Township)	49454	St. Ignace (Mackinac County)	49781	Sharon Hollow	48158
Riverview	48192			Sharps Corners	48653
Rives (Township)	49277	St. Ignace (Mackinac County) (Township)	49781	Shawnee Shores	49036
Rives Junction	49277			Shelby (Macomb County) (Township)	48315-16
Roberts Corners	49868	St. Jacques	49878		
Roberts Landing	48001	St. James	49782	For specific Shelby Zip Codes call (313) 731-9412	
Robinson (Township)	49460	St. James (Township)	49782		
Rochester	48306-09	St. Johns	48879	Shelby	49455
For specific Rochester Zip Codes call (313) 651-8551		Saint John's Provincial Seminary	48170	Shelby (Oceana County) (Township)	49455
Rochester Hills	48309	St. Joseph (Berrien County)	49085	Shelbyville	49344
Rock	49880	St. Joseph (Berrien County) (Township)	49022	Sheldon	48111
Rockford	49341			Shepardsville	48866
Rockland	49960	St. Louis	48880	Shepherd	48883
Rockland (Township)	49960	St. Marys Lake	49017	Sheridan (Calhoun County) (Township)	49224
Rock River (Township)	49825	St. Nicholas	49880		
Rockwood	48173	Salem (Allegan County) (Township)	49314	Sheridan (Clare County) (Township)	48617
Rodney	49342				
Rogers (Township)	49779	Salem (Washtenaw County) (Township)	48178	Sheridan (Huron County) (Township)	48413
Rogers City	49779				
Roger's Plaza (Part of Wyoming)	49509	Salem	48175	Sheridan (Mason County) (Township)	49410
		Saline (Washtenaw County)	48176		
Rolland (Township)	49310	Saline (Washtenaw County) (Township)	49236	Sheridan (Mecosta County) (Township)	49305
Rollin	49278				
Rollin (Township)	49278	Salisbury (Part of Ishpeming)	49849	Sheridan (Montcalm County)	48884
Rome (Township)	49221			Sheridan Charter (Township)	49412
Rome Center	49221	Samaria	48177	Sherman (Gladwin County) (Township)	48624
Romeo	48065	Sanborn (Township)	49766		
Romulus	48174	Sand Beach (Township)	48441	Sherman (Huron County) (Township)	48456
Ronald (Township)	48846	Sand Creek	49279		
Rondo	49799	Sand Lake (Iosco County)	48748	Sherman (Iosco County) (Township)	48748
Roosevelt Park	49441	Sand Lake (Kent County)	49343		
Roscommon (Roscommon County)	48653	Sand Lake Corners	49265	Sherman (Isabella County) (Township)	48632
		Sand River	49822		
Roscommon (Roscommon County) (Township)	48653	Sands	49841	Sherman (Keweenaw County) (Township)	49928
		Sands (Township)	49841		
Rose (Oakland County) (Township)	48442	Sandstone (Township)	49201	Sherman (Mason County) (Township)	49410
		Sandusky	48471		
Rose (Ogemaw County) (Township)	48654	Sandy Beach	49091	Sherman (Newaygo County) (Township)	49412
		Sanford	48657		
Roseburg	48097	Sanilac (Township)	48469		
Rosebush	48878	San Souci Beach	49036	Sherman (Osceola County) (Township)	49688
Rose Center	48442	Santiago	48765		
Rose City	48654	Saranac	48881	Sherman (St. Joseph County) (Township)	49091
Rosedale	49783	Sauble (Township)	49402		
Rose Island	48759	Saugatuck	49453	Sherman (Wexford County)	49668
Rose Lake (Township)	49655	Saugatuck (Township)	49453	Sherman City	48632
Roseville	48066	Sault Ste. Marie	49783	Sherwood	49089
Roseville Plaza (Part of Roseville)	48066	Sault Ste. Marie Air Force Station	49783	Sherwood (Township)	49089
				Sherwood Corners	48647

282 MICHIGAN Shiawassee-Trombly

Name	ZIP
Shiawassee (Township)	48429
Shiawasseetown	48429
Shields	48603
Shiloh	48865
Shingleton	49884
Shoreham	49085
Shore Line Junction (Part of Hancock)	49930
Shorewood Hills	49125
Shorewood-Tower Hills-Harbert	49115
Sibley (Part of Trenton)	48183
Sidnaw	49961
Sidney	48885
Sidney (Township)	48885
Sid Town	48750
Sigel (Township)	48441
Silver City	49953
Silver Creek (Township)	49047
Silverwood	48760
Simar	49948
Sims (Township)	48703
Sister Lakes	49047
Sitka	49412
Six Lakes	48886
Skandia (Township)	49885
Skandia	49885
Skanee	49962
Skeels	48624
Skidway Lake	48756
Slagle (Township)	49638
Slapneck	49816
Sleepy Hollow	49912
Slocum	49451
Smith Corners	49420
Smiths Creek	48074
Smyrna	48887
Snover	48472
Snyderville	48062
Sodus	49126
Sodus (Township)	49126
Sokol Camp	49117
Solon (Township)	49621
Solon (Kent County) (Township)	49319
Solon (Leelanau County)	49621
Somerset	49281
Somerset (Township)	49281
Somerset Center	49282
Somerset Mall (Part of Troy)	48084
Sonoma	49017
Soo (Township)	49783
South Arm (Township)	49727
South Blendon	49426
South Boardman	49680
South Branch (Crawford County) (Township)	48653
South Branch (Ogemaw County)	48761
South Branch (Wexford County) (Township)	49641
South Butler	49082
Southfield	48075-76
For specific Southfield Zip Codes call (313) 357-3310	
Southfield (Oakland County)	48034
Southfield (Oakland County) (Township)	48009
South Flint Plaza (Part of Flint)	48507
Southgate	48195
Southgate Shopping Center (Part of Southgate)	48192
South Haven (Van Buren County)	49090
South Haven (Van Buren County) (Township)	49090
South Ionia	48846
Southland Mall (Part of Portage)	49081
Southland Shopping Center (Part of Taylor)	48180
South Lyon	48178
South Manitou	49654
South Monroe (Monroe County)	48161
South Monterey	49010
South Range	49963
South Riley	48820
South Rockwood	48179
Spalding	49886
Spalding (Township)	49886
Sparlingville	48060
Sparr	49735
Sparta	49345
Sparta (Township)	49345
Spaulding (Township)	48655
Speaker (Township)	48454
Spencer (Kalkaska County)	49646
Spencer (Kent County) (Township)	49326

Name	ZIP
Spinks Corners	49022
Spratt	49753
Spring Arbor	49283
Spring Arbor (Township)	49283
Spring Beach	49031
Springdale (Township)	49683
Springfield (Township)	48346
Springfield (Calhoun County)	49015
Springfield (Kalkaska County) (Township)	49680
Springfield (Oakland County)	48346
Springfield Place (Part of Battle Creek)	49015
Spring Grove	49416
Spring Lake	49456
Spring Lake (Township)	49456
Springport	49284
Springport (Township)	49284
Springvale (Township)	49770
Springville (Lenawee County)	49265
Springville (Wexford County) (Township)	49668
Springwells (Part of Detroit)	48209
Spruce	48762
Spurr (Township)	49861
Stalwart	49789
Stambaugh (Iron County)	49964
Stambaugh (Iron County) (Township)	49935
Standale (Part of Walker)	49504
Standish (Arenac County)	48658
Standish (Arenac County) (Township)	48658
Stannard (Township)	49912
Stanton (Houghton County) (Township)	49931
Stanton (Montcalm County)	48888
Stanwood	49346
Star (Township)	49611
Star Corners (Manistee County)	49660
Star Corners (Menominee County)	49887
Starville	48039
Steamburg	49242
Stephenson (Menominee County)	49887
Stephenson (Menominee County) (Township)	49887
Sterling	48659
Sterling Heights	48310-14
For specific Sterling Heights Zip Codes call (313) 268-2880	
Steuben	49854
Stevensville	49127
Stockbridge	49285
Stockbridge (Township)	49285
Stonington	49878
Stony Creek	48197
Stony Lake	49455
Stony Point	48166
Strasburg	48161
Strathmoor (Part of Detroit)	48227
Strawberry Point	49456
Stronach	49660
Stronach (Township)	49660
Strongs	49790
Strongs Corners	49790
Stuart Lake	49068
Sturgeon Point	48740
Sturgeon River	49864
Sturgis (St. Joseph County)	49091
Sturgis (St. Joseph County) (Township)	49091
Sugar Island (Township)	49783
Sugar Rapids	48624
Sullivan	49451
Sullivan (Township)	49451
Summerfield (Clare County) (Township)	48625
Summerfield (Monroe County) (Township)	49270
Summit (Jackson County) (Township)	49203
Summit (Mason County) (Township)	49431
Summit City	49649
Summit Heights	48629
Summit Place	48328
Sumner	48889
Sumner (Township)	48889
Sumnerville	49120
Sumpter (Township)	48111
Sun	49327
Sunfield	48890
Sunfield (Township)	48890
Sunrise Heights	49015
Sunset Beach	49230

Name	ZIP
Superior (Chippewa County) (Township)	49715
Superior (Washtenaw County) (Township)	48197
Surrey (Township)	48622
Suttons Bay	49682
Suttons Bay (Township)	49682
Swains Lake	49237
Swan Creek (Township)	48655
Swanson	49821
Swartz Creek	48473
Swedetown	49913
Sweetwater (Township)	49304
Sylvan (Osceola County) (Township)	49631
Sylvan (Washtenaw County) (Township)	48118
Sylvan Center	48118
Sylvan Lake	48320
Sylvester	49332
Talbot	49821
Tallmadge	49504
Tallmadge (Township)	49504
Tallman	49410
Tamarack	49913
Tapiola	49916
Tawas (Township)	48763
Tawas Centre	48730
Tawas City	48763-64
For specific Tawas City Zip Codes call (517) 362-2471	
Taylor	48180
Taymouth (Township)	48417
Teapot Dome	49079
Tecumseh (Lenawee County)	49286
Tecumseh (Lenawee County) (Township)	49286
Tekonsha	49092
Tekonsha (Township)	49092
Teleford (Part of Dearborn Heights)	48128
Tel-Twelve Mall (Part of Southfield)	48034
Temperance	48182
Temple	48625
Texas (Township)	49009
Texas Corners	49009
The Fingerboard Corner	49705
The Heights	49230
Theodore	49801
Thetford (Township)	48420
Thomas (Oakland County)	48371
Thomas (Saginaw County) (Township)	48603
Thomaston	49968
Thompson	49854
Thompson (Township)	49854
Thompsonville	49683
Thornapple (Township)	49333
Thornville	49455
Three Lakes	49861
Three Mile Lake	49079
Three Oaks	49128
Three Oaks (Township)	49128
Three Rivers	49093
Thunder Mountain	49038
Tilden (Township)	49849
Tipton	49287
Tittabawassee (Township)	48623
Tobacco (Township)	48612
Tobico Beach	48706
Tobin Location	49920
Tobins Harbor	55605
Toivola	49965
Tompkins (Jackson County)	49277
Tompkins (Jackson County) (Township)	49277
Topaz	49925
Topinabee	49791
Toquin	49057
Torch Lake (Township)	49648
Torch Lake (Antrim County)	49627
Torch Lake (Houghton County) (Township)	49934
Torch River	49676
Towar Gardens	48823
Tower	49792
Tower Hill	49125
Town Corners	49446
Traunik	49890
Traverse Bay	49945
Traverse City	49684
Tremaine Corners	48846
Trenary	49891
Trent	49303
Trenton	48183
Triangle Park	48653
Trimountain	49905
Trolley (Part of Detroit)	48231
Trombly	49880

Ubly-Wolf Lake **MICHIGAN** 283

Name	ZIP
Ubly	48475
Unadilla	48137
Unadilla (Township)	48137
Union (Branch County) (Township)	49094
Union (Cass County)	49130
Union (Grand Traverse County) (Township)	49633
Union (Isabella County) (Township)	48858
Union City	49094
Union Lake	48386-87
Union Pier	49129
Unionville	48767
Universal Mall (Part of Warren)	48092
Upjohn (Part of Portage)	49081
Urbandale (Part of Battle Creek)	49017
Utica	48310-18
For specific Utica Zip Codes call (313) 731-9412	
Valley (Township)	49010
Valley Center	48416
Valley Farms	48906
Van	49755
Van Buren (Township)	48111
Vandalia	49095
Vanderbilt	49795
Vandercook Lake	49203
Van Meer	49884
Vantown	48892
Vassar (Tuscola County)	48768
Vassar (Tuscola County) (Township)	48768
Venice (Township)	48817
Vergennes (Township)	49331
Vermontville	49096
Vermontville (Township)	49096
Vernon (Township)	48429
Vernon (Isabella County) (Township)	48617
Vernon (Shiawassee Co.)	48476
Vernon City	48617
Verona (Township)	48413
Verona (Calhoun County)	49017
Verona (Gogebic County)	49968
Verona (Huron County)	48413
Verona Park	49017
Vestaburg	48891
Veterans Administration Hospital (Part of Iron Mountain)	49801
Vevay (Township)	48854
Vickery Landing	49050
Vickeryville	48884
Vicksburg	49097
Victor (Township)	48848
Victoria	49960
Victory (Township)	49454
Vienna (Genesee County) (Township)	48420
Vienna (Montmorency County) (Township)	49751
Virginia Park	49423
Vogel Center	49657
Volinia	49045
Volinia (Township)	49045
Volney	49309
Vriesland	49464
Vulcan	49892
Wabaningo	49463
Wacousta	48837
Wadhams	48060
Wagarville	48624
Wahjamega	48723
Wainola	49948
Wakefield (Gogebic County) (Township)	49968
Wakefield (Gogebic County)	49968
Wakelee	49067
Wakeshma (Township)	49052
Waldenburg	48044
Waldron	49288
Wales (Township)	48074
Walhalla	49458
Walker (Cheboygan County) (Township)	49705
Walker (Kent County)	49504
Walkers Point	49721
Walkerville	49459
Wallace	49893
Walled Lake	48390
Wallin	49683
Wall Lake	49046
Walloon Lake	49796
Walnut Lake	48010
Walnut Point	49068
Walters	48346
Walton (Township)	49076

Name	ZIP
Waltz	48164
Wardcliff	48823
Warner (Township)	49730
Warren	48089-93
For specific Warren Zip Codes call (313) 751-4900	
Warren (Township)	48618
Wasepi	49032
Washington (Gratiot County) (Township)	48806
Washington (Macomb County) (Township)	48094
Washington (Sanilac County) (Township)	48401
Washington (Macomb County)	48094
Washington Harbor	55605
Washington Heights (Part of Battle Creek)	49017
Waterford	48327-29
For specific Waterford Zip Codes call (313) 623-0020	
Waterloo	49240
Waterloo (Township)	49240
Watermill Lake	49642
Waters	49797
Watersmeet	49969
Watersmeet (Township)	49969
Watertown (Sanilac County) (Township)	48471
Watertown (Tuscola County) (Township)	48435
Watertown (Clinton County) (Township)	48820
Watertown (Sanilac County)	48471
Watervale	49613
Watervliet (Berrien County)	49098
Watervliet (Berrien County) (Township)	49098
Watrousville	48768
Watson	49078
Watson (Township)	49078
Watson Corners	49078
Wattles Park	49017
Watton	49970
Waucedah	49892
Waucedah (Township)	49892
Waverly (Cheboygan County) (Township)	49765
Waverly (Eaton County)	48917
Waverly (Van Buren County) (Township)	49079
Wawatam (Township)	49701
Wawatam Beach (Part of Mackinaw City)	49701
Wayland (Allegan County)	49348
Wayland (Allegan County) (Township)	49348
Wayne	48184-88
For specific Wayne Zip Codes call (313) 728-4100	
Wayne (Township)	49047
Weadlock	49755
Weale	48720
Weare (Township)	49420
Webber (Township)	49304
Webberville	48892
Webster (Township)	48130
Weesaw (Township)	49128
Weidman	48893
Welcome Corners	49058
Weldon (Township)	49683
Wellington (Township)	49753
Wells	49894
Wells (Township)	49894
Wells (Marquette County) (Township)	49818
Wells (Tuscola County) (Township)	48723
Wellston	49689
Wellsville	49228
Wenona Beach	49707
Wequetonsing	49740
West Bloomfield	48322-25
For specific West Bloomfield Zip Codes call (313) 682-0222	
West Bloomfield Township	48323-24
For specific West Bloomfield Township Zip Codes call (313) 682-0222	
West Branch (Township)	48661
West Branch (Dickinson County) (Township)	49877
West Branch (Marquette County) (Township)	49885
West Branch (Missaukee County) (Township)	49667
West Branch (Ogemaw County)	48661

Name	ZIP
Westchester Village	48010
Western Wayne Correctional Facility	48170
West Ishpeming	49849
Westland	48185
Westland Shopping Center (Part of Westland)	48185
West Leroy	49051
West Millbrook	49310
West Olive	49460
Weston	49289
Westphalia	48894
Westphalia (Township)	48894
West Sebewa	48875
West Side (Part of Saginaw)	48603
West Traverse (Township)	49740
Westville	48888
West Willow	48198
West Windsor	48813
Westwood	49007
Westwood Heights	48504
Wetmore	49895
Wetzel	49659
Wexford (Township)	49668
Wheatfield (Township)	48895
Wheatland (Hillsdale County) (Township)	49220
Wheatland (Mecosta County) (Township)	49340
Wheatland (Sanilac County) (Township)	48427
Wheeler	48662
Wheeler (Township)	48662
White	49952
White Cloud	49349
Whitefish (Township)	49728
Whitefish Point	49768
Whiteford (Township)	49267
Whiteford Center	49267
Whitehall (Muskegon Co.)	49461
Whitehall (Muskegon County) (Township)	49461
White Lake	48383
White Lake (Township)	48383
White Lake-Seven Harbors	48383
White Oak (Township)	49285
White Pigeon	49099
White Pigeon (Township)	49099
White Pine	49971
White River (Township)	49437
Whites Beach	48658
Whitewater (Township)	49690
Whitmore Lake	48189
Whitney (Township)	48765
Whittaker	48190
Whittemore	48770
Wickware	48726
Wilber (Township)	48730
Wilcox (Township)	49349
Wildwood (Cheboygan Co.)	49706
Wildwood (Manistee Co.)	49614
Willard	48611
Williams (Township)	48611
Williamsburg	49690
Williamston (Ingham Co.)	48895
Williamston (Ingham County) (Township)	48895
Williamsville (Cass County)	49095
Williamsville (Livingston County)	48137
Willis	48191
Willow	48164
Willow Run	48198
Willwalk	49783
Wilmot (Cheboygan County) (Township)	49799
Wilmot (Tuscola County)	48729
Wilson (Alpena County) (Township)	49707
Wilson (Charlevoix County) (Township)	49729
Wilson (Menominee County)	49896
Windemere	48917
Windsor (Township)	48821
Winegars	48624
Winfield (Township)	48850
Winn	48896
Winona	49965
Winsor (Township)	48755
Winterfield (Township)	49665
Winters	49878
Winthrop Junction (Part of Ishpeming)	49849
Wise (Township)	48618
Wisner (Tuscola County)	48701
Wisner (Tuscola County) (Township)	48733
Witch Lake	49879
Wixom	48393
Wolf Lake (Jackson County)	49201

MICHIGAN Williamsburg-Zutphen

Name	ZIP
Williamsburg	49690
Williamston (Ingham County)	48895
Williamston (Ingham County) (Township)	48895
Williamsville (Cass County)	49095
Williamsville (Livingston County)	48137
Willis	48191
Willow	48164
Willow Run	48198
Willwalk	49783
Wilmot (Cheboygan County) (Township)	49799
Wilmot (Tuscola County)	48729
Wilson (Alpena County) (Township)	49707
Wilson (Charlevoix County) (Township)	49729
Wilson (Menominee County)	49896
Windemere	48917
Windsor (Township)	48821
Winegars	48624
Winfield (Township)	48850
Winn	48896
Winona	49965
Winsor (Township)	48755
Winterfield (Township)	49665
Winters	49878
Winthrop Junction (Part of Ishpeming)	49849
Wise (Township)	48618
Wisner (Tuscola County)	48701

Name	ZIP
Wisner (Tuscola County) (Township)	48733
Witch Lake	49879
Wixom	48393
Wolf Lake (Jackson County)	49201
Wolf Lake (Muskegon County)	49442
Wolverine	49799
Wolverine Lake	48390
Wonderland Mall (Part of Livonia)	48150
Woodard Lake	48834
Woodbridge (Township)	49242
Woodbury	48849
Wooden Shoe Village	48624
Woodhaven	48183
Woodhull (Township)	48872
Woodland	48897
Woodland (Township)	48897
Woodland (Part of Kentwood)	49508
Woodland Beach	48161
Woodland Lake	48116
Woodland Park	49309
Woods Corner	48622
Wood Spur	49953
Woodstock (Township)	49220
Woodville	49349
Wooster	49412
Worth (Arenac County)	48650
Worth (Sanilac County) (Township)	48422
Wright (Township)	49403

Name	ZIP
Wright (Hillsdale County) (Township)	49271
Wright (Ottawa County)	49403
Wurtsmith AFB	48753
Wurtsmith Air Force Base	48753
Wyandotte	48192
Wyman	49310
Wyoming	49509
Wyoming Park (Part of Wyoming)	49509
Yale (Gogebic County)	49911
Yale (St. Clair County)	48097
Yankee Springs (Township)	49333
Yates (Township)	49642
Yellow Jacket	49913
York (Township)	48160
Yorkville	49083
Ypsilanti	48197-98
For specific Ypsilanti Zip Codes call (313) 482-6905	
Ypsilanti Regional Psychiatric Hospital	48197
Yuba	49690
Yuma	49668
Zeba	49946
Zeeland (Ottawa County)	49464
Zeeland (Ottawa County) (Township)	49464
Zilwaukee (Saginaw County)	48604
Zilwaukee (Saginaw County) (Township)	48604
Zutphen	49426

Ada-Carver **MINNESOTA** 285

Name	ZIP
Ada	56510
Adams (Mower County)	55909
Adolph (Part of Hermantown)	55701
Adrian (Nobles County)	56110
Afton	55001
Ah-Gwah-Ching	56430
Aitkin	56431
Akeley	56433
Albany (Stearns County)	56307
Alberta (Stevens County)	56207
Albert Lea	56007
Albertville	55301
Albion Center	55302
Alborn	55702
Alden	56009
Aldrich (Wadena County)	56434
Alexandria	56308
Alida	56676
Allen Junction (Part of Hoyt Lakes)	55750
Alma City	56048
Almelund	55002
Almora	56551
Alpha	56111
Altura	55910
Alvarado	56710
Alvwood	56630
Amboy (Blue Earth County)	56010
Amherst	55922
Amiret	56112
Amor	56515
Andover (Anoka County)	55304
Andree	55006
Andyville	55912
Angle Inlet	56711
Angora	55703
Angus	56712
Annandale	55302
Anoka	55303-04
For specific Anoka Zip Codes call (612) 421-1114	
Antlers Park (Part of Lakeville)	55044
Apache Mall (Part of Rochester)	55902
Apache Plaza (Part of St. Anthony)	55421
Appleton (Swift County)	56208
Apple Valley	55124
Arco	56113
Arcturus (Part of Taconite)	55786
Arden Hills	55112
Arendahl	55962
Argonne (Part of Lakeville)	55044
Argyle	56713
Arlington (Sibley County)	55307
Armstrong	56009
Arnesen	56673
Arnold	55803
Arthyde	56350
Artichoke Lake	56227
Ashby	56309
Ashcreek	56173
Ash Lake (St. Louis County)	55771
Askov	55704
Aspelund	55946
Assumption	55338
Atkinson	55718
Atwater	56209
Atwood (Part of Edina)	55424
Audubon	56511
Augusta (Carver County)	55318
Aure	56676
Aurora (St. Louis County)	55705
Austin (Mower County)	55912
Austin Acres	55912
Auto Club (Part of Bloomington)	55420
Automba	55757
Averill	56547
Avoca	56114
Avon	56310
Babbitt	55706
Backus	56435
Badger (Roseau County)	56714
Bagley	56621
Baker (Clay County)	56513
Balaton	56115
Bald Eagle	55110
Balkan	55719
Ball Bluff	55752
Ball Club	56636
Balmoral	56515
Bancroft	56007
Barden (Part of Shakopee)	55379
Barnesville	56514
Barnum	55707
Barr	55992
Barrett	56311
Barrows	56401

Name	ZIP
Barry (Big Stone County)	56210
Bassett	55602
Basswood	56576
Basswood Grove	55033
Battle Lake	56515
Battle River	56630
Baudette	56623
Baudette Air Force Station, 692nd Air Force Defence	56623
Baxter (Crow Wing County)	56425
Bay Lake	56444
Bayport	55003
Bayview	56359
Beardsley	56211
Bear River	55723
Bear Valley	55041
Beauford	56065
Beaulieu	56557
Beaver (Winona County)	55910
Beaver Bay (Lake County)	55601
Beaver Creek (Rock County)	56116
Beaver Falls (Renville County)	56270
Bechyn	56283
Becida	56625
Becker (Sherburne County)	55308
Beckville	55355
Bejou	56516
Belgrade (Stearns County)	56312
Bellaire	55110
Bellechester	55027
Belle Creek (Goodhue County)	55009
Belle Plaine (Scott County)	56011
Belle Prairie	56345
Belleriver	56319
Bellingham	56212
Beltrami	56517
Belview	56214
Bemidji	56601-19
For specific Bemidji Zip Codes call (218) 751-5600	
Bena	56626
Benedict	56436
Bennettville	56431
Benson	56215
Bergen (Jackson County)	56101
Berville	56661
Bernadotte	56054
Berne	55985
Berner	56644
Berning Mill	55376
Beroun	55004
Bertha (Todd County)	56437
Bethany	55910
Bethel	55005
Big Bend City	56262
Bigelow (Nobles County)	56117
Big Falls	56627
Bigfork	56628
Big Island (Part of Orono)	55331
Big Lake (Sherburne County)	55309
Big Spring	55939
Big Stone City (Part of Ortonville)	56278
Big Woods (Marshall County)	56747
Bingham Lake	56118
Birch Beach	56686
Birchdale (Koochiching County)	56629
Birchwood Village	55110
Bird Island (Renville County)	55310
Biscay	55336
Biwabik	55708
Bixby	55917
Blackberry	55744
Blackduck	56630
Black Hammer	55974
Blaine	55433
Blakeley	56011
Blomford	55040
Blomkest	56216
Bloom Dale (Part of Bloomington)	55431
Blooming Prairie (Steele County)	55917
Bloomington	55420
Blue Earth	56013
Blue Grass	56477
Bluffton (Otter Tail County)	56518
Bock	56313
Bodum	55040
Boisberg	56296
Bois Fort	55772
Bombay	55946
Bonanza Grove	56211
Bongards	55368
Bonnie Glen	55013

Name	ZIP
Border	56629
Borup	56519
Bovey	55709
Bovey-Coleraine (Part of Bovey)	55709
Bowlus	56314
Bowstring	56631
Boyd	56218
Boy River	56632
Bradford (Isanti County)	55040
Braham	55006
Brainerd	56401
Brainerd Regional Human Services Center	56401
Branch	55056
Brandon	56315
Bratsberg	55971
Breckenridge (Wilkin County)	56520
Breezy Point	56472
Bremen (Wabasha County)	55957
Brennyville	56329
Brevik	56655
Brewster	56119
Bricelyn	56014
Bridge Court (Part of Anoka)	55303
Bridgeman	56473
Bridgewater (Rice County)	55021
Brimson	55602
Bristol	55939
Britt	55710
Brookdale Shopping Center (Part of Brooklyn Center)	55430
Brooklyn (Part of Hibbing)	55746
Brooklyn Center	55429
Brooklyn Park	55443
Brook Park (Pine County)	55007
Brooks	56715
Brookston	55711
Brooten	56316
Browerville	56438
Brownsdale	55918
Browns Valley (Traverse County)	56219
Brownsville (Houston County)	55919
Brownton	55312
Bruno	55712
Brunswick (Kanabec County)	55051
Brush Creek	56014
Brushvale	56520
Buckman (Morrison County)	56317
Buffalo (Wright County)	55313
Buffalo Lake	55314
Buhl	55713
Bunde	56222
Burchard	56115
Burnett	55727
Burnsville	55337
Burnsville Center (Part of Burnsville)	55337
Burr	56220
Burschville (Part of Corcoran)	55357
Burtrum	56318
Butler	56567
Butterfield (Watonwan County)	56120
Butternut	56055
Buyck	55771
Bygland (Polk County)	56721
Byron (Olmsted County)	55920
Cable	56301
Caledonia	55921
Callaway	56521
Calumet	55716
Cambria	56073
Cambridge	55008
Camden Place (Part of Minneapolis)	55412
Campbell (Wilkin County)	56522
Camp Lacupolis	55041
Camp Ripley	56345
Canby	56220
Cannon City	55021
Cannon Falls	55009
Cannon Lake	55021
Canton	55922
Canyon	55717
Cardigan Junction (Part of Shoreview)	55112
Caribou (Kittson County)	56735
Carimona	55965
Carlisle	56537
Carlos	56319
Carlton	55718
Carp	56623
Carver	55315

286 MINNESOTA

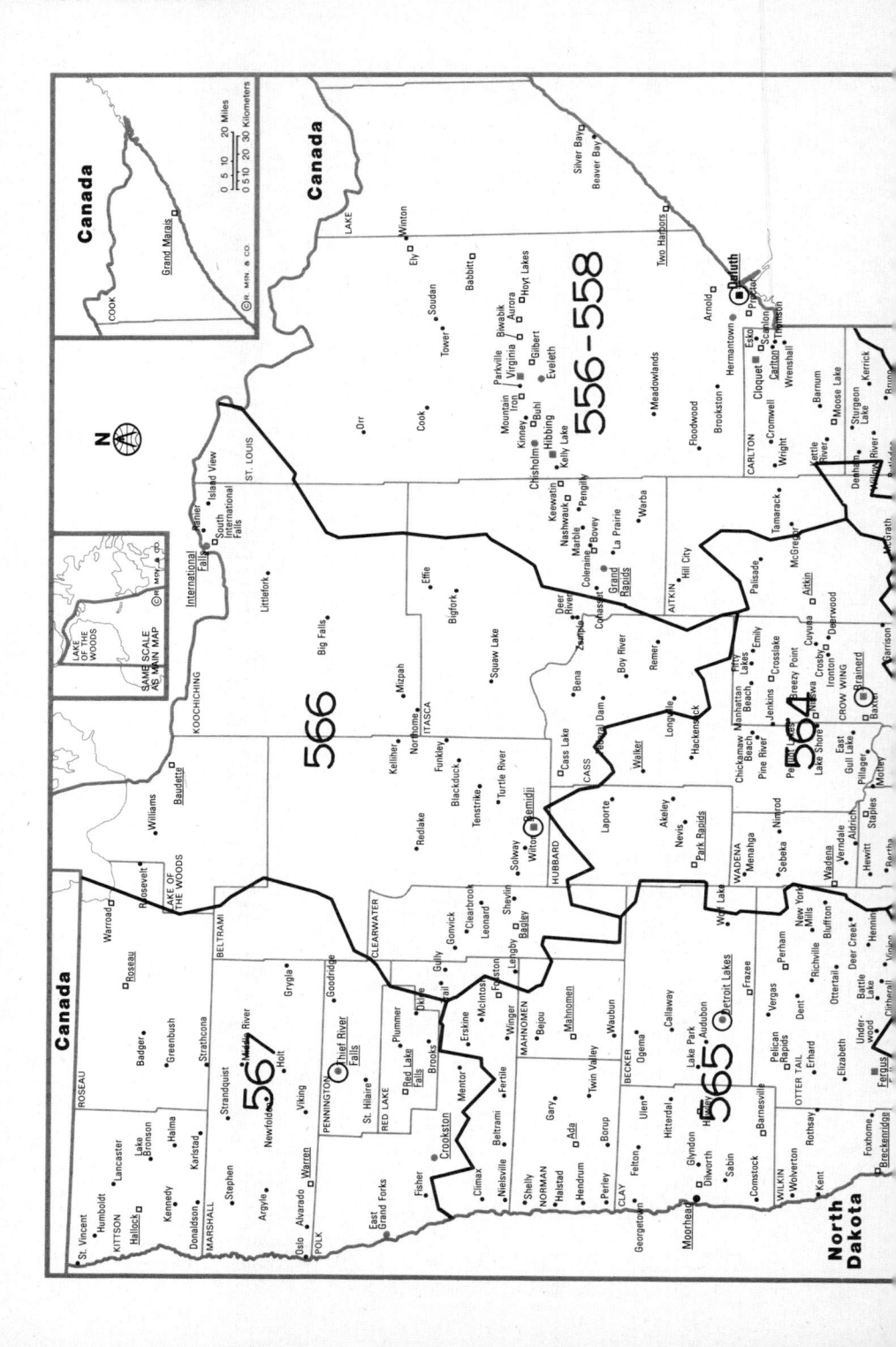

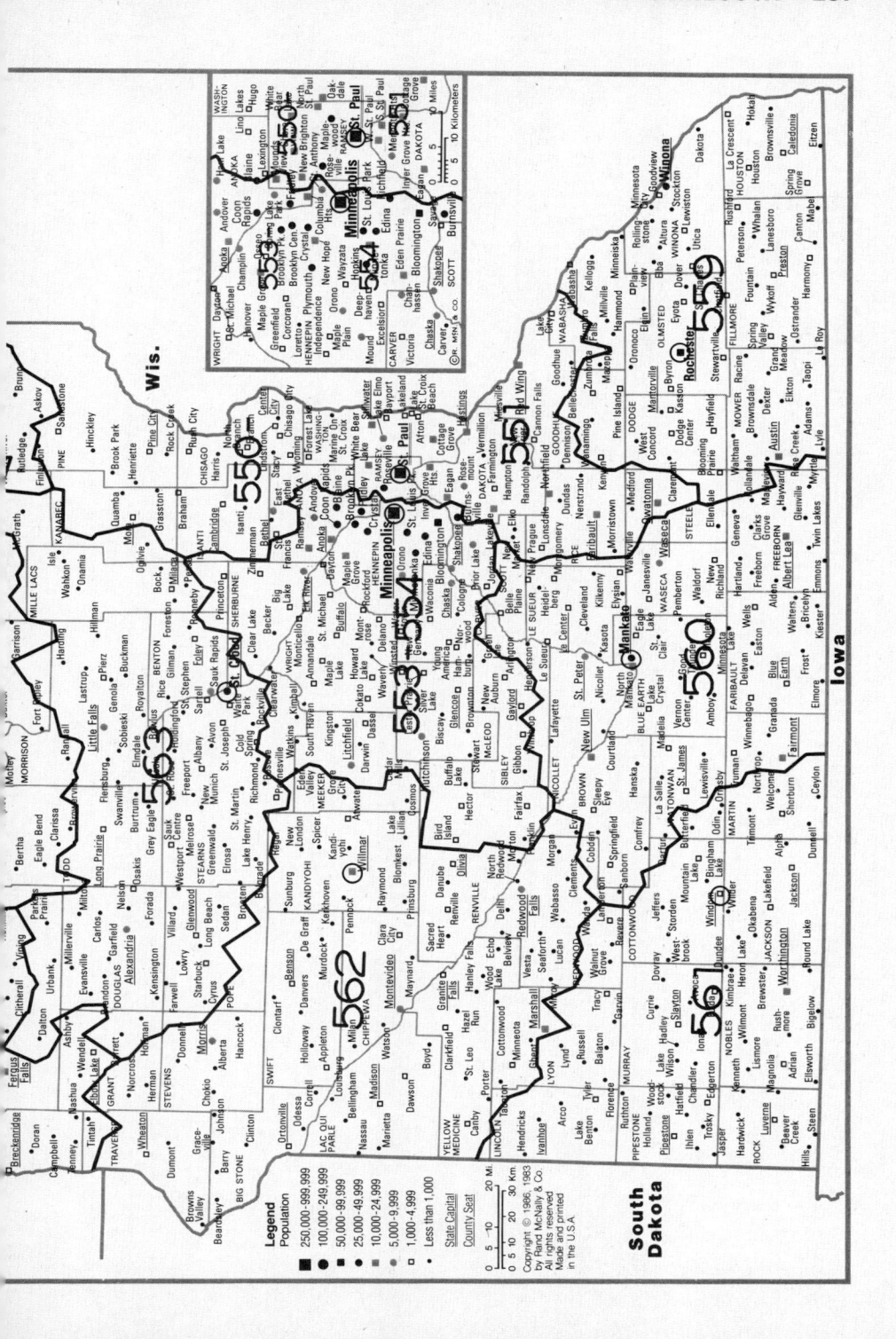

MINNESOTA

288 MINNESOTA Cashtown-Felton

Name	ZIP
Cashtown (Part of Ortonville)	56278
Casino	56473
Cass Lake	56633
Castle Danger	55616
Castle Rock	55010
Cedar (Anoka County)	55011
Cedar Beach	55960
Cedar Grove (Part of Eagan)	55111
Cedar Mills (Meeker County)	55350
Cedar Riverside (Part of Minneapolis)	55440
Celina	55788
Center City	55012
Centerville (Anoka County)	55038
Centerville (Winona County)	55987
Central	56481
Central Lakes	55734
Ceylon	56121
Champlin	55316
Chandler	56122
Chanhassen	55317
Charlesville	56583
Chaska	55318
Chatfield	55923
Cherry	55751
Cherry Grove (Fillmore County)	55975
Chester (Olmsted County)	55904
Chicago Bay	55606
Chickamaw Beach	56474
Chisago City	55013
Chisholm	55719
Choice	55954
Chokio	56221
Chowens Corner (Part of Deephaven)	55391
Circle Pines	55014
City (Part of Rochester)	55904
City Center (Part of Minneapolis)	55402
Civic Center (Part of Duluth)	55802
Clara City	56222
Claremont	55924
Clarissa	56440
Clarkfield	56223
Clarks Grove	56016
Clearbrook	56634
Clear Lake (Sherburne County)	55319
Clearwater	55320
Clements	56224
Clementson	56623
Cleveland	56017
Cliff (Part of Lilydale)	55118
Climax	56523
Clinton (Big Stone County)	56225
Clinton Falls	55060
Clitherall (Otter Tail County)	56524
Clontarf (Swift County)	56226
Cloquet	55720
Clotho	56347
Cloverdale	55037
Cloverton	55048
Clyde	55979
Coates	55068
Cobden	56085
Cohasset	55721
Coin	56358
Cokato (Wright County)	55321
Colby (Part of Hoyt Lakes)	55750
Cold Spring	56320
Coleraine	55722
Collegeville	56321
Collis	56236
Cologne	55322
Columbia Heights	55421
Comfrey	56019
Commerce (Part of Minneapolis)	55415
Como (Ramsey County)	55108
Comstock (Clay County)	56525
Conception	55945
Concord	55985
Conger	56020
Constance (Part of Andover)	55303
Cook	55723
Cooley	55769
Coon Lake Beach (Part of East Bethel)	55092
Coon Rapids	55433
Copas	55073
Corcoran	55340
Cordova (Le Sueur County)	56057
Cormorant	56572
Corning	55912
Correll	56227
Corvuso	56228

Name	ZIP
Cosmos (Meeker County)	56228
Cottage Grove	55016
Cotton	55724
Cottonwood (Lyon County)	56229
Courtland (Nicollet County)	56021
Cove	56359
Craigville	56639
Crane Lake	55725
Credit River	55372
Croftville	55604
Cromwell (Carlton County)	55726
Crookston (Polk County)	56716
Crosby (Crow Wing County)	56441
Crosby Beach	56444
Crosslake	56442
Crown	55070
Crow River (Meeker County)	56243
Crow Wing	56401
Crystal	55428
Crystal Bay (Hennepin County)	55323
Crystal Shopping Center (Part of Crystal)	55428
Culver	55727
Cummingsville	55923
Currie	56123
Cushing	56443
Cusson	55771
Cutler	56431
Cuyuna	56444
Cyrus	56323
Dakota	55925
Dalbo	55017
Dale (Clay County)	56549
Dalton	56324
Danube	56230
Danvers	56231
Darfur	56022
Darling	56345
Darwin (Meeker County)	55324
Dassel (Meeker County)	55325
Dawson	56232
Day	55006
Dayton (Anoka County)	55303
Dayton (Hennepin County)	55327
Daytons Bluff (Part of St. Paul)	55106
Debs	56676
Deephaven	55391
Deer Creek (Otter Tail County)	56527
Deerfield (Steele County)	55049
Deer River (Itasca County)	56636
Deerwood	56444
De Graff	56233
Delano	55328
Delavan	56023
Delft	56124
Delhi (Redwood County)	56283
Dell	56013
Dellwood	55110
Denham	55728
Dennison	55018
Dent	56528
Detroit Lakes	56501-02
For specific Detroit Lakes Zip Codes call (218) 847-8379	
Dexter (Mower County)	55926
Diamond Lake (Hennepin County)	55419
Dilworth	56529
Dinkytown (Part of Minneapolis)	55414
Dodge Center	55927
Donaldson	56720
Donnelly (Stevens County)	56235
Dora Lake	56661
Doran	56522
Dorothy	56750
Dorset	56470
Douglas (Olmsted County)	55960
Douglas Lodge	56460
Dover (Olmsted County)	55929
Dovray	56125
Downer	56514
Dresbach	55947
Duelm	56329
Duluth	55801-16
For specific Duluth Zip Codes call (218) 626-2959	
Duluth International Airport, 4787th Air Base Group	55814
Dumfries	55981
Dumont	56236
Dundas	55019
Dundee	56126
Dunnell	56127
Dunvilla	56572
Duquette	55729
Duxbury	55048
Eagan	55121

Name	ZIP
Eagle Bend	56446
Eagle Lake (Blue Earth County)	56024
East Beaver Bay	55601
East Bethel	55005
East Chain	56031
East Cottage Grove (Part of Cottage Grove)	55016
Eastern Heights (Part of St. Paul)	55119
East Grand Forks	56721
East Gull Lake	56401
East Hastings (Part of Hastings)	55033
East Lake	55760
East Lake Francis Shores	55040
Easton	56025
East Prairieville	55021
Eastside (Hennepin County)	55418
East Union	55315
Ebro	56621
Echo (Yellow Medicine County)	56237
Echols	56081
Eddsville	55310
Eden (Dodge County)	55927
Eden Prairie	55344
Eden Prairie Center (Part of Eden Prairie)	55344
Eden Valley	55329
Edgerton	56128
Edgewood	55008
Edina	55424
Effie	56639
Eidswold	55020
Eitzen	55931
Elba (Winona County)	55910
Elbow Lake (Grant County)	56531
Eldes Corner	55810
Eldred	56523
Elgin (Wabasha County)	55932
Elizabeth (Otter Tail County)	56533
Elkland	55021
Elko	55020
Elk River	55330
Elkton (Mower County)	55933
Ellendale	56026
Ellsworth (Nobles County)	56129
Elmdale (Morrison County)	56314
Elmer (St. Louis County)	55765
Elmore	56027
Elmwood (Hennepin County)	55416
Elrosa	56325
Elway (Part of St. Paul)	55116
Ely	55731
Ely Lake	55734
Elysian	56028
Embarrass	55732
Emco (Part of Hoyt Lakes)	55750
Emily	56447
Emmons	56029
Empire (Dakota County)	55024
Enfield	55362
Englund	56758
Erdahl	56531
Erhard	56534
Ericsonville	56359
Ericsburg	56649
Erie (Pennington County)	56725
Erskine	56535
Esden	56444
Esko	55733
Essig	56030
Estes Brook	56357
Etna	55975
Etter	55089
Euclid	56722
Evan	56238
Evansville	56326
Eveleth	55734
Everdell	56520
Evergreen	56544
Excelsior	55331
Eyota (Olmsted County)	55934
Fairbanks	55602
Fairfax (Renville County)	55332
Fairhaven	55382
Fairmont (Martin County)	56031
Faith	56584
Falcon Heights	55113
Faribault	55021
Farming	56368
Farmington (Dakota County)	55024
Farris	56633
Farwell	56327
Federal Correctional Institution	55072
Federal Dam	56641
Felton	56536

Fergus Falls-Ironton **MINNESOTA** **289**

	ZIP		ZIP		ZIP
Fergus Falls	56537-38	Glyndon	56547	Hayward	56043
For specific Fergus Falls Zip Codes call (218) 736-7840		Godahl	56081	Hazel Run (Yellow Medicine County)	56247
Fernando	55385	Golden Hill	55901	Hazelwood	55057
Fertile	56540	Golden Hills (Part of St. Louis Park)	55416	Heatwole	55350
Fifty Lakes	56448	Golden Valley (Hennepin County)	55427	Hector (Renville County)	55342
Fillmore (Fillmore County)	55990	Gonvick	56644	Heiberg	56584
Finland	55603	Goodhue	55027	Heidelberg	56071
Finland Air Force Station, 756th Radar Squadron	55603	Goodland (Itasca County)	55742	Heinola	56567
Finlayson (Pine County)	55735	Goodridge (Pennington County)	56725	Henderson	56044
Fisher	56723	Good Thunder	56037	Hendricks	56136
Flensburg	56328	Goodview	55987	Hendrum (Norman County)	56550
Fletcher	55369	Gordon (Freeborn County)	56036	Henning (Otter Tail County)	56551
Flintwood Hills (Part of Ramsey)	55303	Gotha	55322	Henriette	55036
Flom	56541	Graceton	56686	Henrytown	55939
Floodwood	55736	Graceville	56240	Herman	56248
Florence (Lyon County)	56130	Granada	56039	Hermantown	55811
Florenton	55792	Grand Falls	56627	Heron Lake (Jackson County)	56137
Florian	56758	Grand Marais	55604	Hewitt	56453
Foley	56329	Grand Meadow (Mower County)	55936	Hiawatha Spur (Part of Eagan)	55111
Fond du Lac Indian Reservation	55720	Grand Portage	55605	Hibbing	55746-47
Forada	56308	Grand Portage Indian Reservation	55605	For specific Hibbing Zip Codes call (218) 263-4086	
Forbes	55738	Grand Rapids	55744	Hidden Creek (Part of Andover)	55303
Fordson (Part of Eagan)	55121	Grand View Heights	56573	High Forest	55976
Forest City	55355	Grandy	55029	Highland (Fillmore County)	55986
Forest Grove	56660	Granger	55937	Highland (Hennepin County)	55411
Forest Lake (Washington County)	55025	Granite Falls	56241	Highland (Lake County)	55616
Forest Mills	55992	Grass Lake (Kanabec County)	55006	Highland (Wright County)	55349
Foreston	56330	Grasston	55030	High Landing	56725
Fork (Marshall County)	56744	Grattan (Itasca County)	56661	Highland Park (Part of St. Paul)	55116
Fort Ripley	56449	Greaney	55740	Hill City	55748
Fort Snelling	55111	Greater Leech Lake Indian Reservation	56633	Hillman (Morrison County)	56338
Fosston	56542	Greenbush (Roseau County)	56726	Hills	56138
Fossum	56584	Greenfield (Hennepin County)	55357	Hilltop	55421
Fountain	55935	Green Isle (Sibley County)	55338	Hillview	56477
Four Corners	55811	Greenland	56028	Hinckley (Pine County)	55037
Fourtown	56727	Greenleaf	55355	Hines	56647
Foxhome	56543	Greenleafton	55965	Hitterdal	56552
Fox Lake	56181	Green Valley (Lyon County)	56258	Hoffman	56339
Franconia	55074	Greenwald	56335	Hoffmans Corners (Part of Gem Lake)	55110
Franklin (Renville County)	55333	Greenwood (Hennepin County)	55331	Hokah	55941
Franklin (St. Louis County)	55792	Grey Eagle (Todd County)	56336	Holdingford	56340
Franklin Avenue (Part of Minneapolis)	55404	Grogan	56081	Holland (Pipestone County)	56139
Frazee	56544	Groningen	55072	Hollandale	56045
Freeborn	56032	Grove City	55975	Holloway	56249
Freeburg	55921	Grove Lake (Pope County)	56316	Hollywood (Carver County)	55388
Freedhem	56345	Grygla	56727	Holmes City (Douglas County)	56341
Freeport	56331	Guckeen	56013	Holt (Marshall County)	56738
Fremont	55979	Gully	56646	Holyoke	55749
French Lake	55302	Gutches Grove	56347	Homer	55942
French River	55804	Guthrie	56461	Hoot Lake (Part of Fergus Falls)	56537
Fridley	55432	Hackensack	56452	Hope (Steele County)	56046
Friesland	55037	Hackett	56623	Hopkins	55343-47
Frontenac	55026	Hader	55992	For specific Hopkins Zip Codes call (612) 935-8606	
Frost	56033	Hadley	56133	Hopper (Part of Mountain Iron)	55792
Fulda	56131	Hagan	56262	Houston (Houston County)	55943
Funkley	56630	Hallock	56728	Hovland	55606
Garden City	56034	Halma	56729	Howard Lake	55349
Garfield (Douglas County)	56332	Halstad (Norman County)	56548	Hoyt Lakes	55750
Garrison	56450	Hamburg	55339	Hubbard	56470
Garvin	56132	Hamel	55340	Hugo	55038
Gary	56545	Hamilton	55975	Humboldt	56731
Gatzke	56724	Ham Lake	55304	Huntersville (Wadena County)	56464
Gaylord	55334	Hammond (Wabasha County)	55938	Huntley	56047
Gem Lake	55110	Hampton	55031	Husby Spur (Part of Arden Hills)	55112
Gemmell	56660	Hancock (Stevens County)	56244	Hutchinson (McLeod County)	55350
Geneva	56035	Hanley Falls	56245	Hydes Lake	55322
Genoa (Olmsted County)	55920	Hanover	55341	Ideal Corners	56472
Genoa (St. Louis County)	55734	Hanska	56041	Idington	55703
Genola	56364	Happyland	56653	Ihlen	56140
Gentilly	56716	Harding	56364	Illgen City	55614
Georgetown	56546	Hardwick	56134	Imogene	56039
Georgeville	56312	Har-Mar Mall (Part of Roseville)	55113	Independence (Hennepin County)	55359
Gheen	55740	Harmony	55939	Independence (St. Louis County)	55727
Gheen Corner	55740	Harnell Park	55779	Indus	56629
Ghent	56239	Harris (Chisago County)	55032	Industrial (Ramsey County)	55104
Gibbon	55335	Hart	55971	Inger	56636
Giese	55735	Hartland	56042	Inguadona	56655
Gilbert	55741	Hassan (Hennepin County)	55374	International Falls	56649
Gilfillan	56283	Hassman	56431	Inver Grove Heights	55076-77
Gilman	56333	Hastings	55033	For specific Inver Grove Heights Zip Codes call (612) 451-1243	
Gladstone (Part of Maplewood)	55109	Hasty	55320	Iona (Murray County)	56141
Glen (Aitkin County)	56431	Hatfield	56135	Iron	55751
Glencoe	55336	Havana	55060	Ironhub	56431
Glendale	55771	Hawick	56246	Ironton	56455
Glendorado	55371	Hawley	56549		
Glen Lake (Part of Minnetonka)	55343	Hay Creek	55066		
Glenville	56036	Haydenville	56256		
Glenwood (Pope County)	56334	Hayfield	55940		
Glenwood Junction (Part of Golden Valley)	55427	Haypoint	55748		
Glory	56431				
Gloster (Part of Maplewood)	55109				
Gluek	56260				

290 MINNESOTA Isabella-Middle River

	ZIP		ZIP		ZIP
Isabella	55607	Lake Shore (Cass County)	56401	Luverne (Rock County)	56156
Isanti	55040	Lake Shore Park (Part of White Bear Lake)	55110	Luxemburg (Stearns County)	56301
Island Lake (Beltrami County)	56667	Lakeside (Renville County)	55314	Lydia	55352
Island Park (Part of Mound)	55364	Lakeside (St. Louis County)	55804	Lyle (Mower County)	55953
Island View	56649	Lake St. Croix Beach	55043	Lynd	56157
Isle	56342	Lake Street (Part of Minneapolis)	55408	Lyndale (Part of Independence)	55359
Ivanhoe	56142	Lakeville	55044	Lynwood (Part of Hibbing)	55746
Iverson	55718	Lake Wilson	56151	Mabel	55954
Jackson (Jackson County)	56143	Lamberton (Redwood County)	56152	McCauleyville	56553
Jacobson	55752	Lamoille	55987	McGrath	56350
Jacobs Prairie	56320	Lamson	55325	McGregor	55760
Jakeville	56329	Lancaster	56735	McHugh	56501
Jameson	56649	Landfall Village	55128	McIntosh	56556
Janesville (Waseca County)	56048	Lanesboro	55949	McKee (Part of Eagan)	55121
Jarretts	55957	Langdon (Part of Cottage Grove)	55016	McKinley (St. Louis County)	55761
Jasper	56144	Lansing	55950	Madelia (Watonwan County)	56062
Jeffers	56145	Laporte	56461	Madison	56256
Jenkins	56456	La Prairie (Itasca County)	55744	Madison East (Part of Mankato)	56001
Jennie	55325	Larsmont	55616	Madison Lake	56063
Jessenland	56044	La Salle	56056	Magnolia (Rock County)	56158
Jessie Lake	56637	Lastrup	56344	Mahkonce	56557
Johnsburg	55909	Lauderdale	55113	Mahnomen	56557
Johnson (Big Stone County)	56250	Lavinia	55746	Mahtomedi	55115
Johnsville (Part of Blaine)	55433	Lawler	55760	Mahtowa	55762
Jonathan (Part of Chaska)	55318	Lawndale	56579	Maine	56586
Jordan (Scott County)	55352	Lax Lake	55614	Maine Prairie (Stearns County)	55353
Judson	56055	Leader	56466	Makinen	55763
Kabekona	56461	Leaf Lake	56551	Mall (Part of Fairmont)	56031
Kabetogama	56669	Leaf Valley	56332	Malmo	56431
Kanaranzi	56146	Leavenworth (Brown County)	56085	Manannah	56243
Kandi Mall Shopping Center (Part of Willmar)	56201	Le Center	56057	Manchester	56064
Kandiyohi	56251	Leetonia (Part of Hibbing)	55746	Manhattan Beach	56463
Karlstad	56732	Le Hillier	56001	Manitou	56629
Kasota	56050	Lengby	56651	Mankato	56001-02
Kasson	55944	Lenora	55922	For specific Mankato Zip Codes call (507) 625-1781	
Katrine	56444	Leonard	56652	Mansfield	56009
Keewatin	55753	Leonidas	55734	Mantorville	55955
Kelliher	56650	Leota	56153	Maple (Carver County)	55387
Kellogg	55945	Lerdal	56007	Maple Bay	56736
Kelly Lake (Part of Hibbing)	55754	Le Roy (Mower County)	55951	Maple Grove (Hennepin County)	55369
Kelsey (St. Louis County)	55755	Lester Prairie	55354	Maple Hill	55604
Kennedy	56733	Le Sueur	56058	Maple Island	56045
Kenneth	56147	Lewis Lake	55006	Maple Lake (Wright County)	55358
Kensington	56343	Lewiston	55952	Maple Plain	55359
Kent	56553	Lewisville	56060	Mapleton	56065
Kenwood (Hennepin County)	55403	Lexington (Anoka County)	55112	Mapleview	55912
Kenwood (St. Louis County)	55811	Lexington (Le Sueur County)	56057	Maplewood (Ramsey County)	55109
Kenyon	55946	Libby	55760	Maplewood Mall (Part of Maplewood)	55109
Kerkhoven (Swift County)	56252	Lilydale	55118	Marble (Itasca County)	55764
Kerr (Part of Hibbing)	55746	Lime Creek	56131	Marcell	56657
Kerrick (Pine County)	55756	Lincoln (Morrison County)	56443	Margie	56658
Kettle River (Carlton County)	55757	Linden Grove	55723	Marietta	56257
Kiester	56051	Lindford	56653	Marine On St. Croix	55047
Kilkenny	56052	Lindstrom	55045	Marion	55901
Kimball (Stearns County)	55353	Lino Lakes	55014	Markham	55763
Kimberly (Aitkin County)	56431	Linwood	55005	Markville	55048
Kinbrae	56126	Lismore (Nobles County)	56155	Marshall (Lyon County)	56258
Kingsdale	55048	Litchfield (Meeker County)	55355	Martin Lake	55079
Kings Park	55960	Litomysl	55060	Marysburg	56063
Kingston (Meeker County)	55326	Little Canada	55110	Marystown	55379
Kinmount	55771	Little Chicago	55057	Matawan	56072
Kinney	55758	Little Falls (Morrison County)	56345	Mattson	56728
Kitzville (Part of Hibbing)	55746	Littlefork	56653	Max (Itasca County)	56659
Kjellberg Park	55362	Little Marais	55614	Mayer	55360
Klossner	56053	Little Pine (Crow Wing County)	56431	Mayhew	56379
Knapp	55321	Little Rock (Morrison County)	56373	Mayhew Lake (Benton County)	56379
Knife River	55609	Little Sauk	56346	Maynard	56260
Knollwood Mall (Part of St. Louis Park)	55426	Little Swan (Part of Hibbing)	55746	Mayville (Mower County)	55912
Komensky	55350	Local	56501	Mazeppa (Wabasha County)	55956
Kragnes	56560	Lockhart	56510	M&D Junction (Part of White Bear Lake)	55110
Kroschel	55037	Loman	56654	Meadowlands (St. Louis County)	55765
Lac Qui Parle	56265	London	56061	Medford (Steele County)	55049
La Crescent	55947	Long Beach	56334	Medicine Lake	55441
Lafayette (Nicollet County)	56054	Long Lake (Hennepin County)	55356	Meire Grove	56352
Lagoona Beach	56278	Long Point	56686	Melby	56326
Lake Benton	56149	Long Prairie (Todd County)	56347	Melrose (Stearns County)	56352
Lake Bronson	56734	Long Siding	55371	Melrude	55766
Lake Center	56511	Longville	56655	Menahga	56464
Lake City	55041	Lonsdale	55046	Mendota	55150
Lake Crystal	56055	Loop (Part of Minneapolis)	55402	Mendota Heights	55118
Lake Elmo	55042	Loretto	55357	Mentor	56736
Lake Eunice	56501	Loring (Part of Minneapolis)	55403	Meriden	56067
Lakefield	56150	Louisburg	56254	Merrifield	56465
Lake George	56458	Louriston (Chippewa County)	56260	Merton	55060
Lake Henry	56362	Lower Sioux Indian Reservation	56270	Mesaba (Part of Hoyt Lakes)	55750
Lake Hubert	56459	Lowry	56349	Middle River (Marshall County)	56737
Lake Itasca	56460	Lucan	56255		
Lakeland	55043	Lude	56686		
Lakeland Shores	55043	Lutsen	55612		
Lake Lillian	56253				
Lake Netta (Part of Ham Lake)	55303				
Lake Nichols	55717				
Lake Park (Becker County)	56554				
Lake Sarah (Hennepin County)	55357				

Midway-Pillsbury **MINNESOTA** **291**

	ZIP		ZIP		ZIP
Midway (Becker County)	56464	Montevideo	56265	Northtown Shopping Center	
Midway (Ramsey County)	55104	Montgomery	56069	(Part of Blaine)	55434
Midway (St. Louis County)	55792	Monticello (Wright County)	55362	Northwest Terminal (Part of	
Midway Center (Part of St.		Montrose	55363	Minneapolis)	55418
Paul)	55104	Moorhead	56560-61	Norway Lake (Kandiyohi	
Miesville	55009	For specific Moorhead Zip Codes		County)	56289
Milaca (Mille Lacs County)	56353	call (218) 236-6001		Norwood	55368
Milan	56262	Moose Lake (Carlton		Nowthen	55303
Mille Lacs Indian		County)	55767	Noyes	56740
Reservation	56359	Moose Lake State Hospital	55767	Oak Center	55041
Miller Hill (Part of Duluth)	55811	Mora	55051	Oakdale	55128
Miller Hill Mall (Part of		Morgan (Redwood County)	56266	Oakhill	56347
Duluth)	55811	Morgan Park (Part of		Oak Island	56741
Millersburg	55021	Duluth)	55808	Oak Knoll (Part of	
Millerville	56315	Morningside (Part of Edina)	55424	Minnetonka)	55343
Millville	55957	Morrill	56329	Oakland	56076
Milroy	56263	Morris (Stevens County)	56267	Oak Park (Anoka County)	55433
Miltona	56354	Morristown (Rice County)	55052	Oak Park (Benton County)	56357
Mineral Center	55605	Morton	56270	Oak Park Heights	55082
		Moscow	55912	Oak Ridge	55910
Minneapolis	55401-80	Motley (Morrison County)	56466	Odessa	56276
For specific Minneapolis Zip		Mound (Hennepin County)	55364	Odin (Watonwan County)	56160
Codes call (612) 452-3800		Mounds View	55432	Ogema (Becker County)	56569
COLLEGES & UNIVERSITIES		Mountain Iron	55768	Ogilvie	56358
Augsburg College	55454	Mountain Lake (Cottonwood		Okabena	56161
North Central Bible College	55404	County)	56159	Oklee	56742
University of Minnesota-		Mount Royal (Part of		Old Frontenac	55041
Twin Cities	55455	Duluth)	55803	Olga	56646
FINANCIAL INSTITUTIONS		Munger	55806	Olivia	56277
First Bank National		Murdock	56271	Onamia (Mille Lacs County)	56359
Association	55420	Murphy City	55603	Onigum	56484
First Minnesota Savings		Muskoda	56549	Opole	56340
Bank, FSB	55402	Myrtle	56070	Orchard Lake (Part of	
IDS Bank and Trust	55402	Nashua	56565	Lakeville)	55044
Investors Savings Bank,		Nashwauk	55769	Org	56187
F.S.B.	55402	Nassau	56272	Orleans	56735
Marquette Bank		Navarre (Part of Orono)	55392	Ormsby	56162
Minneapolis, National		Naytahwaush	56566	Orono	55323
Association	55480	Nebish	56667	Oronoco (Olmsted County)	55960
First Star MetroBank	55425	Nelson (Douglas County)	56355	Orr	55771
Midwest Federal Savings &		Nerstrand	55053	Orrock	55309
Loan Association of		Nett Lake	55772	Ortonville	56278
Minneapolis	55402	Nett Lake Indian		Osage	56570
National City Bank of		Reservation	55772	Osakis	56360
Minneapolis	55402	Nevis	56467	Oshawa	56082
Norwest Bank Minnesota,		New Auburn (Sibley		Oslo (Dodge County)	55940
National Association	55479	County)	55366	Oslo (Marshall County)	56744
Park National Bank of St.		New Brighton	55112	Oslund	56680
Louis Park	55416	Newburg	55954	Osseo	55369
Richfield Bank & Trust Co	55423	Newfolden (Marshall		Ostrander	55961
TCF Banking & Savings,		County)	56738	Otisco	56077
F.A.	55402	New Germany	55367	Otisville	56073
HOSPITALS		New Hartford	55925	Ottawa	56058
Abbott-Northwestern		New Hope	55428	Otter Creek	55718
Hospital	55407	Newhouse	55954	Ottertail (Otter Tail County)	56571
Fairview Riverside Hospital	55454	New London	56273	Outing	56662
Fairview Southdale Hospital	55435	New Market	55054	Owatonna (Steele County)	55060
Health Metropolitan		New Munich	56356	Oxlip	55040
Hospitals	55430	Newport	55055	Oylen	56481
Hennepin County Medical		New Prague	56071	Padua	56378
Center	55415	New Richland (Waseca		Palisade	56469
Metropolitan Mt. Sinai		County)	56072	Palmdale	55084
Medical Center	55404	New Rome	55307	Palmers	55804
University of Minnesota		Newry (Freeborn County)	56045	Palo	55705
Hospital and Clinic	55455	New Trier	55031	Parent	56329
Veterans Administration		New Ulm	56073	Parkers Prairie (Otter Tail	
Medical Center	55417	New York Mills	56567	County)	56361
HOTELS/MOTELS		Nickerson	55797	Park Rapids	56470
Hyatt Regency Minneapolis		Nicollet (Nicollet County)	56074	Park View (Part of	
Nicollet Mall	55403	Nicols (Part of Eagan)	55121	Crookston)	56716
Sheraton Park Place Hotel	55416	Nicolville	55912	Parkville (Part of Mountain	
The Vista Marquette	55402	Nielsville	56568	Iron)	55773
MILITARY INSTALLATIONS		Nimrod	56478	Payne	55765
Minneapolis-St. Paul		Nininger (Dakota County)	55033	Payne Avenue (Part of St.	
International Airport,		Nisswa	56468	Paul)	55101
934th Tactical Airlift		Nodine	55925	Paynesville (Stearns County)	56362
Group	55450	Nokomis (Part of		Pearl Lake	55353
Minnehaha (Part of		Minneapolis)	55417	Pease	56363
Minneapolis)	55406	Nopeming	55810	Pelican Rapids	56572
Minneiska (Wabasha		Norcross	56274	Pelland	56649
County)	55910	Normandale (Part of Edina)	55435	Pemberton	56078
Minneota (Lyon County)	56264	Norseland	56082	Pencer	56751
Minnesota City	55959	North Benton	56329	Pengilly	55775
Minnesota Lake	56068	North Branch (Chisago		Pennington	56663
Minnesota Transfer (Part of		County)	55056	Pennock	56279
St. Paul)	55114	Northcote	56728	Pequaywan Lake	55801
Minnetonka	55345	Northdale (Part of Coon		Pequot Lakes	56472
Minnetonka Beach	55361	Rapids)	55433	Perham (Otter Tail County)	56573
Minnetonka Mills (Part of		North Douglas (Part of		Perkins	55943
Minnetonka)	55343	Crystal)	55422	Perley	56574
Minnetrista	55364	Northfield (Rice County)	55057	Petersburg	56143
Minnewawa	55760	North Mankato	56001	Peterson	55962
Mizpah	56660	North Oaks	55110	Petran	56043
Moland (Rice County)	55946	Northome	56661	Phelps	56586
Money Creek	55943	North Prairie	56314	Philbrook	56466
		North Redwood	56283	Pickwick	55987
		Northrop	56075	Pierz (Morrison County)	56364
		Northside (Part of Albert		Pigeon River	55605
		Lea)	56007	Pike Lake	55811
		North St. Paul	55109	Pillager	56473
				Pillsbury (Todd County)	56382

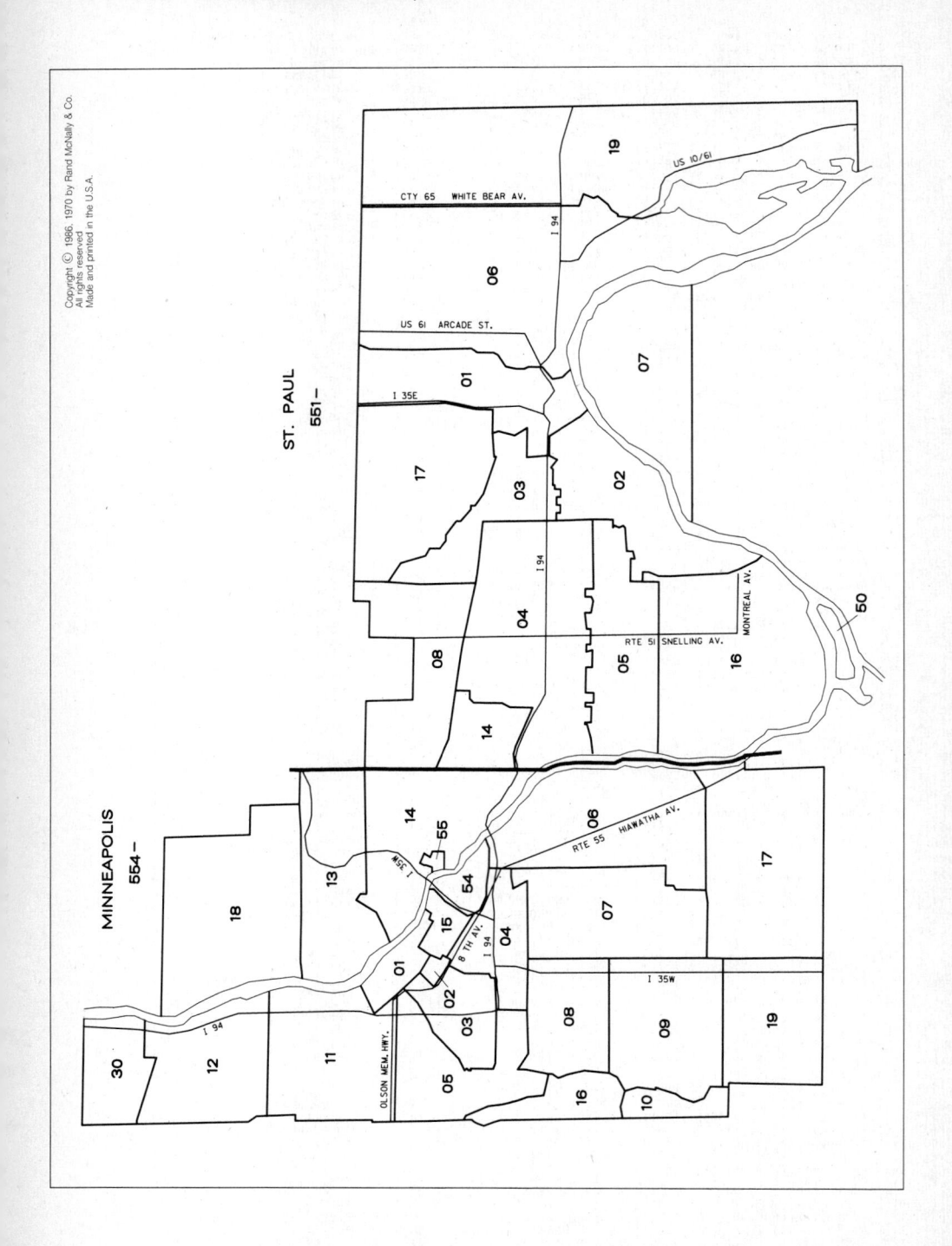

MINNESOTA Minneapolis

MINNESOTA 293

Location	ZIP
Pilot Grove	56027
Pilot Mound	55923
Pine Bend (Dakota County)	55068
Pine Bend (Mahnomen County)	56651
Pine Brook	55008
Pine Center	56401
Pine City (Pine County)	55063
Pinecreek	56751
Pine Island	55963
Pine River (Cass County)	56474
Pine Springs	55115
Pineville	55705
Pinewood	56676
Pioneer (Part of St. Paul)	55101
Pipestone	56164
Pitt	56665
Plainview (Wabasha County)	55964
Plato	55370
Pleasant Grove	55976
Pleasant Lake	56301
Plummer	56748
Plymouth	55441
Point Douglas	55033
Ponemah	56666
Ponsford	56575
Poplar (Cass County)	56479
Popple Creek	56379
Port Cargill (Part of Savage)	55378
Porter	56280
Post Town	55920
Potsdam	55932
Powderhorn (Part of Minneapolis)	55407
Prairie Island Indian Reservation	55089
Prairieville (Rice County)	55021
Pratt	55060
Predmore	55934
Preston	55965
Priam	56282
Princeton (Mille Lacs County)	55371
Prinsburg	56281
Prior Lake	55372
Prior Lake Indian Reservation	55372
Proctor	55810
Prosit	55702
Prosper	55954
Pulaski Lake Shores	55313
Puposky	56667
Quamba	55007
Racine (Mower County)	55967
Radium	56762
Rainy Junction (Part of Virginia)	55792
Ramey	56329
Ramsey (Anoka County)	55303
Ramsey (Mower County)	55912
Randall	56475
Randolph	55065
Ranier	56668
Rapidan	56001
Rassat	55313
Rauch	55740
Ray	56669
Raymond (Kandiyohi County)	56282
Reading	56165
Reads Landing	55968
Redby	56670
Redlake	56671
Red Lake Falls (Red Lake County)	56750
Red Lake Indian Reservation	56671
Red Rock (Cook County)	55605
Red Top	56342
Red Wing	55066
Redwood Falls (Redwood County)	56283
Reformatory (Part of St. Cloud)	56301
Regal	56312
Remer	56672
Reno (Houston County)	55919
Renville	56284
Revere	56166
Rice (Benton County)	56367
Riceford	55954
Rice Street (Part of St. Paul)	55117
Richfield	55423
Richfield Hub Shopping Center (Part of Richfield)	55423
Richmond (Stearns County)	56368
Rich Valley (Dakota County)	55075
Richville	56576
Richwood	56577

Location	ZIP
Ridgedale Shopping Center (Part of Minnetonka)	55343
Ridgeway	55943
Rindal	56540
Riverside (Hennepin County)	55454
Riverside Heights	56013
Riverton (Crow Wing County)	56455
Riverview (Part of St. Paul)	55107
Robbin	58225
Robbinsdale	55422
Robinson	55731
Rochert	56578
Rochester	55901-04
For specific Rochester Zip Codes call (507) 282-3811	
Rock Creek	55067
Rock Dell	55920
Rockford (Wright County)	55373
Rockville	56369
Rogers (Hennepin County)	55374
Rollag	56549
Rollingstone (Winona County)	55969
Rollins	55602
Ronneby	56329
Roosevelt (Roseau County)	56673
Roscoe	55983
Roscoe	56371
Roseau	56751
Rose City	56446
Rose Creek	55970
Roseland	56216
Rosemount (Dakota County)	55068
Rosen	56212
Rosendale (Meeker County)	56243
Roseport (Part of Inver Grove Heights)	55075
Roseville (Ramsey County)	55113
Rosewood (Marshall County)	56701
Ross	56751
Rossburg	56431
Rothsay	56579
Round Lake (Nobles County)	56167
Round Prairie	56347
Rowena	56293
Royalton (Morrison County)	56373
Roy Lake	56557
Ruby Junction (Part of Hibbing)	55746
Rush City	55069
Rushford	55971
Rushford Village	55962
Rushmore	56168
Rush Point	55080
Rush River	56058
Ruskin	55021
Russell	56169
Rustad	56560
Ruthton	56170
Rutledge	55778
Sabin	56580
Sacred Heart (Renville County)	56285
Saga Hill (Part of Orono)	55323
Saginaw	55779
St. Anna	56310
St. Anthony (Hennepin County)	55418
St. Anthony (Stearns County)	56307
St. Augusta (Stearns County)	56301
Saint Benedict	56071
St. Bonifacius	55375
St. Charles (Winona County)	55972
St. Clair (Blue Earth County)	56080
St. Clair (Ramsey County)	55116
St. Cloud	56301-04
For specific St. Cloud Zip Codes call (612) 251-8220	
St. Croix Junction (Part of Hastings)	55033
St. Francis (Anoka County)	55070
St. Francis (Stearns County)	56331
St. George (Nicollet County)	56073
St. Henry	56057
St. Hilaire	56754
St. James (Watonwan County)	56081
St. Joseph (Stearns County)	56374
St. Killian	56185
St. Leo	56286
St. Louis Park	55426
St. Martin	56376
St. Mary's Point	55043

Location	ZIP
St. Mathias (Crow Wing County)	56449
St. Michael	55376
St. Nicholas	55389
St. Patrick	56071
St. Paul	55101-89
For specific St. Paul Zip Codes call (612) 452-3800	

COLLEGES & UNIVERSITIES

Bethel College	55112
College of St. Catherine	55105
College of St. Thomas	55105
Macalester College	55105
Metropolitan State University	55101
William Mitchell College of Law	55105

FINANCIAL INSTITUTIONS

American National Bank & Trust Company	55101
Commercial State Bank in St. Paul	55102
Eastern Heights State Bank of St. Paul	55119
First Star Roseville Bank	55113
Liberty State Bank	55104
Midway National Bank	55104

HOSPITALS

Healtheast Bethesda Lutheran Hospital	55103
St. Paul-Ramsey Medical Center	55101
United Hospital	55102

HOTELS/MOTELS

Holiday Inn St. Paul/East	55119
Ramada Hotel St. Paul	55119
The Saint Paul	55102

MILITARY INSTALLATIONS

Fort Snelling	55111
Minnesota Air National Guard, 133rd Tacitcal Airlift Wing	55111
Twin Cities Army Ammunition Plant (Semiactive)	55112
United States Army Engineer District, St. Paul	55101
United States Army Transportation Office, Minneapolis-St. Paul Area	55111

Location	ZIP
St. Paul Park	55071
St. Peter	56082
St. Rosa	56331
St. Thomas	56058
St. Vincent	56755
St. Wendel	56310
Salem Corners	55920
Salol	56756
Sanborn	56083
Sandstone (Pine County)	55072
Santiago	55377
Saratoga (Winona County)	55972
Sargeant (Mower County)	55973
Sartell	56377
Sauk Centre (Stearns County)	56378
Sauk Rapids	56379
Saum	56674
Savage	55378
Sawyer	55780
Scandia (Washington County)	55073
Scandia Valley (Morrison County)	56443
Scanlon	55720
Schley	56633
Schroeder	55613
Scotts Corner	55718
Seaforth	56287
Searles	56084
Sebeka	56477
Section Thirty	55731
Sedan	56380
Seven-Hi Shopping Center (Part of Minnetonka)	55343
Shafer	55074
Shakopee	55379
Shaw	55717
Sheffield Mill (Part of Faribault)	55021
Sheldon	55921
Shelly (Norman County)	56581
Sherack	56722
Sherburn	56171
Sheshebee	55760

MINNESOTA St. Paul

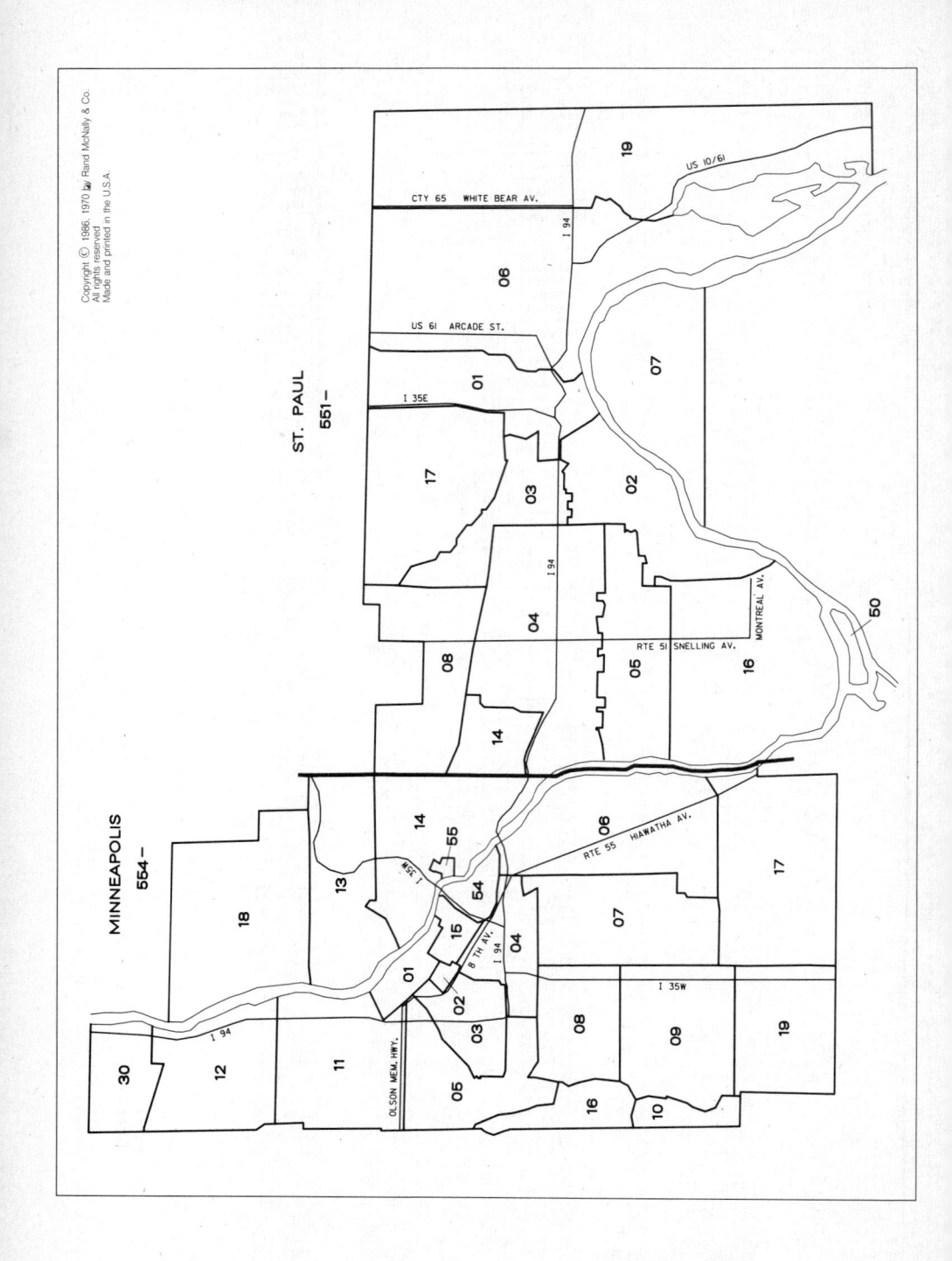

Shevlin-Willernie MINNESOTA 295

Name	ZIP
Shevlin	56676
Shieldsville (Rice County)	55021
Shooks	56661
Shoreham	56501
Shoreview	55112
Shorewood	55331
Shotley (Beltrami County)	56650
Shovel Lake	55785
Side Lake	55781
Signal Hills Shopping Center (Part of West St. Paul)	55118
Silica	55746
Silo	55952
Silver Bay	55614
Silver Creek (Lake County)	55616
Silver Creek (Wright County)	55380
Silverdale	55740
Silver Lake (McLeod County)	55381
Simpson	55901
Sioux Valley	51347
Skibo	55750
Skyburg	55946
Skyline	56001
Slayton (Murray County)	56172
Sleepy Eye	56085
Sletten	56556
Smiths Mill	56048
Snellman	56570
Sobieski	56345
Soderville (Part of Ham Lake)	55304
Sogn	55018
Solway (Beltrami County)	56678
Soudan	55782
South Bend (Blue Earth County)	56001
South Branch	56081
Southdale (Part of Edina)	55435
Southdale Center (Part of Edina)	55424
South Haven	55382
South International Falls	56679
South Minneapolis (Part of Minneapolis)	55408
South St. Paul	55075-77
For specific South St. Paul Zip Codes call (612) 451-1243	
Southtown Center (Part of Bloomington)	55420
Spafford	56187
Spectacle Lake	55008
Spicer	56288
Springfield (Brown County)	56087
Spring Grove	55974
Spring Hill	56352
Spring Lake (Isanti County)	55056
Spring Lake (Itasca County)	56680
Spring Lake Park	55432
Spring Park	55384
Springsteel Island	56763
Springvale	55080
Spring Valley	55975
Spruce Center	56354
Squaw Lake	56681
Stacy	55079
Stanchfield	55080
Stanley (Isanti County)	55008
Stanton	55018
Staples (Todd County)	56479
Starbuck	56381
Stark (Chisago County)	55032
Steele Center	55060
Steelton (Part of Duluth)	55808
Steen	56173
Stephen	56757
Sterling Center	56010
Stewart (Lake County)	55616
Stewart (McLeod County)	55385
Stewartville	55976
Stillwater	55082-83
For specific Stillwater Zip Codes call (612) 439-4232	
Stockholm	55321
Stockton	55988
Storden	56174
Strandquist	56758
Strathcona	56759
Strout	55355
St Stephen	56375
Stubbs Bay (Part of Orono)	55356
Sturgeon (St. Louis County)	55703
Sturgeon Lake	55783
Sugar Loaf (Part of Winona)	55987
Summit (Steele County)	55917
Sunburg	56289
Sundal	56545
Sunfish Lake	55118
Sunrise (Chisago County)	55056
Svea (Kandiyohi County)	56290

Name	ZIP
Sveadahl	56081
Swanburg	56474
Swan River (Itasca County)	55784
Swanville (Morrison County)	56382
Swatara	55785
Swift	56673
Swift Falls	56215
Sylvan (Cass County)	56473
Syre	56584
Tabor	56712
Taconite	55786
Taconite Harbor	55613
Talmoon	56637
Tamarack	55787
Taopi	55977
Taunton	56291
Tawney	55954
Taylors Falls	55084
Tenney	56583
Tenstrike	56683
Terrace	56380
Terrebonne	56750
The Arches	55952
Theilman	55978
Thief River Falls	56701
Third Crow Wing Lake	56467
Thompson Grove (Part of Cottage Grove)	55016
Thompson Heights (Part of Coon Rapids)	55433
Thompson Heights Shopping Center (Part of Coon Rapids)	55433
Thompson Park (Part of Coon Rapids)	55433
Thompson Riverview Terrace (Part of Coon Rapids)	55433
Thomson	55718
Thor	56431
Thorhult	56727
Tintah (Traverse County)	56583
Toad Lake	56544
Tofte	55615
Togo	55788
Toimi	55602
Toivola	55789
Tonka Bay	55331
Tower	55790
Tracy	56175
Traffic (Part of Minneapolis)	55403
Trail	56684
Trails End	55604
Traverse (Nicollet County)	56082
Trimont	56176
Trommald	56441
Trosky	56177
Troy (Winona County)	55972
Truman	56088
Turtle River (Beltrami County)	56601
Twig	55791
Twin Cities (Part of Richfield)	55111
Twin Lakes (Freeborn County)	56089
Twin Valley	56584
Two Harbors	55616
Two Inlets	56470
Tyler	56178
Ulen	56585
Underwood (Otter Tail County)	56586
Union Hill	56071
University (Part of Minneapolis)	55414
Upper Sioux Indian Reservation	56241
Upsala	56384
Uptown (Part of St. Paul)	55102
Urbank	56361
U.S. Air Force	55814
Utica	55979
Vadnais Heights	55110
Valley Ridge (Part of Burnsville)	55378
Valley West Shopping Center (Part of Bloomington)	55420
Vasa	55089
Verdi	56179
Vergas	56587
Vermillion	55085
Vermillion Dam	55771
Verndale	56481
Vernon Center	56090
Veseli	55046
Vesta (Redwood County)	56292
Victoria	55386
Viking (Marshall County)	56760

Name	ZIP
Village North Shopping Center (Part of Brooklyn Park)	55429
Villard (Pope County)	56385
Vineland (Mille Lacs County)	56359
Vining	56588
Viola	55934
Virginia	55792
Vista	55077
Wabasha	55981
Wabasso	56293
Wabedo (Cass County)	56655
Waconia	55387
Wacouta	55066
Wadena (Wadena County)	56482
Wahkon	56386
Waite Park	56387
Walbo	55008
Waldo	55616
Waldorf	56091
Wales	55616
Walker	56484
Walnut Grove	56180
Walters	56092
Waltham (Mower County)	55982
Wanamingo	55983
Wanda	56294
Wannaska	56761
Warba	55793
Ward Springs	55336
Warman	55051
Warren (Marshall County)	56762
Warroad	56763
Warsaw (Rice County)	55087
Waseca	56093
Washington (Fillmore County)	55975
Wasioja (Dodge County)	55927
Waskish	56685
Wastedo	55009
Waterford	55057
Watertown	55388
Waterville	56096
Watkins	55389
Watson	56295
Waubun	56589
Waverly (Wright County)	55390
Wawina	55794
Wayzata	55391
Wayzata Boulevard (Part of St. Louis Park)	55416
Wealthwood	56431
Weaver	55910
Weber	55056
Webster	55088
Wegdahl	56265
Welch	55089
Welcome	56181
Wells (Faribault County)	56097
Weme	56634
Wendell	56590
West Albany (Wabasha County)	55957
West Albion	55302
Westbrook	56183
Westbury	56501
West Concord	55985
West Duluth (Part of Duluth)	55807
West End (Part of St. Paul)	55102
West Lake Francis Shores	55040
West Lynn	55350
West Newton (Wabasha County)	55945
West Point	55008
Westport (Pope County)	56385
West Rock	55063
West St. Paul	55118
West Union (Todd County)	56389
West Virginia (Part of Mountain Iron)	55792
Whalan	55986
Wheatland (Rice County)	56069
Wheaton	56296
Whipholt	56485
White Bear Beach	55110
White Bear Lake (Ramsey County)	55110
White Earth	56591
White Earth Indian Reservation	56591
Whiteface	55766
White Rock	55009
Whyte	55616
Wig Wam Bay	56359
Wilbert	56121
Wilder	56184
Wildwood	56661
Wilkinson	56633
Willernie	55090

MINNESOTA Williams-Zumbrota

Name	ZIP
Williams (Lake of the Woods County)	56686
Willmar	56201
Willmar State Hospital	56201
Willow Creek	56010
Willow River	55795
Wilmington	55921
Wilmont (Nobles County)	56185
Wilno	56142
Wilpen (Part of Hibbing)	55746
Wilson (Winona County)	55987
Wilton (Beltrami County)	56687
Wilton (Waseca County)	56093
Windom (Cottonwood County)	56101
Winger (Polk County)	56592
Winnebago (Faribault County)	56098
Winnebago (Houston County)	55921
Winnipeg Junction	56549
Winona (Winona County)	55987
Winsted	55395
Winthrop	55396
Winton	55796
Wirock	56141
Wirt	56688
Withrow	55082
Witoka	55987
Wolf	55751
Wolf Lake	56593
Wolford (Crow Wing County)	56441
Wolverton	56594
Woodbury (Washington County)	55125
Wood Lake (Yellow Medicine County)	56297
Woodland (Hennepin County)	55391
Woodland (Kanabec County)	56342
Woodland (St. Louis County)	55803
Woodland Park	56551
Woodland Terrace (Part of Andover)	55303
Woodstock	56186
Worthington (Nobles County)	56187
Wrenshall (Carlton County)	55797
Wright (Carlton County)	55798
Wrightstown	56453
Wyattville	55952
Wykoff	55990
Wylie	56750
Wyman (Part of Hoyt Lakes)	55750
Wyoming	55092
Yorktown (Part of Edina)	55435
Young America	55397
Yucatan	55943
Zemple	56636
Zerkel	56621
Zim	55799
Zimmerman	55398
Zumbra Heights (Part of Victoria)	55386
Zumbro Falls	55991
Zumbrota	55992

Abbeville-Cedars MISSISSIPPI 297

	ZIP		ZIP		ZIP
Abbeville	38601	Beech Springs	38866	Branch	39117
Abbott	39773	Beechwood	39645	Brandon	39042
Aberdeen	39730	Beelake	39169	Branyan	38828
Ackerman	39735	Belden	38826	Brasfield	39096
Acona	39095	Belen	38609	Braxton	39044
Adams	39175	Bellefontaine	39737	Brazil	38963
Adaton	39759	Belle Isle	39572	Brentwood (Part of Gulfport)	39501
Agricola	39452	Belleville	39462	Brewer (Clarke County)	39355
Airey	39574	Bellewood	38754	Brewer (Lee County)	38868
Albin	38966	Bells School	39759	Brewer (Perry County)	39476
Alcorn State University	39096	Belmont	38827	Bright	38632
Aldridge	38756	Belzoni	39038	Bristers Store	39641
Alesville	38655	Benjoe	39456	Brockton (Part of Meridian)	39301
Algoma	38820	Benndale	39456	Brody	38603
Allen	39083	Benoit	38725	Brookhaven	39601
Alligator	38720	Benson	39437	Brook Hollow	39212
Alpine	38849	Bentley	39751	Brooklyn	39425
Altitude	38829	Bent Oak	39701	Brooks	38737
Alva	38925	Benton	39039	Brooksville	39739
Amory	38821	Bentonia	39040	Brownfield	38683
Anchor	39776	Benwood	38922	Browning	38930
Anchorage	39194	Berclair	38941	Brownsville	39041
Anding	39040	Berwick	39645	Brown Town	39452
Anguilla	38721	Bethany	38849	Brozville	39095
Anse	39073	Betheden	39339	Bruce	38915
Ansley	39558	Bethel	39345	Brunswick	39180
Antioch	39440	Bethlehem (Marshall County)	38659	Bryant	38922
Apple Ridge (Part of Jackson)	39204	Bethlehem (Pontotoc County)	38863	Buchannan	38863
Arcola	38722	Bethsaida	39350	Buckatunna	39322
Ariel	39638	Bett	38618	Buckhorn	38864
Arkabutla	38602	Beulah (Bolivar County)	38726	Bude	39630
Arlington (Lincoln County)	39629	Beulah (Newton County)	39337	Buelah	39337
Arlington (Neshoba County)	39350	Bexley	39452	Buelah Hubbard	39337
Arm	39663	Bigbee	38821	Buena Vista (Chickasaw County)	38851
Arnold Line	39401	Bigbee Valley	39738	Buena Vista (Tippah County)	38663
Artesia	39736	Big Creek	38914	Buena Vista Lakes	38632
Ashland	38603	Biggersville	38834	Bunker Hill	39429
Askew	38621	Big Level	39573	Bunkley	39653
Athens	39730	Bigpoint	39567	Burgess	38655
Atlanta	39776	Billups	39701	Burns	39153
Atway	38635	Biloxi	39530-35	Burnside	39350
Auburn (Lee County)	38801	For specific Biloxi Zip Codes call (601) 432-0311		Burnsville	38833
Auburn (Lincoln County)	39664			Burrell	38628
Austin	38676			Burrow	38674
Avalon	38912	Binford	39730	Burtons	38829
Avera	39451	Binnsville	39358	Bush	39149
Avon	38723	Birdie	38617	Busy Corner	39638
Bailey	39320	Birmingham	38828	Butler	39169
Baird	38751	Bissell	38801	Byhalia	38611
Baker	38652	Black Hawk	38923	Byram	39212
Baldwyn	38824	Blackjack	39759	Cadamy	38876
Ballard	39046	Blackland	38829	Cadaretta	38929
Ballardsville	38801	Blackwater (Kemper County)	39326	Caesar	39466
Ballentine	38621	Blackwater (Lafayette County)	38685	Caile	38754
Ball Ground	39156			Cairo	38873
Baltzer	38614	Blaine	38778	Caledonia	39740
Banks	38664	Blair	38849	Calhoun (Jones County)	39440
Bankston	39772	Blakely	39180	Calhoun (Newton County)	39345
Banner	38913	Blanton	39159	Calhoun City	38916
Barlow	39083	Blodgett	39464	Calyx	39361
Barnes	39051	Bloody Springs	38827	Cam	39601
Barnesville	38109	Bloomfield (Kemper County)	39328	Cambridge	38601
Barnett	39347	Bloomfield (Neshoba County)	39350	Camden	39045
Barr	38668			Cameron	39146
Barrontown	39401	Blue Hills	39144	Cameta	39159
Bartahatchie	39740	Blue Lake	38737	Campbell (Part of Ripley)	38663
Barth	39470	Blue Mountain	38610	Canaan	38603
Barto	39648	Blue Springs	38828	Candlestick (Part of Jackson)	39212
Barton (George County)	39452	Bluff Springs (Kemper County)	39328	Candlestick Park (Part of Jackson)	39212
Barton (Marshall County)	38017	Bluff Springs (Panola County)	38666	Canton	39046
Basic	39330			Cardsville	38858
Basin	39452	Bobo (Coahoma County)	38614	Carlisle	39049
Bassfield	39421	Bobo (Quitman County)	38606	Carlos	39191
Batesville	38606	Boggan Bend	38849	Carmack	39176
Batson	39401	Bogue Chitto	39629	Carmichael (Clarke County)	39360
Battlefield (Hinds County)	39204	Boice	39367	Carmichael (Hinds County)	39175
Battle Field (Newton County)	39325	Bolatusha	39160	Carmichael (Perry County)	39423
Battles	39362	Bolivar	38725	Carnes	39455
Baugh	38669	Bolton	39041	Carolina	38858
Baxter	39338	Bond (Neshoba County)	39350	Carpenter	39086
Baxterville	39455	Bond (Stone County)	39577	Carriere	39426
Bayou Oaks (Part of Gulfport)	39501	Bon Homme	39401	Carrollton	38917
Bay Saint Louis	39520-21	Bonita (Part of Meridian)	39301	Carson	39427
For specific Bay Saint Louis Zip Codes call (601) 467-5788		Boon	39339	Carter	39194
		Boone	38614	Carterville (Part of Petal)	39465
Bayside Park	39520	Booneville	38829	Carthage	39051
Bay Springs	39422	Bothwell	39476	Cary	39054
Beacon Hill	38652	Bounds Crossroads	35582	Cascilla	38920
Beans Ferry	38843	Bourbon	38756	Caseyville	39191
Bear Garden	38748	Bovina	39180	Cato	39042
Bear Town	39648	Bowdre	38664	Cayce	38017
Beasley	39755	Bowles	38753	Cayuga	39175
Beatline	39350	Bowling Green	39063	Cedarbluff	39741
Beatrice	39330	Bowman	38618	Cedar Hill (Madison County)	39071
Beatty	39176	Boyer	38751	Cedar Hill (Montgomery County)	38925
Beaumont	39423	Boyette	39160		
Beauregard	39191	Boyle	38730		
Becker	38825	Bradley	39759	Cedars	39180

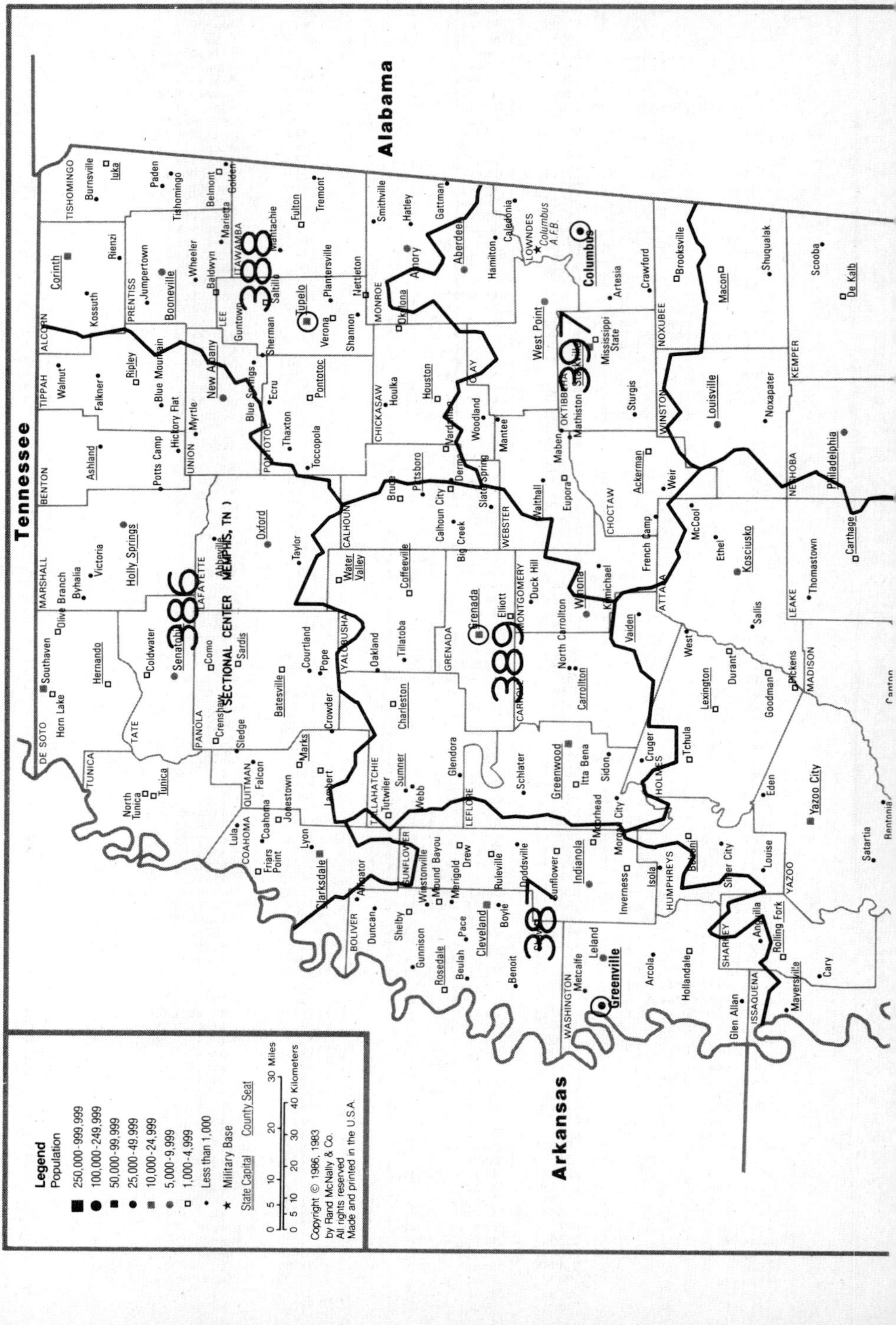
Tennessee
Alabama
Arkansas
(SECTIONAL CENTER MEMPHIS, TN)
386
387
388
389
397
TISHOMINGO
ALCORN
TIPPAH
BENTON
MARSHALL
DE SOTO
TUNICA
TATE
PANOLA
LAFAYETTE
UNION
PRENTISS
LEE
ITAWAMBA
PONTOTOC
CALHOUN
YALOBUSHA
QUITMAN
COAHOMA
TALLAHATCHIE
MONROE
CHICKASAW
CLAY
LOWNDES
OKTIBBEHA
WEBSTER
GRENADA
MONTGOMERY
CARROLL
LEFLORE
SUNFLOWER
BOLIVER
WASHINGTON
HUMPHREYS
HOLMES
ATTALA
CHOCTAW
WINSTON
NOXUBEE
KEMPER
NESHOBA
LEAKE
MADISON
YAZOO
SHARKEY
ISSAQUENA
Burnsville
Iuka
Paden
Tishomingo
Belmont
Golden
Marietta
Corinth
Rienzi
Kossuth
Jumpertown
Booneville
Wheeler
Baldwyn
Mantachie
Fulton
Tremont
Walnut
Ripley
Falkner
Blue Mountain
Blue Springs
Guntown
Sherman
Saltillo
Tupelo
Plantersville
Verona
Shannon
Nettleton
Ecru
Pontotoc
Thaxton
Toccopola
Ashland
Hickory Flat
Myrtle
New Albany
Potts Camp
Smithville
Hatley
Gattman
Amory
Aberdeen
Okolona
Houlka
Houston
Hamilton
Caledonia
Columbus A.F.B.
Columbus
West Point
Artesia
Crawford
Brooksville
Macon
Shuqualak
Scooba
De Kalb
Mississippi State
Starkville
Mathiston
Sturgis
Louisville
Noxapater
Philadelphia
Woodland
Mantee
Vardaman
Derma
Slate Spring
Maben
Eupora
Walthall
Ackerman
Weir
McCool
Ethel
Kosciusko
Carthage
Thomastown
Pittsboro
Bruce
Calhoun City
Big Creek
Water Valley
Coffeeville
Taylor
Oxford
Abbeville
Holly Springs
Victoria
Byhalia
Olive Branch
Southaven
Horn Lake
Hernando
Coldwater
Senatobia
Como
Sardis
Crenshaw
Sledge
Batesville
Courtland
Pope
Crowder
Marks
Lambert
Falcon
Jonestown
Lula
Coahoma
Lyon
Friars Point
Clarksdale
Alligator
North Tunica
Tunica
Oakland
Tillatoba
Charleston
Grenada
Elliott
Duck Hill
Winona
Kilmichael
French Camp
Vaiden
North Carrollton
Carrollton
West
Lexington
Durant
Goodman
Pickens
Sallis
Canton
Tchula
Cruger
Greenwood
Itta Bena
Sidon
Schlater
Glendora
Sumner
Tutwiler
Webb
Moorhead
Morgan City
Belzoni
Silver City
Louise
Eden
Yazoo City
Satartia
Bentonia
Drew
Ruleville
Doddsville
Sunflower
Indianola
Inverness
Isola
Winstonville
Mound Bayou
Merigold
Cleveland
Boyle
Shelby
Duncan
Gunnison
Pace
Rosedale
Beulah
Benoit
Leland
Metcalfe
Greenville
Arcola
Hollandale
Anguilla
Rolling Fork
Cary
Mayersville
Glen Allan
Legend
Population
250,000-999,999
100,000-249,999
50,000-99,999
25,000-49,999
10,000-24,999
5,000-9,999
1,000-4,999
Less than 1,000
Military Base
State Capital
County Seat
0 5 10 20 30 Miles
0 5 10 20 30 40 Kilometers

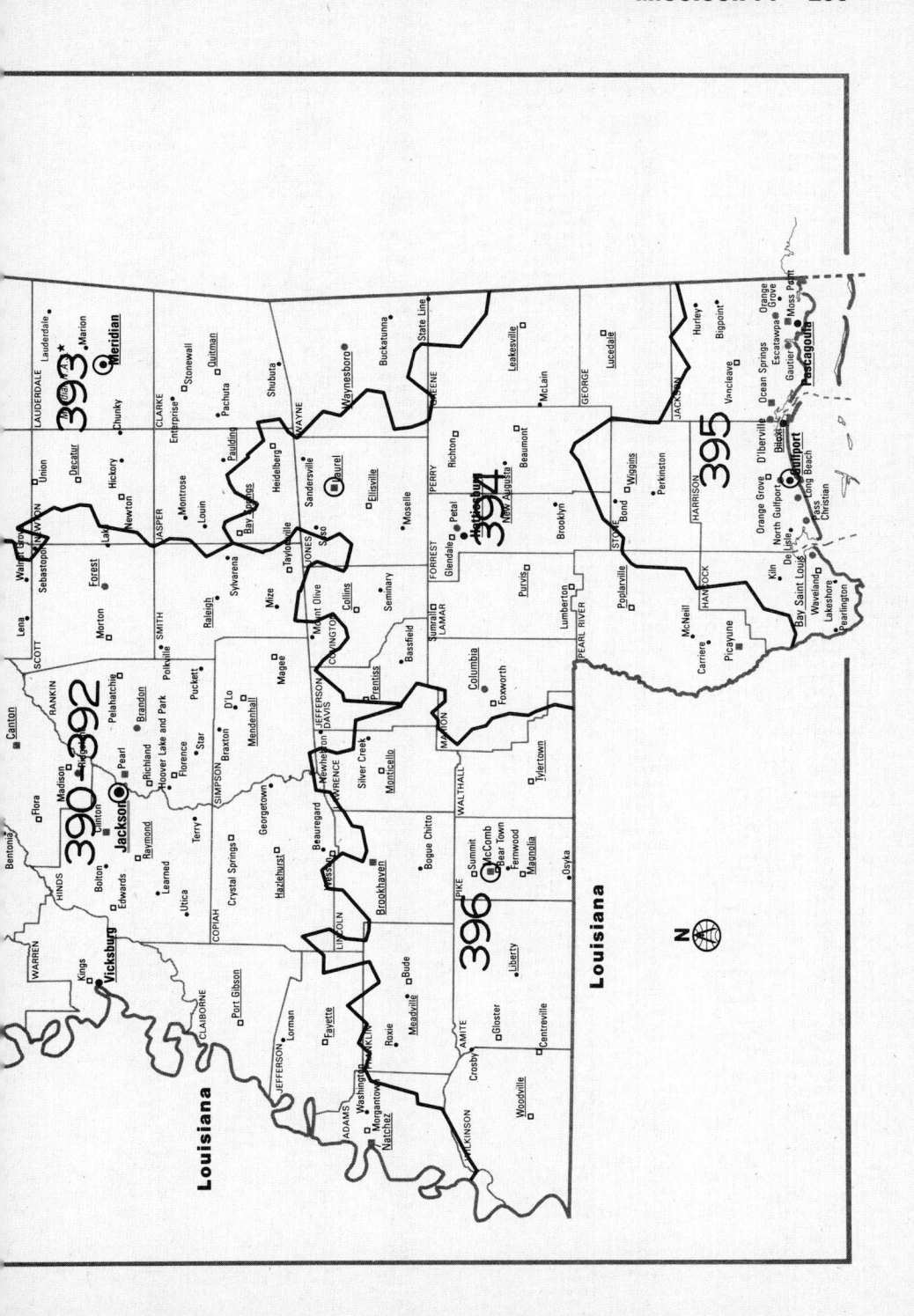

MISSISSIPPI 299

300 MISSISSIPPI Cedarview-Fame

Place	ZIP
Cedarview	38654
Center (Attala County)	39090
Center (Union County)	38652
Center Hill	39301
Center Point	39083
Center Ridge (Smith County)	39168
Center Ridge (Winston County)	39339
Centerville	38855
Centralgrove	38858
Centreville	39631
Chalybeate	38683
Champion Hill	39066
Chapel Hill	39175
Charleston	38921
Chatawa	39632
Chatham	38731
Cheraw	39483
Cherrycreek	38828
Chester	39735
Chesterville	38801
Chicora	39322
Choctaw (Bolivar County)	38773
Choctaw (Jones County)	39440
Choctaw Indian Reservation	39350
Chulahoma	38635
Chunky	39323
Church Hill	39055
Clack	38664
Clara	39324
Claremont	38614
Clarksburg	39117
Clarksdale	38614
Clarkson	39752
Clay	38843
Clayrysville	38663
Clayton	38626
Clayton Village	39759
Claytown	39339
Cleo	39440
Clermont Harbor	39520
Cleveland (Bolivar County)	38732-33
For specific Cleveland Zip Codes call (601) 843-4031	
Cleveland (Kemper County)	39328
Clifton	39074
Cliftonville	39739
Clinton	39056
Clinton Plaza (Part of Clinton)	39056
Cloverdale	39120
Clover Hill	38645
Cloverleaf Mall (Part of Hattiesburg)	39401
Coahoma	38617
Coats	39119
Cobbs	39601
Cobbville	39046
Cockrum	38632
Coffeeville	38922
Cohay	39153
Coila	38923
Colby	39088
Coldwater (Neshoba County)	39350
Coldwater (Tate County)	38618
Coles	39633
College (Part of Columbus)	39701
College Hill (Lafayette County)	38655
Collins	39428
Collinsville	39325
Colonial (Part of Jackson)	39211
Colony Town	38941
Colsub (Part of Amory)	38821
Columbia	39429
Columbus	39701-05
For specific Columbus Zip Codes call (601) 328-6171	
Columbus AFB	39701
Columbus Air Force Base	39701
Commerce	38664
Como	38619
Conehatta	39057
Conway	39051
Cooksville	39341
Cooperville	39117
Coosa	39051
Corinth	38834
Cornersville	38633
Corrona	38849
Cotton Plant	38610
Cottonville	38618
Counts	38614
County Line	39362
Courthouse (Part of Gulfport)	39501
Courtland	38620
Cowart	38921
Coxburg	39095

Place	ZIP
Coxs Ferry	39041
Coy	39354
Craigside	38930
Craig Springs	39769
Crandall	39355
Crane Creek	39573
Cranfield	39661
Crawford	39743
Crenshaw	38621
Crockett	38668
Crosby	39633
Crossgates (Part of Brandon)	39042
Crossroad	39051
Crossroads (George County)	39452
Crossroads (Neshoba County)	39350
Crossroads (Pearl River County)	39470
Cross Roads (Rankin County)	39145
Crossroads (Washington County)	38703
Crotts	39437
Crowder	38622
Cruger	38924
Crupp	39194
Crystal Springs	39059
Cuba	38834
Cub Lake	38632
Cuevas	39571
Cumberland	39750
Curtis Station	38606
Cybur	39466
Cynthia	39206
Dahomey	38725
Daisy-Vestry	39573
Daleville	39326
Damascus (Kemper County)	39328
Damascus (Scott County)	39189
Dancy	39751
Daniel	39151
Darbun	39643
Darden	38650
Darling	38623
Darlove	38748
Darracott	39730
Darrington	39633
Davenport	38614
Davis	39046
Days	38641
Deans Corner	38641
Deasonville	39179
Decatur	39327
Deemer	39350
Deemer Station	39320
Deerbrook	39739
Deeson	38740
De Kalb	39328
De Lay	38655
De Lisle	39571
Delta	38621
Delta City	39061
Delta Drive (Part of Jackson)	39213
Delta State University (Part of Cleveland)	38733
Denham	39367
Denmark	38655
Dennis	38838
Dennis Settlement	39092
Dentontown	38916
Dentville	39086
Derby	39470
Derma	38839
De Soto	39360
Deweese	39350
Dexter	39667
Diamondhead	39520
D'Iberville	39532
Dinsmore	39341
Dixie	39401
Dixie Pine	39401
Dixon	39350
D'Lo	39062
Doddsville	38736
Dogtown	38655
Doloroso	39669
Domascus	39328
Donegal	39669
Doolittle	39345
Dorsey	38843
Doskie	38852
Dossville	39051
Dover (Neshoba County)	39365
Dover (Yazoo County)	39040
Dowdville	39350
Downtown (Harrison County)	39501
Downtown (Lee County)	38801

Place	ZIP
Downtown (Warren County)	39181
Drew	38737
Dry Creek	39428
Dubard	38901
Dubbs	38626
Dublin	38739
Ducitt	39451
Duck Hill	38925
Duffee	39337
Dumas	38625
Duncan	38740
Dundee	38626
Dunleith	38756
Durant	39063
Dwiggins	38737
Dwyer	38778
Eagle Lake	39180
Earlygrove	38642
East Aberdeen	39730
Eastabuchie	39436
East Canton (Part of Canton)	39046
Eastfork	39664
East Heights (Part of Tupelo)	38801
East Hillsboro	39074
Eastlawn (Part of Pascagoula)	39567
East Lincoln	39601
East Moss Point (Part of Moss Point)	39563
Eastport	38852
East Side	39476
East Tupelo (Part of Tupelo)	38801
Eatonville	39401
Ebenezer	39064
Ecru	38841
Eddiceton	39647
Eden	39194
Edgewater Plaza (Part of Biloxi)	39531
Edinburg	39051
Edwards	39066
Effie	38921
Eggville	38801
Egremont	39159
Egypt	38860
Eldorado	39156
Electric Mills	39358
Elizabeth	38756
Ellard	38915
Elliott	38926
Ellistown	38838
Ellisville	39437
Ellisville Junction	39437
Elsie	38878
Elton (Part of Jackson)	39212
Elwood	39355
Eminence	39479
Emory	39095
Endville	38828
Energy	39301
Enid	38927
Enon	39641
Enondale	39352
Enterprise (Amite County)	39645
Enterprise (Clarke County)	39330
Enterprise (Lincoln County)	39601
Enterprise (Union County)	38650
Enzor	39301
Errata	39440
Erwin	38731
Escatawpa	39552
Eset	39362
Eskridge	38925
Estes	39339
Estesmill	39051
Estill	38748
Ethel	39067
Etta	38627
Eucutta	39360
Eudora	38632
Eupora	39744
Eureka Springs	38620
Evansville (Tate County)	38618
Evansville (Tunica County)	38676
Everett	39114
Evergreen	38843
Expose	39429
Fairfield	38828
Fairground	39350
Fairhaven	38654
Fairhill	39361
Fairlane (Part of Columbus)	39701
Fair Oaks Springs	39601
Fair River	39601
Fairview (Itawamba County)	38847
Fairview (Sunflower County)	38751
Falcon	38628
Falkner	38629
Fame	39744

Fannin-King and Anderson MISSISSIPPI 301

Name	ZIP	Name	ZIP	Name	ZIP
Fannin	39042	Grange	39140	Hinze	39108
Farmhaven	39046	Grange Hall	39180	Hiwannee	39367
Farmington	38834	Grapeland	38725	Hobo Station	38829
Farrell	38630	Gravel Hill	38930	Hohenlinden	39751
Fayette	39069	Graves	38828	Holcomb	38940
Fenton	39571	Gravestown	38663	Holcut	38852
Fentress	39735	Greenbrier Park	39466	Hollandale	38748
Fenwick	39120	Greenfield (Newton County)	39057	Hollis	38878
Fernwood	39635	Greenfield (Rankin County)	39042	Holly Bluff	39088
Fikestown	39092	Greenfield Addition (Part of Greenville)	38701	Holly Grove	38954
Fitler	39070	Green Grove	38767	Holly Ridge	38749
Fitzhugh	38737	Greenland	39365	Holly Springs	38635
Flora	39071	Greenville	38701	Hollywood	38676
Florence	39073	Greenville Mall (Part of Greenville)	38701	Holmesville	39648
Flowerdale (Part of Tupelo)	38801	Greenville North (Part of Greenville)	38701	Homewood	39152
Floweree	39156	Greenwood (Itawamba County)	38843	Homochitto	39638
Flowood	39208	Greenwood (Leflore County)	38930	Honey Island	39038
Floyd	38603	Greenwood Springs	38848	Hoover Lake and Park	39073
Fondren (Part of Jackson)	39216	Grenada	38901	Hope	39350
Fontainebleau	39564	Griffith	39741	Hopedale	39113
Foote	38748	Gulde	39042	Hopewell (Benton County)	38067
Fords Creek	39470	Gulf Hills	39564	Hopewell (Copiah County)	39059
Fordyke	39039	Gulf Hills Country Club	39564	Horn Lake	38637
Forest	39074	Gulf Park Estates	39564	Horseshoe (Holmes County)	39169
Forestdale	39365	Gulfport	39501-07	Horse Shoe (Scott County)	39189
Forest Hill (Part of Jackson)	39212	For specific Gulfport Zip Codes call (601) 832-4131		Hortontown	38863
Forkville	39076	Gum Grove	39169	Hot Coffee	39428
Fort Adams	39669	Gums	38922	Houlka	38850
Fort Stephens	39320	Gum Springs	39074	House	39365
Four Corners	39090	Gunn	39111	Houston	38851
Four Mile	39038	Gunnison	38746	Howard	39095
Foxworth	39483	Guntown	38849	Howell	39452
Francis	38740	Gwin (Part of Tchula)	39169	Howison	39574
Frankstown	38824	Gwinville	39140	Hoy	39440
Freeny	39051	Hale	39360	Hub	39429
Freerun	39194	Halltown	38849	Hubbard	39066
Freetrade	39051	Hamburg	39661	Hudsonville	38635
Freeze Corner	38632	Hamilton	39746	Humber	38614
French Camp	39745	Hampton	38744	Hurley	39555
Friars Point	38631	Hand	39320	Hurricane	38863
Friendship (Lincoln County)	39601	Handle	39339	Hurricane Creek	39301
Friendship (Pontotoc County)	38841	Handsboro (Part of Gulfport)	39501	Hushpuckena	38774
Frog Island	38801	Handy Corner	38654	Improve	39429
Frostbridge	39367	Hard Cash	39038	Increase	39301
Fruitland Park	39577	Hardy	39452	Inda	39573
Fugate	39039	Harleston	38619	Independence (Scott County)	39117
Fulton	38843	Harmontown	38619	Independence (Tate County)	38638
Furrs	38863	Harmony	39355	Indian Hills	38866
Futheyville	38901	Harperville	39080	Indianola	38751
Gallman	39077	Harriston	39081	Indian Springs	39401
Gandsi	39479	Harrisville	39082	Industrial	39466
Garden City	39661	Harvey (Part of Petal)	39465	Ingomar	38652
Garlandville	39345	Hathorn	39429	Ingrams Mill	38611
Gaston	38865	Hatley	38821	Inverness	38753
Gatesville	39059	Hattiesburg	39401-07	Irene	39666
Gatewood	38922	For specific Hattiesburg Zip Codes call (601) 268-0888		Isola	38754
Gattman	38844	Hayes Crossing	38666	Itta Bena	38941
Gautier	39553	Haynes Bluff	39156	Iuka	38852
Geeslin Corner	38901	Hays	39057	Jacinto	38865
Geeville	38829	Hazel	39092	Jack	39175
Geneill	38756	Hazlehurst	39083	Jackson	39201-98
Georgetown	39078	Heads	38756	For specific Jackson Zip Codes call (601) 968-0572	
Germania	39162	Heathman	38751	Jackson Mall (Part of Jackson)	39213
Gholson	39354	Hebron (Jefferson Davis County)	39140	Jackson Square (Part of Jackson)	39204
Gibson	39730	Hebron (Jones County)	39168	Jago	38671
Gift	38834	Heidelberg	39439	Jaketown	39038
Giles	39358	Helena	39567	James	38748
Gill	39051	Helm	38756	Jamestown	39483
Gillsburg	39657	Henderson's Point	39571	Jayess	39641
Gitano	39168	Hendrix	39747	Jeff Davis	39180
Glade	39440	Henleyfield	39426	Jefferson	38917
Glancy	39083	Herbert Springs	39325	Jeffries	38626
Glen	38846	Hermanville	39086	Jenkins	39437
Glen Allan	38744	Hernando	38632	Jericho	38824
Glendale	39401	Hero	38345	Johns	39042
Glendora	38928	Hesterville	39192	Johnston	39437
Glenfield (Part of New Albany)	38652	Heucks Retreat	39191	Jonathan	39451
Glenwild	38901	Hickory	39332	Jonestown (Coahoma County)	38639
Gloster	39638	Hickory Flat	38633	Jonestown (Yazoo County)	39194
Glover	38680	Hideaway Hills	38666	Jug Fork	38828
Gluckstadt	39110	Hidi	39166	Jumpertown	38829
Golden	38847	Higgins	39482	Junction City	39355
Golden Grove	39365	High Hill	39350	Kalem	39117
Goldfield	38737	Highlandale	38852	Katzenmeyer	39156
Gooden Lake	39038	High Point	39339	Keirn	38924
Good Hope (Leake County)	39094	Hightown	38834	Kellis Store	39354
Good Hope (Neshoba County)	39350	Hillhouse	38720	Kelona	39366
Good Hope (Perry County)	39476	Hillman	39451	Kendrick	38834
Goodman	39079	Hillsboro	39087	Keownville	38652
Goodwater	39366	Hillsdale	39470	Kewanee	39364
Goodyear (Part of Picayune)	39466	Hinchcliff	38646	Key Field (Part of Meridian)	39301
Gore Springs	38929	Hinkle	38865	Kilmichael	39747
Goshen Springs	39042	Hintonville	39423	Kiln	39556
Goss	39429			King and Anderson	38614
Grace	38745				
Grady	39744				
Graham	38824				
Grand Gulf	39150				

302 MISSISSIPPI Kings-Murry

Name	ZIP
Kings	39180
Kinlock	38751
Kirby	39661
Kirkville	38843
Klem	39074
Klondike	39320
Knobtown	39362
Knoxo	39667
Knoxville	39661
Kokomo	39643
Kola	39428
Kolola Springs	39740
Kosciusko	39090
Kossuth	38834
Kreole (Part of Moss Point)	39563
Lackey	39730
Lafayette Springs	38655
Lake	39092
Lake Center	38659
Lake City	38829
Lake Como	39422
Lake Cormorant	38641
Lakeland (Part of Richland)	39218
Lake of Hills	38632
Lakeshore	39558
Lake View	38680
Lamar	38642
Lamar Park	39401
Lambert	38643
Lamkin	39166
Lamont	38755
Lampton	39429
Landon	39501
Laneheart	39669
Langford	39042
Langsdale	39360
Larue	39564
Latimer	39564
Latonia	39452
Lauderdale	39335
Laurel	39440-42
For specific Laurel Zip Codes call (601) 425-1408	
Laurelhill	39350
Lawrence	39336
Laws Hill	38685
Leaf	39456
Leakesville	39451
Learned	39154
Lebanon (Hinds County)	39154
Lebanon (Marshall County)	38659
Lee Donald	39366
Leedy	38833
Leesburg	39117
Leesdale	39661
Leeville	39401
Leflore	38940
Leigh Mall (Part of Columbus)	39701
Leland	38756
Lemon	39074
Lena	39094
Lessley	39669
Le Tourneau	39180
Leverett	38920
Lewisburg	38654
Lexie	39667
Lexington	39095
Liberty (Amite County)	39645
Liberty (Kemper County)	39328
Lightsey	39440
Lillian	39074
Limbert (Part of Laurel)	39440
Linn	38736
Linwood (Neshoba County)	39365
Linwood (Yazoo County)	39179
Little Creek	39423
Little Italy	39092
Little Rock	39337
Little Texas	38676
Little Yazoo	39040
Litton	38773
Lizana	39501
Lobdell	38726
Lobutcha	39108
Loch Leven	39669
Locke Station	38606
Lockhart	39335
Lodi (Humphreys County)	39166
Lodi (Montgomery County)	39767
Lombardy	38774
Long	38756
Long Beach	39560
Longino	39350
Long Lake (Coahoma County)	38617
Long Lake (Warren County)	39180
Longshot	38773
Longstreet	38643
Longtown	38665

Name	ZIP
Longview (Oktibbeha County)	39759
Longview (Pontotoc County)	38863
Longwood	38748
Looxahoma	38668
Lorens	39074
Lorenzen	39159
Lorman	39096
Louin	39338
Louise	39097
Louisville	39339
Love	38632
Loyd	38878
Loyd Star	39601
Lucas	39474
Lucedale	39452
Lucern	39365
Lucien	39601
Luckney	39208
Ludlow	39098
Lula	38644
Lumberton	39455
Lurand	38614
Lux	39401
Lyman	39503
Lynchburg	38109
Lynn Creek	39739
Lynville	39354
Lyon	38645
Maben	39750
McAdams	39107
McBride	39144
McCall Creek	39647
McCallum	39401
McCarley	38943
McComb	39648
McCondy	38854
McCool	39108
McCrary	39701
McCutcheon	38722
Mc Donald (Leake County)	39094
McDonald (Neshoba County)	39365
Macedonia (Forrest County)	39401
Macedonia (Lee County)	38801
Macedonia (Union County)	38650
Macel	38950
McElveen	39666
McHenry	39561
McLain	39456
McLaurin	39401
McLaurin Heights (Part of Pearl)	39208
McLeod	39341
McMillan	39339
McNair	39069
McNeal	39338
McNeill	39457
Macon	39341
McSwain	39476
McVille	39090
McWillie (Part of Jackson)	39206
Madden	39109
Madison	39110
Madisonville	39046
Magee	39111
Magnolia	39652
Mahned	39462
Malone	38685
Malvina	38769
Mannassa	39355
Mantachie	38855
Mantee	39751
Marcella	39169
Marianna	38635
Marie	38751
Marietta	38856
Marion	39342
Maris Town (Part of Canton)	39046
Markette	38655
Markham	38761
Marks	38646
Mars Hill	39666
Martin	39325
Martinsville	39083
Martintown	38652
Martinville	39114
Marydell	39051
Mashulaville	39341
Matherville	39360
Mathiston	39752
Mattson	38758
Maxie	39425
Maybank	39401
Maybell	39437
Mayersville	39113
Mayhew	39753
Mayton	39042
Maywood	38654
Meadville	39653

Name	ZIP
Mechanicsburg	39040
Meehan	39301
Meeks	38924
Melba	39482
Meltonville	39046
Memphis	38680
Mendenhall	39114
Meridian	39301-09
For specific Meridian Zip Codes call (601) 693-2581	
Meridian Naval Air Station	39309
Meridian Station	39301
Merigold	38759
Merit	39114
Merrill	39452
Mesa	39667
Metcalfe	38760
Metrocenter (Part of Jackson)	39204
Meyers	39401
Michigan City	38647
Midnight	39115
Midway (Copiah County)	39191
Midway (Hinds County)	39170
Midway (Scott County)	39074
Midway (Tishomingo County)	38852
Midway (Yazoo County)	39039
Mileston	39169
Mill Creek (Jones County)	39440
Mill Creek (Pearl River County)	39426
Mill Creek (Rankin County)	39042
Millcreek (Winston County)	39339
Mill Creek Cabin Area	38852
Miller	38654
Millington	39358
Mill Town (Part of Canton)	39046
Mimms	38606
Mineral Wells	38648
Mingo	38873
Minter City	38944
Missionary	39356
Mississippi City (Part of Gulfport)	39501
Mississippi College (Part of Clinton)	39058
Mississippi State	39762
Mississippi Valley State University	38941
Mitchell	38663
Mize	39116
Money	38945
Monroe	39653
Monterey	39073
Monte Vista	39771
Montgomery	39191
Monticello	39654
Montpelier	39754
Montrose	39338
Moon	38662
Moores Mill	38838
Mooreville	38857
Moorhead	38761
Morgan City	38846
Morgans	39170
Morgantown (Adams County)	39120
Morgantown (Marion County)	39484
Morgantown (Oktibbeha County)	39769
Morning Star	39066
Morriston	39401
Morton	39117
Moscow	39328
Moselle	39459
Moss	39460
Moss Point	39563
Mound Bayou	38762
Mound City (Bolivar County)	38826
Mound City (Union County)	38828
Mount Carmel	39474
Mount Olive (Amite County)	39664
Mount Olive (Covington County)	39119
Mount Olive (Franklin County)	39653
Mount Olive (Jones County)	39440
Mount Pleasant (Itawamba County)	38876
Mount Pleasant (Marshall County)	38649
Mount Vernon	38801
Mount Zion	39111
Movella	39452
Muldon	39730
Mullins Store	38655
Murphreesboro	38961
Murphy	38748
Murry	38663

MISSISSIPPI 303

Place	ZIP
Muskegon	39092
Myrick	39440
Myrleville	39040
Myrtle	38650
Nancy	39366
Nason	38940
Natchez	39120-22
For specific Natchez Zip Codes call (601) 442-4361	
National Cemetery (Part of Vicksburg)	39180
Necaise	39573
Neely	39461
Negro Crossroads	39059
Nellieburg	39301
Nesbit	38651
Neshoba	39365
Nettleton	38858
Nevada	39041
New Albany	38652
New Augusta	39462
New Byram	39212
New Canaan	38603
New Fitler	39070
New Harmony	38828
New Hebron	39140
New Hope	39701
Newman	39066
Newmans	39180
Newmans Grove	39154
Newport (Attala County)	39160
Newport (DeSoto County)	38641
New Salem	38843
New Sight	39601
New Site	38859
Newton	39345
New Town	38668
New Wren	39730
Nicholson	39463
Nida	39172
Nitta Yuma	38763
Nixon (Humphreys County)	39115
Nixon (Pontotoc County)	38863
Nod	39039
Nola	39665
Norfield	39629
Norris	39074
North (Hinds County)	39206
North (Lauderdale County)	39305
North Bay	39532
North Bend	39350
North Carrollton	38947
North Crossroads	38852
North Greenville (Part of Greenville)	38701
North Gulfport (Harrison County)	39501
North Haven	38652
North Long Beach	39560
Northpark Mall (Part of Ridgeland)	39157
North Tunica	38676
Northwest Junior College (Part of Senatobia)	38668
Northwood Hills	39501
Norton	38663
Noxapater	39346
Oak Bowery	39437
Oak Grove (Holmes County)	39169
Oak Grove (Jones County)	39437
Oak Grove (Lamar County)	39401
Oakland (Itawamba County)	38843
Oakland (Pike County)	39666
Oakland (Yalobusha County)	38948
Oakley	39154
Oak Ridge	39180
Oak Vale	39656
Obadiah	39320
Ocean Springs	39564-65
For specific Ocean Springs Zip Codes call (601) 875-4431	
Ocobla	39350
Ofahoma	39051
Oil City	39040
Okahola	39475
Oklahoma	38917
Okolona	38860
Oktoc	39759
Old Cairo	38829
Oldenburg	39661
Oldham	38852
Old Hamilton	39746
Old Houlka	38850
Old Red Star	39601
Old Union	38868
Olive Branch	38654
Oloh	39482
Oma	39654
Omega	39169
Onward	39159

Place	ZIP
Ora	39428
Orange	39347
Orange Grove (Harrison County)	39503
Orange Grove (Harrison County)	39501
Orange Grove (Jackson County)	39567
Orange Hill	39041
O'Reilly	38730
Orwood	38655
Osborn	39759
Osborne Creek	38829
Osyka	39657
Ovett	39464
Owens Wells	39095
Oxberry	38940
Oxford (Amite County)	39638
Oxford (Lafayette County)	38655
Ozona	39426
Pace	38764
Pachuta	39347
Paden	38873
Palmer	39401
Palmetto	38801
Panther Burn	38765
Parchman	38738
Parham	38848
Paris	38949
Parks	38652
Parksplace	38619
Pascagoula	39567-68
For specific Pascagoula Zip Codes call (601) 762-5722	
Pascagoula River Estates	39456
Pass Christian	39571
Patosi	39194
Pattison	39144
Paul	38920
Paulding	39348
Paulette	39341
Paynes	38920
Pearl (Rankin County)	39208
Pearl (Simpson County)	39073
Pearl City (Part of Pearl)	39208
Pearlhaven (Part of Brookhaven)	39601
Pearlington	39572
Pearl River	39350
Pearson	39208
Pecan	39567
Pecan Grove	39437
Pelahatchie	39145
Penalty	39356
Pendorff	39640
Penns Station	39743
Penton	38664
Peoples	38663
Peoria	39560
Percy	38748
Perdue	39337
Perkinston	39573
Perrytown	39633
Perth	39069
Perthshire	38746
Petal	39465
Peyton	39144
Pheba	39755
Philadelphia	39350
Philipp	38950
Phillipstown	38954
Phoenix	39040
Piave	39476
Picayune	39466
Pickens	39146
Pickwick	39483
Pierce Crossroads	39194
Piggtown	39094
Piketown	39074
Pinckneyville	39669
Pinebluff	39751
Pinebur	39429
Pinedale	38627
Pine Flat	38965
Pine Grove (Benton County)	38633
Pine Grove (Lamar County)	39475
Pine Grove (Lee County)	38868
Pine Grove (Tippah County)	38829
Pine Ridge (Adams County)	39120
Pine Ridge (Lamar County)	39475
Pine Springs	39301
Pine Valley	38965
Pineview	39440
Pineville	39074
Piney Woods	39148
Pinola	39149
Pisgah (Greene County)	39452
Pisgah (Prentiss County)	38865
Pisgah (Rankin County)	39042
Pistol Ridge	39455
Pittman	39483

Place	ZIP
Pittsboro	38951
Plainview (Part of Richland)	39218
Plantersville	38862
Plattsburg	39350
Pleasant Grove	38657
Pleasant Hill (Copiah County)	39668
Pleasant Hill (DeSoto County)	38651
Pleasant Hill (Union County)	38652
Pleasant Ridge (Jones County)	39440
Pleasant Ridge (Union County)	38625
Pluto	39169
Poagville	38618
Pocahontas	39072
Pokal	39140
Polfrey	39564
Polkville	39117
Pollock	38751
Ponta	39301
Pontotoc	38863
Poolville	38650
Pope	38658
Poplar Corners	38680
Poplar Creek	39747
Poplar Springs (Holmes County)	39063
Poplar Springs (Montgomery County)	39747
Poplar Springs (Newton County)	39345
Poplarville	39470
Porterville	39352
Port Gibson	39150
Posey Mound	38623
Post	39325
Potts Camp	38659
Powell	38626
Powers	39440
Prairie	39756
Prairie Point	39353
Prentiss	39474
Presidential Hills (Part of Jackson)	39213
Preston	39354
Pricedale	39666
Prichard	38676
Prince Chapel	39354
Priscilla	38701
Prismatic	39320
Progress (Jefferson Davis County)	39474
Progress (Pike County)	39648
Prospect	39057
Puckett	39151
Pulaski	39152
Pumpkin Center	38652
Purvis	39475
Pyland	38851
Quentin	39647
Quincy	38848
Quitman	39355
Quito	38941
Quofaloma	39169
Rainey	39459
Raleigh	39153
Ramsey Springs	39573
Randolph	38864
Rankin	39042
Ras	39338
Ratliff	38855
Rawls Springs	39401
Raworth	39117
Raymond	39154
Raytown	39046
Red Banks	38661
Redbone	39180
Reddoch	39168
Red Lick	39096
Redstar	39191
Redwood	39156
Reedtown	39175
Reform	39757
Refuge	38701
Reid	38878
Remus	39051
Rena Lara	38767
Renfroe	39051
Renova	38732
Revive	39045
Rexburg	38756
Rexford	39073
Rhodes	39476
Riceville	39573
Rich	38662
Richardson	39466
Richey	39159
Richland (Holmes County)	39079

304 MISSISSIPPI Richland-Turnetta

Location	ZIP
Richland (Humphreys County)	39166
Richland (Rankin County)	39218
Richmond	38801
Richton	39476
Ridgeland	39157-58
For specific Ridgeland Zip Codes call (601) 957-9800	
Rienzi	38865
Ripley	38663
Rising Sun	38954
Riverton (Part of Clarksdale)	38614
Riverview Estates	39456
Robbs	38864
Roberts	39336
Robinson Gin	38632
Robinsonville	38664
Robinwood	39654
Rochdale	38740
Rock Creek	39365
Rock Hill (Alcorn County)	38834
Rock Hill (Forrest County)	39475
Rock Hill (Oktibbeha County)	39759
Rock Hill (Rankin County)	39042
Rockport	39083
Rocky Springs	39049
Rodney	39096
Roebuck	38954
Rogerslacy	39477
Rolling Fork	39159
Rome	38768
Roseacres	38617
Rosebloom	38920
Rosebud	39189
Rosedale	38769
Rose Hill	39356
Rosella	39654
Rosemary	39170
Rosetta	39633
Rough Edge	38863
Roundaway	38614
Roundlake	38740
Rounsaville	39452
Roxie	39661
Ruby	38945
Rudyard	38617
Rufus	39145
Ruleville	38771
Runnelstown	39401
Rural Hill	39108
Russell	39301
Russum	39096
Ruth	39662
Ryan	38843
Sabino	38646
Sabougla	38916
Sago	38745
St. Martin	39533
Salem (Leake County)	39189
Salem (Walthall County)	39667
Sallis	39160
Saltillo	38866
Sanatorium	39112
Sandersville	39477
Sand Hill (Copiah County)	39191
Sand Hill (Greene County)	39476
Sand Hill (Jones County)	39437
Sandhill (Rankin County)	39161
Sandpoint	39153
Sandtown	39350
Sandy Hook	39478
Sanford	39479
Sapa	39744
Sarah	38665
Saratoga	39111
Sardis (Copiah County)	39083
Sardis (Panola County)	38666
Sarepta	38864
Sartinsville	39641
Satartia	39162
Saucier	39574
Saukum	39633
Sauls	39662
Savage	38665
Savannah	39470
Savannah Grove (Part of Meridian)	39301
Savoy	39301
Schamberville	39325
Schlater	38952
Schley	39140
Scobey	38953
Scooba	39358
Scotland	39040
Scotland Forks	39040
Scott	38772
Sebastopol	39359
Sellers	39573
Sels Prairie	39360
Seminary	39479

Location	ZIP
Senatobia	38668
Senatobia Lakes	38668
Seneca	39455
Sessums	39759
Seven Springs	39154
Shackleford	39169
Shady Grove (Copiah County)	39083
Shady Grove (Jones County)	39440
Shannon	38868
Sharkey	38921
Sharon (Jones County)	39440
Sharon (Madison County)	39163
Sharpsburg	39146
Shaw	38773
Shelby	38774
Shellmound	38930
Shelton	39459
Sherard	38669
Sherman	38869
Sherwood	39752
Sherwood Forest	39042
Shiloh (Itawamba County)	38855
Shiloh (Rankin County)	39145
Shipman	39452
Shivers	39149
Shoccoe	39046
Shrock	39079
Shubuta	39360
Shucktown	39301
Shuford	38620
Shuqualak	39361
Sibley	39165
Sibleyton	39747
Sidon	38954
Signal	39180
Silver City	39166
Silver Creek	39663
Silver Run	39573
Singleton	39051
Singleton Settlement	39074
Skene	38775
Skuna	38915
Skyline	38801
Slate Spring	38955
Slayden	38642
Sledge	38670
Sloan	39046
Smith (Covington County)	39428
Smith (Lauderdale County)	39364
Smithdale	39664
Smiths	39066
Smithville	38870
Smyrna (Attala County)	39090
Smyrna (Copiah County)	39083
Snell	39301
Snow Lake Shores	38603
Somerville	38944
Sonora	38851
Sontag	39665
Soso	39480
South Amory (Part of Amory)	38821
Southaven	38671
Southern (Part of Hattiesburg)	39401
South McComb (Part of McComb)	39648
Spanish Fort	39088
Sparta	39776
Splinter	38673
Splunge	38848
Spring Cottage	39429
Spring Creek	39350
Springdale	38965
Spring Hill (Benton County)	38647
Springhill (Jones County)	39440
Spring Hill (Lafayette County)	38655
Spring Hill (Neshoba County)	39350
Springville	38863
Stallo	39350
Stampley	39069
Standing Pine	39051
Stanton	39120
Star	39167
Starkville	39759
State Line	39362
Steele	39074
Steens	39766
Steiner	38773
Stewart	39767
Stokes	39046
Stoneville	38776
Stonewall (Clarke County)	39363
Stonewall (DeSoto County)	38611
Stonewall (Holmes County)	39169
Stovall	38614
Straight Bayou	38721

Location	ZIP
Stratton	39365
Strayhorn	38665
Strengthford	39440
Strickland	38834
Stringer	39441
Stringtown	38725
Stronghope	39191
Strongs	39730
Sturgis	39769
Sucarnochee	39352
Success	39574
Sumbax	39483
Summerland	39168
Summit	39666
Sumner	38957
Sumrall	39482
Sunflower (Prentiss County)	38829
Sunflower (Sunflower County)	38778
Sunnycrest	38901
Sunnyside	38944
Sunrise (Forrest County)	39401
Sunrise (Leake County)	39051
Suqualena	39301
Swan Lake	38958
Sweatman	38925
Swiftown	38959
Swiftwater	38701
Sylvarena	39153
Symonds	38769
Tallula	39159
Talowah	39455
Tandy	38921
Taylor	38673
Taylorsville	39168
Tchula	39169
Teasdale	38927
Ted	39338
Teoc	38917
Terrell	39474
Terry	39170
Terza	38666
Thaxton	38871
Theadville	39355
The Mall (Part of Vicksburg)	39180
Theo	38683
Thomastown	39171
Thomasville	39073
Thompson	39664
Thompsonville	39059
Thorn	38851
Thornton	39172
Thrashers	38829
Three Rivers	39567
Thyatira	38668
Tibbee	39773
Tibbs	38670
Tie Plant	38901
Tilden	38843
Tillatoba	38961
Tillman	39150
Tilton	39654
Tinsley	39173
Tiplersville	38674
Tippah	38603
Tippo	38962
Tishomingo	38873
Toccopola	38874
Tocowa	38620
Tomnolen	39744
Toomsuba	39364
Topeka	39641
Topisaw	39662
Topton	39301
Touchstone	39044
Tougaloo (Part of Jackson)	39174
Townsend	39352
Tracetown (Part of Natchez)	39120
Tralake	38756
Trapp	39350
Traxler	39111
Trebloc	38875
Tremont	38876
Trenton	39152
Triangle (Part of Biloxi)	39534
Tribbett	38779
Trinity (DeSoto County)	38632
Trinity (Lowndes County)	39743
Troy	38863
Truitt	39146
Tucker	39350
Tuckers Crossing	39440
Tula	38675
Tunica	38676
Tupelo	38801-03
For specific Tupelo Zip Codes call (601) 842-4482	
Tupelo Mall (Part of Tupelo)	38801
Turnbull	39669
Turnerville	39338
Turnetta	39046

MISSISSIPPI Turon–Zumbro 305

Name	ZIP	Name	ZIP	Name	ZIP
Turon	38870	Wakefield	38618	Whitehead	38928
Tuscola	39094	Wakeland	38930	Whites (Clay County)	39773
Tutwiler	38963	Waldrup	39422	Whites (Rankin County)	39073
Twin	39478	Wallerville	38652	Whitesand (Jefferson Davis County)	39140
Twin Lakes	38680	Wallhill	38618	White Sand (Pearl River County)	39470
Tylertown	39667	Walls	38680	Whites Crossing	39577
Tyro	38668	Walnut (Quitman County)	38964	Whitfield (Jones County)	39464
Union (Jones County)	39437	Walnut (Tippah County)	38683	Whitfield (Rankin County)	39193
Union (Lee County)	38862	Walnut Grove (Coahoma County)	38767	Whitney	38737
Union (Newton County)	39365	Walnut Grove (Leake County)	39189	Whynot	39301
Union (Simpson County)	39149	Walters	39437	Wickware	39345
Union Church	39668	Waltersville	39180	Wiggins (Leake County)	39051
Union Hall	39601	Walthall	39771	Wiggins (Stone County)	39577
Unity	38849	Wanilla	39654	Wilco Estates	38632
University (Part of Oxford)	38677	Wardwell	38878	Wildwood	38930
University Medical Center (Part of Jackson)	39216	Warrenton	39180	Wilkinson	39669
University of Mississippi	38677	Warsaw	38611	Willet	38748
Usrytown	39074	Washington	39190	Williamsburg	39428
Utica	39175	Waterford	38685	Williamsville (Attala County)	39090
Utica Junior College	39175	Water Oak	39367	Williamsville (Neshoba County)	39350
Vaiden	39176	Water Valley	38965	Willis Heights (Part of Tupelo)	38801
Valewood	38744	Watson (Forrest County)	39401	Willowood	39212
Valley	39194	Watson (Marshall County)	38611	Willows	39150
Valley Hill	38917	Wautubbee	39330	Winborn	38633
Valley Park	39177	Waveland	39576	Winchester	39367
Value (Part of Brandon)	39042	Waxhaw	38746	Windsor Park	39564
Van Buren	38858	Way	39046	Wingate (Part of New Augusta)	39462
Vance	38964	Waynesboro	39367	Winona	38967
Vancleave (Jackson County)	39564	Wayside	38780	Winstonville	38781
Van Cleave (Jackson County)	39564	Weathersby	39114	Winterville	38782
Van Vleet	38877	Webb	38966	Wolf Springs	39301
Vardaman	38878	Weir	39772	Woodburn	38751
Vaughan	39179	Wells (Part of Caledonia)	39740	Woodland (Chickasaw County)	39776
Vaughn	39601	Wells Town	39455	Woodland (Pontotoc County)	38863
Velma	38965	Wenasoga	38834	Woodland Lake	38632
Vernal	39452	Wesson	39191	Woodville	39669
Vernon (Madison County)	39339	West (Holmes County)	39192	Woodwards	39367
Vernon (Winston County)	39339	West (Lauderdale County)	39305	Woolmarket	39532
Verona	38879	West Biloxi (Part of Biloxi)	39531	Wortham	39574
Veterans Administration Center (Part of Biloxi)	39531	West Days	38641	Wren	39730
Vickland	38763	West Gulfport	39501	Wright	38746
Vicksburg	39180-82	West Hill	39063	Wyatte	38668
For specific Vicksburg Zip Codes call (601) 636-1071		West Jackson (Part of Jackson)	39207	Yazoo City	39194
Victoria	38679	Westland (Part of Jackson)	39209	Yocona	38655
Vidalia	39571	Westland Plaza (Part of Jackson)	39209	Yokena	39180
Village Fair Mall (Part of Meridian)	39301	West Lincoln	39601	Youngs	38922
Vimville	39301	West Marks	38646	Zama	39090
Virlilia	39046	West Point	39773	Zemuly	39160
Vossburg	39366	West Poplarville	39470	Zero	39301
Waco	38753	Westside	39150	Zetus	39601
Waddell	39741	West Union	38650	Zieglerville	39039
Wade (Jackson County)	39567	Wheeler	38880	Zion	38863
Wade (Sunflower County)	38737	Whistler	39367	Zumbro	38732
Wahalak	39358	White Apple	39661		
		Whitebluff	39483		
		White Cap	39638		

MISSOURI

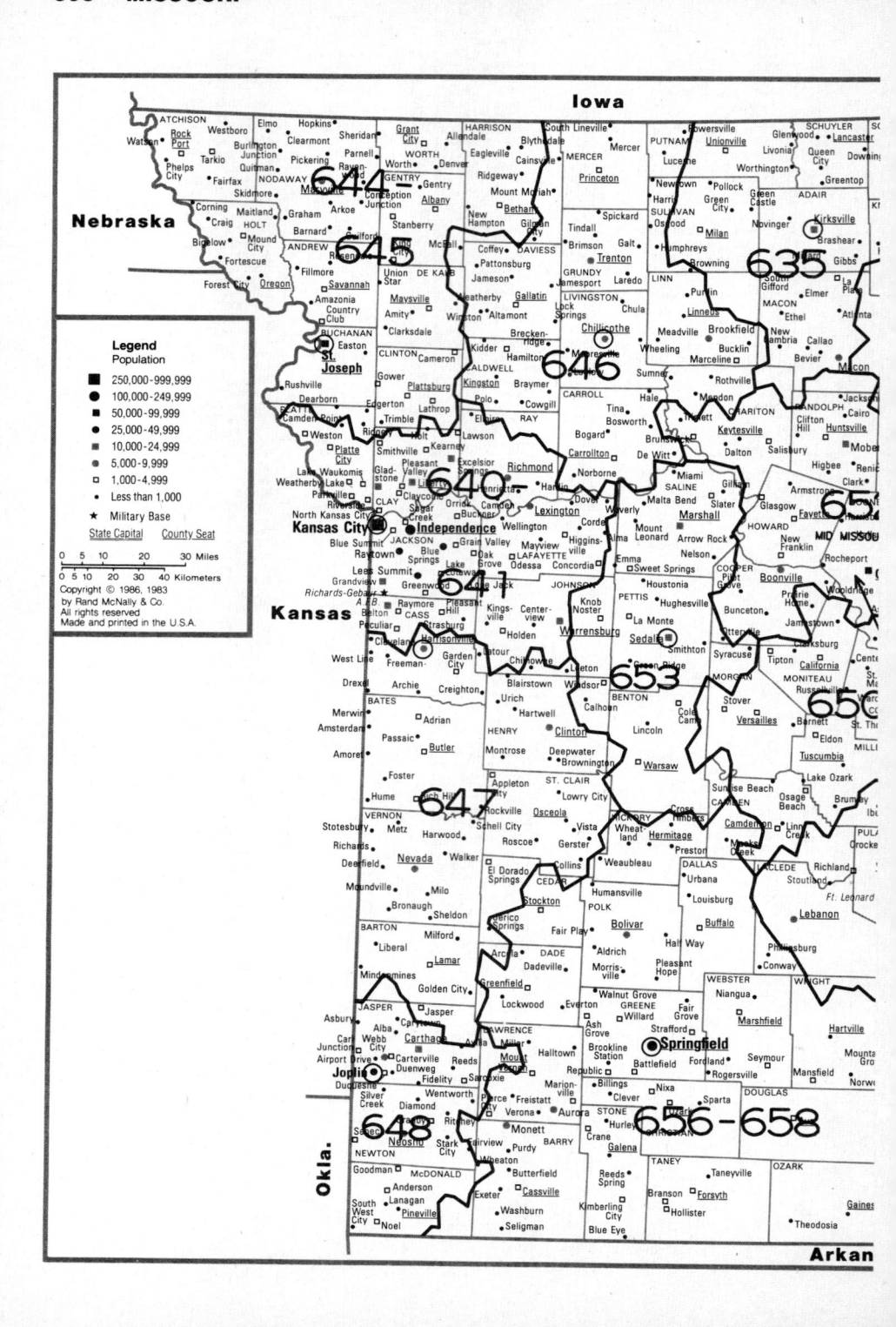

MISSOURI 307

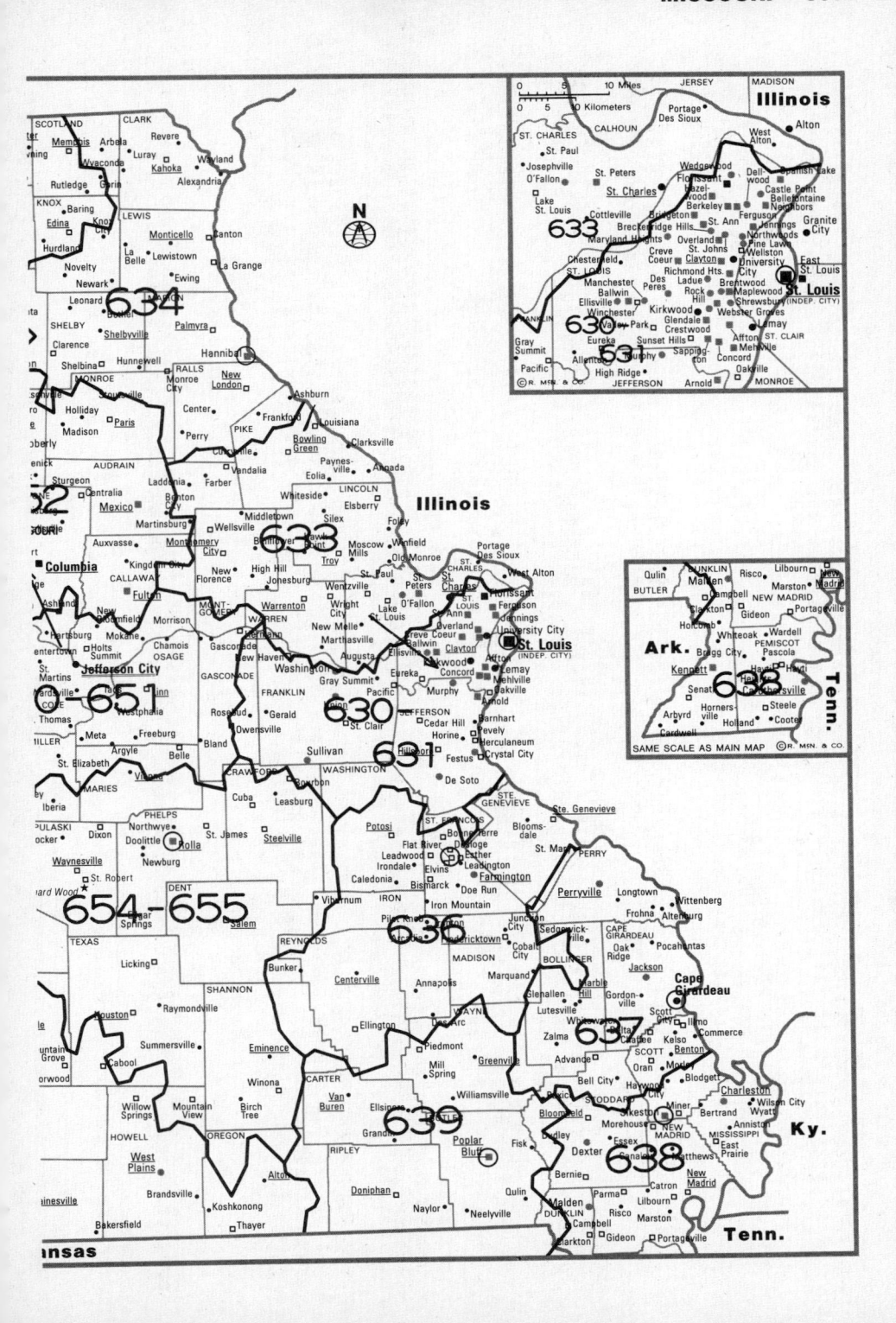

MISSOURI Aaron-Bowers Mill

Name	ZIP
Aaron	64720
Abesville	65656
Abo	65536
Acorn Corner	63877
Acornridge	63960
Adair (Adair County)	63533
Adrian	64720
Advance	63730
Affton	63123
Agency	64401
Aid	63825
Airline Acres	63834
Airport Drive	64801
Alanthus	64489
Alba	64830
Albany (Gentry County)	64402
Albany (Ray County)	64077
Aldrich	65601
Alexandria	63430
Alfalfa Center	63834
Algonquin (Part of Webster Groves)	63119
Allbright	63655
Allendale	64420
Allenton	63001
Allerville	63740
Alley Spring	65466
All Saints Village	63376
Alma	64001
Almartha	65773
Almon	65732
Alpha	64652
Altamont	64620
Altenburg	63732
Altheim	63141
Alton	65606
Altoona	64720
Amazonia	64421
Americus	65069
Amity	64422
Amoret	64722
Amsterdam	64723
Amy	65626
Anabel	63431
Anaconda	63077
Anderson	64831
Annada	63330
Annapolis	63620
Anniston	63820
Anson	52626
Anthonies Mill	65441
Antioch (Clark County)	63445
Antioch (Clay County)	64119
Antioch Center (Part of Kansas City)	64119
Antonia	63052
Anutt	65540
Apache Flats	65101
Apple Creek (Perry County)	63775
Appleton City	64724
Aquilla	63825
Arab	63733
Arbela	63432
Arbor	63740
Arbor Terrace (Part of Northwoods)	63121
Arbyrd	63821
Arcadia	63621
Archie	64725
Arcola	65603
Ardeola	63730
Arditta	65626
Ardmore	65247
Argo	65441
Argyle	65001
Arkmo	63821
Arkoe	64468
Arley	64060
Arlington	65550
Armstrong	65230
Arnold	63010
Aroma	64844
Arroll	65571
Arrowhead Beach (Part of Lake Ozark)	65049
Arrowhead Lake Estates	65326
Arrow Rock	65320
Arthur	64779
Asbury	64832
Ashburn	63433
Asherville	63960
Ash Grove	65604
Ash Hill	63940
Ashland	65010
Ashley	63334
Ashley Creek	65555
Ashton	63453
Aspenhoff	63357
Athens (Clark County)	63465
Atherton	64050
Atlanta	63530

Name	ZIP
Atlas	64836
Atwater Terrace	63136
Auburn	63343
Augusta	63332
Aullville	64037
Aurora	65605
Aurora Springs	65026
Austin (Cass County)	64725
Auxvasse (Callaway County)	65231
Ava	65608
Avalon	64621
Avenue City	64505
Avert	63825
Avery	65355
Avilla	64833
Avon	63640
Avondale	64117
Azen	63432
Babbtown	65085
Bacon (Moniteau County)	65046
Baden (Part of St. Louis)	63147
Baderville	63862
Bado	65689
Bagnell	65026
Bahner	65350
Baker (Stoddard County)	63846
Bakersfield	65609
Bakersville	63827
Baldwin Lake	64080
Baldwin Park	64080
Ballard	64730
Ballwin	63011
	63021-22
For specific Ballwin Zip Codes call (314) 436-4454	
Bancroft	64642
Banner	63623
Bannister	65786
Bannister Mall (Part of Kansas City)	64137
Bardley	63935
Baring	63531
Barnard	64423
Barnesville	63530
Barnett	65011
Barnhart	63012
Barretts	63122
Barry (Part of Kansas City)	64155
Bartlett	65438
Barwick	64649
Baryties	63626
Bates City	64011
Batesville	63932
Battlefield	65619
Battlefield Mall (Part of Springfield)	65804
Baxter	65681
Bay	65041
Baydy Peak	65065
Bayshore (Part of Arnold)	63010
Beach	65632
Beaman	65350
Bean Lake	64484
Bearcreek (Cedar County)	65649
Bearfield	65201
Beaufort	63013
Beckville (Part of Piedmont)	63957
Bedford (Livingston County)	64643
Bedison	64434
Belews Creek	65050
Belgique	63775
Belgrade	63622
Bellair	65237
Bellamy	64784
Bella Villa	63125
Bell City	63735
Belle	65013
Belle Center	64801
Bellefontaine (St. Louis County)	63017
Bellefontaine (Washington County)	63630
Bellefontaine Neighbors	63137
Bellerive	63121
Bellerive Estates	63141
Belleview (Iron County)	63623
Belleville	64801
Bellflower	63333
Bel-Nor	63133
Bel-Ridge	63133
Belton	64012
Belvidere (Part of Grandview)	64030
Bem	65066
Ben Avis (Part of Ferguson)	63135
Benbow	63440
Benbush	63141
Bendavis	65433
Benjamin	63435
Bentley Farms	63088

Name	ZIP
Benton (Scott County)	63736
Benton City	65232
Benton Park (Part of St. Louis)	63104
Bentonville	65355
Berger	63014
Berkeley	63134
Berlin	64463
Bermott	65706
Bernheimer	63357
Bernie	63822
Berryman	65565
Bertrand	63823
Berwick	65723
Bessville	63762
Bethany	64424
Bethel	63434
Bethlehem (McDonald County)	64861
Bethpage	64867
Beulah (Madison County)	63636
Beulah (Phelps County)	65536
Beverly	64079
Beverly Hills	63121
Bevier	63532
Biblegrove	63531
Biehle	63775
Bigelow	64425
Big Lake	64425
Big Piney	65550
Big River Mills	63628
Bigspring	63363
Billings	65610
Billingsville	65233
Billmore	65690
Birch Tree	65438
Birds Corners	63846
Birdtown	65637
Birmingham	64161
Bismarck	63624
Bixby	65439
Black	63625
Blackburn	65321
Blackjack (St. Clair County)	65785
Black Jack (St. Louis County)	63031
Black Walnut	63301
Blackwater	65322
Blackwell	63626
Blairstown	64726
Bland	65014
Blendville (Part of Joplin)	64801
Bliss	63626
Blodgett	63824
Blomeyer	63740
Bloomfield	63825
Blooming Rose	65436
Bloomington (Macon County)	63532
Bloomsdale	63627
Blosser	65339
Blue Branch	65355
Blue Eye	65611
Blue Lick	65350
Blue Mound	64638
Blue Ridge	64424
Blue Ridge Mall (Part of Kansas City)	64119
Blue Springs	64014-15
For specific Blue Springs Zip Codes call (816) 229-6900	
Blue Summit	64126
Blue Vue (Part of Kansas City)	64133
Bluffton	65069
Blythedale	64426
Boaz	65631
Boekerton	63873
Bogard (Carroll County)	64622
Bois D'Arc	65612
Bolckow	64427
Boles	63055
Bolivar	65613
Bona	65601
Bonanza	64650
Bongor Lake Estate	65202
Bonham	65605
Bonne Terre	63628
Bonnots Mill	65016
Boonesboro	65250
Boonville	65233
Bosky Dell (Part of Lanagan)	64831
Boss	65440
Boston	64759
Bosworth	64623
Boulder City	64844
Bourbon (Crawford County)	65441
Bowen	65360
Bowers Mill	64848

Bowling Green-Commerce MISSOURI 309

Name	ZIP
Bowling Green (Pike County)	63334
Boydsville	65251
Boynton	63556
Boys Ranch	65617
Boys Town	65559
Bracken	65706
Bradfield	65705
Bradleyville	65614
Braggadocio	63826
Bragg City	63827
Braley	64477
Branch	65786
Brandon	65360
Brandsville	65688
Branson	65616
Brashear	63533
Braymer	64624
Brays	65486
Brazeau (Perry County)	63737
Brazil	63664
Brazito	65101
Breckenridge	64625
Breckenridge Hills	63114
Breen Acres (Part of Kansas City)	64152
Brentwood	63144
Brewer	63775
Briar	63931
Brickeys	63627
Bridgeton	63044
Bridlecroft	64083
Brighton	65617
Brimson	64642
Brinktown	65443
Briscoe	63379
Bristow	64772
Brixey	65618
Broadway (Part of St. Louis)	63147
Brock	63555
Bronaugh	64728
Brookdale	63141
Brookfield	64628
Brooking Park	65301
Brookline Station	65619
Brooklyn	64481
Brooklyn Heights	64836
Broseley	63932
Brownbranch	65608
Brownfield	65556
Browning	64630
Brownington	64740
Browns	65202
Browns Spring	65610
Brownwood	63738
Brumley	65017
Bruner	65620
Brunot	63636
Brunswick	65236
Brushcreek (Laclede County)	65536
Brushyknob	65608
Buck Donic	65829
Buckhart	65638
Buckhorn (Madison County)	63655
Buckhorn (Pulaski County)	65583
Bucklin	64631
Buckner	64016
Bucoda	63876
Bucyrus	65444
Buell	63361
Buffalo (Dallas County)	65622
Buffington	63846
Bullion	63501
Bunceton	65237
Bunker	63629
Bunker Hill	65257
Burbank	63944
Burdett	64720
Burfordville	63739
Burgess	64769
Burke City	63135
Burksville	63434
Burlington Junction	64428
Burnham	65793
Burns	65613
Burr	72741
Burton	65248
Burtville	65336
Butcher	65774
Butler (Bates County)	64730
Butler Hill Estates	63128
Butterfield	65623
Butts	65441
Bynumville	65281
Byron	65013
Cabanne (Part of St. Louis)	63112
Cabool	65689
Caddo	65706
Cadet	63630
Cainsville	64632

Name	ZIP
Cairo	65239
Caledonia	63631
Calhoun	65323
California	65018
Callao	63534
Calm	63942
Calton Mill	65769
Calumet	63336
Calverton Park	63136
Calwood	65251
Cambridge	65330
Camden (Ray County)	64017
Camden Point	64018
Camdenton	65020
Cameron	64429
Campbell (Dunklin County)	63933
Campbellton	63068
Camp Clark	64772
Canaan (Gasconade County)	65014
Canalou	63828
Cane Hill	65635
Caney Creek	63771
Cannon Mines	63630
Canton (Part of Desloge)	63435
Cantwell (Part of Desloge)	63601
Cape Fair	65624
Cape Girardeau	63701-02
For specific Cape Girardeau Zip Codes call (314) 335-5501	
Capital Mall (Part of Jefferson City)	65101
Capitol Hill	63136
Caplinger Mills	65607
Cappeln	63348
Capps	65082
Cardwell	63829
Carl Junction	64834
Carlow	64648
Carmack	64402
Carola	63961
Carondelet (Part of St. Louis)	63111
Carr (Part of Florissant)	63031
Carrington	65251
Carr Lane	72616
Carrollton	64633
Carsonville	63121
Carterville	64835
Carthage	64836
Caruth	63857
Caruthersville	63830
Carytown	64836
Cascade	63632
Case	65041
Cash	63534
Cassel Addition	65785
Cassidy	65714
Cassville	65625
Castle Point	63136
Castle Rock (Part of Joplin)	64801
Castlewood	63011
Catawba	64624
Catawissa	63015
Catherine Place	63645
Cato	65605
Catron	63833
Caulfield	65626
Cave	63379
Cave Hill	65041
Caverna	72739
Cave Spring	65770
Cawood	64427
Cedar City	65022
Cedarcreek	65627
Cedar Gap	65746
Cedar Hill	63016
Cedar Hill Lakes	63016
Cedar Lake (Boone County)	65201
Cedar Lake (Jefferson County)	63070
Cedar Ridge	65590
Cedar Springs	64744
Cedar Valley	63901
Cedarville	64756
Celt	65764
Center (Ralls County)	63436
Center Square (Part of Kansas City)	64196
Centertown	65023
Centerview	64019
Centerville	63633
Central (Jackson County)	64142
Central (Madison County)	63645
Central City	64801
Centralia	65240
Central Missouri Correctional Center	65101
Centropolis (Part of Kansas City)	64126
Chadwick	65629

Name	ZIP
Chaffee	63740
Chain of Rocks	63369
Chain-O-Lakes	65625
Chambersburg	63445
Chamois	65024
Champ	63042
Champion (Douglas County)	65717
Champion City	63056
Chandler	64060
Channel	63877
Chapel Hill	64011
Chapel Hills	65785
Chariton (Putnam County)	63565
Charity	65644
Charlack	63114
Charles Nagel (Part of St. Louis)	63115
Charleston	63834
Charteroak	63833
Cherokee Pass	63645
Cherry Box	63451
Cherry Valley Estates	65804
Cherryville	65446
Chesapeake	65712
Chesterfield	63005-06
	63017
For specific Chesterfield Zip Codes call (314) 532-3482	
Chestnutridge	65630
Chicopee	63965
Chilhowee	64733
Chillicothe	64601
Chilton	63965
Chitwood (Part of Joplin)	64801
Chloride	63646
Chouteau	63110
Chula	64635
Circle City	63846
Civic Center (Part of Kansas City)	64106
Civil Bend	64670
Clapper	63456
Clara	65483
Clarence	63437
Clark (Randolph County)	65243
Clark City	63445
Clarksburg	65025
Clarksdale	64430
Clarkson Valley	63017
Clarksville	63336
Clarkton	63837
Claryville	63775
Claycomo	64119
Claysvill	65039
Clayton	63105
Clear Creek (Cooper County)	65276
Clearmont	64431
Clear Spring	63965
Clear Springs	65793
Clearview	65202
Clearwater	63670
Cleavesville	65014
Cleveland (Cass County)	64734
Clever	65631
Cliff Village	64801
Clifton City	65348
Clifton Hill	65244
Climax Springs	65324
Clines Island	63846
Clinton (Henry County)	64735
Cliquot	65640
Clover Bottom	63090
Cloverdale	65590
Clubb	63934
Clyde	64432
Coal (Henry County)	64735
Coal Hill	64744
Coatsville	63535
Cobalt City	63645
Cody	65742
Coffey	64636
Coffeyton	65441
Coffman	63670
Coldspring (Douglas County)	65717
Cold Springs	65355
Coldwater (Wayne County)	63964
Cole Camp	65325
Cole Camp Junction	65325
College Mound	65247
Collins	64738
Coloma	64622
Colony	63563
Columbia	65201-05
For specific Columbia Zip Codes call (314) 876-7829	
Columbia Mall (Part of Columbia)	65201
Columbus	64019
Commerce	63742

MISSOURI Commerce Tower-Erie

Name	ZIP
Commerce Tower (Part of Kansas City)	64199
Commercial (Part of Springfield)	65803
Competition	65470
Conception	64433
Conception Junction	64434
Conclay (Part of Ladue)	63124
Concord	63128
Concord (Callaway County)	65231
Concord Hill	63357
Concordia	64020
Connelsville	63559
Conran	63838
Converse	64465
Conway	65632
Cook Station	65449
Cool Valley	63135
Cooper Hill	65014
Cooter	63839
Cora	63556
Corder	64021
Cornelia	64093
Corning	64435
Cornwall	63645
Corridon	63633
Corry	65635
Corsicana (Barry County)	65734
Corso	63377
Corticelli	65074
Cosby	64436
Cossville	64849
Cottage Farm	63050
Cottleville	63338
Cotton Plant	63855
Cottonwood Point	63830
Couch	65690
Coulstone	65542
Country Club (Andrew County)	64505
Country Club (Jackson County)	64113
Country Club Hills	63136
Country Club Plaza (Part of Kansas City)	64113
Country Lake Woods (St. Louis County)	63011
Country Life Acres	63131
Countryside (Part of Kansas City)	64152
Courtney (Part of Sugar Creek)	64050
Courtois (Washington County)	65451
Cowgill	64637
Coy	64831
Crabbs	65746
Craig	64437
Crane	65633
Creighton	64739
Crescent	63025
Crescent Hill	64720
Crescent Lake (Part of Excelsior Springs)	64024
Crestwood	63126
Crestwood Plaza (Part of Crestwood)	63126
Cretcher	65351
Creve Coeur	63141
Crider	65790
Crites Corner	63937
Crocker	65452
Cross Keys	63031
Cross Keys Shopping Center (Part of Florissant)	63033
Cross Roads (Douglas County)	65608
Cross Roads (Ozark County)	65637
Cross Timbers	65634
Crosstown	63775
Cross Way	65706
Crowder	63801
Crown	65706
Cruise Mill	63626
Crump	63785
Crystal City	63019
Crystal Lake Park	63131
Crystal Lakes	64024
Cuba	65453
Cunningham	64681
Curdton	63960
Cureall	65790
Currentview	63935
Curryville	63339
Custer	65501
Cyclone	64856
Cyrene	63334
Dadeville	65635
Daisy	63743
Daleview	64446

Name	ZIP
Dalton	65246
Damascus	64776
Dameron	63343
Damsel (Part of Osage Beach)	65065
Danby	63627
Danforth	63559
Danville	63361
Dardenne	63366
Dardenne Prairie	63366
Darien	65560
Daris Crossing	63601
Darksville	65259
Darlington	64438
Daugherty	64701
Davis (Lincoln County)	63379
Davis (St. Francois County)	63601
Davis Store	63932
Davisville	65456
Dawn	64638
Dawson (Wright County)	65711
Dawsonville	64428
Dawt	65760
Dayton	64747
Daytown (St. Francois County)	63653
Daytown (St. Francois County)	63601
Dearborn	64439
Decaturville	65536
Deckard-Y	65690
Dederick	64744
Deepwater (Henry County)	64740
Deerfield	64741
Deering	63840
Deer Land	63857
Deer Park	65201
Deer Ridge	63447
Deer Run	63965
Defiance	63341
Deicke	63025
De Kalb	64440
De Lassus	63640
Delaware	65438
Delbridge	63664
Dell Junction	65355
Dellwood	63136
Delmar	64735
Delmo	63801
Delta	63744
Dennis Acres	64801
Denton	63877
Denver	64441
Derby	63601
Des Arc	63636
Desloge	63601
De Soto	63020
Des Peres	63131
Dessa	64850
Detmold	63068
Devils Elbow	65457
De Witt	64639
Dexter	63841
Diamond	64840
Dickens	65759
Diehlstadt	63834
Diggins	65636
Dikeland	64083
Dillard	65456
Dillon	65401
Dissen	63068
Dittmer	63023
Dixie	65063
Dixon	65459
Dockery	64085
Doc Long Estates	65355
Doe Run	63637
Dogwood (Douglas County)	65746
Dogwood (Mississippi County)	63845
Dolly Siding (Part of Bonne Terre)	63628
Dongola	63730
Doniphan	63935
Doolittle	65401
Dora	65637
Dorena	63845
Doss	65560
Dotham	64446
Dove	65536
Dover	64022
Dover (Lewis County)	63448
Downing	63536
Drake (Gasconade County)	65066
Dresden	65301
Drexel	64742
Dripping Spring	65202
Drury	65638
Dudenville	64748
Dudley	63936
Duenweg	64841

Name	ZIP
Dugginsville	65761
Duke	65461
Duncans Bridge	63437
Duncans Point	65324
Dundee	63090
Dunksburg	65351
Dunlap	64683
Dunn	65711
Dunnegan	65640
Duquesne	64801
Durham	63438
Dutchtown	63745
Dutzow	63342
Dye	64098
Dykes	65444
Eagle Rock	65641
Eagleville	64442
Easley (Boone County)	65203
East Bonne Terre	63628
East End	63623
East Hills Mall (Part of St. Joseph)	64506
East Independence (Part of Independence)	64056
East Kirkwood (Part of Kirkwood)	63122
East Leavenworth	64079
East Lynne	64743
East Mexico (Part of Mexico)	65265
Easton	64443
East Prairie	63845
East Purdy	65734
Eastwood	63965
Ebenezer	65803
Ebo (Washington County)	63664
Eccles	65261
Echo Valley	65065
Economy	63530
Ectonville	64089
Edgar Springs	65462
Edge Acres	65785
Edgehill	63625
Edgerton	64444
Edgerton Junction	64439
Edgewater Beach	65653
Edgewood	63334
Edina	63357
Edinburg	64683
Edmonson	65338
Edmundson	63134
Edwards	65326
Egypt Grove	65626
Egypt Mills	63701
El Chaparral	65201
Eldon	65026
El Dorado Springs	64744
Eldridge	65463
Elgin	63434
Elijah	65626
Elk Creek (Texas County)	65464
Elkhead	65753
Elkhorn (Ray County)	64077
Elkhurst	65201
Elkland	65644
Elk Springs	64854
Elkton	65650
Ellington	63638
Ellis	64772
Ellis Prairie	65444
Ellisville	63011
Elsinore	63937
Elm (Johnson County)	64061
Elmdale Village (Part of St. Johns)	63114
Elmer	63538
Elmira	64062
Elmo	64445
Elmont	63080
Elmwood	65321
Elsberry	63343
Elsey	65633
Elston	65101
Elvins	63601
Elwood	65802
Ely	63461
Emden	63439
Emerald Beach	65658
Emerson	63454
Eminence	65466
Emma	65327
Empire Prairie	64463
Englewood (Boone County)	65010
Englewood (Jackson County)	64052
Enon (Moniteau County)	65074
Enon (St. Charles County)	63385
Enyart	64453
Eolia	63344
Epworth	63469
Erie (McDonald County)	64843

Ernestville-Guilford **MISSOURI** 311

	ZIP		ZIP		ZIP
Ernestville	64020	Folk	65085	Gipsy	63750
Essex	63846	Foose	65622	Girdner	65608
Estes	63359	Forbes	64473	Gladden	65560
Esther	63601	Ford City	64463	Gladstone	64118
Estill	65274	Fordland	65652	Glasgow	65254
Ethel	63539	Forest City	64451	Glasgow Village	63137
Ethlyn	63369	Forest Green	65281	Glenaire	64068
Etlah	63014	Forest Hills	65355	Glenallen	63751
Etterville	65031	Foristell	63348	Glencoe	63038
Eudora	65645	Forker	64651	Glendale (Putnam County)	63551
Eugene (Cole County)	65032	Forkners Hill	65632	Glendale (St. Louis County)	63122
Eunice	65468	Forrest Mill	64859	Glen Echo Park	63121
Eureka	63025	Forsyth	65653	Glennon	63762
Evans	65608	Fortescue	64452	Glennonville	63933
Evansville (Buchanan County)	64507	Fort Henry	65259	Glen Park	63070
Evansville (Monroe County)	65270	Fort Leonard Wood (Pulaski County)	65473	Glensted	65084
Eve	64741	Fortuna	65034	Glenstone (Part of Springfield)	65804
Eveningshade	65552	Fort Zumwalt	63366	Glenwood	63541
Everett	64725	Foster	64745	Glenwood Junction (Part of Glenwood)	63541
Eversonville	64688	Fountain Grove	64659	Glidewell	65803
Everton	65646	Fox Creek (St. Louis County)	63069	Glover	63646
Ewing	63440	Fox Haven	64083	Gobler	63849
Excello	65247	Foxwood Springs	64083	Golden	65658
Excelsior	65084	Frailie	63848	Golden City	64748
Excelsior Springs	64024	Frankclay	63644	Golden Oak (Part of Kansas City)	64117
Excelsior Springs Junction	64077	Frankenstein	65016	Goldman	63050
Exeter	65647	Frankford	63441	Goldsberry (Macon County)	63539
Fagus	63938	Franklin (Howard County)	65250	Gooch Mill	65068
Fairdealing	63939	Franks	65459	Goodhope	65608
Fairfax	64446	Frazier	64401	Goodland	63623
Fairgrounds (Part of St. Louis)	63107	Fredericksburg	65061	Goodman	64843
Fair Grove	65648	Fredericktown	63645	Goodson	65659
Fair Haven	64750	Fredville	64850	Gordonville	63752
Fairleigh (Part of St. Joseph)	64506	Freeburg	65035	Gorin	63543
Fairmont	63474	Freedom (Camden County)	65052	Goshen	64673
Fairmount (Part of Independence)	64053	Freedom (Osage County)	65024	Gospel Ridge (Part of St. Robert)	65583
Fair Play	65649	Freeman	64746	Gower	64454
Fairport	64447	Freistatt	65654	Graff	65660
Fairview (Newton County)	64842	Fremont	63941	Graham	64455
Fairview (Taney County)	65744	Fremont Hills	65721	Grain Valley	64029
Fairview (Texas County)	65689	French Village	63036	Granby	64844
Fairview Acres (Part of Flat River)	63601	Friedheim	63747	Grand Center	63534
Falcon	65470	Friendly Valley	63775	Grand Falls	64801
Fanchon	65788	Frisbee	63852	Grandin	63943
Fanning	65453	Frisco	63846	Grand Pass	65339
Farber	63345	Fristoe	65355	Grandview (Benton County)	65355
Farewell	64478	Frohna	63748	Grandview (Jackson County)	64030
Farley	64028	Frontenac	63131	Granger	63442
Farmer	63339	Fruitland (Cape Girardeau County)	63755	Graniteville	63650
Farmersville	64683	Fruitland (Greene County)	65648	Grant (St. Louis County)	63123
Farmington	63640	Fulton	65251	Grant City	64456
Farmington Correctional Center	63640	Gaines	64735	Grantwood Village	63123
Farrar	63746	Gainesville	65655	Granville	65275
Farrenberg	63869	Galena (Stone County)	65656	Grassy	63753
Faucett	64448	Galesburg	64855	Gravelhill	63739
Fayette	65248	Gallatin (Daviess County)	64640	Gravelton	63655
Fayetteville	64093	Galloway (Part of Springfield)	65804	Gravois	63116
Federal	63601	Galmey	65779	Gravois Mills	65037
Fee Fee	63141	Galt	64641	Grayridge	63850
Femme Osage	63332	Gamburg	63955	Grayson	64492
Fenton	63026	Game	63830	Grays Point	65707
Ferguson	63135	Gamma	63333	Gray Summit	63039
Fern Ridge	63141	Garden City	64747	Graysville	63551
Fernview Estates	63141	Gardenview	63033	Green Acres	64801
Ferrelview	64163	Garfield	65690	Green Bay Terrace	65079
Fertile	63630	Garland	64735	Greenbrier	63730
Festus	63028	Garrison	65657	Green Castle	63544
Fidelity	64836	Garwood	63957	Green City	63545
Field (Part of St. Louis)	63108	Gasconade (Gasconade County)	65036	Greendale	63133
Filley	64744	Gascondy	65013	Greenfield	65661
Fillmore (Andrew County)	64449	Gashland (Part of Kansas City)	64155	Green Forest	63901
Fisk	63940	Gateway Drive (Part of Joplin)	64801	Green Grove	63559
Flag Springs (Andrew County)	64494	Gateway South	65201	Green Lawn	63462
Flag Springs (Phelps County)	65559	Gatewood	63942	Green-Mar	63026
Flat	65550	Gaynor	64475	Green Mound Ridge	65669
Flat River	63601	Gazette	63359	Green Mountain	65711
Flatwood	65466	Geneva	72438	Green Oaks	63936
Fleming	64077	Gentry	64453	Green Ridge	65332
Flemington	65650	Gentryville (Douglas County)	65608	Greensburg	63531
Fletcher	63030	Gentryville (Gentry County)	64402	Greenstreet	63013
Flinthill	63346	Georgetown (Boone County)	65203	Greentop	63546
Flordell Hills	63136	Georgetown (Pettis County)	65301	Green Trail	63026
Florence (Buchanan County)	64504	Gerald	63037	Greenville (Clay County)	64060
Florence (Morgan County)	65329	Germantown	64770	Greenville (Wayne County)	63944
Florida	65283	Gerster	64776	Greenwood	64034
Florissant	63031-34	Gibbs	63540	Greer	65606
For specific Florissant Zip Codes call (314) 837-1810		Gibson	63847	Gregory	63435
		Gideon	63848	Gregory Heights	65202
		Gilbert	63855	Gretna	65616
Floyd	64077	Gilliam	65330	Grimmett	65775
Flucom	63020	Gilman City	64642	Grisham	63762
Foil	65755	Gilmore	63385	Grogan	65464
Foley	63347	Ginger Blue	64854	Grover (St. Louis County)	63040
				Grovespring	65662
				Grubville	63041
				Guilford	64457

312 MISSOURI Gumbo-Kimberling City

Name	ZIP
Gumbo	63601
Gunn City	64760
Guthrie	65063
Hagers Grove	63437
Hahatonka	65020
Hahn	63762
Hailey	65605
Hale	64643
Half Rock	64679
Half Way	65663
Halls	64504
Hallsville	65255
Halltown	65664
Hamilton	64644
Hammond	65762
Hams Prairie	65251
Hancock	65452
Handy	63941
Hanley Hills	63133
Hannibal	63401
Hannon	64762
Happy Hollow	63630
Hardeman	65340
Hardenville	65666
Hardin (Ray County)	64035
Harg	65201
Harper	64776
Harris (Sullivan County)	64645
Harrisburg	65256
Harrisonville	64701
Harry S. Truman (Part of Independence)	64055
Hart (McDonald County)	64865
Hartford (Putnam County)	63565
Hartsburg	65039
Hartshorn	65479
Hartville	65667
Hartwell	64788
Hartzell	63848
Harvester	63302
Harviell	63945
Harwood	64750
Haseltine	65802
Hassard	63456
Hastain	65326
Hatfield	64458
Hatton	65231
Havenhurst	64856
Hawkeye	65452
Hawk Point	63349
Hayden	65459
Hayes Park (Part of Sibley)	64088
Hayti	63851
Hayti Heights	63851
Hayward	63873
Haywood City	63736
Hazelgreen	65556
Hazel Run	63628
Hazelwood	63042-45
For specific Hazelwood Zip Codes call (314) 436-4454	
Heatonville	65707
Hebron	65775
Hecla	64653
Hedge City	63460
Helena	64459
Helm	65459
Heman Park (Part of University City)	63130
Hematite	63047
Hemple	64490
Henderson	65742
Hendrickson	63967
Henley	65040
Henrietta	64036
Henry's Acres	65338
Henry Winfield Wheeler (Part of St. Louis)	63101
Herbs	65338
Herculaneum	63048
Hercules	65614
Heritage Hills	64083
Hermann	65041
Hermitage	65668
Hermondale	63877
Hickman Mills (Part of Kansas City)	64134
Hickory Creek	64683
Hickory Hill	65040
Higbee	65257
Higdon	63645
Higginsville	64037
High Gate	65559
High Hill	63350
Highland (Perry County)	63775
Highlandville	65669
Highley Heights (Part of Desloge)	63601
High Point	65042
High Ridge	63049
Hilda	65680

Name	ZIP
Hill City	65625
Hillhouse Addition (Part of Richland)	65556
Hilliard	63901
Hillsboro	63050
Hillsdale	63133
Hill Top	63935
Hinch	65441
Hinton	65202
Hiram	63947
Hoberg	65712
Hobson	65560
Hocomo	65626
Hodge	64096
Hoene Spring	63025
Hoffman Junction	63628
Holcomb	63852
Holden	64040
Holiday Shores	65326
Holland	63853
Holliday	65258
Holliday Landing	63944
Hollister	65672
Hollow	63069
Hollywood	63821
Holman	65757
Holmes Park (Part of Kansas City)	64131
Holstein	63357
Holt	64048
Holts Summit	65043
Homestead	64024
Homestown	63879
Honey Creek (Cole County)	65101
Hooker (Pulaski County)	65550
Hoover	64079
Hopewell (Warren County)	63357
Hopewell (Washington County)	63660
Hopkins	64461
Horine	63070
Hornersville	63855
Hornet	64865
Hortense	64735
Horton	64751
House Creek	63965
House Springs	63051
Houston	65483
Houstonia	65333
Houston Lake	64152
Howards Ridge	65655
Howardville	63869
Howell (St. Charles County)	63303
Howes Mill	65560
H. S. Jewell (Part of Springfield)	65802
Hudson	64724
Huggins (Texas County)	64484
Hughesville	65334
Hugo	65052
Humansville	65674
Hume	64752
Humphreys	64646
Hunnewell	63443
Hunter	63943
Hunters Mill	63664
Hunterville	63846
Huntingdale	64735
Huntington	63456
Huntleigh	63131
Huntsdale	65203
Huntsville	65259
Hurdland	63547
Hurley	65675
Hurlingen	64443
Huron	65613
Hurricane (Bollinger County)	63762
Hurricane Deck	65079
Hurryville	63640
Hutton Valley	65793
Iantha	64759
Iatan	64098
Iberia	65486
Iconium	64776
Idalia	63825
Idlewild	63960
Ike	65737
Ilasco	63401
Illmo	63780
Imperial	63052
Independence	64050-58
For specific Independence Zip Codes call (816) 836-1440	
Independence Center (Part of Independence)	64057
Indian Creek	63456
Indian Ford	65582
Indian Grove	65236
Indian Hills (Part of Kansas City)	64114
Indian Lake	65453

Name	ZIP
Indian Springs	64783
Ink	65466
Ionia	65335
Irena	64456
Irondale	63648
Iron Gates	64801
Iron Mountain	63650
Iron Mountain Lake	63624
Ironton	63650
Irwin	64759
Isabella	65676
Isadora	64456
Ishmael	63664
Ives	63936
Jack	65560
Jacket	65745
Jackson (Benton County)	65355
Jackson (Cape Girardeau County)	63755
Jacksonville	65260
Jadwin	65501
James Crews (Part of Kansas City)	64127
Jameson	64647
Jamesport	64648
Jamestown	65046
Jamesville	65631
Jane	64856
Japan	63080
Jarvis	63050
Jasper (Jasper County)	64755
Jaudon	64012
Jawdea	64083
Jaywye	63873
Jedburg	63011
Jefferson City	65101-10
For specific Jefferson City Zip Codes call (314) 636-4186	
Jefferson Memorial (Part of St. Louis)	63102
Je-Ke-Ki	65326
Jenkins	65605
Jennings	63136
Jerico	65746
Jerico Springs	64756
Jerk Tail	65667
Jerome	65529
Jesse M. Donaldson (Part of Kansas City)	64195
Jewett	63620
J&G Junction (Part of Joplin)	64801
Johnson City	64724
Johnstown (Bates County)	64770
Johnstown (Jasper County)	64835
Jonesburg	63351
Joplin	64801-04
For specific Joplin Zip Codes call (417) 623-6176	
Jordan	65634
Jordan W Chambers (Part of St. Louis)	63106
Josephville	63385
Judge	65051
Junction City	63645
Junland	63901
Kahoka	63445
Kaiser	65047
Kampville	63301
Kampville Beach	63301
Kampville Court	63301
Kansas City	64101-99
For specific Kansas City Zip Codes call (816) 842-2800	
Karr's	65355
Kaseyville	63534
Kearney	64060
Keener Cave	63967
Keenland	64083
Keethtown	65486
Keightley's Beach	65355
Kellerville	63469
Kelso	63758
Keltner	65720
Kendricktown	64836
Kennett	63857
Kenoma	64759
Keota	63532
Kerr	64429
Kersey Coates (Part of Kansas City)	64105
Ketterman	64790
Kewanee	63860
Keys Summit	63122
Keysville	65565
Keytesville	65261
Kidder	64649
Kiel	63068
Killarney Shores	63650
Kilwinning	63555
Kimberling City	65686

Kimberling Hills-Marvin MISSOURI 313

	ZIP		ZIP		ZIP
Kimberling Hills (Part of Kimberling City)	65686	La Monte	65337	Long Lane	65590
Kimble	65542	Lampe	65681	Longrun	65761
Kime	63944	Lanagan	64847	Longtown	63775
Kimmswick	63053	Lancaster	63548	Longview (Jackson County)	64138
Kinder (Stoddard County)	63960	Langdon	64446	Longview (McDonald County)	64861
Kinderpost	65542	Lanton	65775	Loose Creek	65054
Kinfolks Ridge	63830	La Plata	63549	Loughboro	63601
King City	64463	Laquey	65534	Louisburg	65685
Kingdom City	65262	Laredo	64652	Louisiana	63353
Kings Lake	63347	Larimore	63138	Louisville	63334
Kings Point	65682	La Russell	64848	Lowground	63559
Kingston	64650	Latham	65050	Lowndes	63951
Kingsville	64061	Lathrop (Clinton County)	64465	Lowry City	64763
Kingsway Mall (Part of Sikeston)	63801	Latour	64760	Low Wassie	65588
Kinloch	63140	Latty	63664	Lucas	64788
Kinsey	63627	Laurel Heights (Part of Raytown)	64133	Lucas and Hunt Village	63121
Kirbyville	65679	Laurie	65038	Lucerne	64655
Kirksville	63501	La Valle	63833	Ludlow	64656
Kirkwood	63122	Lawrenceburg	65646	Luebbering	63061
Kirschner (Part of St. Joseph)	64504	Lawrenceton	63627	Lulu	65606
Kissee Mills	65680	Lawson	64062	Luna	65555
Kliever	65018	Leadington	63601	Lupus	65046
Knobby	65326	Lead Mine	65764	Luray	63453
Knob Lick	63651	Leadwood	63653	Lutesville (Part of Marble Hill)	63762
Knob Noster	65336	Leann	65605	Luystown	65016
Knobtown (Part of Kansas City)	64138	Leasburg	65535	Lynchburg	65543
Knolls	65065	Leawood	64801	Lyon	63068
Knox City	63446	Lebanon (Laclede County)	65536	Mc Allister Springs	65333
Knoxville	64084	Lebo	65775	McBaine	65203
Kodiak	64485	Lecoma	65540	McBride	63776
Koeltztown	65048	Leeds (Part of Kansas City)	64129	McCarty	63830
Koenig	65013	Leemon	63755	McClurg	65701
Koshkonong	65692	Leeper	63957	McCracken	65753
Krakow	63090	Lees Summit	64063-64 64081-82	McCurry	64438
Kurreville	63766	For specific Lees Summit Zip Codes call (816) 524-0199		McDowell	65769
Labadie	63055	Leesville	64735	Macedonia	65401
La Belle	63447	Leeton	64761	McFall	64657
Lac du Bois	63141	Lemay	63125	McGee	63763
Laclede	64651	Lemons	63565	McGirk	65055
Lacyville	64720	Lenox	65541	Machens	63373
Laddonia	63352	Lentner	63450	McKenna Villa	65326
La Due (Henry County)	64735	Leonard	63451	Mackenzie	63123
Ladue (St. Louis County)	63124	Leon Mercer Jordan (Part of Kansas City)	64128	McKinley (Lawrence County)	65705
Laflin	63760	Leopold	63760	McKittrick	65056
La Forge	63869	Leora	63825	Macks Camp	65355
Lagonda	63558	Leota	65626	Macks Creek	65786
La Grange	63448	Leslie (Franklin County)	63056	McMullin	63801
Laguna Beach (Part of Osage Beach)	65065	Lesterville	63654	McNatt	64867
Lake Adelle	63016	Levasy	64066	Macomb	65702
Lake Annette	64746	Lewis (Henry County)	64735	Macon	63552
Lake Arrowhead	63060	Lewis and Clark Village	64484	Madison (Monroe County)	65263
Lake City (Part of Independence)	64016	Lewistown	63452	Madisonville	63436
Lake Contrary	64504	Lexington	64067	Madry	65605
Lake Creek (Benton County)	65325	Liberal	64762	Magnolia	64040
Lake Forest Estates	63670	Liberty (Callaway County)	65063	Main City	64742
Lake Junction (Part of Webster Groves)	63119	Liberty (Clay County)	64068	Maitland	64466
Lake Kah-Tan-Da	63775	Libertyville	63640	Majorville	65355
Lakeland	65026	Lick	65233	Makalu Estates	65065
Lake Lotawana	64063	Licking	65542	Malden	63863
Lake Mykee Town	65043	Liguori	63057	Malta Bend	65339
Lakenan	63468	Lilbourn	63862	Mammoth	65655
Lake of the Woods (Boone County)	65201	Lilly	64477	Manchester	63011
Lake-of-the-Woods (Grundy County)	64683	Lincoln (Benton County)	65338	Mandeville	64622
Lake Ozark	65049	Lindbergh	65202	Manes	65711
Lake Sherwood	63357	Linden (Christian County)	65742	Mano	65625
Lakeshire	63125	Lindenlure Lake	65742	Mansfield	65704
Lakeside (Benton County)	65338	Lindley (Grundy County)	64652	Many Springs	65606
Lakeside (Boone County)	65256	Lingo	64631	Mapaville	63065
Lakeside (Jasper County)	64801	Linkville (Part of Kansas City)	64152	Maplegrove	64748
Lakeside (Miller County)	65026	Linn (Osage County)	65051	Maples	65542
Lake Spring	65532	Linn Creek	65052	Maplewood (Cass County)	64083
Lake St. Louis	63367	Linneus	64653	Maplewood (St. Louis County)	63143
Lake Tapawingo	64015	Lisbon	65254	Marble Hill	63764
Lake Tekakwitha	63069	Lisle	64742	Marceline	64658
Lake Timberline	63628	Lithium	63775	March	65644
Lake Valle	63020	Little Blue (Part of Kansas City)	64133	Marco	63870
Lakeview (Cass County)	64083	Little Village (Part of Kansas City)	64118	Margona Village (Part of St. Johns)	63114
Lakeview (Miller County)	65026	Livonia	63551	Marion (Cole County)	65023
Lakeview (Stone County)	65737	Lock Springs	64654	Marionville	65705
Lakeview Heights	65338	Lockview Estates	65785	Mark Twain Mall (Part of St. Charles)	63301
Lake Viking	64640	Lockwood	65682	Marlborough	63123
Lake Ware	63020	Locust Hill	63460	Marling	63359
Lake Waukomis	64152	Lodi	63950	Marquand	63655
Lake Wauwanoka	63050	Logan (Lawrence County)	65705	Marshall (Saline County)	65340
Lake Winnebago	64034	Lohman	65053	Marshall Junction	65340
Lake Wittona	64683	Loma Linda	63901	Marshfield	65706
Lakewood	65201	Lonedell	63060	Marston	63866
Lamar (Barton County)	64759	Lone Elm (Cooper County)	65237	Marthasville	63357
Lamar Heights	64759	Lone Elm (Jasper County)	64801	Martin City (Part of Kansas City)	64145
Lambert	63736	Lone Hill	63901	Martinsburg	65264
Lamine	65233	Lone Jack	64070	Martinstown	63565
		Lone Star	63862	Martinsville	64467
		Lone Tree	64701	Marvel Cave Park	65616
		Long Beach	65616	Marvin	65084

314 MISSOURI Marvin Terrace-Old Fredonia

	ZIP		ZIP		ZIP
Marvin Terrace (Part of St. Johns)		Moline Acres	63136	New Market	64439
		Molino	63265	New Melle	63365
Maryden	63624	Monark Springs	64850	New Offenburg	63661
Maryknoll	63369	Monegaw Springs	64776	New Piper	64788
Maryland Heights	63043	Monett	65708	New Point	64473
Marys Home	65032	Monkey Run	63401	Newport	64759
Maryville	64468	Monroe City	63456	New Santa Fe (Part of Kansas City)	64145
Maryville College-Saint Louis	63141	Montague	65669		
Maryville Gardens (Part of St. Louis)	63118	Montague Hill	65340	New Survey	63877
		Montevallo	64767	Newtonia	64853
Masters	65649	Montgomery City	63361	Newtown	64667
Matson	63341	Monticello	63457	New Truxton	63381
Mattese	63129	Montier (Shannon County)	65546	New Wells	63768
Matthews	63867	Montreal	65591	New Woolam	65066
Maud	63437	Montrose	64770	New York	64644
Maupin	63061	Montserrat	65336	Niangua	65713
Mayesburg	64788	Moody	65777	Niangua Junction	65713
Mayfield (Bollinger County)	63662	Mooresville	64664	Nichols (Part of Springfield)	65802
Maysville	64469	Mora	65345	Nind	63501
Mayview	64071	Morehouse	63868	Ninnescah Park	64740
Maywood	63454	Morgan (Laclede County)	65632	Nishnabotna (Atchison County)	64482
Meacham Park (Part of Kirkwood)	63122	Morgan Heights	64836		
		Morley	63767	Nixa	65714
Meadowbrook Acres	64083	Morrison	65061	Noble	65715
Meadowbrook Downs (Part of Overland)	63114	Morrisville	65710	Nodaway	64421
		Morse Mill	63066	Noel	64854
Meadowbrook West	65203	Morton	64085	Norborne	64668
Meadville	64659	Mosby	64073	Normandy	63121
Mecca	64492	Moscow Mills	63362	Normandy Shopping Center (Part of Northwoods)	63121
Medford	64040	Moselle	63084		
Medill	63445	Mosher	63670	Norris	64726
Medoc	64855	Mound City	64470	North Boonville	65274
Mehlville	63129	Moundville	64771	North County	63138
Meinert	65682	Mountain (McDonald County)	65772	Northeast (Part of Kansas City)	64123
Melbourne	64642				
Melrose	63069	Mountain Grove	65711	Northern Heights (Part of Kansas City)	64152
Memphis	63555	Mountain View	65548		
Mendon	64660	Mount Airy	65259	North Kansas City	64116
Menfro	63765	Mount Freedom	65050	Northland Shopping Center (Part of Jennings)	63136
Mentor	65742	Mount Hope	63077		
Mercer	64661	Mount Hulda	65325	North Lilbourn	63862
Mercyville	63538	Mount Leonard	65339	Northmoor	64152
Merriam Woods	65653	Mount Moriah	64665	North Noel (Part of Noel)	64854
Merritt	65720	Mount Pleasant (Miller County)	65026	North Park Mall (Part of Joplin)	64801
Merwin	64723				
Mesler	63772	Mount Shira	64854	North Patton	63662
Meta	65058	Mount Sterling	65062	North Salem	63566
Metro North Mall (Part of Kansas City)	64155	Mount Vernon	65712	North Shores	65355
		Mount Zion (Douglas County)	65608	Northview	65706
Metz	64765			North Wardell	63879
Mexico	65265	Mount Zion (Henry County)	64740	Northwest Plaza (Part of St. Ann)	63074
Miami (Saline County)	65344	Mulberry (Barton County)	66756		
Michelles Corner	65444	Mulberry (Bates County)	64722	Northwood Acres	64152
Micola	63877	Mullendike	64083	Northwoods	63121
Middle Brook	63656	Munsell	65588	Northwye	65401
Middle Grove	65263	Murphy	63026	Norwood	65717
Middletown	63359	Murry	65255	Norwood Court	63121
Mid Rivers Mall (Part of St. Peters)	63376	Musicks Ferry	63034	Nottinghill	65762
		Musselfork	65261	Novelty	63460
Midvale	65571	Myrtle (Oregon County)	65778	Novinger	63559
Midway	65202	Mystic	63545	Number Eight	63532
Mike	64658	Napier	64451	Nyhart	64730
Milan	63556	Napoleon	64074	Nyssa	63932
Mildred	65679	Napton	65340	Oak	64422
Milford	64766	Nashua (Part of Kansas City)	64155	Oak Grove (Franklin County)	63080
Millard	63501				
Millcreek (Madison County)	63645	Nashville	64855	Oak Grove (Jackson County)	64075
Miller (Lawrence County)	65707	Naylor	63953		
Millersburg	65251	Nebo	65470	Oak Grove Heights	65801
Millersville	63766	Neck City	64849	Oak Hill	65453
Mill Grove	64673	Neelys	63755	Oakland (Laclede County)	65536
Millheim	63775	Neelyville	63954	Oakland (St. Louis County)	63122
Mill Spring	63952	Neeper	63445	Oakland Park	64870
Millville	64085	Neier	63084	Oak Leaf	65065
Millwood (Lincoln County)	63377	Nelson	65347	Oak Ridge	63769
Milo	64767	Nelsonville	63440	Oaks	64118
Milton (Atchison County)	64446	Nemo	65724	Oakside	65548
Milton (Randolph County)	65270	Neola	65661	Oakton	64759
Mincy	65679	Neosho	64850	Oakview	64118
Mindenmines	64769	Netherlands	63851	Oakville	63129
Mine La Motte	63645	Nettleton	64644	Oakwood (Clay County)	64116
Mineola	63361	Nevada	64772	Oakwood (Marion County)	63401
Miner	63801	Newark	63458	Oakwood Park	64116
Mineral Point	63660	New Bloomfield	65063	Oasis	63347
Mineral Spring	65625	New Boston	63557	Oates	63625
Mineville (Part of Kansas City)	64161	Newburg	65550	Ocie	65761
		New Cambria	63558	Octa	63876
Mingo (Stoddard County)	63960	New Florence	63363	Odessa	64076
Minimum	63620	New Frankfort	65549	Odin	65667
Mint Hill	65024	New Franklin	65274	O'Fallon	63366
Mirabile	64671	New Hamburg	63736	Ogborn	63640
Missionary Acres	63944	New Hampton	64471	Oglesville	63961
Missouri City	64072	New Harmony	65339	Ohio (St. Clair County)	64763
Missouri Eastern Correctional Center	63069	New Hartford	63364	Okete	63379
		New Haven (Franklin County)	63068	Olathia	65704
Missouri Training Center for Men	65270			Old Appleton	63770
		New Hope	63343	Old Bland	65014
Mitchell	63601	New Lebanon	65237	Old Chilhowee	64733
Moberly	65270	New Liberty	65588	Olden	65789
Modena	64673	New London	63459	Oldfield	65720
Mokane	65059	New Madrid	63869	Old Fredonia	65355

Oldham-Ritchey **MISSOURI** 315

Name	ZIP
Oldham	65010
Old Linn Creek	65052
Old Merritt	65720
Old Mines	63630
Old Monroe	63369
Old Orchard (Part of Webster Groves)	63119
Old Post Office (Part of St. Louis)	63169
Old Success	65570
Old Woollam	65066
Olean	65064
Olive (Dallas County)	65648
Olive (St. Louis Indep. City)	63101
Olivette	63132
Olivewood	64083
Olney	63370
Olympia	64744
Olympian Village	63020
Omaha	63565
Ongo	65753
Opolis	66760
Oran	63771
Orange	65605
Orchard Farm	63301
Orchard Lakes	63141
Orearville	65349
Oregon	64473
Oriole	63701
Orla	65536
Oronogo	64855
Orrick	64077
Orrsburg	64475
Osage (Cole County)	65101
Osage Beach	65065
Osage Bend	65101
Osage Bluff	65101
Osage Hill (Part of Kirkwood)	63122
Osborn	64474
Oscar	65542
Osceola	64776
Osgood	64641
Osiris	64756
Oskaloosa	64762
Otterville	65348
Otto	63052
Overland	63114
Overton	65233
Owens	65717
Owensville	65066
Owsley	65332
Oxford	64475
Oxly	63955
Oyer	64744
Ozark (Christian County)	65721
Ozark Beach	65653
Ozark Correctional Center	65652
Ozark Springs	65583
Ozark View	63122
Pacific	63069
Pack	64854
Pagedale	63133
Painton	63772
Palisades	63011
Palmer	63664
Palmyra	63461
Palopinto	65338
Papin	63020
Papinsville	64780
Paradise	64089
Paradise Point	65355
Paris	65275
Paris Springs	65646
Parkcrest Village (Part of Springfield)	65807
Parkdale (Part of Kansas City)	64152
Parker Lake	63775
Parkers Park	63347
Park Forest (Part of Kansas City)	64152
Parksdale	63049
Parkville	64152
Parkway (Franklin County)	63077
Parkway (Jackson County)	64130
Parma	63870
Parnell	64475
Pasadena Hills	63121
Pasadena Park	63121
Pascola	63871
Passaic	64777
Passo	65355
Patterson	63956
Patton	63662
Patton Junction	63662
Pattonsburg	64670
Paulding	63821
Paulina Hills	63010
Paydown	65582
Paynesville	63371

Name	ZIP
Peace Valley	65788
Peach Orchard	63848
Peaksville	63465
Pea Ridge	63080
Pebble Acres	63141
Peculiar (Cass County)	64078
Peerless Park	63088
Peers	63357
Pendleton (Warren County)	63383
Penermon	63846
Pennsboro	65752
Pennville	63545
Peoria	63622
Pepsin	64844
Perkins	63774
Perrin	64477
Perry (Ralls County)	63462
Perryville	63775
Pershing	65061
Peru	64730
Peruque	63301
Petersburg	65250
Petersville	63055
Pevely	63070
Phelps	64848
Phelps City	64482
Philadelphia	63463
Phillipsburg	65722
Pickering	64476
Piedmont	63957
Pierce City	65723
Pierpont	65201
Pierre Laclede (Part of St. Louis)	63108
Pilot Grove	65276
Pilot Knob	63663
Pinckney	63357
Pine	63935
Pine Cove	65324
Pine Crest	65571
Pine Lawn	63120
Pineville	64856
Piney Park	63077
Pinhook	63845
Pioneer	65734
Piper	64770
Pisgah	65237
Pittsburg	65724
Pittsville	64040
Plad	65764
Plato	65552
Platte City	64079
Platte Woods	64152
Plattin	63028
Plattsburg	64477
Plaza (Part of Kansas City)	64112
Plaza Shopping Center (Part of Springfield)	65804
Pleasant Gap	64730
Pleasant Green	65276
Pleasant Grove	65068
Pleasant Hill	64080
Pleasant Hope	65725
Pleasant Ridge (Barry County)	65769
Pleasant Ridge (Bates County)	64780
Pleasant Valley (Clay County)	64068
Pleasant Valley (Jasper County)	64836
Plevna	63464
Plew	64848
Plymouth	64624
Pocahontas	63779
Point Lookout	65726
Point Pleasant	63873
Polk (Polk County)	65727
Pollock	63560
Polo	64671
Pomona	65789
Pom-o-sa Heights	65355
Ponce de Leon	65728
Pond	63038
Pondfork	65762
Pontiac	65729
Pony Express (Part of St. Joseph)	64503
Poplar	65355
Poplar Bluff	63901
Portage Des Sioux	63373
Portageville	63873
Port Hudson	63068
Portland	65067
Possumwalk	64428
Post Oak	64761
Potosi	63664
Pottersville	65790
Powe	63822
Powell	65730
Powersite	65731

Name	ZIP
Powersville	64672
Poynor	63959
Prairie City	64780
Prairie Hill	65281
Prairie Home	65068
Prairie Meadows Estate	65201
Prathersville (Boone County)	65202
Prathersville (Clay County)	64024
Pratt	63935
Prescott	65483
Preston (Hickory County)	65732
Preston (Jasper County)	64836
Princeton	64673
Principia	63131
Prospect	65713
Prospect Hill (Part of Riverview)	63137
Prosperity	64801
Protem	65733
Pulaski	63935
Pulaskifield	65708
Pumpkin Center	64423
Purcell	64857
Purdin	64674
Purdy	65734
Pure Air	63559
Purina Farm	63039
Purman	63935
Purvis	65079
Puxico	63960
Pyletown	63841
Pyrmont	65078
Quarles	64735
Queen City	63561
Quincy	65735
Quitman	64478
Qulin	63961
Racine	64858
Racket	64735
Racola	63630
Radar	65582
Rader	65713
Ralls	63401
Randles	63740
Randolph (Clay County)	64116
Ravanna	64673
Ravena (Part of Pleasant Valley)	64068
Ravena Gardens (Part of Pleasant Valley)	64068
Ravenwood	64479
Raymondville	65555
Raymore	64083
Raytown	64133
Rayville	64084
Rea	64480
Readsville	65067
Rector	65560
Redbird	65014
Red Bridge (Part of Kansas City)	64131
Redford	63665
Redings Mill	64801
Redman	63431
Red Oak	64848
Red Top	65757
Reeds	64859
Reeds Spring	65737
Regal	64624
Reger	63556
Renick	65278
Rensselaer	63401
Renz Correctional Center	65022
Republic	65738
Rescue	64848
Revere	63465
Reynolds	63666
Rhineland	65069
Rhyse	65560
Richards	64778
Richards-Gebaur Air Force Base	64030
Rich Fountain	65035
Rich Hill (Bates County)	64779
Richland (Pulaski County)	65556
Richmond (Ray County)	64085
Richmond Heights	63117
Richville (Douglas County)	65637
Richville (Holt County)	64473
Richwoods	63071
Ridgedale	65739
Ridgely	64444
Ridgeway	64481
Ridgley	65647
Riggs	65284
Rimby	65659
Ripley (Part of Independence)	64056
Risco	63874
Rise Branch	65324
Ritchey	64844

316 MISSOURI River Aux Vases-Shearwood

	ZIP
River Aux Vases	63670
River Bend Estates	63017
Rivermines	63601
River Roads (Part of Jennings)	63136
Riverside (Dunklin County)	63829
Riverside (Platte County)	64150
Riverside Inn	64854
Riverton	65606
Riverview	63137
Rives	63875
Roach	65787
Roads	64668
Roanoke	65230
Roanridge (Part of Kansas City)	64152
Robertson	63042
Robertsville	63072
Robinwood East	63141
Robinwood West	63141
Roby	65557
Rocheport	65279
Rochester	64459
Rockaway Beach	65740
Rockbridge	65741
Rockbridge Estate	65201
Rock Hill	63124
Rockingham	64035
Rock Port	64482
Rock Springs	63601
Rockview	63740
Rockville	64780
Rocky Comfort	64861
Rocky Mount	65072
Rocky Ridge	63670
Rogersville	65742
Rolla	65401
Rolling Hills	64083
Rombauer	63962
Rome	65608
Rondo	65650
Roosterville (Part of Liberty)	64068
Rosati	65559
Roscoe	64781
Rosebud	63091
Rosedale (Part of St. Louis)	63112
Roseland	65323
Roselle	63650
Rosendale	64483
Rothville	64676
Roubidoux (Texas County)	65444
Round Grove (Lawrence County)	65707
Round Spring	65466
Rover	65775
Rowena	65240
Royal	65559
Royal Heights (Part of Joplin)	64801
Royal Oak	65606
Ruble	63638
Rucker	65243
Rueter	65744
Running Deer	65065
Rush Hill	65280
Rush Tower	63028
Rushville	64484
Russ	65536
Russellville (Cole County)	65074
Russellville (Ray County)	64035
Rutledge	63563
Sabula	63620
Saco	63645
Sac Valley Estates	65785
Safe	65559
Sage Hill	65605
Saginaw	64864
St. Albans	63073
St. Ann	63074
St. Ann Shopping Center	63074
St. Anthony	65486
St. Catharine	64677
St. Charles	63301-03
For specific St. Charles Zip Codes call (314) 724-4810	
St. Clair	63077
St. Clement	63334
St. Cloud	65441
St. Elizabeth	65075
St. Francisville	63430
St. Francois (St. Francois County)	63601
Ste. Genevieve	63670
St. George (St. Louis County)	63125
St. George (Wright County)	65667
St. James (Phelps County)	65559
St. Johns (St. Louis County)	63114
St. Johns Station (Part of St. Johns)	63114

	ZIP
St. Joseph	64501-08
For specific St. Joseph Zip Codes call (816) 364-3503	
St. Joseph Stock Yards (Part of St. Joseph)	64501
St. Louis	63101-88
For specific St. Louis Zip Codes call (314) 436-4454	
COLLEGES & UNIVERSITIES	
Harris-Stowe State College	63103
Maryville College	63141
St. Louis University	63103
University of Missouri-St. Louis	63121
Washington University	63130
Webster University	63119
FINANCIAL INSTITUTIONS	
The Boatmen's National Bank of St. Louis	63102
Cass Bank & Trust Company	63101
Citizens National Bank of Greater St. Louis	63143
Commerce Bank of St. Louis, National Association	63110
Community Federal Savings & Loan Association	63129
The First National Bank of St. Louis County	63105
Heartland Savings Bank, F.S.B.	63101
Home Federal Savings & Loan Association of St. Louis County	63141
Jefferson Bank & Trust Co.	63103
Landmark Bank	63101
Lemay Bank and Trust Company	63125
Mark Twain Bank	63101
Mercantile Bank of St. Louis National Association	63101
Missouri Savings Association	63109
Pulaski Savings & Loan Association	63141
St. Johns Bank and Trust Company	63114
Southern Commercial Bank	63111
South Side National Bank In St. Louis	63116
Southwest Bank of St. Louis	63110
United Missouri Bank of St. Louis, National Association	63101
United Postal Savings Association	63122
HOSPITALS	
Barnes Hospital	63110
Christian Hospitals Northeast-Northwest	63136
Deaconess Hospital	63139
Jewish Hospital of St. Louis	63110
Lutheran Medical Center	63118
Normandy Osteopathic Medical Center	63131
St. Anthony's Medical Center	63128
St. John's Mercy Medical Center	63141
St. Mary's Health Center	63117
University Hospital, St. Louis University Medical Center	63104
Veterans Administration Medical Center	63125
HOTELS/MOTELS	
The Breckenridge Frontenac	63131
Harley Hotel of St. Louis	63045
Holiday Inn Southwest-Viking	63127
Marriott Pavilion Hotel	63102
The Mayfair	63101
The Radisson Hotel	63105
Sheraton St. Louis Hotel	63101
Stouffer Concourse Hotel	63134
MILITARY INSTALLATIONS	
Aviation Systems Command	63120
Coast Guard Base, St. Louis	63111
Defense Mapping Agency, Aerospace Center, Installation One	63118

	ZIP
Defense Mapping Agency, Aerospace Center, Installation Two	63125
St. Louis Army Ammunition Plant	63120
United States Army Aviation Systems and Troop Support Command	63120
United States Army Engineer District, St. Louis	63101
United States Army Publications Center	63114
United States Army Reserve Personnel Center	63132
St. Louis Centre (Part of St. Louis)	63102
St. Louis Galleria (Part of Richmond Heights)	63147
St. Luke	65632
St. Martins	65101
St. Mary	63673
St. Patrick	63466
St. Paul	63366
St. Peters	63376
St. Robert	65583
St. Thomas	65076
Salcedo	63801
Salem (Dent County)	65560
Saline (Mercer County)	64632
Saline City	65349
Salisbury	65281
Salt Springs	65340
Samford	63877
Sampsel	64601
Sampson	65713
San Antonio	64443
Sandhills	63563
Sandstone	64767
Sandy Hook	65046
Santa Fe	65282
Santa Rosa	64670
Sapp	65203
Sappington	63126
Saratoga	64854
Sarcoxie	64862
Sarvis Point	65746
Savannah	64485
Saverton	63467
Saxton	64507
Schell City	64783
Schlatitz	63730
Schluersburg	63332
Schofield	65663
Scholten	65605
Schubert	65101
Schuermann Heights (Part of Woodson Terrace)	63114
Scobeville	63857
Scopus	63762
Scotland	64836
Scotsdale	63051
Scott City	63780
Scotts Corner	63352
Scrivner	65074
Scrub Ridge	63873
Seaton	65560
Sedalia	65301-02
For specific Sedalia Zip Codes call (816) 826-8887	
Sedgewickville	63781
Seligman	65745
Sellers	63457
Selma	63028
Selmore	65721
Selsa (Part of Independence)	64057
Senate Grove	63068
Senath	63876
Seneca (Newton County)	64865
Sequoita (Part of Springfield)	65804
Sereno	63775
Seymour	65746
Shackelford	65340
Shade	63851
Shady Dell	63901
Shady Grove (Christian County)	65753
Shady Grove (Pulaski County)	65583
Shady Slope	65065
Shamrock	63361
Shannondale	65560
Sharon	65349
Shaw	65202
Shawnee Mound	64733
Shawneetown	63755
Shearwood	64648

Sheffield-Ulman MISSOURI 317

Place	ZIP
Sheffield (Part of Kansas City)	64125
Shelbina	63468
Shelbyville	63469
Sheldon	64784
Shell Knob	65747
Sheridan (Worth County)	64486
Sherrill	65542
Shibboleth	63630
Shibleys Point	63559
Shirley	63664
Shoal Creek Drive	64801
Shoal Creek Estates	64801
Shook	63963
Short Bend (Dent County)	65560
Shoveltown	63031
Shrewsbury	63119
Sibley	64088
Sigsbee	63434
Sikeston	63801
Silex	63377
Silica	63028
Siloam Springs	65775
Silva	63964
Silver Creek (Newton County)	64801
Silver Dollar City	65616
Silver Lake (Cass County)	64083
Silver Lake (Perry County)	63775
Silver Mine	63645
Simcoe	64861
Simmons	65689
Sinsabaugh	63953
Sitze Store	63753
Skidmore	64487
Slabtown	65542
Slagle	65613
Slater	65349
Sleeper	65536
Sligo	65560
Smallett	65608
Smelter Hill (Part of Joplin)	64801
Smithfield	64834
Smithton	65350
Smithville	64089
Smoky Hollow	65560
Sni Mills	64075
Snow Hollow Lake	63656
Snyder	65286
Solo	65564
Souder	65751
Soulard (Part of St. Louis)	63157
South Carrollton (Part of Carrollton)	64633
South Cedar City (Part of Cedar City)	65022
South County Center	63129
Southeast (Part of Kansas City)	64132
Southeast Missouri Mental Health Center	63640
Southern Hills	65301
South Fork (Howell County)	65776
Southgate Shopping Center (Part of Springfield)	65804
South Gifford	63549
South Greenfield	65752
South Lee (Part of Lees Summit)	64063
South Liberty (Part of Liberty)	64068
South Lineville	50147
South Mall (Part of Warrensburg)	64093
South Point (Part of Washington)	63090
South Saint Joseph (Part of St. Joseph)	64504
South Shore	63301
South Side (Part of Springfield)	65806
South Troost (Part of Kansas City)	64131
South Troy	63379
South Van Buren	63965
Southwest	63139
South West City	64863
Spalding	63401
Spanish Lake	63138
Sparta	65753
Speed	65233
Spencerburg	63339
Sperry	63501
Spickard	64679
Splitlog	64843
Spokane	65754
Sprague	64779
Spring Bluff	63080
Spring City	64801
Spring Creek (Phelps County)	65461

Place	ZIP
Springfield	65801-99
For specific Springfield Zip Codes call (417) 864-0101	
Spring Garden	65032
Springhill	64601
Spring Lake	63501
Springtown	63660
Spring Valley (Camden County)	65065
Spring Valley (McDonald County)	64854
Sprott	63670
Spruce (Bates County)	64730
Spurgeon	64850
Squires	65755
Stahl	63559
Stanberry	64489
Stanhope	65339
Stanley	63851
Stanton	63079
Star City	65734
Stark (Pike County)	63353
Stark City	64866
Starkenburg	65069
State Correctional Pre-release Center	65081
Steedman	65077
Steele	63877
Steeles	63935
Steelville	65565
Steffenville	63470
Steinmetz	65254
Stella	64867
Stephens (Boone County)	65202
Stephens (Callaway County)	65201
Stet	64680
Stewartsville	64490
Stillings	64079
Stinson	65707
Stockton	65785
Stockton Hills	65785
Stockyards (Buchanan County)	64504
Stockyards (Jackson County)	64102
Stone Hill	65560
Stoneridge	65737
Stony Hill	63068
Stotesbury	64752
Stotts City	65756
Stoutland	65567
Stoutsville	65283
Stover	65078
Strafford	65757
Strain	63080
Strasburg	64090
Stringtown (Butler County)	63901
Stringtown (Cole County)	65053
Stringtown (Jasper County)	64834
Stults	65737
Stultz	65464
Sturdivant	63782
Sturgeon	65284
Sturges	64601
Sublette	63546
Success	65570
Sugar Creek (Jackson County)	64054
Sugar Lake	64484
Sugartree	64668
Sullivan	63080
Sulphur Springs	63083
Sumach	63852
Summerfield	65013
Summerset Lake	63020
Summersville	65571
Summit (Washington County)	63660
Summit Shopping Center (Part of Lees Summit)	64063
Sumner	64681
Sundown	65761
Sunland Hills	63031
Sunlight	63622
Sunny Slope (Part of Kansas City)	64110
Sunnyvale (Part of Joplin)	64801
Sunrise	63855
Sunrise Beach	65079
Sunrise Lake	63020
Sunset Hills	63127
Sutherland	65360
Swan (Taney County)	65759
Swedeborg	65572
Sweden	65608
Sweet Springs	65351
Sweetwater (Newton County)	64850
Sweetwater (Reynolds County)	63638
Swift	63851

Place	ZIP
Swinton	63730
Swiss	65041
Sycamore	65758
Sycamore Hills	63114
Sycamore Valley	65355
Syenite	63651
Sylvania (Dade County)	65682
Syracuse	65354
Taberville	64780
Table Rock	65616
Taitsville	64671
Tallapoosa	63878
Taneyville	65759
Tanner	63801
Tan Tar Estates	65065
Tanyard	64801
Taos (Buchanan County)	64448
Taos (Cole County)	65101
Tara	63123
Tarkio	64491
Tarrants	63334
Tarsney Lakes	64075
Taskee	63967
Tauria	65737
Taylor (Marion County)	63471
Tea	63091
Teal Bend	65355
Tebbetts	65080
Tecumseh	65760
Tempo	63141
Ten Brook (Part of Arnold)	63010
Tenmile	63552
Ten Mile Corner	64784
Teresita	65573
Terre DuLac	63628
Thayer	65791
Theodosia	65761
Thomas Hill	65244
Thomasville	65438
Thompson	65285
Thornfield	65762
Thorpe	65644
Thox Rock	65550
Thrush	64735
Tiff	63674
Tiffany Springs (Part of Kansas City)	64152
Tiff City	64868
Tiffin	64744
Tightwad	64735
Tillman	63730
Tilsit	63755
Timber	65560
Times Beach	63025
Tina	64682
Tindall	64683
Tinkerville	63857
Tin Town	65622
Tipperary	63559
Tipton	65081
Tipton Ford	64801
Tip Top (Benton County)	65355
Tip Top (Iron County)	63621
Toga	63730
Toledo	65755
Tolona	63452
Torch	63953
Tower Grove (Part of St. Louis)	63163
Town and Country	63131
Tracy	64079
Trask	65548
Treloar	63378
Trenton	64683
Trimble	64492
Triplett	65286
Troutt	63664
Troy	63379
Truesdail	63383
Truman Corners (Part of Grandview)	64030
Truxton	63381
Tuckahoe	64801
Tucker	63942
Tuckers Corner	64849
Tunas	65764
Turners	65765
Turnerville	65548
Turney	64493
Turtle	65560
Tuscumbia	65082
Tuxedo Park (Part of Webster Groves)	63119
Twelve Mile	63645
Twin	65355
Twin Oaks	63011
Twin Springs	63079
Tyler (Pemiscot County)	63877
Tyrone	65483
Udall	65766
Ulman	65083

318 MISSOURI Umber-Zora

	ZIP		ZIP		ZIP
Umber	65785	Ware	63050	Wilbur Park	63123
Umberland	65785	Warren (Marion County)	63456	Wilcox	64468
Umber View	65785	Warrensburg	64093	Wilderness	63941
Umber View Heights	65785	Warrenton	63383	Wildwood	64424
Union (Ray County)	64062	Warsaw	65355	Wildwood Estates	65804
Union (Franklin County)	63084	Warson Woods	63122	Wildwood Lake (Part of Raytown)	64133
Union City	65610	Washburn	65772	Wilhelmina	63933
Union Star	64494	Washington (Franklin County)	63090	Willard	65781
Uniontown	63783	Washington Center	64467	William M Chick (Part of Kansas City)	64124
Unionville	63565	Wasola	65773	Williamsburg	63388
Unity Village	64063	Waterloo	64097	Williamstown	63473
University City	63130	Watson	64496	Williamsville	63967
Uplands Park	63121	Waverly (Lafayette County)	64096	Willmathsville	63546
Upton	65552	Wayland (Clark County)	63472	Willow Brook	64448
Urbana	65767	Wayne (Barry County)	65772	Willow Springs	65793
Urbandale (Part of Moberly)	65270	Waynesville	65583	Wilson City	63882
Urich	64788	Weatherby	64497	Wilton	65039
Useful (Osage County)	65051	Weatherby Lake	64152	Winchester (Clark County)	63435
Utica	64686	Weaubleau	65774	Winchester (St. Louis County)	63011
Vale (Part of Kansas City)	64138	Webb City	64870	Winchester Gap	65536
Valles Mines	63087	Weber Hill	63051	Windsor	65360
Valley City	65336	Webster Groves	63119	Windsor Springs (Part of Kirkwood)	63122
Valley Park	63088	Webster Park (Part of Webster Groves)	63119	Windyville	65783
Valley View (Benton County)	65355	Wedgewood	63031	Winfield	63389
Valley View (Ste. Genevieve County)	63627	Wedgewood Green	63031	Winigan	63566
Valley Water Mills	65803	Weingarten	63670	Winnwood (Part of Kansas City)	64117
Van	65613	Wela	64865	Winnwood Gardens (Part of Kansas City)	64117
Van Buren (Carter County)	63965	Weldon Spring	63301	Winnwood Lake (Part of Kansas City)	64117
Vance	65713	Weldon Springs Heights	63301	Winona	65588
Vancleve	65058	Wellington	64097	Winston	64689
Vandalia	63382	Wellston (St. Louis County)	63112	Winthrop	64484
Vandiver	65265	Wellston (St. Louis Indep. City)	63112	Wisdom	65355
Vanduser	63784	Wellsville	63384	Wishart	65710
Vanzant	65768	Wentworth	64873	Withers Mill	63401
Vastus	63954	Wentzville	63385	Wittenberg	63786
Velda Village	63133	Wesco	65586	Wolf Island	63881
Velda Village Hills	63121	West Alton	63386	Womack	63645
Vera	63334	West Aurora	65026	Woodbine Heights (Part of Kirkwood)	63122
Verdella	64762	Westboro	64498	Woodcliffe	65804
Verona	65769	Westbrooke	65201	Woodland	63461
Verona Hills (Part of Kansas City)	64145	West County Center (Part of Des Peres)	63131	Woodland Park	65026
Versailles	65084	West Ely	63401	Woodland Shores	65355
Veterans Hospital (Part of Kansas City)	64128	West Eminence	65466	Woodlandville	65279
Vibbard	64062	West Hermondale	63877	Woodridge	63033
Viburnum	65566	West Line	64734	Woodruff	64098
Vichy	65580	Weston	64098	Woods Heights	64024
Victoria	63020	West Park Mall (Part of Cape Girardeau)	63701	Woodson Terrace	63134
Vida	65401	Westphalia	65085	Woodville	65247
Vienna	65582	West Plains	65775	Woolam	65014
Vigus	63042	Westport (Part of Kansas City)	64111	Wooldridge	65287
Village of Charlack	63114	West Quincy	63471	Worland	64752
Village of Four Seasons	65049	Westview	64850	Worlds of Fun (Part of Kansas City)	64161
Villa Heights (Part of Joplin)	64801	Westville	64658	Wornall (Part of Kansas City)	64114
Villa Ridge	63089	Westwood	63131	Worth	64499
Vineland	63020	Wet Glaize	65567	Wortham	63601
Vinita Park	63114	Wheatland	65779	Worthington	63567
Vinita Terrace	63114	Wheaton	64874	Wright City	63390
Vinson	63841	Wheelerville	65605	Wyaconda	63474
Viola	65747	Wheeling	64688	Wyatt	63882
Virgil City	64744	Whispering Hills	63141	Wyatt Park (Part of St. Joseph)	64507
Virginia (Bates County)	64730	Whispering Pines	65401	Wyeth	64483
Vista	64789	Whitakerville	65355	Yacht Club Harbor	65065
Vulcan	63675	White Branch	65355	Yarrow	63501
Waco	64869	White Church	65789	Yates	65257
Wagoner	65785	White City	65020	Yonkerville	65723
Wainwright	65043	White Cloud (Hickory County)	65779	Youngstown	63559
Wakenda (Carroll County)	64687	White Hall Fields (Part of Liberty)	64068	Yount	63775
Waldo (Part of Kansas City)	64114	Whiteman AFB	65305	Yukon	65589
Waldron	64092	Whiteman Air Force Base	65305	Zalma	63787
Walker (Vernon County)	64790	Whiteoak (Dunklin County)	63880	Zanoni	65784
Wallace	64439	Whiteside	63387	Zell	63670
Wall Street	65590	Whitesville	64480	Zion	63645
Walnut Grove	65770	Whitewater (Cape Girardeau County)	63785	Zion Hill	65559
Walnut Shade	65771	Whiting	63845	Zora	65078
Wanamaker	65340	Whitman	65286		
Wanda	64866	Wien	63558		
Wappapello	63966				
Wardell	63879				
Ward Parkway Center (Part of Kansas City)	64114				
Wardsville	65101				

Absarokee-Harlem **MONTANA** 319

	ZIP		ZIP		ZIP
Absarokee	59001	Canyon Ferry	59601	East Glacier Park	59434
Acton	59002	Capitol	57724	East Helena	59635
Adel	59421	Cardwell	59721	East Missoula	59801
Agawam	59422	Carlyle	59353	Ekalaka	59324
Agency	59831	Carter	59420	Elkhorn Hot Springs	59746
Alberton	59820	Carterville	59347	Elliston	59728
Albion	59311	Cascade	59421	Elmdale	59213
Alder	59710	Castle Rock	59327	Elmo	59915
Alhambra	59634	Castner Falls	59421	Emigrant	59027
Alloy (Part of Butte)	59701	Cat Creek	59017	Enid	59243
Alpine	59071	Centerville (Cascade		Ennis	59729
Alzada	59311	County)	59472	Epsie	59317
Amazon	59632	Centerville (Silver Bow		Essex	59916
Amsterdam	59741	County)	59701	Ethridge	59435
Anaconda	59711	Central Park	59714	Eureka	59917
Anceney	59741	Champion (Part of		Evaro	59801
Andes	59218	Anaconda)	59722	Evergreen	59901
Angela	59312	Chapman	59537	Everson	59430
Antelope	59211	Charles M. Russell (Part of		Fairfield	59436
Apgar	59936	Great Falls)	59405	Fairview	59221
Argenta	59725	Charlo	59824	Fallon	59326
Arlee	59821	Charlos Heights	59840	Farmington	59422
Armington	59412	Checkerboard	59053	Feely (Part of Butte)	59727
Ashland	59003	Chester	59522	Ferdig	59466
Ashuelot	59443	Chico Hot Springs	59065	Fergus	59451
Augusta	59410	Chinook	59523	Findon	59053
Avon	59713	Choteau	59422	First Creek	59538
Babb	59411	Christina	59451	Fishtail	59028
Bainville	59212	Church Hill	59741	Flathead Indian Reservation	59831
Baker	59313	Circle	59215	Flatwillow	59087
Ballantine	59006	Clancy	59634	Flaxville	59222
Bannack	59725	Clinton	59825	Floral Park (Part of Butte)	59701
Basin	59631	Clyde Park	59018	Florence	59833
Bearcreek	59007	Coalridge	59219	Floweree	59440
Bearmouth	59832	Coalwood	59351	Forestgrove	59441
Bear Spring	59430	Cobden	59872	Forest Park	59330
Beaverton	59261	Coffee Creek	59424	Forsyth	59327
Beehive	59061	Cohagen	59322	Fort Belknap Agency	59526
Belfry	59008	Colorado Gulch	59601	Fort Belknap Indian	
Belgrade	59714	Colstrip	59323	Reservation	59526
Belknap	59874	Columbia Falls	59912	Fort Benton	59442
Belle Creek	59317	Columbia Gardens (Part of		Fortine	59918
Belmont	59046	Butte)	59701	Fort Keogh	59301
Belt	59412	Columbia Heights	59912	Fort Kipp	59213
Beltower	59324	Columbus	59019	Fort Peck	59223
Benchland	59462	Comanche	59015	Fort Peck Indian	
Benteen	59031	Condon	59826	Reservation	59255
Biddle	59314	Conner	59827	Fort Shaw	59443
Big Arm	59910	Conrad	59425	Four Buttes	59224
Bigfork	59911	Cooke City	59020	Fourchette	59538
Bighorn	59010	Coram	59913	Four Corners	59466
Big Sandy	59520	Corbin	59638	Frazer	59225
Big Sky	59716	Corvallis	59828	Frenchtown	59834
Big Timber	59011	Corwin Springs	59021	Froid	59226
Billings	59101-07	Crackerville (Part of		Fromberg	59029
For specific Billings Zip Codes call		Anaconda)	59711	Galata	59444
(406) 657-5709		Craig	59648	Galen (Part of Anaconda)	59722
Billings Heights	59105	Crane	59217	Gallatin Gateway	59730
Birch Creek Colony	59486	Creston	59902	Gardiner	59030
Birney	59012	Crow Agency	59022	Garland	59301
Black Eagle	59414	Crow Indian Reservation	59022	Garneill	59445
Blackfeet Indian Reservation	59417	Crow Rock	59301	Garrison	59731
Blackfoot	59417	Culbertson	59218	Garryowen	59031
Bloomfield	59315	Cushman	59046	Georgetown (Part of	
Blossburg	59728	Custer	59024	Anaconda)	59711
Bonner	59823	Cut Bank	59427	Geraldine	59446
Bonner-West Riverside	59801	Dagmar	59219	Geyser	59447
Boulder	59632	Danvers	59457	Gibson Flats	59401
Box Elder	59521	Darby	59829	Gildford	59525
Boyd	59013	Dawson (Part of Butte)	59748	Gilt Edge	59457
Boyes	59316	Dayton	59914	Glacier Colony	59427
Bozeman	59715	Dearborn	59648	Glasgow	59230
	59771-72	De Borgia	59830	Glasgow Air Base	59231
For specific Bozeman Zip Codes		Decker	59025	Glen	59732
call (406) 586-1508		Deerfield Colony	59457	Glendive	59330
Brady	59416	Deer Lodge	59722	Glentana	59240
Brandenberg	59301	Del Bonita	59427	Goldcreek	59733
Brandon	59749	Dell	59724	Golden Ridge	59436
Bridger (Carbon County)	59014	Delphia	59073	Goldstone	59540
Bridger (Gallatin County)	59722	Dempsey	59722	Grace (Part of Butte)	59759
Broadus	59317	Denton	59430	Grant	59725
Broadview	59015	Dentons Point (Part of		Grantsdale	59835
Brock Creek	59731	Anaconda)	59711	Grass Range	59032
Brockton	59213	Devon	59474	Great Falls	59401-06
Brockway	59214	Dewey	59727	For specific Great Falls Zip Codes	
Brooks	59457	Dillon	59725	call (406) 761-4894	
Brown (Part of Anaconda)	59711	Divide (Part of Butte)	59727	Greenfield	59436
Brown Addition	59472	Dixon	59831	Greenough	59836
Browning	59417	Dodson	59524	Gregson (Part of Butte)	59748
Brusett	59318	Donald (Part of Butte)	59759	Greycliff	59033
Buffalo	59418	Dover	59479	Hackney (Part of Butte)	59748
Busby	59016	Dovetail	59087	Half Moon	59912
Butte	59701-03	Downtown (Part of Billings)	59101	Hall	59837
For specific Butte Zip Codes call		Drummond	59832	Hamilton	59840
(406) 494-2107		Dublin Gulch (Part of Butte)	59701	Hammond	59332
Buxton (Part of Butte)	59750	Dunkirk	59474	Hammond Valley	59327
Bynum	59419	Dupuyer	59432	Happys Inn	59923
Camas	59845	Durant (Part of Butte)	59748	Happy Valley	59937
Camas Prairie	59859	Dutton	59433	Hardin	59034
Cameron	59720	Eagleton	59520	Hardy	59421
Canyon Creek	59633	East Butte (Part of Butte)	59701	Harlem	59526

MONTANA

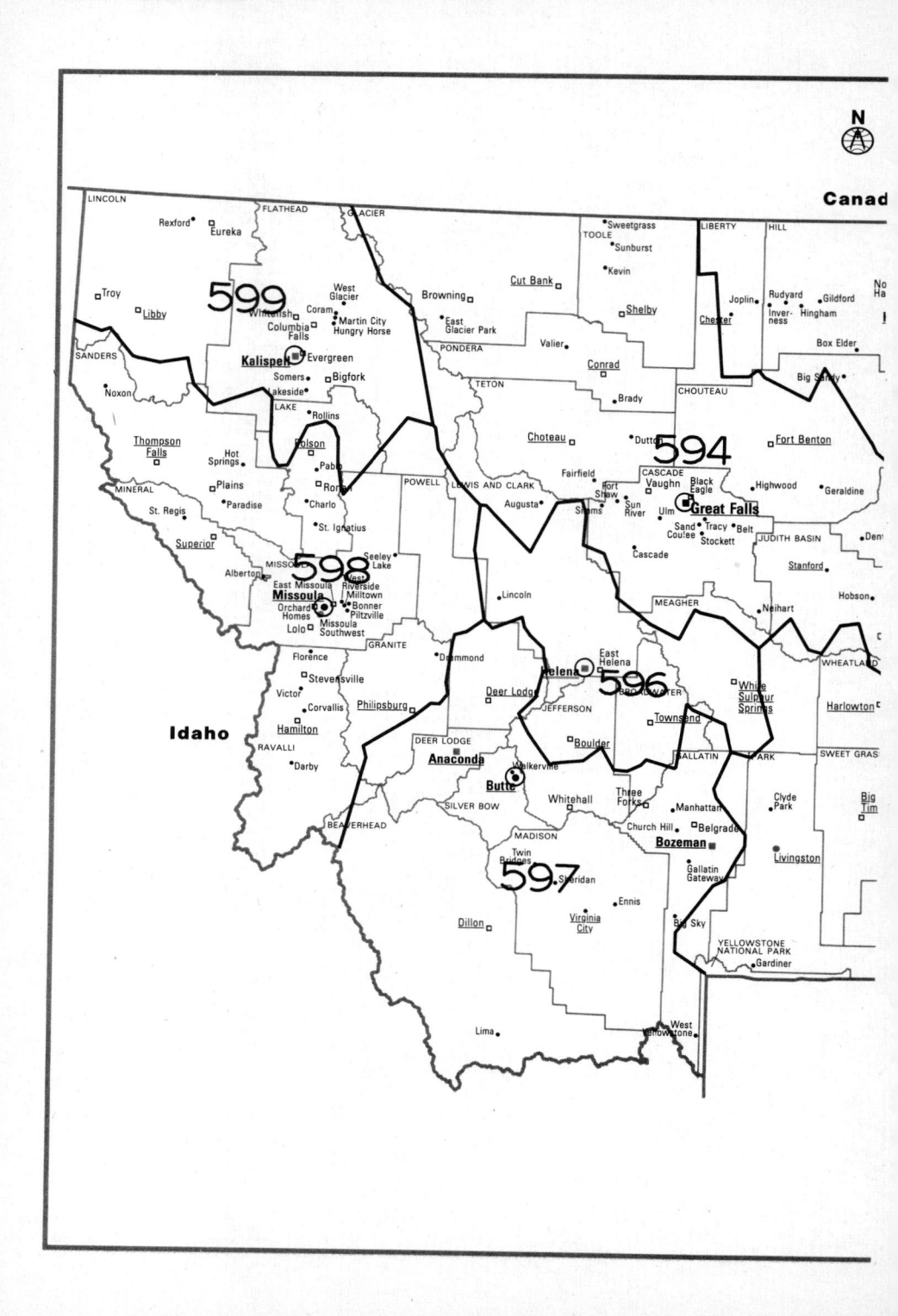

MONTANA 321

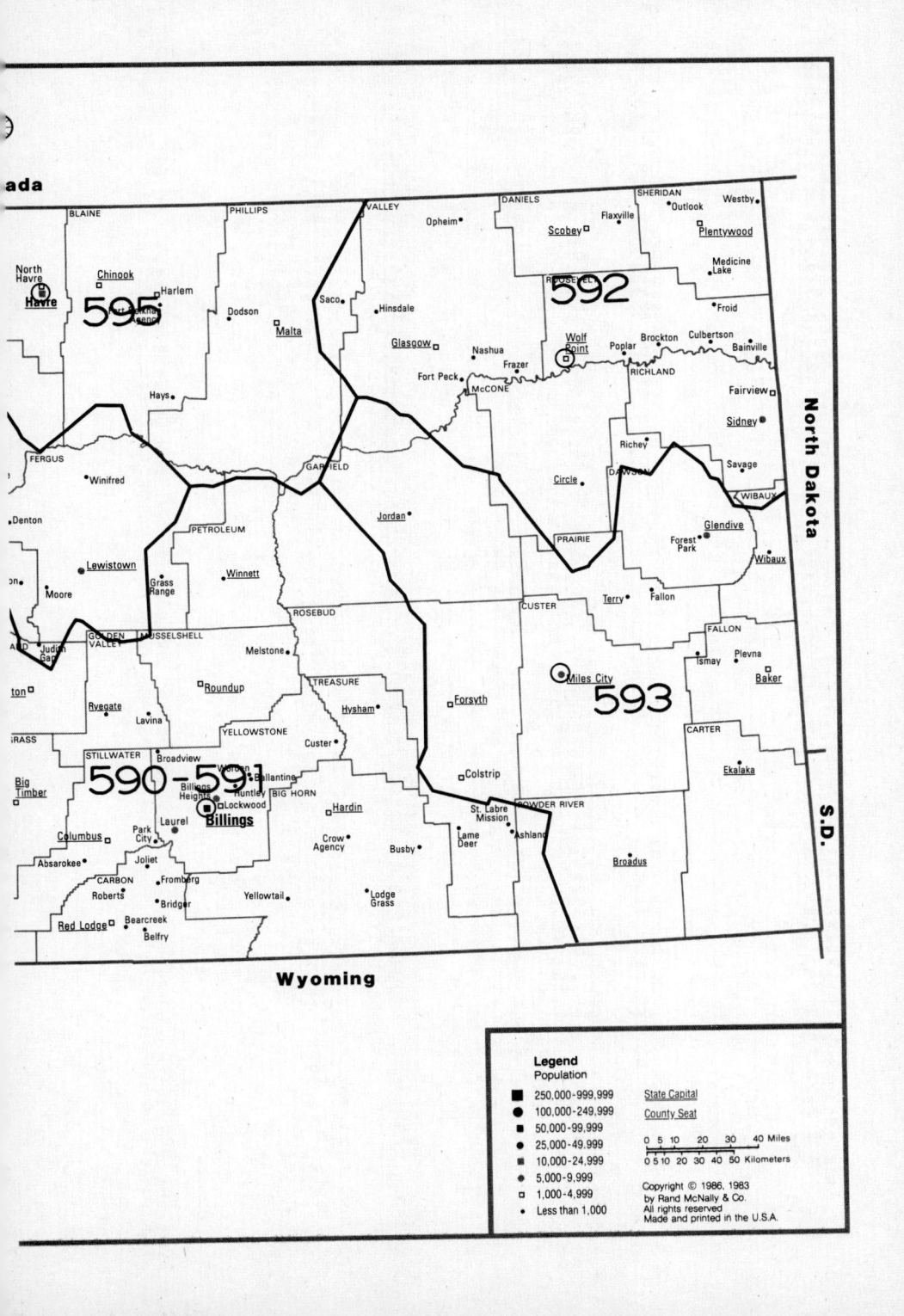

322 MONTANA Harlowton-Sand Coulee

Location	ZIP
Harlowton	59036
Harrison	59735
Hathaway	59333
Haugan	59842
Havre	59501
Havre Air Force Station 778th Aircraft Control	59501
Havre North	59501
Hays	59527
Heart Butte	59448
Heath	59457
Hedgesville	59078
Helena	59601-26
For specific Helena Zip Codes call (406) 443-3304	
Hellgate (Part of Missoula)	59802
Helmville	59843
Heron	59844
Herron Park	59501
Hesper	59106
Highwood	59450
Hilger	59451
Hingham	59528
Hinsdale	59241
Hobson	59452
Hodges	59353
Hogeland	59529
Holiday Village (Part of Great Falls)	59405
Holter Dam	59648
Homestead	59242
Hopp	59520
Hot Springs	59845
Howard	59327
Hughesville	59463
Hungry Horse	59919
Huntley	59037
Huson	59846
Hysham	59038
Iliad	59520
Ingomar	59039
Inverness	59530
Ismay	59336
Jackson	59736
Janney (Part of Butte)	59701
Jardine	59030
Jeffers	59729
Jefferson City	59638
Jefferson Island	59721
Jellison Place	59085
Joliet	59041
Joplin	59531
Jordan	59337
Judith Gap	59453
Kalispell	59901
Kenilworth	59520
Kevin	59454
Kila	59920
Kingsbury Colony	59486
Kinsey	59338
Kirby	59016
Klein	59072
Kolin	59451
Kremlin	59532
Lake McDonald	59921
Lakeside	59922
Lakeview	59739
Lambert	59243
Lame Deer	59043
Landusky	59524
Larslan	59244
LaSalle	59912
Last Chance (Part of Helena)	59601
Laurel	59044
Laurin	59749
Lavina	59046
Lavon	59732
Lebo	59053
Ledger	59456
Lennep	59053
Lewistown	59457
Libby	59923
Lima	59739
Limestone	59061
Lincoln	59639
Lindsay	59339
Livingston	59047
Lloyd	59535
Lockwood	59101
Lodge Grass	59050
Lodge Pole	59524
Logan	59741
Lohman	59523
Lolo	59847
Lolo Hot Springs	59847
Loma	59460
Lonepine	59848
Loring	59537
Lost Creek (Part of Anaconda)	59711

Location	ZIP
Lothair	59461
Lower Sun River (Part of Great Falls)	59401
Lustre	59225
Luther	59051
McAllister	59740
McCabe	59245
McClellans Creek	59635
McGlone Heights (Part of Butte)	59701
McLeod	59052
McQueen (Part of Butte)	59701
Madoc	59222
Maiden	59457
Maiden Rock (Part of Butte)	59743
Malmström AFB	59402
Malmstrom Air Force Base	59402
Malta	59538
Manhattan	59741
Many Glacier Hotel	59411
Marion	59925
Marsh	59326
Martin City	59926
Martinsdale	59053
Marysville	59640
Maudlow	59714
Maxville	59858
Medicine Lake	59247
Medicine Springs	59827
Melrose (Part of Butte)	59743
Melstone	59054
Melville	59055
Mildred	59341
Miles City	59301
Milford Colony	59648
Mill Creek (Part of Anaconda)	59711
Miller Colony	59422
Mill Iron	59342
Milltown	59851
Miner	59027
Missoula	59801-07
For specific Missoula Zip Codes call (406) 329-2200	
Missoula South	59801
Missoula Southwest	59801
Mizpah	59301
Moccasin	59462
Moffit Canyon	59715
Moiese	59824
Molt	59057
Mona	59213
Monarch	59463
Monida	59739
Montague	59442
Montana City	59634
Montanapolis Springs	59065
Moore	59464
Morel (Part of Anaconda)	59711
Morgan	59537
Mosby	59058
Moulton	59451
Mount Ellis	59715
Musselshell	59059
Myers	59038
Nashua	59248
Navajo	59222
Neihart	59465
Nevada City	59755
New Chicago	59832
Newcomb (Part of Butte)	59701
New Miami Colony	59425
New Rockport Colony	59422
Niarada	59852
Nibbe	59088
Nickwall	59201
Nine Mile	59846
Nissler (Part of Butte)	59701
Nohle	59221
Norris	59745
Northern Cheyenne Indian Reservation	59043
Northridge Heights (Part of Kalispell)	59901
Noxon (Sanders County)	59853
Nye	59061
Oilmont	59466
Olive	59343
Ollie	59313
Olney	59927
Opheim	59250
Opportunity (Part of Anaconda)	59711
Orchard Homes (Missoula County)	59801
Ossette	59244
Oswego	59201
Otter	59062
Outlook	59252
Ovando	59854
Pablo	59855

Location	ZIP
Paradise	59856
Park City	59063
Park Grove	59248
Peerless	59253
Pendroy	59467
Perma	59859
Petrolia	59087
Philipsburg	59858
Piegan	59411
Piltzville	59801
Pine Creek	59047
Pinegrove	59801
Pinesdale	59841
Pinnacle	59916
Pioneer (Silver Bow County)	59701
Pioneer (Yellowstone County)	59102
Pioneer Junction	59923
Plains	59859
Pleasant Prairie	59222
Pleasant Valley	59925
Pleasant View	59330
Plentywood	59254
Plevna	59344
Plum Creek	59457
Polaris	59746
Polebridge	59928
Polson	59860
Pompeys Pillar	59064
Pony	59747
Poplar	59255
Portage	59440
Post Creek	59865
Potomac	59823
Powderville	59345
Power	59468
Pray	59065
Proctor	59929
Pryor	59066
Quinn (Part of Butte)	59743
Racetrack	59722
Radersburg	59641
Ramsay (Part of Butte)	59748
Rapelje	59067
Rattlesnake	59801
Ravalli	59863
Ravenna	59825
Raymond	59256
Raynesford	59469
Red Bluff	59745
Red Lodge	59068
Redstone	59257
Reedpoint	59069
Regina	59538
Reserve	59258
Rexford	59930
Richey	59259
Richland	59260
Ridgelawn	59270
Ridgway	59332
Rimini	59601
Rimrock Mall (Part of Billings)	59102
Ringling	59642
Rising Sun	59434
Riverside	59840
Rivulet	59820
Roberts	59070
Rocker (Part of Butte)	59701
Rockport Colony	59467
Rock Springs (Rosebud County)	59312
Rock Springs (Sheridan County)	59258
Rockvale	59800
Rocky Boy	59521
Rocky Boys Indian Reservation	59521
Rollins	59931
Ronan	59864
Roosville	59917
Roscoe	59071
Rosebud	59347
Rossfork	59457
Roundup	59072
Roy	59471
Ruby	59710
Rudyard	59540
Ryegate	59074
Saco	59261
Sage Creek	59522
St. Ignatius	59865
St. Labre Mission	59004
St. Marie	59230
St. Mary	59417
St. Peter	59421
St. Regis	59866
St. Xavier	59075
Salmon Prairie	59911
Saltese	59867
Sand Coulee	59472

MONTANA 323
Sand Creek-Zurich

Name	ZIP	Name	ZIP	Name	ZIP
Sand Creek	59201	Sula	59871	Warmsprings (Part of Anaconda)	59756
Sanders	59076	Sumatra	59083	Warren	82423
Sand Springs	59077	Summit	59434	Warrick	59520
Santa Rita	59473	Summit Valley	59721	Washoe	59007
Sapphire Village	59452	Sunburst	59482	Waterloo	59759
Savage	59262	Sunnyside (Part of Anaconda)	59711	Wayne	59412
Savoy	59526	Sun Prairie	59538	Webster	59313
Scobey	59263	Sun River	59483	Weldon	59215
Seaver Park	59601	Sunset	59836	Westby	59275
Sedan	59086	Superior	59872	West Glacier	59936
Seeley Lake	59868	Swan Lake	59911	West Lewistown	59457
Shawmut	59078	Sweetgrass	59484	West Park Plaza (Part of Billings)	59102
Shelby	59474	Swiftcurrent	59411	West Riverside	59801
Shepherd	59079	Tampico	59230	West Valley (Part of Anaconda)	59711
Sheridan	59749	Tarkio	59872	West Yellowstone	59758
Shonkin	59476	Teigen	59084	Whately	59248
Sidney	59270	Terry	59349	Wheeler	59230
Silesia	59080	The Pines	59859	Whitefish	59937
Silver Bow (Part of Butte)	59750	Thompson Falls	59873	Whitehall	59759
Silver Bow Park (Part of Butte)	59701	Three Forks	59752	White Haven	59923
Silver Gate	59081	Toston	59643	Whitepine	59874
Silver Star	59751	Townsend	59644	White Sulphur Springs	59645
Simms	59477	Tracy	59472	Whitetail	59276
Simpson	59501	Trego	59934	Whitewater	59544
Sipple	59464	Trident	59752	Whitlash	59545
Sleeping Buffalo	59261	Trout Creek	59874	Wibaux	59353
Smelter Hill	59414	Troy	59935	Wickes	59638
Somers	59932	Truly	59485	Willard	59354
Sonnette	59348	Turah	59825	Williamsburg (Part of Butte)	59701
Southern Cross (Part of Anaconda)	59711	Turner	59542	Willow Creek	59760
Southgate Mall (Part of Missoula)	59801	Turner Colony	59542	Wilsall	59086
Spring Creek Colony	59457	Twin Bridges	59754	Windham	59479
Springdale	59082	Twin Creeks	59823	Winifred	59489
Springdale Colony	59645	Twodot	59085	Winnett	59087
Square Butte	59442	Ulm	59485	Winston	59647
Stanford	59479	Unionville	59601	Wisdom	59761
Stark	59846	Utica	59452	Wise River	59762
Starr School	59417	Valier	59486	Wolf Creek	59648
State Capitol (Part of Helena)	59601	Vandalia	59273	Wolf Point	59201
Staton (Part of Anaconda)	59711	Varney	59729	Woods Bay	59911
Stemple	59633	Vaughn	59487	Woodside	59875
Stevensville	59870	Victor	59875	Woodworth	59836
Stockett	59480	Vida	59274	Worden	59088
Stone	59837	Virgelle	59520	Wyola	59089
Straw	59418	Virginia City	59755	Yaak Valley	59935
Stryker	59933	Volborg	59351	Yellowtail	59035
Stuart (Part of Anaconda)	59711	Volt	59201	York	59601
Suffolk	59451	Wagner	59538	Zortman	59546
		Walkerville	59701	Zurich	59547
		Wan-i-gan	59065		
		Ware	59457		

NEBRASKA

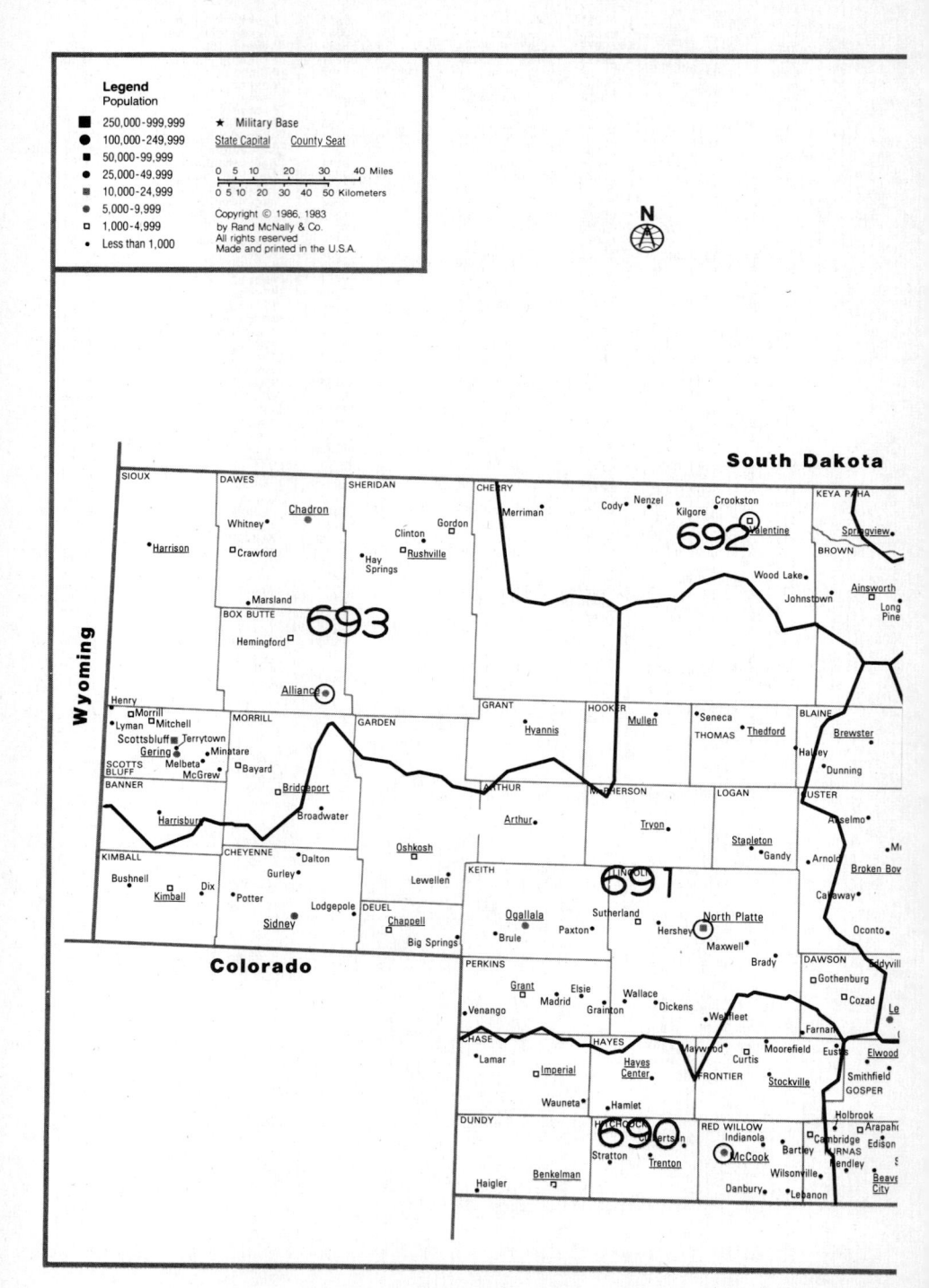

Legend
Population
- ■ 250,000-999,999
- ● 100,000-249,999
- ● 50,000-99,999
- ● 25,000-49,999
- ■ 10,000-24,999
- ● 5,000-9,999
- □ 1,000-4,999
- • Less than 1,000

★ Military Base
State Capital   County Seat

0 5 10   20   30   40 Miles
0 5 10 20   30   40 50 Kilometers

Copyright © 1986, 1983
by Rand McNally & Co.
All rights reserved
Made and printed in the U.S.A.

N

South Dakota

SIOUX — DAWES — SHERIDAN — CHERRY — KEYA PAHA
- Harrison
- Whitney
- Chadron
- Crawford
- Hay Springs
- Clinton
- Rushville
- Gordon
- Merriman
- Cody
- Nenzel
- Kilgore
- Crookston
- Valentine **692**
- Springview
- BROWN
- Wood Lake
- Johnstown
- Ainsworth
- Long Pine
- Marsland
- BOX BUTTE
- Hemingford
- **693**
- Alliance
- GRANT — HOOKER — BLAINE
- Hyannis
- Mullen
- Seneca
- THOMAS — Thedford
- Brewster
- Halsey
- Dunning

Wyoming

- Henry
- Morrill
- Lyman
- Mitchell
- Scottsbluff
- Terrytown
- Gering
- Minatare
- Melbeta
- Bayard
- McGrew
- SCOTTS BLUFF
- BANNER
- MORRILL
- GARDEN
- ARTHUR
- McPHERSON
- LOGAN
- CUSTER
- Anselmo
- Bridgeport
- Broadwater
- Arthur
- Tryon
- Stapleton
- Gandy
- Arnold
- Broken Bow
- Harrisburg
- KIMBALL — CHEYENNE
- Bushnell
- Kimball
- Dix
- Dalton
- Gurley
- Potter
- Lodgepole
- DEUEL
- Sidney
- Chappell
- Big Springs
- Oshkosh
- Lewellen
- KEITH
- LINCOLN
- **691**
- Ogallala
- Sutherland
- Paxton
- Brule
- Hershey
- North Platte
- Maxwell
- Brady
- Callaway
- DAWSON
- Oconto
- Gothenburg
- Cozad

Colorado

- PERKINS
- Grant
- Elsie
- Wallace
- Venango
- Madrid
- Grainton
- Dickens
- Wellfleet
- Farnam
- CHASE — HAYES
- Lamar
- Imperial
- Hayes Center
- Wauneta
- Hamlet
- Maywood
- Curtis
- Moorefield
- Eustis
- FRONTIER
- Stockville
- Elwood
- Smithfield
- GOSPER
- Holbrook
- DUNDY — HITCHCOCK — RED WILLOW
- Haigler
- Benkelman
- Stratton
- Trenton
- **690**
- McCook
- Indianola
- Bartley
- FURNAS
- Cambridge
- Arapahoe
- Edison
- Wilsonville
- Hendley
- Danbury
- Lebanon
- Beaver City

NEBRASKA 325

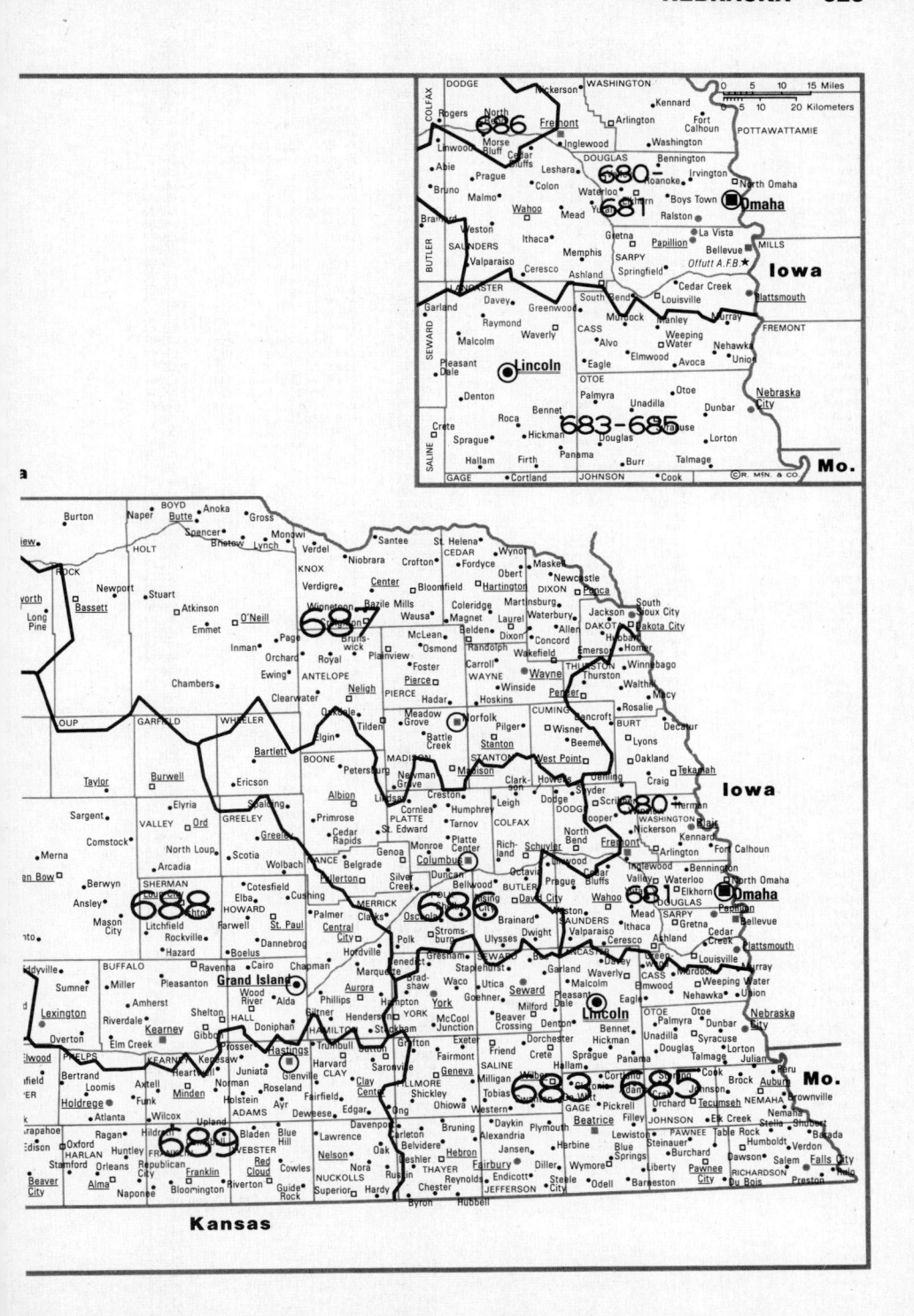

326 NEBRASKA Abie-Gross

Place	ZIP
Abie	68001
Adams	68301
Agnew	68428
Ainsworth	69210
Air Mail Facility (Part of Omaha)	68119
Air Park West	68524
Akron	68620
Albion	68620
Alda	68810
Alexandria	68303
Allen	68710
Alliance	69301
Alma (Harlan County)	68920
Almeria	68879
Aloys	68788
Altona	68787
Alvo	68304
Amelia	68711
Ames	68621
Ames Avenue (Part of Omaha)	68111
Amherst	68812
Angora	69331
Angus	68961
Anoka	68722
Anselmo	68813
Ansley	68814
Antioch	69340
Arapahoe	68922
Arcadia	68815
Archer	68816
Arlington	68002
Arnold	69120
Arthur	69121
Ashby	69333
Ashland	68003
Ashton	68817
Assumption	68955
Aten	68730
Atkinson	68713
Atlanta	68923
Auburn	68305
Aurora	68818
Autumn Hills (Part of Omaha)	68134
Avoca	68307
Axtell	68924
Ayr	68925
Bancroft	68004
Barada	68355
Barneston	68309
Bartlett	68622
Bartley	69020
Bassett	68714
Battle Creek	68715
Bayard	69334
Bazile Mills	68729
Beatrice	68310
Beaver City	68926
Beaver Crossing	68313
Bee	68314
Beemer	68716
Belden	68717
Belgrade	68623
Bellevue	68005
Bellwood	68624
Belvidere	68315
Benedict	68316
Benkelman	69021
Bennet	68317
Bennington	68007
Benson (Part of Omaha)	68104
Berea	69301
Bertrand	68927
Berwyn	68819
Bignell	69151
Big Springs	69122
Bingham	69335
Bixby	68979
Bladen	68928
Blair (Washington County)	68008
Bloomfield	68718
Bloomington	68929
Blue Hill	68930
Blue River Lodge	68333
Blue Springs	68318
Boelus	68820
Boone	68625
Bostwick	68978
Bow Valley	68739
Boys Town	68010
Bradshaw	68319
Brady	69123
Brainard	68626
Brandon	69140
Breslau	68765
Brewster	68821
Bridgeport	69336
Briggs	68122
Bristol	68719

Place	ZIP
Broadwater	69125
Brock	68320
Broken Bow (Custer County)	68822
Brownlee	69166
Brownson	69162
Brownville	68321
Brule	69127
Bruning	68322
Bruno	68014
Brunswick	68720
Burchard	68323
Burkett (Part of Grand Island)	68801
Burr	68324
Burress	68354
Burton	68778
Burwell	68823
Bushnell	69128
Butte	68722
Byron	68325
Cadams	68978
Cairo	68824
Callaway	68825
Cambridge	69022
Campbell	68932
Carleton	68326
Carroll	68723
Cedar Bluffs	68015
Cedar Creek	68016
Cedar Rapids	68627
Center (Knox County)	68724
Central City	68826
Ceresco	68017
Chadron	69337
Chalco	68046
Chambers	68725
Champion	69023
Chapman	68827
Chappell	69129
Cheneys	68506
Chester (Thayer County)	68327
Clarks	68628
Clarkson	68629
Clatonia	68328
Clay Center	68933
Clearwater	68726
Clinton	69343
Cody	69211
Coleridge	68727
College View (Part of Lincoln)	68506
Colon	68018
Colton	69162
Columbus (Platte County)	68601
Comstock	68828
Concord	68728
Conestoga Mall (Part of Grand Island)	68801
Constance	68730
Cook	68329
Cordova	68330
Cornlea	68642
Cortland	68331
Cotesfield	68829
Cowles	68930
Cozad	69130
Crab Orchard	68332
Craig	68019
Crawford (Dawes County)	69339
Creighton (Knox County)	68729
Creston	68631
Crete	68333
Crofton	68730
Crookston	69212
Crossroads Mall (Part of Omaha)	68114
Crowell	68057
Crown Point (Part of Omaha)	68122
Culbertson	69024
Curtis	69025
Cushing	68873
Dakota City	68731
Dalton	69131
Dana College	68008
Danbury	69026
Dannebrog	68831
Darr	69130
Davenport	68335
Davey	68336
David City	68632
Dawson	68337
Daykin	68338
DeBolt (Part of Omaha)	68152
Decatur	68020
Denman	68956
Denton	68339
Deshler	68340
De Soto	68023
Deweese	68934

Place	ZIP
De Witt	68341
Dickens	69132
Diller	68342
Dix	69133
Dixon	68732
Dodge	68633
Doniphan	68832
Dorchester	68343
Douglas (Otoe County)	68344
Downtown (Part of Omaha)	68102
Du Bois	68345
Dunbar	68346
Duncan	68634
Dunning	68833
Dwight	68635
Eagle	68347
Eddyville	68834
Edgar	68935
Edison	68936
Elba	68835
Elgin	68636
Eli	69201
Elk City	68064
Elk Creek (Johnson County)	68348
Elkhorn (Douglas County)	68022
Ellis	68310
Ellsworth (Sheridan County)	69340
Elm Creek	68836
Elmwood	68349
Elmwood Park (Part of Omaha)	68106
Elsie	69134
Elsmere	69135
Elwood	68937
Elyria	68837
Emerald	68502
Emerson	68733
Emmet	68734
Enders	69027
Endicott	68350
Enola	68701
Ericson	68637
Ericson Lake	68637
Eustis	69028
Ewing	68735
Exeter	68351
Fairbury	68352
Fairfield	68938
Fairmont	68354
Falls City	68355
Farnam	69029
Farwell	68838
Filley	68357
Firth	68358
Florence (Part of Omaha)	68112
Fontanelle	68044
Fordyce	68736
Fort Calhoun	68023
Fort Robinson	69339
Foster	68737
Franklin (Franklin County)	68939
Fremont	68025
Friend	68359
Fullerton (Nance County)	68638
Funk	68940
Gandy	69163
Garland	68360
Garrison	68632
Gates	68822
Gateway Shopping Center (Part of Lincoln)	68505
Geneva	68361
Genoa	68640
Gering	69341
Gibbon	68840
Gilead	68362
Giltner	68841
Gladstone	68352
Glen	69339
Glenover (Part of Beatrice)	68310
Glenvil	68941
Glenwood Park	68847
Goehner	68364
Good Samaritan Village (Part of Hastings)	68901
Gordon	69343
Gothenburg	69138
Grafton	68365
Grainton	69169
Grand Island	68801-03
For specific Grand Island Zip Codes call (308) 381-5551	
Grand Island Mall (Part of Grand Island)	68801
Grant (Perkins County)	69140
Greeley	68842
Green Meadows	68164
Greenwood	68366
Gresham	68367
Gretna	68028
Gross	68719

Grover-Roanoke **NEBRASKA** 327

	ZIP		ZIP		ZIP
Grover	68405	Lemoyne	69146	North Oaks	68122
Guide Rock	68942	Leshara	68035	North Omaha (Part of	
Gurley	69141	Lewellen	69147	Omaha)	68112
Hadar	68738	Lewiston	68380	North Platte	69101-03
Haig	69357	Lexington	68850	For specific North Platte Zip	
Haigler	69030	Liberty (Gage County)	68381	Codes call (308) 532-3144	
Hallam	68368	Lincoln	68501-72	Northport	69336
Halsey	69142	For specific Lincoln Zip Codes call		North Shore	
Hamlet	69031	(402) 473-1695		Northwest (Part of Omaha)	68134
Hampton	68843	Lindsay	68644	Oak	68964
Hansen	68901	Lindy	68718	Oakdale	68761
Harbine	68377	Linwood	68036	Oakland (Burt County)	68045
Hardy	68943	Lisco	69148	Obert	68762
Harrisburg	69345	Litchfield	68852	Oconto	68860
Harrison (Sioux County)	69346	Lodgepole	69149	Octavia	68650
Hartington	68739	Loma	68626	Odell	68415
Harvard	68944	Long Pine	69217	Odessa	68861
Hastings	68901-02	Loomis	68958	Offutt AFB West	68113
For specific Hastings Zip Codes		Lorenzo	69162	Offutt Air Force Base	68113
call (402) 463-3107		Loretto	68620	Ogallala	69153
Havelock (Part of Lincoln)	68529	Lorton	68382	Ohiowa	68416
Havens	68628	Louisville	68037	Old Mill (Part of Omaha)	68134
Hayes Center	69032	Loup City	68853	Olean	68633
Hay Springs	69347	Lowell	68840	Omaha	68101-72
Hazard	68844	Lushton	68371	For specific Omaha Zip Codes call	
Heartwell	68945	Lyman	69352	(402) 348-2861	
Hebron	68370	Lynch	68746	Omaha Indian Reservation	68039
Hemingford	69348	Lyons	68038	O'Neill	68763
Henderson	68371	McCook	69001	Ong	68452
Hendley	68946	McCool Junction	68401	Orchard	68764
Henry	69349	McGrew	69353	Ord (Valley County)	68862
Herman	68029	McLean	68747	Orleans	68966
Hershey	69143	Macon	68939	Orum	68008
Hickman	68372	Macy	68039	Osceola	68651
Hideaway Acres	68730	Madison (Madison County)	68748	Oshkosh	69154
Hildreth	68947	Madrid	69150	Osmond	68765
Hillerage	69361	Magnet	68749	Otoe	68417
Holbrook	68948	Malcolm	68402	Overton	68863
Holdrege	68949	Malmo	68040	Oxford	68967
Holland	68372	Manley	68403	Page	68766
Hollinger	68967	Maple Hills (Part of Omaha)	68134	Palisade	69040
Holmesville	68374	Marion (Red Willow County)	69026	Palmer	68864
Holstein	68950	Marquette	68854	Palmyra	68418
Homer	68030	Marsland	69354	Panama	68419
Hooper	68031	Martell	68404	Papillion	68046
Hordville	68846	Martinsburg	68770	Papillion-La Vista (Part of	
Hoskins	68740	Mascot	68967	Papillion)	68128
Howe	68305	Maskell	68751	Parks	69041
Howells	68641	Mason City	68855	Parkview (Part of Grand	
Hubbard	68741	Max	69037	Island)	68801
Hubbell	68375	Maxwell	69151	Paul	68410
Humboldt	68376	Maywood	69038	Pauline	68941
Humphrey	68642	Mead (Saunders County)	68041	Pawnee City	68420
Huntley	68951	Meadow Grove	68752	Paxton	69155
Hyannis	69350	Melbeta	69355	Pender	68047
Imperial	69033	Memphis	68042	Peru	68421
Imperial Mall (Part of		Menominee	68736	Petersburg	68652
Hastings)	68901	Merna	68856	Phillips	68865
Inavale	68952	Merriman	69218	Pickrell	68422
Indianola	69034	Milford	68405	Pierce	68767
Inglewood	68025	Millard (Part of Omaha)	68137	Pilger	68768
Inland	68954	Miller (Buffalo County)	68858	Plainview	68769
Inman	68742	Milligan	68406	Platte Center	68653
Irvington	68134	Mills	68753	Plattsmouth	68048
Ithaca	68033	Milton	68858	Pleasant Dale	68423
Jacinto	69133	Minatare	69356	Pleasant Hill	68343
Jackson (Dakota County)	68743	Minden	68959	Pleasanton	68866
Jamison	68759	Mitchell	69357	Plymouth	68424
Jansen	68377	Monowi	68746	Polk	68654
Johnson	68378	Monroe	68647	Ponca (Dixon County)	68770
Johnson Lake	68937	Monterey	68788	Ponce Indian Reservation	68071
Johnstown	69214	Moorefield	69039	Potter	69156
Julian	68379	Morrill	69358	Powell	68352
Juniata	68955	Morse Bluff	68648	Prague	68050
Kearney	68847-48	Mount Michael	68022	Prairie Home	68527
For specific Kearney Zip Codes		Mullen (Hooker County)	69152	Precept	68977
call (308) 234-2051		Murdock	68407	Preston	68355
Keene	68924	Murphy	68855	Primrose	68655
Kenesaw	68956	Murray	68409	Princeton	68404
Kennard	68034	Mynard	68048	Prosser	68868
Keystone	69144	Naper	68755	Purdum	69157
Kilgore	69216	Naponee	68960	Raeville	68652
Kimball	69145	Nashville	68112	Ragan	68969
King Lake	68064	Nebraska City	68410	Ralston	68127
Kingsley	69153	Nehawka	68413	Randolph	68771
Knievels Corner	68735	Neligh (Antelope County)	68756	Ravenna	68869
Kohles Acres	68730	Nelson	68961	Raymond (Lancaster	
Kramer	68333	Nemaha (Nemaha County)	68414	County)	68428
Kronborg	68854	Nenzel	69219	Red Cloud	68970
Kuesters Lake	68801	Newcastle	68757	Redington	69336
Lake Forest Estates	68134	Newman Grove	68758	Regency (Part of Omaha)	68114
Lakeside	69351	Newport	68759	Republican City	68971
Lamar	69035	Nickerson	68044	Reynolds	68429
Lanham	68415	Niobrara	68760	Richfield	68054
La Platte	68123	Nora	68961	Richland (Colfax County)	68601
Laurel	68745	Norfolk	68701	Ringgold	69167
La Vista	68128	Norman	68963	Rising City	68658
Lawrence	68957	North Auburn (Part of		Riverdale	68870
Lebanon	69036	Auburn)	68305	Riverside Lakes	68069
Lee Valley (Part of Omaha)	68134	North Bend	68649	Riverton	68972
Leigh	68643	North Loup	68859	Roanoke (Part of Omaha)	68134

328 NEBRASKA Roca-Yutan

	ZIP		ZIP		ZIP
Roca	68430	Sprague	68438	Verdel	68782
Rockford	68310	Springfield	68059	Verdigre	68783
Rockville	68871	Springview	68778	Verdon	68457
Rogers	68659	Stamford	68977	Vesta	68450
Rosalie	68055	Stanton (Stanton County)	68779	Veterans' Administration	
Roscoe	69153	Staplehurst	68439	Hospital (Part of Omaha)	68105
Rose	68772	Stapleton	69163	Virginia	68458
Roseland	68973	State House (Part of		Wabash	68407
Rosemont	68930	Lincoln)	68509	Waco	68460
Rosenburg	68644	Steele City	68440	Wagners Lake	68601
Royal	68773	Steinauer	68441	Wahoo (Saunders County)	68066
Rulo	68431	Stella	68442	Wakefield	68784
Rushville	69360	Sterling	68443	Walkers Valley View	68730
Ruskin	68974	Still Meadow (Part of		Wallace	69169
Saddle Creek (Part of		Omaha)	68122	Walthill	68067
Omaha)	68132	Stockham	68818	Walton	68461
St. Bernard	68644	Stockville	69042	Wann	68003
St. Columbans	68056	Stock Yards (Part of		Washington (Washington	
St. Edward	68660	Omaha)	68107	County)	68068
St. Helena	68774	Strang	68444	Waterbury	68785
St. James	68792	Stratton	69043	Waterloo	68069
St. Libory	68872	Stromsburg	68666	Wauneta	69045
St. Mary	68432	Stuart	68780	Wausa	68786
St. Paul	68873	Sumner	68878	Waverly	68462
St. Stephens	68957	Sunnyslope (Part of Omaha)	68134	Wayne (Wayne County)	68787
Salem (Richardson County)	68433	Sunol	69149	Wayside	69337
Santee	68760	Superior	68978	Weeping Water	68463
Santee Indian Reservation	68760	Surprise	68667	Weissert	68880
Sarben	69155	Sutherland	69165	Wellfleet	69170
Sargent	68874	Sutton (Clay County)	68879	Western (Saline County)	68464
Saronville	68975	Swanton	68445	Westerville	68881
Schaupps	68817	Swedeburg	68666	West Omaha (Part of	
Schuyler	68661	Syracuse	68446	Omaha)	68114
Scotia	68875	Table Rock	68447	Weston	68070
Scottsbluff	69361-63	Talmage	68448	West Point	68788
For specific Scottsbluff Zip Codes		Tamora	68434	Westroads Shopping Center	
call (308) 635-1121		Tarnov	68642	(Part of Omaha)	68114
Scribner	68057	Taylor	68879	Westwood Plaza (Part of	
Seneca	69161	Tecumseh	68450	Omaha)	68144
Seward	68434	Tekamah	68061	Whiteclay	69365
Seymour Park (Part of		Telbasta	68002	Whitman	69366
Ralston)	68127	Terrytown	69341	Whitney	69367
Shelby	68662	Thayer (York County)	68460	Wilber	68465
Shelton	68876	Thedford	69166	Wilcox	68982
Shickley	68436	Thompson	68352	Willis	68743
Sholes	68771	Thurston	68062	Willow Island	69171
Shubert	68437	Tilden	68781	Wilsonville	69046
Sidney	69162	Tobias	68453	Winnebago	68071
Silver Creek (Merrick		Touhy	68065	Winnebago Indian	
County)	68663	Trenton	69044	Reservation	68071
Smithfield	68976	Trumbull	68980	Winnetoon	68789
Snyder	68664	Tryon	69167	Winside	68790
South Bend	68058	Uehling	68063	Winslow	68072
South Minden (Part of		Ulysses	68669	Wisner (Cuming County)	68791
Minden)	68959	Unadilla	68454	Wolbach	68882
South Omaha (Part of		Union (Cass County)	68455	Wood Lake	69221
Omaha)	68107	University Place (Part of		Woodland Park	68701
Southroads Shopping		Lincoln)	68504	Wood River (Hall County)	68883
Center (Part of Bellevue)	68005	Upland	68981	Worms	68872
South Sioux City	68776	Utica	68456	Wymore	68466
South Yankton	57078	Valentine	69201	Wynot	68792
Spalding	68665	Valley (Douglas County)	68064	York	68467
Sparks	69220	Valparaiso	68065	Yossem's Paradise Valley	
Sparta	68783	Venango	69168	(Part of Omaha)	68134
Spencer	68777	Venice	68069	Yutan	68073
Spencer Park (Part of					
Hastings)	68901				

Alamo-Spanish Springs Valley NEVADA 329

	ZIP		ZIP		ZIP
Alamo	89001	Galena (Part of Reno)	89502	Mountain View Estates (Part of Elko)	89801
Amargosa Valley	89020	Galena Forest Estates	89511	Mount Montgomery	93512
Arthur	89833	Gardnerville	89410	Mustang	89431
Ash Springs	89017	Gardnerville-Minden	89410	Naval Ammunition Depot	89415
Atlanta	89043	Gardnerville Ranchos	89410	Nellis AFB	89191
Austin	89310	Garside (Part of Las Vegas)	89102	Nellis Air Force Base	89191
Baker	89311	Genoa	89411	Nelson	89046
Basalt	93512	Gerlach	89412	New Empire (Part of Carson City)	89701
Battle Mountain	89820	Glenbrook	89413	New Washoe City	89701
Beatty	89003	Glendale (Clark County)	89025	Nixon	89424
Belmont	89022	Glendale (Washoe County)	89431	North Battle Mountain	89820
Beowawe	89821	Golconda	89414	North 7 Estates (Part of Elko)	89801
Black Springs	89506	Golden Valley	89501	North Fork	89801
Blue Diamond	89004	Goldfield	89013	North Las Vegas	89030
Bluffs (Part of Elko)	89801	Gold Hill	89440	Northridge (Part of Elko)	89801
Bonanza (Part of Las Vegas)	89106	Gold Point	89013	North Valley (Part of Reno)	89501
Boulder City	89005-06	Goodsprings	89019	Oasis	89835
For specific Boulder City Zip Codes call (702) 293-2618		Goshute Indian Reservation (NV part)	84034	Oreana	89419
Boulevard Mall	89109	Greenbrae (Part of Sparks)	89431	Orovada	89425
Buckeye	89410	Halleck	89824	Overton	89040
Bunkerville	89007	Hawthorne	89415-16	Owyhee	89832
Cactus Springs	89101	For specific Hawthorne Zip Codes call (702) 945-2850		Pahrump	89041
Caliente	89008	Hazen	89408	Palomino Valley	89433
Cal-Nev-Ari	89039	Henderson	89015-16	Panaca	89042
Carlin	89822	For specific Henderson Zip Codes call (702) 565-8388		Panther Valley (Part of Reno)	89501
Carlton Square (Part of North Las Vegas)	89030	Hidden Valley	89502	Paradise	89109
Carp	89008	Highland Estates	89705	Paradise Hill	89445
Carson City	89701-21	Hiko	89017	Paradise Valley (Clark County)	89119
For specific Carson City Zip Codes call (702) 887-7000		Horizon Hills	89501	Paradise Valley (Humboldt County)	89426
Carson Meadows (Part of Carson City)	89701	Huffakers (Part of Reno)	89501	Park Lane Center (Part of Reno)	89502
Carvers	89045	Humboldt	89418	Park Terrace (Part of Carson City)	89701
Caselton	89043	Huntridge (Part of Las Vegas)	89104	Patrick	89431
Centerville	89410	Imlay	89418	Pinenut	89410
Chambers Field	89410	Incline Village	89450	Pioche	89043
Chaparral Ridge (Part of Elko)	89801	Incline Village-Crystal Bay	89450	Pittman (Part of Henderson)	89044
Charleston	89801	Indian Hills	89705	Pleasant Valley	89511
Charleston Park	89108	Indian Springs	89018	Preston	89301
Charleston Plaza (Part of Las Vegas)	89104	Indian Springs Air Force Auxiliary Field	89018	Pyramid Lake Indian Reservation	89424
Cherry Creek	89301	Ione	89310	Quail Ridge	89403
Circus Circus	89114	Jackpot	89825	Rachel	89001
Clover Hills (Part of Elko)	89801	Jacks Valley	89705	Raleigh Heights (Part of Reno)	89506
Coaldale	89049	Jarbidge	89826	Rancho Estates	89410
Cobre	89835	Jean	89019	Rancho Haven	89501
Cold Springs	89406	Jiggs	89801	Rancho Vista	89403
Contact	89825	Johnson Lane	89423	Red Rock Estates	89501
Cottonwood Cove	89046	Kingsbury	89449	Reno	89501-70
Country Lane Estates	89410	Kingston	89310	For specific Reno Zip Codes call (702) 788-0600	
Crescent Valley	89821	Lake Mead Base	89191	Rhyolite	89003
Crystal Bay	89402	Lakeridge	89448	Ridgeview Estates	89705
Currant	89301	Lake Village	89449	Riverside	89007
Currie	89301	Lamoille	89828	River Village	89403
Dayton	89403	Lane	89301	Rixie's	89820
Deep Creek	89801	Las Vegas	89101-99	Round Hill Village	89448
Deeth	89823	For specific Las Vegas Zip Codes call (702) 361-9212		Round Mountain	89045
Denio	89404	Las Vegas Highlands (Part of North Las Vegas)	89030	Rowland	83604
Dixie Valley	89406	Laughlin	89029	Ruby Valley	89833
Downtown (Clark County)	89101	Lawton	89503	Ruby Valley Indian Reservation	89701
Downtown (Washoe County)	89501	Lee	89801	Ruhenstroth	89410
Dresslerville	89410	Lemmon Valley	89501	Ruth	89319
Duck Valley Indian Reservation (NV part)	89832	Lida	89013	Sagecrest Complex (Part of Elko)	89801
Duckwater	89314	Lincoln Park	89413	Sage Hills 2 (Part of Elko)	89801
Duckwater Indian Reservation	89314	Lockwood	89431	Sandy	89019
Dunphy	89820	Logandale	89021	San Jacinto	89825
Dyer	89010	Lovelock	89419	Satalite Hills (Part of Sparks)	89431
East Ely (Part of Ely)	89315	Lower Kingsbury	89449	Schurz	89427
Eastland Hills (Part of Elko)	89801	Lund	89317	Searchlight	89029
East Las Vegas	89112	Luning	89420	Shafter	89835
Echo Bay	89040	McDermitt	89421	Sheridan	89410
Edgewood	89449	McGill	89318	Sheridan Acres	89410
Elburz	89824	Majors Place	89301	Shoshone	89301
Eldorado Lakes	89403	Manhattan	89022	Sierra (Part of Reno)	89506
Elgin	89008	Mason	89447	Silverada Mall (Part of Reno)	89431
Elko	89801	Mayberry-Highland Park (Part of Reno)	89501	Silverado Heights	89705
Elk Point	89448	Meadowood Mall (Part of Reno)	89502	Silver City	89428
Ely	89301	Meadows, The (Part of Las Vegas)	89107	Silverpeak	89047
Empire	89405	Mercury	89023	Silver Springs	89429
Etna	89008	Mesquite	89024	Skyland	89448
Eureka	89316	Metropolis	89835	Sloan	89103
Fallon	89406	Midas	89414	Smith	89430
Fallon Indian Reservation	89406	Mill City	89418	Southern Nevada Correctional Center	89019
Fallon Naval Air Station	89406	Mina	89422	South Fork Indian Reservation	89801
Fallon Station	89406	Minden	89423	Southgate	89801
Federal (Part of Las Vegas)	89101	Moapa	89025	South Hills	89501
Fernley	89408	Moapa River Indian Reservation	89025	Spanish Springs Valley	89433
Fish Spring	89410	Mogul	89502		
Flanigan	89501	Montello	89830		
Fort McDermitt Indian Reservation (NV part)	89421	Mottsville	89410		
Fort Mojave Indian Reservation (NV part)	92363	Mountain City	89831		
Gabbs	89409	Mountain Springs	89101		

NEVADA

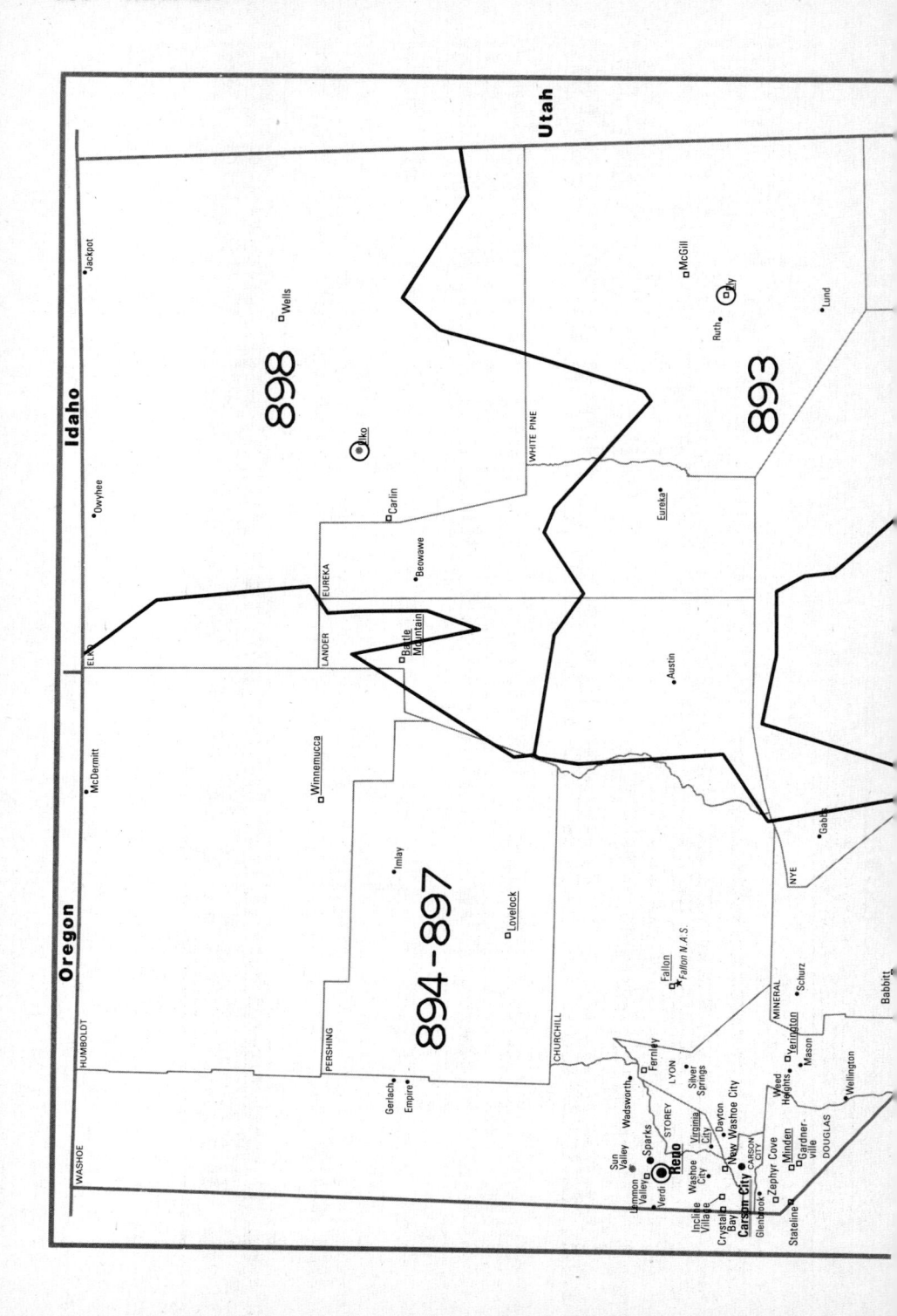

NEVADA 331

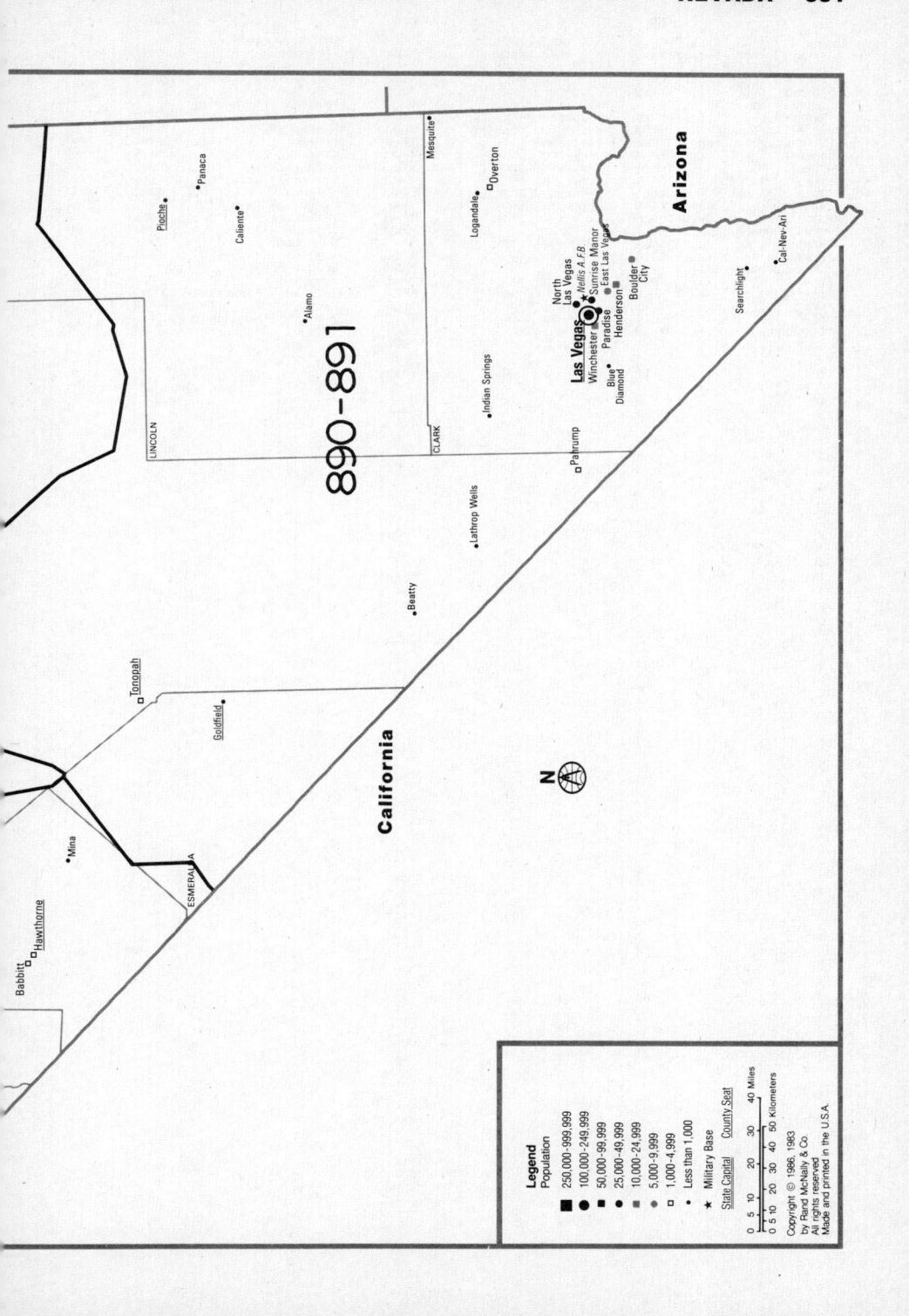

890-891

NEVADA — Sparks-Zephyr Cove-Round Hill Village

Location	ZIP
Sparks	89431-36
For specific Sparks Zip Codes call (702) 359-1161	
Spring Creek	89801
Stagecoach	89429
Stanton Park (Part of Carson City)	89701
Stateline (Clark County)	89019
Stateline (Douglas County)	89449
Steamboat	89511
Steptoe	89318
Stewart (Part of Carson City)	89701
Stewarts Point	89040
Stillwater	89406
Summit Lake Indian Reservation	89701
Suncrest (Part of Elko)	89801
Sundance Estates (Part of Elko)	89801
Sunrise Manor	89110
Sun Valley	89433
Sutcliffe	89501
Tahoe Village	89449
Tempiute	89001

Location	ZIP
Thomas Creek Estates	89501
Thousand Springs	89835
Timberline Estates (Part of Carson City)	89703
Tonopah	89049
Topaz Junction	89410
Topaz Lake	89410
Topaz Ranch Estates	89444
Tracy-Clark	89431
Tuscarora	89834
Tyrolean Village	89450
Unionville	89418
University (Part of Reno)	89507
Upper Kingsbury	89449
Ursine	89043
Valmy	89438
Vegas View (Part of North Las Vegas)	89030
Verdi	89439
Virginia City	89440
Vista (Part of Sparks)	89434
Vya	96104
Wabuska	89447
Wadsworth	89442
Walker Lake	89415

Location	ZIP
Walker River Indian Reservation	89427
Warm Springs	89049
Washington (Part of Reno)	89503
Washoe City	89701
Washoe-Dresslerville Indian Reservation	89410
Weed Heights	89447
Wellington	89444
Wells	89835
Wendover	89883
Westland Mall (Part of Las Vegas)	89102
Westwood Village	89423
Willow Beach	89005
Winchester	89101
Winnemucca	89445
Yerington	89447
Yerington Indian Reservation	89447
Yomba Indian Reservation	89310
Zephyr Cove	89448
Zephyr Cove-Round Hill Village	89448

Ackerman's Trailer Park-Forest Ridge NEW HAMPSHIRE 333

Name	ZIP
Ackerman's Trailer Park	03079
Acworth	03601
Acworth (Town)	03601
Albany	03818
Albany (Town)	03818
Alexandria	03222
Alexandria (Town)	03222
Allenstown	03275
Allenstown (Town)	03275
Alstead	03602
Alstead (Town)	03602
Alstead Center	03602
Alton	03809
Alton (Town)	03809
Alton Bay	03810
Amherst	03031
Amherst (Town)	03031
Andover	03216
Andover (Town)	03216
Antrim	03440
Antrim (Town)	03440
Arlington Park	03073
Ashland	03217
Ashland (Town)	03217
Ashuelot	03441
Atkinson	03811
Atkinson (Town)	03811
Atkinson and Gilmanton Academy (Town)	03579
Atkinson Heights	03811
Auburn	03032
Auburn (Town)	03032
Baboosic Lake	03031
Bagley	03278
Bank Village	03048
Barnstead	03218
Barnstead (Town)	03218
Barrington	03825
Barrington (Town)	03825
Barryvilla (Part of Rochester)	03867
Bartlett	03812
Bartlett (Town)	03812
Base	03595
Bath	03740
Bath (Town)	03740
Bayside	03840
Beans Grant (Town)	03595
Beans Island	03077
Beans Purchase (Town)	03581
Beaver Lake	03041
Bedford	03102
Bedford (Town)	03102
Beebe River	03223
Belmont	03220
Belmont (Town)	03220
Bennington	03442
Bennington (Town)	03442
Benton	03785
Benton (Town)	03785
Berlin	03570
Berlin Mills (Part of Berlin)	03570
Bethlehem	03574
Bethlehem (Town)	03574
Bethlehem Junction	03598
Birch Hill	03855
Blair	03264
Blais Park (Part of Berlin)	03570
Blodgett Landing	03255
Bonds Corner	03458
Boscawen	03301
Boscawen (Town)	03301
Bow	03301
Bow (Town)	03301
Bow Center	03301
Bowkerville	03465
Box Corner	03220
Bradford	03221
Bradford (Town)	03221
Bradford Center	03221
Brentwood	03042
Brentwood (Town)	03042
Brentwood Corner	03848
Bretton Woods	03575
Bridgewater	03222
Bridgewater (Town)	03222
Bristol	03222
Bristol (Town)	03222
Broad Acres (Part of Nashua)	03060
Brookfield	03872
Brookfield (Town)	03872
Brookline	03033
Brookline (Town)	03033
Brook Village North (Part of Nashua)	03060
Bungy	03576
Burkehaven	03782
Cambridge (Town)	03588
Camp Hedding	03042
Campton	03223

Name	ZIP
Campton (Town)	03223
Campton Hollow	03264
Campton Lower Village	03223
Campton Upper Village	03223
Canaan	03741
Canaan (Town)	03741
Canaan Center	03741
Canaan Street	03741
Candia	03034
Candia (Town)	03034
Candia Four Corners	03034
Candia Village	03034
Canobie Lake	03079
Canterbury (Town)	03224
Canterbury (Merrimack County)	03224
Carroll (Town)	03595
Cascade	03581
Cedar Pond	03570
Center Barnstead	03225
Center Conway	03813
Center Effingham	03882
Center Harbor	03226
Center Harbor (Town)	03226
Center Haverhill	03774
Center Ossipee	03814
Center Sandwich	03227
Center Strafford	03815
Center Tuftonboro	03816
Central Park (Part of Somersworth)	03878
Chandlers Purchase (Town)	03595
Charlestown	03603
Charlestown (Town)	03603
Chase Village	03281
Chateau Richelieu (Part of Nashua)	03060
Chatham	04058
Chatham (Town)	04058
Cheever	03266
Chesham	03455
Chester	03036
Chester (Town)	03036
Chesterfield	03443
Chesterfield (Town)	03443
Chichester	03263
Chichester (Town)	03263
Chicks Corner	03259
Chocorua	03817
Christian Hollow	03608
Cilleyville	03265
Claremont	03743
Claremont Center (Part of Claremont)	03743
Claremont Junction (Part of Claremont)	03743
Clarks Landing	03226
Clarksville (Town)	03576
Clinton	03440
Clinton Grove	03281
Clovelly (Part of Nashua)	03060
Coburn Woods (Part of Nashua)	03060
Cold Regions Research and Engineering Laboratory	03755
Cold River	03608
Colebrook	03576
Colebrook (Town)	03576
Collettes Grove	03841
Columbia (Town)	03576
Columbia Valley	03576
Concord	03301-03
For specific Concord Zip Codes call (603) 225-5536	
Contoocook	03229
Contoocook Lake	03452
Converseville	03461
Conway	03818
Conway (Town)	03818
Cornish	03746
Cornish Center	05089
Cornish City	05089
Cornish Flat	03746
Cornish Mills	05089
Cotton Mountain	03894
Crawford Notch	03595
Crawfords Purchase (Town)	03595
Cricket Corner	03031
Croydon	03773
Croydon (Town)	03773
Croydon Flat	03773
Crystal	03570
Cushman	03598
Cutts Grant (Town)	03595
Dalton	03598
Dalton (Town)	03598
Danbury	03230
Danbury (Town)	03230
Danville	03819
Danville (Town)	03819
Davisville	03229

Name	ZIP
Deerfield	03037
Deerfield (Town)	03037
Deerfield Parade	03037
Deering	03244
Deering (Town)	03244
Derry	03038
Derry (Town)	03038
Derry Village	03038
Dixs Grant (Town)	03576
Dixville (Town)	03576
Dixville Notch	03576
Dorchester	03266
Dorchester (Town)	03266
Dover	03820
Dover Point (Part of Dover)	03820
Drewsville	03604
Dublin	03444
Dublin (Town)	03444
Dummer (Town)	03588
Dunbarton	03301
Dunbarton (Town)	03301
Durham	03824
Durham (Town)	03824
East Alstead	03602
East Alton	03809
East Andover	03231
East Candia	03040
East Concord (Part of Concord)	03301
East Conway	04037
East Deering	03244
East Derry	03041
East Dummer	03588
East Grafton	03240
East Grantham	03753
East Hampstead	03826
East Haverhill	03780
East Hebron	03232
East Holderness	03217
East Kingston	03827
East Kingston (Town)	03827
East Lempster	03605
East Merrimack	03054
East Milford	03055
Easton	03580
Easton (Town)	03580
East Plainfield	03766
East Rindge	03461
East Rochester (Part of Rochester)	03867
East Sandwich	03226
East Sullivan	03445
East Sutton	03278
East Swanzey	03446
East Tilton	03252
East Unity	03773
Eastview	03450
East Wakefield	03830
East Washington	03244
East Westmoreland	03467
East Wilder (Part of Lebanon)	03784
East Wolfeboro	03894
Eaton (Town)	03832
Eaton Center	03832
Effingham	03814
Effingham (Town)	03814
Effingham Falls	03814
Elkins	03233
Ellsworth (Town)	03264
Elmwood (Hillsborough County)	03449
Elmwood (Merrimack County)	03230
Enfield	03748
Enfield (Town)	03748
Enfield Center	03749
Epping	03042
Epping (Town)	03042
Epsom	03234
Epsom (Town)	03234
Errol	03579
Errol (Town)	03579
Ervings Location (Town)	03576
Etna	03750
Exeter	03833
Exeter (Town)	03833
Exeter Hampton Mobile Village	03833
Exeter Villa	03833
Exeter West	03833
Fabyan	03595
Farmington	03835
Farmington (Town)	03835
Fitzwilliam	03447
Fitzwilliam (Town)	03447
Fitzwilliam Depot	03447
Forest Lake	03470
Forest Ridge (Part of Nashua)	03060

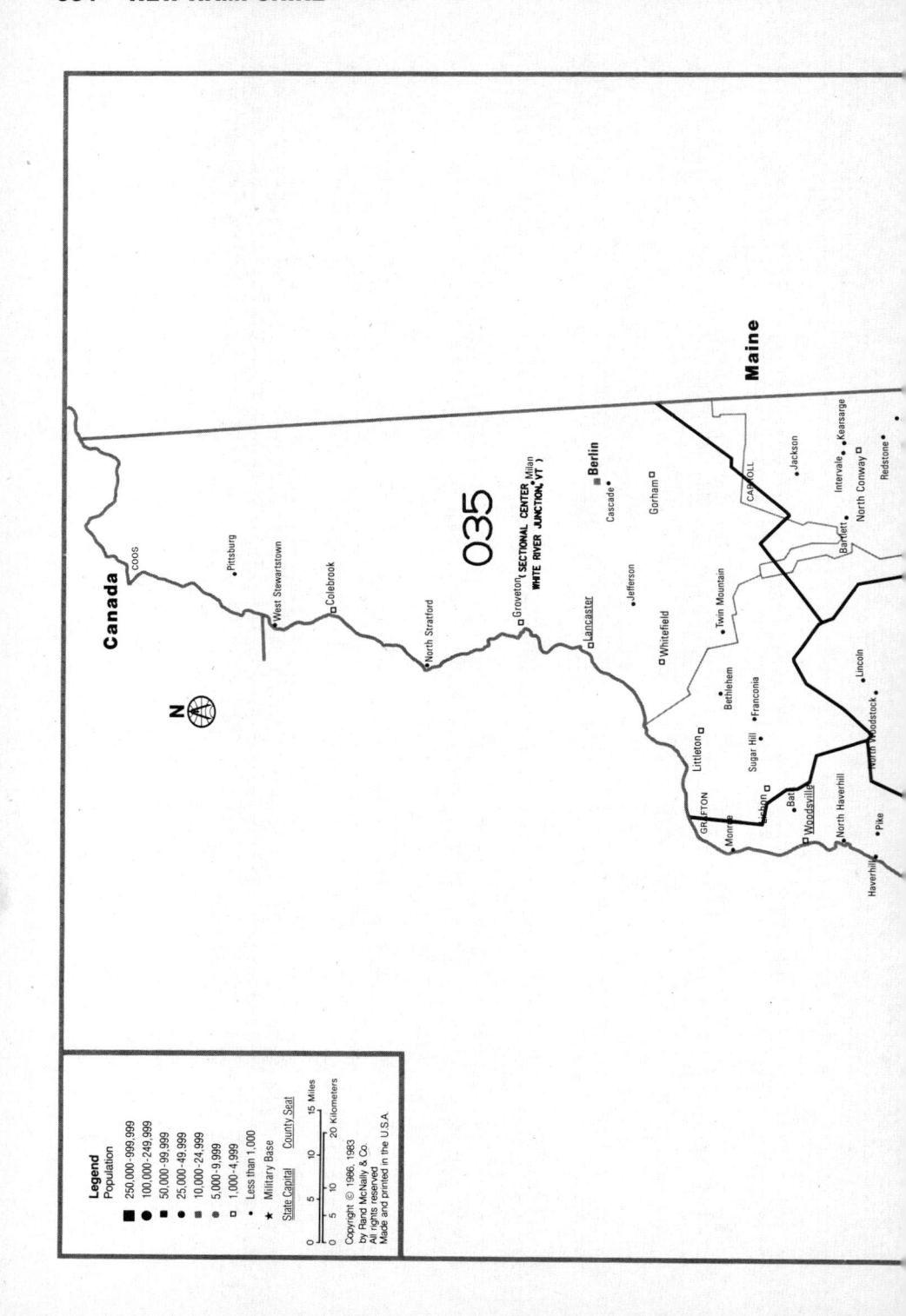

NEW HAMPSHIRE

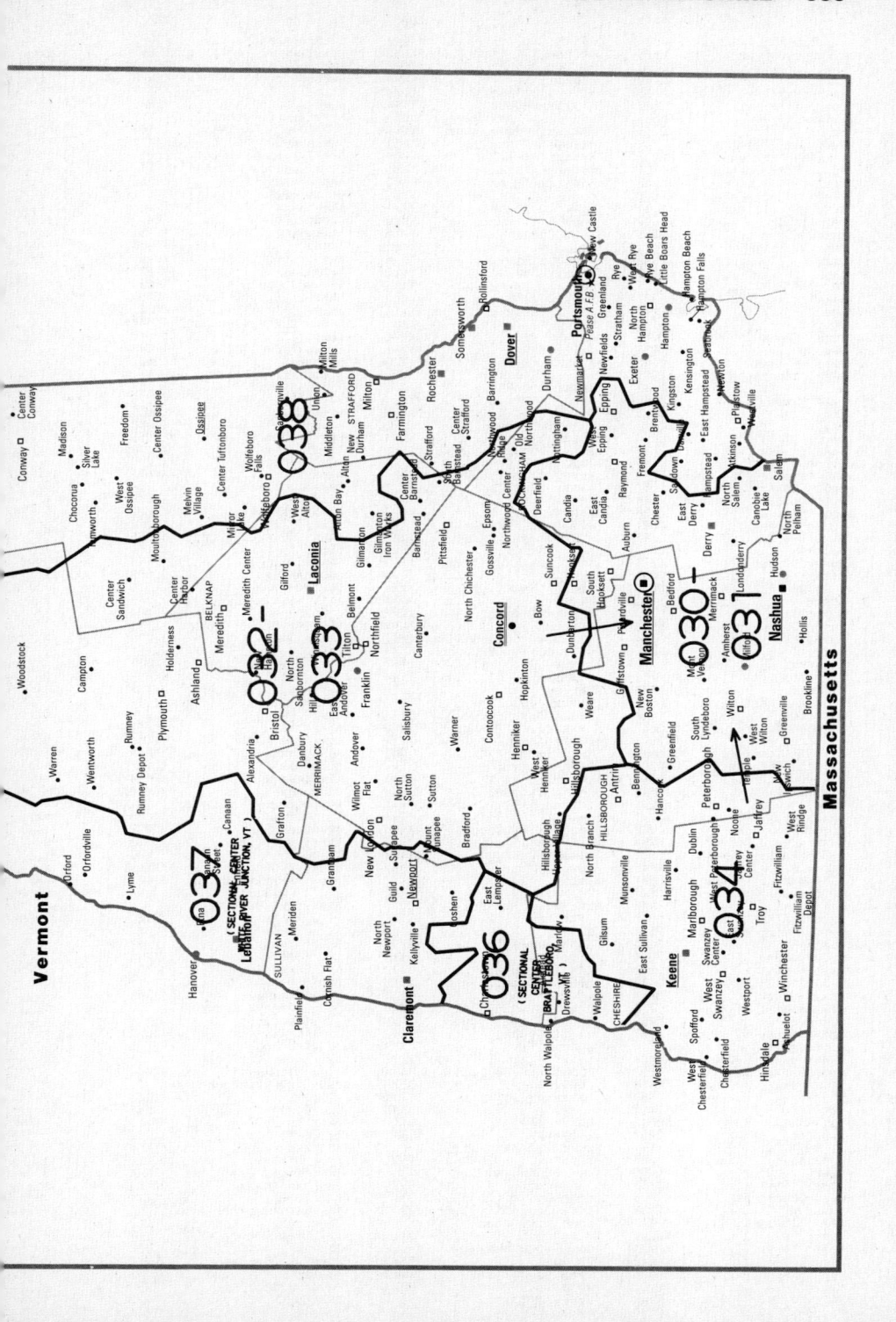

NEW HAMPSHIRE 335

336 NEW HAMPSHIRE Foundry-Newton

	ZIP		ZIP		ZIP
Foundry (Part of Somersworth)	03878	Hill	03243	Lyndeborough	03082
Foyes Corner	03870	Hill (Town)	03243	Lyndeborough (Town)	03082
Francestown	03043	Hill Center	03243	Madbury	03820
Francestown (Town)	03043	Hillsboro	03244	Madbury (Town)	03820
Franconia	03580	Hillsborough (Town)	03244	Madison	03849
Franconia (Town)	03580	Hillsborough Center	03244	Madison (Town)	03849
Franklin	03235	Hillsborough Lower Village	03244	Mall of New Hampshire, The (Part of Manchester)	03103
Franklin Falls (Part of Franklin)	03235	Hillsborough Upper Village	03244	Manchester	03101-08
Franklin Pierce College	03461	Hinsdale	03451	For specific Manchester Zip Codes call (603) 644-4111	
Freedom	03836	Hinsdale (Town)	03451	Maple Haven (Part of Portsmouth)	03801
Freedom (Town)	03836	Holderness	03245	Maplewood	03281
Fremont	03044	Holderness (Town)	03245	Marlborough	03455
Fremont (Town)	03044	Hollis	03049	Marlborough (Town)	03455
Gardners Grove	03252	Hollis (Town)	03049	Marlow	03456
Gates Corner (Part of Dover)	03820	Hooksett	03106	Marlow (Town)	03456
Gaza	03269	Hooksett (Town)	03106	Marshall Corner	03833
Georges Mills	03751	Hopkinton	03229	Marshall Farms	03833
Gerrish	03301	Hopkinton (Town)	03229	Martin	03106
Gilford	03246	Horses Corner	03263	Martins Location (Town)	03581
Gilford (Town)	03246	Hudson	03051	Mascoma (Part of Lebanon)	03748
Gilmans Corner	03777	Hudson (Town)	03051	Mason	03048
Gilmanton	03237	Hudson Center	03051	Mason (Town)	03048
Gilmanton (Town)	03237	Intervale	03845	Meadows	03587
Gilmanton Iron Works	03837	Jackson	03846	Melrose Corner (Part of Rochester)	03867
Gilsum	03448	Jackson (Town)	03846	Melvin Mills	03278
Gilsum (Town)	03448	Jady Hill	03833	Melvin Village	03850
Glen	03838	Jaffrey	03452	Meredith	03253
Glencliff	03238	Jaffrey (Town)	03452	Meredith (Town)	03253
Glendale	03246	Jaffrey Center	03454	Meredith Center	03246
Glenmere Village	03857	Jefferson	03583	Meriden	03770
Goffstown	03045	Jefferson (Town)	03583	Merrimack	03054
Goffstown (Town)	03045	Jenness Beach	03871	Merrimack (Town)	03054
Gonic (Part of Rochester)	03867	Jones Corner	03461	Middleton	03887
Goodrich Falls	03846	Joslin (Part of Keene)	03431	Middleton (Town)	03887
Goose Hollow	03223	Kearsarge	03847	Milan	03588
Gorham	03581	Keene	03431	Milan (Town)	03588
Gorham (Town)	03581	Kelleys Corner	03263	Milford	03055
Goshen	03752	Kellyville	03743	Milford (Town)	03055
Goshen (Town)	03752	Kelwyn Park (Part of Somersworth)	03878	Mill Hollow	03602
Gosport	03801	Kensington	03827	Millsfield (Town)	03579
Gossville	03234	Kensington (Town)	03827	Mill Village (Cheshire County)	03464
Grafton	03240	Kidderville	03576	Mill Village (Sullivan County)	03781
Grafton (Town)	03240	Kilkenny (Town)	03584	Millville Lake	03079
Grafton Center	03240	Kingston	03848	Milton	03851
Grange	03584	Kingston (Town)	03848	Milton (Town)	03851
Granite	03864	Laconia	03246-47	Milton Mills	03852
Grantham	03753	For specific Laconia Zip Codes call (603) 524-6271		Mirror Lake	03853
Grantham (Town)	03753	Lakeport (Part of Laconia)	03246	Monroe	03771
Grasmere	03045	Lancaster	03584	Monroe (Town)	03771
Great Boars Head	03842	Lancaster (Town)	03584	Mont Vernon	03057
Greenfield	03047	Landaff	03585	Mont Vernon (Town)	03057
Greenfield (Town)	03047	Landaff Center	03585	Moultonboro	03254
Greenland	03840	Langdon	03602	Moultonborough (Town)	03254
Greenland (Town)	03840	Langdon (Town)	03602	Moultonborough Falls	03254
Greens Grant (Town)	03581	Langs Corner	03870	Moultonville	03814
Greenville	03048	Laskey Corner	03887	Mountain View Estates (Part of Nashua)	03060
Greenville (Town)	03048	Laurel Lake	03447	Mount Sunapee	03772
Groton	03241	Leavitts Hill	03034	Mount Washington	03589
Groton (Town)	03241	Lebanon	03766	Munsonville	03457
Groveton	03582	Lee	03824	Nashua	03060-63
Guild	03754	Lee (Town)	03857	For specific Nashua Zip Codes call (603) 882-2646	
Hadleys Purchase (Town)	03595	Lee's	03833	Nashua Mall (Part of Nashua)	03060
Hale's Location (Town)	03845	Lempster	03606	Nelson	03457
Hampstead	03841	Lempster (Town)	03606	Nelson (Town)	03457
Hampstead (Town)	03841	Lincoln	03251	New Boston	03070
Hampton	03842	Lincoln (Town)	03251	New Boston (Town)	03070
Hampton (Town)	03842	Lincoln Park (Part of Nashua)	03060	New Boston Air Force Tracking Station, Detachment 2, Second Satellite Tracking Group	03103
Hampton Beach	03842	Lisbon	03585		
Hampton Falls	03844	Lisbon (Town)	03585		
Hampton Falls (Town)	03844	Litchfield	03051		
Hampton Landing	03842	Litchfield (Town)	03051	Newbury	03255
Hancock	03449	Little Boars Head	03862	Newbury (Town)	03255
Hancock (Town)	03449	Little Island Pond	03076	New Castle (Rockingham County) (Town)	03854
Hanover	03755	Littleton	03561		
Hanover (Town)	03755	Littleton (Town)	03561	New Castle (Rockingham County)	03854
Hanover Center	03750	Livermore (Town)	03251		
Hanover Street (Part of Manchester)	03101	Livermore Falls	03264	New Durham	03855
Happy Corner	03592	Lochmere	03252	New Durham (Town)	03855
Happy Valley	03458	Lockehaven	03748	Newfields	03856
Harrisville	03450	Londonderry	03053	Newfields (Town)	03856
Harrisville (Town)	03450	Londonderry (Town)	03053	New Hampton	03256
Hart's Location (Town)	03812	Loudon	03301	New Hampton (Town)	03256
Hastings	03257	Loudon (Town)	03301	Newington (Town)	03801
Haven Hill (Part of Rochester)	03867	Loudon Center	03301	New Ipswich	03071
Haverhill	03765	Louisburg Square (Part of Nashua)	03060	New Ipswich (Town)	03071
Haverhill (Town)	03765	Low And Burbanks Grant (Town)	03581	New London	03257
Hayes (Rockingham County)	03833	Lower Bartlett	03845	New London (Town)	03257
Hayes (Strafford County)	03867	Lower Gilmanton	03263	Newmarket	03857
Hebron	03241	Lower Village (Cheshire County)	03448	Newmarket (Town)	03857
Hebron (Town)	03241	Lower Village (Merrimack County)	03278	Newport	03773
Hedding	03042			Newport (Town)	03773
Hell Hollow	03746	Lyman (Town)	03585	New Rye	03275
Henniker	03242	Lyme	03768	Newton	03858
Henniker (Town)	03242	Lyme (Town)	03768		
High Bridge	03048	Lyme Center	03769		

Newton-Webster Lake **NEW HAMPSHIRE** 337

Place	ZIP
Newton (Town)	03858
Newton Junction	03859
Noone	03458
North Barnstead	03225
North Beach	03842
North Branch	03440
North Brookline	03055
North Charlestown	03603
North Chatham	04058
North Chichester	03263
North Conway	03860
North Danville	03044
Northfield	03276
Northfield (Town)	03276
North Grantham	03766
North Groton	03266
North Hampton (Town)	03862
North Hampton	03862
North Hampton Center	03862
North Haverhill	03774
North Holderness	03264
North Londonderry	03053
North Newport	03773
North Pelham	03076
North Pembroke	03301
North Richmond	03470
North Salem	03073
North Sanbornton	03269
North Sandwich	03259
North Stratford	03590
North Sutton	03260
North Swanzey	03431
Northumberland	05905
Northumberland (Town)	05905
North Village	03458
North Walpole	03609
North Wilmot	03230
North Wolfeboro	03894
Northwood	03261
Northwood (Town)	03261
Northwood Center	03261
Northwood Ridge	03261
North Woodstock	03262
Nottingham	03290
Nottingham (Town)	03290
Noyes Terrace	03079
Nuttings Beach	03222
Odell	03582
Old Millstream Estates	03833
Old Northwood	03261
Onway Lake	03077
Orange	03741
Orange (Town)	03741
Orford	03777
Orford (Town)	03777
Orfordville	03777
Ossipee	03864
Ossipee (Town)	03864
Pages Corner	03301
Pannaway Manor (Part of Portsmouth)	03801
Parker Hill	03585
Park Hill	03467
Partridge Lake	03561
Passaconaway	03818
Pearls Corner	03301
Pelham	03076
Pelham (Town)	03076
Pembroke (Town)	03275
Penacook (Part of Concord)	03303
Pendleton Beach (Part of Laconia)	03246
Pequawket	03875
Percy	03582
Peterborough	03458
Peterborough (Town)	03458
Pheasant Lane Mall (Part of Nashua)	03063
Pickering (Part of Rochester)	03867
Pickpocket Woods	03833
Piermont	03779
Piermont (Town)	03779
Pike	03780
Pinardville	03045
Pine Brook Estates	03833
Pinecrest	03833
Pine Valley	03086
Pinkhams Grant (Town)	03581
Pittsburg	03592
Pittsburg (Town)	03592
Pittsfield	03263
Pittsfield (Town)	03263
Plaice Cove	03842
Plainfield	03781
Plainfield (Town)	03781
Plaistow	03865
Plaistow (Town)	03865
Plymouth	03264
Plymouth (Town)	03264
Ponemah	03055

Place	ZIP
Portsmouth	03801
Post Office Annex (Part of Portsmouth)	03801
Potter Place	03265
Puckershire (Part of Claremont)	03743
Quaker City	03603
Quincy	03266
Quintown	03777
Rand	03461
Randolph	03570
Randolph (Town)	03570
Raymond	03077
Raymond (Town)	03077
Redstone	03813
Reeds Ferry	03054
Richardson	03055
Richmond	03470
Richmond (Town)	03470
Rindge	03461
Rindge (Town)	03461
Rivercrest	03755
Riverdale	03045
Riverhill (Part of Concord)	03301
Riverside	03874
Riverside Plaza (Part of Keene)	03431
Robinson Corner	03240
Roby	03278
Rochester	03867
Rockwoid	03245
Rollinsford	03869
Rollinsford (Town)	03869
Roxbury (Town)	03431
Royal Crest Estates (Part of Nashua)	03060
Rumney	03266
Rumney (Town)	03266
Rumney Depot	03266
Ryder Corner	03773
Rye	03870
Rye (Town)	03870
Rye Beach	03871
Rye North Beach	03870
Sachem Village (Part of Lebanon)	03784
Salem	03079
Salem (Town)	03079
Salem Center	03079
Salem Depot	03079
Salisbury	03268
Salisbury (Town)	03268
Salisbury Heights	03268
Sanbornton	03269
Sanbornton (Town)	03269
Sanbornville	03872
Sandown	03873
Sandown (Town)	03873
Sandwich	03227
Sandwich (Town)	03227
Sargents Purchase (Town)	03589
Sawyers (Part of Dover)	03820
Scotland	03470
Seabrook	03874
Seabrook (Town)	03874
Seabrook Beach	03874
Seacrest Village (Part of Portsmouth)	03801
Second College Grant (Town)	03576
Severance	03105
Sharon	03458
Sharon (Town)	03458
Shelburne (Town)	03581
Sherwood Forest	03833
Shirley Hill	03045
Short Falls	03234
Silver Lake	03875
Simoneau Plaza (Part of Nashua)	03060
Smiths Point	03246
Smithtown	03874
Smithville	03071
Snowville	03849
Snumshire	03603
Somersworth	03878
Soo Nipi	03257
South Acworth	03607
South Barnstead	03225
South Brookline	03033
South Charlestown	03603
South Chatham	04037
South Conway	03813
South Cornish	05089
South Danville	03819
South Deerfield	03037
South Effingham	03882
South Hampton	01913
South Hampton (Town)	01913
South Hooksett	03106

Place	ZIP
South Keene (Part of Keene)	03431
South Kingston	03848
South Lee	03857
South Lyndeboro	03082
South Merrimack	03060
South Milford	03055
South Newbury	03272
South Pittsfield	03263
South Stoddard	03464
South Sutton	03273
South Tamworth	03883
South Weare	03281
South Wolfeboro	03894
Spofford	03462
Spofford Lake	03462
Springfield	03284
Springfield (Town)	03284
Squantum	03452
Stark	03582
Stark (Town)	03582
State Line	03447
Stewartstown	03576
Stewartstown (Town)	03576
Stewartstown Hollow	03576
Stinson Lake	03274
Stoddard	03464
Stoddard (Town)	03464
Strafford (Strafford County)	03884
Strafford (Strafford County) (Town)	03884
Strafford (Coos County)	03590
Strafford (Coos County) (Town)	03590
Stratham	03885
Stratham (Town)	03885
Strawbery Banke (Part of Portsmouth)	03801
Success (Town)	03570
Sugar Hill	03585
Sugar Hill (Town)	03585
Sullivan	03431
Sullivan (Town)	03431
Sunapee	03782
Sunapee (Town)	03782
Suncook	03275
Surry	03431
Surry (Town)	03431
Sutton	03221
Sutton (Town)	03221
Swanzey (Town)	03431
Swanzey Center	03431
Swiftwater	03785
Tamworth	03886
Tamworth (Town)	03886
Temple	03084
Temple (Town)	03084
The Glen	03592
Thomas	03461
Thompson And Meserves Purchase (Town)	03595
Thornton	03285
Thornton (Town)	03285
Tilton	03276
Tilton (Town)	03276
Tilton-Northfield	03276
Tinkerville	03585
Trapshire	03603
Troy	03465
Troy (Town)	03465
Tuftonboro	03864
Tuftonboro (Town)	03864
Twin Mountain	03595
Union	03887
Unity	03603
Unity (Town)	03603
Upper Kidderville	03576
Wadley Falls	03857
Wakefield	03872
Wakefield (Town)	03872
Wallis Sands	03870
Walpole	03608
Walpole (Town)	03608
Warner	03278
Warner (Town)	03278
Warren	03279
Warren (Town)	03279
Washington	03280
Washington (Town)	03280
Waterloo	03278
Water Village	03864
Waterville Estates	03223
Waterville Valley	03223
Waterville Valley (Town)	03223
Wawbeek	03853
Weare	03281
Weare (Town)	03281
Webster	03301
Webster (Town)	03301
Webster Lake (Part of Franklin)	03235

338 NEW HAMPSHIRE Webster Place-Woodsville

	ZIP		ZIP		ZIP
Webster Place (Part of Franklin)	03235	West Henniker	03242	Whittier	03890
Weirs Beach (Part of Laconia)	03246	West Hopkinton	03229	Willey House	03812
Wendell	03782	West Lebanon (Part of Lebanon)	03784	Wilmot	03287
Wentworth (Town)	03282	West Milan	03570	Wilmot (Town)	03287
Wentworth (Coos County) (Town)	03579	Westmoreland	03467	Wilmot Flat	03287
Wentworth (Grafton County)	03282	Westmoreland (Town)	03467	Wilton (Hillsborough County)	03086
Wentworth By The Sea	03854	West Nottingham	03291	Wilton (Hillsborough County) (Town)	03086
West Alton	03246	West Ossipee	03890	Wilton Center	03086
West Andover	03265	West Peterborough	03468	Winchester	03470
West Brentwood	03848	West Plymouth	03264	Winchester (Town)	03470
West Campton	03223	Westport	03469	Windham (Town)	03087
West Canaan	03741	West Rindge	03461	Windham (Rockingham County)	03087
West Center Harbor	03217	West Rumney	03266	Windsor (Town)	03244
West Chesterfield	03466	West Rye	03870	Winnisquam	03289
West Claremont (Part of Claremont)	03743	West Salisbury	03216	Winona	03217
West Deering	03440	West Springfield	03284	Wolfeboro	03894
West Dummer	03570	West Stewartstown	03597	Wolfeboro (Town)	03894
West Epping	03042	West Swanzey	03469	Wolfeboro Center	03894
West Franklin (Part of Franklin)	03235	West Thornton	03285	Wolfeboro Falls	03896
West Gonic (Part of Rochester)	03867	West Unity	03743	Wonalancet	03897
West Hampstead	03841	Westville	03865	Woodman	03830
		West Wilton	03086	Woodmere	03452
		West Windham	03087	Woodstock	03293
		Whiteface	03259	Woodstock (Town)	03293
		Whitefield	03598	Woodsville	03785
		Whitefield (Town)	03598		

Aberdeen-Brookside **NEW JERSEY** 339

Name	ZIP
Aberdeen (Township)	07747
Aberdeen Township	07747
Absecon	08201
Absecon Heights	08201
Absecon Highlands	08201
Academy Estates	07981
Ackors Corner	08534
A Country Place	08701
Adams	08902
Adamston	08723
Adelphia	07710
Agasote	08618
Ajax Park	08618
Albion	08009
Albion Place (Part of Clifton)	07013
Aldene (Part of Roselle)	07203
Aldine	08318
Aldrich Estates	07731
Alexandria (Township)	08848
Allaire	07727
Allamuchy	07820
Allamuchy (Township)	07820
Allendale	07401
Allenhurst	07711
Allentown	08501
Allenwood	08720
Allerton	08833
Alloway	08001
Alloway (Township)	08001
Allwood (Part of Clifton)	07012
Almolind	08096
Almonesson	08096
Alpha	08865
Alphano	07838
Alpine	07620
Amber Terrace (Part of Pine Hill)	08021
Amon Heights	08110
Ampere (Part of East Orange)	07017
Ancora (Camden County)	08037
Anderson	07882
Andover (Sussex County)	07821
Andover (Sussex County) (Township)	07860
Andover Junction (Part of Andover)	07821
Andrews	08081
Anglesea (Part of North Wildwood)	08260
Annandale	08801
Anthony	08826
Applegarth	08512
Apple Hill	08002
Apshawa	07405
Arbor	08854
Arbors	08857
Arcola (Part of Paramus)	07652
Ardena	07728
Arlington (Part of Kearny)	07032
Arneys Mount	08068
Arneytown	08501
Arrowhead Park	08723
Arrowhead Village	08723
Asbury	08802
Asbury Gardens	07753
Asbury Park	07712
Ashland	08043
Atco	08004
Atlantic City	08401-06
For specific Atlantic City Zip Codes call (609) 345-4212	
Atlantic Highlands	07716
Atlantis	08087
Atsion	08088
Auburn	08085
Audubon	08106
Audubon Park	08106
Augusta	07822
Aura	08028
Avalon	08202
Avenel	07001
Avis Mills	08098
Avon By The Sea	07717
Avondale	07110
Awosting	07421
Babbitt	07047
Bacons Neck	08302
Bakersville (Atlantic County)	08225
Bakersville (Mercer County)	08638
Baldwins Corner	08534
Baleville	07860
Baltusrol	07081
Bamber Lake	08731
Baptistown	08803
Barbertown	08825
Barclay Farm	08002
Bargaintown	08221
Barkers Corner	07838
Barley Sheaf	08822
Barlow	08002

Name	ZIP
Barnegat	08005
Barnegat (Township)	08005
Barnegat Beach	08758
Barnegat Light	08006
Barnegat Pines	08731
Barnsboro	08080
Barrington	08007
Barrington Manor (Part of Barrington)	08033
Bartley	07836
Basking Ridge	07920
Bassett Park	07801
Bass River (Township)	08224
Bates Mill	08037
Batesville	08002
Batsto	08037
Battentown (Part of Swedesboro)	08085
Bay Harbor Estates	08723
Bay Head	08742
Bay Head Junction (Part of Bay Head)	08742
Bayonne	07002
Bay Shore West	08204
Bay Side (Cumberland County)	08302
Bay Side (Ocean County)	08050
Bayview Heights	08753
Bayview Shores	08738
Bayville	08721
Bayville Park	08721
Bayway (Part of Elizabeth)	07202
Baywood	08723
Beach Creek (Part of North Wildwood)	08260
Beach Glen	07866
Beach Haven	08008
Beach Haven Crest	08008
Beach Haven Gardens	08008
Beach Haven Heights	08008
Beach Haven Terrace	08008
Beach Haven West	08050
Beach View	08005
Beachwood	08722
Beatyestown	07840
Beaufort (Part of Roseland)	07068
Beaver Dam	08070
Beaver Lake	07416
Beckerville	08733
Bedminster	07921
Bedminster (Township)	07921
Beechwood Heights	07876
Beemerville	07461
Beesleys Point	08223
Belcher Creek	07480
Belcoville	08330
Belford	07718
Belle Mead	08502
Belleplain	08270
Belleville (Essex County)	07109
Belleville (Essex County) (Township)	07109
Belleville Annex (Part of Newark)	07109
Bellmawr	08031
Bellmawr Park (Part of Bellmawr)	08030
Bells Crossing (Part of Glen Gardner)	08826
Bells Lake	08012
Bellview	08077
Bellwood Park (Part of Bellmawr)	08030
Belmar	07719
Belmar Gardens	07719
Belvidere	07823
Belwood Park	07109
Bennett	08204
Bennetts Mills	08527
Bergen (Part of Jersey City)	07304
Bergenfield	07621
Bergenline (Part of Union City)	07087
Bergen Mall (Part of Paramus)	07652
Bergen Point (Part of Bayonne)	07002
Berkeley (Township)	08721
Berkeley Heights (Union County) (Township)	07922
Berkeley Heights (Union County)	07922
Berkeley Shore Estates	08721
Berlin (Camden County)	08009
Berlin (Camden County) (Township)	08091
Berlin Estates	08009
Berlin Heights (Part of Berlin)	08009
Bernards (Township)	07920
Bernardsville	07924

Name	ZIP
Bertrand Island (Part of Mount Arlington)	07856
Bethlehem (Township)	08802
Betsytown (Part of Elizabeth)	07201
Beverly	08010
Billingsport (Part of Paulsboro)	08066
Birches	08012
Birches West	08071
Birch Hills	07981
Birchwood Lakes	08055
Birchwood Park	08723
Birmingham	08011
Bishops	08009
Bivalve	08349
Black Horse Pike Shopping Center (Part of Audubon)	08106
Blackwells Mills	08873
Blackwood	08012
Blackwood Terrace	08096
Blairstown	07825
Blairstown (Township)	07825
Blawenburg	08504
Blenheim	08012
Bloomfield (Essex County)	07003
Bloomfield (Essex County) (Township)	07003
Bloomfield Terrace	08816
Bloomingdale (Morris County)	07457
Bloomingdale (Passaic County)	07403
Bloomsbury	08804
Blue Anchor	08037
Blue Bell	08344
Blue Star Shopping Center (Part of Watchung)	07060
Bogota	07603
Bon Air	08110
Bonhamton	08817
Boonton (Morris County)	07005
Boonton (Morris County) (Township)	07005
Bordentown (Burlington County)	08505
Bordentown (Burlington County) (Township)	08505
Bossert Estates	08505
Bound Brook (Camden County)	08002
Bound Brook (Somerset County)	08805
Bowman Manor	08251
Braddock	08037
Bradley Beach	07720
Bradley Gardens	08876
Bradley Park	07753
Braeburn Heights	08638
Braeburn Park	08638
Brainards	08865
Brainy Boro (Part of Metuchen)	08840
Branchburg (Township)	08876
Branchport (Part of Long Branch)	07740
Branchville	07826
Brant Beach	08008
Brass Castle	07882
Breton Woods	08723
Brick	08723-24
For specific Brick Zip Codes call (201) 477-0100	
Brick Church (Part of East Orange)	07018
Bricksboro	08332
Brick Township	08723
Bridgeboro	08075
Bridgeport	08014
Bridgeton	08302
Bridgeton Junction (Part of Bridgeton)	08302
Bridgeville	07823
Bridgewater	08807
Bridgewater (Township)	08807
Brielle	08730
Brigadoon	08096
Brigantine	08203
Brighton Beach	08008
Broad Lane	08094
Broad Street Annex (Part of Newark)	07102
Broadway (railroad station)	08886
Broadway	08808
Brookdale (Camden County)	08002
Brookdale (Essex County)	07003
Brookfields	08002
Brooklawn	08030
Brookmeade	08002
Brookside	07926

340 NEW JERSEY

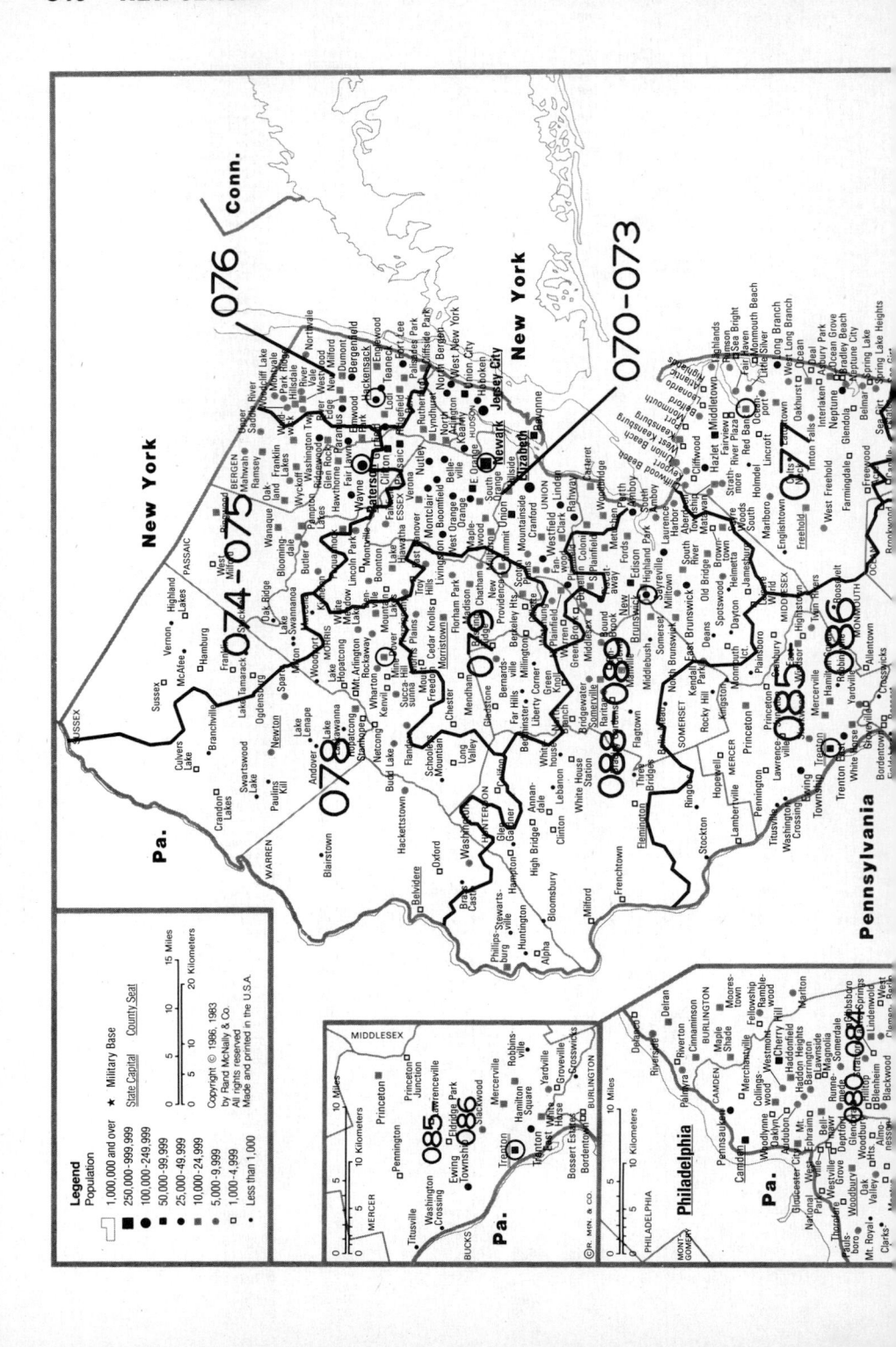

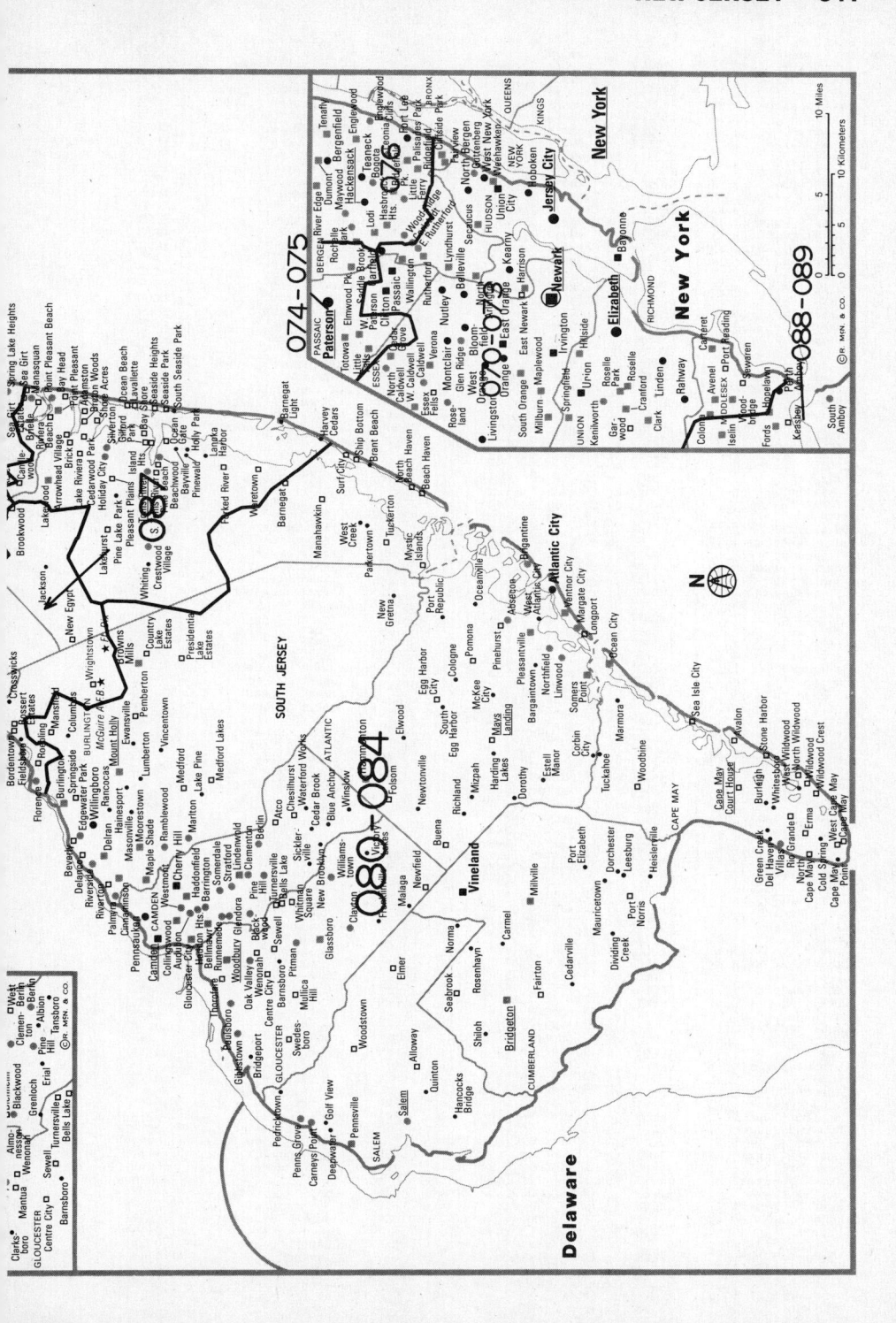

NEW JERSEY 341

342 NEW JERSEY Brook Tree-Deal

Name	ZIP
Brook Tree	08520
Brook Valley (Part of Kinnelon)	07405
Brookville (Hunterdon County)	08559
Brookville (Ocean County)	08005
Brookwood	08527
Brotmanville	08302
Browns Mills	08015
Browntown	08857
Brunswick Acres	08852
Brunswick Gardens	08857
Brunswick Shopping Center (Part of New Brunswick)	08902
Brunswick Square	08816
Brush Hollow	08053
Buckingham Village	08080
Buckshutem	08332
Budd Lake	07828
Buddtown	08088
Buena	08310
Buena Vista (Township)	08360
Bulltown	08215
Bunker Hill	08080
Bunnvale	07830
Burcliff Farms	08638
Burleigh	08210
Burlington (Burlington County)	08016
Burlington (Burlington County) (Township)	08016
Burnt Mills	07921
Bustleton	08016
Butler	07405
Butler Park	07882
Butlers Park	07882
Butterworth Farms	07801
Buttzville	07829
Byram (Hunterdon County)	08559
Byram (Sussex County) (Township)	07821
Byram Cove (Part of Hopatcong)	07843
Caldwell (Essex County)	07006
Caldwell (Essex County) (Township)	07004
Califon	07830
Callahans	07849
Cambridge	08075
Cambridge Park	08053
Camden	08101-10
For specific Camden Zip Codes call (609) 757-0330	
Camp Tecumseh	08867
Candlewood (census area only)	07731
Candlewood (census area only)	08701
Canton	08079
Cape Breton	08723
Cape May	08204
Cape May Court House	08210
Cape May Point	08212
Capitol Hill	08010
Cardiff	08232
Carlls Corner	08302
Carlstadt	07072
Carlton Hill (Part of Rutherford)	07073
Carmel	08332
Carmerville	07719
Carneys Point (Township)	08069
Carneys Point (Salem County)	08069
Carpenterville	08865
Carteret	07008
Cassville	08527
Castle Point (Part of Hoboken)	07030
Cecil	08094
Cedar Beach (Monmouth County)	07758
Cedar Beach (Ocean County)	08721
Cedar Bonnet Island	08050
Cedar Bridge Manor	08723
Cedar Brook	08018
Cedar Crest Manor	08069
Cedar Croft	08723
Cedar Glen Homes East	08757
Cedar Glen Lakes	08759
Cedar Glen West	08733
Cedar Grove (Cape May County)	08210
Cedar Grove (Essex County) (Township)	07009
Cedar Grove (Essex County)	07009
Cedar Heights	08801
Cedar Knolls	07927
Cedar Lake	07834

Name	ZIP
Cedar Ridge	08857
Cedar Run	08092
Cedarville (Cumberland County)	08311
Cedarville (Salem County)	08098
Cedarwood Park	08723
Centennial Lake	08053
Center (Part of Trenton)	08608
Center Grove	07869
Center Square	08085
Centerton (Burlington County)	08054
Centerton (Salem County)	08318
Centerville (Mercer County)	08534
Centerville (Somerset County)	08853
Central (Part of East Orange)	07018
Central Park	08070
Centre City	08051
Centre Grove	08332
Ceramics	08817
Chadwick Beach	08739
Chairville	08055
Chambersburg (Part of Trenton)	08611
Chambers Corner	08060
Changewater	07831
Chapel Heights	08080
Charlotteburg	07435
Charlton Village	07747
Chatham (Morris County)	07928
Chatham (Morris County) (Township)	07928
Chatsworth	08019
Cheesequake	08857
Cheesequake Estates	07747
Cherry Hill	08002-03
For specific Cherry Hill Zip Codes call (609) 424-4324	
Cherry Hill Estates	08002
Cherry Hill Mall	08002
Cherry Quay	08723
Cherry Ridge	08002
Cherry Valley	08002
Cherryville	08822
Cherrywood	08012
Chesilhurst	08089
Chester (Morris County)	07930
Chester (Morris County) (Township)	07930
Chesterfield	08650
Chesterfield (Township)	08650
Chestnut	07083
Chewalla Park	08619
Chews Landing	08012
Chrome (Part of Carteret)	07008
Churchtown	08070
Cinnaminson (Burlington County) (Township)	08077
Cinnaminson (Burlington County)	08077
Clark (Union County) (Township)	07066
Clark (Union County)	07066
Clarksboro	08020
Clarksburg	08510
Clarks Landing (Part of Point Pleasant)	08742
Clarktown	08330
Clayton	08312
Claytons Corner	07746
Clayville (Part of Vineland)	08360
Clearbrook Park	08831
Clear View Lake	07860
Clementon	08021
Clermont (Burlington County)	08060
Clermont (Cape May County)	08210
Cliffdale Park	07865
Cliff Park (Part of Cliffside Park)	07010
Cliffside Park	07010
Cliffwood	07721
Cliffwood Beach (Middlesex County)	08879
Cliffwood Beach (Monmouth County)	07735
Cliffwood Lake	07460
Clifton	07011-15
For specific Clifton Zip Codes call (201) 472-7900	
Clinton (Hunterdon County)	08809
Clinton (Hunterdon County) (Township)	08801
Clinton Hill (Part of Newark)	07108
Closter	07624
Cloverdale (Camden County)	08030

Name	ZIP
Cloverdale (Cumberland County)	08332
Cloverhill (Hunterdon County)	08822
Clover Hill (Monmouth County)	07722
Clover Hill at Holmdel	07733
Clover Leaf Lakes	08330
Coffins Corner	08026
Cohansey	08302
Cokesbury	08833
Cold Indian Springs	07712
Cold Spring	08204
Colesville	07461
Collings Lakes	08094
Collingswood	08108
Collingwood Park	07727
Collinsville	07960
Cologne	08213
Colonia	07067
Colonial Arms	08527
Colonial Manor	08096
Colonial Park	08520
Colonial Terrace	07712
Colts Neck	07722
Colts Neck (Township)	07722
Columbia	07832
Columbia Lakes	08002
Columbus	08022
Colwick	08002
Commercial (Township)	08349
Concordia	08512
Congressional Estates	08002
Conklintown (Part of Ringwood)	07465
Conovertown	08201
Constable Hook (Part of Bayonne)	07002
Constable Junction (Part of Bayonne)	07002
Convent Station	07961
Cookstown	08511
Coontown	07060
Cooper Park Village	08002
Cooper Village	08096
Copper Hill	08551
Corbin City	08270
Cornish	07823
Country Farms	07733
Country Lake Estates	08015
Country Manor	08857
Country Woods	07733
Coytesville (Part of Fort Lee)	07024
Cozy Lake	07438
Cragmere Park	07430
Cranberry Lake	07821
Cranbury (Township)	08512
Cranbury (Middlesex County)	08512
Cranbury Manor	08512
Crandon Lakes	07860
Cranford (Union County) (Township)	07016
Cranford (Union County)	07016
Cranford Junction	07016
Creamridge	08514
Crescent Heights	08068
Crescent Park (Part of Bellmawr)	08030
Cresskill	07626
Crestmoor	07853
Creston	08619
Crestwood Village	08759
Cropwell	08053
Cross Keys	08080
Crossroads	08055
Crosswicks	08515
Croton	08822
Crowfoot	08004
Crystal Lake (Bergen County)	07436
Crystal Lake (Ocean County)	08721
Culvers Lake	07826
Cumberland	08332
Cumberland Mall (Part of Vineland)	08360
Cuthbert Manor	08108
Cyn-Wyd	08016
Da Costa (Part of Hammonton)	08037
Danceys Corner	08069
Daretown	08318
Darlington Heights	08088
Darts Mills	08822
Davis	08514
Davis Bridge	07946
Dayton	08810
Deacons	08060
Deal	07723

Deal Park-Franklin **NEW JERSEY** 343

	ZIP		ZIP		ZIP
Deal Park	07723	East Orange	07017-19	Fairfield (Essex County)	
Deans	08852	For specific East Orange Zip		(Township)	07101
Deauville Beach	08739	Codes call (201) 673-5555		Fairfield (Essex County)	07004
De Cou Village	08610	East Pennsauken	08110	Fairfield (Monmouth County)	07728
Deepwater	08023	East Riverton	08077	Fair Haven	07704
Deerfield (Township)	08352	East Rutherford	07073	Fair Lawn	07410
Deerfield Park	08087	East Side (Part of		Fairmount	07830
Deerfield Street	08313	Bridgeton)	08302	Fairton	08320
Deer Park	08002	East Spotswood (railroad		Fairview (Bergen County)	07022
Deer Trail Lake	07460	station)	08884	Fairview (mail Riverside)	
Delair	08110	East Spotswood	08857	(Burlington County)	08075
Delanco (Burlington County)		East Trenton Heights	08638	Fairview (mail Medford)	
(Township)	08075	East Vineland (Part of		(Burlington County)	08055
Delanco (Burlington County)	08075	Vineland)	08360	Fairview (Gloucester	
Delawanna (Part of Clifton)	07014	East Wenonah	08090	County)	08080
Delaware (Hunterdon		East Windsor	08520	Fairview (Hudson County)	07047
County) (Township)	08822	East Windsor (Township)	08520	Fairview (Monmouth	
Delaware (Warren County)	07833	East Woodbury	08096	County)	07701
Delaware Gardens	08110	Eatontown	07724	Falcon Courts North	08562
Delaware Park	08865	Echelon	08043	Fanwood	07023
Delcrest	08075	Echo Lake	07435	Far Hills	07931
Del Haven	08251	Edgar	07095	Farmersville	07830
Delmont	08314	Edgebrook (Part of New		Farmingdale	07727
Delran (Burlington County)		Brunswick)	08901	Farmington	08232
(Township)	08075	Edgewater	07020	Farrington Lake Heights	08816
Delran (Burlington County)	08075	Edgewater Park (Burlington		Fashion Center, The (Part	
Delwood	08002	County) (Township)	08010	of Paramus)	07652
Demarest	07627	Edgewater Park (Burlington		Fawn Lakes	08050
Dennis (Township)	08214	County)	08010	Fayson Lakes (Part of	
Dennisville	08214	Edgewater Park Estates	08016	Kinnelon)	07405
Denville (Morris County)	07834	Edgewood	08210	Fellowship	08057
Denville (Morris County)		Edgewood Park	08527	Fenwick	08098
(Township)	07834	Edinburg	08691	Fernwood Terrace	08618
Deptford	08096	Edison	08817-20	Ferrell	08343
Deptford (Township)	08096	For specific Edison Zip Codes call		Ferry Road Manor	08628
Deptford Mall	08096	(201) 287-4311		Fieldsboro	08505
Deptford Terrace	08097	Egg Harbor (Township)	08221	Fieldstone	07920
Devonshire	08215	Egg Harbor City	08215	Finderne	08807
Dias Creek	08210	Eilers Corner	08520	Finesville	08865
Dicktown	08081	Elberon (Part of Long		Firthtown (Part of	
Dividing Creek	08315	Branch)	07740	Phillipsburg)	08865
Doddtown (Part of East		Elberon Park	07755	Fish House	08110
Orange)	07017	Eldora	08270	Fish House Junction	08110
Dolphin (Part of Northfield)	08225	Eldridge Park	08638	Fishing Creek	08204
Dorchester	08316	Eldridges Hill	08098	Five Corners (Part of Jersey	
Dorothy	08317	Elizabeth	07201-08	City)	07308
Dover (Morris County)	07801	For specific Elizabeth Zip Codes		Five Points (Salem County)	08067
Dover (Ocean County)		call (201) 352-8400		Five Points (Sussex County)	07860
(Township)	08753	Elizabethport (Part of		Flagtown	08821
Dover Hills	07801	Elizabeth)	07206	Flanders	07836
Dover Shores	08753	Elk (Township)	08028	Flatbrookville	07832
Dover Walk	08753	Elks Terrace	08079	Flemington	08822
Downe (Township)	08315	Ellisburg	08002	Flemington Junction	08822
Downer	08094	Ellisdale	08501	Floral Hill	07928
Downs Farms	08002	Elm	08037	Florence (Township)	08518
Downtown (Part of Trenton)	08608	Elmer	08318	Florence	08009
Drakestown	07840	Elmora (Part of Elizabeth)	07202	Florence (Burlington Co.)	08554
Drew University (Part of		Elmwood Park	07407	Florence (Burlington Co.)	08518
Madison)	07940	Elsinboro (Township)	08079	Florence-Roebling	08518
Dumont	07628	Elsmere (Part of Glassboro)	08028	Florham Park	07932
Dunbarton	08004	Elwood	08217	Folsom	08037
Dundee (Part of Passaic)	07055	Elwood-Magnolia	08217	Ford Estates	08096
Dunellen	08812	Emerson	07630	Ford Landing	08065
Dunham's Corner	08816	Emmelville	08330	Fords	08863
Dunham Siding	07047	Englewood	07631-32	Forest Grove	08360
Dunns Mills	08505	For specific Englewood Zip Codes		Forest Hill (Camden County)	08002
Durham	08817	call (201) 568-0086		Forest Hill (Ocean County)	08721
Durham Park	08854	Englewood Cliffs	07632	Forked River	08731
Dutch Neck	08550	English Creek	08330	Forked River Beach	08731
Dutchtown	08802	Englishtown	07726	Forrest Lake Estates	08328
Eagleswood (Township)	08092	Erial	08081	Fort Dix (Burlington County)	08640
Earle	07722	Erlton	08002	Fort Elfsborg	08079
East (Part of Paterson)	07514	Erma (Cape May County)	08204	Fortescue	08321
Eastampton (Township)	08060	Erma Park	08204	Fort Hancock	07732
East Amwell (Township)	08551	Ernston (Part of Sayreville)	08859	Fort Lee	07024
East Berlin	08009	Erskine (Part of Ringwood)	07456	Fort Mercer (Part of	
East Bound Brook (Part of		Erskine Lakes (Part of		National Park)	08063
Middlesex)	08846	Ringwood)	07456	Fort Mott	08079
East Bridgeton (Part of		Essex Fells (Essex County)	07021	Fort Plains	07728
Bridgeton)	08302	Essex Fells (Essex County)		Forty-third Street (Part of	
East Brunswick (Middlesex		(Township)	07021	Union City)	07087
County)	08816	Essex Green Mall	07052	Fostertown	08060
East Brunswick (Middlesex		Estell Manor	08319	Foster Village (Part of	
County) (Township)	08816	Estelville (Part of Estell		Bergenfield)	07621
East Burlington (Part of		Manor)	08319	Foul Rift	07823
Burlington)	08016	Estling Lake	07834	Four Bridges	07853
East Camden (Part of		Etra	08520	Foxborough Village	08857
Camden)	08105	Everett	07735	Fox Chase	08088
East Freehold	07728	Everittstown	08867	Fox Hills (Part of Mountain	
East Greenwich (Township)	08020	Evesboro	08053	Lakes)	07046
East Hanover (Morris Co.)		Evesham (Township)	08053	Fox Hollow Woods	08002
(Township)	07936	Ewan	08025	Francis Mills	08527
East Hanover (Morris		Ewansville	08060	Frankford (Township)	07826
County)	07936	Ewing (Township)	08618	Franklin (Gloucester County)	
East Keansburg	07734	Ewing Park	08638	(Township)	08322
East Long Branch (Part of		Ewing Township	08618	Franklin (Hunterdon	
Long Branch)	07740	Ewingville	08638	County) (Township)	08822
East Millstone	08873	Extonville	08501	Franklin (Somerset County)	
East Newark	07029	Fairfield (Cumberland		(Township)	08873
		County) (Township)	08320	Franklin (Sussex County)	07416

344 NEW JERSEY Franklin-Hootens Hollow

	ZIP		ZIP		ZIP
Franklin (Warren County) (Township)	08808	Green Grove	07712	Harrisonville (Salem County)	08079
Franklin Lakes	07417	Green Haven	08002	Hartford	08057
Franklin Park	08823	Green Hills	08876	Harvey Cedars	08008
Franklinville	08322	Green Hut Park	07801	Hasbrouck Heights	07604
Frazier Park	08008	Green Island	08753	Haskell (Part of Wanaque)	07420
Fredon (Township)	07860	Green Knoll	08876	Haven Beach	08008
Free Acres	07922	Greenland (Part of Magnolia)	08049	Haworth	07641
Freehold (Monmouth County)	07728	Green Pond	07435	Hawthorne	07506
Freehold (Monmouth County) (Township)	07728	Green Pond Junction (Part of Kinnelon)	07405	Hazen	07823
Freewood Acres	07727	Greensand	08817	Hazlet (Monmouth County)	07730
Frelinghuysen (Township)	07821	Greens Bridge (Part of Phillipsburg)	08865	Hazlet (Monmouth County) (Township)	07730
Frenchtown	08825	Green Village	07935	Head Of River (Part of Estell Manor)	08270
Freneau (Part of Matawan)	07747	Greenville (Hudson County)	07305	Headquarters	08557
Friendship	08343	Greenville (Ocean County)	08701	Heather Hills	07439
Friendship (Friendship Station)	08069	Greenville (Salem County)	08318	Hedding	08505
Fries Mill	08322	Greenwich	08323	Heislerville	08324
Galilee (Part of Monmouth Beach)	07750	Greenwich (Township)	08323	Helmetta	08828
Galloping Hill	07920	Greenwich (Gloucester County) (Township)	08027	Helmetta Park	08828
Galloway (Township)	08213	Greenwich (Warren County) (Township)	08886	Hensfoot	08827
Gandys Beach	08345	Greenwich Pier	08323	Herbertsville	08723
Garden City	08096	Greenwood Park	08071	Heritage Village	08053
Gardendale	08079	Grenloch	08032	Herman	08215
Garden Lake (Part of Lindenwold)	08021	Grenloch Terrace	08032	Herwood	08002
Gardens (Part of Ocean City)	08226	Greystone Park	07950	Hesstown	08332
Gardens of Pleasant Plains	08753	Griggstown	08540	Hewitt	07421
Garden State (Part of Paramus)	07652	Grove	07003	Heyden	07095
Garden State Plaza (Part of Paramus)	07652	Grove Chapel (Part of Vineland)	08344	Hibernia	07842
Gardenville	08096	Grovers Mill	08550	Hibernia Junction (Part of Rockaway)	07866
Gardenville Center	08096	Groveville	08620	Hickory Acres	08520
Garfield	07026	Gum Tree Corner	08302	Hickory Tree	07928
Garwood	07027	Guttenberg	07093	Hickstown	08012
Genasco	08861	Hackensack	07601-08	Higbee Town	08201
General Lafayette (Part of Jersey City)	07304	For specific Hackensack Zip Codes call (201) 440-7820		High Bridge	08829
Georgetown	08022	Hackettstown	07840	High Crest Lake	07480
Georgetowne	08053	Haddon (Township)	08108	Highland Beach (Part of Sea Bright)	07760
Georgia	07728	Haddonfield	08033	Highland Lakes	07422
Germania	08215	Haddon Heights	08035	Highland Park (Camden County)	08030
Germania Gardens	08213	Haddon Hills	08033	Highland Park (Camden County)	08012
Gibbsboro	08026	Haddon Leigh	08033	Highland Park (Middlesex County)	08904
Gibbstown	08027	Haddontowne	08002	Highlands	07732
Giffordtown	08057	Hainesburg	07832	High Point (Part of Harvey Cedars)	08008
Gilford Park (Ocean County)	08753	Haines Corner	08620	High Point Manor	08857
Gillespie (Part of Sayreville)	08872	Hainesport	08036	Highs Beach	08210
Gillette	07933	Hainesport (Township)	08036	Hightstown	08520
Gilman Lake	08343	Hainesville	07826	Hightstown Heights	08520
Glacier Hills	07950	Haledon	07508	Highview Park	08736
Gladstone	07934	Haledon-North Haledon (Part of Haledon)	07508	Hillcrest (Camden County)	08109
Glassboro	08028	Haleyville	08349	Hillcrest (Passaic County)	07502
Glasser (Part of Hopatcong)	07837	Halsey	07860	Hillcrest (Warren County)	08865
Glen Cove	08721	Hamburg	07419	Hilliard	08050
Glendale (Camden County)	08043	Hamden	08801	Hillsborough (Township)	08853
Glendale (Mercer County)	08618	Hamilton (Atlantic County) (Township)	08330	Hillsdale	07642
Glendola	07719	Hamilton (Mercer County) (Township)	08619	Hillsdale Manor (Part of Hillsdale)	07642
Glendora	08029	Hamilton (Monmouth County)	07753	Hillside (Union County)	07205
Glen Gardner	08826	Hamilton Square	08690	Hillside (Union County) (Township)	07205
Glen Oaks	08021	Hammond Heights	08090	Hilltop	08012
Glen Ridge (Essex County)	07028	Hammonton	08037	Hilltop Terrace	08816
Glen Ridge (Essex County) (Township)	07028	Hampton (Hunterdon County)	08827	Hilltown	07885
Glen Rock	07452	Hampton (Sussex County) (Township)	07860	Hillwood Lakes	08638
Glenside	08070	Hancocks Bridge	08038	Hilton (Part of Atlantic Highlands)	07716
Glenview	08002	Hanover (Township)	07981	Hinchman	08002
Glenwood	07418	Hanover Neck	07936	Hi-Nella	08083
Gloucester (Township)	08012	Hanover Township	07981	Hoboken	07030
Gloucester City	08030	Harbourton	08530	Hoffmans	07830
Godfrey Manor	08723	Harding (Township)	07940	Hoffner	08518
Golf Hill	07876	Harding Lakes	08330	Ho Ho Kus	07423
Golf Manor	08069	Hardingville	08343	Holgate	08008
Golf View	08069	Hardistonville (Part of Hamburg)	07419	Holiday City	08753
Gordon Lakes	07405	Hardwick (Township)	07825	Holiday City at Berkeley	08757
Gordon's Corner	07728	Hardyston (Township)	07460	Holiday City-Berkeley (census area only)	08753
Goshen	08218	Harfield	08527	Holiday City West	08757
Gouldtown	08302	Harker Village	08096	Holiday on the Bay	08753
Grandin	08801	Harlingen	08502	Holland (Township)	08848
Granton Junction	07047	Harmersville	08079	Holland	08848
Grasselli (Part of Linden)	07036	Harmony (Township)	08865	Holly Brook	08060
Grassy Sound	08260	Harmony (Monmouth County)	07748	Holly Crest	08723
Gravel Hill	07726	Harmony (Ocean County)	08527	Holly Hills	08060
Great Meadows	07838	Harmony (Warren County)	08865	Holly Park	08721
Great Notch	07424	Harrington Park	07640	Holmansville	08527
Green (Township)	07821	Harrison (Gloucester County) (Township)	08062	Holmdel	07733
Green Acres	08618	Harrison (Hudson County)	07029	Holmdel (Township)	07733
Green Bank	08215	Harrison Mountain Lake (Part of Ringwood)	07456	Holmdel Village	07733
Green Brook (Township)	08812	Harrisonville (Gloucester County)	08039	Holmeson	08526
Green Brook	08812			Homes Mills	08514
Green Creek	08219			Homestead	07047
Green Curve Heights	08638			Homestead Park	07933
Greendell	07839			Homestead Run	08753
Greenfield	08230			Homestead Village	07920
Greenfield Heights	08096			Hootens Hollow	08002
Greenfields Village	08096				

Hoover Village-Lows Hollow   NEW JERSEY   345

Name	ZIP
Hoover Village	08302
Hopatcong	07843
Hopatcong Heights (Part of Hopatcong)	07843
Hopatcong Hills (Part of Hopatcong)	07843
Hope	07844
Hope (Township)	07844
Hopelawn	08861
Hopewell (Cumberland County) (Township)	08302
Hopewell (Mercer County)	08525
Hopewell (Mercer County) (Township)	08560
Hornerstown	08514
Howell (Township)	07727
Howell	07728
	07731
For specific Howell Zip Codes call (201) 364-5288	
Hudson City (Part of Jersey City)	07307
Hudson Heights	07047
Hudson Shopping Plaza (Part of Jersey City)	07304
Hughesville	08848
Huntington	08865
Huntsburg	07860
Hunt Tract	08002
Hurdtown	07885
Hurffville	08080
Hutchinson	08865
Hutchinson Mills	08619
Hyson	08527
Ideal Beach	07734
Imlaystown (railroad station)	08501
Imlaystown	08526
Immaculate Conception Seminary	07430
Imperial Manor	08002
Independence (Township)	07840
Independence Corner	07461
Indian Lake	07834
Indian Mills	08088
Industrial-Hillside	07205
Interlaken	07712
Interlaken Estates	07712
Interstate Shopping Center (Part of Ramsey)	07446
Iona	08322
Ironbound (Part of Newark)	07105
Ironia	07845
Iron Rock	08109
Irven Heights	08638
Irvington (Essex County)	07111
Irvington (Essex County) (Township)	07111
Iselin	08830
Island Beach	08752
Island Heights	08732
Ivystone Farms	08004
Ivywood	08077
Jackson (Township)	08527
Jackson (Camden County)	08004
Jackson (Ocean County)	08527
Jackson Avenue (Part of Jersey City)	07305
Jacksonburg	07825
Jackson Estates	08527
Jacksons Mills	08527
Jacksonville (Burlington County)	08505
Jacksonville (Morris County)	07035
Jacobstown	08562
Jamesburg	08831
Janvier	08322
Jefferson (Gloucester County)	08062
Jefferson (Morris County) (Township)	07849
Jeffrey Lane Estates	08721
Jenkins	08019
Jericho	08096
Jersey City	07301-11
For specific Jersey City Zip Codes call (201) 915-7033	
Jerseyville	07728
Jobstown	08041
Johnsonburg	07846
Jones Island	08311
Jordantown	08109
Journal Square (Part of Jersey City)	07306
Juliustown	08042
Jutland	08827
Kampfe Lake (Part of Bloomingdale)	07403
Karrsville	07865
Kay Gardens	08067
Keansburg	07734
Kearny	07032

Name	ZIP
Kearny Junction (Part of Kearny)	07032
Keasbey	08832
Keasbey Heights	08832
Kemah Lake	07860
Kendall Park	08824
Kenilworth	07033
Kenvil	07847
Kenwood	08002
Keswick Grove	08759
Keyport	07735
Kingfisher Cove	08723
Kings Hill	08002
Kingsland	07071
Kingston	08528
Kingston Estates	08002
Kingsway Village	08002
Kingswood	08002
Kingwood (Township)	08825
Kinkora	08505
Kinnelon	07405
Kirbys Mill	08055
Kirkwood	08043
Kitchell Lake	07480
Kittatinny Lake	07826
Klinesville	08822
Knollwood	08002
Knowlton	07832
Knowlton (Township)	07832
Kresson	08053
Lacey (Township)	08731
Lafayette	07848
Lafayette (Township)	07848
La Gorce Square	08016
Lake	08344
Lake Arrowhead	07834
Lake Como (Part of Spring Lake Heights)	07762
Lake Denmark	07801
Lake Forest	07849
Lake Grinnell	07871
Lake Hiawatha	07034
Lake Hopatcong	07849
Lakehurst	08733
Lakehurst Naval Air Station	08733
Lake Iliff	07860
Lake Intervale	07005
Lake Lackawanna	07874
Lakeland	08012
Lake Lenape	07860
Lake Lookover	07421
Lake Neepaulin	07461
Lake Nelson	08854
Lake Owassa	07860
Lake Pine	08053
Lakeridge	07747
Lake Riviera	08723
Lake Rogerine (Part of Mount Arlington)	07856
Lake Shawnee	07885
Lakeside	07421
Lakeside Park	08610
Lake Stockholm	07460
Lake Swannanoa	07438
Lake Tamarack	07460
Lake Telemark	07866
Lakeview (Burlington Co.)	08060
Lakeview (Monmouth Co.)	08501
Lake Villa Estates	08009
Lakewood (Township)	08701
Lakewood	08701
Lambertville	08530
Lambs Terrace	08081
Lamington	07921
Landing	07850
Landisville (Part of Buena)	08326
Land of Pines	08701
Landsdown	08801
Lanes Mills	08701
Lanoka Harbor	08734
Lanoka Harbor Estates	08734
Larger Cross Roads	07921
Larison's Corner	08551
Larrabees	08701
Laurel Acres	08723
Laureldale	08330
Laurel Harbor	08734
Laurel Hill	08021
Laurel Homes	08861
Laurelhurst	08723
Laurel Lake (Part of Millville)	08332
Laurel Manor (Camden Co.)	08021
Laurel Manor (Ocean Co.)	08723
Laurel Springs	08021
Laurel Springs Gardens	08021
Laurelton Acres	08723
Laurelton Heights	08723
Laurelton Park	08723
Laurence Harbor (Middlesex County)	08879

Name	ZIP
Lavallette	08735
Lawnside	08045
Lawrence (Cumberland County) (Township)	08311
Lawrence (Mercer County) (Township)	08638
Lawrence Brook	08816
Lawrenceville	08648
Layton	07851
Lebanon (Hunterdon County)	08833
Lebanon (Hunterdon County) (Township)	07830
Lebanon Lake Estates	08015
Lebanon Park	08088
Ledgewood	07852
Ledgewood Mall	07852
Leeds Point	08220
Leektown	08215
Leesburg	08327
Leisuretowne	08088
Leisure Village	08701
Leisure Village West	08733
Lenola	08057
Leonardo	07737
Leonia	07605
Lewisville	08638
Liberty (Township)	07863
Liberty Corner	07938
Libertyville	07461
Lincoln	08062
Lincoln Park	07035
Lincroft	07738
Linden	07036
Linden Junction (Part of Linden)	07036
Lindenwold	08021
Lindy Lake	07405
Linvale	08551
Linwood	08221
Little Egg Harbor (Township)	08087
Little Falls (Passaic County)	07512
Little Falls (Passaic County) (Township)	07424
Little Falls (Passaic County)	07424
Little Ferry	07643
	07660
For specific Little Ferry Zip Codes call (201) 641-2106	
Little Ferry Junction (Part of Ridgefield Park)	07657
Little Rocky Hill	08540
Little Silver	07739
Little Silver Point (Part of Little Silver)	07739
Littleton (Part of Morris Plains)	07950
Little York	08834
Livingston (Essex County) (Township)	07039
Livingston (Essex County)	07039
Livingston Mall	07039
Loch Arbour	07711
Locktown	08822
Locust	07760
Locust Corner	08512
Lodi	07644
Logan (Township)	08014
Lommasons Glen	07823
London Terrace	08859
Long Beach	08008
Long Beach (Township)	08008
Long Branch	07740
Long Bridge	07838
Long Hill	07928
Longport	08403
Long Valley	07853
Longwood Lake	07438
Lopatcong (Township)	08865
Lorillard Beach (Part of Union Beach)	07735
Lorraine (Part of Roselle Park)	07204
Louden	08004
Loveladies	08008
Lower (Township)	08204
Lower Alloways Creek (Township)	08038
Lower Bank	08215
Lower Berkshire Valley	07885
Lower Harmony	08865
Lower Longwood Lake	07438
Lower Montville	07045
Lower Squankum	07731
Lower Valley (Part of Califon)	07830
Low Moor (Part of Sea Bright)	07760
Lows Hollow	08886

346 NEW JERSEY Low Moor-Mystic Islands

	ZIP		ZIP		ZIP
Low Moor (Part of Sea Bright)	07760	Matawan	07747	Monmouth Park (Part of Oceanport)	07757
Lows Hollow	08886	Maurice River (Township)	08327	Monroe (Gloucester County) (Township)	08094
Lozier Park (Part of Oradell)	07649	Mauricetown	08329	Monroe (Middlesex County) (Township)	08520
Lucaston (Part of Lindenwold)	08009	Maxim	08701	Monroe (Morris County)	07981
Lumberton	08048	Mayetta	08092	Monroe (Sussex County)	07871
Lumberton (Township)	08048	Mayfair at Marlton	08053	Monroeville	08343
Lyndhurst (Bergen County) (Township)	07071	Mayfair Gardens	08080	Montague	07827
Lyndhurst (Bergen County)	07071	Mays Landing	08330	Montague (Township)	12771
Lynn Oaks	07067	Mayville	08210	Montana	08865
Lyons	07920	Maywood	07607	Montclair	07042-44
	07939	Meadowbrook	08109	For specific Montclair Zip Codes call (201) 744-2660	
For specific Lyons Zip Codes call (201) 647-2626		Meadowbrook Village	08527	Montgomery (Township)	08558
Lyonsville	08005	Meadowview	07047	Montrose	07722
McAfee	07428	Meadow Village	07009	Montvale	07645
McCoys Corner	07461	Mechanicsville (Middlesex County)	08879	Montville	07045
McDonoughs (Part of South Amboy)	08879	Mechanicsville (Monmouth County)	07730	Montville (Township)	07045
McGuire AFB	08641	Medford	08055	Moonachie	07074
McGuire Air Force Base	08641	Medford (Township)	08055	Moores Corner	08079
McKee City	08232	Medford Farms	08088	Moores Meadows	08088
Macopin	07405	Medford Lakes	08055	Moorestown (Burlington County)	08057
Madison	07940	Melrose (Burlington County)	08055	Moorestown (Burlington County) (Township)	08057
Madison Park (Middlesex County)	08859	Melrose (Middlesex County)	08879	Moorestown-Lenola	08057
Madisonville	07920	Menantico (Part of Millville)	08332	Moorestown Mall	08057
Magnolia (Burlington County)	08068	Mendham (Morris County)	07945	Moosepack Lake	07439
Magnolia (Camden County)	08049	Mendham (Morris County) (Township)	07926	Morehousetown	07039
Mahoneyville	08070	Menlo Park	08837	Morgan (Part of Sayreville)	08879
Mahwah	07430	Menlo Park Mall	08817	Morgan Beach	08879
Mahwah (Township)	07430	Menlo Park Terrace	08840	Morganville	07751
Main Avenue (Cumberland County)	08360	Mercerville	08619	Morris (Camden County)	08110
Main Avenue (Passaic County)	07011	Mercerville-Hamilton Square	08619	Morris (Morris County) (Township)	07961
Malaga	08328	Merchantville	08109	Morris Beach	08330
Malapardis	07981	Meriden	07005	Morris Park	08865
Mall at Short Hills, The	07078	Metedeconk	08723	Morris Plains	07950
Manahawkin	08050	Metedeconk Park	08723	Morris Street (Part of Morristown)	07960
Manalapan	07728	Metedeconk Pines	08723	Morristown (Morris County)	07960-63
Manalapan (Township)	07728	Metropark	07095	For specific Morristown Zip Codes call (201) 539-5890	
Manasquan	08736	Mettler	08873	Morristown (Middlesex County)	07747
Manasquan Park	08736	Metuchen	08840	Morrisville	08110
Manasquan Shores	08736	Meyersville	07933	Morsemere (Part of Ridgefield)	07657
Manchester (Township)	08759	Miami Beach	08251	Morses Creek (Part of Linden)	07036
Mandalay	08723	Mickleton	08056	Mountain Lake	07823
Mannington (Township)	08079	Middle (Township)	08210	Mountain Lakes	07046
Manor Park	08723	Middlebush	08873	Mountainside	07092
Mansfield	08022	Middlesex	08846	Mountain Spring Lakes	07405
Mansfield (Burlington County) (Township)	08022	Middletown (Township)	07748	Mountain Station	07079
Mansfield (Warren County) (Township)	07863	Middletown (Morris County)	07866	Mountain View	07470
Mansfield Square	08022	Middletown (Monmouth County)	07748	Mountainville	08833
Mantoloking	08738	Middletown (census area only) (Monmouth County)	07718	Mount Airy	08530
Mantua	08051	Middle Valley	07853	Mount Arlington	07856
Mantua (Township)	08051	Middleville	07855	Mount Bethel	07865
Mantua Grove	08061	Midland Park	07432	Mount Ephraim	08059
Mantua Heights	08051	Midstreams	08723	Mount Fern	07801
Mantua Terrace	08051	Midstreams Park	08723	Mount Freedom	07970
Manunka Chunk	07832	Midtown (Part of Newark)	07102	Mount Hermon	07825
Manville	08835	Midvale (Part of Wanaque)	07465	Mount Holly (Burlington County)	08060
Maplecrest	07040	Mile Hollow	08505	Mount Holly (Burlington County) (Township)	08060
Maple Glen	08527	Milford	08848	Mount Hope	07885
Maple Shade (Burlington County) (Township)	08052	Military Ocean Terminal (Part of Bayonne)	07002	Mount Hope Mineral Junction (Part of Wharton)	07885
Maple Shade (Burlington County)	08052	Millbridge	08021	Mount Kemble Lake	07960
Maple Tree	08753	Millbrook (Morris County)	07869	Mount Laurel	08054
Maple View	08857	Millbrook (Warren County)	07832	Mount Laurel (Township)	08054
Maplewood (Essex County) (Township)	07040	Millburn (Essex County) (Township)	07041	Mount Olive (Township)	07828
Maplewood (Essex County)	07040	Millburn (Essex County)	07041	Mount Pleasant (Cape May County)	08270
Marcella	07866	Millhurst	07728	Mount Pleasant (Hunterdon County)	08848
Margate City	08402	Millington	07946	Mount Pleasant (Warren County)	07832
Marksboro	07825	Millside Heights	08075	Mount Rose	08525
Marlboro (Township)	07746	Millside Manor	08075	Mount Royal	08061
Marlboro (Burlington County)	08053	Millstone (Monmouth County) (Township)	08510	Mount Salem	07461
Marlboro (Cumberland County)	08302	Millstone (Somerset County)	08876	Mounts Mills	08831
Marlboro (Monmouth County)	07746	Milltown (Middlesex County)	08850	Mount Tabor (Morris County)	07878
Marlboro Heights	07726	Milltown (Union County)	07081	Mount Tabor (Morris County)	07834
Marlton (Burlington County)	08053	Millville	08332	Mount Vernon	07832
Marlton Heights	08098	Milmay	08340	Muhlenberg (Part of Plainfield)	07060
Marlton Hills	08053	Milton	07438	Mullica (Township)	08217
Marlton Lakes	08004	Mimosa Lake	08053	Mullica Hill	08062
Marlyn Manor	08242	Mine Brook (Part of Bernardsville)	07931	Murray Hill (Part of New Providence)	07974
Marmora	08223	Mine Hill (Township)	07801	Myrtle Grove	07860
Marshalls Corner	08525	Mine Hill	07801	Mystic Islands	08087
Marshalltown	08079	Minotola (Part of Buena)	08341		
Martins Beach	08045	Miramar	08223		
Martinsville	08836	Mizpah	08342		
Maryland	08527	Money Island	08753		
Maskell Mill	08079	Monitor (Part of West New York)	07093		
Masonville	08054	Monksville (Part of Ringwood)	07465		
		Monmouth (Part of Eatontown)	07724		
		Monmouth Beach	07750		
		Monmouth Heights	07746		
		Monmouth Hills	07732		
		Monmouth Junction	08852		

Mystic Shores-Pellettown   NEW JERSEY   347

Name	ZIP
Mystic Shores	08087
Natco (Part of Union Beach)	07735
National Park	08063
Naughright	07853
Naval Air Propulsion Test Center	08628
Navesink	07752
Navesink Beach (Part of Sea Bright)	07760
Nejecho Beach	08723
Neptune (Monmouth County)	07753
Neptune (Monmouth County) (Township)	07753
Neptune City	07753
Nesco	08037
Neshanic	08853
Neshanic Station	08853
Netcong	07857
Netherwood (Part of Plainfield)	07062
New Albany	08077
New Amsterdam Village	08879
Newark	**07101-75**

For specific Newark Zip Codes call (201) 596-5177

COLLEGES & UNIVERSITIES

Rutgers-The State University of New Jersey	07102
University of Medicine and Dentistry of New Jersey	07103

FINANCIAL INSTITUTIONS

Broad National Bank, Newark	07102
Carteret Savings Bank	07102
First Fidelity Bank, National Association, New Jersey	07192
The Howard Savings Bank	07101
Midlantic National Bank	07102
Nutley Savings & Loan Association	07110
Penn Federal Savings Bank	07105

HOSPITALS

Newark Beth Israel Medical Center	07112
Saint Michael's Medical Center	07102
United Hospitals Medical Center	07107
University of Medicine and Dentistry of New Jersey-University Hospital	07103

Newark Heights	07040
Newbakers Corners	07825
New Bedford	07719
Newbolds Corner	08060
New Bridge (Part of New Milford)	07646
New Brooklyn	08081
New Brunswick	08901-06

For specific New Brunswick Zip Codes call (201) 819-3200

New Canton	08501
New Durham	07047
New Egypt	08533
Newfield	08344
Newfoundland	07435
New Freedom	08009
New Gretna	08224
New Hampton	08827
New Hanover (Township)	08511
New Italy (Part of Vineland)	08360
New Jersey & New York Junction (Part of East Rutherford)	07073
New Jersey State Prison	08327
New Lisbon	08064
New Milford (Bergen County)	07649
New Milford (Bergen County)	07646
New Monmouth	07748
Newport (Cumberland County)	08345
Newport (Hunterdon County)	08826
New Providence	07974
New Sharon (Gloucester County)	08080
New Sharon (Mercer County)	08691
Newton	07860
Newton Heights	08816
Newtonville	08346
New Vernon	07976
New Village	08886

Name	ZIP
New York & Greenwood Lake Junction (Part of Kearny)	07032
Nixon	08817
Norma	08347
Normandie (Part of Sea Bright)	07760
Normandy Beach	08739
Normandy Harbor	08739
North (Part of Newark)	07104
North Arlington	07032
North Asbury Park (Part of Asbury Park)	07712
North Beach	08008
North Beach Haven	08008
North Bergen (Hudson County)	07047
North Bergen (Hudson County) (Township)	07047
North Branch	08876
North Brunswick (Middlesex County) (Township)	08902
North Brunswick (Middlesex County)	08902
North Caldwell (Essex County)	07006
North Caldwell (Essex County) (Township)	07006
North Cape May	08204
North Cedarville	08311
North Center	07003
North Church	07416
North Church Estates	07416
North Crosswicks	08515
North Dennis	08214
North Edison	08817
North Elizabeth (Part of Elizabeth)	07208
Northfield (Atlantic County)	08225
Northfield (Essex County)	07039
North Hackensack (Part of River Edge)	07661
North Haledon	07508
North Hanover (Township)	08562
North Hawthorne (Part of Hawthorne)	07507
North Highlands Beach	08251
North Long Branch (Part of Long Branch)	07740
North Merchantville (Part of Merchantville)	08109
Northmont (Part of Mount Ephraim)	08059
North Plainfield	07060
North Port Norris	08349
North Stelton	08854
Northvale	07647
North Vineland (Part of Vineland)	08360
North Wildwood	08260
North Woodbury (Part of Woodbury)	08096
Norton	08827
Nortonville	08085
Norwood	07648
Nottingham	08619
Nugentown	08087
Nutley (Essex County)	07110
Nutley (Essex County) (Township)	07110
Oak Dale	08060
Oak Glen	07731
Oak Hill	07748
Oakhurst	07755
Oakland	07436
Oaklyn	08107
Oak Ridge (Ocean County)	08753
Oak Ridge (Passaic County)	07438
Oak Ridge Lake	07438
Oak Shades	07747
Oak Tree (Middlesex County)	08817
Oak Tree (Ocean County)	08527
Oak Valley	08090
Oakview	08096
Oakwood	06055
Oakwood Beach	08079
Oakwood Park (Part of New Providence)	07974
Ocean (Monmouth County) (Township)	07755
Ocean (Ocean County) (Township)	08758
Ocean Acres	08050
Ocean Beach	08735
Ocean City	08226
Ocean City Gardens	08226
Ocean County Mall	08753
Ocean Gate	08740
Ocean Grove	07756

Name	ZIP
Ocean Heights (Part of Linwood)	08221
Oceanport	07757
Ocean Township	07712
Ocean View	08230
Oceanville	08231
Ogdensburg	07439
Old Bridge	08857
Old Bridge (Township)	08857
Old Bridge	08857
Old Charleston Woods	08002
Old Forge Village	07960
Old Manor	07730
Oldmans (Township)	08067
Old Orchard	08002
Old Tappan	07675
Oldwick	08858
Olivet	08318
Oradell	07649
Orange	**07050-52**

For specific Orange Zip Codes call (201) 673-2372

Orchard Center	08302
Orchard View	08016
Orston (Part of Audubon)	08106
Ortley Beach	08751
Osage	08043
Osbornsville	08723
Othello	08302
Outcalt	08831
Outwater (Part of Garfield)	07026
Overbrook (Camden County)	08021
Overbrook (Essex County)	07009
Owens	07461
Oxford	07863
Oxford (Township)	07863
Oyster Creek	08220
Packanack Lake	07470
Pahaquarry (Township)	07832
Palatine	08318
Palermo	08223
Palisade (Part of Fort Lee)	07024
Palisades Park	07650
Palmer Square (Part of Princeton)	08540
Palmyra (Burlington County)	08065
Palmyra (Hunterdon County)	08867
Pamrapo (Part of Bayonne)	07002
Pancoast	08310
Panther Lake	07821
Paradise Lakes	08001
Paramus	**07652-53**

For specific Paramus Zip Codes call (201) 262-6886

Paramus Park Shopping Center (Part of Paramus)	07652
Park (Part of Paterson)	07513
Park Avenue	07087
Parker	07853
Parkertown	08087
Park Ridge	07656
Park Ridge Farms	08505
Parkside	08865
Park Village	07016
Parkway Pines	08701
Parkway Village	08628
Parlin (Part of Sayreville)	08859
Parry	08077
Parsippany (Morris County)	07046
	07054

For specific Parsippany Zip Codes call (201) 335-2300

Parsippany-Troy Hills (Township)	07054
Parsippany-Troy Hills Township (census area only)	07005
Pasadena	08759
Passaic (Morris County) (Township)	07946
Passaic (Passaic County)	07055
Passaic Junction	07662
Passaic Park (Part of Passaic)	07055
Paterson	**07501-44**

For specific Paterson Zip Codes call (201) 977-4738

Patricks Corner	08816
Pattenburg	08802
Paulina	07825
Paulins Kill	07860
Paulsboro	08066
Peahala Park	08008
Peapack (Part of Gladstone)	07977
Pedricktown	08067
Peermont (Part of Avalon)	08202
Pelican Island	08751
Pellet Pond	07480
Pellettown	07822

348 NEW JERSEY Pemberton-Rutherford

	ZIP
Pemberton (Burlington County)	08068
Pemberton (Burlington County) (Township)	08015
Pemberton Heights	08068
Penbryn	08009
Penekum	08021
Pennington	08534
Pennsauken (Camden County)	08110
Pennsauken (Camden County) (Township)	08110
Pennsauken (Camden County)	08110
Penns Beach	08070
Penns Grove	08069
Penns Neck	08540
Pennsville	08070
Pennsville (Township)	08070
Penny Pot (Part of Folsom)	08037
Penton	08079
Penwell	07865
Peppermill Farms	08002
Pequannock (Morris County)	07440
Pequannock (Morris County) (Township)	07440
Pequest	07863
Perrineville	08535
Perth Amboy	08861-63
For specific Perth Amboy Zip Codes call (201) 826-2090	
Petersburg	08270
Philips Mills	07734
Phillipsburg	08865
Phoenix	08817
Picatinny Arsenal	07806
Pierces Point	08210
Piersonville	08620
Pilesgrove (Township)	08093
Pine Acres (Part of Woodbury Heights)	08090
Pine Beach	08741
Pine Brook (Monmouth County)	07724
Pine Brook (Morris County)	07058
Pine Brook (Somerset County)	08502
Pine Cliff Lake	07480
Pine Grove	08053
Pine Hill	08021
Pinehurst	08201
Pine Lake Park	08753
Pine Ridge	08857
Pine Ridge at Crestwood	08759
Pines Lake	07470
Pine Terrace	08753
Pinetree Village	08857
Pine Valley	08021
Pinewald	08721
Pinewold Village	08016
Piscataway	08854-55
For specific Piscataway Zip Codes call (201) 981-0740	
Pitman	08071
Pittsgrove (Salem County)	08318
Pittsgrove (Salem County) (Township)	08347
Pittstown	08867
Plainfield	07059-60
For specific Plainfield Zip Codes call (201) 756-5200	
Plainsboro	08536
Plainsboro (Township)	08536
Plainville	08502
Plauderville (Part of Garfield)	07026
Plaza (Part of Secaucus)	07094
Plaza Park	08016
Pleasant Gardens	08527
Pleasant Grove (Morris County)	07853
Pleasant Grove (Ocean County)	08527
Pleasant Hill	07876
Pleasant Mills	08037
Pleasant Plains (Morris County)	07980
Pleasant Plains (Ocean County)	08753
Pleasant Run (Burlington County)	08077
Pleasant Run (Hunterdon County)	08822
Pleasant Terrace	08314
Pleasant Valley	07882
Pleasant View	08502
Pleasantville (Atlantic County)	08232
Pleasantville (Cumberland County)	08360

	ZIP
Pleasure Bay (Part of Long Branch)	07740
Pluckemin	07978
Plumbsock	07461
Plumsted (Township)	08533
Pohatcong (Township)	08804
Pointers	08079
Point Pleasant	08742
Point Pleasant Beach	08742
Point Pleasant Manor	08723
Polkville	07832
Pomona	08240
Pompton Junction (Part of Pompton Lakes)	07442
Pompton Lakes	07442
Pompton Plains	07444
Porchtown	08344
Port-au-Peck (Part of Oceanport)	07757
Port Colden	07882
Port Elizabeth	08348
Portertown	08098
Port Johnson (Part of Bayonne)	07002
Port Monmouth	07758
Port Morris	07850
Port Murray	07865
Port Norris	08349
Port Reading	07064
Port Reading Junction (Part of Manville)	08835
Port Republic	08241
Port Warren	08886
Possumtown	08854
Post Brook Farms Lake	07480
Potter	08817
Potterstown	08833
Pottersville	07979
Powerville	07005
Prallsville (Part of Stockton)	08559
Presidential Lakes Estates	08015
Princeto Ivy East	08520
Princeton	08540-43
For specific Princeton Zip Codes call (609) 452-9044	
Princeton (Mercer County) (Township)	08540
Princeton (Mercer County)	08540
Princeton Junction	08550
Princeton North	08540
Prospect Heights	08638
Prospect Highlands	08638
Prospect Park (Mercer County)	08638
Prospect Park (Passaic County)	07508
Prospect Plains	08512
Prospect Point	07849
Prospertown	08514
Pullentown	08501
Quaker Gardens	08619
Quakertown	08868
Quarryville	07461
Quinton	08072
Quinton (Township)	08072
Racoon Island	07849
Radburn (Part of Fair Lawn)	07410
Rahway	07065-67
For specific Rahway Zip Codes call (201) 388-1110	
Rainbow Lakes	07834
Raines Corner	08069
Ralston	07945
Ramblewood	08054
Ramsey	07446
Ramseysburg	07832
Rancocas	08073
Rancocas Heights	08060
Rancocas Woods	08060
Randolph (Morris County)	07869
Randolph (Morris County) (Township)	07970
Raritan (Hunterdon County) (Township)	08822
Raritan (Somerset County)	08869
Raven Rock	08559
Readington	08870
Readington (Township)	08870
Reaville	08822
Rebel Hill	07920
Red Bank (Monmouth County)	07701-04
For specific Red Bank Zip Codes call (201) 741-9200	
Red Bank (Gloucester County)	08063
Red Lion	08088
Reed Crossing (Part of Berlin)	08009
Reeds Beach	08210

	ZIP
Reevytown (Part of Tinton Falls)	07753
Repaupo (railroad station)	08085
Repaupo	08066
Retreat	08088
Richard Mine	07885
Richland	08350
Richwood	08074
Rider College	08648
Ridgefield	07657
Ridgefield Park	07660
Ridgeway	08733
Ridgewood	07450-52
For specific Ridgewood Zip Codes call (201) 444-5400	
Ridgewood Junction (Part of Glen Rock)	07452
Riegel Ridge	08848
Riegelsville	08848
Ringoes	08551
Ringwood	07456
Rio Grande	08242
Ritz (Part of Garfield)	07026
River Bank	08741
Riverdale	07457
River Edge	07661
River Edge Manor (Part of New Milford)	07646
River Plaza	07701
River Road (Part of Fair Lawn)	07410
Riverside (Burlington County) (Township)	08075
Riverside (Burlington County)	08075
Riverside Park	08075
Riverside Square (Part of Hackensack)	07601
River Street (Part of Paterson)	07524
Riverton	08077
River Vale (Bergen County) (Township)	07675
River Vale (Bergen County)	07675
Riverview Manor	08854
Riverwood	08753
Riviera Beach	08723
Roadstown	08302
Robbinsville	08691
Robertsville (census area only)	07746
Robertsville	07726
Robin Hood Homes	08010
Robins Estates	08527
Rochelle Park (Bergen County) (Township)	07662
Rochelle Park (Bergen County)	07662
Rockaway (Morris County)	07866
Rockaway (Morris County) (Township)	07866
Rockaway Neck	07054
Rockaway Valley	07005
Rockleigh	07647
Rockport	07840
Rock Ridge Lake	07834
Rocktown	08551
Rocky Hill	08553
Roebling	08554
Roosevelt	08555
Roosevelt City	08759
Roosevelt Park (Part of Millville)	08332
Rosedale (Part of Hammonton)	08037
Rosegate	08857
Rose Hill Heights	08865
Roseland	07068
Roselle	07203
Roselle Park	07204
Rosemont (Hunterdon County)	08556
Rosemont (Mercer County)	08619
Rosenhayn	08352
Roseville (Part of Newark)	07107
Ross Corner	07822
Rossmoor	08831
Rowe Street	07003
Roxburg	08865
Roxbury (Township)	07876
Rudeville	07419
Rumson	07760
Runnemede	08078
Runyon	08857
Russia	07438
Rutgers Village (Part of New Brunswick)	08901
Rutherford	07070-75
For specific Rutherford Zip Codes call (201) 933-1213	

Saddle Brook-Town Bank NEW JERSEY 349

Name	ZIP
Saddle Brook (Bergen County) (Township)	07662
Saddle Brook (Bergen County)	07662
Saddle River	07458
St. Cloud	07052
St. Josephs Village (Part of Rockleigh)	07647
Salem	08079
Salem Hills	08701
Salina	08080
Sand Brook	08559
Sand Hills (mail Perth Amboy)	08861
Sand Hills (mail Monmouth Junction)	08852
Sands Point (Part of Oceanport)	07757
Sandy Point	08723
Sandyston (Township)	07851
Saxton Falls	07874
Sayres Neck	08311
Sayreville	08872
Sayre Woods (Part of Sayreville)	08859
Sayre Woods South	08857
Schelllengers Landing (Part of Cape May)	08204
Schooleys Mountain	07870
Scobeyville	07724
Scotch Bonnet	08210
Scotch Plains (Union County) (Township)	07076
Scotch Plains (Union County)	07076
Scudders Falls	08628
Scullville	08330
Seaboard (Part of Kearny)	07032
Sea Breeze	08302
Sea Bright	07760
Seabrook	08302
Sea Girt	08750
Sea Girt Estates	08750
Sea Isle City	08243
Seaside Heights	08751
Seaside Park	08752
Seaview Park	08201
Seaview Square	07712
Seaville	08230
Secaucus	07094
Sedgefield	07950
Sergeantsville	08557
Seven Stars	08701
Sewaren	07077
Sewell	08080
Shady Lakes	07480
Shafto Corners (Part of Tinton Falls)	07727
Shamong (Township)	08088
Shark River Hills	07753
Shark River Manor	07719
Sharptown	08098
Shaw Crest	08260
Shelter Cove	08753
Sherbrook Estates	08520
Sherwood on the Green	08096
Sherwood West	08066
Shiloh	08353
Shimer Manor	08865
Ship Bottom	08008
Shippenport	07850
Shirley	08318
Shongum	07970
Shore Acres	08723
Shore Crest	07067
Short Hills	07078
Shrewsbury (Monmouth County)	07702
Shrewsbury (Monmouth County) (Township)	07724
Shrewsbury Road	08501
Sicklerville	08081
Sidney	08867
Siloam	07728
Silver Bay	08753
Silver Lake (Essex County)	07109
Silver Lake (Warren County)	07825
Silver Ridge	08753
Silver Ridge Park	08757
Silver Ridge Park West	08757
Silver Springs	07850
Silverton (Ocean County)	08753
Sim Place	08005
Singac	07424
Sinnickson Landing	08079
Six Points	08302
Skillman	08558
Skylands (Part of Ringwood)	07456
Sky Line Lake (Part of Ringwood)	07465

Name	ZIP
Slackwoods	08638
Sloop Creek Estates	08721
Sloping Hills	07920
Smithburg	07728
Smiths Mills	07405
Smith Tract	08008
Smithville (Atlantic County)	08201
Smithville (Burlington County)	08060
Smoke Rise (Part of Kinnelon)	07405
Snow Hill (Part of Lawnside)	08045
Society Hill	08857
Soho	07109
Somerdale	08083
Somerset (Somerset County)	08873-75
For specific Somerset Zip Codes call (201) 846-0732	
Somerset (Mercer County)	08628
Somers Point	08244
Somerville	08876-77
For specific Somerville Zip Codes call (201) 725-0570	
South (Part of Newark)	07114
South Amboy	08879
Southampton (Township)	08088
Southard	08701
South Belmar	07719
South Bound Brook (Middlesex County)	08846
South Bound Brook (Somerset County)	08880
South Branch	08876
South Brunswick	08540
South Brunswick (Township)	08852
South Camden (Part of Camden)	08104
South Dennis	08245
South Egg Harbor	08215
Southern State 1 & 2	08314
South Glassboro (Part of Glassboro)	08028
South Hackensack (Bergen County) (Township)	07606
South Hackensack (Bergen County)	07606
South Harrison (Township)	08039
South Kearny (Part of Kearny)	07032
South Lakewood	08701
South Livingston	07039
South Mantoloking	08738
South Merchantville (Part of Merchantville)	08109
South Ogdensburg (Part of Ogdensburg)	07439
South Orange	07079
South Orange Village (Township)	07079
South Paterson (Part of Paterson)	07503
South Pemberton (Part of Pemberton)	08068
South Penns Grove	08069
South Plainfield	07080
South River	08882
South Seaside Park	08752
South Seaville	08246
South Toms River	08757
South Vineland (Part of Vineland)	08360
South Westville (Part of Westville)	08093
Southwest Vinland (Part of Vineland)	08360
Southwind	08527
Southwood	08857
South Woodstown (Part of Woodstown)	08098
Sparta	07871
Sparta (Township)	07871
Sparta Junction	07871
Sparta Lake	07871
Sperry Springs (Part of Hopatcong)	07843
Spotswood	08884
Spray Beach	08008
Springdale (Camden County)	08002
Springdale (Sussex County)	07860
Springfield (Burlington County) (Township)	08041
Springfield (Union County) (Township)	07081
Springfield (Union County)	07081
Spring Gardens	08618
Spring Lake	07762
Spring Lake Heights	07762
Spring Mills	08848
Springside	08016

Name	ZIP
Springtown (Cumberland County)	08302
Springtown (Warren County)	08865
Springville	08057
Squire Village	08753
Stafford (Township)	08050
Staffordville	08092
Stanhope	07874
Stanton	08885
Stanton Station	08822
Stanwick	08057
Stanwick Glen	08057
Star Cross	08322
State Hospital	08625
Staten Island Junction	07016
Steelmantown	08270
Steelmanville	08221
Stephensburg	07865
Stevens	08016
Stewartsville	08886
Still Valley	08865
Stillwater	07875
Stillwater (Township)	07875
Stirling	07980
Stockholm	07460
Stockton	08559
Stockton State College	08240
Stone Harbor	08247
Stone House	07946
Stone Tavern	08514
Stonetown (Part of Ringwood)	07465
Stoney Brook Estates	08096
Stony Hill	07922
Stoutsburg	08525
Stow Creek (Township)	08302
Stow Creek Landing	08302
Stratford	08084
Strathmere	08248
Strathmore	07747
Styertowne Shopping Center (Part of Clifton)	07012
Suburban	07701
Succasunna	07876
Succasunna-Kenvil	07876
Summerfield	07823
Summit	07901
Summit Avenue (Part of Union City)	07087
Sunbury	08068
Sunnyside	08801
Sunrise Beach	08731
Sunrise Park	07876
Sunset Hills	08540
Surf City	08008
Sussex	07461
Sutton Park	07836
Swainton	08210
Swartswood	07877
Swartswood Lake	07860
Swedesboro	08085
Sweet Briar	07733
Sweetwater	08037
Sykesville	08562
Sylvan Glen	08505
Sylvan Lake	08016
Tabernacle	08088
Tabernacle (Township)	08088
Tanglewood Farms	07733
Tanners Corner	08816
Tansboro	08004
Taunton Lakes	08053
Taurus (Part of West New York)	07093
Tavistock	08033
Taylortown	07005
Teabo	07885
Teaneck (Bergen County) (Township)	07666
Teaneck (Bergen County)	07666
Tenafly	07670
Tennent	07763
Teterboro	07608
Tewksbury (Township)	08833
The Acres (Part of Glassboro)	08028
The Dunes	08008
The Orchards	08619
Thompson Beach	08324
Thorofare	08086
Three Bridges	08887
Timber Lakes	08094
Timbuctoo	08060
Tinton Falls	07724
Titusville	08560
Toms River	08753-57
For specific Toms River Zip Codes call (201) 349-0710	
Totowa	07512
Towaco	07082
Town Bank	08204

350 NEW JERSEY Town Brook-Wonder Lake

Name	ZIP
Town Brook	07748
Town Center	07052
Town Estates	08016
Townley	07083
Townsbury	07863
Townsends Inlet (Part of Sea Isle City)	08243
Tranquility	07879
Tremley (Part of Linden)	07036
Tremley Point (Part of Linden)	07036
Trenton	08601-91
For specific Trenton Zip Codes call (609) 581-3030	
Trenton Gardens	08610
Trenton Highlands	08619
Troy Hills	07054
Tuckahoe	08250
Tuckerton	08087
Tuckerton Shores (Part of Tuckerton)	08087
Turkey Point Corner	08349
Turnersville	08012
Tuttles Corner	07826
Twin Rivers	08520
Tyler Park	07047
Undercliff (Part of Edgewater)	07020
Union (Hunterdon County) (Township)	08802
Union (Union County) (Township)	07083
Union (Union County)	07083
Union Beach	07735
Union Center	07083
Union City	07087
Union Hill	07801
Union Mills	08060
Union Square (Part of Elizabeth)	07201
Uniontown	08865
Union Valley	08512
Unionville	08600
Upper (Township)	08250
Upper Berkshire Valley	07885
Upper Deerfield (Township)	08313
Upper Freehold (Township)	08501
Upper Greenwood Lake	07421
Upper Harmony	08865
Upper Mohawk	07871
Upper Montclair	07043
Upper Montvale (Part of Montvale)	07645
Upper Pittsgrove (Township)	08318
Upper Saddle River	07458
Uptown (Part of Hoboken)	07030
V.A. Hospital (Part of East Orange)	07018
Vail Homes	07724
Vails	07832
Vailsburg (Part of Newark)	07106
Valley (Middlesex County)	08817
Valley (Passaic County)	07470
Vanada Woods	08723
Vanhiseville	08527
Van Marters Corner	07730
Vasa Home	07840
Vauxhall	07088
Ventnor City	08406
Ventnor Heights (Part of Ventnor City)	08406
Verga	08093
Vernon	07462
Vernon (Township)	07462
Vernon Valley Lake	07418
Vernoy	07830
Verona (Essex County)	07044
Verona (Essex County) (Township)	07044
Victoria	08344
Victory Gardens	07801
Victory Lakes	08094
Vienna	07880
Vienna Gardens	08213
Villas	08251
Vincentown	08088
Vineland	08360
Voken Tract	08002
Voorhees (Township)	08043
Voorhees Corner	08822
Vulcanite (Part of Alpha)	08865
Wading River	08215
Waldwick	07463
Wall (Monmouth County)	07719
Wall (Monmouth County) (Township)	07719
Wallington	07057
Wallkill Lake	07461
Wallpack Center	07881
Wallworth Park	08002
Walnford	08501

Name	ZIP
Walnut Valley	07832
Walpack (Township)	07881
Walt Whitman Homes	08086
Wanamassa	07712
Wanaque	07465
Wantage (Township)	07461
Waretown	08758
Warners (Part of Linden)	07036
Warren	07059
Warren (Township)	07060
Warren Glen	08886
Warren Grove	08005
Warren Point (Part of Fair Lawn)	07410
Warrington	07832
Washington (Bergen County) (Township)	07675
Washington (Burlington County) (Township)	08215
Washington (Gloucester County) (Township)	08080
Washington (Mercer County) (Township)	08691
Washington (Morris County) (Township)	07853
Washington (Warren County)	07882
Washington (Warren County) (Township)	07882
Washington Crossing	08560
Washington Park (Part of Newark)	07102
Washington Street (Part of Hoboken)	07030
Washington Township	07675
Washington Valley	07960
Washingtonville (Part of Watchung)	07060
Watchung	07060
Waterford (Township)	08004
Waterford Works	08089
Waterloo	07874
Watsessing	07003
Watsontown (Part of Clementon)	08021
Wayne	07470-74
For specific Wayne Zip Codes call (201) 694-3325	
Wayside	07712
Wedgewood	08071
Weehawken (Hudson County) (Township)	07087
Weehawken (Hudson County)	07087
Weekstown	08037
Weequahic (Part of Newark)	07112
Wellwood (Part of Merchantville)	08109
Wenonah	08090
West (Part of Newark)	07103
West Allenhurst	07711
Westampton (Township)	08073
West Amwell (Township)	08530
West Arlington (Part of Kearny)	07032
West Atco	08004
West Atlantic City	08232
West Belmar	07719
West Belt Mall	07470
West Berlin	08091
Westboro (Part of Red Bank)	07701
West Brunswick	08873
West Caldwell (Essex County) (Township)	07006
West Caldwell (Essex County)	07004
West Cape May	08204
West Carteret (Part of Carteret)	07008
West Carteret-Woodbridge (Part of Carteret)	07008
West Collingswood (Part of Collingswood)	08107
West Collingswood Heights	08059
West Creek	08092
West Deal	07712
West Deptford (Township)	08086
West End (Gloucester County)	08096
West End (Monmouth County)	07740
West Englewood	07666
West Farms	07731
Westfield	07090-92
For specific Westfield Zip Codes call (201) 233-1167	
West Fort Lee (Part of Fort Lee)	07024
West Freehold	07728
West Grove	07753

Name	ZIP
West Haddonfield (Part of Haddonfield)	08033
West Hoboken (Part of Union City)	07087
West Hoboken (Part of Hoboken)	07030
West Hudson (Part of Kearny)	07032
West Keansburg	07734
West Long Branch	07764
West Mahwah	07430
West Mantoloking	08723
West Milford	07480
West Milford (Township)	07480
Westmont	08108
West Moorestown	08057
West New York	07093
West Norwood (Part of Norwood)	07648
West Ocean City	08223
West Ocean Grove	07753
Weston (Part of Manville)	08835
Westons Mills (Part of New Brunswick)	08816
West Orange (Essex County)	07052
West Orange (Essex County) (Township)	07052
West Paterson	07424
West Point Island	08735
West Point Pleasant (Part of Point Pleasant)	08742
West Portal	08802
West Side (Part of Hoboken)	07030
West Side (Part of Jersey City)	07304
West Trenton	08628
West Tuckerton	08087
West View (Part of Ridgefield Park)	07660
West Village	08302
Westville	08093
Westville Grove	08093
Westville Oaks	08093
West Wildwood	08260
West Windsor (Township)	08550
Westwood	07675
Weymouth (Atlantic County)	08330
Weymouth (Atlantic County) (Township)	08317
Whale Beach	08248
Wharton	07885
Wheat Road (Part of Buena)	08341
Whiglane	08343
Whippany	07981
White (Township)	07829
White Horse	08610
Whitehouse	08888
White House Station	08889
White Meadow Lake	07866
Whiteoak Ridge	07078
White Rock Lake	07439
Whitesbog	08015
Whitesboro	08252
Whitesboro-Burleigh	08252
Whitesville (Monmouth County)	07753
Whitesville (Ocean County)	08527
Whiting	08759
Whitman Square	08012
Wickatunk	07765
Wilburtha	08628
Wilburtha Manor	08628
Wilderness Acres	08002
Wildwood	08260
Wildwood Crest	08260
Wildwood Gables (Part of Wildwood Crest)	08260
Wildwood Highlands Beach	08251
Williamstown	08094
Williamstown Junction	08009
Willingboro (Burlington County) (Township)	08046
Willingboro (Burlington County)	08046
Willingboro Mall	08046
Willington Park	08077
Willowbrook Mall	07470
Willowdale	08002
Willow Grove	08344
Windsor	08561
Windsor Park	08753
Winfield (Union County) (Township)	07036
Winfield (Union County)	07036
Winslow	08095
Winslow (Township)	08095
Winslow Junction	08095
Winston Park	07727
Wonder Lake	07480

Wood Acres-Zion NEW JERSEY 351

Name	ZIP
Wood Acres	07731
Woodbine	08270
Woodbridge (Middlesex County)	07095
Woodbridge (Middlesex County) (Township)	07095
Woodbridge Center	07095
Woodbridge Oaks	08830
Woodbridge Township	07095
Woodbury	08096
Woodbury Gardens	08096
Woodbury Heights	08097
Woodcliff	07047
Woodcliff Lake	07675
Woodcrest	08003
Woodglen	07830
Woodland (Township)	08019
Woodland Ridge	07801
Woodlynne	08107
Woodmere (Ocean County)	08527

Name	ZIP
Woodmere (Salem County)	08079
Woodport	07885
Wood-Ridge	07075
Woodruffs	08302
Woods Tavern	08876
Woodstown	08098
Woodstream	08053
Woodsville	08525
Woolwich (Township)	08085
Wortendyke (Part of Midland Park)	07432
Wrights Mill	08343
Wrightstown	08562
Wrightsville (Burlington County)	08077
Wrightsville (Monmouth County)	08526
Wyckoff (Bergen County) (Township)	07481

Name	ZIP
Wyckoff (Bergen County)	07481
Wyckoff Mills	07728
Wyckoffs Mills	08512
Wynnewood	08854
Yardville	08620
Yardville-Groveville	08620
Yellow Frame	07860
York Estates	08520
Yorketown	07726
Yorktown	08098
Youth Correctional Institution (Burlington County)	08505
Youth Correctional Institution (Hunterdon County)	08801
Zarephath	08890
Zion	08558

352 NEW MEXICO

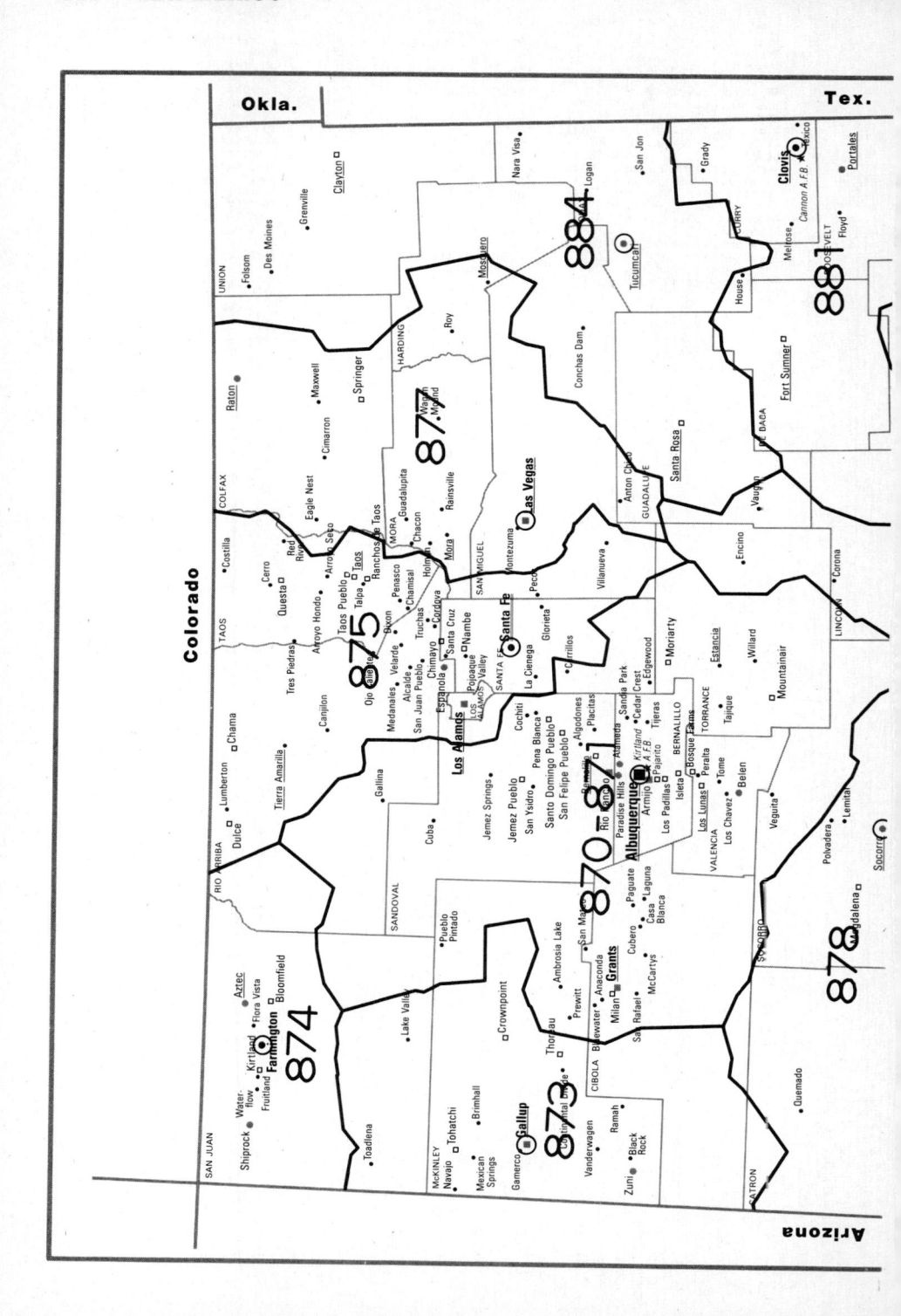

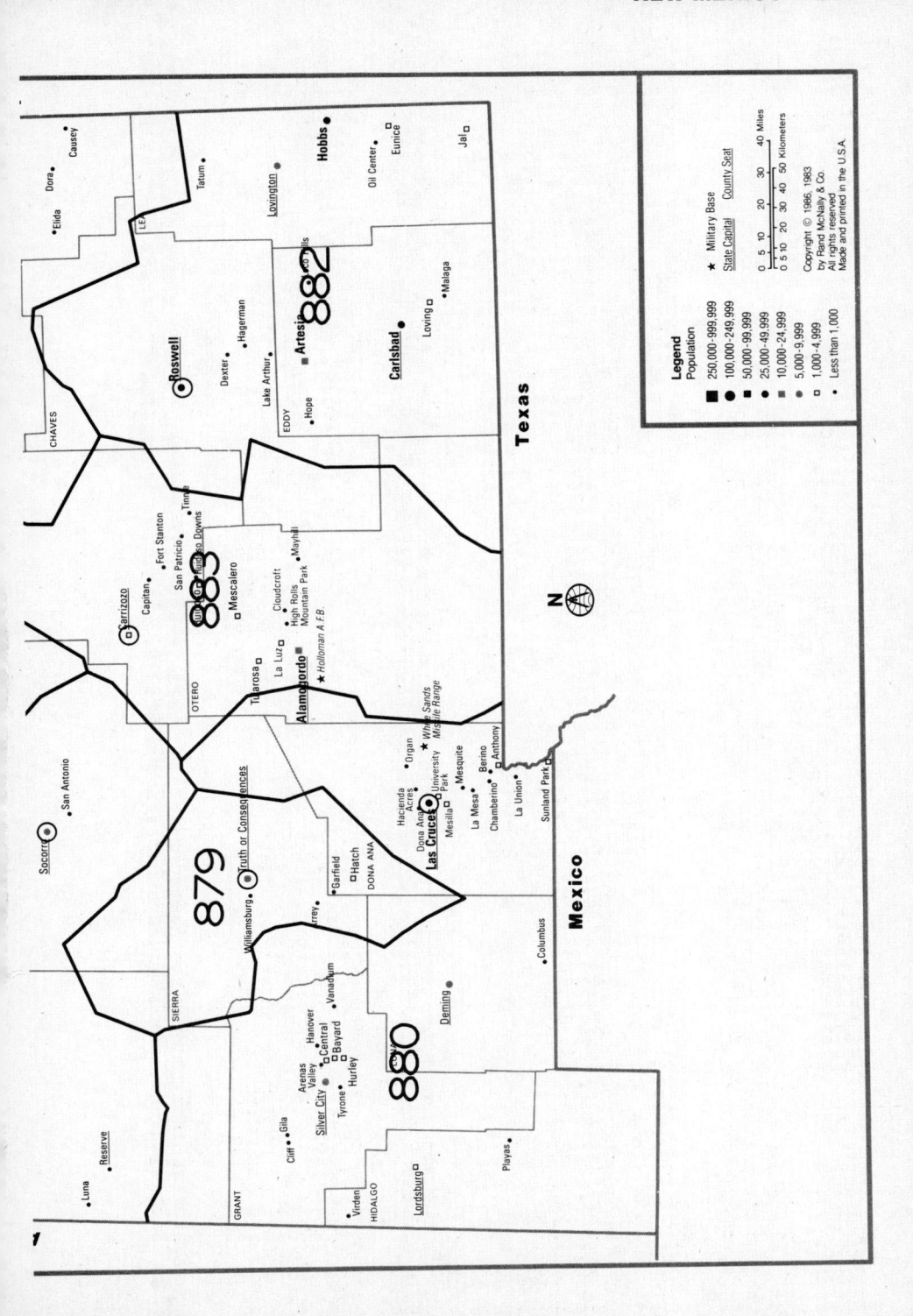

NEW MEXICO 353

354 NEW MEXICO Abbott-Emplazado

	ZIP		ZIP		ZIP
Abbott	87747	Boles	88311	Cochiti Lake	87041
Abeytas	87006	Boles Acres	88311	Colonias	88435
Abiquiu	87510	Bonito	88341	Columbine	87556
Abo	87036	Bosque	87006	Columbus	88029
Abuelo	87732	Bosque Farms	87068	Conchas Dam	88416
Acoma	87049	Boys Ranch	87002	Continental Divide	87312
Acoma Indian Reservation	87031	Brazos	87551	Contreras	87028
Acomita	87034	Bread Springs	87301	Coolidge	87312
Adelino	87031	Brimhall	87310	Corazon	87701
Adobe Acres	87105	Broadmoor (Part of Roswell)	88201	Cordova	87523
Agua Fria	87501	Broadview	88112	Corona	88318
Air Mail Facility (Part of Albuquerque)	87119	Broadview Acres	87020	Coronado (Part of Santa Fe)	87501
Alameda	87114	Buckeye	88260	Coronado Center (Part of Albuquerque)	87110
Alamillo	87831	Buckhorn	88025	Corrales	87048
Alamo	87825	Buena Vista	87712	Coruco	87560
Alamogordo	88310-11	Bueyeros	88412	Costilla	87524
For specific Alamogordo Zip Codes call (505) 437-9390		Burnham	87401	Cotton City	88020
		Butterfield Park	88001	Counselor	87018
Alamo Indian Reservation	87825	Caballo	87931	Country Club Estates (Bernalillo County)	87114
Albert	87733	Cameron	88120		
Albuquerque	87101-99	Campus (Part of Socorro)	87801	Country Club Estates (Lincoln County)	88345
For specific Albuquerque Zip Codes call (505) 848-3872		Canada de los Alamos	87501		
		Canjilon	87515	Country Club Heights (Part of Ruidoso)	88345
Alcalde	87511	Cannon AFB	88101		
Algodones	87001	Cannon Air Force Base	88103	Cowles	87573
Alire	87518	Canon	87571	Coyote	87012
Allison	87301	Canoncito (rural) (Bernalillo County)	87008	Cree Meadows Heights (Part of Ruidoso)	88345
Alma	88039				
Alpine Village	88345	Canoncito (Bernalillo County)	87026	Crossroads	88114
Alto	87312			Crownpoint	87313
Alto Crest (Part of Ruidoso)	88345	Canoncito (Rio Arriba County)	87527	Cruzville	87830
Amalia	87512			Crystal	87328
Ambrosia Lake	87020	Canoncito (San Miguel County)	87745	Cuba	87013
Amistad	88410			Cubero	87014
Anaconda	87020	Canoncito (Santa Fe County)	87505	Cuchillo	87932
Ancho	88301			Cuervo	88417
Angel Fire	87710	Canoncito Indian Reservation	87026	Cundiyo	87522
Angostura (Dona Ana County)	87940			Cuyamungue	87501
		Canones	87516	Dahlia	87711
Angostura (Taos County)	87579	Canon Plaza	87581	Dalies	87031
Angus	88316	Canova	87582	Dalton Pass	87313
Animas	88020	Canyon	87024	Datil	87821
Animas Valley Mall (Part of Farmington)	87401	Canyoncito	87535	Del Norte (Part of Ruidoso)	88345
		Capitan	88316	Deming	88030-31
Anthony	88021	Caprock	88213	For specific Deming Zip Codes call (505) 546-9461	
Anton Chico	87711	Capulin	88414		
Apache Creek	87830	Carlsbad	88220-21	Derry	87933
Apache Park	88345	For specific Carlsbad Zip Codes call (505) 885-5717		Des Moines	88418
Apodaca	87527			De Vargas Shopping Center (Part of Santa Fe)	87501
Arabela	88351	Carlsbad North	88220		
Aragon	87820	Carnuel	87112	Dexter	88230
Arch	88130	Carrizo	88345	Dilia	87724
Arenas Valley	88022	Carrizozo	88301	Dixon	87527
Arkansas Junction	88240	Carson	87517	Dog Canyon Estates	88310
Armijo	87105	Casa Blanca	87007	Domingo	87052
Arrey	87930	Causey	88113	Dona Ana	88032
Arroyo del Agua	87012	Cebolla	87518	Dora	88115
Arroyo Hondo	87513	Cedar Creek	88345	Downtown (Part of Albuquerque)	87103
Arroyo Seco	87514	Cedar Crest	87008		
Artesia	88210-11	Cedar Grove	87056	Dulce	87528
For specific Artesia Zip Codes call (505) 746-4412		Cedar Hill	87410	Dunken	88344
		Cedarvale	87009	Duran	88319
Artesia Camp	88347	Cedro Village	87059	Dusty	87943
Atoka	88210	Central	88026	Eagle Nest	87718
Atrisco (Part of Albuquerque)	87105	Central NM Correctional Facility	87031	East Grand Plains	88201
				East Pecos	87552
Aurora (Mora County)	87734	Cerrillos	87010	Edgewood	87015
Aurora (San Miguel County)	87583	Cerro	87519	El Ancon	87560
Aztec	87410	Chacon	87713	El Cerrito	87583
Bacaville (Part of Belen)	87002	Chama	87520	El Cerro	87031
Bard	88411	Chamberino	88027	Eldorado (Part of Albuquerque)	87111
Barelas (Part of Albuquerque)	87102	Chamisal	87521		
		Chamita	87566	Eldorado at Santa Fe	87505
Barranca	87510	Chaparral	88021	El Duende	87537
Bayard	88023	Chapelle	87569	Elephant Butte	87935
Becenti	87313	Chaperito	87701	Elephant Butte Estates	87935
Beclabito	87420	Chelwood Park (Part of Albuquerque)	87112	El Gauche	87566
Belen	87002			El Guique	87566
Bell Ranch	88441	Chical	87031	Elida	88116
Bellview	88111	Chi Chil Tah	87326	Elk	88339
Bennett	88252	Chili	87537	Elkins	88201
Bent	88314	Chilili	87059	El Llano	87004
Berino	88024	Chimayo	87522	El Llano (Rio Arriba County)	87532
Bernal	87569	Chippeway Park	88317		
Bernalillo	87004	Chloride	87943	El Llano (San Miguel County)	87701
Bernardo	87006	Chupadero	87501		
Beulah	87745	Church Rock	87311	El Morro	87034
Bibo	87055	Cimarron	87714	El Portero	87522
Bingham	87815	Claunch	87011	El Porvenir	87731
Bisti	87401	Clayton	88415	El Prado	87529
Black Forest (Part of Ruidoso)	88345	Cleveland	87715	El Pueblo	87560
		Cliff	88028	El Rancho	87532
Black Lake	87734	Clines Corners	87070	El Rancho Loma Linda	87579
Black River Village	88220	Cloud Country Estates	88317	El Renz-O-Ranch	87718
Black Rock	87327	Cloudcroft	88317	El Rincon de los Trujillos	87522
Blanchard	87569	Cloverdale	88020	El Rito	87530
Blanco	87412	Clovis	88101-03	El Turquillo	87722
Bloomfield	87413	For specific Clovis Zip Codes call (505) 763-5556		El Vado	87575
Bluewater (Cibola County)	87005			El Valle	87521
Bluewater (Lincoln County)	88351	Cochiti	87041	Embudo	87531
		Cochiti Indian Reservation	87041	Emplazado	87745

Enchanted Hills-Milnesand NEW MEXICO 355

Name	ZIP
Enchanted Hills (Part of Ruidoso)	88345
Encinal	87014
Encino	88321
Engel	87935
Ensenada	87575
Escabosa	87059
Escondida	87801
Espanola	87532
Estaca	87566
Estancia	87016
Eunice	88231
Fairacres	88033
Fairview (Part of Espanola)	87533
Farley	88422
Farmington	87401
Faywood	88034
Faywood Hot Springs	88034
Fence Lake	87315
Field	88124
Fierro	88041
First Plaza (Part of Albuquerque)	87102
Five Points	87105
Flora Vista	87415
Florida	87801
Floyd	88118
Flume Canyon (Part of Ruidoso)	88345
Flying H	88322
Folsom	88419
Forest Heights (Part of Ruidoso)	88345
Forest Park	87008
Forrest	88427
Fort Bliss	79916
Fort Stanton	88323
Fort Sumner	88119
Fort Wingate	87316
Fort Wingate Depot Activity	87301
French Corners	87747
Fruitland	87416
Gabaldon	87701
Galisteo	87010
Gallegos	88426
Gallina	87017
Gallina Plaza	87017
Gallinas	87731
Gallup	87301-05
For specific Gallup Zip Codes call (505) 863-3491	
Gamerco	87317
Garanbuio	87568
Garfield	87936
Garita	88421
Garrison	88132
Gascon	87742
Gavilan	87029
Gila	88038
Gila Hot Springs	88061
Gladstone	88422
Glencoe	88324
Glen Grove (Part of Ruidoso)	88345
Glenrio	88423
Glenwood	88039
Glorieta	87535
Gobernador	87412
Golden	87047
Golondrinas	87712
Gonzales Ranch	87536
Grady	88120
Gran Quivira	87036
Grants	87020
Greenfield	88230
Green Meadows (Part of Ruidoso)	88345
Grenville	88424
Grier	88101
Guachupangue	87532
Guadalupita	87722
Hachita	88040
Hacienda Acres	88001
Hagerman	88232
Hamilton Terrace (Part of Ruidoso)	88345
Hanover	88041
Happy Valley	88220
Hatch	87937
Hayden	88410
Hernandez	87537
Highland (Part of Albuquerque)	87108
High Rolls	88325
Hill	88005
Hillburn City	88260
Hillsboro	88042
Hobbies	87059
Hobbs	88240-41
For specific Hobbs Zip Codes call (505) 393-2912	

Name	ZIP
Hoffman Town (Part of Albuquerque)	87112
Holiday Acres (Part of Ruidoso)	88345
Hollene	88101
Holloman AFB	88330
Holloman Air Force Base	88330
Hollywood (Part of Ruidoso)	88345
Holman	87723
Hondo	88336
Hooverville	88416
Hope	88250
Horse Springs	87821
Hospah	87313
Hot Springs	87731
Hot Springs Landing	87935
House	88121
Humble City	88240
Hurley	88043
Hyde Park Estates	87501
Idlewild	87718
Ilfeld	87538
Indian Hills (Part of Ruidoso)	88345
Isleta	87022
Isleta Indian Reservation	87022
Isleta Pueblo	87022
Iyanbito	87316
Jacona	87501
Jal	88252
Jarales	87023
Jemez Indian Reservation	87024
Jemez Pueblo	87024
Jemez Springs	87025
Jicarilla Apache Indian Reservation	87528
Jordan	88427
Kenna	88122
Kingston	88042
Kingswood (Part of Ruidoso)	88345
Kirtland	87417
Kirtland Air Force Base (Bernalillo County)	87115
Kirtland Air Force Base East (Bernalillo County)	87115
Knowles	88240
La Bolsa	87531
La Cienega	87501
La Constancia	87002
La Cueva (Mora County)	87712
La Cueva (Santa Fe County)	87535
La Fraqua	87568
Laguna	87026
Laguna Indian Reservation	87026
Lagunita	87560
La Huerta	88220
La Jara	87027
La Joya (Santa Fe County)	87535
Lajoya (Socorro County)	87028
La Junta	87531
Lake Arthur	88253
Lake Valley	87313
Lake View Pines	87718
Lakewood	88254
La Ladera	87031
La Loma	87724
La Luz	88337
Lama	87556
La Madera (Rio Arriba County)	87539
La Madera (Sandoval County)	87047
La Manga	87701
La Mesa	88044
La Mesilla	87532
Lamy	87540
La Plata	87418
La Puebla	87532
La Puente	87575
Las Cruces	88001-08
For specific Las Cruces Zip Codes call (505) 525-2841	
Las Mochas	87579
Las Nutrias	87062
Las Palomas	87942
Las Placitas	87530
Las Tablas	87541
Las Tusas	87745
Las Vegas	87701
La Union	88021
La Villita	87511
Ledoux	87725
Lemitar	87823
Levy	87752
Leyba	87560
Lincoln	88338
Linda Vista (Part of Roswell)	88201
Lindrith	87029
Lingo	88123
Little Walnut Village	88061

Name	ZIP
Littlewater	87461
Llano	87543
Llano del Medio	87724
Llano Largo	87561
Llano Quemado	87557
Llaves	87027
Loco Hills	88255
Logan	88426
Lordsburg	88045
Los Alamos (Los Alamos County)	87544
Los Alamos (San Miguel County)	87745
Los Candelarias (Part of Albuquerque)	87107
Los Chavez	87002
Los Cordovas	87571
Los Duranes (Part of Albuquerque)	87104
Los Febres	87734
Los Griegos (Part of Albuquerque)	87107
Los Huecos	87734
Los Lentes (Part of Los Lunas)	87031
Los Luceros	87511
Los Lunas	87031
Los Lunas Correctional Center	87031
Los Lunas Hospital and Training School	87031
Los Montoyas	87701
Los Ojos	87551
Los Pachecos	87522
Los Padillas	87105
Los Pinos	81120
Los Ranchos	87101
Los Ranchos de Albuquerque	87107
Lost Lodge	88317
Los Trujillos	87002
Los Vigiles	87701
Lourdes	87701
Lovato	87568
Loving	88256
Lovington	88260
Lower La Posada	87552
Lower Nutria	87327
Lower Pueblo	87560
Lower Ranchito	87581
Lower Rociada	87742
Lower San Francisco Plaza	87830
Lucero	87736
Lucy	87063
Luis Lopez	87801
Lumberton	87547
Luna	87824
Lyden	87582
McAlister	88427
McCartys (Cibola County)	87049
McCartys (Harding County)	88430
McDonald	88262
McGaffey	87316
McIntosh	87032
Madrid	87010
Maes	87701
Magdalena	87825
Malaga	88263
Maljamar	88264
Mangas	87821
Mangas Springs	88061
Manuelitas	87745
Manuelito	87319
Manzano (Bernalillo County)	87112
Manzano (Torrance County)	87036
Mariano Lake	87301
Maxwell	87728
Mayhill	88339
Meadow Lake	87031
Medanales	87548
Melrose	88124
Mentmore	87319
Mesa Poleo	87012
Mescalero	88340
Mescalero Apache Indian Reservation	88340
Mesilla	88046
Mesilla Park (Part of Las Cruces)	88047
Mesilla Valley Mall (Part of Las Cruces)	88001
Mesita	87026
Mesquite	88048
Mexican Springs	87320
Miami	87729
Midway	88201
Milagro	88321
Milan	87021
Mills	87730
Milnesand	88125

356 NEW MEXICO Mimbres-Silver City

	ZIP		ZIP		ZIP
Mimbres	88049	Pintada	88435	San Antonio (Bernalillo County)	87008
Mimbres Hot Springs	88041	Placita	87579	San Antonio (San Miguel County)	87701
Mineral Hill	87701	Placitas (Dona Ana County)	87937	San Antonio (Socorro County)	87832
Mission Park	87031	Placitas (Rio Arriba County)	87515	San Antonio de Padua del Rancho	87501
Mogollon	88039	Placitas (Sandoval County)	87043	San Antonito (Bernalillo County)	87047
Monero	87547	Placitas (Sierra County)	87939	San Antonito (Socorro County)	87832
Monte Aplanado	87732	Playas	88009	Sanchez	87746
Monte Verde (Part of Angel Fire)	87718	Plaza Blanca	87563	San Cristobal	87564
Montezuma	87731	Pleasant Hill	88135	Sanctuario	87522
Montgomery Plaza Mall (Part of Albuquerque)	87110	Pleasanton	88039	Sandia	87047
Monticello	87939	Pojoaque Indian Reservation	87501	Sandia Base	87115
Montoya	88401	Pojoaque Valley	87501	Sandia Indian Reservation	87004
Monument	88265	Polvadera	87828	Sandia Knolls	87047
Moqino	87040	Ponderosa	87044	Sandia Park	87047
Mora	87732	Ponderosa Heights (Part of Ruidoso)	88345	Sandia Pueblo	87004
Moriarty	87035	Ponderosa Pines	87059	San Felipe Indian Reservation	87004
Mosquero	87733	Portales	88130	San Felipe Pueblo	87001
Mountainair	87036	Pot Creek	87571	San Fidel	87049
Mountain Park	88325	Prairie Dog Trading Post	87013	San Francisco	87006
Mountain View (Bernalillo County)	87105	Prairieview	88260	San Francisco Plaza	87830
Mountain View (Chaves County)	88201	Prewitt	87045	San Geronimo	87701
Mount Dora	88429	Progresso	87063	San Ignacio	87745
Mule Creek	88051	Pueblito	87566	San Ildefonso Indian Reservation	87502
Nadine	88240	Pueblitos	87002	San Ildefonso Pueblo	87501
Nageezi	87037	Pueblo de Acoma	87034	San Jon	88434
Nambe	87501	Pueblo Pintado	87013	San Jose (Bernalillo County)	87102
Nambe Indian Reservation	87501	Puerto de Luna	88432	San Jose (Rio Arriba County)	87537
Nambe Pueblo	87501	Punta de Agua	87036	San Jose (San Miguel County)	87565
Nara Visa	88430	Quarris Acres	88317	San Juan	87565
Naschitti	87325	Quarteles	87532	San Juan Indian Reservation	87566
Navajo	87328	Quay	88433	San Juan Pueblo	87566
Navajo Dam	87419	Queen	88220	San Lorenzo	88041
Navajo Estates	87375	Quemado	87829	San Mateo	87050
Navajo Indian Reservation	86515	Questa	87556	San Miguel (Dona Ana County)	88058
Navajo Wingate Village	87311	Radium Springs	88054	San Miguel (Rio Arriba County)	81120
Newcomb	87455	Rainsville	87736	San Miguel (San Miguel County)	87560
Newkirk	88431	Ramah	87321	Sanostee	87461
New Laguna	87038	Ramah Navajo Indian Reservation	87327	San Pablo	87701
New York	87014	Ramon	88136	San Patricio	88348
Nogal	88341	Ranchito	87571	San Pedro	87532
North Carmen	87732	Ranchitos	87532	San Rafael (Cibola County)	87051
North Hurley	88043	Rancho Grande Estates	87830	San Rafael (San Miguel County)	88439
North San Ysidro	87538	Ranchos de Taos	87557	San Sebastian	87501
North Valley	87107	Ranchos Lake Conchas	88416	Santa Ana Indian Reservation	87004
Nutrias	87575	Ranchvale	88101	Santa Ana Pueblo	87004
Ocate	87734	Raton	87740	Santa Clara Indian Reservation	87532
Oil Center	88266	Red Hill	87829	Santa Clara Pueblo	87532
Ojito (Rio Arriba County)	87029	Red River	87558	Santa Cruz	87567
Ojito (Taos County)	87521	Redrock (Grant County)	88055	Santa Fe	87501-06
Ojitos Frios	87701	Red Rock (McKinley County)	87420	For specific Santa Fe Zip Codes call (505) 988-6351	
Ojo Caliente (Cibola County)	87327	Regina	87046	Santa Rosa	88435
Ojo Caliente (Taos County)	87549	Rehoboth	87322	Santa Teresa	88008
Ojo Feliz	87735	Rencona	87562	Santo Domingo Indian Reservation	87052
Ojo Sarco	87550	Reserve	87830	Santo Domingo Pueblo	87052
Old Albuquerque (Part of Albuquerque)	87104	Ribera	87560	Santo Nino	87567
Old Picacho	88033	Rincon	87940	Santo Tomas	88044
Omega	87829	Rinconada	87531	San Ysidro	87053
Organ	88052	Rincon Montoso	87745	Sapello	87745
Orogrande	88342	Rio Chiquito	87522	Seama	87014
Oscura	88301	Rio Communities	87002	Seboyeta	87055
Otis	88220	Rio Grande Estates	87002	Sedan	88436
Paguate	87040	Rio Lucio	87553	Sedillo Hill	87059
Pajarito (Bernalillo County)	87105	Rio Puerco	87064	Sena	87568
Pajarito (Santa Fe County)	87532	Rio Rancho	87124	Seneca	88437
Paradise Hills	87114	Rio West Mall (Part of Gallup)	87301	Separ	88045
Paraje	87007	Rito de las Sillas	87064	Serafina	87569
Park Springs	87701	Riverside (Eddy County)	88210	Servilleta Plaza	87539
Pastura	88435	Riverside (Lincoln County)	88201	Seton Village	87501
Paxton Springs	87020	Robin Hood Park	88317	Seven Lakes	87313
Pecos	87552	Rociada	87742	Seven Rivers	88254
Pena Blanca	87041	Rock Canyon	87935	Seven Springs	87025
Penasco	87553	Rock Springs	87301	Shady Brook	87571
Penasco Blanco	87742	Rodarte	87561	Sheep Springs	87364
Pendaries	87742	Rodeo	88056	Sherman	88041
Penitentiary of New Mexico	87501	Rodey	87937	Shiprock	87420
Pep	88126	Rogers	88132	Sierra Vista	88312
Peralta	87042	Romeroville	87701	Sierra Vista Estates	87008
Perea	87316	Rosebud	88410	Sile	87041
Pescado	87327	Roswell	88201-02	Silver Acres	88061
Petaca	87554	For specific Roswell Zip Codes call (505) 622-3741		Silver City	88061-62
Philadelphia	87014	Roswell Mall (Part of Roswell)	88201	For specific Silver City Zip Codes call (505) 538-2831	
Philmont	87714	Rowe	87562		
Picacho	88343	Roy	87743		
Picuris	87553	Ruidoso	88345		
Picuris Indian Reservation	87553	Ruidoso Downs	88346		
Pie Town	87827	Rutheron	87563		
Pilar	87571	Sabinal	87006		
Pine	87552	Sabinoso	87746		
Pinedale	87301	Sacramento	88347		
Pine Hill	87321	St. Vrain	88133		
Pine View	87579	Salem	87941		
Pineywoods Estates	88317	San Acacia	87831		
Pinon	88344	San Andres-Alameda Estates	88001		
Pinos Altos	88053				
Pinoswells	87009				

Sipapu-Zuni Indian Reservation NEW MEXICO 357

	ZIP		ZIP		ZIP
Sipapu	87579	Tocito	87461	Vaughn	88353
Sixteen Springs	88317	Tohatchi	87325	Veguita	87062
Smith Lake	87323	Tohlakai	87301	Velarde	87582
Socorro	87801	Tolar	88134	Ventero	87512
Sofia	88424	Tome	87060	Vermejo Park	87740
Soham	87565	T-O Ranch	87740	Villa Linda Mall (Part of	
Solano	87746	Torreon (Sandoval County)	87013	Santa Fe)	87505
Sombrillo	87532	Torreon (Torrance County)	87061	Villa Madonna	88312
South Carmen	87725	Tortugas	88047	Villanueva	87583
Southern New Mexico		Totavi	87544	Virden	85534
Correctional Facility	88004	Trampas	87576	Volcano Cliffs (Part of	
South San Ysidro	87565	Trechado	87315	Albuquerque)	87120
South Springs Acres	88201	Trementina	88439	Wagon Mound	87752
South Valley	87102	Tres Piedras	87577	Walker (Part of Roswell)	88201
Spencerville	87410	Tres Ritos	87579	Waterfall	88317
Springer	87747	Truchas	87578	Waterflow	87421
Springstead	87311	Trujillo	87701	Watrous	87753
Squirrel Springs	87325	Truth or Consequences	87901	Weed	88354
Standing Rock	87313	Tse Bonito	86515	Western New Mexico	
Stanley	87056	Tucumcari	88401	Correctional Facility	87020
Star Lake	87013	Tularosa	88352	Westgate Heights (Part of	
Stead	88438	Turley	87412	Albuquerque)	87105
Sumner Lake State Park	88119	Turn	87002	West Las Vegas (Part of	
Sunland Park	88063	Twin Forks Estates	88317	Las Vegas)	87701
Sunshine	88030	Twin Lakes	87301	White Horse	87013
Sunspot	88349	Two Gray Hills	87325	White Lakes	87056
Sun Valley	88312	Two Wells	87326	White Oaks	88301
Taiban	88134	Tyrone	88065	White Rock (Los Alamos	
Tajique	87057	University (Bernalillo County)	87106	County)	87544
Talpa	87557	University (Roosevelt		White Rock (San Juan	
Taos	87571	County)	88130	County)	87313
Taos Indian Reservation	87571	University Park	88003	White Sands	88002
Taos Pueblo	87571	Upper Anton Chico	87711	White Sands Missile Range	88002
Taos Ski Valley	87571	Upper Dilia	87724	Whites City	88268
Tatum	88267	Upper Pueblo	87560	White Signal	88061
Tecolote	87701	Upper Rociada	87742	Willard	87063
Tecolotito	87711	Uptown (Part of		Williams Acres	87301
Tererro	87573	Albuquerque)	87110	Williamsburg	87942
Tesuque	87574	Ute Mountain Indian		Willow Creek	88039
Tesuque Indian Reservation	87574	Reservation	81334	Winrock Center (Part of	
Tesuque Pueblo	87501	Ute Park	87749	Albuquerque)	87110
Texico	88135	Vadito	87579	Winston	87943
Thoreau	87323	Vado	88072	Wyoming Mall, The (Part of	
Three Rivers	88352	Valdez	87580	Albuquerque)	87112
Tierra Amarilla	87575	Valencia	87031	Yah-Ta-Hey	87375
Tierra Monte	87742	Vallecitos	87581	Yeso	88136
Tijeras	87059	Vallecitos de los Indios	87025	Youngsville	87064
Timberon	88350	Valle Escondido	87571	Zamora	87059
Tinian	87401	Valmora	87750	Zia Indian Reservation	87053
Tinnie	88351	Val Verde	87718	Zia Pueblo	87053
Tiptonville	87753	Vanadium	88023	Zuni	87327
Toadlena	87324	Vanderwagen	87326	Zuni Indian Reservation	87327

358   NEW YORK

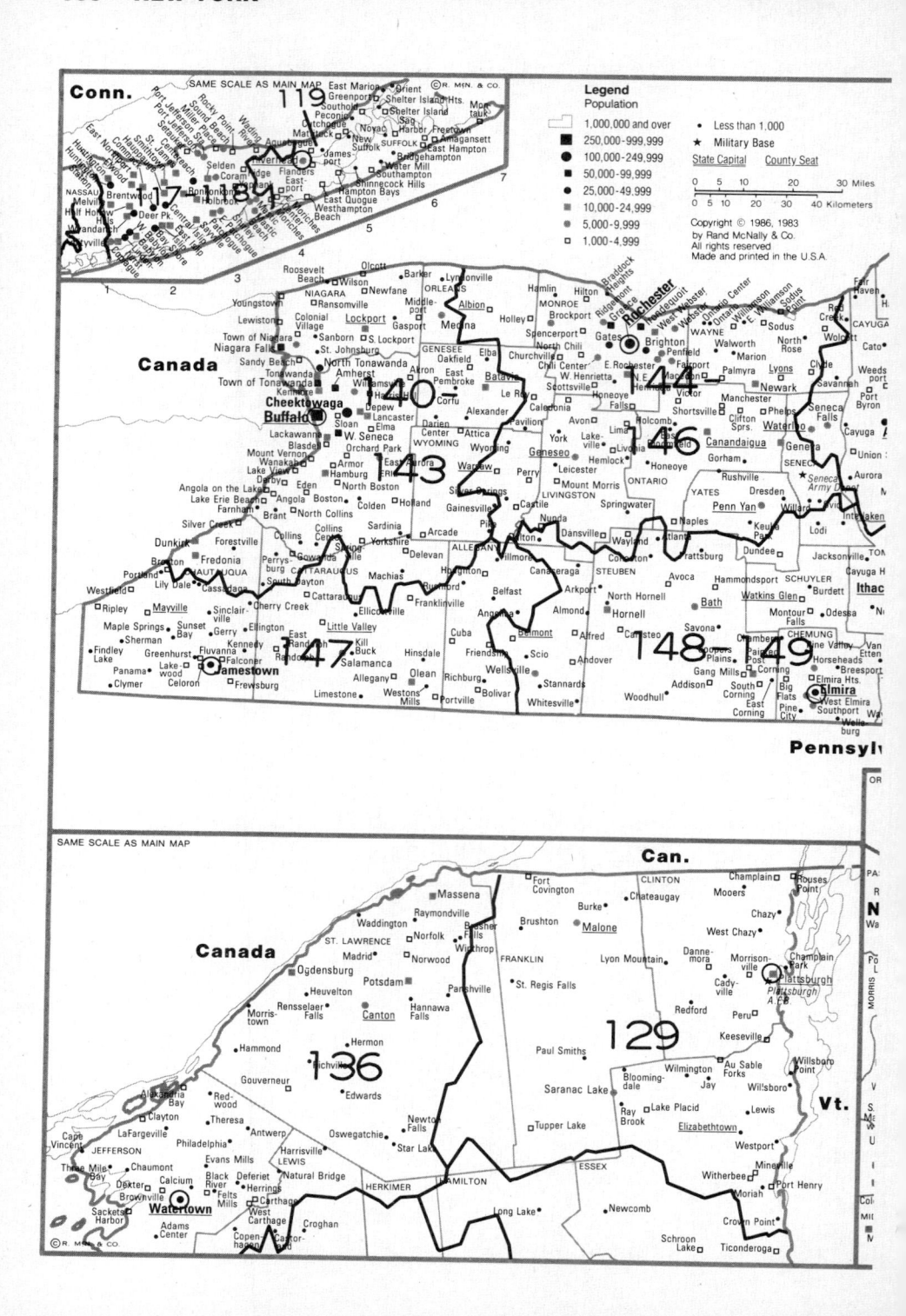

NEW YORK 359

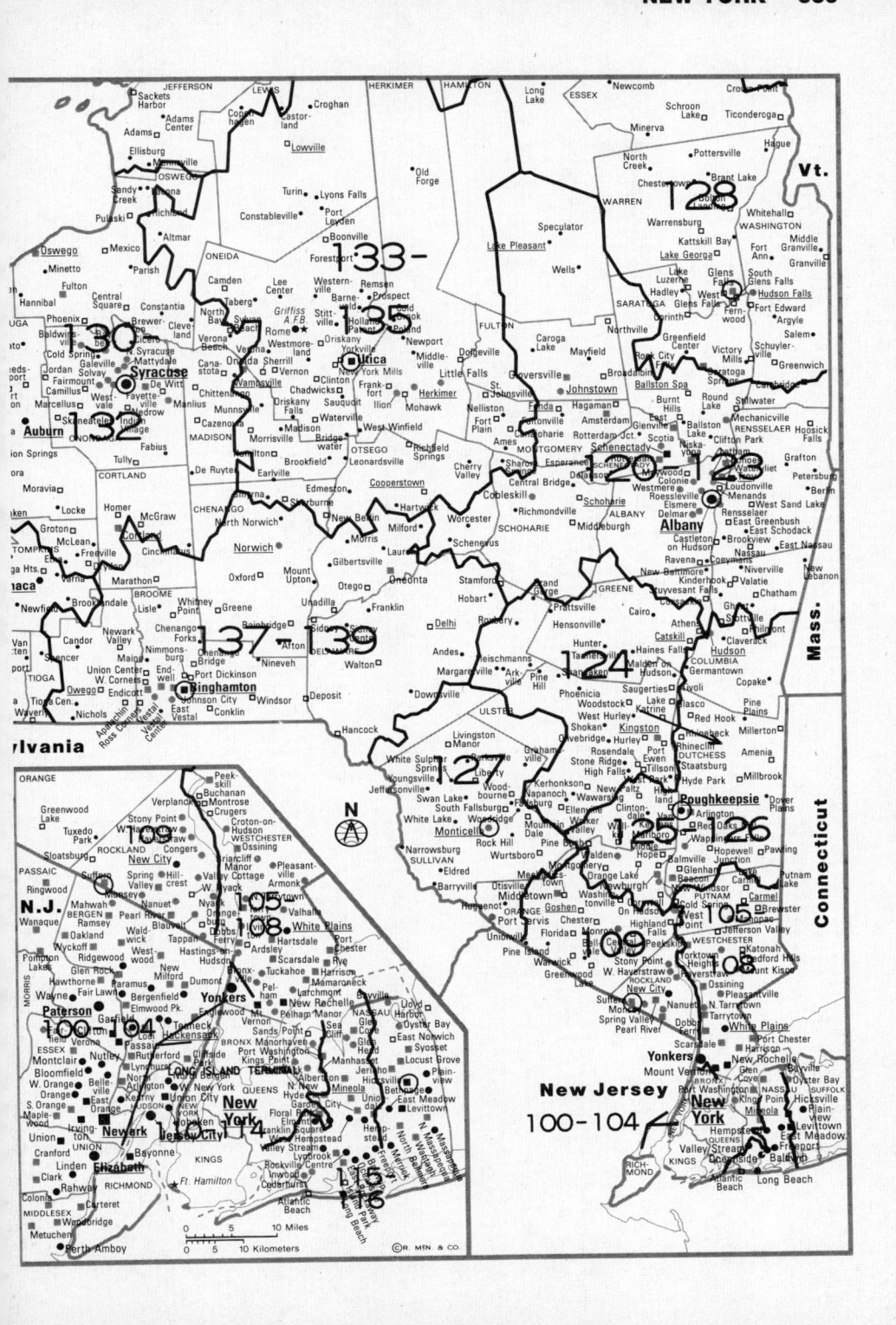

360 NEW YORK Abbotts-Basom

	ZIP
Abbotts	14727
Academy (Albany County)	12208
Academy (Ontario County)	14424
Accord	12404
Acidalia	12760
Acra	12405
Adams	13605
Adams (Town)	13605
Adams Basin	14410
Adams Center	13606
Adams Corners	10579
Adams Cove	13634
Adamsville	12827
Addison	14801
Addison (Town)	14801
Addison Hill	16920
Adelphi (Part of New York)	11238
Adirondack	12808
Adrian	14823
Afton	13730
Afton (Town)	13730
Afton Lake	13730
Airmont	10901
Airmont Heights	10901
Akins Corners	12563
Akron	14001
Alabama	14003
Alabama (Town)	14003
Albany	12201-60
For specific Albany Zip Codes call (518) 452-2499	
Albany Medical Center (Part of Albany)	12208
Albertson	11507
Albia (Part of Troy)	12180
Albion	14411
Albion (Orleans County) (Town)	14411
Albion (Oswego County) (Town)	13302
Albion Correctional Facility	14411
Alcove	12007
Alden	14004
Alden (Town)	14004
Alden Bend	12910
Alden Center	14004
Alden Manor	11003
Alder Creek	13301
Alexander	14005
Alexander (Town)	14005
Alexander Corners	13650
Alexander Shopping Center (Part of Yonkers)	10710
Alexandria (Town)	13607
Alexandria Bay	13607
Alfred (Town)	14802
Alfred	14802
Alfred Station	14803
Allaben	12480
Allard Corners	12586
Allegany	14706
Allegany (Town)	14706
Allegany Indian Reservation (Cattaraugus County) (Town)	14081
Allegany Indian Reservation (Cattaraugus County)	14081
Allen (Town)	14709
Allen Center	14735
Allens Hill	14469
Allentown	14707
Allenwood	11021
Allerton (Part of New York)	10467
Alligerville	12440
Alloway	14489
Alma	14708
Alma (Town)	14708
Almond	14804
Almond (Town)	14804
Aloquin	14561
Alpine	14805
Alplaus	12008
Alps	12018
Alsen	12415
Altamont (Albany County)	12009
Altamont (Franklin County) (Town)	12986
Altay	14837
Altmar	13302
Alton	14413
Altona	12910
Altona (Town)	12910
Amagansett	11930
Amawalk	10501
Amber	13110
Amberville	13843
Amboy (Onondaga County)	13031
Amboy (Oswego County) (Town)	13493
Amboy Center	13493
Amchir (Part of Middletown)	10940

	ZIP
Amenia	12501
Amenia (Town)	12501
Amenia Union	12501
Ames	13317
Amherst	14226
Amherst (Town)	14226
Amity (Allegany County) (Town)	14813
Amity (Orange County)	10990
Amity Harbor	11701
Amityville	11701
Amsdell Heights	14075
Amsterdam (Montgomery County)	12010
Amsterdam (Montgomery County) (Town)	12010
Ancram	12502
Ancram (Town)	12502
Ancramdale	12503
Andes	13731
Andes (Town)	13731
Andover	14806
Andover (Town)	14806
Andrea Park Estates	10598
Angelica	14709
Angelica (Town)	14709
Angola	14006
Angola on the Lake	14006
Annandale-on-Hudson	12504
Annsville (Oneida County) (Town)	13471
Annsville (Westchester County)	10566
Ansonia (Part of New York)	10023
Antwerp	13608
Antwerp (Town)	13608
Apalachin	13732
Apex	13783
Appleton	14008
Apulia	13159
Apulia Station	13020
Aquebogue	11931
Aqueduct	12308
Aquetuck	12143
Arcade	14009
Arcade (Town)	14009
Arcade Junction (Part of Arcade)	14009
Arcadia (Town)	14513
Archdale	12834
Archville	10510
Arden	10910
Ardonia	12515
Ardsley	10502
Ardsley-on-Hudson (Part of Irvington)	10503
Argusville	13459
Argyle	12809
Argyle (Town)	12809
Arietta (Town)	12139
Arkport	14807
Arkville	12406
Arkwright (Town)	14718
Arlington	12603
Arlyn Oaks	11758
Armonk	10504
Armor	14075
Arnolds Mill	12037
Arrochar (Part of New York)	10305
Arthur Manor (Part of Scarsdale)	10583
Arthursburg	12533
Arverne (Part of New York)	11692
Asharoken	11768
Ashford (Cattaraugus County)	14731
Ashford (Cattaraugus County) (Town)	14171
Ashford Hollow	14171
Ashland (Town)	12407
Ashland (Chemung County) (Town)	14894
Ashland (Greene County)	12407
Ashokan	12481
Ashville (Chautauqua County)	14710
Ashville Bay	14710
Ashwood	14098
Aspenwood	12065
Aspinwall Corners	13650
Assembly Point	12845
Association Island	13651
Astoria (Part of New York)	11102
Athens	12015
Athens (Town)	12015
Athol	12810
Athol Springs	14010
Atlanta	14808
Atlantic (Part of New York)	10307
Atlantic Beach	11509
Atlantique	11706

	ZIP
Attica	14011
Attica (Town)	14011
Attica Center	14011
Attica Correctional Facility	14011
Attlebury	12581
Atwater	13081
Atwell	13338
Atwood	12484
Auburn	13021-24
For specific Auburn Zip Codes call (315) 252-9554	
Audubon (Part of New York)	10032
Augusta	13425
Augusta (Town)	13425
Aurelius (Town)	13034
Auriesville	12016
Aurora (Cayuga County)	13026
Aurora (Erie County) (Town)	14052
Aurora Tract	13088
Au Sable (Town)	12944
Au Sable Chasm	12944
Au Sable Forks	12912
Austerlitz	12017
Austerlitz (Town)	12017
Ava	13303
Ava (Town)	13303
Averill Park	12018
Avoca	14809
Avoca (Town)	14809
Avon	14414
Avon (Town)	14414
Axeville	14726
Babcock Hill	13318
Babcock Lake	12138
Babylon	11702-04
For specific Babylon Zip Codes call (516) 669-1318	
Bacon Hill	12871
Baggs Corner	13601
Bainbridge	13733
Bainbridge (Town)	13733
Baiting Hollow	11933
Bakers Mills	12811
Bakerstand	14101
Balcom	14138
Balcom Beach	14777
Bald Mountain	12834
Baldwin (Chemung County) (Town)	14861
Baldwin (Nassau County)	11510
Baldwin Heights (Part of Olean)	14760
Baldwin Place	10505
Baldwin Place Shopping Center	10505
Baldwinsville	13027
Ballina	13035
Ballston (Town)	12019
Ballston Center	12020
Ballston Lake	12019
Ballston Spa	12020
Balltown	14062
Balmat	13609
Balmville	12550
Baltimore	13141
Bangall (Dutchess County)	12506
Bangall (Onondaga County)	13112
Bangor	12966
Bangor (Town)	12966
Bangor Station	12966
Bank Plaza	11566
Barberville	12018
Barcelona	14787
Barclay Heights (Part of Saugerties)	12477
Bardonia	10954
Barker (Broome County) (Town)	13746
Barker (Niagara County)	14012
Barkers Grove	12154
Barkersville	12850
Barkertown	14836
Barnegat	12603
Barnerville	12092
Barnes Corners	13610
Barnes Hole	11930
Barneveld	13304
Barnum Island	11558
Barre (Town)	14411
Barre Center	14411
Barrington (Town)	14837
Barrytown	12507
Barryville	12719
Bartlett	13440
Bartlett Corners	14468
Bartlett Hollow	13775
Barton	13734
Barton (Town)	13734
Basket	12760
Basom	14013

Batavia-Brant **NEW YORK** 361

	ZIP		ZIP		ZIP
Batavia	14020-21	Bellevue	14225	Blauvelt	10913
For specific Batavia Zip Codes call (716) 343-0491		Bellevue Gardens	12151	Bleecker	12078
		Bellmont (Town)	12917	Bleecker (Town)	12078
Batchellerville	12134	Bellmont Center	12920	Blenheim (Town)	12131
Bates	12469	Bellmore	11710	Bliss	14024
Bath	14810	Bellona	14415	Blockville	14710
Bath (Town)	14810		14527	Blodgett Mills	13738
Bath Beach (Part of New York)	11214	For specific Bellona Zip Codes call (716) 526-5500		Bloomfield (Part of New York)	10314
Battenville	12834	Bellow Corners	14171	Bloomingburg	12721
Battery Park City (Part of New York)	10007	Bellport	11713	Bloomingdale	12913
		Bellvale	10912	Blooming Grove	10914
Baxter Estates	11050	Bellville	14717	Blooming Grove (Town)	10914
Bay (Part of New York)	11235	Belmont	14813	Bloomington	12411
Bayberry	13088	Belvidere	14813	Bloomington-Hickory Bush	12401
Bayberry Dunes	11772	Bemis Heights	12170	Bloomville	13739
Bayberry-Lynelle Meadows	13088	Bemus Point	14712	Blossvale	13308
Bayberry Park (Part of New Rochelle)	10804	Benedict Beach	14464	Blue Mountain	12477
		Bennett Bridge	13302	Blue Mountain Lake	12812
Bayberry Shopping Center	13088	Bennettsburg	14818	Blue Point	11715
Baychester (Part of New York)	10469	Bennettsville	13733	Blue Ridge	12534
		Bennington	14011	Blue Stores	12526
Bay Park	11518	Bennington (Town)	14011	Bluff Point	14478
Bay Point	11963	Benson	12134	Blythebourne (Part of New York)	11219
Bayport	11705	Benson (Town)	12134		
Bay Ridge (Part of New York)	11220	Benson Mines	13690	Boardmanville (Part of Olean)	14760
		Benton (Town)	14527		
Bay Shore (Suffolk County)	11706	Benton Center	14527	Boerum Hill (Part of New York)	11201
Bay Shores	13110	Berea	12549		
Bayside (Part of New York)	11360	Bergen	14416	Boght Corners	12047
		Bergen (Town)	14416	Bohemia	11716
Bay Terrace (Queens County)	11360	Bergen Beach	14847	Boiceville	12412
		Bergen Park	11746	Bolivar	14715
Bay Terrace (Richmond County)	10306	Bergholtz	14304	Bolivar (Town)	14715
		Berkshire (Town)	13736	Bolton	12824
Bay View (Erie County)	14075	Berkshire (Fulton County)	12078	Bolton (Town)	12824
Bayview (Suffolk County)	11971	Berkshire (Onondaga County)	13066	Bolton Landing	12814
Bayville	11709			Bolts Corners	13147
Beach Hampton	11930	Berkshire (Tioga County)	13736	Bombay	12914
Beach Ridge	14120	Berkshire Terrace	10512	Bombay (Town)	12914
Beach Shopping Center (Part of Peekskill)	10566	Berlin	12022	Bon Air Heights (Part of Suffern)	10901
		Berlin (Town)	12022		
Beachville	14807	Berne	12023	Bonney	13464
Beacon	12508	Berne (Town)	12023	Bonni Castle	14590
Beacon Hill	12508	Bernhards Bay	13028	Bonnie Crest (Part of New Rochelle)	10804
Beantown	14859	Berryville	12068		
Bear Mountain	10911	Berwyn	13084	Bonny Lee Estates	12184
Bearsville	12409	Best	12018	Boonville	13309
Beaver Brook	12764	Bethany	14054	Boonville (Town)	13309
Beavertown Lake	12550	Bethany (Town)	14054	Borden	14801
Beaver Dams	14812	Bethel (Town)	12720	Border City (Ontario County)	14456
Beaver Falls	13305	Bethel (Dutchess County)	12567		
Beaverkill	12758	Bethel (Sullivan County)	12720	Border City (Seneca County)	14456
Beaver Meadow	13832	Bethel Corners	13111		
Beaver River	13367	Bethel Grove	14850	Borodino	13152
Beckers Corners	12158	Bethford	14219	Borough Hall (Part of New York)	11424
Becks Grove (Part of Rome)	13308	Bethlehem (Town)	12054		
		Bethlehem Center	12077	Boston	14025
Bedell	12430	Bethlehem Heights	12161	Boston (Town)	14025
Bedford (Town)	10506	Bethpage	11714	Boston Corners	12546
Bedford (Kings County)	11210	Beukendaal	12302	Botanical (Part of York)	10458
Bedford (Westchester County)	10506	Beverly Inn Corners	13315		
		Bible School Park (Part of Johnson City)	13737	Bouckville	13310
Bedford Hills	10507			Boughton Hill	14564
Bedford Hills Correctional Facility	10507	Bidwell (Part of Buffalo)	14222	Boulevard (Part of New York)	10459
		Big Brook	13486		
Bedford-Stuyvesant (Part of New York)	11233	Big Flats	14814	Boulevard Mall	14226
		Big Flats (Town)	14814	Boultons Beach (Part of Sackets Harbor)	13685
Beecher Corners	12442	Big Fresh Pond	11968		
Beechertown	13697	Big H Shopping Center	11743	Bouquet	12936
Beech Hill (Part of Yonkers)	10710	Big Indian	12410	Bournes Beach	14787
Beechmont (Part of New Rochelle)	10804	Big Island	10924	Bovina (Town)	13740
		Big Moose	13331	Bovina Center	13740
Beechmont Woods (Part of New Rochelle)	10804	Big Tree	14219	Bowen	14772
		Big Wolf Lake	12986	Bowens Corners	13069
Beechurst (Part of New York)	11357	Billings	12510	Bowerstown	13326
		Billington Bay	13030	Bowling Green (Part of New York)	10004
Beechwood (Part of Rochester)	14609	Billington Heights	14052		
		Biltmore Shores	11758	Bowmansville	14026
Beehive Crossing	12090	Bingham Mills	12526	Boylston (Town)	13083
Beekman	12533	Binghamton	13901-05	Boyntonville	12090
Beekman (Town)	12570	For specific Binghamton Zip Codes call (607) 729-3726		Boysen Bay (Onondaga County)	13039
Beekman Corners	13459				
Beekmantown	12901	Binghamton (Town)	13902	Braddock Heights	14612
Beekmantown (Town)	12901	Binghamton Plaza (Part of Binghamton)	13901	Bradford	14815
Beixedon Estates	11971			Bradford (Town)	14815
Belair Road (Part of New York)	10305	Bingley	13035	Bradley	12754
		Binnewater	12401	Braeside	12123
Belcher	12865	Birchwood Estates	12184	Brainard	12024
Belcoda	14546	Birdsall	14709	Brainards Corners	13315
Belden	13787	Birdsall (Town)	14709	Brainardsville	12915
Belfast	14711	Bishopville	14807	Braman Corners	12053
Belfast (Town)	14711	Black Brook	12912	Bramans Corners	12186
Belfort	13327	Black Brook (Town)	12912	Bramanville	12092
Belgium	13027	Black Creek	14714	Brambler Ridge	14450
Belle Isle	13209	Blackmans Corners	12959	Branchport	14418
Bellerose (Nassau County)	11426	Black River	13612	Brandon (Town)	12966
Bellerose (Queens County)	11426	Black Rock (Part of Buffalo)	14207	Brandon Center	12966
Bellerose Terrace	11426	Blackwatch Hills	14450	Brandreth	12847
Belle Terre	11777	Blakeley	14052	Brant	14027
Belleview	14712	Blasdell	14219	Brant (Town)	14027
Belleville	13611				

362 NEW YORK Brantingham-Calverton

Name	ZIP
Brantingham	13312
Brant Lake	12815
Brasher (Town)	13613
Brasher Center	13613
Brasher Falls	13613
Brasher Falls-Winthrop	13613
Brasie Corners	13642
Breakabeen	12122
Breesport	14816
Breezy Point (Part of New York)	11697
Brentwood	11717
Brevoort (Part of New York)	11216
Brewerton	13029
Brewster	10509
Brewster Heights	10509
Brewster Hill	10509
Briarcliff Manor	10510
Briar Park	11793
Bridge (Part of Niagara Falls)	14305
Bridgehampton	11932
Bridgeport	13030
Bridgeville	12701
Bridgewater	13313
Bridgewater (Town)	13313
Brier Hill	13614
Brighton (Franklin County) (Town)	12970
Brighton (Kings County)	11235
Brighton (Monroe County) (Town)	14610
Brighton (Monroe County)	14610
Brighton (Otsego County)	13439
Brighton Beach (Part of New York)	11235
Brightside	13436
Brightwaters	11718
Brinckerhoff	12524
Brisben	13830
Briscoe	12783
Bristol	14469
Bristol (Town)	14469
Bristol Center	14424
Bristol Springs	14512
Broadacres	13905
Broadalbin	12025
Broadalbin (Town)	12025
Broad Channel (Part of New York)	11693
Broadway (Part of New York)	11106
Brockport	14420
Brockville	14411
Brockway	12508
Brocton	14716
Brodhead	12494
Bronx	10401-75

For specific Bronx Zip Codes call (212) 960-5006

COLLEGES & UNIVERSITIES

City University of New York-Herbert H. Lehman College	10468
Fordham University	10458
Manhattan College	10471
State University of New York Maritime College	10465

FINANCIAL INSTITUTIONS

North Side Savings Bank	10463
Tremont Federal Savings & Loan Association	10467
Yorkville Federal Savings & Loan Association	10461

HOSPITALS

Bronx Municipal Hospital Center	10461
Bronx-Lebanon Hospital Center	10457
Bronx Psychiatric Center	10461
Hebrew Hospital for Chronic Sick	10475
Lincoln Medical and Mental Health Center	10451
Montefiore Medical Center	10467
North Central Bronx Hospital	10467
Our Lady of Mercy Medical Center	10466
St. Barnabas Hospital	10457
Veterans Administration Medical Center	10468

Bronxville	10708
Bronxville Heights (Part of Yonkers)	10708
Brookdale	13668

Name	ZIP
Brookfield	13314
Brookfield (Town)	13314
Brookhaven	11719
Brookhaven (Town)	11719
Brooklyn	11201-56
	13775

For specific Brooklyn Zip Codes call (718) 834-3000

COLLEGES & UNIVERSITIES

Brooklyn Law School	11201
City University of New York-Brooklyn College	11210
City University of New York-Medgar Evers College	11225
City University of New York-New York City Technical College	11201
Long Island University-Brooklyn Campus	11201
Polytechnic University	11201
Pratt Institute	11205
St. Francis College	11201
State University of New York Health Science Center at Brooklyn	11203

FINANCIAL INSTITUTIONS

Bay Ridge Federal Savings & Loan Association	11209
Brooklyn Federal Savings & Loan Association	11201
Crossland Savings, FSB	11201
Dime Savings Bank of Williamsburgh	11211
East New York Savings Bank	11207
Flatbush Federal Savings & Loan Association	11210
The Green Point Savings Bank	11222
Hamilton Federal Savings & Loan Association	11209
The Home Savings Bank	11237
Independence Savings Bank	11202
Nassau Federal Savings & Loan Association	11207
The Williamsburgh Savings Bank	11243

HOSPITALS

Brookdale Hospital Medical Center	11212
Brooklyn Hospital-Caledonian Hospital	11201
Catholic Medical Center of Brooklyn and Queens	11217
Coney Island Hospital	11235
Interfaith Medical Center	11238
Kings County Hospital Center	11203
Kingsbrook Jewish Medical Center	11203
Long Island College Hospital	11201
Lutheran Medical Center	11220
Maimonides Medical Center	11219
Methodist Hospital	11215
University Hospital of Brooklyn-State University of N.Y. Health Sciences Center at Brooklyn	11203
Veterans Administration Medical Center	11209
Victory Memorial Hospital	11228
Woodhull Medical and Mental Health Center	11206
Wyckoff Heights Hospital	11237

MILITARY INSTALLATIONS

Coast Guard Supply Center, Brooklyn	11232
Fort Hamilton and New York Area Command	11252
Naval Station, Brooklyn	11251
Supervisor of Shipbuilding, Conversion and Repair, 3rd Naval District, Brooklyn	11251

Brooks Avenue Station (Part of Rochester)	14624
Brooksburg	12496
Brooks Grove	14510
Brooktondale	14817
Brookview	12026
Brookville	11545
Brookville Park	11751
Broome (Town)	12122

Name	ZIP
Broome Center	12076
Broughton Park	13760
Browns Bridge	13625
Browns Hollow	13317
Brownsville (Kings County)	11212
Brownsville (Ontario County)	14564
Brownville	13615
Brownville (Town)	13615
Bruceville	12440
Brunswick (Town)	12180
Brushton	12916
Brutus (Town)	13166
Bruynswick	12589
Bryant (Part of New York)	10036
Bryn Mawr Park (Part of Yonkers)	10701
Buchanan	10511
Buckingham Estates	10989
Buckleyville	12037
Bucks Bridge	13660
Buckton	13697
Buel	13317
Buellville	13104
Buena Vista	14823
Buffalo	14201-40

For specific Buffalo Zip Codes call (716) 855-2414

Buffalo Creek (Part of Buffalo)	14224
Buffalo Junction (Part of Buffalo)	14201
Buffalo Lake (Part of Buffalo)	14222
Bull Hill	13324
Bulls Head (Monroe County)	14611
Bulls Head (Richmond County)	10314
Bullville	10915
Bundys	13126
Burden Lake	12018
Burdett	14818
Burgoyne	12871
Burke	12917
Burke (Town)	12917
Burke Center	12917
Burlingham	12722
Burlington	13315
Burlington (Town)	13315
Burlington Flats	13315
Burnhams (Part of Cassadaga)	14718
Burns	14807
Burns (Town)	14807
Burnside	12543
Burns-Whitney Estates	12110
Burnt Hills	12027
Burnwood	13756
Burrs Mills	13601
Burt	14028
Burtonsville	12066
Bushes Landing	13367
Bushnell Basin	14534
Bushnellsville	12480
Bush Terminal (Part of New York)	11232
Bushville (Genesee County)	14020
Bushville (Sullivan County)	12701
Bushwick (Part of New York)	11221
Buskirk	12028
Busti	14701
Busti (Town)	14701
Butler (Town)	14590
Butler Center	14590
Butlerville	10519
Butterfield (Part of Utica)	13503
Butternut Grove	12776
Butternuts (Town)	13776
Byersville	14517
Byrden	12526
Byron	14422
Byron (Town)	14422
Cabinhill	13752
Cadiz	14737
Cadosia	13783
Cadyville	12918
Cahoonzie	12780
Cairo	12413
Cairo (Town)	12413
Calcium	13616
Calcutta	12064
Caldor Shopping Center (Part of Port Chester)	10573
Caledonia	14423
Caledonia (Town)	14423
Calico Colony	12065
Callicoon (Sullivan County)	12723
Callicoon (Sullivan County) (Town)	12791
Callicoon Center	12724
Calverton	11933

Calverton-Roanoke-City Island NEW YORK 363

Name	ZIP
Calverton-Roanoke	11933
Cambria (Town)	14094
Cambria Heights (Part of New York)	11411
Cambridge	12816
Cambridge (Town)	12816
Camden	13316
Camden (Town)	13316
Cameron	14819
Cameron (Town)	14819
Cameron Mills	14820
Camillus	13031
Camillus (Town)	13031
Camillus Plaza	13031
Campbell	14821
Campbell (Town)	14821
Campbell Hall	10916
Camp Hemlock	12721
Camp Hill (Part of Pomona)	10970
Camps Mills	13601
Campville	13760
Camroden	13440
Canaan	12029
Canaan (Town)	12029
Canaan Center	12029
Canada Lake	12032
Canadice	14560
Canadice (Town)	14560
Canajoharie	13317
Canajoharie (Town)	13317
Canal Street (Part of New York)	10013
Canandaigua	14424-25
For specific Canandaigua Zip Codes call (716) 394-1500	
Canarsie (Part of New York)	11236
Canaseraga	14822
Canastota	13032
Canawaugus	14423
Candor	13743
Candor (Town)	13743
Caneadea	14717
Caneadea (Town)	14717
Canisteo	14823
Canisteo (Town)	14823
Cannon Corners	12959
Canoe Place	11946
Canoga	13148
Canterbury Hill (Part of Rome)	13440
Canterbury Woods	13116
Canton	13617
Canton (Town)	13617
Cape Vincent	13618
Cape Vincent (Town)	13618
Capitol (Part of Albany)	12224
Capitol Annex (Part of Albany)	12225
Capitol Hills	10950
Cardiff	13084
Carle Place	11514
Carle Terrace	12449
Carlisle	12031
Carlisle (Town)	12031
Carlisle Center	12035
Carlisle Gardens	14094
Carlton	14411
Carlton (Town)	14411
Carman	12303
Carmel (Putnam County)	10512
Carmel (Putnam County) (Town)	10512
Carmel Park Estates	10512
Carnegie	14075
Caroga (Town)	12032
Caroga Lake	12032
Caroline	14817
Caroline (Town)	14817
Caroline Center	14817
Carroll (Town)	14738
Carroll Gardens (Part of New York)	11231
Carrollton (Cattaraugus County)	14748
Carrollton (Cattaraugus County) (Town)	14753
Carson	14823
Carthage	13619
Cascade	13118
Case	13084
Casowasco	13118
Cassadaga	14718
Cassville	13318
Castile	14427
Castile (Town)	14427
Castile Center	14427
Castle (Part of New Rochelle)	10801
Castle Creek	13744
Castle Hill (Part of New York)	10462

Name	ZIP
Castle Point	12511
Castleton Corners (Part of New York)	10314
Castleton on Hudson	12033
Castorland	13620
Catatonk	13827
Catharine	14869
Catharine (Town)	14869
Cathedral (Part of New York)	10025
Catlin (Town)	14812
Cato	13033
Cato (Town)	13033
Caton	14830
Caton (Town)	14830
Catskill	12414
Catskill (Town)	12414
Cattaraugus	14719
Cattaraugus Indian Reservation (Cattaraugus County) (Town)	14081
Cattaraugus Indian Reservation (Cattaraugus County)	14081
Cattaraugus Indian Reservation (Chautauqua County) (Town)	14081
Cattaraugus Indian Reservation (Erie County) (Town)	14081
Cattown	13337
Caughdenoy	13036
Cayuga	13034
Cayuga Heights	14850
Cayuta	14824
Cayuta (Town)	14805
Cayutaville	14860
Caywood	13035
Cazenovia	13035
Cazenovia (Town)	13035
Cecil Park (Part of Yonkers)	10707
Cedar Cliff	12542
Cedarcrest	14487
Cedar Flats	10980
Cedar Hill	12158
Cedarhurst	11516
Cedar Knolls (Part of Yonkers)	10708
Cedarvale	13215
Cedarville	13357
Celoron	14720
Cementon	12415
Centenary	10956
Center Avenue (Part of East Rockaway)	11518
Center Brunswick	12180
Centereach	11720
Center Falls	12834
Centerfield	14424
Centerlisle	13797
Center Moriches	11934
Centerport (Cayuga County)	13166
Centerport (Suffolk County)	11721
Centerville	14029
Centerville (Town)	14029
Centerville	13756
Center White Creek	12057
Central (Part of New York)	11435
Central Bridge	12035
Centralia	14782
Central Islip (Suffolk County)	11722
Central Nyack	10960
Central Park (Part of Buffalo)	14215
Central Park Shopping Center (Part of Buffalo)	14214
Central Square	13036
Central Valley	10917
Centre Island	11771
Centre Village	13787
Centuck (Part of Yonkers)	10710
Ceres	14721
Chadwicks	13319
Chaffee	14030
Chamberlain Corners	13660
Chambers	14812
Champion	13619
Champion (Town)	13619
Champion Huddle	13619
Champlain	12919
Champlain (Town)	12919
Champlain Park	12901
Chapel Hill Estates	10598
Chapin	14424
Chappaqua	10514
Charleston (Montgomery County) (Town)	12066
Charleston (Richmond County)	10301
Charleston Four Corners	12166

Name	ZIP
Charlotte (Chautauqua County) (Town)	14782
Charlotte (Monroe County)	14612
Charlotte Center	14782
Charlotteville	12036
Charlton	12019
Charlton (Town)	12019
Charwood Manor	12065
Chase Lake	13343
Chase Mills	13621
Chaseville	12116
Chasm Falls	12953
Chateaugay	12920
Chateaugay (Town)	12920
Chatham	12037
Chatham (Town)	12037
Chatham Center	12184
Chaumont	13622
Chauncey (Part of Dobbs Ferry)	10502
Chautauqua	14722
Chautauqua (Town)	14722
Chautauqua Mall (Part of Lakewood)	14750
Chazy	12921
Chazy (Town)	12921
Chazy Lake	12935
Chazy Landing	12921
Chedwel	14712
Cheektowaga (Town)	14225
Cheektowaga	14225
Cheektowaga Northwest	14225
Cheektowaga Southwest	14227
Chelsea (Dutchess County)	12512
Chelsea (Richmond County)	10314
Chemung	14825
Chemung (Town)	14825
Chemung Center	14825
Chenango (Town)	13745
Chenango Bridge	13745
Chenango Forks	13746
Chenango Lake	13815
Cheneys Point	14710
Cheningo	13158
Cherokee (Part of New York)	10028
Cherry Creek	14723
Cherry Creek (Town)	14723
Cherry Grove	11782
Cherry Lane (Part of Fredonia)	14063
Cherry Plain	12040
Cherrytown	12446
Cherry Valley	13320
Cherry Valley (Town)	13320
Cherry Valley Junction	12043
Cheshire	14424
Chester	10918
Chester (Orange County) (Town)	10918
Chester (Warren County) (Town)	12860
Chesterfield (Town)	12944
Chester Heights (Part of Yonkers)	10701
Chester Hill Park (Part of Mount Vernon)	10550
Chestertown	12817
Chestnut Hill	13088
Chestnut Ridge (Niagara County)	14094
Chestnut Ridge (Rockland County)	10952
Cheviot	12526
Chichester	12416
Childs	14411
Childwold	12922
Chili (Town)	14428
Chili Center	14624
Chilson	12883
Chinatown (Part of New York)	10013
Chipmonk	14706
Chippewa Bay	13623
Chittenango	13037
Chittenango Falls	13035
Choconut Center	13905
Church Street (Part of New York)	10007
Churchtown	12521
Churchville (Monroe County)	14428
Churchville (Oneida County)	13478
Churubusco	12923
Cicero	13039
Cicero (Town)	13039
Cicero Center	13041
Cincinnatus	13040
Cincinnatus (Town)	13040
Circleville	10919
City Island (Part of New York)	10464

364 NEW YORK Clairemont Farms-Crescent Estates North

Place	ZIP
Clairemont Farms	13088
Clare (Town)	13684
Claremont Park (Part of New York)	10457
Clarence	14031
Clarence (Town)	14031
Clarence Center	14032
Clarendon	14429
Clarendon (Town)	14429
Clark Heights	12569
Clark Mills	13321
Clarksburg	14057
Clarks Corners	14747
Clarks Mills	12834
Clarkson	14430
Clarkson (Town)	14430
Clarkstown (Town)	10956
Clarksville (Albany County)	12041
Clarksville (Allegany County) (Town)	14786
Claryville	12725
Clason Point (Part of New York)	10473
Classon (Part of New York)	11238
Claverack	12513
Claverack (Town)	12513
Claverack-Red Mills	12513
Clay	13041
Clay (Town)	13041
Clayburg	12981
Clayton	13624
Clayton (Town)	13624
Clayville	13322
Clear Creek	14726
Clearfield	14221
Clemons	12819
Clermont	12526
Clermont (Town)	12526
Cleveland	13042
Cleveland Hill	14225
Cleverdale	12820
Cliff Haven	12901
Clifford	13069
Cliffside	12116
Clifton (Monroe County)	14428
Clifton (Richmond County)	10304
Clifton (St. Lawrence County) (Town)	13666
Clifton Gardens	12065
Clifton Heights	14085
Clifton Knolls (Saratoga County)	12065
Clifton Park	12065
Clifton Park (Town)	12065
Clifton Park Center	12065
Clifton Springs	14432
Climax	12042
Clinton (Clinton County) (Town)	12923
Clinton (Dutchess County) (Town)	12514
Clinton (Oneida County)	13323
Clinton Corners	12514
Clintondale	12515
Clinton Heights	12144
Clinton Hollow	12578
Clinton Park	12144
Clintonville	12924
Clockville	13043
Clough Corners	13862
Clove	12043
Clover Bank	14075
Cloverville	12430
Clyde	14433
Clymer	14724
Clymer (Town)	14724
Cobb	11976
Cobble Hill (Part of New York)	11201
Cobleskill	12043
Cobleskill (Town)	12043
Cochecton	12726
Cochecton (Town)	12726
Cochecton Center	12727
Coeymans	12045
Coeymans (Town)	12045
Coeymans Hollow	12046
Coffins Mills	13670
Cohocton	14826
Cohocton (Town)	14826
Cohoes	12047
Cokertown	12571
Colchester (Delaware County)	13856
Colchester (Delaware County) (Town)	13755
Cold Brook (Herkimer County)	13324
Coldbrook (Schenectady County)	12303
Colden	14033

Place	ZIP
Colden (Town)	14033
Coldenham	12549
Colden Hill	12550
Coldspring (Cattaraugus County) (Town)	14783
Cold Spring (Putnam County)	10516
Cold Spring Harbor	11724
Cold Springs (Onondaga County)	13027
Cold Springs (Steuben County)	14810
Cold Spring Terrace	11743
Coldwater	14624
Colemans Mills	13492
Colesville (Town)	13787
Colgate (Part of Hamilton)	13346
Collabar	12549
Collamer	13057
College (Part of New York)	10030
College Park	12571
College Point (Part of New York)	11356
Colliersville	13747
Collingwood	13084
Collingwood Estates	14174
Collins	14034
Collins (Town)	14034
Collins Center	14035
Collins Correctional Facility	14079
Collins Landing	13607
Collinsville	13433
Colonial Acres	12077
Colonial Green	12188
Colonial Heights (Dutchess County)	12603
Colonial Heights (Westchester County)	10708
Colonial Park (Part of New York)	10039
Colonial Springs	11798
Colonial Village (Part of Lewiston)	14092
Colonie	12212
Colonie (Town)	12212
Colonie Center	12205
Colosse	13131
Colton	13625
Colton (Town)	13625
Columbia (Town)	13357
Columbia Center	13357
Columbia University (Part of New York)	10025
Columbia University Extension	10926
Columbiaville	12050
Columbus	13411
Columbus (Town)	13411
Columbus Circle (Part of New York)	10023
Colvin Elmwood (Part of Syracuse)	13205
Commack	11725
Commack Corners Shopping Center	11725
Comstock	12821
Comstock Tract	13027
Concord (Erie County) (Town)	14141
Concord (Richmond County)	10304
Conesus	14435
Conesus (Town)	14435
Conesville	12076
Conesville (Town)	12076
Conewango	14726
Conewango (Town)	14726
Conewango Valley	14726
Coney Island (Part of New York)	11224
Conger Corners	13480
Congers	10920
Conifer	12986
Conklin	13748
Conklin (Town)	13748
Conklin Forks	13903
Conklingville	12835
Connelly	12417
Connelly Park	14710
Conquest	13140
Conquest (Town)	13140
Constable	12926
Constable (Town)	12926
Constableville	13325
Constantia	13044
Constantia (Town)	13044
Constantia Center	13028
Continental Village	10566
Cook Corners	13625
Cooksburg	12469
Cooks Falls	12776

Place	ZIP
Cookville	14036
Coolidge Beach	14172
Coonrod (Part of Rome)	13440
Co-op City (Part of New York)	10475
Cooper (Part of New York)	10003
Coopers Plains	14827
Cooperstown	13326
Cooperstown Junction	12116
Coopersville (Clinton County)	12919
Coopersville (Livingston County)	14517
Copake	12516
Copake (Town)	12516
Copake Falls	12517
Copake Lake	12521
Copenhagen	13626
Copiague	11726
Coram	11727
Coram Hill	11763
Corbett	13755
Corbettsville	13749
Coreys	12986
Corfu	14036
Corinth	12822
Corinth (Town)	12822
Cornell (Part of New York)	10473
Corners (Part of Cayuga Heights)	14850
Corning (Steuben County)	14830
Corning (Steuben County) (Town)	14830
Corning Manor	14830
Cornwall (Orange County)	12518
Cornwall (Orange County) (Town)	12518
Cornwall On Hudson	12520
Cornwallville	12418
Corona-A (Part of New York)	11368
Corona-Elmhurst (Part of New York)	11373
Cortland	13045
Cortlandt (Town)	10520
Cortlandville (Town)	13045
Cortland West	13045
Cosmos Heights	13045
Cossayuna	12823
Coss Corners	14810
Cottage	14138
Cottage City	14424
Cottage Park	14750
Cottam Hill	12590
Cottekill	12419
Cottonwood Point	14435
Council Meadows	12027
Country Knolls	12151
Country Knolls (census area only)	12019
Country Knolls South	12065
Country Life Press (Part of Garden City)	11530
Country Ridge Estates	10573
County Line	14098
Cove Neck	11771
Coventry	13778
Coventry (Town)	13778
Coventryville	13733
Covert	14847
Covert (Town)	14847
Coveytown Corners	12917
Covington	14525
Covington (Town)	14525
Cowlesville	14037
Coxsackie	12051
Coxsackie (Town)	12051
Coxsackie Correctional Facility	12192
Crafts	10512
Cragsmoor	12420
Craigville	10918
Crains Mills	13158
Cranberry Creek	12117
Cranberry Lake	12927
Crandall Corners	12154
Cranes Corners	13340
Cranesville	12010
Cranford (Part of New York)	10470
Crary Mills	13617
Craryville	12521
Craterclub	12936
Crawford (Town)	12566
Creek Locks	12411
Crescent	12188
Crescent Beach (Monroe County)	14612
Crescent Beach (Richmond County)	10301
Crescent Estates	12065
Crescent Estates North	12065

Crestview Heights-East Hills NEW YORK 365

Name	ZIP
Crestview Heights	13760
Crestwood (Part of Tuckahoe)	10707
Crestwood (Part of Yonkers)	10710
Crestwood Gardens (Part of Yonkers)	10710
Crittenden	14038
Crocketts	13156
Crofts Corners	10579
Croghan	13327
Croghan (Town)	13327
Crompond	10517
Cropseyville	12052
Cross Country Center (Part of Yonkers)	10704
Crossgates Mall	12203
Cross River	10518
Cross Roads Estates	10598
Croton	14864
Crotona Park (Part of New York)	10460
Croton Falls	10519
Croton Heights	10598
Croton-on-Hudson	10520
Crotonville	10562
Crown Heights	12603
Crown Point	12928
Crown Point (Town)	12928
Crown Point Center	12928
Crown Village	11762
Crugers	10521
Crum Creek	13452
Crystal Brook	11766
Crystal Dale	13367
Crystal Lake (Albany County)	12147
Crystal Lake (Cattaraugus County)	14060
Cuba	14727
Cuba (Town)	14727
Cuddebackville	12729
Cullen	13439
Cummingsville	14437
Curriers	14009
Curry	12765
Currytown	12166
Curtis	14821
Cutchogue	11935
Cutchoque-New Suffolk	11935
Cutting	14724
Cuyler	13050
Cuyler (Town)	13050
Cuyler Hill	13050
Cuylerville	14481
Cypress Hills (Part of New York)	11208
Dadville	13367
Dahlia	12758
Dairyland	12435
Dale	14039
Dalton	14836
Damascus	13865
Danby	14850
Danby (Town)	14850
Dannemora	12929
Dannemora (Town)	12929
Dansville (Livingston County)	14437
Dansville (Steuben County) (Town)	14807
Danube (Town)	13365
Darien	14040
Darien (Town)	14040
Darien Center	14040
Darrowsville	12817
Davenport	13750
Davenport (Town)	13750
Davenport Center	13751
Davis Park	11772
Daws	14020
Day (Town)	12835
Days Rock	13407
Dayton (Town)	14041
Dayton	14041
Daytonville	13480
Deansboro	13328
Debruce	12758
Decatur	12197
Decatur (Town)	12197
Deck	13407
Deckertown	12758
Deerfield (Town)	13503
Deerland	12847
Deerpark (Orange County) (Town)	12729
Deer Park (Suffolk County)	11729
Deer River	13627
Deferiet	13628
Defreestville	12144
Degrass	13684

Name	ZIP
De Kalb	13630
De Kalb (Town)	13630
De Kalb Junction	13630
De Lancey	13752
Delanson	12053
Delaware (Albany County)	12209
Delaware (Sullivan County) (Town)	12723
Delevan	14042
Delhi	13753
Delhi (Town)	13753
Delmar	12054
Delphi Falls	13051
Delray	14224
Dempster Beach	13126
Demster	13126
Denmark	13631
Denmark (Town)	13631
Dennies Hollow	12117
Denning	12725
Denning (Town)	12725
Dennison Corners	13407
Denton	10958
Denton Hills	11721
Denver	12421
Depauville	13632
Depew	14043
De Peyster	13633
De Peyster (Town)	13633
Deposit	13754
Deposit (Town)	13754
Derby	14047
Dering Harbor	11964
De Ruyter	13052
DeRuyter (Town)	13052
Deuels Corners	14127
Devereux	14731
Devon	11930
Dewey (Part of Rochester)	14613
Dewey Bridge	12827
De Witt	13214
De Witt (Town)	13214
Dewittville	14728
Dexter	13634
Dexterville	13069
Diamond Point	12824
Diana (Town)	13648
Dibbletown	13308
Dickersonville	14131
Dickinson (Broome County) (Town)	13905
Dickinson (Franklin County) (Town)	12930
Dickinson Center	12930
Dick Urban	14043
Dimmick Corners	12831
Dineharts	14810
Divine Corners	12759
Dix (Town)	14891
Dix Hills (Suffolk County)	11746
Dobbs Ferry	10522
Dolgeville	13329
Dongan Hills (Part of New York)	10304
Doraville	13813
Doris Park	13044
Dorloo	12043
Dormansville	12055
Dorwood Park	14131
Douglass	12944
Douglaston (Part of New York)	11363
Dover (Town)	12522
Dover Furnace	12522
Dover Plains	12522
Downstate Correctional Facility	12524
Downsville	13755
Downtown (Chemung County)	14901
Downtown (Monroe County)	14603
Downtown (Onondaga County)	13201
Doyle	14206
Dreiser Loop (Part of New York)	10475
Dresden (Washington County) (Town)	12887
Dresden (Yates County)	14441
Dresden Station	12887
Dresserville	13118
Drews Corner	13694
Dryden	13053
Dryden (Town)	13053
Duane (Town)	12953
Duane Center	12968
Duanesburg	12056
Duanesburg (Town)	12056
Dublin	14433
Dugway	13131
Dunbar	13865

Name	ZIP
Dundee	14837
Dunewood	11706
Dunham Hollow	12018
Dunham Manor	13492
Dunkirk (Chautauqua County)	14048
Dunkirk (Chautauqua County) (Town)	14048
Dunnsville	12009
Dunraven	12455
Dunsbach Ferry	12047
Dunwoodie (Part of Yonkers)	10701
Dunwoody Heights (Part of Yonkers)	10701
Durham	12422
Durham (Town)	12422
Durhamville	13054
Durkeetown	12828
Durlandville	10924
Dutchess Junction	12508
Dutch Flats	14167
Dutch Meadows	12065
Dwaar Kill	12566
Dyke	14830
Dykemans	10509
Dyker Heights (Part of New York)	11228
Eagle	14009
Eagle (Town)	14009
Eagle Bay	13331
Eagle Bridge	12057
Eagle Center	14024
Eagle Harbor	14442
Eagle Lake	12883
Eagle Mills	12180
Eagle Point	14454
Eagle Village	13104
Eagleville	12873
Earlton	12058
Earlville (Franklin County)	12920
Earlville (Madison County)	13332
East (Part of Yonkers)	10704
East Amherst	14051
East Arcade	14009
East Atlantic Beach	11509
East Aurora	14052
East Avon	14414
East Bay	14590
East Beekmantown	12901
East Bend Park	12603
East Berkshire	13736
East Berne	12059
East Bethany	14054
East Bloomfield	14443
East Bloomfield (Town)	14443
East Branch	13756
East Brentwood	11717
East Buffalo	14225
East Buskirk	12028
East Campbell	14870
East Cayuga Heights	14850
East Chatham	12060
Eastchester (Town)	10709
East Chester (Orange County)	10918
Eastchester (Westchester County)	10709
East Cobleskill	12157
East Coldenham	12550
East Concord	14055
East Corning	14830
East De Kalb	13630
East Durham	12423
East Eden	14057
East Elmhurst (Part of New York)	11369
Eastern Hills Mall	14221
Eastern New York Correctional Facility	12458
East Farmingdale	11735
East Fishkill (Town)	12533
East Floyd	13354
East Frankfort	13340
East Freetown	13055
East Gaines	14411
East Galway	12850
East Genoa	13092
East Glenville	12302
East Greenbush	12061
East Greenbush (Town)	12061
East Greenlawn	11731
East Greenwich	12826
East Half Hollow Hills	11746
East Hampton	11937
East Hampton (Town)	11937
East Hartford	12832
East Hebron	12865
East Herkimer	13350
East Hill	14850
East Hills	11576

366 NEW YORK East Hillsdale-Fernwood

	ZIP
East Hillsdale	12529
East Homer	13056
East Hoosick	12090
East Hounsfield	13610
East Huntington	11743
East Irvington	10533
East Islip	11730
East Jewett	12424
East Kingston	12401
East Koy	14536
East Lake Ronkonkoma	11779
East Lansing	14852
East Leon	14719
East Line	12020
East Marion	11939
East Martinsburg	13367
East Masonville	13839
East Massapequa (Nassau County)	11758
East Mattituck	11952
East McDonough	13830
East Meadow	11554
East Meredith	13757
East Middletown	10940
Eastmor	12180
East Moriches	11940
East Nassau	12062
East Neck	11743
East New York (Part of York)	11207
East Nichols	13812
East Northport	11731
East Norwich	11732
East Olean (Part of Olean)	14760
Easton (Town)	12834
East Otto	14729
East Otto (Town)	14729
East Palermo	13036
East Palmyra	14444
East Park	12538
East Part	13697
East Patchogue (Suffolk County)	11772
East Pembroke	14056
East Penfield	14450
East Pharsalia	13758
East Pitcairn	13648
East Pittstown	12028
East Poestenkill	12018
Eastport	11941
East Quogue	11942
East Randolph	14730
East Ripley	14775
East River	13056
East Rochester	14445
East Rockaway	11518
East Rodman	13601
East Salamanca (Part of Salamanca)	14779
East Schodack	12063
East Schuyler	13340
East Seneca	14224
East Setauket	11733
East Shelby	14103
East Shoreham	11786
East Side (Broome County)	13904
Eastside (Suffolk County)	11937
East Sidney	13775
East Springfield	13333
East Steamburg	14886
East Stone Arabia	13428
East Syracuse	13057
East Taghkanic	12502
East Varick	14541
East Vestal	13902
East Victor	14564
East View	10595
East Watertown	13601
East Wawarsing	12489
East White Plains (Part of Harrison)	10604
East Williamson	14449
East Williston	11596
East Windham	12439
East Windsor	13865
East Winfield	13491
Eastwood (Part of Syracuse)	13206
East Worcester	12064
Eaton	13334
Eaton (Town)	13334
Eatons Neck	11768
Eavesport	12490
Ebenezer	14224
Ebenezer Junction	14224
Echota (Part of Niagara Falls)	14302
Eddy	13617
Eddyville (Cattaraugus County)	14755
Eddyville (Ulster County)	12401

	ZIP
Eden	14057
Eden (Town)	14057
Edenville	10990
Edgemere (Part of New York)	11691
Edgemont	10583
Edgewater Beach	13308
Edgewater Park	13669
Edgewood (Greene County)	12450
Edgewood (Suffolk County)	11717
Edgewood Garden	13164
Edinburg	12134
Edinburg (Town)	12134
Edmeston	13335
Edmeston (Town)	13335
Edson	13865
Edwards	13635
Edwards (Town)	13635
Edwards Hill	12811
Edwards Park	12029
Edwardsville	13646
Egbertville (Part of New York)	10306
Eggertsville	14226
Egypt	14450
Einstein Loop (Part of New York)	10475
Elayne Meadows	12188
Elba	14058
Elba (Town)	14058
Elbridge	13060
Elbridge (Town)	13060
Eldred	12732
Elizabethtown	12932
Elizabethtown (Town)	12932
Elizaville	12523
Elka Park	12427
Elk Brook	12776
Elk Creek	12155
Elkdale	14779
Ellenburg	12933
Ellenburg (Town)	12933
Ellenburg Center	12934
Ellenburg Depot	12935
Ellenville	12428
Ellery (Town)	14756
Ellery Center	14712
Ellicott (Chautauqua County) (Town)	14733
Ellicott (Part of Buffalo)	14203
Ellicott	14127
Ellicottville	14731
Ellicottville (Town)	14731
Ellington	14732
Ellington (Town)	14732
Ellisburg	13636
Ellisburg (Town)	13636
Ellis Hollow	14850
Ellistown	14892
Elma	14059
Elma (Town)	14059
Elmdale	13642
Elm Grove	13808
Elmhurst	14701
Elmhurst-A (Part of New York)	11373
Elmira	14901-05
For specific Elmira Zip Codes call (607) 737-5100	
Elmira (Town)	14902
Elmira Heights	14903
Elmira Heights North	14903
Elmont	11003
Elm Park (Part of New York)	10303
Elmsford	10523
Elm Valley	14895
Elnora	12065
Elsmere	12054
Eltingville (Part of New York)	10312
Elton	14042
Elton Station	14042
Elwood (Suffolk County)	11731
Elwood Farms	11731
Embogcht	12414
Emerson	13140
Emerson Hill	10301
	10304
For specific Emerson Hill Zip Codes call (718) 816-2790	
Emeryville	13642
Eminence	12175
Emmons	13820
Empeyville	13316
Empire State (Part of New York)	10001
Empire State Plaza (Part of Albany)	12220
Endicott	13760
Endwell	13760
Enfield	14850

	ZIP
Enfield (Town)	14850
Ensenore	13118
Ephratah	13339
Ephratah (Town)	13339
Erieville	13061
Erin	14838
Erin (Town)	14838
Erwin (Town)	14870
Erwins	14870
Escarpment	14092
Esopus	12429
Esopus (Town)	12429
Esperance	12066
Esperance (Town)	12066
Esplanade (Part of New York)	10469
Essex	12936
Essex (Town)	12936
Etna	13062
Euclid	13041
Evans (Town)	14006
Evans Center	14006
Evans Mills	13637
Exeter (Town)	13315
Exeter Center	13315
Fabius	13063
Fabius (Town)	13063
Factory Village	12020
Factoryville	12928
Fairdale	13074
Fairfield	13336
Fairfield (Town)	13336
Fairfield Farms	13066
Fairfield Gardens	12205
Fair Harbor	11706
Fair Haven	13064
Fairlawn Estates	12110
Fairmount	13219
Fairmount (census area only)	13031
Fairmount Fair Mall	13219
Fair Oaks	10940
Fairport	14450
Fairview (Allegany County)	14060
Fairview (Dutchess County)	12601
Fairview (Westchester County)	10603
Fairview (Wyoming County)	14427
Falconer	14733
Falcon Manor	14304
Falconwood	14072
Falls (Part of Niagara Falls)	14303
Fallsburg	12733
Fallsburg (Town)	12733
Fancher	14452
Fargo	14036
Farleys Point	13160
Farmers Mills	10512
Farmersville (Town)	14060
Farmersville Center	14737
Farmersville Station	14060
Farmingdale	11735
Farmington	14425
Farmington (Town)	14425
Farmingville	11738
Farnham	14061
Farragut (Part of New York)	11203
Far Rockaway	11601-97
For specific Far Rockaway Zip Codes call (718) 327-7700	

HOSPITALS

Peninsula Hospital Center	11691
St. John's Episcopal Hospital-South Shore	11691

MILITARY INSTALLATIONS

Fort Tilden	11695
Fawn Ridge	13027
Fayette	13065
Fayette (Town)	13065
Fayetteville	13066
Federal (Part of Rochester)	14614
Federal Correctional Institution	10963
Federal Reserve (Part of New York)	10045
Felts Mills	13638
Fenimore	12801
Fenner (Town)	13035
Fenton (Town)	13833
Ferenbaugh	14830
Fergusons Corners	14456
Fergusonville	12155
Ferndale	12734
Fernwood (Oswego County)	13142
Fernwood (Saratoga County)	12801
Fernwood (Sullivan County)	12760

Ferry Village-Gedney NEW YORK 367

	ZIP
Ferry Village	14072
Feura Bush	12067
Fieldston (Part of New York)	10463
Filer Corners	13808
Fillmore	14735
Finchville	10940
Findley Lake	14736
Fine	13639
Fine (Town)	13639
Fineview	13640
Finger Lakes Manor (Part of Canandaigua)	14424
Fink Basin	13365
Finnegans Corners	10924
Fire Island Pines	11782
Firthcliffe Heights	12584
Fish Creek (Lewis County)	13325
Fish Creek (Ulster County)	12477
Fish Creek Landing	13308
Fishers	14453
Fishers Island	06390
Fishers Landing	13641
Fisherville	14903
Fish House	12025
Fishkill	12524
Fishkill (Town)	12524
Fishkill Plains	12590
Fishs Eddy	13774
Five Corners (Madison County)	13421
Five Corners (Oneida County)	13480
Fivemile Point	13795
Five Points	14456
Five Town Plaza	11598
Flackville	13669
Flanders	11901
Flatbrook	12029
Flatbush (Kings County)	11226
Flatbush (Ulster County)	12477
Flat Creek (Montgomery County)	13317
Flat Creek (Schoharie County)	12076
Fleetwood (Part of Mount Vernon)	10552
Fleischmanns	12430
Fleming	13021
Fleming (Town)	13021
Flemingville	13827
Flint	14561
Floral Park	11001-05

For specific Floral Park Zip Codes call (516) 354-3297

Floral Park (Part of New York)	11001
Florence	13316
Florence (Town)	13316
Florida (Montgomery County) (Town)	12010
Florida (Orange County)	10921
Floridaville	13033
Flowerfield Estates (Part of Lake Grove)	11755
Flower Hill	11050
Flowers	13865
Floyd	13440
Floyd (Town)	13440
Flushing	11301-86

For specific Flushing Zip Codes call (718) 670-4743

COLLEGES & UNIVERSITIES

City University of New York- Queens College	11367

FINANCIAL INSTITUTIONS

Asia Bank, National Association	11354
Bayside Federal Savings & Loan Association	11361
Cross-County Federal Savings Bank	11379
Flushing Savings Bank	11354
Maspeth Federal Savings & Loan Association	11378
Pioneer Savings & Loan Association	11357
Queens County Savings Bank	11354
Whitestone Savings, F.A.	11357

HOSPITALS

Booth Memorial Medical Center	11355
City Hospital Center at Elmhurst	11373
Flushing Hospital and Medical Center	11355
LaGuardia Hospital	11375

	ZIP
HOTELS/MOTELS	
Best Western Midway Hotel	11368
Metropole Hotel Best Western	11368
Pan American Motor Inn	11373
MILITARY INSTALLATIONS	
Fort Totten	11359
Fluvanna	14701
Fly Creek	13337
Flying Point	11976
Fly Summit	12834
Fonda	12068
Foots Corners	14435
Fordham (Part of New York)	10458
Forest	12935
Forestburgh	12777
Forestburgh (Town)	12701
Forest Glen (Part of Hamburg)	14075
Forest Hills (Part of New York)	11375
Forest Home	14850
Forest Knolls (Part of New Rochelle)	10804
Forest Lawn	14580
Forest Park (Chautauqua County)	14787
Forest Park (Dutchess County)	12572
Forestport	13338
Forestport (Town)	13338
Forestport Station	13338
Forestville	14062
Forge Hollow	13328
Forks	14225
Forsonville	10524
Forsyth	14775
Fort Ann	12827
Fort Ann (Town)	12827
Fort Covington	12937
Fort Covington (Town)	12937
Fort Covington Center	12937
Fort Drum	13612
Fort Edward	12828
Fort Edward (Town)	12828
Fort George (Part of New York)	10040
Fort Herkimer	13407
Fort Hunter (Albany County)	12303
Fort Hunter (Montgomery County)	12069
Fort Jackson	12938
Fort Johnson	12070
Fort Miller	12828
Fort Montgomery	10922
Fort Niagara Beach	14174
Fort Plain	13339
Fort Salonga (Suffolk County)	11768
Fortsville	12831
Fort Washington (Part of New York)	10032
Foster	13827
Fosterdale	12726
Fosterville	13021
Foster-Wheeler Junction (Part of Dansville)	14437
Fourth Lake	12846
Fowler	13642
Fowler (Town)	13642
Fowlersville	13433
Fowlerville	14423
Fox Hill	12134
Fox Meadows (Part of Scarsdale)	10583
Frankfort	13340
Frankfort (Town)	13340
Frankfort Center	13340
Franklin	13775
Franklin (Delaware County) (Town)	13775
Franklin (Franklin County) (Town)	12913
Franklin Correctional Facility	12953
Franklin D. Roosevelt (Part of New York)	10022
Franklin Park	13057
Franklin Springs	13341
Franklin Square	11010
Franklinton	12122
Franklinville	14737
Franklinville (Town)	14737
Franks Corner	13045
Fraser	13753
Fredonia	14063
Freedom	14065
Freedom (Town)	14065
Freedom Plains	12569

	ZIP
Freehold	12431
Freeman	14801
Freeport	11520
Freetown (Cortland County) (Town)	13803
Freetown (Suffolk County)	11937
Freetown Corners	13803
Freeville	13068
Fremont (Steuben County) (Town)	14807
Fremont (Sullivan County) (Town)	12736
Fremont Center	12736
Fremont Heights	13057
Fremont Hills	13057
French Creek (Town)	14724
Frenchville	13486
French Woods	13783
Fresh Meadows (Part of New York)	11365
Fresh Pond (Part of York)	11385
Frewsburg	14738
Friend	14527
Friendship	14739
Friendship (Town)	14739
Friends Point	12836
Frontenac	13624
Fruitland	14519
Fruit Valley	13126
Fullerville	13642
Fulmer Valley	14806
Fulton (Oswego County)	13069
Fulton (Schoharie County) (Town)	12122
Fultonham	12071
Fultonville	12072
Furnace Brook	10925
Furnaceville	14519
Furnace Woods	10566
Furniss	13126
Fyler Settlement	13082
Gabriels	12939
Gaines	14411
Gaines (Town)	14411
Gainesville	14066
Gainesville (Town)	14066
Galatia	13803
Gale	12973
Galen (Town)	14433
Galeville (Onondaga County)	13088
Galeville (Ulster County)	12589
Gallatin	12567
Gallatin (Town)	12567
Galleria of White Plains (Part of White Plains)	10601
Gallupville	12073
Galway	12074
Galway (Town)	12074
Galway Lake	12025
Ganahgote	12525
Gang Mills	14870
Gansevoort	12831
Garbutt	14546
Garden City	11530
Garden City Park	11040
Garden City South	11530
Garden Park Estates	12203
Gardenville	14224
Gardiner	12525
Gardiner (Town)	12525
Gardiner Manor Mall	11706
Gardiners Bay Estates	11939
Gardnersville	12043
Gardnertown	12550
Gardnertown (census area only)	12250
Garfield	12168
Garland	14420
Garnerville (Part of West Haverstraw)	10923
Garnet Lake	12843
Garoga	12095
Garrattsville	13342
Garrison	10524
Garrison Four Corners	10524
Garwoods	14822
Gaskill	13827
Gasport	14067
Gates (Monroe County) (Town)	14624
Gates (Monroe County)	14624
Gates Center	14611
Gates-North Gates	14626
Gayhead	12533
Gay Ridge Estates	10598
Gayville	13044
Geddes (Town)	13209
Gedney (Part of White Plains)	10605

368 NEW YORK Geers Corners-Hamilton Park

Name	ZIP
Geers Corners	13648
Genegantslet	13778
Genesee (Town)	14754
Genesee Falls (Town)	14536
Geneseo	14454
Geneseo (Town)	14454
Geneva (Ontario County)	14456
Geneva (Ontario County) (Town)	14456
Genoa	13071
Genoa (Town)	13071
Georgetown	13072
Georgetown (Town)	13072
Georgetown	14450
Georgetown Square (Part of Williamsville)	14221
Georgtown Station	13334
German	13040
German (Town)	13040
German Flatts (Town)	13407
Germantown	12526
Germantown (Town)	12526
Germantown (Part of Port Jervis)	12771
German Village	14617
Germonds	10956
Gerry	14740
Gerry (Town)	14740
Getzville	14068
Geyser Crest	12866
Ghent	12075
Ghent (Town)	12075
Gibson (Nassau County)	11580
Gibson (Steuben County)	14830
Gifford	12056
Gilbert Mills	13135
Gilbertsville	13776
Gilboa	12076
Gilboa (Town)	12076
Gilgo Beach	11702
Gilmantown	12190
Gimbels Number One	11581
Glasco	12432
Glass Lake	12018
Glen	12072
Glen (Town)	12072
Glen Aubrey	13777
Glen Castle	13901
Glenclyffe	10524
Glenco Mills	12534
Glen Cove	11542
Glendale (Lewis County)	13343
Glendale (Queens County)	11385
Glendale Manor (Part of Rome)	13440
Glenerie	12477
Glenfield	13343
Glenford	12433
Glenham	12527
Glen Haven (Monroe County)	14617
Glenhaven (Oneida County)	13492
Glen Head	11545
Glen Island	12814
Glen Lake	12801
Glenmark	14516
Glenmont	12077
Glen Oaks (Part of New York)	11004
Glenora	14837
Glen Park	13601
Glenridge	12148
Glens Falls	12801
Glens Falls North	12801
Glen Spey	12737
Glen Street (Part of Sea Cliff)	11579
Glenville (Schenectady County) (Town)	12302
Glenville (Westchester County)	10591
Glen Wild	12738
Glenwood (Erie County)	14069
Glenwood (Westchester County)	10701
Glenwood Landing	11547
Gloversville	12078
Godeffroy	12739
Golden Glow Heights	14905
Goldens Bridge	10526
Goodman Street (Part of Rochester)	14607
Goodyears Corners	13081
Goose Bay Estates	11971
Goose Island	12809
Gordon Heights	11727
Gorham	14461
Gorham (Town)	14461
Goshen	10924
Goshen (Town)	10924
Goshen Hills	10924
Gothicville	12197
Goulds	12760
Goulds Mill	13368
Gouverneur	13642
Gouverneur (Town)	13642
Governors Island (Part of New York)	10004
Gowanda	14070
Gracie (Cortland County)	13045
Gracie (New York County)	10028
Grafton	12082
Grafton (Town)	12082
Graham Hill	10537
Grahamsville	12740
Granby (Town)	13069
Granby Center	13069
Grand Central (Part of New York)	10017
Grand Gorge	12434
Grand Island	14072
Grand Island (Town)	14072
Grand Station (Part of New York)	11103
Grand View Beach	14612
Grand View Heights	14612
Grand View-on-Hudson	10960
Grandview Park	13692
Grandyle Village	14072
Granger (Town)	14735
Grangerville	12871
Granite	12446
Granite Springs	10527
Graniteville (Part of New York)	10301
Grant	13324
Grant Avenue (Part of Auburn)	13021
Grant Hollow	12121
Grant Park	11557
Granville	12832
Granville (Town)	12832
Grapeville	12042
Graphite	12836
Grassy Point	10980
Gravesend (Part of New York)	11223
Gravesville	13431
Gray	13324
Graymoor	10524
Gray Oaks (Part of Yonkers)	10703
Great Bend	13643
Great Kills (Part of New York)	10308
Great Neck	11020-27
For specific Great Neck Zip Codes call (516) 482-5010	
Great Neck Estates	11021
Great River	11730
	11739
For specific Great River Zip Codes call (516) 581-2130	
Great South Bay (Part of Lindenhurst)	11702
Great Valley	14741
Great Valley (Town)	14741
Greece (Town)	14616
Greece (census area only)	14626
Greece	14616
Greece Towne Mall	14626
Greeley Square (Part of New York)	10001
Green Acres (Part of Fredonia)	14063
Green Acres Shopping Center (Part of Valley Stream)	11581
Greenburgh (Town)	10591
Green Corners	12010
Green Crest	14063
Greendale	12534
Greene	13778
Greene (Town)	13778
Greene Correctional Facility	12051
Greenfield (Town)	12833
Greenfield Center	12833
Greenfield Park	12435
Greenhaven (Part of Rye)	10580
Green Haven Correctional Facility	12570
Greenhurst	14742
Green Island	12183
Green Island (Town)	12183
Greenlawn	11740
Greenpoint (Part of New York)	11222
Greenport (Columbia County) (Town)	12534
Greenport (Suffolk County)	11944
Greenport West	11944
Green River	12529
Greenvale	11548
Greenville	12083
Greenville (Town)	12083
Greenville (Orange County) (Town)	12771
Greenville (Westchester County)	10583
Greenville Center	12083
Greenway (Part of Rome)	13440
Greenwich	12834
Greenwich (Town)	12834
Greenwood	14839
Greenwood (Town)	14839
Greenwood Lake	10925
Gregorytown	13755
Greig	13345
Greig (Town)	13345
Greigsville	14533
Greigsville Station	14533
Grenell	13624
Greycourt (Part of Chester)	10918
Greystone (Part of Yonkers)	10701
Gridleyville	13864
Grindstone	13624
Grooms Corners	12148
Grossinger	12734
Groton	13073
Groton (Town)	13073
Groton City	13073
Grove (Town)	14884
Groveland	14462
Groveland (Town)	14462
Grover	14226
Grover Hills	12956
Grovernor Corners	12035
Groveville	12508
Grymes Hill (Part of New York)	10301
Guilderland	12084
Guilderland (Town)	12084
Guilderland Center	12085
Guilderland Gardens	12203
Guilford	13780
Guilford (Town)	13780
Guilford Center	13780
Gulf Summit	13865
Gunther Park (Part of Yonkers)	10708
Gurn Spring	12831
Guymard	12739
Gypsum	14432
Hadley	12835
Hadley (Town)	12835
Hadley Bay	14785
Hagaman	12086
Hagedorns Mills	12074
Hagerman	11713
Hague	12836
Hague (Town)	12836
Hailesboro	13645
Haines Falls	12436
Halcott (Town)	12430
Halcott Center	12430
Halcottsville	12438
Hales Eddy	13783
Halesite	11743
Half Acre	13021
Half Hollow Hills	11746
Halfmoon	12188
Halfmoon (Town)	12188
Halfway	13060
Halfway House Corners	13660
Hall	14463
Hallow	13413
Halls Corners (Seneca County)	14847
Halls Corners (Wyoming County)	14569
Hallsport	14895
Hallsville	13339
Halsey (Part of New York)	11233
Halseys (Part of Plattsburgh)	12901
Halsey Valley	14883
Hambletville	13754
Hamburg	14075
Hamburg (Town)	14075
Hamburg	12414
Hamburg-on-the-Lake	14075
Hamden	13782
Hamden (Town)	13782
Hamilton	13346
Hamilton (Town)	13346
Hamilton Beach (Part of New York)	11414
Hamilton Center	13346
Hamilton College	13323
Hamilton Grange (Part of New York)	10031
Hamilton Park (Part of New York)	10301

Hamlet-Howlett Hill NEW YORK 369

Name	ZIP
Hamlet	14138
Hamlin (Town)	14464
Hamlin	14464
Hammertown	12567
Hammond	13646
Hammond (Town)	13646
Hammondsport	14840
Hampshire	14855
Hampton	12837
Hampton (Town)	12837
Hampton Bays (Suffolk County)	11946
Hamptonburgh (Town)	10916
Hampton Manor	12144
Hampton Park (Suffolk County)	11968
Hancock	13783
Hancock (Town)	13783
Hankins	12741
Hannacroix	12087
Hannawa Falls	13647
Hannibal	13074
Hannibal (Town)	13074
Hannibal Center	13074
Hanover (Town)	14136
Hanover Hill	14136
Harbor Acres (Part of Sands Point)	11050
Harbor Heights Park	11743
Harbor Hills	11023
Harbor Isle	11558
Hardenburgh (Town)	12455
Hardys	14066
Harford	13784
Harford (Town)	13784
Harford Mills	13785
Harkness	12972
Harlem (Part of New York)	10030
Harlemville	12075
Harmon Park	12302
Harmony (Town)	14767
Harmony Corners	12020
Harpersfield	13786
Harpersfield (Town)	13786
Harpursville	13787
Harriet	14223
Harrietstown (Town)	12983
Harriman	10926
Harriman South	10926
Harris	12742
Harrisburg (Cattaraugus County)	14753
Harrisburg (Lewis County) (Town)	13367
Harrisburg (Warren County)	12878
Harris Corners	14145
Harris Hill	14221
Harrison (Westchester County)	10528
Harrison (Westchester County) (Town)	10528
Harrisville	13648
Harrower	12010
Hartfield	14728
Hartford	12838
Hartford (Town)	12838
Hartland	14067
Hartland (Town)	14067
Hartmans Corners	12009
Hartsdale	10530
Harts Hill	13492
Hartson Point	14487
Hartsville	14843
Hartsville (Town)	14843
Hartwick	13348
Hartwick (Town)	13348
Hartwick Seminary	13349
Hartwood	12729
Harvard	13756
Hasbrouck	12788
Haskell Flats	14727
Haskinville	14826
Hastings	13076
Hastings (Town)	13076
Hastings Center	13036
Hastings-on-Hudson	10706
Hatch's Corner	13684
Hauppauge	11788
Haven	12790
Haverstraw	10927
Haverstraw (Town)	10927
Haviland	12538
Hawkeye	12912
Hawkins Corner	13440
Hawkinsville	13309
Hawleys	13856
Hawleyton	13903
Hawthorne	10532
Hawthorne Hill	12309
Hawthorne Park	14787
Hawversville	12122

Name	ZIP
Hay Beach Point	11964
Haydenville	14760
Hayt Corners	14521
Hazel	12758
Head of the Harbor	11780
Heathcote (Part of Scarsdale)	10583
Heathcote (Part of New Rochelle)	10801
Heatherwood North	11733
Heatherwood South	11720
Heath Grove	13110
Heavenly Valley	12466
Hebron (Town)	12832
Hecla	13490
Hector	14841
Hector (Town)	14841
Hedgesville	14801
Helena	13649
Hell Gate (Part of New York)	10029
Helmuth	14079
Hemlock	14466
Hempstead	11550-54
For specific Hempstead Zip Codes call (516) 560-1700	
Hempstead Gardens	11552
Hemstreet Park	12118
Henderson	13650
Henderson (Town)	13650
Henderson Harbor	13651
Hendy Creek	14871
Henrietta	14467
Henrietta (Town)	14467
Hensonville	12439
Heritage (Part of Schenectady)	12303
Heritage Hills	12020
Heritage Knolls	12020
Herkimer	13350
Herkimer (Town)	13350
Hermitage (Steuben County)	14810
Hermitage (Wyoming County)	14066
Hermon	13652
Hermon (Town)	13652
Herrick Grove	13622
Herricks (Nassau County)	11040
Herrings	13653
Hertel (Part of Buffalo)	14216
Herthum Heights	13492
Hervey Street	12418
Hessville	13339
Heuvelton	13654
Hewittville	13668
Hewlett	11557
Hewlett Bay Park	11557
Hewlett Harbor	11557
Hewlett Neck	11598
Hickeys Corners (Part of Saratoga Springs)	12866
Hickorybush	12401
Hickory Grove	13126
Hicks	14859
Hicksville	11801-05
For specific Hicksville Zip Codes call (516) 933-2476	
Higgins	14065
Higgins Bay	12108
Higginsville	13054
High Bank	12981
High Bridge (Bronx County)	10452
High Bridge (Onondaga County)	13066
High Falls	12440
High Flats	13625
Highland (Sullivan County) (Town)	12732
Highland (Ulster County)	12528
Highland Falls	10928
Highland Lake	12743
Highland Mills	10930
Highland-on-the-Lake	14047
Highlands (Town)	10928
Highlawn (Part of New York)	11223
High Mills	12027
Highmount	12441
High View	12721
High Woods	12477
Hiler	14223
Hillburn	10931
Hillcrest (Broome County)	13901
Hillcrest (Rockland County)	10977
Hiller Heights	13041
Hillis	12603
Hillsboro	13316
Hillsdale	12529
Hillsdale (Town)	12529
Hillside (Part of New York)	10469
Hillside Heights	11040

Name	ZIP
Hillside Lake	12590
Hillside Manor	11040
Hillside Park (Part of Johnstown)	12095
Hillview	12144
Hilton	14468
Himrod	14842
Hinckley	13352
Hinckleyville	14559
Hindsburg	14411
Hinmans Corners	13905
Hinmansville	13135
Hinsdale	14743
Hinsdale (Town)	14743
Hoag Corners	12062
Hobart	13788
Hoboken	13411
Hoffmans	12302
Hoffmeister	13353
Hogansburg	13655
Hogtown	12827
Holbrook	11741
Holcomb	14469
Holcombville	12853
Holiday Manor (Part of Geneva)	14456
Holland	14080
Holland (Town)	14080
Holland Cove	14589
Holland Patent	13354
Holley	14470
Hollis (Part of New York)	11423
Hollis Court (Part of New York)	11429
Holliswood (Part of New York)	11352
Hollowville	12530
Hollywood	12922
Holmes	12531
Holmesville	13789
Holton Beach	14847
Holtsville (Suffolk County)	11742
Homecrest (Part of New York)	11229
Homer	13077
Homer (Town)	13077
Homer Hill (Part of Olean)	14760
Homestead Park (Part of New Rochelle)	10801
Homestead Village	11727
Homewood	13066
Homewood Park	14225
Honeoye	14471
Honeoye Falls	14472
Honest Hill	14470
Honeywell Corners	12025
Honk Hill	12458
Honnedaga Lake	13338
Hoosick	12089
Hoosick (Town)	12089
Hoosick Falls	12090
Hoosick Junction	12133
Hope (Town)	12134
Hope Falls	12134
Hope Farm	12545
Hope Valley	12134
Hopewell (Town)	14424
Hopewell Center	14424
Hopewell Junction	12533
Hopkinton	12940
Hopkinton (Town)	12940
Horace Harding (Part of New York)	11362
Horicon (Town)	12815
Hornby	14812
Hornby (Town)	14812
Hornell	14843
Hornellsville (Town)	14807
Horseheads	14844-45
For specific Horseheads Zip Codes call (607) 739-0371	
Horseheads (Town)	14845
Horseheads North	14845
Horton	12776
Horton Estates	10587
Hortonville	12745
Hospital (Part of Binghamton)	13904
Houghton	14744
Hounsfield (Town)	13685
Houseville	13473
Housons Corners	12122
Howard (Town)	14809
Howard (New York County)	10013
Howard (Steuben County)	14809
Howard Beach (Part of New York)	11414
Howardville	13302
Howells	10932
Howes Cave	12092
Howlett Hill	13031

370 NEW YORK Hub-Kingsway

Name	ZIP
Hub (Part of New York)	10455
Hubbardsville	13355
Hubbardtown	13743
Hudson	12534
Hudson Falls	12839
Hudson Upper (Part of Hudson)	12534
Hughsonville	12537
Huguenot (Orange County)	12746
Huguenot (Richmond County)	10301
Huguenot Park (Part of New Rochelle)	10801
Hulberton	14470
Huletts Landing	12841
Hullsville	13827
Hume	14745
Hume (Town)	14745
Humphrey (Town)	14741
Humphrey Center	14741
Hungerford Corners	13650
Hunt	14846
Hunter	12442
Hunter (Town)	12442
Hunter Lake	12768
Huntersland	12122
Huntington (Town)	11743
Huntington (Suffolk County)	11743
Huntington Bay	11743
Huntington Beach	11721
Huntington Square	11731
Huntington Station	11746
Huntingtonville	13601
Hunts Corners (Cortland County)	13803
Hunts Corners (Erie County)	14031
Hunts Corners (Sullivan County)	12764
Hurd Corners	12564
Hurley (Town)	12443
Hurley	12443
Hurleyville	12747
Huron (Town)	14590
Hyde Park (Dutchess County)	12538
Hyde Park (Town)	12538
Hyde Park (Otsego County)	13326
Hylan Shopping Plaza (Part of New York)	10306
Hyndsville	12043
Idle Hour	11769
Idlewood	14085
Ilion	13357
Imperial Plaza (Part of Wappingers Falls)	12590
Inavale	14739
Independence	14806
Independence (Town)	14806
Index	13326
Indian Castle	13365
Indian Cove	13118
Indian Falls	14036
Indian Kettles	12836
Indian Lake	12842
Indian Lake (Town)	12842
Indian Park	10925
Indian River	13327
Indian Springs	13027
Indian Village	13120
Industry	14474
Ingham Mills	13365
Ingleside	14512
Ingraham	12992
Inlet	13360
Inlet (Town)	13360
Inman	12968
Inter County Shopping Center	11758
Interlaken	14847
Interlaken Beach	14847
International Junction	14223
Inwood (Nassau County)	11696
Inwood (New York County)	10034
Ionia (Onondaga County)	13112
Ionia (Ontario County)	14475
Ira	13033
Ira (Town)	13033
Ira Station	13033
Ireland Corners	12525
Irelandville	14891
Irish Settlement	13625
Irona	12910
Irondequoit (Monroe County) (Town)	14617
Irondequoit (Monroe County)	14617
Irondequoit Manor	14617
Irongate	13088
Ironville	12928
Irving	14081
Irvington	10533

Name	ZIP
Ischua	14743
Ischua (Town)	14743
Island (Part of New York)	10044
Island Cottage Beach	14612
Islandia	11722
Island Park	11558
Isle of San Souci (Part of New Rochelle)	10805
Islip	11751
Islip (Town)	11751
Islip Manor	11751
Islip Terrace	11752
Italy	14512
Italy (Town)	14512
Itaska	13862
Ithaca	14850-52

For specific Ithaca Zip Codes call (607) 272-5454

Name	ZIP
Ithaca College	14850
Ivanhoe	13839
Ives Corner	12018
Jackson (Town)	12816
Jacksonburg	13407
Jackson Corners	12571
Jackson Heights (Part of New York)	11372
Jackson Summit	12117
Jacksonville (Onondaga County)	13135
Jacksonville (Tompkins County)	14854
Jacks Reef	13112
Jamaica	11401-36

For specific Jamaica Zip Codes call (718) 990-1111

COLLEGES & UNIVERSITIES

Name	ZIP
City University of New York-York College	11451

FINANCIAL INSTITUTIONS

Name	ZIP
Chase Manhattan Bank, N.A.	11432

HOSPITALS

Name	ZIP
Jamaica Hospital	11418
Queens Hospital Center	11432

HOTELS/MOTELS

Name	ZIP
JFK Airport Hilton	11436
Marriott JFK Airport	11436
Kennedy Inn	11434

MILITARY INSTALLATIONS

Name	ZIP
John F. Kennedy International Airport, Air Force Facility	11430

Name	ZIP
Jamesport (Suffolk County)	11947
Jamestown	14701-02

For specific Jamestown Zip Codes call (716) 488-0785

Name	ZIP
Jamestown West	14701
Jamesville	13078
Janesville	12043
Jasper	14855
Jasper (Town)	14855
Java (Town)	14082
Java Center	14082
Java Lake	14009
Java Village	14083
Jay	12941
Jay (Town)	12941
Jeddo	14103
Jefferson	12093
Jefferson (Town)	12093
Jefferson Heights	12414
Jefferson Park	13698
Jefferson Valley	10535
Jefferson Valley Mall	10598
Jefferson Valley-Yorktown	10535
Jeffersonville	12748
Jenksville	13736
Jericho (Clinton County)	12910
Jericho (Nassau County)	11753
Jericho (Suffolk County)	11937
Jerome Avenue (Part of New York)	10468
Jersey Colony	11971
Jerusalem (Town)	14418
Jerusalem Corners	14047
Jewell	13042
Jewel Manor	13088
Jewett	12444
Jewett (Town)	12444
Jewett Center	12442
Jewettville	13634
John F. Kennedy Airport (Part of New York)	11430
Johnsburg	12843

Name	ZIP
Johnsburg (Town)	12843
Johnson	10933
Johnsonburg	14167
Johnson City	13790
Johnson Creek	14067
Johnsonville	12094
Johnstown (Fulton County) (Town)	12078
Johnstown (Fulton County)	12095
Jones Point	10986
Jonesville	12065
Jordan	13080
Jordanville	13361
Junction Boulevard (Part of New York)	11372
Junius (Town)	13165
Kabob	14782
Kaisertown	12549
Kanona	14856
Kasoag	13302
Katonah	10536
Katsbaan	12477
Kattelville	13901
Kattskill Bay	12844
Kauneonga Lake	12749
Kaydeross Park (Part of Saratoga Springs)	12866
Kayuta Lake	13338
Kecks Center	12095
Keefers Corners	12067
Keene	12942
Keene (Town)	12942
Keene Valley	12943
Keeseville	12944
Kelleys	12056
Kelloggsville	13118
Kelly Corners	12455
Kelsey	13783
Kendaia	14541
Kendall	14476
Kendall (Town)	14476
Kendall Mills	14470
Kenilworth (Part of Kings Point)	11024
Kenmore	14217
Kennedy	14747
Kenoza Lake	12750
Kensington (Erie County)	14215
Kensington (Kings County)	11218
Kensington (Nassau County)	11021
Kent (Orleans County)	14477
Kent (Putnam County) (Town)	10512
Kent Cliffs	10512
Kents Corners	13630
Kenwood (Part of Oneida)	13421
Kenwood Estates	10512
Kenyonville	14571
Kerhonkson	12446
Kerleys Corners	12571
Kernan (Part of Utica)	13502
Ketchums Corner	12170
Ketchumville	13736
Keuka	14837
Keuka Park	14478
Kew Gardens (Part of New York)	11415
Kew Gardens Hills (Part of New York)	11366
Kiamesha Lake	12751
Kiantone	14701
Kiantone (Town)	14701
Kidders	14847
Killawog	13794
Kill Buck	14748
Kimball Stand	14701
Kinderhook	12106
Kinderhook (Town)	12106
King Ferry	13081
Kings Bridge (Part of New York)	10463
Kingsbury	12839
Kingsbury (Town)	12839
Kings Ferry	13081
Kings Park (Suffolk County)	11754
Kings Park Psychiatric Center	11754
Kings Plaza Shopping Center and Marina (Part of New York)	11234
Kings Point	11024
Kings Settlement	13815
Kings Station	12831
Kingston (Ulster County)	12401
Kingston (Ulster County) (Town)	12401
Kingston Plaza (Part of Kingston)	12401
Kingsway (Part of New York)	11229

Kipps-Locust Grove NEW YORK 371

Name	ZIP
Kipps	10924
Kirk	13844
Kirkland	13323
Kirkland (Town)	13323
Kirkville	13082
Kirkwood	13795
Kirkwood (Town)	13795
Kirschnerville	13327
Kiryas Joel	10950
Kisco Park	10549
Kiskatom	12414
Kismet	11706
Kitchawan	10562
Knapp Creek	14749
Knapps Corner	12603
Knickerbocker (Part of New York)	10002
Knights Creek	14880
Knights Eddy	12780
Knowelhurst	12878
Knowlesville	14479
Knox	12107
Knox (Town)	12107
Knoxboro	13362
Koenig's Point	13021
Komar Park	12019
Kortright	13739
Kortright (Town)	13739
Kossuth	14715
Kringsbush	13452
Kripplebush	12484
Krumville	12461
Kyserike	12440
Lackawanna	14218
Lacona	13083
Ladentown (Part of Pomona)	10970
LaFargeville	13656
La Fayette	13084
LaFayette (Town)	13084
Lafayetteville	12571
La Grange (Dutchess County) (Town)	12540
Lagrange (Wyoming County)	14525
Lagrangeville	12540
La Guardia Airport (Part of New York)	11371
Lairdsville	13323
Lake	10990
Lake Bluff	14590
Lake Bonaparte	13648
Lake Carmel	10512
Lake Charles	12563
Lake Clear	12945
Lake Como	13045
Lake Delta	13440
Lake Erie Beach	14006
Lake Gardens	10541
Lake George	12845
Lake George (Town)	12845
Lake Grove	11755
Lake Hill	12448
Lake Huntington	12752
Lake Katonah	10536
Lake Katrine	12449
Lake Kitchawan	10590
Lakeland (Onondaga County)	13209
Lakeland (Suffolk County)	11779
Lake Lincolndale	10541
Lake Lucille	10956
Lake Luzerne	12846
Lake Luzerne (Town)	12846
Lake Luzerne-Hadley	12835
Lake Mahopac	10541
Lakemont	14857
Lake Moraine	13346
Lake Muskoday	12776
Lake Osceola	10535
Lake Osiris Colony	12586
Lake Panamoka	11961
Lake Peekskill	10537
Lake Placid	12946
Lake Placid Club Resort (Part of Lake Placid)	12946
Lake Pleasant	12108
Lake Pleasant (Town)	12108
Lakeport	13037
Lake Purdy	10578
Lake Ronkonkoma (Suffolk County)	11779
Lake Ronkonkoma Heights	11779
Lake Secor	10541
Lakeside (Orange County)	10930
Lakeside (Wayne County)	14519
Lakeside Park (Albany County)	12205
Lakeside Park (Orleans County)	14571
Lake Station	10990
Lake Success	11040
Lake Success Shopping Center	11040
Lake Sunnyside	12845
Lake Vanare	12846
Lake View (Erie County)	14085
Lakeview (Nassau County)	11552
Lakeview (Oswego County)	13126
Lakeville (Livingston County)	14480
Lakeville (Nassau County)	11040
Lakeville Estates	11040
Lakewood	14750
Lamberton	14063
Lambs Corner	12083
Lamont	14427
Lamson	13135
Lancaster	14086
Lancaster (Town)	14086
Lane (Part of Batavia)	14020
Lanesville	12450
Langdon	13795
Langdon Corners	13617
Langford	14057
Lansing (Town)	14882
Lansing (Oswego County)	13126
Lansing (Tompkins County)	14882
Lansingburg (Part of Troy)	12182
Laona	14063
Lapala	12401
Lapeer (Town)	13803
Laphams Mills	12972
Larchmont	10538
Larchmont North	10538
La Salle	14304
Lassellsville	13452
Latham	12110
Latham Circle Mall	12110
Lathams Corners	13843
Lattingtown	11560
Laughing Waters	11971
Laurel	11948
Laurel Hollow	11791
Laurelton (Monroe County)	14617
Laurelton (Queens County)	11431
Laurens	13796
Laurens (Town)	13796
Lava	12764
Lawrence (Nassau County)	11559
Lawrence (St. Lawrence County) (Town)	12965
Lawrence Farms	10514
Lawrence Park (Part of Yonkers)	10708
Lawrenceville	12949
Lawtons	14091
Lawyersville	12113
Lebanon	13085
Lebanon (Town)	13085
Lebanon Center	13332
Lebanon Springs	12114
Ledyard	13081
Ledyard (Town)	13026
Lee	13440
Lee (Town)	13440
Lee Center	13363
Leeds	12451
Leedsville	12501
Leeside	10512
Leesville	13459
Lefever Falls	12472
Lefferts (Part of New York)	11225
Leibhardt	12404
Leicester	14481
Leicester (Town)	14481
LeMarr Estates	12184
Lenox (Town)	13032
Lenox Furnace	13032
Lenox Hill (Part of New York)	10021
Lenox Park	14456
Leon	14751
Leon (Town)	14751
Leonardsville	13364
Leonta	13775
Le Ray (Town)	13637
Le Roy	14482
Le Roy (Town)	14482
Le Roy Island	14590
Levanna	13026
Levant	14733
Levittown	11756
Lewbeach	12753
Lewis	12950
Lewis (Essex County) (Town)	12950
Lewis (Lewis County) (Town)	13489
Lewisboro (Town)	10590
Lewiston	14092
Lewiston (Town)	14092
Lewiston Heights (Part of Lewiston)	14092
Lewiston Manor	13224
Lexington	12452
Lexington (Town)	12452
Leyden (Town)	13433
Liberty	12754
Liberty (Town)	12754
Liberty Gardens (Part of Rome)	13440
Libertypole	14437
Lido Beach	11561
Lily Dale	14752
Lima	14485
Lima (Town)	14485
Lime Lake	14042
Lime Lake-Machias	14042
Limerick	13657
Lime Rock	14482
Limestone	14753
Limestreet	12414
Lincklaen	13052
Lincklaen (Town)	13052
Lincoln (Madison County) (Town)	13043
Lincoln (Wayne County)	14502
Lincolndale	10540
Lincoln Park (Erie County)	14223
Lincoln Park (Monroe County)	14611
Lincoln Park (Ulster County)	12401
Lincolnshire	13760
Lincolnton (Part of New York)	10037
Lindbergh Court (Part of Colonie)	12205
Linden	14054
Linden Acres	12571
Linden Hill (Part of New York)	11354
Lindenhurst	11757
Lindley	14858
Lindley (Town)	14858
Linlithgo	12526
Linwood	14486
Lisbon	13658
Lisbon (Town)	13658
Lisle	13797
Lisle (Town)	13797
Litchfield (Town)	13456
Lithgow	12545
Little America	13144
Little Bow	13642
Little Britain	12575
Little Canada	14054
Little Falls (Herkimer County)	13365
Little Falls (Herkimer County) (Town)	13407
Little Falls Park (Part of Wappingers Falls)	12590
Little France	13036
Little Genesee	14754
Little Neck (Part of New York)	11363
Little Plains	11731
Little Ram Island	11964
Little Utica	13135
Little Valley	14755
Little Valley (Town)	14755
Littleville	14424
Little York (Cortland County)	13087
Little York (Orange County)	10969
Liverpool	13088-90
For specific Liverpool Zip Codes call (315) 451-3060	
Livingston	12541
Livingston (Town)	12541
Livingston (Part of New York)	11201
Livingston Manor	12758
Livingstonville	12122
Livonia	14487
Livonia (Town)	14487
Livonia Center	14488
Lloyd (Town)	12528
Lloyd Harbor	11743
Lochada Lake	12719
Loch Muller	12857
Loch Sheldrake	12759
Lock Berlin	14489
Locke	13092
Locke (Town)	13092
Lockport (Niagara County)	14094
Lockport (Niagara County) (Town)	14094
Locksley Park	14075
Lockwood	14859
Locust Grove (Lewis County)	13309

372 NEW YORK Locust Grove-Meadows

	ZIP		ZIP		ZIP
Locust Grove (Nassau County)	11791	Lysander (Town)	13094	Maplecrest	12454
Locust Manor (Part of New York)	11431	Mabbettsville	12545	Mapledale	12406
Locust Point (Part of New York)	10465	McClure	13754	Maple Grove (Hamilton County)	12134
Locust Valley	11560	McConnellsville	13401	Maple Grove (Otsego County)	13808
Lodi	14860	MacDonnell Heights	12603	Maple Hill	12401
Lodi (Town)	14860	McDonough	13801	Maplehurst	14743
Lodi Center	14860	McDonough (Town)	13801	Maples	14755
Lodi Point	14860	MacDougall	14541	Maple Springs	14756
Logan	14818	Macedon	14502	Mapleton	13021
Logtown	12771	Macedon (Town)	14502	Mapletown	13317
Lomala	12533	Macedon Center	14502	Maple Transit	14221
Lombard	14775	McGraw	13101	Maple Valley	13488
Lomond Shore	14476	McGrawville	14777	Maple View	13107
Lomontville	12401	Machias (Town)	14101	Maplewood (Albany County)	12189
London Terrace (Part of New York)	10011	Machias (Cattaraugus County)	14101	Maplewood (Sullivan County)	12701
Lonelyville	11706	McKeever	13338	Marathon	13803
Long Beach	11561	Mackey	12076	Marathon (Town)	13803
Long Branch	13088	McKinley	13428	Marble Hill (Part of New York)	10463
Long Branch Manor	13088	McKinstry Hollow	14042	Marbletown	12401
Long Bridge	13153	McKown Park	12203	Marbletown (Town)	12401
Long Eddy	12760	McKownville	12203	Marbletown	14513
		McKownville Estates	12203	Marcellus	13108
Long Island City	11101-06	McLaughlin Acres	10541	Marcellus (Town)	13108
For specific Long Island City Zip Codes call (718) 349-4626		McLean	13102	Marcellus Falls	13108
		McMasters Corners	13201	Marcy (Kings County)	11206
FINANCIAL INSTITUTIONS		McNalls	14067	Marcy (Oneida County)	
		Macomb (Town)	13642		13503
Astoria Federal Savings & Loan Association	11103	McPherson Point	14487	Marengo	14433
Financial Federal Savings & Loan Association	11104	Madison	13402	Margaretville	12455
The Long Island City Savings & Loan Association	11103	Madison (Town)	13402	Mariaville	12137
		Madison Park	11731	Marietta	13110
		Madison Square (Part of New York)	10010	Marilla	14102
HOSPITALS		Madrid	13660	Marilla (Town)	14102
		Madrid (Town)	13660	Marine Hospital (Part of New York)	10301
Long Island Jewish Medical Center	11042	Magnolia	14757	Mariners Harbor (Part of New York)	10303
		Mahopac	10541	Marion	14505
Long Island University Southampton Center	11968	Mahopac Falls	10542	Marion (Town)	14505
Long Lake	12847	Mahopac Hills	10541	Mariposa	13155
Long Lake (Town)	12847	Mahopac Point	10541	Markhams	14070
Long Ridge Mall	14626	Mahopac Ridge	10541	Marlboro	12542
Long View	14710	Maidstone Park	11937	Marlborough (Town)	12542
Longwood (Part of New York)	10459	Maine	13802	Marshall (Allegany County)	14711
Loomis	12754	Maine (Town)	13802	Marshall (Oneida County) (Town)	13328
Loomises	14710	Main Settlement	14770	Marshfield	14091
Loon Lake	12968	Main Village (Part of Williamsville)	14221	Marshland Heights	13760
Loon Lake Junction	12968	Malden Bridge	12115	Marshville (Montgomery County)	13317
Lordville	13783	Malden on Hudson	12453	Marshville (St. Lawrence County)	13652
Lorenz Park	12534	Mall	11706	Martindale Depot	12521
Lorings	13045	Mall at New Rochelle, The (Part of New Rochelle)	10801	Martinsburg	13404
Lorraine	13659	Mallory	13103	Martinsburg (Town)	13404
Lorraine (Town)	13659	Malone	12953	Martisco	13108
Lost Valley	12010	Malone (Town)	12953	Martville	13111
Loudonville	12211	Malta	12020	Maryknoll	10545
Louisville	13662	Malta (Town)	12020	Maryland	12116
Louisville (Town)	13662	Malta Ridge	12020	Maryland (Town)	12116
Lounsberry	13812	Maltaville	12020	Marymount (Part of Tarrytown)	10591
Lower Chateaugay Lake	12920	Maltbie Heights	14070	Masonville	13804
Lower Cincinnatus	13040	Malverne	11565	Masonville (Town)	13804
Lower Genegantslet Corner	13778	Malvic Manor	13088	Maspeth (Part of New York)	11378
Lower Melville	11747	Mamakating (Town)	12790	Massapequa	11758
Lower Oswegatchie	13670	Mamakating Park	12790	Massapequa Park	11762
Lower Rotterdam	12306	Mamaroneck	10543	Massawepie	12986
Lower South Bay	13041	Mamaroneck (Town)	10543	Massena	13662
Low Hampton	05743	Manchester	14504	Massena (Town)	13662
Lowman	14861	Manchester (Town)	14504	Massena Center	13662
Lowville	13367	Manchester Bridge	12603	Massena Springs (Part of Massena)	13662
Lowville (Town)	13367	Mandana	13152	Masten Lake	12790
Ludingtonville	12531	Manhasset	11030	Mastic	11950
Ludlow (Part of Yonkers)	10705	Manhasset Hills	11040	Mastic Beach	11951
Ludlowville	14882	Manhattan (Part of New York)	10027	Matinecock	11560
Lumberland (Town)	12770	Manhattan Park (Part of White Plains)	10601	Matteawan (Part of Beacon)	12508
Luther	12061	Manhattanville (Part of New York)	10027	Mattituck	11952
Lutheranville	12064	Manhattanville College (Part of Harrison)	10577	Mattydale	13211
Lycoming	13093	Manheim (Town)	13329	Maybrook	12543
Lyell (Part of Rochester)	14606	Manheim Center	13365	Mayfair	12302
Lykers	12166	Manitou	10524	Mayfair Shopping Center	11725
Lyme (Town)	13693	Manitou Beach	14468	Mayfield	12117
Lynbrook	11563	Manlius	13104	Mayfield (Town)	12117
Lyncourt	13208	Manlius (Town)	13104	Mayville	14757
Lyndon (Cattaraugus County) (Town)	14737	Manlius Center	13066	Maywood (Albany County)	12205
Lyndon (Onondaga County)	13066	Mannetto Hills	11747	Maywood (Suffolk County)	11701
Lyndonville	14098	Manning	14470	Meacham	11003
Lynelle Meadows	13088	Mannsville	13661	Meadowbrook	12550
Lyon Mountain	12952	Mannville	12189	Meadowdale	12009
Lyons	14489	Manny Corners	12010	Meadow Hill	12550
Lyons (Town)	14489	Manor	13413	Meadow Lane Estates	12184
Lyonsdale	13368	Manorhaven	11050	Meadowmere Park	11598
Lyonsdale (Town)	13368	Manorkill	12076	Meadow Run (Part of Hamburg)	14075
Lyons Falls	13368	Manors	11507	Meadows	14420
Lyonsville	12404	Manorville (Suffolk County)	11949		
Lysander	13094	Manorville (Ulster County)	12477		
		Mansfield (Town)	14755		
		Maple Bay	14710		

Meads-Naples **NEW YORK** 373

	ZIP		ZIP		ZIP
Meads		Millertown	12094	Morris (Town)	13808
Meads Creek	14870	Mill Grove	14770	Morrisania (Part of New York)	10456
Mechanicville	12118	Mill Hook	12404		
Mecklenburg	14863	Mill Neck	11765	Morris Heights (Part of New York)	10453
Meco	12078	Mill Point	12010		
Medford	11763	Millport	14864	Morrison Heights	12549
Medina	14103	Millsburgh	10933	Morrisonville	12962
Medusa	12120	Mills Mills	14735	Morris Park (Part of New York)	10461
Medway	12042	Millville	14103		
Melcourt (Part of New York)	10451	Millwood	10546	Morristown	13664
Mellenville	12544	Milo (Town)	14527	Morristown (Town)	13664
Melrose	12121	Milo Center	14527	Morrisville	13408
Melrose Park	13021	Milton	12020	Morrisville Station	13408
Melville	11747	Milton (Town)	12020	Morsston	12758
Memphis	13112	Milton (Saratoga County)	12020	Morton (Monroe County)	14464
Menands	12204	Milton (Ulster County)	12547	Morton (Orleans County)	14508
Mendon	14506	Milton Point (Part of Rye)	10580	Mosherville	12074
Mendon (Town)	14506	Mina	14781	Mosholu (Part of New York)	10467
Mendon Center	14472	Mina (Town)	14781	Mosquito Point	12468
Mendon Farms	14506	Minaville	12010	Mott Haven (Part of New York)	10454
Menteth Point	14424	Minden (Town)	13339		
Mentz (Town)	13140	Mindenville	13339	Mottville	13119
Meredith	13753	Mineola	11501	Mountain Dale	12763
Meredith (Town)	13753	Mineral Springs	12043	Mountain Lodge	10950
Meridale	13806	Minerva	12851	Mountain View (Franklin County)	12969
Meridian	13113	Minerva (Town)	12851		
Merillon Avenue (Part of Garden City)	11530	Minetto	13115	Mountain View (Rensselaer County)	12180
		Minetto (Town)	13115		
Merrick	11566	Mineville	12956	Mountain View East	10989
Merrickville	13839	Mineville-Witherbee	12956	Mountainville	10953
Merriewold	12701	Minisink (Town)	10998	Mount Carmel (Part of New York)	10458
Merriewold Lake	10950	Minisink Ford	12719		
Merrifield	13147	Minklers Corners	13662	Mount Eve	10924
Merrill	12955	Minoa	13116	Mount Hope	10940
Merrillsville	13421	Mitchellsville	14810	Mount Hope (Town)	10940
Merrilville	12986	Model City	14107	Mount Hope (Part of Hastings-on-Hudson)	10706
Merriweather Campus (Part of Brookville)	11548	Modena	12548		
		Moffitsville	12981	Mount Ivy	10970
Mertensia	14564	Mohawk (Herkimer County)	13407	Mount Kisco (Westchester County)	10549
Messengerville	13803	Mohawk (Montgomery County) (Town)	12068		
Metropolitan (Part of New York)	11206			Mount Kisco (Westchester County) (Town)	10549
		Mohawk Hill	13309		
Mettacahonts	12404	Mohawk Mall	12304	Mount Loretto (Part of New York)	10309
Mews	11507	Mohawk View	12110		
Mexico	13114	Mohawk Village	12303	Mount Marion	12456
Mexico (Town)	13114	Mohegan Heights (Part of Yonkers)	10708	Mount McGregor Correctional Facility	12866
Middle Bridge	13730				
Middleburgh	12122	Mohegan Lake	10547	Mount Merion Park	12456
Middleburgh (Town)	12122	Mohonk Lake	12561	Mount Morris	14510
Middlebury (Town)	14591	Moira	12957	Mount Morris (Town)	14510
Middle Falls	12848	Moira (Town)	12957	Mount Pleasant (Oswego County)	13069
Middlefield	13450	Mombaccus	12446		
Middlefield (Town)	13450	Mongaup	12780	Mount Pleasant (Ulster County)	12457
Middlefield Center	13320	Mongaup Valley	12762		
Middle Granville	12849	Monroe	10950	Mount Pleasant (Westchester County) (Town)	10591
Middle Grove	12850	Monroe (Town)	10950		
Middle Hope	12550	Monroe Southwest	10950		
Middle Island	11953	Monsey	10952	Mount Prosper	12790
Middleport (Madison County)	13346	Monsey Heights	10952	Mount Ross	12567
		Montague (Town)	13367	Mount Sinai	11766
Middleport (Niagara County)	14105	Montario Point	13661	Mount Tremper	12457
Middlesex	14507	Montauk	11954	Mount Upton	13809
Middlesex (Town)	14507	Montauk Beach	11954	Mount Vernon (Westchester County)	10550-53
Middletown (Delaware County) (Town)	12455	Montclair Colony	11964		
		Montebello	10901	For specific Mount Vernon Zip Codes call (914) 964-7201	
Middletown (Orange County)	10940	Monterey	14812		
		Monterey Estates	10989	Mount Vernon (Erie County)	14075
Middletown Psychiatric Center (Part of Middletown)	10940	Montezuma	13117	Mount View Acres	12184
		Montezuma (Town)	13117	Mount View Estates	12184
		Montgomery	12549	Mount Vision	13810
Middle Village (Part of New York)	11379	Montgomery (Town)	12549	Mud Mills	14513
		Monticello	12701	Muitzeskill	12156
Middleville (Herkimer County)	13406	Montour (Town)	14865	Mumford	14511
		Montour Falls	14865	Mungers Corners	13069
Middleville (Suffolk County)	11768	Montrose	10548	Municipal Building (Part of New York)	11201
Mid-Island Mall	11801	Montville	13118		
Midland Beach (Part of New York)	10306	Moody	12986	Munnsville	13409
		Mooers	12958	Munsey Park	11030
Mid-Orange Correctional Facility	10990	Mooers (Town)	12958	Munsons Corners	13045
		Mooers Forks	12959	Murdochs Crossing	14098
Mid-State Correctional Facility	13403	Moores Mill	12569	Murdock Woods	10583
		Moorhouse Corner	12037	Murray	14470
Midtown (Part of New York)	10018	Moose River	13433	Murray (Town)	14470
		Moravia	13118	Murray Hill (New York County)	10016
Midtown Plaza (Part of Rochester)	14604	Moravia (Town)	13118		
Midway	14864	Moreau (Town)	12801	Murray Hill (Queens County)	11354
Midwood (Part of New York)	11230	Morehouse (Town)	13324	Murray Hill (Westchester County)	10583
		Morehouseville	13324		
Milan (Town)	12571	Moreland	14812	Murray Isle	13624
Mileses	12741	Morey Park	12123	Muttontown	11791
Milford	13807	Morgan (Part of New York)	10001	Myers	14882
Milford (Town)	13807	Morgan Hill	12401	Myers Corner	12590
Milford Center	13820	Morganville	14143	Myers Grove	12739
Mill Brook (Bronx County)	10454	Moriah	12960	Nanticoke	13802
Millbrook (Dutchess County)	12545	Moriah (Town)	12960	Nanticoke (Town)	13803
Millen Bay	13618	Moriah Center	12961	Nanuet	10954
Miller Place	11764	Moriches	11955	Nanuet Mall	10954
Millers	14098	Morley	13617	Napanoch	12458
Millers Mills	13491	Morningside (Part of New York)	10026	Napeague	11930
Millersport	14051			Naples	14512
Millerton	12546	Morris	13808		

374 NEW YORK Naples-New York

	ZIP
Naples (Town)	14512
Napoli	14755
Napoli (Town)	14755
Narrowsburg	12764
Nashville	14062
Nassau	12123
Nassau (Town)	12123
Nassau Lake (Rensselaer County)	12123
Nassau Mall	11756
Nassau Shores	11758
Natural Bridge	13665
Natural Dam	13642
Naumburg	13620
Nauraushaun	10965
Navarino	13108
Nazareth College of Rochester	14610
Nedrow	13120
Neiam (Part of New York)	11212
Nelliston	13410
Nelson	13035
Nelson (Town)	13035
Nelsonville	10516
Nepera Park (Part of Yonkers)	10710
Neponsit (Part of New York)	11694
Nepperhan (Part of Yonkers)	10703
Nesconset	11767
Neversink	12765
Neversink (Town)	12765
New Albion	14719
New Albion (Town)	14719
Newark	14513
Newark Valley	13811
Newark Valley (Town)	13811
New Baltimore	12124
New Baltimore (Town)	12124
New Berlin	13411
New Berlin (Town)	13411
New Berlin Junction	13733
New Bremen	13367
New Bremen (Town)	13367
New Brighton (Part of New York)	10310
Newburg	14550
Newburgh (Orange County)	12550
Newburgh (Orange County) (Town)	12550
Newburgh West	12550
New Cassel	11590
New Castle (Town)	10514
New City	10956
New City Park	10956
Newcomb	12852
Newcomb (Town)	12852
New Concord	12060
New Dorp (Part of New York)	10306
New Dorp Beach (Part of New York)	10306
New Ebenezer	14224
New Falconwood	14072
Newfane	14108
Newfane (Town)	14108
Newfield	14867
Newfield (Town)	14867
New Hackensack	12590
New Hamburg	12590
New Hampton	10958
New Hampton-Denton	10958
New Hartford	13413
New Hartford (Town)	13413
New Hartford Shopping Center (Part of New Hartford)	13413
New Haven	13121
New Haven (Town)	13121
New Hempstead	10977
New Hope	13118
New Hudson (Town)	14714
New Hurley	12525
New Hyde Park	11040
New Ireland	13905
New Kingston	12459
Newkirk (Part of New York)	11226
New Lebanon	12125
New Lebanon (Town)	12125
New Lebanon Center	12125
New Lisbon	13415
New Lisbon (Town)	13415
New Lots (Part of New York)	11208
New Market (Part of Niagara Falls)	14301
New Milford	10959
New Oregon	14057
New Paltz	12561
New Paltz (Town)	12561
Newport	13416

	ZIP
Newport (Town)	13416
Newport (Monroe County)	14617
Newport (Onondaga County)	13164
New Rochelle	10801-05
For specific New Rochelle Zip Codes call (914) 632-5906	
New Russia	12964
New Salem (Albany County)	12186
New Salem (Ulster County)	12401
New Scotland	12127
New Scotland (Town)	12127
Newsday	11747
New Springville (Part of New York)	10314
New Square	10977
Newstead (Town)	14001
New Suffolk	11956
Newton Falls	13666
Newton Hook	12173
Newtonville	12128
Newtown	11946
New Vernon	10940
Newville	13365
New Windsor	12550
New Windsor (Town)	12550
New Windsor West	12550
New Woodstock	13122
New York	10001-99
	10101-99
	10201-82
For specific New York Zip Codes call (212) 967-8585	

COLLEGES & UNIVERSITIES

	ZIP
Barnard College	10027
City University of New York-Bernard M. Baruch College	10010
City University of New York-City College	10031
City University of New York-Graduate School and University Center	10036
City University of New York-Hunter College	10021
City University of New York-John Jay College of Criminal Justice	10019
College of Insurance	10007
Columbia University-Columbia College	10027
Cooper Union	10003
Fashion Institute of Technology	10001
The Juilliard School	10023
Marymount Manhattan College	10021
New School for Social Research-Eugene Lang College	10011
New York Institute of Technology-Metropolitan Center	10023
New York Law School	10013
New York University	10012
School of Visual Arts	10010
Touro College	10036
Yeshiva University	10033

FINANCIAL INSTITUTIONS

	ZIP
Amalgamated Bank of New York	10003
Apple Bank for Savings	10017
Atlantic Bank of New York	10001
Banco Central of New York	10004
Banco de Bogota Trust Company	10152
Bank Audi (USA)	10020
Bankers Federal Savings, FSB	10038
Bankers Trust Company	10017
Bank Leumi Trust Company of New York	10017
The Bank of New York	10286
The Bank of Tokyo Trust Company	10005
Barclays Bank of New York, National Association	10265
Bowery Savings Bank	10017
Brown Brothers Harriman & Co	10005
Canadian Imperial Bank of Commerce (New York)	10005
Capital National Bank	10033
Carver Federal Savings Bank	10027
The Chase Manhattan Bank, N.A.	10081
Chemical Bank	10172

	ZIP
The Chinese American Bank	10038
Citibank, N.A.	10043
Daiwa Bank Trust Company	10019
The Depository Trust Company	10004
East River Savings Bank	10007
Edison Federal Savings & Loan Association	10276
Emigrant Savings Bank	10017
Ensign Bank, F.S.B.	10022
European American Bank	10005
Fiduciary Trust Company International	10048
First American Bank of New York	10022
The First New York Bank for Business	10022
Fourth Federal Savings & Loan Association	10021
Freedom National Bank of New York	10027
French American Banking Corporation	10022
The Fuji Bank and Trust Company	10048
The Greater New York Savings Bank	10119
IBJ Schroder Bank & Trust Company	10004
The Industrial Bank of Japan Trust Company	10167
Israel Discount Bank of New York	10017
LTCB Trust Company	10006
The Manhattan Savings Bank	10017
Manufacturers Hanover Trust Company	10017
The Merchants Bank of New York	10013
Mitsubishi Trust & Banking Corporation (USA)	10281
Morgan Guaranty Trust Company of New York	10015
National Westminster Bank USA	10038
Nationar	10017
Republic National Bank of New York	10018
Safra National Bank of New York	10036
Security Pacific National Trust Company	10006
State Street Bank and Trust Company, National Association	10006
Sterling National Bank & Trust Company of New York	10022
Sumitomo Bank & Trust Co. (U.S.A.)	10022
UBAF Arab American Bank	10022
UMB Bank and Trust Company	10020
Union Chelsea National Bank	10017
United States Trust Company of New York	10005

HOSPITALS

	ZIP
Bellevue Hospital Center	10016
Beth Isreal Medical Center	10003
Cabrini Medical Center	10003
Coler Memorial Hospital	10044
Doctors Hospital	10128
Goldwater Memorial Hospital	10044
Harlem Hospital Center	10037
Lenox Hill Hospital	10021
Memorial Hospital for Cancer and Allied Diseases	10021
Metropolitan Hospital Center	10029
Mount Sinai Medical Center	10029
New York Infirmary-Beekman Downtown Hospital	10038
New York University Medical Center	10016
Presbyterian Hospital in the City of New York	10032
Society of the New York Hospital	10021
St. Clare's Hospital and Health Center	10019
St. Luke's-Roosevelt Hospital Center	10019
St. Vincent's Hospital and Medical Center of New York	10011

New York **NEW YORK** 375

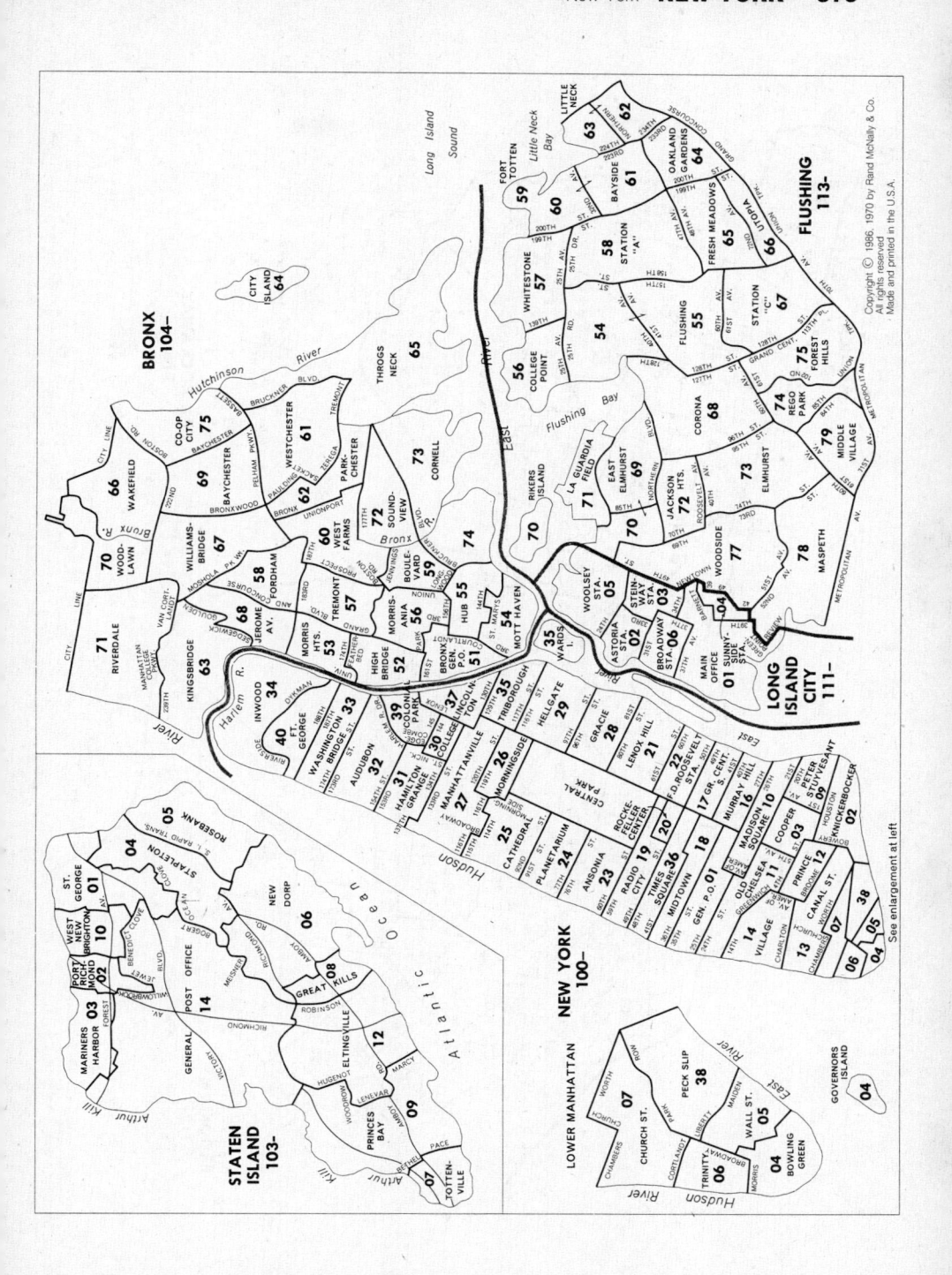

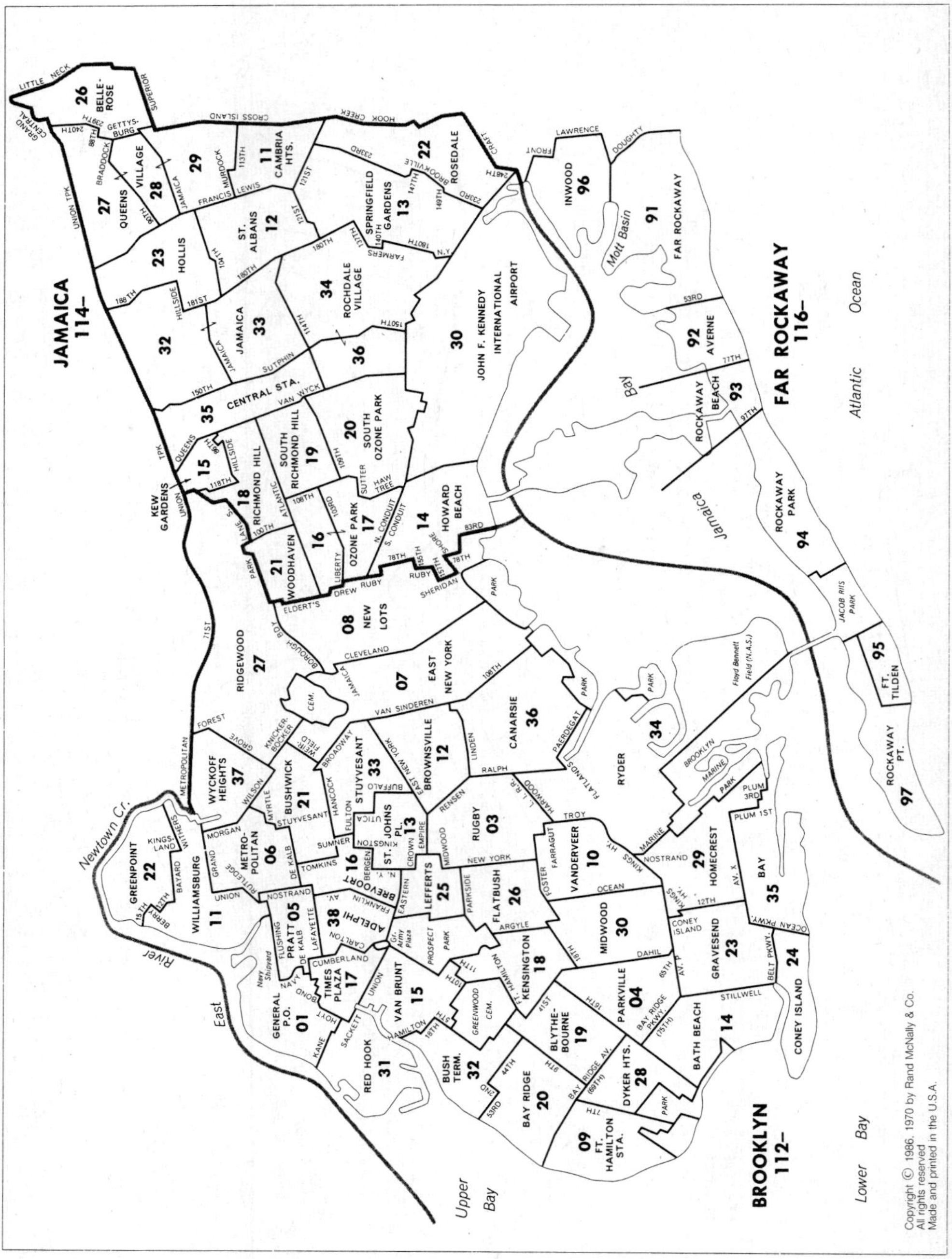
JAMAICA
114–
FAR ROCKAWAY
116–
BROOKLYN
112–
26 BELLE-ROSE
27 QUEENS
28 QUEENS VILLAGE
29
11 CAMBRIA HTS.
12 ST. ALBANS
13 SPRINGFIELD GARDENS
22 ROSEDALE
23 HOLLIS
32
33 JAMAICA
34 ROCHDALE VILLAGE
36
35 CENTRAL STA.
30 JOHN F. KENNEDY INTERNATIONAL AIRPORT
15
18 RICHMOND HILL
19 SOUTH RICHMOND HILL
20 SOUTH OZONE PARK
21 WOODHAVEN
16
17 OZONE PARK
14 HOWARD BEACH
KEW GARDENS
96 INWOOD
91 FAR ROCKAWAY
92 AVERNE
93 ROCKAWAY BEACH
94 ROCKAWAY PARK
95 FT. TILDEN
97 ROCKAWAY PT.
Mott Basin
Jamaica Bay
Atlantic Ocean
27 RIDGEWOOD
08 NEW LOTS
07 EAST NEW YORK
36 CANARSIE
34 RYDER
Floyd Bennett Field (N.A.S.)
37 WYCKOFF HEIGHTS
21 BUSHWICK
33 STUYVESANT
12 BROWNSVILLE
03 RUGBY
10 VANDERVEER
29 HOMECREST
35 BAY
22 GREENPOINT
11 WILLIAMSBURG
06 METRO-POLITAN
05 PRATT
38 ADELPHI
16 BREVOORT
13 ST. JOHNS PL.
25 LEFFERTS
26 FLATBUSH
30 MIDWOOD
23 GRAVESEND
24 CONEY ISLAND
01 GENERAL P.O.
17 TIMES PLAZA
15 VAN BRUNT
18 KENSINGTON
04 PARKVILLE
14 BATH BEACH
31 RED HOOK
32 BUSH TERM.
19 BLYTHE-BOURNE
28 DYKER HTS.
20 BAY RIDGE
09 FT. HAMILTON STA.
Newtown Cr.
East River
Upper Bay
Lower Bay

New York-Old Forge **NEW YORK** 377

	ZIP		ZIP		ZIP
Veterans Administration Medical Center	10010	North Chemung	14861	North Valley Stream	11580
		North Chili	14514	North Victory	13111
HOTELS/MOTELS		North Chittenango	13037	Northview Gardens	14094
		North Clymer	14759	Northville (Fulton County)	12134
Algonquin	10036	North Cohocton	14868	Northville (Suffolk County)	11901
Doral Park Avenue	10016	North Collins	14111	North Wantagh	11793
The Drake Swissotel	10022	North Collins (Town)	14111	North Waverly	14892
Essex House	10019	North Corners	13658	Northway Mall/Off-Price	
Grand Hyatt New York	10017	North Country Shopping		Center, The	12205
The Helmsley Middletowne Hotel	10017	Center (Part of Plattsburgh)	12901	Northway Plaza	12801
The Helmsley Palace Hotel	10022	North Creek	12853	North Western	13419
Hotel Inter-Continental New		Northcrest	12065	Northwest Harbor	11937
York	10017	North Cuba	14727	North White Plains (Westchester County)	10603
Hotel Parker Meridien	10019	North Dansville (Town)	14437	North Wilmurt	13438
The New York Hilton at Rockefeller Center	10019	North Darien	14036	North Wilna	13608
The Pierre	10021	North East (Town)	12546	North Winfield	13491
Ritz Carlton	10019	Northeast Center	12546	North Wolcott	14590
United Nations Plaza Hotel	10017	Northeast Henrietta	14534	Northwood	12188
The Waldorf-Astoria	10022	North Easton	12834	North Woodmere	11581
The Westin Plaza	10019	North Elba (Town)	12946	Norton Hill	12135
The Wyndham Hotel	10019	North End	10940	Norway	13416
		North Evans	14112	Norway (Town)	13416
MILITARY INSTALLATIONS		North Fair Haven (Part of Fair Haven)	13064	Norwich (Chenango County)	13815
United States Army Engineer District, New		North Fenton	13746	Norwich (Chenango County) (Town)	13815
York	10278	Northfield	13856	Norwich Corners	13456
		North Franklin	13820	Norwood	13668
New York Mills	13417	North Gage	13502	Nostrand (Part of New York)	11235
New York Mills Gardens	13492	North Gainesville	14550	Nottingham Estates	14094
Niagara (Town)	14302	Northgate Estates (Part of Rome)	13440	Noxon	12603
Niagara Falls	14301-05	North Germantown	12526	Noyac	11963
For specific Niagara Falls Zip Codes call (716) 285-7561		North Granville	12854	Number Forty (Part of New York)	10001
Niagara Falls International Airport (AFB 6670) 914	14304	North Great River	11722	Number Four	13367
Niagara Square (Part of Buffalo)	14202	North Greece	14515	Nunda	14517
Niagara Town	14302	North Greenbush (Town)	12198	Nunda (Town)	14517
Niagara University	14109	North Greenwich	12834	Nyack	10960
Nichols	13812	North Hamlin	14464	Oak Beach	11702
Nichols (Steuben County)	16920	North Hannibal	13126	Oakdale	11769
Nichols (Tioga County)	13812	North Harmony (Town)	14785	Oakdale Mall (Part of Johnson City)	13790
Nichols Plaza (Part of Watertown)	13601	North Harpersfield	12093	Oakfield	14125
Nichols Run	14749	North Hartland	14008	Oakfield (Town)	14125
Nicholville	12965	North Haven	11963	Oak Hill	12460
Niets Crest	14710	North Hebron	12832	Oakland	14517
Nile	14739	North Hempstead (Town)	11040	Oakland Gardens (Part of New York)	11364
Niles	13152	North Highland	10516	Oak Orchard	14103
Niles (Town)	13152	North Hills	11040	Oak Point (Bronx County)	10455
Nimmonsburg	13901	North Hillsdale	12529	Oak Point (St. Lawrence County)	13646
Nineveh	13813	North Hoosick	12133	Oak Ridge (Montgomery County)	12066
Nineveh Junction	13730	North Hornell	14843	Oakridge (Onondaga County)	13088
Niobe	14758	North Hudson	12855	Oaks Corners	14518
Niskayuna (Schenectady County) (Town)	12309	North Hudson (Town)	12855	Oaksville	13337
Niskayuna (Schenectady County)	12309	North Hudson Falls	12839	Oakwood (Cayuga County)	13021
Nissequogue	11780	North Ilion	13340	Oakwood (Richmond County)	10301
Niverville (Columbia County)	12130	North Jasper	14819	Oakwood Beach (Part of New York)	10301
Noblesboro	13324	North Java	14113	Oakwood Heights (Part of New York)	10301
Norfolk	13667	North Jay	12941	Obernburg	12767
Norfolk (Town)	13667	North Kortright	13739	Obi	14715
Normansville	12054	North Lansing	14852	Occanum	13865
North (Part of Yonkers)	10703	North Lawrence	12967	Ocean Bay Park	11706
North Afton	13730	North Lindenhurst	11757	Ocean Beach	11770
North Amityville	11701	North Litchfield	13340	Oceanside	11572
Northampton (Fulton County) (Town)	12134	North Lynbrook	11563	Odessa	14869
Northampton (Suffolk County)	11901	North Manlius	13082	Ogden (Bronx County)	10452
North Argyle	12809	North Massapequa	11758	Ogden (Monroe County) (Town)	14559
North Babylon	11703	North Merrick	11566	Ogden Center	14559
North Bailey	14226	North New Hyde Park	11040	Ogdensburg	13669
North Baldwin	11510	North Norwich	13814	O'Hara Corners	12083
North Ballston Spa	12020	North Norwich (Town)	13814	Ohio	13324
North Bangor	12966	North Olean (Part of Olean)	14760	Ohio (Town)	13324
North Bay	13123	North Patchogue	11772	Ohioville	12561
North Bay Shore	11706	North Pembroke	14020	Oil Springs Indian Reservation (Allegany County) (Town)	14081
North Beach (Part of New York)	11369	North Petersburg	12138	Oil Springs Indian Reservation (Allegany County)	14081
North Bellmore	11710	North Pharsalia	13844		
North Bellport (Suffolk County)	11713	North Pitcher	13124		
North Bergen	14416	North Pole	12946		
North Bethlehem	12203	Northport	11768		
North Blenheim	12131	North River	12856		
North Bloomfield	14472	North Rockville Centre	11570		
North Boston	14110	North Rose	14516	Oil Springs Indian Reservation (Cattaraugus County) (Town)	14081
North Branch	12766	North Rush	14543	Olcott	14126
North Bridgewater	13318	North Russell	13617	Old Bethpage	11804
North Broadalbin	12025	North Salem	10560	Old Brookville	11545
North Brookfield	13418	North Salem (Town)	10560	Old Central Bridge	12035
North Burke	12917	North Sanford	13754	Old Chatham	12136
Northbush	12095	North Sea	11968	Old Chelsea (Part of New York)	10011
North Cameron	14819	North Selden	11784	Old Field	11733
North Castle (Town)	10504	North Settlement	12496	Old Field South	11790
North Centereach	11720	North Shore Beach	11778	Old Forge	13420
North Chatham	12132	Northside (Part of Corning)	14830		
		North Smithtown	11787		
		North Spencer	14883		
		North Stephentown	12168		
		North Stockholm	13668		
		North Syracuse	13212		
		North Tarrytown	10591		
		North Tonawanda	14120		
		Northtown Plaza	14226		
		Northumberland	12871		
		Northumberland (Town)	12871		

NEW YORK Old Mastic-Pine Bush

Name	ZIP
Old Mastic	11951
Old Orchard Point	14487
Old Stony Brook	11790
Old Village	11023
Old Westbury	11568
Olean (Cattaraugus County)	14760
Olean (Cattaraugus County) (Town)	14760
Olean Center Mall (Part of Olean)	14760
Olive (Town)	12461
Olivebridge	12461
Oliverea	12462
Olmstedville	12857
Omar	13607
Omi	12075
Onativia	13084
Onchiota	12968
One Hundred Thirty Eight (Part of New York)	10001
Oneida	13421
Oneida Castle	13421
Oneonta (Otsego County)	13820
Oneonta (Otsego County) (Town)	13861
Onesquethaw	12067
Oniontown	12522
Onleys Station	10940
Onondaga	13215
Onondaga (Town)	13215
Onondaga Indian Reservation (Onondaga County) (Town)	13120
Onondaga Indian Reservation (Onondaga County)	13120
Ontario	14519
Ontario (Town)	14519
Ontario Center	14520
Ontario on the Lake	14519
Onteo Beach	14464
Onteora Park	12485
Oot Park	13057
Open Meadows	14710
Oppenheim	13329
Oppenheim (Town)	13329
Oquaga Lake	13754
Oramel	14711
Oran	13125
Orange (Town)	14812
Orangeburg	10962
Orange Lake (Orange County)	12550
Orangeport	14067
Orangetown (Town)	10960
Orangeville (Town)	14569
Orangeville Center	14011
Orangeville Corners	14167
Orchard Knoll	14845
Orchard Park	14127
Orchard Park (Town)	14127
Orchard Village	13031
Oregon	11952
Orient	11957
Orienta (Part of Mamaroneck)	10543
Oriental Park	14712
Orient Point	11957
Oriskany	13424
Oriskany Falls	13425
Orlando	14755
Orleans (Jefferson County) (Town)	13656
Orleans (Ontario County)	14432
Orleans Four Corners	13656
Orwell	13426
Orwell (Town)	13426
Oscawana Corners	10579
Oscawana Lake	10579
Osceola	13316
Osceola (Town)	13316
Ossian (Town)	14437
Ossian Center	14437
Ossining	10562
Ossining (Town)	10562
Oswegatchie (St. Lawrence County)	13670
Oswegatchie (St. Lawrence County) (Town)	13654
Oswego (Oswego County)	13126
Oswego (Oswego County) (Town)	13126
Oswego Bitter	13031
Oswego Center	13126
Otego	13825
Otego (Town)	13825
Otisco	13159
Otisco (Town)	13159
Otisco Valley	13110
Otisville	10963
Otisville Correctional Facility	10963
Otsego (Town)	13337
Otselic	13129
Otselic (Town)	13129
Otselic Center	13129
Otter Creek	13343
Otter Lake	13338
Ott Meadows	13088
Otto	14766
Otto (Town)	14766
Ouaquaga	13826
Overlook	12822
Ovid	14521
Ovid (Town)	14521
Ovid Center	14847
Ovington (Part of New York)	11220
Owasco	13130
Owasco (Town)	13130
Owego	13827
Owego (Town)	13827
Owens Mills	14825
Owls Head	12969
Oxbow	13671
Oxford (Town)	13830
Oxford (Chenango County)	13830
Oxford (Orange County)	10918
Oyster Bay	11771
Oyster Bay (Town)	11771
Oyster Bay Cove	11771
Ozone Park (Part of New York)	11416
Pacama	12401
Pace University Pleasantville-Briarcliff Campus	10570
Paddlefords	14424
Paddy Hill	13615
Paines Hollow	13407
Painted Post	14870
Palatine (Town)	13428
Palatine Bridge	13428
Palentown	12446
Palenville	12463
Palermo	13069
Palermo (Town)	13069
Palisades	10964
Palmyra	14522
Palmyra (Town)	14522
Pamelia (Town)	13637
Pamelia	13637
Panama	14767
Panorama	14625
Panther Lake	13028
Pantigo	11937
Paradise Hill	12051
Paradox	12858
Parcells Corner	14062
Paris	13429
Paris (Town)	13429
Parish	13131
Parish (Town)	13131
Parishville	13672
Parishville (Town)	13672
Parishville Center	13676
Paris Station	13456
Parkchester (Part of New York)	10462
Park Hill (Onondaga County)	13057
Park Hill (Westchester County)	10705
Parkside (Part of New York)	11375
Park Slope (Part of New York)	11215
Parkston	12758
Parksville	12768
Park Terrace	13903
Parkville (Part of New York)	11204
Parkway (Part of New York)	10462
Parma (Town)	14468
Parma Center	14468
Parma Corners	14559
Parson Farms	13031
Pastime Park	14456
Pataukunk	12446
Patchin (Part of New York)	10011
Patchinville	14572
Patchogue	11772
Patchogue Highlands	11772
Patria	12187
Patroon (Part of Albany)	12204
Patterson	12563
Patterson (Town)	12563
Pattersonville	12137
Paul Smiths	12970
Pavilion	14525
Pavilion (Town)	14525
Pavilion Center	14525
Pawling	12564
Pawling (Town)	12564
Payne Beach	14468
Peabrook	12760
Peach Lake	10509
Peakville	13756
Pearl Creek	14591
Pearl River	10965
Peas Eddy	13783
Peasleeville	12985
Peat Corners	13036
Pebble Beach	14480
Peck Slip (Part of New York)	10038
Peconic	11958
Peekskill	10566
Pekin	14132
Pelham	10803
Pelham (Town)	10803
Pelham Manor	10803
Pelham Parkway (Part of New York)	10462
Pellets Island	10958
Pembroke	14036
Pembroke (Town)	14036
Penataquit	11706
Pendleton	14094
Pendleton (Town)	14094
Pendleton Center	14094
Penfield	14526
Penfield (Town)	14526
Pennellville	13132
Penn Yan	14527
Peoria	14525
Perch River	13601
Perinton (Town)	14450
Perkinsville	14529
Perry	14530
Perry (Town)	14530
Perry Center	14530
Perry City	14886
Perrysburg	14129
Perrysburg (Town)	14129
Perrys Mills	12919
Perryville	13133
Persia (Town)	14070
Perth (Town)	12010
Perth (Cattaraugus County)	14741
Perth (Fulton County)	12010
Peru	12972
Peru (Town)	12972
Peru	13112
Peruville	13073
Peterboro	13134
Petersburg	12138
Petersburg (Town)	12138
Peter Stuyvesant (Part of New York)	10009
Petries Corners	13367
Petrolla	14895
Pharsalia (Town)	13758
Phelps	14532
Phelps (Town)	14532
Philadelphia	13673
Philadelphia (Town)	13673
Philipse Manor (Part of North Tarrytown)	10591
Philipstown (Town)	10516
Phillipsburg	10940
Phillips Creek	14813
Phillips Mills	14712
Phillipsport	12769
Philmont	12565
Phoenicia	12464
Phoenix	13135
Phoenix Mills	13326
Picketts Corners	12981
Pickettsville	13672
Piercefield	12973
Piercefield (Town)	12973
Pierces Corner	13642
Pierceville	13334
Piermont	10968
Pierrepont	13617
Pierrepont (Town)	13617
Pierrepont Manor	13674
Pierstown	13326
Piffard	14533
Pike	14130
Pike (Town)	14130
Pike Five Corners	14024
Pilgrim (Part of New York)	10461
Pilgrim Corners (Part of Middletown)	10940
Pilgrimport	14489
Pillar Point	13634
Pilot Knob	12844
Pinckney (Town)	13610
Pine (Part of Albany)	12203
Pine Aire	11706
Pinebrook (Part of New Rochelle)	10804
Pinebrook Heights (Part of New Rochelle)	10804
Pine Bush	12566

Pine City-Remsen **NEW YORK** 379

Name	ZIP
Pine City	14871
Pine Grove (Lewis County)	13343
Pine Grove (Schoharie County)	12122
Pinegrove Park	12205
Pine Hill (Erie County)	14225
Pine Hill (Oneida County)	13471
Pine Hill (Ulster County)	12465
Pinehill Estates	12303
Pinehurst	14085
Pine Island	10969
Pine Knolls	13760
Pine Lake	12032
Pine Meadows	13302
Pine Neck	11963
Pine Plains	12567
Pine Plains (Town)	12567
Pine Ridge	12203
Pine Ridge Estates	10573
Pine Valley (Chemung County)	14872
Pine Valley (Suffolk County)	11901
Pineville (Delaware County)	13856
Pineville (Oswego County)	13302
Pinewood Estates	12303
Pine Woods	13310
Pioneer	12020
Piseco	12139
Pitcairn	13648
Pitcairn (Town)	13648
Pitcher	13136
Pitcher (Town)	13136
Pitcher Hill	13212
Pitt (Part of New York)	10002
Pittsfield	13411
Pittsfield (Town)	13411
Pittsford	14534
Pittsford (Town)	14534
Pittstown	12094
Pittstown (Town)	12094
Place Corners	12431
Plainedge	11714
Plainfield (Town)	13491
Plainfield Center	13491
Plainview	11803
Plainview Shopping Center	11803
Plainville	13137
Plandome	11030
Plandome Heights	11030
Plandome Manor	11030
Planetarium (Part of New York)	10024
Plato	14171
Platte Clove	12427
Plattekill	12568
Plattekill (Town)	12568
Platten	14098
Plattsburgh (Clinton County)	12901
Plattsburgh (Clinton County) (Town)	12918
Plattsburgh AFB	12903
Plattsburgh Air Force Base	12903
Plattsburgh West	12962
Plaza (Part of New York)	11101
Pleasantbrook	13320
Pleasantdale	12182
Pleasant Plains (Dutchess County)	12580
Pleasant Plains (Richmond County)	10309
Pleasant Point	13126
Pleasantside	10566
Pleasant Valley	12569
Pleasant Valley (Town)	12569
Pleasant Valley (Oneida County)	13480
Pleasant Valley (Steuben County)	14810
Pleasantville	10570-72
For specific Pleasantville Zip Codes call (914) 769-1517	
Plessis	13675
Plymouth	13832
Plymouth (Town)	13832
Pocantico Hills	10591
Poestenkill	12140
Poestenkill (Town)	12140
Point Au Rouche	12901
Point Breeze	14477
Point Chautauqua	14728
Point Lookout	11569
Point O'Woods	11706
Point Peninsula	13693
Point Pleasant	14622
Point Rochester	14512
Point Rock	13471
Point Stockholm	14742
Point Vivian	13607
Poland (Chautauqua County) (Town)	14747
Poland (Herkimer County)	13431

Name	ZIP
Poland Center	14747
Polkville	13101
Pomfret (Town)	14063
Pomona	10970
Pomona Heights (Part of Pomona)	10901
Pomonok (Part of New York)	11365
Pompey	13138
Pompey (Town)	13138
Pompey Center	13104
Ponck Hockie (Part of Kingston)	12401
Pond Eddy	12770
Ponquogue	11946
Poolville	13432
Poospatuck Indian Reservation (Suffolk County) (Town)	11950
Poospatuck Indian Reservation (Suffolk County)	11950
Pope Mills	13654
Poplar Beach	14541
Poplar Ridge	13139
Poquott	11733
Portage	14846
Portage (Town)	14846
Portageville	14536
Port Authority (Part of New York)	10011
Port Byron	13140
Port Chester	10573
Port Crane	13833
Port Dickinson	13901
Porter (Town)	14131
Porter Center	14131
Porter Corners	12859
Porterville	14052
Port Ewen	12466
Port Gibson	14537
Port Henry	12974
Port Jefferson	11777
Port Jefferson Station (Suffolk County)	11776
Port Jervis	12771
Port Kent	12975
Portland	14769
Portland (Town)	14769
Portlandville	13834
Port Leyden	13433
Port Richmond (Part of New York)	10302
Portville	14770
Portville (Town)	14770
Port Washington	11050
Port Washington North	11050
Post Corners	12057
Post Creek	14812
Potsdam	13676
Potsdam (Town)	13676
Potter	14527
Potter (Town)	14527
Potter Hollow	12469
Pottersville	12860
Poughkeepsie	12601-03
For specific Poughkeepsie Zip Codes call (914) 452-3446	
Poughkeepsie (Town)	12602
Poughquag	12570
Pound Ridge	10576
Pound Ridge (Town)	10576
Pratt (Part of New York)	11205
Pratt Corners	13087
Prattsburg	14873
Prattsburg (Town)	14873
Pratts Hollow	13434
Prattsville	12468
Prattsville (Town)	12468
Preble	13141
Preble (Town)	13141
Prendergast Point	14757
Presho	14858
Preston	13830
Preston (Town)	13830
Preston Hollow	12469
Prince (Part of New York)	10012
Princes Bay (Part of New York)	10309
Princetown	12056
Princetown (Town)	12056
Progress	12078
Prospect	13435
Prospect Heights	12144
Prospect Hill	12188
Prospect Park West (Part of New York)	11215
Providence (Town)	12850
Pulaski	13142
Pulteney	14874
Pulteney (Town)	14874

Name	ZIP
Pultneyville	14538
Pulvers	12075
Pulvers Corners	12567
Pumpkin Hill	14422
Pumpkin Hollow	12529
Purchase (Part of Harrison)	10577
Purdys	10578
Purdys Mills	12910
Purling	12470
Putnam (Town)	12861
Putnam Lake	10509
Putnam Station	12861
Putnam Valley	10579
Putnam Valley (Town)	10579
Pyramid Mall Ithaca (Part of Lansing)	14850
Pyrites	13677
Quackenbush Hill	14830
Quackenkill	12052
Quail (Part of Albany)	12206
Quaker Basin	13052
Quaker Hill	12564
Quaker Ridge (Part of New Rochelle)	10801
Quaker Springs	12871
Quaker Street	12141
Quarry Heights	10603
Quarryville	12477
Queechy	12029
Queensbridge (Part of New York)	11101
Queensbury	12801
Queensbury (Town)	12801
Queens Center (Part of New York)	11373
Queens Village (Part of New York)	11428
Quigley Park	14710
Quinneville	13746
Quioque	11978
Quogue	11959
Raceville	05764
Radio City (Part of New York)	10019
Radison	13027
Rainbow Lake	12976
Ralmar Park	12302
Ramapo	10931
Ramapo (Town)	10931
Ram Island	11964
Rampasture	11946
Randall	12072
Randallsville	13346
Randolph	14772
Randolph (Town)	14772
Ransomville	14131
Rapids	14094
Raquette Lake	13436
Rathbone	14801
Rathbone (Town)	14801
Ravena	12143
Ravenwood (Part of Colonie)	12205
Rawson	14727
Ray Brook	12977
Raymertown	12180
Raymondville	13678
Rayville	12136
Reading (Town)	14876
Reading Center	14876
Reber	12996
Red Creek (Suffolk County)	11946
Red Creek (Wayne County)	13143
Redfalls	12468
Redfield	13437
Redfield (Town)	13437
Redford	12978
Red Hook	12571
Red Hook (Town)	12571
Red Hook (Part of New York)	11231
Red House (Town)	14779
Red Mills (Columbia County)	12513
Red Mills (St. Lawrence County)	13669
Red Oaks Mill	12603
Red Rock (Columbia County)	12060
Red Rock (Onondaga County)	13027
Redwood (Jefferson County)	13679
Redwood (Suffolk County)	11963
Reeds Corner	14437
Reeds Corners	14437
Reeves Park	11901
Rego Park (Part of New York)	11374
Reidsville	12186
Remsen	13438

380 NEW YORK   Remsen-Sand Hill

	ZIP		ZIP		ZIP
Remsen (Town)	13438	Rochester (Town)	12404	Roundout Harbor	12466
Remsenburg	11960	Rockaway Beach (Part of		Round Top	12473
Remsenburg-Speonk	11960	New York)	11693	Rouses Point	12979
Rensselaer	12144	Rockaway Park (Part of		Roxbury	12474
Rensselaer Falls	13680	New York)	11694	Roxbury (Town)	12474
Rensselaerville	12147	Rockaway Point (Part of		Roxbury (Part of New York)	11697
Rensselaerville (Town)	12147	New York)	11697	Royalton	14067
Residence Park (Part of		Rock City (Cattaraugus		Royalton (Town)	14067
New Rochelle)	10805	County)	14760	Ruby	12475
Retsof	14539	Rock City (Dutchess		Ruby Corner	13646
Rexford	12148	County)	12571	Rugby (Part of New York)	11203
Rexville	14877	Rock City Falls	12863	Rumsey Ridge	14092
Reydon Shores	11971	Rock Cut	13078	Rural Grove	12166
Reynoldsville	14818	Rockdale	13809	Rural Hill	13698
Rheims	14840	Rockefeller Center (Part of		Rush	14543
Rhinebeck	12572	New York)	10020	Rush (Town)	14543
Rhinebeck (Town)	12572	Rock Glen	14550	Rushford	14777
Rhinecliff	12574	Rock Hill	12775	Rushford (Town)	14777
Ricard	13302	Rockhurst	12801	Rushford Lake	14717
Rice Grove	13110	Rockland (Town)	12776	Rushville	14544
Riceville (Cattaraugus		Rockland (Rockland		Russell	13684
County)	14171	County)	10962	Russell (Town)	13684
Riceville (Fulton County)	12078	Rockland (Sullivan County)	12776	Russell Gardens	11021
Riceville Station	14171	Rockland Lake	10989	Russia	13431
Richburg	14774	Rockland Psychiatric Center	10962	Russia (Town)	13431
Richfield	13439	Rock Stream	14878	Rutland (Town)	13638
Richfield (Town)	13439	Rock Tavern	12575	Rutland Center	13601
Richfield Springs	13439	Rockton	12010	Ryder (Part of New York)	11234
Richford	13835	Rock Valley	12760	Rye (Westchester County)	10580
Richford (Town)	13835	Rockville (Allegany County)	14711	Rye (Westchester County)	
Richland	13144	Rockville (Orange County)	10940	(Town)	10573
Richland (Town)	13144	Rockville Centre	11570-71	Rye Brook	10573
Richmond (Town)	14471	For specific Rockville Centre Zip		Rye Hills	10573
Richmond Hill (Part of New		Codes call (516) 766-0479		Sabael	12864
York)	11418	Rockville Lake	14711	Sabattis	12847
Richmond Valley (Part of		Rockwells Mills	13843	Sabbath Day Point	12874
New York)	10307	Rockwood	12095	Sacandaga	12134
Richmondville	12149	Rocky Point (Clinton		Sackets Harbor	13685
Richmondville (Town)	12149	County)	12901	Sacketts Lake	12701
Richs Corners	14411	Rocky Point (Suffolk		Saddle Rock	11023
Richville (St. Lawrence		County)	11778	Saddle Rock Estates	11021
County)	13681	Rodman	13682	Sagaponack	11962
Riders Mills	12024	Rodman (Town)	13682	Sages Cottages	11944
Ridge (Livingston County)	14510	Roe Park	10566	Sagetown	14871
Ridge (Suffolk County)	11961	Roessleville	12205	Sag Harbor	11963
Ridgebury	10973	Rolling Acres	14559	Sailors Snug Harbor (Part of	
Ridgelea Heights	14094	Rolling Hills (Monroe		New York)	10301
Ridge Mills (Part of Rome)	13440	County)	14450	St. Albans (Part of New	
Ridgemont Plaza	14626	Rolling Hills (Nassau		York)	11412
Ridgeway	14103	County)	11507	St. Andrew	12586
Ridgeway (Town)	14103	Rolling Meadows	12401	St. Armand (Town)	12913
Ridgeway (Part of White		Romanoff	10512	St. Bonaventure	14778
Plains)	10601	Rombout Ridge	12603	St. George (Part of New	
Ridgewood (Niagara		Rome	13440	York)	10301
County)	14094	Romulus	14541	St. Huberts	12943
Ridgewood (Oneida		Romulus (Town)	14541	St. James	11780
County)	13501	Rondaxe	13420	St. James Heights	11780
Ridgewood (Queens		Rondout (Part of Kingston)	12401	St. John Fisher College	14618
County)	11385	Ronkonkoma	11779	St. Johnsburg	14302
Rifton	12471	Ronkonkoma West	11779	St. Johns Place (Part of	
Riga (Town)	14428	Roosa Gap	12721	New York)	11213
Rigney Bluff	14612	Roosevelt	11575	St. Johnsville	13452
Riley Cove	12020	Roosevelt Beach	14172	St. Johnsville (Town)	13452
Ringdahl Court (Part of		Roosevelt Field (Part of		St. Josephs	12701
Rome)	13440	Garden City)	11530	St. Lawrence Park	13607
Rio	12780	Rooseveltown	13683	St. Mary's Park (Part of	
Riparius	12862	Root (Town)	12166	New York)	10455
Ripley	14775	Roscoe	12776	St. Regis Falls	12980
Ripley (Town)	14775	Rose	14542	St. Regis Indian Reservation	
Rippleton	13035	Rose (Town)	14542	(Franklin County)	13655
Risingville	14820	Rosebank (Part of New		St. Regis Indian Reservation	
River (Part of Rochester)	14627	York)	10305	(Franklin County) (Town)	13655
Riverdale (Part of New		Roseboom	13450	St. Remy	12401
York)	10471	Roseboom (Town)	13450	Saintsville	13116
Riverhead	11901	Rosecrans Park	12123	Salamanca (Cattaraugus	
Riverhead (Town)	11901	Rosedale (Part of New		County)	14779
Riverside (Broome County)	13795	York)	11422	Salamanca (Cattaraugus	
Riverside (Erie County)	14207	Rose Grove	11968	County) (Town)	14779
Riverside (Otsego County)	13838	Rose Hill	13110	Salem	12865
Riverside (Saratoga County)	12118	Rosemont Park (Part of		Salem (Town)	12865
Riverside (Steuben County)	14830	Rensselaer)	12144	Salem Center	10578
Riverside (Suffolk County)	11901	Rosendale	12472	Salina (Onondaga County)	13208
Riverside Estates	11901	Rosendale (Town)	12472	Salina (Onondaga County)	
Riverside-Flanders	11901	Roseton	12550	(Town)	13088
Riverside Mall (Part of Utica)	13502	Rosiere	13618	Salisbury	13365
Riverside Manors	14172	Roslyn	11576	Salisbury (Town)	13365
Riverside Park	12401	Roslyn Estates	11576	Salisbury Center	13454
Riverview	12981	Roslyn Harbor	11576	Salisbury Mills	12577
Roanoke	14143	Roslyn Heights	11577	Salmon River	12901
Robbins Rest	11770	Rossburg	14776	Saltaire	11706
Roberts Corner	13650	Ross Corners	13850	Salt Point	12578
Rochdale	12603	Rossie	13646	Salt Springville	13320
Rochdale Village (Part of		Rossie (Town)	13646	Sammonsville	12095
New York)	11434	Rossman	12173	Samsondale (Part of West	
Rochelle Heights (Part of		Ross Mill	14733	Haverstraw)	10993
New Rochelle)	10801	Rosstown	14871	Samsonville	12481
Rochelle Park (Part of New		Rossville (Part of New York)	10309	Sanborn	14132
Rochelle)	10801	Rotterdam	12303	Sandford Boulevard (Part of	
Rochester	14601-92	Rotterdam (Town)	12303	Mount Vernon)	10550
For specific Rochester Zip Codes		Rotterdam Junction	12150	Sandfordville	13676
call (716) 272-8090		Round Lake	12151	Sand Hill (Erie County)	14001

Sand Hill-South Amsterdam **NEW YORK** 381

	ZIP
Sand Hill (Montgomery County)	13339
Sand Lake	12153
Sand Lake (Town)	12153
Sand Ridge	13132
Sands Point	11050
Sandusky	14133
Sandy Beach	14072
Sandy Creek	13145
Sandy Creek (Town)	13145
Sandy Harbour Beach	14464
Sanford (Town)	13754
Sangerfield	13455
Sangerfield (Town)	13455
Sanitaria Springs	13833
San Remo	11754
Santa Clara	12980
Santa Clara (Town)	12980
Santapoque	11707
Saranac	12981
Saranac (Town)	12981
Saranac Inn	12982
Saranac Lake	12983
Saratoga (Town)	12871
Saratoga Springs	12866
Sardinia	14134
Sardinia (Town)	14134
Saugerties	12477
Saugerties (Town)	12477
Saugerties South	12477
Sauquoit	13456
Savannah	13146
Savannah (Town)	13146
Savona	14879
Sawkill	12401
Sawyers Corners	13021
Saxon Park	11706
Sayville	11782
Scarborough (Part of Briarcliff Manor)	10510
Scarsdale (Westchester County)	10583
Scarsdale (Westchester County) (Town)	10583
Schaghticoke	12154
Schaghticoke (Town)	12154
Schaghticoke Hill	12154
Schenectady	12301-09
For specific Schenectady Zip Codes call (518) 395-5400	
Schenevus	12155
Schermerhorn Corners	14747
Schodack (Town)	12033
Schodack Center	12033
Schodack Landing	12156
Schoharie	12157
Schoharie (Town)	12157
Schonowe	12306
Schroeppel (Town)	13135
Schroon (Town)	12870
Schroon Lake	12870
Schultzville	12572
Schuluski Estates	12188
Schuyler (Town)	13340
Schuyler Falls	12985
Schuyler Falls (Town)	12985
Schuyler Lake	13457
Schuylerville	12871
Scio	14880
Scio (Town)	14880
Sciota	12992
Scipio (Town)	13147
Scipio Center	13147
Scipioville	13147
Sconondoa	13421
Scotchbush (Fulton County)	13452
Scotch Bush (Montgomery County)	12010
Scotchtown	10940
Scotia	12302
Scott	13077
Scott (Town)	13077
Scottsburg	14545
Scottsville	14546
Scranton	14075
Scriba (Town)	13126
Scriba Center	13126
Sea Breeze	14617
Sea Cliff	11579
Seaford	11783
Seager	12406
Searingtown	11507
Searsburg	14886
Sears Corners	10509
Searsville	12549
Seaview	11770
Second Milo	14527
Seeley Creek	14871
Selden	11784
Selkirk	12158
Selkirk Beach	13142

	ZIP
Sellecks Corners	13625
Sempronius	13118
Sempronius (Town)	13118
Seneca (Town)	14561
Seneca Army Depot	14541
Seneca Castle	14547
Seneca Falls	13148
Seneca Falls (Town)	13148
Seneca Hill	13126
Seneca Knolls	13209
Seneca Mall (Erie County)	14224
Seneca Mall (Onondaga County)	13088
Seneca Point	14512
Sennett	13150
Sennett (Town)	13150
Sentinel Heights	13078
Setauket	11733
Setauket-East Setauket	11733
Settlers Hill	10509
Seven Hills	10512
Seventh Day Hollow	13129
Severance	12872
Seward	12043
Seward (Town)	12043
Shackport	13757
Shadigee	14098
Shady	12409
Shandaken	12480
Shandaken (Town)	12480
Shandelee	12758
Sharon	13459
Sharon (Town)	13459
Sharon Springs	13459
Shawangunk (Town)	12589
Shawnee	14132
Sheds	13151
Shekomeko	12546
Shelby	14103
Shelby (Town)	14103
Shelby Basin	14103
Shelby Center	14103
Sheldon (Wyoming County)	14145
Sheldon (Wyoming County) (Town)	14145
Sheldrake	14521
Sheldrake Springs	14847
Shelter Island	11964
Shelter Island (Town)	11964
Shelter Island Heights	11965
Shenandoah	12533
Shenorock	10587
Sherburne	13460
Sherburne (Town)	13460
Sheridan	14135
Sheridan (Town)	14135
Sheridan Park (Part of Geneva)	14456
Sherman	14781
Sherman (Town)	14781
Sherman Park	10594
Shermerhorn Landing	13646
Sherrill	13461
Sherwood Forest	12065
Sherwood Knolls	13031
Sherwood Park	12144
Shinhopple	13837
Shinnecock Hills	11946
Shinnecock Indian Reservation (Suffolk County) (Town)	11968
Shinnecock Indian Reservation (Suffolk County)	11968
Shirewood	12065
Shirley	11967
Shokan	12481
Sholam	12458
Shongo	16923
Shooktown (Part of Lockport)	14094
Shoppingtown Mall	13214
Shore Acres (Chautauqua County)	14712
Shore Acres (Monroe County)	14468
Shore Acres (Suffolk County)	11952
Shore Acres (Westchester County)	10543
Shoreham	11786
Shore Haven	14787
Shorelands	14728
Shore Oaks	13126
Shorewood	11721
Shortsville	14548
Short Tract	14735
Shrub Oak	10588
Shumla	14063
Shushan	12873
Shutter Corners	12157

	ZIP
Shutts Corners	12043
Sibleyville	14472
Sidney	13838
Sidney (Town)	13838
Sidney Center	13839
Siena	12211
Sillimans Corners	14030
Silver Bay	12874
Silver Creek	14136
Silver Lake (Orange County)	10940
Silver Lake (Wyoming County)	14549
Silver Lake Village	10940
Silver Springs	14550
Simmons Island (Part of Cohoes)	12047
Simpsonville	12155
Sinclairville	14782
Sissonville	13676
Skaneateles	13152
Skaneateles (Town)	13152
Skaneateles Falls	13153
Skaneateles Junction	13060
Skerry	12966
Skinnerville	13697
Sky Meadow Farms	10573
Slab City (Cortland County)	13141
Slab City (St. Lawrence County)	13676
Slate Hill	10973
Slaterville Springs	14881
Sleightsburg	12401
Slingerlands	12159
Sloan	14225
Sloansville	12160
Sloatsburg	10974
Slyboro	12832
Smallwood	12778
Smartville	13083
Smithboro	13840
Smith Corners	13407
Smithfield (Dutchess County)	12501
Smithfield (Madison County) (Town)	13134
Smith Haven Mall (Part of Lake Grove)	11755
Smiths Basin	12827
Smiths Corner	12120
Smiths Mills	14062
Smithtown (Town)	11787
Smithtown (Suffolk County)	11787
Smithtown Branch	11787
Smithtown Pines	11787
Smithtown Shopping Center	11787
Smith Valley	14805
Smithville (Chenango County) (Town)	13778
Smithville (Jefferson County)	13605
Smithville Center	13778
Smithville Flats	13841
Smyrna	13464
Smyrna (Town)	13464
Snooks Corners	12010
Snufftown	10924
Snyder	14226
Snyder Crossing	13116
Snyders Corners	12180
Snyders Lake	12180
Sodom (Putnam County)	10509
Sodom (Warren County)	12853
Sodus	14551
Sodus (Town)	14551
Sodus Center	14554
Sodus Point	14555
Solon	13055
Solon (Town)	13055
Solsville	13465
Solvay	13209
Somers	10589
Somers (Town)	10589
Somerset	14012
Somerset (Town)	14012
Somerset Lake	13783
Somerville	13642
Sonora	14879
Sonyea	14556
Sound Beach	11789
Soundview (Part of New York)	10472
South (Part of Yonkers)	10705
South Addison	14801
South Alabama	14013
South Albion	13302
South Amenia	12592
Southampton	11968-69
For specific Southampton Zip Codes call (516) 283-0268	
Southampton College	11946
South Amsterdam (Part of Amsterdam)	12010

382 NEW YORK   South Apalachin-Stone Church

	ZIP		ZIP		ZIP
South Apalachin	13732	South Ripley	14775	Stanwood	10549
South Argyle	12809	South Russell	13684	Stapleton (Part of New	
South Bay (Madison		South Rutland	13688	York)	10304
County)	13032	South Salem	10590	Starbuckville	12817
South Bay (Onondaga		South Schodack	12162	Stark (Town)	13339
County)	13041	South Schroon	12877	Starkey	14837
South Bay Shopping Center	11702	South Setauket	11733	Starkey (Town)	14837
South Bay Village	12827	South Shore Mall	11706	Starks Knob	12871
South Bethlehem	12161	South Side (Part of Elmira)	14904	Starkville	13339
South Bloomfield	14469	South Sodus	14489	Star Lake	13690
South Bolivar	14715	South St. Johnsville		State Bridge	13054
South Bombay	12957	(Montgomery County)	13339	State Line	14775
South Bradford	14879	South Stockton	14782		
South Bristol	14512	South Stony Brook	11790	**Staten Island**	10301-14
South Bristol (Town)	14512	South Trenton	13304	For specific Staten Island Zip	
South Brookfield	13485	South Utica (Part of Utica)	13501	Codes call (718) 816-2790	
South Buffalo (Part of		South Valley (Cattaraugus		*COLLEGES & UNIVERSITIES*	
Buffalo)	14210	County) (Town)	14779	City University of New York-	
South Butler	13154	South Valley (Otsego		College of Staten Island	10301
South Byron	14557	County)	13320	Wagner College	10301
South Cairo	12482	South Valley Stream	11581		
South Cambridge	12028	South Vandalia	14706	*FINANCIAL INSTITUTIONS*	
South Canisteo	14823	South Vestal	13850	Community National Bank &	
South Centereach	11720	Southview (Part of		Trust Company of New	
South Chili	14546	Binghamton)	13903	York	10306
South Colton	13687	South Wales	14139	Gateway State Bank	10304
South Columbia	13439	South Warsaw	14569	Northfield Savings Bank,	
South Corinth	12822	South Westbury	11590	F.S.B.	10314
South Corning	14830	South Westerlo	12163	Richmond County Savings	
South Cortland	13045	Southwest Oswego	13126	Bank	10314
South Danby	13864	Southwood	13078	Staten Island Savings Bank	10304
South Dansville	14807	South Worcester	12197	Westerleigh Savings, A	
South Dayton	14138	Spackenkill	12603	Federal Savings & Loan	
South Dover	12522	Spafford	13077	Association	10314
South Durham	12405	Spafford (Town)	13077		
Southeast (Town)	10509	Sparkill	10976	*HOSPITALS*	
Southeast Owasco	13118	Sparkle Lake	10598	St. Vincent's Medical	
South Edmeston	13466	Sparrow Bush	12780	Center of Richmond	10310
South Edwards	13635	Sparta (Livingston County)		Staten Island Hospital	10305
South Fallsburg	12779	(Town)	14437	Staten Island Mall (Part of	
South Farmingdale	11735	Sparta (Westchester		New York)	10314
Southfields	10975	County)	10562	State School	10990
South Floral Park	11001	Spawn Hollow	12161	State University (Part of Old	
South Flushing (Part of New		Speculator	12164	Westbury)	11568
York)	11365	Speedsville	13736	State University of New	
Southgate Plaza	14224	Speigletown	12182	York at Binghamton	
Southgate Shopping Center		Spencer	14883	(Broome County)	13901
(Part of Massapequa		Spencer (Town)	14883	State University of New	
Park)	11762	Spencerport	14559	York at Stony Brook	
South Gilboa	12167	Spencer Settlement	13440	(Suffolk County)	11794
South Glens Falls	12801	Spencertown	12165	Steamburg	14783
South Granville	12832	Speonk	11972	Steam Valley	14760
South Greece	14626	Split Rock	13031	Stears Corners	13659
South Hamilton	13332	Spragueville	13642	Steelton	14219
South Hannibal	13074	Sprakers	12166	Steinway (Part of New York)	11103
South Hartford (Otsego		Spring Brook	14140	Stella	13905
County)	13810	Spring Creek (Part of New		Stella Niagara	14144
South Hartford (Washington		York)	11239	Stephens Mills	14843
County)	12838	Springfield (Town)	13468	Stephentown	12168
South Haven	11719	Springfield Center	13468	Stephentown (Town)	12168
South Hempstead	11550	Springfield Gardens (Part of		Stephentown Center	12168
South Highland	10524	New York)	11413	Sterling	13156
South Hill	14850	Spring Glen	12483	Sterling (Town)	13156
South Holbrook	11741	Spring Lake	13140	Sterling Forest	10979
South Horicon	12815	Spring Mills	14897	Sterling Valley	13156
South Hornell	14843	Springport (Town)	13160	Stetsonville	13415
South Hudson Falls	12828	Springs	11937	Steuben (Town)	13354
South Huntington	11746	Springtown	12561	Steuben Valley	13354
South Ilion	13357	Springvale	13815	Stever Mill	12025
South Jamesport	11970	Spring Valley (Rockland		Stewart	12550
South Jefferson	12167	County)	10977	Stewart Air Force Base	12550
South Jewett	12442	Spring Valley (Westchester		Stewart Manor	11530
South Kortright	13842	County)	10562	Stilesville	13754
South Lake	10512	Springville (Erie County)	14141	Stillman Village	12138
South Lebanon	13332	Springville (Suffolk County)	11946	Stillwater (Town)	12170
South Lima	14558	Springwater	14560	Stillwater (Chautauqua	
South Livonia	14487	Springwater (Town)	14560	County)	14701
South Lockport	14094	Springwood Village	12538	Stillwater (Putnam County)	10541
South Millbrook	12545	Sprout Brook	13317	Stillwater (Saratoga County)	12170
South New Berlin	13843	Sproutville	12533	Stillwater Hill	10562
South Newstead	14001	Spruceton	12492	Stirling	11944
South Nineveh	13787	Spuyten Duyvil (Part of New		Stissing	12581
South Nyack	10960	York)	10463	Stittville	13469
Southold	11971	Squiretown	11946	Stockbridge	13409
Southold (Town)	11971	Staatsburg	12580	Stockbridge (Town)	13409
South Olean (Part of Olean)	14760	Stacy Basin	13054	Stockholm (Town)	13697
South Onondaga	13120	Stadium (Part of New York)	10452	Stockholm Center	13697
South Otselic	13155	Stafford	14143	Stockport (Columbia	
South Owego	13827	Stafford (Town)	14143	County)	12171
South Oxford	13830	Stamford	12167	Stockport (Town)	12171
South Ozone Park (Part of		Stamford (Town)	12167	Stockport (Delaware	
New York)	11420	Standish	12952	County)	13783
South Park (Part of Buffalo)	14220	Stanford (Town)	12581	Stockport Station	12534
South Plainedge	11758	Stanford Heights	12301	Stockton	14784
South Plymouth	13844	Stanfordville	12581	Stockton (Town)	14784
South Pole (Part of New		Stanley	14561	Stockwell	13480
York)	10090	Stanley Manor	13031	Stokes	13363
Southport	14904	Stannards	14895	Stone Arabia	13339
Southport (Town)	14904	Stanwix (Part of Rome)	13440	Stone Church	14416
South Richmond Hill (Part of		Stanwix Heights (Part of			
New York)	11419	Rome)	13440		

Name	ZIP	Name	ZIP	Name	ZIP
Stonedam	16923	Tanglewood Hills	11727	Tonawanda Indian Reservation (Genesee County) (Town)	14150
Stone Gate	10950	Tannersville	12485		
Stone Mills	13656	Tappan (Rockland County)	10983		
Stone Ridge (Montgomery County)	12072	Tarrytown	10591	Tonawanda Junction	14223
		Tarrytown Heights (Part of Tarrytown)	10591	Torrey (Town)	14441
Stone Ridge (Ulster County)	12484			Tottenville (Part of New York)	10307
Stony Brook (Suffolk County)	11790	Taunton	13219		
		Taylor	13040	Towerville Corners	14701
Stony Creek	12878	Taylor (Town)	13040	Towlesville	14810
Stony Creek (Town)	12878	Taylor Center	13040	Town (Part of Newburgh)	12550
Stony Creek Estates	12065	Teall (Part of Syracuse)	13217	Towners	12531
Stony Hollow	12401	Teboville	12953	Town Line	14086
Stony Point	10980	Ten Mile River	12764	Town Pump	14559
Stony Point (Town)	10980	Tennanah	12776	Townsend	14891
Stormville	12582	Tennanah Lake	12776	Townsendville	14847
Stottville	12172	Terminal (Part of New York)	10301	Tracy Creek	13850
Stow	14785	Terrace Park	13669	Trainsmeadow (Part of New York)	11370
Straits Corners	13827	Terry's Corners	14067		
Stratford	13470	Terryville	11776	Transitown	14221
Stratford (Town)	13470	Texas	13114	Travis (Part of New York)	10301
Strathmore	11030	Texas Valley	13803	Travis Corners	10524
Streeters Corners	14094	Thayer Corners	12917	Treadwell	13846
Streetroad	12883	The Bridges	14477	Tremont (Part of New York)	10457
Strykersville	14145	The Forge	12920	Trenton (Town)	13304
Stuyvesant	12173	The Forks	14030	Trenton Assembly Park	13304
Stuyvesant (Town)	12173	The Glen	12885	Trenton Falls	13304
Stuyvesant (Part of New York)	11233	The Hook	12809	Triangle	13778
		The Narrows	14737	Triangle (Town)	13778
Stuyvesant Falls	12174	Thendara	13472	Triangle Lake	12122
Suffern	10901	Theresa	13691	Tribes Hill	12177
Suffern Park	10901	Theresa (Town)	13691	Triborough (Part of York)	10035
Sugarbush	12968	The Terrace	11050		
Sugar Loaf	10981	The Vly	12484	Triphammer Mall (Part of Lansing)	14852
Sugartown	14741	Thiells	10984		
Sullivan	13037	Thomaston	11021	Tripoli	12827
Sullivan (Town)	13037	Thompson (Ontario County)	14489	Troupsburg	14885
Sullivanville	14845	Thompson (Sullivan County) (Town)	12701	Troupsburg (Town)	14885
Summerhill	13092			Troutburg	14464
Summerhill (Town)	13092	Thompson Ridge	10985	Trout Creek	13847
Summit	12175	Thompsons Lake	12009	Trout River	12926
Summit (Town)	12175	Thompsonville	12784	Troy	12180-83
Summit Park	10977	Thomson	12834	For specific Troy Zip Codes call (518) 272-7300	
Summit Park Mall (Part of Niagara Falls)	14304	Thornton	14723		
		Thornton Grove	13152	Truesdale Lake	10590
Summitville	12781	Thornton Heights	13152	Trumansburg	14886
Sun	12917	Thornwood (Westchester County)	10594	Trumbulls Corners	14867
Sundown	12782			Truthville	12854
Sun Haven (Part of New Rochelle)	10801	Thousand Island Park	13692	Truxton	13158
		Three Mile Bay	13693	Truxton (Town)	13158
Sunmount (Part of Tupper Lake)	12986	Three Rivers	13041	Tuckahoe (Suffolk County)	11968
		Throgg's Neck (Part of New York)	10465	Tuckahoe (Westchester County)	10707
Sunny Side (Chautauqua County)	14701				
		Throop (Town)	13021	Tucker Heights	12019
Sunnyside (Columbia County)	12106	Throopsville	13021	Tucker Terrace	13662
		Thruway Mall	14225	Tudor (Part of New York)	10017
Sunnyside (Queens County)	11104	Thurman (Town)	12885	Tully	13159
Sunrise Mall	11758	Thurston	14821	Tully (Town)	13159
Sunrise Terrace	13902	Thurston (Town)	14821	Tunnel	13848
Sunset (Part of New York)	11220	Thurston Road (Part of Rochester)	14619	Tupper Lake	12986
Sunset Bay (mail Irving)	14081			Turin	13473
		Tiana	11946	Turin (Town)	13473
Sunset Bay (mail Bemus Point)	14712	Tiana Shores	11942	Turnwood	12758
		Ticonderoga (Town)	12883	Tuscan	12197
Sunset Beach	14712	Ticonderoga	12883	Tuscarora (Livingston County)	14510
Sunset City Shopping Center	11703	Tillson	12486		
		Times Plaza (Part of New York)	11217	Tuscarora (Steuben County) (Town)	14801
Sunset Manor	13492				
S U N Y (State University of New York) (Part of Albany)	12203	Times Square (Part of New York)	10036	Tuscarora Indian Reservation (Niagara County) (Town)	14094
		Timothy Heights	12569		
Surprise	12176	Tinkertown	14803		
Surrey Meadows	10918	Tioga (Town)	13845	Tuscarora Indian Reservation (Niagara County)	14094
Svahn Manor	10989	Tioga Center	13845		
Swain	14884	Tioga Terrace	13732	Tusten (Town)	12764
Swan Lake	12783	Tiona	13811	Tuthill	12525
Swartwood	14889	Titusville	12603	Tuxedo (Town)	10987
Swastika	12985	Tivoli	12583	Tuxedo Park	10987
Swazy Acres	12188	Toddsville	13326	Twelve Corners	14618
Sweden (Town)	14420	Toddville	10566	Twilight Park	12436
Sweden Center	14420	Todt Hill (Part of New York)	10301	Twin Lakes Village	10590
Sweet Meadows	12401			Twin Orchards	13850
Swenson Drive (Part of Wappingers Falls)	12590	Toll Gate Corner	14770	Tyner	13830
		Tomhannock	12185	Tyre	13148
Swifts Mills	14001	Tomkins Cove	10986	Tyre (Town)	13148
Swormville	14051	Tompkins Corners	13754	Tyrone	14887
Sycaway	12180	Tompkins Corners	14845	Tyrone (Town)	14887
Sylvan Beach	13157	Tompkins Square (Part of New York)	10009	Ulster (Town)	12401
Sylvan Lake	12533			Ulster Heights	12428
Syosset	11791	Tompkinsville (Part of New York)	10301	Ulster Landing	12477
Syracuse	13201-61			Ulster Park	12487
For specific Syracuse Zip Codes call (315) 470-3486		Tonawanda	14150-51	Ulsterville	12566
		For specific Tonawanda Zip Codes call (716) 693-4560		Ulysses (Town)	14886
Taberg	13471			Unadilla	13849
Tabor Corners	14572	Tonawanda (Erie County) (Town)	14150	Unadilla (Town)	13849
Taborton	12153			Unadilla Forks	13491
Taconic Correctional Facility	10507	Tonawanda (census area only)	14223	Underwood Club	12964
Taconic Lake	12138			Union (Broome County)	13760
Taghkanic	12502	Tonawanda Indian Reservation (Erie County) (Town)	14150	Union (Broome County) (Town)	13760
Taghkanic (Town)	12502				
Talcottville	13309			Union Center	13760
Talcville	13635	Tonawanda Indian Reservation (Erie County)	14150	Uniondale	11553
Tallman	10982				

384 NEW YORK Union Falls-Westbrookville

Name	ZIP
Union Falls	12912
Union Hill	14563
Union Mills	12025
Union Shopping Center (Part of Endicott)	13760
Union Springs	13160
Union Vale (Town)	12585
Union Valley	13052
Unionville (Albany County)	12054
Unionville (Ontario County)	14532
Unionville (Orange County)	10988
Unionville (St. Lawrence County)	13676
United Nations New York (Part of New York)	10017
University (Part of Syracuse)	13210
University Gardens	11020
University Heights (Part of New York)	10452
Upper Benson	12134
Upper Brookville	11545
Upper Grand View	10960
Upper Hollowville	12530
Upper Jay	12987
Upper Lisle	13862
Upper Little York	13087
Upper Little York Lake	13141
Upper Mongaup	12737
Upper Nyack	10960
Upper Red Hook	12571
Upper St. Regis	12945
Upper Union	12309
Upperville	13464
Upton Lake	12514
Uptonville (Part of Rochester)	14617
Uptown (Part of Kingston)	12401
Urbana (Town)	14840
USCC (United States Cadet Corps)	10997
Ushers	12151
U.S. Military Academy	10996
Utica	13501-05
For specific Utica Zip Codes call (315) 738-5354	
Utopia (Part of New York)	11366
Vail Mills	12025
Vails Gate	12584
Vail's Grove	10509
Valatie	12184
Valcour	12972
Valhalla	10595
Valley Cottage	10989
Valley Falls	12185
Valley Mills	13409
Valley Pond Estates	10536
Valley Stream	11580-82
For specific Valley Stream Zip Codes call (516) 825-2220	
Valley View Manor (Part of Rome)	13440
Vallonia Springs	13813
Valois	14888
Van Brunt (Part of New York)	11215
Van Buren (Town)	13027
Van Buren Bay	14048
Van Buren Point	14166
Van Burenville	10940
Van Cortlandtville	10566
Van Cott (Part of New York)	10467
Vandalia	14706
Van Del (Part of Kenmore)	14217
Van Deusenville	13317
Vandever (Part of New York)	11210
Van Etten	14889
Van Etten (Town)	14889
Van Fleet	16920
Van Hornesville	13475
Van Nest (Part of New York)	10462
Van Schaick Island (Part of Cohoes)	12047
Varick (Town)	14541
Varna	14850
Varysburg	14167
Vaughs Corners	12839
Vega	12455
Venice	13147
Venice (Town)	13147
Venice Center	13147
Verbank	12585
Verbank Village	12585
Verdoy	12110
Vermilion	13114
Vermontville	12989
Vernon	13476
Vernon (Town)	13476
Vernon Center	13477
Vernon Valley	11768

Name	ZIP
Verona	13478
Verona (Town)	13478
Verona Beach	13162
Verona Mills	13440
Verplanck	10596
Versailles	14168
Vesper	13159
Vestal	13850-51
For specific Vestal Zip Codes call (607) 798-1772	
Vestal Center	13850
Vestal Gardens	13850
Veteran (Chemung County) (Town)	14864
Veteran (Ulster County)	12477
Veterans Administration Hospital (Erie County)	14215
Veterans Administration Facility (Genesee County)	14020
Veterans Hospital (Part of Syracuse)	13210
Victor	14564
Victor (Town)	14564
Victoria	14710
Victory	13033
Victory (Town)	13033
Victory Mills	12884
Victory Park (Part of New Rochelle)	10804
Vienna	13308
Vienna (Town)	13308
Viewmonte	12526
Village (New York County)	10014
Village (Niagara County)	14094
Village Green (Onondaga County)	13027
Village Green (Saratoga County)	12065
Village of the Branch	11787
Villenova (Town)	14138
Vincent	14424
Vine Valley	14507
Vintonton	12187
Viola	10952
Viola Park	10952
Virgil	13045
Virgil (Town)	13045
Vischer Ferry	12148
Vista	06840
Voak	14527
Volney	13069
Volney (Town)	13069
Volusia	14787
Voorheesville	12186
Vukote	14710
Waccabuc	10597
Waddington	13694
Waddington (Town)	13694
Wadhams	12990
Wadhams Park	13669
Wading River	11792
Wainscott	11975
Waits	13827
Wakefield (Part of New York)	10466
Walden (Erie County)	14225
Walden (Orange County)	12586
Wales (Town)	14139
Wales Center	14169
Wales Hollow	14139
Walesville	13492
Walker	14468
Walker Lane	12801
Walker Valley	12588
Wallace	14809
Wallington	14551
Wallins Corner	12010
Wallkill (Orange County) (Town)	10919
Wallkill (Ulster County)	12589
Wallkill Correctional Facility	12589
Walloomsac	12090
Wall Street (Part of New York)	10005
Walton	13856
Walton (Town)	13856
Walton Park	10950
Walt Whitman Mall	11746
Walworth	14568
Walworth (Town)	14568
Wampsville	13163
Wanakah	14075
Wanakena	13695
Wantagh	11793
Wappinger (Town)	12590
Wappinger Falls North	12590
Wappingers Falls	12590
Wappingers Falls East	12590
Ward (Town)	14880
Wards Island (Part of New York)	10035

Name	ZIP
Warners	13164
Warnerville	12187
Warren	13439
Warren (Town)	13439
Warrensburg	12885
Warrensburg (Town)	12885
Warrens Corners	14094
Warsaw	14569
Warsaw (Town)	14569
Warwick	10990
Warwick (Town)	10990
Washington (Town)	12545
Washington Bridge (Part of New York)	10033
Washington Heights	10940
Washington Lake	12550
Washington Mills	13479
Washingtonville	10992
Wassaic	12592
Waterboro	14747
Waterburg	14886
Waterford (Town)	12188
Waterford	12188
Water Island	11772
Waterloo	13165
Waterloo (Town)	13165
Waterman Corners	14728
Water Mill	11976
Waterport	14571
Waterside Park	11768
Watertown	13601-03
For specific Watertown Zip Codes call (315) 788-0900	
Watertown Junction (Part of Watertown)	13601
Watervale	13104
Water Valley	14075
Waterville	13480
Watervliet	12189
Watkins Glen	14891
Watson	13367
Watson (Town)	13367
Watsonville	12122
Wattlesburg	14775
Watts Flats	14710
Wautoma Beach	14468
Wave Crest (Part of New York)	11691
Waverly (Franklin County) (Town)	12980
Waverly (Tioga County)	14892
Wawarsing	12489
Wawarsing (Town)	12489
Wawayanda (Town)	10973
Wayland	14572
Wayland (Town)	14572
Wayne (Schuyler County)	14893
Wayne (Steuben County) (Town)	14840
Wayne Center	14489
Webb (Town)	13420
Webbs Mills	14871
Webster	14580
Webster (Town)	14580
Webster Crossing	14584
Websters Corners	14127
Wedgewood	14891
Weedsport	13166
Wegatchie	13608
Welcome	13810
Wells	12190
Wells (Town)	12190
Wells Bridge	13859
Wellsburg	14894
Wellsville	14895
Wellsville (Town)	14895
Weltonville	13811
Wende Correctional Facility	14004
Wendelville	14120
Wesley	14070
Wesley Chapel	10901
Wesley Hills	10901
West Almond	14804
West Almond (Town)	14804
West Amboy	13167
West Amityville	11758
West Babylon	11704
West Bainbridge	13733
West Bangor	12991
West Barre	14411
West Batavia	14020
West Bay Shore	11706
West Bellport	11772
West Berne	12023
West Bethany	14054
West Bloomfield	14585
West Bloomfield (Town)	14585
West Branch	13303
West Brentwood	11717
Westbrookville	12785

West Burlington-Wolcottsville NEW YORK 385

Place	ZIP
West Burlington	13482
Westbury (Cayuga County)	13143
Westbury (Nassau County)	11590
West Bush	12078
West Cameron	14819
West Camp	12490
West Candor	13743
West Carthage	13619
West Caton	14830
West Charlton	12010
West Chazy	12992
West Chenango	13905
Westchester (Part of New York)	10461
Westchester Heights (Part of New York)	10461
West Chili	14514
West Clarksville	14786
West Colesville	13904
West Conesville	12076
West Copake	12593
West Corners	13760
West Coxsackie (Part of Coxsackie)	12192
Westdale	13483
West Danby	14896
West Davenport	13860
West Dryden	13068
West Durham	12422
West Eaton	13484
West Edmeston	13485
West Elmira	14905
West End	13820
West Endicott	13760
Westerlea	13031
Westerleigh (Part of New York)	10314
Westerlo	12193
Westerlo (Town)	12193
Western (Town)	13419
Western Lights Shopping Center (Part of Syracuse)	13219
Western Pine Knolls	12203
Westernville	13486
West Exeter	13487
West Falls	14170
West Farms (Part of New York)	10460
Westfield	14787
Westfield (Town)	14787
Westford	13488
Westford (Town)	13488
West Fort Ann	12827
West Fort Salonga	11768
West Frankfort	13340
West Fulton	12194
West Gaines	14411
West Galway	12010
Westgate	14624
West Genesee Terrace	13031
West Ghent	12075
West Gilgo Beach	11702
West Glens Falls	12801
West Glenville	12010
West Greece	14626
West Greenwood	14839
West Groton	13073
Westhampton	11977
Westhampton Beach	11978
West Harpersfield	13786
West Haverstraw	10993
West Hebron	12865
West Hempstead	11552
West Henrietta	14586
West Hill	12301
West Hills (Suffolk County)	11743
West Hoosick	12028
West Huntington	11743
West Hurley	12491
West Islip	11795
West Jewett	12444
West Kendall	14476
West Kill	12492
West Latham	12110
West Laurens	13796
Westlawn	12203
West Lebanon	12195
West Lee	13363
West Leyden	13489
West Lowville	13367
West Mahopac	10541
West Martinsburg	13367
Westmere	12203
West Meredith	13757
West Middleburg	12122
West Middlebury	14054
West Milton	12020
Westminster Park	13607
West Monroe	13167
West Monroe (Town)	13167
Westmore Estates	12203

Place	ZIP
Westmoreland (Oneida County)	13490
Westmoreland (Town)	13490
Westmoreland (Suffolk County)	11965
West Newark	13811
West New Brighton (Part of New York)	10310
West Newburgh (Part of Newburgh)	12550
West Nyack (census area only)	10960
West Nyack	10994
Weston	14837
West Oneonta	13861
Westons Mills	14788
Westover	13790
West Park	12493
West Pawling	12564
West Perrysburg	14129
West Perth	12010
West Phoenix	13135
West Pierrepont	13617
West Point	10996-97
For specific West Point Zip Codes call (914) 446-2010	
Westport	12993
Westport (Town)	12993
West Portland	14787
West Potsdam	13676
West Ridge (Part of Rochester)	14615
West Ronkonkoma	11779
West Rush	14543
West Salamanca (Part of Salamanca)	14779
West Sand Lake	12196
West Saugerties	12477
West Sayville	11796
West Schuyler	13502
West Seneca (Erie County)	14224
West Seneca (Erie County) (Town)	14224
West Shelby	14103
West Shokan	12494
West Side (Part of Elmira)	14905
West Slaterville	14881
West Smithtown	11787
West Somerset	14008
West Sparta (Town)	14437
West Stephentown	12168
West St. James	11787
West Stockholm	13696
West Taghkanic	12502
West Tiana	11946
Westtown	10998
West Turin (Town)	13325
West Union (Town)	14877
West Utica (Part of Utica)	13501
Westvale	13219
West Valley	14171
West Valley Falls (Part of Valley Falls)	12185
Westview (Broome County)	13905
Westview (Livingston County)	14437
West Village (Part of New York)	10014
Westville	12926
Westville (Town)	12926
Westville	12155
Westville Center	12926
West Walworth	14502
West Waterford (Part of Waterford)	12188
West Webster	14580
West Windsor	13865
West Winfield	13491
West Yaphank	11980
Wethersfield (Town)	14569
Wethersfield Springs	14569
Wevertown	12886
Whaley Lake	12531
Whallonsburg	12994
Wheatfield (Town)	14150
Wheatland (Town)	14546
Wheatley (Part of Old Westbury)	11568
Wheatley Heights	11798
Wheatville	14013
Wheeler	14810
Wheeler (Town)	14810
Wheeler Estates	12019
Wheelers	14469
Wheelerville	12032
Whig Corners	13326
Whippleville	12995
Whippoorwill	10504
White Bay	13650
White Creek	12057
White Creek (Town)	12057

Place	ZIP
White Fathers	12968
Whitehall	12887
Whitehall (Town)	12887
White Lake (Oneida County)	13494
White Lake (Sullivan County)	12786
Whitelaw	13032
White Plains	10601-07
For specific White Plains Zip Codes call (914) 287-2500	
Whiteport	12401
Whitesboro	13492
Whites Store	13843
Whitestone (Part of New York)	11357
Whitestone Shopping Center (Part of New York)	11357
Whitestown (Town)	13492
White Sulphur Springs	12787
Whitesville	14897
Whitfield	12404
Whitman	13804
Whitney Country	14450
Whitney Farms	14450
Whitney Highlands	14450
Whitney Point	13862
Wiccopee	12533
Wickham Knolls	10990
Wickham Village	10990
Wilbur (Part of Kingston)	12401
Wildwood	11792
Wileyville	14877
Willard	14588
Willet	13863
Willet (Town)	13863
Williams Bridge (Part of New York)	10467
Williamsburg (Part of New York)	11211
Williams Grove	13110
Williams Lake	12472
Williamson	14589
Williamson (Town)	14589
Williamstown	13493
Williamstown (Town)	13493
Williamsville	14221
Willing (Town)	14895
Williston Park	11596
Willoughby	14741
Willow	12495
Willow Brook (Chautauqua County)	14712
Willowbrook (Richmond County)	10301
Willow Brook Estates	12303
Willow Brook Park	12302
Willowemac	12758
Willow Glen (Saratoga County)	12118
Willow Glen (Tompkins County)	13053
Willow Grove	13140
Willow Point	13850
Willow Ridge Estates	14150
Willsboro	12996
Willsboro (Town)	12996
Willsboro Point	12996
Willseyville	13864
Wilmington	12997
Wilmington (Town)	12997
Wilna (Town)	13619
Wilson	14172
Wilson (Town)	14172
Wilton	12866
Wilton (Town)	12866
Winchester (Erie County)	14224
Winderest Park	13031
Windham	12496
Windham (Town)	12496
Windham Ridge	12496
Winding Ways	13152
Windmill Farms	10504
Windom	14219
Windsor	13865
Windsor (Town)	13865
Windsor Beach	14617
Winebrook Hills	12852
Winfield (Town)	13491
Wingdale	12594
Winona Lake	12550
Winthrop	13697
Wirt (Town)	14774
Wiscoy	14536
Wisner	10990
Witherbee	12998
Wittenberg	12409
Wolcott	14590
Wolcott (Town)	14590
Wolcottsburg	14032
Wolcottsville	14001

NEW YORK Woodberry Hills-Zoar

Name	ZIP
Woodberry Hills	13413
Woodbourne	12788
Woodbury (Nassau County)	11797
Woodbury (Orange County) (Town)	10930
Woodbury Falls	10930
Woodcliff Park	11933
Woodgate	13494
Wood Haven (Part of New York)	11421
Woodhull	14898
Woodhull (Town)	14898
Woodinville	12564
Woodland	12464
Woodland Hills	12065
Woodlands	10607
Woodlawn (Bronx County)	10470
Woodlawn (Chautauqua County)	14710
Woodlawn Beach	14219
Woodmere	11598
Woodridge	12789
Woodrow (Part of New York)	10309
Woodruff Heights	12302
Woodsburgh	11598
Woods Corners	13815
Woods Falls	12910
Woodside (Part of New Rochelle)	11377
Woods Mill	13608
Woods Mills	12918
Woodstock	12498

Name	ZIP
Woodstock (Town)	12498
Woodsville	14437
Woodville (Jefferson County)	13698
Woodville (Ontario County)	14512
Wooglin	14728
Woolsey (Part of New York)	11105
Worcester	12197
Worcester (Town)	12197
Worley Heights	10950
Worth	13659
Worth (Town)	13659
Worthington (Part of White Plains)	10607
Wright (Town)	12073
Wright Park Manor (Part of Rome)	13440
Wrights Corners (Niagara County)	14094
Wrights Corners (Onondaga County)	13135
Wurtemburg	12572
Wurtsboro	12790
Wurtsboro Hills	12790
Wyandanch	11798
Wyatts	12302
Wycoff Heights (Part of New York)	11237
Wykagyl (Part of New Rochelle)	10804
Wykagyl Park (Part of New Rochelle)	10804

Name	ZIP
Wynantskill	12198
Wyomanock	12168
Wyoming	14591
Yaddo	12866
Yagerville	12458
Yaleville	13668
Yankee Lake	12790
Yaphank	11980
Yates (Town)	14098
Yates Center	14098
Yatesville	14527
Yonkers	10701-10
For specific Yonkers Zip Codes call (914) 378-3600	
York	14592
York (Town)	14592
York Corners	14895
Yorkshire	14173
Yorkshire (Town)	14173
Yorktown	10598
Yorktown (Town)	10598
Yorktown Heights (Westchester County)	10598
Yorkville	13495
Yosts	12068
Young Hickory	14885
Youngstown	14174
Youngstown Estates	14174
Youngsville	12791
Yulan	12792
Zena	12498
Zoar	13682

Aarons Corner-Bethesda NORTH CAROLINA 387

Name	ZIP
Aarons Corner	27053
Abbottsburg	28320
Aberdeen	28315
Abner	27356
Abshers	28635
Acme	28456
Acorn Hill	27979
Acorn Woods	28079
Acre	27865
Addie	28779
Addor	28315
Adoniram	24598
Advance	27006
Advent Crossroads	28601
Afton	27589
Aho	28607
Ahoskie	27910
Ai	27583
Airboro	27530
Airlie	27850
Airport (Part of Charlotte)	28219
Alamance	27201
Alamance Correctional Center	27253
Alarka	28713
Albemarle	28001-02
For specific Albemarle Zip Codes call (704) 982-4114	
Albemarle Beach	27970
Albertson	28508
Albrittons	28501
Alert	27589
Alexander	28701
Alexander Correctional Center	28681
Alexander Mills	28043
Alexis	28006
Alfordsville	28383
Allen	28212
Allen Grove	27839
Allen Jay (Part of High Point)	27263
Allens Crossroads	28174
Allensville	27573
All Healing Springs	28681
Alliance	28509
Alligator	27925
Allison	27326
Allreds	27356
Alma	28364
Almond	28702
Altamahaw	27202
Altamont	28657
Altan	28110
Altapass	28777
Amantha	28679
Amerotron Mill (Part of Red Springs)	28377
AMF (Part of Greensboro)	27425
Amity	27013
Amity Gardens (Part of Charlotte)	28205
Ammon	28337
Anderson (Caswell County)	27215
Anderson (Dare County)	27949
Anderson Creek	28323
Anderson Crossroads	27850
Andrews	28901
Angier	27501
Anson Correctional Center	28135
Ansonville	28007
Antioch (Brunswick County)	28422
Antioch (Hoke County)	28377
Antioch (Madison County)	28753
Apex	27502
Appie	27888
Apple Grove	28643
Aquadale	28128
Aquone	28703
Arabia	28376
Arapahoe	28510
Ararat	27007
Arba	28580
Arcadia	27292
Archdale	27263
Archer	27520
Arcola	27589
Arden	28704
Ardmore (Part of Winston-Salem)	27113
Ardulusa	28301
Argura	27783
Arlington	28642
Armour	28456
Arnold	27292
Arran Hills	28304
Arrowhead Beach	27932
Arrowhead Place	28025
Arrowood (Part of Charlotte)	28273
Artesia	28442
Asbury	27330

Name	ZIP
Ash	28420
Asheboro	27203
Asheboro South	27203
Asheboro West	27203
Asheville	28801-16
For specific Asheville Zip Codes call (704) 257-4112	
Asheville Mall, The (Part of Asheville)	28805
Ashford	28752
Ash Hill	27007
Ashland (Ashe County)	28615
Ashland (Bertie County)	27957
Ashland (Caswell County)	27320
Ashland (Rockingham County)	27320
Ashley Heights	28315
Ashton	28425
Ashton Forrest	28304
Ashwood	28571
Askewville	27983
Askin	28527
Aspen	27850
Atkinson	28421
Atlantic	28511
Atlantic Beach	28512
Atlantic Christian College (Part of Wilson)	27893
Auburn	27610
Audubon (Part of Wilmington)	28403
Aulander	27805
Aurelian Springs	27850
Aurora	27806
Austin	28621
Autryville	28318
Avalon Valley	27253
Avent Ferry Road (Part of Raleigh)	27606
Aventon	27891
Averasboro	28334
Avery Correctional Center	28657
Avery Creek	28704
Avery Shores	27974
Avon	27915
Axtell	27563
Ayden	28513
Aydlett	27916
Ayersville	27027
Azalea (Buncombe County)	28805
Azalea (New Hanover County)	28403
Bachelor	28532
Badin	28009
Bagley	27542
Bahama	27503
Bailey	27807
Bailey Town	27052
Baker Rhyne Apartments	28150
Bakers	28110
Bakersville	28705
Bald Creek	28714
Bald Head Island	28461
Bald Mountain	28714
Baldwin (Ashe County)	28694
Baldwin (Moore County)	27341
Baldwin Woods (Part of Whiteville)	28472
Balfour	28706
Ballantree	28803
Ballard	27840
Ballards Crossroads	27834
Ballew Store	28714
Balm	28604
Balsam	28707
Balsam Grove	28708
Baltic	28398
Baltimore	28434
Bamboo	28605
Bandana	28705
Bandy	28609
Banks Creek	28714
Banner Elk	28604
Bannertown	27030
Banoak	28168
Barber	27008
Barclaysville	27501
Barco	27917
Barham	27587
Barium Springs	28010
Barker Heights	28739
Barkers Creek	28789
Barnard	28753
Barnardsville	28709
Barnesfield	28570
Barnesville	28319
Barrett	28623
Barriers Mill	28124
Bass Crossroads	27882
Basstown	28328
Bat Cave	28710

Name	ZIP
Batchelor Crossroads	27882
Bath	27808
Baton	28630
Battleboro	27809
Bay	27925
Bayboro	28515
Bayleaf	27609
Baynes	27302
Baytree	27609
Bayview	27808
Beach Spring	27944
Bear Creek (Chatham County)	27207
Bear Creek (Onslow County)	28539
Beard	28301
Bear Grass	27892
Bearpond	27536
Bear Poplar	28125
Bearskin	28328
Bearwallow	28735
Beatties Ford	28216
Beaufort	28516
Beaufort Heights	27889
Beaver Creek	28694
Beaverdam (Buncombe County)	28715
Beaver Dam (Cleveland County)	28150
Beaver Dam (Columbus County)	28431
Beaverdam (Cumberland County)	28318
Beaverdam (Halifax County)	27823
Beaverdam (Haywood County)	28716
Beckwith	27865
Beech	28787
Beech Bottom	28657
Beechbrook	28012
Beech Creek	28604
Beechertown	28781
Beech Mountain	28604
Beechwood Shores	27958
Bee Log	28714
Beesons Crossroads	27284
Belair	28306
Belcross	27921
Belews Creek	27009
Belfast	27530
Belgrade	28555
Belhaven	27810
Bellarthur	27811
Belle Mead	28601
Bellemont	27216
Bell Island	27929
Bells Cross Roads	28166
Bells Fork (Onslow County)	28546
Bells Fork (Pitt County)	27858
Belltown	27565
Bell View	28906
Belmont (Gaston County)	28012
Belmont (Halifax County)	27870
Belmont Abbey College	28012
Belva	28753
Belvedere	27834
Belvidere	27919
Belville	28451
Belvoir	27834
Belwood	28090
Benham	28621
Bennett	27208
Benson	27504
Bent Creek	28806
Benton Heights (Part of Monroe)	28110
Bentons Crossroad	28110
Berea	27565
Berkeley (Part of Goldsboro)	27534
Bertha	27965
Bertie (Part of Windsor)	27983
Bessemer (Part of Greensboro)	27405
Bessemer City	28016
Bests	28551
Beta	28779
Bethabara (Part of Winston-Salem)	27116
Bethania	27010
Bethany	27320
Bethel (Caswell County)	27311
Bethel (Columbus County)	28432
Bethel (Haywood County)	28716
Bethel (Hoke County)	28376
Bethel (Perquimans County)	27944
Bethel (Pitt County)	27812
Bethel Hill	27573
Bethesda (Davidson County)	27292
Bethesda (Durham County)	27703

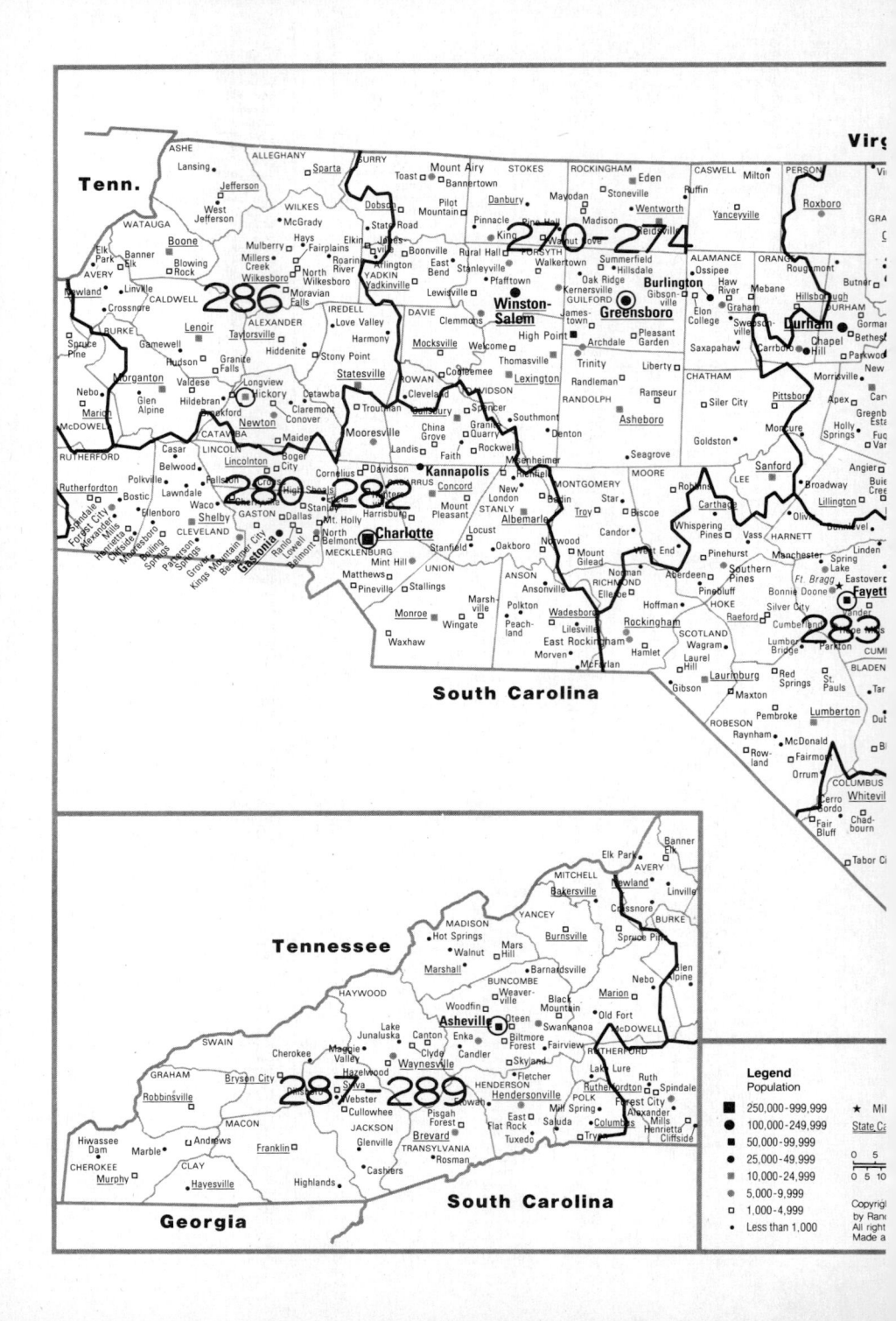

NORTH CAROLINA

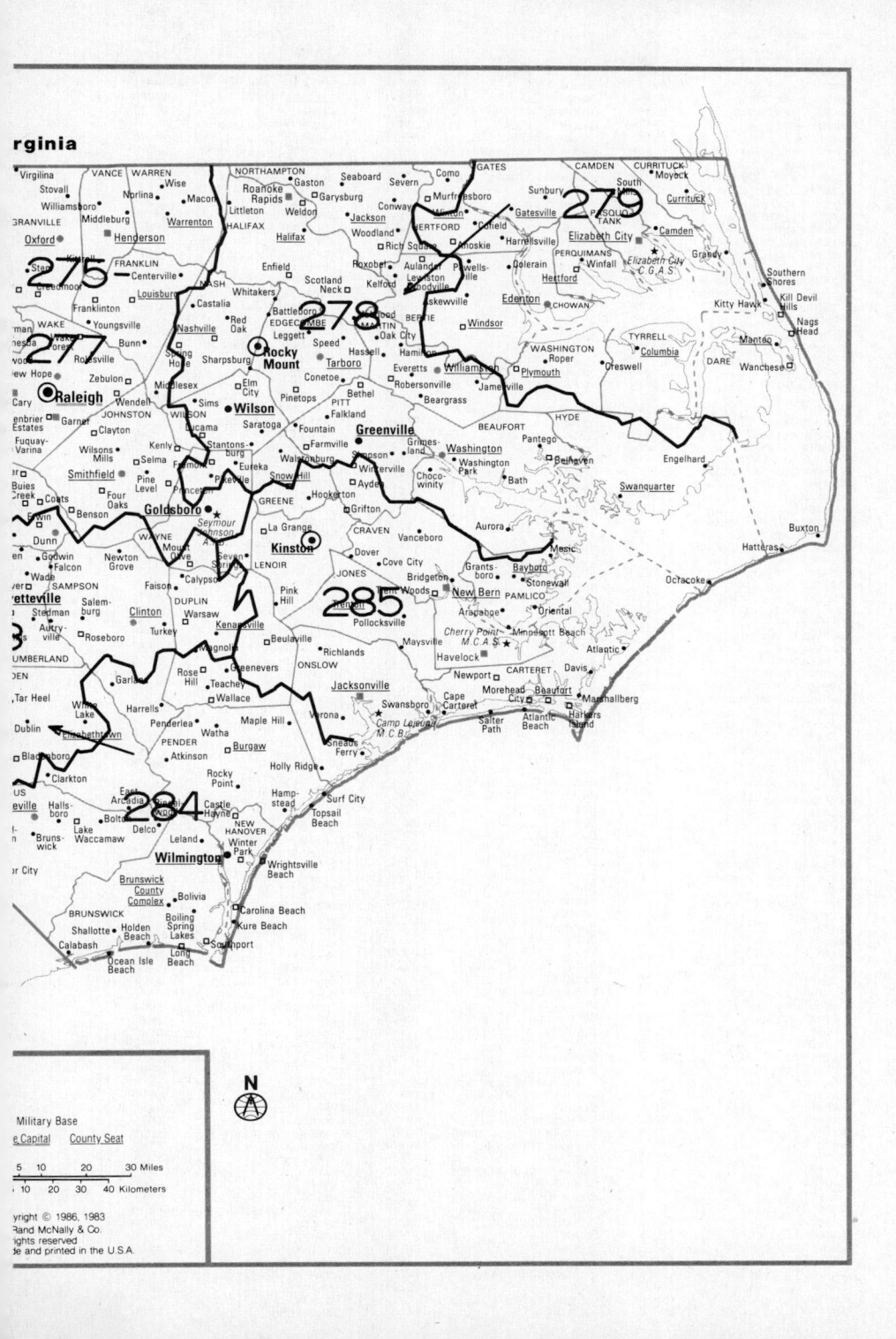

NORTH CAROLINA 389

390 NORTH CAROLINA Bethlehem-Catherine Square

Location	ZIP
Bethlehem (Alexander County)	28601
Bethlehem (Hertford County)	27922
Bettie	28516
Beulah (Hyde County)	27875
Beulah (Polk County)	28756
Beulahtown	27542
Beulaville	28518
Beverly Woods (Part of Charlotte)	28210
Bexley (Part of Wilmington)	28403
Biddleville (Part of Charlotte)	28216
Big Cove	28719
Biggs Park (Part of Lumberton)	28358
Big Laurel	28753
Big Lick	28129
Big Pine	28753
Big Ridge (Carteret County)	28570
Big Ridge (Jackson County)	28736
Biltmore (Part of Asheville)	28803
Biltmore Forest	28803
Birchwood	27215
Bird Cage	28431
Birdtown	28719
Biscoe	27209
Bishops Cross	27860
Bixby	27006
Blackburn	28658
Black Creek	27813
Black Jack	27858
Blackman	27524
Black Mountain	28711
Black Mountain Sanatorium	28711
Blackwell	27311
Blackwood	27514
Bladenboro	28320
Bladenboro North (Part of Bladenboro)	28320
Bladen Correctional Center	28337
Bladen Springs	28434
Blaine	27239
Blanch	27212
Blantyre	28768
Blevins Crossroads	28675
Blevins Store	27017
Blizzards Crossroads	28365
Bloomingdale	28369
Blossomtown	28734
Blounts Creek	27814
Blowing Rock	28605
Blue Ridge (Buncombe County)	28711
Blue Ridge (Henderson County)	28739
Blue Ridge Mall (Part of Hendersonville)	28739
Bluff	28743
Boardman	28438
Boat Club Road	28012
Bobbitt	27544
Boddies Pond	27856
Boger City	28092
Bogue	28570
Boiling Spring Lakes	28461
Boiling Springs (Cherokee County)	28906
Boiling Springs (Cleveland County)	28017
Bolivia	28422
Bolton	28423
Bolyston Creek	28768
Bon Air (Part of Winston-Salem)	27105
Bonaparte Landing	28459
Bonham Heights (Part of Morehead City)	28557
Bonlee	27213
Bonnerton	27806
Bonnetsville	28328
Bonnie Doone (Cumberland County)	28303
Bonsal	27562
Boomer	28606
Boone	28607
Boones Crossroads	27845
Boone Trail	27552
Boonford	28705
Boonville	27011
Bordeaux (Part of Fayetteville)	28304
Bostian Heights	28023
Bostic	28018
Bostwood Estates	28025
Botany Woods	28805
Bottom	27030
Boulevard (Part of Eden)	27288
Bowdens	28398
Bowditch	28714
Bowman	28376

Location	ZIP
Boyles Chapel	27021
Bracey	28383
Bradfords Cross Roads	28677
Braggtown (Part of Durham)	27704
Branon	27055
Brantleys Grove	27910
Brasstown	28902
Braswell	28431
Brendletown	28734
Brentwood (Cumberland County)	28304
Brentwood (Wake County)	27604
Brettonwood	28311
Brevard	28712
Briarwood Terrace	28144
Brices Crossroads	28458
Brickhaven	27559
Bricks	27891
Brickton	28732
Bridgersville	27852
Bridgeton	28519
Brief	28107
Briertown	28781
Brigand Bay	27920
Brightwood (Part of Greensboro)	27214
Brindle Town	28655
Brinkleyville (Hertford County)	27910
Brinkleyville (Lee County)	27823
British Acres	27215
Broad Acres	27253
Broad Creek	28570
Broadway	27505
Brocks	28574
Brogden	27530
Brook Cove	27052
Brookdale	28739
Brookford	28601
Brookhaven	27609
Brookland Manor	28739
Brooks Cross Roads	27020
Brooksdale	27573
Brookside (Part of Goldsboro)	27530
Brookston	27536
Brook Valley	27858
Broughton Hospital	28655
Browns Summit	27214
Brown Town	28012
Brownwood	28684
Bruce	27834
Brunswick	28424
Brutonville	27229
Bryantown	27869
Bryantville Park	27818
Bryson City	28713
Buckhorn	27243
Buckhorn Cross Roads	27542
Buckland	27937
Bucklesberry	28551
Buckner	28754
Buck Shoals	27020
Buena Vista	27983
Buffalo Cove	28645
Bug Hill	28455
Buie	28377
Buies Creek	27506
Buladean	28705
Bullhead	27863
Bullock	27507
Bunn	27508
Bunnlevel	28323
Bunyan	27889
Burbage Crossroads	27808
Burden	27805
Burgaw	28425
Burgess	27944
Burke Chapel	28601
Burkemont	28655
Burlington	27215-17
For specific Burlington Zip Codes call (919) 227-4293	
Burney	28399
Burningtown	28734
Burnsville (Anson County)	28135
Burnsville (Yancey County)	28714
Burnt Mills	27976
Busbee (Part of Asheville)	28803
Bushy Fork	27541
Busick (Guilford County)	27214
Busick (Yancey County)	28714
Butlers Crossroads	28328
Butner	27509
Butters	28324
Buxton	27920
Buzzards Crossroads	27924
Bynum	27228
Byrum Crossroads	27980
Cabarrus	28107

Location	ZIP
Cabarrus Correctional Center	28124
Cabin	28572
Cairo	28119
Cajah's Mountain	28645
Calabash	28459
Calahaln	27028
Caldwell (Mecklenburg County)	28078
Caldwell (Orange County)	27572
Caldwell Correctional Center	28638
Caledonia Correctional Center	27887
California (Dare County)	27954
California (Hertford County)	27986
California (Pitt County)	27828
Callisons	28571
Cal-Vel	27573
Calvert	28712
Calvin Heights	28570
Calypso	28325
Camden	27921
Camelot	27529
Cameron	28326
Cameron Village (Part of Raleigh)	27605
Campbell Creek	27806
Camp Glenn (Part of Morehead City)	28557
Camp Leach	27889
Camp Lejeune (Onslow County)	28542
Camp Lejeune Central	28542
Camp MacKall	28347
Camp Springs	27320
Camp Sutton (Part of Monroe)	28110
Cana	27028
Candler	28715
Candler Heights	28715
Candlewick Estates	27834
Candor	27229
Cane Creek	28167
Cane Mountain	27349
Cane River	28714
Cannon Ferry	27980
Canto	28748
Canton	28716
Cape Carteret	28584
Cape Colony	27932
Cape Fear	27562
Capella	27021
Capelsie	27229
Carbonton	27330
Carmel (Part of Charlotte)	28227
Caroleen	28019
Carolina	27217
Carolina Beach	28428
Carolina Circle Mall (Part of Greensboro)	27405
Carolina East Mall (Part of Greenville)	27834
Carolina Forest	27371
Carolina Mall (Part of Concord)	28025
Carolina Pines	28303
Carolina Trace	27330
Carolina Village	28739
Carova Beach	27927
Carpenter	27560
Carpenter Bottom	28657
Carr	27302
Carrboro	27510
Carr Creek	27330
Carroll	28398
Carter	27938
Carteret Correctional Center	28570
Cartersville	28466
Carthage	28327
Cartoogechaye	28734
Carvers	28434
Cary	27511
Cary Village Mall (Part of Cary)	27511
Casar	28020
Cashiers	28717
Cason Old Field	28170
Castalia	27816
Castle Hayne	28429
Castoria	27888
Casville	27326
Caswell Beach	28461
Caswell Correctional Center	27379
Catawba	28609
Catawba Correctional Center	28658
Catawba Heights	28012
Catawba Mall (Part of Hickory)	28601
Catherine Lake	28574
Catherine Square	28518

Cat Square-Crumpler **NORTH CAROLINA** 391

	ZIP
Cat Square	28168
Ca-Vel (Part of Roxboro)	27573
Cayton	28527
Cedar Creek	28301
Cedar Croft	28081
Cedar Falls	27230
Cedar Fork	28518
Cedar Grove (Orange County)	27231
Cedar Grove (Randolph County)	27203
Cedar Hill (Anson County)	28170
Cedar Hill (Brunswick County)	28451
Cedar Island	28520
Cedar Lodge	27360
Cedar Mountain	28718
Cedar Point	28584
Cedarrock	27816
Ceffo	27573
Celeste Hinkle	28677
Celo	28714
Celotex	28333
Center (Davie County)	27028
Center (Yadkin County)	27055
Center Pigeon	28716
Centerview (Part of Kannapolis)	28081
Centerville	27549
Central	28677
Central Falls (Part of Asheboro)	27203
Central Heights	28025
Century (Part of Raleigh)	27601
Cerro Gordo	28430
Chadbourn	28431
Chadwick Acres	28460
Chalybeate Springs	27526
Champion	28624
Chantilly (Camden County)	27921
Chantilly (Mecklenburg County)	28205
Chapanoke	27944
Chapel Hill	27514-16

For specific Chapel Hill Zip Codes call (919) 942-4179

Charity	28458
Charles	28677
Charlotte	28201-41
	28256-99

For specific Charlotte Zip Codes call (704) 393-4555

COLLEGES & UNIVERSITIES

Johnson C. Smith University	28216
Queens College	28274
University of North Carolina at Charlotte	28223

FINANCIAL INSTITUTIONS

First Federal Savings & Loan Association of Charlotte	28233
First Union National Bank of North Carolina	28288
Home Federal Savings & Loan Association	28202
Mutual Savings & Loan Association of Charlotte, N.C.	28202
NCNB National Bank	28255
North Carolina Federal Savings & Loan Association	28202
Republic Bank & Trust Company	28204
Southeastern Savings & Loan Company	28284

HOSPITALS

Charlotte Memorial Hospital and Medical Center	28203
Mercy Hospital	28207
Presbyterian Hospital	28204

HOTELS/MOTELS

Adam's Mark Charlotte	28204
Guest Quarters Charlotte	28211
Holiday Inn-Woodlawn	28210
The Park Hotel	28211
Ramada Inn-Downtown	28204

MILITARY INSTALLATIONS

Naval Marine Corps Reserve Center, Charlotte	28256
North Carolina Air National Guard, FB6331	28208
Charlotte Correctional Center	28208

	ZIP
Chatham	27514
Cheeks	27316
Cherokee	28719
Cherokee Indian Reservation	28719
Cherry	27928
Cherryfield	28712
Cherry Grove	28430
Cherry Lane	28627
Cherry Oaks	27858
Cherry Point	28533
Cherry Springs	28762
Cherryville	28021
Chesterfield	28655
Chestnut Dale	28657
Chestnut Grove	27021
Chestnut Hill (Ashe County)	28617
Chestnut Hill (Henderson County)	28735
Chimney Rock	28720
China Grove	28023
China Grove Cotton Mill Village	28023
Chinquapin	28521
Chip (Craven County)	28586
Chip (Montgomery County)	27306
Choco Village	27817
Chocowinity	27817
Chowan Beach (Chowan County)	27932
Chowan Beach (Hertford County)	27855
Chublake	27573
Church Crossroads	27871
Churchill	27551
Churchland	27292
Cid	27292
Cisco	27980
City View (Part of Winston-Salem)	27101
Claremont	28610
Clarendon	28432
Clark	28562
Clarkton	28433
Clarrissa	28705
Clay	27565
Clayroot	28513
Clayton	27520
Clear Creek	28212
Clear Run	28441
Clegg	27560
Clemmons	27012
Clemont	28318
Cleveland	27013
Cleveland Correctional Center	28150
Cleveland Springs	28150
Clifdale	28304
Cliffside	28024
Clifton	28693
Climax	27233
Clinchfield	28752
Clingman	28670
Clinton	28328
Cloverdale (Part of Garner)	27529
Clover Garden	27217
Cloverleaf	28304
Club Pines	27834
Clyde	28721
Coakley	27886
Coalville	28901
Coats	27521
Coats Cross Roads	27504
Cobb Town	27829
Cofield	27922
Cognac	28363
Coinjock	27923
Cokesbury (Harnett County)	27526
Cokesbury (Vance County)	27536
Cold Springs	28025
Cold Water	28025
Cole Park	27514
Colerain	27924
Coleridge	27234
Colewood Acres	27604
Colfax	27235
Colington	27948
College (Part of Durham)	27708
College Downs	28213
College Lakes	28301
College Park (Cabarrus County)	28075
College Park (Guilford County)	27403
College Park (Richmond County)	28345
Collettsville	28611
Collinstown	24171
Colly	28448
Colon	27330

	ZIP
Colonial Heights (Beaufort County)	27889
Colonial Heights (Wake County)	27603
Colony Park (Part of Durham)	27705
Columbia	27925
Columbia Heights (Part of Winston-Salem)	27107
Columbus	28722
Columbus Correctional Center	28424
Comfort	28522
Commodore Peninsula	28115
Como	27818
Concord (Cabarrus County)	28025-26

For specific Concord Zip Codes call (704) 786-3161

Concord (Duplin County)	28453
Concord (Person County)	27573
Concord (Rutherford County)	28018
Concord (Sampson County)	28382
Conetoe	27819
Congleton	27871
Connarista	27805
Connelly Springs	28612
Conover	28613
Conway	27820
Cooksville	28168
Cooktown	28705
Cooleemee	27014
Cool Spring	27013
Cool Springs	27330
Cooper Estates	27253
Copeland	27017
Coral Bay	28557
Corapeake	27926
Corbett	27302
Cordova	28330
Core Creek	28516
Core Point	27814
Corinth (Chatham County)	27559
Corinth (Nash County)	27856
Corinth (Rutherford County)	28040
Cornatzer	27028
Cornelius	28031
Cornwall	27565
Corolla	27927
Correll Park	28144
Corriher Heights	28023
Costin	28421
Cotswold Mall (Part of Charlotte)	28211
Cottonade	28303
Cotton Grove	27292
Cottonville	28128
Council	28434
Country Club Estates	28472
Country Hills	27529
Country Homes Estates	27258
Countyline	28634
Courtney	27055
Cove City	28523
Cove Creek	28786
Covington	27306
Cowee	28734
Cox Crossing	27858
Coxville	28513
Cozart	27522
Crab Point	28557
Crabtree	28721
Crabtree Valley Mall (Part of Raleigh)	27612
Craggy	28804
Craggy Correctional Center	28802
Cramerton	28032
Cranberry	28614
Cranberry Gap	28657
Crater Park	28213
Creedmoor	27522
Creeksville	27820
Cremo	27924
Crescent	28138
Crestmont	28601
Creston	28615
Crestview	27344
Creswell	27928
Cricket	28659
Crisp	27852
Croatan	28562
Cross Landing	27925
Cross Mill	28752
Crossnore	28616
Cross Road	27030
Crossway	28352
Crosswinds	27609
Crouse	28033
Crowders	28052
Crowells	27839
Crumpler	28617

392 NORTH CAROLINA Crump Town-Ernul

	ZIP
Crump Town (Part of Wagram)	28396
Cruso	28716
Crusoe Island	28472
Crutchfield Crossroads	27344
Crystal Park	28306
Culberson	28903
Culbreth	27565
Cullasaja	28734
Cullowhee	28723
Cumberland	28331
Cumnock	27237
Cunningham	27343
Currie	28435
Currituck	27929
Currituck Correctional Center	27956
Currytown	27292
Cutshalltown	28753
Cycle	27020
Cypress Creek (Columbus County)	28472
Cypress Creek (Duplin County)	28466
Cyrus	28540
Dabney	27536
Dallas	28034
Dalton	27043
Dana	28724
Danbury	27016
Danieltown	28043
Dan River Shores	27016
Dan Valley	27048
Darby	28624
Darden	27846
Dark Ridge	28622
Darlington	27839
Davenport Forks	27970
Davidson	28036
Davidson Correctional Center	27292
Davidson River	28768
Davie Correctional Center	27028
Davie Crossroads	27028
Davis	28524
Davistown (Edgecombe County)	27864
Davistown (McDowell County)	28762
Dawson Crossroads	27823
Day Book	28740
Days Crossroads	27839
Deep Creek	28133
Deep Gap	28618
Deep River (Part of High Point)	27260
Deep Run	28525
Deerfield	28607
Deerwood	28532
Dehart	28635
Delco	28436
Delight	28090
Dellview	28021
Dellwood	28786
Delway	28458
Democrat	28787
Dennis	27052
Dennys Store	27573
Denton	27239
Denver	28037
Deppe	28555
Derby	28338
Derita (Part of Charlotte)	28213
Devonshire	28081
Devotion	27017
Dewey Pier	27925
Dexter	27565
Dickens Park	28570
Dickerson	27565
Diggs	28379
Dillard	27025
Dillsboro	28725
Dilworth (Part of Charlotte)	28203
Dixon	28445
Dixon Crossroad	27590
Dobbersville	28365
Dobbins Heights	28345
Dobson	27017
Dockery	28635
Dodgetown	27025
Dodsons Crossroads	27278
Dogwood Acres (Durham County)	27704
Dogwood Acres (Randolph County)	27203
Dogwood Park	28025
Don Lee Heights	28532
Donnaha	27050
Doolie	28115
Dortches	27801
Dosier	27040

	ZIP
Dothan	29569
Double Shoals	28090
Douglas Crossroads	27889
Dover (Cleveland County)	28150
Dover (Craven County)	28526
Downtown (Buncombe County)	28802
Downtown (Mecklenburg County)	28202
Downtown (Rowan County)	28144
Downtown (Watauga County)	28607
Draco	28645
Drake	27809
Drake Park	28304
Draper (Part of Eden)	27288
Draughn	27891
Drewry	27553
Drexel	28619
Druid Hills (Part of Hendersonville)	28739
Drum Hill	27337
Drums Crossroads	28609
Dry Creek	27229
Duan	28658
Duart	28384
Dublin	28332
Duck	27949
Dudley	28333
Dudley Heights (Part of Greensboro)	27401
Dudley Shoals	28630
Duff Creek	28464
Duffies	28377
Duke (Part of Durham)	27706
Dulah	28463
Dula Springs	28787
Duncan	27526
Dundarrach	28386
Dunn	28334-35
For specific Dunn Zip Codes call (919) 892-3452	
Dunn Crossroads	27822
Dunns Rock	28712
Dunns Store	27874
Duplin Correctional Center	28349
Dupree Crossroads	27829
Durants Neck	27930
Durham	27701-22
For specific Durham Zip Codes call (919) 683-1976	
Dutchess Downs	27529
Dysartville	28761
Eagle	27020
Eagle Rock	27523
Eagle's Nest	28570
Eagle Springs	27242
Eagletown	27869
Earl	28038
Earley	27910
Earpsboro	27597
Easonburg	27801
Easons Crossroads	27938
East Arcadia	28455
East Bend	27013
East Carolina University (Part of Greenville)	27834
Eastcrest Ridge	28025
East Durham (Part of Durham)	27703
Eastern Correctional Center	28554
East Fayetteville	28301
East Flat Rock	28726
East Franklin (Part of Franklin)	28734
East Lake	27953
Eastland Mall (Part of Charlotte)	28212
East Laport	28723
East Laurinburg	28352
East Lumberton (Part of Lumberton)	28358
East Marion	28752
East Monbo	28677
Easton (Part of Winston-Salem)	27107
Eastover (Cumberland County)	28301
Eastover (Mecklenburg County)	28207
Eastridge Mall (Part of Gastonia)	28054
East Rockingham (Richmond County)	28379
East Rocky Mount (Part of Rocky Mount)	27801
East Side Park (Richmond County)	28379
East Side Park (Robeson County)	28340
East Spencer	28039

	ZIP
East Tabor	28463
Eastway (Part of Charlotte)	28205
East Wilmington (Part of Wilmington)	28405
Eastwood	28327
Ebenezer	28906
Echo	28383
Echo Heights	27603
Eck Reece	28642
Eden	27288
Edenhouse	27957
Edenton	27932
Edgar	27350
Edgemont	28645
Edgewood Acres	28016
Edmonds	28623
Edneyville	28727
Edward	27821
Edwards Crossroads (Alleghany County)	28675
Edwards Crossroads (Nash County)	27882
Edwards Crossroads (Northampton County)	27820
Edwards Fork	27874
Efland	27243
Ela	28713
Elams	23845
Elberon	27589
Eldorado	27371
Eleanors Crossroads	27937
Eleazer	27371
Elf	28904
Eliah	28451
Eli Whitney	27253
Elizabeth (Part of Charlotte)	28204
Elizabeth City	27906-09
For specific Elizabeth City Zip Codes call (919) 338-3869	
Elizabeth City Coast Guard Air Station	27909
Elizabeth Heights	27893
Elizabethtown	28337
Elkin	28621
Elk Mountain (Part of Woodfin)	28804
Elk Park	28622
Elk Valley	28604
Ellenboro	28040
Ellendale (Alexander County)	28681
Ellendale (Wake County)	27545
Eller	27107
Ellerbe	28338
Ellerbe Grove	28379
Ellijay	28734
Elliott	28393
Ellis Crossroads	28144
Ellis Store	27983
Elm City	27822
Elm Grove (Bertie County)	27924
Elm Grove (Lenoir County)	28501
Elmore	28352
Elmwood	28677
Elon College	27244
Elroy	27534
Embro	27551
Emerald Gardens	28304
Emerald Isle	28594
Emerald Village	27610
Emerson (Bladen County)	28433
Emerson (Columbus County)	28463
Emerywood (Part of High Point)	27262
Emit	27557
Emma	28806
Enderly Park (Part of Charlotte)	28208
Endy	28001
Enfield	27823
Engelhard	27824
Englewood (Part of Rocky Mount)	27801
English Woods	28025
Enka	28728
Enka Village	28728
Ennice	28623
Eno	27278
Enochville	28023
Enola	28655
Enon	27018
Eno Valley (Part of Durham)	27712
Enterprise (Davidson County)	27292
Enterprise (Warren County)	27850
Ephesus	27028
Epsom	27536
Erastus	28723
Erect	27341
Ernul	28527

Ervintown-Goldrock NORTH CAROLINA 393

Name	ZIP
Ervintown	28574
Erwin	28339
Erwin Heights (Part of Thomasville)	27360
Essex	27844
Estatoe	28777
Estelle	27305
Ether	27247
Etowah	28729
Eufola	28677
Eure	27935
Eureka	27830
Eureka Springs	28301
Eutaw (Part of Fayetteville)	28303
Evansdale	27893
Everetts	27825
Everetts Crossroads	27865
Evergreen (Beaufort County)	27817
Evergreen (Columbus County)	28438
Evergreen Estates	28304
Exum	28420
Exway	27306
Fair Bluff	28439
Fairfield (Hyde County)	27826
Fairfield (Union County)	28103
Fair Field Estate	28150
Fairfield Harbour	28560
Fairfield Sapphire Valley	28774
Fair Grove	27360
Fairlane	28303
Fairmont	28340
Fairmont Junction	28383
Fairplains	28659
Fairport	27544
Fairview (Buncombe County)	28730
Fairview (Orange County)	27278
Fairview (Rockingham County)	27288
Fairview (Union County)	28110
Fairview Cross Roads	27017
Fairview Park	28636
Fairway Hills	28786
Faison	28341
Faisons	27876
Faith	28041
Falcon	28342
Falkland	27827
Fall Creek	27018
Falling Creek	28501
Falling Creek Estates	28601
Falls	27609
Fallston	28042
Far Away Place	28025
Farmer	27203
Farmington	27028
Farmville (Chatham County)	27330
Farmville (Pitt County)	27828
Faro	27883
Farrington	27514
Faust	28754
Fayblock (Part of Fayetteville)	28301
Fayetteville	28301-14
For specific Fayetteville Zip Codes call (919) 486-2311	
Fayetteville North (Part of Fayetteville)	28311
Fearrington Post	27312
Federal Building (Part of Elizabeth City)	27909
Federal Correctional Institution	27509
Feezor	27292
Feltonville	27502
Ferguson	28624
Ferncliff Estates	28025
Fibreville (Part of Canton)	28716
Fields	28551
Fines Creek	28721
Finger	28124
Fires Creek	28904
First Union (Part of Charlotte)	28202
Fisher Park (Part of Greensboro)	27401
Fisher Town	28081
Fitch	27379
Five Forks (Person County)	27573
Five Forks (Rowan County)	28023
Five Forks (Warren County)	27551
Five Point (Part of Raleigh)	27608
Five Points (Beaufort County)	27889
Five Points (Columbus County)	28431
Five Points (Hoke County)	28376
Five Points (Richmond County)	28379

Name	ZIP
Flat Branch (Gates County)	27938
Flat Branch (Harnett County)	27546
Flat Creek	28787
Flat Rock (Henderson County)	28731
Flat Rock (Stokes County)	27043
Flat Rock (Surry County)	27030
Flats	28781
Flat Shoals	27019
Flat Springs	28622
Flay	28021
Fleetwood	28626
Fleetwood Acres	28052
Fletcher	28732
Flint Hill (Montgomery County)	27371
Flint Hill (Randolph County)	27350
Flint Hill (Yadkin County)	27018
Florence	28556
Florence Town	27302
Flowes Store	28025
Floytan Crossroads	27536
Folkstone	28445
Folly	27979
Fontana Dam	28733
Footsville	27055
Forbes	28740
Forestburg	27944
Forest City	28043
Forest Hills (Cumberland County)	28303
Forest Hills (Forsyth County)	27105
Forest Hills (Gaston County)	28120
Forest Hills (New Hanover County)	28403
Forest Hills (Rockingham County)	27320
Forest Oaks	27406
Forest Ridge	28150
Forestville (Anson County)	28091
Forestville (Wake County)	27587
Fork Church	27028
Fort Barnwell	28526
Fort Bragg (Cumberland County)	28307
Fort Caswell	28461
Fort Junction	28307
Fort Landing	27925
Fort Macon Coast Guard Base	28512
Fort Point	27817
Foscoe	28604
Foster Creek	28753
Fountain (Duplin County)	28521
Fountain (Pitt County)	27829
Fountain Hill	28133
Four Oaks	27524
Four Seasons (Part of Hendersonville)	28739
Four Seasons Towncenter (Part of Greensboro)	27407
Fourway	28538
Fox Fire (Cumberland County)	28303
Foxfire (Moore County)	27281
Foxwood Acres	28025
Francisco	27053
Francis Mill	27805
Francktown	28574
Frank	28657
Franklin (Macon County)	28734
Franklin (Rowan County)	28144
Franklin Correctional Center	27508
Franklin Grove	28713
Franklin Street (Part of Chapel Hill)	27514
Franklinton	27525
Franklinville	27248
Frazier Crossroads	27557
Fraziers Crossroads	27910
Frederick	27817
Freedom (Part of Charlotte)	28208
Freedom Mall (Part of Charlotte)	28208
Freeland	28420
Freeman	28423
Fremont	27830
Friendly Acres	28025
Friendly Center-Forum VI (Part of Greensboro)	27404
Friendship (Cherokee County)	28906
Friendship (Duplin County)	28398
Friendship (Guilford County)	27410
Friendship (Wake County)	27502
Friendship (Yadkin County)	27018
Frisco	27936
Frog Level	27834
Frog Pond	28129

Name	ZIP
Frogsboro	27314
Fruitland	28739
Fulchers Landing	28460
Fullers	27360
Fulp	27052
Funston	28479
Fuquay Springs (Part of Fuquay-Varina)	27526
Fuquay-Varina	27526
Furches	28644
Furnitureland (Part of High Point)	27264
Galatia	27876
Gales Creek	28570
Galloway Crossroads	27858
Gallup Acres	28304
Gamble Hill	28016
Gamewell	28645
Garden Creek	28752
Garden Homes (Part of Greensboro)	27408
Gardnerville	28513
Gardner Webb College (Part of Boiling Springs)	28017
Garland	28441
Garner	27529
Garysburg	27831
Gaston	27832
Gaston Correctional Center	28034
Gastonia	28052-54
For specific Gastonia Zip Codes call (704) 867-6311	
Gaston Mall (Part of Gastonia)	28054
Gates	27937
Gates Correctional Center	27938
Gates Four	28306
Gatesville	27938
Gateway	28789
Gause Landing	28459
Gay	28779
Gaylord	27808
Gela	27582
Gentry Store	27573
George	27897
Georgetown (Buncombe County)	28748
Georgetown (Davidson County)	27284
Georgetown (Lenoir County)	28501
Georgeville	28025
Germanton	27019
Germantown	27875
Gerton	28735
Gethsemane	27891
Gibson	28343
Gibsontown	28716
Gibsonville	27249
Giddensville	28341
Gilkey	28139
Gill	27536
Gillburg	27536
Glade Valley	28627
Glady	28715
Glass (Part of Kannapolis)	28081
Glen Alpine	28628
Glen Ayre	28705
Glenbrook	28304
Glencoe	27217
Glendale Acres (Part of Fayetteville)	28304
Glendale Springs	28629
Glendon	27251
Glenhaven	28304
Glen Lennox (Part of Chapel Hill)	27514
Glenn	27705
Glenola	27263
Glen Raven	27215
Glenview	27823
Glenville	28736
Glenwood (Guilford County)	27403
Glenwood (McDowell County)	28737
Glenwood (Richmond County)	28379
Globe	28645
Gloucester	28528
Gneiss	28734
Goat Neck	27925
Godwin	28344
Golden Forest	27604
Golden Gate (Part of Greensboro)	27405
Gold Hill (Rockingham County)	27025
Gold Hill (Rowan County)	28071
Gold Mine	28741
Gold Point	27871
Goldrock	27891

394 NORTH CAROLINA Goldsboro-Holly Ridge

	ZIP
Goldsboro	27530-34
For specific Goldsboro Zip Codes call (919) 734-3521	
Goldsboro Northwest	27530
Goldston	27252
Gold Valley Crossroads	27557
Goodsonville	28092
Goose Creek	27974
Gooseneck	28456
Goose Pond	27924
Gordonton	27541
Gordontown	27292
Gorman	27704
Goshen	28697
Governors Island	28713
Grace (Part of Asheville)	28814
Grace Chapel	28630
Gradys	28365
Graham	27253
Graingers	28501
Grandfather	28646
Grandview	28906
Grandview Heights (Part of Boone)	28607
Grandy	27939
Granite Falls	28630
Granite Quarry	28072
Grantham	27530
Granthams	28560
Grantsboro	28529
Grape Creek	28906
Grapevine	28753
Graphite	28762
Grassy Creek (Ashe County)	28631
Grassy Creek (Mitchell County)	28777
Grays Chapel	27248
Grayson	28632
Great Neck Landing	28539
Green Acres (Alamance County)	27217
Green Acres (Gaston County)	28012
Green Acres (Wake County)	27603
Green Acres Park	28025
Greenbrier Estates	27603
Greene Correctional Center	28554
Greene Cove	28705
Greenevers	28458
Green Farm	27834
Greenfield	27932
Greenhill (Haywood County)	28716
Green Hill (Rutherford County)	28139
Greenlee	28762
Green Level (Alamance County)	27217
Green Level (Wake County)	27502
Greenmountain	28740
Greenriver	28722
Greensboro	27401-95
For specific Greensboro Zip Codes call (919) 271-5481	
Greens Creek	28779
Green Valley	28615
Greenville	27834-36
For specific Greenville Zip Codes call (919) 752-2153	
Greenwood Homes (Part of Fayetteville)	28303
Gregory	27973
Gregory Crossroads (Bertie County)	27957
Gregory Crossroads (Onslow County)	28574
Greystone	27536
Griffins Crossroads	27312
Grifton	28530
Grimesdale	28739
Grimesland	27837
Grissettown	28459
Grissom	27522
Grist	28431
Grove Hill	27551
Grovemont	28778
Grove Park (Part of Charlotte)	28215
Grover	28073
Grovestone	28778
Growers Crossroads	27924
Guide	28463
Guideway	28463
Guilford (Part of Greensboro)	27409
Guilford College (Part of Greensboro)	27410
Guilford Correctional Center	27301
Guilford Hills (Part of Greensboro)	27408
Gulf	27256

	ZIP
Gull Rock	27824
Gumberry	27838
Gumbranch	28540
Gum Neck	27925
Gum Springs	27312
Guntertown	28753
Gupton	27549
Guthrie	27284
Guyton	28320
Haddocks Crossroads	28590
Hairtown	28302
Half Hell	28422
Half Moon	28540
Halifax	27839
Halifax Correctional Institution	27839
Hallsboro	28442
Halls Ferry Junction	28127
Halls Mills	28649
Halls Store	28385
Hallsville	28518
Hamer	27212
Hamilton	27840
Hamilton Lakes (Part of Greensboro)	27408
Hamlet	28345
Hampstead	28443
Hamptonville	27020
Hamrick	28714
Hancheys Store	28466
Hancock	27932
Handy	27239
Hanes Mall (Part of Winston-Salem)	27103
Hanrahans	28530
Happy Valley (Buncombe County)	28805
Happy Valley (Caldwell County)	28645
Harbinger	27941
Harbor Island (Part of Wrightsville Beach)	28480
Hardees Cross Road	27504
Hardins	28034
Hare	28627
Hargetts Cross Roads	28574
Harkers Island	28531
Harlem Heights	28170
Harlowe	28570
Harmony	28634
Harper's Crossroads	27207
Harrells	28444
Harrellsville	27942
Harrelsonville	28472
Harris (Moore County)	28327
Harris (Rutherford County)	28074
Harrisburg	28075
Harrisburg Estates	28075
Harris Crossroads (Franklin County)	27596
Harris Crossroads (Vance County)	27536
Harris Landing	27932
Harrison Cross Roads	27320
Hartland	28645
Hartman	27016
Hartsease	27886
Harveytown	28501
Hassell	27841
Hastings Corner	27921
Hasty	28352
Hatteras	27943
Havelock	28532
Havelock Station (Part of Havelock)	28532
Haw Branch (Moore County)	27330
Haw Branch (Onslow County)	28574
Haw Creek (Part of Asheville)	28805
Hawfields	27302
Hawk	28705
Haw River	27258
Haws Run	28454
Hayesville	28904
Haymount (Part of Fayetteville)	28305
Hayne	28318
Hays	28635
Hayti (Part of Durham)	27701
Haywood	27559
Haywood Road (Part of Asheville)	28806
Hazelwood	28738
Hazelwood Park	27864
Healing Springs	27239
Heathsville	27823
Heaton	28622
Hedrick Grove	27292
Helens Crossroads	28513

	ZIP
Helton	28631
Hemby Acres	28079
Hemby Bridge	28079
Henderson	27536
Henderson Correctional Center	28739
Hendersonville	28739
Hendrix Estates	28144
Henrico	27842
Henrietta	28076
Henry	28168
Henry River	28602
Hepco	28721
Heritage Hill	27516
Heritage Woods	28025
Herrings Crossroads (Duplin County)	28508
Herrings Crossroads (Greene County)	27888
Hertford	27944
Hester	27581
Hesters Store	27541
Hestertown	28358
Hewitt	28781
Hexlena	27805
Hibbs Acres	28570
Hickmans Crossroads	28459
Hickory	28601-03
For specific Hickory Zip Codes call (704) 328-5503	
Hickory Crossroads	27919
Hickory Grove (Cumberland County)	28304
Hickory Grove (Gaston County)	28054
Hickory Grove (Mecklenburg County)	28215
Hickory Knoll	28734
Hickory North	28601
Hickory Point	27806
Hickory Rock	27549
Hicks Crossroads (Mecklenburg County)	28078
Hicks Crossroads (Vance County)	27565
Hiddenite	28636
Higdonville	28734
Higgins	28714
High Crossroads	27807
Highfalls	27259
High Hampton	28717
Highland Park	28345
Highland Park West (Part of Greensboro)	27407
Highlands	28741
High Point	27260-64
For specific High Point Zip Codes call (919) 884-8344	
High Rock	27239
High Shoals	28077
Highsmiths	28382
Hightowers	27379
Hildebran	28637
Hillcrest (Hoke County)	28376
Hill Crest (Moore County)	28327
Hilliardston	27856
Hillsborough	27278
Hills Crossroads	27839
Hillsdale (Davie County)	27006
Hillsdale (Guilford County)	27405
Hillsville	27350
Hilltop (Guilford County)	27417
Hilltop (Lincoln County)	28092
Hilltop Acres	28570
Hill View	28580
Hines Crossroad	27834
Hinsons Crossroads	28439
Hiwassee Dam	28906
Hobbsville	27946
Hobbton	28366
Hobgood	27843
Hobucken	28537
Hodges Gap	28607
Hodman	27028
Hoffman	28347
Hog Island	28394
Ho-Ho Village	28570
Holden Beach	28462
Holdens Cross Roads	27893
Holiday Island	27944
Holiday Shores	27371
Holland	27526
Hollemans Crossroads	27562
Hollis	28040
Hollister	27844
Holly Grove (Davidson County)	27292
Holly Grove (Gates County)	27926
Holly Hill Mall (Part of Burlington)	27215
Holly Ridge	28445

Holly Springs-Laurel NORTH CAROLINA 395

Place	ZIP
Holly Springs (Macon County)	28734
Holly Springs (Wake County)	27540
Holly View Forest-Highland Park	27030
Hollyville	28515
Hollywood	28304
Hollywood Crossroads	27858
Homestead (Part of Charlotte)	28214
Homestead Heights (Part of Durham)	27704
Honey Hill	28442
Honey Island	28420
Honey Town	28379
Honolulu	28530
Hood Swamp	27534
Hookerton	28538
Hooper Hill	28451
Hoopers Creek	28732
Hootentown	27889
Hopedale	28217
Hope Mills	28348
Hope Valley (Part of Durham)	27707
Hopewell (Rutherford County)	28040
Hopewell (Wayne County)	28365
Hopkins	27597
Horner	27565
Horse Shoe	28742
Hosiery Mill	28170
Hoskins (Part of Charlotte)	28214
Hothouse	28906
Hot Springs	28743
Houston	28110
Houstonville	28634
Howland Parkway	28516
Hubert	28539
Hudson	28638
Hudsons Crossroads	27858
Huffmantown	28574
Hughes	28657
Hugo	28530
Hulls Crossroads	28168
Huntdale	28740
Hunters Bridge	27865
Huntersville	28078
Hunting Creek	28659
Hunts	27882
Huntsboro	27565
Huntsville (Rockingham County)	27025
Huntsville (Yadkin County)	27028
Hurdle Mills	27541
Husk	28639
Hyatt Creek	28786
Hyde Park Estates	28216
Hymans	28562
Icard	28666
Icaria	27980
Ida	28351
Idlewild (Ashe County)	28694
Idlewild (Mecklenburg County)	28212
Idlewild Annex (Part of Charlotte)	28227
Ijames Crossroads	27028
Independence (Part of Charlotte)	28212
Independence Mall (Part of Wilmington)	28403
Index	28694
Indian Beach	28557
Indian Hills	28789
Indian Springs	28578
Indian Town	27973
Indian Trail	28079
Indian Valley	27217
Inez	27589
Ingalls	28657
Ingieside	27549
Ingold	28446
Institute	28551
Intelligence	27025
Iotla	28734
Iredell Correctional Center	28677
Iris Gardens	28306
Ironduff	28786
Irongate	28306
Ironhill	28463
Iron Station	28080
Irving Park (Part of Greensboro)	27408
Isenhour	28127
Island View Shores	27808
Isle of Pines	28115
Ita	27823
Ivanhoe	28447
Ivy	28754

Place	ZIP
Ivy Hills	28786
Jackson (Moore County)	28315
Jackson (Northampton County)	27845
Jackson Hill	27239
Jackson Line	28713
Jackson Park (Cabarrus County)	28081
Jackson Park (Cabarrus County)	28025
Jacksons Creek	27239
Jacksons Crossroads (Duplin County)	28518
Jacksons Crossroads (Lenoir County)	28501
Jackson Springs	27281
Jacksons Store	28518
Jacksontown	27556
Jacksonville	28540-46
For specific Jacksonville Zip Codes call (919) 346-4135	
Jacksonville East	28546
Jacktown	28752
Jakesville	27292
James City (Craven County)	28560
Jamestown	27282
Jamesville	27846
Janeiro	28510
Jarman Forks	28574
Jarvisburg	27947
Jason	28551
Jasper	28562
Jefferson	28640
Jefferson Park	28379
Jenkins Heights	28052
Jenny Lind	28551
Jericho	27379
Jerome	28399
Jerusalem	27028
Joe	28743
Johns	28352
Johnson Crossroad	27501
Johnsons Corner	27976
Johnsontown (Davidson County)	27360
Johnsontown (Sampson County)	28328
Johnsonville (Cherokee County)	28906
Johnsonville (Harnett County)	28326
Johnston Correctional Center	27577
Johnstown	28021
John Umstead Hospital	27509
Jonas Ridge	28641
Jonathan	28786
Jones	27311
Jonesboro Heights (Part of Sanford)	27330
Jones Chapel	27545
Jonestown	28572
Jonesville	28642
Joppa	27919
Joyceton (Part of Hudson)	28638
Joyland (Part of Durham)	27703
Joyners Crossroads	27801
Joynes	28685
Jubilee	27299
Jugtown	28715
Julian	27283
Juno	28806
Jupiter	28787
Justice	27549
Kalmia	28777
Kannapolis	28081
Kappa	27028
Kapps Mill	27017
Katesville	27525
Keane	27707
Keener	28328
Kelford	27847
Kellersville	28604
Kellogs Fork	27979
Kellum	28540
Kellumtown	28539
Kelly	28448
Kenansville	28349
Kendale Shopping Center (Part of Sanford)	27330
Kenilworth (Part of Asheville)	28805
Kenly	27542
Kenmure	28731
Kennebec	27592
Kennells Beach	28529
Kentwood	28081
Kernersville	27284-85
For specific Kernersville Zip Codes call (919) 993-3812	
Kerr	28444

Place	ZIP
Kershaw	28571
Keys Crossroads	27946
Kikers	28133
Kilby Island	27808
Kill Devil Hills	27948
Kimesville	27298
King	27021
King Charles (Part of Raleigh)	27610
Kingsboro	27801
Kings Creek	28645
Kings Crossroads (Guilford County)	27284
Kings Crossroads (Pitt County)	27829
Kings Forest	28144
Kings Grant	28405
Kings Mountain	28086
King Whites Fork	27843
Kinston	28501-03
For specific Kinston Zip Codes call (919) 527-6123	
Kinton Fork	27565
Kipling	27543
Kirbys Crossing	27851
Kirkwood (Part of Greensboro)	27408
Kittrell	27544
Kitty Fork	28328
Kitty Hawk	27949
Knightdale	27545
Knob Hill	28379
Knollwood (Part of Southern Pines)	28387
Knotts Island	27950
Kona	28705
Kornbow	28303
Kornegay	28508
Kure Beach	28449
Kyle	28781
Laboratory	28092
Lackey Hill	28713
Lackey Town	28762
Ladonia	27030
Lafayette	28304
Lagoon	26448
La Grange (Cumberland County)	28303
La Grange (Lenoir County)	28551
Lakecrest	28301
Lakedale (Part of Fayetteville)	28306
Lake Daniel (Part of Greensboro)	27408
Lake Ellsworth	27834
Lake Gaston Estates	27551
Lake Glenwood	27858
Lake in the Pine	27371
Lake Junaluska	28745
Lake Landing	27824
Lake Lure	28746
Lake Lynn	28306
Lake Montonia	28086
Lakemont Park	28601
Lakeside (Forsyth County)	27105
Lakeside (Stanly County)	28001
Lake Toxaway	28747
Lakeview (Alamance County)	27215
Lakeview (Davidson County)	27299
Lakeview (Moore County)	28350
Lakeview Estates (Alamance County)	27215
Lakeview Estates (Henderson County)	28739
Lake View Park	27870
Lake Waccamaw	28450
Lakewood (Cabarrus County)	28025
Lakewood (Henderson County)	28739
Lambert	28163
Lambs Corner	27921
Lamm	27893
Lamms Crossroads	27882
Lancaster Crossroads	27816
Landis	28088
Langley Store	27801
Lansdowne (Part of Charlotte)	28226
Lansing	28643
Lanvale	28451
Lasker	27848
Last Chance	27824
Latham Town (Part of Greensboro)	27407
Lattimore	28089
Lauada	28713
Laurel	28753

396 NORTH CAROLINA Laurel Hill-Midway

	ZIP		ZIP		ZIP
Laurel Hill (Buncombe County)	28715	Longcreek	28457	Mansfield Park	28557
Laurel Hill (Scotland County)	28351	Longisland	28648	Manson	27553
Laurel Hills	27609	Long John Mountain Estates	28739	Manteo	27954
Laurel Park	28739	Longleaf	28570	Maple	27956
Laurel Springs	28644	Long Leaf Park (Part of Wilmington)	28403	Maple Cypress	28530
Laurinburg	28352-53	Long Pine	28170	Maple Hill	28454
For specific Laurinburg Zip Codes call (919) 276-0911		Long Ridge	28754	Maple Springs	28665
Lawndale (Cleveland County)	28090	Long Shoals	28092	Mapleton	27855
Lawndale (Guilford County)	27408	Longs Store	27573	Mapleville	27549
Lawrence	27886	Longtown (Burke County)	28761	Maplewood (Part of Rockingham)	28379
Lawsonville (Rockingham County)	27320	Longtown (Yadkin County)	27011	Marble	28905
Lawsonville (Stokes County)	27022	Long View (Bladen County)	28448	Marcus	27281
Laytown	28645	Longview (Catawba County)	28601	Maready	28521
Leaksville (Part of Eden)	27288	Longview (Cumberland County)	28301	Margaretsville	27853
Leaman	27325	Longwood	28452	Maribel	28515
Leasburg	27291	Longwood Park	28345	Marietta	28362
Leatherman	28734	Loray	28677	Marion	28752
Ledbetter	28379	Louisburg	27549	Mariposa	28164
Ledger	28705	Love Field	28779	Marlboro	27828
Leechville	27810	Lovejoy	27371	Marler	27020
Lee's Ridge (Buncombe County)	28806	Love Valley	28677	Marlwood Acres (Part of Charlotte)	28212
Leewood Acres	28092	Lowell	28098	Mar-Mac	27530
Leggett	27886	Lowes Grove	27713	Mar-Man	28532
Leicester	28748	Lowesville	28164	Marshall	28753
Leland	28451	Lowgap	27024	Marshallberg	28553
Lemon Springs	28355	Lowland	28552	Mars Hill	28754
Lennon Crossroads	28422	Luart	27546	Marshville	28103
Lennons Crossroads	28438	Lucama	27851	Marston	28363
Lennoxville	28516	Lucia	28120	Martel Village (Part of Woodfin)	28804
Lenoir	28645	Luck	28743	Martin Correctional Center	27892
Lenoir Mall (Part of Lenoir)	28645	Lumber Bridge	28357	Martins Creek	28906
Lenoir Rhyne (Part of Hickory)	28601	Lumberton	28358-59	Marvin	28173
Letitia	28906	For specific Lumberton Zip Codes call (919) 738-2451		Marys Grove	28086
Level Cross (Randolph County)	27317	Luther	28715	Mashoes	27953
Level Cross (Surry County)	27017	Lyman	28521	Masonboro	28403
Levels	27925	Lynchs Corner	27909	Masons Crossroads	28343
Lewis	27565	Lynn	28750	Mason Store	27546
Lewisburg	28714	Lynndale	27853	Masontown	28581
Lewiston Woodville	27849	Lynnwood Jr. Estate	28025	Massapoag (Part of Lincolnton)	28092
Lewisville	27023	Lynwood Lakes	27420	Mast	28692
Lexington	27292-93	Mabel	28698	Mathews Crossroads	27816
For specific Lexington Zip Codes call (704) 249-8196		McAdenville	28101	Matkins	27249
Liberia	27589	McAdoo Heights (Part of Greensboro)	27405	Matney	28604
Liberty (Cherokee County)	37391	McArthers Crossroads	28352	Matthews	28105-06
Liberty (Randolph County)	27298	Macclesfield	27852	For specific Matthews Zip Codes call (704) 847-9185	
Liberty (Rowan County)	28071	McConnell (Beaufort County)	27814	Maury	28554
Liberty Hill	27306	McConnell (Moore County)	27325	Mavaton	27932
Liddell	28578	McCray	27215	Maxton	28364
Liledown	28681	McCullen	28328	Mayfair	28304
Lilesville	28091	McCullers	27603	Mayfield	27326
Lillington	27546	Mc Cutcheon Field	28545	Mayhew	28115
Lilly	27976	McDade	27231	Mayodan	27027
Lincoln Correctional Center	28092	McDaniel	28382	Maysville	28555
Lincolnton	28092	McDonald	28340	Mazeppa	28115
Lindell	27883	McDowell Correctional Center	28752	Meadow (Johnston County)	27504
Linden	28356	Macedonia (Wake County)	27606	Meadow (Stokes County)	27052
Lindley Park (Part of Greensboro)	27403	Macedonia (Washington County)	27962	Meadowood	28379
Lineberry	27233	McFarlan	28102	Meadowood Lakes	27302
Linville	28646	MacGee Crossroads	27501	Meadow Summit (Part of Eden)	27288
Linville Falls	28647	McGehees Mill	27343	Meadow Wood	28304
Linwood	27299	McGinnis Crossroads	28722	Meat Camp	28607
Lisbon	28434	McGowans Crossroads	27858	Mebane	27302
Little Creek	28754	McGrady	28649	Mecklenburg Correctional Center	28078
Littlefield	28513	Machpelah	28080	Medfield	27607
Little Horse Creek	28643	Mackeys	27970	Melanchton	27298
Little Mountain	28761	Macks Village	27526	Melrose	28773
Little Pinecreek	28753	McLamb Crossroads	28366	Melville	27302
Little Richmond	28621	McLeansville	27301	Melvin Hill	28722
Little River (Alexander County)	28681	Maco	28451	Menola	27910
Little River (Transylvania County)		Macon	27551	Meredith College (Part of Raleigh)	27601
Madison	27025	Merrimon	28516
Little Switzerland	28749	Maggie Valley	28751	Merritt	28556
Littleton	27850	Magnolia	28453	Merry Hill	27957
Livingstons Quarters	28351	Maiden	28650	Merry Oaks	27559
Lizard Lick	27591	Maine	27028	Mesic	28515
Lizzie	28580	Main Street (Part of Garner)	27529	Metcalf	28150
Lloyd Crossroads	27942	Makatoka	28420	Method (Part of Raleigh)	27606
Loafers Glory	28705	Makleyville	27875	Methodist College	28301
Lobelia	28394	Malmo	28451	Mewborns Crossroads	28501
Lochlommond	28304	Malpass Corner	28425	Micaville	28755
Locust	28097	Maltby	28905	Micro	27555
Locust Grove	28740	Malvern Hills (Part of Asheville)	28806	Middleburg	27556
Locust Hill	27320	Mamers	27552	Middle Fork	28712
Loftins Crossroads	28501	Mamie	27966	Middlesex	27557
Logan	28139	Manchester (Part of Spring Lake)	28390	Middletown	27824
Lola	28520	Mangum	27306	Midland	28107
Lomax	28669	Manly	28387	Midpine	28086
Lone Hickory	27055	Manns Harbor	27953	Midway (Alexander County)	28636
Long Acres (Part of Jacksonville)	28546	Manor Station (Part of Winston-Salem)	27114	Midway (Beaufort County)	27808
				Midway (Bertie County)	27957
				Midway (Brunswick County)	28422
Long Beach	28461	Mansfield	28557	Midway (Cabarrus County)	28081
				Midway (Richmond County)	28379

Midway-Norton **NORTH CAROLINA** 397

	ZIP		ZIP		ZIP
Midway (Rockingham County)	27320	Mount Carmel Acres	28806	New Hanover Correctional Center	28401
Midway Park	28544	Mount Energy	27522	New Haven	28675
Midwood (Part of Charlotte)	28205	Mount Gilead (Avery County)	28622	New Hill	27562
Milburnie	27604	Mount Gilead (Cabarrus County)	28025	New Holland	27885
Mildred	27886	Mount Gilead (Montgomery County)	27306	New Hope (Chatham County)	27559
Miles	27302	Mount Gould	27957	New Hope (Franklin County)	27549
Millboro	27248	Mount Herman	28638	New Hope (Iredell County)	28689
Mill Branch	28420	Mount Holly	28120	New Hope (Orange County)	27514
Millbridge	28144	Mount Mourne	28123	New Hope (Randolph County)	27239
Millbrook (Part of Raleigh)	27658	Mount Olive (Bladen County)	28337	New Hope (Wake County)	27604
Mill Creek (Ashe County)	28684	Mount Olive (Columbus County)	28472	New Hope (Wayne County)	27534
Mill Creek (Brunswick County)	28479	Mount Olive (Hyde County)	27810	New Hope (Wilson County)	27893
Mill Creek (Carteret County)	28570	Mount Olive (Stokes County)	27021	New House	28150
Mill Crossroads	27932	Mount Olive (Wayne County)	28365	Newland	28657
Millennium Church	27805	Mount Pleasant (Avery County)	28657	New Lands	27925
Millers Creek	28651	Mount Pleasant (Cabarrus County)	28124	New Leaksville	27288
Millersville	28681	Mount Pleasant (Cherokee County)	28906	Newlife	28635
Millingport	28001	Mount Pleasant (Moore County)	28326	New London	28127
Mill Spring	28756	Mount Pleasant (Nash County)	27807	New Market	27350
Mills River	28742	Mount Pleasant (Richmond County)	28338	Newport	28570
Milltown	28771	Mount Pleasant (Yadkin County)	27011	New River Marine Corps Air Station	28540
Milton	27305	Mount Sterling	37821	New River Plaza (Part of Jacksonville)	28540
Milwaukee	27854	Mount Tabor (Forsyth County)	27106	New River Station	28542
Mimosa Shores	27889	Mount Tabor (Washington County)	27928	New Salem (Randolph County)	27317
Mineral Springs (Anson County)	28135	Mount Tirzah	27583	New Salem (Union County)	28103
Mineral Springs (Union County)	28108	Mount Ulla	28125	Newsom	27239
Mingo	28334	Mount Vernon (Rowan County)	27013	Newton	28658
Minneapolis	28652	Mount Vernon (Rutherford County)	28139	Newton Grove	28366
Minnesott Beach	28510	Mount Vernon Springs	27344	Newton Park	27893
Minpro	28777	Mount Zion (Part of Greensboro)	27406	Newtons Crossroads	28478
Mint Hill	28212	Moxley	28635	Newtowne Plaza (Part of Statesville)	28677
Mintons Store	27897	Moyock	27958	Niagara	28387
Mintonsville	27946	Mt. Pleasant	27592	Nixons Beach	27932
Mintz	28382	Muddy Cross	27946	Nixonton	27909
Mirror Lake	28741	Mulberry	28659	Nobles Cross Roads	28525
Misenheimer	28109	Murdocksville	28374	Nocarva	27551
Mitchells Fork	27946	Murfreesboro	27855	Nocho Park (Part of Greensboro)	27406
Mitchell Village	28557	Murphey	28458	Norfleet	27874
Mitcheners Crossroads	27525	Murphy	28906	Norlina	27563
Mocksville	27028	Murray Hills	28081	Norman	28367
Moffitt Hill	28762	Murrays Mills	28609	Norrington Crossroads	27546
Mollie	28432	Murraysville	28405	North (Part of Winston-Salem)	27115
Moltonville	28328	Murray Town	28425	North Albemarle (Part of Albemarle)	28001
Momeyer	27856	Musgraves Crossroads	27863	North Asheboro (Part of Asheboro)	27203
Moncure	27559	Myers Park (Part of Charlotte)	28207	North Belmont (Gaston County)	28012
Monks Crossroads	28366	Myrick Estates	27850	North Brevard	28712
Monroe	28110	Myrtle Grove	28403	North Burlington (Part of Burlington)	27215
Monroe Mall (Part of Monroe)	28110	Nags Head	27959	North Charlotte (Part of Charlotte)	28225
Monroetown (Moore County)	28374	Nahunta	27863	North Chase (Part of Wilmington)	28405
Monroetown (Rockingham County)	27320	Nakina	28455	North Concord (Cabarrus County)	28025
Montague	28435	Nantahala	28781	North Cooleemee (Part of Cooleemee)	27014
Montclair	28304	Naples	28760	North Cove	28752
Montezuma	28653	Nashville	27856	North Durham (Part of Durham)	27704
Montgomery Correctional Center	27371	Nathans Creek	28617	North Elkin	28621
Monticello	27214	Naval Hospital	28542	Northgate (Part of Durham)	27701
Montreat	28757	Navassa	28404	Northgate Mall (Part of Durham)	27701
Montrose	28376	Nebo (McDowell County)	28761	North Harbor	28516
Moores Beach	27810	Nebo (Yadkin County)	27011	North Harlowe	28532
Mooresboro	28114	Nebraska	27824	North Henderson	27536
Moores School House	27542	Needmore (Rowan County)	27054	North Hills (Part of Raleigh)	27619
Moores Springs	27053	Needmore (Swain County)	28713	North Lumberton (Part of Lumberton)	28358
Mooresville	28115	Neel Estates	28144	Northmoor	28601
Mooresville Junction (Part of Mooresville)	28115	Nelson	27560	North Point (Part of Winston-Salem)	27106
Moravian Falls	28654	Neuse	27661	North Raeford	28376
Mordecai (Part of Raleigh)	27604	Neuse Crossroads	27661	North River	28516
Morehead City	28557	Neuse Forest	28560	North River Corner	28516
Morgans Corner	27909	Neverson	27880	North Roxboro (Part of Roxboro)	27573
Morganton	28655	New Bern	28560-64	Northside (Granville County)	27564
Morgantown	27215	For specific New Bern Zip Codes call (919) 638-6111		Northside (Wilson County)	27822
Moriah	27572	New Bern Junction (Part of Wilmington)	28405	Northview	27330
Morlan Park	28144	New Bethel	27572	North West	28451
Morning Star	28716	Newbold (Part of Fayetteville)	28301	Northwest Cabarrus Woods	28081
Morris Landing	28445	New Bridge (Part of Woodfin)	28804	North Wilkesboro	28659
Morrisville	27560	Newdale	28714	North Winston (Part of Winston-Salem)	27105
Mortimer	28645	Newell	28126	Northwoods (Part of Jacksonville)	28540
Morven	28119	Newfound	28748	Norton (Jackson County)	28723
Moss	28127			Norton (Macon County)	28763
Moss Hill	28501				
Mother Vineyard	27954				
Motleta	27203				
Mountain Home	28758				
Mountain Island	28120				
Mountain Park	28676				
Mountain Valley	28790				
Mountain View (Gaston County)	28086				
Mountain View (Orange County)	27278				
Mountain View (Stokes County)	27021				
Mount Airy	27030				
Mount Carmel	27306				

398 NORTH CAROLINA Norwood-Poplar

Place	ZIP
Norwood (Rockingham County)	27320
Norwood (Stanly County)	28128
Norwood Beach	28128
Norwood Hollow	28604
Oakboro	28129
Oak City	27857
Oak Crest (Part of Fayetteville)	28301
Oakdale (Guilford County)	27282
Oakdale (Iredell County)	28677
Oak Forest	28803
Oak Grove (Brunswick County)	28462
Oak Grove (Cleveland County)	28086
Oak Grove (Guilford County)	27406
Oak Grove (Macon County)	28734
Oak Grove (Surry County)	27030
Oak Hill (Burke County)	28655
Oak Hill (Caldwell County)	28645
Oakhurst (Part of Charlotte)	28205
Oakland (Nash County)	27882
Oakland (Rutherford County)	28160
Oakley (Part of Asheville)	28803
Oak Park (Buncombe County)	28704
Oak Park (Cherokee County)	28906
Oak Ridge	27310
Oak Ridge Park	28379
Oaks	28560
Oaksmith Acres	28557
Oakview (Part of High Point)	27260
Oak Villa	27986
Oakville	27589
Oakwillow	27910
Oakwood (Part of Greensboro)	27407
Oakwood Acres	27292
Occoneechee	27278
Ocean	28570
Ocean Isle Beach	28459
Ocracoke	27960
Odom Correctional Institution	27845
Ogburn (Part of Winston-Salem)	27105
Ogden	28405
Ogreeta	28906
Oine	27563
Okeewemee	27371
Okisko	27909
Old Bethlehem	27589
Old Dock	28472
Olde Farm	28390
Old Farm	28025
Old Ford	27889
Old Fort	28762
Old Fort Shores	27817
Old Hundred	28351
Old Providence (Part of Charlotte)	28226
Old Sparta	27852
Old Spring Hope	27882
Oldtown (Part of Winston-Salem)	27106
Old Trap	27974
Olin	28660
Olive Branch	28103
Olive Crossroads	28573
Olivehill	27573
Olivers Crossroads	28658
Olivia	28368
Olympia	28560
Olyphic	28463
Onvil	27306
Ophir	27371
Ora Mill	28150
Orange Correctional Center	27278
Orange Grove	27278
Oregon Hill	27326
Oriental	28571
Ormondsville	28513
Orrum	28369
Osborne	28345
Osceola	27214
Osgood	27330
Osmond	27291
Ossipee	27244
Oswalt	28166
Oteen	28805
Othello	28694
Otto	28763
Otway	28516
Outlaws Bridge	28508
Overhills Park	28390
Oxford	27565
Oxford Park	28610

Place	ZIP
Pacolet Valley	28782
Pactolus	27834
Padgett	28454
Paint Fork	28754
Paint Rock	28743
Pala Alto	28555
Palestine	28001
Palmerville	28127
Palmyra	27859
Pamlico	28571
Pamlico Beach	27810
Pantego	27860
Panther Creek	28721
Paradise Point	28012
Parkersburg	28441
Parkers Fork	27926
Park Road (Part of Charlotte)	28209
Parks Crossroads	27316
Park Spring	27315
Parkstone (Part of Charlotte)	28210
Parkstown	28551
Parkton	28371
Parktown	27589
Park View (Part of Kinston)	28501
Parkville	27944
Parkway Forest (Part of Asheville)	28805
Parkwood (Cabarrus County)	28025
Parkwood (Durham County)	27713
Parkwood (Moore County)	28327
Parkwood (Wilson County)	27893
Parmele	27861
Parrott Fork	28501
Parsonville	28665
Paschall	27589
Pates	28372
Patetown	27534
Patterson	28661
Patterson Grove	28086
Patterson Springs	28150
Pauls Crossing	28137
Paw Creek (Part of Charlotte)	28130
Paynes Tavern	27573
Peace Haven Estates	27104
Peachland	28133
Peachtree	28906
Peacock Crossing	28431
Pearce Crossroads	27597
Pea Ridge (Polk County)	28756
Pea Ridge (Yadkin County)	27020
Pecan Grove	28774
Peden	28672
Pee Dee	27306
Pekin	27306
Peletier	28584
Pelham	27311
Pembroke	28372
Pender Correctional Center	28425
Pender Crossroad	27822
Penderlea	28478
Pendleton	27862
Penelope	28655
Penland	28765
Penrose	28766
Pensacola	28714
Perch	27043
Perfection	28523
Perkinsville (Part of Boone)	28607
Perry's Beach	27924
Perrytown	27924
Peru	28460
Petersburg (Madison County)	28753
Petersburg (Onslow County)	28574
Petersville	27292
Pettys Shore	27922
Pfafftown	27040
Philadelphia	27974
Philadelphus	28377
Phillips Cross Roads	28585
Phillipsville	28716
Phoenix	28451
Piedmont Crescent Country Club	27253
Piedmont Heights (Part of Greensboro)	27403
Pierceville	27976
Pigeon Roost	28740
Pike Crossroads	27863
Pike Road	27860
Pikeville	27863
Pilands Crossroads	27922
Pilot (Davidson County)	27306
Pilot (Franklin County)	27597
Pilot Mountain	27041
Pinebluff	28373
Pine Crest	27808
Pinecrest Acres	28301

Place	ZIP
Pinecroft (Part of Greensboro)	27407
Pine Hall	27042
Pine Haven	27239
Pine Hill (Hoke County)	28315
Pine Hill (Surry County)	27011
Pinehurst	28374
Pinehurst Park	27529
Pine Knoll (Part of Hope Mills)	28348
Pine Knoll Shores	28557
Pine Lakes	27030
Pine Level	27568
Pinelog	28472
Pineola	28662
Pine Ridge (Cabarrus County)	28201
Pine Ridge (Franklin County)	27597
Pine Ridge (Surry County)	27030
Pine Ridge (Washington County)	27970
Pinetops	27864
Pinetown	27865
Pine Valley	28403
Pine View	27330
Pineville	28134
Piney Creek	28663
Piney Green (Onslow County)	28544
Piney Green (Sampson County)	28328
Piney Green-White Oak	28540
Piney Grove (Brunswick County)	28422
Piney Grove (Craven County)	28532
Piney Grove (Orange County)	27278
Piney Ridge	28328
Pin Hook	28466
Pink Hill	28572
Pinkney	27830
Pinnacle	27043
Pireway	28463
Pisgah Forest	28768
Pisgah View (Part of Asheville)	28806
Pittmans Store	27891
Pittsboro	27312
Plainview	28383
Plateau	28658
Plaza (Guilford County)	27408
Plaza (Mecklenburg County)	28299
Plaza, The (Part of Greenville)	27834
Pleasant Acres	28301
Pleasant Garden	27313
Pleasant Gardens	28752
Pleasant Grove (Alamance County)	27217
Pleasant Grove (Buncombe County)	28787
Pleasant Grove (Caswell County)	27379
Pleasant Grove (Duplin County)	28365
Pleasant Grove (Northampton County)	27831
Pleasant Grove (Washington County)	27970
Pleasant Hill (Jones County)	28572
Pleasant Hill (Northampton County)	27866
Pleasant Hill (Wilkes County)	28621
Pleasant Plains	27910
Pleasant View	27925
Pleasantville	27025
Plott Farm Addition	28716
Plumtree	28664
Plyler	28001
Plymouth	27962
Pocomoke	27525
Point Caswell	28421
Point Harbor	27964
Pole Creek	28715
Polks Landing	27514
Polkton	28135
Polkville	28136
Pollocksville	28573
Pomona (Part of Greensboro)	27407
Ponderosa (Cumberland County)	28303
Ponderosa (Harnett County)	28334
Ponzer	27810
Pooletown	28137
Poor Town	27910
Pope Air Force Base	28308
Poplar	28740

Poplar Branch-Samarcand **NORTH CAROLINA 399**

	ZIP		ZIP		ZIP
Poplar Branch	27965	Red Cross (Randolph		Rock Hill	28025
Poplar Grove	28341	County)	27233	Rockingham	28379
Poplar Springs	27021	Red Cross (Stanly County)	28129	Rockingham Correctional	
Poplar Tent	28025	Reddies River	28696	Center	27320
Porter	28128	Red Hill (Bladen County)	28433	Rockingham Lake	27320
Portsmouth	27960	Red Hill (Edgecombe		Rock Ridge	27893
Postell	28906	County)	27891	Rockwell	28138
Potecasi	27867	Red Hill (Mitchell County)	28705	Rockwell Park (Part of	
Pot Neck	28551	Redland	27006	Charlotte)	28213
Potters Curve	28431	Red Oak (Nash County)	27868	Rocky Cross	27557
Potters Hill	28572	Red Oak (Pitt County)	27834	Rocky Ford	27544
Pottertown	28684	Red Springs	28377	Rockyhock	27932
Powell Crossroads	27946	Reeds Cross Roads	27292	Rocky Mount	27801-04
Powells Point	27966	Reedy Creek	27292	For specific Rocky Mount Zip	
Powells Store	27326	Reelsboro	28560	Codes call (919) 977-3123	
Powellsville	27967	Reepsville	28168	Rocky Pass	28761
Powhatan	27520	Reese	28692	Rocky Point	28457
Prentiss	28734	Reeves Ferry	28455	Rocky River	28025
Prestonville	27025	Regal	28906	Rocky Springs	28636
Price	27048	Regan	28420	Rodanthe	27968
Price Creek	28714	Register	28458	Roduco	27969
Princeton	27569	Rehoboth	27845	Roiesville	27571
Princeville	27886	Reidsville	27320-23	Rollingwood	28301
Proctors Corner	27910	For specific Reidsville Zip Codes		Rominger	28604
Proctorville	28375	call (919) 342-0391		Ronda	28670
Propst Crossroads	28601	Relief	28740	Rooks	28421
Prospect	28462	Rena	27020	Roper	27970
Prospect Hill	27314	Rennert	28386	Rose Bay	27885
Prosper	28436	Renston	28513	Roseboro	28382
Providence (Caswell		Republican	27983	Roseborough	28646
County)	27315	Rest Haven	27808	Rosebud (Stokes County)	27052
Providence (Granville		Revolution (Part of		Rosebud (Wilson County)	27822
County)	27565	Greensboro)	27405	Rose Hill (Duplin County)	28458
Providence (McDowell		Rex (Gaston County)	28054	Rose Hill (Warren County)	27553
County)	28752	Rex (Robeson County)	28378	Roseland (Columbus	
Providence (Mecklenburg		Reynolda (Part of Winston-		County)	28432
County)	28105	Salem)	27109	Roseland (Lincoln County)	28092
Providence Square (Part of		Reynolda Park (Part of		Roseland (Moore County)	28315
Charlotte)	28211	Winston-Salem)	27107	Rosemary	27870
Proximity (Part of		Rheasville	27870	Rosemary Park	28079
Greensboro)	27405	Rhems	28562	Rosemead	27924
Pumpkin Center (Lincoln		Rhems Landing	28562	Rosemont (Part of Winston-	
County)	28092	Rhodes	27805	Salem)	27107
Pumpkin Center (Onslow		Rhodes-Rhyne	28092	Roseneath	27874
County)	28540	Rhodhiss	28667	Roseville	27573
Pumpkintown	28779	Rhodo	28901	Rosewood	27530
Pungo	27860	Rhyne Crossroads	28425	Rosindale	28434
Pungo Stores	27810	Riceville	28805	Rosman	28772
Purlear	28665	Richardson	28320	Ross Store	27052
Purley	27379	Richfield	28137	Rougemont	27572
Purnell	27587	Richlands	28574	Roughedge	28110
Purvis	28383	Richmond Hill (Alamance		Round Peak	27030
Putnam	28327	County)	27215	Roundtree	28513
Pyatte	28657	Richmond Hill (Yadkin		Rowan Correctional Center	28144
Quail Corners (Part of		County)	27011	Rowan Mill	28144
Charlotte)	28210	Richmond Mills	28351	Rowes Corner	28560
Quail Ridge (Craven		Rich Square	27869	Rowland	28383
County)	28532	Rico	28472	Roxboro	27573
Quail Ridge (Cumberland		Riddle	27973	Roxobel	27872
County)	28306	Ridgecrest	28770	Royal	27806
Quail Ridge (Lee County)	27330	Ridge Haven	27591	Royal Oaks (Part of	
Quaker Gap	27019	Ridge Run	28025	Kannapolis)	28081
Qualla	28789	Ridgeville	27314	Royal Pines	28704
Quebec	28747	Ridgeway	27570	Royster	28451
Queen	27371	Ridgewood	28379	Rudd	27214
Quick	27326	Riegelwood	28456	Ruffin	27326
Quinerly	28530	Riley	27596	Rural Hall	27045
Quinns Store	28518	Rimer	28025	Ruskin	28399
Quitsna	27983	Ringwood	27823	Russtown	28420
Rabbit Corner	27909	River Acres	27889	Ruth	28139
Radical	28649	River Bend	28562	Rutherford College	28671
Radio Island	28516	Riverdale	28560	Rutherford Correctional	
Raeford	28376	River Hills	27758	Center	28043
Raemon	28364	Rivermont	28501	Rutherfordton	28139
Rainbow Springs	28734	River Neck	27925	Rutherwood	28607
Raleigh	27601-61	Riverside (Craven County)	28530	Ryland	27980
For specific Raleigh Zip Codes			28560	Saddle Mountain	28623
call (919) 831-3661		For specific Riverside Zip Codes		Saddletree	28358
Rama Woods	28025	call (919) 638-6111		Sadler	27320
Ramseur	27316	Riverside (Yancey County)	28714	St. Helena	28425
Ramseytown	28714	Riverton	27932	St. John	27910
Randleman	27317	Roanoke Rapids	27870	St. Johns	27932
Randolph (Mecklenburg		Roaring Creek	28657	St. Lewis	27852
County)	28211	Roaring Gap	28668	St. Martin	28001
Randolph (Pitt County)	27834	Roaring River	28669	St. Pauls	28384
Randolph Correctional		Robbins	27325	St. Stephens	28601
Center	27203	Robbinsville	28771	Salem (Burke County)	28655
Randolph Mall (Part of		Roberdel	28379	Salem (Forsyth County)	27108
Asheboro)	27203	Roberdo	27306	Salem (Lincoln County)	28092
Ranger	28906	Roberson Store	27892	Salem (Nash County)	27891
Rangewood	27603	Robersonville	27871	Salem (Randolph County)	27317
Rankin (Guilford County)	27405	Roberta Mill	28025	Salem (Surry County)	27030
Rankin (Pender County)	28421	Robeson Correctional		Salemburg	28385
Ranlo	28054	Center	28358	Salisbury	28144-45
Ransomville	27810	Robin Hood Forest	27545	For specific Salisbury Zip Codes	
Rawls	27526	Robinson's	28570	call (704) 636-0231	
Rayconda	28304	Rock Creek	27349	Salter Path	28575
Raynham	28383	Rockdale (Part of Belwood)	28090	Salty Shores	28570
Rebel Acres	27604	Rockefeller Estates	28326	Saluda	28773
Red Banks	28364	Rockfish	28376	Salvo	27972
Redbug	28442	Rockford	27011	Samarcand	27242

NORTH CAROLINA Samaria-Southwood

Place	ZIP
Samaria	27557
Sampson Correctional Center	28328
Sand Hill (Buncombe County)	28806
Sandhill (Pamlico County)	28560
Sandhill Acres	27229
Sands	28607
Sandy Bottom	28501
Sandy Bottoms	28352
Sandy Cross (Gates County)	27946
Sandy Cross (Nash County)	27856
Sandy Cross (Rockingham County)	27320
Sandy Grove (Davidson County)	27292
Sandy Grove (Hoke County)	28376
Sandymush (Buncombe County)	28753
Sandy Mush (Rutherford County)	28043
Sandy Plain (Columbus County)	28463
Sandy Plain (Duplin County)	28572
Sandy Plains	28782
Sandy Ridge (Guilford County)	27235
Sandy Ridge (Stokes County)	27046
Sandy Ridge Correctional Center	27260
Sanford	27330-31
For specific Sanford Zip Codes call (919) 774-7044	
Santeetlah	28771
Sapona	28301
Sapphire	28774
Saratoga	27873
Sarecta	28349
Sarecta Junction	28349
Sarvis Heights	28052
Sassers Mill	28526
Satterwhite	27565
Saulston	27534
Saunook	28786
Savannah	28779
Saw	28023
Sawmills	28630
Saxapahaw	27340
Sayles Village (Part of Asheville)	28803
Scalesville	27358
Scaly Mountain	28775
Schley	27278
Scholl	28345
Schrams Beach	27810
Scotch Grove	28352
Scotland Correctional Center	28396
Scotland Neck	27874
Scotsdale (Cumberland County)	28304
Scotsdale (Scotland County)	28352
Scott Acres	27302
Scott Park (Part of Greensboro)	27401
Scotts (Iredell County)	28699
Scotts (Wilson County)	27851
Scotts Hill	28405
Scotts Store (Duplin County)	28365
Scotts Store (Pamlico County)	28560
Scottville	28672
Scranton	27875
Scuffleton	28513
Scuppernong	27928
Seaboard	27876
Seabreeze	28403
Seagate	28403
Seagate IV	28516
Seagrove	27341
Sealevel	28577
Seaside	28459
Sedalia	27342
Sedgefield (Guilford County)	27407
Sedgefield (Mecklenburg County)	28203
Sedgefield Lakes	27407
Sedgefield Park	27407
Sedges Garden	27105
Selica	28712
Selma	27576
Selwin	27946
Selwyn Park (Part of Charlotte)	28209
Seminole	27505
Semora	27343
Senia	28657
Seven Devils	28604
Seven Lakes	27376
Seven Paths	27549
Seven Springs	28578
Severn	27977
Seversville (Part of Charlotte)	28208
Sevier	28752
Seward	27040
Seymour Johnson Air Force Base	27531
Shacktown	27055
Shadey Oaks Acres	28150
Shady Banks	27889
Shady Brook (Part of Kannapolis)	28081
Shady Forest	28459
Shady Grove	28501
Shale Brick	27360
Shallotte	28459
Shallotte Point	28459
Shallowell	27330
Shanghai (Cleveland County)	28150
Shanghai (Sampson County)	28458
Shankletown	28025
Shannon	28386
Shannon Plaza (Part of Durham)	27717
Sharon (Camden County)	27976
Sharon (Iredell County)	28677
Sharonbrook (Part of Charlotte)	28210
Sharp Point	27829
Sharpsburg	27878
Shatley Springs	28617
Shawboro	27973
Shaw Heights	28303
Sheffield	27028
Shelby	28150-51
For specific Shelby Zip Codes call (704) 487-4324	
Shell Rock Landing	28539
Shelmerdine	28513
Shelter Neck	28425
Shelton	27311
Shelton Town	27030
Shepard (Part of Durham)	27707
Shepherds	28115
Sherrills Ford	28673
Sherron Acres (Part of Durham)	27703
Sherwood	28692
Sherwood Forest (Buncombe County)	28805
Sherwood Forest (Buncombe County)	28778
Sherwood Forest (Forsyth County)	27104
Sherwood Forest (Transylvania County)	28712
Sherwood Forrest	27893
Sherwood Park	28306
Sherwood Terrace	28712
Sherwood Village (Part of High Point)	27260
Shields Commissary	27874
Shiloh (Buncombe County)	28803
Shiloh (Camden County)	27974
Shiloh (Rutherford County)	28043
Shines Crossroads	28580
Shingle Hollow	28139
Shinnville	28115
Shoal	27043
Shoofly	27581
Shooting Creek	28904
Shopton	28210
Short Off	28741
Shotwell	27545
Shuffletown	28214
Shulls Mills	28607
Shupings Mill	28138
Sidestown	28025
Sidney (Beaufort County)	27810
Sidney (Columbus County)	28472
Signal Hill Mall (Part of Statesville)	28677
Sign Pine	27980
Siler City	27344
Silk Hope	27344
Siloam	27047
Silver City	28376
Silverdale	28539
Silver Hill (Davidson County)	27292
Silver Hill (Pamlico County)	28560
Silver Lake	28403
Silverstone	28698
Silver Valley	27292
Simpson	27879
Sims	27880
Sioux	28740
Sivey Town	28462
Six Forks (Part of Raleigh)	27615
Six Forks (rural)	27609
Skibo	28304
Skinnersville	27970
Skyco	27954
Skycrest Village	27604
Skyland	28776
Skyline	28394
Skyway Terrace	28364
Sladesville	27875
Slatestone Hills	27889
Sligo	27958
Sloan	28466
Slocomb	28356
Slocum	27824
Small	27806
Small Cross Roads	27932
Smallwood (Part of Washington)	27889
Smethport	28694
Smith Crossing	28442
Smithfield	27577
Smith Grove	27028
Smithtown (Beaufort County)	27810
Smithtown (Perquimans County)	27944
Smithtown (Yadkin County)	27018
Smyre	28054
Smyrna	28579
Sneads Ferry	28460
Sneads Grove	28352
Snow Camp	27349
Snowden	27958
Snow Hill (Chowan County)	27980
Snow Hill (Greene County)	28580
Snow Hill (Sampson County)	28382
Snug Harbor	27944
Soapstone Mountain	27355
Sodom	28753
Somerset (Chowan County)	27932
Somerset (Person County)	27573
Somerset Hills	27604
Sophia	27350
Soul City	27553
Sound Side (Dare County)	27959
Sound Side (Tyrrell County)	27925
South Albemarle (Part of Albemarle)	28001
South Aulander	27805
South Belmont	28012
South Creek	27806
Southern Correctional Center	27371
Southern Hills	28025
Southern Pines	28387-88
For specific Southern Pines Zip Codes call (704) 692-2431	
Southern Shores (Dare County)	27949
Southern Shores (Perquimans County)	27944
South Fork (Part of Winston-Salem)	27104
South Gastonia (Gaston County)	28052
Southgate	28304
South Goldsboro	27530
South Henderson	27536
South Hills Elizabethtown	28337
South Hills Outlet Mall (Part of Cary)	27511
South Hominy	28715
South Lexington (Part of Lexington)	27292
South Lumberton (Part of Lumberton)	28358
South Mills	27976
Southmont	27351
Southpark Shopping Center (Part of Charlotte)	28211
Southport	28461
South River	28516
South Rocky Mount (Part of Rocky Mount)	27801
South Salisbury	28144
Southside (Henderson County)	28739
Southside (Lincoln County)	28092
South Square (Part of Durham)	27707
South Tunis	27986
South Wadesboro	28170
South Weldon	27890
Southwest	28540
South Whiteville (Part of Whiteville)	28472
Southwood	28501

Southwood Apartments-Upton NORTH CAROLINA 401

	ZIP		ZIP		ZIP
Southwood Apartments	28304	Summerlins Crossroads	28365	Tin City	28466
Sparta	28675	Summit (Guilford County)	27405	Tiny Oak Fork	27885
Spear	28657	Summit (Halifax County)	27850	Tipton Hill	28740
Speed	27881	Summit (Wilkes County)	28665	Toast	27049
Speedwell	28723	Sunbury	27979	Tobaccoville	27050
Speights Bridge	27888	Sunny Point Military Ocean		Tobemory	28384
Spencer	28159	Terminal (U.S. Army)	28471	Todd	28684
Spencer Mountain	28054	Sunnyside (Burke County)	28655	Todds Crossroads	27983
Spences Corner	27921	Sunny Side (Dare County)	27954	Toddy	27828
Spies	27325	Sunnyside (Forsyth County)	27107	Toecane	28705
Spindale	28160	Sunnyside (Gaston County)	28016	Tolarsville	28384
Spivey's Corner	28334	Sunny Side (Halifax County)	27850	Toledo	28740
Spokane	27341	Sunny View	28756	Toluca	28090
Spot	27966	Sunset Beach	28459	Tomahawk	28444
Spout Springs	28326	Sunset Harbor	28422	Tomotla	28905
Spray (Part of Eden)	27288	Sunset Hills (Catawba		Toms Creek	28752
Spring Creek	28743	County)	28601	Topia	28672
Springdale	28054	Sunset Hills (Guilford		Topnot	27379
Springfield	28635	County)	27403	Topsail Beach	28445
Springfield Mills	28351	Sunset Hills (Rockingham		Topton	28781
Spring Garden	28562	County)	27288	Town and Country Woods	27030
Spring Hill	27874	Sunshine	28018	Town Creek (Brunswick	
Spring Hope	27882	Supply	28462	County)	28451
Spring Lake	28390	Surf City	28445	Town Creek (Wilson	
Spring Valley (Guilford		Surl	27583	County)	27322
County)	27416	Sutherlands	28615	Town Forest	28739
Spring Valley (Mecklenburg		Sutton Park (Part of		Town Mountain Estates	28804
County)	28210	Monroe)	28110	Townsville	27584
Springwood	28052	Suttons Corner	28337	Tradingford	28144
Spruce Pine	28777	Suttontown	28341	Tramway	27330
Stackhouse	28753	Swain	27970	Tranquility	28081
Stacy	28581	Swainsville	28150	Trap	27924
Stag Park	28425	Swancreek	28642	Traphill	28685
Staley	27355	Swann	27330	Travis	27925
Stallings	28105	Swannanoa (Buncombe		Trayton Woods	28025
Stamey Branch	28657	County)	28778	Tree Haven	28739
Stanfield	28163	Swanns	27330	Trenholm Woods	28739
Stanhope	27882	Swanquarter	27885	Trenton	28585
Stanley	28164	Swansboro	28584	Trent Woods	28562
Stanleyville	27045	Sweet Gum	28771	Triangle (Lincoln County)	28164
Stantonsburg	27883	Swepsonville	27359	Triangle (Wake County)	27709
Star	27356	Swindell's Fork	27885	Trinity (Randolph County)	27370
Starmount (Part of		Swiss	28714	Trinity (Union County)	28110
Charlotte)	28210	Sylva	28779	Triple Springs	27573
Starmount Forest (Part of		Tabor City	28463	Triplett	28618
Greensboro)	27403	Talleys Crossing	27284	Trotville	27946
Startown	28658	Tanglewood	28306	Troutman	28166
State Road	28676	Tapoco	28780	Troy	27371
Statesville	28677	Tarawa Terrace	28543	Trust	28743
Statesville West	28677	Tarboro	27886	Tryon (Gaston County)	28016
State University (Part of		Tar Corner	27976	Tryon (Polk County)	28782
Raleigh)	27607	Tar Heel (Bladen County)	28392	Tryon Mall (Part of	
Stecoah	28771	Tarheel (Gates County)	27935	Charlotte)	28213
Stedman	28391	Tar Landing	28540	Tuckasegee	28783
Steeds	27341	Tar River	27565	Tuckerdale	28643
Steen Town	28345	Tarrytown Mall (Part of		Tungsten	27536
Stella	28582	Rocky Mount)	27804	Tunis	27986
Stem	27581	Tate Street (Part of		Turkey	28393
Sterling (Part of Charlotte)	28134	Greensboro)	27435	Turkey Knob	28675
Stevens Mill	27530	Taylor Cross Roads	27856	Turlington	28334
Stocksville	28787	Taylors Bridge	28328	Turnersburg	28688
Stokes	27884	Taylors Corners	28585	Turners Crossroads	27853
Stokes Correctional Center	27052	Taylors Store (Bertie		Turnpike	28715
Stokesdale	27357	County)	27957	Tuscarora	28562
Stokestown	26513	Taylors Store (Nash County)	27856	Tuscarora Beach	27986
Stonebridge	27609	Taylorsville	28681	Tusk	28579
Stonehaven (Part of		Taylorsville Beach	28681	Tuskeegee	28771
Charlotte)	28211	Taylortown	28374	Tusquitee	28904
Stoneville	27048	Teachey	28464	Tuxedo	28784
Stonewall	28583	Teer	27516	Twin Lake (Part of Sunset	
Stoneybrook	28144	Temple Point	28532	Beach)	28459
Stoneycrest	28739	Temple's	28570	Twin Oaks	28675
Stoney Knob	28787	Terrace Gardens (Part of		Tyner	27980
Stonycreek	27244	Hendersonville)	28739	Tyro	27292
Stony Fork (Buncombe		Terra Ceia	27860	Ulah	27203
County)	28715	Terra Cotta (Part of		Unaka	28906
Stony Fork (Watauga		Greensboro)	27407	U N C C (University of	
County)	28618	Terrell	28682	North Carolina-Charlotte)	28223
Stony Hill	27587	Texaco Beach	27974	Union (Hertford County)	27910
Stony Knoll	27017	Texana	28906	Union (Macon County)	28734
Stony Point	28678	Texas	27974	Union (Rutherford County)	28139
Storys	27935	Thankful	28606	Union Cross	27284
Stotts Cross Roads	27880	The Black Cat	28516	Union Grove (Davidson	
Stouts	28110	The Borough	28435	County)	27292
Stovall	27582	The Bottom	27924	Union Grove (Iredell County)	28689
Stowe Park	28034	Thelma	27850	Union Hill	27018
Straits	28516	Thomasboro	28459	Union Mills	28167
Stratford	28675	Thomas Landing	28445	Union Ridge	27215
Strickland Cross Roads	27882	Thomas Valley	28904	Unionville	28110
Stubbs	28150	Thomasville	27360-61	University Estates	
Stumpy Point	27978	For specific Thomasville Zip		(Cumberland County)	28301
Sturgills	28643	Codes call (919) 472-7344		University Estates	
Sugar Grove	28679	Three Mile	28657	(Rockingham County)	27320
Sugar Hill	28752	Thruway Shopping Center		University Mall and Plaza	
Sugarloaf Shores	27371	(Part of Winston-Salem)	27103	(Part of Chapel Hill)	27514
Sugar Mountain	28604	Thurman	28560	University of North Carolina	
Sugar Town	28135	Thurmond	28683	(Part of Wilmington)	28403
Sulphur Springs	27030	Tillery	27887	University Park (Part of	
Summerfield	27358	Timberlake	27583	Charlotte)	28297
Summerhaven	28778	Timber Ridge	28081	Upchurch	27502
Summer Hill	28303	Timothy	28334	Upton	28645

402 NORTH CAROLINA Upward-Winston-Salem

Name	ZIP
Upward	28731
Uwharie	27371
Valdese	28690
Vale	28168
Valhalla (Chowan County)	27932
Valhalla (Polk County)	28782
Valle Crucis	28691
Valley	28657
Valley Hill	28739
Valley Hills Mall (Part of Hickory)	28601
Vanceboro	28586
Vance Correctional Center	27536
Vandemere	28587
Vander	28301
Vannoy	28696
Varnamtown	28462
Vashti	28636
Vass	28394
Vaughan	27586
Vein Mountain	28752
Venable	28803
Venters	28513
Vernon Park Mall (Part of Kinston)	28501
Verona	28540
Vests	28906
Vicksboro	27536
Vienna	27040
Viewmont (Part of Hickory)	28601
Vilas	28692
Villa Heights (Part of Charlotte)	28205
Vinegar Hill	28463
Vineland Park	28306
Vinton Woods	28034
Violet	28906
Virgilina	24598
Vista	28443
Vixen	28714
Volunteer	27043
Waccamaw	28420
Waco	28169
Wade	28395
Wade Mills (Part of Wadesboro)	28170
Wadesboro	28170
Wades Point	27810
Wadeville	27306
Wagoner	28640
Wagram	28396
Wake Crossroads	27604
Wakefield	27597
Wake Forest	27587-88
For specific Wake Forest Zip Codes call (919) 556-3575	
Wakelon	27924
Wakulla	28397
Walkers Crossroads	27587
Walkertown (Forsyth County)	27051
Walkertown (Harnett County)	28356
Wallace	28466
Walla Watta	27865
Wallburg	27373
Walnut	28753
Walnut Cove	27052
Walnut Creek (Madison County)	28753
Walnut Creek (Wayne County)	27534
Walstonburg	27888
Wananish (Part of Lake Waccamaw)	28450
Wanchese	27981
Warbler	27826
Wards	28431
Wards Corner	28425
Wards Store	27891
Wardville	27979
Warne	28909
Warren Plains	27589
Warrensville	28693
Warrenton	27589
Warren Wilson College	28778
Warrior	28645
Warsaw	28398
Washburn	28150
Washburn Store	28018
Washington	27889
Washington Correctional Center	27928
Washington Forks	28560
Washington Park	27889
Watauga	28734
Watauga Correctional Center	28607
Waterlily	27923
Waterville	37821
Watha	28471

Name	ZIP
Watson Crossroads	27542
Watts Crossroads	28025
Waughtown (Part of Winston-Salem)	27117
Waverly	28754
Waves	27982
Waxhaw	28173
Waycross	28453
Wayne Correctional Center	27533
Waynesville	28786
Wayside	28376
Weaversford	28617
Weaverville	28787
Webster	28788
Weddington	28173
Wedgewood Lakes	27958
Weeksville	27909
Wehutty	37391
Welcome	27374
Weldon	27890
Wellons Village (Part of Durham)	27703
Wells	28304
Welmar Heights	28304
Wendell	27591
Wenona	27860
Wentworth	27375
Wesleyan College	27804
Wesley Chapel	28110
Wesley Heights (Part of Charlotte)	28208
Wesser	28713
West	28398
West Asheville (Part of Asheville)	28806
West Brook (Part of Kannapolis)	28081
Westchester Mall (Part of High Point)	27260
Westcliff	28144
West Concord (Cabarrus County)	28025
West Cramerton (Part of Cramerton)	28032
West Durham (Part of Durham)	27705
West Edgecombe	27801
Westend (Guilford County)	27260
West End (Moore County)	27376
Western Prong	28472
Westerwood (Part of Greensboro)	27403
Westfield	27053
West Gastonia (Part of Gastonia)	28052
Westhaven	27834
West Highlands (Part of Winston-Salem)	27104
West Jefferson	28694
West Lumberton (Part of Lumberton)	28358
West Marion	28752
West Market Street (Part of Greensboro)	27402
Westminster	28139
Westmont (Part of Asheboro)	27203
Westmore	27341
West New Bern (Part of New Bern)	28562
Westover (Wake County)	27606
Westover (Washington County)	27962
West Philadelphia	27209
Westridge (Part of Rocky Mount)	27801
West Rockingham	28379
West Rocky Mount (Part of Rocky Mount)	27801
Westry	27801
West Salem (Part of Winston-Salem)	27101
Westside	28023
Wests Mill	28734
West Smithfield	27577
West Statesville (Part of Statesville)	28677
West Trade Street (Part of Charlotte)	28202
Westview (Part of Winston-Salem)	27114
Westwood (Scotland County)	28352
Westwood (Surry County)	27049
West Yanceyville	27379
Wexford	28213
Whalebone (Part of Nags Head)	27959
Whaley	28622
Wharton	27889
Whichard	27884

Name	ZIP
Whichard Beach	27817
Whispering Pines	28327
Whitakers	27891
White Cross	27516
Whitehall Shores	27921
Whitehead	28695
White Hill	27330
Whitehouse	28167
Whitehurst	27871
Whitehurst Park	28025
White Lake	28337
White Oak (Bladen County)	28399
White Oak (Gates County)	27935
White Oak (Guilford County)	27405
White Oak (Halifax County)	27823
White Oak (Nash County)	27856
White Oaks Acres	27893
White Oaks Acres West	27893
White Pines	27049
White Plains (Hyde County)	27824
White Plains (Surry County)	27031
Whitepost	27808
Whiterock	28753
White's Beach	27924
Whites Chapel Church	27292
Whites Crossroads	27924
White Stocking	28425
Whiteston	27919
White Store	28133
Whiteville	28472
Whitfield Crossroads	28578
Whitley Heights	27520
Whitnel (Part of Lenoir)	28645
Whitsett	27377
Whittier	28789
Whitt Town	27573
Whortonville	28556
Whynot	27341
Wilbanks	27822
Wilbar	28696
Wilbon	27526
Wilbourns Store	24598
Wilders Grove	27604
Wildwood (Carteret County)	28557
Wildwood (Henderson County)	28732
Wildwood Estate	28570
Wilgrove (Part of Charlotte)	28212
Wilkerson Cross Roads	27542
Wilkesboro	28697
Wilkes Mall (Part of Wilkesboro)	28697
Wilkinson	27860
Willard	28478
Willeyton	27937
Williams	28472
Williamsboro	27536
Williamsburg (Iredell County)	28634
Williamsburg (Rockingham County)	27320
Williamson Crossroads	28431
Williamston	27892
Willis Landing	28539
Williston	28589
Willits	28779
Wil-Lotta Acres	28025
Willow	27946
Willow Green	28513
Willow Spring	27592
Wilmar	28586
Wil-Mar Park (Part of Concord)	28025
Wilmington	28401-12
For specific Wilmington Zip Codes call (919) 762-3700	
Wilmington Beach	28428
Wilmore (Part of Charlotte)	28203
Wilmot	28789
Wilshire Park (Part of Asheville)	28806
Wilson	27893-95
For specific Wilson Zip Codes call (919) 237-4161	
Wilsons Mills	27593
Wilsonville	27502
Wilton	27525
Wind Blow	27281
Windemere	28405
Winders Cross Roads	27020
Windom	28714
Windsor	27983
Windy Gap	28659
Winfall	27985
Wing	28705
Wingate	28174
Winnabow	28479
Winstead Crossroads	27822
Wnsteadville	27810
Winston-Salem	27101-27
For specific Winston-Salem Zip Codes call (919) 721-6000	

Wintergreen-Zirconia **NORTH CAROLINA** 403

	ZIP		ZIP		ZIP
Wintergreen	28523	Woodlawn (McDowell County)	28752	Worthville	27317
Winter Park	28403	Woodlea	28304	Wrightsboro	28401
Winterville	28590	Woodleaf	27054	Wrightsville	28480
Winton	27986	Woodrow (Craven County)	28560	Wrightsville Beach	28480
Wise	27594	Woodrow (Haywood County)	28716	Yadkin	28144
Wise Forks	28526	Woodrun	27306	Yadkin Correctional Center	27055
Witherspoon Crossroads	28610	Woodsdale	27573	Yadkin Valley	28645
Wittys Crossroads	27320	Woodside	28081	Yadkinville	27055
Wolf Creek	37317	Woodside Hills	28715	Yamacraw	28435
Wolf Laurel	28754	Woodville (Bertie County)	27849	Yanceyville	27379
Wolf Mountain	28783	Woodville (Perquimans County)	27944	Yancy Correctional Center	28714
Wood	27549	Woodville (Surry County)	27030	Yaupon Beach	28461
Woodard (Bertie County)	27983	Woodworth	27536	Yeatsville	27808
Woodard (Wilson County)	27893	Wootens Crossroads (Columbus County)	28433	Yellow Creek	28771
Woodburn	28451	Wootens Crossroads (Greene County)	27888	Yeopim	27932
Wood Crest	28570	Wootens Crossroads (Lenoir County)	28501	Yorick	28399
Wood Dale	28401	Worley	28753	Yorkmont Park (Part of Charlotte)	28217
Woodfin	28804	Worthingtons Crossroads	27858	Yorkwood	28052
Woodford	28684			Youngsville	27596
Woodington	28501			Zebulon	27597
Woodland	27897			Zephyr	28621
Woodland Acres	27892			Zionville	28698
Woodland Hills	28804			Zirconia	28790
Woodlawn (Alamance County)	27302				

404 NORTH DAKOTA

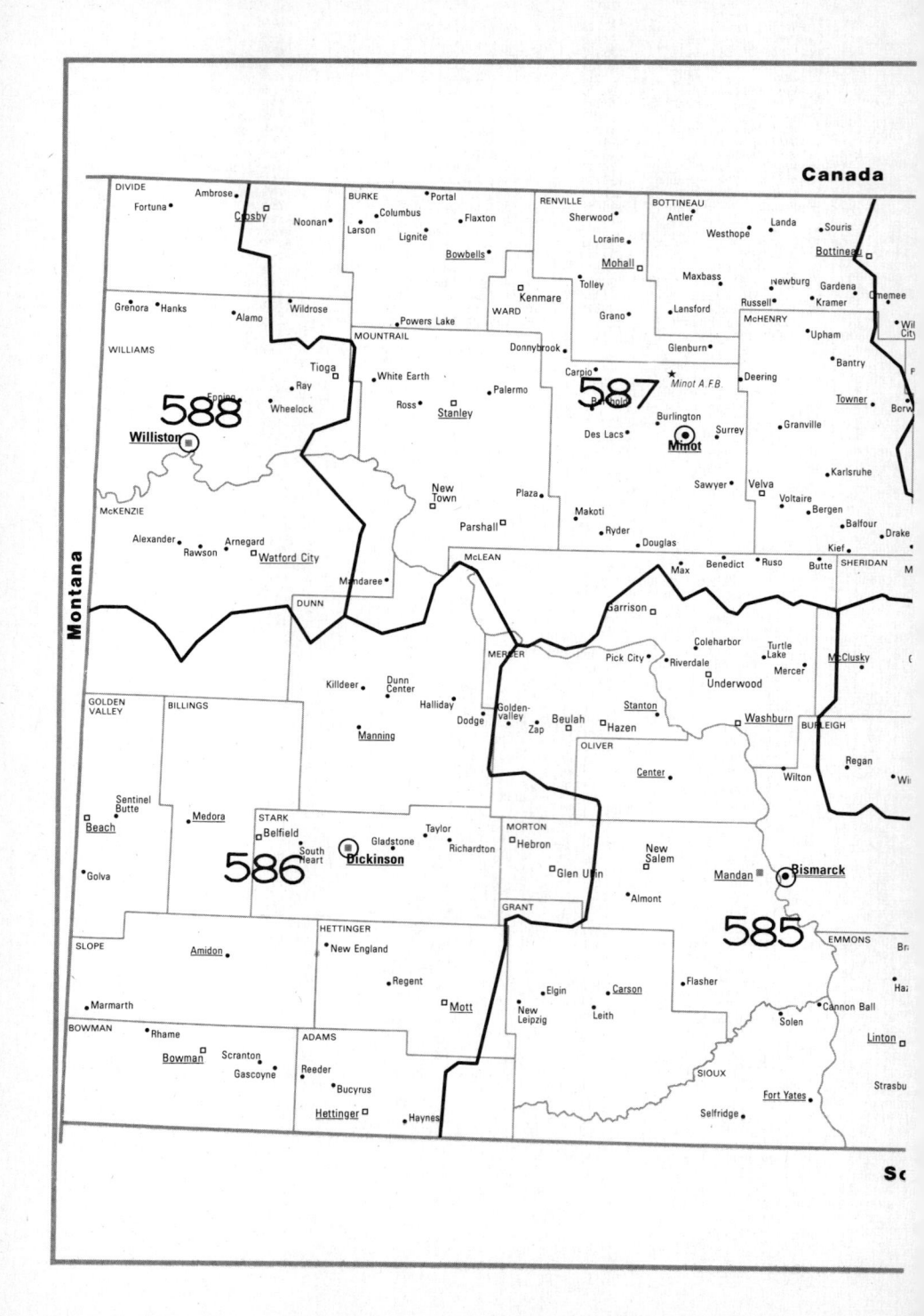

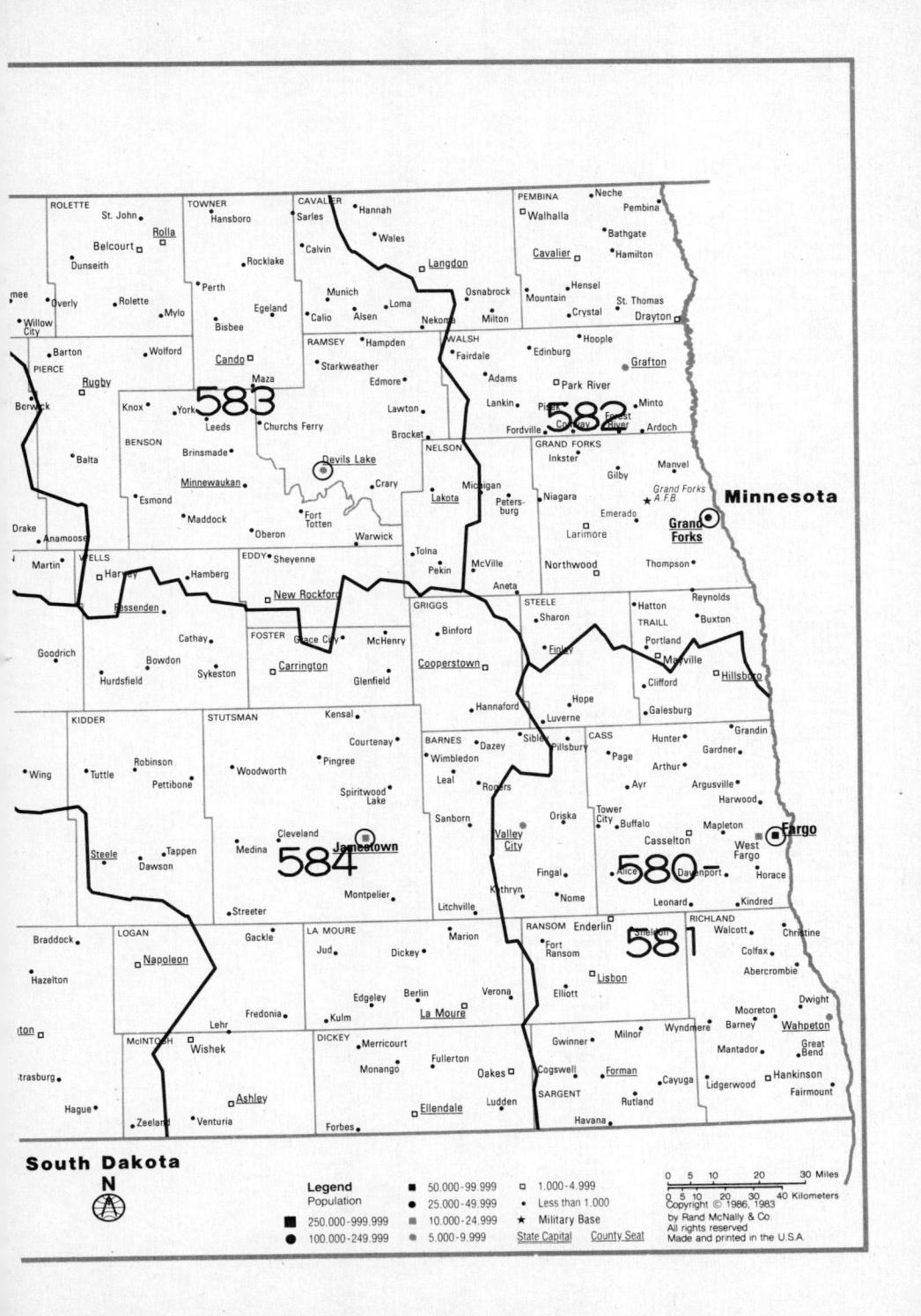

NORTH DAKOTA

NORTH DAKOTA Abercrombie-Golden Valley

	ZIP
Abercrombie	58001
Absaraka	58002
Acres A-Plenty	58504
Adams	58210
Adrian	58472
Agate	58310
Akra	58220
Alamo	58830
Alexander (McKenzie County)	58831
Alfred	58411
Alice	58003
Alkabo	58832
Almont	58520
Alpha	58654
Alsen	58311
Ambrose (Divide County)	58833
Amenia (Cass County)	58004
Amidon	58620
Anamoose (McHenry County)	58710
Anderson Acres	58504
Aneta	58212
Anselm	58068
Antler (Bottineau County)	58711
Appam	58830
Apple Creek Country Club	58501
Apple Creek Estates	58558
Apple Valley	58558
Ardoch	58213
Arena	58412
Argusville	58005
Arnegard	58835
Arthur (Cass County)	58006
Arvilla	58214
Ashley	58413
Ashlund Estates	58504
Auburn	58237
Aurelia	58734
Ayr (Cass County)	58007
Backoo	58282
Baker (Benson County)	58386
Baldwin (Burleigh County)	58521
Balfour (McHenry County)	58712
Balta	58313
Bantry (McHenry County)	58713
Bar-D Estates	58504
Barks Spur	58331
Barlow	58421
Barney	58008
Bartlett	58344
Barton	58315
Bathgate	58216
Battleground Addition	58701
Battleview	58714
Bayshore	58072
Beach (Golden Valley County)	58621
Belcourt	58316
Belden	58784
Belfield	58622
Benedict	58716
Bentley	58562
Berea	58072
Bergen (McHenry County)	58792
Berlin (La Moure County)	58415
Berthold	58718
Berwick (McHenry County)	58788
Beulah	58523
Big Bend (McLean County)	58531
Binford	58416
Bisbee	58317
Bismarck	58501-04
For specific Bismarck Zip Codes call (701) 221-6517	
Blabon	58046
Blacktail Lake	58801
Blaisdell	58720
Blanchard	58009
Bluffview Estates	58504
Bonetraill (Williams County)	58801
Bordulac	58417
Bottineau	58318
Bowbells (Burke County)	58721
Bowdon	58418
Bowesmont	58225
Bowman (Bowman County)	58623
Braddock	58524
Brampton	58017
Brantford	58356
Breen's Addition	58501
Breien	58570
Brekke Addition	58701
Bremen	58319
Brentwood Estates	58501
Briardale	58504
Briarwood	58104
Bridgeview Addition	58701
Brinsmade	58320
Brocket	58321
Brookfield Estates	58501

	ZIP
Brooks Addition	58701
Brooktree Park	58042
Buchanan	58420
Bucyrus (Adams County)	58639
Buffalo (Cass County)	58011
Buffalo Springs	58623
Burke Addition	58201
Burlington	58722
Burnstad	58495
Burt (Hettinger County)	58646
Butte (McLean County)	58723
Buttzville	58054
Buxton	58218
Caledonia	58219
Calio	58322
Calvin	58323
C and L Estates	58504
Cando	58324
Cannon Ball (Sioux County)	58528
Carbury	58783
Carlsbad	58504
Carolville	58801
Carpio	58725
Carrington (Foster County)	58421
Carson	58529
Cartwright	58838
Cashel	58225
Casselton (Cass County)	58012
Cathay	58422
Cavalier	58220
Cayuga	58013
Center (Oliver County)	58530
Chaffee	58014
Charbonneau	58831
Charlson	58763
Chaseley	58423
Chrisan	58102
Christine	58015
Churchs Ferry	58325
Circle K Estates	58501
City View Heights	58504
Cleveland (Stutsman County)	58424
Clifford	58016
Clyde	58352
Cogswell	58017
Coleharbor	58531
Colfax	58018
Colgan	58844
Colgate	58046
Columbia Mall (Part of Grand Forks)	58201
Columbus	58727
Concrete	58220
Conway	58233
Cooperstown (Griggs County)	58425
Corinth	58830
Coteau	58728
Coulee (Mountrail County)	58736
Country Acres	58047
Country-Side Addition	58201
Courtenay	58426
Crary	58327
Crested Butte Addition	58501
Crete	58040
Crosby	58730
Crystal	58222
Crystal Springs	58427
Cuba	58072
Cummings	58223
Dahlen	58224
Dakota Boys Ranch	58701
Dakota Square (Part of Minot)	58701
Davenport (Cass County)	58021
Dawson	58428
Dazey (Barnes County)	58429
Decker	58601
Deering (McHenry County)	58731
De Lamere	58060
Denbigh	58788
Denhoff	58430
Des Lacs	58733
Devils Lake	58301
Dickey	58431
Dickinson	58601-02
For specific Dickinson Zip Codes call (701) 225-6701	
Dodge	58625
Donnybrook	58734
Douglas (Ward County)	58735
Doyon	58328
Drake	58736
Drayton	58225
Dresden (Cavalier County)	58249
Driscoll (Burleigh County)	58532
Dunn Center	58626
Dunning	58760
Dunseith	58329
Durbin	58059

	ZIP
Dwight	58075
Eagle Bend Estates	58301
Eastdale	58601
East Fairview	59221
Eastside Estates	58701
East Valley City	58072
Eckelson	58432
Eckman	58760
Edgeley	58433
Edinburg	58227
Edmore	58330
Edmunds	58476
Egeland	58331
El Dorado Acres	58601
Eldridge	58401
Elgin (Grant County)	58533
Ellendale (Dickey County)	58436
Elliott	58033
Embden	58079
Emerado	58228
Emmet	58540
Emrick	58422
Enderlin	58027
Englevale	58033
Epping	58843
Erie	58029
Esmond (Benson County)	58332
Evergreen (Cass County)	58051
Faiman's Sunrise Addition	58504
Fairdale	58229
Fairfield (Billings County)	58627
Fairmount	58030
Falconer Estates	58504
Falkirk	58577
Fargo	58102-09
For specific Fargo Zip Codes call (701) 241-6100	
Fessenden	58438
Fillmore (Benson County)	58333
Fingal	58031
Finley	58230
Finley Air Force Station, 785th Radar Squadron	58230
Flasher	58535
Flaxton	58737
Flora	58348
Fonda	58366
Forbes	58439
Fordville	58231
Forest River (Cass County)	58102
Forest River (Walsh County)	58233
Forest River Colony	58231
Forman	58032
Fort Berthold Indian Reservation	58763
Fort Buford	58853
Fort Clark	58530
Fort Ransom	58033
Fort Rice	58537
Fort Totten	58335
Fort Totten Indian Reservation	58335
Fortuna	58844
Fortuna Air Force Station, 780th Radar Squadron	59275
Fort Yates	58538
Four Bears Village	58763
Four K's Estates	58501
Foxholm	58738
Fox Island	58504
Fradet	58047
Frazier (Barnes County)	58492
Fredonia	58440
Fried (Stutsman County)	58401
Frison	58301
Frontier	58104
Fryburg	58622
Fullerton	58441
Gackle	58442
Galchutt	58075
Galesburg	58035
Gardar	58227
Gardena	58739
Gardner (Cass County)	58036
Garrison	58540
Garske	58382
Gascoyne (Bowman County)	58653
Geneseo	58053
Gilby (Grand Forks County)	58235
Gladstone (Stark County)	58630
Glasser	58504
Glasston	58236
Glenburn	58740
Glenfield (Foster County)	58443
Glen Ullin	58631
Glenwood Estates	58501
Glover	58474
Golden Valley (Mercer County)	58541

Goldfines Shopping Center-Palm Beach NORTH DAKOTA 407

	ZIP		ZIP		ZIP
Goldfines Shopping Center (Part of Grand Forks)	58201	Joliette	58246	Martin	58758
Golva	58632	Juanita	58443	Mary College	58501
Goodrich	58444	Jud	58454	Max	58759
Gorham	58627	Judson (Morton County)	58563	Maxbass	58760
Grace City	58445	Karlsruhe (McHenry County)	58744	Mayville	58257
Grafton	58237	Kathryn	58049	Maza	58324
Grandberg	58102	Keene	58847	Meadowbrook	58701
Grand Forks	58201-06	Kelso	58045	Meadow View (Part of Bismarck)	58504
For specific Grand Forks Zip Codes call (701) 775-5329		Kelvin	58329	Medina	58467
		Kempton	58267	Medora	58645
Grand Forks AFB	58205	Kenaston	58746	Mee's Country Home Estates	58558
Grand Forks Air Force Base	58201	Kenmare	58746		
Grandin	58038	Kensal	58455	Mekinock (Grand Forks County)	58258
Grand Prairie Estates	58501	Kief	58747		
Grand Rapids (La Moure County)	58458	Killdeer	58640	Melville	58421
		Kindred	58051	Menoken	58558
Grandview (Williams County)	58801	Kings Court	58701	Mercer	58559
		Kintyre	58549	Merricourt	58469
Grano	58750	Kirkwood Plaza (Part of Bismarck)	58501	Michigan (Nelson County)	58259
Granville (McHenry County)	58741			Millarton	58472
Grassy Butte	58634	Kloten	58254	Mills	58504
Great Bend	58039	KMK Estates	58501	Milnor	58060
Green Acres Estates	58501	Knox (Benson County)	58343	Milton	58260
Greene (Renville County)	58787	Kongsberg	58792	Minnewaukan (Benson County)	58351
Greenvale	58601	Kralicek	58601		
Grenora	58845	Kramer	58748	Minot	58701-02
Guelph	58447	Kubishta	58601	For specific Minot Zip Codes call (701) 852-3296	
Guthrie	58736	Kulm	58456		
Gwinner	58040	Lake Jessie	58801	Minot AFB	58701
Hague	58542	Lake Metigoshe	58318	Minot Air Force Base	58704
Halliday	58636	Lake Park	58801	Minot Air Force Station, 786th Radar Squadron	58759
Hallson	58220	Lake Side Estate	58401		
Hamar	58380	Lake Tschida	58533	Minto (Walsh County)	58261
Hamberg	58337	Lake Williams	58478	Mirror Lake	58639
Hamilton	58238	Lakewood Park	58301	Missouri River Estates	58504
Hamlet (Williams County)	58795	Lakota	58344	Moffit	58560
Hampden	58338	Lamoine Addition	58201	Mohall	58761
Hankinson	58041	La Moure (La Moure County)	58458	Monango	58471
Hanks	58856			Montpelier	58472
Hanks Corner	58220	Landa	58749	Mooreton	58061
Hannaford	58448	Langdon (Cavalier County)	58249	Mott (Hettinger County)	58646
Hannah	58239	Lankin	58250	Mountain	58262
Hannover	58563	Lansford (Bottineau County)	58750	Mount Carmel	58249
Hansboro	58339	Larimore (Grand Forks County)	58251	Mouse River Park	58787
Happy Valley	58701			Mr. B's	58501
Harlow	58346	Lark	58535	Munich	58352
Hartland	58725	Larson	58727	Mylo	58353
Harvey (Wells County)	58341	Lawton	58345	Nanson	58366
Harwood	58042	Leal	58479	Napoleon	58561
Hastings (Barnes County)	58049	Leeds (Benson County)	58346	Nash (Walsh County)	58264
Hatton	58240	Lefor	58641	Neche	58265
Havana	53043	Lehigh	58601	Nekoma (Cavalier County)	58355
Havelock	58647	Lehr	58460	Newburg	58762
Hay Creek (Burleigh County)	58501	Leisure World Estates	58504	New England (Hettinger County)	58647
		Leith	58551		
Hay Creek Pines	58501	Leonard (Cass County)	58052	New Hradec	58601
Haynes (Adams County)	58639	Leroy	58282	New Leipzig	58562
Hazelton (Emmons County)	58544	Lewis and Clark Estates	58504	New Rockford (Eddy County)	58356
Hazen	58545	Leyden	58282		
Heaton	58450	Lidgerwood	58053	New Salem	58563
Hebron (Morton County)	58638	Lignite	58752	New Town	58763
Heil	58533	Lincoln (Burleigh County)	58501	Niagara (Grand Forks County)	58266
Heimdal	58342	Lincoln Valley (Sheridan County)	58430		
Hensel	58241			Niobe	58746
Hensler	58547	Linka Addition	58701	Nome	58062
Heritage Hills Estates	58102	Linton (Emmons County)	58552	Noonan (Divide County)	58765
Hesper	58348	Lisbon	58054	Norma (Renville County)	58746
Hettinger (Adams County)	58639	Litchville (Barnes County)	58461	North Dakota Penitentiary	58501
Hickson	58047	Little Ponderosa	58701	North Dakota State University (Part of Fargo)	58105
Hi-Land Heights	58801	Logan (Ward County)	58701		
Hillcrest Acres	58501	Loma	58311	North Forty Estates	58501
Hillsboro	58045	Lone Tree (Ward County)	58718	Northgate	58737
Holiday Colony	58701	Loraine	58761	North Grand Forks	58201
Holmes (Grand Forks County)	58275	Lostwood	58784	North Lemmon	57638
		Lucca	58027	North River	58102
Home on the Range for Boys	58654	Ludden	58447	North Star Acres	58501
		Lunds Valley	58784	North Valley City	58072
Honeyford	58235	Luverne	58056	Northwood (Cass County)	58102
Hoople	58243	Lynchburg	58059	Northwood (Grand Forks County)	58267
Hope (Steele County)	58046	McCanna	58253		
Horace	58047	McClusky	58463	Northwood Estates	58501
Horseshoe Bend	58102	McGregor	58755	Nortonville	58473
Hove Mobile Park	58229	McHenry (Foster County)	58464	Norwich	58768
Huff	58537	McKenzie	58553	Oakes	58474
Hull	58542	McLeod	58057	Oak Ridge	58270
Hunter (Cass County)	58048	McVille	58254	Oakwood	58237
Hurdsfield	58451	Maddock	58348	Oberon (Benson County)	58357
Hutterite Colony	58458	Maida	58255	Olga	58249
Imperial Manor	58701	Makoti	58756	Omemee	58384
Imperial Valley	58504	Mandan (Morton County)	58554	Oriska (Barnes County)	58063
Inkster (Grand Forks County)	58244	Mandaree	58757	Orr	58244
		Manfred	58465	Orrin	58359
Jamestown	58401-02	Manitou	58776	Osnabrock (Cavalier County)	58269
For specific Jamestown Zip Codes call (701) 252-2970		Manning (Dunn County)	58642		
		Mantador	58058	Overly	58360
Jessie	58452	Manvel	58256	Oxbow	58047
Jewett Landing	58072	Mapes	58344	Page (Cass County)	58064
Jiran	58504	Mapleton (Cass County)	58059	Palermo	58769
Johnsons Corner	58847	Marion (La Moure County)	58466	Palm Beach	58601
Johnstown	58245	Marmarth	58643		
		Marshall (Dunn County)	58644		

408 NORTH DAKOTA Park Manor-Zeeland

Name	ZIP
Park Manor (Part of Grand Forks)	58201
Park River	58270
Parshall	58770
Patterson Lake	58601
Pekin	58361
Pembina	58271
Penn	58362
Perth (Towner County)	58363
Petersburg	58272
Pettibone (Kidder County)	58475
Pheasant Lake	58436
Picardville	58463
Pick City	58545
Pillsbury	58065
Pingree	58476
Pisek	58273
Pitcher Park	58301
Plaza	58771
Pleasant Lake	58368
Ponderosa Riverside Village	58501
Porcupine	58568
Portal (Burke County)	58772
Portland	58274
Powell	58201
Powers Lake (Burke County)	58773
Prairie Rose	58104
Prairie View Acres	58501
Price	58547
Prosper	58042
Raleigh	58564
Raub	58779
Raulston	58801
Rawson	58831
Ray (Williams County)	58849
Raymond Lee	58801
Red Willow Lake	58416
Reeder (Adams County)	58649
Regan	58477
Regent	58650
Reile's Acres	58102
Reynolds	58275
Rhame (Bowman County)	58651
Richards West (Part of Grand Forks)	58201
Richardton	58652
Ridgeview Acres	58504
Rio Vista Heights	58801
River Bend	58047
Riverdale (McLean County)	58565
Riverside (Cass County)	58078
River View Acres	58504
Robinson (Kidder County)	58478
Rocklake (Towner County)	58365
Rogers (Barnes County)	58479
Rolette	58366
Rolla	58367
Rolling Meadows	58501
Roseglen	58775
Roshau	58601
Ross	58776
Roth	58783
Round Hill Estates	58102
Rugby	58368
Ruso	58778
Russell (Bottineau County)	58762
Ruthville	58701
Rutland	58067
Ryder	58779
Sabot's First	58501
St. Anthony	58566
St. Benedict	58047
St. Gertrude	58564
St. John	58369
St. Michael	58370
St. Thomas	58276
Sanborn	58480
San Haven	58329
Sanish	58763
Sarles	58372
Sawdust	58270
Sawyer	58781
Scenic East	58801
Schefield	58647
Scranton (Bowman County)	58653
Secluded Acres	58504
Selfridge	58568
Selz	58373
Sentinel Butte	58654
Shamrock Acres	58501
Sharon	58277
Sheldon (Ransom County)	58068
Shepard	58425
Sherwood	58782
Sheyenne (Eddy County)	58374
Sheyenne Valley Addition	58072
Shields	58569
Shryock	58801
Sibley (Barnes County)	58429
Sibley Island Estates	58504
Silva	58368
Simcoe	58741
Sims	58520
Sioux Village	58538
Sisseton Indian Reservation	57262
Skyline Estates	58501
Sleepy Hollow	58047
Solen	58570
Sorenson Addition	58701
Souris	58783
Southam	58327
South Forks Plaza (Part of Grand Forks)	58201
South Heart	58655
Southview	58801
Southview Estates	58601
Spiritwood	58481
Spiritwood Lake	58401
Spring Brook	58843
Standing Rock Indian Reservation (ND part)	58538
Stanley (Mountrail County)	58784
Stanton	58571
Starkweather	58377
State Hospital (Part of Jamestown)	58401
Steele	58482
Sterling	58572
Stirum	58069
Strasburg	58573
Straubville	58017
Streeter	58483
Stromquist (Part of Devils Lake)	58301
Strong (Ramsey County)	58301
Sunnyside Addition	58102
Sunny Slope (Ward County)	58701
Surrey	58785
Sutton	58484
Swansonville	58504
Sykeston	58486
Taft (Traill County)	58045
Tagus	58718
Talbotts	58701
Tappen (Kidder County)	58487
Tatley Meadows	58504
Taylor (Stark County)	58656
Temvik	58552
Thompson	58278
Thorne	58366
Tilden	58351
Timber Lake Place	58504
Tioga	58852
TJ Ranch Estates	58501
Tokio	58379
Tolley	58787
Tolna	58380
Tower City	58071
Town and Country	58801
Town and Country Estates	58504
Town And Country Shopping Center (Part of Minot)	58701
Towner	58788
Trenton	58853
Trestle Valley	58701
Trotters	58657
Turtle Lake (McLean County)	58575
Turtle Mountain Indian Reservation	58316
Tuttle (Kidder County)	58488
Twin Butte (Burleigh County)	58504
Twin Buttes	58636
Underwood	58576
Union (Cavalier County)	58279
University of North Dakota (Part of Grand Forks)	58202
Upham	58789
Urbana	58481
Valley City	58072
Velva (McHenry County)	58790
Venturia	58489
Verona	58490
Veseleyville	58237
Vista South	58504
Vohs Dapplegrey	58801
Voltaire (McHenry County)	58792
Voss	58261
Wabek	58771
Wahpeton	58074-75
For specific Wahpeton Zip Codes call (701) 642-6174	
Walcott	58077
Wales	58281
Walhalla	58282
Walum	58448
Warren	58021
Warsaw	58261
Warwick (Benson County)	58381
Washburn (McLean County)	58577
Watford City	58854
Webster	58382
Welle	58501
Wellsburg	58341
West Acres Estates	58801
Westbrook	58047
West Fargo	58078
Westfield (Emmons County)	58542
West Heart Estates	58504
Westhope (Bottineau County)	58793
West Industrial Park	58601
West Jamestown	58401
West Oakwood	58237
West Town	58401
Westwood on the River	58501
Wheatland	58079
Wheelock	58849
White Earth	58794
White Shield	58540
Whitman	58259
Wild Rice	58047
Wildrose (Williams County)	58795
Williston	58801-02
For specific Williston Zip Codes call (701) 572-3121	
Williston Park	58801
Willow City	58384
Wilton	58579
Wimbledon	58492
Windsor	58424
Wing (Burleigh County)	58494
Wishek	58495
Wolford	58385
Wolseth	58740
Woodland	58051
Woods	58052
Woodworth	58496
Wutzke	58501
Wyndmere	58081
York (Benson County)	58386
Ypsilanti	58497
Zahl	58856
Zap	58580
Zeeland	58581

Abanaka-Beachwood OHIO 409

Name	ZIP
Abanaka	45874
Abbottsville	45304
Aberdeen	45101
Academia	43050
Achor	44441
Acme	44281
Ada	45810
Acair	44625
Adams (Champaign County) (Township)	43070
Adams (Clinton County) (Township)	45177
Adams (Coshocton County) (Township)	43832
Adams (Darke County) (Township)	45308
Adams (Defiance County) (Township)	43512
Adams (Guernsey County) (Township)	43725
Adams (Monroe County) (Township)	43914
Adams (Muskingum County) (Township)	43821
Adams (Seneca County) (Township)	44867
Adams (Washington County) (Township)	45744
Adams Mills	43801
Adamsville (Gallia County)	45614
Adamsville (Muskingum County)	43802
Adario	44837
Addison	45631
Addison (Township)	45631
Addyston	45001
Adelphi	43101
Adena	43901
Adrian	44801
Africa	43021
Afton	45103
Aid	45645
Aid (Township)	45645
Ainger	43543
Air Mail Facility (Part of Dayton)	45490
Air Material Command	45433
Airport (Cuyahoga County)	44181
Airport (Franklin County)	43219
Airway	45431
Akron	44301-98
For specific Akron Zip Codes call (216) 379-0600	
Albany	45710
Al Bar Meadows (Part of The Village of Indian Hill)	45243
Albion	44287
Alcony	45373
Alexander (Township)	45701
Alexanders (Part of Independence)	44131
Alexandersville (Part of West Carrollton City)	45449
Alexandria	43001
Alexis Place (Part of Toledo)	43612
Alfred	45723
Alger	45812
Alikanna	43952
Alledonia	43902
Allen (Darke County) (Township)	45362
Allen (Hancock County) (Township)	45889
Allen (Ottawa County) (Township)	43412
Allen (Union County) (Township)	43070
Allen Center	43040
Allensburg	45133
Allensville	45651
Allentown (Allen County)	45807
Allentown (Scioto County)	45694
Alliance	44601
Alma	45690
Alpha	45301
Alpine Terrace	45230
Alpine Village (Part of Valley Hi)	43360
Alta	44903
Altamont Hills	43938
Altamont Park (Part of Mingo Junction)	43938
Alton	43119
Altoona	45692
Alvada	44802
Alvordton	43501
Amanda (Allen County) (Township)	45807
Amanda (Fairfield County) (Township)	43102

Name	ZIP
Amanda (Fairfield County)	43102
Amanda (Hancock County) (Township)	45867
Amberley	45213
Amberly	43227
Amboy (Ashtabula County)	44030
Amboy (Fulton County) (Township)	43540
Amelia	45102
American (Township)	45807
Ames (Township)	45711
Amesville	45711
Amherst	44001
Amherst (Township)	44001
Amity (Hamilton County)	45236
Amity (Knox County)	43050
Amity (Madison County)	43064
Amity (Montgomery County)	45309
Amlin	43002
Amlin Heights	45385
Amsden	44803
Amsterdam (Jefferson County)	43903
Amsterdam (Licking County)	43076
Anderson (Hamilton County) (Township)	45230
Anderson (Ross County)	45601
Andersonville	45601
Andis	45645
Andover	44003
Andover (Township)	44003
Ankenytown	43019
Anna	45302
Annapolis	43910
Ansonia	45303
Antioch	43793
Antiquity	45771
Antrim (Guernsey County)	43773
Antrim (Wyandot County) (Township)	43323
Antwerp	45813
Apple Creek	44606
Apple Grove	45771
Appleton	43031
Aquilla	44024
Arabia	45659
Arborcrest Acres (Part of Amberley)	45236
Arcadia	44804
Arcanum	45304
Archbold	43502
Archer (Township)	43986
Archers Fork	45767
Arion	45642
Arlington (Hancock County)	45814
Arlington (Montgomery County)	45309
Arlington Heights	45215
Armstrongs Mills	43933
Arnheim	45121
Arnold	43064
Arrow Head (Part of Xenia)	45385
Artanna	43022
Arthur	43512
Arwold	45383
Ashland	44805
Ashley	43003
Ashley Corner	45694
Ash Ridge	45121
Ashtabula	44004
Ashtabula (Township)	44004
Ashville	43103
Assumption	43558
Athalia	45669
Athens	45701
Athens (Athens County) (Township)	45701
Athens (Harrison County) (Township)	43981
Atlanta	43145
Atlas	43713
Attica	44807
Attica Junction	44807
Atwater	44201
Atwater (Township)	44201
Atwater Center	44201
Auburn (Butler County)	45013
Auburn (Crawford County) (Township)	44887
Auburn (Geauga County) (Township)	44255
Auburn (Tuscarawas County) (Township)	44681
Auburn Center (Crawford County)	44875
Auburn Center (Geauga County)	44022
Auburn Corners	44021
Augersburg	44266

Name	ZIP
Auglaize (Allen County) (Township)	45850
Auglaize (Paulding County) (Township)	43512
Augusta	44607
Augusta (Township)	44607
Ault	43947
Aultman	44630
Aurelius (Township)	45746
Aurora	44202
Aurora East	44240
Aurora Meadows	44202
Austin	45628
Austinburg	44010
Austinburg (Township)	44010
Austintown (Township)	44515
Austintown (Mahoning County)	44512
Austintown Plaza	44515
Austin Village (Part of Warren)	44481
Autumn Acres	45239
Ava	43711
Avalon (Butler County)	45042
Avalon (Perry County)	43107
Avalon Heights (Part of Lebanon)	45036
Avon	44011
Avondale (Belmont County)	43906
Avondale (Hamilton County)	45229
Avondale (Licking County)	43076
Avondale (Logan County)	43331
Avondale (Montgomery County)	45404
Avondale (Muskingum County)	43777
Avondale (Stark County)	44708
Avon Lake	44012
Avon Park (Part of Girard)	44420
Axtel	44089
Ayersville	43512
Bachman	45309
Badgertown	43719
Bailey Lakes	44805
Baileys Mills	43713
Bainbridge (Geauga County) (Township)	44022
Bainbridge (Ross County)	45612
Bainbridge Center	44022
Bairdstown	45872
Bakersville	43803
Ballville	43420
Ballville (Township)	43420
Baltic	43804
Baltimore	43105
Bangs	43050
Bannock	43972
Bantam	45103
Barberton	44203
Bardwell	45154
Barlow	45712
Barlow (Township)	45712
Barnesburg	45239
Barnesville	43713
Barnhill	44663
Barr	44681
Barretts Mills	45612
Bartles	45659
Bartlett	45713
Bartley Estates	45414
Bartlow (Township)	43516
Barton	43905
Bartramville	45669
Bascom	44809
Bashan	45743
Bass Lake	44024
Batavia	45103
Batavia (Township)	45103
Batemantown	43019
Batesville	43773
Bath (Township)	44210
Bath (Allen County) (Township)	45801
Bath (Greene County) (Township)	45324
Bath (Summit County)	44210
Battlesburg	44626
Baughman (Township)	44667
Bay (Township)	43452
Bayard	44657
Bay Bridge	44870
Bays	43462
Bay View	44870
Bay Village	44140
Bazetta	44410
Bazetta (Township)	44410
Beach City	44608
Beachland (Part of Cleveland)	44119
Beachwood	44122

OHIO

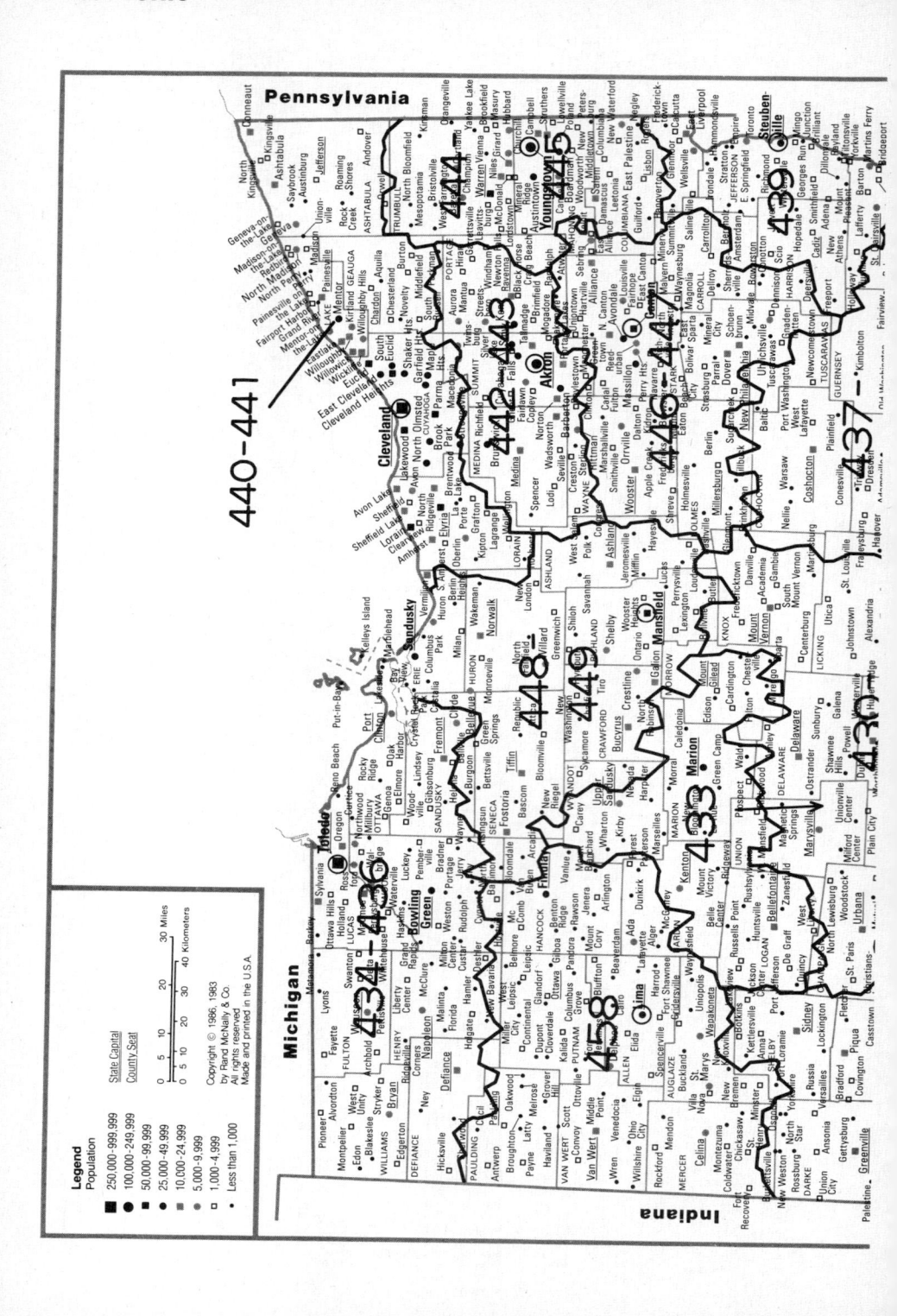

OHIO 411

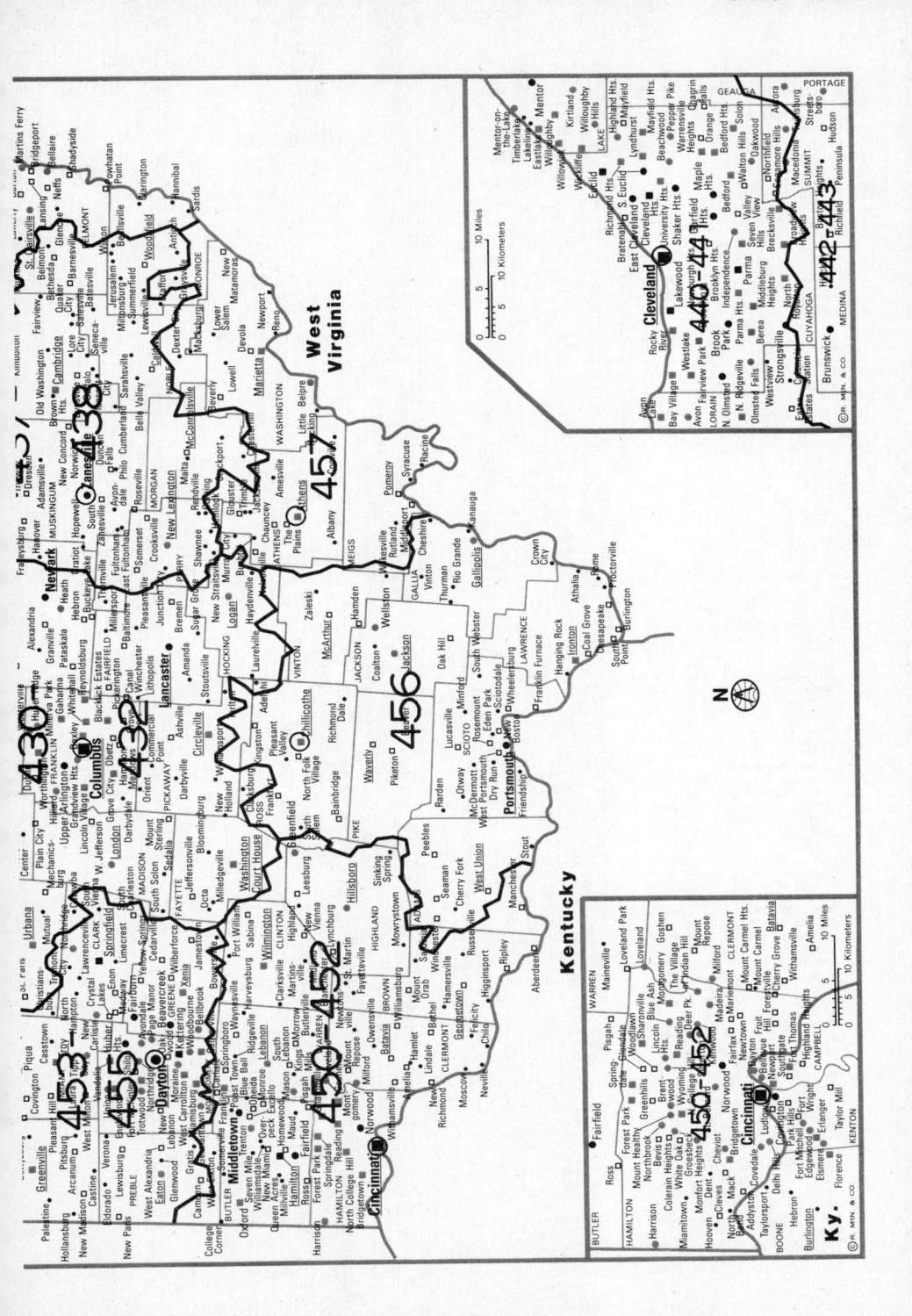

412 OHIO Beachwood Place-Brentwood

Name	ZIP
Beachwood Place (Part of Beachwood)	44122
Beacon Hill	45241
Beallsville	43716
Beals (Part of Pickerington)	43147
Beamsville	45303
Bearfield (Township)	43730
Beartown	44622
Beatty	45506
Beaumont	45701
Beaver (Township)	45690
Beaver (Mahoning County) (Township)	44408
Beaver (Noble County) (Township)	43773
Beaver (Pike County)	45613
Beavercreek (Greene County)	45385
Beavercreek (Greene County) (Township)	45401
Beaverdam	45808
Beaver Park (Part of Lorain)	44052
Beavertown (Montgomery County)	45429
Beavertown (Washington County)	45767
Becker Highlands (Part of Steubenville)	43952
Becks Mills	44654
Bedford (Coshocton County) (Township)	43812
Bedford (Cuyahoga County)	44146
Bedford (Meigs County) (Township)	45769
Bedford Heights	44146
Beechcrest	44240
Beechview Estates (Part of Cincinnati)	45201
Beechwold (Part of Columbus)	43214
Beechwood (Jefferson County)	43952
Beechwood (Preble County)	45064
Beechwood (Stark County)	44601
Bel-Air Mobile Homes	44420
Belden	44044
Belfast (Clermont County)	45122
Belfast (Highland County)	45133
Belfort	44641
Bellaire	43906
Bellaire Gardens	43302
Bellbrook	45305
Belle Center	43310
Bellefontaine	43311
Bellepoint	43015
Belle Valley	43717
Belle Vernon	44882
Belleview Acres (Part of Bellbrook)	45305
Belleview Heights (Preble County)	45347
Belleview Heights (Ross County)	45601
Bellevue	44811
Bellview	45305
Bellview Estates	45305
Bellview Heights	43906
Bellville	44813
Belmont (Allen County)	45801
Belmont (Belmont County)	43718
Belmont (Butler County)	45015
Belmont Park	44420
Belmont Ridge	43983
Belmore	45815
Beloit	44609
Belpre (Washington County)	45714
Belpre (Washington County) (Township)	45714
Belvedere	43952
Bennington (Licking County) (Township)	43011
Bennington (Morrow County) (Township)	43334
Bentley (Part of Lowellville)	44436
Bentleyville	44022
Benton (Crawford County)	44882
Benton (Hocking County) (Township)	43152
Benton (Holmes County)	44654
Benton (Monroe County) (Township)	45767
Benton (Ottawa County) (Township)	43432
Benton (Paulding County) (Township)	45880
Benton (Pike County) (Township)	45690
Benton Ridge	45816
Bentonville	45105
Berea	44130
Berea (Part of Middleburg Heights)	44017
Bergholz	43908
Berkey	43504
Berkley Heights (Part of Kettering)	45429
Berkshire	43074
Berkshire (Township)	43074
Berlin (Township)	44610
Berlin (Knox County) (Township)	43019
Berlin (Mahoning County) (Township)	44401
Berlin (Delaware County) (Township)	43015
Berlin (Erie County) (Township)	44814
Berlin (Holmes County)	44610
Berlin Center	44401
Berlin Heights	44814
Berlinville	44814
Bern (Township)	45770
Berne (Township)	43155
Bernice	43832
Berryman	45805
Berrysville	45133
Berwick	44853
Bessemer	45764
Bethany	45042
Bethel (Clark County) (Township)	45344
Bethel (Clermont County)	45106
Bethel (Miami County) (Township)	45371
Bethel (Monroe County) (Township)	45745
Bethesda	43719
Bethlehem (Coshocton County) (Township)	43812
Bethlehem (Richland County)	44875
Bethlehem (Stark County) (Township)	44662
Bettsville	44815
Beulah Beach	44089
Beverly	45715
Beverly Gardens	45431
Bevis	45239
Bexley	43209
Bidwell	45614
Big Island	43302
Big Island (Township)	43302
Biglick (Township)	44802
Big Plain	43140
Big Prairie	44611
Big Rock	45613
Big Run	45724
Big Spring (Township)	44853
Big Springs	43347
Birds Run	43749
Birmingham (Erie County)	44816
Birmingham (Guernsey County)	43749
Bishopville	45732
Bismarck	44811
Blachleyville	44691
Black Creek (Township)	45882
Blackfork	45656
Black Fork Junction	45656
Black Horse	44266
Blacklick	43004
Blacklick Estates	43227
Black Run	43830
Blacktop	43755
Bladen	45623
Bladensburg	43005
Blaine	43909
Blainesville	43937
Blairmont	43901
Blakeslee	43505
Blanchard (Hancock County) (Township)	45816
Blanchard (Hardin County) (Township)	45836
Blanchard (Putnam County) (Township)	45875
Blanchard (Hardin County)	45836
Blanches Addition	43062
Blanchester	45107
Blendon (Township)	43081
Blissfield	43805
Bloom (Fairfield County) (Township)	43136
Bloom (Morgan County) (Township)	43756
Bloom (Scioto County) (Township)	45682
Bloom (Seneca County) (Township)	44818
Bloom (Wood County) (Township)	44817
Bloom Center (Logan County)	43318
Bloom Center (Wood County)	43413
Bloomdale	44817
Bloomer	45318
Bloomfield (Columbiana County)	43920
Bloomfield (Jackson County) (Township)	45640
Bloomfield (Logan County) (Township)	43333
Bloomfield (Morrow County)	43011
Bloomfield (Muskingum County)	43762
Bloomfield (Trumbull County) (Township)	44450
Bloomfield (Washington County)	45774
Bloomingburg	43106
Bloomingdale	43910
Blooming Grove (Morrow County)	44833
Blooming Grove (Richland County) (Township)	44878
Bloomington	45169
Bloomingville	44870
Bloomville	44818
Blue Ash	45242
Blue Ball	45005
Blue Bell	43772
Bluebird Beach (Part of Vermilion)	44089
Blue Creek (Adams County)	45616
Blue Creek (Paulding County) (Township)	45886
Blue Rock	43720
Blue Rock (Township)	43720
Blue Valley Acres	43130
Bluffton	45817
Boardman	44512
Boardman (Township)	44512
Bobo	45613
Boden	43762
Bokes Creek (Township)	43358
Bolivar	44612
Bolton	44601
Boneta	44274
Bonn	45788
Bono	43445
Bookwalter	43128
Booth (Lucas County)	43618
Booth (Tuscarawas County)	43832
Borromeo College of Ohio	44092
Boston (Highland County)	45133
Boston (Summit County) (Township)	44264
Boston Heights	44236
Boston Mill	44264
Botkins	45306
Boudes Ferry	45121
Boughtonville	44890
Bourneville	45617
Bowerston	44695
Bowersville	45307
Bowling Green (Licking County) (Township)	43076
Bowling Green (Marion County) (Township)	43332
Bowling Green (Wood County)	43402
Bowlusville	43078
Boydsville	43912
Braceville	44444
Braceville (Township)	44444
Braceville Ridge	44444
Bradbury	45760
Bradford	45308
Bradley (Clermont County)	45122
Bradley (Jefferson County)	43917
Bradner	43406
Bradrick	45619
Brady (Township)	43570
Brady Lake	44211
Brady Lake Addition	44211
Bradyville	45144
Braffettsville	45347
Brailey	43558
Branch Hill	45140
Brandon	43050
Brandt	45371
Brandywine	44820
Bratenahl	44108
Bratton (Township)	45660
Brecksville	44141
Brecon	45242
Bremen	43107
Brentwood (Hamilton County)	45231
Brentwood (Jefferson County)	43952

Brentwood-Center **OHIO** 413

Name	ZIP
Brentwood (Lake County)	44060
Brentwood Estates	43952
Brentwood Lake	44044
Brewster	44613
Briarwood Beach	44215
Brice	43109
Briceton	45879
Bridgeport (Belmont County)	43912
Bridgeport (Hardin County)	45843
Bridgetown	45211
Bridgewater (Township)	43543
Bridgewater Center	43543
Brigglesville	43731
Briggs (Cuyahoga County)	44134
Briggs (Washington County)	45714
Briggsdale	43223
Brighton (Township)	44090
Brighton (Clark County)	45369
Brighton (Lorain County)	44090
Brightwood	44663
Brilliant	43913
Brimfield	44240
Brimfield (Township)	44240
Brinkhaven	43006
Bristol (Morgan County) (Township)	43756
Bristol (Perry County)	43764
Bristol (Trumbull County) (Township)	44402
Bristol Village (Part of Waverly)	45690
Bristolville	44402
Broadacre	43910
Broadview Acres (Clark County)	45504
Broadview Acres (Muskingum County)	43701
Broadview Heights	44141
Broadway	43007
Broadwell	45778
Brock	45380
Brokaw	43787
Brokensword	44820
Brokes	45672
Bronson (Township)	44857
Brookfield (Township)	44403
Brookfield (Noble County) (Township)	43732
Brookfield (Trumbull County)	44403
Brookhill	45224
Brook Hollow	45324
Brooklyn	44144
Brooklyn Heights	44131
Brook Park	44142
Brookside	43912
Brookside Estates	43085
Brookview	43912
Brookville	45309
Brookwood (Part of Amberley)	45237
Broughton	45879
Brown (Carroll County) (Township)	44644
Brown (Darke County) (Township)	45303
Brown (Delaware County) (Township)	43015
Brown (Franklin County) (Township)	43026
Brown (Knox County) (Township)	43014
Brown (Miami County) (Township)	45317
Brown (Paulding County) (Township)	45873
Brown (Vinton County) (Township)	45654
Brown Heights	43725
Brownhelm (Lorain County)	44089
Brownhelm (Lorain County) (Township)	44001
Brownstown	45171
Brownsville (Licking County)	43721
Brownsville (Monroe County)	45767
Brownsville (Ross County)	45601
Brunersburg	43512
Bruno	43076
Brunswick	44212
Brunswick Hills (Township)	44280
Brush Creek (Adams County) (Township)	45650
Brush Creek (Highland County) (Township)	45172
Brush Creek (Jefferson County) (Township)	43945
Brush Creek (Muskingum County) (Township)	43777
Brush Creek (Scioto County) (Township)	45657

Name	ZIP
Brush Ridge	43302
Bryan	43506
Buchanan	45690
Buchtel	45716
Buck (Township)	43326
Buckeye	43701
Buckeye Addition	43050
Buckeye Lake	43008
Buckeye Road (Part of Cleveland)	44102
Buckeyeville	43725
Buckhorn	45694
Buckingham	43730
Buckland	45819
Bucks (Township)	43824
Buckskin (Township)	45647
Bucyrus	44820
Bucyrus (Township)	44820
Buena Vista (Butler County)	45042
Buena Vista (Fayette County)	43160
Buena Vista (Hocking County)	43149
Buena Vista (Scioto County)	45684
Buffalo (Guernsey County)	43722
Buffalo (Noble County) (Township)	43772
Buford	45110
Bulah	44047
Bunker Hill (Butler County)	45013
Bunker Hill (Holmes County)	44654
Burbank	44214
Burghill	44404
Burgoon	43407
Burkettsville	45310
Burkhart	43754
Burlingham	45776
Burlington (Fulton County)	43502
Burlington (Lawrence County)	45680
Burlington (Licking County) (Township)	43027
Burnetts Corners	44691
Burnet Woods (Part of Cincinnati)	45220
Burr Oak	45732
Burr Oaks	43143
Burton (Township)	44021
Burton	44021
Burton (rural)	44062
Burton City	44667
Burton Lake	44021
Burtonville	45177
Busenbark (Part of Trenton)	45011
Bushnell	44030
Businessburg	44933
Business Corners	43542
Butler (Columbiana County) (Township)	44460
Butler (Darke County) (Township)	45346
Butler (Knox County) (Township)	43843
Butler (Mercer County) (Township)	45828
Butler (Montgomery County) (Township)	45337
Butler (Richland County)	44822
Butler (Richland County) (Township)	44837
Butlerville	45162
Byers Junction	45692
Byesville	43723
Byhalia	43344
Byington	45646
Byrd (Township)	45115
Byron	45385
Cable	43009
Cadiz	43907
Cadiz (Township)	43907
Cadiz Junction	43976
Cadmus	45658
Caesars Creek (Township)	45385
Cain Heights	43920
Cairo (Allen County)	45820
Cairo (Stark County)	44721
Calais	43773
Calcutta	43920
Caldwell	43724
Caledonia	43314
California	45503
Calla	44406
Cambridge (Township)	43725
Cambridge	43725
Cambridge Mental Health and Development Center	43725
Camden (Lorain County) (Township)	44049
Camden (Preble County)	45311
Cameron	43914
Campbell	44405

Name	ZIP
Campbellsport	44266
Campbellstown	45320
Camp Creek (Pike County) (Township)	45671
Camp Creek (Stark County)	44613
Camp Dennison	45111
Camp Ground	43130
Camp Luther (Part of North Kingsville)	44068
Campus (Part of Cincinnati)	45221
Canaan (Township)	44217
Canaan (Athens County) (Township)	45701
Canaan (Madison County) (Township)	43064
Canaan (Morrow County) (Township)	43320
Canaan (Wayne County)	44217
Canaanville	45701
Canal Fulton	44614
Canal Lewisville	43812
Canal Winchester	43110
Candy Town	45764
Canfield	44406
Canfield (Township)	44406
Cannelville	43777
Cannons Creek	45659
Cannons Mills	43920
Canton	44701-99
For specific Canton Zip Codes call (216) 438-6432	
Canyon Park	44429
Carbondale	45717
Carbon Hill	43111
Cardinal Lake	44085
Cardington	43315
Cardington (Township)	43315
Carey	43316
Carlisle (Lorain County) (Township)	44035
Carlisle (Noble County)	43724
Carlisle (Warren County)	45005
Carmel	45133
Caroline	44807
Carpenter	45710
Carriage	45502
Carroll (Fairfield County)	43112
Carroll (Ottawa County) (Township)	43449
Carrollton	44615
Carrothers	44823
Carryall (Township)	45813
Carthage (Township)	45735
Carthagena	45822
Carysville	45317
Cass (Hancock County) (Township)	44804
Cass (Muskingum County) (Township)	43821
Cass (Richland County) (Township)	44878
Cassell	43725
Cassella	45883
Cassinelli Square (Part of Springdale)	45246
Casstown	45312
Castalia	44824
Castine	45304
Catawba (Champaign County)	43044
Catawba (Clark County)	43010
Catawba Island	43452
Catawba Island (Township)	43452
Causeway Manor	44003
Cavallo	43843
Cavett	45891
Caywood	45750
Cecil	45821
Cedar Center Plaza (Part of University Heights)	44125
Cedarhill	43102
Cedar Mills	45616
Cedar Point (Part of Sandusky)	44870
Cedar Valley	44214
Cedarville	45314
Cedarville (Township)	45314
Cedron	45121
Celeryville	44890
Celina	45822
Centenary	45631
Center (Township)	43725
Center (Mercer County) (Township)	45822
Center (Monroe County) (Township)	43793
Center (Morgan County) (Township)	45715
Center (Noble County) (Township)	43724

414 OHIO Center-Cleveland

	ZIP
Center (Williams County) (Township)	43506
Center (Wood County) (Township)	43402
Center (Carroll County) (Township)	44615
Center (Columbiana County) (Township)	44432
Center (Guernsey County)	43725
Centerburg	43011
Centerfield	45123
Centerpoint	45656
Center Station	45659
Centerton	44890
Center Village	43021
Centerville (Belmont County)	43718
Centerville (Brown County)	45154
Centerville (Marion County)	43342
Centerville (Montgomery County)	45459
Centerville (Wayne County)	44676
Central (Part of Toledo)	43604
Central College (Part of Westerville)	43081
Cessna (Township)	43326
Ceylon	44839
Chagrin Falls (Cuyahoga County)	44022
Chagrin Falls (Cuyahoga County) (Township)	44022
Chagrin Falls Park	44022
Chagrin Harbor (Part of Eastlake)	44094
Chalfants	43739
Chambersburg (Columbiana County)	44657
Chambersburg (Gallia County)	45631
Champion	44481
Champion (Township)	44481
Chandler	43910
Chandlersville	43727
Chapel Hill Shopping Center (Part of Akron)	44310
Chapmans	45692
Chardon	44024
Chardon (Township)	44024
Charity Rotch (Part of Massillon)	44646
Charlestown	44266
Charlestown (Township)	44266
Charloe	45873
Charm	44617
Chasetown	45118
Chaseville	43772
Chaska Beach (Part of Huron)	44839
Chateau Estates	45502
Chateau Ridge (Part of Marion)	43302
Chatfield	44825
Chatfield (Township)	44825
Chatham (Township)	44275
Chatham (Licking County)	43055
Chatham (Medina County)	44256
Chattanooga	45882
Chauncey	45719
Chautauqua	45342
Cherokee	43324
Cherry Fork	45618
Cherry Grove	45230
Cherry Grove Plaza	45230
Cherry Valley	44003
Cherry Valley (Township)	44003
Chesapeake	45619
Cheshire (Township)	45620
Cheshire (Delaware County)	43021
Cheshire (Gallia County)	45620
Chesswood Acres	45239
Chester (Township)	45720
Chester (Morrow County) (Township)	43338
Chester (Wayne County) (Township)	44691
Chester (Clinton County) (Township)	45177
Chester (Geauga County) (Township)	44026
Chester (Meigs County)	45720
Chester Center	44026
Chesterfield (Township)	43567
Chesterhill	43728
Chesterland	44026
Chesterville	43317
Cheviot	45211
Cheviot Hills	45502
Chevy Chase	44833
Chickasaw	45826
Chickwan	43901
Chili	43824

	ZIP
Chillicothe	45601
Chillicothe Correctional Institute	45601
Chillicothe Manor	45601
Chilo	45112
Chipman	45805
Chippewa (Township)	44230
Chippewa Lake	44215
Chippewa Lake Park	44215
Chocktaw Lake	43140
Christiansburg	45389
Chuckery	43029
Churchill	44505
Churchills (Part of Sylvania)	43560
Churchtown	45750
Cincinnati	**45201-75**

For specific Cincinnati Zip Codes call (513) 684-5571

COLLEGES & UNIVERSITIES

God's Bible School and College	45210
University of Cincinnati	45221
Xavier University	45207

FINANCIAL INSTITUTIONS

Centennial Savings & Loan Company	45239
The Central Trust Company, N.A.	45202
Century Bank	45209
Charter Oak Federal Savings Bank	45242
The Cheviot Building & Loan Company	45211
Cottage Savings Association, F.A.	45230
Fidelity Federal Savings & Loan Association	45212
The Fifth Third Bank	45263
First Financial Savings Association, F.A.	45209
Franklin Savings & Loan Company	45202
Gateway Federal Savings & Loan Association	45202
Hunter Savings Association	45236
Merit Savings Association	45213
North Side Bank & Trust Co.	45223
Oak Hills Savings & Loan Company	45211
The Provident Bank	45202
Star Bank, National Association, Cincinnati	45202
Suburban Federal Savings & Loan Association	45242
Thrift Savings & Loan Company	45202
Winton Savings & Loan Company	45239

HOSPITALS

Bethesda North Hospital	45242
Bethesda Oak Hospital	45206
Children's Hospital Medical Center	45229
Christ Hospital	45219
Daniel Drake Memorial Hospital	45216
Deaconess Hospital	45219
Good Samaritan Hospital	45220
Jewish Hospital of Cincinnati	45229
Providence Hospital	45239
St. Francis-St. George Hospital	45238
University of Cincinnati Hospital	45267
Veterans Administration Medical Center	45220

HOTELS/MOTELS

Clarion Hotel	45202
The Hampshire House Hotel	45246
Harley of Cincinnati	45236
Holiday Inn-Downtown	45203
Hyatt Regency Cincinnati-Saks Fifth Avenue Center	45202
Omni Netherland Plaza	45202
Ramada Hotel	45242
The Vernon Manor Hotel	45219

MILITARY INSTALLATIONS

United States Army Engineer Division, Ohio River	45201
Circle Green	43908
Circle Hill (Athens County)	45764

	ZIP
Circle Hill (Miami County)	45308
Circleville	43113
Circleville (Township)	43113
Circleville Bible College	43113
City View Heights	45011
Claiborne	43344
Claiborne (Township)	43344
Claridon	44024
Claridon (Geauga County) (Township)	44024
Claridon	43314
Claridon (Marion County) (Township)	43314
Clarington	43915
Clark (Coshocton County) (Township)	43844
Clark (Holmes County) (Township)	43804
Clark (Brown County) (Township)	45130
Clark (Clinton County) (Township)	45146
Clark (Coshocton County)	43812
Clark Corners (Ashtabula County)	44030
Clark Corners (Medina County)	44281
Clarksburg (Belmont County)	43960
Clarksburg (Ross County)	43115
Clarksfield	44889
Clarksfield (Township)	44889
Clarks Lake	43143
Clarkson	44455
Clarksville (Clinton County)	45113
Clarksville (Perry County)	43748
Clarktown	45648
Clay (Auglaize County) (Township)	45895
Clay (Gallia County) (Township)	45631
Clay (Highland County) (Township)	45171
Clay (Jackson County)	45656
Clay (Knox County) (Township)	43080
Clay (Montgomery County) (Township)	45354
Clay (Muskingum County) (Township)	43777
Clay (Ottawa County) (Township)	43430
Clay (Scioto County) (Township)	45662
Clay (Tuscarawas County) (Township)	44629
Clay Center	43408
Clay Lick	43055
Claysville	43725
Clayton (Adams County)	45144
Clayton (Montgomery County)	45315
Clayton (Perry County) (Township)	43764
Clear Creek (Ashland County) (Township)	44874
Clear Creek (Fairfield County) (Township)	43102
Clear Creek (Warren County) (Township)	45066
Clearport	43130
Clearview (Athens County)	45701
Clearview (Lorain County)	44055
Clearview (Stark County)	44646
Clermontville	45157
Clertoma (Part of Milford)	45150
Cleveland	**44101-99**

For specific Cleveland Zip Codes call (216) 443-4444

COLLEGES & UNIVERSITIES

Case Western Reserve University	44106
Cleveland State University	44115
Dyke College	44115
John Carroll University	44118
Ursuline College	44124

FINANCIAL INSTITUTIONS

AmeriTrust Company National Association	44115
Bank One, Cleveland, National Association	44115
The First Federal Savings Bank	44114
First Federal Savings & Loan Association of Lakewood	44107
Home Federal Savings Bank, Northern Ohio	44107

Cleveland Heights-Crescent Gardens **OHIO** 415

	ZIP
National City Bank	44114
Ohio Savings Bank	44114
Security Federal Savings & Loan Association of Cleveland	44115
Society National Bank	44114
The Strongsville Savings Bank	44136
Third Federal Savings & Loan Association of Cleveland	44105
TransOhio SavingsBank	44114
Western Reserve Savings Bank of Cleveland	44114
Women's Federal Savings Bank	44113

HOSPITALS

Cleveland Clinic Hospital	44195
Deaconess Hospital of Cleveland	44109
Fairview General Hospital	44111
Meridia Huron Hospital	44112
Mt. Sinai Medical Center	44106
Saint Luke's Hospital	44104
St. Vincent Charity Hospital and Health Center	44115
University Hospitals of Cleveland	44106
Veterans Administration Medical Center	44106

HOTELS/MOTELS

Cleveland Hilton South	44131
Sheraton Hopkins Airport Hotel	44135

MILITARY INSTALLATIONS

Naval Finance Center	44199

Cleveland Heights	44118
Cleves	45002
Clifton	45316
Clifton Farms (Part of Middletown)	45042
Climax	43320
Clinton (Franklin County) (Township)	43224
Clinton (Fulton County) (Township)	43567
Clinton (Knox County) (Township)	43050
Clinton (Seneca County) (Township)	44883
Clinton (Shelby County) (Township)	45365
Clinton (Summit County)	44216
Clinton (Vinton County) (Township)	45634
Clinton (Wayne County) (Township)	44676
Clintonville (Part of Columbus)	43202
Clipper Mills	45631
Cloverdale	45827
Cloverhill	43764
Cluff	45244
Clyde	43410
Coach Lite Village	43528
Coal (Jackson County) (Township)	45621
Coal (Perry County) (Township)	43766
Coalburg	44425
Coal Grove	45638
Coalport (Part of Newcomerstown)	43832
Coalridge	43711
Coal Run	45721
Coalton	45621
Coddingville	44256
Coffee Corners	44062
Coitsville (Township)	44436
Coitsville Center	44505
Colby	43410
Cold Springs	45502
Coldwater	45828
Colebrook	44076
Colebrook (Township)	44076
Colerain	43916
Colerain (Township)	43916
Colerain (Hamilton County) (Township)	45251
Colerain (Ross County) (Township)	45644
Colerain Heights	45239
Coles Park	45662
Coletown	45331
College (Township)	43022
College Corner	45003

	ZIP
College Hill (Guernsey County)	43725
College Hill (Hamilton County)	45224
College Hills	45324
Collins	44826
Collinsville	45004
Collinwood (Part of Cleveland)	44110
Collville Station	45723
Colonial Hills (Part of Worthington)	43085
Colony Square (Part of Zanesville)	43701
Colton	43510
Columbia (Hamilton County) (Township)	45243
Columbia (Lorain County) (Township)	44028
Columbia (Meigs County) (Township)	45710
Columbia (Stark County)	44646
Columbia (Tuscarawas County)	44622
Columbia (Williams County)	43518
Columbia Center (Licking County)	43062
Columbia Center (Lorain County)	44028
Columbia Hills Corners	44028
Columbiana	44408
Columbia Station	44028
Columbus	**43201-91**
For specific Columbus Zip Codes call (614) 469-4332	

COLLEGES & UNIVERSITIES

Capital University	43209
Columbus College of Art and Design	43215
DeVry Institute of Technology-Columbus	43209
Ohio Dominican College	43219
Ohio State University	43210

FINANCIAL INSTITUTIONS

BancOhio National Bank	43265
Bank One, Columbus, National Association	43271
Buckeye Federal Savings & Loan Association	43215
City Loan Bank	43220
The Fifth Third Bank of Columbus	43215
Freedom Federal Savings & Loan Association	43221
The Huntington National Bank	43215
Mid-America Federal Savings & Loan Association	43215
Society Bank	43215
Star Bank, Central Ohio	43215
State Savings Bank	43215

HOSPITALS

Children's Hospital	43205
Doctors Hospital	43201
Grant Medical Center	43215
Mount Carmel Health Center	43222
Ohio State University Hospitals	43210
Riverside Methodist Hospital	43214
St. Anthony Medical Center	43207

HOTELS/MOTELS

The Christopher Inn	43215
Columbus Marriott North	43229
Harley of Columbus	43229
Holiday Inn at Ohio Center	43215
Hyatt on Capitol Square-Columbus, Ohio	43215
Parke Hotel	43229
Ramada Inn-North	43229

MILITARY INSTALLATIONS

Defense Construction Supply Center	43215
Port Columbus International Airport, Air Force Facility	43219
Rickenbacker Air Force Base	43217

Columbus Circle (Part of Ashland)	44805
Columbus Grove	45830
Columbus Park	44870
Comet	44216
Commercial Point	43116

	ZIP
Compton Park	45231
Compton Woods (Part of Wyoming)	45215
Conant	45887
Concept	45807
Concord (Township)	44077
Concord (Licking County)	43031
Concord (Miami County) (Township)	45373
Concord (Ross County) (Township)	45628
Concord (Champaign County) (Township)	43072
Concord (Delaware County) (Township)	43015
Concord (Fayette County) (Township)	43160
Concord (Highland County) (Township)	45697
Concord (Lake County)	44060
Condit	43074
Conesville	43811
Congo	43730
Congress (Township)	44287
Congress (Morrow County) (Township)	43338
Congress (Wayne County)	44287
Congress Lake	44632
Conneaut	44030
Conneaut Harbor (Part of Conneaut)	44030
Connett	45764
Connor	43943
Conotton	44695
Conover	45317
Constitution	45750
Continental	45831
Converse	45887
Convoy	45832
Conway Addition	43731
Cooks	43143
Cool Ridge Heights	44905
Coolville	45723
Coonville	45654
Cooperdale	43821
Coopersville	45648
Copley	44321
Copley (Township)	44321
Copley Center	44321
Corinth	44417
Cork	44041
Corner	45714
Cornersburg (Part of Youngstown)	44511
Cornerville	45773
Corning	43730
Corryville (Hamilton County)	45219
Corryville (Lawrence County)	45619
Cortland	44410
Cortsville	45368
Corwin	45068
Coryville	45638
Coshocton	43812
Cottage Grove	44319
Country Acres (Greene County)	45430
Country Acres (Greene County)	45324
Country Club Estates (Part of Steubenville)	43952
Country Club Highlands (Part of Fairfield)	45011
Country Club Hills	45801
Country Estates	45371
Cove	45640
Covedale	45238
Coventry (Township)	44319
Covington	45318
Cozaddale	45122
Craig Beach	44429
Craigton	44676
Cranberry (Township)	44854
Cranberry Prairie	45883
Crandenbrook	43551
Crane (Paulding County) (Township)	45821
Crane (Wyandot County) (Township)	43351
Cranwood (Part of Cleveland)	44128
Crawford (Township)	43316
Crawford (Coshocton County) (Township)	43804
Crawford (Wyandot County)	43316
Crawford Corners	44235
Cream City (Part of Irondale)	43932
Creola	45622
Crescent	43950
Crescent Gardens	44646

416 OHIO Crescentville-East Orwell

	ZIP
Crescentville (Part of Sharonville)	45241
Crestline	44827
Creston	44217
Crestwood Hills (Part of Vandalia)	45377
Cridersville	45806
Crissey	43528
Cromers	44883
Crooked Tree	45727
Crooksville	43731
Crosby (Township)	45030
Cross Creek (Township)	43952
Crossenville	43107
Croton	43013
Crown City	45623
Crystal Lake	44003
Crystal Lakes	45341
Crystal Rock Park	43464
Crystal Springs	44614
Cuba	45114
Cumberland	43732
Cumminsville (Part of Cincinnati)	45223
Curtice	43412
Custar	43511
Cutler	45724
Cuyahoga Falls	44221-24
For specific Cuyahoga Falls Zip Codes call (216) 379-0611	
Cuyahoga Heights	44125
Cygnet	43413
Cynthian (Township)	45845
Cynthiana	45624
Dabel (Part of Dayton)	45420
Dadsville	45381
Dailyville	45690
Dale	43787
Dalewood	45069
Dallas (Township)	44849
Dallasburg	45140
Dalton	44618
Dalzell	45745
Daman Park	45042
Damascus (Henry County) (Township)	43534
Damascus (Mahoning County)	44619
Danbury (Township)	43452
Danville (Highland County)	45133
Danville (Knox County)	43014
Danville (Meigs County)	45741
Darby (Madison County) (Township)	43064
Darby (Pickaway County) (Township)	43146
Darby (Union County) (Township)	43064
Darby Crest	43119
Darbydale	43123
Darbyville	43136
Darlington (Muskingum County)	43701
Darlington (Richland County)	44813
Darrowville (Part of Stow)	44224
Darrtown	45056
Dart	45773
Darwin	45769
Davisville	45692
Dawn	45303
Dawson	45333
Day Heights	45150
Dayton	45401-90
For specific Dayton Zip Codes call (513) 227-1100	
Dayton View (Part of Dayton)	45406
Dean Dale (Part of Mingo Junction)	43938
Deavertown	43731
Decatur (Brown County)	45115
Decatur (Lawrence County) (Township)	45659
Decatur (Washington County) (Township)	45742
Decaturville	45712
Decrow Corners	43031
Dee	44824
Deep Run	43935
Deer Creek (Madison County) (Township)	43140
Deer Creek (Pickaway County) (Township)	43164
Deerfield (Portage County) (Township)	44411
Deerfield (Ross County) (Township)	43115
Deerfield (Warren County) (Township)	45040
Deerfield (Morgan County) (Township)	43758

	ZIP
Deerfield (Portage County)	44411
Deering	45638
Deer Park	45236
Deersville	44693
Defiance	43512
Defiance (Township)	43512
Defiance Junction (Part of Defiance)	43512
De Forest	44484
De Graff	43318
Dekalb	44887
Delaware (Delaware County) (Township)	43015
Delaware (Hancock County) (Township)	45897
Delaware (Defiance County) (Township)	43556
Delaware (Delaware County)	43015
Delhi (Township)	45238
Delhi Hills	45238
Delightful	44470
Delisle	45304
Dellroy	44620
Delmont	43130
Delphi	44890
Delphos	45833
Delta	43515
Denmark (Ashtabula County) (Township)	44047
Denmark (Morrow County)	43320
Denmark Center	44047
Dennison	44621
Densons	43533
Dent	45211
Denver	45690
Derby	43117
Derwent	43733
Deshler	43516
Deunquat	44882
Devil Town	44691
Devola	45750
Deweyville	45858
Dexter	45741
Dexter City	45727
Deyarmonville	43917
Dialton	45502
Diamond	44412
Dicken	43138
Dille	43947
Dillon Falls	43701
Dillonvale (Hamilton County)	45236
Dillonvale (Jefferson County)	43917
Dilworth	44417
Dinsmore (Township)	45306
Dixie	43782
Dixie Heights (Butler County)	45042
Dixie Heights (Montgomery County)	45414
Dixon (Preble County) (Township)	45320
Dixon (Van Wert County)	45832
Dixonville	43920
Doanville	45764
Dobbston	45678
Dodds	45036
Dodgeville	44085
Dodson (Highland County) (Township)	45142
Dodson (Montgomery County)	45309
Dodsonville	45142
Dola	45835
Dolly Varden	45368
Donald L Marrs (Part of Cincinnati)	45258
Doneys (Part of Whitehall)	43213
Donnelsville	45319
Donnersville	43950
Dorcas	45771
Dornbusch	45239
Dorset	44032
Dorset (Township)	44032
Dover (Tuscarawas County) (Township)	44622
Dover (Union County) (Township)	43040
Dover (Athens County) (Township)	45761
Dover (Fulton County) (Township)	43567
Dover (Tuscarawas County)	44622
Dowling	43551
Downtown (Franklin County)	43215
Downtown (Summit County)	44308
Doylestown	44230
Drakes	43730
Drakesburg	44288
Dresden	43821
Drexel	45427

	ZIP
Driftwood (Ashtabula County)	44041
Driftwood (Lake County)	44041
Drinkle	43102
Dry Ridge (Part of Cincinnati)	45249
Dry Run	45662
Dublin (Franklin County)	43017
Dublin (Mercer County) (Township)	45882
Dublin Village Center (Part of Dublin)	43017
Duchouquet (Township)	45895
Dudley (Township)	43326
Duffy	43946
Duke	45657
Dull	45874
Dumontville	43130
Dunbridge	43414
Duncan Falls	43734
Dundas	45634
Dundee	44624
Dungannon (Columbiana County)	44423
Dungannon (Noble County)	45721
Dunglen	43917
Dunham (Township)	45784
Dunkinsville	45660
Dunkirk	45836
Dunlap	45239
Dupont	45837
Durbin (Clark County)	45502
Durbin (Mercer County)	45822
Duvalls	43137
Dyesville	45769
Eagle (Brown County) (Township)	45171
Eagle (Hancock County) (Township)	45881
Eagle (Vinton County) (Township)	43152
Eagle Beach	43452
Eagle City	45504
Eagle Mills	45647
Eagle Point Colony (Part of Rossford)	43460
Eagleport	43756
Eagleville (Ashtabula County)	44047
Eagleville (Wood County)	44817
Earl Peters	43130
East (Township)	44427
East Akron (Part of Akron)	44305
East Alliance	44601
East Ashtabula (Part of Ashtabula)	44004
East Bass Lake	44024
East Batavia Heights	45103
East Cadiz	43907
East Canton	44730
East Carlisle	44035
East Claridon	44033
East Clayton	45764
East Cleveland	44112
East Conneaut (Part of Conneaut)	44030
East Danville	45133
East Defiance (Part of Defiance)	43512
East Delphos (Part of Delphos)	45833
East End (Columbiana County)	43920
East End (Hamilton County)	45226
East Fairfield	44408
East Fultonham	43735
Eastgate Shopping Center (Part of Mayfield Heights)	44125
East Goshen	44609
East Greenville	44666
Eastlake	44094
Eastland Shopping Center (Part of Columbus)	43232
East Lawn	43447
East Lewistown	44408
East Liberty (Logan County)	43319
East Liberty (Summit County)	44319
East Liverpool	43920
East Mansfield	44905
East Mecca	44410
East Millersport	43046
East Millfield	45761
East Monroe	45135
East Norwalk	44857
East Norwood (Hamilton County)	45212
East Norwood (Washington County)	45750
Easton	44270
East Orwell (Part of Orwell)	44076

East Side-Fountain Park **OHIO** 417

	ZIP
East Side (Part of Youngstown)	44506
East Sparta	44626
East Springfield	43925
East Townsend	44826
East Trumbull	44084
East Union (Noble County)	43779
East Union (Wayne County) (Township)	44606
East View (Jefferson Co.)	43938
Eastview (Montgomery County)	45431
Eastwood	45154
Eastwood Mall (Part of Niles)	44446
Eaton (Lorain County) (Township)	44035
Eaton (Preble County)	45320
Eaton Estates	44044
Eber	43160
Echo	43940
Echo Glen Lake	44233
Eckmansville	45697
Eden (Licking County) (Township)	43071
Eden (Seneca County) (Township)	44845
Eden (Wyandot County) (Township)	44849
Eden Park	45662
Edenton	45122
Edenville	44849
Edgefield (Fayette County)	43128
Edgefield (Stark County)	44709
Edgemont	45216
Edgerton	43517
Edgewater (Part of Lakewood)	44107
Edgewater Beach	43076
Edgewater Park	43227
Edgewood	44004
Edgwood Estates	45805
Edinburg (Township)	44272
Edinburg	44272
Edison	43320
Edon	43518
Egypt (Auglaize County)	45865
Egypt (Belmont County)	43713
Eifort	45682
Eileen Gardens	45238
Elba	45746
Elberta Beach (Part of Vermilion)	44089
Eldean	45373
Eldon	44773
Eldorado (Butler County)	45042
Eldorado (Preble County)	45321
Elery	43535
Elgin	45838
Elida	45807
Elizabeth (Lawrence County) (Township)	45659
Elizabeth (Miami County) (Township)	45312
Elizabethtown (Hamilton County)	45052
Elizabethtown (Warren County)	45005
Elk (Noble County) (Township)	45745
Elk (Vinton County) (Township)	45651
Elkrun (Township)	44415
Elkton	44415
Ellerton	45342
Ellet (Part of Akron)	44312
Elliot	43728
Elliottville	45701
Ellis	43701
Ellisonville	45638
Elliston	43432
Ellsberry	45101
Ellsworth	44416
Ellsworth (Township)	44416
Elm Acres	44646
Elm Grove	45661
Elmira	43502
Elmore	43416
Elmville	45133
Elmwood Place	45216
Elroy	45303
Elton	44662
Elyria	44035-39
For specific Elyria Zip Codes call (216) 323-7400	
Emerald (Adams County)	45697
Emerald (Paulding County) (Township)	45879
Emerson	43917
Emerson Heights (Part of Marietta)	45750

	ZIP
Emery Chapel	45502
Empire	43926
Enchanted Hills	45133
England Station	44805
Englewood	45322
Enoch (Township)	43724
Enon	45323
Enterprise (Hocking County)	43138
Enterprise (Preble County)	45381
Epworth	44903
Epworth Heights	45140
Era	43143
Erastus	45822
Erhart	44256
Erie (Township)	43439
Erieview (Part of Cleveland)	44199
Eris	43078
Erlin	43420
Espyville	45302
Essex	43344
Etna	43018
Etna (Township)	43018
Euclid	44117
Euclid Heights (Part of Middletown)	45042
Euclid Square Mall (Part of Euclid)	44132
Eureka	44408
Evansport	43519
Evansville	44440
Evendale	45241
Everett	44264
Evergreen (Gallia County)	45614
Evergreen (Washington County)	45750
Ewing	43138
Ewington	45686
Excello	45044
Fairborn	45324
Fairbrondt	44833
Fairdale	43725
Fairfax (Hamilton County)	45227
Fairfax (Highland County)	45133
Fairfield	45014
Fairfield (Township)	45014
Fairfield (Columbiana County) (Township)	44408
Fairfield (Highland County) (Township)	45135
Fairfield (Huron County) (Township)	44855
Fairfield (Jefferson County)	43944
Fairfield (Madison County) (Township)	43162
Fairfield (Tuscarawas County) (Township)	44678
Fairfield (Washington County) (Township)	45724
Fairfield Beach	43076
Fairground Acres	45107
Fairhaven	45003
Fairhope	44641
Fairlawn	44313
Fairlawn Heights	44484
Fair Oaks	45102
Fairplay (Butler County)	45014
Fairplay (Jefferson County)	43910
Fairpoint	43927
Fairport Harbor	44077
Fairview (Guernsey County)	43736 43772
For specific Fairview (Guernsey County) Zip Codes call (614) 679-2702	
Fairview (Highland County)	45133
Fairview Heights (Jefferson County)	43964
Fairview Heights (Washington County)	45750
Fairview Lanes	44870
Fairview Park	44126
Fairway Terrace	45341
Fairway View Estates	45805
Fairwind Acres (Part of Montgomery)	45242
Falls (Hocking County) (Township)	43138
Falls (Muskingum County) (Township)	43701
Fallsburg	43822
Fallsbury (Township)	43822
Fargo	43074
Farmdale	44417
Farmer	43520
Farmer (Township)	43520
Farmers	45146
Farmerstown	43804
Farmersville	45325
Farmington (Belmont Co.)	43912
Farmington (Trumbull County) (Township)	44491

	ZIP
Farnham (Part of Conneaut)	44030
Farrington	45373
Fashion Heights	45238
Fawcett	45616
Fayette (Fulton County)	43521
Fayette (Lawrence County) (Township)	45680
Fayetteville	45118
Fay Gardens	45140
Fearing (Township)	45788
Federal Reserve (Part of Cleveland)	44101
Feed Springs	44683
Feesburg	45119
Felicity	45120
Fernald	45030
Fernell Heights	45244
Fernwood	43952
Ferry (Erie County)	44870
Ferry (Greene County)	45068
Fields Terrace	45619
Filburns Island	45865
Fincastle	45171
Findlater Garden (Part of Cincinnati)	45232
Findlay	45839-40
For specific Findlay Zip Codes call (419) 423-1264	
Findley Gardens	43964
Finneytown	45224
Fire Brick	45656
Fireside	44811
Firestone Park (Part of Akron)	44301
Fishack	43452
Fitchville (Township)	44851
Fitchville	44851
Five Forks	43945
Five Mile	45154
Five Points (Greene County)	45324
Five Points (Mahoning County)	44452
Five Points (Pickaway County)	43143
Five Points (Trumbull County)	44404
Flatiron (Perry County)	43731
Flat Iron (Warren County)	45005
Flatrock (Henry County) (Township)	43545
Flat Rock (Seneca County)	44828
Fleatown	43055
Fleetwood Addition	43040
Fleming	45712
Fletcher	45326
Flint	43085
Floral Acres	45317
Florence (Township)	44814
Florence (Noble County)	43724
Florence (Williams County) (Township)	43518
Florence (Belmont County)	43935
Florence (Erie County)	44814
Florida	43545
Flushing	43977
Flushing (Township)	43977
Fly	45730
Footville	44084
Foraker	45812
Forest	45843
Forestdale	45638
Forest Hills	45502
Forest Hills Estates	45230
Forest Park (Hamilton County)	45240
Forest Park (Montgomery County)	45405
Forest Park Plaza	45405
Forest View	43952
Forestville	45230
Fort Jefferson	45331
Fort Jennings	45844
Fort Loramie	45845
Fort McKinley (Montgomery County)	45426
Fort Meigs Place	43551
Fort Miami Addition (Part of Maumee)	43537
Fort Recovery	45846
Fort Scott Camps	45030
Fort Seneca	44829
Fort Shawnee	45806
Fort Steuben Mall (Part of Steubenville)	43952
Fosters	45039
Fosterville (Part of Youngstown)	44511
Fostoria	44830
Fountain Park	43084

418 OHIO Fort Steuben Mall-Greasy Ridge

Name	ZIP
Fort Steuben Mall (Part of Steubenville)	43952
Fosters	45039
Fosterville (Part of Youngstown)	44511
Fostoria	44830
Fountain Park	43084
Fountain Square (Part of Cincinnati)	45202
Fowler	44418
Fowler (Township)	44418
Fowlers Mill	44024
Fox (Carroll County) (Township)	43945
Fox (Pickaway County)	43113
Foxboro Manor (Part of Vandalia)	45377
Foxborough Commons	44870
Fox Chase	43081
Frank	44811
Frankfort	45628
Franklin (Warren County) (Township)	45005
Franklin (Wayne County) (Township)	44627
Franklin (Adams County) (Township)	45660
Franklin (Brown County) (Township)	45121
Franklin (Clermont County) (Township)	45120
Franklin (Columbiana County) (Township)	43962
Franklin (Coshocton County) (Township)	43811
Franklin (Darke County) (Township)	45304
Franklin (Franklin County) (Township)	43204
Franklin (Fulton County) (Township)	43502
Franklin (Harrison County) (Township)	44699
Franklin (Jackson County) (Township)	45640
Franklin (Licking County) (Township)	43055
Franklin (Mercer County) (Township)	45866
Franklin (Monroe County) (Township)	43754
Franklin (Morrow County) (Township)	43338
Franklin (Portage County) (Township)	44240
Franklin (Richland County) (Township)	44875
Franklin (Ross County) (Township)	45601
Franklin (Shelby County) (Township)	45363
Franklin (Summit County) (Township)	44216
Franklin (Tuscarawas County) (Township)	44680
Franklin (Warren County)	45005
Franklin Furnace	45629
Franklin Park Mall (Part of Toledo)	43623
Franklin Square	44431
Frazeysburg	43822
Frederick (Miami County)	45371
Frederick (Scioto County)	45694
Fredericksburg	44627
Fredericksdale	43779
Fredericktown (Columbiana County)	43920
Fredericktown (Knox County)	43019
Fredonia	43023
Freeburg	44669
Freedom (Portage County) (Township)	44288
Freedom (Wood County) (Township)	43450
Freedom (Henry County) (Township)	43545
Freedom (Portage County)	44288
Freeport	43973
Freeport (Township)	43973
Fremont	43420
Frenchtown (Darke County)	45380
Frenchtown (Seneca County)	43316
Fresno	43824
Friendship	45630
Frischkorn Heights	43968
Frontier Park	45239
Frontier Town	44514
Frost	45723
Fruitdale	45123

Name	ZIP
Fruit Hill	45230
Fryburg (Auglaize County)	45895
Fryburg (Holmes County)	44654
Frys Corners	45331
Frytown	45418
Fulda	43724
Fulton (Fulton County) (Township)	43558
Fulton (Morrow County)	43321
Fultonham	43738
Funk	44691
Fursville	43062
Gabels Corner	43420
Gage	45658
Gageville	44048
Gahanna	43230
Galatea	45872
Galaxy Acres	45239
Galena	43021
Galion	44833
Gallia	45658
Gallipolis	45631
Gallipolis (Township)	45631
Galloway	43119
Gambier	43022
Ganges	44875
Gano	45241
Garden	45735
Garden Acres (Clark County)	45503
Garden Acres (Jefferson County)	43952
Garden City	45694
Garden Hill Top (Part of Cincinnati)	45232
Garden Isle	44254
Garden Terrace (Part of Steubenville)	43952
Garfield	44460
Garfield Heights	44125
Garrettsville	44231
Gaslight Village	45122
Gasper (Township)	45320
Gates Mills	44040
Gath	45171
Gavers	44432
Geauga Lake (Part of Aurora)	44202
Geeburg	44406
Geneva	44041
Geneva (Township)	44041
Geneva	43107
Geneva-on-the-Lake	44041
Genntown	45036
Genoa (Delaware County) (Township)	43081
Genoa (Ottawa County)	43430
Genung Corners	44057
Georges Run	43938
Georgesville	43123
Georgetown	45121
Gepharts	45694
Gerald	43545
German (Auglaize County) (Township)	45869
German (Clark County) (Township)	45504
German (Fulton County) (Township)	43502
German (Harrison County) (Township)	43976
German (Montgomery County) (Township)	45327
Germano	43986
Germantown (Montgomery County)	45327
Germantown (Washington County)	45745
Getaway	45619
Gettysburg (Darke County)	45328
Gettysburg (Preble County)	45347
Geyer	45884
Ghent	44313
Gibisonville	43149
Gibson (Guernsey County)	43778
Gibson (Mercer County) (Township)	45846
Gibsonburg	43431
Gilboa	45875
Gilead (Township)	43338
Gillivan	43140
Gilmore	43837
Ginghamsburg	45371
Girard	44420
Girton	43457
Gist Settlement	45159
Givens	45690
Glade	45613
Gladstone	45314
Glandorf	45848

Name	ZIP
Glasgow (Columbiana County)	43968
Glasgow (Tuscarawas County)	43837
Glass Rock	43739
Glenbrook Acres	45305
Glencoe (Belmont County)	43928
Glencoe (Hamilton County)	45231
Glendale	45246
Glendwell (Part of Steubenville)	43952
Glen Este	45103
Glenford	43739
Glengary Heights	43081
Glen Karn	45332
Glenmary (Part of Fairfield)	45246
Glenmont	44628
Glenmoor	43920
Glenmore	45874
Glenns Run	43935
Glen Robbins	43943
Glen Roy	45692
Glenwillow	44139
Glenwood	45381
Glenwood Acres	44087
Gloria Glens Park	44215
Glouster	45732
Glynwood	45895
Gnadenhutten	44629
Goes	45387
Golden Corners	44214
Golden Gate Shopping Center (Part of Mayfield Heights)	44124
Goldsboro	45692
Golf Manor	45237
Golfway Acres	45239
Gomer	45809
Good Hope (Fayette County)	43160
Good Hope (Hocking County) (Township)	43149
Goodland Acres	44688
Gordon	45329
Gore	43138
Gorham (Clermont County) (Township)	43521
Goshen (Tuscarawas County) (Township)	45122
Goshen (Township)	44663
Goshen (Hardin County) (Township)	43326
Goshen (Mahoning County) (Township)	44460
Goshen (Tuscarawas County)	44663
Goshen (Auglaize County) (Township)	43331
Goshen (Belmont County) (Township)	43719
Goshen (Champaign County) (Township)	43044
Goshen (Clermont County)	45122
Gould Park	43230
Goulds	43938
Graceland Shopping Center (Part of Columbus)	43214
Grafton	44044
Grafton (Township)	44044
Grand (Township)	45843
Grand Prairie (Township)	43302
Grand Rapids	43522
Grand Rapids (Township)	43522
Grand River	44045
Grandview	45767
Grandview (Township)	45767
Grandview Estates (Delaware County)	43015
Grandview Estates (Marion County)	43302
Grandview Heights (Champaign County)	43072
Grandview Heights (Franklin County)	43212
Grandview Homes (Part of Lima)	45804
Grange Hall	43143
Granger	44256
Granger (Township)	44256
Grants	45843
Granville (Licking County)	43023
Granville (Mercer County) (Township)	43023
Granville (Township)	45883
Grape Grove	45335
Gratiot	43740
Gratis (Township)	45330
Gratis	45330
Graysville	45734
Graytown	43432
Greasy Ridge	45678

Greater State Road Shopping Center-Hiett **OHIO** 419

Name	ZIP
Greater State Road Shopping Center (Part of Cuyahoga Falls)	44223
Great Lakes Mall (Part of Mentor)	44060
Great Northern Mall (Part of North Olmsted)	44070
Great Southern Shoppers City (Part of Columbus)	43207
Great Western Shoppers Mart (Part of Columbus)	43213
Green (Adams County) (Township)	45684
Green (Ashland County) (Township)	44842
Green (Brown County) (Township)	45154
Green (Clark County) (Township)	45502
Green (Clinton County) (Township)	45159
Green (Fayette County) (Township)	45135
Green (Gallia County) (Township)	45658
Green (Hamilton County) (Township)	45211
Green (Harrison County) (Township)	43976
Green (Hocking County) (Township)	43138
Green (Mahoning County) (Township)	44406
Green (Monroe County) (Township)	43793
Green (Ross County) (Township)	45644
Green (Scioto County) (Township)	45629
Green (Shelby County) (Township)	45365
Green (Summit County) (Township)	44720
Green (Wayne County) (Township)	44667
Green Acres	45042
Greenbush	45064
Green Camp (Township)	43322
Green Camp	43322
Greencastle	43112
Green Creek (Township)	43410
Greendale	43138
Greene (Township)	44450
Greenfield (Fairfield County) (Township)	43130
Greenfield (Gallia County) (Township)	45658
Greenfield (Highland County)	45123
Greenfield (Huron County) (Township)	44855
Greenfield Village	45224
Greenford	44422
Green Hills (Greene County)	45324
Greenhills (Hamilton County)	45218
Greenland	43115
Greenlex	43302
Green Meadows	45323
Greenmount (Part of Kettering)	45429
Greensburg (Putnam County) (Township)	45875
Greensburg (Summit County)	44232
Green Springs	44836
Greens Run	45732
Greens Store	45640
Greentown (Jefferson County)	43948
Greentown (Stark County)	44630
Greenview	45415
Greenville	45331
Greenville (Township)	45331
Greenwich	44837
Greenwich (Township)	44837
Greenwood	43780
Greer	44628
Grelton	43523
Griffith (Part of North Bend)	45052
Griggs	44047
Grimms Bridge	43920
Groesbeck	45239
Groton (Township)	44839
Grove City	43123
Groveport	43125
Grover Hill	45849
Guerne	44691
Guernsey	43749
Guilford (Columbiana County)	44432
Guilford (Medina County) (Township)	44273
Gunnerville	45335
Gurneyville	45177
Gustavus	44417
Gustavus (Township)	44417
Gutman	45884
Guyan (Township)	45623
Guysville	45735
Gypsum	43433
Hackney	45715
Hagan Addition	43901
Hageman Junction	45036
Hale (Township)	43340
Haley's Subdivision	44622
Hallock	43506
Halisville	45633
Hambden	44024
Hambden (Township)	44024
Hamburg (Fairfield County)	43130
Hamburg (Preble County)	45321
Hamden	45634
Hamer (Township)	45133
Hamersville	45130
Hametown (Part of Norton)	44203
Hamilton	45011-15
For specific Hamilton Zip Codes call (513) 867-8877	
Hamilton (Franklin County) (Township)	43137
Hamilton (Jackson County) (Township)	45656
Hamilton (Lawrence County) (Township)	45638
Hamilton (Warren County) (Township)	45039
Hamilton Meadows	43207
Hamler	43524
Hamlet	45102
Hamley Run	45701
Hammansburg	43413
Hammondsville	43930
Hampton Woods	45502
Hanersville	45631
Hanging Rock	45638
Hanley Village	44904
Hanna Hills	44266
Hannibal	43931
Hanover (Township)	43055
Hanover	43055
Hanover (Ashland County) (Township)	44842
Hanover (Butler County) (Township)	45013
Hanover (Columbiana County) (Township)	44625
Hanover (Harrison County)	43988
Hanoverton	44423
Hanville Corners	44855
Happy Hollow	44626
Harbor (Part of Ashtabula)	44004
Harbor Hills	43025
Harbor Point	45822
Harbor View	43434
Hardin (Shelby County)	45365
Harding (Lucas County) (Township)	43558
Harding (Muskingum County)	43701
Hardy (Township)	44654
Harewood Acres	45236
Harlan (Township)	45162
Harlan Park (Part of Middletown)	45042
Harlem	43021
Harlem (Township)	43021
Harlem Springs	44631
Harmer (Part of Marietta)	45750
Harmon	44662
Harmons Landing	45885
Harmony	45502
Harmony (Clark County) (Township)	45502
Harmony (Morrow County) (Township)	43315
Harper	43311
Harpersfield	44041
Harpersfield (Township)	44041
Harpster	43323
Harriett (Guernsey County)	43725
Harriett (Highland County)	45133
Harriettsville	45745
Harris (Township)	43416
Harrisburg (Franklin County)	43126
Harrisburg (Gallia County)	45614
Harrisburg (Stark County)	44641
Harrison (Carroll County) (Township)	44615
Harrison (Champaign County) (Township)	43357
Harrison (Darke County) (Township)	45346
Harrison (Gallia County) (Township)	45631
Harrison (Hamilton County) (Township)	45030
Harrison (Henry County) (Township)	43545
Harrison (Knox County) (Township)	43022
Harrison (Licking County) (Township)	43033
Harrison (Logan County) (Township)	43311
Harrison (Montgomery County) (Township)	45415
Harrison (Muskingum County) (Township)	43771
Harrison (Paulding County) (Township)	45880
Harrison (Perry County) (Township)	43731
Harrison (Pickaway County) (Township)	43103
Harrison (Preble County) (Township)	45338
Harrison (Ross County) (Township)	45601
Harrison (Scioto County) (Township)	45653
Harrison (Van Wert County) (Township)	45891
Harrison (Vinton County) (Township)	45647
Harrison (Hamilton County)	45030
Harrison Mills	45682
Harrisonville	45769
Harrisville (Harrison County)	43974
Harrisville (Medina County) (Township)	44214
Harrod	45850
Harshasville	45660
Hartford (Township)	44424
Hartford (Licking County) (Township)	43013
Hartford (Trumbull County)	44424
Hartland	44826
Hartland (Township)	44857
Hartland Center	44826
Hartsgrove	44085
Hartsgrove (Township)	44085
Hartshorn	45734
Hartville	44632
Harveysburg	45032
Haskins	43525
Hasting Hill	45662
Hatch	45661
Hatton	43457
Havana	44890
Havens Corners	43004
Havensport	43112
Haven View	45373
Haverhill	45636
Haviland	45851
Hayden	43002
Haydenville	43127
Hayes Colony (Part of Delaware)	43015
Hayes Corners	44062
Hayesville	44838
Haynes	43135
Hazelwood (Part of Blue Ash)	45242
Heath	43056
Heatherdowns (Part of Toledo)	43614
Hebbardsville	45701
Hebron	43025
Hecla	45638
Hegemans Landing	45865
Heidelburg Beach	44089
Helena	43435
Helmick	43844
Hemlock	43730
Hemlock Grove	45769
Hempstead (Part of Kettering)	45429
Hendrysburg	43713
Henley	45652
Henrietta (Township)	44889
Henry (Township)	45872
Hepburn	43326
Heritage	45805
Heritage Hills	44087
Heritage Park	44212
Hessville	43431
Hickman	43055
Hicksville	43526
Hicksville (Township)	43526
Hide-A-Way Hills	43107
Hiett	45101

420 OHIO Higginsport-Jamestown

	ZIP
Higginsport	45131
Highland (Defiance County) (Township)	43512
Highland (Highland County)	45132
Highland (Muskingum County) (Township)	43762
Highland Heights	44124
Highland Holliday	45133
Highland Park (Hamilton County)	45238
Highland Park (Mercer County)	45822
Highland Park (Scioto County)	45629
Highland Park (Stark County)	44646
Highland Park (Warren County)	45065
Highlands (Part of Springfield)	45503
Highland Terrace	43950
Highlandtown	43945
Highland Trails	45133
Highpoint	45242
High Water	43055
Hill Addition	43920
Hill And Hollow (Part of Oxford)	45056
Hillcrest (Columbiana County)	43968
Hillcrest (Warren County)	45036
Hillcrest (Williams County)	43543
Hill Grove	45390
Hilliar (Township)	43011
Hilliard	43026
Hills and Dales (Montgomery County)	45429
Hills and Dales (Stark County)	44708
Hillsboro (Highland County)	45133
Hillsboro (Jefferson County)	43938
Hilltop (Franklin County)	43204
Hilltop (Trumbull County)	44437
Hilltop Acres (Part of Wyoming)	45215
Hinckley	44233
Hinckley (Township)	44233
Hiram	44234
Hiram (Township)	44234
Hiram Rapids	44234
Hiramsburg	43732
Hitchcock	45656
Hoagland	45133
Hoaglin (Township)	45891
Hobson	45760
Hocking (Township)	43130
Hocking Correctional Facility	45764
Hockingport	45739
Hoke	45383
Holden	45896
Holgate	43527
Holiday Acres	45236
Holiday Hills	45502
Holiday Lakes	44890
Holiday Valley	45324
Holland	43528
Hollansburg	45332
Hollister	45732
Holloway	43985
Hollowtown	45171
Holman-Stonybrook Shopping Center (Part of Loveland)	45140
Holmes (Township)	44820
Holmesville	44633
Home Acres (Butler County)	45042
Home Acres (Miami County)	45373
Homedale (Part of Columbus)	43085
Homer (Licking County)	43027
Homer (Medina County) (Township)	44235
Homer (Morgan County) (Township)	45732
Homerville	44235
Homeside	43950
Homeville	44870
Homewood	45015
Homeworth	44634
Honeytown	44691
Hooker	43130
Hooksburg	43787
Hooring	45766
Hooven	45033
Hopedale	43976
Hopetown	45601
Hopewell (Township)	43746
Hopewell (Perry County) (Township)	43739
Hopewell (Seneca County) (Township)	44809

	ZIP
Hopewell (Jefferson County)	43943
Hopewell (Licking County) (Township)	43740
Hopewell (Mercer County) (Township)	45822
Hopewell (Muskingum County)	43746
Hopkinsville	45039
Horatio	45331
Horns Mill	43130
Hoskinsville	43724
Houcktown	45814
Houston	45333
Howard	43028
Howard (Township)	43028
Howenstein	44626
Howland	44484
Howland (Township)	44484
Hoytville	43529
Hubbard	44425
Hubbard (Township)	44425
Huber Heights	45424
Huber Ridge	43081
Huber South	45439
Hudson	44236
Hudson (Township)	44236
Hue	45622
Hughes	45042
Hulington	45106
Humboldt	45612
Hume	45806
Hunt	45050
Hunter (Belmont County)	43719
Hunter (Warren County)	45005
Hunterdon	45732
Huntington (Lorain County) (Township)	44090
Huntington (Ross County) (Township)	45601
Huntington (Brown County) (Township)	45101
Huntington (Gallia County) (Township)	45686
Huntington (Lorain County)	44090
Huntington Park (Part of Aberdeen)	45101
Hunting Valley	44022
Huntsburg	44046
Huntsburg (Township)	44046
Hunts Corners	44811
Huntsville (Butler County)	45042
Huntsville (Logan County)	43324
Hurford	43901
Huron	44839
Huron (Township)	44839
Hustead	45502
Hyatts	43065
Hyde Park (Hamilton County)	45208
Hyde Park (Montgomery County)	45429
Hyde Park Plaza (Part of Cincinnati)	45209
Iberia	43325
Idaho	45661
Iler	44830
Ilesboro	43138
Immergrun (Part of Oregon)	43618
Independence (Cuyahoga County)	44131
Independence (Defiance County)	43512
Independence (Washington County) (Township)	45767
Indian Camp	43725
Indian Knolls (Part of Milford)	45150
Indian Ridge	45231
Indianview	45147
Ingle Mann (Part of New Paris)	45347
Ingomar	45381
Ink	44883
Ira	44313
Iradale	44313
Irondale (Jefferson County)	43932
Irondale (Muskingum County)	43821
Ironspot	43777
Ironton	45638
Irvington	45414
Irwin	43029
Island Creek (Township)	43964
Island View	43331
Isle Saint George	43436
Isleta	43845
Israel (Township)	45003
Ithaca	45304
Ivorydale (Part of St. Bernard)	45217

	ZIP
Ivorydale Junction (Part of St. Bernard)	45217
Jackson (Allen County) (Township)	45854
Jackson (Ashland County) (Township)	44287
Jackson (Auglaize County) (Township)	45865
Jackson (Brown County) (Township)	45697
Jackson (Champaign County) (Township)	45389
Jackson (Clermont County) (Township)	45145
Jackson (Coshocton County) (Township)	43812
Jackson (Crawford County) (Township)	44827
Jackson (Darke County) (Township)	45390
Jackson (Franklin County) (Township)	43123
Jackson (Guernsey County) (Township)	43723
Jackson (Hancock County) (Township)	45814
Jackson (Hardin County) (Township)	45843
Jackson (Highland County) (Township)	45133
Jackson (Jackson County)	45640
Jackson (Jackson County) (Township)	45640
Jackson (Knox County) (Township)	43005
Jackson (Mahoning County) (Township)	44451
Jackson (Monroe County) (Township)	45730
Jackson (Montgomery County) (Township)	45325
Jackson (Muskingum County) (Township)	43822
Jackson (Noble County) (Township)	45727
Jackson (Paulding County) (Township)	45855
Jackson (Perry County) (Township)	43748
Jackson (Pickaway County) (Township)	43113
Jackson (Pike County) (Township)	45690
Jackson (Preble County) (Township)	45320
Jackson (Putnam County) (Township)	45844
Jackson (Richland County) (Township)	44875
Jackson (Sandusky County) (Township)	43407
Jackson (Seneca County) (Township)	44830
Jackson (Shelby County) (Township)	45334
Jackson (Stark County) (Township)	44646
Jackson (Union County) (Township)	43344
Jackson (Van Wert County) (Township)	45863
Jackson (Vinton County) (Township)	45651
Jackson (Wood County) (Township)	43529
Jackson (Wyandot County) (Township)	45843
Jackson Belden	44718
Jacksonburg	45067
Jackson Center (Mahoning County)	44451
Jackson Center (Shelby County)	45334
Jackson Heights (Clark County)	45504
Jackson Heights (Jackson County)	45640
Jackson Heights (Jefferson County)	43943
Jackson Lake	45656
Jacksontown	43030
Jacksonville (Adams County)	45660
Jacksonville (Athens County)	45740
Jacksonville (Clark County)	45502
Jacktown	45042
Jacobsburg	43933
Jaite (Part of Brecksville)	44141
Jamestown	45335

Jasper-Lee **OHIO** **421**

	ZIP		ZIP		ZIP
Jasper (Fayette County) (Township)	43128	Kamms (Part of Cleveland)	44111	La Croft	43920
Jasper (Pike County)	45642	Kanauga	45631	Lafayette (Township)	44256
Jasper Mills	43160	Kansas	44841	Lafayette (Allen County)	45854
Jays	45331	Kay	45005	Lafayette (Coshocton County) (Township)	43845
Jefferson (Adams County) (Township)	45684	Keays (Part of Middletown)	45042	Lafayette (Madison County)	43140
Jefferson (Ashtabula County) (Township)	44047	Keene	43828	Lafayette (Medina County)	44256
Jefferson (Brown County) (Township)	45168	Keene (Township)	43828	Lafferty	43951
Jefferson (Clinton County) (Township)	45148	Keist Manor	44130	Lagrange (Township)	44050
Jefferson (Coshocton County) (Township)	43844	Keith	43724	La Grange (Lawrence County)	45638
Jefferson (Crawford County) (Township)	44827	Kelleys Island	43438	Lagrange (Lorain County)	44050
Jefferson (Fairfield County)	43112	Kellogg Corners	44410	Laings	43752
Jefferson (Fayette County) (Township)	43128	Kelloggsville	44030	Lake (Ashland County) (Township)	44628
Jefferson (Franklin County) (Township)	43004	Kemp	45806	Lake (Logan County) (Township)	43311
Jefferson (Greene County) (Township)	45335	Kendall Heights	44646	Lake (Stark County) (Township)	44720
Jefferson (Guernsey County) (Township)	43755	Kenmore (Part of Akron)	44314	Lake (Wood County) (Township)	43447
Jefferson (Jackson County) (Township)	45656	Kennard	44009	Lake Cable	44718
Jefferson (Knox County) (Township)	44628	Kennonsburg	43773	Lake Darby	43204
Jefferson (Logan County) (Township)	43311	Keno	45743	Lake Fork	44840
Jefferson (Madison County) (Township)	43162	Kenridge (Part of Blue Ash)	45242	Lakeline	44094
Jefferson (Mercer County) (Township)	45822	Kensington	44427	Lake Lorelei	45118
Jefferson (Montgomery County) (Township)	45345	Kensington Park	45305	Lake Lucerne	44022
Jefferson (Muskingum County) (Township)	43821	Kent (Portage County)	44240	Lake Milton	44429
Jefferson (Noble County) (Township)	43724	Kenton	43326	Lakemore	44250
Jefferson (Preble County) (Township)	45347	Kenwood (Hamilton County)	45236	Lake of the Woods	43021
Jefferson (Richland County) (Township)	44813	Kenwood (Harrison County)	43901	Lake O'Springs	44718
Jefferson (Ross County) (Township)	45601	Kenwood (Lucas County)	43606	Lake Seneca	43543
Jefferson (Scioto County) (Township)	45648	Kenwood Heights (Part of Springfield)	45505	Lakeside (Butler County)	45042
Jefferson (Tuscarawas County) (Township)	43840	Kenwood Knolls	45236	Lakeside (Fairfield County)	43046
Jefferson (Ashtabula County)	44047	Kenwood Mall	45236	Lakeside (Licking County)	43008
Jefferson (Wayne County)	44691	Kenwood Towne Center	45236	Lakeside (Ottawa County)	43440
Jefferson (Williams County) (Township)	43543	Kerr	45643	Lakeside-Marblehead (Part of Marblehead)	43440
Jefferson Estates	43113	Kessler	45383	Lake Slagle	44720
Jefferson Heights	43938	Kettering	45429	Lake Sylvan	45369
Jeffersonville	43128	Kettlersville	45336	Lake View (Knox County)	43019
Jelloway	43014	Key	43906	Lakeview (Logan County)	43331
Jenera	45841	Kidron	44636	Lakeview Heights	45690
Jenkins Addition	43701	Kieferville	45831	Lakeville (Ashtabula County)	44030
Jennings (Putnam County) (Township)	45844	Kilbourne	43032	Lakeville (Holmes County)	44638
Jennings (Van Wert County) (Township)	45894	Kile	43064	Lake Waynoka	45171
Jep	45659	Kilgore	43988	Lakewood	44107
Jericho	45042	Killbuck	44637	Lakota Hills	45069
Jerome	43064	Killbuck (Township)	44637	Lamira	43718
Jerome (Township)	43064	Kilvert	45778	Lancaster	43130
Jeromesville	44840	Kimball	44847	Landeck	45833
Jerry City	43437	Kimberly	45764	Landen	45040
Jersey	43062	Kimbolton	43749	Langsville	45741
Jersey (Township)	43062	King Mines	45177	Lanier (Township)	45381
Jerusalem (Lucas County) (Township)	43412	Kings Corners	43755	Lansing	43934
Jerusalem (Monroe County)	43747	Kings Creek	44904	LaPorte	44035
Jewell	43530	Kingsgate	43078	La Rue	43332
Jewett	43986	Kings Mills	45231	Latcha	43447
Jobs	45732	Kingston (Delaware County) (Township)	45034	Latham	45646
Johnson (Township)	43072	Kingston (Ross County)	43074	Latimer	44428
Johnsons Corners (Part of Barberton)	44203	Kingsville	45644	Lattasburg	44287
Johnston	44417	Kingsville (Township)	44048	Lattasville	45628
Johnston (Township)	44417	Kingsville On-the-Lake (Part of North Kingsville)	44048	Latty (Paulding County)	45855
Johnston	44622	Kingsway	44068	Latty (Paulding County) (Township)	45849
Johnstown	43031	Kinnickinnick	43420	Laura	45337
Johnsville (Part of New Lebanon)	45345	Kinsman (Township)	45601	Laurel (Clermont County)	45157
Jonesboro (Clinton County)	45146	Kinsman (Belmont County)	44428	Laurel (Hocking County) (Township)	43149
Jonesboro (Fayette County)	43160	Kinsman (Trumbull County)	43950	Laurel Creek	44212
Jonestown	45894	Kiousville	44428	Laurel Ridge	44721
Jordanville	44432	Kipling	43143	Laurelville	43135
Joy	43728	Kipton	43750	Lawco Lake	45659
Jug Run	43917	Kirby	44049	Lawndale (Part of Massillon)	44646
Jump	43326	Kirkersville	43330	Lawrence (Lawrence County)	45659
Junction	43512	Kirkpatrick	43033	Lawrence (Lawrence County) (Township)	45645
Junction City	43748	Kirkwood (Belmont County) (Township)	43302	Lawrence (Stark County) (Township)	44614
Justus	44662	Kirkwood (Shelby County)	43713	Lawrence (Tuscarawas County) (Township)	44612
Kalida	45853	Kirkwood Heights	45365	Lawrence (Washington County) (Township)	45750
		Kirtland	43912	Lawrenceville	45502
		Kirtland Hills	44094	Lawshe	45660
		Kitchen	44060	Layhigh	45013
		Kitts Hill	45656	Layland	44637
		Kiwanis Lake	45645	Layman	45724
		Klondike	44065	Leavittsburg	44430
		Knollwood (Part of Beavercreek)	44410	Leavittsville	44614
		Knollwood Village	45432	Lebanon (Meigs County) (Township)	45770
		Knox (Columbiana County) (Township)	43113	Lebanon (Monroe County)	45745
		Knox (Guernsey County) (Township)	44634	Lebanon (Warren County)	45036
		Knox (Holmes County) (Township)	43725	Lebanon Correctional Institution	45036
		Knox (Jefferson County) (Township)	44638	Lecta	45678
		Knox (Vinton County) (Township)	43964	Lee (Athens County) (Township)	45710
		Knoxville	45710		
		Kolmont	43964		
		Kossuth	43938		
		Kunkle	45883		
		Kyger	43531		
		Kylesburg	45620		
		Lacarne	43025		
			43439		

422 OHIO Lee-Madeira

Name	ZIP
Lee (Carroll County) (Township)	44615
Lee (Cuyahoga County)	44120
Lee (Monroe County) (Township)	43946
Leesburg (Highland County)	45135
Leesburg (Union County) (Township)	43040
Lees Creek	45138
Leesville	44639
Leesville Cross Roads	44827
Leetonia	44431
Lehmkuhl Landing	45865
Leipsic	45856
Leipsic Junction (Part of Leipsic)	45856
Leistville	43113
Lemert	44882
Lemon (Township)	45050
Lemoyne	43441
Lena	45317
Lenox	44047
Lenox (Township)	44047
Leo	45640
Leon	44032
Leonardsburg	43015
Lerado	45176
Leroy (Township)	44077
Le Sourdsville	45042
Lester	44256
Letart (Township)	45771
Letart Falls	45771
Levanna	45167
Lewis (Township)	45121
Lewis Addition	43952
Lewisburg	45338
Lewis Center	43035
Lewistown	43333
Lewisville	43754
Lexington (Township)	44601
Lexington (Richland County)	44904
Lexington (Stark County)	44601
Liberty (Adams County) (Township)	45693
Liberty (Butler County) (Township)	45011
Liberty (Clinton County) (Township)	45177
Liberty (Crawford County) (Township)	44881
Liberty (Darke County) (Township)	45352
Liberty (Delaware County) (Township)	43065
Liberty (Fairfield County) (Township)	43105
Liberty (Guernsey County) (Township)	43725
Liberty (Hancock County) (Township)	45840
Liberty (Hardin County) (Township)	45810
Liberty (Henry County) (Township)	43532
Liberty (Highland County) (Township)	45133
Liberty (Jackson County) (Township)	45640
Liberty (Knox County) (Township)	43050
Liberty (Licking County) (Township)	43031
Liberty (Logan County) (Township)	43357
Liberty (Mercer County) (Township)	45882
Liberty (Montgomery County)	45418
Liberty (Putnam County) (Township)	45856
Liberty (Ross County) (Township)	45647
Liberty (Seneca County) (Township)	44841
Liberty (Trumbull County) (Township)	44420
Liberty (Union County) (Township)	43040
Liberty (Van Wert County) (Township)	45891
Liberty (Washington County) (Township)	45745
Liberty (Wood County) (Township)	43462
Liberty Center	43532
Liberty Plaza	44505
Lick (Township)	45640
Licking (Licking County) (Township)	43076
Licking (Muskingum County) (Township)	43830

Name	ZIP
Licking View	43701
Lickskillet	45647
Liebs Island	43046
Lightsville	45362
Lilly Chapel	43140
Lima	45801-09
For specific Lima Zip Codes call (419) 228-7765	
Lima (Township)	43073
Limaville	44640
Lime City	43551
Limecrest	45502
Limerick	45601
Limestone	43432
Limestone City	45506
Lincoln (Morrow County) (Township)	43321
Lincoln (Richland County)	44905
Lincoln Heights (Hamilton County)	45215
Lincoln Heights (Richland County)	44903
Lincoln Village	43228
Lindair Estates	45502
Lindale	45102
Lindentree	44656
Lindenwald (Part of Hamilton)	45015
Lindsey	43442
Lindsley-Gay	44003
Linndale	44111
Linneman	45804
Linnville (Lawrence County)	45696
Linnville (Licking County)	43076
Linton (Township)	43836
Linworth	43085
Lippincotts	43078
Lisbon (Clark County)	45368
Lisbon (Columbiana County)	44432
Lisman	45659
Litchfield	44253
Litchfield (Township)	44253
Lithopolis	43136
Little Farms	43228
Little Hocking	45742
Little Sandusky	43323
Little Walnut	43113
Little Washington	44903
Little York	45414
Liverpool (Columbiana County) (Township)	43920
Liverpool (Medina County) (Township)	44280
Livingston (Part of Columbus)	43227
Lloydsville	43950
Lock	43011
Lockbourne	43137
Lockington	45356
Lockland	45215
Lock Two	45869
Lockville	43112
Lockwood	44450
Lockwood Corners	44319
Locust Corner	45245
Locust Grove (Adams County)	45660
Locust Grove (Butler County)	45042
Locust Grove (Mahoning County)	44460
Locust Lake	45102
Locust Point	43449
Locust Ridge	45176
Lodi (Athens County) (Township)	45735
Lodi (Medina County)	44254
Logan (Auglaize County) (Township)	45887
Logan (Hocking County)	43138
Logan Elm Village	43113
Logansville	43318
Logtown	43432
Lombardsville	45652
London (Madison County)	43140
London (Richland County)	44875
London Correctional Institution	43140
Londonderry (Guernsey County)	43973
Londonderry (Township)	43973
Londonderry (Ross County)	45647
Long	45331
Long Beach	43449
Long Bottom	45743
Long Lake	44638
Long Run	43917
Longs Crossing	44431
Longstreth	45764

Name	ZIP
Longview Heights (Part of Athens)	45701
Longvue (Part of Marietta)	45750
Loomis	43718
Lorain	44052-55
For specific Lorain Zip Codes call (216) 244-4221	
Loramie (Township)	45363
Lordstown	44481
Lore City	43755
Lostcreek (Township)	45312
Lost Creek Addition	45804
Lottridge	45723
Louden (Adams County)	45660
Louden (Tuscarawas County)	44622
Loudon (Carroll County) (Township)	44615
Loudon (Seneca County) (Township)	44830
Loudonville	44842
Louisville (Adams County)	45660
Louisville (Stark County)	44641
Loveland	45140
Loveland Park	45140
Lovell	43351
Lowell	45744
Lowellville	44436
Lowellville Junction (Part of Lowellville)	44436
Lower Salem	45745
Loyal Oak (Part of Norton)	44203
Lucas	44843
Lucasburg	43723
Lucasville	45648
Lucerne	43019
Luckey	43443
Ludington	43730
Ludlow (Township)	45774
Ludlow Falls	45339
Lugbill Addition (Part of Archbold)	43502
Lumberton	45177
Luray	43025
Lush Addition	43302
Lykens	44818
Lykens (Township)	44818
Lyme (Township)	44811
Lynchburg (Columbiana County)	44427
Lynchburg (Highland County)	45142
Lyndhurst	44124
Lyndhurst-Mayfield Heights (Part of Mayfield Heights)	44124
Lyndon	45681
Lynn (Township)	43326
Lynns Corners	44406
Lynx	45650
Lyons	43533
Lyra	45694
Lytle	45068
McArthur (Logan County) (Township)	43324
McArthur (Vinton County)	45651
McCance	44627
Mc Cappin Mill	45133
McCartyville	45302
McClaimsville	43143
McClainville	43906
McClintocksburg	44444
McClure	43534
McComb	45858
McConnelsville	43756
McCracken Corners	44460
McCuneville	43782
McCutchenville	44844
McDermott	45652
McDonald (Hardin County) (Township)	43326
McDonald (Trumbull County)	44437
McDonaldsville	44720
Macedon	45828
Macedonia	44056
McGill	45880
McGonigle	45013
Mc Gough	43050
McGuffey	45859
McIntyre	43910
Mack	45211
McKay	44842
McKean (Township)	43055
McKinley Heights	44446
Macksburg	45746
Mackstown	43081
McLean (Township)	45845
McLuney	43731
Macon	45697
McZena	44638
Madeira	45243

Madison-Middleton **OHIO** **423**

	ZIP
Madison (Butler County) (Township)	45042
Madison (Clark County) (Township)	45368
Madison (Columbiana County) (Township)	43968
Madison (Fairfield County) (Township)	43130
Madison (Fayette County) (Township)	43160
Madison (Franklin County) (Township)	43125
Madison (Guernsey County) (Township)	43773
Madison (Hancock County) (Township)	45814
Madison (Highland County) (Township)	45123
Madison (Jackson County) (Township)	45656
Madison (Lake County) (Township)	44057
Madison (Licking County) (Township)	43055
Madison (Montgomery County) (Township)	45426
Madison (Muskingum County) (Township)	43821
Madison (Perry County) (Township)	43760
Madison (Pickaway County) (Township)	43103
Madison (Richland County) (Township)	44903
Madison (Sandusky County) (Township)	43435
Madison (Scioto County) (Township)	45653
Madison (Vinton County) (Township)	45698
Madison (Williams County) (Township)	43554
Madison (Lake County)	44057
Madisonburg	44691
Madison Correctional Institution	43140
Madison Golf Lakelands	44057
Madison Lake Area	43140
Madison Mills	43143
Madison-on-the-Lake	44057
Madisonville (Part of Cincinnati)	45227
Mad River (Champaign County) (Township)	43083
Mad River (Clark County) (Township)	45324
Mad River (Montgomery County) (Township)	45424
Magnetic Springs	43036
Magnolia	44643
Mahoning	44231
Maineville	45039
Mainsville	43764
Malaga	43757
Malaga (Township)	43757
Malinta	43535
Mallet Creek	44256
Malta	43758
Malta (Township)	43758
Malvern	44644
Manchester	45144
Manchester (Township)	45144
Manchester (Morgan County) (Township)	43756
Manchester (Summit County)	44216
Mandale	45827
Manhattan (Part of Steubenville)	43952
Mannhassett Village (Part of Mason)	45040
Mansfield	44901-07
For specific Mansfield Zip Codes call (419) 755-4621	
Mantua	44255
Mantua (Township)	44255
Mantua Center	44255
Mantua Corners	44255
Maple Corner	45385
Maple Grove (Geauga County)	44231
Maple Grove (Ross County)	45601
Maple Grove (Seneca County)	44883
Maple Heights (Cuyahoga County)	44137
Maple Heights (Noble County)	43724
Maple Lake	43944
Maple Park	45040
Maple Ridge	44601

	ZIP
Mapleshade (Part of Gallipolis)	45631
Mapleton	44730
Maple Valley (Part of Akron)	44320
Maplewood	45340
Marathon	45145
Marble Cliff	43212
Marble Furnace	45660
Marblehead	43440
Marchand	44720
Marcy	43110
Marengo	43334
Margaretta (Township)	44824
Maria Stein	45860
Mariemont	45227
Marietta (Washington County) (Township)	45750
Marietta (Washington County)	45750
Marion	43301-02
For specific Marion Zip Codes call (614) 389-4621	
Marion (Allen County) (Township)	45833
Marion (Clinton County) (Township)	45107
Marion (Fayette County) (Township)	43145
Marion (Hancock County) (Township)	45840
Marion (Hardin County) (Township)	45812
Marion (Henry County) (Township)	43524
Marion (Hocking County) (Township)	43138
Marion (Marion County) (Township)	43302
Marion (Mercer County) (Township)	45883
Marion (Morgan County) (Township)	43728
Marion (Noble County) (Township)	43788
Marion (Pike County) (Township)	45613
Marion Correctional Institution	43302
Marion East	43302
Mark (Township)	43556
Mark Center	43536
Marlain Acres	45231
Marlboro (Township)	44601
Marlboro (Delaware County) (Township)	43015
Marlboro (Stark County)	44601
Marne	43055
Marquis	44406
Marr	43789
Marseilles	43351
Marseilles (Township)	43351
Marshall	45133
Marshall (Township)	45133
Marshallville	44645
Martel	43335
Martin	43445
Martinsburg	43037
Martins Ferry	43935
Martinsville	45146
Mary Ann (Township)	43055
Marygrove	43558
Marysville	43040
Mason (Lawrence County) (Township)	45696
Mason (Warren County)	45040
Mason Heights (Part of Mason)	45040
Massie (Township)	45032
Massieville	45601
Massillon	44646-48
For specific Massillon Zip Codes call (216) 837-8323	
Massillon State Hospital	44646
Masury	44438
Matville	43146
Mauds	45069
Maumee	43537
Maustown	45011
Maximo	44650
Maxville	43748
Mayfield (Butler County)	45042
Mayfield (Cuyahoga County)	44143
Mayfield Heights	44124
Mayflower Village (Part of Massillon)	44646
May Hill	45679
Maynard	43937
Maysville (Allen County)	45810
Maysville (Wayne County)	44606
Mead (Township)	43947
Meade	45644

	ZIP
Meadowbrook	43701
Meadowbrook Lake (Part of Stow)	44224
Meadow Lawn (Part of Middletown)	45042
Mecca	44410
Mecca (Township)	44410
Mechanic (Township)	43804
Mechanicsburg (Champaign County)	43044
Mechanicsburg (Crawford County)	44887
Mechanicsburg (Monroe County)	43793
Mechanicsburg (Wayne County)	44691
Mechanicstown	44651
Mechanicsville	44041
Medina (Medina County)	44256
Medina (Medina County) (Township)	44256
Medway	45341
Meeker	43302
Meigs (Adams County) (Township)	45660
Meigs (Morgan County)	43756
Meigs (Muskingum County) (Township)	43727
Meigsville (Township)	43756
Melbern	43506
Mellett Mall (Part of Canton)	44708
Melmore	44845
Melody Lake	43701
Melrose	45861
Melvin	45177
Memphis	45135
Mendon	45862
Mentor	44060-61
For specific Mentor Zip Codes call (216) 255-9724	
Mentor Headlands (Part of Mentor)	44060
Mentor-on-the-Lake	44060
Mercer	45862
Mercerville	45631
Merrill	43451
Mesopotamia	44439
Mesopotamia (Township)	44439
Metamora	43540
Methodist Theological School of Ohio	43015
Metzger	45601
Mexico	44882
Meyers Lake	44730
Miami (Clermont County) (Township)	45147
Miami (Greene County) (Township)	45387
Miami (Hamilton County)	45041
Miami (Hamilton County) (Township)	45002
Miami (Logan County) (Township)	43343
Miami (Montgomery County) (Township)	45342
Miami Heights	45002
Miamisburg	45342-43
For specific Miamisburg Zip Codes call (513) 866-4551	
Miami Shores (Part of Moraine)	45439
Miamitown	45041
Miami University (Part of Oxford)	45056
Miami Villa (Part of Huber Heights)	45424
Miamiville	45147
Michael Manor	45371
Mid City (Part of Dayton)	45402
Middle Bass	43446
Middleboro	45152
Middlebourne	43773
Middlebranch	44652
Middleburg (Jefferson County)	43903
Middleburg (Logan County)	43336
Middleburg (Noble County)	43724
Middleburg Heights	44130
Middlebury (Knox County) (Township)	43019
Middlebury (Van Wert County)	45832
Middlefield	44062
Middlefield (Township)	44062
Middle Point	45863
Middleport	45760
Middleton (Columbiana County)	44408
Middleton (Columbiana County) (Township)	44455
Middleton (Jackson County)	45692

424 OHIO Middleton-Murdock

Name	ZIP
Middleton (Wood County) (Township)	43525
Middleton Corner	45385
Middletown	45042-44
For specific Middletown Zip Codes call (513) 422-6316	
Middletown (Champaign County)	43009
Middletown (Crawford County)	44833
Middletown South	45050
Midland	45148
Midpark (Part of Parma Heights)	44130
Midtown (Part of Zanesville)	43701
Midvale	44653
Midway	43950
Midway Mall (Part of Elyria)	44035
Mifflin	44805
Mifflin (Ashland County) (Township)	44805
Mifflin (Franklin County) (Township)	43230
Mifflin (Pike County) (Township)	45646
Mifflin (Richland County) (Township)	44843
Mifflin (Wyandot County) (Township)	43351
Milan	44846
Milan (Township)	44846
Milford (Butler County) (Township)	45004
Milford (Clermont County)	45150
Milford (Defiance County) (Township)	43526
Milford (Knox County) (Township)	43011
Milford Center	43045
Mill (Township)	44683
Millbrook	44691
Millbury	43447
Mill Creek (Coshocton County) (Township)	44654
Millcreek (Union County) (Township)	43040
Mill Creek (Williams County) (Township)	43501
Milledgeville	43142
Millens	45383
Miller (Knox County) (Township)	43050
Miller (Lawrence County)	45623
Miller City	45864
Millersburg	44654
Millersport	43046
Millerstown	43072
Millersville	43435
Millertown	43730
Millfield	45761
Milligan	43731
Millport (Columbiana County)	44427
Millport (Pickaway County)	43103
Millville (Butler County)	45013
Millville (Mahoning County)	44460
Millwood (Guernsey County) (Township)	43773
Millwood (Knox County)	43014
Milton (Ashland County) (Township)	44805
Milton (Jackson County) (Township)	45692
Milton (Mahoning County) (Township)	44429
Milton (Wayne County) (Township)	44270
Milton (Wood County) (Township)	43441
Milton Center	43541
Miltonsburg	43793
Miltonville	45042
Mineral	45766
Mineral City	44656
Mineral Ridge	44440
Minersville	45769
Minerva	44657
Minerva Park	43229
Mineyahta on-The-Bay	43440
Minford	45653
Mingo	43047
Mingo Junction	43938
Minster	45865
Misco	43731
Mishler	44260
Mississinawa (Township)	45390
Mitiwanga	44839
Mizer Addition	43832
Modest	45122
Modoc	45732
Moffit Heights	44646

Name	ZIP
Mogadore	44260
Mohawk	43844
Mohawk Lake	44883
Mohican (Township)	44840
Mohicanville	44840
Moline	43465
Momeneetown (Part of Oregon)	43616
Monclova	43542
Monclova (Township)	43542
Monclova Gardens (Part of Maumee)	43537
Monday	45764
Monday Creek (Township)	43138
Monfort Heights	45239
Monnette	43302
Monroe (Adams County) (Township)	45144
Monroe (Allen County) (Township)	45807
Monroe (Ashtabula County) (Township)	44030
Monroe (Butler County)	45050
Monroe (Carroll County) (Township)	44620
Monroe (Clermont County) (Township)	45148
Monroe (Coshocton County) (Township)	43844
Monroe (Darke County) (Township)	45358
Monroe (Guernsey County) (Township)	43749
Monroe (Harrison County) (Township)	44695
Monroe (Henry County) (Township)	43535
Monroe (Holmes County) (Township)	44654
Monroe (Knox County) (Township)	43050
Monroe (Licking County) (Township)	43031
Monroe (Logan County) (Township)	43360
Monroe (Madison County) (Township)	43140
Monroe (Miami County) (Township)	45371
Monroe (Muskingum County) (Township)	43762
Monroe (Perry County) (Township)	43730
Monroe (Pickaway County) (Township)	43143
Monroe (Preble County) (Township)	45338
Monroe (Putnam County) (Township)	45831
Monroe (Richland County) (Township)	44843
Monroe Center	44030
Monroe Mills	43028
Monroeville (Huron County)	44847
Monroeville (Jefferson County)	43945
Monterey (Clermont County)	45103
Monterey (Putnam County) (Township)	45833
Montezuma	45866
Montgomery (Ashland County) (Township)	44805
Montgomery (Hamilton County)	45242
Montgomery (Marion County) (Township)	43332
Montgomery (Wood County) (Township)	43466
Montgomery Heights (Part of Montgomery)	45242
Monticello	45887
Montpelier	43543
Montra	45302
Montrose	44313
Montville	44064
Montville (Geauga County) (Township)	44064
Montville (Medina County) (Township)	44256
Moorefield	45502
Moorefield (Township)	45502
Moorefield	43907
Moorefield (Township)	43907
Moores Fork	45107
Moores Junction	43731
Mooresville	45601
Moraine	45439
Moran (Part of Streetsboro)	44202
Moreland	44691
Moreland Hills	44022

Name	ZIP
Morgan (Ashtabula County) (Township)	44084
Morgan (Butler County) (Township)	45053
Morgan (Gallia County) (Township)	45686
Morgan (Knox County) (Township)	43050
Morgan (Morgan County) (Township)	43756
Morgan (Scioto County) (Township)	45648
Morgan Center	45686
Morgandale	44481
Morgan Place (Part of Englewood)	45322
Morgansville	43758
Morgantown (Mahoning County)	44514
Morgantown (Pike County)	45612
Morges	44643
Morning Sun	45311
Morral	43337
Morris (Township)	43019
Morris Apartments	45414
Morrisons	43701
Morristown (Athens County)	45761
Morristown (Belmont County)	43759
Morrisville	45146
Morrow	45152
Moscow	45153
Moss Run	45750
Moulton	45895
Moulton (Township)	45895
Moultrie	44657
Moundbuilders (Part of Newark)	43055
Moundsville	43724
Mount Air	43085
Mount Blanchard	45867
Mount Carmel (Clermont County)	45244
Mount Carmel (Sandusky County)	43410
Mount Carmel Heights	45244
Mount Cory	45868
Mount Eaton	44659
Mount Ephraim	43779
Mount Everett (Part of Marietta)	45750
Mount Forest Trails	45244
Mount Gilead	43338
Mount Healthy	45231
Mount Healthy Heights (Part of Mount Healthy)	45231
Mount Holly (Clermont County)	45102
Mount Holly (Warren County)	45068
Mount Hope	44660
Mount Jefferson	45333
Mount Joy	45657
Mount Liberty	43048
Mount Olive	45106
Mount Orab	45154
Mount Perry	43760
Mount Pisgah	45157
Mount Pleasant (Township)	43939
Mount Pleasant (Sandusky County)	44811
Mount Pleasant (Stark County)	44720
Mount Pleasant (Hocking County)	43138
Mount Pleasant (Jefferson County)	43939
Mount Repose	45140
Mount Sterling	43143
Mount St. Joseph	45051
Mount Union (Part of Alliance)	44601
Mount Vernon	43050
Mount Vernon Avenue (Part of Columbus)	43203
Mount Victory	43340
Mount View	45133
Mountville	45732
Mount Washington (Part of Cincinnati)	45230
Mowrystown	45155
Moxahala	43761
Mudsock (Franklin County)	43026
Mudsock (Gallia County)	45658
Muhlenberg (Township)	43146
Mulberry	45150
Mule Town	45653
Muncie Hollow	43420
Munroe Falls	44262
Munson (Township)	44024
Murdock	45140

Murlin Heights-Nova OHIO 425

	ZIP		ZIP		ZIP
Murlin Heights	45414	New Lexington (Perry County)	43764	North Benton (Portage County)	44449
Murray City	43144	New Lexington (Preble County)	45381	North Bloomfield (Morrow County) (Township)	44833
Museville	43720	New Liberty	44413	North Bloomfield (Trumbull County)	44450
Muskingum (Muskingum County) (Township)	43830	New London	44851	North Brewster (Part of Brewster)	44613
Muskingum (Washington County) (Township)	45744	New London (Township)	44851	North Bristol	44402
Mutual	43044	New Lyme (Township)	44066	Northbrook	45231
Myersville	44685	New Lyme (Ashtabula County)	44085	North Canton	44720
Myrtle Brook	45140	New Lyme (Ashtabula County)	44066	North Clippinger (Part of The Village of Indian Hill)	45243
Myrtle Village	45140	New Madison	45346	North College Hill	45239
Nankin	44848	Newman (Marion County)	43342	North Condit	43074
Napoleon	43545	Newman (Stark County)	44646	North Creek	45831
Napoleon (Township)	43545	New Market	45133	North Dayton (Part of Dayton)	45404
Nashport	43830	New Market (Township)	45133	Northeast (Part of Columbus)	43231
Nashville (Darke County)	45331	New Marshfield	45766	North Eaton	44044
Nashville (Holmes County)	44661	New Martinsburg	45123	North Fairfield	44855
Nashville (Miami County)	45373	New Matamoras	45767	North Feesburg	45130
National Road	43025	New Miami	45011	Northfield (Summit County)	44067
Navarre	44662	New Middletown	44442	Northfield Center (Summit County) (Township)	44067
Neapolis	43547	New Moscow	43812	Northfield Center (Summit County)	44067
Neave (Township)	45331	New Palestine	45157	North Findlay	45840
Needmore	45833	New Paris	45347	North Fork Village (Part of Chillicothe)	45601
Neel	45167	New Petersburg	45123	North Georgetown	44665
Neelysville	43756	New Philadelphia	44663	North Greenfield	43358
Neffs	43940	New Pittsburg	44691	North Hampton	45349
Negley	44441	New Pittsburgh	44865	North Hill (Part of Akron)	44310
Nellie	43844	New Plymouth	45654	North Hills (Part of Logan)	43138
Nelson	44231	New Plymouth Heights	45629	North Hills Estates	45224
Nelson (Township)	44231	Newport (Township)	45768	North Houston	45333
Nelsonville	45764	Newport (Madison County)	43140	North Industry	44707
Neptune	45822	Newport (Shelby County)	45845	North Jackson	44451
Nettle Lake	43543	Newport (Tuscarawas County)	44683	North Kenova (Part of South Point)	45680
Nevada	44849	Newport (Washington County)	45768	North Kingsville	44068
Neville	45156	New Reading	43783	Northland (Part of Columbus)	43229
New Albany (Franklin County)	43054	New Richland	43310	Northland Mall (Part of Columbus)	43229
New Albany (Mahoning County)	44460	New Richmond	45157	North Lawrence	44666
New Alexander	44625	New Riegel	44853	North Lewisburg	43060
New Alexandria	43938	New Rochester	43450	North Liberty	44822
New Antioch	45177	New Rome	43228	North Lima	44452
Newark	43055-56	New Rumley	43984	North Madison (Lake County)	44057
For specific Newark Zip Codes call (614) 345-4021		New Salem	43148	North Monroeville	44847
Newark Air Force Station	43057	New Salisbury	43930	Northmoor	45315
New Athens	43981	New Somerset	43964	North Mount Vernon	43050
New Baltimore (Hamilton County)	45030	New Springfield	44443	North Olmsted	44070
New Baltimore (Stark County)	44601	New Stark	45897	North Perry	44081
New Bavaria	43548	New Straitsville	43766	North Randall	44128
New Bedford	43804	New Strasburg	43102	North Richmond	44003
Newberry (Township)	45318	Newton (Licking County) (Township)	43055	Northridge (Clark County)	45502
New Bloomington	43341	Newton (Miami County) (Township)	45339	Northridge (Montgomery County)	45414
New Boston	45662	Newton (Muskingum County) (Township)	43735	North Ridgeville	44039
New Bremen	45869	Newton (Pike County) (Township)	45661	North Robinson	44856
New Buffalo	44406	Newton (Trumbull County) (Township)	44444	North Royalton	44133
Newburg (Part of Cleveland)	44105	Newton Falls	44444	North Sagamore Heights (Part of Deer Park)	45236
Newburgh Heights	44105	Newtonsville	45158	North Salem	43749
New Burlington	45231	Newtown (Hamilton County)	45244	North Side (Part of Youngstown)	44504
Newbury	44065	New Town (Hocking County)	43144	North Star	45350
Newbury (Township)	44065	Newtown (Jefferson County)	43917	North Towne Square Mall (Part of Toledo)	43612
New California	43064	Newtowne Mall (Part of New Philadelphia)	44663	North Uniontown	45133
New Carlisle	45344	New Vienna	45159	Northup	45658
Newcastle (Township)	43843	Newville	44864	Northview	45322
New Castle	45638	New Washington	44854	Northwest (Franklin County)	43220
New Castle (Belmont County)	43716	New Waterford	44445	Northwest (Williams County) (Township)	43518
Newcastle (Coshocton County)	43843	New Weston	45348	Northwood (Logan County)	43310
New Cleveland	45875	New Westville	47374	Northwood (Wood County)	43619
Newcomerstown	43832	New Winchester	44820	North Woodbury	44813
New Concord	43762	Ney	43549	North Zanesville	43701
New Cumberland	44656	Nicholsville	45106	Norton (Delaware County)	43356
New Dover	43040	Nile (Township)	45630	Norton (Summit County)	44203
Newell	43941	Niles	44446	Norwalk (Huron County)	44857
Newell Run	45768	Nimishillen (Township)	44641	Norwalk (Huron County) (Township)	44857
New England	45778	Nimisila	44216	Norwich (Franklin County) (Township)	43026
New Floodwood	45764	Nipgen	45612	Norwich (Huron County)	
New Franklin	44657	Noble (Auglaize County) (Township)	45885	Norwich (Huron County) (Township)	44890
New Garden	44423	Noble (Cuyahoga County)	44132	Norwich (Muskingum County)	43767
New Germany (Part of Beavercreek)	45431	Noble (Defiance County) (Township)	43512	Norwood (Hamilton County)	45212
New Guilford	43843	Noble (Noble County) (Township)	43724	Norwood (Washington County)	45750
New Hagerstown	44695	Normandy Heights	45015	Nottingham (Township)	43907
New Hampshire	45870	Norris	45383	Nova	44859
New Harrisburg	44615	North (Township)	43988		
New Harrison	45308	Northampton (Township)	44221		
New Haven (Township)	44850	North Auburn	44887		
New Haven (Hamilton County)	45030	North Baltimore	45872		
New Haven (Huron County)	44850	North Bend	45052		
New Holland	43145	North Benton (Mahoning County)	44449		
Newhope (Brown County)	45121				
New Hope (Preble County)	45320				
New Jasper (Darke County)	45385				
New Jasper (Greene County)	45385				
New Knoxville	45871				
New Lebanon	45345				

426 OHIO Novelty-Perry

Name	ZIP
Novelty	44072
Oakdale (Athens County)	45732
Oakdale (Montgomery County)	45429
Oakdale (Stark County)	44646
Oakfield (Perry County)	43731
Oakfield (Trumbull County)	44450
Oak Grove	45750
Oak Harbor	43449
Oak Hill	45656
Oakland (Butler County)	45050
Oakland (Clinton County)	45177
Oakland (Fairfield County)	43102
Oakland Park	43224
Oakley (Part of Cincinnati)	45209
Oakmont	43920
Oak Park	43907
Oak Run (Township)	43143
Oak Shade	43567
Oakview	45805
Oakwood (Cuyahoga County)	44146
Oakwood (Montgomery County)	45419
Oakwood (Paulding County)	45873
Oberlin	44074
Oberlin Beach	44839
Obetz	43207
Oceola	44860
Oco	43950
O'Connor Landing	43310
Octa	43160
Ogden	45177
Ogontz	44814
Ohio (Clermont County) (Township)	45157
Ohio (Gallia County) (Township)	45623
Ohio (Monroe County) (Township)	43931
Ohio City	45874
Ohio Junction (Part of Martins Ferry)	43935
Ohio Reformatory for Women	43040
Ohio Soldiers and Sailors Home	44870
Ohio State Reformatory	44901
Ohio State University Lima Branch	45804
Okeana	45053
Okolona	43550
Old Fort	44861
Old Gore	43138
Old Mill Creek	44212
Old Plymouth Heights	45629
Old Straitsville	43766
Oldtown	45385
Old Washington	43768
Old West End (Part of Toledo)	43610
Olena	44857
Olive (Meigs County) (Township)	45743
Olive (Noble County)	43724
Olive (Noble County) (Township)	43724
Olive Branch	45103
Olive Green (Delaware County)	43074
Olivegreen (Noble County)	43724
Oliver (Township)	45693
Olivesburg	44805
Olivett	43713
Olmsted (Township)	44138
Olmsted Falls	44138
Olszeski	43917
Omega	45690
Oneida (Butler County)	45042
Oneida (Carroll County)	44644
Ontario	44862
Opperman	43732
Oran	45333
Orange (Ashland County) (Township)	44805
Orange (Carroll County) (Township)	44639
Orange (Coshocton County)	43832
Orange (Cuyahoga County)	44022
Orange (Delaware County) (Township)	43021
Orange (Hancock County) (Township)	45817
Orange (Meigs County) (Township)	45723
Orange (Shelby County) (Township)	45365
Orangeville	44453
Orbiston	45732
Orchard Beach	44089
Orchard Island	43331

Name	ZIP
Orchard Park Heights	44904
Oregon	43616
Oregonia	45054
Oreville	43766
Orient	43146
Orland	45654
Orrville	44667
Orwell	44076
Orwell (Township)	44076
Osgood	45351
Osnaburg (Township)	44730
Ostrander	43061
Otsego	43762
Ottawa	45875
Ottawa (Township)	45875
Ottawa Hills	43606
Otterbein Home	45036
Ottokee	43567
Ottoville	45876
Otway	45657
Outville	43062
Overlook	45431
Overlook Court	43906
Overlook Hills	43952
Overlook Homes	45431
Overlook-Page Manor	45431
Overpeck	45055
Over The Rhine (Part of Cincinnati)	45210
Overton	44691
Owens Hill	43701
Owensville	45160
Oxford	45056
Oxford (Township)	45056
Oxford (Coshocton County) (Township)	43845
Oxford (Delaware County) (Township)	43003
Oxford (Erie County) (Township)	44870
Oxford (Guernsey County) (Township)	43773
Oxford (Tuscarawas County) (Township)	43832
Ozark	43716
Padanaram	44003
Padua	45846
Page Manor	45431
Pagetown	43334
Pageville	45710
Painesville (Lake County)	44077
Painesville (Lake County) (Township)	44077
Painesville on the Lake	44077
Painesville Shopping Center (Part of Painesville)	44077
Paint (Fayette County) (Township)	43106
Paint (Highland County) (Township)	45612
Paint (Holmes County) (Township)	44690
Paint (Madison County) (Township)	43140
Paint (Ross County) (Township)	45612
Paint (Wayne County) (Township)	44659
Painters Creek	45304
Paintersville	45335
Paint Valley	44654
Palermo	44615
Palestine	45352
Palmer (Putnam County) (Township)	45831
Palmer (Washington County) (Township)	43787
Palmyra (Township)	44412
Palmyra (Knox County)	43019
Palmyra (Portage County)	44412
Palos	45732
Pancoastburg	43160
Pandora	45877
Pansy	45107
Paradise	44406
Paradise Hill	44805
Paris (Portage County) (Township)	44266
Paris (Stark County) (Township)	44669
Paris (Union County) (Township)	43040
Paris (Portage County)	44266
Paris (Stark County)	44669
Parkdale (Part of Forest Park)	45240
Parkertown	44824
Park Layne (Clark County)	45344
Park Layne (Montgomery County)	45431
Parkman	44080

Name	ZIP
Parkman (Township)	44080
Park Place (Part of Wyoming)	45215
Park Ridge Acres	45506
Parkview (Part of Fairview Park)	44126
Parkview Heights	45224
Parlett	43907
Parma	44129
Parma Heights	44130
Parmatown Mall (Part of Parma)	44129
Parral	44622
Parrott	43160
Pasadena (Part of Kettering)	45429
Pasco	45365
Pataskala	43062
Patmos	44460
Patriot	45658
Patterson (Darke County) (Township)	45388
Patterson (Hardin County)	45843
Pattersonville	44657
Pattin Addition (Part of Marietta)	45750
Pattonville	45640
Paulding	45879
Paulding (Township)	45879
Paul Laurence Dunbar (Part of Dayton)	45417
Pavonia	44903
Pawnee	44254
Paxton (Township)	45612
Payne	45880
Pearlbrook (Part of Cleveland)	44109
Pease (Township)	43935
Pebble (Township)	45690
Pedro	45659
Peebles	45660
Pee Pee (Township)	45690
Pekin (Carroll County)	44657
Pekin (Jefferson County)	43952
Pekin (Warren County)	45036
Pemberton	45353
Pemberville	43450
Penfield	44052
Penfield (Township)	44090
Peniel	45658
Peninsula	44264
Penn (Highland County) (Township)	45135
Penn (Morgan County) (Township)	43787
Pennsville	43787
Penn View	44003
Peoli	43832
Peoria (Butler County)	45056
Peoria (Union County)	43067
Pepper Pike	44124
Perintown	45150
Perkins (Township)	44870
Perry (Allen County) (Township)	45806
Perry (Ashland County) (Township)	44866
Perry (Brown County) (Township)	45118
Perry (Carroll County) (Township)	43988
Perry (Columbiana County) (Township)	44460
Perry (Coshocton County) (Township)	43843
Perry (Fayette County) (Township)	45135
Perry (Franklin County) (Township)	43017
Perry (Gallia County) (Township)	45658
Perry (Hocking County) (Township)	43135
Perry (Lake County) (Township)	44081
Perry (Lawrence County) (Township)	45638
Perry (Licking County) (Township)	43055
Perry (Logan County) (Township)	43319
Perry (Monroe County) (Township)	43793
Perry (Montgomery County) (Township)	45309
Perry (Morrow County) (Township)	44904
Perry (Muskingum County) (Township)	43701
Perry (Pickaway County) (Township)	43145

Perry-Rathbone OHIO 427

Name	ZIP
Perry (Pike County) (Township)	45616
Perry (Putnam County) (Township)	45837
Perry (Richland County) (Township)	44813
Perry (Shelby County) (Township)	45353
Perry (Stark County) (Township)	44708
Perry (Tuscarawas County) (Township)	44699
Perry (Wood County) (Township)	44817
Perry (Lake County)	44081
Perry Addition	45648
Perry Heights	44646
Perrysburg (Wood County)	43551
Perrysburg (Wood County) (Township)	43551
Perrysburg Heights	43551
Perrysville (Ashland County)	44864
Perrysville (Carroll County)	43988
Perryton	43822
Peru (Huron County)	44847
Peru (Huron County) (Township)	44847
Peru (Morrow County) (Township)	43334
Petersburg (Carroll County)	44615
Petersburg (Jackson County)	45640
Petersburg (Mahoning County)	44454
Petrea	45640
Petroleum	44438
Pettisville	43553
Pfeiffer Station	43326
Phalanx	44470
Pharisburg	43040
Phillippstown (Part of Columbus)	43201
Phillipsburg	45354
Philo	43771
Philothea	45828
Phoneton	45371
Pickaway (Township)	43113
Pickerington	43147
Pickrelltown	43357
Piedmont	43983
Pierce (Township)	45245
Pierpont	44082
Pierpont (Township)	44082
Pigeon Run	44646
Pike (Brown County) (Township)	45176
Pike (Clark County) (Township)	45502
Pike (Coshocton County) (Township)	43822
Pike (Fulton County) (Township)	43515
Pike (Knox County) (Township)	44822
Pike (Madison County) (Township)	43029
Pike (Perry County) (Township)	43764
Pike (Stark County) (Township)	44626
Piketon	45661
Pikeville	45331
Pine Grove	45638
Pinehurst	45750
Pine Valley (Part of Dillonvale)	43917
Piney Fork	43941
Pinkerman	45682
Pioneer	43554
Piqua	45356
Piqua East Mall (Part of Piqua)	45356
Pisgah (Butler County)	45069
Pitchin	45502
Pitsburg	45358
Pitt (Township)	43323
Pittlime (Part of Norton)	44203
Pittsburgh Junction	43986
Pittsfield	44090
Pittsfield (Township)	44090
Placid Meadows	45238
Plain (Franklin County) (Township)	43081
Plain (Stark County) (Township)	44708
Plain (Wayne County) (Township)	44691
Plain (Wood County) (Township)	43402
Plain City	43064
Plainfield	43836

Name	ZIP
Plain View	43793
Plankton	44882
Planktown	44878
Plantation Acres	45224
Plants	45771
Plantsville	43728
Plattsburg	45368
Plattsville	45365
Playhouse Square (Part of Cleveland)	44115
Pleasant (Brown County) (Township)	45121
Pleasant (Clark County) (Township)	43010
Pleasant (Fairfield County) (Township)	43130
Pleasant (Franklin County) (Township)	43123
Pleasant (Hancock County) (Township)	45858
Pleasant (Hardin County) (Township)	43326
Pleasant (Henry County) (Township)	43527
Pleasant (Knox County) (Township)	43050
Pleasant (Logan County) (Township)	43318
Pleasant (Madison County) (Township)	43143
Pleasant (Marion County) (Township)	43302
Pleasant (Perry County) (Township)	43731
Pleasant (Putnam County) (Township)	45830
Pleasant (Seneca County) (Township)	44861
Pleasant (Van Wert County) (Township)	45891
Pleasant Bend	43548
Pleasant City	43772
Pleasant Corners	43123
Pleasant Grove (Belmont County)	43901
Pleasant Grove (Muskingum County)	43701
Pleasant Heights (Columbiana County)	43920
Pleasant Heights (Jefferson County)	43952
Pleasant Hill (Athens County)	45701
Pleasant Hill (Jefferson County)	43952
Pleasant Hill (Miami County)	45359
Pleasant Hills	45231
Pleasant Home	44287
Pleasant Lea	44130
Pleasant Plain	45162
Pleasant Run	45231
Pleasant Run Farms	45240
Pleasant Valley (Coshocton County)	43812
Pleasant Valley (Pike County)	45661
Pleasant Valley (Ross County)	45601
Pleasant Valley (Vinton County)	45601
Pleasant View (Fayette County)	43128
Pleasant View (Stark County)	44705
Pleasantville	43148
Plumwood	43140
Plymouth (Township)	44865
Plymouth (Ashtabula County) (Township)	44004
Plymouth (Ashtabula County)	44004
Plymouth (Richland County)	44865
Plymouth Center	44004
Poast Town	45042
Poetown	45130
Point (Part of Columbus)	43223
Point Isabel	45153
Point Place (Part of Toledo)	43611
Point Pleasant	45153
Poland	44514
Poland (Township)	44514
Poland Center	44436
Polk (Ashland County)	44866
Polk (Crawford County) (Township)	44833
Pomeroy	45769
Pond Run	45684
Poplargrove	45660
Portage (Township)	43451
Portage (Hancock County) (Township)	45872

Name	ZIP
Portage (Ottawa County) (Township)	43452
Portage (Wood County)	43451
Portage Lakes	44319
Port Clinton	43452
Porter (Delaware County) (Township)	43074
Porter (Gallia County)	45614
Porter (Scioto County) (Township)	45694
Porterfield	45714
Portersville	43730
Port Homer	43964
Port Jefferson	45360
Portland	45770
Portsmouth	45662
Port Union	45015
Port Washington	43837
Port William	45164
Possum Woods	45506
Post Town	45042
Post Town Heights	45042
Potsdam	45361
Pottery Additon	43952
Powell	43065
Powellsville	45629
Powhatan Point	43942
Prairie (Franklin County) (Township)	43119
Prairie (Holmes County) (Township)	44633
Prairie Meadows	43812
Pratts Fork	45776
Prattsville	45651
Prentiss	45856
Preston Addition	45648
Price Hill (Part of Cincinnati)	45205
Pricetown (Highland County)	45133
Pricetown (Trumbull County)	44429
Pride	45601
Princeton	45015
Proctor	44266
Proctorville	45669
Prospect	43342
Prospect (Township)	43342
Providence (Township)	43504
Provident	43950
Provincial Point	45244
Public Square (Part of Cleveland)	44114
Pulaski	43506
Pulaski (Township)	43506
Pulaskiville	43338
Pulse	45118
Pultney (Township)	43906
Puntenneyville	45684
Puritas Park (Part of Cleveland)	44135
Purity	43071
Pusheta (Township)	45895
Put-in-Bay	43456
Put-in-Bay (Township)	43456
Putnam Place (Part of Marietta)	45750
Pymatuning Shores	44003
Pyrmont	45309
Pyro	45656
Quaker City	43773
Quaker Hill	44672
Qualey	45724
Queen Acres	45011
Quincy	43343
Raccoon (Township)	45685
Racine	45771
Radcliff	45670
Radford Road	45701
Radio Heights	43920
Radnor	43066
Radnor (Township)	43066
Ragersville	44681
Rainsboro	45165
Ramsey	43917
Ranchwood	44870
Randall Park (Part of North Randall)	44128
Randolph (Township)	44265
Randolph (Montgomery County) (Township)	45322
Randolph (Portage County)	44265
Range	43143
Range (Township)	43143
Ransom	45381
Rarden	45671
Rarden (Township)	45671
Rathbone (Delaware County)	43015
Rathbone (Washington County)	45750

428 OHIO Rathbone Heights-Rye Beach

Name	ZIP
Rathbone Heights (Part of Marietta)	45750
Ravenna	44266
Ravenna (Township)	44266
Ravenna Army Ammunition Plant	44266
Rawson	45881
Ray	45672
Rayland	43943
Raymond	43067
Rays Corners	44047
Reading (Columbiana County)	44665
Reading (Hamilton County)	45215
Reading (Perry County) (Township)	43783
Recker Heights (Part of Piqua)	45356
Recovery (Township)	45846
Red Bank (Part of Fairfax)	45227
Redbird	44057
Redbush	45742
Red Coach Farm (Part of Centerville)	45429
Redfield	43764
Red Fox	44240
Redhaw	44866
Red Lion	45005
Redoak	45167
Red River	45308
Redtown	45732
Reed (Township)	44807
Reedsburg	44691
Reedsmills	43910
Reedsville	45772
Reedtown	44807
Reedurban	44710
Reese Station	43207
Reesville	45166
Rehoboth	43764
Reily	45056
Reily (Township)	45056
Reinersville	43756
Reminderville	44202
Remington	45140
Remsen Corners	44256
Rendville	43730
Reno	45773
Reno Beach	43412
Rensselaer Park	45216
Republic	44867
Resaca	43140
Revenge	43130
Reynoldsburg	43068
Reynolds Corners (Part of Toledo)	43615
Rialto	45069
Rice (Putnam County)	45831
Rice (Sandusky County) (Township)	43420
Riceland	44667
Richfield (Henry County) (Township)	43516
Richfield (Lucas County) (Township)	43504
Richfield (Summit County) (Township)	44286
Richfield (Summit County)	44286
Richfield Center	43504
Richfield Heights (Part of Richfield)	44286
Rich Hill (Knox County)	43011
Rich Hill (Muskingum County) (Township)	43727
Richland (Allen County) (Township)	45817
Richland (Belmont County) (Township)	43950
Richland (Clinton County) (Township)	45169
Richland (Darke County) (Township)	45380
Richland (Defiance County) (Township)	43512
Richland (Fairfield County) (Township)	43150
Richland (Guernsey County) (Township)	43780
Richland (Holmes County) (Township)	44628
Richland (Logan County) (Township)	43310
Richland (Marion County) (Township)	43302
Richland (Montgomery County)	45431
Richland (Vinton County) (Township)	45651
Richland (Wyandot County) (Township)	43359

Name	ZIP
Richmond Mall (Part of Ontario)	44906
Richmond (Ashtabula County) (Township)	44032
Richmond (Huron County) (Township)	44890
Richmond (Jefferson County)	43944
Richmond Center	44003
Richmond Dale	45673
Richmond Heights	44143
Richmond Mall (Part of Richmond Heights)	44143
Richville	44706
Richwood	43344
Rickard Acres	45005
Rickenbacker AFB	43217
Rickenbacker Air Force Base	43217
Ridge (Van Wert County) (Township)	45891
Ridge (Wyandot County) (Township)	43316
Ridgefield (Township)	44847
Ridgeland	45640
Ridgeton	44820
Ridgeview (Part of North Ridgeville)	44035
Ridgeville (Henry County) (Township)	43555
Ridgeville (Warren County)	45036
Ridgeville Corners	43555
Ridgeway	43345
Ridgewood (Allen County) (Township)	43701
Ridgewood (Muskingum County)	43801
Ridgewood Heights	45427
Rigrish	45662
Riley (Putnam County) (Township)	45877
Riley (Sandusky County) (Township)	43420
Rimer	45830
Rinard Mills	45774
Ringgold	43758
Rio Grande	45674
Ripley (Brown County)	45167
Ripley (Holmes County) (Township)	44676
Ripley (Huron County) (Township)	44837
Risingsun	43457
Rittman	44270
River Corners	44275
Riverdale	45661
Riveredge (Cuyahoga County) (Township)	44135
Riveredge (Cuyahoga County)	44135
Riverlea	43085
Riverside (Montgomery County)	45424
Riverside (Shelby County)	45365
Riverside Park	44683
River Styx	44256
Riverview (Belmont County)	43906
Riverview (Washington County)	45750
Rix Mills	43762
Roachester	45152
Roads	45640
Roaming Rock Shores	44085
Roaming Shores	44085
Roanoke	44683
Robertsville	44670
Robins	43723
Robtown	43103
Robyville	43901
Rochester	44090
Rochester (Township)	44090
Rochester Place (Part of Northwood)	43616
Rockbridge	43149
Rock Camp (Columbiana County)	44432
Rock Camp (Lawrence County)	45675
Rock Creek	44084
Rockdale	45015
Rockford	45882
Rockhill	43977
Rockland (Part of Belpre)	45714
Rock Mills	43160
Rockport	45830
Rockville	45684
Rock Way	45504
Rockwood (Erie County)	44824
Rockwood (Lawrence County)	45619
Rocky Fall Estates	45133
Rockyhill	45640

Name	ZIP
Rocky Ridge	43458
Rocky River	44116
Rodney	45631
Rogers	44455
Rokeby Lock	43756
Rolandus	45771
Rollersville	43431
Rolling Acres Mall (Part of Akron)	44322
Rolling Mill Park	45042
Rome (Ashtabula County)	44085
Rome (Lawrence County)	45669
Rome (Richland County)	44878
Rome (Ashtabula County) (Township)	44085
Rome (Athens County) (Township)	45723
Rome (Lawrence County) (Township)	45669
Rome Station	44085
Romohr Acres	45244
Rootstown (Township)	44272
Rootstown (Portage County)	44272
Rose (Township)	44643
Rosedale	43029
Rose Farm	43731
Rose Hill	45348
Roseland	44906
Roselawn (Part of Cincinnati)	45237
Roselms	45849
Rosemont	44451
Rosemount	45662
Roseville	43777
Rosewood	43070
Roslyn (Part of Kettering)	45429
Ross	45061
Ross (Butler County) (Township)	45061
Ross (Greene County) (Township)	43153
Ross (Jefferson County) (Township)	43944
Rossburg	45362
Rossford	43460
Rossmoyne	45236
Rossville (Part of Hamilton)	45013
Roswell	44663
Round Bottom	43915
Roundhead	43346
Roundhead (Township)	43346
Rousculp	45806
Rowsburg	44866
Roxabell	45628
Roxanna	45068
Roxbury	43787
Royalton (Fairfield County)	43130
Royalton (Fulton County) (Township)	43533
Royersville	45638
Rubyville	45662
Rudolph	43462
Ruggles	44837
Ruggles (Township)	44851
Ruggles Beach	44839
Rumley (Harrison County) (Township)	43986
Rumley (Shelby County)	45302
Rural	45120
Ruraldale	43720
Rush (Champaign County) (Township)	43084
Rush (Scioto County) (Township)	45652
Rush (Tuscarawas County) (Township)	44683
Rush Creek (Fairfield County) (Township)	43107
Rushcreek (Logan County) (Township)	43347
Rushmore	45844
Rush Run	43943
Rushsylvania	43347
Rushtown	45652
Rushville	43150
Russell (Geauga County) (Township)	44072
Russell (Highland County)	45133
Russell Center	44072
Russell Heights	43968
Russells	43701
Russells Point	43348
Russellville	45168
Russia (Lorain County) (Township)	44074
Russia (Shelby County)	45363
Rustic Hills	44256
Rutland	45775
Rutland (Township)	45775
Rye Beach (Part of Huron)	44839

Sabina-Skyview Acres OHIO 429

Name	ZIP
Sabina	45169
Sagamore Hills	44067
Sagamore Hills (Township)	44067
Sahara Sands	44646
St. Albans (Township)	43062
St. Bernard	45217
St. Clair (Butler County) (Township)	45011
St. Clair (Columbiana County) (Township)	43920
St. Clairsville	43950
St. Henry	45883
St. Joe	43906
St. Johns	45884
St. Joseph (Mercer County)	45846
St. Joseph (Portage County)	44201
St. Joseph (Williams County) (Township)	43517
St. Louisville	43071
St. Martin	45118
St. Marys	45885
St. Marys (Township)	45885
St. Paris	43072
St. Pauls	43103
St. Peters	45846
St. Rosa	45886
St. Sebastian	45826
St. Stephens	44807
St. Wendelin	45883
Salem (Auglaize County) (Township)	45887
Salem (Champaign County) (Township)	43078
Salem (Columbiana County) (Township)	44431
Salem (Highland County) (Township)	45133
Salem (Jefferson County) (Township)	43944
Salem (Meigs County) (Township)	45741
Salem (Monroe County) (Township)	43915
Salem (Muskingum County) (Township)	43802
Salem (Ottawa County) (Township)	43449
Salem (Shelby County) (Township)	45365
Salem (Tuscarawas County) (Township)	43832
Salem (Warren County) (Township)	45152
Salem (Washington County) (Township)	45745
Salem (Wyandot County) (Township)	43351
Salem (Columbiana County)	44460
Salem Center	45741
Salem Heights	44460
Salem Plaza (Part of Trotwood)	45402
Salesville	43778
Saline (Township)	43932
Salineville	43945
Salisbury (Township)	45769
Saltair	45106
Salt Creek (Hocking County) (Township)	43135
Salt Creek (Holmes County) (Township)	44660
Salt Creek (Muskingum County) (Township)	43727
Salt Creek (Pickaway County) (Township)	43113
Salt Creek (Wayne County) (Township)	44627
Saltillo	43764
Salt Lick (Township)	43782
Salt Rack (Township)	43337
Salt Run	43943
Samantha	45135
Sand Beach	43449
Sand Hill (Erie County)	44870
Sand Hill (Scioto County)	45694
Sand Hill (Washington County)	45773
Sand Ridge	45761
Sandrun	45764
Sandusky	44870-71
For specific Sandusky Zip Codes call (419) 626-5525	
Sandusky (Crawford County) (Township)	44887
Sandusky (Richland County) (Township)	44827
Sandusky (Sandusky County) (Township)	43420
Sandusky South	44870

Name	ZIP
Sandy (Stark County) (Township)	44688
Sandy (Tuscarawas County) (Township)	44656
Sandy Beach	45885
Sandy Springs	45684
Sandyville	44671
San Margherita	43204
Santa Fe	45895
Santoy	43730
Sarahsville	43779
Sardinia	45171
Sardis	43946
Savannah	44874
Saville Estates	45431
Savona	45331
Sawyerwood	44313
Saybrook	44004
Saybrook (Township)	44004
Saybrook-on-the-Lake	44004
Sayler Park (Part of Cincinnati)	45233
Sayre	43731
Scenic Hills	43162
Schauers Acres	45341
Schley	45768
Schoenbrunn	44663
Schooleys	45601
Schrader	45601
Schumm	45898
Scio	43988
Scioto (Delaware County) (Township)	43061
Scioto (Jackson County) (Township)	45640
Scioto (Pickaway County) (Township)	43103
Scioto (Pike County) (Township)	45687
Scioto (Ross County) (Township)	45601
Sciotodale	45662
Scioto Furnace	45677
Sciotoville (Part of Portsmouth)	45662
Scipio (Butler County)	45053
Scipio (Meigs County) (Township)	45710
Scipio (Seneca County) (Township)	44867
Scotch Ridge	43450
Scott (Adams County) (Township)	45679
Scott (Brown County) (Township)	45121
Scott (Marion County) (Township)	43302
Scott (Sandusky County) (Township)	43435
Scott (Van Wert County)	45886
Scottown	45678
Scotts Crossing	45833
Scotty's Beauty Beach	45822
Scroggsfield	44615
Scrub Ridge	45616
Seal (Pike County) (Township)	45661
Seal (Wyandot County)	44849
Seaman	45679
Seasons Four	45140
Sebring	44672
Secedar Corners	44425
Sedalia	43151
Seilcrest Acres	45140
Sellers Point	43046
Selma	45368
Seneca (Monroe County) (Township)	43754
Seneca (Noble County) (Township)	43779
Seneca (Seneca County) (Township)	44853
Senecaville	43780
Senior	45152
Sentinel	44032
Settlement	44875
Seven Hills (Cuyahoga County)	44131
Seven Hills (Hamilton County)	45231
Seven Mile	45062
Seventeen	44629
Severance Center (Part of Cleveland Heights)	44118
Seville	44273
Seward	43533
Sewellsville	43713
Shade	45776
Shademore	45244
Shadeville	43137
Shady Bend	43832

Name	ZIP
Shady Glen (Jefferson County)	43964
Shady Glen (Ross County)	45601
Shady Grove	45324
Shadyside (Belmont County)	43947
Shadyside (Columbiana County)	43920
Shaker Crossing (Part of Kettering)	45429
Shaker Heights	44120
Shalersville (Township)	44266
Shalersville	44255
Shandon (Butler County)	45063
Shanesville (Part of Sugarcreek)	44681
Shannon	43821
Sharon (Franklin County) (Township)	43085
Sharon (Medina County) (Township)	44274
Sharon	43724
Sharon (Noble County) (Township)	43724
Sharon (Richland County) (Township)	44875
Sharon Center	44274
Sharon Hills	43085
Sharon Park (Allen County)	45805
Sharon Park (Butler County)	45011
Sharonville	45241
Sharon West	44438
Sharpeye	45331
Sharpsburg	45777
Shartz Road	45005
Shauck	43349
Shawnee (Allen County) (Township)	45805
Shawnee (Perry County)	43782
Shawnee Hills (Delaware County)	43065
Shawnee Hills (Greene County)	45335
Shawnee Meadows	45806
Shawtown	45858
Shawville (Part of North Ridgeville)	44035
Shay	45767
Sheffield (Ashtabula County) (Township)	44048
Sheffield (Lorain County) (Township)	44054
Sheffield (Lorain County)	44054
Sheffield Lake	44054
Shelby	44875
Shelby Junction (Part of Shelby)	44875
Shell Beach	43076
Shenandoah	44837
Shepard (Part of Columbus)	43219
Sheridan	45680
Sherman (Huron County) (Township)	44847
Sherman (Richland County)	44906
Sherman (Summit County)	44203
Sherritts	45688
Sherrodsville	44675
Sherwood	43556
Sherwood Park	45805
Shillings Mill	44429
Shiloh (Clermont County)	45122
Shiloh (Montgomery County)	45415
Shiloh (Richland County)	44878
Shinrock	44839
Shore (Part of Euclid)	44123
Shoregate Shopping Center (Part of Willowick)	44094
Short Creek (Township)	43901
Short Creek	43989
Short Hills (Part of Kettering)	45429
Shreve	44676
Sidney	45365
Siebold Addition	43162
Signal	44432
Silica	43560
Silver Creek (Greene County) (Township)	45335
Silver Creek (Medina County)	44281
Silver Lake	44221
Silverton	45236
Simons	44093
Singing Hills	45449
Sinking Spring	45172
Sitka	45750
Six Corners	43526
Skyline Acres	45231
Skypark	44281
Skyview Acres	43968

430 OHIO Slabtown-Summit

Name	ZIP
Slabtown	45801
Slate Mills	45601
Slaters	43724
Slickaway	45101
Sligo	45177
Slocums	45662
Smith (Belmont County) (Township)	43718
Smith (Mahoning County) (Township)	44672
Smith Corners	44515
Smithfield (Township)	43948
Smithfield (Jefferson County)	43948
Smithfield (Jefferson County)	43943
Smithville (Wayne County)	44677
Smithville (Wyandot County)	43351
Smyrna	43973
Snodes	44609
Snyder Terrace (Part of Springfield)	45504
Snyderville	45502
Soaptown	44440
Socialville	45050
Soldiers Home	44870
Solon	44139
Somerdale	44678
Somerford (Township)	43044
Somers (Township)	45311
Somerset (Belmont County) (Township)	43713
Somerset (Perry County)	43783
Somerton	43713
Somerville	45064
Sonora	43701
South Amherst	44001
South Arlington (Part of Akron)	44306
South Bay	43019
South Bloomfield (Morrow County) (Township)	43050
South Bloomfield (Pickaway County)	43103
South Bloomingville	43152
South Boy	43019
Southbrook	45429
South Charleston	45368
South Condit	43074
Southdale (Part of Kettering)	45429
Southern Hills (Part of Kettering)	45429
Southern Knoll (Part of Oxford)	45056
Southern Ohio Correctional Facility	45648
Southern Park Mall	44512
South Euclid	44121
South Excello	45042
Southfield Park (Part of Columbus)	43201
Southgate (Part of Springfield)	45506
Southgate Acres	44870
Southgate Shopping Center (Part of Newark)	43055
Southgate U.S.A. (Part of Maple Heights)	44137
South Highlands (Part of Middletown)	45042
South Hill Park	43528
Southington (Township)	44470
Southington	44470
South Kingman	45177
Southland Shopping Center (Cuyahoga County)	44130
Southland Shopping Center (Lucas County)	43614
South Lebanon	45065
South Logan (Part of Logan)	43138
South Lorain (Part of Lorain)	44055
South Madison	44057
South Milford (Part of Milford)	45150
South Moor Shores	45885
South Mount Vernon	43050
South Newbury	44021
South Olive	43724
South Park (Allen County)	45804
South Park (Cuyahoga County)	44131
South Park (Wyandot County)	43351
South Perry	43135
South Plymouth	43160
South Point	45680
Southridge	45505
South Russell	44022
South Salem	45681
South Shore Acres	45885
South Shore Park (Part of Oregon)	43616
South Side (Mahoning County)	44507
South Side (Tuscarawas County)	44663
South Solon	43153
South Vienna	45369
South Webster	45682
Southwest (Part of Mansfield)	44907
South West Hubbard	44425
Southwood	45805
South Woodbury	43334
Southworth	45833
Southwyck Shopping Center (Part of Toledo)	43614
South Zanesville	43701
Spargursville	45612
Sparta	43350
Speaker's Addition	43952
Speidel	43719
Spencer (Allen County) (Township)	45887
Spencer (Guernsey County) (Township)	43732
Spencer (Lucas County) (Township)	43528
Spencer (Medina County) (Township)	44275
Spencer (Medina County)	44275
Spencerville	45887
Spokane	44402
Spreading Oaks	45701
Sprigg (Township)	45144
Springboro	45066
Springbrook	43464
Springcreek (Township)	45356
Springdale	45246
Springfield	45501-06
For specific Springfield Zip Codes call (513) 323-6496	
Springfield (Clark County) (Township)	45505
Springfield (Gallia County) (Township)	45614
Springfield (Hamilton County) (Township)	45239
Springfield (Jefferson County) (Township)	43903
Springfield (Lucas County) (Township)	43528
Springfield (Mahoning County) (Township)	44442
Springfield (Muskingum County) (Township)	43701
Springfield (Richland County) (Township)	44906
Springfield (Ross County) (Township)	45601
Springfield (Summit County) (Township)	44312
Springfield (Williams County) (Township)	43557
Springhills	43318
Spring Meadows	45231
Spring Mill	44903
Spring Mountain	43844
Springvale	45140
Spring Valley (Township)	45370
Spring Valley (Greene County)	45370
Spring Valley (Lorain County)	44035
Spring Valley (Lucas County)	43528
Springville (Seneca County)	43316
Springville (Wayne County)	44676
Springwood	45056
Squirrel Town	45684
Stafford	43786
Standardsburg	44847
Standley	43527
Stanleyville	45788
Stanwood	44662
Starbucktown	45177
Starlight Plaza (Part of Sylvania)	43560
Starr (Township)	45764
Starr	45654
Starrs Corners	44406
State Road (Part of Cuyahoga Falls)	44223
Staunton	43160
Staunton (Township)	45373
Staunton	45373
Steam Corners	44904
Steinersville	43942
Stella	45622
Stelvideo	45331
Sterling (Brown County) (Township)	45154
Sterling (Wayne County)	44276
Sterling Heights	45005
Steuben	44847
Steubenville (Jefferson County) (Township)	43952
Steubenville (Jefferson County)	43952
Stewart	45778
Stewartsville	43960
Stillwater	44679
Stillwell	44637
Stiversville	45770
Stock (Harrison County) (Township)	43988
Stock (Noble County) (Township)	43724
Stockdale	45613
Stockham	45694
Stockport	43787
Stockton (Part of Fairfield)	45014
Stock Yards (Part of Cincinnati)	45225
Stokes (Logan County) (Township)	43331
Stokes (Madison County) (Township)	43153
Stone	43720
Stone Creek	43840
Stonelick (Township)	45103
Stonelick	45103
Stony Lake	44615
Stony Prairie	43420
Stony Ridge	43463
Stonyrill	45005
Stout	45684
Stoutsville	43154
Stovertown	43701
Stow	44224
Strasburg	44680
Stratford	43015
Stratton	43961
Streetsboro	44241
Stringtown (Athens County)	45701
Stringtown (Brown County)	45167
Stringtown (Clermont County)	45120
Stringtown (Perry County)	43731
Strongs Ridge	44811
Strongsville	44136
Struthers	44471
Stryker	43557
Stuart Manor	43952
Suffield (Township)	44260
Suffield	44260
Sugar Bush Knolls	44240
Sugar Creek (Allen County) (Township)	45807
Sugar Creek (Athens County)	45701
Sugar Creek (Greene County) (Township)	45305
Sugar Creek (Putnam County) (Township)	45830
Sugar Creek (Stark County) (Township)	44662
Sugar Creek (Tuscarawas County) (Township)	44681
Sugar Creek (Wayne County) (Township)	44618
Sugarcreek (Tuscarawas County)	44681
Sugar Grove (Crawford County)	44820
Sugar Grove (Fairfield County)	43155
Sugar Grove (Jefferson County)	43964
Sugar Grove (Miami County)	45318
Sugar Grove (Scioto County)	45662
Sugar Grove Hill	45506
Sugar Ridge	43402
Sugar Tree Ridge	45133
Sugar Valley	45320
Sullivan	44880
Sullivan (Township)	44880
Sulphurgrove (Part of Huber Heights)	45424
Sulphur Springs	44881
Summerfield	43788
Summerford	43140
Summerside	45244
Summerside Estates	45244
Summersville	43067
Summit (Hamilton County)	45238
Summit (Monroe County) (Township)	43754
Summit (Ross County)	45601

Summit-Unionport **OHIO** **431**

Name	ZIP
Summit (Trumbull County)	44420
Summit Mall (Part of Fairlawn)	44313
Summit Station	43073
Summitville	43962
Sumner	45720
Sunbury (Delaware County)	43074
Sunbury (Montgomery County)	45327
Sundale	43767
Sunfish (Township)	45661
Sunny Acres	43952
Sunnyland	44502
Sunny Meade	43725
Sunnyside Beach (Part of Vermilion)	44089
Sunsbury (Township)	43716
Sunset Beach	44429
Sunset Heights	43912
Sunset Point	44077
Sunshine	45684
Sunshine Park	43952
Sun Valley	43227
Sun Valley Estates	45505
Superior (Township)	43543
Surrey Hill	44484
Sutton (Township)	45771
Swan (Township)	45622
Swan Creek (Township)	43558
Swanders	45369
Swanktown	45309
Swanton (Fulton County)	43558
Swanton (Lucas County) (Township)	43558
Swickards Additions	43952
Swifton Commons (Part of Cincinnati)	45237
Switzerland (Township)	43942
Sybene	45680
Sycamore (Hamilton County) (Township)	45242
Sycamore (Wyandot County) (Township)	44882
Sycamore	44882
Sycamore Valley	43789
Sychar Road	43050
Sylvania (Township)	43560
Sylvania	43560
Symmes (Butler County)	45014
Symmes (Hamilton County) (Township)	45242
Symmes (Lawrence County) (Township)	45688
Syracuse	45779
Taborville	44022
Tacoma	43713
Taft	45236
Tallmadge	44278
Tama	45822
Tarlton	43135
Tate (Township)	45106
Tatmans	43730
Tawawa	45365
Taylor (Franklin County)	43230
Taylor (Union County) (Township)	43344
Taylor Creek (Township)	43326
Taylor Farm Acres	44614
Taylorsburg	45315
Taylors Creek	45239
Taylorsville	45133
Taylortown (Jefferson County)	43964
Taylortown (Richland County)	44875
Tedrow	43567
Teegarden	44432
Temperanceville	43713
Ten Hills	45805
Tennyson	45661
Terminal Junction (Part of Martins Ferry)	43935
Terrace Park	45174
Terre Haute	43078
Terry Acres	43524
Texas (Crawford County) (Township)	44882
Texas (Henry County)	43532
Thackery	43078
Thatcher	43113
The Avenue	44438
The Bend	43512
The Eastern	43908
Thelma City	44601
The Plains	45780
The Village of Indian Hill	45243
Thompson (Delaware County) (Township)	43066
Thompson (Geauga County) (Township)	44086

Name	ZIP
Thompson (Geauga County)	44086
Thompson (Seneca County) (Township)	44828
Thorn (Township)	43076
Thornville (Perry County)	43076
Thorny Acres	45042
Three Locks	45601
Thrifton	45123
Thurman	45685
Thurston	43157
Tiffin (Adams County) (Township)	45693
Tiffin (Defiance County) (Township)	43512
Tiffin (Seneca County)	44883
Tiltonsville	43963
Timberlake	44094
Tinny	43435
Tipp City	45371
Tippecanoe	44699
Tipton	45851
Tiro	44887
Tiverton (Township)	43006
Tiverton	43006
Toboso	43055
Tod (Township)	44882
Todds	43728
Toledo	43601-99
For specific Toledo Zip Codes call (419) 245-6811	
Toledo Dock (Part of Oregon)	43618
Toledo Great Eastern Shopping Center (Part of Northwood)	43616
Toledo Miracle Mile Shopping Center (Part of Toledo)	43613
Tom Corwin	45692
Tomlison Addition	45648
Tontogany	43565
Torch	45781
Toronto	43964
Town and Country Estates	45429
Town and Country Shopping Center (Part of Whitehall)	43213
Townsend (Huron County) (Township)	44826
Townsend (Sandusky County) (Township)	43464
Townview	45427
Townwood	45856
Tradersville	43044
Trail	44624
Trail Run	43946
Tranquility	45679
Traschel	43302
Trebein (Part of Beavercreek)	45385
Tremont City	45372
Trenton (Butler County)	45067
Trenton (Delaware County) (Township)	43021
Triadelphia	43758
Tri-County Mall (Part of Springdale)	45246
Trimble	45782
Trimble (Township)	45782
Trinway	43842
Tri-Village (Part of Columbus)	43212
Trotwood	45426
Trowbridge	43432
Troy (Ashland County) (Township)	44859
Troy (Athens County) (Township)	45723
Troy (Delaware County) (Township)	43015
Troy (Geauga County) (Township)	44021
Troy (Miami County)	45373
Troy (Morrow County) (Township)	44901
Troy (Richland County) (Township)	44904
Troy (Wood County) (Township)	43443
Truetown	45761
Trumbull	44041
Trumbull (Township)	44041
Truro (Franklin County)	43227
Truro (Franklin County) (Township)	43068
Tuckaho	44003
Tucson	45601
Tully (Marion County) (Township)	43314

Name	ZIP
Tully (Van Wert County) (Township)	45832
Tunnel	45750
Tunnel Hill	43844
Tuppers Plains	45783
Turpin Hills	45244
Turtle Creek (Shelby County) (Township)	45365
Turtle Creek (Warren County) (Township)	45036
Tuscarawas (Coshocton County) (Township)	43812
Tuscarawas (Stark County) (Township)	44646
Tuscarawas (Tuscarawas County)	44682
Twain	44212
Twenty Mile Stand	45140
Twightwee	45140
Twin (Darke County) (Township)	45304
Twin (Preble County) (Township)	45381
Twin (Ross County) (Township)	45617
Twin Lakes (Allen County)	45804
Twin Lakes (Portage County)	44240
Twinsburg (Summit County)	44087
Twinsburg (Summit County) (Township)	44087
Twinsburg Heights	44087
Twin Valley	45662
Two Hundred Ten Row	45701
Tymochtee (Township)	44882
Tymochtee	43351
Tyndall	43812
Uhrichsville	44683
Union (Athens County)	45766
Union (Auglaize County) (Township)	45895
Union (Belmont County) (Township)	43759
Union (Brown County) (Township)	45167
Union (Butler County) (Township)	45069
Union (Carroll County) (Township)	44615
Union (Champaign County) (Township)	43009
Union (Clermont County) (Township)	45245
Union (Clinton County) (Township)	45177
Union (Fayette County) (Township)	43160
Union (Hancock County) (Township)	45881
Union (Highland County) (Township)	45133
Union (Knox County) (Township)	43014
Union (Lawrence County) (Township)	45619
Union (Licking County) (Township)	43025
Union (Logan County) (Township)	43311
Union (Madison County) (Township)	43140
Union (Mercer County) (Township)	45862
Union (Miami County) (Township)	45383
Union (Montgomery County)	45322
Union (Morgan County) (Township)	43758
Union (Muskingum County) (Township)	43762
Union (Pike County) (Township)	45648
Union (Putnam County) (Township)	45844
Union (Ross County) (Township)	45628
Union (Scioto County) (Township)	45652
Union (Tuscarawas County) (Township)	44621
Union (Union County) (Township)	43045
Union (Van Wert County) (Township)	45891
Union (Warren County) (Township)	45036
Union City	45390
Union Furnace	43158
Union Landing Siding	45638
Union Plains	45154
Unionport	43966

432 OHIO Uniontown-Waterford

	ZIP		ZIP		ZIP
Uniontown (Belmont County)	43950	Vernon (Scioto County) (Township)	45694	Warrensburg	43061
Uniontown (Stark County)	44685	Vernon (Lawrence County)	45659	Warrensville (Township)	44122
Unionvale	43907	Vernon (Trumbull County)	44428	Warrensville Heights	44122
Unionville (Ashtabula County)	44088	Vernon Heights (Part of Marion)	43302	Warrenton	43943
Unionville (Morgan County)	43756	Verona	45378	Warsaw	43844
Unionville Center	43077	Versailles	45380	Warwick (Summit County)	44216
Uniopolis	45888	Vesuvius	45659	Warwick (Tuscarawas County) (Township)	44663
Unity (Township)	44413	Veterans Administration (Montgomery County)	45428	Washington (Auglaize County) (Township)	45871
Unity (Adams County)	45693	Veterans Administration Medical Center (Ross County)	45601	Washington (Belmont County) (Township)	43716
Unity (Columbiana County)	44413	Veto	45714	Washington (Brown County) (Township)	45171
University (Part of Columbus)	43210	Vickery	43464	Washington (Carroll County) (Township)	44615
University Center (Part of Cleveland)	44106	Vicksville	45732	Washington (Clermont County) (Township)	45153
University Heights (Allen County)	45804	Vienna	44473	Washington (Clinton County) (Township)	45114
University Heights (Cuyahoga County)	44118	Vienna (Township)	44473	Washington (Columbiana County) (Township)	43945
University View	43212	Vigo	45601	Washington (Coshocton County) (Township)	43842
Upland Heights	43943	Viking Village	45244	Washington (Darke County) (Township)	47390
Upper (Township)	45645	Villa	45503	Washington (Defiance County) (Township)	43549
Upper Arlington (Butler County)	45042	Villa Nova	45885	Washington (Franklin County) (Township)	43017
Upper Arlington (Franklin County)	43221	Vincent (Lorain County)	44035	Washington (Guernsey County) (Township)	43749
Upper Fox Hollow	45502	Vincent (Washington County)	45784	Washington (Hancock County) (Township)	45830
Upper Lowell	45744	Vinton	45686	Washington (Hardin County) (Township)	45835
Upper Sandusky	43351	Vinton (Township)	45670	Washington (Harrison County) (Township)	44699
Urbana (Champaign County)	43078	Violet (Township)	43147	Washington (Henry County) (Township)	43532
Urbana (Champaign County) (Township)	43078	Virginia (Township)	43811	Washington (Highland County) (Township)	45133
Urbancrest	43123	Vo-Ash Lake	44615	Washington (Hocking County) (Township)	43138
Utica (Licking County)	43080	Volunteer Bay	44089	Washington (Holmes County) (Township)	44638
Utica (Warren County)	45036	Vore Ridge	45780	Washington (Jackson County) (Township)	45692
Utopia	45121	Wabash (Darke County) (Township)	45380	Washington (Lawrence County) (Township)	45656
Valley (Columbiana County)	44460	Wabash (Mercer County)	45822	Washington (Licking County) (Township)	43080
Valley (Guernsey County) (Township)	43772	Wacker Heights	43130	Washington (Logan County) (Township)	43348
Valley (Scioto County) (Township)	45648	Waco	44707	Washington (Lucas County) (Township)	43612
Valley City	44280	Wade	45767	Washington (Mercer County) (Township)	45828
Valley City Station	44280	Wadsworth (Medina County)	44281	Washington (Miami County) (Township)	45356
Valley Crossing (Part of Columbus)	43207	Wadsworth (Medina County) (Township)	44281	Washington (Monroe County) (Township)	45734
Valleydale (Part of Cincinnati)	45216	Waggoner Place	43551	Washington (Montgomery County) (Township)	45459
Valley Forge	44212	Wagram	43062	Washington (Morrow County) (Township)	43338
Valley Glen	43938	Wahlsburg	45121	Washington (Muskingum County) (Township)	43701
Valley Hi	43360	Wainwright (Jackson County)	45692	Washington (Paulding County) (Township)	45859
Valley View (Cuyahoga County)	44131	Wainwright (Tuscarawas County)	44663	Washington (Pickaway County) (Township)	43113
Valleyview (Franklin County)	43204	Waite Hill	44094	Washington (Preble County) (Township)	45320
Valley View (Jefferson County)	43910	Wakatomika	43821	Washington (Richland County) (Township)	44906
Valley View (Scioto County)	45662	Wakefield (Darke County)	45331	Washington (Sandusky County) (Township)	43442
Valley View Estates	44403	Wakefield (Pike County)	45687	Washington (Scioto County) (Township)	45662
Valley View Heights	45244	Wakeman	44889	Washington (Shelby County) (Township)	45365
Valley View Village	43701	Wakeman (Township)	44889	Washington (Stark County) (Township)	44601
Valleywood (Part of Beavercreek)	45430	Walbridge	43465	Washington (Tuscarawas County) (Township)	43832
Vanatta	43055	Waldo	43356	Washington (Union County) (Township)	43344
Van Buren (Darke County) (Township)	45304	Waldo (Township)	43356	Washington (Van Wert County) (Township)	45833
Van Buren (Hancock County) (Township)	45897	Walhonding (Coshocton County)	43843	Washington (Warren County) (Township)	45054
Van Buren (Hancock County)	45889	Walhonding (Guernsey County)	43772	Washington (Wood County) (Township)	43565
Vanburen (Licking County)	43055	Wallace Heights	43964	Washington Court House	43160
Van Buren (Putnam County) (Township)	45856	Walnut (Fairfield County) (Township)	43046	Washingtonville	44490
Van Buren (Shelby County) (Township)	45336	Walnut (Gallia County) (Township)	45658	Waterford (Township)	45786
Vandalia	45377	Walnut (Pickaway County) (Township)	43103	Waterford (Knox County)	43019
Vanderhook	45723	Walnut Creek	44687	Waterford (Washington County)	45786
Vanlue	45890	Walnut Creek (Township)	44687		
Van Wert	45891	Walnut Hills (Hamilton County)	45206		
Vaughan (Part of Evendale)	45241	Walnut Hills (Jackson County)	45640		
Vaughnsville	45893	Walnut Hills (Stark County)	44646		
Vega	45685	Walnutrun	43140		
Venedocia	45894	Walton Hills	44146		
Venice (Erie County)	44870	Wamsley	45657		
Venice (Seneca County) (Township)	44807	Wapakoneta	45895		
Venice Heights	44484	Ward (Township)	43144		
Vera Cruz	45118	Wardwood Acres	45239		
Vermilion (Erie County)	44089	Warner	45745		
Vermilion (Erie County) (Township)	44089	Warnock	43967		
Vermilion-on-the-Lake (Part of Vermilion)	44089	Warren	44481-85		
Vermilion (Township)	44805	For specific Warren Zip Codes call (216) 392-1571			
Vernon (Township)	44428	Warren (Belmont County) (Township)	43713		
Vernon (Clinton County) (Township)	45113	Warren (Jefferson County) (Township)	43943		
Vernon (Richland County)	44875	Warren (Trumbull County) (Township)	44430		
Vernon (Crawford County) (Township)	44827	Warren (Tuscarawas County) (Township)	44656		
		Warren (Washington County) (Township)	45750		
		Warren Correctional Institution	45036		

Wayne-Windy Acres **OHIO** 433

Name	ZIP
Wayne (Adams County) (Township)	45618
Wayne (Ashtabula County)	44093
Wayne (Knox County) (Township)	43019
Wayne (Monroe County) (Township)	45734
Wayne (Muskingum County) (Township)	43701
Wayne (Noble County) (Township)	43773
Wayne (Pickaway County) (Township)	43113
Wayne (Tuscarawas County) (Township)	44624
Wayne (Warren County) (Township)	45068
Wayne (Wayne County) (Township)	44691
Wayne (Wood County)	43466
Wayne Lakes	45331
Waynesburg (Crawford County)	44887
Waynesburg (Stark County)	44688
Waynesfield	45896
Waynesville	45068
Weathersfield (Township)	44420
Weaver Station	45331
Webb Heights	43947
Webb Summit	43138
Webster (Darke County)	45308
Webster (Wood County) (Township)	43450
Wegee	43947
Weller (Township)	44903
Wellington	44090
Wellington (Township)	44090
Wellington Park	45231
Wells (Township)	43913
Wellston	45692
Wellsville	43968
Welshfield	44021
Welshtown	45769
Wengerlawn	45309
Wernert (Part of Toledo)	43613
Wesley (Township)	45713
Wesleyan Woods (Part of Delaware)	43015
West (Township)	44625
West Akron (Part of Akron)	44307
West Alexandria	45381
West Andover	44003
West Austintown	44515
West Bass Lake	44024
West Bedford	43844
West Bellaire (Part of Bellaire)	43906
West Berlin	43015
Westboro	45148
West Brookfield (Part of Massillon)	44646
West Carlisle (Coshocton County)	43822
West Carlisle (Lorain Co.)	44035
West Carrollton City	45449
West Charleston	45371
West Chesapeake	45619
West Chester (Butler County)	45069
West Chester (Tuscarawas County)	44699
West Clarksfield	44889
West Covington	45318
West Elkton	45070
West End (Part of Ashtabula)	44004
West Enon Estates	45323
Westerly Park	45805
Western Hills (Hamilton County)	45238
Western Hills (Washington County)	45750
Western Hills Plaza (Part of Cincinnati)	45211
Western Reserve Estates	44236
Westerville	43081
West Fairport (Part of Grand River)	44045
West Farmington	44491
Westfield (Township)	43003
Westfield (Columbiana County)	43920
Westfield (Medina County) (Township)	44251
Westfield (Morrow County)	43003
Westfield Center	44251
West Florence	45320
Westgate Mall (Part of Fairview Park)	44126
Westgate Village (Part of Toledo)	43606

Name	ZIP
Westhope	43516
West Independence	44802
West Jefferson (Madison County)	43162
West Jefferson (Williams County)	43543
West Lafayette	43845
Westlake	44145
West Lakeville (Part of Conneaut)	44030
West Lancaster	43128
Westland (Township)	43725
West Lebanon	44618
West Leipsic	45856
West Liberty (Crawford Co.)	44827
West Liberty (Logan Co.)	43357
West Liberty (Morrow Co.)	43334
West Lodi	44811
West Logan	43138
West London (Part of London)	43140
West Manchester	45382
West Mansfield	43358
West Marietta (Part of Marietta)	45750
West Marysville (Part of Marysville)	43040
West Mecca	44410
West Middletown	45042
West Millgrove	43467
West Milton	45383
Westminster	45850
Westmoor	44833
West Newton	45850
West Oberlin (Part of Oberlin)	44074
Weston	43569
Weston (Township)	43569
West Park (Cuyahoga County)	44111
West Park (Hancock County)	45840
West Park (Jefferson County)	43952
West Park (Stark County)	44646
West Point (Columbiana County)	44492
West Point (Morrow County)	44833
West Portsmouth	45662
West Powhatan (Part of Powhatan Point)	43942
West Richfield (Part of Richfield)	44286
West Rushville	43163
West Salem	44287
West Side (Part of Youngstown)	44509
West Sonora	45338
West Toledo (Part of Toledo)	43612
West Union	45693
West Unity	43570
Westview	44028
Westville (Champaign County)	43083
Westville (Columbiana County)	44609
Westville Lake	44609
West Warren (Part of Warren)	44485
West Wheeling	43906
West Williamsfield	44093
Westwood (Hamilton County)	45211
Westwood (Jefferson County)	43952
Westwood (Wayne County)	44691
Westwood Estates (Part of Steubenville)	43952
West Woodville	45107
Wetzel	45863
Weymouth	44256
Wharton	43359
Wheat Ridge	45693
Wheelersburg	45694
Wheeling (Belmont County) (Township)	43927
Wheeling (Guernsey County) (Township)	43749
Whetstone (Township)	44820
Whigville	43788
Whipple	45788
Whisler	45644
White Cottage	43791
White Eyes (Township)	43824
White Hall (Athens County)	45701
Whitehall (Franklin County)	43213
Whitehouse	43571
White Oak (Brown County)	45154
Whiteoak (Fayette County)	43143

Name	ZIP
White Oak (Hamilton County)	45239
White Oak (Highland County) (Township)	45133
White Oak Meadows	45239
White Oaks (Part of Steubenville)	43952
White Oak Valley (Brown County)	45121
White Pond	44321
White's Landing	43464
White Sulphur	43061
Whitetree (Part of Cincinnati)	45236
Whiteville	43540
Whitewater	45002
Whitewater (Township)	45002
Whitfield	45342
Wick	44093
Wickliffe (Lake County)	44092
Wickliffe (Mahoning County)	44515
Widowville	44805
Wiggonsville	45106
Wightmans Grove	43420
Wilberforce	45384
Wildare	44410
Wildbrook Acres	45231
Wildwood (Part of Middletown)	45042
Wilgus	45695
Wilkesville	45695
Wilkesville (Township)	45695
Wilkins Corners	43055
Willard	44890
Willetsville	45133
Williamsburg	45176
Williamsburg (Township)	45176
Williams Center	43506
Williams Corner	45103
Williamsdale	45011
Williamsfield	44093
Williamsfield (Township)	44093
Williamsport (Columbiana County)	44432
Williamsport (Morrow County)	43338
Williamsport (Pickaway County)	43164
Williamstown	45897
Williston	43468
Willobee (Part of Willoughby)	44094
Willoughby	44094-95
For specific Willoughby Zip Codes call (216) 942-9420	
Willoughby Hills	44092
Willow (Cuyahoga County)	44125
	44127
For specific Willow (Cuyahoga County) Zip Codes call (216) 443-4183	
Willow Brook Heights	44721
Willowcrest	44452
Willowdale Lake	44720
Willowdell	45380
Willow Grove	43906
Willowick	44094
Willow Lakes	43701
Willowville	45103
Willow Wood	45696
Wills (Township)	43755
Wills Creek	43811
Willshire	45898
Willshire (Township)	45898
Wilmington	45177
Wilmot	44689
Wilshire	45122
Wilshire Heights	45005
Wilson (Clinton County) (Township)	45169
Wilson (Monroe County)	43716
Wiltondale	45224
Winameg	43515
Winchester	45697
Winchester (Township)	45697
Winchester	45640
Windfall Heights	44256
Windham	44288
Windham (Township)	44288
Windor Park (Part of Xenia)	45385
Windsor	44099
Windsor (Township)	44099
Windsor (Lawrence County) (Township)	45678
Windsor (Morgan County) (Township)	43787
Windsor (Richland County)	44903
Windsor (Warren County)	45162
Windsor Mills	44099
Windy Acres	45502

434 OHIO Winesburg-Zone

	ZIP
Winesburg	44690
Winfield	44622
Wingett Run	45789
Wingston	43462
Winona	44493
Winterdale (Part of Wintersville)	43952
Winterhaven	45305
Winterset	43755
Wintersville	43952
Wintondale	45231
Winton Terrace (Part of Cincinnati)	45232
Wisterman	45831
Withamsville	45245
Wolf	43832
Wolfhurst	43912
Wolf Run	43970
Woodbourne	45459
Woodbourne-Hyde Park	45429
Woodhaven	45005
Woodington	45331
Woodlawn (Hamilton County)	45215
Woodlawn (Miami County)	45373
Woodlawn Village	45373
Woodmere	44122
Woodridge Plaza (Part of Fairfield)	45014
Woods	45056
Woodsdale	45067
Woodsfield	43793
Woodside	43406
Woodstock	43084
Woodville	43469
Woodville (Township)	43469
Woodville Gardens	43616
Woodville Mall (Part of Northwood)	43619
Woodworth	44512
Woodworth Corners	44473
Wooster (Wayne County)	44691
Wooster (Wayne County) (Township)	44691

	ZIP
Wooster Heights	44903
Worstville	45880
Worthington (Franklin County)	43085
Worthington (Richland County) (Township)	44822
Wren	45899
Wright Brothers (Part of Oakwood)	45409
Wright-Patterson Air Force Base	45433
Wrightsville	45144
Wrightview (Part of Fairborn)	45324
Wrightview Heights (Part of Fairborn)	45324
Wyandot	44849
Wyoming	45215
Wyoming Meadows	45231
Xavier (Part of Cincinnati)	45207
Xenia (Greene County)	45385
Xenia (Greene County) (Township)	45385
Yale (Ottawa County)	43468
Yale (Portage County)	44411
Yankeeburg	45768
Yankee Hills	44403
Yankee Lake	44403
Yankeetown	45130
Yatesville	43106
Yellowbud	45601
Yellow Creek (Township)	43968
Yellow Springs	45387
Yoder	45806
York (Athens County) (Township)	45764
York (Belmont County) (Township)	43942
York (Darke County) (Township)	45380
York (Fulton County) (Township)	43515

	ZIP
York (Jefferson County)	43901
York (Medina County) (Township)	44256
York (Morgan County) (Township)	43731
York (Sandusky County) (Township)	44811
York (Tuscarawas County) (Township)	44663
York (Union County) (Township)	43067
York (Van Wert County) (Township)	45874
York Center	43067
Yorkshire	45388
Yorkshire Estates	43302
Yorkville	43971
Youba Ridge	45723
Young Hickory	43732
Youngs	45657
Youngs Corners	44256
Youngstown	44501-15
For specific Youngstown Zip Codes call (216) 744-6822	
Youngsville	45679
Zahns Corners	45690
Zaleski	45698
Zane (Township)	43336
Zane Addition	45601
Zanesfield	43360
Zanesville	43701-02
For specific Zanesville Zip Codes call (614) 455-2802	
Zenz City	45846
Zimmer Estates	45431
Zimmerman (Part of Beavercreek)	45385
Ziontown	43076
Zoar (Tuscarawas County)	44697
Zoar (Warren County)	45152
Zoarville	44656
Zone	43521

Achille-Corum **OKLAHOMA** **435**

	ZIP		ZIP		ZIP
Achille	74720	Binger	73009	Carnegie	73015
Acme	73082	Bison	73720	Carney	74832
Ada	74820-21	Bixby	74008	Carpenter	73644
For specific Ada Zip Codes call (405) 332-6118		Blackburn	74058	Carriage Hills (Part of Lawton)	73501
		Blackgum	74962		
Adair	74330	Blackwell	74631	Carrier	73727
Adams	73901	Blair	73526	Carson	74850
Adamson	74547	Blanchard	73010	Carter (Beckham County)	73627
Addington	73520	Blanco	74528	Carter (Cherokee County)	74451
Afton	74331	Blocker	74529	Cartersville	74941
Agawam	73067	Blue	74701	Cartwright	74731
Agra	74824	Bluejacket	74333	Cashion	73016
Ahloso	74820	Bluff	74759	Castle	74833
Ahpeatone	73572	Boatman	74361	Catale	74332
Akins	74955	Boehler	74727	Catoosa	74015
Albany	74721	Boggy Depot	74525	Cedar Crest	74352
Albert	73001	Bois D'Arc	74601	Cedar Ridge (Part of Cleveland)	74020
Albion	74521	Boise City	73933		
Alderson	74522	Bokchito	74726	Cedar Valley	73044
Aledo	73654	Bokhoma	74740	Cement	73017
Alex	73002	Bokoshe	74930	Center	74820
Alfalfa	73015	Boley	74829	Center City (Part of Oklahoma City)	73102
Aline	73716	Bond	74426		
Allen	74825	Boone	73006	Centerview	74801
Allison	74730	Boss	74745	Centrahoma	74534
Alluwe	74048	Boswell	74727	Centralia	74336
Alma	73533	Boulevard (Part of Norman)	73069	Central Mall (Part of Lawton)	73501
Altus	73521-23	Bowden	74107		
For specific Altus Zip Codes call (405) 482-3339		Bowlegs	74830	Ceres	74651
		Bowling Spring	74016	Cerrogordo	74740
Alva	73717	Bowring	74009	Cestos	73859
Amber	73004	Box	74962	Chandler	74834
Ames	73718	Boynton	74422	Chase	74401
Amorita	73719	Braden	74959	Chattanooga	73528
Anadarko	73005	Bradley	73011	Checotah	74426
Antioch	73035	Brady	73098	Chelsea	74016
Antlers	74523	Braggs	74423	Cherokee	73728
Apache	73006	Braman	74632	Cherry Tree	74960
Apperson	74633	Bray	73012	Chester	73838
Apple	74760	Breckenridge	73701	Chewey	74964
Arapaho	73620	Brent	74955	Cheyenne	73628
Arcadia	73007	Briartown	74455	Chickasha	73018
Ardmore	73401-03	Bridgeport	73047	Childers	74027
For specific Ardmore Zip Codes call (405) 223-8383		Briggs	74464	Chilli	74578
		Brinkman	73673	Chilocco	74647
Arkoma	74901	Bristow	74010	Chitwood	73067
Arlington	74864	Britton (Part of Oklahoma City)	73114	Choctaw	73020
Armstrong	74729			Chouteau	74337
Arnett (Ellis County)	73832	Brock	73401	Christie	74965
Arnett (Harmon County)	73550	Broken Arrow	74011-14	Cimarron (Part of Oklahoma City)	73111
Arpelar	74548	For specific Broken Arrow Zip Codes call (918) 258-6626			
Artillery Village	73503			Cimmaron City	73028
Asher	74826	Broken Bow	74728	Cisco	74745
Ashland	74570	Bromide	74530	Citra	74825
Atoka	74525	Brooken	74462	Claremore	74017-18
Atwood	74827	Brooksville	74873	For specific Claremore Zip Codes call (918) 341-0614	
Avant	74001	Brown	74701		
Avard	73717	Broxton	73006	Clarita	74535
Avery	74023	Brush Hill	74426	Clarksville	74454
Bache	74526	Brushy	74955	Clayton	74536
Bacone (Part of Muskogee)	74401	Bryant	74880	Clayton Lake	74536
Bailey	73055	Buffalo (Harper County)	73834	Clear Lake	73849
Baker	73950	Buffalo (McCurtain County)	74963	Clearview	74835
Baldhill	74447	Bunch	74931	Clebit	74728
Balko	73931	Burbank	74633	Clemscot	73437
Ballard	74964	Burlington	73722	Cleora	74331
Banner (Part of El Reno)	73036	Burmah	73659	Cleo Springs	73729
Banty	74723	Burneyville	73430	Cleveland	74020
Barber	74471	Burns Flat	73624	Clinton	73601
Barnsdall	74002	Burwell	74754	Clothier (Part of Oklahoma City)	73160
Baron	74965	Bushyhead	74016		
Bartlesville	74003-06	Butler	73625	Cloud Chief	73632
For specific Bartlesville Zip Codes call (918) 336-0947		Butner	74884	Cloudy	74562
		Byars	74831	Clyde	73759
Battiest	74722	Byng	74820	Coalgate	74538
Baugh	74020	Byron	73723	Coalton	74437
Baum	73401	Cache	73527	Cobb	74701
Beachton	71945	Caddo	74729	Cogar	73059
Bearden	74859	Cairo	74538	Colbert	74733
Beaver	73932	Calera	74730	Colcord	74338
Bee	74748	Calhoun	74956	Cole	73010
Beggs	74421	Calida	74020	Coleman	73432
Beland	74401	Calumet	73014	College (Part of Stillwater)	74074
Bell	74960	Calvin	74531	Collinsville	74021
Bellemont	74864	Camargo	73835	Colony	73021
Belvin	74563	Cambria	74578	Comanche	73529
Belzoni	74523	Cameron	74932	Commerce	74339
Bengal	74966	Cameron University (Part of Lawton)	73505	Concho (Part of El Reno)	73022
Bennington	74723			Conner Correctional Center	74035
Bentley	74525	Camp Houston	73842	Connerville	74836
Berlin	73662	Canadian	74425	Conser	74937
Bernice	74331	Caney	74533	Cookietown	73562
Bessie	73622	Caney Ridge	74471	Cookson	74427
Bethany	73008	Canton	73724	Cooperton	73564
Bethel (Comanche County)	73501	Canute	73626	Copan	74022
Bethel (McCurtain County)	74724	Capitol Hill (Part of Oklahoma City)	73109	Corbett	73051
Bethel Acres	74801			Cordell	73632
Big Cabin	74332	Capron	73725	Corinne	74735
Big Cedar	74939	Cardin	74335	Corn	73024
Big Spring	74883	Carleton	73772	Cornish	73456
Billings	74630	Carmen	73726	Corum	73529

436 OKLAHOMA

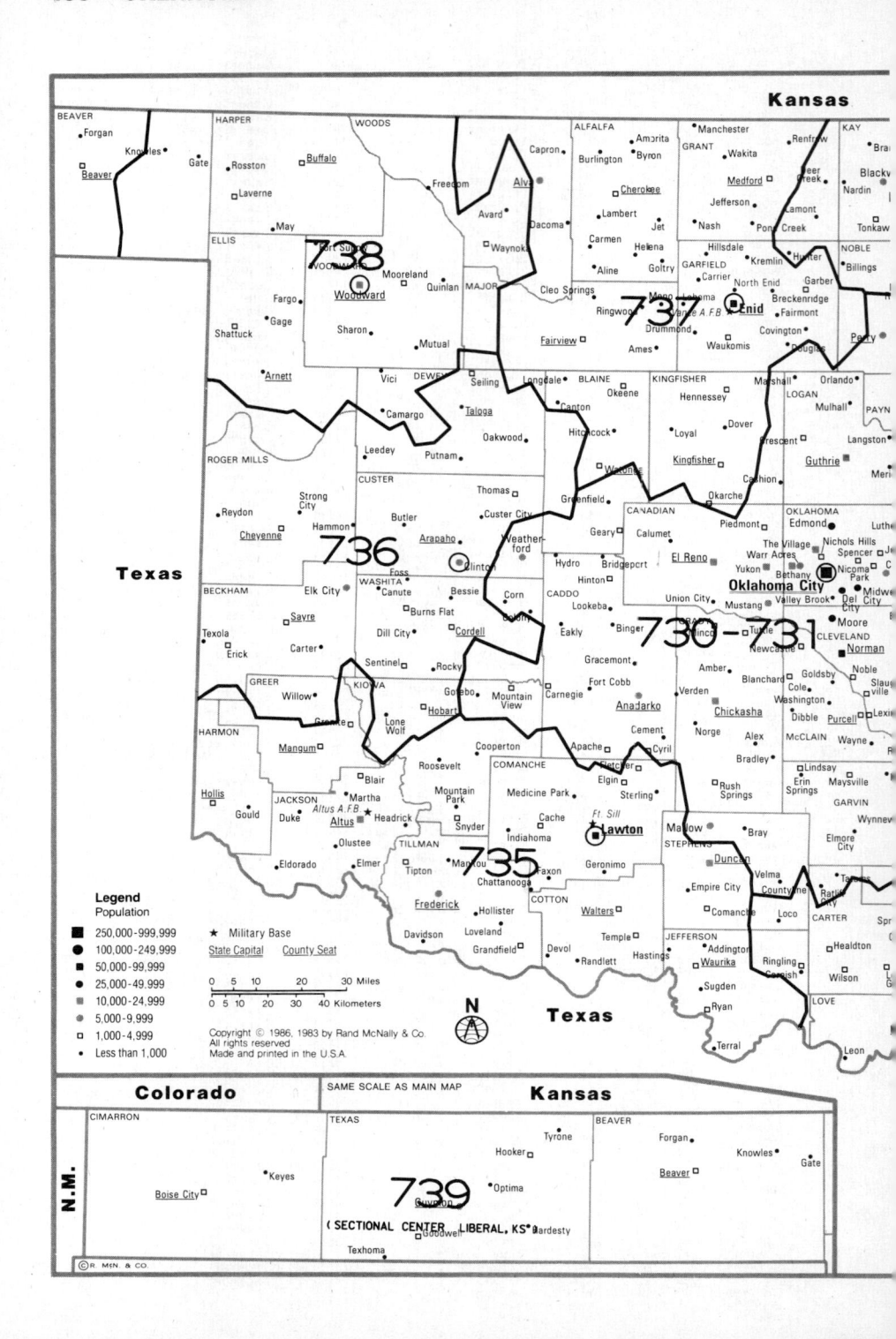

OKLAHOMA 437

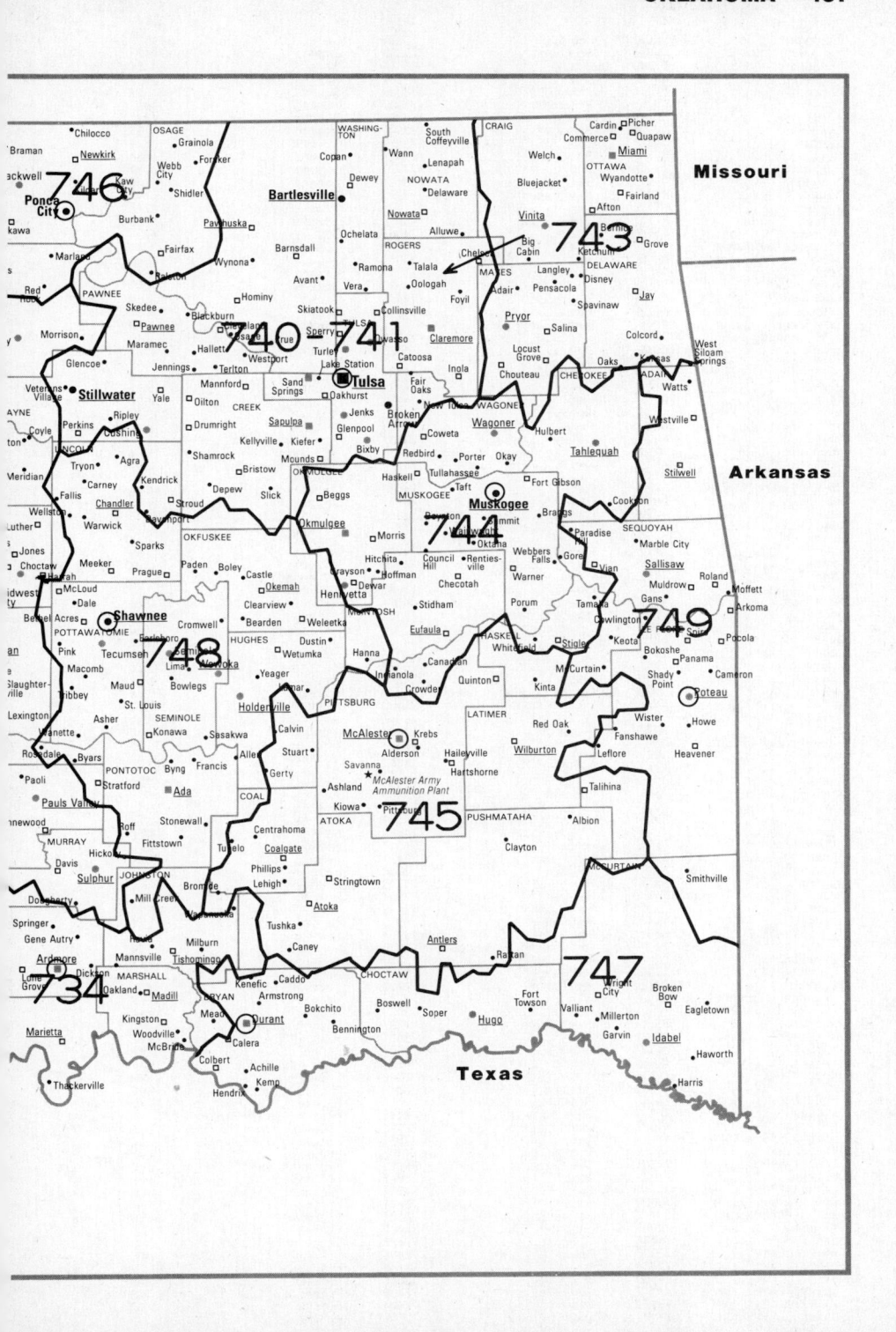

438 OKLAHOMA Cottonwood-Hollister

Name	ZIP
Cottonwood	74538
Council Hill	74428
Countyline	73025
Courtney	73456
Covington	73730
Cowden	73632
Coweta	74429
Cowlington	74941
Cox City	73082
Coyle	73027
Cravens	74563
Crawford	73638
Creosote	74743
Crescent	73028
Criner	73080
Cromwell	74837
Crossroads Mall (Part of Oklahoma City)	73149
Crowder	74430
Crystal Lakes	73718
Cumberland	73446
Curchece	74020
Curt's Shopping Center (Part of Muskogee)	74401
Cushing	74023
Custer City	73639
Cyril	73029
Dacoma	73731
Daisy	74540
Dale	74838
Damon	74578
Darwin	74523
Davenport	74026
Davidson	73530
Davis	73030
Dawson (Part of Tulsa)	74115
Deer Creek	74636
Degnan	74578
Delaware	74027
Del City	73115
Delhi	73662
Dempsey	73628
Dennis	74336
Depew	74028
Depot	74501
Devol	73531
Dewar	74431
Dewey	74029
Dibble	73031
Dickson	73401
Dighton	74437
Dillard	73463
Dill City	73641
Disney	74340
Dixon	74884
Donaldson (Part of Tulsa)	74104
Dotyville	74354
Dougherty	73032
Douglas	73733
Dover	73734
Dow	74501
Doyle	73039
Drake	73086
Driftwood	73728
Drumb	74578
Drummond	73735
Drumright	74030
Duke	73532
Dunbar	73448
Duncan	73533-34
For specific Duncan Zip Codes call (405) 255-7226	
Dunjee Park (Part of Oklahoma City)	73084
Durant	74701-02
For specific Durant Zip Codes call (405) 924-6464	
Durham	73642
Durwood (Part of Dickson)	73401
Dustin	74839
Eagle City	73658
Eagletown	74734
Eakly	73033
Earl	73447
Earlsboro	74840
Eastborough	74014
Eastern Oklahoma A&M College	74578
Eastern State Hospital	74301
East Jessie	74871
Eastland Mall (Part of Tulsa)	74114
Eastside (Custer County)	73096
East Side (Washington County)	74006
Eddy	74643
Edgewater Park	73006
Edmond	73034
Edna	74010
Eighty Ninth Street (Part of Oklahoma City)	73159
Eldon	74464

Name	ZIP
Eldorado	73537
Elgin	73538
Elk City	73644
Elmer	73539
Elmore City	73035
Elmwood	73932
El Reno	73036
Emerson Center	73572
Emet	73450
Empire City	73533
Empy	74020
Enid	73701-06
For specific Enid Zip Coces call (405) 237-4331	
Enos	73439
Enterprise	74561
Enville	73448
Erick	73645
Erin Springs	73052
Ethel	74523
Etta	74471
Eucha	74342
Euchee Creek (Part of Sand Springs)	74063
Eufaula	74432
Eva	73939
Ewing (Part of Clinton)	73601
Fairfax	74637
Fairland	74343
Fairmont	73736
Fair Oaks	74015
Fairview	73737
Falconhead	73430
Falfa	74571
Fallis	74881
Fame	74432
Fanshawe	74935
Fargo	73840
Farley (Part of Oklahoma City)	73107
Farmers Hill	74736
Farris	74542
Faxon	73540
Fay	73646
Featherston	74561
Federal Correctional Institution	73036
Felker	74764
Felt	73937
Fillmore	73432
Finley	74543
First National Bank (Part of Oklahoma City)	73102
Fisher (Part of Sand Springs)	74063
Fittstown	74842
Fitzhugh	74843
Fletcher	73541
Floris	73938
Folsom	73432
Fontana Shopping Center (Part of Tulsa)	74145
Foraker	74652
Forest Hill	74937
Forest Park	73121
Forgan	73938
Forney	74743
Forrester	74937
Fort Cobb	73038
Fort Coffee	74959
Fort Gibson	74434
Fort Reno (Part of El Reno)	73036
Fort Sill (Comanche County)	73503
Fort Supply	73841
Fort Towson	74735
Foss	73647
Foster	73039
Four Corners	74437
Fox	73435
Foyil	74031
Francis	74844
Frederick	73542
Freedom	73842
French Market (Part of Oklahoma City)	73116
Friendship	73521
Frisco	74871
Frogville	74743
Gaar Corner	74820
Gage	73843
Gans	74936
Garber	73738
Garden Grove	74801
Garland	74462
Garvin	74736
Gate	73844
Gay	74743
Geary	73040
Gene Autry	73436
Georgetown	74434
Geronimo	73543

Name	ZIP
Gerty	74531
Gibson	74467
Gideon	74464
Gilcrease (Part of Tulsa)	74127
Gilmore	74953
Glencoe	74032
Glendale	74940
Glenpool	74033
Glover	74728
Golden	74737
Goldsby	73093
Goltry	73739
Goodland	74743
Goodwater	74740
Goodwell	73939
Gore	74435
Gotebo	73041
Gould	73544
Gowen	74545
Gracemont	73042
Grady	73569
Graham	73437
Grainola	74652
Grandfield	73546
Grand Lake Towne	74301
Granite	73547
Grant	74738
Gray Horse	74637
Grayson	74437
Greasy	74931
Greenfield	73043
Green Pastures (Part of Oklahoma City)	73084
Green Valley Estates	74962
Greenville	73448
Greenwood	74523
Grimes	73628
Grove	74344
Guthrie	73044
Guymon	73942
Haileyville	74546
Hall Addition (Part of Sand Springs)	74063
Hallett	74034
Hall Park	73069
Hammon	73650
Hanna	74845
Hanson	74955
Happyland	74820
Harden City	74871
Hardesty	73944
Harmon	73832
Harrah	73045
Harris	74740
Harrison	74955
Hartshorne	74547
Haskell	74436
Hastings	73548
Haw Creek	74939
Hawley	73761
Haworth	74740
Hayward	73730
Haywood	74548
Headrick	73549
Healdton	73438
Heavener	74937
Helena	73741
Hendrix	74741
Hennepin	73046
Hennessey	73742
Henryetta	74437
Heritage Hills	73507
Heritage Park Mall (Part of Midwest City)	73110
Hess	73539
Hester	73554
Hewitt (Part of Wilson)	73463
Hext	73645
Hickory	74865
Hicks Addition (Part of Spencer)	73084
Hill	74932
Hillsdale	73743
Hillsdale Free Will Baptist College	73160
Hill Top	74570
Hinton	73047
Hissom Memorial Center	74063
Hitchcock	73744
Hitchita	74438
Hobart	73651
Hockerville	74363
Hodgen	74939
Hodge Podge (Part of Tulsa)	74105
Hoffman	74437
Holdenville	74848
Holley Creek	74728
Hollis	73550
Hollister	73551

Homer-Non **OKLAHOMA** 439

Name	ZIP	Name	ZIP	Name	ZIP
Homer	74820	Lambert	73728	Marland	74644
Homestead	73763	La Mesa (Part of Enid)	73701	Marlow	73055
Hominy	74035	Lamont	74643	Marshall	73056
Honobia	74549	Lane	74555	Martha	73556
Hontubby	74937	Langley	74350	Martin	74401
Hooker	73945	Langston	73050	Mason	74859
Hoot Owl	74365	Lark	73439	Matoy	74729
Hopeton	73746	Last Chance	74859	Maud	74854
Hough	73942	Latta	74820	Maxwell	74820
Howard C. McLeod Correctional Center	74542	Laverne	73848	May	73851
Howe	74940	Lawrence Creek	74044	Mayfield	73656
Hoyt	74440	Lawton	73501-07	May Ridge (Part of Oklahoma City)	73119
Hugo	74743	For specific Lawton Zip Codes call (405) 353-1500		Maysville	73057
Hulbert	74441	Leach	74364	Mazie	74353
Hulen	73572	Leader	74825	Mead	73449
Humphreys	73521	Leander	74020	Medford	73759
Hunter	74640	Lebanon	73440	Medicine Park	73557
Hyde Park (Part of Muskogee)	74401	Leedey	73654	Meeker	74855
Hydro	73048	Leflore	74942	Meers	73558
Idabel	74745	Lehigh	74556	Mehan	74074
Independence	74937	Leisure Square (Part of Tulsa)	74112	Mellette	74432
Indiahoma	73552	Lenapah	74042	Melvin	74441
Indian Meadows	74464	Lenna	74432	Meno	73760
Indianola	74442	Lenora	73667	Meridian	73058
Ingalls	74074	Leon	73441	Merritt	73644
Ingersoll	73728	Leonard	74043	Messer	74743
Inola	74036	Lequire	74943	Miami	74354-55
Iona	73086	Leroy	74020	For specific Miami Zip Codes call (918) 542-8325	
Iron Stob Corner	74736	Lewisville	74552	Micawber	74882
Irving	73565	Lexington	73051	Middleberg	73010
Isabella	73747	Lexington Assessment and Recption Center	73051	Midlothian	74834
Jackson	74723			Midway	74538
Jacktown	74855	Liberty (Bryan County)	74741	Midwest City	73110
Jamestown	74080	Liberty (Sequoyah County)	74948	Milburn	73450
Jay	74346	Liberty (Tulsa County)	74101	Milfay	74046
Jefferson	73759	Lighthouse (Part of Tulsa)	74136	Mill Creek	74856
Jenks	74037	Lima	74884	Miller	74557
Jennings	74038	Limestone (Latimer County)	74578	Millerton	74750
Jesse	74871	Limestone (Rogers County)	74017	Milo	73401
Jet	73749	Lincolnville	74363	Milton	74944
Jimtown	73430	Lindsay	73052	Minco	73059
Joburn	74556	Little	74868	Moffett	74946
Joe Harp Correctional Center	73051	Little Chief	74637	Monroe	74947
		Little City	73446	Montclair Addition (Part of Heavener)	74937
John H. Lilley Correctional Center	74829	Little Ponderosa	67901		
		Loco	73442	Moodys	74444
Johnson	74801	Locust Grove	74352	Moon	74740
Jollyville	73030	Logan	73849	Moore	73160
Jones	73049	Lona	74552	Mooreland	73852
Joy	73098	Lone Grove	73443	Moorewood	73650
Juby's	74020	Lone Oak	74948	Morris	74445
Jumbo	74557	Lone Wolf	73655	Morrison	73061
Kansas	74347	Long	74948	Mound Grove	74764
Karen Park (Part of Midwest City)	73110	Longdale	73755	Mounds	74047
		Lookeba	73053	Mountain Park	73559
Katie	73035	Lotsee	74063	Mountain View	73062
Kaw City	74641	Loveland	73553	Mount Herman	74728
Keefeton	74401	Lovell	73028	Mount Zion	74736
Keetonville	74037	Loving	74937	Moyers	74557
Kellond	74523	Loyal	73756	Mudsand	74759
Kellyville (Creek County)	74039	Lucien	73757	Muldrow	74948
Kellyville (Ottawa County)	74370	Lugert	73655	Mule Barn (Part of Cleveland)	74101
Kemp	74747	Lula	74825		
Kendrick	74079	Luther	73054	Mulhall	73063
Kenefic	74748	Lutie	74578	Murphy	74352
Kensington Center (Part of Tulsa)	74103	Lynn Addition	74056	Muse	74949
		Lyons	74960	Muskogee	74401-03
Kent	74759	McAlester	74501-02	For specific Muskogee Zip Codes call (918) 682-7846	
Kenton	73946	For specific McAlester Zip Codes call (918) 423-4048			
Kenwood	74365			Mustang	73064
Keota	74941	McAlester Army Ammunition Plant	74501	Mutual	73853
Ketchum	74349			Nani-Chito	74957
Keyes	73947	MacArthur Park (Part of Lawton)	73507	Narcissa	74354
Kiamichi	74574			Nardin	74646
Kiefer	74041	McBride	73439	Nash	73761
Kildare	74601	McCurtain	74944	Nashoba	74558
Kingfisher	73750	McKey	74962	Natura	74421
Kingston	73439	Mack H. Alford Correctional Center	74569	Navina	73044
Kinta	74552			Nebo	73086
Kiowa	74553	McKiddyville	73051	Needmore	73068
Knowles	73847	McKnight	73550	Neff	74953
Konawa	74849	McLain	74401	Nelagony	74056
Kosoma	74557	McLoud	74851	Newalla (Part of Oklahoma City)	74857
Krebs	74554	McMillan	73446		
Kremlin	73753	Macomb	74852	Newcastle	73065
Kulli	74745	McWillie	73716	Newkirk	74647
Kusa	74437	Madill	73446	New Liberty	73662
Lacey	73742	Maguire (Part of Slaughterville)	73068	New Lima	74884
Lahoma	73754			New Oberlin	74727
Lake Aluma	73121	Manard	74434	Newport	73401
Lake Creek	73547	Manchester	73758	New Tulsa	74429
Lake Hiwasse	73007	Mangum	73554	Nichols Hills	73116
Lake Humphreys	73055	Manitou	73555	Nicoma Park	73066
Lakeside Village	73538	Mannford	74044	Nicut	74948
Lake Station (Part of Sand Springs)	74127	Mannsville	73447	Nida	74748
		Maple	74948	Ninnekah	73067
Lake Valley	73041	Maramec	74045	Noble	73068
Lake West	74727	Marble City	74945	Nobletown	74884
Lamar	74850	Marietta	73448	Non	74531

440 OKLAHOMA Norge-Sequoyah

Name	ZIP
Norge	73018
Norman	73069-72
For specific Norman Zip Codes call (405) 321-2484	
Norris	74563
Northeast (Part of Tulsa)	74115
North Enid	73701
North McAlester (Part of McAlester)	74501
North Miami	74358
Northside (Part of Tulsa)	74106
Northwest (Part of Oklahoma City)	73106
Nowata	74048
Nuyaka	74447
Oak Grove (Murray County)	73032
Oak Grove (Pawnee County)	74020
Oak Grove (Payne County)	74030
Oak Hill	74728
Oakhurst	74050
Oakland	73446
Oakman	74820
Oak Park (Part of Bartlesville)	74003
Oaks	74359
Oakwood	73658
Oberlin	74727
Owasso	74051
Ochelata	74957
Octavia	74061
Oglesby	74061
Oil Center	74820
Oil City	73463
Oilton	74052
Okarche	73762
Okay	74446
Okeene	73763
Okemah	74859
Okesa	74003
Okfuskee	74859
Oklahoma City	**73101-80**
For specific Oklahoma City Zip Codes call (405) 278-6122	

COLLEGES & UNIVERSITIES

Name	ZIP
Oklahoma Christian College	73136
Oklahoma City University	73106
University of Oklahoma Health Sciences Center	73190

FINANCIAL INSTITUTIONS

Name	ZIP
Central Bank of Oklahoma City	73106
Continental Federal Savings & Loan Association	73134
First Interstate Bank of Oklahoma, National Association	73102
The First National Bank of Midwest City	73110
First Western Federal Savings & Loan Association	73109
Founders Bank & Trust Company	73112
Friendly Bank of Oklahoma City	73159
Guaranty Bank & Trust Co.	73127
Liberty National Bank and Trust Company of Oklahoma City	73102
Local Federal Savings & Loan Association	73116
MidFirst Savings & Loan Association	73108
The Oklahoma Bank	73108

HOSPITALS

Name	ZIP
Baptist Medical Center of Oklahoma	73112
HCA Presbyterian Hospital	73104
Mercy Health Center	73120
South Community Hospital	73109
St. Anthony Hospital	73101
Veterans Administration Medical Center	73104

HOTELS/MOTELS

Name	ZIP
Embassy Suites	73108
Hilton Inn Northwest	73112
Hilton Inn West	73108
Skirvin Plaza Hotel	73102
Waterford Hotel	73118

MILITARY INSTALLATIONS

Name	ZIP
Oklahoma Air National Guard, FB6562	73179
Oklahoma City Air Logistics Command, Tinker Air Force Base	73145

Name	ZIP
United States Property and Fiscal Office for Oklahoma	73111
Oklahoma State Penitentiary	74501
Okmulgee	74447
Oktaha	74450
Oleta	74735
Olive	74030
Olney	74538
Olustee	73560
Omega	73764
Oneta	74012
Oologah	74053
Optima	73945
Orienta	73737
Orlando	73073
Orr	73546
Osage	74054
Osage Hills Estates (Part of Sand Springs)	74063
Osage Indian Reservation	74056
Oscar	73561
Ouachita Correctional Center	74939
Overbrook	73453
Owasso	74055
Paden	74860
Page	74939
Panama	74951
Panola	74559
Paoli	73074
Paradise Hill	74955
Paradise View	74337
Park Hill	74451
Parkland	74824
Park Lane (Part of Lawton)	73501
Patterson	74578
Pauls Valley	73075
Pawhuska	74056
Pawnee	74058
Paw Paw	74948
Payson	74855
Pearson	74826
Pearsonia	74056
Peckham	74647
Peggs	74452
Penn Square Mall (Part of Oklahoma City)	73118
Pensacola	74301
Peoria	74363
Perkins	74059
Pernell	73076
Perry	73077
Pershing	74002
Peterman Ridge	74420
Petersburg	73456
Petros	74937
Pettit	74451
Pettit Bay	74451
Pharoah	74862
Phillips	74538
Picher	74360
Pickens	74752
Pickett	74820
Piedmont	73078
Pierce	74426
Piney	74960
Pink	74873
Pin Oaks Acres	74337
Pittsburg	74560
Platter	74753
Pleasant Hill	74740
Plunkettville	74963
Pocasset	73079
Pocola	74902
Pollard	74740
Ponca City	74601-04
For specific Ponca City Zip Codes call (405) 762-2485	
Pond Creek	73766
Pontotoc	74863
Pooleville	73458
Porter	74454
Porter Hill	73538
Porum	74455
Poteau	74953
Powell	73439
Prague	74864
Prattville (Part of Sand Springs)	74063
Preston	74456
Proctor	74457
Prue	74060
Pruitt City	73081
Pryor	74361-62
For specific Pryor Zip Codes call (918) 825-0912	
Pumpkin Center (Comanche County)	73501

Name	ZIP
Pumpkin Center (Okmulgee County)	74445
Purcell	73080
Purdy	73052
Putnam	73659
Pyramid Corners	74333
Quail Creek (Part of Oklahoma City)	73120
Quail Springs Mall (Part of Oklahoma City)	73134
Qualls	74451
Quapaw	74363
Quay	74085
Quinlan	73852
Quinton	74561
Rabornville	74020
Raiford	74432
Ralston	74650
Ramona	74061
Ranchwood Manor (Part of Oklahoma City)	73160
Randlett	73562
Ratliff City	73081
Rattan	74562
Ravia	73455
Reagan	73460
Reck	73463
Redbird	74458
Red Hill	74941
Red Horse (Part of Midwest City)	73110
Redland	74948
Red Oak	74563
Red Rock	74651
Reed	73554
Regal (Part of Lawton)	73501
Reichert	74937
Remus	74801
Renfrow	73759
Rentiesville	74459
Retrop	73627
Reydon	73660
Rhea	73654
Richards Spur	73538
Richland	73099
Richville	74501
Rigsby	74020
Ringling	73456
Ringold	74754
Ringwood	73768
Ripley	74062
Roberta	74701
Rock Island	74932
Rocky	73661
Rocky Mountain	74960
Rocky Point	74467
Roff	74865
Roland	74954
Roll	73628
Roosevelt	73564
Rose	74364
Rosedale	74831
Rosston	73855
Rossville	74881
Rubottom	73463
Rufe	74755
Rush Springs	73082
Russell	73554
Russellville	74561
Russett	73447
Ryan	73565
Sacred Heart	74849
Sageeyah	74017
St. Louis	74866
Salem	74437
Salina	74365
Sallisaw	74955
Salt Fork	74640
Sams Point	74501
Sandbluff	74759
Sand Point	73449
Sand Springs	74063
Sansbois	74552
Sapulpa	74066-67
For specific Sapulpa Zip Codes call (918) 224-0733	
Sardis	74536
Sasakwa	74867
Savanna	74565
Sawyer	74756
Sayre	73662
Schulter	74460
Scipio	74501
Scraper	74464
Scullin	73086
Scullyville	74959
Seiling	73663
Selman	73834
Seminole	74868
Sentinel	73664
Sequoyah	74017

Seward-Yale **OKLAHOMA** 441

Name	ZIP
Seward	73044
Shady Grove (Pawnee County)	74112
Shady Grove (Sequoyah County)	74954
Shady Point	74956
Shamrock	74068
Sharon	73857
Shartel (Part of Oklahoma City)	73118
Sha-To-She	74020
Shattuck	73858
Shawnee	74801-02
For specific Shawnee Zip Codes call (405) 273-2204	
Shay	73439
Shepherd Mall (Part of Oklahoma City)	73107
Sheridan (Comanche County)	73505
Sheridan (Tulsa County)	74135
Sherwood	74728
Shidler	74652
Shinewell	74740
Short	72955
Shults	74745
Sickles	73053
Silo	74701
Silver City	74038
Skedee	74058
Skiatook	74070
Slapout	73848
Slaughterville	73051
Slick	74071
Smith Village	73115
Smithville	74957
Snow	74567
Snyder	73566
Sobol	74735
Sooner Fashion Mall (Part of Norman)	73072
Soper	74759
Southard	73770
South Coffeyville	74072
South East (Oklahoma County)	73109
Southeast (Tulsa County)	74145
Southroads Mall (Part of Tulsa)	74135
Southside (Part of Tulsa)	74136
Southwest (Part of Oklahoma City)	73119
Sparks	74869
Spaulding	74848
Spavinaw	74366
Speer	74743
Spelter City	74437
Spencer	73084
Spencerville	74760
Sperry	74073
Spiro	74959
Sportsmen Acres	74361
Springer	73458
Springlake Park (Part of Oklahoma City)	73111
Stafford	73601
Stanley	74536
Stapp	74939
Star	74941
State Capitol (Part of Oklahoma City)	73105
Stealy	73080
Stecker	73006
Steedman	74825
Steel Junction	74728
Steen (Part of Enid)	73701
Sterling	73567
Stidham	74461
Stigler	74462
Stillwater	74074-76
For specific Stillwater Zip Codes call (405) 377-3867	
Stilwell	74960
Stockyards (Part of Oklahoma City)	73108
Stonebluff	74436
Stonewall	74871
Stony Point (Adair County)	74960
Stony Point (Le Flore County)	74959
Story	73057
Straight	73942
Strang	74367
Stratford	74872
Stringtown	74569
Strong City	73628
Stroud	74079
Stuart	74570
Sugden	73573
Sullivan Village (Part of Lawton)	73501

Name	ZIP
Sulphur	73086
Summerfield	74966
Summit	74401
Sumner	73077
Sungate (Part of Lawton)	73501
Sunkist	74727
Sunray	73529
Sweetwater	73666
Swink	74761
Tabler	73018
Tablerville	74734
Taft	74463
Tahlequah	74464-65
For specific Tahlequah Zip Codes call (918) 456-2381	
Tahona	74932
Tailholt	74471
Talala	74080
Talihina	74571
Tallant	74002
Taloga	73667
Tamaha	74462
Tangier	73801
Tatums	73087
Taylor	73562
Tecumseh	74873
Temple	73568
Teresita	74364
Terlton	74081
Terral	73569
Texanna	74426
Texhoma	73949
Texola	73668
Thackerville	73459
Thirty-Fourth Street (Part of Woodward)	73801
Thirty-Ninth Street (Part of Oklahoma City)	73112
Thomas	73669
Ti	74528
Tiawah	74017
Timber Brook	74014
Timberlane	74020
Tiner	74728
Tipton	73570
Tishomingo	73460
Titanic	74960
Tom	74740
Tonkawa	74653
Topsy	74366
Tribbey	74852
Trousdale	74878
Troy	74856
Trusty Unit	74501
Tryon	74875
Tucker	74959
Tullahassee	74466
Tulsa	74101-94
For specific Tulsa Zip Codes call (918) 599-6965	
Tulsa Promenade (Part of Tulsa)	74135
Tupelo	74572
Turley	74156
Turner	73430
Turpin	73950
Tushka	74525
Tuskahoma	74574
Tuskegee	74010
Tussy	73088
Tuttle	73089
Tuxedo (Part of Bartlesville)	74003
Twin Hills	74447
Twin Oaks	74368
Tyrone	73951
Unger	74727
Union (Part of Tulsa)	74012
Union City	73090
Union Valley	74871
University (Garfield County)	73701
University (Pottawatomie County)	74801
University of Science and Arts (Part of Chickasha)	73018
Uptown Shopping Center (Part of Midwest City)	73110
Utica	74726
Utica Square (Part of Tulsa)	74152
Valley Brook	73149
Valley Park	74017
Valliant	74764
Vamoosa	74849
Vance Air Force Base	73701
Vanoss	74820
Velma	73091
Vera	74082
Verden	73092
Verdigris	74017
Vernon	74877
Vian	74962

Name	ZIP
Vici	73859
Victory	73560
Village	73120
Vinco	74059
Vinita	74301
Vinson	73571
Virgil	74756
Vista	74849
Vivian	74432
Wade	74723
Wagoner	74467
Wainwright	74468
Wakita	73771
Wallville	73052
Walters	73572
Wanette	74878
Wann	74083
Wapanucka	73461
Wardville	74576
Warner	74469
Warr Acres	73132
Warren	73526
Warwick	74834
Washington	73093
Washita	73094
Waterloo	73034
Watonga	73772
Watova	74048
Watson	74963
Watts	74964
Wauhillau	74960
Waukomis	73773
Waurika	73573
Wayne	73095
Waynoka	73860
Weatherford	73096
Webb	73835
Webb City	74652
Webbers Falls	74470
Welch	74369
Weleetka	74880
Welling	74471
Wellston	74881
Welty	74882
Wes	74020
West Nichols Hills (Part of Oklahoma City)	73116
West Park (Part of Oklahoma City)	73123
Westport	74020
Westside (Part of Oklahoma City)	73127
West Siloam Springs	72761
West Tulsa (Part of Tulsa)	74107
Westville	74965
Wetumka	74883
Wewoka	74884
Wheatland (Part of Oklahoma City)	73097
Wheeless	73933
Whippoorwill	74009
White Bead	73075
White Eagle	74601
Whitefield	74472
White Oak (Cherokee County)	74451
White Oak (Craig County)	74301
Whitesboro	74577
Whittier (Part of Tulsa)	74150
Wichita Mountains Estates	73501
Wilburton	74578
Wildcat Point	74451
Wild Horse	74035
Williams	74932
Willis	73439
Willow	73673
Wilson (Carter County)	73463
Wilson (Okmulgee County)	74437
Winchester	74421
Winganon	74016
Wister	74966
Wolco	74002
Wolf	74854
Woodford	73458
Woodland Hills Mall (Part of Tulsa)	74133
Woodland View (Part of Tulsa)	74145
Woodlawn Park	73008
Woodville	73439
Woodward	73801-02
For specific Woodward Zip Codes call (405) 256-7138	
Woody Chapel	73095
Wright City	74766
Wyandotte	74370
Wybark	74401
Wye	74852
Wynnewood	73098
Wynona	74084
Yale	74085

OKLAHOMA Yanush-Zoe

	ZIP
Yanush	74574
Yarnaby	74741
Yeager	74848
Yewed	73728

	ZIP
Yost Lake	74032
Yuba	74721
Yukon	73099
Zafra	71945

	ZIP
Zena	74346
Zincville	66713
Zion	74960
Zoe	74939

Acorn Park-Dorena **OREGON** 443

Name	ZIP
Acorn Park (Part of Eugene)	97402
Ada	97493
Adair Village	97330
Adams	97810
Adel	97620
Adrian	97901
Agate Beach (Part of Newport)	97365
Agency Lake	97624
Agness	97406
Aims	97019
Airlie	97361
Ajax	97823
Albany	97321
Albany Yard (Part of Albany)	97321
Alder Creek	97055
Aldrich Point	97103
Alfalfa	97701
Alicel	97824
Alkali Lake	97758
Allegany	97407
Allston	97048
Aloha (Washington County)	97007
Aloha Annex	97007
Alpine	97456
Alsea	97324
Altamont	97601
Alvadore	97409
Amity	97101
Andrews	97720
Anlauf	97435
Annex	83672
Antelope	97001
Apiary	97048
Applegate	97530
Apple Valley	97056
Arago	97458
Arch Cape	97102
Arlington	97812
Arock	97902
Ashland	97520
Ashwood	97711
Astoria	97103
Astoria Coast Guard Base	97103
Athena	97813
Aumsville	97325
Aurora	97002
Austin	97817
Austin Junction	97817
Avon (Part of Rainier)	97048
Azalea	97410
Bakeoven	97037
Baker City	97814
Ballston	97378
Bandon	97411
Banks	97106
Barlow	97013
Barton	97009
Barview (Coos County)	97420
Barview (Tillamook County)	97136
Basque	89421
Bates	97817
Battin	97266
Bay City	97107
Bay Park	97420
Bayshore	97394
Bayside Garden	97131
Bayview	97394
Beatty	97621
Beaver	97108
Beavercreek	97004
Beaver Homes	97048
Beaver Marsh	97731
Beaver Springs	97048
Beaverton	97005-07, 97075-76
For specific Beaverton Zip Codes call (503) 646-3196	
Belleview (Part of Ashland)	97520
Bellevue	97128
Bellfountain	97456
Bend	97701-09
For specific Bend Zip Codes call (503) 388-1971	
Berlin	97355
Bethany	97123
Bethel Heights	97304
Beulah	97911
Beverly Beach	97365
Biggs	97065
Bingham Springs	97810
Birkenfeld	97016
Blachly	97412
Black Butte Ranch	97759
Blaine	97108
Blalock	97812
Blodgett	97326
Blooming	97113
Blue River	97413
Bly	97622

Name	ZIP
Boardman	97818
Bolton (Part of West Linn)	97068
Bonanza	97623
Bonneville	97014
Bonny Slope	97229
Boring	97009
Boyd	97021
Boyer	97347
Bradwood	97016
Breitenbush	97342
Brickerville	97453
Bridal Veil	97010
Bridge	97458
Bridgeport (Baker County)	97819
Bridgeport (Polk County)	97338
Brighton	97136
Brightwood	97011
Broadacres	97002
Broadbent	97414
Brockway	97496
Brogan	97903
Brookings	97415
Brooklyn (Part of Portland)	97266
Brooks	97305
Brothers	97712
Brownlee	97840
Brownsboro	97524
Brownsmead	97016
Brownsville	97327
Bryant (Part of Lake Oswego)	97034
Buchanan	97720
Buck Fork	97457
Buckley	97029
Buena Vista	97351
Bulrun	97055
Bunker Hill	97420
Buoy Depot (Part of Astoria)	97103
Burington	97231
Burns	97720
Burnside	97103
Burns Junction	97910
Burnt Woods	97326
Butte Falls	97522
Butteville	97002
Buxton	97109
Cages	97739
Cairo	97914
Calapooya	97386
Camas Valley	97416
Camp Clatsop	97146
Camp Polk	97759
Camp Sherman	97730
Camp Twelve	97391
Campus Station (Part of Corvallis)	97331
Canaan	97054
Canary	97493
Canby	97013
Canemah (Part of Oregon City)	97045
Cannon Beach	97110
Cannon Beach Junction	97138
Canterbury Square (Part of Tigard)	97224
Canyon City	97820
Canyonville	97417
Cape Meares	97141
Carlton	97111
Carnation (Part of Forest Grove)	97116
Carpenterville	97415
Carson	97834
Carus	97045
Carver	97015
Cascade Gorge	97536
Cascade Locks	97014
Cascade Summit	97425
Cascadia	97329
Cave Junction	97523
Cayuse	97821
Cecil	97843
Cedar Dale	97038
Cedar Hills (Washington County)	97005
Cedar Hills (Washington County)	97225
Cedarhurst Park	97023
Cedar Mill	97229
Celilo	97058
Centennial	97203
Central (Part of Portland)	97204
Central Point	97502
Central Point West	97502
Chapman	97056
Charleston	97420
Charlestown	97838
Chemawa Indian School	97303
Chemult	97731
Chenoweth	97058
Cherry Grove	97119

Name	ZIP
Cherry Heights	97058
Cherryville	97055
Cheshire	97419
Chiloquin	97624
Chitwood	97391
Christmas Valley	97641
City Farm	97823
Clackamas	97015
Clackamas Heights	97045
Clarkes	97004
Clarno	97830
Clatskanie	97016
Clear Lake	97303
Clifton	97016
Cloverdale (Deschutes County)	97756
Cloverdale (Lane County)	97426
Cloverdale (Tillamook County)	97112
Clow Corner	97338
Coaledo	97420
Coburg	97401
College Crest (Part of Eugene)	97401
Colton	97017
Columbia City	97018
Concord	97222
Condon	97823
Cook (Part of Lake Oswego)	97034
Coos Bay	97420
Cooston	97459
Coquille	97423
Corbett	97019
Cornelius	97113
Cornelius Pass	97231
Coronado Shores	97388
Corvallis	97330-33
For specific Corvallis Zip Codes call (503) 758-1412	
Cottage Grove	97424
Cottrell	97009
Courtrock	97864
Cove	97824
Cove Orchard	97119
Crabtree	97335
Crane	97732
Crater Lake	97604
Crawfordsville	97336
Crescent	97733
Crescent Lake	97425
Crescent Lake Junction	97425
Creston (Part of Portland)	97206
Creswell	97426
Crooked River Ranch	97760
Crow	97401
Crowfoot	97355
Cully	97203
Culp Creek	97427
Culver	97734
Currinsville	97023
Curtin	97428
Cutler City (Part of Lincoln City)	97367
Dairy	97625
Dale	97880
Daley	97701
Dallas	97338
Damascus	97009
Damascus Heights	97009
Dammasch State Hospital	97070
Danner	97910
Days Creek	97429
Dayton	97114
Dayville	97825
Deadwood	97430
Dee	97031
Deer Island	97054
Delena	97016
Dellwood	97420
Delmoor	97146
Denmark	97450
Depoe Bay	97341
Deschutes Junction	97701
Detroit	97342
Dever	97321
Dew Valley	97411
Dexter	97431
Diamond	97722
Diamond Lake	97731
Diamond Lake Junction	97731
Dickey Prairie	97038
Dillard	97432
Dilley	97116
Dixonville	97470
Dodge	97023
Dodson	97014
Dolph Corner	97338
Donald	97020
Dora	97458
Dorena	97434

OREGON

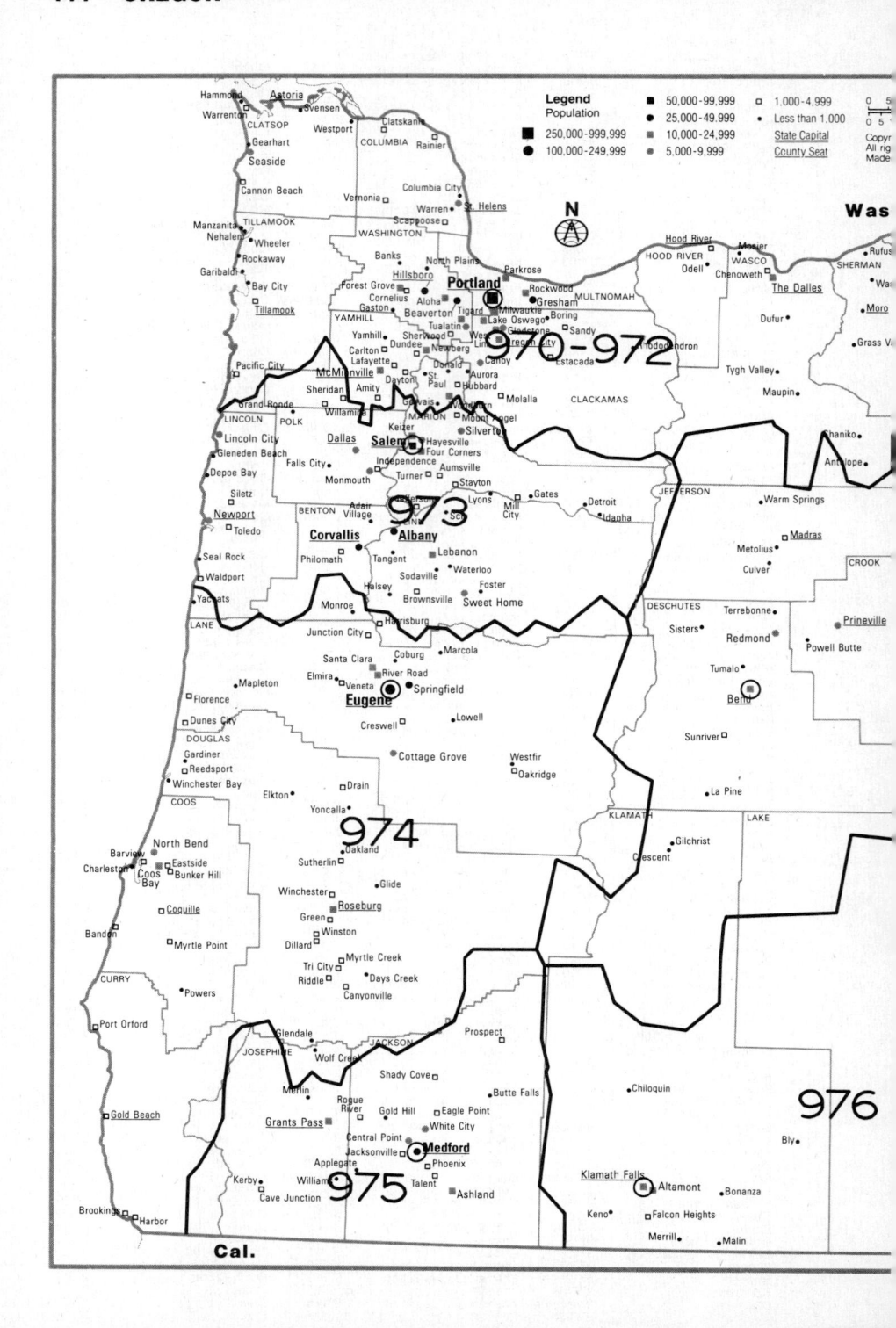

OREGON 445

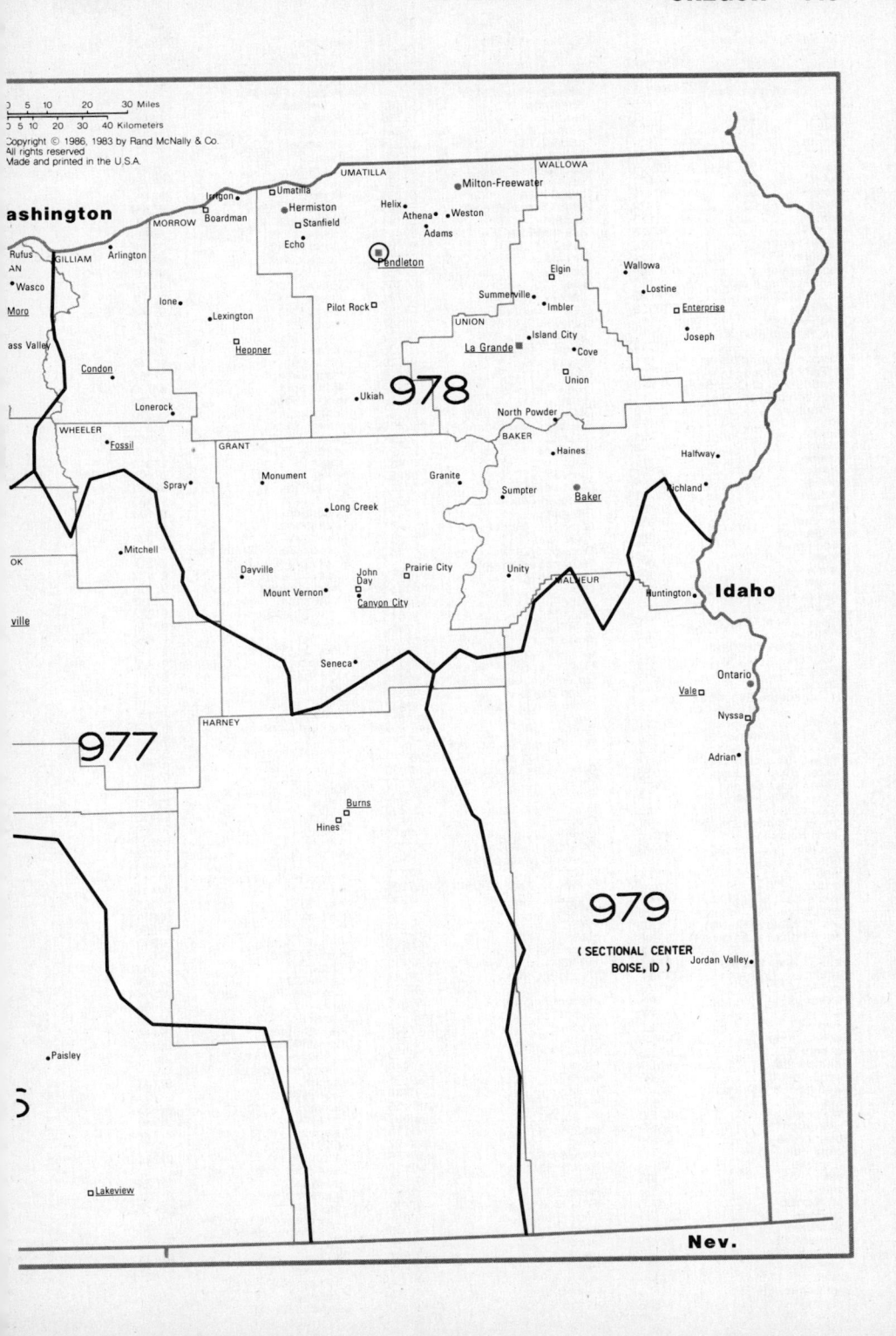

446 OREGON Douglas Gardens-Langell Valley

Name	ZIP
Douglas Gardens (Part of Springfield)	97477
Dover	97055
Downing	97016
Downtown (Part of Bend)	97701
Drain	97435
Draperville	97321
Drew	97484
Drewsey	97904
Drift Creek	97394
Dufur	97021
Dukes Valley	97031
Dundee	97115
Dunes City	97439
Durham	97223
Durkee	97905
Eagle Creek	97022
Eagle Point	97524
East Gardiner	97467
East Gresham (Part of Gresham)	97030
East Lake	97739
East Parkrose	97230
East Portland (Part of Portland)	97214
Eastport Shopping Center (Part of Beaverton)	97005
Eastside (Part of Coos Bay)	97420
Eastwood (Part of Roseburg)	97470
Echo	97826
Eckman Lake	97394
Eddyville	97343
Elgarose	97470
Elgin	97827
Elk City	97391
Elk Lake	97701
Elkton	97436
Ellendale	97338
Ellingson Mill	97884
Elliott Prairie	97071
Elmira	97437
Elsie	97138
Elwood	97017
Emerald Heights (Part of Astoria)	97103
Empire (Part of Coos Bay)	97420
Enterprise	97828
Errol Heights (Multnomah County)	97266
Estacada	97023
Eugene	97401-05
For specific Eugene Zip Codes call (503) 341-3611	
Fairfield	97026
Fair Oaks (Clackamas County)	97222
Fairoaks (Douglas County)	97479
Fairview (Coos County)	97423
Fairview (Lake County)	97630
Fairview (Multnomah County)	97024
Fairview (Tillamook County)	97141
Falcon Heights	97601
Fall Creek	97438
Falls City	97344
Fargo	97002
Faubion	97049
Fayetteville	97377
Fern Corner	97338
Fern Hill (Clatsop County)	97103
Fern Hill (Columbia County)	97048
Ferns	97338
Fields (Harney County)	97710
Fields (Lane County)	97463
Finn Rock	97488
Fir Grove	97401
Fir Villa	97338
Firwood	97055
Fishers Corner	97045
Fishers Mill	97045
Fish Lake Resort	97524
Five Corners	97630
Flavel (Part of Warrenton)	97146
Flora	97828
Floras Lake	97450
Florence	97439
Forest Grove	97116
Forest Park (Part of Portland)	97210
Forfar	97366
Fort Hill	97396
Fort Klamath	97626
Fort Rock	97735
Fort Stevens (Part of Hammond)	97121
Fortune Branch	97442
Fossil	97830
Foster	97345
Four Corners (Jackson County)	97502

Name	ZIP
Four Corners (Marion County)	97301
Fox	97831
Franklin	97448
Freewater (Part of Milton-Freewater)	97862
Frenchglen	97736
Friend	97021
Fruitdale	97526
Fruitvale	97365
Gales Creek	97117
Galice	97532
Garden Home	97223
Garden Home-Whitford	97223
Gardiner	97441
Gardiner Ridge	97415
Garfield	97023
Garibaldi	97118
Gaston	97119
Gates	97346
Gateway	97741
Gaylord	97458
Gazley	97457
Gearhart	97138
George	97023
Gervais	97026
Gibbon	97810
Gibson Hill	97321
Gilbert	97266
Gilchrist	97737
Gillespie Corners	97405
Gilliams	97338
Gladstone	97027
Glasgow	97459
Glenada	97439
Glendale	97442
Gleneden Beach	97388
Glengary	97470
Glenmorrie (Part of Lake Oswego)	97034
Glenwood (Lane County)	97401
Glenwood (Washington County)	97116
Glide	97443
Globe	97490
Goble	97048
Gold Beach	97444
Gold Hill	97525
Gooseberry	97843
Goshen	97401
Government Camp	97028
Grand Ronde	97347
Grand Ronde Agency	97347
Granite	97347
Grants Pass	97526-27
For specific Grants Pass Zip Codes call (503) 479-7526	
Grass Valley	97029
Green	97470
Green Acres	97420
Greenberry	97330
Greenhorn	97877
Greenleaf	97445
Greenville (Linn County)	97386
Greenville (Washington County)	97116
Greenway (Part of Tigard)	97223
Gresham	97030
Haines	97833
Halfway	97834
Halsey	97348
Hammond	97121
Hampton	97712
Hamricks Corner	97013
Happy Valley	97236
Harbeck-Fruitdale	97526
Harbor	97415
Hardman	97836
Harlan	97343
Harney	97720
Harper	97906
Harriman	97601
Harrisburg	97446
Hauser	97459
Hayesville	97303
Hazelwood	97230
Hebo	97122
Heceta Beach	97439
Heceta Junction	97439
Helix	97835
Helvetia	97123
Hemlock (Part of Westfir)	97492
Henley	97601
Henrice	97045
Heppner	97836
Hereford	97837
Hermiston	97838
Highland	97004
Hildebrand	97623
Hilgard	97850

Name	ZIP
Hillsboro	97123-24
For specific Hillsboro Zip Codes call (503) 294-2308	
Hines	97738
Holladay Park (Part of Portland)	97212
Holley	97386
Hollywood (Part of Salem)	97303
Homestead (Baker County)	97840
Homestead (Deschutes County)	97701
Hood River	97031
Horton	97412
Hoskins	97370
Hot Lake	97850
Hubbard	97032
Hugo	97526
Hunter Creek	97444
Huntington	97907
Idanha	97350
Idaville	97107
Idleyld Park	97447
Illahe	97406
Illinois Valley	97523
Imbler	97841
Imnaha	97842
Independence	97351
Indian Ford	97759
Indian Village	97720
Inglis	97016
Interlachen	97060
Ione	97843
Ironside	97908
Irrigon	97844
Irving	97401
Island City	97850
Ivy	97103
Ivy Station	97103
Jacksonville	97530
Jamieson	97909
Jantzen Beach Center (Part of Portland)	97217
Jasper	97438
Jeffers Garden	97103
Jefferson	97352
Jennings Lodge	97222
Jewell	97138
Jimtown	97834
John Day	97845
Johnson City	97222
Jonesboro	97911
Jordan	97374
Jordan Valley	97910
Joseph	97846
Junction City	97448
Juntura	97911
Kahneeta Hot Springs	97761
Kamela	97859
Kansas City	97116
Keating	97814
Keizer	97303
Kellogg	97462
Kelso	97009
Kendall	97206
Keno	97627
Kent	97033
Kenton (Part of Portland)	97217
Kerby	97531
Kernville	97367
Kimberly	97848
King City	97224
Kingman Kolory	97913
Kingsley Field	97601
Kingston	97383
Kings Valley	97361
Kingwood (Part of Salem)	97304
Kinton	97005
Kinzua	97830
Kiwanda Beach	97149
Klamath Falls	97601-03
For specific Klamath Falls Zip Codes call (503) 884-9226	
Knappa	97103
Knoll Heights	97701
Lacomb	97355
Ladd Hill	97070
Lafayette	97127
La Grande	97850
Lakecreek	97524
Lake Grove (Part of Lake Oswego)	97035
Lake of the Woods	97601
Lake Oswego	97034-35
For specific Lake Oswego Zip Codes call (503) 294-2308	
Lakeside	97449
Lakeview	97630
Lancaster	97448
Lancaster Mall (Part of Salem)	97301
Langell Valley	97623

Langlois-Prineville Southeast OREGON 447

Name	ZIP
Langlois	97450
Langrell	97834
La Pine	97739
Larwood	97374
Latham	97424
Latourell Falls	97014
Laurel	97123
Laurel Grove	97411
Laurelwood	97119
Lawen	97740
Leaburg	97489
Lebanon	97355
Lee's Camp	97141
Leland	97497
Lents (Part of Portland)	97266
Lewisburg	97330
Lexington	97839
Libby	97420
Liberal	97038
Liberty	97386
Lime	97907
Lincoln	97520
Lincoln Beach	97341
Lincoln City	97367
Lindbergh	97048
Little Albany	97390
Little Sweden	97346
Lloyd Center (Part of Portland)	97232
Locoda	97016
Logsden	97357
London	97424
Lone Elder	97013
Lonerock	97823
Long Creek	97856
Lookingglass (Douglas County)	97470
Looking Glass (Union County)	97827
Lorane	97451
Lorella	97623
Lostine (Wallowa County)	97857
Lowell	97452
Lower Bridge	97760
Lower Highland	97007
Lower Logan	97045
Lynch (Part of Portland)	97236
Lyons	97358
McCoy	97371
McEwen	97877
McKee	97071
McKee Bridge	97530
Mc Kenzie Bridge	97413
Macksburg	97013
McMinnville	97128
McNary (Part of Umatilla)	97882
McNary Mobile Manor (Part of Umatilla)	97882
McNulty	97051
Madras	97741
Malin	97632
Mall 205 (Part of Portland)	97216
Manhattan Beach (Part of Rockaway)	97136
Manning	97125
Manzanita	97130
Mapleton	97453
Marcola	97454
Marion	97359
Marion Forks	97350
Marlene Village	97005
Marquam	97362
Marshland	97016
Martin Manor	97225
Marylhurst	97036
Mason Additions (Part of Prineville)	97754
Maupin	97037
Mayger	97016
May Park	97850
Mayville	97830
Maywood Park	97220
Meacham	97859
Meadowbrook	97038
Meadow View	97448
Meda	97112
Medford	97501-04
For specific Medford Zip Codes call (503) 776-1326	
Medford Center (Part of Medford)	97504
Medford Mall (Part of Medford)	97501
Medical Springs	97814
Mehama	97384
Melrose	97470
Melrose Acres	97754
Melville	97103
Menlo Park (Part of Portland)	97230
Merlin	97532

Name	ZIP
Merrill	97633
Metolius	97741
Metzger	97223
Midland	97634
Midway (Multnomah County)	97233
Midway (Washington County)	97123
Mikkalo	97861
Miles Crossing	97103
Mill City	97360
Millersburg	97321
Millican	97701
Millington	97420
Milo	97429
Milton (Part of Milton-Freewater)	97862
Milton-Freewater	97862
Milwaukie	97222
Minam	97885
Mission	97801
Mist	97016
Mitchell	97750
Modeville	97351
Modoc Point	97624
Mohawk	97477
Mohawk Junction (Part of Springfield)	97477
Mohler	97131
Mclalla	97038
Mcnitor	97071
Monmouth	97361
Monroe	97456
Monument	97864
Moody	97391
Morgan	97843
Moro	97039
Mosier	97040
Mountaindale	97113
Mount Angel	97362
Mount Hebron	97801
Mount Hood	97041
Mount Hood-Parkdale	97041
Mount Pleasant (Part of Oregon City)	97045
Mount Vernon	97865
Mulino	97042
Mulloy	97140
Multnomah (Part of Portland)	97219
Murkers	97374
Murphy	97533
Myrick	97810
Myrtle Creek	97457
Myrtle Point	97458
Narrows	97721
Nashville	97326
Natal	97064
Neahkahnie	97131
Nedonna	97136
Needy	97013
Nehalem	97131
Nelscott (Part of Lincoln City)	97367
Neotsu	97364
Nesika Beach	97444
Neskowin	97149
Netarts	97143
Newberg	97132
New Bridge	97870
New Era	97013
New Hope	97527
New Idaho	97630
New Idanha	97350
New Pine Creek	97635
Newport	97365
Newton Creek	97470
Ninety One	97013
Nonpareil	97479
North Albany	97321
North Bend	97459
North Bend Coast Guard Air Station	97459
North Fork	97467
North Howell	97381
North Plains	97133
North Powder	97867
North Roseburg (Part of Roseburg)	97470
North Santiam	97325
North Side (Part of Silverton)	97301
North Springfield	97477
North Umpqua Village	97447
Norway	97460
Norwood	97062
Noti	97461
Nottingham	97701
Nyssa	97913
Nyssa Heights	97913

Name	ZIP
Oak Grove (Clackamas County)	97267
Oak Grove (Hood River County)	97031
Oakland	97462
Oakridge	97463
Oakville	97377
Oakway Mall (Part of Eugene)	97401
O'Brien	97534
Oceanside	97134
Odell	97044
Odessa	97601
Oklahoma Hill	97016
Old Colton	97017
Old Town	97462
Olene	97601
Olex	97812
Olney	97103
Ontario	97914
Ophir	97464
Ordnance	97838
Oregon City	97045
Orenco	97123
Oretech (Part of Klamath Falls)	97601
Oretown	97112
Orient	97030
Orleans	97321
Otis	97368
Otter Rock	97369
Owyhee	97913
Oxbow	97840
Pacific City	97135
Page (Part of Albany)	97321
Paisley	97636
Palestine	97321
Paradise Park	97023
Parkdale	97041
Parker	97351
Parkersburg	97411
Park Place	97045
Parkrose	97230
Patterson Junction	97844
Paulina	97751
Pedee	97361
Peel	97443
Pendair Heights (Part of Pendleton)	97801
Pendleton	97801
Pendleton Junction (Part of Pendleton)	97801
Peoria	97377
Perry	97850
Perrydale	97101
Philomath	97370
Phoenix	97535
Piedmont (Part of Portland)	97211
Pigeon Point	97420
Pike	97148
Pilot Rock	97868
Pine	97834
Pine Grove (Hood River County)	97031
Pine Grove (Wasco County)	97037
Pioneer (Part of Portland)	97204
Pistol River	97444
Pittsburg	97064
Plainview (Deschutes County)	97701
Plainview (Linn County)	97377
Pleasant Hill	97455
Pleasant Valley (Baker County)	97814
Pleasant Valley (Josephine County)	97532
Pleasant Valley (Tillamook County)	97141
Plush	97637
Pocahontas	97814
Polk Station	97338
Pony Village (Part of North Bend)	97459
Porter Creek	97481
Portland	97201-99
For specific Portland Zip Codes call (503) 294-2308	
Port Orford	97465
Post	97752
Powell Butte	97753
Powellhurst (Multnomah County)	97236
Powers	97466
Prairie City	97869
Pratum	97301
Prescott	97048
Princeton	97721
Prineville	97754
Prineville Southeast (Part of Prineville)	97754

448 OREGON — Pringle Park Plaza-West Rainier

Name	ZIP
Pringle Park Plaza (Part of Salem)	97301
Progress	97005
Prospect	97536
Prosper	97411
Quinaby	97303
Quincy	97016
Quines Creek	97442
Rainier	97048
Rajneeshpuram	97741
Raleigh Hills	97225
Ramsey	97701
Randolph	97411
Redland	97045
Redmond	97756
Redwood	97526
Reedsport	97467
Remote	97468
Rhododendron	97049
Rice Hill	97462
Richardson	97490
Richland	97870
Rickreall	97371
Riddle	97469
Rieth	97801
Riley	97758
Ritter	97872
River Crest (Part of Oregon City)	97045
Rivergrove	97034
River Road	97404
Riverside (Linn County)	97321
Riverside (Malheur County)	97917
Riverside (Umatilla County)	97801
Riverton	97423
Riverview (Columbia County)	97064
Riverview (Lane County)	97448
Roans Estate	97739
Robinwood (Part of West Linn)	97068
Rockaway	97136
Rock Creek (Baker County)	97833
Rock Creek (Gilliam County)	97812
Rockford	97031
Rockie Four Corners	97375
Rockwood	97233
Rocky Point	97601
Rogue River	97537
Rogue Valley Mall (Part of Medford)	97501
Rome	97910
Roseburg	97470
Rose City Park (Part of Portland)	97213
Rose Lodge	97372
Rosemont	97068
Rowena	97058
Roy	97106
Ruch	97530
Rufus	97050
Ruggs	97836
Rural Dell	97032
Russellville	97216
Rye Valley	97907
Saginaw	97472
St. Benedict	97373
St. Helens	97051
St. Johns (Part of Portland)	97203
St. Louis	97026
St. Paul	97137
Salem	97301-14
For specific Salem Zip Codes call (503) 370-4700	
Salmon Harbor	97467
Salt Creek	97338
Sams Valley	97525
Sand Lake	97112
Sandy	97055
San Marine	97498
Santa Clara	97404
Saunders Lake	97459
Scappoose	97056
Scholls	97123
Scio	97374
Scofield	97109
Scottsburg	97473
Scotts Mills	97375
Seal Rock	97376
Seaside	97138
Seghers	97119
Sellwood Moreland (Part of Portland)	97202
Selma	97538
Seneca	97873
Shadowood	97068
Shady Cove	97539
Shady Dell	97038
Shaniko	97057
Shasta Plaza (Part of Klamath Falls)	97601

Name	ZIP
Shaw	97325
Shedd	97377
Shelburn	97374
Sheridan	97378
Sherwood	97140
Shiloh Basin	97051
Shorewood	97459
Siletz	97380
Siltcoos	97493
Silver Lake	97638
Silverton	97381
Silvies	97720
Simnasho	97761
Sisters	97759
Six Corners (Part of Sherwood)	97140
Sixes	97476
Skelley	97499
Smithfield	97338
Smock	97063
Sodaville	97355
Southbeach	97366
Southgate (Part of Portland)	97266
South Junction	97037
South Lebanon	97355
South Medford	97501
South Scappoose	97056
Southside (Part of Eugene)	97405
Spicer	97355
Sprague River	97639
Spray	97874
Springbrook	97132
Springdale	97060
Springfield	97477-78
For specific Springfield Zip Codes call (503) 747-3383	
Springwater	97023
Stafford	97068
Staleys Junction	97109
Stanfield	97875
Stayton	97383
Steamboat	97447
Stewart Lennox Addition	97601
Stimson Mill	97119
Sublimity	97385
Summer Lake	97640
Summer Lake Hot Springs	97636
Summerville	97876
Summit	97326
Sumner	97420
Sumpter	97877
Sunnycrest	97132
Sunnyside (Clackamas County)	97015
Sunnyside (Umatilla County)	97862
Sunny Valley	97497
Sun Park South	97009
Sunriver	97707
Sunset (Part of West Linn)	97068
Sunset Beach	97146
Sunset Hills (Part of Seaside)	97138
Suntex Valley	97758
Suplee	97751
Surf Pines	97146
Surprise Valley	97457
Sutherlin	97479
Suver	97361
Suver Junction	97361
Svensen	97103
Sweet Home	97386
Swisshome	97480
Table Rock	97501
Taft (Part of Lincoln City)	97367
Takilma	97523
Talbot	97352
Talent	97540
Tallman	97355
Tangent	97389
Taylorville	97016
Telocaset	97883
Tenmile	97481
Terrebonne	97760
Thatcher	97116
The Dalles	97058
Thornhollow	97810
Three Lynx	97023
Thurston (Part of Springfield)	97482
Tide	97480
Tidewater	97390
Tiernan	97453
Tierra Del Mar	97112
Tigard	97223
Tillamook	97141
Tiller	97484
Tillican	97701
Timber	97144
Timber Grove	97004
Timberline Lodge	97028
Toketee Falls	97447

Name	ZIP
Toledo	97391
Tollgate	97886
Tolovana Park	97145
Tongue Point Village	97103
Top	97864
Tophill	97109
Town Center (Part of Portland)	97229
Trail	97541
Trent	97431
Triangle Lake	97412
Tri-City	97457
Trout Creek	97710
Troutdale	97060
Troy	97828
Tualatin	97062
Tumalo	97701
Turner	97392
Twelve Mile	97030
Twickenham	97750
Twin Rocks	97136
Twomile	97411
Tygh Valley	97063
Ukiah	97880
Umapine	97862
Umatilla	97882
Umatilla Indian Reservation	97801
Umpqua	97486
Union	97883
Union Creek	97536
Union Gap	97462
Union Mills	97042
Union Point	97327
Unionvale	97114
Unity (Baker County)	97884
Unity (Lane County)	97438
University (Lane County)	97401
University (Multnomah County)	97201
Upper Farm	97357
Upper Highland	97004
Vale	97918
Valley Falls	97630
Valley Junction	97396
Valley River Center (Part of Eugene)	97401
Valley View	97321
Valsetz	97380
Vaughn	97487
Veneta	97487
Verboort	97116
Vernonia	97064
Vida	97488
Vinemaple	97138
Viola	97023
Vista (Part of Salem)	97302
Waconda	97026
Wagontire	97720
Wagon Trail Ranch	97739
Wakonda Beach	97394
Walden	97424
Waldport	97394
Walker	97426
Wallace Bridge	97396
Wallowa	97885
Wallowa Lake Resort	97846
Walterville	97489
Walton	97490
Wamic	97063
Wapato	97119
Warm Springs	97761
Warm Springs Indian Reservation	97761
Warner Valley	97620
Warren	97053
Warrendale	97014
Warrenton	97146
Wasco	97065
Waterloo	97355
Watseco	97136
Weatherby	97905
Wecoma Beach (Part of Lincoln City)	97367
Wedderburn	97491
Welches	97067
Wemme	97067
Western Evangelical Seminary	97045
Westfall	97920
Westfir	97492
West Haven	97225
Westlake (Part of Dunes City)	97493
West Linn	97068
West Oak (Part of Oakridge)	97463
Weston	97886
Westport	97016
West Powelhurst	97266
West Rainier	97048

OREGON 449

Name	ZIP
West Scio	97374
West Side (Lake County)	97630
West Side (Lane County)	97402
West Slope	97225
West Stayton	97325
West St. Helens (Part of St. Helens)	97051
West Union	97123
Wetmore	97830
Weyerhaeuser Townsite	97601
Wheeler	97147
Wheeler Heights (Part of Wheeler)	97147
Whiskey Hill	97032
White City	97503
Whiteson	97101
Wilbur	97494
Wilderville	97543
Wildwood	97049
Wilkes-Rockwood	97236
Willamette (Part of West Linn)	97068
Willamette City (Part of Oakridge)	97463
Willamina	97396
Williams	97544
Willowcreek	97918
Willsburg Junction (Part of Milwaukie)	97222
Wilson Beach	97141
Wilsonville	97070
Wimer	97537
Winchester	97495
Winchester Bay	97467
Windmaster Corner	97031
Winema Beach	97112
Wingville	97814
Winston	97496
Winterville	97411
Wistful Vista	97741
Witch Hazel	97123
Wocus	97601
Wolf Creek	97497
Women's Release Unit	97301
Wonder	97543
Woodburn	97071
Woods	97112
Woodson	97016
Wood Village	97060
Worden	97601
Wren	97370
Wyeth	97014
Yachats	97498
Yamhill	97148
Yankton	97051
Yaquina	97365
Yoder	97032
Yoncalla	97499
Yonna	97623
Zigzag	97049

450 PENNSYLVANIA

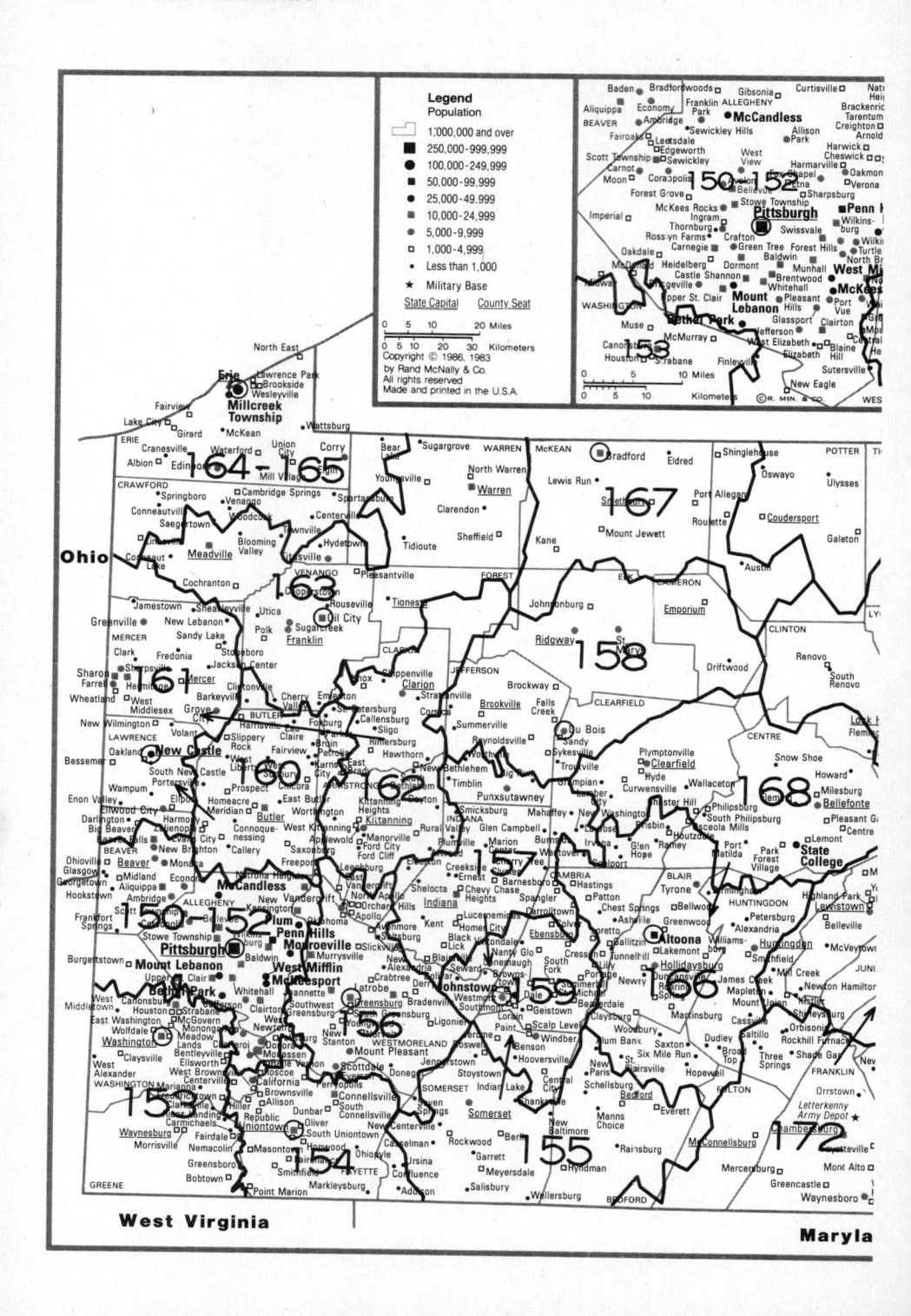

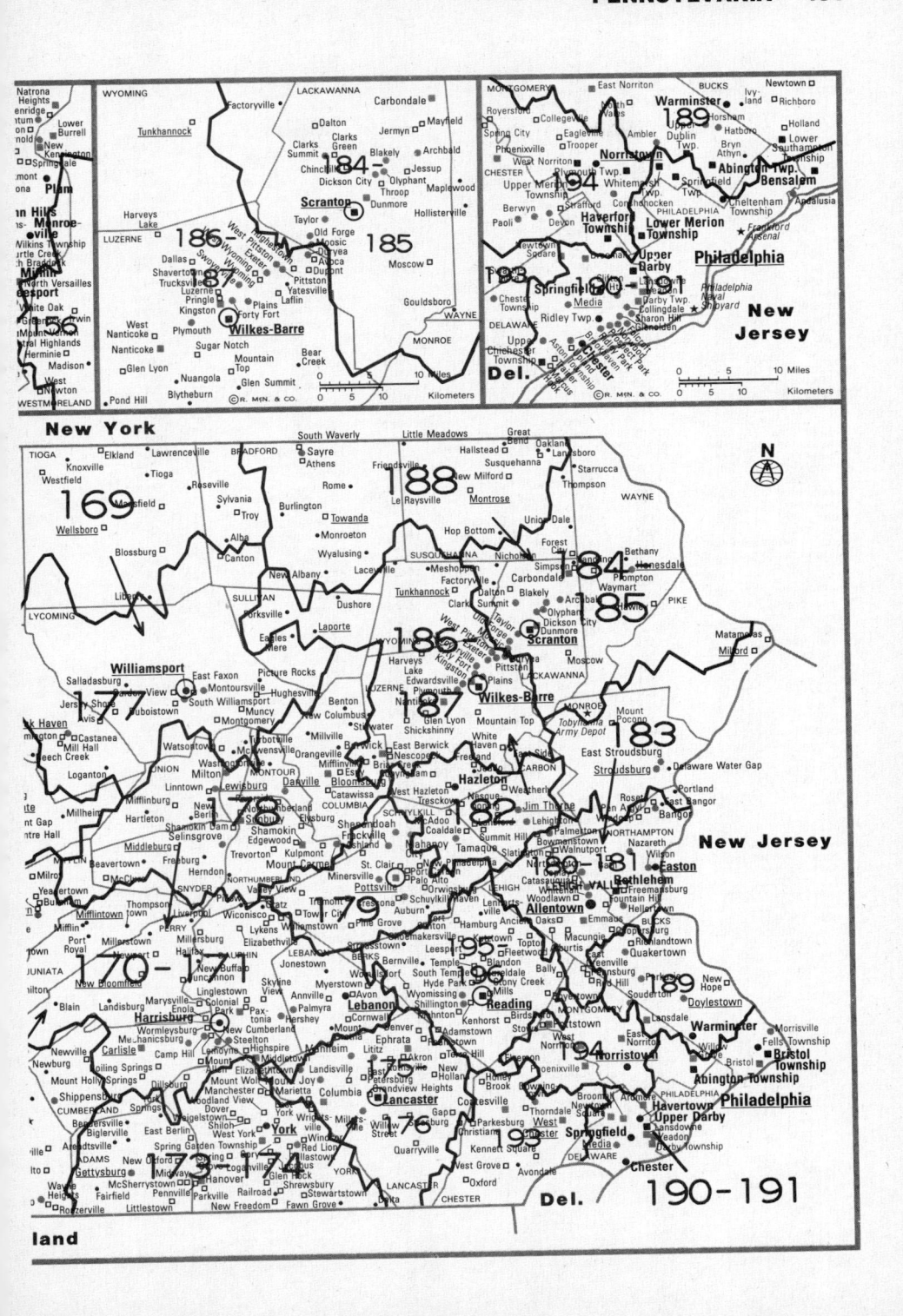

PENNSYLVANIA 451

452 PENNSYLVANIA Aaronsburg-Ashtola

Name	ZIP
Aaronsburg	16820
Abbot (Township)	16922
Abbottstown	17301
Aberdeen	18444
Abington (Lackawanna County) (Township)	18471
Abington (Montgomery County)	19001
Abington (Montgomery County) (Township)	19001
Abrahamsville	12723
Abrams	19406
Academia	17082
Academy Corners	16928
Academy Gardens (Part of Philadelphia)	19154
Acahela	18610
Accomac	17406
Ache	15454
Ackermanville	18010
Acme	15610
Acmetonia	15024
Acosta	15520
Acre Pond	18826
Adah	15410
Adams (Armstrong County)	16028
Adams (Butler County) (Township)	16046
Adams (Cambria County) (Township)	15955
Adams (Snyder County) (Township)	17813
Adams (Somerset County)	15541
Adamsburg	15611
Adams Corner	16057
Adamsdale	17972
Adams Hill	15642
Adamstown	19501
Adamsville	16110
Addingham	19026
Addison (Somerset County)	15411
Addison (Somerset County) (Township)	15540
Adelaide	15425
Adio Institute of Straight Chiropractic	19058
Admire	17364
Adrian	16210
Adrian Furnace	15801
Advance	15732
Africa	17236
Afton Village	18034
Aiden Lair	19025
Aiken	16744
Airville	17302
Airydale	17060
Aitch	16693
Ajax	16323
Akeley	16345
Akersville	15536
Akron	17501
Aladdin	15656
Alaska	15825
Alba	16910
Albany	19529
Albany (Township)	19529
Albany (Bradford County) (Township)	18833
Albany (Fayette County)	15417
Albidale	19006
Albion (Erie County)	16401
Albion (Jefferson County)	15767
Albrightsville	18210
Alburtis	18011
Alcoa Center	15069
Aldan	19018
Alden	18634
Aldenville	18401
Alderson (Part of Harveys Lake)	18618
Aldham	19460
Aleppo (Allegheny County)	15310
Aleppo (Allegheny County) (Township)	15143
Aleppo (Greene County)	15310
Alexander Springs	17004
Alexandria	16611
Alfarata	17841
Alford	18826
Alice	15610
Alicia (Fayette County)	15417
Alicia (Greene County)	15338
Alinda	17040
Aline	17853
Aliquippa	15001
Allandale	17011
Allegany (Township)	16915
Allegheny (Allegheny County)	15212
Allegheny (Blair County) (Township)	16635

Name	ZIP
Allegheny (Butler County) (Township)	16049
Allegheny (Cambria County) (Township)	15940
Allegheny (Somerset County) (Township)	15538
Allegheny (Venango County) (Township)	16341
Allegheny (Westmoreland County) (Township)	15656
Allegheny Acres	15024
Allegheny College (Part of Meadville)	16335
Allegheny Furnace (Part of Altoona)	16602
Allegheny Springs	16371
Alleghenyville	19540
Allemans	16639
Allen (Cumberland County)	17007
Allen (Northampton County) (Township)	18067
Allen Crest	18052
Allen Lane (Part of Philadelphia)	19119
Allenport (Huntingdon County)	17066
Allenport (Washington County)	15412
Allens Mills	15851
Allensville	17002
Allentown	18101-95
For specific Allentown Zip Codes call (215) 821-8450	
Allenvale	15501
Allenwood	17810
Allis Hollow	18837
Allison (Clinton County) (Township)	17751
Allison (Fayette County)	15413
Allison Heights	15413
Allison Park	15101
Allport (Cambria County)	15714
Allport (Clearfield County)	16821
Almaden	16680
Almedia	17815
Almont	18960
Alpha (Part of Windgap)	18091
Alpine	17339
Alsace (Township)	19606
Alsace Manor	19560
Altamont	17931
Altenwald	17268
Althom	16351
Alton	19380
Alton Park (Part of Allentown)	18103
Altoona	16601-03
For specific Altoona Zip Codes call (814) 944-4505	
Alum Bank	15521
Alum Rock	16373
Aluta	18064
Alverda	15710
Alverton	15612
Amaranth	17267
Amasa	18433
Ambau	17362
Amberson	17210
Ambler	19002
Ambler Highlands	19034
Ambridge	15003
Ambridge Heights	15003
Ambrose	15759
Amend	15401
American Philatelic Building (Part of State College)	16801
Amesville	16651
Amity (Berks County) (Township)	19518
Amity (Erie County) (Township)	16438
Amity (Washington County)	15311
Amity Gardens	19518
Amity Hall	17020
Amsbry	16641
Amsterdam	16127
Amwell (Township)	15345
Analomink	18320
Ancient Oaks	18062
Ancient Oaks South	18062
Ancient Oaks West	18062
Andalusia	19020
Anderson	17044
Andersonburg	17047
Anderson Park	15235
Anderson Road	15001
Andersontown	17055
Andreas	18211
Andrews Bridge	17509
Andrews Plan	15001
Andrews Settlement	16923

Name	ZIP
Angelica	19540
Angels	18445
Angora (Part of Philadelphia)	19143
Anita	15711
Ankeny	15547
Annaline Village	19061
Annin (Township)	16743
Annisville	16049
Annville (Lebanon County) (Township)	17003
Annville (Lebanon County)	17003
Anselma	19425
Ansonia	16901
Ansonville	16656
Antes Fort	17720
Anthony (Lycoming County) (Township)	17728
Anthony (Montour County) (Township)	17772
Anthracite (Part of Cornwall)	17016
Antis (Township)	16617
Antrim (Franklin County) (Township)	17225
Antrim (Tioga County)	16901
Apolacon (Township)	18830
Apollo	15613
Appenzell	18360
Applebachsville	18951
Appletree Hill	19007
Appleville	19380
Applewold	16201
Aquashicola	18012
Aqueduct	17020
Aquetong	18938
Ararat	18465
Ararat (Township)	18465
Arbor	17356
Arbuckle	16438
Arcadia (Indiana County)	15712
Arcadia (Lancaster County)	17563
Archbald	18403
Arch Rock	17059
Arch Spring	16686
Arcola	19420
Ardara	15615
Arden	15301
Ardenheim	16652
Arden Mines	15301
Ardmore (Delaware County)	19003
Ardmore (Montgomery County)	19003
Ardmore Manor	19003
Ardmore Park	19003
Ardsley	19038
Arendtsville	17303
Arensberg	15433
Argentine	16040
Argus	18960
Aristes	17920
Arlingham	19031
Arlingham Hills	19031
Arlington	18436
Arlington Heights (Monroe County)	18360
Arlington Knolls	18052
Arlington Park	15137
Armagh (Indiana County)	15920
Armagh (Mifflin County) (Township)	17063
Armbrust	15616
Armenia (Township)	16947
Armstrong (Indiana County) (Township)	15774
Armstrong (Lycoming County) (Township)	17701
Arnold	15068
Arnold City	15012
Arnot	16911
Arnots Addition (Part of St. Clair)	17970
Arona	15617
Aroninink	19026
Aronwald	19073
Arrowhead Lake	18347
Arsenal (Part of Pittsburgh)	15201
Artemas	17211
Arundel Village	19044
Arwin Acres	17036
Asaph	16901
Asbury (Columbia County)	17859
Asbury (Erie County)	16509
Ashcom	15537
Asherton	17801
Ashfield	18212
Ashland (Clarion County) (Township)	16232
Ashland (Clearfield County)	16666
Ashland (Schuylkill County)	17921
Ashley	18706
Ashtola	15963

Ashville-Bendersville **PENNSYLVANIA** 453

Name	ZIP
Ashville	16613
Askam	18706
Aspers	17304
Aspinwall	15215
Aston (Delaware County)	19014
Aston (Delaware County) (Township)	19014
Asylum (Township)	18848
Atco	12764
Atglen	19310
Athens (Bradford County)	18810
Athens (Bradford County) (Township)	18810
Athens (Crawford County) (Township)	16360
Athol	19519
Atkinsons Mills	17051
Atlantic (Clearfield County)	16651
Atlantic (Crawford County)	16111
Atlantic (Westmoreland County)	15671
Atlas	17851
Atlasburg	15004
Atwood	16249
Auburn (Schuylkill County)	17922
Auburn (Susquehanna County) (Township)	18630
Auburn Center	18623
Auburn Four Corners	18630
Audenried	18201
Audubon	19407
Aughwick	17066
Augustaville	17801
Aultman	15713
Austin	16720
Austinburg	16928
Austinville	16914
Avalon	15202
Avella	15312
Avella Heights	15312
Avella Highlands	15312
Avis	17721
Avoca	18641
Avon	17042
Avondale	19311
Avondale Knolls	19086
Avon Heights	17042
Avonia	16423
Avonmore	15618
Axemann	16823
Ayr (Township)	17212
Bachmanville	17033
Baden	15005
Baederwood	19046
Bagdad	15656
Baggaley	15650
Bailey	17074
Baileys Corner	16926
Baileyville	16865
Bainbridge	17502
Bair	17405
Bairdford	15006
Bairdstown	15717
Bakers Crossroads	16668
Bakers Summit	16614
Baker Station	19390
Bakerstown (Allegheny County)	15044
Bakerstown (Allegheny County)	15007
Bakersville	15501
Bala	19004
Bala-Cynwyd	19004
Bala-Cynwyd Shopping Center	19004
Bald Eagle (Blair County)	16686
Bald Eagle (Clinton County) (Township)	17751
Bald Hill (Clearfield County)	16850
Bald Hill (Greene County)	15327
Baldwin (Allegheny County)	15234
Baldwin (Allegheny County) (Township)	15234
Baldwin (Delaware County)	19013
Baldwin Township	15234
Balliettsville	18037
Balls Eddy	18461
Balls Mills	17728
Balltown	16347
Bally	19503
Balsinger	15484
Banbury Crossing	17036
Bando	15501
Banetown	15301
Baney Settlement	16830
Bangor	18013
Banian Junction	16661
Banks (Carbon County) (Township)	18254
Banks (Indiana County) (Township)	15742

Name	ZIP
Banksville (Part of Pittsburgh)	15216
Banner Ridge	15757
Bannerville	17841
Banning	15428
Baptist Bible College and School of Theology	18411
Barbours	17701
Bard	15534
Baresville	17331
Bareville	17540
Barkeyville	16038
Barlow	17325
Barnards	16222
Barnes (Cambria County)	15737
Barnes (Jefferson County)	15825
Barnes (Warren County)	16347
Barnesboro	15714
Barneston	19344
Barnesville	18214
Barnett (Forest County) (Township)	15828
Barnett (Jefferson County) (Township)	15860
Barneytown	17052
Barnitz	17013
Barnsley	19363
Barr (Township)	15760
Barree (Huntingdon County)	16611
Barree (Huntingdon County) (Township)	16669
Barren Hill	19444
Barret Plan	15001
Barrett (Clearfield County)	16830
Barrett (Monroe County) (Township)	18342
Barronvale	15557
Barr Slope	15734
Barrville	17084
Barry (Township)	17921
Barry Heights (Part of Norristown)	19401
Bart	17503
Bart (Township)	17562
Barto	19504
Bartonsville	18321
Bartville	17509
Basket	19547
Bassards Corners	18038
Bastress (Township)	17701
Bath	18014
Bath Addition	19007
Bath Manor	19007
Bauerstown	15209
Baumgardner	17584
Baumstown	19508
Bausman	17504
Bavington	15019
Baxter	15829
Beachdale	15530
Beach Haven	18601
Beach Lake	18405
Beachly	15424
Beading	15241
Beale (Township)	17082
Beallsville	15313
Beans Cove	15535
Bear Creek	18602
Bear Creek (Township)	18602
Bear Creek Lake	18229
Bear Gap	17824
Bear Lake	16402
Bear Rocks	15610
Beartown (Franklin County)	17268
Beartown (Lancaster County)	17555
Bear Valley	17872
Beatty	15650
Beatty Hills	19008
Beaufort Farms	17110
Beaumont	18618
Beaver (Beaver County)	15009
Beaver (Clarion County) (Township)	16232
Beaver (Columbia County) (Township)	17815
Beaver (Crawford County) (Township)	16406
Beaver (Jefferson County) (Township)	15864
Beaver (Snyder County) (Township)	17813
Beaver Acres	15136
Beaver Brook	18201
Beaver Center	16435
Beaverdale (Cambria County)	15921
Beaverdale (Northumberland County)	17851
Beaverdale-Lloydell	15921
Beaver Dam	16407

Name	ZIP
Beaver Falls	15010
Beaver Lake	17758
Beaver Meadows	18216
Beaver Springs	17812
Beavertown (Blair County)	16662
Beavertown (Huntingdon County)	16685
Beavertown (Snyder County)	17813
Beavertown (York County)	17019
Beaver Valley	16640
Beccaria	16616
Beccaria (Township)	16627
Bechtelsville	19505
Beckersville	19540
Becks	17901
Becks Run (Part of Pittsburgh)	15201
Bedford (Bedford County) (Township)	15522
Bedford (Bedford County)	15522
Bedminster	18910
Bedminster (Township)	18910
Beech Creek (Clinton County)	16822
Beech Creek (Clinton County) (Township)	16822
Beecherstown	17307
Beech Flats	17724
Beech Glen	17758
Beech Grove	15822
Beechmont	15071
Beechton	15824
Beechview (Part of Pittsburgh)	15216
Beechwood	15834
Beechwood Park	19014
Beechwoods	15840
Beersville	18067
Beesons	15445
Beham	15376
Bela	16049
Belair	17601
Belair Park	17601
Belardley	19007
Belden	15522
Belfast (Fulton County) (Township)	17238
Belfast (Northampton County)	18064
Belfast Junction	18042
Belfry	19401
Belknap	16222
Bell (Clearfield County) (Township)	16627
Bell (Jefferson County) (Township)	15767
Bell (Westmoreland County) (Township)	15650
Bell Acres	15143
Bella Vista	17754
Belle Bridge (Part of Lincoln)	15037
Bellefield (Part of Pittsburgh)	15213
Bellefonte	16823
Bellegrove	17003
Bellemont	17562
Belle Valley	16509
Belle Vernon (Fayette County)	15012
Belle Vernon (Washington County)	15012
Belleville	17004
Bellevue	15202
Bell Mountain (Part of Dickson City)	18508
Bell Point	15613
Bellrun	16748
Bells Camp	16727
Bells Landing	15757
Bells Mills	15767
Belltown	17841
Bellview	15301
Bellwood	16617
Belmar	16323
Belmont	15904
Belmont Corner	18453
Belmont Hills	19020
Belmont Homes	15904
Belmont Terrace	19406
Belsano	15922
Belsena Mills	16661
Belton	16117
Beltzhoover (Part of Pittsburgh)	15210
Ben Avon (Allegheny County)	15202
Ben Avon (Indiana County)	15701
Ben Avon Heights	15202
Bencetown	15734
Bendersville	17306

454 PENNSYLVANIA Bendertown-Bower Hill

	ZIP		ZIP		ZIP
Bendertown	17859	Bidwell	15464	Bloomfield (Bedford County) (Township)	16673
Benedicks	17315	Biesecker Gap	17268	Bloomfield (Crawford County) (Township)	16438
Benezett	15821	Big Beaver	15010	Bloomingdale (Carbon County)	18250
Benezette (Township)	15821	Big Cove Tannery	17212	Bloomingdale (Lancaster County)	17601
Benfer	17812	Biggertown	17774	Bloomingdale (Luzerne County)	18655
Benjamin (Part of Perkasie)	18944	Bigler (Clearfield County)	16825	Blooming Glen	18911
Benner (Township)	16823	Bigler (Clearfield County) (Township)	16661	Blooming Grove (Pike County)	18428
Bensalem (Bucks County)	19020	Biglerville	17307	Blooming Grove (Township)	18464
Bensalem (Bucks County) (Township)	19020	Big Meadow Run	15417	Blooming Grove (York County)	17331
Benscreek (Cambria County)	15905	Big Mine Run	17921	Bloomington (Clearfield County)	16833
Bens Creek (Cambria County)	15938	Bigmount	17315	Bloomington (Lackawanna County)	18444
Benson	15935	Big Pond	16914	Blooming Valley	16335
Bentley Creek	14894	Big Run	15715	Bloomsburg	17815
Bentleyville	15314	Big Shanty	16738	Bloomsdale Gardens	19058
Benton (Columbia County)	17814	Bimber Corners	16351	Bloserville	17241
Benton (Columbia County) (Township)	17814	Bingen	18015	Bloss (Township)	16911
Benton (Lackawanna County) (Township)	18420	Bingham (McKean County)	16726	Blossburg	16912
Benvenue	17020	Bingham (Potter County) (Township)	16923	Blosser Hill	15451
Benzinger (Township)	15857	Bingham Center	16948	Blossom Hill	17601
Bergey	19438	Binnstown (Part of Centerville)	15417	Blossom Valley	17601
Berkeley Hills	15237	Bino	17225	Blough	15936
Berkley	19605	Birchardville	18801	Blue Ball	17506
Berkleys Mill	15552	Birchrunville	19421	Blue Bell	19422
Berkshire Heights (Part of Wyomissing)	19610	Birch Valley	19058	Blue Bell Farms	19422
Berkshire Mall (Part of Wyomissing)	19610	Birchwood Lakes	18328	Blue Bell Gardens	19422
Berlin (Somerset County)	15530	Birdell	19344	Blue Bell Knoll	19422
Berlin (Wayne County) (Township)	18431	Bird in Hand	17505	Blue Heron Pond	18328
Berlin Junction	17350	Birdsboro	19508	Blue Hill	17870
Berlinsville	18088	Birdville	17052	Blue Jay	16347
Bermudian	17019	Birmingham	19380	Blueknob	15946
Bern (Township)	19605	Birmingham (Township)	19380	Blue Ridge	19058
Berne	19526	Birmingham (Delaware County) (Township)	19317	Blue Ridge Summit	17214
Bernharts	19605	Birmingham (Huntingdon County)	16686	Bluff	15341
Bernice	18632	Bishop	15057	Blythe (Township)	17930
Bernville	19506	Bitner	15431	Blytheburn	18707
Berrysburg	17005	Bittersville	17366	Blythedale	15018
Berrytown	16925	Bitumen	17778	Blythewood	18901
Bertha	15021	Bixler	17047	Boaba	18457
Berwick (Adams County) (Township)	17316	Black (Bradford County)	18848	Boalsburg	16827
Berwick (Columbia County)	18603	Black (Somerset County) (Township)	15557	Boardman	16863
Berwinsdale	16656	Blackash	16327	Bobbys Corners (Part of Hermitage)	16159
Berwyn	19312	Black Bear (Part of St. Lawrence)	19606	Bobtown	15315
Besco	15322	Blackburn (Part of Trafford)	15085	Bocktown	15001
Bessemer (Allegheny County)	15104	Black Creek (Township)	18246	Bodines	17722
Bessemer (Lawrence County)	16112	Black Diamond (Part of Monongahela)	15063	Boggs (Armstrong County) (Township)	16259
Bessemer (Westmoreland County)	15666	Blackfield	15542	Boggs (Centre County) (Township)	16823
Bessemer Terrace (Part of East Pittsburgh)	15112	Blackgap	17222	Boggs (Clearfield County) (Township)	16878
Best (Part of West Mifflin)	15122	Blackhawk	15010	Boggstown	17221
Best Station	18080	Blackhorse (Chester County)	19365	Boggsville	16055
Bethany	18431	Black Horse (Delaware County)	19063	Bohrmans Mill	17972
Bethayres	19006	Black Horse (Montgomery County)	19401	Boiling Springs	17007
Bethel (Township)	19507	Blacklick (Cambria County) (Township)	15922	Bolde Point	18428
Bethel (Cambria County)	15931	Black Lick (Indiana County)	15716	Bolivar	15923
Bethel (Delaware County) (Township)	19061	Black Lick (Indiana County) (Township)	15717	Bolivar Run	16701
Bethel (Fulton County) (Township)	17267	Blacklog	17243	Boltz	15954
Bethel (Lebanon County) (Township)	17026	Blackman	18702	Bon Air (Cambria County)	15909
Bethel (Mercer County)	16159	Black Ridge	15235	Bon Air (Delaware County)	19083
Bethel (Westmoreland County)	15687	Blackrock	21088	Bon Aire	16001
Bethel (Armstrong County) (Township)	16226	Blacktown	16137	Bondsville	19335
Bethel (Berks County)	19507	Black Walnut	18623	Bonnair	17327
Bethelboro	15401	Blackwell	16938	Bonneauville	17325
Bethel Park	15102	Blain	17006	Bonus	16049
Bethesda	17532	Blain City	16627	Bocker	16661
Bethlehem	18015-18	Blaine (Township)	13565	Boone	15926
For specific Bethlehem Zip Codes call (215) 866-0911		Blaine Hill	15037	Booneville	17747
Bethlehem (Clearfield County)	15757	Blainesburg (Part of West Brownsville)	15417	Boon Terrace	15342
Bethlehem (Northampton County) (Township)	18017	Blainsport	17569	Booth Corner	19061
Bethlehem Annex	18017	Blair (Township)	16635	Boothwyn	19061
Bethton	18964	Blairs	16232	Boothwyn Highlands	19061
Betula	16749	Blairs Mills	17213	Boot Jack	15853
Betz	16661	Blairsville	15717	Boquet	15644
Betzwood	19401	Blairtown	15370	Bordnersville	17038
Beulah	16661	Blakely	18447	Borland Manor	15317
Beverly Estates	17601	Blakes	16912	Bortondale	19063
Beverly Heights	17042	Blakeslee	18610	Boston	15135
Beverly Hills (Blair County)	16601	Blanchard (Allegheny County)	15084	Boston Run	17948
Beverly Hills (Delaware County)	19082	Blanchard (Centre County)	16826	Boswell	15531
Beyer	16211	Blanco	16249	Boulevard (Part of Philadelphia)	19149
Biddle	15692	Blandburg	16619	Bourne	18850
		Blandon	19510	Bovard (Butler County)	16020
		Blanket Hill	16201	Bovard (Westmoreland County)	15619
		Blawnox	15238	Bowdertown	15724
		Bloom (Township)	16838	Bower	15757
		Bloomfield (Allegheny County)	15224	Bower Hill (Allegheny County)	15017

Bower Hill-Buck Run **PENNSYLVANIA** 455

Name	ZIP
Bower Hill (Washington County)	15367
Bowers	19511
Bowie	16133
Bowling Green	19063
Bowman Addition	17331
Bowman Heights	17201
Bowmans	17948
Bowmansdale	17008
Bowmans Store	17329
Bowmanstown (Carbon County)	18030
Bowmansville	17507
Bowser Plan	16201
Boyce	15241
Boyds Mills	18443
Boydstown	16025
Boydtown	17872
Boyers	16020
Boyers Junction	19522
Boyertown	19512
Boynton	15532
Brackenridge	15014
Brackney	18812
Bradbury Plan	15001
Braddock (Allegheny County)	15104
Braddock (Washington County)	15301
Braddock Hills	15221
Braden Plan	15322
Bradenville	15620
Bradford (Clearfield County) (Township)	16881
Bradford (McKean County)	16701
Bradford (McKean County) (Township)	16701
Bradford Hills	19335
Bradford Park (Part of Economy)	15005
Bradfordwoods	15015
Bradley Junction	15931
Bradleytown	16317
Brady (Butler County) (Township)	16057
Brady (Clarion County) (Township)	16248
Brady (Clearfield County)	15801
Brady (Clearfield County) (Township)	15848
Brady (Huntingdon County) (Township)	17002
Brady (Lycoming County) (Township)	17752
Bradys Bend	16028
Bradys Bend (Township)	16028
Braeburn (Part of Lower Burrell)	15068
Braintrim (Township)	18623
Braman	18417
Bramcote	19464
Branch (Township)	17901
Branch Dale	17923
Branchton	16021
Branchville	16426
Brandamore	19316
Brandon	16374
Brandonville	17967
Brandt	18847
Brandtsville	17055
Brandy Camp	15822
Brandywine Hills	19380
Brandywine Homes	19320
Brandywine Manor	19343
Brandywine Summit	19342
Brandywine Village	19406
Bratton (Township)	17044
Brave	15316
Braznell	15442
Breakneck	15425
Brecknock (Berks County) (Township)	19540
Brecknock (Lancaster County) (Township)	17517
Breezewood (Allegheny County)	15237
Breezewood (Bedford County)	15533
Breezy Corner	19522
Breinigsville	18031
Brenizer	15717
Brent	16156
Brentwood	15227
Breslau	18702
Bressler	17113
Bretonville	16656
Briarbrook	18707
Briarcliff	19036
Briar Creek (Columbia County)	18603

Name	ZIP
Briar Creek (Columbia County) (Township)	18603
Briar Hill (Armstrong County)	16201
Briar Hill (Wayne County)	18438
Briarwood (Part of New Britain)	18901
Brickchurch	16226
Brickerville	17543
Brick Tavern	18951
Bridesburg (Part of Philadelphia)	19137
Bridgeburg	18210
Bridgeport (Adams County)	17307
Bridgeport (Carbon County)	18661
Bridgeport (Clearfield County)	16833
Bridgeport (Lancaster County)	17602
Bridgeport (Montgomery County)	19405
Bridgeport (Perry County)	17040
Bridgeport (Westmoreland County)	15666
Bridgeton (Bucks County) (Township)	18972
Bridgeton (York County)	17352
Bridgetown	19047
Bridge Valley	18925
Bridgeville	15017
Bridgewater (Bucks County)	19020
Bridgewater (Susquehanna County) (Township)	18801
Bridgewater Farms	19014
Brier Hill	15415
Briggsville	18635
Brighton (Township)	15009
Brightside	19007
Brightwood (Part of Bethel Park)	15102
Brilhart	17403
Brinkerton	15601
Brintons	19380
Briquette (Part of Duquesne)	15110
Brisbin	16620
Briscoe Springs	16127
Bristol (Bucks County)	19007
Bristol (Bucks County) (Township)	19020
Bristol Heights	19007
Bristol Park	19007
Bristol Township	19007
Bristoria	15337
Brittany Farms	18914
Britton Run	16434
Broad Acres	16127
Broad Axe	19002
Broad Ford	15425
Broadford Junction	15425
Broadlawn Highlands	15241
Broad Street (Part of Hazleton)	18201
Broad Top (Bedford County) (Township)	16633
Broad Top (Huntingdon County)	16621
Broadview	15084
Broadway	18655
Broadway Manor	19007
Brock	15362
Brockie	17403
Brockport	15823
Brockton	17925
Brockway	15824
Brodbeck	17329
Brodhead	18017
Brodheadsville	18322
Brogue	17309
Brogueville	17322
Brokenstraw (Township)	16340
Brommerstown	17922
Brookdale (Cambria County)	15942
Brookdale (Susquehanna County)	18822
Brookes Mills	16635
Brookfield (Township)	16950
Brookhaven	19015
Brookland	16948
Brookline (Allegheny County)	15226
Brookline (Delaware County)	19083
Brooklyn	18813
Brooklyn (Township)	18813
Brookside (Cumberland County)	17257
Brookside (Erie County)	16510
Brookside (Lycoming County)	17771
Brookside (Schuylkill County)	17963

Name	ZIP
Brookside (York County)	17315
Brookside Farms	15241
Brookside Villa	18101
Brookston	16347
Brookthorpe Hills	19008
Brookvale	15425
Brookville	15825
Brookwater Park	19426
Broomall	19008
Brothersvalley (Township)	15530
Brotherton	15530
Broughton	15236
Brown (Lycoming County) (Township)	17727
Brown (Mifflin County) (Township)	17084
Brownbacks	19475
Browndale	18421
Brownfield	15416
Brownhill	16403
Brown Row	15431
Browns (Part of Avoca)	18641
Brownsburg	18938
Browns Crossroads	16218
Brownsdale	16053
Brownstown (Armstrong County)	15630
Brownstown (Cambria County)	15906
Brownstown (Fayette County)	15438
Brownstown (Lancaster County)	17508
Brownsville (Berks County)	19565
Brownsville (Fayette County)	15417
Brownsville (Fayette County) (Township)	15417
Brownsville (Fayette County)	15417
Brownsville (Franklin County)	17222
Brownsville (Schuylkill County)	17976
Brownsville Junction	15417
Browntown (Bradford County)	18853
Browntown (Luzerne County)	18640
Browntown (Washington County)	15312
Bruceton	15236
Bruin	16022
Brunnerville	17543
Brunots Island (Part of Pittsburgh)	15204
Brush Creek (Township)	15536
Brushmeadway	16648
Brushtown (Adams County)	17331
Brushtown (Cumberland County)	17241
Brush Valley	15720
Brush Valley (Township)	15701
Brushville	18847
Bryan (Armstrong County)	16222
Bryan (Fayette County)	15428
Bryan Hill	15701
Bryan Mills	17737
Bryansville	17314
Bryant	15101
Bryn Athyn	19009
Bryn Gweled	18966
Bryn Mawr (Allegheny County)	15221
Bryn Mawr (Montgomery County)	19010
Brysonia	17307
Bucher	16661
Buck (Lancaster County)	17566
Buck (Luzerne County) (Township)	18610
Buckeye	15666
Buck Hill Falls	18323
Buckhorn (Cambria County)	16613
Buckhorn (Columbia County)	17815
Buckingham (Township)	18912
Buckingham (Bucks County)	18437
Buckingham (Bucks County)	18938
Buckingham (Bucks County)	18912
Buckingham Valley	18938
Buckland Valley Farms	18977
Buckman Village (Part of Chester)	19013
Buckmanville	18938
Buck Mountain	18255
Buck Mountain Colliery	18214
Buck Run (Chester County)	19320
Buck Run (Indiana County)	15728
Buck Run (Schuylkill County)	17901

456 PENNSYLVANIA Buckstown-Cedarbrook Hills

Name	ZIP
Buckstown	15563
Bucksville	18930
Bucktown	19464
Buck Valley	17267
Buells Corners	16434
Buena Vista (Allegheny County)	15018
Buena Vista (Butler County)	16025
Buena Vista (Fayette County)	15486
Buena Vista (Franklin County)	17268
Buena Vista (Lancaster County)	17527
Buena Vista Springs	17268
Buffalo (Butler County) (Township)	16055
Buffalo (Perry County) (Township)	17045
Buffalo (Union County) (Township)	17837
Buffalo (Washington County)	15301
Buffalo (Washington County) (Township)	15323
Buffalo Cross Roads	17837
Buffalo Mills	15534
Buffalo Springs	17042
Buffalo Valley	16262
Buffington (Fayette County)	15468
Buffington (Indiana County) (Township)	15961
Buhl (Part of Sharon)	16146
Buhls	16033
Bulger	15019
Bullion	16374
Bullis Mill	16731
Bullskin (Township)	15666
Bully Hill	16323
Bunches	17070
Bungalow Park	18104
Bunker Hill (Cumberland County)	17055
Bunker Hill (Lebanon County)	17042
Bunker Hill (Schuylkill County)	17901
Bunkertown	17049
Bunola	15020
Burbank	16749
Burd Coleman Village (Part of Cornwall)	17016
Burgettstown	15021
Burholme (Part of Philadelphia)	19111
Burlington (Bradford County)	18814
Burlington (Bradford County) (Township)	18848
Burnham	17009
Burning Well	16735
Burnside (Centre County) (Township)	16845
Burnside (Clearfield County)	15721
Burnside (Clearfield County) (Township)	16692
Burnside (Northumberland County)	17872
Burnstown	16117
Burnt Cabins	17215
Burnwood	18465
Burrell (Armstrong County)	16226
Burrell (Indiana County) (Township)	15716
Burrous	16922
Burson Plan	15322
Bursonville	18077
Burtville	16743
Bush Addition	16823
Bushkill (Northampton County) (Township)	18064
Bushkill (Pike County)	18324
Bushkill Center	18064
Bush Patch (Part of Old Forge)	18518
Bustleton (Part of Philadelphia)	19115
Bute	15489
Butler	16001-03
For specific Butler Zip Codes call (412) 287-1706	
Butler (Adams County) (Township)	17307
Butler (Butler County) (Township)	16045
Butler (Luzerne County) (Township)	18222
Butler (Schuylkill County) (Township)	17921
Butler Junction	16229

Name	ZIP
Buttermilk Falls	15658
Buttonwood (Luzerne County)	18702
Buttonwood (Lycoming County)	17771
Buttonwood Glen	18901
Buttonwood Manor	18901
Butztown	18017
Buyerstown	17535
Buzzingtown	15642
Byberry (Part of Philadelphia)	19116
Bycot	18928
Byers	19480
Byersdale	15005
Byrnedale	15827
Byrnesville	17927
Byromtown	16239
Bywood	19082
Bywood Heights	19082
Cabbage Hill	15106
Cabot	16023
Cacoossing	19608
Cadis	18837
Cadogan (Armstrong County) (Township)	16212
Cadogan (Armstrong County)	16212
Caernarvon (Berks County) (Township)	19543
Caernarvon (Lancaster County) (Township)	17555
Cains	17527
Cairnbrook	15924
Caldwell	17745
Caledonia	15868
Caledonia Park	17222
California (Bucks County)	18951
California (Washington County)	15419
Calkins	18443
Callapoose	18444
Callensburg	16213
Callery	16024
Callimont	15552
Caln	19320
Caln (Township)	19320
Calumet	15621
Calumet-Norvelt	15621
Calvert	17771
Calvert Hills (Part of Altoona)	16601
Calvin	16622
Camargo	17566
Cambra	18611
Cambria (Township)	15931
Cambridge (Chester County)	19344
Cambridge (Crawford County) (Township)	16403
Cambridge Springs	16403
Camden Hill (Part of West Mifflin)	15122
Cameron	15834
Cammal	17723
Camp Akiba	18352
Campbelltown (Lebanon County)	17010
Campbelltown (McKean County)	16735
Camp Bnai Brith	18461
Camp Curtin (Part of Harrisburg)	17110
Camp Grove	17830
Camp Hill (Allegheny County)	15106
Camp Hill (Cumberland County)	17011
Camp Hill Shopping Mall (Part of Camp Hill)	17011
Camp Indian Run	19344
Camp Jo-Ann	15668
Camp Mystic	16403
Camp Perry	16114
Camp Starlight	18461
Camptown	18815
Camp Westmont	18449
Canaan	18472
Canaan (Township)	18472
Canadensis	18325
Canadohta Lake	16438
Canal (Township)	16314
Canan Station	16601
Candlebrook	19406
Candor	15019
Cannelton	16115
Canoe (Township)	15772
Canoe Camp	16933
Canoe Creek	16648
Canoe Ridge	15772
Canonsburg	15317

Name	ZIP
Canton (Bradford County)	17724
Canton (Bradford County) (Township)	17724
Canton (Washington County) (Township)	15301
Capital City Plaza (Cumberland County)	17011
Caprivi	17013
Carbon (Huntingdon County) (Township)	16678
Carbon (Mercer County)	16154
Carbon (Westmoreland County)	15601
Carbon Center	16001
Carbondale (Lackawanna County)	18407
Carbondale (Lackawanna County) (Township)	18407
Cardale	15420
Cardiff	15943
Cardington	19082
Carlisle	17013
Carlisle Barracks (Cumberland County)	17013
Carlisle Springs	17013
Carlson	16735
Carlton	16311
Carlton Heights	17252
Carmichaels	15320
Carnegie	15106
Carnot	15108
Carnot-Moon	15108
Carnwath	16861
Carol Acres	17036
Carpenter Corner	16153
Carpenter Town (Lackawanna County)	18414
Carpentertown (Westmoreland County)	15666
Carriage Hill	19067
Carrick (Part of Pittsburgh)	15210
Carrier (Part of Summerville)	15864
Carroll (Clinton County)	17747
Carroll (Perry County) (Township)	17090
Carroll (Washington County) (Township)	15063
Carroll (York County) (Township)	17019
Carroll Park (Columbia County)	17815
Carroll Park (Montgomery County)	19151
Carrolltown	15722
Carroll Valley	17320
Carson (Part of Pittsburgh)	15203
Carsontown	17776
Carson Valley	16635
Carsonville	17032
Carter Camp	16922
Cartwright	15823
Carver Court	19320
Carversville	18913
Carverton	18644
Casanova	16860
Cascade (Township)	17771
Cashtown (Adams County)	17310
Cashtown (Franklin County)	17201
Cass (Huntingdon County) (Township)	16623
Cass (Schuylkill County) (Township)	17901
Cassandra	15925
Casselman	15557
Cassville	16623
Castanea (Clinton County)	17726
Castanea (Clinton County) (Township)	17726
Castanea (Clinton County)	17726
Caste Village (Part of Whitehall)	15236
Castle Garden	15832
Castle Rock	19073
Castle Shannon	15234
Castle Valley	18914
Castlewood	16101
Castor (Part of Philadelphia)	19149
Cataract	16871
Catasauqua	18032
Catawissa (Columbia County)	17820
Catawissa (Columbia County) (Township)	17820
Caterbury Manor	15061
Catharine (Township)	16693
Cavettsville	15085
Ceasetown	18612
Cecil	15321
Cecil (Township)	15057
Cedarbrook	19095
Cedarbrook Hills	19095

Cedarbrook Mall-Clayton **PENNSYLVANIA** 457

Name	ZIP
Cedarbrook Mall	19095
Cedar Cliff Manor	17011
Cedar Creek	15012
Cedar Heights	19428
Cedar Hollow	19355
Cedarhurst	15243
Cedar Knoll	19320
Cedar Lane	17519
Cedar Ledge	17724
Cedar Ridge (Adams County)	17350
Cedar Ridge (Beaver County)	15061
Cedar Run	17727
Cedars	19423
Cedar Springs	19464
Cedarville	16123
Celia	18052
Cementon	18052
Centennial (Adams County)	17331
Centennial (Centre County)	16870
Centennial Hills	18974
Center (Beaver County) (Township)	15001
Center (Butler County) (Township)	16001
Center (Greene County) (Township)	15359
Center (Indiana County) (Township)	15748
Center (Juniata County)	17059
Center (Perry County)	17062
Center Bridge	18938
Center City (Part of Williamsport)	17701
Center Hill	16201
Center Manor	15061
Center Mills	17304
Center Moreland	18657
Centerport	19516
Center Road	16424
Center Square	19422
Centertown	16127
Center Union	16652
Center Valley	18034
Centerville (Bedford County)	15522
Centerville (Crawford County)	16404
Centerville (Lancaster County)	17602
Centerville (Perry County)	17045
Centerville (Washington County)	15417
Centerville (York County)	17327
Central (Allegheny County)	15132
Central (Columbia County)	17814
Central (Washington County)	15301
Central (Westmoreland County)	15688
Central City (Centre County)	16853
Central City (Somerset County)	15926
Central Highlands	15037
Centralia	17927
Central Manor	17582
Central Oak Heights	17886
Central Park	15037
Central Square Greens	19401
Central Wharf (Part of Munhall)	15120
Centre (Berks County) (Township)	19541
Centre (Perry County)	17047
Centre (Perry County) (Township)	17068
Centre (Snyder County) (Township)	17842
Centre Hall	16828
Centre Hill	16828
Century	15417
Century III Mall (Part of West Mifflin)	15122
Ceres (Township)	16748
Cessna	15522
Cetronia	18104
Ceylon	15320
Chadds Ford	19317
Chadville	15401
Chain	17960
Chain Bridge	18940
Chaintown	15428
Chalfant	15112
Chalfont	18914
Chalkhill	15421
Challenge	15823
Chalybeate	15522
Chambersburg	17201
Chambers Hill	17111
Chambers Mill	15301
Chambersville	15723

Name	ZIP
Champion	15622
Chanceford (Township)	17309
Chandler Plan	16226
Chandlers Valley	16312
Chaneysville	15535
Chapel	18070
Chapel Downs	15024
Chapel Hill	19006
Chapel Valley	15001
Chapman (Township)	17864
Chapman (Clinton County) (Township)	17760
Chapman (Lehigh County)	18106
Chapman (Northampton County)	18014
Chapman (Snyder County)	17864
Chapman Lake	18433
Charleroi	15022
Charleston (Mercer County)	16146
Charleston (Tioga County) (Township)	16901
Charlestown (Chester County)	19460
Charlestown (Township)	19460
Charlestown (Franklin County)	17236
Charlesville	15522
Charlottsville	16686
Charlton (Clinton County)	17745
Charlton (Dauphin County)	17112
Charmian	17214
Charming Forge	19551
Charteroak	16669
Charter Oaks	16509
Charterwood	15237
Chartiers (Township)	15342
Chartiers Terrace	15106
Chase	18708
Chatham (Chester County)	19318
Chatham (Tioga County) (Township)	16935
Chatham Park	19083
Chatham Village	19083
Chatwood	19380
Checkerville	16925
Chelsea	19013
Chelten Avenue (Part of Philadelphia)	19144
Cheltenham (Montgomery County)	19012
Cheltenham (Montgomery County) (Township)	19012
Cheltenham Shopping Center	19095
Cheltenham Square	19150
Cherokee Ranch	19560
Cherry (Butler County) (Township)	16057
Cherry (Sullivan County) (Township)	18614
Cherry City	15209
Cherrydale	19444
Cherry Flats	16917
Cherry Grove (Township)	16313
Cherry Grove (Huntingdon County)	17264
Cherry Grove (Warren County)	16313
Cherry Hill (Erie County)	16401
Cherryhill (Indiana County) (Township)	15765
Cherry Hill (Lancaster County)	17563
Cherry Hill (Northampton County)	18064
Cherry Hill (York County)	17070
Cherry Lane	15613
Cherry Ridge (Township)	18431
Cherry Run	17885
Cherrytown	16657
Cherrytree (Township)	16354
Cherry Tree (Indiana County)	15724
Cherry Tree (Venango County)	16354
Cherry Valley (Butler County)	16373
Cherry Valley (Washington County)	15021
Cherryville (Northampton County)	18035
Cherryville (Schuylkill County)	17966
Chest (Cambria County) (Township)	16668
Chest (Clearfield County) (Township)	16656
Chester	19013-16
For specific Chester Zip Codes call (215) 876-1613	
Chesterfield	16627

Name	ZIP
Chester Heights	19017
Chester Hill	16866
Chester Plaza	19014
Chester Springs	19425
Chester Township	19013
Chester Valley Knoll	19355
Chesterville	19350
Chestnut Grove	16838
Chestnut Hill (Erie County)	16509
Chestnut Hill (Lancaster County)	17512
Chestnuthill (Monroe County) (Township)	18331
Chestnut Hill (Northampton County)	18042
Chestnut Hill (Philadelphia County)	19118
Chestnut Level	17566
Chestnut Ridge (Fayette County)	15422
Chestnut Ridge (Lancaster County)	17603
Chestnut View	17603
Chest Springs	16624
Cheswick	15024
Chevy Chase Heights	15701
Chewton	16157
Cheyney	19319
Chickasaw	16259
Chickory	15909
Chicora	16025
Childs	18407
Chillisquaque	17850
Chinchilla	18410
Chippewa (Township)	15010
Choconut	18812
Choconut (Township)	18818
Christiana	17509
Christian Springs	18064
Christmas	18229
Christy Manor	16226
Chrome	19362
Chrystal	16748
Church Hill (Fayette County)	15458
Church Hill (Forest County)	16321
Church Hill (Franklin County)	17236
Church Hill Manor	17084
Churchill	15235
Churchill Plan	16117
Churchill Valley	15235
Churchtown	17555
Churchville (Bedford County)	16667
Churchville (Bucks County)	18966
Cinnamon Hills	19406
Circleville	15642
Cisna Run	17047
Cito	17233
City View	17044
Clair Manor	15012
Clairton	15025
Clairton Junction (Part of West Mifflin)	15122
Clamtown	18252
Clappertown	16693
Clapp Farm	16301
Clara (Township)	16748
Clarence	16829
Clarendon	16313
Clarendon Heights (Warren County)	16313
Claridge	15623
Clarington	15828
Clarion (Clarion County)	16214
Clarion (Clarion County) (Township)	15829
Clark	16113
Clark Manor	15001
Clarksburg	15725
Clarks Green	18411
Clarks Mills	16114
Clarks Summit	18411
Clarks Summit State Hospital	18501
Clarkstown	17756
Clarksville	15322
Clarksville Hill	15322
Claussville	18069
Clay (Township)	17578
Clay (Butler County) (Township)	16061
Clay (Huntingdon County) (Township)	17264
Clay (Lancaster County)	17522
Clay Hill	17201
Claylick	17236
Claypoole Heights	15701
Claysburg	16625
Claysville	15323
Clayton	19503

458 PENNSYLVANIA Claytonia-Cooper Settlement

Place	ZIP
Claytonia	16057
Clearbrook	19050
Clearbrook Village	19040
Clearfield (Butler County) (Township)	16034
Clearfield (Cambria County) (Township)	16668
Clearfield (Clearfield County)	16830
Clearfield (Northampton County)	18064
Clear Ridge	17229
Clear Run	15801
Clear Spring	17019
Clearview	17601
Clearview Estates (Beaver County)	15001
Clearview Estates (Cumberland County)	17011
Clearview Manor	18101
Clearville	15535
Cleona	17042
Clermont	16740
Cleveland (Township)	17820
Cleversburg	17257
Cliff Mine	15108
Clifford (Township)	18413
Clifford (Snyder County)	17870
Clifford (Susquehanna County)	18413
Clifton (Dauphin County)	17057
Clifton (Lackawanna County) (Township)	18424
Clifton Heights	19018
Climax (Armstrong County)	16216
Climax (Clarion County)	16216
Climax (Indiana County)	15944
Clinton (Allegheny County)	15026
Clinton (Armstrong County)	16229
Clinton (Butler County) (Township)	16001
Clinton (Fayette County)	15469
Clinton (Lycoming County) (Township)	17752
Clinton (Venango County) (Township)	16373
Clinton (Wayne County) (Township)	18472
Clinton (Wyoming County) (Township)	18419
Clintondale	17751
Clintonville	16372
Cloe	15767
Clonmell	19390
Clover (Township)	15829
Cloverdale Park	18915
Clover Hill	15423
Clover Run	15757
Clune	15727
Cly	17370
Clyde	15944
Clyde No. 3	15322
Clymer (Indiana County)	15728
Clymer (Tioga County) (Township)	16943
Coal (Township)	17872
Coal Bluff	15332
Coal Brook	15425
Coal Cabin Beach	17314
Coal Castle	17901
Coal Center	15423
Coal City	16374
Coaldale (Dauphin County)	17048
Coaldale (Schuylkill County)	18218
Coal Glen	15824
Coal Hill	16301
Coal Hollow	15846
Coal Junction	15531
Coalmont	16678
Coalport (Carbon County)	18229
Coalport (Clearfield County)	16627
Coal Run (Clearfield County)	16666
Coal Run (Northumberland County)	17866
Coal Run (Somerset County)	15552
Coaltown (Butler County)	16057
Coaltown (Lawrence County)	16101
Coatesville	19320
Cobalt Ridge	19058
Cobblerville	17218
Cobbs Corners	16434
Cobham	16351
Coburn (Blair County)	16601
Coburn (Centre County)	16832
Cocalico	17517
Cochran Acres	15001
Cochrans Mills	16226
Cochranton	16314

Place	ZIP
Cochranville	19330
Cocolamus	17014
Codorus (York County)	17311
Codorus (York County) (Township)	17327
Coffeetown (Lebanon County)	17078
Coffeetown (Lehigh County)	18069
Coffeetown (Northampton County)	18042
Cogan House (Township)	17771
Cogan Station	17728
Cokeburg	15324
Cokeburg Junction	15331
Cold Point	19462
Cold Run	19508
Cold Spring (Franklin County)	17222
Cold Spring (Huntingdon County)	16652
Cold Spring (Lebanon County) (Township)	17028
Cold Spring (York County)	17360
Cold Spring Park	19464
Cold Springs Crossing	19426
Colebrook (Clinton County) (Township)	17734
Colebrook (Lebanon County)	17015
Colebrookdale (Berks County)	19512
Colebrookdale (Berks County) (Township)	19512
Colegrove	16749
Coleman	15541
Colemanville	17565
Colerain (Bedford County) (Township)	15522
Colerain (Huntingdon County)	16683
Colerain (Lancaster County) (Township)	17536
Coles	17948
Colesburg	16915
Coles Creek	17814
Colesville	18015
Coleville (Centre County)	16823
Coleville (McKean County)	16749
Colfax	16652
College (Beaver County)	15010
College (Centre County) (Township)	16801
College (Northampton County)	18042
College A (Part of East Stroudsburg)	18301
College Heights	19605
College Hill (Part of Beaver Falls)	15010
College Manor	18612
College Misericordia	18612
College Park (Montgomery County)	19031
College Park (Union County)	17837
College View Heights	18016
Collegeville	19426
Colley (Township)	18614
Collier (Allegheny County) (Township)	15106
Collier (Fayette County)	15401
Collingdale	19023
Collins	17566
Collinsburg	15089
Collinsville	17302
Collinswood Acres	15017
Collomsville	17701
Colmar	18915
Colona (Part of Monaca)	15061
Colonial Crest	17111
Colonial Hills (Berks County)	19608
Colonial Hills (Mifflin County)	17044
Colonial Manor	17603
Colonial Park (Dauphin County)	17109
Colonial Park (Delaware County)	19064
Colonial Park (Lancaster County)	17540
Colonial Park (Northumberland County)	17847
Colonial Village	19087
Colony Park	19608
Columbia (Bradford County) (Township)	16914
Columbia (Lancaster County)	17512
Columbia Cross Roads	16914
Columbus	16405
Columbus (Township)	16405
Colver	15927

Place	ZIP
Colwyn	19023
Comly	17772
Commerce (Part of Philadelphia)	19108
Commodore	15729
Compass	17527
Conashaugh Lake	18337
Concord (Butler County) (Township)	16025
Concord (Delaware County) (Township)	19331
Concord (Erie County) (Township)	16407
Concord (Franklin County)	17217
Concord (Westmoreland County)	15012
Concord Park	19047
Concordville	19331
Conemaugh (Cambria County) (Township)	15902
Conemaugh (Indiana County) (Township)	15725
Conemaugh (Somerset County) (Township)	15905
Conestoga (Township)	17516
Conestoga (Chester County)	19520
Conestoga (Lancaster County)	17516
Conestoga Farms	19317
Conestoga Woods	17602
Coneville	16748
Conewago (Adams County) (Township)	17331
Conewago (Dauphin County) (Township)	17022
Conewago (York County) (Township)	17404
Conewago Heights	17345
Conewango (Township)	16365
Confluence	15424
Congo	19504
Congruity	15601
Conifer	15864
Connaughton	19428
Conneaut (Crawford County) (Township)	16424
Conneaut (Erie County) (Township)	16401
Conneaut Lake	16316
Conneaut Lake Park	16316
Conneautville	16406
Connellsville (Fayette County)	15425
Connellsville (Fayette County) (Township)	15425
Connersville	17851
Connerton	17935
Connoquenessing (Butler County)	16027
Connoquenessing (Butler County) (Township)	16053
Conoy (Township)	17502
Conrad	16720
Conshohocken	19428
Continental (Part of Philadelphia)	19106
Conway	15027
Conyngham (Columbia County) (Township)	17851
Conyngham (Luzerne County)	18219
Conyngham (Luzerne County) (Township)	18655
Cook (Township)	15687
Cooke (Township)	17241
Cookport	15729
Cooksburg	16217
Cookseytown	18707
Cooks Mills	15545
Cooks Run	17778
Coolbaugh (Township)	18466
Coolbaughs	18324
Coolspring (Fayette County)	15445
Coolspring (Jefferson County)	15730
Coolspring (Mercer County) (Township)	16137
Cool Valley (Washington County)	15317
Cool Valley (Westmoreland County)	15601
Coon Hunter	17842
Coontown	16735
Cooper (Clearfield County) (Township)	16839
Cooper (Montour County) (Township)	17821
Coopersburg	18036
Cooper Settlement	16834

Cooperstown-Dearth PENNSYLVANIA 459

Name	ZIP
Cooperstown (Butler County)	16059
Cooperstown (Venango County)	16317
Cooperstown (Westmoreland County)	15650
Coopersville	17509
Copella	18014
Copesville	19380
Coplay	18037
Coral	15731
Coraopolis	15108
Coraopolis Heights	15108
Corinne	19380
Cork Lane	18640
Corliss (Part of Pittsburgh)	15204
Corner Ketch	19335
Corner Store	19460
Corning	18092
Cornish	15451
Cornog	19343
Cornplanter (Township)	16301
Cornpropst	16652
Cornwall	17016
Cornwall Center (Part of Cornwall)	17016
Cornwells Heights	19020
Corrine	19380
Corry	16407
Corsica	15829
Cortez (Jefferson County)	15767
Cortez (Lackawanna County)	18436
Corwins Corners	16701
Corydon (Township)	16701
Coryville	16731
Costello	16720
Cosytown	17225
Coterell Lake	18470
Cottage	16669
Cottage Grove	16105
Cottage Hill	16242
Cottageville	18901
Cotton Town	16625
Couchtown	17047
Coudersport	16915
Coulters	15028
Council Crest	18201
Country Club Estates (Armstrong County)	16201
Country Club Estates (Lancaster County)	17601
Country Club Estates (Montgomery County)	19444
Country Club Heights	17601
Country Gardens	17540
Country Hills	15642
Countryside	17011
County Line	18966
County Line Park	18914
Coupon	16629
Court at King of Prussia, The	19406
Courtdale	18704
Courtney	15029
Cove	17020
Covedale	16693
Cove Gap	17236
Coventryville	19464
Coverdale (Part of Bethel Park)	15102
Coveville	18325
Covington (Township)	16917
Covington (Clearfield County) (Township)	16836
Covington (Lackawanna County) (Township)	18424
Covington (Tioga County)	16917
Covode	15767
Cowan	17844
Cowanesque	16918
Cowansburg	15642
Cowanshannock (Township)	16222
Cowans Village	17224
Cowansville	16218
Cowden	15057
Coxeville	18216
Coy	15748
Coy Junction	15748
Coylesburg	16034
Coyleville	15380
Crabapple	15624
Crabtree	15624
Crabtree Hollow	19053
Crackersport	18104
Crafton	15205
Craig	18414
Craigheads	17013
Craigs	17948
Craigs Meadow	18301
Craigsville	16262
Craley	17312

Name	ZIP
Cramer	15954
Cranberry (Township)	16319
Cranberry (Butler County) (Township)	16046
Cranberry (Luzerne County)	18201
Cranberry (Venango County)	16319
Cranberry Estates	16046
Cranberry Ridge	18201
Cranesville	16410
Crates	16240
Crawford (Township)	17740
Crawfordtown	15733
Creamery	19430
Creekside	15732
Creighton	15030
Crenshaw	15824
Crescent (Township)	15046
Crescentdale (Part of Wampum)	16157
Crescent Heights	15427
Crescent Lake (Monroe County)	18332
Crescent Lake (Pike County)	18337
Crescent Township	15046
Cresco	18326
Creslo	15951
Cresmont	17931
Cresmont Farms	19335
Cress	17268
Cresson (Cambria County)	16630
Cresson (Cambria County) (Township)	16630
Cressona	17929
Crestmont (Clinton County)	17745
Crestmont (Montgomery County)	19090
Crestmont Village	15001
Crestview	19040
Crestwood	18444
Creswell	17516
Crete	15701
Criders Corners	16046
Crimson Maple	18837
Croft	16830
Cromby	19460
Cromwell (Township)	17260
Crooked Creek	16652
Crookham	15332
Crosby	16724
Cross Creek	15021
Cross Creek (Township)	15312
Cross Fork	17729
Crossgrove	17841
Crossingville	16412
Cross Keys (Adams County)	17350
Cross Keys (Blair County)	16635
Cross Keys (Bucks County)	18901
Cross Keys (Juniata County)	17021
Crossroads (Northampton County)	18014
Cross Roads (York County)	17322
Crosswicks	19046
Crown	16220
Croydon	19020
Croydon Acres	19020
Croydon Crest	19020
Croydon Heights	19020
Croydon Manor	19020
Croydon Park	19020
Croyle (Township)	15955
Crozer Park Gardens (Part of Chester)	19013
Crucible	15325
Crum Creek Manor	19013
Crum Lynne (Delaware County)	19078
Crum Lynne (Delaware County)	19022
Crystal	15439
Crystal Lake	18407
Crystal Spring	15536
Crystal View	15084
Cuba Mills	17059
Cuddy	15031
Cuddy Hill	15031
Culbertson	17201
Culmerville	15084
Culp	16601
Culpepper Woods	19444
Cumberland (Adams County) (Township)	17325
Cumberland (Greene County) (Township)	15320
Cumberland Park	17011
Cumberland Valley (Township)	15522
Cumberland Village	15320

Name	ZIP
Cumbola	17930
Cummings (Township)	17776
Cummingstown	17013
Cummingswood Park	15610
Cumru (Township)	19540
Cupola	19344
Curllsville	16221
Curren Terrace (Part of Norristown)	19401
Curry Run	15757
Curryville	16631
Curtin (Centre County)	16841
Curtin (Centre County) (Township)	16841
Curtis Hills	19095
Curtis Park (Centre County)	16866
Curtis Park (Delaware County)	19079
Curtisville	15032
Curwensville	16833
Cush Creek (Indiana County)	15712
Cussewago (Township)	16433
Custards	16314
Custer City	16725
Custis Woods	19038
Cutler Summit	16923
Cyclone	16726
Cymbria Mine	15714
Cynwyd Estates	19004
Cynwyd Hills	19004
Cypher	16650
Daggett	16936
Dagus	15846
Daguscahonda	15853
Dagus Mines	15831
Daisytown (Cambria County)	15902
Daisytown (Washington County)	15427
Dale (Cambria County)	15902
Dale (Clearfield County)	16881
Dale Summit	16801
Daleville (Chester County)	19330
Daleville (Lackawanna County)	18424
Dalevue	16801
Daley	15924
Dallas (Luzerne County)	18612
Dallas (Luzerne County) (Township)	18612
Dallas City	16701
Dallastown	17313
Dalmatia	17017
Dalton	18414
Damascus	18415
Damascus (Township)	18415
Danboro	18916
Danielsville	18038
Dannersville	18067
Danville	17821
Danville State Hospital	17821
Darby (Delaware County)	19023
Darby (Delaware County) (Township)	19036
Darby Township	19036
Darlington (Beaver County)	16115
Darlington (Beaver County) (Township)	16115
Darlington (Delaware County)	19063
Darlington (Westmoreland County)	15658
Darlington Corners	19380
Darragh	15625
Darthmouth Farms	17036
Dartmouth Hills	19406
Dauberville	19517
Daugherty (Township)	15066
Dauphin	17018
Davidsburg	17315
Davidson (Township)	17758
Davidson Heights	15001
Davidsville	15928
Davis Grove	19044
Davistown (Fayette County)	15446
Davistown (Greene County)	15349
Dawson	15428
Dawson Manor	19040
Dawson Ridge	15009
Dawson Run	16370
Day	16258
Daylesford	19312
Dayton (Armstrong County)	16222
Dayton (Dauphin County)	17098
Deal	15552
Dean	16636
Dean (Township)	16636
Deanville	16242
Dearth	15401

460 PENNSYLVANIA Decatur-Earl

	ZIP
Decatur (Clearfield County) (Township)	16666
Decatur (Mifflin County) (Township)	17841
Deckard	16314
Deckers Point	15759
Deckertown	18446
Deemers Cross Roads	15851
Deemston	15333
Deep Dale East	19058
Deep Dale West	19058
Deep Run	18944
Deep Valley	15352
Deer Creek (Township)	16145
Deercroft	19444
Deerfield (Tioga County) (Township)	16928
Deerfield (Warren County) (Township)	16351
Deer Lake (Fayette County)	15421
Deer Lake (Schuylkill County)	17961
Deer Mt. Lake (Monroe County)	18355
Deer Mt. Lake (Monroe County)	18370
Deer Park	18938
Defiance	16633
Degolia	16701
Deiblers Station	17821
Delabole	18072
De Lancey	15733
Delano	18220
Delano (Township)	18220
Delaware (Juniata County) (Township)	17094
Delaware (Mercer County) (Township)	16125
Delaware (Northumberland County) (Township)	17777
Delaware (Pike County) (Township)	18328
Delaware Grove	16124
Delaware Valley College (Part of New Britain)	18901
Delaware Water Gap	18327
Dellville	17020
Delmar (Township)	16901
Delmont	15626
Delphi	19473
Delps	18038
Delroy	17406
Delta	17314
Delta Manor	18017
Demmler	15137
Demmler Transfer	15137
Dempseytown	16317
Denbeau Heights (Part of Centerville)	15417
Denbo (Part of Centerville)	15429
Denholm	17059
Dennison (Township)	18661
Dennys Mill	16023
Dents Run	15832
Denver	17517
Deodate	17022
Deringer	18241
Derrick City	16727
Derrs	17814
Derry (Dauphin County) (Township)	17033
Derry (Mifflin County) (Township)	17099
Derry (Montour County) (Township)	17821
Derry (Westmoreland County)	15627
Derry (Westmoreland County) (Township)	15627
Derwood Park	19094
Derwyn	19004
Deshon Manor	16001
Desire	15851
Detters Mill	17315
De Turksville	17963
Devault	19432
Devon	19333
Devon-Berwyn	19312
Dewart	17730
Dewey Heights	18052
De Young	16728
Diamond (Clarion County)	16248
Diamond (Venango County)	16354
Diamondton	17851
Diamondville	15728
Dice	17844
Dickerson Run	15430
Dickey	17236
Dickinson (Cumberland County)	17218

	ZIP
Dickinson (Cumberland County) (Township)	17065
Dicksonburg	16406
Dickson City	18519
Dieners Hall	17901
Dilliner	15327
Dillinger	18049
Dillingersville	18092
Dillontown	18417
Dillsburg	17019
Dilltown	15929
Dilworthtown	19380
Dimeling	16830
Dimock	18816
Dimock (Township)	18816
Dimock Corners	18430
Dingman (Township)	18337
Dingmans Ferry	18328
Dipple Manor	18201
Distant	16223
District (Township)	19512
Divide	17814
Dividing Ridge	15530
Dixmont	15143
Dixon	18657
Dixonville	15734
D&M Junction	17019
Doe Run	19320
Dogtown (Columbia County)	17815
Dogtown (Luzerne County)	18655
Dogtown (Snyder County)	17870
Dogwood Acres	18966
Dogwood Hollow	19053
Dolington	18940
Dombach Manor	17601
Donald Son	17981
Donaldson Crossroads	15317
Donation	16652
Donegal (Butler County) (Township)	16025
Donegal (Washington County) (Township)	15323
Donegal (Westmoreland County)	15628
Donegal (Westmoreland County) (Township)	15646
Donegal Heights	17552
Donegal Springs	17552
Donerville	17603
Donnally Mills	17062
Donnelly	15612
Donnellytown	17013
Donohoe	15650
Donora	15033
Dooleyville	17851
Dora (Greene County)	15338
Dora (Jefferson County)	15767
Dormont	15216
Dorneyville	18104
Dornsife	17823
Dorothy	15650
Dorrance	18707
Dorrance (Township)	18707
Dorset	17960
Dorseyville	15238
Dott	17267
Dotters Corners	18058
Doubling Gap	17241
Douglass (Berks County) (Township)	19464
Douglass (Montgomery County) (Township)	19525
Douglassville	19518
Doutyville	17872
Dover (York County)	17315
Dover (York County) (Township)	17315
Down East	19355
Downey	15530
Downieville	16059
Downingtown	19335
Downtown (Erie County)	16501
Downtown (Fayette County)	15401
Downtown (Lancaster County)	17603
Doylesburg	17219
Doyles Mills	17058
Doylestown (Bucks County)	18901
Doylestown (Bucks County) (Township)	18901
Drake	16156
Drakes Mills	16403
Draketown	15424
Drane	16666
Draper	16901
Drauckers	15848
Dravosburg	15034
Dreher (Township)	18445
Drehersville	17961
Drennen	15068
Dresher	19025

	ZIP
Drexelbrook	19026
Drexel Heights	18067
Drexel Hill	19026
Drexel Hills (Part of New Cumberland)	17070
Drexeline Shopping Center	19026
Drexel Plaza	19050
Drexlewood	19610
Drifting	16834
Drifton	18221
Driftwood	15832
Drinker	18444
Drocton (Part of Renovo)	17764
Dromgold	17090
Druid Hills (Part of Dallas)	18708
Drummond	15823
Drumore	17518
Drumore (Township)	17563
Drums	18222
Drury Run	17764
Dry Hill	15425
Dry Ridge	15601
Dry Run	17220
Dry Tavern	15357
Dry Valley Crossroads	17889
Dryville	19539
Dublin (Bucks County)	18917
Dublin (Fulton County) (Township)	17223
Dublin (Huntingdon County) (Township)	17239
Dublin Mills	17229
Du Bois	15801
Duboistown	17701
Dudley	16634
Duffield	17201
Duffs Junction (Part of Pittsburgh)	15230
Duhring	16239
Duke Center	16729
Dumas	15424
Dunbar (Fayette County)	15431
Dunbar (Fayette County) (Township)	15425
Duncan (Township)	16901
Duncan Circle	15009
Duncannon	17020
Duncansville	16635
Duncott	17901
Dundaff	18407
Dundore	17864
Dungarvin	16877
Dunkard	15327
Dunkard (Township)	15315
Dunkelbergers	17872
Dunlap Creek Village	15475
Dunlevy	15432
Dunlo	15930
Dunminning	19073
Dunmore	18512
Dunn	15329
Dunningsville	15330
Dunningtown	15632
Dunns Eddy	16371
Dunnstable (Township)	17751
Dunnstown	17745
Dupont	18641
Duquesne	15110
Duquesne Heights (Part of Pittsburgh)	15211
Duquesne Wharf (Part of Duquesne)	15110
Durbin	15380
Durham	18039
Durham (Township)	18039
Durham Furnace	18930
Durlach	17522
Durrell	18848
Duryea	18642
Dushore	18614
Dutch Hill (Clarion County)	16049
Dutch Hill (Fayette County)	15450
Dutch Hill (Mercer County)	16148
Dutch Settlement	15946
Dutchtown	17236
Dutton Mill	19380
Dyberry (Township)	18431
Dysart	16636
Eagle Foundry	16621
Eaglehurst	16509
Eagle Point	19530
Eagle Rock	16301
Eagles Mere	17731
Eagles Mere Park (Part of Eagles Mere)	17731
Eagleville (Centre County)	16826
Eagleville (Montgomery County)	19408
Earl (Berks County) (Township)	19512

Earl-Eldred PENNSYLVANIA 461

Name	ZIP
Earl (Lancaster County) (Township)	17557
Earlington	18918
Earlston	15537
Earlville	19519
Earlyville	15846
Earnest	19401
Earnestville	16666
East Allen (Township)	18067
East Altoona	16601
East Ararat	18465
East Athens	18810
East Bangor	18013
East Benton	18414
East Berlin	17316
East Berwick	18603
East Bethlehem (Township)	15322
East Bradford (Chester County) (Township)	19380
East Bradford (McKean County)	16701
East Brady	16028
East Branch (Jefferson County)	15767
East Branch (Warren County)	16434
East Brandywine (Township)	19335
Eastbrook	16101
East Brunswick (Township)	17960
East Buffalo (Union County) (Township)	17837
East Buffalo (Washington County)	15301
East Butler	16029
East Caln (Township)	19341
East Cameron (Township)	17872
East Canton	17724
East Carnegie (Part of Pittsburgh)	15230
East Carroll (Township)	15722
East Chillisquaque (Township)	17847
East Cocalico (Township)	17517
East Conemaugh	15909
East Connellsville	15425
East Coventry (Township)	19457
East Deer (Township)	15030
East Donegal (Township)	17547
East Drumore (Township)	17566
East Du Bois (Part of Du Bois)	15801
East Du Bois Junction (Part of Du Bois)	15801
East Earl	17519
East Earl (Township)	17519
East End (Blair County)	16602
East End (Luzerne County)	18702
East Fairfield (Township)	16314
East Fallowfield (Chester County) (Township)	19320
East Fallowfield (Crawford County) (Township)	16111
East Falls (Part of Philadelphia)	19129
East Faxon	17701
East Finley	15377
East Finley (Township)	15377
East Franklin (Township)	16201
East Fredericktown	15450
East Freedom	16637
East Germantown (Part of Philadelphia)	19138
East Goshen (Township)	19380
East Greenville	18041
East Hanover (Dauphin County) (Township)	17028
East Hanover (Lebanon County) (Township)	17028
East Hempfield (Township)	17603
East Herrick	18853
East Hickory	16321
East Hills (Part of Doylestown)	18901
East Hills Center	15235
East Honesdale (Part of Honesdale)	18431
East Hopewell (Township)	17322
East Huntingdon (Township)	15612
East Kane	16735
East Keating (Township)	17778
East Kendall	17356
East Kittanning	16201
East Lackawannock (Township)	16137
East Lampeter (Township)	17602
Eastland	19362
Eastland Hills (Franklin County)	17268
Eastland Hills (Lancaster County)	17602
Eastland Shopping Plaza	15137

Name	ZIP
East Lansdowne	19050
East Lawn	18064
Eastlawn Gardens (Northampton County)	18064
East Lawrence	16929
East Lemon	18657
East Lenox	18470
East Lewisburg	17847
East Liberty (Part of Pittsburgh)	15206
East Mahoning (Township)	15759
East Manchester (Township)	17347
East Marianna	15345
East Marlborough (Township)	19348
East McKeesport	15035
East Mead (Township)	16335
East Millsboro	15433
East Mines (Part of St. Clair)	17970
Eastmont (Allegheny County)	15235
Eastmont (Cambria County)	15902
Eastmont (York County)	17315
East Nantmeal (Township)	19421
East New Castle	16101
East Newport	17074
East Norriton (Montgomery County) (Township)	19401
East Norriton (Montgomery County)	19401
East Norwegian (Township)	17901
East Nottingham (Township)	19363
East Oakmont (Part of Plum)	15131
Easton	18042-44
For specific Easton Zip Codes call (215) 252-9987	
Easton	16255
East Oreland	19075
East Penn (Township)	18235
East Pennsboro (Township)	17025
East Petersburg	17520
East Pike	15701
East Pikeland (Township)	19460
East Pittsburgh	15112
Eastpoint	17765
East Prospect	17317
East Providence (Township)	15533
East Riverside	15433
East Rochester	15074
East Rockhill (Township)	18944
Eastrun	15759
East Rush	18801
East Salem	17059
East Saxton	16678
East Sharon	16748
East Sharpsburg	16673
East Side	18661
East Smethport	16730
East Smithfield	18817
East Springfield	16411
East St. Clair (Township)	15554
East Stroudsburg	18301
East Taylor (Township)	15909
East Texas	18046
East Titusville	16354
East Towanda	18848
Easttown (Township)	19312
Easttown Woods	19312
East Troy	16947
East Union (Township)	18248
East Uniontown (Fayette County)	15401
Eastvale	15010
East Vandergrift	15629
East View	15370
Eastville	17747
East Vincent (Township)	19475
East Washington	15301
East Waterford	17021
East Weissport	18235
East Wheatfield (Township)	15920
East Whiteland (Township)	19355
Eastwicks (Part of Philadelphia)	19153
East William Penn	17976
Eastwood (Allegheny County)	15235
Eastwood (Westmoreland County)	15601
East Yoe	17356
East York	17402
Eaton (Township)	18657
Eatonville	18657
Eau Claire	16030
Ebenezer	17042
Ebensburg	15931
Ebensburg Junction	15931
Eberhardt (Allegheny County)	15101

Name	ZIP
Eberhardt (Butler County)	16001
Eberlys Mill	17011
Ebervale	18223
Echo (Armstrong County)	16222
Echo (Cambria County)	15942
Echo Lake	18301
Echo Valley (Delaware County)	19073
Echo Valley (Schuylkill County)	17981
Eckenrode Mill	16668
Eckley	18255
Eckville	19529
Economy (Part of Ambridge)	15003
Economy	15005
Eddington	19020
Eddington Gardens	19020
Eddystone	19013
Eddyville	16242
Edelman	18064
Eden (Clearfield County)	16836
Eden (Lancaster County)	17601
Eden (Lancaster County) (Township)	17566
Edenborn	15458
Edenburg	19526
Eden Croft	19006
Edendale	16666
Eden Heights	17601
Edenville	17201
Edgebrook (Part of Pittsburgh)	15226
Edgecliff (Part of Lower Burrell)	15068
Edgegrove	17331
Edge Hill	19038
Edgely	19007
Edgemont (Dauphin County)	17109
Edgemont (Delaware County)	19028
Edgemont (Northampton County)	18088
Edgemont Farms	19073
Edges Mill	19335
Edgewater (Part of Oakmont)	15139
Edgewater Terrace	15650
Edgewood (Allegheny County)	15218
Edgewood (Indiana County)	15701
Edgewood (Northumberland County)	17872
Edgewood (Somerset County)	15501
Edgewood Acres (Part of Forest Hills)	15221
Edgewood Grove (Part of Somerset)	15501
Edgewood Park (Bucks County)	19067
Edgewood Park (Delaware County)	19008
Edgeworth	15143
Edgmont (Township)	19028
Edie	15501
Edinboro	16412
Edinburg	16116
Edison	18901
Edisonville	17579
Edmon	15630
Edna	15611
Edwardsville	18704
Effort	18330
Egypt (Clearfield County)	16881
Egypt (Jefferson County)	15824
Egypt (Lehigh County)	18052
Ehrenfeld	15956
Eichelbergertown	16650
Eidenau	16037
Eighty Four	15330
Ekastown	16055
Elam	19342
Elberta	16601
Elbon	15823
Elbrook	17268
Elco	15434
Elder (Township)	16646
Elders Ridge	15681
Eldersville	15036
Elderton	15736
El-Do-Lake	18058
Eldora (Lancaster County)	17563
Eldora (Washington County)	15063
Eldorado (Blair County)	16602
Eldorado (Butler County)	16049
Eldred (Jefferson County) (Township)	15860

462 PENNSYLVANIA Eldred-Falling Spring

Name	ZIP
Eldred (Lycoming County) (Township)	17754
Eldred (McKean County)	16731
Eldred (McKean County) (Township)	16731
Eldred (Monroe County) (Township)	18058
Eldred (Schuylkill County) (Township)	17964
Eldred (Warren County) (Township)	16340
Eldredsville	18616
Eleven Mile	16923
Elfinwild	15101
Elgin	16413
Elgin Park	19073
Elim	15905
Elimsport	17810
Elizabeth (Allegheny County)	15037
Elizabeth (Allegheny County) (Township)	15018
Elizabeth (Lancaster County) (Township)	17543
Elizabethtown	17022
Elizabethville	17023
Elk (Chester County) (Township)	19351
Elk (Clarion County) (Township)	16232
Elk (Tioga County) (Township)	16921
Elk (Warren County) (Township)	16345
Elk City	16232
Elk Creek (Township)	16401
Elkdale (Chester County)	19352
Elkdale (Susquehanna County)	18470
Elk Grove	17814
Elkins Park	19117
Elk Lake (Susquehanna County)	18801
Elk Lake (Wayne County)	18472
Elkland (Sullivan County) (Township)	18616
Elkland (Tioga County)	16920
Elkland (Tioga County) (Township)	16920
Elk Lick (Township)	15565
Elk Run Junction (Part of Punxsutawney)	15767
Elkview	19390
Ellen Gowan	17976
Ellenton	17724
Ellerslie	19020
Elliger Park	19034
Elliott (Part of Pittsburgh)	15220
Elliott Heights (Part of Bethlehem)	18015
Elliottsburg	17024
Elliotts Mills	16057
Elliottson	17013
Elliottsville	15437
Ellisburg	16923
Ellport	16117
Ellrod (Part of Versailles)	15132
Ellsworth	15331
Ellwood City	16117
Elm	17521
Elmdale	18436
Elmer	16950
Elmhurst (Lackawanna County) (Township)	18416
Elmhurst (Lackawanna County)	18416
Elmo	16232
Elmora	15737
Elmwood (Philadelphia County)	19142
Elmwood (York County)	17403
Elmwood Terrace	18444
Elora	16057
Elrama	15038
Elrico	15684
Elroy	18964
Elstie	16613
Elstonville	17545
Elton	15934
Elverson	19520
Elwood Park	15301
Elwyn	19063
Elwyn Terrace	17545
Elysburg	17824
Emanuelville	18014
Emblem (Part of White Oak)	15131
Embreeville	19320
Embreeville State Hospital	19320
Emeigh	15738
Emerald (Greene County)	15322
Emerald (Lehigh County)	18080

Name	ZIP
Emerickville	15825
Emigh Run (Part of Cherry Tree)	15724
Emigsville (York County)	17318
Emlenton	16373
Emmaus	18049
Emmaville	15536
Emporium	15834
Emporium Junction (Part of Emporium)	15834
Emsworth	15202
Endeavor	16322
Enders	17032
Energy	16101
Enfield	19075
Engleside (Part of Lancaster)	17602
Engles Lake	18370
Englesville	19512
Englewood	17931
English Center	17776
Enhaut	17113
Enid	16691
Enlow	15126
Ennisville	16652
Enola	17025
Enon (Greene County)	15377
Enon (Washington County)	15377
Enon Valley	16120
Enterline	17032
Enterprise (Mercer County)	16127
Enterprise (Warren County)	16354
Entlerville	17241
Entriken	16638
Ephrata (Lancaster County)	17522
Ephrata (Lancaster County) (Township)	17522
Equinunk	18417
Ercildoun	19320
Erdenheim	19118
Erdman	17048
Erhard	16861
Erie	16501-65
For specific Erie Zip Codes call (814) 898-7317	
Erie Heights (Part of Erie)	16501
Erlen	19126
Erly	17024
Ernest	15739
Erney	17315
Erwinna	18920
Eshbach	19505
Eshcol	17062
Esplen (Part of Pittsburgh)	15204
Espy	17815
Espyville Station	16424
Essington	19029
Estella	18616
Esterly (Part of St. Lawrence)	19606
Estherton	17110
Etna	15223
Etters	17319
Euclid	16001
Eulalia (Township)	16915
Eureka (Cambria County)	15963
Eureka (Westmoreland County)	15479
Evans	15401
Evansburg	19426
Evans City	16033
Evans Falls	18657
Evanston	15625
Evansville (Berks County)	19522
Evansville (Columbia County)	18603
Evendale	17086
Everett	15537
Evergreen	18833
Evergreen Park	18052
Everhartville	17074
Everson	15631
Ewalt (Part of Pittsburgh)	15212
Ewings Mill	15765
Ewingsville	15106
Excelsior	17825
Exchange	17821
Exeter (Berks County) (Township)	19606
Exeter (Luzerne County)	18643
Exeter (Luzerne County) (Township)	18643
Exeter (Wyoming County) (Township)	18615
Export	15632
Exton	19341
Exton Square Mall	19341
Eyers Grove	17846
Eynon (Part of Archbald)	18403
Factoryville (Northampton County)	18013

Name	ZIP
Factoryville (Wyoming County)	18419
Fagleysville	19525
Fagundus	16351
Fair Acres	17070
Fairbank	15435
Fairbrook	16865
Fairchance	15436
Fairdale (Greene County)	15320
Fairdale (Susquehanna County)	18801
Fairfield (Adams County)	17320
Fairfield (Crawford County) (Township)	16314
Fairfield (Erie County)	16510
Fairfield (Lycoming County) (Township)	17754
Fairfield (Washington County)	15345
Fairfield (Westmoreland County) (Township)	15923
Fair Grounds	15344
Fairhaven Heights	15137
Fairhill (Bucks County)	19440
Fairhill (Philadelphia County)	19133
Fairhope (Township)	15538
Fairhope (Fayette County)	15012
Fairhope (Somerset County)	15538
Fairhope-Arnold City	15012
Fairland	17543
Fairlane Village Mall (Part of Pottsville)	17901
Fairlawn	17728
Fairless	19030
Fairless Hills	19030
Fairmont	15642
Fairmount (Lancaster County)	17566
Fairmount (Luzerne County) (Township)	17814
Fairmount (Philadelphia County)	19121
Fairmount (Wayne County)	18462
Fairmount City	16224
Fairmount Springs	17814
Fairoaks (Allegheny County)	15003
Fairoaks (Montgomery County)	19044
Fairplay	17325
Fairview (Township)	16137
Fairview (Mifflin County)	17044
Fairview (Northumberland County)	17872
Fairview (York County) (Township)	17070
Fairview (Beaver County)	15052
Fairview (Blair County)	16601
Fairview (Butler County)	16050
Fairview (Butler County) (Township)	16025
Fairview (Clearfield County)	16858
Fairview (Erie County)	16415
Fairview (Erie County) (Township)	16415
Fairview (Franklin County)	17268
Fairview (Jefferson County)	15767
Fairview (Luzerne County) (Township)	18707
Fairview (Mercer County)	16124
Fairview Drive	17331
Fairview-Ferndale	17872
Fairview Heights (Allegheny County)	15238
Fairview Heights (Berks County)	19533
Fairview Heights (Luzerne County)	18707
Fairview Heights (McKean County)	16701
Fairview Hills	18707
Fairview Knolls	18042
Fairview Park (Chester County)	19380
Fairview Park (Luzerne County)	18707
Fairview Park (York County)	17070
Fairview Village	19409
Fairville (Chester County)	19317
Fairville (Union County)	17837
Fairway Park	17603
Fairways of Brookside	18062
Fairywood (Part of Pittsburgh)	15205
Falconcrest	19380
Fallentimber	16639
Fallen Timbers	15451
Falling Spring (Franklin County)	17201
Falling Spring (Perry County)	17040

Fallowfield-Foxtown Hill **PENNSYLVANIA** 463

Name	ZIP
Fallowfield (Township)	15022
Falls (Township)	18615
Falls (Bucks County) (Township)	19054
Falls (Wyoming County)	18615
Falls Creek	15840
Fallsington	19054
Fallston	15066
Falls Township	19054
Falmouth	17502
Fannett (Township)	17220
Fannettsburg	17221
Faraday Park	19070
Farmbrook	19007
Farmdale	17552
Farmers	17364
Farmers Mills	16875
Farmers Valley (Bradford County)	16947
Farmers Valley (McKean County)	16749
Farmersville (Lancaster County)	17522
Farmersville (Northampton County)	18042
Farmington (Berks County)	19539
Farmington (Clarion County) (Township)	16220
Farmington (Fayette County)	15437
Farmington (Lehigh County)	18103
Farmington (Tioga County) (Township)	16946
Farmington (Warren County) (Township)	16345
Farmington Hill	16946
Farquhar Estates	17403
Farragut	17754
Farrandsville	17734
Farrell	16121
Farview	19607
Farwell	17764
Fassett	16925
Faunce	16863
Fawn (Allegheny County) (Township)	15084
Fawn (York County) (Township)	17321
Fawn Grove	17321
Faxon	17701
Fayette (Juniata County) (Township)	17049
Fayette (Lawrence County)	16156
Fayette City	15438
Fayetteville	17222
Fayfield	17402
Fay Terrace	16125
Fearnot	17968
Feasterville	19047
Feasterville Gardens	19047
Feasterville Heights	19047
Feasterville-Trevose	19047
Federal	15071
Federal Penitentiary	17837
Federal Prison Camp	17810
Federal Reserve (Part of Pittsburgh)	15230
Federal Square (Part of Harrisburg)	17108
Fell (Township)	18421
Fellsburg	15012
Fellwick	19034
Felton	17322
Feltonville	19013
Fenelton	16034
Ferguson (Centre County) (Township)	16801
Ferguson (Clearfield County) (Township)	16833
Ferguson (Fayette County)	15431
Fergusonville	19007
Fermanagh (Township)	17059
Fern	16319
Fern Brook	18612
Ferndale (Bucks County)	18921
Ferndale (Cambria County)	15905
Ferndale (Northumberland County)	17872
Ferndale (Schuylkill County)	17985
Fern Glen	18241
Fern Hill	19380
Fernridge	18610
Fern Village	19040
Fernville	17815
Fernway	16063
Fernwood (Clearfield County)	16680
Fernwood (Delaware County)	19050
Fernwood-Yeadon	19050
Ferrelton	15563

Name	ZIP
Fertigs	16364
Fertility	17602
Fetterville	17555
Fiddle Lake	18465
Fiddlers Green	15946
Fidelity (Part of Philadelphia)	19109
Fieldmore Springs	16354
Fife Shire Acres	15317
Fifficktown	15956
Fiketown	15459
Filbert	15435
Fillmore	16823
Finch Hill	18407
Findlay (Township)	15026
Findley (Township)	16137
Finland	18073
Finleyville (Bedford County)	16679
Finleyville (Washington County)	15332
Fireside Terrace (Part of York)	17404
Fisher	16225
Fisherdale	17824
Fisher-Eldora	15063
Fisher Heights (Butler County)	16001
Fisher Heights (Washington County)	15063
Fishers Corner	19013
Fishers Ferry	17801
Fishertown (Bedford County)	15539
Fishertown (Cambria County)	15956
Fisherville	17032
Fishing Creek (Township)	17859
Fiske	16639
Fitch Corner	18615
Fitz Henry	15479
Five Corners	16404
Five Forks	17268
Five Points (Part of Ohioville)	15059
Five Points (Beaver County)	15001
Five Points (Berks County)	19606
Five Points (Butler County)	16057
Five Points (Chester County)	19348
Five Points (Clearfield County)	15753
Five Points (Erie County)	16509
Five Points (Indiana County)	15732
Five Points (Luzerne County)	18249
Five Points (Mercer County)	16133
Five Points (rural)	16150
Five Points (Northumberland County)	17772
Five Points (Venango County)	16342
Five Points (Westmoreland County)	15601
Fivepointville	17517
Flat Rock (Centre County)	16870
Flat Rock (Fayette County)	15459
Flatwoods	15486
Fleetville	18420
Fleetwing Estates	19057
Fleetwood	19522
Fleming	16835
Flemington	17745
Flicksville	18050
Flinton	16640
Flintville	17042
Floradale	17307
Floreffe (Part of Jefferson)	15025
Florence	15021
Florida Park	19073
Florin (Part of Mount Joy)	17552
Flourtown	19031
Flourtown Gardens	19031
Flying Hills	19607
FM Corners (Part of Hermitage)	16148
Fogelsville	18051
Folcroft	19032
Foleys Siding (Part of Castle Shannon)	15234
Folsom	19033
Folstown	18707
Fombell	16123
Font	19335
Fontana	17042
Footedale	15468
Foot of Ten	16635
Forbes Road	15633
Force	15841
Ford City	16226
Ford Cliff	16228
Fordham	15767
Ford View	16226

Name	ZIP
Fordville	17364
Fordyce	15370
Forest	16879
Forest Castle (Part of Exeter)	18643
Forest City	18421
Forest Grove (Allegheny County)	15108
Forest Grove (Bucks County)	18922
Foresthill (Union County)	17844
Forest Hill (York County)	17356
Forest Hills (Allegheny County)	15221
Forest Hills (Lancaster County)	17540
Forest Hills Manor	19006
Forest Inn	18235
Forest Lake	18801
Forest Lake (Township)	18801
Forest Park (Bucks County)	18914
Forest Park (Luzerne County)	18702
Forestville (Butler County)	16035
Forestville (Schuylkill County)	17901
Forge	16686
Forks (Columbia County)	17859
Forks (Northampton County) (Township)	18042
Forks (Sullivan County) (Township)	18614
Forkston	18629
Forkston (Township)	18629
Forksville	18616
Forsythia Gate	19053
Fort Allen Plan	15601
Fortenia	18431
Fort Fetter	16648
Fort Hill (Somerset County)	15540
Fort Hill (Westmoreland County)	15687
Fort Hunter	17110
Fort Indiantown Gap	17003
Fort Littleton	17223
Fort Loudon	17224
Fortney	17339
Fort Roberston	17047
Fortuna	18915
Fort Washington	19034
Forty Fort	18704
Forward (Allegheny County) (Township)	15063
Forward (Butler County) (Township)	16033
Fossilville	15534
Foster (Indiana County)	15681
Foster (Luzerne County) (Township)	18224
Foster (McKean County) (Township)	16701
Foster (Schuylkill County) (Township)	17901
Foster Brook	16701
Fostoria	16617
Foundryville	18603
Fountain	17938
Fountain Dale	17320
Fountain Hill	18015
Fountain House Corners	16433
Fountain Springs	17921
Fountainville	18923
Fourth Avenue (Part of Pittsburgh)	15222
Foustown	17404
Foustwell	15953
Fowler Heights	15701
Fowlersville	18603
Fox (Elk County) (Township)	15846
Fox (Sullivan County) (Township)	17724
Foxburg (Cambria County)	15773
Foxburg (Clarion County)	16036
Foxburg (Jefferson County)	15767
Fox Chapel	15238
Fox Chase (Lancaster County)	17601
Fox Chase (Philadelphia County)	19111
Fox Chase Manor	19117
Foxcroft (Delaware County)	19008
Foxcroft (Montgomery County)	19046
Foxdale (Part of New Stanton)	15672
Fox Hill (Franklin County)	17268
Fox Hill (Luzerne County)	18702
Fox Run	16046
Foxton Lake	18847
Foxtown	15697
Foxtown Hill	18360

464 PENNSYLVANIA Frackville-Gladstone

Name	ZIP	Name	ZIP	Name	ZIP
Frackville	17931	Frenchville	16836	Gaysport (Part of Hollidaysburg)	16648
Frailey (Township)	17981	Freysville	17356	Gay Street (Part of West Chester)	19380
Francis	16417	Fricks	18927	Gearhartville	16866
Francis Mine	15021	Fricks Lock	19464	Geeseytown	16648
Franconia	18924	Friedens (Lehigh County)	18080	Geiger	15501
Franconia (Township)	18924	Friedens (Somerset County)	15541	Geigertown	19523
Frank	15018	Friedensburg	17933	Geistown	15904
Frankford (Part of Philadelphia)	19124	Friedensville	18017	Gelatt	18825
Frankfort Springs	15050	Friendship Heights	15467	General Warren Village	19355
Franklin (Adams County) (Township)	17307	Friendship Village	19320	Genesee	16923
Franklin (Beaver County) (Township)	16123	Friendsville	18818	Genesee (Township)	16923
Franklin (Bradford County) (Township)	18848	Friesville	16625	Geneva	16316
Franklin (Butler County) (Township)	16052	Frisbie	17961	Geneva Hill	15010
Franklin (Cambria County)	15909	Frisco	16117	Georges (Township)	15401
Franklin (Carbon County) (Township)	18235	Fritztown	19608	George School (Part of Newtown)	18940
Franklin (Chester County) (Township)	19350	Frogtown (Armstrong County)	16028	Georgetown (Adams County)	17340
Franklin (Columbia County) (Township)	17820	Frogtown (Clarion County)	16224	Georgetown (Armstrong County)	15656
Franklin (Erie County) (Township)	16412	Frogtown (Huntingdon County)	16877	Georgetown (Beaver County)	15043
Franklin (Fayette County) (Township)	15486	Frogtown (York County)	17070	Georgetown (Luzerne County)	18702
Franklin (Greene County) (Township)	15370	Froman	15332	Georgetown (Northampton County)	18064
Franklin (Huntingdon County) (Township)	16865	Frostburg	15740	Georgeville	15759
Franklin (Luzerne County) (Township)	18640	Frosts	16239	German (Township)	15458
Franklin (Lycoming County) (Township)	17742	Frugality	16639	German Corners	18053
Franklin (Snyder County) (Township)	17861	Fruitville (Lancaster County)	17601	Germania	16922
Franklin (Susquehanna County) (Township)	18801	Fruitville (Montgomery County)	19473	Germans	18235
Franklin (Venango County)	16323	Frutcheys	18301	Germansville	18053
Franklin (York County) (Township)	17019	Fryburg	16326	Germantown (Adams County)	17340
Franklin Acres	16046	Frystown	17067	Germantown (Franklin County)	17222
Franklin Center (Delaware County)	19063	Fuhrmans Mill	17331	Germantown (Philadelphia County)	19144
Franklin Center (Erie County)	16412	Fulmor Heights	19040	Germantown (Pike County)	18428
Franklindale	18832	Fulton (Township)	17563	Germany (Township)	17340
Franklin Farms	15301	Fulton Run	15701	Geryville	18073
Franklin Forks	18801	Furlong	18925	Getty Heights	15701
Franklin Hill	18822	Furnace Hill (Fayette County)	15431	Gettysburg	17325
Franklin Park	15143	Furnace Hill (Mercer County)	16159	Ghenne Heights	15063
Franklintown	17323	Furnace Run	16210	Ghennes Heights	15063
Franklinville	16683	Furniss	17563	Ghent	18850
Frankstown	16648	Gabby Heights	15301	Giant Oaks	15317
Frankstown (Township)	16648	Gabelsville	19512	Gibbon Glade	15440
Frazer (Allegheny County) (Township)	15084	Gahagen	15926	Gibbs Hill	16735
Frazer (Chester County)	19355	Gaibleton	15747	Gibraltar	19508
Frederick	19435	Gaines	16921	Gibson (Township)	18842
Fredericksburg (Armstrong County)	16041	Gaines (Township)	16921	Gibson	15314
Fredericksburg (Blair County)	16625	Galeton	16922	Gibson (Cameron County) (Township)	15832
Fredericksburg (Clovercreek) (Blair County)	16662	Galilee	18415	Gibson (Susquehanna County)	18820
Fredericksburg (Crawford County)	16335	Gallagher (Township)	17745	Gibsonia	15044
Fredericksburg (Lebanon County)	17026	Gallagherville	19335	Gibsonton	15012
Fredericksville	19539	Gallatin	15063	Gifford	16732
Fredericktown	15333	Gallery at Market East, The (Part of Philadelphia)	19107	Gilbert	18331
Fredericktown Hill	15333	Gallitzin (Cambria County)	16641	Gilberton	17934
Fredonia	16124	Gallitzin (Cambria County) (Township)	16641	Gilbertsville	19525
Freeburg	17827	Galloway (Part of Sugarcreek)	16323	Gilfoyl	16239
Freedom (Adams County) (Township)	17307	Gamble (Township)	17771	Gillespie	15438
Freedom (Beaver County)	15042	Ganister	16693	Gillett	16925
Freedom (Blair County) (Township)	16637	Gans	15439	Gillingham	16836
Freehold (Township)	16402	Gap	17527	Gilmore (Fayette County)	15401
Freeland	18224	Gapsville	15533	Gilmore (Greene County) (Township)	15352
Freemansburg	18017	Garards Fort	15334	Gilmore (McKean County)	16727
Freemansburg Heights	18017	Gardeau	16720	Gilmore (Washington County)	15057
Freemansville	19607	Garden City (Allegheny County)	15146	Gilmore Acres	15235
Freeport (Armstrong County)	16229	Garden City (Delaware County)	19013	Gilpin (Township)	15656
Freeport (Erie County)	16428	Gardendale	19061	Ginger Hill	15063
Freeport (Greene County) (Township)	15352	Garden Heights (Part of Altoona)	16602	Ginter	16651
Freeport Junction (Part of Freeport)	16229	Garden Hills	17603	Ginther	18252
French Creek (Mercer County) (Township)	16311	Garden View (Lycoming County)	17701	Gipsy	15741
Frenchcreek (Venango County) (Township)	16323	Gardenview (Mifflin County)	17084	Girard (Clearfield County) (Township)	16836
Frenchs Corners	16210	Gardenville	18926	Girard (Erie County)	16417
Frenchtown	16327	Gardner	16101	Girard (Erie County) (Township)	16417
		Gardners	17324	Girard Avenue (Part of Philadelphia)	19122
		Garfield	19506	Girardville	17935
		Garland	16416	Girty	15686
		Garman	15714	Gitts Run	17331
		Garrett	15542	Gladden	15057
		Garrett Hill	19010	Gladden Heights	15057
		Garretts Run	16201	Glade (Somerset County)	15530
		Garrison	15352	Glade (Warren County)	16365
		Gascola	15235	Glade (Warren County) (Township)	16365
		Gaskill (Township)	15715	Glade City	15552
		Gastonville	15336	Glades	17402
		Gastown	15774	Gladhill	17320
		Gatchellville	17352	Gladstone (Part of Lansdowne)	19050
		Gates	15410		
		Gatesburg	16877		
		Gateway Center (Part of Pittsburgh)	15222		
		Gateway Shopping Center (Part of Edwardsville)	18704		
		Gauff Hill	18017		
		Gayly	15146		

Gladwyne-Greenwood PENNSYLVANIA 465

Name	ZIP
Gladwyne	19035
Glanford (Part of Pittsburgh)	15230
Glasgow (Beaver County)	15059
Glasgow (Cambria County)	16644
Glasgow (Montgomery County)	19464
Glass City	16866
Glasser	15061
Glassmere	15030
Glassport	15045
Glassworks	15338
Glatfelter	17360
Gleason	17724
Gleasonton	17760
Glen Acres	19380
Glen Ashton Farms	19020
Glenburn (Township)	18414
Glenburn	18414
Glen Campbell	15742
Glen Carbon	17901
Glencoe	15538
Glendale (Allegheny County)	15106
Glendale (Luzerne County)	18641
Glendale Gardens (Part of Glenolden)	19036
Glendale Manor	18701
Glendon (Northampton County)	18042
Glendon (Schuylkill County)	17948
Glen Dower	17901
Glen Eden (Butler County)	16033
Glenfield	15143
Glen Forney	17268
Glen Gormley	15071
Glenhall	19380
Glen Hazel	15870
Glen Hope	16645
Glenhurst (Part of Bryn Athyn)	19009
Gleniron	17845
Glenloch	19380
Glen Lyon	18617
Glen Mawr	17737
Glen Mills	19342
Glenmoore (Chester County)	19343
Glen Moore (Lancaster County)	17601
Glenolden	19036
Glen Richey	16863
Glen Riddle	19037
Glen Riddle-Lima	19037
Glen Rock	17327
Glen Rose	19320
Glen Roy	19362
Glenruadh	16505
Glen Savage	15538
Glenshaw	15116
Glenside	19038
Glenside Gardens	19038
Glenside Heights	19038
Glen Summit	18707
Glenville	17329
Glenwall Village	15001
Glenwillard	15046
Glenwood (Allegheny County)	15230
Glenwood (Dauphin County)	17109
Glenwood (Erie County)	16501
Glenwood (Mifflin County)	17044
Glenwood (Susquehanna County)	18446
Glenwood Junction (Part of Pittsburgh)	15230
Glenworth	17901
Glosser View	17701
Glyde	15301
Glyndon	16434
Gnatstown	17331
Goat Hill	15301
Godfrey	15656
Goff	16020
Goheenville	16259
Gold	16923
Golden Hill	18623
Golden Key Lake	18337
Goldenridge	19057
Golden Rod Farms	16830
Good	17268
Goodhope	17055
Good Hope Farms	17055
Good Intent	15323
Goodmans Corners	16364
Goods Corner	15906
Good Spring	17981
Goodtown	15530
Goodville	17528
Goodyear	17324
Goosetown	19320
Gordon	17936

Name	ZIP
Gordonville	17529
Goshen	16830
Goshen (Township)	16873
Goshenville	19380
Gosser Hill	15656
Gouglersville	19608
Gouldsboro	18424
Gourley	15061
Gowen	18241
Gowen City	17828
Grace Park	19081
Graceton	15748
Graceville	15537
Gracey	17228
Gradwohl Terrace	18017
Gradyville	19039
Grafton (Indiana County)	15716
Graham (Clearfield County)	16866
Graham (Clearfield County) (Township)	16858
Grampian	16838
Grampian Hills (Part of Williamsport)	17701
Grand Valley	16420
Grandview (Armstrong County)	16201
Grandview (Butler County)	16045
Grahdview (Elk County)	15857
Grandview (Indiana County)	15701
Grandview (Washington County)	15063
Grandview Heights	17601
Grandview Park (Elk County)	15857
Grand View Park (Montgomery County)	19426
Grange	15767
Grange Corners	16433
Grange Hall Center	16433
Grangeville	17331
Granite	17325
Granite Run Mall	19063
Grant (Elk County)	15821
Grant (Indiana County) (Township)	15759
Grant City	16051
Grantham	17027
Grant Street (Part of Pittsburgh)	15219
Grantville	17028
Granville (Township)	17044
Granville (Part of California)	15423
Granville (Bradford County) (Township)	16926
Granville (Mifflin County)	17029
Granville Center	16926
Granville Summit	16926
Grapeville	15634
Grassflat	16839
Grassmere	17814
Grassy (Part of Olyphant)	18447
Graterford	19426
Gratz	17030
Gratztown	15089
Gravity	18436
Gray (Clearfield County)	16881
Gray (Greene County) (Township)	15337
Gray (Somerset County)	15544
Graydon	17322
Grays Landing	15461
Gray Station	15717
Graysville (Greene County)	15337
Graysville (Huntingdon County)	16865
Grazier	15953
Grazierville	16686
Greason	17013
Great Bend (Susquehanna County)	18821
Great Bend (Susquehanna County) (Township)	18822
Greater Pittsburgh International Airport 911th Tactical Airlift Group	15231
Greater Point Marion	15474
Greble	17067
Greece City	16025
Greeley	18425
Green (Forest County) (Township)	16353
Green (Indiana County) (Township)	15724
Greenawalds	18104
Greenbank	17557
Greenbrae	16201
Greenbrier (Centre County)	16875
Greenbrier (Dauphin County)	17036
Greenbrier (Delaware County)	19073

Name	ZIP
Greenbrier (Northumberland County)	17867
Greenbrook	19007
Greenburr	17747
Greencastle	17225
Green Circle	18451
Greencrest Park	16125
Greendale	16735
Greendown Acres	16635
Greene (Beaver County) (Township)	15050
Greene (Clinton County) (Township)	17747
Greene (Erie County) (Township)	16509
Greene (Franklin County) (Township)	17254
Greene (Greene County) (Township)	15320
Greene (Lancaster County)	17518
Greene (Mercer County) (Township)	16125
Greene (Pike County) (Township)	18426
Greene Junction (Part of South Connellsville)	15425
Greenfield (Allegheny County)	15217
Greenfield (Blair County) (Township)	16625
Greenfield (Cambria County)	16613
Greenfield (Erie County) (Township)	16428
Greenfield (Lackawanna County) (Township)	18407
Greenfield (Mercer County)	16137
Greenfields (Berks County)	19605
Green Fields (Dauphin County)	17098
Green Hill	19380
Green Hills (Delaware County)	19079
Green Hills (Washington County)	15301
Green Lane	18054
Green Lane Farms	17011
Greenlawn Park	19007
Greenmount	17325
Green Oaks	16301
Greenock	15047
Green Park	17031
Green Point	17038
Green Ridge (Delaware County)	19014
Green Ridge (Lackawanna County)	18509
Green Ridge (Luzerne County)	18201
Greenridge (Westmoreland County)	15642
Greenridge Farms	19006
Greensboro	15338
Greensburg	15601
Greens Landing	18810
Greenspring	17241
Green Springs	17331
Greentown	18426
Green Tree (Allegheny County)	15220
Green Tree (Chester County)	19355
Green Valley (Allegheny County)	15137
Green Valley (Jefferson County)	15825
Green Village	17201
Greenville (Clearfield County)	16839
Greenville (Mercer County)	16125
Greenville (Somerset County) (Township)	15552
Greenville East	16125
Greenwald	15670
Greenwich (Berks County) (Township)	19530
Greenwich (Cambria County)	15714
Greenwood (Township)	17859
Greenwood (Crawford County) (Township)	16316
Greenwood (Juniata County) (Township)	17094
Greenwood (Perry County) (Township)	17062
Greenwood (Blair County)	16601
Greenwood (Clearfield County) (Township)	15757
Greenwood (Columbia County)	17846

466 PENNSYLVANIA Greenwood Hills-Heidelberg

Name	ZIP
Greenwood Hills (Dauphin County)	17109
Green Wood Hills (Franklin County)	17222
Greenwood Village	16001
Gregg (Allegheny County)	15071
Gregg (Centre County) (Township)	16875
Gregg (Union County) (Township)	17810
Gregory (Part of Larksville)	18704
Grenoble	18974
Gresham	16354
Greshville	19512
Gretna	15301
Grey Nuns	19067
Grier City	18214
Griesemersville	19512
Griffiths	16735
Grill	19607
Grimesville	17701
Grimms Crossroads	17356
Grimville	19530
Grindstone	15442
Gringo	15001
Grisemore	15728
Groffdale	17557
Grovania	17821
Grove (Cameron County) (Township)	15861
Grove (Chester County)	19380
Grove Chapel	15701
Grove City	16127
Grover	17735
Groveton	15108
Grugan (Township)	17745
Gruvertown	18013
Guenot Settlement	16836
Guernsey	17307
Guffey (McKean County)	16740
Guffey (Westmoreland County)	15642
Guilford	17201
Guilford (Township)	17201
Guilford Hills	17201
Guilford Springs	17201
Guitonville	16239
Guldens	17325
Gulich (Township)	16671
Gulph	19406
Gulph Mills	19428
Gump	15370
Gum Tree	19320
Guth	18104
Guthriesville	19335
Guthsville	18069
Guys Mills	16327
Gwynedd	19436
Gwynedd Square	19446
Gwynedd Valley	19437
Haafsville	18031
Habrenfield Hills	18612
Hackelbernie (Part of Jim Thorpe)	18229
Hackett	15367
Haddenville	15401
Haddock	18201
Hadley	16130
Haffey	15147
Hagersville	18944
Hahnstown	17522
Hahntown	15642
Haines (Township)	16820
Haines Acres	17402
Haleeka	17728
Halfmoon (Township)	16877
Halford Hills	19401
Halfville	17543
Halfway	17042
Halfway House	19464
Halifax (Dauphin County)	17032
Halifax (Dauphin County) (Township)	17032
Hall (Allegheny County)	15146
Hall (Beaver County)	15061
Hallowell	19044
Halls	17756
Hallstead	18822
Hallston	16057
Halliton	15860
Hallwood	18621
Halsey	16735
Hamburg	19526
Hametown	17327
Hamilton (Adams County) (Township)	17316
Hamilton (Franklin County) (Township)	17201
Hamilton (Jefferson County)	15744
Hamilton (McKean County) (Township)	16333

Name	ZIP
Hamilton (Monroe County) (Township)	18354
Hamilton (Northumberland County)	17801
Hamilton (Tioga County) (Township)	16912
Hamiltonban (Township)	17325
Hamilton Heights	17201
Hamilton Mall (Part of Allentown)	18101
Hamilton Park	17603
Hamlin (Lebanon County)	17026
Hamlin (McKean County) (Township)	16733
Hamlin (Wayne County)	18427
Hammersley Fork	17764
Hammett	16510
Hammond	16946
Hammondville	15666
Hamorton	19348
Hampden (Berks County)	19604
Hampden (Cumberland County) (Township)	17055
Hampden Heights (Part of Reading)	19604
Hampshire Heights	15601
Hampton (Adams County)	17350
Hampton (Allegheny County) (Township)	15101
Hampton Station	16301
Hancock	19539
Haneyville	17745
Hankey Farms	15071
Hanlin	15021
Hannah	16870
Hannahstown	16023
Hannastown	15635
Hannaville	16314
Hann Hill (Part of Hermitage)	16159
Hanover (Township)	18017
Hanover (Washington County) (Township)	15021
Hanover (York County)	17331
Hanover (Beaver County) (Township)	15026
Hanover (Lehigh County) (Township)	18103
Hanover (Luzerne County)	18634
Hanover (Luzerne County) (Township)	18702
Hanover (Northampton County)	18017
Hanoverdale	17036
Hanover Green	18702
Hanover Heights	19464
Hanover Hills	17036
Hanover Junction	17360
Hanover Township	18103
Hansotte Plan	16226
Happy Valley (Part of Exeter)	18643
Harbor	16101
Harborcreek	16421
Harborcreek (Township)	16421
Harding	18615
Hardy Hill	15431
Harford	18823
Harford (Township)	18823
Harford Heights	15642
Harlan	15829
Harlansburg	16101
Harleigh	18225
Harlem	18062
Harleysville	19438
Harmar (Township)	15024
Harmar Heights	15024
Harmarville	15238
Harmonsburg	16422
Harmonville	19428
Harmony (Beaver County) (Township)	15003
Harmony (Butler County)	16037
Harmony (Clearfield County)	16692
Harmony (Forest County) (Township)	16370
Harmony (Jefferson County)	15767
Harmony (Susquehanna County) (Township)	18847
Harmony Grove	17315
Harmony Hill	19335
Harmony Township	15003
Harmonyville	19464
Harnedsville	15424
Harpers	18088
Harper Tavern	17003
Harper Village	15001
Harris (Township)	16827
Harris Acres	16801

Name	ZIP
Harrisburg	17101-13
For specific Harrisburg Zip Codes call (717) 257-2150	
Harrison (Allegheny County) (Township)	15065
Harrison (Bedford County) (Township)	15550
Harrison (Potter County) (Township)	16927
Harrison City	15636
Harrison Valley	16927
Harrisonville	17228
Harristown	17562
Harrisville	16038
Harrity	18235
Harrow	18942
Harshaville	15026
Hartleton	17829
Hartley (Township)	17835
Hartranft	19401
Hartsfield	16930
Hartstown	16131
Hartsville	18974
Harvey Plan	15042
Harveys Lake	18618
Harveyville	18655
Harwick	15049
Harwood	18201
Harwood Park	19082
Hasentab's	16635
Hasson Heights	16301
Hastings	16646
Hatboro	19040
Hatfield (Fayette County)	15401
Hatfield (Montgomery County)	19440
Hatfield (Montgomery County) (Township)	19440
Hauto (Part of Nesquehoning)	18240
Haverford (Delaware County) (Township)	19083
Haverford (Montgomery County)	19041
Haverford Township	19083
Havertown	19083
Hawkeye	15612
Hawk Run	16840
Hawksville	17566
Hawley	18428
Hawleywood	18428
Hawstone	17044
Hawthorn	16230
Haycock (Township)	18951
Haydentown	15478
Hayesville	19363
Hayfield (Township)	16433
Haymaker	16731
Haynie	16254
Hays (Allegheny County)	15230
Hays (Fayette County)	15401
Hays Creek	18661
Hays Grove	17241
Hays Mills	15552
Haysville (Allegheny County)	15143
Haysville (Butler County)	16041
Hayti	19320
Hazel Hurst	16733
Hazel Kirk	15063
Hazelwood (Part of Pittsburgh)	15207
Hazen	15825
Hazle (Township)	18201
Hazlebrook	18201
Hazleton	18201
Hazle Village (Part of Hazleton)	18201
Hazzard (Part of Monongahela)	15063
Heacock Meadows	19067
Headlee Heights	15334
Heart Lake	18801
Heath (Township)	15860
Heatherwold	19086
Heathvilla	15864
Hebe	17830
Heberlig	17241
Hebron (Lebanon County)	17042
Hebron (Potter County) (Township)	16915
Hebron Center	16915
Heckscherville	17901
Hecktown	18017
Hecla	17960
Hector (Township)	16948
Hegarty Crossroads	16671
Hegins	17938
Hegins (Township)	17938
Heidelberg (Allegheny County)	15106

Heidelberg-Hopewell PENNSYLVANIA 467

Name	ZIP
Heidelberg (Berks County) (Township)	19567
Heidelberg (Lebanon County) (Township)	17088
Heidelberg (Lehigh County) (Township)	18053
Heidelberg (York County) (Township)	17362
Heidlersburg	17372
Heights Plaza	15065
Heilmandale	17042
Heilwood	15745
Heise Run	16901
Heistersburg	15433
Helen Furnace	16214
Helen Mills (Elk County)	15823
Helfenstein	17939
Helixville	15559
Hellam (York County)	17406
Hellam (York County) (Township)	17368
Hellertown	18055
Helvetia	15848
Hemlock (Columbia County) (Township)	17815
Hemlock (Warren County)	16365
Hemlock Grove (Pike County)	18426
Hemlock Grove (Sullivan County)	17758
Hempfield (Mercer County) (Township)	16125
Hempfield (Westmoreland County) (Township)	15601
Hempfield Manor	15601
Henderson (Clearfield County)	16651
Henderson (Huntingdon County) (Township)	16652
Henderson (Jefferson County) (Township)	15767
Henderson (Mercer County)	16153
Henderson Park	19406
Hendersonville (Butler County)	16046
Hendersonville (Washington County)	15339
Hendleton	19607
Hendricks	18979
Henningsville	18011
Henrietta	16662
Henry·Clay (Township)	15424
Henrys Bend	16301
Henrys Mill	16347
Henryville	18332
Hensel	17566
Hensingerville	18011
Hepburn (Township)	17728
Hepburn Heights	17728
Hepburnia	16838
Hepburnville	17728
Hephzibah	19320
Hepler	17941
Herbert	15435
Hercules (Part of Stockertown)	18083
Hereford	18056
Hereford (Township)	18056
Heritage Hills	16117
Herman	16039
Hermine No. 2	15642
Herminie	15637
Hermitage	16148
Herndon	17830
Hero	15341
Herrick (Bradford County) (Township)	18853
Herrick (Susquehanna County) (Township)	18430
Herrick Center	18430
Herrick Corner	18430
Herrickville	18853
Herrs Island (Part of Pittsburgh)	15230
Hershey	17033
Hershey Heights	17331
Heshbon	15717
Heshbon Park	17701
Hessdale	17560
Hesston	16647
Hetlerville	18635
Hettesheimer Corners	18636
Hiawatha	18462
Hibbs	15443
Hickernell	16435
Hickman	15071
Hickory (Forest County) (Township)	16322
Hickory (Lawrence County) (Township)	16105
Hickory (Washington County)	15340
Hickory Corners (Mercer County)	16146
Hickory Corners (Northumberland County)	17017
Hickory Grove	18847
Hickory Heights	16101
Hickory Hill (Bedford County)	16679
Hickoryhill (Chester County)	19363
Hickory Hills	19067
Hickory Run Forest	18229
Hickorytown (Cumberland County)	17013
Hickorytown (Montgomery County)	19401
Hickox	16923
Hicks Hill	15618
Hidden Valley	19406
Hidden Valley Estates	18062
Higgins Corners	16040
High Bridge	17044
Highcliff	15229
High House	15478
Highland (Adams County) (Township)	17325
Highland (Allegheny County)	15237
Highland (Beaver County)	15010
Highland (Chester County) (Township)	19320
Highland (Clarion County) (Township)	16214
Highland (Elk County) (Township)	16728
Highland (Luzerne County)	18224
Highland (Westmoreland County)	15633
Highland Acres	17602
Highland Corners	16735
Highland Meadows (Allegheny County)	15037
Highland Meadows (Cambria County)	15904
Highland Park (Bucks County)	19053
Highland Park (Cambria County)	15904
Highland Park (Cumberland County)	17011
Highland Park (Delaware County)	19082
Highland Park (Erie County)	16506
Highland Park (Mifflin County)	17044
Highland Park (Northampton County)	18042
Highland Woods	18701
High Meadows	19063
Highmount	17406
High Park	19040
High Rock	17302
Highspire	17034
Highville	17516
Hileman Heights (Part of Altoona)	16602
Hillchurch (Berks County)	19512
Hill Church (Washington County)	15317
Hill City	16319
Hillcrest (Allegheny County)	15102
Hillcrest (Beaver County)	15001
Hill Crest (Fayette County)	15425
Hillcrest (Mercer County)	16146
Hill Crest (Montgomery County)	19126
Hillcrest (York County)	17403
Hillcroft	17403
Hilldale	18702
Hiller	15444
Hilliards	16040
Hillman	15767
Hillsboro	15963
Hills Creek Lake	16901
Hillsdale	15746
Hillsgrove	18619
Hillsgrove (Township)	18619
Hillside (Lehigh County)	18069
Hillside (Luzerne County)	18708
Hillside (Schuylkill County)	17901
Hillside (Westmoreland County)	15627
Hillside Junction (Part of Moosic)	18507
Hills Terrace	17948
Hillsview	15658
Hillsville	16132
Hill Top Acres (Armstrong County)	16226
Hilltop Acres (Lancaster County)	17603
Hilltown (Township)	18911
Hilltown (Adams County)	17307
Hilltown (Bucks County)	18927
Hillville	16041
Hilton	17315
Hines Corners	18449
Hinkle	18947
Hinkletown	17522
Hinkson Corner	19086
Hiyasota	15935
Hoadleys	18431
Hoban Heights	18657
Hobart	17331
Hobbie	18660
Hoblitzell	15545
Hockersville	17241
Hoernerstown	17036
Hoffer	17864
Hoffmansville	19435
Hogestown	17055
Hog Island	19029
Hoguetown	16630
Hokendauqua	18052
Hokes	17327
Holbrook	15341
Holicong	18928
Holiday	16935
Holiday Hills	18106
Holiday Park (Part of Plum)	15239
Holiday Pocono	18210
Holland	18966
Hollenback (Township)	18660
Hollentown	16639
Hollers Hill	18201
Holley Heights	17404
Hollidaysburg	16648
Hollinger	17603
Hollisterville	18444
Hollsopple	15935
Hollywood (Clearfield County)	15849
Hollywood (Luzerne County)	18201
Hollywood (Montgomery County)	19117
Hollywood (York County)	17403
Hollywood Heights	17403
Holmes	19043
Holmesburg (Part of Philadelphia)	19136
Holtwood	17532
Home	15747
Homeacre	16001
Homeacre-Lyndora	16001
Home Camp	15856
Homeland	17601
Home Park	18052
Homer (Township)	16915
Homer City	15748
Homer Gap	16601
Homestead	15120
Homestead Park (Part of Munhall)	15120
Homesville	17921
Hometown	18252
Homets Ferry	18853
Homeville	19330
Homewood (Allegheny County)	15208
Homewood (York County)	17019
Honeoye	16748
Honesdale	18431
Honey Brook (Chester County)	19344
Honeybrook (Chester County) (Township)	19344
Honey Creek	17084
Honey Grove	17035
Honey Pot (Part of Nanticoke)	18634
Hooker	16041
Hookstown	15050
Hoover	15458
Hooverhurst	15742
Hooversville	15936
Hop Bottom	18824
Hopeland	17533
Hope Mills	16137
Hopewell (Beaver County) (Township)	15001
Hopewell (Bedford County)	16650
Hopewell (Bedford County) (Township)	15537
Hopewell (Chester County)	19363
Hopewell (Cumberland County) (Township)	17240
Hopewell (Huntingdon County) (Township)	16678
Hopewell (Washington County) (Township)	15301
Hopewell (York County) (Township)	17363

	ZIP		ZIP		ZIP
Hoppenville	18073	Hutchinson (Westmoreland		Jacks Creek	17044
Hopwood	15445	County)	15640	Jacks Mountain	17320
Horatio	15767	Hyde	16843	Jackson (Susquehanna	
Hormtown	15851	Hyde Park (Berks County)	19605	County) (Township)	18825
Horn Brook	18848	Hyde Park (Westmoreland		Jackson (Tioga County)	
Hornby	16428	County)	15641	(Township)	16936
Horning (Part of Baldwin)	15236	Hydetown	16328	Jackson (Venango County)	
Horseshoe Heights	17602	Hyde Villa	19605	(Township)	16317
Horsham	19044	Hyndman	15545	Jackson (York County)	
Horsham (Township)	19044	Hynemansville	18066	(Township)	17362
Horton (Township)	15823	Hyner	17738	Jackson (Butler County)	
Hosensack	18092	Icedale	19344	(Township)	16063
Hosensock	18214	Ickesburg	17037	Jackson (Cambria County)	
Hospital (Part of Norristown)	19401	Idaho	15774	(Township)	15909
Host	19567	Idamar	15734	Jackson (Columbia County)	
Hostetter	15638	Idaville	17337	(Township)	17814
Hottelville	16239	Idetown (Part of Harveys		Jackson (Dauphin County)	
Houserville	16801	Lake)	18612	(Township)	17032
Houston	15342	Idlewood (Part of Crafton)	15205	Jackson (Greene County)	
Houston City	18641	Imler	16655	(Township)	15341
Houtzdale	16651	Imlertown	15522	Jackson (Huntingdon	
Hovey (Township)	16049	Immaculata	19345	County) (Township)	16669
Howard (Cameron County)	15834	Imperial	15126	Jackson (Lebanon County)	
Howard (Centre County)	16841	Imperial-Enlow	15126	(Township)	17042
Howard (Centre County)		Independence	15001	Jackson (Luzerne County)	
(Township)	16841	Independence (Beaver		(Township)	18708
Howard Siding	15834	County) (Township)	15026	Jackson (Lycoming County)	
Howe (Forest County)		Independence (Washington		(Township)	17765
(Township)	16239	County) (Township)	15312	Jackson (Mercer County)	
Howe (Perry County)		Independence (Snyder		(Township)	16133
(Township)	17074	County)	17864	Jackson (Monroe County)	
Howell Park	15037	Independence (Washington		(Township)	18352
Howellville	19132	County)	15312	Jackson (Northumberland	
Howersville	18088	Indiana (Allegheny County)		County) (Township)	17830
Howerton	18067	(Township)	15051	Jackson (Perry County)	
Hoytdale (Part of Big		Indiana (Indiana County)	15701	(Township)	17006
Beaver)	16157	Indian Creek (Bucks		Jackson (Snyder County)	
Hoytville	16938	County)	19057	(Township)	17889
Hublersburg	16823	Indian Creek (Cumberland		Jackson (Susquehanna	
Hubley (Township)	17968	County)	17055	County)	18825
Huckenberry	16849	Indian Crossing	16731	Jackson Center	16133
Hudson (Clearfield County)	16866	Indian Head (Erie County)	16441	Jackson Corner	16652
Hudson (Luzerne County)	18702	Indian Head (Fayette		Jackson Crossing	16365
Hudsondale	18255	County)	15446	Jackson Hall	17201
Huefner	16235	Indian Hills	16201	Jackson Knolls	16101
Huey	16248	Indian King	19380	Jackson Summit	16936
Huff	15944	Indian Lake (Luzerne		Jacksonville (Centre	
Huffs Church	18011	County)	18661	County)	16841
Hughes Park	19406	Indian Lake (Somerset		Jacksonville (Lehigh	
Hughestown	18640	County)	15926	County)	18066
Hughesville	17737	Indianland	18088	Jacksonville (Northampton	
Hughs	18621	Indian Mountain Lake	18210	County)	18014
Hulltown	15428	Indianola	15051	Jacksonwald	19606
Hulmeville	19047	Indian Orchard	18431	Jacksville	16057
Hulton (Part of Oakmont)	15139	Indian Pines	15205	Jacktown	15642
Humbolt	18201	Indian Springs Estates	15701	Jacktown Acres	15642
Hummelstown	17036	Industry	15052	Jacobs Creek	15448
Hummels Wharf	17831	Inez	16915	Jacobs Mills	17331
Humphreys	15601	Ingleby	16882	Jacobus	17407
Humphreyville	19320	Inglenook	17032	Jalappa	19526
Hungerford (Part of		Inglesmith	17211	James City	16734
Shrewsbury)	17361	Ingomar	15127	James Creek	16657
Hungry Hollow	15656	Ingram	15205	Jamestown (Cambria	
Hunker	15639	Inkerman	18640	County)	15946
Hunlock (Township)	18621	Intercourse	17534	Jamestown (Carbon	
Hunlock Creek	18621	Iola	17846	County)	18235
Hunlock Gardens	18621	Iona	17042	Jamestown (Mercer County)	16134
Hunter	17872	Irishtown (Adams County)	17350	Jamesville	18014
Hunter Hill	19462	Irishtown (Clearfield County)	16838	Jamison (Bucks County)	18929
Hunters Run	17324	Irishtown (Fayette County)	15431	Jamison (Fayette County)	15401
Hunterstown	17325	Irishtown (McKean County)	16738	Jamison (Forest County)	16370
Huntersville	17756	Irishtown (Mercer County)	16137	Jamison City	17814
Huntingdon	16652	Iron Bridge	15666	Japan	18224
Huntingdon Furnace	16686	Iron Springs	17320	Jarrettown	19025
Huntingdon Heights	15642	Ironton	18037	Jay (Township)	15827
Ironville (Blair County)	16686	Jeanesville	18201
Huntingdon Manor	17540	Ironville (Lancaster County)	17512	Jeannette	15644
Huntingdon Meadows	19006	Irvin (Part of West Mifflin)	15122	Jeddo	18224
Huntingdon Valley	19006	Irvine	16329	Jednota	17057
Hunting Park (Part of		Irving	17963	Jefferis Crossing	15401
Philadelphia)	19140	Irvona	16656	Jefferson (Township)	15021
Huntington (Adams County)		Irwin (Venango County)		Jefferson	15687
(Township)	17372	(Township)	16038	Jefferson (Allegheny	
Huntington (Luzerne		Irwin (Westmoreland		County)	15025
County) (Township)	18655	County)	15642	Jefferson (Berks County)	
Huntington Mills	18622	Isabella	15447	(Township)	19506
Huntley	15832	Iselin	15681	Jefferson (Butler County)	
Huntsdale	17013	Iselin Heights	15801	(Township)	16001
Huntsville	18612	Island Lake	18462	Jefferson (Dauphin County)	
Husband	15501	Island Park	17801	(Township)	17032
Huston (Blair County)		Ithan	19085	Jefferson (Fayette County)	
(Township)	16693	Itley	16412	(Township)	15473
Huston (Centre County)		Iva	17562	Jefferson (Greene County)	15344
(Township)	16844	Ivarea	16410	Jefferson (Greene County)	
Huston (Clearfield County)		Ivyland	18974	(Township)	15344
(Township)	15849	Ivy Mills (Part of Chester		Jefferson (Lackawanna	
Huston Run	15332	Heights)	19342	County) (Township)	18436
Hustontown	17229	Ivy Ridge (Part of		Jefferson (Mercer County)	
Hutchins	16740	Philadelphia)	19101	(Township)	16150
Hutchinson (Fayette		Ivy Rock	19401	Jefferson (Schuylkill County)	17922
County)	15401	Ivywood	18451		

468 PENNSYLVANIA Hoppenville-Jefferson

Jefferson-Knobsville **PENNSYLVANIA** 469

Name	ZIP
Jefferson (Somerset County) (Township)	15501
Jefferson (Washington County)	15312
Jefferson Center	16001
Jeffersonville	19408
Jenkins (Township)	18640
Jenkintown	19046
Jenkintown Manor	19117
Jenks (Township)	16239
Jenner (Township)	15531
Jenners	15546
Jenners Crossroads	15531
Jennerstown	15547
Jennersville	19390
Jenningsville	18629
Jericho	15861
Jericho Mills	17059
Jermyn	18433
Jerome	15937
Jerome Junction (Part of Benson)	15935
Jersey Mills	17739
Jersey Shore	17740
Jerseytown	17815
Jessup (Lackawanna County)	18434
Jessup (Susquehanna County) (Township)	18801
Jessup-Peckville (Part of Jessup)	18434
Jewtown	15745
Jim Thorpe	18229
Jimtown	15501
Joanna	19543
Joanna Heights	19543
Jobs Corners	16936
Joffre	15053
Johnsonburg (Elk County)	15845
Johnsonburg (Indiana County)	15772
Johnsons Corner	19317
Johnstown	15901-09
For specific Johnstown Zip Codes call (814) 533-4915	
Johnstown	17844
Johnsville	18974
John Wanamaker (Part of Philadelphia)	19107
Jo Jo	16735
Joliett	17981
Joller	16674
Jollytown	15352
Jonas	18058
Jonathan Point	18210
Jones (Township)	15870
Jones Mills	15646
Jones Terrace	18042
Jonestown (Columbia County)	17859
Jonestown (Lebanon County)	17038
Jonestown (Schuylkill County)	17901
Jonestown (Washington County)	15022
Jordan (Clearfield County) (Township)	16833
Jordan (Lehigh County)	18053
Jordan (Lycoming County) (Township)	17774
Jordan (Northumberland County) (Township)	17830
Jordan Valley	18053
Josephine	15750
Jugtown (Bucks County)	18920
Jugtown (Franklin County)	17268
Julian	16844
Jumonville	15445
Juneau	15751
Junedale	18230
June Meadows	19006
Junewood	19007
Juniata (Bedford County) (Township)	15534
Juniata (Blair County)	16601
Juniata (Blair County) (Township)	16655
Juniata (Fayette County)	15431
Juniata (Huntingdon County) (Township)	16652
Juniata (Perry County) (Township)	17074
Juniata Gap	16601
Juniata Terrace	17044
Just A Farm	19006
Justus	18411
Kaiserville	18630
Kalinoski	15061
Kammerer	15330
Kane	16735

Name	ZIP
Kanesholm	16735
Kaneville	16301
Kantner	15548
Kantz	17870
Kaolin	19374
Kapp Heights	17857
Karns City	16041
Karthaus	16845
Karthaus (Township)	16845
Kaseville	17821
Kasiesville	17236
Kaska	17959
Kasson	16749
Kauffman	17201
Kaufmann	15464
Kaybrook Manor	18101
Kaylor	16025
Kaywood	16827
Kearney	16679
Kearsarge	16509
Keating (Clinton County)	17778
Keating (McKean County) (Township)	16730
Keating (Potter County) (Township)	16720
Keating Summit	16720
Kecksburg	15666
Kedron Park	19070
Keelersburg	18657
Keelersville	18944
Keeneyville	16935
Keepville	16401
Keewaydin	16836
Keffer (Schuylkill County)	17981
Keffer (Westmoreland County)	15658
Keifertown	15683
Keisters	16057
Keisterville	15449
Kelayres	18231
Kellersburg	16259
Kellers Church	18944
Kellersville	18360
Kellettville	16353
Kelley (Part of Pittsburgh)	15230
Kelly (Armstrong County)	16226
Kelly (Union County) (Township)	17837
Kelly Crossroads	17837
Kelly Point	17837
Kellytown (Clearfield County)	16863
Kellytown (Tioga County)	16933
Kellyville	19026
Kelton	19346
Kemblesville	19347
Kempton	19529
Kendall (Beaver County)	15043
Kendall (York County)	17356
Kendall Creek (Part of Bradford)	16701
Kendrick	16651
Kenhorst	19607
Kenilworth	19464
Kenmar	17701
Kenmawr	15136
Kennard	16125
Kennedy (Allegheny County) (Township)	15108
Kennedy (Tioga County)	16901
Kennedy Mill	16051
Kennedy Township	15108
Kennells Mills	15545
Kennerdell	16374
Kennett (Township)	19348
Kennett Square	19348
Kenney Yard (Part of West Mifflin)	15122
Kenny Row	15468
Kennywood (Part of West Mifflin)	15122
Kensington (Part of Philadelphia)	19125
Kensington Heights	17201
Kent	15752
Kenwick Village	17601
Kenwood (Bucks County)	19007
Kenwood (Indiana County)	15728
Kepner	17960
Kepple Hill	15690
Kepples Corner	16025
Kernsville	18069
Kerr	16830
Kerrmoor	16833
Kerrs Corners	16127
Kerrsville	17013
Kerrtown	16335
Kerrwood Farms	15208
Kersey	15846
Kesslerville	18064
Keys	17322

Name	ZIP
Keystone (Elk County)	15823
Keystone (Luzerne County)	18702
Keystone (Somerset County)	15552
Keystone (Westmoreland County)	15637
Khedive	15320
Kidder (Township)	18624
Kilbuck (Allegheny County)	15233
Kilbuck (Allegheny County) (Township)	15237
Kilbuck Township	15233
Kilgore	16153
Killam Park	18451
Killinger	17061
Kimberton	19442
Kimbles	18428
Kimmell (Township)	16655
Kimmelton	15563
Kim Plan	15642
Kinderhook	17512
Kindts Corner	19555
King (Bedford County)	16655
King (Bedford County) (Township)	16667
King of Prussia	19406
King of Prussia Plaza	19406
Kingsdale	17340
Kingsessing (Part of Philadelphia)	19143
Kingsley (Forest County) (Township)	16353
Kingsley (Susquehanna County)	18826
Kings Manor	19406
Kingston (Luzerne County)	18704
Kingston (Luzerne County) (Township)	18708
Kingston (Westmoreland County)	15650
Kingston-Forty Fort (Part of Kingston)	18704
Kingsville	15864
Kingswood Park	19007
Kingview	15683
Kingwood	15551
Kinlock (Part of Lower Burrell)	15069
Kinney	16923
Kinport	15724
Kintersburg (Indiana County)	15701
Kintigh Plan	15601
Kintnersville	18930
Kinzers	17535
Kipps Run	17821
Kirby	15370
Kirbyville	19522
Kirks Mills	19362
Kirkwood	17536
Kirwan Heights	15017
Kiser Corners	16353
Kishacoquillas	17004
Kiskimere	15690
Kiskiminetas (Township)	15613
Kis-Lyn	18222
Kissel Hill	17543
Kissimmee	17842
Kissingers Mill	16248
Kistler (Mifflin County)	17066
Kistler (Perry County)	17047
Kitches Corners	16125
Kittanning (Armstrong County)	16201
Kittanning (Armstrong County) (Township)	16226
Kittanning Heights (Part of West Kittanning)	16201
Kladder Station	16648
Klahr	16625
Klecknersville	18014
Kleinfeltersville	17039
Kline (Township)	18237
Klines Corner	19539
Klines Grove	17801
Klinesville (Berks County)	19534
Klinesville (Lancaster County)	17512
Kline Village (Part of Harrisburg)	17104
Klingerstown	17941
Klondike	16738
Klondyke	17044
Knapp	16901
Knauers	19540
Knauertown	19464
Kneedler	19446
Knepper	17268
Knightsbridge	15205
Knightsville	17052
Knobsville	17233

470 PENNSYLVANIA Knoebel's Grove-Lehigh Furnace

Name	ZIP
Knoebel's Grove	17824
Knousetown	17062
Knowltonwood	19065
Knox (Beaver County)	16117
Knox (Clarion County)	16232
Knox (Clarion County) (Township)	16235
Knox (Clearfield County) (Township)	16863
Knox (Jefferson County) (Township)	15825
Knox Dale	15847
Knoxlyn	17325
Knox Run	16858
Knoxville (Allegheny County)	15210
Knoxville (Fayette County)	15417
Knoxville (Tioga County)	16928
Koonsville	18655
Koppel	16136
Korn Krest	18702
Kossuth	16331
Kralltown	17316
Kratzerville	17870
Krayn	15963
Kreamer	17833
Kregar	15622
Kreidersville	18067
Kremis	16125
Kresgeville	18333
Kreutz Creek	17406
Kricktown	19608
Krings	15904
Krocksville	18104
Krumrine (Part of State College)	16801
Krumsville	19534
Kuhn	15501
Kuhnsville	18103
Kuhntown	15341
Kulp	17820
Kulpmont	17834
Kulps Corner	18944
Kulpsville	19443
Kulptown	19518
Kunkle	18612
Kunkletown	18058
Kushequa	16735
Kutztown (Berks County)	19530
Kutztown (Lebanon County)	17067
Kylers Corners	15846
Kylertown	16847
Kyleville	17302
La Anna	18326
La Belle	15450
Laboratory	15301
Labott	17364
Lacey Park	18974
Laceyville	18623
Lack (Township)	17021
Lackawannock (Township)	16137
Lackawaxen	18435
Lackawaxen (Township)	18425
Lacock	15301
Laddsburg	18833
Lafayette	16738
Lafayette (Township)	16738
Lafayette Hill	19444
Lafayette Park	19444
Lafferty Hill (Part of Baldwin)	15227
Laflin	18702
La Gonda	15301
Lahaska	18931
Laings Garden	19007
Lairds Crossing	16262
Lairdsville	17742
La Jose	15753
Lake (Luzerne County) (Township)	18621
Lake (Mercer County) (Township)	16153
Lake (Wayne County) (Township)	18436
Lake Ariel	18436
Lake Carey	18657
Lake City	16423
Lake Como	18437
Lake Donegal	15610
Lake Harmony	18624
Lake Heritage	17325
Lake Idlewild	18470
Lake Jo-Ann	15367
Lakeland	18436
Lake Lynn	15451
Lake Meade	17316
Lake Monroe	18335
Lakemont	16602
Lakemont Terrace (Part of Altoona)	16602
Lake Naomi	18350

Name	ZIP
Lake Pleasant	16438
Lake Quinn	18472
Lake Sheridan	18446
Lakeside (Bucks County)	19053
Lakeside (Susquehanna County)	18834
Lake Stonycreek	15541
Laketon Heights	15235
Lakeview	18847
Lakeview Heights	17111
Lakeville	18438
Lake Waynewood	18436
Lake Wesauking	18848
Lake Winola	18625
Lakewood (Erie County)	16505
Lakewood (Wayne County)	18439
Lamar (Clinton County)	16848
Lamar (Clinton County) (Township)	17750
Lamartine	16375
Lamberton	15458
Lambertsville	15563
Lambs Creek	16933
Lamonts Corners (Part of Hermitage)	16150
La Mott	19012
Lampeter	17537
Lanark	17601-05
Lancaster	
For specific Lancaster Zip Codes call (717) 394-9035	
Lancaster (Butler County) (Township)	16037
Lancaster (Lancaster County) (Township)	17603
Lancaster Avenue (Part of Philadelphia)	19104
Lancaster Bible College	17601
Lancaster Junction	17545
Landenberg	19350
Lander	16345
Landingville	17942
Landisburg	17040
Landis Farms	17601
Landis Store	19512
Landis Valley	17604
Landisville	17538
Landreth Manor	19007
Landstreet	15935
Lane (Part of Freeport)	16229
Lanesboro	18827
Lanes Mills	15824
Langdon	17763
Langdondale	16650
Langeloth	15054
Langhorne	19047
Langhorne Gables	19047
Langhorne Gardens	19047
Langhorne Manor	19047
Langhorne Terrace	19047
Lansdale	19446
Lansdowne	19050
Lansdowne Park Gardens (Part of Collingdale)	19023
Lanse	16849
Lansford	18232
Lantz Corners	16740
Lapidea Hills	19013
La Plume	18440
La Plume (Township)	18440
Laporte (Sullivan County)	18626
Laporte (Sullivan County) (Township)	17758
Larabee	16731
Lardintown	16055
Large (Part of Jefferson)	15025
Larimer (Somerset County) (Township)	15552
Larimer (Westmoreland County)	15647
Larke	16693
Larksville	18704
Larrys Creek	17740
Larryville	17740
Larue	17327
Lashley	17267
Lathrop (Township)	18446
Latimore	17372
Latimore (Township)	17372
Latrobe	15650
Latrobe Shopping Center	15650
Lattimer Mines	18234
Laughlin Corner	15043
Laughlin Junction (Part of Pittsburgh)	15207
Laughlintown	15655
Laurel (Cumberland County)	17324
Laurel (York County)	17322
Laurel Bend	19007
Laureldale	19605
Laurel Falls	15552

Name	ZIP
Laurel Gardens	15229
Laurel Hill (Fayette County)	15431
Laurel Hill (Washington County)	15057
Laurel Lake (Luzerne County)	18707
Laurel Lake (Susquehanna County)	18812
Laurel Mountain	15655
Laurel Park	17845
Laurel Ridge	15009
Laurel Run	18702
Laurelton	17835
Laurelville (Fayette County)	15666
Laurelville (Lancaster County)	17557
Laurys Station	18059
Lausanne (Township)	18255
Lavansville	15501
Lavelle	17943
Laverock	19118
Lawn	17041
Lawnherst	18042
Lawnton	17111
Lawrence (Clearfield County) (Township)	16830
Lawrence (Tioga County) (Township)	16946
Lawrence (Washington County)	15055
Lawrence Park (Delaware County)	19008
Lawrence Park (Erie County) (Township)	16511
Lawrence Park (Erie County)	16511
Lawrenceville (Allegheny County)	15201
Lawrenceville (Lackawanna County)	18642
Lawrenceville (Tioga County)	16929
Lawsonham	16248
Lawson Heights	15650
Lawsville Center	18801
Lawton	18828
Layfield	19525
Layton	15473
Leacock (Lancaster County)	17540
Leacock (Lancaster County) (Township)	17572
Leaders Heights	17403
Leaf Park	17603
Leak Run (Part of Monroeville)	15146
Leaman Place	17562
Leamersville	16635
Learn Settlement	15729
Leasuresville	16055
Leather Corner Post	18069
Leatherwood	16242
Lebanon (Lebanon County)	17042
Lebanon (Wayne County) (Township)	18431
Lebanon Plaza	17042
Lebanon South	17042
Lebo	17040
Le Boeuf (Township)	16441
Le Boeuf Gardens	16441
Leck Kill	17836
Leckrone	15454
Lecontes Mills	16850
Lederach	19450
Ledgedale	18463
Lee	18617
Leechburg	15656
Leech Hill	16943
Leedon Estates	19078
Leedon Gardens	19078
Lee Mine	18634
Lee Park	18702
Leeper	16233
Leesburg	16156
Leesburg Station	16156
Lees Cross Roads	17257
Leesport	19533
Leet (Township)	15003
Leetonia	17727
Leetsdale	15056
Lehigh (Carbon County) (Township)	18255
Lehigh (Lackawanna County) (Township)	18424
Lehigh (Northampton County) (Township)	18088
Lehigh (Wayne County) (Township)	18424
Lehigh Furnace	18080

Lehigh Gap-Longsdale **PENNSYLVANIA** 471

Place	ZIP
Lehigh Gap (Carbon County)	18071
Lehigh Gap (Lehigh County)	18080
Lehighton	18235
Lehigh University (Part of Bethlehem)	18015
Lehigh Valley Facility	18001
Lehigh Valley Mall	18052
Lehman	18627
Lehman (Township)	18612
Lehman (Pike County) (Township)	18324
Lehman (York County)	17362
Leibeyville	17960
Leidy (Township)	17764
Leinbachs	19605
Leisenring	15455
Leith	15401
Leith-Hatfield	15401
Leithsville	18055
Lemasters	17231
Lemon (Wyoming County)	18657
Lemon (Wyoming County) (Township)	18657
Lemont	16851
Lemont Furnace	15456
Lemoyne	17043
Lenape	19380
Lenape Heights (Armstrong County)	16226
Lenape Park	16226
Lenhartsville	19534
Lenker Manor	17111
Lenkerville	17061
Lenni	19052
Lenni Heights	19037
Lennox Park (Part of Trainer)	19015
Lenover	19365
Lenox (Township)	18446
Lenoxville	18441
Lenwood Heights	17236
Leola	17540
Leolyn	17765
Leona	16914
Leopard	19312
Leopard Lakes	19312
Le Raysville	18829
Le Roy	17743
Leroy (Township)	17724
Lester	19113
Letort	17582
Letterkenny (Township)	17244
Letterkenny Army Depot	17201
Level Corner	17744
Level Green	15085
Levittown	19053-59
For specific Levittown Zip Codes call (215) 949-3131	
Levittown Center (Part of Tullytown)	19054
Levittown Discount World (Part of Tullytown)	19055
Levittown-Tullytown	19007
Lewis (Lycoming County) (Township)	17771
Lewis (Northumberland County) (Township)	17772
Lewis (Union County) (Township)	17880
Lewisberry	17339
Lewisburg	17837
Lewis Crossing	15458
Lewis Run	16738
Lewistown (Mifflin County)	17044
Lewistown (Schuylkill County)	18252
Lewistown Junction	17044
Lewisville (Chester County)	19351
Lewisville (Indiana County)	15725
Lexington	17543
Liberty (Adams County) (Township)	17320
Liberty (Allegheny County)	15133
Liberty (Bedford County) (Township)	16678
Liberty (Centre County) (Township)	16826
Liberty (McKean County) (Township)	16749
Liberty (Mercer County) (Township)	16127
Liberty (Montour County) (Township)	17821
Liberty (Susquehanna County) (Township)	18801
Liberty (Tioga County)	16930
Liberty (Tioga County) (Township)	16930
Liberty Corners	18848
Liberty Square	17518

Place	ZIP
Library	15129
Lickdale	17038
Licking (Township)	16049
Licking Creek (Township)	17228
Lickingville	16332
Lightner	17404
Light Street	17839
Ligonier (Westmoreland County)	15658
Ligonier (Westmoreland County) (Township)	15658
Lilly	15938
Lillyville	16123
Lima	19037
Limehill	18853
Limekiln	19535
Limeport	18060
Limerick	19468
Limerick (Township)	19468
Lime Ridge	17815
Lime Rock	17543
Limestone	16234
Limestone (Township)	16234
Limestone (Lycoming County) (Township)	17740
Limestone (Montour County) (Township)	17821
Limestone (Union County) (Township)	17844
Limestone (Warren County) (Township)	16365
Limestoneville	17847
Lime Valley	17584
Limeville	17527
Lincoln (Allegheny County)	15037
Lincoln (Bedford County) (Township)	15521
Lincoln (Huntingdon County) (Township)	16638
Lincoln (Lancaster County)	17522
Lincoln (Somerset County) (Township)	15501
Lincoln Acres	15642
Lincoln Beach	15068
Lincoln Colliery	17963
Lincoln Falls	18616
Lincoln Heights (Berks County)	19508
Lincoln Heights (Westmoreland County)	15644
Lincoln Hill	15301
Lincoln Park (Allegheny County)	15235
Lincoln Park (Berks County)	19609
Lincoln Park (Delaware County)	19079
Lincoln Place (Part of Pittsburgh)	15122
Lincoln Terrace	18042
Lincoln University	19352
Lincolnville	16404
Lincolnway	17404
Linconia	19047
Lindaville	18824
Linden (Lycoming County)	17744
Linden (Washington County)	15317
Linden Hall	16828
Lindenhurst	19067
Linds Crossing	16648
Lindsey (Part of Punxsutawney)	15767
Line Lexington	18932
Line Mountain	17941
Linesville	16424
Linfield	19468
Linglestown	17112
Linn	15442
Linntown	17837
Linville Circle (Part of Lancaster)	17602
Linwood	19061
Linwood Park	19061
Linwood Terrace	19061
Lionville	19353
Lippincott	15370
Lisbon	16373
Lisburn	17055
Listie	15549
Listonburg	15424
Litchfield	18810
Litchfield (Township)	18810
Lithia Springs	17857
Lithia Valley (Part of Factoryville)	18419
Lititz	17543
Little Beaver (Township)	16141
Little Britain (Township)	19363
Little Chicago	15320
Little Cooley	16404
Little Corners	16335

Place	ZIP
Little Gap	18058
Little Hickory	16353
Little Hope	16428
Little Italy	18956
Little Kansas	17051
Little Mahanoy (Township)	17823
Little Marsh	16950
Little Meadows	18830
Littlestown	17340
Little Summit	15431
Little Washington (Chester County)	19335
Little Washington (Cumberland County)	17241
Live Easy	15320
Liverpool (Perry County)	17045
Liverpool (Perry County) (Township)	17045
Livonia	16872
Llandrilla	19004
Llanfair	15930
Llangelan Hills	19073
Llewellyn	17944
Llewelyn Corners	18602
Lloydell	15921
Lloydesville	15650
Llyswen (Part of Altoona)	16602
Loag	19520
Lobachsville	19547
Lochiel	17837
Lochvale	15742
Locke Mills	17063
Lock Haven	17745
Lock No. 4 (Part of Charleroi)	15022
Lockport (Clinton County)	17745
Lockport (Mifflin County)	17044
Lockport (Westmoreland County)	15923
Locksley	19342
Lockview	15022
Locust (Columbia County) (Township)	17820
Locust (Indiana County)	15771
Locustdale	17945
Locust Gap	17840
Locust Grove	17402
Locust Grove Gardens	17402
Locust Lakes Village	18347
Locust Point	17055
Locust Ridge	15116
Locust Run	17094
Locust Summit	17840
Locust Valley (Lehigh County)	18036
Locust Valley (Schuylkill County)	18214
Lofty	18201
Logan (Blair County) (Township)	16602
Logan (Clinton County) (Township)	17747
Logan (Huntingdon County) (Township)	16611
Logan (Indiana County)	15742
Logan (Philadelphia County)	19141
Logan Mills	17747
Logans Ferry (Part of Plum)	15068
Logans Ferry Heights (Part of Plum)	15068
Logan Square (Part of Norristown)	19401
Loganton	17747
Loganville	17342
Log Pile	15301
London	16127
London Britain (Township)	19350
Londonderry (Bedford County) (Township)	15545
Londonderry (Chester County) (Township)	19330
Londonderry (Dauphin County) (Township)	17057
London Grove (Chester County)	19348
London Grove (Chester County) (Township)	19390
Lonely Acres	15722
Lone Pine	15301
Lonewood	15145
Long Acre Park (Part of Yeadon)	19050
Long Branch	15423
Long Bridge	15658
Longbrook	17758
Longfellow	17044
Longlevel	17368
Long Pond	18334
Long Run	18235
Longs Crossroad	16661
Longsdale	19539

PENNSYLVANIA Longsdorf-Manchester

Name	ZIP
Longsdorf	17241
Longstown	17402
Longswamp	19539
Longswamp (Township)	19539
Longview (Part of Bethel Park)	15102
Longwood	19348
Lookout	18417
Loomis Park	18702
Loop Station	16648
Lopez	18628
Lorain	15902
Lorane	19606
Lorberry	17963
Lords Valley	18428
Lorenton	16938
Loretto	15940
Loretto Road	15931
Loshs Run	17020
Lost Creek	17746
Lottsville	16402
Loux Corner	18927
Lovedale	15037
Lovejoy	15729
Lovell	16407
Lovelton	18629
Lovely	15521
Lover	15022
Lowber (Fayette County)	15438
Lowber (Westmoreland County)	15660
Lowe Lake	18470
Lower Allen (Township)	17011
Lower Alsace (Township)	19606
Lower Askam	18706
Lower Augusta (Township)	17801
Lower Brownville	17976
Lower Burrell	15068
Lower Chanceford (Township)	17302
Lower Chichester (Township)	19061
Lower Frankford (Township)	17013
Lower Frederick (Township)	19492
Lower Gwynedd (Township)	19437
Lower Heidelberg (Township)	19604
Lower Longswamp	19539
Lower Macungie (Township)	18062
Lower Mahanoy (Township)	17017
Lower Makefield (Township)	19067
Lower Merion (Township)	19003
Lower Merion Township	19003
Lower Mifflin (Township)	17241
Lower Milford (Township)	18036
Lower Moreland (Township)	19006
Lower Moreland Township	19006
Lower Mount Bethel (Township)	18063
Lower Nazareth (Township)	18017
Lower Orchard	19058
Lower Oxford (Township)	19363
Lower Paxton (Dauphin County)	17109
Lower Paxton (Dauphin County) (Township)	17109
Lower Peanut	15480
Lower Pottsgrove (Township)	19464
Lower Providence (Township)	19401
Lower Sagon	17877
Lower Salford (Township)	19438
Lower Saucon (Township)	18015
Lower Southampton (Township)	19047
Lower Southampton Township	19047
Lower Swatara (Township)	17057
Lower Towamensing (Township)	18071
Lower Turkeyfoot (Township)	15424
Lower Tyrone (Township)	15428
Lower Windsor (Township)	17368
Lower Yoder (Township)	15906
Lowhill (Lehigh County) (Township)	18069
Low Hill (Washington County)	15429
Lowville	16442
Loyalhanna (Westmoreland County)	15661
Loyalhanna (Westmoreland County) (Township)	15681
Loyalhanna Woodlands No. 1	15670
Loyalsock (Township)	17701
Loyalsockville	17754
Loyalton	17048
Loyalville	18612

Name	ZIP
Loysburg	16659
Loysville	17047
Lucernemines	15754
Lucesco	15656
Lucinda	16235
Luciusboro	15748
Lucknow	17110
Lucky	17322
Lucon	19473
Lucy Crossing (Part of Glendon)	18042
Lucy Furnace	17066
Ludlow	16333
Ludwigs Corner	19343
Luke Fidler	17872
Lumber (Township)	15834
Lumber City (Clearfield County)	16833
Lumber City (Mifflin County)	17084
Lumberville	18933
Lumstead	16201
Lundys Lane	16401
Lungerville	17774
Lurgan	17232
Lurgan (Township)	17240
Luthersburg	15848
Luthers Mills	18848
Lutztown	17013
Lutzville	15537
Luxor	15662
Luzerne	15433
Luzerne (Township)	15417
Luzerne	18709
Lycippus	15650
Lycoming (Township)	17728
Lykens (Dauphin County)	17048
Lykens (Dauphin County) (Township)	17048
Lyleville	16627
Lynch	16347
Lynchville	15857
Lyndell	19354
Lyndon	17602
Lyndora	16045
Lynn (Lehigh County) (Township)	19529
Lynn (Susquehanna County)	18844
Lynnewood	19150
Lynnewood Gardens	19012
Lynnport	18066
Lynnville	18066
Lynnwood (Fayette County)	15012
Lynnwood (Luzerne County)	18702
Lynnwood-Pricedale	15012
Lyon Station	19536
Lyon Valley	18066
Mable	17921
Mable Hill	15327
McAdoo	18237
McAdoo Heights	18237
McAlevys Fort	16652
McAlisters Crossroads	15086
McAlisterville	17049
MacArthur (Part of Aliquippa)	15001
McCalmont (Township)	15711
McCandless (Allegheny County)	15237
McCandless (Allegheny County) (Township)	15237
McCartney	16661
McCauley	16651
McChesneytown	15650
McChesneytown-Loyalhanna	15620
McClarran	15650
Mc Cleary	15050
McClellan	17032
McClellandtown	15458
McClellan Heights	17403
McClintock	16301
McClure (Fayette County)	15666
McClure (Snyder County)	17841
McConnellsburg	17233
McConnells Mill	15301
McConnellstown	16660
McCormick (mail Smicksburg)	16256
McCormick (mail Marion Center)	15759
McCoysville	17058
McCullocks Mills	17035
McCullough	15636
McDonald	15057
Macdonaldton	15530
Macedonia (Bradford County)	18848
Macedonia (Juniata County)	17059
McElhattan	17748
McEwensville	17749

Name	ZIP
McGareys	15825
McGees Mills	15757
McGillstown	17003
McGovern	15342
McGrann	16236
McGregor	16222
McHenry (Township)	17723
McIlhaney	18322
McIntyre (Indiana County)	15756
McIntyre (Lycoming County) (Township)	17763
McKean (Erie County)	16426
McKean (Erie County) (Township)	16426
McKean Corners	16351
McKeansburg	17960
McKee	16637
McKee Half Falls	17864
McKeesport	15130-35
For specific McKeesport Zip Codes call (412) 672-9721	
McKees Rocks	15136
Mackeyville	17750
McKinley	19117
McKinley Hill (Part of Point Marion)	15474
McKinney	17232
McKnight	15237
McKnightstown	17343
McKnight Village	15237
McLane	16426
McMichaels	18360
McMurray	15317
McNett (Township)	17765
McPherron	15753
McSherrystown	17344
Macungie	18062
McVeytown	17051
McVille	16229
McWilliams	16242
Maddensville	17229
Madera	16661
Madge	16735
Madison (Armstrong County) (Township)	16259
Madison (Clarion County) (Township)	16248
Madison (Columbia County) (Township)	17846
Madison (Lackawanna County) (Township)	18444
Madison (Westmoreland County)	15663
Madisonburg	16852
Madisonville	18444
Madley	15534
Magee	16351
Magill Heights	15024
Magnolia Gardens	19007
Magnolia Hill	19007
Mahaffey	15757
Mahanoy (Township)	17976
Mahanoy City	17948
Mahanoy Plane (Part of Gilberton)	17949
Mahoning (Armstrong County)	16259
Mahoning (Armstrong County) (Township)	16242
Mahoning (Carbon County) (Township)	18235
Mahoning (Lawrence County) (Township)	16132
Mahoning (Montour County) (Township)	17821
Mahoning Manor	17847
Mahoningtown (Part of New Castle)	16102
Maiden Creek	19510
Maidencreek (Township)	19605
Main (Township)	17815
Mainesburg	16932
Mainland	19451
Mainsville	17257
Mainville	17815
Maitland	17044
Maizeville (Part of Gilberton)	17934
Majeriks Corners	16441
Malden Place (Part of Centerville)	15417
Mall (Part of Monroeville)	15146
Malta	17017
Malvern	19355
Mammoth	15664
Mamont	15632
Manada Gap	17112
Manatawny	19547
Manayunk (Part of Philadelphia)	19127
Manchester (Allegheny County)	15233

Place	ZIP
Manchester (Wayne County) (Township)	18417
Manchester (York County)	17345
Manchester (York County) (Township)	17402
Mandata	17830
Manheim (Lancaster County)	17545
Manheim (Lancaster County) (Township)	17601
Manheim (York County) (Township)	17329
Manifold	15301
Manito	15650
Mann (Township)	17211
Mannitto Haven	15670
Manns Choice	15550
Mannsville	17074
Manoa	19083
Manor (Armstrong County) (Township)	16226
Manor (Lancaster County) (Township)	17603
Manor (Westmoreland County)	15665
Manor Hill	16652
Manor Hills (Part of Yeadon)	19050
Manor Park Terrace	16226
Manor Ridge	17603
Manor Shopping Center	17603
Manorville	16238
Manown	15063
Mansfield	16933
Mantzville	18252
Manver	15765
Maple Beach	19007
Mapledale	16323
Maple Glen (Montgomery County)	19002
Maple Glen (Washington County)	15417
Maple Grove (Berks County)	18011
Maple Grove (Chester County)	19363
Maple Grove (Clarion County)	16248
Maple Grove (Fayette County)	15622
Maple Grove Park	19540
Maple Hill (Lycoming County)	17752
Maple Hill (Montgomery County)	19422
Maple Hill (Schuylkill County)	17976
Maple Hills	17319
Maple Hollow	16635
Maplelake	18444
Maple Manor	18201
Maple Ridge	15935
Maple Shade	19020
Mapleton Depot	17052
Mapletown	15338
Maplewood (Bucks County)	18901
Maplewood (Wayne County)	18436
Maplewood Heights	18612
Maplewood Park	19018
Maplewood Terrace	15601
Marble	16334
Marble Hall	19444
Marcel Lake Estates	18328
Marchand	15758
Marchwood	19341
Marcus Hook	19061
Marengo	16877
Margaret	16201
Margaretta Furnace	17406
Margo Gardens	19007
Marguerite	15650
Marianna	15345
Mariasville	16373
Marienville	16239
Marietta	17547
Marion (Beaver County) (Township)	15066
Marion (Berks County) (Township)	19567
Marion (Butler County) (Township)	16020
Marion (Centre County) (Township)	16841
Marion (Franklin County)	17235
Marion Center	15759
Marion Heights	17832
Mark Acres	15642
Markelsville	17074
Markes	17236
Market Square (Part of Philadelphia)	19118
Market Street (Part of West Chester)	19380
Markle	15613
Markleton	15551
Markleysburg	15459
Markton	15764
Markvue Manor	15642
Marlboro (Chester County)	19348
Marlboro (Montgomery County) (Township)	18084
Mar Lin	17951
Marple (Township)	19008
Marron	16833
Mars	16046
Marsh (Chester County)	19520
Marsh (Franklin County)	17268
Marshall (Township)	15086
Marshall Heights	15716
Marshalls Creek	18335
Marshall Terrace	19061
Marshallton (Chester County)	19380
Marshallton (Northumberland County)	17872
Marshbrook	18414
Marshburg	16738
Marsh Hill	17771
Marshlands	16921
Marsh Run	17070
Marshview	18848
Marshwood (Part of Olyphant)	18434
Marsteller	15760
Marstown	17963
Martha Furnace	16870
Martic (Township)	17565
Martic Forge	17565
Marticville	17565
Martin	15460
Martindale (Cambria County)	15946
Martindale (Lancaster County)	17549
Martinsburg	16662
Martins Corner	19320
Martins Creek	18063
Martinsville	17366
Martzville	18603
Marvel Gardens	19094
Marvindale	16749
Marwood	16023
Mary D	17952
Marysville	17053
Marywood College (Part of Scranton)	18509
Mascot	17572
Mason-Dixon	17225
Masontown	15461
Masseyburg	16669
Mastersonville	17545
Mast Hope	18435
Matamoras (Dauphin County)	17032
Matamoras (Pike County)	18336
Mather	15346
Mattawana	17054
Mattey Plan	15012
Matthews Run	16371
Mausdale	17821
Maxatawny	19538
Maxatawny (Township)	19538
Maxwell	15450
Mayberry (Township)	17821
Mayburg	16347
Mayfair (Part of Philadelphia)	19136
Mayfield	18433
Mayfield East	17405
Mayport	16240
Maysville (Armstrong County)	15618
Maysville (Mercer County)	16125
Maytown (Lancaster County)	17550
Maytown (York County)	17339
Mayview	15017
Mayville	16105
Maze	17094
Mazeppa	17837
Mead (Township)	16313
Meadia Heights	17602
Meadowbrook (Fayette County)	15401
Meadowbrook (Montgomery County)	19046
Meadowbrook Manor	19341
Meadow Gap	17243
Meadow Lands	15347
Meadowood	16045
Meadowview Estates	17540
Meadow Wood	15001
Meadville	16335
Mechanicsburg	17055
Mechanics Grove	17566
Mechanicsville (Bucks County)	18934
Mechanicsville (Clarion County)	16214
Mechanicsville (Lancaster County)	17545
Mechanicsville (Lehigh County)	18104
Mechanicsville (Montour County)	17821
Mechanicsville (Schuylkill County)	17901
Meckesville	18210
Mecks Corner	17068
Media	19063-65
For specific Media Zip Codes call (215) 566-3196	
Medix Run	15868
Meeker	18612
Megargee	19320
Mehoopany	18629
Mehoopany (Township)	18629
Meiser	17842
Meiserville	17853
Melcroft	15462
Mellingertown	15666
Melrose (Fayette County)	15450
Melrose (Susquehanna County)	18847
Melrose Park	19012
Menallen (Adams County) (Township)	17304
Menallen (Fayette County) (Township)	15401
Mench	15537
Mendenhall	19357
Mendon	15679
Menges Mills	17346
Menno	17004
Menno (Township)	17004
Mentcle	15761
Mercer (Butler County) (Township)	16038
Mercer (Mercer County)	16137
Mercersburg	17236
Mercur	18854
Meredith	16249
Meridian	16001
Merion Park	19066
Merion Square	19035
Merion Station	19066
Merion View	19406
Meriwether Farms	19380
Merlin	19460
Mermaid Estates	19401
Merrian	17851
Merrill (Part of Industry)	15052
Merrittstown	15463
Merryall	18853
Mertztown	19539
Merwinsburg	18330
Meshoppen (Wyoming County)	18630
Meshoppen (Wyoming County) (Township)	18630
Messiah College	17027
Messmore	15458
Metal	17224
Metal (Township)	17221
Mexico	17056
Meyersdale	15552
Meyersville	18104
Middleburg (Luzerne County)	18661
Middleburg (Snyder County)	17842
Middlebury (Township)	16935
Middlebury Center	16935
Middle Churches	15666
Middle City (Part of Philadelphia)	19103
Middle Creek (Snyder County)	17813
Middlecreek (Snyder County) (Township)	17833
Middlecreek (Somerset County) (Township)	15557
Middle Lancaster	16037
Middle Paxton (Township)	17018
Middleport	17953
Middlesex (Township)	17013
Middlesex (Butler County) (Township)	16059
Middlesex (Cumberland County)	17013
Middle Smithfield (Township)	18301
Middle Spring	17257
Middle Taylor (Township)	15906

474 PENNSYLVANIA Middleton-Mosgrove

Name	ZIP
Middleton	15757
Middletown (Bucks County) (Township)	19056
Middletown (Dauphin County)	17057
Middletown (Delaware County) (Township)	19037
Middletown (McKean County)	16749
Middletown (Northampton County)	18017
Middletown (Susquehanna County) (Township)	18818
Middletown (Westmoreland County)	15601
Middletown Center	18818
Middletown Heights	19063
Middletown Township	19037
Midland (Beaver County)	15059
Midland (Washington County)	15342
Midvale	18705
Midvale Manor	19608
Midvalley	17888
Midway (Adams County)	17331
Midway (Lebanon County)	17042
Midway (Washington County)	15060
Midway (Westmoreland County)	15601
Mifflin (Columbia County) (Township)	18631
Mifflin (Dauphin County) (Township)	17061
Mifflin (Juniata County)	17058
Mifflin (Lycoming County) (Township)	17740
Mifflinburg	17844
Mifflin Junction (Part of West Mifflin)	15236
Mifflintown	17059
Mifflinville	18631
Milan	18831
Milanville	18443
Mildred	18632
Mile Run	17801
Miles (Township)	16872
Milesburg	16853
Milesville	15063
Milford (Township)	15557
Milford (Bucks County) (Township)	18968
Milford (Juniata County) (Township)	17062
Milford (Pike County)	18337
Milford (Pike County) (Township)	18337
Milford (Somerset County)	15501
Milford Manor	19067
Milford Square	18935
Milfred Terrace	15348
Militia Hill	19034
Millardsville	17067
Millbach	17073
Millbank	15658
Millbourne	19082
Millbrook (Centre County)	16801
Millbrook (Mercer County)	16133
Mill Brook (Pike County)	18426
Millburn	16137
Mill City	18414
Millcreek (Clarion County) (Township)	16225
Millcreek (Erie County) (Township)	16506
Millcreek (Erie County)	16505
Mill Creek (Huntingdon County)	17060
Millcreek (Lebanon County) (Township)	17073
Mill Creek (Lycoming County) (Township)	17756
Mill Creek (Mercer County) (Township)	16145
Mill Creek (Schuylkill County)	17901
Mill Creek Falls	19007
Millcreek Mall	16509
Milledgeville	16311
Miller (Huntingdon County) (Township)	16652
Miller (Perry County) (Township)	17094
Miller Heights	18017
Miller Manor	18067
Miller Plan	15042
Miller Run	15936
Millers	16403
Millersburg	17061
Miller Shaft	15946

Name	ZIP
Millerstown (Allegheny County)	15084
Millerstown (Blair County)	16662
Millerstown (Clarion County)	16334
Millerstown (Perry County)	17062
Millersville	17551
Millerton	16936
Millertown	15446
Mill Grove	17820
Mill Hall	17751
Millheim	16854
Milligantown	15069
Millmont	17845
Millport (Lancaster County)	17540
Millport (Potter County)	16748
Millrift	18340
Mill Run (Blair County)	16601
Mill Run (Fayette County)	15464
Mills	16937
Millsboro	15348
Millstone (Township)	15860
Milltown (Bradford County)	18840
Milltown (Chester County)	19380
Millvale	15209
Millview	18616
Mill Village	16427
Millville	17846
Millway	17543
Millwood	15627
Millwood Manor	15068
Milmont Park	19033
Milnesville	18239
Milnor	17225
Milroy	17063
Milton (Armstrong County)	16222
Milton (Northumberland County)	17847
Milton Grove	17552
Milwaukee	18411
Mina	16915
Mineral (Township)	16342
Mineral Point	15942
Mineral Springs	16855
Miners Mills (Part of Wilkes-Barre)	18705
Miners Village (Part of Cornwall)	17016
Minersville	17954
Minesite (Part of Allentown)	18103
Mingoville	16856
Minisink Hills	18341
Minister	16347
Minnequa	17724
Miola	16214
Miquon	19452
Miquon Hills	19452
Mission Hill	17601
Mitchell Park (Part of Hatboro)	19040
Mix Run	15832
Mocanaqua	18655
Moc-A-Tek Lake	18436
Mocking Bird Hill	15642
Modena	19358
Moffit	15327
Mogees	19401
Mohns Hill	19608
Mohnton	19540
Mohrsville	19541
Molino	17961
Mollenauer (Part of Bethel Park)	15102
Mollitown	19522
Monaca	15061
Monaghan (Township)	17404
Monarch	15431
Monessen	15062
Mongul	17257
Moninger	15342
Moniteau	16061
Monocacy Station	19542
Monongahela (Greene County) (Township)	15338
Monongahela (Washington County)	15063
Monongahela Junction (Part of Duquesne)	15110
Monroe (Bedford County) (Township)	15537
Monroe (Bradford County) (Township)	18848
Monroe (Clarion County)	16232
Monroe (Clarion County) (Township)	16255
Monroe (Cumberland County) (Township)	17055
Monroe (Juniata County) (Township)	17086
Monroe (Snyder County) (Township)	17831

Name	ZIP
Monroe (Wyoming County) (Township)	18657
Monroe Heights (Part of Monroeville)	15146
Monroeton	18832
Monroeville	15146
Monroeville Mall (Part of Monroeville)	15146
Mont Alto	17237
Montandon	17850
Mont Clare	19453
Montdale	18447
Montello	19608
Monterey (Berks County)	19530
Monterey (Franklin County)	17214
Monterey (Lancaster County)	17540
Montgomery (Franklin County) (Township)	17236
Montgomery (Indiana County) (Township)	15712
Montgomery (Lycoming County)	17752
Montgomery (Montgomery County) (Township)	18936
Montgomerys Ferry	17074
Montgomery Square	18936
Montgomeryville	18936
Montour (Allegheny County)	15244
Montour (Columbia County) (Township)	17815
Montour Junction (Part of Coraopolis)	15108
Montoursville	17754
Montrose (Berks County)	19607
Montrose (Susquehanna County)	18801
Montrose Hill	15238
Montsera	17013
Monument	16822
Moon	15108
Moon (Township)	15108
Moon Crest	15108
Moon Run	15136
Moore (Township)	18014
Mooredale	17013
Mooresburg	17821
Moores Corners	16057
Moorestown	18014
Moorheadville	16428
Moosic	18507
Moosic Lake	18416
Morado (Part of Beaver Falls)	15010
Morann	16663
Moravia	16157
Moravian (Part of Bethlehem)	18018
Mordansville	17815
Morea	17948
Moreland (Township)	17756
Moreland Farms	19040
Moreland Manor	19040
Morewood	19040
Morgan (Allegheny County)	15064
Morgan (rural)	15456
Morgan	15425
Morgan (Greene County) (Township)	15346
Morgan Hill	15031
Morgans Hill	18042
Morgantown	19543
Morningside (Part of Pittsburgh)	15206
Morrell	15431
Morris (Tioga County) (Township)	16938
Morris (Washington County) (Township)	15329
Morris (Clearfield County) (Township)	16821
Morris (Greene County) (Township)	15364
Morris (Huntingdon County) (Township)	16611
Morris (Tioga County)	16938
Morris Cross Roads	15451
Morrisdale	16858
Morris Run	16939
Morrisville (Bucks County)	19067
Morrisville (Greene County)	15370
Morrows Corner	16210
Morstein	19380
Morton	19070
Mortonville	19320
Morwood	18969
Morysville	19512
Moscow	18444
Moselem	19526
Moselem Springs	19522
Mosgrove	16259

Moshannon-New Britain PENNSYLVANIA 475

Name	ZIP
Moshannon	16859
Mosherville	16925
Mosiertown	16433
Mosserville	18066
Moss Plan	15074
Mostoller	15563
Mottarns Mill	15771
Moudy Hill	15946
Moulstown	17331
Mount Aetna	19544
Mountaindale (Cambria County)	16639
Mountain Dale (Dauphin County)	17110
Mountain Grove	17815
Mountainhome	18342
Mountain Lake	18848
Mountain Top (Lancaster County)	17555
Mountain Top (Luzerne County)	18707
Mountain Valley Lake	17921
Mount Airy (Clarion County)	16255
Mount Airy (Lancaster County)	17578
Mount Airy (Philadelphia County)	19119
Mount Airy Terrace	18708
Mount Allen	17055
Mount Alton	16738
Mount Bethel	18343
Mount Braddock	15465
Mount Carbon	17901
Mount Carmel (Northumberland County)	17851
Mount Carmel (Northumberland County) (Township)	17851
Mount Chestnut	16001
Mount Chestnut Springs	16001
Mount Cobb	18436
Mount Eagle	16841
Mount Etna	16693
Mount Gretna	17064
Mount Gretna Heights	17064
Mount Holly Springs	17065
Mount Hope	17320
Mount Independence	15456
Mount Jackson	16101
Mount Jewett	16740
Mount Joy (Adams County) (Township)	17340
Mount Joy (Clearfield County)	16830
Mount Joy (Lancaster County)	17552
Mount Joy (Lancaster County) (Township)	17022
Mount Joy (Westmoreland County)	15666
Mount Laffee	17901
Mount Laurel	18201
Mount Lebanon (Allegheny County) (Township)	15228
Mount Lebanon (Allegheny County)	15228
Mount Misery	17350
Mount Morris	15349
Mount Nebo (Allegheny County)	15143
Mount Nebo (Lancaster County)	17565
Mount Oliver	15210
Mount Patrick	17045
Mount Penn	19606
Mount Pleasant (Adams County)	17331
Mount Pleasant (Adams County) (Township)	17325
Mount Pleasant (Berks County)	19506
Mount Pleasant (Columbia County) (Township)	17815
Mount Pleasant (Delaware County)	19087
Mount Pleasant (Juniata County)	17059
Mount Pleasant (Lebanon County)	17042
Mount Pleasant (Mifflin County)	17063
Mount Pleasant (Northampton County)	18013
Mount Pleasant (Northumberland County)	17801
Mount Pleasant (Perry County)	17006
Mount Pleasant (Schuylkill County)	17901
Mount Pleasant (Tioga County)	16938

Name	ZIP
Mount Pleasant (Washington County) (Township)	15340
Mount Pleasant (Wayne County) (Township)	18472
Mount Pleasant (Westmoreland County)	15666
Mount Pleasant (Westmoreland County) (Township)	15664
Mount Pleasant (York County)	17019
Mount Pleasant Mills	17853
Mount Pocono	18344
Mountrock (Cumberland County)	17013
Mount Rock (Franklin County)	17257
Mount Rock (Mifflin County)	17044
Mount Royal	17315
Mount Sterling	15461
Mount Tabor	17324
Mount Troy	15212
Mount Union (Franklin County)	17222
Mount Union (Huntingdon County)	17066
Mount Vernon (Allegheny County)	15135
Mount Vernon (Chester County)	19363
Mount Vernon (Lancaster County)	17527
Mount Vernon (Westmoreland County)	15601
Mountville	17554
Mount Washington (Allegheny County)	15211
Mount Washington (Beaver County)	15010
Mount Wilson	17042
Mount Wolf	17347
Mount Zion (Cumberland County)	17055
Mount Zion (Cumberland County)	17013
Mount Zion (Lebanon County)	17042
Mount Zion (Luzerne County)	18643
Mount Zion (Monroe County)	18301
Mount Zion (York County)	17402
Moween	15681
Mowersville	17257
Mowry	17921
Moyer	15425
Moylan	19065
Mozart	18925
Mt Pocahontas	18210
Muddycreek (Township)	16051
Muddy Creek Forks	17302
Muhlenberg (Berks County) (Township)	19560
Muhlenberg (Luzerne County)	18621
Muhlenberg Park	19605
Muir	17957
Mullertown	17331
Mumbauersville	18073
Mummasburg	17325
Muncy (Lycoming County)	17756
Muncy (Lycoming County) (Township)	17756
Muncy Creek (Township)	17756
Muncy Valley	17758
Munderf	15825
Mundys Corner	15909
Munhall	15120
Munson	16860
Munster	15940
Munster (Township)	15938
Murdock	15501
Murdocksville	15026
Murphy Siding	15425
Murraysville (Part of Murrysville)	15668
Murrell	17522
Murrinsville	16020
Murry Hill	15317
Murrysville	15668
Muse	15350
Mustard	15037
Mutual	15601
Myersburg	18854
Myerstown (Cumberland County)	17324
Myerstown (Lebanon County)	17067
Mylo Park	15931
Myobeach	18630

Name	ZIP
Myoma	16046
Myrtle	14721
Mystic Park	16404
Naces Corner	18927
Naceville	18960
Nadine	15147
Naginey	17063
Nagles Crossroad	16668
Nan Lynn Gardens	18974
Nansen	16735
Nanticoke	18634
Nantmeal Village	19343
Nanty Glo	15943
Naomi	15438
Napier (Township)	15559
Napierville	17522
Narberth	19072
Narbrook Park (Part of Narberth)	19072
Narrows Creek	15801
Narrows Shopping Center (Part of Edwardsville)	18704
Narrowsville	18972
Narvon	17555
Nashua	16101
Nashville (Indiana County)	15771
Nashville (York County)	17362
Nassau Village	19078
Natalie	17851
National Hill	15031
Natrona	15065
Natrona Heights	15065
Nauvoo	16938
Naval Air Development Center	18974
Nazareth	18064
Nealmont	16686
Neason Hill	16335
Neath	18829
Nebo	15622
Nectarine	16038
Ned	15352
Needful	16881
Needmore	17238
Neelyton	17239
Neffs	18065
Neffs Mills	16669
Neffsville	17601
Neiffer	19473
Neiltown	16341
Neiman	17327
Nellie	15486
Nelson	16940
Nelson (Township)	16940
Nemacolin	15351
Nemanie	18451
Nescopeck (Luzerne County)	18635
Nescopeck (Luzerne County) (Township)	18635
Neshaminy	18976
Neshaminy Falls	19047
Neshaminy Hills	19047
Neshaminy Valley	19020
Neshaminy Woods	19047
Neshannock (Lawrence County)	16105
Neshannock (Lawrence County) (Township)	16105
Neshannock Falls	16156
Nesquehoning	18240
Nether Providence (Township)	19086
Nether Providence Township	19013
Neville (Township)	15225
Neville Island	15225
New Albany	18833
New Alexandria	15670
New Athens	16248
New Baltimore (Somerset County)	15553
New Baltimore (York County)	17331
New Beaver	16141
New Bedford	16140
New Berlin	17855
New Berlinville	19545
Newberry (Lycoming County)	17701
Newberry (York County) (Township)	17370
Newberrytown	17319
New Bethlehem	16242
New Bloomfield	17068
Newboro	15468
New Boston	17948
New Bridgeville	17356
New Brighton	15066
New Britain (Bucks County)	18901

476 PENNSYLVANIA New Britain-North Wales

Name	ZIP
New Britain (Bucks County) (Township)	18914
New Buena Vista	15550
New Buffalo	17069
Newburg (Blair County)	16601
Newburg (Cumberland County)	17240
Newburg (Northampton County)	18017
Newburg Homes	18042
New Castle	16101-08
For specific New Castle Zip Codes call (412) 656-7200	
New Castle (Township)	17970
New Castle Northwest	16105
New Centerville	15557
Newchester	17350
New Columbia	17856
New Columbus (Carbon County)	18240
New Columbus (Luzerne County)	17878
Newcomer	15401
New Cumberland	17070
New Cumberland Army Depot	17105
New Danville	17603
New Derry	15671
New Eagle	15067
Newell	15466
New England	18252
New Enterprise	16664
New Era	18833
Newfield (Allegheny County)	15147
Newfield (Potter County)	16948
New Florence	15944
Newfoundland	18445
New Franklin	17201
New Freedom	17349
New Freeport	15352
New Galena	18914
New Galilee	16141
New Garden	19374
New Garden (Township)	19350
New Geneva	15467
New Germantown	17071
New Germany	15946
New Grass Manor	18612
New Grenada	16674
New Hamburg	16124
New Hanover	19525
New Hanover (Township)	19525
New Hanover Square	19525
Newhard	18080
New Holland	17557
New Homestead (Part of Pittsburgh)	15120
New Hope	18938
New Ireland	16438
New Jerusalem	19522
New Kensington	15068
New Kingstown	17072
Newkirk	18252
New Lebanon	16145
New Lexington	15557
Newlin (Chester County) (Township)	19380
Newlin (Columbia County)	17820
New London (Township)	19360
New London (Chester County)	19360
New London (Warren County)	16351
Newlonsburg (Part of Murrysville)	15668
New Mahoning	18235
Newmanstown	17073
Newmansville	16353
New Market	17070
New Milford (Susquehanna County)	18834
New Milford (Susquehanna County) (Township)	18834
New Millport	16681
New Mines	17923
New Oxford	17350
New Paris	15554
New Park	17352
New Philadelphia	17959
Newport (Lawrence County)	16157
Newport (Luzerne County) (Township)	18634
Newport (Perry County)	17074
Newportville	19056
Newportville Terrace	19020
New Providence	17560
New Richmond	16327
New Ringgold	17960
Newry	16665
New Salem	15468
New Salem-Buffington	15468

Name	ZIP
New Schaefferstown	19506
New Sewickley (Township)	15074
New Sheffield	15001
Newside	18080
New Smithville	19530
New Stanton	15672
New Street	17901
New Texas	17563
Newton (Township)	18411
Newtonburg	15757
Newton Hamilton	17075
Newton Lake	18407
Newtown (Bucks County)	18940
Newtown (Bucks County) (Township)	18940
New Town (Centre County)	16666
Newtown (Clearfield County)	16878
Newtown (Delaware County) (Township)	19073
Newtown (Lancaster County)	17512
Newtown (Lehigh County)	18031
Newtown (Luzerne County)	18706
Newtown Square	19073
New Tripoli	18066
New Vernon	16145
New Vernon (Township)	16145
Newville (Bucks County)	18914
Newville (Cumberland County)	17241
Newville (Lancaster County)	17023
New Virginia (Part of Hermitage)	16146
New Washington	15757
New Wilmington	16142
Niagara	18453
Niantic	19504
Nicetown (Part of Philadelphia)	19140
Nichola	16262
Nicholson (Fayette County) (Township)	15461
Nicholson (Wyoming County)	18446
Nicholson (Wyoming County) (Township)	18446
Nickel Mines	17562
Nickleville	16373
Nicklin	16323
Nicktown	15762
Nilan	15474
Niles	16323
Niles Valley	16935
Ninepoints	17509
Nine Row	15927
Nineveh (Clarion County)	16232
Nineveh (Greene County)	15353
Nippenose (Township)	17720
Nisbet	17759
Nittany	16841
Niverton	15558
Nixon	16001
Noble	19046
Noble Hill	15215
Noblestown	15071
Nockamixon (Township)	18930
Noll Acres	17055
Nolo	15765
Nook	17058
Nordmont	17758
Normal Square	18235
Normalville	15469
Norman	15825
Norristown	19401-09
For specific Norristown Zip Codes call (215) 275-9780	
Norrisville	16406
North Abington (Township)	18414
Northampton (Bucks County) (Township)	18954
Northampton (Northampton County)	18067
Northampton (Somerset County) (Township)	15538
Northampton Hills	18966
North Annville (Township)	17038
North Apollo	15673
North Aronimink	19082
North Bangor	18013
North Barnesboro (Part of Barnesboro)	15714
North Beaver (Township)	16102
North Belle Vernon	15012
North Bend	17760
North Bessemer	15235
North Bethlehem (Township)	15360
North Bingham	16923
North Braddock	15104
North Branch (Township)	18629
Northbrook	19380

Name	ZIP
Northbrook Hills	17601
North Buffalo (Township)	16201
North Butler	16001
North Catasauqua	18032
North Centre (Township)	18603
North Charleroi	15022
North Codorus (Township)	17362
North Connellsville	15425
North Cornwall (Lebanon County)	17016
North Cornwall (Lebanon County) (Township)	17042
North Coventry (Township)	19464
North East (Erie County)	16428
North East (Erie County) (Township)	16428
Northeast Madison (Township)	17047
North Edinburg	16116
North End (Part of Wilkes-Barre)	18705
Northern Lights Shopping Center (Part of Economy)	15005
North Essington	19029
North Fayette (Township)	15071
North Fork	16950
North Franklin (Township)	15301
North Fredericktown	15333
North Freedom	16240
North Hamilton (Part of Doylestown)	18901
North Hanover Mall (Part of Hanover)	17331
North Heidelberg (Township)	19506
North Hills (Montgomery County)	19038
North Hills (Northumberland County)	17847
North Hopewell (Township)	17322
North Huntingdon (Township)	15642
North Irwin	15642
North Jackson	18847
North Larchmont	19073
North Lebanon (Township)	17042
North Liberty	16127
North Londonderry (Township)	17078
North Mahoning (Township)	15771
North Mall Factory Outlet Center (Part of York)	17404
North Manheim (Township)	17901
North McKees Rocks	15136
North Mehoopany	18629
North Middleton (Township)	17013
Northmoreland (Township)	18612
North Mountain	17758
North Newton (Township)	17241
North Oakland	16025
North Orwell	18837
North Philadelphia (Part of Philadelphia)	19132
North Philipsburg	16866
North Pine Grove	16260
North Point (Bedford County)	16679
Northpoint (Indiana County)	15763
North Radcliffe	19007
North Rochester	15074
North Rome	18854
North Scottdale	15683
North Scranton (Part of Scranton)	18508
North Sewickley (Beaver County)	15010
North Sewickley (Beaver County) (Township)	15010
North Sherango (Township)	16424
North Springfield	16430
North Strabane (Township)	15317
North Towanda	18848
North Towanda (Township)	18848
Northumberland	17857
North Union (Fayette County) (Township)	15401
North Union (Schuylkill County) (Township)	18241
North Vandergrift	15690
North Vandergrift-Pleasant View	15690
North Versailles (Allegheny County) (Township)	15137
North Versailles (Allegheny County)	15137
Northview Heights (Part of Economy)	15005
Northview Homes (Part of Economy)	15005
Northvue	16001
North Wales	19454

North Warren-Palmyra PENNSYLVANIA 477

Name	ZIP
North Warren	16365
North Washington (Butler County)	16048
North Washington (Westmoreland County)	15613
Northway Mall	15237
North Waynesburg	17268
North Weissport	18235
Northwest Harborcreek	16510
North Whitehall (Township)	18037
Northwood	16686
North Woodbury (Township)	16662
Northwood Heights	18042
North York	17404
Norvelt	15674
Norwegian (Township)	17951
Norwich (Township)	16724
Norwin Heights	15642
Norwood (Allegheny County)	15136
Norwood (Delaware County)	19074
Nossville	17213
Nottingham (Bucks County)	19020
Nottingham (Chester County)	19362
Nottingham (Washington County) (Township)	15332
Nowrytown	15681
Noxen	18636
Noxen (Township)	18636
Noyes (Township)	17764
Nuangola	18637
Nuangola Station	18707
Number Five Mine	16137
Number Thirty Seven	15963
Numidia	17858
Nu Mine	16244
Nuremberg	18241
Nutts Corners	16127
Nyesville	17201
Oakbottom	17566
Oakdale (Allegheny County)	15071
Oakdale (Luzerne County)	18224
Oakdale Manor	19067
Oakeola	19036
Oakford	19047
Oak Forest	15370
Oak Grove (Clearfield County)	16858
Oak Grove (Schuylkill County)	17963
Oakgrove (Westmoreland County)	15658
Oak Hall	16827
Oak Hill (mail Turtle Creek)	15145
Oak Hill (mail North Versailles)	15137
Oak Hill (Clearfield County)	16845
Oakland (Allegheny County)	15213
Oakland (Butler County) (Township)	16061
Oakland (Cambria County)	15904
Oakland (Lawrence County)	16101
Oakland (Mercer County)	16137
Oakland (Susquehanna County)	18847
Oakland (Susquehanna County) (Township)	18847
Oakland (Venango County) (Township)	16317
Oakland Beach	16316
Oakland Hills I	18016
Oakland Mills	17076
Oakland Park	18101
Oak Lane (Part of Philadelphia)	19126
Oaklane Manor	19012
Oakleigh	17111
Oaklyn	17801
Oakmont (Allegheny County)	15139
Oakmont (Cambria County)	15904
Oakmont Villa	17036
Oak Park (Montgomery County)	19446
Oak Park (Montgomery County)	19440
Oak Park (Northumberland County)	17857
Oak Ridge (Armstrong County)	16245
Oak Ridge (Clearfield County)	16661
Oakryn	17563
Oaks	19456
Oak Shade	17566
Oaktree Hollow	19007
Oakview	19026
Oakview Park	19026
Oakville (Cumberland County)	17257

Name	ZIP
Oakville (Westmoreland County)	15650
Oakwood	16101
Oakwood Park (Part of Laflin)	18702
Obelisk	19492
Oberlin	17113
Oberlin Gardens	17113
Observatory (Part of Pittsburgh)	15214
Odenthal	15946
Odenwelder (Part of West Easton)	18042
Odin	16915
Ogden	19061
Ogdensburg	17765
Ogle (Butler County)	16046
Ogle (Somerset County) (Township)	15963
Ogletown	15963
Ogontz	19012
Ogontz Campus	19001
O'Hara (Township)	15238
Ohio (Township)	15237
Ohiopyle	15470
Ohio Township	15143
Ohioview (Part of Industry)	15052
Ohioville	15059
Ohl	15864
Oil City (Cambria County)	15925
Oil City (Venango County)	16301
Oil Creek (Crawford County) (Township)	16354
Oil Creek (Venango County)	16301
Oilcreek (Venango County) (Township)	16341
Oklahoma (Clearfield County)	15801
Oklahoma (Westmoreland County)	15613
Okome	17739
Olanta	16863
Old Bethany	15688
Old Boston	18640
Old Clarendon (Part of Clarendon)	16313
Old Concord	15329
Old Crabtree	15650
Old Enon	16120
Old Forge	18518
Oldframe	15478
Old Junction (Part of Somerset)	15501
Old Line	17545
Old Lycoming (Township)	17701
Old Meadow	15683
Old Orchard (Monroe County)	18370
Old Orchard (Northampton County)	18042
Old Port	17082
Old Stanton (Part of New Stanton)	15672
Old Zionsville	18068
Oleopolis	16301
Oley	19547
Oley (Township)	19547
Oley Furnace	19547
Oliphant Furnace	15401
Oliveburg	15764
Oliver (Fayette County)	15472
Oliver (Jefferson County) (Township)	15825
Oliver (Mifflin County) (Township)	17044
Oliver (Perry County) (Township)	17074
Oliver No. 2 (Fayette County)	15401
Oliver No. 3 (Fayette County)	15401
Olivers Mills (Part of Laurel Run)	18702
Olivet	15618
Olney (Part of Philadelphia)	19120
Olwen Heights	18444
Olyphant	18447
Oneida (Butler County)	16001
Oneida (Huntingdon County) (Township)	16652
Oneida (Schuylkill County)	18242
Onnalinda	15955
Ono	17077
Ontario	15330
Ontelaunee (Township)	19605
Opp	17756
Oppermans Corner	19425
Option (Part of Baldwin)	15236
Orange (Columbia County) (Township)	17859
Orange (Luzerne County)	18612

Name	ZIP
Orangeville	17859
Orbisonia	17243
Orchard Beach	16428
Orchard Crossing	16686
Orchard Hill (Part of Mount Pleasant)	15666
Orchard Hills	15613
Orefield	18069
Oregon (Lancaster County)	17540
Oregon (Wayne County) (Township)	18431
Oregon Hill	16938
Ore Hill	16673
Oreland	19075
Oreland Gardens	19075
Oreminea	16693
Ore Valley	17403
Orient	15420
Oriental	17045
Oriole	17740
Ormrod	18037
Ormsby	16726
Orners Corner	16601
Orrstown	17244
Orrtanna	17353
Orrville	15144
Orson	18449
Orvilla	19440
Orviston	16864
Orwell	18837
Orwell (Township)	18837
Orwigsburg	17961
Orwin	17980
Osborne	15143
Osceola	16942
Osceola (Township)	16942
Osceola Mills	16666
Osgood	16125
Oshanter	16830
Ostend	15757
Osterburg	16667
Osterhout	18657
Oswayo (Potter County)	16915
Oswayo (Potter County) (Township)	16748
Ottawa	17821
Otter Creek (Township)	16125
Otto (Township)	16745
Ottsville	18942
Ott Town	15537
Outcrop	15478
Outlet	18612
Outwood	17963
Oval	17740
Overbrook (Allegheny County)	15210
Overbrook (Philadelphia County)	19151
Overbrook Hills	19151
Overfield (Township)	18414
Overholt Acres	15642
Overleigh	19004
Overlook	17601
Overlook Heights	16801
Overlook Springs	18049
Overton	18833
Overton (Township)	18833
Overview	17053
Owensdale	15425
Oxbow Meadows	18914
Oxford (Adams County) (Township)	17350
Oxford (Chester County)	19363
Oxford Valley	19030
Oyster Point	17602
Packer (Township)	18255
Packerton	18235
Paddytown	15551
Pageville	16401
Paint (Clarion County) (Township)	16254
Paint (Somerset County)	15963
Paint (Somerset County) (Township)	15963
Paintersville (Mifflin County)	17044
Paintersville (Westmoreland County)	15672
Paintertown	15642
Paisley	15320
Paletown	18944
Palm	18070
Palmdale	17033
Palmer (Township)	18042
Palmer Heights	18042
Palmer Park	18042
Palmerton	18071
Palmerton East (Part of Palmerton)	18071
Palmertown	15716
Palmyra (Lebanon County)	17078

478 **PENNSYLVANIA** Palmyra-Philadelphia

Name	ZIP
Palmyra (Pike County) (Township)	18451
Palmyra (Wayne County) (Township)	18428
Palo Alto (Bedford County)	15545
Palo Alto (Schuylkill County)	17901
Palomino Farms	18976
Pancoast	15851
Panic	15851
Panorama Village	16801
Pansy	15864
Pansy Hill	17042
Panther	18445
Paoli (Chester County)	19301
Paper Mills (Part of Bryn Athyn)	19009
Paradise	17562
Paradise (Township)	17562
Paradise (Monroe County) (Township)	18326
Paradise (Schuylkill County)	17963
Paradise (York County) (Township)	17301
Paradise Falls	18326
Paradise Valley	18326
Pardee	16866
Pardeesville	18243
Pardoe	16137
Pardus	15851
Paris	15021
Park (Part of Vandergrift)	15690
Parkchester	19380
Park Crest	18214
Parker (Armstrong County)	16049
Parker (Butler County) (Township)	16001
Parker Ford	19457
Parkersville	19380
Parkesburg	19365
Park Forest Village	16801
Park Gate	16117
Park Heights	17331
Parkhill	15945
Park Hills (Centre County)	16801
Park Hills (York County)	17331
Parkland	19047
Park Manor	19607
Park Meadows	15642
Park Place	17948
Parks (Township)	15690
Parkside	19015
Parkside Courts	18104
Parkside Manor (Part of Parkside)	19015
Parkstown	16101
Parktown Estates	19067
Parkview	15215
Parkview Gardens	18052
Park View Heights (Part of Bellefonte)	16823
Parkville (York County)	17331
Parkway Center (Part of Green Tree)	15220
Parkway Center Mall (Part of Pittsburgh)	15220
Park Way Manor	18104
Parkwood	15774
Parnassus (Part of New Kensington)	15068
Parryville	18244
Parsonville (Butler County)	16050
Parsonville (Clearfield County)	16651
Parvin	17751
Paschall (Part of Philadelphia)	19142
Passer	18036
Patchel Run (Part of Sugarcreek)	16323
Patchinville	15724
Patterson (Township)	15010
Patterson Grove	18655
Patterson Heights	15010
Patterson Hill (Part of Lincoln)	15037
Pattersons Mill	15312
Patterson Township	15010
Pattersonville	17967
Patton (Cambria County)	16668
Patton (Centre County) (Township)	16801
Patton (Washington County)	15301
Pattonville	16226
Paulton	15613
Paupack (Pike County)	18451
Paupack (Wayne County) (Township)	18428
Paupack Gardens	18451
Pavia	16655
Paxinos	17860
Paxtang	17111

Name	ZIP
Paxtang Manor	17111
Paxton	17017
Paxtonia	17111
Paxtonville	17861
Peacedale	19363
Peach Bottom (Lancaster County)	17563
Peach Bottom (York County) (Township)	17314
Peach Bottom Village	17563
Peach Glen	17306
Pealertown	17859
Peanut (Lawrence County)	16116
Peanut (Westmoreland County)	15627
Pearl	16342
Pebble Hill	18901
Pecan	16342
Pechin	15431
Pecks Pond	18328
Peckville (Part of Blakely)	18452
Pemberton	16683
Pen Argyl	18072
Penarth	19004
Penbrook	17103
Penbryn	17765
Pendle Hill	19086
Penfield	15849
Penfield Downs	19151
Penllyn	19422
Pen Mar	17268
Penn (Berks County) (Township)	19506
Penn (Butler County) (Township)	16001
Penn (Centre County) (Township)	16832
Penn (Chester County) (Township)	19390
Penn (Clearfield County) (Township)	16838
Penn (Cumberland County) (Township)	17257
Penn (Huntingdon County) (Township)	16647
Penn (Lancaster County) (Township)	17545
Penn (Lycoming County) (Township)	17737
Penn (Perry County) (Township)	17020
Penn (Snyder County) (Township)	17870
Penn (Westmoreland County)	15675
Penn (Westmoreland County) (Township)	15636
Penn (York County) (Township)	17331
Penn Allen	18064
Pennbrook (Part of Lansdale)	19446
Penn Center (Part of Philadelphia)	19102
Penncraft	15433
Penndel	19047
Pennersville	17268
Penn Estates	18320
Pennfield	19007
Penn Five	16666
Penn Forest (Township)	18210
Penn Glyn (Part of Irwin)	15642
Pennhall	16875
Penn Heights (Part of Hanover)	17331
Penn Hill	17563
Penn Hill Homes	19022
Penn Hills (Allegheny County) (Township)	15235
Penn Hills (Allegheny County)	15235
Penn Hills Shopping Center	15235
Pennhurst Center	19475
Penn Lake Park	18661
Pennline	16424
Penn Pines	19018
Penn Pitt	15338
Penn Rose Park	17601
Penn Run	15765
Pennsburg	18073
Pennsbury (Township)	19317
Pennsbury Heights	19067
Pennsbury Village	15205
Penns Creek	17862
Pennsdale	17756
Pennside (Berks County)	19606
Pennside (Erie County)	16401
Penns Park	18943
Penn Square Village	19401
Pennsville (Fayette County)	15425

Name	ZIP
Pennsville (Northampton County)	18067
Penns Woods	15642
Pennsylvania Furnace	16865
Penn Taft (Part of West Mifflin)	15222
Pennvale	17701
Penn Valley	19072
Penn Valley Terrace	19047
Penn Village (Part of Pottstown)	19464
Pennville	17331
Pennwyn	19607
Penn Wynne	19151
Penobscot	18707
Penowa	15312
Penryn	17564
Pequea (Lancaster County)	17565
Pequea (Lancaster County) (Township)	17584
Percy	15456
Perdix	17020
Perkasie	18944
Perkiomen (Township)	19426
Perkiomen Heights	18073
Perkiomen Junction	19460
Perkiomen Village	19426
Perkiomenville	18074
Perrine Corners	16153
Perry (Armstrong County) (Township)	16041
Perry (Berks County) (Township)	19526
Perry (Clarion County) (Township)	16049
Perry (Fayette County) (Township)	15482
Perry (Greene County) (Township)	15349
Perry (Jefferson County) (Township)	15767
Perry (Lawrence County) (Township)	16117
Perry (Mercer County) (Township)	16130
Perry (Snyder County) (Township)	17853
Perrymont	15237
Perryopolis	15473
Perry Square (Part of Erie)	16507
Perrysville (Allegheny County)	15237
Perrysville (Westmoreland County)	15618
Perryville (Clarion County)	16049
Perryville (Lycoming County)	17728
Perulack	17021
Peters (Franklin County) (Township)	17236
Peters (Washington County) (Township)	15317
Petersburg	16669
Peters Corner	18934
Peters Creek (Part of Clairton)	15025
Petersville	18067
Petrolia	16050
Pettis	16335
Pheasant Hill	17601
Pheasant Ridge	18901
Philadelphia	19101-96

For specific Philadelphia Zip Codes call (215) 895-9000

COLLEGES & UNIVERSITIES

Name	ZIP
Chestnut Hill College	19118
Drexel University	19104
Hahnemann University	19102
Holy Family College	19114
LaSalle University	19141
Philadelphia Colleges of Art	19102
Philadelphia College of Pharmacy and Science	19104
Philadelphia College of Textiles and Science	19144
St. Joseph's University	19131
Temple University	19122
University of Pennsylvania	19104

FINANCIAL INSTITUTIONS

Name	ZIP
Beneficial Mutual Savings Bank	19107
Brown Brothers Harriman & Co	19102
Cheltenham Bank	19111
Cheltenham Federal Savings & Loan Association	19111

Philadelphia **PENNSYLVANIA** 479

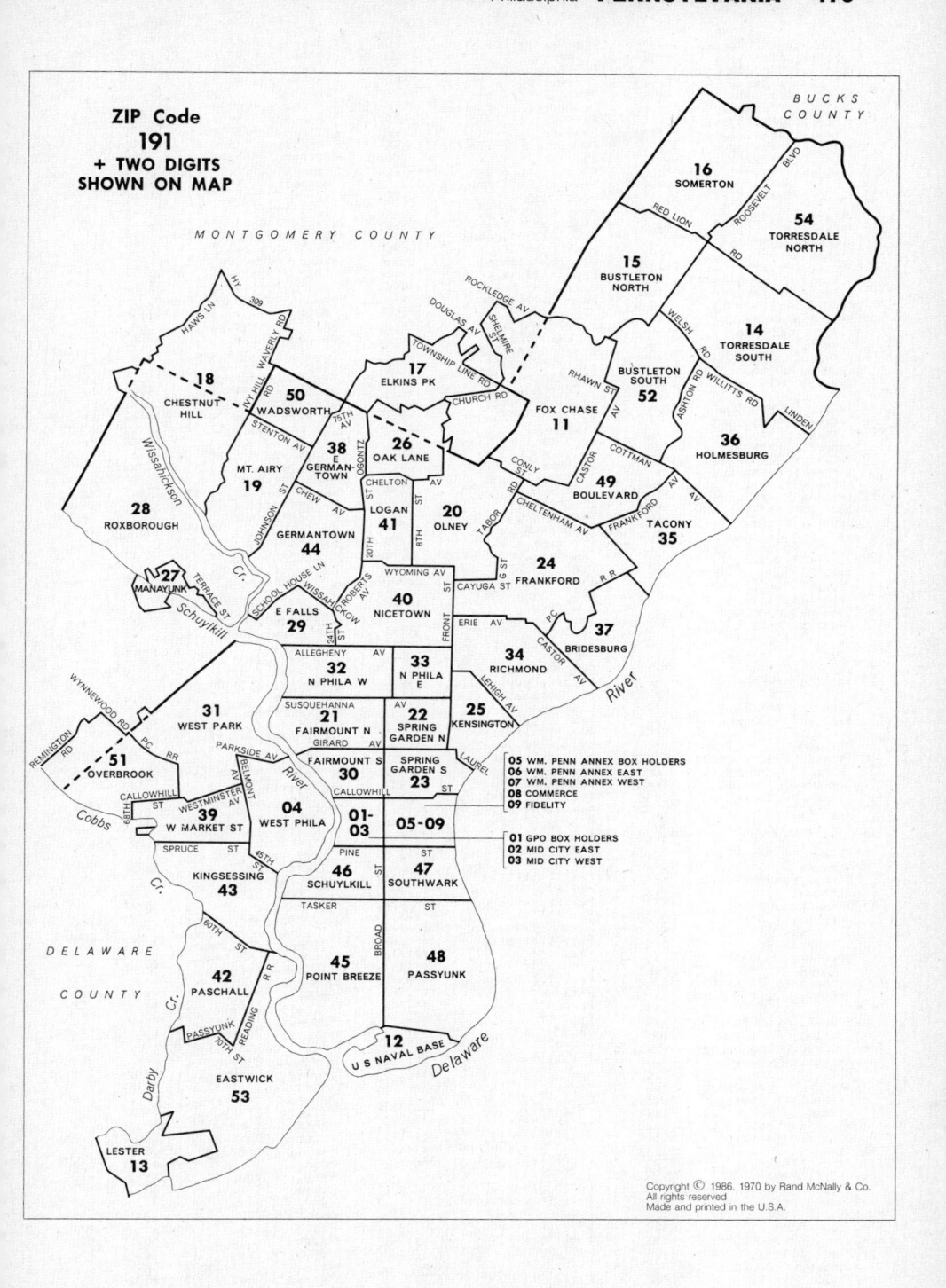

480 PENNSYLVANIA Philatelic-Pleasant Corners

	ZIP
Fidelity Federal Savings & Loan Association	19375
Fox Chase Federal Savings & Loan Association	19111
Frankford Trust Company	19124
Roxborough-Manayunk Federal Savings & Loan Association	19128
Third Federal Savings & Loan Association of Philadelphia	19124

HOSPITALS

	ZIP
Albert Einstein Medical Center	19141
Children's Hospital of Philadelphia	19104
Episcopal Hospital	19125
Frankford Hospital of the City of Philadelphia	19114
Friedman Hospital of the Home for the Jewish Aged	19141
Germantown Hospital and Medical Center	19144
Graduate Hospital	19103
Hahnemann University Hospital	19102
Hospital of Philadelphia College of Osteopathic Medicine	19131
Hospital of the Medical College of Pennsylvania	19129
Hospital of the University of Pennsylvania	19104
Lankenau Hospital	19151
Methodist Hospital	19148
Nazareth Hospital	19152
Pennsylvania Hospital	19107
Presbyterian Medical Center of Philadelphia	19104
Temple University Hospital	19140
Thomas Jefferson University Hospital	19107
Veterans Administration Medical Center	19104

HOTELS/MOTELS

	ZIP
The Barclay Hotel	19103
Four Seasons Hotel Philadelphia	19103
Guest Quarters	19153
Holiday Inn-Independence Mall	19106
The Latham	19103
Philadelphia Airport Marriott	19153
Quality Inn Airport	19145
The Warwick	19103
Wyndham Franklin Plaza Hotel	19103

MILITARY INSTALLATIONS

	ZIP
Defense Industrial Aviation Supply Center	19111
Defense Personnel Support Center	19101
Fort Mifflin Engineer Reservation	19153
Naval Publications and Forms Center	19120
Naval Regional Medical Center	19145
Naval Station, Philadelphia	19112
Philadelphia Naval Shipyard	19112

	ZIP
Philatelic (Part of State College)	16801
Philipsburg (Centre County)	16866
Philipsburg (Washington County)	15419
Phillips (Fayette County)	15401
Phillips (Tioga County)	16918
Phillipston	16248
Phillipsville (Chester County)	19320
Phillipsville (Erie County)	16442
Philmont	19006
Philmont Manor	19006
Philmont Park	19006
Phoenix Park	17901
Phoenixville	19460
Piatt (Township)	17740
Picture Rocks	17762
Pierce (Allegheny County)	15025
Pierce (Armstrong County)	16240
Pierceville	17327
Pigeon	16239
Pike (Berks County) (Township)	19547
Pike (Bradford County) (Township)	18829
Pike (Clearfield County) (Township)	16833
Pike (Potter County) (Township)	16922
Pikeland	19425
Pikes Peak	15765
Piketown	17112
Pikeville	19547
Pilgrim Gardens	19026
Pilgrimham	16232
Pillow	17080
Pine (Allegheny County) (Township)	15090
Pine (Armstrong County) (Township)	16259
Pine (Clearfield County) (Township)	15849
Pine (Clinton County)	17748
Pine (Columbia County) (Township)	17846
Pine (Crawford County) (Township)	16424
Pine (Indiana County) (Township)	15745
Pine (Lycoming County) (Township)	16938
Pine (Mercer County) (Township)	16127
Pine Bank	15352
Pine Beach	18428
Pinebrook	17011
Pine Creek (Clinton County) (Township)	17721
Pinecreek (Jefferson County) (Township)	15825
Pinecrest	19047
Pinecroft	16601
Pinedale (Part of Deer Lake)	17961
Pine Flats	15728
Pine Forge	19548
Pine Glen (Centre County)	16845
Pine Glen (Mifflin County)	17044
Pine Grove (Perry County)	17047
Pine Grove (Schuylkill County)	17963
Pine Grove (Schuylkill County) (Township)	17963
Pine Grove (Susquehanna County)	18446
Pinegrove (Venango County) (Township)	16301
Pine Grove (Warren County) (Township)	16345
Pine Grove Furnace	17324
Pine Grove Mills	16868
Pine Hill (Armstrong County)	16201
Pine Hill (Schuylkill County)	17901
Pine Hill (Somerset County)	15530
Pine Ridge	19063
Pine Run (Bucks County)	18901
Pine Run (Lycoming County)	17744
Pine Summit	17846
Pine Swamp	19520
Pinetown	17339
Pinetree (Part of Scottdale)	15683
Pine Valley	16405
Pine Valley Estates	18901
Pine View	18707
Pineville (Bucks County)	18946
Pineville (Warren County)	16420
Pinewood	19054
Piney	16214
Piney (Township)	16255
Piney Fork	15129
Pinola	17257
Pipersville	18947
Pitcairn	15140
Pitman	17964
Pitt Gas	15322
Pittock	15136
Pitts	16901
Pittsburgh	15201-90
	15122-23

For specific Pittsburgh Zip Codes call (412) 359-7860

COLLEGES & UNIVERSITIES

	ZIP
Carlow College	15213
Carnegie-Mellon University	15213
Duquesne University	15282
La Roche College	15237
Point Park College	15222
University of Pittsburgh	15260

FINANCIAL INSTITUTIONS

	ZIP
Allegheny Valley Bank of Pittsburgh	15201
Bell Federal Savings & Loan Association of Bellevue	15222
Dollar Bank, A Federal Savings Bank	15222
First Federal Savings & Loan Association of Pittsburgh	15222
First Home Savings Association	15222
First South Savings Association	15203
Great American Federal Savings & Loan Association	15236
Landmark Savings Association	15222
North Side Deposit Bank	15212
Peoples Bank of Unity-Penn Hills	15239
Pittsburgh Home Savings & Loan Association	15222
Pittsburgh National Bank	15222
The Union National Bank of Pittsburgh	15278
West View Savings & Loan Association	15237

HOSPITALS

	ZIP
Allegheny General Hospital	15212
Magee-Womens Hospital	15213
Mercy Hospital of Pittsburgh	15219
Montefiore Hospital	15213
North Hills Passavant Hospital	15237
Presbyterian-University Hospital	15213
Shadyside Hospital	15232
St. Clair Memorial Hospital	15243
St. Francis Medical Center	15201
St. Margaret Memorial Hospital	15215
Veterans Administration Medical Center	15240
Western Pennsylvania Hospital	15224

HOTELS/MOTELS

	ZIP
Airport Hilton Inn	15231
Best Western Parkway Center Inn	15220
Days Inn-Redwood	15216
Harley of Pittsburgh	15235
Hyatt Pittsburgh at Chatham Center	15219
Pittsburgh Green Tree Marriott	15205
Sheraton Hotel at Station Square	15219

MILITARY INSTALLATIONS

	ZIP
Greater Pittsburgh International Airport, 911th TAG (AFRES)	15231
Hays Army Ammunition Plant	15207
Pennsylvania Air National Guard, FB6381	15231
United States Army Engineer District for Pittsburgh	15222
United States Army Support Element and Maintenance Division, Neville Island	15225

	ZIP
Pittsburgh Plate Plan	16226
Pittsburgh Valley	17516
Pittsfield	16340
Pittsfield (Township)	16340
Pittston	18640-44

For specific Pittston Zip Codes call (717) 654-3313

	ZIP
Pittston Junction (Part of Wilkes-Barre)	18705
Pittsville	16374
Plainfield (Cumberland County)	17081
Plainfield (Northampton County) (Township)	18064
Plain Grove (Township)	16156
Plains	18705
Plains (Township)	18705
Plainsville	18705
Plainview	17325
Planebrook	19355
Plank	16938
Platea	16417
Plateau Heights	16335
Plattsville	16646
Plaza (Part of Butler)	16001
Plaza Heights (Part of Hanover)	17331
Pleasant (Township)	16365
Pleasant Corners	18235

Pleasant Gap-Radebaugh **PENNSYLVANIA** **481**

Name	ZIP
Pleasant Gap	16823
Pleasant Grove (Lancaster County)	17563
Pleasant Grove (Washington County)	15323
Pleasant Hall	17246
Pleasant Hill (Cambria County)	15738
Pleasant Hill (mail Grassflat)	16839
Pleasant Hill (mail Philipsburg)	16866
Pleasant Hill (Delaware County)	19063
Pleasant Hill (Fayette County)	15425
Pleasant Hill (Indiana County)	15701
Pleasant Hill (Lawrence County)	16123
Pleasant Hill (Lebanon County)	17042
Pleasant Hill (York County)	17331
Pleasant Hills (Allegheny County)	15236
Pleasant Hills (Dauphin County)	17112
Pleasant Mount	18453
Pleasant Union	15552
Pleasant Unity	15676
Pleasant Valley (Blair County)	16602
Pleasant Valley (Bucks County)	18951
Pleasant Valley (Lancaster County)	17604
Pleasant Valley (Potter County) (Township)	16743
Pleasant Valley (Schuylkill County)	17963
Pleasant Valley (Westmoreland County)	15642
Pleasant Valley Estates	18058
Pleasant View (Armstrong County)	15690
Pleasantview (Beaver County)	15010
Pleasant View (Centre County)	16823
Pleasant View (Franklin County)	17201
Pleasantview (Juniata County)	17082
Pleasant View (York County)	17356
Pleasant Village (Part of Altoona)	16602
Pleasantville	16341
Pleasureville	17402
Pleasureville Heights	17402
Plowville	19540
Plum (Township)	16354
Plum (Allegheny County)	15239
Plum (Venango County)	16354
Plumbridge	19056
Plumb Sock	15329
Plum Creek (Allegheny County)	15239
Plumcreek (Armstrong County) (Township)	15774
Plumer	16301
Plummer	15458
Plum Run	17238
Plumsock	19073
Plumstead (Township)	18923
Plumsteadville	18949
Plumville	16246
Plunketts Creek (Township)	17701
Plymouth (Luzerne County)	18651
Plymouth (Luzerne County) (Township)	18651
Plymouth (Montgomery County) (Township)	19401
Plymouth Junction (Part of Larksville)	18651
Plymouth Meeting	19462
Plymouth Meeting Mall	19462
Plymouth Township	19401
Plymouth Valley	19401
Plymptonville	16830
Pocahontas	15552
Pocono (Township)	18372
Pocono Country Place	18466
Pocono Farms	18466
Pocono Farms East	18466
Pocono Heights	18301
Pocono Lake	18347
Pocono Lake Preserve	18348
Pocono Manor	18349
Pocono Mt. Lake Forest	18328
Pocono Park	18360
Pocono Pines	18350

Name	ZIP
Pocono Summit	18346
Pocono Summit Estates	18346
Pocopson	19366
Pocopson (Township)	19366
Poets Village	15701
Pogue	17264
Point (Bedford County)	15559
Point (Northumberland County) (Township)	17857
Point Breeze (Allegheny County)	15208
Point Breeze (Philadelphia County)	19145
Point Marion	15474
Point Phillip	18014
Point Pleasant	18950
Point Ridge Farms	17011
Point View	16693
Pokeytown	15563
Poland	15327
Polk (Jefferson County) (Township)	15825
Polk (Monroe County) (Township)	18333
Polk (Venango County)	16342
Polktown	17268
Polk Valley	18055
Pomeroy	19367
Pomeroy Heights	19320
Pond Bank	17201
Pond Creek	18661
Pond Eddy	12770
Ponderosa	18451
Pond Hill	18660
Pont	16401
Poplar Grove (Fayette County)	15425
Poplar Grove (Lancaster County)	17543
Porkey	16347
Portage (Cambria County)	15946
Portage (Cambria County) (Township)	15946
Portage (Cameron County) (Township)	15834
Portage (Potter County) (Township)	16720
Portage Creek	16743
Port Allegany	16743
Port Barnett	15825
Port Blanchard	18640
Port Carbon	17965
Port Clinton	19549
Porter (Township)	16222
Porter (Lycoming County) (Township)	17740
Porter (Pike County) (Township)	18301
Porter (Schuylkill County) (Township)	17980
Porter (Clarion County) (Township)	16242
Porter (Clinton County) (Township)	17751
Porter (Huntingdon County) (Township)	16611
Porter (Jefferson County)	15767
Porters Sideling	17354
Portersville	16051
Port Griffith	18640
Port Indian	19401
Port Jenkins	18661
Port Kennedy	19406
Portland	18351
Portland Mills	15853
Port Matilda	16870
Port Providence	19453
Port Royal	17082
Port Trevorton	17864
Port Vue	15133
Possum Hollow (Part of New Beaver)	16157
Potetown	16673
Potosi	17327
Potter (Beaver County) (Township)	15061
Potter (Centre County) (Township)	16875
Potter Brook	16950
Pottersdale	16871
Potters Mills	16875
Potterville	18837
Pottsgrove (Montgomery County)	19464
Potts Grove (Northumberland County)	17865
Pottstown	19464
Pottstown Landing	19464
Pottsville	17901
P&OV Junction	15136
Powder Mill Village	15687

Name	ZIP
Powder Valley	18092
Powell	18832
Powells Valley	17032
Powelton	16677
Powys	17728
Poyntelle	18454
Prentisvale	16731
Prescott	17042
Prescottville	15851
President	16353
President (Township)	16301
Presidential Heights (Allegheny County)	15237
Presidential Heights (Franklin County)	17201
Presque Isle	16505
Presston	15136
Presto	15142
Preston (Luzerne County)	18706
Preston (Wayne County) (Township)	18455
Preston Hill	17935
Preston Park	18455
Pretoria	15935
Price (Township)	18301
Priceburg (Part of Dickson City)	18519
Pricedale	15072
Pricetown	19522
Priceville	18417
Primos	19018
Primos-Secane	19018
Primrose (Schuylkill County)	17901
Primrose (Washington County)	15057
Princeton	16101
Pringle	18704
Pritchards Corner	16150
Prittstown	15666
Proctor	17701
Progress	17109
Prompton	18456
Prospect	16052
Prospect Gardens	17602
Prospect Heights	18017
Prospect Park (Cameron County)	15834
Prospect Park (Delaware County)	19076
Prospectville	19002
Prosperity	15329
Providence (Township)	17560
Providence Downe	19063
Providence Square	19426
Providence Village	19086
Provins Works	15461
Pughtown	19464
Puite	17110
Pulaski (Township)	16143
Pulaski (Beaver County) (Township)	15066
Pulaski (Lawrence County)	16143
Pulaski Township	15066
Punxsutawney	15767
Purcell	15535
Purchase Line	15729
Puritan (Cambria County)	15946
Puritan (Fayette County)	15458
Putnam (Township)	16917
Putneyville	16242
Puttstown	16678
Puzzletown	16635
Pymatuning (Township)	16125
Pyra	16226
Quakake	18245
Quaker Hills (Part of Millersville)	17551
Quaker Lake	18812
Quakertown	18951
Quaker Valley	17307
Quarryville	17566
Quecreek	15555
Queen (Bedford County)	16670
Queen (Forest County)	16321
Queen City	17820
Queensgate Shopping Center (Part of York)	17404
Queens Grant	19067
Queens Run	17745
Queenstown	16041
Quemahoning (Township)	15563
Quentin	17083
Quicks Bend	18846
Quicktown	18444
Quiggleville	17728
Quincy	17247
Quincy (Township)	17247
Quincy Hollow	19057
Raccoon (Township)	15001
Racine	15010
Radebaugh	15601

482 PENNSYLVANIA Radnor-Rockdale

	ZIP		ZIP		ZIP
Radnor (Township)	19087	Reflection Lakes	18417	Ridgeview	17112
Radnor Township	19087	Refton	17568	Ridgeview Park	15627
Rahns	19426	Regency Park (Part of Plum)	15239	Ridgeville	17821
Railroad	17355			Ridgewood (Berks County)	19508
Raineytown	15428	Regional Correctional Facility at Greensburg	15601	Ridgewood (Luzerne County)	18705
Rainsburg	15522	Register	17878	Ridgewood Farm	19380
Ralpho (Township)	17872	Rehrersburg	19550	Ridgway (Elk County)	15853
Ralphton	15563	Reidsburg	16214	Ridgway (Elk County) (Township)	15853
Ralston	17763	Reiffton	19606	Ridley (Township)	19033
Ramblewood	16865	Reightown	16686	Ridley Farms	19070
Ramey	16671	Reilly (Township)	17923	Ridley Gardens	19043
Ramona	17067	Reillys	16668	Ridley Park (Cumberland County)	17011
Ramsay Terrace (Part of Mount Pleasant)	15666	Reinerton	17980	Ridley Park (Delaware County)	19078
Ramsaytown	15825	Reinholds	17569	Ridley Parkview	19078
Ramsey	17740	Reinoeldville	17042	Ridley Township	19018
Ranavilla	17011	Reistville	17067	Riegelsville	18077
Rand (Part of Baldwin)	15227	Reitz	15824	Rienze	18853
Randolph (Township)	16327	Reitz No. 2	15924	Rife	17061
Rankin	15104	Relay	17313	Riggles Gap	16601
Ranshaw	17866	Reliance	18964	Riggs	18850
Ransom	18653	Rembrant	15728	Rillton	15678
Ransom (Township)	18411	Renfrew	16053	Rimer	16259
Rapho (Township)	17545	Rennerdale	15106	Rimersburg	16248
Rasler Run	15425	Reno (Part of Sugarcreek)	16343	Rimerton	16259
Rasleytown	18072	Renovo	17764	Rinely	17363
Rasselas	15870	Renton (Part of Plum)	15239	Ringdale	18614
Rathbun	15834	Republic	15475	Ringgold	15770
Rathmel	15851	Republican (Part of California)	15419	Ringgold (Township)	15770
Rattigan	16025	Republic-Merrittstown	15463	Ringing Hill	19464
Raubsville	18042	Reserve (Township)	15212	Ringing Rock Park	19464
Rauchtown	17740	Reserve Township	15212	Ringtown (Berks County)	19539
Rauschs	17960	Reservoir	16648	Ringtown (Schuylkill County)	17967
Raven Creek	17814	Retort	16677	Risher Mine Siding (Part of West Mifflin)	15122
Raven Run	17946	Retreat	18621	Rising Sun	18080
Ravine	17966	Revere	18953	Riterville	16738
Rawlinsville	17532	Revloc	15948	Ritzie Village	17112
Rayburn (Township)	16201	Rew	16744	River Hill	15063
Raymilton	16342	Reward	17062	Riverside (Cambria County)	15904
Raymond	16923	Rexford	16921	Riverside (Lackawanna County)	18403
Rayne (Township)	15747	Rexis	15961	Riverside (Northumberland County)	17868
Raytown	15742	Rexmont (Part of Cornwall)	17085	Riverton	18013
Rea	15356	Rextown	18080	River Valley	15024
Reade (Township)	16619	Reyburn	18655	River View (Armstrong County)	15690
Reading	19601-12	Reynolds	18252	Riverview (Beaver County)	15010
For specific Reading Zip Codes call (215) 921-7050		Reynoldsdale	15554	Riverview (Clearfield County)	16830
Reading (Township)	17350	Reynolds Heights	16125	Riverview (Clinton County)	17745
Reading Mines	15563	Reynoldsville	15851	River View (Washington County)	15067
Reagantown	15679	Rheems	17570	Riverview Acres	18080
Reamstown	17567	Rhone (Part of Nanticoke)	18634	Riverview Heights	17011
Reamstown Heights	17567	Ribot	16669	River View Park	19605
Rebel Hill	19406	Rice (Township)	18707	Rixford	16745
Rebersburg	16872	Rices Landing	15357	Roadside	17268
Rebuck	17867	Riceville	16432	Roaring Branch	17765
Rector	15677	Richards Grove	17774	Roaring Brook (Township)	18444
Redbank (Armstrong County) (Township)	16240	Richardsville	15825	Roaring Brook Estates	18444
Redbank (Clarion County) (Township)	16224	Richboro	18954	Roaring Creek (Columbia County)	17820
Red Bank (Union County)	17844	Richboro Manor	18954	Roaring Creek (Columbia County) (Township)	17820
Redbird	15946	Richeyville (Part of Centerville)	15358	Roaring Spring	16673
Red Bridge (Franklin County)	17201	Richfield	17086	Robb	15944
Red Bridge (McKean County)	16735	Richfol (Part of Canonsburg)	15317	Robert Bruce West	19040
Redclyffe	16239	Rich Hill (Bucks County)	18951	Robert Morris College	15108
Red Cross	17823	Richhill (Greene County) (Township)	15377	Robertsdale	16674
Redds Mill	15022	Rich Hill (Washington County)	15347	Robertsville	15767
Red Gate Farms	18901	Richland (Allegheny County) (Township)	15044	Robeson (Township)	19508
Red Hill (Blair County)	16601	Richland (Bucks County) (Township)	18951	Robeson Crossing	19508
Red Hill (Montgomery County)	18076	Richland (Cambria County) (Township)	15904	Robeson Extension	16693
Redington	18055	Richland (Cambria County)	16636	Robesonia	19551
Red Lion (Berks County)	18062	Richland (Clarion County) (Township)	16049	Robindale	15954
Red Lion (Chester County)	19348	Richland (Lebanon County)	17087	Robin Hood Lakes	18058
Red Lion (York County)	17356	Richland (Venango County) (Township)	16373	Robinson (Allegheny County) (Township)	15136
Red Mill	15840	Richlandtown	18955	Robinson (Indiana County)	15949
Red Oak	18436	Richmond (Berks County) (Township)	19530	Robinson (Lawrence County)	16132
Red Rock (Luzerne County)	17814	Richmond (Crawford County) (Township)	16327	Robinson (Washington County) (Township)	15057
Red Rock (McKean County)	16727	Richmond (Northampton County)	18013	Rocherty	17042
Red Rose Gate	19056	Richmond (Philadelphia County)	19134	Rochester (Beaver County)	15074
Redrun	17517	Richmond (Tioga County) (Township)	16933	Rochester (Beaver County) (Township)	15074
Redstone	15438	Richmondale	18421	Rochester Mills	15771
Redstone (Township)	15442	Richmond Furnace	17224	Rock	17972
Redstone Junction	15472	Richview Manor	15904	Rockdale (Bucks County)	19007
Reduction	15479	Riddlesburg	16672	Rockdale (Crawford County) (Township)	16403
Reed (Dauphin County) (Township)	17032	Riddlewood	19063	Rockdale (Delaware County)	19014
Reed (Northumberland County)	17860	Riderville	16738	Rockdale (Jefferson County)	15840
Reeder	18938	Ridgebury	14894		
Reeders	18352	Ridgebury (Township)	16914		
Reeds Gap	17035	Ridge Valley	18960		
Reeds Road	19335				
Reedsville	17084				
Reels Corners	15926				
Reemersville	18426				
Reese	16648				
Reesedale	16210				
Reevesdale	18252				

PENNSYLVANIA 483

Place	ZIP
Rockdale (Lehigh County)	18080
Rockefeller (Township)	17801
Rock Glen	18246
Rock Hill (Bucks County)	18960
Rockhill (Lancaster County)	17516
Rockhill Furnace	17249
Rockingham	15924
Rock Lake	18453
Rockland (Township)	16374
Rockland (Berks County) (Township)	19522
Rockland (Venango County)	16374
Rockledge	19111
Rockport	18255
Rockrimmin Ridge	17540
Rock Run	19320
Rocksprings	16865
Rockton (Clearfield County)	15856
Rocktown	15688
Rockview	16823
Rockville (Armstrong County)	16226
Rockville (Cambria County)	15956
Rockville (Chester County)	19344
Rockville (Clarion County)	16242
Rockville (Dauphin County)	17110
Rockville (Juniata County)	17059
Rockville (Mifflin County)	17004
Rockville (Northampton County)	18038
Rockwood (Lebanon County)	17042
Rockwood (Somerset County)	15557
Rock Works	15461
Rocky Forest	18623
Rocky Grove (Part of Sugarcreek)	16323
Rocky Hill	19380
Rodman	16673
Roedersville	17963
Rogers Mills	15469
Rogers Stop	15022
Rogerstown	15425
Rogersville	15359
Rogertown	16313
Rohrerstown	17603
Rohrsburg	17859
Roler	17315
Rolfe (Part of Johnsonburg)	15845
Rolling Glen	19341
Rolling Hills (Beaver County)	15061
Rolling Hills (Berks County)	19607
Rolling Hills (Lehigh County)	18052
Rolling Meadows	15370
Romansville	19320
Romar	15943
Rome (Bradford County)	18837
Rome (Bradford County) (Township)	18850
Rome (Crawford County) (Township)	16354
Romney	15446
Ronco	15476
Ronks	17572
Rook (Part of Green Tree)	15220
Roosevelt Mall (Part of Philadelphia)	19149
Roots Crossing	16686
Rosas	12770
Roscoe	15477
Rose (Township)	15825
Roseann	17063
Rose Bud	16627
Roseburg	17074
Rosecrans	17747
Rose Crest (Part of Monroeville)	15146
Rosedale (Allegheny County)	15147
Rosedale (Chester County)	19317
Rosedale (Fayette County)	15401
Rosedale (Greene County)	15327
Rosedale Heights	15147
Roseglen	17020
Rosehill (Part of Philadelphia)	19140
Rose Hollow	19067
Rosemont (Delaware County)	19010
Rosemont (Montgomery County)	19010
Rose Point	16101
Roses	16239
Roseto	18013
Rose Valley (Delaware County)	19063
Rose Valley (Montgomery County)	19002
Rose Valley Acres	19063
Roseville (Jefferson County)	15825
Roseville (Tioga County)	16933
Rosewood Gardens	18974
Roslyn (Chester County)	19380
Roslyn (Montgomery County)	19001
Ross (Allegheny County) (Township)	15237
Ross (Luzerne County) (Township)	18656
Ross (Monroe County) (Township)	18353
Ross Common	18353
Rossford	16226
Rossiter	15772
Rosslyn Farms	15106
Rossmere	17601
Rossmoyne	17011
Ross Siding	17723
Rosston	16226
Ross Township	15237
Rossville	17358
Rostraver	15012
Rostraver (Township)	15012
Rote	17751
Rothsville	17543
Rough and Ready	17941
Roulette	16746
Roulette (Township)	16746
Round Top (Adams County)	17325
Round Top (Bedford County)	16679
Roundtown	17404
Rouseville	16344
Rouzerville	17250
Rowes Run	15442
Rowland	18457
Rowland Park	19012
Rowles	15757
Roxborough (Part of Philadelphia)	19128
Roxbury (Cumberland County)	17055
Roxbury (Franklin County)	17251
Roxbury (Somerset County)	15530
Royal (Fayette County)	15422
Royal (Susquehanna County)	18441
Royalton	17057
Royer	16693
Royersford	19468
Roystone	16347
Roytown	15501
Rozel Park	18966
Ruble	15478
Ruchsville	18037
Rudytown	17070
Ruffcreek	15329
Ruffs Dale	15679
Ruggles	18636
Rummel	15963
Rummerfield	18853
Rundell	16406
Running Brooke	15701
Runville	16823
Rupert	17815
Ruppsville	18106
Rural Ridge	15075
Rural Valley	16249
Ruscombmanor (Township)	19522
Rush (Township)	18801
Rush (Centre County) (Township)	16866
Rush (Dauphin County) (Township)	17980
Rush (Northumberland County) (Township)	17821
Rush (Schuylkill County) (Township)	18252
Rush (Susquehanna County)	18801
Rushland	18956
Rushtown	17821
Rushville	18839
Russell	16345
Russell Hill	18657
Russellton	15076
Russellville (Chester County)	19363
Russellville (Huntingdon County)	16657
Rutan	15341
Rutherford	17111
Rutherford Park	17036
Ruthford	15955
Ruthfred Acres (Part of Bethel Park)	15102
Rutland (Township)	16933
Rutledge	19070
Rutledgedale	18469
Ryan (Township)	18214
Ryans Corner	18940
Rydal	19046
Ryde	17051
Rye (Township)	17053
Ryerson Station	15380
Ryot	15521
Rywal Park	19020
Sabinsville	16943
Sabula	15801
Saco (Bradford County)	18848
Saco (Lackawanna County)	18436
Sacramento	17968
Saddle Brook	18101
Saddlebrook Village I and II	19565
Sadlers Corner	16301
Sadsbury (Chester County) (Township)	19369
Sadsbury (Crawford County) (Township)	16316
Sadsbury (Lancaster County) (Township)	17509
Sadsburyville	19369
Saegersville	18053
Saegertown	16433
Safe Harbor	17516
Sagamore (Armstrong County)	16250
Sagamore (Fayette County)	15446
Sagamore Hills	18101
Saginaw	17347
Sagon	17872
St. Augustine	16636
St. Benedict	15773
St. Boniface	16675
St. Charles	16242
St. Clair (Schuylkill County)	17970
St. Clair (Westmoreland County)	15601
St. Clair (Westmoreland County) (Township)	15954
St. Clairsville	16667
St. Davids	19087
St. George	16374
St. Johns	18247
St. Joseph	18818
St. Lawrence (Berks County)	19606
St. Lawrence (Cambria County)	16668
St. Leonard	18940
St. Marys	15857
St. Michael	15951
St. Michael-Sidman	15951
St. Nicholas	17948
St. Paul	15552
St. Peters	19470
St. Petersburg	16054
St. Thomas	17252
St. Thomas (Township)	17201
St. Vincent College	15650
St. Vincent Shaft	15650
Salco	15530
Salem (Clarion County) (Township)	16232
Salem (Clearfield County)	15801
Salem (Franklin County)	17201
Salem (Luzerne County) (Township)	18603
Salem (Mercer County)	16125
Salem (Mercer County) (Township)	16130
Salem (Snyder County)	17870
Salem (Wayne County) (Township)	18444
Salem (Westmoreland County) (Township)	15601
Salem Harbor	19020
Salemville	16664
Salford (Montgomery County)	18957
Salford (Montgomery County) (Township)	18969
Salford Heights	19438
Salfordville	18958
Salida (Part of Baldwin)	15227
Salina	15680
Salisbury (Lancaster County) (Township)	17535
Salisbury (Lehigh County) (Township)	18103
Salisbury (Somerset County)	15558
Salisbury Heights	17527
Salix	15952
Salladasburg	17740
Salona	17767
Saltillo	17253
Saltlick (Township)	15446
Saltsburg	15681
Salunga	17538
Saluvia	17228
Sample Heights	15116

484 PENNSYLVANIA Sample Run-Shirks Corner

Name	ZIP
Sample Run (Part of Clymer)	15728
Sampson	15063
Sanatoga	19464
Sanatoga Park	19464
Sanbourn	16651
Sandbeach	17033
Sand Hill (Lebanon County)	17042
Sandhill (Monroe County)	18354
Sand Hill (Westmoreland County)	15666
Sand Patch	15552
Sand Springs	18222
Sandts Eddy	18042
Sandy	15801
Sandy (Township)	15801
Sandy Bank	19063
Sandy Creek (Allegheny County)	15147
Sandy Creek (Mercer County) (Township)	16125
Sandycreek (Venango County) (Township)	16323
Sandy Hill	19401
Sandy Hollow	16248
Sandy Lake (Mercer County)	16145
Sandy Lake (Mercer County) (Township)	16153
Sandy Plains	15322
Sandy Ridge	16677
Sandy Ridge Acres	18901
Sandy Run (Bucks County)	19067
Sandy Run (Greene County)	15338
Sandy Run (Luzerne County)	18224
Sandy Shore	18428
Sandy Valley	15851
Sandyville	18324
Sanford	16340
Sankertown	16630
Sarah Furnace	16248
Sardis (Part of Murrysville)	15668
Sartwell	16731
Sarver	16055
Sarversville	16055
Sassamansville	19472
Satterfield	18614
Satterfield Junction	18614
Saucon Acres	18034
Saulsburg	16652
Saville	17074
Saville (Township)	17037
Sawtown	16301
Saxonburg (Butler County)	16056
Saxton	16678
Saybrook	16347
Saylorsburg	18353
Sayre	18840
Scalp Level	15963
Scammells Corner	19067
Scandia	16345
Scenery Hill	15360
Schaefferstown	17088
Schellsburg	15559
Schenley	15682
Schnecksville	18078
Schoeneck (Lancaster County)	17578
Schoeneck (Northampton County)	18064
Schoentown (Part of Port Carbon)	17965
Schofer	19530
Schollard	16137
School Lane	17603
School Lane Hills	17604
School Valley Farms	17520
Schubert	19507
Schultzville	19504
Schulzville	18411
Schuster Heights	16229
Schuyler	17772
Schuylkill (Chester County) (Township)	19460
Schuylkill (Philadelphia County)	19146
Schuylkill (Schuylkill County) (Township)	17952
Schuylkill Haven	17972
Schuylkill Hills	19401
Schwenksville	19473
Sciota	18354
Sconnelltown	19380
Scotch Hill	16233
Scotch Hollow	16666
Scotia (Part of Jefferson)	15025
Scotland	17254
Scotrun	18355
Scott (Allegheny County) (Township)	15106

Name	ZIP
Scott (Columbia County) (Township)	17815
Scott (Lackawanna County) (Township)	18447
Scott (Lawrence County) (Township)	16101
Scott (Wayne County) (Township)	18462
Scott Center	18462
Scottdale	15683
Scott Haven	15083
Scottsville	15001
Scott Township	15106
Scranton	18501-19
For specific Scranton Zip Codes call (717) 969-5100	
Scrubgrass (Township)	16373
Scullton	15557
Scyoc	17021
Seamentown	15729
Seanor	15953
Searights	15401
Sebring	16930
Secane	19018
Secane Highlands	19018
Seek (Part of Coaldale)	18218
Seelyville	18431
Seemsville	18067
Seger	15627
Seidersville	18015
Seipstown	18031
Seisholtzville	18062
Seitzland	17327
Seitzville	17360
Selea	17264
Selinsgrove	17870
Sellersville	18960
Seltzer	17974
Seminole	16253
Seneca	16346
Seneca Valley	15642
Sereno	17846
Sergeant (McKean County)	16735
Sergeant (McKean County) (Township)	16740
Seven Fields	16046
Seven Hills	18837
Seven Pines	17082
Sevenpoints	17801
Seven Springs	15622
Seven Stars (Adams County)	17325
Seven Stars (Juniata County)	17062
Seven Valleys	17360
Seward	15954
Sewickley (Allegheny County)	15143
Sewickley (Westmoreland County) (Township)	15637
Sewickley Heights	15143
Sewickley Hills	15143
Seybertown	16028
Seyfert	19508
Shade (Township)	15924
Shade Gap	17255
Shadeland	16435
Shades Glen	18661
Shade Valley	17213
Shadle	17853
Shado-wood Village	15701
Shady Acres	17834
Shady Grove	17256
Shady Plain	15613
Shadyside (Part of Pittsburgh)	15232
Shaffer	15801
Shaffers Corner	15401
Shaffersville	16652
Shaft (Schuylkill County)	17976
Shaft (Somerset County)	15530
Shafton	15642
Shaler (Township)	15116
Shalercrest	15223
Shaler Township	15116
Shamokin (Northumberland County)	17872
Shamokin (Northumberland County) (Township)	17860
Shamokin Dam	17876
Shamrock (Fayette County)	15401
Shamrock (Somerset County)	15557
Shamrock Station	15539
Shaner	15642
Shaners Crossroads	15656
Shanesville	19512
Shankles (Part of Du Bois)	15801
Shanksville	15560
Shanktown	15777
Shannondale	16240

Name	ZIP
Shannon Heights	15235
Shanor Heights	16001
Sharon (Mercer County)	16146
Sharon (Potter County) (Township)	16748
Sharon Center	16748
Sharon Hill	19079
Sharon North (Part of Hermitage)	16146
Sharon Park (Par. of Sharon Hill)	19079
Sharpsburg (Allegheny County)	15215
Sharpsburg (Huntingdon County)	17060
Sharps Hill	15215
Sharpsville	16150
Sharrertown	15427
Shartlesville	19554
Shavertown (Delaware County)	19061
Shavertown (Luzerne County)	18708
Shawanese (Part of Harveys Lake)	18654
Shaw Mine	15057
Shawmut	15823
Shawnee on Delaware	18356
Shawtown	15642
Shawville	16873
Shay	16226
Sheakleyville	16151
Shearersburg	15656
Sheatown	18634
Sheffield	16347
Sheffield (Township)	16347
Sheffield Heights	15001
Sheffield Terrace	15001
Sheffield Village	19401
Shehawken	18462
Shellsville	17028
Shelly	18951
Shellytown	16693
Shelocta	15774
Sheltontown	16403
Shelvey	15846
Shenandoah	17976
Shenandoah Heights	17976
Shenango (Lawrence County) (Township)	16101
Shenango (Mercer County)	16125
Shenango (Mercer County) (Township)	16159
Shenango Valley Mall (Part of Hermitage)	16146
Shenkel	19464
Shenks Ferry	17309
Shepherd Hills	18101
Shepherdstown	17055
Sheppton	18248
Sherersville	18104
Sheridan (Lebanon County)	17073
Sheridan (Schuylkill County)	17980
Sherman	18847
Shermans Dale	17090
Shermansville	16316
Sherrett	16218
Sherwood Acres	15061
Sheshequin	18850
Sheshequin (Township)	18848
Shetters Grove	17405
Shickshinny	18655
Shields (Part of Edgeworth)	15143
Shieldsburg	15670
Shillington	19607
Shiloh (Clearfield County)	16881
Shiloh (York County)	17404
Shiloh East	17405
Shimerville	18049
Shimpstown	17236
Shindle	17841
Shinglehouse	16748
Shingletown	16801
Shintown	17764
Shipmans Eddy	16365
Shippen (Cameron County) (Township)	15834
Shippen (Tioga County) (Township)	16901
Shippensburg (Cumberland County)	17257
Shippensburg (Cumberland County) (Township)	17257
Shippensburg State College	17257
Shippenville	16254
Shippingport	15077
Ships Parts Control Center, USN	17055
Shiremanstown	17011
Shire Oaks	15322
Shirks Corner	19473

Shirley-South Union **PENNSYLVANIA** **485**

	ZIP		ZIP		ZIP
Shirley (Township)	17066	Smallwood (Part of California)	15423	Southampton (Bucks County)	18966
Shirleysburg	17260	Smethport	16749	Southampton (Cumberland County) (Township)	17257
Shoaf	15478	Smicksburg	16256	Southampton (Franklin County) (Township)	17244
Shocks Mills	17547	Smiley	15401	Southampton (Somerset County) (Township)	15552
Shoemaker	15946	Smith (Blair County)	16665	South Annville (Township)	17042
Shoemakers (Monroe County)	18301	Smith (Indiana County)	15717	South Auburn	18630
Shoemakers (Schuylkill County)	17948	Smith (Washington County) (Township)	15078	South Beaver (Township)	16115
Shoemakersville	19555	Smith Bridge	15380	South Bend	15686
Shoenberger	16686	Smithdale	15089	South Bend (Township)	15774
Shoenersville	18103	Smithfield (Bradford County) (Township)	18831	South Bethlehem	16242
Shohola	18458	Smithfield (Fayette County)	15478	South Bradford	16701
Shohola (Township)	18458	Smithfield (Huntingdon County) (Township)	16652	South Buffalo (Township)	16229
Shope Gardens	17057	Smithfield (Huntingdon County)	16652	South Burgettstown (Part of Burgettstown)	15021
Shorbes Hill	17331	Smithfield (Monroe County) (Township)	18335	South Canaan	18459
Shortsville	16935	Smithfield Center	16652	South Canaan (Township)	18472
Shraders	17084	Smith Gardens	17345	South Carnegie	15106
Shrewsbury (Lycoming County) (Township)	17737	Smithland	16242	South Centre (Township)	17815
Shrewsbury (Sullivan County) (Township)	17758	Smithmill	16680	South Clarksville	15322
Shrewsbury (York County)	17361	Smithport	15742	South Clearfield (Part of Clearfield)	16830
Shrewsbury (York County) (Township)	17327	Smiths	17362	South Coatesville	19320
Shumans	17815	Smiths Corner	18950	South Connellsville	15425
Shunk	17768	Smiths Corners	16374	South Coventry (Township)	19464
Shy Beaver	16657	Smiths Ferry (Part of Ohioville)	15059	South Creek (Township)	16925
Sickles Corner	16601	Smithton	15479	Southdale	18655
Siddonsburg	17019	Smithtown (Bucks County)	18947	South Duquesne (Part of Duquesne)	15110
Sidman	15955	Smithtown (Jefferson County)	15840	Southeastern	19397-99
Siegfried (Part of Northampton)	18067	Smithville	17560	For specific Southeastern Zip Codes call (215) 964-6448	
Sigel	15860	Smock	15480	Southeastern Facility	19399
Siglerville	17063	Smokeless	15944	South Easton (Part of Easton)	18042
Sigmund	18092	Smokerun	16681	South Eaton	18657
Silkworth	18621	Smoketown (Bucks County)	18951	South Enola	17025
Silvara	18623	Smoketown (Franklin County)	17222	South Erie (Part of Erie)	16508
Silver Creek	17959	Smoketown (Lancaster County)	17576	Southerwood	15610
Silverdale	18962	Smullton	16854	South Fayette (Township)	15064
Silver Ford Heights	17066	Smyerstown	15772	South Fork	15956
Silver Lake (Township)	18812	Smyrna	17509	South Franklin (Township)	15301
Silver Lake (Wayne County)	18469	Snake Spring Valley (Township)	15522	South Gibson	18842
Silver Lake (York County)	17339	Snedekerville	16914	South Greensburg	15601
Silver Lake (Bucks County)	18940	Snively Corners	16232	South Hanover (Township)	17033
Silver Lake (Susquehanna County)	18812	Snowball Gate	19056	South Heidelberg (Township)	19565
Silver Spring (Cumberland County) (Township)	17055	Snowden	15129	South Heights	15081
Silver Spring (Lancaster County)	17575	Snowdenville	19475	South Hermitage	17555
Silverville	16055	Snow Shoe (Centre County)	16874	South Hills (Allegheny County)	15216
Simmonstown	17527	Snow Shoe (Centre County) (Township)	16829	South Hills (Mifflin County)	17044
Simpson	18407	S. N. P. J. (Slovene National Benefit Society)	16120	South Hills Village	15241
Singersville	17018	Snyder (Blair County)		South Huntingdon (Township)	15089
Sinking Spring	19608	Snyder (Jefferson County) (Township)	16686	South Lakemont	16602
Sinking Valley	16601	Snyder Corner	15824	Southland 4 Seasons Centre (Part of Pleasant Hills)	15236
Sinnamahoning	15861	Snyders	17356	South Lebanon (Township)	17042
Sinsheim	17362	Snydersburg	17960	South Londonderry (Township)	17010
Sipesville	15561	Snydersville	16257	South Mahoning (Township)	15747
Sitka	15431	Snydertown (Centre County)	18360	South Manheim (Township)	17972
Six Mile Run	16679	Snydertown (Fayette County)	16841	South Meadville	16335
Six Points	16049	Snydertown (Northumberland County)	15425	South Media	19063
Sixty-Ninth Street Center	19082	Snydertown (Westmoreland County)	17877	South Middleton (Township)	17007
Sizerville	15834	Snyderville	15620	Southmont	15905
Skelp	16601	Social Island	16222	South Montrose	18843
Skidmore	16101	Soho (Part of Pittsburgh)	17201	South Mountain	17261
Ski Haven Lake Estates	18326	Soldier	15219	South Mountain Restoration Center	17261
Skinners Eddy	18623	Solebury	15851	South New Castle	16101
Skippack	19474	Solebury (Township)	18963	South Newton (Township)	17266
Skippack (Township)	19474	Somerset (Somerset County) (Township)	18963	South Oil City (Part of Oil City)	16301
Skyline Heights	17402	Somerset (Somerset County)	15501	South Park (Township)	15129
Skyline View	17112	Somerset (Washington County) (Township)	15501	South Philipsburg	16866
Skytop	18357	Somers Lane	15330	South Pottstown (Chester County)	19464
Sky View	18426	Somerton (Part of Philadelphia)	16929	South Pymatuning (Township)	16150
Slabtown (Clearfield County)	15724	Somerville	19116	South Renovo	17764
Slabtown (Franklin County)	17268	Sonestown	16028	South Rockwood	15557
Slackwater	17551	Sonman	17770	South Shenango (Township)	16134
Slatedale	18079	Soradoville	15946	South Side (Allegheny County)	15203
Slateford	18038	Soudersburg	17841	South Side (Butler County)	16045
Slateford	18343	Souderton	17577	South Side (Lackawanna County)	18505
Slateford Junction	18343	Soukesburg	18964	Southside (Northampton County)	18015
Slate Hill	17314	South Abington (Township)	15956	South Sterling	18460
Slate Lick	16229	South Altoona (Part of Altoona)	18410	South Strabane (Township)	15301
Slate Run	17769	Southampton (Bedford County) (Township)	16602	South Tamaqua	18252
Slate Valley	18038		17211	South Temple	19560
Slateville	19529			South Towanda	18848
Slatington	18080			South Union (Township)	15401
Slickport	16646				
Slickville	15684				
Sligo	16255				
Slippery Rock (Butler County)	16057				
Slippery Rock (Butler County) (Township)	16057				
Slippery Rock (Lawrence County) (Township)	16101				
Slippery Rock Park	16057				
Slocum (Township)	18660				
Slocum Corners	18660				
Slovan	15078				

486 PENNSYLVANIA South Uniontown-Stormstown

	ZIP
South Uniontown	15401
South Versailles (Township)	15028
Southview	15361
Southwark (Part of Philadelphia)	19147
South Waverly	14892
Southwest (Warren County) (Township)	16354
Southwest (Westmoreland County)	15685
Southwest Greensburg	15601
Southwest Madison (Township)	17047
South Whitehall (Township)	18104
South Williamsport	17701
South Woodbury (Township)	16664
Southwood Hills	17403
Spaces Corners	16201
Spangenberg Lake	18436
Spangler	15775
Spangsville	19512
Sparta (Crawford County) (Township)	16434
Sparta (Washington County)	15329
Spartansburg	16434
Spears Grove	17021
Speedwell	17543
Speers	15012
Spike Island	16666
Spillway Lake	15473
Spindley City	16641
Spinnerstown	18968
Spinnlers Point	18464
Split Rock	18624
Sporting Hill (Cumberland County)	17055
Sporting Hill (Lancaster County)	17545
Sportsburg	15767
Spraggs	15362
Sprankle Mills	15767
Spring (Berks County) (Township)	19609
Spring (Centre County) (Township)	16823
Spring (Crawford County) (Township)	16406
Spring (Perry County) (Township)	17040
Spring (Snyder County) (Township)	17812
Spring Bank	16872
Springboro	16435
Spring Brook (Township)	18444
Spring Church	15686
Spring City	19475
Spring Creek (Township)	16436
Spring Creek (Elk County) (Township)	15853
Spring Creek (Lehigh County)	18011
Spring Creek (Warren County)	16436
Springdale (Allegheny County)	15144
Springdale (Allegheny County) (Township)	15049
Springdell	19320
Springettsbury (Township)	17402
Springfield	16914
Springfield (Township)	18831
Springfield (Bucks County) (Township)	18951
Springfield (Cumberland County)	17241
Springfield (Delaware County) (Township)	19064
Springfield (Delaware County)	19064
Springfield (Erie County) (Township)	16443
Springfield (Fayette County) (Township)	15464
Springfield (Huntingdon County) (Township)	17243
Springfield (Mercer County) (Township)	16137
Springfield (Montgomery County) (Township)	19118
Springfield (York County) (Township)	17327
Springfield Falls	16137
Springfield Mall	19064
Springfield Township	19118
Spring Garden (Bucks County)	18940
Spring Garden (Lancaster County)	17535
Spring Garden (Philadelphia County)	19122

	ZIP
Spring Garden (Schuylkill County)	17972
Spring Garden (Union County)	17810
Spring Garden (Westmoreland County)	15666
Spring Garden (York County) (Township)	17403
Spring Garden (York County)	17403
Spring Glen	17978
Spring Grove	17362
Springhaven Estates	19086
Springhill (Bradford County)	18853
Spring Hill (Cambria County)	15946
Spring Hill (Delaware County)	19018
Springhill (Fayette County) (Township)	15478
Springhill (Greene County) (Township)	15352
Springhope	15559
Spring House	19477
Springhouse Farms	18104
Spring Meadow	15554
Spring Meadows	19565
Spring Mill	19428
Spring Mills	16875
Springmont	19609
Spring Mount (Huntingdon County)	16877
Spring Mount (Montgomery County)	19478
Spring Run	17262
Springs	15562
Springtown (Bucks County)	18081
Springtown (Franklin County)	17221
Springtown (Luzerne County)	18707
Springtown (Northumberland County)	17777
Springvale	17356
Spring Valley (Berks County)	19560
Spring Valley (Bucks County)	18901
Spring Valley (Clearfield County)	16878
Spring Valley (Northampton County)	18015
Spring Valley Estates	17201
Spring Valley Farms	18901
Springville (Township)	18844
Springville	16342
Springville (Cumberland County)	17007
Springville (Lancaster County)	17535
Springville (Susquehanna County)	18844
Sproul	16682
Spruce Creek	16683
Spruce Creek (Township)	16683
Spruce Hill	17082
Spruce Hill (Township)	17082
Sprucetown	15474
Spry	17403
Squab Hollow	15846
Square Corner	17325
Squirrel Hill (Part of Pittsburgh)	15217
Stack Town	17502
Stafore Estates	18017
Stahlstown	15687
Stairville	18660
Stalker	12741
Stambaugh	15456
Standard	15666
Standard Shaft	15666
Standing Stone	18854
Standing Stone (Township)	18853
Stanhope	17963
Stanley	15801
Stanton (Jefferson County)	15825
Stanton (Luzerne County)	15825
Stanton Heights (Allegheny County)	15201
Stanton Heights (Westmoreland County)	15672
Stanwood Gardens	19020
Star Brick	16365
Starford	15777
Star Junction	15482
Starkville	18657
Starlight	18461
Starners Station	17324
Starr (Forest County)	16353
Starr (Warren County)	16420
Starrucca	18462
Starview	17347

	ZIP
Starview Heights	17402
State College	16801-05
For specific State College Zip Codes call (814) 238-2435	
State Correctional Institution at Dallas (Luzerne County)	18612
State Correctional Institution (Lycoming County)	17756
State Correctional Institution (Montgomery County)	19426
State Correction Institution	17011
State Hill (Berks County)	19608
State Hill (Chester County)	17527
State Line (Bedford County)	15545
Stateline (Erie County)	16428
State Line (Franklin County)	17263
Steamburg	16424
Steel City	18015
Steelstown	17003
Steelton	17113
Steelville	19370
Steene	18472
Steffins Hill	15010
Steinbachs Corner	18847
Steinsburg	18951
Steinsville	19529
Stemlersville	18235
Sterling (Township)	18445
Sterling (Clearfield County)	16651
Sterling (Wayne County)	18463
Sterling Run	15832
Sterlingworth	18104
Sterrettania	16415
Stetlersville	18069
Steuben (Township)	16404
Stevens (Bradford County) (Township)	18854
Stevens (Lancaster County)	17578
Stevens Point	18847
Stevenstown	17019
Stevensville	18845
Stewardson (Township)	17729
Stewart (Township)	15470
Stewart Run	16341
Stewartstown	17363
Stewartsville	15642
Stickney	16701
Sticks	17329
Stiefler Corner	16670
Stier	18013
Stifflertown	15724
Stiles	18052
Stiles Hill	16943
Still Creek	18252
Stilleys Siding (Part of Jefferson)	15025
Stillwater	17878
Stillwater Lake Estates	18346
Stiltz	17327
Stines Corner	18066
Stobo	15061
Stockdale	15483
Stockertown	18083
Stockton	18201
Stockton Number Eight	18201
Stockton Number Seven	18201
Stockton Number Six	18201
Stoddartsville	18610
Stokesdale	16901
Stoneboro	16153
Stone Church	18343
Stone Glen	17018
Stoneham	16313
Stone Hill	17516
Stone House	16258
Stonehurst	19006
Stonerstown	16678
Stonersville	19508
Stonetown	19508
Stonevilla	15601
Stoneybreak	17267
Stonington	17801
Stonybrook	17402
Stonybrook Heights	17402
Stonycreek (Cambria County) (Township)	15906
Stonycreek (Somerset County) (Township)	15541
Stony Creek Mills	19606
Stonyfork	16901
Stony Point (Bucks County)	18930
Stony Point (Crawford County)	16316
Stony Point (Franklin County)	17262
Stony Point (Greene County)	15344
Stony Run	19557
Stoopville	18940
Stormstown	16870

Stormville-Thornbury PENNSYLVANIA 487

Name	ZIP
Stormville	18360
Stottsville	19367
Stouchsburg	19567
Stoufferstown	17201
Stoughstown	17257
Stover	16686
Stoverdale	17036
Stoverstown	17362
Stowe (Allegheny County) (Township)	15136
Stowe (Montgomery County)	19464
Stowell	18623
Stowe Township	15136
Stoystown	15563
Straban (Township)	17325
Strabane	15363
Strafford	19087
Strangford	15717
Strasburg (Lancaster County)	17579
Strasburg (Lancaster County) (Township)	17602
Strattanville	16258
Strausstown	19559
Strawberry Ridge	17821
Strawbridge	17758
Straw Pump	15642
Street Road	18966
Strickhousers	17360
Stricklerstown	17073
Strinestown	17345
Stringtown (Armstrong County)	16226
Stringtown (Greene County)	15320
Strobleton	16353
Strodes Mills	17044
Stronach	16833
Strong	17851
Strongstown	15957
Stroud (Township)	18360
Stroudsburg	18360
Stroudsburg West	18360
Strum	15478
Studa	15312
Stull	18636
Stump Creek	15863
Stumptown	16666
Sturgeon	15082
Sturgeon-Noblestown	15071
Sturgis (Part of Archbald)	18447
Suburban Village	19380
Sudan	15063
Suedburg	17963
Sugarcreek (Armstrong County) (Township)	16218
Sugarcreek (Venango County)	16323
Sugar Grove (Greene County)	15380
Sugar Grove (Mercer County) (Township)	16125
Sugargrove (Warren County)	16350
Sugar Grove (Warren County) (Township)	16350
Sugar Hill	15824
Sugarloaf (Township)	18251
Sugarloaf (Columbia County) (Township)	17814
Sugarloaf (Luzerne County)	18249
Sugar Notch	18706
Sugar Run	18846
Sugartown	19355
Sullivan (Township)	16932
Summerdale	17093
Summerhill (Cambria County)	15958
Summerhill (Cambria County) (Township)	15921
Summer Hill (Columbia County)	18603
Summerhill (Crawford County) (Township)	16406
Summerson	15821
Summerville (Jefferson County)	15864
Summerville (Susquehanna County)	18822
Summit (Butler County) (Township)	16001
Summit (Cambria County)	16630
Summit (Crawford County) (Township)	16424
Summit (Erie County) (Township)	16509
Summit (McKean County)	16701
Summit (Potter County) (Township)	16720
Summit (Somerset County) (Township)	15552
Summit (Susquehanna County)	18834
Summit Grove Camp (Part of New Freedom)	17349
Summit Hill	18250
Summit Lawn	18103
Summit Mills	15552
Summit Station	17979
Sumneytown	18084
Sunbeam	17201
Sunbrook	16635
Sunbury	17801
Suncliff	15765
Sundale	18920
Sunderlinville	16943
Sunnybrook	19075
Sunnyburn	17302
Sunny Point	18428
Sunny Side (Allegheny County)	15063
Sunnyside (Lawrence County)	16101
Sunnyside (Lebanon County)	17042
Sunnyside (Northumberland County)	17872
Sunrise Lake	18337
Sunset Acres	15701
Sunset Grove	19380
Sunset Hills (Part of Economy)	15042
Sunset Manor	17405
Sunset Pines (Part of Lock Haven)	17745
Sunset Valley	15642
Sunset Village	18451
Sunshine (Fayette County)	15461
Sunshine (Luzerne County)	18655
Sun Valley	18330
Sun Village (Part of Chester)	19013
Sunville	16317
Superior (Fayette County)	15417
Superior (Westmoreland County)	15627
Suplee	19371
Surveyor Mine	16830
Suscon	18641
Susquehanna (Cambria County) (Township)	15714
Susquehanna (Dauphin County) (Township)	17109
Susquehanna (Juniata County) (Township)	17045
Susquehanna (Lycoming County) (Township)	17701
Susquehanna (Susquehanna County)	18847
Susquehanna Bridge	16830
Susquehanna Valley Mall	17831
Sutersville	15083
Swales	17049
Swamproot	16127
Swan Acres	15237
Swanville	16415
Swart	15364
Swarthmore	19081
Swarthmorwood	19081
Swartzville	17569
Swatara (Dauphin County) (Township)	17111
Swatara (Lebanon County) (Township)	17038
Swatara Station	17033
Swatara Township	17111
Swede Hill	15601
Swedeland	19401
Sweden (Township)	16915
Sweden Valley	16915
Swedesburg	19405
Swedetown (Cambria County)	16646
Swedetown (Westmoreland County)	15683
Sweeney Plan	15012
Sweet Valley	18656
Sweitzer	15061
Swengel	17880
Swiftwater	18370
Swineford (Part of Middleburg)	17842
Swissdale	17745
Swissmont	15857
Swissvale	15218
Switzer	18066
Swoyerville	18704
Sybertsville	18251
Sycamore	15364
Sygan	15017
Sygan Hill	15017
Sykesville	15865
Sylmar	19362
Sylvan	17236
Sylvan Crest	15061
Sylvan Dell	17701
Sylvan Grove	16858
Sylvan Hills	16648
Sylvania (Bradford County)	16945
Sylvania (Potter County) (Township)	16720
Sylvis	16692
Syner	17003
Table Rock	17307
Tacony (Part of Philadelphia)	19135
Tafton	18464
Tait	15825
Talmage	17580
Talmar	17814
Tamanend	18252
Tamaqua	18252
Tamarack	17764
Tamiment	18371
Tanglewood Lakes	18426
Tanguy	19342
Tank	18249
Tannersville	18372
Tannery (Carbon County)	18661
Tannery (Luzerne County)	18661
Tanoma	15728
Tarentum	15084
Tarrs	15688
Tarrtown	16210
Tatamy	18085
Tatesville	15537
Taylor (Blair County) (Township)	16673
Taylor (Centre County) (Township)	16686
Taylor (Fulton County) (Township)	16689
Taylor (Lackawanna County)	18517
Taylor (Lawrence County) (Township)	16160
Taylor Highlands (Part of Huntingdon)	16652
Tayloria	19363
Taylor-Old Forge (Part of Taylor)	18517
Taylorstown (Washington County)	15323
Taylorstown (Washington County)	15365
Taylorsville	15729
Taylorville	17921
Teagarden Homes	15322
Tearing Run	15748
Teedyskung Lake	18457
Teepleville	16403
Telescope	16922
Telford	18969
Tell (Township)	17213
Temple	19560
Templeton	16259
Ten Mile	15311
Tenmile Bottom	16346
Tenth Avenue (Part of Bethlehem)	18018
Terminal	19082
Terrace Acres	18052
Terre Hill	17581
Terry (Township)	18853
Terrytown	18853
Texas (Township)	18431
Tharptown	17872
The Hideout	18436
The Meadows	16865
The Pines	17350
The Woodlands	16046
Thieleman Crossroads	16046
Thomas	15330
Thomasdale	15935
Thomas Mills	15935
Thomasville	17364
Thompson (Fulton County) (Township)	17236
Thompson (Susquehanna County)	18465
Thompson (Susquehanna County) (Township)	18462
Thompson No. 1 (Fayette County)	15475
Thompson No. 2 (Fayette County)	15468
Thompsontown (Clearfield County)	15753
Thompsontown (Juniata County)	17094
Thompsonville	15317
Thornburg	15205
Thornbury (Chester County) (Township)	19395

488 PENNSYLVANIA Thornbury-Unity House

Name	ZIP
Thornbury (Delaware County) (Township)	19373
Thorndale	19372
Thorndale Heights	19335
Thornhurst	18424
Thornridge	19054
Thornton	19373
Threemile	16728
Three Springs	17264
Three Springs Run	16938
Three Tuns	19002
Throop	18512
Thumptown	16901
Thurston	18657
Tidal	16259
Tide	15748
Tidioute	16351
Tiffany	18801
Tilden (Township)	19526
Tillotson	16438
Timber Lakes	19067
Timberly Heights	16001
Timblin	15778
Timbuck	16738
Time	15353
Tinicum	18947
Tinicum (Bucks County) (Township)	18947
Tinicum (Delaware County) (Township)	19029
Tinicum Township	19029
Tioga (Tioga County)	16946
Tioga (Tioga County) (Township)	16946
Tioga Junction	16946
Tiona	16352
Tionesta (Forest County)	16353
Tionesta (Forest County) (Township)	16353
Tippecanoe	15480
Tipton	16684
Tire Hill	15959
Titusville	16354
Tivoli	17737
Toboyne (Township)	17071
Toby (Clarion County) (Township)	16248
Toby (Elk County)	15846
Toby Farms (Part of Chester)	19015
Tobyhanna (Monroe County)	18466
Tobyhanna (Monroe County) (Township)	18350
Tobyhanna Army Depot	18466
Tod (Township)	16685
Todd (Fulton County) (Township)	17233
Todd (Huntingdon County)	16685
Toddesville	17325
Todmorron	19086
Toftrees	16803
Toland	17324
Tolna	17349
Tomb	17740
Tompkins	16940
Tompkinsville	18433
Tomstown	17268
Tooley Corners	18444
Topton	19562
Torpedo	16340
Torrance	15779
Torrance State Hospital	15779
Torresdale (Part of Philadelphia)	19114
Torresdale Manor	19020
Torrey	18473
Toughkenamon	19374
Towamencin (Township)	19443
Towamensing (Township)	18071
Towamensing Trails	18210
Towanda (Bradford County)	18848
Towanda (Bradford County) (Township)	18848
Tower City	17980
Tower Hill	18914
Tower Hill No. One	15475
Tower Hill No. Two	15417
Towerville	19320
Town Hill	18655
Town Line	18655
Townville	16360
Traces of Lattimore	18328
Trade City	16256
Trafford	15085
Trailwood	18702
Trainer	19013
Transfer	16154
Trappe	19426
Trauger	15650
Traymore	18974

Name	ZIP
Traymore Manor	18974
Tredyffrin (Township)	19312
Treehaven (Part of Bethel Park)	15102
Trees Mills	15601
Treichlers	18086
Tremont (Schuylkill County)	17981
Tremont (Schuylkill County) (Township)	17963
Trent	15622
Trenton	17948
Tresckow	18254
Tresslarville	18436
Trevorton	17881
Trevose	19047
Trevose Heights	19047
Trexler	19529
Trexler Mall	18087
Trexlertown	18087
Trimmer Manor	17405
Trindle Spring	17055
Trinity Park	15301
Triumph (Township)	16340
Trooper	19401
Trotter	15425
Trotwood	15241
Trout Run	17771
Trouts Corners (Part of Hermitage)	16148
Trouts Crossing	15666
Troutville	15866
Troxelville	17882
Troy (Bradford County)	16947
Troy (Bradford County) (Township)	16947
Troy (Clearfield County)	16866
Troy (Crawford County) (Township)	16354
Troy Center	16404
Troy Hill	16201
Truce	17566
Trucksville	18708
Trucksville Gardens	18708
Truemans	16347
Truesdale Terrace	18706
Truittsburg	16224
Truman	15834
Trumbauersville	18970
Trunkeyville	16351
Truxall	15613
Tryonville	16404
Tuckerton	19605
Tullytown	19007
Tulpehocken (Township)	19550
Tuna	16701
Tunkhannock (Monroe County) (Township)	18610
Tunkhannock (Wyoming County)	18657
Tunkhannock (Wyoming County) (Township)	18657
Tunnel	18661
Tunnelhill	16641
Tunnelton	15681
Turbett (Township)	17082
Turbot (Township)	17847
Turbotville	17772
Turkey City	16058
Turkeyfoot (Franklin County)	17201
Turkeyfoot (Washington County)	15332
Turkey Run (Part of Shenandoah)	17976
Turkeytown	15089
Turnersville	16134
Turnip Hole	16373
Turnpike (Part of Shrewsbury)	17361
Turtle Creek	15145
Turtlepoint	16750
Tuscarora (Bradford County) (Township)	18623
Tuscarora (Juniata County)	17082
Tuscarora (Juniata County) (Township)	17035
Tuscarora (Perry County) (Township)	17062
Tuscarora (Schuylkill County)	17982
Tusculum	17257
Tusseyville	16828
Twenty Row	15927
Twickinham Village	19038
Twilight	15022
Twin Bridge Farm	19380
Twin Bridges	15022
Twin Brooks	17405
Twin Lakes	18458
Twin Oaks (Adams County)	17325
Twin Oaks (Bucks County)	19056

Name	ZIP
Twin Oaks (Delaware County)	19014
Twin Oaks Farms	19014
Twin Rocks	15960
Two Taverns	17325
Tyler	15849
Tylerdale (Part of Washington)	15301
Tyler Hill	18469
Tylersburg	16361
Tylersport	18971
Tylersville	17773
Tyre	15126
Tyrone (Adams County) (Township)	17325
Tyrone (Blair County)	16686
Tyrone (Blair County) (Township)	16686
Tyrone (Perry County) (Township)	17040
Uhlerstown	18920
Uledi	15484
Ulhers	18042
Ulster	18850
Ulster (Township)	18850
Ulysses (Potter County)	16948
Ulysses (Potter County) (Township)	16948
Unicorn	17566
Union (Adams County) (Township)	17331
Union (Bedford County) (Township)	16655
Union (Berks County) (Township)	19508
Union (Centre County) (Township)	16844
Union (Clearfield County) (Township)	15856
Union (Crawford County) (Township)	16335
Union (Erie County) (Township)	16438
Union (Fulton County) (Township)	17267
Union (Huntingdon County) (Township)	17052
Union (Jefferson County) (Township)	15829
Union (rural) (Lancaster County)	17560
Union (Lancaster County)	17536
Union (Lawrence County) (Township)	16101
Union (Lebanon County) (Township)	17038
Union (Luzerne County) (Township)	18655
Union (Mifflin County) (Township)	17004
Union (Schuylkill County) (Township)	17967
Union (Snyder County) (Township)	17864
Union (Tioga County) (Township)	17724
Union (Union County) (Township)	17889
Union (Washington County) (Township)	15332
Union Center	17724
Union City	16438
Union Dale	18470
Union Depcsit	17033
Union Furnace	16686
Union Grove	17519
Union Hill	18235
Union Mills	17004
Union Square	17545
Uniontown (Fayette County)	15401
Uniontown (Indiana County)	15724
Uniontown (York County)	17019
Uniontown Heights	16323
Uniontown North	15401
Uniontown Shopping Center (Part of Uniontown)	15401
Union Trust (Part of Pittsburgh)	15219
Union Valley (Lawrence County)	16157
Union Valley (Washington County)	15332
Unionville (Beaver County)	15066
Unionville (Berks County)	19518
Unionville (Butler County)	16001
Unionville (Chester County)	19375
Union Water Works	17003
United	15689
Unity (Township)	15650
Unity House	18373

Unity Junction-Wandin **PENNSYLVANIA** 489

Name	ZIP
Unity Junction (Part of Plum)	15239
Unityville	17774
Universal	15235
University City (Part of Philadelphia)	19104
University Heights	18015
University Park (Part of State College)	16802
Upland	19015
Upland Terrace	19004
Upper Allen (Township)	17055
Upper Augusta (Township)	17801
Upper Bern (Township)	19506
Upper Black Eddy	18972
Upper Brownville	17976
Upper Burrell (Township)	15068
Upper Chichester (Township)	19061
Upper Chichester Township	19061
Upper Darby	19082-83
For specific Upper Darby Zip Codes call (215) 352-0800	
Upper Dublin (Township)	19034
Upper Dublin Township	19002
Upper Exeter	18643
Upper Fairfield (Township)	17754
Upper Frankford (Township)	17241
Upper Frederick (Township)	18074
Upper Glasgow	19464
Upper Gwynedd (Township)	19454
Upper Hanover (Township)	18041
Upper Hillville	16248
Upper Lawn	17078
Upper Leacock (Township)	17540
Upper Lehigh	18224
Upper Macungie (Township)	18087
Upper Mahanoy (Township)	17836
Upper Mahantango (Township)	17941
Upper Makefield (Township)	18940
Upper Merion (Township)	19406
Upper Merion Township	19406
Upper Middletown	15480
Upper Mifflin (Township)	17241
Upper Milford (Township)	18092
Upper Mill (Part of Mount Holly Springs)	17065
Upper Moreland (Township)	19090
Upper Moreland Township	19090
Upper Mount Bethel (Township)	18013
Upper Nazareth (Township)	18064
Upper Orchard	19056
Upper Oxford (Township)	19363
Upper Paxton (Township)	17061
Upper Peanut	15480
Upper Pottsgrove (Township)	19464
Upper Providence (Delaware County) (Township)	19063
Upper Providence (Montgomery County) (Township)	19456
Upper Providence Township	19063
Upper Reese	16648
Upper Sagon	17877
Upper Salford (Township)	18957
Upper Saucon (Township)	18034
Upper Southampton (Township)	18966
Upper Southampton Township	19006
Upper St. Clair (Allegheny County) (Township)	15241
Upper St. Clair (Allegheny County)	15241
Upperstrasburg	17265
Upper Tulpehocken (Township)	19559
Upper Turkeyfoot (Township)	15557
Upper Two Lick	15721
Upper Tyrone (Township)	15683
Upper Uwchlan (Township)	19335
Upper Yoder (Township)	15905
Upton	17225
Uptown (Part of Pittsburgh)	15219
Urban	17830
Urey	15742
Uriah	17324
Ursina	15485
Ursina Junction (Part of Confluence)	15424
Utahville	16627
Utica	16362
Utopia	15613
Uwchlan (Township)	19353
Uwchland	19480
Vail	16686

Name	ZIP
Valencia	16059
Valier	15780
Vallamont Hills (Part of Williamsport)	17701
Valley (Armstrong County) (Township)	16201
Valley (Chester County) (Township)	19320
Valley (Montour County) (Township)	17821
Valley Falls	19006
Valley Forge	19481-82
For specific Valley Forge Zip Codes call (215) 783-0232	
Valley Forge Christian College	19460
Valley Forge Estates	19087
Valley Forge Homes	19406
Valley Forge Manor	19460
Valley Furnace	17959
Valley Green	19026
Valley Green Estates	17319
Valley Green Heights	17319
Valley Green West	17319
Valley-Hi	15533
Valley Stream	18707
Valley View (Cambria County)	15906
Valley View (Centre County)	16823
Valley View (Chester County)	19344
Valley View (Lancaster County)	17545
Valley View (Schuylkill County)	17983
Valley View Farms	19006
Valley View Heights	16226
Van	16319
Van Buren	15329
Vance	15301
Vances Mills	15401
Vanceville	15330
Vanderbilt	15486
Vandergrift	15690
Vandergrift Heights (Part of Vandergrift)	15690
Vandling	18421
Vandyke	17082
Vankirk	15301
Van Meter	15479
Van Ormer	16639
Vanport (Beaver County) (Township)	15009
Vanport (Beaver County)	15009
Van Voorhis	15366
Van Wert	17059
Varden	18436
Vaux Town (Part of New Britain)	18901
Vawter	18810
Venango (Butler County) (Township)	16049
Venango (Crawford County)	16440
Venango (Crawford County) (Township)	16440
Venango (Erie County) (Township)	16442
Venetia	15367
Venice	15057
Venturetown	16365
Venus	16364
Vera Cruz	18049
Verdilla	17870
Vere Cruz	17569
Vermilion Hill	19054
Vernfield	19438
Vernon (Crawford County) (Township)	16335
Vernon (Wyoming County)	18657
Vernondale	16509
Vernon Park (Part of Philadelphia)	19144
Verona	15147
Versailles	15132
Vestaburg	15368
Vesta Heights	15333
Vesta No 6 (Part of Centerville)	15429
Veterans Administration Hospital (Blair County)	16602
Veterans Administration Hospital (Butler County)	16001
Veterans Administration Medical Center (Lebanon County)	17042
Veterans Hospital (Allegheny County)	15240
Veterans Hospital (Chester County)	19320
Veterans Hospital (Luzerne County)	18702

Name	ZIP
Vicksburg (Blair County)	16648
Vicksburg (Union County)	17883
Victory (Township)	16342
Victory Heights	16323
Victory Hills	15063
Vienna	15376
Viennese Woods	15209
Viewmont Mall (Part of Dickson City)	18519
Village	15241
Village Green	19013
Village of Cross Creek	17402
Village of Olde Hickory	17601
Village of the Four Seasons	18470
Village of Westover	17055
Villa Green	17403
Villa Maria	16155
Villanova	19085
Vinco	15909
Vinemont	17569
Vintage	17562
Vintondale	15961
Violet Hill	17403
Violet Wood	19057
Vira	17044
Virginia Farms	15717
Virginia Hills West	15126
Virginia Mills	17320
Virginville	19564
Voganville	17522
Vogleyville	16001
Volant	16156
Vosburg	18657
Vowinckel	16260
Vulcan	18214
Wabash (Part of Pittsburgh)	15220
Wadesville	17901
Wadsworth (Part of Philadelphia)	19150
Wagner	17841
Wagnersville	18042
Wagontown	19376
Wahlville	16033
Wahnetah (Part of Jim Thorpe)	18229
Wakena	15681
Walbert	18104
Walcksville	18235
Walden Woods	15126
Walkchalk	16201
Walker (Centre County) (Township)	16841
Walker (Huntingdon County) (Township)	16660
Walker (Juniata County) (Township)	17059
Walker (Schuylkill County) (Township)	18252
Walkers Mill	15106
Walkertown	15427
Wall	15148
Wallace (Township)	19343
Wallace Junction (Part of Girard)	16417
Wallaceton	16876
Wallaceville	16354
Wallenpaupack Lake Estates	18436
Waller	17814
Wallingford	19086
Wallingford Hills	19086
Wallis Run	17771
Walls Corners	18414
Wallsville	18414
Walltown	16838
Walmo	16101
Walnut	17082
Walnut Bend	16301
Walnut Bottom	17266
Walnut Gardens	18052
Walnut Grove	17074
Walnut Hill (Fayette County)	15401
Walnut Hill (Greene County)	15327
Walnut Hill (Montgomery County)	19001
Walnutport	18088
Walnuttown	19522
Walsall	15904
Walston	15781
Walston Junction (Part of Punxsutawney)	15767
Walters	18042
Waltersburg	15488
Waltonville	17036
Waltz	15679
Waltz Landing	18428
Waltzvale	16671
Wampum	16157
Wanamakers	19529
Wanamie	18634
Wandin	15729

490 PENNSYLVANIA Wanneta-West Fallowfield

Name	ZIP
Wanneta	16401
Wapwallopen	18660
Ward (Delaware County)	19331
Ward (Tioga County) (Township)	17724
Warfordsburg	17267
Warminster (Bucks County) (Township)	18974
Warminster (Bucks County)	18974
Warner (Bucks County)	19007
Warner (Washington County)	15022
Warren (Bradford County) (Township)	18851
Warren (Franklin County) (Township)	17236
Warren (Warren County)	16365
Warren Center	18851
Warrendale	15086
Warren South	16365
Warren State Hospital	16365
Warrensville	17701
Warrington	18976
Warrington (Bucks County) (Township)	18976
Warrington (York County) (Township)	17019
Warrior Ridge	16669
Warrior Run	18706
Warriors Mark	16877
Warriors Mark (Township)	16686
Warsaw (Jefferson County) (Township)	15851
Warsaw (Lackawanna County)	18512
Warsaw (Luzerne County)	18702
Warwick (Bucks County) (Township)	18929
Warwick (Chester County) (Township)	19520
Warwick (Lancaster County) (Township)	17543
Warwick (Chester County)	19470
Washington (Armstrong County) (Township)	16218
Washington (Berks County) (Township)	19512
Washington (Butler County) (Township)	16061
Washington (Cambria County) (Township)	15938
Washington (Clarion County) (Township)	16326
Washington (Dauphin County) (Township)	17048
Washington (Erie County) (Township)	16412
Washington (Fayette County) (Township)	15012
Washington (Franklin County) (Township)	17268
Washington (Greene County) (Township)	15370
Washington (Indiana County) (Township)	15732
Washington (Jefferson County) (Township)	15840
Washington (Lawrence County) (Township)	16156
Washington (Lehigh County) (Township)	18080
Washington (Lycoming County) (Township)	17810
Washington (Northampton County) (Township)	18010
Washington (Northumberland County) (Township)	17867
Washington (Schuylkill County) (Township)	17963
Washington (Snyder County) (Township)	17842
Washington (Washington County)	15301
Washington (Westmoreland County) (Township)	15613
Washington (Wyoming County) (Township)	18657
Washington (York County) (Township)	17316
Washington Boro	17582
Washington Crossing	18977
Washington Heights (Part of Lemoyne)	17043
Washington Hill (Part of Pottstown)	19464
Washington Square Gardens	19401
Washingtonville	17884
Wassergass	18055
Waterfall	16689
Waterford (Erie County)	16441
Waterford (Erie County) (Township)	16411
Waterford (Westmoreland County)	15658
Waterford (York County)	17402
Waterloo	17021
Waterloo Mills	19333
Waterman	15748
Waterside	16695
Waterson	16258
Water Street	16611
Waterton	18655
Waterville	17776
Waterworks, The (Part of Pittsburgh)	15212
Watkins	15722
Watrous	16921
Watson (Lycoming County) (Township)	17740
Watson (Warren County) (Township)	16351
Watson Farm	16239
Watson Run	16316
Watsontown	17777
Watters	16033
Wattersonville	16218
Watts (Township)	17020
Wattsburg	16442
Waverly	18471
Wawa (Part of Chester Heights)	19017
Wawaset	19380
Wayland Corners	16335
Waymart	18472
Wayne (Armstrong County) (Township)	16222
Wayne (Clinton County) (Township)	17748
Wayne (Crawford County) (Township)	16314
Wayne (Dauphin County) (Township)	17032
Wayne (Delaware County)	19087
Wayne (Erie County) (Township)	16407
Wayne (Greene County) (Township)	15362
Wayne (Lawrence County) (Township)	16117
Wayne (Mifflin County) (Township)	17051
Wayne (Schuylkill County) (Township)	17933
Waynecastle	17225
Wayne Heights	17268
Waynesboro	17268
Waynesburg	15370
Waynesburg Lakes	15329
Waynesville	17032
Weatherly	18255
Weaverland	17519
Weaversville	18067
Weavertown (Berks County)	19518
Weavertown (Lancaster County)	17505
Weavertown (Lebanon County)	17042
Weavertown (Washington County)	15317
Weber City	15834
Webster	15087
Webster Mills	17233
Weedville	15868
Wegley	15642
Wehnwood (Part of Altoona)	16601
Weidasville	18078
Weidmanville	17522
Weigelstown	17315
Weigh Scale	17872
Weikert	17885
Weilersville	18011
Weinel's Crossroads	15656
Weir Lake	18058
Weisel	18944
Weisenberg (Township)	18066
Weishample	17938
Weissport	18235
Weissport East	18235
Weldbank	16313
Weldon	19006
Wellersburg	15564
Wellington Estates	18901
Welliversville	17815
Wellmans Corners	18834
Wells (Bradford County) (Township)	16925
Wells (Fulton County) (Township)	16691
Wellsboro	16901
Wellsboro Junction	16901
Wellscreek	15541
Wells Tannery	16691
Wellsville	17365
Welsh Hill	18470
Welsh Run	17225
Welty	15666
Wendel	15691
Wendover	15601
Wenks	17304
Wentlings Corners	16232
Werleys Corner	18066
Wernersville	19565
Wernersville Heights	19565
Wernersville State Hospital	19565
Wertz	16693
Wertzville	17055
Wescosville	18106
Wesley	16038
Wesley Chapel	15909
Wesleyville	16510
Wessex Hills	15108
West (Township)	16669
West Abington (Township)	18419
West Acres	17837
West Alexander	15376
West Aliquippa (Part of Aliquippa)	15001
West Ambler	19002
West Annville	17003
West Apollo (Part of Oklahoma)	15613
West Auburn	18623
Westaway	19444
West Bangor (Northampton County)	18072
West Bangor (York County)	17314
West Beaver (Township)	17841
West Belt Junction (Part of Pittsburgh)	15230
West Bend	15433
West Berwick (Part of Berwick)	18603
West Bethlehem (Township)	15345
West Bingham	16923
West Bolivar	15923
West Bradford (Township)	19335
West Branch (Cambria County)	15714
West Branch (Potter County) (Township)	16922
West Brandywine (Township)	19320
West Bridgewater	15009
West Bristol	19007
West Brownsville	15417
West Brunswick (Township)	17961
West Buffalo (Township)	17844
West Burlington	16947
West Burlington (Township)	16914
Westbury	15071
West Caln (Township)	19376
West Cameron	17872
West Cameron (Township)	17872
West Carroll (Township)	15737
West Catasauqua	18052
West Chester	19380-82
For specific West Chester Zip Codes call (215) 696-4808	
West Chillisquaque (Township)	17850
West Clifford	18470
West Cocalico (Township)	17578
Westcolang	18428
West Conshohocken	19428
West Cornwall (Township)	17042
West Creek	15834
West Creek Hills	17011
West Cressona (Part of Cressona)	17929
West Damascus	18469
West Decatur	16878
West Deer (Township)	15076
West Derry	15627
West Donegal (Township)	17022
West Earl (Township)	17508
West Easton	18042
West Elcred	16731
West Elizabeth	15088
West Ellwood Junction (Part of Koppel)	16136
West End (Dauphin County)	17102
West End (Washington County)	15301
West Enola	17025
West Export (Part of Export)	15632
West Fairfield	15944
West Fairview	17025
Westfall (Township)	18336
West Fallowfield (Chester County) (Township)	19330

West Fallowfield-Wilcox PENNSYLVANIA 491

Name	ZIP
West Fallowfield (Crawford County) (Township)	16131
West Falls	18615
West Fayetteville	17222
Westfield (Tioga County)	16950
Westfield (Tioga County) (Township)	16950
Westfield Terrace	17070
West Finley	15377
West Finley (Township)	15377
Westford	16134
West Franklin (Armstrong County) (Township)	16262
West Franklin (Bradford County)	18832
West Freedom	16049
Westgate Hills	18017
West Goshen (Chester County)	19380
West Goshen (Chester County) (Township)	19380
West Goshen Hills	19380
West Goshen Park	19380
West Grove	19390
West Hamburg	19526
West Hanover (Township)	17112
West Hazleton	18201
West Hemlock (Township)	17821
West Hempfield (Township)	17601
West Hickory	16370
West Hill	17013
West Hills Estates	17701
West Hoffman	15101
West Homestead	15120
Westinghouse Village	19029
West Jeannette (Part of Jeannette)	15644
West Jonestown	17038
West Keating (Township)	16871
West Kittanning	16201
West Lampeter (Township)	17537
West Lancaster	17603
Westland	15378
West Lawn (Berks County)	19609
West Lawn (Union County)	17837
West Lebanon (Indiana County)	15783
West Lebanon (Lebanon County) (Township)	17042
West Lebanon (Lebanon County)	17042
West Leechburg	15656
West Leisenring	15489
West Lenox	18826
West Leroy	17724
West Liberty (Butler County)	16057
West Liberty (Clearfield County)	15801
West Library (Part of Bethel Park)	15102
Westline	16740
West Mahanoy (Township)	17976
West Mahoning (Township)	16256
West Manayunk	19151
West Manchester (Township)	17404
West Manchester Mall (Part of York)	17345
West Manheim (Township)	17331
West Market (Part of Philadelphia)	19139
West Marlborough (Township)	19348
West Mayfield	15010
West Mead (Township)	16335
West Meyersdale (Part of Meyersdale)	15552
West Middlesex	16159
West Middletown	15379
West Mifflin	15122-23
For specific West Mifflin Zip Codes call (412) 466-5120	
West Milton	17886
Westminster (Erie County)	16506
Westminster (Luzerne County)	18702
Westminster Manor	15241
West Monocacy	19518
Westmont (Cambria County)	15905
Westmont (Lebanon County)	17042
West Monterey	16049
Westmont Plan	16201
Westmoreland City	15692
West Moshannon	16651
West Myerstown	17067
West Nanticoke	18634
West Nantmeal (Township)	19520
West New Kensington	15030
West Newton	15089

Name	ZIP
West Nicholson	18446
West Norriton (Montgomery County) (Township)	19401
West Norriton (Montgomery County)	19401
West Nottingham (Township)	19362
Weston	18256
Weston Place	17976
Westover (Bucks County)	19067
Westover (Clearfield County)	16692
West Overton	15683
Westover Woods	19401
West Park (Allegheny County)	15136
West Park (Philadelphia County)	19131
West Pen Argyl	18072
West Penn (Township)	17960
West Pennsboro (Township)	17241
West Perry (Township)	17086
West Pike	16922
West Pikeland (Township)	19425
West Pike Run (Township)	15427
West Pittsburg	16160
West Pittston	18643
West Point (Cambria County)	15942
West Point (Montgomery County)	19486
West Point (Westmoreland County)	15601
Westport	17778
West Pottsgrove (Montgomery County)	19464
West Pottsgrove (Montgomery County) (Township)	19464
West Providence (Township)	15537
West Reading	19611
West Renovo	17764
West Ridge	17603
West Rockhill (Township)	18960
West Sadsbury (Township)	19365
West Salem (Township)	16125
West Salisbury	15565
West Scranton (Part of Scranton)	18504
West Shenango (Township)	16134
West Side (Part of West Newton)	15089
West Spring Creek	16407
West Springfield	16443
West St. Clair (Township)	15521
West Sunbury	16061
West Tarentum (Part of Tarentum)	15084
West Taylor (Township)	15906
West Telford (Part of Telford)	18969
Westtown	19395
Westtown (Township)	19395
Westtown Acres	19380
West Union	15364
West Valley	16201
West Vandergrift (Part of Vandergrift)	15690
West View (Allegheny County)	15229
Westview (Beaver County)	15009
Westville	15824
West Vincent (Township)	19425
West Warren	13812
West Wayne (Delaware County)	19087
West Waynesburg	15370
West Wheatfield (Township)	15944
West Whiteland (Township)	19341
West William Penn	17976
West Willow	17583
West Wilmerding	15137
West Winfield	16023
Westwood (Cambria County)	15905
Westwood (Chester County)	19320
Westwood Park	19083
West Wyoming	18644
West Wyomissing	19609
West York	17404
West Zollarsville	15345
Wetherills Corner	19460
Wetmore (McKean County)	16735
Wetmore (McKean County) (Township)	16735
Wetona	16914
Wexford	15090
Weyant	16655
Wharton (Township)	16720

Name	ZIP
Wharton (Fayette County) (Township)	15437
Wharton (Potter County)	16720
Wheatfield (Township)	17020
Wheatland	16161
Wheatland Hills	17604
Wheat Sheaf	19067
Wheeler	15425
Wheelerville	17768
Whig Hill	16353
Whipkeys-Dam	15551
Whiskerville	16040
Whitaker	15120
White (Beaver County) (Township)	15010
White (Cambria County) (Township)	15906
White (Fayette County)	15490
White (Indiana County)	15681
White (Indiana County) (Township)	15701
White Bear	19508
White Cottage	15341
White Deer	17887
White Deer (Township)	17887
Whitehall (Township)	18052
White Hall	17821
Whitehall (Adams County)	17340
Whitehall (Allegheny County)	15227
White Hall (Dauphin County)	17110
Whitehall (Lehigh County)	18052
Whitehall Mall	18052
Whitehall Park	19401
White Haven	18661
White Hill	17011
White Horse (Chester County)	19073
White Horse (Lancaster County)	17527
White House	15478
Whiteland Crest	19341
Whiteland Farms	19355
Whiteley (Township)	15370
Whitemarsh (Township)	19428
Whitemarsh Downs	19075
Whitemarsh Estates	19444
Whitemarsh Greens	19444
Whitemarsh Hills	19444
Whitemarsh Township	19428
Whitemarsh Valley Farms	19444
White Mills	18473
White Oak (Allegheny County)	15131
White Oak (Lancaster County)	17545
White Oak (Westmoreland County)	15068
White Oak Manor	18042
White Oaks	18701
White Pine	17771
Whitesburg	16201
Whites Corner	16927
Whites Crossing	18407
Whites Ferry	18657
Whiteside	16651
Whitesprings	17844
White Squaw Mission	17353
Whitestown	16052
Whites Valley	18453
White Township	15010
White Valley (Part of Murrysville)	15632
Whitewood	19057
Whitfield	19609
Whitford Hills	19341
Whitney	15693
Whitney Lake	18428
Whitneyville	16901
Whitpain (Township)	19422
Whitsett	15473
Wick	16057
Wickerham Manor	15063
Wickerton	19390
Wickham Village	15001
Wickhaven	15492
Wiconisco	17097
Wiconisco (Township)	17097
Widener College (Part of Chester)	19013
Widnoon	16261
Wiegletown	16101
Wiester (Part of Murrysville)	15632
Wiggans	17948
Wigwam	16731
Wila	17074
Wilawana	18840
Wilbur	15563
Wilburton	17888
Wilco Hill	15087
Wilcox	15870

492 PENNSYLVANIA Wild Acres Country Club-Youngsville

	ZIP		ZIP		ZIP
Wild Acres Country Club	18328	Windsor Farms	17110	Worman	19518
Wildcat	16248	Windsor Park (Cumberland		Wormleysburg	17043
Wilden Acres	18042	County)	17055	Worth (Butler County)	
Wildwood	15091	Windsor Park (York County)	17403	(Township)	16057
Wildwood Terrace	18701	Windward Heights	16001	Worth (Centre County)	
Wiley	17363	Winfield (Butler County)		(Township)	16870
Wiley Heights	15320	(Township)	16023	Worth (Mercer County)	
Wilgus	15742	Winfield (Union County)	17889	(Township)	16133
Wilkes-Barre	18701-73	Wingate	16880	Worthington	16262
For specific Wilkes-Barre Zip		Wingerton	17268	Worthville	15784
Codes call (717) 829-5468		Winslow	15767	Woxall	18979
Wilkes-Barre (Township)	18702	Winslow (Township)	15851	Wright (Township)	18707
Wilkes-Barre Township	18702	Winstead	15474	Wrights	16743
Wilkes Manor	18977	Winterburne	15849	Wrights Corners	16749
Wilkins (Township)	15145	Winterdale	18461	Wrightsdale	17563
Wilkinsburg	15221	Winterstown	17356	Wrightstown	18940
Wilkins Township	15145	Wintersville	17087	Wrightstown (Township)	18980
Willet	15732	Wiscasset	18344	Wrightsville (Warren County)	16340
William Penn Annex (Part of		Wishaw	15851	Wrightsville (York County)	17368
Philadelphia)	19107	Wismer	18947	Wurtemburg	16117
William Penn Manor	18017	Wissahickon Village	19444	Wurtemburg Heights	16117
Williams (Dauphin County)		Wissinoming (Part of		Wyalusing (Bradford	
(Township)	17098	Philadelphia)	19135	County)	18853
Williams (Montgomery		Witinski Villa	18706	Wyalusing (Bradford	
County)	19444	Witmer	17585	County) (Township)	18853
Williams (Northampton		Wittmer	15116	Wyano	15695
County) (Township)	18042	Wolf (Township)	17737	Wyattville (Part of	
Williamsburg (Blair County)	16693	Wolf Creek (Township)	16127	Sugarcreek)	16323
Williamsburg (Clarion		Wolfdale	15301	Wycombe	18980
County)	16214	Wolf Run	16749	Wydnor	18015
Williams Grove	17055	Wolfsburg	15522	Wyebrooke	19344
Williamson	17270	Wolfs Corner	16353	Wylandville	15330
Williamsport	17701-03	Wolfs Crossroads	17801	Wylie (Part of Clairton)	15025
For specific Williamsport Zip		Wolftown (Part of North		Wylie (Part of Pittsburgh)	15219
Codes call (717) 323-6103		Braddock)	15104	Wylie (Allegheny County)	15037
Williamstown	17098	Womelsdorf	19567	Wyncote	19095
Willistown (Township)	19355	Wood	16694	Wyncote Hills	19095
Willock (Part of Baldwin)	15236	Wood (Township)	16674	Wyncroft	19063
Willopenn	18966	Woodale	18301	Wyndham Hills	17403
Willowbrook	19061	Woodbine	17302	Wyndmoor	19118
Willowburn	19085	Woodbourne	19047	Wyndmoor Valley	19075
Willowdale	19348	Woodbridgetown	15478	Wynn	15401
Willow Grove (Lawrence		Woodbury (Bedford County)	16695	Wynnewood (Bucks	
County)	16101	Woodbury (Bedford County)		County)	19067
Willow Grove (Montgomery		(Township)	16695	Wynnewood (Montgomery	
County)	19090	Woodbury (Blair County)		County)	19096
Willow Grove Naval Air		(Township)	16693	Wynnewood Shopping	
Station	19090	Woodchoppertown	19512	Center	19096
Willow Grove Park	19090	Woodcock (Crawford		Wyoming	18644
Willow Hill	17271	County)	16433	Wyoming Camp Ground	18643
Willow Lake	17901	Woodcock (Crawford		Wyoming Valley Mall	
Will-O-Wood	19007	County) (Township)	16433	(Luzerne County)	18702
Willow Springs (Columbia		Woodcock Grange	16433	Wyomissing	19610
County)	17815	Woodcrest	19380	Wyomissing Hills	19609
Willow Springs		Wooddale	15425	Wyomissing Junction (Part	
(Westmoreland County)	15642	Woodglen	15442	of Wyomissing)	19610
Willow Street	17584	Woodhaven Estates	15001	Wysox	18854
Willow View Heights	17584	Woodhill	18940	Wysox (Township)	18854
Wills Creek	15545	Woodland (Clearfield		Yardley	19067
Wilmer	19460	County)	16881	Yardley Farms	19067
Wilmerding	15148	Woodland (Mifflin County)	17084	Yardley Hunt	19067
Wilmington (Lawrence		Woodland Heights		Yarnell	16823
County) (Township)	16105	(Venango County)	16301	Yatesboro	16263
Wilmington (Mercer County)		Woodland Park	17701	Yatesville (Luzerne County)	18640
(Township)	16142	Woodland View	17402	Yatesville (Schuylkill County)	17976
Wilmore	15962	Woodlawn (Lancaster		Yeadon	19050
Wilmore Heights	15958	County)	17603	Yeagertown	17099
Wilmot (Township)	18846	Woodlawn (Lehigh County)	18104	Yellow Creek	16650
Wilpen	15658	Woodlawn (Westmoreland		Yellow Hammer	16322
Wilshire Hills (Lancaster		County)	15644	Yellow House	19518
County)	17603	Woodlawn Park	15001	Yellowwood	19007
Wilshire Hills (York County)	17402	Woodlyn	19094	Yerkes	19426
Wilson (Allegheny County)	15025	Woodlyn Manor	19094	Yocumtown	17319
Wilson (Berks County)	19608	Woodlyn Park	19094	Yoe	17313
Wilson (Northampton		Woodrow	15340	York	17401-07
County)	18042	Woodruff	15341	For specific York Zip Codes call	
Wilson Creek	15557	Woodside (Bucks County)	19067	(717) 848-2381	
Wilson Heights	18426	Woodside (Fayette County)	15478	York (Township)	17403
Wilsons Corners	19460	Woodside (Luzerne County)	18224	Yorkana	17402
Wimmers	18436	Woodside-Drifton	18221	York County (Part of York)	17402
Winburne	16879	Woods of Sandy Ridge	18901	York Haven	17370
Windber	15963	Woodstown	15935	Yorklyn	17402
Winder Village	19007	Woodvale Heights	15901	York New Salem	17371
Windfall	17724	Woodville	15106	York Road (Bucks County)	18974
Windgap	18091	Woodville State Hospital	15106	York Road (York County)	17331
Windham (Bradford County)		Woodward (Centre County)	16882	York Run	15401
(Township)	18837	Woodward (Clearfield		Yorkshire	17402
Windham (Wyoming		County) (Township)	16651	York Springs	17372
County) (Township)	18623	Woodward (Clinton County)		Yostville	18444
Windham Center	18837	(Township)	17745	Young (Indiana County)	
Winding Brook Manor	18062	Woodward (Lycoming		(Township)	15725
Winding Hill	17055	County) (Township)	17744	Young (Jefferson County)	
Winding Hill Heights	17055	Woodward Acres	15601	(Township)	15767
Windom	17603	Woodycrest	16801	Youngdale	17748
Wind Ridge	15380	Woolrich	17779	Youngsburg	19320
Windsor (Berks County)		Wopsononock	16636	Youngstown (Luzerne	
(Township)	19526	Worcester	19490	County)	18221
Windsor (York County)	17366	Worcester (Township)	19490	Youngstown (Westmoreland	
Windsor (York County)		Worden Place (Part of		County)	15696
(Township)	17356	Harveys Lake)	18618	Youngsville (Northampton	
Windsor Castle	19526	Worleytown	17225	County)	18038

Location	ZIP	Location	ZIP	Location	ZIP
Youngsville (Warren County)	16371	Zerbe (Schuylkill County)	17981	Zionsville	18092
Youngwood	15697	Zieglerville	19492	Zollarsville	15345
Yukon	15698	Zimmerman	15501	Zooks Corner	17602
Zebleys Corner	19061	Zion (Centre County)	16823	Zooks Dam	17059
Zehners	17960	Zion (Luzerne County)	18643	Zora	17320
Zelienople	16063	Zion Grove	17985	Zucksville	18042
Zerbe (Northumberland County) (Township)	17881	Zionhill	18981	Zullinger	17272
		Zions View	17404		

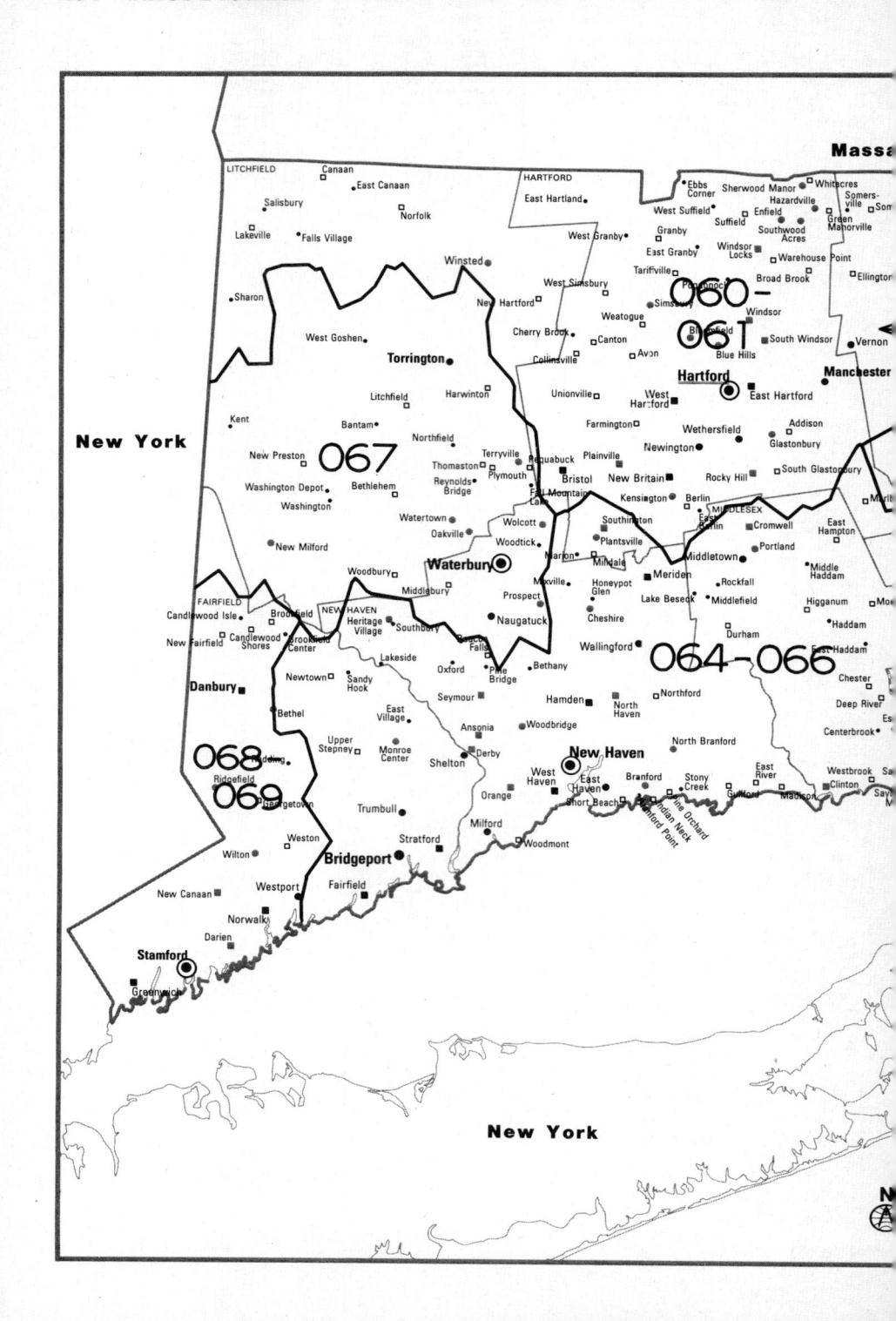

RHODE ISLAND

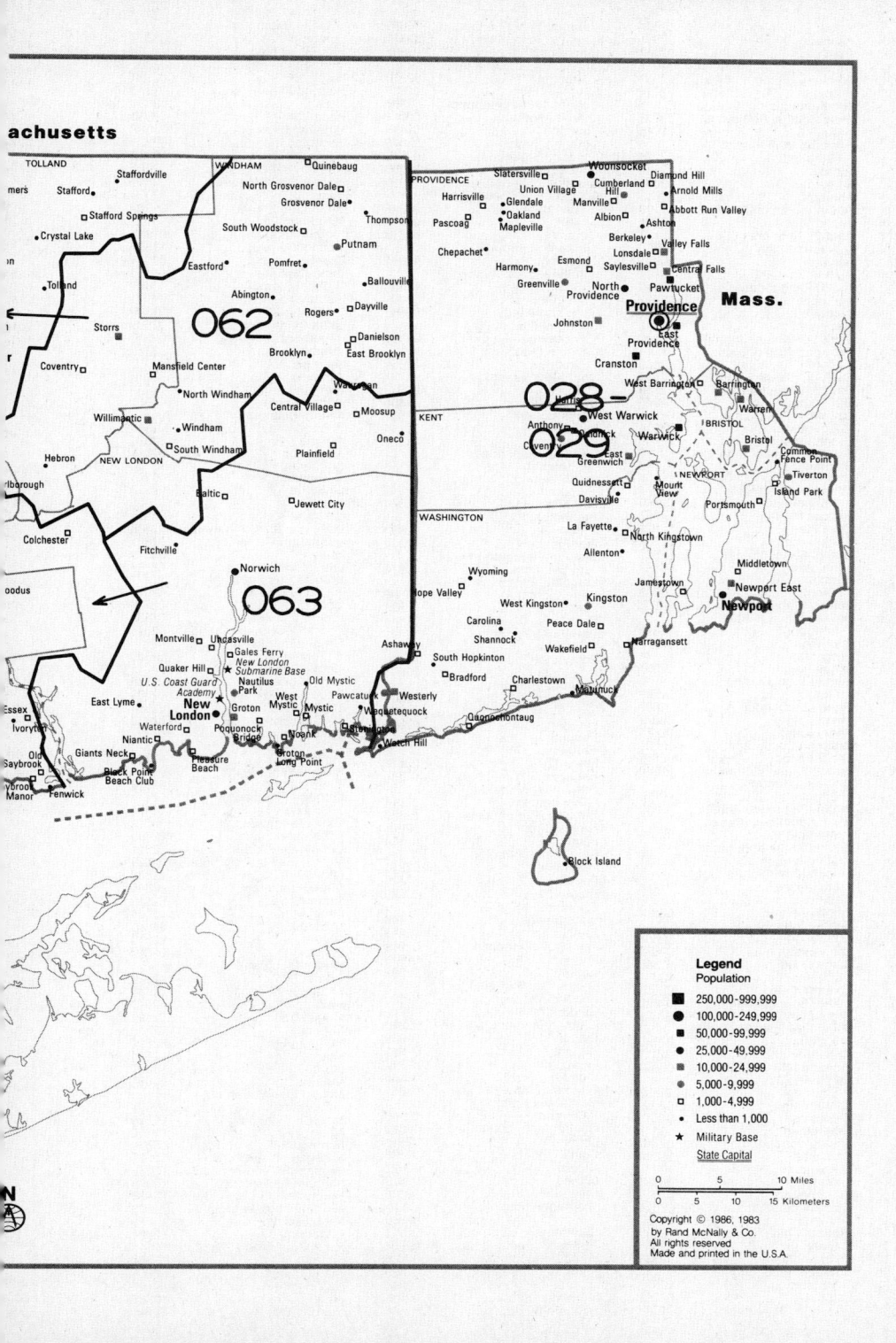

RHODE ISLAND

Legend
Population
- ■ 250,000-999,999
- ● 100,000-249,999
- ■ 50,000-99,999
- ● 25,000-49,999
- ■ 10,000-24,999
- ● 5,000-9,999
- □ 1,000-4,999
- · Less than 1,000
- ★ Military Base
- State Capital

0   5   10 Miles
0   5   10   15 Kilometers

Copyright © 1986, 1983
by Rand McNally & Co.
All rights reserved
Made and printed in the U.S.A.

496 RHODE ISLAND — Abbott Run Valley-Newport East

Place	ZIP
Abbott Run Valley	02864
Adamsville	02801
Albion	02802
Allendale	02911
Allenton	02852
Alton	02894
Annawomscutt	02806
Annex (Part of Providence)	02903
Anthony	02816
Apple Blossom (Part of Cranston)	02920
Arcadia	02832
Arctic	02893
Arkwright	02816
Arlington (Part of Cranston)	02920
Arnold Mills	02864
Arnold's Neck (Part of Warwick)	02886
Ashaway	02804
Ashton	02864
Auburn (Part of Cranston)	02910
Austin	02822
Avondale	02891
Barberville	02832
Barrington (Bristol County)	02806
Barrington (Bristol County) (Town)	02806
Bayridge (Part of Warwick)	02818
Bayside (Part of Warwick)	02889
Bay Spring	02806
Bay View (Part of East Providence)	02914
Beach Terrace	02809
Bellefonte (Part of Cranston)	02920
Belleville	02852
Berkeley	02864
Beverage Hill (Part of Pawtucket)	02860
Bishops Heights	02857
Black Plain	02822
Block Island	02807
Bonnet Shores	02882
Boon Lake	02822
Bowdish Lake	02814
Bradford	02808
Branch Village	02895
Brenton Village (Part of Newport)	02840
Bridgeport	02878
Bridgetown	02874
Briggs Beach	02837
Bristol (Bristol County) (Town)	02809
Bristol (Bristol County)	02809
Bristol Colony	02872
Bristol Ferry	02871
Bristol Highlands	02809
Bristol Narrows	02809
Broadway (Part of Newport)	02840
Brookfield (Part of Cranston)	02920
Brown (Part of Providence)	02912
Brush Neck Cove (Part of Warwick)	02886
Bryant College of Business Administration	02917
Bullocks Point (Part of East Providence)	02914
Burdickville	02808
Burrillville (Town)	02830
Buttonwoods (Part of Warwick)	02886
Canonchet	02832
Carnegie Heights	02865
Carolina	02812
Carpenters Beach	02879
Cedar Grove Estates	02822
Cedar Point	02835
Cedar Tree Point (Part of Warwick)	02886
Centerdale	02911
Centerville (Kent County)	02893
Centerville (Washington County)	02832
Central Falls	02863
Charlestown	02813
Charlestown (Town)	02813
Charlestown Beach	02813
Chepachet	02814
Chepiwanoxet (Part of Warwick)	02886
Cherry Valley	02814
Cherry Valley Beach	02814
Chopmist	02857
Clarke's Village	02835
Clayville	02815
Clyde	02893
Coasters Harbor (Part of Newport)	02840
Coggeshall	02885
Coles (Part of Warwick)	02889

Place	ZIP
Columbia Heights	02875
Common Fence Point	02871
Commons	02837
Comstock Gardens (Part of Cranston)	02910
Conanicut Park	02835
Conimicut (Part of Warwick)	02889
Corey's Lane	02871
Coventry	02816
Coventry (Town)	02816
Coventry Center	02816
Cowesett (Part of Warwick)	02886
Cranston	02910
Crescent Park (Part of East Providence)	02914
Crompton	02893
Cross Mills	02813
Cumberland (Providence County)	02864
Cumberland (Providence County) (Town)	02864
Cumberland Hill	02864
Curtis Corners	02883
Darlington (Part of Pawtucket)	02861
Davisville (Washington County)	02854
Davisville (Washington County)	02852
Diamond Hill	02864
Dunns Corners	02891
Durfee Hill	02814
Eagleville	02878
East Greenwich (Kent County) (Town)	02818
East Greenwich (Kent County)	02818
East Matunuck	02879
East Natick (Part of Warwick)	02893
East Providence	02914
East Providence Wharf (Part of East Providence)	02914
East Side (Part of Providence)	02906
East Warren	02885
Echo Lake	02814
Eden Park (Part of Cranston)	02920
Edgewood (Part of Cranston)	02905
Elmwood (Part of Providence)	02907
Enos (Part of Cranston)	02920
Escoheag	02821
Esmond	02917
Exeter	02822
Exeter (Town)	02822
Fairbanks Corner	02827
Finast (Part of East Providence)	02914
Fiskeville (Part of Cranston)	02823
Fogland Point	02878
Forestdale	02824
Fort Adams (Part of Newport)	02840
Foster	02825
Foster (Town)	02825
Fox Point (Part of Providence)	02906
Frenchtown	02818
Friar (Part of Providence)	02918
Fruit Hill	02911
Galilee	02882
Garden City (Part of Cranston)	02920
Garden City Shopping Center (Part of Cranston)	02920
Gazzaville	02839
Geneva	02911
Georgiaville	02917
Glendale	02826
Glocester (Town)	02814
Goat Island (Part of Newport)	02840
Goulds	02883
Graniteville	02911
Grants Mills	02838
Greene	02827
Green Hill	02879
Greenville	02828
Greenwood (Part of Warwick)	02886
Greystone	02911
Hamilton	02852
Hampden Meadows	02806
Harmony	02829
Harris	02816
Harrisville	02830
Haversham	02891

Place	ZIP
Highland Beach (Part of Warwick)	02889
Hill's Grove (Part of Warwick)	02886
Hog Island	02809
Homestead	02872
Hope	02831
Hope Valley	02832
Hopkins Hollow	02827
Hopkinton	02833
Hopkinton (Town)	02833
Howard (Part of Cranston)	02920
Hoxsie (Part of Warwick)	02889
Hughesdale	02919
Indian Lake Shores	02879
India Point (Part of Providence)	02903
Island Park	02871
Jackson	02823
Jamestown (Newport County) (Town)	02835
Jamestown (Newport County)	02835
Jamestown Center	02835
Jamestown Shores	02835
Jerusalem	02879
Johnston (Town)	02919
Johnston	02919
Kent Corner (Part of East Providence)	02914
Kent Heights (Part of East Providence)	02914
Kenyon	02836
Kingston	02881
Knightsville (Part of Cranston)	02920
La Fayette	02852
Lake Bel Air	02895
Lake Mishnock	02816
Lakewood (Part of Warwick)	02888
Langworthy Corner	02891
Laurel Hill	02859
Laurel Park	02885
Leonard Corner (Part of East Providence)	02914
Liberty	02877
Limerock	02865
Lincoln (Providence County)	02865
Lincoln (Providence County) (Town)	02860
Lincoln Park (Part of Warwick)	02888
Lippit	02893
Lippitt Estate	02864
Little Compton	02837
Little Compton (Town)	02837
Lockwood Corner (Part of Warwick)	02889
Longmeadow (Part of Warwick)	02889
Lonsdale (Providence County)	02864
Lonsdale (Providence County)	02865
Lymansville	02911
Manton (Part of Providence)	02909
Manville	02838
Maple Root Village	02816
Mapleville	02839
Marieville	02904
Matunuck	02879
Mellville	02840
Melville	02840
Meshanticut (Part of Cranston)	02920
Middletown (Town)	02840
Middletown	02840
Misquamicut	02891
Mohegan	02830
Mohegan Bluffs	02807
Mooresfield	02874
Moosup Valley	02827
Moscow	02832
Mount Pleasant (Part of Providence)	02908
Mount Vernon	02825
Mount View	02852
Nannaquaket	02878
Narragansett	02882
Narragansett (Town)	02882
Narragansett Heights	02878
Nasonville	02830
Natick (Part of Warwick)	02893
Nausauket (Part of Warwick)	02886
Naval Construction Battalion Center	02854
Nayatt	02806
New Harbor	02807
Newport	02840
Newport East	02840

RHODE ISLAND 497

Location	ZIP
New Shoreham (Town)	02807
Nichols Corner	02818
Nooseneck	02816
North (Part of Providence)	02908
North Foster	02825
North Kingstown	02852-54
For specific North Kingstown Zip Codes call (401) 294-4641	
North Providence (Providence County) (Town)	02911
North Providence (Providence County)	02911
North Quidnessett	02852
North Scituate	02857
North Smithfield (Town)	02876
Norwood (Part of Warwick)	02888
Oakland	02830
Oakland Beach (Part of Warwick)	02886
Oak Lawn (Part of Cranston)	02920
Old Harbor	02807
Olney Arnold Estates (Part of Cranston)	02920
Olneyville (Part of Providence)	02909
Palace Garden (Part of Warwick)	02888
Parcel Post Annex	02891
Pascoag	02859
Pawtucket	02860-65
For specific Pawtucket Zip Codes call (401) 722-1073	
Peace Dale	02883
Perryville	02879
Pettaquamscutt Lake Shores	02874
Phenix	02893
Phillipsdale (Part of East Providence)	02914
Pilgrim (Part of Warwick)	02888
Pine Hill	02822
Pleasant View (Part of Pawtucket)	02860
Plum Beach	02874
Plum Point	02874
Poccasett Heights	02871
Point Judith	02882
Pontiac (Part of Warwick)	02886
Popasquash Point	02809
Portsmouth	02871
Portsmouth (Town)	02871
Potowomut (Part of Warwick)	02818
Potter Hill	02891
Primrose	02895
Print Works (Part of Cranston)	02920
Providence	02901-40
For specific Providence Zip Codes call (401) 276-6850	
Prudence Island	02872
Prudence Park	02872
Quidnessett	02852
Quidnick	02816
Quinnville	02865
Quonochontaug	02813
Rhode Island Mall (Part of Warwick)	02886
Rice City	02827
Rice Plat	02857
Richmond (Town)	02812
River Point	02893
Riverside (Part of East Providence)	02915
River Vue (Part of Warwick)	02889
Rockville	02873
Rocky Point (Part of Warwick)	02889
Rumford (Part of East Providence)	02916
Rumstick Point	02806
Sakonnet	02837
Sandy Point (Kent County)	02818
Sandy Point (Washington County)	02807
Saunderstown	02874
Saundersville	02857
Saylesville	02865
Scituate (Town)	02857
Shady Harbor	02891
Shannock	02875
Shawomet (Part of Warwick)	02889
Shelter Harbor	02891
Shores Acres	02852
Silver Lake (Part of Providence)	02909
Simmonsville	02919
Slatersville	02876
Slocum	02877
Smithfield (Town)	02917
Smith Hill (Part of Providence)	02908
Sockanosset (Part of Cranston)	02920
South Foster	02825
South Hopkinton	02813
South Kingstown (Town)	02879
South Providence (Part of Providence)	02905
South Warren	02885
Spragueville	02828
Spring Green (Part of Warwick)	02888
Spring Grove	02814
Spring Lake Beach	02826
Squantum (Part of East Providence)	02914
Stillwater	02917
Summit	02827
Tarkiln	02830
The Anchorage	02840
The Hummocks	02871
Thornton	02919
Tiverton	02878
Tiverton (Town)	02878
Tiverton Four Corners	02878
Tockwotten (Part of Providence)	02903
Tonomy Hill (Part of Newport)	02840
Touisset Highlands	02885
Tuckertown	02879
Tunipus	02837
Union Village	02895
Usquepaug	02892
Valley Falls	02864
Vaughn Hollow	02827
Wakefield	02879-83
For specific Wakefield Zip Codes call (401) 783-2691	
Wakefield-Peacedale	02883
Walnut Hill (Part of Woonsocket)	02895
Warren (Bristol County) (Town)	02885
Warren (Bristol County)	02885
Warren Point	02837
Warwick	02886-89
For specific Warwick Zip Codes call (401) 737-6200	
Warwick Mall (Part of Warwick)	02886
Warwick Neck (Part of Warwick)	02889
Washington Park (Part of Cranston)	02905
Watch Hill	02891
Watchmocket Square (Part of East Providence)	02914
Waterford	01504
Waterman Four Corners	02857
Weekapaug	02891
West Barrington	02806
Westcott (Part of Warwick)	02893
Westcott Beach	02814
Westerly	02891
Westerly (Town)	02891
West Glocester	06260
West Greenville	02828
West Greenwich (Town)	02816
West Greenwich Center	02827
West Kingston	02892
West Warwick (Kent County)	02893
West Warwick (Kent County) (Town)	02893
Weybosset Hill (Part of Providence)	02903
Whipple	02830
White Rock	02891
Wickford Junction	02852
Wildes Corner (Part of Warwick)	02886
Wood Estates	02816
Wood River Junction	02894
Woodville (Providence County)	02911
Woodville (Washington County)	02832
Woonsocket	02895
Wyoming	02898
Yorktown Manor	02852

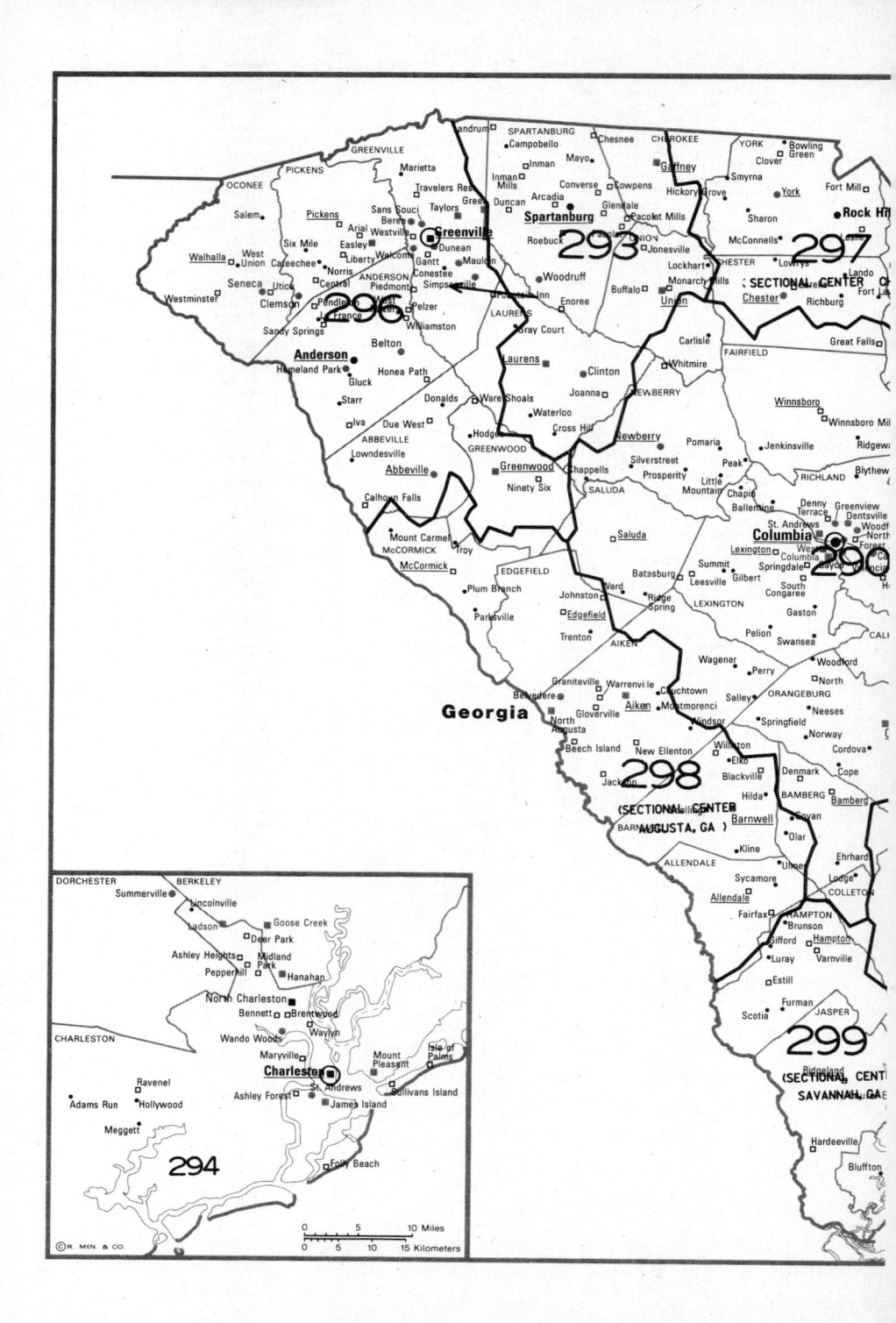

SOUTH CAROLINA

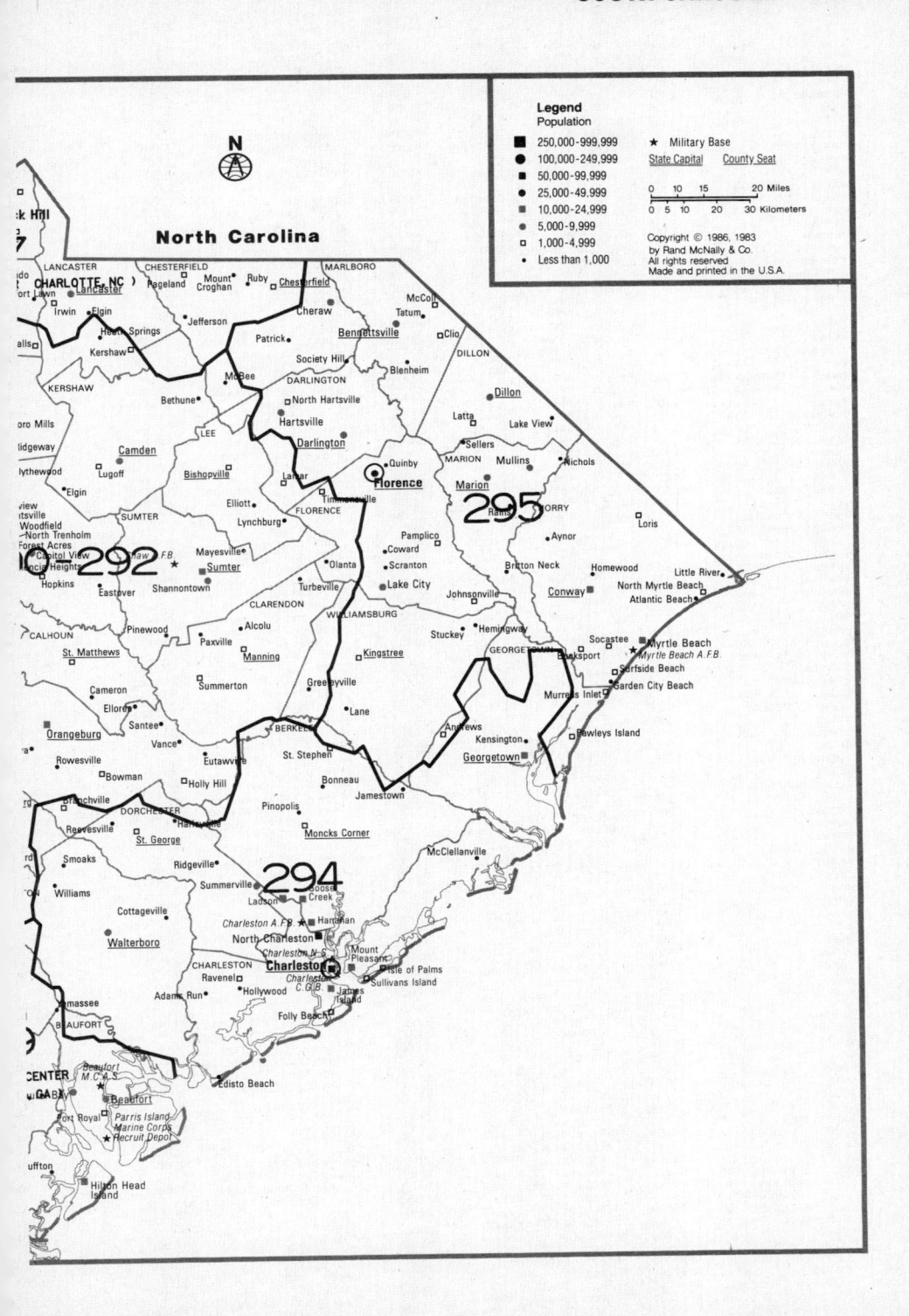

SOUTH CAROLINA 499

500 SOUTH CAROLINA   Abbeville-Chicora Place

	ZIP		ZIP		ZIP
Abbeville	29620	Belle Meade (Greenville County)	29603	Brownsville (Marlboro County)	29516
Abney	29067	Belle Meade (Lexington County)	29169	Brownway	29526
Adamsburg	29379	Bellinger	29927	Bruner	29061
Adams Run	29426	Bells	29475	Brunson	29911
Adamsville	29570	Belmont	29203	Brunsons Crossroads	29554
Adger	29180	Belton	29627	Buck Hall	29429
Adrian	29526	Belvedere (Aiken County)	29841	Buckingham Landing (Part of Hilton Head Island)	29928
Aiken	29801	Belvedere (Richland County)	29204	Bucksport	29527
Aiken Estates	29801	Ben Avon	29302	Bucksville	29526
Aiken West	29801	Bendale (Part of Columbia)	29203	Buffalo	29321
Alcolu	29001	Bennett	29405	Buford Crossroads	29720
Alcot	29010	Bennettsville	29512	Bufords Bridge	29843
Alice Mill (Part of Easley)	29640	Bennettsville Southwest	29512	Bullock Creek	29742
Allen	29511	Berea (Greenville County)	29611	Bunker Hill	29536
Allendale	29810	Berlin	29137	Burgess	29576
Allsbrook	29569	Bethany	29710	Burnettown	29834
Alvin	29479	Bethcar	29164	Burnt Church Crossroads	29452
Anderson	29621-25	Bethera	29430	Burton	29902
For specific Anderson Zip Codes call (803) 226-1595		Bethesda	29584	Bynum	29556
Anderson Mall (Part of Anderson)	29621	Bethune	29009	Byrd	29477
Andrews	29510	Beufordtown	29453	Byrds Crossroads	28114
Angelus	29718	Beverly Hills	29445	Cades	29518
Angle Siding	29902	Biddle	29180	Caesars Head	28718
Ansel	29651	Bingham	29565	Caldwell Street (Part of Rock Hill)	29731
Antioch (Kershaw County)	29020	Bird Town	29550	Calhoun (Part of Clemson)	29631
Antioch (Lancaster County)	29720	Bishopville	29010	Calhoun Falls	29628
Antreville	29655	Blacks	29166	Callison	29819
Appleton	29810	Blacksburg	29702	Camden	29020
Appleton Mills	29621	Blackstock	29014	Cameron	29030
Aragon Mills (Chester County)	29706	Blackville	29817	Campbell Work Release Center	29210
Aragon Mills (York County)	29730	Blair	29015	Camp Creek	29720
Arcadia	29320	Blairville	29742	Camp Croft	29302
Arcadia Lakes	29206	Blakedale	29646	Campobello	29322
Arial	29640	Blenheim	29516	Campton	29349
Ariel Cross Roads	29574	Bloomingvale	29510	Canaan (Orangeburg County)	29038
Arkwright (Spartanburg County)	29301	Bloomville	29102	Canaan (Spartanburg County)	29302
Arlington	29651	Blossom	29583	Canadys	29433
Armenia	29706	Blue Brick	29571	Cane Savannah	29150
Arthurtown	29201	Blue Heaven	29638	Canterbury	29673
Asbury	29340	Blue Ridge Community Pre-Release Center	29609	Capitol (Part of Columbia)	29211
Ashepoo	29446	Blue Town	29512	Capitol View (Richland County)	29209
Ashland	29010	Bluff Estates	29209	Carlisle	29031
Ashleigh	29817	Bluffton	29910	Carmel	29058
Ashley Forest	29407	Blythewood	29016	Caromi Village	29456
Ashley Hall (Part of Charleston)	29401	Bob Jones University (Part of Greenville)	29614	Cartersville	29161
Ashley Heights	29405	Boiling Springs	29316	Carver Heights	29204
Ashley Junction (Part of North Charleston)	29406	Bolen	29115	Carvers Bay	29554
Ashton	29082	Bon Air Terrace	29150	Cash	29520
Ashwood	29150	Bonham	29379	Cashville	29388
Atkins	29080	Bonneau	29431	Cassatt	29032
Atlantic Beach	29582	Bonniview Estates	29801	Catarrh	29718
Auburn	29550	Boones Creek	29676	Catawba	29704
Augusta Road (Part of Greenville)	29604	Bordeaux	29835	Cateechee	29667
Avondale	29407	Borden	29017	Cave	29810
Avondale-Moorland	29407	Boulder Bluff (Part of Goose Creek)	29445	Cayce	29033
Awendaw	29429	Bounty Land	29678	Cayce-West Columbia (Part of West Columbia)	29169
Aynor	29511	Bowling Green	29703	Cedar Grove	29526
Badham	29471	Bowman	29018	Cedar Springs	29455
Baileys Landing	29936	Bowyer	29059	Cedar Terrace	29209
Baker Crossroads	29569	Boyden Arbor	29206	Celriver	29730
Bald Rock	29379	Boykin	29128	Cementon	29059
Baldwin	29706	Boykins	28343	Centenary	29519
Ballentine	29002	Bradley	29819	Centerville	29565
Balltown	29801	Bradleyville	29841	Central	29630
Bamberg	29003	Branchville	29432	Central Pacolet	29372
Barefoot	29006	Brand	29360	Challedon	29210
Barkersville	29916	Brandon	29611	Chapin	29036
Barksdale	29360	Branwood (Part of Greenville)	29610	Chappells	29037
Barnes	29655	Brattonsville	29726	Charleston	29401-20
Barnwell	29812	Brazen Crossroads	29583	For specific Charleston Zip Codes call (803) 745-4350	
Barrineau	29560	Breeze Hill	29834	Charleston Heights (Part of North Charleston)	29405
Barton	29827	Brentwood	29405	Charles Towne Square (Part of North Charleston)	29406
Bascomville	29729	Brewerton	29692	Chartwell	29210
Batesburg	29006	Briarcliffe Acres	29577	Cheddar	29627
Bath	29816	Brighton	29922	Cheraw	29520
Baton Rouge	29706	Brighton Beach	29910	Cherokee	29302
Battlecreek	29658	Brightsville	28343	Cherokee Falls	29705
Baxter Forks	29569	Bristow	29516	Cherokee Forest	29687
Bayboro	29569	Britton	29150	Cherry Grove Beach (Part of North Myrtle Beach)	29582
Bay Springs	29584	Britton Neck	29546	Cherry Road (Part of Rock Hill)	29730
Bay View	29204	Broad Street (Part of Sumter)	29150	Cherryville	29150
Beaufort (Beaufort County)	29901-03	Broadway	29125	Chesnee	29323
For specific Beaufort Zip Codes call (803) 524-4746		Broadway Lake	29621	Chester	29706
Beaufort (Lancaster County)	29720	Brockington	29556	Chesterfield	29709
Beaufort Marine Corps Air Station	29904	Brogdon	29150	Chestnut Hills	29605
Beaufort Station	29904	Brookdale (Orangeburg County)	29115	Chickasaw Point	29643
Beckhamville	29055	Brook Forest	29605	Chicora Place (Part of North Charleston)	29405
Beech Island	29841	Brook Green Park	29501		
Bel-Clear Heights	29841	Brooklyn	29720		
Beldoc	29836	Brooksville	29582		
Belle Isle Gardens	29440	Brownsville (Dorchester County)	29483		

Choppee-Gardens Corner **SOUTH CAROLINA** **501**

Name	ZIP
Choppee	29440
Citadel (Part of Charleston)	29409
Citadel Mall (Part of Charleston)	29407
City View	29611
Claremont	29150
Clarks Hill	29821
Claussen	29505
Clayton	29015
Clearmont	29693
Clear Pond	29003
Clearspring	29681
Clearwater	29822
Clemson	29631-33
For specific Clemson Zip Codes call (803) 654-2531	
Clemson University	29631
Cleora	29824
Cleveland	29635
Clifton	29324
Clinton	29325
Clio	29525
Clover	29710
Clubhouse Crossroads (Dorchester County)	29472
Club House Crossroads (Lexington County)	29054
Clyde	29101
Coastal (Part of North Myrtle Beach)	29582
Coastal Work Release Center	29405
Cochrantown	29526
Cokesbury	29653
Cold Point	29360
Coldstream	29210
College Acres	29801
Colliers	29838
Collins	29712
Columbia	29201-92
For specific Columbia Zip Codes call (803) 733-4646	
Columbia Bible College	29203
Columbia Mall	29204
Coneross	29693
Conestee	29636
Congaree	29044
Converse	29329
Conway	29526
Cooks Crossroads	29644
Cool Branch	29031
Cooley Springs	29323
Cool Spring	29511
Coosaw	29940
Coosawhatchie	29912
Cope	29038
Cordesville	29434
Cordova	29039
Cornaca	29646
Cornwell	29014
Cottageville	29435
Couchtown	29801
Country Club Estates	29730
Courtenay	29678
Coward	29530
Cowpens	29330
Crafts-Farrow	29203
Crane Forest	29203
Crescent	29388
Crescent Beach (Part of North Myrtle Beach)	29582
Creston	29030
Crestview	29501
Crocketts Crossroads	29720
Crocketville	29913
Crosland Park (Part of Aiken)	29801
Cross	29436
Cross Anchor	29331
Cross Anchor Correctional Institution	29335
Crosscreek Mall (Part of Greenwood)	29646
Cross Hill	29332
Cross Keys	29379
Crosswell	29640
Cummings	29944
Cusaac Crossroads	29541
Cypress Crossroads	29069
Cypress Fork	29001
Dacusville	29640
Daisy	29569
Dale	29914
Dalewood	29655
Dalzell	29040
Danwood	29541
Darlington	29532
Daufuskie Island	29915
Davis Crossroads	29148
Davis Station	29041
Deans	29684

Name	ZIP
Deer Park	29405
De Kalb	29175
Delemar Crossroads	29470
Delmae	29501
Delmar	29070
Delphia	29745
Delphos	29726
Delta	29178
Denmark	29042
Denny Terrace	29203
Dentsville (Richland County)	29204
Denver	29621
Deweys Hill (Part of North Charleston)	29406
Dillon	29536
Dinkins	29150
Dinkins Mill	29128
Dixiana	29169
Dixie	29720
Dog Bluff	29511
Donalds	29638
Doneraile	29532
Dongola	29526
Dorange	29471
Dorchester	29437
Dorchester Estates	29485
Dorchester Terrace	29405
Dorchester Terrace-Brentwood	29405
Dorchester-Waylyn	29405
Douglass	29014
Dovesville	29540
Drake	29516
Drawdy	29488
Drayton (Charleston County)	29407
Drayton (Spartanburg County)	29333
Draytonville	29340
Drexel Lake Hills	29206
Dry Branch	29801
Dubose	29150
Du Bose Crossroads	29150
Du Bose Park	29020
Dudley	29728
Due West	29639
Duford	29581
Dunbar (Georgetown County)	29440
Dunbar (Marlboro County)	29525
Duncan	29334
Dunean	29601
Dunes (Part of Myrtle Beach)	29577
Dupont	29407
Dusty Bend	29020
Dutch Fork	29210
Dutchman	29374
Dutchman Correctional Institution	29335
Dutch Square	29210
Dutch Village	29063
Dyson	29666
Eadytown	29468
Earle Homes	29621
Earles	29510
Earlwood Park	29532
Early Branch	29916
Easley	29640-42
For specific Easley Zip Codes call (803) 859-9411	
East Gaffney	29340
East Gantt	29609
East Greer	29651
East Hartsville	29550
Eastmont	29209
Eastover	29044
East Sumter	29150
East View	29669
Eau Claire (Part of Columbia)	29203
Ebenezer (Florence County)	29501
Ebenezer (York County)	29732
Eden	29645
Edenwood	29033
Edgefield	29824
Edgemoor	29712
Edgewood (Part of Columbia)	29204
Edisto	29038
Edisto Beach	29438
Edisto Island	29438
Edmund	29072
Effingham	29541
Ehrhardt	29081
Elgin (Kershaw County)	29045
Elgin (Lancaster County)	29720
Elko	29826
Elliott	29046
Elloree	29047
Elmwood Park	29801
Emerald Valley	29210

Name	ZIP
Emory	29138
Enoree	29335
Epworth	29666
Equinox Mill	29621
Estill	29918
Eulala	29138
Eureka (Aiken County)	29847
Eureka (Chester County)	29706
Eutaw Springs	29048
Eutawville	29048
Evans Crossroad	29720
Evergreen	29541
Evergreen Hills	29621
Fairfax	29827
Fairfield (Part of Hilton Head Island)	29928
Fairfield Terrace	29203
Fairforest	29336
Fairmont	29301
Fair Play	29643
Fairview	29651
Fairview (rural)	29644
Fairview Crossroads	29070
Farrel Crossroads	29432
Farrow Terrace	29203
Fechtig	29916
Federal (Florence County)	29503
Federal (Greenville County)	29603
Felderville	29047
Fenwick Hills	29455
Ferndale (Part of North Charleston)	29406
Filbert	29710
Fingerville	29338
Finklea	29569
Finland	29042
Five Forks (Anderson County)	29621
Five Forks (Greenville County)	29681
Five Forks (Pickens County)	29657
Five Points (Oconee County)	29693
Five Points (Richland County)	29205
Flat Rock	29621
Flat Shoals	29691
Fletcher	29570
Florence	29501-06
For specific Florence Zip Codes call (803) 667-9501	
Florence Mall (Part of Florence)	29501
Floyd Dale	29542
Floyds Crossroads	29581
Folly Beach	29439
Folly Field (Part of Hilton Head Island)	29928
Forest	29437
Forest Acres	29206
Forest Beach (Part of Hilton Head Island)	29928
Forestbrook	29577
Forest Lake (Richland County)	29206
Forest Lake (York County)	29715
Foreston	29102
Fork	29543
Fork Shoals	29644
Forrest Hills	29565
Fort Lawn	29714
Fort Mill	29715
Fort Motte	29135
Fountain Inn	29644
Four Holes	29115
Four Mile	29464
Fowler	29556
Foxtown	29801
Francis Marion College	29506
Fraserville (Part of Pawleys Island)	29585
Friarsgate	29063
Friendfield	29591
Friendship	29678
Fripp Island	29920
Fruit Hill	29138
Furman	29921
Furman University	29613
Gable	29051
Gadsden	29052
Gaffney	29340-42
For specific Gaffney Zip Codes call (803) 489-7144	
Gaillard Crossroads	29040
Galavon	29536
Galaxy	29209
Galivants Ferry	29544
Gantt (Greenville County)	29605
Gapway	29574
Garden City Beach	29576
Gardens Corner	29945

502 SOUTH CAROLINA Garnett-Lodge

Name	ZIP
Garnett	29922
Gaston	29053
Georgetown	29440
Gifford	29923
Gilbert	29054
Gillisonville	29936
Givhans	29472
Glass Hill	29526
Glendale	29346
Glenn Springs	29374
Glenwood (Part of Easley)	29640
Gloverville	29828
Gluck	29621
Glymphville	29126
Godsey	29666
Golden Grove	29673
Golightly	29302
Gooches	29720
Goodwins Crossroads	29325
Goose Creek	29445
Goretown	29569
Gourdin	29564
Govan	29843
Gowensville	29322
Grace	29720
Grahamville (Horry County)	29526
Grahamville (Jasper County)	29936
Gramling	29348
Graniteville	29829
Graves	29440
Gray Court	29645
Grays	29916
Grays Hill	29902
Great Falls	29055
Greeleyville	29056
Green Bay	29450
Greenbrier	29180
Green Pond (Colleton County)	29446
Greenpond (Greenville County)	29645
Green Pond (Spartanburg County)	29388
Green Sea	29545
Greenview	29203
Greenville	29601-16
For specific Greenville Zip Codes call (803) 282-4801	
Greenwood	29646-49
For specific Greenwood Zip Codes call (803) 223-2321	
Greenwood Shores	29666
Greer	29650-52
For specific Greer Zip Codes call (803) 877-6423	
Greer Mill (Part of Greer)	29651
Grenadier	29210
Gresham	29546
Grice Ferry	29574
Grover	29447
Guess	29727
Gurley	29569
Guthries	29726
Hagood	29128
Hamburg	29841
Hamer	29547
Hammond	29621
Hammond Crossroads	29135
Hampton	29924
Hampton Heights	29687
Hampton Park Terrace (Part of Charleston)	29403
Hanahan	29406
Hannah	29583
Harbour Town (Part of Hilton Head Island)	29928
Hardeeville	29927
Harleyville	29448
Harmony (Edgefield County)	29832
Harmony (York County)	29704
Harris	29646
Hartsville	29550
Harveytown	29365
Haskell Heights	29203
Hayne	29301
Hayne Junction	29301
Hazelwood Acres	29209
H & B Village (Part of Hampton)	29924
Heathley Wood (Part of Sumter)	29150
Heath Springs	29058
Hebron	29518
Helena	29108
Hemingway	29554
Hendersonville	29488
Hendricks Corner	29526
Hibernia	29105
Hickory Grove (Horry County)	29526

Name	ZIP
Hickory Grove (York County)	29717
Hickory Tavern	29645
High Point	29627
Hilda	29813
Hillbrook	29302
Hillcrest (Part of Spartanburg)	29302
Hillcrest Acres	29627
Hillcrest Heights (Part of Williamston)	29697
Hillcrest Mall (Part of Spartanburg)	29302
Hilton	29036
Hilton Head Island	29925-26
	29928
For specific Hilton Head Island Zip Codes call (803) 785-2179	
Hobcaw Point	29464
Hodges	29653
Hollands Store	29684
Holly Hill	29059
Holly Springs (Oconee County)	29693
Holly Springs (Spartanburg County)	29349
Hollywood (Charleston County)	29449
Hollywood (Saluda County)	29138
Hollywood Hills	29203
Holmesville	29563
Holtson Crossroads	29006
Homeland Park	29621
Homewood	29526
Honea Path	29654
Honey Hill	29480
Hoodtown	29742
Hopewell	29717
Hopkins	29061
Horatio	29062
Horeb	29180
Horrel Hill	29061
Horry	29511
Horsegall	29944
Howard	29569
Hudsontown	29477
Huger	29450
Hunley Park (Part of North Charleston)	29404
Hyman	29583
Independents	29209
Industrial (Part of Rock Hill)	29730
Ingleside	29356
Inman	29349
Inman Mills	29349
Irmo	29063
Irvines Landing	29646
Irwin	29720
Islandton	29929
Isle of Palms	29451
Italy	29510
Iva	29655
Jackson	29831
Jacksonboro	29452
Jacksonham	28173
Jackson Mill	29385
Jacksonville	29834
Jalapa	29108
James Island	29412
Jamestown (Berkeley County)	29453
Jamestown (Horry County)	29526
Jamison	29115
Jedburg	29483
Jefferson	29718
Jenkinsville	29065
Jennys	29827
Jericho	29426
Joanna	29351
Jocassee	29676
Johns Island	29455-57
For specific Johns Island Zip Codes call (803) 559-0622	
Johnson City	29301
Johnson Crossroads	29809
Johnsonville	29555
Johnston	29832
Johnstown	29816
Johnsville	29481
Jones Crossroads (Aiken County)	29105
Jones Crossroads (Lancaster County)	29720
Jonesville	29353
Jordan	29102
Jordania	29678
Jordanville	29544
Judson	29611
Judson No. 2	29611
Juniper Bay	29526

Name	ZIP
Kathwood (Part of West Columbia)	29169
Kelly	29379
Kellytown	29550
Kelton	29353
Kemper	29563
Kensington	29440
Keowee	29678
Kershaw	29067
Ketchuptown	29544
Kiawah Island	29455
Kilgore	29335
Killian	29203
Kinards	29355
King Circle	29720
Kingsburg	29555
Kings Creek	29719
Kingstree	29556
Kingswood	29210
Kirkland	29020
Kirkland Correctional Institute	29210
Kirksey	29848
Kitchings Mill	29137
Kittredge	29434
Kline	29814
Klondike Crossroads	29526
Kneece	29006
Knightsville	29483
Knox	29706
Ladson	29456
La France	29656
Lake City	29560
Lake Forest	29606
Lake Lanier	29356
Lakemont	29635
Lake Murray Shores	29070
Lake Shores	29646
Lake View	29563
Lakewood	29732
Lamar	29069
Lambertown	29510
Lambs (Part of North Charleston)	29405
Lancaster	29720-21
For specific Lancaster Zip Codes call (803) 283-4969	
Lancaster Mills	29720
Lando	29724
Landrum	29356
Lands End	29920
Landsford	29704
Lane	29564
Lanford	29335
Langley	29834
Lathem	29640
Latta	29565
Laurel Bay	29902
Laurens	29360
Leawood	29601
Lebanon (Anderson County)	29621
Lebanon (Fairfield County)	29180
Leeds	29031
Leesburg (Part of Columbia)	29209
Leesville	29070
Legareville	29455
Lena	29918
Leo	29560
Lesslie	29730
Lester	29512
Level Land	29655
Lewis	29706
Lewis Cross Roads	29532
Lexington	29072
Liberty	29657
Liberty Hill (Charleston County)	29406
Liberty Hill (Kershaw County)	29074
Liberty Hill (McCormick County)	29835
Lieber Correctional Institution	29472
Limehouse	29927
Limestone	29115
Lincoln Shire	29203
Lincolnville	29483
Lions Beach	29461
Litchfield Beach (Part of Pawleys Island)	29585
Little Africa	29323
Little Camden	29201
Little Eastatoe	29685
Little Mountain	29075
Little River	29566
Little Rock	29567
Livingston	29076
Lobeco	29931
Lockhart	29364
Lockhart Junction	29353
Lodge	29082

Lone Star-Piedmont **SOUTH CAROLINA** **503**

Name	ZIP
Lone Star	29077
Long Bay Estates	29577
Long Branch	29853
Longcreek	29658
Long Point	29569
Longs	29568
Longtown	29130
Loris	29569
Lowndesville	29659
Lowrys	29706
Lucknow	29010
Lugoff	29078
Luray	29932
Lydia	29079
Lydia Mills	29325
Lykesland	29061
Lyman	29365
Lynchburg	29080
Lyndhurst	29812
Lynwood	29816
McAlister Square (Part of Greenville)	29607
Mac Arthurs Junction	29638
McBee	29101
McBeth	29431
McClellanville	29458
McColl	29570
McConnells	29726
McCormick	29835
McCormick Correctional Institution	29835
McCormick Crossroads	29536
McCutchen Crossroads	29010
MacDougall Youth Correction Center	29472
McKenzie Crossroads	29114
McPhersonville	29916
Maddens	29360
Madison (Aiken County)	29829
Madison (Oconee County)	29693
Magnolia Park	29853
Manning	29102
Manning Crossroads	29536
Manville	29010
Maple Crossroads	29526
Marietta	29661
Marine Corps Air Station	29904
Marion	29571
Marlboro	29512
Mars Bluff	29506
Martin	29836
Maryville (Charleston County)	29407
Maryville (Georgetown County)	29440
Masons Crossroads	29621
Mathews Heights (Part of Greenwood)	29646
Mauldin	29662
May	29563
Mayesville	29104
Mayfair	29687
Mayfair Mill (Part of Pickens)	29671
Mayo	29368
Mayo Mills	29368
Mayson	29169
Meadowlake	29203
Meadows	29379
Mechanicsville (Darlington County)	29532
Mechanicsville (Lee County)	29010
Meeting Street	29824
Meggett	29449
Melrose	29809
Merchant	29138
Middendorf	29550
Midland Park	29405
Midland Valley	29829
Midway (Bamberg County)	29003
Midway (Kershaw County)	29032
Midway (Lancaster County)	29720
Midway Village	29577
Miley	29933
Millers Crossroads	29838
Millett	29836
Mill Village (Part of Bennettsville)	29512
Millwood (Sumter County)	29150
Millwood (Williamsburg County)	29556
Millwood Gardens	29150
Milton	29325
Minturn	29573
Mitchellville	29936
Mitford	29055
Modoc	29838
Monaghan	29611
Monarch Mills	29379
Moncks Corner	29461
Monetta	29105
Mont Clare	29532

Name	ZIP
Monticello	29106
Montmorenci	29839
Montrose	29520
Moore	29369
Moores Crossroads	29518
Moreland	29407
Morgan	29927
Morningside	29607
Morris Acres	29455
Moselle	29929
Mountain Brook	29209
Mountain Rest	29664
Mountain View	29323
Mount Carmel	29840
Mount Croghan	29727
Mount Gallagher	29692
Mount Holly	29643
Mount Olive	29581
Mount Pleasant	29464-65
For specific Mount Pleasant Zip Codes call (803) 884-8221	
Mount View	29687
Mountville	29370
Mulberry	29150
Mullins	29574
Murrells Inlet	29576
Myrtle Beach	29577-78
For specific Myrtle Beach Zip Codes call (803) 626-9533	
Myrtle Beach Air Force Base	29579
Myrtle Island	29910
Myrtle Square (Part of Myrtle Beach)	29577
Naval Hospital	29902
Naval Weapons	29445
Naval Weapons Station	29408
Neeses	29107
Nesmith	29580
Nevitt Forest	29621
Newberry	29108
New Cut	29720
New Easley Highway (Part of Greenville)	29611
New Ellenton	29809
New Holland Crossroads	29006
New Hope	29530
Newport	29730
New Prospect	29349
New Road	29945
Newry	29665
Newtonville	29512
New Town	29536
New Zion	29111
Nichols	29581
Nicholson Village	29801
Nimmons	29685
Nine Times	29685
Ninety Six	29666
Nixons Crossroads	29582
Nixonville	29526
Nixville	29944
Nob Hill	29505
Norris	29667
North	29112
North Aiken (Part of Aiken)	29801
North Anderson (Part of Anderson)	29623
North Augusta	29841
Northbridge (Part of Charleston)	29407
North Bridge Terrace (Part of Charleston)	29405
North Charleston	29406
North Conway (Part of Conway)	29526
North Forest Beach (Part of Hilton Head Island)	29928
Northgate	29501
North Greenwood	29646
North Hartsville	29550
North Litchfield Beach (Part of Pawleys Island)	29585
North Mullins (Part of Mullins)	29574
North Myrtle Beach	29582, 29597-98
For specific North Myrtle Beach Zip Codes call (803) 249-1023	
North Orangeburg	29112
North Pacolet	29322
North Rock Hill	29730
North Santee	29440
Northside Correctional Center	29303
North Summerville	29483
North Trenholm (Richland County)	29206
North Winyah Heights (Part of Georgetown)	29440
Northwood Estates	29405

Name	ZIP
Northwoods Mall (Part of Charleston)	29405
Norway	29113
Oak Dale (Clarendon County)	29111
Oakdale (Florence County)	29501
Oak Grove (Dillon County)	29565
Oak Grove (Lexington County)	29072
Oak Hill	29801
Oakland (Beaufort County)	29902
Oakland (Sumter County)	29150
Oakland Crossroads	29547
Oakland Mill (Part of Newberry)	29108
Oakley	29461
Oak Ridge	29058
Oaks Crossroads	29142
Oakvale	29673
Oakway	29693
Oakwood	29801
Oatland	29440
Oats	29069
Ocean Drive Beach (Part of North Myrtle Beach)	29582
Ocean Forest (Part of North Myrtle Beach)	29577
Oceanview	29412
Oconee Station	29691
Ogden	29730
Olanta	29114
Olar	29843
Old House	29936
Old Madison	29693
Olympia	29201
Ora	29360
Orangeburg	29115-17
For specific Orangeburg Zip Codes call (803) 536-1720	
Orr Mill	29621
Orrville	29621
Orum	29583
Osborn	29426
Osceola	29744
Oswego	29150
Otranto	29405
Outland	29554
Owings	29645
Oyster Point	29412
Pacolet	29372
Pacolet Mills	29373
Pacolet Park	29373
Padgetts	29481
Pageland	29728
Palmer Work Release Center	29501
Palmetto	29532
Palmetto Fort	29464
Pamplico	29583
Panola (Clarendon County)	29125
Panola (Greenwood County)	29646
Paramount Park	29605
Paris	29609
Parkers Ferry	29426
Parkersville (Part of Pawleys Island)	29585
Park Place	29609
Parksville	29844
Parler	29142
Parris Island	29905
Parris Island Marine Corps Recruit Depot	29905
Parrot Point	29412
Patrick	29584
Pauline	29374
Pawleys Island	29585
Paxville	29102
Peach Valley	29303
Peak	29122
Pearman	29621
Pecan Terrace	29605
Pecan Way Terrace (Part of Orangeburg)	29115
Peedee	29571
Pelham	29651
Pelion	29123
Pelzer	29669
Pelzer North (Part of Pelzer)	29669
Pelzer South (Part of Pelzer)	29669
Pendleton	29670
Peniel Crossroads	29161
Pepperhill	29418
Percival Crossroads	29693
Perry	29124
Perry Correctional Institution	29669
Philip	29464
Phoenix	29646
Pickens	29671
Pickensville (Part of Easley)	29642
Pickett Post	29691
Piedmont	29673

504 SOUTH CAROLINA Piercetown-Springfield

Name	ZIP
Piercetown	29697
Pierpont (Charleston County)	29407
Pimlico	29461
Pinehurst (Dorchester County)	29483
Pinehurst (Greenwood County)	29646
Pinehurst-Sheppard Park	29483
Pine Island	29577
Pineland (Charleston County)	29429
Pineland (Jasper County)	29934
Pineridge (Darlington County)	29101
Pineridge (Lexington County)	29169
Pine Valley	29210
Pineville	29468
Pinewood (Spartanburg County)	29303
Pinewood (Sumter County)	29125
Pinopolis	29469
Pisgah	29128
Plains	29718
Plantersville	29440
Plaza (Part of Sumter)	29150
Pleasantburg (Part of Greenville)	29606
Pleasant Grove	29635
Pleasant Grove Community	29635
Pleasant Hill	29058
Pleasant Lane	29824
Pleasant Valley	29605
Plum Branch	29845
Pocataligo	29945
Poe	29609
Polaris Missile Facility Atlantic	29408
Polk Village	29902
Pomaria	29126
Pontiac	29045
Poovey Farm	29720
Poplar Springs	29369
Port Royal	29935
Port Royal Plantation (Part of Hilton Head Island)	29928
Poston	29588
Powdersville	29673
Pregnall	29437
Primus	29720
Princeton	29674
Pritchardville	29910
Promised Land	29819
Prospect Crossroads	29560
Prosperity	29127
Providence	29059
Pumpkintown	29671
Puncheon Creek	29510
Purysburg Landing	29927
Quail Hollow	29169
Quinby	29506
Quinby Estates (Part of Quinby)	29506
Quinby Forest (Part of Quinby)	29506
Rabon Crossroads	29511
Rains	29589
Rantowles	29449
Ravenel	29470
Ravenwood	29206
Red Bank	29072
Red Bluff Crossroads	29569
Red Hill (Horry County)	29526
Red Hill (rural) (Horry County)	29544
Red Hill (Lee County)	29020
Red Top	29455
Reevesville	29471
Rehobeth	29544
Reid Park	29520
Reidville	29375
Rembert	29128
Remount (Part of North Charleston)	29406
Renfrew	29690
Renno	29325
Retreat	29693
Return	29678
Reynold	29817
Rhems	29440
Ribault Park	29902
Richburg	29729
Rich Hill Crossroads	29058
Richland	29675
Richland Mall (Part of Forest Acres)	29206
Richland Springs	29138
Richmond Hills	29609
Richtex	29180
Ridgecrest	29801

Name	ZIP
Ridge Cut	29916
Ridgeland	29936
Ridge Spring	29129
Ridgeville	29472
Ridgeway	29130
Ridgewood (Charleston County)	29456
Ridgewood (Richland County)	29203
Rimini	29131
Rion	29132
Ritter	29488
Riverdale	29536
River Falls	29661
Riverland	29412
Riverland Terrace	29412
Rivermont	29210
Rivers Annex (Part of North Charleston)	29411
Riverside (Abbeville County)	29692
Riverside (Anderson County)	29624
Riverside (Greenville County)	29611
Riverside (Lancaster County)	29720
Riverside Park	29210
Riverview	29715
Robat	29379
Robbins	29831
Robbins Circle	29706
Robertville	29922
Robinson	29101
Rock Bluff	29556
Rockbridge	29206
Rock Hill	29730-33
For specific Rock Hill Zip Codes call (803) 327-4187	
Rockton	29180
Rockville	29487
Rocky Bottom	29685
Rocky River	29655
Roddy	29704
Rodman	29706
Roebuck	29376
Rogers Fallout	29511
Roseida	29902
Rosinville	29477
Round O	29474
Rowell	29704
Rowesville	29133
Ruby	29741
Ruffin	29475
Russellville	29476
St. Andrews (Charleston County)	29407
St. Andrews (Richland County)	29210
St. Charles	29104
St. George	29477
St. Helenas Island	29920
St. Matthews	29135
St. Paul	29148
St. Paul Forks	29526
St. Stephen	29479
Salak	29646
Salem (Florence County)	29583
Salem (Oconee County)	29676
Salem Crossroads	29015
Salley	29137
Salters	29590
Saluca	29646
Saluda	29138
Saluda Gardens (Part of West Columbia)	29169
Saluda Terrace	29169
Samaria	29006
Sampit	29440
Sanders Corner	29062
Sandridge (Berkeley County)	29059
Sand Ridge (Horry County)	29526
Sandwood	29206
Sandy Flat	29687
Sandy Ridge	29666
Sandy Springs	29677
Sans Souci	29609
Sans Souci Heights	29609
Santee	29142
Santee Circle	29461
Santuc	29031
Sardinia	29143
Sardis	29161
Satchel Ford Terrace	29206
Sato (Part of Denmark)	29042
Savannah Bluff	29526
Sawyerdale	29112
Saxon	29301
Saylors Crossroads	29627
Scanlonville	29464

Name	ZIP
Schofield	29843
Schultz Hill (Part of North Augusta)	29841
Scotia	29939
Scottsville	29104
Scranton	29591
Seabrook	29940
Seabrook Island	29455
Sea Pines (Part of Hilton Head Island)	29928
Seaside	29412
Secessionville	29412
Sedalia	29379
Seiglers Crossroads	29801
Seigling	29810
Seivern	29164
Sellers	29592
Selma	29536
Seneca	29678-79
For specific Seneca Zip Codes call (803) 882-8422	
Seven Mile (Part of North Charleston)	29405
Seven Mile	29464
Seven Oaks (Lexington County)	29210
Shady Rest (Part of Bennettsville)	29512
Shannon Hill	29010
Shannontown	29150
Sharon	29742
Shaw AFB	29152
Shaw Air Force Base	29152
Shaw Heights	29152
Sheldon	29941
Shell	29526
Shell Point	29902
Shepard	29032
Sheppard Park	29483
Sherwood Acres	29301
Shiloh (Oconee County)	29678
Shiloh (Sumter County)	29080
Shipyard Plantations (Part of Hilton Head Island)	29928
Shirley	29922
Shoals Junction	29638
Shulerville	29480
Silver	29102
Silver Bluff Estates	29801
Silverstreet	29145
Simpson	29130
Simpsonville	29681
Singleton	29135
Six Mile	29682
Six Points	29801
Skyview Terrace	29210
Slansville	29483
Slater	29683
Slater-Marietta	29661
Smallwood	29130
Smith	29730
Smithboro	29574
Smith Mills	29554
Smoaks	29481
Smyrna	29743
Snelling	29812
Sniders Crossroads	29475
Snowden	29464
Socastee	29577
Society Hill	29593
Sol Legare Island	29401
South Bennettsville	29512
South Congaree	29169
Southern Shops	29303
South Forest Estates	29605
South Greenwood (Part of Greenwood)	29646
South Hartsville	29550
South Hills	29379
South Lynchburg	29080
South Mullins (Part of Mullins)	29574
South Park (Part of Florence)	29505
Southpark Shopping Center (Part of Florence)	29505
Southside	29505
South Sumter	29150
South Windermere (Part of Charleston)	29407
Spartanburg	29301-18
For specific Spartanburg Zip Codes call (803) 585-0301	
Spiderweb	29841
Springdale (Lancaster County)	29720
Springdale (Lexington County)	29169
Springfield (Orangeburg County)	29146

Springfield-Zion SOUTH CAROLINA 505

Name	ZIP
Springfield (Spartanburg County)	29349
Spring Hill (Lee County)	29128
Spring Hill (Richland County)	29177
Springmaid Beach	29577
Spring Mills	29067
Springwood	29204
Stallsville	29485
Stark Terrace	29203
Starmount	29169
Starr	29684
Startex	29377
Stateburg	29150
State College (Part of Orangeburg)	29115
State Farm	29128
Steedman	29070
Stiefeltown	29851
Stokes	29488
Stokes Bridge	29010
Stomp Springs	29325
Stoneboro	29058
Stoney Hill	29127
Stono	29412
Stover	29014
Stratton Capers	29405
Strawberry	29461
Stuart Point	29940
Stuckey	29554
Sullivans Island	29482
Summer Hill (Part of North Augusta)	29841
Summerland (Part of Batesburg)	29006
Summerton	29148
Summerville	29483-85
For specific Summerville Zip Codes call (803) 873-3571	
Summit	29070
Sumter	29150-54
For specific Sumter Zip Codes call (803) 773-9312	
Sumter Southwest	29150
Sunnyside	29651
Sunset	29685
Surfside Beach	29575
Suttons	29510
Swansea	29160
Sweden	29042
Sweetwater (Aiken County)	29841
Sweetwater (Barnwell County)	29812
Switzer	29369
Switzerland	29936
Sycamore	29846
Syracuse	29532
Talatha	29809
Tamassee	29686
Tanglewood	29611
Tarboro	29943
Tatum	29594
Taxahaw	29067
Taylors (Greenville County)	29687
Tega Cay	29715
Temperance	29571
Temperance Hill	29571
Ten Mile (Part of Charleston)	29406
Ten Mile (Whitehall Terrace)	29464
Terrells Crossroads	29518
Texas	29477
The Dunes (Part of Myrtle Beach)	29577
The Farms (Part of Hanahan)	29410
The Groves	29464
Thor	29123
Three Trees	29412
Tibwin	29458
Tigerville	29688
Tillman	29943
Timmonsville	29161

Name	ZIP
Tirzah	29745
Toddville	29526
Tokeena Crossroads	29678
Toney Creek	29627
Townville	29689
Toxaway (Part of Anderson)	29621
Tradesville	29720
Tranquil Acres	29483
Travelers Rest	29690
Trenton	29847
Triangle	29627
Trio	29595
Troy	29848
Tuckertown	29031
Tugtown	29059
Turbeville	29162
Twin Lake Hill	29209
Ulmer	29849
Una (Darlington County)	29069
Una (Spartanburg County)	29378
Union	29379
Union Bleachery	29609
Union Crossroads	29111
Unity	28173
University (Part of Columbia)	29208
University of South Carolina at Coastal Carolina	29526
Utica	29678
Valencia Heights	29205
Valley Falls	29303
Vance	29163
Van Wyck	29744
Varnville	29944
Vaucluse	29850
Verdery	29819
Victor Mills Village (Part of Greer)	29651
Virginia Acres	29801
Voorhees College	29042
Waddell Gardens	29902
Wade Hampton	29607
Wadmalaw Island	29487
Wagener	29164
Walden Correctional Institute	29210
Walhalla	29691
Wallace	29596
Walnut Grove	29374
Walterboro	29488
Wampee	29568
Wando	29492
Wando Woods	29405
Ward	29166
Ware Place	29669
Ware Shoals	29692
Warren Crossroads	29470
Warrenville	29851
Warsaw	29510
Wateree	29044
Waterloo	29384
Watkins Store	29801
Watsonia	29105
Watts Mills	29360
Waverly Mills (Part of Pawleys Island)	29585
Waylyn	29405
Wedgefield	29168
Welcome (Anderson County)	29621
Welcome (Greenville County)	29611
Wellford	29385
Wesleyan	29630
West Andrews (Part of Andrews)	29510
West Columbia	29169-71
For specific West Columbia Zip Codes call (803) 796-0455	
West Gantt	29605
Westgate Mall (Part of Spartanburg)	29301

Name	ZIP
West Greenwood	29646
Westminster	29693
West Orangeburg	29115
Westover Acres	29169
West Pelzer	29669
West Springs	29353
West Union	29696
West View	29301
Westville	29611
West Warrenville	29851
Whetstone	29664
Whipper Barony (Part of North Charleston)	29405
White Bluff	29067
White Hall (Colleton County)	29446
Whitehall (Greenwood County)	29646
Whitehall (Lexington County)	29210
White Oak	29176
White Plains	29697
White Pond	29853
White Rock	29177
White Stone	29386
Whitesville	29461
Whitmire	29178
Whitney (Spartanburg County)	29303
Whitney Heights	29303
Wilder	29431
Wiles Crossroads	29135
Wilkinson Heights	29115
Wilkinsville	29340
Wilksburg	29706
Williams	29493
Williams Estate	29720
Williamston	29697
Willington	29835
Williston	29853
Willowbrook	29445
Wilson	29102
Wilson Mill	29102
Wilsons Cross Roads	29532
Windsor	29856
Windsor Estates	29204
Windsor Lake Park	29206
Windsor Park	29520
Windy Hill	29506
Windy Hill Beach (Part of North Myrtle Beach)	29582
Winnsboro	29180
Winnsboro Mills	29180
Winona	29506
Winthrop College (Part of York)	29733
Wisacky	29183
Wolfton	29112
Women's Correctional Center	29210
Woodburn Hills	29301
Woodfield (Richland County)	29206
Woodfields	29605
Woodford	29112
Woodland Hills	29210
Woodrow	29040
Woodruff	29388
Woodside	29610
Woodville	29669
Woodward	29014
Workman	29111
Yauhannah	29440
Yeamans Hall (Part of Hanahan)	29410
Yemassee	29945
Yenome	29814
Yonges Island	29449
Yorba Village	29941
York	29745
Yorkshire	29209
Youngs	29388
Zion	29574

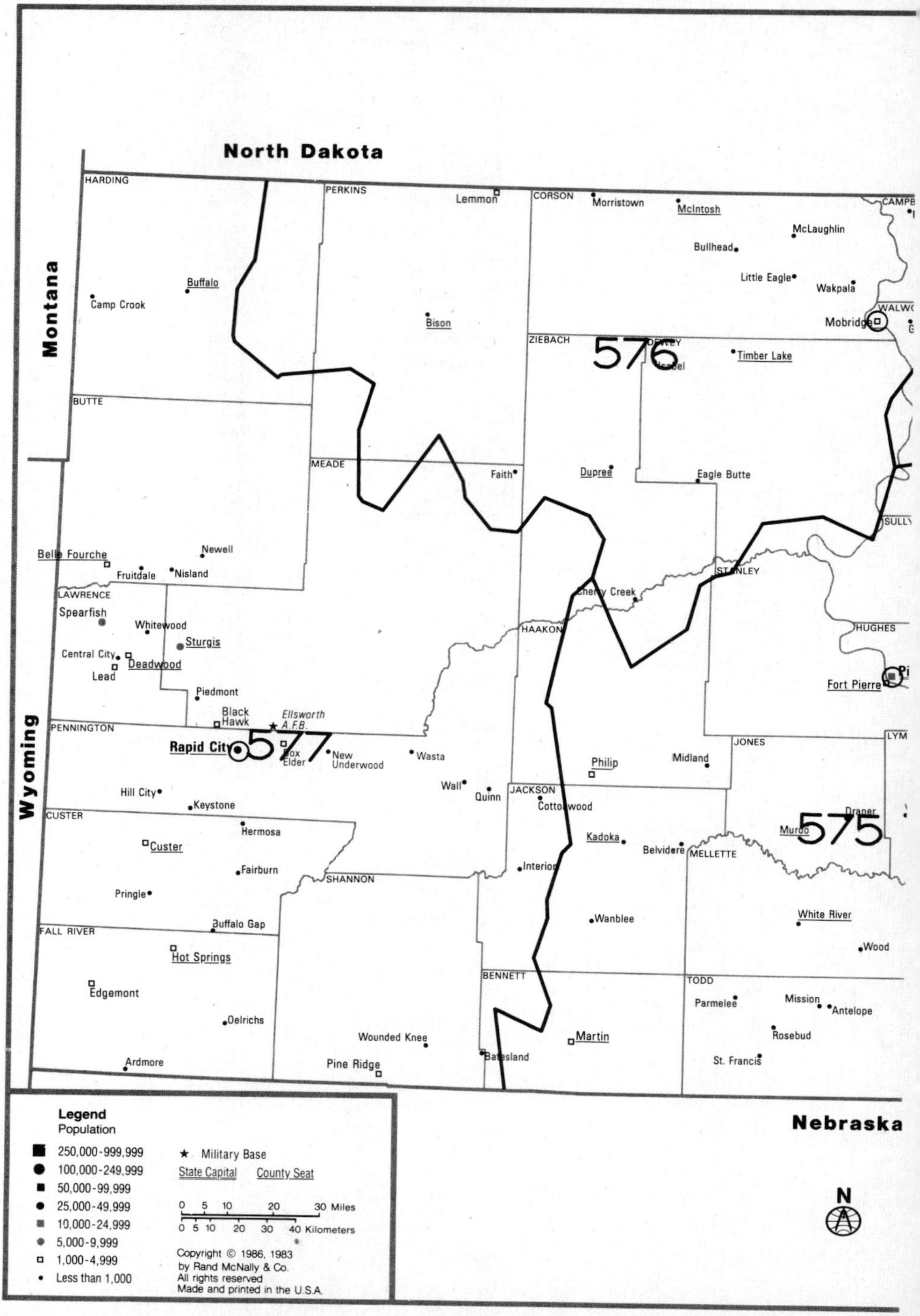

North Dakota
Montana
Wyoming
Nebraska
HARDING
PERKINS
CORSON
CAMPB
WALWO
ZIEBACH
DEWEY
BUTTE
MEADE
LAWRENCE
PENNINGTON
HAAKON
STANLEY
SULLY
HUGHES
JONES
LYM
JACKSON
MELLETTE
CUSTER
SHANNON
FALL RIVER
BENNETT
TODD
Lemmon
Morristown
McIntosh
McLaughlin
Bullhead
Little Eagle
Wakpala
Mobridge
Camp Crook
Buffalo
Bison
Timber Lake
Faith
Dupree
Eagle Butte
Belle Fourche
Newell
Fruitdale
Nisland
Cherry Creek
Spearfish
Whitewood
Sturgis
Central City
Deadwood
Lead
Piedmont
Black Hawk
Ellsworth A.F.B.
Fort Pierre
Rapid City
Box Elder
New Underwood
Wasta
Philip
Midland
Wall
Quinn
Hill City
Keystone
Cottonwood
Draper
Murdo
Hermosa
Custer
Kadoka
Belvidere
Fairburn
Interior
Pringle
Wanblee
White River
Buffalo Gap
Wood
Hot Springs
Edgemont
Parmelee
Mission
Antelope
Oelrichs
Rosebud
Wounded Knee
Martin
Batesland
Ardmore
Pine Ridge
St. Francis
576
577
575
Legend
Population
250,000-999,999
100,000-249,999
50,000-99,999
25,000-49,999
10,000-24,999
5,000-9,999
1,000-4,999
Less than 1,000
Military Base
State Capital
County Seat
0 5 10 20 30 Miles
0 5 10 20 30 40 Kilometers
Copyright © 1986, 1983
by Rand McNally & Co.
All rights reserved
Made and printed in the U.S.A.
N

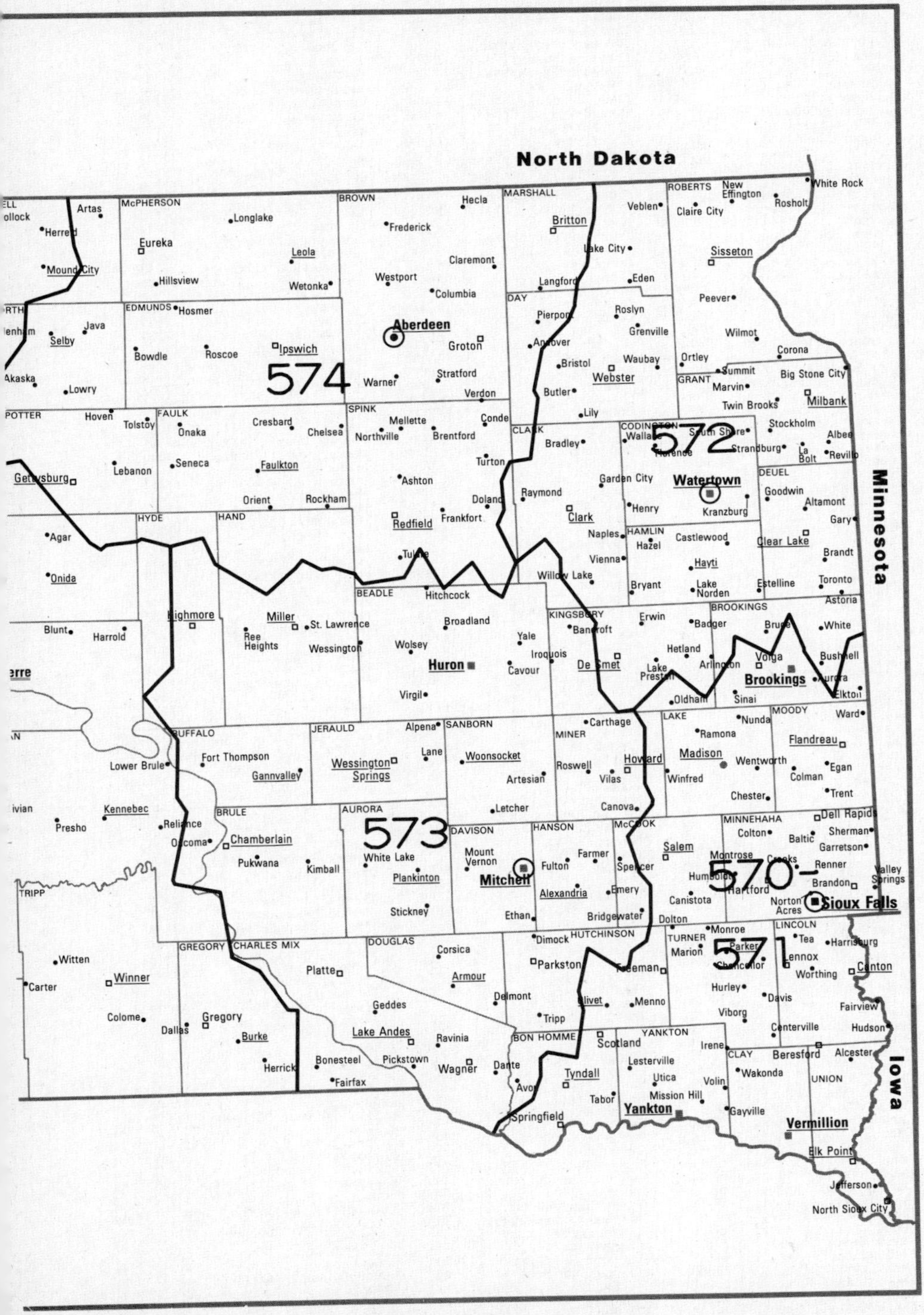
North Dakota
Minnesota
Iowa
574
572
573
570–571
McPHERSON
BROWN
MARSHALL
ROBERTS
EDMUNDS
DAY
GRANT
POTTER
FAULK
SPINK
CLARK
CODINGTON
DEUEL
HYDE
HAND
HAMLIN
BEADLE
KINGSBURY
BROOKINGS
BUFFALO
JERAULD
SANBORN
MINER
LAKE
MOODY
BRULE
AURORA
DAVISON
HANSON
McCOOK
MINNEHAHA
TRIPP
GREGORY
CHARLES MIX
DOUGLAS
HUTCHINSON
TURNER
LINCOLN
BON HOMME
YANKTON
CLAY
UNION
Artas
Herreid
Mound City
Eureka
Longlake
Leola
Hillsview
Wetonka
Frederick
Hecla
Claremont
Westport
Columbia
Britton
Lake City
Langford
Veblen
Claire City
New Effington
Rosholt
White Rock
Sisseton
Eden
Peever
Hosmer
Java
Selby
Bowdle
Roscoe
Ipswich
Aberdeen
Groton
Stratford
Warner
Verdon
Akaska
Lowry
Pierpont
Andover
Bristol
Butler
Roslyn
Grenville
Waubay
Webster
Wilmot
Ortley
Summit
Marvin
Corona
Big Stone City
Milbank
Twin Brooks
Hoven
Tolstoy
Onaka
Cresbard
Chelsea
Mellette
Northville
Brentford
Conde
Lily
Bradley
Wallace
South Shore
Florence
Stockholm
Strandburg
La Bolt
Albee
Revillo
Gettysburg
Lebanon
Seneca
Faulkton
Ashton
Turton
Garden City
Watertown
Goodwin
Altamont
Gary
Orient
Rockham
Redfield
Frankfort
Doland
Raymond
Clark
Henry
Kranzburg
Agar
Onida
Naples
Hazel
Castlewood
Clear Lake
Brandt
Tulare
Vienna
Willow Lake
Hayti
Bryant
Lake Norden
Estelline
Toronto
Astoria
Hitchcock
Highmore
Miller
St. Lawrence
Ree Heights
Wessington
Broadland
Blunt
Harrold
Bancroft
Erwin
Badger
Bruce
White
Wolsey
Yale
Iroquois
Hetland
Arlington
Volga
Bushnell
Huron
Cavour
De Smet
Lake Preston
Brookings
Aurora
Elkton
Virgil
Oldham
Sinai
Ward
Alpena
Carthage
Ramona
Nunda
Flandreau
Fort Thompson
Lower Brule
Gannvalley
Wessington Springs
Lane
Woonsocket
Roswell
Howard
Madison
Wentworth
Egan
Artesian
Vilas
Winfred
Colman
Trent
Chester
Kennebec
Presho
Reliance
Oacoma
Chamberlain
Letcher
Canova
Dell Rapids
Colton
Baltic
Sherman
Garretson
Pukwana
Kimball
White Lake
Plankinton
Mount Vernon
Mitchell
Fulton
Farmer
Spencer
Salem
Montrose
Crooks
Renner
Humboldt
Hartford
Brandon
Valley Springs
Alexandria
Emery
Canistota
Norton Acres
Sioux Falls
Stickney
Ethan
Bridgewater
Dolton
Monroe
Tea
Harrisburg
Witten
Winner
Carter
Platte
Corsica
Dimock
Parkston
Freeman
Marion
Parker
Chancellor
Lennox
Worthing
Canton
Armour
Delmont
Hurley
Davis
Colome
Dallas
Gregory
Burke
Geddes
Olivet
Menno
Tripp
Viborg
Fairview
Lake Andes
Ravinia
Scotland
Irene
Centerville
Hudson
Beresford
Alcester
Herrick
Bonesteel
Fairfax
Pickstown
Wagner
Dante
Avon
Tyndall
Lesterville
Utica
Mission Hill
Volin
Wakonda
Tabor
Yankton
Gayville
Springfield
Vermillion
Elk Point
Jefferson
North Sioux City

508 SOUTH DAKOTA Aberdeen-Kennebec

Name	ZIP
Aberdeen	57401-02
For specific Aberdeen Zip Codes call (605) 226-2555	
Academy	57369
Agar	57520
Agency Village	57262
Akaska	57420
Albee	57210
Alcester (Union County)	57001
Alexandria	57311
Allen (Bennett County)	57714
Alpena (Jerauld County)	57312
Altamont (Deuel County)	57226
Ames	57362
Amherst	57421
Andover (Day County)	57422
Antelope (Todd County)	57555
Ardmore	57715
Arlington	57212
Arlington Beach	57212
Armour	57313
Arpan	57762
Artas	57437
Artesian	57314
Ashton	57424
Astoria	57213
Athol	57425
Aurora (Brookings County)	57002
Aurora Center	57375
Avon (Bon Homme County)	57315
Badger (Kingsbury County)	57214
Baltic	57003
Bancroft	57316
Barnard	57426
Batesland	57716
Bath	57427
Bear Butte	57785
Bear Creek	57636
Belle Fourche	57717
Belvidere	57521
Bemis	57238
Beresford	57004
Bethlehem	57708
Big Bend	57702
Big Springs	57001
Big Stone City	57216
Bijou Hills	57370
Bison (Perkins County)	57620
Black Hawk	57718
Blacktail	57754
Blumengard Colony	57438
Blunt	57522
Bonesteel	57317
Bon Homme Colony	57063
Bonilla	57348
Bowdle (Edmunds County)	57428
Box Elder	57719
Bradley	57217
Brandon	57005
Brandt (Deuel County)	57218
Brentford	57429
Bridger	57748
Bridgewater (McCook County)	57319
Bristol (Day County)	57219
Britton	57430
Broadland (Beadle County)	57350
Brookings (Brookings County)	57006
Brownsville	57754
Bruce	57220
Bryant (Hamlin County)	57221
Buffalo (Harding County)	57720
Buffalo Gap	57722
Buffalo Ridge	57115
Buffalo Trading Post	57018
Bullhead	57621
Burbank	57010
Burke (Gregory County)	57523
Bushnell	57276
Butler (Day County)	57219
Cactus Flat	57567
Camp Crook	57724
Canistota (McCook County)	57012
Canova (Miner County)	57321
Canton (Lincoln County)	57013
Capa	57552
Caputa	57725
Carpenter	57322
Carter (Tripp County)	57526
Carthage (Miner County)	57323
Castle Rock	57760
Castlewood (Hamlin County)	57223
Cavour (Beadle County)	57324
Cedarbutte	57527
Cedar Grove Colony	57369
Center (McCook County)	57058
Center Point	57070
Centerville (Turner County)	57014
Central City	57754

Name	ZIP
Chamberlain (Brule County)	57325
Chancellor	57015
Chautauqua	57042
Chelsea	57465
Cherry Creek	57622
Chester (Lake County)	57016
Cheyenne Crossing	57754
Cheyenne River Indian Reservation	57625
Claire City	57224
Claremont (Brown County)	57432
Clark (Clark County)	57225
Clark Colony	57258
Clayton	57332
Clearfield	57580
Clear Lake (Deuel County)	57226
Colman (Moody County)	57017
Colome (Tripp County)	57528
Colton	57018
Columbia (Brown County)	57433
Conde (Spink County)	57434
Corn Creek	57560
Corona	57227
Corsica	57328
Corson	57005
Cottonwood (Jackson County)	57775
Crandall	57434
Crazy Horse	57730
Creighton	57729
Cresbard	57435
Crocker	57229
Crooks	57020
Crow Creek Indian Reservation	57339
Crow Lake	57382
Custer (Custer County)	57730
Dallas	57529
Dante	57329
Davis	57021
Deadwood	57732
De Grey	57501
Dell Rapids (Minnehaha County)	57022
Delmont	57330
Dempster	57230
Denby	57716
De Smet (Kingsbury County)	57231
Dimock	57331
Dixon	57533
Doland	57436
Dolton (Turner County)	57023
Downtown (Part of Aberdeen)	57401
Draper (Jones County)	57531
Dupree	57623
Eagle Butte	57625
East Sioux Falls	57101
Eden (Marshall County)	57232
Edgemont	57735
Egan (Moody County)	57024
Elk Point (Union County)	57025
Elkton	57026
Ellis	57101
Ellsworth AFB	57706
Ellsworth Air Force Base	57706
Elmore	57754
Elm Springs	57736
Elm Springs Colony	57334
Emery (Hanson County)	57332
Empire	57788
Empire Mall, The (Part of Sioux Falls)	57101
Enning	57737
Epiphany	57321
Erwin	57233
Esmond (Kingsbury County)	57353
Estelline (Hamlin County)	57234
Ethan	57334
Eureka (McPherson County)	57437
Fairburn	57738
Fairfax (Gregory County)	57335
Fairpoint	57787
Fairview (Lincoln County)	57027
Faith	57626
Farmer	57336
Farmingdale	57725
Faulkton	57438
Fedora	57337
Ferney	57439
Firesteel (Dewey County)	57628
Flandreau (Moody County)	57028
Flandreau Indian Reservation	57028
Fleetwood (Part of Brandon)	57005
Florence (Codington County)	57235
Forestburg	57338
Fort Pierre	57532
Fort Thompson	57339

Name	ZIP
Frankfort (Spink County)	57440
Franklin (Lake County)	57042
Frederick (Brown County)	57441
Freeman	57029
Froehlich Addition	57104
Fruitdale	57742
Fulton	57340
Galena	57732
Gannvalley	57341
Garden City	57236
Garretson	57030
Gary	57237
Gayville (Yankton County)	57031
Geddes	57342
Gettysburg (Potter County)	57442
Glad Valley	57629
Glencross	57630
Glendale Colony	57440
Glenham	57631
Goodwin (Deuel County)	57238
Graceville Colony	57076
Greenfield (Clay County)	57010
Green Grass	57625
Greenwood (Charles Mix County)	57380
Gregory	57533
Grenville (Day County)	57239
Groton (Brown County)	57445
Grover	57201
Hamill	57534
Hammer	57255
Hanna	57754
Harrington	57551
Harrisburg	57032
Harrison (Douglas County)	57344
Harrold (Hughes County)	57536
Hartford (Minnehaha County)	57033
Hartford Beach	57227
Hayes	57537
Hayti (Hamlin County)	57241
Hayward Addition	57106
Hazel	57242
Hecla (Brown County)	57446
Henry (Codington County)	57243
Hereford	57785
Hermosa	57744
Herreid	57632
Herrick (Gregory County)	57538
Hetland	57244
Hiawatha Beach	57279
Hidden Timber	69201
Highmore (Hyde County)	57345
Hill City	57745
Hillhead	57270
Hillside (Douglas County)	57328
Hillside Colony	57436
Hillsview	57437
Hisega	57701
Hisle	57577
Hitchcock	57348
Holabird	57540
Holmquist	57274
Hooker	57070
Hoover	57760
Hosmer (Edmunds County)	57448
Hot Springs	57747
Houghton	57449
Hoven (Potter County)	57450
Howard (Miner County)	57349
Howes	57748
Hub City	57069
Hudson (Lincoln County)	57034
Huffton	57432
Humboldt (Minnehaha County)	57035
Hurley (Turner County)	57036
Huron (Beadle County)	57350
Huron Colony	57350
Ideal	57541
Igloo	57735
Imlay	57780
Interior (Jackson County)	57750
Iona	57542
Ipswich (Edmunds County)	57451
Irene	57037
Iron Lightning	57623
Iroquois (Kingsbury County)	57353
Isabel	57633
James	57445
Java	57452
Jefferson (Union County)	57038
Johnson Siding	57701
Joubert	57344
Junction City	57010
Junius	57042
Kadoka (Jackson County)	57543
Kaylor	57354
Keldron	57634
Kenel	57642
Kennebec (Lyman County)	57544

Keyapaha-Valley View SOUTH DAKOTA 509

Name	ZIP
Keyapaha	57545
Keystone	57751
Kidder (Marshall County)	57430
Kimball (Brule County)	57355
Kingsburg	57062
Kones Corner	57223
Kranzburg (Codington County)	57245
Kyle	57752
La Bolt	57246
Ladner	57720
Lake Andes	57356
Lake Campbell	57006
Lake City	57247
Lake Norden	57248
Lake Preston	57249
Lane	57358
Langford	57454
Lantry	57636
La Plant	57652
Lead	57754
Lebanon	57455
Lemmon	57638
Lennox	57039
Leola (McPherson County)	57456
Lesterville	57040
Letcher (Sanborn County)	57359
Lily	57274
Linden Beach	57227
Littleburg	57555
Little Eagle	57639
Lodgepole	57640
Lone Tree (Moody County)	57024
Longlake	57457
Long Lake Colony	57481
Longvalley	57547
Loomis	57301
Lower Brule	57548
Lower Brule Indian Reservation	57548
Lowry	57472
Lucas (Gregory County)	57523
Ludlow	57755
Lyons	57041
McCook Lake	57038
McIntosh	57641
McLaughlin	57642
Madison (Lake County)	57042
Madsen Beach	57279
Mahto	57643
Manchester	57353
Manderson	57756
Mansfield	57460
Marcus	57757
Marcy Colony	57366
Marion (Turner County)	57043
Marlow	57270
Martin (Bennett County)	57551
Marty	57361
Marvin	57251
Maurine	57626
Maxwell Colony	57059
Mayfield (Yankton County)	57037
Meadow	57644
Meckling	57044
Mellette (Spink County)	57461
Menno	57045
Midland (Haakon County)	57552
Midway	57037
Milbank	57252
Milesville	57553
Millboro	57580
Miller (Hand County)	57362
Miller Dale Colony	57362
Milltown	57366
Mina	57462
Miranda	57438
Mission (Todd County)	57555
Mission Hill (Yankton County)	57046
Mission Ridge	57532
Mitchell (Davison County)	57301
Mobridge	57601
Monroe (Turner County)	57047
Montrose (McCook County)	57048
Morningside (Beadle County)	57350
Morristown	57645
Mosher	57580
Mound City	57646
Mount Vernon	57363
Mud Butte	57758
Murdo	57559
Mystic	57745
Naples	57271
Nemo	57759
New Effington	57255
Newell	57760
New Holland	57364
New Underwood	57761
Nisland	57762

Name	ZIP
Nora	57001
Norbeck	57438
Norris	57560
North Eagle Butte	57625
North Sioux City	57049
Northville (Spink County)	57465
Norton Acres	57104
Nunda (Lake County)	57050
Oacoma (Lyman County)	57365
Oelrichs	57763
Ogala Lakota College	57752
Oglala	57764
Okaton	57562
Okreek	57563
Ola	57325
Oldham	57051
Olivet	57052
Olsonville	69201
Onaka	57466
Onida	57564
Opal	57765
Oral	57766
Ordway	57433
Orient (Faulk County)	57467
Orland	57042
Ortley (Roberts County)	57256
Osceola (Kingsbury County)	57316
Owanka	57767
Parade	57647
Parker (Turner County)	57053
Parkston	57366
Parmelee	57566
Patricia	57551
Pearl Creek Colony	57353
Pearsons Corner	57070
Pedro	57729
Peever	57257
Peninsula Park	57075
Perkins	57062
Philip	57567
Pickerel	57239
Pickstown	57367
Piedmont	57769
Pierpont	57468
Pierre	57501
Pine Ridge	57770
Pine Ridge Indian Reservation	57770
Plainview (Meade County)	57748
Plainview Colony	57451
Plankinton (Aurora County)	57368
Plano	57340
Platte (Charles Mix County)	57369
Platte Colony	57369
Pluma	57732
Pollock	57648
Polo	57467
Porcupine	57772
Potato Creek	57750
Prairie City	57649
Prairie Village	57042
Presho (Lyman County)	57568
Pringle	57773
Promise	57601
Provo	57774
Pukwana (Brule County)	57370
Pumpkin Center	57035
Putney	57445
Quinn (Pennington County)	57775
Quinn Table	57790
Ralph	57650
Ramona	57054
Rapid City	57701-09
For specific Rapid City Zip Codes call (605) 394-8600	
Rapid Valley	57701
Ravinia (Charles Mix County)	57357
Raymond (Clark County)	57258
Red Elm	57623
Redfield (Spink County)	57469
Redig	57776
Redowl	57777
Red Scaffold	57626
Red Shirt	57744
Ree Heights (Hand County)	57371
Reliance (Lyman County)	57569
Renner	57055
Reva	57651
Revillo	57259
Richland (Union County)	57025
Ridgeview	57652
Riverside Colony	57350
Rochford	57778
Rockerville	57701
Rockham	57470
Rockport	57311
Roscoe	57471
Rosebud (Todd County)	57570
Rosebud Indian Reservation	57570
Rosedale Colony	57301

Name	ZIP
Rosholt	57260
Roslyn	57261
Roswell (Miner County)	57349
Roubaix	57754
Rowena	57056
Rumford	57774
Rumpus Ridge	57012
Running Water	57062
Rushmore Mall (Part of Rapid City)	57701
Rutland	57057
St. Charles (Gregory County)	57571
St. Francis	57572
St. Lawrence (Hand County)	57373
St. Onge	57779
Salem (McCook County)	57058
Sanator	57730
Savoy	57754
Scenic	57780
Scotland (Bon Homme County)	57059
Selby	57472
Seneca	57473
Shadehill	57653
Shady Beach	57227
Sherman (Minnehaha County)	57060
Silver City	57701
Sinai	57061
Sioux Falls	57055-57, 57101-18
For specific Sioux Falls Zip Codes call (605) 332-8360	
Sisseton (Roberts County)	57262
Sisseton Indian Reservation	57262
Smiths Park	57075
Smithwick	57782
So Dak Park	57279
Soldier Creek	57555
Sorum	57620
South Shore	57263
Spearfish	57783
Spencer	57374
Spink (Union County)	57025
Spink Colony	57440
Spring Creek (Todd County)	57572
Spring Creek Colony	58439
Springfield (Bon Homme County)	57062
Spring Valley (Turner County)	57036
Spring Valley Colony	57382
Standing Rock Indian Reservation (SD part)	58538
Stanley Corner	57319
Stephan	57346
Stickney	57375
Stockholm (Grant County)	57264
Stone Bridge	57223
Stoneville	57787
Storla	57359
Strandburg	57265
Stratford	57474
Sturgis	57785
Summit (Roberts County)	57266
Sunnyview	57006
Swett	57551
Tabor (Bon Homme County)	57063
Tacoma Park	57433
Tea	57064
Thomas	57241
Thunder Butte	57623
Thunder Hawk	57638
Tilford	57769
Timber Lake	57656
Tolstoy	57475
Toronto	57268
Trail City	57657
Trent	57065
Tripp	57376
Trojan	57754
Troy (Grant County)	57265
Tschetter Colony	57052
Tulare (Spink County)	57476
Turkey Ridge	57036
Turton (Spink County)	57477
Tuthill	57574
Twin Brooks (Grant County)	57269
Tyndall	57066
Union Center	57787
Unityville	57058
University (Part of Brookings)	57007
Usta	57626
Utica (Yankton County)	57067
Vale	57788
Valley Springs (Minnehaha County)	57068
Valley View	57072

510 SOUTH DAKOTA Vayland-Zeona

Name	ZIP
Vayland	57381
Veblen (Marshall County)	57270
Vedin Corner	57037
Verdon	57434
Vermillion (Clay County)	57069
Vetal	57551
Viborg	57070
Victor (Roberts County)	57260
Vienna	57271
Vilas	57349
Villa Ranchaero	57706
Villa Trailer Court	57706
Virgil (Beadle County)	57379
Vivian	57576
Volga (Brookings County)	57071
Volin (Yankton County)	57072
Wagner	57380
Wakonda	57073
Wakpala	57658
Wakpamani	57716
Walker	57601
Wall (Pennington County)	57790
Wallace	57272
Wanblee	57577
Ward (Moody County)	57074

Name	ZIP
Warner	57479
Wasta	57791
Watauga	57660
Watertown	57201
Waubay (Day County)	57273
Waverly (Codington County)	57202
Webster (Day County)	57274
Webster Grove	57106
Wecota	57438
Wentworth (Lake County)	57075
Wessington (Beadle County)	57381
Wessington Springs (Jerauld County)	57382
Western Mall (Part of Sioux Falls)	57105
Westerville	57069
Westport	57481
Wetonka	57481
Wewela	57578
White (Brookings County)	57276
White Butte	57638
Whitehorse	57661
White Lake (Aurora County)	57383

Name	ZIP
White Owl	57792
White River	57579
White Rock (Roberts County)	57260
Whitewood (Lawrence County)	57793
Wicksville	57767
Willow Lake (Clark County)	57278
Wilmot	57279
Winfred	57076
Winner	57580
Witten	57584
Wolf Creek Colony	57052
Wolsey (Beadle County)	57384
Wood	57585
Woonsocket (Sanborn County)	57385
Worthing	57077
Wounded Knee	57794
Yale	57386
Yankton	57078
Yankton Indian Reservation	57380
Zell	57483
Zeona	57795

Acklen-Beulah **TENNESSEE** 511

	ZIP		ZIP		ZIP
Acklen (Part of Nashville)	37212	Asbury (Pickett County)	38577	Beech Bluff	38313
Acton	38357	Asbury (Stewart County)	37175	Beech Bottom	37083
Adair	38301	Asbury Estates	37801	Beech Fork	37714
Adams	37010	Ashburn	37172	Beech Grove (Anderson County)	37769
Adams Crossroads	37055	Ash Hill	37046		
Adamsville	38310	Ashland	38485	Beechgrove (Coffee County)	37018
Aetna	37033	Ashland City	37015		
Afton	37616	Ashport	38063	Beech Grove (Grainger County)	37881
Airport	37110	Ashwood	38401		
Airport Estates (Part of Nashville)	37217	Asia	37398	Beech Grove (Hawkins County)	37711
		Aspen Hill	38478		
Airport Mail Facility (Davidson County)	37217	Athendale	38401	Beech Grove (Trousdale County)	37074
		Athens	37303		
Airport Mail Facility (Shelby County)	38130	Atkins	37079	Beech Grove (Weakley County)	38230
		Atoka	38004		
Air View	37301	Atwood	38220	Beech Hill (Franklin County)	37398
Akard Addition	37620	Auburntown	37016	Beech Hill (Giles County)	38478
Alamo	38001	Aulon (Part of Memphis)	38101	Beech Hill (Macon County)	37074
Alanthus Hill	37879	Austin Peay State University (Part of Clarksville)	37040	Beechnut	37617
Albany	37743			Beech Springs	37764
Albright	37066	Austin Springs (Washington County)	37601	Beechwood	37020
Alcoa	37701			Beersheba Springs	37305
Alder Branch	37862	Austin Springs (Weakley County)	38226	Bel Air	38261
Alder Springs (Campbell County)	37766			Bel Aire (Coffee County)	37388
		Avoca (Part of Bristol)	37620	Bel Aire (Rutherford County)	37130
Alder Springs (Union County)	37807	Avondale (Grainger County)	37861	Bel-Aire Heights (Part of Winchester)	37398
		Avondale (Sumner County)	37075		
Alexander Springs	38456	Avondale Springs	37861	Belfast	37019
Alexandria	37012	Ayers	38030	Belinda City	37122
Algood	38501	Bacchus	37879	Belk	37166
Allardt	38504	Bacon Gap	37763	Bella Mara Estates	37854
Allens	38012	Bagdad	37145	Bell Buckle	37020
Allens Chapel	37166	Baggettsville	37172	Bell Campground	37849
Allensville	37862	Bailey	38017	Belle Aire (Knox County)	37922
Allisona	37046	Baileyton	37743	Belle Aire (White County)	38583
Allons	38541	Bailey Town	37821	Belle Brook Estate (Part of Bristol)	37620
Alloway	37337	Bain	38320		
Allred	38542	Bairds Mills	37087	Belle Eagle	38012
Almaville	37014	Baker Crossroads	38555	Belle Founte	37311
Almira	38011	Bakers (Part of Nashville)	37072	Belle Meade (Blount County)	37801
Almy	37755	Bakers Crossroads	38583		
Alpha	37814	Bakersworks	37029	Belle Meade (Davidson County)	37205
Alpha Heights	37814	Bakerton	37150		
Alpine	38543	Bakertown (Davidson County)	37013	Belleville	37334
Altamont	37301			Bellevue (Part of Nashville)	37221
Alto	37324	Bakertown (Moore County)	37352	Bellevue Estates	37331
Alton Park (Part of Chattanooga)	37409	Bakerville	38185	Beil Mill	37363
		Bakewell	37304	Bels	38006
Altonville	37857	Bald Point	37881	Bellsburg	37036
Alumwell	37857	Ball Camp	37921	Bell Town (Cheatham County)	37082
Alynwick	37804	Ballplay (Monroe County)	37385		
Amherst (Part of Knoxville)	37931	Ball Play (Polk County)	37362	Belltown (Monroe County)	37385
Amity Heights	37620	Balltown	37331	Belltown (Polk County)	37317
Amqui (Part of Nashville)	37115	Baltimore	37843	Bellview (Bledsoe County)	37367
Anark	38344	Baneberry	37890	Bellview (Lincoln County)	37334
Anderson (Franklin County)	37376	Bangham	38501	Bellwood	37087
Anderson (Overton County)	38574	Banner	37738	Belmont (Anderson County)	37705
Anderson Heights	37617	Banner Hill (Unicoi County)	37650	Belmont (Coffee County)	37355
Andersonville	37705	Banner Springs	38556	Belmont (Jefferson County)	37725
Anes	37091	Baptist (Part of Nashville)	37203	Belmont West	37919
Angeltown	37022	Baptist Ridge	38568	Belvidere	37306
Anglea	37022	Barefoot	37186	Bemis (Part of Jackson)	38314
Anglers Cove	37763	Barfield	37129	Bending Chestnut	37064
Annadale (Part of Cleveland)	37311	Bargerton	38351	Benton (Polk County)	37307
		Barkertown	37365	Benton Springs	37307
Annadel	37770	Barnardsville	37763	Berclair (Part of Memphis)	38117
Anthony Hill	38460	Barnes	38573	Berea (Giles County)	38478
Antioch (Davidson County)	37013	Barnesville	38483	Berea (Warren County)	38581
Antioch (De Kalb County)	37166	Barr	38040	Berlin	37091
Antioch (Jackson County)	38562	Barren Plain	37172	Berry Hill	37204
Antioch (Loudon County)	37771	Barretville	38053	Berrys Chapel	37064
Antioch (Polk County)	37307	Barthelia	37031	Bertha	37765
Antioch (Tipton County)	38058	Bartlebaugh	37416	Bessie	38079
Apison	37302	Bartlett	38134	Bethany	37110
Appleton	38457	Barton Springs	37814	Bethel (Anderson County)	37716
Arcadia	37660	Bates Hill	37110	Bethel (Benton County)	38320
Archer	37091	Bath Springs	38311	Bethel (Blount County)	37882
Archville	37369	Batley	37716	Bethel (Carroll County)	38344
Arcott	38551	Battlewood Estates	37064	Bethel (Cheatham County)	37015
Ardmore	38449	Baugh	38449	Bethel (De Kalb County)	37166
Arkland	38487	Baugh Spring	37353	Bethel (Giles County)	38477
Arlington (Houston County)	37061	Baxter	38544	Bethel (Haywood County)	38012
Arlington (Knox County)	37917	Bazel Town (Part of Harriman)	37748	Bethel (Maury County)	38482
Arlington (Shelby County)	38002			Bethel (Perry County)	37096
Armathwaite	38504	Beacon	38363	Bethel Springs	38315
Armona	37804	Beamswitch	38230	Bethesda (Greene County)	37641
Armour	38401	Beans Creek	37345	Bethesda (Williamson County)	37046
Arms Mill	37807	Bean Station	37708		
Arno	37046	Bear Creek	37892	Bethlehem (Bedford County)	37160
Arnold Air Force Base	37389	Beardstown (Part of Lobelville)	37097		
Arnold Engineering Development Center	37389			Bethlehem (Campbell County)	37766
		Bear Spring	37058		
Arnolds Chapel	38544	Beartown	37660	Bethlehem (Hardin County)	38310
Arp	38063	Bearwallow	37015	Bethlehem (Henry County)	38222
Arrington	37014	Beasley	37034	Bethlehem (Monroe County)	37354
Arrowhead	37920	Beauty Hill	38315	Bethlehem (Williamson County)	37064
Arthur	37707	Beaver	38011		
Asbury (Coffee County)	37355	Beaverdam Springs	37147	Bethpage	37022
Asbury (Haywood County)	38069	Beaver Ridge	37921	Betsy Willis	37342
Asbury (Knox County)	37914	Beckwith	37122	Beulah (Greene County)	37810
Asbury (Lauderdale County)	38063	Bedford	37160	Beulah (Union County)	37807

TENNESSEE

Legend
Population
- ■ 250,000-999,999
- ● 100,000-249,999
- ▪ 50,000-99,999
- • 25,000-49,999
- ▪ 10,000-24,999
- • 5,000-9,999
- ▫ 1,000-4,999
- · Less than 1,000
- ★ Military Base

State Capital   County Seat

0 5 10   20   30   40 Miles
0 5 10   20   30   40 50 Kilometers

Copyright © 1986, 1983
by Rand McNally & Co.
All rights reserved
Made and printed in the U.S.A.

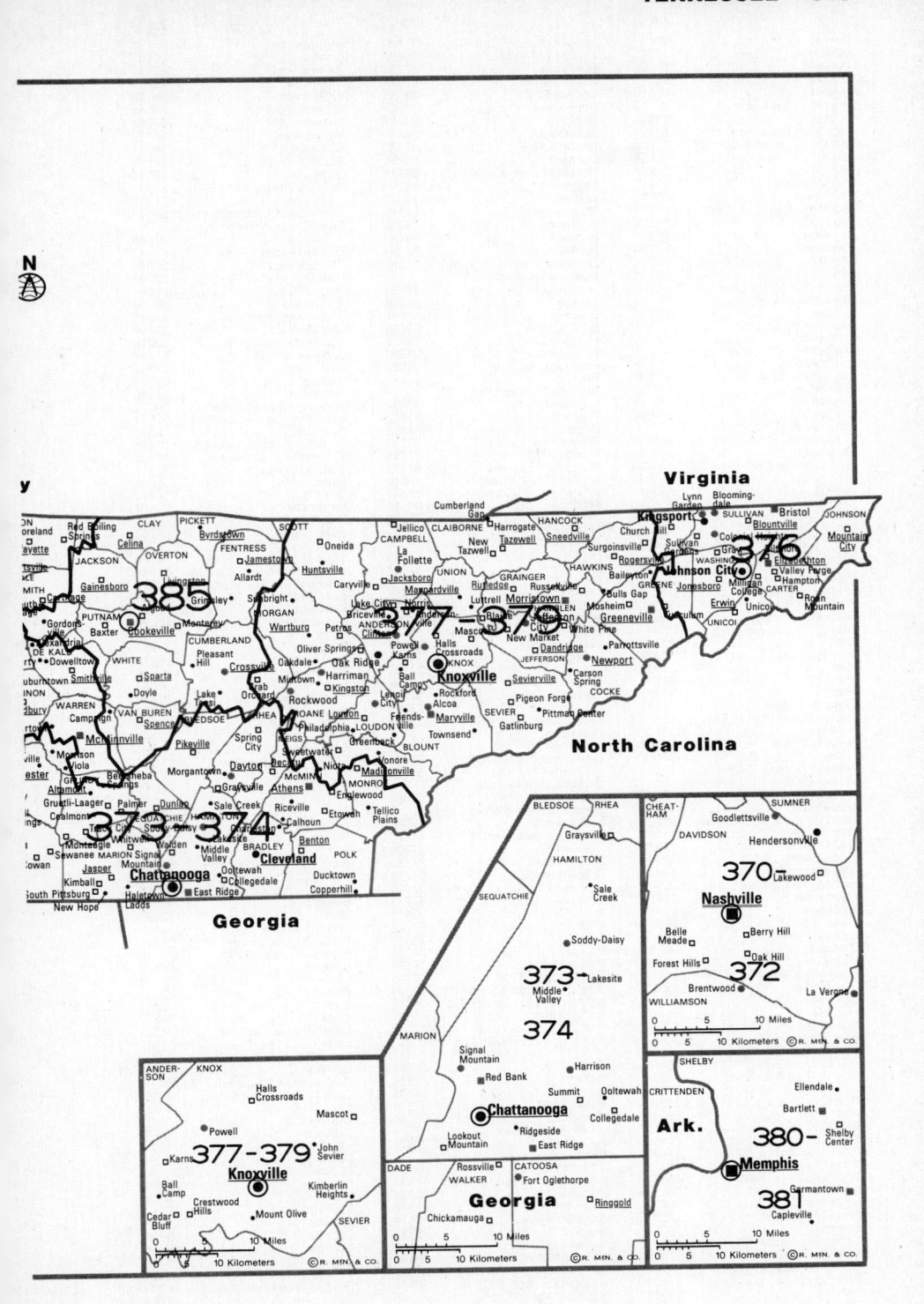

TENNESSEE 513

514 TENNESSEE Beverly-Camp Austin

Name	ZIP
Beverly	37918
Bible Hill	38363
Bidwell	37144
Big Boy Junction	38030
Bigbyville	38401
Big Creek (Hancock County)	37869
Big Creek (Hawkins County)	37857
Big Creek (Monroe County)	37354
Big Ivy	38372
Big Lick	38555
Big Mountain	37840
Big Piney	37774
Big Ridge Park	37807
Big Rock	37023
Big Sandy	38221
Big Sinks	37866
Big Spring (Blount County)	37737
Big Spring (Carter County)	37643
Big Spring (Meigs County)	37322
Big Springs (Hancock County)	37731
Big Springs (Overton County)	38570
Big Springs (Rutherford County)	37037
Big Spring Union	37752
Biltmore	37643
Binfield	37804
Bingham	37064
Binghamton (Part of Memphis)	38112
Birchwood	37308
Bird Crossroad	37862
Bird Song	38320
Bishop	38024
Bivens	38472
Black Center	38320
Black Creek	37852
Black Fox (Bradley County)	37311
Black Fox (Grainger County)	37888
Black Jack	37355
Blackman	37129
Black Oak	37841
Blackwell	37861
Blaine	37709
Blair	37748
Blair Gap	37660
Blair Lane	37087
Blakeville	37144
Blanche	38488
Blanche Chapel	38449
Blaney Forest (Part of East Ridge)	37412
Blanton Chapel	37355
Bledsoe (Lincoln County)	37144
Bledsoe (Sumner County)	37022
Block City (Part of Mount Carmel)	37642
Blockhouse	37801
Blondy (Part of Hohenwald)	38462
Bloomingdale (Sullivan County)	37660
Bloomington	38549
Bloomington Heights	37660
Bloomington Springs	38545
Blount Hills	37804
Blountville	37617
Blowing Cave Mill	37862
Blowing Springs	37716
Bluebank	38079
Blue Creek	38472
Bluefields (Part of Nashville)	37214
Blue Goose	38351
Bluegrass	37722
Blue Hill	37110
Blue Ridge (Part of Bristol)	37620
Blue Spring	37643
Blue Springs (De Kalb County)	37166
Blue Springs (Hamilton County)	37341
Bluff City	37618
Bluff Creek	38547
Bluff Springs	37110
Bluhmtown	37166
Blunts Landing	37096
Blythe Ferry	37321
Board Valley	38583
Boatland	38556
Bodenham	38478
Boggs	37861
Bogota	38007
Bohannon Addition (Part of Athens)	37303
Boiling Springs	38544
Bold Spring	37101
Bolivar	38008
Bolton	38002
Boma	38544

Name	ZIP
Bon Air (Sumner County)	37022
Bon Air (White County)	38583
Bon Aqua	37025
Bon Aqua Junction	37098
Bon De Croft	38583
Bone Cave	38581
Bonicord	38024
Bonnertown	38457
Bonny Kate	37920
Bonsack	38554
Bonwood (Part of Jackson)	38301
Boom	38573
Boone	37601
Boones Creek	37615
Booneville	37334
Boonshill	38459
Boothspoint	38030
Bordeaux (Part of Nashville)	37218
Borden Mills (Part of Kingsport)	37660
Boston	37064
Bowen	37861
Bowling	38555
Bowman	38555
Bowmantown	37690
Boxwood Hills	37922
Boyd	37722
Boyd Mill Estates (Part of Franklin)	37064
Boyds Creek	37862
Brace	38483
Brackentown	37148
Bradburn Hill	37743
Bradbury	37763
Braden (Fayette County)	38010
Braden (Union County)	37870
Bradford	38316
Bradleytown	38030
Bradshaw	38459
Bradyville	37026
Braemar	37658
Braid Cove	37087
Brainerd (Part of Chattanooga)	37411
Brakebill	37354
Bransford	37022
Bratcher's	37110
Brattontown	37083
Braxton	37190
Bray	37881
Brayton	37338
Braytown	37710
Brazil	38382
Breckinredge South	37064
Brentlawn (Part of Springfield)	37172
Brentwood (Hamblen County)	37814
Brentwood (Williamson County)	37027
Brentwood Mall (Part of Brentwood)	37027
Brewer Addition (Part of Athens)	37303
Brewstertown	37852
Briar Thicket	37713
Briarwood	37040
Briceville	37710
Brick Church	38478
Brick Mill	37742
Bride	38019
Bridgeport	37821
Bridwell Heights	37617
Bright Hope	37743
Brighton (Lincoln County)	37335
Brighton (Tipton County)	38011
Brims Corner	38001
Bristol	37620-25
For specific Bristol Zip Codes call (615) 968-2355	
Britton Ford	38256
Brittontown	37616
Brittsville	37336
Broad Acres	37849
Broadmoor	38024
Broad Street (Part of Cookeville)	38501
Broadview (Crockett County)	38034
Broadview (Franklin County)	37398
Broadway	38351
Brockdell	37367
Brockland Acres	37814
Brock's	38230
Brookhaven (Part of Crossville)	38555
Brotherton	38501
Browder (Loudon County)	37771
Browder (Marion County)	37347
Brown Cross Roads	38469
Brown Ellis	37748

Name	ZIP
Brownington	37398
Browns	37083
Browns Shop	37144
Brownsville	38012
Browntown	38578
Brownwood Acres	37064
Broylesville	37681
Bruceton	38317
Bruceville	38024
Bruner Grove	37713
Brunswick	38014
Brush Creek (Sequatchie County)	37327
Brush Creek (Smith County)	38547
Brush Creek (Williamson County)	37062
Brushy Mountain State Penitentiary	37845
Bryan Hill (Part of Dayton)	37321
Bryant Station	37091
Bryson	38453
Bryson Mountain	40965
Brysonville	37190
Buchanan	38222
Buckeye	37847
Buck Lodge	37148
Buckner	37166
Bucksnort	37140
Bucktown (Hardin County)	38372
Bucktown (Loudon County)	37771
Buena Vista	38318
Buffalo (Humphreys County)	37078
Buffalo (Scott County)	37756
Buffalo Springs	37861
Buffalo Valley	38548
Bufords	38472
Bugscuffle	37183
Buladeen	37643
Bullards Gap	38562
Bull Creek	37756
Bullet Creek	37369
Bull Run (Anderson County)	37849
Bull Run (Davidson County)	37015
Bulls Gap	37711
Bumpass Cove	37650
Bumpus Mills	37028
Buncombe	37617
Bungalow Town	37804
Bunker Hill	38478
Buntontown	37640
Burbank	37687
Burchfield Heights	37830
Burem	37857
Burgen	37026
Burke	37367
Burlington (Part of Knoxville)	37914
Burlington Heights (Part of Cleveland)	37311
Burlison	38015
Burns	37029
Burnt Church	38372
Burristown	38562
Burrville	37872
Burt	37190
Burton (Part of Rogersville)	37857
Burwood	37179
Busby (Part of Loretto)	38469
Busselltown	37771
Butler	37640
Butlers Landing	38551
Bybee (Cocke County)	37713
Bybee (Warren County)	37110
Byrdstown	38549
Cabin Row	37171
Cabo	38332
Cades	38358
Cades Cove	37882
Cadet (Part of Franklin)	37064
Cagle	37327
Cain Mill	37860
Cainsville	37085
Cairo (Crockett County)	38001
Cairo (Sumner County)	37066
Cairo Bend	37087
Calderwood	37801
Calfkiller	38574
Calhoun	37309
Calico	37322
Calistia	37049
Callins	38230
Calls	37330
Camargo	37334
Cambria	37325
Cambridge	38581
Camden	38320
Camelot (Cumberland County)	38555
Camelot (Hawkins County)	37857
Camilla Homes	38004
Campaign	38550
Camp Austin	37829

Campbell Army Airfield-Coal Chute TENNESSEE 515

Name	ZIP
Campbell Army Airfield	42223
Campbell Junction	38555
Campbells	38451
Campbellsville	38478
Camp Creek	37743
Camp Ground	38237
Camp Marymount	37062
Camp Monterey Lake	38574
Camp Nakanawa	38555
Camp Relax	37166
Camps	37869
Camp Ta-Pa-Win-Go	37694
Camp Woodlee	37110
Canadaville	38028
Cane Ridge (Part of Nashville)	37013
Caney Branch	37743
Caney Creek	37891
Caney Ford	37748
Caney Spring	37091
Caney Valley	37879
Cantrell	38485
Capitol Hill (Franklin County)	37330
Capitol Hill (Scott County)	37756
Capleville	38118
Caravelle Estates	37122
Cardiff	37854
Carlisle	37058
Carlock	37331
Carnegie (Part of Johnson City)	37601
Carpenter Campground	37804
Carroll	37087
Carroll Reece (Part of Johnson City)	37601
Carrs Branch	37825
Carson Spring	37821
Carter	37643
Carters Creek	38401
Carthage	37030
Carthage Junction (Part of Gordonsville)	38567
Cartwright (Sequatchie County)	37397
Cartwright (Smith County)	37145
Caryville	37714
Cash Point	38449
Cassville	38583
Castalian Springs	37031
Castle Heights	37821
Cat Corner	38240
Cates	38079
Cates Trailor	37764
Catlettsburg	37862
Cato	37057
Catons Grove	37722
Catoosa	37770
Cave	38559
Cave Spring	37879
Cavvia	38341
Cedar Bluff (Knox County)	37722
Cedar Bluff (Sevier County)	37862
Cedarbluff (Trousdale County)	37087
Cedar Bluff Two	37722
Cedar Chapel	38075
Cedar Creek	37743
Cedar Creek Landing	37096
Cedarcrest	37857
Cedarfork (Claiborne County)	37879
Cedar Fork (Loudon County)	37846
Cedar Grove (Bedford County)	37034
Cedar Grove (Carroll County)	38321
Cedar Grove (Carter County)	37601
Cedar Grove (Henderson County)	38371
Cedar Grove (Humphreys County)	37078
Cedar Grove (Pickett County)	38577
Cedar Grove (Roane County)	37763
Cedar Grove (Rutherford County)	37060
Cedar Grove (Sullivan County)	37660
Cedar Grove (Sullivan County)	37618
Cedar Grove (Wilson County)	37087
Cedar Hill (Putnam County)	38544
Cedar Hill (Robertson County)	37032
Cedar Springs	37303
Cedar Valley (Part of Bristol)	37620
Celina	38551

Name	ZIP
Center (Crockett County)	38337
Center (Lawrence County)	38464
Center (Monroe County)	37385
Center Grove (Franklin County)	37388
Center Grove (Jackson County)	38562
Center Hill (Cannon County)	37190
Center Hill (Warren County)	37110
Center Point (Chester County)	38332
Center Point (Giles County)	38478
Center Point (Hardeman County)	38042
Center Point (Lawrence County)	38468
Center Point (Sequatchie County)	37327
Center Point (Stewart County)	37058
Center Point (White County)	38587
Center Star	38454
Centersville	37742
Centertown	37110
Centerville (Hickman County)	37033
Centerville (Wilson County)	37087
Central (Carter County)	37601
Central (Gibson County)	38382
Central (Lauderdale County)	38063
Central (Obion County)	38253
Central Heights	37617
Central Point	37861
Central State Psychiatric Hospital (Part of Nashville)	37217
Central View	38587
Cerro Gordo	38372
Chable	30708
Chalklevel (Benton County)	38320
Chalk Level (Hawkins County)	37857
Champ	37359
Chanceytown	37391
Chandler	37777
Chantay Acres (Part of Columbia)	38401
Chanute	38577
Chapel Hill (Marshall County)	37034
Chapel Hill (Maury County)	38474
Chapman Grove	37763
Chapmans	38478
Chapmansboro	37035
Charity	37334
Charles Creek Estates	37110
Charleston (Bradley County)	37310
Charleston (Tipton County)	38069
Charleys Branch	37710
Charlotte	37036
Charlotte Park (Part of Nashville)	37209
Charlton Green (Part of Franklin)	37064
Chaska	37766
Chattanooga	37401-22
For specific Chattanooga Zip Codes call (615) 499-8256	
Cherokee (Decatur County)	38380
Cherokee (Washington County)	37659
Cherokee Harshaw	37743
Cherokee Heights	37801
Cherokee Hills (Roane County)	37763
Cherokee Hills (Part of Sevierville) (Sevier County)	37865
Cherokee Hills (Sevier County)	37862
Cherry	38041
Cherry Acres (Part of Gruetli-Laager)	37339
Cherrybrook	37912
Cherry Chapel	38372
Cherry Grove	38333
Cherry Hill	38582
Cherry Valley	37184
Chesney	37848
Chester Estates (Part of Fairview)	37062
Chesterfield	38351
Chestnut Bluff	38040
Chestnut Glade	38237
Chestnut Grove (Jefferson County)	37725
Chestnut Grove (Perry County)	37096
Chestnut Grove (Stewart County)	37058

Name	ZIP
Chestnut Grove (Sumner County)	37148
Chestnut Grove (Union County)	37807
Chestnut Hill (Cumberland County)	38555
Chestnut Hill (Jefferson County)	37725
Chestnut Hill (Sumner County)	37148
Chestnut Mound	38552
Chestnut Orchard	37172
Chestnut Ridge (Greene County)	37641
Chestnutridge (Lincoln County)	37144
Chestoa	37650
Chestua	37354
Chestuee	37311
Chewalla	38393
Chic	38030
Chickamauga (Part of Chattanooga)	37421
Chickasaw Heights (Part of Paris)	38242
Childers Hill	38326
Chilhowee View	37801
China Grove	38233
Chinquapin Grove	37618
Chinubee	38486
Chipman	37022
Chittum	37879
Choptack	37857
Chota	37801
Chotham	38382
Choto	37922
Choto Hills	37777
Christiana	37037
Christian Bend	37642
Christianburg	37874
Christie Hill	37801
Christmasville (Carroll County)	38201
Christmasville (Haywood County)	38012
Chuckey	37641
Church Hill	37642
Churchton	38059
Citico Beach	37885
Clacks Gap	37748
Clairfield	37715
Clark Addition	37804
Clarkrange	38553
Clarksburg	38324
Clarksville	37040-43
For specific Clarksville Zip Codes call (615) 647-3392	
Clarksville Base	42223
Clarktown	38583
Claxton (Anderson County)	37849
Claxton (McMinn County)	37303
Claybrook	38301
Clay Hill	37892
Claylick	37187
Clayton	38260
Clearbranch	37650
Clear Creek Mill	37332
Clearmont	37110
Clear Springs (Greene County)	37681
Clear Springs (Knox County)	37806
Clear Springs (McMinn County)	37309
Clearwater	37303
Clements Lake Estates (Part of Fairview)	37062
Clementsville	37150
Cleveland	37311-12
For specific Cleveland Zip Codes call (615) 472-6597	
Clevenger	37821
Cliff Springs	38574
Clifftops	37356
Clifton (Clifton City)	38425
Clifton	38485
Clifty	38583
Clinton	37716
Clopton	38011
Cloud Creek	37857
Clouds	37879
Clouse Hill	37387
Clovercroft	37064
Cloverdale (Obion County)	38240
Cloverdale (Shelby County)	38053
Cloverdale (White County)	38583
Clover Hill (Blount County)	37804
Cloverhill (Davidson County)	37214
Cloverport	38381
Club Springs	38560
Coal Chute	37643

516 TENNESSEE Coalfield-Dodson Estates

	ZIP
Coalfield	37719
Coal Hill (Morgan County)	37748
Coal Hill (Scott County)	37872
Coaling	37051
Coalmont	37313
Cobbs	38006
Coble	37033
Coffee Landing	38310
Coffee Ridge	37650
Cog Hill	37325
Cokercreek	37314
Cold Spring (Bledsoe County)	37367
Cold Spring (Johnson County)	37683
Cold Springs (Blount County)	37886
Cold Springs (Hawkins County)	37873
Coldwater	37334
Colesburg	37055
Coles Ferry	37087
Coles Store	38544
Coletown	37317
College (Bledsoe County)	37327
College (Blount County)	37801
Collegedale	37315
College Grove	37046
College Grove Estates	37854
College Hill (Part of Dayton)	37321
College Park	37601
College Park Estates	37801
Colliers Corner	37760
Collierville	38017
Collins (Grundy County)	37365
Collins (Hawkins County)	37857
Collinwood	38450
Colonial Acres	38225
Colonial Circle	37865
Colonial Heights	37663
Colonial Village (Part of Knoxville)	37920
Columbia	38401-02
For specific Columbia Zip Codes call (615) 388-6161	
Columbus Hill	38574
Columbus Hill	38562
Comfort	37380
Commerce	37184
Community Acres	37180
Como	38223
Compton	37130
Conasauga	37316
Concord (Carroll County)	38344
Concord (Gibson County)	38382
Concord (Humphreys County)	37185
Concord (Knox County)	37922
Concord (census area only) (Knox County)	37901
Concord (Rhea County)	37332
Concord (Rutherford County)	37153
Concord-Farragut	37922
Conklin	37659
Conner Heights (Part of Pigeon Forge)	37863
Conyersville	38251
Cookeville	38501-02
For specific Cookeville Zip Codes call (615) 526-7141	
Cool Springs	38259
Cooper	38556
Coopers	38317
Coopertown	37172
Copperhill	37317
Corbin Hill	37840
Cordell	37756
Corder Cross Roads	37348
Cordova	38018
Corinth (Knox County)	37918
Corinth (Sumner County)	37148
Cornersville	37047
Coro Lake	38109
Corona	72338
Corryton	37721
Cortner	37360
Cosby	37722
Coster (Part of Knoxville)	37917
Cottage Grove	38224
Cottage Home	37095
Cottonport	37322
Cottontown	37048
Cottonwood Estates	37064
Cottonwood Grove	38080
Cotula	37766
Couchville (Part of Nashville)	37214
Coulterville	37373
Counce	38326
Country Club	38008

	ZIP
Country Haven Estates	37179
Country Roads	37064
Countrywood Estates	37064
Countyline (Moore County)	37352
County Line (Sevier County)	37865
Courtland	37172
Cove Creek (Campbell County)	37714
Cove Creek (Carter County)	37687
Cove Creek Cascades	37862
Cove Lake Estates	37714
Covington	38019
Cowan	37318
Cowanstown	37640
Cowards	37921
Cowenville	38567
Coxville	38343
Cozyette	38380
Crab Orchard	37723
Crabtree	37687
Crackers Neck	37683
Craggie Hope	37082
Craigfield	37025
Crandull	37688
Cranmore Cove	37321
Cravenstown	38589
Crawfish Valley	38464
Crawford	38554
Creekwood (Bedford County)	37160
Creekwood (Wilson County)	37122
Crenshaw	37920
Crescent	37129
Creson (Part of Fayetteville)	37334
Creston	38555
Crestwood	37763
Crestwood Hills	37918
Crewstown	38464
Crieve Hall (Part of Nashville)	37211
Crippen Gap	37918
Crisp Spring	37357
Crockett	38253
Crockett Mills	38021
Cronanville	38079
Cross	37617
Cross Anchor	37743
Cross Bridges	38474
Cross Keys	37046
Crossland	42049
Cross Lanes	37186
Cross Plains	37049
Cross Road	37841
Crossroads (Benton County)	38320
Cross Roads (Cannon County)	37190
Crossroads (Crockett County)	38006
Cross Roads (De Kalb County)	37059
Cross Roads (Dyer County)	38034
Cross Roads (Fentress County)	38556
Crossroads (Hardin County)	38372
Cross Roads (Lawrence County)	38456
Crossroads (Lawrence County)	38468
Cross Roads (Macon County)	37186
Crossroads (Shelby County)	38017
Cross Roads (Stewart County)	37178
Crossroads (Wayne County)	38450
Crosstown (Shelby County)	38104
Crosstown (Tipton County)	38004
Crossville	38555
Crosswinds	37122
Crowley Store	38230
Crown Point Estates	37122
Crucifer	38345
Crump	38327
Crunk	37073
Crystal	38261
Crystal Springs	37348
Cuba (Hawkins County)	37811
Cuba (Shelby County)	38053
Cuba Landing	37185
Cub Creek	38562
Culleoka	38451
Culpepper	37149
Cumberland City	37050
Cumberland Estates (Part of Knoxville)	37921
Cumberland Furnace	37051
Cumberland Gap	37724
Cumberland Heights (Grundy County)	37313
Cumberland Heights (Montgomery County)	37040

	ZIP
Cumberland Springs	37321
Cumberland View	37757
Cumberland View Estates	37769
Cummings	38583
Cummingsville	38585
Cunningham	37052
Cupp Mill	37825
Curlee	37190
Curve	38063
Cusick	37865
Cuzick	37771
Cypress	38001
Cypress Creek	38222
Cypress Inn	38452
Daisy (Part of Socdy-Daisy)	37379
Dale Hollow	38551
Dalewood (Part of Nashville)	37207
Dallas Gardens	37379
Dallas Hills	37379
Dalton Heights (Part of Morristown)	37814
Dancyville	38069
Dandridge	37725
Dante	37921
Darden	38328
Darks Mill	38401
Daugherty Estates	37062
Daus	37327
Davenport	37110
Davidson	38589
Davidson Chapel	38382
Davis Chapel (Campbell County)	37766
Davis Chapel (Carroll County)	38344
Davis Springs	37692
Daylight	37110
Daysville	37854
Dayton	37321
Dayton Spur	38555
Deanburg	38366
Deans	37033
DeArmond	37748
Deason	37020
De Busk	37743
Decatur	37322
Decaturville	38329
Decherd	37324
Deep Springs	37725
Deerfield (Lawrence County)	38464
Deerfield (Williamson County)	37064
Deerfield Acres	37620
Deer Lodge	37726
Deermont	37829
Defeated	37030
Defense Depot (Part of Memphis)	38114
Delano	37325
Delina	37047
Dellrose	38453
Dellwood	37804
Del Rio	37727
Demory	37766
Denmark	38391
Dennis Cove	37658
Denton	37722
Dentville	37325
Denver (Cannon County)	37149
Denver (Humphreys County)	37054
De Priest Bend (Part of Lobelville)	37097
De Rossett	38583
Detroit	38015
Devonia	37710
Diana	37047
Dibrell	37110
Dickel	37388
Dickey Bluff Peninsula	37381
Dickson	37055
Dickson Town	38455
Difficult	37145
Dill	37367
Dilley	37730
Dillton	37130
Disco	37737
Dismal	37095
Disney	37769
Dixie	38261
Dixie Lee Junction (Part of Farragut)	37771
Dixon Springs	37057
Dixonville	38053
Doaks Crossroads	37087
Dockery	37310
Dodson (Roane County)	37748
Dodson (White County)	38583
Dodson Estates (Part of Nashville)	37076

Dodsons-Federal Correctional Institution **TENNESSEE 517**

Name	ZIP
Dodsons	38472
Doeville	37640
Dog Hill	38050
Dogtown (Carter County)	37643
Dog Town (Grundy County)	37313
Dogtown (Polk County)	37391
Dogwood	37763
Dogwood Heights	37879
Dollar	38313
Donelson (Part of Nashville)	37214
Donnels Chapel	37149
Donoho	37030
Doran Addition	37660
Dorton	38555
Dossett	37716
Dotson	37888
Dotson Branch	38501
Dotson's Camp Ground	37888
Dotsontown	37681
Dotsonville	37191
Doty Chapel	37616
Double Bridges	38040
Double Springs (McMinn County)	37303
Double Springs (Putnam County)	38544
Douglas	37064
Douglas Estates	37725
Dover (Hamblen County)	37814
Dover (Stewart County)	37058
Dowelltown	37059
Dowler Heights	37377
Downtown (Blount County)	37801
Downtown (Bradley County)	37311
Downtown (Hamilton County)	37402
Doyle	38559
Drapers Crossroads	37083
Dresden	38225
Driftwood (Part of Bristol)	37620
Dripping Springs	37398
Drop	38583
Drummonds	38023
Drycreek	37659
Dry Hill (Johnson County)	37640
Dry Hill (Lauderdale County)	38040
Dry Hollow (Part of Kingsport)	37660
Duck Creek	37869
Duck River	38454
Ducktown (Polk County)	37326
Ducktown (Washington County)	37681
Dudney Hill	38562
Due West (Part of Nashville)	37115
Duff	37766
Dukedom	38226
Dulaney	37743
Dull	37036
Dumplin	37820
Dunbar	38311
Duncantown	37330
Dunlap	37327
Duplex	37064
Du Pont	37865
Durhamville	38063
Dutch	37888
Dutch Valley	37716
Dyer	38330
Dyersburg	38024-25
For specific Dyersburg Zip Codes call (901) 285-5491	
Dykes Crossroads	38555
Dyllis	37748
Dyson Grove	37640
Eads	38028
Eagan	37730
Eagle Creek	38341
Eagle Furnace	37854
Eagle Hill	38242
Eagleton Village (Blount County)	37801
Eagleton Village (Blount County)	37804
Eagleville	37060
Earleyville	37110
East (Part of Nashville)	37206
East Acres	38053
Eastbrook (Part of Estill Springs)	37330
East Chattanooga (Part of Chattanooga)	37406
East Cleveland	37311
East Cyruston	37334
East Due West (Part of Nashville)	37115
Easter Seal	37087
East Etowah	37331
East Fork	37862
Eastgate Mall (Part of Chattanooga)	37411

Name	ZIP
Eastgate Shopping Center (Part of Memphis)	38117
East Jamestown	38556
East Junction (Part of Memphis)	38101
East Lake (Part of Chattanooga)	37407
Eastland	38583
East Memphis (Part of Memphis)	38111
East Miller's Cove	37886
East Ridge	37412
Eastside (Cannon County)	37190
East Side (Carter County)	37643
East Side (Dickson County)	37029
Eastside (Sullivan County)	37664
Eastside (Warren County)	38581
East Springbrook (Part of Alcoa)	37701
East Sweetwater	37874
East Union	38301
Eastview (Greene County)	37743
Eastview (McNairy County)	38367
East View (Meigs County)	37336
Eastwood (Part of La Vergne)	37086
Eaton	38331
Eaton Crossroad	37771
Eaton Forest	37771
Ebenezer	37347
Echo Hills	37743
Eddie Hill	37087
Edenwold (Part of Nashville)	37115
Edgefield (Part of Bristol)	37620
Edgemont (Cocke County)	37821
Edgemont (Sullivan County)	37620
Edgemoor	37716
Edgewater (Rhea County)	37321
Edgewater (Wilson County)	37122
Edgewood (Dyer County)	38059
Edgewood (Sullivan County)	37660
Edgewood Acres	37804
Edgewood Heights	37849
Edison	38343
Edith	38063
Edwards Point	37377
Edwina	37821
Egam	37334
Egypt (Part of Memphis)	38128
Eidson	37731
Elba	38066
Elbethel	37160
Elbridge	38227
Elgin	37732
Elizabeth	38034
Elizabethton	37643-44
For specific Elizabethton Zip Codes call (615) 543-5801	
Elkhead	37366
Elkhorn	38242
Elk Mills	37640
Elk Mill Village (Part of Fayetteville)	37334
Elkmont	37738
Elkmont Springs	38449
Elkton	38455
Elk Valley	37847
Ellejoy	37865
Ellendale	38029
Ellington Park	37064
Ellis Mills	37050
Ellisville	38004
Elm Grove	38015
Elm Springs	37888
Elmwood	38560
Elora	37328
Elverton	37748
Elza	37830
Embreeville	37650
Emerald Acres	37814
Emerts Cove	37862
Emery Mill	37367
Emmanuel School of Religion	37601
Emmett	37620
Emory Gap (Part of Harriman)	37748
Emory Heights (Part of Harriman)	37748
Englewood (McMinn County)	37329
Englewood (Obion County)	38261
English Mountain Resort	37862
Enigma	38548
Eno	37055
Enon	37150
Ensor	38544
Enterprise (Hawkins County)	37857
Enterprise (Maury County)	38474
Enville	38332
Epperson	37385

Name	ZIP
Erasmus	38555
Erie	37846
Erin	37061
Erlanger (Part of Chattanooga)	37403
Ernestville	37650
Erwin	37650
Essary Springs	38061
Estes Kefauver (Part of Johnson City)	37601
Estill Springs	37330
Ethridge	38456
Etowah	37331
Etter	38549
Euchee	37880
Eulia	37186
Eureka (Bradley County)	37311
Eureka (Hardin County)	38372
Eureka (Roane County)	37854
Eurekaton	38075
Eva	38333
Evansville	38024
Evensville	37332
Evergreen	37687
Evins Mill	37166
Ewingville (Part of Franklin)	37064
Excell	37040
Factory	38485
Fair Acres (Hickman County)	37025
Fair Acres (Sullivan County)	37660
Fairfield (Bedford County)	37183
Fairfield (Hamblen County)	37814
Fairfield (Hickman County)	37033
Fairfield (Sumner County)	37186
Fairfield Glade	38555
Fair Garden	37862
Fairgrounds (Part of Shelbyville)	37160
Fairlane Estates (Part of Shelbyville)	37160
Fairmont (Part of Bristol)	37620
Fairmount	37377
Fairview (Blount County)	37801
Fairview (Bradley County)	37311
Fairview (Carroll County)	38201
Fairview (Carter County)	37658
Fairview (Clay County)	38541
Fairview (Coffee County)	37360
Fairview (Fentress County)	38556
Fairview (Gibson County)	38233
Fairview (Greene County)	37810
Fairview (Greene County)	37616
Fairview (Lawrence County)	38469
Fair View (Lincoln County)	37334
Fairview (Macon County)	37186
Fairview (Madison County)	38343
Fairview (McMinn County)	37303
Fairview (Meigs County)	37322
Fairview (Pickett County)	38549
Fairview (Putnam County)	38501
Fairview (Roane County)	37763
Fairview (Scott County)	37756
Fairview (Stewart County)	37058
Fairview (Warren County)	37110
Fairview (Washington County)	37659
Fairview (Wayne County)	38463
Fairview (White County)	38583
Fairview (Williamson County)	37062
Fairview Heights (Jefferson County)	37725
Fairview Heights (Williamson County)	37062
Fairyland	38555
Faix	38549
Falcon	38375
Fall Branch	37656
Fall Creek	37160
Falling Water	37343
Fallriver	38468
Falls Mill	37306
Fanchers Mills	38583
Fancy Meadows	37871
Farmers Exchange	38462
Farmers Valley	38458
Farmington (Marshall County)	37091
Farmington (Williamson County)	37064
Farner	37333
Farragut	37922
Farris Chapel	37398
Farrport (Part of Alcoa)	37701
Faulkner Springs	37110
Faxon	38221
Fayette Corners	38075
Fayetteville	37334
Federal Correctional Institution	38116

518 TENNESSEE Federal Reserve-Greenbrier

Name	ZIP
Federal Reserve (Part of Nashville)	37203
Fellowship	37122
Fennel Store	37709
Fernvale	37064
Fernwood	37814
Few Chapel	37101
Fielden Store	37820
Fincastle	37766
Findlay (Part of Sparta)	38583
Finger	38334
Finley	38030
Fisherville	38017
Fishery	37650
Fish Springs	37640
Fisk University (Part of Nashville)	37203
Five Points (Lawrence County)	38457
Five Points (Madison County)	38366
Five Points (Rhea County)	37321
Flag Branch	37743
Flag Pond	37657
Flat Branch Junction	37387
Flat Creek (Bedford County)	37160
Flat Creek (Overton County)	38570
Flat Gap (Hancock County)	37881
Flatgap (Jefferson County)	37760
Flat Hollow	37870
Flat Rock (Morgan County)	37726
Flat Rock (Smith County)	37087
Flattop	37379
Flatwood (Tipton County)	38015
Flatwood (Warren County)	37110
Flatwoods (Lawrence County)	38456
Flatwoods (Perry County)	38458
Flewellyn	37172
Flintville	37335
Flippin	38063
Floraton	37149
Florence	37129
Flourville	37659
Flowertown	37360
Fly	38482
Flynns Lick	38562
Foothills Mall (Part of Maryville)	37804
Forbus	38577
Ford	37771
Ford Chapel	37825
Fordtown (Campbell County)	37766
Fordtown (Sullivan County)	37663
Forest Chapel	37186
Forest Grove (Davidson County)	37080
Forest Grove (Meigs County)	37322
Forest Hill (Blount County)	37801
Forest Hill (Shelby County)	38138
Forest Hills (Bedford County)	37160
Forest Hills (Davidson County)	37215
Forest Hills (Knox County)	37919
Forest Hills (Sullivan County)	37620
Forest Home	37064
Forest Home Farms	37064
Forest Mills	37355
Forge Ridge	37752
Forked Deer	38037
Fork Mountain	37710
Fork of Pike	37095
Fork Ridge	40965
Forrest Park (Part of Tullahoma)	37388
Forsythe (Part of Memphis)	38101
Fort Campbell	42223
Fort Campbell South	42223
Fort Donelson Shores	37058
Fort Henry Mall (Part of Kingsport)	37664
Fort Loudon Estates	37771
Fort Pillow Prison and State Farm	38041
Fort Robinson (Part of Kingsport)	37660
Fosterville	37063
Foundry Hill	38251
Fountain City (Part of Knoxville)	37918
Fountain Head	37148
Fountain Heights	38401
Fourmile Board Hill	38485
Four Points	37820
Fowler Grove	37713
Fowlers	38320
Fowlkes	38033

Name	ZIP
Fox Bluff	37015
Foxbranch	37765
Foxfire	38555
Frankewing	38459
Frankfort	37770
Franklin	37064-65
For specific Franklin Zip Codes call (615) 794-2784	
Franklin East	37064
Fraterville	37769
Frayser (Part of Memphis)	38127
Fredonia (Coffee County)	37355
Fredonia (Montgomery County)	37040
Free Communion	38573
Free Hills	38551
Freeland	38222
Free State	38562
Freewill	38562
Fremont	38261
French Broad	37727
Frettin	38052
Friendship (Bledsoe County)	37381
Friendship (Crockett County)	38034
Friendship (Hamilton County)	37341
Friendship (Hawkins County)	37881
Friendship (Sullivan County)	37620
Friends Station	37820
Friendsville	37737
Frisco	37642
Frog Jump (Crockett County)	38040
Frog Jump (Gibson County)	38382
Frog Level	37731
Front Street (Part of Memphis)	38103
Frost Bottom	37840
Fruitland	38343
Fruitvale	38336
Fruit Valley	37153
Fulton	38041
Gabtown	37766
Gadsden	38337
Gainesboro	38562
Gainsville	38049
Gaitherville	38464
Galaxy Heights (Part of Chattanooga)	37343
Galbraith Springs	37811
Galen	37083
Gallatin	37066
Gallaway	38036
Gandy	38464
Gann	38358
Gapcreek	37643
Gardner	38237
Garland	38019
Garretts	38329
Gassaway	37095
Gates	38037
Gath	37110
Gatlinburg	37738
Gattistown	37359
Gause	37035
Gay	37110
Gentry	38544
Georgetown (Gibson County)	38382
Georgetown (Hamilton County)	37336
Georgetown (McMinn County)	37370
George W. Lee (Part of Memphis)	38126
Georgia Crossing	37398
Germantown (Davidson County)	37189
Germantown (Shelby County)	38138
Gerren Heights	37367
Gibbs (Part of Union City)	38261
Gibbs Crossroads	37145
Gibson	38338
Gibson Hall	37879
Gibsontown (Part of Memphis)	37660
Gibson Wells	38343
Gift	38019
Gilchrist	38310
Gildfield	38002
Gilfield	37686
Gillises Mills	38372
Gilmore	38301
Gilt Edge	38015
Gin House Lake	38058
Gladdice	38562
Glade Creek	38583
Glades (Morgan County)	37726

Name	ZIP
Glades (Sevier County)	37738
Gladeville	37071
Glass	38240
Gleason	38229
Glen	37342
Glen Alice	37854
Glencliff (Part of Nashville)	37211
Glendale (Hamilton County)	37405
Glendale (Lawrence County)	38469
Glendale (Loudon County)	37742
Glendale (Maury County)	38401
Glendale Estates	38478
Glen Del Acres	37860
Glenhaven (Part of Fairview)	37062
Glen Mary	37852
Glenmore Estates	37853
Glen Oaks	37122
Glenobey	38556
Glenview (Part of Nashville)	37217
Glenwood	37185
Glenwylde	37051
Glimp	38041
Glover	37172
Glover Hill	37347
Glynnwood Lake	38028
Gnat Hill	37355
Goat City	38355
Godwin	38401
Goffton	38501
Goin	37825
Golddust	38063
Goldpoint	37343
Goodbars	38581
Goodfield	37322
Good Hope (Campbell County)	37762
Good Hope (Dyer County)	38059
Goodlettsville	37072
Good Luck	38369
Goodspring	38460
Good Springs	37331
Goose Horn	38588
Gooseneck (Anderson County)	37705
Gooseneck (Blount County)	37737
Gordon (Part of Pulaski)	38478
Gordonsburg	38462
Gordonsville	38563
Gorman	37101
Goshen	37642
Gossburg	37018
Graball (Gibson County)	38358
Graball (Marshall County)	37047
Graball (Sumner County)	37148
Graham	37137
Grammer Estates	37062
Grand Junction	38039
Grand Valley	38067
Grandview (Greene County)	37641
Grandview (Knox County)	37920
Grandview (Rhea County)	37337
Grandview Estates	37764
Grandview Terrace	37620
Granite	37716
Grannys Branch	38221
Grant	38563
Grantsboro	37766
Granville	38564
Grasshopper	37308
Grassland	37064
Grassy Cove	38555
Grassy Creek	37317
Grassy Fork	37753
Grassy Valley	37743
Gratio	38240
Gravel Hill (McNairy County)	38339
Gravel Hill (Washington County)	37681
Gravelly Hill (Part of Jefferson City)	37760
Graveltown	37145
Graveston	37721
Gray	37615
Gray Acres	37620
Graysville	37338
Graytown	37033
Graywinds	37122
Green Ack	37840
Green Acres (Giles County)	38478
Green Acres (Knox County)	37921
Green Acres (Roane County)	37763
Green Acres (Sullivan County)	37660
Greenback	37742
Greenbriar	37185
Greenbriar Village (Part of Crossville)	38555
Greenbrier (Cheatham County)	37015

Green Brier-Holiday Hills TENNESSEE 519

	ZIP		ZIP		ZIP
Green Brier (Pickett County)	38549	Happy Valley	37878	Hickory Grove (Gibson County)	38382
Greenbrier (Robertson County)	37073	Harbin	37854	Hickory Grove (Sumner County)	37031
Greenbrier (Williamson County)	37064	Harbison	37721	Hickory Grove (Warren County)	37110
Greenbrier Lake	37087	Harbor Town	38221	Hickory Hill (Part of Lynchburg)	37352
Greeneville	37743-44	Harbour Island	37138	Hickory Hill Estates (Part of Tullahoma)	37388
For specific Greeneville Zip Codes call (615) 638-2221		Harbuck	37391	Hickory Hills	37064
Greenfield	38230	Hardin Estates	37771	Hickory Hollow Mall (Part of Nashville)	37211
Greenfield Bend	38487	Hardy	38501	Hickory Point	37040
Greenfields (Part of Kingsport)	37660	Harmon	37688	Hickory Star Landing	37807
Green Grove	37074	Harmony (Franklin County)	37398	Hickory Tree	37618
Green Harbor	37138	Harmony (Jackson County)	38562	Hickory Valley (Hardeman County)	38042
Greenhaw	37324	Harmony (Washington County)	37659	Hickory Valley (Union County)	37807
Green Hill (Jefferson County)	37725	Harmony Grove	37727	Hickory Withe	38043
Green Hill (Warren County)	37110	Harmony Hills	37660	Hicks Chapel	37397
Green Hill (Wilson County)	37138	Harms	37334	Hicksville (Part of Jackson)	38301
Green Hills (Part of Nashville)	37215	Harpeth	37064	Hico	38344
Greenland	37642	Harpeth Estates	37064	Hico Station (Carroll County)	38344
Green Meadow (Blount County)	37701	Harpeth Hills	37064	Hide-A-Way Hills	38555
Green Meadow (Bradley County)	37311	Harpeth Meadows (Part of Franklin)	37064	Highcliff	37762
Green Meadows	38556	Harpeth Valley	37187	Highgate	37064
Green Pond	38554	Harpeth Valley Park (Part of Nashville)	37221	Highland (De Kalb County)	37166
Greens	37110	Harrill Hills (Part of Knoxville)	37918	Highland (Jackson County)	38562
Greens Mill	37343	Harriman	37748	Highland (Overton County)	38570
Greentown	37387	Harriman Junction (Part of Harriman)	37748	Highland (Wayne County)	38450
Greenvale	37184	Harris	38261	Highland Academy	37148
Green Valley (Knox County)	37919	Harrisburg	37862	Highland Acres	37804
Green Valley (Macon County)	37083	Harrison	37341	Highland Forest (Part of Rockwood)	37854
Green Valley (Williamson County)	37064	Harrison Hills	37771	Highland Heights (Davidson County)	37207
Green Village (Part of Church Hill)	37642	Harrogate	37752	Highland Heights (Giles County)	38478
Greenwood (Macon County)	37150	Harrogate-Shawnee	37752	Highland Heights (Shelby County)	38122
Greenwood (Rutherford County)	37046	Harrtown	37617	Highland Junction	38589
Greenwood (Wilson County)	37087	Hartford	37753	Highland Manor	37341
Greystone	37743	Hartmantown	37659	Highland Park (Campbell County)	37766
Griffith	37367	Hartsville	37074	Highland Park (Hamilton County)	37404
Griffith Creek	37397	Haskins Chapel	37091	Highland Park (Loudon County)	37771
Grimsley	38565	Hatchertown	37862	Highland Park (Sullivan County)	37660
Grinders	37033	Hatchie	38392	Highland Springs	37709
Gronanville	38079	Havley Springs (Part of Morristown)	37814	Highlandview	37920
Gruetli (Part of Gruetli-Laager)	37339	Havron Chapel	37347	High Point (Campbell County)	37714
Gruetli-Laager	37339	Hawkinsville	38034	High Point (Scott County)	37841
Gudger	37354	Hawthorne	37160	Hilham	38568
Guild	37340	Haydenburg	38588	Hillcrest (Cumberland County)	38555
Gulf Park	37919	Hayes	38583	Hillcrest (Hamblen County)	37814
Gum	37130	Hayes Fork	37058	Hillcrest (Part of Kingsport)	37660
Gum Creek	37324	Haynes	38077	Hillcrest	37618
Gum Flat	38006	Haynesfield (Part of Bristol)	37620	Hilldale (Part of Clarksville)	37043
Gum Spring	37821	Hays	38057	Hill Estates (Part of Franklin)	37064
Gum Springs (Lawrence County)	38468	Haysboro (Part of Nashville)	37214	Hilliard	38344
Gum Springs (Macon County)	37145	Haysville	37083	Hillsboro	37342
Guntown	37857	Head of Barren	37825	Hillsboro Acres	37064
Guys	38339	Heard	38573	Hillsdale	37057
Habersham	37766	Heatherwood Hill	37064	Hillside	38237
Hackberry	37142	Heatoncreek	37687	Hills View	37370
Hales Crossroads	37814	Hebbertsburg	37723	Hilltop (Bedford County)	37160
Hales Point	38040	Hebron	38052	Hilltop (Montgomery County)	37040
Halesville	37095	Heiskell	37754	Hilltop (Rutherford County)	37167
Haletown-Ladds	37340	Helena	38556	Hill Top (Washington County)	37601
Haley	37183	Helenwood	37755	Hill Town	38482
Half Acre	37166	Heloise	38030	Hillvale	37716
Halls (Knox County)	37918	Helton	37012	Hillville	38075
Halls (Lauderdale County)	38040	Helton Springs	37861	Hillwood (Part of Nashville)	37205
Halls Creek	37185	Heltonville	37708	Himesville	37160
Halls Crossroads	37918	Hemlock Hills	37650	Hindscreek	37716
Hallshare Estates	38320	Henard Mill	37857	Hinds Creek Valley	37807
Halls Hill	37118	Henardtown	37857	Hinkle	38371
Halls Mills	37160	Henderson	38340	Hinkledale	38201
Hall Town (Sumner County)	37148	Hendersonville	37075	Hitchcox	37367
Halltown (Trousdale County)	37074	Hendon	37338	Hiwassee College	37354
Hallview Meadows (Part of Fairview)	37062	Hendron	37920	Hiwassee Hills	37354
Hamburg	38376	Henley (Part of Decherd)	37324	Hixon	37301
Hamillville (Part of Chattanooga)	37343	Henning	38041	Hixson (Part of Chattanooga)	37343
Hamilton Mill	38453	Henrietta	37015	Hobbs Hill	37387
Hamilton Place (Part of Chattanooga)	37421	Henry	38231	Hodges	37820
Hamlin Town	37715	Henrys Crossroads	37764	Hoggtown	37030
Hammon Chapel	37683	Henry Street (Part of Morristown)	37814	Hohenwald	38462
Hampshire	38461	Henryville	38483	Holiday City (Part of Memphis)	38118
Hampton	37658	Hensley Chapel	38583	Holiday Hills (Cumberland County)	38555
Hamptons Crossroads	38583	Herbert Domain	37367		
Hampton Station	37040	Heritage Estates	38555		
Handleyton	37148	Heritage Hills	37801		
Hanging Limb	38554	Hermitage (Part of Nashville)	37076		
Happy Hill	38478	Hermitage Hills (Part of Nashville)	37076		
Happy Top	37337	Hermitage Springs	37150		
		Hermon	37616		
		Hiawassee	37357		
		Hickerson	37388		
		Hickey	38582		
		Hickman	38567		
		Hickory Bend (Part of Nashville)	37214		
		Hickory Flat	38321		
		Hickory Flats	38310		

520 TENNESSEE Holiday Hills-Kyles Ford

Name	ZIP
Holiday Hills (Roane County)	37763
Holiday Shores	37028
Holladay (Benton County)	38341
Holladay (Putnam County)	38501
Holland Mill	37616
Hollow Rock	38342
Hollow Springs	37026
Holly Grove (Haywood County)	38006
Holly Grove (Marshall County)	37091
Holly Grove (Tipton County)	38011
Holly Leaf	38258
Holly Springs	38570
Hollywood (Maury County)	38451
Hollywood (Shelby County)	38108
Hollywood Hills	37066
Holston Army Ammunition Plant	37662
Holston Heights (Part of Kingsport)	37660
Holston Hills (Knox County)	37914
Holston Hills (Sullivan County)	37620
Holston Institute	37617
Holston Valley	37620
Holts Corner	37034
Holttown	37821
Holy Hill	37683
Homestead	38555
Honeycutt	37857
Hood Lake (Part of Lawrenceburg)	38464
Hoodoo	37018
Hookers Bend	38361
Hoop	37879
Hoovers Gap	37037
Hopewell (Bradley County)	37311
Hopewell (Carroll County)	38348
Hopewell (Claiborne County)	37879
Hopewell (Davidson County)	37138
Hopewell (Gibson County)	38389
Hopewell (Tipton County)	38011
Hopewell Springs	37354
Hopper Bluff	37861
Hopson	37687
Hornbeak	38232
Horner	37096
Hornertown	37147
Hornsby	38044
Horn Springs	37087
Horse Creek (Greene County)	37641
Horse Creek (Sullivan County)	37660
Horse Shoe	37643
Horseshoe Bend	38560
Horsleys	37074
Housley Addition (Part of Athens)	37303
Houston	38471
Houston Valley	37743
Howard (Monroe County)	37885
Howard (Sevier County)	37865
Howard Chapel	38570
Howard Hill (Part of Kingsport)	37660
Howard Quarter	37879
Howard Springs	38583
Howell (Lincoln County)	37334
Howell (White County)	38583
Howell Hill	37334
Howley	38321
Hubbard	37801
Hubertville	37172
Hudson	38464
Hugarth	38556
Hughes Loop	38358
Hughett	37852
Hughey	37334
Hulan Hollow (Part of Erwin)	37650
Humboldt	38343
Humphrey	37865
Hunter	37643
Hunter Hills	37379
Hunters Point	37087
Hunters Ridge	37064
Huntersville	38301
Hunting Creek Farms	37064
Huntingdon	38344
Huntland	37345
Huntsville (Loudon County)	37771
Huntsville (Scott County)	37756
Hurdlow (Part of Lynchburg)	37306
Hurley	38357
Hurley Acres	37814
Huron	38345
Hurricane (Houston County)	37175
Hurricane (Jackson County)	38562

Name	ZIP
Hurricane (Wilson County)	37087
Hurricane Hill	38063
Hurricane Mills	37078
Hustburg	37134
Hutsell (Part of Athens)	37303
Hygeia Springs	37073
Hyndsver	37073
Hyndsver	38237
Iconium	37190
Idaho	38468
Idaville	38004
Ideal Valley	37381
Idlewild (Gibson County)	38346
Idlewild (McMinn County)	37303
Idlewood (Part of Franklin)	37064
Ilemar	37122
Imperial Estates	37921
Independence (Hancock County)	37731
Independence (Overton County)	38573
Independence Estates	37087
India	38242
Indian Bluff	37710
Indian Cave	37709
Indian Creek	37757
Indian Hills	37087
Indian Mound (De Kalb County)	38583
Indian Mound (Stewart County)	37079
Indian Ridge (Grainger County)	37709
Indian Ridge (Washington County)	37601
Indian Springs	37617
Ingleside Hill (Part of Athens)	37303
Inglewood (Part of Nashville)	37216
Inskip (Part of Knoxville)	37912
Interstate Park	37032
Irish Cut	37821
Iron City	38463
Ironsburg	37385
Irving College	37110
Irwinton Shores	37880
Isabella	37346
Isham	37892
Island Home (Part of Knoxville)	37920
Island Park	37618
Isoline	38555
Isom	38461
Ivy	37369
Ivy Bluff	37110
Ivydell	37766
Ivy Point (Part of Nashville)	37072
Ivyton	38543
Jacksboro	37757
Jacks Creek	38347
Jackson	38301-08
For specific Jackson Zip Codes call (901) 422-5369	
Jackson Heights (Part of Murfreesboro)	37129
Jackson Ridge	37060
Jacksons Chapel	37036
Jackson Square (Part of Oak Ridge)	37830
Jacobs Hill	37087
Jakestown	37130
Jamestown (Fentress County)	38556
Jamestown (Tipton County)	38015
Jarrell	38201
Jasper	37347
Jaybird (Cocke County)	37821
Jaybird (Hamblen County)	37814
Jeannette	38363
Jearoldstown	37641
Jefferson	37166
Jefferson City	37760
Jefferson Estates	37877
Jefferson Springs	37167
Jellico	37762
Jena	37742
Jenkins Hill (Part of Sevierville)	37862
Jenkinsville	38024
Jere Baxter (Part of Nashville)	37216
Jernigan Town	37188
Jersey (Part of Chattanooga)	37416
Jessie	37110
Jewell	38225
Jewett	37337
Jimtown	37821
Joelton (Part of Nashville)	37080
John Sevier	37914
Johnson Bible College	37920

Name	ZIP
Johnson City	37601-15
For specific Johnson City Zip Codes call (615) 461-8251	
Johnsons	37048
Johnsons Chapel	38583
Johnsons Grove	38006
Johntown	37074
Jones	38006
Jonesborough	37659
Jones Chapel	38549
Jones Cove	37862
Jones Mill	38224
Jones Valley	38482
Jonesville (Fentress County)	38553
Jonesville (Roane County)	37840
Joppa (Grainger County)	37861
Joppa (White County)	38587
Jordonia (Part of Nashville)	37218
Jug Town	37130
Juno	38351
Kagley	37801
Kansas (Jefferson County)	37760
Kansas (Sumner County)	37066
Karns	37921
Kaywood (Part of Tullahoma)	37388
Kedron (Giles County)	38477
Kedron (Maury County)	37174
Keefe	38080
Keeling	38069
Keenburg	37643
Keese (Part of Decherd)	37324
Keith Springs	37398
Kellertown	37183
Kelley Town (Part of Oliver Springs)	37840
Kelso	37348
Keltonburg	37166
Kemmer Hill (Part of Spring City)	37381
Kempville	37030
Kendricks Creek	37663
Kennedy Creek	37016
Kennnytown	37743
Kenton	38233
Kepler	37857
Kerrville	38053
Kettle Mills	38461
Key	38583
Keystone (Part of Johnson City)	37601
Killians Chapel (Part of Altamont)	37301
Kilsyth	37766
Kimball	37347
Kimberlin Heights	37920
Kimberly Acres	37122
Kimbrough Crossroad	37890
Kimery	38230
Kimmins	38462
Kimsey	37391
Kin Cove	37087
Kinderhook	38482
King	37715
Kingfield	37064
Kingsport	37660-65
For specific Kingsport Zip Codes call (615) 245-5111	
King Springs	37601
Kings Ridge (Part of Chattanooga)	37343
Kingston	37763
Kingston Heights	37763
Kingston Hills	37919
Kingston Mill	37160
Kingston Springs	37082
Kingston Woods	37919
Kinzel Springs	37882
Kirk	38017
Kirkland (Lincoln County)	38488
Kirkland (Williamson County)	37046
Kite	37857
Kittrell	37149
Kleburne	37174
Kline	37398
Klondike	37857
Knapp	37769
Knob Creek (Lauderdale County)	38063
Knob Creek (Sevier County)	37865
Knoxville	37901-50
For specific Knoxville Zip Codes call (615) 558-4528	
Knoxville College (Part of Knoxville)	37921
Kodak	37764
Kodak Estates	37764
KoKo	38069
Kontika	37087
Kyles Ford	37765

Laager-McIllwain TENNESSEE 521

Name	ZIP
Laager (Part of Gruetli-Laager)	37339
Laconia	38045
Lacy	38052
Lafayette	37083
La Follette	37766
La Grange	38046
Laguardo	37087
Lake City	37769
Lake Colonial Estates	37014
Lake Crest	37663
Lake Drive	38079
Lake Farm Estates	37167
Lake Forest (Grainger County)	37861
Lake Forest (Hamilton County)	37343
Lake Forest (Knox County)	37920
Lakeharbor	37763
Lake Harbor Estates	37416
Lake Haven	37087
Lake Hills (Part of Tullahoma)	37388
Lakeland	38002
Lakemont	37777
Lakemont Cabin Area	37811
Lakemont Heights (Part of Rockwood)	37854
Lakemoor	37920
Lakemoore (Part of Morristown)	37814
Lake Placid	38340
Lake Road (Part of Fairview)	37062
Lakeshore Estates	37416
Lake Side (Hamilton County)	37343
Lakeside (Monroe County)	37885
Lakeside Estates (Part of Estill Springs)	37330
Lakeside Heights	37890
Lakesite	37379
Lake Tansi Village	38555
Lake Tullahoma Estates (Part of Tullahoma)	37388
Lakeview (Blount County)	37777
Lakeview (Claiborne County)	37825
Lakeview (Hamblen County)	37814
Lakeview (McMinn County)	37303
Lakeview (Roane County)	37763
Lakeview (Robertson County)	37172
Lakeview Commercial Park (Part of Franklin)	37064
Lakeview Estates	37777
Lake View Heights (Part of Harriman)	37748
Lakeview Manor	38256
Lakeview Park (Part of Dandridge)	37725
Lakewood	37138
Lakewood Village	37381
Lamar (Part of Memphis)	38114
Lambert	38068
Lamont	37172
Lamontville	37309
Lancaster	38569
Lancaster Hill	38567
Lancelot Acres	38478
Lancing	37770
Lane	38240
Laneview	38382
Langford Farms	37138
Lanier	37801
Lantana	38555
Lapata	38059
Lascassas	37085
Lassiter Corner	38232
Latham	38225
Laurel (Anderson County)	37716
Laurel (Sevier County)	37862
Laurel Bloomery	37680
Laurel Bluff	37763
Laurel Brook	37321
Laurelburg	38581
Laurel Cove	38585
Laurel Grove	37710
La Vergne	37086
Lavinia	38348
Law	38351
Law Chapel	37801
Lawnville	37763
Lawrenceburg	38464
Lawson Crossroad	37882
Lawton	38375
Leach	38344
Leadvale (Cocke County)	37821
Leadvale (Jefferson County)	37890
Leana	37129
Leapwood	38310

Name	ZIP
Lea Springs	37709
Leatherwood	38485
Lebanon	37087-88
For specific Lebanon Zip Codes call (615) 444-2672	
Ledgemere	37160
Lee	37367
Lee College (Part of Cleveland)	37311
Leeland	37064
Leemans Corner	37087
Leesburg	37659
Lee Valley	37869
Leeville	37087
Leewood (Part of Memphis)	38101
Leftwich	38401
Legate	37079
Leighs Chapel	38019
Leighton	38391
Leinart	37716
Leipers Fork	37064
Lenoir City	37771
Lenow	38018
Lenox	38047
Leoma	38468
Leonard	37620
Leoni	37190
Lewisburg	37091
Lewis Chapel	37327
Lexie	37306
Lexie Crossroads	37306
Lexington	38351
Liberty (Benton County)	38320
Liberty (De Kalb County)	37095
Liberty (Decatur County)	38374
Liberty (Franklin County)	37398
Liberty (Giles County)	38477
Liberty (Jackson County)	38564
Liberty (Johnson County)	37683
Liberty (Lincoln County)	37334
Liberty (Morgan County)	37887
Liberty (Sumner County)	37066
Liberty (Sumner County)	37022
Liberty (Washington County)	37641
Liberty (Weakley County)	38229
Liberty Grove	38469
Liberty Hill (Grainger County)	37888
Liberty Hill (Greene County)	37641
Liberty Hill (McMinn County)	37329
Liberty Hill (Williamson County)	37025
Liberty Hill (Wilson County)	37012
Lick Creek (Benton County)	38221
Lick Creek (Decatur County)	38363
Lickskillet	37807
Lickton (Part of Nashville)	37189
Lightfoot	38063
Lillamay	37015
Lillydale	37650
Lily Grove	37825
Limbs	38255
Limestone	37681
Limestone Cove	37692
Linary	38555
Lincoln	37334
Lincoln Park (Part of Knoxville)	37917
Lincoya Hills (Part of Nashville)	37214
Linden	37096
Lindsay Mill	37769
Link	37037
Linsdale	37325
Linton (Part of Nashville)	37216
Linwood	37087
Lisbon	38052
Little Barren (Claiborne County)	37825
Little Barren (Union County)	37825
Littlebrook (Part of Rockford)	37853
Littlecrab	38556
Little Creek	37752
Little Doe	37640
Little Emory	37748
Little Hope (Rutherford County)	37129
Little Hope (Wayne County)	38485
Littlelot	38454
Little Milligan	37640
Little River	37804
Little White Oak	37766
Litton	37367
Litz Manor (Part of Kingsport)	37660
Liverwort	37040
Livingston	38570
Lobelville	37097

Name	ZIP
Locke	38053
Lockertsville	37015
Lockmiller Addition (Part of Athens)	37303
Locust Grove	38059
Locust Mount	37659
Locust Springs	37616
Lodge	37380
Lodi	38486
Logans Lake	38334
Lois (Part of Lynchburg)	37359
Lomax Crossroads	38462
Lone Mountain (Claiborne County)	37773
Lone Mountain (Scott County)	37852
Lone Oak	37377
Lone Oaks (Part of Atoka)	38004
Lone Star	37660
Long Branch (Hamilton County)	37343
Long Branch (Lawrence County)	38464
Long Creek	37843
Long Hollow (Part of La Follette)	37766
Long Island	37660
Long Rock	38344
Longs Mills	37303
Longtown	38049
Longview	37020
Longwood	37064
Lonsdale (Part of Knoxville)	37921
Lookout Mountain	37350
Lookout Valley (Part of Chattanooga)	37419
Loon Bay	37028
Loonewood	38585
Loretto	38469
Lorraine	37381
Lost Creek	38583
Lost Mountain	37743
Loudon	37774
Louise	37051
Louisville	37777
Love Joy	38574
Lovelace	37641
Love Lady	38549
Loveland (Part of Knoxville)	37924
Lovell Heights	37922
Love Station	37650
Lovetown	38474
Lower Mill	37343
Lower Mockeson	38468
Lowland	37778
Lowryville	38372
Luckett	38063
Lucky	37110
Lucy	38053
Luna	37019
Lunns Store	37034
Lupton City (Part of Chattanooga)	37351
Luray	38352
Lusk	37327
Luskville	37309
Luther	37869
Luttrell (Loudon County)	37846
Luttrell (Union County)	37779
Lutts	38471
Lyles	37098
Lynchburg	37352
Lynn Garden (Sullivan County)	37665
Lynnville	38472
Lyons View (Part of Knoxville)	37919
McAllister Hill	37346
McAllisters Crossroads	37171
McAnna	38260
McBurg	38459
McCains	38401
McClamerys Stand (Part of Collinwood)	38450
McCloud	37857
McClures Bend	37030
McCoinsville	38562
McConnell	38237
McCullough	38024
McDonald	37353
McDonald Hill	37857
Macedonia (Carroll County)	38201
Macedonia (McMinn County)	37329
Macedonia (Obion County)	38233
Macedonia (White County)	38583
McElroy	38559
Mace's Hill	37057
McEwen	37101
McGeetown	37317
McIllwain	38341

522 TENNESSEE McKenzie-Montgomery Junction

	ZIP
McKenzie	38201
McKinley	37601
McKinnon	37175
McKnight	38482
McLemoresville	38235
McLin's Corner	38034
McMahan (Sevier County)	37862
McMillan	37914
McMinnville	37110
McNairy	38315
Macon	38048
McPheeter Bend	37642
Maddox	38372
Madge	38002
Madie	38080
Madison (Part of Nashville)	37115
Madison College (Part of Nashville)	37115
Madison Hall	38301
Madison Square (Part of Nashville)	37115
Madisonville	37354
Maggart	38560
Magnolia	37175
Magnolia Place (Part of Franklin)	37064
Major	37087
Malesus (Part of Jackson)	38301
Mall (Part of Cookeville)	38501
Mall, The (Part of Johnson City)	37601
Mall of Memphis, The (Part of Memphis)	38118
Mallory (Part of Memphis)	38109
Mallorys (Part of Franklin)	37064
Maloney Heights	37920
Maloneyville	37918
Manchester	37355
Mankinville	37130
Manlyville	38256
Mansfield	38236
Mansfield Gap	37877
Mansford	37398
Manson	38556
Maple Grove (Clay County)	38541
Maple Grove (Macon County)	37083
Maple Grove (Meigs County)	37880
Maple Hill	37620
Maplehurst	37618
Maplewood (Part of Nashville)	37216
Marble City (Part of Knoxville)	37919
Marbledale	37914
Marble Hall	37857
Marble Hill (Blount County)	37737
Marble Hill (Moore County)	37398
Marble Plains	37398
Marbleton	37692
Marguerite	37814
Marion (Claiborne County)	37715
Marion (Montgomery County)	37051
Market Square Mall (Part of Knoxville)	37902
Markham	38079
Marlborough	38317
Marlow	37716
Marlyn Hills (Part of Bristol)	37620
Marrowbone	37015
Mars Hill	38464
Martel Estates	37771
Martha	37087
Martha Washington	38553
Martin	38237
Martin Creek	38544
Martin Springs	37380
Marvin	37818
Marys Grove	38488
Maryville	37801-04
For specific Maryville Zip Codes call (615) 983-7801	
Mascot	37806
Mason	38049
Mason Grove	38343
Masonhall	38233
Masseyville	38315
Maupin Row	37601
Maury City	38050
Maxey	38059
Maxwell	37306
Maxwell Chapel	38568
May Acres	37877
Mayhome	37184
Mayland	38555
Maynardville	37807
Mayview Heights	37849
Meacham	38024

	ZIP
Meades Quarry (Part of Knoxville)	37920
Meadorville	37083
Meadow	37742
Meadowbrook (Blount County)	37804
Meadowbrook (Greene County)	37616
Meadow Brook (Warren County)	37110
Meadow Green Acres	37064
Meadow Mead (Part of Paris)	38242
Meadow View (Hamilton County)	37336
Meadowview (Lawrence County)	38464
Meadowview Gardens (Part of Harriman)	37748
Meadowwood Acres (Part of Fairview)	37062
Mechanicsville	37190
Medford	37769
Medina	38355
Medon	38356
Melrose (Blount County)	37886
Melrose (Davidson County)	37204
Melville Hill (Part of Soddy-Daisy)	37379
Melvine	37367
Melwood	38315
Memorial	37150
Memphis	38101-87
For specific Memphis Zip Codes call (901) 775-3872	
COLLEGES & UNIVERSITIES	
Christian Brothers College	38104
Memphis State University	38152
Rhodes College	38112
University of Tennessee Center for the Health Sciences	38163
FINANCIAL INSTITUTIONS	
Bank of Bartlett	38134
Boatmen's Bank of Tennessee	38103
The Community Bank of Germantown	38119
First American National Bank	38103
First Tennessee Bank National Association	38103
Germantown Trust Savings Bank	38138
Leader Federal Savings & Loan Association	38104
National Bank of Commerce	38150
Sovran Bank/Memphis	38112
Union Planters National Bank	38103
United American Bank of Memphis	38117
HOSPITALS	
Baptist Memorial Hospital	38146
Methodist Hospital-Central Unit	38104
Regional Medical Center at Memphis	38103
St. Francis Hospital	38119
St. Joseph Hospital	38101
Veterans Administration Medical Center	38104
HOTELS/MOTELS	
Holiday Inn Medical Center	38104
Holiday Inn Memphis Airport	38116
Holiday Inn Overton Square	38104
Ramada Hotel	38115
Ramada Hotel Convention Center	38103
MILITARY INSTALLATIONS	
Defense Depot, Memphis	38114
Tennessee Air National Guard, FB6422	38181
United States Army Engineer District, Memphis	38103
Memphis State University (Part of Memphis)	38111
Mengelwood	38047
Mentor	37777
Mercer	38392
Meredith Cave	37766
Merry Oaks (Part of Nashville)	37214

	ZIP
Michie	38357
Middlebrook Heights (Part of Knoxville)	37919
Middleburg (Hardeman County)	38008
Middleburg (Henderson County)	38374
Middle City	38024
Middle Creek	37862
Middle Fork	38352
Middle Settlement	37777
Middleton	38052
Middle Valley (Hamilton County)	37343
Middle Valley Estates	37343
Midfields	37665
Midland	37020
Midland Shopping Center (Part of Alcoa)	37701
Midtown	37748
Midtown Heights	37748
Midway (Cannon County)	37026
Midway (Cocke County)	37727
Midway (Cumberland County)	38555
Midway (De Kalb County)	37166
Midway (Dyer County)	38030
Midway (Franklin County)	37375
Midway (Greene County)	37818
Midway (Johnson County)	37640
Midway (Knox County)	37871
Midway (Obion County)	38261
Midway (Roane County)	37763
Midway (Warren County)	37110
Midway (Washington County)	37601
Mifflin	38352
Milan	38358
Milan Army Ammunition Plant	38358
Milburnton	37681
Miles Crossroads	37150
Mile Straight (Part of Soddy-Daisy)	37379
Milky Way	38478
Mill Brook	37681
Mill Creek (Anderson County)	37705
Mill Creek (Hickman County)	37098
Mill Creek (Morgan County)	37872
Mill Creek (Putnam County)	38501
Milldale	37172
Milledgeville	38359
Miller's Store	38225
Millersville	37072
Millertown	37914
Millican	37862
Milligan College	37682
Millington	38053
Millsfield	38024
Mill Spring	37820
Milltown (Humphreys County)	37101
Milltown (Jackson County)	38588
Milltown (Macon County)	37150
Milltown (Marshall County)	37091
Millview	37064
Milo	37381
Milton	37118
Mimms (Part of Nashville)	37211
Mimosa	37334
Mimosa Estates	37777
Mimosa Heights	37777
Mineral Park	37353
Mineral Springs	38574
Mink	38485
Minnick	38240
Minor Hill	38473
Mint	37801
Miser Station	37777
Miston	38056
Mitchell	37148
Mitchellville	37119
Mixie	38342
Moccasin	38485
Mohawk	37810
Mohawk Crossroad	37711
Molino	37334
Mon	37087
Mona	37129
Monoville	37121
Monroe	38573
Monsanto	38402
Montague (Davidson County)	37216
Montague (Rhea County)	37321
Monteagle	37356
Monterey	38574
Montezuma	38340
Montgomery Junction	37756

Monticello-Newton **TENNESSEE** **523**

Name	ZIP
Monticello (Williamson County)	37064
Monticello (Wilson County)	37122
Montpier Farms	37064
Montvale	37801
Moodyville	38549
Mooneyham	38585
Moons	38256
Moon Shadows	37341
Mooreland Heights (Part of Knoxville)	37920
Mooresburg	37811
Mooresburg Springs	37811
Moores Chapel	38358
Moores College	38581
Mooresville	37091
Mooretown	37190
Mooring	38080
Morgan Springs	37321
Morganton	37742
Morgantown	37321
Morganville	37397
Morley (Part of Nashville)	37766
Morny (Part of Nashville)	37080
Morris Chapel (Benton County)	38320
Morris Chapel (Hardin County)	38361
Morrison	37357
Morrison City	37660
Morrison Creek	38562
Morristown	37813-16

For specific Morristown Zip Codes call (615) 586-1291

Name	ZIP
Moscow	38057
Mosheim	37818
Moss	38575
Mossy Grove	37748
Mountain City	37683
Mountain Dale	37650
Mountain Home (Part of Johnson City)	37684
Mountain View (Part of Dayton)	37321
Mountain View Acres (Part of Winchester)	37398
Mount Airy	37327
Mount Ararat	37095
Mount Carmel (Decatur County)	38329
Mount Carmel (Greene County)	37711
Mount Carmel (Hawkins County)	37642
Mount Carmel (Tipton County)	38019
Mount Carmel (Washington County)	37641
Mount Crest	37367
Mount Cumberland	37329
Mount Denson	37172
Mount Gilead (Henderson County)	38321
Mount Gilead (White County)	38583
Mount Harmony (McMinn County)	37826
Mount Harmony (Monroe County)	37385
Mount Helen	38504
Mount Herman (Bedford County)	37160
Mount Herman (Weakley County)	38230
Mount Hope	38485
Mount Horeb	37760
Mount Joy	38474
Mount Juliet	37122
Mount Lebanon	38464
Mount Leo	37110
Mount Moriah	38320
Mount Nebo	38463
Mount Olive (Grundy County)	37110
Mount Olive (Knox County)	37920
Mount Olive (Marion County)	37397
Mount Olive (Rutherford County)	37130
Mount Pelia	38237
Mount Pisgah	38587
Mount Pleasant (Greene County)	37743
Mount Pleasant (Henry County)	38222
Mount Pleasant (Maury County)	38474
Mount Pleasant (Putnam County)	38501
Mount Pleasant (Scott County)	37852

Name	ZIP
Mount Tabor	37804
Mount Tucker Addition	37617
Mount Union (Jackson County)	38564
Mount Union (Pickett County)	38549
Mount Vernon (Monroe County)	37358
Mount Vernon (Rutherford County)	37153
Mount Vernon (Sumner County)	37022
Mount View (Davidson County)	37211
Mount View (Grundy County)	37356
Mount View (Scott County)	37852
Mount Vinson	38379
Mount Zion (Cheatham County)	37015
Mount Zion (Monroe County)	37885
Mount Zion (Montgomery County)	37051
Mount Zion (Obion County)	38232
Mount Zion (Warren County)	37110
Mourberry	38583
Mowbray	37379
Mud Creek (McNairy County)	38310
Mud Creek (Warren County)	38581
Muddy Pond	38574
Mudsink	37064
Mulberry	37359
Mulberry Gap	37869
Mulberry Hill	37058
Mulloy	37048
Munford	38058
Murfreesboro	37129-33

For specific Murfreesboro Zip Codes call (615) 893-2201

Name	ZIP
Murray-Lake Hills (Part of Chattanooga)	37416
Murray Store	37826
Myers (Part of Winchester)	37398
Nameless	38545
Nance	38001
Nance Ferry	37709
Nances Grove	37820
Nankipoo	38040
Napier	38462
Narrow Valley	37861
Nash	38544
Nashville	37201-37

For specific Nashville Zip Codes call (615) 885-1005

COLLEGES & UNIVERSITIES

Name	ZIP
Belmont College	37212
David Lipscomb College	37204
Tennessee State University	37203
Vanderbilt University	37212

FINANCIAL INSTITUTIONS

Name	ZIP
Dominion Bank of Middle Tennessee	37201
Fidelity Federal Savings & Loan Association of Tennessee	37219
First American National Bank of Nashville	37237
Metropolitan Federal Savings & Loan Association	37219
Security Federal Savings & Loan Association	37204
Sovran Bank/Central South	37219
Third National Bank in Nashville	37219

HOSPITALS

Name	ZIP
Baptist Hospital	37236
Park View Medical Center	37202
Nashville Metropolitan Bordeaux Hospital	37218
St. Thomas Hospital	37205
Vanderbilt University Hospital and Clinic	37232
Veterans Administration Medical Center	37203

HOTELS/MOTELS

Name	ZIP
Doubletree Hotel	37219
Holiday Inn-Briley Parkway	37210
Hyatt Regency Nashville	37219
Maxwell House, A Clarion Hotel	37228
Nashville Marriott	37210
Sheraton Music City	37214

Name	ZIP
Vanderbilt Plaza Hotel	37203

MILITARY INSTALLATIONS

Name	ZIP
Tennessee Air National Guard, FB6421	37217
United States Army Engineer District, Nashville	37202
United States Property and Fiscal Office for Tennessee	37204
Natco (Part of Columbia)	38401
National Cemetery (Part of Memphis)	38122
Natural Bridge	37843
Nauvoo	38024
Neapolis	38401
Neboville	38059
Needmore (Hamblen County)	37891
Needmore (Marshall County)	37091
Needmore (Maury County)	38474
Needmore (Montgomery County)	37079
Needmore (Wilson County)	37138
Neely	38391
Neely Crossroads	38551
Nelsontown (Part of Kingsport)	37660
Nemo	37887
Nenny	37891
Neptune	37015
Netherland	38501
Neubert	37920
Neva	37683
Newbern	38059
New Bethel	37331
New Canton	37642
New Castle	38075
Newcomb	37762
New Corinth	37861
New Deal	37048
New Dellrose	38453
New Due West (Part of Nashville)	37115
Newell Station	37865
New Era	38555
New Harmony (Bledsoe County)	37367
New Harmony (Macon County)	37074
New Haven (Lawrence County)	38464
New Haven (Scott County)	37841
New Herman	37160
New Hope (Cheatham County)	37080
New Hope (Hancock County)	37869
New Hope (Hardin County)	38310
New Hope (Hawkins County)	37857
New Hope (Houston County)	37175
New Hope (Humphreys County)	37101
New Hope (Jackson County)	38568
New Hope (Lincoln County)	37334
New Hope (Marion County)	37380
New Hope (McNairy County)	38339
New Hope (Roane County)	37854
New Hope (Williamson County)	37062
New Hope (Wilson County)	37087
New Johnsonville	37134
New Line	37814
New Loyston	37705
Newmansville	37616
New Market	37820
New Markham	38079
New Middleton	38563
New Midway	37763
Newport	37821
New Prospect	38464
New Providence (Loudon County)	37771
New Providence (Montgomery County)	37042
New River	37755
New Salem (Hamilton County)	37379
New Salem (Jackson County)	38562
New Salem (Scott County)	37841
New Tazewell	37825
Newton	38555

524 TENNESSEE New Town-Pigeon Roost

Name	ZIP
New Town (Marshall County)	37047
New Town (Maury County)	37174
Newtown (Polk County)	37317
New Union	37355
New Victory	37659
New Zion (Carroll County)	38344
New Zion (Macon County)	37186
Nickletown	37347
Nicks Creek	37756
Nine Mile	37367
Ninth Model	37382
Niota	37826
Nixon	38372
Noah	37355
Nolensville	37135
Nonaburg	37329
Nonaville	37122
Nonconnah (Part of Memphis)	38116
Norene	37136
Norma	37756
Normandy	37360
Norris	37828
North (Davidson County)	37208
North (Shelby County)	38107
North Chattanooga (Part of Chattanooga)	37405
Northcott	37660
Northcutts Cove (Grundy County)	37110
Northcutt's Cove (Warren County)	37110
Northeast (Part of Nashville)	37207
Northern Hills (Part of Chattanooga)	37343
Northgate Shopping Center (Part of Memphis)	38107
North Glen Estates (Part of Chattanooga)	37343
North Hills (Part of Knoxville)	37917
North Johnson City (Part of Johnson City)	37601
North Knoxville (Part of Knoxville)	37917
Northpoint	37874
North Riverside	38462
Northside (Part of Jackson)	38301
North Springs	38588
Norwood (Anderson County)	37840
Norwood (Knox County)	37912
Notchy Creek	37354
Nough	37727
Nubia	37186
Nucarbon	38468
Number One (Part of Gallatin)	37066
Nunnelly	37137
Nutbush	38012
Oak City	37865
Oakdale (Hawkins County)	37873
Oakdale (Macon County)	37186
Oakdale (Morgan County)	37829
Oak Dale (Overton County)	38573
Oakdale (White County)	38583
Oakfield	38362
Oak Grove (Campbell County)	37779
Oak Grove (Carter County)	37643
Oak Grove (Claiborne County)	37752
Oak Grove (Clay County)	38575
Oak Grove (Dickson County)	37055
Oak Grove (Franklin County)	37324
Oak Grove (Giles County)	38460
Oak Grove (Hardin County)	38372
Oak Grove (Henry County)	38222
Oak Grove (Jefferson County)	37725
Oak Grove (Lewis County)	38462
Oak Grove (Madison County)	38301
Oak Grove (Marion County)	37397
Oak Grove (Monroe County)	37354
Oak Grove (Overton County)	38570
Oak Grove (Overton County)	38568
Oakgrove (Pickett County)	38573
Oak Grove (Polk County)	37307
Oak Grove (Sumner County)	37022
Oak Grove (Tipton County)	38019
Oak Grove (Union County)	37866
Oak Grove (Warren County)	37357

Name	ZIP
Oak Grove (Washington County)	37615
Oak Grove (Weakley County)	38237
Oak Grove Heights	37921
Oakhaven (Part of Memphis)	38116
Oak Hill (Carter County)	37658
Oak Hill (Cocke County)	37843
Oak Hill (Cumberland County)	38555
Oak Hill (Davidson County)	37220
Oak Hill (Overton County)	38580
Oak Hill (Pickett County)	38549
Oak Hill (Sullivan County)	37620
Oak Hill (Washington County)	37659
Oakhurst (Part of Maryville)	37801
Oakland (Fayette County)	38060
Oakland (Grainger County)	37861
Oakland (Henry County)	38242
Oakland (Jefferson County)	37760
Oakland (Knox County)	37918
Oakland (Robertson County)	37172
Oakland (Warren County)	37110
Oakland (Washington County)	37690
Oaklawn	37166
Oakleigh Estates	37620
Oakley	38541
Oaklyn	38555
Oak Park (Part of Tullahoma)	37388
Oakplain	37015
Oak Plains	37040
Oak Ridge	37830
Oak Tree	37062
Oak View	37886
Oakville (Part of Memphis)	38118
Oakwood (Knox County)	37917
Oakwood (Montgomery County)	37191
Oakwood Estates	37064
Obion	38240
Ocana	37075
Ocoee	37361
O'Connors	38583
Odd Fellows Hall	38478
Odens Bend	37066
Officers Chapel	38501
Offutt	37716
Ogden	37321
Okalona	38570
Okolona (Carter County)	37601
Okolona (Hawkins County)	37642
Old Antioch	38562
Old Chihowee	37865
Olde Mill	37343
Oldfort	37362
Old Glory	37804
Old Hickory (Part of Nashville)	37138
Old Hickory Mall (Part of Jackson)	38301
Old Kingsport (Part of Kingsport)	37660
Old Laguardo	37122
Old Lawton	38375
Old Salem	37345
Old Springville	38256
Old Sweetwater	37874
Old Washington	37321
Old Winesap	38555
Old Zion	38583
Olivehill	38475
Oliver Springs	37840
Olivet	38372
One Hundred Oaks Regional Mall (Part of Nashville)	37204
Oneida	37841
Only	37140
Ooltewah	37363
Opossum	38063
Opossum Creek Pines	37379
Oral	37771
Orchard View	37840
Orebank	37664
Ore Spring	38225
Orlinda	37141
Orme	37380
Orysa	38063
Osage	38242
Osemont Chapel	37190
Ostella	37091
Oswego	37762
Otes	37857
Otter Creek	38555
Ottway	37743
Overall	37130

Name	ZIP
Overlook	37804
Ovilla	38464
Ovoca	37388
Owens	37172
Owl City	38079
Owlhollow	37398
Owl Hoot	38080
Ozone	37842
Pactolus	37663
Pailo	37327
Paint Rock (Loudon County)	37846
Paint Rock (Roane County)	37846
Palestine (Henderson County)	38351
Palestine (Robertson County)	37172
Pall Mall	38577
Palmer	37365
Palmersville	38241
Palmyra	37142
Pandora	37640
Paperville (Part of Bristol)	37620
Paradise Acres	37122
Paragon Mills (Part of Nashville)	37211
Paris	38242
Parkburg	38366
Park City (Knox County)	37914
Park City (Lincoln County)	37334
Parker	38577
Parker's Cross Roads	38388
Parkey	37869
Park Grove	38464
Park Settlement	37862
Park Shore	37343
Parkshore Estates	37343
Parksville	37307
Parkview	37854
Parkway Village (Part of Memphis)	38118
Parrottsville	37843
Parsons	38363
Paschall	37064
Pasquo (Part of Nashville)	37221
Pate Hill	37818
Patterson	37153
Patterson Crossroads	37752
Patty	37325
Paulette	37807
Paw Paw Ridge	38030
Payne Cove	37366
Paynes Store	37022
Peabody	37766
Peak	37716
Peakland	37322
Peanut	37843
Pea Ridge (De Kalb County)	37095
Pea Ridge (Lawrence County)	38464
Pearl City	37334
Peavine	38555
Pebble Hill	38357
Peckerwood Point	38004
Peeled Chestnut	38583
Pegram	37143
Pelham	37366
Penile Hill	37324
Pennine	37381
Pennington Bend (Part of Nashville)	37214
Pennington Chapel	37888
Peppertown	38469
Perrin Hollow	37709
Perry	38301
Perryville	38363
Persia	37857
Petersburg (Hawkins County)	37857
Petersburg (Lincoln County)	37144
Peters Landing	38425
Petros	37845
Petway	37015
Peytonsville	37064
Philadelphia (Jackson County)	38545
Philadelphia (Loudon County)	37846
Philadelphia (Washington County)	37641
Philippi	37166
Phillippy	38079
Pickwatina Place (Part of Athens)	37303
Pickwick Dam	38365
Piedmont	37725
Pierce	38257
Pigeon Forge	37863
Pigeon River Estates (Part of Sevierville)	37862
Pigeon Roost	37185

Pikeville-Richland TENNESSEE 525

Name	ZIP
Pikeville	37367
Pillowville	38201
Pilot Knob (Greene County)	37711
Pilot Knob (Sumner County)	37066
Pilot Mountain	37770
Pine Bluff	37398
Pinebrook Estates	37341
Pinecrest (Campbell County)	37757
Pine Crest (Carter County)	37601
Pine Grove (Greene County)	37743
Pine Grove (Loudon County)	37774
Pine Grove (Sevier County)	37862
Pine Grove (Van Buren County)	38585
Pine Haven (Fentress County)	38556
Pinehaven (Shelby County)	38053
Pine Hill (Bradley County)	37353
Pine Hill (Clay County)	38575
Pine Hill (Marion County)	37397
Pine Hill (Scott County)	37841
Pineland	37322
Pine Orchard	37829
Pine Point	38256
Pine Ridge (Jefferson County)	37890
Pine Ridge (Polk County)	37333
Pine Top	37771
Pine Tree Estates	37343
Pine View	37096
Pineville (Part of Morristown)	37814
Pinewood	37137
Piney (Loudon County)	37774
Piney (Morgan County)	37892
Piney (Van Buren County)	38585
Piney Flats	37686
Piney Grove (McMinn County)	37303
Piney Grove (Scott County)	37892
Piney Grove (Washington County)	37601
Piney Shores Estates	37381
Pinhook (Putnam County)	38574
Pin Hook (Union County)	37807
Pinnacle (Part of Pittman Center)	37862
Pinson	38366
Pioneer	37847
Pipers	37148
Piperton	38017
Pisgah (De Kalb County)	37166
Pisgah (Giles County)	38478
Pisgah (Shelby County)	38018
Pittman Center	37738
Plainfield (Part of Maryville)	37801
Plain Grove	38573
Plainview (Rutherford County)	37037
Plainview (Union County)	37779
Plant	37134
Plantation Hills (Part of Knoxville)	37917
Plateau	38555
Pleasant Green	37726
Pleasant Grove (Bedford County)	37160
Pleasant Grove (Cocke County)	37821
Pleasant Grove (Lincoln County)	37334
Pleasant Grove (Marion County)	37347
Pleasant Grove (Scott County)	37892
Pleasant Grove (Sumner County)	37186
Pleasant Hill (Claiborne County)	37870
Pleasant Hill (Clay County)	38541
Pleasant Hill (Cumberland County)	38578
Pleasant Hill (Greene County)	37641
Pleasant Hill (Hawkins County)	37711
Pleasant Hill (Lauderdale County)	38041
Pleasant Hill (Meigs County)	37880
Pleasant Hill (Moore County)	37352
Pleasant Hill (Obion County)	38253
Pleasant Hill (Polk County)	37317
Pleasant Hill (Rutherford County)	37060
Pleasant Hill (Sevier County)	37862
Pleasant Hill (Weakley County)	38237
Pleasant Point (Claiborne County)	37825

Name	ZIP
Pleasant Point (Lawrence County)	38469
Pleasant Ridge (Cannon County)	37190
Pleasant Ridge (Knox County)	37921
Pleasant Shade	37145
Pleasant Valley (Macon County)	37074
Pleasant Valley (Sumner County)	37048
Pleasant Valley (Washington County)	37659
Pleasant View (Cannon County)	37190
Pleasant View (Cheatham County)	37146
Pleasant View (Claiborne County)	37879
Pleasant View (Fentress County)	38556
Pleasantville	37147
Plunkets Creek	38563
Pocahontas (Coffee County)	37357
Pocahontas (Hardeman County)	38061
Poga	37640
Point Pleasant	37821
Polk	38253
Pollard	37061
Pomona (Cumberland County)	38555
Pomona (Dickson County)	37055
Pomona Road	38555
Pond	37055
Ponderosa	37763
Ponderosa Hills	37849
Ponders Gap	37880
Pond Grove	37854
Pond Hill	37303
Pondville	37022
Pope	37096
Poplar	37716
Poplar Corner	38006
Poplar Grove (Claiborne County)	37752
Poplar Grove (Humphreys County)	37101
Poplar Grove (Lauderdale County)	38040
Poplar Grove (Putnam County)	38501
Poplar Hill (Giles County)	38477
Poplar Hill (McMinn County)	37303
Poplar Plaza Shopping Center (Part of Memphis)	38111
Poplar Springs (Henderson County)	38351
Poplar Springs (Loudon County)	37774
Poplar Springs (Overton County)	38501
Poplar Springs (Roane County)	37763
Poplins Crossroads	37180
Porter Court (Part of Paris)	38242
Porterfield	37118
Porter Gap	38040
Porters Chapel	38474
Portland	37148
Port Royal	37010
Port Serena	37343
Postelle	37317
Post Oak (Putnam County)	38501
Post Oak (Roane County)	37854
Poteet	38543
Pottsville	38401
Powder Springs	37748
Powell	37849
Powell Chapel	38478
Powells Chapel	38044
Powells Crossroads	37397
Powell Valley	37766
Prairie Creek	37379
Prairie Peninsula	37343
Prairie Plains	37342
Prater	37190
Preston Woods (Part of Kingsport)	37660
Price (Lauderdale County)	38041
Price (White County)	38583
Pride	38261
Primm Springs	38476
Princeton (Part of Johnson City)	37601
Proctor City	38079
Prospect (Blount County)	37886
Prospect (Bradley County)	37311
Prospect (Giles County)	38477
Prospect (Lincoln County)	37334
Prospect (Loudon County)	37774

Name	ZIP
Prospect (McMinn County)	37329
Prosperity (Macon County)	37150
Prosperity (Wilson County)	37016
Protemus	38260
Providence (Davidson County)	37211
Providence (Grundy County)	37324
Providence (Madison County)	38301
Providence (Sumner County)	37186
Providence (Trousdale County)	37074
Pruden	37851
Pryor Ridge	37387
Puckett	37153
Pulaski	38478
Pumpkintown	37083
Punch	37030
Puncheon Camp	37888
Punkton	37727
Purdy	38375
Puryear	38251
Push	38232
Pyburns	38372
Quail Meador	37087
Quebeck	38579
Quercus	38483
Quincy	38001
Quito	38053
Raccoon Valley	37807
Rader	37743
Rafter	37385
Ragsdale	37355
Raines (Part of Memphis)	38116
Raleigh (Part of Memphis)	38128
Raleigh Springs Mall (Part of Memphis)	38128
Rally Hill	38401
Ralston	38237
Ramah	38468
Ramer	38367
Ramsey (Knox County)	37914
Ramsey (Wilson County)	37087
Randolph	38023
Range	37694
Rankin	37821
Rankin Cove	37347
Rascal Town	38469
Rathburn (Part of Soddy-Daisy)	37379
Raus	37388
Raven Branch	37753
Raven Hill	37879
Ravenscroft	38583
Rayon City (Part of Nashville)	37138
Rays Chapel	37034
Raysville (Part of Lynchburg)	37388
Readyville	37149
Reagan	38368
Rebel Acres (Part of Pulaski)	38478
Rebel Meadows (Part of Franklin)	37064
Red Ash	37714
Red Bank	37415
Red Boiling Springs	37150
Red Hill (Bradley County)	37311
Red Hill (Claiborne County)	37752
Red Hill (Coffee County)	37355
Red Hill (Fentress County)	38556
Red Hill (Lawrence County)	38464
Red Hill (Marion County)	37397
Red Hill (Pickett County)	38549
Red Hill (Weakley County)	38225
Red House	37709
Red Row	38474
Redwing Farms	37064
Reeds Lake	38004
Reed Spring	37846
Reeds Store	37046
Reedtown	37821
Reel Cove	37397
Reesetown	37391
Rehoboth	38024
Reliance	37369
Reubensville	37148
Reverie	72395
Revilo	38468
Rheatown	37641
Rialto	38019
Rice Bend	37657
Riceville	37370
Rich	38472
Rich Acres (Part of Johnson City)	37601
Richard City	37380
Richardson	38023
Richland (Davidson County)	37209

526 TENNESSEE Richland-Sharon

Name	ZIP
Richland (Grainger County)	37709
Richmond	37144
Richview Acres	37865
Richwood	38024
Rickman	38580
Riddleton	37151
Ridenour	37705
Ridge	37879
Ridgedale (Knox County)	37931
Ridgedale (Sullivan County)	37620
Ridgefield (Part of Kingsport)	37660
Ridge Lake North (Part of Chattanooga)	37343
Ridgely	38080
Ridgeside	37411
Ridgetop (Lewis County)	38461
Ridgetop (Robertson County)	37152
Ridgeview	37814
Ridgeville (Part of Lynchburg)	37352
Ridgewood	37714
Ridley	38401
Riggs	37046
Riggs Crossroads	37046
Right	38361
Rim Rock Mesa	38583
Rinda	38230
Rinnie	38555
Riovista (Part of Elizabethton)	37643
Ripley	38063
Ritchie	37879
Ritta	37918
Riva Lake Camp	37398
Riverdale	37914
Rivergate Mall (Part of Nashville)	37072
River Hill	37650
River Oaks	37341
River Rest	37064
Riversburg	38478
Riverside (Claiborne County)	37879
Riverside (Coffee County)	37355
Riverside (Davidson County)	37218
Riverside (Decatur County)	38363
Riverside (Shelby County)	38113
Riverside (Sullivan County)	37618
Riverton	38556
Riverview (Claiborne County)	37752
Riverview (Sullivan County)	37660
Riverview (Unicoi County)	37650
Riverview Estates	37033
Rives	38253
Roan Mountain	37687
Roaring Springs	37616
Roarks Cove	37324
Robbins (Pickett County)	38549
Robbins (Scott County)	37852
Roberts	38582
Robertson Fork	38472
Robinson Crossroads	37921
Rockbridge	37022
Rock City (Smith County)	37030
Rock City (Sullivan County)	37664
Rock Creek (Pickett County)	38556
Rock Creek (Unicoi County)	37650
Rockdale	38474
Rockford	37853
Rock Haven	37708
Rock Hill (Hancock County)	37765
Rock Hill (Henderson County)	38351
Rock Hill (Sullivan County)	37694
Rock House	37075
Rock Island	38581
Rockland (Part of Hendersonville)	37075
Rock Ledge Estates	37363
Rock Springs (Dickson County)	37036
Rock Springs (Dyer County)	38024
Rock Springs (Henderson County)	38388
Rock Springs (Rutherford County)	37167
Rock Springs (Sullivan County)	37663
Rock Station	38581
Rockvale	37153
Rockville	37874
Rockwood	37854
Rockwood Hill	37743
Rocky Branch	37886
Rocky Creek	37031
Rocky Fork (Rutherford County)	37167

Name	ZIP
Rocky Fork (Unicoi County)	37657
Rocky Grove	37722
Rocky Hill (Part of Knoxville)	37919
Rocky Mound	37186
Rocky Point (Hamblen County)	37860
Rocky Point (Putnam County)	38501
Rocky Ridge	38573
Rocky Spring (Monroe County)	37354
Rocky Spring (Sullivan County)	37686
Rocky Valley	37820
Roddy	37381
Roe Junction	37814
Roellen	38024
Rogana	37022
Rogers Creek	37303
Rogers Spring	38052
Rogersville	37857
Rolling Acres (Jefferson County)	37877
Rolling Acres (Williamson County)	37062
Rolling Hills (Hickman County)	37025
Rolling Hills (Marshall County)	37091
Rolling Hills (Unicoi County)	37650
Rolling Hills (Warren County)	37110
Rolling Meadows (Part of Franklin)	37064
Rome	37030
Romeo	37711
Rose Creek	38375
Rosedale	37710
Rose Hill (Madison County)	38301
Rose Hill (Union County)	37807
Rosemark	38053
Rose Valley	37079
Roseville	37183
Roslin	38556
Ross Camp Ground	37642
Rosser	38344
Rossview	37040
Rossville	38066
Rotherwood	37642
Round Pond	37040
Round Rock	37714
Round Top	37012
Routon	38231
Rover	37060
Rowland	38581
Royal	37160
Royal Blue	37847
Royal Oak (Part of Manchester)	37355
Royal Oaks (Williamson County)	37064
Royal Oaks (Wilson County)	37122
Royer Estates (Part of Murfreesboro)	37130
Rucker	37130
Rudderville	37064
Rudolph	38012
Rugby	37733
Rugby Hills (Part of Memphis)	38127
Rural Hill (Part of Nashville)	37217
Rural Vale	37385
Russel Fork	37766
Russell Crossroad	37743
Russell Hill	38145
Russellville	37860
Rusty (Part of Fairview)	37062
Rutherford	38369
Rutherford Estates	38401
Ruthton	37620
Ruthville	38237
Rutledge	37861
Rutledge Falls	37355
Rutledge Hill	37342
Ryall Springs	37421
Sadie	37643
Sadlers	37010
Safford	38328
Safley	37110
Sagewood Estates	38401
Sailors Rest	37050
St. Andrews	37372
St. Bethlehem	37155
St. Clair (Hawkins County)	37711
Saint Clair (Rhea County)	37381
St. James	37743
St. Joseph	38481
St. Paul	38023
Saint Peters	38012
Sainville	37355
Sale Creek	37373

Name	ZIP
Salem (Cocke County)	37843
Salem (Lewis County)	37033
Salem (Montgomery County)	37040
Salem (Tipton County)	38004
Salem (Weakley County)	38255
Saltillo	38370
Samburg	38254
Sampson	37367
Sanders	37387
Sand Hill	38229
Sandlick	37825
Sand Ridge	38351
Sand Springs	38574
Sand Switch	37375
Sandy	38589
Sandy Hook	38474
Sandy Lane	37385
Sandy Point	38320
Sandy Ridge	37725
Sandy Spring	37032
Sanford	37370
Sanford Hill (Part of Henderson)	38340
Sango	37040
Santa Fe	38482
Saratoga Springs	37367
Sardis	38371
Saulsbury	38067
Saundersville (Part of Hendersonville)	37075
Savannah	38372
Sawdust	38401
Sawyers Mill	38320
Scandlyn	37840
Scarboro (Part of Oak Ridge)	37830
Scattersville	37148
Scenic Point Estates	37777
Scoot Mill	37810
Scottsboro (Part of Nashville)	37218
Scotts Hill	38374
Screamer	38474
Seeber Flats	37710
Selmer	38375
Sentinel Heights (Part of Dayton)	37363
Sequatchie	37374
Sequoia Grove (Part of Cleveland)	37311
Sequoia Hills	37743
Sequoyah Estates (Part of Madisonville)	37354
Sequoyah Hills	37343
Sequoyah Village (Part of Madisonville)	37354
Serles	38008
Settlers Point	37064
Seven Islands	37920
Seven Oaks	37922
Sevier Home	37920
Sevierville	37862
Sewanee	37375
Sewee	37826
Seymour	37865
Shackle Island	37075
Shacklett	37082
Shades Bridge	38230
Shadowlawn	38002
Shady Grove (Coffee County)	37357
Shady Grove (Hamilton County)	37379
Shady Grove (Jefferson County)	37725
Shady Grove (Knox County)	37922
Shady Grove (Lincoln County)	37335
Shady Grove (Montgomery County)	37040
Shady Grove (Morgan County)	37770
Shady Grove (Putnam County)	38574
Shady Grove (Trousdale County)	37074
Shady Grove (White County)	38587
Shady Grove Shores	37379
Shady Hill	38351
Shady Rest	37110
Shady Valley	37688
Shafter	38230
Shake Rag Hill	38485
Shallowford	37650
Shandy	38008
Shannondale (Part of Knoxville)	37918
Shannon Hills	37343
Sharon	38255

Sharondale-Summit **TENNESSEE** **527**

	ZIP		ZIP		ZIP
Sharondale (Part of Tullahoma)	37388	Smithville	37166	Spurgeon (Washington County)	37659
Sharp Place	38556	Smithwood (Part of Knoxville)	37918	Staffords Store	38230
Sharps Chapel	37866	Smoky Junction	37756	Staffordtown	37317
Sharpsville	37130	Smoky View Estates	37804	Stainville	37710
Shaver Town	38563	Smyrna (Carroll County)	38318	Stanfill	37847
Shawanee	37867	Smyrna (Pickett County)	38549	Stanley Junction	37841
Shawnette	38450	Smyrna (Rutherford County)	37167	Stanton	38069
Shawtown	38232	Smyrna (Warren County)	37110	Stantonville	38379
Shelby Center	38134	Sneed Forest Estates	37064	Star Point	38549
Shelby Farms (Part of Memphis)	38101	Sneed Glen	37064	State (Part of Nashville)	37219
Shelbyville	37160	Sneedville	37869	State Line	37334
Shelbyville Mills	37160	Snell	37130	Statesville	37184
Shell Creek	37687	Snow Hill	37363	State University (Part of Johnson City)	37601
Shellmound	37380	Snows Hill	37059	Static	38549
Shellsford	37110	Soddy-Daisy	37379	Station Camp	37048
Shenandoah Heights	37601	Solo	38019	Stayton	37051
Shennendoah	37865	Solway	37931	Stella	38460
Shepp	38069	Somerville	38068	St Elmo (Part of Chattanooga)	37409
Sherrill Heights (Part of Madisonville)	37354	South (Davidson County)	37210	Stephen Holston (Part of Bristol)	37620
Sherrilltown	37184	South (Hamilton County)	37409	Stephens	37840
Sherwood	37376	Southall	37064	Stephenson	37342
Sherwood Estates	37716	South Berlin	37091	Steppsville	37710
Sheybogan	37190	South Carthage	37030	Sterling Park	37343
Shiloh (Bedford County)	37183	South Cleveland	37311	Stewart (Houston County)	37175
Shiloh (Cumberland County)	38555	South Clinton	37716	Stewart (Warren County)	37110
Shiloh (Grainger County)	37861	South Columbia (Part of Columbia)	38401	Stewart Chapel	37335
Shiloh (Hardin County)	38376	South Covington (Part of Covington)	38019	Stinking Creek	37766
Shiloh (Hawkins County)	37869	South Daisy (Part of Soddy-Daisy)	37379	Stiversville	38451
Shiloh (Humphreys County)	37101	South Dyersburg	38024	Stock Creek	37920
Shiloh (Jackson County)	38501	Southeastern Tennessee State Regional Correctional	37367	Stockton	38556
Shiloh (Montgomery County)	37051	Southern Hills (Part of Columbia)	38401	Stockton Valley	37774
Shiloh (Overton County)	38554	South Etowah	37331	Stokes	38034
Shiloh (Rutherford County)	37130	South Fulton	38257	Stone	38562
Shiloh (Sumner County)	37066	Southgate Shopping Center (Part of Memphis)	38109	Stonebrook	37135
Shiloh (Wilson County)	37138	South Green	37743	Stone River (Part of Nashville)	37076
Shingleton	37683	South Hall (Part of Alcoa)	37701	Stone River Estates (Part of Nashville)	37214
Shining Rock	37166	South Harriman (Part of Harriman)	37748	Stones River Homes (Part of Smyrna)	37167
Shipetown	37806	South Johnson City	37601	Stonewall	38560
Shipley	38501	South Knoxville (Part of Knoxville)	37920	Stoney Fork	37714
Shipps Bend	37033	Southland Mall (Part of Memphis)	38116	Stoney Point	37181
Shirley	38504	South Liberty	37370	Stony Gap	37869
Shirleyton	37397	South Pittsburg	37380	Stony Point	37873
Shooks Gap	37920	Southport	38451	Strahl	37857
Shop Springs	37184	Southside (Hardin County)	38326	Straight Fork	37847
Shore Acres	37379	Southside (Montgomery County)	37171	Strawberry Plains (Jefferson County)	37871
Short Creek	37037	South Tunnel	37066	Striggersville	37857
Short Mountain	37190	Spain's Hill	37085	Stringtown (Gibson County)	38233
Short Tail Springs	37341	Sparkman	38559	Stringtown (Montgomery County)	37191
Shouns	37683	Sparta	38583	Stroudsville	37032
Shubert	38462	Speedwell	37870	Suburban Hills (Knox County)	37901
Siam	37643	Spencer	38585	Suburban Hills (McMinn County)	37370
Sideview	37066	Spencer Creek	37064	Suck Creek	37405
Sidonia	38255	Spencer Hill	38474	Sugar Creek (Jackson County)	38562
Signal Hills (Part of Chattanooga)	37405	Spencers Mill	37029	Sugar Creek (Johnson County)	37683
Signal Mountain	37377	Sportman Acres	37122	Sugar Forks (Part of Dandridge)	37725
Silerton	38377	Spot	37140	Sugar Grove (Bradley County)	37311
Silica	37714	Spout Springs	38232	Sugar Grove (Roane County)	37748
Siloam	37186	Springbrook (Part of Alcoa)	37701	Sugar Grove (Sumner County)	37186
Silvacola	37617	Spring City	37381	Sugarlimb	37774
Silver City	37860	Spring Creek (Hardeman County)	38067	Sugar Tree	38380
Silver Grove	37618	Spring Creek (Madison County)	38378	Suggs Creek	37122
Silverhill	37087	Spring Creek (McMinn County)	37370	Sullivan Gardens	37663
Silver Point	38582	Spring Creek (Perry County)	37096	Sulphur	38570
Silver Ridge (Part of Lenoir City)	37771	Spring Creek (Wilson County)	37087	Sulphura	37148
Silver Springs	37122	Springdale (Claiborne County)	37879	Sulphur Creek	37147
Silvertop	37101	Springdale (Sullivan County)	37663	Sulphur Springs (Anderson County)	37716
Simonton	38011	Springfield	37172	Sulphur Springs (Hamblen County)	37814
Sims Spring	37160	Spring Hill (Anderson County)	37716	Sulphur Springs (Lincoln County)	37334
Singleton (Bedford County)	37160	Spring Hill (Henderson County)	38345	Sulphur Springs (Marion County)	37397
Singleton (Blount County)	37777	Spring Hill (Maury County)	37174	Sulphur Springs (Washington County)	37659
Singtown	37148	Spring Hill (White County)	38583	Sumac	38478
Sinking Cove	37376	Spring Lake	38134	Summer City	37367
Sitka	38358	Springmont	37138	Summerfield	37387
Sixmile	37801	Spring Place	37914	Summer Shade	38541
Skaggston	37806	Springtown	37369	Summertown (Hamilton County)	37377
Skinem	37334	Springvale	37814	Summertown (Lawrence County)	38483
Skinner Crossroad	37810	Spring View (Blount County)	37801		
Skullbone	38316	Springview (Williamson County)	37064		
Skyline	38063	Springville	38256		
Skyline Park (Part of Signal Mountain)	37377	Spruce Pine	37811	Summit (Hamilton County)	37363
Slayden	37165				
Slick Rock	37852				
Slide	37857				
Smartt	37378				
Smith Chapel	38501				
Smithfield	37385				
Smithland	37348				
Smith Mill	37334				
Smiths Chapel	37150				
Smiths Fork	38475				
Smith Springs (Part of Nashville)	37217				
Smithtown (Bledsoe County)	37338				
Smithtown (Marion County)	37380				

528 TENNESSEE Summit-Volunteer Heights

Name	ZIP
Summit (Hawkins County)	37711
Summitville	37382
Sunbright	37872
Sunkist Beach	38079
Sunny Brook (Part of Bristol)	37620
Sunny Hill	38012
Sunny Hills	37620
Sunnyside (Greene County)	37743
Sunnyside (Hancock County)	37869
Sunnyside (Sullivan County)	37617
Sunrise (Hickman County)	37033
Sunrise (Macon County)	37150
Sunset (Grainger County)	37861
Sunset (Pickett County)	38549
Sunset Gap	37722
Sunset Hills (Hamblen County)	37814
Sunset Hills (Sullivan County)	37660
Surgoinsville	37873
Sutherland	24236
Swan Bluff	37033
Swann Chapel	37725
Swannsylvania	37725
Sweet Lips	38340
Sweeton Hill (Part of Coalmont)	37313
Sweetwater (Lewis County)	38462
Sweetwater (Monroe County)	37874
Swift	38372
Sycamore (Cheatham County)	37015
Sycamore (Putnam County)	38501
Sycamore Hall	37879
Sycamore Landing	37185
Sykes	38547
Sylvia	37055
Tabernacle (Haywood County)	38012
Tabernacle (Tipton County)	38019
Tabor	38555
Tackett Creek	37766
Taft	38488
Talbott	37877
Tallassee	37878
Talley	37144
Tampico	37861
Tanglewood (Monroe County)	37874
Tanglewood (Smith County)	37030
Tara Estates (Part of Tullahoma)	37388
Tarbett	37853
Tarlton	37110
Tarpley	38478
Tarsus	37142
Tasso	37311
Tate	38344
Tate Springs	37708
Tatesville	37365
Tatumville	38059
Taylor	37058
Taylor Crossroads	37160
Taylor Hill (Part of Dayton)	37321
Taylor Place	38556
Taylors Cross Roads	38573
Taylorsville (Maury County)	38461
Taylorsville (Wilson County)	37087
Taylortown	38459
Tazewell	37879
Teague	38356
Tekoa	37931
Telford	37690
Tellico Hills (Part of Athens)	37303
Tellico Plains	37385
Temperance Hall	37095
Temple Hill	37650
Temple Hills Country Club Estates	37064
Templeton	38059
Templow	37022
Ten Mile	37880
Tennemo	38056
Tennessee City	37055
Tennessee Hills (Part of Bristol)	37620
Tennessee Ridge	37178
Tennessee Tech (Part of Cookeville)	38501
Terrace Hills	37122
Terrell	38237
Terry	38321
Terry Creek	37847
Theta	38401
The Wye	37769
Thick	37034
Thomas	38544
Thomas Addition	37665
Thomas Bridge	37618
Thomasville	37015
Thompsons Station	37179
Thompsons Store	38551
Thorngrove	37871
Thorn Hill	37881
Thornton Heights	37722
Three Churches	38450
Three Oaks	38456
Three Point	38041
Three Points	37918
Three Springs	37860
Three Way	38343
Throckmorton	37079
Thula	37810
Thurman Addition (Part of Pigeon Forge)	37862
Tibbs	38012
Tidwell	37025
Tiftona (Part of Chattanooga)	37419
Tiger Valley	37658
Tigrett	38070
Tilghman	38233
Timberlake (Hawkins County)	37857
Timberlake (Henderson County)	38351
Timesville	37377
Timothy	38568
Tinch	38556
Tin Cup	38320
Tinsleys Bottom	38551
Tiprell	37724
Tipton (Knox County)	37920
Tipton (Tipton County)	38071
Tiptonville	38079
Tishamingo	37122
Tobaccoport	37028
Tom Murray (Part of Jackson)	38301
Toone	38381
Top of the World Estates	37878
Topside	37920
Topsy	38485
Toqua	37885
Tottys	38454
Toulon	38063
Towee	37369
Town Acres (Part of Greeneville)	37743
Town Creek	37870
Towne Hills (Part of Chattanooga)	37343
Townsend	37882
Trace End Estates	37064
Traceview	37064
Tracy City	37387
Trade	37691
Tradewinds	37122
Trails End	37122
Tranquility	37303
Travisville	38577
Treadway	37881
Treeville	37849
Trenton	38382
Trent Valley	37869
Trentville	37871
Trevecca-College (Part of Nashville)	37210
Trezevant	38258
Tri-Angle	37160
Trigonia	37801
Trimble	38259
Trinity	37064
Triune	37014
Trousdale	37357
Troy	38260
Trundel Crossroad	37865
Tuckahoe	37871
Tuckers Crossroads	37087
Tucker Springs	37353
Tullahoma	37388
Tulu	38357
Tumbling	38201
Tuppertown (Part of Oliver Springs)	37840
Turley	37714
Turnbull	37029
Turners Station	37186
Turnersville	37032
Turnpike	38012
Turtletown	37391
Tusculum (Part of Nashville)	37211
Tusculum College	37743
Twin Bridges	37726
Twin Cove	37714
Twin Oak	38544
Twin Oaks	37665
Twinton	38554
Twomey (Part of Centerville)	37033
Tylersville	38030
Tyner Hills (Part of Chattanooga)	37421
Tyson	38233
Uceba	37865
Una (Part of Nashville)	37217
Unaka Springs	37650
Underwood	37764
Unicoi	37692
Union (Hardin County)	38310
Union (Haywood County)	38012
Union (Morgan County)	37840
Union (Roane County)	37763
Union (Union County)	37866
Union (Warren County)	38581
Union Central	38358
Union City	38261
Union Grove (Blount County)	37737
Union Grove (McMinn County)	37826
Union Grove (Meigs County)	37322
Union Heights	37814
Union Hill (Clay County)	38575
Union Hill (Davidson County)	37080
Union Hill (Henderson County)	38368
Union Hill (Lawrence County)	38468
Union Hill (Sumner County)	37066
Union Hill (Tipton County)	38004
Union McMinn	37826
Union Ridge	37183
Union Temple	37616
Union Valley	37865
Unionville (Bedford County)	37180
Unionville (Dyer County)	38040
Unitia	37771
University (Part of Knoxville)	37916
University of Tennessee (Part of Martin)	38238
University of the South	37375
Upchurch	37616
Upper Mockeson	38468
Upper Shell Creek	37687
Upper Sinking	37147
Uptonville	38392
Uptown (Part of Knoxville)	37902
Uptown Nashville (Part of Nashville)	37219
Vale	38317
Valleybrook (Hamilton County)	37343
Valley Brook (Wilson County)	37122
Valley Creek	37715
Valley Forge	37643
Valley Hills (Part of Bristol)	37620
Valley View Heights	37716
Van Buren	38042
Vandever	38555
Van Dyke	38242
Van Hill	37857
Vanleer	37181
Vannatta	37160
Vanntown	37335
Vardy	37869
Vasper	37714
Vaughn's Gap (Part of Nashville)	37205
Vaughns Grove	38382
Verdun	37841
Vernon	37137
Vernon Heights	37664
Verona	37091
Verona Hills	37122
Versailles	37153
Vesta	37087
Vestal (Part of Knoxville)	37920
Veterans Administration (Part of Murfreesboro)	37129
Veto	38477
Viar	38024
Victoria	37397
Victory	37766
Vildo	38075
Villa Gardens (Part of Knoxville)	37918
Village Green (Part of Farragut)	37922
Vine	37087
Vinegar Hill	37620
Vine Ridge	38554
Vinson	37110
Viola	37394
Virtue (Part of Farragut)	37922
Vise	38329
Volunteer Heights (Part of Crossville)	38555

Vonore-Yorkville **TENNESSEE** 529

	ZIP		ZIP		ZIP
Vonore	37885	West Forest (Part of Knoxville)	37919	Widow Town	37862
Vose (Part of Alcoa)	37701	West Fork	38543	Wilder	38589
Waco	38472	West Greene (Part of Greeneville)	37743	Wilder Chapel	37324
Walden	37377	West Harpeth	37064	Wildersville	38388
Walden Creek	37862	Westhaven Village (Part of Knoxville)	37921	Wild Plum	38555
Waldens Ridge (Bledsoe County)	37381	West Hills (Jefferson County)	37820	Wildwood	37801
Waldens Ridge (Rhea County)	37321	West Hills (Knox County)	37919	Wildwood Lake	37311
Wales	38478	West Hills (Monroe County)	37354	Wilhite	38501
Walkertown (Greene County)	37616	West Hills (Roane County)	37748	Wilkinsville	38004
Walkertown (Hardin County)	38372	West Johnson City	37659	Willard	37074
Walland	37886	West Junction (Part of Memphis)	38101	Willette	37150
Walling	38587	West Knoxville (Part of Knoxville)	37919	Williams (Lauderdale County)	38063
Walnut Acres	37064	West Maryville (Part of Maryville)	37801	Williams (Macon County)	37083
Walnut Grove (Gibson County)	38233	West Meade (Part of Nashville)	37205	Williamsburg	37331
Walnut Grove (Hardin County)	38372	West Miller Cove	37886	Williams Creek	37841
Walnut Grove (Lauderdale County)	38063	Westmoreland	37186	Williams Crossroads	38544
Walnut Grove (Meigs County)	37322	Westmoreland Heights (Part of Knoxville)	37919	Williamsport	38487
Walnut Grove (Sevier County)	37862	West Nashville (Part of Nashville)	37209	Williams Springs	37888
Walnut Grove (Sullivan County)	37618	West Oneida (Part of Oneida)	37841	Willis	37765
Walnut Grove (Sumner County)	37048	Westover	38301	Willis Spring	37362
Walnut Grove (Tipton County)	38015	Westpoint	38486	Williston	38076
Walnut Grove (Trousdale County)	37074	Westport	38387	Willow Grove (Bedford County)	37360
Walnut Hill (Crockett County)	38006	West Robbins	37852	Willow Grove (Clay County)	38541
Walnut Hill (Roane County)	37748	West Shiloh	38379	Willow Grove (Haywood County)	38012
Walnut Hill (Sullivan County)	37620	Westside Heights (Part of Tullahoma)	37388	Wilmore Estates	37890
Walnut Log	38261	West Springbrook (Part of Alcoa)	37701	Wilson Station	37329
Walnut Shade	37150	West Town Mall (Part of Knoxville)	37919	Wilsonville	37821
Walter Crossroad	37743	West Union	38225	Winchester	37398
Walterhill	37129	West View (Knox County)	37921	Winchester Springs	37398
Wa-Ni Village	37861	Westview (Weakley County)	38237	Windle	38570
Ware Branch	37341	West View Acres	37087	Windletown	38554
Warren	38068	West View Park	37660	Windrock	37840
Warrens Bluff	38351	Westwood	38401	Windrow	37153
Warrensburg	37818	Westwood Gardens (Part of Jackson)	38301	Windy City	38343
Wartburg	37887	Westwood Hills	37801	Windy Hill (Part of Bristol)	37620
Wartrace	37183	Westwood Homes	37355	Winesap	38555
Warwicktown	37807	Wetmore	37325	Winfield	37892
Washburn	37888	Wheel	37160	Wingo	38258
Washington	37321	Wheelerton	38453	Winklers	37150
Washington College	37681	Whispering Hills	38261	Winner	37643
Washington Heights (Part of Chattanooga)	37406	Whispering Pine	37601	Winona	37756
Watauga	37694	Whitaker	37160	Winton Town	37355
Watauga Flats	37601	White (Shelby County)	38117	Wirmingham	38573
Watauga Point (Part of Elizabethton)	37643	White (Warren County)	37110	Withamtown	37022
Waterstown	37886	White Bluff (Dickson County)	37187	Witt	37814
Watertown	37184	White Bluff (Trousdale County)	37074	Wixtown	37186
Water Valley	38487	White City	37387	Wolf Creek (Cocke County)	37727
Waterville	37311	White Fern	38313	Wolf Creek (De Kalb County)	38582
Watkins (De Kalb County)	37166	Whitehaven (Part of Memphis)	38116	Wolf Creek (Rhea County)	37381
Watkins (Tipton County)	38019	Whitehaven Plaza (Part of Memphis)	38116	Wolf Hill	37022
Watt Heights (Part of Calhoun)	37309	Whitehead Hills	37687	Wolf River	38577
Watts Bar Dam	37395	White Hill (Robertson County)	37072	Womack (Sumner County)	37066
Watts Bar Estates	37381	White Hill (Van Buren County)	38581	Womack (Warren County)	37110
Waverly	37185	White Horn	37711	Woodbine (Part of Nashville)	37211
Wayland Springs	38463	White House	37188	Woodbury	37190
Waynesboro	38485	White Oak (Campbell County)	37766	Woodcliff	38574
Wayside	37110	White Oak (Morgan County)	37829	Wooddale	37914
Weakly Creek	38464	Whiteoak Crossing	38425	Wooded Acres (Part of Knoxville)	37921
Wear Valley	37862	White Oak Flat	37036	Woodland (Davidson County)	37206
Weaver	37620	White Oaks (Part of Manchester)	37355	Woodland (Haywood County)	38012
Webber City	38456	White Pine	37890	Woodland Acres	37919
Webbs Chapel	37166	White Rock	37687	Woodland Mills	38271
Webbtown	37083	Whitesand	37743	Woodlawn (Cumberland County)	38555
Webster	37854	Whitesburg	37891	Woodlawn (Montgomery County)	37191
Wedgewood Hills	37922	White Schoolhouse Corners	37840	Woodlawn (Washington County)	37659
Welch Crossroad	37866	Whites Creek (Davidson County)	37189	Woodlawn (Wayne County)	38450
Welchland	38585	White's Creek (Rhea County)	37381	Woodmont (Part of Nashville)	37215
Welch's Camp	37714	Whiteside	37396	Woodrow	37617
Well Spring	37870	Whiteville	38075	Woods Ferry	37066
Wells Station (Part of Memphis)	38122	Whitleyville	38588	Woodstock	38053
Wellsville	37801	Whitlock	38242	Woods Valley	37051
Wellwood	38006	Whitthorne	38348	Woodville	38063
Wesleyanna	37303	Whittle Springs (Part of Knoxville)	37917	Woody	38555
West (Davidson County)	37209	Whitway	38358	Wooldridge	37762
West (Gibson County)	38358	Whitwell	37397	Wrigley	37098
West Cyruston	37334			Wyatts Chapel	37058
Westel	37854			Wyatt Village	37708
West Emory	37922			Wyly	38320
Western Heights	37857			Wynn	37766
Western Institute (Part of Bolivar)	38074			Wynnburg	38077
Westfield Estates (Part of Franklin)	37064			Yager	37110
				Yankeetown	38583
				Yell	37091
				Yellow Store	37873
				Yett Addition	37862
				Yettland (Part of Sevierville)	37862
				Yorkely	38472
				Yorktown (Part of Franklin)	37064
				Yorkville	38389

TENNESSEE Young Bend-Zion Hill

	ZIP		ZIP		ZIP
Young Bend	37166	Yukon	38488	Zion Grove	37862
Youngs	38301	Yuma	38390	Zion Hill (Part of Surgoinsville)	37857
Youngville	37172	Yum Yum	38068		
Y Section	37601	Zack	38320		

Abbott-Bandera **TEXAS** **531**

	ZIP		ZIP		ZIP
Abbott	76621	Alsdorf	75119		76010-18
Aberfoyle	75496	Altair	77412	For specific Arlington Zip Codes call (214) 647-2996	
Abernathy	79311	Alta Loma (Part of Santa Fe)	77510	Arlington Downs (Part of Arlington)	76010
Abilene	79601-08	Alto	75925		
For specific Abilene Zip Codes call (915) 673-6485		Altoga	75069	Arlington Heights (Part of Fort Worth)	76107
Abilene Christian College (Part of Abilene)	79601	Alton	78572	Armstrong	78338
		Alto Springs	76653	Arneckeville	77954
Ables Springs	75160	Alum	78160	Arnett (Coryell County)	76528
Abram	78572	Alum Creek	78957	Arnett (Hockley County)	79336
Acala	79839	Alvarado	76009	Arp	75750
Ace	77326	Alvin	77511-12	Arrowhead Lake	77378
Ackerly	79713	For specific Alvin Zip Codes call (713) 331-4747		Arrowhead Shores	76048
Acton	76048			Arrowhead Village	78130
Acuff	79401	Alvord	76225	Arroyo (Part of Harlingen)	78550
Acworth	75426	Amarillo	79101-76	Arsenal (Part of San Antonio)	78283
Adams	76936	For specific Amarillo Zip Codes call (806) 379-2140			
Adams Gardens	78550			Art	76820
Adams Oaks	77365	Ambrose	75414	Artesian Forest	77304
Adamsville	76550	American Technological University	76541	Artesia Wells	78001
Addicks	77079			Arthur City	75411
Addicks Barker (Part of Houston)	77218	Ames (Coryell County)	76528	Arvana	79331
		Ames (Liberty County)	77575	Asa	76707
Addielou	75412	Amherst	79312	Ash (Henderson County)	75751
Addison	75001	Amigoland Mall (Part of Brownsville)	78520	Ash (Houston County)	75835
Addran	75482			Ashby	77465
Adell	76086	Ammansville	78945	Asherton	78827
Ad Hall	76520	Amy	75432	Ashland	75640
Adina	78947	Anadarko	75667	Ashmore	79342
Adkins	78101	Anahuac	77514	Ashtola	79226
Admiral	79504	Anchor	77515	Ashworth	75142
Adrian	79001	Anchorage	78065	Asia	75939
Adsul	75956	Ander	77963	Aspermont	79502
Ady	79010	Anderson	77830	Astrodome (Part of Houston)	77025
Afton	79220	Andice	78628		
Aggieland (Part of College Station)	77844	Andrews	79714	Astro Hills	78130
		Andrewsville	75683	Atascocita (Part of Humble)	77346
Agnes	76082	Angelo State University (Part of San Angelo)	76909	Atascosa	78002
Agua Dulce	78330			Ater	76528
Agua Nueva	78361	Angleton	77515-16	Athens	75751
Aguilares	78369	For specific Angleton Zip Codes call (409) 849-7500		Atlanta	75551
Aiken (Floyd County)	79221			Atlas	75460
Aiken (Shelby County)	75935	Angleton South	77515	Atlee	78019
Airlawn (Part of Dallas)	75235	Angus	75110	Atoy	75785
Airport City	78108	Angus Valley	78758	Atreco (Part of Port Arthur)	77640
Airport Mail Facility (Part of Houston)	77205	Anna	75003	Attoyac	75961
		Annarose	78022	Atwell	76437
Air Terminal (Part of Midland)	79703	Annetta	76008	Aubrey	76227
		Annetta North	76086	Auburn	76050
Airville	76501	Annetta South	76086	Audobon Park (Part of Houston)	77338
Airway Acres	79760	Anneville	76023		
Alamo	78516	Annona	75550	Augusta	75844
Alamo Alto	79853	Anson	79501	Aurora	76078
Alamo Beach	77979	Anson Jones (Part of Houston)	77009	Austin	78701-89
Alamo Heights	78209			For specific Austin Zip Codes call (512) 929-1255	
Alamo Ranchettos	79735	Antelope	76350		
Alanreed	79002	Anthony	79821	Austin Lake Estates	78759
Alazan	75961	Anthony Harbor	75929	Austonio	75835
Alba	75410	Antioch (Cass County)	75551	Austwell	77950
Albany	76430	Antioch (Delta County)	75432	Authon	76086
Albert	78601	Antioch (Henderson County)	75758	Autumn Woods	77362
Albert Thomas (Part of Nassau Bay)	77058	Antioch (Houston County)	75851	Avalon	76623
		Antioch (Jasper County)	77612	Avery	75554
Albion	75426	Antioch (Madison County)	75852	Avinger	75630
Alco	75949	Antioch (Rusk County)	75652	Avoca	79503
Aldine (Harris County)	77018	Antioch (mail Timpson) (Shelby County)	75975	Avonbell (Part of Amarillo)	79106
Aldine (Harris County)	77039			Avondale	76179
Aldine Estates	77039	Antioch (mail Center) (Shelby County)	75935	Avon Park	76708
Aldine Gardens	77039			Axtell	76624
Aldine Meadows	77039	Anton	79313	Azle	76020
Aledo	76008	Apache Addition (Part of Seguin)	78155	Bacliff	77518
Aleman	76531			Bader	78009
Alexander	76446	Apache Court	76028	Bagby	75446
Aley	75143	Apache Shores	78759	Bagwell	75412
Alfred	78332	Apolonia	77830	Bahia Mar	78597
Algerita	76877	Apparel Mart (Part of Dallas)	75207	Bailey	75413
Algoa	77511	Appelt Hill	77964	Baileyboro	79371
Alice	78332-33	Appleby	75961	Baileys Prairie	77515
For specific Alice Zip Codes call (512) 664-5541		Apple Springs	75926	Baileyville	75670
		Aqua Verde	78759	Bainer	79339
Alief (Part of Houston)	77411	Aquilla	76622	Bainville	78119
Allamore	79855	Aransas Pass	78336	Baird	79504
Allen	75002	Arbala	75482	Baker	76086
Allendale	76301	Arbor	75847	Bakersfield	79752
Allenfarm	77868	Arbor Oaks (Part of Houston)	77088	Balch	79358
Allenhurst	77414			Balch Springs	75180
Allens Chapel	75492	Arcadia (Galveston County)	77517	Balcones (Part of Austin)	78759
Allens Point	75446	Arcadia (Shelby County)	75935	Balcones Heights	78201
Alleyton	78935	Archer City	76351	Balcones Village	78750
Allison	79003	Arcola	77583	Bald Hill	75901
Allmon	79250	Arden	76901	Bald Prairie	77756
Alma	75119	Argenta	78368	Baldwin	75661
Almeda (Part of Houston)	77045	Argo	75558	Ballinger	76821
Almeda Mall (Part of Houston)	77034	Argyle	76226	Balmorhea	79718
		Argyle Plaza (Part of Houston)	77035	Balsora	76026
Almont	75559			Bammel	77040
Aloe	77901	Ariola	77625	Bammel Timbers	77040
Alpine	79830-31	Arizona	77367	Banana Junction	76708
For specific Alpine Zip Codes call (915) 837-2524		Arlam	75946	Bancroft (Part of Pinehurst)	77630
Alsa	75169	Arlington	76003-07	Bandera	78003

532 TEXAS

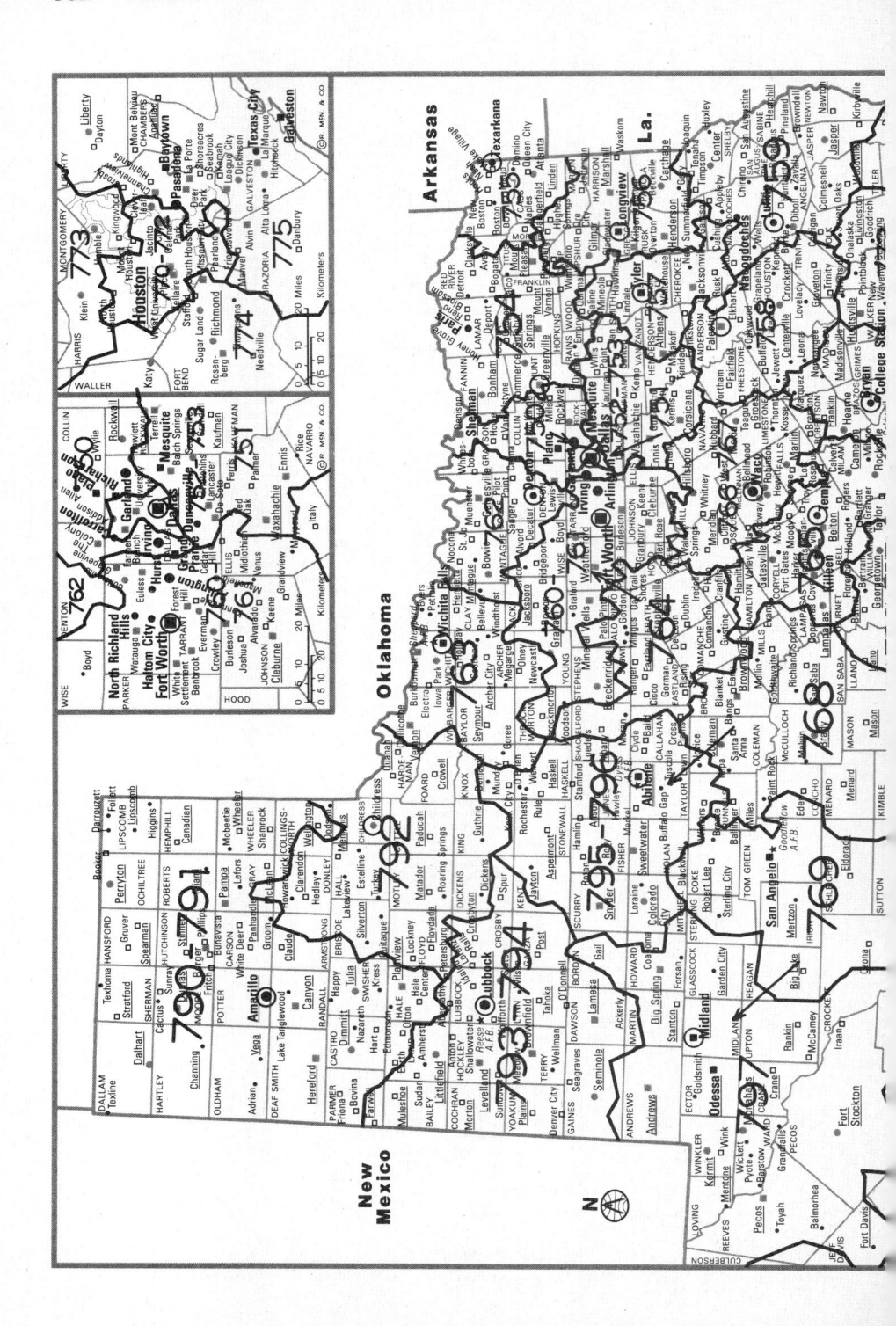

TEXAS 533

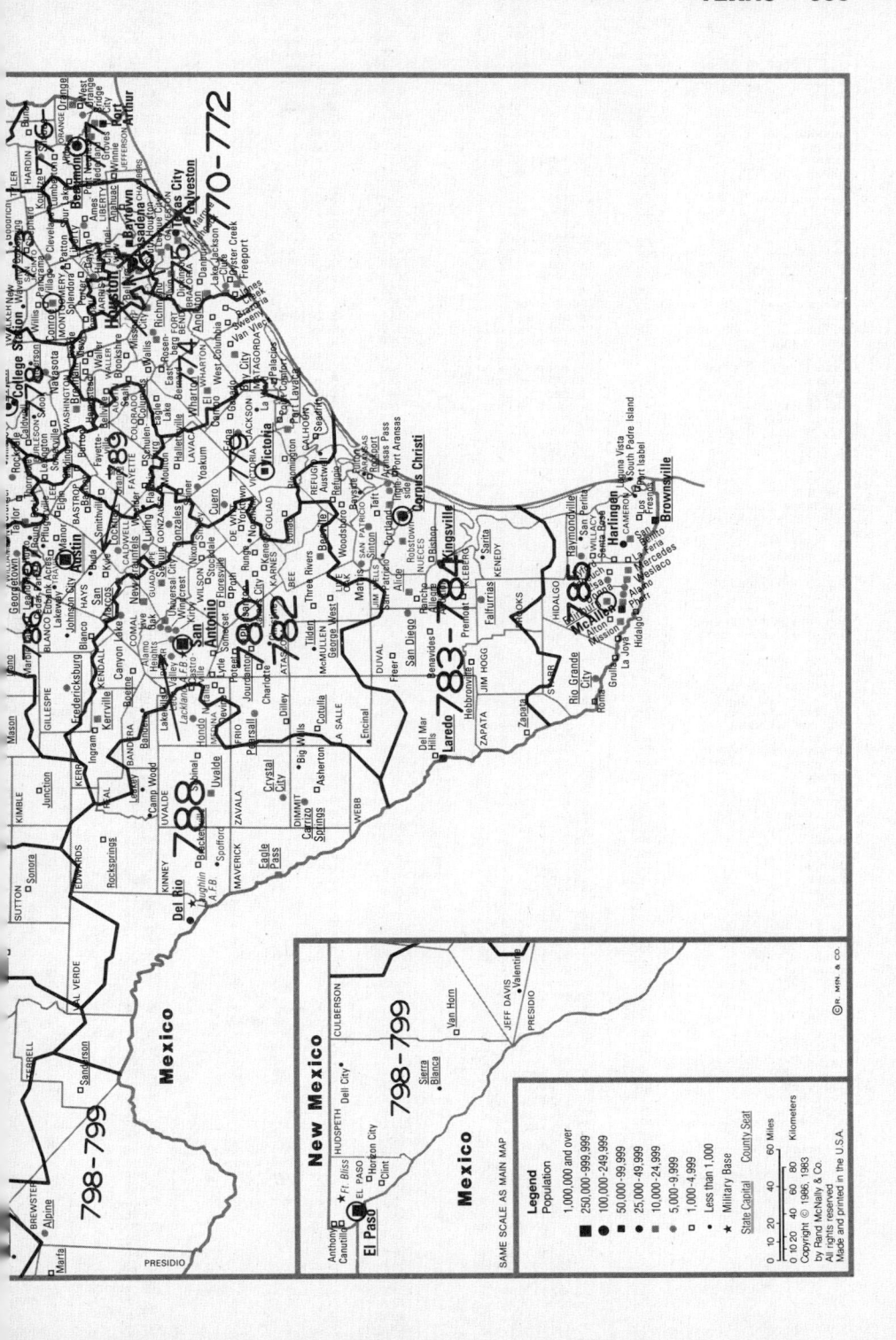

534 TEXAS Bandera Falls-Branchville

Name	ZIP
Bandera Falls	78063
Bangs	76823
Banquete	78339
Barbarosa	78130
Barclay	76656
Bardwell	75101
Barker	77413
Barksdale	78828
Barnes	75960
Barnhart	76930
Barnum	75939
Barrett	77532
Barrington Oaks	78759
Barry	75102
Barstow	79719
Bartlett	76511
Bartley Woods	75492
Barton Creek Square (Part of Austin)	78746
Bartons Chapel	76056
Bartonville	76226
Barwise	79235
Bascom	75705
Basin Springs	76264
Bassett	75574
Bassett Center (Part of El Paso)	79925
Bastrop	78602
Bastrop Bayou	77515
Bastrop Beach	77515
Bateman	78662
Batesville	78829
Batson	77519
Battle	76664
Baxter	75751
Bay City	77414
Bay Harbor	77553
Baylor University (Part of Waco)	76706
Bay Oaks	77571
Bayou Bend (Part of Houston)	77088
Bayou Chantilly (Part of Dickinson)	77539
Bayou Vista	77563
Bay Plaza (Part of Baytown)	77520
Bayport (Part of Houston)	77058
Bayside	78340
Bayside Terrace	77571
Baytown	77520-22
For specific Baytown Zip Codes call (713) 420-2508	
Bayview (Cameron County)	78566
Bay View (Galveston County)	77518
Bayway (Part of Baytown)	77520
Baywood (Part of Seabrook)	77586
Bazette	75144
Beach	77301
Beach City	77520
Beacon Hill (Part of San Antonio)	78201
Beadle	77414
Bear Grass	75846
Beasley	77417
Beattie	76442
Beaukiss	78621
Beaumont	77701-26
For specific Beaumont Zip Codes call (409) 842-7200	
Beaumont Place	77028
Beauxart Gardens	77705
Beaver Dam	75559
Bebe	78603
Beck	79371
Becker	75142
Beckville	75631
Becton	79343
Bedford	76021-22
For specific Bedford Zip Codes call (214) 647-2996	
Bedias	77831
Bee Cave	78746
Beech Grove	75951
Beechnut (Harris County)	77072
Beechwood	75948
Bee House	76525
Beeville	78102-04
For specific Beeville Zip Codes call (512) 358-3727	
Belcherville	76255
Belew	76258
Belfalls	76579
Belgrade	75928
Belk	75411
Bellaire	77401-02
For specific Bellaire Zip Codes call (713) 668-3121	
Bellaire Addition	75704
Bellaire West (Part of Houston)	77072

Name	ZIP
Bellevue	76228
Bellmead	76705
Bells	75414
Bellview	75410
Bellville	77418
Belmar (Part of Amarillo)	79106
Belmont	78604
Belott	75835
Belton	76513
Ben Arnold	76517
Benavides	78341
Ben Bolt	78342
Benbrook	76126
Benchley	77801
Bend	76824
Bending Bough	77373
Ben Franklin	75415
Ben Hur	76664
Benjamin	79505
Bennett	76066
Bennett Estates	77302
Benoit	76882
Bent Tree (Part of Dallas)	75287
Ben Wheeler	75754
Berclair	78107
Berea (Houston County)	75835
Berea (Marion County)	75657
Bergheim	78004
Bergstrom Air Force Base	78743
Berlin	77833
Bernardo	78933
Berry Street (Part of Fort Worth)	76109
Berryville	75763
Bertram	78605
Bessmay	77612
Bessmay-Buna	77612
Best	76932
Bethany	71007
Bethel (Anderson County)	75861
Bethel (Ellis County)	75165
Bethel (Henderson County)	75751
Bethel (Runnels County)	76821
Bethlehem (Bowie County)	75559
Bethlehem (Upshur County)	75644
Betner (Part of Paris)	75460
Beto Unit (Anderson County)	75861
Beto 2 Unit (Anderson County)	75801
Bettie	75644
Beulah	75941
Beverly	76711
Beverly Hills (Part of Dallas)	75211
Beversville	78615
Bevil Oaks	77706
Bevilport	75951
Beyersville	78615
Biardstown	75460
Big Bend National Park	79834
Bigfoot	78005
Biggs Field	79908
Big Lake	76932
Big Oaks	75630
Big Sandy	75755
Big Spring	79720-21
For specific Big Spring Zip Codes call (915) 263-7391	
Big Square	79027
Big Thiket	77369
Big Town Shopping Center (Part of Mesquite)	75149
Big Wells	78830
Billington	76624
Billpark (Part of Houston)	77012
Biloxi	75928
Birch	77879
Bird Farm Crossing	79839
Birdville (Part of Haltom City)	76117
Birnam Woods	77379
Birome	76625
Birthright	75482
Biry	78016
Bisbee	76063
Bishop	78343
Bishop Hills	79106
Bivins	75555
Black	79035
Blackfoot	75853
Black Jack (Cherokee County)	75789
Black Jack (Robertson County)	77859
Blackland	75089
Blackoak	75431
Blackwell	79506
Blakeney	75412
Blanchard	77351
Blanco	78606
Blanconia	78102

Name	ZIP
Bland (Part of West Orange)	77630
Blandlake	75972
Blanket	76432
Blanton	76821
Bleakwood	75956
Bledsoe	79314
Bleiblerville	78931
Blessing	77419
Blevins	76524
Blewett	78801
Blocker	75670
Blodgett	75686
Bloomburg	75556
Bloomdale	75069
Bloomfield	76258
Blooming Grove	76626
Bloomington	77951
Blossom	75416
Blue	78947
Bluegrove	76352
Blue Haven Estates	75169
Blue Lake Estates	78654
Blue Mound	76131
Blue Ridge (Collin County)	75004
Blue Ridge (Falls County)	76680
Blueroan	77434
Bluetown	78592
Blue Water Key	75758
Bluff Dale	76433
Bluff Springs (Parker County)	76020
Bluff Springs (Travis County)	78744
Bluffton	78607
Blum	76627
Blumenthal	78624
Bluntzer	78380
Board	76442
Bob Harris (Part of Pasadena)	77506
Bob Lyons (Part of Galveston)	77550
Bobo	75974
Bobville	77333
Boca Chica (Part of Brownsville)	78520
Boerne	78006
Bogata	75417
Bois D'Arc	75801
Boling	77420
Boling-lago	77420
Bolivar	76266
Bolton	75686
Bomarton	76380
Bon Ami	75956
Bonanza (Hill County)	76692
Bonanza (Hopkins County)	75420
Bonham	75418
Bonita	76255
Bonney	77583
Bonnie View	78393
Bono	76031
Bon Wier	75928
Booker	79005
Boonsville	76026
Booth	77469
Boquillas	79834
Borden	78962
Borderland	79932
Bordersville (Part of Houston)	77338
Borger	79007-08
For specific Borger Zip Codes call (806) 273-3761	
Bosqueville	76708
Boston (Part of New Boston)	75557
Boswell	77340
Bovina	79009
Bowie	76230
Bowser	76872
Box Church	76642
Boxelder	75550
Boxwood	75683
Boyce	75165
Boyd (Fannin County)	75418
Boyd (Wise County)	76023
Boys Ranch	79010
Boz	75165
Brachfield	75681
Bracken	78218
Brackettville	78832
Brad	76475
Bradfield	75656
Bradford	75853
Bradshaw	76945
Brady (McCulloch County)	76825
Brady (Shelby County)	75935
Branch	75069
Branchville	76520

Brandon-Cedar Point TEXAS 535

Name	ZIP
Brandon	76628
Bransford (Part of Colleyville)	76034
Branton	76471
Brashear	75420
Braun Station West	78250
Brazoria	77422
Brazos	76472
Brazos Mall (Part of Lake Jackson)	77566
Brazos Point	76652
Breckenridge	76024
Bremond	76629
Brenham	77833
Brentwood Manor	77901
Breslau	77964
Briar	76020
Briarcliff	78746
Briaroaks	76028
Briary	76570
Brice	79226
Bridge City	77611
Bridgeport	76026
Brierwood Bay	75763
Briggs	78608
Bright Star (Rains County)	75410
Bright Star (Van Zandt County)	75169
Briscoe	79011
Bristol	75119
Britton	76063
Broaddus	75929
Broadway (Crosby County)	79243
Broadway (Lamar County)	75460
Broadway Junction	75460
Broadway Square (Part of Tyler)	75701
Brock	76086
Brock Junction	76086
Brogado	79718
Bronco	79355
Bronson	75930
Bronte	76933
Brookeland	75931
Brookesmith	76827
Brook Forest	77357
Brook Glen Addition (Part of La Porte)	77571
Brookhollow (Part of Dallas)	75247
Brookshier	76933
Brookshire	77423
Brookside Village	77581
Brookston	75421
Broom City	75839
Broome	76951
Brown College	77880
Browndell	75931
Brownfield	79316
Browning	75705
Brownsboro (Caldwell County)	78644
Brownsboro (Henderson County)	75756
Brownsville	78520-26
For specific Brownsville Zip Codes call (512) 546-2411	
Brownwood	76803-04
For specific Brownwood Zip Codes call (915) 646-0656	
Brownwood (Part of Orange)	77630
Broyles	75801
Bruceville (Part of Bruceville-Eddy)	76630
Bruceville-Eddy	76630
Brumley	75686
Brundage	78834
Bruner (Part of West Orange)	77630
Bruni	78344
Brunswick	75925
Brushie Prairie	76641
Brushy	77801
Brushy Creek	75801
Bryan	77801-06
For specific Bryan Zip Codes call (409) 779-3000	
Bryans Mill	75560
Bryson	76027
Buchanan Dam	78609
Buchanan Lake Village	78672
Buck Creek	75949
Buckeye	77414
Buckholts	76518
Buckhorn (Austin County)	77418
Buckhorn (Newton County)	75928
Buckingham	75080
Buckner	76462
Buda	78610
Buena Vista (Bexar County)	78221

Name	ZIP
Buena Vista (Shelby County)	75975
Buffalo	75831
Buffalo Gap (Taylor County)	79508
Buffalo Gap (Travis County)	78734
Buffalo Springs	76228
Buford	79512
Bugbee Heights	79078
Bug Tussle	75449
Bula	79320
Bullard	75757
Bullock	76470
Bulverde	78163
Buna	77612
Bunavista	79007
Buncomb	75633
Bunger	76046
Bunker Hill (Harris County)	77024
Bunker Hill (Lamar County)	75486
Bunyan	76446
Burgess	75669
Burkburnett	76354
Burke	75941
Burkett	76828
Burkeville	75932
Burleigh	77418
Burleson	76028
Burlington	76519
Burnell	78119
Burnet	78611
Burns (Bowie County)	75561
Burns (Cooke County)	76258
Burr	77488
Burris Crossing	79853
Burrow	75089
Burton	77835
Busby	79543
Bushland	79012
Bushwhacker Peninsula	75147
Bustamante	78361
Busterville	79358
Butler (Bastrop County)	78621
Butler (Freestone County)	75855
Byers	76357
Bynum	76631
Byrd	75119
Byrds	76801
Cable Hole Crossing	79853
Cabot Kingsmill	79065
Cactus	79013
Caddo	76029
Caddo Mills	75005
Cadiz	78102
Caesar	78119
Cain City	78624
Calaveras	78114
Caldwell	77836
Caledonia	75946
Calf Creek	76825
Call (Jasper County)	75933
Call (Newton County)	75933
Calliham	78007
Callisburg	76240
Calvary	75773
Calvert	77837
Camden	75934
Camelot Two	78239
Cameron	76520
Camey	75034
Camp Air	76856
Camp Alzafar	78006
Campbell	75422
Campbellton	78008
Camp Dallas	75034
Camp Maxey	75473
Campo Alto	78516
Camp Ruby	77351
Camp San Saba	76825
Camp Springs	79526
Camp Stanley	78206
Camp Strake	77301
Campti	75935
Camp Valley	78140
Camp Verde	78010
Camp Wood	78833
Cana	75169
Canada Verde	78114
Canadian	79014
Canal City	77617
Candelaria	79843
Candlelight Oaks (Part of Houston)	77088
Cane Creek	78624
Caney	75148
Caney City	77357
Caney Creek Estates	75095
Cannon	75103
Canton	75103
Canutillo	79835
Canyon (Lubbock County)	79408
Canyon (Randall County)	79015

Name	ZIP
Canyon Creek (Part of Richardson)	75080
Canyon Creek Estates	78130
Canyon Lake	78130
Canyon Lake Acres	78130
Canyon Lake Estates	78130
Canyon Lake Forest	78130
Canyon Lake Hills	78130
Canyon Lake Island	78130
Canyon Lake Mobile Home Estates	78130
Canyon Lake Shores	78130
Canyon Lake Village West	78130
Canyon Springs Resort	78130
Canyon Valley	79356
Canyon View Acres	78163
Capital Plaza (Part of Austin)	78723
Capitol (Part of Austin)	78701
Caplen	77617
Capps Corner	76265
Cap Rock	79357
Caprock Shopping Center (Part of Lubbock)	79404
Caps	79605
Caradan	76844
Carancahua	77465
Carbon	76435
Carbondale	75567
Cardinal (Part of Athens)	75751
Carey	79222
Carey Estates (Part of Seabrook)	77586
Carlisle (Lubbock County)	79407
Carlisle (Trinity County)	75862
Carlos	77830
Carl Range (Part of Irving)	75062
Carlsbad	76934
Carl's Corner	76645
Carlton	76436
Carmine	78932
Carmona	75939
Caro	75961
Carolina Cove	77367
Carpenter	78101
Carpenters Bluff	75020
Carricitos	78586
Carrizo Springs	78834
Carroll	75771
Carroll Springs	75853
Carrollton	75006-08
	75010-11
For specific Carrollton Zip Codes call (214) 418-7858	
Carson	75488
Carta Valley	78835
Carterville	75563
Carthage	75633
Cartwright (Kaufman County)	75142
Cartwright (Wood County)	75494
Casa Piedra	79843
Casa View (Part of Dallas)	75228
Casey	79836
Cash	75401
Cason	75636
Cass	75556
Castell	76831
Castle Hill Estates (Part of Azle)	76020
Castle Hills	78213
Castlewood	77039
Castlewood Forest	78745
Castolon	79834
Castroville	78009
Catarina	78836
Cat Spring	78933
Causeway Beach	75143
Cave Springs	75670
Caviness	75460
Cawthon	77868
Cayote	76689
Cayuga	75832
Cedar Branch	75147
Cedar Creek (Anderson County)	75839
Cedar Creek (Bastrop County)	78612
Cedar Grove (Cass County)	75560
Cedar Grove (El Paso County)	79915
Cedar Grove (Harris County)	77532
Cedar Hill (Dallas County)	75104
Cedar Hill (Floyd County)	79241
Cedar Hills	78621
Cedar Lake	77414
Cedar Lane	77415
Cedar Mills Resort	76245
Cedar Park	78613
Cedar Point	77520

536 TEXAS Cedar Shores Estates-Coughran

	ZIP
Cedar Shores Estates	76671
Cedar Springs (Falls County)	76570
Cedar Springs (Upshur County)	75683
Cedar Valley	78736
Cedarview	75104
Cee Vee	79223
Cego	76524
Cele	78653
Celeste	75423
Celina	75009
Center (Limestone County)	76642
Center (Shelby County)	75935
Center City	76844
Center Grove	75455
Center Line	77879
Center Point (Camp County)	75686
Center Point (Ellis County)	76651
Center Point (Howard County)	79720
Center Point (Kerr County)	78010
Center Point (Panola County)	75691
Center Point (Parker County)	76086
Center Point (Parker County)	76020
Center Point (Titus County)	75455
Center Point (Upshur County)	75755
Centerview	75833
Centerville (Dallas County)	75040
Centerville (Leon County)	75833
Centerville (Trinity County)	75845
Centex (Part of San Marcos)	78666
Central (Angelina County)	75969
Central (Cherokee County)	75925
Central (Tarrant County)	76102
Central Gardens	77627
Central Heights (Jefferson County)	77627
Central Heights (Nacogdoches County)	75961
Centralia	75834
Central Mall (Bowie County)	75501
Central Mall (Jefferson County)	77640
Central Park (Bexar County)	78216
Central Park (Harris County)	77011
Central Unit	77478
Cestohowa	78113
Chaffee Village	76544
Chalk	79224
Chalk Bluff	76705
Chalk Mountain	76401
Chalybeate	75494
Chambersville	75069
Chambliss	75003
Champion Forest	77303
Champions	77034
Chandler	75758
Channelview	77530
Channelwood	77530
Channing	79018
Chapman	75652
Chapman Ranch	78347
Chappel	76877
Chappell Hill	77426
Charco	77963
Charleston	75450
Charlie	76308
Charlotte	78011
Chat	76645
Chateau Woods	77301
Chatfield	75105
Cheapside	77952
Cheek	77705
Cherokee	76832
Cherry Spring	78624
Chester	75936
Chesterville	77435
Chico	76030
Chicota	75425
Chief	75142
Chihuahua	78572
Childress	79201
Chillicothe	79225
Chilton	76632
China	77613
China Grove (Bexar County)	78223
China Grove (Scurry County)	79526
China Spring	76633
Chinati	79843
Chireno	75937
Chita	75862
Choate	78119
Chocolate Bayou	77511

	ZIP
Choice	75935
Chriesman	77838
Christine	78012
Christoval	76935
C H Rouse Estates	77365
Church Hill (Cherokee County)	75766
Church Hill (Rusk County)	75652
Churchill Bridge	77422
Cibolo	78108
Cielo Vista Mall (Part of El Paso)	79925
Circle	79064
Circle Back	79371
Circleville	76574
Cisco	76437
Cistern	78941
Citrus City	78572
Citrus Grove	77465
Civic Center (Part of Houston)	77208
Clairemont	79549
Clairette	76457
Clardy	75468
Clarendon	79226
Clareville	78102
Clark	77327
Clarks	77979
Clarksville	75426
Clarksville City	75647
Clarkwood (Part of Corpus Christi)	78406
Claude	79019
Clauene	79336
Clawson	75901
Clay	77839
Clayton (Jefferson County)	77627
Clayton (Panola County)	75637
Claytonville (Fisher County)	79556
Claytonville (Swisher County)	79052
Clear Creek	76544
Clear Lake City (Part of Houston)	77062
Clear Lake Shores	77565
Clear Spring	78130
Clearview	78602
Clearwater	75480
Cleburne	76031-33
For specific Cleburne Zip Codes call (817) 645-3991	
Clegg	78022
Clemens Unit	77422
Clemons	77423
Clemville	77414
Cleveland	77327-28
For specific Cleveland Zip Codes call (713) 592-3951	
Clever Creek	75935
Cliffside	79106
Clifton (Bosque County)	76634
Clifton (Van Zandt County)	75169
Climax	75077
Cline	78801
Clint	79836
Clinton (De Witt County)	77954
Clinton (Hunt County)	75005
Clodine	77469
Close City	79356
Cloverleaf	77015
Club Lake Estates	75708
Clute	77531
Clyde	79510
Coady	77520
Coahoma	79511
Coal Mine (Part of Lytle)	78052
Cobb Creek	75852
Cobb Switch	75160
Cocenter (Part of Pampa)	79065
Cochran	77418
Cockrell Hill	75211
Coffee City	75763
Coffeeville	75683
Coffield Unit	75861
Coit	76653
Coke	75431
Coldhill	75708
Coldspring	77331
Coleman	76834
Coleman Cove	75929
Colfax	75103
College Country Estates	75020
College Hill	75559
Collegeport	77428
College Station	77840-45
For specific College Station Zip Codes call (409) 693-4152	
Colleyville	76034
Collin Creek Mall (Part of Plano)	75075
Collinsville	76233

	ZIP
Colmesneil	75938
Cologne	77901
Colonial (Part of Waco)	76707
Colonies North (Part of San Antonio)	78201
Colony	78941
Colorado City	79512
Colton	78744
Columbus	78934
Comal	78130
Comanche	76442
Comanche Cove	76048
Comanche Harbor	76048
Combes	78535
Combine	75159
Comfort	78013
Commerce	75428
Como	75431
Comstock	78837
Comyn	76444
Concan	78838
Concepcion	78349
Concho	76866
Concord (Cherokee County)	75789
Concord (Leon County)	77850
Concord (Morris County)	75571
Concord (Rusk County)	75681
Concrete	77954
Cone	79321
Congress Square (Part of Austin)	78745
Conlen	79022
Connor	77864
Conroe	77301-05
	77384-85
For specific Conroe Zip Codes call (409) 756-8908	
Constitution Village (Part of Sherman)	75095
Content	79519
Converse	78109
Conway	79068
Cooks Point	77836
Cookville	75558
Cool	76086
Coolidge	76635
Cooper	75432
Cooper Creek	76201
Copano Village	78382
Copeland	75701
Copeville	75018
Coppell	75019
Copperas Cove	76522
Copper Canyon	76226
Corbet	75110
Cordele	77957
Corine	75766
Corinth (Denton County)	76201
Corinth (Eastland County)	76437
Corinth (Jones County)	79553
Corinth (Leon County)	75831
Corinth (Van Zandt County)	75140
Corley	75567
Cornersville	75494
Cornett	75568
Cornudas	79847
Coronado (Part of El Paso)	79912
Coronado Center (Part of Pampa)	79065
Corpus Christi	78401-82
For specific Corpus Christi Zip Codes cal (512) 657-8302	
Corral City	76226
Corrigan	75939
Corry	79041
Corsicana	75110
Corsicana Junction (Part of Corsicana)	75110
Coryell	76689
Cost	78614
Cotton Center (Fannin County)	75418
Cotton Center (Hale County)	79021
Cottondale	76073
Cotton Flat	79701
Cotton Gin	75860
Cotton Mill Spur (Part of Denison)	75020
Cottonwood (Calahan County)	79504
Cottonwood (Falls County)	76655
Cottonwood (Kaufman County)	75158
Cottonwood (Lamar County)	75460
Cottonwood (Madison County)	77864
Cottonwood Shores	78654
Cotulla	78014
Coughran	78064

Country Campus-De Soto **TEXAS** **537**

	ZIP		ZIP		ZIP
Country Campus	77340	Curvitas	78565	Hyatt Regency Dallas	75207
Country Club Estates (Part of Odessa)	79760	Cushing	75760	Lexington Hotel Suites	75237
		Cusseta	75566	Loews Anatole Hotel	75207
Country Club Terrace (Potter County)	79106	Cut	75835	Plaza of the Americas Hotel	75201
		Cut and Shoot	77302	Preston House All Suites Hotel	75240
Country Club Terrace (Victoria County)	77901	Cuthand	75417	Sheraton Dallas Hotel	75201
		Cuthbert	79512	Sheraton Park Central Hotel & Towers	75251
Country Colony	77372	Cyclone	76519	
Country Place Acres	77355	Cypress (Franklin County)	75494	Stouffer Dallas Hotel	75207
Countryside Plaza (Part of San Antonio)	78216	Cypress (Harris County)	77429	The Summit Hotel	75234
		Cypress Bend	77040	
Country Squire Estates	77630	Cypress Cove	78130	*MILITARY INSTALLATIONS*
County Line (Camp County)	75686	Cypress Creek	78028	
County Line (Cochran County)	79346	Cypress Creek Estates	77429	Naval Air Station, Dallas	75211
		Cypress Mill	78654	Texas Air National Guard, FB6431	75211
County Line (Hale County)	79363	Dabney	78801	
Coupland	78615	Da Costa	77901	United States Army Corp. of Engineers, Southwestern Division	75242
Courtney	77868	Dacus	77356	
Cove	77520	Daingerfield	75638	
Cove City (Part of Orange)	77630	Daisetta	77533	
Cove Spring	75766	Dalby Springs	75559	Dallas-Fort Worth Airport (Part of Coppell)	75261
Covington	76636	Dale	78616	
Covington Woods	77478	Dalhart	79022	Dalrock	75088
Cox	75644	Dallardsville	77332	Dalton	75568
Coyanosa	79730			Dalworthington Gardens	76010
Coy City	78118	**Dallas**	75201-99 75301-98	Dalys	75844
Cozy Corner	78945			Dam B	75979
Crabb	77469	For specific Dallas Zip Codes call (214) 647-2996		Damon	77430
Crabbs Prairie	77340			Danbury	77534
Craft	75766	*COLLEGES & UNIVERSITIES*		Danciger	77431
Crafton	76030			Danevang	77432
Crandall	75114	Bishop College	75241	Danville (Collin County)	75069
Crane	79731	Dallas Baptist University	75211	Danville (Gregg County)	75662
Cranfills Gap	76637	Dallas Theological Seminary	75204	Daphne	75455
Crawford	76638	Southern Methodist University	75275	Darco	75670
Creagleville	75140			Darrouzett	79024
Creechville	75119	University of Texas Health Science Center at Dallas	75235	Daugherty	75440
Creedmoor	78747			Davenport	75412
Creekwood Acres	77375	*FINANCIAL INSTITUTIONS*		Davila	76523
Creekwood Addition	77372			Davisville (Angelina County)	75901
Crennelland	77650	Bright Banc Savings Association	75207	Davisville (Leon County)	75833
Crescent	77488			Dawn	79025
Crescent Heights	75751	Capital Bank	75206	Dawson	76639
Cresson	76035	Continental Bank	75214	Dayton	77535
Cresthaven (Part of San Antonio)	78213	Cullen/Frost Bank of Dallas, N.A.	75201	Dayton Lakes	77535
				Deadwood	75633
Crestwood (Ector County)	79762	Deposit Insurance Bridge Bank, N.A.	75201	Dean (Clay County)	76301
Crestwood (Marion County)	75630			Dean (Hockley County)	79363
Crestwood Farms	77356	First City Bank of Dallas	75228	Deanville	77852
Crews	79567	First City, Texas-Dallas	75201	De Berry	75639
Crimcrest (Part of Henderson)	75652	First Interstate Bank of Texas, N.A.	75214	Decatur	76234
				Decker (Nolan County)	79506
Cripple Creek Farms (Montgomery County)	77355	Grand Bank	75201	Decker (Travis County)	78653
		Hibernia National Bank in Dallas	75201	Decker Prairie	77355
Cripple Creek Farms (Montgomery County)	77362			De Cordova Bend Estates	76048
		Inwood National Bank	75209	Deep Water Point Estates	75018
Cripple Creek Farms West	77362	Metropolitan Financial Savings & Loan Association	75206	Deer Creek	76365
Cripple Creek North	77355			Deer Haven	78654
Crisp	75119			Deer Park	77536
Crockett	75835	Montfort Savings Association, F.S.A.	75240	De Kalb	75559
Crosby	77532			Delbert L. Atkinson (Part of Pasadena)	77505
Crosbyton	79322	Murray Savings Association	75240	
Cross (Grimes County)	77861	North Dallas Bank & Trust Company	75230	De Leon	76444
Cross (McMullen County)	78026			Delhi	78953
Cross Cut	76801	Northpark National Bank of Dallas	75225	Delia	76635
Crossing (Part of De Soto)	75115			Dell City	79837
Cross Plains	76443	Southwest Savings Association	75201	Del Mar Hills	78040
Crossroads (Camp County)	75686			Delmita	78536
Cross Roads (Cass County)	75656	Texas American Bridge Bank, National Association	75235	Del Monte	77627
Crossroads (Cass County)	77962			Delray	75633
Cross Roads (Delta County)	75432			Del Rio	78840-42
Cross Roads (Denton County)	76227	Texas Commerce Bank- Dallas, National Association	75201	For specific Del Rio Zip Codes call (512) 775-3571	
Crossroads (Harrison County)	75670			Delrose	75644
		United National Bank	75201	Del Valle	78617
Cross Roads (Henderson County)	75148	*HOSPITALS*		Demi-John Island	77541
				Democrat (Comanche County)	76442
Cross Roads (Milam County)	76520	Baylor University Medical Center	75246	Democrat (Mills County)	76442
				De Moss (Part of Houston)	77074
Cross Roads (Rusk County)	75662	Dallas County Hospital District-Parkland Memorial Hospital	75235	Denhawken	78160
Croton	79232			Denison	75020-21
Crow	75765			For specific Denison Zip Codes call (214) 465-1464	
Crowell	79227	Humana Hospital-Medical City Dallas	75230	
Crowley	76036			Denning	75972
Cruz Calle	78349	Methodist Medical Center	75208	Dennis	76037
Cryer Creek	75102	Presbyterian Hospital	75231	Denny	76653
Crystal Beach	77650	RHD Memorial Medical Center	75234	Denson Springs	75844
Crystal City	78839			Denton (Denton County)	76201-06
Crystal Creek Forest	77301	St. Paul Medical Center	75235	For specific Denton Zip Codes call (817) 387-8555	
Crystal Lake	75801	Veterans Administration Medical Center	75216	
Crystal Lakes Estates	77351			Denton (Callahan County)	79510
Cuadrilla	79836	*HOTELS/MOTELS*		Denver City	79323
Cuero	77954			Denver Harbor (Part of Houston)	77020
Cullen Mall (Part of Corpus Christi)	78412	Adolphus Hotel	75202	
		Dallas Hilton Inn	75206	Deport	75435
Culleoka	75069	Dallas Marriott Market Center	75207	Derby	78017
Cumby	75433			Dermott	79549
Cundiff	76056	Doubletree Hotel	75206	Desdemona	76445
Cuney	75759	Fairmont Hotel at the Dallas Arts District	75201	Desert	75004
Cunningham	75434			De Soto	75115
Curtis	75951	Holiday Inn Brook Hollow	75247		

538 TEXAS Dallas

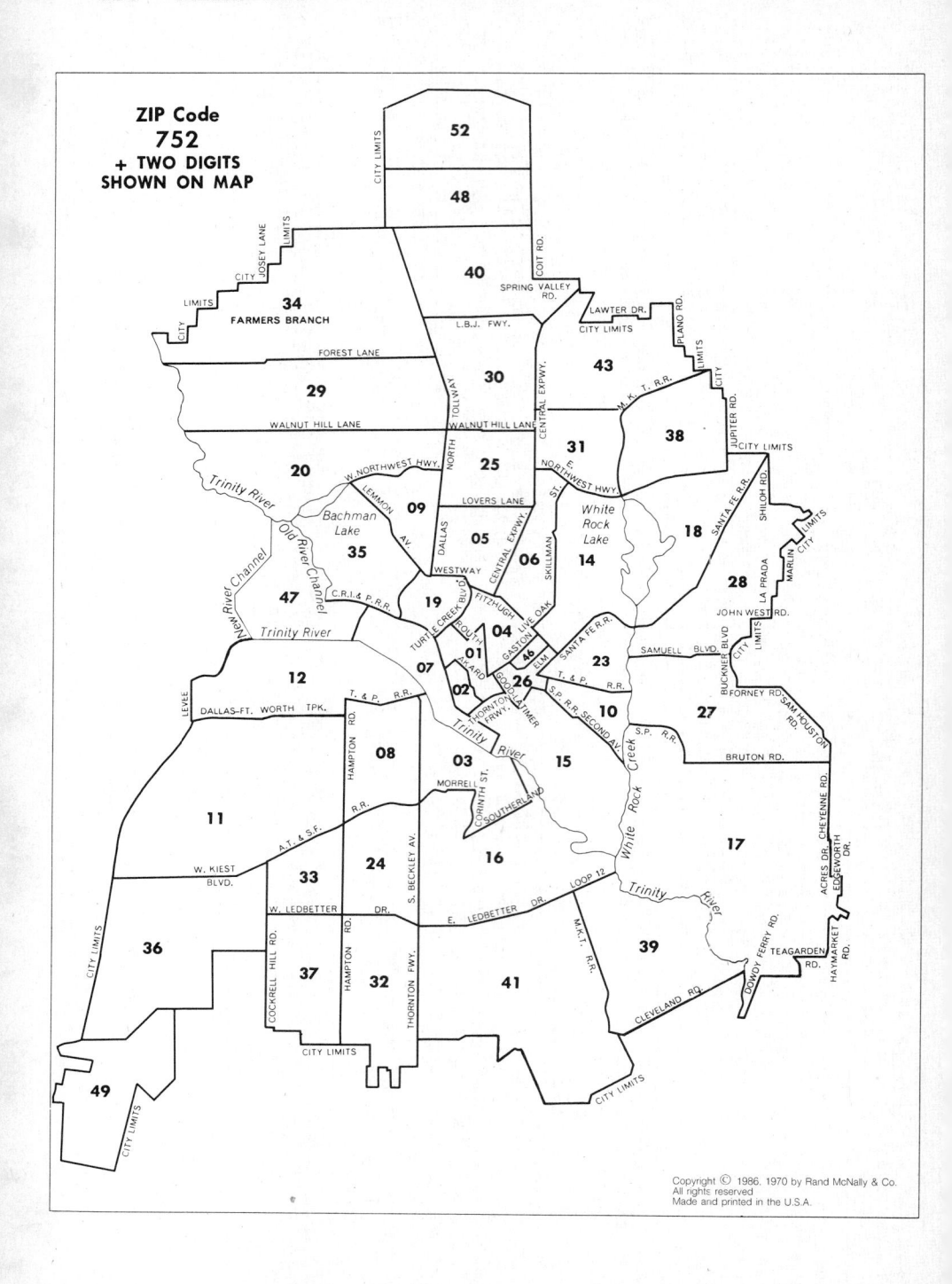

ZIP Code 752 + TWO DIGITS SHOWN ON MAP

Dessau-Enloe **TEXAS** 539

	ZIP		ZIP		ZIP
Dessau	78751	Driners	75937	Edmonson	79032
Detmold	76577	Dripping Springs	78620	Edna	77957
Detroit	75436	Driscoll	78351	Edna Hill	76446
Devers	77538	Drop	76247	Edom	75756
Devils Pocket	77612	Dryden	78851	Edroy	78352
Devine	78016	Dubina	78956	Egan	76031
Dew	75860	Dublin	76446	Egypt (Leon County)	75833
Dewalt	77478	Dudley	79601	Egypt (Montgomery County)	77355
Dewees	78114	Duffau	76447	Egypt (Wharton County)	77436
Deweyville	77614	Dugas Addition	77611	Elam Springs	75755
Dewville	78140	Dugger	78155	Elbert	76359
Dexter	76240	Dumas	79029	El Calmino	75948
Dextra	75760	Dumont	79232	El Campo	77437
D'Hanis	78850	Dunbar	75440	El Campo Club	77465
Dial (Fannin County)	75446	Duncanville	75116	El Campo South	77437
Dial (Hutchinson County)	79007		75137-38	El Centro (Part of Laredo)	78040
Dialville	75785	For specific Duncanville Zip Codes call (214) 298-3603		El Centro Mall (Part of Pharr)	78577
Diamondhead	77356			Eldorado	76936
Diana	75640	Dundee	76366	Eldorado Center	76639
Diboll	75941	Dunlap	79248	Eldridge (Part of Sugar Land)	77478
Dicey	76086	Dunlay	78861		
Dickens	79229	Dunn	79516	Electra	76360
Dickinson	77539	Dunnan (Part of Houston)	77022	Electric City	79007
Dido	76179	Duplex	75447	Elevation	76556
Dies	75979	Durango	76656	El Gato	78516
Dike	75437	Durwood Hills (Part of Grapevine)	76051	Elgin	78621
Dilley	78017			Eliasville	76038
Dilworth	78629	Duster	76444	El Indio	78860
Dime Box	77853	Dye Mound	76265	El Jardin (Part of Brownsville)	78520
Dimmitt	79027	Dyersdale	77016		
Dimple	75426	Eagle Lake	77434	El Jardin Del Mar (Part of Pasadena)	77586
Dinero	78350	Eagle Mountain	76135		
Ding Dong	76541	Eagle Mountain Acres	76020	Elk	76624
Dinsmore	77488	Eagle Pass	78852-53	Elkhart	75839
Direct	75486	For specific Eagle Pass Zip Codes call (512) 773-3210		El Lago	77586
Dirgin	75691			Ellinger	78938
Divide	75420	Earles Chapel	75764	Ellington Air Force Base (Part of Houston)	77209
Divot	78017	Earlis Camp	79521		
Dixie (Grayson County)	76273	Early	76801	Elliott (Robertson County)	77859
Dixie (Jasper County)	75951	Earlywine	77833	Elliott (Wilbarger County)	76364
Dixon	75401	Earth	79031	Ellis Unit	77340
Doans	76384	East Afton	79220	Elmaton	77440
Dobbin	77333	East Amarillo (Part of Amarillo)	79104	Elmdale	79605
Dobrowolski	78026			Elmendorf	78112
Dodd	79347	East Austin (Part of Austin)	78702	Elm Flat	75144
Dodd City	75438	East Bernard	77435	Elm Grove (Cherokee County)	75785
Dodge	77334	East Caney	75482		
Dodson	79230	East Columbia	77486	Elm Grove (Fayette County)	78959
Dogwood	75979	East Delta	75450	Elm Grove (San Saba County)	76872
Dogwood Acres (Part of Houston)	77022	East Direct	75486		
		East Donna (Part of Donna)	78537	Elm Grove (Wharton County)	77434
Dolen	77327	Easterly	77856		
Domino	75572	Eastex Oaks Village (Part of Houston)	77338	Elm Mott	76640
Donie	75838			Elmo	75118
Donna	78537	East Fork	75069	Elmont	75095
Doole	76836	Eastgate	77535	Elm Ridge (Grayson County)	75020
Dorchester	75059	East Grand (Part of Dallas)	75223		
Doss	78618	East Hamilton	75973	Elm Ridge (Milam County)	76520
Dot	76524	East Houston (Part of Houston)	77028	Elmwood (Anderson County)	75801
Dothan	76437				
Dotson	75669	Eastland	76448	Elmwood (Guadalupe County)	78155
Double Bayou	77514	East Liberty	75935		
Double Diamond Estates	79036	East Mayfield (Part of Hemphill)	75948	Eloise	76680
Double Oak	76226			El Oso	78119
Doucette	75942	East Mountain	75644	El Paso (El Paso County)	79901-99
Dougherty	79231	Easton	75641	For specific El Paso Zip Codes call (915) 775-7542	
Douglass	75943	East Point	75494		
Douglassville	75560	East Ridge (Part of Amarillo)	79107	El Paso (Fisher County)	79543
Downing	76442	East Side	75639	El Pinon Estates	75929
Downsville	76706	East Tawakoni	75453	El Rancho	79760
Downtown (Bexar County)	78205	East Tempe	77351	El Rancho Estates	76008
Downtown (Brazoria County)	77541	East Texas (Part of Commerce)	75428	El Refugio	78582
				Elroy	78617
Downtown (Brazos County)	77801	East View (Part of Kilgore)	75662	Elsa	78543
Downtown (Cameron County)	78520	Eastview Terrace	78101	El Sauz	78582
		Eastwood (El Paso County)	79925	Elstone	78861
Downtown (Part of Irving) (Dallas County)	75060	Eastwood (Harris County)	77023	El Toro	77957
		Eaton	77856	Elwood (Fannin County)	75447
Downtown (Part of Dallas) (Dallas County)	75201	Ebenezer (Camp County)	75686	Elwood (Madison County)	75852
		Ebenezer (Jasper County)	75951	Ely	75439
Downtown (El Paso County)	79901	Ebony	76864	Elysian Fields	75642
Downtown (Gregg County)	75601	Echo (Coleman County)	76834	Emberson	75486
Downtown (Hidalgo County)	78501	Echo (Orange County)	77630	Emblem	75482
Downtown (Lubbock County)	79401	Echo Hills	75763	Emerald Valley	78250
		Eckert	78675	Emhouse	75110
Downtown (McLennan County)	76701	Ecleto	78111	Emmett	76641
		Ector	75439	Emory	75440
Downtown (Nueces County)	78401	Edcouch	78538	Encantada	78586
Downtown (Potter County)	79105	Eddy (Part of Bruceville-Eddy)	76524	Enchanted Oaks (Harris County)	77373
Downtown (Smith County)	75702				
Doyle	76642	Eden	76837	Enchanted Oaks (Henderson County)	75147
Dozier	79079	Edgar	77954		
Drane	75110	Edge	77801	Encinal	78019
Drasco	79567	Edgecliff	76134	Encino	78353
Draw	79373	Edgewater Estates	78368	Energy	76452
Dreka	75973	Edgewood	75117	Engle	78956
Dresden	75102	Edgeworth	76569	English	75426
Dreyer	77984	Edhube	75418	Enloe	75441
Driftwood (Hays County)	78619	Edinburg	78539-40		
Driftwood (Henderson County)	75143	For specific Edinburg Zip Codes call (512) 383-3866			

540 TEXAS Ennis-Franklin

Name	ZIP
Ennis	75119-20
For specific Ennis Zip Codes call (214) 875-3894	
Enoch	75644
Enochs	79324
Ensign	75119
Enterprise (Cherokee County)	75766
Enterprise (Van Zandt County)	75169
Eola	76937
Eolian	76024
Era	76238
Erath	76708
Erin	75951
Erwin	77830
Esbon	76885
Escobares	78584
Escobas	78361
Eskota	79561
Esmond Estates (Part of Odessa)	79762
Esperanza	79839
Esperanza Crossing	79838
Esquire Estates	75147
Esseville	78008
Estacado (Crosby County)	79343
Estacado (Lubbock County)	79250
Estelline	79233
Estes	78382
Estes Addition	76071
Ethel	76233
Etoile	75944
Etter	79029
Eubank Acres	78753
Eula	79510
Eulalie	75975
Euless	76039-40
For specific Euless Zip Codes call (817) 283-6316	
Eulogy	76652
Eureka	75110
Eustace	75124
Evadale	77615
Evant	76525
Evergreen (Grimes County)	77861
Evergreen (San Jacinto County)	77327
Evergreen Park	77662
Everitt	77327
Everman	76140
Ewell	75644
Exchange Park (Part of Dallas)	75245
Exell	79058
Eylau	75501
Ezzell	77964
Fabens	79838
Fairbanks (Part of Houston)	77040
Fairchilds	77461
Fairfield	75840
Fairgreen	77039
Fairland	78654
Fairlie	75428
Fairmount	75948
Fairoaks	75838
Fair Oaks Ranch	78006
Fair Park (Part of Dallas)	75210
Fair Play	75631
Fairview (Bailey County)	79371
Fairview (Bosque County)	76689
Fairview (Brazos County)	77801
Fairview (Cass County)	75563
Fairview (Collin County)	75069
Fairview (Gaines County)	79360
Fairview (Harris County)	77006
Fairview (Howard County)	79720
Fairview (Nacogdoches County)	75961
Fairview (Rusk County)	75784
Fairview (Wilson County)	78114
Fairview (Wise County)	76078
Fairy	76457
Faker	75686
Falcon	78564
Falcon Heights	78545
Falcon Village	78545
Falfurrias	78355
Fallon	76667
Falls City	78113
Famuliner	79346
Fannett	77705
Fannin	77960
Fargo	76384
Farmer	76062
Farmers Branch	75234
Farmers Valley	76384
Farmersville	75031
Farmington	75058
Farnsworth	79033
Farr Addition	79756

Name	ZIP
Farrar	75838
Farrsville	75977
Farwell	79325
Fashing	78008
Fate	75032
Faught	75460
Faulkner	75416
Fawil	75928
Fayburg	75004
Fayetteville	78940
Faysville	78539
Federal Correctional Institution (Bastrop County)	78602
Federal Correctional Institution (Bowie County)	75501
Federal Correctional Institution (Dallas County)	75159
Federal Correctional Institution (Tarrant County)	76119
Federal Prison Camp	79720
Fedor	78947
Fellowship	75961
Fentress	78622
Ferris	75125
Fetzer	77363
Fiddlers Green	75034
Field Creek	76869
Fieldton	79326
Fife	76825
Files Valley	76055
Fincastle	75763
Fink	75076
Finney (Hale County)	79072
Finney (King County)	79248
Fischer	78623
Fish Branch	77371
Fisk	76834
Fitze	75946
Fitzhugh	78703
Five Points (El Paso County)	79903
Five Points (Ellis County)	75165
Flagg	79027
Flamingo Bay (Part of Seabrook)	77586
Flanagan	75691
Flat	76526
Flat Fork	75974
Flatonia	78941
Flat Prairie	77835
Flats	75472
Fleetwood Oaks	77079
Fletcher	77656
Flint	75762
Flint Creek	76046
Flo	75831
Flomot	79234
Flora	75437
Florence	76527
Florence Hill (Part of Grand Prairie)	75052
Floresville	78114
Florey	79714
Florine (Part of San Antonio)	78209
Flour Bluff (Part of Corpus Christi)	78418
Flowella	78355
Flower Mound	75067
Floy	78941
Floyd	75401
Floydada	79235
Fluvanna	79517
Flynn	77855
Fodice	75851
Follett	79034
Folley	79255
Foncine	75069
Fondren (Part of Webster)	77598
Foot	75069
Fords Corner	75972
Fordtran	77995
Forest	75925
Forestburg	76239
Forest Chapel	75411
Forest Glade	76667
Forest Grove (Collin County)	75069
Forest Grove (Henderson County)	75758
Forest Heights	77630
Forest Hill (Lamar County)	75446
Forest Hill (Potter County)	79107
Forest Hill (Tarrant County)	76119
Forest Hill (Wood County)	75783
Forest Hills (Part of Tyler)	75702
Forney	75126
Forreston	76041
Forsan	79733

Name	ZIP
Fort Bliss (census area only)	79916
Fort Bliss (U.S. Army)	79906
Fort Davis	79734
Fort Gates	76528
Fort Griffin	76430
Fort Hancock	79839
Fort Hood (Bell County)	76544
Fort McKavett	76841
Fort Ringgold	78582
Fort Spunky	76031
Fort Stockton	79735
Fort Worth	76101-85
For specific Fort Worth Zip Codes call (817) 625-3628	

COLLEGES & UNIVERSITIES

Name	ZIP
Southwestern Baptist Theological Seminary	76122
Texas Christian University	76129
Texas Wesleyan College	76105

FINANCIAL INSTITUTIONS

Name	ZIP
American Bank of Haltom City	76117
Bank of Commerce	76102
Central Bank & Trust	76104
Deposit Insurance Bridge Bank, N.A.	76102
First Interstate Bank of Texas, Nationa Association	76180
Landmark Bank of Fort Worth	76102
North Fort Worth Bank	76106
Nowlin Savings Association	76180
Overton Park National Bank	76109
Southwest Bank	76133
Summit National Bank	76102
Texas American Bridge Bank, N.A.	76113
Texas Commerce Bank-Fort Worth, National Association	76102

HOSPITALS

Name	ZIP
All Saints Episcopal Hospital of Fort Worth	76104
Harris Methodist-Fort Worth	76104
Medical Plaza Hospital	76104
Saint Joseph Hospital	76104
Tarrant County Hospital District	76104

HOTELS/MOTELS

Name	ZIP
Fort Worth Hilton	76102
Residence Inn by Marriott	76107
The Worthington	76102

MILITARY INSTALLATIONS

Name	ZIP
Carswell Air Force Base	76127
United States Army Engineer District, Fort Worth	76102
United States Property and Fiscal Office for Fort Worth	76108

Name	ZIP
Fort Worth Town Center (Part of Fort Worth)	76115
Forum 303 Mall (Part of Arlington)	76010
Foster (Fort Bend County)	77469
Foster (Terry County)	79316
Foster Hills	75951
Foster Place (Part of Houston)	77021
Foster Store	77836
Fouke	75765
Fountain View	77032
Four Corners (Brazoria County)	77422
Four Corners (Fort Bend County)	77469
Four Corners (Montgomery County)	77301
Four Points	78710
Four Way	79018
Fowlerton	78021
Fox	76086
Fox Landing	75938
Fox Run	77373
Foxwood	77362
Frame Switch	76574
Francis (Part of West Orange)	77630
Francitas	77961
Frankel City	79714
Frankell	76470
Franklin	77856

Frankston-Grosvenor TEXAS 541

Name	ZIP
Frankston	75763
Fred	77616
Fredericksburg	78624
Fredonia (Gregg County)	75662
Fredonia (Mason County)	76842
Fredonia Hill (Part of Nacogdoches)	75961
Freedom (Part of-Lubbock)	79412
Freeland	76031
Freeneytown	75667
Freeport	77541
Freer	78357
Freestone	75838
Freeway Oaks Estates	77365
Freheit	78130
Frelsburg	78950
French Creek Village (Part of San Antonio)	78229
Frenstat	77836
Fresenius	77656
Fresno	77545
Freyburg	78956
Friday	75845
Friendship (Jasper County)	75966
Friendship (Lamb County)	79371
Friendship (Leon County)	75846
Friendship (Smith County)	75647
Friendship (Upshur County)	75644
Friendship (Van Zandt County)	75140
Friendswood	77546
Friona	79035
Frio Town	78061
Frisco	75034
Fritch	79036
Frog	75160
Frognot	75004
Frontier Lakes	77378
Fronton	78584
Frosa	76678
Frost	76641
Fruitland	76230
Fruitvale	75127
Frydek	77474
Frys Gap	75766
Fulbright	75436
Fuller Springs	75901
Fulshear	77441
Fulton	78358
Fulton Beach (Part of Fulton)	78358
Funston	79501
Furney Richardson	75860
Gail	79738
Gainesville	76240
Galena Park	77547
Galilee	77340
Gallatin	75764
Gallaway	71049
Galle	78638
Galleon Bay	78418
Galleria (Part of Dallas)	75240
Galleria, The (Part of Houston)	77056
Galveston	77550-54
For specific Galveston Zip Codes call (409) 763-1819	
Galvez Mall (Part of Galveston)	77551
Ganado	77962
Gano	76577
Garceno	78584
Garciasville	78547
Garden Acres (Part of Fort Worth)	76028
Garden City (Glasscock County)	79739
Garden City (Harris County)	77018
Gardendale (Ector County)	79758
Gardendale (La Salle County)	78014
Garden Oaks (Part of Houston)	77206
Garden Ridge	78218
Garden Valley (Childress County)	79238
Garden Valley (Smith County)	75771
Garden Villas	77901
Garfield (De Witt County)	78164
Garfield (Travis County)	78617
Garland	75040-48
For specific Garland Zip Codes call (214) 272-5541	
Garland (Bowie County)	75559
Garland (Red River County)	75550
Garner	76086
Garrett	75119
Garretts Bluff	75411
Garrison	75946
Garth	77520

Name	ZIP
Garvin	76023
Garwood	77442
Gary	75643
Garza Place	78745
Gasoline	79255
Gastonia	75114
Gatesville	76528
Gatesville Unit	76528
Gateway Shopping City (Part of Beaumont)	77701
Gatewood	77039
Gause	77857
Gay Hill (Fayette County)	78945
Gay Hill (Washington County)	77833
Geneva	75947
Geneva Estates	78736
Genoa (Part of Houston)	77034
George	77871
Georges Creek	76031
Georgetown	78626-28
For specific Georgetown Zip Codes call (512) 863-2325	
George West	78022
George W. Singer (Part of Lubbock)	79424
Georgia	75486
Gerald	76640
Germantz	78539
Geronimo	78115
Gethsemane	75657
Gholson	76705
Gibtown	76075
Giddings	78942
Gilchrist	77617
Giles	79237
Gill	75670
Gillett	78116
Gilliland	79260
Gilmer	75644
Gilpin	79370
Ginger	75410
Girard	79518
Girvin	79740
Givens	75460
Gladewater (Gregg County)	75647
Gladewater (Titus County)	75455
Glass	76690
Glaze City	77984
Glazier	79014
Glen Cove (Coleman County)	76834
Glen Cove (Galveston County)	77565
Glencrest (Part of Fort Worth)	76119
Glendale	75862
Glenfawn	75760
Glen Flora	77443
Glenn Heights	75115
Glenrio	88423
Glen Rose	76043
Glenwood (Potter County)	79103
Glenwood (Upshur County)	75644
Glidden	78943
Globe	75486
Glory	75460
Gober	75443
Godley	76044
Gold	78624
Golden	75444
Golden Beach	78643
Golden Triangle Mall (Part of Denton)	76201
Goldfinch	78005
Goldsboro	79519
Goldsmith	79741
Goldthwaite	76844
Goliad	77963
Golinda	76655
Gomez	79316
Gonzales	78629
Goober Hill	75973
Good Hope (Lavaca County)	77964
Good Hope (Shelby County)	75935
Goodland	79371
Goodlett	79252
Goodlow	75110
Goodlow Park	75144
Goodnight (Armstrong County)	79226
Goodnight (Navarro County)	75144
Goodrich	77335
Good Springs	75667
Goodville	76632
Gordon (Lynn County)	79356
Gordon (Palo Pinto County)	76453
Gordonville	76245
Goree	76363

Name	ZIP
Goree Unit	77340
Gorman	76454
Goshen	77340
Gossett	75143
Gouldbusk	76845
Grace	77422
Graceton	75644
Graford	76045
Graham (Garza County)	79356
Graham (Jasper County)	75951
Graham (Young County)	76046
Granbury	76048-49
For specific Granbury Zip Codes call (817) 573-5515	
Grand Bluff	75631
Grandfalls	79742
Grand Prairie	75050-53
For specific Grand Prairie Zip Codes call (214) 264-5751	
Grand Saline	75140
Grandview (Dawson County)	79351
Grandview (Gray County)	79039
Grandview (Johnson County)	76050
Grange Hall	75670
Granger	76530
Grangerland	77302
Granite Shoals	78654
Granjeno	78572
Granville W. Elder (Part of Houston)	77013
Grapeland	75844
Grapetown	78624
Grapevine	76051
Grassland	79356
Graves (Part of Midland)	79707
Gray	75657
Grayback	76360
Grayburg	77659
Grays Chapel	75801
Grays Prairie	75158
Graytown	78114
Green	78119
Green Acres	77058
Greenfield Acres	79762
Green Hill	75455
Green Lake	77979
Greenridge (Part of Houston)	77022
Greens Bayou (Part of Houston)	77015
Greens Camp	79521
Greenshores	78759
Greenspoint Mall (Part of Houston)	77018
Green Valley	76227
Greenview	75420
Greenview Hills (Part of Irving)	75062
Greenview Manor	77032
Greenville	75401
Greenville Avenue (Part of Dallas)	75206
Greenvine	77835
Greenway	78223
Greenway Plaza (Part of Houston)	77046
Greenwood (Hopkins County)	75478
Greenwood (Midland County)	79701
Greenwood (Parker County)	76086
Greenwood (Wise County)	76246
Greenwood Acres (Llano County)	78609
Greenwood Acres (Orange County)	77626
Greenwood Village	77093
Gregg	78653
Greggton (Part of Longview)	75601
Gregory	78359
Gresham	75703
Grey Forest	78023
Gribble (Part of Farmers Branch)	75234
Grice	75644
Griffin	75789
Griffing (Part of Port Arthur)	77640
Griffing Park (Part of Port Arthur)	77640
Griffith (Cochran County)	79346
Griffith (Ellis County)	76084
Grigsby	75935
Grit (Mason County)	76856
Grit (Rains County)	75410
Groceville	77301
Groesbeck	76642
Groom	79039
Grosvenor	76801

542 TEXAS Groves-Honey Grove

Name	ZIP
Groves	77619
Groveton	75845
Grow	79248
Gruenau	78164
Gruene	78130
Grulla	78548
Gruver	79040
Guadalupe	77901
Guadalupe Heights	78028
Guajillo	78332
Guerra	78360
Guilbeau (Part of San Antonio)	78204
Gulf Camp	79756
Gulfgate Shopping Center (Part of Houston)	77087
Gulfway (Part of Corpus Christi)	78412
Gum Springs (Cass County)	75560
Gum Springs (Harrison County)	75601
Gun Barrel City	75147
Gunsight	76437
Gunter (Grayson County)	75058
Gunter (Wood County)	75410
Gussettville	78022
Gustine	76455
Guthrie	79236
Guy	77444
Guys Store	75833
Hacienda Heights (Part of El Paso)	79915
Hackberry (Bexar County)	78210
Hackberry (Cottle County)	79248
Hackberry (Denton County)	75068
Hackberry (Garza County)	79356
Hackberry (Lavaca County)	78956
Hagansport	75487
Hagerville	75847
Hail	75492
Hainesville	75773
Halbert	75973
Hale Center	79041
Halesboro	75417
Halfway	79072
Hall (Marion County)	75657
Hall (Morris County)	75638
Hall (San Saba County)	76871
Hallettsville	77964
Halloway Heights	77047
Halls Bluff	75835
Hallsburg	76705
Halls Store	71007
Hallsville	75650
Haltom City	76117
Hamby	79601
Hamilton	76531
Hamlin	79520
Hamon	78629
Hampton	75936
Hamshire	77622
Hancock Oak Hills	78130
Hancock Shopping Center (Part of Austin)	78751
Handley (Part of Fort Worth)	76112
Hankamer	77560
Hannibal	76401
Hanover	76520
Hansford	79081
Hanson	75954
Happy	79042
Happy Hill	76009
Happy Hollow	78801
Happy Landing	75954
Happy Union	79072
Happy Valley	79756
Harbin	76446
Harbor Grove (Part of Hickory Creek)	75065
Harborlight	75948
Hardin	77561
Hardin-Simmons (Part of Abilene)	79601
Hardy	76265
Hare	76574
Hargill	78549
Harker Heights	76543
Harkeyville	76877
Harlandale (Part of San Antonio)	78214
Harlem	77469
Harleton	75651
Harlingen	78550-52
For specific Harlingen Zip Codes call (512) 423-1464	
Harmon	75446
Harmony (Anderson County)	75801
Harmony (Nacogdoches County)	75943
Harmony (Parker County)	76086
Harmony (Rusk County)	75684
Harmony Grove	77340
Harmony Hill	75691
Harper	78631
Harriet	76901
Harrisburg (Harris County)	77012
Harrisburg (Jasper County)	75951
Harrisdale	79760
Harrison	76682
Harrold	76364
Hart	79043
Hartburg	77630
Hart Camp	79339
Hartley	79044
Hart Spur (Part of Hurst)	76053
Hartzo	75657
Harvard	75686
Harvest Acres	77372
Harvest Heights	77088
Harvey	77801
Harveytown	75951
Harwood	78632
Haskell	79521
Haslam	75954
Haslet	76052
Hasse	76456
Hatchel	79567
Hatchetville	75437
Havana	78572
Hawkins	75765
Hawkinsville	77414
Hawley	79525
Hawthorne	77358
Hayden	75169
Haynesville	76360
Hays	78666
Hazy Hollow	77355
Headlea Estates (Part of Odessa)	79762
Headsville	76653
Heald	79057
Hearne	77859
Heath	75087
Hebbronville	78361
Hebco (Part of San Antonio)	78218
Hebron	75067
Heckville	79329
Hedley	79237
Hedwig Village	77024
Hefner	76363
Heidelberg	78570
Heidenheimer	76533
Heights (Galveston County)	77590
Heights (Harris County)	77008
Helena	78118
Helmic	75845
Helotes	78023
Helotes Park Estates	78023
Helotes Ranch Acres	78023
Hemphill	75948
Hempstead	77445
Henderson	75652-53
For specific Henderson Zip Codes call (214) 657-1481	
Henderson Chapel	76866
Henderson Heights	79763
Henkhaus	77984
Henly	78620
Henning	75946
Henrietta	76365
Henrys Chapel	75789
Hereford	79045
Heritage Northwest	78245
Heritage Oaks	77365
Hermleigh	79526
Herring (Part of San Angelo)	76901
Herty (Part of Lufkin)	75901
Hester	75110
Hewitt	76643
Hext	76848
Hickey	75667
Hickory	75929
Hickory Creek (Denton County)	75065
Hickory Creek (Hunt County)	75423
Hickory Hill	75686
Hickory Hills	77356
Hickston	78959
Hico	76457
Hidalgo	78557
Hidden Echo	77336
Hidden Forest	78232
Hidden Hill	75065
Hidden Hills Harbor	75147
Hidden Valey	78759
Hidden Valley (Part of Houston)	77088
Higginbotham	79360
Higgins	79046
Highbank	76680
High Hill	78956
High Island	77623
Highland (Erath County)	76446
Highland (Johnson County)	76031
Highland Acres (Grayson County)	75076
Highland Acres (Harris County)	77018
Highland Acres (Hunt County)	75453
Highland Addition (Harris County)	77018
Highland Addition (Parker County)	76082
Highland Bayou	77563
Highland Estates (Part of Victoria)	77901
Highland Hills (Bexar County)	78223
Highland Hills (Dallas County)	75241
Highland Mall (Part of Austin)	78757
Highland Oaks	78758
Highland Park	75205
Highlands	77562
Highland Village	75067
Highland Waters	78003
Highpoint	77093
Highsaw	75763
Hi Ho	77630
Hiland Shores	75076
Hill	78602
Hill and Dale Acres	77372
Hill City	76476
Hill Country Village	78232
Hillcrest	77511
Hillebrandt	77705
Hillister	77624
Hillje	77455
Hills	78659
Hillsboro	76645
Hillside Estates	75763
Hillside Gardens	77039
Hilltop (Coryell County)	76528
Hilltop (Gillespie County)	78624
Hilltop (Grayson County)	75020
Hilltop Lakes	77871
Hilshire Village	77055
Hinckley	75460
Hindes	78026
Hines	76384
Hinkles Ferry	77422
Hiram	75169
Hitchcock	77563
Hitchland	73942
Hoard	75773
Hobbs	79526
Hobson	78117
Hochheim	77967
Hockley	77447
Hodges	79525
Hodgson	75559
Hoen	76691
Hogan Acres	76028
Hogansville	75410
Hogg	77836
Holiday Estates	75169
Holiday Harbor	75630
Holiday Hills	75453
Holiday Lake Estates	77335
Holiday Lakes	77515
Holiday Oaks	77372
Holland (Bell County)	76534
Holland (Hardin County)	77625
Holland Quarters	75633
Holliday	76366
Hollis	77864
Holly	75851
Holly Grove	77351
Holly Springs (Camp County)	75686
Holly Springs (Jasper County)	75951
Holly Springs (Nacogdoches County)	75946
Holly Springs (Van Zandt County)	75754
Holly Terrace	77365
Hollywood Addition	77627
Hollywood Heights	77627
Hollywood Park	78232
Holman	78962
Holt	76872
Homer (Angelina County)	75901
Homer (Jasper County)	75951
Homewood	75951
Hondo	78861
Honea	77356
Honey Grove (Cass County)	75551

Honey Grove-Jarrell **TEXAS** 543

	ZIP
Honey Grove (Fannin County)	75446
Honey Island	77625
Hood	76240
Hooks	75561
Hoover	79065
Hoovers Valley	78611
Hope	77995
Hopewell (Franklin County)	75457
Hopewell (Houston County)	75835
Hopewell (Leon County)	75833
Horizon City	79917
Horn Hill	76642
Hornsby Bend	78725
Horseshoe Bay	78654
Hortense	77351
Horton (Delta County)	75428
Horton (Jasper County)	75951
Horton (Panola County)	75639
Hostetter Creek Estates	77358
Hostyn	78945
Hot Wells	79851
Houmont Park	77044
Houseman Addition	77662
Houston	77001-99
	77101-99
	77201-93
For specific Houston Zip Codes call (713) 227-1474	

COLLEGES & UNIVERSITIES

Houston Baptist University	77074
Rice University	77251
South Texas College of Law	77002
Texas Southern University	77004
University of Houston-Clear Lake	77058
University of Houston-Downtown	77002
University of Houston-University Park	77004
University of St. Thomas	77006
University of Texas Health Science Center at Houston	77225

FINANCIAL INSTITUTIONS

American Bank	77002
BancPlus Savings Association	77002
BancTEXAS-Houston, National Association	77063
Bank of Houston	77002
Benjamin Franklin Savings Association	77056
Charter National Bank-Houston	77018
Commonwealth Savings Association	77024
Cullen Center Bank & Trust	77002
Deposit Guaranty Bank	77008
Deposit Insurance Bridge Bank, N.A.	77023
Enterprise Bank-Houston	77023
First Capital Savings Association of Texas	77240
First City, Texas-Houston, N.A.	77002
Guardian Savings & Loan Association	77057
Harrisburg Bank, Houston, Texas	77012
Home Savings Association	77056
Lockwood National Bank of Houston	77020
Med Center Bank	77030
Merchants Bank-Houston	77008
NCNB Texas National Bank	77002
Northwest Bank	77092
Post Oak Bank	77056
River Oaks Bank	77019
South Main Bank	77002
Texas American Bridge Bank, N.A.	77056
Texas Commerce Bank, National Association	77002
Texas Western Federal Savings & Loan Association	77027
United Savings Association of Texas	77027
Universal Savings Association	77229
University Savings Association	77079
University State Bank	77005
Village Savings Bank, FSB	77046

HOSPITALS

AMI Park Plaza Hospital	77004

	ZIP
AMI Twelve Oaks Hospital	77027
Harris County Hospital District	77019
Hermann Hospital	77030
Houston Northwest Medical Center	77090
Memorial City Medical Center	77024
Memorial Hospital System	77074
The Methodist Hospital	77030
HCA Spring Branch Memorial Hospital	77055
St. Joseph Hospital	77002
St. Luke's Episcopal Hospital	77030
Texas Children's Hospital	77030
University of Texas M.D. Anderson Cancer Center	77030
Veterans Administration Medical Center	77030

HOTELS/MOTELS

Adam's Mark Hotel	77042
Embassy Suites Hotel	77074
Four Seasons Hotel, Houston Center	77010
Holiday Inn Crowne Plaza-Galleria	77027
Holiday Inn-Intercontinental Airport	77032
Hotel Luxeford	77054
Hotel Sofitel	77060
Houston Airport Marriott	77032
Hyatt Regency Houston	77002
The Marriott Houston Galleria	77056
Quality Inn-Intercontinental Airport	77205
The Remington On Post Oak Park	77027
Residence Inn Astrodome	77030
Sheraton Crown Hotel & Conference Center	77032
The Westchase Hilton & Towers	77042
The Westin Galleria	77056
The Westin Oaks	77056

MILITARY INSTALLATIONS

Ellington Air National Guard Base	77034
Ellington Field, Texas Air National Guard, FB6433	77034
Lyndon B. Johnson Space Center (NASA)	77058

Howard	75165
Howardwick	79226
Howe	75059
Howland	75460
Hoxie	76574
Hoyt (Part of Alba)	75410
Hoyte	76520
Hub	79035
Hubbard	76648
Huckabay	76401
Hudson	75901
Hudson Oaks	76086
Huffines	75555
Huffman	77336
Hufsmith	77337
Hughes Springs	75656
Hughey	75662
Hulen Mall (Part of Fort Worth)	76132
Hulen Park (Part of Texas City)	77590
Hull	77564
Humble	77338-39
	77345-47
For specific Humble Zip Codes call (713) 446-3152	
Humble Camp	78377
Humble Heights (Part of Houston)	77338
Hungerford	77448
Hunt	78024
Hunter	78130
Hunters Creek Village	77024
Hunters Retreat	77355
Huntington	75949
Huntsville	77340-44
For specific Huntsville Zip Codes call (409) 295-7741	
Hurlwood	79407
Hurnville	76365
Huron	76627
Hurst	76053-54
For specific Hurst Zip Codes call (817) 647-2996	
Hurstown	75973

	ZIP
Hurst Springs	76634
Hutchins	75141
Hutto	78634
Huxley	75973
Huxley Bay	75973
Hye	78635
Hylton	79506
Iago	77420
Iatan	79565
Ida	75491
Idalou	79329
Idyle Hour Acres	78664
Ike	75165
Illinois Bend	76265
Impact	79603
Imperial	79743
Imperial Valley (Part of Houston)	77022
Inadale	79545
Independence	77833
India	75125
Indian Creek	76801
Indian Gap	76531
Indian Harbor Estates	76048
Indian Hill	75977
Indian Hills	78006
Indian Lake (Cameron County)	78586
Indian Lake (Newton County)	77630
Indian Lodge	76652
Indian Oaks	75163
Indianola	77979
Indian Rock	75644
Indian Shores	77532
Indian Springs	77351
Indian Trails (Part of Victoria)	77901
Indian Village	77351
Indian Woods	77355
Indio	79845
Industrial (Part of Dallas)	75207
Industry	78944
Inez	77968
Ingleside	78362
Ingleside on the Bay	78362
Ingram	78025
Ingram Park Mall (Part of San Antonio)	78238
Inks Lake Village	78609
Inwood (Part of Dallas)	75209
Inwood Forest (Part of Houston)	77088
Inwood Place	77016
Iola	77861
Iowa Colony	77583
Iowa Park	76367
Ira	79527
Iraan	79744
Irby	79521
Iredell	76649
Ireland	76538
Irene	76650
Ironton	75766
Irving	75015-16
	75038-39
	75060-63
For specific Irving Zip Codes call (214) 647-2996	
Irving Mall (Part of Irving)	75062
Irvington (Part of Houston)	77022
Isla	75959
Island (Galveston County)	77550
Island (Madison County)	75852
Italy	76651
Itasca	76055
Ivan	76024
Ivanhoe	75447
Iveys Crossing	79853
Ivy	76854
Izoro	76522
Jacinto City	77029
Jacksboro	76056
Jackson (Marion County)	75657
Jackson (Shelby County)	75954
Jackson (Van Zandt County)	75103
Jacksonville	75766
Jacobia	75401
Jacobs	75684
Jamaica Beach	77551
James	75935
James Moody (Part of Victoria)	77901
Jamestown (Newton County)	75966
Jamestown (Smith County)	75140
Jaques Spur (Part of Denison)	75020
Jardin	75428
Jarrell	76537

544 TEXAS Jarvis Christian College-Lakeview Estates

	ZIP		ZIP		ZIP
Jarvis Christian College	75765	Kelton	79096	Kyote	78005
Jasper	75951	Keltys (Part of Lufkin)	75901	Labatt	78114
Jasper Heights (Part of Marshall)	75670	Kemah	77565	La Blanca	78558
Jayton	79528	Kemp	75143	La Casita	78582
Jean	76374	Kempner	76539	Laceola	77864
Jeddo	78953	Kendalia	78027	Lackland AFB	78236
Jefferson	75657	Kendleton	77451	Lackland Heights	78227
Jefferson City Shopping Center (Part of Port Arthur)	77640	Kenedy	78119	La Coste	78039
		Kenefick	77535	La Cuchilla (Part of Mission)	78572
		Kennard	75847	Lacy	75845
Jenkins	75638	Kennedale	76060	Lacy-Lakeview	76705
Jennings	75460	Kennedy Shores	78520	Ladonia	75449
Jensen Drive (Part of Houston)	77026	Kenney	77452	LaFayette	75686
		Kensing	75450	La Feria	78559
Jensens Point	77465	Kent	79855	La Gloria	78591
Jericho	79226	Kentuckytown	75491	Lago	78586
Jermyn	76057	Kenwood Place	77339	Lago Vista	78645
Jerrys Quarters	77833	Kerens	75144	La Grange	78945
Jersey Village	77040	Kermit	79745	Laguna Heights	78578
Jerusalem	77422	Kerrick	79051	Laguna Park	76634
Jester Unit	77469	Kerrville	78028-29	Laguna Tres Estates	76048
Jewett	75846	For specific Kerrville Zip Codes call (512) 257-5040		Laguna Vista	78578
J. Frank Dobie (Part of San Antonio)	78220			Laguna Vista Estates	75751
		Kevin	77327	La Hacienda Estates	78759
Jiba	75142	Key	79331	Laird Hill	75666
Joaquin	75954	Key Ranch Estates	75163	La Isla	79838
Joe Pool (Part of Dallas)	75224	Kickapoo	75763	Lajitas	79852
John Allen (Part of Houston)	77007	Kildare	75562	La Joya	78560
John Foster (Part of Pasadena)	77502	Kildare Junction	75555	La Junta (Part of Reno)	76020
		Kilgore	75662-63	Lake Air Center (Part of Waco)	76710
Johnson	79316	For specific Kilgore Zip Codes call (214) 984-2313			
Johnson City	78636			Lake Barbara (Part of Clute)	77531
Johnsons Station (Part of Arlington)	76015	Killeen	76540-47	Lake Bonanza	77356
		For specific Killeen Zip Codes call (817) 634-0281		Lake Bridgeport	76026
Johnstown	75169			Lake Brownwood	76801
Johnsville	76401	Killeen Army Base	76544	Lake Chateau Woods	77302
Johntown	75417	Kilowatt (Part of Orange)	77630	Lake Cherokee	75652
Joiner	78945	Kimball	76652	Lake City	78387
Joinerville	75658	Kimbro	78653	Lake Conroe Forrest	77301
Joliet	78648	Kinard Estates	77630	Lake Conroe West	77301
Jolly	76301	King (Coryell County)	76528	Lake Corsicana (Part of Corsicana)	75110
Jollyville	78664	King (Red River County)	75550		
Jonah	78626	King City (Part of Cleveland)	77327	Lake Creek	75450
Jones	75140			Lake Creek Estates	77355
Jonesboro	76538	King Ranch	78363	Lake Dallas	75065
Jones Creek (Brazoria County)	77541	Kingsbury	78638	Lake Halbert (Part of Corsicana)	75110
		Kingsland	78639		
Jones Creek (Wharton County)	77437	Kingsland Estates	78639	Lakehills	78063
		Kingsley (Part of Garland)	75041	Lake Jackson	77566
Jones Prairie	76520	Kings Mill	79065	Lake Jackson Farms	77566
Jonestown	78645	Kingston	75401	Lake Kiowa	76240
Jonesville	75659	Kings Village	78664	Lakeland (Jasper County)	75931
Joplin	76056	Kingsville	78363-64	Lakeland (Montgomery County)	77302
Joppa	78605	For specific Kingsville Zip Codes call (512) 592-2801			
Josephine	75064			Lakeland Heights (Part of Grand Prairie)	75050
Joshua	76058	Kingsville Naval Station	78363		
Josserand	75845	Kingswood	75104	Lakeland Park	78759
Jot 'Em Down	75449	Kingtown	75961	Lake Livingston	77376
Jourdanton	78026	Kingwood	77339	Lake Meredith Estates	79036
Joy (Clay County)	76365	Kinkler	77964	Lake Pauline	79252
Joy (Smith County)	75647	Kiomatia	75436	Lake Placid	78155
Jozye	77864	Kirby	78219	Lakeport	75601
Jubilee Springs	76501	Kirbyville	75956	Lake Rolling Wood	77301
Jud	79544	Kirkland	79238	Lake Sam Raybum Estates	75968
Judson	75660	Kirkpatrick Addition	75704	Lake Shadows	77532
Juliff	77583	Kirtley	78957	Lake Shore	76801
Julius Melcher (Part of Houston)	77027	Kirvin	75848	Lakeshore Estates	75630
		Kittrell	75862	Lakeshore Estates West	75630
Junction	76849	Kleberg (Part of Dallas)	75253	Lake Shore Gardens	78368
Juno	76943	Klein	77379	Lakeside (Bexar County)	78222
Jupiter Pharmacy (Part of Richardson)	75080	Klondike (Dawson County)	79331	Lakeside (Galveston County)	77565
		Klondike (Delta County)	75448		
Justiceburg	79330	Klump	77833	Lakeside (Tarrant County)	76108
Justin	76247	Knapp	79527	Lakeside Beach	78669
Kadane Corner	76360	Knickerbocker	76939	Lakeside City	76308
Kalgary	79370	Knippa	78870	Lakeside Heights	78639
Kamay	76369	Knob Hill	75034	Lakeside Park	77530
Kamey	77979	Knollwood	75090	Lakeside Village	76671
Kanawha	75436	Knott	79748	Lake Splendora	77372
Karen	77355	Knox City	79529	Lake Tanglewood	79105
Karnack	75661	Knoxville	78631	Lake Tejas	77371
Karnes City	78118	Koerth	77964	Lake Thomas	79527
Katemcy	76850	Kohrville	77040	Laketon	79065
Katy	77449-50	Kokomo	76454	Lake Victor	76550
	77491-94	Komensky	77975	Lakeview (Cherokee County)	75766
For specific Katy Zip Codes call (713) 391-7958		Kona Kai	77650		
		Kopernik Shores	78520	Lakeview (Floyd County)	79235
Kaufman	75142	Kopperl	76652	Lakeview (Hall County)	79239
Kayare (Part of Harlingen)	78550	Kosciusko	78160	Lakeview (Jefferson County)	77640
Keechi	75831	Kosse	76653		
Keenan	77356	Kountze	77625	Lakeview (Lynn County)	79345
Keene	76059	Kovar	78941	Lakeview (McLennan County)	76705
Keeter	76023	Kress	79052		
Keith	77861	Kreutzberg	78006	Lakeview (Orange County)	77662
Keller	76248	Krugerville	76227		
Kellerville	79057	Krum	76249	Lakeview (Swisher County)	79088
Kelly	75003	Kubala Store	78164	Lakeview (Tarrant County)	76135
Kellyville	75657	Kurten	77862	Lakeview Estates (Johnson County)	76031
Kelsey (Jim Hogg County)	78353	Kuykendahl Village (Part of Houston)	77068		
Kelsey (Upshur County)	75644	Kyle	78640	Lakeview Estates (Orange County)	77662

Lakeview Estates-Lovelace   TEXAS   545

	ZIP		ZIP		ZIP
Lakeview Estates (Van Zandt County)	75169	League City	77573-74	Lively	75143
Lakeview Hills	78641	For specific League City Zip Codes call (713) 554-6281		Live Oak (Bexar County)	78233
Lakeview Park	78130			Liveoak (Palo Pinto County)	76462
Lakeway	78734	Leagueville	75778	Liverpool	77577
Lake Whitney Estates	76692	Leakey	78873	Livingston	77351
Lake Wildwood	77302	Leander	78641	Llano	78643
Lakewood (Dallas County)	75214	Leary	75501	Lobo	79855
Lakewood (Harris County)	75520	Lebanon	75034	Locker	76871
Lakewood (Orange County)	77662	Ledbetter	78946	Lockett	76384
Lakewood (San Augustine County)	75929	Ledbetter Hills (Part of Dallas)	75211	Lockettville	79358
Lakewood Estates	77304	Leedale	76569	Lockhart	78644
Lakewood Harbor	76634	Lees	79720	Lockney	79241
Lakewood Heights (Part of Houston)	77336	Leesburg	75451	Loco	79201
Lakewood Hills (Comal County)	78130	Leesville	78122	Locust	75076
		Lefors	79054	Locust Grove	79014
		Leggett	77350	Lodi	75564
		Legion (Part of Kerrville)	78028	Loeb	77656
Lakewood Hills (Hood County)	76048	Lehman	79346	Loebau	78948
		Leigh	75661	Logan (Marion County)	75657
Lakewood Village (Denton County)	76201	Lela	79079	Logan (Panola County)	71049
		Lelia Lake	79240	Log Cabin	75148
Lakewood Village (Travis County)	78731	Leming	78050	Log Cabin Estates	75148
		Lenorah	79749	Lohn	76852
Lake Worth	76135	Lenz	78118	Loire	78064
Lamar (Aransas County)	78382	Leo (Cooke County)	76234	Lois	76272
Lamar (Shelby County)	75935	Leo (Lee County)	78947	Lolaville	75034
Lamar Park (Part of Corpus Christi)	78411	Leona	75850	Lolita	77971
		Leonard	75452	Lollipop	75763
La Marque	77568	Leon Junction	76552	Loma	77876
Lamar University (Part of Beaumont)	77710	Leon Springs	78229	Loma Alta	78840
		Leon Valley	78238	Lomas de Arena	79843
Lamasco	75488	Leroy	76654	Loma Terrace (Part of El Paso)	79907
Lamesa	79331	Lesley	79259	Loma Vista	78829
Lamkin	76455	Letney Park	75951	Lomax (Harris County)	77571
Lampasas	76550	Le Tourneau (Part of Longview)	75601	Lomax (Howard County)	79720
Lamplight Village	78758			Lometa	76853
Lancaster	75146	Levelland	79336-38	Lomo Alta	78072
Landa Park Highlands (Part of New Braunfels)	78130	For specific Levelland Zip Codes call (806) 894-3250		London	76854
				Lone Camp	76072
Lane	75423	Leveretts Chapel	75684	Lone Cedar	76626
Lane City	77453	Levi	76655	Lone Elm	75165
Lanely	75831	Levita	76528	Lone Grove	78643
Laneport	76574	Lewis Addition	77465	Lone Mountain	75644
Lane Prairie	76031	Lewisville	75028-29 75056-57 75067	Lone Oak (Bexar County)	78101
Laneville	75667			Lone Oak (Colorado County)	78940
Langtry	78871			Lone Oak (Hunt County)	75453
Lanham	76538	For specific Lewisville Zip Codes call (214) 221-2755		Lone Pine	75801
Lanier	75563			Lone Star (Floyd County)	79241
Lannius	75438	Lexington	78947	Lone Star (Morris County)	75668
La Paloma	78586	Lexington Woods	77373	Lone Star (Titus County)	75558
La Plaza (Part of McAllen)	78501	Libby	75961	Long Branch (Eastland County)	76435
La Porte	77571-72	Liberty (Hamilton County)	76525		
For specific La Porte Zip Codes call (713) 471-0284		Liberty (Liberty County)	77575	Long Branch (Panola County)	75669
		Liberty (Lubbock County)	79401		
La Presa Crossing	79846	Liberty (Newton County)	75966	Longfellow	79848
La Pryor	78872	Liberty (Rusk County)	75652	Longford Place	77630
La Puerta	78582	Liberty City	75647	Long Hollow	77865
Laredo	78040-44	Liberty Grove	75098	Long Lake (Anderson County)	75801
For specific Laredo Zip Codes call (512) 723-2043		Liberty Hill (Houston County)	75844		
				Long Lake (Montgomery County)	77355
La Reforma	78536	Liberty Hill (Milam County)	76567		
Lariat	79325	Liberty Hill (Titus County)	75455	Long Mott	77972
Larue	75770	Liberty Hill (Williamson County)	78642	Long Point (Harris County)	77055
La Salle (Calhoun County)	77979			Long Point (Harrison County)	75661
La Salle (Jackson County)	77969	Liggett (Part of Irving)	75060		
Lasara	78561	Lilac	76577	Long Point (Washington County)	77835
Las Milpas	78577	Lilbert	75760		
Las Milpas-Hidalgo Park	78577	Lillian	76061	Longview	75601-15
Las Palmas (Part of San Antonio)	78237	Lily Grove	75961	For specific Longview Zip Codes call (214) 753-7644	
		Lily Island	75934		
Las Rusias	78586	Lincoln	78948	Longview Heights	75601
Lassater	75630	Lincoln Park	76227	Longview Mall (Part of Longview)	75601
Latch	75644	Lindale	75771		
Latexo	75849	Linden	75563	Longworth	79543
La Tijera	78537	Lindenau	77954	Lonoke Place	77093
La Tina	78586	Lindenwood	77630	Looneyville	75760
Latium	77835	Lindsay	76250	Loop	79342
Latonia	77422	Lindsay Addition	79772	Lopeno	78564
La Tuna	79821	Lingleville	76461	Lopezville	78589
Laughlin AFB	78840	Link Five (Part of La Porte)	77571	Loraine	79532
Laughlin Air Force Base	78840	Linkwood (Part of Leon Valley)	78229	Lorena	76655
Laureles	78586			Lorenzo	79343
Laurel Heights (Part of San Antonio)	78212	Linkwood Addition	76008	Los Angeles	78014
		Linn	78563	Los Barreras	78582
La Vernia	78121	Linn Flat	75961	Los Coyotes	78569
La Villa	78562	Linwood	75925	Los Ebanos	78565
Lavon	75066	Lipan	76462	Los Fresnos	78566
Lavon Beach Estates	75031	Lipscomb	79056	Los Indios	78567
La Ward	77970	Lissie	77454	Los Jardines (Part of San Antonio)	78237
Lawn	79530	Littig	78621		
Lawrence	75160	Little Boy	77662	Losoya	78221
Lawrence Park (Part of Amarillo)	79109	Little Elm	75068	Los Saenz (Part of Roma City)	78584
		Littlefield	79339		
Lawrence Springs	75140	Little Flock	77879	Lost Lakes	77357
Lawson	75149	Little Hope	75494	Los Velas	78582
Lazare	79252	Little Mexico	79735	Lott	76656
Lazbuddie	79053	Little New York	78629	Louise	77455
Leaday	76888	Little Ridge	75018	Love Chapel	75656
		Little River	76554	Lovelace	76645
		Little River-Academy	76513		

546 TEXAS Lovelady-Millett

	ZIP		ZIP		ZIP
Lovelady	75851	Mahl	75961	Megargel	76370
Lovell Lake	77706	Mahomet	78605	Megaron (Part of Lubbock)	79423
Loving	76062	Mahoney	75482	Melear (Part of Arlington)	76015
Lowake	76855	Main Place (Part of Dallas)	75202	Melissa	75071
Lowry Crossing	75069	Majors	75457	Melody Hills (Part of Fort Worth)	76111
Loyola Beach	78379	Malakoff	75148	Melrose (Gregg County)	75662
Lozano	78568	Mallard	76251	Melrose (Nacogdoches County)	75961
Lubbock	79401-99	Mall Del Norte (Part of Laredo)	78040	Melrose Heights	77018
For specific Lubbock Zip Codes call (806) 762-7804		Mall of Abilene (Part of Abilene)	79605	Melvin	76858
Lucas	75069	Malone	76660	Melwood Place	77016
Luckenbach	78624	Malta	75570	Memorial City Shopping Center (Part of Houston)	77024
Lucky Ridge	76023	Mambrino	76048	Memorial Park (Part of Houston)	77024
Lueders	79533	Manchaca	78652	Memphis	79245
Luella	75090	Manchester	75412	Menard	76859
Lufkin	75901-03	Manda	78653	Mendoza	78644
For specific Lufkin Zip Codes call (409) 634-7749		Manheim	78659	Menlow	76621
Luling	78648	Mankin	75163	Mentone	79754
Lull	78539	Mankins	76366	Mentz	78935
Lumberton	77711	Manor	78653	Mercedes	78570
Lums Chapel	79339	Manor East Shopping Center (Part of Bryan)	77801	Mercer's Gap	76442
Lund	78621	Mansfield	76063	Merchandise Mart (Part of Dallas)	75201
Luther	79720	Manvel	77578	Mercury	76872
Lutie	79079	Maple (Bailey County)	79344	Mereta	76940
Lydia	75554	Maple (Red River County)	75417	Meridian	76665
Lyford	78569	Maple Crest Acres (Part of Vidor)	77662	Merit	75072
Lynchburg	77520	Maple Springs	75455	Merkel	79536
Lyncrest	77086	Mapleton	75835	Merle	77879
Lyndon B. Johnson Space Center	77058	Marathon	79842	Mertens	76666
Lynn Grove	77868	Marble Falls	78654	Mertzon	76941
Lyons	77863	March Trailer Court	75169	Mesa	79838
Lytle	78052	Marfa	79843	Mesa Verde (Part of Amarillo)	79107
Lytton Springs	78616	Margaret	79227	Mesilla Park	79107
Mabank	75147	Marie	76933	Meskill (Part of Texas City)	77590
Mabelle	76380	Marietta	75566	Mesquite (Dallas County)	75149-50 75180-85
Mabry	75426	Marilee	75058	For specific Mesquite Zip Codes call (214) 288-4476	
McAdoo	79243	Marion	78124	Mesquite (Borden County)	79351
McAllen	78501-04	Markham	77456	Metcalf Gap	76475
For specific McAllen Zip Codes call (512) 686-1771		Markley	76062	Meusebach Creek	78624
McBeth	77515	Marlin	76661	Mexia	76667
McCamey	79752	Marquez	77865	Mexico	75474
Mc Caskills Crossing	79839	Marshall	75670-71	Meyerland Plaza Mall (Part of Houston)	77096
McCaulley	79534	For specific Marshall Zip Codes call (214) 938-4086		Meyersville	77974
McClanahan	76661	Marshall Creek	76262	Miami	79059
McCook	78539	Marshall Ford	78732	Michael Unit	75861
McCoy (Atascosa County)	78053	Marshall Meadows	78229	Mickey	79241
McCoy (Floyd County)	79235	Mart	76664	Mico	78056
McCoy (Panola County)	75643	Martindale	78655	Midcity	75473
McCreless Mall (Part of San Antonio)	78223	Martinez	78220	Middleton	75833
McDade	78650	Martin Luther King (Part of Houston)	77033	Middletowne (Part of Seguin)	78155
McDade Estates	77304	Martins Mills	75754	Middle Water	79022
Macdona	78054	Martin Springs	75482	Midfield	77458
Macedonia (Austin County)	77474	Martinsville	75958	Midkiff	79755
Macedonia (Bowie County)	75501	Marvin	75460	Mid Lake Village	75948
Macedonia (Brazoria County)	77422	Mary Hardin-Baylor (Part of Belton)	76513	Midland	79701-12
McElroy	75968	Maryneal	79535	For specific Midland Zip Codes call (915) 560-5105	
McFaddin	77973	Marysville	76252	Midline	77327
McGalin	77612	Mason	76856	Midlothian	76065
McGee Landing	75948	Mason Lake Estates	77327	Midway (Dawson County)	79331
McGregor	76657	Massey Lake	75861	Midway (Fannin County)	75418
McKenzie	75630	Masterson	79058	Midway (Hill County)	76645
McKibben	79081	Matador	79244	Midway (Jim Wells County)	78372
McKinney	75069-70	Matagorda	77457	Midway (Lavaca County)	77984
For specific McKinney Zip Codes call (214) 542-5031		Matagorda Beach	77457	Midway (Lubbock County)	79364
McLean	79057	Mathis	78368	Midway (Madison County)	75852
McLendon (Part of McLendon-Chisholm)	75087	Matinburg	75686	Midway (Montgomery County)	77327
McLendon-Chisholm	75087	Maud	75567	Midway (San Patricio County)	78390
McLeod	75565	Mauriceville	77626	Midway (Scurry County)	79526
McMahan	78616	Maverick	78865	Midway (Smith County)	75792
McMillin	76877	Maxdale	76544	Midway (Titus County)	75455
McMurray (Part of Abilene)	79605	Maxey	75421	Midway (Upshur County)	75644
McNair	77520	Maxwell	78656	Midway (Van Zandt County)	75754
McNair Village	76544	May	76857	Midyett	75639
McNary	79839	Maydelle	75772	Miguel	78005
McNeil (Caldwell County)	78648	Mayfair (Part of Houston)	77022	Milam	75959
McNeil (Travis County)	78651	Mayfield (Hale County)	79041	Milano	76556
McQueeney	78123	Mayfield (Hill County)	76055	Milburn	76872
Mc Rea Lake	77302	Mayflower (Newton County)	75977	Mildred	75110
Macune	75972	Mayflower (Rusk County)	75691	Mile High	79851
Macy	77882	Mayhill	76201	Miles	76861
Madero	78572	Maynard	77358	Milford	76670
Madisonville	77864	Maypearl	76064	Mill Creek	77833
Magasco	75968	Maysfield	76555	Mill Creek Forest	77355
Magic (Part of San Antonio)	78229	Meador Grove	76557	Miller Grove (Camp County)	75686
Magnet	77488	Meadow	79345	Miller Grove (Hopkins County)	75433
Magnolia	77355	Meadows	77477	Miller's Cove	75455
Magnolia Beach	77979	Meadow Village	78227	Millersview	76862
Magnolia Bend	77302	Meadow Wood Acres	78227	Millett	78014
Magnolia Gardens	77044	Mecca	77871		
Magnolia Grove	77371	Medicine Mound	79252		
Magnolia Hills	77355	Medill	75460		
Magnolia Springs	75957	Medina	78055		
Magpetco (Part of Port Neches)	77651	Medio (Part of Houston)	77022		
		Meek Estates	75163		
		Meeks	76519		

Millheim-Northeast TEXAS 547

Name	ZIP
Millheim	77474
Millican	77866
Milligan	75069
Millsap	76066
Millsville	78362
Millwood	75089
Milton	75435
Minden	75680
Mineola	75773
Mineral	78125
Mineral Wells	76067
Minerva	76567
Mings Chapel	75644
Mingus	76463
Minimaz (Part of Alvin)	77511
Minter	75468
Mirando City	78369
Mission	78572
Mission Valley	77901
Missouri City	77459
Mitchell Avenue (Part of Waco)	76708
Mixon	75789
Mobeetie	79061
Mobile Meadows Park	77630
Moffat	76501
Moffett	75901
Monadale	78634
Monahans	79756
Monaville	77445
Monkstown	75488
Monroe	75662
Monroe City	77514
Monroe Street (Part of Wichita Falls)	76309
Mont	77964
Montague	76251
Montalba	75853
Mont Belvieu	77580
Monte Alto	78538
Montell	78801
Monte Oaks	77357
Monteola	78119
Montfort	75110
Montgomery	77356
Montgomery Gardens	75708
Monthalia	78614
Monticello	75455
Moody	76557
Moonshine Hill	77338
Moore (Frio County)	78057
Moore (Jasper County)	75951
Moore's Chapel	75418
Moores Crossing	78617
Moore Station	75770
Mooresville	76632
Mooring	77801
Morales	77957
Moran	76464
Moravia	78956
Morgan	76671
Morgan Mill	76465
Morgan's Point	77571
Morgan's Point Resort	76513
Morrill	75925
Morris Ranch	78624
Morse	79062
Morton (Cochran County)	79346
Morton (Harrison County)	75640
Moscow	75960
Mosheim	76689
Moss Bluff	77575
Moss Hill	77575
Mostyn	77355
Moulton	77975
Mound	76558
Mound City	75844
Mountain	76528
Mountain City	78610
Mountain Home	78058
Mountain Peak	76065
Mountain Springs (Cooke County)	76258
Mountain Springs (Hill County)	76645
Mountain Valley Estates	76058
Mountain View Unit	76528
Mount Blanco	79322
Mount Calm	76673
Mount Carmel	76360
Mount Enterprise (Rusk County)	75681
Mount Enterprise (Wood County)	75773
Mount Haven	75766
Mount Houston	77016
Mount Joy	75432
Mount Lucas	78350
Mount Mitchell	75571
Mount Olive	77995
Mount Pleasant	75455

Name	ZIP
Mount Selman	75757
Mount Sylvan	75771
Mount Union	75956
Mount Vernon	75457
Mozelle	76834
Muddig	75449
Mudville	77801
Muellersville	77833
Muenster	76252
Mulberry	75476
Muldoon	78949
Muleshoe	79347
Mulkey	79027
Mullin	76864
Mullins Prairie	78945
Mumford	77867
Muncy	79241
Munday	76371
Munson	75089
Murchison	75778
Murphy	75073
Murray	76046
Murray (Part of Lubbock)	79413
Musgrove	75494
Mustang (Denton County)	76258
Mustang (Navarro County)	75110
Mustang Mott Store	77954
Mykawa Road (Part of Houston)	77033
Myra	76253
Myrtle Springs	75169
Naaman (Part of Garland)	75040
Nacalina	75944
Nacogdoches	75961-63
For specific Nacogdoches Zip Codes call (409) 564-3737	
Nada	77460
Nadeau (Part of Texas City)	77590
Nancy	75980
Naples	75568
Naruna	76550
Nash (Bowie County)	75569
Nash (Ellis County)	75165
Nassau Bay (Harris County)	77058
Nassau Bay (Hood County)	76048
Nat	75760
Natalia	78059
Natural Bridge Caverns	78218
Naval Air (Part of Corpus Christi)	78419
Naval Air Station	78102
Navarro	75151
Navarro Mills	76679
Navasota	77868-69
For specific Navasota Zip Codes call (409) 825-6812	
Navo	75034
Nazareth	79063
Neals Valley	75119
Nebgen	78624
Necessity	76024
Nechanitz	78946
Neches	75779
Neches Indian Village	75925
Neches Junction (Part of Port Arthur)	77640
Nederland	77627
Needmore	79371
Needville	77461
Negley	75426
Neinda	79520
Nell	78119
Nelson City	78006
Nelsonville	77418
Nelta	75437
Nemo	76070
Nesbitt (Harrison County)	75670
Nesbitt (Robertson County)	76629
Neuville	75935
Nevada	75073
Newark	76071
New Baden	77870
New Berlin	78121
New Bielau	78962
New Birthright	75482
New Boston	75570
New Braunfels	78130-33
For specific New Braunfels Zip Codes call (512) 625-7736	
New Bremen	78950
Newburg	76442
Newby	75846
New Caney	77357
New Caney Heights	77357
Newcastle	76372
New Chapel Hill	75701
New Clarkson	76570
New Colony	75563
New Corn Hill	76537
New Deal	79350
New Fountain	78861

Name	ZIP
Newgulf	77462
New Harmony (Shelby County)	75973
New Harmony (Smith County)	75704
Newharp	76239
New Hebron	75685
New Home	79383
New Hope (Cherokee County)	75766
New Hope (Collin County)	75069
New Hope (Dallas County)	75149
New Hope (Henderson County)	75756
New Hope (Jones County)	79553
New Hope (Rusk County)	75662
New Hope (San Jacinto County)	77327
New Hope (Smith County)	75703
New Hope (Wood County)	75773
Newlin	79245
New London	75682
New Lynn	79373
Newman	79934
New Mine	75686
New Moore	79351
Newport (Clay County)	76254
Newport (Harris County)	77532
New Prospect (Rusk County)	75652
New Prospect (Shelby County)	75975
New River Lake Estates	77327
New Salem (Falls County)	76570
New Salem (Palo Pinto County)	76472
New Salem (Rusk County)	75652
Newsome	75686
New Summerfield	75780
New Sweden (McCulloch County)	76825
New Sweden (Travis County)	78653
New Taiton	77437
Newton	75966
New Ulm	78950
New Waverly	77358
New Wehdem	77833
New Willard	77351
New York	75770
Neylandville	75401
Nickel	78629
Nickel Creek	88220
Niederwald	78640
Nigton	75926
Nile	76577
Nimitz (Part of San Antonio)	78216
Nimrod	76437
Nineveh	75833
Nix	76550
Nixon	78140
Noack	76574
Nobility	75004
Noble	75470
Nockenut	78160
Nocona	76255
Nogalus	75845
Nolan	79537
Nolanville	76559
Nome	77629
Noodle	79536
Noonday	75762
Nopal	78164
Nordheim	78141
Norias	78338
Norman Crossing	76574
Normandy	78877
Normangee	77871
Normanna	78142
Norse	76634
North Abilene	79525
North Amarillo (Part of Amarillo)	79107
Northampton	77379
North Austin (Part of Austin)	78751
Northaven (Part of Dallas)	75229
North Bonami	75956
North Broadway (Part of San Antonio)	78217
North Caney	75482
North Caplen	77617
North Cedar	75926
North Cleveland	77327
North College (Part of Lubbock)	79417
Northcrest	76705
Northcrest Estates (Part of Victoria)	77901
Northcross Mall (Part of Austin)	78757
Northeast (Part of Austin)	78752

548 TEXAS North East Mall-Parkdale Mall

Name	ZIP
North East Mall (Part of Hurst)	76053
Northern Hills	75020
Northfield	79201
North Garland (Part of Garland)	75044
North Gate (Ector County)	79760
Northgate (El Paso County)	79924
Northgate (Victoria County)	77901
North Grant Gardens	79762
North Groesbeck	79252
North Heights (Part of Amarillo)	79107
North Hills Mall (Part of North Richland Hills)	76118
North Houston	77086
North Houston Heights	77039
North Jericho	75935
North Lake (Dallas County)	75238
Northlake (Denton County)	76247
North Line Oaks	77301
Northline Shopping Center (Part of Houston)	77022
Northline Terrace	77093
North Mesquite (Part of Mesquite)	75187
North Oaks	78753
North Orange Heights	77630
Northpark (Part of Dallas)	75225
North Pleasanton (Part of Pleasanton)	78064
North Port Arthur (Part of Port Arthur)	77642
North Redland	75961
North Richland Hills	76118
Northrup	78942
North Rusk (Part of Rusk)	75785
North San Pedro	78380
North Shepherd (Part of Houston)	77088
Northside Village (Part of Houston)	77015
North Springs	77373
North Star Mall (Part of San Antonio)	78216
North Talpa	76882
Northtown Mall (Part of Dallas)	75234
North Uvalde (Part of Uvalde)	78801
Northview Hills	78759
Northwest (Part of Austin)	78757
Northwest Mall (Part of Houston)	77292
Northwest Park	77086
Northwood	78758
North Zulch	77872
Norton	76865
Norwood	75972
Notla	79070
Notrees	79759
Nottingham Forest	77630
Nottingham Woods	75835
Novice (Coleman County)	79538
Novice (Lamar County)	75460
Novohrad	77975
Noxville	78631
Nugent	79601
Number Two (Part of Paris)	75460
Nursery	77976
Nuway	79821
Oakalla	76541
Oak Canyon	77302
Oak Creek Addition (Part of Grapevine)	76051
Oak Dale (Erath County)	76401
Oakdale (Hopkins County)	75482
Oak Flat (Angelina County)	75949
Oak Flat (Nacogdoches County)	75760
Oak Flat (Rusk County)	75681
Oak Forest (Harris County)	77018
Oak Forest (Travis County)	78759
Oak Grove (Bowie County)	75554
Oak Grove (Camp County)	75686
Oak Grove (Ellis County)	75119
Oak Grove (Kaufman County)	75142
Oak Grove (Morris County)	75638
Oak Grove (Tarrant County)	76028
Oak Grove (Wood County)	75783
Oak Hill (Jasper County)	75951
Oak Hill (Johnson County)	76031
Oak Hill (Rusk County)	75652
Oak Hill (Travis County)	78735
Oak Hills Acres	77362
Oakhurst	77359
Oak Island	77514
Oak Knoll (Part of Haltom City)	76117
Oak Lake	76705

Name	ZIP
Oakland (Cherokee County)	75785
Oakland (Colorado County)	78951
Oakland (Orange County)	77630
Oakland (Rusk County)	75652
Oakland (Van Zandt County)	75103
Oak Lawn (Part of Dallas)	75219
Oaklawn Village (Part of Texarkana)	75501
Oak Point	75034
Oak Ridge (Bowie County)	75559
Oak Ridge (Cooke County)	76240
Oak Ridge (Kaufman County)	75160
Oak Ridge (Llano County)	78654
Oak Ridge (Nacogdoches County)	75961
Oak Ridge (Parker County)	76086
Oak Ridge North	77302
Oaks (Bee County)	78119
Oaks (Tarrant County)	76114
Oak Terrace	77365
Oak Trail Shores	76048
Oak Valley (Gonzales County)	78140
Oak Valley (Navarro County)	75110
Oakview	77611
Oakville	78060
Oakwilde	77093
Oakwood	75855
Oakwood Village and Westwood Plaza (Part of Abilene)	79603
Oatmeal	78605
O'Brien	79539
Oceanshore	77550
Ocee	76638
Odell	79247
Odell Addition (Part of Grapevine)	76051
Odem	78370
Odessa	79760-68
For specific Odessa Zip Codes call (915) 332-6436	
Odom	75147
O'Donnell	79351
Oenaville	76501
O'Farrell	75551
Oglesby	76561
Oilla	77630
Oilton	78371
Oklahoma	77355
Oklahoma Flat	79339
Oklahoma Lane	79325
Oklaunion	76373
Okra	76435
Ola	75142
Old Boston	75570
Old Bowling	77865
Old Brazoria (Part of Brazoria)	77422
Old Dime Box	77853
Olden	76466
Oldenburg	78945
Old Glory	79540
Old Ivy	75847
Old Kinkler	77964
Old Larissa	75757
Old London	75682
Old Mill (Part of Leon Valley)	78238
Old Mobeetie (Part of Mobeetie)	79061
Old Moulton	77975
Old Ocean	77463
Old River Lake	77327
Old River Terrace	77530
Old River-Winfree	77520
Old Round Rock (Part of Round Rock)	78664
Olds	75951
Old Sabinetown	75948
Old Salem	75933
Old Union (Bowie County)	75574
Old Union (Limestone County)	76687
Old Union (Titus County)	75455
Old Waverly	77358
Oletha	76687
Olfen	76875
Olin	76457
Oline	77625
Olivia	77979
Olmito	78575
Olmos (Bee County)	78389
Olmos (Starr County)	78582
Olmos Park	78212
Olney	76374
Olton	79064

Name	ZIP
Omaha	75571
Omen	75789
Onalaska	77360
One Meta Place (Part of Odessa)	79760
One Seventy Seven Lake Estates	77356
Opdyke	79336
Opdyke West	79336
Opelika	75778
Oplin	79510
O'Quinn	78945
Ora	75949
Oran	76045
Orange	77630-31
For specific Orange Zip Codes call (409) 883-9351	
Orangedale	78102
Orangefield	77639
Orange Grove (Harris County)	77039
Orange Grove (Jim Wells County)	78372
Orangeville	75491
Orchard	77464
Ore City	75683
Orient	76901
Orla	79770
Orme (Part of Arlington)	76010
Osage	76528
Oscar	76501
Osceola	76055
Ottine	78658
Otto	76675
Ovalo	79541
Overland Plaza (Part of Arlington)	76017
Overton	75684
Ovilla	75154
Owens (Brown County)	76801
Owens (Crosby County)	79357
Owensville	77856
Owentown	75708
Oyster Creek	77541
Ozona	76943
Pacio	75450
Pack Unit	77868
Padgett	76374
Padre-Staples Mall (Part of Corpus Christi)	78411
Paducah	79248
Pagoda	75862
Paige	78659
Paint Rock	76866
Paisano Annex (Part of El Paso)	79905
Pakan	79079
Palacios	77465
Palava	79556
Palestine (Anderson County)	75801-02
For specific Palestine Zip Codes call (214) 729-2435	
Palestine (Polk County)	75936
Palito Blanco	78332
Palmer	75152
Palmetto (Part of Oakhurst)	77359
Palmhurst	78572
Palm Valley	78550
Palmview	78539
Palo Alto	78343
Paloduro	79226
Palo Pinto	76072
Paluxy	76467
Pampa	79065-66
For specific Pampa Zip Codes call (806) 665-5713	
Pancake	76528
Pandale	76943
Pandora	78143
Panhandle	79068
Panna Maria	78144
Panola	75685
Panorama Estates	75169
Panorama Village	77301
Pantego	76013
Pantex	79068
Papalote	78387
Paradise	76073
Paradise Bay	75143
Paradise Hills	75929
Paris	75460-61
For specific Paris Zip Codes call (214) 784-3381	
Park	78945
Park Cities (Part of University Park)	75205
Parkdale (Part of Dallas)	75227
Parkdale Mall (Part of Beaumont)	77706

Parkdale Plaza-Port Bolivar TEXAS 549

Name	ZIP
Parkdale Plaza (Part of Corpus Christi)	78411
Parker (Collin County)	75002
Parker (Johnson County)	76050
Parker Point	75980
Parker Square (Part of Wichita Falls)	76308
Park Glen (Part of Houston)	77072
Park Place (Part of Houston)	77017
Park Row (Part of Katy)	77449
Parks at Arlington, The (Part of Arlington)	76015
Park Springs	76270
Parkview Estates	78155
Parkwood	77612
Parkwood Estates	77032
Parmer Lane Heights	78758
Parnell	79233
Parvin	75009
Pasadena	77501-08
For specific Pasadena Zip Codes call (713) 475-5140	
Pasadena Town Square (Part of Pasadena)	77506
Patilo	76462
Patrich	75652
Patricia	79331
Patrick	75125
Patroon	75973
Pattison	77466
Patton (McLennan County)	76689
Patton (Montgomery County)	77372
Pattonfield	75644
Pattonville	75468
Pauline	75124
Pauls Store	75973
Pawelekville	78113
Pawnee	78145
Paxton	75954
Paynes Corner	79360
Payne Springs	75124
Payton Colony	78606
Peach Creek	77488
Peach Creek Estates	77372
Peach Tree (Brazos County)	77801
Peachtree (Jasper County)	75951
Peacock	79542
Peadenville	76067
Pearl	76528
Pearland	77581
Pearl City	77995
Pear Ridge (Part of Port Arthur)	77640
Pearsall	78061
Pearsons Chapel	75851
Pear Valley	76867
Peaster	76074
Pebble Beach	75018
Pebble Hills (Part of El Paso)	79925
Pecan Acres (Orange County)	77662
Pecan Acres (Wise County)	76071
Pecan Gap	75469
Pecangrove	76528
Pecan Hill	75154
Pecan Lake Area	77835
Pecan Plantation	76048
Pecos	79772
Peeltown	75158
Peerless	75482
Peggy	78062
Pelham	76648
Pelican Bay	76020
Pendleton	76564
Pendleton Harbor	75948
Penelope	76676
Peniel (Part of Greenville)	75401
Penitas	78576
Pennington	75856
Penwell	79776
Peoria	76645
Pep	79353
Percilla	75844
Perezville	78572
Perico	79087
Pernitas Point	78383
Perrin	76075
Perrin Field	75020
Perrin Heights	75020
Perry	76677
Perry Landing (Part of Jones Creek)	77541
Perryton	79070
Perryville	75494
Pershing (Part of Austin)	78702
Personville	76642
Pert	75801
Peters	77474

Name	ZIP
Petersburg	79250
Peterson	77627
Peters Prairie	75426
Petersville	77995
Petrolia	76377
Petronila	78380
Petteway	76629
Pettibone	76520
Pettit (Comanche County)	76455
Pettit (Hockley County)	79336
Pettus	78146
Petty (Lamar County)	75470
Petty (Lynn County)	79373
Petty's Chapel	75110
Pflugerville	78660
Phalba	75147
Pharr	78577
Phelan	78602
Phelps	77340
Phillips	79007
Phillipsburg	77426
Philview Camp	79007
Pickens	75751
Pickett	75110
Pickton	75471
Pidcoke	76528
Piedmont (Grimes County)	77830
Piedmont (Upshur County)	75644
Pierce	77467
Pierces Chapel	75766
Piggly Wiggly (Part of Bryan)	77801
Pike	75004
Pilgrim Ridge	77367
Pilgrims Rest	75410
Pilot Grove	75491
Pilot Knob	78744
Pilot Point	76258
Pine	75686
Pine Acres	77357
Pine Branch	75417
Pine Crest	77301
Pine Forest (Hopkins County)	75471
Pine Forest (Orange County)	77662
Pine Grove (Cherokee County)	75766
Pine Grove (Newton County)	75966
Pine Grove (Orange County)	77630
Pine Hill (Cherokee County)	75766
Pinehill (Rusk County)	75652
Pinehurst (Montgomery County)	77362
Pinehurst (Orange County)	77630
Pine Island	77484
Pine Lake	77356
Pineland	75968
Pine Mills	75773
Pine Park	75948
Pine Prairie	77340
Pine Ridge	77625
Pine Springs (Culberson County)	88220
Pine Springs (Smith County)	75702
Pine Trail Estates	75762
Pine Valley (Angelina County)	75941
Pine Valley (San Jacinto County)	77358
Pine Valley (Walker County)	77358
Pineview	75494
Pinewood (Part of Longview)	75601
Pinewood Estates (Hardin County)	77706
Pinewood Estates (Montgomery County)	77372
Pinewood Village	77093
Piney	77418
Piney Grove (Cass County)	75551
Piney Grove (Upshur County)	75451
Piney Point (Harris County)	77024
Piney Point (Montgomery County)	77301
Piney Point (Sabine County)	75959
Piney Woods	75951
Pinnacle	75644
Pioneer	76471
Pioneer Town	78676
Pioneer Trails	77302
Pipe Creek	78063
Pirtle	75684
Pisgah	75929
Pitner Junction	75684
Pitts	77338
Pittsburg	75686
Placation Estates	75959

Name	ZIP
Placedo	77977
Placid	76872
Plains (Borden County)	79351
Plains (Yoakum County)	79355
Plainview (Hale County)	79072-73
For specific Plainview Zip Codes call (806) 296-2744	
Plainview (Denton County)	76249
Plainview (Sabine County)	75968
Plainview (Wharton County)	77455
Plano	75023-26
	75074-75
	75093-94
For specific Plano Zip Codes call (214) 647-2996	
Plantersville	77363
Plaska	79245
Plateau	79855
Pleak	77469
Pleasant Farms	79763
Pleasant Grove (Dallas County)	75217
Pleasant Grove (Falls County)	76570
Pleasant Grove (Upshur County)	75755
Pleasant Grove (Wood County)	75494
Pleasant Hill (Blanco County)	78636
Pleasant Hill (Eastland County)	76437
Pleasant Hill (Nacogdoches County)	75946
Pleasant Hill (Polk County)	75939
Pleasant Hill (Washington County)	77833
Pleasanton	78064
Pleasant Point	76009
Pleasant Ridge (Henderson County)	75763
Pleasant Ridge (Leon County)	75833
Pleasant Ridge (Montague County)	76230
Pleasant Ridge (Panola County)	75633
Pleasant Springs	75833
Pleasant Valley (Dallas County)	75040
Pleasant Valley (Garza County)	79356
Pleasant Valley (Lamb County)	79031
Pleasant Valley (Potter County)	79107
Pleasant Valley (Wichita County)	76301
Pleasant Valley Acres	77355
Pledger (Fisher County)	79543
Pledger (Matagorda County)	77468
Pluck	75939
Plum	78952
Plum Creek	75831
Plum Grove	77327
Plum Ridge	75980
Plymouth Park (Part of Irving)	75061
Poe Prairie	76066
Poesville	76671
Poetry	75160
Point	75472
Pointblank	77364
Point Comfort	77978
Point Enterprise	76667
Point Loma	78368
Point Royal	75758
Point Venture	78641
Polar	79549
Pollok	75969
Polvo	79846
Polytechnic (Part of Fort Worth)	76105
Ponder	76259
Pone	75667
Ponta	75766
Pontotoc	76869
Pony	76821
Poole	75440
Poolville	76076
Porfirio	78580
Port Acres (Part of Port Arthur)	77640
Portairs (Part of Corpus Christi)	78415
Port Alto	77979
Port Aransas	78373
Port Arthur	77640-43
For specific Port Arthur Zip Codes call (409) 983-3266	
Port Bolivar	77650

550 TEXAS Porter-River Ridge

	ZIP		ZIP		ZIP
Porter	77365	Pumpkin	77358	Red Springs (Baylor County)	76378
Porter Heights	77365	Pumpkin Center	79331	Red Springs (Bowie County)	75501
Porter Springs	75835	Pumpville	78851	Red Springs (Smith County)	75701
Porterville Timbers	77365	Punkin Center	76086	Red Top	76046
Port Isabel	78578	Purdon	76679	Redtown (Anderson County)	75839
Portland	78374	Purley	75457	Red Town (Angelina County)	75901
Port Lavaca	77979	Purmela	76566	Redwater	75573
Port Mansfield	78598	Pursley	76679	Redwood	78666
Port Neches	77651	Purves	76446	Reedville	78656
Port O'Connor	77982	Putnam	76469	Reese	75766
Porvenir	79854	Pyote	79777	Reese AFB	79401
Posey (Hopkins County)	75482	Pyron	79545	Reese Air Force Base	79489
Posey (Lubbock County)	79364	Quail	79251	Refugio	78377
Possum Kingdom	76045	Quanah	79252	Regency	76864
Post	79356	Quarry	77833	Rehburg	77835
Post Oak (Blanco County)	78636	Queen City	75572	Rehobeth	75633
Post Oak (Delta County)	75432	Quemado	78877	Reilly Springs	75482
Postoak (Freestone County)	75840	Quicksand	75966	Rek Hill	78940
Post Oak (Houston County)	75851	Quihi	78861	Reklaw	75784
Postoak (Jack County)	76230	Quinlan	75474	Relampago	78570
Postoak (Lamar County)	75416	Quintana	77541	Reliance	77801
Post Oak (Robertson County)	76629	Quitaque	79255	Remolino	78582
Post Oak Bend City	75142	Quite Village	77662	Rendon	76028
Post Oak Mall (Part of College Station)	77840	Quitman	75783	Reno (Lamar County)	75460
Post Oak Point	78950	Rabb	78380	Reno (Parker County)	76020
Poteet	78065	Rabbit Center	76401	Retreat (Grimes County)	77868
Poth	78147	Rabbs	77964	Retreat (Hill County)	76627
Potosi	79601	Rabbs Prairie	78945	Retreat (Navarro County)	75110
Potters Point	75657	Rachal	78353	Retrieve Unit	77515
Pottsboro	75076	Radium	79501	Retta	76028
Pottsville	76565	Ragtown	75411	Rhea	79035
Powderly	75473	Rainbow	76077	Rhea Mills	75069
Powell	75153	Rainbow Hills	78227	Rhineland	76371
Powell Point	77451	Raisin	77901	Rhome	76078
Poynor	75782	Raleigh	76641	Rhonesboro	75494
Prade Ranch	78058	Ralls	79357	Ricardo	78363
Praesel	76567	Ramah	75974	Rice (Navarro County)	75155
Praha	78941	Rambo	75555	Rice (Smith County)	75701
Prairie Dell	76571	Ramireno	78067	Rices Crossing	76574
Prairie Grove (Angelina County)	75941	Ramirez	77376	Richards	77873
Prairie Grove (Limestone County)	76667	Ranch Harbor Estates	76692	Richardson	75080-83
Prairie Hill (Limestone County)	76678	Ranchito	78586	For specific Richardson Zip Codes call (214) 235-8353	
Prairie Hill (Washington County)	77833	Ranchland (Part of El Paso)	79915	Richardson Square (Part of Richardson)	75081
Prairie Lea	78661	Ranchland Acres	79701	Richland (Dallas County)	75243
Prairie Mountain	78643	Rancho Allegre Addition	78332	Richland (Navarro County)	76681
Prairie Point	76239	Rancho Dela Parita	78372	Richland (Rains County)	75472
Prairie Valley (Fayette County)	78952	Rancho Viejo (Cameron County)	78520	Richland Hills	76118
Prairie Valley (Montague County)	76255	Rancho Viejo (Jim Hogg County)	78361	Richland Mall (Part of Waco)	76710
Prairieview (Hale County)	79072	Randolph	75475	Richland Park (Part of Fort Worth)	76118
Prairie View (Waller County)	77446	Randolph Air Force Base	78148	Richland Plaza (Part of North Richland Hills)	76118
Prairieville	75147	Ranger	76470	Richland Springs	76871
Prattville	75432	Rangerville	78586	Richmond	77469
Preiss Heights	78130	Rankin (Ellis County)	75119	Richwood	77531
Premont	78375	Rankin (Upton County)	79778	Ridge (Mills County)	76864
Presidio	79845	Ransom Canyon	79366	Ridge (Robertson County)	77856
Preston (Part of Dallas)	75225	Ratama	78017	Ridgecrest (Orange County)	77630
Preston Shores	75076	Ratcliff (Houston County)	75858	Ridgecrest (Randall County)	79109
Prestonwood (Part of Arlington)	76012	Ratcliff (San Augustine County)	75972	Ridgecrest Addition	77630
Prestonwood Town Center (Part of Dallas)	75240	Ratcliffe	78164	Ridgeheights	79701
Price (Jefferson County)	77627	Ratibor	76501	Ridgemere (Part of Amarillo)	79107
Price (Rusk County)	75687	Rattan	75432	Ridgeway	75482
Priddy	76870	Ravenna	75476	Ridglea (Part of Fort Worth)	76116
Prietos Bar	79843	Rayburn	77327	Ridgmar Mall (Part of Fort Worth)	76116
Primera	78550	Rayburn Hideaway	75937	Ridings	75476
Primrose	75754	Rayford	77373	Riesel	76682
Princeton	75077	Rayland	76384	Rimwick Forrest	77355
Pringle	79083	Raymondville	78580	Rincon	78582
Pritchett	75644	Ray Point	78071	Ringgold	76261
Proctor	76468	Raywood	77582	Rio Farms	78538
Proffitt	76372	Reagan	76680	Rio Frio	78879
Progreso	78579	Reagan Wells	78801	Rio Grande City	78582
Progress (Bailey County)	79347	Reagor Springs	75165	Rio Hondo	78583
Progress (Palo Pinto County)	76067	Realitos	78376	Riomedina	78066
Progresso Lakes	78579	Redbank	75561	Rio Pecos	79740
Promenade (Part of Richardson)	75080	Red Bird Addition	75116	Rios	78349
Prospect	75657	Red Bird Mall (Part of Dallas)	75237	Rio Vista	76093
Prosper	75078	Red Bluff	79770	Rising Star	76471
Providence (Angelina County)	75901	Red Branch	75855	Rita	77857
Providence (Hardin County)	77625	Redford	79846	River Bend (Newton County)	75932
Providence (Polk County)	77351	Red Gate	78539	River Bend (Sabine County)	75948
Providence (Van Zandt County)	75140	Red Hill (Cass County)	75560	River Brook	77302
Provident City	77455	Red Hill (Lamar County)	75473	Riverby	75488
Pruett	75657	Red Hill (Wharton County)	77437	Riverdrive Mall (Part of Laredo)	78040
Pruitt	75140	Red Lake	75855	Riverland	76365
Puerto Rico	78563	Redland (Angelina County)	75901	River Oak Lake Estates	78758
Pullman	79109	Redland (Leon County)	75833	River Oaks (Harris County)	77019
Pumphrey	79567	Redland (Van Zandt County)	75754	River Oaks (Tarrant County)	76114
		Redlawn	75925	River Plantation	77302
		Redlick	75501	River Ridge	75951
		Redmond Terrace (Part of College Station)	77840		
		Red Oak (Ellis County)	75154		
		Red Oak (Kaufman County)	75142		
		Red Ranger	76569		
		Red River Army Depot	75501		
		Red Rock	78662		

Riverside-Sandy Corner **TEXAS** 551

Location	ZIP
Riverside (Hudspeth County)	79839
Riverside (Tarrant County)	76111
Riverside (Walker County)	77367
Riverside Crest (Part of Houston)	77338
River Woods Estates	77050
Riviera	78379
Riviera Beach	78379
Roach Town	75758
Roane	75110
Roanoke	76262
Roans Prairie	77875
Roaring Springs	79256
Robbins	75846
Robert Lee	76945
Robertson	79343
Robinson	76706
Robinson Plaza (Part of Robinson)	76706
Robstown	78380
Roby	79543
Rochelle	76872
Rochester	79544
Rock Creek	76708
Rockdale	76567
Rockett	75165
Rockford	75460
Rock Harbor	76048
Rockhill (Collin County)	75069
Rock Hill (Jasper County)	75951
Rock Hill (Wood County)	75783
Rockhouse	78950
Rock Island (Colorado County)	77470
Rock Island (Polk County)	75939
Rockland	75970
Rockne	78602
Rockport	78382
Rock Prairie	77801
Rocksprings	78880
Rockwall	75087
Rockwood	76873
Rocky Branch	75638
Rocky Creek Park	77835
Rocky Hill	76661
Rocky Mound	75686
Rocky Springs (Angelina County)	75949
Rocky Springs (Tyler County)	75970
Roddy	75147
Rodney	76639
Roganville	75956
Rogers	76569
Rolling Hills (Hunt County)	75453
Rolling Hills (Potter County)	79108
Rolling Hills (Waller County)	77445
Rolling Hills Shores	76086
Rolling Hills West	78746
Rolling Meadows	75601
Rolling Oaks	75169
Rolling Oaks Park Mall (Part of San Antonio)	78209
Rollingwood	78746
Roma City	78584
Roman Forest	77357
Roman Hills	77356
Romayor	77368
Romero	79022
Romney	76471
Roosevelt (Kimble County)	76874
Roosevelt (Lubbock County)	79401
Ropesville	79358
Rosalie	75417
Rosanky	78953
Roscoe	79545
Rosebud	76570
Rose City	77662
Rosedale	76680
Rose Hill	77375
Rose Hill Acres	77656
Rosenberg	77471
Rosenthal	76655
Rosevine	75930
Rosewood	75644
Rosharon	77583
Rosita (Duval County)	78384
Rosita (Starr County)	78582
Ross	76684
Rosser	75157
Rosston	76263
Rossville	78065
Rotan	79546
Round Mountain	78663
Round Prairie	75144
Round Rock	78664
	78680-81
For specific Round Rock Zip Codes call (512) 255-3516	

Location	ZIP
Round Timber	76380
Round Top (Fayette County)	78954
Round Top (Fisher County)	79520
Roundup	79313
Routt Point	77461
Rowden	79504
Rowena	76875
Rowlett	75088
Roxton	75477
Royal Forest	77303
Royal Lane (Part of Dallas)	75230
Royal Oaks (Henderson County)	75143
Royal Oaks (Llano County)	78639
Royal Oaks (Orange County)	77626
Royalty	79779
Royalwood	77028
Roy Miller (Part of Corpus Christi)	78405
Roy Royall (Part of Houston)	77093
Royse City	75089
Royston	79543
Rucker	76444
Rugby	75435
Ruidosa	79843
Rule	79547
Rumley	76539
Run	78537
Runaway Bay	76234
Runge	78151
Rural Shade	75144
Rushwood	77067
Rusk	75785
Rutersville	78945
Ruth Springs	75163
Ryanville	78377
Rye	77369
Rylie (Part of Balch Springs)	75149
Sabanna	76437
Sabathany	76086
Sabinal	78881
Sabine	77640
Sabine Pass	77655
Sabine Sands	75928
Sabinetown	75948
Sachse	75040
Sacul	75788
Saddle and Surrey	77356
Sadler	76264
Sagerton	79548
Saginaw	76179
St. Claire Cove	77650
St. Francis	79107
St. Francis Village	76036
St. Hedwig	78152
St. Jo	76265
Saint John	78956
Saint John Colony	78616
St. Lawrence	79739
St. Louis (Part of Tyler)	75702
St. Paul (Brazoria County)	77422
St. Paul (Collin County)	75098
St. Paul (Falls County)	76661
St. Paul (San Patricio County)	78387
Salado	76571
Salem (Bastrop County)	78953
Salem (Milam County)	76520
Salem (Smith County)	75789
Salesville	76067
Salineno	78585
Salmon	75839
Salona	76230
Salt Flat	79847
Salt Gap	76836
Saltillo	75478
Salty	76577
Sam Houston (Part of Houston)	77002
Sam Houston College (Part of Huntsville)	77341
Samnorwood	79077
Sam Rayburn	75951
San Angelo	76901-06
For specific San Angelo Zip Codes call (915) 655-5681	
San Antonio	78201-99
For specific San Antonio Zip Codes call (512) 657-8302	
COLLEGES & UNIVERSITIES	
Incarnate Word College	78209
Our Lady of the Lake University of San Antonio	78285
St. Mary's University of San Antonio	78284
Trinity University	78284

Location	ZIP
University of Texas Health Science Center at San Antonio	78284
University of Texas at San Antonio	78285
FINANCIAL INSTITUTIONS	
Alamo Savings Association of Texas	78209
The Bank of San Antonio	78205
Bexar Savings Association	78217
Broadway National Bank	78209
Commerce Savings Association	78209
Deposit Insurance Bridge Bank, N.A.	78205
First City, Texas-San Antonio, N.A.	78216
First Federal Savings and Loan Association	78209
First State Savings Association	78216
Frost National Bank	78205
Groos Bank, National Association	78205
Jefferson State Bank	78201
Kelly Field National Bank	78238
National Bank of Fort Sam Houston	78286
NBC Bank-San Antonio, National Association	78205
San Pedro Bank	78232
Texas Commerce Bank-San Antonio	78209
Travis Savings & Loan Association	78215
Union Bank	78211
U.S.A.A. Federal Savings Bank	78230
Westside Bank	78285
HOSPITALS	
Audie L. Murphy Memorial Veterans Hospital	78284
Baptist Medical Center	78286
Bexar County Hospital District	78284
Humana Hospital-San Antonio	78229
Santa Rosa Medical Center	78207
Southwest Texas Methodist Hospital	78229
HOTELS/MOTELS	
Embassy Suites Hotel NW	78230
The Hilton Palacio del Rio	78205
Holiday Inn Downtown	78204
Ramada Inn Airport	78209
San Antonio Inn	78233
San Antonio Marriott Riverwalk	78205
St. Anthony Inter-Continental	78205
MILITARY INSTALLATIONS	
Brooks Air Force Base	78235
Camp Bullis	78234
Camp Stanley Storage Activity	78269
Fort Sam Houston	78234
Kelly Air Force Base	78241
Lackland Air Force Base	78236
Texas Air National Guard, FB6432	78241
San Augustine	75972
San Benito	78586
San Carlos	78539
Sanco	76945
Sanctuary	76020
Sand	79331
Sanderson	79848
Sand Flat (Rains County)	75440
Sandflat (Smith County)	75706
Sand Flat (Van Zandt County)	75140
Sand Hill (Floyd County)	79235
Sand Hill (Upshur County)	75644
Sandia	78383
San Diego	78384
Sandjack	75928
Sand Lake	75119
Sandoval	76574
Sand Ridge (Houston County)	75835
Sand Ridge (Wharton County)	77434
Sand Springs	79720
Sandusky	76245
Sandy	78665
Sandy Acres	79701
Sandy Corner	77437

552 TEXAS Sandy Ridge-South End

	ZIP
Sandy Ridge	77351
San Elizario	79849
San Felipe	77473
Sanford	79078
Sanford Estates	79036
San Gabriel	76577
Sanger	76266
San Geromino	78023
San Isidro	78588
San Jacinto (Part of Amarillo)	79106
San Jose	78332
San Juan	78539
	78589
For specific San Juan Zip Codes call (512) 787-2491	
San Juan (Nueces County)	78406
San Leanna	78767
San Leon (Galveston Co.)	77539
San Marcos	78666-67
For specific San Marcos Zip Codes call (512) 392-3451	
San Patricio	78368
San Pedro	78520
San Perlita	78590
San Saba	76877
Sansom Park	76114
Santa Anna	76878
Santa Catarina	78582
Santa Cruz	78582
Santa Elena	78591
Santa Fe	77510
Santa Maria	78592
Santa Monica	78580
Santa Rosa	78593
Santo	76472
San Ygnacio	78067
Saragosa	79780
Saratoga	77585
Sarco	77963
Sardis (Cass County)	75656
Sardis (Ellis County)	76065
Sargent	77414
Sarita	78385
Sash	75446
Sasparrico	78112
Satin	76685
Satsuma	77040
Sattler	78130
Saturn	78959
Sauney Stand	77426
Savage	79357
Savoy	75479
Sayers	78602
Scallorn	76853
Scenic Heights	78130
Scenic Terrace	78130
Schattel	78005
Schertz	78154
Schicke Point	77465
Schoolerville	76531
School Land	78140
Schroeder	77963
Schulenburg	78956
Schumansville	78130
Schwab City	77351
Schwertner	76573
Scotland	76379
Scotsdale (Ector County)	79762
Scotsdale (El Paso County)	79925
Scott	75169
Scott Park	79521
Scottsville	75688
Scranton	76437
Scrappin Valley	75977
Scroggins	75480
Scurry	75158
Seabrook	77586
Sea Crest Park	77520
Seadrift	77983
Seagoville	75159
Seagraves	79359
Sea Isle	77551
Seale	76687
Sealy	77474
Seaton	76501
Seawillow	78644
Sebastian	78594
Sebastopol	75862
Seco Mines	78852
Security	77327
Sedalia	75095
Segno	77351
Segovia	76849
Seguin	78155-56
For specific Seguin Zip Codes call (512) 379-2594	
Sejita	78376
Selden	76401
Selfs	75446
Selma	78209

	ZIP
Selman City	75689
Seminary Hill (Part of Fort Worth)	76115
Seminole	79360
Senate	76056
Senior	78073
Sequoia Estates	77032
Serbin	78942
Serna (Part of San Antonio)	78218
Seth Ward	79072
Seven Oaks	77350
Seven Pines	75601
Seven Points	75143
Seven Sisters	78357
Sexton	75972
Sexton City	75684
Seymore	75482
Seymour	76380
Shadow Glen	77530
Shadow Lake Estates	77365
Shadowland	75435
Shadowland Retreat	77365
Shady Acres	77422
Shady Brook Acres	77355
Shady Grove (Angelina County)	75941
Shady Grove (Cherokee County)	75785
Shady Grove (Dallas Co.)	75050
Shady Grove (Kerr County)	78028
Shady Grove (Marion Co.)	75657
Shady Grove (Nacogdoches County)	75961
Shady Grove (Navarro County)	76679
Shady Grove (Rains County)	75440
Shady Grove (Smith County)	75706
Shady Grove (Upshur County)	75755
Shady Oaks (Part of Hurst)	76053
Shady Shores (Denton County)	76201
Shady Shores (Henderson County)	75147
Shady Trees (Part of Houston)	77338
Shafter	79850
Shallowater	79363
Shamrock	79079
Shamrock Shores	76801
Shanklerville	75932
Shannon	76365
Sharon	75701
Sharp	76518
Sharpstown (Part of Houston)	77036
Sharpstown Center (Part of Houston)	77036
Sharyland (Part of Mission)	78572
Shavano Park	78213
Shaw Bend	76877
Shawnee	75949
Shawnee Shores	75948
Shawnee Shores Estates	75474
Sheffield	79781
Shelby	78940
Shelbyville	75973
Sheldon	77028
Shenandoah	77301
Shep	79566
Shepherd	77371
Sheppard	77612
Shepton	75073
Sher-Den Mall (Part of Sherman)	75090
Sheridan	77475
Sherman	75090-91
For specific Sherman Zip Codes call (214) 892-3462	
Sherman-Hansford Plant	79040
Sherman Junction (Part of Denison)	75020
Sherwood	76941
Sherwood Place	77016
Sherwood Shores	78654
Shields	76845
Shiloh (Bastrop County)	78602
Shiloh (Delta County)	75448
Shiloh (Leon County)	75855
Shiloh (Liberty County)	77575
Shiloh (Limestone County)	76667
Shiloh (Williamson County)	76578
Shiner	77984
Shipman Camp	79521
Shirley	75482
Shirley Creek	75937
Shiro	77876
Shive	76531
Shoreacres	77571

	ZIP
Short	75935
Shovel Mountain	78654
Sidney	76474
Sierra Blanca	79851
Siesta Shores (Travis County)	78669
Siesta Shores (Zapata County)	78076
Sikes Center (Part of Wichita Falls)	76308
Silas	75975
Siloam (Bowie County)	75559
Siloam (Comanche County)	76455
Siloam (Williamson County)	78621
Silsbee	77656
Silver	76949
Silver City (Milam County)	76520
Silver City (Navarro County)	76679
Silver Hills	78006
Silver Lake	75140
Silverton	79257
Silver Valley	76834
Simmons	78071
Simms	75574
Simonton	77476
Simpsonville	77465
Simsboro	75860
Sinclair City	75789
Singing Sands	77617
Singletary Sites	75956
Singleton	77831
Sinton	78387
Sipe Springs	76442
Sisterdale	78006
Six Flags Mall (Part of Arlington)	76010
Six Mile	77979
Six Points (Part of Corpus Christi)	78404
Skellytown	79080
Skidmore	78389
Sky Harbor	76048
Slabtown	75460
Slate Shoals	75460
Slaton	79364
Slay	76641
Sleepy Hollow	79121
Slide	79413
Slidell	76267
Sloan	76877
Slocum	75839
Small	75117
Smeltertown (Part of El Paso)	79927
Smetana	77801
Smiley	78159
Smithfield (Part of North Richland Hills)	76180
Smith Grove	75851
Smith Hill	75561
Smithland	75657
Smith Oaks	75090
Smith Point	77514
Smiths Bend	76634
Smith Springs	76401
Smithville	78957
Smithwick	78654
Smitty (Part of Athens)	75751
Smyer	79367
Smyrna	75551
Snook	77878
Snow Hill (Collin County)	75031
Snow Hill (Polk County)	75939
Snyder	79549
Socorro	79927
Soda	77351
Soda Springs	76066
Sodville	78387
Solms	78130
Somerset	78069
Somerville	77879
Sonoma (Part of Ennis)	75119
Sonora	76950
Soules Chapel	75644
Sour Lake	77659
South (Part of College Station)	77840
South Amarillo (Part of Amarillo)	79109
South Austin (Part of Austin)	78704
South Bend	76081
South Bosque	76710
South Brice	79226
South Dallas (Part of Dallas)	75215
Southeast (Part of Austin)	78744
Southeast Crossing (Part of Tyler)	75701
South Elm	76518
South End (Part of Beaumont)	77705

Southeast-Tehuacana **TEXAS 553**

Place	ZIP
Southeast (Part of Austin)	78744
Southeast Crossing (Part of Tyler)	75701
South Elm	76518
South End (Part of Beaumont)	77705
Southern Methodist University (Part of University Park)	75275
South Gale	75020
South Groveton (Part of Groveton)	75845
South Hanen	79720
South Houston	77587
South Jericho	75935
Southlake	76092
Southland (Garza County)	79368
Southland (Wharton County)	77437
Southland Acres (Part of Arlington)	76010
South Liberty (Part of Liberty)	77575
Southmayd	76268
Southmore (Part of Houston)	77004
South Oak Cliff (Part of Dallas)	75216
South Padre Island	78597
South Park Mall (Part of San Antonio)	78224
South Plains	79258
South Plains Mall (Part of Lubbock)	79414
South Post Oak (Part of Houston)	77035
South Purmela	76566
Southridge Plaza (Part of Austin)	78745
South San Antonio (Part of San Antonio)	78211
South San Pedro	78380
Southside Estates (Part of Amarillo)	79110
Southside Place	77005
South Sulphur	75496
South Temple (Part of Temple)	76501
South Texarkana (Part of Texarkana)	75501
South Texas Medical Center (Part of San Antonio)	78229
Southton	78221
South View Estates	78737
Southwestern Baptist Theological Seminary (Part of Fort Worth)	76122
Southwest Freeway (Part of Houston)	77057
Sowells Bluff	75476
Sowers (Part of Irving)	75060
Spade	79369
Spanish Camp	77488
Spanish Fort	76255
Spanish Trail	76048
Sparenberg	79331
Sparks	76534
Speaks	77985
Spearman	79081
Speegleville	76710
Spicewood	78669
Spicewood At Balcones Village	78759
Spicewood Beach	78669
Spillers Store	75850
Spillview Estates	75147
Spinwick Addition (Part of La Porte)	77571
Splendora	77372
Splendora Farms	77372
Spofford	78877
Spooner (Part of Pinehurst)	77630
Spraberry	79702
Spring	77373
	77379-83
	77386-91
For specific Spring Zip Codes call (713) 288-6652	
Spring Branch	78070
Spring Creek (Gillespie County)	78624
Spring Creek (San Saba County)	76871
Spring Creek (Throckmorton County)	76370
Spring Creek Acres (Part of Victoria)	77901
Spring Creek Estates	77355
Springdale	75572
Spring Dell	77373
Springfield (Anderson County)	75801

Place	ZIP
Springfield (Limestone County)	76667
Spring Forest	77373
Spring Hill (Bowie County)	75559
Spring Hill (Camp County)	75686
Spring Hill (Gregg County)	75601
Spring Hill (Guadalupe County)	78155
Spring Hill (Jasper County)	75951
Springhill (Navarro County)	76639
Spring Hills	77373
Springlake	79082
Spring Seat	75846
Springtown	76082
Spring Valley (Harris County)	77024
Spring Valley (McLennan County)	76655
Sprinkle	78751
Spur	79370
Spurger	77660
Stacy	76836
Stafford	77477
Stagecoach	77355
Stage Coach Farms	77355
Stage Coach Hills	78229
Stairtown	78648
Stamford	79553
Stamps	75644
Stanfield	76365
Stanton	79782
Staples	78670
Star	76880
Star Harbor	75148
Star Route	79346
Starrville	75792
Startzville	78130
Steeltown (Part of Groves)	77619
Steep Hollow	77801
Stegall	79371
Stellar	78949
Stephen F. Austin University (Part of Nacogdoches)	75962
Stephenville	76401
Sterley	79241
Sterling City	76951
Sterlings Island	77367
Sterrett	75165
Stewards Mill	75840
Stewart	75691
Stewart Heights (Part of Baytown)	77520
Stieren	78632
Stilson	77535
Stinnett	79083
Stith	79536
Stockard	75751
Stockdale	78160
Stockholm	78569
Stockman	75975
Stock Yards (Part of Fort Worth)	76106
Stoneburg	76230
Stoneham	77868
Stonewall	78671
Stonewall Mall (Part of Corpus Christi)	78410
Stony	76259
Stout	75494
Stowell	77661
Stranger	76653
Stratford	79084
Stratton	77954
Stratton Ridge	77531
Strawn	76475
Streetman	75859
Strickland	75968
String Prairie	78953
Stringtown	77371
Structure	78621
Stuart Place	78550
Study Butte	79852
Stumptown	75931
Sturdivant	76067
Sturgeon	76273
Styx	75143
Sublett (Part of Arlington)	76063
Sublime	77986
Sudan	79371
Suffolk	75644
Sugar Land	77478-79
For specific Sugar Land Zip Codes call (713) 494-2042	
Sugar Valley	77480
Sullivan City	78595
Sulphur Bluff	75481
Sulphur Springs (Angelina County)	75980
Sulphur Springs (Hopkins County)	75482

Place	ZIP
Sulphur Springs (Rusk County)	75760
Sul Ross (Part of Alpine)	79830
Summerall	75147
Summerfield (Castro County)	79085
Summerfield (Upshur County)	75644
Summer Hill	75751
Summit Heights (Part of El Paso)	79930
Sumner	75486
Sun (Part of Denison)	75020
Sundown	79372
Sunnyside (Castro County)	79027
Sunny Side (Waller County)	77445
Sunnyvale	75149
Sunray	79086
Sunrise (El Paso County)	79904
Sunrise (Falls County)	76661
Sunrise Acres (Part of El Paso)	79904
Sunrise Beach	78643
Sunrise Mall (Part of Corpus Christi)	78412
Sunset (Lubbock County)	79407
Sunset (Montague County)	76270
Sunset Heights	79762
Sunset Marketown (Part of Amarillo)	79102
Sunset Ridge	77301
Sunset Valley	78745
Suntide	78409
Sun Valley (El Paso County)	79924
Sun Valley (Lamar County)	75460
Surf Oaks (Part of Seabrook)	77586
Surfside Beach	77541
Sutherland Springs	78161
Swamp City	75647
Swan	75706
Swan Lagoon (Part of Nassau Bay)	77058
Swanson Hill	75801
Sweeny	77480
Sweeny Switch	78368
Sweet Home (Guadalupe County)	78155
Sweet Home (Lavaca County)	77987
Sweetwater (Comanche County)	76442
Sweetwater (Nolan County)	79556
Swenson	79502
Swift	75961
Swiss Alp	78956
Sycamore	75932
Sylvan	75460
Sylvan Beach (Part of La Porte)	77571
Sylvester	79560
Tabor	77801
Tacoma	75633
Tadmor	75847
Taft	78390
Taft Southwest	78390
Tahoka	79373
Taiton	77437
Talco	75487
Tall Pines	75630
Talpa	76882
Talty	75160
Tamega	78605
Tamina	77302
Tandy Center (Part of Fort Worth)	76102
Tanglewood	78947
Tanglewood Manor	77357
Tankersly	76901
Tarkington Acres	77327
Tarkington Prairie	77327
Tarleton (Part of Stephenville)	76402
Tarpley	78883
Tarrant (Part of Fort Worth)	76039
Tarzan	79783
Tatum	75691
Tavener	77435
Taylor	76574
Taylor Lake Village	77586
Taylorsville	78662
Taylor Town	75460
Taylorville	75452
T C U (Texas Christian University) (Part of Fort Worth)	76129
Teague	75860
Teaselville	75757
Tecula	75766
Teepee	79762
Tehuacana	76686

554 TEXAS Telegraph-Verhelle

	ZIP		ZIP		ZIP
Telegraph	76883	Todd City	75801	Union Bluff	76645
Telephone	75488	Todd Mission	77363	Union Bower (Part of Irving)	75060
Telferner	77988	Togo	78957	Union Center	76471
Telico	75119	Tokio	79376	Union Grove (Bell County)	76513
Tell	79259	Tolar	76476	Union Grove (Cherokee	
Temple	76501-05	Tolbert	76384	County)	75766
For specific Temple Zip Codes call (817) 773-0792		Toledo Village (Newton County)	75932	Union Grove (Upshur County)	75647
Temple Mall (Part of		Toledo Village (Sabine		Union High	76639
Temple)	76501	County)	75948	Union Hill (Bosque County)	76652
Temple Springs	75951	Tolosa	75143	Union Hill (Upshur County)	75644
Tenaha	75974	Toluca	78579	Union Springs	75961
Tennessee Colony	75861	Tomball	77375	Union Valley (Hurt County)	75089
Tennyson	76953	Tom Bean	75489	Union Valley (Wilson	
Terlingua	79852	Tool	75143	County)	78140
Terrell	75160	Topsey	76522	United States Automobile	
Terrell Hills	78209	Tornillo	79853	Association (Part of San	
Terrell Station	79781	Tours	76691	Antonio)	78284
Terrell Wells (Part of San		Tow	78672	Unity	75486
Antonio)	78221	Town and Country Center		Universal City	78148
Terrys Chapel	76570	(Part of Houston)	77024	University (Part of Austin)	78712
Terryville	77995	Town Bluff Estates	75979	University of Dallas (Part of	
Texarkana	75501-05	Towne and Country		Irving)	75061
For specific Texarkana Zip Codes call (214) 838-9537		Shopping Center (Part of Temple)	76501	University of Texas at El Paso (Part of El Paso)	79902
Texas City	77590-92	Town East Mall (Part of		University Park (Bexar	
For specific Texas City Zip Codes call (409) 948-2591		Mesquite)	75149	County)	78228
		Towne West	77478	University Park (Dallas	
Texas City Terminal		Town North (Part of Austin)	78758	County)	75205
Junction (Part of Hitchcock)	77563	Town North Addition (Part of Sherman)	75095	University Park (Wichita County)	76308
Texas City Junction (Part of		Town Oaks (Part of		University Place (Part of	
Texas City)	77590	Marshall)	75670	Nacogdoches)	75961
Texas Lutheran (Part of		Town Plaza (Part of		Upper Meyersville	78164
Seguin)	78155	Victoria)	77901	Upshaw	75943
Texhoma	73949	Toyah	79785	Upton	78957
Texline	79087	Toyahvale	79786	Urbana	77371
Texon	76932	Tracy	76567	Utility (Part of San Antonio)	78219
Thalia	79227	Tradewinds	75143	Utley	78602
Thayer	78570	Trammells	77045	Utopia	78884
The Colony	75056	Travis	76656	Uvalde	78801-02
Thedford	75771	Travis Country	78735	For specific Uvalde Zip Codes call (512) 278-3911	
The Grove	76576	Travis Peak	78654		
The Heights (Part of Alvin)	77511	Trawick	75961	Valdasta	75004
The Knobbs	78650	Trent	79561	Valentine	79854
Thelma (Bexar County)	78221	Trenton	75490	Valera	76884
Thelma (Limestone County)	76642	Trevat	75845	Valle de Oro	79010
The Meadows (Part of		Tri Cities	75751	Valle Vista Mall (Part of	
Meadows)	77477	Trickham	76878	Harlingen)	78550
The Oaks	78130	Tri-Lake Estates	77356	Valleycreek	75452
Theon	76537	Trimmier Friendship	76541	Valley-Hi (Part of San	
Thermo	75482	Trinidad	75163	Antonio)	78227
The Woodlands	77380	Trinity	75862	Valley Lodge (Part of	
The Y	75551	Trinity Park	75098	Simonton)	77476
Thicket	77374	Tripp (Part of Sunnyvale)	75149	Valley Mills	76689
Thomas	75644	Trophy Club	76262	Valley Spring	76885
Thomas Manor (Part of El		Tropical Acres	77901	Valley View (Comal County)	78130
Paso)	79915	Troup	75789	Valley View (Cooke County)	76272
Thomaston	77989	Trout Creek	75933	Valley View (McLennan	
Thompson	77040	Troy	76579	County)	76701
Thompson Heights	75020	Truby	79525	Valley View (Midland	
Thompsons	77481	Truce	76230	County)	79702
Thompsonville	78959	Trumbull	75125	Valley View (Mitchell	
Thornberry	76308	Truscott	79260	County)	79512
Thorndale	76577	Tucker	75801	Valley View (Runnels	
Thornton	76687	Tuleta	78162	County)	76821
Thorntonville	77756	Tulia	79088	Valley View (Upshur	
Thorp Spring	76048	Tulip	75447	County)	75644
Thousand Oaks (Part of		Tulsita	78119	Valley View (Wichita	
San Antonio)	78270	Tundra	75103	County)	76367
Thrall	76578	Tunis	77836	Valley View Center (Part of	
Three Leagues	79331	Tupelo	75155	Dallas)	75240
Three Point	78664	Turkey	79261	Valley Wells	78830
Three Rivers	78071	Turkey Creek	75656	Val Verde	76518
Thrifty	76801	Turlington	75840	Van	75790
Throckmorton	76083	Turnersville (Coryell County)	76528	Van Alstyne	75095
Thurber	76463	Turnersville (Travis County)	78610	Vance	78828
Tidwell	75401	Turnertown	75689	Vancourt	76955
Tidwell Prairie	76629	Turney	75766	Vandalia	75426
Tigertown	75446	Turtle Bayou	77514	Vanderbilt	77991
Tiki Island	77551	Tuscola	79562	Vanderpool	78885
Tilden	78072	Tuttle Addition	77488	Vandyke	76442
Tilmon	78616	Tuxedo	79553	Vanetia	77865
Timber Cove (Part of Taylor		Twine Cedar Retreat	75948	Van Horn	79855
Lake Village)	77586	Twin Shores	77378	Van Vleck	77482
Timbercreek Canyon	79118	Twitty	79090	Varisco	77801
Timberlake	77429	T.W.U (Part of Denton)	76204	Vasco	75450
Timberlake Acres	77365	Tye	79563	Vashti	76228
Timber Lakes Estates	77380	Tyler	75701-13	Vattmannville	78379
Timber Ridge	77380	For specific Tyler Zip Codes call (214) 595-8621		Vaughan	76645
Timothy	75105			Vealmoor	79720
Timpson	75975	Tynan	78391	Veal Station	76082
Tin Top	76086	Type	78621	Vedas Camp	79521
Tioga	76271	Uhland	78640	Vega	79092
Tira	75482	Umbarger	79091	Ventura	77355
Tivoli	77990	Uncertain	75661	Venus	76084
Tivydale	78624	Union (Brazos County)	77862	Vera	76383
Tobe Hahn (Part of		Union (Franklin County)	75478	Verbena	79356
Beaumont)	77706	Union (Lubbock County)	79364	Verdi	78064
Toco	75421	Union (Scurry County)	79549	Verhalen	79772
Tod (Part of Seabrook)	77586	Union (Terry County)	79316	Verhelle	77954

Veribest-Wild Peach Village **TEXAS** 555

	ZIP		ZIP		ZIP
Veribest	76886	Waskom	75692	West Orange	77630
Vernon	76384	Wastella	79545	Westover (Baylor County)	76380
Verona	75004	Watauga	76137	Westover (Ector County)	79760
Veterans Administration		Water Front Park	78130	Westover Hills	76107
(Part of Waco)	76711	Waterloo (Grayson County)	75020	Westphalia	76656
Viboras	78361	Waterloo (Williamson		West Point (Fayette County)	78963
Vick	76937	County)	76574	West Point (Lynn County)	79373
Vickers	75959	Waterman	75935	West Sinton	78370
Vickery (Part of Dallas)	75231	Waters Bluff	75792	West Tawakoni	75474
Victoria (Victoria County)	77901-05	Water Valley	76958	West Texas (Part of	
For specific Victoria Zip Codes		Waterwood	77359	Canyon)	79016
call (512) 575-2363		Watkins	75103	West Texas State University	
Victoria (Limestone County)	76664	Watson	76550	(Part of Canyon)	79016
Victoria Square (Part of		Watsonville	76063	West University Place	77005
Victoria)	77904	Watt	76664	West Vernon (Part of	
Victory City	75561	Waxahachie	75165	Vernon)	76384
Victory Gardens	77630	Wayside	79094	Westview (Part of Waco)	76710
Vidauri	78377	Wealthy	77871	Westville	75862
Vidor	77662	Weatherford	76086-87	West Waco (Part of Waco)	76710
Vienna	77964	For specific Weatherford Zip		Westway	79835
View	79605	Codes call (817) 594-3072		Westwood	75951
Vigo Park	79088	Weaver	75478	Westwood Mall (Part of	
Vilas	76534	Webberville	78653	Houston)	77036
Villa Cavazos	78520	Webbville	76828	Westworth Village	76114
Village (Dallas County)	75205	Webster (Harris County)	77598	Wetmore (Part of San	
Village (Midland County)	79705	Webster (Wood County)	75494	Antonio)	78163
Village Mills	77663	Weches	75844	Wetsel	75069
Village Shores	78130	Wedgewood (Part of Fort		Wexford Park	77662
Village West	78759	Worth)	76133	Whaley	75570
Villa Nueva	78520	Weedhaven	77979	Wharton	77488
Villareales	78582	Weeping Mary	75925	Whatley	75657
Vincent	79511	Weesatche	77993	Wheatland	76116
Vineyard	76056	Weimar	78962	Wheeler	79096
Vinton	79821	Weinert	76388	Wheeler Springs	75835
Viola	78409	Weir	78674	Wheelock	77882
Violet	78380	Weirville	75482	Whispering Oaks	75453
Virginia Point	77550	Welch	79377	Whispering Pines	
Vistula	75851	Welch Store	75973	(Montgomery County)	77302
Voca	76887	Welcome	78944	Whispering Pines (Walker	
Volente	78641	Weldon	75851	County)	77358
Von Ormy	78073	Welfare	78006	Whisperwood (Part of	
Voss	76888	Wellborn	77881	Lubbock)	79416
Votaw	77376	Wellington	79095	White City (San Augustine	
Voth (Part of Beaumont)	77709	Wellman	79378	County)	75929
Vsetin	77964	Wells (Cherokee County)	75976	White City (Wilbarger	
Waco	76701-16	Wells (Lynn County)	79351	County)	76384
For specific Waco Zip Codes call		Wellswood	75929	White City (Wise County)	76234
(817) 757-6585		Wentworth	75103	White Deer	79097
Wade	78372	Weser	77963	Whiteface	79379
Wadsworth	77483	Weslaco	78596	Whiteflat	79234
Waelder	78959	Weslaco Farm Labor Center		White Hall (Bell County)	76557
Wainwright (Part of San		(Part of Weslaco)	78596	White Hall (Coryell County)	76528
Antonio)	78208	Weslayan (Part of Houston)	77005	White Hall (Grimes County)	77868
Waka	79093	Wesley	77833	Whitehall (Kaufman County)	75147
Wake	79243	Wesley Grove	77831	Whitehouse	75791
Wakefield (Morris County)	75638	West	76691	Whiteland	76858
Wakefield (Polk County)	75939	West Austin (Part of Austin)	78703	White Mound	75090
Wake Village	75501	West Baytown (Part of		White Oak (Gregg County)	75693
Walburg	78673	Baytown)	77520	White Oak (Montgomery	
Waldeck	78946	West Bluff	77630	County)	77365
Walden	77356	Westbrook	79565	White Oak Valley Estates	77301
Walden Place	77093	West Camp	79325	White Rock (Dallas County)	75218
Walden Woods (Part of		Westchase (Part of		White Rock (Grayson	
Houston)	77012	Houston)	77042	County)	75491
Waldrip	76852	West Cliff	76513	White Rock (Hunt County)	75423
Walhalla	78954	West Columbia	77486	White Rock (Red River	
Walkers Mill	75650	West Delta	75448	County)	75426
Wall	76957	Western Plaza Mall (Part of		White Rock (San Augustine	
Wallace	75103	Amarillo)	79101	County)	75972
Wallace Chapel	75686	Westfield	77090	Whitesboro	76273
Waller	77484	Westfield Estates	77093	White Settlement	76108
Wallis	77485	West Fort Hood	76544	Whitestar	79234
Wallisville	77597	West Galveston (Part of		White Stone (Part of Cedar	
Walnut Bend	76273	Jamaica Beach)	77551	Park)	78641
Walnut Creek	77355	Westgate	77429	Whiteway	76538
Walnut Forest	78753	Westgate Acres	79763	Whitewright	75491
Walnut Grove (Collin		Westgate Mall (Potter		Whitharral	79380
County)	75069	County)	79121	Whitman	77833
Walnut Grove (Smith		Westgate Mall (Travis		Whitney	76692
County)	75703	County)	78704	Whitsett	78075
Walnut Hill (Part of Dallas)	75220	Westgate Towne Center		Whitt	76090
Walnut Hills	77303	(Part of Abilene)	79605	Whitton	75103
Walnut Springs (Bosque		Westhaven	78130	Whon	76889
County)	76690	Westhaven Park (Part of		Wichita Falls	76301-11
Walnut Springs		Amarillo)	79109	For specific Wichita Falls Zip	
(Montgomery County)	77355	Westheimer (Part of		Codes call (817) 766-4188	
Walston Springs	75801	Houston)	77042	Wichita Valley Farms	76301
Walton (Cass County)	71082	Westhill Addition	77437	Wickett	79788
Walton (Van Zandt County)	75751	Westhoff	77994	Wiedeville	77833
Wamba	75503	West Lake (Jasper County)	75951	Wieland	75401
Waples	76048	Westlake (Tarrant County)	76248	Wiergate	75977
Warda	78960	Westlake (Travis County)	78746	Wiggins	75555
Ward Prairie	75840	West Lake Highlands	78746	Wigginsville	77301
Wards Creek	75574	West Lake Hills	78716	Wilcox	77879
Waring	78074	Westlawn	77630	Wildcat (Part of Plano)	75023
Warren	77664	West Mineola (Part of		Wilderville	76570
Warren City	75647	Mineola)	75773	Wild Horse	79855
Warrenton	78961	Westminster	75096	Wild Hurst	75925
Warsaw	75142	West Mountain	75647	Wildorado	79098
Washburn	79019	West Odessa	79763	Wild Peach Village	77422
Washington	77880	Weston	75097		

TEXAS Wildwood-Zybach

Place	ZIP
Wildwood (Bexar County)	78240
Wildwood (Hardin County)	77663
Wildwood (Walker County)	77367
Wilford Hall U.S.A.F. Hospital (Part of San Antonio)	78236
Wilkins	75755
Wilkinson	75455
Willacy County Housing Authority	78580
Willamar	78580
William Beaumont Army Medical Center	79920
William Beaumont Hospital (Part of El Paso)	79920
William Penn	77833
William Rice (Part of Houston)	77005
Williams	76471
Williamsburg (Lamar County)	75460
Williamsburg (Lavaca County)	77964
William Spear Addition	75704
Willis	77378
Willow City	78675
Willow Grove	75954
Willow Park	76086
Willow Place (Part of Houston)	77070
Willow Point	76026
Willow Springs (Fayette County)	78940
Willow Springs (Rains County)	75440
Wills Point	75169
Wilmer	75172
Wilmeth	79567
Wilson (Falls County)	76519
Wilson (Lynn County)	79381
Wimberley	78676
Winchell	76827
Winchester	78964
Windcrest	78239
Windom	75492
Windsor Estates	78284
Windsor Park Mall (Part of San Antonio)	78218
Windthorst	76389
Winedale	77835
Winfield	75493
Winfree (Chambers County)	77535
Winfree (Orange County)	77630
Wingate	79566
Wink	79789
Winkler	75859
Winnie	77665
Winningkoff (Part of Lucas)	75069
Winnsboro	75494
Winona	75792
Winter Haven	78839
Winters	79567
Winter Valley Estates	77535
Winwood Mall (Part of Odessa)	79760
Witting	77975
Wizard Wells	76056
Woden	75978
Wolfe City	75496
Wolf Flat	79261
Wolfforth	79382
Womack	76634
Wonderland (Part of San Antonio)	78201
Woodal Farm	76520
Woodbine	76240
Woodbranch	77357
Woodbury	76645
Wood-Canyon Waters	75147
Woodcrest	77301
Woodhaven Estates	77304
Wood Hollow	77365
Woodlake (Bexar County)	78244
Woodlake (Grayson County)	75020
Woodlake (Trinity County)	75865
Woodland	75436
Woodland Estates	75948
Woodland Heights (Part of Brownwood)	76801
Woodland Hills (Henderson County)	75143
Woodland Hills (Hill County)	76692
Woodland Lakes	77355
Woodland Shores	75630
Woodlawn (Angelina County)	75901
Woodlawn (Harrison County)	75694
Woodlawn Lakes	77355
Woodley	75670
Woodloch	77301
Woodrow (Fort Bend County)	77430
Woodrow (Lubbock County)	79401
Woods	75974
Woodsboro	78393
Woods of Shavano	78249
Woodson	76091
Wood Springs	75701
Woodville	75979
Woodway (McLennan County)	76710
Woodway (Victoria County)	77901
Woody Acres	77365
Woosley	75472
World Trade Center (Part of Dallas)	75207
Wortham	76693
Worthing	77964
Wright City	75684
Wrightsboro	78677
Wylie (Collin County)	75098
Wylie (Franklin County)	75494
Wylie (Taylor County)	79605
Wynne Rock Estates	78737
Wynne Unit	77340
Wynnewood Village (Part of Dallas)	75224
Yale	75457
Yancey	78886
Yantis	75497
Yarboro	77868
Yard	75861
Yarrelton	76518
Yaupon Cove	77351
Ybanez	79331
Yellowpine	75948
Yescas	78586
Yoakum	77995
Yorktown	78164
Young	75840
Youngsport	76544
Yowell	75428
Ysleta (Part of El Paso)	79907
Zabcikville	76501
Zapata	78076
Zavalla	75980
Zephyr	76890
Zionsville	77833
Zipp City (Part of Balch Springs)	75149
Zippville	78155
Zorn	78666
Zuehl	78124
Zunkerville	78119
Zybach	79011

Abraham-Loa **UTAH** **557**

Name	ZIP
Abraham	84635
Adamsville	84713
Alpine	84003
Alta	84092
Altamont	84001
Alton	84710
Altonah	84002
Amalga	84335
American Fork	84003-04
For specific American Fork Zip Codes call (801) 756-3241	
Aneth	84510
Angle	84712
Annabella	84711
Antimony	84712
Arcadia	84012
Arsenal (Part of Sunset)	84015
Aspen Acres	84055
Atwood (Part of Murray)	84107
Aurora	84620
Austin	84754
Avon	84328
Axtell	84621
Ballard	84066
Bauer	84071
Bear River City	84301
Beaver	84713
Beaverdam	84306
Belmont Heights	84070
Benjamin	84660
Ben Lomond (Part of Ogden)	84404
Bennion (Salt Lake County)	84118
Benson	84335
Beryl	84714
Beryl Junction	84714
Bicknell	84715
Big Water	84741
Bingham Canyon	84006
Birdseye	84629
Blanding	84511
Bloomington	84770
Bluebell	84007
Bluff	84512
Bluffdale	84065
Bonanza	84078
Boneta	84051
Bonnie (Part of Orem)	84057
Bothwell	84337
Boulder	84716
Bountiful	84010-11
For specific Bountiful Zip Codes call (801) 295-5589	
Bowery Haven	84701
Brendel	84540
Brian Head	84719
Bridgeland	84012
Brigham City	84302
Brighton	84121
Brooklyn	84754
Bryce	84764
Bryce Canyon	84717
Burbank	84751
Burmester	84029
Burrville	84701
Bushnell (Part of Brigham City)	84302
Cache Junction	84304
Cache Valley Mall (Part of Logan)	84321
Caineville	84775
Callao	84034
Call Fort	84302
Cannonville	84718
Carbonville	84501
Castle Dale	84513
Castleton	84532
Castle Valley	84532
Cedar City	84720-22
For specific Cedar City Zip Codes call (801) 586-6701	
Cedar Hills	84062
Cedar Valley	84013
Cedarview	84066
Center Creek	84032
Centerfield	84622
Centerville	84014
Central (Sevier County)	84754
Central (Washington County)	84722
Charleston	84032
Chester	84623
Circleville	84723
Cisco	84515
Clarkston	84305
Clawson	84516
Clear Creek (Box Elder County)	83342
Clear Creek (Carbon County)	84526
Clearfield	84015

Name	ZIP
Cleveland	84518
Clinton	84015
Clover	84069
Clyde (Part of Orem)	84057
Coalville	84017
College Ward	84321
Collinston	84306
Columbia	84520
Columbia Junction (Part of East Carbon)	84520
Copperton	84006
Corinne	84307
Cornish	84308
Cottonwood	84121
Cottonwood Heights (Salt Lake County)	84121
Cottonwood Mall	84112
Cove	84320
Crescent	84070
Croydon	84018
Cushing (Part of Midvale)	84047
Daniel	84032
Defas Park	84031
Delta	84624
Deseret	84624
Devils Slide	84050
Deweyville	84309
Downtown (Part of Salt Lake City)	84101
Draper	84020
Dry Fork	84078
Duchesne	84021
Dugway (Tooele County)	84022
Dugway Proving Ground	84022
Dutch John	84023
East Bay (Part of Provo)	84605
East Carbon	84520
Eastland Township	84535
East Layton (Part of Layton)	84041
East Midvale	84047
East Portal	84032
Eastwood Hills	84106
Echo	84024
Eden	84310
Elberta	84626
Elgin	84525
Elk Ridge	84660
Elmo	84521
Elsinore	84724
Elwood	84337
Emery	84522
Emory	84024
Enoch	84720
Enterprise (Morgan County)	84050
Enterprise (Washington County)	84725
Ephraim	84627
Erda	84074
Escalante	84726
Esk Dale	84728
Etna	84313
Eureka	84628
Fairfield	84013
Fairgrounds (Part of Salt Lake City)	84116
Fairview	84629
Farmington	84025
Farr West	84404
Fashion Place (Part of Murray)	84107
Faust	84080
Fayette	84630
Ferron	84523
Fielding	84311
Fillmore	84631
Fish Lake	84701
Flowell	84631
Foothill (Part of Salt Lake City)	84108
Fort Duchesne	84026
Fountain Green	84632
Francis	84036
Freedom	84646
Freeport Center (Part of Clearfield)	84016
Fremont	84747
Fruita	84775
Fruit Heights	84037
Fruitland	84027
Gandy	84728
Garden City	84028
Garland	84312
Garrison	84728
Genola	84655
Glendale	84729
Glenwood	84730
Gorder (Part of Ogden)	84403
Goshen	84633
Goshute Indian Reservation	84034
Gouldings Trading Post	86033
Grand Vu	84515

Name	ZIP
Granger (Part of West Valley City)	84119
Granite	84092
Granite Park	84106
Grantsville	84029
Greendale	84023
Green Lake	84023
Green River	84525
Greenville	84731
Greenwich	84732
Grouse Creek	84313
Grover	84773
Gunlock	84733
Gunnison	84634
Gusher	84030
Hailstone	84032
Hamilton Fort	84720
Hanksville	84734
Hanna	84031
Hardy (Part of Lindon)	84062
Harrisburg Junction	84770
Harrisville	84404
Hatch	84735
Hatton	84637
Hayden	84053
Heber City	84032
Helper	84526
Henefer	84033
Henrieville	84736
Herriman	84065
Hiawatha	84527
Hidden Lake	84055
Highland	84003
Highlands	84050
Hildale	84784
Hill Air Force Base	84056
Hinckley	84635
Holden	84636
Holiday Park	84055
Holladay	84117
Honeyville	84314
Hooper	84315
Hoovers	84750
Howell	84316
Hoytsville	84017
Hunter (Part of West Valley City)	84120
Huntington	84528
Huntsville	84317
Hurricane	84737
Hyde Park	84318
Hyrum	84319
Ibapah	84034
Indianola	84629
Ioka	84066
Ivins	84738
Jensen	84035
Jerusalem	84646
Joseph	84739
Junction	84740
Kamas	84036
Kanab	84741
Kanarraville	84742
Kanesville	84315
Kanosh	84637
Kaysville	84037
Kearns	84118
Keetley	84032
Kelton	84336
Kenilworth	84529
Kimball Junction	84060
Kingston	84743
Koosharem	84744
Lake Point	84074
Lake Shore	84660
Lakeside Resort	84701
Laketown	84038
Lakeview	84601
Lapoint	84039
Lark	84065
La Sal	84530
La Verkin	84745
Lawrence	84528
Layton	84040-41
For specific Layton Zip Codes call (801) 544-1203	
Layton Hills Mall (Part of Layton)	84041
Leamington	84638
Leeds	84746
Leeton	84066
Lehi	84043
Leland	84660
Levan	84639
Lewiston	84320
Liberty	84310
Lincoln	84074
Lindon	84042
Little Bonanza	84008
Littleton	84050
Loa	84747

UTAH

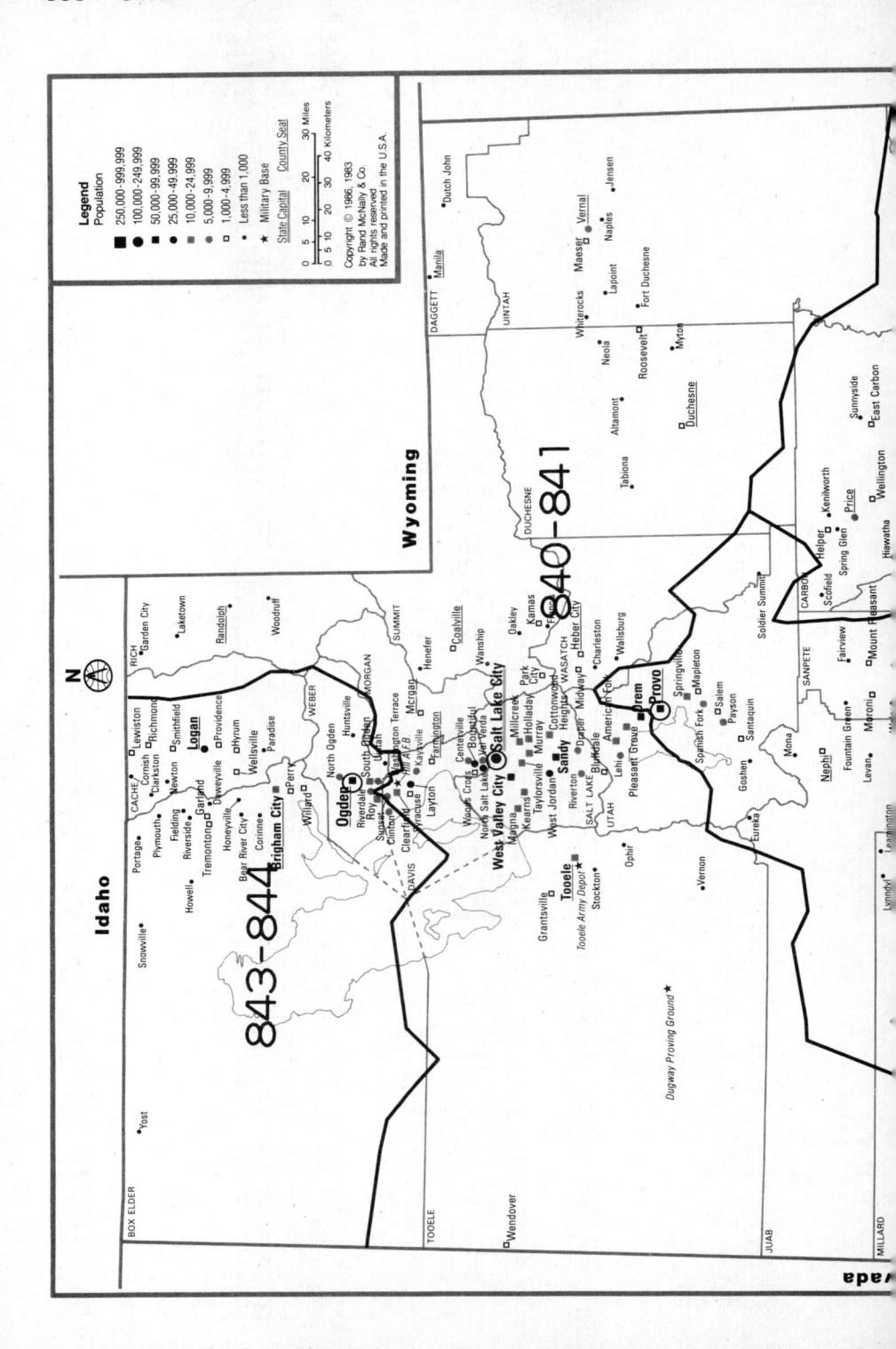

UTAH 559

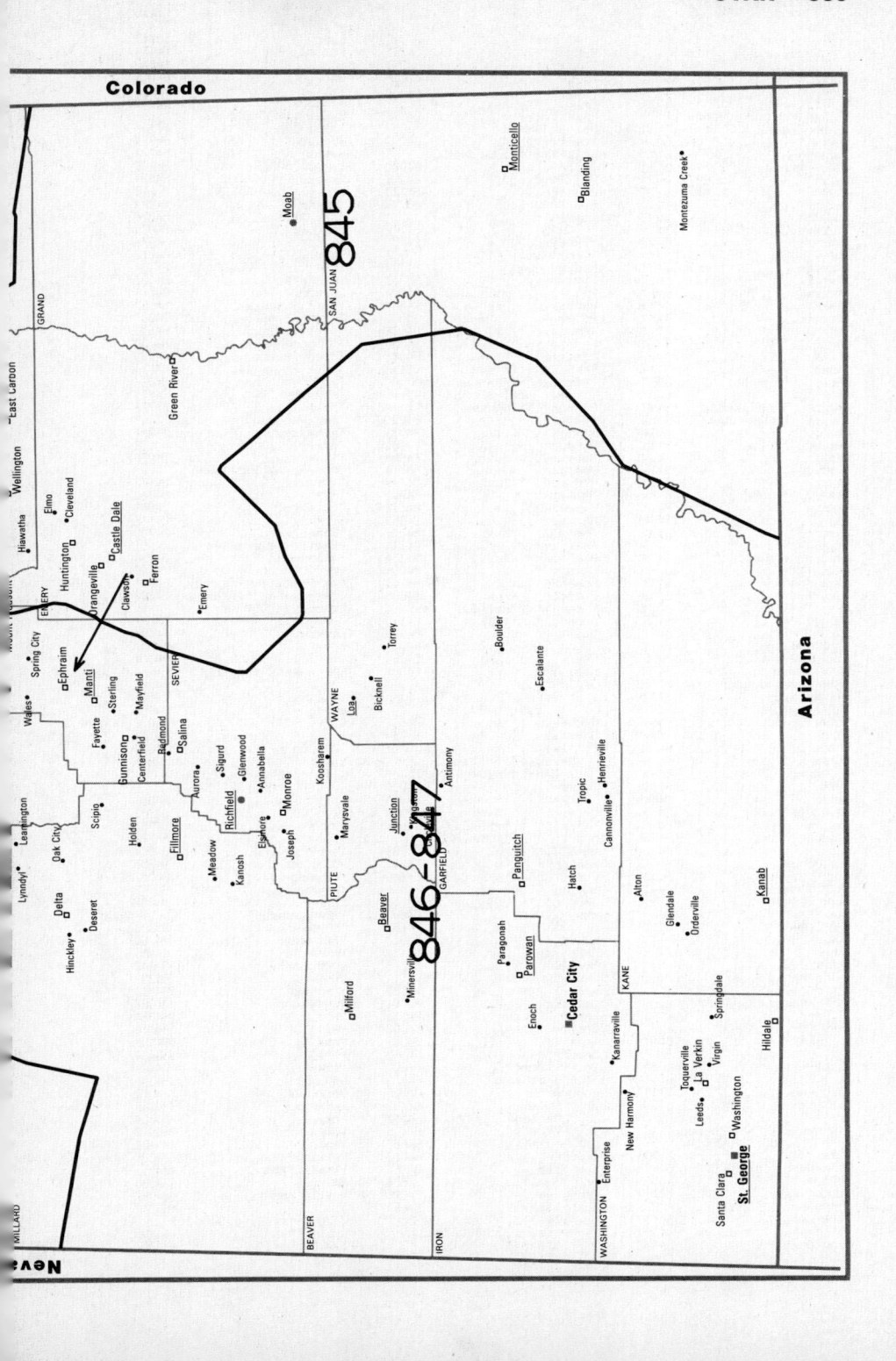

560 UTAH Logan-Zion National Park

Location	ZIP
Logan	84321
Long Valley Junction	84758
Lund	84720
Lyman	84749
Lynn	83346
Lynndyl	84640
Madsen (Part of Honeyville)	84314
Maeser	84078
Magna	84044
Mammoth	84601
Manderfield	84713
Manila	84046
Manti	84642
Mantua	84302
Mapleton	84663
Marion	84036
Marriott	84404
Martin	84526
Marysvale	84750
Mayfield	84643
Meadow	84644
Meadowville	84038
Mendon	84325
Mexican Hat	84531
Middleton	84770
Midvale	84047
Midway	84049
Milburn	84629
Milford	84751
Millcreek (Grand County)	84515
Millcreek (Salt Lake County)	84109
Mills	84639
Millville	84326
Milton	84050
Minersville	84752
Moab	84532
Modena	84753
Molen	84523
Mona	84645
Monarch	84066
Monroe	84754
Montezuma Creek	84534
Monticello	84535
Monti Verdi	84050
Monument Valley	84536
Moore	84523
Morgan	84050
Moroni	84646
Mountain Green	84050
Mountain Home	84051
Mount Carmel	84755
Mount Carmel Junction	84755
Mount Emmons	84001
Mount Olympus	84117
Mount Pleasant	84647
Murray	84107
Myton	84052
Naples	84078
Navajo Indian Reservation	86515
Neola	84053
Nephi	84648
Newcastle	84756
New Harmony	84757
Newton	84327
Nibley	84321
North Creek	84713
North Logan	84321
North Ogden	84404
North Salt Lake	84054
Oak City	84649
Oak Creek	84629
Oakley	84055
Oasis	84650
Ogden	84401-14
For specific Ogden Zip Codes call (801) 627-4437	
Ogden ALC Hardness Test Center	84401
Ogden City Mall (Part of Ogden)	84401
Oljato	86033
Olmstead	84604
Ophir	84071
Orangeville	84537
Orderville	84758
Orem	84057-59
For specific Orem Zip Codes call (801) 225-2071	
Ouray	84063
Pallas (Part of Murray)	84107
Palmyra	84660
Panguitch	84759
Paradise	84328
Paragonah	84760
Park City	84060
Park Terrace	84106

Location	ZIP
Park Valley	84329
Parowan	84761
Partoun	84083
Payson	84651
Penrose	84337
Peoa	84061
Perry	84302
Peruvian Park	84093
Peterson	84050
Pickelville (Part of Garden City)	84028
Pine Mountain	84055
Pine Valley	84722
Pintura	84720
Pioneer (Part of Salt Lake City)	84147
Plain City	84404
Pleasant Grove	84062
Pleasant View	84404
Plymouth	84330
Polls	84050
Portage	84331
Portersville	84050
Price	84501
Promontory	84307
Providence	84332
Provo	84601-06
For specific Provo Zip Codes call (801) 374-2000	
Provo Junction (Part of Provo)	84601
Randlett	84063
Randolph	84064
Redmond	84652
Red Wash	84078
Redwood	84119
Richfield	84701
Richmond	84333
Richville	84050
Riverdale	84405
River Heights	84321
Riverside	84334
Riverton	84065
Rockville	84763
Roosevelt	84066
Roper (Part of South Salt Lake)	84115
Rosette	84329
Round Valley	84038
Roy	84067
Rush Valley	84069
St. George	84770-71
For specific St. George Zip Codes call (801) 673-3312	
Salem	84653
Salina	84654
Salt Lake City	84101-90
For specific Salt Lake City Zip Codes call (801) 974-2200	
Samak	84036
Sandy	84070
	84090-94
For specific Sandy Zip Codes call (801) 255-3442	
Santa Clara	84765
Santaquin	84655
Scipio	84656
Scofield	84526
Sevier	84766
Sherwood Park	84093
Shivwits	84765
Sigurd	84657
Silver Fork	84121
Silver Reef	84746
Skull Valley Indian Reservation	84029
Slaterville	84404
Smithfield	84335
Snowbird	84092
Snowville	84336
Snyderville	84060
Soldier Summit	84601
South Cottonwood	84120
South Jordan	84065
South Ogden	84403
South Salt Lake	84115
South Weber	84405
Spanish Fork	84660
Spring City	84662
Springdale	84767
Springdell	84604
Spring Glen	84526
Spring Lake	84651
Springville	84663-64
For specific Springville Zip Codes call (801) 489-4561	

Location	ZIP
Standrod	83342
Stansbury Park	84074
Starr	84645
Sterling	84665
Stockton	84071
Stoddard	84050
Sugar House (Part of Salt Lake City)	84106
Sugarville	84624
Summit	84772
Summit Point	84535
Sunnyside	84539
Sunset	84015
Sutherland	84624
Swan Creek	84028
Syracuse	84075
Tabiona	84072
Talmage	84073
Taylor	84401
Taylorsville	84107
Teasdale	84773
Terra	84022
Thatcher	84337
Thompson	84540
Thompsonville	84750
Ticaboo	84533
Tooele	84074
Tooele Army Depot	84074
Toquerville	84774
Torrey	84775
Town (Part of Ogden)	84401
Tremonton	84337
Trenton	84338
Tridell	84076
Trolley Square (Part of Salt Lake City)	84102
Tropic	84776
Trout Creek	84083
Ucolo	84535
Uintah	84405
Uintah and Ouray Indian Reservation	84026
Union	84047
Union-East Midvale	84047
University (Part of Provo)	84602
University Mall (Part of Orem)	84057
Upalco	84007
Upton	84017
Utah State Prison	84020
Utah State University (Part of Logan)	84322
Utida (Part of Cornish)	84308
Uvada	84753
Val Verda	84010
Venice	84701
Vermillion	84657
Vernal	84078-79
For specific Vernal Zip Codes call (801) 789-2393	
Vernon	84080
Veyo	84782
Vineyard	84057
Virgin	84779
Vivian Park	84604
Wales	84667
Wallsburg	84082
Wanship	84017
Warren	84404
Washakie Indian Reservation	83203
Washington	84780
Washington Terrace	84403
Wellington	84542
Wellsville	84339
Wendover	84083
West Bountiful	84087
West Jordan	84084
West Point	84015
West Valley City	84120
West Warren	84404
West Weber	84401
Wheelon	84306
White City	84070
Whiterocks	84085
Wildwood	84604
Willard	84340
Wilson	84401
Woodland	84036
Woodland Hills	84653
Woodruff	84086
Woods Cross	84087
Yost	83342
ZCMI Center (Part of Salt Lake City)	84106
Zion National Park	84767

Abnaki-Essex Junction **VERMONT** 561

	ZIP		ZIP		ZIP
Abnaki	05474	Bridgewater Center	05035	Craftsbury	05826
Adamant	05640	Bridgewater Corners	05035	Craftsbury (Town)	05826
Addison	05491	Bridport	05734	Craftsbury Common	05827
Addison (Town)	05491	Bridport (Town)	05734	Cream Hill	05734
Albany	05820	Brighton (Town)	05846	Crystal Beach	05732
Albany (Town)	05820	Brimstone Corner	05083	Cuttingsville	05738
Albany Center	05845	Brimstone Corners	05761	Danby	05739
Alburg	05440	Bristol	05443	Danby (Town)	05739
Alburg (Town)	05440	Bristol (Town)	05443	Danby Corners	05739
Alburg Center	05440	Brockways Mills	05143	Danville	05828
Alburg Springs	05440	Brookfield	05036	Danville (Town)	05828
Alfrecha	05759	Brookfield (Town)	05036	Danville Center	05828
Alpine Village	05674	Brookfield Center	05036	Derby	05829
Ames Hill	05344	Brookline (Town)	05345	Derby (Town)	05829
Amsden	05151	Brookside (Chittenden County)	05494	Derby Line	05830
Andover (Town)	05143			Deweys Mills	05059
Arlington	05250	Brookside (Windham County)	05341	Dorset	05251
Arlington (Town)	05250			Dorset (Town)	05251
Arlington	05250	Brooksville	05753	Dover	05341
Arnold Bay	05491	Brownington	05860	Dover (Town)	05341
Ascutney	05030	Brownington (Town)	05860	Downers	05151
Athens	05143	Brownington Center	05860	Downingville	05443
Athens (Town)	05143	Brownsville	05037	Dows Crossing	05836
Avalon Beach	05750	Brunswick (Town)	03590	Dowsville	05660
Averill (Essex County)	05901	Buck Hollow	05454	Dummerston	05346
Averill (Essex County) (Town)	05901	Buels Gore (Town)	05487	Dummerston (Town)	05346
		Burke	05871	Duxbury (Town)	05676
Averys Gore (Town)	05903	Burke (Town)	05871	Duxbury	05676
Bailey's Mills	05062	Burke Mountain	05832	Eagle Point	05855
Bakersfield	05441	Burlington	05401-04	East Albany	05845
Bakersfield (Town)	05441	For specific Burlington Zip Codes call (802) 863-6033		East Alburgh	05440
Baltimore (Town)	05144			East Arlington	05252
Barnard	05031	Burnham Hill	05843	East Barnard	05068
Barnard (Town)	05031	Burnham Hollow	05757	East Barre	05649
Barnet	05821	Butlers Corners	05452	East Berkshire	05447
Barnet (Town)	05821	Butternut Bend	05761	East Bethel	05032
Barnet Center	05821	Button Bay	05491	East Braintree	05060
Barnumtown	05472	Cabot	05647	East Brookfield	05036
Barre (Washington County)	05641	Cabot (Town)	05647	East Burke	05832
Barre (Washington County) (Town)	05678	Cadys Falls	05661	East Cabot	05647
		Calais	05648	East Calais	05650
Barre Transfer (Part of Montpelier)	05602	Calais (Town)	05648	East Cambridge	05464
		Cambridge	05444	East Charleston	05833
Barton	05822	Cambridge (Town)	05444	East Charlotte	05445
Barton (Town)	05822	Cambridge Junction	05464	East Clarendon	05759
Bartonsville	05143	Cambridgeport	05141	East Concord	05906
Basin Harbor	05491	Canaan	05903	East Corinth	05040
Bayside	05404	Canaan (Town)	05903	East Craftsbury	05826
Beanville	05060	Castleton	05735	East Dorset	05253
Beaulieu's Corner	05459	Castleton (Town)	05735	East Dover	05341
Beebe Plain	05823	Cavendish	05142	East Dummerston	05346
Beecher Falls	05902	Cavendish (Town)	05142	East Enosburg	05450
Bellows Falls	05101	Cavendish Center	05142	East Fairfield	05448
Belmont	05730	Cedar Beach	05445	East Fletcher	05464
Belvidere (Town)	05442	Center Rutland	05736	East Franklin	05457
Belvidere Center	05492	Centerville (Lamoille County)	05655	East Granville	05669
Belvidere Corners	05492	Centerville (Windsor County)	05001	East Hardwick	05836
Belvidere Junction	05492			East Haven	05837
Bennington	05201	Champlain (Part of South Burlington)	05401	East Haven (Town)	05837
Bennington (Town)	05201			East Highgate	05459
Bennington College (Part of North Bennington)	05201	Charleston (Town)	05872	East Hubbardton	05735
		Charlotte	05445	East Jamaica	05343
Benson	05731	Charlotte (Town)	05445	East Johnson	05656
Benson (Town)	05731	Checkerberry	05468	East Lyndon	05851
Benson Landing	05743	Chelsea	05038	East Middlebury	05740
Berkshire	05447	Chelsea (Town)	05038	East Monkton	05443
Berkshire (Town)	05450	Chelsea West Hill	05041	East Montpelier	05651
Berlin (Town)	05602	Chester	05143	East Montpelier (Town)	05651
Berlin Corners	05602	Chester (Town)	05143	East Montpelier Center	05602
Bethel	05032	Chester-Chester Depot	05143	East Orange	05086
Bethel (Town)	05032	Chester Depot	05144	East Peacham	05862
Bethel Gilead	05060	Chimney Corner	05446	East Pittsford	05701
Binghamville	05444	Chimney Point	05491	East Poultney	05741
Birdland	05474	Chipman Lake	05739	East Putney	05346
Bliss Pond	05640	Chipmans Point	05760	East Randolph	05041
Blissville	05764	Chippenhook	05777	East Richford	05476
Bloomfield	03590	Chiselville	05250	East Roxbury	05663
Bloomfield (Town)	03590	Chittenden	05737	East Rupert	05761
Blossoms Corners	05775	Chittenden (Town)	05737	East Ryegate	05042
Bolton	05676	Clarendon	05759	East Sheldon	05450
Bolton (Town)	05676	Clarendon (Town)	05759	East Shoreham	05770
Bolton Valley	05477	Clarendon Springs	05777	East St. Johnsbury	05838
Boltonville	05081	Cleveland Corner	05661	East Sutton Ridge	05867
Bomoseen (Rutland County)	05732	Cloverdale	05489	East Thetford	05043
Bondville	05340	Colbyville	05676	East Wallingford	05742
Bordoville	05450	Colchester	05446	East Warren	05674
Bowlsville	05742	Colchester (Town)	05446	Eden	05652
Bradford	05033	Cold River	05738	Eden (Town)	05652
Bradford (Town)	05033	Concord	05824	Eden Mills	05653
Bragg	05055	Concord (Town)	05824	Egypt	05448
Braintree	05060	Concord Corner	05824	Elmore (Town)	05657
Braintree (Town)	05060	Copperfield	05079	Ely	05044
Braintree Hill	05060	Corinth	05039	Enosburg (Town)	05450
Brandon	05733	Corinth (Town)	05039	Enosburg Center	05450
Brandon (Town)	05733	Corinth Center	05039	Enosburg Falls	05450
Brattleboro	05301	Corinth Corners	05039	Essex	05451
Brattleboro (Town)	05301	Cornwall	05753	Essex (Town)	05451
Brattleboro Center	05301	Cornwall (Town)	05753	Essex Junction	05452-53
Bread Loaf	05753	Coventry	05825	For specific Essex Junction Zip Codes call (802) 878-3085	
Bridgewater	05034	Coventry (Town)	05825		
Bridgewater (Town)	05034				

562 VERMONT

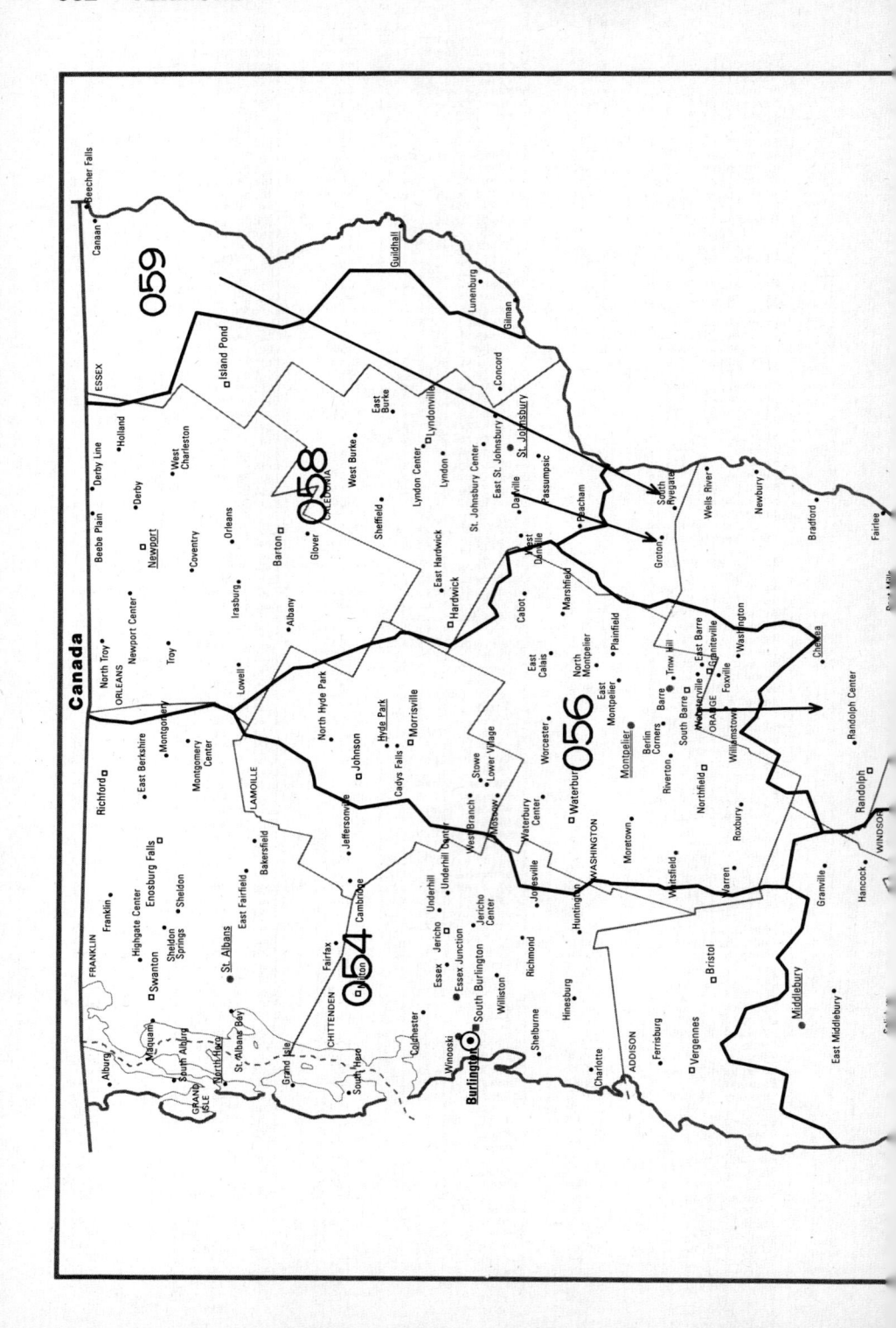

VERMONT 563

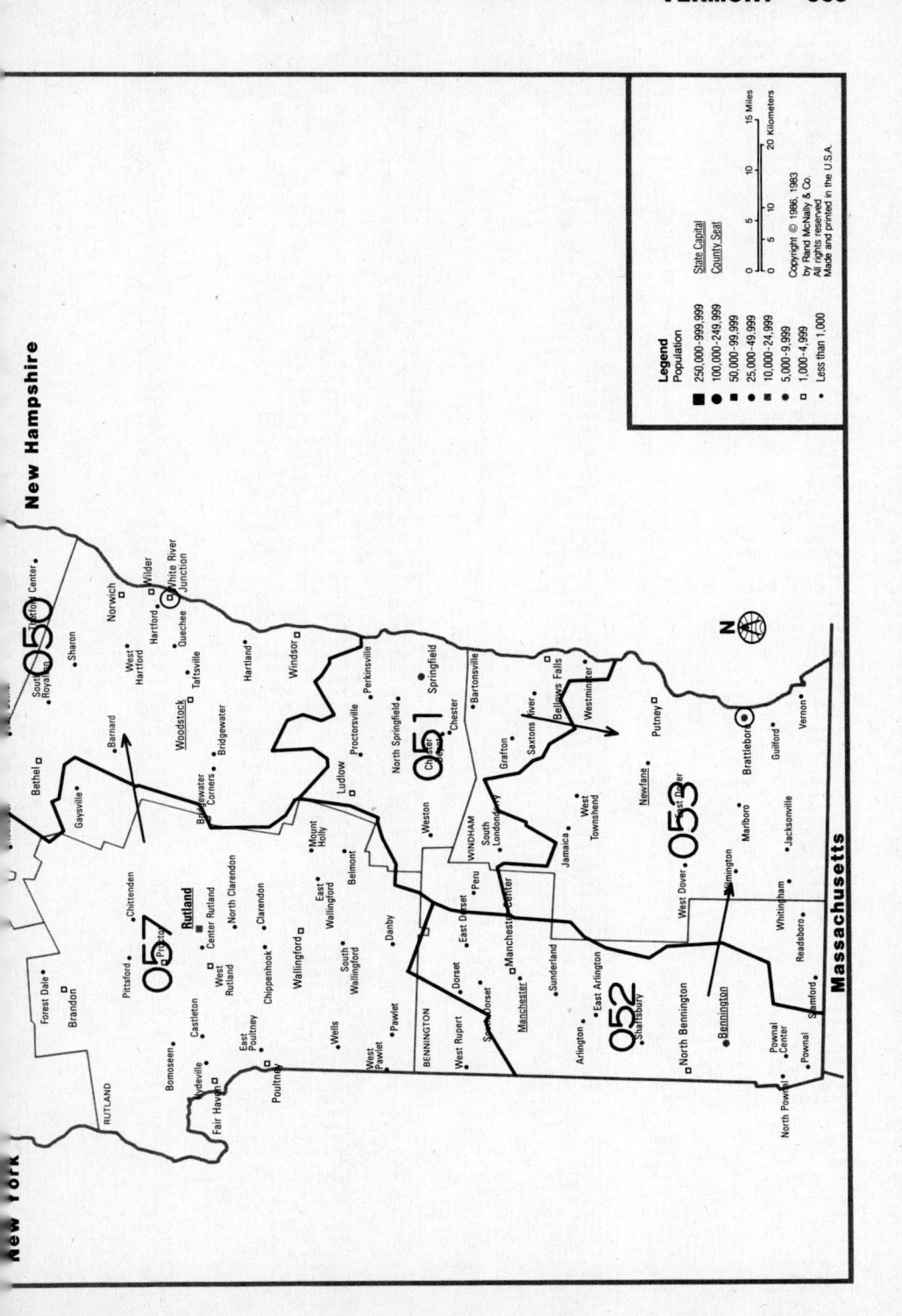

564 VERMONT Ethan Allen Shopping Center-North Clarendon

	ZIP		ZIP		ZIP
Ethan Allen Shopping Center (Part of Burlington)	05404	Highgate Center	05459	Lyndon	05849
Evansville	05860	Highgate Falls	05459	Lyndon (Town)	05849
Fairfax	05454	Highgate Springs	05460	Lyndon Center	05850
Fairfax (Town)	05454	Hinesburg	05461	Lyndon Corners	05849
Fairfax Falls	05454	Hinesburg (Town)	05461	Lyndon State College	05851
Fairfield	05455	Hinesburg	05301	Lyndonville	05851
Fairfield (Town)	05455	Holden	05763	McIndoe Falls	05050
Fairfield Station	05455	Holland	05830	Mackville	05843
Fair Haven (Rutland County) (Town)	05743	Holland (Town)	05830	Mad River Glen	05673
Fair Haven (Rutland County)	05743	Hortonia	05760	Maidstone (Town)	05905
Fairlee	05045	Hortonville	05758	Maidstone Lake	03590
Fairlee (Town)	05045	Houghtonville	05146	Mallets Bay	05404
Fays Corner	05477	Hubbard Corner	05478	Manchester (Town)	05254
Fayston (Town)	05660	Hubbardton	05732	Manchester (Bennington County)	05254
Ferdinand (Town)	05905	Hubbardton (Town)	05732	Manchester (Bennington County)	05255
Fernville	05733	Huntington	05462	Manchester Center	05255
Ferrisburg	05456	Huntington (Town)	05462	Maple Dell	05156
Ferrisburg (Town)	05456	Huntington Center	05462	Maquam	05488
Fieldsville	05089	Huntville	05454	Marlboro (Town)	05344
Fletcher	05444	Hutchins	05471	Marlboro	05344
Fletcher (Town)	05444	Hyde Park	05655	Marshfield	05658
Florence	05744	Hyde Park (Town)	05655	Marshfield (Town)	05658
Fonda	05488	Hydeville	05750	Mary Meyer	05353
Forest Dale	05745	Indian Point (Part of Newport)	05855	Mechanicsville	05477
Foxville	05654	Inwood	05821	Medburyville	05363
Franklin	05457	Ira	05777	Melville	05478
Franklin (Town)	05457	Ira (Town)	05777	Mendon	05701
Freedleyville	05253	Irasburg	05845	Mendon (Town)	05701
Gallup Mills	05858	Irasburg (Town)	05845	Merrill Corner	05845
Garfield	05661	Irasville	05673	Middlebury	05753
Gassetts	05144	Island Pond	05846	Middlebury (Town)	05753
Gaysville	05746	Isle La Motte	05463	Middlesex	05602
Georgia	05454	Isle La Motte (Town)	05463	Middlesex (Town)	05602
Georgia (Town)	05478	Jacksonville	05342	Middlesex Center	05602
Georgia Center	05478	Jamaica	05343	Middletown	05143
Georgia Plain	05468	Jamaica (Town)	05343	Middletown Springs	05757
Gilman	05904	Jay	05859	Middletown Springs (Town)	05757
Glastenbury (Town)	05262	Jay (Town)	05859	Mile Point	05491
Glover	05839	Jay Peak	05859	Miles Pond	05858
Glover (Town)	05839	Jeffersonville	05464	Millbrook	05053
Goodrich Four Corners	05055	Jenneville	05089	Mill Village (Orange County)	05079
Goose City	05341	Jericho	05465	Mill Village (Orleans County)	05827
Goose Green	05039	Jericho (Town)	05465	Milton	05468
Gordon Landing	05458	Jericho Center	05465	Milton (Town)	05468
Goshen	05733	Jerusalem	05443	Miltonboro	05468
Goshen (Town)	05733	Joes Pond	05873	Monkton	05469
Goulds Mills	05156	Johnson	05656	Monkton (Town)	05469
Grafton	05146	Johnson (Town)	05656	Monkton Ridge	05473
Grafton (Town)	05146	Jonesville	05466	Montgomery	05470
Grahamville	05149	Kansas	05252	Montgomery (Town)	05470
Granby	05840	Keeler Bay	05486	Montgomery Center	05471
Granby (Town)	05840	Kendall	05043	Montpelier	05601-02
Grand Isle	05458	Kendricks Corner	05150	For specific Montpelier Zip Codes call (802) 823-4404	
Grand Isle (Town)	05458	Killington	05751		
Graniteville	05654	Kimball	05822	Moretown	05660
Graniteville-East Barre	05654	Kirby (Town)	05824	Moretown (Town)	05660
Granville (Town)	05747	Kirby Corner	05495	Moretown Common	05660
Granville	05747	Lake Dunmore	05769	Morgan	05853
Green Acres	05477	Lake Elmore	05657	Morgan (Town)	05853
Green Bay	05046	Lake Fairlee	05044	Morgan Center	05855
Greenbush	05151	Lake Hortonia	05743	Morristown	05661
Green River	05301	Lake Morey	05045	Morristown (Town)	05661
Greensboro	05841	Lake Park	05855	Morrisville	05661
Greensboro (Town)	05841	Lake Raponda	05363	Moscow	05662
Greensboro Bend	05842	Lake Rescue	05149	Mosquitoville	05042
Greens Corners	05478	Lake St. Catherine	05764	Mount Holly	05758
Groton	05046	Lakewood	05488	Mount Holly (Town)	05758
Groton (Town)	05046	Landgrove	05148	Mount Snow	05356
Guildhall	05905	Landgrove (Town)	05148	Mount Tabor	05739
Guildhall (Town)	05905	Lapham Bay	05734	Mount Tabor (Town)	05739
Guilford	05301	Larrabees Point	05770	Nashville	05465
Guilford (Town)	05301	Leicester	05733	Neshobe Beach	05732
Guilford Center	05301	Leicester (Town)	05733	Newark	05871
Halifax	05358	Leicester Junction	05778	Newark (Town)	05871
Halifax (Town)	05358	Lemington	03576	Newark Hollow	05871
Halls Lake	05081	Lemington (Town)	03576	New Boston (Windsor County)	05772
Hammondsville	05062	Lewis (Town)	05905		
Hancock	05748	Lewiston	05055	New Boston (Windsor County)	05055
Hancock (Town)	05748	Lilliesville	05032	Newbury	05051
Hanksville	05487	Lincoln	05443	Newbury (Town)	05051
Hardscrabble	05156	Lincoln (Town)	05443	Newbury Center	05081
Hardwick	05843	Lindsay Beach	05855	Newfane	05345
Hardwick (Town)	05843	Londonderry	05148	Newfane (Town)	05345
Hardwick Center	05843	Londonderry (Town)	05148	New Haven (Town)	05472
Hardwick Steet	05836	Long Point	05473	New Haven (Addison County)	05472
Harmonyville	05353	Lowell	05847		
Harrisville	05301	Lowell (Town)	05847	New Haven Mills	05443
Hartford	05047	Lower Branch	05060	Newport (Orleans County)	05855
Hartford (Town)	05047	Lower Cabot	05658	Newport (Orleans County) (Town)	05857
Hartland	05048	Lower Granville	05747		
Hartland (Town)	05048	Lower Plain	05033	Newport Center	05857
Hartland Four Corners	05049	Lower Village	05672	North Bennington	05257
Harvey	05828	Lower Waterford	05848	North Burlington (Part of Burlington)	05401
Healdville	05758	Lower Websterville	05641		
Heartwellville	05350	Ludlow	05149	North Calais	05650
Hectorville	05471	Ludlow (Town)	05149	North Cambridge	05464
Hewitts Corners	05053	Lunenburg	05906	North Chester	05144
Highgate (Town)	05459	Lunenburg (Town)	05906	North Clarendon	05759
		Lyman	05001		
		Lympus	05032		

North Concord-Union Village **VERMONT** 565

Name	ZIP	Name	ZIP	Name	ZIP
North Concord	05858	Queen City Park (Part of South Burlington)	05401	Smugglers Notch	05464
North Danville	05819			Sodom	05257
North Derby	05855	Ralston Corner	05824	Somerset (Town)	05345
North Dorset	05253	Randolph	05060	South Albany	05875
North Duxbury	05676	Randolph (Town)	05060	South Alburg	05440
North Fairfax	05454	Randolph Center	05061	South Barre	05670
North Fayston	05660	Rawsonville	05155	South Burlington	05403
North Ferrisburg (Addison County)	05473	Reading	05062	South Cabot	05658
		Reading (Town)	05062	South Cambridge	05464
Northfield	05663	Reading Center	05062	South Corinth	05039
Northfield (Town)	05663	Readsboro	05350	South Danville	05828
Northfield Center	05663	Readsboro (Town)	05350	South Dorset	05251
Northfield Falls	05664	Readsboro Falls	05350	South Duxbury	05660
North Hartland	05052	Red Village	05851	South End	05739
North Hero	05474	Reedville	05143	South Hero	05486
North Hero (Town)	05474	Rhode Island Corner	05477	South Hero (Town)	05486
North Hyde Park	05665	Rices Mills	05075	South Lincoln	05443
North Montpelier	05666	Richford	05476	South Londonderry	05155
North Orwell	05760	Richford (Town)	05476	South Lunenburg	05906
North Pomfret	05053	Richmond	05477	South Newbury	05051
North Pownal	05260	Richmond (Town)	05477	South Newfane	05351
North Randolph	05041	Ricker Mills	05046	South Northfield	05663
North Royalton	05068	Ripton	05766	South Peacham	05821
North Rupert	05761	Ripton (Town)	05766	South Pomfret	05067
North Sheldon	05485	Riverton	05663	South Poultney	05764
North Sherburne	05751	Robinson	05767	South Randolph	05041
North Shrewsbury	05738	Rochester	05767	South Reading	05153
North Springfield	05150	Rochester (Town)	05767	South Richford	05476
North Thetford	05054	Rockingham	05101	South Royalton	05068
North Troy	05859	Rockingham (Town)	05101	South Ryegate	05069
North Tunbridge	05077	Rockville	05443	South Starksboro	05487
North Vernon	05354	Rocky Dale	05443	South Strafford	05070
North Westminster	05101	Round Pond	05069	South Tunbridge	05068
North Windham	05148	Roxbury	05669	South Vershire	05079
North Wolcott	05680	Roxbury (Town)	05669	South Walden	05843
Norton	05907	Roxbury Flat	05669	South Wallingford	05773
Norton (Town)	05907	Royalton	05068	South Wardsboro	05355
Norwich	05055	Royalton (Town)	05068	South Washington	05675
Norwich (Town)	05055	Rupert	05768	South Wheelock	05851
Norwich University (Part of Northfield)	05663	Rupert (Town)	05768	South Windham	05359
		Russellville	05738	South Woodbury	05681
Oakland	05478	Russtown	05001	South Woodstock	05071
Oil City	05072	Rutland	05701-02	Spoonerville	05144
Old Bennington	05201	For specific Rutland Zip Codes call (802) 773-0222		Springfield	05156
Old Church	05060			Springfield (Town)	05156
Orange	05641	Ryegate	05042	Stamford	05352
Orange (Town)	05641	Ryegate (Town)	05042	Stamford (Town)	05352
Orchard Lane	05156	St. Albans (Franklin County)	05478	Stannard	05842
Orleans	05860	St. Albans (Franklin County) (Town)	05481	Stannard (Town)	05842
Orwell	05760			Starksboro	05487
Orwell (Town)	05760	St. Albans Bay	05481	Starksboro (Town)	05487
Panton	05491	St. Albans Hill	05478	Stevens Mills	05476
Panton (Town)	05491	St. Albans Shopping Center (Part of St. Albans)	05478	Stevensville	05489
Paper Mill Village	05257			Stockbridge	05772
Passumpsic	05861	St. George (Town)	05495	Stockbridge (Town)	05772
Pawlet	05761	St. Johnsbury	05819	Stowe	05672
Pawlet (Town)	05761	St. Johnsbury (Town)	05819	Stowe (Town)	05672
Peacham	05862	St. Johnsbury Center	05863	Strafford	05072
Peacham (Town)	05862	Saint Michael's College	05404	Strafford (Town)	05072
Pearl	05458	St. Rocks	05478	Stratton (Town)	05360
Peaseville	05143	Salisbury (Town)	05769	Stratton Mountain	05155
Pedden Acres	05156	Salisbury (Addison County)	05769	Sudbury	05733
Pekin	05667	Samsonville	05450	Sudbury (Town)	05733
Perkinsville	05151	Sanderson Corner	05454	Sugarbush Valley	05674
Peru	05152	Sandgate	05250	Summer Point	05491
Peru (Town)	05152	Sandgate (Town)	05250	Summit	05758
Peth	05060	Saxtons River	05154	Sunderland	05250
Pierces Corner	05759	Scottsville	05739	Sunderland (Town)	05250
Pikes Falls	05343	Searsburg	05363	Sutton	05867
Pittsfield	05762	Searsburg (Town)	05363	Sutton (Town)	05867
Pittsfield (Town)	05762	Seymour Lake	05853	Swanton	05488
Pittsford	05763	Shadow Lake	05839	Swanton (Town)	05488
Pittsford (Town)	05763	Shady Rill	05602	Tafts Corner	05495
Plainfield	05667	Shaftsbury	05262	Taftsville	05073
Plainfield (Town)	05667	Shaftsbury (Town)	05262	Talcville	05767
Pleasant Valley	05458	Shaftsbury Center	05262	Tarbellville	05742
Plymouth	05056	Sharon	05065	The Bluffs (Part of Newport)	05855
Plymouth (Town)	05056	Sharon (Town)	05065	The Island	05161
Plymouth Kingdom	05149	Shawville	05457	Thetford	05074
Plymouth Union	05056	Sheddsville	05089	Thetford (Town)	05074
Pomfret	05053	Sheffield	05866	Thetford Center	05075
Pomfret (Town)	05053	Sheffield (Town)	05866	Thompsonburg	05148
Post Mills	05058	Sheffield Square	05866	Thompson's Point	05445
Potash Bay	05491	Shelburne	05482	Tinmouth	05773
Potash Point	05491	Shelburne (Town)	05482	Tinmouth (Town)	05773
Pottersville	05680	Shelburne Falls	05482	Topsham	05076
Poultney	05764	Shelburne Road Section (Part of South Burlington)	05401	Topsham (Town)	05076
Poultney (Town)	05764			Topsham Four Corners	05040
Pownal (Town)	05261	Sheldon	05483	Townshend	05353
Pownal	05261	Sheldon (Town)	05483	Townshend (Town)	05353
Pownal Center	05261	Sheldon Junction	05483	Trow Hill	05641
Prindle Corner	05445	Sheldon Springs	05485	Troy	05868
Proctor (Rutland County) (Town)	05765	Sherburne (Town)	05751	Troy (Town)	05868
		Shoreham	05770	Tunbridge	05077
Proctor (Rutland County)	05765	Shoreham (Town)	05770	Tunbridge (Town)	05077
Proctorsville	05153	Shoreham Center	05770	Tyson	05149
Prosper	05091	Shrewsbury	05738	Una Bella	05201
Putnamville	05602	Shrewsbury (Town)	05738	Underhill	05489
Putney	05346	Simonsville	05143	Underhill (Town)	05489
Putney (Town)	05346	Simpsonville	05353	Underhill Center	05490
Quechee	05059	Smithville	05149	Union Village	05043

VERMONT University Mall-Wrightsville

Location	ZIP
University Mall (Part of South Burlington)	05401
University of Vermont (Part of Burlington)	05405
Upper Graniteville	05654
Vergennes	05491
Vernon	05354
Vernon (Town)	05354
Vershire	05079
Vershire (Town)	05079
Vershire Center	05079
Vershire Heights	05079
Victory (Town)	05858
Waitsfield	05673
Waitsfield (Town)	05673
Waitsfield Common	05673
Waits River	05086
Walden	05873
Walden (Town)	05873
Walden Heights	05873
Wallace Pond	05903
Wallingford	05773
Wallingford (Town)	05773
Waltham (Town)	05491
Wardsboro	05355
Wardsboro (Town)	05355
Wardsboro Center	05355
Warners Grant (Town)	05903
Warren	05674
Warren (Town)	05674
Warrens Gore (Town)	05903
Washington	05675
Washington (Town)	05675
Washington Heights	05657
Waterbury	05676
Waterbury (Town)	05676
Waterbury Center	05677
Waterford (Town)	05848
Waterville	05492
Waterville (Town)	05492
Weathersfield (Town)	05151
Weathersfield Bow	05156
Weathersfield Center	05151
Websterville	05678
Wells	05774
Wells (Town)	05774
Wells River	05081
West Addison	05491
West Arlington	05250
West Barnet	05821
West Berkshire	05450

Location	ZIP
West Bolton	05465
West Branch	05672
West Brattleboro	05301
West Bridgewater	05035
West Bridport	05734
West Brookfield	05060
West Burke	05871
West Castleton	05743
West Charleston	05872
West Corinth	05039
West Cornwall	05753
West Danville	05873
West Dover	05356
West Dummerston	05357
West Enosburg	05450
West Fairlee	05083
West Fairlee (Town)	05083
West Fairlee Center	05044
Westfield	05874
Westfield (Town)	05874
Westford	05494
Westford (Town)	05494
West Georgia	05478
West Glover	05875
West Groton	05046
West Halifax	05358
West Hartford	05084
West Haven	05743
West Haven (Town)	05743
West Hill	05450
West Lincoln	05443
West Milton	05468
Westminster	05158
Westminster (Town)	05158
Westminster Station (Part of Westminster)	05159
Westminster West	05346
Westmore	05860
Westmore (Town)	05860
West Newbury	05085
West Norwich	05055
Weston	05161
Weston (Town)	05161
Weston Priory	05161
West Pawlet	05775
West Rupert	05776
West Rutland (Rutland County) (Town)	05777
West Rutland (Rutland County)	05777
West Salisbury	05769

Location	ZIP
West Springfield	05156
West Swanton	05488
West Topsham	05086
West Townshend	05359
West Wardsboro	05360
West Waterford	05819
West Windsor (Town)	05037
West Woodstock	05091
Weybridge	05753
Weybridge (Town)	05753
Weybridge Hill	05753
Wheelock	05851
Wheelock (Town)	05851
White River Junction	05001
Whitesville	05142
Whiting	05778
Whiting (Town)	05778
Whitingham	05361
Whitingham (Town)	05361
Wilder	05088
Williamstown	05679
Williamstown (Town)	05679
Williamsville	05362
Williston (Town)	05495
Williston (Chittenden County)	05495
Williston Road Section (Part of South Burlington)	05401
Wilmington	05363
Wilmington (Town)	05363
Windham	05359
Windham (Town)	05359
Windsor (Windsor County) (Town)	05089
Windsor (Windsor County)	05089
Winhall (Town)	05340
Winooski	05404
Winooski Park	05404
Wolcott	05680
Wolcott (Town)	05680
Woodbury	05681
Woodbury (Town)	05681
Woodford	05201
Woodford (Town)	05201
Woodford Hollow	05201
Woodstock	05091
Woodstock (Town)	05091
Worcester	05682
Worcester (Town)	05682
Wrightsville (Part of Montpelier)	05602

Aarons Creek-Beechwood Hills **VIRGINIA** 567

	ZIP		ZIP		ZIP
Aarons Creek	24598	Apple Blossom Mall (Part of		Ballentine Place (Part of	
Abbey Oaks	22180	Winchester)	22601	Norfolk)	23509
Abbott	24127	Apple Grove	23117	Balls Hills	22101
Abilene	23923	Appomattox	24522	Ballston	22203
Abingdon	24210	Aqua	24435	Ballston Common	22203
Accomac	23301	Aquia Harbor	22554	Ballsville	23139
Accotink	22060	Aragona Village (Part of		Baltimore Corner	23850
Accotink Heights	22003	Virginia Beach)	23455	Balty	22546
Achilles	23001	Ararat	24053	Banco	22711
Achsah	22727	Arbor Estates (Part of		Bandy	24602
Acorn	22469	Suffolk)	23434	Bane	24134
Acredale (Part of Virginia		Arborhill	24401	Banner	24230
Beach)	23464	Arcadia	24066	Banners Corner	24224
Acree Acres	23690	Arch Mills	24066	Barbours Creek	24127
Ada	22115	Arcola	22010	Barboursville	22923
Addison Heights	22202	Arcturus	22308	Barcroft	22204
Aden	22123	Ardmore (Part of Fairfax)	22030	Barfoot	24151
Adial	22938	Argyle Heights	22405	Barham	23881
Adkins Store	23140	Ark	23003	Barhamsville	23011
Adner	23149	Arlington	22201-16	Barley	23847
Adria	24630	For specific Arlington Zip Codes		Barnesville	23964
Adsit	23856	call (703) 525-4838		Barnett	24266
Advance Mills	22968	Arlington (Part of Hopewell)	23860	Barnetts	23030
Adwolf	24354	Arlington Forest	22203	Barracks Road (Part of	
Afton	22920	Arlington Hall	22212	Charlottesville)	22903
Agricola	24574	Arlington Heights	22204	Barren Ridge	24401
Aiken Summit	24054	Arlington Village	22204	Barren Springs	24313
Aily	24237	Arlingwood	22207	Barrett Acres (Part of	
Air Mail Facility (Part of		Armel	22601	Suffolk)	23434
Norfolk)	23519	Armistead Forest (Part of		Bartlett	23314
Airmont	22141	Portsmouth)	23703	Bartlick	24256
Ajax	24161	Armstrong	24460	Bartons Crossroad	24378
Alanthus	22714	Armstrong Gardens (Part of		Bartonville	22601
Alanton (Part of Virginia		Hampton)	23669	Barytes (Part of Bristol)	24201
Beach)	23450	Aroda	22709	Basham	24138
Albemarle (Part of Norfolk)	23503	Arrington	22222	Basic (Part of Waynesboro)	22980
Alberene	22959	Arrowhead (Part of Virginia		Baskerville	23915
Alberta	23821	Beach)	23462	Baskerville Correctional Unit	23915
Albin	22601	Arthur	24162	Bassett	24055
Alcoma	23921	Artillery Ridge	22401	Bassett Forks	24055
Aldie	22001	Artrip	24225	Bastian	24314
Alexander Corner (Part of		Arvonia	23004	Basye	22810
Portsmouth)	23707	Asberrys	24377	Batesville	22924
Alexandria	22301-20	Ashburn	22011	Bath Alum	24460
For specific Alexandria Zip Codes		Ashby	23040	Battersea (Part of	
call (703) 549-4201		Ashland	23005	Petersburg)	23803
Alfonso	22421	Ashton Glen	22110	Battery	22560
Algonquin Park (Part of		Ashton Heights	22201	Battery Park (Henrico	
Norfolk)	23505	Ashville	22115	County)	23228
Alhambra	22951	Ashwood	24445	Battery Park (Isle of Wight	
Alice Heights	23234	Aspen	23959	County)	23304
Alleghany	24426	Aspenwall	24528	Battle Beach	23851
Alleghany Spring	24162	Assawoman	23302	Battle Creek	22851
Allen	24226	Atkins	24311	Battlefield Green	22401
Allencrest	22207	Atlantic (Accomack County)	23303	Battlefield Park (Part of	
Allens Creek	24553	Atlantic (Virginia Beach		Petersburg)	23805
Allenslevel	23936	Indep. City)	23458	Bavon	23013
Allentown	23301	Atlantic Park (Part of		Bayberry Estates	22485
Allison Gap	24370	Virginia Beach)	23451	Bay Colony (Part of Virginia	
Allisonia	24347	Atlee	23111	Beach)	23451
Allmondsville	23061	Atoka	22115	Bayford	23354
Allwood	24521	Attoway	24354	Bay Island (Part of Virginia	
Alma	22851	Auburn	22019	Beach)	23451
Almagro (Part of Danville)	24541	Augusta Correctional Center	24430	Bay Lake Beach (Part of	
Almira (Part of Pound)	24279	Augusta Springs	24411	Virginia Beach)	23455
Alonzaville	22644	Aurora Hills	22202	Baylake Pines (Part of	
Alpha	23936	Austinville	24312	Virginia Beach)	23455
Alpine	22003	Avalon	22473	Baynesville	22520
Alps	22514	Avalon Terrace (Part of		Bayport	23079
Alsop	22553	Virginia Beach)	23462	Bayside (Accomack	
Altavista	24517	Averett	24580	County)	23417
Alto	24483	Avon	22920	Bayside (Virginia Beach	
Alton	24520	Avondale	23111	Indep. City)	23455
Alum Ridge	24091	Avon Forest	22039	Bay View	23310
Alvarado	24210	Axtel	24562	Bayville Park (Part of	
Amburg	23043	Axton	24054	Virginia Beach)	23455
Amelia Court House	23002	Aylett	23009	Baywood	24333
Amherst (Amherst County)	24521	Aylor	22727	Beach	23832
Amherst (Fairfax County)	22015	Azalea Acres (Part of		Beach Grove	22967
Amissville	22002	Norfolk)	23518	Beaconsdale (Part of	
Ammon	23822	Azalea Court	23227	Newport News)	23607
Amonate	24601	Azalea Gardens (Part of		Bealeton	22712
Ampthill	23234	Hampton)	23669	Beamantown (Part of Big	
Ampthill Heights (Part of		Bachelors Hall	24541	Stone Gap)	24219
Richmond)	23234	Backbay (Part of Virginia		Beamon (Part of Suffolk)	23434
Amsterdam	24175	Beach)	23457	Bear Wallow	24622
Andersonville	23911	Bacons Castle	23883	Beaufont Hills (Part of	
Andover	24215	Bacons Fork	23950	Richmond)	23225
Andrew Lewis Place	24153	Bacova	24412	Beaumont	23014
Angola	23901	Bacova Junction	24445	Beaverdam	23015
Ankum	23868	Baden	24228	Beaverlett	23016
Annalee Heights	22042	Bagby	22514	Beazley	22560
Annandale (Fairfax County)	22003	Bagleys Mills	23970	Beckham	24538
Annandale Acres	22003	Bailey	24605	Bedford	24523
Annandale Gardens	22003	Baileys Crossroads (Fairfax		Bee	24217
Annandale Terrace	22003	County)	22041	Beech Fork	23974
Annex	24401	Bailey's Crossroads (Fairfax		Beech Springs	24263
Ante	23847	County)	22041	Beechwood	23919
Antioch	24590	Balcony Falls (Part of		Beechwood Hills (Arlington	
Appalachia	24216	Glasgow)	24555	County)	22207
		Ballards Crossroads	23315		

568 VIRGINIA

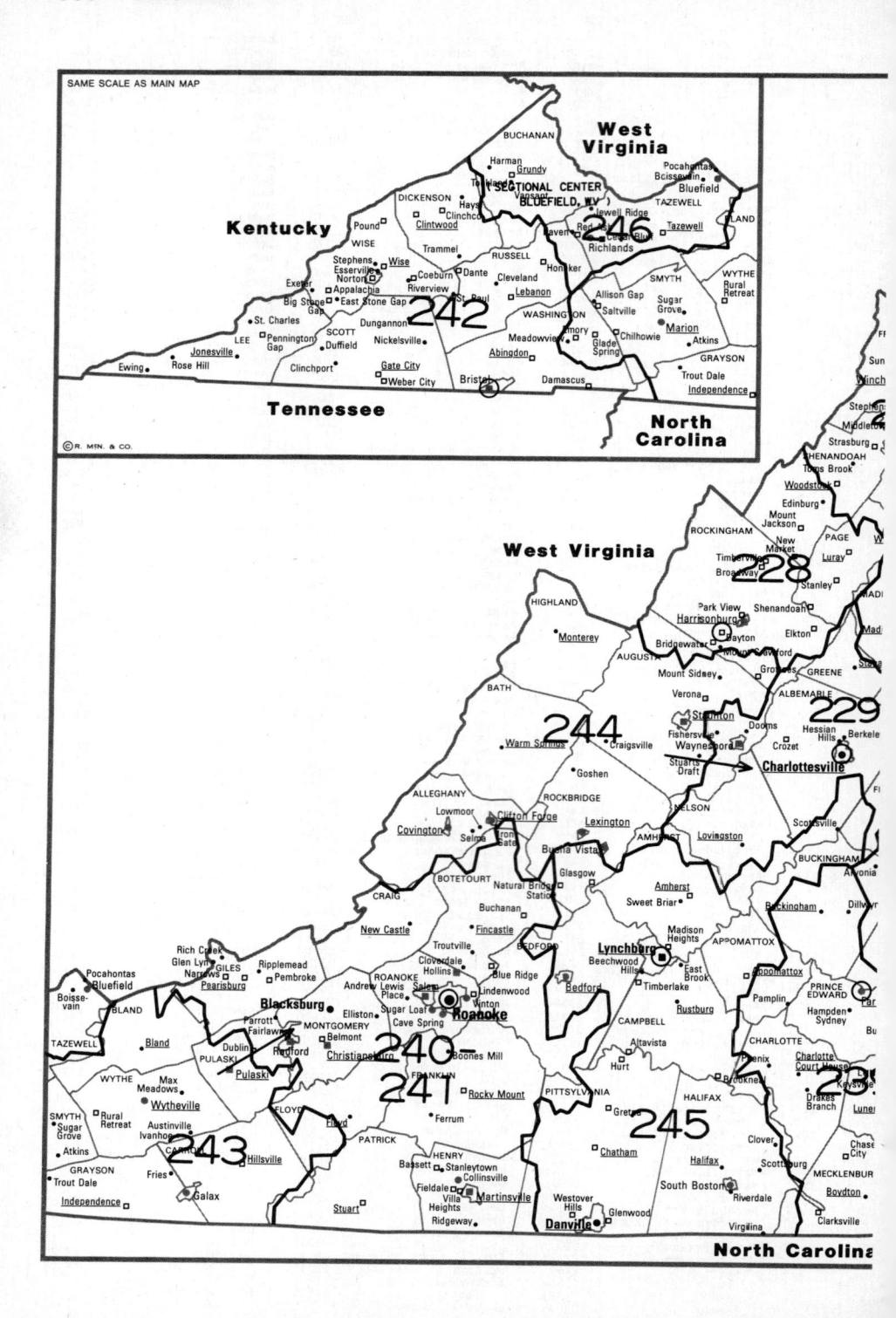

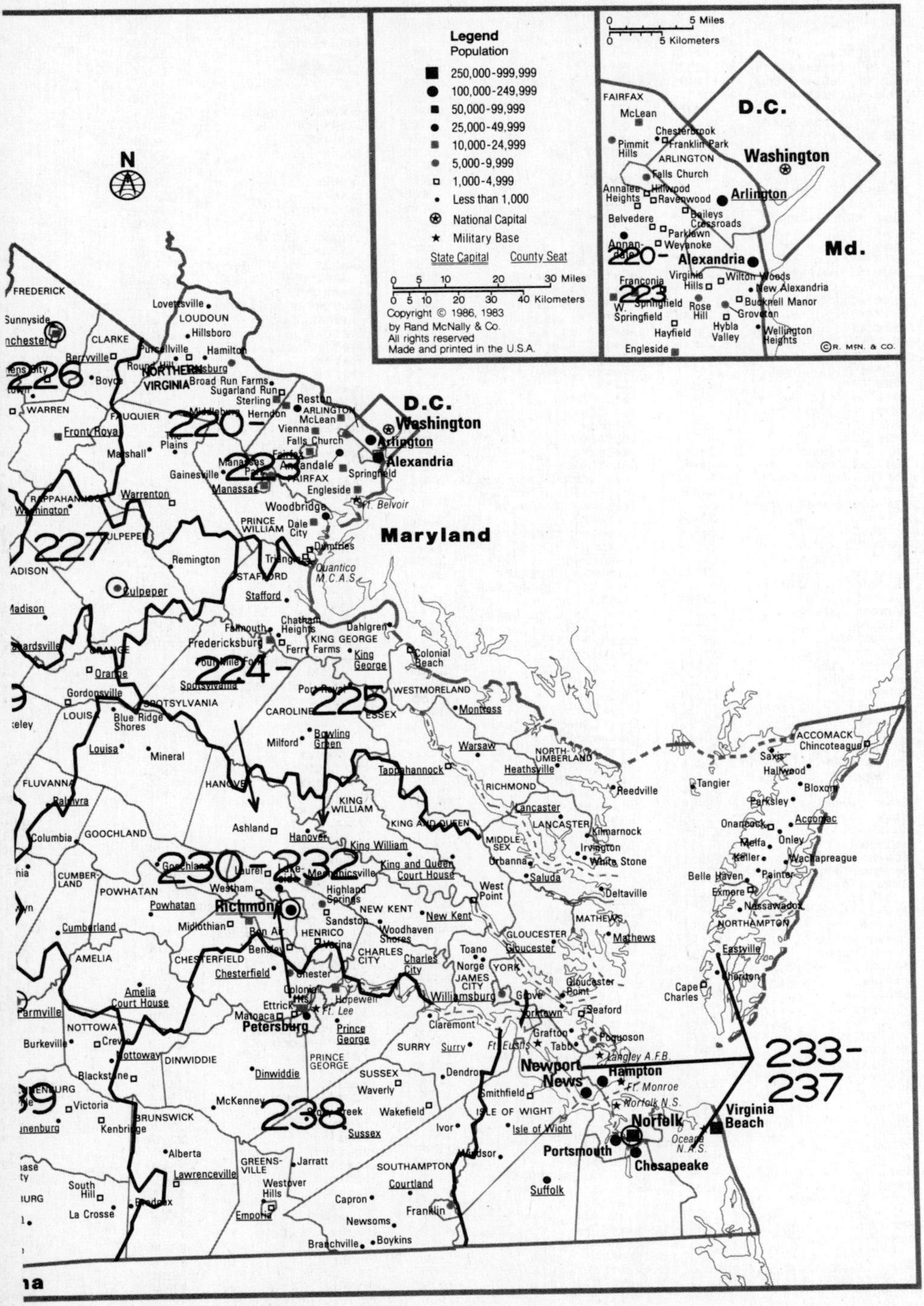
Legend
Population
250,000-999,999
100,000-249,999
50,000-99,999
25,000-49,999
10,000-24,999
5,000-9,999
1,000-4,999
Less than 1,000
National Capital
Military Base
State Capital
County Seat
0 5 10 20 30 Miles
0 5 10 20 30 40 Kilometers
Copyright © 1986, 1983
by Rand McNally & Co.
All rights reserved
Made and printed in the U.S.A.
0 5 Miles
0 5 Kilometers
FAIRFAX
McLean
Chesterbrook
Franklin Park
Pimmit Hills
ARLINGTON
D.C.
Washington
Falls Church
Annalee Heights
Hillwood
Ravenwood
Arlington
Baileys Crossroads
Belvedere
Parklawn
Weyanoke
Md.
220-
Alexandria
Franconia
223
Virginia Hills
Wilton Woods
New Alexandria
W. Springfield
Springfield
Rose Hill
Bucknell Manor
Groveton
Hayfield
Hybla Valley
Wellington Heights
Engleside
©R. McN. & CO.
N
FREDERICK
Sunnyside
Lovettsville
LOUDOUN
Hillsboro
CLARKE
Purcellville
Hamilton
Berryville
226
Boyce
NORTHERN VIRGINIA
Broad Run Farms
Sugarland Run
Sterling
Reston
WARREN
FAUQUIER
220-
Herndon
ARLINGTON
McLean
D.C.
Washington
Front Royal
The Plains
Vienna
Falls Church
Arlington
Alexandria
Marshall
Manassas
223
Annandale
Springfield
Gainesville
FAIRFAX
Manassas
Engleside
RAPPAHANNOCK
Warrenton
Ft. Belvoir
Washington
Woodbridge
PRINCE WILLIAM
Dale City
227
CULPEPER
Dumfries
Maryland
MADISON
Remington
Triangle
Quantico M.C.A.S.
STAFFORD
Culpeper
Madison
Stafford
Falmouth
Chatham Heights
Dahlgren
Fredericksburg
KING GEORGE
ORANGE
Ferry Farms
King George
Colonial Beach
224-
Orange
Spotsylvania
Port Royal
225
WESTMORELAND
Gordonsville
SPOTSYLVANIA
CAROLINE
ESSEX
LOUISA
Blue Ridge Shores
Montross
Bowling Green
ACCOMACK
Louisa
Milford
Chincoteague
Mineral
Warsaw
NORTHUMBERLAND
Saxis
Hallwood
FLUVANNA
HANOVER
Tappahannock
Heathsville
Tangier
Bloxom
Palmyra
Reedville
KING WILLIAM
RICHMOND
Parksley
Lancaster
Accomac
Ashland
LANCASTER
Columbia
GOOCHLAND
KING AND QUEEN
Onancock
Kilmarnock
Onley
Hanover
MIDDLESEX
Melfa
Irvington
King William
Keller
Wachapreague
230-232
White Stone
Goochland
King and Queen Court House
Urbanna
CUMBERLAND
Laurel
Lakeside
Mechanicsville
Belle Haven
Painter
Saluda
West Point
Highland Springs
Westham
Exmore
POWHATAN
Deltaville
Richmond
Nassawadox
NEW KENT
Powhatan
Sandston
New Kent
MATHEWS
NORTHAMPTON
Midlothian
Woodhaven Shores
Cumberland
Bon Air
HENRICO
GLOUCESTER
Mathews
Bensley
Varina
Toano
Gloucester
Eastville
AMELIA
CHARLES CITY
CHESTERFIELD
YORK
Norge
Charles City
Chester
Chesterfield
JAMES CITY
Cheriton
Gloucester Point
Amelia Court House
Colonial Hts.
Hopewell
Williamsburg
Cape Charles
Grove
Ettrick
Ft. Lee
Seaford
Matoaca
Farmville
Yorktown
Petersburg
Claremont
NOTTOWAY
Prince George
Grafton
Poquoson
Crewe
Ft. Eustis
Tabb
Burkeville
SURRY
Surry
Langley A.F.B.
233-
Nottoway
DINWIDDIE
PRINCE GEORGE
Newport News
Hampton
Blackstone
Dinwiddie
SUSSEX
Dendron
Ft. Monroe
237
LUNENBURG
Waverly
McKenney
Smithfield
Norfolk N.S.
Victoria
238
Virginia Beach
Stony Creek
Wakefield
ISLE OF WIGHT
Norfolk
Lunenburg
BRUNSWICK
Ivor
Isle of Wight
Kenbridge
Sussex
Oceana N.A.S.
Portsmouth
Chesapeake
Alberta
Windsor
GREENSVILLE
Jarratt
SOUTHAMPTON
Lawrenceville
Courtland
Suffolk
South Hill
Westover Hills
Capron
Franklin
La Crosse
Brodnax
Emporia
Newsoms
Branchville
Boykins

570 VIRGINIA Beechwood Hills-Brookhaven

	ZIP
Beechwood Hills (Campbell County)	24502
Beechwood Manor	23860
Bel Air	22042
Belaire (Part of Norfolk)	23518
Beldor	22827
Belfast Mills	24609
Bellair (Albemarle County)	22901
Bell Air (Stafford County)	22405
Bellamy (Gloucester County)	23017
Bellamy (Scott County)	24251
Bellamy Manor (Part of Virginia Beach)	23464
Bellbluff (Chesterfield County)	23219
Bellbluff (Chesterfield County)	23234
Belle Haven (Accomack County)	23306
Belle Haven (Fairfax County)	22307
Belle Haven (Virginia Beach Indep. City)	23452
Belle Meade (Fauquier County)	22642
Bellemeade (Richmond Indep. City)	23224
Belle Meadows (Part of Bristol)	24201
Belle View	22307
Belleville (Part of Suffolk)	23435
Bellevue (Part of Richmond)	23227
Bellevue Forest	22207
Bells Cross Road	22553
Bells Cross Roads	23093
Bell Spur (Carroll County)	24120
Bell Spur (Patrick County)	24120
Bells Valley	24439
Bellwood (Chesterfield County)	23234
Bellwood Manor	23234
Belmont (Loudoun County)	22011
Belmont (Montgomery County)	24073
Belmont (Prince William County)	22191
Belmont (Spotsylvania County)	22553
Belmont Acres	23234
Belmont Circle	23901
Belmont Estates	24073
Belmont Farms	24073
Belmont Park	22079
Belmont Place (Part of Norfolk)	23505
Belona	23139
Belspring	24058
Belvedere (Fairfax County)	22041
Belvedere (Norfolk Indep. City)	23504
Belvidere Beach	22401
Belvoir	22115
Bena	23018
Benhams	24201
Ben Hur	24218
Benmoreel (Part of Norfolk)	23505
Bennetts Creek (Part of Suffolk)	23435
Bennetts Harbor (Part of Suffolk)	23434
Bennett Springs	24153
Benns Church	23430
Bensley (Chesterfield County)	23234
Bent Creek	24553
Bent Mountain	24059
Bentonville	22610
Bergton	22811
Berkeley	22901
Berkeley (Part of Norfolk)	23523
Berkshire	22207
Berlin	23866
Berryville	22611
Berton	24134
Bestland	22454
Betana Park	22090
Bethany	24312
Bethel (Fauquier County)	22186
Bethel (Halifax County)	24589
Bethel (Prince William County)	22191
Bethel (Warren County)	22630
Bethel Manor (Part of Hampton)	23665
Beulah Church	22560
Beulah Village	23234
Beulahville	23009
Beverley Hills (Part of Alexandria)	22305
Beverly Forest	22150

	ZIP
Beverly Heights (Part of Salem)	24153
Beverly Hills	23229
Beverly Manor	22101
Beverlyville	22539
Big Bethel (Part of Hampton)	23666
Big Fork	23970
Big Island	24526
Big Laurel	24293
Big River	24439
Big Rock	24603
Big Spring	22650
Big Stone Gap	24219
Big Vein	24635
Biltmore	23060
Binns Hall	23030
Birch	24592
Birchett Estate	23875
Birchland Park	24592
Birchleaf	24220
Birch Town	23336
Birchwood Park	23185
Birdneck Acres (Part of Virginia Beach)	23451
Birdsnest	23307
Birmingham	24609
Biscoe	23148
Bishop	24604
Bishops Corner	23938
Blackberry	24055
Black Branch	23924
Black Creek	23851
Blackford	24260
Blacklick	24368
Blackridge	23950
Blacksburg	24060-63
For specific Blacksburg Zip Codes call (703) 552-2751	
Blacksburg (Rockbridge County)	24416
Blacksburg (Washington County)	24340
Blackstone	23824
Blackwater (Lee County)	24221
Blackwater (Virginia Beach Indep. City)	23457
Blackwater Bridge (Part of Virginia Beach)	23457
Blackwells Chapel	24361
Blackwood	24273
Blainville	22835
Blairs	24527
Blakes	23035
Bland	24315
Bland Correctional Center	24315
Blandford (Part of Petersburg)	23803
Blanks Store	23030
Blanks Tavern	23030
Bleak	22728
Blevinstown	22030
Bloomfield	20120
Bloomingdale	23228
Blowing Rock	24228
Bloxom	23308
Bluefield	24605
Blue Grass	24413
Bluemont	22012
Blue Mountain	22630
Blue Ridge	24064
Blue Ridge Mountain Estates	22630
Blue Ridge Shores	23093
Bluestone	23927
Blundon Corner	22456
Bocock	24501
Body Camp	24523
Bohannon	23021
Boiling Spring	24426
Boissevain	24606
Bolar	24484
Bolsters Store	23882
Bolton	24266
Bon Air (Arlington County)	22205
Bon Air (Chesterfield County)	23235
Bonbrook	24065
Bondtown (Part of Coeburn)	24230
Bonny Blue	24282
Bonsack	24012
Boones Mill	24065
Boonesville	22932
Boonsboro	24503
Bordeaux	22090
Boston (Accomack County)	23420
Boston (Culpeper County)	22713
Boston (Suffolk Indep. City)	23434
Boswells Tavern	22942
Botha	22186
Bottoms Bridge	23150

	ZIP
Boudar Gardens	23228
Boulevard Estates	22031
Bowers Corner	23893
Bowers Hill (Part of Chesapeake)	23321
Bowlers Wharf	22560
Bowling	24263
Bowling Green	22427
Bowling Park (Part of Norfolk)	23504
Bowmans Crossing	22824
Boxley Hills	24012
Boxwood	24054
Boyce	22620
Boyd Tavern	22947
Boydton	23917
Boykins	23827
Boys Home	24426
Bracey	23919
Braddock (Part of Alexandria)	22302
Braddock Heights (Part of Alexandria)	22302
Braddock Hills	22003
Bradford Acres (Part of Virginia Beach)	23455
Bradley Acres	23150
Bradley Forest	22110
Bradshaw	24087
Brambleton (Part of Norfolk)	23504
Branchville	23828
Brand	24401
Brandon	23881
Brandon Heights (Part of Newport News)	23601
Brandon Place (Part of Norfolk)	23513
Brandons Store	23824
Brandon Village	22203
Brandy Creek Estates	23111
Brandy Station	22714
Brattons Bridge	24460
Brays	22560
Brayshore Park	23072
Breaks	24607
Brecon Ridge	22030
Bremo Bluff	23022
Bren Mar Park	22312
Brentsville	22013
Brentwood	23234
Brentwood Forest (Part of Norfolk)	23518
Briarcliff (Part of Vinton)	24179
Briarwood (Bristol Indep. City)	24201
Briarwood (Portsmouth Indep. City)	23703
Bridgetown	23405
Bridgewater	22812
Bridle Creek	24348
Briery	23947
Briery Branch	22821
Briggs	22611
Brights	24557
Brightwood	22715
Brilyn Park	22046
Brink	23847
Bristol	24201-03
For specific Bristol Zip Codes call (615) 968-2355	
Bristol Mall (Part of Bristol)	24201
Bristow (Fairfax County)	22003
Bristow (Prince William County)	22013
Britain	22080
Britton Hills Farms	23230
Brittonwood	23234
Broad Bay Colony (Part of Virginia Beach)	23451
Broad Creek (Part of Norfolk)	23502
Broadford	24316
Broad Meadows	23060
Broad Rock (Part of Richmond)	23224
Broad Run	22014
Broad Run Farms	22170
Broadway	22815
Brockroad	22553
Brodnax	23920
Brokenburg	22553
Broken Hill	22065
Brookbury (Part of Richmond)	23234
Brooke	22430
Brookeshire	23181
Brookfield (Fairfax County)	22021
Brookfield (Stafford County)	22405
Brookfield Park (Part of Norfolk)	23503
Brookhaven	22101

Brook Hill-Charity **VIRGINIA** 571

Name	ZIP
Brook Hill	23227
Brookland Estates	22310
Brookland Gardens	23228
Brooklyn	24594
Brookneal	24528
Brook Vale	22503
Brookville (Part of Alexandria)	22304
Brookwood (Part of Virginia Beach)	23452
Brookwood Manor	23141
Brosville	24541
Brown Field (Part of Quantico)	22134
Brown Grove	23005
Brownsburg	24415
Browns Corner	23141
Browns Cove	22932
Browns Store	22473
Brown Town (Amherst County)	24521
Browntown (Warren County)	22610
Broyhill Crest	22003
Broyhill Forest	22207
Broyhill Park	22042
Brucetown	22622
Bruington	23023
Brumley Gap	24210
Bruno	24258
Brunswick	23868
Brush Tavern	24502
Bryan Park	23228
Bryan Parkway	23228
Bryant	22967
Bryants Corner	23847
Bryn Mawr	22101
Buchanan	24066
Buckhall	22110
Buckingham (Arlington County)	22203
Buckingham (Buckingham County)	23921
Buckingham (Chesterfield County)	23112
Buckingham Circle	22901
Buckland	22065
Bucknell Heights	22307
Bucknell Manor	22307
Buckner	23024
Buckroe Beach (Part of Hampton)	23664
Buckton	22657
Buena	22733
Buena Vista	24416
Buffalo Forge	24555
Buffalo Gap	24479
Buffalo Hill	24521
Buffalo Hills	22044
Buffalo Junction	24529
Buffalo Ridge	24171
Buffalo Springs	24529
Buford Cross Roads	23847
Bull Run Mountain Estates	22069
Bumpass	23024
Bundy	24265
Bunker Hill	24523
Burdette	23851
Burgess	22432
Burgundy Village	22303
Burke (Fairfax County)	22015
Burke Heights	22015
Burke Hills	22015
Burkes Garden	24608
Burkes Shop	22580
Burketown	24486
Burkeville	23922
Burks Garden (Part of Tazewell)	24651
Burnam Woods	23168
Burnleys	22923
Burnside Farms	23111
Burnsville	24487
Burnt Chimney	24184
Burnt Store	23950
Burnt Tree	22960
Burr Hill	22433
Burrowsville	23842
Burson Place	24201
Burton (Part of Virginia Beach)	23455
Burtons Shop	24651
Bush Hill Woods	22310
Bush Mill	24271
Busthead	24609
Bustleburg	24450
Butterworth	23840
Butts Corner	22039
Butylo	22504
Bybee	22963
Byllesby	24350
Bynum Store	23924

Name	ZIP
Byrdton	22482
Cabin Point	23881
Cadet (Part of Big Stone Gap)	24219
Cady	23069
Caira	23040
Caiedonia	23038
Callaghan	24426
Callands	24530
Callao	22435
Callaville	23856
Callaway	24067
Callison	22445
Calno	23069
Calvary	22664
Calverton	22016
Cambria (Part of Christiansburg)	24073
Cambridge	23235
Camden Heights (Part of Norfolk)	23502
Camellia Shores (Part of Norfolk)	23518
Camelot	22003
Cameron Station (Part of Alexandria)	22304
Cameron Valley (Part of Alexandria)	22314
Camp	24375
Camp Barrett	22134
Campbell	22947
Camp Creek	24091
Campostella Heights (Part of Norfolk)	23523
Camps Mill (Part of Suffolk)	23434
Camptown	24528
Cana	24317
Candlewax	24260
Cannady	24656
Canova	22110
Canterburg	22655
Canterbury	23229
Canterbury Hills	22901
Canterbury Woods	22003
Canton	24221
Capahosic	23061
Cape Charles	23310
Cape Henry (Part of Virginia Beach)	23454
Cape Henry Shores (Part of Virginia Beach)	23451
Cape Story by the Sea (Part of Virginia Beach)	23451
Capeville	23313
Capitol (Part of Richmond)	23219
Capon Road	22657
Capron	23829
Captain's Cove	23356
Carbo	24225
Cardinal	23025
Cardinal Forest	22152
Cardova	22701
Cardwell	22039
Cardwell Town	24370
Caret	22436
Carfax	24230
Carloover	24445
Carolanne Farms (Part of Virginia Beach)	23462
Caroline Correctional Unit	23069
Caroline Pines	22546
Carriage Hill (Fairfax County)	22181
Carriage Hill (Virginia Beach Indep. City)	23452
Carrie	24225
Carrollton	23314
Carrsbrook	22901
Carrsville	23315
Carsley	23890
Carson	23830
Carsonville	24348
Carters Mills	24053
Cartersville	23027
Carterton	24266
Carver Court (Part of Hampton)	23669
Carver Gardens	23185
Carysbrook	23055
Casanova	22017
Cascade	24069
Cash	23061
Cash Corner	22942
Cashville	23417
Caskie	24553
Castle Craig	24550
Castle Heights	23917
Castleton	22716
Castlewood	24224
Catalpa	22701
Catawba (Halifax County)	24577

Name	ZIP
Catawba (Roanoke County)	24070
Catharpin	22018
Catherton (Part of Manassas)	22110
Catlett	22019
Cats Bridge	23420
Cauthornville	23029
Cavalcade	22003
Cavalier Park (Part of Virginia Beach)	23451
Cave Mountain	24579
Cave Spring (Roanoke County)	24018
Cavetown	22835
Caylor	24248
Cedar Bluff (Tazewell County)	24609
Cedar Bluff (Washington County)	24236
Cedar Branch (Part of Saltville)	24370
Cedar Forest	24569
Cedar Fork	22546
Cedar Green	24401
Cedar Grove (Halifax County)	24520
Cedar Grove (Mecklenburg County)	23970
Cedar Grove (Northampton County)	23310
Cedar Grove Acres (Part of Chesapeake)	23320
Cedarhill	24565
Cedar Lawn	23231
Cedar Level (Part of Hopewell)	23860
Cedar Point	23063
Cedar Springs	24368
Cedarville (Warren County)	22630
Cedarville (Washington County)	24361
Cedon	22580
Celt	22973
Centenary	24590
Center Cross	22437
Center Star	23841
Centerville (Accomack County)	23412
Centerville (Augusta County)	22812
Centerville (Bedford County)	24523
Centerville (Goochland County)	23103
Centerville (Halifax County)	24592
Centerville (James City County)	23185
Centerville (Louisa County)	23117
Central (Arlington County)	22203
Central (Richmond Indep. City)	23219
Central Facility	22079
Central Garage	23086
Central Gardens	23223
Central Hill	23487
Centralia	23831
Centralia Gardens	23234
Central Martinsville (Part of Martinsville)	24112
Central Plains	22963
Central Point	22514
Central State Hospital	23803
Centre Heights	22020
Centreville (Fairfax County)	22020
Centreville Farms	22020
Ceres	24318
Chadswyck (Part of Chesapeake)	23321
Chalet Woods	22020
Chalk Level	24557
Chamberlain Village	22134
Chamberlayne	23227
Chamberlayne Farms	23227
Chamberlayne Heights	23227
Chamberlayne North	23227
Chamblissburg	24179
Champlain	22438
Chance	22439
Chancellor	22401
Chancellors Green	22401
Chancellorsville	22553
Chaneys	24565
Chantilly (Fairfax County)	22021
Chantilly Estates	22021
Chapel	24124
Chapel Acres	22153
Chapel Hill (Part of Alexandria)	22302
Chapel Park (Part of Newport News)	23606
Chapel Square	22003
Charity	24185

572 VIRGINIA Charlemont-Crescent Hills

	ZIP
Charlemont	24526
Charles City	23030
Charlie Hope	23920
Charlotte Court House	23923
Charlottesville	22901-08
For specific Charlottesville Zip Codes call (804) 286-2282	
Chase City	23924
Chatham	24531
Chatham Heights	22405
Chatham Hill	24370
Chatmoss	24112
Cheapside	23310
Check	24072
Cheriton	23316
Cherokee Heights (Part of Norfolk)	23518
Cherry Acres (Part of Hampton)	23669
Cherrydale	22207
Cherry Hill (Charles City County)	23030
Cherry Hill (Dinwiddie County)	23872
Cherry Hill (Prince William County)	22026
Chesapeake	23310
	23320-25
For specific Chesapeake Zip Codes call (804) 629-2198	
Chesapeake Beach (Northumberland County)	22539
Chesapeake Beach (Virginia Beach Indep. City)	23455
Chesapeake Heights (Part of Hampton)	23664
Chesapeake Manor (Part of Norfolk)	23513
Chesconessex	23417
Chesdin Manor	23885
Chesopeian Colony (Part of Virginia Beach)	23452
Chesswood	23234
Chester	23831
Chesterbrook	22101
Chesterbrook Gardens	22101
Chesterbrook Woods	22101
Chester Estates (Part of Bristol)	24201
Chesterfield	23832
Chesterfield Heights (Part of Norfolk)	23504
Chester Gap	22623
Chestnut Hill (Fairfax County)	22003
Chestnut Hill (King George County)	22485
Chestnut Knob	24112
Chestnut Level	24527
Chestnut Yard	24381
Chevalle	22110
Chewings Corner	22534
Chickahominy Haven	23089
Chickahominy Shores	23089
Childress	24073
Childry	24577
Chilesburg	22546
Chilhowie	24319
Chiltons	22520
Chimney Run	24484
Chincoteague	23336
Chinquapin Village (Part of Alexandria)	22302
Chisford	22520
Christchurch	23031
Christensons Corner	23185
Christians	24479
Christiansburg	24073
Christie	24598
Chuckatuck (Part of Suffolk)	23432
Chula	23002
Church Hill (Part of Richmond)	23223
Churchill	22043
Churchland (Part of Portsmouth)	23703
Church Road	23833
Church View	23032
Churchville	24421
Cifax	24556
Circlewoods	22031
Cismont	22947
Civic Center (Part of Richmond)	23240
Clam	23308
Clancie	23156
Claraville	22473
Claremont (Arlington County)	22206
Claremont (Surry County)	23899
Clarendon	22201

	ZIP
Claresville	23847
Clarkes Gap	22075
Clarksville (Mecklenburg County)	23927
Clarksville (Washington County)	24340
Clarkton	24577
Clary	22657
Claudville	24076
Clay Bank	23061
Claypool Hill	24609
Clays Mill	24589
Clayville	23139
Clear Brook (Frederick County)	22624
Clearbrook (Roanoke County)	24014
Clearfield	22151
Clearfork	24314
Clearview Manor	22101
Clearwater Park	24426
Clell	24631
Clermont Woods	22310
Cleveland	24225
Cliffield	24637
Clifford	24533
Cliffview	24333
Clifton (Fairfax County)	22024
Clifton (Orange County)	22733
Cliftondale	24422
Clifton Forge	24422
Climax	24531
Clinchburg	24321
Clinchco	24226
Clinchport	24244
Clintwood	24228
Clito	24330
Clover (Alexandria Indep. City)	22314
Clover (Halifax County)	24534
Cloverdale (Botetourt County)	24077
Cloverdale (Fluvanna County)	23022
Clover Hill	22821
Club Court	23227
Cluster Springs	24555
Coalcreek	24333
Coaldan	24641
Coal Kiln	23420
Coal Mine	22657
Coan Stage	22473
Cobbdale (Part of Fairfax)	22030
Cobbs Creek	23035
Cobham	22929
Cobham Park	22572
Cobham Wharf	23883
Cochran	23821
Cody	24577
Coeburn	24230
Coffee	24551
Cohasset	23055
Cohoke	23181
Coke	23072
Colchester	22079
Cold Harbor Farms	23111
Coldwater	23108
Coleman Falls	24536
Coleman Place (Part of Norfolk)	23502
Coles Creek	24151
Coles Point	22442
Coliseum Mall (Part of Hampton)	23666
Colleen	22922
College (Part of Fredericksburg)	22401
College Park (Alexandria Indep. City)	22314
College Park (Staunton Indep. City)	24401
College Park (Suffolk Indep. City)	23703
Colley	24220
Collierstown	24450
Collingwood	22308
Collins Crossing	22580
Collinsville	24078
Collinwood	24266
Cologne	23037
Colonial Beach	22443
Colonial Forest	23111
Colonial Heights (Colonial Heights Indep. City)	23834
Colonial Heights (Hampton Indep. City)	23664
Colonial Heights (Norfolk Indep. City)	23518
Colonial Heights (Washington County)	24201

	ZIP
Colonial Place (Part of Norfolk)	23508
Colonial Village	22201
Colonial Williamsburg (Part of Williamsburg)	23185
Colosse	23315
Colthurst	22901
Coltons Mill	24523
Columbia	23038
Columbia Forest	22204
Columbia Furnace	22824
Columbia Heights	22204
Columbia Park (Part of Hopewell)	23860
Columbia Pines	22003
Colvin Run	22066
Comans Well	23897
Comers Rock	24326
Comet	23430
Commodore Park (Part of Norfolk)	23503
Commonwealth	22901
Commonwealth Acres	23875
Community	22306
Comorn	22401
Compton	22650
Conaway	24603
Concord (Brunswick County)	23876
Concord (Campbell County)	24538
Concord Heights	22401
Conde	22115
Confederate Heights	23222
Coniceville	22842
Conners Grove	24380
Conners Valley	24324
Contra	22437
Cookstown	22553
Cool Spring	22308
Coolwell	24521
Cooper	23092
Cootes Store	22815
Copper Hill	24079
Copper Valley	24141
Corbin	22446
Corinth	23866
Corn Valley	24260
Cornwall	24416
Coronado (Part of Norfolk)	23513
Cottage Heights (Part of Norfolk)	23504
Cottage Park (Part of Norfolk)	23503
Cottage Road Park (Part of Norfolk)	23505
Coulson	24381
Coulwood	24260
Council	24260
Countis Corner	24201
Country Club Hills (Arlington County)	22207
Country Club Hills (Fairfax Indep. City)	22030
Country Club Lake	22026
Country Club Manor	22207
Country Club View	22032
Country Creek	22181
Counts	24237
County Line Cross Roads	23923
Court House	22216
Courtland	23837
Courtland Park	22041
Courtney	23060
Cove Colony	22503
Cove Creek (Bland County)	24314
Cove Creek (Tazewell County)	24651
Covesville	22931
Covingston Corner	23047
Covington	24426
Cox's Chapel	24363
Crab Orchard	24230
Crackers Neck (Scott County)	24271
Crackers Neck (Wise County)	24219
Craddockville	23341
Cradock (Part of Portsmouth)	23702
Craigs Mills	24201
Craig Springs	24127
Craigsville	24430
Crandon	24315
Cranes Nest	24230
Craney Island Estates	23111
Creeds (Part of Virginia Beach)	23457
Crescent Hill (Part of Hopewell)	23860
Crescent Hills	22207

Cresthill-Ebenezer VIRGINIA 573

Name	ZIP
Cresthill	22639
Crestview (Henrico County)	23226
Crestview (Prince Edward County)	23901
Crestwood Manor	22003
Crewe	23930
Criders	22820
Criglersville	22727
Crimora	24431
Cripple Creek	24322
Crittenden (Part of Suffolk)	23433
Critz	24082
Croaker	23185
Croatan Beach (Part of Virginia Beach)	23451
Crockett	24323
Crockett Springs	24162
Crofton	24179
Cromwell (Part of Norfolk)	23509
Crooked Oak	24343
Crossbrook	24215
Crosses Corner	23069
Cross Junction	22625
Crosskeys	22841
Crossroads (Albemarle County)	22959
Crossroads (Halifax County)	24577
Crossroads Mall (Part of Roanoke)	24012
Crosswinds	22153
Crouch	22437
Crows	24426
Crozet	22932
Crozier	23039
Crymes Store	23974
Crystal Hill	24539
Crystal Spring Knolls	22207
Cuckoo	23117
Cullen	23934
Culmore	22041
Culpeper	22701
Cumberland	23040
Cummings Heights	24210
Cumnor	23085
Cunningham	22963
Curdsville	23936
Currioman Landing	22520
Currituck Farms	23150
Cuscowilla	23917
Customhouse (Part of Norfolk)	23514
Cypress Chapel (Part of Suffolk)	23434
Cypress Manor	23851
Cypress Point (James City County)	23089
Cypress Point (Surry County)	23899
Dabney Estates	23885
Dabneys	23042
Dahlgren	22448
Dahlia	27866
Dalbys	23310
Dale City	22193
Dalecrest (Part of Alexandria)	22304
Dale Enterprise	22801
Daleville	24083
Damascus	24236
Dam Neck (Part of Virginia Beach)	23461
Dam Neck Corner (Part of Virginia Beach)	23454
Danbury Forest	22151
Dandy	23690
Daniel	22960
Daniel Boone	24251
Danieltown	23821
Danripple	24592
Dante	24237
Danville	24540-43
For specific Danville Zip Codes call (804) 792-3766	
Dare	23690
Darlington Heights	23935
Darnell Town	24265
Darvills	23824
Darwin	24228
Daugherty	23301
Davenport	24239
Davis	24472
Davis Corner (Part of Virginia Beach)	23462
Davis Wharf	23345
Dawley Corner (Part of Virginia Beach)	23457
Dawn	23047
Dayton	22821
Deans (Part of Suffolk)	23435
Deatonville	23083
De Bree (Part of Norfolk)	23517

Name	ZIP
De Busk Mill	24340
Deel	24656
Deep Bottom	23075
Deep Creek (Accomack County)	23417
Deep Creek (Chesapeake Indep. City)	23323
Deep Creek (Newport News Indep. City)	23606
Deep Hole	23336
Deerborne (Part of Richmond)	23234
Deerfield	24432
Deerfield Correctional Center	23829
Deerfield Estates	23832
Deer Park (Part of Manassas)	22110
Deer Park Groove (Part of Newport News)	23607
Deerrock	22938
Defense General Supply Center	23234
De Jarnett	22514
Delaplane	22025
Delaware	23851
Delmar	24236
Del Ray (Part of Alexandria)	22301
Delta (Part of Alexandria)	22304
Deltaville	23043
Delton	24324
Denaro	23002
Denbigh (Part of Newport News)	23602
Denby Park (Part of Norfolk)	23505
Dendron	23839
Denmark	24450
Denniston	24520
Dentons Corner	23921
Derby	24216
Desha	22560
Detrick	22664
Devon Manor (Part of Norfolk)	23503
Devonshire Gardens	22042
Dewey	24279
DeWitt	23840
Dewitt Hospital	22060
Diamond Springs (Part of Virginia Beach)	23455
Diascund	23089
Dickensdale	23230
Dickensonville	24224
Diggs	23045
Diggs Park (Part of Norfolk)	23523
Dillard's Landing	23140
Dillwyn	23936
Dinwiddie	23841
Dinwiddie Gardens	23803
Disputanta	23842
Ditchley	22482
Dixie (Fluvanna County)	23055
Dixie (Mathews County)	23050
Dixie Hill	22030
Dockery	23970
Doe Hill	24433
Dogtown	23063
Dogue	22451
Dogue Creek Village	22060
Dogwood Hill (Part of Staunton)	24401
Dogwood Knoll	23111
Dolphin	23843
Donna Lee Gardens	22046
Dooms	22980
Doran	24612
Dorchester (Richmond Indep. City)	23234
Dorchester (Wise County)	24273
Dorchester Junction	24273
Dorset Woods	23075
Doswell	23047
Dot	24277
Double Tollgate	22663
Douglas Park (Part of Portsmouth)	23701
Douglass Park	22204
Doveville	22032
Dowden Terrace	22311
Downings	22460
Downtown (Charlottesville Indep. City)	22902
Downtown (Loudoun County)	22075
Downtown (Lynchburg Indep. City)	24505
Downtown (Manassas Indep. City)	22110
Downtown (Montgomery County)	24063

Name	ZIP
Downtown (Roanoke Indep. City)	24001
Doylesville	22932
Drakes Branch	23937
Dranesville	22070
Draper	24324
Drewryville	23844
Drill	24260
Driver (Part of Suffolk)	23435
Drouin Hill	23075
Drum Bay	22469
Dry Branch	24132
Dryburg	24589
Dryden	24243
Dry Fork (Pittsylvania County)	24549
Dry Fork (Wise County)	24230
Drytown	24630
Duane	23009
Dublin	24084
Dudley	24558
Duffield	24244
Dugspur	24325
Dugwell	24151
Duke Gardens (Part of Alexandria)	22304
Dumbarton (Henrico County)	23228
Dumfries	22026
Dumont	22401
Dunavant	24216
Dunbar	
Dunbar Gardens (Part of Hampton)	23666
Dunbrooke	22560
Duncan Gap	24293
Duncans Mills	22435
Duncanville	24210
Dundalow (Part of Suffolk)	23434
Dundas	23938
Dunford Town	24602
Dungadin Heights	22630
Dungannon	24245
Dunlop (Part of Colonial Heights)	23834
Dunn Loring (Fairfax County)	22027
Dunn Loring Woods	22180
Dunnsville	22454
Durrett Town	22920
Dutton	23050
Duty	24217
Dwale	24228
Dwina	24230
Dye	24649
Dyers Store	24112
Dyke	22935
Eads	22202
Eagle Rock	24085
Earlhurst	24426
Earls	23002
Earlysville	22936
East Aberdeen Gardens (Part of Hampton)	23666
East Brook	24501
East End (Part of Richmond)	23223
Eastern Park (Part of Virginia Beach)	23452
Eastern State Hospital	23185
East Falls Church	22205
Eastham	22901
East Hampton (Part of Hampton)	23669
East Highland Park (Henrico County)	23222
East Hilton (Part of Newport News)	23607
East Lexington	24450
Eastmoreland	23231
East Norton (Part of Norton)	24273
East Norview (Part of Norfolk)	23513
East Ocean View (Part of Norfolk)	23503
Easton Place (Part of Norfolk)	23502
Eastover (Part of Suffolk)	23434
Eastover Gardens	23231
East Point (Accomack County)	23417
East Point (Rockingham County)	22827
East Radford (Part of Radford)	24141
East Stone Gap	24246
East Suffolk Gardens (Part of Suffolk)	23434
Eastville	23347
Eastville Station (Part of Eastville)	23347
Ebenezer	24565

574　VIRGINIA　Ebony-Fort Lee

	ZIP
Ebony	23845
Eclipse (Part of Suffolk)	23433
Edge	24554
Edgehill (King George County)	22485
Edgehill (Southampton County)	23851
Edgehill Park	23803
Edgemont (Part of Covington)	24426
Edgemont Park	24210
Edgerton	23868
Edgewater (Part of Norfolk)	23508
Edgewood (Part of Petersburg)	23805
Edinburg	22824
Ednam Forest	22901
Edom	22834
Edsall Park	22151
Edwards Shop	22718
Edwardsville	22456
Effinger	24450
Eggleston	24086
Eheart	22923
Elam	23960
Elberon	23846
Elephant Fork (Part of Suffolk)	23434
Elevon	22438
Elizabeth Park (Part of Norfolk)	23502
Elizabeth River Shores (Part of Virginia Beach)	23464
Elizabeth River Terrace (Part of Virginia Beach)	23464
Elk Creek	24326
Elk Garden	24266
Elk Hill	23063
Elko	23150
Elkrun	22728
Elkton	22827
Elkwood	22718
Ellett	24073
Elliston	24087
Elliston-Lafayette	24087
Ellisville	23093
Ellsworth (Part of Norfolk)	23505
Elma	22971
Elmhurst (Part of Norfolk)	23513
Elmo	24592
Elmont	23005
Elmwood Estates	22101
El-Nido	22101
Elon	24572
Elsom	23181
Eltham	23181
Elysian Woods	22192
Emmerton	22572
Emory	24327
Emory-Meadow View	24327
Emporia	23847
Endicott	24088
Enfield	23106
Engleside	22309
English Hills	23228
Enonville	23936
Eppes Fork	27584
Erica	22520
Esmont	22937
Esnon	23924
Esserville	24273
Estabrook (Part of Norfolk)	23509
Estabrook Park (Part of Norfolk)	23513
Estaline	24430
Estes	22716
Ethel	22572
Ethridge Estates	23805
Etlan	22719
Ettrick	23803
Euclid (Part of Virginia Beach)	23462
Euclid Place (Part of Virginia Beach)	23462
Euclid Terrace (Part of Virginia Beach)	23462
Eureka	23947
Eureka Park (Part of Virginia Beach)	23452
Eustaces Corner	22728
Euwanee Park (Part of Norfolk)	23503
Everets (Part of Suffolk)	23434
Evergreen	23939
Evergreen Hills	24201
Evergreen Shores	23696
Evington	24550
Ewell	23185
Ewing	24248
Exeter	24249
Exmore	23350

	ZIP
Faber	22938
Fagg	24073
Fairchester (Part of Fairfax)	22030
Fair City Mall (Part of Fairfax)	22031
Fairfax	22030-39
For specific Fairfax Zip Codes call (703) 273-5571	
Fairfax Acres	22030
Fairfax Circle (Part of Fairfax)	22031
Fairfax Forest	22031
Fairfax Station	22039
Fairfax Villa	22030
Fairfax Woods (Part of Fairfax)	22030
Fairfield (Essex County)	22454
Fairfield (Rockbridge County)	24435
Fairhaven	22303
Fair Hill	22031
Fairland	22312
Fairlawn (Covington Indep. City)	24426
Fairlawn (Pulaski County)	24141
Fairlawn Estates (Part of Norfolk)	23502
Fairlawn Heights	22075
Fairlee	22031
Fair Meadows (Part of Virginia Beach)	23462
Fair Meadows Estates (Part of Virginia Beach)	23462
Fairmont Manor (Part of Norfolk)	23509
Fairmount Park (Part of Norfolk)	23509
Fair Oaks (Fairfax Indep. City)	22032
Fair Oaks (Henrico County)	23075
Fair Port	22539
Fairview (Fairfax County)	22031
Fairview (Fairfax Indep. City)	22031
Fairview (Mecklenburg County)	23924
Fairview (Montgomery County)	24149
Fairview (Northampton County)	23310
Fairview (Page County)	22835
Fairview (Scott County)	24244
Fairview Beach	22401
Fairview Heights (Clifton Forge Indep. City)	24422
Fairview Heights (Lexington Indep. City)	24450
Fairwood	24378
Fairwood Acres	22039
Falconbridge	23234
Falconerville	24521
Falling Creek	23234
Falling Spring	24445
Falls Church	22040-46
For specific Falls Church Zip Codes call (703) 532-8822	
Falls Hill	22043
Falls Mills	24613
Fallville	24326
Falmouth (Stafford County)	22405
Fancy Gap	24328
Fancy Hill	24521
Farmers	22580
Farmers Fork (Essex County)	22509
Farmers Fork (Richmond County)	22572
Farmers Store	24360
Farmingdale (Part of Hopewell)	23860
Farmington (Albemarle County)	22903
Farmington (Henrico County)	23229
Farmville	23901
Farnham	22460
Fauquier Springs	22186
Favonia	24382
Fawcett Gap	22601
Fayette Park	23222
FBPO (Fleet Branch Post Office) (Part of Norfolk)	23593
Featherstone	22191
Featherstone Shores	22191
Federal Correctional Institution	23803
Federal Reserve (Part of Richmond)	23219
Fentress (Chesapeake Indep. City)	23322
Fentress (Virginia Beach Indep. City)	23451

	ZIP
Fenwick Park	22042
Fergusonville	23930
Ferncliff	23084
Ferndale Gardens	23803
Ferndale Park	23803
Ferrum	24088
Ferry Farms	22405
Fieldale	24089
Fife	23054
Figsboro	24112
File	22427
Fincastle	24090
Finchley	23927
Fine Creek Mills	23139
Finneywood	23924
First Colony	23185
First Street (Part of Radford)	24141
Fishers Hill	22626
Fishersville	22939
Five Forks (Amherst County)	24521
Five Forks (Bedford County)	24523
Five Forks (Carroll County)	24343
Five Forks (Dinwiddie County)	23833
Five Forks (Halifax County)	24592
Five Forks (Hopewell Indep. City)	23860
Five Forks (James City County)	23185
Five Forks (Madison County)	22960
Five Forks (Nelson County)	24553
Five Forks (Prince Edward County)	23958
Five Lakes	23141
Five Mile Fork	22401
Five Oaks	24630
Flactem Manor	23805
Flagpond	24221
Flat Gap	24279
Flat Iron	22520
Flatridge	24378
Flat Rock (Powhatan County)	23139
Flatrock (Russell County)	24260
Flat Run	22508
Flat Spur	24237
Flat Top	24230
Flatwood	24312
Flatwoods	24090
Fleeburg	22849
Fleenors	24201
Fleenortown	24263
Fleet (Part of Norfolk)	23511
Fleeton	22539
Flemington	22228
Fletcher	22973
Fletcherville	22186
Flint Hill (Bedford County)	24121
Flint Hill (Rappahannock County)	22627
Flood	24458
Floris	22071
Floyd	24091
Foneswood	22461
Fontaine	24148
Ford	23850
Fordham (Part of Hampton)	23663
Forest	24551
Forest Acres	23805
Forest Hill (Part of Richmond)	23225
Forest Hills (Part of Virginia Beach)	23450
Forest Lake Hills	23111
Forest Park (Hampton Indep. City)	23666
Forest Park (Norfolk Incep. City)	23518
Forestville (Fairfax County)	22066
Forestville (Shenandoah County)	22847
Fork Ridge	24639
Forks of Buffalo	24521
Forks Of Water	24413
Forksville	23950
Fork Union	23055
Formosa	23962
Fort Belvoir (Fairfax County)	22060
Fort Blackmore	24250
Fort Chiswell	24360
Fort Defiance	24437
Fortener Addition	24354
Fort Hill (Henrico County)	23226
Fort Hill (Lynchburg Indep. City)	24502
Fort Hunt	22306
Fort Lee (Henrico County)	23075
Fort Lee (Prince George County)	23801

Fort Lewis Terrace-Gum Tree **VIRGINIA** 575

Name	ZIP
Fort Lewis Terrace (Part of Salem)	24153
Fort Mitchell	23941
Fort Myer	22211
Fort Myer Heights	22209
Fort Pickett	23824
Fort Valley	22652
Foster	23056
Fosters Falls	24329
Four Corners	22182
Four Mile Fork	24401
Fourway (Part of Tazewell)	24630
Fox	24348
Foxhall (Part of Norfolk)	23502
Fox Hill (Part of Hampton)	23664
Fox Mill Estates	22070
Foxwells	22578
Fractionville	24210
Fraleytown	24244
Franconia	22310
Franconia Commons	22310
Franklin	23851
Franklin Farms	23805
Franklin Forest	22101
Franklin Heights	24151
Franklin Junction (Part of Suffolk)	23438
Franklin Park	22101
Franks Mill	24401
Franktown	23354
Frederick Hall	23117
Frederick Heights	22601
Fredericksburg (Independent City)	22401-05
For specific Fredericksburg Zip Codes call (703) 373-6543	
Fredericksburg (Rockbridge County)	24473
Freeman	23856
Freemont	24343
Freeport	23061
Freeshade Corner	23071
Free Union	22940
Fremac (Part of Virginia Beach)	23451
Friendship	24340
Fries	24330
Fringer	24066
Frogtown	22012
Front Royal	22630
Frytown	22186
Fugua Farms	23234
Fulks Run	22830
Fulton (Part of Richmond)	23231
Furnace	22827
Furnace Hill	24354
Furnace Mountain	22075
Gainesboro	22601
Gaines Mill Estates	23111
Gainesville	22065
Gala	24085
Galax	24333
Gallops Corner (Part of Virginia Beach)	23464
Galts Mill	24572
Gammons Store	23042
Garden City (Arlington County)	22207
Garden City (Hampton Indep. City)	23661
Garden Wood Park (Part of Virginia Beach)	23455
Gardner	24260
Gardners Crossroads	23117
Garfield Estates	22191
Gargatha	23421
Garland Heights	23234
Garrisonville	22463
Garrisonville Estates	22554
Garysville	23860
Gasburg	23857
Gate City	24251
Gatewood	22534
Gatewood Park (Part of Virginia Beach)	23454
Gaylord	22611
Gaynor Heights	24112
Gayton	23075
Geer	22973
Genito	23139
Genoa	22830
George Mason University	22030
Georges Fork	24228
Georges Mill	22080
Georges Tavern	23063
Georgetown	22842
Georgetown South (Part of Manassas)	22110
Georgetown Village	22191
George Washington (Part of Alexandria)	22305

Name	ZIP
George Washington Village	22060
Georgian Hamlet	22110
Gether	22514
Getz	22842
Ghent (Part of Norfolk)	23517
Gholsonville	23893
Gibson Station	24248
Gidsville	24521
Gilbert Gardens	23231
Gilmore Mills	24579
Ginter Park (Part of Richmond)	23227
Gladehill	24092
Gladesboro	24343
Glade Spring	24340
Gladstone	24553
Gladys	24554
Glamorgan	24293
Glasgow	24555
Glass	23072
Glebe Point	22432
Gleedsville	22075
Glen Alden	22030
Glen Allen (Henrico County)	23060
Glenbrook Hills	23075
Glencarlyn	22204
Glendale (Part of Newport News)	23607
Glendale Acres	23030
Glen Echo	23223
Glenford	24210
Glen Forest	22041
Glenita	24244
Glen Lyn	24093
Glenmore	24562
Glenns	23149
Glen Oaks	22015
Glenrochie	24210
Glen Rock (Part of Norfolk)	23502
Glen Roy Estates	23061
Glenshellah (Part of Portsmouth)	23707
Glenvar	24153
Glen Wilton	24438
Glenwood	24541
Glenwood Farms	23223
Glenwood Park (Part of Norfolk)	23505
Gloucester	23061
Gloucester Banks	23062
Gloucester Courthouse	23061
Gloucester Point (Gloucester County)	23062
Goblintown	24171
Goddin Hill	23005
Gogginsville	24151
Goldbond	24094
Golddale	22568
Gold Hill	23123
Goldvein	22720
Gonyon	22473
Goochland	23063
Goodall	23192
Goode	24556
Goods Mills	24471
Goodview	24095
Goodwins Ferry	24128
Goose Pimple Junction	24201
Gordonsville	22942
Gore	22637
Goshen	24439
Goshen Cross Road	23015
Gossan Mines	24333
Gouldin	23192
Gowrie Park (Part of Norfolk)	23509
Grady	24530
Grafton	23692
Grafton Village	22405
Grahams Forge	24360
Granby Shores (Part of Norfolk)	23503
Grandin Road (Part of Roanoke)	24015
Grand View (Part of Hampton)	23664
Grangeville	23410
Granite Hills (Part of Richmond)	23225
Granite Springs	22553
Grant	24378
Grant's Field	23803
Granville	23030
Grapefield	24314
Grassland	22733
Grass Ridge	22101
Grassy Creek (Henry County)	24112
Grassy Creek (Russell County)	24224
Gratton	24651

Name	ZIP
Gravel Hill (Part of Richmond)	23225
Graves Mill	22721
Graves Store	24104
Gray	23897
Graysontown	24141
Gray's Pointe	22033
Graysville	23301
Great Bridge (Part of Chesapeake)	23320
Great Falls	22066
Great Neck Manor (Part of Virginia Beach)	23450
Green Acres (Part of Fairfax)	22030
Greenbackville	23356
Green Bay	23942
Greenbriar (Chesterfield County)	23831
Greenbriar (Fairfax County)	22033
Greenbrier Mall (Part of Chesapeake)	23320
Greenbush	23357
Green Cove	24236
Greendale (Henrico County)	23228
Greendale (Washington County)	24210
Greendale Manor	23230
Greenes Corner	23024
Greenfield (Nelson County)	22920
Greenfield (Pittsylvania County)	24557
Greenfield (Washington County)	24361
Greenfield Farms (Part of Portsmouth)	23703
Greenlee	24579
Greenmount	22801
Green Oaks (Part of Newport News)	23601
Green Pond	24531
Greens Folly Apartments	24592
Green Spring	22601
Green Springs (Louisa County)	22942
Green Springs (Washington County)	24210
Green Valley (Part of Bristol)	24201
Greenville (Augusta County)	24440
Greenville (Fauquier County)	22123
Greenville Correctional Unit	24440
Greenway Downs	22042
Greenway Hills (Part of Fairfax)	22030
Greenwich (Prince William County)	22123
Greenwich (Virginia Beach Indep. City)	23462
Greenwood (Albemarle County)	22943
Greenwood (Henrico County)	23060
Greenwood (Norfolk Indep. City)	23513
Greenwood (Rockingham County)	22827
Greenwood Farms (Part of Hampton)	23666
Gregory Corner	23968
Gressitt	23137
Gretna	24557
Griffinsburg	22701
Griffith	24422
Grimes	22624
Grimsleyville	24639
Grimstead	23064
Grindall Creek	23234
Grit	24563
Grizzard	23879
Groseclose	24368
Grotons	23399
Groton Town	23359
Grottoes	24441
Grove	23185
Grove Hill	22849
Grove Park (Part of Portsmouth)	23707
Groveton	22306
	22303
For specific Groveton Zip Codes call (703) 549-4201	
Groveton Gardens	22303
Groveton Heights	22306
Grundy	24614
Guilford (Accomack County)	23308
Guilford (Fairfax County)	22310
Guilford Heights	23899
Guinea	22580
Guinea Mills	23040
Gum Spring	23065
Gum Tree	23005

576 VIRGINIA Gunn Hall Manor-Huske

	ZIP
Gunn Hall Manor (Part of Virginia Beach)	23454
Gunston Heights	22079
Gunston Manor	22079
Gunton Park	24360
Gwathmey	23005
Gwynn	23066
Hacksneck	23358
Haddonfield	24279
Hadensville	23067
Hagans	22463
Hague	22469
Hale Creek	24634
Halemhurst (Part of Fairfax)	22032
Hales Bottom	24605
Halfway	22171
Halifax	24558
Halifax Correctional Unit	24558
Hall Addition	24354
Hallieford	23068
Hallowing Point Estates	22079
Hallsboro	23113
Halls Hill	22207
Hallwood (Accomack County)	23359
Hallwood (Hampton Indep. City)	23664
Hamburg (Page County)	22835
Hamburg (Shenandoah County)	22824
Hamilton	22068
Hamiltontown	24273
Hamlin	24224
Hampden Sydney	23943
Hampton	23651-70
For specific Hampton Zip Codes call (804) 826-7585	
Hampton Institute (Part of Hampton)	23668
Hampton Terrace (Part of Hampton)	23669
Hanckel	24361
Handsom	23859
Hanging Rock	24153
Hanover	23069
Hanover Heights	23111
Hansonville	24266
Happy Creek	22630
Harbors of Newport	22191
Harborton	23389
Harbor View	22079
Hardings	22482
Hardware	24590
Hardwood	24245
Hardy	24101
Hardyville	23070
Hare Valley	23350
Harless	24073
Harman (Buchanan County)	24618
Harman (Tazewell County)	24602
Harman Junction	24614
Harmony (Halifax County)	24520
Harmony (Shenandoah County)	22824
Harpersville (Part of Newport News)	23607
Harrell Siding (Part of Suffolk)	23434
Harris Grove	23690
Harrisonburg	22801
Harriston	24441
Harrisville	22660
Harrowgate	23831
Harryhogan	22435
Hartfield	23071
Harts Shop	23117
Hartwood	22471
Harvey	24219
Hassen Heights (Part of Bristol)	24201
Hatchers	23139
Hat Creek	24528
Hatton	24590
Haven Heights (Part of Virginia Beach)	23462
Hawkinstown	22842
Hawthorne (Part of Norton)	24273
Hayes	23702
Hayfield (Fairfax County)	22310
Hayfield (Frederick County)	22638
Haymarket	22069
Haynesville	22472
Haynesville Correctional Unit	22472
Haysi	24256
Hayters Gap	24210
Haywood	22722
Hazel	24237
Hazel Heights (Part of Bristol)	24201
Head Waters	24442
Healing Springs	24445

	ZIP
Health Science (Part of Richmond)	23219
Healys	23071
Heards	22920
Heathsville	22473
Hebron (Augusta County)	24401
Hebron (Carroll County)	24333
Hebron (Dinwiddie County)	23894
Hechler Village	23223
Heights (Part of Petersburg)	23803
Helmet	23148
Hematite	24426
Hendricks Store	24121
Henry	24102
Henry Clay Heights	23111
Henry Fork	24151
Henrytown (Part of Saltville)	24370
Hepners	22842
Herald	24230
Heritage Court	23228
Heritage Square	22003
Heritage Village	22003
Herman	23967
Hermitage	22980
Hermitage Farms	23228
Hermitage Park	23228
Hermosa	24577
Herndon	22070-71 22090-94
For specific Herndon Zip Codes call (703) 437-3740	
Hessian Hills (Albemarle County)	22901
Hewlett	22546
Hickory Flat	24333
Hickory Ground (Part of Chesapeake)	23322
Hickory Grove Acres	22069
Hickory Haven	23103
Hickory Hill	22901
Hickory Junction	24260
Hicks Island	23089
Hicksville	24314
Hiddenbrook	22070
Hideaway Park	22031
Hidenwood (Part of Newport News)	23606
High Knob	22630
Highland	24084
Highland Gardens	23222
Highland Homes	22405
Highland Park (Arlington County)	22205
Highland Park (Hopewell Indep. City)	23860
Highland Park (Portsmouth Indep. City)	23707
Highland Park (Prince William County)	22110
Highland Park (Richmond Indep. City)	23222
Highlands	22201
Highland Springs (Henrico County)	23075
High Meadows	24201
High Point (Part of Hopewell)	23860
Hightown (Highland County)	24444
Hightown (Rockingham County)	22834
Highview Park	22207
Hilander Park	24201
Hill	24251
Hillbrook	22003
Hillcrest	23040
Hillcrest Estates	22110
Hillsboro	22132
Hillsdale (Part of Suffolk)	23434
Hillsman Corner	24502
Hillsville	24343
Hill Top (Martinsville Indep. City)	24112
Hilltop (Suffolk Indep. City)	23451
Hilltop Manor (Part of Virginia Beach)	23454
Hilltop-Oceana (Part of Virginia Beach)	23454
Hilltown	24330
Hillwood	22042
Hiltons	24258
Hilton Village (Part of Newport News)	23601
Hinesville	24549
Hinnom	22520
Hinton	22831
Hitesburg	24598
Hiwassee	24347
Hixburg	23958
Hoadly	22191
Hobson (Part of Suffolk)	23436
Hockley	23137

	ZIP
Hockman (Part of Bluefield)	24605
Hodges	24554
Hodges Manor (Part of Portsmouth)	23701
Hodgesville	24151
Hoges Chapel	24136
Holcomb Rock	24503
Holdcroft	23030
Holiday Hills (Part of Richmond)	23235
Holiday Point Estates (Part of Suffolk)	23434
Holland (Part of Suffolk)	23437
Hollindale	22306
Hollin Hall	22308
Hollin Hills	22307
Hollins	24019
Hollins College	24020
Holly Brook	24315
Holly Forest	22039
Holly Forks	23011
Holly Grove	23024
Holly Hills	23139
Hollymead (Albemarle County)	22901
Holly Park	22032
Holly Point	23430
Hollywood (Part of Suffolk)	23434
Holman	22853
Holmes Run Acres	22042
Holmes Run Heights	22003
Holmes Run Park	22042
Holston	24210
Holston Mill	24354
Holts Crossing	24554
Home Creek	24614
Homeville	23890
Homewood	22015
Honaker	24260
Honey Branch	24283
Honeyville	22851
Hood	22723
Hopeton	23421
Hopewell (Hopewell Indep. City)	23860
Hopewell (Pittsylvania County)	24549
Hopkins	23421
Horizon Hills (Part of Bristol)	24201
Horners	22520
Hornsbyville	23690
Horntown	23395
Horse Gap (Part of Pound)	24279
Horse Head	22473
Horse Pasture	24112
Horsepen	24619
Horsey	23396
Hotchkiss	24460
Hot Springs	24445
Howardsville (Albemarle County)	24562
Howardsville (Loudour County)	22012
Howellsville	22630
Howertons	22454
Howland	22473
Hubbard Springs	24263
Huckleberry Hills	23805
Huddle	24382
Huddleston	24104
Hudgins	23076
Hudson Crossroads	22842
Hudson Terrace (Part of Newport News)	23607
Huffman	24128
Huffville	24138
Hughes Store	23030
Hull Street (Part of Richmond)	23224
Hume	22639
Hunterdale	23851
Hunter Estates	22079
Hunters Valley	22181
Huntersville (Norfolk Indep. City)	23504
Huntersville (Suffolk Indep. City)	23435
Huntingcreek Hills	23234
Huntington (Fairfax County)	22303
Huntington (Henrico County)	23229
Huntington Heights (Part of Newport News)	23607
Huntly	22640
Hunton	23060
Hunts Village	22032
Hupp	22853
Hurley	24620
Hurricane	24293
Hurt	24563
Huske	23882

Hupp-Larchmont **VIRGINIA** 577

	ZIP		ZIP		ZIP
Hupp	22853	Jetersville	23083	Kingsland	23234
Hurley	24620	Jewell Hollow	22835	Kings Park	22151
Hurricane	24293	Jewell Ridge	24622	Kings Park West	22032
Hurt	24563	Jewell Valley	24622	Kings Point	23185
Huske	23882	Johnsontown	23405	Kings Store	24091
Hustle	22476	Joliff (Part of Chesapeake)	23321	Kingston	24550
Hyacinth	22477	Jolivue	24401	Kingston Chase	22070
Hybla Valley (Fairfax County)	22306	Jollett	22827	Kingstown	24019
Hybla Valley Farms	22306	Jones	22553	Kingsville	23901
Hyco	24592	Jonesboro	23824	Kingswood	23185
Hylas	23146	Jones Corner	22427	Kingswood Court	23111
Hylton Park	23235	Jones Creek (Part of Martinsville)	24112	Kingtown (Part of Bristol)	24201
Iberis	22503	Jonesville	24263	King William	23086
Ida	22835	Jordan Mines	24449	Kino	22560
Idlewilde (Part of Covington)	24426	Josephine	24273	Kinsale	22488
Idylwood (Fairfax County)	22043	Joyce Heights (Part of Fairfax)	22030	Kiptopeke	23310
Igo	22401	Joyner	23829	Kire	24094
Imboden	24216	Justisville	23421	Kirkside	22306
Independence	24348	Ka	24245	Klotz	24150
Independent Hill	22110	Karo	22630	Knightly	24437
Index	22485	Kathmoor	22310	Knob Hill (Part of Virginia Beach)	23464
Indian Field	22572	Keats	27553	Koehler	24112
Indian Gap	24656	Kecoughtan (Part of Hampton)	23667	Konnarock	24236
Indian Neck	23148	Keeling	24566	Laburnum Manor	23222
Indian River (Part of Chesapeake)	23325	Keene	22946	Lacey Forest	22205
Indian River Estates (Part of Virginia Beach)	23462	Keene Mill Manor	22152	Lacey Spring	22833
Indian Rock	24066	Keen Mountain	24624	Lackey	23694
Indian Run Park	22312	Keezletown	22832	La Crosse	23950
Indian Springs (Chesterfield County)	23234	Keith	23009	Ladd	22980
Indian Springs (Fairfax County)	22312	Keller	23401	Ladysmith	22501
Indian Valley	24105	Kells Corner	23924	Lafayette	24087
Indika	23487	Kelsa	24620	Lafayette Boulevard (Part of Norfolk)	23509
Ingham	22849	Kemmerer Gem No. 2	24282	Lafayette Park (Part of Norfolk)	23509
Ingleside (Part of Norfolk)	23502	Kemp's Place	23231	Lahore	22502
Ingram	24597	Kempsville (Part of Virginia Beach)	23462	Lake	22511
Inlet	22701	Kempsville Colony (Part of Virginia Beach)	23464	Lake Barcroft	22041
Inman	24216	Kempsville Gardens (Part of Virginia Beach)	23462	Lake Barcroft (census area only)	22044
Ino	22437	Kempsville Heights (Part of Virginia Beach)	23462	Lake Caroline	22546
Interior	24094	Kenbridge	23944	Lake Crystal Farms	23235
Intervale	24426	Kendall Acres	23234	Lake Jackson	22110
Ira	24620	Kendall Grove	23347	Lake Of The Woods	22508
Irisburg	24054	Kenilworth (Part of Norfolk)	23503	Lake Ridge	22192
Irondale	24219	Kennard	22572	Lakeside (Henrico County)	23228
Iron Gate (Alleghany County)	24448	Kennelworth (Part of Petersburg)	23803	Lakeside (Newport News Indep. City)	23606
Irongate (Prince William County)	22110	Kent	24382	Lakeside (Salem Indep. City)	24153
Ironto	24087	Kent Gardens	22101	Lakeside Heights	23690
Irving	24174	Kent Park (Part of Norfolk)	23509	Lakeside Hills	23228
Irvington	22480	Kents Store	23084	Lakeside Village	23038
Irwin	23063	Kentuck	24586	Lakeview Acres	23901
Isaac	23851	Kenwood (Hanover County)	23005	Lakeville Estates (Part of Virginia Beach)	23464
Island Creek	24343	Kenwood (Hopewell Indep. City)	23860	Lakewood (Fairfax County)	22041
Island Farm	22560	Keokee	24265	Lakewood (James City County)	23185
Island Ford	22827	Kerfoot	22025	Lakewood (Norfolk Indep. City)	23509
Isle of Wight	23397	Kermit	24251	Lakewood (Pittsylvania County)	24541
Isom	24228	Kerns	24250	Lamberts Point (Part of Norfolk)	23508
Ivakota	22024	Kernstown (Part of Winchester)	22601	Lambsburg	24351
Ivanhoe	24350	Kerrs Creek	24450	Lanahan	24088
Ivondale	22572	Keswick	22947	Lancaster	22503
Ivor	23866	Keysville	23947	Landmark Center (Part of Alexandria)	22304
Ivy	22945	Key West	22901	Landmark Plaza (Part of Alexandria)	22312
Jacksons Ferry	24312	Kibler	24053	Landmark Square (Part of Manassas)	22110
Jamaica	23079	Kidds Fork	22514	Land of Promise (Part of Virginia Beach)	23457
James River Estates	23233	Kidd's Store	24590	Land O'Pines	23832
James Store	23080	Kidville	22939	Landtown (Part of Virginia Beach)	23456
Jamesville	23398	Kiels Gardens	22030	Lanes Corner (Hanover County)	23005
Janaf Shopping Center (Part of Norfolk)	23502	Kiger Hill	24450	Lanes Corner (Spotsylvania County)	22553
Janey	24631	Kilby (Part of Suffolk)	23434	Lanesville	23086
Jarratt	23867	Kilby Shores (Part of Suffolk)	23434	Laneview	22504
Jasper	24244	Kildare Annex	23230	Lanexa	23089
Java	24565	Kilmarnock	22482	Langhorne Acres	22031
Jefferson (Fairfax County)	22042	Kilmarnock Wharf	22482	Langley	22101
Jefferson (Powhatan County)	23139	Kimages	23030	Langley Forest	22101
Jefferson Manor	22303	Kimballton	24150	Langley Research Center (Part of Hampton)	23665
Jefferson Mews (Part of Herndon)	22070	Kimberley Hills	23901	Langley View (Part of Hampton)	23669
Jefferson Park	23860	Kimberling	24315	Lankford Corner	22473
Jeffersonton	22724	Kimberly Acres	23234	Lantz Mills	22824
Jefferson Village	22042	Kinderhook	22973	Lara	22503
Jeffress	23927	Kindrick	24382	Larchmont (Arlington County)	22201
Jenkins Bridge	23399	King and Queen Court House	23085		
Jenkins Neck	23072	King George	22485		
Jennings	23930	Kingsbury Manor	22980		
Jennings Gap	24421	Kings Corner	23089		
Jennings Mission	24251	Kings Crossroads	23964		
Jennings Store	24244	Kingsdale	23851		
Jericho (Carroll County)	24381	Kings Fork (Part of Suffolk)	23434		
Jericho (Suffolk Indep. City)	23434	Kings Grant (Part of Virginia Beach)	23452		
Jerome	22824	Kings Hill	23231		
Jersey	22481				
Jessup Farms	23234				
Jester Gardens (Part of Chesapeake)	23320				

578 VIRGINIA Laswell-Marcem

Name	ZIP
Laswell	24360
Latanes	22443
Laurel (Henrico County)	23060
Laurel (Russell County)	24260
Laurel Branch	24091
Laureldale	24236
Laurel Dell	23228
Laurel Fork	24352
Laurel Grove	24594
Laurel Grove Estates	23111
Laurel Hill (Augusta County)	24482
Laurel Hill (Shenandoah County)	22641
Laurel Manor (Part of Virginia Beach)	23451
Laurel Mills	22716
Laurel Oak	23234
Laurel Park	23228
Lawndale Farms	23231
Lawrenceville	23868
Lawrenceville Hills	23868
Lawson	23430
Lawson Forest (Part of Virginia Beach)	23455
Lawson's Store (Mecklenburg County)	23924
Lawsons Store (Russell County)	24224
Lawyers	24501
LC Page (Part of Norfolk)	23518
Leaksville	22835
Leatherwood	24112
Lebanon	24266
Lebanon Church	22641
Leck	24230
Leda	24577
Lee	23039
Lee Acres	23875
Lee Boulevard Heights	22044
Leedstown	22443
Lee Forest	22030
Lee Hall (Part of Newport News)	23603
Lee Heights	22207
Lee-Hi Village	22030
Leemaster	24656
Lee Meadows	22032
Lee Mont	23403
Lee Park	23150
Leesburg	22075
Leesville	24571
Lee Town	24614
Leewood	22151
Lenah	22001
Lennig	24577
Lenox (Norfolk Indep. City)	23503
Lenox (Virginia Beach Indep. City)	23451
Leon	22725
Lerty	22520
Lester Manor	23086
Level Run	24563
Lewinsville	22101
Lewinsville Heights	22101
Lewisetta	22505
Lewis Gardens	23150
Lewis Park	22030
Lewiston	23005
Lewisville	22611
Lexington	24450
Liberia Woods (Part of Manassas)	22110
Liberty (Halifax County)	24577
Liberty (Tazewell County)	24651
Lick Fork	24230
Lick Run	24085
Lick Skillet	24370
Lightfoot	23090
Lignum	22726
Lilian	22539
Lilly	22821
Lime Hill	24201
Limeton	22610
Lincoln	22078
Lincolnia (Fairfax County)	22312
Lincolnia Heights	22312
Lincolnia Park	22312
Lincoln Park (Fairfax County)	22030
Lincoln Park (Norfolk Indep. City)	23513
Lindell	24210
Linden	22642
Lindenwood	24179
Lindsay	22942
Linkhorn (Part of Virginia Beach)	23454
Linkhorn Estates (Part of Virginia Beach)	23454
Linkhorn Shores (Part of Virginia Beach)	23451

Name	ZIP
Linlier (Part of Virginia Beach)	23451
Linville	22834
Lipps	24273
Lithia	24066
Little Haven (Part of Virginia Beach)	23452
Little Plymouth	23091
Little River Hills (Part of Fairfax)	22031
Little River Pines	22031
Little River Shopping Center	22003
Little Rocky Run	22024
Littleton	23890
Little Vienna Estates	22181
Litwalton	22503
Litz	24340
Lively	22507
Lloyd Place (Part of Suffolk)	23434
Loch Laird (Part of Buena Vista)	24416
Loch Lomond	22110
Lockhart Flats	24228
Locust Creek	23024
Locust Dale	22948
Locust Grove	22508
Locust Hill (Middlesex County)	23092
Locust Hill (Wythe County)	24360
Locust Mound	23410
Locustville	23404
Lodge	22435
Lodi	24340
Lodore	23002
Lofton	24472
Logan	22553
Loisdale Estates	22150
Lombardy Grove	23970
London Bridge (Part of Virginia Beach)	23454
London Towne	22020
Lone Fountain	24421
Lone Gum	24104
Longbottom (Part of Grundy)	24614
Long Branch	24237
Long Dale (Alleghany County)	24422
Longdale (Henrico County)	23060
Longdale Furnace	24422
Long Island	24569
Long Point (Part of Portsmouth)	23703
Longshop	24060
Long Spur	24084
Longview	23430
Looney's Creek	24614
Loretto	22509
Lorfax Heights	22079
Lorne	22546
Lorraine	23075
Lorton	22079
Lost Corner	22663
Lost Forest	23234
Lottsburg	22511
Loudoun Heights	25425
Louisa	23093
Love	22952
Loves Mill	24319
Loves Shop	24558
Lovettsville	22080
Lovingston	22949
Lower Brandon	23881
Lower Elk Creek	24326
Lower Exeter	24249
Lowery Hills	24201
Lowesville	22951
Lowmoor	24457
Lowry	24570
Loxley Place (Part of Portsmouth)	23702
Luck	24565
Lucketts	22075
Lumberton	23890
Lummis (Part of Suffolk)	23434
Lunenburg	23952
Luray	22835
Lurich	24124
Lusters Gate	24060
Luttrellville	22435
Lydia	22973
Lyells	22572
Lyman Park	22134
Lynchburg	24501-06
For specific Lynchburg Zip Codes call (804) 528-8900	
Lynch Station	24571
Lyndhurst	22952
Lynhaven (Part of Alexandria)	22305
Lynn Grove	23222

Name	ZIP
Lynnhaven (Hampton Indep. City)	23666
Lynnhaven (Virginia Beach Indep. City)	23450
Lynnhaven Acres (Part of Virginia Beach)	23452
Lynnhaven Colony (Part of Virginia Beach)	23451
Lynnhaven Mall (Part of Virginia Beach)	23452
Lynn Shores (Part of Virginia Beach)	23452
Lynn Spring	24649
Lynnwood (Rockingham County)	24471
Lynnwood (Virginia Beach Indep. City)	23452
Lynwood	22191
Lyon Park	22201
Lyon Village	22201
Mabe	24244
McAdam	24301
Macanie	22842
McCall Gap	24340
McChesney Heights (Fart of Bristol)	24201
McClung	24460
McClure	24269
McConnell	24251
McCoy	24111
McCrady	24370
McDonalds Mill	24060
McDonald's Small Farms	23060
McDowell	24458
Macedonia	24308
Maces Springs	24258
McGaheysville	22840
McHenry	22553
Machipongo	23405
McKendree	24558
McKenney	23872
McKinley	24459
McLean	22101-06
For specific McLean Zip Codes call (703) 790-9100	
McLean Estates	22101
McLean Hamlet	22102
McLean Manor	22101
McMullen	22973
McNeals Corner	22503
Macon	23101
Madison	22727
Madison College (Part of Harrisonburg)	22801
Madison Heights	24572
Madison Manor	22205
Madison Mills	22953
Madison Run	22942
Madisonville	23958
Madrid	22980
Madrillon Farms	22182
Maggie	24127
Magnolia (Part of Suffolk)	23434
Magnolia Gardens (Part of Suffolk)	23434
Maidens	23102
Major	24526
Makemie Park	23442
Malbrook	22044
Malcolm	24201
Malibu (Part of Virginia Beach)	23452
Mallow	24426
Malmaison	24527
Manakin	23103
Manakin Farms	23103
Manakin Sabot	23103
Manry	23888
Manassas	22110-11
For specific Manassas Zip Codes call (703) 368-2145	
Manassas Park	22111
Manchester Mills	23875
Maness	24282
Mangohick	23104
Mannboro	23105
Manquin	23106
Mantua (Fairfax County)	22031
Mantua Hills	22031
Manville	24251
Maple Grove (Rockbridge County)	24450
Maple Grove (Spotsylvania County)	22401
Maple Grove (Westmoreland County)	22443
Maplewood	23002
Mappsburg	23420
Mappsville	23407
Marble Valley	24432
Marcem (Part of Gate City)	24251

Marengo-Murphy VIRGINIA 579

Name	ZIP
Marengo	23950
Margo	22553
Marion	24354
Marion Hill	23231
Marionville	23408
Markham (Fauquier County)	22643
Markham (Pittsylvania County)	24557
Mark Haven Beach	22454
Marksville	22851
Marlan Forest	22307
Marlbank	23690
Marlboro	23224
Marlbrook	24483
Marrowbone Heights	24148
Marshall	22115
Marshall Heights	23072
Marsh Run	22712
Marstella Estates	22186
Martha Gap	24256
Martin Siding	23405
Martins Store	22920
Martinsville	24112-15
For specific Martinsville Zip Codes call (703) 632-4745	
Marumsco Acres	22191
Marumsco Hills	22191
Marumsco Plaza	22191
Marumsco Village	22191
Marumsco Woods	22191
Marvin	24639
Marye	22553
Marysville	24554
Maryus	23107
Mascot	23108
Mason Cove	24153
Mason Creek (Part of Salem)	24153
Masonville	22003
Massanetta Springs	22801
Massaponax	22401
Massies Mill	22954
Mathews	23109
Matoaca	23803
Mattaponi	23110
Maurertown	22644
Maury Place (Part of Newport News)	23601
Mavisdale	24627
Max Creek	24347
Maxie	24628
Maximum Security Facility	22079
Max Meadows	24360
Maxwell	24651
Mayberry	24120
Maybrook	24136
Mayfair Place	23223
Mayfield	23230
Mayfield Farms	23111
Mayflower	24521
Mayo (Halifax County)	24598
Mayo (Henry County)	24165
Maytown (Part of Coeburn)	24230
Meade	22560
Meadowbrook (Chesterfield County)	23234
Meadowbrook (Norfolk Indep. City)	23505
Meadowbrook Forest (Part of Norfolk)	23518
Meadowcrest (Part of Bristol)	24201
Meadowood	23227
Meadows of Dan	24120
Meadows of Newgate	22020
Meadow View (Chesterfield County)	23234
Meadowview (Washington County)	24361
Meadville	24558
Mears	23409
Mears Station	23409
Mearsville	23409
Mechanicsburg	24315
Mechanicsville (Hanover County)	23111
Mechanicsville (Rockingham County)	22853
Mechums River	22901
Mecklenburg Correctional Center	23917
Media Park	23231
Meetze	22186
Meherrin	23954
Melfa	23410
Melrose (Campbell County)	24554
Melrose (Roanoke Indep. City)	24017
Melrose Gardens	22172
Melton	22942
Memorial Heights	22306

Name	ZIP
Mendota	24270
Mentow	24104
Meredithville	23873
Meridian Park	22046
Merrifield	22031
Merrimac	24060
Merrimack Park (Part of Norfolk)	23503
Merrimac Shores (Part of Hampton)	23669
Merry Point	22513
Messongo	23399
Metomkin	23421
Mew	24224
Michaux	23139
Midcity Shopping Center (Part of Portsmouth)	23707
Middlebrook	24459
Middleburg	22117
Middleridge	22032
Middleton	23228
Middleton Gardens (Part of Salem)	24153
Middletown (Frederick County)	22645
Middletown (Northampton County)	23413
Middletowne Farms	23185
Midland	22728
Midlothian	23112-13
For specific Midlothian Zip Codes call (804) 794-5177	
Midway (Halifax County)	24598
Midway (Mecklenburg County)	23915
Midway (Tazewell County)	24609
Mike	24538
Mila	22473
Milan (Part of Norfolk)	23508
Miles	23025
Milford	22514
Military Circle (Part of Norfolk)	23502
Millboro	24460
Millboro Spring	24460
Mill Creek Park	22003
Millenbeck	22503
Miller Park (Part of Lynchburg)	24501
Millers Tavern	23115
Mill Gap	24465
Mill Garden	22553
Milltown	22080
Millwood	22646
Milteer Acres (Part of Suffolk)	23434
Mineral	23117
Mine Run	22568
Minimum Security Facility	22079
Minnieville	22193
Minor	22560
Mint Spring	24463
Miona	23415
Miskimon	22473
Mission Home	22940
Mitchells	22729
Mitchelltown	24445
Mobjack	23118
Modern (Part of Hampton)	23666
Modest Town	23412
Moffats Creek	24459
Mogarts Beach	23430
Mollusk	22517
Monaskon	22503
Moneta	24121
Moneys Corner	22070
Monroe	24574
Monroe Gardens (Part of Hampton)	23669
Monroe Hall	22443
Montague	22504
Montclair	22026
Montebello	24464
Monterey	24465
Montevideo	22840
Montezuma	22821
Montezuma Gardens	23223
Montford	22960
Montgomery	24023
Monticello Park (Part of Alexandria)	22305
Monticello Village (Part of Norfolk)	23509
Monticello Woods	22150
Montpelier (Charles City County)	23030
Montpelier (Hanover County)	23192
Montpelier Station	22957
Montrose (Henrico County)	23231

Name	ZIP
Montrose Heights (Part of Richmond)	23231
Montrose Terrace	23231
Montross	22520
Montvale	24122
Montvue	22901
Monument Heights	23226
Moon	23119
Mooreland	23075
Mooreland Farms	23229
Moores Corner	22554
Moorings	23839
Moran	23966
Morattico	22523
Morefield	24283
Morningside Hills	24210
Morning Star	22835
Morrisdale	23831
Morrison (Part of Newport News)	23601
Morrisonville	22080
Morrisville	22712
Morven	23002
Mosby	22042
Mosby Woods (Part of Fairfax)	22030
Moscow	22843
Moseley	23120
Moss Run	24426
Mossy Creek	22812
Motley	24563
Motleys Mill	24531
Motorun	23163
Mountain Falls	22601
Mountain Gap	22075
Mountain Grove	24484
Mountain Hill	24586
Mountain Lake	24136
Mountain Valley	24112
Mountain View (Giles County)	24134
Mountain View (King George County)	22401
Mountain View (Pulaski County)	24084
Mountain View (Rockbridge County)	24416
Mountain View (Washington County)	24210
Mount Airy	24557
Mount Alto	22937
Mount Carmel (Halifax County)	24520
Mount Carmel (Smyth County)	24354
Mountcastle	23140
Mount Clifton	22842
Mount Clinton	22801
Mount Crawford	22841
Mountfair	22932
Mount Garland	23117
Mount Hermon	24541
Mount Heron	24631
Mount Holly	22524
Mount Jackson	22842
Mount Landing	22560
Mount Laurel	24534
Mount Meridian	24441
Mount Nebo	23235
Mount Olive	22660
Mount Pisgah	24467
Mount Pleasant	24521
Mount Pleasant Estates	24405
Mount Sidney	24467
Mount Solon	22843
Mount Vernon	22121
Mount Vernon Forest	22309
Mount Vernon Park	22309
Mount Vernon Square	22306
Mount Vernon Terrace	22309
Mount Vernon Valley	22309
Mount Vernon Woods	22309
Mountville	22117
Mount Vinco	23921
Mount Williams	22601
Mount Zephyr	22309
Mount Zion	24554
Mouth of Laurel	24609
Mouth of Wilson	24363
Mt. Ararat	23927
Mt. Cross	24540
Mt. View	24354
Mud Fork	24630
Mulch	22460
Munden (Part of Virginia Beach)	23457
Mundy Point	22435
Munson Hill	22041
Murat	24450
Murpheyville	24368
Murphy	24656

580 VIRGINIA Murrayfield-Oldtown

Name	ZIP
Murrayfield	24319
Museville	24531
Mustoe	24468
Mutton Hunk	23421
Myndus	22949
Myrtle (Part of Suffolk)	23434
Nace	24175
Naffs	24065
Nahor	22963
Nain	22601
Namozine Store	23833
Nancy Wrights Corner	22580
Nandua	23420
Nansemond (Part of Suffolk)	23434
Nansemond Shores (Part of Suffolk)	23434
Naola	24574
Narrows	24124
Naruna	24576
Nash Ford	24225
Nasons	22733
Nassawadox	23413
Nathalie	24577
National Airport	20001
National Heights	23231
Natural Bridge	24578
Natural Bridge Station	24579
Natural Well	24445
Naval Base (Part of Norfolk)	23511
Naval Weapons Laboratory	22448
Naval Weapons Station	23691
Navy Annex	20370
Naxera	23122
Naylors Beach	22572
Nealy Ridge	24226
Nebo	24318
Needmore (Smyth County)	24319
Needmore (Wise County)	24273
Neenah	22520
Neersville	22132
Negro Foot	23192
Nellysford	22958
Nelson	24580
Nelson Estates	23231
Nelsonia	23414
Nelson Park	23185
Nesting	23079
Nethers	22740
Nettleridge	24171
New Alexandria	22307
New Baltimore	22186
Newbern	24126
Newberry	22170
New Birchett Estates	23875
New Bohemia	23842
New Canton	23123
New Castle	24127
New Church	23415
Newcomb Hall (Part of Charlottesville)	22904
New Design (Part of Danville)	24541
New Ellett	24060
New Glasgow	24521
New Gosport (Part of Portsmouth)	23702
New Hampden	24413
New Hope (Augusta County)	24469
New Hope (Charles City County)	23030
Newington	22122
Newington Station	22153
Newington Woods	22153
New Kent	23124
Newland	22572
New London	24551
New Market	22844
Newmarket North (Part of Hampton)	23605
Newmarket South (Part of Newport News)	23605
New Point	23125
Newport (Giles County)	24128
Newport (Page County)	22849
Newport News	23601-09
For specific Newport News Zip Codes call (804) 247-5341	
New Post	22401
New River	24129
News Ferry	24592
Newsoms	23874
Newstead Farm	23875
New Store	23901
Newton Park (Part of Norfolk)	23523
Newtown (King and Queen County)	23126
Newtown (Lancaster County)	22503

Name	ZIP
Newtown (Rockbridge County)	24450
Newtown (Rockingham County)	22827
Newville (Prince George County)	23842
Newville (Sussex County)	23890
Niceleytown	24422
Nickelsville	24271
Niday	24124
Nimrod Hall	24460
Ninde	22526
Nineveh	22630
Nokesville	22123
Nomini Grove	22552
Nora	24272
Norfolk	**23501-93**
For specific Norfolk Zip Codes call (804) 629-2198	
COLLEGES & UNIVERSITIES	
Norfolk State University	23504
FINANCIAL INSTITUTIONS	
New Atlantic Bank, N.A.	23510
Dominion Bank of Greater Hampton Roads, National Association	23510
First Virginia Bank of Tidewater	23510
Life Federal Savings Bank	23510
HOSPITALS	
DePaul Medical Center	23505
Lake Taylor Hospital	23502
Sentara Leigh Hospital	23502
Sentara Norfolk General Hospital	23507
HOTELS/MOTELS	
Admiralty Motor Hotel	23515
Best Western Center Inn	23502
Days Inn-Norfolk	23502
Holiday Inn-Ocean View	23503
Holiday Inn-Waterside	23510
Norfolk Airport Hilton	23502
Quality Inn-Lake Wright	23502
Ramada Inn-Newtown	23502
MILITARY INSTALLATIONS	
Armed Forces Staff College	23511
Material Department, Naval Supply Center	23512
Naval Air Station, Norfolk	23511
Naval Amphibious Base, Little Creek	23521
Naval Supply Center, Freight Terminal Department, Air Terminal	23512
Naval Supply Center, Freight Terminal Department, Ocean Terminal	23512
Special Materials Supply Department, Naval Supply Center	23512
United States Army Engineer District, Norfolk	23510
Norge	23127
Norland	24228
Norman	22701
North (Arlington County)	22207
North (Mathews County)	23128
North Bristol (Part of Bristol)	24201
North Fairlington	22206
Northfields	22901
North Fork	22132
North Gap	24366
North Garden	22959
North Halifax	24577
North Holston	24370
North Jericho (Part of Suffolk)	23434
North Linkhorn Park (Part of Virginia Beach)	23451
North Post	22060
North Rolleston (Part of Norfolk)	23502
North Run Hills	23228
Northside (Part of Richmond)	23222
North Springfield (Fairfax County)	22151
North Stanton	24577
North Tazewell (Part of Tazewell)	24630
North View	23973
North Virginia Beach (Part of Virginia Beach)	23451

Name	ZIP
North Weems	22576
North Wellville	23824
Northwest (Part of Chesapeake)	23322
North Woodley	22042
Norton	24273
Nortonsville	22935
Norvello	23917
Norview (Part of Norfolk)	23513
Norwood (Bedford County)	24551
Norwood (Nelson County)	24581
Nottingham (Richmond Indep. City)	23235
Nottingham (Scott County)	24251
Nottoway	23955
Nottoway Correctional Center	23922
Novelty	24137
Novum	22735
Nurney (Part of Suffolk)	23434
Nurneysville (Part of Suffolk)	23434
Nutbush	23942
Nuttall	23061
Nuttsville	22528
Oakcrest (Alexandria Indep. City)	22302
Oakcrest (Arlington County)	22202
Oakdale	24450
Oakdale Farms (Part of Norfolk)	23505
Oak Forest	23040
Oak Grove (Carroll County)	24381
Oak Grove (Loudoun County)	22170
Oak Grove (Spotsylvania County)	22401
Oak Grove (Washington County)	24201
Oak Grove (Westmoreland County)	22443
Oak Hall	23416
Oak Hill (Augusta County)	22980
Oak Hill (Grayson County)	24363
Oak Hill (Henrico County)	23223
Oak Hill (Page County)	22650
Oak Hill Estates	23005
Oakhurst (Part of Petersburg)	23805
Oakland (Part of Suffolk)	23432
Oakland Park	23350
Oakleaf Terrace (Part of Norfolk)	23523
Oak Level (Halifax County)	24558
Oaklevel (Henry County)	24055
Oakley	22437
Oakpark	22730
Oak Ridge (Fairfax County)	22180
Oakridge (Suffolk Indep. City)	23434
Oakridge Estates (Prince William County)	22110
Oakridge Estates (Suffolk Indep. City)	23434
Oakton (Fairfax County)	22124
Oak Valley Estates	22181
Oakville	24522
Oakwood (Arlington County)	22213
Oakwood (Buchanan County)	24631
Oakwood (Fairfax County)	22310
Oakwood (Norfolk Indep. City)	23513
Oakwood Forest	24426
Oatlands	22075
Occoquan	22125
Occoquan Facility	22079
Occupacia	22476
Oceana (Part of Virginia Beach)	23454
Ocean Park (Part of Virginia Beach)	23455
Ocean View (Part of Norfolk)	23503
Ocoonita	24263
Ocran	22578
Oilville	23129
Old Courthouse	22182
Old Creek Estates	22032
Old Dominion	22969
Old Dominion Gardens	22101
Olde Forge	22032
Oldewood	22043
Oldfield (Part of Virginia Beach)	23451
Old Glade Spring	24340
Old Hampton (Part of Hampton)	23669
Oldhams	22529
Old Somerset	22972
Old Tavern	22171
Oldtown	24333

Old Well-Potomac Mills **VIRGINIA** 581

	ZIP
Old Well	23959
Olinger	24219
Olive (Part of Portsmouth)	23701
Omaha	24228
Omega	24592
Onancock	23417
Onemo	23130
Onley	23418
Ontario	23937
Opal	22186
Opequon	22601
Ophelia	22530
Oranda	22657
Orange	22960
Orange Hunt	22153
Orapax Farms	23141
Orbit	23487
Orchard Hill	23234
Orchid	23117
Orchid Lake	23065
Ordinary	23131
Oregon Acres (Part of Portsmouth)	23707
Oreton	24219
Oriskany	24130
Orkney Springs	22845
Orlando (Part of Suffolk)	23434
Orlean	22128
Orleans Village	22312
Oronoco	24483
Osaka	24216
Osbornes Chapel	24221
Osborns Gap	24228
Osceola	24210
Osso	22401
Othma	23153
Otter Hill	24523
Otter River	24571
Otterville	24523
Ottobine	22821
Ottoman	22503
Overall	22610
Overbrook (Part of Norfolk)	23513
Overlee Knolls	22205
Owens	22485
Owens Brooke (Part of Manassas)	22110
Owenton	23148
Oxford (Part of Richmond)	22235
Oyster	23419
Oyster Point (Part of Newport News)	23606
Ozeana	22454
Paces	24592
Paeonian Springs	22129
Page	24631
Page Hollow	24370
Paige	22580
Paineville	23083
Paint Bank	24131
Painter	23420
Paint Lick	24637
Palls	23086
Palmer	22578
Palmer Crossroads	27563
Palmer Springs	23917
Palmyra (Fluvanna County)	22963
Palmyra (Suffolk Indep. City)	23434
Pamlico (Part of Norfolk)	23503
Pamplin	23958
Panoramic Hills	22003
Pardee	24216
Paris	22130
Park (Part of Waynesboro)	22980
Parker	22508
Parkers Shores	22577
Parkfairfax (Part of Alexandria)	22302
Parkglen	22204
Parklawn	22312
Park Lee Place	23234
Park Place (Part of Norfolk)	23504
Parksley	23421
Parkview (Newport News Indep. City)	23605
Park View (Portsmouth Indep. City)	23707
Parkview (Rockingham County)	22801
Parkview Hills	22101
Parkwood	22401
Parnassus	24421
Parrott	24132
Parsonage	24224
Partlow	22534
Passapatanzy	22401
Passing	22427
Pastoria	23421
Patna	24487
Patrician Manor (Part of Hampton)	23666

	ZIP
Patrick Henry Correctional Unit	24148
Patrick Henry Heights	23111
Patrick Henry Mall (Part of Newport News)	23607
Patrick Springs	24133
Patterson (Buchanan County)	24633
Patterson (Wythe County)	24343
Pattonsville	24244
Pauls Cross Roads	22560
Paynes Store	22553
Paytes	22553
Peach Bottom	24333
Peaks	23069
Peapatch	24622
Pearisburg (Giles County)	24134
Pearly	24614
Peary	23138
Pedlar Mills	24574
Pedro	22559
Pemberton	23063
Pembroke	24136
Pembroke Mall (Part of Virginia Beach)	23450
Pembroke Manor (Part of Virginia Beach)	23455
Pender	22033
Penderbrook	22033
Pendleton	23117
Penhook	24137
Penn Acres	23235
Penn Daw	22303
Penn Daw Terrace	22307
Pennington Gap	24277
Penn Laird	22846
Penn Lee	24282
Penns Store	24165
Pennsytown (Part of Norfolk)	23513
Penola	22546
Pentagon	20301
Penvir	24124
Peola Mills	22740
Pepper	24141
Perrin	23072
Perrowville	24551
Perryville (Part of Saltville)	24370
Perth	24577
Petersburg	23801-05
For specific Petersburg Zip Codes call (804) 732-4631	
Peterson Chapel	24244
Petunia	24382
Peytonsburg	24565
Phenix	23959
Philadelphia (Part of Suffolk)	23434
Philbeck Crossroads	23968
Phillip	24201
Phillis	23917
Philomont	22131
Philpott	24055
Phoebus (Part of Hampton)	23663
Piankatank Shores	23071
Pickaway	24597
Pico	24066
Piedmont	24441
Pierces Corner	22503
Pierces Shop	22960
Pigeon Hill	22611
Pilgrams Knob	24634
Pilot	24138
Pimmit	22043
Pimmit Hills	22043
Pine	24324
Pineaire (Part of Suffolk)	23434
Pine Chapel Village (Part of Hampton)	23666
Pinecrest	22312
Pinecrest Heights	22003
Pinedale	23229
Pine Grove (Clarke County)	22012
Pine Grove (Page County)	22851
Pine Grove (Washington County)	24270
Pine Grove Court (Part of Hampton)	23669
Pine Grove Terrace (Part of Hampton)	23669
Pine Hill	23111
Pinehurst (Part of Portsmouth)	23703
Pine Ridge (mail Annandale) (Fairfax County)	22003
Pine Ridge (mail Fairfax) (Fairfax County)	22031
Pinero	23061
Pine Springs	22042
Pine Tree	23027
Pinetta	23061
Pineville	22840

	ZIP
Pinewood Lake	22309
Pinewood Lawns	22309
Pinewood Park (Part of Manassas Park)	22110
Pinewood South	22309
Piney Grove	24589
Piney River	22964
Pinners Point (Part of Portsmouth)	23707
Pipers Gap	24333
Pisgah	24651
Pitmans Corner	22576
Pittmantown (Part of Suffolk)	23438
Pittsville	24139
Pizarro	24091
Plain View	23137
Plantersville	23937
Plasterco	24370
Plaza, The (Part of Lynchburg)	24501
Pleasant Gap	24549
Pleasant Grove (Henry County)	24112
Pleasant Grove (Lunenburg County)	23947
Pleasant Grove (Mecklenburg County)	23970
Pleasant Grove Estates	23920
Pleasant Heights	24370
Pleasant Hill (Harrisonburg Indep. City)	22801
Pleasant Hill (Suffolk Indep. City)	23434
Pleasant Ridge (Fairfax County)	22003
Pleasant Ridge (Virginia Beach Indep. City)	23451
Pleasant Shade	23847
Pleasant Valley (Buckingham County)	23936
Pleasant Valley (Fairfax County)	22021
Pleasant Valley (Rockingham County)	22848
Pleasantview	24574
Plum Creek	24340
Plum Point	23181
Plum Tree	23024
Plymouth	23974
Poages Mill	24018
Pocahontas (Petersburg Indep. City)	23803
Pocahontas (Tazewell County)	24635
Pocahontas Correctional Unit	23832
Pocket	24282
Poetown (Part of Grundy)	24614
Poff	24091
Pohick Estates	22079
Point Breeze	22454
Point Eastern	22546
Point Pleasant	24315
Pons	23866
Poole Siding	23833
Pope	23829
Poplar Camp	24360
Poplar Cove	23417
Poplar Heights	22046
Poplar Hill (Fairfax County)	22003
Poplar Hill (Giles County)	24134
Poplar Inn	22546
Poplar Springs	23075
Poquoson	23662
Porter	22937
Porters Cross Roads	24382
Port Haywood	23138
Portlock (Part of Chesapeake)	23324
Port Norfolk (Part of Portsmouth)	23707
Port-O-Dumfries	22172
Port Republic	24471
Port Royal	22535
Portsmouth	23701-09
For specific Portsmouth Zip Codes call (804) 397-4607	
Portsmouth Heights (Part of Portsmouth)	23707
Post Oak	22553
Potato Creek	24363
Potomac (Part of Alexandria)	22301
Potomac Beach (Part of Colonial Beach)	22443
Potomac Farms	22011
Potomac Hills	22101
Potomac Mills (Prince William County)	22192

582 VIRGINIA Potomac Mills-Ruark

Location	ZIP
Potomac Mills (Westmoreland County)	22520
Potters Flats	41522
Pound	24279
Pounding Mill	24637
Powcan	23023
Powells Store (Albemarle County)	22937
Powells Store (Bedford County)	24526
Powhatan	23139
Prater	24656
Pratts	22731
Premier	24640
Prentiss Place (Part of Portsmouth)	23707
Preston	24112
Preston Hills	24201
Preston King	22205
Prices Fork	24073
Prices Store	24572
Prilliman	24088
Prince George	23875
Prince George Woods Estates	23875
Princess Anne (Part of Virginia Beach)	23456
Proffit	22901
Prospect	23960
Prospectdale	24134
Providence (Grayson County)	24330
Providence (Halifax County)	24577
Providence Church (Part of Suffolk)	23434
Providence Forge	23140
Providence Park	23222
Provost	23139
Public Fork	23967
Pughsville (Part of Suffolk)	23435
Pulaski	24301
Pulaski North	24301
Pumpkin Center	24315
Pungo (Part of Virginia Beach)	23456
Pungoteague	23422
Purcell	24225
Purcellville	22132
Purchase	24244
Purdy	23847
Purvis (Part of Suffolk)	23437
Puryear Corner	23927
Putnam	24260
Quail Oaks	23234
Quantico	22134
Quantico Marine Corps Air Station (Prince William County)	22134
Quantico Station	22134
Quarry	24370
Quebec	24354
Queens Lake	23185
Quicksburg	22847
Quicks Mill	24401
Quinby	23423
Quinque	22965
Quinton	23141
Rabat	24577
Raccoon Ford	22701
Racefield	23168
Radford	24141-43
For specific Radford Zip Codes call (703) 639-3531	
Radford Army Ammunition Plant	24141
Radford University (Part of Radford)	24142
Radiant	22732
Radnor Heights	22209
Ragged Point Beach	22442
Raines Tavern	23901
Rainswood	22473
Raketown	24350
Raleigh Place (Part of Chesapeake)	23320
Raleigh Terrace (Part of Hampton)	23661
Ramoth	22554
Ramsey (Part of Norton)	24273
Randolph	23962
Random Hills	22030
Rangeley	24089
Ransons	23936
Raphine	24472
Rapidan	22733
Rappahannock Academy	22538
Rappahannock Estates	22454
Rappahannock Shores	22454
Rapps Mill	24450
Raven	24639
Ravensworth	22151

Location	ZIP
Ravensworth Grove	22003
Ravensworth Park	22003
Ravenwood (Fairfax County)	22044
Ravenwood (Prince William County)	22110
Ravenwood Park	22044
Rawhide	24265
Rawley Springs	22831
Rawlings	23876
Raymondale	22042
Raynor	23866
Rayon Terrace (Part of Covington)	24426
Readus	22824
Reams	23803
Reba	24523
Rectortown	22140
Red Apple Orchard	22971
Redart	23142
Red Ash	24640
Red Bank (Halifax County)	24598
Red Bank (Northampton County)	23408
Redd Shop	23901
Red Eye	24531
Red Fox Forest	22003
Red Hill (Albemarle County)	22959
Red Hill (Charlotte County)	24528
Red House	23963
Red Lane	23139
Redlawn	23919
Red Mills	24431
Red Oak	23964
Red Top (Part of Suffolk)	23434
Red Valley	24065
Redwood	24146
Reed Creek	24265
Reedville	22539
Reesedale	24087
Reese Shop	23967
Refuge	22655
Regina	22540
Rehoboth	23974
Rehoboth Church	22482
Reids Ferry (Part of Suffolk)	23434
Reids Grove	22101
Reliance	22649
Remington	22734
Remlik	23175
Remo	22579
Renan	24557
Republican Grove	24585
Rescue	23424
Reservoir Hill (Part of Covington)	24426
Rest	22624
Reston	22090
Retreat	24151
Reva	22735
Revis	23175
Rexburg	22560
Reynolds Store	22625
Rhoadesville	22542
Rice	23966
Riceville	24565
Richardson	24343
Richardsville	22736
Rich Creek	24147
Richlands	24641
Richmond	23201-94
For specific Richmond Zip Codes call (804) 775-6140	
Richmond Beach	22560
Richmond Heights	23231
Rich Neck	22472
Richpatch	24426
Rich Valley	24370
Ridge	23229
Ridgecrest	22124
Ridgelea Estates	22031
Ridge View	22310
Ridgeway (Halifax County)	24597
Ridgeway (Henry County)	24148
Ridgeway (Pittsylvania County)	24139
Riggs	22435
Rileyville	22650
Riner	24149
Ringgold	24586
Rio	22901
Ripplemead	24150
Rip Rap	24598
Rivanna	22936
River Bend Estates	22190
Riverdale (Halifax County)	24592
Riverdale (Hampton Indep. City)	23666
Riverdale (Southampton County)	23851
Riverhill	24333
River Hills	23075

Location	ZIP
Rivermont (Augusta County)	24477
Rivermont (Chesterfield County)	23831
Rivermont (Covington Indep. City)	24426
Rivermont (Lynchburg Indep. City)	24503
Rivermont (Newport News Indep. City)	23601
River Oaks	22101
River Park (Part of Portsmouth)	23707
River Ridge Mall (Part of Lynchburg)	24502
Rivers Edge	23860
Riverside	24416
Riverside Estates	22309
Riverside Gardens	22308
Riverton (Part of Front Royal)	22651
Riverview (Norfolk Indep. City)	23504
Riverview (Wise County)	24230
Riverville	24553
Riverwood	22207
Rixeyville	22737
Roanes	23061
Roanoke	24001-38
For specific Roanoke Zip Codes call (703) 985-8765	
Roaringfork	24216
Roaring Run	24066
Robbins Chapel	24265
Roberts Mill	24375
Robertsons	24523
Robin Ridge	23111
Robinwood	23231
Robley	22460
Robnel (Part of Manassas)	22110
Rochelle	22738
Rockbridge Baths	24473
Rock Castle	23063
Rockfish	22971
Rockland	22630
Rockland Village	22021
Rock Mills	22716
Rock Springs (Chesterfield County)	23234
Rock Springs (Fauquier County)	22186
Rocktown	24201
Rockville	23146
Rocky Bar	22827
Rocky Gap	24366
Rocky Mount	24151
Roda	24216
Rodden	24577
Rodophil	23083
Roebuck	24210
Roetown	24236
Rogers	24073
Roland Park (Part of Norfolk)	23509
Rolling Brook	22192
Rolling Hills	22309
Rolling Meadows	23875
Rolling Valley	22152
Rollins Fork	22544
Rondo	24531
Roosevelt Gardens (Part of Norfolk)	23513
Roseann	24614
Rose Bower	24522
Rosedale	24280
Rose Hill (Fairfax County)	22310
Rose Hill (Lee County)	24281
Rose Hill Farms	22310
Roseland	22967
Rosemont (Alexandria Indep. City)	22301
Rosemont (Fairfax County)	22101
Rosemont (Suffolk Indep. City)	23434
Rosemont (Virginia Beach Indep. City)	23452
Roseville	22554
Roslyn Hills	23229
Rosslyn	22209
Roth	24633
Rough Creek	23959
Round Bottom	24124
Round Hill	22141
Round Top	24293
Roundtree	22042
Rowe	24646
Roxbury (Charles City County)	23140
Roxbury (Henrico County)	23229
Royal City (Part of Grundy)	24614
Royal Court	22003
Ruark	23043

Rubermont-Speedwell VIRGINIA 583

Name	ZIP
Rubermont	23974
Ruby	22545
Ruckersville	22968
Rudee Inlet (Part of Virginia Beach)	23451
Rue	23421
Ruff	23016
Rugby	24363
Rural Retreat	24368
Rushmere	23430
Rushmere Shores	23430
Russell	24260
Russell Creek	24283
Rustburg	24588
Rustburg Correctional Unit	24588
Rustic	23030
Rutherford	22032
Ruther Glen	22546
Ruthland	23228
Ruthville	23147
Ryan	22011
Rye Cove	24244
Sabot	23103
Sadler Heights (Part of Suffolk)	23434
Sago	24137
St. Brides (Part of Chesapeake)	23322
St. Charles	24282
St. Clair	24605
St. Clair Bottom	24319
St. Davids Church	22652
St. Elmo (Part of Alexandria)	22305
St. Joy	23921
St. Just	22567
St. Luke	22664
St. Paul	24283
St. Stephens	22019
St. Stephens Church	23148
Salem (Culpeper County)	22701
Salem (Salem Indep. City)	24153
Salem Woods	23234
Salisbury	23113
Salona Village	22101
Saltpetre	24085
Saltville	24370
Saluda	23149
Salvia	23148
Samos	23180
Sanburne Park	23150
Sand Bridge (Part of Virginia Beach)	23456
Sandidges	24521
Sands	23874
Sandston	23150
Sandy Bottom (Part of Suffolk)	23432
Sandy Fork	23927
Sandy Hook	23153
Sandy Level	24161
Sandy Point	22579
Sandy River	24054
Sanford	23426
Sangerville	22812
Sanville	24055
Sarah	23130
Saratoga	22153
Saratoga Place (Part of Suffolk)	23434
Saumsville	22644
Saunders (Part of Richmond)	23220
Savage Crossing (Part of Suffolk)	23434
Savageville	23417
Savedge	23881
Saxe	23967
Saxis	23427
Sayersville	24602
Scarborough Neck	23330
Scenic Park (Part of Bristol)	24201
Schley	23154
Schoolfield (Part of Danville)	24541
Schuyler	22969
Scotland	23883
Scott Addition	24210
Scottie Farms	23075
Scottsburg	24589
Scotts Crossroads	23924
Scotts Fork	23002
Scottsville	24590
Scottswood	23851
Scrabble	22749
Scruggs	24121
Seaboard	24641
Seaford	23696
Seaford Shores	23696
Sealston	22547
Seapines (Part of Virginia Beach)	23451
Searcy	23831
Seatack (Part of Virginia Beach)	23451
Seaview	23429
Seawright Spring	24467
Sebrell	23837
Sedalia	24526
Sedgefield (Part of Newport News)	23607
Sedgefield Manor	23228
Sedley	23878
Selden	23061
Selma	24474
Seminary	24219
Seminary Valley (Part of Alexandria)	22304
Senora	22503
Seven Corners	22044
Seven Corners Shopping Center	22044
Seven Fountains	22652
Seven Mile Ford	24373
Seven Pines	23150
Seven Pines Villa	23150
Severn	23155
Severn Manor	23072
Shacklefords	23156
Shacklefords Fork	23156
Shadow	23163
Shadow Valley (Part of Bristol)	24201
Shadwell	22947
Shady Grove (Greene County)	22940
Shady Grove (Halifax County)	24598
Shady Grove (Washington County)	24210
Shady Oak	22066
Shadyside	23405
Shanghai	23110
Shannondale	24630
Shannon Hills	24148
Shannon Park	22577
Sharps	22548
Shawnee Land	22601
Shawsville	24162
Shawver Mill	24651
Shea Terrace (Part of Portsmouth)	23707
Sheep Town	24312
Sheffield Court	23235
Sheffield Terrace	24148
Shelby	22727
Shelfar	23117
Shelors Mill	24091
Shelton (Part of Virginia Beach)	23455
Shenandoah (Hopewell Indep. City)	23860
Shenandoah (Page County)	22849
Shenandoah Farms	22630
Shenandoah Place	23226
Shenandoah Retreat	22012
Shenandoah Shores	22630
Shepherds Hill	24265
Shepherds Store	23038
Sheppards	23901
Sherando	22952
Sherwill	24538
Sherwood Forest	24401
Sherwood Hall	22306
Sheva	24531
Shields	23306
Shiloh (Southampton County)	23827
Shiloh (King George County)	22549
Shiny Rock	23927
Shipman	22971
Shirley	23030
Shirley Duke (Part of Alexandria)	22304
Shirley Gate Park	22030
Shirlington	22206
Shockoe	24531
Shores	22963
Short Lane	23061
Short Pump	23060
Shorts Creek	24312
Shortt Gap	24647
Shoulders Hill (Part of Suffolk)	23435
Shrevewood	22043
Shumansville	22514
Shumate	24124
Siddon	24580
Sigma (Part of Virginia Beach)	23456
Signpine	23061
Siler	22601
Silva	23415
Silver Beach	23398
Silver Springs	22310
Silverwood (Part of Chesapeake)	23320
Simeon	22901
Simmonsville	24127
Simons Corner	22572
Simonsdale (Part of Portsmouth)	23701
Simonson	22460
Simpkins	23310
Simpsons	24072
Sinai	24592
Sinclair Farms (Part of Hampton)	23669
Singers Glen	22850
Sinking Creek	24127
Sinnickson	23395
Sissons Corner	22473
Sixmile Post	24151
Skeetrock	24228
Skeggs	24646
Skinquarter	23120
Skippers	23879
Skipwith	23968
Skipwith Farms (Henrico County)	23229
Skipwith Farms (Williamsburg Indep. City)	23185
Skyland	22835
Skyland Estates	22642
Skymont (Part of Staunton)	24401
Slabtown	24251
Slate	24614
Slate Mills	22740
Sleepy Hole (Part of Suffolk)	23435
Sleepy Hollow	22042
Sleepy Hollow Estates (Fairfax County)	22044
Sleepy Hollow Estates (Henrico County)	23229
Sleepy Hollow Manor	22044
Sleepy Hollow Run	22003
Sleepy Hollow Woods	22003
Sliders	23936
Sloantown	22244
Smithfield	23430
Smiths Cross Roads	23970
Smoky Ordinary	23868
Snake Creek	24343
Snapp	24340
Snell	22553
Snowden (Amherst County)	24526
Snowden (Fairfax County)	22308
Snowflake	24251
Snow Hill	23156
Snowville	24347
Soles	23050
Solomons Store	23060
Solsburg	22827
Somers	22503
Somerset	22972
Somerton (Part of Suffolk)	23438
Somerville	22739
Sonans	24531
Sorocco (Part of Suffolk)	23434
Soudan	23927
South	22204
Southampton (Part of Hampton)	23669
Southampton Correctional Center	23829
South Anna	23117
South Boston	24592
South Chesconessex	23417
South Clinchfield	24225
Southern Estates	23805
Southern Pine	23803
South Fairlington	22206
South Garden	22959
South Hill	23970
South Jackson	22842
South Martinsville (Part of Martinsville)	24112
South Norfolk (Part of Chesapeake)	23324
South Plains (Part of Petersburg)	23805
Southport	22191
Southridge	22101
South Roanoke (Part of Roanoke)	24014
Southside (Part of Richmond)	23224
South Suffolk (Part of Suffolk)	23434
South Woodley	22042
Spainville	23824
Sparkling Springs	22834
Sparta	22552
Speedwell	24374

584 VIRGINIA Speegleville-Town and Country Estates

	ZIP		ZIP		ZIP
Speegleville (Part of Hampton)	23666	Stony Battery	24354	Syringa	23169
Spencer	24165	Stony Creek	23882	Tabb	23602
Sperryville	22740	Stony Man	22835	Tabscott	23038
Spivey Store	24251	Stony Point	22901	Tacoma	24230
Splash Dam	24256	Stony Point Mills	23040	Taft	22578
Spotsylvania	22553	Stony Ridge	24630	Talbot Park (Part of Norfolk)	23505
Spottswood	24475	Stormont	23149	Tall Oaks	22003
Spout Spring	24593	Story	23837	Tallysville	23124
Springbrook Forest	22003	Stott	23898	Tamworth	23027
Spring City	24225	Stovall	24577	Tangier	23440
Springcreek	22812	Stover	24421	Tannersville	24377
Springdale (Bristol Indep. City)	24201	Straightstone	24569	Tappahannock	22560
Springdale (Henrico County)	23222	Strasburg	22657	Tara	22205
Springfield (Fairfax County)	22150-53	Strasburg Junction	22657	Taro	23934
For specific Springfield Zip Codes call (703) 451-3333		Stratford (Fairfax County)	22308	Tarpon	24228
		Stratford (Westmoreland County)	22558	Tasley	23441
Springfield (Page County)	22835	Stratford Hills (Arlington County)	22207	Tatum	22567
Springfield (Rockbridge County)	24066	Stratford Hills (Richmond Indep. City)	23225	Tauxemont	22308
Springfield Estates	22150	Stratford Landing	22308	Taylors Store	24184
Springfield Forest	22150	Stratford-on-the-Potomac	22308	Taylorstown	22075
Springfield Mall Regional Shopping Center	22150	Stratford Village	23222	Taylors Valley	24236
Springfield Plaza	22150	Strathmeade Springs	22003	Taylorsville	23047
Spring Garden (Bristol Indep. City)	24201	Strathmore	23022	Tazewell	24651
Spring Garden (Pittsylvania County)	24527	Stringtown	22611	Tazewell Correctional Unit	24651
Spring Grove	23881	Stroupes Store	24382	Teas	24375
Springhaven Estates	22102	Stuart	24171	Temperanceville	23442
Spring Hill	24401	Stuarts Draft	24477	Temple Hall Estates	23168
Spring Meadows	23111	Stubbs	22553	Temple Hill	24224
Spring Mills	24538	Studley	23162	Templeman	22520
Springvale	22066	Stukeley Hall Farms	23227	Tenso	24226
Spring Valley (Grayson County)	24330	Stumptown (Loudoun County)	22075	Tenth Legion	22815
Spring Valley (Stafford County)	22405	Stumptown (Northampton County)	23347	Terrys Fork	24138
Springville	24630	Suburban Apartments	23230	Tetotum	22485
Springwood	24066	Sudley	22110	Thaxton	24174
Sprouses Corner	23936	Sudley Manor	22110	The English Hills	22039
Stacy	24616	Suffolk	23432-38	The Hollow	24053
Stafford	22554	For specific Suffolk Zip Codes call (804) 539-5191		The Knolls	22191
Stafford Correctional Unit	22554			Thelma	22942
Staffordshire	23235	Sugar Grove	24375	The Manors	22192
Staffordsville	24167	Sugar Hill	24528	Theological Seminary (Part of Alexandria)	22304
Stage Junction	23038	Sugarland Run	22170	The Plains	22171
Staleys Cross Roads	24368	Sugar Loaf	24018	The Ridge	23917
Stanardsville	22973	Suiter	24314	Thessalia	24134
Stanley	22851	Sulgrave Manor	22309	The Timbers	22152
Stanleytown (Henry County)	24168	Sumerduck	22742	The Villas	22191
Stanleytown (Scott County)	22435	Summerdeon	24479	Thomas Bridge	24354
Stapleton	24572	Summit (Smyth County)	24375	Thomas Corner (Part of Norfolk)	23502
Starkey	24018	Summit (Spotsylvania County)	22401	Thomasson Park	22134
Starnes	24250	Sun	24224	Thomas Terrace	24501
Star Tannery	22654	Sunbeam	23851	Thomastown	24445
Statesville	23874	Sunnybank	22539	Thompson Valley	24651
Station Hills	22039	Sunnybrook	22182	Thornburg	22565
Staunton	24401	Sunnybrook Estates	22110	Thornhill	22960
Staunton Park (Part of Staunton)	24401	Sunnyside (Cumberland County)	23040	Thoroughfare	22014
Steeleburg	24609	Sunnyside (Frederick County)	22601	Thoroughgood (Part of Virginia Beach)	23455
Steeles Tavern	24476	Sunny View	22309	Three Forks	24588
Steinman	24226	Sunset Heights	23231	Threemile Corner	23117
Stella	24133	Sunset Hills	22090	Three Spring	24201
Stemphleytown	22821	Sunset Manor	22312	Three Square (Goochland County)	23063
Stephens	22293	Sunset Village (Part of Salem)	24153	Three Square (Louisa County)	23024
Stephens City	22655	Supply	22559	Threeway	22469
Stephenson	22656	Surrey Square	22032	Tibbstown	22942
Sterling	22170	Surry	23883	Tibitha	22539
Sterling Point (Part of Portsmouth)	23703	Susan	23163	Ticktown	23301
Stevensburg	22741	Sussex	23884	Tidemill	23072
Stevens Creek (Grayson County)	24330	Sussex Hilton (Part of Newport News)	23605	Tidewater	22572
Stevensville	23161	Sutherland (Dinwiddie County)	23885	Tidwells	22520
Stewart (Part of Richmond)	23221	Sutherland (Wise County)	24273	Tight Squeeze	24531
Stewartsburg	24416	Sutherland Manor	23885	Tignor	22514
Stewartsville	24179	Sutherlin	24594	Timberlake (Campbell County)	24502
Stickleyville	24244	Sutton Place	22031	Timberly Heights (Part of Petersburg)	23803
Stingray Point	23043	Sutton Woods	22180	Timber Ridge	24450
Stith	24534	Swansea Manor (Part of Newport News)	23601	Timberville	22853
St Louis	22131	Swansonville	24549	Timothy Park	22309
Stockton	24054	Sweet Briar	24595	Tiny	24220
Stoddert	23901	Sweet Briar Park	23075	Tiptop	24630
Stokesland (Part of Danville)	24541	Sweet Chalybeate	24426	Tito	24244
Stokesville	22843	Sweet Hall	23181	Tivis	24256
Stone Bridge	22663	Swift Creek (Part of Colonial Heights)	23834	Toano	23168
Stone Creek	24277	Swift Run	22827	Tobaccoville	23139
Stonega	24285	Switch Back	24445	Todds Tavern	22553
Stone Mountain	24523	Swoope	24479	Toga	23936
Stones Mill	24382	Swords Creek	24649	Tola	23959
Stone Springs (Part of Harrisonburg)	22801	Sycamore	24557	Toms Bottom	24256
Stonewall	24538	Sydnorsville	24151	Toms Brook	22660
Stonewall Acres	22110	Sylvania Heights	22401	Toms Creek	24230
Stonewall Manor	22180	Sylvatus	24343	Tookland	24614
Stoneybrook	22553	Syria	22743	Topnot	22657
Stony	24245			Topping	23169
				Toshes	24139
				Totaro	23856
				Tower Mall (Part of Portsmouth)	23703
				Town and Country Estates	22180

Townsend-Westover **VIRGINIA** **585**

	ZIP		ZIP		ZIP
Townsend	23443	Vera	24522	Warsaw	22572
Trade Center (Part of Alexandria)	22304	Verbena	22827	Warwick (Part of Newport News)	23601
Trammel	24289	Verdi	22435	Warwick on the James (Part of Newport News)	23601
Trapp	22176	Vernon Hill	24597	Warwick Village (Part of Alexandria)	22305
Treemont	23234	Verona	24482	Washington	22747
Treherneville	23307	Vertain Park	22032	Washington Corner	22580
Tremont Gardens	22042	Vesta	24177	Washington Gardens (Part of Hampton)	23669
Trenholm	23139	Vests Store	23139	Washington National Airport	22201
Trents Mill	23040	Vesuvius	24483	Washington Park	23847
Trevilians	23170	Vicey	24256	Watauga	24210
Triangle	22172	Vicker	24073	Waterford	22190
Trigg	24134	Vicker Heights	24073	Waterlick	22657
Trinity	24175	Vicksville	23878	Waterloo	22663
Triplet	23868	Victoria	23974	Water View (Middlesex County)	23180
Trout Dale	24378	Vienna	22180-83	Waterview (Portsmouth Indep. City)	23707
Troutville	24175	For specific Vienna Zip Codes call (703) 938-2125		Watson	22075
Trower	23480	Viers	24256	Wattsville	23483
Troy	22974	Viewtown	22746	Waugh	24526
Trueblue	22701	Village	22570	Waverly	23890
Truxillo	23002	Villa Heights	24112	Waverly Hills	22207
Tuckahoe	23229	Villamay	22307	Waverly Village	22401
Tuckahoe Park	23229	Villamont	24178	Waxpool	22010
Tuckahoe Village	23229	Villboro	22580	Wayland	23235
Tucker Hill	22488	Vint Hill Farms	22186	Waynesboro	22980
Tuggle	23901	Vint Hill Farms Station	22186	Waynewood	22308
Tunstall	23124	Vinton	24179	Wayside	23030
Turbeville	24596	Virgilina	24598	Weal	24531
Turnbull	22186	Virginia Beach	23450-64	Webbtown	22611
Turners Crossroads	23879	For specific Virginia Beach Zip Codes call (804) 340-6227		Weber City (Fluvanna County)	23022
Turner Store	23873	Virginia City	24283	Weber City (Scott County)	24251
Turnpike (Part of Fairfax)	22031	Virginia Forest (Part of Falls Church)	22046	Wedgewood	23229
Tuscarora	22454	Virginia Gardens (Part of Norfolk)	23505	Weedonville	22485
Twin Pines (Part of Portsmouth)	23703	Virginia Heights (Arlington County)	22204	Weems	22576
Twin Poplars	22938	Virginia Heights (Henrico County)	23231	Weirwood	23484
Twin Springs	24271	Virginia Highlands	22202	Welchs	22580
Twymans Mill	22727	Virginia Hills (Bristol Indep. City)	24201	Welcome	22485
Tye River	22922	Virginia Hills (Fairfax County)	22310	Wellford	22572
Tyler Gardens (Part of Falls Church)	22046	Virginia State University (Part of Petersburg)	23803	Wellington (Fairfax County)	22308
Tyler Park	22042	Virginia Union University (Part of Richmond)	23220	Wellington (Prince William County)	22110
Tylerton	22405	Vir-Mar Beach	22473	Wellington Heights	22308
Tyro	22976	Volens	24577	West Arlington	22213
Tysons Corner	22102	Volney	24379	West Augusta	24485
Tysons Corner (shopping center)	22103	Vulcan	22567	West Bottom	23022
Tysons Green	22182	Wabun	24153	Westbourne	23230
Union (Bedford County)	24174	Wachapreague	23480	Westbriar	23075
Union (Floyd County)	24380	Wadesville	22611	Westchester (Chesterfield County)	23235
Union Hall	24176	Wake	23176	Westchester (Fairfax County)	22031
Union Level	23973	Wakefield (Alexandria Indep. City)	22304	Westdale	23229
Unionville	22567	Wakefield (Sussex County)	23888	West Dante	24272
Unison	22141	Wakefield Chapel	22003	West End Manor	23229
United States Marine Reservation	22134	Wakefield Forest	22003	Western (Part of Petersburg)	23803
Unity	23898	Wake Forest	24060	West Falls Church (Part of Falls Church)	22046
University (Part of Charlottesville)	22903	Wakenva	24237	Westfield (Part of Bristol)	24201
University Heights (Albemarle County)	22901	Waldrop	22942	West Fork	24069
University Heights (Henrico County)	23229	Walhaven	22310	West Fredericksburg (Part of Fredericksburg)	22401
University of Richmond (Part of Richmond)	23173	Walkers	23089	West Galax (Part of Galax)	24333
Uno	22738	Walker Store	23924	West Gate	22110
Upper Brandon	23881	Walkers Well	24531	West Gate of Lomond	22110
Upperville	22176	Walkerton	23177	West Ghent (Part of Norfolk)	23507
Upright	22454	Wallace	24201	Westgrove	22307
Upshaw	23009	Wallaces Store	23937	Westham	23229
Urbanna	23175	Wallops Flight Center	23337	Westhampton (Fairfax County)	22043
Vails Mill	24236	Wallops Island	23337	Westhampton (Richmond Indep. City)	23226
Vale	22124	Walnut Grove	24270	Westhaven (Part of Portsmouth)	23707
Valentine Hills	23228	Walnut Hill (Part of Petersburg)	23805	West Hope	23882
Valentines	23887	Walters	23315	Westland	22578
Valley Brook	22042	Walters Woods	22044	West Langley	22101
Valley Creek	24271	Walton	24141	Westlawn	22042
Valley Mall (Harrisonburg Indep. City)	22801	Walton Furnace	24360	West Leigh	22901
Valley Mills	24479	Walton Park	23112	West Lexington (Part of Covington)	24450
Valley Ridge	24426	Waltons Store	24104	Westmoreland (Albemarle County)	22901
Valley View	22306	Wan	23061	Westmoreland (Westmoreland County)	22577
Valley View Mall (Part of Roanoke)	24012	Ward	24620	Westmoreland Heights	22043
Valleywood	22191	Wardell	24609	Westmoreland Park	22046
Van Buren Furnace	22644	Wards Corner (Part of Norfolk)	23505	West Norfolk (Part of Portsmouth)	23703
Vanderpool	24465	Wards Mill	24333	Westover (Arlington County)	22205
Vandola	24541	Wardtown	23482	Westover (Charles City County)	23030
Vandyke (Buchanan County)	24639	Ware Neck	23178	Westover (Pittsylvania County)	24541
Van Dyke (Tazewell County)	24609	Wares Crossroads	23117		
Vannoy Acres	22030	Wares Wharf	22454		
Vannoy Park	22024	Warfield	23889		
Vansant	24656	Warminster	24599		
Varina	23231	Warm Springs	24484		
Varina Grove	23075	Warner	23179		
Vaucluse	22655	Warren	24590		
Vaughn	22835	Warrenton	22186		
Vawter Corner	23093	Warren Woods (Part of Fairfax)	22030		
Velma	23108				
Venia	24260				

586 VIRGINIA Westover Hills-Zuni

	ZIP		ZIP		ZIP
Westover Hills (Augusta County)	22980	Willard Park (Part of Norfolk)	23509	Woodlawn (Hopewell Indep. City)	23860
Westover Hills (Greensville County)	23847	Williamsburg	23185-87	Woodlawn Manor	22309
Westover Hills (Richmond Indep. City)	23225	For specific Williamsburg Zip Codes call (804) 229-4668		Woodlawn Mansion	22060
West Petersburg	23803	Williamsburg Manor	22308	Woodlawn Park	22309
West Piney	24382	Williams Mill	24251	Woodlawn Terrace (Fairfax County)	22309
West Point	23181	Williamson Road (Part of Roanoke)	24012	Woodlawn Terrace (Henrico County)	23150
West Raven	24639	Williamsville	24487	Woodlawn Village	22060
West Springfield (Fairfax County)	22152	Willis	23380	Woodlee (Part of Staunton)	24401
Wests Store	24577	Willisville	22176	Woodley Hills	22309
Westview (Augusta County)	24479	Willis Wharf	23486	Woodley Hills (mobile home park)	22306
West View (Goochland County)	23063	Willoughby Terrace (Part of Norfolk)	23503	Woodman Terrace	23228
Westview Hills	22152	Willow	24521	Woodmont (Arlington County)	22207
West Warm Springs	24484	Willowbrook	23024	Woodmont (Chesterfield County)	23235
Westwood	23226	Willow Hill	23881	Woodridge	24590
Westwood Estates	24210	Willow Lakes (Part of Chesapeake)	23320	Woodrow Wilson	22939
Westwood Forest	22182	Willow Lawn	23230	Woodrum (Part of Staunton)	24401
Westwood Park	22046	Willow Run	22003	Woods Cross Roads	23190
Westwood Place	24426	Willow Spring	24266	Woodside Estates	22102
Weyanoke	22312	Willow Woods	22003	Woods Mill	22938
Weyers Cave	24486	Wills Corner	23430	Woodson	22951
Whaley (Part of Suffolk)	23438	Willston	22044	Woods Store	24091
Whaleyville (Part of Suffolk)	23438	Wilmington	22963	Woodstock	22664
Wheatfield	22641	Wilroy (Part of Suffolk)	23434	Woodville	22749
Wheatland	22132	Wilsons	23894	Woodway	24277
Wheeler	24248	Wilson Springs	24473	Woolwine	24185
Whitacre	22625	Wilton Woods	22310	Worlds	24530
White City	23847	Winchester	22601	Worsham	23901
White Gate	24134	Windmill Point	22578	Worshams	23139
White Hall (Albemarle County)	22987	Windsor	23487	Wren	23959
Whitehall (Frederick County)	22601	Windsordale	23229	Wright (Part of Norfolk)	23505
White Head Hall	23828	Windsor Estates	22310	Wrights Shop	24572
White Hill	24477	Windsor Farms (Part of Richmond)	23221	Wrightsville	22427
White House	24580	Windsor Park	22310	Wurno	24301
White Marsh	23183	Windsor Place	23075	Wylliesburg	23976
White Mill	24210	Windsor Shades	23140	Wyndale	24210
White Oak (Halifax County)	24558	Windy Hill Estates	23111	Wythe (Part of Hampton)	23661
White Oak (Stafford County)	22405	Winesap	24572	Wytheville	24382
White Oaks	22307	Winfall	24554	Yacht Haven Estates	22309
White Oak Swamp	23150	Wingina	24599	Yale	23897
White Plains	23893	Winona (Part of Norfolk)	23509	Yancey Mills	22932
White Post	22663	Winslow Hills	22310	Yanceyville	23093
White Shop	23086	Winston	22701	Yards	24659
White Stone	22578	Wintergreen	22958	Yellow Branch	24550
Whitesville	23421	Winterham	23002	Yellow Springs	24361
Whitethorne	24060	Winterpock	23832	Yellow Sulphur Springs	24073
Whitetop	22292	Wirtz	24184	Yellow Tavern	23060
Whiteville	23040	Wise	24293	York Manor	23075
Whitewood	24657	Wisharts Point	23303	Yorkshire (Prince William County)	22110
Whitley	23487	Wistar Farms	23228	Yorkshire Acres	22110
Whitlock	22942	Witch Duck (Part of Suffolk)	23462	Yorkshire Park	22110
Whitmell	24549	Withams	23488	York Terrace	23185
Whittle	24531	Wittens Mills	24630	Yorktown	23690-92
Wickford	22310	Wolfglade	24333	For specific Yorktown Zip Codes call (804) 898-3098	
Wicomico	23184	Wolford	24658	Yorktown Naval Weapons Station	23691
Wicomico Church	22579	Wolftown	22748	Yost	24460
Wide Water	22554	Wolf Trap (Fairfax County)	22182	Youngers Store	24558
Widewater Beach	22554	Wolf Trap (Halifax County)	24592	Yuma	24251
Wightman	23924	Womacks	23923	Zacata	22581
Wilburdale	22003	Wood	24250	Zack	24459
Wilda	24477	Woodberry Forest	22989	Zanoni	23191
Wilde Acres	22601	Woodberry Hills (Part of Danville)	24541	Zenda	22801
Wilderness	22553	Woodbridge	22191-94	Zepp	22644
Wilderness Corner	22553	For specific Woodbridge Zip Codes call (703) 494-6427		Zion	22942
Wildwood (Fluvanna County)	22963	Woodbrook	22901	Zion Crossroads	22942
Wildwood (Henrico County)	23227	Woodford	22580	Ziontown	23075
Wildwood Farms	23842	Woodhaven Shores	23141	Zuni	23898
Wilkinsons Store	23833	Woodland Hills	24210		
Wilkinson Terrace	23234	Woodlawn (Carroll County)	24381		

Aberdeen-Columbia Valley Gardens WASHINGTON 587

Name	ZIP
Aberdeen	98520
Aberdeen Gardens	98520
Academy	99031
Acme	98220
Addy	99101
Adelaide	98003
Adelma Beach	98368
Adna	98522
Adrian	98851
Aeneas	98855
Agnew	98362
Ahtanum	98903
Airway Heights	99001
Ajlune	98564
Albion	99102
Alder	98328
Alderton	98371
Alderwood	98225
Alderwood Manor (census area only)	98011
Alderwood Manor	98036
Alexander Beach	98221
Alger	98233
Algona	98002
Allen	98232
Allentown	98178
Allyn	98524
Almira	99103
Aloha	98571
Alpental	98068
Alpha	98570
Altoona	98643
Amanda Park	98526
Amber	99004
Amboy	98601
American Lake	98493
Anacortes	98221
Anatone	99401
Anderson Island	98303
Angle Lake	98188
Annapolis (Part of Port Orchard)	98366
Appleton	98602
Arden	99114
Ardenvoir	98811
Argyle	98250
Ariel	98603
Arletta	98335
Arlington	98223
Arlington Heights	98223
Armar	98270
Arnada Park Annex (Part of Vancouver)	98663
Arrowhead (King County)	98011
Arrowhead (Pierce County)	98498
Artic	98537
Ashford	98304
Asotin	99402
Auburn	98001-03
For specific Auburn Zip Codes call (206) 833-0540	
Ault Field	98277
Avon	98273
Avondale	98052
Ayer	99348
Ayer Junction	99348
Azwell	98846
Baby Island Heights	98260
Bainbridge Island Winslow	98110
Baird	99115
Ballard (Part of Seattle)	98107
B and G	98201
Bangor	98345
Bangor Submarine Base	98315
Barberton	98665
Baring	98224
Barstow	99141
Basin City	99343
Battle Ground	98604
Battle Point	98110
Bay Center	98527
Bay City	98520
Bayne	98022
Bay Shore	98584
Bay View (Island County)	98260
Bayview (Skagit County)	98273
Beacon Hill	98632
Beaux Arts	98004
Beaver	98305
Beaver Valley	98365
Beckett Point	98368
Belfair (Kitsap County)	98310
Belfair (Mason County)	98528
Bellevue	98004-09
For specific Bellevue Zip Codes call (206) 454-2489	
Bellevue Square (Part of Bellevue)	98004
Bellingham	98225-27
For specific Bellingham Zip Codes call (206) 676-8303	

Name	ZIP
Belmont	99104
Belvidere	99116
Bench Drive (Part of Aberdeen)	98520
Benge	99105
Benson Hill	98055
Benton City	99320
Bethel	98366
Beverly	99321
Beverly Beach	98249
Beverly Park (Part of Everett)	98201
Beverly Park South (Part of Everett)	98201
Bickleton	99322
Big Lake	98273
Bingen	98605
Birch Bay	98230
Birchfield	98901
Birdsview	98237
Bitter Lake (Part of Seattle)	98133
Black Diamond	98010
Black Lake	99114
Black River (Part of Renton)	98055
Black River	98178
Black River Junction (Part of Renton)	98055
Blaine	98230
Blakely Island	98222
Blanchard	98232
Blewett	98826
Blue Creek	99109
Blueslide	99180
Blyn	98382
Boise	98022
Bonneville Spur (Part of Bellingham)	98225
Bonney Lake	98390
Bossburg	99126
Boston Harbor	98501
Bothell	98011-12
For specific Bothell Zip Codes call (206) 486-3243	
Boulevard Park	98188
Bow	98232
Boyds	99107
Brady	98563
Breidablick	98370
Bremerton	98310-15
For specific Bremerton Zip Codes call (206) 373-1456	
Brewster	98812
Briarwood	98031
Bridgeport	98813
Bridle Trail	98033
Brief	98822
Brier	98036
Brinnon	98320
Broadway (Part of Seattle)	98102
Brookdale	98444
Brooklyn	98537
Browns Point	98422
Brownstown	98920
Brownsville	98310
Brush Prairie	98606
Bryant	98223
Bryn Mawr	98178
Bryn Mawr-Skyway	98178
Buckhorn	98245
Buckley	98321
Bucoda	98530
Buena	98921
Buena Vista	98292
Bunker	98532
Burbank	99323
Burbank Heights	99301
Burien (King County)	98166
Burley	98322
Burlington	98233
Burnett	98321
Burton	98013
Bush Point	98249
BZ Corner	98623
Camano City	98292
Camano Country Club	98292
Camas	98607
Camelot	98002
Camp Murray	98498
Camp Union	98310
Campus (Part of Bellingham)	98225
Capital Mall (Part of Olympia)	98502
Capitol Hill (Part of Seattle)	98102
Cap Sante (Part of Anacortes)	98221
Carbonado	98323
Carlisle	98536
Carlsborg	98324
Cariton	98814
Carlyle	98011

Name	ZIP
Carnation	98014
Carriage Hill	98366
Carrier Annex (Part of Everett)	98204
Carrolls	98609
Carson	98610
Cascade-Fairwood	98055
Cascade Mall	98055
Cascade Vista	98055
Cashmere	98815
Castle Rock	98611
Cathcart	98290
Cathlamet	98612
Cavelero Beach	98292
Cedar Creek Corrections Center	98556
Cedardale	98273
Cedar Falls	98045
Cedar Grove	98038
Cedarhome	98292
Cedar Mountain	98055
Cedar Park Addition	98362
Cedarview	98390
Cedarville	98568
Cedonia	99137
Center	98376
Centerville	98613
Central (Part of Yakima)	98901
Centralia	98531
Central Park	98520
Central Valley	98370
Ceres	98532
Charleston (Part of Bremerton)	98312
Charter Oak	98604
Chattaroy	99003
Chehalis	98532
Chehalis Indian Reservation	98568
Chelan (Chelan County)	98816
Chelan Falls	98817
Chelatchie	98601
Chelsea Park	98166
Cheney	99004
Chenowith	98651
Cherokee Bay Park	98042
Cherry Crest (Part of Bellevue)	98004
Cherry Gardens	98019
Cherry Grove	98604
Cherry Point (mail Blaine)	98230
Cherry Point (mail Ferndale)	98248
Chesaw	98844
Chewelah	99109
Chico	98310
Chimacum	98325
Chinook	98614
Christopher	98002
Chuckanut Village (Part of Bellingham)	98225
Chumstick	98826
Cicero	98223
Cinebar	98533
City Center (Part of Bellingham)	98225
Clallam Bay	98326
Claquato	98532
Claremont (Part of Everett)	98201
Clarkston	99403
Clarkston Heights	99403
Clayton	99110
Clearbrook	98247
Clearlake	98235
Clearview	98290
Clearwater	98331
Cle Elum	98922
Cleveland	99356
Cliffdell	98937
Cline (Part of Springdale)	99173
Clinton	98236
Clipper	98244
Cloverdale	98625
Cloverland	99402
Clover Park	98499
Clyde Hill	98004
Coal Creek	98632
Coalfield	98055
Cohasset Beach	98595
Colbert	99005
Colby	98366
Colchester	98366
Coles Corner	98826
Colfax	99111
College (Part of Pullman)	99163
College Place	99324
Colton	99113
Columbia (Part of Seattle)	98118
Columbia Beach	98236
Columbia Heights	98632
Columbia Shopping Center (Part of Kennewick)	99336
Columbia Valley Gardens	98626

588 WASHINGTON

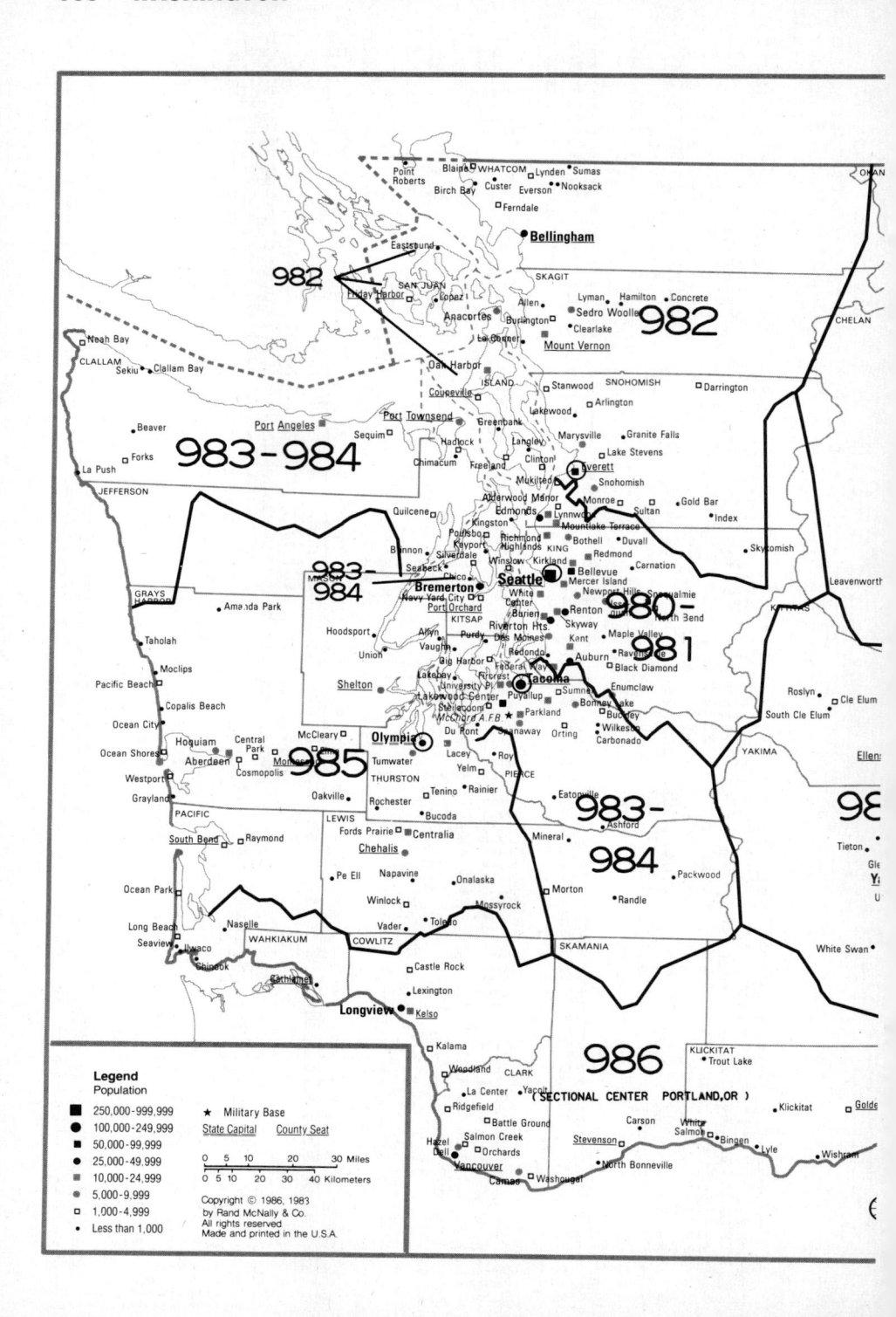

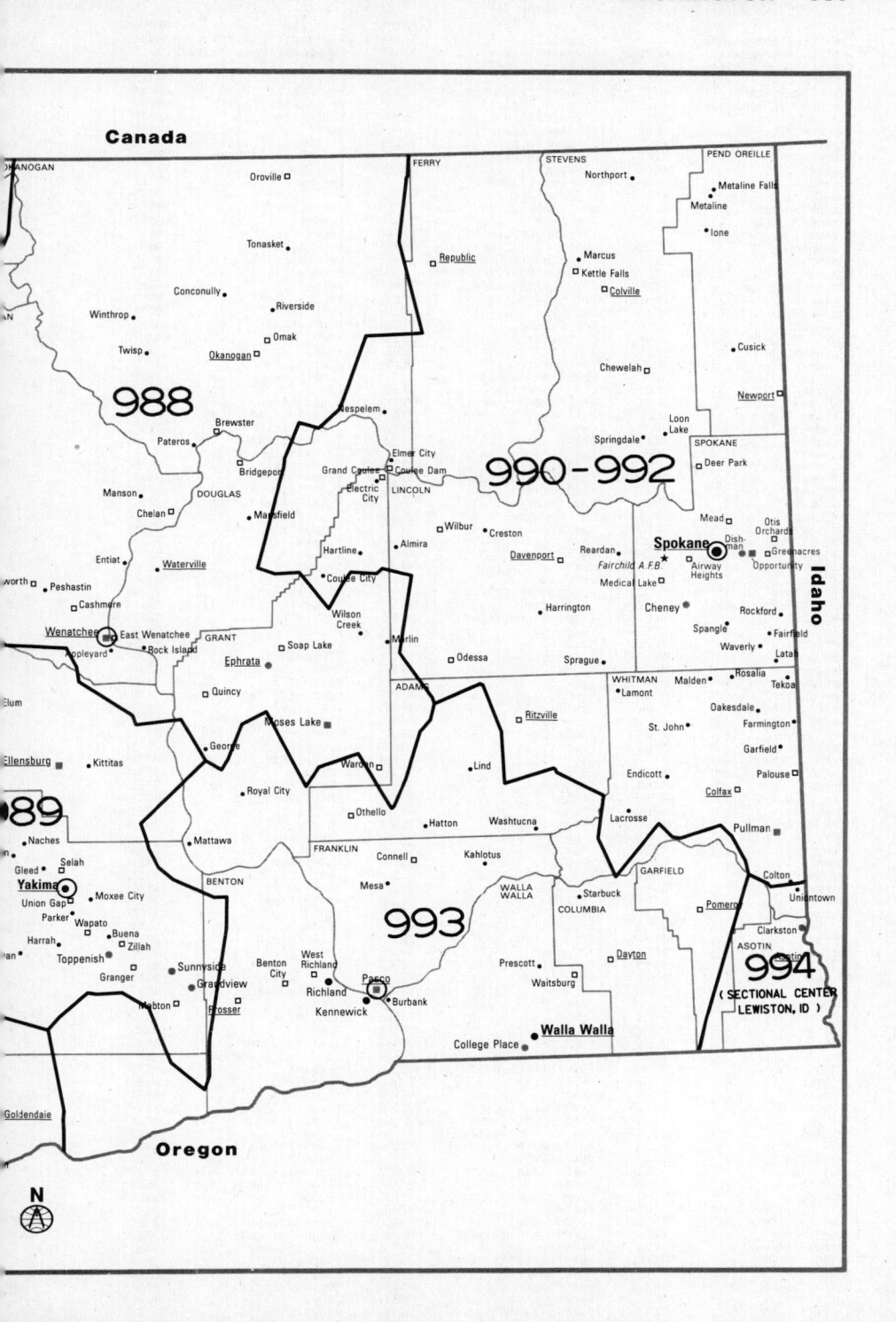

WASHINGTON 589

590 WASHINGTON Columbia Shopping Center-Grays Landing

Name	ZIP
Columbia Shopping Center (Part of Kennewick)	99336
Columbia Valley Gardens	98626
Colville	99114
Colville Indian Agency	99155
Colville Indian Reservation	99155
Conconully	98819
Concora (Part of Tukwila)	98188
Concrete	98237
Conifer View	98011
Connell	99326
Conway	98238
Cook	98605
Copalis Beach	98535
Copalis Crossing	98536
Cornwall (Part of Bellingham)	98225
Cosmopolis	98537
Cottage Lake (King County)	98072
Cottonwood Beach	98230
Cougar	98616
Coulee City	99115
Coulee Dam	99116
Country Homes	99218
Coupeville	98239
Coveland	98239
Covington	98042
Cowiche	98923
Cozy Nook	99109
Crescent Valley	98335
Creston	99117
Crocker	98360
Cromwell	98335
Crossroads (Part of Bellevue)	98008
Crystal Mountain	98022
Crystal Springs	98466
Cumberland	98022
Cunningham	99327
Curlew	99118
Curtis	98538
Cushman Dam	98548
Cusick	99119
Custer (Pierce County)	98413
Custer (Whatcom County)	98240
Dabob	98376
Daisy	99167
Dalkena	99156
Dallesport	98617
Danville	99121
Darlington (Part of Everett)	98201
Darrington	98241
Dash Point	98402
Davenport	99122
Day Creek	98284
Day Island	98466
Dayton (Columbia County)	99328
Dayton (Mason County)	98584
Decatur	98221
Deep Creek	99022
Deep River	98638
Deer Harbor	98243
Deer Lake	99148
Deer Park	99006
Delano	99133
Dellesta Park	98225
Deming	98244
Denison	99006
Denny Creek	98045
Denny Park	98033
Des Moines	98188
Devereaux Lake	98528
Dewey	98221
Dexter by the Sea	98590
Diablo	98283
Diamond	99111
Diamond Lake	99156
Dieringer	98390
Dines Point	98253
Disautel	98841
Discovery Bay	98368
Dishman	99213
Dixie	99329
Dockton	98070
Dodge	99347
Doe Bay	98279
Dollar's Corner	98604
Donald	98951
Doty	98539
Douglas	98858
Downing	98812
Downtown (Clark County)	98660
Downtown (Pierce County)	98402
Draper Spring	98619
Driftwood Shores	98292
Dryad	98532
Dryden	98821
Dumas Bay-Twin Lakes	98002
Dungeness	98382
Du Pont	98327
Dusty	99143

Name	ZIP
Duvall	98019
Duwamish	98188
Eagledale	98110
Eagle Mount	98368
Earlington (Part of Renton)	98055
Earlmount (Part of Redmond)	98052
East Aberdeen (Part of Aberdeen)	98520
East Auburn (Part of Auburn)	98002
East Coulee Dam (Part of Coulee Dam)	99116
East Everett	98201
East Farms	99025
Eastgate (King County)	98004
	98007
For specific Eastgate Zip Codes call (206) 454-2489	
Eastgate (Walla Walla Co.)	99362
East Hoquiam	98550
Eastmont	98204
East Olympia	98540
Easton	98925
East Port Orchard	98366
East Quilcene	98376
East Redmond (Part of Redmond)	98052
East Renton Highlands	98024
East Selah	98901
Eastsound	98245
East Spokane	99211
East Stanwood (Part of Stanwood)	98292
East Union (Part of Seattle)	98122
Eastview Hills	98204
East Wenatchee	98801
East Wenatchee Bench	98801
Eatonville	98328
Echo	99114
Echo Lake	98133
Eden	98643
Edgecomb	98223
Edgemoor (Part of Bellingham)	98225
Edgewater (Part of Everett)	98201
Edgewood	98371
Edison	98232
Edmonds	98020
Edwall	99008
Eglon	98346
Elbe	98330
Elberton	99130
Eldon	98555
Electric City	99123
Elgin	98335
Elk	99009
Elk Plain	98387
Ellensburg	98926
Ellisford	98855
Ellisport	98070
Ellsworth	98662
Elma	98541
Elmer City	99124
Eltopia	99330
Emerald Hills (Part of Bellevue)	98004
Endicott	99125
Enetai	98310
Enterprise	99129
Entiat	98822
Enumclaw	98022
Ephrata	98823
Erlands Point	98310
Espanola	99022
Esperance	98043
Ethel	98542
Etna	98674
Eufaula Heights	98632
Eureka (Walla Walla County)	99348
Eureka (Whatcom County)	98225
Evaline	98596
Evans	99126
Everett	98201-08
For specific Everett Zip Codes call (206) 355-8366	
Everett Mall (Part of Everett)	98204
Evergreen (Part of Vancouver)	98662
Everson	98247
Ewan	99127
Factoria	98006
Fairchild AFB	99011
Fairchild Air Force Base	99011
Fairfield	99012
Fairhaven (Part of Bellingham)	98225
Fairmont-Intercity	98204
Fairview (Kitsap County)	98393
Fairview (Yakima County)	98901
Fairview-Sumach	98903

Name	ZIP
Fairwood (King County)	98055
Fairwood (Spokane County)	99218
Fall City	98024
Fargher Lake	98601
Farmington	99128
Federal (Part of Seattle)	98104
Federal Way	98003
Felida	98665
Ferndale	98248
Fern Hill (Part of Tacoma)	98412
Fern Prairie	98607
Fernwood	98366
Fife	98424
Fife Heights	98424
Fircrest	98466
Firdale	98577
Firgrove	98204
Fir Tree	98540
Firwood	98371
Fisher	98607
Fletcher Bay	98110
Florence	98292
Fobes Hill	98205
Foothill	99207
Ford	99013
Fordair	99115
Fords Prairie	98531
Forest	98532
Forest Beach	98335
Forest City (Part of Port Orchard)	98366
Forest Hills Addition	99208
Forest Park (Part of Lake Forest Park)	98155
Forks	98331
Fort Lewis (Pierce County)	98433
Foster (Part of Tukwila)	98188
Four Lakes	99014
Fox Island	98333
Fragaria	98359
Frances	98577
Freeland	98249
Freeman	99015
Friday Harbor	98250
Frisken Wye	98541
Fruitland	99129
Fruitvale	98902
Furport	99156
Gales Addition	98362
Galvin	98544
Gardena	99360
Garden City (Part of McCleary)	98557
Gardenville (Part of Fife)	98422
Gardiner	98334
Garfield	99130
Garland (Part of Spokane)	99209
Garrett	99362
Gate	98579
Geiger Heights	99220
Geneva	99225
George	98824
Georgetown (Part of Seattle)	98108
Georgetown	98051
Getchell	98223
Gibraltar	98221
Gibson Creek	98568
Gifford	99131
Gig Harbor	98335
Gilberton	98310
Glacier	98244
Gleed	98904
Glen Cove (Jefferson Co.)	98368
Glencove (Pierce County)	98335
Glendale	98236
Glenoma	98336
Glenrose	99203
Glenwood (Kitsap County)	98366
Glenwood (Klickitat County)	98619
Gold Bar	98251
Goldendale	98620
Gooseprairie	98937
Gorst	98337
Govan	99185
Graham	98338
Grand Coulee	99133
Grand Mound	98501
Grandview (Clallam County)	98362
Grandview (Yakima County)	98930
Granger	98932
Granite Falls	98252
Grant Orchards	98851
Grant Road Addition	98801
Granville Grange	98252
Grapeview	98546
Grassmere	98237
Gravelly Lake	98499
Grayland	98547
Grays Harbor City	98550
Grays Landing	99009

Greenacres-Makah Air Force Station 758th Radar Squadron   WASHINGTON   591

Name	ZIP
Greenacres	99016
Greenbank	98253
Green Bluff	99003
Green Mountain	98674
Green River	98022
Greenwater	98022
Greenwood (Grays Harbor County)	98520
Greenwood (King County)	98103
Greenwood (Stevens County)	99141
Greenwood (Whatcom County)	98264
Grisdale	98563
Grotto	98288
Guemes	98221
Hadlock	98339
Hamilton	98255
Hansville	98340
Happy Valley (Part of Bellingham)	98225
Harbor Center	98249
Harbor Heights (Part of Gig Harbor)	98338
Harmon Heights	98045
Harmony	98585
Harper	98366
Harrah	98933
Harrington	99134
Harstine	98584
Hartford (Part of Lake Stevens)	98258
Hartland	98635
Hartline	99135
Harwood	98902
Hatton	99332
Havillah	98855
Hay	99136
Hayford	99204
Hays Park (Part of Spokane)	99207
Hazel	98223
Hazel Dell	98660
	98665
For specific Hazel Dell Zip Codes call (206) 695-4446	
Hazelwood	98055
Heather Downs	98055
Heisson	98622
Herron Island	98349
Highland (Asotin County)	99403
Highland (Clark County)	98629
Highland (Snohomish County)	98258
Highlands (Part of Renton)	98056
High Point	98027
High Valley	98027
Hillgrove (Part of McCleary)	98557
Hilltop	98004
Hillyard (Part of Spokane)	99207
Hintzville	98312
Hobart	98025
Hockinson	98606
Hoh Indian Reservation	98331
Hoko	98326
Holcomb	98577
Holden Village	98816
Holly	98310
Hollywood	98072
Holman	98644
Home	98349
Home Acres	98201
Home Valley	98648
Hood	98651
Hoodsport	98548
Hoogdal	98284
Hooper	99333
Hope	98333
Hoquiam	98550
Horizon View	98004
Horseshoe Lake	98366
Houghton (Part of Kirkland)	98033
Humptulips	98552
Hunters	99137
Hunts Point	98004
Huntsville	99328
Husum	98623
Hyak	98068
Illahee (Grays Harbor County)	98550
Illahee (Kitsap County)	98310
Ilwaco	98624
Image	98662
Impach	99138
Inchelium	98138
Index	98256
Indian Beach	98292
Indianola	98342
Indian Village	98221
Inglewood (King County)	98011
Innis Arden	98160

Name	ZIP
	98177
For specific Innis Arden Zip Codes call (206) 285-1650	
Intercity	98201
Interlaken	98438
International (Part of Seattle)	98104
Ione	99139
Irby	99159
Irondale	98368
Island Center	98110
Island Lake	98370
Island View (Part of Richland)	99352
Issaquah	98027
Jared	99180
Johnson	99113
Jorden	98223
Jovita	98371
Joyce	98343
Juanita (Part of Sun Village)	98011
Juanita	98033
Junction City	98520
Juniper Beach	98292
Kahlotus	99335
Kalama	98625
Kalispel Indian Reservation	99180
Kamilche	98584
Kanaskat	98051
Kangley	98051
Kapowsin	98344
Keller	99140
Kellogg Marsh	98223
Kellys Korner	98501
Keiso	98626
Kendall	98244
Kenmore	98028
Kennard Corner	98011
Kennedys Lagoon	98239
Kennewick	99336-37
For specific Kennewick Zip Codes call (509) 582-5000	
Kennydale	98055
Kenroy	98801
Kent	98031-32
For specific Kent Zip Codes call (206) 852-3950	
Kettle Falls	99141
Kewa	99138
Key Center	98335
Keyport	98345
Keyport Naval Torpedo Station	98345
Keystone	98849
Kid Valley	98649
Kingsgate	98011
Kingston	98346
Kiona	99320
Kirkland	98033-34
For specific Kirkland Zip Codes call (206) 822-2292	
Kitsap Lake	98310
Kittitas	98934
Klaber	98538
Klickitat	98628
Klipsan Beach	98640
Knab	98591
Krain	98022
Kruse	98270
Kruse Junction	98270
K Street (Part of Tacoma)	98405
Kummer	98010
Lacamas	98570
La Center	98629
Lacey	98503
La Conner	98257
Lacrosse	99143
Lagoon Point	98253
La Grande	98341
Lake Alice	98024
Lakebay	98110
Lake City (Part of Seattle)	98125
Lake Crescent	98362
Lake Dolloff	98002
Lake Forest North	98155
Lake Forest Park	98155
Lake Goodwin	98292
Lake Heights	98002
Lake Hills (Part of Bellevue)	98007
Lake Howard	98292
Lake Joy	98014
Lake Kathleen	98055
Lake Ki	98223
Lakeland North	98002
Lakeland South	98002
Lakeland Village (Part of Medical Lake)	99022
Lake Leota	98072
Lake Loma	98270
Lake Louise	98498
Lake Lucerne	98038
Lake Marta	98292

Name	ZIP
Lake McDonald	98055
Lake Meridian	98042
Lake Retreat	98051
Lakeridge	98178
Lake Sawyer	98042
Lakes District	98499
Lake Shore	98665
Lakeside (Part of Chelan)	98816
Lake Stevens	98258
Lake Stickney	98036
Lakeview	98499
Lakeview Park	98851
Lake Wilderness	98038
Lakewood	98259
Lakota	98003
Lamona	99144
Lamont	99017
Langley	98260
La Push	98350
Larch Corrections Center	98675
Larchmont (Part of Tacoma)	98409
Larimers Corner	98290
Latah	99018
Laurel (Klickitat County)	98619
Laurel (Whatcom County)	98225
Laurel Heights (Part of Everett)	98201
Laurier	99146
Lawrence (Pierce County)	98409
Lawrence (Whatcom County)	98247
Laws Corner	98672
Leadpoint	99114
Leavenworth	98826
Lebam	98554
Leland	98368
Lemolo	98370
Lexington	98626
Liberty	98922
Liberty Lake	99019
Liberty Park (Part of Spokane)	99202
Lilliwaup	98555
Lincoln	99147
Lind	99341
Lindberg	98356
Littell	98532
Little Boston	98346
Little Falls	99013
Littlerock	98556
Lochsloy	98258
Locke	99119
Lofall	98370
Lone Oak	98632
Lone Pine	99116
Long Beach	98631
Longbranch	98349
Long Lake (Kitsap County)	98366
Long Lake (Lincoln County)	99013
Longmire	98397
Longview	98632
Loomis	98827
Loon Lake	99148
Lopez	98261
Lost Creek	99180
Lost Lake	98292
Loveland	98387
Lowden	99360
Lowell (Part of Everett)	98203
Lucerne	98816
Lummie Point	98262
Lummi Indian Reservation	98225
Lummi Island	98262
Lyle	98635
Lyman	98263
Lynden	98264
Lynnwood	98036-37
For specific Lynnwood Zip Codes call (206) 778-2154	
Lynwood Center	98110
Mabana	98292
Mabton	98935
McChord AFB	98438
McChord Air Force Base	98438
McCleary	98557
McDonald	98837
McGowan	98614
Machias	98290
McKees Beach	98292
McKenna	98558
McMicken Heights	98188
McMillin	98352
McNeil Island	98388
Madigan Hospital	98431
Madrona Beach	98292
Madrona Point (Part of Bremerton)	98312
Mae	98837
Magnolia (Part of Seattle)	98199
Makah Air Force Station 758th Radar Squadron	98357

592 WASHINGTON Makah Indian Reservation-Point Roberts

Name	ZIP
Makah Indian Reservation	98357
Malaga	98828
Malden	99149
Malo	99150
Malone	98559
Malott	98829
Maltby	98290
Manchester	98353
Manette (Part of Bremerton)	98310
Manito (Part of Spokane)	99203
Manito Club Estates	99203
Manitou Beach	98061
Manor	98604
Mansfield	98830
Manson	98831
Manzanita	98110
Maple Beach	98281
Maple Falls	98266
Maple Grove	98362
Maple Hills	98031
Maple Valley	98038
Maple Valley Heights	98055
Maplewood (King County)	98055
Maplewood (Pierce County)	98371
Maplewood Heights	98055
Marblemount	98267
Marcus	99151
Marengo	99169
Marietta	98225
Marietta-Alderwood	98225
Marine Drive (Part of Bremerton)	98310
Marine Hills	98003
Marine View Estates	98003
Marketown	98277
Markham	98520
Marlin	98832
Marshall	99020
Martha Lake (Snohomish County)	98011
Maryhill	98620
Marys Corner	98532
Marysville	98270
Mason City (Part of Coulee Dam)	99116
Matlock	98560
Matneys Spur	99141
Mattawa	99344
Maxwelton	98236
Mays Pond	98011
Maytown	98501
Mazama	98833
Mead	99021
Meadow Brook (Part of Snoqualmie)	98065
Meadowdale (Kitsap County)	98310
Meadowdale (Snohomish County)	98020
Meadow Glade	98604
Medical Lake	99022
Medina	98039
Meeker (Part of Puyallup)	98371
Melbourne	98563
Menlo	98561
Menlo Park	98466
Mercer Island	98040
Meredith (Part of Auburn)	98002
Meridan Heights	98042
Merritt	98826
Mesa	99343
Metaline	99152
Metaline Falls	99153
Methow	98834
Metreco	98438
Miami Beach	98380
Mica	99023
Midland	98444
Midland Acres (Part of Camas)	98607
Midvale Corner	98236
Midway (King County)	98035
Midway (Pierce County)	98335
Milan	99003
Milco (Part of Kelso)	98626
Miles	99122
Mill A	98605
Mill Creek	98011
Miller River	98288
Millwood	99212
Milton	98354
Mineral	98355
Minnehaha	98661
Mirror Lake	98002
Mirrormont	98027
Mission Beach	98270
Misty Meadows	98011
Mobase	98433
Moclips	98562
Mohler	99134
Mold	99115

Name	ZIP
Molson	98844
Mondovi	99122
Monitor	98836
Monohon	98027
Monroe	98272
Monse	98812
Monta Vista	98499
Montborne	98273
Montesano	98563
Moorlands	98011
Moran Prairie	99203
Morgan Acres	99207
Morganville (Part of Black Diamond)	98010
Morton	98356
Moses Lake	98837
Moses Lake North	98837
Mossyrock	98564
Mountain View Beach	98292
Mount Brook	98672
Mount Hope	99012
Mountlake Terrace	98043
Mount Pleasant	98362
Mount Vernon	98273
Moxee City	98936
Muckleshoot Indian Reservation	98002
Mukilteo	98275
Murphy's Corner	98011
Naches	98937
Nahcotta	98637
Napavine	98565
Naselle	98638
National	98304
Naval Supply Center Puget Sound	98314
Naval Torpedo Station	98345
Navy Yard City	98310
Neah Bay	98357
Neilton	98566
Nemah	98586
Nespelem	99155
Newaukum	98002
Newcastle	98055
Newhalem	98283
New London	98550
Newman Lake	99025
Newport (King County)	98004
Newport (Pend Oreille County)	99156
Newport Hills (census designated place)	98002
Newport Hills	98006
Newport Shores	98006
Newton	98550
Nighthawk	98827
Nile	98937
Nine Mile Falls	99026
Nisqually	98501
Nisqually Indian Reservation	98597
Nisson	98550
Nooksack	98276
Nordland	98358
Norma Beach	98020
Norman	98292
Normandy Park	98166
North Bend	98045
North Bonneville	98639
North City	98155
North City-Ridgecrest	98155
North Cove	98590
North Fort Lewis	98434
Northgate (Part of Seattle)	98125
Northgate Shopping Center (Part of Seattle)	98125
North Hill	98166
North Lake	98002
North Lynnwood	98036
North Marysville (Snohomish County)	98270
North Marysville (Snohomish County)	98201
Northport	99157
North Prosser	99350
North Puyallup	98371
Northrup (Part of Bellevue)	98004
North Selah	98942
Northtown Mall (Part of Spokane)	99207
Northwood	98264
Norwood Village (Part of Bellevue)	98004
Novelty	98019
Oakbrook	98497
Oakesdale	99158
Oak Harbor	98277
Oakland (Part of Tacoma)	98409
Oak Park (Part of Camas)	98607
Oakville	98568
O'Brien (Part of Kent)	98032
Ocean Beach	98632

Name	ZIP
Ocean City	98569
Ocean City/Shores	98569
Ocean Park	98640
Ocean Shores	98569
Ocean Shores Estates (Part of Ocean Shores)	98569
Ocosta	98520
Odessa	99159
Offutt Lake	98501
Okanogan	98840
Olalla	98359
Olalla Valley	98359
Old Tacoma (Part of Tacoma)	98466
Old Willapa	98577
Olga	98279
Olympia	98501-07
For specific Olympia Zip Codes call (206) 753-9474	
Olympia (Part of Bellevue)	98004
Olympic Corrections Center	98331
Olympic View	98383
Omak	98841
Onalaska	98570
Onion Creek	99114
Opportunity	99214
Orcas	98280
Orchard Avenue	99211
Orchard Prairie	99207
Orchards (Clark County)	98662
Orient	99160
Orillia (Part of Kent)	98032
Orin	99114
Orondo	98843
Oroville	98844
Orting	98360
Osceola	98022
Oso	98223
Ostrander	98626
Othello	99344
Otis Orchards	99027
Otis Orchards-East Farms	99025
Outlook	98938
Overlook	98366
Oyhut	98550
Oysterville	98641
Ozette	98326
Pacific	98047
Pacific Beach	98571
Packwood	98361
Palisades	98845
Palmer	98051
Palouse	99161
Paradise Inn	98398
Park	98284
Parker	98939
Parkland	98444
Park Orchard	98031
Park Rapids	99114
Parkwater (Spokane County)	99211
Parkway Plaza (Part of Tukwila)	98188
Parkwood	98366
Pasadena Park	99206
Pasco	99301-02
For specific Pasco Zip Codes call (509) 547-8481	
Pataha City	99347
Pateros	98846
Paterson	99345
Peach Acres	98465
Pearcot	98801
Pearson	98370
Pe Ell	98572
Pend Orielle Village	99153
Penn Cove Park	98277
Peone	99021
Perrinville (Part of Edmonds)	98020
Peshastin	98847
Picnic Point	98335
Pillar Rock	98643
Pinebrook (Part of Vancouver)	98660
Pine City	99170
Pinecliff	98937
Pinecroft	99214
Pinehurst (Part of Everett)	98203
Pine Lake	98027
Ping	99347
Pioneer Square (Part of Seattle)	98104
Pipe Lake	98038
Plain	98826
Plaza	99170
Pleasant Prairie	99207
Pleasant Valley (Part of Vancouver)	98665
Plymouth	99346
Pocahontas Bay	99009
Point Roberts	98281

Point White-Snohomish WASHINGTON 593

Name	ZIP
Point White	98110
Pomeroy	99347
Pomona	98908
Ponder	98499
Ponderosa Estates	98390
Pontius Park	98011
Portage	98013
Port Angeles	98362
Port Angeles East	98362
Port Blakely	98110
Port Discovery	98368
Porter	98541
Port Gamble	98364
Port Gamble Indian Reservation	98364
Port Ludlow	98365
Port Madison	98110
Port Madison Indian Reservation	98310
Port Orchard	98366
Port Stanley	98261
Port Townsend	98368
Possession	98236
Potlatch	98584
Poulsbo	98370
Poverty Bay	98003
Prairie	98284
Prairie Center (Part of Coupeville)	98239
Prairie Ridge	98390
Prescott	99348
Preston	98050
Proctor (Part of Tacoma)	98407
Proebstel (Part of Vancouver)	98662
Prosser	99350
Puget Island	98612
Puget Sound Naval Base	98314
Puget Sound Naval Shipyard	98314
Pullman	99163-65
For specific Pullman Zip Codes call (509) 334-3212	
Purdy	98335
Purdy Treatment Center for Women	98335
Puyallup	98371-74
For specific Puyallup Zip Codes call (206) 845-2334	
Queen Anne (Part of Seattle)	98109
Queensborough	98011
Queensgate	98011
Queets	98331
Quendall (Part of Renton)	98055
Quilcene	98376
Quillayute Indian Reservation	98350
Quinault	98575
Quinault Indian Reservation	98587
Quincy	98848
Rainer Valley (Part of Seattle)	98118
Rainier	98576
Rainier Beach (Part of Seattle)	98102
Ralston	99169
Rambler Park	98908
Randle	98377
Raugust	98837
Ravensdale	98051
Raymond	98577
Reardan	99029
Redmond	98052-53
For specific Redmond Zip Codes call (206) 885-1296	
Redondo	98054
Rees Corner	98290
Renton	98055-58
For specific Renton Zip Codes call (206) 255-8920	
Renton Village (Part of Renton)	98055
Republic	99166
Retsil	98378
Rhodena Beach	98239
Rhododendron Park	98390
Rice	99167
Richland	99352
Richmond Beach	98160
Richmond Beach-Innis Arden	98160
Richmond Highlands	98133
Ridgecrest	98155
Ridgefield	98642
Riiho Park	98640
Rimrock	98937
Ritzville	99169
Rivercrest	98204
Riverside (Okanogan County)	98849

Name	ZIP
Riverside (Spokane County)	99201
Riverton Heights	98188
Robe	98252
Robinswood (Part of Bellevue)	98004
Roche Harbor	98250
Rochester	98579
Rockford	99030
Rock Island	98850
Rockport	98283
Rocky Butte	98812
Rocky Point (Cowlitz County)	98626
Rocky Point (Island County)	98292
Rocky Point	98310
	98312
For specific Rocky Point Zip Codes call (206) 373-1456	
Rocky Woods	98387
Rollingbay	98061
Ronald	98940
Roosevelt (Klickitat County)	99356
Roosevelt (Snohomish County)	98290
Rosalia	99170
Rosario	98245
Rosburg	98643
Rosedale	98335
Rose Hill (King County)	98033
Rose Valley	98626
Rosewood	99208
Roslyn	98941
Roy	98580
Royal	99344
Royal City	99357
Ruby	99119
Ruff	98832
Ruston	98407
Ryderwood	98581
St. Andrews	99115
St. John	99171
St. Urbans	98596
Salkum	98582
Salmon Beach (Part of Tacoma)	98424
Salmon Creek	98665
Saltwater	98188
Samish Island	98232
Samish Lake	98225
Sammamish Camp	98004
San de Fuca	98239
Sandy Hook Park	98370
Sandy Shores	98070
Sappho	98305
Sara	98642
Saratoga Shores	98292
Satsop	98583
Sawyer	98951
Scandia	98370
Schawana	99321
Schneiders Prairie	98501
Schwarder	98903
Scopa (Part of Renton)	98055
Seabeck	98380
Seabold	98110
Sea First (Part of Seattle)	98104
Seahurst	98062
Seatac Mall	98003
Seatons Grove	99116
Seattle	98101-99
For specific Seattle Zip Codes call (206) 285-1650	

COLLEGES & UNIVERSITIES

Name	ZIP
Griffin College	98121
Seattle University	98122
University of Washington	98195

FINANCIAL INSTITUTIONS

Name	ZIP
American Marine Bank	98110
Family Savings & Loan Association	98105
First Interstate Bank of Washington, N.A.	98104
Key Bank of Puget Sound	98104
Metropolitan Federal Savings & Loan Association of Seattle	98101
Olympic Savings Bank	98101
Seattle-First National Bank	98124
Security Pacific Bank Washington, N.A.	98124
U.S. Bank of Washington, National Association	98101
Washington Federal Savings & Loan Association	98101
Washington Mutual Savings Bank	98101

HOSPITALS

Name	ZIP
Group Health Cooperative Central Hospital	98112
Harborview Medical Center	98104
Providence Medical Center	98122
Swedish Hospital Medical Center	98104
University of Washington Medical Center	98195
Veterans Administration Medical Center	98108
Virginia Mason Hospital	98101

HOTELS/MOTELS

Name	ZIP
Edgewater Inn	98121
Holiday Inn Crowne Plaza	98101
Marriott Hotel-Seattle Airport	98188
Ramada Inn	98133
Red Lion Inn-SeaTac	98188
Seattle Airport Hilton	98188
The Seattle Hilton	98101
Seattle Sheraton Hotel & Towers	98101
The Sorrento Hotel	98104
The Westin Hotel	98101

MILITARY INSTALLATIONS

Name	ZIP
Coast Guard Support Center, Seattle	98134
Fort Lawton	98199
Material Traffic Management Command (MTMC) Pacific Northwest Outport	98134
Naval Station, Seattle	98115
Seattle-Tacoma International Airport Air Force Facility	98110
Supervisor of Shipbuilding, Conversion and Repair Seattle	98115
United States Air Force Water Port Logistics Office	98134
United States Army Engineer District, Seattle	98124
13th Coast Guard District, Seattle	98174

Name	ZIP
Seattle Heights	98036
Seaview	98644
Sedro Woolley	98284
Sekiu	98381
Selah	98942
Selleck	98051
Sequim	98382
Sequioa	98031
Seven Mile	99026
Shadle Center (Part of Spokane)	99205
Shandle-Garland (Part of Spokane)	99205
Shaw Island	98286
Shawnee	99111
Shelton	98584
Sheridan Beach	98155
Sheridan Park (Part of Bremerton)	98310
Sherwood Forest (Part of Bellevue)	98004
Shine	98325
Shoalwater Indian Reservation	98590
Shore Acres	98335
Shorewood	98106
Shorewood Beach	98333
Shuwah	98331
Sifton	98662
Sightly	98649
Silvana	98287
Silvana Terraces	98292
Silver Beach (Part of Bellingham)	98225
Silver Creek	98585
Silverdale	98383
Silverlake (Cowlitz County)	98645
Silver Lake (Snohomish County)	98201
Silver Lake-Firecrest	98201
Similk Beach	98221
Sisco Heights	98223
Skamania	98648
Skamokawa	98647
Skokomish Indian Reservation	98584
Skykomish	98288
Skyway	98178
Sleepy Hollow	98647
Smokey Point	98223
Smyrna	99357
Snee-oosh-Beach	98257
Snohomish	98290

594 WASHINGTON Snoqualmie-Wiley

	ZIP
Snoqualmie	98065
Snoqualmie Pass	98068
Soap Lake	98851
South Aberdeen (Part of Aberdeen)	98520
South Bay	98501
South Beach	98281
South Bellingham (Part of Bellingham)	98225
South Bend	98586
South Broadway	98902
Southcenter (Part of Tukwila)	98188
South Cle Elum	98943
South Colby	98384
South Elma	98541
Southgate (Pierce County)	98499
Southgate (Thurston County)	98501
South Hill	98373
South Montesano	98563
South Park Village	98366
South Point	98365
South Prairie	98385
South Seattle (Part of Seattle)	98102
Southshore Mall (Part of Aberdeen)	98520
Southside (Part of Everett)	98208
South Snohomish	98290
South Sound (Part of Lacey)	98503
South Tacoma (Part of Tacoma)	98409
South Wenatchee	98801
Southworth	98386
Spanaway	98387
Spangle	99031
Spear	99213
Special Offender Center	98272
Spokane	99201-28
For specific Spokane Zip Codes call (509) 459-0222	
Spokane Indian Reservation	99040
Sprague	99032
Springdale	99173
Spring Glen	98024
Squaxin Island Indian Reservation	98584
Stanwood	98292
Starbuck	99359
Star Lake	98002
Startup	98293
Stehekin	98852
Steilacoom	98388
Steptoe	99174
Sterling	98284
Stevenson	98648
Stickney Lake	98036
Stiebels Corner	98346
Stillwater	98014
Strandell (Part of Everson)	98247
Stratford	98853
Stringtown	98624
Sultan	98294
Sumach	98295
Sumas	98295
Summit	98371
Summit Park	98221
Sumner	98390
Sundale	99356
Sundins Beach	98292
Sunlight Beach	98236
Sunny Bay	98335
Sunnydale	98155
Sunnyside (Snohomish County)	98201
Sunnyside (Yakima County)	98944
Sunnyside Beach (Part of Steilacoom)	98388
Sunnyslope (Chelan County)	98801
Sunnyslope (Kitsap County)	98366
Sunrise Beach	98335
Sunrise Point	98292
Sunset	99171
Sunset Bay	99026
Sunset Beach (Grays Harbor County)	98562
Sunset Beach (Island County)	98292
Sunset Beach (Mason County)	98528
Sunset Beach (Pierce County)	98465
Sun Village	98011
Suquamish	98392
Swan Trail	98201
Swinomish Indian Reservation	98257
Swofford	98564

	ZIP
Sylvan	98333
Synarep	98849
Tacoma	98397-99
	98401-99
For specific Tacoma Zip Codes call (206) 756-6175	
Tacoma Junction (Part of Fife)	98424
Tacoma Mall (Part of Tacoma)	98409
Tacoma Point	98390
Tahlequah	98013
Taholah	98587
Tahuya	98588
Tampico	98901
Tanglewilde	98501
Tanglewilde-Thompson Place	98501
Tanner	98045
Teanaway	98922
Tekoa	99033
Telma	98826
Tenino	98589
Terminal Annex (King County)	98134
Terminal Annex (Spokane County)	99220
Terrace Heights	98901
Terry Avenue (Part of Seattle)	98109
Terrys Corner	98292
The Four Seasons	98362
Thomas	98032
Thompson Place	98501
Thornton	99176
Thorp	98946
Thrashers Corner	98011
Three Lakes	98290
Three Rivers Mall (Part of Kelso)	98626
Thrift	98338
Tieton	98947
Tiger	99180
Tillicum	98492
Tillicum Beach	98292
Tillicum Siding	98492
Timberlane	98042
Tokeland	98590
Toledo	98591
Tonasket	98855
Toppenish	98948
Totem Lake (Part of Kirkland)	98033
Touchet	99360
Toutle	98649
Town and Country	99210
Tracyton	98393
Trafton	98223
Trend	99033
Trentwood	99215
Triangle Shopping Mall (Part of Longview)	98632
Tri-Cities (Part of Pasco)	99302
Trinidad	98848
Triton	98555
Trout Lake	98650
Tukwila	98188
Tulalip	98270
Tulalip Indian Reservation	98270
Tumtum	99034
Tumwater	98502
Turner Corner	98072
Twin Rivers Corrections Center	98272
Twisp	98856
Tyler	99004
Umtanum	98926
Underwood	98651
Union	98592
Union Gap	98903
Union Mills	98501
Uniontown	99179
University (Part of Seattle)	98105
University Place	98465
Upper Preston	98027
Urban	98221
Usk	99180
Utsalady	98292
Vader	98593
Valhalla (Part of Bothell)	98011
Valley	99181
Valleyford	99036
Valley Mall (Part of Union Gap)	98903
Valley Ridge (King County)	98188
Van Buren	98247
Vancouver	98660-68
	98682-86
For specific Vancouver Zip Codes call (206) 695-4462	
Van Horn	98237

	ZIP
Vantage	98950
Van Zandt	98244
Vashon	98070
Vashon Center	98070
Vashon Heights	98070
Vaughn	98394
Veazey	98002
Venersborg	98604
Venice	98110
Veradale	99037
Verlot	98252
Vesta	98537
Veterans Administration Hospital (Part of Vancouver)	98661
View	98629
View Park	98366
Villa Beach	98303
Villa Plaza	98499
Virginia	98370
Wabash	98022
Wahkiacus	98628
Waitsburg	99361
Waldron	98297
Walla Walla	99362
Walla Walla East	99362
Wallicut	98624
Wallingford (Part of Seattle)	98103
Wallula	99363
Wallula Junction	99363
Walnut Grove	98662
Wanapum Village	99321
Wapato	98951
Warden	98857
Warm Beach	98292
Warren	98335
Washington Corrections Center	98584
Washington State Reformatory	98272
Washington State University (Part of Pullman)	99164
Washougal	98671
Washtucna	99371
Waterman	98366
Waterville	98858
Wauconda	98859
Waukon	99008
Wauna	98395
Waunch Prairie (Part of Centralia)	98531
Wautauga Beach	98366
Waverly	99039
Wawawai	99113
Wedgwood (Part of Seattle)	98115
Wegoe	98433
Weikel	98902
Welcome	98244
Wellpinit	99040
Wenatchee	98801-07
For specific Wenatchee Zip Codes call (509) 662-7663	
Wenatchee Heights	98802
West Beach	98245
West Blakely	98110
West Clarkston	99403
West Clarkston-Highland	99403
West Coulee (Part of Coulee Dam)	99116
Westfair	98023
Westhaven (Part of Westport)	98595
West Park (Part of Bremerton)	98310
West Pasco	99301
Westport	98595
West Richland	99352
West Seattle (Part of Seattle)	98116
West Side (Part of Yakima)	98902
West Sound	98245
Westward Siding (Part of Tacoma)	98406
West Wenatchee	98802
Westwood (King County)	98126
Westwood (Kitsap County)	98110
Wheeler	98837
Whidbey Island Naval Air Station	98278
White Center	98126
White Center-Shorewood	98106
White Pass	98937
Whites	98541
White Salmon	98672
White Swan	98952
Whitstran	99350
Wickersham	98220
Wilbur	99185
Wilburton (Part of Bellevue)	99004
Wildcat Lake	98310
Wiley	98903

	ZIP		ZIP		ZIP
Wilkeson	98396	Wollochet	98335	Yakima	98901-09
Willada	99171	Woodinville	98072	For specific Yakima Zip Codes call (509) 575-5827	
Willapa	98577	Woodland (Cowlitz County)	98674		
Willard	98605	Woodland (Snohomish County)	98292	Yakima Indian Reservation	98948
Willow Grove	98632			Yakima Mall (Part of Yakima)	98901
Wilson Creek	98860	Woodland Beach	98292		
Winchester	98848	Woodlawn (Part of Hoquiam)	98550	Yale	96603
Winlock	98596			Yardley	99211
Winona	99125	Woodmont Beach	98032	Yarrow Point	98004
Winthrop	98862	Wood Run	98072	Yelm	98597
Winton	98826	Woodway	98020	Yoman Ferry	98303
Wishkah	98520	Wycoff (Part of Bremerton)	98312	Zenith	98188
Wishram	98673	Wye Lake	98366	Zenith-Saltwater	98188
Wishram Heights	98673	Yacht Haven	98250	Zillah	98953
Withrow	98858	Yacolt	98675		

596 WEST VIRGINIA

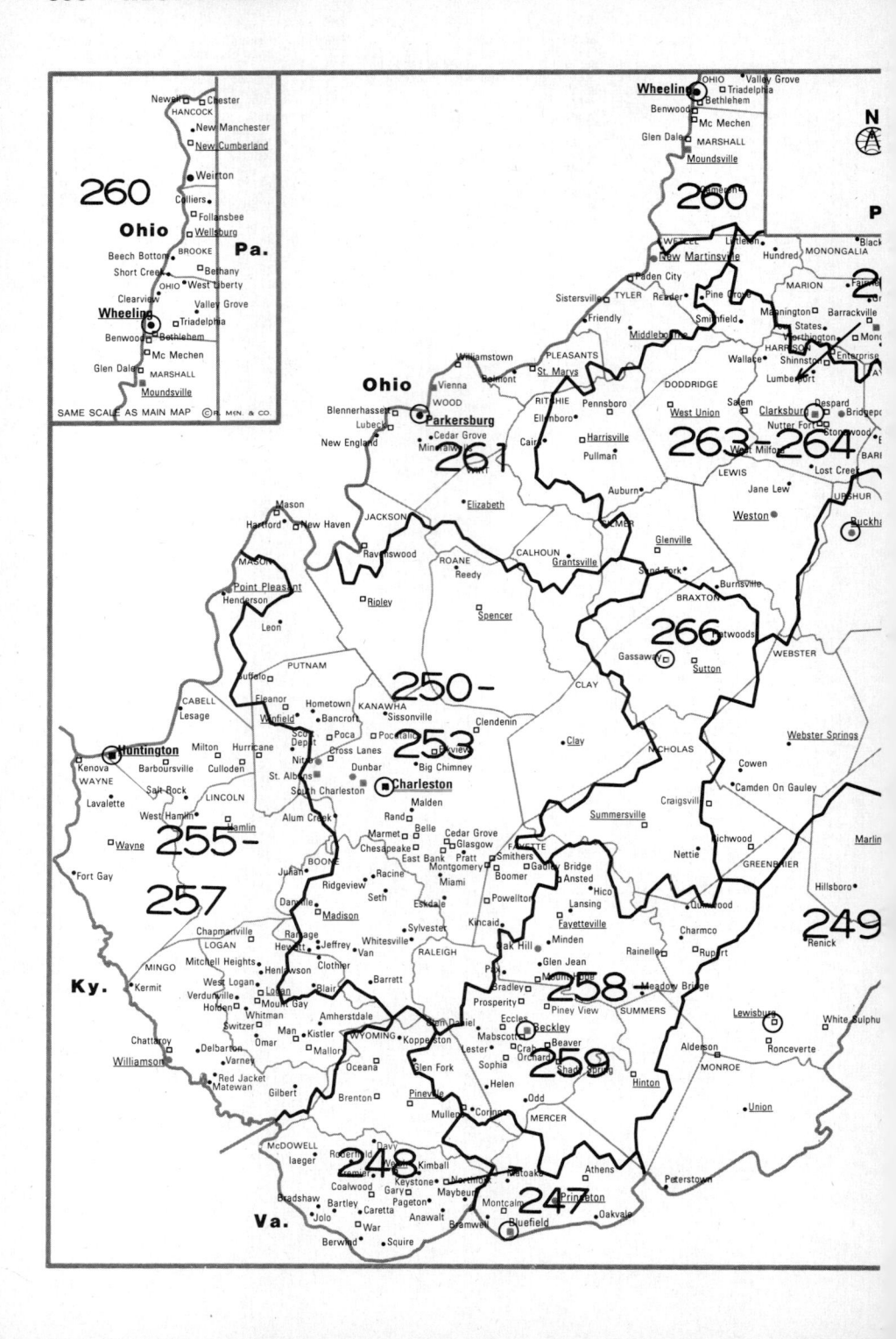

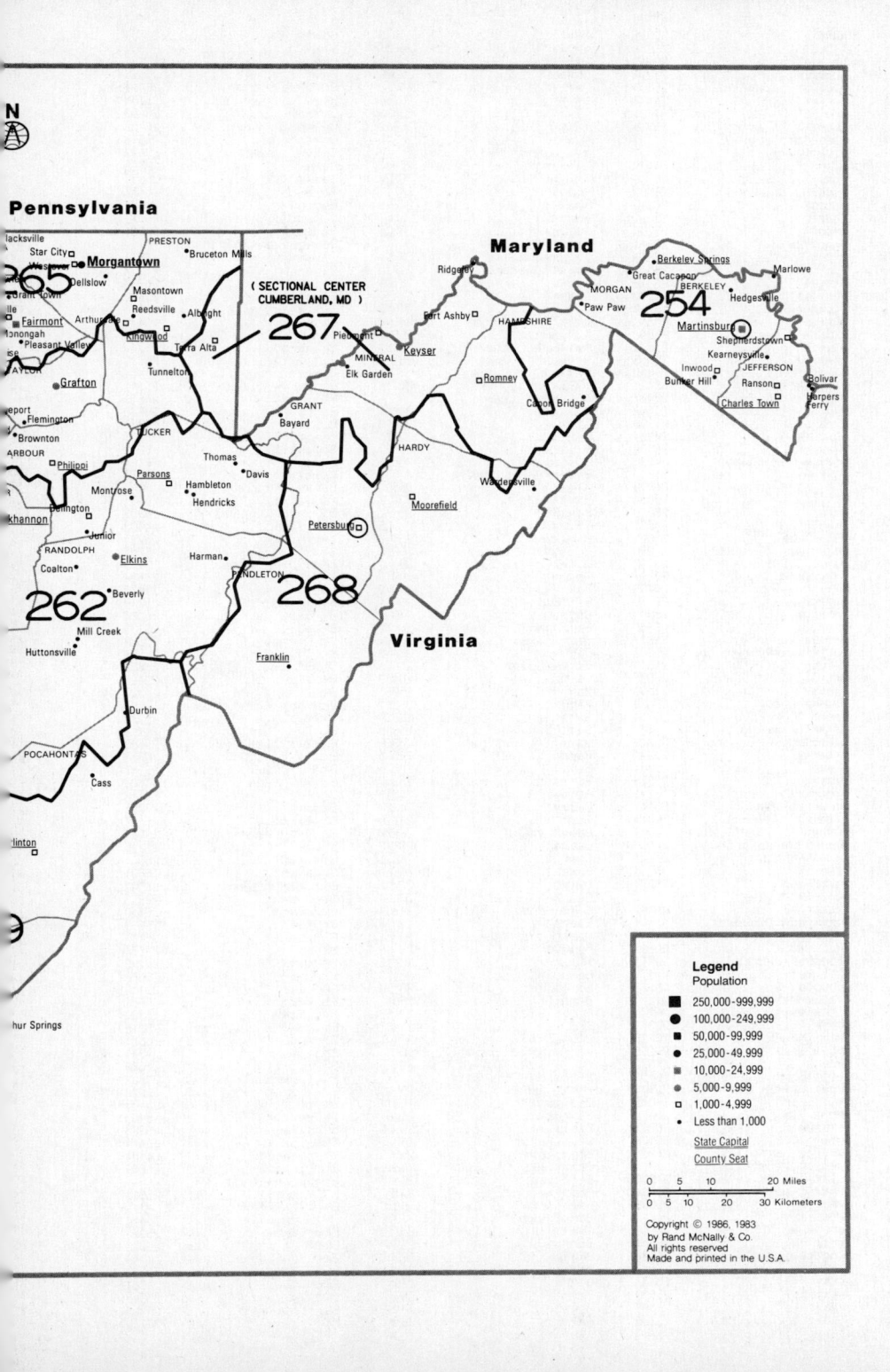

WEST VIRGINIA 597

WEST VIRGINIA Aarrons Fork-Blue Rock

	ZIP
Aarrons Fork	25071
Abbott	26201
Abney	25847
Abraham	25918
Accoville	25606
Acme	25122
Ada	24701
Adaline	26033
Adamston (Part of Clarksburg)	26301
Adamsville	26431
Adlai	26170
Adolph	26280
Adrian	26210
Advent	25231
Afton	26764
Aggregate	26241
Airport Road	25813
Ajax	25676
Albright	26519
Alderson	24910
Alexander	26218
Algoma	24868
Alice	26342
Alkol	25501
Allendale	26003
Allen Junction	25810
Allensville	25427
Allister	26167
Alloy	25002
Alma	25320
Alpena	26254
Alpha	26408
Alpheus (Part of Gary)	24836
Alpoca	24710
Alta	26656
Altizer	25234
Alton	26210
Alum Bridge	26321
Alum Creek	25003
Alvon	24986
Alvy	26322
Amandaville	25177
Amboy	26705
Ambrosia	25550
Ameagle	25004
Amelia	25160
Amherstdale	25607
Amherstdale-Robinette	25607
Amigo	25811
Amma	25005
Anawalt	24808
Andersonville	26033
Andrew	25154
Angel Terrace (Part of Charleston)	25303
Angerona	25241
Anjean	25984
Anmoore	26323
Annamoriah	26141
Annamoriah Flats	26141
Ansted	25812
Anthony	24914
Antioch (Doddridge County)	26456
Antioch (Mineral County)	26743
Aplin	25244
Apple Farm	25274
Apple Grove (Mason County)	25502
Apple Grove (McDowell County)	24844
Aracoma	25601
Arborland Acres	25177
Arbovale	24915
Arbuckle	25123
Arbutus Park (Part of Clarksburg)	26301
Archer	26377
Archer Heights	26035
Arcola	26206
Ardel	25570
Arden (Barbour County)	26405
Arden (Berkeley County)	25401
Argonne	25649
Argyle	25654
Arkansas	26801
Arlee	25106
Arlington (Harrison County)	26301
Arlington (McDowell County)	24810
Arlington (Upshur County)	26234
Arnett	25007
Arnette	26619
Arnettsville	26505
Arnold Hill	26241
Arnoldsburg	25234
Arroyo	26047
Arthur	26816
Arthurdale	26520
Artie	25008
Arvilla	26135

	ZIP
Asbury	24916
Asbury Church	26801
Asco	24828
Ashford	25009
Ashland	24810
Ashley	26456
Ashton	25503
Aspinall	26412
Astor	26347
Astor Junction (Part of Flemington)	26347
Atenville	25524
Athens	24712
Atwell	24813
Atwood	26167
Auburn	26325
Augusta (Hampshire County)	26704
Augusta (Mercer County)	24740
Aurora	26705
Austen	26410
Auto	24917
Auville (Part of Iaeger)	24844
Auviltown	26290
Avis (Part of Hinton)	25951
Avon	26411
Avondale (Doddridge County)	26456
Avondale (McDowell County)	24811
Bablin	26376
Backus	25976
Baden	25123
Baisden (Logan County)	25652
Baisden (Mingo County)	25608
Baker	26801
Baker Heights	25401
Baker Park	25177
Baker Ridge	26505
Bakerton	25410
Bald Knob	25010
Baldwin	26351
Ballard	24918
Ballengee	24919
Balls Gap	25541
Bancroft	25011
Bandytown	25012
Barboursville	25504
Bardane	25430
Bargers Springs	24935
Barker	26419
Barksdale	25951
Barn	25841
Barnabus	25638
Barnet Run	26610
Barrackville	26559
Barrett	25013
Barrs	25276
Barry Mine	26347
Bartley	24813
Bartow	24920
Basin	24726
Basnettsville	26570
Basore	26812
Bass	26836
Baxter	26560
Bayard	26707
Bear Creek	26624
Beard Heights	24954
Beards Fork	25014
Bear Mountain Mine	26334
Bearsville	26149
Beason	26415
Beatrice	26178
Beatysville	26133
Beaver	25813
Bebee	26155
Becco	25607
Beckley	25801-02
For specific Beckley Zip Codes call (304) 252-4202	
Beckley Junction (Part of Mabscott)	25871
Beckwith	25814
Bedington	25401
Beebe	25625
Beech Bottom	26030
Beech Creek	25682
Beech Glen	26656
Beechgrove	26415
Beech Hill	25187
Beechwood	25810
Beelick Knob	25976
Beeson	24714
Belgrove	25248
Belington	26250
Bellburn	25958
Belle	25015
Bellepoint (Part of Hinton)	25951
Belleville	26133
Bellmeade	25550

	ZIP
Bellview (Part of Fairmont)	26554
Bellwood	25962
Belmont	26134
Belva	26656
Belvedere Heights	25414
Bemis	26268
Benbush	26292
Bendale	26452
Ben Lomond	25515
Bennett	26423
Benson	26378
Benson Park	25302
Bens Run	26135
Benton Ferry	26554
Bentree	25018
Benwood	26031
Benwood Junction (Part of Benwood)	26031
Berea	26327
Bergoo	26298
Berkeley	25401
Berkeley Springs	25411
Berlin	26452
Bernie	25521
Berryburg	26347
Berry Siding	26621
Berryville	25411
Bertha Hill	26541
Berwind	24815
Beryl	26726
Besoco	25857
Bessemer	25401
Bethany	26032
Bethel Place	26181
Bethesda	25570
Bethlehem (Harrison County)	26431
Bethlehem (Ohio County)	26003
Betty Zane	26003
Beverly	26253
Beverly Hills (Cabell County)	25705
Beverly Hills (Marion County)	26554
Bias	25670
Bickmore	25019
Big Battle	26426
Bigbend	26136
Big Chimney	25302
Big Creek	25505
Big Four	24853
Big Isaac	26426
Big Moses	26320
Big Mountain (Part of Cedar Grove)	25039
Big Otter	25113
Big Run (Marion Ccunty)	26582
Big Run (Marshall County)	26033
Big Run (Webster County)	26217
Big Run (Wetzel Ccunty)	26561
Big Sandy	24816
Bigson	22206
Big Springs	26137
Big Sycamore	25111
Billings	25270
Bim	25021
Bingamon	26591
Bingamon Junction	26591
Bingham	25958
Birch River	26610
Birchton	25209
Birds Creek	26410
Bishop	24604
Bismarck	26739
Blackberry City	25678
Black Betsy	25159
Black Bottom	25601
Black Eagle	25882
Blackhawk	25306
Blacksville	26521
Black Wolf	24871
Blaine	21538
Blair (Jefferson Courty)	25432
Blair (Logan County)	25022
Blairton	25401
Blakeley	25160
Blandville	26328
Blaser	26444
Blennerhassett	26101
Blocton	25685
Bloomery (Hampshire County)	26817
Bloomery (Jefferson County)	25414
Bloomingrose	25024
Blount	25025
Blue	26149
Blue Creek	25026
Bluefield	24701
Blue Jay	25816
Blue Ridge Acres	25425
Blue Rock	26280

Bluestone-Congo **WEST VIRGINIA** 599

Name	ZIP
Bluestone	24701
Blue Sulphur Springs	24910
Blueville (Part of Grafton)	26354
Bluewell	24701
Blundon	25071
Board	25253
Boaz	26187
Bob White	25028
Boggs	26299
Bolair	26288
Bolivar	25425
Bolt	25817
Bomont	25030
Bona Vista (Part of Charleston)	25311
Bonnie	26619
Bonnivale	26150
Booher	26320
Boomer	25031
Boonesborough (Part of Gauley Bridge)	25057
Booth	26522
Boothsville	26554
Borderland	25665
Boreman	26101
Borgman	26444
Bottom Creek	24853
Boulder	25701
Bowan Ridge	25701
Bowden	26254
Bowlby	26541
Bowles	25523
Boyd	26234
Boyer	24915
Bozoo	24923
Bradley (Boone County)	25051
Bradley (Raleigh County)	25818
Bradshaw	24817
Braeholm	25607
Bragg	25918
Bramwell	24715
Branchland	25506
Brandonville	26523
Brandywine	26802
Braxton	26619
Bream	25071
Breeden	25666
Brenton	24818
Bretz (Preston County)	26524
Bretz (Tucker County)	26287
Brewsterdale	24619
Briarwood Estates	26101
Brick Church	25514
Bridgeport	26330
Bridgeport Hill (Part of Bridgeport)	26330
Bridgeway	26149
Brink	26582
Bristol	26332
Broaddus (Part of Philippi)	26416
Broadmoor	26181
Broad Oaks (Part of Clarksburg)	26301
Brohard	26138
Brookhaven (Kanawha County)	25143
Brookhaven (Monongalia County)	26505
Brooklyn	25840
Brooklyn Junction (Part of New Martinsville)	26155
Brooks	25957
Brookside	26705
Brounland	25314
Brown	26448
Brownlow	26354
Brownsburg	24954
Browns Mills	26505
Brownsville (Fayette County)	25085
Brownsville (Lewis County)	26452
Brownton	26334
Brownwood	25864
Bruceton Mills	26525
Bruno	25611
Brush Fork	24701
Brushy Run	26866
Brydon	26435
Bryson	25865
Bubbling Spring	26885
Buck	25951
Buckeye	24924
Buckhannon	26201
Bud	24716
Buena Vista	25320
Buffalo	25033
Buffalo Creek	25530
Buff Lick	25039
Bula	26521
Bulger	25501
Bull	25669
Bull Run	26547

Name	ZIP
Bulltown	26631
Bunker Hill (Berkeley County)	25413
Bunker Hill (Kanawha County)	25309
Bunners Ridge	26554
Burchfield	26562
Burlington	26710
Burning Springs (Kanawha County)	25015
Burning Springs (Wirt County)	26141
Burnsville	26335
Burnsville Junction (Part of Burnsville)	26335
Burnt Factory	25411
Burnt House	26178
Burnwell	25034
Burton	26562
Butchersville	26452
Cabell	25871
Cabin Creek	25035
Cabins	26855
Cabot	25163
Cabot Station	26147
Cairo	26337
Caldwell	24925
Calis	26033
Callaway	25880
Calvert (Part of St. Albans)	25177
Calvin	26660
Cambria	26386
Camden	26338
Camden On Gauley	26208
Cameron	26033
Camp	26320
Campbelltown	24954
Camp Creek	25820
Campus	24827
Canaan	26234
Canaan Heights	26260
Canaan Valley	26260
Canebrake	24819
Cane Fork	25075
Canfield (Braxton County)	26601
Canfield (Randolph County)	26241
Cannelton	25036
Canton	26456
Cantwell	26362
Canvas	26662
Canyon	26505
Capehart	25123
Capels	24820
Capitol (Part of Charleston)	25311
Capon Bridge	26711
Capon Springs	26823
Carbon	25122
Carbondale	25036
Caretta	24821
Carl	26676
Carlisle	25917
Carl Lee Ray	26181
Carlos	24844
Carolina	26563
Carolina Heights	25177
Carrollton	26238
Carswell	24853
Carter	26218
Cascade	26547
Cashmere	24918
Cass	24927
Cassity	26278
Cassville	26527
Catawba	26554
Cave	26807
Cazy	25028
Cedar Grove (Kanawha County)	25039
Cedar Grove (Wood County)	26101
Cedarville	26611
Center Hill	26143
Center Point	26339
Centerville	25555
Central	26101
Centralia	26612
Central Station	26456
Century	26214
Century No. 2	26238
Ceredo	25507
Ceres	24701
Cham	25654
Chapel	26624
Chapman (Braxton County)	26412
Chapman (Webster County)	26288
Chapman Addition	26070
Chapmanville	25508
Charleston	25301-75
For specific Charleston Zip Codes call (304) 357-4152	

Name	ZIP
Charleston Ordnance Center (Part of South Charleston)	25303
Charleston Town Center (Part of Charleston)	25375
Charles Town	25414
Charlton Heights (Part of Gauley Bridge)	25040
Charmco	25958
Chatham Hill	26571
Chattaroy	25667
Chauncey	25612
Cheat Neck	26505
Chelyan	25035
Cherokee	25122
Cherry Falls	26288
Cherry Grove	26804
Cherry Run	25427
Chesapeake (Kanawha County)	25315
Chesapeake (Marion County)	26554
Chester	26034
Chesterville	26150
Chestnut Heights	26070
Chestnut Hill (Part of Weirton)	26062
Chestnut Ridge	26505
Chiefton	26301
Childs	26162
Chimney Corner	25085
Chloe	25235
Christian	25611
Churchville	26338
Cicerone	25243
Cinco	25306
Cinderella	25661
Circleville	26804
Cirtsville	25801
Cisco	26161
Claremont	25936
Clarence	25244
Clarksburg	26301-02
For specific Clarksburg Zip Codes call (304) 623-7700	
Clay	25043
Claypool (Logan County)	25617
Claypool (Summers County)	25976
Claysville	26743
Clayton	24910
Clear Creek	25044
Clear Fork	24822
Clearview	26003
Clem	26623
Clemtown	26405
Clendenin	25045
Cleveland	26215
Clifftop	25831
Clifton	25237
Clifton Mills	26525
Clinton (Boone County)	25013
Clinton (Ohio County)	26059
Clintonville	24928
Clio	25046
Clothier	25047
Clouston	26033
Clover	25276
Cloverdale	24963
Clover Lick	24927
Clyde (Kanawha County)	25302
Clyde (Wetzel County)	26186
Coal Branch Heights (Part of Charleston)	25301
Coalburg	25035
Coal City	25823
Coaldale	24717
Coal Fork (Part of Ohley)	25147
Coal Fork (Part of Malden)	25306
Coal Mountain	24823
Coalton	26257
Coal Valley	25047
Coalwood	24824
Coburn	26562
Coco	25071
Cofoco	25147
Coketon	26292
Colcord	25048
Cold Stream	26711
Coldwater	26411
Colebank	26405
Coleman	25517
Colfax	26566
Colliers	26035
Collinsdale	25034
Columbia	25118
Combs Addition	25617
Comfort	25049
Conaway	26149
Concord	26410
Confidence	25168
Congo	26050

600 WEST VIRGINIA Conings-Everettville

Name	ZIP
Conings	26443
Cool Ridge	25825
Cooper (Part of Bramwell)	24715
Coopertown	25148
Copen	26615
Copley	26452
Cora	25614
Cordova	24966
Core	26529
Corinne	25826
Corinth	26713
Corley (Barbour County)	26250
Corley (Braxton County)	26621
Corliss	25962
Cornstalk	24901
Cornwallis	26337
Cortland	26260
Corton	25045
Costa	25051
Cottageville	25239
Cottle	26207
Cotton	25046
Cottontown	26562
Country Club Acres (Part of South Charleston)	25309
Countsville	25243
Courtright	26330
Cove (Part of Weirton)	26062
Cove Creek	25534
Cove Gap	25534
Covel	24719
Cowen	26206
Cox Landing	25537
Coxs Mills	26342
Coxtown (Part of Weston)	26452
Crab Orchard	25827
Crag	25962
Craigmoor	26408
Craigsville	26205
Cranberry	25828
Craneco	25630
Cranesville	26764
Crany	24870
Crawford	26343
Crawley	24931
Creamery	24910
Crede	25302
Cremo	26141
Crescent	25136
Cressmont	25043
Creston	26141
Crichton	25961
Crickmer	25831
Crooked Creek	25639
Crosby	25125
Cross Lanes	25313
Crossroads	26589
Crow	25813
Crown (Logan County)	25606
Crown (Monongalia County)	26508
Crown Hill	25052
Crow Summit	26164
Crum	25669
Crumpler	24825
Crystal	24747
Crystal Lake	26456
Crystal Springs (Randolph County)	26241
Crystal Springs (Wood County)	26181
Cubana	26237
Cucumber	24826
Culloden	25510
Cumberland Heights	24701
Cunard	25840
Curtin	26204
Curtisville	26582
Cusicks Crossing	26562
Custer Addition	26301
Cutlips	26619
Cuzzart	26530
Cyclone	24827
Cyrus	25530
Czar	26224
Dabney	25654
Dahmer	26807
Dailey	26259
Daisy	25505
Dakota	26554
Dale	26377
Dallas	26036
Dallison	26180
Dameron	25849
Danese	25831
Daniels	25832
Dans Run	26763
Danville	25053
Darkesville	25428
Dartmont	25009
Dartmoor	26250
Davenport	26175

Name	ZIP
Davin	25617
Davis (Logan County)	25625
Davis (Tucker County)	26260
Davis Creek	25003
Davisville	26142
Davy	24828
Dawes	25054
Dawmont	26344
Dawson	24910
Daybrook	26570
Daysville	26201
Deansville	26201
Deanville	26452
Decota	25122
Deep Valley (Marion County)	26582
Deep Valley (Tyler County)	26360
Deep Water	25057
Deer Creek	24927
Deer Run	26807
Deer Walk	26180
Dehue	25654
Delbarton	25670
Dellslow	26531
Delong	26170
Delray	26714
Dempsey	25840
Denver (Marshall County)	26033
Denver (Preston County)	26444
Denver Heights	26033
Derryhale	25846
Despard (Harrison County)	26301
Dessie	26623
Devon	25682
Dewitt	25901
Diamond (Kanawha County)	25015
Diamond (Logan County)	25625
Diana	26217
Dickinson	25015
Dickson	25535
Dille	26617
Dingess	25671
Dingy	26623
Dink	25113
Dixie	25059
Doane	25511
Dobra	25183
Dock	25177
Dog Patch	25636
Dog Run	25043
Dola	26386
Donaldson	26206
Doortown	26288
Dorcas	26847
Dorothy	25060
Dothan	25833
Dott	24736
Douglas (Calhoun County)	25235
Douglas (Tucker County)	26292
Downtown (Cabell County)	25701
Downtown (Ohio County)	26003
Drennen	26667
Drews Creek	25140
Droop	24946
Drybranch	25061
Dry Creek	25062
Dryfork	26263
Dry Hill	25801
Duck	25063
Dudeon	25248
Dudley Gap	25541
Duffields	25442
Duffy	26376
Duhring	24747
Dukes	25252
Dunbar	25064
Duncan	25252
Dundon	25043
Dunloup	25880
Dunlow	25511
Dunmore	24934
Dunns	25841
Duo	25841
Dupont Circle	26181
Dupont City	25015
Durbin	26264
Durgon	26836
Dutchman	26148
Dutch Ridge	25045
Dyer	26206
Eagle	25136
Earling	25632
Earnshaw	26585
East Bank	25067
East Beckley (Part of Beckley)	25801
East Dailey	26253
East Gulf	25915
East Huntington (Part of Huntington)	25702
East Kermit	25674

Name	ZIP
East Lynn	25512
East Nitro (Part of Nitro)	25143
East Oak Hill	25901
Easton	26505
East Pea Ridge	25705
East Salem	26426
East Side (Kanawha County)	25301
Eastside (Marion County)	26554
East View	26301
East Vivian	24891
East Williamson (Part of Williamson)	25661
Eaton	26180
Eccles	25836
Echo	25570
Eckman	24829
Eden (Ohio County)	26003
Eden (Upshur County)	26234
Edgarton	25672
Edgemont (Part of Fairmont)	26554
Edgewood (Harrison County)	26301
Edgewood (Kanawha County)	25302
Edgewood (Ohio County)	26003
Edgewood Acres (Part of Charleston)	25302
Edison	24701
Edmond	25837
Edna	26505
Edray	24954
Edwight	25189
Effie	25514
Egeria (Mercer County)	25841
Egeria (Raleigh County)	25902
Eggleton	25523
Eglon	26716
Elana	25266
Elbert (Part of Gary)	24830
Eldora	26554
Eleanor	25070
Elgood	24740
Elizabeth	26143
Elk	26271
Elk City	26416
Elk Forest	25311
Elk Garden	26717
Elkhorn	24831
Elkhurst	25164
Elkins	26241
Elkridge (Fayette County)	25161
Elkridge (McDowell County)	24868
Elk Run Junction	25209
Elkview	25071
Elkwater	26273
Ella	26055
Ellamore	26267
Ellenboro	26346
Elliber Spring	26852
Ellison	25969
Elm Grove (Ohio County)	26003
Elmira	26618
Elm Terrace (Part of Wheeling)	26003
Elmwood (Mason County)	25123
Elmwood (Wayne County)	25570
Elmwood Heights	26187
Eloise	25511
Elton	25965
Emma	25124
Emmart	26447
Emmett	25620
Emmons	25009
Emoryville	26717
Endicott	26581
Engle	25425
English	24832
Ennis	24887
Enoch	25043
Enon	26651
Enterprise (Harrison County)	26568
Enterprise (Wirt County)	26160
Entry Mountain	26807
Epperly	25823
Erbacon	26203
Erie	26301
Erwin	26705
Eskdale	25075
Esty	24966
Etam	26425
Ethel	25076
Eunice	25209
Eureka	26144
Evans	25241
Evansdale (Part of Morgantown)	26505
Evansville	26440
Evenwood	26254
Everettville	26533

Evergreen-Hampden **WEST VIRGINIA** 601

	ZIP		ZIP		ZIP
Evergreen	26218	Fort Spring	24936	Glen Ferris	25090
Evergreen Hills	25239	Foster	25081	Glen Fork	25845
Everson	26554	Fosterville	25181	Glengary	25421
Excelsior (McDowell County)	24892	Four Mile	26419	Glenhayes	25519
		Four States	26572	Glen Jean	25846
Excelsior (Upshur County)	26201	Frame	25071	Glenmore	26241
Exchange	26619	Frametown	26623	Glen Morgan	25847
Extra	25033	Francis (Harrison County)	26554	Glenray	24910
Factory	25411	Francis (Raleigh County)	25915	Glen Rogers	25848
Fairdale	25839	Frank	24920	Glen View	25827
Fairfax Estates (Part of Charleston)	25314	Frankford	24938	Glenville	26351
		Franklin (Brooke County)	26070	Glen White	25849
Fairlea	24902	Franklin (Pendleton County)	26807	Glenwood (Mason County)	25520
Fairmont	26554-55	Franklintown	25441	Glenwood (Ohio County)	26003
For specific Fairmont Zip Codes call (304) 366-1610		Fraziers Bottom	25082	Glenwood Park	24701
		Freed	26138	Glover Gap	26585
Fairmor (Part of Westover)	26505	Freeman (Part of Bramwell)	24724	Gluck	24844
Fairplain	25271	Freemansburg	26452	Godby	25508
Fairview (Jackson County)	25252	Freeport (Preston County)	26764	Godfrey	24735
Fairview (Marion County)	26570	Freeport (Wirt County)	26180	Goffs	26362
Fairview (Marshall County)	26055	Freeze Fork	25076	Goldtown	25248
Fairview (Mason County)	25253	French Creek	26218	Goodhope	26378
Fairview (Mingo County)	25661	Frenchton	26219	Goodman	25667
Fairview (Wood County)	26181	Frew	26149	Goodwill	24747
Fallen Timber	26437	Friars Hill	24939	Gordon	25093
Falling Rock	25079	Friendly	26146	Gore	26301
Falling Waters	25419	Friendly View	25062	Gormania	26720
Falls	26833	Frogtown	25625	Gormley	26267
Falls Mill	26620	Frost	24954	Goshen	26234
Falls Mills	26146	Frozen Camp	25252	Gould	26218
Fallsview	25002	Fry	25524	Grace	25270
Fanco	25606	Fulton (Part of Wheeling)	26003	Grafton	26354
Fanny	24834	Gaines	26234	Graham	25253
Fanrock	24834	Gallagher	25083	Graham Heights	26554
Far	26167	Gallipolis Ferry	25515	Grand Central Mall (Part of Vienna)	26105
Farley	25979	Galloway	26349		
Farmington	26571	Galloway Junction	26349	Grandview	25813
Farnum	26369	Galmish	26167	Grangeville	26582
Faulkner	26241	Gandeeville	25243	Grantsville	26147
Fayetteville	25840	Gap Mills	24941	Grant Town	26574
Federal (Part of Bluefield)	24701	Gap of the Ridge	24701	Granville	26534
Federal Correctional Institute (Monroe County)	24910	Gardner	24740	Grape Island	26170
		Garland	24811	Grapevine	24844
Federal Correctional Institution (Summers County)	24910	Garretts Bend	25564	Grassy Meadows	24943
		Garrison	25209	Grave Creek	26041
		Garten	25840	Graydon	25938
Federal Mine (Part of Grant Town)	26574	Garwood	24726	Graysville	26055
		Gary	24836	Great Cacapon	25422
Federal Ridge	26170	Gassaway	26624	Green Bank	24944
Fellowsville	26410	Gaston	26452	Green Bottom	25537
Fenwick	26202	Gaston Junction (Part of Fairmont)	26554	Greenbrier	24810
Ferguson	25511			Green Castle	26180
Ferrellsburg	25524	Gates	24983	Greendale	26656
Fetterman (Part of Grafton)	26354	Gatewood	25840	Green Hill	26155
Filbert (Part of Gary)	24835	Gauley Bridge	25085	Greenland (Grant County)	26833
Finch	26170	Gauley Mill	26208	Greenland (Wood County)	26181
Finley	25003	Gawthrop	26201	Green Spring	26722
Fireco	25856	Gay	25244	Greenstown	25901
Fisher	26818	Gaymont	25938	Green Sulphur Springs	25966
Fitzpatrick	25801	Gem	26625	Green Valley (Mercer County)	24701
Five Block	25022	Genoa	25517		
Five Forks (Calhoun County)	26145	Georges Run	26456	Green Valley (Nicholas County)	25981
		Georgetown (Lewis County)	26372		
Five Forks (Preston County)	26525	Georgetown (Marshall County)	26033	Greenview	25053
Five Forks (Ritchie County)	26362			Greenville	24945
Fivemile (Kanawha County)	25306	Georgetown (Monongalia County)	26505	Greenwood (Boone County)	25010
Fivemile (Mason County)	25106			Greenwood (Doddridge County)	26360
Flat Rock	25123	Gerrardstown	25420		
Flats	25140	Ghent	25843	Greer (Mason County)	25550
Flat Top	25841	Giatto	24736	Greer (Monongalia County)	26505
Flat Top Lake	25843	Gilbert	25621	Greggsville (Part of Wheeling)	26003
Flatwoods (Braxton County)	26621	Gilboa	26671		
Flatwoods (Jackson County)	26164	Giles	25054	Grey Eagle	25674
		Gilkerson	25512	Griffithsville	25521
Flemington	26347	Gill	25557	Grimms Landing	25095
Flinderation	26332	Gilliam	24897	Grippe	25314
Flint	26456	Gillman Bottom	25617	Grove	26411
Flipping	24747	Gilman	26241	Groves	25063
Floe	25242	Gilmer	26350	Grubbs Corner	25401
Flower	26611	Gip	26618	Guardian	26217
Flowing Acres	25414	Given	25245	Gum Spring	26505
Fola	25080	Glace	24942	Gunville	25123
Follansbee	26037	Glade Farms	26525	Guthrie	25312
Folsom	26348	Glade Springs	25832	Guyandotte (Part of Huntington)	25702
Forest Hill	24935	Gladesville	26374		
Forest Hills (Kanawha County)	25314	Glade View	26206	Guyan Estates	25504
		Gladwin	26241	Guyan Terrace	25601
Forest Hills (Ohio County)	26003	Glady	26268	Gypsy	26361
Forks of Cacapon	25434	Glady Creek	26554	Hacker Valley	26222
Forks of Coal	25003	Glasgow	25086	Hagans	26529
Forks of Hurricane	25514	Glen	25088	Hager	25563
Fort Ashby	26719	Glen Alum	25651	Hales Gap	24701
Fort Branch	25076	Glencoe	25119	Hall	26201
Fort Gay	25514	Glen Dale	26038	Hallburg	25063
Fort Grand	26533	Glendale Heights	26038	Halleck	26505
Fort Hill (Part of Charleston)	25303	Glen Daniel	25844	Halltown	25423
Fort Martin	26541	Glendon	26623	Halo	26206
Fort Neal (Part of Parkersburg)	26103	Glen Easton	26039	Hambleton	26269
		Glen Elk (Part of Clarksburg)	26301	Hamlin	25523
Fort Run	26836			Hammond	26566
Fort Seybert	26806	Glen Falls	26301	Hampden	25623

602 WEST VIRGINIA Hampton-Kincaid

Name	ZIP
Hampton	26201
Hampton Heights (Part of Charleston)	25314
Hancock	25411
Handley	25102
Hanna	26180
Hannahsville	26290
Hanover	24839
Hansford	25103
Hany	25511
Harding	26250
Hardy	24740
Harewood Mine	25031
Harlin	26456
Harman	26270
Harmco (Part of Mullens)	25882
Harmony	25246
Harmony Grove	26505
Harper (Pendleton County)	26807
Harper (Raleigh County)	25851
Harper Heights	25801
Harpers Ferry	25425
Harpertown	26241
Harris Ferry	26181
Harrison (Clay County)	25105
Harrison (Mineral County)	26717
Harrisville	26362
Harters Hill	26591
Hartford	25247
Hartland	25043
Hartmansville	26717
Harts	25524
Harvey	25901
Harveytown (Part of Huntington)	25704
Hastings	26377
Hatcher (Mercer County)	24740
Hatcher (Wyoming County)	24870
Hatfield Bottom (Part of Matewan)	25678
Havaco	24841
Haywood	26366
Haywood Junction	26431
Hazelgreen	26367
Hazelton	26535
Hazelwood	26241
Hazy	25188
Headsville	26710
Heaters	26627
Heatherfield	25443
Heavener Grove	26201
Hebron	26346
Hedgesville	25427
Hedgeview	25637
Heizer	25159
Helen	25853
Helens Run	26591
Helvetia	26224
Hemlock	26224
Hemphill (Part of Welch)	24842
Henderson	25106
Hendricks	26271
Henlawson	25624
Henning	24938
Henrietta	26147
Hensley	24843
Hensley Heights	25635
Hepzibah (Harrison County)	26369
Hepzibah (Taylor County)	26330
Hereford	25252
Herndon	24726
Herndon Heights	24726
Hernshaw	25107
Herold	26601
Herring	26547
Hettie	26376
Hetzel	25076
Hewett	25108
Hiawatha	24729
Hickman Run	26554
Hickory Chapel	25550
Hico	25854
Highland	26346
Highland Lake Terrace	26181
Highland Park	26241
Highlawns (Part of Rivesville)	26588
High View	26808
Hildebrand	26505
Hillcrest (Part of Fairmont)	26554
Hilldale	25951
Hillsboro	24946
Hillsdale	24976
Hilltop	25760
Hillview (Cabell County)	25702
Hillview (Marion County)	26554
Hillview Terrace	26041
Hilton Village	25962
Hinch	25682
Hines	25967
Hinkleville	26201

Name	ZIP
Hinton	25951
Hiorra	26410
Hite	26588
Hitop	25160
Hix	25951
Hodgesville	26201
Hogsett	25515
Hokes Mill	24970
Holbrook	26456
Holcomb	26261
Holden (Logan County)	25625
Holly	25122
Holly Grove	25103
Hollywood	24983
Homeland	26378
Hometown	25109
Homewood	26452
Hominy Falls	26679
Hoodsville	26588
Hoo Hoo	25865
Hookersville	26651
Hooverson Heights	26037
Hoover Town	26218
Hopemont	26764
Hopeville	26855
Hopewell (Barbour County)	26416
Hopewell (Fayette County)	25938
Hopewell (Marion County)	26554
Hopewell (Preston County)	26525
Hopkins Fork	25181
Horner	26372
Horsepen	24619
Horse Shoe Run	26769
Horton	26296
Hosterman	26264
Hotchkiss	25920
Hoult	26554
Howells Mill	25545
Howesville	26444
Hoy	26704
Hubball	25506
Hubbardstown	25555
Hudson	26519
Huff Junction	25634
Hughart	24928
Hughes	26404
Hugheston	25110
Hugo	25168
Hull	24844
Humphrey	26133
Hundred	26575
Hunt	25635
Hunter's Ridge (Part of Charleston)	25314
Huntersville	24954
Hunting Ground	26804
Huntington	25701-79
For specific Huntington Zip Codes call (304) 526-9600	
Huntington Mall (Part of Barboursville)	25504
Hur	26151
Hurricane	25526
Hurst	26445
Hutchinson	26591
Huttonsville	26273
Huttonsville Correctional Center	26273
Iaeger	24844
Idamay	26576
Ikes Fork	24845
Independence (Clay County)	25125
Independence (Jackson County)	25275
Independence (Preston County)	26374
Indian (Part of St. Albans)	25177
Indian Meadows	25545
Indian Mills	24935
Indore	25111
Industrial (Part of Clarksburg)	26301
Industrial	26375
Industry	26152
Ingleside	24740
Ingram Branch	25119
Inkerman	26801
Institute	25112
Intermont	26851
Inwood	25428
Ireland	26376
Irona	26537
Iroquis	25928
Isaban	24846
Isom	25121
Israel	26444
Itmann	24847
Iuka	26149
Ivy	26201
Ivydale	25113

Name	ZIP
Jacksonburg	26377
Jackson Flats	24873
Jacksons Mills	26452
Jacobs Fork	24884
Jacox	24946
Jamestown	25446
Jamison Mine No. Nine	26571
Jane Lew	26378
Janie	25209
Jarrolds Valley (Part of Whitesville)	25209
Jarvisville	26332
Jawood	25811
Jayenn	26554
Jeffrey	25114
Jenkinjones	24848
Jenks	25563
Jenningston	26254
Jenny Gap	25865
Jere	26546
Jerrys Run	26133
Jesse	24849
Jimtown (Harrison County)	26386
Jimtown (Morgan County)	25411
Job	26270
Jockeycamp Run	26456
Jodie	26674
Joetown	26582
Johnnycake	24844
Johnsontown (Berkeley County)	25427
Johnsontown (Jefferson County)	25430
Johnstown	26385
Joker	26141
Jolo	24850
Jonben	25856
Jones Springs	25427
Jordan	26554
Jordan Run	26833
Josephine	25857
Josephs Mills	26320
Joy	26456
Judson	24910
Judy Gap	26814
Julia	24966
Julian	25529
Jumping Branch	25969
Junction	26824
Junior	26275
Justice	24851
Justice Addition	25601
Kabletown	25414
Kalamazoo	26416
Kanawha	26142
Kanawha City (Part of Charleston)	25304
Kanawha Drive	26351
Kanawha Estates (Part of Charleston)	25304
Kanawha Falls	25115
Kanawha Head	26228
Kanawha Station	26142
Kansooth	26033
Kasson	26405
Katy	26554
Katy Lick	26301
Kayford	25122
Kearneysville	25430
Kedron	26201
Keeler Glade	26525
Keenan	24983
Kegley	24731
Keister	24901
Keith	25148
Kelly	25022
Kelly Hill	25045
Kellysville	24732
Kenna	25248
Kenova	25530
Kent	26055
Kentuck	25249
Kera Landing	25262
Kerens	26276
Kermit	25674
Keslers Cross Lanes	26675
Kessler	25984
Kettle	25243
Key	26814
Keyrock	24874
Keyser	26726
Keystone	24852
Kiahsville	25534
Kidwell	26149
Kieffer	24950
Kilarney Junction	26554
Killarney	25915
Kilsyth	25859
Kimball	24853
Kimberly	25118
Kincaid	25119

Kincheloe-Meadow Bridge WEST VIRGINIA 603

Name	ZIP
Kincheloe	26378
Kinder	25540
Kingmont	26578
Kingston	25120
Kingstown	26561
Kingsville	26257
Kingwood	26537
Kirby	26729
Kirby Addition	24740
Kirbyton	25181
Kirk	25671
Kirt	26283
Kistler	25628
Kitchen	25508
Kitsonville (Part of Weston)	26452
Kline	26866
Klines Gap	26833
Knawl	26447
Knob Fork	25581
Knobs	24983
Knollwood	25302
Knottsville	26354
Kodol	26186
Kopperston	24854
Kyle	24855
Lacoma	24827
La Frank (Part of Richwood)	26261
Lahmansville	26731
Lake	25121
Lake Floyd	26332
Lake Ridge	26330
Lake Ron	26181
Lake Washington	25526
Lakin	25250
Lamberton	26346
Lanark	25860
Landes	26847
Landgraff	24829
Landisburg	25831
Lando Mines	25670
Landville	25635
Laneville	26263
Lanham	25159
Lansing	25862
Largent	25422
Larkmead	26101
Lashmeet	24733
Lauckport (Part of Parkersburg)	26101
Laura Lee Mine	26386
Laurel Branch	24131
Laurel Dale	26743
Laurel Fork	26601
Laurel Iron Works	26505
Laurel Park	26301
Laurel Point	25505
Laurel Valley	26301
Lavalette	25535
Lawn	25976
Lawrenceville (Part of Chester)	26034
Layland	25864
Leachtown	26143
Lead Mine	26290
Leadsville	26241
Leander	25912
Leckie	24856
Lee	25880
Lee Creek	26181
Leet	25536
Leetown	25430
Leevale	25209
Leewood	25122
Leewood Park	26003
Left Hand	25251
Lego	25857
Lehew	26865
Leivasy	26676
Lenore	25676
Lenox	26519
Leon	25123
Leonard	24966
Leopold	26443
Lerona	25971
Le Roy	25252
Lesage	25537
Leslie	25972
Lester	25865
Letart	25253
Letherbark	25234
Letter Gap	25255
Levels	25431
Lewisburg	24901
Lex	24817
Liberty (Harrison County)	26301
Liberty (Putnam County)	25124
Lick Creek	25979
Lick Fork	25840
Lico	25314
Lightburn	26378
Lila	24808

Name	ZIP
Lilac Hills	24740
Lillybrook	25857
Lillydale (Monroe County)	24945
Lillydale (Wyoming County)	24822
Lilly Grove	24740
Lillyhaven	24854
Lilly Park	25962
Lima	26383
Limestone (Marshall County)	26041
Limestone (Mineral County)	26726
Limestone Hill	26143
Linden	25256
Lindside	24951
Lindytown	25204
Link	26167
Linn	26384
Linwood	26291
Little	26146
Little Birch	26629
Little Falls	26505
Little Italy (Clay County)	25113
Little Italy (Randolph County)	26296
Little Laurel Creek (Part of Richwood)	26261
Little Pittsburg	26434
Littlesburg	24701
Littleton	26581
Lively	25917
Liverpool	25252
Livingston	25083
Lizemores	25125
Lloydsville	26619
Lobata	25678
Lobelia	24946
Lochgelly	25866
Lockbridge	25973
Lockhart	25275
Lockney	25258
Lockwood	26651
Lodgeville	26330
Logan	25601
Logansport	26582
Lomax	24899
London	25126
Lonetree	26149
Longacre	25186
Long Branch (Fayette County)	25867
Long Branch (Wyoming County)	24882
Longdale	25253
Longpole	24844
Long Run	26426
Longview	26238
Lookout	25868
Loom	26704
Looneyville	25259
Lorado	25630
Lorentz	26229
Lorton Lick	24701
Lost City	26810
Lost Creek	26385
Lost River	26811
Loudenville	26033
Loudon Heights (Part of Charleston)	25314
Louise	25070
Loveridge	24966
Lovern	24740
Lowdell	26169
Lowell	24962
Lower Belle	25015
Lower Falls	25177
Lower Nicut	26633
Low Gap	25130
Lowney	25666
Lowsville	26533
Lubeck	26101
Lucas	25938
Lucretia	26354
Lumberport	26386
Lundale	25631
Lyburn	25632
Lynco	24857
Lynn	25678
Lynn Camp	26039
Lynwinn	25823
Lyonsville	26651
Maben	25870
Mabie	26278
Mabscott	25871
MacAlpin	25921
MacArthur	25873
McCauley	26801
McClellan	26582
McCloud	25671
Mc Comas	24735
Mc Connell	25633
McCorkle	25564
McCreery	25934

Name	ZIP
Macdale	26521
Macdonald	25880
Mc Dowell	24810
MacDunn	25161
Mace	26294
Macfarlan	26148
McGee	26354
Mc Graws	25875
McGuire Park	26452
McIntire	26369
McKeefrey	26041
McKinleyville	26070
Macksville	26884
Mc Mechen	26040
Macomber	26425
McRoss	25962
Mc Whorter	26401
Madam Creek	25951
Madeline	25811
Madison	25130
Madison Run	26705
Magnolia (Morgan County)	25422
Magnolia (Upshur County)	26218
Mahan	25131
Maher	25661
Mahone	26362
Maidsville	26541
Maitland	24886
Majorsville	26036
Malcom Spring Heights	25541
Malden	25306
Mallory	25634
Mallory (Part of Davin)	25617
Mammoth	25132
Man	25635
M and K Junction (Part of Rowlesburg)	26425
Manheim	26425
Manila	25508
Manleys Church	26554
Mannings	25425
Mannington	26582
Manown	26537
Mansfield (Part of Philippi)	26416
Manus	25649
Maple Acres	24701
Maple Fork	25880
Maple Lake	26330
Maple Meadow	25865
Maple Point (Part of Barrackville)	26559
Maple View	24701
Maplewood	25874
Marfrance	25981
Margaret	26448
Marianna	24859
Marie	24918
Marie Heights	26101
Marine	24828
Market	26411
Markwood	26710
Marlaing Addition	25177
Marlinton	24954
Marlowe	25419
Marmet	25315
Marquess	26444
Marrtown	26101
Marshall	25252
Marshall Terrace	26070
Marshall University (Part of Huntington)	25703
Marshville	26332
Martha	25504
Martin	26743
Martinsburg	25401
Marvel	25812
Maryland Junction	26767
Marytown	24889
Mason	25260
Masontown	26542
Masonville	26847
Masseyville	25174
Matewan	25678
Matheny (Wood County)	26181
Matheny (Wyoming County)	24860
Mathias	26812
Matoaka	24736
Maud	26155
Maxine	25049
Maxwell	26170
Maxwell Acres	26041
Maxwelton	24957
Maybeury	24861
Maynor	25801
Maysel	25133
Maysville	26833
Mead	25915
Meadland	26330
Meador	25682
Meadow Bluff	24958
Meadow Bridge	25976

604 WEST VIRGINIA Meadowbrook-Osbornes Mills

	ZIP		ZIP		ZIP
Meadowbrook (Harrison County)	26404	Morgansville	26456	Newburg	26410
Meadowbrook (Kanawha County)	25311	Morgantown	26502-07	New Creek	26743
		For specific Morgantown Zip Codes call (304) 291-1035		New Cumberland	26047
Meadowbrook (Mason County)	25550	Morning Star	25276	Newdale	26155
Meadow Creek	25977	Morrall Mine	26416	Newell	26050
Meadowdale	26554	Morristown	26143	New England	26181
Meadowville	26250	Morrisvale	25565	New England Heights	26181
Meadville	26135	Mossy	25917	New Era	25275
Mechanicstown	25414	Moundsville	26041	Newhall	24866
Mechlenberg Heights	25443	Mountain	26407	New Hamlin	25523
Medina	26164	Mountain Cove	25938	New Haven	25265
Medley	26734	Mountaindale	26525	New Hill (Marion County)	26591
Melissa	25504	Mountaineer Mall (Part of Morgantown)	26505	New Hill (Monongalia County)	26527
Mellin	26362	Mountain Mission	25425	New Hope	24740
Melrose (Mercer County)	24712	Mountain View	26444	Newlon	26236
Melrose (Wood County)	26181	Mount Alto	25264	New Manchester	26056
Melville	25646	Mount Carbon	25139	New Martinsville	26155
Mercers Bottom	25123	Mount Clare	26408	New Milton	26411
Meredith Springs	26554	Mount De Chantel (Part of Wheeling)	26003	New Richmond	24867
Meriden	26416	Mount Echo	26060	New Thacker	25694
Merrimac	25661	Mount Gay	25637	Newton	25266
Metz	26585	Mount Gay-Shamrock	25601	Newtown	25686
Meyerstown	25414	Mount Harmony	26554	Newville	26601
Miami	25134	Mount Home	25113	Next	26175
Micco	25647	Mount Hope (Fayette County)	25880	Nicolette	26101
Middlebourne	26149	Mount Hope (Roane County)	25286	Nicut	26633
Middle Grave Creek	26041	Mount Hope (Wood County)	26160	Nimitz	25978
Middle Run	26623	Mount Liberty	26416	Nitro	25143
Middletown (Part of Richwood)	26261	Mount Lookout	26678	Nitro Park Addition	25143
Midkiff	25540	Mount Nebo	26679	Nobe	26137
Midland	26241	Mount Olive (Mason County)	25503	Nolan	25687
Midway (Barbour County)	26250	Mount Olive (Roane County)	25276	Nollville	25401
Midway (Mercer County)	24701	Mount Olivet (Marshall County)	26003	Normantown	25267
Midway (Putnam County)	25168	Mount Olivet (Mercer County)	24747	North Berkeley	25411
Midway (Raleigh County)	25878	Mount Pleasant	25446	North Charleston (Part of Charleston)	25312
Mifflin	25047	Mount Storm	26739	North Fairmont (Part of Fairmont)	26554
Milam (Hardy County)	26838	Mount Tabor	25801	Northfork	24868
Milam (Wyoming County)	25875	Mount Vernon (Preston County)	26547	North Hills	26101
Mile Branch	24811	Mount Vernon (Putnam County)	25526	North Matewan	25688
Millard	25276	Mountview	25825	North Mitchell Heights	25601
Millbrook	26711	Mount Welcome	25286	North Mountain	25427
Mill Creek	26280	Mount Zion (Calhoun County)	26151	North Parkersburg (Part of Parkersburg)	26104
Millersville	26554	Mount Zion (Tucker County)	26290	North River Mills	26711
Millertown	26354	Moyers	26813	North Spring	24869
Milliken	25071	Mozart	26003	North View (Part of Clarksburg)	26301
Mill Point	24959	Mozer	26866	Norton	26285
Mill Run	26271	Mud	25565	Norway	26554
Millstone (Calhoun County)	25261	Muddlety	26651	Norwood (Part of Fairmont)	26554
Millstone (Mingo County)	25670	Mudfork (Calhoun County)	25235	Numan	26426
Milltown	25163	Mudfork (Logan County)	25649	Nuriva (Part of Mullens)	25882
Millville	25432	Mullens	25882	Nursery Gap	25514
Millwood	25262	Mullensville	24874	Nutter Farm	26161
Milo	25256	Munday	26152	Nutter Fort	26301
Milton	25541	Munson	24883	Nutter Fort Stonewood (Part of Nutter Fort)	26301
Minden	25879	Murphy	26201	Nutterville	25981
Mineral City	25617	Murphytown	26142	Oak Acres	26181
Mineralwells	26150	Murraysville	26153	Oakdale	26582
Mingo	26294	Muses Bottom	26153	Oak Flat	26802
Mink Shoals	25302	Mustang Acres (Part of Parkersburg)	26101	Oak Hill	25901
Minnehaha Springs	24954	Myra	25544	Oakmont (Mineral County)	26717
Minnie	26155	Myrtle (Boone County)	25165	Oakmont (Ohio County)	26003
Minnora	25268	Myrtle (Mingo County)	25684	Oakvale	24739
Miracle Run	26570	Nabob	25122	Oakview Heights	25530
Missouri Branch	25511	Nallen	26680	Oakwood Estates	26101
Mitchell	26807	Nancys Run	25276	O'Brion	25063
Mitchell Branch	25692	Naoma	25140	Oceana	24870
Mitchell Heights	25601	Napier	26631	Odaville	25275
Moatstown	26813	National	26505	Odd	25902
Moatsville	26405	Natrium	26055	Ohley	25147
Mobley	26437	Naugatuck	25685	Olcott	25314
Mohawk	24862	Neal	25530	Old Arthur	26816
Mohegan	24820	Neals Run	25444	Old Fields	26845
Moler Crossroads	25443	Nebo (Clay County)	25141	Omps	25638
Monarch	25039	Nebo (Upshur County)	26201	Ona	25545
Monaville	25636	Needmore	26801	Onego	26886
Monclo	25183	Neibert	25632	O'Neil	26461
Monitor	24976	Nellis	25142	Oney Gap	24740
Monkeytown	26814	Nelson	25163	Onoto	24954
Monongah	26554	Nemours	24738	Opekiska	26554
Monson	24836	Neola	24961	Oral Lake	26330
Montana Mines	26586	Neptune	26153	Orchard	24918
Montcalm	24737	Nestlow	25512	Orchard Hill	25438
Montcoal	25135	Nestorville	26405	Organ Cave	24970
Monterville	26282	Nethkin	26726	Orgas	25148
Montgomery	25136	Nettie	26681	Orient Hill	25958
Montgomery Heights	25057	Neville (Part of Beckley)	25801	Orlando	26412
Montpelier (Part of Clarksburg)	26301	New	25918	Orleans Road	25422
Montrose (Kanawha County)	25303	Newark	26143	Orma	25268
Montrose (Randolph County)	26283	Newberne	26409	Orr	26764
Moore	26283			Ortin Heights	25143
Moorefield	26836			Orville	25654
Mooresville	26529			Osage	26543
Morgan	26153			Osborne	25045
Morgan Heights (Part of Westover)	26505			Osbornes Mills	25045

Oscar-Rocksdale WEST VIRGINIA 605

Name	ZIP
Oscar	24966
O'Toole	24808
Otsego	25882
Ottawa	25149
Otto	25276
Ovapa	25150
Overfield	26416
Owings	26431
Oxford	26456
Packs Branch	25880
Packsville	25209
Pad	25286
Paden City	26159
Page	25152
Pageton	24871
Paint Creek Junction (Part of Pratt)	25162
Palace Valley	26224
Palermo	25546
Palestine (Greenbrier County)	24910
Palestine (Wirt County)	26160
Pansy	26847
Panther	24872
Paradise	25124
Parchment Valley	25271
Parcoal	26288
Pardee	25630
Park Addition	26070
Parkersburg	26101-06
For specific Parkersburg Zip Codes call (304) 485-7770	
Parkview (Ohio County)	26003
Parkview (Taylor County)	26354
Par Metta Crest	26184
Parsley Bottom	25676
Parsons	26287
Patterson Creek	26753
Paw Paw	25434
Pax	25904
Paynesville	24873
Peach Creek	25639
Peanut	26582
Pear	25918
Pecks Mill	25547
Pecks Run	26201
Peeltree	26238
Peewee	25252
Pemberton	25905
Pence Springs	24962
Peniel	25270
Pennsboro	26415
Pentress	26544
Peora	26431
Pepper	26330
Perkins	26634
Perry	26851
Persinger	26651
Petersburg	26847
Peterson	26423
Peterstown	24963
Petroleum	26161
Pettit Heights	26070
Pettry	24712
Pettry Bottom	25189
Pettus	25209
Pettyville	26101
Peytona	25154
Pharoah	25555
Pheasant Run	26276
Phico	25508
Philippi	26416
Piatt	25015
Pickaway	24976
Pickens	26230
Pickle Street	26321
Pickshin	25857
Pie	25670
Piedmont	26750
Pierce	26292
Pierpont (Monongalia County)	26505
Pierpont (Wyoming County)	25870
Pigeon	25164
Pike	26346
Pikeside	25401
Pinch	25156
Pine Bluff	26431
Pine Creek	25625
Pine Grove (Kanawha County)	25143
Pine Grove (Marion County)	26554
Pine Grove (Wetzel County)	26419
Pineknob	25140
Pineville	24874
Piney	26167
Piney View	25906
Pinoak	24733
Pipestem	25979
Pisgah	26525
Pleasant Creek	26416

Name	ZIP
Pleasant Dale	26704
Pleasant Hill	26147
Pleasant Home	26133
Pleasant Valley (Hancock County)	26062
Pleasant Valley (Marion County)	26554
Pleasant Valley (Marshall County)	26033
Pleasant Valley (Monongalia County)	26505
Pleasant Valley (Ohio County)	26003
Pleasant View (Jackson County)	26164
Pleasant View (Lincoln County)	25506
Pleasant View (Marion County)	26588
Pleasure Valley	26283
Pliny	25158
Plum Orchard	25271
Pluto	25951
Plymouth	25011
Poca	25159
Pocatalico	25320
Poe	26683
Point Lick Junction	25306
Point Mills (Part of Valley Grove)	26059
Point Pleasant	25550
Points	25437
Polard	26149
Polemic	26601
Polk Gap	25870
Pondco	25208
Pond Creek	26133
Pond Gap	25160
Pond Junction (Part of Madison)	25130
Pool	26684
Port Amherst	25306
Porters Falls	26162
Porterwood	26283
Porto Rico	26411
Posey	25180
Potomac	15376
Potomac Manor	21538
Potomac Park	25419
Powell	26554
Powell Creek	25130
Powellton	25161
Powhatan	24877
Pratt	25162
Premier	24878
Prenter	25163
Price	25540
Price Hill (Boone County)	25130
Price Hill (Raleigh County)	25818
Price Hill Junction (Part of Mount Hope)	25880
Pricetown (Lewis County)	26452
Pricetown (Wetzel County)	26437
Prichard	25555
Priestly	25003
Prince	25907
Princeton	24740
Princewick	25908
Procious	25164
Proctor	26055
Propstburg	26802
Prospect Valley	26431
Prosperity	25909
Prudence	25901
Pruntytown	26354
Pullman	26421
Pumpkintown	26257
Purgitsville	26852
Puritan	25670
Pursglove	26546
Pursley	26175
Quaker	25511
Quarrier	25122
Queens	26237
Queen Shoals	25045
Quick	25045
Quiet Dell	26408
Quinland	25205
Quinnimont	25910
Quinwood	25981
Rachel	26587
Racine	25165
Racy	26161
Rada	26852
Radnor	25517
Ragland	25690
Rainelle	25962
Raines Corner	24951
Raintown	24959
Raleigh	25911
Ramage	25166

Name	ZIP
Ramp	25985
Ramsey	25912
Rand	25306
Randall	26543
Ranger	25557
Ranson	25438
Raven	26651
Ravencliff	25913
Raven Rock	26170
Raven Rocks	26763
Ravenswood	26164
Rawl	25691
Rayburn	25550
Raymond City	25159
Raysal	24879
Reader	26167
Ream (Part of Gary)	24836
Reamer	25045
Red Creek	26289
Redhill	26101
Red House	25168
Red Jacket	25692
Red Run	26271
Red Spring	25976
Redstar	25914
Red Sulphur Springs	24918
Red Warrior Junction	25122
Reedson	25442
Reedsville	26547
Reedy	25270
Reedyville	25276
Reeses Mill	26726
Reger	26201
Renick	24966
Renicks Valley	24966
Rensford	25306
Replete	26222
Reston	25130
Reynoldsville	26422
Rhodell	25915
Richard	26505
Richardson	25234
Richland	24901
Richwood	26261
Rider	26385
Ridersville	25411
Ridgedale	26505
Ridge Farms	26588
Ridgeley	26753
Ridgeview (Boone County)	25169
Ridgeview (Logan County)	25637
Ridgeville	26710
Ridgeway	25440
Riffle	26601
Rift	24892
Rig	26836
Riley	25927
Rinehart	26448
Ringold	26505
Rio	26755
Ripley	25271
Ripley Landing	25262
Ripling Waters	25248
Rippon	25441
Rita	25632
Riverbend	25177
Riverlake Estates	25177
Riverlawn (Part of St. Albans)	25177
Riverside (Kanawha County)	25086
Riverside (Monongalia County)	26505
Riverton	26814
Rivesville	26588
Rivesville Junction (Part of Rivesville)	26588
Roach	25504
Roanoke	26423
Roberts	26456
Robertsburg	25172
Robey	26386
Robinette	25607
Robson	25173
Rock	24747
Rock Camp	24951
Rock Castle	25272
Rock Cave	26234
Rock Creek	25174
Rockford	26385
Rock Forge	26505
Rock Gap	25411
Rock Lake	26554
Rock Lake Village (Part of South Charleston)	25309
Rock Lick (Fayette County)	25879
Rocklick (Marshall County)	26033
Rock Oak	26801
Rockport	26169
Rockridge	24873
Rock Run	26456
Rocksdale	25234

606 WEST VIRGINIA Rockton-Summers

	ZIP		ZIP		ZIP
Rockton	26623	Security Hills	25414	South Park (Kanawha County)	25304
Rock View	24880	Sedalia	26426	South Park (Lewis County)	26378
Rockville	25540	Seebert	24946	South Parkersburg (Part of Parkersburg)	26101
Rocky Fork	25312	Selbyville	26236
Rodemer	26764	Seminole	26361
Roderfield	24881	Seneca Rocks	26884	South Ruffner (Part of Charleston)	25304
Rohr	26547	Seng Creek	25209
Rolfe	24897	Servia	25063	Southside	25187
Rollins Branch	24870	Seth	25181	South Side Junction (Part of Thurmond)	25936
Romance	25248	Seven Pines	26582
Romines Mills	26385	Shadow Lawn (Part of Charleston)	25311	South Worthington	26591
Romney	26757			Spangler	25160
Romont	25812	Shady Brook (Part of Weston)	26452	Spanishburg	25922
Ronceverte	24970			Spaulding	25666
Ronda	25182	Shady Spring	25918	Spears	25540
Roneys Point	26059	Shafer	26290	Speed	25276
Rosebud	26386	Shamrock	25614	Speedway	24712
Roseby Rock	26041	Shanghai	25427	Spelter	26438
Rosedale (Fayette County)	25901	Shanks	26761	Spencer	25276
Rosedale (Gilmer County)	26636	Shannondale	25425	Spencer Hospital	25276
Rosedale (Monongalia County)	26541	Sharon	25182	Spice	24946
		Sharon Heights	25621	Sprague	25926
Rosemont	26424	Sharples	25183	Sprattsville	25621
Roseville Addition	25177	Shawvers Crossing	24931	Spread	25043
Rossmore	25643	Shegon	25649	Sprigg	25693
Rough Run	26866	Shenandoah Junction	25442	Spring Creek	24966
Round Bottom	26575	Shepherdstown	25443	Spring Dale (Fayette County)	25986
Round Knob	25033	Sheridan	25506
Rowlesburg	26425	Sherman	26173	Springdale (Ohio County)	26003
Roxalana (Kanawha County)	25064	Sherrard	26003	Springfield	26763
Roxalana (Roane County)	25259	Sherwood	26456	Spring Gap	25444
Ruddle	26807	Shiloh (Raleigh County)	25844	Spring Hill (Harrison County)	26301
Rumble	25009	Shiloh (Tyler County)	26146	Spring Hill (Kanawha County)	25309
Runa	26688	Shinnston	26431
Rupert	25984	Shirley	26434	Springton	24736
Rush Creek	25276	Shively	25508	Spring Valley	25701
Rush Run	25274	Shoals	25562	Spurlockville	25565
Rusk	26161	Shock	26638	Squire	24884
Russelldale	26710	Short Creek	26058	Stanaford (Raleigh County)	25927
Russellville	26680	Short Creek Valley	26003	Standard	25083
Russellville Road	25981	Short Gap	26726	Star City	26505
Russett	26147	Short Line Junction (Part of Clarksburg)	26301	Staten	25274
Ruth	25314			Statler Run	26570
Ruthbelle	26519	Shrewsbury	25015	Statts Mills	25279
Rutherford	26362	Shriver	26546	Stealey (Part of Clarksburg)	26301
Rutledge	25311	Sias	25563	Steeles	24844
Ryanville	26330	Sidneyville	25271	Steelton (Part of New Martinsville)	26155
Rymer	26582	Sigman	25168
Sabine	25916	Silver Grove	25425	Steep Gut Hollow	25687
Sabraton (Part of Morgantown)	26505	Silver Hill	26155	Stephenson	25928
		Silver Lake	26769	Steptown	25674
Sago	26201	Silverton	26164	Stevenboro	26444
St. Albans	25177	Simoda	26814	Stewart	26101
St. Clara	26445	Simon	24882	Stewart Chapel	26301
St. Cloud	26575	Simpson	26435	Stewartstown	26505
St. George	26290	Sinclair	26405	Stickney	25188
St. Joe (Part of Albright)	26519	Sinks Grove	24976	Stillman	26234
St. Joseph	26055	Sir Johns Run	25411	Stinson	25235
St. Marys	26170	Sissonville	25320	Stirrat	25645
Salem	26426	Sistersville	26175	Stohrs Cross Roads	25411
Salt Hill	25271	Six	24824	Stollings	25646
Saltlick Bridge	26627	Six Mile	25053	Stone Branch	25508
Saltpetre	25514	Skeetersville	25442	Stonecoal	25674
Salt Rock	25559	Skelton	25919	Stoneville	24834
Salt Sulphur Springs	24983	Skygusty	24883	Stonewall (Part of Charleston)	25302
Saltwell	26330	Slab Fork	25920
Sam Black Church	24928	Slabtown	25621	Stonewood	26301
Sanderson	25045	Slagle	25654	Stony Bottom	24927
Sand Fork	26430	Slanesville	25444	Stony River	26739
Sand Hill	26003	Slate	26143	Stotesbury	25921
Sandlick	24701	Slatyfork	26291	Stotlers Crossroads	25411
Sand Lick Junction	26435	Sleepy Creek	25411	Stouts Mills	26439
Sand Ridge	25274	Smithburg	26436	Stover	25844
Sand Run	26201	Smith Crossroads	25411	Stowe	25607
Sandstone	25985	Smithers	25186	Strange Creek	26639
Sandy Huff	26844	Smithfield (Jefferson County)	25430	Streby	26833
Sandy Summit	25252			Streeter	25969
Sandyville	25275	Smithfield (Wetzel County)	26437	Stringtown (Barbour County)	26250
Sanford	26554	Smithtown	26505	Stringtown (Marion County)	26582
Sanger	25901	Smithville (Marion County)	26588	Stringtown (Randolph County)	26263
Sanoma	26160	Smithville (Ritchie County)	26178
Sarah Ann	25644	Smoke Hole	26866	Stringtown (Roane County)	25276
Sardis	26301	Smoot	24977	Strouds	26208
Sarton	24973	Snider	26537	Stumptown	25280
Sassafras	25287	Snowden	25573	Sturgisson	26505
Sattes (Part of Nitro)	25143	Snow Flake	24936	Sugar Camp	26411
Saulsbury	26150	Snow Hill	25311	Sugar Grove	26815
Saulsville	25876	Snowshoe	26209	Sugar Tree	25521
Saunders	25630	Sod	25564	Sugar Valley (Pleasants County)	26135
Saxman	26202	Sodom	25183
Saxon	25180	Somerville	26181	Sugar Valley (Preston County)	26525
Scarbro	25917	Sophia	25921
Scarlet	25670	South Charleston	25303	Sullivan (Raleigh County)	25847
Scary	25177	South Fork Junction	24883	Sullivan (Randolph County)	26241
Scherr	26726	South Hills (Kanawha County)	25314	Sully	26254
Schrader	25071			Sulphur	26717
Schultz	26170	South Hills (Monongalia County)	26505	Sulphur Spring	25625
Scott Depot	25560			Sumerco	25567
Scrabble	25443	South Madison (Part of Madison)	25130	Summerlee	25931
Seaman	25252		
Secondcreek	24974	South Malden	25306	Summers	26456

Summersville-Whites Creek **WEST VIRGINIA 607**

Name	ZIP
Summersville	26651
Summit (Lincoln County)	25567
Summit (Wood County)	26101
Summit Park	26301
Summit Point	25446
Sun	25846
Sunbeam	25076
Suncrest (Part of Morgantown)	26505
Sundial	25189
Sun Flower	25252
Sun Hill	24822
Sunlight	24982
Sunset Acres	26452
Sunset Beach	26505
Sunset Court	25508
Sunshine	26582
Sun Valley (Hancock County)	26062
Sun Valley (Harrison County)	26301
Sun Valley (Kanawha County)	25177
Superior	24886
Superior Bottom	25638
Surosa	25678
Surveyor	25932
Sutton	26601
Swamp Run	26201
Swandale	25043
Sweeneysburg	25801
Sweetland	25568
Sweet Run	25530
Sweet Springs	24980
Swiss	26690
Switchback	24887
Switzer	25647
Sycamore (Calhoun County)	25261
Sycamore (Harrison County)	26301
Sycamore (Logan County)	25625
Sydnor Addition	25694
Sylvester	25193
Tablerock	25813
Tablers	25428
Tacy	26416
Tad	25201
Tague	26623
Talbott	26250
Talcott	24981
Tallmansville	26237
Tamcliff	25621
Tams	25921
Tango	25523
Tanner	26179
Tannery	26836
Taplin	25648
Tappan	26354
Tarico Heights	25413
Tariff	25281
Tate	26623
Taylorville	25670
Teaberry	24901
Teays	25569
Tekram	25670
Tempa	24910
Ten Mile	26237
Tennerton	26201
Tera Rosa	26181
Terra Alta	26764
Terry	25934
Tesla	26629
Teter	26238
Teterton	26886
Thacker	25694
Thacker Mines	25694
Thayer	25936
The Mileground	26505
The Y	25275
Thoburn	26554
Thomas	26292
Thompson Town	25637
Thornhill	24735
Thornton	26440
Thornwood	24920
Thorpe (Part of Gary)	24888
Thousand Oaks (Part of Charleston)	25303
Three Churches	26765
Threefork Bridge	26374
Three Mile	25071
Thurmond	25936
Thursday	26178
Tichenal	26385
Tidewater	24853
Tilden	25847
Tioga	26691
Tolleys (Part of Beckley)	25801
Toll Gate	26415
Tomahawk	25427
Toney	25524
Toneyfork	24870

Name	ZIP
Tophet	25979
Topins Grove	26153
Tornado	25202
Tourison	25840
Town Hill (Part of Petersburg)	26847
Trace	25671
Trace Fork	25320
Trace Junction	25625
Tralee	24710
Traphill	25932
Triadelphia	26059
Tribble	25123
Triplett	25043
Tripp	25669
Triune	26505
Trout	24982
Troy	26443
Troy Town	25649
Trubada	26351
True	25988
Tuckahoe	24986
Tunnelton	26444
Turkey Gap	24736
Turkey Knob (Fayette County)	25880
Turkey Knob (Marion County)	26591
Turner Douglass	21550
Turnertown	26452
Turtle Creek	25203
Twilight	25204
Twin Branch	24889
Two Lick	26378
Two Mile (Part of Charleston)	25301
Two Run	26160
Tygart (Part of Parkersburg)	26101
Tyler	26320
Tyler Heights	25312
Tyler Mountain	25312
Tyrone	26505
Uffington	26505
Uler	25266
Uneeda	25205
Unger	25411
Union	24983
Union Addition	25136
Union City	24844
Union Ridge	25520
United	25122
Unus	24938
Upland (Mason County)	25082
Upland (McDowell County)	24877
Upper Addis Run	26362
Upperglade	26266
Upper Leatherwood	25019
Upper Mingo	26294
Upper Tract	26866
Upton Creek	25177
Ury	25853
Utica	26133
Uvilla	25442
Vadis	26445
Vago	24938
Vaie	25976
Valley Bend (Barbour County)	26250
Valley Bend (Randolph County)	26293
Valley Chapel	26446
Valley Falls	26566
Valley Fork	25283
Valley Furnace	26405
Valley Grove	26060
Valley Head	26294
Valley Point	26519
Vallscreek	24819
Van	25206
Vanclevesville	25401
Vandalia (Kanawha County)	25303
Vandalia (Lewis County)	26423
Van Junction	25206
Vanville	25401
Van Vorhis	26505
Varney	25696
Vaucluse	26170
Vaughan	26656
Vedra	24862
Vegan	26267
Venus (Part of Gary)	24836
Verdunville	25649
Verner	25650
Victor	25938
Victoria	26374
Vienna	26105
Villa	25311
Viola (Marion County)	26554
Viola (Marshall County)	26003
Virginia Heights	25177
Virginville	26035

Name	ZIP
Viropa	26431
Vivian	24891
Volcano	26180
Volga	26238
Vulcan	25697
Wadestown	26589
Wadeville	26133
Wahoo	26554
Wainville	26206
Waiteville	24984
Waldeck	26452
Walker	26180
Walker Lanes	26181
Walkersville	26447
Wallace	26448
Wallace Heights	25312
Wallback	25285
Walnut	25235
Walnut Bottom	26818
Walnut Grove	25414
Walnut Hill	25652
Walnut Valley Acres	25312
Walton	25286
Wana	26590
Wanda	25076
War	24892
Ward	25039
Warden	25927
Wardensville	26851
War Eagle	24844
Warriormine (Part of War)	24894
Warwood (Part of Wheeling)	26003
Washburn	26362
Washington	26181
Washington Gardens	26181
Washington Heights	25130
Washington Lake	26181
Waterloo	25123
Watson (Part of Fairmont)	26554
Waverly	26184
Wayne	25570
Wayside	24985
Weaver	26250
Webb	25669
Weberwood (Part of South Charleston)	25303
Webster	26354
Webster Springs	26288
Weircrest (Part of Weirton)	26062
Weirton	26062
Weirton Heights (Part of Weirton)	26062
Welch	24801
Wellford	25045
Wellington Heights	26416
Wellsburg	26070
Wendel	26347
Werner	26250
Werth	26651
West Charleston (Part of Charleston)	25302
West Columbia	25287
West Dunbar	25064
West End	26444
West Gilbert (Part of Gilbert)	25621
West Grafton (Part of Grafton)	26354
West Hamlin	25571
West Huntington (Part of Huntington)	25704
West Junction	25206
West Liberty	26074
West Logan	25601
West Milford	26451
Weston	26452
Westover	26505
West Pea Ridge	25705
West Raleigh	25911
West Romney	26757
West Union	26456
West Van Voorhis	26541
West Williamson (Part of Williamson)	25661
Weyanoke	24736
Wharncliffe	25651
Wharton	25208
Wheeler	26222
Wheeling	26003
Wheeling Island (Part of Wheeling)	26003
Whipple	25917
Whirlwind	25524
Whitby	25823
Whitehall	26554
White Oak (Raleigh County)	25989
Whiteoak (Ritchie County)	26421
White Oak Springs	26764
White Pine	26147
White Rock	26554
Whites Addition	25637
Whites Creek	25555

WEST VIRGINIA White Sulphur Springs-Zion

Name	ZIP
White Sulphur Springs	24986
Whitesville	25209
Whitman	25652
Whitman Junction	25652
Whitmer	26296
Whittaker	25083
Wick	26185
Wickham	25871
Widemouth	24736
Widen	25211
Wikel	24945
Wilbur (Logan County)	25632
Wilbur (Tyler County)	26320
Wilcoe (Part of Gary)	24895
Wildcat	26376
Wilding	26164
Wiley Ford	26767
Wileyville	26186
Wilkinson	25653
Willard	26431
William	26292
Williamsburg	24991
Williams Mountain	25163
Williamson	25661
Williamsport	26710
Williamstown	26187
Willis Branch	25880
Willow Bend	24983
Willow Island	26190
Willowton	24740
Wilmore	24844
Wilsie	26641
Wilson	26707
Wilsonburg	26461
Wilsondale	25699
Wilsontown	26234
Winding Gulf	25823
Windom	24859
Windsor Heights	26075
Windy	26143
Winebrenners Crossroad	25401
Winfield (Marion County)	26554
Winfield (Putnam County)	25213
Wingrove	25917
Winifrede	25214
Winifrede Junction (Part of Chesapeake)	25315
Winona	25942
Wiseburg	25275
Witcher	25015
Wolfcreek	24993
Wolfe	24751
Wolf Pen	24896
Wolf Run	26033
Wolf Summit	26462
Wood	25123
Woodcliff Acres	26181
Woodland	26055
Woodland Heights (Part of Charleston)	25314
Woodland Park (Part of Parkersburg)	26101
Woodrow	24954
Woodruff	26033
Woodville	25572
Woodward Woods (Part of Charleston)	25312
Worth	24897
Worthington	26591
Wriston	25840
Wyatt	26463
Wyco	25943
Wylo	25611
Wymer	26297
Wyoma	25515
Wyoming	24898
Yards	24659
Yates Crossing	25545
Yawkey	25573
Yellow Creek	26136
Yellow Spring	26865
Yolyn	25654
Youngs Bottom	25071
Yukon	24899
Zela	26651
Zerith	24951
Zevely	26537
Zigler	26807
Zinnia	26426
Zion	26218

Abbotsford-Bell Heights WISCONSIN 609

Name	ZIP
Abbotsford	54405
Abells Corners	53121
Abrams	54101
Abrams (Town)	54101
Ackerville	53086
Ackley (Town)	54409
Ada	53020
Adams (Adams County)	53910
Adams (Adams County) (Town)	53934
Adams (Green County) (Town)	53504
Adams (Jackson County) (Town)	54615
Adams (Walworth County)	53120
Adams Beach	54929
Addison	53002
Addison (Town)	53002
Adell	53001
Adrian (Town)	54648
Advance	54111
Afton	53501
Agenda (Town)	54514
Ahnapee (Town)	54201
Ainsworth (Town)	54462
Air Mail Facility (Part of Milwaukee)	53237
Akan (Town)	54655
Alaska	54216
Alban (Town)	54473
Albany (Green County)	53502
Albany (Green County) (Town)	53502
Albany (Pepin County) (Town)	54755
Albertville	54730
Albion	53534
Albion (Town)	53534
Albion (Jackson County) (Town)	54615
Albion (Trempealeau County) (Town)	54738
Alden (Town)	54017
Alderley	53066
Algoma (Kewaunee County)	54201
Algoma (Winnebago County) (Town)	54901
Allen	54770
Allens Grove	53114
Allenton	53002
Allenville	54904
Allouez (Brown County) (Town)	54301
Allouez (Brown County)	54301
Alma (Buffalo County)	54610
Alma (Buffalo County)	54610
Alma (Jackson County) (Town)	54611
Alma Center	54611
Almena (Barron County)	54805
Almena (Barron County) (Town)	54826
Almon (Town)	54416
Almond (Portage County)	54909
Almond (Portage County) (Town)	54909
Alpha	54840
Alto	53919
Alto (Town)	53919
Altoona	54720
Alvin	49936
Alvin (Town)	49936
Amberg	54102
Amberg (Town)	54102
Amery	54001
Amherst (Portage County)	54406
Amherst (Portage County) (Town)	54977
Amherst Junction	54407
Amnicon (Town)	54874
Amnicon Falls	54874
Anacker	53901
Anderson (Burnett County) (Town)	54840
Anderson (Iron County) (Town)	54565
Angelica	54162
Angelica (Town)	54162
Angelo	54656
Angelo (Town)	54656
Angus	54817
Aniwa (Shawano County)	54408
Aniwa (Shawano County) (Town)	54414
Annaton	53825
Anson	54729
Anson (Town)	54748
Anston	54301
Anthony	54755
Antigo (Langlade County)	54409

Name	ZIP
Antigo (Langlade County) (Town)	54409
Applecreek	54911
Apple River (Town)	54810
Appleton	54911-15
For specific Appleton Zip Codes call (414) 734-7141	
Applewood	53711
Arbor Vitae	54568
Arbor Vitae (Town)	54568
Arcade Acres	54971
Arcadia (Trempealeau County)	54612
Arcadia (Trempealeau County) (Town)	54612
Arena (Iowa County)	53503
Arena (Iowa County) (Town)	53503
Argonne	54511
Argonne (Town)	54511
Argyle (Lafayette County)	53504
Argyle (Lafayette County) (Town)	53504
Arkansaw	54721
Arkdale	54613
Arland	54004
Arland (Town)	54004
Arlington (Columbia County)	53911
Arlington (Columbia County) (Town)	53555
Armenia (Town)	54646
Armstrong (Fond du Lac County)	53079
Armstrong (Oconto County) (Town)	54149
Armstrong Creek	54103
Armstrong Creek (Town)	54103
Arnott	54481
Arpin	54410
Arpin (Town)	54410
Artesia Beach	53049
Arthur (Chippewa County) (Town)	54727
Arthur (Grant County)	53818
Ashford	53010
Ashford (Town)	53010
Ashippun	53003
Ashippun (Town)	53003
Ashland (Ashland County)	54806
Ashland (Ashland County) (Town)	54846
Ash Ridge	54664
Ashton	53562
Ashton Corners	53562
Ashwaubenon	54304
Askeaton	54126
Astico	53912
Athelstane	54104
Athelstane (Town)	54104
Athens	54411
Atlanta (Town)	54819
Atlas	54853
Attica	53502
Atwater	53922
Atwood	54460
Auburn (Chippewa County) (Town)	54757
Auburn (Fond du Lac County) (Town)	53040
Auburndale (Wood County)	54412
Auburndale (Wood County) (Town)	54412
Auburn Lake	53010
Augusta	54722
Aurora	49801
Aurora (Town)	49801
Aurora (Taylor County) (Town)	54433
Aurora (Waushara County) (Town)	54923
Auroraville	54923
Avalanche	54665
Avalon	53505
Avoca	53506
Avon (Town)	53520
Avon (Lafayette County)	53530
Avon (Rock County)	53520
Aztalan (Town)	53038
Babcock	54413
Badger Army Ammunition Plant (Sauk County)	53913
Bad River Indian Reservation	54806
Bagley (Grant County)	53801
Bagley (Oconto County) (Town)	54161
Baileys Harbor	54202
Baileys Harbor (Town)	54202
Bakerville	54449
Baldwin (St. Croix County)	54002
Baldwin (St. Croix County) (Town)	54028

Name	ZIP
Balsam Lake (Polk County)	54810
Balsam Lake (Polk County) (Town)	54024
Bancroft	54921
Bangor (La Crosse County)	54614
Bangor (La Crosse County) (Town)	54653
Baraboo (Sauk County)	53913
Baraboo (Sauk County) (Town)	53951
Barksdale	54806
Barksdale (Town)	54806
Barnes (Town)	54873
Barneveld	53507
Barnum	54631
Barre (Town)	54601
Barre Mills	54601
Barron (Barron County)	54812
Barron (Barron County) (Town)	54812
Barronett (Barron County)	54813
Barronett (Washburn County) (Town)	54871
Barron Junction (Part of Barron)	54812
Bartelme (Town)	54416
Barton (Washington County)	53095
Barton (Washington County) (Town)	53095
Basco	53508
Bashaw (Burnett County)	54871
Bashaw (Washburn County) (Town)	54871
Bass Bay (Part of Muskego)	53150
Bassett	53101
Bass Lake (Sawyer County) (Town)	54843
Bass Lake (Washburn County) (Town)	54875
Basswood	53573
Batavia	53001
Bateman	54729
Bay City	54723
Bayfield (Bayfield County)	54814
Bayfield (Bayfield County) (Town)	54814
Bay Park Square (Part of Ashwaubenon)	54304
Bay Settlement (Part of Green Bay)	54301
Bay Shore Shopping Center (Part of Glendale)	53217
Bayside	53217
Bayview (Bayfield County) (Town)	54891
Bay View (Milwaukee County) (Town)	53207
Beachs Corners	54627
Bear Bluff (Town)	54666
Bear Creek (Outagamie County)	54922
Bear Creek (Sauk County) (Town)	53577
Bear Creek (Waupaca County) (Town)	54922
Bear Lake (Barron County) (Town)	54868
Bear Lake (Rusk County)	54728
Bear Valley	53937
Beaver (Clark County) (Town)	54446
Beaver (Marinette County) (Town)	54114
Beaver (Polk County) (Town)	54889
Beaver (Marinette County)	54114
Beaver Brook (Town)	54871
Beaver Dam (Dodge County)	53916
Beaver Dam (Dodge County) (Town)	53916
Beaver Edge	53916
Beecher (Town)	54156
Beecher	54156
Beecher Lake	54156
Beechwood	53001
Beetown	53802
Beetown (Town)	53802
Beldenville	54003
Belgium (Ozaukee County)	53004
Belgium (Ozaukee County) (Town)	53004
Bell (Town)	54827
Bell Center	54631
Belle Plaine	54166
Belle Plaine (Town)	54166
Belleville	53508
Bellevue	54311
Bellevue (Town)	54311
Bell Heights (Part of Appleton)	54911

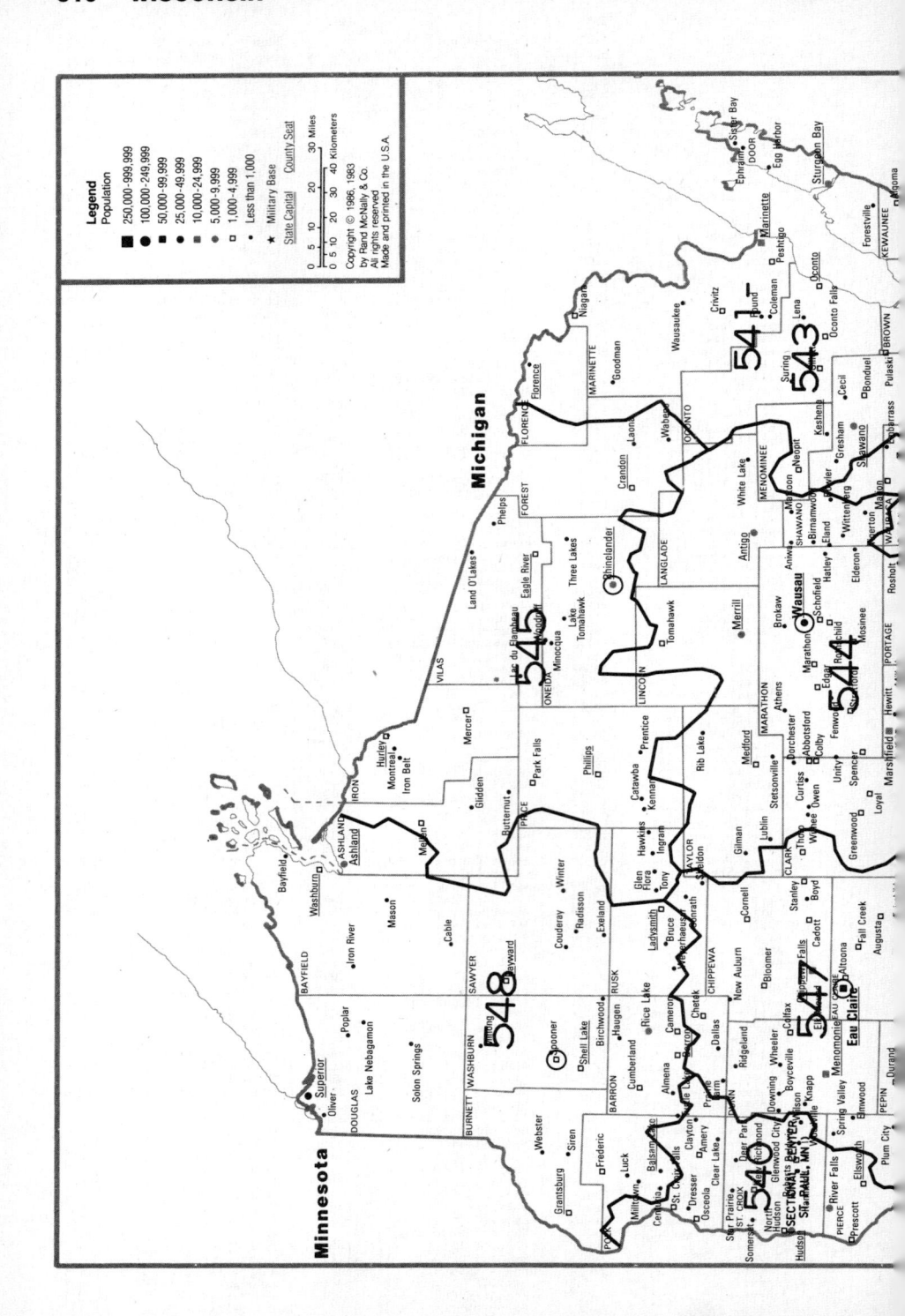

WISCONSIN

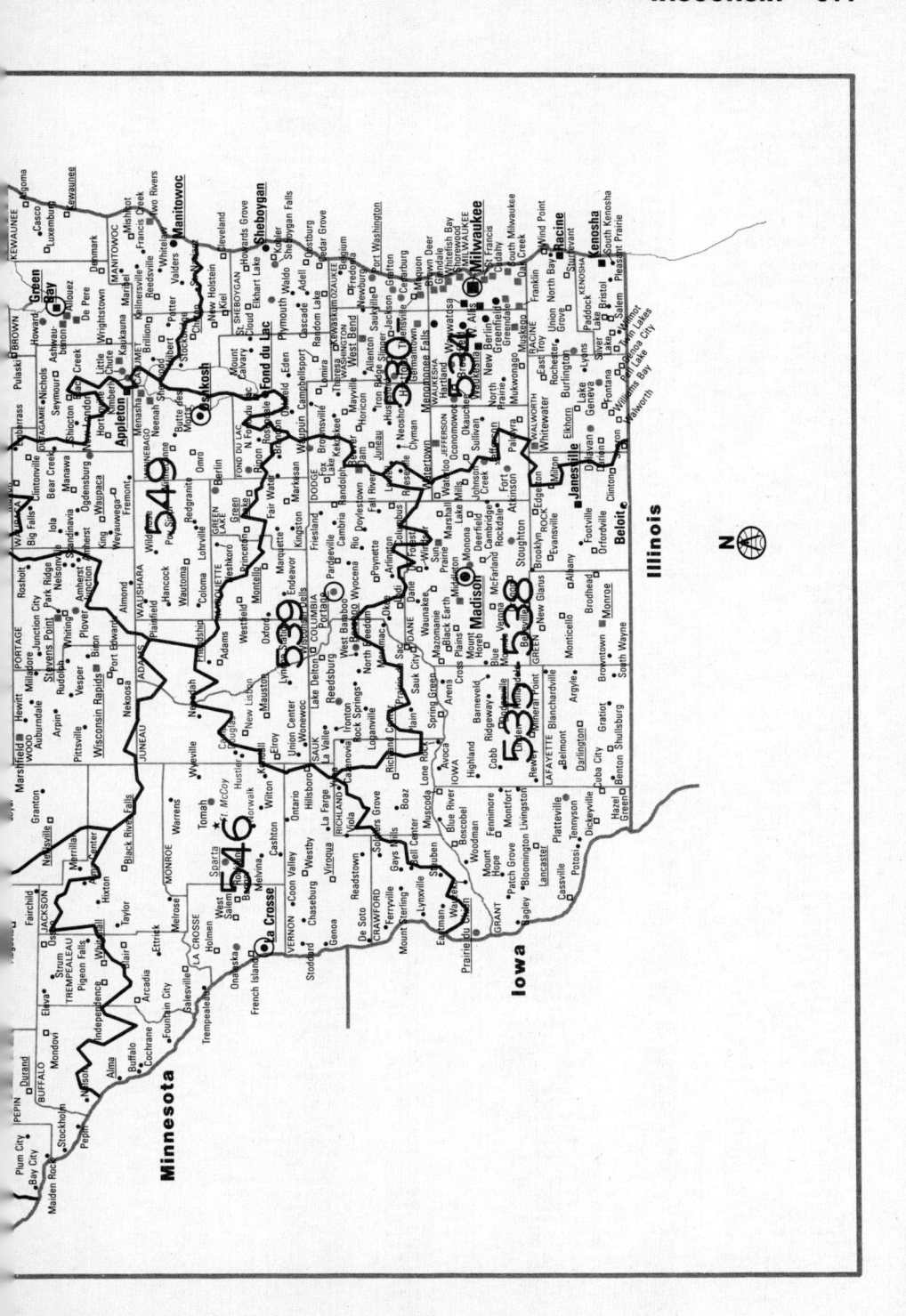

WISCONSIN 611

612 WISCONSIN Bellinger-Carter

Name	ZIP
Bellinger	54771
Bellwood	54820
Belmont (Lafayette County)	53510
Belmont (Lafayette County) (Town)	53818
Belmont (Portage County) (Town)	54909
Beloit (Rock County)	53511
Beloit (Rock County) (Town)	53511
Beloit Mall (Part of Beloit)	53511
Beloit North	53511
Belvidere (Town)	54610
Benderville	54301
Benet Lake	53102
Bennett	54873
Bennett (Town)	54873
Benoit	54816
Benton (Lafayette County)	53803
Benton (Lafayette County) (Town)	53803
Bergen (Marathon County) (Town)	54455
Bergen (Vernon County) (Town)	54658
Berlin (Green Lake County)	54923
Berlin (Green Lake County) (Town)	54923
Berlin (Marathon County) (Town)	54401
Bern (Town)	54411
Barry (Town)	54528
Bethel	54410
Bethesda	53186
Bevent	54440
Bevent (Town)	54440
Big Bend (Rusk County) (Town)	54819
Big Bend (Waukesha County)	53103
Big Falls (Rusk County) (Town)	54848
Big Falls (Waupaca County)	54926
Big Flats	53934
Big Flats (Town)	54613
Big Patch	53818
Big Spring	53965
Billings Park (Part of Superior)	54880
Binghamton	54106
Birch (Ashland County)	54559
Birch (Lincoln County) (Town)	54442
Birch Creek (Town)	54745
Birchwood (Washburn County)	54817
Birchwood (Washburn County) (Town)	54817
Birchwood Lake	53010
Birnamwood (Shawano County)	54414
Birnamwood (Shawano County) (Town)	54414
Biron	54494
Black Erook (Town)	54005
Black Creek (Outagamie County)	54106
Black Creek (Outagamie County) (Town)	54106
Black Earth (Dane County)	53515
Black Earth (Dane County) (Town)	53560
Black Hawk	53588
Black River	53081
Black River Falls	54615
Blackwell	54541
Blackwell (Town)	54541
Black Wolf (Town)	54901
Blaine (Burnett County) (Town)	55048
Blaine (Portage County)	54909
Blair	54616
Blanchard (Town)	53516
Blanchardville	53516
Blenker	54415
Bloom (Town)	54639
Bloom City	54617
Bloomer (Chippewa County)	54724
Bloomer (Chippewa County) (Town)	54724
Bloomfield (Walworth County) (Town)	53128
Bloomfield (Waushara County) (Town)	54965
Bloomingdale	54667
Blooming Grove (Town)	53701
Bloomington (Grant County)	53804
Bloomington (Grant County) (Town)	53810
Bloomville	54435
Blueberry	54854
Blue Mounds (Dane County)	53517

Name	ZIP
Blue Mounds (Dane County) (Town)	53572
Blue River	53518
Bluff Siding	54629
Bluffview	53913
Boardman	54017
Boaz	53581
Bohners Lake	53105
Bolt	54208
Boltonville	53040
Bonduel	54107
Bone Lake (Town)	54837
Borth	54923
Boscobel (Grant County)	53805
Boscobel (Grant County) (Town)	53805
Bosstown	53581
Boulder Junction	54512
Boulder Junction (Town)	54512
Bovina (Town)	54170
Bowers	53121
Bowler	54416
Boyceville	54725
Boyd	54726
Boydtown	53826
Brackett	54742
Bradford (Town)	53505
Bradley	54487
Bradley (Town)	54487
Bradley (Part of Milwaukee)	53223
Branch	54203
Brandon	53919
Branstad	54840
Brant	53014
Brantwood	54513
Braund Addition	54660
Brazeau (Town)	54161
Breed	54174
Breed (Town)	54174
Briarcrest Estates	53545
Briarton	54162
Briarwood	53575
Brickson Park	53558
Bridge Creek (Town)	54722
Bridgeport	53821
Bridgeport (Town)	53821
Briggsville	53920
Brigham (Town)	53507
Brighton	53139
Brighton (Kenosha County) (Town)	53139
Brigton (Marathon County) (Town)	54488
Brill	54818
Brillion (Calumet County)	54110
Brillion (Calumet County) (Town)	54110
Bristol (Dane County)	53104
Bristol (Dane County) (Town)	53590
Bristol (Kenosha County)	53104
Bristow	54665
Brockway (Town)	54615
Brodhead	53520
Brodtville	53801
Brokaw	54417
Brookfield (Waukesha County)	53005
Brookfield (Waukesha County) (Town)	53186
Brookfield Square (Part of Brookfield)	53005
Brookhaven	54494
Brooklyn (Green County)	53521
Brooklyn (Green County) (Town)	53521
Brooklyn (Green Lake County) (Town)	54941
Brooklyn (Washburn County) (Town)	54888
Brooks	53921
Brookside (Adams County)	53910
Brookside (Oconto County)	54101
Brookwood (Part of Madison)	53711
Brothertown	53014
Brothertown (Town)	53014
Brown Deer	53209
Browning (Town)	54451
Browns Lake	53105
Brownsville	53006
Browntown	53522
Bruce	54819
Bruemmerville	54201
Brule	54820
Brule (Town)	54820
Brunswick (Town)	54701
Brushville	54965
Brussels	54204
Brussels (Town)	54204
Bryant	54418

Name	ZIP
Buchanan (Town)	54911
Buck Creek	53581
Buckhorn Corner	53916
Buckman	54208
Budd	54665
Budsin	54960
Buena Park	53185
Buena Vista (Portage County) (Town)	54467
Buena Vista (Richland County) (Town)	53556
Buena Vista (Waukesha County)	53072
Buffalo (Buffalo County)	54622
Buffalo (Buffalo County) (Town)	54629
Buffalo (Marquette County) (Town)	53949
Buffalo Estates	53949
Bundy	54435
Bunker Hill	53924
Burke	53590
Burke (Town)	53590
Burkhardt	54016
Burlington (Racine County)	53105
Burlington (Racine County) (Town)	53105
Burnett	53922
Burnett (Town)	53922
Burnett Corners	53922
Burns (Town)	54614
Burns	54614
Burnside (Town)	54747
Burr Oak	54644
Burton	53820
Busseyville	53534
Butler (Clark County) (Town)	54771
Butler (Milwaukee County)	53213
Butler (Waukesha County)	53007
Butte des Morts	54927
Butternut	54514
Butternut Island	53039
Byrds Creek	53518
Byron	53009
Byron (Fond du Lac County) (Town)	53009
Byron (Monroe County) (Town)	54618
Cable (Bayfield County)	54821
Cable (Bayfield County) (Town)	54821
Caddy Vista	53108
Cadiz (Town)	53522
Cadott	54727
Cady (Town)	54027
Cainville	53536
Calamine	53565
Calamus (Town)	53916
Caldwell	53149
Caledonia (Town)	53108
Caledonia (Trempealeau County) (Town)	54630
Caledonia (Waupaca County) (Town)	54940
Caledonia (Columbia County) (Town)	53901
Caledonia (Racine County)	53108
Calhoun (Part of New Berlin)	53151
Calumet (Town)	53049
Calumetville	53049
Calvary	53057
Cambria	53923
Cambridge	53523
Cameron (Barron County)	54822
Cameron (Wood County) (Town)	54449
Campbell (Town)	54601
Campbellsport	53010
Camp Douglas	54618
Campia	54868
Camp Lake (Kenosha County)	53109
Camp Leonard	53558
Canton (Barron County)	54868
Canton (Buffalo County) (Town)	54736
Capitol (Part of Madison)	53701
Capitol Court (Part of Milwaukee)	53216
Carey (Town)	54534
Carlsville	54235
Carlton (Town)	54216
Carnot	54213
Carol Beach Estates	53140
Caroline	54928
Carrollville (Part of Oak Creek)	53154
Carson (Town)	54443
Carter	54566

Carthage College-Deer Creek WISCONSIN 613

Name	ZIP
Carthage College	53140
Cary (Town)	54466
Caryville	54701
Cascade	53011
Casco (Kewaunee County)	54205
Casco (Kewaunee County) (Town)	54216
Casey (Town)	54801
Cashton	54619
Cassel (Town)	54426
Cassian (Town)	54529
Cassville (Grant County)	53806
Cassville (Grant County) (Town)	53806
Castle Rock (Town)	53809
Castle Rock	53569
Caswell (Town)	54511
Cataract	54620
Catawba (Price County)	54515
Catawba (Price County) (Town)	54459
Cato (Town)	54206
Cato	54206
Cavour	54511
Cayuga	54546
Cazenovia	53924
Cecil	54111
Cedar	54559
Cedarburg (Ozaukee County)	53012
Cedarburg (Ozaukee County) (Town)	53012
Cedar Creek	53095
Cedar Falls	54751
Cedar Grove	53013
Cedar Lake (Town)	54868
Cedar Rapids (Town)	54526
Center (Outagamie County) (Town)	54911
Center (Rock County) (Town)	53545
Center House	53946
Center Lake Woods	53179
Center Ninety (Part of Onalaska)	54650
Center Valley	54106
Centerville (Manitowoc County) (Town)	53015
Centerville (Trempealeau County)	54630
Central Avenue (Part of Superior)	54880
Central Park (Part of Superior)	54880
Centuria	54824
Chaffey	54836
Chambers Island	54212
Champion	54229
Chapel Ridge Heights	54301
Charlesburg	53014
Charlestown (Town)	53014
Charlie Bluff	53563
Chase	54171
Chase (Town)	54171
Chaseburg	54621
Chelsea	54419
Chelsea (Town)	54419
Chenequa	53029
Cherokee	54421
Cherrywood	53593
Chester (Town)	53963
Chetek (Barron County)	54728
Chetek (Barron County) (Town)	54728
Chicago Corners	54115
Chicog (Town)	54888
Chili	54420
Chilton (Calumet County)	53014
Chilton (Calumet County) (Town)	53014
Chimney Rock (Town)	54770
Chippewa (Town)	54514
Chippewa Falls	54729
Chiwaukee	53140
Christiana (Dane County) (Town)	53523
Christiana (Vernon County) (Town)	54667
Christie	54456
Cicero	54165
Cicero (Town)	54165
City Point	54466
City Point (Town)	54466
Clam Falls (Town)	54837
Clam Falls	54837
Clam Lake	54517
Clark	54498
Clark Mills	54206
Clarks Point	54986
Clarno	53566
Clarno (Town)	53566

Name	ZIP
Claybanks (Town)	54201
Clayton (Crawford County) (Town)	54655
Clayton (Polk County)	54004
Clayton (Polk County) (Town)	54004
Clayton (Winnebago County) (Town)	54956
Clear Creek (Town)	54770
Clearfield (Town)	53950
Clear Lake (Polk County)	54005
Clear Lake (Polk County) (Town)	54005
Clear Lake (Rock County)	53563
Clearwater Lake	54521
Cleghorn	54738
Cleveland (Chippewa County) (Town)	54732
Cleveland (Jackson County) (Town)	54741
Cleveland (Manitowoc County)	53015
Cleveland (Marathon County) (Town)	54484
Cleveland (Taylor County) (Town)	54433
Clifford	54564
Clifton (Monroe County) (Town)	54618
Clifton (Pierce County) (Town)	54022
Clifton (Grant County) (Town)	53554
Clifton (Monroe County) (Town)	54618
Clinton (Barron County) (Town)	54805
Clinton (Rock County)	53525
Clinton (Rock County) (Town)	53525
Clinton (Vernon County) (Town)	54619
Clintonville	54929
Clover (Bayfield County) (Town)	54844
Clover (Manitowoc County)	54220
Cloverdale	54646
Cloverland (Douglas County) (Town)	54854
Cloverland (Vilas County) (Town)	54521
Clyde (Town)	53506
Clyde	53506
Clyman (Dodge County)	53016
Clyman (Dodge County) (Town)	53039
Cobb	53526
Cobban	54732
Cochrane	54622
Coddington	54467
Colburn (Town)	54726
Colburn (Adams County) (Town)	54943
Colburn (Chippewa County)	54726
Colby (Clark County)	54421
Colby (Clark County) (Town)	54421
Cold Spring	53538
Cold Spring (Town)	53538
Coleman	54112
Colfax (Dunn County)	54730
Colfax (Dunn County) (Town)	54730
Colgate	53017
Collins	54207
Coloma (Waushara County)	54930
Coloma (Waushara County) (Town)	54930
Coloma Corners	54930
Columbia	54456
Columbus (Columbia County)	53925
Columbus (Columbia County) (Town)	53925
Combined Locks	54113
Commonwealth	54121
Commonwealth (Town)	54121
Como	53147
Comstock	54826
Concord	53066
Concord (Town)	53066
Connorsville	54725
Conover	54519
Conover (Town)	54519
Conrath	54731
Cooks Valley (Town)	54724
Cooksville	53536
Coomer	54837
Coon (Town)	54621
Coon Rock	53503
Coon Valley	54623
Cooperstown	54208

Name	ZIP
Cooperstown (Town)	54227
Coral City	54773
Corinth	54411
Cormier (Part of Howard)	54301
Cornelia	53818
Cornell	54732
Corning (Town)	54452
Cornucopia	54827
Cottage Grove (Dane County)	53527
Cottage Grove (Dane County) (Town)	53527
Cottonville	53934
Couderay (Sawyer County)	54828
Couderay (Sawyer County) (Town)	54835
Country Estates	53105
County Line	54153
Courtland (Town)	53932
Crandon (Forest County)	54520
Crandon (Forest County) (Town)	54520
Cranmoor	54494
Cranmoor (Town)	54494
Cream	54610
Crescent (Chippewa County)	54727
Crescent (Oneida County) (Town)	54501
Crescent Park	53558
Crestview	53402
Crivitz	54114
Cross (Town)	54629
Cross Lake	60002
Cross Plains (Dane County)	53528
Cross Plains (Dane County) (Town)	53528
Crystal (Town)	54801
Crystal Lake (Barron County) (Town)	54826
Crystal Lake (Marquette County) (Town)	54960
Crystal Lake Corners	54981
Cuba City	53807
Cudahy	53110
Cumberland (Barron County)	54829
Cumberland (Barron County) (Town)	54829
Curran (Jackson County) (Town)	54635
Curran (Kewaunee County)	54208
Curtiss	54422
Cushing	54006
Custer	54423
Cutler	54646
Cutler (Town)	54618
Cylon	54017
Cylon (Town)	54017
Czechville	54629
Dacada	53075
Dairyland	54830
Dairyland (Town)	54830
Dakota	54982
Dakota (Town)	54982
Dale	54931
Dale (Town)	54931
Daleyville	53572
Dallas (Barron County)	54733
Dallas (Barron County) (Town)	54733
Dalton	53926
Danbury	54830
Dancy	54455
Dane (Dane County)	53529
Dane (Dane County) (Town)	53555
Daniels (Town)	54872
Danville	53925
Darboy	54911
Darien (Walworth County)	53114
Darien (Walworth County) (Town)	53115
Darlington (Lafayette County)	53530
Darlington (Lafayette County) (Town)	53530
Davis Corners	53965
Day (Town)	54484
Dayton (Green County)	53508
Dayton (Richland County) (Town)	53581
Dayton (Waupaca County) (Town)	54981
Deansville	53559
Decatur (Town)	53520
Deckers Corner	53012
Decorah Prairie	54630
Dedham	54836
Deerbrook	54424
Deer Creek (Outagamie County) (Town)	54170

WISCONSIN Deer Creek-Farmington

	ZIP
Deer Creek (Taylor County) (Town)	54480
Deerfield (Dane County)	53531
Deerfield (Dane County) (Town)	53531
Deerfield (Waushara County) (Town)	54943
Deer Park (Eau Claire County)	54742
Deer Park (St. Croix County)	54007
De Forest	53532
Dekorra (Town)	53955
Delafield (Waukesha County)	53018
Delafield (Waukesha County) (Town)	53072
Delavan (Walworth County)	53115
Delavan (Walworth County) (Town)	53115
Delavan Lake	53115
Dell	54667
Dellona (Town)	53965
Dell Prairie (Town)	53965
Dellwood	53927
Delmar (Town)	54726
Delta (Town)	54856
Delton (Town)	53959
Denmark	54208
Denoon (Part of Muskego)	53150
Denzer	53951
De Pere (Brown County)	54115
De Pere (Brown County) (Town)	54301
Deronda	54001
De Soto	54624
Dewey (Burnett County) (Town)	54845
Dewey (Douglas County)	54880
Dewey (Portage County) (Town)	54481
Dewey (Rusk County) (Town)	54563
Dewhurst (Town)	54456
Dexter (Town)	54466
Dexterville	54466
Diamond Bluff	54014
Diamond Bluff (Town)	54014
Dickeyville	53808
Diefenbach Corners	53086
Dilly	54634
Disco	54615
Dobie	54868
Dodge (Town)	54625
Dodge (Town)	54625
Dodge Correctional Institution	53963
Dodges Corners	53149
Dodgeville (Iowa County)	53533
Dodgeville (Iowa County) (Town)	53533
Doering	54435
Donald	54433
Dorchester	54425
Doty (Town)	54149
Dotyville	53057
Douglas (Town)	53930
Dousman	53118
Dover (Buffalo County) (Town)	54755
Dover (Racine County) (Town)	53182
Dovre (Town)	54757
Downing	54734
Downing Junction (Part of Downing)	54734
Downsville	54735
Downtown (Part of Oshkosh)	54901
Doyle (Town)	54868
Doylestown	53928
Drammen (Town)	54739
Draper (Town)	54896
Draper	54896
Dresser	54009
Drummond (Town)	54832
Drummond	54832
Drywood	54727
Duck Creek (Part of Howard)	54301
Dudley	54435
Dunbar	54119
Dunbar (Town)	54156
Dunbarton	53586
Dundas	54130
Dundee	53010
Dunkirk (Town)	53589
Dunkirk	53589
Dunn (Dane County) (Town)	53558
Dunn (Dunn County) (Town)	54751
Duplainville	53186

	ZIP
Dupont (Town)	54950
Durand (Pepin County)	54736
Durand (Pepin County) (Town)	54736
Durham (Part of Muskego)	53130
Durham Hill (Part of Franklin)	53132
Duvall	54217
Dyckesville	54217
Eagle (Richland County) (Town)	53573
Eagle (Waukesha County)	53119
Eagle (Waukesha County) (Town)	53119
Eagle Corners	53573
Eagle Lake	53139
Eagle Lake Manor	53139
Eagle Point (Town)	54729
Eagle River	54521
Eagleton	54724
Eagleville	53149
Earl	54875
East Bristol	53925
East Delavan	53115
East Ellsworth (Part of Ellsworth)	54010
East End (Part of Superior)	54880
East Farmington	54020
East Friesland	53956
East Krok	54216
Eastman (Crawford County)	54626
Eastman (Crawford County) (Town)	53826
Easton	53910
Easton (Adams County) (Town)	53910
Easton (Marathon County) (Town)	54471
East Side (Part of Madison)	53704
East Towne Mall (Part of Madison)	53704
East Troy (Walworth County)	53120
East Troy (Walworth County) (Town)	53120
East Waupun	53963
Eastwood	54494
Eaton (Brown County) (Town)	54217
Eaton (Clark County) (Town)	54437
Eaton (Manitowoc County) (Town)	53042
Eau Claire	54701-03
For specific Eau Claire Zip Codes call (715) 836-6470	
Eau Galle	54737
Eau Galle (Dunn County) (Town)	54737
Eau Galle (St. Croix County) (Town)	54028
Eau Pleine (Marathon County) (Town)	54484
Eau Pleine (Portage County) (Town)	54443
Eden (Fond du Lac County)	53019
Eden (Fond du Lac County) (Town)	53010
Eden (Iowa County) (Town)	53526
Edgar	54426
Edgerton	53534
Edgewater	54834
Edgewater (Town)	54834
Edgewood	53072
Edithton Beach	53140
Edmund	53535
Edson	54726
Edson (Town)	54726
Edwards	53015
Edwards Park (Part of McFarland)	53558
Egg Harbor (Door County)	54209
Egg Harbor (Door County) (Town)	54209
Eidsvold	54768
Eileen (Town)	54806
Eisenstein (Town)	54552
Eland	54427
Elba (Town)	53925
Elcho	54428
Elcho (Town)	54428
Elderon (Marathon County)	54429
Elderon (Marathon County) (Town)	54440
Eldorado	54932
Eldorado (Town)	54932
Eleva	54738
Elk (Town)	54555
Elk Creek	54747
Elk Grove (Town)	53807
Elk Grove	53807

	ZIP
Elkhart Lake	53020
Elkhorn	53121
Elk Mound (Dunn County)	54739
Elk Mound (Dunn County) (Town)	54739
Ella	54721
Ellenboro (Town)	53813
Elington (Town)	54944
Ellis	54481
Ellison Bay	54210
Ellisville	54217
Ellsworth (Pierce County)	54011
Ellsworth (Pierce County) (Town)	54003
Elm Grove	53122
Elmhurst	54409
Elm Island	53185
Elmore	53010
Elm Tree Corners (Part of Howard)	54301
Elmwood	54740
Elmwood Park	53405
Elmwood Plaza (Part of Racine)	53403
El Paso	54003
El Paso (Town)	54003
Elroy	53929
Elton	54430
Embarrass	54933
Emerald	54012
Emerald (Town)	54012
Emerald Grove	53545
Emery (Town)	54513
Emmet (Dodge County) (Town)	53094
Emmet (Marathon County) (Town)	54426
Empire (Town)	54935
Enchanted Valley Estates	53562
Endeavor	53930
Enterprise	54463
Enterprise (Town)	54463
Ephraim	54211
Erdman	53083
Erin (St. Croix County)	54017
Erin (Washington County) (Town)	53027
Erin Prairie (Town)	54002
Esadore Lake	54451
Esdaile	54723
Esofea	54667
Estella (Town)	54732
Ettrick (Trempealeau County)	54627
Ettrick (Trempealeau County) (Town)	54627
Eureka (Polk County) (Town)	54024
Eureka (Winnebago County)	54934
Eureka Center	54024
Euren	54205
Evansville	53536
Evergreen (Langlade County) (Town)	54491
Evergreen (Marathon County)	54455
Evergreen (Washburn County) (Town)	54801
Excelsior (Richland County)	53518
Excelsior (Sauk County) (Town)	53961
Exeland	54835
Exeter (Town)	53508
Exile	54761
Fahey Heights	53575
Fairbanks (Town)	54486
Fairburn	54923
Fairchild (Eau Claire County)	54741
Fairchild (Eau Claire County) (Town)	54741
Fairfield (Rock County)	53114
Fairfield (Sauk County) (Town)	53913
Fairplay	53811
Fairview (Crawford County)	54628
Fairview (Milwaukee County)	53219
Fairview Beach	54901
Fair Water	53931
Fall City	54739
Fall Creek	54742
Fall River	53932
Falun	54840
Fargo	54665
Farmersville	53050
Farmhill	54740
Farmington	53094
Farmington (Town)	53094
Farmington (La Crosse County) (Town)	54644

WISCONSIN Farmington-Grover

Name	ZIP
Farmington (Polk County) (Town)	54017
Farmington (Washington County) (Town)	53040
Farmington (Waupaca County) (Town)	54981
Fayette	53530
Fayette (Town)	53530
Federal Correctional Institution	53952
Fence	54120
Fence (Town)	54120
Fennimore (Grant County)	53809
Fennimore (Grant County) (Town)	53809
Fenwood	54426
Fern (Town)	54121
Ferron Park	54801
Ferryville	54628
Fifield	54524
Fifield (Town)	54524
Fillmore	53021
Finley	54646
Finley (Town)	54646
Fish Creek	54212
Fisk	54904
Fitchburg	53713
Five Corners (Outagamie County)	54911
Five Corners (Ozaukee County)	53012
Five Points	53518
Flambeau (Price County) (Town)	54555
Flambeau (Rusk County)	54745
Flambeau (Rusk County) (Town)	54848
Flintville	54301
Florence	54121
Florence (Town)	54121
Folsom	54655
Fond du Lac	54935-36
For specific Fond du Lac Zip Codes call (414) 921-9300	
Fontana	53125
Fontenoy	54208
Footville	53537
Ford (Town)	54433
Forest (St. Croix County) (Town)	54012
Forest (Vernon County) (Town)	54639
Forest (Fond du Lac County) (Town)	54935
Forest (Richland County) (Town)	54664
Forest (St. Croix County)	54012
Forest Junction	54123
Forest Mall (Part of Fond du Lac)	54935
Forestville (Door County)	54213
Forestville (Door County) (Town)	54213
Fort Atkinson	53538
Fort McCoy	54656
Fort Winnebago (Town)	53901
Forward	53572
Foster (Clark County) (Town)	54493
Foster (Eau Claire County)	54758
Fountain (Town)	53929
Fountain City	54629
Fountain Prairie (Town)	53932
Four Corners (Burnett County)	54837
Four Corners (Douglas County)	54880
Foxboro	54836
Fox Creek	54810
Fox Lake (Dodge County)	53933
Fox Lake (Dodge County) (Town)	53933
Fox Lake Correctional Institution	53933
Fox Point	53217
Fox River	53105
Fox River Mall (Part of Appleton)	54911
Francis Creek	54214
Frankfort (Marathon County) (Town)	54426
Frankfort (Pepin County) (Town)	54721
Franklin	54659
Franklin (Town)	54659
Franklin (Kewaunee County) (Town)	54216
Franklin (Manitowoc County) (Town)	54230
Franklin (Milwaukee County)	53132
Franklin (Sauk County) (Town)	53943
Franklin (Sheboygan County)	53073
Franklin (Vernon County) (Town)	54665
Franksville	53126
Franzen (Town)	54499
Frazer	54162
Frederic	54837
Fred John (Part of Milwaukee)	53225
Fredonia (Ozaukee County)	53021
Fredonia (Ozaukee County) (Town)	53075
Freedom (Outagamie County) (Town)	54131
Freedom (Sauk County) (Town)	53951
Freedom (Forest County) (Town)	54566
Freedom (Outagamie County)	54131
Freeman (Town)	54628
Freistadt (Part of Mequon)	53092
Fremont (Clark County) (Town)	54420
Fremont (Waupaca County)	54940
Fremont (Waupaca County) (Town)	54940
French Island	54601
Frenchville	54627
Friendship (Adams County)	53934
Friendship (Fond du Lac County) (Town)	54935
Friesland	53935
Frog Creek (Town)	54859
Fulton	53534
Fulton (Town)	53534
Fussville (Part of Menomonee Falls)	53051
Gale (Town)	54630
Galesville	54630
Galloway	54432
Garden Valley (Town)	54611
Garden Village	53511
Gardner (Town)	54204
Garfield (Jackson County) (Town)	54758
Garfield (Polk County) (Town)	54001
Garfield (Portage County)	54407
Garnet	53049
Gays Mills	54631
Genesee	53149
Genesee (Town)	53149
Genesee Depot	53127
Geneva (Town)	53121
Genevista	53147
Genoa (Vernon County)	54632
Genoa (Vernon County) (Town)	54624
Genoa City	53128
Georgetown (Grant County)	53807
Georgetown (Polk County) (Town)	54853
Georgetown (Price County) (Town)	54537
Germania (Iron County)	54550
Germania (Marquette County)	54960
Germania (Shawano County) (Town)	54486
Germantown (Juneau County) (Town)	53948
Germantown (Washington County)	53022
Germantown (Washington County) (Town)	53076
Gibbsville	53070
Gibraltar (Town)	54212
Gibson (Town)	54228
Gilbert	54487
Gile (Part of Montreal)	54525
Gillett (Oconto County)	54124
Gillett (Oconto County) (Town)	54124
Gillingham	53581
Gills Rock	54210
Gilman (Pierce County) (Town)	54767
Gilman (Taylor County)	54433
Gilmanton	54743
Gilmanton (Town)	54743
Gingles (Town)	54806
Glasgow	54627
Gleason	54435
Glenbeulah	53023
Glencoe (Town)	54629
Glendale (Town)	54638
Glendale (Milwaukee County)	53209
Glendale (Monroe County)	54638
Glen Flora	54526
Glen Haven	53810
Glen Haven (Town)	53810
Gienmore (Town)	54208
Glenwood (Town)	54012
Glenwood City	54013
Glidden	54527
Globe	54456
Goetz (Town)	54727
Goodman	54125
Goodman (Town)	54125
Goodnow	54529
Goodrich (Town)	54451
Goodrich	54411
Gooseville	53075
Gordon (Town)	54838
Gordon (Ashland County) (Town)	54527
Gordon (Douglas County)	54838
Gotham	53540
Grafton (Ozaukee County)	53024
Grafton (Ozaukee County) (Town)	53024
Grand Avenue, The (Part of Milwaukee)	53203
Grand Chute (Town)	54911
Grand Marsh	53936
Grand Rapids (Town)	54494
Grand View	54839
Grand View (Town)	54839
Granite Heights	54401
Grant (Clark County) (Town)	54436
Grant (Dunn County) (Town)	54730
Grant (Monroe County) (Town)	54666
Grant (Portage County) (Town)	54494
Grant (Rusk County) (Town)	54848
Grant (Shawano County) (Town)	54950
Granton	54436
Grantsburg (Burnett County)	54840
Grantsburg (Burnett County) (Town)	54840
Gratiot (Lafayette County)	53541
Gratiot (Lafayette County) (Town)	53541
Gravesville	53014
Green Acres	53121
Green Bay	54301-24
For specific Green Bay Zip Codes call (414) 498-3993	
Green Bay (Town)	54229
Green Bay Plaza (Part of Green Bay)	54303
Greenbush	53026
Greenbush (Town)	53026
Greendale	53129
Greenfield (La Crosse County) (Town)	54623
Greenfield (Milwaukee County)	53220
Greenfield (Monroe County) (Town)	54660
Greenfield (Sauk County) (Town)	53913
Greenfield Park (Part of Fitchburg)	53711
Green Grove (Town)	54460
Green Lake (Green Lake County)	54941
Green Lake (Green Lake County) (Town)	54941
Green Lake Terrace	54941
Greenleaf	54126
Greenridge Park	53558
Greenstreet	54227
Green Valley (Town)	54127
Green Valley (Marathon County) (Town)	54455
Green Valley (Shawano County)	54127
Greenville	54942
Greenville (Town)	54942
Greenwood (Clark County)	54437
Greenwood (Taylor County) (Town)	54451
Greenwood (Vernon County) (Town)	54634
Gregorville	54201
Grellton	53094
Gresham	54128
Grimms	54230
Grover (Marinette County) (Town)	54157
Grover (Taylor County) (Town)	54451

616 WISCONSIN Grow-Jewett

	ZIP		ZIP		ZIP
Grow (Town)	54563	Helena	53503	Hubbard (Dodge County)	
Guenther (Town)	54455	Helenville	53137	(Town)	53032
Gull Lake (Town)	54875	Helvetia (Town)	54962	Hubbard (Rusk County)	
Gurney	54528	Hendren (Town)	54493	(Town)	54848
Gurney (Town)	54528	Henrietta (Town)	53934	Hubbelton	53094
Hackett (Town)	54555	Henrysville	54217	Hub City	53581
Hager City	54014	Herbster	54844	Hubertus	53033
Halder	54455	Herman (Dodge County)		Hudson (St. Croix County)	54016
Hale	54758	(Town)	53078	Hudson (St. Croix County)	
Hale (Town)	54758	Herman (Shawano County)		(Town)	54016
Hales Corners	53130	(Town)	54166	Hughes (Town)	54820
Hallie	54729	Herman (Sheboygan		Huilsburg	53078
Hallie (Town)	54729	County) (Town)	53085	Hull (Marathon County)	
Halsey (Town)	54411	Herman Center	53050	(Town)	54421
Harold	54411	Herold	54610	Hull (Portage County)	
Hamburg		Hersey	54027	(Town)	54481
Hamburg (Marathon		Hertel	54845	Humbird	54746
County) (Town)	54411	Hewett (Town)	54456	Humboldt (Town)	54217
Hamburg (Vernon County)		Hewitt (Marathon County)		Humboldt	54229
(Town)	54621	(Town)	54401	Hunter (Town)	54843
Hamilton (Town)	54669	Hewitt (Wood County)	54441	Hunting	54486
Hammel (Town)	54451	Hiawatha Trail Estates	53934	Huntington	54017
Hammond (St. Croix		Hickory Corners	54174	Hurley	54534
County)	54015	Hickory Grove (Town)	53805	Huron	54768
Hammond (St. Croix		Hickory Hill	53593	Hurricane	53813
County) (Town)	54002	Hickory Hill Estates	53562	Husher	53108
Hampden (Town)	53960	Hickory Meadows	53597	Hustisford (Dodge County)	53034
Hamples Corners	54911	High Bridge	54846	Hustisford (Dodge County)	
Hampton (Part of		High Cliff	54952	(Town)	53039
Milwaukee)	53218	Highland (Douglas County)		Hustler	54637
Hancock (Waushara		(Town)	54849	Hutchins (Town)	54414
County)	54943	Highland (Iowa County)	53543	Hyde	53582
Hancock (Waushara		Highland (Iowa County)		Idlewild	54235
County) (Town)	54943	(Town)	53543	Iduna	54627
Haney (Town)	54631	Highland Park	53049	Imalone	54819
Hannibal	54439	Highland Shore	54904	Independence	54747
Hanover	53542	Hika (Part of Cleveland)	53015	Indian Creek	54837
Hansen (Town)	54489	Hilbert	54129	Indianford	53534
Hansonville	54822	Hilbert Junction (Part of		Indian Shores	54986
Happy Corners	53807	Hilbert)	54129	Ingram	54526
Harbor (Part of Milwaukee)	53204	Hiles	54511	Inlet	53115
Harding (Town)	54452	Hiles (Forest County)		Ino	54856
Harmony (Marinette County)	54143	(Town)	54511	Institute	54235
Harmony (Price County)		Hiles (Wood County) (Town)	54466	Iola (Waupaca County)	54945
(Town)	54515	Hill (Town)	54459	Iola (Waupaca County)	
Harmony (Rock County)		Hilldale (Part of Madison)	53705	(Town)	54945
(Town)	53545	Hilldale Shopping Center		Irma	54442
Harmony (Vernon County)		(Part of Madison)	53705	Iron Belt	54536
(Town)	54665	Hillpoint	53937	Iron Ridge	53035
Harmony Grove	53555	Hillsboro (Vernon County)	54634	Iron River	54847
Harris (Town)	53949	Hillsboro (Vernon County)		Iron River (Town)	54847
Harrison (Town)	54435	(Town)	54638	Ironton (Sauk County)	53941
Harrison (Marathon County)		Hillsdale	54744	Ironton (Sauk County)	
(Town)	54409	Hillside	53523	(Town)	53959
Harrison (Waupaca County)		Hilltop (Part of Milwaukee)	53205	Irving (Town)	54615
(Town)	54945	Hines	54874	Irvington	54751
Harrison (Calumet County)		Hingham	53031	Isaar	54165
(Town)	54911	Hintz	54124	Isabelle (Town)	54723
Harrison (Grant County)		Hixon (Town)	54498	Island Beach	54901
(Town)	53818	Hixton (Jackson County)	54635	Island Lake	54757
Harrison (Lincoln County)	54435	Hixton (Jackson County)		Island Park	54963
Harrisville	53949	(Town)	54635	Itasca (Part of Superior)	54880
Harshaw	54529	Hoard (Town)	54422	Ithaca	53581
Hartford (Washington		Hobart (Town)	54303	Ithaca (Town)	53581
County)	53027	Hofa Park	54165	Ives (Part of Racine)	53404
Hartford (Washington		Hoffman Corners	54638	Ives Grove	53177
County) (Town)	53027	Hogarty	54408	Ixonia	53036
Hartland (Pierce County)		Holcombe	54745	Ixonia (Town)	53036
(Town)	54011	Holiday Heights	53934	Jackson (Adams County)	
Hartland (Shawano County)		Holiday Hills	53511	(Town)	53952
(Town)	54107	Holland	54130	Jackson (Burnett County)	
Hartland (Waukesha		Holland (Town)	54130	(Town)	54893
County)	53029	Holland (La Crosse County)		Jackson (Washington	
Harvey Estates	53589	(Town)	54636	County)	53037
Hatchville	54751	Holland (Sheboygan		Jackson (Washington	
Hatfield	54754	County) (Town)	53070	County) (Town)	53037
Hatley	54440	Hollandale	53544	Jacksonport	54235
Hauer	54876	Hollister	54491	Jacksonport (Town)	54235
Haugen	54841	Holmen	54636	Jacobs (Town)	54527
Haven	53083	Holton (Town)	54405	Jamestown (Town)	53807
Hawkins (Rusk County)	54530	Holway (Town)	54451	Janesville	53545-47
Hawkins (Rusk County)		Holy Cross	53074	For specific Janesville Zip Codes	
(Town)	54530	Homestead (Town)	54121	call (608) 754-5555	
Hawthorne	54842	Honey Creek (Sauk County)		Janesville Mall (Part of	
Hawthorne (Town)	54842	(Town)	53577	Janesville)	53545
Hayes	54174	Honey Creek (Walworth		Jefferson (Green County)	
Hay River (Town)	54725	County)	53138	(Town)	53550
Hayton	53014	Honey Lake	53105	Jefferson (Jefferson	
Hayward (Sawyer County)	54843	Hoopers Mill	53551	County)	53549
Hayward (Sawyer County)		Hope	53527	Jefferson (Jefferson	
(Town)	54843	Horicon	53032	County) (Town)	53137
Hazel Green (Grant County)	53811	Horns Corners	53012	Jefferson (Monroe County)	
Hazel Green (Grant County)		Horse Creek	54026	(Town)	54619
(Town)	53811	Hortonia (Town)	54961	Jefferson (Vernon County)	
Hazelhurst	54531	Hortonville	54944	(Town)	54667
Hazelhurst (Town)	54531	Houlton	55082	Jefferson Junction	53549
Heafford Junction	54532	How (Town)	54174	Jenkynsville	53807
Heart Prairie	53190	Howard (Brown County)	54303	Jennings	54463
Hebel	54208	Howard (Chippewa County)		Jericho (Calumet County)	53014
Hebron	53538	(Town)	54730	Jericho (Waukesha County)	53119
Hebron (Town)	53538	Howards Grove-Millersville	53083	Jewett	54017
Hegg	54627				

Jim Falls-Lincoln WISCONSIN 617

Name	ZIP
Jim Falls	54748
Joel	54001
Johannesburg	54017
John P. Cofrin (Part of Green Bay)	54302
Johnsburg	53049
Johnson (Town)	54411
Johnson Creek	53038
Johnsonville	53085
Johnstown (Town)	53505
Johnstown (Polk County) (Town)	54889
Johnstown (Rock County)	53505
Johnstown Center	53545
Jonesdale	53565
Jordan (Green County) (Town)	53504
Jordan (Portage County)	54481
Jordan Center	53504
Jordan Lake	53965
Juda	53550
Jump River (Town)	54434
Jump River	54434
Junction City	54443
Juneau (Dodge County)	53039
Juneau (Milwaukee County)	53202
Kaiser	54552
Kansasville	53139
Kaukauna (Outagamie County)	54130
Kaukauna (Outagamie County) (Town)	54130
Keene	54921
Keenville	54901
Kekoskee	53050
Kellner	54494
Kellnersville	54215
Kelly (Bayfield County) (Town)	54856
Kelly (Marathon County)	54476
Kempster	54444
Kendall (Lafayette County) (Town)	53530
Kendall (Monroe County)	54638
Kennan (Price County)	54537
Kennan (Price County) (Town)	54537
Kenosha	53140-43
For specific Kenosha Zip Codes call (414) 657-3188	
Keshena	54135
Keshena Falls	54135
Kettle Moraine Correctional Institution	53073
Kettle Moraine Lake	53010
Kewaskum (Washington County)	53040
Kewaskum (Washington County) (Town)	53040
Kewaunee	54216
Keyeser	53532
Keyesville	53937
Keystone (Bayfield County) (Town)	54806
Keystone (Chippewa County)	54732
Kickapoo (Town)	54652
Kickapoo Center	54664
Kiel	53042
Kieler	53812
Kildare (Town)	53944
Kimball (Town)	54534
Kimberly	54136
King (Lincoln County) (Town)	54487
King (Waupaca County)	54946
Kingsbridge	54241
Kingston (Green Lake County)	53939
Kingston (Green Lake County) (Town)	53926
Kingston (Juneau County) (Town)	54641
Kinnickinnic (Town)	54022
Kirby	54666
Kirchhayn	53012
Klevenville	53572
Klondike	54112
Kloten	53014
Knapp (Dunn County)	54749
Knapp (Jackson County) (Town)	54666
Kneeland	53108
Knellsville	53074
Knight (Town)	54536
Knowles	53048
Knowlton	54455
Knowlton (Town)	54455
Knox (Town)	54513
Kodan	54201
Kohler	53044

Name	ZIP
Kohlsville	53095
Kolberg	54213
Komensky (Town)	54754
Koshkonong (Jefferson County) (Town)	53538
Koshkonong (Rock County)	53538
Kossuth (Town)	54220
Krakow	54137
Kroghville	53594
Krok	54216
Kronenwetter (Town)	54455
Kunesh	54162
Lac Courte Oreilles Indian Reservation	54876
Lac du Flambeau	54538
Lac du Flambeau (Town)	54538
Lac du Flambeau Indian Reservation	54538
Lac La Belle	53066
La Crosse	54601-03
For specific La Crosse Zip Codes call (608) 782-6034	
La Crosse Mall (Part of La Crosse)	54601
Ladoga	53963
Ladysmith	54848
La Farge	54639
Lafayette (Chippewa County) (Town)	54729
Lafayette (Monroe County) (Town)	54656
Lafayette (Walworth County) (Town)	53121
La Follette (Town)	54872
La Grange (Town)	53190
La Grange (Monroe County) (Town)	54660
La Grange (Walworth County)	53190
Lake (Marinette County) (Town)	54159
Lake (Price County) (Town)	54552
Lake Beulah	53120
Lake Camelot	54475
Lake Church	53004
Lake Como Beach	53147
Lake Delton	53940
Lake Eau Claire	54722
Lake Emily	54407
Lakefield	53024
Lake Five	53017
Lake Geneva	53147
Lake George (Kenosha County)	53104
Lake George (Oneida County)	54501
Lake Hallie	54729
Lake Holcombe (Town)	54745
Lake Ivanhoe	53147
Lake Keesus	53029
Lakeland (Town)	54813
Lakeland College	53081
Lake Lorraine	53115
Lake Mills (Jefferson County)	53551
Lake Mills (Jefferson County) (Town)	53551
Lake Nebagamon	54849
Lake Shangrila	60002
Lake Sherwood	54457
Lakeside (Town)	54874
Lake Tomahawk (Town)	54539
Lake Tomahawk	54539
Laketown (Town)	54006
Lake Wazeecha	54494
Lake Windsor	53598
Lake Wissota	54729
Lakewood	54138
Lakewood (Town)	54138
Lamartine	53065
Lamartine (Town)	53065
Lamont	53530
Lamont (Town)	53530
Lampson	54888
Lanark (Town)	54981
Lancaster	53813
Land O'Lakes	54540
Land O'Lakes (Town)	54540
Landstad	54107
Langes Corners	54208
Langlade (Langlade County)	54491
Langlade (Langlade County) (Town)	54465
Lannon	53046
Laona	54541
Laona (Town)	54541
La Pointe	54850
La Pointe (Town)	54850
La Prairie (Town)	53545
Lark	54126

Name	ZIP
Larrabee (Manitowoc County)	54241
Larrabee (Waupaca County) (Town)	54929
Larsen	54947
LaRue	53951
Lasleys Point	54986
Lauderdale	53121
La Valle (Sauk County)	53941
La Valle (Sauk County) (Town)	53941
LaVerne Dilweg (Part of Green Bay)	54303
Lawrence (Brown County) (Town)	54115
Lawrence (Marquette County)	53964
Lawrence (Rusk County) (Town)	54526
Lawton	54003
Layton Park (Part of Milwaukee)	53215
Leadmine	53807
Lebanon	53047
Lebanon (Dodge County) (Town)	53047
Lebanon (Waupaca County) (Town)	54961
Ledges	53532
Leeds	53571
Leeds (Town)	53571
Leeds Center	53911
Leeman	54170
Leipsig	53916
Leland	53951
Lemington	54835
Lemonweir (Town)	53948
Lena (Oconto County)	54139
Lena (Oconto County) (Town)	54139
Lenroot (Town)	54843
Leola (Town)	54921
Leon	54656
Leon (Monroe County) (Town)	54646
Leon (Waushara County) (Town)	54965
Leonards Point	54904
Leopolis	54948
LeRoy	53048
LeRoy (Town)	53048
Leslie	53510
Lessor (Town)	54107
Levis (Town)	54456
Lewis	54851
Lewiston	53965
Lewiston (Town)	53965
Leyden	53545
Liberty (Grant County) (Town)	53825
Liberty (Manitowoc County) (Town)	54245
Liberty (Outagamie County) (Town)	54170
Liberty (Vernon County) (Town)	54664
Liberty Grove (Town)	54202
Liberty Pole	54665
Liddell	54729
Lilly Lake	53105
Lily	54445
Lima (Grant County) (Town)	53818
Lima (Pepin County) (Town)	54736
Lima (Rock County) (Town)	53190
Lima (Sheboygan County) (Town)	53085
Lima Center	53190
Limeridge	53942
Lincoln (Town)	54205
Lincoln (Monroe County) (Town)	54666
Lincoln (Polk County) (Town)	54001
Lincoln (Trempealeau County) (Town)	54773
Lincoln (Vilas County) (Town)	54521
Lincoln (Wood County) (Town)	54449
Lincoln (Adams County) (Town)	53964
Lincoln (Bayfield County) (Town)	54856
Lincoln (Buffalo County) (Town)	54610
Lincoln (Burnett County) (Town)	54893
Lincoln (Eau Claire County) (Town)	54722
Lincoln (Forest County) (Town)	54520

618 WISCONSIN Lincoln-Milladore

Place	ZIP
Lincoln (Kewaunee County)	54205
Lind (Town)	54983
Lind Center	54981
Linden (Iowa County)	53553
Linden (Iowa County) (Town)	53565
Lindina (Town)	53948
Lindsey	54449
Linn (Town)	60034
Linton	53147
Linwood (Town)	54481
Lisbon (Juneau County) (Town)	53950
Lisbon (Waukesha County) (Town)	53089
Little Black	54451
Little Black (Town)	54451
Little Chicago	54448
Little Chute	54140
Little Fall (Town)	54656
Little Falls	54001
Little Grant (Town)	53813
Little Hope	54981
Little Kohler	53021
Little Prairie	53119
Little Rapids	54115
Little Rice (Town)	54564
Little River (Town)	54153
Little Rose	54484
Little Sturgeon	54235
Little Suamico	54141
Little Suamico (Town)	54141
Little Wolf (Town)	54949
Livingston	53554
Loddes Mill	53583
Lodi (Columbia County)	53555
Lodi (Columbia County) (Town)	53555
Loganville	53943
Lohrville	54970
Lombard	54771
Lomira (Dodge County)	53048
Lomira (Dodge County) (Town)	53006
London	53523
London Square Mall (Part of Eau Claire)	54701
Lone Rock (Juneau County)	54618
Lone Rock (Richland County)	53556
Long Lake	54542
Long Lake (Town)	54542
Long Lake (Fond du Lac County)	53011
Long Lake (Washburn County) (Town)	54817
Longwood	54498
Longwood (Town)	54498
Lookout	54755
Loomis	54159
Lorain (Town)	54837
Loretta	54896
Lost Lake	53956
Louisburg	53807
Louis Corners	53042
Lowell (Dodge County)	53557
Lowell (Dodge County) (Town)	53579
Lower Nemahbin Lake	53066
Lowville (Town)	53955
Loyal (Clark County)	54446
Loyal (Clark County) (Town)	54446
Loyd	53924
Lublin	54447
Lucas (Town)	54751
Luck (Polk County)	54853
Luck (Polk County) (Town)	54837
Ludington	54742
Ludington (Town)	54742
Lugerville	54555
Lund	54769
Lunds	54166
Luxemburg (Kewaunee County)	54217
Luxemburg (Kewaunee County) (Town)	54217
Lykens	54810
Lymantown	54552
Lyndhurst	54128
Lyndon (Juneau County) (Town)	53944
Lyndon (Sheboygan County) (Town)	53073
Lyndon Station	53944
Lynn	54436
Lynn (Town)	54436
Lynne (Town)	54564
Lynxville	54640
Lyons	53148
Lyons (Town)	53148
McAllister	54177
McCartney	53806
McFarland	53558
Mackford (Town)	53946
McKinley (Town)	54829
McKinley (Polk County)	54829
McKinley (Taylor County) (Town)	54766
Mackville (Outagamie County)	54911
McMillan (Town)	54449
McNaughton	54543
Madge (Town)	54870
Madison	53701-19
For specific Madison Zip Codes call (608) 246-1249	
Madsen	54220
Magenta (Part of Eau Claire)	54701
Magnolia	53536
Magnolia (Town)	53536
Maiden Rock (Pierce County)	54750
Maiden Rock (Pierce County) (Town)	54750
Maine (Marathon County) (Town)	54401
Maine (Outagamie County) (Town)	54170
Mallwood	53534
Malone	53049
Manawa	54949
Manchester	53945
Manchester (Green Lake County) (Town)	53945
Manchester (Jackson County) (Town)	54615
Manitowish	54547
Manitowish Waters (Town)	54545
Manitowish Waters	54545
Manitowoc	54220-21
For specific Manitowoc Zip Codes call (414) 682-6166	
Manitowoc Rapids (Town)	54220
Manitowoc Rapids (Part of Manitowoc)	54220
Maple	54854
Maple (Town)	54854
Maple Bluff	53704
Maple Creek (Town)	54961
Maple Grove (Barron County) (Town)	54744
Maple Grove (Manitowoc County)	54230
Maple Grove (Manitowoc County) (Town)	54110
Maple Grove (Shawano County) (Town)	54162
Maple Heights	53014
Maple Hills	53125
Maplehurst (Town)	54498
Maple Plain (Town)	54829
Mapleton	53066
Maple Valley (Town)	54174
Maplewood	54226
Marathon (Marathon County)	54448
Marathon (Marathon County) (Town)	54448
Marblehead	53019
Marcellon (Town)	53901
March Rapids	54484
Marengo (Ashland County)	54855
Marengo (Ashland County) (Town)	54855
Maribel	54227
Marietta (Town)	53805
Marinette	54143
Marion (Grant County) (Town)	53805
Marion (Juneau County) (Town)	53948
Marion (Waupaca County)	54950
Marion (Waushara County) (Town)	54960
Markesan	53946
Marquette (Green Lake County)	53947
Marquette (Green Lake County) (Town)	53946
Marshall (Dane County)	53559
Marshall (Richland County) (Town)	53581
Marshall (Rusk County) (Town)	54731
Marshfield (Fond du Lac County) (Town)	53057
Marshfield (Wood County)	54449
Marshfield (Wood County) (Town)	54449
Marshland	54629
Martell	54767
Martell (Town)	54767
Martinsville	53528
Martintown	61089
Marxville	53560
Mary Lake	53597
Marytown	53061
Mason (Bayfield County)	54856
Mason (Bayfield County) (Town)	54856
Mather	54641
Matteson (Town)	54929
Mattoon	54450
Mauston	53948
Maxville	54736
Maxville (Town)	54736
May Corner	54157
Mayfair Mall (Part of Wauwatosa)	53213
Mayfield	53037
Mayville (Clark County) (Town)	54425
Mayville (Dodge County)	53050
Mazomanie (Dane County)	53560
Mazomanie (Dane County) (Town)	53560
Mead (Town)	54437
Meadowbrook (Town)	54835
Mecan (Town)	53949
Medary (Town)	54650
Medford (Taylor County)	54451
Medford (Taylor County) (Town)	54451
Medina (Dane County) (Town)	53559
Medina (Outagamie County)	54951
Meeker (Part of Germantown)	53022
Meeme (Town)	53063
Meeme	53063
Meenon (Town)	54893
Meggers	53061
Mellen	54546
Melnik	54247
Melrose (Jackson County)	54642
Melrose (Jackson County) (Town)	54642
Melrose Park	54901
Melvina	54619
Memorial Mall (Part of Sheboygan)	53081
Menasha (Winnebago County)	54952
Menasha (Winnebago County) (Town)	54952
Menchalville	54206
Menekaunee (Part of Marinette)	54143
Menominee (Town)	54150
Menomonee Falls	53051
Menomonie (Dunn County)	54751
Menomonie (Dunn County) (Town)	54751
Menomonie Junction (Part of Menomonie)	54751
Mentor (Town)	54746
Mequon	53092
Mercer	54547
Mercer (Town)	54547
Meridean	54755
Merrill (Lincoln County)	54452
Merrill (Lincoln County) (Town)	54452
Merrillan	54754
Merrimac (Sauk County)	53561
Merrimac (Sauk County) (Town)	53561
Merton (Waukesha County)	53056
Merton (Waukesha County) (Town)	53029
Meteor (Town)	54835
Metomen (Town)	54971
Metz	54940
Mid-City (Part of Milwaukee)	53208
Middle Inlet	54114
Middle Inlet (Town)	54114
Middle Ridge	54614
Middleton (Dane County)	53562
Middleton (Dane County) (Town)	53562
Middleton Junction	53562
Midway (Brown County)	54301
Midway (La Crosse County)	54650
Mifflin	53580
Mifflin (Town)	53580
Mikana	54857
Mikesville	54901
Milan	54453
Milford	53551
Milford (Town)	53551
Milladore (Wood County)	54454

Milladore-Norrie WISCONSIN 619

	ZIP
Milladore (Wood County) (Town)	54412
Millard	53121
Mill Center	54301
Millersville (Part of Howards Grove-Millersville)	53083
Millhome	53042
Millston	54643
Millston (Town)	54643
Millstone Heights	53532
Milltown (Polk County)	54858
Milltown (Polk County) (Town)	54858
Millville	53827
Millville (Town)	53827
Milton (Buffalo County) (Town)	54629
Milton (Rock County)	53563
Milton (Rock County) (Town)	53563
Milton Junction (Part of Milton)	53563
Milwaukee	**53201-95**
For specific Milwaukee Zip Codes call (414) 291-2444	

COLLEGES & UNIVERSITIES

Alverno College	53215
Cardinal Stritch College	53217
Marquette University	53233
Milwaukee School of Engineering	53201
Mount Mary College	53222
University of Wisconsin-Milwaukee	53201

FINANCIAL INSTITUTIONS

Associated Commerce Bank	53203
Badger Savings Association	53211
Continental Savings & Loan Association	53202
First Bank (N.A.)-Milwaukee	53259
First Bank Southeast, National Association	53202
First Wisconsin National Bank of Milwaukee	53202
First Wisconsin Trust Company	53202
Great American Savings & Loan Association	53226
Guaranty Savings & Loan Association	53223
Hopkins Savings & Loan Association	53226
Kinnickinnic Federal Savings & Loan Association	53207
Lincoln Savings & Loan Association	53215
Marine Bank, National Association	53202
M&I Marshall & Ilsley Bank	53202
M&I Wauwatosa State Bank	53213
Mutual Savings & Loan Association of Wisconsin	53202
St. Francis Savings & Loan Association	53207
Security Savings & Loan Association	53203
Wauwatosa Savings & Loan Association	53213
West Allis Savings & Loan Association	53221

HOSPITALS

Columbia Hospital	53211
Milwaukee County Medical Complex	53226
St. Francis Hospital	53215
St. Joseph's Hospital	53210
St. Luke's Medical Center	53215
St. Mary's Hospital	53201
St. Michael Hospital	53209
Sinai Samaritan Medical Center	55233
Veterans Administration Medical Center	53295

HOTELS/MOTELS

The Astor Hotel	53202
Best Western Midway Motor Lodge	53226
Holiday Inn-South Airport	53221
Howard Johnson Executive Hotel	53203
Hyatt Regency Milwaukee	53203
The Marc Plaza Hotel	53203
The Pfister Hotel	53202
Red Carpet Hotel	53207

	ZIP
MILITARY INSTALLATIONS	
Coast Guard Base, Milwaukee	53207
General Billy Mitchell Field, 440th Tactical Airlift Wing	53207
Wisconsin Air National Guard, FB6491	53207
84th Division (Training)	53218
Mindoro	54644
Mineral Point (Iowa County)	53565
Mineral Point (Iowa County) (Town)	53565
Minnesota Junction	53032
Minocqua	54548
Minocqua (Town)	54548
Minong (Washburn County)	54859
Minong (Washburn County) (Town)	54859
Mishicot (Manitowoc County)	54228
Mishicot (Manitowoc County) (Town)	54228
Mitchell (Town)	53093
Modena	54755
Modena (Town)	54755
Moeville	54011
Mole Lake	54520
Mole Lake Indian Reservation	54520
Molitor (Town)	54451
Monches	53029
Mondovi (Buffalo County)	54755
Mondovi (Buffalo County) (Town)	54755
Monico (Town)	54501
Monico	54501
Monona	53716
Monroe (Adams County) (Town)	54613
Monroe (Green County)	53566
Monroe (Green County) (Town)	53566
Monroe Center	54613
Montana	54747
Montana (Town)	54747
Montello (Marquette County)	53949
Montello (Marquette County) (Town)	53949
Monterey	53066
Montfort	53569
Monticello (Green County)	53570
Monticello (Lafayette County) (Town)	54810
Montpelier (Town)	54217
Montreal	54550
Montrose (Town)	53508
Moon	54455
Moose Junction	55048
Moquah	54806
Morgan (Town)	54154
Morgan (Oconto County)	54154
Morgan (Shawano County)	54128
Morris (Town)	54486
Morrison	54126
Morrison (Town)	54126
Morrisonville	53571
Morris Park	53558
Morse (Ashland County)	54527
Morse (Ashland County) (Town)	54546
Moscow (Town)	53507
Mosel (Town)	53015
Mosinee (Marathon County)	54455
Mosinee (Marathon County) (Town)	54455
Mosling	54124
Moundville (Town)	53930
Mountain	54149
Mount Calvary	53057
Mount Hope (Grant County)	53816
Mount Hope (Grant County) (Town)	53816
Mount Horeb	53572
Mount Ida	53809
Mount Ida (Town)	53809
Mount Morris	54982
Mount Morris (Town)	54982
Mount Pleasant (Green County) (Town)	53502
Mount Pleasant (Racine County) (Town)	53401
Mount Sterling	54645
Mount Tabor	54638
Mount Vernon	53572
Mount Zion	53805
Mukwa (Town)	54961
Mukwonago (Waukesha County)	53149

	ZIP
Mukwonago (Waukesha County) (Town)	53149
Murphy Corner	54130
Murry (Town)	54819
Muscoda (Grant County)	53573
Muscoda (Grant County) (Town)	53573
Muskego	53150
Myra	53095
Nabob	53095
Namakagon (Town)	54821
Namur	54204
Naples (Town)	54755
Nasbro	53006
Nasewaupee (Town)	54235
Nashotah	53058
Nashville (Town)	54520
Nasonville	54449
Navarino	54107
Navarino (Town)	54107
Necedah (Juneau County)	54646
Necedah (Juneau County) (Town)	54646
Neda	53035
Neenah	54956-57
For specific Neenah Zip Codes call (414) 725-4818	
Neillsville	54456
Nekimi (Town)	54901
Nekoosa	54457
Nelma	49935
Nelson	54756
Nelson (Town)	54756
Nelsonville	54458
Nenno	53002
Neopit	54150
Neosho	53059
Nepeuskun (Town)	54971
Neshkoro (Marquette County)	54960
Neshkoro (Marquette County) (Town)	54960
Neuern	54217
Neva (Town)	54424
Neva Corners	54424
Newald	54511
New Amsterdam	54636
Newark	53511
Newark (Town)	53511
New Auburn	54757
New Berlin	53151
Newbold (Town)	54501
Newburg	53060
Newburg Corners	54614
New Centerville	54002
New Chester (Town)	53936
New Denmark (Town)	54208
New Diggings	61075
New Diggings (Town)	61075
New Fane	53040
New Franken	54229
New Glarus (Green County)	53574
New Glarus (Green County) (Town)	53574
New Haven (Adams County) (Town)	53920
New Haven (Dunn County) (Town)	54005
New Holstein (Calumet County)	53061
New Holstein (Calumet County) (Town)	53061
New Hope (Town)	54407
New Lisbon	53950
New London	54961
New Lyme (Town)	54656
New Miner	54646
New Munster	53152
New Odanah	54861
Newport (Town)	53965
New Post	54828
New Prospect	53010
New Richmond	54017
New Rome	54457
Newry	54619
Newton	53063
Newton (Town)	53063
Newton (Marquette County) (Town)	53964
Newton (Vernon County)	54665
Newtonburg	54220
Newville	53534
Niagara (Marinette County)	54151
Niagara (Marinette County) (Town)	49870
Nichols	54152
Nippersink Manor	53128
Nokomis (Town)	54487
Nora	53531
Norman	54216
Norrie	54414

620 WISCONSIN Norrie-Point Loomis Shopping Center

Name	ZIP
Norrie (Town)	54414
Norske	54945
North Andover	53810
North Bay (Door County)	54202
North Bay (Racine County)	53402
North Bend	54642
North Bend (Town)	54642
North Branch	54611
North Bristol	53590
North Cape	53126
Northeim	53063
Northfield	54635
Northfield (Town)	54635
North Fond du Lac	54935
North Freedom	53951
North Hudson	54016
North Lake (Walworth County)	53121
North Lake (Waukesha County)	53064
North Lancaster (Town)	53813
Northland	54945
Northland Mall (Part of Milwaukee)	53209
North Leeds	53911
North Lowell	53039
North Menomonie (Part of Menomonie)	54751
North Park	53402
Northport (Door County)	54210
Northport (Waupaca County)	54961
North Prairie	53153
Northridge (Part of Milwaukee)	53223
North Shore (Part of Glendale)	53217
North Tomah	54660
Northway Mall (Part of Marshfield)	54449
Northwoods Beach	54843
North York	54846
Norton	54730
Norwalk	54648
Norway (Town)	53182
Norway Grove	53532
Norwegian Bay	54940
Norwood (Town)	54401
Nutterville	54401
Nye	54020
Oak Center	53065
Oak Creek	53154
Oakdale	54649
Oakdale (Town)	54649
Oakfield (Fond du Lac County)	53065
Oakfield (Fond du Lac County) (Town)	53065
Oak Grove (Dodge County) (Town)	53039
Oak Grove (Pierce County) (Town)	54021
Oak Grove (Barron County) (Town)	54868
Oak Grove (Dodge County)	53039
Oak Hill	53156
Oakhill Correctional Institution	53575
Oakland (Town)	53538
Oakland	53538
Oakland (Burnett County) (Town)	54893
Oakland (Douglas County) (Town)	54874
Oakley	53550
Oakridge	53179
Oak Shores	53125
Oakwood (Part of Oak Creek)	53154
Oakwood Mall (Part of Eau Claire)	54703
Oasis (Town)	54966
Oconomowoc (Waukesha County)	53066
Oconomowoc (Waukesha County) (Town)	53069
Oconomowoc Lake	53066
Oconto (Oconto County)	54153
Oconto (Oconto County) (Town)	54139
Oconto Falls (Oconto County)	54154
Oconto Falls (Oconto County) (Town)	54154
Odanah	54861
Ogdensburg	54962
Ogema	54459
Ogema (Town)	54459
Oil City	54648
Ojibwa	54862
Ojibwa (Town)	54862

Name	ZIP
Okauchee	53069
Okauchee Lake (Waukesha County)	53058
Okee	53555
Old Albertville	54730
Old Ashippun	53003
Old Lebanon	53094
Oliver	54880
Olivet	54767
Oma (Town)	54534
Omro (Winnebago County)	54963
Omro (Winnebago County) (Town)	54901
Onalaska (La Crosse County)	54650
Onalaska (La Crosse County) (Town)	54650
Oneida	54155
Oneida (Town)	54155
Oneida Indian Reservation	54155
Ono	54750
Ontario	54651
Oostburg	53070
Orange (Town)	54618
Orange Mill	54618
Oregon (Dane County)	53575
Oregon (Dane County) (Town)	53575
Orfordville	53576
Orienta (Town)	54865
Orihula	54940
Orion	53573
Orion (Town)	53573
Osborn (Town)	54165
Osceola (Fond du Lac County) (Town)	53010
Osceola (Polk County)	54020
Osceola (Polk County) (Town)	54020
Oshkosh	54901-04
For specific Oshkosh Zip Codes call (414) 236-0200	
Osman	53063
Osseo	54758
Ostrander	54961
Otsego	53925
Otsego (Town)	53925
Ottawa (Town)	53118
Otter Creek (Dunn County) (Town)	54772
Otter Creek (Eau Claire County) (Town)	54722
Oulu (Town)	54847
Ourtown	53085
Owen	54460
Oxbo	54552
Oxford (Marquette County)	53952
Oxford (Marquette County) (Town)	53952
Pacific (Town)	53954
Packwaukee (Town)	53953
Packwaukee	53953
Paddock Lake	53168
Padus	54566
Palmyra (Jefferson County)	53156
Palmyra (Jefferson County) (Town)	53156
Paoli	53508
Pardeeville	53954
Parfreyville	54981
Paris (Grant County) (Town)	53807
Paris (Kenosha County) (Town)	53182
Paris	53182
Park Falls	54552
Parkland (Town)	54874
Parklawn (Part of Milwaukee)	53216
Park Plaza (Part of Oshkosh)	54902
Park Ridge	54481
Parrish	54435
Parrish (Town)	54435
Patch Grove (Grant County)	53817
Patch Grove (Grant County) (Town)	53821
Patzau	54836
Pearson	54462
Peck (Town)	54424
Pecks Station	53121
Peebles	54935
Peeksville (Town)	54527
Pelican (Town)	54501
Pelican Lake	54463
Pella	54950
Pella (Town)	54950
Pell Lake	53157
Pembine	54156
Pembine (Town)	54156
Pence	54550
Pence (Town)	54550

Name	ZIP
Peninsula Center	54202
Pensaukee	54153
Pensaukee (Town)	54153
Pepin (Pepin County)	54759
Pepin (Pepin County) (Town)	54759
Peplin	54455
Perkinstown	54451
Perry (Town)	53572
Pershing (Town)	54433
Peru (Dunn County) (Town)	54764
Peru (Portage County)	54407
Peshtigo (Marinette County)	54157
Peshtigo (Marinette County) (Town)	54143
Petersburg	54631
Petty Acres	53589
Pewaukee (Waukesha County)	53072
Pewaukee (Waukesha County) (Town)	53072
Phantom Lake	53149
Pheasant Branch (Part of Middleton)	53562
Phelps	54554
Phelps (Town)	54554
Phillips	54555
Phipps	54843
Phlox	54464
Piacenza	54986
Pickerel	54465
Pickett	54964
Piehl (Town)	54501
Pierce (Town)	54216
Pigeon (Town)	54773
Pigeon Falls	54760
Pike Lake	54440
Pilsen (Bayfield County) (Town)	54806
Pilsen (Kewaunee County)	54217
Pine Bluff	53528
Pine Creek	54625
Pine Grove (Brown County)	54301
Pine Grove (Portage County) (Town)	54921
Pine Lake (Iron County)	54534
Pine Lake (Oneida County) (Town)	54501
Pine River (Lincoln County) (Town)	54452
Pine River (Waushara County)	54965
Pine Tree Mall (Part of Marinette)	54143
Pine Valley (Town)	54456
Pipe	53049
Pipersville	53094
Pittsfield (Town)	54301
Pittsville	54466
Plain	53577
Plainfield (Waushara County)	54966
Plainfield (Waushara County) (Town)	54966
Plainville	53965
Plat	53017
Platteville (Grant County)	53818
Platteville (Grant County) (Town)	53818
Plaza 8 (Part of Sheboygan)	53081
Pleasant Prairie	53158
Pleasant Ridge	53533
Pleasant Springs (Town)	53589
Pleasant Valley (Eau Claire County) (Town)	54701
Pleasant Valley (St. Croix County) (Town)	54015
Pleasant Valley (Vernon County)	54658
Pleasant View	54615
Pleasantville	54758
Plover (Marathon County) (Town)	54414
Plover (Portage County)	54467
Plover (Portage County) (Town)	54467
Plugtown	53805
Plum City	54761
Plum Lake (Town)	54560
Plymouth (Juneau County) (Town)	53929
Plymouth (Rock County)	53545
Plymouth (Sheboygan County)	53073
Plymouth (Sheboygan County) (Town)	53073
Point Loomis Shopping Center (Part of Milwaukee)	53221

Poland-Rushford WISCONSIN 621

Name	ZIP
Poland	54301
Polar	54418
Polar (Town)	54418
Polifka Corners	54247
Polk (Town)	53076
Polley	54433
Polonia	54423
Poniatowski	54426
Poplar	54864
Popple Lake	54729
Popple River	54542
Popple River (Town)	54542
Porcupine	54721
Portage	53901
Port Andrew	53518
Port Edwards (Wood County)	54469
Port Edwards (Wood County) (Town)	54457
Porter (Town)	53545
Porterfield	54159
Porterfield (Town)	54159
Portland (Dodge County)	53594
Portland (Dodge County) (Town)	53594
Portland (Monroe County)	54619
Portland (Monroe County) (Town)	54619
Port Plaza Mall (Part of Green Bay)	54308
Port Washington (Ozaukee County)	53074
Port Washington (Ozaukee County) (Town)	53074
Port Wing	54865
Port Wing (Town)	54865
Poskin	54866
Post Lake	54428
Postville	53516
Potawatomi Indian Reservation	54520
Potosi (Grant County)	53820
Potosi (Grant County) (Town)	53820
Potter	54160
Potter Lake	53120
Potts Corners	54639
Pound (Marinette County)	54161
Pound (Marinette County) (Town)	54139
Powell	54547
Powers Lake	53159
Poygan (Town)	54963
Poynette	53955
Poy Sippi	54967
Poysippi (Town)	54967
Praag	54610
Prairie Corners	53807
Prairie du Chien (Crawford County)	53821
Prairie du Chien (Crawford County) (Town)	53821
Prairie du Sac (Sauk County)	53578
Prairie du Sac (Sauk County) (Town)	53583
Prairie Farm (Barron County)	54762
Prairie Farm (Barron County) (Town)	54762
Prairie Lake (Town)	54728
Pray	54466
Preble (Part of Green Bay)	54302
Prentice (Price County)	54556
Prentice (Price County) (Town)	54556
Prescott	54021
Presque Isle	54557
Presque Isle (Town)	54557
Preston (Adams County) (Town)	53934
Preston (Grant County)	53809
Preston (Trempealeau County) (Town)	54616
Price (Jackson County)	54741
Price (Langlade County) (Town)	54418
Primrose (Town)	53593
Princeton (Green Lake County) (Town)	54968
Princeton (Green Lake County)	54968
Prospect (Part of New Berlin)	53151
Pukwana Beach	53049
Pulaski (Brown County)	54162
Pulaski (Iowa County) (Town)	53506
Pulcifer	54164
Purdy	54665
Quarry	54230

Name	ZIP
Quincy (Town)	53910
Quincy Details	53934
Quinney	53014
Racine	53401-08
For specific Racine Zip Codes call (414) 632-1661	
Radisson (Sawyer County)	54867
Radisson (Sawyer County) (Town)	54867
Randall (Burnett County)	54840
Randall (Kenosha County) (Town)	60071
Randolph (Columbia County) (Town)	53923
Randolph (Dodge County)	53956
Random Lake	53075
Range	54001
Rankin	54201
Rantoul (Town)	53014
Rattman Heights	53701
Ravenoaks	53575
Rawson (Part of Oak Creek)	53172
Raymond	53126
Raymond (Town)	53126
Readfield (Waupaca County)	54969
Readstown	54652
Red Banks	54940
Red Cedar (Town)	54751
Red Cliff	54814
Red Cliff Indian Reservation	54806
Redgranite	54970
Red Mound	54624
Red River (Kewaunee County) (Town)	54205
Red River (Shawano County)	54166
Red Springs (Town)	54128
Redville	54498
Reedsburg (Sauk County)	53959
Reedsburg (Sauk County) (Town)	53959
Reedsville	54230
Reeseville	53579
Reeve	54004
Regency Mall (Part of Racine)	53406
Reid (Town)	54440
Reighmoor	54963
Remington (Town)	54413
Reseburg (Town)	54437
Reserve	54876
Retreat	54624
Rewey	53580
Rhine	53020
Rhine (Town)	53020
Rhinelander	54501
Rib Falls	54426
Rib Falls (Town)	54426
Rib Lake (Taylor County)	54470
Rib Lake (Taylor County) (Town)	54470
Rib Mountain (Town)	54401
Rice Lake (Barron County)	54868
Rice Lake (Barron County) (Town)	54868
Richardson	54004
Richfield (Washington County) (Town)	53076
Richfield (Wood County) (Town)	54449
Richfield (Adams County) (Town)	53934
Richfield (Washington County)	53076
Richford	54930
Richford (Town)	54930
Richland (Richland County) (Town)	53581
Richland (Rusk County) (Town)	54526
Richland Center	53581
Richmond (Town)	53115
Richmond (Shawano County) (Town)	54166
Richmond (St. Croix County) (Town)	54017
Richmond (Walworth County)	53115
Richwood (Dodge County)	53094
Richwood (Richland County) (Town)	53518
Ridgeland	54763
Ridgeville (Town)	54648
Ridgeway (Iowa County)	53582
Ridgeway (Iowa County) (Town)	53582
Rief's Mills	54247
Rietbrock (Town)	54411
Rileys	53593
Rileys Point	54235

Name	ZIP
Ringle	54471
Ringle (Town)	54471
Rio	53960
Rio Creek	54231
Riplinger	54479
Ripon (Fond du Lac County)	54971
Ripon (Fond du Lac County) (Town)	54971
Rising Sun	54628
River Falls (Pierce County)	54022
River Falls (Pierce County) (Town)	54022
River Hills	53217
Rivermoor	54963
Riverside	53541
Riverview (Town)	54149
Riverwood	54613
River Wood Estates	53589
Roberts	54023
Robinson	53147
Rochester (Racine County)	53167
Rochester (Racine County) (Town)	53105
Rock (Rock County) (Town)	53545
Rock (Wood County) (Town)	54466
Rockbridge	53581
Rockbridge (Town)	53581
Rock Creek (Town)	54764
Rockdale	53523
Rock Elm	54740
Rock Elm (Town)	54740
Rock Falls (Dunn County)	54764
Rock Falls (Lincoln County) (Town)	54442
Rockfield	53077
Rock Lake	53179
Rockland (Brown County) (Town)	54115
Rockland (La Crosse County)	54653
Rockland (Manitowoc County) (Town)	54207
Rock Springs	53961
Rockton	54639
Rockville (Grant County)	53820
Rockville (Manitowoc County)	53042
Rockwood	54220
Rocky Run	54481
Rodell	54722
Rogersville	54974
Rolling (Town)	54409
Rolling Acres	53589
Rolling Ground	54655
Rolling Prairie	53039
Rolling View	53589
Romance	54632
Rome (Adams County) (Town)	54457
Rome (Jefferson County)	53178
Roosevelt (Burnett County) (Town)	54813
Roosevelt (Oneida County)	54501
Roosevelt (Taylor County) (Town)	54447
Root River (Part of Milwaukee)	53227
Rose (Town)	54984
Rosecrans	54227
Rose Lawn	54165
Rosemere (Part of Manitowoc)	54220
Rosendale (Fond du Lac County)	54974
Rosendale (Fond du Lac County) (Town)	54964
Rosholt	54473
Rosiere	54205
Ross (Forest County) (Town)	54511
Ross (Vernon County)	54665
Ross D. Sills	53125
Rostok	54216
Rothschild	54474
Round Lake (Town)	54843
Rowleys Bay	54210
Roxbury	53583
Roxbury (Town)	53583
Royalton	54975
Royalton (Town)	54975
Rozellville	54484
Rubicon (Town)	53078
Rubicon	53078
Ruby (Town)	54745
Rudolph (Wood County)	54475
Rudolph (Wood County) (Town)	54475
Rural	54981
Rushford (Town)	54963

622 WISCONSIN Rush Lake-Spring Green

Place	ZIP
Rush Lake	54971
Rush River (Town)	54002
Rusk (Burnett County) (Town)	54801
Rusk (Dunn County)	54751
Rusk (Rusk County) (Town)	54728
Russell (Bayfield County) (Town)	54814
Russell (Lincoln County) (Town)	54435
Russell (Sheboygan County) (Town)	53079
Russell (Trempealeau County)	54747
Rutland (Town)	53589
Sabin	53581
Sacred Heart School of Theology	53130
St. Anna	53061
St. Anthony	53002
St. Cloud	53079
St. Croix Falls (Polk County)	54024
St. Croix Falls (Polk County) (Town)	54824
St. Croix Indian Reservation	54830
St. Francis	53207
Saint George	53085
St. Germain	54558
St. Germain (Town)	54558
St. John	54129
St. Joseph (Fond du Lac County)	53079
St. Joseph (La Crosse County)	54601
St. Joseph (St. Croix County) (Town)	54016
St. Kilian	53010
St. Lawrence (Washington County)	53027
St. Lawrence (Waupaca County) (Town)	54962
St. Marie (Town)	54968
St. Martins (Part of Franklin)	53132
St. Marys	54619
St. Michaels	53040
St. Nazianz	54232
St. Peter	53049
St. Wendel (Part of Cleveland)	53015
Salem	53168
Salem (Kenosha County) (Town)	53168
Salem (Pierce County) (Town)	54750
Salem Oaks	53168
Salvatorian Center (Part of New Holstein)	53062
Sampson (Chippewa County) (Town)	54757
Sampson (Oconto County)	54171
Sanborn (Ashland County)	54806
Sanborn (Ashland County) (Town)	54861
Sand Bay (Bayfield County)	54814
Sand Bay (Door County)	54235
Sand Creek	54765
Sand Creek (Town)	54765
Sand Lake (Burnett County) (Town)	54893
Sandlake (Polk County)	54009
Sand Lake (Sawyer County) (Town)	54876
Sand Prairie	53518
Sandusky	53937
Saratoga (Town)	54494
Sarona	54870
Sarona (Town)	54870
Sauk City	53583
Saukville (Ozaukee County)	53080
Saukville (Ozaukee County) (Town)	53074
Saxeville	54976
Saxeville (Town)	54976
Saxon	54559
Saxon (Town)	54559
Saylesville (Dodge County)	53078
Saylesville (Waukesha County)	53186
Sayner	54560
Scandinavia (Waupaca County)	54977
Scandinavia (Waupaca County) (Town)	54977
Scarboro	54217
Schleswig (Town)	53042
Schley (Town)	54452
Schnappsville	54411
Schoepke (Town)	54463
Schofield	54476
School Hill	53042
Schraven Circle	54935
Scott (Brown County) (Town)	54229
Scott (Burnett County) (Town)	54893
Scott (Columbia County) (Town)	53923
Scott (Crawford County) (Town)	53518
Scott (Lincoln County) (Town)	54452
Scott (Monroe County) (Town)	54666
Scott (Sheboygan County) (Town)	53001
Sechlerville	54635
Seeleys	54843
Seif (Town)	54456
Seneca	54654
Seneca (Town)	54654
Seneca (Green Lake County) (Town)	54923
Seneca (Shawano County) (Town)	54978
Seneca (Wood County) (Town)	54494
Sevastopol (Town)	54235
Seven Mile Creek (Town)	53944
Sextonville	53584
Seymour (Eau Claire County) (Town)	54701
Seymour (Lafayette County) (Town)	53586
Seymour (Outagamie County)	54165
Seymour (Outagamie County) (Town)	54165
Shamrock	54615
Shanagolden	54527
Shanagolden (Town)	54527
Shantytown	54473
Sharon (Portage County) (Town)	54473
Sharon (Walworth County)	53585
Sharon (Walworth County) (Town)	53585
Shawano	54166
Shawano North Beach	54166
Sheboygan	53081-83
For specific Sheboygan Zip Codes call (414) 458-3741	
Sheboygan Falls (Sheboygan County)	53085
Sheboygan Falls (Sheboygan County) (Town)	53085
Sheil	53575
Shelby (Town)	54601
Sheldon (Monroe County) (Town)	54651
Sheldon (Rusk County)	54766
Shell Lake	54871
Shennington	54618
Shepley	54499
Sheridan (Dunn County) (Town)	54725
Sheridan (Waupaca County)	54981
Sherman (Clark County) (Town)	54479
Sherman (Dunn County) (Town)	54751
Sherman (Iron County) (Town)	54552
Sherman (Sheboygan County) (Town)	53075
Sherman Center	53075
Sherry	54454
Sherry (Town)	54454
Sherwood (Calumet County)	54169
Sherwood (Clark County) (Town)	54466
Shields (Dodge County) (Town)	53094
Shields (Marquette County) (Town)	53949
Shiocton	54170
Shirley	54115
Shopiere	53511
Shoreview	53179
Shorewood	53211
Shorewood Hills	53705
Shortville	54456
Shoto	54241
Shullsburg (Lafayette County)	53586
Shullsburg (Lafayette County) (Town)	53586
Sidney	54456
Sigel (Chippewa County) (Town)	54727
Sigel (Wood County) (Town)	54494
Silica	53049
Silver Cliff (Town)	54104
Silver Creek	53075
Silver Lake (Kenosha County)	53170
Silver Lake (Walworth County)	53121
Silver Lake (Waushara County)	54982
Sinsinawa	53824
Sioux	54891
Sioux Creek (Town)	54728
Siren (Burnett County)	54872
Siren (Burnett County) (Town)	54872
Sister Bay	54234
Skanawan (Town)	54442
Slab City	54107
Slabtown	53549
Slades Corner	53105
Slinger	53086
Slovan	54205
Smelser (Town)	53807
Sobieski	54171
Sobieski Corners	54141
Soldiers Grove	54655
Solon Springs (Douglas County)	54873
Solon Springs (Douglas County) (Town)	54873
Somers	53171
Somers (Town)	53171
Somerset (St. Croix County)	54025
Somerset (St. Croix County) (Town)	55082
Somo (Town)	54564
Soperton	54566
South Beaver Dam	53916
South Byron	53006
South Chase	54162
South Chippewa (Part of Chippewa Falls)	54729
South Fork (Town)	54530
Southgate Mall (Part of Milwaukee)	53215
South Itasca (Part of Superior)	54880
South Janesville (Part of Janesville)	53545
South Kenosha	53140
South Lancaster (Town)	53813
South Luxemburg (Part of Luxemburg)	54217
South Milwaukee	53172
South Necedah (Part of Necedah)	54646
South Randolph	53956
South Range	54874
Southridge (Part of Greendale)	53129
South Side (Part of Madison)	53715
South Wayne	53587
Sparta (Monroe County)	54656
Sparta (Monroe County) (Town)	54656
Spaulding	54466
Spencer (Marathon County)	54479
Spencer (Marathon County) (Town)	54479
Spider Lake (Town)	54843
Spirit	54513
Spirit (Town)	54513
Spirit Falls	54564
Split Rock	54486
Spokeville	54479
Spooner (Washburn County)	54801
Spooner (Washburn County) (Town)	54801
Sprague	54646
Spread Eagle	54121
Spring Bluff	54930
Springbrook (Town)	54875
Spring Brook (Dunn County) (Town)	54751
Springbrook (Washburn County)	54875
Springdale (Town)	53593
Springfield (Dane County) (Town)	53528
Springfield (Jackson County) (Town)	54659
Springfield (Marquette County) (Town)	53964
Springfield (St. Croix County) (Town)	54013
Springfield (Walworth County)	53176
Springfield Corners	53529
Spring Green (Sauk County)	53588

Spring Green-Valley **WISCONSIN** 623

Name	ZIP
Spring Green (Sauk County) (Town)	53588
Spring Grove (Town)	53550
Spring Hill Edition	53589
Spring Lake (Pierce County) (Town)	54767
Spring Lake (Waushara County)	54960
Spring Prairie	53121
Spring Prairie (Town)	53121
Springstead	54552
Springvale (Columbia County) (Town)	53960
Springvale (Fond du Lac County) (Town)	54974
Spring Valley (Manitowoc County)	53063
Spring Valley (Pierce County)	54767
Spring Valley (Rock County) (Town)	53576
Springville (Adams County) (Town)	53965
Springville (Vernon County)	54665
Springwater (Town)	54984
Spruce	54139
Spruce (Town)	54139
Stanbery	54875
Standart	53533
Stanfold (Town)	54812
Stangelville	54208
Stanley (Barron County) (Town)	54822
Stanley (Chippewa County)	54768
Stanton (Dunn County) (Town)	54725
Stanton (St. Croix County) (Town)	54017
Stark (Town)	54639
Starks	54501
Starlake	54561
Star Prairie (St. Croix County)	54026
Star Prairie (St. Croix County) (Town)	54025
Star Valley	54655
Starview Heights	53545
State Line	53142
State Street (Part of Racine)	53404
Steffenrud Addition	54656
Stella (Town)	54501
Stephenson (Town)	54114
Stephenson Island (Part of Marinette)	54143
Stephensville	54944
Sterling (Polk County) (Town)	54006
Sterling (Vernon County) (Town)	54624
Stetsonville	54480
Stettin (Town)	54401
Steuben	54657
Stevens Point	54481
Stevenstown	54636
Stiles	54139
Stiles (Town)	54139
Stiles Junction	54139
Stinnett (Town)	54875
Stitzer	53825
Stockbridge (Calumet County)	53088
Stockbridge (Calumet County) (Town)	53014
Stockbridge-Munsee Indian Reservation	54416
Stockholm (Pepin County)	54769
Stockholm (Pepin County) (Town)	54769
Stockton (Town)	54481
Stockton	54481
Stoddard	54658
Stonebank	53066
Stone Lake (Washburn County)	54876
Stone Lake (Washburn County) (Town)	54876
Stoughton	53589
Strader	54722
Stratford	54484
Strickland (Town)	54895
Strongs Prairie (Town)	54613
Strum	54770
Stubbs (Town)	54819
Sturgeon Bay (Door County)	54235
Sturgeon Bay (Door County) (Town)	54235
Sturtevant	53177
Suamico	54173
Suamico (Town)	54173
Sugar Bush (Brown County)	54217

Name	ZIP
Sugar Bush (Outagamie County)	54961
Sugar Camp	54501
Sugar Camp (Town)	54501
Sugar Creek (Town)	53121
Sugar Grove	54655
Sugar Island	53094
Sullivan (Jefferson County)	53178
Sullivan (Jefferson County) (Town)	53549
Summit (Douglas County) (Town)	54836
Summit (Juneau County) (Town)	53948
Summit (Langlade County) (Town)	54435
Summit (Waukesha County) (Town)	53058
Summit Corners	53066
Summit Lake	54485
Sumner (Town)	54868
Sumner (Barron County)	54822
Sumner (Jefferson County) (Town)	53538
Sumner (Trempealeau County) (Town)	54758
Sumpter (Town)	53951
Sunburst	53701
Sunnyslope (Part of New Berlin)	53151
Sun Prairie (Dane County)	53590
Sun Prairie (Dane County) (Town)	53559
Sunset	54401
Sunset Beach	53916
Superior (Douglas County)	54880
Superior (Douglas County) (Town)	54880
Superior (Douglas County)	54880
Suring	54174
Sussex	53089
Swiss (Town)	54830
Sylvan	54664
Sylvan (Town)	54664
Sylvania	53177
Sylvester (Town)	53550
Symco	54949
Tabor	53404
Taegesville	54401
Taft (Town)	54771
Tainter (Town)	54730
Tamarack	54612
Tarrant	54736
Taus	54206
Taycheedah	54935
Taycheedah (Town)	54935
Taycheedah Correctional Institution	54935
Taylor	54659
Teegarden	54751
Tell	54610
Tennyson	53820
Terrace Park	53532
Tess Corners (Part of Muskego)	53130
Teutonia (Part of Milwaukee)	53206
Texas (Town)	54401
Theresa (Dodge County)	53091
Theresa (Dodge County) (Town)	53050
Thiensville	53092
Thiry Daems	54217
Thompson	53027
Thompsonville	53126
Thornapple (Town)	54819
Thornton	54166
Thorp (Clark County)	54771
Thorp (Clark County) (Town)	54768
Three Lakes	54562
Three Lakes (Town)	54562
Tibbets	53121
Tichigan Lake	53185
Tiffany (Dunn County) (Town)	54725
Tiffany (Rock County)	53511
Tigerton	54486
Tilden	54729
Tilden (Town)	54729
Tilleda	54978
Tipler	49935
Tipler (Town)	49935
Tisch Mills	54240
Token Creek	53532
Tomah (Monroe County)	54660
Tomah (Monroe County) (Town)	54660
Tomahawk (Lincoln County)	54487
Tomahawk (Lincoln County) (Town)	54487

Name	ZIP
Tonet	54217
Tony	54563
Towerville	54655
Townsend	54175
Townsend (Town)	54175
Trade Lake	54837
Trade Lake (Town)	54837
Trade River	54840
Trego	54888
Trego (Town)	54888
Trempealeau (Trempealeau County)	54661
Trempealeau (Trempealeau County) (Town)	54661
Trenton (Dodge County) (Town)	53916
Trenton (Pierce County) (Town)	54014
Trenton (Washington County) (Town)	53095
Trevor	53179
Tri City (Part of Oak Creek)	53154
Trimbelle	54011
Trimbelle (Town)	54011
Tripoli	54564
Tripp (Town)	54847
Troy (Town)	53120
Troy (Sauk County) (Town)	53583
Troy (St. Croix County) (Town)	54022
Troy (Walworth County)	53121
Troy Center	53120
True (Town)	54526
Truesdell	53140
Truman	53530
Trusler Circle	53575
Tuckaway (Part of Milwaukee)	53221
Tuleta Hills	53946
Tunnel City	54662
Turtle (Town)	53511
Turtle Lake (Barron County)	54889
Turtle Lake (Barron County) (Town)	54004
Turtle Lake (Walworth County)	53115
Tustin	54940
Twelfth Street Junction (Part of Superior)	54880
Twelve Corners	54106
Twenty-Eighth Street Junction (Part of Superior)	54880
Twin Bluffs	53581
Twin Grove	53550
Twin Lakes	53181
Two Creeks	54241
Two Creeks (Town)	54241
Two Rivers (Manitowoc County)	54241
Two Rivers (Manitowoc County) (Town)	54241
Ubet	54009
Underhill	54176
Underhill (Town)	54176
Union (Town)	53536
Union (Vernon County) (Town)	54634
Union (Waupaca County) (Town)	54949
Union (Burnett County) (Town)	54830
Union (Door County) (Town)	54204
Union (Eau Claire County) (Town)	54701
Union (Grant County)	53818
Union (Pierce County) (Town)	54750
Union (Rock County)	53536
Union Center	53962
Union Church	53126
Union Grove	53182
Unity (Clark County) (Town)	54488
Unity (Marathon County)	54488
Unity (Trempealeau County) (Town)	54770
University (Part of Madison)	53715
Upham (Town)	54485
Upper Third Street (Part of Milwaukee)	53212
Upson	54565
Uptown (Part of Racine)	53403
Urne	54736
Utica (Crawford County) (Town)	54655
Utica (Dane County)	53523
Utica (Waukesha County)	53066
Utica (Winnebago County) (Town)	54964
Valders	54245
Valley	54639

624 WISCONSIN Upham-Winter

	ZIP
Upham (Town)	54485
Upper Third Street (Part of Milwaukee)	53212
Upson	54565
Uptown (Part of Racine)	53403
Urne	54736
Utica (Crawford County) (Town)	54655
Utica (Dane County)	53523
Utica (Waukesha County)	53066
Utica (Winnebago County) (Town)	54964
Valders	54245
Valley	54639
Valley Junction	54660
Valley View Mall (Part of La Crosse)	54601
Valmy	54235
Valton	53968
Van Buskirk	54534
Vance Creek (Town)	54868
Vandenbroek (Town)	54130
Vandyne	54979
Vaudreuil	54615
Veedum	54466
Vermont (Town)	53515
Vernon (Town)	53103
Verona (Dane County)	53593
Verona (Dane County) (Town)	53593
Vesper	54489
Veterans Administration Hospital (Part of Shorewood Hills)	53705
Victory	54624
Vienna (Town)	53532
Vignes	54235
Vilas (Dane County)	53527
Vilas (Langlade County) (Town)	54424
Villard (Part of Milwaukee)	53209
Vineyard	53575
Vinland (Town)	54901
Viola	54664
Viroqua (Vernon County)	54665
Viroqua (Vernon County) (Town)	54665
Voltz Lake	53179
Wabeno	54566
Wabeno (Town)	54566
Wagner (Town)	54177
Waino	54820
Waldo	53093
Waldwick	53565
Waldwick (Town)	53565
Wales	53183
Walhain	54217
Walsh	54159
Walworth (Walworth County)	53184
Walworth (Walworth County) (Town)	53184
Wandawega	53121
Wanderoos	54001
Warner (Town)	54437
Warren (St. Croix County) (Town)	54023
Warren (Waushara County) (Town)	54923
Warrens	54666
Warrentown	54750
Wascott (Town)	54890
Wascott	54890
Washburn (Bayfield County)	54891
Washburn (Bayfield County) (Town)	54891
Washburn (Clark County) (Town)	54456
Washington (Door County) (Town)	54246
Washington (Eau Claire County) (Town)	54742
Washington (Green County) (Town)	53570
Washington (La Crosse County) (Town)	54619
Washington (Rusk County) (Town)	54819
Washington (Sauk County) (Town)	53937
Washington (Shawano County) (Town)	54107
Washington (Vilas County) (Town)	54521
Washington Island	54246
Waterford (Racine County)	53185
Waterford (Racine County) (Town)	53185
Waterford Woods	53185
Waterloo (Grant County) (Town)	53820
Waterloo (Jefferson County)	53594

	ZIP
Waterloo (Jefferson County) (Town)	53551
Watertown (Jefferson Co.)	53094
Watertown (Jefferson County) (Town)	53094
Waterville (Pepin County) (Town)	54721
Waterville (Waukesha Co.)	53066
Watterstown (Town)	53805
Waubeek (Town)	54736
Waubeesee	53185
Waubeka	53021
Waubesa Heights	53558
Waucousta	53010
Waukau	54980
Waukechon (Town)	54166
Waukesha	53186-88
For specific Waukesha Zip Codes call (414) 542-5377	
Waumandee	54622
Waumandee (Town)	54622
Waunakee	53597
Waupaca (Waupaca Co.)	54981
Waupaca (Waupaca County) (Town)	54981
Waupun (Dodge County)	53963
Waupun (Fond du Lac County) (Town)	53963
Wausau	54401-02
For specific Wausau Zip Codes call (715) 842-5791	
Wausau Center (Part of Wausau)	54401
Wausaukee (Marinette County)	54177
Wausaukee (Marinette County) (Town)	54177
Wausau West-Rib Mountain	54401
Wautoma (Waushara County)	54982
Wautoma (Waushara County) (Town)	54982
Wauwatosa	53213
Wauzeka (Crawford County)	53826
Wauzeka (Crawford County) (Town)	53826
Waverly	54740
Wayne (Town)	53010
Wayne (Lafayette County) (Town)	53587
Wayne (Washington Co.)	53010
Wayside	54126
Webb Lake	54830
Webb Lake (Town)	54830
Webster (Burnett County)	54893
Webster (Vernon County) (Town)	54639
Weirgor (Sawyer County)	54835
Weirgor (Sawyer County) (Town)	54835
Wellington (Town)	54651
Wells (Town)	54656
Wentworth	54874
Werley	53809
Wescott (Town)	54166
West Allis	53214
West Baraboo	53913
West Bend (Washington County)	53095
West Bend (Washington County) (Town)	53095
West Bloomfield	54983
Westboro	54490
Westboro (Town)	54490
Westby	54667
West De Pere (Part of De Pere)	54115
Western (Part of Milwaukee)	53210
Westfield (Marquette County)	53964
Westfield (Marquette County) (Town)	53964
Westfield (Sauk County) (Town)	53943
Westford (Dodge County) (Town)	53916
Westford (Richland County) (Town)	53924
West Jacksonport	54209
West Kewaunee (Town)	54216
West Lima	54639
Westlyn	54494
West Marshland (Town)	54840
West Milwaukee	53214
Weston (Town)	54751
Weston	54476
Weston (Town)	54476
Weston (Clark County) (Town)	54456
Weston (Dunn County)	54751

	ZIP
West Plainfield	54966
West Point (Town)	53555
Westport (Dane County) (Town)	53597
Westport (Richland County)	53518
West Prairie	54665
West Racine (Part of Racine)	53405
West Rosendale	54974
West Salem	54669
West Sweden (Town)	54837
West Towne Mall (Part of Madison)	53719
Weyauwega (Waupaca County)	54983
Weyauwega (Waupaca County) (Town)	54983
Weyerhaeuser	54895
Wheatland	53105
Wheatland (Vernon County) (Town)	54624
Wheatland (Kenosha County) (Town)	53105
Wheaton (Town)	54739
Wheeler	54772
Whitcomb	54486
White Creek	53965
Whitefish Bay (Door County)	54235
Whitefish Bay (Milwaukee County)	53217
Whitehall	54773
White Lake	54491
Whitelaw	54247
White Oak Springs (Town)	53586
White River (Town)	54855
Whitestown (Town)	54639
Whitewater (Walworth County)	53190
Whitewater (Walworth County) (Town)	53190
Whiting	54481
Whittlesey	54451
Wien (Town)	54426
Wild Rose	54984
Wildwood	54028
Wilkinson (Town)	54895
Willard (Clark County)	54493
Willard (Rusk County) (Town)	54731
Williams Bay	53191
Williamstown (Town)	53032
Willow (Town)	53924
Willow Springs (Lafayette County) (Town)	53565
Willow Springs (Waukesha County)	53051
Wilmore Heights	54971
Wilmot	53192
Wilson (Dunn County) (Town)	54733
Wilson (Eau Claire County) (Town)	54726
Wilson (Lincoln County) (Town)	54487
Wilson (Rusk County) (Town)	54817
Wilson (Sheboygan County) (Town)	53081
Wilson (Eau Claire County)	54726
Wilson (St. Croix County)	54027
Wilton (Monroe County)	54670
Wilton (Monroe County) (Town)	54670
Winchester (Villas County)	54545
Winchester (Villas County) (Town)	54545
Winchester (Winnebago County)	54947
Winchester (Winnebago County) (Town)	54947
Wind Lake	53185
Wind Point	53402
Windsor	53598
Windsor (Town)	53598
Windsor Hills	53532
Windsor Prairie	53532
Winfield (Town)	53959
Wingville (Town)	53569
Winnebago	54985
Winnebago Heights	53049
Winnebago Indian Reservation	53965
Winnebago Mission	54615
Winneboujou	54820
Winneconne (Winnebago County)	54986
Winneconne (Winnebago County) (Town)	54927
Winter (Sawyer County)	54896

Name	ZIP
Withee (Clark County) (Town)	54771
Wittenberg (Shawano County)	54499
Wittenberg (Shawano County) (Town)	54499
Witwen	53583
Wolfcreek	54024
Wolf Lake	53079
Wolf River (Langlade County) (Town)	54491
Wolf River (Winnebago County) (Town)	54940
Wonewoc (Juneau County)	53968
Wonewoc (Juneau County) (Town)	53929
Wood (Milwaukee County)	53193
Wood (Wood County) (Town)	54466
Woodboro	54501
Woodboro	54501
Wooddale	54817
Woodford	53599
Woodhull	54932
Woodland (Dodge County)	53099
Woodland (Sauk County) (Town)	53968
Woodman (Grant County)	53827
Woodman (Grant County) (Town)	53827
Woodmohr (Town)	54724
Wood River (Town)	54840
Woodruff	54568
Woodruff (Town)	54568
Woodstock	53581
Woodville (Calumet County) (Town)	54129
Woodville (St. Croix County)	54028
Woodworth	53194
Worcester (Town)	54555
Worden (Town)	54771
Wrightstown (Brown County)	54180
Wrightstown (Brown County) (Town)	54115
Wuertsburg	54411
Wyalusing	53801
Wyalusing (Town)	53801
Wyeville	54671
Wyocena (Columbia County)	53969
Wyocena (Columbia County) (Town)	53960
Wyoming (Iowa County) (Town)	53588
Wyoming (Waupaca County) (Town)	54945
Yahara Heights	53597
Yellow Lake	54830
York (Clark County) (Town)	54436
York (Dane County) (Town)	53925
York (Green County) (Town)	53516
York (Jackson County)	54758
York Center	53559
Yorkville	53182
Yorkville (Town)	53182
Young America	53095
Yuba	54639
Zachow	54182
Zander	54208
Zenda	53195
Zittau	54940

626 WYOMING

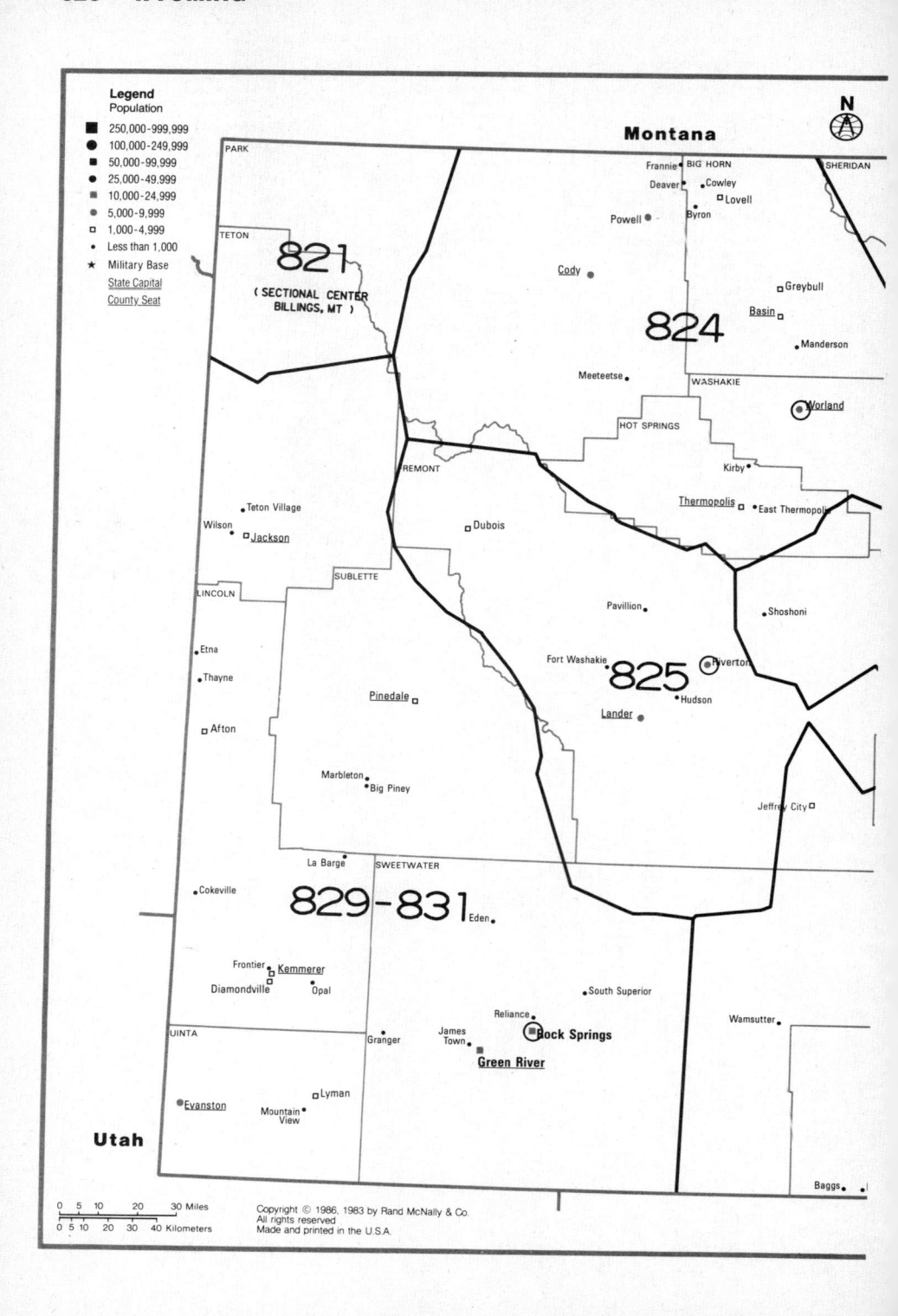

Legend
Population
- ■ 250,000-999,999
- ● 100,000-249,999
- ■ 50,000-99,999
- ● 25,000-49,999
- ■ 10,000-24,999
- ● 5,000-9,999
- □ 1,000-4,999
- · Less than 1,000
- ★ Military Base
- <u>State Capital</u>
- <u>County Seat</u>

Montana

821 (SECTIONAL CENTER BILLINGS, MT)

PARK — TETON

BIG HORN — SHERIDAN
Frannie
Deaver • Cowley
 • Lovell
Powell • Byron

Cody

Greybull □
824
Basin □
 • Manderson

Meeteetse
WASHAKIE
◎ Worland
HOT SPRINGS
Kirby •
Thermopolis □ • East Thermopolis

FREMONT
Dubois □

• Teton Village
Wilson •
 □ Jackson
SUBLETTE

Pavillion •
 • Shoshoni

LINCOLN

• Etna
• Thayne

Fort Washakie
825 ◎ Riverton
 • Hudson
Lander ◎

□ Afton

Pinedale □

Marbleton •
 • Big Piney

 • Jeffrey City □

La Barge • SWEETWATER

• Cokeville

829-831 Eden •

Frontier •■ Kemmerer
Diamondville □ • Opal
UINTA

Granger •
James Town ■

Reliance •
 • South Superior
◉ Rock Springs
■ Green River

 • Wamsutter

◉ Evanston
 □ Lyman
 Mountain View □

Utah

 • Baggs

0 5 10 20 30 Miles
0 5 10 20 30 40 Kilometers

Copyright © 1986, 1983 by Rand McNally & Co.
All rights reserved
Made and printed in the U.S.A.

WYOMING 627

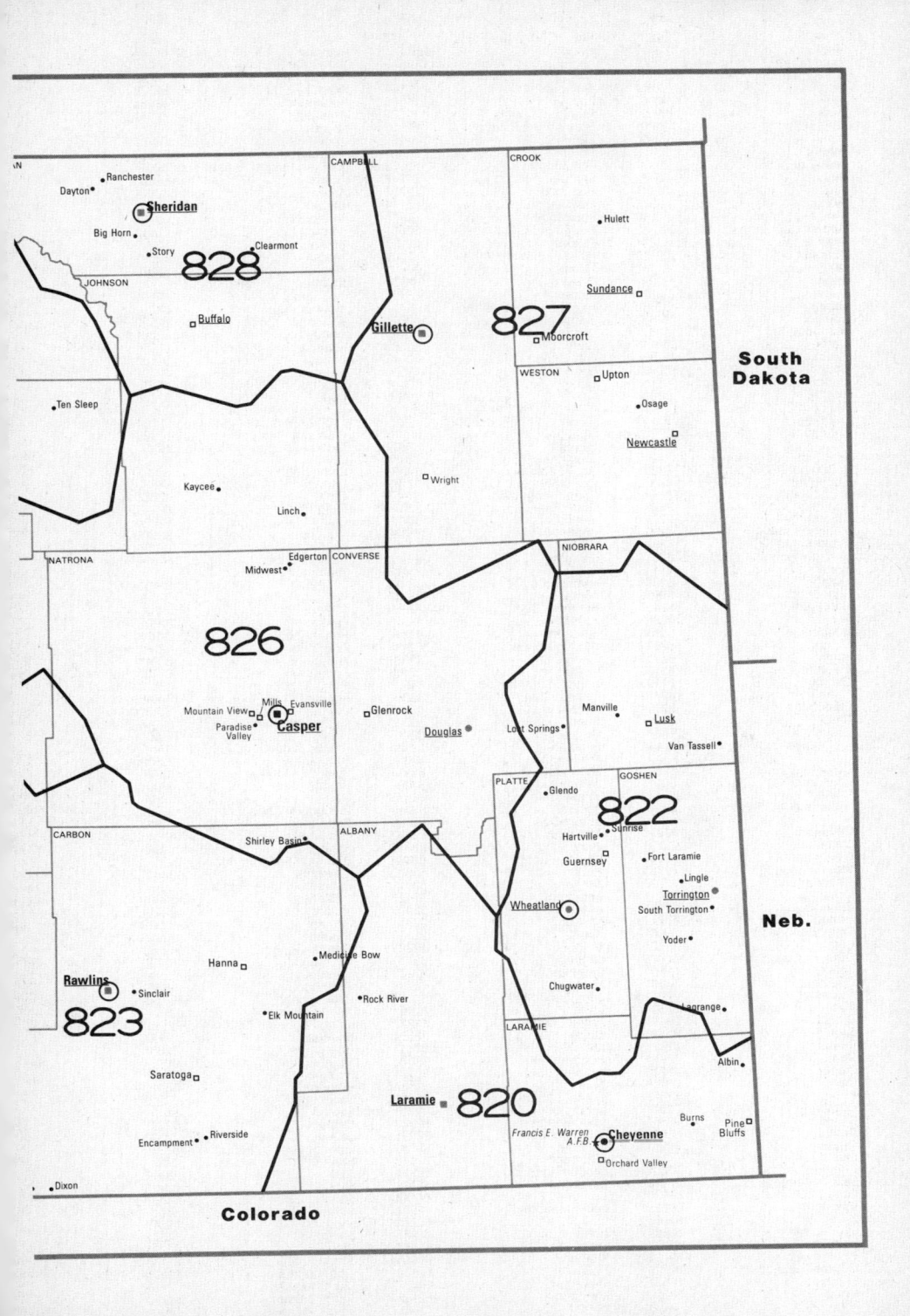

628 WYOMING Acme-South Torrington

	ZIP		ZIP		ZIP
Acme	82839	Etna	83118	Mantua	82435
Afton	83110	Evanston	82930-31	Manville	82227
Airport (Part of Cheyenne)	82001	For specific Evanston Zip Codes call (307) 789-2912		Marbleton	83113
Aladdin	82710			Mayoworth	82639
Albany	82070	Evansville	82636	Medicine Bow	82329
Albin	82050	Fairview	83119	Meeteetse	82433
Alcova	82620	Farson	82932	Meriden	82081
Allendale	82601	Fishing Bridge	82190	Merna	83115
Almy	82930	Flattop	82220	Midvale	82501
Alpine	83128	Fontenelle	83101	Midwest	82643
Alpine Junction	83127	Fort Bridger	82933	Midwest Heights	82601
Alta	83422	Fort Laramie	82212	Milford	82520
Alva	82711	Fort Steele	82301	Mills	82644
Arapahoe	82510	Fort Washakie	82514	Moneta	82601
Arminto	82630	Four Corners	82715	Moorcroft	82721
Arrow Head Lodge	82836	Fox Farm	82001	Moose	83012
Arvada	82831	Foxpark	82057	Moran	83013
Atlantic City	82520	Francis E. Warren A F B	82001	Morton	82501
Auburn	83111	Frannie	82423	Mountain Home	82070
Baggs	82321	Freedom	83120	Mountain View (Natrona County)	82601
Bairoil	82322	Frontier	83121		
Banner	82832	Frontier Mall (Part of Cheyenne)	82001	Mountain View (Uinta County)	82939
Barnum	82639				
Bar Nunn	82601	Garland	82435	Muddy Gap	82301
Basin	82410	Garrett	82083	Museum (Part of Cheyenne)	82001
Bear Lodge	82836	Gas Camp 1	82643	Natrona	82601
Beckton	82801	Gas Hills	82501	Newcastle	82701
Bedford	83112	Gebo	82443	New Haven	82720
Beulah	82712	Gillette	82716-17	Node	82228
Big Horn	82833	For specific Gillette Zip Codes call (307) 682-3727		Number One (Part of Cheyenne)	82001
Big Piney	83113				
Big Sandy	82923	Glendo	82213	O'Donnell Spur	82435
Bill	82631	Glenrock	82637	Old Faithful	82190
Blairtown (Part of Rock Springs)	82901	Granger	82934	Opal	83124
		Granite Canon	82059	Orchard Valley	82001
Bondurant	82922	Grants Village	82190	Orin	82633
Bonneville	82649	Grass Creek	82443	Orpha	82633
Bordeaux	82201	Green River	82935	Osage	82723
Bosler	82051	Greybull	82426	Oshoto	82724
Bosler Junction	82051	Grover	83122	Osmond	83110
Boulder	82923	Grovont	83011	Otto	82434
Boxelder	82637	Guernsey	82214	Pahaska	82414
Bronx	83115	Halfway	83113	Paradise Valley (Part of Casper)	82601
Buffalo	82834	Hamilton Dome	82427		
Buford	82052	Hanna	82327	Parkerton	82637
Burlington	82411	Harriman	82059	Parkman	82838
Burns	82053	Hartville	82215	Pavillion	82523
Burntfork	82938	Hawk Springs	82217	Piedmont	82933
Burris	82512	Heart Mountain	82435	Pine Bluffs	82082
Byron	82412	Hiland	82638	Pinedale	82941
Calpet	83123	Hillsdale	82060	Pine Haven	82721
Canyon	82190	Hilltop (Part of Casper)	82609	Point of Rocks	82942
Carlile	82713	Horse Creek	82061	Powder River	82648
Carpenter	82054	Hudson	82515	Powell	82435
Carter	82937	Hulett	82720	Prospector-Rawhide Village	82716
Casper	82601-15	Huntley	82218	Quealy	82901
For specific Casper Zip Codes call (307) 266-4000		Hyattville	82428	Ralston	82440
		Iron Mountain	82062	Ranchester	82839
Centennial	82055	Ishawooa	82414	Rawhide Village	82716
Chatham	82401	Jackson	83001	Rawlins	82301
Cheyenne	82001-09	James Town	82935	Recluse	82725
For specific Cheyenne Zip Codes call (307) 772-6583		Jay Em	82219	Red Buttes Village	82601
		Jeffrey City	82310	Red Desert	82336
Chugwater	82210	Jelm	82063	Red Lane	82443
Clareton	82701	Jenny Lake	83012	Reliance	82943
Clark	59008	Kaycee	82639	Reno Junction (Part of Wright)	82732
Clay	82723	Keeline	82220		
Clearmont	82835	Kelly	83011	Richardson Acres (Part of Bar Nunn)	82601
Cody	82414	Kemmerer	83101		
Cokeville	83114	Keystone	82070	Riddle	82414
Colony	57717	Kinnear	82516	Riovista	82935
Colter Bay	83001	Kirby	82430	Riverside	82325
Cora	82925	Kirtley	82225	Riverton	82501
Cowley	82420	La Barge	83123	Riverview	57735
Creston	82301	Lagrange	82221	Robertson	82344
Creston Junction	82301	Lake	82190	Rock River	82083
Crowheart	82512	Lake Creek Resort	82057	Rock Springs	82901-02
Cy (Part of Casper)	82604	Lamont	82301	For specific Rock Springs Zip Codes call (307) 362-9792	
Daniel	83115	Lance Creek	82222		
Dayton	82836	Lander	82520	Rockypoint	82724
Deaver	82421	LaPrele	82633	Rolling Hills	82637
Devils Tower	82714	Laramie	82070	Rozet	82727
Diamond	82210	Leiter	82837	Ryan Park	82331
Diamondville	83116	Leo	82327	Ryegrass	83115
Dixon	82323	Linch	82640	Saddlestring	82840
Douglas	82633	Lingle	82223	Sand Draw	82501
Downer	82801	Little America	82929	Saratoga	82331
Dubois	82513	Little Bear	82001	Savery	82332
Dwyer	82201	Lonetree	82936	Seminoe Dam	82334
Eastridge Mall (Part of Casper)	82601	Lost Cabin	82642	Shawnee	82229
		Lost Springs	82224	Shell	82441
East Thermopolis	82443	Lovell	82431	Sheridan	82801
Eden	82926	Lucerne	82443	Sheridan Gardens	82801
Edgerton	82635	Lucky MacCamp	82501	Shirley Basin	82615
Egbert	82053	Lusk	82225	Shoshoni	82649
Elk Mountain	82324	Lyman	82937	Sinclair	82334
Elmo (Part of Hanna)	82327	Lysite	82642	Slater	82201
Emblem	82422	McFadden	82080	Smoot	83126
Encampment	82325	McKinley	82633	South Laramie	82070
Esterbrook	82633	McKinnon	82938	South Pass City	82520
Ethete	82520	Manderson	82432	South Torrington	82240

	ZIP		ZIP		ZIP
Spotted Horse	82831	Tower Junction	82190	West Lance Creek	82222
Story	82842	Turnerville	83112	West Laramie	82070
Sundance	82729	Ucross	82835	Weston	82731
Sunrise	82215	Ulm	82835	West Thumb	82190
Sunshine	82433	University (Part of Laramie)	82071	Wheatland	82201
Superior	82945	Upton	82730	Willwood	82435
Sussex	82639	Urie	82937	Wilson	83014
Sussex Unit	82640	Uva	82201	Wind River Indian	
Sweetwater Station	82520	Valley	82414	Reservation	82514
Taylor	82643	Van Tassell	82242	Wolf	82844
Ten Sleep	82442	Veteran	82243	Woods Landing	82063
Teton Village	83025	Walcott	82335	Worland	82401
Thayne	83127	Wamsutter	82336	Wright	82732
Thermopolis	82443	Wapiti	82450	Wyarno	82845
Three Forks	82301	Warren AFB	82005	Wyodak	82716
Tie Siding	82084	Western Hills (Part of			
Torrington	82240	Cheyenne)	82001		

NOTES

NOTES

NOTES

NOTES

NOTES

NOTES

NOTES

NOTES

NOTES

NOTES

NOTES

NOTES

NOTES

NOTES

NOTES

NOTES

NOTES

NOTES

NOTES